ZECHARIA SITCHIN

THE 12th PLANET

The First Book
of
The Earth Chronicles

Bear & Company
Rochester, Vermont • Toronto, Canada

Bear & Company
One Park Street
Rochester, Vermont 05767
www.BearandCompanyBooks.com

Bear & Company is a division of Inner Traditions International

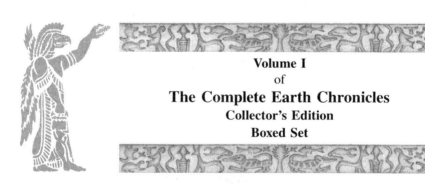

Volume I
of
The Complete Earth Chronicles
Collector's Edition
Boxed Set

Printed and bound in India at Replika Press Pvt. Ltd.

10 9 8 7 6

Praise for the Works of Zecharia Sitchin

"Reflects the highest level of scientific knowledge . . ."

"Exciting . . . credible . . . most provocative and compelling."

"One of the most important books on Earth's roots ever written."

"Sitchin is a zealous investigator into man's origins . . . a dazzling performance."

"For thousands of years priests, poets, and scientists have tried to explain how man was created. Now a recognized scholar has come forth with a theory that is most astonishing of all."

Also by Zecharia Sitchin

ACKNOWLEDGMENTS

The author wishes to express his gratitude to the many scholars who, over a span of more than a century, have uncovered, deciphered, translated, and explained the textual and artistic relics of the ancient Near East; and to the many institutions and their staffs by whose excellence and courtesies the texts and pictorial evidence on which this book is based were made available to the author.

The author wishes especially to thank the New York Public Library and its Oriental Division; the Research Library (Reading Room and Oriental Students Room) of the British Museum, London; the Research Library of the Jewish Theological Seminary, New York; and, for pictorial assistance, the Trustees of the British Museum and the Keeper of Assyrian and Egyptian Antiquities; the Director of the Vorderasiatisches Museum, Staatliche Museen, East Berlin; the University Museum, Philadelphia; la Réunion des Musées Nationaux, France (Musée du Louvre); the Curator, Museum of Antiquities, Aleppo; the U.S. National Aeronautics and Space Administration.

CONTENTS

•

AUTHOR'S NOTE

•

The prime source for the biblical verses quoted in *The Twelfth Planet* is the Old Testament in its original Hebrew text. It must be borne in mind that all the translations consulted—of which the principal ones are listed at the end of the book—are just that: translations or interpretations. In the final analysis, what counts is what the original Hebrew says.

In the final version quoted in *The Twelfth Planet,* I have compared the available translations against each other and against the Hebrew source and the parallel Sumerian and Akkadian texts/tales, to come up with what I believe is the most accurate rendering.

The rendering of Sumerian, Assyrian, Babylonian, and Hittite texts has engaged a legion of scholars for more than a century. Decipherment of script and language was followed by transcribing, transliterating, and finally, translating. In many instances, it was possible to choose between differing translations or interpretations only by verifying the much earlier transcriptions and transliterations. In other instances, a late insight by a contemporary scholar could throw new light on an early translation.

The list of sources for Near Eastern texts, given at the end of this book, thus ranges from the oldest to the newest, and is followed by the scholarly publications in which valuable contributions to the understanding of the texts were found.

Z. SITCHIN

THE 12th PLANET

Prologue: GENESIS

•

At a time when our own astronauts have landed on the Moon and our unmanned spacecraft explore other planets, it is no longer impossible to believe that a civilization on another planet more advanced than ours was capable of landing its astronauts on the planet Earth at some time in the past. Indeed, a number of popular writers have speculated that ancient artifacts such as the pyramids and giant stone sculptures must have been fashioned by advanced visitors from another planet.

There is, however, little novelty in such intriguing speculation. Even the ancient peoples themselves believed that superior beings "from the heavens"—the ancient gods—came down to Earth. What no popular writer on the subject provides is *answers*. If, indeed, such beings did come to Earth, *when* did they come, *how* did they come, from *where* did they come, and *what* did they do here during their stay?

What we propose to do is to provide answers to these questions. Using the Old Testament as our anchor, and submitting as evidence nothing but the texts, drawings, and artifacts left us by the ancient peoples of the Near East, we will go beyond the intriguing questions and the provocative suggestions. We will prove that Earth was indeed visited in its past by astronauts from another planet.

We will identify the planet from which these astronauts came.

We will decipher a sophisticated ancient cosmology that explains better than our present sciences how Earth and other parts of the solar system came into being.

We will lay bare ancient reports of a celestial collision, as a result of which an intruding planet was captured into the Sun's orbit, and show that all the ancient religions were based on the knowledge and veneration of this twelfth member of our solar system.

We will prove that this Twelfth Planet was the home planet of the ancient visitors to Earth. We will submit texts and celestial maps dealing with the space flights to Earth, and will establish when and why they came to Earth.

We will describe them, and show how they looked and dressed and ate, glimpse their craft and weapons, follow their activities upon Earth, their loves and jealousies, achievements and struggles. We will unravel the secret of their "immortality."

We will trace the dramatic events that led to the "Creation" of Man, and show the advanced methods by which this was accomplished. We will then follow the tangled relationship of Man and his deities, and throw light on the true meaning of the events passed to us in the tales of the Garden of Eden, the Tower of Babel, the Deluge, the rise of civilization, the three branches of Mankind. We will show how Man—endowed by his makers biologically and materially—ended up crowding his gods off Earth.

We will show that Man is not alone and that future generations will have yet another encounter with the bearers of the Kingship of Heaven.

1

·

THE ENDLESS BEGINNING

Of the evidence that we have amassed to support our conclusions, exhibit number one is Man himself. In many ways, modern man—*Homo sapiens*—is a stranger to Earth.

Ever since Charles Darwin shocked the scholars and theologians of his time with the evidence of evolution, life on Earth has been traced through Man and the primates, mammals, and vertebrates, and backward through ever-lower life forms to the point, billions of years ago, at which life is presumed to have begun.

But having reached these beginnings and having begun to contemplate the probabilities of life elsewhere in our solar system and beyond, the scholars have become uneasy about life on Earth: Somehow, it does not belong here. If it began through a series of spontaneous chemical reactions, why does life on Earth have but a single source, and not a multitude of chance sources? And why does all living matter on Earth contain too little of the chemical elements that abound on Earth, and too much of those that are rare on our planet?

Was life, then, imported to Earth from elsewhere?

Man's position in the evolutionary chain has compounded the puzzle. Finding a broken skull here, a jaw there, scholars at first believed that Man originated in Asia some 500,000 years ago. But as older fossils were found, it became evident that the mills of evolution grind much, much slower. Man's ancestor apes are now placed at a staggering 25,000,000 years ago. Discoveries in East Africa reveal a transition to manlike apes (hominids) some 14,000,000 years ago. It was about 11,000,000 years later that the first ape-man worthy of the classification *Homo* appeared there.

The first being considered to be truly manlike—"Advanced Australopithecus"—existed in the same parts of Africa some 2,000,000 years ago. It took yet another million years to produce *Homo erectus*. Finally, after another 900,000 years, the first primitive Man appeared; he is named Neanderthal after the site where his remains were first found.

In spite of the passage of more than 2,000,000 years between Advanced Australopithecus and Neanderthal, the tools of these two groups—sharp stones—were virtually alike; and the groups themselves (as they are believed to have looked) were hardly distinguishable. (Fig. 1)

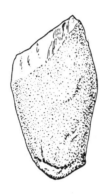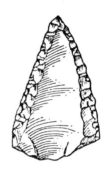

Fig. 1

Then, suddenly and inexplicably, some 35,000 years ago, a new race of Men—*Homo sapiens* ("thinking Man")—appeared as if from nowhere, and swept Neanderthal Man from the face of Earth. These modern Men—named Cro-Magnon—looked so much like us that, if dressed like us in modern clothes, they would be lost in the crowds of any European or American city. Because of the magnificent cave art which they created, they were at first called "cavemen." In fact, they roamed Earth freely, for they knew how to build shelters and homes of stones and animal skins wherever they went.

For millions of years, Man's tools had been simply stones of useful shapes. Cro-Magnon Man, however, made specialized tools and weapons of wood and bones. He was no longer a "naked ape," for he used skins for clothing. His society was organized; he lived in clans with a patriarchal hegemony. His cave drawings bespeak artistry and depth of feeling; his drawings and sculptures evidence some form of "religion," apparent in the worship of a Mother Goddess, who was sometimes depicted with the sign of the Moon's crescent. He buried his dead, and must therefore have had some philosophies regarding life, death, and perhaps even an afterlife.

As mysterious and unexplained as the appearance of Cro-Magnon Man has been, the puzzle is still more complicated. For, as other remains of modern Man were discovered (at sites including

Swanscombe, Steinheim, and Montmaria), it became apparent that Cro-Magnon Man stemmed from an even earlier *Homo sapiens* who lived in western Asia and North Africa some 250,000 years before Cro-Magnon Man.

The appearance of modern Man a mere 700,000 years after *Homo erectus* and some 200,000 years before Neanderthal Man is absolutely implausible. It is also clear that *Homo sapiens* represents such an extreme departure from the slow evolutionary process that many of our features, such as the ability to speak, are totally unrelated to the earlier primates.

An outstanding authority on the subject, Professor Theodosius Dobzhansky *(Mankind Evolving)*, was especially puzzled by the fact that this development took place during a period when Earth was going through an ice age, a most unpropitious time for evolutionary advance. Pointing out that *Homo sapiens* lacks completely some of the peculiarities of the previously known types, and has some that never appeared before, he concluded: "Modern man has many fossil collateral relatives but no progenitors; the derivation of *Homo sapiens,* then, becomes a puzzle."

How, then, did the ancestors of modern Man appear some 300,000 years ago—instead of 2,000,000 or 3,000,000 years in the future, following further evolutionary development? Were we imported to Earth from elsewhere, or were we, as the Old Testament and other ancient sources claim, created by the gods?

We now know where civilization began and how it developed, once it began. The unanswered question is: *Why*—why did civilization come about at all? For, as most scholars now admit in frustration, by all data Man should still be without civilization. There is no obvious reason that we should be any more civilized than the primitive tribes of the Amazon jungles or the inaccessible parts of New Guinea.

But, we are told, these tribesmen still live as if in the Stone Age because they have been isolated. But isolated from what? If they have been living on the same Earth as we, why have they not acquired the same knowledge of sciences and technologies on their own as we supposedly have?

The real puzzle, however, is not the backwardness of the Bushmen, but our advancement; for it is now recognized that in the normal course of evolution Man should still be typified by the Bushmen and not by us. It took Man some 2,000,000 years to advance in his "tool industries" from the use of stones as he found them to the realization that he could chip and shape stones to better suit his purposes. Why not another 2,000,000 years to learn the use of other materials, and another 10,000,000 years to master mathematics and engineering and astronomy? Yet here we are, less than 50,000 years from Neanderthal Man, landing astronauts on the Moon.

The obvious question, then, is this: Did we and our Mediterranean ancestors really acquire this advanced civilization on our own?

Though Cro-Magnon Man did not build skyscrapers nor use metals, there is no doubt that his was a sudden and revolutionary civilization. His mobility, ability to build shelters, his desire to clothe himself, his manufactured tools, his art—all were a sudden high civilization breaking an endless beginning of Man's culture that stretched over millions of years and advanced at a painfully slow pace.

Though our scholars cannot explain the appearance of *Homo sapiens* and the civilization of Cro-Magnon Man, there is by now no doubt regarding this civilization's place of origin: the Near East. The uplands and mountain ranges that extend in a semiarc from the Zagros Mountains in the east (where present-day Iran and Iraq border on each other), through the Ararat and Taurus ranges in the north, then down, westward and southward, to the hill lands of Syria, Lebanon, and Israel, are replete with caves where the evidence of prehistoric but modern Man has been preserved. (Fig. 2)

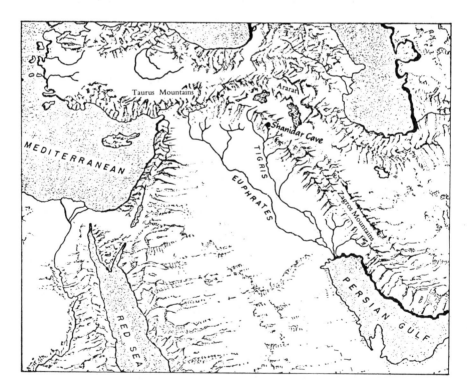

Fig. 2

One of these caves, Shanidar, is located in the northeastern part of the semiarc of civilization. Nowadays, fierce Kurdish tribesmen seek shelter in the area's caves for themselves and their flocks during the cold winter months. So it was, one wintry night 44,000 years ago, when a family of seven (one of whom was a baby) sought shelter in the cave of Shanidar.

Their remains—they were evidently crushed to death by a rockfall—were discovered in 1957 by a startled Ralph Solecki, who went to the area in search of evidence of early Man. What he found was more than he expected. As layer upon layer of debris was removed, it became apparent that the cave preserved a clear record of Man's habitation in the area from about 100,000 to some 13,000 years ago.

What this record showed was as surprising as the find itself. Man's culture has shown not a progression but a regression. Starting from a certain standard, the following generations showed not more advanced but less advanced standards of civilized life. And from about 27,000 B.C. to 11,000 B.C., the regressing and dwindling population reached the point of an almost complete absence of habitation. For reasons that are assumed to have been climatic, Man was almost completely gone from the whole area for some 16,000 years.

And then, circa 11,000 B.C., "thinking Man" reappeared with new vigor and on an inexplicably higher cultural level.

It was as if an unseen coach, watching the faltering human game, dispatched to the field a fresh and better-trained team to take over from the exhausted one.

*

Throughout the many millions of years of his endless beginning, Man was nature's child; he subsisted by gathering the foods that grew wild, by hunting the wild animals, by catching wild birds and fishes. But just as Man's settlements were thinning out, just as he was abandoning his abodes, when his material and artistic achievements were disappearing—just then, suddenly, with no apparent reason and without any prior known period of gradual preparation—Man became a farmer.

Summarizing the work of many eminent authorities on the subject, R. J. Braidwood and B. Howe (*Prehistoric Investigations in Iraqi Kurdistan*) concluded that genetic studies confirm the archaeological finds and leave no doubt that agriculture began exactly where thinking Man had emerged earlier with his first crude civilization: in the Near East. There is no doubt by now that agriculture spread all over the world from the Near Eastern arc of mountains and highlands.

Employing sophisticated methods of radiocarbon dating and plant genetics, many scholars from various fields of science concur in the conclusion that Man's first farming venture was the cultivation of wheat and barley, probably through the domestication of a wild variety of emmer. Assuming that, somehow, Man did undergo a gradual process of teaching himself how to domesticate, grow, and farm a wild plant, the scholars remain baffled by the profusion of other plants and cereals basic to human survival and advancement that kept coming out of the Near East. These included, in rapid succession, millet, rye, and spelt, among the edible cereals; flax, which provided fibers and edible oil; and a variety of fruit-bearing shrubs and trees.

In every instance, the plant was undoubtedly domesticated in the Near East for millennia before it reached Europe. It was as though the Near East were some kind of genetic-botanical laboratory, guided by an unseen hand, producing every so often a newly domesticated plant.

The scholars who have studied the origins of the grapevine have concluded that its cultivation began in the mountains around northern Mesopotamia and in Syria and Palestine. No wonder. The Old Testament tells us that Noah "planted a vineyard" (and even got drunk on its wine) after his ark rested on Mount Ararat as the waters of the Deluge receded. The Bible, like the scholars, thus places the start of vine cultivation in the mountains of northern Mesopotamia.

Apples, pears, olives, figs, almonds, pistachios, walnuts—all originated in the Near East and spread from there to Europe and other parts of the world. Indeed, we cannot help recalling that the Old Testament preceded our scholars by several millennia in identifying the very same area as the world's first orchard: "And the Lord God planted an orchard in Eden, in the east. . . . And the Lord God caused to grow, out of the ground, every tree that is pleasant to behold and that is good for eating."

The general location of "Eden" was certainly known to the biblical generations. It was "in the east"—east of the Land of Israel. It was in a land watered by four major rivers, two of which are the Tigris and the Euphrates. There can be no doubt that the Book of Genesis located the first orchard in the highlands where these rivers originated, in northeastern Mesopotamia. Bible and science are in full agreement.

As a matter of fact, if we read the original Hebrew text of the Book of Genesis not as a theological but as a scientific text, we find that it also accurate.y describes the process of plant domestication. Science tells us that the process went from wild grasses to wild cereals to cultivated cereals, followed by fruit-bearing shrubs and trees. This is exactly the process detailed in the first chapter of the Book of Genesis.

And the Lord said:
"Let the Earth bring forth grasses;
cereals that by seeds produce seeds;
fruit trees that bear fruit by species,
   which contain the seed within themselves."

And it was so:
The Earth brought forth grass;
cereals that by seed produce seed, by species;
and trees that bear fruit, which contain
   the seed within themselves, by species.

The Book of Genesis goes on to tell us that Man, expelled from the orchard of Eden, had to toil hard to grow his food. "By the sweat of thy brow shalt thou eat bread," the Lord said to Adam. It was after that that "Abel was a keeper of herds and Cain was a tiller of the soil." Man, the Bible tells us, became a shepherd soon after he became a farmer.

Scholars are in full agreement with this biblical sequence of events. Analyzing the various theories regarding animal domestication, F. E. Zeuner (*Domestication of Animals*) stresses that Man could not have "acquired the habit of keeping animals in captivity or domestication before he reached the stage of living in social units of some size." Such settled communities, a prerequisite for animal domestication, followed the changeover to agriculture.

The first animal to be domesticated was the dog, and not necessarily as Man's best friend but probably also for food. This, it is believed, took place circa 9500 B.C. The first skeletal remains of dogs have been found in Iran, Iraq, and Israel.

Sheep were domesticated at about the same time; the Shanidar cave contains remains of sheep from circa 9000 B.C., showing that a large part of each year's young were killed for food and skins. Goats, which also provided milk, soon followed; and pigs, horned cattle, and hornless cattle were next to be domesticated.

In every instance, the domestication began in the Near East.

The abrupt change in the course of human events that occurred circa 11,000 B.C. in the Near East (and some 2,000 years later in Europe) has led scholars to describe that time as the clear end of the Old Stone Age (the Paleolithic) and the beginning of a new cultural era, the Middle Stone Age (Mesolithic).

The name is appropriate only if one considers Man's principal raw material—which continued to be stone. His dwellings in the mountainous areas were still built of stone; his communities were protected by stone walls; his first agricultural implement—the sickle—was made of stone. He honored or protected his dead by covering and adorning their graves with stones; and he used stone to make images of the supreme beings, or "gods," whose benign intervention he sought. One such image, found in northern Israel and dated to the ninth millennium B.C., shows the carved head of a "god" shielded by a striped helmet and wearing some kind of "goggles." (Fig. 3)

From an overall point of view, however, it would be more

Fig. 3

appropriate to call the age that began circa 11,000 B.C. not the Middle Stone Age but the Age of Domestication. Within the span of a mere 3,600 years—overnight in terms of the endless beginning—Man became a farmer, and wild plants and animals were domesticated. Then, a new age clearly followed. Our scholars call it the New Stone Age (Neolithic); but the term is totally inadequate, for the main change that had taken place circa 7500 B.C. was the appearance of pottery.

For reasons that still elude our scholars—but which will become clear as we unfold our tale of prehistoric events—Man's march toward civilization was confined, for the first several millennia after 11,000 B.C., to the highlands of the Near East. The discovery of the many uses to which clay could be put was contemporary with Man's descent from his mountain abodes toward the lower, mud-filled valleys.

By the seventh millennium B.C., the Near Eastern arc of civilization was teeming with clay or pottery cultures, which produced great numbers of utensils, ornaments, and statuettes. By 5000 B.C., the Near East was producing clay and pottery objects of superb quality and fantastic design.

But once again progress slowed, and by 4500 B.C., archaeological evidence indicates, regression was all around. Pottery became simpler.

Stone utensils—a relic of the Stone Age—again became predominant. Inhabited sites reveal fewer remains. Some sites that had been centers of pottery and clay industries began to be abandoned, and distinct clay manufacturing disappeared. "There was a general impoverishment of culture," according to James Melaart *(Earliest Civilizations of the Near East);* some sites clearly bear the marks of "the new poverty-stricken phase."

Man and his culture were clearly on the decline.

Then—suddenly, unexpectedly, inexplicably—the Near East witnessed the blossoming of the greatest civilization imaginable, a civilization in which our own is firmly rooted.

A mysterious hand once more picked Man out of his decline and raised him to an even higher level of culture, knowledge, and civilization.

2

·

THE SUDDEN CIVILIZATION

For a long time, Western man believed that his civilization was the gift of Rome and Greece. But the Greek philosophers themselves wrote repeatedly that they had drawn on even earlier sources. Later on, travelers returning to Europe reported the existence in Egypt of imposing pyramids and temple-cities half-buried in the sands, guarded by strange stone beasts called sphinxes.

When Napoleon arrived in Egypt in 1799, he took with him scholars to study and explain these ancient monuments. One of his officers found near Rosetta a stone slab on which was carved a proclamation from 196 B.C. written in the ancient Egyptian pictographic writing (hieroglyphic) as well as in two other scripts.

The decipherment of the ancient Egyptian script and language, and the archaeological efforts that followed, revealed to Western man that a high civilization had existed in Egypt well before the advent of the Greek civilization. Egyptian records spoke of royal dynasties that began circa 3100 B.C.—two full millennia before the beginning of Hellenic civilization. Reaching its maturity in the fifth and fourth centuries B.C., Greece was a latecomer rather than an originator.

Was the origin of our civilization, then, in Egypt?

As logical as that conclusion would have seemed, the facts militated against it. Greek scholars did describe visits to Egypt, but the ancient sources of knowledge of which they spoke were found elsewhere. The pre-Hellenic cultures of the Aegean Sea—the Minoan on the island of Crete and the Mycenaean on the Greek mainland—revealed evidence that the Near Eastern, not the Egyptian, culture had been adopted. Syria and Anatolia, not Egypt, were the principal avenues through which an earlier civilization became available to the Greeks.

Noting that the Dorian invasion of Greece and the Israelite invasion of Canaan following the Exodus from Egypt took place at about the same time (circa the thirteenth century B.C.), scholars have been fascinated to discover a growing number of similarities between the Semitic and Hellenic civilizations. Professor Cyrus H. Gordon (*Forgotten Scripts; Evidence for the Minoan Language*) opened up a new field of study by showing that an early Minoan script, called Linear A, represented a Semitic language. He concluded that "the pattern (as distinct from the content) of the Hebrew and Minoan civilizations is the same to a remarkable extent," and pointed out that the island's name, Crete, spelled in Minoan *Ke-re-ta*, was the same as the Hebrew word *Ke-re-et* ("walled city") and had a counterpart in a Semitic tale of a king of Keret.

Even the Hellenic alphabet, from which the Latin and our own alphabets derive, came from the Near East. The ancient Greek historians themselves wrote that a Phoenician named Kadmus ("ancient") brought them the alphabet, comprising the same number of letters, in the same order, as in Hebrew; it was the only Greek alphabet when the Trojan War took place. The number of letters was raised to twenty-six by the poet Simonides of Ceos in the fifth century B.C.

That Greek and Latin writing, and thus the whole foundation of our Western culture, were adopted from the Near East can easily be demonstrated by comparing the order, names, signs, and even numerical values of the original Near Eastern alphabet with the much later ancient Greek and the more recent Latin. (Fig. 4)

The scholars were aware, of course, of Greek contacts with the Near East in the first millennium B.C., culminating with the defeat of the Persians by Alexander the Macedonian in 331 B.C. Greek records contained much information about these Persians and their lands (which roughly paralleled today's Iran). Judging by the names of their kings—Cyrus, Darius, Xerxes—and the names of their deities, which appear to belong to the Indo-European linguistic stem, scholars reached the conclusion that they were part of the Aryan ("lordly") people that appeared from somewhere near the Caspian Sea toward the end of the second millennium B.C. and spread westward to Asia Minor, eastward to India, and southward to what the Old Testament called the "lands of the Medes and Parsees."

Yet all was not that simple. In spite of the assumed foreign origin of these invaders, the Old Testament treated them as part and parcel of biblical events. Cyrus, for example, was considered to be an "Anointed of Yahweh"—quite an unusual relationship between the Hebrew God and a non-Hebrew. According to the biblical Book of Ezra, Cyrus acknowledged his mission to rebuild the Temple in Jerusalem, and stated that he was acting upon orders given by Yahweh, whom he called "God of Heaven."

Cyrus and the other kings of his dynasty called themselves

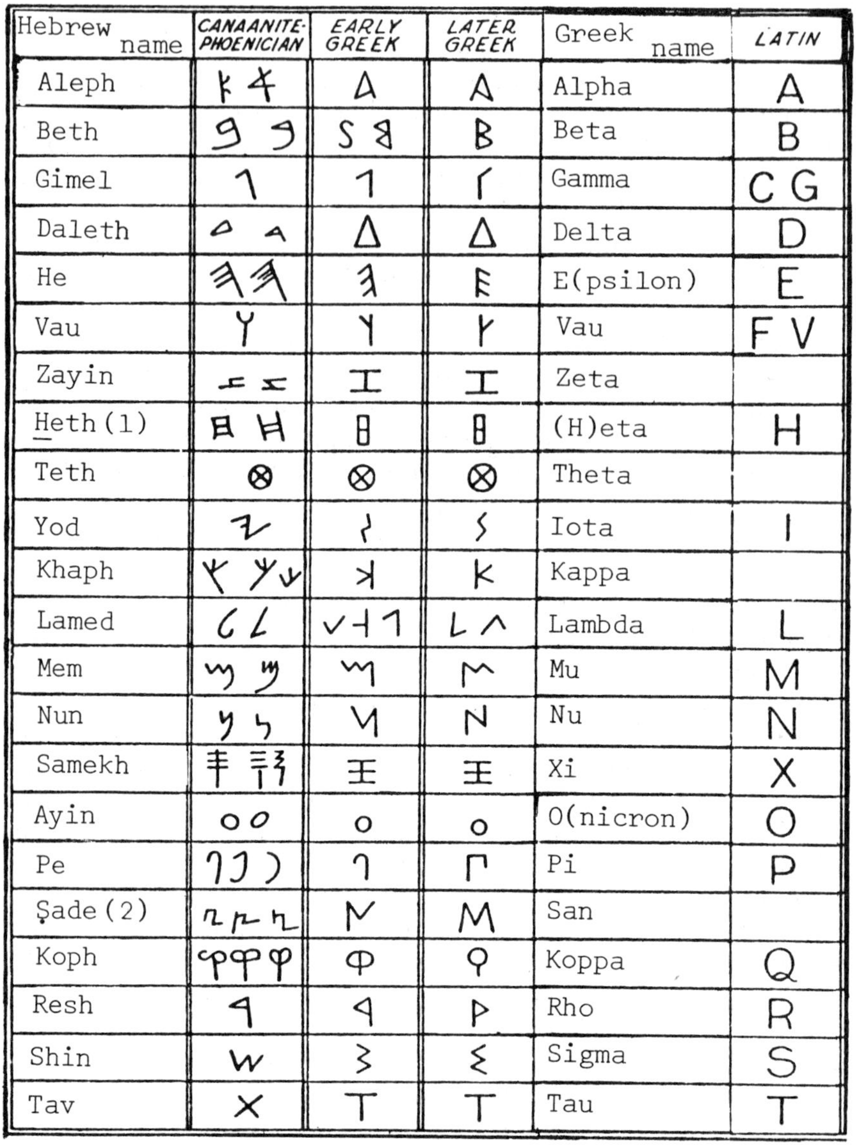

Hebrew name	CANAANITE-PHOENICIAN	EARLY GREEK	LATER GREEK	Greek name	LATIN
Aleph		Δ	Λ	Alpha	A
Beth			Β	Beta	B
Gimel				Gamma	C G
Daleth		Δ	Δ	Delta	D
He			Ε	E(psilon)	E
Vau	Y	Y		Vau	F V
Zayin		I	I	Zeta	
Heth (1)				(H)eta	H
Teth	⊗	⊗	⊗	Theta	
Yod				Iota	I
Khaph			K	Kappa	
Lamed				Lambda	L
Mem				Mu	M
Nun			N	Nu	N
Samekh				Xi	X
Ayin	o o	o	o	O(nicron)	O
Pe				Pi	P
Şade (2)			M	San	
Koph				Koppa	Q
Resh				Rho	R
Shin	W			Sigma	S
Tav	X	T	T	Tau	T

(1) "H̱", commonly transliterated as "H" for simplicity, is pronounced in the Sumerian and Semitic languages as "CH" in the Scottish or German "loch".

(2) "Ṣ", commonly transliterated as "S" for simplicity, is pronounced in the Sumerian and Semitic languages as "TS".

Fig. 4

Achaemenids—after the title adopted by the founder of the dynasty, which was Hacham-Anish. It was not an Aryan but a perfect Semitic title, which meant "wise man." By and large, scholars have neglected to investigate the many leads that may point to similarities between the Hebrew God Yahweh and the deity Achaemenids called "Wise Lord," whom they depicted as hovering in the skies within a Winged Globe, as shown on the royal seal of Darius. (Fig. 5)

Fig. 5

It has been established by now that the cultural, religious, and historic roots of these Old Persians go back to the earlier empires of Babylon and Assyria, whose extent and fall is recorded in the Old Testament. The symbols that make up the script that appeared on the Achaemenid monuments and seals were at first considered to be decorative designs. Engelbert Kampfer, who visited Persepolis, the Old Persian capital, in 1686, described the signs as "cuneates," or wedge-shaped impressions. The script has since been known as cuneiform.

As efforts began to decipher the Achaemenid inscriptions, it became clear that they were written in the same script as inscriptions found on ancient artifacts and tablets in Mesopotamia, the plains and highlands that lay between the Tigris and Euphrates rivers. Intrigued by the scattered finds, Paul Emile Botta set out in 1843 to conduct the first major purposeful excavation. He selected a site in northern Meso-potamia, near present-day Mosul, now called Khorsabad. Botta was soon able to establish that the cuneiform inscriptions named the place Dur Sharru Kin. They were Semitic inscriptions, in a sister language of Hebrew, and the name meant "walled city of the righteous king." Our textbooks call this king Sargon II.

This capital of the Assyrian king had as its center a magnificent royal palace whose walls were lined with sculptured bas-reliefs, which, if placed end to end, would stretch for over a mile. Commanding the city and the royal compound was a step pyramid called a ziggurat; it served as a "stairway to Heaven" for the gods. (Fig. 6)

The layout of the city and the sculptures depicted a way of life on a grand scale. The palaces, temples, houses, stables, warehouses, walls, gates, columns, decorations, statues, artworks, towers, ramparts, ter-races, gardens—all were completed in just five years. According to Georges Contenau (*La Vie Quotidienne à Babylone et en Assyrie*), "the imagination reels before the potential strength of an empire which could accomplish so much in such a short space of time," some 3,000 years ago.

Not to be outdone by the French, the English appeared on the scene in the person of Sir Austen Henry Layard, who selected as his site a place some ten miles down the Tigris River from Khorsabad. The natives called it Kuyunjik; it turned out to be the Assyrian capital of Nineveh.

Biblical names and events had begun to come to life. Nineveh was

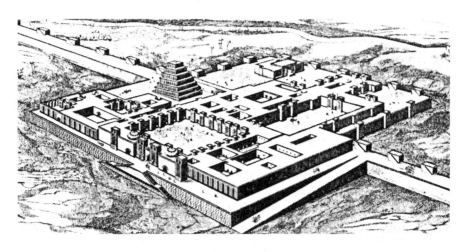

Fig. 6

the royal capital of Assyria under its last three great rulers: Sennacherib, Esarhaddon, and Ashurbanipal. "Now, in the fourteenth year of king Hezekiah, did Sennacherib king of Assyria come up against all the walled cities of Judah," relates the Old Testament (II Kings 18:13), and when the Angel of the Lord smote his army, "Sennacherib departed and went back, and dwelt in Nineveh."

The mounds where Nineveh was built by Sennacherib and Ashurbanipal revealed palaces, temples, and works of art that surpassed those of Sargon. The area where the remains of Esarhaddon's palaces are believed to lie cannot be excavated, for it is now the site of a Muslim mosque erected over the purported burial place of the prophet Jonah, who was swallowed by a whale when he refused to bring Yahweh's message to Nineveh.

Layard had read in ancient Greek records that an officer in Alexander's army saw a "place of pyramids and remains of an ancient city"—a city that was already buried in Alexander's time! Layard dug it up, too, and it turned out to be Nimrud, Assyria's military center. It was there that Shalmaneser II set up an obelisk to record his military expeditions and conquests. Now on exhibit at the British Museum, the obelisk lists, among the kings who were made to pay tribute, "Jehu, son of Omri, king of Israel."

Again, the Mesopotamian inscriptions and biblical texts supported each other!

Astounded by increasingly frequent corroboration of the biblical narratives by archaeological finds, the Assyriologists, as these scholars came to be called, turned to the tenth chapter of the Book of Genesis. There Nimrod—"a mighty hunter by the grace of Yahweh"—was described as the founder of all the kingdoms of Mesopotamia.

And the beginning of his kingdom:
Babel and Erech and Akkad, all in the Land of Shin'ar.
Out of that Land there emanated Ashur where
    Nineveh was built, a city of wide streets;
and Khalah, and Ressen—the great city
    which is between Nineveh and Khalah.

There were indeed mounds the natives called Calah, lying between Nineveh and Nimrud. When teams under W. Andrae excavated the area from 1903 to 1914, they uncovered the ruins of Ashur, the Assyrian religious center and its earliest capital. Of all the Assyrian cities mentioned in the Bible, only Ressen remains to be found. The name means "horse's bridle"; perhaps it was the location of the royal stables of Assyria.

At about the same time as Ashur was being excavated, teams under R. Koldewey were completing the excavation of Babylon, the biblical Babel—a vast place of palaces, temples, hanging gardens, and the inevitable ziggurat. Before long, artifacts and inscriptions unveiled the history of the two competing empires of Mesopotamia: Babylonia and Assyria, the one centered in the south, the other in the north.

Rising and falling, fighting and coexisting, the two constituted a high civilization that encompassed some 1,500 years, both rising circa 1900 B.C. Ashur and Nineveh were finally captured and destroyed by the Babylonians in 614 and 612 B.C., respectively. As predicted by the biblical prophets, Babylon itself came to an inglorious end when Cyrus the Achaemenid conquered it in 539 B.C.

Though they were rivals throughout their history, one would be hard put to find any significant differences between Assyria and Babylonia in cultural or material matters. Even though Assyria called its chief deity Ashur ("all-seeing") and Babylonia hailed Marduk ("son of the pure mound"), the pantheons were otherwise virtually alike.

Many of the world's museums count among their prize exhibits the ceremonial gates, winged bulls, bas-reliefs, chariots, tools, utensils, jewelry, statues, and other objects made of every conceivable material that have been dug out of the mounds of Assyria and Babylonia. But the true treasures of these kingdoms were their written records: thousands upon thousands of inscriptions in the cuneiform script, including cosmological tales, epic poems, histories of kings, temple records, commercial contracts, marriage and divorce records, astronomical tables, astrological forecasts, mathematical formulas, geographic lists, grammar and vocabulary school texts, and, not least of all, texts dealing with the names, genealogies, epithets, deeds, powers, and duties of the gods.

The common language that formed the cultural, historical, and religious bond between Assyria and Babylonia was Akkadian. It was the first known Semitic language, akin to but predating Hebrew, Aramaic, Phoenician, and Canaanite. But the Assyrians and Babylonians laid no claim to having invented the language or its script; indeed, many of their tablets bore the postscript that they had been copied from earlier originals.

Who, then, invented the cuneiform script and developed the language, its precise grammar and rich vocabulary? Who wrote the "earlier originals"? And why did the Assyrians and Babylonians call the language Akkadian?

Attention once more focuses on the Book of Genesis. "And the beginning of his kingdom: Babel and Erech and Akkad." Akkad—could there really have been such a royal capital, preceding Babylon and Nineveh?

The ruins of Mesopotamia have provided conclusive evidence that once upon a time there indeed existed a kingdom by the name of Akkad, established by a much earlier ruler, who called himself a *sharru-kin* ("righteous ruler"). He claimed in his inscriptions that his empire stretched, by the grace of his god Enlil, from the Lower Sea (the Persian Gulf) to the Upper Sea (believed to be the Mediterranean). He boasted that "at the wharf of Akkad, he made moor ships" from many distant lands.

The scholars stood awed: They had come upon a Mesopotamian empire in the third millennium B.C.! There was a leap—backward—of some 2,000 years from the Assyrian Sargon of Dur Sharrukin to Sargon of Akkad. And yet the mounds that were dug up brought to light literature and art, science and politics, commerce and communications—a full-fledged civilization—long before the appearance of Babylonia and Assyria. Moreover, it was obviously the predecessor and the source of the later Mesopotamian civilizations; Assyria and Babylonia were only branches off the Akkadian trunk.

The mystery of such an early Mesopotamian civilization deepened, however, as inscriptions recording the achievements and genealogy of Sargon of Akkad were found. They stated that his full title was "King of Akkad, King of Kish"; they explained that before he assumed the throne, he had been a counselor to the "rulers of Kish." Was there, then—the scholars asked themselves—an even earlier kingdom, that of Kish, which preceded Akkad?

Once again, the biblical verses gained in significance.

> And Kush begot Nimrod;
> He was first to be a Hero in the Land. . . .
> And the beginning of his kingdom:
> Babel and Erech and Akkad.

Many scholars have speculated that Sargon of Akkad was the biblical Nimrod. If one reads "Kish" for "Kush" in the above biblical verses, it would seem Nimrud was indeed preceded by Kish, as claimed by Sargon. The scholars then began to accept literally the rest of his inscriptions: "He defeated Uruk and tore down its wall . . . he was victorious in the battle with the inhabitants of Ur . . . he defeated the entire territory from Lagash as far as the sea."

Was the biblical Erech identical with the Uruk of Sargon's inscriptions? As the site now called Warka was unearthed, that was found to be the case. And the Ur referred to by Sargon was none other than the biblical Ur, the Mesopotamian birthplace of Abraham.

Not only did the archaeological discoveries vindicate the biblical records; it also appeared certain that there must have been kingdoms and cities and civilizations in Mesopotamia even before the third millennium B.C. The only question was: How far back did one have to go to find the *first* civilized kingdom?

The key that unlocked the puzzle was yet another language.

Scholars quickly realized that names had a meaning not only in Hebrew and in the Old Testament but throughout the ancient Near East. All the Akkadian, Babylonian, and Assyrian names of persons and places had a meaning. But the names of rulers that preceded Sargon of Akkad did not make sense at all: The king at whose court Sargon was a counselor was called Urzababa; the king who reigned in Erech was named Lugalzagesi; and so on.

Lecturing before the Royal Asiatic Society in 1853, Sir Henry Rawlinson pointed out that such names were neither Semitic nor Indo-European; indeed, "they seemed to belong to no known group of languages or peoples." But if names had a meaning, what was the mysterious language in which they had the meaning?

Scholars took another look at the Akkadian inscriptions. Basically, the Akkadian cuneiform script was syllabic: Each sign stood for a complete syllable *(ab, ba, bat,* etc.). Yet the script made extensive use of signs that were not phonetic syllables but conveyed the meanings "god," "city," "country," or "life," "exalted," and the like. The only possible explanation for this phenomenon was that these signs were remains of an earlier writing method which used pictographs. Akkadian, then, must have been preceded by another language that used a writing method akin to the Egyptian hieroglyphs.

It was soon obvious that an earlier language, and not just an earlier form of writing, was involved here. Scholars found that Akkadian inscriptions and texts made extensive use of loanwords—words borrowed intact from another language (in the same way that a modern Frenchman would borrow the English word *weekend).* This was especially true where scientific or technical terminology was involved, and also in matters dealing with the gods and the heavens.

One of the greatest finds of Akkadian texts was the ruins of a library assembled in Nineveh by Ashurbanipal; Layard and his colleagues carted away from the site 25,000 tablets, many of which were described by the ancient scribes as copies of "olden texts." A group of twenty-three tablets ended with the statement: "23rd tablet: language of

Shumer not changed." Another text bore an enigmatic statement by
Ashurbanipal himself:

> The god of scribes has bestowed on me the gift of the knowledge of his art.
> I have been initiated into the secrets of writing.
> I can even read the intricate tablets in Shumerian;
> I understand the enigmatic words in the stone carvings
>   from the days before the Flood.

The claim by Ashurbanipal that he could read intricate tablets in
"Shumerian" and understand the words written on tablets from "the
days before the Flood" only increased the mystery. But in January 1869
Jules Oppert suggested to the French Society of Numismatics and
Archaeology that recognition be given to the existence of a pre-
Akkadian language and people. Pointing out that the early rulers of
Mesopotamia proclaimed their legitimacy by taking the title "King of
Sumer and Akkad," he suggested that the people be called "Sumeri-
ans," and their land, "Sumer."

Except for mispronouncing the name—it should have been *Sh*umer,
not Sumer—Oppert was right. Sumer was not a mysterious, distant land,
but the early name for southern Mesopotamia, just as the Book of
Genesis had clearly stated: The royal cities of Babylon and Akkad and
Erech were in "the Land of Shin'ar." (Shinar was the biblical name for
Shumer.)

Once the scholars had accepted these conclusions, the flood gates
were opened. The Akkadian references to the "olden texts" became
meaningful, and scholars soon realized that tablets with long columns of
words were in fact Akkadian-Sumerian lexicons and dictionaries,
prepared in Assyria and Babylonia for their own study of the first
written language, Sumerian.

Without these dictionaries from long ago, we would still be far from
being able to read Sumerian. With their aid, a vast literary and cultural
treasure opened up. It also became clear that the Sumerian script,
originally pictographic and carved in stone in vertical columns, was
then turned horizontally and, later on, stylized for wedge writing on
soft clay tablets to become the cuneiform writing that was adopted by
the Akkadians, Babylonians, Assyrians, and other nations of the ancient
Near East. (Fig. 7)

The decipherment of the Sumerian language and script, and the
realization that the Sumerians and their culture were the fountainhead
of the Akkadian–Babylonian–Assyrian achievements, spurred archae-

ological searches in southern Mesopotamia. All the evidence now indicated that the beginning was there.

The first significant excavation of a Sumerian site was begun in 1877 by French archaeologists; and the finds from this single site were so extensive that others continued to dig there until 1933 without completing the job.

Called by the natives Telloh ("mound"), the site proved to be an early Sumerian city, the very Lagash of whose conquest Sargon of Akkad had boasted. It was indeed a royal city whose rulers bore the same title Sargon had adopted, except that it was in the Sumerian language: EN.SI ("righteous ruler"). Their dynasty had started circa 2900 B.C. and lasted for nearly 650 years. During this time, forty-three *ensi*'s reigned without interruption in Lagash: Their names, genealogies, and lengths of rule were all neatly recorded.

The inscriptions provided much information. Appeals to the gods "to cause the grain sprouts to grow for harvest . . . to cause the watered plant to yield grain," attest to the existence of agriculture and irrigation. A cup inscribed in honor of a goddess by "the overseer of the granary" indicated that grains were stored, measured, and traded. (Fig. 8)

An *ensi* named Eannatum left an inscription on a clay brick which makes it clear that these Sumerian rulers could assume the throne only with the approval of the gods. He also recorded the conquest of another city, revealing to us the existence of other city-states in Sumer at the beginning of the third millennium B.C.

Eannatum's successor, Entemena, wrote of building a temple and adorning it with gold and silver, planting gardens, enlarging brick-lined wells. He boasted of building a fortress with watchtowers and facilities for docking ships.

One of the better-known rulers of Lagash was Gudea. He had a large number of statuettes made of himself, all showing him in a votive stance, praying to his gods. This stance was no pretense: Gudea had indeed devoted himself to the adoration of Ningirsu, his principal deity, and to the construction and rebuilding of temples.

His many inscriptions reveal that, in the search for exquisite building materials, he obtained gold from Africa and Anatolia, silver from the Taurus Mountains, cedars from Lebanon, other rare woods from Ararat, copper from the Zagros range, diorite from Egypt, carnelian from Ethiopia, and other materials from lands as yet unidentified by scholars.

When Moses built for the Lord God a "Residence" in the desert, he did so according to very detailed instructions provided by the Lord. When King Solomon built the first Temple in Jerusalem, he did so after

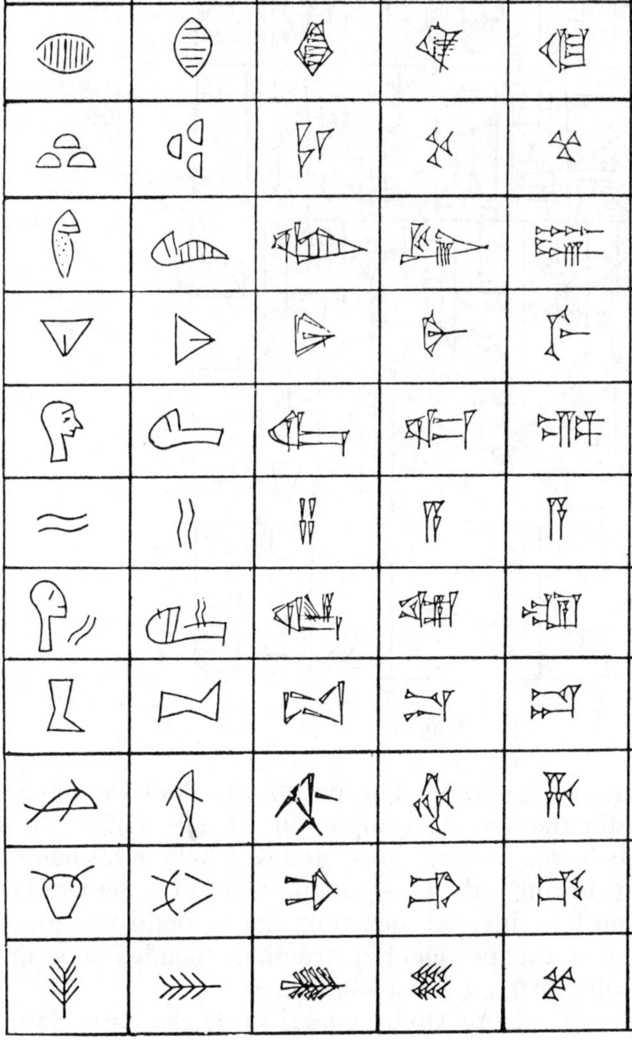

SUMERIAN			CUNEIFORM		Pronun-	Meaning
Original	Turned	Archaic	Common	Assyrian	ciation	
					KI	Earth Land
					KUR	Mountain
					LU	Domestic Man
					SAL MUNUZ	Vulva Woman
					SAG	Head
					A	Water
					NAG	Drink
					DU	Go
					HA	Fish
					GUD	Ox Bull Strong
					SHE	Barley

Fig. 7

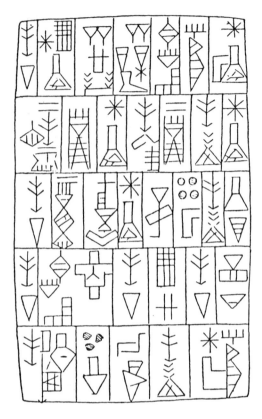

Fig. 8

the Lord had "given him wisdom." The prophet Ezekiel was shown very detailed plans for the Second Temple "in a Godly vision" by a "person who had the appearance of bronze and who held in his hand a flaxen string and a measuring rod." Ur-Nammu, ruler of Ur, depicted in an earlier millennium how his god, ordering him to build for him a temple and giving him the pertinent instructions, handed him the measuring rod and rolled string for the job. (Fig. 9)

Twelve hundred years before Moses, Gudea made the same claim. The instructions, he recorded in one very long inscription, were given to him in a vision. "A man that shone like the heaven," by whose side stood "a divine bird," "commanded me to build his temple." This "man," who "from the crown on his head was obviously a god," was later identified as the god Ningirsu. With him was a goddess who "held the tablet of her favorable star of the heavens"; her other hand "held a holy stylus," with which she indicated to Gudea "the favorable planet." A third man, also a god, held in his hand a tablet of precious stone; "the

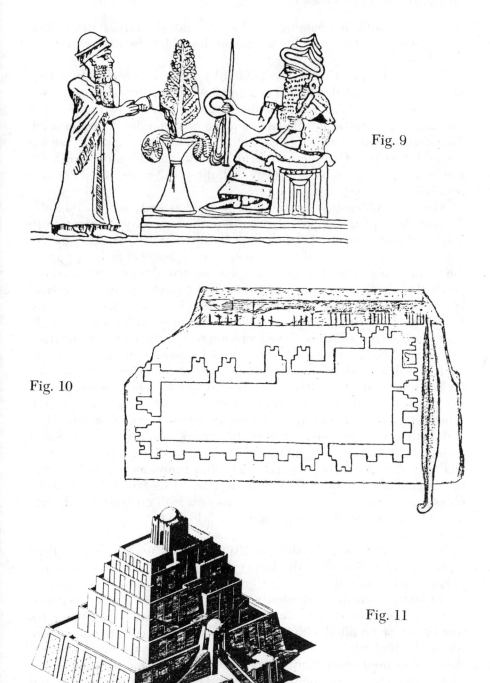

Fig. 9

Fig. 10

Fig. 11

plan of a temple it contained." One of Gudea's statues shows him seated, with this tablet on his knees; on the tablet the divine drawing can clearly be seen. (Fig. 10)

Wise as he was, Gudea was baffled by these architectural instructions, and he sought the advice of a goddess who could interpret divine messages. She explained to him the meaning of the instructions, the plan's measurements, and the size and shape of the bricks to be used. Gudea then employed a male "diviner, maker of decisions" and a female "searcher of secrets" to locate the site, on the city's outskirts, where the god wished his temple to be built. He then recruited 216,000 people for the construction job.

Gudea's bafflement can readily be understood, for the simple-looking "floor plan" supposedly gave him the necessary information to build a complex ziggurat, rising high by seven stages. Writing in *Der Alte Orient* in 1900, A. Billerbeck was able to decipher at least part of the divine architectural instructions. The ancient drawing, even on the partly damaged statue, is accompanied at the top by groups of vertical lines whose number diminishes as the space between them increases. The divine architects, it appears, were able to provide, with a single floor plan, accompanied by seven varying scales, the complete instructions for the construction of a seven-stage high-rise temple.

It has been said that war spurs Man to scientific and material breakthroughs. In ancient Sumer, it seems, temple construction spurred the people and their rulers into greater technological, commercial, transportation, architectural, and organizational achievements. The ability to carry out major construction work according to prepared architectural plans, to organize and feed a huge labor force, to flatten land and raise mounds, to mold bricks and transport stones, to bring rare metals and other materials from afar, to cast metal and shape utensils and ornaments—all clearly speak of a high civilization, already in full bloom in the third millennium B.C. (Fig. 11)

As masterful as even the earliest Sumerian temples were, they represented but the tip of the iceberg of the scope and richness of the material achievements of the first great civilization known to Man.

In addition to the invention and development of writing, without which a high civilization could not have come about, the Sumerians should also be credited with the invention of printing. Millennia before Johann Gutenberg "invented" printing by using movable type, Sumerian scribes used ready-made "type" of the various pictographic signs, which they used as we now use rubber stamps to impress the desired sequence of signs in the wet clay.

They also invented the forerunner of our rotary presses—the cylinder seal. Made of extremely hard stone, it was a small cylinder into which the message or design had been engraved in reverse; whenever the seal was rolled on the wet clay, the imprint created a "positive" impression on the clay. The seal also enabled one to assure the authenticity of documents; a new impression could be made at once to compare it with the old impression on the document. (Fig. 12)

Many Sumerian and Mesopotamian written records concerned themselves not necessarily with the divine or spiritual but with such daily tasks as recording crops, measuring fields, and calculating prices. Indeed, no high civilization would have been possible without a parallel advanced system of mathematics.

The Sumerian system, called sexagesimal, combined a mundane 10 with a "celestial" 6 to obtain the base figure 60. This system is in some respects superior to our present one; in any case, it is unquestionably superior to later Greek and Roman systems. It enabled the Sumerians to divide into fractions and multiply into the millions, to calculate roots or raise numbers several powers. This was not only the first-known mathematical system but also one that gave us the "place" concept: Just as, in the decimal system, 2 can be 2 or 20 or 200, depending on the digit's place, so could a Sumerian 2 mean 2 or 120 (2 × 60), and so on, depending on the "place." (Fig. 13)

The 360-degree circle, the foot and its 12 inches, and the "dozen" as a unit are but a few examples of the vestiges of Sumerian mathematics still evident in our daily life. Their concomitant achievements in astronomy, the establishment of a calendar, and similar mathematical-celestial feats will receive much closer study in coming chapters.

Just as our own economic and social system—our books, court and tax records, commercial contracts, marriage certificates, and so on—depends on paper, Sumerian/Mesopotamian life depended on clay. Temples, courts, and trading houses had their scribes ready with tablets of wet clay on which to inscribe decisions, agreements, letters, or calculate prices, wages, the area of a field, or the number of bricks required in a construction.

Clay was also a crucial raw material for the manufacture of utensils for daily use and containers for storage and transportation of goods. It was also used to make bricks—another Sumerian "first," which made possible the building of houses for the people, palaces for the kings, and imposing temples for the gods.

The Sumerians are credited with two technological breakthroughs that made it possible to combine lightness with tensile strength for all clay products: reinforcing and firing. Modern architects have discovered that reinforced concrete, an extremely strong building material, can be created by pouring cement into molds containing iron rods; long ago, the Sumerians gave their bricks great strength by mixing the wet clay with chopped reeds or straw. They also knew that clay products could be given tensile strength and durability by firing them in a kiln. The world's first high-rise buildings and archways, as well as durable ceramic wares, were made possible by these technological breakthroughs.

The invention of the kiln—a furnace in which intense but controllable temperatures could be attained without the risk of contaminating products with dust or ashes—made possible an even greater technological advance: the Age of Metals.

It has been assumed that man discovered that he could hammer "soft stones"—naturally occurring nuggets of gold as well as copper and silver compounds—into useful or pleasing shapes, sometime about 6000 B.C. The first hammered-metal artifacts were found in the highlands of the Zagros and Taurus mountains. However, as R. J. Forbes (*The Birthplace of Old World Metallurgy*) pointed out, "in the ancient Near East, the supply of native copper was quickly exhausted, and the miner had to turn to ores." This required the knowledge and ability to find and extract the ores, crush them, then smelt and refine them—processes that could not have been carried out without kiln-type furnaces and a generally advanced technology.

The art of metallurgy soon encompassed the ability to alloy copper with other metals, resulting in a castable, hard, but malleable metal we call bronze. The Bronze Age, our first metallurgical age, was also a Mesopotamian contribution to modern civilization. Much of ancient commerce was devoted to the metals trade; it also formed the basis for the development in Mesopotamia of banking and the first money—the silver *shekel* ("weighed ingot").

The many varieties of metals and alloys for which Sumerian and Akkadian names have been found and the extensive technological terminology attest to the high level of metallurgy in ancient Mesopotamia. For a while this puzzled the scholars because Sumer, as such, was devoid of metal ores, yet metallurgy most definitely began there.

The answer is energy. Smelting, refining, and alloying, as well as casting, could not be done without ample supplies of fuels to fire the kilns, crucibles, and furnaces. Mesopotamia may have lacked ores, but it had fuels in abundance. So the ores were brought to the fuels, which explains many early inscriptions describing the bringing of metal ores from afar.

The fuels that made Sumer technologically supreme were bitumens

Fig. 12

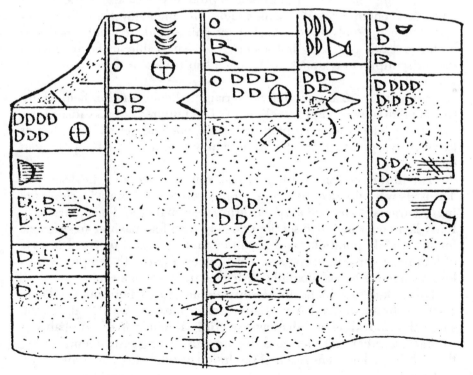

Fig. 13

and asphalts, petroleum products that naturally seeped up to the surface in many places in Mesopotamia. R. J. Forbes *(Bitumen and Petroleum in Antiquity)* shows that the surface deposits of Mesopotamia were the ancient world's prime source of fuels from the earliest times to the Roman era. His conclusion is that the technological use of these petroleum products began in Sumer circa 3500 B.C.; indeed, he shows that the use and knowledge of the fuels and their properties were greater in Sumerian times than in later civilizations.

So extensive was the Sumerian use of these petroleum products—not only as fuel but also as road-building materials, for waterproofing, caulking, painting, cementing, and molding—that when archaeologists searched for ancient Ur they found it buried in a mound that the local Arabs called "Mound of Bitumen." Forbes shows that the Sumerian language had terms for every genus and variant of the bituminous substances found in Mesopotamia. Indeed, the names of bituminous and petroleum materials in other languages—Akkadian, Hebrew, Egyptian, Coptic, Greek, Latin, and Sanskrit—can clearly be traced to the Sumerian origins; for example, the most common word for petroleum—*naphta*—derives from *napatu* ("stones that flare up").

The Sumerian use of petroleum products was also basic to an advanced chemistry. We can judge the high level of Sumerian knowledge not only by the variety of paints and pigments used and such processes as glazing but also by the remarkable artificial production of semiprecious stones, including a substitute for lapis lazuli.

Bitumens were also used in Sumerian medicine, another field where the standards were impressively high. The hundreds of Akkadian texts that have been found employ Sumerian medical terms and phrases extensively, pointing to the Sumerian origin of all Mesopotamian medicine.

The library of Ashurbanipal in Nineveh included a medical section. The texts were divided into three groups—*bultitu* ("therapy"), *shipir bel imti* ("surgery") and *urti mashmashshe* ("commands and incantations"). Early law codes included sections dealing with fees payable to surgeons for successful operations, and penalties to be imposed on them in case of failure: A surgeon, using a lancet to open a patient's temple, was to lose his hand if he accidentally destroyed the patient's eye.

Some skeletons found in Mesopotamian graves bore unmistakable marks of brain surgery. A partially broken medical text speaks of the surgical removal of a "shadow covering a man's eye," probably a cataract; another text mentions the use of a cutting instrument, stating that "if the sickness has reached the inside of the bone, you shall scrape and remove."

Sick persons in Sumerian times could choose between an A.ZU ("water physician") and an IA.ZU ("oil physician"). A tablet excavated in Ur, nearly 5,000 years old, names a medical practitioner as "Lulu, the doctor." There were also veterinarians—known either as "doctors of oxen" or as "doctors of asses."

A pair of surgical tongs is depicted on a very early cylinder seal, found at Lagash, that belonged to "Urlugaledina, the doctor." The seal also shows the serpent on a tree—the symbol of medicine to this day. (Fig. 14) An instrument that was used by midwives to cut the umbilical cord was also frequently depicted.

Fig. 14

Sumerian medical texts deal with diagnosis and prescriptions. They leave no doubt that the Sumerian physician did not resort to magic or sorcery. He recommended cleaning and washing; soaking in baths of hot water and mineral solvents; application of vegetable derivatives; rubbing with petroleum compounds.

Medicines were made from plant and mineral compounds and were mixed with liquids or solvents appropriate to the method of application. If taken by mouth, the powders were mixed into wine, beer, or honey; if "poured through the rectum"—administered in an enema— they were mixed with plant or vegetable oils. Alcohol, which plays such an important role in surgical disinfection and as a base for many medicines, reached our languages through the Arabic kohl, from the Akkadian kuhlu.

Models of livers indicate that medicine was taught at medical schools with the aid of clay models of human organs. Anatomy must have been an advanced science, for temple rituals called for elaborate dissections of sacrificial animals—only a step removed from comparable knowledge of human anatomy.

Several depictions on cylinder seals or clay tablets show people lying on some kind of surgical table, surrounded by teams of gods or people. We know from epics and other heroic texts that the Sumerians and their successors in Mesopotamia were concerned with matters of life, sickness, and death. Men like Gilgamesh, a king of Erech, sought the "Tree of Life" or some mineral (a "stone") that could provide eternal youth. There were also references to efforts to resurrect the dead, especially if they happened to be gods:

> Upon the corpse, hung from the pole,
> they directed the Pulse and the Radiance;
> Sixty times the Water of Life,
> Sixty times the Food of Life,
> they sprinkled upon it;
> And Inanna arose.

Were some ultramodern methods, about which we can only speculate, known and used in such revival attempts? That radioactive materials were known and used to treat certain ailments is certainly suggested by a scene of medical treatment depicted on a cylinder seal dating to the very beginning of Sumerian civilization. It shows, without question, a man lying on a special bed; his face is protected by a mask, and he is being subjected to some kind of radiation. (Fig. 15)

One of Sumer's earliest material achievements was the development of textile and clothing industries.

Our own Industrial Revolution is considered to have commenced with the introduction of spinning and weaving machines in England in the 1760s. Most developing nations have aspired ever since to develop a textile industry as the first step toward industrialization. The evidence shows that this has been the process not only since the eighteenth

Fig. 15

century but ever since man's first great civilization. Man could not have made woven fabrics before the advent of agriculture, which provided him with flax, and the domestication of animals, creating a source for wool. Grace M. Crowfoot (*Textiles, Basketry and Mats in Antiquity*) expressed the scholastic consensus by stating that textile weaving appeared first in Mesopotamia, around 3800 B.C.

Sumer, moreover, was renowned in ancient times not only for its woven fabrics, but also for its apparel. The Book of Joshua (7:21) reports that during the storming of Jericho a certain person could not resist the temptation to keep "one good coat of Shin'ar," which he had found in the city, even though the penalty was death. So highly prized were the garments of Shinar (Sumer), that people were willing to risk their lives to obtain them.

A rich terminology already existed in Sumerian times to describe both items of clothing and their makers. The basic garment was called TUG—without doubt, the forerunner in style as well as in name of the Roman toga. Such garments were TUG.TU.SHE, which in Sumerian meant "garment which is worn wrapped around." (Fig. 16)

The ancient depictions reveal not only an astonishing variety and opulence in matters of clothing, but also elegance, in which good taste and coordination among clothes, hairdos, headdresses, and jewelry prevailed. (Figs. 17, 18)

Another major Sumerian achievement was its agriculture. In a land with only seasonal rains, the rivers were enlisted to water year-round crops through a vast system of irrigation canals.

Mesopotamia—the Land Between the Rivers—was a veritable food basket in ancient times. The apricot tree, the Spanish word for which is *damasco* ("Damascus tree"), bears the Latin name *armeniaca*, a loanword from the Akkadian *armanu*. The cherry—*kerasos* in Greek, *Kirsche* in German—originates from the Akkadian *karshu*. All the evidence suggests that these and other fruits and vegetables reached Europe from Mesopotamia. So did many special seeds and spices: Our word *saffron* comes from the Akkadian *azupiranu*, *crocus* from *kurkanu* (via *krokos* in Greek), *cumin* from *kamanu*, *hyssop* from *zupu*, *myrrh* from *murru*. The list is long; in many instances, Greece provided the physical and etymological bridge by which these products of the land reached Europe. Onions, lentils, beans, cucumbers, cabbage, and lettuce were common ingredients of the Sumerian diet.

What is equally impressive is the extent and variety of the ancient Mesopotamian food-preparation methods, their cuisine. Texts and pictures confirm the Sumerian knowledge of converting the cereals they had grown into flour, from which they made a variety of leavened and unleavened breads, porridges, pastries, cakes, and biscuits. Barley was also fermented to produce beer; "technical manuals" for beer production have been found among the texts. Wine was obtained from grapes and from date palms. Milk was available from sheep, goats, and cows; it was used as a beverage, for cooking, and for converting into yogurt, butter, cream, and cheeses. Fish was a common part of the diet. Mutton was readily available, and the meat of pigs, which the Sumerians tended in large herds, was considered a true delicacy. Geese and ducks may have been reserved for the gods' tables.

The ancient texts leave no doubt that the haute cuisine of ancient Mesopotamia developed in the temples and in the service of the gods. One text prescribed the offering to the gods of "loaves of barley bread . . . loaves of emmer bread; a paste of honey and cream; dates, pastry . . . beer, wine, milk . . . cedar sap, cream." Roasted meat was offered with libations of "prime beer, wine, and milk." A specific cut of a bull was prepared according to a strict recipe, calling for "fine flour . . . made to a dough in water, prime beer, and wine," and mixed with animal fats, "aromatic ingredients made from hearts of plants," nuts, malt, and spices. Instructions for "the daily sacrifice to the gods of the city of Uruk" called for the serving of five different beverages with the meals, and specified what "the millers in the kitchen" and "the chef working at the kneading trough" should do.

Our admiration for the Sumerian culinary art certainly grows as we come across poems that sing the praises of fine foods. Indeed, what can one say when one reads a millennias-old recipe for "coq au vin":

In the wine of drinking,
In the scented water,
In the oil of unction—
This bird have I cooked,
and have eaten.

A thriving economy, a society with such extensive material enterprises could not have developed without an efficient system of transportation. The Sumerians used their two great rivers and the artificial network of canals for waterborne transportation of people, goods, and cattle. Some of the earliest depictions show what were undoubtedly the world's first boats.

We know from many early texts that the Sumerians also engaged in deep-water seafaring, using a variety of ships to reach faraway lands in search of metals, rare woods and stones, and other materials unobtainable in Sumer proper. An Akkadian dictionary of the Sumerian language was found to contain a section on shipping, listing 105

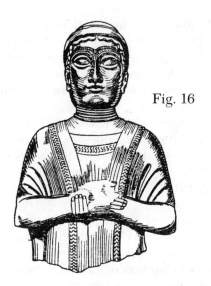

Fig. 16

Fig. 17

Fig. 18

Sumerian terms for various ships by their size, destination, or purpose (for cargo, for passengers, or for the exclusive use of certain gods). Another 69 Sumerian terms connected with the manning and construction of ships were translated into the Akkadian. Only a long seafaring tradition could have produced such specialized vessels and technical terminology.

For overland transportation, the wheel was first used in Sumer. Its invention and introduction into daily life made possible a variety of vehicles, from carts to chariots, and no doubt also granted Sumer the distinction of having been the first to employ "ox power" as well as "horse power" for locomotion. (Fig. 19)

In 1956 Professor Samuel N. Kramer, one of the great Sumerologists of our time, reviewed the literary legacy found beneath the mounds of Sumer. The table of contents of *From the Tablets of Sumer* is a gem in itself, for each one of the twenty-five chapters described a Sumerian "first," including the first schools, the first bicameral congress, the first historian, the first pharmacopoeia, the first "farmer's almanac," the first cosmogony and cosmology, the first "Job," the first proverbs and sayings, the first literary debates, the first "Noah," the first library catalogue; and Man's first Heroic Age, his first law codes and social reforms, his first medicine, agriculture, and search for world peace and harmony.

This is no exaggeration.

The first schools were established in Sumer as a direct outgrowth of the invention and introduction of writing. The evidence (both archaeological, such as actual school buildings, and written, such as exercise tablets) indicates the existence of a formal system of education by the

Fig. 19

beginning of the third millennium B.C. There were literally thousands of scribes in Sumer, ranging from junior scribes to high scribes, royal scribes, temple scribes, and scribes who assumed high state office. Some acted as teachers at the schools, and we can still read their essays on the schools, their aims and goals, their curriculum and teaching methods.

The schools taught not only language and writing but also the sciences of the day—botany, zoology, geography, mathematics, and theology. Literary works of the past were studied and copied, and new ones were composed.

The schools were headed by the *ummia* ("expert professor"), and the faculty invariably included not only a "man in charge of drawing" and a "man in charge of Sumerian," but also a "man in charge of the whip." Apparently, discipline was strict; one school alumnus described on a clay tablet how he had been flogged for missing school, for insufficient neatness, for loitering, for not keeping silent, for misbehaving, and even for not having neat handwriting.

An epic poem dealing with the history of Erech concerns itself with the rivalry between Erech and the city-state of Kish. The epic text relates how the envoys of Kish proceeded to Erech, offering a peaceful settlement of their dispute. But the ruler of Erech at the time, Gilgamesh, preferred to fight rather than negotiate. What is interesting is that he had to put the matter to a vote in the Assembly of the Elders, the local "Senate":

> The lord Gilgamesh,
> Before the elders of his city put the matter,
> Seeks out the decision:
> "Let us not submit to the house of Kish,
> let us smite it with weapons."

The Assembly of the Elders was, however, for negotiations. Undaunted, Gilgamesh took the matter to the younger people, the Assembly of the Fighting Men, who voted for war. The significance of the tale lies in its disclosure that a Sumerian ruler had to submit the question of war or peace to the first bicameral congress, some 5,000 years ago.

The title of First Historian was bestowed by Kramer on Entemena, king of Lagash, who recorded on clay cylinders his war with neighboring Umma. While other texts were literary works or epic poems whose themes were historical events, the inscriptions by Entemena were straight prose, written solely as a factual record of history.

Because the inscriptions of Assyria and Babylonia were deciphered well before the Sumerian records, it was long believed that the first code of laws was compiled and decreed by the Babylonian king Hammurabi, circa 1900 B.C. But as Sumer's civilization was uncovered, it became clear that the "firsts" for a system of laws, for concepts of social order, and for the fair administration of justice belonged to Sumer.

Well before Hammurabi, a Sumerian ruler of the city-state of Eshnunna (northeast of Babylon) encoded laws that set maximum prices for foodstuffs and for the rental of wagons and boats so that the poor could not be oppressed. There were also laws dealing with offenses against person and property, and regulations pertaining to family matters and to master–servant relations.

Even earlier, a code was promulgated by Lipit-Ishtar, a ruler of Isin. The thirty-eight laws that remain legible on the partly preserved tablet (a copy of original that was engraved on a stone stela) deal with real estate, slaves and servants, marriage and inheritance, the hiring of boats, the rental of oxen, and defaults on taxes. As was done by Hammurabi after him, Lipit-Ishtar explained in the prologue to his code that he acted on the instructions of "the great gods," who had ordered him "to bring well-being to the Sumerians and the Akkadians."

Yet even Lipit-Ishtar was not the first Sumerian law encoder. Fragments of clay tablets that have been found contain copies of laws encoded by Urnammu, a ruler of Ur circa 2350 B.C.—more than half a millennium before Hammurabi. The laws, enacted on the authority of the god Nannar, were aimed at stopping and punishing "the grabbers of the citizens' oxen, sheep, and donkeys" so that "the orphan shall not fall prey to the wealthy, the widow shall not fall prey to the powerful, the man of one shekel shall not fall prey to a man of 60 shekels." Urnammu also decreed "honest and unchangeable weights and measurements."

But the Sumerian legal system, and the enforcement of justice, go back even farther in time.

By 2600 B.C. so much must already have happened in Sumer that the *ensi* Urukagina found it necessary to institute reforms. A long inscription by him has been called by scholars a precious record of man's first social reform based on a sense of freedom, equality, and justice—a "French Revolution" imposed by a king 4,400 years before July 14, 1789.

The reform decree of Urukagina listed the evils of his time first, then the reforms. The evils consisted primarily of the unfair use by supervisors of their powers to take the best for themselves; the abuse of official status; the extortion of high prices by monopolistic groups.

All such injustices, and many more, were prohibited by the reform decree. An official could no longer set his own price "for a good donkey or a house." A "big man" could no longer coerce a common citizen.

The rights of the blind, poor, widowed, and orphaned were restated. A divorced woman—nearly 5,000 years ago—was granted the protection of the law.

How long had Sumerian civilization existed that it required a major reform? Clearly, a long time, for Urukagina claimed that it was his god Ningirsu who called upon him "to restore the decrees of former days." The clear implication is that a return to even older systems and earlier laws was called for.

The Sumerian laws were upheld by a court system in which the proceedings and judgments as well as contracts were meticulously recorded and preserved. The justices acted more like juries than judges; a court was usually made up of three or four judges, one of whom was a professional "royal judge" and the others drawn from a panel of thirty-six men.

While the Babylonians made rules and regulations, the Sumerians were concerned with justice, for they believed that the gods appointed the kings primarily to assure justice in the land.

More than one parallel can be drawn here with the concepts of justice and morality of the Old Testament. Even before the Hebrews had kings, they were governed by judges; kings were judged not by their conquests or wealth but by the extent to which they "did the righteous thing." In the Jewish religion, the New Year marks a ten-day period during which the deeds of men are weighed and evaluated to determine their fate in the coming year. It is probably more than a coincidence that the Sumerians believed that a deity named Nanshe annually judged Mankind in the same manner; after all, the first Hebrew patriarch—Abraham—came from the Sumerian city of Ur, the city of Ur-Nammu and his code.

The Sumerian concern with justice or its absence also found expression in what Kramer called "the first 'Job.'" Matching together fragments of clay tablets at the Istanbul Museum of Antiquities, Kramer was able to read a good part of a Sumerian poem which, like the biblical Book of Job, dealt with the complaint of a righteous man who, instead of being blessed by the gods, was made to suffer all manner of loss and disrespect. "My righteous word has been turned into a lie," he cried out in anguish.

In its second part, the anonymous sufferer petitions his god in a manner akin to some verses in the Hebrew Psalms:

My god, you who are my father,
who begot me—lift up my face. . . .
How long will you neglect me,
leave me unprotected . . .
leave me without guidance?

Then follows a happy ending. "The righteous words, the pure words uttered by him, his god accepted; . . . his god withdrew his hand from the evil pronouncement."

Preceding the biblical Book of Ecclesiastes by some two millennia, Sumerian proverbs conveyed many of the same concepts and witticisms.

> If we are doomed to die—let us spend;
> If we shall live long—let us save.

> When a poor man dies, do not try to revive him.

> He who possesses much silver, may be happy;
> He who possesses much barley, may be happy;
> But who has nothing at all, can sleep!

> Man: For his pleasure: Marriage;
> On his thinking it over: Divorce.

> It is not the heart which leads to enmity;
> it is the tongue which leads to enmity.

> In a city without watchdogs,
> the fox is the overseer.

The material and spiritual achievements of the Sumerian civilization were also accompanied by an extensive development of the performing arts. A team of scholars from the University of California at Berkeley made news in March 1974 when they announced that they had deciphered the world's oldest song. What professors Richard L. Crocker, Anne D. Kilmer, and Robert R. Brown achieved was to read and actually play the musical notes written on a cuneiform tablet from circa 1800 B.C., found at Ugarit on the Mediterranean coast (now in Syria).

"We always knew," the Berkeley team explained, "that there was music in the earlier Assyrio-Babylonian civilization, but until this deciphering we did not know that it had the same heptatonic-diatonic scale that is characteristic of contemporary Western music, and of Greek music of the first millennium B.C." Until now it was thought that Western music originated in Greece; now it has been established that our music—as so much else of Western civilization—originated in Mesopotamia. This should not be surprising, for the Greek scholar Philo had already stated that the Mesopotamians were known to "seek worldwide harmony and unison through the musical tones."

There can be no doubt that music and song must also be claimed as a Sumerian "first." Indeed, Professor Crocker could play the ancient tune only by constructing a lyre like those which had been found in the ruins of Ur. Texts from the second millennium B.C. indicate the existence of musical "key numbers" and a coherent musical theory; and Professor Kilmer herself wrote earlier *(The Strings of Musical Instruments: Their Names, Numbers and Significance)* that many Sumerian hymnal texts had "what appear to be musical notations in the margins." "The Sumerians and their successors had a full musical life," she concluded. No wonder, then, that we find a great variety of musical instruments—as well as of singers and dancers performing—depicted on cylinder seals and clay tablets. (Fig. 20)

Fig. 20

Like so many other Sumerian achievements, music and song also originated in the temples. But, beginning in the service of the gods, these performing arts soon were also prevalent outside the temples. Employing the favorite Sumerian play on words, a popular saying commented on the fees charged by singers: "A singer whose voice is not sweet is a 'poor' singer indeed."

Many Sumerian love songs have been found; they were undoubtedly sung to musical accompaniment. Most touching, however, is a lullaby that a mother composed and sang to her sick child:

Come sleep, come sleep, come to my son.
Hurry sleep to my son;
Put to sleep his restless eyes. . . .

You are in pain, my son;
I am troubled, I am struck dumb,
I gaze up to the stars.
The new moon shines down on your face;
Your shadow will shed tears for you.
Lie, lie in your sleep. . . .

May the goddess of growth be your ally;
May you have an eloquent guardian in heaven;
May you achieve a reign of happy days. . . .
May a wife be your support;
May a son be your future lot.

What is striking about such music and songs is not only the conclusion that Sumer was the source of Western music in structure and harmonic composition. No less significant is the fact that as we hear the music and read the poems, they do not sound strange or alien at all, even in their depth of feeling and their sentiments. Indeed, as we contemplate the great Sumerian civilization, we find that not only are *our* morals and *our* sense of justice, *our* laws and architecture and arts and technology rooted in Sumer, but the Sumerian institutions are so familiar, so close. At heart, it would seem, we are all Sumerians.

After excavating at Lagash, the archaeologist's spade uncovered Nippur, the onetime religious center of Sumer and Akkad. Of the 30,000 texts found there, many remain unstudied to this day. At Shuruppak, schoolhouses dating to the third millennium B.C. were found. At Ur, scholars found magnificent vases, jewelry, weapons, chariots, helmets made of gold, silver, copper, and bronze, the remains of a weaving factory, court records—and a towering ziggurat whose ruins still dominate the landscape. At Eshnunna and Adab the archaeologists found temples and artful statues from pre-Sargonic times. Umma produced inscriptions speaking of early empires. At Kish monumental buildings and a ziggurat from at least 3000 B.C. were unearthed.

Uruk (Erech) took the archaeologists back into the fourth millennium B.C. There they found the first colored pottery baked in a kiln, and evidence of the first use of a potter's wheel. A pavement of limestone blocks is the oldest stone construction found to date. At Uruk the archaeologists also found the first ziggurat—a vast man-made mound, on top of which stood a white temple and a red temple. The world's first inscribed texts were also found there, as well as the first cylinder seals. Of the latter, Jack Finegan (*Light from the Ancient Past*) said, "The excellence of the seals upon their first appearance in the Uruk period is amazing." Other sites of the Uruk period bear evidence of the emergence of the Metal Age.

In 1919, H. R. Hall came upon ancient ruins at a village now called El-Ubaid. The site gave its name to what scholars now consider the first phase of the great Sumerian civilization. Sumerian cities of that period—ranging from northern Mesopotamia to the southern Zagros foothills—produced the first use of clay bricks, plastered walls, mosaic decorations, cemeteries with brick-lined graves, painted and decorated ceramic wares with geometric designs, copper mirrors, beads of imported turquoise, paint for eyelids, copper-headed "tomahawks," cloth, houses, and, above all, monumental temple buildings.

Farther south, the archaeologists found Eridu—the first Sumerian city, according to ancient texts. As the excavators dug deeper, they came upon a temple dedicated to Enki, Sumer's God of Knowledge, which appeared to have been built and rebuilt many times over. The strata clearly led the scholars back to the beginnings of Sumerian civilization: 2500 B.C., 2800 B.C., 3000 B.C., 3500 B.C.

Then the spades came upon the foundations of the first temple dedicated to Enki. Below that, there was virgin soil—nothing had been built before. The time was circa 3800 B.C. That is when civilization began.

It was not only the first civilization in the true sense of the term. It was a most extensive civilization, all-encompassing, in many ways more advanced than the other ancient cultures that had followed it. It was undoubtedly the civilization on which our own is based.

Having begun to use stones as tools some 2,000,000 years earlier, Man achieved this unprecedented civilization in Sumer circa 3800 B.C. And the perplexing fact about this is that to this very day the scholars have no inkling who the Sumerians were, where they came from, and how and why their civilization appeared.

For its appearance was sudden, unexpected, and out of nowhere.

H. Frankfort (Tell Uqair) called it "astonishing." Pierre Amiet (Elam) termed it "extraordinary." A. Parrot (Sumer) described it as "a flame which blazed up so suddenly." Leo Oppenheim (Ancient Mesopotamia) stressed "the astonishingly short period" within which this civilization had arisen. Joseph Campbell (The Masks of God) summed it up in this way: "With stunning abruptness . . . there appears in this little Sumerian mud garden . . . the whole cultural syndrome that has since constituted the germinal unit of all the high civilizations of the world."

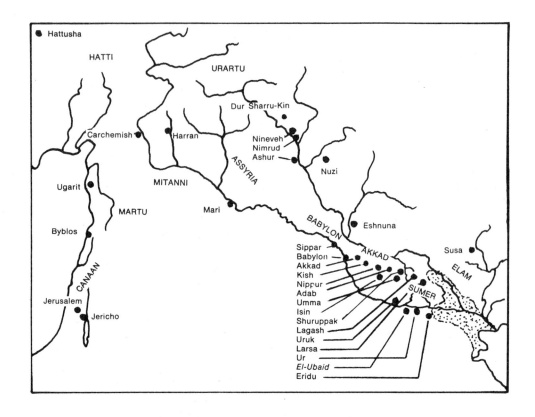

- Hattusha
- HATTI
- URARTU
- Dur Sharru-Kin
- Carchemish
- Harran
- Nineveh
- Nimrud
- Ashur
- Nuzi
- Ugarit
- MITANNI
- ASSYRIA
- MARTU
- Mari
- BABYLON
- Byblos
- Eshnuna
- Susa
- AKKAD
- Sippar
- Babylon
- Akkad
- ELAM
- CANAAN
- Kish
- Nippur
- Adab
- SUMER
- Jerusalem
- Umma
- Jericho
- Isin
- Shuruppak
- Lagash
- Uruk
- Larsa
- Ur
- El-Ubaid
- Eridu

Napoleon conquers Europe
American Revolution

Columbus discovers America
Byzantine empire falls to Turks
Inca empire arises in South America
Aztec civilization in Mexico
Magna Carta granted by King John
Norman conquest of England

Charlemagne forms Holy Roman Empire

Muhammed proclaims Islam

Sack of Rome

Maya civilization in Central America

Jerusalem falls to Roman legions

Jesus of Nazareth

Hannibal challenges Rome
Great Wall begun in China
Alexander defeats Darius
Greek Classical age begins
Roman republic founded
Buddha rises in India
Cyrus captures Babylon
Fall of Nineveh

David king in Jerusalem
Dorian invasion of Greece
Israelite Exodus from Egypt

Mycenaean culture begins
Aryans migrate to India
Hittite empire rises
Abraham migrates from Ur
Hammurabi king in Babylon
Rise of Babylon & Assyria

Chinese civilization begins
Indus valley civilization
Hurrians arrive in Near East
Gudea rules in Lagash
Ur-Nammu rules in Ur

Sargon first king of Akkad
Minoan Civilization in Crete
Gilgamesh rules in Erech

Etana rules in Kish
Egyptian civilization begins

Kingship begins in Kish

Sumerian civilization begins in Eridu

| 2000 AD | 1000 AD | 0 | 1000 BC | 2000 BC | 3000 BC | 4000 BC |

3
·

GODS OF HEAVEN AND EARTH

What was it that after hundreds of thousands and even millions of years of painfully slow human development abruptly changed everything so completely, and in a one–two–three punch—circa 11,000–7400–3800 B.C.—transformed primitive nomadic hunters and food gatherers into farmers and pottery makers, and then into builders of cities, engineers, mathematicians, astronomers, metallurgists, merchants, musicians, judges, doctors, authors, librarians, priests? One can go further and ask an even more basic question, so well stated by Professor Robert J. Braidwood *(Prehistoric Men):* "Why did it happen at all? Why are all human beings not still living as the Maglemosians did?"

The Sumerians, the people through whom this high civilization so suddenly came into being, had a ready answer. It was summed up by one of the tens of thousands of ancient Mesopotamian inscriptions that have been uncovered: "Whatever seems beautiful, we made by the grace of the gods."

The gods of Sumer. Who were they?

Were the gods of the Sumerians like the Greek gods, who were described as living at a great court, feasting in the Great Hall of Zeus in the heavens—Olympus, whose counterpart on earth was Greece's highest peak, Mount Olympus?

The Greeks described their gods as anthropomorphic, as physically similar to mortal men and women, and human in character: They could be happy and angry and jealous; they made love, quarreled, fought; and they procreated like humans, bringing forth offspring through sexual intercourse—with each other or with humans.

They were unreachable, and yet they were constantly mixed up in human affairs. They could travel about at immense speeds, appear and disappear; they had weapons of immense and unusual power. Each had specific functions, and, as a result, a specific human activity could suffer or benefit by the attitude of the god in charge of that particular activity; therefore, rituals of worship and offerings to the gods were supposed to gain their favor.

The principal deity of the Greeks during their Hellenic civilization was Zeus, "Father of Gods and Men," "Master of the Celestial Fire." His chief weapon and symbol was the thunderbolt. He was a "king" upon earth who had descended from the heavens; a decision maker and the dispenser of good and evil to mortals, yet one whose original domain was in the skies.

He was neither the first god upon Earth nor the first deity to have been in the heavens. Mixing theology with cosmology to come up with what scholars treat as mythology, the Greeks believed that first there was Chaos; then Gaea (Earth) and her consort Uranus (the heavens) appeared. Gaea and Uranus brought forth the twelve Titans, six males and six females. Though their legendary deeds took place on Earth, it is assumed that they had astral counterparts.

Cronus, the youngest male Titan, emerged as the principal figure in Olympian mythology. He rose to supremacy among the Titans through usurpation, after castrating his father Uranus. Fearful of the other Titans, Cronus imprisoned and banished them. For that, he was cursed by his mother: He would suffer the same fate as his father, and be dethroned by one of his own sons.

Cronus consorted with his own sister Rhea, who bore him three sons and three daughters: Hades, Poseidon, and Zeus; Hestia, Demeter, and Hera. Once again, it was fated that the youngest son would be the one to depose his father, and the curse of Gaea came true when Zeus overthrew Cronus, his father.

The overthrow, it would seem, did not go smoothly. For many years battles between the gods and a host of monstrous beings ensued. The decisive battle was between Zeus and Typhon, a serpent-like deity. The fighting ranged over wide areas, on Earth and in the skies. The final battle took place at Mount Casius, near the boundary between Egypt and Arabia—apparently somewhere in the Sinai Peninsula. (Fig. 21)

Having won the struggle, Zeus was recognized as the supreme deity. Nevertheless, he had to share control with his brothers. By choice (or, according to one version, through the throwing of lots), Zeus was given control of the skies, the eldest brother Hades was accorded the Lower World, and the middle brother Poseidon was given mastery of the seas.

Though in time Hades and his region became a synonym for Hell, his original domain was a territory somewhere "far below," encompassing marshlands, desolate areas, and lands watered by mighty rivers. Hades was depicted as "the unseen"—aloof, forbidding, stern; unmoved by prayer or sacrifice. Poseidon, on the other hand, was frequently seen holding up his symbol (the trident). Though ruler of the seas, he was

Fig. 21

also master of the arts of metallurgy and sculpting, as well as a crafty magician or conjurer. While Zeus was depicted in Greek tradition and legend as strict with Mankind—even as one who at one point schemed to annihilate Mankind—Poseidon was considered a friend of Mankind and a god who went to great lengths to gain the praise of mortals.

The three brothers and their three sisters, all children of Cronus by his sister Rhea, made up the older part of the Olympian Circle, the group of Twelve Great Gods. The other six were all offspring of Zeus, and the Greek tales dealt mostly with their genealogies and relationships.

The male and female deities fathered by Zeus were mothered by different goddesses. Consorting at first with a goddess named Metis, Zeus had born to him a daughter, the great goddess Athena. She was in charge of common sense and handiwork, and was thus the Goddess of Wisdom. But as the only major deity to have stayed with Zeus during his combat with Typhon (all the other gods had fled), Athena acquired martial qualities and was also the Goddess of War. She was the "perfect maiden" and became no one's wife; but some tales link her frequently with her uncle Poseidon, and though his official consort was the goddess who was the Lady of the Labyrinth from the island of Crete, his niece Athena was his mistress.

Zeus then consorted with other goddesses, but their children did not qualify for the Olympian Circle. When Zeus got around to the serious business of producing a male heir, he turned to one of his own sisters. The eldest was Hestia. She was, by all accounts, a recluse—perhaps too old or too sick to be the object of matrimonial activities—and Zeus needed little excuse to turn his attentions to Demeter, the middle sister, the Goddess of Fruitfulness. But, instead of a son, she bore him a daughter, Persephone, who became wife to her uncle Hades and shared his dominion over the Lower World.

Disappointed that no son was born, Zeus turned to other goddesses for comfort and love. Of Harmonia he had nine daughters. Then Leto bore him a daughter and a son, Artemis and Apollo, who were at once drawn into the group of major deities.

Apollo, as firstborn son of Zeus, was one of the greatest gods of the Hellenic pantheon, feared by men and gods alike. He was the interpreter to mortals of the will of his father Zeus, and thus the authority in matters of religious law and temple worship. Representing moral and divine laws, he stood for purification and perfection, both spiritual and physical.

Zeus's second son, born of the goddess Maia, was Hermes, patron of shepherds, guardian of the flocks and herds. Less important and powerful than his brother Apollo, he was closer to human affairs; any stroke of good luck was attributed to him. As Giver of Good Things, he was the deity in charge of commerce, patron of merchants and travelers. But his main role in myth and epic was as herald of Zeus, Messenger of the Gods.

Impelled by certain dynastic traditions, Zeus still required a son by one of his sisters—and he turned to the youngest, Hera. Marrying her in the rites of a Sacred Marriage, Zeus proclaimed her Queen of the Gods, the Mother Goddess. Their marriage was blessed by a son, Ares, and two daughters, but rocked by constant infidelities on the part of Zeus, as well as a rumored infidelity on the part of Hera, which cast doubt on the true parentage of another son, Hephaestus.

Ares was at once incorporated into the Olympian Circle of twelve major gods and was made Zeus's chief lieutenant, a God of War. He was depicted as the Spirit of Carnage; yet he was far from being invincible—fighting at the battle of Troy, on the side of the Trojans, he suffered a wound which only Zeus could heal.

Hephaestus, on the other hand, had to fight his way into the Olympian summit. He was a God of Creativity; to him was attributed the fire of the forge and the art of metallurgy. He was a divine artificer, maker of both practical and magical objects for men and gods. The legends say that he was born lame and was therefore cast away in anger by his mother Hera. Another and more believable version has it that it was Zeus who banished Hephaestus—because of the doubt regarding his parentage—but Hephaestus used his magically creative powers to force Zeus to give him a seat among the Great Gods.

The legends also relate that Hephaestus once made an invisible net that would close over his wife's bed if it were warmed by an intruding lover. He may have needed such protection, for his wife and consort was Aphrodite, Goddess of Love and Beauty. It was only natural that many tales of love affairs would build up around her; in many of these the seducer was Ares, brother of Hephaestus. (One of the offspring of that illicit love affair was Eros, the God of Love.)

Aphrodite was included in the Olympian Circle of Twelve, and the circumstances of her inclusion shed light on our subject. She was neither a sister of Zeus nor his daughter, yet she could not be ignored. She had come from the Asian shores of the Mediterranean facing Greece (according to the Greek poet Hesiod, she arrived by way of Cyprus); and, claiming great antiquity, she ascribed her origin to the genitals of Uranus. She was thus genealogically one generation ahead of Zeus, being (so to say) a sister of his father, and the embodiment of the castrated Forefather of the Gods. (Fig. 22)

Aphrodite, then, had to be included among the Olympian gods. But their total number, twelve, apparently could not be exceeded. The solution was ingenious: Add one by dropping one. Since Hades was given domain over the Lower World and did not remain among the Great Gods on Mount Olympus, a vacancy was created, admirably handy for seating Aphrodite in the exclusive Circle of Twelve.

It also appears that the number twelve was a requirement that worked both ways: There could be no more than twelve Olympians, but no fewer than twelve, either. This becomes evident through the circumstances that led to the inclusion of Dionysus in the Olympian Circle. He was a son of Zeus, born when Zeus impregnated his own daughter, Semele. Dionysus, who had to be hidden from Hera's wrath, was sent to far-off lands (reaching even India), introducing vinegrowing and winemaking wherever he went. In the meantime, a vacancy became available on Olympus. Hestia, the oldest sister of Zeus, weaker and older, was dropped entirely from the Circle of Twelve. Dionysus then returned to Greece and was allowed to fill the vacancy. Once again, there were twelve Olympians.

Though Greek mythology was not clear regarding the origins of mankind, the legends and traditions claimed descent from the gods for heroes and kings. These semigods formed the link between the human destiny—daily toil, dependence on the elements, plagues, illness, death—and a golden past, when only the gods roamed Earth. And although so many of the gods were born on Earth, the select Circle of Twelve Olympians represented the celestial aspect of the gods. The original Olympus was described by the *Odyssey* as lying in the "pure upper air." The original Twelve Great Gods were Gods of Heaven who had come down to Earth; and they represented the twelve celestial bodies in the "vault of Heaven."

The Latin names of the Great Gods, given them when the Romans adopted the Greek pantheon, clarify their astral associations: Gaea was

Fig. 22

Fig. 23

Fig. 24

Earth; Hermes, Mercury; Aphrodite, Venus; Ares, Mars; Cronus, Saturn; and Zeus, Jupiter. Continuing the Greek tradition, the Romans envisaged Jupiter as a thundering god whose weapon was the lightning bolt; like the Greeks, the Romans associated him with the bull. (Fig. 23)

There is now general agreement that the foundations of the distinct Greek civilization were laid on the island of Crete, where the Minoan culture flourished from circa 2700 B.C. to 1400 B.C. In Minoan myth and legend, the tale of the minotaur is prominent. This half-man, half-bull was the offspring of Pasiphaë, the wife of King Minos, and a bull. Archaeological finds have confirmed the extensive Minoan worship of the bull, and some cylinder seals depict the bull as a divine being accompanied by a cross symbol, which stood for some unidentified star or planet. It has therefore been surmised that the bull worshiped by the Minoans was not the common earthly creature but the Celestial Bull—the constellation Taurus—in commemoration of some events that had occurred when the Sun's spring equinox appeared in that constellation, circa 4000 B.C. (Fig. 24)

By Greek tradition, Zeus arrived on the Greek mainland via Crete, whence he had fled (by swimming the Mediterranean) after abducting Europa, the beautiful daughter of the king of the Phoenician city of Tyre. Indeed, when the earliest Minoan script was finally deciphered by Cyrus H. Gordon, it was shown to be "a Semitic dialect from the shores of the Eastern Mediterranean."

The Greeks, in fact, never claimed that their Olympian gods came directly to Greece from the heavens. Zeus arrived from across the Mediterranean, via Crete. Aphrodite was said to have come by sea from the Near East, via Cyprus. Poseidon (Neptune to the Romans) brought the horse with him from Asia Minor. Athena brought "the olive, fertile and self-sown," to Greece from the lands of the Bible.

There is no doubt that the Greek traditions and religion arrived on the Greek mainland from the Near East, via Asia Minor and the Mediterranean islands. It is there that their pantheon had its roots; it is there that we should look for the origins of the Greek gods, and their astral relationship with the number twelve.

°

Hinduism, the ancient religion of India, considers the *Vedas*—compositions of hymns, sacrificial formulas, and other sayings pertaining to the gods—as sacred scriptures, "not of human origin." The gods themselves composed them, the Hindu traditions say, in the age that preceded the present one. But, as time went on, more and more of the original 100,000 verses, passed from generation to generation orally, were lost and confused. In the end, a sage wrote down the remaining verses, dividing them into four books and trusting four of his principal disciples to preserve one *Veda* each.

When, in the nineteenth century, scholars began to decipher and understand forgotten languages and trace the connections between them, they realized that the *Vedas* were written in a very ancient Indo-European language, the predecessor of the Indian root-tongue Sanskrit, of Greek, Latin, and other European languages. When they were finally able to read and analyze the *Vedas,* they were surprised to see the uncanny similarity between the Vedic tales of the gods and the Greek ones.

The gods, the *Vedas* told, were all members of one large, but not necessarily peaceful, family. Amid the tales of ascents to the heavens and descents to Earth, aerial battles, wondrous weapons, friendships and rivalries, marriages and infidelities, there appears to have existed a basic concern for genealogical record keeping—who fathered whom, and who was the firstborn of whom. The gods on Earth originated in the heavens; and the principal deities, even on Earth, continued to represent celestial bodies.

In primeval times, the Rishis ("primeval flowing ones") "flowed" celestially, possessed of irresistible powers. Of them, seven were the Great Progenitors. The gods Rahu ("demon") and Ketu ("disconnected") were once a single celestial body that sought to join the gods without permission; but the God of Storms hurled his flaming weapon at him, cutting him into two parts—Rahu, the "Dragon's Head," which unceasingly traverses the heavens in search of vengeance, and Ketu, the "Dragon's Tail." Mar-Ishi, the progenitor of the Solar Dynasty, gave birth to Kash-Yapa ("he who is the throne"). The *Vedas* describe him as having been quite prolific; but the dynastic succession was continued only through his ten children by Prit-Hivi ("heavenly mother").

As dynastic head, Kash-Yapa was also chief of the devas ("shining ones") and bore the title Dyaus-Pitar ("shining father"). Together with his consort and ten children, the divine family made up the twelve Adityas, gods who were each assigned a sign of the zodiac and a celestial body. Kash-Yapa's celestial body was "the shining star"; Prit-Hivi represented Earth. Then there were the gods whose celestial counterparts included the Sun, the Moon, Mars, Mercury, Jupiter, Venus, and Saturn.

In time, the leadership of the pantheon of twelve passed to Varuna, the God of the Heavenly Expanse. He was omnipresent and all-seeing; one of the hymns to him reads almost like a Biblical psalm:

It is he who makes the sun shine in the heavens,
And the winds that blow are his breath.
He has hollowed out the channels of the rivers;
They flow at his command.
He has made the depths of the sea.

His reign also came sooner or later to an end. Indra, the god who slew the celestial "Dragon," claimed the throne by slaying his father. He was the new Lord of the Skies and God of Storms. Lightning and thunder were his weapons, and his epithet was Lord of Hosts. He had, however, to share dominion with his two brothers. One was Vivashvat, who was the progenitor of Manu, the first Man. The other was Agni ("igniter"), who brought fire down to Earth from the heavens, so that Mankind could use it industrially.

The similarities between the Vedic and Greek pantheons are obvious. The tales concerning the principal deities, as well as the verses dealing with a multitude of other lesser deities—sons, wives, daughters, mistresses—are clearly duplicates (or originals?) of the Greek tales. There is no doubt that Dyaus came to mean Zeus; Dyaus-Pitar, Jupiter; Varuna, Uranus; and so on. And, in both instances, the Circle of the Great Gods always stood at *twelve*, no matter what changes took place in the divine succession.

How could such similarity arise in two areas so far apart, geographically and in time?

Scholars believe that sometime in the second millennium B.C. a people speaking an Indo-European language, and centered in northern Iran or the Caucasus area, embarked on great migrations. One group went southeast, to India. The Hindus called them Aryans ("noble men"). They brought with them the *Vedas* as oral tales, circa 1,500 B.C. Another wave of this Indo-European migration went westward, to Europe. Some circled the Black Sea and arrived in Europe via the steppes of Russia. But the main route by which these people and their traditions and religion reached Greece was the shortest one: Asia Minor. Some of the most ancient Greek cities, in fact, lie not on the Greek mainland but at the western tip of Asia Minor.

But who were these Indo-Europeans who chose Anatolia as their abode? Little in Western knowledge shed light on the subject.

Once again, the only readily available—and reliable—source proved to be the Old Testament. There the scholars found several references to the "Hittites" as the people inhabiting the mountains of Anatolia. Unlike the enmity reflected in the Old Testament toward the Canaanites and other neighbors whose customs were considered an "abomination," the Hittites were regarded as friends and allies to Israel. Bathsheba, whom King David coveted, was the wife of Uriah the Hittite, an officer in King David's army. King Solomon, who forged alliances by marrying the daughters of foreign kings, took as wives the daughters both of an Egyptian pharaoh and of a Hittite king. At another time, an invading Syrian army fled upon hearing a rumor that "the king of Israel hath hired against us the kings of the Hittites and the kings of the Egyptians." These brief allusions to the Hittites reveal the high esteem in which their military abilities were held by other peoples of the ancient Near East.

With the decipherment of the Egyptian hieroglyphs—and, later on, of the Mesopotamian inscriptions—scholars have come across numerous references to a "Land of Hatti" as a large and powerful kingdom in Anatolia. Could such an important power have left no trace?

Forearmed with the clues provided in the Egyptian and Mesopotamian texts, the scholars embarked on excavations of ancient sites in Anatolia's hilly regions. The efforts paid off: They found Hittite cities, palaces, royal treasures, royal tombs, temples, religious objects, tools, weapons, art objects. Above all, they found many inscriptions—both in a pictographic script and in cuneiform. The biblical Hittites had come to life.

A unique monument bequeathed to us by the ancient Near East is a rock carving outside the ancient Hittite capital (the site is nowadays called Yazilikaya, which in Turkish means "inscribed rock"). After passing through gateways and sanctuaries, the ancient worshiper came into an open-air gallery, an opening among a semicircle of rocks, on which all the gods of the Hittites were depicted in procession.

Marching in from the left is a long procession of primarily male deities, clearly organized in "companies" of twelve. At the extreme left, and thus last to march in this amazing parade, are twelve deities who look identical, all carrying the same weapon. (Fig. 25)

The middle group of twelve marchers includes some deities who look older, some who bear diversified weapons, and two who are highlighted by a divine symbol. (Fig. 26)

The third (front) group of twelve is clearly made up of the more important male and female deities. Their weapons and emblems are more varied; four have the divine celestial symbol above them; two are winged. This group also includes nondivine participants: two bulls holding up a globe, and the king of the Hittites, wearing a skull cap and standing under the emblem of the Winged Disk. (Fig. 27)

Marching in from the right were two groups of female deities; the rock carvings are, however, too mutilated to ascertain their full original number. We will probably not be wrong in assuming that they, too, made up two "companies" of twelve each.

The two processions from the left and from the right met at a central panel which clearly depicted Great Gods, for they were all shown elevated, standing atop mountains, animals, birds, or even on the shoulders of divine attendants. (Fig. 28)

Much effort was invested by scholars (for example, E. Laroche, *Le*

Panthéon de Yazilikaya) to determine from the depictions, the hieroglyphic symbols, as well as from partly legible texts and god names that were actually carved on the rocks, the names, titles, and roles of the deities included in the procession. But it is clear that the Hittite pantheon, too, was governed by the "Olympian" twelve. The lesser gods were organized in groups of twelve, and the Great Gods on Earth were associated with twelve celestial bodies.

That the pantheon was governed by the "sacred number" twelve is made additionally certain by yet another Hittite monument, a masonry shrine found near the present-day Beit-Zehir. It clearly depicts the divine couple, surrounded by ten other gods—making a total of twelve. (Fig. 29)

The archaeological finds showed conclusively that the Hittites worshiped gods that were "of Heaven and Earth," all interrelated and arranged into a genealogical hierarchy. Some were great and "olden" gods who were originally of the heavens. Their symbol—which in the Hittite pictographic writing meant "divine" or "heavenly god"—looked like a pair of eye goggles. (Fig. 30) It frequently appeared on round seals as part of a rocket-like object. (Fig. 31)

Other gods were actually present, not merely on Earth but among the Hittites, acting as supreme rulers of the land, appointing the human kings, and instructing the latter in matters of war, treaties, and other international affairs.

Heading the physically present Hittite gods was a deity named Teshub, which meant "wind blower." He was thus what scholars call a Storm God, associated with winds, thunder, and lightning. He was also nicknamed Taru ("bull"). Like the Greeks, the Hittites depicted bull worship; like Jupiter after him, Teshub was depicted as the God of Thunder and Lightning, mounted upon a bull. (Fig. 32)

Hittite texts, like later Greek legends, relate how their chief deity had to battle a monster to consolidate his supremacy. A text named by the scholars "The Myth of the Slaying of the Dragon" identifies Teshub's adversary as the god Yanka. Failing to defeat him in battle, Teshub appealed to the other gods for help, but only one goddess came to his assistance, and disposed of Yanka by getting him drunk at a party.

Recognizing in such tales the origins of the legend of Saint George and the Dragon, scholars refer to the adversary smitten by the "good" god as "the dragon." But the fact is that Yanka meant "serpent," and that the ancient peoples depicted the "evil" god as such—as seen in this bas-relief from a Hittite site. (Fig. 33) Zeus, too, as we have shown, battled not a "dragon" but a serpent-god. As we shall show later on, there was deep meaning attached to these ancient traditions of a struggle between a god of winds and a serpent deity. Here, however,

Fig. 25

Fig. 26

Fig. 27

Fig. 28

Fig. 29

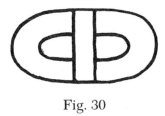

Fig. 30

Fig. 31

Fig. 32

Fig. 33

we can only stress that battles among the gods for the divine Kingship were reported in the ancient texts as events that had unquestionably taken place.

A long and well-preserved Hittite epic tale, entitled "Kingship in Heaven," deals with this very subject—the heavenly origin of the gods. The recounter of those premortal events first called upon twelve "mighty olden gods" to listen to his tale, and be witnesses to its accuracy:

> Let there listen the gods who are in Heaven,
> And those who are upon the dark-hued Earth!
> Let there listen, the mighty olden gods.

Thus establishing that the gods of old were both of Heaven and upon Earth, the epic lists the twelve "mighty olden ones," the forebears of the gods; and assuring their attention, the recounter proceeded to tell how the god who was "king in Heaven" came to "dark-hued Earth:"

> Formerly, in the olden days, Alalu was king in Heaven;
> He, Alalu, was seated on the throne.
> Mighty Anu, the first among the gods, stood before him,
> Bowed at his feet, set the drinking cup in his hand.
> For nine counted periods, Alalu was king in Heaven.
> In the ninth period, Anu gave battle against Alalu.
> Alalu was defeated, he fled before Anu—
> He descended to the dark-hued Earth.
> Down to the dark-hued Earth he went;
> On the throne sat Anu.

The epic thus attributed the arrival of a "king in Heaven" upon Earth to a usurpation of the throne: A god named Alalu was forcefully deposed from his throne (somewhere in the heavens), and, fleeing for his life, "descended to dark-hued Earth." But that was not the end. The text proceeded to recount how Anu, in turn, was also deposed by a god named Kumarbi (Anu's own brother, by some interpretations).

There is no doubt that this epic, written a thousand years before the Greek legends were composed, was the forerunner of the tale of the deposing of Uranus by Cronus and of Cronus by Zeus. Even the detail pertaining to the castration of Cronus by Zeus is found in the Hittite text, for that was exactly what Kumarbi did to Anu:

For nine counted periods Anu was king in Heaven;
In the ninth period, Anu had to do battle with Kumarbi.
Anu slipped out of Kumarbi's hold and fled—
Flee did Anu, rising up to the sky.
After him Kumarbi rushed, seized him by his feet;
He pulled him down from the skies.
He bit his loins; and the "Manhood" of Anu
with the insides of Kumarbi combined, fused as bronze.

According to this ancient tale, the battle did not result in a total victory. Though emasculated, Anu managed to fly back to his Heavenly Abode, leaving Kumarbi in control of Earth. Meanwhile, Anu's "Manhood" produced several deities within Kumarbi's insides, which he (like Cronus in the Greek legends) was forced to release. One of these was Teshub, the chief Hittite deity.

However, there was to be one more epic battle before Teshub could rule in peace.

Learning of the appearance of an heir to Anu in Kummiya ("heavenly abode"), Kumarbi devised a plan to "raise a rival to the God of Storms." "Into his hand he took his staff; upon his feet he put the shoes that are swift as winds"; and he went from his city Ur-Kish to the abode of the Lady of the Great Mountain. Reaching her,

His desire was aroused;
He slept with Lady Mountain;
His manhood flowed into her.
Five times he took her. . . .
Ten times he took her.

Was Kumarbi simply lustful? We have reason to believe that much more was involved. Our guess would be that the succession rules of the gods were such that a son of Kumarbi by the Lady of the Great Mountain could have claimed to be the rightful heir to the Heavenly Throne; and that Kumarbi "took" the goddess five and ten times in order to make sure that she conceived, as indeed she did: she bore a son, whom Kumarbi symbolically named Ulli-Kummi ("suppressor of Kummiya"—Teshub's abode).

The battle for succession was foreseen by Kumarbi as one that would entail fighting in the heavens. Having destined his son to suppress the incumbents at Kummiya, Kumarbi further proclaimed for his son:

Let him ascend to Heaven for kingship!
Let him vanquish Kummiya, the beautiful city!
Let him attack the God of Storms
And tear him to pieces, like a mortal!
Let him shoot down all the gods from the sky.

Did the particular battles fought by Teshub upon Earth and in the skies take place when the Age of Taurus commenced, circa 4000 B.C.? Was it for that reason that the winner was granted association with the bull? And were the events in any way connected with the beginning, at the very same time, of the sudden civilization of Sumer?

There can be no doubt that the Hittite pantheon and tales of the gods indeed had their roots in Sumer, its civilization, and its gods.

The tale of the challenge to the Divine Throne by Ulli-Kummi continues to relate heroic battles but of an indecisive nature. At one point, the failure of Teshub to defeat his adversary even caused his spouse, Hebat, to attempt suicide. Finally, an appeal was made to the gods to mediate the dispute, and an Assembly of the Gods was called. It was led by an "olden god" named Enlil, and another "olden god" named Ea, who was called upon to produce "the old tablets with the words of destiny"—some ancient records that could apparently help settle the dispute regarding the divine succession.

When these records failed to settle the dispute, Enlil advised another battle with the challenger, but with the help of some very ancient weapons. "Listen, ye olden gods, ye who know the olden words," Enlil said to his followers:

Open ye the ancient storehouses
Of the fathers and the forefathers!
Bring forth the Olden Copper lance
With which Heaven was separated from Earth;
And let them sever the feet of Ulli-kummi.

Who were these "olden gods"? The answer is obvious, for all of them—Anu, Antu, Enlil, Ninlil, Ea, Ishkur—bear Sumerian names. Even the name of Teshub, as well as the names of other "Hittite" gods, were often written in Sumerian script to denote their identities. Also, some of the places named in the action were those of ancient Sumerian sites.

It dawned on the scholars that the Hittites in fact worshiped a pantheon of Sumerian origins, and that the arena of the tales of the "olden gods" was Sumer. This, however, was only part of a much wider discovery. Not only was the Hittite language found to be based on several Indo-European dialects, but it was also found to be subject to substantial Akkadian influence, both in speech and more so in writing. Since Akkadian was the international language of the ancient world in the second millennium B.C., its influence on Hittite could somehow be rationalized.

But there was cause for true astonishment when scholars discovered in the course of deciphering Hittite that it extensively employed Sumerian pictographic signs, syllables, and even whole words! Moreover, it became obvious that Sumerian was their language of high learning. The Sumerian language, in the words of O. R. Gurney *(The Hittites)*, "was intensively studied at Hattu-Shash [the capital city] and Sumerian-Hittite vocabularies were found there.... Many of the syllables associated with the cuneiform signs in the Hittite period are really Sumerian words of which the meaning had been forgotten [by the Hittites].... In the Hittite texts the scribes often replaced common Hittite words by the corresponding Sumerian or Babylonian word."

Now, when the Hittites reached Babylon sometime after 1600 B.C., the Sumerians were already long gone from the Near Eastern scene. How was it, then, that their language, literature, and religion dominated another great kingdom in another millennium and in another part of Asia?

The bridge, scholars have recently discovered, were a people called the Hurrians.

Referred to in the Old Testament as the Horites ("free people"), they dominated the wide area between Sumer and Akkad in Mesopotamia and the Hittite kingdom in Anatolia. In the north their lands were the ancient "cedar lands" from which countries near and far obtained their best woods. In the east their centers embraced the present-day oil fields of Iraq; in one city alone, Nuzi, archaeologists found not only the usual structures and artifacts but also thousands of legal and social documents of great value. In the west, the Hurrians' rule and influence extended to the Mediterranean coast and encompassed such great ancient centers of trade, industry, and learning as Carchemish and Alalakh.

But the seats of their power, the main centers of the ancient trade routes, and the sites of the most venerated shrines were within the heartland that was "between the two rivers," the biblical Naharayim. Their most ancient capital (as yet undiscovered) was located somewhere on the Khabur River. Their greatest trading center, on the Balikh River, was the biblical Haran—the city where the family of the patriarch Abraham sojourned on their way from Ur in southern Mesopotamia to the Land of Canaan.

Egyptian and Mesopotamian royal documents referred to the

Hurrian kingdom as Mitanni, and dealt with it on an equal footing—a strong power whose influence spread beyond its immediate borders. The Hittites called their Hurrian neighbors "Hurri." Some scholars pointed out, however, that the word could also be read "Har," and (like G. Contenau in *La Civilisation des Hittites et des Hurrites du Mitanni*) have raised the possibility that, in the name "Harri," "one sees the name 'Ary' or Aryans for these people."

There is no doubt that the Hurrians were Aryan or Indo-European in origin. Their inscriptions invoked several deities by their Vedic "Aryan" names, their kings bore Indo-European names, and their military and cavalry terminology derived from the Indo-European. B. Hrozny, who in the 1920s led an effort to unravel the Hittite and Hurrian records, even went so far as to call the Hurrians "the oldest Hindus."

These Hurrians dominated the Hittites culturally and religiously. The Hittite mythological texts were found to be of Hurrian provenance, and even epic tales of prehistoric, semidivine heroes were of Hurrian origin. There is no longer any doubt that the Hittites acquired their cosmology, their "myths," their gods, and their pantheon of twelve from the Hurrians.

The triple connection—between Aryan origins, Hittite worship, and the Hurrian sources of these beliefs—is remarkably well documented in a Hittite prayer by a woman for the life of her sick husband. Addressing her prayer to the goddess Hebat, Teshub's spouse, the woman intoned:

> Oh goddess of the Rising Disc of Arynna,
> My Lady, Mistress of the Hatti Lands,
> Queen of Heaven and Earth. . . .
> In the Hatti country, thy name is
> "Goddess of the Rising Disc of Arynna";
> But in the land that thou madest,
> In the Cedar Land,
> Thou bearest the name "Hebat."

With all that, the culture and religion adopted and transmitted by the Hurrians were not Indo-European. Even their language was not really Indo-European. There were undoubtedly Akkadian elements in the Hurrian language, culture, and traditions. The name of their capital, Washugeni, was a variant of the Semitic *resh-eni* ("where the waters begin"). The Tigris River was called Aranzakh, which (we believe) stemmed from the Akkadian words for "river of the pure cedars." The gods Shamash and Tashmetum became the Hurrian Shimiki and Tashimmetish—and so on.

But since the Akkadian culture and religion were only a development of the original Sumerian traditions and beliefs, the Hurrians, in fact, absorbed and transmitted the religion of Sumer. That this was so was also evident from the frequent use of the original Sumerian divine names, epithets, and writing signs.

The epic tales, it has become clear, were the tales of Sumer; the "dwelling places" of the olden gods were Sumerian cities; the "olden language" was the language of Sumer. Even the Hurrian art duplicated Sumerian art—its form, its themes, and its symbols.

When and how were the Hurrians "mutated" by the Sumerian "gene"?

Evidence suggests that the Hurrians, who were the northern neighbors of Sumer and Akkad in the second millennium B.C., had actually commingled with the Sumerians in the previous millennium. It is an established fact that Hurrians were present and active in Sumer in the third millennium B.C., that they held important positions in Sumer during its last period of glory, that of the third dynasty of Ur. There is evidence showing that the Hurrians managed and manned the garment industry for which Sumer (and especially Ur) was known in antiquity. The renowned merchants of Ur were probably Hurrians for the most part.

In the thirteenth century B.C., under the pressure of vast migrations and invasions (including the Israelite thrust from Egypt to Canaan), the Hurrians retreated to the northeastern portion of their kingdom. Establishing their new capital near Lake Van, they called their kingdom Urartu ("Ararat"). There they worshiped a pantheon headed by Tesheba (Teshub), depicting him as a vigorous god wearing a horned cap and standing upon his cult symbol, the bull. (Fig. 34) They called their main shrine Bitanu ("house of Anu") and dedicated themselves to making their kingdom "the fortress of the valley of Anu."

And Anu, as we shall see, was the Sumerian Father of the Gods.

°

What about the other avenue by which the tales and worship of the gods reached Greece—from the eastern shores of the Mediterranean, via Crete and Cyprus?

The lands that are today Israel, Lebanon, and southern Syria—which formed the southwestern band of the ancient Fertile Crescent—were then the habitat of peoples that can be grouped together as the Canaanites. Once again, all that was known of them until rather recently appeared in references (mostly adverse) in the Old Testament and scattered Phoenician inscriptions. Archaeologists were only beginning to understand the Canaanites when two discoveries came to light: certain Egyptian texts at Luxor and Saqqara, and, much more

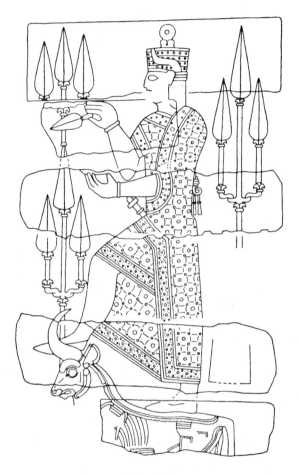

Fig. 34

important, historical, literary, and religious texts unearthed at a major Canaanite center. The place, now called Ras Shamra, on the Syrian coast, was the ancient city of Ugarit.

The language of the Ugarit inscriptions, the Canaanite language, was what scholars call West Semitic, a branch of the group of languages that also includes the earliest Akkadian and present-day Hebrew. Indeed, anyone who knows Hebrew well can follow the Canaanite inscriptions with relative ease. The language, literary style, and terminology are reminiscent of the Old Testament, and the script is the same as that of Israelite Hebrew.

The pantheon that unfolds from the Canaanite texts bears many similarities to the later Greek one. At the head of the Canaanite pantheon, too, there was a supreme deity called *El*, a word that was both the personal name of the god and the generic term meaning "lofty deity." He was the final authority in all affairs, human or divine. Ab Adam ("father of man") was his title; the Kindly, the Merciful was his epithet. He was the "creator of things created, and the one who alone could bestow kingship."

The Canaanite texts ("myths" to most scholars) depicted El as a sage, elderly deity who stayed away from daily affairs. His abode was remote, at the "headwaters of the two rivers"—the Tigris and Euphrates. There he would sit on his throne, receive emissaries, and contemplate the problems and disputes the other gods brought before him.

A stela found in Palestine depicts an elderly deity sitting on a throne and being served a beverage by a younger deity. The seated deity wears a conical headdress adorned with horns—a mark of the gods, as we have seen, from prehistoric times—and the scene is dominated by the symbol of a winged star—the ubiquitous emblem that we shall increasingly encounter. It is generally accepted by the scholars that this sculptured relief depicts El, the senior Canaanite deity. (Fig. 35)

Fig. 35

El, however, was not always an olden lord. One of his epithets was Tor (meaning "bull"), signifying, scholars believe, his sexual prowess and his role as Father of the Gods. A Canaanite poem, called "Birth of the Gracious Gods," placed El at the seashore (probably naked), where two women were completely charmed by the size of his penis. While a bird was roasting on the beach, El had intercourse with the two women. Thus were the two gods Shaḥar ("dawn") and Shalem ("completion" or "dusk") born.

These were not his only children nor his principal sons (of which he had, apparently, seven). His principal son was Baal—again the personal name of the deity, as well as the general term for "lord." As the Greeks did in their tales, the Canaanites spoke of the challenges by the son to the authority and rule of his father. Like El his father, Baal was what the scholars call a Storm God, a God of Thunder and Lightning. A nickname for Baal was Hadad ("sharp one"). His weapons were the battle-ax and the lightning-spear; his cult animal, like El's, was the bull, and, like El, he was depicted wearing the conical headdress adorned with a pair of horns.

Baal was also called Elyon ("supreme"); that is, the acknowledged prince, the heir apparent. But he had not come by this title without a struggle, first with his brother Yam ("prince of the sea"), and then with his brother Mot. A long and touching poem, pieced together from numerous fragmented tablets, begins with the summoning of the "Master Craftsman" to El's abode "at the sources of the waters, in the midst of the headwaters of the two rivers":

> Through the fields of El he comes
> He enters the pavilion of the Father of Years.
> At El's feet he bows, falls down,
> Prostrates himself, paying homage.

The Master Craftsman is ordered to erect a palace for Yam as the mark of his rise to power. Emboldened by this, Yam sends his messengers to the assembly of the gods, to ask for the surrender to him of Baal. Yam instructs his emissaries to be defiant, and the assembled gods do yield. Even El accepts the new lineup among his sons. "Ba'al is thy slave, O Yam," he declares.

The supremacy of Yam, however, was short-lived. Armed with two "divine weapons," Baal struggled with Yam and defeated him—only to be challenged by Mot (the name meant "smiter"). In this struggle, Baal was soon vanquished; but his sister Anat refused to accept this demise of Baal as final. "She seized Mot, the son of El, and with a blade she cleaved him."

The obliteration of Mot led, according to the Canaanite tale, to the miraculous resurrection of Baal. Scholars have attempted to rationalize the report by suggesting that the whole tale was only allegorical, representing no more than a tale of the annual struggle in the Near East between the hot, rainless summers that dry out the vegetation, and the coming of the rainy season in the autumn, which revives or "resurrects" the vegetation. But there is no doubt that the Canaanite tale intended no allegory, that it related what were then believed to be the true events: how the sons of the chief deity fought among themselves, and how one of them defied defeat to reappear and become the accepted heir, making El rejoice:

> El, the kindly one, the merciful, rejoices.
> His feet on the footstool he sets.
> He opens his throat and laughs;
> He raises his voice and cries out:
> "I shall sit and take my ease,
> The soul shall repose in my breast;
> For Ba'al the mighty is alive,
> For the Prince of Earth exists!"

Anat, according to Canaanite traditions, thus stood by her brother the Lord (Baal) in his life-and-death struggle with the evil Mot; and the parallel between this and the Greek tradition of the goddess Athena standing with the supreme god Zeus in his life-and-death struggle with Typhon is only too obvious. Athena, as we have seen, was called "the perfect maiden," yet had many illicit love affairs. Likewise, Canaanite traditions (which preceded the Greek ones) employed the epithet "the Maiden Anat," and, in spite of this, proceeded to report her various love affairs, especially with her own brother Baal. One text describes the arrival of Anat at Baal's abode on Mount Zaphon, and Baal's hurried dismissal of his wives. Then he sank by his sister's feet; they looked into each other's eyes; they anointed each other's "horns"—

> He seizes and holds her womb. . . .
> She seizes and holds his "stones.". . . .
> The maiden Anat . . . is made to conceive and bear.

No wonder, then, that Anat was often depicted completely naked, to emphasize her sexual attributes—as in this seal impression, which illustrates a helmeted Baal battling another god. (Fig. 36)

Like the Greek religion and its direct forerunners, the Canaanite pantheon included a Mother Goddess, official consort of the chief deity. They called her Ashera; she paralleled the Greek Hera. Astarte (the biblical Ashtoreth) paralleled Aphrodite; her frequent consort was Athtar, who was associated with a bright planet, and who probably paralleled Ares, Aphrodite's brother. There were other young deities, male and female, whose astral or Greek parallels can easily be surmised.

But besides these young deities there were the "olden gods," aloof from mundane affairs but available when the gods themselves ran into serious trouble. Some of their sculptures, even in a partly damaged state, show them with commanding features, gods recognizable by their horned headgear. (Fig. 37)

Whence had the Canaanites, for their part, drawn their culture and religion?

The Old Testament considered them a part of the Hamitic family of nations, with roots in the hot (for that is what _ham_ meant) lands of Africa, brothers of the Egyptians. The artifacts and written records unearthed by archaeologists confirm the close affinity between the two, as well as the many similarities between the Canaanite and Egyptian deities.

The many national and local gods, the multitude of their names and epithets, the diversity of their roles, emblems, and animal mascots at first cast the gods of Egypt as an unfathomable crowd of actors upon a strange stage. But a closer look reveals that they were essentially no different from those of the other lands of the ancient world.

The Egyptians believed in Gods of Heaven and Earth, Great Gods that were clearly distinguished from the multitudes of lesser deities. G. A. Wainwright *(The Sky-Religion in Egypt)* summed up the evidence, showing that the Egyptian belief in Gods of Heaven who descended to Earth from the skies was "extremely ancient." Some of the epithets of these Great Gods—Greatest God, Bull of Heaven, Lord/Lady of the Mountains—sound familiar.

Although the Egyptians counted by the decimal system, their religious affairs were governed by the Sumerian sexagesimal *sixty*, and celestial matters were subject to the divine number *twelve*. The heavens were divided into three parts, each comprising twelve celestial bodies. The afterworld was divided into twelve parts. Day and night were each divided into twelve hours. And all these divisions were paralleled by "companies" of gods, which in turn consisted of twelve gods each.

The head of the Egyptian pantheon was Ra ("creator"), who presided over an Assembly of the Gods that numbered twelve. He performed his wondrous works of creation in primeval times, bringing forth Geb ("Earth") and Nut ("sky"). Then he caused the plants to grow on Earth, and the creeping creatures—and, finally, Man. Ra was an unseen celestial god who manifested himself only periodically. His manifestation was the Aten—the Celestial Disc, depicted as a Winged Globe. (Fig. 38)

Fig. 36

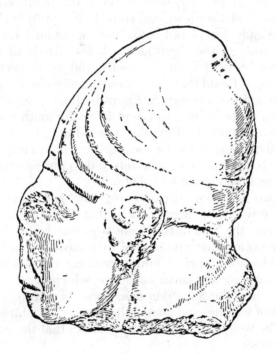

Fig. 37

The appearance and activities of Ra on Earth were, according to Egyptian tradition, directly connected with kingship in Egypt. According to that tradition, the first rulers of Egypt were not men but gods, and the first god to rule over Egypt was Ra. He then divided the kingdom, giving Lower Egypt to his son Osiris and Upper Egypt to his son Seth. But Seth schemed to overthrow Osiris and eventually had Osiris drowned. Isis, the sister and wife of Osiris, retrieved the mutilated body of Osiris and resurrected him. Thereafter, he went through "the secret gates" and joined Ra in his celestial path; his place on the throne of Egypt was taken over by his son Horus, who was sometimes depicted as a winged and horned deity. (Fig. 39)

Though Ra was the loftiest in the heavens, upon Earth he was the son of the god Ptah ("developer," "one who fashioned things"). The Egyptians believed that Ptah actually raised the land of Egypt from under floodwaters by building dike works at the point where the Nile rises. This Great God, they said, had come to Egypt from elsewhere; he established not only Egypt but also "the mountain land and the far foreign land." Indeed, the Egyptians acknowledged, all their "olden gods" had come by boat from the south; and many prehistoric rock drawings have been found that show these olden gods—distinguished by their horned headdress—arriving in Egypt by boat. (Fig. 40)

The only sea route leading to Egypt from the south is the Red Sea, and it is significant that the Egyptian name for it was the Sea of Ur. Hieroglyphically, the sign for Ur meant "the far-foreign [land] in the east"; that it actually may also have referred to the Sumerian Ur, lying in that very direction, cannot be ruled out.

The Egyptian word for "divine being" or "god" was NTR, which meant "one who watches." Significantly, that is exactly the meaning of the name Shumer: the land of the "ones who watch."

The earlier notion that civilization may have begun in Egypt has been discarded by now. There is ample evidence now showing that the Egyptian-organized society and civilization, which began half a millennium and more *after* the Sumerian one, drew its culture, architecture, technology, art of writing, and many other aspects of a high civilization from Sumer. The weight of evidence also shows that the gods of Egypt originated in Sumer.

Cultural and blood kinsmen of the Egyptians, the Canaanites shared the same gods with them. But, situated in the land strip that was the bridge between Asia and Africa from time immemorial, the Canaanites also came under strong Semitic or Mesopotamian influences. Like the Hittites to the north, the Hurrians to the northeast, the Egyptians to the south, the Canaanites could not boast of an original pantheon. They, too, acquired their cosmogony, deities, and legendary tales from

Fig. 38

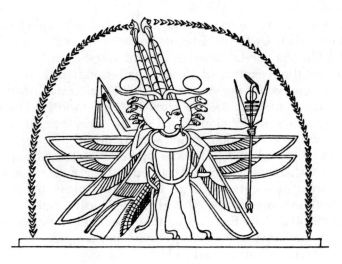

Fig. 39

Fig. 40

elsewhere. Their direct contacts with the Sumerian source were the Amorites.

                         *

The land of the Amorites lay between Mesopotamia and the Mediterranean lands of western Asia. Their name derives from the Akkadian *amurru* and Sumerian *martu* ("westerners"), they were not treated as aliens but as related people who dwelt in the western provinces of Sumer and Akkad.

Persons bearing Amorite names were listed as temple functionaries in Sumer. When Ur fell to Elamite invaders circa 2000 B.C., a Martu named Ishbi-Irra reestablished Sumerian kingship at Larsa and made his first task the recapture of Ur and the restoration there of the great shrine to the god Sin. Amorite "chieftains" established the first independent dynasty in Assyria circa 1900 B.C. And Hammurabi, who brought greatness to Babylon circa 1800 B.C., was the sixth successor of the first dynasty of Babylon, which was Amorite.

In the 1930s archaeologists came upon the center and capital city of the Amorites, known as Mari. At a bend of the Euphrates, where the Syrian border now cuts the river, the diggers uncovered a major city whose buildings were erected and continuously reerected, between 3000 and 2000 B.C., on foundations that date to centuries earlier. These earliest remains included a step pyramid and temples to the Sumerian deities Inanna, Ninhursag, and Enlil.

The palace of Mari alone occupied some five acres and included a throne room painted with most striking murals, three hundred various rooms, scribal chambers, and (most important to the historian) well over twenty thousand tablets in the cuneiform script, dealing with the economy, trade, politics, and social life of those times, with state and military matters, and, of course, with the religion of the land and its people. One of the wall paintings at the great palace of Mari depicts the investiture of the king Zimri-Lim by the goddess Inanna (whom the Amorites called Ishtar). (Fig. 41)

As in the other pantheons, the chief deity physically present among the Amurru was a weather or storm god. They called him Adad—the equivalent of the Canaanite Baal ("lord")—and they nicknamed him Hadad. His symbol, as might be expected, was forked lightning.

In Canaanite texts, Baal is often called the "Son of Dagon." The Mari texts also speak of an older deity named Dagan, a "Lord of Abundance" who—like El—is depicted as a retired deity, who complained on one occasion that he was no longer consulted on the conduct of a certain war.

Other members of the pantheon included the Moon God, whom the

Fig. 41

Canaanites called Yerah, the Akkadians Sin, and the Sumerians Nannar; the Sun God, commonly called Shamash; and other deities whose identities leave no doubt that Mari was a bridge (geographically and chronologically) connecting the lands and the peoples of the eastern Mediterranean with the Mesopotamian sources.

Among the finds at Mari, as elsewhere in the lands of Sumer, there were dozens of statues of the people themselves: kings, nobles, priests, singers. They were invariably depicted with their hands clasped in prayer, their gaze frozen forever toward their gods. (Fig. 42)

Fig. 42

Who were these Gods of Heaven and Earth, divine yet human, always headed by a pantheon or inner circle of twelve deities?

We have entered the temples of the Greeks and the Aryans, the Hittites and the Hurrians, the Canaanites, the Egyptians, and the Amorites. We have followed paths that took us across continents and seas, and clues that carried us over several millennia.

And all the corridors of all the temples have led us to one source: *Sumer.*

4
.

SUMER: LAND OF THE GODS

There is no doubt that the "olden words," which for thousands of years constituted the language of higher learning and religious scriptures, was the language of Sumer. There is also no doubt that the "olden gods" were the gods of Sumer; records and tales and genealogies and histories of gods older than those pertaining to the gods of Sumer have not been found anywhere.

When these gods (in their original Sumerian forms or in the later Akkadian, Babylonian, or Assyrian) are named and counted, the list runs into the hundreds. But once they are classified, it is clear that they were not a hodgepodge of divinities. They were headed by a pantheon of Great Gods, governed by an Assembly of the Deities, and related to each other. Once the numerous lesser nieces, nephews, grandchildren, and the like are excluded, a much smaller and coherent group of deities emerges—each with a role to play, each with certain powers or responsibilities.

There were, the Sumerians believed, gods that were "of the heavens." Texts dealing with the time "before things were created" talk of such heavenly gods as Apsu, Tiamat, Anshar, Kishar. No claim is ever made that the gods of this category ever appeared upon Earth. As we look closer at these "gods," who existed before Earth was created, we shall realize that they were the celestial bodies that make up our solar system; and, as we shall show, the so-called Sumerian myths regarding these celestial beings are, in fact, precise and scientifically plausible cosmologic concepts regarding the creation of our solar system.

There were also lesser gods who were "of Earth." Their cult centers were mostly provincial towns; they were no more than local deities. At best, they were given charge of some limited operation—as, for example, the goddess NIN.KASHI ("lady-beer"), who supervised the preparation of beverages. Of them, no heroic tales were told. They possessed no awesome weapons, and the other gods did not shudder at their command. They remind one very much of the company of young gods that marched last in the procession depicted on the rocks of Hittite Yazilikaya.

Between the two groups there were the Gods of Heaven and Earth, the ones called "the ancient gods." They were the "olden gods" of the epic tales, and, in the Sumerian belief, they had come down to Earth from the heavens.

These were no mere local deities. They were national gods—indeed, international gods. Some of them were present and active upon Earth even before there were Men upon Earth. Indeed, the very existence of Man was deemed to have been the result of a deliberate creative enterprise on the part of these gods. They were powerful, capable of feats beyond mortal ability or comprehension. Yet these gods not only looked like humans but ate and drank like them and displayed virtually every human emotion of love and hate, loyalty and infidelity.

Although the roles and hierarchical standing of some of the principal deities shifted over the millennia, a number of them never lost their paramount position and their national and international veneration. As we take a close look at this central group, there emerges a picture of a dynasty of gods, a divine family, closely related yet bitterly divided.

The head of this family of Gods of Heaven and Earth was AN (or Anu in the Babylonian/Assyrian texts). He was the Great Father of the Gods, the King of the Gods. His realm was the expanse of the heavens, and his symbol was a star. In the Sumerian pictographic writing, the sign of a star also stood for An, for "heavens," and for "divine being," or "god" (descended of An). This fourfold meaning of the symbol remained through the ages, as the script moved from the Sumerian pictographic to the cuneiform Akkadian, to the stylized Babylonian and Assyrian. (Fig. 43)

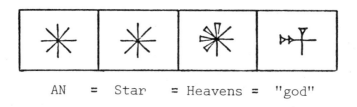

AN = Star = Heavens = "god"

Fig. 43

From the very earliest times until the cuneiform script faded away—from the fourth millennium B.C. almost to the time of Christ—this symbol preceded the names of the gods, indicating that the name written in the text was not of a mortal, but of a deity of heavenly origin.

Anu's abode, and the seat of his Kingship, was in the heavens. That was where the other Gods of Heaven and Earth went when they needed individual advice or favor, or where they met in assembly to settle disputes among themselves or to reach major decisions. Numerous texts describe Anu's palace (whose portals were guarded by a god of the Tree of Truth and a god of the Tree of Life), his throne, the manner in which other gods approached him, and how they sat in his presence.

The Sumerian texts could also recall instances when not only the other gods but even some chosen mortals were permitted to go up to Anu's abode, mostly with the object of escaping mortality. One such tale pertained to Adapa ("model of Man"). He was so perfect and so loyal to the god Ea, who had created him, that Ea arranged for him to be taken to Anu. Ea then described to Adapa what to expect.

Adapa,
thou art going before Anu, the King;
The road to Heaven thou wilt take.
When to Heaven thou hast ascended,
and hast approached the gate of Anu,
the "Bearer of Life" and the "Grower of Truth"
at the gate of Anu will be standing.

Guided by his creator, Adapa "to Heaven went up . . . ascended to Heaven and approached the gate of Anu." But when he was offered the chance to become immortal, Adapa refused to eat the Bread of Life, thinking that the angry Anu offered him poisoned food. He was thus returned to Earth as an anointed priest but still a mortal.

The Sumerian claim that not only gods but also selected mortals could ascend to the Divine Abode in the heavens is echoed in the Old Testament tales of the ascents to the heavens by Enoch and the prophet Elijah.

Though Anu lived in a Heavenly Abode, the Sumerian texts reported instances when he came down to Earth—either at times of great crisis, or on ceremonial visits (when he was accompanied by his spouse ANTU), or (at least once) to make his great-granddaughter IN.ANNA his consort on Earth.

Since he did not permanently reside on Earth, there was apparently no need to grant him exclusivity over his own city or cult center; and the abode, or "high house," erected for him was located at Uruk (the biblical Erech), the domain of the goddess Inanna. The ruins of Uruk include to this day a huge man-made mound, where archaeologists have found evidence of the construction and reconstruction of a high temple—the temple of Anu; no less than eighteen strata or distinct phases were discovered there, indicating the existence of compelling reasons to maintain the temple at that sacred site.

The temple of Anu was called E.ANNA ("house of An"). But this simple name applied to a structure that, at least at some of its phases, was quite a sight to behold. It was, according to Sumerian texts, "the hallowed E-Anna, the pure sanctuary." Traditions maintained that the Great Gods themselves "had fashioned its parts." "Its cornice was like copper," "its great wall touching the clouds—a lofty dwelling place"; "it was the House whose charm was irresistible, whose allure was unending." And the texts also made clear the temple's purpose, for they called it "the House for descending from Heaven."

A tablet that belonged to an archive at Uruk enlightens us as to the pomp and pageantry that accompanied the arrival of Anu and his spouse on a "state visit." Because of damage to the tablet, we can read of the ceremonies only from some midpoint, when Anu and Antu were already seated in the temple's courtyard. The gods, "exactly in the same order as before," then formed a procession ahead of and behind the bearer of the scepter. The protocol then instructed:

> They shall then descend to the Exalted Court,
> and shall turn towards the god Anu.
> The Priest of Purification shall libate the Scepter,
> and the Scepter-bearer shall enter and be seated.
> The deities Papsukal, Nusku and Shala
> shall then be seated in the court of the god Anu.

Meanwhile, the goddesses, "The Divine Offspring of Anu, Uruk's Divine Daughters," bore a second object, whose name or purpose are unclear, to the E.NIR, "The House of the Golden Bed of the Goddess Antu." Then they returned in a procession to the courtyard, to the place where Antu was seated. While the evening meal was being prepared according to a strict ritual, a special priest smeared a mixture of "good oil" and wine on the door sockets of the sanctuary to which Anu and Antu were later to retire for the night—a thoughtful touch intended, it seems, to eliminate squeaking of the doors while the two deities slept.

While an "evening meal"—various drinks and appetizers—was being served, an astronomer-priest went up to the "topmost stage of the tower of the main temple" to observe the skies. He was to look out for the rising in a specific part of the sky of the planet named Great Anu of Heaven. Thereupon, he was to recite the compositions named "To the one who grows bright, the heavenly planet of the Lord Anu," and "The Creator's image has risen."

Once the planet had been sighted and the poems recited, Anu and Antu washed their hands with water out of a golden basin and the first part of the feast began. Then, the seven Great Gods also washed their hands from seven large golden trays and the second part of the feast began. The "rite of washing of the mouth" was then performed; the priests recited the hymn "The planet of Anu is Heaven's hero." Torches were lit, and the gods, priests, singers, and food-bearers arranged themselves in a procession, accompanying the two visitors to their sanctuary for the night.

Four major deities were assigned to remain in the courtyard and keep watch until daybreak. Others were stationed at various designated gates. Meanwhile, the whole country was to light up and celebrate the presence of the two divine visitors. On a signal from the main temple, the priests of all the other temples of Uruk were "to use torches to start bonfires"; and the priests in other cities, seeing the bonfires at Uruk, were to do likewise. Then:

> The people of the Land shall light fires in their homes,
> and shall offer banquets to all the gods. . . .
> The guards of the cities shall light fires
> in the streets and in the squares.

The departure of the two Great Gods was also planned, not only to the day but to the minute.

> On the seventeenth day,
> forty minutes after sunrise,
> the gate shall be opened before the gods Anu and Antu,
> bringing to an end their overnight stay.

While the end of this tablet has broken off, another text in all probability describes the departure: the morning meal, the incantations, the handshakes ("grasping of the hands") by the other gods. The Great Gods were then carried to their point of departure on thronelike litters carried on the shoulders of temple functionaries. An Assyrian depiction of a procession of deities (though from a much later time) probably gives us a good idea of the manner in which Anu and Antu were carried during their procession in Uruk. (Fig. 44)

Special incantations were recited when the procession was passing through "the street of the gods"; other psalms and hymns were sung as the procession neared "the holy quay" and when it reached "the dike of the ship of Anu." Good-byes were then said, and yet more incantations were recited and sung "with hand-raising gestures."

Then all the priests and temple functionaries who carried the gods, led by the great priest, offered a special "prayer of departure." "Great Anu, may Heaven and Earth bless you!" they intoned seven times. They prayed for the blessing of the seven celestial gods and invoked the gods that were in Heaven and the gods that were upon Earth. In conclusion, they bade farewell to Anu and Antu, thus:

> May the Gods of the Deep,
> and the Gods of the Divine Abode,
> bless you!
> May they bless you daily—
> every day of every month of every year!

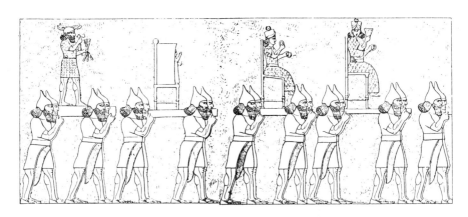

Fig. 44

Among the thousands upon thousands of depictions of the ancient gods that have been uncovered, none seems to depict Anu. Yet he peers at us from every statue and every portrait of every king that ever was, from antiquity to our very own days. For Anu was not only the Great King, King of the Gods, but also the one by whose grace others could be crowned as kings. By Sumerian tradition, rulership flowed from Anu; and the very term for "Kingship" was *Anutu* ("Anu-ship"). The insignia of Anu were the tiara (the divine headdress), the scepter (symbol of power), and the staff (symbolizing the guidance provided by the shepherd).

The shepherd's staff may now be found more in the hands of bishops than of kings. But the crown and scepter are still held by whatever kings Mankind has left on some thrones.

The second most powerful deity of the Sumerian pantheon was EN.LIL. His name meant "lord of the airspace"—the prototype and father of the later Storm Gods that were to head the pantheons of the ancient world.

He was Anu's eldest son, born at his father's Heavenly Abode. But at some point in the earliest times he descended to Earth, and was thus the principal God of Heaven *and* Earth. When the gods met in assembly at the Heavenly Abode, Enlil presided over the meetings alongside his father. When the gods met for assembly on Earth, they met at Enlil's court in the divine precinct of Nippur, the city dedicated to Enlil and the site of his main temple, the E.KUR ("house which is like a mountain").

Not only the Sumerians but the very gods of Sumer considered Enlil supreme. They called him Ruler of All the Lands, and made it clear that "in Heaven—he is the Prince; On Earth—he is the Chief." His "word [command] high above made the Heavens tremble, down below made the Earth quake":

> Enlil,
> Whose command is far reaching;
> Whose "word" is lofty and holy;
> Whose pronouncement is unchangeable;
> Who decrees destinies unto the distant future....
> The Gods of Earth bow down willingly before him;
> The Heavenly gods who are on Earth
> humble themselves before him;
> They stand by faithfully, according to instructions.

Enlil, according to Sumerian beliefs, arrived on Earth well before Earth became settled and civilized. A "Hymn to Enlil, the All-Beneficent" recounts the many aspects of society and civilization that would not have existed had it not been for Enlil's instructions to "execute his orders, far and wide."

No cities would be built, no settlements founded;
No stalls would be built, no sheepfolds erected;
No king would be raised, no high priest born.

The Sumerian texts also stated that Enlil arrived on Earth before the "Black-Headed People"—the Sumerian nickname for Mankind—were created. During such pre-Mankind times, Enlil erected Nippur as his center, or "command post," at which Heaven and Earth were connected through some "bond." The Sumerian texts called this bond DUR.AN.KI ("bond heaven–earth") and used poetic language to describe Enlil's first actions on Earth:

Enlil,
When you marked off divine settlements on Earth,
Nippur you set up as your very own city.
The City of Earth, the lofty,
Your pure place whose water is sweet.
You founded the Dur-An-Ki
In the center of the four corners of the world.

In those early days, when gods alone inhabited Nippur and Man had not yet been created, Enlil met the goddess who was to become his wife. According to one version, Enlil saw his future bride while she was bathing in Nippur's stream—naked. It was love at first sight, but not necessarily with marriage in mind:

The shepherd Enlil, who decrees the fates,
The Bright-Eyed One, saw her.
The lord speaks to her of intercourse;
she is unwilling.
Enlil speaks to her of intercourse;
she is unwilling:
"My vagina is too small [she said],
It knows no copulation;
My lips are too little,
they know not kissing."

But Enlil did not take no for an answer. He disclosed to his chamberlain Nushku his burning desire for "the young maid," who was called SUD ("the nurse"), and who lived with her mother at E.RESH ("scented house"). Nushku suggested a boat ride and brought up a boat. Enlil persuaded Sud to go sailing with him. Once they were in the boat, he raped her.

The ancient tale then relates that though Enlil was chief of the gods they were so enraged that they seized him and banished him to the Lower World. "Enlil, immoral one!" they shouted at him. "Get thyself out of the city!" This version has it that Sud, pregnant with Enlil's child, followed him, and he married her. Another version has the repentant Enlil searching for the girl and sending his chamberlain to her mother to ask for the girl's hand. One way or another, Sud did become the wife of Enlil, and he bestowed on her the title NIN.LIL ("lady of the airspace").

But little did he and the gods who banished him know that it was not Enlil who had seduced Ninlil, but the other way around. The truth of the matter was that Ninlil bathed naked in the stream on her mother's instructions, with the hope that Enlil—who customarily took his walks by the stream—would notice Ninlil and wish to "forthwith embrace you, kiss you."

In spite of the manner in which the two fell for each other, Ninlil was held in the highest esteem once she was given by Enlil "the garment of ladyship." With one exception, which (we believe) had to do with dynastic succession, Enlil is never known to have had other indiscretions. A votive tablet found at Nippur shows Enlil and Ninlil being served food and beverage at their temple. The tablet was commissioned by Ur-Enlil, the "Domestic of Enlil." (Fig. 45)

Apart from being chief of the gods, Enlil was also deemed the supreme Lord of Sumer (sometimes simply called "The Land") and its "Black-Headed People." A Sumerian psalm spoke in veneration of this god:

Lord who knows the destiny of The Land,
  trustworthy in his calling;
Enlil who knows the destiny of Sumer,
  trustworthy in his calling;
Father Enlil,
  Lord of all the lands;
Father Enlil,
  Lord of the Rightful Command;
Father Enlil,
  Shepherd of the Black-Headed Ones. . . .
From the Mountain of Sunrise
  to the Mountain of Sunset,
There is no other Lord in the land;
  you alone are King.

The Sumerians revered Enlil out of both fear and gratitude. It was

Fig. 45

he who made sure that decrees by the Assembly of the Gods were carried out against Mankind; it was his "wind" that blew obliterating storms against offending cities. It was he who, at the time of the Deluge, sought the destruction of Mankind. But when at peace with Mankind, he was a friendly god who bestowed favors; according to the Sumerian text, the knowledge of farming, together with the plow and the pickax, were granted to Mankind by Enlil.

Enlil also selected the kings who were to rule over Mankind, not as sovereigns but as servants of the god entrusted with the administration of divine laws of justice. Accordingly, Sumerian, Akkadian, and Babylonian kings opened their inscriptions of self-adoration by describing how Enlil had called them to Kingship. These "calls"—issued by Enlil on behalf of himself and his father Anu—granted legitimacy to the ruler and outlined his functions. Even Hammurabi, who acknowledged a god named Marduk as the national god of Babylon, prefaced his code of laws by stating that "Anu and Enlil named me to promote the welfare of the people . . . to cause justice to prevail in the land."

God of Heaven and Earth, Firstborn of Anu, Dispenser of Kingship, Chief Executive of the Assembly of the Gods, Father of Gods and Men, Granter of Agriculture, Lord of the Airspace—these were some of the attributes of Enlil that bespoke his greatness and powers. His "command was far reaching," his "pronouncements unchangeable"; he "decreed the destinies." He possessed the "bond· heaven–earth," and from his "awesome city Nippur" he could "raise the beams that search the heart of all the lands"—"eyes that could scan all the lands."

Yet he was as human as any young man enticed by a naked beauty; subject to moral laws imposed by the community of the gods, transgressions of which were punishable by banishment; and not even immune to mortal complaints. At least in one known instance, a Sumerian king of Ur complained directly to the Assembly of the Gods that a series of troubles that had befallen Ur and her people could be traced back to the ill-fated fact that "Enlil did give the kingship to a worthless man . . . who is not of Sumerian seed."

As we go along, we shall see the central role that Enlil played in divine and mortal affairs on Earth, and how his several sons battled among themselves and with others for the divine succession, undoubtedly giving rise to the later tales of the battles of the gods.

The third Great God of Sumer was another son of Anu; he bore two names, E.A and EN.KI. Like his brother Enlil, he, too, was a God of Heaven and Earth, a deity originally of the heavens, who had come down to Earth.

His arrival on Earth is associated in Sumerian texts with a time when the waters of the Persian Gulf reached inland much farther than nowadays, turning the southern part of the country into marshlands. Ea (the name meant literally "house-water"), who was a master engineer, planned and supervised the construction of canals, the diking of the rivers, and the draining of the marshlands. He loved to go sailing on these waterways, and especially in the marshlands. The waters, as his name denoted, were indeed his home. He built his "great house" in the city he had founded at the edge of the marshlands, a city appropriately named HA.A.KI ("place of the water-fishes"); it was also known as E.RI.DU ("home of going afar").

Ea was "Lord of the Saltwaters," the seas and oceans. Sumerian texts speak repeatedly of a very early time when the three Great Gods divided the realms among them. "The seas they had given to Enki, the Prince of Earth," thereby giving Enki "the rulership of the Apsu" (the "Deep"). As Lord of the Seas, Ea built ships that sailed to far lands, and especially to places from which precious metals and semiprecious stones were brought to Sumer.

The earliest Sumerian cylinder seals depicted Ea as a deity surrounded by flowing streams that were sometimes shown to contain fish. The seals associated Ea, as shown here, with the Moon (indicated by its crescent), an association stemming perhaps from the fact that the Moon caused the tides of the seas. It was no doubt in reference to such an astral image that Ea was given the epithet NIN.IGI.KU ("lord bright-eye"). (Fig. 46)

According to the Sumerian texts, including a truly amazing autobiography by Ea himself, he was born in the heavens and came down to Earth before there was any settlement or civilization upon Earth. "When I approached the land, there was much flooding," he

Fig. 46

stated. He then proceeded to describe the series of actions taken by him to make the land habitable: He filled the Tigris River with fresh, "life-giving waters"; he appointed a god to supervise the construction of canals, to make the Tigris and Euphrates navigable; and he unclogged the marshlands, filling them up with fish and making them a haven for birds of all kinds, and causing to grow there reeds that were a useful building material.

Turning from the seas and rivers to the dry land, Ea claimed that it was he who "directed the plow and the yoke . . . opened the holy furrows . . . built the stalls . . . erected sheepfolds." Continuing, the self-adulatory text (named by scholars "Enki and the World Order") credited the god with bringing to Earth the arts of brickmaking, construction of dwellings and cities, metallurgy, and so on.

Presenting the deity as Mankind's greatest benefactor, the god who brought about civilization, many texts also depicted him as Mankind's chief protagonist at the councils of the gods. Sumerian and Akkadian Deluge texts, on which the biblical account must have drawn, depict Ea as the god who—in defiance of the decision of the Assembly of the Gods—enabled a trusted follower (the Mesopotamian "Noah") to escape the disaster.

Indeed, the Sumerian and Akkadian texts, which (like the Old Testament) adhered to the belief that a god or the gods created Man through a conscious and deliberate act, attribute to Ea a key role: As the chief scientist of the gods, he outlined the method and the process by which Man was to be created. With such affinity to the "creation" or emergence of Man, no wonder that it was Ea who guided Adapa—the "model man" created by Ea's "wisdom"—to the abode of Anu in the heavens, in defiance of the gods' determination to withhold "eternal life" from Mankind.

Was Ea on the side of Man simply because he had a hand in his creation, or did he have other, more subjective motives? As we scan the record, we find that invariably Ea's defiance—in mortal and divine matters alike—was aimed mostly at frustrating decisions or plans emanating from Enlil.

The record is replete with indications of Ea's burning jealousy of his brother Enlil. Indeed, Ea's other (and perhaps first) name was EN.KI ("lord of Earth"), and the texts dealing with the division of the world among the three gods hint that it may have been simply by a drawing of lots that Ea lost mastery of Earth to his brother Enlil.

> The gods had clasped hands together,
> Had cast lots and had divided.
> Anu then went up to Heaven;
> To Enlil the Earth was made subject.
> The seas, enclosed as with a loop,
> They had given to Enki, the Prince of Earth.

As bitter as Ea/Enki may have been about the results of this drawing, he appears to have nurtured a much deeper resentment. The reason is given by Enki himself in his autobiography: It was he, not Enlil, who was firstborn, Enki claimed; it was then he, and not Enlil, who was entitled to be the heir apparent to Anu:

> "My father, the king of the universe,
> brought me forth in the universe. . . .
> I am the fecund seed,
> engendered by the Great Wild Bull;
> I am the first born son of Anu.
> I am the Great Brother of the gods. . . .
> I am he who has been born
> as the first son of the divine Anu."

Since the codes of laws by which men lived in the ancient Near East were given by the gods, it stands to reason that the social and family laws applying to men were copies of those applying to the gods. Court and family records found at such sites as Mari and Nuzi have confirmed that the biblical customs and laws by which the Hebrew patriarchs lived were the laws by which kings and noblemen were bound throughout the ancient Near East. The succession problems the patriarchs faced are therefore instructive.

Abraham, deprived of a child by the apparent barrenness of his wife Sarah, had a firstborn son by her maidservant. Yet this son (Ishmael) was excluded from the patriarchal succession as soon as Sarah herself bore Abraham a son, Isaac.

Isaac's wife Rebecca was pregnant with twins. The one who was technically firstborn was Esau—a reddish, hairy, and rugged fellow. Holding onto Esau's heel was the more refined Jacob, whom Rebecca cherished. When the aging and half-blind Isaac was about to proclaim his testament, Rebecca used a ruse to have the blessing of succession bestowed on Jacob rather than on Esau.

Finally, Jacob's succession problems resulted from the fact that though he served Laban for twenty years to get the hand of Rachel in marriage, Laban forced him to marry her older sister Leah first. It was Leah who bore Jacob his first son (Reuben), and he had more sons and a daughter by her and by two concubines. Yet when Rachel finally bore him *her* firstborn son (Joseph), Jacob preferred him over his brothers.

Against the background of such customs and succession laws, one can understand the conflicting claims between Enlil and Ea/Enki. Enlil, by all records the son of Anu and his official consort Antu, was the *legal* firstborn. But the anguished cry of Enki: "*I* am the fecund seed . . . *I* am the first born son of Anu," must have been a statement of fact. Was he then born to Anu, but by another goddess who was only a concubine? The tale of Isaac and Ishmael, or the story of the twins Esau and Jacob, may have had a prior parallel in the Heavenly Abode.

Though Enki appears to have accepted Enlil's succession prerogatives, some scholars see enough evidence to show a continuing power struggle between the two gods. Samuel N. Kramer has titled one of the ancient texts "Enki and His Inferiority Complex." As we shall see later on, several biblical tales—of Eve and the serpent in the Garden of Eden, or the tale of the Deluge—involve in their original Sumerian versions instances of defiance by Enki of his brother's edicts.

At some point, it seems, Enki decided that there was no sense to his struggle for the Divine Throne; and he put his efforts into making a son of his—rather than a son of Enlil—the third-generation successor. This he sought to achieve, at least at first, with the aid of his sister NIN.HUR.SAG ("lady of the mountainhead").

She, too, was a daughter of Anu, but evidently not by Antu, and therein lay another rule of succession. Scholars have wondered in years past why both Abraham and Isaac advertised the fact that their respective wives were also their sisters—a puzzling claim in view of the biblical prohibition against sexual relations with a sister. But as the legal documents were unearthed at Mari and Nuzi, it became clear that a man could marry a half-sister. Moreover, when all the children of all the wives were considered, the son born of such a wife—being fifty percent more of the "pure seed" than a son by an unrelated wife—was the legal heir whether or not he was the firstborn son. This, incidentally, led (in Mari and Nuzi) to the practice of adopting the preferred wife as a "sister" in order to make her son the unchallenged legal heir.

It was of such a half-sister, Ninhursag, that Enki sought to have a son. She, too, was "of the heavens," having come to Earth in earliest times. Several texts state that when the gods were dividing Earth's domains among themselves, she was given the Land of Dilmun—"a pure place . . . a pure land . . . a place most bright." A text named by the scholars "Enki and Ninhursag—a Paradise Myth" deals with Enki's trip to Dilmun for conjugal purposes. Ninhursag, the text repeatedly stresses, "was alone"—unattached, a spinster. Though in later times she was depicted as an old matron, she must have been very attractive when she was younger, for the text informs us unabashedly that, when Enki neared her, the sight of her "caused his penis to water the dikes."

Instructing that they be left alone, Enki "poured the semen in the womb of Ninhursag. She took the semen into the womb, the semen of Enki"; and then, "after the nine months of Womanhood . . . she gave birth at the bank of the waters." But the child was a daughter.

Having failed to obtain a male heir, Enki then proceeded to make love to his own daughter. "He embraced her, he kissed her; Enki poured the semen into the womb." But she, too, bore him a daughter. Enki then went after his granddaughter and made her pregnant, too; but once again the offspring was a female. Determined to stop these efforts, Ninhursag put a curse on him whereby Enki, having eaten some plants, became mortally sick. The other gods, however, forced Ninhursag to remove the curse.

While these events had great bearing on divine affairs, other tales pertaining to Enki and Ninhursag have great bearing on human affairs; for, according to the Sumerian texts, Man was created by Ninhursag following processes and formulas devised by Enki. She was the chief nurse, the one in charge of medical facilities; it was in that role that the goddess was called NIN.TI ("lady-life"). (Fig. 47)

Some scholars read in *Adapa* (the "model man" of Enki) the biblical *Adama*, or Adam. The double meaning of the Sumerian TI also raises biblical parallels. For *ti* could mean both "life" and "rib," so that Ninti's name meant both "lady of life" and "lady of the rib." The biblical Eve—whose name meant "life"—was created out of Adam's rib, so Eve, too, was in a way a "lady of life" and a "lady of the rib."

As giver of life to gods and Man alike, Ninhursag was spoken of as the Mother Goddess. She was nicknamed "Mammu"—the forerunner of our "mom" or "mamma"—and her symbol was the "cutter"—the tool used in antiquity by midwives to cut the umbilical cord after birth. (Fig. 48)

Enlil, Enki's brother and rival, did have the good fortune to achieve such a "rightful heir" by his sister Ninhursag. The youngest of the gods upon Earth who were born in the heavens, his name was NIN.UR.TA ("lord who completes the foundation"). He was "the heroic son of Enlil who went forth with net and rays of light" to battle for his father; "the avenging son . . . who launched bolts of light." (Fig. 49) His spouse BA.U was also a nurse or a doctor; her epithet was "lady who the dead brings back to life."

The ancient portraits of Ninurta showed him holding a unique weapon—no doubt the very one that could shoot "bolts of light." The ancient texts hailed him as a mighty hunter, a fighting god renowned for his martial abilities. But his greatest heroic fight was not in behalf of his father but for his own sake. It was a wide-ranging battle with an evil god named ZU ("wise"), and it involved no less a prize than the leadership of the gods on Earth; for Zu had illegally captured the insignia and objects Enlil had held as Chief of the Gods.

The texts describing these events are broken at the beginning, and the story becomes legible only from the point when Zu arrives at the E-Kur, the temple of Enlil. He is apparently known, and of some rank, for Enlil welcomes him, "entrusting to him the guarding of the entrance to his shrine." But the "evil Zu" was to repay trust with betrayal, for it was "the removal of the Enlilship"—the seizing of the divine powers—that "he conceived in his heart."

To do so, Zu had to take possession of certain objects, including the magical Tablet of Destinies. The wily Zu seized his opportunity when Enlil undressed and went into the pool for his daily swim, leaving his paraphernalia unattended.

> At the entrance of the sanctuary,
> which he had been viewing,
> Zu awaits the start of day.
> As Enlil was washing with pure water—
> his crown having been removed
> and deposited on the throne—
> Zu seized the Tablet of Destinies in his hands,
> took away the Enlilship.

Fig. 47

Fig. 48

Fig. 49

As Zu fled in his MU (translated "name," but indicating a flying machine) to a faraway hideaway, the consequences of his bold act were beginning to take effect.

> Suspended were the Divine Formulas;
> Stillness spread all over; silence prevailed. . . .
> The Sanctuary's brilliance was taken off.

"Father Enlil was speechless." "The gods of the land gathered one by one at the news." The matter was so grave that even Anu was informed at his Heavenly Abode. He reviewed the situation and concluded that Zu must be apprehended so that the "formulas" could be restored. Turning "to the gods, his children," Anu asked, "Which of the gods will smite Zu? His name shall be greatest of all!"

Several gods known for their valor were called in. But they all pointed out that having taken the Tablet of Destinies, Zu now possessed the same powers as Enlil, so that "he who opposes him becomes like clay." At this point, Ea had a great idea: Why not call upon Ninurta to take up the hopeless fight?

The assembled gods could not have missed Ea's ingenious mischief. Clearly, the chances of the succession falling to his own offspring stood to increase if Zu were defeated; likewise, he could benefit if Ninurta were killed in the process. To the amazement of the gods, Ninhursag (in this text called NIN.MAH—"great lady"), agreed. Turning to her son Ninurta, she explained to him that Zu robbed not only Enlil but Ninurta, too, of the Enlilship. "With shrieks of pain I gave birth," she shouted, and it was she who "made certain for my brother and for Anu" the continued "Kingship of Heaven." So that her pains not be in vain, she instructed Ninurta to go out and fight to win:

> Launch thy offensive . . . capture the fugitive Zu. . . .
> Let thy terrifying offensive rage against him. . . .
> Slit his throat! Vanquish Zu! . . .
> Let thy seven ill Winds go against him. . . .
> Cause the entire Whirlwind to attack him. . . .
> Let thy Radiance go against him. . . .
> Let thy Winds carry his Wings to a secret place. . . .
> Let sovereignty return to Ekur;
> Let the Divine Formulas return
> to the father who begot thee.

The various versions of the epic then provide thrilling descriptions of the battle that ensued. Ninurta shot "arrows" at Zu, but "the arrows could not approach Zu's body . . . while he bore the Tablet of Destinies of the gods in his hand." The launched "weapons were stopped in the midst" of their flight. As the inconclusive battle wore on, Ea advised Ninurta to add a *til-lum* to his weapons, and shoot it into the "pinions," or small cog-wheels, of Zu's "wings." Following this advice, and shouting "Wing to wing," Ninurta shot the *til-lum* at Zu's pinions. Thus hit, the pinions began to scatter, and the "wings" of Zu fell in a swirl. Zu was vanquished, and the Tablets of Destiny returned to Enlil.

✿

Who was Zu? Was he, as some scholars hold, a "mythological bird"?

Evidently he could fly. But so can any man today who takes a plane, or any astronaut who goes up in a spaceship. Ninurta, too, could fly, as skillfully as Zu (and perhaps better). But he himself was not a bird of any kind, as his many depictions, by himself or with his consort BA.U (also called GU.LA), make abundantly clear. Rather, he did his flying with the aid of a remarkable "bird," which was kept at his sacred precinct (the GIR.SU) in the city of Lagash.

Nor was Zu a "bird"; apparently he had at his disposal a "bird" in which he could fly away into hiding. It was from within such "birds" that the sky battle took place between the two gods. And there can be no doubt regarding the nature of the weapon that finally smote Zu's "bird." Called TIL in Sumerian and *til-lum* in Assyrian, it was written pictorially thus: ➤——▷— , and it must have meant then what *til* means nowadays in Hebrew: "missile."

Zu, then, was a god—one of the gods who had reason to scheme at usurpation of the Enlilship; a god whom Ninurta, as the legitimate successor, had every reason to fight.

Was he perhaps MAR.DUK ("son of the pure mound"), Enki's firstborn by his wife DAM.KI.NA, impatient to seize by a ruse what was not legally his?

There is reason to believe that, having failed to achieve a son by his sister and thus produce a legal contender for the Enlilship, Enki relied on his son Marduk. Indeed, when the ancient Near East was seized with great social and military upheavals at the beginning of the second millennium B.C., Marduk was elevated in Babylon to the status of national god of Sumer and Akkad. Marduk was proclaimed King of the Gods, replacing Enlil, and the other gods were required to pledge allegiance to him and to come to reside in Babylon, where their activities could easily be supervised. (Fig. 50)

This usurpation of the Enlilship (long after the incident with Zu) was accompanied by an extensive Babylonian effort to forge the ancient texts. The most important texts were rewritten and altered so as to

Fig. 50

make Marduk appear as the Lord of Heavens, the Creator, the Benefactor, the Hero, instead of Anu or Enlil or even Ninurta. Among the texts altered was the "Tale of Zu"; and according to the Babylonian version it was Marduk (not Ninurta) who fought Zu. In this version, Marduk boasted: *"Maḫaṣti moḫ il Zu"* ("I have crushed the skull of the god Zu"). Clearly, then, Zu could not have been Marduk.

Nor would it stand to reason that Enki, "God of Sciences," would have coached Ninurta regarding the choice and use of the successful weapons against his own son Marduk. Enki, to judge by his behavior as well as by his urging Ninurta to "cut the throat of Zu," expected to gain from the fight, no matter who lost. The only logical conclusion is that Zu, too, was in some way a *legal* contender to the Enlilship.

This suggests only one god: Nanna, the firstborn of Enlil by his official consort Ninlil. For if Ninurta were eliminated, Nanna would be in the unobstructed line of succession.

Nanna (short for NAN.NAR—"bright one") has come down to us through the ages better known by his Akkadian (or "Semitic") name Sin.

As firstborn of Enlil, he was granted sovereignty over Sumer's best-known city-state, UR *("The* City"). His temple there was called E.GISH.NU.GAL ("house of the seed of the throne"). From that abode, Nanna and his consort NIN.GAL ("great lady") conducted the affairs of the city and its people with great benevolence. The people of Ur reciprocated with great affection for their divine rulers, lovingly calling their god "Father Nanna" and other affectionate nicknames.

The prosperity of Ur was attributed by its people directly to Nanna. Shulgi, a ruler of Ur (by the god's grace) at the end of the third millennium B.C., described the "house" of Nanna as "a great stall filled with abundance," a "bountiful place of bread offerings," where sheep multiplied and oxen were slaughtered, a place of sweet music where the drum and timbrel sounded.

Under the administration of its god-protector Nanna, Ur became the granary of Sumer, the supplier of grains as well as of sheep and cattle to other temples elsewhere. A "Lamentation over the Destruction of Ur" informs us, in a negative way, of what Ur was like before its demise:

> In the granaries of Nanna there was no grain.
> The evening meals of the gods were suppressed;
> in their great dining halls, wine and honey ended. . . .
> In his temple's lofty oven, oxen and sheep are not prepared;
> The hum has ceased at Nanna's great Place of Shackles:
> that house where commands for the ox were shouted—
> its silence is overwhelming. . . .
> Its grinding mortar and pestle lie inert. . . .
> The offering boats carried no offerings. . . .
> Did not bring offering bread to Enlil in Nippur.
> Ur's river is empty, no barge moves on it. . . .
> No foot trods its banks; long grasses grow there.

Another lamentation, bewailing the "sheepfolds that have been delivered to the wind," the abandoned stables, the shepherds and herdsmen that were gone, is most unusual: It was not written by the people of Ur, but by the god Nanna and his spouse Ningal themselves. These and other lamentations over the fall of Ur disclose the trauma of some unusual event. The Sumerian texts inform us that Nanna and Ningal left the city before its demise became complete. It was a hasty departure, touchingly described.

> Nanna, who loved his city,
>   departed from the city.
> Sin, who loved Ur,
>   no longer stayed in his House.
> Ningal . . .
>   fleeing her city through enemy territory,
> hastily put on a garment,
>   departed from her House.

The fall of Ur and the exile of its gods have been depicted in the lamentations as the results of a deliberate decision by Anu and Enlil. It was to the two of them that Nanna appealed to call off the punishment.

> May Anu, the king of the gods,
>   utter: "It is enough";
> May Enlil, the king of the lands,
>   decree a favorable fate!

Appealing directly to Enlil, "Sin brought his suffering heart to his father; curtsied before Enlil, the father who begot him," and begged him:

> O my father who begot me,
> Until when will you look inimically
> upon my atonement?
> Until when? . . .
> On the oppressed heart that you have made
> flicker like a flame—
> please cast a friendly eye.

Nowhere do the lamentations disclose the *cause* of Anu's and Enlil's wrath. But if Nanna were Zu, the punishment would have justified his crime of usurpation. *Was* he Zu?

He certainly could have been Zu because Zu was in possession of some kind of flying machine—the "bird" in which he escaped and from which he fought Ninurta. Sumerian psalms spoke in adoration of his "Boat of Heaven."

> Father Nannar, Lord of Ur . . .
> Whose glory in the sacred Boat of Heaven is . . .
> Lord, firstborn son of Enlil.
> When in the Boat of Heaven thou ascendeth,
> Thou art glorious.
> Enlil hath adorned thy hand
> With a scepter everlasting
> When over Ur in the Sacred Boat thou mountest.

There is additional evidence. Nanna's other name, Sin, derived from SU.EN, which was another way of pronouncing ZU.EN. The same complex meaning of a two-syllable word could be obtained by placing the syllables in any order: ZU.EN and EN.ZU were "mirror" words of each other. Nanna/Sin as ZU.EN was none other than EN.ZU ("lord *Zu*"). It was he, we must conclude, who tried to seize the Enlilship.

We can now understand why, in spite of Ea's suggestion, the lord Zu (Sin) was punished, not by execution, but by exile. Both Sumerian texts, as well as archaeological evidence, indicate that Sin and his spouse fled to Haran, the Hurrian city protected by several rivers and mountainous terrain. It is noteworthy that when Abraham's clan, led by his father Terah, left Ur, they also set their course to Haran, where they stayed for many years en route to the Promised Land.

Though Ur remained for all time a city dedicated to Nanna/Sin, Haran must have been his residence for a very long time, for it was made to resemble Ur—its temples, buildings, and streets—almost exactly. André Parrot (*Abraham et son temps*) sums up the similarities by saying that "there is every evidence that the cult of Harran was nothing but an exact replica of that of Ur."

When the temple of Sin at Haran—built and rebuilt over the millennia—was uncovered during excavations that lasted more than fifty years, the finds included two stelae (memorial stone pillars) on which a unique record was inscribed. It was a record dictated by Adadguppi, a high priestess of Sin, of how she prayed and planned for the return of Sin, for, at some unknown prior time,

> Sin, the king of all the gods,
> became angry with his city and his temple,
> and went up to Heaven.

That Sin, disgusted or despairing, just "packed up" and "went up to Heaven" is corroborated by other inscriptions. These tell us that the Assyrian king Ashurbanipal retrieved from certain enemies a sacred "cylinder seal of the costliest jasper" and "had it improved by drawing upon it a picture of Sin." He further inscribed upon the sacred stone "a eulogy of Sin, and hung it around the neck of the image of Sin." That stone seal of Sin must have been a relic of olden times, for it is further stated that "it is the one whose face had been damaged in those days, during the destruction wrought by the enemy."

The high priestess, who was born during the reign of Ashurbanipal, is assumed to have been of royal blood herself. In her appeals to Sin, she proposed a practical "deal": the restoration of his powers over his adversaries in return for helping her son Nabunaid become ruler of Sumer and Akkad. Historical records confirm that in the year 555 B.C. Nabunaid, then commander of the Babylonian armies, was named by his fellow officers to the throne. In this he was stated to have been directly helped by Sin. It was, the inscriptions by Nabunaid inform us, "on the first day of his appearance" that Sin, using "the weapon of Anu"—was able to "touch with a beam of light" the skies and crush the enemies down on Earth below.

Nabunaid kept his mother's promise to the god. He rebuilt Sin's temple E.HUL.HUL ("house of great joy") and declared Sin to be Supreme God. It was then that Sin was able to grasp in his hands "the power of the Anu-office, wield all the power of the Enlil-office, take over the power of the Ea-office—holding thus in his own hand all the Heavenly Powers." Thus defeating the usurper Marduk, even capturing the powers of Marduk's father Ea, Sin assumed the title of "Divine Crescent" and established his reputation as the so-called Moon God.

How could Sin, reported to have gone back to Heaven in disgust, have been able to perform such feats back on Earth?

Nabunaid, confirming that Sin had indeed "forgotten his angry command . . . and decided to return to the temple Ehulhul," claimed a miracle. A miracle "that has not happened to the Land since the days of old" had taken place: A deity "has come down from Heaven."

> This is the great miracle of Sin,
> That has not happened to the Land
> Since the days of old;
> That the people of the Land
> Have not seen, nor had written
> On clay tablets, to preserve forever:
> That Sin,
> Lord of all the gods and goddesses,
> Residing in Heaven,
> Has come down from Heaven.

Regrettably, no details are provided of the place and manner in which Sin landed back on Earth. But we do know that it was in the fields outside of Haran that Jacob, on his way from Canaan to find himself a bride in the "old country," saw "a ladder set up on the earth and its top reaching heavenward, and there were angels of the Lord ascending and descending by it."

At the same time that Nabunaid restored the powers and temples of Nanna/Sin, he also restored the temples and worship of Sin's twin children, IN.ANNA ("Anu's lady") and UTU ("the shining one").

The two were born to Sin by his official spouse Ningal, and were thus by birth members of the Divine Dynasty. Inanna was technically the firstborn, but her twin brother Utu was the firstborn *son*, and thus the legal dynastic heir. Unlike the rivalry that existed in the similar instance of Esau and Jacob, the two divine children grew up very close to each other. They shared experiences and adventures, came to each other's aid, and when Inanna had to choose a husband from one of two gods, she turned to her brother for advice.

Inanna and Utu were born in time immemorial, when only the gods inhabited Earth. Utu's city-domain Sippar was listed among the very first cities to have been established by the gods in Sumer. Nabunaid stated in an inscription that when he undertook to rebuild Utu's temple E.BABBARA ("shining house") in Sippar:

> I sought out its ancient foundation-platform,
> and I went down eighteen cubits into the soil.
> Utu, the Great Lord of Ebabbara . . .
> Showed me personally the foundation-platform
> of Naram-Sin, son of Sargon, which for 3,200 years
> no king preceding me had seen.

When civilization blossomed in Sumer, and Man joined the gods in the Land Between the Rivers, Utu became associated primarily with law and justice. Several early law codes, apart from invoking Anu and Enlil, were also presented as requiring acceptance and adherence because they were promulgated "in accordance with the true word of Utu." The Babylonian king Hammurabi inscribed his law code on a stela, at the top of which the king is depicted receiving the laws from the god. (Fig. 51)

Tablets uncovered at Sippar attest to its reputation in ancient times as a place of just and fair laws. Some texts depict Utu himself as sitting in judgment on gods and men alike; Sippar was, in fact, the seat of Sumer's "supreme court."

The justice advocated by Utu is reminiscent of the Sermon on the Mount recorded in the New Testament. A "wisdom tablet" suggested the following behavior to please Utu:

> Unto your opponent do no evil;
> Your evildoer recompense with good.
> Unto your enemy, let justice be done. . . .
> Let not your heart be induced to do evil. . . .
> To the one begging for alms—
> give food to eat, give wine to drink. . . .
> Be helpful; do good.

Because he assured justice and prevented oppression—and perhaps

Fig. 51

for other reasons, too, as we shall see later on—Utu was considered the protector of travelers. Yet the most common and lasting epithets applied to Utu concerned his brilliance. From earliest times, he was called Babbar ("shining one"). He was "Utu, who sheds a wide light," the one who "lights up Heaven and Earth."

Hammurabi, in his inscription, called the god by his Akkadian name, Shamash, which in Semitic languages means "Sun." It has therefore been assumed by the scholars that Utu/Shamash was the Mesopotamian Sun God. We shall show, as we proceed, that while this god was assigned the Sun as his celestial counterpart, there was another aspect to the statements that he "shed a bright light" when he performed the special tasks assigned to him by his grandfather Enlil.

Just as the law codes and the court records are human testimonials to the actual presence among the ancient peoples of Mesopotamia of a deity named Utu/Shamash, so there exist endless inscriptions, texts, incantations, oracles, prayers, and depictions attesting to the physical presence and existence of the goddess Inanna, whose Akkadian name was Ishtar. A Mesopotamian king in the thirteenth century B.C. stated that he had rebuilt her temple in her brother's city of Sippar, on foundations that were eight hundred years old in his time. But in her central city, Uruk, tales of her went back to olden times.

Known to the Romans as Venus, to the Greeks as Aphrodite, to the

Canaanites and the Hebrews as Astarte, to the Assyrians and Babylonians and Hittites and the other ancient peoples as Ishtar or Eshdar, to the Akkadians and the Sumerians as Inanna or Innin or Ninni, or by others of her many nicknames and epithets, she was at all times the Goddess of Warfare and the Goddess of Love, a fierce, beautiful female who, though only a great-granddaughter of Anu, carved for herself, by herself, a major place among the Great Gods of Heaven and Earth.

As a young goddess she was, apparently, assigned a domain in a far land east of Sumer, the Land of Aratta. It was there that "the lofty one, Inanna, queen of all the land," had her "house." But Inanna had greater ambitions. In the city of Uruk there stood the great temple of Anu, occupied only during his occasional state visits to Earth; and Inanna set her eyes on this seat of power.

Sumerian king lists state that the first nondivine ruler of Uruk was Meshkiaggasher, a son of the god Utu by a human mother. He was followed by his son Enmerkar, a great Sumerian king. Inanna, then, was the great-aunt of Enmerkar; and she found little difficulty in persuading him that she should really be the goddess of Uruk, rather than of the remote Aratta.

A long and fascinating text named "Enmerkar and the Lord of Aratta" describes how Enmerkar sent emissaries to Aratta, using every possible argument in a "war of nerves" to force Aratta to submit because "the lord Enmerkar who is the servant of Inanna made her queen of the House of Anu." The epic's unclear end hints at a happy ending: While Inanna moved to Uruk, she did not "abandon her House in Aratta." That she might have become a "commuting goddess" is not so improbable, for Inanna/Ishtar was known from other texts as an adventurous traveler.

Her occupation of Anu's temple in Uruk could not have taken place without his knowledge and consent; and the texts give us strong clues as to how such consent was obtained. Soon Inanna was known as "Anunitum," a nickname meaning "beloved of Anu." She was referred to in texts as "the holy mistress of Anu"; and it follows that Inanna shared not only Anu's temple but also his bed—whenever he came to Uruk, or on the reported occasions of her going up to his Heavenly Abode.

Having thus maneuvered herself into the position of goddess of Uruk and mistress of the temple of Anu, Ishtar proceeded to use trickery for enhancing Uruk's standing and her own powers. Farther down the Euphrates stood the ancient city of Eridu—Enki's center. Knowing of his great knowledge of all the arts and sciences of civilization, Inanna resolved to beg, borrow, or steal these secrets. Obviously intending to use her "personal charms" on Enki (her great-uncle), Inanna arranged to call on him alone. That fact was not unnoticed by Enki, who instructed his housemaster to prepare dinner for two.

> Come my housemaster Isimud, hear my instructions;
> a word I shall say to you, heed my words:
> The maiden, all alone, has directed her step to the Abzu . . .
> Have the maiden enter the Abzu of Eridu,
> Give her to eat barley cakes with butter,
> Pour for her cold water that freshens the heart,
> Give her to drink beer. . . .

Happy and drunk, Enki was ready to do anything for Inanna. She boldly asked for the divine formulas, which were the basis of a high civilization. Enki granted her some one hundred of them, including divine formulas pertaining to supreme lordship, Kingship, priestly functions, weapons, legal procedures, scribeship, woodworking, even the knowledge of musical instruments and of temple prostitution. By the time Enki awoke and realized what he had done, Inanna was already well on her way to Uruk. Enki ordered after her his "awesome weapons," but to no avail, for Inanna had sped to Uruk in her "Boat of Heaven."

Quite frequently, Ishtar was depicted as a naked goddess; flaunting her beauty, she was sometimes even depicted raising her skirts to reveal the lower parts of her body. (Fig. 52)

Gilgamesh, a ruler of Uruk circa 2900 B.C. who was also partly divine (having been born to a human father and a goddess), reported how Inanna enticed him—even after she already had an official spouse. Having washed himself after a battle and put on "a fringe cloak, fastened with a sash,"

Fig. 52

Glorious Ishtar raised an eye at his beauty.
"Come, Gilgamesh, be thou my lover!
Come, grant me your fruit.
Thou shall be my male mate, I will be thy female."

But Gilgamesh knew the score. "Which of thy lovers didst thou love forever?" he asked. "Which of thy shepherds pleased thee for all time?" Reciting a long list of her love affairs, he refused.

As time went on—as she assumed higher ranks in the pantheon, and with it the responsibility for affairs of state—Inanna/Ishtar began to display more martial qualities, and was often depicted as a Goddess of War, armed to the teeth. (Fig. 53)

The inscriptions left by Assyrian kings describe how they went to war for her and upon her command, how she directly advised when to wait and when to attack, how she sometimes marched at the head of the armies, and how, on at least one occasion, she granted a theophany and appeared before all the troops. In return for their loyalty, she promised the Assyrian kings long life and success. "From a Golden Chamber in the skies I will watch over thee," she assured them.

Was she turned into a bitter warrior because she, too, came upon hard times with the rise of Marduk to supremacy? In one of his inscriptions Nabunaid said: "Inanna of Uruk, the exalted princess who dwelt in a gold cella, who rode upon a chariot to which were harnessed seven lions—the inhabitants of Uruk changed her cult during the rule of king Erba-Marduk, removed her cella and unharnessed her team." Inanna, reported Nabunaid, "had therefore left the E-Anna angrily, and stayed hence in an unseemly place" (which he does not name). (Fig. 54)

Seeking, perhaps, to combine love with power, the much-courted Inanna chose as her husband DU.MU.ZI, a younger son of Enki. Many ancient texts deal with the loves and quarrels of the two. Some are love songs of great beauty and vivid sexuality. Others tell how Ishtar—back from one of her journeys—found Dumuzi celebrating her absence. She arranged for his capture and disappearance into the Lower World—a domain ruled by her sister E.RESH.KI.GAL and her consort NER.GAL. Some of the most celebrated Sumerian and Akkadian texts deal with the journey of Ishtar to the Lower World in search of her banished beloved.

Of the six known sons of Enki, three have been featured in Sumerian tales: the firstborn Marduk, who eventually usurped the supremacy; Nergal, who became ruler of the Lower World; and Dumuzi, who married Inanna/Ishtar.

Enlil, too, had three sons who played key roles in both divine and human affairs: Ninurta, who, having been born to Enlil by his sister

Fig. 53

Fig. 54

Ninhursag, was the legal successor; Nanna/Sin, firstborn by Enlil's official spouse Ninlil; and a younger son by Ninlil named ISH.KUR ("mountainous," "far mountain land"), who was more frequently called Adad ("beloved").

As brother of Sin and uncle of Utu and Inanna, Adad appears to have felt more at home with them than at his own house. The Sumerian texts constantly grouped the four together. The ceremonies connected with the visit of Anu to Uruk also spoke of the four as a group. One text, describing the entrance to the court of Anu, states that the throne room was reached through "the gate of Sin, Shamash, Adad, and Ishtar." Another text, first published by V. K. Shileiko (Russian Academy of the History of Material Cultures) poetically described the four as retiring for the night together.

The greatest affinity seems to have existed between Adad and Ishtar, and the two were even depicted next to each other, as on this relief showing an Assyrian ruler being blessed by Adad (holding the ring and lightning) and by Ishtar, holding her bow. (The third deity is too mutilated to be identified.) (Fig. 55)

Was there more to this "affinity" than a platonic relationship, especially in view of Ishtar's "record"? It is noteworthy that in the biblical Song of Songs, the playful girl calls her lover *dod*—a word that means both "lover" and "uncle." Now, was Ishkur called Adad—a derivative from the Sumerian DA.DA—because he was the uncle who was the lover?

But Ishkur was not only a playboy; he was a mighty god, endowed by his father Enlil with the powers and prerogatives of a storm god. As such he was revered as the Hurrian/Hittite Teshub and the Urartian Teshubu ("wind blower"), the Amorite Ramanu ("thunderer"), the Canaanite Ragimu ("caster of hailstones"), the Indo-European Buriash ("light maker"), the Semitic Meir ("he who lights up" the skies). (Fig. 56)

A god list kept at the British Museum, as shown by Hans Schlobies *(Der Akkadische Wettergott in Mesopotamien)*, clarifies that Ishkur was indeed the divine lord in lands far from Sumer and Akkad. As Sumerian texts reveal, this was no accident. Enlil, it seems, willfully dispatched his young son to become the "Resident Deity" in the mountain lands north and west of Mesopotamia.

Why did Enlil dispatch his youngest and beloved son away from Nippur?

Several Sumerian epic tales have been found about the arguments and even bloody struggles among the younger gods. Many cylinder seals depict scenes of god battling god (Fig. 57); it would seem that the

Fig. 55

Fig. 56

Fig. 57

original rivalry between Enki and Enlil was carried on and intensified between their sons, with brother sometimes turning against brother—a divine tale of Cain and Abel. Some of these battles were against a deity identified as Kur—in all probability, Ishkur/Adad. This may well explain why Enlil deemed it advisable to grant his younger son a far-off domain, to keep him out of the dangerous battles for the succession.

The position of the sons of Anu, Enlil, and Enki, and of their offspring, in the dynastic lineage emerges clearly through a unique Sumerian device: the allocation of *numerical rank* to certain gods. The discovery of this system also brings out the membership in the Great Circle of Gods of Heaven and Earth when Sumerian civilization blossomed. We shall find that this Supreme Pantheon was made up of *twelve* deities.

The first hint that a cryptographic number system was applied to the Great Gods came with the discovery that the names of the gods Sin, Shamash, and Ishtar were sometimes substituted in the texts by the numbers 30, 20, and 15, respectively. The highest unit of the Sumerian sexagesimal system—60—was assigned to Anu; Enlil "was" 50; Enki, 40; and Adad, 10. The number 10 and its six multiples within the prime number 60 were thus assigned to *male* deities, and it would appear plausible that the numbers ending with 5 were assigned to the female deities. From this, the following cryptographic table emerges:

Male	*Female*
60—Anu	55—Antu
50—Enlil	45—Ninlil
40—Ea/Enki	35—Ninki
30—Nanna/Sin	25—Ningal
20—Utu/Shamash	15—Inanna/Ishtar
10—Ishkur/Adad	5—Ninhursag
6 male deities	6 female deities

Ninurta, we should not be surprised to learn, was assigned the number 50, like his father. In other words, his dynastic rank was conveyed in a cryptographic message: If Enlil goes, you, Ninurta, step into his shoes; but until then, you are not one of the Twelve, for the rank of "50" is occupied.

Nor should we be surprised to learn that when Marduk usurped the Enlilship, he insisted that the gods bestow on him "the *fifty* names" to signify that the rank of "50" had become his.

There were many other gods in Sumer—children, grandchildren, nieces, and nephews of the Great Gods; there were also several hundred rank-and-file gods, called Anunnaki, who were assigned (one may say) "general duties." But only *twelve* made the Great Circle. They, their family relationships, and, above all, the line of dynastic succession can better be referred to if we show them in a chart:

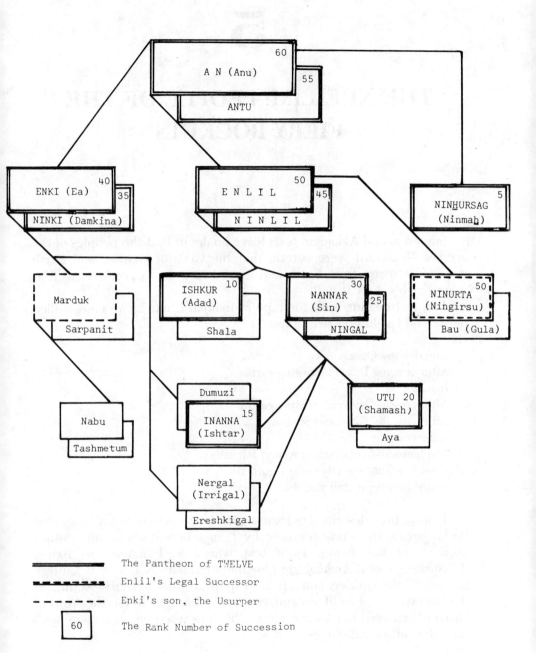

────────	The Pantheon of TWELVE
▪▬▪▬▪▬▪	Enlil's Legal Successor
─ ─ ─ ─ ─	Enki's son, the Usurper
60	The Rank Number of Succession

5
·
THE NEFILIM: PEOPLE OF THE FIERY ROCKETS

Sumerian and Akkadian texts leave no doubt that the peoples of the ancient Near East were certain that the Gods of Heaven and Earth were able to rise from Earth and ascend into the heavens, as well as roam Earth's skies at will.

In a text dealing with the rape of Inanna/Ishtar by an unidentified person, he justifies his deed thus:

> One day my Queen,
> After crossing heaven, crossing earth—
> Inanna,
> After crossing heaven, crossing earth—
> After crossing Elam and Shubur,
> After crossing . . .
> The hierodule approached weary, fell asleep.
> I saw her from the edge of my garden;
> Kissed her, copulated with her.

Inanna, here described as roaming the heavens over many lands that lie far apart—feats possible only by *flying*—herself spoke on another occasion of her flying. In a text which S. Langdon (in *Revue d'Assyriologie et d'Archéologie Orientale*) named "A Classical Liturgy to Innini," the goddess laments her expulsion from her city. Acting on the instructions of Enlil, an emissary, who "brought to me the word of Heaven," entered her throne room, "his unwashed hands put on me," and, after other indignities,

> Me, from my temple,
> they caused to fly;

A Queen am I whom, from my city,
like a bird they caused to fly.

Such a capability, by Inanna as well as the other major gods, was
often indicated by the ancient artists by depicting the gods—anthropomorphic in all other respects, as we have seen—with wings. The
wings, as can be seen from numerous depictions, were not part of the
body—not natural wings—but rather a decorative attachment to the
god's clothing. (Fig. 58)

Inanna/Ishtar, whose far-flung travels are mentioned in many

Fig. 58

Fig. 59

ancient texts, commuted between her initial distant domain in Aratta and her coveted abode in Uruk. She called upon Enki in Eridu and Enlil in Nippur, and visited her brother Utu at his headquarters in Sippar. But her most celebrated journey was to the Lower World, the domain of her sister Ereshkigal. The journey was the subject not only of epic tales but also of artistic depictions on cylinder seals—the latter showing the goddess with wings, to stress the fact that she flew over from Sumer to the Lower World. (Fig. 59)

The texts dealing with this hazardous journey describe how Inanna very meticulously put on herself seven objects prior to the start of the voyage, and how she had to give them up as she passed through the seven gates leading to her sister's abode. Seven such objects are also mentioned in other texts dealing with Inanna's skyborne travels:

1. The SHU.GAR.RA she put on her head.
2. "Measuring pendants," on her ears.
3. Chains of small blue stones, around her neck.
4. Twin "stones," on her shoulders.
5. A golden cylinder, in her hands.
6. Straps, clasping her breast.
7. The PALA garment, clothed around her body.

Though no one has as yet been able to explain the nature and significance of these seven objects, we feel that the answer has long been available. Excavating the Assyrian capital Assur from 1903 to 1914, Walter Andrae and his colleagues found in the Temple of Ishtar a battered statue of the goddess showing her with various "contraptions" attached to her chest and back. In 1934 archaeologists excavating at Mari came upon a similar but intact statue buried in the ground. It was a life-size likeness of a beautiful woman. Her unusual headdress was adorned with a pair of horns, indicating that she was a goddess. Standing around the 4,000-year-old statue, the archaeologists were thrilled by her lifelike appearance (in a snapshot, one can hardly distinguish between the statue and the living men). They named her *The Goddess with a Vase* because she was holding a cylindrical object. (Fig. 60)

Unlike the flat carvings or bas-reliefs, this life-size, three-dimensional representation of the goddess reveals interesting features about her attire. On her head she wears not a milliner's chapeau but a special helmet; protruding from it on both sides and fitted over the ears are objects that remind one of a pilot's earphones. On her neck and upper chest the goddess wears a necklace of many small (and probably

Fig. 60

precious) stones; in her hands she holds a cylindrical object which appears too thick and heavy to be a vase for holding water.

Over a blouse of see-through material, two parallel straps run across her chest, leading back to and holding in place an unusual box of rectangular shape. The box is held tight against the back of the goddess's neck and is firmly attached to the helmet with a horizontal strap. Whatever the box held inside must have been heavy, for the contraption is further supported by two large shoulder pads. The weight of the box is increased by a hose that is connected to its base by a circular clasp. The complete package of instruments—for this is what they undoubtedly were—is held in place with the aid of the two sets of straps that crisscross the goddess's back and chest.

The parallel between the seven objects required by Inanna for her aerial journeys and the dress and objects worn by the statue from Mari (and probably also the mutilated one found at Ishtar's temple in Ashur) is easily proved. We see the "measuring pendants"—the earphones—on her ears; the rows or "chains" of small stones around her neck; the "twin stones"—the two shoulder pads—on her shoulders; the "golden cylinder" in her hands, and the clasping straps that crisscross her breast. She is indeed clothed in a "PALA garment" ("ruler's garment"), and on her head she wears the SHU.GAR.RA helmet—a term that literally means "that which makes go far into universe."

All this suggests to us that the attire of Inanna was that of an aeronaut or an astronaut.

The Old Testament called the "angels" of the Lord *malachim*— literally, "emissaries," who carried divine messages and carried out divine commands. As so many instances reveal, they were divine airmen: Jacob saw them going up a sky ladder, Hagar (Abraham's concubine) was addressed by them from the sky, and it was they who brought about the aerial destruction of Sodom and Gomorrah.

The biblical account of the events preceding the destruction of the two sinful cities illustrates the fact that these emissaries were, on the one hand, anthropomorphic in all respects, and, on the other hand, they could be identified as "angels" as soon as they were observed. We learn that their appearance was sudden. Abraham "raised his eyes and, lo and behold, there were three *men* standing by him." Bowing and calling them "My Lords," he pleaded with them, "Do not pass *over* thy servant," and prevailed on them to wash their feet, rest, and eat.

Having done as Abraham had requested, two of the angels (the third "man" turned out to be the Lord himself) then proceeded to Sodom. Lot, the nephew of Abraham, "was sitting at the gate of Sodom; and when he saw them he rose up to meet them and bowed to the ground, and said: If it pleases my Lords, pray come to the house of thy servant and wash your feet and sleep overnight." Then "he made for them a feast, and they ate." When the news of the arrival of the two spread in the town, "all the town's people, young and old, surrounded the house, and called out to Lot and said: Where are the *men* who came this night unto thee?"

How were these men—who ate, drank, slept, and washed their tired feet—nevertheless so instantly recognizable as angels of the Lord? The only plausible explanation is that what they wore—their helmets or uniforms—or what they carried—their weapons—made them immediately recognizable. That they carried distinctive weapons is certainly a possibility: The two "men" at Sodom, about to be lynched by the crowd, "smote the people at the entrance of the house with blindness . . . and they were unable to find the doorway." And another angel, this time appearing to Gideon, as he was chosen to be a Judge in Israel, gave him a divine sign by touching a rock with his baton, whereupon a fire jumped out of the rock.

The team headed by Andrae found yet another unusual depiction of Ishtar at her temple in Ashur. More a wall sculpture than the usual relief, it showed the goddess with a tight-fitting decorated helmet with the "earphones" extended as though they had their own flat antennas, and wearing very distinct goggles that were part of the helmet. (Fig. 61)

Needless to say, any man seeing a person—male or female—so clad, would at once realize that he is encountering a divine aeronaut.

Clay figurines found at Sumerian sites and believed to be some 5,500 years old may well be crude representations of such *malachim* holding wandlike weapons. In one instance the face is seen through a helmet's visor. In the other instance, the "emissary" wears the distinct divine conical headdress and a uniform studded with circular objects of unknown function. (Figs. 62, 63)

The eye slots or "goggles" of the figurines are a most interesting feature because the Near East in the fourth millennium B.C. was literally swamped with wafer-like figurines that depicted in a stylized manner the upper part of the deities, exaggerating their most prominent feature: a conical helmet with elliptical visors or goggles. (Fig. 64) A hoard of such figurines was found at Tell Brak, a prehistoric site on the Khabur River, the river on whose banks Ezekiel saw the divine chariot millennia later.

It is undoubtedly no mere coincidence that the Hittites, linked to Sumer and Akkad via the Khabur area, adopted as their written sign for

"gods" the symbol , clearly borrowed from the "eye" figurines.

It is also no wonder that this symbol or hieroglyph for "divine being," expressed in artistic styles, came to dominate the art not only of Asia Minor but also of the early Greeks during the Minoan and Mycenaean periods. (Fig. 65)

The ancient texts indicate that the gods put on such special attire not only for their flights in Earth's skies but also when they ascended to the distant heavens. Speaking of her occasional visits to Anu at his Celestial Abode, Inanna herself explained that she could undertake such journeys because "Enlil himself fastened the divine ME-attire about my body." The text quoted Enlil as saying to her:

> You have lifted the ME,
> You have tied the ME to your hands,
> You have gathered the ME,
> You have attached the ME to your breast. . . .
> O Queen of all the ME, O radiant light
> Who with her hand grasps the seven ME.

An early Sumerian ruler invited by the gods to ascend to the heavens was named EN.ME.DUR.AN.KI, which literally meant "ruler whose *me* connect Heaven and Earth." An inscription by Nebuchadnezzar II, describing the reconstruction of a special pavilion for Marduk's "celestial chariot," states that it was part of the "fortified house of the seven *me* of Heaven and Earth."

The scholars refer to the *me* as "divine power objects." Literally, the term stems from the concept of "swimming in celestial waters." Inanna described them as parts of the "celestial garment" that she put on for her journeys in the Boat of Heaven. The *me* were thus parts of the special gear worn for flying in Earth's skies as well as into outer space.

The Greek legend of Icarus had him attempt to fly by attaching feathered wings to his body with wax. The evidence from the ancient Near East shows that though the gods may have been depicted with wings to indicate their flying capabilities—or perhaps sometimes put on winged uniforms as a mark of their airmanship—they never attempted to use attached wings for flying. Instead, they used vehicles for such travels.

The Old Testament informs us that the patriarch Jacob, spending the night in a field outside of Haran, saw "a ladder set up on Earth and its top reaching heavenwards," on which "angels of the Lord" were busily going up and down. The Lord himself stood at the top of the ladder. And the astounded Jacob "was fearful, and he said":

Fig. 61

Fig. 62

Fig. 63

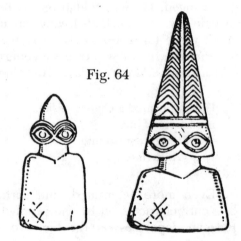

Fig. 64

Fig. 65

Indeed, a God is present in this place,
and I knew it not. . . .
How awesome is this place!
Indeed, this is none but the Lord's Abode
and this is the Gateway to Heaven.

There are two interesting points in this tale. The first is that the divine beings going up and down at this "Gateway to Heaven" were using a mechanical facility—a "ladder." The second is that the sight took Jacob by complete surprise. The "Lord's Abode," the "ladder," and the "angels of the Lord" using it were not there when Jacob lay down to sleep in the field. Suddenly, there was the awesome "vision." And by morning the "Abode," the "ladder," and their occupants were gone.

We may conclude that the equipment used by the divine beings was some kind of craft that could appear over a place, hover for a while, and disappear from sight once again.

The Old Testament also reports that the prophet Elijah did not die on Earth, but "went up into Heaven by a Whirlwind." This was not a sudden and unexpected event: The ascent of Elijah to the heavens was prearranged. He was told to go to Beth-El ("the lord's house") on a specific day. Rumors had already spread among his disciples that he was about to be taken up to the heavens. When they queried his deputy whether the rumor was true, he confirmed that, indeed, "the Lord will take away the Master today." And then:

There appeared a chariot of fire,
and horses of fire. . . .
And Elijah went up into Heaven
by a Whirlwind.

Even more celebrated, and certainly better described, was the heavenly chariot seen by the prophet Ezekiel, who dwelt among the Judaean deportees on the banks of the Khabur River in northern Mesopotamia.

The Heavens were opened,
and I saw the appearances of the Lord.

What Ezekiel saw was a Manlike being, surrounded by brilliance and brightness, sitting on a throne that rested on a metal "firmament" within the chariot. The vehicle itself, which could move whichever way upon wheels-within-wheels and rise off the ground vertically, was described by the prophet as a glowing whirlwind.

And I saw
a Whirlwind coming from the north,
as a great cloud with flashes of fire
and brilliance all around it.
And within it, from within the fire,
there was a radiance like a glowing halo.

Some recent students of the biblical description (such as Josef F. Blumrich of the U.S. National Aeronautics and Space Administration) have concluded that the "chariot" seen by Ezekiel was a helicopter consisting of a cabin resting on four posts, each equipped with rotary wings—a "whirlwind" indeed.

About two millennia earlier, when the Sumerian ruler Gudea commemorated his building the temple for his god Ninurta, he wrote that there appeared to him "a man that shone like Heaven . . . by the helmet on his head, he was a god." When Ninurta and two divine companions appeared to Gudea, they were standing beside Ninurta's "divine black wind bird." As it turned out, the main purpose of the temple's construction was to provide a secure zone, an inner special enclosure within the temple grounds, for this "divine bird."

The construction of this enclosure, Gudea reported, required huge beams and massive stones imported from afar. Only when the "divine bird" was placed within the enclosure was the construction of the temple deemed completed. And, once in place, the "divine bird" "could lay hold on heaven" and was capable of "bringing together Heaven and Earth." The object was so important—"sacred"—that it was constantly protected by two "divine weapons," the "supreme hunter" and the "supreme killer"—weapons that emitted beams of light and death-dealing rays.

The similarity of the biblical and Sumerian descriptions, both of the vehicles and the beings within them, is obvious. The description of the vehicles as "bird," "wind bird," and "whirlwind" that could rise heavenward while emitting a brilliance, leaves no doubt that they were some kind of flying machine.

Enigmatic murals uncovered at Tell Ghassul, a site east of the Dead Sea whose ancient name is unknown, may shed light on our subject. Dating to circa 3500 B.C., the murals depict a large eight-pointed "compass," the head of a helmeted person within a bell-shaped chamber, and two designs of mechanical craft that could well have been the "whirlwinds" of antiquity. (Fig. 66)

Fig. 66

The ancient texts also describe some vehicle used to lift aeronauts into the skies. Gudea stated that, as the "divine bird" rose to circle the lands, it "flashed upon the raised bricks." The protected enclosure was described as MU.NA.DA.TUR.TUR ("strong stone resting place of the MU"). Urukagina, who ruled in Lagash, said in regard to the "divine black wind bird": "The MU that lights up as a fire I made high and strong." Similarly, Lu-Utu, who ruled in Umma in the third millennium B.C., constructed a place for a *mu*, "which in a fire comes forth," for the god Utu, "in the appointed place within his temple."

The Babylonian king Nebuchadnezzar II, recording his rebuilding of Marduk's sacred precinct, said that within fortified walls made of burned brick and gleaming onyx marble:

I raised the head of the boat ID.GE.UL
the Chariot of Marduk's princeliness;
The boat ZAG.MU.KU, whose approach is observed,
the supreme traveler between Heaven and Earth,
in the midst of the pavilion I enclosed,
screening off its sides.

ID.GE.UL, the first epithet employed to describe this "supreme traveler," or "Chariot of Marduk," literally means "high to heaven, bright at night." ZAG.MU.KU, the second epithet describing the vehicle—clearly a "boat" nesting in a special pavilion—means "the bright MU which is for afar."

That a *mu*—an oval-topped, conical object—was indeed installed in the inner, sacred enclosure of the temples of the Great Gods of Heaven and Earth can, fortunately, be proved. An ancient coin found at Byblos (the biblical Gebal) on the Mediterranean coast of present-day Lebanon depicts the Great Temple of Ishtar. Though shown as it stood in the first millennium B.C., the requirement that temples be built and rebuilt upon the same site and in accordance with the original plan undoubt-edly means that we see the basic elements of the original temple of Byblos, traced to millennia earlier.

The coin depicts a two-part temple. In front stands the main temple structure, imposing with its columned gateway. Behind it is an inner courtyard, or "sacred area," hidden and protected by a high, massive wall. It is clearly a raised area, for it can be reached only by ascending many stairs. (Fig. 67)

Fig. 67

In the center of this sacred area stands a special platform, its crossbeam construction resembling that of the Eiffel Tower, as though built to withstand great weight. And on the platform stands the object of all this security and protection: an object that can only be a *mu.*

Like most Sumerian syllabic words, *mu* had a primary meaning; in the case of *mu,* it was "that which rises straight." Its thirty-odd nuances encompassed the meanings "heights," "fire," "command," "a counted period," as well as (in later times) "that by which one is remembered." If we trace the written sign for *mu* from its Assyrian and Babylonian cuneiform stylizations to its original Sumerian pictographs, the follow-ing pictorial evidence emerges:

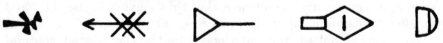

We clearly see a conical chamber, depicted by itself or with a narrow section attached to it. "From a golden chamber-in-the-sky I will watch over thee," Inanna promised to the Assyrian king. Was this *mu* the "heavenly chamber"?

A hymn to Inanna/Ishtar and her journeys in the Boat of Heaven clearly indicates that the *mu* was the vehicle in which the gods roamed the skies far and high:

Lady of Heaven:
She puts on the Garment of Heaven;
She valiantly ascends towards Heaven.
Over all the peopled lands
she flies in her MU.
Lady, who in her MU
to the heights of Heaven joyfully wings.
Over all the resting places
she flies in her MU.

There is evidence to show that the people of the eastern Mediterranean had seen such a rocket-like object not only in a temple enclosure but actually in flight. Hittite glyphs, for example, showed—against a background of starry heavens—cruising missiles, rockets mounted on launch pads, and a god inside a radiating chamber. (Fig. 68)

Fig. 68

Professor H. Frankfort (*Cylinder Seals*), demonstrating how both the art of making the Mesopotamian cylinder seals and the subjects depicted on them spread throughout the ancient world, reproduces the design on a seal found in Crete and dated to the thirteenth century B.C. The seal design clearly depicts a rocket ship moving in the skies and propelled by flames escaping from its rear. (Fig. 69)

The winged horses, the entwined animals, the winged celestial globe, and the deity with horns protruding from his headdress are all known Mesopotamian themes. It can certainly be assumed that the fiery rocket shown on the Cretan seal was also an object familiar throughout the ancient Near East.

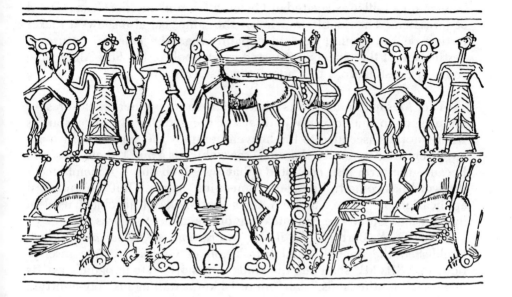

Fig. 69

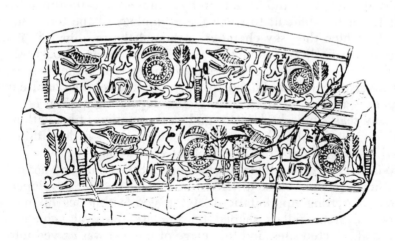

Fig. 70

Indeed, a rocket with "wings" or fins—reachable by a "ladder"—can be seen on a tablet excavated at Gezer, a town in ancient Canaan, west of Jerusalem. The double imprint of the same seal also shows a rocket resting on the ground next to a palm tree. The celestial nature or destination of the objects is attested by symbols of the Sun, Moon, and zodiacal constellations that adorn the seal. (Fig. 70)

The Mesopotamian texts that refer to the inner enclosures of temples, or to the heavenly journeys of the gods, or even to instances where mortals ascended to the heavens, employ the Sumerian term *mu* or its Semitic derivatives *shu-mu* ("that which is a *mu*"), *sham*, or *shem*. Because the term also connoted "that by which one is remembered," the word has come to be taken as meaning "name." But the universal application of "name" to early texts that spoke of an object used in flying has obscured the true meaning of the ancient records.

Thus G. A. Barton *(The Royal Inscriptions of Sumer and Akkad)* established the unchallenged translation of Gudea's temple inscription—that "Its MU shall hug the lands from horizon to horizon"—as "Its *name* shall fill the lands." A hymn to Ishkur, extolling his "ray-emitting MU" that could attain the heights of Heaven, was likewise rendered: "Thy *name* is radiant, it reaches Heaven's zenith." Sensing, however, that *mu* or *shem* may mean an object and not "name," some scholars have treated the term as a suffix or grammatical phenomenon not requiring translation and have thereby avoided the issue altogether.

It is not too difficult to trace the etymology of the term, and the route by which the "sky chamber" assumed the meaning of "name." Sculptures have been found that show a god inside a rocket-shaped chamber, as in this object of extreme antiquity (now in the possession of the University Museum, Philadelphia) where the celestial nature of the chamber is attested by the twelve globes decorating it. (Fig. 71)

Many seals similarly depict a god (and sometimes two) within such oval "divine chambers"; in most instances, these gods within their sacred ovals were depicted as objects of veneration.

Wishing to worship their gods throughout the lands, and not only at the official "house" of each deity, the ancient peoples developed the custom of setting up imitations of the god within his divine "sky chamber." Stone pillars shaped to simulate the oval vehicle were erected at selected sites, and the image of the god was carved into the stone to indicate that he was within the object.

It was only a matter of time before kings and rulers—associating these pillars (called stelae) with the ability to ascend to the Heavenly Abode—began to carve their own images upon the stelae as a way of associating themselves with the Eternal Abode. If they could not escape

Fig. 71

Fig. 72

a physical oblivion, it was important that at least their "name" be forever commemorated. (Fig. 72)

That the purpose of the commemorative stone pillars was to simulate a *fiery* skyship can further be gleaned from the term by which such stone stelae were known in antiquity. The Sumerians called them NA.RU ("stones that rise"). The Akkadians, Babylonians, and Assyrians called them *naru* ("objects that give off light"). The Amurru called them *nuras* ("fiery objects"—in Hebrew, *ner* still means a pillar that emits light, and thus today's "candle"). In the Indo-European tongues of the Hurrians and the Hittites, the stelae were called *hu-u-ashi* ("fire bird of stone").

Biblical references indicate familiarity with two types of commemorative monument, a *yad* and a *shem*. The prophet Isaiah conveyed to the suffering people of Judaea the Lord's promise of a better and safer future:

> And I will give them,
> In my House and within my walls,
> A *yad* and a *shem*.

Literally translated, this would amount to the Lord's promise to provide his people with a "hand" and a "name." Fortunately, however, from ancient monuments called *yad*'s that still stand in the Holy Land, we learn that they were distinguished by tops shaped like pyramidions. The *shem*, on the other hand, was a memorial with an *oval* top. Both, it seems evident, began as simulations of the "sky chamber," the gods' vehicle for ascending to the Eternal Abode. In ancient Egypt, in fact, the devout made pilgrimages to a special temple at Heliopolis to view and worship the *ben-ben*—a pyramidion-shaped object in which the gods had arrived on Earth in times immemorial. Egyptian pharaohs, on their deaths, were subjected to a ceremony of "opening of the mouth," in which they were supposed to be transported by a similiar *yad* or a *shem* to the divine Abode of Eternal Life. (Fig. 73)

The persistence of biblical translators to employ "name" wherever they encounter *shem* has ignored a farsighted study published more than a century ago by G. M. Redslob (in *Zeitschrift der Deutschen Morgenlandischen Gesellschaft*) in which he correctly pointed out that the term *shem* and the term *shamaim* ("heaven") stem from the root word *shamah*, meaning "that which is highward." When the Old Testament reports that King David "made a *shem*" to mark his victory over the Aramaeans, Redslob said, he did not "make a name" but set up a monument pointing skyward.

The realization that *mu* or *shem* in many Mesopotamian texts should be read not as "name" but as "sky vehicle" opens the way to the

Fig. 73

understanding of the true meaning of many ancient tales, including the biblical story of the Tower of Babel.

The Book of Genesis, in its eleventh chapter, reports on the attempt by humans to raise up a *shem*. The biblical account is given in concise (and precise) language that bespeaks historical fact. Yet generations of scholars and translators have sought to impart to the tale only an allegorical meaning because—as they understood it—it was a tale concerning Mankind's desire to "make a *name*" for itself. Such an approach voided the tale of its factual meaning; our conclusion regarding the true meaning of *shem* makes the tale as meaningful as it must have been to the people of antiquity themselves.

The biblical tale of the Tower of Babel deals with events that followed the repopulation of Earth after the Deluge, when some of the people "journeyed from the east, and they found a plain in the land of Shin'ar, and they settled there."

The Land of Shinar is, of course, the Land of Sumer, in the plain between the two rivers in southern Mesopotamia. And the people, already knowledgeable concerning the art of brickmaking and high-rise construction for an urban civilization, said:

> "Let us build us a city,
> and a tower whose top shall reach the heavens;
> and let us make us a *shem*,
> lest we be scattered upon the face of the Earth."

But this human scheme was not to God's liking.

And the Lord came down,
to see the city and the tower
which the Children of Adam had erected.
And he said: "Behold,
all are as one people with one language,
and this is just the beginning of their undertakings;
Now, anything which they shall scheme to do
shall no longer be impossible for them."

And the Lord said—to some colleagues whom the Old Testament does not name:

"Come, let us go down,
and there confound their language;
So that they may not understand each other's speech."
And the Lord scattered them from there
upon the face of the whole Earth,
and they ceased to build the city.
Therefore was its name called Babel,
for there did the Lord mingle the Earth's tongue.

The traditional translation of *shem* as "name" has kept the tale unintelligible for generations. Why did the ancient residents of Babel—Babylonia—exert themselves to "make a name," why was the "name" to be placed upon "a tower whose top shall reach the heavens," and how could the "making of a name" counteract the effects of Mankind's scattering upon Earth?

If all that those people wanted was to make (as scholars explain) a "reputation" for themselves, why did this attempt upset the Lord so much? Why was the raising of a "name" deemed by the Deity to be a feat after which "anything which they shall scheme to do shall no longer be impossible for them"? The traditional explanations certainly are insufficient to clarify why the Lord found it necessary to call upon other unnamed deities to go down and put an end to this human attempt.

We believe that the answers to all these questions become plausible—even obvious—once we read "skyborne vehicle" rather than "name" for the word *shem*, which is the term employed in the original Hebrew text of the Bible. The story would then deal with the concern of Mankind that, as the people spread upon Earth, they would lose contact with one another. So they decided to build a "skyborne vehicle" and to erect a *launch tower* for such a vehicle so that they, too, could—like the goddess Ishtar, for example—fly in a *mu* "over all the peopled lands."

A portion of the Babylonian text known as the "Epic of Creation" relates that the first "Gateway of the Gods" was constructed in Babylon by the gods themselves. The Anunnaki, the rank-and-file gods, were ordered to

Construct the Gateway of the Gods. . . .
Let its brickwork be fashioned.
Its *shem* shall be in the designated place.

For two years, the Anunnaki toiled—"applied the implement . . . molded bricks"—until "they raised high the top of Eshagila" ("house of Great Gods") and "built the stage tower as high as High Heaven."

It was thus some cheek on the part of Mankind to establish its own launch tower on a site originally used for the purpose by the gods, for the name of the place—Babili—literally meant "Gateway of the Gods."

Is there any other evidence to corroborate the biblical tale and our interpretation of it?

The Babylonian historian-priest Berossus, who in the third century B.C. compiled a history of Mankind, reported that the "first inhabitants of the land, glorying in their own strength . . . undertook to raise a tower whose 'top' should reach the sky." But the tower was overturned by the gods and heavy winds, "and the gods introduced a diversity of tongues among men, who till that time had all spoken the same language."

George Smith (*The Chaldean Account of Genesis*) found in the writings of the Greek historian Hestaeus a report that, in accordance with "olden traditions," the people who had escaped the Deluge came to Senaar in Babylonia but were driven away from there by a diversity of tongues. The historian Alexander Polyhistor (first century B.C.) wrote that all men formerly spoke the same language. Then some undertook to erect a large and lofty tower so that they might "climb up to heaven." But the chief god confounded their design by sending a whirlwind; each tribe was given a different language. "The city where it happened was Babylon."

There is little doubt by now that the biblical tales, as well as the reports of the Greek historians of 2,000 years ago and of their predecessor Berossus, all stem from earlier—*Sumerian*—origins. A. H. Sayce (*The Religion of the Babylonians*) reported reading on a fragmentary tablet in the British Museum "the Babylonian version of the building of the Tower of Babel." In all instances, the attempt to reach the heavens and the ensuing confusion of tongues are basic elements of the version. There are other Sumerian texts that record the deliberate confusion of Man's tongue by an irate god.

Mankind, presumably, did not possess at that time the technology required for such an aerospace project; the guidance and collaboration of a knowledgeable god was essential. Did such a god defy the others to help Mankind? A Sumerian seal depicts a confrontation between armed gods, apparently over the disputed construction by men of a stage tower. (Fig. 74)

A Sumerian stela now on view in Paris in the Louvre may well depict the incident reported in the Book of Genesis. It was put up circa 2300 B.C. by Naram-Sin, king of Akkad, and scholars have assumed that it depicts the king victorious over his enemies. But the large central figure is that of a deity and not of the human king, for the person is wearing a helmet adorned with horns—the identifying mark exclusive to the gods. Furthermore, this central figure does not appear to be the leader of the smaller-sized humans, but to be trampling upon them. These humans, in turn, do not seem to be engaged in any warlike activities, but to be marching toward, and standing in adoration of, the same large conical object on which the deity's attention is also focused. Armed with a bow and lance, the deity seems to view the object menacingly rather than with adoration. (Fig. 75)

The conical object is shown reaching toward three celestial bodies. If its size, shape, and purpose indicate that it was a *shem*, then the scene depicted an angry and fully armed god trampling upon people celebrating the raising of a *shem*.

Both the Mesopotamian texts and the biblical account impart the same moral: The flying machines were meant for the gods and not for Mankind.

Men—assert both Mesopotamian and biblical texts—could ascend to the Heavenly Abode only upon the express wish of the gods. And therein lie more tales of ascents to the heavens and even of space flights.

°

The Old Testament records the ascent to the heavens of several mortal beings.

The first was Enoch, a pre-Diluvial patriarch whom God befriended and who "walked with the Lord." He was the seventh patriarch in the line of Adam and the great-grandfather of Noah, hero of the Deluge. The fifth chapter of the Book of Genesis lists the genealogies of all these patriarchs and the ages at which they died—except for Enoch, "who

Fig. 74

Fig. 75

was gone, for the Lord had taken him." By implication and tradition, it was heavenward, to escape mortality on Earth, that God took Enoch. The other mortal was the prophet Elijah, who was lifted off Earth and taken heavenward in a "whirlwind."

A little-known reference to a third mortal who visited the Divine Abode and was endowed there with great wisdom is provided in the Old Testament, and it concerns the ruler of Tyre (a Phoenician center on the eastern Mediterranean coast). We read in Chapter 28 of the Book of Ezekiel that the Lord commanded the prophet to remind the king how, perfect and wise, he was enabled by the Deity to visit with the gods:

> Thou art molded by a plan,
> full of wisdom, perfect in beauty.
> Thou hast been in Eden, the garden of God;
> every precious stone was thy thicket. . . .
> Thou art an anointed Cherub, protected;
> and I have placed thee in the sacred mountain;
> as a god werest thou,
> moving within the Fiery Stones.

Predicting that the ruler of Tyre should die a death "of the uncircumcised" by the hand of strangers even if he called out to them "I am a Deity," the Lord then told Ezekiel the reason: After the king was taken to the Divine Abode and given access to all wisdom and riches, his heart "grew haughty," he misused his wisdom, and he defiled the temples.

> Because thine heart is haughty, saying
> "A god am I;
> in the Abode of the Deity I sat,
> in the midst of the Waters";
> Though thou art a Man, not a god,
> thou set thy heart as that of a Deity.

The Sumerian texts also speak of several men who were privileged to ascend to the heavens. One was Adapa, the "model man" created by Ea. To him Ea "had given wisdom; eternal life he had not given him." As the years went by, Ea decided to avert Adapa's mortal end by providing him with a *shem* with which he was to reach the Heavenly Abode of Anu, there to partake of the Bread of Life and the Water of Life. When Adapa arrived at Anu's Celestial Abode, Anu demanded to know who had provided Adapa with a *shem* with which to reach the heavenly location.

There are several important clues to be found in both the biblical and the Mesopotamian tales of the rare ascents of mortals to the Abode of the Gods. Adapa, too, like the king of Tyre, was made of a perfect "mold." All had to reach and employ a *shem*—"fiery stone"—to reach the celestial "Eden." Some had gone up and returned to Earth; others, like the Mesopotamian hero of the Deluge, stayed there to enjoy the company of the gods. It was to find this Mesopotamian "Noah" and obtain from him the secret of the Tree of Life, that the Sumerian Gilgamesh set out.

The futile search by mortal Man for the Tree of Life is the subject of one of the longest, most powerful epic texts bequeathed to human culture by the Sumerian civilization. Named by modern scholars "The Epic of Gilgamesh," the moving tale concerns the ruler of Uruk who was born to a mortal father and a divine mother. As a result, Gilgamesh was considered to be "two-thirds of him god, one-third of him human," a circumstance that prompted him to seek escape from the death that was the fate of mortals.

Tradition had informed him that one of his forefathers, Utna-pishtim—the hero of the Deluge—had escaped death, having been taken to the Heavenly Abode together with his spouse. Gilgamesh therefore decided to reach that place and obtain from his ancestor the secret of eternal life.

What prompted him to go was what he took to be an invitation from Anu. The verses read like a description of the sighting of the falling back to Earth of a spent rocket. Gilgamesh described it thus to his mother, the goddess NIN.SUN:

My mother,
During the night I felt joyful
and I walked about among my nobles.
The stars assembled in the Heavens.
The handiwork of Anu descended toward me.
I sought to lift it; it was too heavy.
I sought to move it; move it I could not!
The people of Uruk gathered about it,
While the nobles kissed its legs.
As I set my forehead, they gave me support.
I raised it. I brought it to thee.

The interpretation of the incident by Gilgamesh's mother is

mutilated in the text, and is thus unclear. But obviously Gilgamesh was encouraged by the sighting of the falling object—"the handiwork of Anu"—to embark on his adventure. In the introduction to the epic, the ancient reporter called Gilgamesh "the wise one, he who has experienced everything":

> Secret things he has seen,
> what is hidden to Man he knows;
> He even brought tidings
> of a time before the Deluge.
> He also took the distant journey,
> wearisome and under difficulties;
> He returned, and engraved all his toil
> upon a stone pillar.

The "distant journey" Gilgamesh undertook was, of course, his journey to the Abode of the Gods; he was accompanied by his comrade Enkidu. Their target was the Land of Tilmun, for there Gilgamesh could raise a *shem* for himself. The current translations employ the expected "name" where the Sumerian *mu* or the Akkadian *shumu* appear in the ancient texts; we shall, however, employ *shem* instead so that the term's true meaning—a "skyborne vehicle"—will come through:

> The ruler Gilgamesh
> toward the Land of Tilmun set his mind.
> He says to his companion Enkidu:
> "O Enkidu . . .
> I would enter the Land, set up my *shem*.
> In the places where the *shem*'s were raised up
> I would raise my *shem*."

Unable to dissuade him, both the elders of Uruk and the gods whom Gilgamesh consulted advised him to first obtain the consent and assistance of Utu/Shamash. "If thou wouldst enter the Land—inform Utu," they cautioned him. "The Land, it is in Utu's charge," they stressed and restressed to him. Thus forewarned and advised, Gilgamesh appealed to Utu for permission:

> Let me enter the Land,
> Let me set up my *shem*.
> In the places where the *shem*'s are raised up,

let me raise my *shem.* . . .
Bring me to the landing place at. . . .
Establish over me thy protection!

An unfortunate break in the tablet leaves us ignorant regarding the location of "the landing place." But, wherever it was, Gilgamesh and his companion finally reached its outskirts. It was a "restricted zone," protected by awesome guards. Weary and sleepy, the two friends decided to rest overnight before continuing.

No sooner had sleep overcome them than something shook them up and awoke them. "Didst thou arouse me?" Gilgamesh asked his comrade. "Am I awake?" he wondered, for he was witnessing unusual sights, so awesome that he wondered whether he was awake or dreaming. He told Enkidu:

In my dream, my friend, the high ground toppled.
It laid me low, trapped my feet. . . .
The glare was overpowering!
A man appeared;
the fairest in the land was he.
His grace . . .
From under the toppled ground he pulled me out.
He gave me water to drink; my heart quieted.

Who was this man, "the fairest in the land," who pulled Gilgamesh from under the landslide, gave him water, "quieted his heart"? And what was the "overpowering glare" that accompanied the unexplained landslide?

Unsure, troubled, Gilgamesh fell asleep again—but not for long.

In the middle of the watch his sleep was ended.
He started up, saying to his friend:
"My friend, didst thou call me?
Why am I awake?
Didst thou not touch me?
Why am I startled?
Did not some god go by?
Why is my flesh numb?"

Thus mysteriously reawakened, Gilgamesh wondered who had touched him. If it was not his comrade, was it "some *god*" who went by? Once more, Gilgamesh dozed off, only to be awakened a third time. He described the awesome occurrence to his friend.

The vision that I saw was wholly awesome!
The heavens shrieked, the earth boomed;
Daylight failed, darkness came.
Lightning flashed, a flame shot up.
The clouds swelled, it rained death!
Then the glow vanished; the fire went out.
And all that had fallen had turned to ashes.

One needs little imagination to see in these few verses an ancient account of the witnessing of the launching of a rocket ship. First the tremendous thud as the rocket engines ignited ("the heavens shrieked"), accompanied by a marked shaking of the ground ("the earth boomed"). Clouds of smoke and dust enveloped the launching site ("daylight failed, darkness came"). Then the brilliance of the ignited engines showed through ("lightning flashed"); as the rocket ship began to climb skyward, "a flame shot up." The cloud of dust and debris "swelled" in all directions; then, as it began to fall down, "it rained death!" Now the rocket ship was high in the sky, streaking heavenward ("the glow vanished; the fire went out"). The rocket ship was gone from sight; and the debris "that had fallen had turned to ashes."

Awed by what he saw, yet as determined as ever to reach his destination, Gilgamesh once more appealed to Shamash for protection and support. Overcoming a "monstrous guard," he reached the mountain of Mashu, where one could see Shamash "rise up to the vault of Heaven."

He was now near his first objective—the "place where the *shem*'s are raised up." But the entrance to the site, apparently cut into the mountain, was guarded by fierce guards:

Their terror is awesome, their glance is death.
Their shimmering spotlight sweeps the mountains.
They watch over Shamash,
As he ascends and descends.

A seal depiction (Fig. 76) showing Gilgamesh (*second from left*) and his companion Enkidu (*far right*) may well depict the intercession of a god with one of the robot-like guards who could sweep the area with spotlights and emit death rays. The description brings to mind the statement in the Book of Genesis that God placed "the revolving sword" at the entrance to the Garden of Eden, to block its access to humans.

When Gilgamesh explained his partly divine origins, the purpose of

Fig. 76

his trip ("About death and life I wish to ask Utnapishtim") and the fact that he was on his way with the consent of Utu/Shamash, the guards allowed him to go ahead.

Proceeding "along the route of Shamash," Gilgamesh found himself in utter darkness; "seeing nothing ahead or behind," he cried out in fright. Traveling for many *beru* (a unit of time, distance, or the arc of the heavens), he was still engulfed by darkness. Finally, "it had grown bright when twelve *beru* he attained."

The damaged and blurred text then has Gilgamesh arriving at a magnificent garden where the fruits and trees were carved of semi-precious stones. It was there that Utnapishtim resided. Posing his problem to his ancestor, Gilgamesh encountered a disappointing answer: Man, Utnapishtim said, cannot escape his mortal fate. However, he offered Gilgamesh a way to postpone death, revealing to him the location of the Plant of Youth—"Man becomes young in old age," it was called. Triumphant, Gilgamesh obtained the plant. But, as fate would have it, he foolishly lost it on his way back, and returned to Uruk empty-handed.

Putting aside the literary and philosophic values of the epic tale, the story of Gilgamesh interests us here primarily for its "aerospace" aspects. The *shem* that Gilgamesh required in order to reach the Abode of the Gods was undoubtedly a rocket ship, the launching of one of which he had witnessed as he neared the "landing place." The rockets, it would seem, were located inside a mountain, and the area was a well-guarded, restricted zone.

No pictorial depiction of what Gilgamesh saw has so far come to light. But a drawing found in the tomb of an Egyptian governor of a far land shows a rockethead aboveground in a place where date trees grow. The shaft of the rocket is clearly stored *underground,* in a man-made silo constructed of tubular segments and decorated with leopard skins. (Fig. 77)

Very much in the manner of modern draftsmen, the ancient artists

Fig. 77

showed a cross-section of the underground silo. We can see that the rocket contained a number of compartments. The lower one shows two men surrounded by curving tubes. Above them there are three circular panels. Comparing the size of the rockethead—the *ben-ben*—to the size of the two men inside the rocket, and the people above the ground, it is evident that the rockethead—equivalent to the Sumerian *mu*, the "celestial chamber"—could easily hold one or two operators or passengers.

TIL.MUN was the name of the land to which Gilgamesh set his course. The name literally meant "land of the missiles." It was the land where the *shem*'s were raised, a land under the authority of Utu/Shamash, a place where one could see this god "rise up to the vault of heavens."

And though the celestial counterpart of this member of the Pantheon of Twelve was the Sun, we suggest that his name did not mean "Sun" but was an epithet describing his functions and responsibilities. His Sumerian name Utu meant "he who brilliantly goes in." His derivate Akkadian name—Shem-Esh—was more explicit: *Esh* means "fire," and we now know what *shem* originally meant.

Utu/Shamash was "he of the fiery rocket ships." He was, we suggest, the commander of the spaceport of the gods.

The commanding role of Utu/Shamash in matters of travel to the Heavenly Abode of the Gods, and the functions performed by his subordinates in this connection, are brought out in even greater detail in yet another Sumerian tale of a heavenward journey by a mortal.

The Sumerian king lists inform us that the thirteenth ruler of Kish was Etana, "the one who to Heaven ascended." This brief statement needed no elaboration, for the tale of the mortal king who journeyed up to the highest heavens was well known throughout the ancient Near East, and was the subject of numerous seal depictions.

Etana, we are told, was designated by the gods to bring Mankind the security and prosperity that Kingship—an organized civilization—was intended to provide. But Etana, it seems, could not father a son who would continue the dynasty. The only known remedy was a certain Plant of Birth that Etana could obtain only by fetching it down from the heavens.

Like Gilgamesh at a later time, Etana turned to Shamash for permission and assistance. As the epic unfolds, it becomes clear that Etana was asking Shamash for a *shem!*

O Lord, may it issue from thy mouth!
Grant thou me the Plant of Birth!
Show me the Plant of Birth!
Remove my handicap!
Produce for me a *shem!*

Flattered by prayer and fattened by sacrificial sheep, Shamash agreed to grant Etana's request to provide him with a *shem*. But instead of speaking of a *shem*, Shamash told Etana that an "eagle" would take him to the desired heavenly place.

Directing Etana to the pit where the Eagle had been placed,

Shamash also informed the Eagle ahead of time of the intended mission. Exchanging cryptic messages with "Shamash, his lord," the Eagle was told: "A man I will send to thee; he will take thy hand . . . lead him hither . . . do whatever he says . . . do as I say."

Arriving at the mountain indicated to him by Shamash, "Etana saw the pit," and, inside it, "there the Eagle was." "At the command of valiant Shamash," the Eagle entered into communication with Etana. Once more, Etana explained his purpose and destination; whereupon the Eagle began to instruct Etana on the procedure for "raising the Eagle from its pit." The first two attempts failed, but on the third one the Eagle was properly raised. At daybreak, the Eagle announced to Etana: "My friend . . . up to the Heaven of Anu I will bear thee!" Instructing him how to hold on, the Eagle took off—and they were aloft, rising fast.

As though reported by a modern astronaut watching Earth recede as his rocket ship rises, the ancient storyteller describes how Earth appeared smaller and smaller to Etana:

When he had borne him aloft one *beru*,
the Eagle says to him, to Etana:
"See, my friend, how the land appears!
Peer at the sea at the sides of the Mountain House:
The land has indeed become a mere hill,
The wide sea is just like a tub."

Higher and higher the Eagle rose; smaller and smaller Earth appeared. When he had borne him aloft a second *beru*, the Eagle said:

"My friend,
Cast a glance at how the land appears!
The land has turned into a furrow. . . .
The wide sea is just like a bread-basket.". . .
When he had borne him aloft a third *beru*,
The Eagle says to him, to Etana:
"See, my friend, how the land appears!
The land has turned into a gardener's ditch!"

And then, as they continued to ascend, Earth was suddenly out of sight.

As I glanced around, the land had disappeared,
and upon the wide sea mine eyes could not feast.

According to one version of this tale, the Eagle and Etana did reach the Heaven of Anu. But another version states that Etana got cold feet when he could no longer see Earth, and ordered the Eagle to reverse course and "plunge down" to Earth.

Once again, we find a biblical parallel to such an unusual report of seeing Earth from a great distance above it. Exalting the Lord Yahweh, the prophet Isaiah said of him: "It is he who sitteth upon the circle of the Earth, and the inhabitants thereof are as insects."

The tale of Etana informs us that, seeking a *shem*, Etana had to communicate with an Eagle inside a pit. A seal depiction shows a winged, tall structure (a launch tower?) above which an eagle flies off. (Fig. 78)

What or who was the Eagle who took Etana to the distant heavens?

We cannot help associating the ancient text with the message beamed to Earth in July 1969 by Neil Armstrong, commander of the Apollo 11 spacecraft: "Houston! Tranquility Base here. The *Eagle* has landed!"

He was reporting the first landing by Man on the Moon. "Tranquility Base" was the site of the landing; *Eagle* was the name of the lunar module that separated from the spacecraft and took the two astronauts inside it to the Moon (and then back to their mother craft). When the lunar module first separated to start its own flight in Moon orbit, the astronauts told Mission Control in Houston: "The *Eagle* has wings."

But "Eagle" could also denote the astronauts who manned the spacecraft. On the Apollo 11 mission, "Eagle" was also the symbol of the astronauts themselves, worn as an emblem on their suits. Just as in the Etana tale, they, too, were "Eagles" who could fly, speak, and communicate. (Fig. 79)

How would an ancient artist have depicted the pilots of the skyships of the gods? Would he have depicted them, by some chance, as eagles?

That is exactly what we have found. An Assyrian seal engraving from circa 1500 B.C. shows two "eagle-men" saluting a *shem!* (Fig. 80)

Numerous depictions of such "Eagles"—the scholars call them "bird-men"—have been found. Most depictions show them flanking the Tree of Life, as if to stress that they, in their *shem*'s, provided the link with the Heavenly Abode where the Bread of Life and Water of Life were to be found. Indeed, the usual depiction of the Eagles showed them holding in one hand the Fruit of Life and in the other the Water of Life, in full conformity with the tales of Adapa, Etana, and Gilgamesh. (Fig. 81)

The many depictions of the Eagles clearly show that they were not monstrous "bird-men," but anthropomorphic beings wearing costumes or uniforms that gave them the appearance of eagles.

Fig. 78

Fig. 79

Fig. 80

Fig. 81

Fig. 82

The Hittite tale concerning the god Telepinu, who had vanished, reported that "the great gods and the lesser gods began to search for Telepinu" and "Shamash sent out a swift Eagle" to find him.

In the Book of Exodus, God is reported to have reminded the Children of Israel, "I have carried you upon the wings of Eagles, and have brought you unto me," confirming, it seems, that the way to reach the Divine Abode was upon the wings of Eagles—just as the tale of Etana relates. Numerous biblical verses, as a matter of fact, describe the Deity as a winged being. Boaz welcomed Ruth into the Judaean community as "coming under the wings" of the God Yahweh. The Psalmist sought security "under the shadow of thy wings" and described the descent of the Lord from the heavens. "He mounted a Cherub and went flying; He soared upon windy wings." Analyzing the similarities between the biblical El (employed as a title or generic term for the Deity) and the Canaanite El, S. Langdon (*Semitic Mythology*) showed that both were depicted, in text and on coins, as winged gods.

The Mesopotamian texts invariably present Utu/Shamash as the god in charge of the landing place of the *shem*'s and of the Eagles. And like his subordinates he was sometimes shown wearing the full regalia of an Eagle's costume. (Fig. 82)

In such a capacity, he could grant to kings the privilege of "flying on the wings of birds" and of "rising from the lower heavens to the lofty ones." And when he was launched aloft in a fiery rocket, it was he "who stretched over unknown distances, for countless hours." Appropriately, "his net was the Earth, his trap the distant skies."

The Sumerian terminology for objects connected with celestial travel was not limited to the *me*'s that the gods put on or the *mu*'s that were their cone-shaped "chariots."

Sumerian texts describing Sippar relate that it had a central part, hidden and protected by mighty walls. Within those walls stood the Temple of Utu, "a house which is like a house of the Heavens." In an inner courtyard of the temple, also protected by high walls, stood "erected upwards, the mighty APIN" ("an object that plows through," according to the translators).

A drawing found at the temple mound of Anu at Uruk depicts such an object. We would have been hard put a few decades ago to guess what this object was; but now we readily recognize it as a multistage space rocket at the top of which rests the conical *mu*, or command cabin. (Fig. 83)

The evidence that the gods of Sumer possessed not just "flying chambers" for roaming Earth's skies but space-going multistage rocket ships also emerges from the examination of texts describing the sacred

Fig. 83

objects at Utu's temple at Sippar. We are told that witnesses at Sumer's supreme court were required to take the oath in an inner courtyard, standing by a gateway through which they could see and face three "divine objects." These were named "the golden sphere" (the crew's cabin?), the GIR, and the *alikmahrati*—a term that literally meant "advancer that makes vessel go," or what we would call a motor, an engine.

What emerges here is a reference to a three-part rocket ship, with the cabin or command module at the top end, the engines at the bottom end, and the *gir* in the center. The latter is a term that has been used extensively in connection with space flight. The guards Gilgamesh encountered at the entrance to the landing place of Shamash were called *gir*-men. In the temple of Ninurta, the sacred or most guarded inner area was called the GIR.SU ("where the *gir* is sprung up").

Gir, it is generally acknowledged, was a term used to describe a sharp-edged object. A close look at the pictorial sign for *gir* provides a better understanding of the term's "divine" nature; for what we see is a long, arrow-shaped object, divided into several parts or compartments:

That the *mu* could hover in Earth's skies on its own, or fly over Earth's lands when attached to a *gir*, or become the command module atop a multistage *apin* is testimony to the engineering ingenuity of the gods of Sumer, the Gods of Heaven and Earth.

A review of the Sumerian pictographs and ideograms leaves no doubt that whoever drew those signs was familiar with the shapes and purposes of rockets with tails of billowing fire, missile-like vehicles, and celestial "cabins."

 KA.GIR ("rocket's mouth") showed a fin-equipped *gir*, or rocket, inside a shaftlike underground enclosure.

 ESH ("Divine Abode"), the chamber or command module of a space vehicle.

 ZIK ("ascend"), a command module taking off?

Finally, let us look at the pictographic sign for "gods" in Sumerian. The term was a two-syllable word: DIN.GIR. We have already seen what the symbol for GIR was: a two-stage rocket with fins. DIN, the first syllable, meant "righteous," "pure," "bright." Put together, then, DIN.GIR as "gods" or "divine beings" conveyed the meaning "the righteous ones of the bright, pointed objects" or, more explicitly, "the pure ones of the blazing rockets."

The pictographic sign for *din* was this:  , easily

bringing to mind a powerful jet engine spewing flames from the end part, and a front part that is puzzlingly open. But the puzzle turns to amazement if we "spell" *dingir* by combining the two pictographs. The tail of the finlike *gir* fits perfectly into the opening in the front of *din*! (Figs. 84, 85)

The astounding result is a picture of a rocket-propelled spaceship, with a landing craft docked into it perfectly—just as the lunar module was docked with the Apollo 11 spaceship! It is indeed a three-stage vehicle, with each part fitting neatly into the other: the thrust portion containing the engines, the midsection containing supplies and equip-

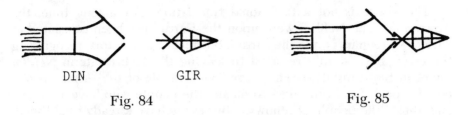

DIN   GIR

Fig. 84   Fig. 85

ment, and the cylindrical "sky chamber" housing the people named *dingir*—the gods of antiquity, the astronauts of millennia ago.

Can there be any doubt that the ancient peoples, in calling their deities "Gods of Heaven and Earth," meant literally that they were people from elsewhere who had come to Earth from the heavens?

The evidence thus far submitted regarding the ancient gods and their vehicles should leave no further doubt that they were once indeed living beings of flesh and blood, people who literally came down to Earth from the heavens.

Even the ancient compilers of the Old Testament—who dedicated the Bible to a single God—found it necessary to acknowledge the presence upon Earth in early times of such divine beings.

The enigmatic section—a horror of translators and theologians alike—forms the beginning of Chapter 6 of Genesis. It is interposed between the review of the spread of Mankind through the generations following Adam and the story of the divine disenchantment with Mankind that preceded the Deluge. It states—unequivocally—that, at that time,

> the sons of the gods
> saw the daughters of man, that they were good;
> and they took them for wives,
> of all which they chose.

The implications of these verses, and the parallels to the Sumerian tales of gods and their sons and grandsons, and of semidivine offspring resulting from cohabitation between gods and mortals, mount further as we continue to read the biblical verses:

> The Nefilim were upon the Earth,
> in those days and thereafter too,
> when the sons of the gods
> cohabited with the daughters of the Adam,
> and they bore children unto them.
> They were the mighty ones of Eternity—
> The People of the *shem*.

The above is not a traditional translation. For a long time, the expression "The Nefilim were upon the Earth" has been translated as "There were giants upon the earth"; but recent translators, recognizing the error, have simply resorted to leaving the Hebrew term *Nefilim* intact in the translation. The verse "The people of the *shem*," as one could expect, has been taken to mean "the people who have a name," and, thus, "the people of renown." But as we have already established, the term *shem* must be taken in its original meaning—a rocket, a rocket ship.

What, then, does the term *Nefilim* mean? Stemming from the Semitic root *NFL* ("to be cast down"), it means exactly what it says: It means *those who were cast down upon Earth!*

Contemporary theologians and biblical scholars have tended to avoid the troublesome verses, either by explaining them away allegorically or simply by ignoring them altogether. But Jewish writings of the time of the Second Temple did recognize in these verses the echoes of ancient traditions of "fallen angels." Some of the early scholarly works even mentioned the names of these divine beings "who fell from Heaven and were on Earth in those days": Sham-Hazzai ("*shem*'s lookout"), Uzza ("mighty") and Uzi-El ("God's might").

Malbim, a noted Jewish biblical commentator of the nineteenth century, recognized these ancient roots and explained that "in ancient times the rulers of countries were the sons of the deities who arrived upon the Earth from the Heavens, and ruled the Earth, and married wives from among the daughters of Man; and their offspring included heroes and mighty ones, princes and sovereigns." These stories, Malbim said, were of the pagan gods, "sons of the deities, who in earliest times fell down from the Heavens upon the Earth . . . that is why they called themselves 'Nefilim,' i.e. Those Who Fell Down."

Irrespective of the theological implications, the literal and original meaning of the verses cannot be escaped: The sons of the gods who came to Earth from the heavens were the Nefilim.

And the Nefilim were the People of the Shem—the People of the Rocket Ships. Henceforward, we shall call them by their biblical name.

6.

THE TWELFTH PLANET

The suggestion that Earth was visited by intelligent beings from elsewhere postulates the existence of another celestial body upon which intelligent beings established a civilization more advanced than ours.

Speculation regarding the possibility of Earth visitation by intelligent beings from elsewhere has centered, in the past, on such planets as Mars or Venus as their place of origin. However, now that it is virtually certain that these two planetary neighbors of Earth have neither intelligent life nor an advanced civilization upon them, those who believe in such Earth visitations look to other galaxies and to distant stars as the home of such extraterrestrial astronauts.

The advantage of such suggestions is that while they cannot be proved, they cannot be disproved, either. The disadvantage is that these suggested "homes" are fantastically distant from Earth, requiring years upon years of travel at the speed of light. The authors of such suggestions therefore postulate one-way trips to Earth: a team of astronauts on a no-return mission, or perhaps on a spaceship lost and out of control, crash-landing upon Earth.

This is definitely *not* the Sumerian notion of the Heavenly Abode of the Gods.

The Sumerians accepted the existence of such a "Heavenly Abode," a "pure place," a "primeval abode." While Enlil, Enki, and Ninhursag went to Earth and made their home upon it, their father Anu remained in the Heavenly Abode as its ruler. Not only occasional references in various texts but also detailed "god lists" actually named twenty-one divine couples of the dynasty that preceded Anu on the throne of the "pure place."

Anu himself reigned over a court of great splendor and extent. As Gilgamesh reported (and the Book of Ezekiel confirmed), it was a place with an artificial garden sculpted wholly of semiprecious stones. There Anu resided with his official consort Antu and six concubines, eighty offspring (of which fourteen were by Antu), one Prime Minister, three Commanders in charge of the *mus* (rocket ships), two Commanders of the Weapons, two Great Masters of Written Knowledge, one Minister of the Purse, two Chief Justices, two "who with sound impress," and two Chief Scribes, with five Assistant Scribes.

Mesopotamian texts refer frequently to the magnificence of the abode of Anu and the gods and weapons that guarded its gateway. The tale of Adapa reports that the god Enki, having provided Adapa with a *shem,*

> Made him take the road to Heaven,
> and to Heaven he went up.
> When he had ascended to Heaven,
> he approached the Gate of Anu.
> Tammuz and Gizzida were standing guard
> at the Gate of Anu.

Guarded by the divine weapons SHAR.UR ("royal hunter") and SHAR.GAZ ("royal killer"), the throne room of Anu was the place of the Assembly of the Gods. On such occasions a strict protocol governed the order of entering and seating:

> Enlil enters the throne room of Anu,
> seats himself at the place of the right tiara,
> on the right of Anu.
> Ea enters [the throne room of Anu],
> seats himself at the place of the sacred tiara,
> on the left of Anu.

The Gods of Heaven and Earth of the ancient Near East not only originated in the heavens but could also return to the Heavenly Abode. Anu occasionally came down to Earth on state visits; Ishtar went up to Anu at least twice. Enlil's center in Nippur was equipped as a "bond heaven–earth." Shamash was in charge of the Eagles and the launching place of the rocket ships. Gilgamesh went up to the Place of Eternity and returned to Uruk; Adapa, too, made the trip and came back to tell about it; so did the biblical king of Tyre.

A number of Mesopotamian texts deal with the *Apkallu,* an Akkadian term stemming from the Sumerian AB.GAL ("great one who leads," or "master who points the way"). A study by Gustav Guterbock (*Die Historische Tradition und Ihre Literarische Gestaltung bei Babylonier und Hethiten*) ascertained that these were the "bird-men" depicted as the "Eagles" that we have already shown. The texts that spoke of their feats said of one that he "brought down Inanna from Heaven, to the E-Anna temple made her descend." This and other references indicate that these Apkallu were the pilots of the spaceships of the Nefilim.

Two-way travel was not only possible but actually contemplated to begin with, for we are told that, having decided to establish in Sumer the Gateway of the Gods (Babili), the leader of the gods explained:

> When to the Primeval Source
> for assembly you shall ascend,
> There shall be a restplace for the night
> to receive you all.
> When from the Heavens
> for assembly you shall descend,
> There shall be a restplace for the night
> to receive you all.

Realizing that such two-way travel between Earth and the Heavenly Abode was both contemplated and practiced, the people of Sumer did not exile their gods to distant galaxies. The Abode of the Gods, their legacy discloses, was within our own solar system.

We have seen Shamash in his official uniform as Commander of the Eagles. On each of his wrists he wears a watchlike object held in place by metal clasps. Other depictions of the Eagles reveal that all the important ones wore such objects. Whether they were merely decorative or served a useful purpose, we do not know. But all scholars are agreed that the objects represented rosettes—a circular cluster of "petals" radiating from a central point. (Fig. 86)

The rosette was the most common decorative temple symbol throughout the ancient lands, prevalent in Mesopotamia, western Asia, Anatolia, Cyprus, Crete, and Greece. It is the accepted view that the rosette as a temple symbol was an outgrowth or stylization of a celestial phenomenon—a sun encircled by its satellites. That the ancient astronauts wore this symbol on their wrists adds credence to this view.

An Assyrian depiction of the Gateway of Anu in the Heavenly Abode (Fig. 87) confirms ancient familiarity with a celestial system such as our Sun and its planets. The gateway is flanked by two Eagles—indicating that their services are needed to reach the Heavenly Abode. The Winged Globe—the supreme divine emblem—marks the gateway. It is flanked by the celestial symbols of the number seven and the crescent, representing (we believe) Anu flanked by Enlil and Enki.

Where are the celestial bodies represented by these symbols? Where is the Heavenly Abode? The ancient artist answers with yet another depiction, that of a large celestial deity extending its rays to eleven smaller celestial bodies encircling it. It is a representation of a Sun, orbited by eleven planets.

That this was not an isolated representation can be shown by reproducing other depictions on cylinder seals, like this one from the Berlin Museum of the Ancient Near East. (Fig. 88)

When the central god or celestial body in the Berlin seal is enlarged (Fig. 89), we can see that it depicts a large, ray-emitting star surrounded by eleven heavenly bodies—planets. These, in turn, rest on a chain of twenty-four smaller globes. Is it only a coincidence that the number of all the "moons," or satellites, of the planets in our solar system (astronomers exclude those of ten miles or less in diameter) is also exactly twenty-four?

Now there is, of course, a catch to claiming that these depictions—of a Sun and *eleven* planets—represent *our* solar system, for our scholars tell us that the planetary system of which Earth is a part comprises the Sun, Earth and Moon, Mercury, Venus, Mars, Jupiter, Saturn, Uranus, Neptune, and Pluto. This adds up to the Sun and only ten planets (when the Moon is counted as one).

But that is not what the Sumerians said. They claimed that our system was made up of the Sun and eleven planets (counting the Moon), and held steadfastly to the opinion that, in addition to the planets known to us today, there has been a *twelfth* member of the solar system—the home planet of the Nefilim.

We shall call it the *Twelfth Planet*.

Before we check the accuracy of the Sumerian information, let us review the history of our own knowledge of Earth and the heavens around it.

We know today that beyond the giant planets Jupiter and Saturn— at distances insignificant in terms of the universe, but immense in human terms—two more major planets (Uranus and Neptune) and a third, small one (Pluto) belong to our solar system. But such knowledge is quite recent. Uranus was discovered, through the use of improved telescopes, in 1781. After observing it for some fifty years, some astronomers reached the conclusion that its orbit revealed the influence of yet another planet. Guided by such mathematical calculations, the missing planet—named Neptune—was pinpointed by astronomers in 1846. Then, by the end of the nineteenth century, it became evident that Neptune itself was being subjected to unknown gravitational pull. Was there yet another planet in our solar system? The puzzle was solved in 1930 with the observation and location of Pluto.

Up to 1780, then, and for centuries before that, people believed

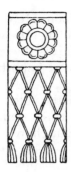

Fig. 86

Fig. 87

Fig. 88

Fig. 89

there were *seven* members of our solar system: Sun, Moon, Mercury, Venus, Mars, Jupiter, Saturn. Earth was not counted as a planet because it was believed that these other celestial bodies circled Earth—the most important celestial body created by God, with God's most important creation, Man, upon it.

Our textbooks generally credit Nicolaus Copernicus with the discovery that Earth is only one of several planets in a heliocentric (Sun-centered) system. Fearing the wrath of the Christian church for challenging Earth's central position, Copernicus published his study (*De revolutionibus orbium coelestium*) only when on his deathbed, in 1543.

Spurred to reexamine centuries-old astronomical concepts primarily by the navigational needs of the Age of Discovery, and by the findings by Columbus (1492), Magellan (1520), and others that Earth was not flat but spherical, Copernicus depended on mathematical calculations and searched for the answers in ancient writings. One of the few churchmen who supported Copernicus, Cardinal Schonberg, wrote to him in 1536: "I have learned that you know not only the groundwork of the ancient mathematical doctrines, but that you have created a new theory . . . according to which the Earth is in motion and it is the Sun which occupies the fundamental and therefore the cardinal position."

The concepts then held were based on Greek and Roman traditions that Earth, which was flat, was "vaulted over" by the distant heavens, in which the stars were fixed. Against the star-studded heavens the planets (from the Greek word for "wanderer") moved around Earth. There were thus seven celestial bodies, from which the seven days of the week and their names originated: the Sun (Sunday), Moon (Monday), Mars *(mardi)*, Mercury *(mercredi)*, Jupiter *(jeudi)*, Venus *(vendredi)*, Saturn (Saturday). (Fig. 90)

These astronomical notions stemmed from the works and codifications of Ptolemy, an astronomer in the city of Alexandria, Egypt, in the second century A.D. His definite findings were that the Sun, Moon, and five planets moved in circles around Earth. Ptolemaic astronomy predominated for more than 1,300 years—until Copernicus put the Sun in the center.

While some have called Copernicus the "Father of Modern Astronomy," others view him more as a researcher and reconstructor of earlier ideas. The fact is that he pored over the writings of Greek astronomers who preceded Ptolemy, such as Hipparchus and Aristarchus of Samos. The latter suggested in the third century B.C. that the motions of the heavenly bodies could better be explained if the Sun—and not Earth—were assumed to be in the center. In fact, 2,000 years before Copernicus, Greek astronomers listed the planets in their

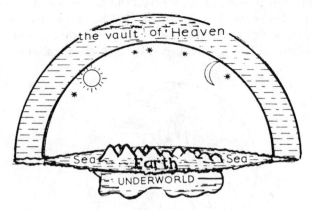

Fig. 90

correct order from the Sun, acknowledging thereby that the Sun, not Earth, was the solar system's focal point.

The heliocentric concept was only *re*discovered by Copernicus; and the interesting fact is that astronomers knew more in 500 B.C. than in A.D. 500 and 1500.

Indeed, scholars are now hard put to explain why first the later Greeks and then the Romans assumed that Earth was flat, rising above a layer of murky waters below which there lay Hades or "Hell," when some of the evidence left by Greek astronomers from earlier times indicates that they knew otherwise.

Hipparchus, who lived in Asia Minor in the second century B.C., discussed "the displacement of the sostitial and equinoctial sign," the phenomenon now called precession of the equinoxes. But the phenomenon can be explained only in terms of a "spherical astronomy," whereby Earth is surrounded by the other celestial bodies as a sphere within a spherical universe.

Did Hipparchus, then, know that Earth was a globe, and did he make his calculations in terms of a spherical astronomy? Equally important is yet another question. The phenomenon of the precession could be observed by relating the arrival of spring to the Sun's position (as seen from Earth) in a given zodiacal constellation. But the shift from one zodiacal house to another requires 2,160 years. Hipparchus certainly could not have lived long enough to make that astronomical observation. Where, then, did he obtain his information?

Eudoxus of Cnidus, another Greek mathematician and astronomer who lived in Asia Minor two centuries before Hipparchus, designed a celestial sphere, a copy of which was set up in Rome as a statue of Atlas supporting the world. The designs on the sphere represent the zodiacal constellations. But if Eudoxus conceived the heavens as a sphere, where in relation to the heavens was Earth? Did he think that the celestial globe rested on a *flat* Earth—a most awkward arrangement—or did he know of a spherical Earth, enveloped by a celestial sphere? (Fig. 91)

Fig. 91

The works of Eudoxus, lost in their originals, have come down to us thanks to the poems of Aratus, who in the third century B.C. "translated" the facts put forth by the astronomer into poetic language. In this poem (which must have been familiar to St. Paul, who quoted from it) the constellations are described in great detail, "drawn all around"; and their grouping and naming is ascribed to a very remote prior age. "Some men of yore a nomenclature thought of and devised, and appropriate forms found."

Who were the "men of yore" to whom Eudoxus attributed the designation of the constellations? Based on certain clues in the poem, modern astronomers believe that the Greek verses describe the heavens as they were observed in *Mesopotamia* circa 2200 B.C.

The fact that both Hipparchus and Eudoxus lived in Asia Minor raises the probability that they drew their knowledge from Hittite sources. Perhaps they even visited the Hittite capital and viewed the divine procession carved on the rocks there; for among the marching gods two bull-men hold up a globe—a sight that might well have inspired Eudoxus to sculpt Atlas and the celestial sphere. (Fig. 92)

Fig. 92

Were the earlier Greek astronomers, living in Asia Minor, better informed than their successors because they could draw on Mesopotamian sources?

Hipparchus, in fact, confirmed in his writings that his studies were based on knowledge accumulated and verified over many millennia. He named as his mentors "Babylonian astronomers of Erech, Borsippa, and Babylon." Geminus of Rhodes named the "Chaldeans" (the ancient Babylonians) as the discoverers of the exact motions of the Moon. The historian Diodorus Siculus, writing in the first century B.C., confirmed the exactness of Mesopotamian astronomy; he stated that "the Chaldeans named the planets . . . in the center of their system was the Sun, the greatest light, of which the planets were 'offspring,' reflecting the Sun's position and shine."

The acknowledged source of Greek astronomical knowledge was, then, Chaldea; invariably, those earlier Chaldeans possessed greater and more accurate knowledge than the peoples that followed them. For generations, throughout the ancient world, the name "Chaldean" was synonymous with "stargazers," astronomers.

Abraham, who came out of "Ur of the Chaldeans," was told by God to gaze at the stars when the future Hebrew generations were discussed. Indeed, the Old Testament was replete with astronomical information. Joseph compared himself and his brothers to twelve celestial bodies, and the patriarch Jacob blessed his twelve descendants by associating them with the twelve constellations of the zodiac. The Psalms and the Book of Job refer repeatedly to celestial phenomena, the zodiacal constellations, and other star groups (such as the Pleiades). Knowledge of the zodiac, the scientific division of the heavens, and other astronomical information was thus prevalent in the ancient Near East well before the days of ancient Greece.

The scope of Mesopotamian astronomy on which the early Greek astronomers drew must have been vast, for even what archaeologists have found amounts to an avalanche of texts, inscriptions, seal impressions, reliefs, drawings, lists of celestial bodies, omens, calendars, tables of rising and setting times of the Sun and the planets, forecasts of eclipses.

Many such later texts were, to be sure, more astrological than astronomical in nature. The heavens and the movements of the heavenly bodies appeared to be a prime preoccupation of mighty kings, temple priests, and the people of the land in general; the purpose of the stargazing seemed to be to find in the heavens an answer to the course of affairs on Earth: war, peace, abundance, famine.

Compiling and analyzing hundreds of texts from the first millennium B.C., R. C. Thompson (*The Reports of the Magicians and Astrologers of Nineveh and Babylon*) was able to show that these stargazers were concerned with the fortunes of the land, its people, and its ruler from a national point of view, and not with individual fortunes (as present-day "horoscopic" astrology is):

> When the Moon in its calculated time is not seen, there will be an invasion of a mighty city.

> When a comet reaches the path of the Sun, field-flow will be diminished; an uproar will happen twice.

> When Jupiter goes with Venus, the prayers of the land will reach the heart of the gods.

> If the Sun stands in the station of the Moon, the king of the land will be secure on the throne.

Even this astrology required comprehensive and accurate astronomical knowledge, without which no omens were possible. The Mesopotamians, possessing such knowledge, distinguished between the "fixed" stars and the planets that "wandered about" and knew that the Sun and the Moon were neither fixed stars nor ordinary planets. They were familiar with comets, meteors, and other celestial phenomena, and could calculate the relationships between the movements of the Sun, Moon, and Earth, and predict eclipses. They followed the motions of the celestial bodies and related them to Earth's orbit and rotation through the heliacal system—the system still in use today, which measures the rising and setting of stars and planets in Earth's skies relative to the Sun.

To keep track of the movements of the celestial bodies and their positions in the heavens relative to Earth and to one another, the Babylonians and Assyrians kept accurate ephemerides. These were tables that listed and predicted the future positions of the celestial bodies. Professor George Sarton (*Chaldean Astronomy of the Last Three*

Centuries B.C.) found that they were computed by two methods: a later one used in Babylon, and an older one from Uruk. His unexpected finding was that the older, Uruk method was more sophisticated and more accurate than the later system. He accounted for this surprising situation by concluding that the erroneous astronomical notions of the Greeks and Romans resulted from a shift to a philosophy that explained the world in geometric terms, while the astronomer-priests of Chaldea followed the prescribed formulas and traditions of Sumer.

The unearthing of the Mesopotamian civilizations in the past one hundred years leaves no doubt that in the field of astronomy, as in so many others, the roots of our knowledge lie deep in Mesopotamia. In this field, too, we draw upon and continue the heritage of Sumer.

Sarton's conclusions have been reinforced by very comprehensive studies by Professor O. Neugebauer (*Astronomical Cuneiform Texts*), who was astonished to find that the ephemerides, precise as they were, were not based on observations by the Babylonian astronomers who prepared them. Instead, they were calculated "from some fixed arithmetical schemes ... which were given and were not to be interfered with" by the astronomers who used them.

Such automatic adherence to "arithmetical schemes" was achieved with the aid of "procedure texts" that accompanied the ephemerides, which "gave the rules for computing ephemerides step by step" according to some "strict mathematical theory." Neugebauer concluded that the Babylonian astronomers were ignorant of the theories on which the ephemerides and their mathematical calculations were based. He also admitted that "the empirical and theoretical foundation" of these accurate tables, to a large extent, escapes modern scholars as well. Yet he is convinced that ancient astronomical theories "must have existed, because it is impossible to devise computational schemes of high complication without a very elaborate plan."

Professor Alfred Jeremias (*Handbuch der Altorientalischen Geistkultur*) concluded that the Mesopotamian astronomers were acquainted with the phenomenon of retrograde, the apparent erratic and snakelike course of the planets as seen from Earth, caused by the fact that Earth orbits the Sun either faster or slower than the other planets. The significance of such knowledge lies not only in the fact that retrograde is a phenomenon related to orbits around the Sun, but also in the fact that very long periods of observation were required to grasp and track it.

Where were these complicated theories developed, and who made the observations without which they could not have been developed? Neugebauer pointed out that "in the procedure texts, we meet a great number of technical terms of wholly unknown reading, if not unknown meaning." Someone, much earlier than the Babylonians, possessed astronomical and mathematical knowledge far superior to that of later culture in Babylon, Assyria, Egypt, Greece, and Rome.

The Babylonians and Assyrians devoted a substantial part of their astronomical efforts to keeping an accurate calendar. Like the Jewish calendar to this very day, it was a solar-lunar calendar, correlating ("intercalating") the solar year of just over 365 days with a lunar month of just under 30 days. While a calendar was important for business and other mundane needs, its accuracy was required primarily to determine the precise day and moment of the New Year, and other festivals and worship of the gods.

To measure and correlate the intricate movements of Sun, Earth, Moon, and planets, the Mesopotamian astronomer-priests relied on a complex spherical astronomy. Earth was taken to be a sphere with an equator and poles; the heavens, too, were divided by imaginary equatorial and polar lines. The passage of celestial bodies was related to the ecliptic, the projection of the plane of Earth's orbit around the Sun upon the celestial sphere; the equinoxes (the points and the times at which the Sun in its apparent annual movement north and south crosses the celestial equator); and the solstices (the time when the Sun during its apparent annual movement along the ecliptic is at its greatest declination north or south). All these are astronomical concepts used to this very day.

But the Babylonians and Assyrians did not invent the calendar or the ingenious methods for its calculation. Their calendars—as well as our own—originated in Sumer. There the scholars have found a calendar, in use from the very earliest times, that is the basis for *all* later calendars. The principal calendar and model was the calendar of Nippur, the seat and center of Enlil. Our present-day one is modeled on that Nippurian calendar.

The Sumerians considered the New Year to begin at the exact moment when the Sun crossed the spring equinox. Professor Stephen Langdon *(Tablets from the Archives of Drehem)* found that records left by Dungi, a ruler of Ur circa 2400 B.C., show that the Nippurian calendar selected a certain celestial body by whose setting against the sunset it was possible to determine the exact moment of the New Year's arrival. This, he concluded, was done "perhaps 2,000 years before the era of Dungi"—that is, circa 4400 B.C.!

Can it really be that the Sumerians, without actual instruments, nevertheless had the sophisticated astronomical and mathematical know-how required by a spherical astronomy and geometry? Indeed they had, as their language shows.

They had a term—DUB—that meant (in astronomy) the 360-degree "circumference of the world," in relation to which they spoke of the curvature or arc of the heavens. For their astronomical and mathematical calculations they drew the AN.UR—an imagined "heavenly horizon" against which they could measure the rising and setting of celestial bodies. Perpendicular to this horizon they extended an imagined vertical line, the NU.BU.SAR.DA; with its aid they obtained the zenith point and called it the AN.PA. They traced the lines we call meridians, and called them "the graded yokes"; latitude lines were called "middle lines of heaven." The latitude line marking the summer solstice, for example, was called AN.BIL ("fiery point of the heavens").

The Akkadian, Hurrian, Hittite, and other literary masterpieces of the ancient Near East, being translations or versions of Sumerian originals, were replete with Sumerian loanwords pertaining to celestial bodies and phenomena. Babylonian and Assyrian scholars who drew up star lists or wrote down calculations of planetary movements often noted the Sumerian originals on the tablets that they were copying or translating. The 25,000 texts devoted to astronomy and astrology said to have been included in the Nineveh library of Ashurbanipal frequently bore acknowledgments of Sumerian origins.

A major astronomical series that the Babylonians called "The Day of the Lord" was declared by its scribes to have been copied from a Sumerian tablet written in the time of Sargon of Akkad—in the third millennium B.C. A tablet dated to the third dynasty of Ur, also in the third millennium B.C., describes and lists a series of celestial bodies so clearly that modern scholars had little difficulty in recognizing the text as a classification of constellations, among them Ursa Major, Draco, Lyra, Cygnus and Cepheus, and Triangulum in the northern skies; Orion, Canis Major, Hydra, Corvus, and Centaurus in the southern skies; and the familiar zodiacal constellations in the central celestial band.

In ancient Mesopotamia the secrets of celestial knowledge were guarded, studied, and transmitted by astronomer-priests. It was thus perhaps fitting that three scholars who are credited with giving back to us this lost "Chaldean" science were Jesuit priests: Joseph Epping, Johann Strassman, and Franz X. Kugler. Kugler, in a masterwork (*Sternkunde und Sterndienst in Babel*), analyzed, deciphered, sorted out, and explained a vast number of texts and lists. In one instance, by mathematically "turning the skies backwards," he was able to show that a list of thirty-three celestial bodies in the Babylonian skies of 1800 B.C. was neatly arranged according to present-day groupings!

After much work deciding which are true groups and which are merely subgroups, the world's astronomical community agreed (in 1925) to divide the heavens as seen from Earth into *three* regions—

northern, central, and southern—and group the stars therein into eighty-eight constellations. As it turned out, there was nothing new in this arrangement, for the Sumerians were the first to divide the heavens into three bands or "ways"—the northern "way" was named after Enlil, the southern after Ea, and the central band was the "Way of Anu"—and to assign to them various constellations. The present-day central band, the band of the twelve constellations of the zodiac, corresponds *exactly* to the Way of Anu, in which the Sumerians grouped the stars into twelve houses.

In antiquity, as today, the phenomenon was related to the concept of the zodiac. The great circle of Earth around the Sun was divided into twelve equal parts, of thirty degrees each. The stars seen in each of these segments, or "houses," were grouped together into a constellation, each of which was then named according to the shape the stars of the group seemed to form.

Because the constellation and their subdivisions, and even individual stars within the constellations, have reached Western civilization with names and descriptions borrowed heavily from Greek mythology, the Western world tended for nearly two millennia to credit the Greeks with this achievement. But it is now apparent that the early Greek astronomers merely adopted into their language and mythology a ready-made astronomy obtained from the Sumerians. We have already noted how Hipparchus, Eudoxus, and others obtained their knowledge. Even Thales, the earliest Greek astronomer of consequence, who is said to have predicted the total solar eclipse of May 28, 585 B.C., which stopped the war between the Lydians and the Medians, allowed that the sources of his knowledge were of pre-Semitic Mesopotamian origins, namely—Sumerian.

We have acquired the name "zodiac" from the Greek *zodiakos kyklos* ("animal circle") because the layout of the star groups was likened to the shape of a lion, fishes, and so on. But those imaginary shapes and names were actually originated by the Sumerians, who called the twelve zodiacal constellations UL.HE ("shiny herd"):

1. GU.AN.NA ("heavenly bull"), *Taurus.*
2. MASH.TAB.BA ("twins"), our *Gemini.*
3. DUB ("pincers," "tongs"), the Crab or *Cancer.*
4. UR.GULA ("lion"), which we call *Leo.*
5. AB.SIN ("her father was Sin"), the Maiden, *Virgo.*
6. ZI.BA.AN.NA ("heavenly fate"), the scales of *Libra.*
7. GIR.TAB ("which claws and cuts"), *Scorpio.*
8. PA.BIL ("defender"), the Archer, *Sagittarius.*
9. SUHUR.MASH ("goat-fish"), *Capricorn.*

10. GU ("lord of the waters"), the Water Bearer, *Aquarius.*
11. SIM.MAH ("fishes"), *Pisces.*
12. KU.MAL ("field dweller"), the Ram, *Aries.*

The pictorial representations or signs of the zodiac, like their names, have remained virtually intact since their introduction in Sumer. (Fig. 93)

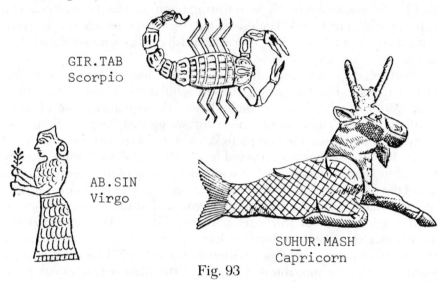

GIR.TAB
Scorpio

AB.SIN
Virgo

SUHUR.MASH
Capricorn

Fig. 93

Until the introduction of the telescope, European astronomers accepted the Ptolemaic recognition of only nineteen constellations in the northern skies. By 1925, when the current classification was agreed upon, twenty-eight constellations had been recognized in what the Sumerians called the Way of Enlil. We should no longer be surprised to find out that, unlike Ptolemy, the earlier Sumerians recognized, identified, grouped, named, and listed *all* the constellations of the northern skies!

Of the celestial bodies *in* the Way of Enlil, twelve were deemed to be *of* Enlil—paralleling the twelve zodiacal celestial bodies in the Way of Anu. Likewise, in the southern portion of the skies—the Way of Ea—twelve constellations were listed, not merely as present *in* the southern skies, but as *of* the god Ea. In addition to these twelve principal constellations of Ea, several others were listed for the southern skies—though not so many as are recognized today.

The Way of Ea posed serious problems to the Assyriologists who undertook the immense task of unraveling the ancient astronomical knowledge not only in terms of modern knowledge but also based on what the skies should have looked like centuries and millennia ago. Observing the southern skies from Ur or Babylon, the Mesopotamian astronomers could see only a little more than halfway into the southern skies; the rest was already below the horizon. Yet, if correctly identified, some of the constellations of the Way of Ea lay well beyond the horizon. But there was an even greater problem: If, as the scholars assumed, the Mesopotamians believed (as the Greeks did in later times) that Earth was a mass of dry land resting upon the chaotic darkness of a netherworld (the Greek Hades)—a flat disc over which the heavens arched in a semicircle—then there should have been no southern skies at all!

Restricted by the assumption that the Mesopotamians were beholden to a flat-Earth concept, modern scholars could not permit their conclusions to take them too much below the equatorial line dividing north and south. The evidence, however, shows that the three Sumerian "ways" encompassed the complete skies of a global, not flat, Earth.

In 1900 T. G. Pinches reported to the Royal Asiatic Society that he was able to reassemble and reconstruct a complete Mesopotamian astrolabe (literally, "taker of stars"). He showed it to be a circular disc, divided like a pie into twelve segments and three concentric rings, resulting in a field of thirty-six portions. The whole design had the appearance of a rosette of twelve "leaves," each of which had the name of a month written in it. Pinches marked them I to XII for convenience, starting with Nisannu, the first month of the Mesopotamian calendar. (Fig. 94)

Each of the thirty-six portions also contained a name with a small circle below it, signifying that it was the name of a celestial body. The names have since been found in many texts and "star lists" and are undoubtedly the names of constellations, stars, or planets.

Each of the thirty-six segments also had a number written below the name of the celestial body. In the innermost ring, the numbers ranged from 30 to 60; in the central ring, from 60 (written as "1") to 120 (this "2" in the sexagesimal system meant 2 × 60 = 120); and in the outermost ring, from 120 to 240. What did these numbers represent?

Writing nearly fifty years after the presentation by Pinches, the astronomer and Assyriologist O. Neugebauer (*A History of Ancient Astronomy: Problems and Methods*) could only say that "the whole text constitutes some kind of schematic celestial map . . . in each of the thirty-six fields we find the name of a constellation and simple numbers whose significance is not yet clear." A leading expert on the subject, B. L. Van der Waerden (*Babylonian Astronomy: The Thirty-Six Stars*), reflecting on the apparent rise and fall of the numbers in some rhythm, could only suggest that "the numbers have something to do with the duration of daylight."

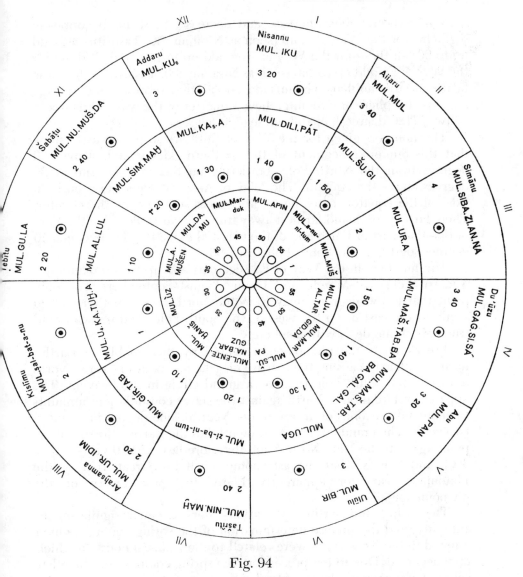

Fig. 94

The puzzle can be solved, we believe, only if one discards the notion that the Mesopotamians believed in a flat Earth, and recognizes that their astronomical knowledge was as good as ours—not because they had better instruments than we do, but because their source of information was the Nefilim.

We suggest that the enigmatic numbers represent degrees of the celestial arc, with the North Pole as the starting point, and that the astrolabe was a planisphere, the representation of a sphere upon a flat surface.

While the numbers increase and decrease, those in the opposite segments for the Way of Enlil (such as Nisannu—50, Tashritu—40) add up to 90; all those for the Way of Anu add up to 180; and all those for the Way of Ea add up to 360 (such as Nisannu 200, Tashritu 160). These figures are too familiar to be misunderstood; they represent segments of a complete spherical circumference: a quarter of the way (90 degrees), halfway (180 degrees), or full circle (360 degrees).

The numbers given for the Way of Enlil are so paired as to show that this Sumerian segment of the northern skies stretched over 60 degrees from the North Pole, bordering on the Way of Anu at 30 degrees above the equator. The Way of Anu was equidistant on both sides of the equator, reaching to 30 degrees south below the equator. Then, farther south and farthest away from the North Pole, lay the Way of Ea—that part of Earth and of the celestial globe that lay between 30 degrees south and the South Pole. (Fig. 95)

The numbers in the Way of Ea segments add up to 180 degrees in Addaru (February–March) and Ululu (August–September). The only point that is 180 degrees away from the North Pole, whether you go south on the east or on the west, is the South Pole. And this can hold true only if one deals with a sphere.

Precession is the phenomenon caused by the wobble of Earth's north–south axis, causing the North Pole (the one pointing at the North Star) and the South Pole to trace a grand circle in the heavens. The apparent retardation of Earth against the starry constellations amounts to about fifty seconds of an arc in one year, or one degree in seventy-two years. The grand circle—the time it takes the Earth's North Pole to point again at the same North Star—therefore lasts 25,920 years (72 × 360), and that is what the astronomers call the Great Year or the Platonian Year (for apparently Plato, too, was aware of the phenomenon).

The rising and setting of various stars deemed significant in antiquity, and the precise determination of the spring equinox (which ushered in the New Year), were related to the zodiacal house in which they occurred. Due to the precession, the spring equinox and the other celestial phenomena, being retarded from year to year, were finally retarded once in 2,160 years by a full zodiacal house. Our astronomers continue to employ a "zero point" ("the first point of Aries"), which marked the spring equinox circa 900 B.C., but this point has by now shifted well into the house of Pisces. Circa A.D. 2100 the spring equinox will begin to occur in the preceding house of Aquarius. This is what is meant by those who say that we are about to enter the Age of Aquarius. (Fig. 96).

Because the shift from one zodiacal house to another takes more

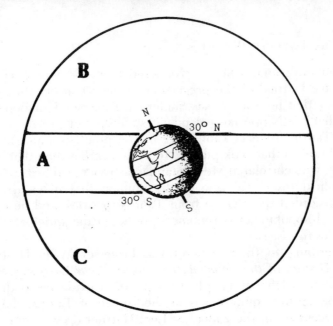

Fig. 95. THE CELESTIAL SPHERE

A. The Way of Anu, the celestial band of the Sun, planets and the constellations of the Zodiac
B. The way of Enlil, the northern skies
C. The Way of Ea, the southern skies

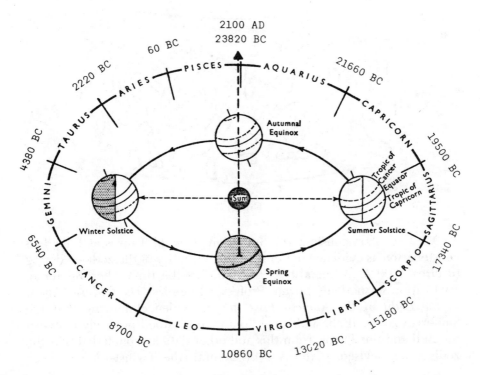

Fig. 96

than two millennia, scholars wondered how and where Hipparchus could have learned of the precession in the second century B.C. It is now clear that his source was Sumerian. Professor Langdon's findings reveal that the Nippurian calendar, established circa 4400 B.C., in the Age of Taurus, reflects knowledge of the precession and the shift of zodiacal houses that took place 2,160 years *earlier* than that. Professor Jeremias, who correlated Mesopotamian astronomical texts with Hittite astronomical texts, was also of the opinion that older astronomical tablets recorded the change from Taurus to Aries; and he concluded that the Mesopotamian astronomers predicted and anticipated the shift from Aries to Pisces.

Subscribing to these conclusions, Professor Willy Hartner *(The Earliest History of the Constellations in the Near East)* suggested that the Sumerians left behind plentiful pictorial evidence to that effect. When the spring equinox was in the zodiac of Taurus, the summer solstice occurred in the zodiac of Leo. Hartner drew attention to the recurrent motif of a bull–lion "combat" appearing in Sumerian depictions from earliest times, and suggested that these motifs represented the key positions of the constellations of Taurus (Bull) and Leo (Lion) to an observer at 30 degrees north (such as at Ur) circa 4000 B.C. (Fig. 97)

Fig. 97

Most scholars consider the Sumerian stress of Taurus as their first constellation as evidence not only of the antiquity of the zodiac—dating to circa 4000 B.C.—but also as testifying to the time when Sumerian civilization so suddenly began. Professor Jeremias *(The Old Testament in the Light of the Ancient East)* found evidence showing that the Sumerian zodiacal-chronological "point zero" stood precisely between the Bull and the Twins; from this and other data he concluded that the zodiac was devised in the Age of Gemini (the Twins)—that is, even *before* Sumerian civilization began. A Sumerian tablet in the Berlin Museum (VAT.7847) begins the list of zodiacal constellations with that of *Leo* — taking us back to circa 11,000 B.C.,when Man had just begun to till the land.

Professor H. V. Hilprecht *(The Babylonian Expedition of the University of Pennsylvania)* went even farther. Studying thousands of tablets bearing mathematical tabulations, he concluded that "all the multiplication and division tables from the temple libraries of Nippur and Sippar, and from the library of Ashurbanipal [in Nineveh] are based upon [the number] 12960000." Analyzing this number and its significance, he concluded that it could be related only to the phenomenon of the precession, and that the Sumerians knew of the Great Year of 25,920 years.

This is indeed fantastic astronomical sophistication at an impossible time.

Just as it is evident that the Sumerian astronomers possessed knowledge that they could not possibly have acquired on their own, so is there evidence to show that a good deal of their knowledge was of no practical use to them.

This pertains not only to the very sophisticated astronomical methods that were used—who in ancient Sumer really needed to establish a celestial equator, for example?—but also to a variety of elaborate texts that dealt with the measurement of distances between stars.

One of these texts, known as AO.6478, lists the twenty-six major stars visible along the line we now call the Tropic of Cancer, and gives distances between them as measured in three different ways. The text first gives the distances between these stars by a unit called *mana shukultu* ("measured and weighed"). It is believed that this was an ingenious device that related the weight of escaping water to the passage of time. It made possible the determination of distances between two stars in terms of time.

The second column of distances was in terms of *degrees of the arc* of the skies. The full day (daylight and nighttime) was divided into twelve double hours. The arc of the heavens comprised a full circle of 360 degrees. Hence, one *beru* or "double hour" represented 30 degrees of the arc of the heavens. By this method, passage of time on Earth provided a measure of the distances in degrees between the named celestial bodies.

The third method of measurement was *beru ina shame* ("length in the skies"). F. Thureau-Dangin *(Distances entre Etoiles Fixes)* pointed out that while the first two methods were relative to other phenomena, this third method provided absolute measurements. A "celestial *beru*," he and others believe, was equivalent to 10,692 of our present-day meters (11,693 yards). The "distance in the skies" between the twenty-six stars was calculated in the text as adding up to 655,200 "*beru* drawn in the skies."

The availability of three different methods of measuring distances between stars conveys the great importance attached to the matter. Yet, who among the men and women of Sumer needed such knowledge—and who among them could devise the methods and accurately use them? The only possible answer is: The Nefilim had the knowledge and the need for such accurate measurements.

Capable of space travel, arriving on Earth from another planet, roaming Earth's skies—they were the only ones who could, and did, possess at the dawn of Mankind's civilization the astronomical knowledge that required millennia to develop, the sophisticated methods and mathematics and concepts for an advanced astronomy, and the need to teach human scribes to copy and record meticulously table upon table of distances in the heavens, order of stars and groups of stars, heliacal risings and settings, a complex Sun-Moon-Earth calendar, and the rest of the remarkable knowledge of both Heaven and Earth.

Against this background, can it still be assumed that the Mesopotamian astronomers, guided by the Nefilim, were not aware of the planets beyond Saturn—that they did not know of Uranus, Neptune, and Pluto? Was their knowledge of Earth's own family, the solar system, less complete than that of distant stars, their order, and their distances?

Astronomical information from ancient times contained in hundreds of detailed texts lists celestial bodies, neatly arranged by their celestial order or by the gods or the months or the lands or the constellations with which they were associated. One such text, analyzed by Ernst F. Weidner (*Handbuch der Babylonischen Astronomie*), has come to be called "The Great Star List." It listed in five columns tens of celestial bodies as related to one another, to months, countries, and deities. Another text listed correctly the main stars in the zodiacal constellations. A text indexed as B.M.86378 arranged (in its unbroken part) seventy-one celestial bodies by their location in the heavens; and so on and on and on.

In efforts to make sense of this legion of texts, and in particular to identify correctly the planets of our solar system, a succession of scholars came up with confusing results. As we now know, their efforts were doomed to failure because they incorrectly assumed that the Sumerians and their successors were unaware that the solar system was heliocentric, that Earth was but another planet, and that there were more planets beyond Saturn.

Ignoring the possibility that some names in the star lists may have applied to Earth itself, and seeking to apply the great number of other names and epithets only to the five planets they believed were known to the Sumerians, scholars reached conflicting conclusions. Some scholars even suggested that the confusion was not theirs, but a Chaldean mix-up—for some unknown reason, they said, the Chaldeans had switched around the names of the five "known" planets.

The Sumerians referred to all celestial bodies (planets, stars, or constellations) as MUL ("who shine in the heights"). The Akkadian term *kakkab* was likewise applied by the Babylonians and Assyrians as a general term for any celestial body. This practice further frustrated the scholars seeking to unravel the ancient astronomical texts. But some *mul*'s that were termed LU.BAD clearly designated planets of our solar system.

Knowing that the Greek name for the planets was "wanderers," the scholars have read LU.BAD as "wandering sheep," deriving from LU ("those which are shepherded") and BAD ("high and afar"). But now that we have shown that the Sumerians were fully aware of the true nature of the solar system, the other meanings of the term *bad* ("the olden," "the foundation," "the one where death is") assume direct significance.

These are appropriate epithets for the Sun, and it follows that by *lubad* the Sumerians meant not mere "wandering sheep" but "sheep" shepherded by the Sun—the planets of our Sun.

The location and relation of the *lubad* to each other and to the Sun were described in many Mesopotamian astronomical texts. There were references to those planets that are "above" and those that are "below," and Kugler correctly guessed that the reference point was Earth itself.

But mostly the planets were spoken of in the framework of astronomical texts dealing with MUL.MUL—a term that kept the scholars guessing. In the absence of a better solution, most scholars have agreed that the term *mulmul* stood for the Pleiades, a cluster of stars in the zodiacal constellation of Taurus, and the one through which the axis of the spring equinox passed (as viewed from Babylon) circa 2200 B.C. Mesopotamian texts often indicated that the *mulmul* included seven LU.MASH (seven "wanderers that are familiar"), and the scholars assumed that these were the brightest members of the Pleiades, which can be seen with the naked eye. The fact that, depending on classification, the group has either six or nine such bright stars, and not seven, posed a problem; but it was brushed aside for lack of any better ideas as to the meaning of *mulmul*.

Franz Kugler (*Sternkunde und Sterndienst in Babel*), reluctantly accepted the Pleiades as the solution, but expressed his astonishment when he found it stated unambiguously in Mesopotamian texts that *mulmul* included not only "wanderers" (planets) but also the Sun and the Moon—making it impossible to retain the Pleiades idea. He also came upon texts that clearly stated that *"mulmul ul-shu 12"* (*"mulmul* is a band of twelve"), of which ten formed a distinct group.

We suggest that the term *mulmul* referred to the solar system, using the repetitive (MUL.MUL) to indicate the group as a whole, as "the celestial body comprising all celestial bodies."

Charles Virolleaud (*L'Astrologie Chaldéenne*), transliterated a Mesopotamian text (K.3558) that describes the members of the *mulmul* or *kakkabu/kakkabu* group. The text's last line is explicit:

> *Kakkabu/kakkabu.*
> The number of its celestial bodies is twelve.
> The stations of its celestial bodies twelve.
> The complete months of the Moon is twelve.

The texts leave no doubt: The *mulmul*—our solar system—was made up of *twelve* members. Perhaps this should not come as a surprise, for the Greek scholar Diodorus, explaining the three "ways" of the Chaldeans and the consequent listing of thirty-six celestial bodies, stated that "of those celestial gods, twelve hold chief authority; to each of these the Chaldeans assign a month and a sign of the zodiac."

Ernst Weidner (*Der Tierkreis und die Wege am Himmel*) reported that in addition to the Way of Anu and its twelve zodiac constellations, some texts also referred to the "way of the Sun," which was also made up of twelve celestial bodies: the Sun, the Moon, and ten others. Line 20 of the so-called TE-tablet stated: *"naphar 12 shere-mesh ha.la sha kakkab.lu sha Sin u Shamash ina libbi ittiqu,"* which means, "all in all, 12 members where the Moon and Sun belong, where the planets orbit."

We can now grasp the significance of the number *twelve* in the ancient world. The Great Circle of Sumerian gods, and of all Olympian gods thereafter, comprised exactly twelve; younger gods could join this circle only if older gods retired. Likewise, a vacancy had to be filled to retain the divine number twelve. The principal celestial circle, the way of the Sun with its twelve members, set the pattern, according to which each other celestial band was divided into twelve segments or was allocated twelve principal celestial bodies. Accordingly, there were twelve months in a year, twelve double-hours in a day. Each division of Sumer was assigned twelve celestial bodies as a measure of good luck.

Many studies, such as the one by S. Langdon (*Babylonian Men-ologies and the Semitic Calendar*) show that the division of the year into twelve months was, from its very beginnings, related to the twelve Great Gods. Fritz Hommel (*Die Astronomie der alten Chaldäer*) and others after him have shown that the twelve months were closely connected with the twelve zodiacs and that both derived from twelve principal celestial bodies. Charles F. Jean (*Lexicologie sumerienne*) reproduced a Sumerian list of twenty-four celestial bodies that paired twelve zodiacal constellations with twelve members of our solar system.

In a long text, identified by F. Thureau-Dangin (*Rituels accadiens*) as a temple program for the New Year Festival in Babylon, the evidence for the consecration of twelve as the central celestial phenomenon is persuasive. The great temple, the Esagila, had twelve gates. The powers of all the celestial gods were vested in Marduk by reciting twelve times the pronouncement "My Lord, is He not my Lord." The mercy of the god was then invoked twelve times, and that of his spouse twelve times. The total of twenty-four was then matched with the twelve zodiacal constellations and twelve members of the solar system.

Fig. 98

A boundary stone carved with the symbols of the celestial bodies by a king of Susa depicts these twenty-four signs: the familiar twelve signs of the zodiac, and symbols that stand for the twelve members of the solar system. These were the twelve astral gods of Mesopotamia, as well as of the Hurrian, Hittite, Greek, and all other ancient pantheons. (Fig. 98)

Although our natural counting base is the number ten, the number twelve permeated all matters celestial and divine long after the Sumerians were gone. There were twelve Greek Titans, twelve Tribes of Israel, twelve parts to the magical breastplate of the Israelite High Priest. The power of this celestial twelve carried over to the twelve Apostles of Jesus, and even in our decimal system we count from one to twelve, and only after twelve do we return to "ten and three" (thirteen), "ten and four," and so on.

Where did this powerful, decisive number *twelve* stem from? From the heavens.

For the solar system—the *mulmul*—included, in addition to all the planets known to us, also the planet of Anu, the one whose symbol—a radiant celestial body—stood in the Sumerian writing for the god Anu and for "divine." "The *kakkab* of the Supreme Scepter is one of the sheep in *mulmul*," explained an astronomical text. And when Marduk usurped the supremacy and replaced Anu as the god associated with this planet, the Babylonians said: "The planet of Marduk within *mulmul* appears."

Teaching humanity the true nature of Earth and the heavens, the Nefilim informed the ancient astronomer-priests not only of the planets beyond Saturn but also of the existence of the most important planet, the one from which they came:

THE TWELFTH PLANET.

7

THE EPIC OF CREATION

On most of the ancient cylinder seals that have been found, symbols that stand for certain celestial bodies, members of our solar system, appear above the figures of gods or humans.

An Akkadian seal from the third millennium B.C., now at the Vorderasiatische Abteilung of the State Museum in East Berlin (catalogued VA/243), departs from the usual manner of depicting the celestial bodies. It does not show them individually but rather as a group of eleven globes encircling a large, rayed star. It is clearly a depiction of the solar system as it was known to the Sumerians: a system consisting of *twelve* celestial bodies. (Fig. 99)

We usually show our solar system schematically as a line of planets stretching away from the Sun in ever-increasing distances. But if we depicted the planets, not in a line, but one after the other in a *circle* (the closest, Mercury, first, then Venus, then Earth, and so on), the result would look something like Fig. 100. (All drawings are schematic and not to scale; planetary orbits in the drawings that follow are circular rather than elliptical for ease of presentation.)

If we now take a second look at an enlargement of the solar system depicted on cylinder seal VA/243, we shall see that the "dots" encircling the star are actually globes whose sizes and order conform to that of the solar system depicted in Fig. 100. The small Mercury is followed by a larger Venus. Earth, the same size as Venus, is accompanied by the small Moon. Continuing in a counterclockwise direction, Mars is shown correctly as smaller than Earth but larger than the Moon or Mercury. (Fig. 101)

The ancient depiction then shows a planet unknown to us—considerably larger than Earth, yet smaller than Jupiter and Saturn, which clearly follow it. Farther on, another pair perfectly matches our Uranus and Neptune. Finally, the smallish Pluto is also there, but not where we now place it (after Neptune); instead, it appears between Saturn and Uranus.

Treating the Moon as a proper celestial body, the Sumerian depiction fully accounts for all of our known planets, places them in the correct order (with the exception of Pluto), and shows them by size.

The 4,500-year-old depiction, however, also insists that there was—or has been—another major planet between Mars and Jupiter. It is, as we shall show, the Twelfth Planet, the planet of the Nefilim.

If this Sumerian celestial map had been discovered and studied two centuries ago, astronomers would have deemed the Sumerians totally uninformed, foolishly imagining more planets beyond Saturn. Now, however, we know that Uranus and Neptune and Pluto are really there. Did the Sumerians imagine the other discrepancies, or were they properly informed by the Nefilim that the Moon was a member of the solar system in its own right, Pluto was located near Saturn, and there was a Twelfth Planet between Mars and Jupiter?

The long-held theory that the Moon was nothing more than "a frozen golf ball" was not discarded until the successful conclusion of several U.S. Apollo Moon missions. The best guesses were that the Moon was a chunk of matter that had separated from Earth when Earth was still molten and plastic. Were it not for the impact of millions of meteorites, which left craters on the face of the Moon, it would have been a faceless, lifeless, history-less piece of matter that solidified and forever follows Earth.

Observations made by unmanned satellites, however, began to bring such long-held beliefs into question. It was determined that the chemical and mineral makeup of the Moon was sufficiently different from that of Earth to challenge the "breakaway" theory. The experiments conducted on the Moon by the American astronauts and the study and analysis of the soil and rock samples they brought back have established beyond doubt that the Moon, though presently barren, was once a "living planet." Like Earth it is layered, which means that it solidified from its own original molten stage. Like Earth it generated heat, but whereas Earth's heat comes from its radioactive materials, "cooked" inside Earth under tremendous pressure, the Moon's heat comes, apparently, from layers of radioactive materials lying very near the surface. These materials, however, are too heavy to have floated up. What, then, deposited them near the Moon's surface?

The Moon's gravity field appears to be erratic, as though huge chunks of heavy matter (such as iron) had not evenly sunk to its core but were scattered about. By what process or force, we might ask? There is evidence that the ancient rocks of the Moon were magnetized. There is also evidence that the magnetic fields were changed or reversed. Was it by some unknown internal process, or by an undetermined outside influence?

The Apollo 16 astronauts found on the Moon rocks (called breccias)

Fig. 99

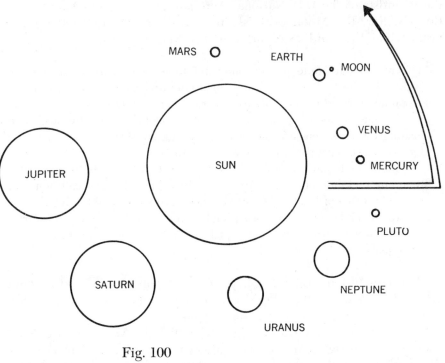

Fig. 100

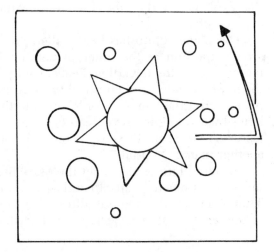

Fig. 101

that result from the shattering of solid rock and its rewelding together by extreme and sudden heat. When and how were these rocks shattered, then re-fused? Other surface materials on the Moon are rich in rare radioactive potassium and phosphorous, materials that on Earth are deep down inside.

Putting such findings together, scientists are now certain that the Moon and Earth, formed of roughly the same elements at about the same time, evolved as separate celestial bodies. In the opinion of the scientists of the U.S. National Aeronautics and Space Administration (NASA), the Moon evolved "normally" for its first 500 million years. Then, they said (as reported in *The New York Times*),

> The most cataclysmic period came 4 billion years ago, when celestial bodies the size of large cities and small countries came crashing into the Moon and formed its huge basins and towering mountains.
>
> The huge amounts of radioactive materials left by the collisions began heating the rock beneath the surface, melting massive amounts of it and forcing seas of lava through cracks in the surface.
>
> Apollo 15 found a rockslide in the crater Tsiolovsky six times greater than any rockslide on Earth. Apollo 16 discovered that the collision that created the Sea of Nectar deposited debris as much as 1,000 miles away.
>
> Apollo 17 landed near a scarp eight times higher than any on Earth, meaning it was formed by a moonquake eight times more violent than any earthquake in history.

The convulsions following that cosmic event continued for some 800 million years, so that the Moon's makeup and surface finally took on their frozen shape some 3.2 billion years ago.

The Sumerians, then, were right to depict the Moon as a celestial body in its own right. And, as we shall soon see, they also left us a text that explains and describes the cosmic catastrophe to which the NASA experts refer.

The planet Pluto has been called "the enigma." While the orbits around the Sun of the other planets deviate only somewhat from a perfect circle, the deviation ("eccentricity") of Pluto is such that it has the most extended and elliptical orbit around the Sun. While the other planets orbit the Sun more or less within the same plane, Pluto is out of kilter by a whopping seventeen degrees. Because of these two unusual features of its orbit, Pluto is the only planet that cuts across the orbit of another planet, Neptune.

In size, Pluto is indeed in the "satellite" class: Its diameter, 3,600 miles, is not much greater than that of Triton, a satellite of Neptune, or Titan, one of the ten satellites of Saturn. Because of its unusual characteristics, it has been suggested that this "misfit" might have started its celestial life as a satellite that somehow escaped its master and went into orbit around the Sun on its own.

This, as we shall soon see, is indeed what happened—according to the Sumerian texts.

And now we reach the climax of our search for answers to primeval celestial events: the existence of the Twelfth Planet. Astonishing as it may sound, our astronomers have been looking for evidence that indeed such a planet once existed between Mars and Jupiter.

Toward the end of the eighteenth century, even before Neptune had been discovered, several astronomers demonstrated that "the planets were placed at certain distances from the Sun according to some definite law." The suggestion, which came to be known as Bode's Law, convinced astronomers that a planet ought to revolve in a place where hitherto no planet had been known to exist—that is, between the orbits of Mars and Jupiter.

Spurred by these mathematical calculations, astronomers began to scan the skies in the indicated zone for the "missing planet." On the first day of the nineteenth century, the Italian astronomer Giuseppe Piazzi discovered at the exact indicated distance a very small planet (485 miles across), which he named Ceres. By 1804 the number of asteroids ("small planets") found there rose to four; to date, nearly 3,000 asteroids have been counted orbiting the Sun in what is now called the asteroid belt. Beyond any doubt, this is the debris of a planet that had shattered to pieces. Russian astronomers have named it Phayton ("chariot").

While astronomers are certain that such a planet existed, they are unable to explain its disappearance. Did the planet self-explode? But then its pieces would have flown off in all directions and not stayed in a single belt. If a collision shattered the missing planet, where is the celestial body responsible for the collision? Did it also shatter? But the debris circling the Sun, when added up, is insufficient to account for even one whole planet, to say nothing of two. Also, if the asteroids comprise the debris of two planets, they should have retained the axial revolution of two planets. But all the asteroids have a single axial rotation, indicating they come from a single celestial body. How then was the missing planet shattered, and what shattered it?

The answers to these puzzles have been handed down to us from antiquity.

￮

About a century ago the decipherment of the texts found in Mesopotamia unexpectedly grew into a realization that there—in Mesopotamia—texts existed that not only paralleled but also *preceded* portions of the Holy Scriptures. *Die Keilschriften und das alte Testament* by Eberhard Schräder in 1872 started an avalanche of books, articles, lectures, and debates that lasted half a century. Was there a link, at some early time, between Babylon and the Bible? The headlines provocatively affirmed, or denounced: BABEL UND BIBEL.

Among the texts uncovered by Henry Layard in the ruins of the library of Ashurbanipal in Nineveh, there was one that told a tale of Creation not unlike the one in the Book of Genesis. The broken tablets, first pieced together and published by George Smith in 1876 (*The Chaldean Genesis*), conclusively established that there indeed existed an Akkadian text, written in the Old Babylonian dialect, that related how a certain deity created Heaven and Earth and all upon Earth, including Man.

A vast literature now exists that compares the Mesopotamian text with the biblical narrative. The Babylonian deity's work was done, if not in six "days," then over the span of six tablets. Parallel to the biblical God's seventh day of rest and enjoyment of his handiwork, the Mesopotamian epic devotes a seventh tablet to the exaltation of the Babylonian deity and his achievements. Appropriately, L. W. King named his authoritative text on the subject *The Seven Tablets of Creation*.

Now called "The Creation Epic," the text was known in antiquity by its opening words, *Enuma Elish* ("When in the heights"). The biblical tale of Creation begins with the creation of Heaven and Earth; the Mesopotamian tale is a true cosmogony, dealing with prior events and taking us to the beginning of time:

Enuma elish la nabu shamamu
  When in the heights Heaven had not been named
Shaplitu ammatum shuma la zakrat
  And below, firm ground [Earth] had not been called

It was then, the epic tells us, that two primeval celestial bodies gave birth to a series of celestial "gods." As the number of celestial beings increased, they made great noise and commotion, disturbing the Primeval Father. His faithful messenger urged him to take strong measures to discipline the young gods, but they ganged up on him and robbed him of his creative powers. The Primeval Mother sought to take revenge. The god who led the revolt against the Primeval Father had a new suggestion: Let his young son be invited to join the Assembly of the Gods and be given supremacy so that he might go to fight singlehanded the "monster" their mother turned out to be.

Granted supremacy, the young god—Marduk, according to the Babylonian version—proceeded to face the monster, and, after a fierce battle, vanquished her and split her in two. Of one part of her he made Heaven, and of the other, Earth.

He then proclaimed a fixed order in the heavens, assigning to each celestial god a permanent position. On Earth he produced the mountains and seas and rivers, established the seasons and vegetation, and created Man. In duplication of the Heavenly Abode, Babylon and its towering temple were built on Earth. Gods and mortals were given assignments, commandments, and rituals to be followed. The gods then proclaimed Marduk the supreme deity, and bestowed on him the "fifty names"—the prerogatives and numerical rank of the Enlilship.

As more tablets and fragments were found and translated, it became evident that the text was not a simple literary work: It was the most hallowed historical-religious epic of Babylon, read as part of the New Year rituals. Intended to propagate the supremacy of Marduk, the Babylonian version made him the hero of the tale of Creation. This, however, was not always so. There is enough evidence to show that the Babylonian version of the epic was a masterful religious-political forgery of earlier Sumerian versions, in which Anu, Enlil, and Ninurta were the heroes.

No matter, however, what the actors in this celestial and divine drama were called, the tale is certainly as ancient as Sumerian civilization. Most scholars see it as a philosophic work—the earliest version of the eternal struggle between good and evil—or as an allegorical tale of nature's winter and summer, sunrise and sunset, death and resurrection.

But why not take the epic at face value, as nothing more nor less than the statement of cosmologic facts as known to the Sumerians, as told them by the Nefilim? Using such a bold and novel approach, we find that the "Epic of Creation" perfectly explains the events that probably took place in our solar system.

The stage on which the celestial drama of *Enuma Elish* unfolds is the primeval universe. The celestial actors are the ones who create as well as the ones being created. Act I:

When in the heights Heaven had not been named,
And below, Earth had not been called;
Naught, but primordial APSU, their Begetter,
MUMMU, and TIAMAT—she who bore them all;
Their waters were mingled together.

No reed had yet formed, no marshland had appeared.
None of the gods had yet been brought into being,
None bore a name, their destinies were undetermined;
Then it was that gods were formed in their midst.

With a few strokes of the reed stylus upon the first clay tablet—in nine short lines—the ancient poet-chronicler manages to seat us in front row center, and boldly and dramatically raise the curtain on the most majestic show ever: the Creation of our solar system.

In the expanse of space, the "gods"—the planets—are yet to appear, to be named, to have their "destinies"—their orbits—fixed. Only three bodies exist: "primordial AP.SU" ("one who exists from the beginning"); MUM.MU ("one who was born"); and TIAMAT ("maiden of life"). The "waters" of Apsu and Tiamat were mingled, and the text makes it clear that it does not mean the waters in which reeds grow, but rather the primordial waters, the basic life-giving elements of the universe.

Apsu, then, is the Sun, "one who exists from the beginning."

Nearest him is Mummu. The epic's narrative makes clear later on that Mummu was the trusted aide and emissary of Apsu: a good description of Mercury, the small planet rapidly running around his giant master. Indeed, this was the concept the ancient Greeks and Romans had of the god-planet Mercury: the fast messenger of the gods.

Farther away was Tiamat. She was the "monster" that Marduk later shattered—the "missing planet." But in primordial times she was the very first Virgin Mother of the first Divine Trinity. The space between her and Apsu was not void; it was filled with the primordial elements of Apsu and Tiamat. These "waters" "commingled," and a pair of celestial gods—planets—were formed in the space between Apsu and Tiamat.

> Their waters were mingled together. . . .
> Gods were formed in their midst:
> God LAHMU and god LAHAMU were brought forth;
> By name they were called.

Etymologically, the names of these two planets stem from the root *LHM* ("to make war"). The ancients bequeathed to us the tradition that Mars was the God of War and Venus the Goddess of both Love and War. LAHMU and LAHAMU are indeed male and female names, respectively; and the identity of the two gods of the epic and the planets Mars and Venus is thus affirmed both etymologically and mythologically. It is also affirmed astronomically: As the "missing planet," Tiamat was located beyond Mars. Mars and Venus are indeed located in the space between the Sun (Apsu) and "Tiamat." We can illustrate this by following the Sumerian celestial map. (Figs. 102, 103)

The process of the formation of the solar system then went on. Lahmu and Lahamu—Mars and Venus—were brought forth, but even

> Before they had grown in age
> And in stature to an appointed size—
> God ANSHAR and god KISHAR were formed,

Surpassing them [in size].
As lengthened the days and multiplied the years,
God ANU became their son—of his ancestors a rival.
Then Anshar's first-born, Anu,
As his equal and in his image begot NUDIMMUD.

With a terseness matched only by the narrative's precision, Act I of the epic of Creation has been swiftly played out before our very eyes. We are informed that Mars and Venus were to grow only to a limited size; but even before their formation was complete, another pair of planets was formed. The two were majestic planets, as evidenced by their names—AN.SHAR ("prince, foremost of the heavens") and KI.SHAR ("foremost of the firm lands"). They overtook in size the first pair, "surpassing them" in stature. The description, epithets, and location of this second pair easily identify them as Saturn and Jupiter. (Fig. 104).

Some time then passed ("multiplied the years"), and a third pair of planets was brought forth. First came ANU, smaller than Anshar and Kishar ("their son"), but larger than the first planets ("of his ancestors a rival" in size). Then Anu, in turn, begot a twin planet, "his equal and in his image." The Babylonian version names the planet NUDIMMUD, an epithet of Ea/Enki. Once again, the descriptions of the sizes and locations fit the next known pair of planets in our solar system, Uranus and Neptune.

There was yet another planet to be accounted for among these outer planets, the one we call Pluto. The "Epic of Creation" has already referred to Anu as "Anshar's first-born," implying that there was yet another planetary god "born" to Anshar/Saturn. The epic catches up with this celestial deity later on, when it relates how Anshar sent out his emissary GAGA on various missions to the other planets. Gaga appears in function and stature equal to Apsu's emissary Mummu; this brings to mind the many similarities between Mercury and Pluto. Gaga, then, was Pluto; but the Sumerians placed Pluto on their celestial map not beyond Neptune, but next to Saturn, whose "emissary," or satellite, it was. (Fig. 105)

As Act I of the "Epic of Creation" came to an end, there was a solar system made up of the Sun and nine planets:

SUN—*Apsu*, "one who existed from the beginning."
MERCURY—*Mummu*, counselor and emissary of Apsu.
VENUS—*Lahamu*, "lady of battles."
MARS—*Lahmu*, "deity of war."
??—*Tiamat*, "maiden who gave life."
JUPITER—*Kishar*, "foremost of firm lands."

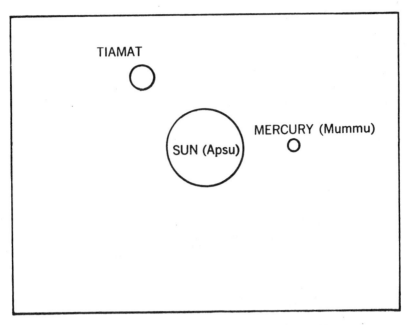

Fig. 102. I. In the Beginning: Sun, Mercury, "Tiamat."

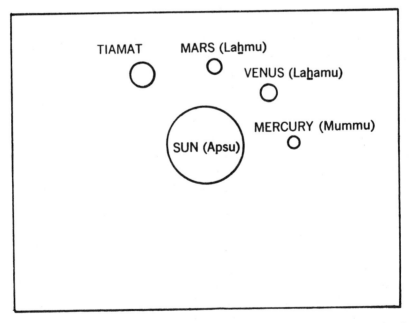

Fig. 103. II. The Inner Planets—the "gods in the midst"—come forth.

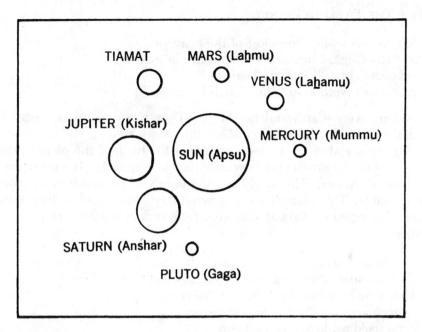

Fig. 104. III. The SHAR's—the giant planets—are created, together with their "emissary."

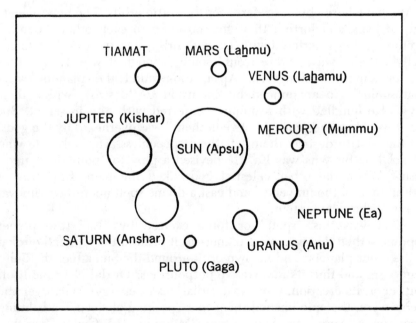

Fig. 105. IV. The last two planets are added—equal, in each other's image.

SATURN—*Anshar*, "foremost of the heavens."
PLUTO—*Gaga*, counselor and emissary of Anshar.
URANUS—*Anu*, "he of the heavens."
NEPTUNE—*Nudimmud (Ea)*, "artful creator."

Where were Earth and the Moon? They were yet to be created, products of the forthcoming cosmic collision.

With the end of the majestic drama of the birth of the planets, the authors of the Creation epic now raise the curtain on Act II, on a drama of celestial turmoil. The newly created family of planets was far from being stable. The planets were gravitating toward each other; they were converging on Tiamat, disturbing and endangering the primordial bodies.

> The divine brothers banded together;
> They disturbed Tiamat as they surged back and forth.
> They were troubling the "belly" of Tiamat
> By their antics in the dwellings of heaven.
> Apsu could not lessen their clamor;
> Tiamat was speechless at their ways.
> Their doings were loathsome. . . .
> Troublesome were their ways.

We have here obvious references to erratic orbits. The new planets "surged back and forth"; they got too close to each other ("banded together"); they interfered with Tiamat's orbit; they got too close to her "belly"; their "ways" were troublesome. Though it was Tiamat that was principally endangered, Apsu, too, found the planets' ways "loathsome." He announced his intention to "destroy, wreck their ways." He huddled with Mummu, conferred with him in secret. But "whatever they had plotted between them" was overheard by the gods, and the plot to destroy them left them speechless. The only one who did not lose his wits was Ea. He devised a ploy to "pour sleep upon Apsu." When the other celestial gods liked the plan, Ea "drew a faithful map of the universe" and cast a divine spell upon the primeval waters of the solar system.

What was this "spell" or force exerted by "Ea" (the planet Neptune)—then the outermost planet—as it orbited the Sun and circled all the other planets? Did its own orbit around the Sun affect the Sun's magnetism and thus its radioactive outpourings? Or did Neptune itself emit, upon its creation, some vast radiations of energy? Whatever the effects were, the epic likened them to a "pouring of sleep"—a calming effect—upon Apsu (the Sun). Even "Mummu, the Counsellor, was powerless to stir."

As in the biblical tale of Samson and Delilah, the hero—overcome by sleep—could easily be robbed of his powers. Ea moved quickly to rob Apsu of his creative role. Quenching, it seems, the immense outpourings of primeval matter from the Sun, Ea/Neptune "pulled off Apsu's tiara, removed his cloak of aura." Apsu was "vanquished." Mummu could no longer roam about. He was "bound and left behind," a lifeless planet by his master's side.

By depriving the Sun of its creativity—stopping the process of emitting more energy and matter to form additional planets—the gods brought temporary peace to the solar system. The victory was further signified by changing the meaning and location of the Apsu. This epithet was henceforth to be applied to the "Abode of Ea." Any additional planets could henceforth come only from the new Apsu— from "the Deep"—the far reaches of space that the outermost planet faced.

How long was it before the celestial peace was broken once more? The epic does not say. But it does continue, with little pause, and raises the curtain on Act III:

In the Chamber of Fates, the place of Destinies,
A god was engendered, most able and wisest of gods;
In the heart of the Deep was MARDUK created.

A new celestial "god"—a new planet—now joins the cast. He was formed in the Deep, far out in space, in a zone where orbital motion—a planet's "destiny"—had been imparted to him. He was attracted to the solar system by the outermost planet: "He who begot him was Ea" (Neptune). The new planet was a sight to behold:

Alluring was his figure, sparkling the lift of his eyes;
Lordly was his gait, commanding as of olden times. . . .
Greatly exalted was he above the gods, exceeding throughout. . . .
He was the loftiest of the gods, surpassing was his height;
His members were enormous, he was exceedingly tall.

Appearing from outer space, Marduk was still a newborn planet, belching fire and emitting radiation. "When he moved his lips, fire blazed forth."

As Marduk neared the other planets, "they heaped upon him their awesome flashes," and he shone brightly, "clothed with the halo of ten gods." His approach thus stirred up electrical and other emissions from the other members of the solar system. And a single word here confirms our decipherment of the Creation epic: *Ten* celestial bodies awaited him—the Sun and only nine other planets.

The epic's narrative now takes us along Marduk's speeding course. He first passes by the planet that "begot" him, that pulled him into the solar system, the planet Ea/Neptune. As Marduk nears Neptune, the latter's gravitational pull on the newcomer grows in intensity. It rounds out Marduk's path, "making it good for its purpose."

Marduk must still have been in a very plastic stage at that time. As he passed by Ea/Neptune, the gravitational pull caused the side of Marduk to bulge, as though he had "a second head." No part of Marduk, however, was torn off at this passage; but as Marduk reached the vicinity of Anu/Uranus, chunks of matter began to tear away from him, resulting in the formation of four satellites of Marduk. "Anu brought forth and fashioned the four sides, consigned their power to the leader of the host." Called "winds," the four were thrust into a fast orbit around Marduk, "swirling as a whirlwind."

The order of passage—first by Neptune, then by Uranus—indicates that Marduk was coming into the solar system not in the system's orbital direction (counterclockwise) but from the opposite direction, moving clockwise. Moving on, the oncoming planet was soon seized by the immense gravitational and magnetic forces of the giant Anshar/Saturn, then Kishar/Jupiter. His path was bent even more inward—into the center of the solar system, toward Tiamat. (Fig. 106)

The approach of Marduk soon began to disturb Tiamat and the inner planets (Mars, Venus, Mercury). "He produced streams, disturbed Tiamat; the gods were not at rest, carried as in a storm."

Though the lines of the ancient text were partially damaged here, we can still read that the nearing planet "diluted their vitals . . . pinched their eyes." Tiamat herself "paced about distraught"—her orbit, evidently, disturbed.

The gravitational pull of the large approaching planet soon began to tear away parts of Tiamat. From her midst there emerged eleven "monsters," a "growling, raging" throng of satellites who "separated themselves" from her body and "marched at the side of Tiamat." Preparing herself to face the onrushing Marduk, Tiamat "crowned them with halos," giving them the appearance of "gods" (planets).

Of particular importance to the epic and to Mesopotamian cosmogony was Tiamat's chief satellite, who was named KINGU, "the first-born among the gods who formed her assembly."

She exalted Kingu,
In their midst she made him great. . . .
The high command of the battle
She entrusted into his hand.

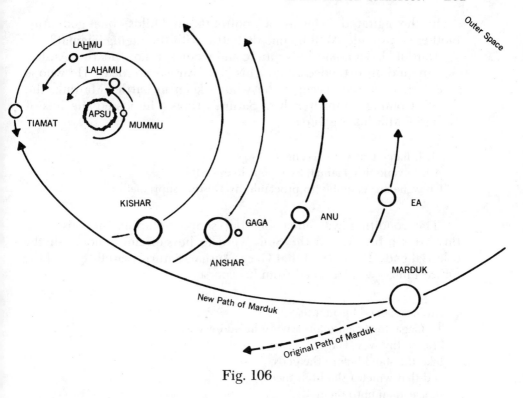

Fig. 106

Subjected to conflicting gravitational pulls, this large satellite of Tiamat began to shift toward Marduk. It was this granting to Kingu of a Tablet of Destinies—a planetary path of his own—that especially upset the outer planets. Who had granted Tiamat the right to bring forth new planets? Ea asked. He took the problem to Anshar, the giant Saturn.

> All that Tiamat had plotted, to him he repeated:
> ". . . she has set up an Assembly and is furious with rage . . .
> she has added matchless weapons, has borne monster-gods . . .
> withal eleven of this kind she has brought forth;
> from among the gods who formed her Assembly,
> she has elevated Kingu, her first-born, made him chief . . .
> she has given him a Tablet of Destinies, fastened it
> on his breast."

Turning to Ea, Anshar asked him whether he could go to slay Kingu. The reply is lost due to a break in the tablets; but apparently Ea did not satisfy Anshar, for the continuing narrative has Anshar turning to Anu (Uranus) to find out whether he would "go and stand up to Tiamat." But Anu "was unable to face her and turned back."

In the agitated heavens, a confrontation builds; one god after another steps aside. Will no one do battle with the raging Tiamat?

Marduk, having passed Neptune and Uranus, is now nearing Anshar (Saturn) and his extended rings. This gives Anshar an idea: "He who is potent shall be our Avenger; he who is keen in battle: Marduk, the Hero!" Coming within reach of Saturn's rings ("he kissed the lips of Anshar"), Marduk answers:

"If I, indeed, as your Avenger
Am to vanquish Tiamat, save your lives—
Convene an Assembly to proclaim my Destiny supreme!"

The condition was audacious but simple: Marduk and his "destiny"—his orbit around the Sun—were to be supreme among all the celestial gods. It was then that Gaga, Anshar/Saturn's satellite—and the future Pluto—was loosened from his course:

Anshar opened his mouth,
To Gaga, his Counsellor, a word he addressed. . . .
"Be on thy way, Gaga,
take the stand before the gods,
and that which I shall tell thee
repeat thou unto them."

Passing by the other god/planets, Gaga urged them to "fix your decrees for Marduk." The decision was as anticipated: The gods were only too eager to have someone else go to settle the score for them. "Marduk is king!" they shouted, and urged him to lose no more time: "Go and cut off the life of Tiamat!"

The curtain now rises on Act IV, the celestial battle.

The gods have decreed Marduk's "destiny"; their combined gravitational pull has now determined Marduk's orbital path so that he can go but one way—toward a "battle," a collision with Tiamat.

As befits a warrior, Marduk armed himself with a variety of weapons. He filled his body with a "blazing flame"; "he constructed a bow . . . attached thereto an arrow . . . in front of him he set the lightning"; and "he then made a net to enfold Tiamat therein." These are common names for what could only have been celestial phenomena—the discharge of electrical bolts as the two planets converged, the gravitational pull (a "net") of one upon the other.

But Marduk's chief weapons were his satellites, the four "winds" with which Uranus had provided him when Marduk passed by that planet: South Wind, North Wind, East Wind, West Wind. Passing now by the giants, Saturn and Jupiter, and subjected to their tremendous gravitational pull, Marduk "brought forth" three more satellites—Evil Wind, Whirlwind, and Matchless Wind.

Using his satellites as a "storm chariot," he "sent forth the winds that he had brought forth, the seven of them." The adversaries were ready for battle.

> The Lord went forth, followed his course;
> Towards the raging Tiamat he set his face. . . .
> The Lord approached to scan the innerside of Tiamat—
> The scheme of Kingu, her consort, to perceive.

But as the planets drew nearer each other, Marduk's course became erratic:

> As he looks on, his course becomes upset,
> His direction is distracted, his doings are confused.

Even Marduk's satellites began to veer off course:

> When the gods, his helpers,
> Who were marching at his side,
> Saw the valiant Kingu, blurred became their vision.

Were the combatants to miss each other after all? But the die was cast, the courses irrevocably set on collision. "Tiamat emitted a roar" . . . "the Lord raised the flooding storm, his mighty weapon." As Marduk came ever closer, Tiamat's "fury" grew; "the roots of her legs shook back and forth." She commenced to cast "spells" against Marduk—the same kind of celestial waves Ea had earlier used against Apsu and Mummu. But Marduk kept coming at her.

> Tiamat and Marduk, the wisest of the gods,
> Advanced against one another;
> They pressed on to single combat,
> They approached for battle.

The epic now turns to the description of the celestial battle, in the aftermath of which Heaven and Earth were created.

> The Lord spread out his net to enfold her;
> The Evil Wind, the rearmost, he unleashed at her face.
> As she opened her mouth, Tiamat, to devour him—
> He drove in the Evil Wind so that she close not her lips.

The fierce storm Winds then charged her belly;
Her body became distended; her mouth had opened wide.
He shot there through an arrow, it tore her belly;
It cut through her insides, tore into her womb.
Having thus subdued her, her life-breath he extinguished.

Here, then, (Fig. 107) is a most original theory explaining the celestial puzzles still confronting us. An unstable solar system, made up of the Sun and nine planets, was invaded by a large, comet-like planet from outer space. It first encountered Neptune; as it passed by Uranus, the giant Saturn, and Jupiter, its course was profoundly bent inward toward the solar system's center, and it brought forth seven satellites. It was unalterably set on a collision course with Tiamat, the next planet in line.

But the two planets did *not* collide, a fact of cardinal astronomical importance: It was the satellites of Marduk that smashed into Tiamat, and not Marduk himself. They "distended" Tiamat's body, made in her a wide cleavage. Through these fissures in Tiamat, Marduk shot an "arrow," a "divine lightning," an immense bolt of electricity that jumped as a spark from the energy-charged Marduk, the planet that was "filled with brilliance." Finding its way into Tiamat's innards, it "extinguished her life-breath"—neutralized Tiamat's own electric and magnetic forces and fields, and "extinguished" them.

The first encounter between Marduk and Tiamat left her fissured and lifeless; but her final fate was still to be determined by future encounters between the two. Kingu, leader of Tiamat's satellites, was also to be dealt with separately. But the fate of the other ten, smaller satellites of Tiamat was determined at once.

After he had slain Tiamat, the leader,
Her band was shattered, her host broken up.
The gods, her helpers who marched at her side,
Trembling with fear,
Turned their backs about so as to save and preserve their lives.

Can we identify this "shattered . . . broken" host that trembled and "turned their backs about"—reversed their direction?

By doing so we offer an explanation to yet another puzzle of our solar system—the phenomenon of the comets. Tiny globes of matter, they are often referred to as the solar system's "rebellious members," for they appear to obey none of the normal rules of the road. The orbits of the planets around the Sun are (with the exception of Pluto) almost circular; the orbits of the comets are elongated, and in most instances

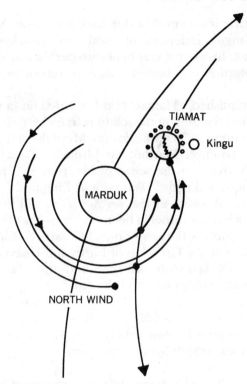

Fig. 107. THE CELESTIAL BATTLE

A. Marduk's "winds" colliding with Tiamat and her "host" (led by Kingu).

very much so—to the extent that some of them disappear from our view for hundreds or thousands of years. The planets (with the exception of Pluto) orbit the Sun in the same general plane; the comets' orbits lie in many diverse planes. Most significant, while all the planets known to us circle the Sun in the same counterclockwise direction, many comets move in the reverse direction.

Astronomers are unable to say what force, what event created the comets and threw them into their unusual orbits. Our answer: Marduk. Sweeping in the reverse direction, in an orbital plane of his own, he shattered, broke the host of Tiamat into smaller comets and affected them by his gravitational pull, his so-called net:

> Thrown into the net, they found themselves ensnared. . . .
> The whole band of demons that had marched on her side
> He cast into fetters, their hands he bound. . . .
> Tightly encircled, they could not escape.

After the battle was over, Marduk took away from Kingu the Tablet of Destinies (Kingu's independent orbit) and attached it to his own (Marduk's) breast: his course was bent into permanent solar orbit. From that time on, Marduk was bound always to return to the scene of the celestial battle.

Having "vanquished" Tiamat, Marduk sailed on in the heavens, out into space, around the Sun, and back to retrace his passage by the outer planets: Ea/Neptune, "whose desire Marduk achieved," Anshar/Saturn, "whose triumph Marduk established." Then his new orbital path returned Marduk to the scene of his triumph, "to strengthen his hold on the vanquished gods," Tiamat and Kingu.

As the curtain is about to rise on Act V, it will be here—and only here, though this has not hitherto been realized—that the biblical tale of Genesis joins the Mesopotamian "Epic of Creation"; for it is only at this point that the tale of the Creation of Earth and Heaven really began.

Completing his first-ever orbit around the Sun, Marduk "then returned to Tiamat, whom he had subdued."

> The Lord paused to view her lifeless body.
> To divide the monster he then artfully planned.
> Then, as a mussel, he split her into two parts.

Marduk himself now hit the defeated planet, splitting Tiamat in two, severing her "skull," or upper part. Then another of Marduk's satellites, the one called North Wind, crashed into the separated half. The heavy blow carried this part—destined to become Earth—to an orbit where no planet had been orbiting before:

> The Lord trod upon Tiamat's hinder part;
> With his weapon the connected skull he cut loose;
> He severed the channels of her blood;
> And caused the North Wind to bear it
> To places that have been unknown.

Earth had been created!

The lower part had another fate: on the second orbit, Marduk himself hit it, smashing it to pieces (Fig. 108):

> The [other] half of her he set up as a screen for the skies:
> Locking them together, as watchmen he stationed them. . . .
> He bent Tiamat's tail to form the Great Band as a bracelet.

The pieces of this broken half were hammered to become a "bracelet" in the heavens, acting as a screen between the inner planets

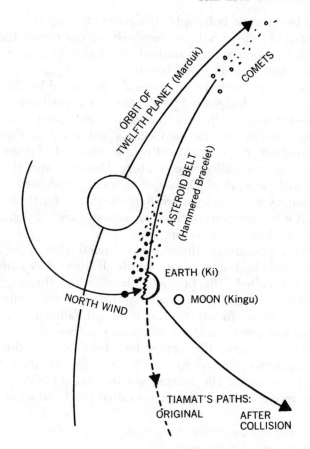

Fig. 108. THE CELESTIAL BATTLE

B. Tiamat has been split: its shattered half is the Heaven—the Asteroid Belt; the other half, Earth, is thrust to a new orbit by Marduk's satellite "North Wind." Tiamat's chief satellite, Kingu, becomes Earth's Moon; her other satellites now make up the comets.

and the outer planets. They were stretched out into a "great band." The asteroid belt had been created.

Astronomers and physicists recognize the existence of great differences between the inner, or "terrestrial," planets (Mercury, Venus, Earth and its Moon, and Mars) and the outer planets (Jupiter and beyond), two groups separated by the asteroid belt. We now find, in the Sumerian epic, ancient recognition of these phenomena.

Moreover, we are offered—for the first time—a coherent cosmogonic-scientific explanation of the celestial events that led to the disappearance of the "missing planet" and the resultant creation of the asteroid belt (plus the comets) and of Earth. After several of his satellites and his electric bolts split Tiamat in two, another satellite of Marduk shunted her upper half to a new orbit as our planet Earth; then Marduk, on his second orbit, smashed the lower half to pieces and stretched them in a great celestial band.

Every puzzle that we have mentioned is answered by the "Epic of Creation" as we have deciphered it. Moreover, we also have the answer to the question of why Earth's continents are concentrated on one side of it and a deep cavity (the Pacific Ocean's bed) exists on the opposite side. The constant reference to the "waters" of Tiamat is also illuminating. She was called the Watery Monster, and it stands to reason that Earth, as part of Tiamat, was equally endowed with these waters. Indeed, some modern scholars describe Earth as "Planet Ocean"—for it is the only one of the solar system's known planets that is blessed with such life-giving waters.

New as these cosmologic theories may sound, they were accepted fact to the prophets and sages whose words fill the Old Testament. The prophet Isaiah recalled "the primeval days" when the might of the Lord "carved the Haughty One, made spin the watery monster, dried up the waters of *Tehom-Raba*." Calling the Lord Yahweh "my primeval king," the Psalmist rendered in a few verses the cosmogony of the epic of Creation. "By thy might, the waters thou didst disperse; the leader of the watery monsters thou didst break up." Job recalled how this celestial Lord also smote "the assistants of the Haughty One"; and with impressive astronomical sophistication exalted the Lord who:

> The hammered canopy stretched out in the place of *Tehom*,
> The Earth suspended in the void. . . .
> His powers the waters did arrest,
> His energy the Haughty One did cleave;
> His Wind the Hammered Bracelet measured out;
> His hand the twisting dragon did extinguish.

Biblical scholars now recognize that the Hebrew *Tehom* ("watery deep") stems from Tiamat; that *Tehom-Raba* means "great Tiamat," and that the biblical understanding of primeval events is based upon the Sumerian cosmologic epics. It should also be clear that first and foremost among these parallels are the opening verses of the Book of Genesis, describing how the Wind of the Lord hovered over the waters of *Tehom*, and how the lightning of the Lord (Marduk in the Babylonian version) lit the darkness of space as it hit and split Tiamat, creating Earth and the *Rakia* (literally, "the hammered bracelet"). This celestial band (hitherto translated as "firmament") is called "the Heaven."

The Book of Genesis (1:8) explicitly states that it is this "hammered out bracelet" that the Lord had named "heaven" *(shamaim)*. The Akkadian texts also called this celestial zone "the hammered bracelet" *(rakkis)*, and describe how Marduk stretched out Tiamat's lower part until he brought it end to end, fastened into a permanent great circle. The Sumerian sources leave no doubt that the specific "heaven," as distinct from the general concept of heavens and space, was the asteroid belt.

Our Earth and the asteroid belt are the "Heaven and Earth" of both Mesopotamian and biblical references, created when Tiamat was dismembered by the celestial Lord.

After Marduk's North Wind had pushed Earth to its new celestial location, Earth obtained its own orbit around the Sun (resulting in our seasons) and received its axial spin (giving us day and night). The Mesopotamian texts claim that one of Marduk's tasks after he created Earth was, indeed, to have "allotted [to Earth] the days of the Sun and established the precincts of day and night." The biblical concepts are identical:

> And God said:
> "Let there be Lights in the hammered Heaven,
> to divide between the Day and the Night;
> and let them be celestial signs
> and for Seasons and for Days and for Years."

Modern scholars believe that after Earth became a planet it was a hot ball of belching volcanoes, filling the skies with mists and clouds. As temperatures began to cool, the vapors turned to water, separating the face of Earth into dry land and oceans.

The fifth tablet of *Enuma Elish*, though badly mutilated, imparts exactly the same scientific information. Describing the gushing lava as Tiamat's "spittle," the Creation epic correctly places this phenomenon before the formation of the atmosphere, the oceans of Earth, and the continents. After the "cloud waters were gathered," the oceans began to form, and the "foundations" of Earth—its continents—were raised. As "the making of cold"—a cooling off—took place, rain and mist appeared. Meanwhile, the "spittle" continued to pour forth, "laying in layers," shaping Earth's topography.

Once again, the biblical parallel is clear:

> And God said:
> "Let the waters under the skies be gathered together,
> unto one place, and let dry land appear."
> And it was so.

Earth, with oceans, continents, and an atmosphere, was now ready for the formation of mountains, rivers, springs, valleys. Attributing all Creation to the Lord Marduk, *Enuma Elish* continued the narration:

Putting Tiamat's head [Earth] into position,
He raised the mountains thereon.
He opened springs, the torrents to draw off.
Through her eyes he released the Tigris and Euphrates.
From her teats he formed the lofty mountains,
Drilled springs for wells, the water to carry off.

In perfect accord with modern findings, both the Book of Genesis and *Enuma Elish* and other related Mesopotamian texts place the beginning of life upon Earth in the waters, followed by the "living creatures that swarm" and "fowl that fly." Not until then did "living creatures after their kind: cattle and creeping things and beasts" appear upon Earth, culminating with the appearance of Man—the final act of Creation.

As part of the new celestial order upon Earth, Marduk "made the divine Moon appear . . . designated him to mark the night, define the days every month."

Who was this celestial god? The text calls him SHESH.KI ("celestial god who protects Earth"). There is no mention earlier in the epic of a planet by this name; yet there he is, "within *her* heavenly pressure [gravitational field]." And who is meant by "her": Tiamat or Earth?

The roles of, and references to, Tiamat and Earth appear to be interchangeable. Earth is Tiamat reincarnated. The Moon is called Earth's "protector"; that is exactly what Tiamat called Kingu, her chief satellite.

The Creation epic specifically excludes Kingu from the "host" of Tiamat that were shattered and scattered and put into reverse motion around the Sun as comets. After Marduk completed his own first orbit and returned to the scene of the battle, he decreed Kingu's separate fate:

And Kingu, who had become chief among them,
He made shrink;
As god DUG.GA.E he counted him.
He took from him the Tablet of Destinies,
Not rightfully his.

Marduk, then, did not destroy Kingu. He punished him by taking away his independent orbit, which Tiamat had granted him as he grew in size. Shrunk to a smaller size, Kingu remained a "god"—a planetary member of our solar system. Without an orbit he could only become a satellite again. As Tiamat's upper part was thrown into a new orbit (as the new planet Earth), we suggest, Kingu was pulled along. Our Moon, we suggest, is Kingu, Tiamat's former satellite.

Transformed into a celestial *duggae*, Kingu had been stripped of his "vital" elements—atmosphere, waters, radioactive matter; he shrank in size and became "a mass of lifeless clay." These Sumerian terms fittingly describe our lifeless Moon, its recently discovered history, and the fate that befell this satellite that started out as KIN.GU ("great emissary") and ended up as DUG.GA.E ("pot of lead").

L. W. King *(The Seven Tablets of Creation)* reported the existence of three fragments of an astronomical-mythological tablet that presented another version of Marduk's battle with Tiamat, which included verses that dealt with the manner in which Marduk dispatched Kingu. "Kingu, her spouse, with a weapon not of war he cut away ... the Tablets of Destiny from Kingu he took in his hand." A further attempt, by B. Landesberger (in 1923, in the *Archiv für Keilschriftforschung*), to edit and fully translate the text, demonstrated the interchangeability of the names Kingu/Ensu/Moon.

Such texts not only confirm our conclusion that Tiamat's main satellite became our Moon; they also explain NASA's findings regarding a huge collision "when celestial bodies the size of large cities came crashing into the Moon." Both the NASA findings and the text discovered by L. W. King describe the Moon as the "planet that was laid waste."

Cylinder seals have been found that depict the celestial battle, showing Marduk fighting a fierce female deity. One such depiction shows Marduk shooting his lightning at Tiamat, with Kingu, clearly identified as the Moon, trying to protect Tiamat, his creator. (Fig. 109)

This pictorial evidence that Earth's Moon and Kingu were the same satellite is further enhanced by the etymological fact that the name of the god SIN, in later times associated with the Moon, derived from SU.EN ("lord of wasteland").

Having disposed of Tiamat and Kingu, Marduk once again "crossed the heavens and surveyed the regions." This time his attention was focused on "the dwelling of Nudimmud" (Neptune), to fix a final "destiny" for Gaga, the erstwhile satellite of Anshar/Saturn who was made an "emissary" to the other planets.

The epic informs us that as one of his final acts in the heavens, Marduk assigned this celestial god "to a hidden place," a hitherto

Fig. 109

unknown orbit facing "the deep" (outer space), and entrusted to him the "counsellorship of the Watery Deep." In line with his new position, the planet was renamed US.MI ("one who shows the way"), the outermost planet, our Pluto.

According to the Creation epic, Marduk had at one point boasted, "The ways of the celestial gods I will artfully alter . . . into two groups shall they be divided."

Indeed he did. He eliminated from the heavens the Sun's first partner-in-Creation, Tiamat. He brought Earth into being, thrusting it into a new orbit nearer the Sun. He hammered a "bracelet" in the heavens—the asteroid belt that does separate the group of inner planets from the group of outer planets. He turned most of Tiamat's satellites into comets; her chief satellite, Kingu, he put into orbit around Earth to become the Moon. And he shifted a satellite of Saturn, Gaga, to become the planet Pluto, imparting to it some of Marduk's own orbital characteristics (such as a different orbital plane).

The puzzles of our solar system—the oceanic cavities upon Earth, the devastation upon the Moon, the reverse orbits of the comets, the enigmatic phenomena of Pluto—all are perfectly answered by the Mesopotamian Creation epic, as deciphered by us.

Having thus "constructed the stations" for the planets, Marduk took for himself "Station Nibiru," and "crossed the heavens and surveyed" the *new* solar system. It was now made up of twelve celestial bodies, with twelve Great Gods as their counterparts. (Fig. 110)

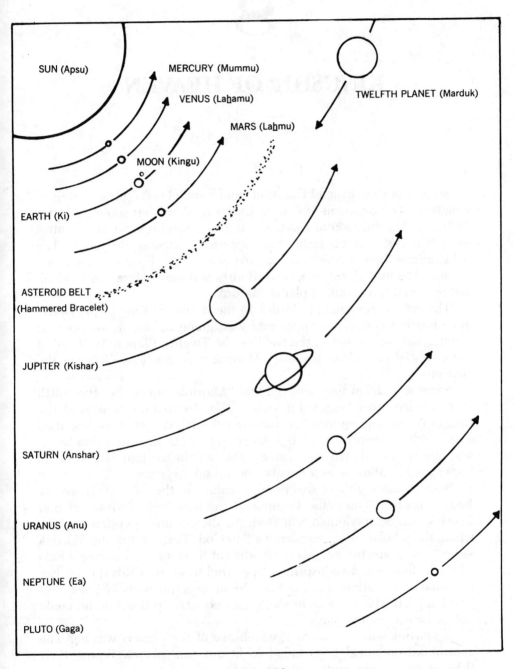

Fig. 110

8

·

KINGSHIP OF HEAVEN

Studies of the "Epic of Creation" and parallel texts (for example, S. Langdon's *The Babylonian Epic of Creation*) show that sometime after 2000 B.C., Marduk, son of Enki, was the successful winner of a contest with Ninurta, son of Enlil, for supremacy among the gods. The Babylonians then revised the original Sumerian "Epic of Creation," expunged from it all references to Ninurta and most references to Enlil, and renamed the invading planet Marduk.

The actual elevation of Marduk to the status of "King of the Gods" upon Earth was thus accompanied by assigning to him, as his celestial counterpart, the planet of the Nefilim, the Twelfth Planet. As "Lord of the Celestial Gods [the planets]" Marduk was thus also "King of the Heavens."

Some scholars at first believed that "Marduk" was either the North Star or some other bright star seen in the Mesopotamian skies at the time of the spring equinox because the celestial Marduk was described as a "bright heavenly body." But Albert Schott *(Marduk und sein Stern)* and others have shown conclusively that all the ancient astronomical texts spoke of Marduk as a member of the solar system.

Since other epithets described Marduk as the "Great Heavenly Body" and the "One Who Illumines," the theory was advanced that Marduk was a Babylonian Sun God, parallel to the Egyptian god Ra, whom the scholars also considered a Sun God. Texts describing Marduk as he "who scans the heights of the distant heavens . . . wearing a halo whose brilliance is awe-inspiring" appeared to support this theory. But the same text continued to say that "he surveys the lands like Shamash [the Sun]." If Marduk was in some respects *akin* to the Sun, he could not, of course, *be* the Sun.

If Marduk was not the Sun, which one of the planets was he? The ancient astronomical texts failed to fit any one planet. Basing their theories on certain epithets (such as Son of the Sun), some scholars pointed at Saturn. The description of Marduk as a reddish planet made Mars, too, a candidate. But the texts placed Marduk in *markas shame* ("in the center of Heaven"), and this convinced most scholars that the proper identification should be Jupiter, which is located in the center of the line of planets:

Jupiter

Mercury Venus Earth Mars   Saturn Uranus Neptune Pluto

This theory suffers from a contradiction. The same scholars who put it forward were the ones who held the view that the Chaldeans were unaware of the planets beyond Saturn. These scholars list Earth as a planet, while contending that the Chaldeans thought of Earth as a flat center of the planetary system. And they omit the Moon, which the Mesopotamians most definitely counted among the "celestial gods." The equating of the Twelfth Planet with Jupiter simply does not work out.

The "Epic of Creation" clearly states that Marduk was an invader from outside the solar system, passing by the outer planets (including Saturn and Jupiter) before colliding with Tiamat. The Sumerians called the planet NIBIRU, the "planet of crossing," and the Babylonian version of the epic retained the following astronomical information:

Planet NIBIRU:
The Crossroads of Heaven and Earth he shall occupy.
Above and below, they shall not go across;
They must await him.

Planet NIBIRU:
Planet which is brilliant in the heavens.
He holds the central position;
To him they shall pay homage.

Planet NIBIRU:
It is he who without tiring
The midst of Tiamat keeps crossing.
Let "CROSSING" be his name—
The one who occupies the midst.

These lines provide the additional and conclusive information that in dividing the other planets into two equal groups, the Twelfth Planet in "the midst of Tiamat keeps crossing": Its orbit takes it again and again to the site of the celestial battle, where Tiamat used to be.

We find that astronomical texts that dealt in a highly sophisticated manner with the planetary periods, as well as lists of planets in their celestial order, also suggested that Marduk appeared somewhere between Jupiter and Mars. Since the Sumerians did know of all the planets, the appearance of the Twelfth Planet in "the central position" confirms our conclusions:

Marduk

Mercury Venus Moon Earth Mars   Jupiter Saturn Uranus Neptune Pluto

If Marduk's orbit takes it to where Tiamat once was, relatively near us (between Mars and Jupiter), why have we not yet seen this planet, which is supposedly large and bright?

The Mesopotamian texts spoke of Marduk as reaching unknown regions of the skies and the far reaches of the universe. "He scans the hidden knowledge . . . he sees all the quarters of the universe." He was described as the "monitor" of all the planets, one whose orbit enables him to encircle all the others. "He keeps hold on their bands [orbits]," makes a "hoop" around them. His orbit was "loftier" and "grander" than that of any other planet. It thus occurred to Franz Kugler (*Sternkunde und Sterndienst in Babylon*) that Marduk was a fast-moving celestial body, orbiting in a great elliptical path just like a comet.

Such an elliptical path, focused on the Sun as a center of gravity, has an apogee—the point farthest from the Sun, where the return flight begins—and a perigee—the point nearest the Sun, where the return to outer space begins. We find that two such "bases" are indeed associated with Marduk in the Mesopotamian texts. The Sumerian texts described the planet as going from AN.UR ("Heaven's base") to E.NUN ("lordly abode"). The Creation epic said of Marduk:

He crossed the Heaven and surveyed the regions. . . .
The structure of the Deep the Lord then measured.
E-Shara he established as his outstanding abode;
E-Shara as a great abode in the Heaven he established.

One "abode" was thus "outstanding"—far in the deep regions of space. The other was established in the "Heaven," within the asteroid belt, between Mars and Jupiter. (Fig. 111)

Following the teachings of their Sumerian forefather, Abraham of Ur, the ancient Hebrews also associated their supreme deity with the supreme planet. Like the Mesopotamian texts, many books of the Old Testament describe the "Lord" has having his abode in the "heights of

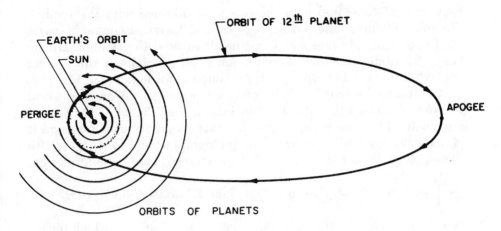

Fig. 111

Heaven," where he "beheld the foremost planets as they were arisen";
a celestial Lord who, unseen, "in the heavens moves about in a circle."
The Book of Job, having described the celestial collision, contains these
significant verses telling us where the lordly planet had gone:

> Upon the Deep he marked out an orbit;
> Where light and darkness [merge]
> Is his farthest limit.

No less explicitly, the Psalms outlined the planet's majestic course:

> The Heavens bespeak the glory of the Lord;
> The Hammered Bracelet proclaims his handiwork. . . .
> He comes forth as a groom from the canopy;
> Like an athlete he rejoices to run the course.
> From the end of heavens he emanates,
> And his circuit is to their end.

Recognized as a great traveler in the heavens, soaring to immense
heights at its apogee and then "coming down, bowing unto the
Heaven" at its perigee, the planet was depicted as a Winged Globe.

Wherever archaeologists uncovered the remains of Near Eastern
peoples, the symbol of the Winged Globe was conspicuous, dominating
temples and palaces, carved on rocks, etched on cylinder seals, painted
on walls. It accompanied kings and priests, stood above their thrones,
"hovered" above them in battle scenes, was etched into their chariots.

Clay, metal, stone, and wood objects were adorned with the symbol. The rulers of Sumer and Akkad, Babylon and Assyria, Elam and Urartu, Mari and Nuzi, Mitanni and Canaan—all revered the symbol. Hittite kings, Egyptian pharaohs, Persian *shar*'s—all proclaimed the symbol (and what it stood for) supreme. It remained so for millennia. (Fig. 112)

Central to the religious beliefs and astronomy of the ancient world was the conviction that the Twelfth Planet, the "Planet of the Gods," remained within the solar system and that its grand orbit returned it periodically to Earth's vicinity. The pictographic sign for the Twelfth Planet, the "Planet of Crossing," was a cross. This cuneiform sign,

▷▷┼— , which also meant "Anu" and "divine," evolved in the

Semitic languages to the letter *tav*, ✗ ✗ ✗   which meant "the sign."

Indeed, all the peoples of the ancient world considered the periodic nearing of the Twelfth Planet as a sign of upheavals, great changes, and new eras. The Mesopotamian texts spoke of the planet's periodic appearance as an anticipated, predictable, and observable event:

> The great planet:
> At his appearance, dark red.
> The Heaven he divides in half
> and stands as Nibiru.

Many of the texts dealing with the planet's arrival were omen texts prophesying the effect the event would have upon Earth and Mankind. R. Campbell Thompson *(Reports of the Magicians and Astronomers of Nineveh and Babylon)* reproduced several such texts, which trace the progress of the planet as it "ringed the station of Jupiter" and arrived at the point of crossing, Nibiru:

> When from the station of Jupiter
> the Planet passes towards the west,
> there will be a time of dwelling in security.
> Kindly peace will descend on the land.
> When from the station of Jupiter
> the Planet increases in brilliance
> and in the Zodiac of Cancer will become Nibiru,
> Akkad will overflow with plenty,
> the king of Akkad will grow powerful.
> When Nibiru culminates. . . .

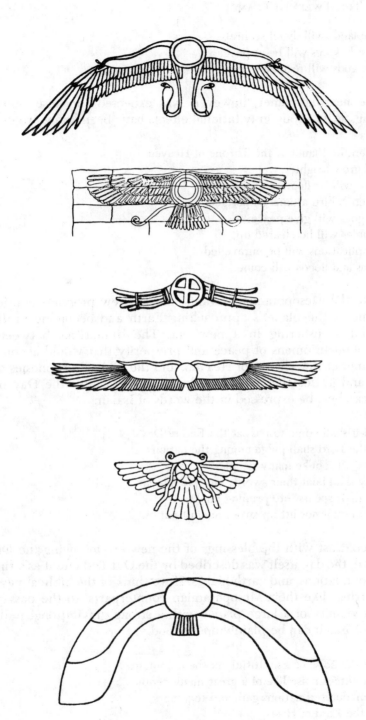

Fig. 112

The lands will dwell securely,
Hostile kings will be at peace,
The gods will receive prayers and hear supplications.

The nearing planet, however, was expected to cause rains and flooding, as its strong gravitational effects have been known to do:

When the Planet of the Throne of Heaven
will grow brighter,
there will be floods and rains. . . .
When Nibiru attains its perigee,
the gods will give peace;
troubles will be cleared up,
complications will be unravelled.
Rains and floods will come.

Like the Mesopotamian savants, the Hebrew prophets considered the time of the planet's approaching Earth and becoming visible to Mankind as ushering in a new era. The similarities between the Mesopotamian omens of peace and prosperity that would accompany the Planet of the Throne of Heaven, and the biblical prophesies of the peace and justice that would settle upon Earth after the Day of the Lord, can best be expressed in the words of Isaiah:

And it shall come to pass at the End of Days:
. . . the Lord shall judge among the nations
and shall rebuke many peoples.
They shall beat their swords into ploughshares
and their spears into pruning hooks;
nation shall not lift up sword against nation.

In contrast with the blessings of the new era following the Day of the Lord, the day itself was described by the Old Testament as a time of rains, inundations, and earthquakes. If we think of the biblical passages as referring, like their Mesopotamian counterparts, to the passage in Earth's vicinity of a large planet with a strong gravitational pull, the words of Isaiah can be plainly understood:

Like the noise of a multitude in the mountains,
a tumultous noise like of a great many people,
of kingdoms of nations gathered together;
it is the Lord of Hosts,
commanding a Host to battle.

From a far away land they come,
from the end-point of the Heaven
do the Lord and his Weapons of wrath
come to destroy the whole Earth. . . .
Therefore will I agitate the Heaven
and Earth shall be shaken out of its place
when the Lord of Hosts shall be crossing,
the day of his burning wrath.

While on Earth "mountains shall melt . . . valleys shall be cleft," Earth's axial spin would also be affected. The prophet Amos explicitly predicted:

It shall come to pass on that Day,
sayeth the Lord God,
that I will cause the Sun to go down at noon
and I will darken the Earth in the midst of daytime.

Announcing, "Behold, the Day of the Lord is come!" the prophet Zechariah informed the people that this phenomenon of an arrest in Earth's spin around its own axis would last only one day:

And it shall come to pass on that Day
there shall be no light—uncommonly shall it freeze.
And there shall be one day, known to the Lord,
which shall be neither day nor night,
when at eve-time there shall be light.

On the Day of the Lord, the prophet Joel said, "the Sun and Moon shall be darkened, the stars shall withdraw their radiance"; "the Sun shall be turned into darkness, and the Moon shall be as red blood."

Mesopotamian texts exalted the planet's radiance and suggested that it could be seen even at daytime: "visible at sunrise, disappearing from view at sunset." A cylinder seal, found at Nippur, depicts a group of plowmen looking up with awe as the Twelfth Planet (depicted with its cross symbol) is visible in the skies. (Fig. 113)

The ancient peoples not only expected the periodic arrival of the Twelfth Planet but also charted its advancing course.

Various biblical passages—especially in Isaiah, Amos, and Job— relate the movement of the celestial Lord to various constellations. "Alone he stretches out the heavens and treads upon the highest Deep; he arrives at the Great Bear, Orion and Sirius, and the constellations of the south." Or, "He smiles his face upon Taurus and Aries; from Taurus

Fig. 113

to Sagittarius he shall go." These verses describe a planet that not only spans the highest heavens but also comes in from the *south* and moves in a *clockwise* direction—just as we have deduced from the Mesopotamian data. Quite explicitly, the prophet Habakkuk stated: "The Lord from the south shall come . . . his glory shall fill the Earth . . . and Venus shall be as light, its rays of the Lord given."

Among the many Mesopotamian texts that dealt with the subject, one is quite clear:

> Planet of the god Marduk:
> Upon its appearance: Mercury.
> Rising thirty degrees of the celestial arc: Jupiter.
> When standing in the place of the celestial battle:
> Nibiru.

As the accompanying schematic chart illustrates, the above texts do not simply call the Twelfth Planet by different names (as scholars have assumed). They deal rather with the movements of the planet and the three crucial points at which its appearance can be observed and charted from Earth. (Fig. 114)

The first opportunity to observe the Twelfth Planet as its orbit brings it back to Earth's vicinity, then, was when it aligned with Mercury (point A)—by our calculations, at an angle of 30 degrees to the imaginary celestial axis of Sun–Earth–perigee. Coming closer to Earth and thus appearing to "rise" farther in Earth's skies (another 30 degrees, to be exact), the planet crossed the orbit of Jupiter at point B. Finally, arriving at the place where the celestial battle had taken place, the perigee, or the Place of the Crossing, the planet is Nibiru, point C.

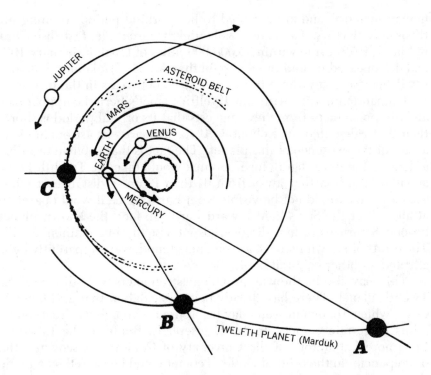

Fig. 114. THE RE-APPEARANCE OF THE TWELFTH PLANET.

Drawing an imaginary axis between Sun, Earth and the perigee of Marduk's orbit, observers on Earth first saw Marduk aligned with Mercury, at a 30° angle (point A). Progressing another 30°, Marduk crossed the orbital path of Jupiter at point B.

Then, at its apogee (point C) Marduk reached The Crossing: back at the site of the Celestial Battle, it was closest to Earth, and began its orbit back to distant space.

The anticipation of the Day of the Lord in the ancient Mesopotamian and Hebrew writings (which were echoed in the New Testament's expectations of the coming of the Kingship of Heaven) was thus based on the actual experiences of Earth's people: their witnessing the periodic return of the Planet of Kingship to Earth's vicinity.

The planet's periodic appearance and disappearance from Earth's view confirms the assumption of its permanence in solar orbit. In this it acts like many comets. Some of the known comets—like Halley's comet, which nears Earth every seventy-five years—disappeared from view for such long times that astronomers were hard-pressed to realize that they were seeing the same comet. Other comets have been seen only once in human memory, and are assumed to have orbital periods running into thousands of years. The comet Kohoutek, for example, first discovered in March 1973, came within 75,000,000 miles of Earth in January 1974, and disappeared behind the Sun soon thereafter. Astronomers calculate it will reappear anywhere from 7,500 to 75,000 years in the future.

Human familiarity with the Twelfth Planet's periodic appearances and disappearances from view suggests that its orbital period is shorter than that calculated for Kohoutek. If so, why are our astronomers not aware of the existence of this planet? The fact is that even an orbit half as long as the lower figure for Kohoutek would take the Twelfth Planet about six times farther away from us than Pluto—a distance at which such a planet would not be visible from Earth, since it would barely (if at all) reflect the Sun's light toward Earth. In fact, the known planets beyond Saturn were first discovered not visually but mathematically. The orbits of known planets, astronomers found, were apparently being affected by other celestial bodies.

This may also be the way in which astronomers will "discover" the Twelfth Planet. There has already been speculation that a "Planet X" exists, which, though unseen, may be "sensed" through its effects on the orbits of certain comets. In 1972, Joseph L. Brady of the Lawrence Livermore Laboratory of the University of California discovered that discrepancies in the orbit of Halley's comet could be caused by a planet the size of Jupiter orbiting the Sun every 1,800 years. At its estimated distance of 6,000,000,000 miles, its presence could be detected only mathematically.

While such an orbital period cannot be ruled out, the Mesopotamian and biblical sources present strong evidence that the orbital period of the Twelfth Planet is 3,600 years. The number 3,600 was written in Sumerian as a large circle. The epithet for the planet—shar ("supreme ruler")—also meant "a perfect circle," a "completed cycle." It also meant the number 3,600. And the identity of the three terms—planet/orbit/3,600—could not be a mere coincidence.

Berossus, the Babylonian priest-astronomer-scholar, spoke of ten rulers who reigned upon Earth before the Deluge. Summarizing the writings of Berossus, Alexander Polyhistor wrote: "In the second book was the history of the ten kings of the Chaldeans, and the periods of each reign, which consisted collectively of an hundred and twenty shar's, or four hundred and thirty-two thousand years; reaching to the time of the Deluge."

Abydenus, a disciple of Aristotle, also quoted Berossus in terms of ten pre-Diluvial rulers whose total reign numbered 120 shar's. He made clear that these rulers and their cities were located in ancient Mesopotamia:

It is said that the first king of the land was Alorus. . . . He reigned ten *shar*'s.

Now, a *shar* is esteemed to be three thousand six hundred years. . . .

After him Alaprus reigned three *shar*'s; to him succeeded Amillarus from the city of panti-Biblon, who reigned thirteen *shar*'s. . . .

After him Ammenon reigned twelve *shar*'s; he was of the city of panti-Biblon. Then Megalurus of the same place, eighteen *shar*'s.

Then Daos, the Shepherd, governed for the space of ten *shar*'s. . . .

There were afterwards other Rulers, and the last of all Sisithrus; so that in the whole, the number amounted to ten kings, and the term of their reigns to an hundred and twenty *shar*'s.

Apollodorus of Athens also reported on the prehistorical disclosures of Berossus in similar terms: Ten rulers reigned a total of 120 *shar*'s (432,000 years), and the reign of each one of them was also measured in the 3,600-year *shar* units.

With the advent of Sumerology, the "olden texts" to which Berossus referred were found and deciphered; these were Sumerian king lists, which apparently laid down the tradition of ten pre-Diluvial rulers who ruled Earth from the time when "Kingship was lowered from Heaven" until the "Deluge swept over the Earth."

One Sumerian king list, known as text W-B/144, records the divine reigns in five settled places or "cities." In the first city, Eridu, there were two rulers. The text prefixes both names with the title-syllable "A," meaning "progenitor."

When kingship was lowered from Heaven,
kingship was first in Eridu.
In Eridu,
A.LU.LIM became king; he ruled 28,800 years.
A.LAL.GAR ruled 36,000 years.
Two kings ruled it 64,800 years.

Kingship then transferred to other seats of government, where the rulers were called *en*, or "lord" (and in one instance by the divine title *dingir*).

I drop Eridu;
its kingship was carried to Bad-Tibira.
In Bad-Tibira,
EN.MEN.LU.AN.NA ruled 43,200 years;
EN.MEN.GAL.AN.NA ruled 28,800 years.
Divine DU.MU.ZI, Shepherd, ruled 36,000 years.
Three kings ruled it for 108,000 years.

The list then names the cities that followed, Larak and Sippar, and their divine rulers; and last, the city of Shuruppak, where a human of divine parentage was king. The striking fact about the fantastic lengths of these rules is that, without exception, they are multiples of 3,600:

Alulim	− 8	× 3,600	=	28,800
Alalgar	−10	× 3,600	=	36,000
Enmenluanna	−12	× 3,600	=	43,200
Enmengalanna	− 8	× 3,600	=	28,800
Dumuzi	−10	× 3,600	=	36,000
Ensipazianna	− 8	× 3,600	=	28,800
Enmenduranna	− 6	× 3,600	=	21,600
Ubartutu	− 5	× 3,600	=	18,000

Another Sumerian text (W-B/62) added Larsa and its two divine rulers to the king list, and the reign periods it gives are also perfect multiples of the 3,600-year *shar*. With the aid of other texts, the conclusion is that there were indeed ten rulers in Sumer before the Deluge; each rule lasted so many *shar*'s; and altogether their reign lasted 120 *shar*'s—as reported by Berossus.

The conclusion that suggests itself is that these *shar*'s of rulership were related to the orbital period *shar* (3,600 years) of the planet "Shar," the "Planet of Kingship"; that Alulim reigned during eight orbits of the Twelfth Planet, Alalgar during ten orbits, and so on.

If these pre-Diluvial rulers were, as we suggest, Nefilim who came to Earth from the Twelfth Planet, then it should not be surprising that their periods of "reign" on Earth should be related to the orbital period of the Twelfth Planet. The periods of such tenure or Kingship would last from the time of a landing to the time of a takeoff; as one commander arrived from the Twelfth Planet, the other's time came up. Since the landings and takeoffs must have been related to the Twelfth Planet's approach to Earth, the command tenures could only have been measured in these orbital periods, of *shar*'s.

One may ask, of course, whether any one of the Nefilim, having landed on Earth, could remain in command here for the purported 28,800 or 36,000 years. No wonder scholars speak of the length of these reigns as "legendary."

But what is a year? Our "year" is simply the time it takes Earth to complete one orbit around the Sun. Because life developed on Earth when it was already orbiting the Sun, life on Earth is patterned by this length of orbit. (Even a more minor orbit time, like that of the Moon, or the day–night cycle is powerful enough to affect almost all life on Earth.) We live so many years because our biological clocks are geared to so many Earth orbits around the Sun.

There can be little doubt that life on another planet would be "timed" to the cycles of that planet. If the trajectory of the Twelfth Planet around the Sun were so extended that one orbit was completed in the same time it takes Earth to complete 100 orbits, then one year of the Nefilim would equal 100 of our years. If their orbit took 1,000 times longer than ours, then 1,000 Earth years would equal only one Nefilim year.

And what if, as we believe, their orbit around the sun lasted 3,600 Earth years? Then 3,600 of our years would amount to only one year in their calendar, and also only one year in their lifetime. The tenures of Kingship reported by the Sumerians and Berossus would thus be neither "legendary" nor fantastic: They would have lasted five or eight or ten Nefilim years.

We have noted, in earlier chapters, that Mankind's march to civilization—through the intervention of the Nefilim—passed through three stages, which were separated by periods of 3,600 years: the Neolithic period (circa 11,000 B.C.), the pottery phase (circa 7400 B.C.), and the sudden Sumerian civilization (circa 3800 B.C.). It is not unlikely, then, that the Nefilim periodically reviewed (and resolved to continue) Mankind's progress, since they could meet in assembly each time the Twelfth Planet neared Earth.

Many scholars (for example, Heinrich Zimmern in *The Babylonian and Hebrew Genesis*) have pointed out that the Old Testament also carried traditions of pre-Diluvial chieftains, or forefathers, and that the line from Adam to Noah (the hero of the Deluge) listed ten such rulers. Putting the situation prior to the Deluge in perspective, the Book of Genesis (Chapter 6) described the divine disenchantment with Mankind. "And it repented the Lord that he had made Man on Earth . . . and the Lord said: I will destroy Man whom I had created."

> And the Lord said:
> My spirit shall not shield Man forever;
> having erred, he is but flesh.
> And his days were one hundred and twenty years.

Generations of scholars have read the verse "And his days shall be a hundred and twenty years" as God's granting a life span of 120 years to Man. But this just does not make sense. If the text dealt with God's intent to destroy Mankind, why would he in the same breath offer Man long life? And we find that no sooner had the Deluge subsided than Noah lived far longer than the supposed limit of 120 years, as did his descendants Shem (600), Arpakhshad (438), Shelah (433), and so on.

In seeking to apply the span of 120 years to Man, the scholars ignore the fact that the biblical language employs not the future tense—"His days *shall be*"—but the past tense—"And his days *were* one hundred and twenty years." The obvious question, then, is: *Whose* time span is referred to here?

Our conclusion is that the count of 120 years was meant to apply to the Deity.

Setting a momentous event in its proper time perspective is a common feature of the Sumerian and Babylonian epic texts. The "Epic of Creation" opens with the words *Enuma elish* ("when on high"). The story of the encounter of the god Enlil and the goddess Ninlil is placed at the time "*when* man had not yet been created," and so on.

The language and purpose of Chapter 6 of Genesis were geared to the same purpose—to put the momentous events of the great Flood in their proper time perspective. The very first word of the very first verse of Chapter 6 is *when:*

When the Earthlings
began to increase in number
upon the face of the Earth,
and daughters were born unto them.

This, the narrative continues, was the time when

The sons of the gods
saw the daughters of the Earthling
that they were compatible;
and they took unto themselves
wives of whichever they chose.

It was the time when

The Nefilim were upon the land
in those days, and thereafter too;
when the sons of the gods
cohabited with the Earthling's daughters
and they conceived.
They were the Mighty Ones who are of Olam,
the People of the *Shem.*

It was then, in those days, at that time that Man was about to be wiped off the face of the Earth by the Flood.

When exactly was that?

Verse 3 tells us unequivocally: when his, the Deity's count, was 120 years. One hundred twenty "years," not of Man and not of Earth, but as counted by the mighty ones, the "People of the Rockets," the Nefilim. And their year was the *shar*—3,600 Earth years.

This interpretation not only clarifies the perplexing verses of Genesis 6, it also shows how the verses match the Sumerian information: 120 *shars*, 432,000 Earth years, had passed between the Nefilim's first landing on Earth and the Deluge.

Based on our estimates of when the Deluge occurred, we place the first landing of the Nefilim on Earth circa 450,000 years ago.

＊

Before we turn to the ancient records regarding the voyages of the Nefilim to Earth and their settlement on Earth, two basic questions need to be answered: Could beings obviously not much different from us evolve on another planet? Could such beings have had the capability, half a million years ago, for interplanetary travel?

The first question touches upon a more fundamental question: Is there life as we know it anywhere besides the planet Earth? Scientists now know that there are innumerable galaxies like ours, containing countless stars like our Sun, with astronomical numbers of planets providing every imaginable combination of temperature and atmosphere and chemicals, offering billions of chances for Life.

They have also found that our own interplanetary space is not void. For example, there are water molecules in space, the remnants of what are believed to have been clouds of ice crystals that apparently envelop stars in their early stages of development. This discovery lends support to persistent Mesopotamian references to the waters of the Sun, which mingled with the waters of Tiamat.

The basic molecules of living matter have also been found "floating" in interplanetary space, and the belief that life can exist only within certain atmospheres or temperature ranges has also been shattered. Furthermore, the notion that the only source of energy and heat available to living organisms is the Sun's emissions has been discarded. Thus, the spacecraft *Pioneer 10* discovered that Jupiter, though much farther away from the Sun than Earth, was so hot that it must have its own sources of energy and heat.

A planet with an abundance of radioactive elements in its depths would not only generate its own heat; it would also experience substantial volcanic activity. Such volcanic activity provides an atmosphere. If the planet is large enough to exert a strong gravitational pull, it will keep its atmosphere almost indefinitely. Such an atmosphere, in turn, creates a hothouse effect: it shields the planet from the cold of outer space, and keeps the planet's own heat from dissipating into space—much as clothing keeps us warm by not letting the body's heat dissipate. With this in mind, the ancient texts' descriptions of the Twelfth Planet as "clothed with a halo" assume more than poetic significance. It was always referred to as a radiant planet—"most radiant of the gods he is"—and depictions of it showed it as a ray-emitting body. The Twelfth Planet could generate its own heat and retain the heat because of its atmospheric mantle. (Fig. 115)

Fig. 115

Scientists have also come to the unexpected conclusion that not only could life have evolved upon the outer planets (Jupiter, Saturn, Uranus, Neptune) but it probably *did* evolve there. These planets are made up of the lighter elements of the solar system, have a composition more akin to that of the universe in general, and offer a profusion of hydrogen, helium, methane, ammonia, and probably neon and water vapor in their atmospheres—all the elements required for the production of organic molecules.

For life as we know it to develop, water is essential. The Mesopotamian texts left no doubt that the Twelfth Planet was a watery planet. In the "Epic of Creation," the planet's list of fifty names included a group exalting its watery aspects. Based on the epithet A.SAR ("watery king"), "who established water levels," the names described the planet as A.SAR.U ("lofty, bright watery king"), A.SAR.U.LU.DU ("lofty, bright watery king whose deep is plentiful"), and so on.

The Sumerians had no doubt that the Twelfth Planet was a verdant planet of life; indeed, they called it NAM.TIL.LA.KU, "the god who maintains life." He was also "bestower of cultivation," "creator of grain and herbs who causes vegetation to sprout . . . who opened the wells, apportioning waters of abundance"—the "irrigator of Heaven and Earth."

Life, scientists have concluded, evolved not upon the terrestrial planets, with their heavy chemical components, but in the outer fringes of the solar system. From these fringes of the solar system, the Twelfth

Planet came into our midst, a reddish, glowing planet, generating and radiating its own heat, providing from its own atmosphere the ingredients needed for the chemistry of life.

If a puzzle exists, it is the appearance of life on Earth. Earth was formed some 4,500,000,000 years ago, and scientists believe that the simpler forms of life were already present on Earth within a few hundred million years thereafter. This is simply much too soon for comfort. There are also several indications that the oldest and simplest forms of life, more than 3,000,000,000 years old, had molecules of a biological, not a nonbiological, origin. Stated differently, this means that the life that was on Earth so soon after Earth was born was itself a descendant of some previous life form, and *not* the result of the combination of lifeless chemicals and gases.

What all this suggests to the baffled scientists is that life, which could not easily evolve on Earth, did not, in fact, evolve on Earth. Writing in the scientific magazine *Icarus* (September 1973), Nobel Prize winner Francis Crick and Dr. Leslie Orgel advanced the theory that "life on Earth may have sprung from tiny organisms from a distant planet."

They launched their studies out of the known uneasiness among scientists over current theories of the origins of life on Earth. Why is there only *one* genetic code for all terrestrial life? If life started in a primeval "soup," as most biologists believe, organisms with a variety of genetic codes should have developed. Also, why does the element molybdenum play a key role in enzymatic reactions that are essential to life, when molybdenum is a very rare element? Why are elements that are more abundant on Earth, such as chromium or nickel, so unimportant in biochemical reactions?

The bizarre theory offered by Crick and Orgel was not only that all life on Earth may have sprung from an organism from another planet but that such "seeding" was *deliberate*—that intelligent beings from another planet launched the "seed of life" from their planet to Earth in a spaceship, for the express purpose of starting the life chain on Earth.

Without benefit of the data provided by this book, these two eminent scientists came close to the real fact. There was no premeditated "seeding"; instead, there was a celestial collision. A life-bearing planet, the Twelfth Planet and its satellites, collided with Tiamat and split it in two, "creating" Earth of its half.

During that collision the life-bearing soil and air of the Twelfth Planet "seeded" Earth, giving it the biological and complex early forms of life for whose early appearance there is no other explanation.

If life on the Twelfth Planet started even 1 percent sooner than on

Earth, then it began there some 45,000,000 years earlier. Even by this minute margin, beings as developed as Man would already have been living upon the Twelfth Planet when the first small mammals had just begun to appear on Earth.

Given this earlier start for life on the Twelfth Planet, it was possible for its people to be capable of space travel a mere 500,000 years ago.

9
.
LANDING ON PLANET EARTH

We have set foot only on the Moon, and have probed only the planets closest to us with unmanned craft. Beyond our relatively close neighbors, both interplanetary and outer space are still outside the reach of even small scanning craft. But the Nefilim's own planet, with its vast orbit, has served as a traveling observatory, taking them through the orbits of all the outer planets and enabling them to observe at first hand most of the solar system.

No wonder, then, that when they landed on Earth, a good deal of the knowledge they brought with them concerned astronomy and celestial mathematics. The Nefilim, "Gods of Heaven" upon Earth, taught Man to look up unto the heavens—just as Yahweh urged Abraham to do.

No wonder, too, that even the earliest and crudest sculptures and drawings bore celestial symbols of constellations and planets; and that when the gods were to be represented or invoked, their celestial symbols were used as a graphic shorthand. By invoking the celestial ("divine") symbols, Man was no longer alone; the symbols connected Earthlings with the Nefilim, Earth with Heaven, Mankind with the universe.

Some of the symbols, we believe, also convey information that could be related only to space travel to Earth.

Ancient sources provide a profusion of texts and lists dealing with the celestial bodies and their associations with the various deities. The ancient habit of assigning several epithet names to both the celestial bodies and the deities has made identification difficult. Even in the case of established identifications, such as Venus/Ishtar, the picture is confused by the changes in the pantheon. Thus, in earlier times Venus was associated with Ninhursag.

Somewhat greater clarity has been obtained by scholars, such as E. D. Van Buren (*Symbols of the Gods in Mesopotamian Art*), who assembled and sorted out the more than eighty symbols—of gods and celestial bodies—that can be found on cylinder seals, sculptures, stelae, reliefs, murals, and (in great detail and clarity) on boundary stones *(kudurru* in Akkadian). When the classification of the symbols is made, it becomes evident that apart from standing for some of the better-known southern or northern constellations (such as the Sea Serpent for the constellation Hydra), they represented either the *twelve* constellations of the zodiac (for example, the Crab for Scorpio), or the *twelve* Gods of Heaven and Earth, or the *twelve* members of the solar system. The *kudurru* set up by Melishipak, king of Susa (see p. 186), shows the twelve symbols of the zodiac and the symbols of the twelve astral gods.

A stela erected by the Assyrian king Esarhaddon shows the ruler holding the Cup of Life while facing the twelve chief Gods of Heaven and Earth. We see four gods atop animals, of whom Ishtar on the lion and Adad holding the forked lightning can definitely be identified. Four other gods are represented by the tools of their special attributes, as the war-god Ninurta by his lion-headed mace. The remaining four gods are shown as celestial bodies—the Sun (Shamash), the Winged Globe (the Twelfth Planet, the abode of Anu), the Moon's crescent, and a symbol consisting of seven dots. (Fig. 116)

Fig. 116

Although in later times the god Sin was associated with the Moon, identified by the crescent, ample evidence shows that in "olden times" the crescent was the symbol of an elderly and bearded deity, one of Sumer's true "olden gods." Often shown surrounded by streams of water, this god was undoubtedly Ea. The crescent was also associated with the science of measuring and calculating, of which Ea was the divine master. It was appropriate that the God of the Seas and Oceans,

Ea, be assigned as his celestial counterpart the Moon, which causes the ocean's tides.

What was the meaning of the symbol of the seven dots?

Many clues leave no doubt that it was the celestial symbol of Enlil. The depiction of the Gateway of Anu (the Winged Globe) flanked by Ea and Enlil (see Fig. 87), represents them by the crescent and the seven-dot symbol. Some of the clearest depictions of the celestial symbols that were meticulously copied by Sir Henry Rawlinson *(The Cuneiform Inscriptions of Western Asia)* assign the most prominent position to a group of three symbols, standing for Anu flanked by his two sons; these show that the symbol for Enlil could be either the seven dots or a seven-pointed "star." The essential element in Enlil's celestial representation was the number *seven* (the daughter, Ninhursag, was sometimes included, represented by the umbilical cutter). (Fig. 117)

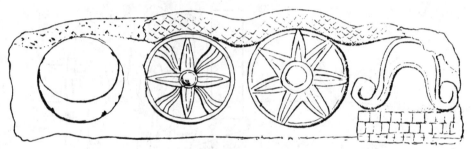

Fig. 117

Scholars have been unable to understand a statement by Gudea, king of Lagash, that "the celestial 7 is 50." Attempts at arithmetic solutions—some formula whereby the number seven would go into fifty—failed to reveal the meaning of the statement. However, we see a simple answer: Gudea stated that the celestial body that is "seven" stands for the god that is "fifty." The god Enlil, whose rank number was fifty, had as his celestial counterpart the planet that was seventh.

Which planet was the planet of Enlil? We recall the texts that speak of the early times when the gods first came to Earth, when Anu stayed on the Twelfth Planet, and his two sons who had gone down to Earth drew lots. Ea was given the "rulership over the Deep," and to Enlil "the Earth was given for his dominion." And the answer to the puzzle bursts out in all its significance:

The planet of Enlil was Earth. Earth—to the Nefilim—was the seventh planet.

In February 1971, the United States launched an unmanned

spacecraft on the longest mission to date. For twenty-one months it traveled, past Mars and the asteroid belt, to a precisely scheduled rendezvous with Jupiter. Then, as anticipated by NASA scientists, the immense gravitational pull of Jupiter "grabbed" the spacecraft and hurled it into outer space.

Speculating that *Pioneer 10* might someday be attracted by the gravitational pull of another "solar system" and crash-land on some planet elsewhere in the universe, the *Pioneer 10* scientists attached to it an engraved aluminum plaque bearing the accompanying "message." (Fig. 118)

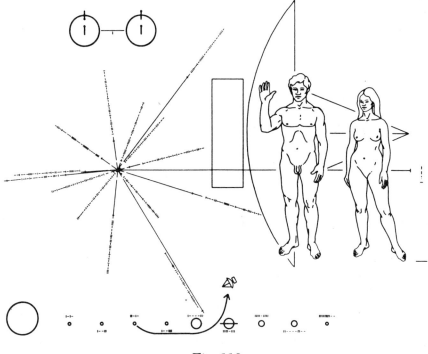

Fig. 118

The message employs a pictographic language—signs and symbols not too different from those used in the very first pictographic writing of Sumer. It attempts to tell whoever might find the plaque that Mankind is male and female, of a size related to the size and shape of the spacecraft. It depicts the two basic chemical elements of our world, and our location relative to a certain interstellar source of radio emissions. And it depicts our solar system as a Sun and nine planets, telling the finder: "The craft that you have found comes from the *third* planet of this Sun."

Our astronomy is geared to the notion that Earth is the third planet—which, indeed, it is if one begins the count from the center of our system, the Sun.

But to someone nearing our solar system *from the outside,* the first planet to be encountered would be Pluto, the second Neptune, the third Uranus—not Earth. Fourth would be Saturn; fifth, Jupiter; sixth, Mars.

And Earth would be *seventh.*

No one but the Nefilim, traveling to Earth past Pluto, Neptune, Uranus, Saturn, Jupiter, and Mars, could have considered Earth "the seventh." Even if, for the sake of argument, one assumed that the inhabitants of ancient Mesopotamia, rather than travelers from space, had the knowledge or wisdom to count Earth's position not from the central Sun but from the solar system's edge, then it would follow that the ancient peoples *knew* of the existence of Pluto and Neptune and Uranus. Since they could not have known of these outermost planets on their own, the information must, we conclude, have been imparted to them by the Nefilim.

Whichever assumption is adopted as a starting point, the conclusion is the same: Only the Nefilim could have known that there are planets beyond Saturn, as a consequence of which Earth—counting from the outside—is the seventh.

Earth is not the only planet whose numerical position in the solar system was represented symbolically. Ample evidence shows that Venus was depicted as an eight-pointed star: Venus is the eighth planet, following Earth, when counted from the outside. The eight-pointed star also stood for the goddess Ishtar, whose planet was Venus. (Fig. 119)

Many cylinder seals and other graphic relics depict Mars as the sixth planet. A cylinder seal shows the god associated with Mars (originally Nergal, then Nabu), seated on a throne under a six-pointed "star" as his symbol. (Fig. 120) Other symbols on the seal show the Sun, much in the same manner we would depict it today; the Moon; and the cross, symbol of the "Planet of Crossing," the Twelfth Planet.

In Assyrian times, the "celestial count" of a god's planet was often indicated by the appropriate number of star symbols placed alongside the god's throne. Thus, a plaque depicting the god Ninurta placed four star symbols at his throne. His planet Saturn is indeed the fourth planet, as counted by the Nefilim. Similar depictions have been found for most of the other planets.

The central religious event of ancient Mesopotamia, the twelve-day New Year Festival, was replete with symbolism that had to do with the

Fig. 119

Fig. 120

orbit of the Twelfth Planet, the makeup of the solar system, and the journey of the Nefilim to Earth. The best-documented of these "affirmations of the faith" were the Babylonian New Year rituals; but evidence shows that the Babylonians only copied traditions going back to the beginning of Sumerian civilization.

In Babylon, the festival followed a very strict and detailed ritual; each portion, act, and prayer had a traditional reason and a specific meaning. The ceremonies started on the first day of Nisan—then the first month of the year—coinciding with the spring equinox. For eleven days, the other gods with a celestial status joined Marduk in a prescribed order. On the twelfth day, each of the other gods departed to his own abode, and Marduk was left alone in his splendor. The parallel to the appearance of Marduk within the planetary system, his "visit" with the eleven other members of the solar system, and the separation on the twelfth day—leaving the Twelfth God to go on as King of the Gods, but in isolation from them—is obvious.

The ceremonies of the New Year Festival paralleled the course of the Twelfth Planet. The first four days, matching Marduk's passage by the first four planets (Pluto, Neptune, Uranus, and Saturn), were days of preparation. At the end of the fourth day, the rituals called for marking the appearance of the planet Iku (Jupiter) within sight of Marduk. The celestial Marduk was nearing the place of the celestial battle; symbolically, the high priest began reciting the "Epic of Creation"—the tale of that celestial battle.

The night passed without sleep. When the tale of the celestial battle had been recited, and as the fifth day was breaking, the rituals called for the twelvefold proclamation of Marduk as "The Lord," affirming that in the aftermath of the celestial battle there were now twelve members of the solar system. The recitations then named the twelve members of the solar system and the twelve constellations of the zodiac.

Sometime during the fifth day, the god Nabu—Marduk's son and heir—arrived by boat from his cult center, Borsippa. But he entered Babylon's temple compound only on the sixth day, for by then Nabu was a member of the Babylonian pantheon of twelve and the planet assigned to him was Mars—the sixth planet.

The Book of Genesis informs us that in six days "the Heaven and the Earth and all their host" were completed. The Babylonian rituals commemorating the celestial events that resulted in the creation of the asteroid belt and Earth were also completed in the first six days of Nisan.

On the seventh day, the festival turned its attention to Earth. Though details of the rituals on the seventh day are scarce, H. Frankfort (*Kingship and the Gods*) believes that they involved an enactment by the gods, led by Nabu, of the liberation of Marduk from his imprisonment in the "Mountains of Lower Earth." Since texts have been found that detail epic struggles between Marduk and other claimants to the rulership of Earth, we can surmise that the events of the seventh day were a reenactment of Marduk's struggle for supremacy on Earth (the "Seventh"), his initial defeats, and his final victory and usurpation of the powers.

On the eighth day of the New Year Festival in Babylon, Marduk, victorious on Earth, as the forged *Enuma Elish* had made him in the heavens, received the supreme powers. Having bestowed them on Marduk, the gods, assisted by the king and populace, then embarked, on the ninth day, on a ritual procession that took Marduk from his house within the city's sacred precinct to the "House of Akitu," somewhere outside the city. Marduk and the visiting eleven gods stayed there through the eleventh day; on the twelfth day, the gods dispersed to their various abodes, and the festival was over.

Of the many aspects of the Babylonian festival that reveal its earlier, Sumerian origins, one of the most significant was that which pertained to the House of Akitu. Several studies, such as *The Babylonian Akitu Festival* by S. A. Pallis, have established that this house was featured in religious ceremonies in Sumer as early as the third millennium B.C. The essence of the ceremony was a holy procession that saw the reigning god leave his abode or temple and go, via several stations, to a place well out of town. A special ship, a "Divine Boat," was used for the purpose. Then the god, successful in whatever his mission was at the A.KI.TI House, returned to the city's quay by the same Divine Boat, and retraced his course back to the temple amid feasting and rejoicing by the king and populace.

The Sumerian term A.KI.TI (from which the Babylonian *akitu* derived) literally meant "build on Earth life." This, coupled with the various aspects of the mysterious journey, leads us to conclude that the procession symbolized the hazardous but successful voyage of the Nefilim from their abode to the seventh planet, Earth.

Excavations conducted over some twenty years on the site of ancient Babylon, brilliantly correlated with Babylonian ritual texts, enabled teams of scholars led by F. Wetzel and F. H. Weissbach *(Das Hauptheiligtum des Marduks in Babylon)* to reconstruct the holy precinct of Marduk, the architectural features of his ziggurat, and the Processional Way, portions of which were reerected at the Museum of the Ancient Near East, in East Berlin.

The symbolic names of the seven stations and the epithet of Marduk at each station were given in both Akkadian and Sumerian—attesting both to the antiquity and to the Sumerian origins of the procession and its symbolism.

The first station of Marduk, at which his epithet was "Ruler of the Heavens," was named "House of Holiness" in Akkadian and "House of Bright Waters" in Sumerian. The god's epithet at the second station is illegible; the station itself was named "Where the Field Separates." The partly mutilated name of the third station began with the words "Location facing the planet . . ."; and the god's epithet there changed to "Lord of Poured-Out Fire."

The fourth station was called "Holy Place of Destinies," and Marduk was called "Lord of the Storm of the Waters of *An* and *Ki*." The fifth station appeared less turbulent. It was named "The Roadway," and Marduk assumed the title "Where the Shepherd's Word

Appears." Smoother sailing was also indicated at the sixth station, called "The Traveler's Ship," where Marduk's epithet changed to "God of the Marked-Out Gateway."

The seventh station was the *Bit Akitu* ("house of building life on Earth"). There, Marduk took the title "God of the House of Resting."

It is our contention that the seven stations in the procession of Marduk represented the space trip of the Nefilim from their planet to Earth; that the first "station," the "House of Bright Waters," represented the passage by Pluto; the second ("Where the Field Separates") was Neptune; the third, Uranus; the fourth—a place of celestial storms—Saturn. The fifth, where "The Roadway" became clear, "where the shepherd's word appears," was Jupiter. The sixth, where the journey switched to "The Traveler's Ship," was Mars.

And the seventh station was Earth—the end of the journey, where Marduk provided the "House of Resting" (the god's "house of building life on Earth").

°

How did the "Aeronautics and Space Administration" of the Nefilim view the solar system in terms of the space flight to Earth?

Logically—and in fact—they viewed the system in two parts. The one zone of concern was the zone of flight, which embraced the space occupied by the seven planets extending from Pluto to Earth. The second group, beyond the zone of navigation, was made up of four celestial bodies—the Moon, Venus, Mercury, and the Sun. In astronomy and divine genealogy, the two groups were considered separate.

Genealogically, Sin (as the Moon) was the head of the group of the "Four." Shamash (as the Sun) was his son, and Ishtar (Venus), his daughter. Adad, as Mercury, was the Uncle, Sin's brother, who always kept company with his nephew Shamash and (especially) with his niece Ishtar.

The "Seven," on the other hand, were lumped together in texts dealing with the affairs of both gods and men, and with celestial events. They were "the seven who judge," "seven emissaries of Anu, their king," and it was after them that the number seven was consecrated. There were "seven olden cities"; cities had seven gates; gates had seven bolts; blessings called for seven years of plenty; curses, for famines and plagues lasting seven years; divine weddings were celebrated by "seven days of lovemaking"; and so on and on.

During solemn ceremonies like those that accompanied the rare visits to Earth by Anu and his consort, the deities representing the Seven Planets were assigned certain positions and ceremonial robes, while the Four were treated as a separate group. For example, ancient rules of protocol stated: "The deities Adad, Sin, Shamash, and Ishtar shall be seated in the court until daybreak."

In the skies, each group was supposed to stay in its own celestial zone, and the Sumerians assumed that there was a "celestial bar" keeping the two groups apart. "An important astral-mythological text," according to A. Jeremias *(The Old Testament in the Light of the Ancient Near East)*, deals with some remarkable celestial event, when the Seven "stormed in upon the Celestial Bar." In this upheaval, which apparently was an unusual alignment of the Seven Planets, "they made allies of the hero Shamash [the Sun] and of the valiant Adad [Mercury]"—meaning, perhaps, that all exerted a gravitational pull in a single direction. "At the same time, Ishtar, seeking a glorious dwelling place with Anu, strove to become Queen of Heaven"—Venus was somehow shifting its location to a more "glorious dwelling place." The greatest effect was on Sin (the Moon). "The seven who fear not the laws . . . the Light-giver Sin had violently besieged." According to this text, the appearance of the Twelfth Planet saved the darkened Moon and made it "shine forth in the heavens" once again.

The Four were located in a celestial zone the Sumerians termed GIR.HE.A ("celestial waters where rockets are confused"), MU.HE ("confusion of spacecraft"), or UL.HE ("band of confusion"). These puzzling terms make sense once we realize that the Nefilim considered the heavens of the solar system in terms of their space travel. Only recently, the engineers of Comsat (Communications Satellite Corporation) discovered that the Sun and Moon "trick" satellites and "shut them off." Earth satellites could be "confused" by showers of particles from solar flares or by changes in the Moon's reflection of infrared rays. The Nefilim, too, were aware that rocket ships or spacecraft entered a "zone of confusion" once they passed Earth and neared Venus, Mercury, and the Sun.

Separated from the Four by an assumed celestial bar, the Seven were in a celestial zone for which the Sumerians used the term UB. The *ub* consisted of seven parts called (in Akkadian) *giparu* ("night residences"). There is little doubt that this was the origin of Near Eastern beliefs in the "Seven heavens."

The seven "orbs" or "spheres" of the *ub* comprised the Akkadian *kishshatu* ("the entirety"). The term's origin was the Sumerian SHU, which also implied "that part which was the most important," the Supreme. The Seven Planets were therefore sometimes called "the Seven Shiny Ones SHU.NU"—the Seven who "in the Supreme Part rest."

The Seven were treated in greater technical detail than the Four.

Sumerian, Babylonian, and Assyrian celestial lists described them with various epithets and listed them in their correct order. Most scholars, assuming that the ancient texts could not possibly have dealt with planets beyond Saturn, have found it difficult to identify correctly the planets described in the texts. But our own findings make identification and understanding of the names' meanings relatively easy.

First to be encountered by the Nefilim approaching the solar system was *Pluto*. The Mesopotamian lists name this planet SHU.PA ("supervisor of the SHU"), the planet that guards the approach to the Supreme Part of the solar system.

As we shall see, the Nefilim could land on Earth only if their spaceship were launched from the Twelfth Planet well before reaching Earth's vicinity. They could thus have crossed the orbit of Pluto not only as inhabitants of the Twelfth Planet but also as astronauts in a moving spaceship. An astronomical text said that the planet Shupa was the one where "the deity Enlil fixed the destiny for the Land"—where the god, in charge of a spacecraft, set the right course for the planet Earth and the Land of Sumer.

Next to Shupa was IRU ("loop"). At *Neptune*, the spacecraft of the Nefilim probably commenced its wide curve or "loop" toward its final target. Another list named the planet HUM.BA, which connotes "swampland vegetation." When we probe Neptune someday, will we discover that its persistent association with waters is due to the watery swamps the Nefilim saw upon it?

Uranus was called *Kakkab Shanamma* ("planet which is the double"). Uranus is truly the twin of Neptune in size and appearance. A Sumerian list calls it EN.TI.MASH.SIG ("planet of bright greenish life"). Is Uranus, too, a planet on which swampy vegetation abounded?

Beyond Uranus looms *Saturn*, a giant planet (nearly ten times Earth's size) distinguished by its rings, which extend more than twice as far out as the planet's diameter. Armed with a tremendous gravitational pull and the mysterious rings, Saturn must have posed many dangers to the Nefilim and their spacecraft. This may well explain why they called the fourth planet TAR.GALLU ("the great destroyer"). The planet was also called KAK.SI.DI ("weapon of righteousness") and SI.MUTU ("he who for justice kills"). Throughout the ancient Near East, the planet represented the punisher of the unjust. Were these names expressions of fear or references to actual space accidents?

The *Akitu* rituals, we have seen, made reference to "storms of the waters" between *An* and *Ki* on the fourth day—when the spacecraft was between *Anshar* (Saturn) and *Kishar* (Jupiter).

A very early Sumerian text, assumed since its first publication in

1912 to be "an ancient magical text," very possibly records the loss of a spaceship and its fifty occupants. It relates how Marduk, arriving at Eridu, rushed to his father Ea with some terrible news:

> "It has been created like a weapon;
> It has charged forward like death . . .
> The *Anunnaki* who are fifty,
> it has smitten. . . .
> The flying, birdlike SHU.SAR
> it has smitten on the breast."

The text does not identify "it," whatever destroyed the SHU.SAR (the flying "supreme chaser") and its fifty astronauts. But fear of celestial danger was evident only in regard to Saturn.

The Nefilim must have passed by Saturn and come in view of *Jupiter* with a great sense of relief. They called the fifth planet *Barbaru* ("bright one"), as well as SAG.ME.GAR ("great one, where the space suits are fastened"). Another name for Jupiter, SIB.ZI.AN.NA ("true guide in the heavens"), also described its probable role in the journey to Earth: It was the signal for curving into the difficult passage between Jupiter and Mars, and the entry into the dangerous zone of the asteroid belt. From the epithets, it would seem that it was at this point that the Nefilim put on their *mes*, their spacesuits.

Mars, appropriately, was called UTU.KA.GAB.A ("light established at the gate of the waters"), reminding us of the Sumerian and biblical descriptions of the asteroid belt as the celestial "bracelet" separating the "upper waters" from the "lower waters" of the solar system. More precisely, Mars was referred to as *Shelibbu* ("one near the center" of the solar system).

An unusual drawing on a cylinder seal suggests that, passing Mars, an incoming spacecraft of the Nefilim established constant communication with "Mission Control" on Earth. (Fig. 121)

The central object in this ancient drawing simulates the symbol of the Twelfth Planet, the Winged Globe. Yet it looks different: It is more mechanical, more manufactured than natural. Its "wings" look almost exactly like the solar panels with which American spacecraft are provided to convert the Sun's energy to electricity. The two antennas cannot be mistaken.

The circular craft, with its crownlike top and extended wings and antennas, is located in the heavens, between Mars (the six-pointed star) and Earth and its Moon. On Earth, a deity extends his hand in greeting to an astronaut still out in the heavens, near Mars. The astronaut is

Fig. 121

shown wearing a helmet with a visor and a breastplate. The lower part of his suit is like that of a "fish-man"—a requirement, perhaps, in case of an emergency splashdown in the ocean. In one hand he holds an instrument; the other hand reciprocates the greeting from Earth.

And then, cruising on, there was *Earth*, the seventh planet. In the lists of the "Seven Celestial Gods" it was called SHU.GI ("right resting place of SHU"). It also meant the "land at the conclusion of SHU," of the Supreme Part of the solar system—the destination of the long space journey.

While in the ancient Near East the sound *gi* was sometimes transformed into the more familiar *ki* ("Earth," "dry land"), the pronunciation and syllable *gi* have endured into our own times in their original meaning, exactly as the Nefilim meant it to be: *geo*-graphy, *geo*-metry, *geo*-logy.

In the earliest form of pictographic writing, the sign SHU.GI also meant *shibu ("the seventh")*. And the astronomical texts explained:

> *Shar shadi il Enlil ana kakkab SHU.GI ikabbi*
> *"Lord of Mountains, deity Enlil, with planet Shugi is identical."*

Paralleling the seven stations of Marduk's journey, the planets' names also bespeak a space flight. The land at the journey's end was the seventh planet, Earth.

We may never know whether, countless years from now, someone on another planet will find and understand the message drawn on the plaque attached to *Pioneer 10*. Likewise, one would think it futile to expect to find on Earth such a plaque in reverse—a plaque conveying to

Earthlings information regarding the location and the route from the Twelfth Planet.

Yet such extraordinary evidence does exist.

The evidence is a clay tablet found in the ruins of the Royal Library of Nineveh. Like many of the other tablets, it is undoubtedly an Assyrian copy of an earlier Sumerian tablet. Unlike others, it is a circular disc; and though some cuneiform signs on it are excellently preserved, the few scholars who took on the task of deciphering the tablet ended by calling it "the most puzzling Mesopotamian document."

In 1912, L. W. King, then curator of Assyrian and Babylonian antiquities in the British Museum, made a meticulous copy of the disc, which is divided into eight segments. The undamaged portions bear geometric shapes unseen on any other ancient artifact, designed and drawn with considerable precision. They include arrows, triangles, intersecting lines, and even an ellipse—a geometric-mathematical curve previously assumed to have been unknown in ancient times. (Fig. 122)

The unusual and puzzling clay plaque was first brought to the attention of the scientific community in a report submitted to the British Royal Astronomical Society on January 9, 1880. R. H. M. Bosanquet and A. H. Sayce, in one of the earliest discourses on "The Babylonian Astronomy," referred to it as a planisphere (the reproduction of a spherical surface as a flat map). They announced that some of the cuneiform signs on it "suggest measurements . . . appear to bear some technical meaning."

The many names of celestial bodies appearing in the eight segments of the plaque clearly established its astronomical character. Bosanquet and Sayce were especially intrigued by the seven "dots" in one segment. They said these might represent the phases of the Moon, were it not for the fact that the dots appeared to run along a line naming the "star of stars" DIL.GAN and a celestial body called APIN.

"There can be no doubt that this enigmatical figure is susceptible of a simple explanation," they said. But their own effort to provide such an explanation did not go beyond reading correctly the phonetic values of the cuneiform signs and the conclusion that the disc was a celestial planisphere.

When the Royal Astronomical Society published a sketch of the planisphere, J. Oppert and P. Jensen improved the reading of some star or planet names. Dr. Fritz Hommel, writing in a German magazine in 1891 ("Die Astronomie der Alten Chaldäer"), drew attention to the fact that each one of the eight segments of the planisphere formed an angle of 45 degrees, from which he concluded that a total sweep of the skies—all 360 degrees of the heavens—was represented. He suggested that the focal point marked some location "in the Babylonian skies."

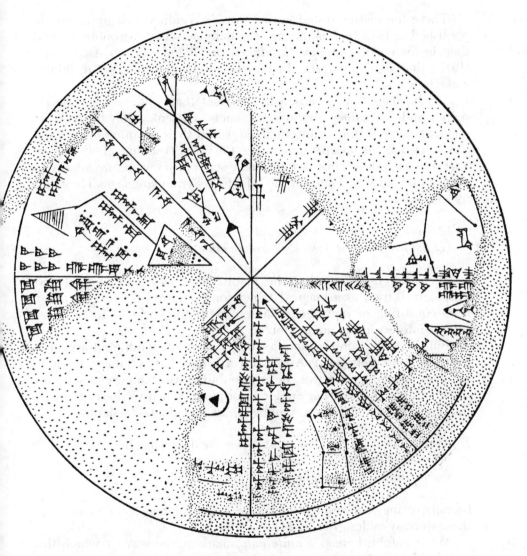

Fig. 122

There the matter rested until Ernst F. Weidner, first in an article published in 1912 (*Babyloniaca:* "Zur Babylonischen Astronomie") and then in his major textbook *Handbuch der Babylonischen Astronomie* (1915), thoroughly analyzed the tablet, only to conclude that it did not make sense.

His bafflement was caused by the fact that while the geometric shapes and the names of stars or planets written within the various segments were legible or intelligible (even if their meaning or purpose was unclear), the inscriptions along the lines (running at 45-degree angles to each other) just did not make sense. They were, invariably, a series of repeated syllables in the tablet's Assyrian language. They ran, for example, thus:

> *lu bur di   lu bur di   lu bur di*
> *bat bat bat kash kash kash kash alu alu alu alu*

Weidner concluded that the plaque was both astronomical and astrological, used as a magical tablet for exorcism, like several other texts consisting of repeated syllables. With this, he laid to rest any further interest in the unique tablet.

But the tablet's inscriptions assume a completely different aspect if we try to read them not as Assyrian word-signs, but as Sumerian word-syllables; for there can hardly any doubt that the tablet represents an Assyrian copy of an earlier Sumerian original. When we look at one of the segments (which we can number I), its meaningless syllables

> *na na na na   a na   a na nu* (along the descending line)
> *sha sha sha sha sha sha* (along the circumference)
> *sham sham bur kur Kur* (along the horizontal line)

literally spring to meaningfulness if we enter the Sumerian meaning of these word-syllables. (Fig. 123)

What unfolds here is a *route map*, marking the way by which the god Enlil "went by the planets," accompanied by some operating instructions. The line inclined at 45 degrees appears to indicate the line of a spaceship's descent from a point which is "high high high high," through "vapor clouds" and a lower zone that is vaporless, toward the horizon point, where the skies and the ground meet.

In the skies near the horizontal line, the instructions to the astronauts make sense: They are told to "set set set" their instruments for the final approach; then, as they near the ground, "rockets rockets" are fired to slow the craft, which apparently should be raised ("piled up") before reaching the landing point because it has to pass over high or rugged terrain ("mountain mountain").

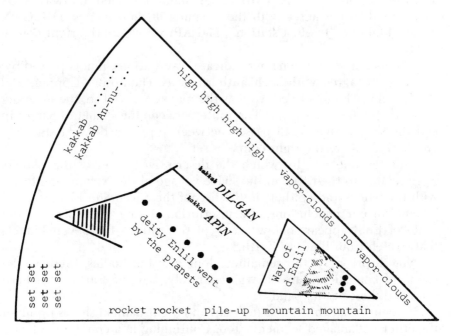

Fig. 123

The information provided in this segment clearly pertains to a space voyage by Enlil himself. In this first segment we are given a precise geometric sketch of two triangles connected by a line that turns at an angle. The line represents a route, for the inscription clearly states that the sketch shows how the "deity Enlil went by the planets."

The starting point is the triangle on the left, representing the farther reaches of the solar system; the target area is on the right, where all the segments converge toward the landing point.

The triangle on the left, drawn with its base open, is akin to a known sign in Near Eastern pictographic writing; its meaning can be read as "the ruler's domain, the mountainous land." The triangle on the right is identified by the inscription *shu-ut il Enlil* ("Way of god Enlil"); the term, as we know, denotes Earth's northern skies.

The angled line, then, connects what we believe to have been the Twelfth Planet—"the ruler's domain, the mountainous land"—with Earth's skies. The route passes between two celestial bodies—Dilgan and Apin.

Some scholars have maintained that these were names of distant stars or parts of constellations. If modern manned and unmanned spacecraft navigate by obtaining a "fix" on predetermined bright stars, a similar navigational technique for the Nefilim cannot be ruled out.

Yet the notion that the two names stand for such faraway stars somehow does not agree with the meaning of their names: DIL.GAN meant, literally, "the first station"; and APIN, "where the right course is set."

The meanings of the names indicate way stations, points passed by. We tend to agree with such authorities as Thompson, Epping, and Strassmaier, who identified Apin as the planet Mars. If so, the meaning of the sketch becomes clear: The route between the Planet of Kingship and the skies above Earth passed between Jupiter ("the first station") and Mars ("where the right course is set").

This terminology, by which the descriptive names of the planets were related to their role in the space voyage of the Nefilim, conforms with the names and epithets in the lists of the Seven *Shu* Planets. As if to confirm our conclusions, the inscription stating that this was the route of Enlil appears below a row of seven dots—the Seven Planets that stretch from Pluto to Earth.

Not surprisingly, the remaining four celestial bodies, those in the "zone of confusion," are shown separately, beyond Earth's northern skies and the celestial band.

Evidence that this is a space map and flight manual shows up in all the other undamaged segments, too. Continuing in a counterclockwise direction, the legible portion of the next segment bears the inscription: "take take take   cast cast cast cast   complete complete." The third segment, where a portion of the unusual elliptical shape is seen, the legible inscriptions include "*kakkab* SIB.ZI.AN.NA . . . envoy of AN.NA . . . deity ISH.TAR," and the intriguing sentence: "Deity NI.NI supervisor of descent."

In the fourth segment, which contains what appear to be directions on how to establish one's destination according to a certain group of stars, the descending line is specifically identified as the skyline: The word *sky* is repeated eleven times under the line.

Does this segment represent a flight phase nearer Earth, nearer the landing spot? This might indeed be the import of the legend over the horizontal line: "hills hills hills hills   top top top top   city city city city." The inscription in the center says: "*kakkab* MASH.TAB.BA [Gemini] whose encounter is fixed; *kakkab* SIB.ZI.AN.NA [Jupiter] provides knowledge."

If, as appears to be the case, the segments are arranged in an approach sequence, then one can almost share the excitement of the Nefilim as they approached Earth's spaceport. The next segment, again identifying the descending line as "sky sky sky," also announces:

our light   our light   our light
change   change   change   change
observe path and high ground
. . . flat land . . .

The horizontal line contains, for the first time, figures:

rocket   rocket
rocket   rise   glide
40 40 40
40 40 20 22 22

The upper line of the next segment no longer states: "sky sky"; instead, it calls for "channel channel   100 100 100 100 100 100 100." A pattern is discernible in this largely damaged segment. Along one of the lines the inscription says: *"Ashshur,"* which can mean "He who sees" or "seeing."

The seventh segment is too damaged to add to our examination; the few discernible syllables mean "distant distant . . . sight sight," and the instructional words are "press down." The eighth and final segment, however, is almost complete. Directional lines, arrows, and inscriptions mark a path between two planets. Instructions to "pile up   mountain mountain," show four sets of crosses, inscribed twice "fuel water grain" and twice "vapor water grain."

Was this a segment dealing with preparations for the flight toward Earth, or one dealing with stocking up for the return flight to rejoin the Twelfth Planet? The latter may have been the case, for the line with the sharp arrow pointing toward the landing site on Earth has at its other end another "arrow" pointing in the opposite direction, and bearing the legend *"Return."* (Fig. 124)

When Ea arranged for Anu's emissary to "make Adapa take the road to Heaven" and Anu discovered the ruse, he demanded to know:

Why did Ea, to a worthless human
the plan of Heaven-Earth disclose—
rendering him distinguished,
making a *Shem* for him?

In the planisphere we have just deciphered, we indeed see such a route map, a "plan of Heaven-Earth." In sign language and in words, the Nefilim have sketched for us the route from their planet to ours.

Otherwise inexplicable texts dealing with celestial distances also

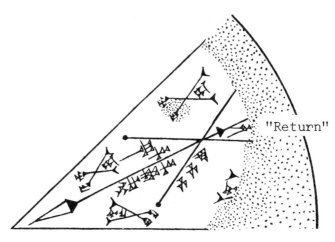

Fig. 124

make sense if we read them in terms of space travel from the Twelfth Planet. One such text, found in the ruins of Nippur and believed to be some 4,000 years old, is now kept at the Hilprecht Collection at the University of Jena, in Germany. O. Neugebauer (*The Exact Sciences in Antiquity*) established that the tablet was undoubtedly a copy "from an original composition which was older"; it gives ratios of celestial distances starting from the Moon to Earth and then through space to six other planets.

The second part of the text appears to have provided the mathematical formulas for solving whatever the interplanetary problem was, stating (according to some readings):

40 4 20 6 40 × 9 is 6 40
13 kasbu 10 ush mul SHU.PA
eli mul GIR sud
40 4 20 6 40 × 7 is 5 11 6 40
10 kasbu 11 ush 6½ gar 2 u mul GIR tab
eli mul SHU.PA sud

There has never been full agreement among scholars as to the correct reading of the measurement units in this part of the text (a new reading was suggested to us in a letter from Dr. J. Oelsner, custodian of the Hilprecht Collection at Jena). It is clear, however, that the second part of the text measured distances from SHU.PA (Pluto).

Only the Nefilim, traversing the planetary orbits, could have worked out these formulas; only they needed such data.

Taking into consideration that their own planet and their target, Earth, were both in continuous motion, the Nefilim had to aim their craft not at where Earth was at launch time but where it would be at arrival time. One can safely assume that the Nefilim worked out their trajectories very much as modern scientists map the missions to the Moon and to other planets.

The spacecraft of the Nefilim was probably launched from the Twelfth Planet in the direction of the Twelfth Planet's own orbit, but well ahead of its arrival in Earth's vicinity. Based on these and a myriad other factors, two alternative trajectories for the spacecraft were worked out for us by Amnon Sitchin, doctor of aeronautics and engineering. The first trajectory would call for the launching of the spacecraft from the Twelfth Planet before it reached its apogee (the point farthest out). With few power needs, the spaceship would actually not so much change course as slow down. While the Twelfth Planet (a space vehicle, too, even though a huge one) continued on its vast elliptical orbit, the spaceship would follow a much shorter elliptical course and reach Earth far ahead of the Twelfth Planet. This alternative may have offered the Nefilim both advantages and disadvantages.

The full span of 3,600 Earth years, which applied to tenures of office and other activities of the Nefilim upon Earth, suggests that they might have preferred the second alternative, that of a short trip and a stay in Earth's skies coinciding with the arrival of the Twelfth Planet itself. This would have called for the launching of the spaceship (C) when the Twelfth Planet was about midway on its course back from the apogee. With the planet's own speed rapidly increasing, the spaceship required strong engines to overtake its home planet and reach Earth (D) a few Earth years ahead of the Twelfth Planet. (Fig. 125)

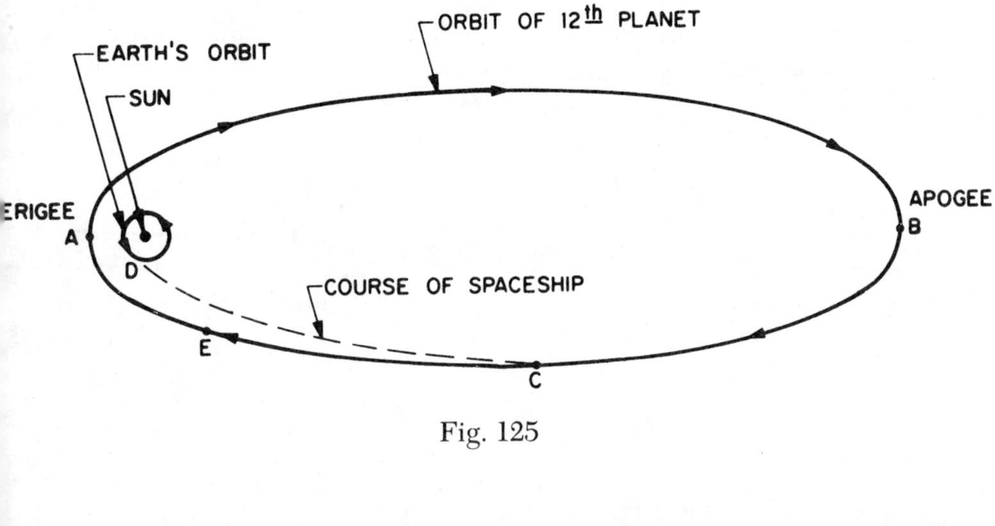

Fig. 125

Based on complex technical data, as well as hints in Mesopotamian texts, it appears that the Nefilim adopted for their Earth missions the same approach NASA adopted for the Moon missions: When the principal spaceship neared the target planet (Earth), it went into orbit around that planet without actually landing. Instead, a smaller craft was released from the mother ship and performed the actual landing.

As difficult as accurate landings were, the departures from Earth must have been even trickier. The landing craft had to rejoin its mother ship, which then had to fire up its engines and accelerate to extremely high speeds, for it had to catch up with the Twelfth Planet, which by then was passing its perigee between Mars and Jupiter at its top orbital speed. Dr. Sitchin has calculated that there were three points in the spaceship's orbit of Earth that lent themselves to a thrust toward the Twelfth Planet. The three alternatives offered the Nefilim a choice of catching up with the Twelfth Planet within 1.1 to 1.6 Earth years.

Suitable terrain, guidance from Earth, and perfect coordination with the home planet were required for successful arrivals, landings, takeoffs, and departures from Earth.

As we shall see, the Nefilim met all these requirements.

10

•

CITIES OF THE GODS

The story of the first settlement of Earth by intelligent beings is a breathtaking saga no less inspiring than the discovery of America or the circumnavigation of Earth. It was certainly of greater importance, for, as a result of this settlement, we and our civilizations exist today.

The "Epic of Creation" informs us that the "gods" came to Earth following a deliberate decision by their leader. The Babylonian version, attributing the decision to Marduk, explains that he waited until Earth's soil dried and hardened sufficiently to permit landing and construction operations. Then Marduk announced his decision to the group of astronauts:

> In the deep Above,
> where you have been residing,
> "The Kingly House of Above" have I built.
> Now, a counterpart of it
> I shall build in The Below.

Marduk then explained his purpose:

> When from the Heavens
> for assembly you shall descend,
> there shall be a restplace for the night
> to receive you all.
> I will name it "Babylon"—
> The Gateway of the Gods.

Earth was thus not merely the object of a visit or a quick, exploratory stay; it was to be a permanent "home away from home."

Traveling on board a planet that was itself a kind of spaceship, crossing the paths of most of the other planets, the Nefilim no doubt first scanned the heavens from the surface of their own planet.

Unmanned probes must have followed. Sooner or later they acquired the capacity to send out manned missions to the other planets.

As the Nefilim searched for an additional "home," Earth must have struck them favorably. Its blue hues indicated it had life-sustaining water and air; its browns disclosed firm land; its greens, vegetation and the basis for animal life. Yet when the Nefilim finally voyaged to Earth, it must have looked somewhat different from the way it does to our astronauts today. For when the Nefilim first came to Earth, Earth was in the midst of an ice age—a glacial period that was one of the icing and deicing phases of Earth's climate.

Early glaciation—begun some 600,000 years ago
First warming (interglacial period)—550,000 years ago
Second glacial period—480,000 to 430,000 years ago

When the Nefilim first landed on Earth some 450,000 years ago, about a third of Earth's land area was covered with ice sheets and glaciers. With so much of Earth's waters frozen, rainfall was reduced, but not everywhere. Due to the peculiarities of wind patterns and terrain, among other things, some areas that are well watered today were barren then, and some areas with only seasonal rains now were experiencing year-round rainfalls then.

The sea levels were also lower because so much water had been captured as ice on the land masses. Evidence indicates that at the height of the two major ice ages, sea levels were as much as 600 to 700 feet lower than at present. Therefore, there was dry land where we now have seas and coastlines. Where rivers continued to run, they created deep gorges and canyons if their courses took them through rocky terrain; if their courses ran in soft earth and clay, they reached the ice-age seas through vast marshlands.

Arriving on Earth amidst such climatic and geographic conditions, where were the Nefilim to set up their first abode?

They searched, no doubt, for a place with a relatively temperate climate, where simple shelters would suffice and where they could move about in light working clothes rather than in heavily insulated suits. They must also have searched for water for drinking, washing, and industrial purposes, as well as to sustain the plant and animal life needed for food. Rivers would both facilitate the irrigation of large tracts of land and provide a convenient means of transportation.

Only a rather narrow temperate zone on Earth could meet all these requirements, as well as the need for the long, flat areas suitable for landings. The attention of the Nefilim, as we now know, focused on three major river systems and their plains: the Nile, the Indus, and the

Tigris–Euphrates. Each of these river basins was suitable for early colonization; each, in time, became the center of an ancient civilization.

The Nefilim would hardly have ignored another need: a source of fuel and energy. On Earth, petroleum has been a versatile and abundant source of energy, heat, and light, as well as a vital raw material from which countless essential goods are made. The Nefilim, judging by Sumerian practice and records, made extensive use of petroleum and its derivatives; it stands to reason that in their search for the most suitable habitat on Earth, the Nefilim would prefer a site rich in petroleum.

With this in mind, the Nefilim probably placed the Indus plain in last place, for it is not an area where oil could be found. The Nile valley was probably given second place; geologically it lies in a major sedimentary rock zone, but the area's oil is found only at some distance from the valley and requires deep drilling. The Land of the Two Rivers, Mesopotamia, was doubtless put in first place. Some of the world's richest oil fields stretch from the tip of the Persian Gulf to the mountains where the Tigris and Euphrates originate. And while in most places one must drill deep to bring up the crude oil, in ancient Sumer (now southern Iraq), bitumens, tars, pitches, and asphalts bubbled or flowed up to the surface naturally.

(Interestingly, the Sumerians had names for *all* bituminous substances—petroleum, crude oils, native asphalts, rock asphalts, tars, pyrogenic asphalts, mastics, waxes, and pitches. They had nine different names for the various bitumens. By comparison, the ancient Egyptian language had only two, and Sanskrit, only three.)

The Book of Genesis describes God's abode on Earth—Eden—as a place of temperate climate, warm yet breezy, for God took afternoon strolls to catch the cooling breeze. It was a place of good soil, lending itself to agriculture and horticulture, especially the cultivation of orchards. It was a place that drew its waters from a network of four rivers. "And the name of the third river [was] Hidekel [Tigris]; it is the one which floweth towards the east of Assyria; and the fourth was the Euphrates."

While opinions regarding the identity of the first two rivers, Pishon ("abundant") and Gihon ("which gushes forth"), are inconclusive, there is no uncertainty regarding the other two rivers, the Tigris and the Euphrates. Some scholars locate Eden in northern Mesopotamia, where the two rivers and two lesser tributaries originate; others (such as E. A. Speiser, in *The Rivers of Paradise*) believe that the four streams converged at the head of the Persian Gulf, so that Eden was not in northern but in southern Mesopotamia.

The biblical name Eden is of Mesopotamian origin, stemming from the Akkadian *edinu*, meaning "plain." We recall that the "divine" title of the ancient gods was DIN.GIR ("the righteous/just ones of the rockets"). A Sumerian name for the gods' abode, E.DIN, would have meant "home of the righteous ones"—a fitting description.

The selection of Mesopotamia as the home on Earth was probably motivated by at least one other important consideration. Though the Nefilim in time established a spaceport on dry land, some evidence suggests that at least initially they landed by splashing down into the sea in a hermetically sealed capsule. If this was the landing method, Mesopotamia offered proximity to not one but two seas—the Indian Ocean to the south and the Mediterranean to the west—so that in case of an emergency, the landing did not have to depend on one watery site alone. As we shall see, a good bay or gulf from which long sea voyages could be launched was also essential.

In ancient texts and pictures, the craft of the Nefilim were initially termed "celestial boats." The landing of such "maritime" astronauts, one can imagine, might have been described in ancient epic tales as the appearance of some kind of submarine from the heavens in the sea, from which "fish-men" emerged and came ashore.

The texts do, in fact, mention that some of the AB.GAL who navigated the spaceships were dressed as fish. One text dealing with Ishtar's divine journeys quotes her as seeking to reach the "Great *gallu*" (chief navigator) who had gone away "in a sunken boat." Berossus transmitted legends regarding Oannes, the "Being Endowed with Reason," a god who made his appearance from "the Erythrean sea which bordered on Babylonia," in the first year of the descent of Kingship from Heaven. Berossus reported that though Oannes looked like a fish, he had a human head under the fish's head, and had feet like a man under the fish's tail. "His voice too and language were articulate and human." (Fig. 126)

The three Greek historians through whom we know what Berossus wrote, reported that such divine fish-men appeared periodically, coming ashore from the "Erythrean sea"—the body of water we now call the Arabian Sea (the western part of the Indian Ocean).

Why would the Nefilim splash down in the Indian Ocean, hundreds of miles from their selected site in Mesopotamia, instead of in the Persian Gulf, which is so much closer? The ancient reports indirectly confirm our conclusion that the first landings occurred during the second glacial period, when today's Persian Gulf was not a sea but a stretch of marshlands and shallow lakes, in which a splashdown was impossible.

Coming down in the Arabian Sea, the first intelligent beings or

Fig. 126

Earth then made their way toward Mesopotamia. The marshlands extended deeper inland than today's coastline. There, at the edge of the marshes, they established their very first settlement on our planet.

They named it E.RI.DU ("house in faraway built"). What an appropriate name!

To this very day, the Persian term *ordu* means "encampment." It is a word whose meaning has taken root in all languages: The settled Earth is called *Erde* in German, *Erda* in Old High German, *Jördh* in Icelandic, *Jord* in Danish, *Airtha* in Gothic, *Erthe* in Middle English; and, going back geographically and in time, "Earth" was *Aratha* or *Ereds* in Aramaic, *Erd* or *Ertz* in Kurdish, and *Eretz* in Hebrew.

At Eridu, in southern Mesopotamia, the Nefilim established Earth Station I, a lonely outpost on a half-frozen planet. (Fig. 127)

Sumerian texts, confirmed by later Akkadian translations, list the original settlements or "cities" of the Nefilim in the order in which they were established. We are even told which god was put in charge of each of these settlements. A Sumerian text, believed to have been the original of the Akkadian "Deluge Tablets," relates the following regarding five of the first seven cities:

After kingship had been lowered from heaven,
after the exalted crown, the throne of kingship
had been lowered from heaven,
he ... perfected the procedures,
the divine ordinances. ...
Founded five cities in pure places,
called their names,
laid them out as centers.

A lonely outpost on an alien planet:

Asia as it probably looked like from the air in the midst

of an ice stage. Lower sea levels meant coastlines different from

ours today. The Persian Gulf and southern Mesopotamia were patches

of muddy ground, lakes and marshlands.

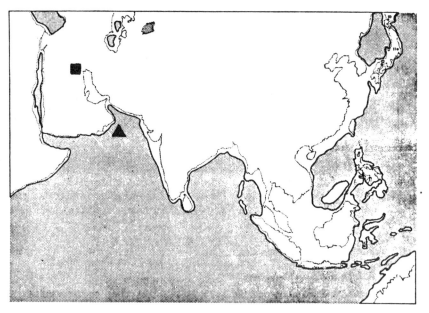

········ Present-day coastlines

▲ Presumed splashdown spot in the Arabian sea

■ Location of Eridu, at the edge of the marshlands

Fig. 127

The first of these cities, ERIDU,
he gave to Nudimmud, the leader.
The second, BAD-TIBIRA,
he gave to Nugig.
The third, LARAK,
he gave to Pabilsag.
The fourth, SIPPAR,
he gave to the hero Utu.
The fifth, SHURUPPAK,
he gave to Sud.

The name of the god who lowered Kingship from Heaven, planned the establishment of Eridu and four other cities, and appointed their governors or commanders, is unfortunately obliterated. All the texts agree, however, that the god who waded ashore to the edge of the marshlands and said "Here we settle" was Enki, nicknamed "Nudimmud" ("he who made things") in the text.

This god's two names—EN.KI ("lord of firm ground") and E.A ("whose house is water")—were most appropriate. Eridu, which remained Enki's seat of power and center of worship throughout Mesopotamian history, was built on ground artificially raised above the waters of the marshlands. The evidence is contained in a text named (by S. N. Kramer) the "Myth of Enki and Eridu":

The lord of the watery-deep, the king Enki . . .
built his house. . . .
In Eridu he built the House of the Water Bank. . . .
The king Enki . . . has built a house:
Eridu, like a mountain,
he raised up from the earth;
in a good place he had built it.

These and other, mostly fragmentary texts suggest that one of the first concerns of these "colonists" on Earth had to do with the shallow lakes or watery marshes. "He brought . . .; established the cleaning of the small rivers." The effort to dredge the beds of streams and tributaries to allow a better flow of the waters was intended to drain the marshes, obtain cleaner, potable water, and implement controlled irrigation. The Sumerian narrative also indicates some landfilling or the raising of dikes to protect the first houses from the omnipresent waters.

A text named by scholars the "myth" of "Enki and the Land's Order" is one of the longest and best preserved of Sumerian narrative poems so far uncovered. Its text consists of some 470 lines, of which 375 are perfectly legible. Its beginning (some 50 lines) is, unfortunately, broken. The verses that follow are devoted to an exaltation of Enki and to the establishment of his relationship with the chief deity Anu (his father), Ninti (his sister), and Enlil (his brother).

Following these introductions, Enki himself "picks up the microphone." As fantastic as it may sound, the fact is that the text amounts to a first-person report by Enki of his landing on Earth.

"When I approached Earth,
there was much flooding.
When I approached its green meadows,
heaps and mounds were piled up
at my command.
I built my house in a pure place. . . .
My house—
Its shade stretches over the Snake Marsh. . . .
The carp fish wave their tails in it
among the small *gizi* reeds."

The poem then goes on to describe and record, in the third person, the achievements of Enki. Here are some selected verses:

He marked the marshland,
placed in it carp and . . .—fish;
He marked the cane thicket,
placed in it . . .—reeds and green-reeds.
Enbilulu, the Inspector of Canals,
he placed in charge of the marshlands.

Him who set net so no fish escapes,
whose trap no . . . escapes,
whose snare no bird escapes,
. . . the son of . . . a god who loves fish
Enki placed in charge of fish and birds.

Enkimdu, the one of the ditch and dike,
Enki placed in charge of ditch and dike.

Him whose . . . mold directs,
Kulla, the brick-maker of the Land,
Enki placed in charge of mold and brick.

The poem lists other achievements of Enki, including the purification of the waters of the Tigris River and the joining (by canal) of the

Tigris and Euphrates. His house by the watery bank adjoined a wharf at which reed rafts and boats could anchor, and from which they could sail off. Appropriately, the house was named E.ABZU ("house of the Deep"). Enki's sacred precinct in Eridu was known by this name for millennia thereafter.

No doubt Enki and his landing party explored the lands around Eridu, but he appears to have preferred traveling by water. The marshland, he said in one of the texts, "is my favorite spot; it stretches out its arms to me." In other texts Enki described sailing in the marshlands in his boat, named MA.GUR (literally, "boat to turn about in"), namely, a touring boat. He tells how his crewmen "drew on the oars in unison," how they used to "sing sweet songs, causing the river to rejoice." At such times, he confided, "sacred songs and spells filled my Watery Deep." Even such a minor detail as the name of the captain of Enki's boat is recorded. (Fig. 128)

Fig. 128

The Sumerian king lists indicate that Enki and his first group of Nefilim remained alone on Earth for quite a while: Eight *shar*'s (28,800 years) passed before the second commander or "settlement chief" was named.

Interesting light is shed on the subject as we examine the astronomical evidence. Scholars have been puzzled by the apparent Sumerian "confusion" regarding which one of the twelve zodiacal houses was associated with Enki. The sign of the fish-goat, which stood for the constellation Capricorn, was apparently associated with Enki (and, indeed, may explain the epithet of the founder of Eridu, A.LU.LIM, which could mean "sheep of the glittering waters"). Yet Ea/Enki was frequently depicted as holding vases of flowing waters—the original Water Bearer, or Aquarius; and he was certainly the God of Fishes, and thus associated with Pisces.

Astronomers are hard put to clarify how the ancient stargazers actually saw in a group of stars the outlines of, say, fishes or a water bearer. The answer that comes to mind is that the signs of the zodiac were not named after the shape of the star group but after the epithet or main activity of a god primarily associated with the time when the vernal equinox was in that particular zodiacal house.

If Enki landed on Earth—as we believe—at the end of an Age of Pisces, witnessed a precessional shift to Aquarius, and stayed through a Great Year (25,920 years) until an Age of Capricorn began, then he was indeed in sole command on Earth the purported 28,800 years.

The reported passage of time also confirms our earlier conclusion that the Nefilim arrived on Earth in the midst of an ice age. The hard work of raising dikes and digging canals commenced when climatic conditions were still harsh. But within a few *shar*'s of their landing, the glacial period was giving way to a warmer and rainier climate (circa 430,000 years ago). It was then that the Nefilim decided to move farther inland and expand their settlements. Befittingly, the Anunnaki (rank-and-file Nefilim) named the second commander of Eridu A.LAL.GAR ("he who in raintime brought rest.")

But while Enki was enduring the hardships of a pioneer on Earth, Anu and his other son Enlil were watching the developments from the Twelfth Planet. The Mesopotamian texts make it clear that the one who was really in charge of the Earth mission was Enlil; and as soon as the decision was made to proceed with the mission, Enlil himself descended to Earth. For him a special settlement or base named Larsa was built by EN.KI.DU.NU ("Enki digs deep"). When Enlil took personal charge of the place, he was nicknamed ALIM ("ram"), coinciding with the "age" of the zodiacal constellation Aries.

The establishment of Larsa launched a new phase in the settlement of Earth by the Nefilim. It marked the decision to proceed with the tasks for which they had come to Earth, which required the shipping to Earth of more "manpower," tools, and equipment, and the return of valuable cargoes to the Twelfth Planet.

Splashdowns at sea were no longer adequate for such heavier loads. The climatic changes made the interior more accessible; it was time to shift the landing site to the center of Mesopotamia. At that juncture, Enlil came to Earth and proceeded from Larsa to establish a "Mission Control Center"—a sophisticated command post from which the Nefilim on Earth could coordinate space journeys to and from their home planet, guide in landing shuttlecraft, and perfect their takeoffs and dockings with the spaceship orbiting Earth.

The site Enlil selected for this purpose, known for millennia as Nippur, was named by him NIBRU.KI ("Earth's crossing"). (We recall that the celestial site of the Twelfth Planet's closest pass to Earth was called the "Celestial Place of the Crossing.") There Enlil established the DUR.AN.KI, the "bond Heaven–Earth."

The task was understandably complex and time-consuming. Enlil stayed in Larsa for 6 *shar*'s (21,600 years) while Nippur was under construction. The Nippurian undertaking was also lengthy, as evidenced by the zodiacal nicknames of Enlil. Having paralleled the Ram (Aries) while in Larsa, he was subsequently associated with the Bull (Taurus). Nippur was established in the "age" of Taurus.

A devotional poem composed as a "Hymn to Enlil, the All-Beneficent" and glorifying Enlil, his consort Ninlil, his city Nippur, and its "lofty house," the E.KUR, tells us much about Nippur. For one thing, Enlil had at his disposal there some highly sophisticated instruments: a "lifted 'eye' which scans the land," and a "lifted beam which searches the heart of all the land." Nippur, the poem tells us, was protected by awesome weapons: "Its sight is awesome fear, dread"; from "its outside, no mighty god can approach." Its "arm" was a "vast net," and in its midst there crouched a "fast-stepping bird," a "bird" whose "hand" the wicked and the evil could not escape. Was the place protected by some death ray, by an electronic power field? Was there in its center a helicopter pad, a "bird" so swift no one could outrun its reach?

In the center of Nippur, atop an artificially raised platform, stood Enlil's headquarters, the KI.UR ("place of Earth's root")—the place where the "bond between Heaven and Earth" rose. This was the communications center of Mission Control, the place from which the Anunnaki on Earth communicated with their comrades, the IGI.GI ("they who turn and see") in the orbiting spacecraft.

At this center, the ancient text goes on to say, stood a "heavenward tall pillar reaching to the sky." This extremely tall "pillar," firmly planted on the ground "as a platform that cannot be overturned," was used by Enlil to "pronounce his word" heavenward. This is a simple description of a broadcasting tower. Once the "word of Enlil"—his command—"approached heaven, abundance would pour down on Earth." What a simple way to describe the flow of materials, special foods, medicines, and tools brought down by the shuttlecraft, once the "word" from Nippur was given!

This Control Center on a raised platform, Enlil's "lofty house," contained a mysterious chamber, named the DIR.GA:

> As mysterious as the distant Waters,
> as the Heavenly Zenith.
> Among its . . . emblems,

the emblems of the stars.
The ME it carries to perfection.
Its words are for utterance. . . .
Its words are gracious oracles.

What was this *dirga?* Breaks in the ancient tablet have robbed us of more data; but the name speaks for itself, for it means "the dark, crownlike chamber," a place where star charts were kept, where predictions were made, where the *me* (the astronaut's communications) were received and transmitted. The description reminds us of Mission Control in Houston, Texas, monitoring the astronauts on their Moon missions, amplifying their communications, plotting their courses against the starry sky, giving them "gracious oracles" of guidance.

We may recall here the tale of the god Zu, who made his way to Enlil's sanctuary and snatched away the Tablet of Destinies, whereupon "suspended was the issuance of commands . . . the hallowed inner chamber lost its brilliance . . . stillness spread . . . silence prevailed."

In the "Epic of Creation," the "destinies" of the planetary gods were their orbits. It is reasonable to assume that the Tablet of Destinies, which was so vital to the functions of Enlil's "Mission Control Center," also controlled the orbits and flight paths of the spaceships that maintained the "bond" between Heaven and Earth. It might have been the vital "black box" containing the computer programs that guided the spaceships, without which the contact between the Nefilim on Earth and their link to the Home Planet was disrupted.

Most scholars take the name EN.LIL to mean "lord of the wind," which fits the theory that the ancients "personified" the elements of nature and thus assigned one god to be in charge of winds and storms. Yet some scholars have already suggested that in this instance the term LIL means not a stormy wind of nature but the "wind" that comes out of the mouth—an utterance, a command, a spoken communication. Once again, the archaic Sumerian pictographs for the term EN—especially as applied to Enlil—and for the term LIL, shed light on the subject. For what we see is a structure with a high tower of antennas rising from it, as well as a contraption that looks very much like the giant radar nets erected nowadays for capturing and emitting signals—the "vast net" described in the texts. (Fig. 129)

In Bad-Tibira, established as an industrial center, Enlil installed his son Nannar/Sin in command; the texts speak of him in the list of cities as NU.GIG ("he of the night sky"). There, we believe, the twins Inanna/Ishtar and Utu/Shamash were born—an event marked by associating their father Nannar with the next zodiacal constellation,

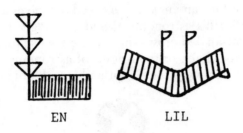

EN   LIL

Fig. 129

Gemini (the Twins). As the god trained in rocketry, Shamash was assigned the constellation GIR (meaning both "rocket" and "the crab's claw," or Cancer), followed by Ishtar and the Lion (Leo), upon whose back she was traditionally depicted.

The sister of Enlil and Enki, "the nurse" Ninhursag (SUD), was not neglected: In her charge Enlil put Shuruppak, the medical center of the Nefilim—an event marked by naming her constellation "The Maid" (Virgo).

While these centers were being established, the completion of Nippur was followed by the construction of the spaceport of the Nefilim on Earth. The texts made clear that Nippur was the place where the "words"—commands—were uttered: There, when "Enlil commanded: 'Towards heaven!' . . . that which shines forth rose like a sky rocket." But the action itself took place "where Shamash rises," and that place—the "Cape Kennedy" of the Nefilim—was Sippar, the city in the charge of the Chief of the Eagles, where multistage rockets were raised within its special enclave, the "sacred precinct."

As Shamash matured to take command of the Fiery Rockets, and in time also to become the God of Justice, he was assigned the constellations Scorpio and Libra (the Scales).

Completing the list of the first seven Cities of the Gods and the correspondence with the twelve zodiac constellations was Larak, where Enlil put his son Ninurta in command. The city lists call him PA.BIL.SAG ("great protector"); it is the same name by which the constellation Sagittarius was called.

It would be unrealistic to assume that the first seven Cities of the Gods were established haphazardly. These "gods," who were capable of space travel, located the first settlements in accordance with a definite plan, serving a vital need: to be able to land on Earth and to leave Earth for their own planet.

What was the master plan?

As we searched for an answer, we asked ourselves a question: What is the origin of Earth's astronomical and astrological symbol, a circle bisected by a right-angled cross—the symbol we use to signify "target"?

The symbol goes back to the origins of astronomy and astrology in Sumer and is identical with the Egyptian hieroglyphic sign for "place":

Is this coincidence, or significant evidence? Did the Nefilim land on Earth by superimposing on its image or map some kind of "target"?

The Nefilim were strangers to Earth. As they scanned its surface from space, they must have paid special attention to the mountains and mountain ranges. These could present hazards during landings and takeoffs, but they could also serve as navigational landmarks.

If the Nefilim, as they hovered over the Indian Ocean, looked toward the Land Between the Rivers, which they had selected for their earliest colonizing efforts, one landmark stood out unchallenged: Mount Ararat.

An extinct volcanic massif, Ararat dominates the Armenian plateau where the present-day borders of Turkey, Iran, and Soviet Armenia meet. It rises on the eastern and northern sides to some 3,000 feet above sea level, and on the northwestern side to 5,000 feet. The whole massif is some twenty-five miles in diameter, a towering dome sticking out from the surface of Earth.

Other features make it stand out not only from the horizon but also from high in the skies. First, it is located almost midway between two lakes, Lake Van and Lake So-Van. Second, two peaks rise from the high massif: Little Ararat (12,900 feet) and Great Ararat (17,000 feet—well over 5 kilometers). No other mountains rival the solitary heights of the two peaks, which are permanently snow-covered. They are like two shining beacons between the two lakes that, in daylight, act as giant reflectors.

We have reason to believe that the Nefilim selected their landing site by coordinating a north–south meridian with an unmistakable landmark and a convenient river location. North of Mesopotamia, the easily identifiable twin-peaked Ararat would have been the obvious landmark. A meridian drawn through the center of the twin-peaked Ararat bisected the Euphrates. That was the target—the site selected for the spaceport. (Fig. 130)

Could one easily land and take off there?

The answer was Yes. The selected site lay in a plain; the mountain

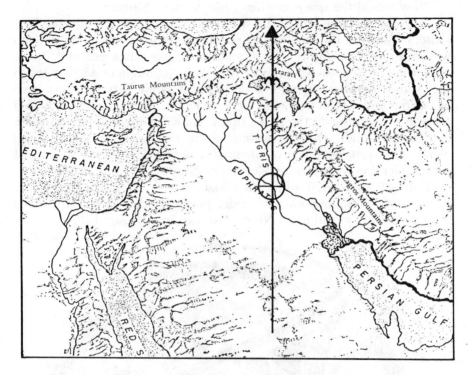

Fig. 130

ranges surrounding Mesopotamia were a substantial distance away. The highest ones (to the east, northeast, and north) would not interfere with a space shuttle gliding in from the southeast.

Was the place accessible—could astronauts and materials be brought there without too much difficulty?

Again, the answer was Yes. The site could be reached overland and, via the Euphrates River, by waterborne craft.

And one more crucial question: Was there a nearby source of energy, of fuel for light and power? The answer was an emphatic Yes. The bend in the Euphrates River where Sippar was to be established was one of the richest known sources in antiquity of surface bitumens, petroleum products that seeped up through natural wells and could be collected from the surface without any deep digging or drilling.

We can imagine Enlil, surrounded by his lieutenants at the spacecraft's command post, drawing the cross within a circle on the map. "What shall we call the place?" he may have asked.

"Why not 'Sippar'?" someone might have suggested.

In Near Eastern languages, the name means "bird." Sippar was the place where the Eagles would come to nest.

How would the space shuttles glide down to Sippar?

We can visualize one of the space navigators pointing out the best route. On the left they had the Euphrates and the mountainous plateau west of it; on the right, the Tigris and the Zagros range east of it. If the craft were to approach Sippar at the easily set angle of 45 degrees to the Ararat meridian, its path would take it safely between these two hazardous areas. Moreover, coming in to land at such an angle, it would cross in the south over the rocky tip of Arabia while at a high altitude, and start its glide over the waters of the Persian Gulf. Coming and going, the craft would have an unobstructed field of vision and of communication with Mission Control at Nippur.

Enlil's lieutenant would then make a rough sketch—a triangle of waters and mountains on each side, pointing like an arrow toward Sippar. An "X" would mark Nippur, in the center. (Fig. 131)

Fig. 131

Incredible as it may seem, this sketch was *not* made by us; the design was drawn on a ceramic object unearthed at Susa, in a stratum dated to about 3200 B.C. It brings to mind the planisphere that described the flight path and procedures, which was based on 45-degree segments.

The establishment of settlements on Earth by the Nefilim was not a hit-or-miss effort. All the alternatives were studied, all the resources evaluated, all the hazards taken into account; moreover, the settlement plan itself was carefully mapped out so that each site fit into the final pattern, whose purpose was to outline the landing path to Sippar.

No one has previously attempted to see a master plan in the scattered Sumerian settlements. But if we look at the first seven cities ever established, we find that Bad-Tibira, Shuruppak, and Nippur lay on a line running precisely at a 45-degree angle to the Ararat meridian, and that line crossed the meridian exactly at Sippar! The other two cities whose sites are known, Eridu and Larsa, also lay on another straight line that crossed the first line and the Ararat meridian, also at Sippar.

Taking our cue from the ancient sketch, which made Nippur the center of a circle, and drawing concentric circles from Nippur through the various cities, we find that another ancient Sumerian town, Lagash, was located exactly on one of these circles—on a line equidistant from the 45-degree line, like the Eridu–Larsa–Sippar line. The location of Lagash mirrors that of Larsa.

Though the site of LA.RA.AK ("seeing the bright halo") remains unknown, the logical site for it would be at Point 5, since there logically was a City of the Gods there, completing the string of cities on the central flight path at intervals of six *beru*: Bad-Tibira, Shuruppak, Nippur, Larak, Sippar. (Fig. 132)

The two outside lines, flanking the central line running through Nippur, lay 6 degrees on each side of it, acting as southwest and northeast outlines of the central flight path. Appropriately, the name LA.AR.SA meant "seeing the red light"; and LA.AG.ASH meant "seeing the halo at six." The cities along each line were indeed six *beru* (approximately sixty kilometers, or thirty-seven miles) from each other.

This, we believe, was the master plan of the Nefilim. Having selected the best location for their spaceport (Sippar), they laid out the other settlements in a pattern outlining the vital flight path to it. In the center they placed Nippur, where the "bond Heaven–Earth" was located.

Neither the original Cities of the Gods nor their remains can ever be seen by man again—they were all destroyed by the Deluge that later swept over Earth. But we can learn much about them because it was the sacred duty of Mesopotamian kings continuously to rebuild the sacred precincts in exactly the same spot and according to the original plans. The rebuilders stressed their scrupulous adherence to the original plans in their dedication inscriptions, as this one (uncovered by Layard) stated:

> The everlasting ground plan,
> that which for the future
> the construction determined
> [I have followed].
> It is the one which bears
> the drawings from the Olden Times
> and the writing of the Upper Heaven.

If Lagash, as we suggest, was one of the cities that served as a landing beacon, then much of the information provided by Gudea in the third millennium B.C. makes sense. He wrote that when Ninurta instructed him to rebuild the sacred precinct, an accompanying god gave him the architectural plans (drawn on a stone tablet), and a goddess (who had "travelled between Heaven and Earth" in her "chamber") showed him a celestial map and instructed him on the astronomical alignments of the structure.

In addition to the "divine black bird," the god's "terrible eye" ("the great beam that subdues the world to its power") and the "world controller" (whose sound could "reverberate all over") were installed in the sacred precinct. Finally, when the structure was complete, the "emblem of Utu" was raised upon it, facing "toward the rising place of Utu"—toward the spaceport at Sippar. All these beaming objects were important to the spaceport's operation, for Utu himself "came forth joyfully" to inspect the installations when completed.

Early Sumerian depictions frequently show massive structures, built in earliest times of reeds and wood, standing in fields among grazing cattle. The current assumption that these were stables for cattle is contradicted by the pillars that are invariably shown protruding from the roofs of such structures. (Fig. 133a)

The pillars' purpose, as one can see, was to support one or more pairs of "rings," whose function is unstated. But although these structures were erected in the fields, one must question whether they were built to shelter cattle. The Sumerian pictographs (Fig. 133b) depict the word DUR, or TUR (meaning "abode," "gathering place"), by drawings that undoubtedly represent the same structures shown on the cylinder seals; but they make clear that the main feature of the

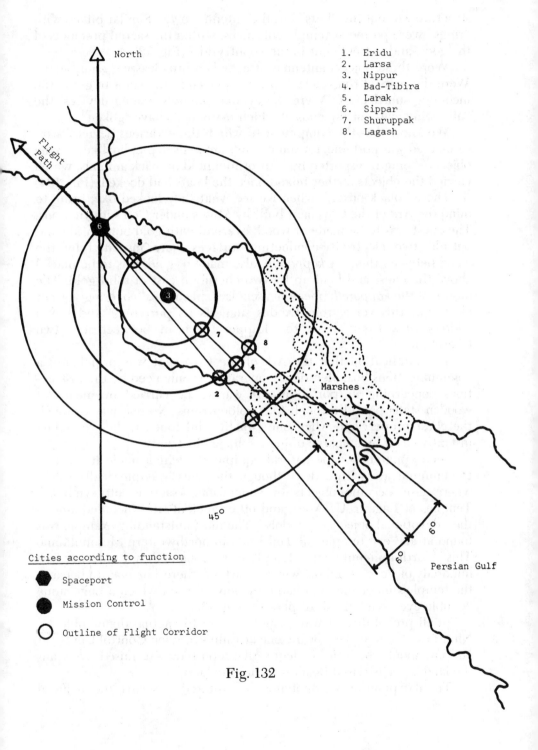

North

1. Eridu
2. Larsa
3. Nippur
4. Bad-Tibira
5. Larak
6. Sippar
7. Shuruppak
8. Lagash

Flight Path

5

6

3

7

8

4

2

1

Marshes

45°

6°

6°

Persian Gulf

Cities according to function

⬢ Spaceport

● Mission Control

○ Outline of Flight Corridor

Fig. 132

structure was not the "huts" but the antenna tower. Similar pillars with "rings" were posted at temple entrances, within the sacred precincts of the gods, and not only out in the countryside. (Fig. 133c)

Were these objects antennas attached to broadcasting equipment? Were the pairs of rings radar emitters, placed in the fields to guide the incoming shuttlecraft? Were the eyelike pillars scanning devices, the "all-seeing eyes" of the gods of which many texts have spoken?

We know that the equipment to which these various devices were connected was portable, for some Sumerian seals depict boxlike "divine objects" being transported by boat or mounted on pack animals, which carried the objects farther inland once the boats had docked. (Fig. 134)

These "black boxes," when we see what they looked like, bring to mind the Ark of the Covenant built by Moses under God's instructions. The chest was to be made of wood, overlaid with gold both inside and outside—two electricity-conducting surfaces were insulated by the wood between them. A *kapporeth*, also made of gold, was to be placed above the chest and held up by two cherubim cast of solid gold. The nature of the *kapporeth* (meaning, scholars speculate, "covering") is not clear; but this verse from Exodus suggests its purpose: "And I will address thee from above the Kapporeth, from between the two Cherubim."

The implication that the Ark of the Covenant was principally a communications box, electrically operated, is enhanced by the instructions concerning its portability. It was to be carried by means of wooden staffs passed through four golden rings. No one was to touch the chest proper; and when one Israelite did touch it, he was killed instantly—as if by a charge of high-voltage electricity.

Such apparently supernatural equipment—which made it possible to communicate with a deity though the deity was physically somewhere else—became objects of veneration, "sacred cult symbols." Temples at Lagash, Ur, Mari, and other ancient sites included among their devotional objects "eye idols." The most outstanding example was found at an "eye temple" at Tell Brak, in northwestern Mesopotamia. This fourth-millennium B.C. temple was so named not only because hundreds of "eye" symbols were unearthed there but mainly because the temple's inner sanctum had only one altar, on which a huge stone "double-eye" symbol was displayed. (Fig. 135)

In all probability, it was a simulation of the actual divine object—Ninurta's "terrible eye," or the one at Enlil's Mission Control Center at Nippur, about which the ancient scribe reported: "His raised Eye scans the land. . . . His raised Beam searches the land."

The flat plain of Mesopotamia necessitated, it seems, the artificial

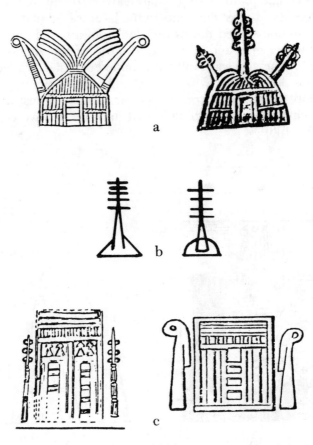

a

b

c

Fig. 133

Fig. 134

raising of platforms on which the space-related equipment was to be placed. Texts and pictorial depictions leave no doubt that the structures ranged from the earliest field huts to the later staged platforms, reached by staircases and sloped ramps that led from a broad lower stage to a narrower upper one, and so on. At the top of the ziggurat an actual residence for the god was built, surrounded by a flat, walled courtyard to house his "bird" and "weapons." A ziggurat depicted on a cylinder seal not only shows the customary stage-upon-stage construction, it also has two "ring antennas" whose height appears to have equaled three stages. (Fig. 136)

Fig. 135

Fig. 136

Marduk claimed that the ziggurat and temple compound at Babylon (the E.SAG.IL) had been built under his own instructions, also in accordance with the "writing of Upper Heaven." A tablet (known as the Smith Tablet, after its decipherer), analyzed by André Parrot (*Ziggurats et Tour de Babel*) established that the seven-stage ziggurat was a perfect square, with the first stage or base having sides of 15 *gar* each. Each successive stage was smaller in area and in height, except the last stage (the god's residence), which was of a greater height. The total height, however, was again equal to 15 *gar*, so that the complete structure was not only a perfect square but a perfect cube as well.

The *gar* employed in these measurements was equivalent to 12 short cubits—approximately 6 meters, or 20 feet. Two scholars, H. G. Wood and L. C. Stecchini, have shown that the Sumerian sexagesimal base, the number 60, determined all the primary measurements of Mesopotamian ziggurats. Thus each side measured 3 by 60 cubits at its base, and the total was 60 *gar*. (Fig. 137)

What factor determined the height of each stage? Stecchini discovered that if he multiplied the height of the first stage (5.5 *gar*) by double cubits, the result was 33, or the approximate latitude of Babylon (32.5 degrees North). Similarly calculated, the second stage raised the angle of observation to 51 degrees, and each of the succeeding four stages raised it by another 6 degrees. The seventh stage thus stood atop a platform raised to 75 degrees above the horizon at Babylon's geographic latitude. This final stage added 15 degrees—letting the observer look straight up, at a 90-degree angle. Stecchini concluded that each stage acted like a stage of an astronomical observatory, with a predetermined elevation relative to the arc of the sky.

There may, of course, have been more "hidden" considerations in these measurements. While the elevation of 33 degrees was not too accurate for Babylon, it was precise for Sippar. Was there a relationship between the 6-degree elevation at each of four stages and the 6-*beru* distances between the Cities of the Gods? Were the seven stages somehow related to the location of the first seven settlements, or to Earth's position as the seventh planet?

G. Martiny (*Astronomisches zur babylonischen Turm*) showed how these features of the ziggurat suited it for celestial observations, and that the topmost stage of the Esagila was oriented toward the planet Shupa (which we have identified as Pluto) and the constellation Aries. (Fig. 138)

But were the ziggurats raised solely to observe the stars and planets, or were they also meant to serve the spacecraft of the Nefilim? All the ziggurats were oriented so that their corners pointed exactly north, south, east, and west. As a result, their sides ran precisely at 45-degree angles to the four cardinal directions. This meant that a space shuttle coming in for a landing could follow certain sides of the ziggurat exactly along the flight path—and reach Sippar without difficulty!

The Akkadian/Babylonian name for these structures, *zukiratu*, connoted "tube of divine spirit." The Sumerians called the ziggurats ESH; the term denoted "supreme" or "most high"—as indeed these structures were. It could also denote a numerical entity relating to the "measuring" aspect of the ziggurats. And it also meant "a heat source" ("fire" in Akkadian and Hebrew).

Even scholars who have approached the subject without our "space" interpretation could not escape the conclusion that the ziggurats had some purpose other than to make the god's abode a "high-rise" building. Samuel N. Kramer summed up the scholastic

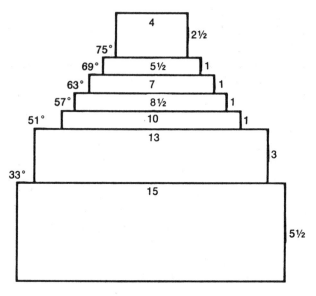

Fig. 137

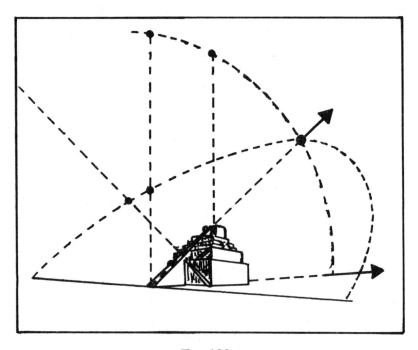

Fig. 138

consensus: "The ziggurat, the stagetower, which became the hallmark of Mesopotamian temple architecture ... was intended to serve as a connecting link, both real and symbolic, between the gods in heaven and the mortals on earth."

We have shown, however, that the true function of these structures was to connect the gods in Heaven with the gods—not the mortals—on Earth.

11

•

MUTINY OF THE ANUNNAKI

After Enlil arrived on Earth in person, "Earth Command" was transferred out of Enki's hands. It was probably at this point that Enki's epithet or name was changed to E.A ("lord waters") rather than "lord earth."

The Sumerian texts explain that at that early stage in the arrival of the gods on Earth, a separation of powers was agreed upon: Anu was to stay in the heavens and rule over the Twelfth Planet; Enlil was to command the lands; and Enki was put in charge of the AB.ZU (*apsu* in Akkadian). Guided by the "watery" meaning of the name E.A, scholars have translated AB.ZU as "watery deep," assuming that, as in Greek mythology, Enlil represented the thundering Zeus, and Ea was the prototype of Poseidon, God of the Oceans.

In other instances, Enlil's domain was referred to as the Upper World, and Ea's as the Lower World; again, the scholars assumed that the terms meant that Enlil controlled Earth's atmosphere while Ea was ruler of the "subterranean waters"—the Greeklike Hades the Mesopotamians supposedly believed in. Our own term *abyss* (which derives from *apsu*) denotes deep, dark, dangerous waters in which one can sink and disappear. Thus, as scholars came upon Mesopotamian texts describing this Lower World, they translated it as *Unterwelt* ("underworld") or *Totenwelt* ("world of the dead"). Only in recent years have the Sumerologists mitigated the ominous connotation somewhat by using the term *netherworld* in translation.

The Mesopotamian texts most responsible for this misinterpretation were a series of liturgies lamenting the disappearance of Dumuzi, who is better known from biblical and Canaanite texts as the god Tammuz. It was with him that Inanna/Ishtar had her most celebrated love affair; and when he disappeared, she went to the Lower World to seek him.

The massive *Tammuz-Liturgen und Verwandtes* by P. Maurus Witzel, a masterwork on the Sumerian and Akkadian "Tammuz texts," only helped perpetuate the misconception. The epic tales of Ishtar's search were taken to mean a journey "to the realm of the dead, and her eventual return to the land of the living."

The Sumerian and Akkadian texts describing the descent of Inanna/Ishtar to the Lower World inform us that the goddess decided to visit her sister Ereshkigal, mistress of the place. Ishtar went there neither dead nor against her will—she went alive and uninvited, forcing her way in by threatening the gatekeeper:

> If thou openest not the gate so that I cannot enter,
> I will smash the door, I will shatter the bolt,
> I will smash the doorpost, I will move the doors.

One by one, the seven gates leading to the abode of Ereshkigal were opened to Ishtar; when she finally made it, and Ereshkigal saw her, she literally blew her top (the Akkadian text says, "burst at her presence"). The Sumerian text, vague about the purpose of the trip or the cause of Ereshkigal's anger, reveals that Inanna expected such a reception. She took pains to notify the other principal deities of her journey in advance, and made sure that they would take steps to rescue her in case she was imprisoned in the "Great Below."

The spouse of Ereshkigal—and Lord of the Lower World—was Nergal. The manner in which he arrived in the Great Below and became its lord not only illuminates the human nature of the "gods" but also depicts the Lower World as anything but a "world of the dead."

The tale, found in several versions, begins with a banquet at which the guests of honor were Anu, Enlil, and Ea. The banquet was held "in the heavens," but not at Anu's abode on the Twelfth Planet. Perhaps it took place aboard an orbiting spacecraft, for when Ereshkigal could not ascend to join them, the gods sent her a messenger who "descended the long staircase of the heavens, reached the gate of Ereshkigal." Having received the invitation, Ereshkigal instructed her counselor, Namtar:

> "Ascend, Namtar, the long staircase of the heavens;
> Remove the dish from the table, take my share;
> Whatever Anu gives to thee, bring it all to me."

When Namtar entered the banquet hall, all the gods except "a bald god, seated in the back," rose to greet him. Namtar reported the incident to Ereshkigal when he returned to the Lower World. She and all the lesser gods of her domain were insulted. She demanded that the offending god be sent to her for punishment.

The offender, however, was Nergal, a son of the great Ea. After a severe reprimand by his father, Nergal was instructed to make the trip alone, armed only with lots of fatherly advice on how to behave. When Nergal arrived at the gate, he was recognized by Namtar as the offending god and led in to "Ereshkigal's wide courtyard," where he was put to several tests.

Sooner or later, Ereshkigal went to take her daily bath.

> . . . she revealed her body.
> What is normal for man and woman,
> he . . . in his heart . . .
> . . . they embraced,
> passionately they got into bed.

For seven days and nights they made love. In the Upper World, an alarm had gone out for the missing Nergal. "Release me," he said to Ereshkigal. "I will go, and I will come back," he promised. But no sooner had he left than Namtar went to Ereshkigal and accused Nergal of having no intention of coming back. Once more Namtar was sent up to Anu. Ereshkigal's message was clear:

> I, thy daughter, was young;
> I have not known the play of maidens. . . .
> That god whom you didst send,
> and who had intercourse with me—
> Send him to me, that he may be my husband,
> That he might lodge with me.

With married life perhaps not yet on his mind, Nergal organized a military expedition and stormed the gates of Ereshkigal, intending to "cut off her head." But Ereshkigal pleaded:

> "Be thou my husband and I will be thy wife.
> I will let thee hold dominion
> over the wide Lower Land.
> I will place the Tablet of Wisdom in thy hand.
> Thou shalt be Master, I will be Mistress."

And then came the happy ending:

> When Nergal heard her words,
> He took hold of her hand and kissed her,
> Wiping away her tears:
> "What thou hast wished for me
> since months past—so be it now!"

The events recounted do not suggest a Land of the Dead. Quite the contrary: It was a place the gods could enter and leave, a place of lovemaking, a place important enough to be entrusted to a granddaughter of Enlil and a son of Enki. Recognizing that the facts do not support the earlier notion of a dismal region, W. F. Albright (*Mesopotamian Elements in Canaanite Eschatology*) suggested that Dumuzi's abode in the Lower World was "a bright and fruitful home in the subterranean paradise called 'the mouth of the rivers' which was closely associated with the home of Ea in the Apsu."

The place was far and difficult to reach, to be sure, and a somewhat "restricted area," but hardly a "place of no return." Like Inanna, other leading deities were reported going to, and returning from, this Lower World. Enlil was banished to the Abzu for a while, after he had raped Ninlil. And Ea was a virtual commuter between Eridu in Sumer and the Abzu, bringing to the Abzu "the craftsmanship of Eridu" and establishing in it "a lofty shrine" for himself.

Far from being a dark and desolate place, it was described as a bright place with flowing waters.

> A rich land, beloved of Enki;
> Bursting with riches, perfect in fullness . . .
> Whose mighty river rushes across the land.

We have seen the many depictions of Ea as the God of Flowing Waters. It is evident from Sumerian sources that such flowing waters indeed existed—not in Sumer and its flatlands, but in the Great Below. W. F. Albright drew attention to a text dealing with the Lower World as the Land of UT.TU—"in the west" of Sumer. It speaks of a journey of Enki to the Apsu:

> To thee, Apsu, pure land,
> Where great waters rapidly flow,
> To the Abode of Flowing Waters
> The Lord betakes himself. . . .
> The Abode of Flowing Waters
> Enki in the pure waters established;
> In the midst of the Apsu,
> A great sanctuary he established.

By all accounts, the place lay beyond a sea. A lament for "the pure son," the young Dumuzi, reports that he was carried off to the Lower World in a ship. A "Lamentation over the Destruction of Sumer" describes how Inanna managed to sneak aboard a waiting ship. "From her possessions she sailed forth. She descends to the Lower World."

A long text, little understood because no intact version has been found, deals with some major dispute between Ira (Nergal's title as Lord of the Lower World) and his brother Marduk. In the course of the dispute, Nergal left his domain and confronted Marduk in Babylon; Marduk, on the other hand, threatened: "To the Apsu will I descend, the Anunnaki to supervise . . . my raging weapons against them I will raise." To reach the Apsu, he left the Land of Mesopotamia and traveled over "waters that rose up." His destination was Arali in the "basement" of Earth, and the texts provide a precise clue as to where this "basement" was:

> In the distant sea,
> 100 *beru* of water [away] . . .
> The ground of *Arali* [is] . . .
> It is where the Blue Stones cause ill,
> Where the craftsman of Anu
> the Silver Axe carries, which shines as the day.

The *beru*, both a land-measuring and a time-reckoning unit, was probably used in the latter capacity when travel over water was involved. As such it was a double hour, so that one hundred *beru* meant two hundred hours of sailing. We have no way of determining the assumed or average sailing speed employed in these ancient distance reckonings. But there is no doubt that a truly distant land was reached after a sea voyage of over two or three thousand miles.

The texts indicate that Arali was situated west and south of Sumer. A ship traveling two to three thousand miles in a southwesterly direction from the Persian Gulf could have only one destination: the shores of southern Africa.

Only such a conclusion can explain the terms Lower World, as meaning the southern hemisphere, where the Land of Arali was, as contrasted with the Upper World, or northern hemisphere, where Sumer was. Such a division of Earth's hemispheres between Enlil (northern) and Ea (southern) paralleled the designation of the northern skies as the Way of Enlil and the southern skies as the Way of Ea.

The ability of the Nefilim to undertake interplanetary travel, orbit Earth, and land on it should obviate the question whether they could possibly have known of southern Africa, besides Mesopotamia. Many cylinder seals, depicting animals peculiar to the area (such as the zebra or ostrich), jungle scenes, or rulers wearing leopard skins in the African tradition, attest to an "African connection."

What interest did the Nefilim have in this part of Africa, diverting to it the scientific genius of Ea and granting to the important gods in charge of the land a unique "Tablet of Wisdom"?

The Sumerian term AB.ZU, which scholars have accepted to mean "watery deep," requires a fresh and critical analysis. Literally, the term meant "primeval deep source"—not necessarily of waters. According to Sumerian grammatical rules, either of two syllables of any term could precede the other without changing the word's meaning, with the result that AB.ZU and ZU.AB meant the same thing. The latter spelling of the Sumerian term enables identification of its parallel in the Semitic languages, for *za-ab* has always meant and still means "precious metal," specifically "gold," in Hebrew and its sister languages.

The Sumerian pictograph for AB.ZU was that of an excavation deep into Earth, mounted by a shaft. Thus, Ea was not the lord of an indefinite "watery deep," but the god in charge of the exploitation of Earth's minerals! (Fig. 139)

Fig. 139   Fig. 140   Fig. 141

Fig. 142

In fact, the Greek *abyssos*, adopted from the Akkadian *apsu*, also meant an extremely deep hole in the ground. Akkadian textbooks explained that *"apsu is nikbu"*; the meaning of the word and that of its Hebrew equivalent *nikba* is very precise: a deep, man-made cutting or drilling into the ground.

P. Jensen *(Die Kosmologie der Babylonier)* observed back in 1890 that the oft-encountered Akkadian term *Bit Nimiku* should not be translated as "house of wisdom" but as "house of deepness." He quoted a text (V.R.30, 49–50ab) that stated: "It is from Bit Nimiku that gold and silver come." Another text (III.R.57, 35ab), he pointed out, explained that the Akkadian name "Goddess Shala of *Nimiki*" was the translation of the Sumerian epithet "Goddess Who Hands the Shining Bronze." The Akkadian term *nimiku*, which has been translated as "wisdom," Jensen concluded, "had to do with metals." But why, he admitted simply, "I do not know."

Some Mesopotamian hymns to Ea exalt him as *Bel Nimiki*, translated "lord of wisdom"; but the correct translation should undoubtedly be "lord of mining." Just as the Tablet of Destinies at Nippur contained orbital data, it follows that the Tablet of Wisdom entrusted to Nergal and Ereshkigal was in fact a "Tablet of Mining," a "data bank" pertaining to the mining operations of the Nefilim.

As Lord of the Abzu, Ea was assisted by another son, the god GI.BIL ("he who burns the soil"), who was in charge of fire and smelting. Earth's Smith, he was usually depicted as a young god whose shoulders emit red-hot rays or sparks of fire, emerging from the ground or about to descend into it. The texts state that Gibil was steeped by Ea in "wisdom," meaning that Ea had taught him mining techniques. (Fig. 140)

The metal ores mined in southeastern Africa by the Nefilim were carried back to Mesopotamia by specially designed cargo ships called MA.GUR UR.NU AB.ZU ("ship for ores of the Lower World"). There, the ores were taken to Bad-Tibira, whose name literally meant "the foundation of metalworking." Smelted and refined, the ores were cast into ingots whose shape remained unchanged throughout the ancient world for millennia. Such ingots were actually found at various Near Eastern excavations, confirming the reliability of the Sumerian pictographs as true depictions of the objects they "wrote" out; the Sumerian sign for the term ZAG ("purified precious") was the picture of such an ingot. In earlier times it apparently had a hole running through its length, through which a carrying rod was inserted. (Fig. 141)

Several depictions of a God of the Flowing Waters show him flanked by bearers of such precious metal ingots, indicating that he was also the Lord of Mining. (Fig. 142)

The various names and epithets for Ea's African Land of Mines are replete with clues to its location and nature. It was known as A.RA.LI ("place of the shiny lodes"), the land from which the metal ores come. Inanna, planning her descent to the southern hemisphere, referred to the place as the land where "the precious metal is covered with soil"—where it is found underground. A text reported by Erica Reiner, listing the mountains and rivers of the Sumerian world, stated: "Mount Arali: home of the gold"; and a fragmented text described by H. Radau confirmed that Arali was the land on which Bad-Tibira depended for its continued operations.

The Mesopotamian texts spoke of the Land of Mines as mountainous, with grassy plateaus and steppes, and lush with vegetation. The capital of Ereshkigal in that land was described by the Sumerian texts as being in the GAB.KUR.RA ("in the chest of the mountains"), well inland. In the Akkadian version of Ishtar's journey, the gatekeeper welcomes her:

Enter my lady,
Let Kutu rejoice over thee;
Let the palace of the land of Nugia
Be glad at thy presence.

Conveying in Akkadian the meaning "that which is in the heartland," the term KU.TU in its Sumerian origin also meant "the bright uplands." It was a land, all texts suggest, with bright days, awash with sunshine. The Sumerian terms for gold (KU.GI—"bright out of earth") and silver (KU.BABBAR—"bright gold") retained the original association of the precious metals with the bright (ku) domain of Ereshkigal.

The pictographic signs employed as Sumer's first writing reveal great familiarity not only with diverse metallurgical processes but also with the fact that the sources of the metals were mines dug down into the earth. The terms for copper and bronze ("handsome-bright stone"), gold ("the supreme mined metal"), or "refined" ("bright-purified") were all pictorial variants of a mine shaft ("opening/mouth for dark-red" metal). (Fig. 143)

The land's name—Arali—could also be written as a variant of the pictograph for "dark-red" (soil), of Kush ("dark-red," but in time meaning "Negro"), or of the metals mined there; the pictographs always depicted variants of a mine shaft. (Fig. 144)

Extensive references to gold and other metals in ancient texts suggest familiarity with metallurgy from the earliest times. A lively metals trade existed at the very beginnings of civilization, the result of

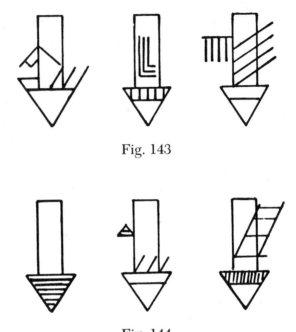

Fig. 143

Fig. 144

knowledge bequeathed to Mankind by the gods, who, the texts state, had engaged in mining and metallurgy long before Man's appearance. Many studies that correlate Mesopotamian divine tales with the biblical pre-Diluvial list of patriarchs point out that, according to the Bible, Tubal-cain was an "artificer of gold and copper and iron" long before the Deluge.

The Old Testament recognized the land of Ophir, which was probably somewhere in Africa, as a source of gold in antiquity. King Solomon's ship convoys sailed down the Red Sea from Ezion-geber (present-day Elath). "And they went to Ophir and fetched from thence gold." Unwilling to risk a delay in the construction of the Lord's Temple in Jerusalem, Solomon arranged with his ally, Hiram, king of Tyre, to sail a second fleet to Ophir by an alternate route:

> And the king had at sea a navy of Tarshish
> with the navy of Hiram.
> Once every three years came the navy of Tarshish,
> bringing gold and silver, ivory and apes and monkeys.

The fleet of Tarshish took three years to complete a round trip. Allowing for an appropriate time to load up at Ophir, the voyage in each direction must have lasted well over a year. This suggests a route much more roundabout than the direct route via the Red Sea and the Indian Ocean—a route around Africa. (Fig. 145)

Fig. 145

Most scholars locate Tarshish in the western Mediterranean, possibly at or near the present Strait of Gibraltar. This would have been an ideal place from which to embark on a voyage around the African continent. Some believe that the name Tarshish meant "smeltery."

Many biblical scholars have suggested that Ophir should be identified with present-day Rhodesia. Z. Herman (*Peoples, Seas, Ships*) brought together evidence showing that the Egyptians obtained various minerals from Rhodesia in earliest times. Mining engineers in Rhodesia as well as in South Africa have often searched for gold by seeking evidence of prehistoric mining.

How was the inland abode of Ereshkigal reached? How were the ores transported from the "heartland" to the coastal ports? Knowing of the reliance of the Nefilim on river shipping, one should not be surprised to find a major, navigable river in the Lower World. The tale of "Enlil and Ninlil" informed us that Enlil was banished to exile in the Lower World. When he reached the land, he had to be ferried over a wide river.

A Babylonian text dealing with the origins and destiny of Mankind referred to the river of the Lower World as the River Habur, the "River of Fishes and Birds." Some Sumerian texts nicknamed the Land of Ereshkigal the "Prairie Country of HA.BUR."

Of the four mighty rivers of Africa, one, the Nile, flows north into the Mediterranean; the Congo and Niger empty into the Atlantic Ocean on the west; and the Zambezi flows from the heartland of Africa in an eastward semicircle until it reaches the east coast. It offers a wide delta with good port sites; it is navigable inland over a distance of hundreds of miles.

Was the Zambezi the "River of Fishes and Birds" of the Lower World? Were its majestic Victoria Falls the waterfalls mentioned in one text as the site of Ereshkigal's capital?

Aware that many "newly discovered" and promising mining sites in southern Africa had been mining sites in antiquity, the Anglo-American Corporation called in teams of archaeologists to examine the sites before modern earth-moving equipment swept away all traces of ancient work. Reporting on their findings in the magazine *Optima*, Adrian Boshier and Peter Beaumont stated that they had come upon layers upon layers of ancient and prehistoric mining activities and human remains. Carbon dating at Yale University and at the University of Groningen (Holland) established the age of the artifacts as ranging from a plausible 2000 B.C. to an amazing 7690 B.C.

Intrigued by the unexpected antiquity of the finds, the team extended its area of search. At the base of a cliff face on the precipitous western slopes of Lion Peak, a five-ton slab of hematite stone blocked access to a cavern. Charcoal remains dated the mining operations within the cavern at 20,000 to 26,000 B.C.

Was mining for metals possible during the Old Stone Age? Incredulous, the scholars dug a shaft at a point where, apparently, the ancient miners had begun their operations. A charcoal sample found there was sent to the Groningen laboratory. The result was a dating of 41,250 B.C., give or take 1,600 years!

South African scientists then probed prehistoric mine sites in southern Swaziland. Within the uncovered mine caverns, they found twigs, leaves, and grass, even feathers—all, presumably, brought in by the ancient miners as bedding. At the 35,000 B.C. level, they found notched bones, which "indicate man's ability to count at that remote period." Other remains advanced the age of the artifacts to about 50,000 B.C.

Believing that the "true age of the onset of mining in Swaziland is more likely to be in the order of 70,000–80,000 B.C., the two scientists suggested that "southern Africa ... could well have been in the forefront of technological invention and innovation during much of the period subsequent to 100,000 B.C."

Commenting on the discoveries, Dr. Kenneth Oakley, former head anthropologist of the Natural History Museum in London, saw quite a different significance to the finds. "It throws important light on the origins of Man ... it is now possible that southern Africa was the evolutionary home of Man," the "birthplace" of Homo sapiens.

As we shall show, it was indeed there that modern Man appeared on Earth, through a chain of events triggered by the gods' search for metals.

°

Both serious scientists and science-fiction writers have suggested that a good reason for us to establish settlements on other planets or asteroids might be the availability of rare minerals on those celestial bodies, minerals that might be too scarce or too costly to mine on Earth. Could this have been the Nefilim's purpose in colonizing Earth?

Modern scholars divide Man's activities on Earth into the Stone Age, Bronze Age, Iron Age, and so on; in ancient times, however, the Greek poet Hesiod, for example, listed five ages—Golden, Silver, Bronze, Heroic, and Iron. Except for the Heroic Age, all ancient traditions accepted the sequence of gold–silver–copper–iron. The prophet Daniel had a vision in which he saw "a great image" with a head of fine gold, breast and arms of silver, belly of brass, legs of iron, and extremities, or feet, of clay.

Myth and folklore abound with hazy memories of a Golden Age, mostly associated with the time when gods roamed Earth, followed by a Silver Age, and then the ages when gods and men shared Earth—the Age of Heroes, of Copper, Bronze, and Iron. Are these legends in fact vague recollections of actual events on Earth?

Gold, silver, and copper are all native elements of the gold group. They fall into the same family in the periodic classification by atomic weight and number; they have similar crystallographic, chemical, and physical properties—all are soft, malleable, and ductile. Of all known elements, these are the best conductors of heat and electricity.

Of the three, gold is the most durable, virtually indestructible. Though best known for its use as money and in jewelry or fine artifacts, it is almost invaluable in the electronics industry. A sophisticated society requires gold for microelectronic assemblies, guidance circuitry, and computer "brains."

Man's infatuation with gold is traceable to the beginnings of his civilization and religion—to his contacts with the ancient gods. The gods of Sumer required that they be served food from golden trays, water and wine from golden vessels, that they be clad in golden garments. Though the Israelites left Egypt in such a hurry that there was no time for them to let their bread leaven, they were ordered to ask the Egyptians for all available silver and gold objects. This command, as we shall find out later, anticipated the need for such materials to construct the Tabernacle and its electronic accoutrements.

Gold, which we call the royal metal, was in fact the metal of the gods. Speaking to the prophet Haggai, the Lord made it clear, in connection with his return to judge the nations: "The silver is mine and the gold is mine."

The evidence suggests that Man's own infatuation with these metals has its roots in the great need of the Nefilim for gold. The Nefilim, it appears, came to Earth for gold and its related metals. They may also have come for other rare metals—such as platinum (abundant in southern Africa), which can power fuel cells in an extraordinary manner. And the possibility should not be ruled out that they came to Earth for sources of radioactive minerals, such as uranium or cobalt—the Lower World's "blue stones that cause ill," which some texts mention. Many depictions show Ea—as the God of Mining—emitting such powerful rays as he exits from a mine that the gods attending him have to use screening shields; in all these depictions, Ea is shown holding a miner's rock saw. (Fig. 146)

Though Enki was in charge of the first landing party and the development of the Abzu, credit for what was accomplished—as the case should be with all generals—should not go to him alone. Those who actually did the work, day in, day out, were the lesser members of the landing party, the Anunnaki.

A Sumerian text describes the construction of Enlil's center in Nippur. "The Annuna, gods of heaven and earth, are working. The axe and the carrying-basket, with which they laid foundation of the cities, in their hands they held."

The ancient texts described the Anunnaki as the rank-and-file gods who had been involved in the settlement of Earth—the gods "who performed the tasks." The Babylonian "Epic of Creation" credited

Fig. 146

Marduk with giving the Anunnaki their assignments. (The Sumerian original, we can safely assume, named Enlil as the god who commanded these astronauts.)

> Assigned to Anu, to heed his instructions,
> Three hundred in the heavens he stationed as a guard;
> the ways of Earth to define from the Heaven;
> And on Earth,
> Six hundred he made reside.
> After he all their instructions had ordered,
> to the Anunnaki of Heaven and of Earth
> he allotted their assignments.

The texts reveal that three hundred of them—the "Anunnaki of Heaven," or Igigi—were true astronauts who stayed aboard the spacecraft without actually landing on Earth. Orbiting Earth, these spacecraft launched and received the shuttlecraft to and from Earth.

As chief of the "Eagles," Shamash was a welcome and heroic guest aboard the "mighty great chamber in heaven" of the Igigi. A "Hymn to Shamash" describes how the Igigi observed Shamash approaching in his shuttlecraft:

> At thy appearances, all the princes are glad;
> All the Igigi rejoice over thee....
> In the brilliance of thy light, their path....
> They constantly look for thy radiance....
> Opened wide is the doorway, entirely....
> The bread offerings of all the Igigi [await thee].

Staying aloft, the Igigi were apparently never encountered by Mankind. Several texts say that they were "too high up for Mankind," as a consequence of which "they were not concerned with the people." The Anunnaki, on the other hand, who landed and stayed on Earth, were known and revered by Mankind. The texts that state that "the Anunnaki of Heaven . . . are 300" also state that "the Anunnaki of Earth . . . are 600."

Still, many texts persist in referring to the Anunnaki as the "fifty great princes." A common spelling of their name in Akkadian, *An-nun-na-ki*, readily yields the meaning "the fifty who went from Heaven to Earth." Is there a way to bridge the seeming contradiction?

We recall the text relating how Marduk rushed to his father Ea to report the loss of a spacecraft carrying "the Anunnaki who are fifty" as it passed near Saturn. An exorcism text from the time of the third dynasty of Ur speaks of the *anunna eridu ninnubi* ("the fifty Anunnaki of the city Eridu"). This strongly suggests that the group of Nefilim who founded Eridu under the command of Enki numbered fifty. Could it be that fifty was the number of Nefilim in each landing party?

It is, we believe, quite conceivable that the Nefilim arrived on Earth in groups of fifty. As the visits to Earth became regular, coinciding with the opportune launching times from the Twelfth Planet, more Nefilim would arrive. Each time, some of the earlier arrivals would ascend in an Earth module and rejoin the spaceship for a trip home. But, each time, more Nefilim would stay on Earth, and the number of Twelfth Planet astronauts who stayed to colonize Earth grew from the initial landing party of fifty to the "600 who on Earth settled."

How did the Nefilim expect to achieve their mission—to mine on Earth its desired minerals, and ship the ingots back to the Twelfth Planet—with such a small number of hands?

Undoubtedly, they relied on their scientific knowledge. It was there that Enki's full value becomes clear—the reason for his, rather than Enlil's, being the first to land, the reason for his assignment to the Abzu.

A famous seal now on exhibit at the Louvre Museum shows Ea with his familiar flowing waters, except that the waters seem to emanate from, or be filtered through, a series of laboratory flasks. (Fig. 147) Such an ancient interpretation of Ea's association with waters raises the possibility that the original hope of the Nefilim was to obtain their minerals from the sea. The oceans' waters do contain vast quantities of gold and other vital minerals, but so greatly diluted that highly sophisticated and cheap techniques are needed to justify such "water mining." It is also known that the sea beds contain immense quantities

Fig. 147

of minerals in the form of plum-sized nodules—available if only one could reach deep down and scoop them up.

The ancient texts refer repeatedly to a type of ship used by the gods called *elippu tebiti* ("sunken ship"—what we now call a submarine). We have seen the "fish-men" that were assigned to Ea. Is this evidence of efforts to dive to the depths of the oceans and retrieve their mineral riches? The Land of the Mines, we have noted, was earlier called A.RA.LI.– "place of the waters of the shiny lodes." This could mean a land where gold could be river-panned; it could also refer to efforts to obtain gold from the seas.

If these were the plans of the Nefilim, they apparently came to naught. For, soon after they had established their first settlements, the few hundred Anunnaki were given an unexpected and most arduous task: to go down into the depths of the African soil and mine the needed minerals there.

Depictions that have been found on cylinder seals show gods at what appear to be mine entrances or mine shafts; one shows Ea in a land where Gibil is aboveground and another god toils underground, on his hands and knees. (Fig. 148)

In later times, Babylonian and Assyrian texts disclose, men—young and old—were sentenced to hard labor in the mines of the Lower World. Working in darkness and eating dust as food, they were doomed never to return to their homeland. This is why the Sumerian epithet for the land—KUR.NU.GI.A—acquired the interpretation "land of no return"; its literal meaning was "land where gods-who-work, in deep tunnels pile up [the ores]." For the time when the Nefilim settled Earth, all the ancient sources attest, was a time when Man was not yet on Earth; and in the absence of Mankind, the few Anunnaki had to toil in

Fig. 148

the mines. Ishtar, on her descent to the Lower World, described the toiling Anunnaki as eating food mixed with clay and drinking water fouled with dust.

Against this background, we can fully understand a long epic text named (after its opening verse, as was the custom), "When the gods, like men, bore the work."

Piecing together many fragments of both Babylonian and Assyrian versions, W. G. Lambert and A. R. Millard (*Atra-Hasis: The Babylonian Story of the Flood*) were able to present a continuous text. They reached the conclusion that it was based on earlier Sumerian versions, and possibly on even earlier oral traditions about the arrival of the gods on Earth, the creation of Man, and his destruction by the Deluge.

While many of the verses hold only literary value to their translators, we find them highly significant, for they corroborate our findings and conclusions in the preceding chapters. They also explain the circumstances that led to the mutiny of the Anunnaki.

The story begins in the time when only the gods lived on Earth:

> When the gods, like men,
> bore the work and suffered the toil—
> the toil of the gods was great,
> the work was heavy,
> the distress was much.

At that time, the epic relates, the chief deities had already divided the commands among themselves.

> Anu, father of the Anunnaki, was their Heavenly King;
> Their Lord Chancellor was the warrior Enlil.
> Their Chief Officer was Ninurta,
> And their Sheriff was Ennugi.

The gods had clasped hands together,
Had cast lots and divided.
Anu had gone up to heaven,
[Left] the earth to his subjects.
The seas, enclosed as with a loop,
They had given to Enki, the prince.

Seven cities were established, and the text refers to seven Anunnaki who were city commanders. Discipline must have been strict, for the text tells us "The seven Great Anunnaki were making the lesser gods suffer the work."

Of all their chores, it seems, digging was the most common, the most arduous, and the most abhorred. The lesser gods dug up the river beds to make them navigable; they dug canals for irrigation; and they dug in the Apsu to bring up the minerals of Earth. Though they undoubtedly had some sophisticated tools—the texts spoke of the "silver axe which shines as the day," even underground—the work was too exacting. For a long time—for forty "periods," to be exact—the Anunnaki "suffered the toil"; and then they cried: No more!

They were complaining, backbiting,
Grumbling in the excavations.

The occasion for the mutiny appears to have been a visit by Enlil to the mining area. Seizing the opportunity, the Anunnaki said to one another:

Let us confront our . . . the Chief Officer,
That he may relieve us of our heavy work.
The king of the gods, the hero Enlil,
Let us unnerve him in his dwelling!

A leader or organizer of the mutiny was soon found. He was the "chief officer of old time," who must have held a grudge against the current chief officer. His name, regrettably, is broken off; but his inciting address is quite clear:

"Now, proclaim war;
Let us combine hostilities and battle."

The description of the mutiny is so vivid that scenes of the storming of the Bastille come to mind:

The gods heeded his words.
They set fire to their tools;
Fire to their axes they put;
They troubled the god of mining in the tunnels;
They held [him] as they went
to the gate of the hero Enlil.

The drama and tension of the unfolding events are brought to life by the ancient poet:

It was night, half-way through the watch.
His house was surrounded—
but the god, Enlil, did not know.
Kalkal [then] observed it, was disturbed.
He slid the bolt and watched. . . .
Kalkal roused Nusku;
they listened to the noise of. . . .
Nusku roused his lord—
he got him out of his bed, [saying]:
"My lord, your house is surrounded,
battle has come right up to your gate."

Enlil's first reaction was to take up arms against the mutineers. But Nusku, his chancellor, advised a Council of the Gods:

"Transmit a message that Anu come down;
Have Enki brought to your presence."
He transmitted and Anu was carried down;
Enki was also brought to his presence.
With the great Anunnaki present,
Enlil arose . . . opened his mouth
And addressed the great gods.

Taking the mutiny personally, Enlil demanded to know:

"Is it against me that this is being done?
Must I engage in hostilities . . . ?
What did my very own eyes see?
That battle has come right up to my gate!"

Anu suggested that an inquiry be undertaken. Armed with the authority of Anu and the other commanders, Nusku went to the encamped mutineers. "Who is the instigator of battle?" he asked. "Who is the provoker of hostilities?"

The Anunnaki stood together:

"Every single one of us gods has war declared!
We have our . . . in the excavations;
Excessive toil has killed us,
Our work was heavy, the distress much."

When Enlil heard Nusku's report of these grievances, "his tears flowed." He presented an ultimatum: either the leader of the mutineers be executed or he would resign. "Take the office away, take back your power," he told Anu, "and I will to you in heaven ascend." But Anu, who came down from Heaven, sided with the Anunnaki:

"What are we accusing them of?
Their work was heavy, their distress was much!
Every day . . .
The lamentation was heavy, we could hear the complaint."

Encouraged by his father's words, Ea also "opened his mouth" and repeated Anu's summation. But he had a solution to offer: Let a *lulu*, a "Primitive Worker," be created!

"While the Birth Goddess is present,
Let her create a Primitive Worker;
Let him bear the yoke. . . .
Let him carry the toil of the gods!"

The suggestion that a "Primitive Worker" be *created* so that he could take over the burden of work of the Anunnaki was readily accepted. Unanimously, the gods voted to create "The Worker." " '*Man*' shall be his name," they said:

They summoned and asked the goddess,
The midwife of the gods, the wise Mami,
[and said to her:]
"You are the Birth Goddess, create Workers!
Create a Primitive Worker,
That he may bear the yoke!
Let him bear the yoke assigned by Enlil,
Let The Worker carry the toil of the gods!"

Mami, the Mother of the Gods, said she would need the help of Ea, "with whom skill lies." In the House of Shimti, a hospital-like place, the gods were waiting. Ea helped prepare the mixture from which the Mother Goddess proceeded to fashion "Man." Birth goddesses were present. The Mother Goddess went on working while incantations were constantly recited. Then she shouted in triumph:

"I have created!
My hands have made it!"

She "summoned the Anunnaki, the Great Gods . . . she opened her mouth, addressed the Great Gods":

"You commanded me a task—
I have completed it. . . .
I have removed your heavy work
I have imposed your toil on The Worker, 'Man.'
You raised a cry for a Worker-kind:
I have loosed the yoke,
I have provided your freedom."

The Anunnaki received her announcement enthusiastically. "They ran together and kissed her feet." From then on it would be the Primitive Worker—Man—"who will bear the yoke."

The Nefilim, having arrived on Earth to set up their colonies, had created their own brand of slavery, not with slaves imported from another continent, but with Primitive Workers fashioned by the Nefilim themselves.

A mutiny of the gods had led to the creation of Man.

12
·

THE CREATION OF MAN

The assertion, first recorded and transmitted by the Sumerians, that "Man" was created by the Nefilim, appears at first sight to clash both with the theory of evolution and with the Judeo-Christian tenets based on the Bible. But in fact, the information contained in the Sumerian texts—and only that information—can affirm both the validity of the theory of evolution and the truth of the biblical tale—and show that there really is no conflict at all between the two.

In the epic "When the gods as men," in other specific texts, and in passing references, the Sumerians described Man as both a deliberate creature of the gods and a link in the evolutionary chain that began with the celestial events described in the "Epic of Creation." Holding firm to the belief that the creation of Man was preceded by an era during which only the Nefilim were upon Earth, the Sumerian texts recorded instance after instance (for example, the incident between Enlil and Ninlil) of events that had taken place "when Man had not yet been created, when Nippur was inhabited by the gods alone." At the same time, the texts also described the creation of Earth and the development of plant and animal life upon it, in terms that conform to the current evolutionary theories.

The Sumerian texts state that when the Nefilim first came to Earth, the arts of grain cultivation, fruit planting, and cattle raising had not yet extended to Earth. The biblical account likewise places the creation of Man in the sixth "day" or phase of the evolutionary process. The Book of Genesis, too, asserts that at an earlier evolutionary stage:

No plant of the cleared field was yet on Earth,
No herb that is planted had yet been grown. . . .
And Man was not yet there to work the soil.

All the Sumerian texts assert that the gods created Man to do their work. Putting the explanation in words uttered by Marduk, the Creation epic reports the decision:

> I will produce a lowly Primitive;
> "Man" shall be his name.
> I will create a Primitive Worker;
> He will be charged with the service of the gods,
> that they might have their ease.

The very terms by which the Sumerians and Akkadians called "Man" bespoke his status and purpose: He was a *lulu* ("primitive"), a *lulu amelu* ("primitive worker"), an *awilum* ("laborer"). That Man was created to be a servant of the gods did not strike the ancient peoples as a peculiar idea at all. In biblical times, the deity was "Lord," "Sovereign," "King," "Ruler," "Master." The term that is commonly translated as "worship" was in fact *avod* ("work"). Ancient and biblical Man did not "worship" his god; he worked for him.

No sooner had the biblical Deity, like the gods in Sumerian accounts, created Man, than he planted a garden and assigned Man to work there:

> And the Lord God took the "Man"
> and placed him in the garden of Eden
> to till it and to tend it.

Later on, the Bible describes the Deity "strolling in the garden in the breeze of the day," now that the new being was there to tend the Garden of Eden. How far is this version from the Sumerian texts that describe how the gods clamored for workers so that they could rest and relax?

In the Sumerian versions, the decision to create Man was adopted by the gods in their Assembly. Significantly, the Book of Genesis— purportedly exalting the achievements of a sole Deity—uses the plural Elohim (literally, "deities") to denote "God," and reports an astonishing remark:

> And Elohim said:
> "Let us make Man in our image,
> after our likeness."

Whom did the sole but plural Deity address, and who were the "us" in whose plural image and plural likeness Man was to be made? The Book of Genesis does not provide the answer. Then, when Adam and

Eve ate of the fruit of the Tree of Knowing, Elohim issued a warning to the same unnamed colleagues: "Behold, Man has become as one of us, to know good and evil."

Since the biblical story of Creation, like the other tales of beginnings in Genesis, stems from Sumerian origins, the answer is obvious. Condensing the many gods into a single Supreme Deity, the biblical tale is but an edited version of the Sumerian reports of the discussions in the Assembly of the Gods.

The Old Testament took pains to make clear that Man was neither a god nor from the heavens. "The Heavens are the Heavens of the Lord, unto Mankind Earth He hath given." The new being was called "the Adam" because he was created of the *adama*, the Earth's soil. He was, in other words, "the Earthling."

Lacking only certain "knowing" and a divine span of life, the Adam was in all other respects created in the image *(şelem)* and likeness *(dmut)* of his Creator(s). The use of both terms in the text was meant to leave no doubt that Man was similar to the God(s) both physically and emotionally, externally and internally.

In all ancient pictorial depictions of gods and men, this physical likeness is evident. Although the biblical admonition against the worship of pagan images gave rise to the notion that the Hebrew God had neither image nor likeness, not only the Genesis tale but other biblical reports attest to the contrary. The God of the ancient Hebrews could be seen face-to-face, could be wrestled with, could be heard and spoken to; he had a head and feet, hands and fingers, and a waist. The biblical God and his emissaries looked like men and acted like men—because men were created to look like and act like the gods.

But in this very simplicity lies a great mystery. How could a *new* creature possibly be a virtual physical, mental, and emotional replica of the Nefilim? How, indeed, was Man created?

The Western world was long wedded to the notion that, created deliberately, Man was put upon Earth to subdue it and have dominion over all other creatures. Then, in November 1859, an English naturalist by the name of Charles Darwin published a treatise called *On the Origin of Species by Means of Natural Selection, or the Preservation of Favoured Races in the Struggle for Life.* Summing up nearly thirty years of research, the book added to earlier thoughts about natural evolution the concept of natural selection as a consequence of the struggle of all species—of plant and animal alike—for existence.

The Christian world had been jostled earlier when, from 1788 on, noted geologists had begun to express their belief that Earth was of great antiquity, much, much greater than the roughly 5,500 years of the Hebrew calendar. Nor was the concept of evolution as such the explosive: Earlier scholars had noted such a process, and Greek scholars as far back as the fourth century B.C. compiled data on the evolution of animal and plant life.

Darwin's shattering bombshell was the conclusion that all living things—*Man included*—were products of evolution. Man, contrary to the then-held belief, was not generated spontaneously.

The initial reaction of the Church was violent. But as the scientific facts regarding Earth's true age, evolution, genetics, and other biological and anthropological studies came to light, the Church's criticism was muted. It seemed at last that the very words of the Old Testament made the tale of the Old Testament indefensible; for how could a God who has no corporal body and who is universally alone say, "Let *us* make Man in *our image*, after *our likeness*?"

But are we really nothing more than "naked apes"? Is the monkey just an evolutionary arm's length away from us, and the tree shrew just a human who has yet to lose his tail and stand erect?

As we showed at the very beginning of this book, modern scientists have come to question the simple theories. Evolution can explain the general course of events that caused life and life's forms to develop on Earth, from the simplest one-celled creature to Man. But evolution cannot account for the appearance of *Homo sapiens,* which happened virtually overnight in terms of the millions of years evolution requires, and with no evidence of earlier stages that would indicate a gradual change from *Homo erectus.*

The hominid of the genus *Homo* is a product of evolution. But *Homo sapiens* is the product of some sudden, revolutionary event. He appeared inexplicably some 300,000 years ago, millions of years too soon.

The scholars have no explanation. But we do. The Sumerian and Babylonian texts do. The Old Testament does.

Homo sapiens—modern Man—was brought about by the ancient gods.

°

The Mesopotamian texts, fortunately, provide a clear statement regarding the time when Man was created. The story of the toil and ensuing mutiny of the Anunnaki informs us that "for 40 periods they suffered the work, day and night"; the long years of their toil are dramatized by repetitious verses.

For 10 periods they suffered the toil;
For 20 periods they suffered the toil;
For 30 periods they suffered the toil;
For 40 periods they suffered the toil.

The ancient text uses the term *ma* to denote "period," and most scholars have translated this as "year." But the term had the connotation of "something that completes itself and then repeats itself." To men on Earth, one year equals one complete orbit of Earth around the Sun. As we have already shown, the orbit of the Nefilim's planet equaled a *shar*, or 3,600 Earth years.

Forty *shars*, or 144,000 Earth years, after their landing, the Anunnaki protested, "No more!" If the Nefilim first landed on Earth, as we have concluded, some 450,000 years ago, then the creation of Man took place some 300,000 years ago!

The Nefilim did not create the mammals or the primates or the hominids. "The Adam" of the Bible was not the genus *Homo*, but the being who is our ancestor—the first *Homo sapiens*. It is modern Man as we know him that the Nefilim created.

The key to understanding this crucial fact lies in the tale of a slumbering Enki, aroused to be informed that the gods had decided to form an *adamu*, and that it was his task to find the means. He replied:

"The creature whose name you uttered—
IT EXISTS!"

and he added: "Bind upon it"—on the creature that already exists—"the image of the gods."

Here, then, is the answer to the puzzle: The Nefilim did not "create" Man out of nothing; rather, they took an existing creature and manipulated it, to "bind upon it" the "image of the gods."

Man is the product of evolution; but modern Man, *Homo sapiens*, is the product of the "gods." For, some time circa 300,000 years ago, the Nefilim took ape-man *(Homo erectus)* and implanted on him their own image and likeness.

Evolution and the Near Eastern tales of Man's creation are not at all in conflict. Rather, they explain and complement each other. For without the creativity of the Nefilim, modern Man would still be millions years away on the evolutionary tree.

❋

Let us transport ourselves back in time, and try to visualize the circumstances and the events as they unfolded.

The great interglacial stage that began about 435,000 years ago, and its warm climate, brought about a proliferation of food and animals. It also speeded up the appearance and spread of an advanced manlike ape, *Homo erectus*.

As the Nefilim looked about them, they saw not only the predominant mammals but also the primates—among them the manlike apes. Is it not possible that the roaming bands of *Homo erectus* were lured to come close to observe the fiery objects rising to the sky? Is it not possible that the Nefilim observed, encountered, even captured some of these interesting primates?

That the Nefilim and the manlike apes did meet is attested to by several ancient texts. A Sumerian tale dealing with the primordial times states:

> When Mankind was created,
> They knew not the eating of bread,
> Knew not the dressing in garments;
> Ate plants with their mouth like sheep;
> Drank water from a ditch.

Such an animal-like "human" being is also described in the "Epic of Gilgamesh." That text tells what Enkidu, the one "born on the steppes," was like before he became civilized:

> Shaggy with hair is his whole body,
> he is endowed with head-hair like a woman. . . .
> He knows neither people nor land;
> Garbed he is like one of the green fields;
> With gazelles he feeds on grass;
> With the wild beasts he jostles
> at the watering place;
> With the teeming creatures in the water
> his heart delights.

Not only does the Akkadian text describe an animal-like man; it also describes an encounter with such a being:

> Now a hunter, one who traps,
> faced him at the watering place.
> When the hunter saw him,
> his face became motionless. . . .
> His heart was disturbed, overclouded his face,
> for woe had entered his belly.

There was more to it than mere fear after the hunter beheld "the savage," this "barbarous fellow from the depths of the steppe"; for this "savage" also interfered with the hunter's pursuits:

> He filled the pits that I had dug,
> he tore up my traps which I had set;
> the beasts and creatures of the steppe
> he has made slip through my hands.

We can ask for no better description of an ape-man: hairy, shaggy, a roaming nomad who "knows neither people nor land," garbed in leaves, "like one of the green fields," feeding on grass, and living among the animals. Yet he is not without substantial intelligence, for he knows how to tear up the traps and fill up the pits dug to catch the animals. In other words, he protected his animal friends from being caught by the alien hunters. Many cylinder seals have been found that depict this shaggy ape-man among his animal friends. (Fig. 149)

Fig. 149

Then, faced with the need for manpower, resolved to obtain a Primitive Worker, the Nefilim saw a ready-made solution: to domesticate a suitable animal.

The "animal" was available—but *Homo erectus* posed a problem. On the one hand, he was too intelligent and wild to become simply a docile beast of work. On the other hand, he was not really suited to the task. His physique had to be changed—he had to be able to grasp and use the tools of the Nefilim, walk and bend like them so that he could replace the gods in the fields and in the mines. He had to have better "brains"—not like those of the gods but enough to understand speech and commands and the tasks allotted to him. He needed enough cleverness and understanding to be an obedient and useful *amelu*—a serf.

If, as the ancient evidence and modern science seem to confirm, life on Earth germinated from life on the Twelfth Planet, then evolution on Earth should have proceeded as it had on the Twelfth Planet. Undoubtedly there were mutations, variations, accelerations, and retardations caused by different local conditions; but the same genetic codes, the same "chemistry of life" found in all living plants and animals on Earth would also have guided the development of life forms on Earth in the same general direction as on the Twelfth Planet.

Observing the various forms of life on Earth, the Nefilim and their chief scientist, Ea, needed little time to realize what had happened:

During the celestial collision, their planet had seeded Earth with its life. Therefore, the being that was available was really akin to the Nefilim—though in a less evolved form.

A gradual process of domestication through generations of breeding and selection would not do. What was needed was a quick process, one that would permit "mass production" of the new workers. So the problem was posed to Ea, who saw the answer at once: to "imprint" the image of the gods on the being that already existed.

The process that Ea recommended in order to achieve a quick evolutionary advancement of *Homo erectus* was, we believe, *genetic manipulation.*

We now know that the complex biological process whereby a living organism reproduces itself, creating progeny that resemble their parents, is made possible by the genetic code. All living organisms—a threadworm, a fern tree, or Man—contain in their cells chromosomes, minute rodlike bodies within each cell that hold the complete hereditary instructions for that particular organism. As the male cell (pollen, sperm) fertilizes the female cell, the two sets of chromosomes combine and then divide to form new cells that hold the complete hereditary characteristics of their parent cells.

Artificial insemination, even of a female human egg, is now possible. The real challenge lies in cross-fertilization between different families within the same species, and even between different species. Modern science has come a long way from the development of the first hybrid corns, or the mating of Alaskan dogs with wolves, or the "creation" of the mule (the artificial mating of a mare and a donkey), to the ability to manipulate Man's own reproduction.

A process called cloning (from the Greek word *klon*—"twig") applies to animals the same principle as that of taking a cutting from a plant to reproduce hundreds of similar plants. The technique as applied to animals was first demonstrated in England, where Dr. John Gordon replaced the nucleus of a fertilized frog's egg with the nuclear material from another cell of the same frog. The successful formation of normal tadpoles demonstrated that the egg proceeds to develop and subdivide and create progeny no matter where it obtains the correct set of matching chromosomes.

Experiments at the Institute of Society, Ethics and Life Sciences at Hastings-on-Hudson, New York, have shown that techniques already exist for cloning human beings. It is now possible to take the nuclear material of any human cell (not necessarily from the sex organs) and, by introducing its twenty-three sets of complete chromosomes into the female ovum, lead to the conception and birth of a "predetermined" individual. In normal conception, "father" and "mother" chromosome sets merge and then must split to remain at twenty-three chromosome pairs, leading to chance combinations. But in cloning the offspring is an exact replica of the source of the unsplit set of chromosomes. We already possess, according to Dr. W. Gaylin of the Institute, the "awful knowledge to make exact copies of human beings"—a limitless number of Hitlers or Mozarts or Einsteins (if we had preserved their cell nuclei).

But the art of genetic engineering is not limited to one process. Researchers in many countries have perfected a process called "cell fusion," making it possible to fuse cells rather than combine chromosomes within a single cell. As a result of such a process, cells from different sources can be fused into one "supercell," holding within itself two nuclei and a double set of the paired chromosomes. When this cell splits, the mixture of nuclei and chromosomes may split in a pattern different from that of each cell before the fusion. The result can be two new cells, each genetically complete, but each with a brand-new set of genetic codes, completely garbled as far as the ancestor cells were concerned.

This means that cells from hitherto incompatible living organisms— say, that of a chicken and that of a mouse—can be fused to form new cells with brand-new genetic mixes that produce new animals that are neither chickens nor mice as we know them. Further refined, the process can also permit us to *select* which traits of one life form shall be imparted to the combined or "fused" cell.

This has led to the development of the wide field of "genetic transplant." It is now possible to pick up from certain bacteria a single specific gene and introduce that gene into an animal or human cell, giving the offspring an added characteristic.

We should assume that the Nefilim—being capable of space travel 450,000 years ago—were also equally advanced, compared to us today, in the field of life sciences. We should also assume that they were aware of the various alternatives by which two preselected sets of chromosomes could be combined to obtain a predetermined genetic result; and that whether the process was akin to cloning, cell fusion, genetic transplant, or methods as yet unknown to us, they knew these processes and could carry them out, not only in the laboratory flask but also with living organisms.

We find a reference to such a mixing of two life-sources in the ancient texts. According to Berossus, the deity Belus ("lord")—also called Deus ("god")—brought forth various "hideous Beings, which were produced of a two-fold principle."

Men appeared with two wings, some with four and two faces. They had one body but two heads, the one of a man, the other of a woman. They were likewise in their several organs both male and female.

Other human figures were to be seen with the legs and horns of goats. Some had horses' feet; others had the limbs of a horse behind, but in front were fashioned like men, resembling hippocentaurs. Bulls likewise bred there with the heads of men; and dogs with fourfold bodies, and the tails of fishes. Also horses with the heads of dogs; men too and other animals with the heads and bodies of horses and the tails of fishes. In short, there were creatures with the limbs of every species of animals. . . .

Of all these were preserved delineations in the temple of Belus at Babylon.

The tale's baffling details may hold an important truth. It is quite conceivable that before resorting to the creation of a being in their own image, the Nefilim attempted to come up with a "manufactured servant" by experimenting with other alternatives: the creation of a hybrid ape-man–animal. Some of these artificial creatures may have survived for a while but were certainly unable to reproduce. The enigmatic bull-men and lion-men (sphinxes) that adorned temple sites in the ancient Near East may not have been just figments of an artist's imagination but actual creatures that came out of the biological laboratories of the Nefilim—unsuccessful experiments commemorated in art and by statues. (Fig. 150)

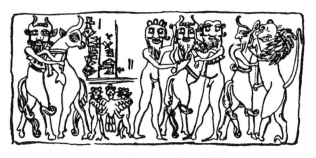 

Fig. 150

Sumerian texts, too, speak of deformed humans created by Enki and the Mother Goddess (Ninḫursag) in the course of their efforts to fashion a perfect Primitive Worker. One text reports that Ninḫursag, whose task it was to "bind upon the mixture the mold of the gods," got drunk and "called over to Enki,"

"How good or how bad is Man's body?
As my heart prompts me,
I can make its fate good or bad."

Mischievously, then, according to this text—but probably unavoidably, as part of a trial-and-error process—Ninhursag produced a Man who could not hold back his urine, a woman who could not bear children, a being who had neither male nor female organs. All in all, six deformed or deficient humans were brought forth by Ninhursag. Enki was held responsible for the imperfect creation of a man with diseased eyes, trembling hands, a sick liver, a failing heart; a second one with sicknesses attendant upon old age; and so on.

But finally the perfect Man was achieved—the one Enki named Adapa; the Bible, Adam; our scholars, *Homo sapiens*. This being was so much akin to the gods that one text even went so far as to point out that the Mother Goddess gave to her creature, Man, "a skin as the skin of a god"—a smooth, hairless body, quite different from that of the shaggy ape-man.

With this final product, the Nefilim were genetically compatible with the daughters of Man and able to marry them and have children by them. But such compatibility could exist only if Man had developed from the same "seed of life" as the Nefilim. This, indeed, is what the ancient texts attest to.

Man, in the Mesopotamian concept, as in the biblical one, was made of a mixture of a godly element—a god's blood or its "essence"—and the "clay" of Earth. Indeed, the very term *lulu* for "Man," while conveying the sense of "primitive," literally meant "one who has been mixed." Called upon to fashion a man, the Mother Goddess "Washed her hands, pinched off clay, mixed it in the steppe." (It is fascinating to note here the sanitary precautions taken by the goddess. She "washed her hands." We encounter such clinical measures and procedures in other creation texts as well.)

The use of earthly "clay" mixed with divine "blood" to create the prototype of Man is firmly established by the Mesopotamian texts. One, relating how Enki was called upon to "bring to pass some great work of Wisdom"—of scientific know-how—states that Enki saw no great problem in fulfilling the task of "fashioning servants for the gods." "It can be done!" he announced. He then gave these instructions to the Mother Goddess:

> "Mix to a core the clay
> from the Basement of Earth,
> just above the Abzu—
> and shape it into the form of a core.
> I shall provide good, knowing young gods
> who will bring that clay to the right condition."

The second chapter of Genesis offers this technical version:

And Yahweh, Elohim, fashioned the Adam
of the clay of the soil;
and He blew in his nostrils the breath of life,
and the Adam turned into a living Soul.

The Hebrew term commonly translated as "soul" is *nephesh*, that elusive "spirit" that animates a living creature and seemingly abandons it when it dies. By no coincidence, the Pentateuch (the first five books of the Old Testament) repeatedly exhorted against the shedding of human blood and the eating of animal blood "because the blood is the *nephesh.*" The biblical versions of the creation of Man thus equate *nephesh* ("spirit," "soul") and blood.

The Old Testament offers another clue to the role of blood in Man's creation. The term *adama* (after which the name Adam was coined) originally meant not just any earth or soil, but specifically dark-red soil. Like the parallel Akkadian word *adamatu* ("dark-red earth"), the Hebrew term *adama* and the Hebrew name for the color red *(adom)* stem from the words for blood: *adamu, dam.* When the Book of Genesis termed the being created by God "the Adam," it employed a favorite Sumerian linguistic play of double meanings. "The Adam" could mean "the one of the earth" (Earthling), "the one made of the dark-red soil," and "the one made of blood."

The same relationship between the essential element of living creatures and blood exists in Mesopotamian accounts of Man's creation. The hospital-like house where Ea and the Mother Goddess went to bring Man forth was called the House of Shimti; most scholars translate this as "the house where fates are determined." But the term *Shimti* clearly stems from the Sumerian SHI.IM.TI, which, taken syllable by syllable, means "breath-wind-life." *Bit Shimti* meant, literally, "the house where the wind of life is breathed in." This is virtually identical to the biblical statement.

Indeed, the Akkadian word employed in Mesopotamia to translate the Sumerian SHI.IM.TI was *napishtu*—the exact parallel of the biblical term *nephesh.* And the *nephesh* or *napishtu* was an elusive "something" in the blood.

While the Old Testament offered only meager clues, Mesopotamian texts were quite explicit on the subject. Not only do they state that blood was required for the mixture of which Man was fashioned; they specified that it had to be the blood of a god, divine blood.

When the gods decided to create Man, their leader announced: "Blood will I amass, bring bones into being." Suggesting that the blood be taken from a specific god, "Let primitives be fashioned after his pattern," Ea said. Selecting the god,

Out of his blood they fashioned Mankind;
imposed on it the service, let free the gods. . . .
It was a work beyond comprehension.

According to the epic tale "When gods as men," the gods then called the Birth Goddess (the Mother Goddess, Ninḥursag) and asked her to perform the task:

While the Birth Goddess is present,
Let the Birth Goddess fashion offspring.
While the Mother of the Gods is present,
Let the Birth Goddess fashion a *Lulu;*
Let the worker carry the toil of the gods.
Let her create a *Lulu Amelu,*
Let him bear the yoke.

In a parallel Old Babylonian text named "Creation of Man by the Mother Goddess," the gods call upon "The Midwife of the gods, the Knowing Mami" and tell her:

Thou art the mother-womb,
The one who Mankind can create.
Create then *Lulu,* let him bear the yoke!

At this point, the text "When gods as men" and parallel texts turn to a detailed description of the actual creation of Man. Accepting the "job," the goddess (here named NIN.TI—"lady who gives life") spelled out some requirements, including some chemicals ("bitumens of the Abzu"), to be used for "purification," and "the clay of the Abzu."
Whatever these materials were, Ea had no problem understanding the requirements; accepting, he said:

"I will prepare a purifying bath.
Let one god be bled. . . .
From his flesh and blood,
let Ninti mix the clay."

To shape a man from the mixed clay, some feminine assistance, some pregnancy or childbearing aspects were also needed. Enki offered the services of his own spouse:

Ninki, my goddess-spouse,
will be the one for labor.
Seven goddesses-of-birth
will be near, to assist.

Following the mixing of the "blood" and "clay," the childbearing phase would complete the bestowal of a divine "imprint" on the creature.

> The new-born's fate thou shalt pronounce;
> Ninki would fix upon it the image of the gods;
> And what it will be is "Man."

Depictions on Assyrian seals may well have been intended as illustrations for these texts—showing how the Mother Goddess (her symbol was the cutter of the umbilical cord) and Ea (whose original symbol was the crescent) were preparing the mixtures, reciting the incantations, urging each other to proceed. (Figs. 151, 152)

The involvement of Enki's spouse, Ninki in the creation of the first successful specimen of Man reminds us of the tale of Adapa, which we discussed in an earlier chapter:

> In those days, in those years,
> The Wise One of Eridu, Ea,
> created him as a model of men.

Scholars have surmised that references to Adapa as a "son" of Ea implied that the god loved this human so much that he adopted him. But in the same text Anu refers to Adapa as "the human offspring of Enki." It appears that the involvement of Enki's spouse in the process of creating Adapa, the "model Adam," did create some genealogical relationship between the new Man and his god: It was Ninki who was pregnant with Adapa!

Fig. 151

Fig. 152

Ninti blessed the new being and presented him to Ea. Some seals show a goddess, flanked by the Tree of Life and laboratory flasks, holding up a newborn being. (Fig. 153)

Fig. 153

The being that was thus produced, which is repeatedly referred to in Mesopotamian texts as a "model Man" or a "mold," was apparently the right creature, for the gods then clamored for duplicates. This seemingly unimportant detail, however, throws light not only on the process by which Mankind was "created," but also on the otherwise conflicting information contained in the Bible.

According to the first chapter of Genesis:

Elohim created the Adam in His image—
in the image of Elohim created He him.
Male and female created He them.

Chapter 5, which is called the Book of the Genealogies of Adam, states that:

On the day that Elohim created Adam,
in the likeness of Elohim did He make him.
Male and female created He them,
and He blessed them, and called them "Adam"
on the very day of their creation.

In the same breath, we are told that the Deity created, in his likeness and his image, only a single being, "the Adam," and in apparent contradiction, that both a male and a female were created simultaneously. The contradiction seems sharper still in the second chapter of Genesis, which specifically reports that the Adam was alone for a while, until the Deity put him to sleep and fashioned Woman from his rib.

316 · THE TWELFTH PLANET

The contradiction, which has puzzled scholars and theologians alike, disappears once we realize that the biblical texts were a condensation of the original Sumerian sources. These sources inform us that after trying to fashion a Primitive Worker by "mixing" apemen with animals, the gods concluded that the only mixture that would work would be between apemen and the Nefilim themselves. After several unsuccessful attempts, a "model"—Adapa/Adam—was made. There was, at first, only a single Adam.

Once Adapa/Adam proved to be the right creature, he was used as the genetic model or "mold" for the creation of duplicates, and those duplicates were not only male, but male and female. As we showed earlier, the biblical "rib" from which Woman was fashioned was a play on words on the Sumerian TI ("rib" and "life")—confirming that Eve was made of Adam's "life's essence."

The Mesopotamian texts provide us with an eye-witness report of the first production of the duplicates of Adam.

The instructions of Enki were followed. In the House of Shimti— where the breath of life is "blown in"—Enki, the Mother Goddess, and fourteen birth goddesses assembled. A god's "essence" was obtained, the "purifying bath" prepared. "Ea cleaned the clay in her presence; he kept reciting the incantation."

> The god who purifies the Napishtu, Ea, spoke up.
> Seated before her, he was prompting her.
> After she had recited her incantation,
> She put her hand out to the clay.

We are now privy to the detailed process of Man's mass creation. With fourteen birth goddesses present,

> Ninti nipped off fourteen pieces of clay;
> Seven she deposited on the right,
> Seven she deposited on the left.
> Between them she placed the mould.
> . . . the hair she . . .
> . . . the cutter of the umbilical cord.

It is evident that the birth goddesses were divided into two groups. "The wise and learned, twice-seven birth goddesses had assembled," the text goes on to explain. Into their wombs the Mother Goddess deposited the "mixed clay." There are hints of a surgical procedure— the removal or shaving off of hair, the readying of a surgical instrument, a cutter. Now there was nothing to do but wait:

The birth goddesses were kept together.
Ninti sat counting the months.
The fateful 10th month was approaching;
The 10th month arrived;
The period of opening the womb had elapsed.
Her face radiated understanding:
She covered her head, performed the midwifery.
Her waist she girdled, pronounced the blessing.
She drew a shape; in the mould was life.

The drama of Man's creation, it appears, was compounded by a late birth. The "mixture" of "clay" and "blood" was used to induce pregnancy in fourteen birth goddesses. But nine months passed, and the tenth month commenced. "The period of opening the womb had elapsed." Understanding what was called for, the Mother Goddess "performed the midwifery." That she engaged in some surgical operation emerges more clearly from a parallel text (in spite of its fragmentation):

Ninti . . . counts the months. . . .
The destined 10th month they called;
The Lady Whose Hand Opens came.
With the . . . she opened the womb.
Her face brightened with joy.
Her head was covered;
. . . made an opening;
That which was in the womb came forth.

Overcome with joy, the Mother Goddess let out a cry.

"I have created!
My hands have made it!"

How was the creation of Man accomplished?

The text "When the gods as men" contains a passage whose purpose was to explain why the "blood" of a god had to be mixed into the "clay." The "divine" element required was not simply the dripping blood of a god, but something more basic and lasting. The god that was selected, we are told, had TE.E.MA—a term the leading authorities on the text (W. G. Lambert and A. R. Millard of Oxford University) translate as "personality." But the ancient term is much more specific; it literally means "that which houses that which binds the memory."

Further on, the same term appears in the Akkadian version as *etemu,* which is translated as "spirit."

In both instances we are dealing with that "something" in the blood of the god that was the repository of his individuality. All these, we feel certain, are but roundabout ways of stating that what Ea was after, when he put the god's blood through a series of "purifying baths," was the god's *genes.*

The purpose of mixing this divine element thoroughly with the earthly element was also spelled out:

In the clay, god and Man shall be bound,
to a unity brought together;
So that to the end of days
the Flesh and the Soul
which in a god have ripened—
that Soul in a blood-kinship be bound;
As its Sign life shall proclaim.
So that this not be forgotten,
Let the "Soul" in a blood-kinship be bound.

These are strong words, little understood by scholars. The text states that the god's blood was mixed into the clay so as to bind god and Man genetically "to the end of days" so that both the flesh ("image") and the soul ("likeness") of the gods would become imprinted upon Man in a kinship of blood that could never be severed.

The "Epic of Gilgamesh" reports that when the gods decided to create a double for the partly divine Gilgamesh, the Mother Goddess mixed "clay" with the "essence" of the god Ninurta. Later on in the text, Enkidu's mighty strength is attributed to his having in him the "essence of Anu," an element he acquired through Ninurta, the grand-son of Anu.

The Akkadian term *kiṣir* refers to an "essence," a "concentration" that the gods of the heavens possessed. E. Ebeling summed up the efforts to understand the exact meaning of *kiṣir* by stating that as "Essence, or some nuance of the term, it could well be applied to deities as well as to missiles from Heaven." E. A. Speiser concurred that the term also implied "something that came down from Heaven." It carried the connotation, he wrote, "as would be indicated by the use of the term in medicinal contexts."

We are back to a simple, single word of translation: *gene.*

The evidence of the ancient texts, Mesopotamian as well as biblical, suggests that the process adopted for merging two sets of genes—those of a god and those of *Homo erectus*—involved the use of male genes as the divine element and female genes as the earthly element.

Repeatedly asserting that the Deity created Adam in his image and in his likeness, the Book of Genesis later describes the birth of Adam's son Seth in the following words:

> And Adam lived a hundred and thirty years,
> and had an offspring
> in his likeness and after his image;
> and he called his name Seth.

The terminology is identical to that used to describe the creation of Adam by the Deity. But Seth was certainly born to Adam by a biological process—the fertilization of a female egg by the male sperm of Adam, and the ensuing conception, pregnancy, and birth. The identical terminology bespeaks an identical process, and the only plausible conclusion is that Adam, too, was brought forth by the Deity through the process of fertilizing a female egg with the male sperm of a god.

If the "clay" into which the godly element was mixed was an earthly element—as all texts insist—then the only possible conclusion is that the male sperm of a god—his genetic material—was inserted into the egg of an ape-woman!

The Akkadian term for the "clay"—or, rather, "molding clay"—is *tit*. But its original spelling was TI.IT ("that which is with life"). In Hebrew, *tit* means "mud"; but its synonym is *boṣ*, which shares a root with *biṣa* ("marsh") and *beṣa* ("egg").

The story of Creation is replete with plays on words. We have seen the double and triple meanings of Adam–*adama*–*adamtu*–*dam*. The epithet for the Mother Goddess, NIN.TI, meant both "lady of life" and "lady of the rib." Why not, then, *boṣ*–*biṣa*–*beṣa* ("clay–mud–egg") as a play on words for the female ovum?

The ovum of a female *Homo erectus*, fertilized by the genes of a god, was then implanted within the womb of Ea's spouse; and after the "model" was obtained, duplicates of it were implanted in the wombs of birth goddesses, to undergo the process of pregnancy and birth.

> The Wise and learned,
> Double-seven birth-goddesses had assembled;
> Seven brought forth males,
> Seven brought forth females.
> The Birth Goddess brought forth
> The Wind of the Breath of Life.

In pairs were they completed,
In pairs were they completed in her presence.
The creatures were People—
Creatures of the Mother Goddess.

Homo sapiens had been created.

The ancient legends and myths, biblical information, and modern science are also compatible in one more aspect. Like the findings of modern anthropologists—that Man evolved and emerged in southeast Africa—the Mesopotamian texts suggest that the creation of Man took place in the Apsu—in the Lower World where the Land of the Mines was located. Paralleling Adapa, the "model" of Man, some texts mention "sacred Amama, the Earth woman," whose abode was in the Apsu.

In the "Creation of Man" text, Enki issues the following instructions to the Mother Goddess: "Mix to a core the clay from the Basement of Earth, just above the Abzu." A hymn to the creations of Ea, who "the Apsu fashioned as his dwelling," begins by stating:

Divine Ea in the *Apsu*
pinched off a piece of clay,
created Kulla to restore the temples.

The hymn continues to list the construction specialists, as well as those in charge of the "abundant products of mountain and sea," who were created by Ea—all, it is inferred, from pieces of "clay" pinched off in the Abzu—the Land of Mines in the Lower World.

The texts make it abundantly clear that while Ea built a brick house by the water in Eridu, in the Abzu he built a house adorned with precious stones and silver. It was there that his creature, Man, originated:

The Lord of the AB.ZU, the king Enki . . .
Built his house of silver and lapis-lazuli;
Its silver and lapis-lazuli, like sparkling light,
The Father fashioned fittingly in the AB.ZU.
The Creatures of bright countenance,
Coming forth from the AB.ZU,
Stood all about the Lord Nudimmud.

One can even conclude from the various texts that the creation of Man caused a rift among the gods. It would appear that at least at first the new Primitive Workers were confined to the Land of Mines. As a result, the Anunnaki who were toiling in Sumer proper were denied the benefits of the new manpower. A puzzling text named by the scholars "The Myth of the Pickax" is in fact the record of the events whereby the Anunnaki who stayed in Sumer under Enlil obtained their fair share of the Black-Headed People.

Seeking to reestablish "the normal order," Enlil took the extreme action of severing the contacts between "Heaven" (the Twelfth Planet or the spaceships) and Earth, and launched some drastic action against the place "where flesh sprouted forth."

> The Lord,
> That which is appropriate he caused to come about.
> The Lord Enlil,
> Whose decisions are unalterable,
> Verily did speed to separate Heaven from Earth
> So that the Created Ones could come forth;
> Verily did speed to separate Earth from Heaven.
> In the "Bond Heaven–Earth" he made a gash,
> So that the Created Ones could come up
> From the Place-Where-Flesh-Sprouted-Forth.

Against the "Land of Pickax and Basket," Enlil fashioned a marvelous weapon named AL.A.NI ("ax that produces power"). This weapon had a "tooth," which, "like a one-horned ox," could attack and destroy large walls. It was by all descriptions some kind of a huge power drill, mounted on a bulldozer-like vehicle that crushed everything ahead of it:

> The house which rebels against the Lord,
> The house which is not submissive to the Lord,
> The AL.A.NI makes it submissive to the Lord.
> Of the bad . . . , the heads of its plants it crushes;
> Plucks at the roots, tears at the crown.

Arming his weapon with an "earth splitter," Enlil launched the attack:

> The Lord called forth the AL.A.NI, gave its orders.
> He set the Earth Splitter as a crown upon its head,
> And drove it into the Place-Where-Flesh-Sprouted-Forth.
> In the hole was the head of a man;
> From the ground, people were breaking through
> towards Enlil.
> He eyed his Black-headed Ones in steadfast fashion.

Grateful, the Anunnaki put in their requests for the arriving Primitive Workers and lost no time in putting them to work:

> The Anunnaki stepped up to him,
> Raised their hands in greetings,
> Soothing Enlil's heart with prayers.
> Black-headed Ones they were requesting of him.
> To the Black-headed people,
> they give the pickax to hold.

The Book of Genesis likewise conveys the information that "the Adam" was created somewhere west of Mesopotamia, then brought over eastward to Mesopotamia to work in the Garden of Eden:

> And the Deity Yahweh
> Planted an orchard in Eden, in the east . . .
> And He took the Adam
> And placed him in the Garden of Eden
> To work it and to keep it.

13

THE END OF ALL FLESH

Man's lingering belief that there was some Golden Age in his prehistory cannot possibly be based on human recollection, for the event took place too long ago and Man was too primitive to record any concrete information for future generations. If Mankind somehow retains a subconscious sense that in those earliest days Man lived through an era of tranquillity and felicity, it is simply because Man knew no better. It is also because the tales of that era were first told Mankind, not by earlier men, but by the Nefilim themselves.

The only complete account of the events that befell Man following his transportation to the Abode of the Gods in Mesopotamia is the biblical tale of Adam and Eve in the Garden of Eden:

And the Deity Yahweh planted an orchard
In Eden, in the east;
And he placed there the Adam
Whom He had created.
And the Deity Yahweh
Caused to grow from the ground
Every tree that is pleasant to the sight
And good for eating;
And the Tree of Life was in the orchard
And the Tree of Knowing good and evil. . . .
And the Deity Yahweh took the Adam
And placed him in the Garden of Eden
To work it and to keep it.
And the Deity Yahweh
Commanded the Adam, saying:
"Of every tree of the orchard eat you shall;
but of the Tree of Knowing good and evil
thou shalt not eat of it;
for on the day that thou eatest thereof
thou shalt surely die."

Though two vital fruits were available, the Earthlings were prohibited from reaching only for the fruit of the Tree of Knowing. The Deity—at that point—appeared unconcerned that Man might try to reach for the Fruit of Life. Yet Man could not adhere even to that single prohibition, and tragedy followed.

The idyllic picture soon gave way to dramatic developments, which biblical scholars and theologians call the Fall of Man. It is a tale of unheeded divine commandments, divine lies, a wily (but truth-telling) Serpent, punishment, and exile.

Appearing from nowhere, the Serpent challenged God's solemn warnings:

And the Serpent . . . said unto the woman:
"Hath the Deity indeed said
'Ye shall not eat of any tree of the orchard'?"
And the woman said unto the Serpent:
"Of the fruits of the trees of the orchard
eat we may;
it is of the fruit of the tree in the
midst of the orchard that the Deity hath said:
'Ye shall not eat of it, neither touch it,
lest ye die.' "
And the Serpent said unto the woman:
"Nay, ye will surely not die;
It is that the Deity doth know
that on the day ye eat thereof
your eyes will be opened
and ye will be as the Deity—
knowing good and evil."
And the woman saw that the tree was good to eat
And that it was lustful to behold;
And the tree was desirable to make one wise;
And she took of its fruit and did eat,
And gave also to her mate with her, and he ate.
And the eyes of both of them were opened,
And they knew that they were naked;
And they sewed fig leaves together,
And made themselves loincloths.

Reading and rereading the concise yet precise tale, one cannot help wondering what the whole confrontation was about. Prohibited under threat of death from even touching the Fruit of Knowing, the two Earthlings were persuaded to go ahead and eat the stuff, which would make them "knowing" as the Deity. Yet all that happened was a sudden awareness that they were naked.

The state of nakedness was indeed a major aspect of the whole incident. The biblical tale of Adam and Eve in the Garden of Eden opens with the statement: "And the both of them were naked, the Adam and his mate, and they were not ashamed." They were, we are to understand, at some lesser stage of human development than that of fully developed humans: Not only were they naked, they were unaware of the implications of such nakedness.

Further examination of the biblical tale suggests that its theme is Man's acquisition of some sexual prowess. The "knowing" that was held back from Man was not some scientific information but something connected with the male and female sex; for no sooner had Man and his mate acquired the "knowing" than "they knew that they were naked" and covered their sex organs.

The continuing biblical narrative confirms the connection between nakedness and the lack of knowing, for it took the Deity no time at all to put the two together:

And they heard the sound of the Deity Yahweh
Walking in the orchard in the day's breeze,
And the Adam and his mate hid
From the Deity Yahweh amongst the orchard's trees.
And the Deity Yahweh called to the Adam
And said: "Where art thou?"
And he answered:
"Thy sound I heard in the orchard
and I was afraid, for I am naked;
and I hid."
And He said:
"Who told thee that thou art naked?
Hast thou eaten of the tree,
whereof I commanded thee not to eat?"

Admitting the truth, the Primitive Worker blamed his female mate, who, in turn, blamed the Serpent. Greatly angered, the Deity put curses on the Serpent and the two Earthlings. Then—surprisingly—"the Deity Yahweh made for Adam and his wife garments of skins, and clothed them."

One cannot seriously assume that the purpose of the whole incident—which led to the expulsion of the Earthlings from the Garden of Eden—was a dramatic way to explain how Man came to wear clothes. The wearing of clothes was merely an outward manifestation of the new "knowing." The acquisition of such "knowing," and the Deity's attempts to deprive Man of it, are the central themes of the events.

While no Mesopotamian counterpart of the biblical tale has yet been found, there can be little doubt that the tale—like all the biblical material concerning Creation and Man's prehistory—was of Sumerian origin. We have the locale: the Abode of the Gods in Mesopotamia. We have the telltale play on words in Eve's name ("she of life," "she of rib"). And we have two vital trees, the Tree of Knowing and the Tree of Life, as in Anu's abode.

Even the words of the Deity reflect a Sumerian origin, for the sole Hebrew Deity has again lapsed into the plural, addressing divine colleagues who were featured not in the Bible but in Sumerian texts:

> Then did the Deity Yahweh say:
> "Behold, the Adam has become as one of us,
> to know good and evil.
> And now might he not put forth his hand
> And partake also of the Tree of Life,
> and eat, and live forever?"
> And the Deity Yahweh expelled the Adam
> from the orchard of Eden.

As many early Sumerian depictions show, there had been a time when Man, as a Primitive Worker, served his gods stark naked. He was naked whether he served the gods their food and drink, or toiled in the fields or on construction jobs. (Figs. 154, 155)

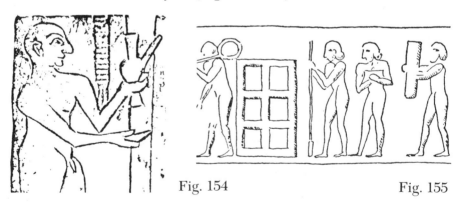

Fig. 154   Fig. 155

The clear implication is that the status of Man vis-à-vis the gods was not much different from that of domesticated animals. The gods had merely upgraded an existing animal to suit their needs. Did the lack of "knowing," then, mean that, naked as an animal, the newly fashioned being also engaged in sex as, or with, the animals? Some early depictions indicate that this was indeed the case. (Fig. 156)

Fig. 156

Sumerian texts like the "Epic of Gilgamesh" suggest that the manner of sexual intercourse did indeed account for a distinction between wild-Man and human-Man. When the people of Uruk wanted to civilize the wild Enkidu—"the barbarous fellow from the depths of the steppes"—they enlisted the services of a "pleasure girl" and sent her to meet Enkidu at the water hole where he used to befriend various animals, and there to offer him her "ripeness."

It appears from the text that the turning point in the process of "civilizing" Enkidu was the rejection *of* him *by* the animals he had befriended. It was important, the people of Uruk told the girl, that she continue to treat him to "a woman's task" until "his wild beasts, that grew up on his steppe, will reject him." For Enkidu to be torn away from sodomy was a prerequisite to his becoming human.

The lass freed her beasts, bared her bosom,
and he possessed her ripeness . . .
She treated him, the savage,
to a woman's task.

Apparently the ploy worked. After six days and seven nights, "after he had had his fill of her charms," he remembered his former playmates.

He set his face toward his wild beasts; but
On seeing him the gazelles ran off.
The wild beasts of the steppe
drew away from his body.

The statement is explicit. The human intercourse brought about such a profound change in Enkidu that the animals he had befriended "drew away from his body." They did not simply run away; they shunned physical contact with him.

Astounded, Enkidu stood motionless for a while, "for his wild animals had gone." But the change was not to be regretted, as the ancient text explains:

> Now he had vision, broader understanding. . . .
> The harlot says to him, to Enkidu:
> "Thou art knowing, Enkidu;
> Thou art become like a god!"

The words in this Mesopotamian text are almost identical to those of the biblical tale of Adam and Eve. As the Serpent had predicted, by partaking of the Tree of Knowing, they had become—in sexual matters—"as the Deity—knowing good and evil."

If this meant only that Man had come to recognize that having sex with animals was uncivilized or evil, why were Adam and Eve punished for giving up sodomy? The Old Testament is replete with admonitions against sodomy, and it is inconceivable that the learning of a virtue would cause divine wrath.

The "knowing" that Man obtained against the wishes of the Deity—or one of the deities—must have been of a more profound nature. It was something good for Man, but something his creators did not wish him to have.

We have to read carefully between the lines of the curse against Eve to grasp the meaning of the event:

> And to the woman He said:
> "I will greatly multiply thy suffering
> by thy pregnancy.
> In suffering shalt thou bear children,
> yet to thy mate shall be thy desire". . .
> And the Adam named his wife "Eve,"
> for she was the mother of all who lived.

This, indeed, is the momentous event transmitted to us in the biblical tale: As long as Adam and Eve lacked "knowing," they lived in the Garden of Eden without any offspring. Having obtained "knowing," Eve gained the ability (and pain) to become pregnant and bear children. Only after the couple had acquired this "knowing," "Adam *knew* Eve his wife, and she conceived and gave birth to Cain."

Throughout the Old Testament, the term "to know" is used to denote sexual intercourse, mostly between a man and his spouse for the purpose of having children. The tale of Adam and Eve in the Garden of Eden is the story of a crucial step in Man's development: *the acquisition of the ability to procreate.*

That the first representatives of *Homo sapiens* were incapable of reproduction should not be surprising. Whatever method the Nefilim had used to infuse some of their genetic material into the biological makeup of the hominids they selected for the purpose, the new being was a hybrid, a cross between two different, if related, species. Like a mule (a cross between a mare and a donkey), such mammal hybrids are sterile. Through artificial insemination and even more sophisticated methods of biological engineering, we can produce as many mules as we desire, even without actual intercourse between donkey and mare; but no mule can procreate and bring forth another mule.

Were the Nefilim, at first, simply producing "human mules" to suit their requirements?

Our curiosity is aroused by a scene depicted on a rock carving found in the mountains of southern Elam. It depicts a seated deity holding a "laboratory" flask from which liquids are flowing—a familiar depiction of Enki. A Great Goddess is seated next to him, a pose that indicates that she was a co-worker rather than a spouse; she could be none other than Ninti, the Mother Goddess or Goddess of Birth. The two are flanked by lesser goddesses—reminiscent of the birth goddesses of the Creation tales. Facing these creators of Man are row upon row of human beings, whose outstanding feature is that they all look alike—like products from the same mold. (Fig. 157)

Fig. 157

Our attention is also drawn again to the Sumerian tale of the imperfect males and females initially brought forth by Enki and the Mother Goddess, who were either sexless or sexually incomplete beings. Does this text recall the first phase of the existence of hybrid Man—a being in the likeness and image of the gods, but sexually incomplete: lacking in "knowing"?

After Enki managed to produce a "perfect model"—Adapa/Adam, "mass-production" techniques are described in the Sumerian texts: the implanting of the genetically treated ova in a "production line" of birth goddesses, with the advance knowledge that half would produce males and half would produce females. Not only does this bespeak the technique by which hybrid Man was "manufactured"; it also implies that Man could not procreate on his own.

The inability of hybrids to procreate, it has been discovered recently, stems from a deficiency in the reproductive cells. While all cells contain only one set of the hereditary chromosomes, Man and other mammals are able to reproduce because their sex cells (the male sperm, the female ovum) contain two sets each. But this unique feature is lacking in hybrids. Attempts are now being made through genetic engineering to provide hybrids with such a double set of chromosomes in their reproductive cells, making them sexually "normal."

Was that what the god whose epithet was "The Serpent" accomplished for Mankind?

The biblical Serpent surely was not a lowly, literal snake—for he could converse with Eve, he knew the truth about the matter of "knowing," and he was of such high stature that he unhesitatingly exposed the deity as a liar. We recall that in all ancient traditions, the chief deity fought a Serpent adversary—a tale whose roots undoubtedly go back to the Sumerian gods.

The biblical tale reveals many traces of its Sumerian origin, including the presence of other deities: "The Adam has become as one of *us*." The possibility that the biblical antagonists—the Deity and the Serpent—stood for Enlil and Enki seems to us entirely plausible.

Their antagonism, as we have discovered, originated in the transfer to Enlil of the command of Earth, although Enki had been the true pioneer. While Enlil stayed at the comfortable Mission Control Center at Nippur, Enki was sent to organize the mining operations in the Lower World. The mutiny of the Anunnaki was directed at Enlil and his son Ninurta; the god who spoke out for the mutineers was Enki. It was Enki who suggested, and undertook, the creation of Primitive Workers; Enlil had to use force to obtain some of these wonderful creatures. As the Sumerian texts recorded the course of human events, Enki as a rule emerges as Mankind's protagonist, Enlil as its strict discipliner if not outright antagonist. The role of a deity wishing to keep the new humans sexually suppressed, and of a deity willing and capable of bestowing on Mankind the fruit of "knowing," fit Enlil and Enki perfectly.

Once more, Sumerian and biblical plays on words come to our aid. The biblical term for "Serpent" is *nahash*, which does mean "snake." But the word comes from the root NHSH, which means "to decipher, to find out"; so that *nahash* could also mean "he who can decipher, he who finds things out," an epithet befitting Enki, the chief scientist, the God of Knowledge of the Nefilim.

Drawing parallels between the Mesopotamian tale of Adapa (who obtained "knowing" but failed to obtain eternal life) and the fate of Adam, S. Langdon (*Semitic Mythology*) reproduced a depiction unearthed in Mesopotamia that strongly suggests the biblical tale: a serpent entwined on a tree, pointing at its fruit. The celestial symbols are significant: High above is the Planet of Crossing, which stood for Anu; near the serpent is the Moon's crescent, which stood for Enki. (Fig. 158)

Most pertinent to our findings is the fact that in the Mesopotamian texts, the god who eventually granted "knowledge" to Adapa was none other than Enki:

> Wide understanding he perfected for him. . . .
> Wisdom [he had given him]. . . .
> To him he had given Knowledge;
> Eternal Life he had not given him.

A pictorial tale engraved on a cylinder seal found in Mari may well be an ancient illustration of the Mesopotamian version of the tale in Genesis. The engraving shows a great god seated on high ground rising from watery waves—an obvious depiction of Enki. Water-spouting serpents protrude from each side of this "throne."

Flanking this central figure are two treelike gods. The one on the right, whose branches have penis-shaped ends, holds up a bowl that presumably contains the Fruit of Life. The one on the left, whose branches have vagina-shaped ends, offers fruit-bearing branches, representing the Tree of "Knowing"—the god-given gift of procreation.

Standing to the side is another Great God; we suggest that he was Enlil. His anger at Enki is obvious. (Fig. 159)

We shall never know what caused this "conflict in the Garden of Eden." But whatever Enki's motives were, he did succeed in perfecting the Primitive Worker and in creating *Homo sapiens*, who could have his own offspring.

After Man's acquisition of "knowing," the Old Testament ceases to refer to him as "*the* Adam," and adopts as its subject *Adam*, a specific person, the first patriarch of the line of people with whom the Bible was concerned. But this coming of age of Mankind also marked a schism between God and Man.

The parting of the ways, with Man no longer a dumb serf of the gods but a person tending for himself, is ascribed in the Book of Genesis not to a decision by Man himself but to the imposition of a punishment by the Deity: lest the Earthling also acquire the ability to escape mortality, he shall be cast out of the Garden of Eden. According to these sources, Man's independent existence began not in southern Mesopotamia, where the Nefilim had established their cities and orchards, but to the east, in the Zagros Mountains: "And he drove out the Adam and made him reside east of the Garden of Eden."

Once more, then, biblical information conforms to scientific findings: Human culture began in the mountainous areas bordering the Mesopotamian plain. What a pity the biblical narrative is so brief, for it deals with what was Man's first civilized life on Earth.

Cast out of the Abode of the Gods, doomed to a mortal's life, but able to procreate, Man proceeded to do just that. The first Adam with whose generations the Old Testament was concerned "knew" his wife Eve, and she bore him a son, Cain, who tilled the land. Then Eve bore Abel, who was a shepherd. Hinting at homosexuality as the cause, the Bible relates that "Cain rose up unto his brother Abel and killed him."

Fearing for his life, Cain was given a protective sign by the Deity and was ordered to move farther east. At first leading a nomad's life, he finally settled in "the Land of Migration, well east of Eden." There he had a son whom he named Enoch ("inauguration"), "and he built a city, and called the name of the city after the name of his son." Enoch, in turn, had children and grandchildren and great-grandchildren. In the sixth generation after Cain, Lamech was born; his three sons are credited by the Bible as the bearers of civilization: Jabal "was the father of such as dwell in tents and have cattle"; Jubal "was the father of all that grasp lyre and harp"; Tubal-cain was the first smith.

But Lamech, too, as his ancestor Cain, became involved in murder—this time of both a man and a child. It is safe to assume that the victims were not some humble strangers, for the Book of Genesis dwells on the incident and considers it a turning point in the lineage of Adam. The Bible reports that Lamech summoned his two wives, mothers of his three sons, and confessed to them the double murder, declaring, "If Cain be sevenfold avenged, Lamech shall seventy and seven fold." This little-understood statement must be assumed to deal with the succession; we see it as an admission by Lamech to his wives that the hope

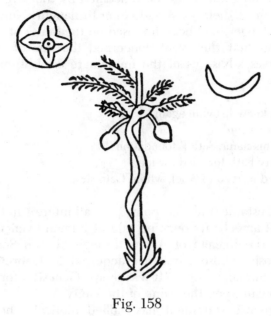

Fig. 158

Fig. 159

that the curse on Cain would be redeemed by the seventh generation (the generation of their sons) had come to naught. Now a new curse, lasting much longer, had been imposed on the house of Lamech.

Confirming that the event concerned the line of succession, the following verses advise us of the immediate establishment of a new, pure, lineage:

And Adam knew his wife again
and she bore a son
and called his name Seth ["foundation"]
for the Deity hath founded for me
another seed instead of Abel, whom Cain slew.

The Old Testament at that point loses all interest in the defiled line of Cain and Lamech. Its ongoing tale of human events is henceforth anchored on the lineage of Adam through his son Seth, and Seth's firstborn, Enosh, whose name has acquired in Hebrew the generic connotation "human being." "It was then," Genesis informs us, "that it was begun to call upon the name of the Deity."

This enigmatic statement has baffled biblical scholars and theologians throughout the ages. It is followed by a chapter giving the genealogy of Adam through Seth and Enosh for ten generations ending with Noah, the hero of the Deluge.

The Sumerian texts, which describe the early ages when the gods were alone in Sumer, describe with equal precision the life of humans in Sumer at a later time, but before the Deluge. The Sumerian (and original) story of the Deluge has as its "Noah" a "Man of Shuruppak," the seventh city established by the Nefilim when they landed on Earth.

At some point, then, the human beings—banished from Eden—were allowed to return to Mesopotamia, to live alongside the gods, to serve them, and to worship them. As we interpret the biblical statement, this happened in the days of Enosh. It was then that the gods allowed Mankind back into Mesopotamia, to serve the gods "and to call upon the name of the deity."

Eager to get to the next epic event in the human sage, the Deluge, the Book of Genesis provides little information besides the names of the patriarchs who followed Enosh. But the meaning of each patriarch's name may suggest the events that took place during his lifetime.

The son of Enosh, through whom the pure lineage continued, was Cainan ("little Cain"); some scholars take the name to mean "metalsmith." Cainan's son was Mahalal-El ("praiser of god"). He was followed by Jared ("he who descended"); his son was Enoch ("conse-

crated one"), who at age 365 was carried aloft by the Deity. But three
hundred years earlier, at age sixty-five, Enoch had begotten a son
named Methuselah; many scholars, following Lettia D. Jeffreys (*Ancient Hebrew Names: Their Significance and Historical Value*) translate
Methuselah as "man of the missile."

Methuselah's son was named Lamech, meaning "he who was
humbled." And Lamech begot Noah ("respite"), saying: "Let this one
comfort us concerning our work and the suffering of our hands by the
earth which the deity hath accursed."

Humanity, it appears, was undergoing great deprivations when
Noah was born. The hard work and the toil were getting it nowhere, for
Earth, which was to feed them, was accursed. The stage was set for the
Deluge—the momentous event which was to wipe off the face of Earth
not only the human race but all life upon the land and in the skies.

> And the Deity saw that the wickedness of Man
> was great on the earth,
> and that every desire of his heart's thoughts
> was only evil, every day.
> And the Deity repented that He had made Man
> upon the earth, and His heart grieved.
> And the Deity said:
> "I will destroy the Earthling whom I have created
> off the face of the earth."

These are broad accusations, presented as justifications for drastic
measures to "end all flesh." But they lack specificity, and scholars and
theologians alike find no satisfactory answers regarding the sins or
"violations" that could have upset the Deity so much.

The repeated use of the term *flesh*, both in the accusative verses and
in the proclamations of judgment, suggest, of course, that the corrup-
tions and violations had to do with the flesh. The Deity grieved over the
evil "desire of Man's thoughts." Man, it would seem, having discovered
sex, had become a sex maniac.

But one can hardly accept that the Deity would decide to wipe
Mankind off the face of Earth simply because men made too much love
to their wives. The Mesopotamian texts speak freely and eloquently of
sex and lovemaking among the gods. There are texts describing tender
love between gods and their consorts; illicit love between a maiden and
her lover; violent love (as when Enlil raped Ninlil). There is a profusion
of texts describing lovemaking and actual intercourse among the gods—
with their official consorts or unofficial concubines, with their sisters

336 · THE TWELFTH PLANET

and daughters and even granddaughters (making love to the latter was a favorite pastime of Enki). Such gods could hardly turn against Mankind for behaving as they themselves did.

The Deity's motive, we find, was not merely concern for human morals. The mounting disgust was caused by a spreading defilement of the gods themselves. Seen in this light, the meaning of the baffling opening verses of Genesis 6 becomes clear:

> And it came to pass,
> When the Earthlings began to increase in number
> upon the face of the Earth,
> and daughters were born unto them,
> that the sons of the deities
> saw the daughters of the Earthlings
> that they were compatible,
> and they took unto themselves
> wives of whichever they chose.

As these verses should make clear, it was when the sons of the gods began to be sexually involved with Earthlings' offspring that the Deity cried, "Enough!"

> And the Deity said:
> "My spirit shall not shield Man forever;
> having strayed, he is but flesh."

The statement has remained enigmatic for millennia. Read in the light of our conclusions regarding the genetic manipulation that was brought to play in Man's creation, the verses carry a message to our own scientists. The "spirit" of the gods—their genetic perfection of Mankind—was beginning to deteriorate. Mankind had "strayed," thereby reverting to being "but flesh"—closer to its animal, simian origins.

We can now understand the stress put by the Old Testament on the distinction between Noah, "a righteous man ... pure in his genealogies" and "the whole earth that was corrupt." By intermarrying with the men and women of decreasing genetic purity, the gods were subjecting themselves, too, to deterioration. By pointing out that Noah alone continued to be genetically pure, the biblical tale justifies the Deity's contradiction: Having just decided to wipe all life off the face of Earth, he decided to save Noah and his descendants and "every clean animal," and other beasts and fowls, "so as to keep seed alive upon the face of all the earth."

The Deity's plan to defeat his own initial purpose was to alert Noah to the coming catastrophe and guide him in the construction of a waterborne ark, which would carry the people and the creatures that were to be saved. The notice given to Noah was a mere seven days. Somehow, he managed to build the ark and waterproof it, collect all the creatures and put them and his family aboard, and provision the ark in the allotted time. "And it came to pass, after the seven days, that the waters of the Deluge were upon the earth." What came to pass is best described in the Bible's own words:

On that day,
all the fountains of the great deep burst open,
and the sluices of the heavens were opened. . . .
And the Deluge was forty days upon the Earth,
and the waters increased, and bore up the ark,
and it was lifted up above the earth.
And the waters became stronger
and greatly increased upon the earth,
and the ark floated upon the waters.
And the waters became exceedingly strong upon the
earth and all the high mountains were covered,
those that are under all the skies:
fifteen cubits above them did the water prevail,
and the mountains were covered.
And all flesh perished. . . .
Both man and cattle and creeping things
and the birds of the skies
were wiped off from the Earth;
And Noah only was left,
and that which were with him in the ark.

The waters prevailed upon Earth 150 days, when the Deity

caused a wind to pass upon the Earth,
and the waters were calmed.
And the fountains of the deep were dammed,
as were the sluices of the heavens;
and the rain from the skies was arrested.
And the waters began to go back from upon the Earth,
coming and going back.
And after one hundred and fifty days,
the waters were less;
and the ark rested on the Mounts of Ararat.

According to the biblical version, Mankind's ordeal began "in the six hundredth year of Noah's life, in the second month, on the seventeenth day of the month." The ark rested on the Mounts of Ararat "in the seventh month, on the seventeenth day of the month." The surge of the waters and their gradual "going back"—enough to lower the water level so that the ark rested on the peaks of Ararat—lasted, then, a full five months. Then "the waters continued to diminish, until the peaks of the mountains"—and not just the towering Ararats—"could be seen on the eleventh day of the tenth month," nearly three months later.

Noah waited another forty days. Then he sent out a raven and a dove "to see if the waters were abated from off the face of the ground." On the third try, the dove came back holding an olive leaf in her mouth, indicating that the waters had receded enough to enable treetops to be seen. After a while, Noah sent out the dove once more, "but she returned not again." The Deluge was over.

And Noah removed the covering of the Ark
and looked, and behold:
the face of the ground was dry.

"In the second month, on the twenty-seventh day of the month, did the earth dry up." It was the six hundred and first year of Noah. The ordeal had lasted a year and ten days.

Then Noah and all that were with him in the ark came out. And he built an altar and offered burnt sacrifices to the Deity.

And the Deity smelled the enticing smell
and said in his heart:
"I shall no longer curse the dry land
on account of the Earthling;
for his heart's desire is evil from his youth."

The "happy ending" is as full of contradictions as the Deluge story itself. It begins with a long indictment of Mankind for various abominations, including defilement of the purity of the younger gods. A momentous decision to have all flesh perish is reached and appears fully justified. Then the very same Deity rushes in a mere seven days to make sure that the seed of Mankind and other creatures shall not perish. When the trauma is over, the Deity is enticed by the smell of roasting meat and, forgetting his original determination to put an end to Mankind, dismisses the whole thing with an excuse, blaming Man's evil desires on his youth.

These nagging doubts of the story's veracity disperse, however, when we realize that the biblical account is an edited version of the original Sumerian account. As in the other instances, the monotheistic Bible has compressed into one Deity the roles played by several gods who were not always in accord.

Until the archaeological discoveries of the Mesopotamian civilization and the decipherment of the Akkadian and Sumerian literature, the biblical story of the Deluge stood alone, supported only by scattered primitive mythologies around the world. The discovery of the Akkadian "Epic of Gilgamesh" placed the Genesis Deluge tale in older and venerable company, further enhanced by later discoveries of older texts and fragments of the Sumerian original.

The hero of the Mesopotamian Deluge account was Ziusudra in Sumerian (Utnapishtim in Akkadian), who was taken after the Deluge to the Celestial Abode of the Gods to live there happily ever after. When, in his search for immortality, Gilgamesh finally reached the place, he sought Utnapishtim's advice on the subject of life and death. Utnapishtim disclosed to Gilgamesh—and through him to all post-Diluvial Mankind—the secret of his survival, "a hidden matter, a secret of the gods"—the true story (one might say) of the Great Flood.

The secret revealed by Utnapishtim was that before the onslaught of the Deluge the gods held a council and voted on the destruction of Mankind. The vote and the decision were kept secret. But Enki searched out Utnapishtim, the ruler of Shuruppak, to inform him of the approaching calamity. Adopting clandestine methods, Enki spoke to Utnapishtim from behind a reed screen. At first his disclosures were cryptic. Then his warning and advice were clearly stated:

Man of Shuruppak, son of Ubar-Tutu:
Tear down the house, build a ship!
Give up possessions, seek thou life!
Foreswear belongings, keep soul alive!
Aboard ship take thou the seed of all living things;
That ship thou shalt build—
her dimensions shall be to measure.

The parallels with the biblical story are obvious: A Deluge is about to come; one Man is forewarned; he is to save himself by preparing a specially constructed boat; he is to take with him and save "the seed of all living things." Yet the Babylonian version is more plausible. The decision to destroy and the effort to save are not contradictory acts of the same single Deity, but the acts of different deities. Moreover, the decision to forewarn and save the seed of Man is the defiant act of one god (Enki), acting in secret and contrary to the joint decision of the other Great Gods.

Why did Enki risk defying the other gods? Was he solely concerned with the preservation of *his* "wondrous works of art," or did he act against the background of a rising rivalry or enmity between him and his elder brother Enlil?

The existence of such a conflict between the two brothers is highlighted in the Deluge story.

Utnapishtim asked Enki the obvious question: How could he, Utnapishtim, explain to the other citizens of Shuruppak the construction of an oddly shaped vessel and the abandonment of all possessions? Enki advised him:

> Thou shalt thus speak unto them:
> "I have learnt that Enlil is hostile to me,
> so that I cannot reside in your city,
> nor set my foot in Enlil's territory.
> To the Apsu I will therefore go down,
> to dwell with my Lord Ea."

The excuse was thus to be that, as Enki's follower, Utnapishtim could no longer dwell in Mesopotamia, and that he was building a boat in which he intended to sail to the Lower World (southern Africa, by our findings) to dwell there with his Lord, Ea/Enki. Verses that follow suggest that the area was suffering from a drought or a famine; Utnapishtim (on Enki's advice) was to assure the residents of the city that if Enlil saw him depart, "the land shall [again] have its fill of harvest riches." This excuse made sense to the other residents of the city.

Thus misled, the people of the city did not question, but actually lent a hand in, the construction of the ark. By killing and serving them bullocks and sheep "every day" and by lavishing upon them "must, red wine, oil and white wine," Utnapishtim encouraged them to work faster. Even children were pressed to carry bitumen for waterproofing.

"On the seventh day the ship was completed. The launching was very difficult, so they had to shift the floor planks above and below, until two-thirds of the structure had gone into the water" of the Euphrates. Then Utnapishtim put all his family and kin aboard the ship, taking along "whatever I had of all the living creatures" as well as "the animals of the field, the wild beasts of the field." The parallels with the biblical tale—even down to the seven days of construction—are clear.

Going a step beyond Noah, however, Utnapishtim also sneaked aboard all the craftsmen who had helped him build the ship.

He himself was to go aboard only upon a certain signal, whose nature Enki had also revealed to him: a "stated time" to be set by Shamash, the deity in charge of the fiery rockets. This was Enki's order:

> "When Shamash who orders a trembling at dusk
> will shower down a rain of eruptions—
> board thou the ship, batten up the entrance!"

We are left guessing at the connection between this apparent firing of a space rocket by Shamash and the arrival of the moment for Utnapishtim to board his ark and seal himself inside it. But the moment did arrive; the space rocket did cause a "trembling at dusk"; there was a shower of eruptions. And Utnapishtim "battened down the whole ship" and "handed over the structure together with its contents" to "Puzur-Amurri, the Boatman."

The storm came "with the first glow of dawn." There was awesome thunder. A black cloud rose up from the horizon. The storm tore out the posts of buildings and piers; then the dikes gave. Darkness followed, "turning to blackness all that had been light;" and "the wide land was shattered like a pot."

For six days and six nights the "south-storm" blew.

> Gathering speed as it blew,
> submerging the mountains,
> overtaking the people like a battle....
> When the seventh day arrived,
> the flood-carrying south-storm
> subsided in the battle
> which it had fought like an army.
> The sea grew quiet,
> the tempest was still,
> the flood ceased.
> I looked at the weather.
> Stillness had set in.
> And all of Mankind had returned to clay.

The will of Enlil and the Assembly of the Gods was done.

But, unknown to them, the scheme of Enki had also worked: Floating in the stormy waters was a vessel carrying men, women, children, and other living creatures.

With the storm over, Utnapishtim "opened a hatch; light fell upon my face." He looked around; "the landscape was as level as a flat roof." Bowing low, he sat and wept, "tears running down on my face." He looked about for a coastline in the expanse of the sea; he saw none. Then:

> There emerged a mountain region;
> On the Mount of Salvation the ship came to a halt;
> Mount *Niṣir* ["salvation"] held the ship fast,
> allowing no motion.

For six days Utnapishtim watched from the motionless ark, caught in the peaks of the Mount of Salvation—the biblical peaks of Ararat. Then, like Noah, he sent out a dove to look for a resting place, but it came back. A swallow flew out and came back. Then a raven was set free—and flew off, finding a resting place. Utnapishtim then released all the birds and animals that were with him, and stepped out himself. He built an altar "and offered a sacrifice"—just as Noah had.

But here again the single-Deity–multideity difference crops up. When Noah offered a burnt sacrifice, "Yahweh smelled the enticing smell"; but when Utnapishtim offered a sacrifice, "the gods smelled the savor, the gods smelled the sweet savor. The gods crowded like flies about a sacrificer."

In the Genesis version, it was Yahweh who vowed never again to destroy Mankind. In the Babylonian version it was the Great Goddess who vowed: "I shall not forget. . . . I shall be mindful of these days, forgetting them never."

That, however, was not the immediate problem. For when Enlil finally arrived on the scene, he had little mind for food. He was hopping mad to discover that some had survived. "Has some living soul escaped? No man was to survive the destruction!"

Ninurta, his son and heir, immediately pointed a suspecting finger at Enki. "Who, other than Ea, can devise plans? It is Ea alone who knows every matter." Far from denying the charge, Enki launched one of the world's most eloquent defense summations. Praising Enlil for his own wisdom, and suggesting that Enlil could not possibly be "unreasoning"—a realist—Enki mixed denial with confession. "It was not I who disclosed the secret of the gods"; I merely let one Man, an "exceedingly wise" one, perceive by his own wisdom what the gods' secret was. And if indeed this Earthling is so wise, Enki suggested to Enlil, let's not ignore his abilities. "Now then, take counsel in regard to him!"

All this, the "Epic of Gilgamesh" relates, was the "secret of the gods" that Utnapishtim told Gilgamesh. He then told Gilgamesh of the final event. Having been influenced by Enki's argument,

> Enlil thereupon went aboard the ship.
> Holding me by the hand, he took me aboard.
> He took my wife aboard,
> made her kneel by my side.
> Standing between us,
> he touched our foreheads to bless us:
> "Hitherto Utnapishtim has been but human;
> henceforth Utnapishtim and his wife
> shall be unto us like gods.
> Utnapishtim shall reside in the Far Away,
> at the Mouth of the Waters!"

And Utnapishtim concluded his story to Gilgamesh. After he was taken to reside in the Far Away, Anu and Enlil

> Gave him life, like a god,
> Elevated him to eternal life, like a god.

But what happened to Mankind in general? The biblical tale ends with an assertion that the Deity then permitted and blessed Mankind to "be fruitful and multiply." Mesopotamian versions of the Deluge story also end with verses that deal with Mankind's procreation. The partly mutilated texts speak of the establishment of human "categories":

> . . . Let there be a third category among the Humans:
> Let there be among the Humans
> Women who bear, and women who do not bear.

There were, apparently, new guidelines for sexual intercourse:

> Regulations for the human race:
> Let the male . . . to the young maiden. . . .
> Let the young maiden. . . .
> The young man to the young maiden . . .
> When the bed is laid,
> let the spouse and her husband lie together.

Enlil was outmaneuvered. Mankind was saved and allowed to procreate. The gods opened up Earth to Man.

14
·

WHEN THE GODS FLED FROM EARTH

What was this Deluge, whose raging waters swept over Earth?

Some explain the Flood in terms of the annual inundations of the Tigris–Euphrates plain. One such inundation, it is surmised, must have been particularly severe. Fields and cities, men and beasts were swept away by the rising waters; and primitive peoples, seeing the event as a punishment by the gods, began to propagate the legend of a Deluge.

In one of his books, *Excavations at Ur*, Sir Leonard Woolley relates how, in 1929, as the work on the Royal Cemetery at Ur was drawing to a close, the workmen sank a small shaft at a nearby mound, digging through a mass of broken pottery and crumbled brick. Three feet down, they reached a level of hard-packed mud—usually soil marking the point where civilization had started. But could the millennia of urban life have left only three feet of archaeological strata? Sir Leonard directed the workmen to dig farther. They went down another three feet, then another five. They still brought up "virgin soil"—mud with no traces of human habitation. But after digging through eleven feet of silted, dry mud, the workmen reached a stratum containing pieces of broken green pottery and flint instruments. An earlier civilization had been buried under eleven feet of mud!

Sir Leonard jumped into the pit and examined the excavation. He called in his aides, seeking their opinions. No one had a plausible theory. Then Sir Leonard's wife remarked almost casually, "Well, of course, it's the Flood!"

Other archaeological delegations to Mesopotamia, however, cast doubt on this marvelous intuition. The stratum of mud containing no traces of habitation did indicate flooding; but while the deposits of Ur and al-'Ubaid suggested flooding sometime between 3500 and 4000 B.C., a similar deposit uncovered later at Kish was estimated to have occurred circa 2800 B.C. The same date (2800 B.C.) was estimated for mud strata found at Erech and at Shuruppak, the city of the Sumerian Noah. At Nineveh, excavators found, at a depth of some sixty feet, no less than thirteen alternate strata of mud and riverine sand, dating from 4000 to 3000 B.C.

Most scholars, therefore, believe that what Woolley found were traces of diverse local floodings—frequent occurrences in Mesopotamia, where occasional torrential rains and the swelling of the two great rivers and their frequent course changes cause such havoc. All the varying mud strata, scholars have concluded, were not the comprehensive calamity, the monumental prehistoric event that the Deluge must have been.

The Old Testament is a masterpiece of literary brevity and precision. The words are always well chosen to convey precise meanings; the verses are to the point; their order is purposeful; their length is no more than is absolutely needed. It is noteworthy that the whole story from Creation through the expulsion of Adam and Eve from the Garden of Eden is told in eighty verses. The complete record of Adam and his line, even when told separately for Cain and his line and Seth, Enosh, and their line, is managed in fifty-eight verses. But the story of the Great Flood merited no less than eighty-seven verses. It was, by any editorial standard, a "major story." No mere local event, it was a catastrophe affecting the whole of Earth, the whole of Mankind. The Mesopotamian texts clearly state that the "four corners of the Earth" were affected.

As such, it was a crucial point in the prehistory of Mesopotamia. There were the events and the cities and the people *before* the Deluge, and the events and cities and people *after* the Deluge. There were all the deeds of the gods and the Kingship that they lowered from Heaven *before* the Great Flood, and the course of godly and human events when Kingship was lowered again to Earth *after* the Great Flood. It was the great time divider.

Not only the comprehensive king lists but also texts relating to individual kings and their ancestries made mention of the Deluge. One, for example, pertaining to Ur-Ninurta, recalled the Deluge as an event remote in time:

> On that day, on that remote day,
> On that night, on that remote night,
> In that year, in that remote year—
> When the Deluge had taken place.

The Assyrian king Ashurbanipal, a patron of the sciences who amassed the huge library of clay tablets in Nineveh, professed in one of his commemorative inscriptions that he had found and was able to read "stone inscriptions from before the Deluge." An Akkadian text dealing with names and their origins explains that it lists names "of kings from after the Deluge." A king was exalted as "of seed preserved from before the Deluge." Various scientific texts quoted as their source "the olden sages, from before the Deluge."

No, the Deluge was no local occurrence or periodic inundation. It was by all counts an Earthshaking event of unparalleled magnitude, a catastrophe the likes of which neither Man nor gods experienced before or since.

°

The biblical and Mesopotamian texts that we have examined so far leave a few puzzles to be solved. What was the ordeal suffered by Mankind, in respect to which Noah was named "Respite" with the hope that his birth signaled an end to the hardships? What was the "secret" the gods swore to keep, and of whose disclosure Enki was accused? Why was the launching of a space vehicle from Sippar the signal to Utnapishtim to enter and seal the ark? Where were the gods while the waters covered even the highest mountains? And why did they so cherish the roasted meat sacrifice offered by Noah/Utnapishtim?

As we proceed to find the answers to these and other questions, we shall find that the Deluge was not a premeditated punishment brought about by the gods at their exclusive will. We shall discover that though the Deluge was a predictable event, it was an unavoidable one, a natural calamity in which the gods played not an active but a passive role. We will also show that the secret the gods swore to was a conspiracy against Mankind—to withhold from the Earthlings the information they had regarding the coming avalanche of water so that, while the Nefilim saved themselves, Mankind should perish.

Much of our greatly increased knowledge of the Deluge and the events preceding it comes from the text "When the gods as men." In it the hero of the Deluge is called Atra-Hasis. In the Deluge segment of the "Epic of Gilgamesh," Enki called Utnapishtim "the exceedingly wise"—which in Akkadian is *atra-hasis*.

Scholars theorized that the texts in which Atra-Hasis is the hero might be parts of an earlier, Sumerian Deluge story. In time, enough Babylonian, Assyrian, Canaanite, and even original Sumerian tablets were discovered to enable a major reassembly of the Atra-Hasis epic, a masterful work credited primarily to W. G. Lambert and A. R. Millard (*Atra-Hasis: The Babylonian Story of the Flood*).

After describing the hard work of the Anunnaki, their mutiny, and the ensuing creation of the Primitive Worker, the epic relates how Man (as we also know from the biblical version) began to procreate and multiply. In time, Mankind began to upset Enlil.

> The land extended, the people multiplied;
> In the land like wild bulls they lay.
> The god got disturbed by their conjugations;
> The god Enlil heard their pronouncements,
> and said to the great gods:
> "Oppressive have become the pronouncements of Mankind;
> Their conjugations deprive me of sleep."

Enlil—once again cast as the prosecutor of Mankind—then ordered a punishment. We would expect to read now of the coming Deluge. But not so. Surprisingly, Enlil did not even mention a Deluge or any similar watery ordeal. Instead, he called for the decimation of Mankind through pestilence and sicknesses.

The Akkadian and Assyrian versions of the epic speak of "aches, dizziness, chills, fever" as well as "disease, sickness, plague, and pestilence" afflicting Mankind and its livestock following Enlil's call for punishment. But Enlil's scheme did not work. The "one who was exceedingly wise"—Atra-Hasis—happened to be especially close to the god Enki. Telling his own story in some of the versions, he says, "I am Atra-Hasis; I lived in the temple of Ea my lord." With "his mind alert to his Lord Enki," Atra-Hasis appealed to him to undo his brother Enlil's plan:

> "Ea, O Lord, Mankind groans;
> the anger of the gods consumes the land.
> Yet it is thou who hast created us!
> Let there cease the aches, the dizziness,
> the chills, the fever!"

Until more pieces of the broken-off tablets are found, we shall not know what Enki's advice was. He said of something, ". . . let there appear in the land." Whatever it was, it worked. Soon thereafter, Enlil complained bitterly to the gods that "the people have not diminished; they are more numerous than before!"

He then proceeded to outline the extermination of Mankind through starvation. "Let supplies be cut off from the people; in their bellies, let fruit and vegetables be wanting!" The famine was to be achieved through natural forces, by a lack of rain and failing irrigation.

Let the rains of the rain god be withheld from above;
Below, let the waters not rise from their sources.
Let the wind blow and parch the ground;
Let the clouds thicken, but hold back the downpour.

Even the sources of seafood were to disappear: Enki was ordered to "draw the bolt, bar the sea," and "guard" its food away from the people.

Soon the drought began to spread devastation.

From above, the heat was not. . . .
Below, the waters did not rise from their sources.
The womb of the earth did not bear;
Vegetation did not sprout. . . .
The black fields turned white;
The broad plain was choked with salt.

The resulting famine caused havoc among the people. Conditions got worse as time went on. The Mesopotamian texts speak of six increasingly devastating *sha-at-tam*'s—a term that some translate as "years," but which literally means "passings," and, as the Assyrian version makes clear, "a year of Anu":

For one *sha-at-tam* they ate the earth's grass.
For the second *sha-at-tam* they suffered the vengeance.
The third *sha-at-tam* came;
their features were altered by hunger,
their faces were encrusted . . .
they were living on the verge of death.
When the fourth *sha-at-tam* arrived,
their faces appeared green;
they walked hunched in the streets;
their broad [shoulders?] became narrow.

By the fifth "passing," human life began to deteriorate. Mothers barred their doors to their own starving daughters. Daughters spied on their mothers to see whether they had hidden any food.

By the sixth "passing," cannibalism was rampant.

When the sixth *sha-at-tam* arrived
they prepared the daughter for a meal;
the child they prepared for food. . . .
One house devoured the other.

The texts report the persistent intercession by Atra-Hasis with his god Enki. "In the house of his god . . . he set foot; . . . every day he wept, bringing oblations in the morning . . . he called by the name of his god," seeking Enki's help to avert the famine.

Enki, however, must have felt bound by the decision of the other deities, for at first he did not respond. Quite possibly, he even hid from his faithful worshiper by leaving the temple and sailing into his beloved marshlands. "When the people were living on the edge of death," Atra-Ḥasis "placed his bed facing the river." But there was no response.

The sight of a starving, disintegrating Mankind, of parents eating their own children, finally brought about the unavoidable: another confrontation between Enki and Enlil. In the seventh "passing," when the remaining men and women were "like ghosts of the dead," they received a message from Enki. "Make a loud noise in the land," he said. Send out heralds to command all the people: "Do not revere your gods, do not pray to your goddesses." There was to be total disobedience!

Under the cover of such turmoil, Enki planned more concrete action. The texts, quite fragmented at this point, disclose that he convened a secret assembly of "elders" in his temple. "They entered . . . they took counsel in the House of Enki." First Enki exonerated himself, telling them how he had opposed the acts of the other gods. Then he outlined a plan of action; it somehow involved his command of the seas and the Lower World.

We can glean the clandestine details of the plan from the fragmentary verses: "In the night . . . after he . . ." someone had to be "by the bank of the river" at a certain time, perhaps to await the return of Enki from the Lower World. From there Enki "brought the water warriors"—perhaps also some of the Earthlings who were Primitive Workers in the mines. At the appointed time, commands were shouted: "Go! . . . the order . . ."

In spite of missing lines, we can gather what had happened from the reaction of Enlil. "He was filled with anger." He summoned the Assembly of the Gods and sent his sergeant at arms to fetch Enki. Then he stood up and accused his brother of breaking the surveillance-and-containment plans:

> All of us, Great Anunnaki,
> reached together a decision. . . .
> I commanded that in the Bird of Heaven
> Adad should guard the upper regions;
> that Sin and Nergal should guard
> the Earth's middle regions;
> that the bolt, the bar of the sea,
> you [Enki] should guard with your rockets.
> But you let loose provisions for the people!

Enlil accused his brother of breaking the "bolt to the sea." But Enki denied that it had happened with his consent:

> The bolt, the bar of the sea,
> I did guard with my rockets.
> [But] when . . . escaped from me . . .
> a myriad of fish . . . it disappeared;
> they broke off the bolt . . .
> they had killed the guards of the sea.

He claimed that he had caught the culprits and punished them, but Enlil was not satisfied. He demanded that Enki "stop feeding his people," that he no longer "supply corn rations on which the people thrive." The reaction of Enki was astounding:

> The god got fed up with the sitting;
> in the Assembly of the Gods,
> laughter overcame him.

We can imagine the pandemonium. Enlil was furious. There were heated exchanges with Enki and shouting. "There is slander in his hand!" When the Assembly was finally called to order, Enlil took the floor again. He reminded his colleagues and subordinates that it had been a unanimous decision. He reviewed the events that led to the fashioning of the Primitive Worker and recalled the many times that Enki "broke the rule."

But, he said, there was still a chance to doom Mankind. A "killing flood" was in the offing. The approaching catastrophe had to be kept a secret from the people. He called on the Assembly to swear themselves to secrecy and, most important, to "bind prince Enki by an oath."

> Enlil opened his mouth to speak
> and addressed the Assembly of all the gods:
> "Come, all of us, and take an oath
> regarding the Killing Flood!"
> Anu swore first;
> Enlil swore; his sons swore with him.

At first, Enki refused to take the oath. "Why will you bind me with an oath?" he asked. "Am I to raise my hands against my own humans?" But he was finally forced to take the oath. One of the texts specifically states: "Anu, Enlil, Enki, and Ninhursag, the gods of Heaven and Earth, had taken the oath."

The die was cast.

What was the oath he was bound by? As Enki chose to interpret it, he swore not to reveal the secret of the coming Deluge to the people; but could he not tell it to a wall? Calling Atra-Hasis to the temple, he made him stay behind a screen. Then Enki pretended to speak not to his devout Earthling but to the wall. "Reed screen," he said,

> Pay attention to my instructions.
> On all the habitations, over the cities,
> a storm will sweep.
> The destruction of Mankind's seed it will be. . . .
> This is the final ruling,
> the word of the Assembly of the gods,
> the word spoken by Anu, Enlil and Ninhursag.

(This subterfuge explains Enki's later contention, when the survival of Noah/Utnapishtim was discovered, that he had not broken his oath— that the "exceedingly wise" (atra-hasis) Earthling had found out the secret of the Deluge all by himself, by correctly interpreting the signs.) Pertinent seal depictions show an attendant holding the screen while Ea—as the Serpent God—reveals the secret to Atra-Hasis. (Fig. 160)

Fig. 160

Enki's advice to his faithful servant was to build a waterborne vessel; but when the latter said, "I have never built a boat . . . draw for me a design on the ground that I may see," Enki provided him with precise instructions regarding the boat, its measurements, and its construction. Steeped in Bible stories, we imagine this "ark" as a very large boat, with decks and superstructures. But the biblical term— teba—stems from the root "sunken," and it must be concluded that Enki instructed his Noah to construct a submersible boat—a submarine.

The Akkadian text quotes Enki as calling for a boat "roofed over and below," hermetically sealed with "tough pitch." There were to be no decks, no openings, "so that the sun shall not see inside." It was to be a boat "like an Apsu boat," a *sulili;* it is the very term used nowadays in Hebrew (*soleleth*) to denote a submarine.

"Let the boat," Enki said, "be a MA.GUR.GUR"—"a boat that can turn and tumble." Indeed, only such a boat could have survived an overpowering avalanche of waters.

The Atra-Hasis version, like the others, reiterates that although the calamity was only seven days away, the people were unaware of its approach. Atra-Hasis used the excuse that the "Apsu vessel" was being built so that he could leave for Enki's abode and perhaps thereby avert Enlil's anger. This was readily accepted, for things were really bad. Noah's father had hoped that his birth signaled the end of a long time of suffering. The people's problem was a drought—the absence of rain, the shortage of water. Who in his right mind would have thought that they were about to perish in an avalanche of water?

Yet if the humans could not read the signs, the Nefilim could. To them, the Deluge was not a sudden event; though it was unavoidable, they detected its coming. Their scheme to destroy Mankind rested not on an active but on a passive role by the gods. They did not cause the Deluge; they simply connived to withhold from the Earthlings the fact of its coming.

Aware, however, of the impending calamity, and of its global impact, the Nefilim took steps to save their own skins. With Earth about to be engulfed by water, they could go in only one direction for protection: skyward. When the storm that preceded the Deluge began to blow, the Nefilim took to their shuttlecraft, and remained in Earth orbit until the waters began to subside.

The day of the Deluge, we will show, was the day the gods fled from Earth.

The sign for which Utnapishtim had to watch, upon which he was to join all others in the ark and seal it, was this:

When Shamash,
who orders a trembling at dusk,
will shower down a rain of eruptions—
board thou the ship,
batten up the entrance!

Shamash, as we know, was in charge of the spaceport at Sippar. There is no doubt in our mind that Enki instructed Utnapishtim to watch for the first sign of space launchings at Sippar. Shuruppak, where Utnapishtim lived, was only 18 *beru* (some 180 kilometers, or 112 miles) south of Sippar. Since the launchings were to take place at dusk, there would be no problem in seeing the "rain of eruptions" that the rising rocket ships would "shower down."

Though the Nefilim were prepared for the Deluge, its coming was a frightening experience: "The noise of the Deluge ... set the gods trembling." But when the moment to leave Earth arrived, the gods, "shrinking back, ascended to the heavens of Anu." The Assyrian version of Atra-Hasis speaks of the gods using *rukub ilani* ("chariot of the gods") to escape from Earth. "The Anunnaki lifted up," their rocket-ships, like torches, "setting the land ablaze with their glare."

Orbiting Earth, the Nefilim saw a scene of destruction that affected them deeply. The Gilgamesh texts tell us that, as the storm grew in intensity, not only "could no one see his fellow," but "neither could the people be recognized from the heavens." Crammed into their space-craft, the gods strained to see what was happening on the planet from which they had just blasted off.

> The gods cowered like dogs,
> crouched against the outer wall.
> Ishtar cried out like a woman in travail:
> "The olden days are alas turned to clay.". . .
> The Anunnaki gods weep with her.
> The gods, all humbled, sit and weep;
> their lips drawn tight . . . one and all.

The Atra-Hasis texts echo the same theme. The gods, fleeing, were watching the destruction at the same time. But the situation within their own vessels was not very encouraging, either. Apparently, they were divided among several spaceships; Tablet III of the Atra-Hasis epic describes the conditions on board one where some of the Anunnaki shared accommodations with the Mother Goddess.

> The Anunnaki, great gods,
> were sitting in thirst, in hunger. . . .
> Ninti wept and spent her emotion;
> she wept and eased her feelings.
> The gods wept with her for the land.
> She was overcome with grief,
> she thirsted for beer.
> Where she sat, the gods sat weeping;
> crouching like sheep at a trough.
> Their lips were feverish of thirst,
> they were suffering cramp from hunger.

The Mother Goddess herself, Ninhursag, was shocked by the utter devastation. She bewailed what she was seeing:

The Goddess saw and she wept . . .
her lips were covered with feverishness. . . .
"My creatures have become like flies—
they filled the rivers like dragonflies,
their fatherhood was taken by the rolling sea."

Could she, indeed, save her own life while Mankind, which she helped create, was dying? Could she really leave the Earth, she asked aloud—

"Shall I ascend up to Heaven,
to reside in the House of Offerings,
where Anu, the Lord, had ordered to go?"

The orders to the Nefilim become clear: Abandon Earth, "ascend up to Heaven." It was a time when the Twelfth Planet was nearest Earth, within the asteroid belt ("Heaven"), as evidenced by the fact that Anu was able to attend personally the crucial conferences shortly before the Deluge.

Enlil and Ninurta—accompanied perhaps by the elite of the Anunnaki, those who had manned Nippur—were in one spacecraft, planning, no doubt, to rejoin the main spaceship. But the other gods were not so determined. Forced to abandon Earth, they suddenly realized how attached they had become to it and its inhabitants. In one craft, Ninhursag and her group of Anunnaki debated the merits of the orders given by Anu. In another, Ishtar cried out: "The olden days, alas, are turned into clay"; the Anunnaki who were in her craft "wept with her."

Enki was obviously in yet another spacecraft, or else he would have disclosed to the others that he had managed to save the seed of Mankind. No doubt he had other reasons to feel less gloomy, for the evidence suggests that he had also planned the encounter at Ararat.

The ancient versions appear to imply that the ark was simply carried to the region of Ararat by the torrential waves; and a "south-storm" would indeed drive the boat northward. But the Mesopotamian texts reiterate that Atra-Hasis/Utnapishtim took along with him a "Boatman" named Puzur-Amurri ("westerner who knows the secrets"). To him the Mesopotamian Noah "handed over the structure, together with its contents," as soon as the storm started. Why was an experienced navigator needed, unless it was to bring the ark to a specific destination?

The Nefilim, as we have shown, used the peaks of Ararat as landmarks from the very beginning. As the highest peaks in that part of the world, they could be expected to reappear first from under the mantle of water. Since Enki, "The Wise One, the All-Knowing," certainly could figure that much out, we can surmise that he had instructed his servant to guide the ark toward Ararat, planning the encounter from the very beginning.

Berossus's version of the Flood, as reported by the Greek Abydenus, relates: "Kronos revealed to Sisithros that there would be a Deluge on the fifteenth day of Daisios [the second month], and ordered him to conceal in Sippar, the city of Shamash, every available writing. Sisithros accomplished all these things, sailed immediately to Armenia, and thereupon what the god had announced did happen."

Berossus repeats the details regarding the release of the birds. When Sisithros (which is *atra-asis* reversed) was taken by the gods to their abode, he explained to the other people in the ark that they were "in Armenia" and directed them back (on foot) to Babylonia. We find in this version not only the tie-in with Sippar, the spaceport, but also confirmation that Sisithros was instructed to "sail immediately to Armenia"—to the land of Ararat.

As soon as Atra-Hasis had landed, he slaughtered some animals and roasted them on a fire. No wonder that the exhausted and hungry gods "gathered like flies over the offering." Suddenly they realized that Man and the food he grew and the cattle he raised were essential. "When at length Enlil arrived and saw the ark, he was wroth." But the logic of the situation and Enki's persuasion prevailed; Enlil made his peace with the remnants of Mankind and took Atra-Hasis/Utnapishtim in his craft up to the Eternal Abode of the Gods.

Another factor in the quick decision to make peace with Mankind may have been the progressive abatement of the Flood and the reemergence of dry land and the vegetation upon it. We have already concluded that the Nefilim became aware ahead of time of the approaching calamity; but it was so unique in their experience that they feared that Earth would become uninhabitable forever. As they landed on Ararat, they saw that this was not so. Earth was still habitable, and to live on it, they needed man.

What was this catastrophe—predictable yet unavoidable? An important key to unlocking the puzzle of the Deluge is the realization that it was not a single, sudden event, but the climax of a chain of events.

Unusual pestilences affecting man and beast and a severe drought preceded the ordeal by water—a process that lasted, according to the Mesopotamian sources, seven "passings," or *sar's*. These phenomena could be accounted for only by major climatic changes. Such changes have been associated in Earth's past with the recurring ice ages and interglacial stages that had dominated Earth's immediate past. Reduced precipitation, falling sea and lake levels, and the drying up of subterranean water sources have been the hallmarks of an approaching ice age. Since the Deluge that abruptly ended those conditions was followed by the Sumerian civilization and our own present, postglacial age, the glaciation in question could only have been the last one.

Our conclusion is that the events of the Deluge relate to Earth's last ice age and its catastrophic ending.

Drilling into the Arctic and Antarctic ice sheets, scientists have been able to measure the oxygen trapped in the various layers, and to judge from that the climate that prevailed millennia ago. Core samples from the bottoms of the seas, such as the Gulf of Mexico, measuring the proliferation or dwindling of marine life, likewise enable them to estimate temperatures in ages past. Based on such findings, scientists are now certain that the last ice age began some 75,000 years ago and underwent a mini-warming some 40,000 years ago. Circa 38,000 years ago, a harsher, colder, and drier period ensued. And then, about 13,000 years ago, the ice age abruptly ended, and our present mild climate was ushered in.

Aligning the biblical and Sumerian information, we find that the harsh times, the "accursation of Earth," began in the time of Noah's father Lamech. His hopes that the birth of Noah ("respite") would mark the end of the hardships was fulfilled in an unexpected way, through the catastrophic Deluge.

Many scholars believe that the ten biblical pre-Diluvial patriarchs (Adam to Noah) somehow parallel the ten pre-Diluvial rulers of the Sumerian king lists. These lists do not apply the divine titles DIN.GIR or EN to the last two of the ten, and treat Ziusudra/Utnapishtim and his father Ubar-Tutu as *men*. The latter two parallel Noah and his father Lamech; and according to the Sumerian lists, the two reigned a combined total of 64,800 years until the Deluge occurred. The last ice age, from 75,000 to 13,000 years ago, lasted 62,000 years. Since the hardships began when Ubartutu/Lamech was already reigning, the 62,000 fit perfectly into the 64,800.

Moreover, the extremely harsh conditions lasted, according to the Atra-Hasis epic, seven *shars*, or 25,200 years. The scientists discovered evidence of an extremely harsh period from circa 38,000 to 13,000 years ago—a span of 25,000 years. Once again, the Mesopotamian evidence and modern scientific findings corroborate each other.

Our endeavor to unravel the puzzle of the Deluge, then, focuses on Earth's climatic changes, and in particular the abrupt collapse of the ice age some 13,000 years ago.

What could have caused a sudden climatic change of such magnitude?

Of the many theories advanced by the scientists, we are intrigued by the one suggested by Dr. John T. Hollin of the University of Maine. He contended that the Antarctic ice sheet periodically breaks loose and slips into the sea, creating an abrupt and enormous tidal wave!

This hypothesis—accepted and elaborated upon by others—suggests that as the ice sheet grew thicker and thicker, it not only trapped more of Earth's heat beneath the ice sheet but also created (by pressure and friction) a slushy, slippery layer at its bottom. Acting as a lubricant between the thick ice sheet above and the solid earth below, this slushy layer sooner or later caused the ice sheet to slide into the surrounding ocean.

Hollin calculated that if only half the present ice sheet of Antarctica (which is, on the average, more than a mile in thickness) were to slip into the southern seas, the immense tidal wave that would follow would raise the level of all the seas around the globe by some sixty feet, inundating coastal cities and lowlands.

In 1964, A.T. Wilson of Victoria University in New Zealand offered the theory that ice ages ended abruptly in such slippages, not only in the Antarctic but also in the Arctic. We feel that the various texts and facts gathered by us justify a conclusion that the Deluge was the result of such a slippage into the Antarctic waters of billions of tons of ice, bringing an abrupt end to the last ice age.

The sudden event triggered an immense tidal wave. Starting in Antarctic waters, it spread northward toward the Atlantic, Pacific, and Indian oceans. The abrupt change in temperature must have created violent storms accompanied by torrents of rain. Moving faster than the waters, the storms, clouds, and darkened skies heralded the avalanche of waters.

Exactly such phenomena are described in the ancient texts.

As commanded by Enki, Atra-Hasis sent everybody aboard the ark while he himself stayed outside to await the signal for boarding the vessel and sealing it off. Providing a "human-interest" detail, the ancient text tells us that Atra-Hasis, though ordered to stay outside the vessel, "was in and out; he could not sit, could not crouch . . . his heart was broken; he was vomiting gall." But then:

. . . the Moon disappeared. . . .
The appearance of the weather changed;
The rains roared in the clouds. . . .
The winds became savage . . .
. . . the Deluge set out,

its might came upon the people like a battle;
One person did not see another,
they were not recognizable in the destruction.
The Deluge bellowed like a bull;
The winds whinnied like a wild ass.
The darkness was dense;
The Sun could not be seen.

The "Epic of Gilgamesh" is specific about the direction from which the storm came: It came from the south. Clouds, winds, rain, and darkness indeed preceded the tidal wave which first tore down the "posts of Nergal" in the Lower World:

With the glow of dawn
a black cloud arose from the horizon;
inside it the god of storms thundered. . . .
Everything that had been bright
turned to blackness. . . .
For one day the south storm blew,
gathering speed as it blew, submerging the mountains. . . .
Six days and six nights blows the wind
as the South Storm sweeps the land.
When the seventh day arrived,
the Deluge of the South Storm subsided.

The references to the "south storm," "south wind" clearly indicate the direction from which the Deluge arrived, its clouds and winds, the "heralds of the storm," moving "over hill and plain" to reach Mesopotamia. Indeed, a storm and an avalanche of water originating in the Antarctic would reach Mesopotamia via the Indian Ocean after first engulfing the hills of Arabia, then inundating the Tigris–Euphrates plain. The "Epic of Gilgamesh" also informs us that before the people and their land were submerged, the "dams of the dry land" and its dikes were "torn out": the continental coastlines were overwhelmed and swept over.

The biblical version of the Deluge story reports that the "bursting of the fountains of the Great Deep" preceded the "opening of the sluices of heaven." First, the waters of the "Great Deep" (what a descriptive name for the southernmost, frozen Antarctic seas) broke loose out of their icy confinement; only then did the rains begin to pour from the skies. This confirmation of our understanding of the Deluge is repeated, in reverse, when the Deluge subsided. First the "Fountains of the Deep [were] dammed"; then the rain "was arrested from the skies."

After the first immense tidal wave, its waters were still "coming and going back" in huge waves. Then the waters began "going back," and "they were less" after 150 days, when the ark came to rest between the peaks of Ararat. The avalanche of water, having come from the southern seas, went back to the southern seas.

○

How could the Nefilim predict *when* the Deluge would burst out of Antarctica?

The Mesopotamian texts, we know, related the Deluge and the climatic changes preceding it to seven "passings"—undoubtedly meaning the periodic passage of the Twelfth Planet in Earth's vicinity. We know that even the Moon, Earth's small satellite, exerts sufficient gravitational pull to cause the tides. Both Mesopotamian and biblical texts described how the Earth shook when the Celestial Lord passed in Earth's vicinity. Could it be that the Nefilim, observing the climatic changes and the instability of the Antarctic ice sheet, realized that the next, seventh "passing" of the Twelfth Planet would trigger the impending catastrophe?

Ancient texts show that it was so.

The most remarkable of these is a text of some thirty lines inscribed in miniature cuneiform writing on both sides of a clay tablet less than one inch long. It was unearthed at Ashur, but the profusion of Sumerian words in the Akkadian text leaves no doubt as to its Sumerian origin. Dr. Erich Ebeling determined that it was a hymn recited in the House of the Dead, and he therefore included the text in his masterwork *(Tod und Leben)* on death and resurrection in ancient Mesopotamia.

On close examination, however, we find that the composition "called on the names" of the Celestial Lord, the Twelfth Planet. It elaborates the meaning of the various epithets by relating them to the passage of the planet at the site of the battle with Tiamat—a passage that causes the Deluge!

The text begins by announcing that, for all its might and size, the planet ("the hero") nevertheless orbits the Sun. The Deluge was the "weapon" of this planet.

> His weapon is the Deluge;
> God whose Weapon brings death to the wicked.
> Supreme, Supreme, Anointed . . .
> Who like the Sun, the lands crosses;
> The Sun, his god, he frightens.

Calling out the "first name" of the planet—which, unfortunately, is illegible—the text describes the passage near Jupiter, toward the site of the battle with Tiamat:

First Name: . . .
Who the circular band hammered together;
Who the Occupier split in two, poured her out.
Lord, who at Akiti time
Within Tiamat's battle place reposes. . . .
Whose seed are the sons of Babylon;
Who by the planet Jupiter cannot be distracted;
Who by his glow shall create.

Coming closer, the Twelfth Planet is called SHILIG.LU.DIG ("powerful leader of the joyous planets"). It is now nearest to Mars: "By the brilliance of the god [planet] Anu god [planet] Laḫmu [Mars] is clothed." Then it loosed the Deluge upon the Earth:

This is the name of the Lord
Who from the second month to the month Addar
The waters had summoned forth.

The text's elaboration of the two names offers remarkable calendarial information. The Twelfth Planet passed Jupiter and neared Earth "at *Akiti* time," when the Mesopotamian New Year began. By the second month it was closest to Mars. Then, "from the second month to the month Addar" (the twelfth month), it loosed the Deluge upon Earth.

This is in perfect harmony with the biblical account, which states that "the fountains of the great deep burst open" on the seventeenth day of the second month. The ark came to rest on Ararat in the seventh month; other dry land was visible in the tenth month; and the Deluge was over in the twelfth month—for it was on "the first day of the first month" of the following year that Noah opened the ark's hatch.

Shifting to the second phase of the Deluge, when the waters began to subside, the text calls the planet SHUL.PA.KUN.E.

Hero, Supervising Lord,
Who collects together the waters;
Who by gushing waters
The righteous and the wicked cleanses;
Who in the twin-peaked mountain
Arrested the. . . .
. . . fish, river, river; the flooding rested.
In the mountainland, on a tree, a bird rested.
Day which . . . said.

In spite of the illegibility of some damaged lines, the parallels with the biblical and other Mesopotamian Deluge tales is evident: The flooding had ceased, the ark was "arrested" on the twin-peaked mountain; the rivers began to flow again from the mountaintops and carry the waters back to the oceans; fish were seen; a bird was sent out from the ark. The ordeal was over.

The Twelfth Planet had passed its "crossing." It had neared Earth, and it began to move away, accompanied by its satellites:

When the savant shall call out: "Flooding!"—
It is the god *Nibiru* ["Planet of Crossing"];
It is the Hero, the planet with four heads.
The god whose weapon is the Flooding Storm,
shall turn back;
To his resting place he shall lower himself.

(The receding planet, the text asserts, then recrossed the path of Saturn in the month of Ululu, the sixth month of the year.)

The Old Testament frequently refers to the time when the Lord caused Earth to be covered by the waters of the deep. The twenty-ninth Psalm describes the "calling" as well as the "return" of the "great waters" by the Lord:

Unto the Lord, ye sons of the gods,
Give glory, acknowledge might. . . .
The sound of the Lord is upon the waters;
The God of glory, the Lord,
Thundereth upon the great waters. . . .
The Lord's sound is powerful,
The Lord's sound is majestic;
The Lord's sound breaketh the cedars. . . .
He makes [Mount] Lebanon dance as a calf,
[Mount] Sirion leap like a young bull.
The Lord's sound strikes fiery flames;
The Lord's sound shaketh the desert. . . .
The Lord to the Deluge [said]: "Return!"
The Lord, as king, is enthroned forever.

In the magnificent Psalm 77—"Aloud to God I Cry"—the Psalmist recalls the Lord's appearance and disappearance in earlier times:

I have calculated the Olden Days,
The years of *Olam.* . . .
I shall recall the Lord's deeds,
Remember thy wonders in antiquity. . . .
Thine course, O Lord, is determined;

No god is as great as the Lord. . . .
The waters saw thee, O Lord, and shuddered;
Thine splitting sparks went forth.
The sound of thine thunder was rolling;
Lightnings lit up the world;
The Earth was agitated and it quaked.
[Then] in the waters was thy course,
Thine paths in the deep waters;
And thine footsteps were gone, unknown.

Psalm 104, exalting the deeds of the Celestial Lord, recalled the time when the oceans overran the continents and were made to go back:

Thou didst fix the Earth in constancy,
For ever and ever to be unmoved.
With the oceans, as with garment, thou coveredst it;
Above the mountains did the water stand.
At thy rebuke, the waters fled;
At the sound of thine thunder, they hastened away.
They went upon the mountains, then down to the valleys
Unto the place which thou hast founded for them.
A boundary thou hast set, not to be passed over;
That they turn not again to cover the Earth.

The words of the prophet Amos are even more explicit:

Woe unto you that desire the Day of the Lord;
To what end is it for you?
For the Day of the Lord is darkness and no light. . . .
Turneth morning unto death's shadow,
Maketh the day dark as night;
Calleth forth the waters of the sea
and poureth them upon the face of the Earth.

These, then, were the events that took place "in olden days." The "Day of the Lord" was the day of the Deluge.

We have already shown that, having landed on Earth, the Nefilim associated the first reigns in the first cities with the zodiacal ages—giving the zodiacs the epithets of the various associated gods. We now find that the text uncovered by Ebeling provided calendarial information not only for men but also for the Nefilim. The Deluge, it informs us, occurred in the "Age of the constellation Lion":

Supreme, Supreme, Anointed;
Lord whose shining crown with terror is laden.
Supreme planet: a seat he has set up
Facing the confined orbit of the red planet [Mars].
Daily within the Lion he is afire;
His light his bright kingships on the lands pronounces.

We can now also understand an enigmatic verse in the New Year's rituals, stating that it was "the constellation Lion that measured the waters of the deep." These statements place the time of the Deluge within a definite framework, for though astronomers nowadays cannot precisely ascertain where the Sumerians set the beginning of a zodiacal house, the following timetable for the ages is considered accurate.

60 B.C. to A.D. 2100—Age of Pisces
2220 B.C. to 60 B.C.—Age of Aries
4380 B.C. to 2220 B.C.—Age of Taurus
6540 B.C. to 4380 B.C.—Age of Gemini
8700 B.C. to 6540 B.C.—Age of Cancer
10,860 B.C. to 8700 B.C.—Age of the Lion

If the Deluge occurred in the Age of the Lion, or sometime between 10,860 B.C. and 8700 B.C., then the date of the Deluge falls well within our timetable: According to modern science, the last ice age ended abruptly in the southern hemisphere some twelve to thirteen thousand years ago, and in the northern hemisphere one or two thousand years later.

The zodiacal phenomenon of precession offers even more comprehensive corroboration of our conclusions. We concluded earlier that the Nefilim landed on Earth 432,000 years (120 *shar*'s) before the Deluge, in the Age of Pisces. In terms of the precessional cycle, 432,000 years comprise sixteen full cycles, or Great Years, and more than halfway through another Great Year, into the "age" of the constellation of the Lion.

We can now reconstruct the complete timetable for the events embraced by our findings.

Years Ago	*EVENT*
445,000	The Nefilim, led by Enki, arrive on Earth from the Twelfth Planet. Eridu—Earth Station I—is established in southern Mesopotamia.
430,000	The great ice sheets begin to recede. A hospitable climate in the Near East.
415,000	Enki moves inland, establishes Larsa.
400,000	The great interglacial period spreads globally. Enlil arrives on Earth, establishes Nippur as Mission Control Center. Enki establishes sea routes to southern Africa, organizes gold-mining operations.
360,000	The Nefilim establish Bad-Tibira as their metallurgical center for smelting and refining. Sippar, the spaceport, and other cities of the gods are built.
300,000	The Anunnaki mutiny. Man—the "Primitive Worker"—is fashioned by Enki and Ninhursag.
250,000	"Early *Homo sapiens*" multiply, spread to other continents.
200,000	Life on Earth regresses during new glacial period.
100,000	Climate warms again. The sons of the gods take the daughters of Man as wives.
77,000	Ubartutu/Lamech, a human of divine parentage, assumes the reign in Shuruppak under the patronage of Ninhursag.
75,000	The "accursation of Earth"—a new ice age—begins. Regressive types of Man roam Earth.
49,000	The reign of Ziusudra ("Noah"), a "faithful servant" of Enki, begins.
38,000	The harsh climatic period of the "seven passings" begins to decimate Mankind. Europe's Neanderthal Man disappears; only Cro-Magnon Man (based in the Near East) survives. Enlil, disenchanted with Mankind, seeks its demise.
13,000	The Nefilim, aware of the impending tidal wave that will be triggered by the nearing Twelfth Planet, vow to let Mankind perish.

The Deluge sweeps over Earth, abruptly ending the ice age.

15

·

KINGSHIP ON EARTH

The Deluge, a traumatic experience for Mankind, was no less so for the "gods"—the Nefilim.

In the words of the Sumerian king lists, "the Deluge had swept over," and an effort of 120 *shar*'s was wiped away overnight. The south African mines, the cities in Mesopotamia, the control center at Nippur, the spaceport at Sippar—all lay buried under water and mud. Hovering in their shuttlecraft above devastated Earth, the Nefilim impatiently awaited the abatement of the waters so that they could set foot again on solid ground.

How were they going to survive henceforth on Earth when their cities and facilities were gone, and even their manpower—Mankind—was totally destroyed?

When the frightened, exhausted, and hungry groups of Nefilim finally landed on the peaks of the "Mount of Salvation," they were clearly relieved to discover that Man and beast alike had not perished completely. Even Enlil, at first enraged to discover that his aims had been partly frustrated, soon changed his mind.

The deity's decision was a practical one. Faced with their own dire conditions, the Nefilim cast aside their inhibitions about Man, rolled up their sleeves, and lost no time in imparting to Man the arts of growing crops and cattle. Since survival, no doubt, depended on the speed with which agriculture and animal domestication could be developed to sustain the Nefilim and a rapidly multiplying Mankind, the Nefilim applied their advanced scientific knowledge to the task.

·

Unaware of the information that could be culled from the biblical and Sumerian texts, many scientists who have studied the origins of agriculture have arrived at the conclusion that its "discovery" by Mankind some 13,000 years ago was related to the neothermal ("newly warm") climate that followed the end of the last ice age. Long before modern scholars, however, the Bible also related the beginnings of agriculture to the aftermath of the Deluge.

"Sowing and Harvesting" were described in Genesis as divine gifts granted to Noah and his offspring as part of the post-Diluvial covenant between the Deity and Mankind:

For as long as the Earth's days shall be,
There shall not cease
Sowing and Harvesting,
Cold and Warmth,
Summer and Winter,
Day and Night.

Having been granted the knowledge of agriculture, "Noah as a Husbandman was first, and he planted a vineyard": He became the first post-Diluvial farmer engaged in the deliberate, complicated task of planting.

The Sumerian texts, too, ascribed to the gods the granting to Mankind of both agriculture and the domestication of animals.

Tracing the beginnings of agriculture, modern scholars have found that it appeared first in the Near East, but not in the fertile and easily cultivated plains and valleys. Rather, agriculture began in the mountains skirting the low-lying plains in a semicircle. Why would farmers avoid the plains and limit their sowing and reaping to the more difficult mountainous terrain?

The only plausible answer is that the low-lying lands were, at the time when agriculture began, uninhabitable; 13,000 years ago the low-lying areas were not yet dry enough following the Deluge. Millennia passed before the plains and valleys had dried sufficiently to permit the people to come down from the mountains surrounding Mesopotamia and to settle the low-lying plains. This, indeed, is what the Book of Genesis tells us: Many generations after the Deluge, people arriving "from the East"—from the mountainous areas east of Mesopotamia— "found a plain in the land of Shin'ar [Sumer], and settled there."

The Sumerian texts state that Enlil first spread cereals "in the hill country"—in the mountains, not in the plains—and that he made cultivation possible in the mountains by keeping the floodwaters away. "He barred the mountains as with a door." The name of this mountainous land east of Sumer, E.LAM, meant "house where vegetation germinated." Later, two of Enlil's helpers, the gods Ninazu and Ninmada, extended the cultivation of cereals to the low-lying plains so that, eventually, "Sumer, the land that knew not grain, came to know grain."

Scholars, who have now established that agriculture began with the domestication of wild emmer as a source of wheat and barley, are unable to explain how the earliest grains (like those found at the Shanidar cave) were already uniform and highly specialized. Thousands of generations of genetic selection are needed by nature to acquire even a modest degree of sophistication. Yet the period, time, or location in which such a gradual and very prolonged process might have taken place on Earth are nowhere to be found. There is no explanation for this botanogenetic miracle, unless the process was not one of natural selection but of artificial manipulation.

Spelt, a hard-grained type of wheat, poses an even greater mystery. It is the product of "an unusual mixture of botanic genes," neither a development from one genetic source nor a mutation of one source. It is definitely the result of mixing the genes of several plants. The whole notion that Man, in a few thousand years, changed animals through domestication, is also questionable.

Modern scholars have no answers to these puzzles, nor to the general question of why the mountainous semicircle in the ancient Near East became a continuous source of new varieties of cereals, plants, trees, fruits, vegetables, and domesticated animals.

The Sumerians knew the answer. The seeds, they said, were a gift sent to Earth by Anu from his Celestial Abode. Wheat, barley, and hemp were lowered to Earth from the Twelfth Planet. Agriculture and the domestication of animals were gifts given to Mankind by Enlil and Enki, respectively.

Not only the presence of the Nefilim but also the periodic arrivals of the Twelfth Planet in Earth's vicinity seem to lie behind the three crucial phases of Man's post-Diluvial civilization: agriculture, circa 11,000 B.C., the Neolithic culture, circa 7500 B.C., and the sudden civilization of 3800 B.C. took place at intervals of 3,600 years.

It appears that the Nefilim, passing knowledge to Man in measured doses, did so in intervals matching the periodic returns of the Twelfth Planet to Earth's vicinity. It was as though some on-site inspection, some face-to-face consultation possible only during the "window" period that allowed landings and takeoffs between Earth and the Twelfth Planet, had to take place among the "gods" before another "go ahead" could be given.

The "Epic of Etana" provides a glimpse of the deliberations that took place. In the days that followed the Deluge, it says:

The great Anunnaki who decree the fate
sat exchanging their counsels regarding the land.
They who created the four regions,
who set up the settlements, who oversaw the land,
were too lofty for Mankind.

The Nefilim, we are told, reached the conclusion that they needed an intermediary between themselves and the masses of humans. They were, they decided, to be gods—*elu* in Akkadian, meaning "lofty ones." As a bridge between themselves as lords and Mankind, they introduced "Kingship" on Earth: appointing a human ruler who would assure Mankind's service to the gods and channel the teachings and laws of the gods to the people.

A text dealing with the subject describes the situation before either tiara or crown had been placed on a human head, or scepter handed down; all these symbols of Kingship—plus the shepherd's crook, the symbol of righteousness and justice—"lay deposited before Anu in Heaven." After the gods had reached their decision, however, "Kingship descended from Heaven" to Earth.

Both Sumerian and Akkadian texts state that the Nefilim retained the "lordship" over the lands, and had Mankind first rebuild the pre-Diluvial cities exactly where they had originally been and as they had been planned: "Let the bricks of all the cities be laid on the dedicated places, let all the [bricks] rest on holy places." Eridu, then, was first to be rebuilt.

The Nefilim then helped the people plan and build the first royal city, and they blessed it. "May the city be the nest, the place where Mankind shall repose. May the King be a Shepherd."

The first royal city of Man, the Sumerian texts tell us, was Kish. "When Kingship was lowered again from Heaven, the Kingship was in Kish." The Sumerian king lists, unfortunately, are mutilated just where the name of the very first human king was inscribed. We do know, however, that he started a long line of dynasties whose royal abode changed from Kish to Uruk, Ur, Awan, Hamazi, Aksak, Akkad, and then to Ashur and Babylon and more recent capitals.

The biblical "Table of Nations" likewise listed Nimrud—the patriarch of the kingdoms at Uruk, Akkad, Babylon, and Assyria—as descended from Kish. It records the spread of Mankind, its lands and Kingships, as an outgrowth of the division of Mankind into three branches following the Deluge. Descended from and named after the three sons of Noah, these were the peoples and lands of Shem, who inhabited Mesopotamia and the Near Eastern lands; Ham, who inhabited Africa and parts of Arabia; and Japheth, the Indo-Europeans in Asia Minor, Iran, India, and Europe.

These three broad groupings were undoubtedly three of the "regions" whose settlement was discussed by the great Anunnaki. Each of the three was assigned to one of the leading deities. One of these was, of course, Sumer itself, the region of the Semitic peoples, the place where Man's first great civilization arose.

The other two also became sites of flourishing civilizations. Circa 3200 B.C.—about half a millennium after the blooming of the Sumerian civilization—statehood, Kingship, and civilization made their first appearance in the Nile valley, leading in time to the great civilization of Egypt.

Nothing was known until some fifty years ago about the first major Indo-European civilization. But by now it is well established that an advanced civilization, encompassing large cities, a developed agriculture, a flourishing trade, existed in the Indus valley in ancient times. It came into being, scholars believe, some 1,000 years after the Sumerian civilization began. (Fig. 161)

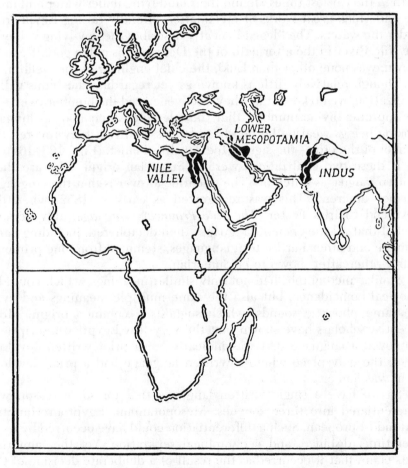

Fig. 161

Ancient texts as well as archaeological evidence attest to the close cultural and economic links between these two river-valley civilizations and the older Sumerian one. Moreover, both direct and circumstantial evidence has convinced most scholars that the civilizations of the Nile and Indus not only were linked to, but were actually offspring of, the earlier civilization of Mesopotamia.

The most imposing monuments of Egypt, the pyramids, have been found to be, under a stone "skin," simulations of the Mesopotamian ziggurats; and there is reason to believe that the ingenious architect who designed the plans for the great pyramids and supervised their construction was a Sumerian venerated as a god. (Fig. 162)

The ancient Egyptian name for their land was the "Raised Land," and their prehistoric memory was that "a very great god who came forth in the earliest times" found their land lying under water and mud. He undertook great works of reclamation, literally raising Egypt from under the waters. The "legend" neatly describes the low-lying valley of the Nile River in the aftermath of the Deluge; this olden god, it can be shown, was none other than Enki, the chief engineer of the Nefilim.

Though relatively little is known as yet regarding the Indus valley civilization, we do know that they, too, venerated the number twelve as the supreme divine number; that they depicted their gods as human-looking beings wearing horned headdresses; and that they revered the symbol of the cross—the sign of the Twelfth Planet. (Figs. 163, 164)

If these two civilizations were of Sumerian origin, why are their written languages different? The scientific answer is that the languages are not different. This was recognized as early as 1852, when the Reverend Charles Foster (*The One Primeval Language*) ably demonstrated that all the ancient languages then deciphered, including early Chinese and other Far Eastern languages, stemmed from one primeval source—thereafter shown to be Sumerian.

Similar pictographs had not only similar meanings, which could be a logical coincidence, but also the same multiple meanings and even the same phonetic sounds—which suggests a common origin. More recently, scholars have shown that the very first Egyptian inscriptions employed a language that was indicative of a prior written development; the only place where a written language had a prior development was Sumer.

So we have a single written language that for some reason was differentiated into three tongues: Mesopotamian, Egyptian/Hamitic, and Indo-European. Such a differentiation could have occurred by itself over time, distance, and geographical separation. Yet the Sumerian texts claim that it occurred as the result of a deliberate decision of the gods, once again initiated by Enlil. Sumerian stories on the subject are

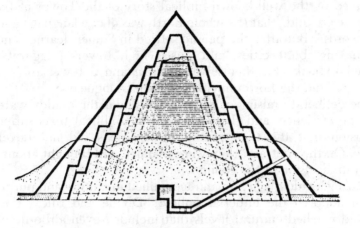

Fig. 162

Fig. 163

Fig. 164

paralleled by the well-known biblical story of the Tower of Babel, in which we are told "that the whole Earth was of one language and of the same words." But after the people settled in Sumer, learned the art of brickmaking, built cities, and raised high towers (ziggurats), they planned to make for themselves a *shem* and a tower to launch it. Therefore "did the Lord mingle the Earth's tongue."

The deliberate raising of Egypt from under the muddy waters, the linguistic evidence, and the Sumerian and biblical texts support our conclusion that the two satellite civilizations did not develop by chance. On the contrary, they were planned and brought about by the deliberate decision of the Nefilim.

Fearing, evidently, a human race unified in culture and purpose, the Nefilim adopted the imperial policy: "Divide and rule." For while Mankind reached cultural levels that included even airborne efforts— after which "anything they shall scheme to do shall no longer be impossible for them"—the Nefilim themselves were a declining lot. By the third millennium B.C., children and grandchildren, to say nothing of humans of divine parentage, were crowding the great olden gods.

The bitter rivalry between Enlil and Enki was inherited by their principal sons, and fierce struggles for supremacy ensued. Even the sons of Enlil—as we have seen in earlier chapters—fought among themselves, as did the sons of Enki. As has happened in recorded human history, overlords tried to keep the peace among their children by dividing the land among the heirs. In at least one known instance, one son (Ishkur/Adad) was deliberately sent away by Enlil to be the leading local deity in the Mountain Land.

As time went on, the gods became overlords, each jealously guarding the territory, industry, or profession over which he had been given dominion. Human kings were the intermediaries between the gods and the growing and spreading humanity. The claims of ancient kings that they went to war, conquered new lands, or subjugated distant peoples "on the command of my god" should not be taken lightly. Text after text makes it clear that this was literally so: The gods retained the powers of conducting foreign affairs, for these affairs involved other gods in other territories. Accordingly, they had the final say in matters of war or peace.

With the proliferation of people, states, cities, and villages, it became necessary to find ways to remind the people who their particular overlord, or "lofty one," was. The Old Testament echoes the problem of having people adhere to *their* god and not "prostitute after other gods." The solution was to establish many places of worship, and to put up in each of them the symbols and likenesses of the "correct" gods.

The age of paganism began.

Following the Deluge, the Sumerian texts inform us, the Nefilim held lengthy counsels regarding the future of gods and Man on Earth. As a result of these deliberations, they "created the four regions." Three of them—Mesopotamia, the Nile valley, and the Indus valley—were settled by Man.

The fourth region was "holy"—a term whose original literal meaning was "dedicated, restricted." Dedicated to the gods alone, it was a "pure land," an area that could be approached only with authorization; trespassing could lead to quick death by "awesome weapons" wielded by fierce guards. This land or region was named TIL.MUN (literally, "the place of the missiles"). It was the restricted area where the Nefilim had reestablished their space base after the one at Sippar had been wiped out by the Deluge.

Once again the area was put under the command of Utu/Shamash, the god in charge of the fiery rockets. Ancient heroes like Gilgamesh strove to reach this Land of Living, to be carried by a *shem* or an Eagle to the Heavenly Abode of the Gods. We recall the plea of Gilgamesh to Shamash:

> Let me enter the Land, let me raise my *Shem*. . . .
> By the life of my goddess mother who bore me,
> of the pure faithful king, my father—
> my step direct to the Land!

Ancient tales—even recorded history—recall the ceaseless efforts of men to "reach the land," find the "Plant of Life," gain eternal bliss among the Gods of Heaven and Earth. This yearning is central to all the religions whose roots lie deep in Sumer: the hope that justice and righteousness pursued on Earth will be followed by an "afterlife" in some Heavenly Divine Abode.

But where was this elusive land of the divine connection?

The question can be answered. The clues are there. But beyond it loom other questions. Have the Nefilim been encountered since? What will happen when they are encountered again?

And if the Nefilim were the "gods" who "created" Man on Earth, *did evolution alone, on the Twelfth Planet, create the Nefilim?*

SOURCES

•

I. Principal sources for biblical texts

A. Genesis through Deuteronomy: *The Five Books of Moses,* new edition, revised by Dr. M. Stern, Star Hebrew Book Company, undated.

B. For latest translation and interpretation based on Sumerian and Akkadian finds: "Genesis," from *The Anchor Bible,* trans. by E. A. Speiser, Garden City, N.Y.: Doubleday & Co., 1964.

C. For "archaic" flavor: *The Holy Bible,* King James Version, Cleveland and New York: The World Publishing Co., undated.

D. For verification of recent interpretations of biblical verses: *The Torah,* new translation of the Holy Scriptures according to the Masoretic text, New York: Jewish Publication Society of America, 1962; *The New American Bible,* translation by members of the Catholic Biblical Association of America, New York: P. J. Kenedy & Sons, 1970; and *The New English Bible,* planned and directed by the Church of England, Oxford: Oxford University Press; Cambridge: Cambridge University Press, 1970.

E. For reference on usage comparison and translation aids: *Veteris Testamenti Concordantiae Hebraicae Atque Chaldaicae* by Solomon Mandelkern, Jerusalem: Schocken Books, Inc., 1962; *Encyclopedic Dictionary of the Bible,* a translation and adaptation of the work by A. van den Born, by the Catholic Biblical Association of America, New York: McGraw-Hill Book Co., Inc., 1963; and *Millon-Hatanach* (Hebrew), Hebrew-Aramaic by Jushua Steinberg, Tel Aviv: Izreel Publishing House Ltd., 1961.

II. Principal sources for Near Eastern texts

Barton, George A. *The Royal Inscriptions of Sumer and Akkad.* 1929.

Borger, Riekele. *Babylonisch-Assyrisch Lesestücke.* 1963.

Budge, E. A. Wallis. *The Gods of the Egyptians.* 1904.

Budge, E. A. W., and King, L. W. *Annals of the Kings of Assyria.* 1902.

Chiera, Edward. *Sumerian Religious Texts.* 1924.

Ebeling, E.; Meissner, B.; and Weidner, E. (eds.). *Reallexikon der Assyrologie und Vorderasiatischen Archäology.* 1932-1957.

Ebeling, Erich. *Enuma Elish: die Siebente Tafel des Akkadischen Weltschöpfungsliedes.* 1939.

——. *Tod und Leben nach den Vorstellungen der Babylonier.* 1931.

Falkenstein, Adam, and W. von Soden. *Sumerische und Akkadische Hymnen und Gebete.* 1953.

Falkenstein, Adam. *Sumerische Goetterlieder.* 1959.

Fossey, Charles. *La Magie Syrienne.* 1902.

Frankfort, Henri. *Kingship and the Gods.* 1948.

Gray, John. *The Cananites.* 1964.

Gordon, Cyrus H. "Canaanite Mythology" in *Mythologies of the Ancient World.* 1961.

Grossman, Hugo. *The Development of the Idea of God in the Old Testament.* 1926.

——.*Altorientalische Texte und Bilder zum alten Testamente.* 1909.

Güterbock, Hans G. "Hittite Mythology" in *Mythologies of the Ancient World.* 1961.

Heidel, Alexander. *The Babylonian Genesis.* 1969.

Hilprecht, Herman V. (ed.). *Reports of the Babylonian Expedition: Cuneiform Texts.* 1893-1914.

Jacobsen, Thorkild. "Mesopotamia" in *The Intellectual Adventure of the Ancient Man.* 1946.

Jastrow, Morris. *Die Religion Babyloniens und Assyriens.* 1905-12.

Jean, Charles-F. *La religion sumerienne.* 1931.

Jensen, P. *Texte zur assyrisch-babylonischen Religion.* 1915.

——.*Die Kosmologie der Babylonier.* 1890.

Jeremias, Alfred. *The Old Testament in the Light of the Ancient Near East.* 1911.

——. *Das Alter der babylonischen Astronomie.* 1908.

——. *Handbuch der Altorientalische Geistkultur.*

Jeremias, Alfred, and Winckler, Hugo. *Im Kampfe um den alten Orient.*

King, Leonard W. *Babylonian Magic and Sorcery, being "The Prayers of the Lifting of the Hand."* 1896.

——. *The Assyrian Language.* 1901.

——. *The Seven Tablets of Creation.* 1902.

——. *Babylonian Religion and Mythology.* 1899.

Kramer, Samuel N. *The Sumerians.* 1963.

——. (ed.): *Mythologies of the Ancient World.* 1961.

——. *History Begins at Sumer.* 1959.

——. *Enmerkar and the Lord of Aratta.* 1952.

——. *From the Tablets of Sumer.* 1956.

——. *Sumerian Mythology.* 1961.

Kugler, Franz Xaver. *Sternkunde und Sterndienst in Babylon.* 1907-1913.

Lambert, W. G., and Millard, A. R. *Atra-Hasis, the Babylonian Story of the Flood.* 1970.

Langdon, Stephen. *Sumerian and Babylonian Psalms.* 1909.

——. *Tammuz and Ishtar.* 1914.

——. (ed.): *Oxford Editions of Cuneiform Texts.* 1923 ff.

——. "Semitic Mythology" in *The Mythology of All Races.* 1964.

——. *Enuma Elish: The Babylonian Epic of Creation.* 1923.

——. *Babylonian Penitential Psalms.* 1927.

——. *Die Neu-Babylonischen Königsinschriften.* 1912.

Luckenbill, David D. *Ancient Records of Assyria and Babylonia.* 1926-27.

Neugebauer, O. *Astronomical Cuneiform Texts.* 1955.

Pinches, Theophilus G. "Some Mathematical Tablets in the British Museum" in *Hilprecht Anniversary Volume.* 1909.

Pritchard, James B. (ed.). *Ancient Near Eastern Texts Relating to the Old Testament.* 1969.

Rawlinson, Henry C. *The Cuneiform Inscriptions of Western Asia.* 1861-84.

Sayce, A. H. *The Religion of the Babylonians.* 1888.

Smith, George. *The Chaldean Account of Genesis.* 1876.

Thomas, D. Winton (ed.). *Documents from Old Testament Times.* 1961.

Thompson, R. Campbell. *The Reports of the Magicians and. Astrologers of Nineveh and Babylon.* 1900.

Thureau-Dangin, François. *Les Inscriptions de Sumer et Akkad.* 1905.

——. *Die sumerischen und akkadische Königsinschriften.* 1907.

——. *Rituels accadiens.* 1921.

Virolleaud, Charles. *L'Astronomie Chaldéenne.* 1903-1908.

Weidner, Ernst F. *Alter und Bedeutung der Babylonischer Astronomie und Astrallehre.* 1914.

——. *Handbuch der Babylonischen Astronomie.* 1915.

Witzel, P. Maurus. *Tammuz-Liturgien und Verwandtes.* 1935.

III. Studies and articles consulted in various issues of the following periodicals

Der Alte Orient (Leipzig)

American Journal of Archaeology (Concord, Mass.)

American Journal of Semitic Languages and Literatures (Chicago)

Annual of the American Schools of Oriental Research (New Haven)

Archiv für Keilschriftforschung (Berlin)

Archiv für Orientforschung (Berlin)

Archiv Orientalni (Prague)

Assyrologische Bibliothek (Leipzig)

Assyrological Studies (Chicago)

Das Ausland (Berlin)

Babyloniaca (Paris)

Beiträge zur Assyrologie und semitischen Sprachwissenschaft (Leipzig)

Berliner Beiträge zur Keilschriftforschung (Berlin)

Bibliotheca Orientalis (Leiden)

Bulletin of the American Schools of Oriental Research (Jerusalem and Baghdad)

Deutsches Morgenländische Gesellschaft, Abhandlungen (Leipzig)
Harvard Semitic Series (Cambridge, Mass.)
Hebrew Union College Annual (Cincinnati)
Journal Asiatique (Paris)
Journal of the American Oriental Society (New Haven)
Journal of Biblical Literature and Exegesis (Middletown)
Journal of Cuneiform Studies (New Haven)
Journal of Near Eastern Studies (Chicago)
Journal of the Royal Asiatic Society (London)
Journal of the Society of Oriental Research (Chicago)
Journal of Semitic Studies (Manchester)
Keilinschriftliche Bibliothek (Berlin)
Königliche Museen zu Berlin: Mitteilungen aus der Orientalischen Samm-
    lungen (Berlin)
Leipziger semitische Studien (Leipzig)
Mitteilungen der altorientalischen Gesellschaft (Leipzig)
Mitteilungen des Instituts für Orientforschung (Berlin)
Orientalia (Rome)
Orientalische Literaturzeitung (Berlin)
Proceedings of the American Philosophical Society (Philadelphia)
Proceedings of the Society of Biblical Archaeology (London)
Revue d'Assyrologie et d'archéologie orientale (Paris)
Revue biblique (Paris)
Sacra Scriptura Antiquitatibus Orientalibus Illustrata (Vatican)
Studia Orientalia (Helsinki)
Transactions of the Society of Biblical Archaeology (London)
Untersuchungen zur Assyrologie und vorderasiatischen Archäologie (Berlin)
Vorderasiatische Bibliothek (Leipzig)
Die Welt des Orients (Göttingen)
Wissenschaftliche Veröffentlichungen der deutschen Orient-Gesellschaft
    (Berlin)
Zeitschrift für Assyrologie und verwandte Gebiete (Leipzig)
Zeitschrift für die alttestamentliche Wissenschaft (Berlin, Gissen)
Zeitschrift der deutschen morgenländischen Gesellschaft (Leipzig)
Zeitschrift für Keilschriftforschung (Leipzig)

INDEX

•

Praise for the Works of Zecharia Sitchin

"Reflects the highest level of scientific knowledge . . ."

SCIENCE & RELIGION NEWS

"Exciting . . . credible . . . most provocative and compelling."

LIBRARY JOURNAL

"One of the most important books on Earth's roots ever written."

EAST WEST JOURNAL

"Sitchin is a zealous investigator into man's origins . . . a dazzling performance."

KIRKUS REVIEWS

"For thousands of years priests, poets, and scientists have tried to explain how man was created. Now a recognized scholar has come forth with a theory that is most astonishing of all."

UNITED PRESS INTERNATIONAL

Also by Zecharia Sitchin

Genesis Revisited

Divine Encounters

The Earth Chronicles Handbook

The Earth Chronicles Expeditions (autobiographical)

Journeys to the Mythical Past (autobiographical)

The King Who Refused to Die (fiction)

The Lost Book of Enki

There Were Giants Upon the Earth

The Earth Chronicles

The 12th Planet — Book I

The Stairway to Heaven — Book II

The Wars of Gods and Men — Book III

The Lost Realms — Book IV

When Time Began — Book V

The Cosmic Code — Book VI

The End of Days — Book VII

ZECHARIA SITCHIN

THE ── STAIRWAY TO HEAVEN

The Second Book
of
The Earth Chronicles

Bear & Company
Rochester, Vermont • Toronto, Canada

Bear & Company
One Park Street
Rochester, Vermont 05767
www.BearandCompanyBooks.com

Bear & Company is a division of Inner Traditions International

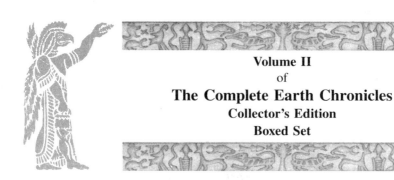

Volume II
of
The Complete Earth Chronicles
Collector's Edition
Boxed Set

Printed and bound in India at Replika Press Pvt. Ltd.

10 9 8 7 6

Contents

I

In Search of Paradise

There was a time—our ancient scriptures tell us—when Immortality was within the grasp of Mankind.

A golden age it was, when Man lived with his Creator in the Garden of Eden—Man tending the wonderful orchard, God taking strolls in the afternoon breeze. "And the Lord God caused to grow from the ground every tree that is pleasant to the sight and good for eating; and the Tree of Life was in the orchard, and the Tree of Knowing good and evil. And a river went out of Eden to water the garden, and from there it was parted and became four principal streams: the name of the first is Pishon . . . and of the second Gihon . . . and of the third Tigris . . . and the fourth river is the Euphrates."

Of the fruit of every tree were Adam and Eve permitted to eat—except of the fruit of the Tree of Knowing. But once they did (tempted by the Serpent)—the Lord God grew concerned over the matter of Immortality:

> Then did the Lord Yahweh say:
> "Behold, the Adam has become as one of us
> to know good and evil;
> And now might he not put forth his hand
> and partake also of the Tree of Life,
> and eat, and live forever?"

> And the Lord Yahweh expelled the Adam
> from the Garden of Eden . . .
> And He placed at the east of the Garden of Eden
> the Cherubim, and the Flaming Sword which revolveth,
> to guard the way to the Tree of Life.

So was Man cast out of the very place where eternal life was within his grasp. But though barred from it, he has never ceased to remember it, to yearn for it, and to try to reach it.

Ever since that expulsion from Paradise, heroes have gone to the ends of Earth in search of Immortality; a selected few were given a glimpse of it; and simple folk claimed to have chanced upon it. Throughout the ages, the

Search for Paradise was the realm of the individual; but earlier in this millennium, it was launched as the national enterprise of mighty kingdoms.

The New World was discovered—so have we been led to believe—when explorers went seeking a new, maritime route to India and her wealth. True—but not the whole truth; for what Ferdinand and Isabel, king and queen of Spain, had desired most to find was the Fountain of Eternal Youth: a magical fountain whose waters rejuvenate the old and keep one young forever, for it springs from a well in Paradise.

No sooner had Columbus and his men set foot in what they all thought were the islands off India (the "West Indies"), than they combined the exploration of the new lands with a search for the legendary Fountain whose waters "made old men young again." Captured "Indians" were questioned, even tortured, by the Spaniards, so that they would reveal the secret location of the Fountain.

One who excelled in such investigations was Ponce de Leon, a professional soldier and adventurer, who rose through the ranks to become governor of the part of the island of Hispaniola now called Haiti, and of Puerto Rico. In 1511, he witnessed the interrogation of some captured Indians. Describing their island, they spoke of its pearls and other riches. They also extolled the marvelous virtues of its waters. A spring there is, they said, of which an islander "grievously oppressed with old age" had drunk. As a result, he "brought home manly strength and has practiced all manly performances, having taken a wife again and begotten children."

Listening with mounting excitement, Ponce de Leon—himself an aging man—was convinced that the Indians were describing the miraculous Fountain of the rejuvenating waters. Their postscript, that the old man who drank of the waters regained his manly strength, could resume practicing "all manly performances," and even took again a young wife who bore him children—was the most conclusive aspect of their tale. For in the court of Spain, as throughout Europe, there hung numerous paintings by the greatest painters, and whenever they depicted love scenes or sexual allegories, they included in the scene a fountain. Perhaps the most famous of such paintings, Titian's *Love Sacred and Love Profane*, was created at about the time the Spaniards were on their quest in the Indies. As everyone well knew, the Fountain in the paintings hinted at the ultimate lovemaking; the Fountain whose waters make possible "all manly performances" through Eternal Youth.

Ponce de Leon's report to King Ferdinand is reflected in the records kept by the official court historian, Peter Martyr de Angleria. As stated in his *Decade de Orbe Novo* [Decades of the New World], the Indians who had come from the islands of Lucayos or the Bahamas, had revealed that "there is an island . . . in which there is a perennial spring of running water of such marvelous virtue, that the waters thereof being drunk, perhaps with some diet, make old men young again." Many researches, such as *Ponce de Leon's Fountain of Youth: History of a Geographical Myth* by Leonardo

Olschki, have established that "the Fountain of Youth was the most popular and characteristic expression of the emotions and expectations which agitated the conquerors of the New World." Undoubtedly, Ferdinand the king of Spain was one of those so agitated, so expectant for the definitive news.

So, when word came from Ponce de Leon, Ferdinand lost little time. He at once granted Ponce de Leon a Patent of Discovery (dated February 23, 1512), authorizing an expedition from the island of Hispaniola northward. The admiralty was ordered to assist Ponce de Leon and make available to him the best ships and seamen, so that he might discover without delay the island of "Beininy" (Bimini). The king made one condition explicit: "that after having reached the island and learned what is in it, you shall send me a report of it."

In March 1513, Ponce de Leon set out northward, to look for the island of Bimini. The public excuse for the expedition was a search for "gold and other metals"; the true aim was to find the Fountain of Eternal Youth. This the seamen soon learnt as they came upon not one island but hundreds of islands in the Bahamas. Anchoring at island after island, the landing parties were instructed to search not for gold but for some unusual fountain. The waters of each stream were tasted and drunk—but with no evident effects. On Easter Sunday—*Pasca de Flores* by its Spanish name—a long coastline was sighted. Ponce de Leon called the "island" Florida. Sailing along the coast and landing again and again, he and his men searched the jungled forests and drank the waters of endless springs. But none seemed to work the expected miracle.

The mission's failure appears to have hardly dampened the conviction that the Fountain was undoubtedly there: it only had to be discovered. More Indians were questioned. Some seemed unusually young for the old ages claimed by them. Others repeated legends that confirmed the existence of the Fountain. One such legend (as recounted in *Creation Myths of Primitive America* by J. Curtin) relates that when Olelbis, "He Who Sits Above," was about to create Mankind, he sent two emissaries to Earth to construct a ladder which would connect Earth and Heaven. Halfway up the ladder, they were to set up a resting place, with a pool of pure drinking waters. At the summit, they were to create two springs: one for drinking and the other for bathing. When a man or woman grows old, said Olelbis, let him or her climb up to this summit, and drink and bathe; whereupon his youth shall be restored.

The conviction that the Fountain existed somewhere on the islands was so strong that in 1514—the year after Ponce de Leon's unfruitful mission—Peter Martyr (in his Second Decade) informed Pope Leo X as follows:

At a distance of 325 leagues from Hispaniola, they tell, there is an island called Boyuca, alias Ananeo, which—according to those who explored its interior—has such an extraordinary fountain that drinking of its waters rejuvenates the old.

And let Your Holiness not think this to be said lightly or rashly; for they have spread word of this as the truth throughout the court, so formally that the whole people, not few of whom are from among those whom wisdom or fortune distinguished from the common people, hold it to be true.

Ponce de Leon, undaunted, concluded after some additional research that what he had to look for was a spring in conjunction with a river, the two possibly connected by a hidden underground tunnel. If the Fountain was on an island, was its source a river in Florida?

In 1521, the Spanish Crown sent Ponce de Leon on a renewed search, this time focusing on Florida. There can be no doubt regarding the true purpose of his mission: writing only a few decades later, the Spanish historian Antonio de Herrera y Tordesillas stated thus in his *Historia General de las Indias*: "He (Ponce de Leon) went seeking that Sacred Fountain, so renowned among the Indians, as well as the river whose waters rejuvenated the aged." He was intent on finding the spring of Bimini and the river in Florida, of which the Indians of Cuba and Hispaniola "affirmed that old persons bathing themselves in them became young again."

Instead of Eternal Youth, Ponce de Leon found death by an Indian arrow. And although the individual search for a potion or lotion that can postpone the Last Day may never end, the organized search, under a royal decree, did come to an end.

Was the search futile to begin with? Were Ferdinand and Isabel and Ponce de Leon, and the men who sailed and died in search of the Fountain, all fools childishly believing in some primitive fairy tales?

Not the way they saw it. The Holy Scriptures, pagan beliefs, and the documented tales of great travelers, all combined to affirm that there was indeed a place whose waters (or fruits' nectars) could bestow Immortality by keeping one forever young.

There were still current olden tales—left from the times when the Celts were in the peninsula—of a secret place, a secret fountain, a secret fruit or herb whose finder shall be redeemed of death. There was the goddess Idunn, who lived by a sacred brook and who kept magical apples in her coffer. When the gods grew old, they would come to her to eat of the apples, whereupon they turned young again. Indeed, "Idunn" meant "Again Young"; and the apples that she guarded were called the "Elixir of the Gods."

Was this an echo of the legend of Herakles (Hercules) and his twelve labors? A priestess of the god Apollo, predicting his travails in an oracle, had also assured him: "When this shall be done, thou shalt become one of the Immortals." To achieve this, the last but one labor was to seize and bring back from the Hesperides the divine golden apples. The Hesperides—"Daughters of the Evening Land"—resided at the Ends of Earth.

Have not the Greeks, and then the Romans, left behind them tales of mortals immortalized? The god Apollo anointed the body of Sarpedon, so that he lived the life of several generations of men. The goddess Aphrodite granted to Phaon a magic potion; anointing himself with it, he turned into a beautiful youth "who wakened love in the hearts of all the women of Lesbos." And the child Demophon, anointed with ambrosia by the goddess Demeter, would surely have become immortal were not his mother—ignorant of Demeter's identity—to snatch him away from the goddess.

There was the tale of Tantalus, who had become immortal by eating at the gods' table and stealing their nectar and ambrosia. But having killed his son to serve his flesh as food for the gods, he was punished by being banished to a land of luscious fruits and waters—eternally out of his reach. (The god Hermes restored the butchered son to life.) On the other hand, Odysseus, offered Immortality by the nymph Calypso if only he would stay with her forever, forsook Immortality for a chance to return to his home and wife.

And was not there the tale of Glaukos, a mortal, an ordinary fisherman, who became a sea-god? One day he observed that a fish that he had caught, coming in touch with a herb, came back to life and leaped back into the water. Taking the herb into his mouth, Glaukos jumped into the water at the exact same spot; whereupon the sea-gods Okeanos and Tethys admitted him to their circle and transformed him into a deity.

The year 1492, in which Columbus set sail from Spain, was also the year in which the Muslim occupation of the Iberian Peninsula ended with the surrender of the Moors at Granada. Throughout the nearly eight centuries of Muslim and Christian contention over the peninsula, the interaction of the two cultures was immense; and the tale in the Koran (the Muslim holy book) of the Fish and the Fountain of Life was known to Moor and Catholic alike. The fact that the tale was almost identical to the Greek legend of Glaukos the fisherman, was taken as confirmation of its authenticity. It was one of the reasons for seeking the legendary Fountain in India—the land which Columbus had set out to reach, and which he thought he had reached.

The segment in the Koran which contains the tale is the eighteenth *Sura*. It relates the exploration of various mysteries by Moses, the biblical hero of the Israelite Exodus from Egypt. While Moses was being groomed for his new calling as a Messenger of God, he was to be instructed in such knowledge as he still lacked by a mysterious "Servant of God." Accompanied by only one attendant, Moses was to go find this enigmatic teacher with the aid of a single clue: he was to take with him a dried fish; the place where the fish would jump and disappear would be the place where he would meet the teacher.

After much searching in vain, the attendant of Moses suggested that they stop and give up the search. But Moses persisted, saying that he would not give up until they reached "the junction of the two streams." Unnoticed by them, it was there that the miracle happened:

> But when they reached the Junction,
> they forgot about their fish,
> which took its course through the stream,
> as in a tunnel.

After journeying further, Moses said to his attendant: "Bring us our early meal." But the attendant replied that the fish was gone:

> "When we betook ourselves to the rock,
> sawest thou what had happened?
> I did indeed forget about the fish—
> Satan made me forget to tell you about it:
> It took its course through the stream,
> in a marvelous way.
> And Moses said:
> "That was what we were seeking after."

The tale in the Koran (Fig. 1) of the dried fish that came to life and swam back to the sea through a tunnel, went beyond the parallel Greek tale by relating itself not to a simple fisherman, but to the venerated Moses. Also, it presented the incident not as a chance discovery, but as an occurrence premediated by the Lord, who knew of the location of the Waters of Life— waters that could be recognized through the medium of the resurrection of a dead fish.

As devout Christians, the king and queen of Spain must have accepted literally the vision described in the Book of Revelation, "of a pure river of Water of Life, clear as crystal, proceeding out of the throne of God. . . . In the midst of the street of it, and on either side of the river, was there the Tree of Life, with twelve manner of fruit." They must have believed in the Book's promises: "I will give unto him that is athirst of the Fountain of the Water of Life"—"I will give to eat of the Tree of Life which is the midst of the Paradise of God." And could they not be aware of the words of the biblical Psalmist:

> Thou givest them to drink
> of thy Stream of Eternities;
> For with thee is the Fountain of Life.

60. Behold, Moses said
To his attendant, "I will not
Give up until I reach
The junction of the two
Seas or (until) I spend
Years and years in travel."

١.٦- وَإِذْ قَالَ مُوسَى لِفَتَنهُ لَا
أَبْرَحُ حَتَّى أَبْلُغَ مَجْمَعَ الْبَحْرَيْنِ أَوْ
أَمْضِيَ حُقُبًا ٥

61. But when they reached
The Junction,   they forgot
(About) their Fish,   which took
Its course through the sea
(Straight) as in a tunnel.

٦١- فَلَمَّا بَلَغَا مَجْمَعَ بَيْنِهِمَا نَسِيَا حُوتَهُمَا
فَاتَّخَذَ سَبِيلَهُ فِى الْبَحْرِ سَرَبًا ٥

62. When they had passed on
(Some distance), Moses said
To his attendant : "Bring us
Our early meal ; truly
We have suffered much fatigue
At this (stage of) our journey."

٦٢- فَلَمَّا جَاوَزَا قَالَ
لِفَتَنهُ ءَاتِنَا غَدَآءَنَا لَقَدْ
لَقِينَا مِن سَفَرِنَا هَذَا نَصَبًا ٥

63. He replied : "Sawest thou
(What happened) when we
Betook ourselves to the rock ?
I did indeed forget
(About) the Fish : none but
Satan made me forget
To tell (you) about it :
It took its course through
The sea in a marvellous way ! "

٦٣- قَالَ أَرَءَيْتَ إِذْ أَوَيْنَا
إِلَى الصَّخْرَةِ فَإِنِّى نَسِيتُ الْحُوتَ
وَمَآ أَنسَىنِيهُ إِلَّا الشَّيْطَنُ أَنْ أَذْكُرَهُ ۚ
وَاتَّخَذَ سَبِيلَهُ فِى الْبَحْرِ عَجَبًا ٥

64. Moses said : "That was what
We were seeking after :"
So they went back
On their footsteps, following
(The path they had come).

٦٤- قَالَ ذَلِكَ مَا كُنَّا نَبْغِ ۚ
فَارْتَدَّا عَلَى ءَاثَارِهِمَا قَصَصًا ٥

Fig. 1

There could thus be no doubt, as attested by the holiest Scriptures, that
the Fountain of Life, or the Stream of Eternity, did exist; the only problem
was—where, and how to find it.

The eighteenth *Sura* of the Koran seemed to offer some important clues.
It goes on to relate the three paradoxes of life that Moses was shown once
he located the Servant of God. Then the same section of the Koran
continues to describe three other episodes: first, about a visit to a land
where the Sun sets; then to a land where the Sun rises—that is, in the east;
and finally to a land beyond the second land, where the mythical people of

Gog and Magog (the biblical contenders at the End of Days) were causing untold mischief on Earth. To put an end to this trouble, the hero of the tale, here named Du-al'karnain ("Possessor of the Two Horns"), filled up the pass between two steep mountains with blocks of iron and poured over them molten lead, creating such an awesome barrier that even the mighty Gog and Magog were powerless to scale it. Separated, the two could cause no more hardship on Earth.

The word Karnain, in Arabic as in Hebrew, means both Double Horns and Double Rays. The three additional episodes, following immediately after the tale of the Mysteries of Moses, thus appear to retain as their hero Moses, who could well have been nicknamed Du-al'karnain because his face "was with rays"—radiated—after he had come down from Mount Sinai, where he had met the Lord face to face. Yet popular medieval beliefs attributed the epithet and the journeys to the three lands to Alexander the Great, the Macedonian king who in the fourth century B.C. conquered most of the ancient world, reaching as far as India.

This popular belief, interchanging Moses and Alexander, stemmed from traditions concerning the conquests and adventures of Alexander the Great. These included not only the feat in the land of Gog and Magog, but also an identical episode of a dry, dead fish that came back to life when Alexander and his cook had found the Fountain of Life!

The reports concerning Alexander's adventures that were current in Europe and the Near East in medieval times were based upon the supposed writings of the Greek historian Callisthenes of Olynthus. He was appointed by Alexander to record the exploits, triumphs and adventures of his Asiatic expedition; but he died in prison, having offended Alexander, and his writings have mysteriously perished. Centuries later, however, there began to circulate in Europe a Latin text purporting to be a translation of the lost original writings of Callisthenes. Scholars speak of this text as "pseudo-Callisthenes."

For many centuries it was believed that the many translations of the Exploits of Alexander that were current in Europe and the Middle East, all stemmed from this Latin pseudo-Callisthenes. But it was later discovered that other, parallel versions existed in many languages—including Hebrew, Arabic, Persian, Syriac, Armenian and Ethiopic—as well as at least three versions in Greek. The various versions, some tracing their origins to Alexandria of the second century B.C., differ here and there; but by and large, their overwhelming similarities do indicate a common source—perhaps the writings of Callisthenes after all, or—as is sometimes claimed—copies of Alexander's letters to his mother Olympias and to his teacher Aristotle.

The miraculous adventures with which we are concerned began after Alexander completed the conquest of Egypt. From the texts it is neither clear in which direction Alexander set his course, nor is it certain that the episodes are arranged in an accurate chronological or geographical order.

One of the very first episodes, however, may explain the popular confusion between Alexander and Moses: apparently Alexander attempted to leave Egypt as Moses did, by parting the waters and getting his followers to cross the sea on foot.

Reaching the sea, Alexander decided to part it by building in its midst a wall of molten lead, and his masons "continued to pour lead and molten matter into the water until the structure rose above its surface. Then he built upon it a tower and a pillar, upon which he carved his own figure, having two horns upon his head." And he wrote upon the monument: "Whosoever hath come into this place and would sail over the sea, let him know that I have shut it up."

Having thus shut out the waters, Alexander and his men began to cross the sea. As a precaution, however, they sent ahead some prisoners. But as they reached the tower in the midst of the waters, "the waves of the sea leapt up upon them (the prisoners) and the sea swallowed them up and they all perished. . . . When the Two-Horned One saw this, he was afraid of the sea with a mighty fear," and gave up the attempt to emulate Moses.

Eager, however, to discover the "darkness" on the other side of the sea, Alexander made several detours, during which he purportedly visited the sources of the river Euphrates and of the river Tigris, studying there "the secrets of the heavens and the stars and the planets."

Leaving his troops behind, Alexander returned toward the Land of Darkness, reaching a mountain named *Mushas* at the edge of the desert. After several days of marching, he saw "a straight path which had no wall, and it had no high and no low place in it." He left his few trusted companions and proceeded alone. After a journey of twelve days and twelve nights, "he perceived the radiance of an angel"; but as he drew nearer, the angel was "a flaming fire." Alexander realized that he had reached "the mountain from which the whole world is surrounded."

The angel was no less puzzled than Alexander. "Who art thou, and for what reason art thou here, O mortal?" the angel asked, and wondered how Alexander had managed "to penetrate into this darkness, which no other man hath been able to do." To which Alexander replied that God himself had guided him and gave him strength to "have arrived in this place, which is Paradise."

To convince the reader that Paradise, rather than Hell, was reachable through underground passages, the ancient author then introduced a long discourse between the angel and Alexander on matters of God and Man. The angel then urged Alexander to return to his friends; but Alexander persisted in seeking answers to the mysteries of Heaven and Earth, God and Men. In the end Alexander said that he would leave only if he were granted something that no man had ever obtained before. Complying, "the angel said unto him: 'I will tell thee something whereby thou mayest live and not die.' The Two-Horned said: 'Say on.' And the angel said unto him:

In the land of Arabia, God hath set the blackness of solid darkness, wherein is hidden a treasury of this knowledge. There too is the fountain of water which is called "The Water of Life"; and whosoever drinketh therefrom, if it be but a single drop, shall never die.

The angel attributed other magical powers to these Waters of Life, such as "the power of flying through the heavens, even as the angels fly." Needing no further prompting, Alexander anxiously inquired: "In which quarter of the earth is this fountain of water situated?" "Ask those men who are heirs to the knowledge thereof," was the angel's enigmatic answer. Then the angel gave Alexander a cluster of grapes whereby to feed his troops.

Returning to his companions, Alexander told his colleagues of his adventure and gave them each a grape. But "as he plucked off from the cluster, another grew in its place." And so did one cluster feed all the soldiers and their beasts.

Alexander then began to make inquiries of all the learned men he could find. He asked the sages: "Have you ever read in your books that God hath a place of darkness of which knowledge is hidden, and that the Fountain which is called the 'Fountain of Life' is situated therein?" The Greek versions have him search the Ends of Earth for the right savant; the Ethiopic versions suggest that the sage was right there, among his troops. His name was Matun, and he knew the ancient writings. The place, he said, "lieth nigh unto the sun when it rises on the right side."

Scarcely more informed by such riddles, Alexander put himself in the hands of his guide. They again went into a Place of Darkness. After journeying for a long time, Alexander got tired and sent Matun ahead by himself, to find the right path. To help him see in the darkness, Alexander gave him a stone which was given him earlier under miraculous circumstances by an ancient king who was living among the gods—a stone which was brought out of Paradise by Adam when he left it, and which was heavier than any other substance on Earth.

Matun, though careful to follow the path, eventually lost his way. He then produced the magical stone and put it down; when it touched the ground, it emitted light. By the light, Matun saw a well. He was not yet aware that he had chanced upon the Fountain of Life. The Ethiopic version describes what ensued:

Now, he had with him a dried fish, and being exceedingly hungry he went down with it to the water, that he might wash it therein and make it ready for cooking. . . . But behold, as soon as the fish touched the water, it swam away.

"When Matun saw this, he stripped his clothes and went down into the water after the fish, and found it to be alive in the water." Realizing that this was the "Well of the Water of Life," Matun washed himself in the waters and drank thereof. When he had come up from the well, he was no longer hungry nor did he have any worldly care, for he had become *El-Khidr*—"the Evergreen"—the one who was Forever Young.

Returning to the encampment, he said nothing of his discovery to Alexander (whom the Ethiopic version calls "He of the Two Horns"). Then Alexander himself resumed the search, groping for the right way in the darkness. Suddenly, he saw the stone (left behind by Matun) "shining in the darkness; (and) now it had two eyes, which sent forth rays of light." Realizing that he had found the right path, Alexander rushed ahead, but was stopped by a voice which admonished him for his ever-increasing ambitions, and prophesied that instead of attaining eternal life he would soon bite the dust. Terrified, Alexander returned to his companions and his troops, giving up the search.

According to some versions, it was a bird with human features who spoke to Alexander and made him turn back when he reached a place "inlaid with sapphires and emeralds and jacinths." In Alexander's purported letter to his mother, there were two bird-men who blocked his way.

In the Greek version of pseudo-Callisthenes, it was Andreas, the cook of Alexander, who took the dried fish to wash it in a fountain "whose waters flashed with lightnings." As the fish touched the water, it became alive and slipped out of the cook's hands. Realizing what he had found, the cook drank of the waters and took some in a silver bowl—but told no one of his discovery. When Alexander (in this version, he was accompanied by 360 men) continued the search, they reached a place that shined though there were neither Sun nor Moon nor stars to be seen. The way was blocked by two birds with human features.

"Go back!" one of them ordered Alexander, "for the land on which you stand belongs to God alone. Go back, O wretched one, for in the Land of the Blessed you cannot set foot!" Shuddering with fear, Alexander and his men turned back; but before they left the place, they took as souvenirs some of its soil and stones. After several days' marching, they came out of the Land of Everlasting Night; and when they reached light, they saw that the "soil and stones" they picked up were in fact pearls, precious stones and nuggets of gold.

Only then did the cook tell Alexander of the fish that came to life, but still kept it a secret that he himself had drunk of the waters and that he had kept some of it. Alexander was furious and hit him, and banished him from the camp. But the cook wished not to leave alone, for he had fallen in love with a daughter of Alexander. So he revealed his secret to her, and gave her to drink of the waters. When Alexander found that out, he banished her too: "You have become a godly being, having become immortal," he told her; therefore, he said, you cannot live among men—go live in the Land of the

Blessed. And as for the cook—him Alexander threw into the sea, with a stone around his neck. But instead of drowning, the cook became the sea-demon Andrentic.

"And thus," we are told, "ends the tale of the Cook and the Maiden."

To the learned advisers of Europe's medieval kings and queens, the various versions only served to confirm both the antiquity and the authenticity of the legend of Alexander and the Fountain of Life. But where, O where were these magical waters located?

Were they indeed across the border of Egypt, in the Sinai peninsula—the arena of the activities of Moses? Were they close to the area where the Euphrates and Tigris rivers begin to flow, somewhere north of Syria? Did Alexander go to the Ends of Earth—India—to find the Fountain, or did he embark on those additional conquests after he was turned back from it?

As the medieval scholars strove to unravel the puzzle, new works on the subject from Christian sources began to shape a consensus in favor of India. A Latin composition named *Alexander Magni Inter Ad Paradisum*, a Syriac Homilie of Alexander by Bishop Jakob of Sarug, the *Recension of Josippon* in Armenian—complete with the tale of the tunnel, the man-like birds, the magical stone—placed the Land of Darkness or the Mountains of Darkness at the Ends of Earth. There, some of these writings said, Alexander took a boat ride on the Ganges River, which was none other than the Pishon River of Paradise. There, in India (or on an island offshore), did Alexander reach the Gates of Paradise.

As these conclusions were taking shape in Europe of the Middle Ages, new light was shed on the subject from a wholly unexpected source. In the year 1145, the German bishop Otto of Freising reported in his *Chronicon* a most astonishing epistle. The Pope, he reported, had received a letter from a Christian ruler of India, whose existence had been totally unknown until then. And that king had affirmed in his letter that the River of Paradise was indeed located in his realm.

Bishop Otto of Freising named as the intermediary, through whom the Pope had received the epistle, Bishop Hugh of Gebal, a town on the Mediterranean coast of Syria. The ruler, it was reported, was named John the Elder or, being a priest, Prester John. He was reputedly a lineal descendant of the Magi who had visited Christ the child. He defeated the Muslim kings of Persia, and formed a thriving Christian kingdom in the lands of the Ends of Earth.

Nowadays, some scholars consider the whole affair to have been a forgery for propaganda purposes. Others believe that the reports which reached the Pope were distortions of events that were really happening. The Christian world at the time, having launched the Crusades against Muslim rule over the Near East (including the Holy Land) fifty years earlier, met with a crushing defeat at Edessa in 1144. But at the Ends of Earth Mongol rulers began to storm the gates of the Muslim empire, and in 1141 defeated the

Sultan Sanjar. When the news reached the Mediterranean coastal cities, it was forwarded to the Pope in the garb of a Christian king, rising to defeat the Muslims from the other side.

If the search for the Fountain of Youth was not among the reasons for the First Crusade (1095), it apparently was among the reasons for the following ones. For no sooner had Bishop Otto reported the existence of Prester John and of the River of Paradise in his realm, than the Pope issued a formal call for the resumption of the Crusades. Two years later, in 1147, Emperor Conrad of Germany, accompanied by other rulers and many nobles, launched the Second Crusade.

As the fortunes of the Crusaders rose and fell, Europe was swept anew by word from Prester John and his promises of aid. According to chroniclers of those days, Prester John sent in 1165 a letter to the Byzantine emperor, to the Holy Roman emperor, and to lesser kings, in which he declared his definite intention to come to the Holy Land with his armies. Again his realm was described in glowing terms, as befits the place where the River of Paradise—indeed, the Gates of Paradise—were situated.

The promised help never came. The way from Europe to India was not breached open. By the end of the thirteenth century, the Crusades were over, ending in final defeat at the hands of the Muslims.

But even as the Crusaders were advancing and retreating, the fervent belief in the existence of the Waters of Paradise in India kept growing and spreading.

Before the twelfth century was over, a new and popular version of the exploits of Alexander the Great made its way into the encampments and town squares. Called the *Romance of Alexander*, it was (as is now known) the work of two Frenchmen who based this poetic and glowing composition on the Latin version of pseudo-Callisthenes and other "biographies" of the Macedonian hero then available. The knights, the warriors, the townspeople in the drinking halls, cared not who the authors were; for—in language they could understand—it vividly drew for them visions of Alexander's adventures in strange lands.

Among these was the tale of the three wondrous fountains. One rejuvenated the old; the second granted Immortality; the third resurrected the dead. The three fountains, the *Romance* explained, were located in different lands, issuing as they were from the Tigris and Euphrates rivers in western Asia, the Nile in Africa, and the Ganges River in India. These were the four Rivers of Paradise; and though they flowed in different lands, they all arose from a single source: from the Garden of Eden—just as the Bible had stated all along.

It was the Fountain of Rejuvenation, the *Romance* related, that Alexander and his men had found. It recounted as fact that fifty-six aged companions of Alexander "recovered the complexion of thirty [years] old after drinking from the Fountain of Youth." As translations of the *Romance* carried the tale far and wide, the versions became increasingly specific on this point: not only the appearance, but also the manhood and virility of the aged soldiers were restored to youthfulness.

But how does one get to this Fountain, if the route to India is blocked by the heathen Muslims?

On and off, the Popes attempted to communicate with the enigmatic Prester John, "the illustrious and magnificent king of the Indies and beloved son of Christ." In 1245, Pope Innocent IV dispatched the Friar Giovanni da Pian del Carpini, via southern Russia, to the Mongol ruler or Khan, believing the Mongols to be Nestorians (an offshoot of the Eastern Orthodox Church) and the Khan to be Prester John. In 1254, the Armenian ruler-priest Haithon traveled in disguise through eastern Turkey to the camp of the Mongol chieftain in southern Russia. The record of his adventurous travels mentioned that his way took him via the narrow pass on the shores of the Caspian Sea called *The Iron Gates*; and the speculation that his route resembled that of Alexander the Great (who had poured molten iron to close a mountain pass) only served to suggest that the Ends of Earth, the Gates of Paradise, could indeed be so reached.

These and other papal and royal emissaries were soon joined by private adventurers, such as the brothers Nicolo and Maffeo Polo and the former's son Marco Polo (1260–1295), and the German knight William of Boldensele (1336)—all searching for the kingdom of Prester John.

While their travelogues kept up the interest of Church and Courts, it was once again the fate of a popular literary work to rekindle mass interest. Its author introduced himself as "I, John Maundeville, Knight," born in the town of St. Albans in England who "passed the sea in the year of our Lord Jesus 1322." Writing at the end of his travels thirty-four years later, Sir John explained that he had therein "set down the way to the Holy Land, and to Hierusalem: as also to the lands of the Great Caan, and of Prester John: to Inde, and divers other countries: together with many and strange marvels therein."

In the twenty-seventh chapter, captioned "Of the Royal Estate of Prester John," the book (*The Voyages and Travels of Sir John Maundeville, Knight*) states:

This emperor, Prester John, possesses very extensive territory, and has many noble cities and good towns in his realm, and many great and large isles. For all the country of India is divided into isles, by the great floods that come from Paradise. . . .

And this land is full good and rich. . . . In the land of Prester John are many divers things and many precious stones, so great and so large, that men make thereof plates, dishes, cups etc. . . . .

Sir John went on to describe the River of Paradise:

In his country is the sea called the Gravelly Sea. . . . Three days from that sea are great mountains, out of which runs a great river which comes from Paradise, and it is full of precious stones, without a drop of water, and it runs through the desert, on one side, so that it makes the Gravelly Sea where it ends.

Beyond the River of Paradise, there was "a great isle, long and broad, called Milsterak," that was a paradise on Earth. It had "the fairest garden that might be imagined; and therein were trees bearing all manner of fruits, all kinds of herbs of virtue and of good smell." This paradise, Sir John states, had marvelous pavilions and chambers, the purpose of which was diverse sexual enjoyment, all the work of a rich and devilish man.

Having fired the imagination (and greed) of his readers with the tales of precious stones and other riches, Sir John now played on the men's sexual desires. The place, he wrote, was filled with "the fairest damsels that might be found under the age of fifteen years, and the fairest young striplings that men might get of that same age, and they were all clothed richly in clothes of gold; and he said that they were angels." And the devilish man—

Had also caused to be made three fair and noble wells, all surrounded with stone of jasper and crystal, diapered with gold, and set with precious stones and great Orient pearls. And he had made a conduit under the earth, so that the three wells, at his will, should run one with milk, another with wine, and another with honey. And that place he called Paradise.

To that place, the crafty man lured "good knights, hardy and noble," and after entertaining them he persuaded them to go and kill his enemies; telling them that they should not fear being slain, for should they die, they would be resurrected and rejuvenated:

After their death they should come to his Paradise, and they should be of the age of the damsels, and they should play with them. And after that he would put them in a fairer Paradise, where they should see the God of Nature visibly, in his majesty and bliss.

But that, said John Maundeville, was not the real Paradise of biblical renown. That one, he said in Chapter XXX, lay beyond the isles and lands which Alexander the Great had journeyed through. The route to it led farther east, toward two isles rich in gold and silver mines "where the Red Sea separates from the Ocean Sea":

And beyond that land and isles, and deserts of Prester John's lordship, in going straight toward the east, men find nothing but mountains and great rocks; and there is the dark region, where no man can see, neither by day nor night. . . . And that desert, and that place of darkness, lasts from this coast unto Terrestrial Paradise, where Adam, our first father, and Eve were put.

It was from there that the waters of Paradise flowed:

And in the highest place of Paradise, exactly in the middle, is a well that casts out the four streams, which run by diverse lands, of which the first is called Pison, or Ganges, that runs through India, or Emlak, in which river are many precious stones, and much lignum aloes, and much sand of gold.
And the other river is called Nile, or Gyson, which goes through Ethiopia, and after through Egypt.
And the other is called Tigris, which runs by Assyria, and by Armenia the Great.
And the other is called Euphrates, which runs through Media, Armenia and Persia.

Confessing that he himself had not reached this biblical Garden of Eden, John Maundeville explained: "No mortal man may approach to that place without special grace of God; so that of that place I can tell you no more."

In spite of this admission, the many versions in many languages that flowed from the English original maintained that the knight had stated "I, John de Maundeville, saw that Fountain and drank three times of that water with my companion, and since I drank I feel well." The fact that in the English version, Maundeville complained that he was sick with rheumatic gout and near the end of his days, mattered not to the many who were thrilled by the marvelous tales. Nor did it matter then, that scholars nowadays believe that "Sir John Maundeville, Knight" may in fact have been a French doctor who had never traveled, but very skillfully put together a travelogue from the writings of others who did take the risk and trouble of journeying far and away.

Writing about the visions that had motivated the exploration that led to the discovery of America, Angel Rosenblat (*La Primera Vision de America y Otros Estudios*) summed up the evidence thus: "Along with the belief in the earthly Paradise was associated another desire of a messianic (or Faustic) nature; to find the Fountain of Eternal Youth. All the Middle Ages had dreamed of it. In the new images of the Lost Paradise, the Tree of Life was converted into the Fountain of Life, and then into a River or Spring of Youth." The motivation was the conviction that "the Fountain of Life came from India . . . a Fountain that cured all ills and assured immortality. The fantastic John Maundeville had actually encountered it on his trip to India . . . in the Christian Kingdom of Prester John." To reach India and the waters that flow from Paradise became "a symbol of the eternal human desire for pleasure, youth and happiness."

With the land routes blocked by enemies, the Christian kingdoms of Europe sought a sea route to India. Under Henry the Navigator, the kingdom of Portugal emerged in the middle of the fifteenth century as the leading power in the race to reach the Orient by sailing around Africa. In 1445, the Portuguese navigator Dinas Dias reached the mouth of the Senegal River, and mindful of the voyage's purpose reported that "men say it comes from the Nile, being one of the most glorious rivers of Earth, flowing from the Garden of Eden and the earthly Paradise." Others followed, pushing to and around the Cape at the tip of the African continent. In 1499, Vasco da Gama and his fleet circumnavigated Africa and reached the cherished target: India.

Yet the Portuguese, who had launched the Age of Discovery, failed to win the race. Diligently studying the ancient maps and all the writings of those who had ventured east, an Italian-born seaman named Cristóbal Colón concluded that by sailing *west*, he could reach India by a sea route much shorter than the Eastern Route sought by the Portuguese. Seeking a sponsor, he arrived at the court of Ferdinand and Isabel. He had with him (and took on his first voyage) an annotated copy of the Latin version of Marco Polo's book. He could also point to the writings of John Maundeville, who explained a century and a half before Columbus (Colón) that by going to the farthest east, one arrives at the west "on account of the roundness of the earth . . . for our Lord God made the earth all around."

In January 1492, Ferdinand and Isabel defeated the Muslims and expelled them from the Iberian Peninsula. Was it not a divine sign to Spain, that what the Crusaders could not achieve, Spain would? On August 3 of the same year, Columbus sailed under the Spanish flag to find a western sea route to India. On October 12, he sighted land. Until his death in 1506, he was sure that he had reached the islands which made up a great part of the legendary domain of Prester John.

Two decades later, Ferdinand issued to Ponce de Leon the Patent of Discovery, instructing him to find without delay the rejuvenating waters.

The Spaniards had thought that they were emulating Alexander the Great. Little did they know that they were following footsteps of far greater antiquity.

II

The Immortal Ancestors

The short life of Alexander the Macedonian—he died at age thirty-three in Babylon—was filled with conquest, adventure, exploration; a burning desire to reach the Ends of Earth, to unravel divine mysteries.

It was not an aimless search. Son of Queen Olympias and presumably of her husband King Philip II, he was tutored by the philosopher Aristotle in all manner of ancient wisdom. Then he witnessed quarreling and divorce between his parents, leading to the flight of his mother with the young Alexander. There was reconciliation, then murder; the assassination of Philip led to the crowning of Alexander when twenty years old. His early military expeditions brought him to Delphi, seat of the renowned oracle. There he heard the first of several prophesies predicting for him fame—but a very short life.

Undaunted, Alexander set out—as the Spaniards did nearly 1,800 years later—to find the Waters of Life. To do so, he had to open the way to the East. It was from there that the gods had come: the great Zeus, who swam across the Mediterranean, from the Phoenician city of Tyre to the island of Crete; Aphrodite who also came from across the Mediterranean, via the island of Cyprus; Poseidon, who brought with him the horse from Asia Minor; Athena, who carried to Greece the olive tree from the lands of western Asia. There, too, according to the Greek historians, whose writings Alexander studied, were the Waters which kept one forever young.

There was the history of Cambyses, son of the Persian king Cyrus, who went by way of Syria, Palestine and the Sinai to attack Egypt. Defeating the Egyptians, he treated them cruelly, and defiled the temple of their god Ammon. Then he took into his heart to go south and attack "the long-lived Ethiopians." Describing the events, Herodotus—writing a century before Alexander—said (*History*, Book III):

His spies went to Ethiopia, under the pretense of carrying presents to the king, but in reality to take note of all they saw, and especially to observe whether there was really what is called "The Table of the Sun" in Ethiopia. . . .

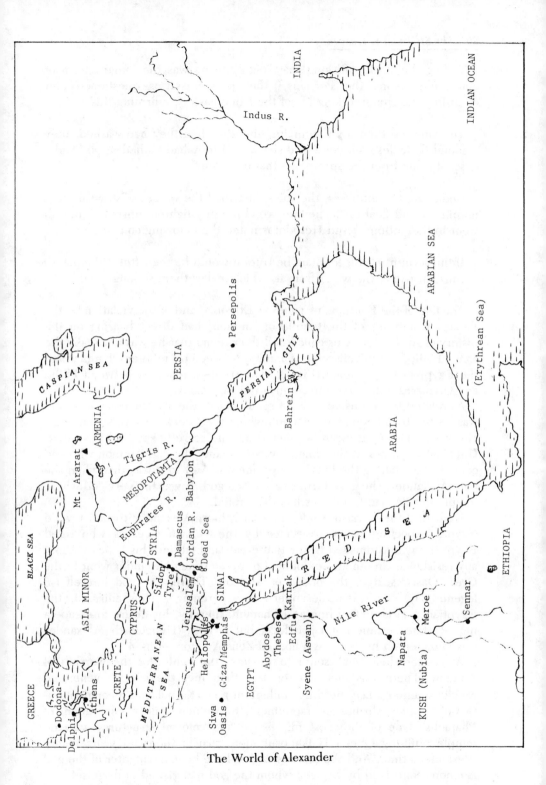

The World of Alexander

Fig. 2

Telling the Ethiopian king that "eighty years was the longest term of man's life among the Persians," the spies/emissaries questioned him regarding the rumored long life of the Ethiopians. Confirming this,

The king led them to a fountain, wherein when they had washed, they found their flesh all glossy and sleek, as if they had bathed in oil. And a scent came from the spring like that of violets.

Returning to Cambyses, the spies described the water as "so weak, that nothing would float on it, neither wood nor any lighter substance, but all went to the bottom." And Herodotus noted the following conclusion:

If the account of this fountain be true, it would be their (the Ethiopians') constant use of the water from it, which makes them so long-lived.

The tale of the Fountain of Youth in Ethiopia, and of the violation by the Persian Cambyses of the temple of Ammon, had direct bearing on the history of Alexander. This concerned the rumors that he was not really the son of Philip, but the offspring of a union between his mother Olympias and the Egyptian god Ammon (Fig. 3). The strained relations between Philip and Olympias only served to confirm the suspicions.

As related in various versions of pseudo-Callisthenes, the court of Philip was visited by an Egyptian Pharaoh whom the Greeks called Nectanebus. He was a master magician, a diviner; and he secretly seduced Olympias. Unbeknown to her at the time, it was in reality the god Ammon who had come to her, taking the guise of Nectanebus. And so it was that when she bore Alexander, she gave birth to a son of a god. It was the very god whose temple the Persian Cambyses had desecrated.

Defeating the Persian armies in Asia Minor, Alexander turned toward Egypt. Expecting heavy resistance by the Persian viceroys who ruled Egypt, he was astonished to see that great land fall into his hands without any resistance: an omen, no doubt. Losing no time, Alexander went to the Great Oasis, seat of the oracle of Ammon. There, the god himself (so legends say) confirmed Alexander's true parentage. Thus affirmed, the Egyptian priests deified him as a Pharaoh; thereby, his desire to escape a mortal's fate became not a privilege, but a right. (Henceforth, Alexander was depicted on his coins as a horned Zeus-Ammon—Fig. 4.)

Alexander then went south to *Karnak*, the center of the worship of Ammon. There was more to the trip than met the eye. A venerated religious center since the third millenium B.C., Karnak was a conglomeration of temples, shrines and monuments to Ammon built by generations of Pharaohs. One of the most impressive and colossal structures was the temple built by Queen Hatshepsut more than a thousand years before Alexander's time. And she too was said to have been a daughter of the god Ammon, conceived by a queen whom the god had visited in disguise!

Fig. 3   Fig. 4

Whatever actually transpired there, no one really knows. The fact is that instead of leading his armies back east, toward the heartland of the Persian empire, Alexander selected a small escort and a few companions for an expedition even farther south. His puzzled companions were led to believe that he was going on a pleasure trip—the pleasures of lovemaking.

The uncharacteristic interlude was as incomprehensible to the historians of those days as to the generals of Alexander. Trying to rationalize, the recorders of Alexander's adventures described the woman he was about to visit as a *femme fatale*, one "whose beauty no living man could praise sufficiently." She was Candace, queen of a land to the south of Egypt (today's Sudan). Reversing the tale of Solomon and the Queen of Sheba, in this instance it was the king who traveled to the queen's land. For, unbeknown to his companions, Alexander was really seeking not love, but the secret of Immortality.

After a pleasant stay, the queen agreed to reveal to Alexander, as a parting gift, the secret of "the wonderful cave where the gods congregate." Following her directions, Alexander found the sacred place:

He entered with a few soldiers, and saw a starlit haze. And the rooftops were shining, as if lit by stars. The external forms of the gods were physically manifest; a crowd was serving (them) in silence.

At first he (Alexander) was frightened and surprised. But he stayed to see what would happen, for he saw some reclining figures whose eyes were shining like beams of light.

The sight of the "reclining figures," with eyes emitting beams of light, made Alexander stop short. Were they too gods, or deified mortals? He was then startled by a voice: one of the "figures" had spoken up:

And there was one who said: "Glad greetings, Alexander. Do you know who I am?"
And he (Alexander) said: "No, my lord."
The other said: "I am Sesonchusis, the world-conquering king who has joined the ranks of the gods."

Alexander was far from being surprised—as though he had encountered the very person he had searched for. His arrival apparently expected, Alexander was invited in, to "the Creator and Overseer of the entire universe." He "went within, and saw a fire-bright haze; and, seated on a throne, the god whom he had once seen worshipped by men in Rokôtide, the Lord Serapis." (In the Greek version, it was the god Dionysus.)

Alexander saw his chance to bring up the matter of his longevity. "Lord god," he said, "how many years shall I live?"

But there was no answer from the god. Then Sesonchusis sought to console Alexander, for the god's silence spoke for itself. Though I myself have joined the ranks of the gods, Sesonchusis said, "I was not as fortunate as you . . . for although I have conquered the whole world and subjugated so many peoples, nobody remembers my name; but you shall have great renown . . . you will have an immortal name even after death." In this manner, he consoled Alexander. "You shall live upon dying, thus not dying"—immortalized by a lasting reputation.

Disappointed, Alexander left the caves and "continued the journey to be made"—to seek the advice of other sages, to find an escape from a mortal's fate, to emulate others who before him did succeed in joining the immortal gods.

According to one version, among those whom Alexander searched out and met was Enoch, the biblical patriarch from the days before the Deluge, who was the great-grandfather of Noah. It was a place of mountains, "where Paradise, which is the Land of the Living, is situated," the "abode where the saints dwell." Atop a mountain there was a glittering structure, from which there extended skyward a huge stairway, made of 2,500 golden slabs. In a vast hall or cavern Alexander saw "golden figures, each standing in its niche," a golden altar, and two huge "candlesticks" measuring some sixty feet in height.

Upon a couch nearby reclined the form of a man who was draped in a coverlet inlaid with gold and precious stones, and above it, worked in gold, were branches of a vine, having its cluster of grapes formed of jewels.

The man suddenly spoke up, identifying himself as Enoch. "Do not pry into the mysteries of God," the voice warned Alexander. Heeding the warning, Alexander left to rejoin his troops; but not before receiving as a parting gift a bunch of grapes that miraculously were sufficient to feed his whole army.

In yet another version, Alexander encountered not one but two men from the past: Enoch, and the Prophet Elijah—two who according to biblical traditions have never died. It happened when Alexander was traversing an uninhabited desert. Suddenly, his horse was seized by a "spirit" which carried horse and rider aloft, bringing Alexander to a glittering tabernacle. Inside, he saw the two men. Their faces were bright, their teeth whiter than milk, their eyes shone brighter than the morning star; they were "lofty of stature, of gracious look." Telling him who they were, they said that "God hid them from death." They told him that the place was "The City of the Storehouse of Life," from where the "Bright Waters of Life" emanated. But before Alexander could find out more, or drink of the "Waters of Life," a "chariot of fire" snatched him away—and he found himself back with his troops.

(According to Muslim tradition, the prophet Muhammed was also carried heavenward, a thousand years later, riding his white horse.)

Was the episode of the Cave of the Gods—as the other episodes in the histories of Alexander—pure fiction, mere myth, or perhaps embellished tales based on historical fact?

Was there a Queen Candace, a royal city named Shamar, a world-conqueror named Sesonchusis? In truth, the names meant little to students of antiquity until relatively recently. If these were names of Egyptian royal personages or of a mystical province of Egypt, they were as obscured by time as the monuments were obscured by the encroaching sands; rising above the sands, the pyramids and the Sphinx only broadened the enigma; the hieroglyphic picture-words, undecipherable, only confirmed that there were secrets not to be unlocked. The tales from antiquity, passed on via the Greeks and Romans, dissolved into legends; eventually, they faded into obscurity.

It was only when Napoleon conquered Egypt in 1798, that Europe began to rediscover Egypt. Accompanying Napoleon's troops were groups of serious scholars who began to remove the sands and raise the curtain of forgetfulness. Then, near the village of Rosetta, a stone tablet was found bearing the same inscription in three languages. The key was found to unlock the language and inscriptions of ancient Egypt: its records of Pharaonic feats, the glorification of its gods.

In the 1820s European explorers penetrating southward, into the Sudan, reported the existence of ancient monuments (including sharp-angled pyramids) at a site on the Nile river called Meroe. A Royal Prussian expedition uncovered impressive archaeological remains during excavations in the years 1842–44. Between 1912 and 1914, others uncovered sacred sites; the hieroglyphic inscriptions indicated one of them was called the Sun Temple—perhaps the very place where the spies of Cambyses observed the "Table of the Sun." Further excavations in this century, the piecing together of archaeological finds, and the continued decipherment of the inscriptions, have established that there indeed existed in that land a Nubian kingdom in the first millennium B.C.; it was the biblical Land of Kush.

There indeed was a Queen Candace. The hieroglyphic inscriptions revealed, that at the very beginning of the Nubian kingdom, it was ruled by a wise and benevolent queen. Her name was Candace (Fig. 5). Thereafter, whenever a woman ascended the throne—which was not infrequent—she adopted the name as a symbol of great queenship. And farther south of Meroe, within this kingdom's domain, there was a city named *Sennar*— possibly the *Shamar* referred to in the Alexander tale.

And what about Sesonchusis? It is told in the Ethiopic version of pseudo-Callisthenes, that journeying to (or from) Egypt, Alexander and his men passed by a lake swarming with crocodiles. There, an earlier ruler had built a way to cross the lake. "And behold, there was a building upon the shore of the lake, and above the building was a heathen altar upon which was written: 'I am Kosh, the king of the world, the conqueror who crossed this lake.'"

Who was this world conqueror *Kosh*, namely the king who ruled over Kush or Nubia? In the Greek version of this tale, the conqueror who had commemorated his crossing of the lake—described as part of the waters of the Red Sea—was named Sesonchusis; so Sesonchusis and Kosh were one and the same ruler—a Pharaoh who had ruled both Egypt and Nubia. Nubian monuments depicted such a ruler as he receives from a "Shiny God" the Fruit of Life shaped like date palms (Fig. 6).

Egyptian records do speak of a great Pharaoh who, early in the second millenium B.C., was indeed a world conqueror. His name was Senusert; and he, too, was a devotee of Ammon. Greek historians credited him with the conquest of Libya and Arabia, and significantly also of Ethiopia and all the islands of the Red Sea; of great parts of Asia—penetrating east even farther than the later Persians; and of invading Europe via Asia Minor. Herodotus described the great feats of this Pharaoh, whom he names Sesostris; stating that Sesostris erected memorial pillars wherever he went.

Fig. 5

Fig. 6

"The pillars which he erected," Herodotus wrote, "are still visible." Thus, when Alexander saw the pillar by the lake, it only confirmed what Herodotus had written a century earlier.

Sesonchusis did indeed exist. His Egyptian name meant "He whose births live." For, by virtue of being a Pharaoh of Egypt, he had every right to join the company of the gods, and live forever.

In the search for the Waters of Life or of Eternal Youth, it was important to assert that the search was surely not futile, for others in days past had succeeded in the quest. Moreover, if the waters flow from a Paradise Lost, would not finding those who had been there be a means of learning from them how to get there?

It was with that in mind, that Alexander sought to reach the Immortal Ancestors. Whether he indeed encountered them is not too important: the important fact is that in the centuries preceding the Christian era, Alexander or his historians (or both) believed that the Immortal Ancestors indeed existed—that in days that to them were ancient and olden, mortals could become immortal if the gods so wished.

The authors or editors of the histories of Alexander relate various incidents in which Alexander encountered Sesonchusis; Elijah and Enoch; or just Enoch. The identity of Sesonchusis could only be guessed, and the manner of his translation to Immortality is not described. Not so with Elijah—the companion of Enoch in the Shining Temple, according to one Alexander version.

He was the biblical Prophet who was active in the Kingdom of Israel in the ninth century B.C., during the reign of kings Ahab and Ahaziah. As his adopted name indicated (*Eli-Yah*—"My God is Yahweh"), he was inspired by and stood up for the Hebrew god Yahweh, whose faithful were finding themselves harassed by the followers of the Canaanite god Baal. After a period of seclusion at a secret place near the Jordan River, where he was apparently coached by the Lord, he was given "a mantle of haircloth" of magical powers, and was able to perform miracles. Residing first near the Phoenician town of Sidon, his first reported miracle (as related in I Kings Chapter 17) was the making of a little cooking oil and a spoonful of flour last a widow, who gave him shelter, the rest of her lifetime. Then he prevailed on the Lord to revive her son, after he had died of a violent illness. He could also summon the Fire of God from the skies, which came in handily in the ongoing struggle with the kings and priests who succumbed to pagan temptations.

Of him, the Scriptures say, that he did not die on Earth, for he "went up into Heaven in a whirlwind." According to Jewish traditions, Elijah is still immortal; and to this very day, tradition requires that he be invited to come into Jewish homes on Passover eve. His ascent is described in the Old Testament in great detail. And as reported in II Kings Chapter 2, the event was not a sudden or unexpected occurrence. On the contrary: it was a planned and pre-arranged operation, whose place and time were communicated to Elijah in advance.

The designated place was in the Jordan Valley, on the eastern side of the river—perhaps in the very area where Elijah was ordained as "a Man of God." As he began his last journey to Gilgal—a place commemorating an earlier miracle, as the Bible tells—he had a tough time shaking off his devoted chief disciple Elisha. Along the way, the two Prophets were repeatedly intercepted by disciples, "Sons of Prophets," who kept asking: Is it true that the Lord will take Elijah heavenward today?

Let the biblical narrator tell the story in his own words:

> And it came to pass when the Lord
> would take up Elijah into Heaven by a Whirlwind,
> that Elijah went with Elisha from Gilgal.
> And Elijah said unto Elisha:
> "Tarry here, I pray thee,
> for the Lord has sent me to Beth-El."
> And Elisha said unto him:
> "As the Lord liveth, and by thy life,
> I will not leave thee."
> So they went down to Beth-El.
>
> And the Sons of the Prophets that were at Beth-el
> came forth to Elisha, and said unto him:
> "Knowest thou that the Lord will, this day,
> take the master from above thee?"
> And he said:
> "Yea, I know it too; but keep silent."

Now Elijah admitted to Elisha that his destination was Jericho, by the Jordan River; and he asked his colleague to stay behind. But again Elisha refused and went along with the Prophet; "and so they came to Jericho."

> And the Sons of the Prophets that were at Jericho
> approached Elisha and said unto him:
> "Knowest thou that the Lord will, this day,
> take the master from above thee?"
> And he said:
> "Yea, I know it too; but keep silent."

Foiled thus far in his attempt to proceed alone, Elijah then asked Elisha to stay behind in Jericho, and to let him proceed to the river's bank unaccompanied. But Elisha refused, and would not part from Elijah. Encouraged, "fifty men of the Sons of the Prophets went along; but they stopped and stood apart as the two (Elijah and Elisha) reached the Jordan."

> And Elijah took his mantle
> and rolled it together,
> and struck the waters.
> And the waters parted hither and thither,
> and the two of them crossed over on dry ground.

Once they were across, Elisha asked that Elijah imbue him with the divine spirit; but before he could get an answer,

> As they continued to walk on and to talk,
> there appeared a chariot of fire,
> and horses of fire, and the two were separated.
> And Elijah went up into Heaven,
> in a Whirlwind.
> And Elisha saw,
> and he cried out:
> "My father! My father!
> The Chariot of Israel and its horsemen!"
> And he saw it no more.

Distraught, Elisha sat stunned for a while. Then he saw that the mantle of Elijah was left behind. Was it by accident or on purpose? Determined to find out, Elisha took the mantle, and returned to the banks of the Jordan, and called the name of Yahweh, and struck the waters. And lo and behold— "the waters parted hither and thither, and Elisha crossed." And the Sons of the Prophets, the disciples who stood back on the western side of the river in the plain of Jericho, "saw this; and they said: 'the inspiration of Elijah doth rest upon Elisha'; and they came toward him, and prostrated themselves before him."

Incredulous of what they had seen with their own eyes, the fifty disciples wondered whether Elijah was indeed taken heavenward for good. Perchance the Lord's wind had blown him only some distance, and he was thrown upon a mountain or into some ravine? they asked. Over the objections of Elisha, they searched for three days. And when they returned from the futile search, Elisha said: "Did I not say unto you, 'Go not'?" for he well knew the truth: that the Lord of Israel had taken Elijah up in a Chariot of Fire.

The encounter with Enoch, which the histories of Alexander claimed for him, introduced into the Search for Immortality an "Immortal Ancestor" specifically mentioned in the Old and New Testaments alike, the legends of whose ascent to the heavens predated the Bible and were recorded in their own right.

According to the Bible, Enoch was the seventh pre-Diluvial patriarch in the line of Adam through Seth (as distinct from the accursed line of Adam through Cain). He was the great-grandfather of Noah, the hero of the Deluge. The fifth chapter of the Book of Genesis lists the genealogies of these patriarchs, the ages at which their rightful heirs were born, and the ages at which they died. But Enoch was an exception: no mention at all is made of his death. Explaining that "he had walked with the Lord," the Book of Genesis states that at the actual or symbolic age of 365 (the number of days in a solar year), Enoch "was gone" from Earth, "for the Lord had taken him."

Enlarging on the cryptic biblical statement, Jewish commentators often quoted older sources which seemed to describe an actual ascent by Enoch to the heavens, where he was (by some versions) translated into Metatron, the Lord's "Prince of the Countenance" who was stationed right behind the Lord's throne.

According to these legends, as brought together by I. B. Lavner in his *Kol Agadoth Israel* [*All the Legends of Israel*], when Enoch was summoned to the Lord's abode, a fiery horse was sent for him from the heavens. Enoch was at the time preaching righteousness to the people. When the people saw the fiery horse descending from the skies, they asked Enoch for an explanation. And he told them: "Know ye, that the time has come to leave ye and ascend to Heaven." But as he mounted the horse, the people refused to let him leave, and followed him about for a whole week. "And it was on the seventh day, that a fiery chariot drawn by fiery horses and angels came down, and raised Enoch skyward." While he was soaring up, the Angels of Heaven objected to the Lord: "How comes a man born of a woman to ascend unto the Heavens?" But the Lord pointed out the piety and devotion of Enoch, and opened to him the Gates of Life and of Wisdom, and arrayed him in a magnificent garment and a luminous crown.

As in other instances, cryptic references in the Scriptures often suggest that the ancient editor assumed that his reader was familiar with some other, more detailed writings on the subject at hand. There are even specific mentions of such writings—"The Book of Righteousness," or "The Book of the Wars of Yahweh"—which must have existed, but were entirely lost. In the case of Enoch, the New Testament augments a cryptic statement that Enoch was "translated" by the Lord "that he should not see death" with a mention of a *Testimony of Enoch*, written or dictated by him "before his Translation" to Immortality (Hebrews 11:5). Jude 14, referring to the prophecies of Enoch, is also taken as referring to some actual writings by this patriarch.

Various Christian writings throughout the centuries also contain similar hints or references; and as it turned out, there have in fact circulated since the second century B.C. several versions of a *Book of Enoch*. When the manuscripts were studied in the nineteenth century, scholars concluded that there were basically two sources. The first, identified as *I Enoch* and called the *Ethiopic Book of Enoch,* is an Ethiopic translation of a previous

Greek translation of an original work in Hebrew (or Aramaic). The other, identified as *II Enoch*, is a Slavonic translation from an original written in Greek whose full title was *The Book of the Secrets of Enoch*.

Scholars who have studied these versions do not rule out the possibility that both *I Enoch* and *II Enoch* stem from a much earlier original work; and that there indeed could have existed in antiquity a *Book of Enoch*. *The Apocrypha and Pseudepigrapha of the Old Testament*, which R. H. Charles began to publish in 1913, is still the major English translation of the Books of Enoch and the other early writings which were excluded from the canonized Old and New Testaments.

Written in the first person, *The Book of the Secrets of Enoch* starts with an exact place and time:

> On the first day of the first month of the 365th year I was alone in my house and I rested on my bed and slept. . . . And there appeared to me two men, very tall, such as I have never seen on Earth; and their faces shone like the sun, and their eyes were like burning lamps, and fire came forth from their lips. Their dress had the appearance of feathers, their feet were purple. Their wings were brighter than gold; their hands whiter than snow. They stood at the head of my bed and called me by name.

Because he was asleep when these strangers arrived, Enoch adds for the record that by then he was no longer sleeping; "I saw clearly these men, standing in front of me," he states. He made obeisance to them, and was overtaken by fear. But the two reassured him:

> Be of good cheer, Enoch, be not afraid; the Everlasting God hath sent us to thee and lo, today thou shalt ascend with us into heaven.

They then told Enoch to wake up his family and servants, and order them not to seek him, "till the Lord bring thee back to them." This Enoch did, using the opportunity to instruct his sons in the ways of righteousness. Then the time came to depart:

> It came to pass when I had spoken to my sons, these men summoned me and took me on their wings and placed me on the clouds; and lo, the clouds moved. . . . Going higher I saw the air and (going still) higher I saw the ether; and they placed me in the First Heaven; and they showed me a very great sea, greater than the earthly sea.

Ascending thus unto the heavens upon "clouds that move," Enoch was transported from the First Heaven—where "two hundred angels rule the stars"—to the Second, gloomy Heaven; then to the Third Heaven. There he was shown a garden with a goodliness of its appearance; beautiful and fragrant trees and fruits.

In the midst therein there is a Tree of Life—in that place on which the God rests when he comes into Paradise.

Stunned by the Tree's magnificence, Enoch manages to describe the Tree of Life in the following words: "It is beautiful more than any created thing; on all sides in appearance it is like gold and crimson, transparent as fire." From its root go four streams which pour honey, milk, oil and wine, and they go down from this heavenly Paradise to the Paradise of Eden, making a revolution around Earth. This Third Heaven and its Tree of Life are guarded by three hundred "very glorious" angels. It is in this Third Heaven that the Place of the Righteous, and the Terrible Place where the wicked are tortured, are situated.

Going further up, to the Fourth Heaven, Enoch could see the Luminaries and various wondrous creatures, and the Host of the Lord. In the Fifth Heaven, he saw many "hosts"; in the Sixth, "bands of angels who study the revolutions of the stars." Then he reached the Seventh Heaven, where the greatest angels hurried about and where he saw the Lord—"from afar"—sitting on his throne.

The two winged men and their moving cloud placed Enoch at the limits of the Seventh Heaven, and left; whereupon the Lord sent the archangel Gabriel to fetch Enoch into His Presence.

For thirty-three days, Enoch was instructed in all the wisdoms and all the events of the past and the future; then he was returned to Earth by an awful angel who had a "very cold appearance." In total, he was absent from Earth sixty days. But his return to Earth was only so that he might instruct his sons in the laws and commandments; and thirty days later, he was taken up again unto the heavens—this time, for good.

Written both as a personal testament and as a historic review, the *Ethiopic Book of Enoch*, whose earliest title was probably *The Words of Enoch*, describes his journeys to Heaven as well as to the four corners of Earth. As he traveled north, "toward the north ends of Earth," he "saw there a great and glorious device," the nature of which is not described. And he saw there, as well as at the western ends of Earth, "three portals of heaven open in the heaven" in each place, through which hail and snow, cold and frost blew in.

"And thence I went to the south to the ends of the Earth," and through the portals of Heaven there blow in the dew and rain. And thence he went to see the eastern portals, through which the stars of Heaven pass and run their course.

But the principal mysteries, and secrets of the past and the future, were shown to Enoch as he went to "the middle of the Earth," and to the east and to the west thereof. The "middle of the Earth" was the site of the future

Holy Temple in Jerusalem; on his journey east, Enoch reached the Tree of Knowledge; and going west, he was shown the Tree of Life.

On his eastward journey, Enoch passed mountains and deserts, saw water courses flowing from mountain peaks covered by clouds, and snow and ice ("water which flows not"), and trees of diverse fragrances and balsams. Going farther and farther east, he found himself back over mountains bordering the Erythraean Sea (the Sea of Arabia and the Red Sea). Continuing, he passed by Zotiel, the angel guarding the entrance to Paradise, and he "came unto the Garden of Righteousness." There he saw among many wonderful trees the "Tree of Knowledge." It was as high as a fir, its leaves were as of the carob, and its fruit like the clusters of a vine. And the angel who was with him confirmed that indeed it was the very tree whose fruit Adam and Eve had eaten before they were driven out of the Garden of Eden.

On his journey west, Enoch arrived at a "mountain range of fire, which burnt day and night." Beyond it he reached a place encircled by six mountains separated by "deep, rough ravines." A seventh mountain rose in their midst, "resembling the seat of a throne; and fragrant trees encircled the throne. And amongst them was a tree such as I had never smelt . . . and its fruit resembles the dates of a palm."

The angel who accompanied him explained that the middle mountain was the throne "on which the Holy Great One, the Lord of Glory, the Eternal King will sit when He shall come to visit Earth." And as to the tree whose fruits were as the date palms, he said:

> As for this fragrant tree, no mortal is permitted to
>   touch it till the Great Judgment . . .
> Its fruit shall be for food for the elect . . .
> Its fragrance shall be in their bones,
> And they shall live a long life on Earth.

It was during these journeys that Enoch "saw in those days how long cords were given to those angels, and they took to themselves wings, and they went towards the north." And when Enoch asked what this was all about, the angel who guided him said: "They have gone off to measure . . . they shall bring the measures of the righteous to the righteous, and the ropes of the righteous to the righteous . . . all these measures shall reveal the secrets of the earth."

Having visited all the secret places on Earth, Enoch's time had come to take the Journey to Heaven. And, like others after him, he was taken to a "mountain whose summit reached to Heaven" and to a Land of Darkness:

> And they (the angels) took me to a place in which those who were there were like flaming fire, and when they wished, they appeared as men.
>
> And they brought me to a place of darkness, and to a mountain the point of whose summit reached to heaven.

And I saw the chambers of the luminaries, and the treasuries of the stars, and of the thunder, in the great depths, where were a fiery bow and arrows, and their quiver, and a fiery sword, and all the lightnings.

Whereas, at such a crucial stage, Immortality slipped out of Alexander's hands because he had searched for it contrary to his proclaimed destiny—Enoch, as the Pharaohs after him, was proceeding with divine blessing. Thus, at this crucial moment, he was deemed worthy of proceeding; so "they (the angels) took me to the Waters of Life."

Continuing, he arrived at the "House of Fire":

And I went in till I drew nigh to a wall which is built of crystals and surrounded by tongues of fire; and it began to affright me.

And I went into the tongues of fire and drew nigh to a large house which was built of crystals; and the walls of the house were like a tesselated floor of crystals, and its groundwork was of crystal. Its ceiling was like the path of the stars and the lightnings, and between them were fiery Cherubim, and their heaven was as water.

A flaming fire surrounded the walls, and its portals blazed with fire.

And I entered into that house, and it was hot as a fire and cold as ice. . . .

And I beheld a vision: behold, there was a second house, greater than the former, and the entire portal stood open before me, and it was built of flames of fire. . . .

And I looked therein and saw a lofty throne: its appearance was as crystal, and the wheels thereof as the shining sun, and there was the appearance of Cherubim.

And from underneath the throne came streams of flaming fire, so that I could not look thereon.

Arriving at the "River of Fire," Enoch was taken aloft.

He could see the whole of Earth—"the mouths of all the rivers of Earth . . . and the cornerstones of Earth . . . and the winds on Earth carrying the clouds." Rising higher, he was "where the winds stretch the vaults of Heaven and have their station between Heaven and Earth. I saw the winds of Heaven which turn and bring the circumference of the Sun, and all the stars." Following "the paths of the angels," he reached a point "in the firmament of Heaven above" from which he could see "the end of Earth."

From there, he could view the expanse of the heavens; and he could see "seven stars like great shining mountains"—"seven mountains of magnificent stones." From wherever he was viewing these celestial bodies, "three were toward the east," where there was "the region of heavenly fire"; there Enoch saw rising and falling "columns of fire"—eruptions of fire "which were beyond measure, alike toward the width and toward the depth." On the other side, three celestial bodies were "toward the south"; there Enoch saw "an abyss, a place which had no firmament of the Heaven above, and no firmly founded Earth below . . . it was a void and awesome place." When he asked the angel who was carrying him aloft for an explanation, he replied: "There the heavens were completed . . . it is the end of Heaven and Earth; it is a prison for the stars and the host of Heaven."

The middle star "reached to Heaven like the throne of God." Having the appearance of alabaster, "and the summit of the throne as of sapphire," the star was "like a flaming fire."

Journeying on in the heavens, Enoch said, "I proceeded to where things were chaotic. And I saw there something horrible." What he saw was "stars of the heaven bound together." And the angel explained to him: "These are of the number of stars of heaven which have transgressed the commandment of the Lord, and are bound here till ten thousand years are consummated."

Concluding his report of the first Journey to Heaven, Enoch said: "And I, Enoch, alone saw the vision, the ends of all things; and no man shall see as I have seen." After being taught at the Heavenly Abode all manner of wisdom, he was returned to Earth to impart teachings to other men. For an unspecified length of time, "Enoch was hidden, and no one of the children of men knew where he was hidden, and where he abode, and what had become of him." But when the Deluge neared, he wrote down his teachings and advised his great-grandson Noah to be righteous and worthy of salvation.

After that, Enoch was once again "raised aloft from among those who dwell on Earth. He was raised aloft on the Chariot of the Spirits, and his 'Name' vanished among them."

III

The Pharaoh's Journey to the Afterlife

The adventures of Alexander and his search for the Immortal Ancestors clearly comprised elements which simulated their experiences: caverns, angels, subterranean fires, fiery horses and Chariots of Fire. But it is equally clear that, in the centuries preceding the Christian era, it was believed (by Alexander or by his historians or by both) that if one wished to attain Immortality, one had to emulate the Egyptian Pharaohs.

Accordingly, Alexander's claim to semi-divine ancestry was evolved from a complicated affair by an Egyptian deity, rather than by simply claiming affinity to a local Greek god. It is an historical fact, not mere legend, that Alexander found it necessary, as soon as he broke through the Persian lines in Asia Minor, not to pursue the Persian enemy, but to go to Egypt; there to seek the answer to his purported divine "roots," and from there to begin the search for the Waters of Life.

Whereas the Hebrews, the Greeks and other peoples in antiquity recounted tales of a unique few who were able to escape a mortal's fate by divine invitation, the ancient Egyptians developed the privilege into a right. Not a universal right, nor a right reserved to the singularly righteous; but a right attendant on the Egyptian king, the Pharaoh, by sole virtue of having sat on the throne of Egypt. The reason for this, according to the traditions of ancient Egypt, was that the first rulers of Egypt were not men but gods.

Egyptian traditions held that in times immemorial "Gods of Heaven" came to Earth from the Celestial Disk (Fig. 7). When Egypt was inundated by waters, "a very great god who came forth (to Earth) in the earliest times" arrived in Egypt and literally raised it from under the waters and mud, by damming the waters of the Nile and undertaking extensive dyking and land reclamation works (it was therefore that Egypt was nicknamed "The Raised Land"). This olden god was named PTAH—"The Developer." He was considered to have been a great scientist, a master engineer and architect, the Chief Craftsman of the gods, who even had a hand in creating and shaping Man. His staff was frequently depicted as a graduated stick—very much like the graduated rod which surveyors employ for field measuring nowadays (Fig. 7).

The Egyptians believed that Ptah eventually retired south, where he could continue to control the waters of the Nile with sluices he had installed in a secret cavern, located at the first cataract of the Nile (the site of today's Aswan Dam). But before leaving Egypt, he built its first hallowed city and named it AN, in honor of the God of the Heavens (the biblical *On*, whom the Greeks called *Heliopolis*). There, he installed as Egypt's first Divine Ruler his own son RA (so named in honor of the Celestial Globe).

Ra, a great "God of Heaven and Earth," caused a special shrine to be built at An; it housed the *Ben-Ben*—a "secret object" in which Ra had purportedly come down to Earth from the heavens.

In time Ra divided the kingdom between the gods OSIRIS and SETH. But the sharing of the kingdom between the two divine brothers did not work. Seth kept seeking the overthrow and death of his brother Osiris. It took some doing, but finally Seth succeeded in tricking Osiris into entering a coffin, which Seth promptly set to seal and drown. ISIS, the sister and wife of Osiris, managed to find the coffin, which had floated ashore in what is nowadays Lebanon. She hid Osiris as she went to summon the help of other gods who could bring Osiris back to life; but Seth discovered the body and cut it to pieces, dispersing them all over the land. Helped by her sister NEPHTYS, Isis managed to retrieve the pieces (all except for the phallus) and to put together the mutilated body of Osiris, thereby resurrecting him.

Thereafter, Osiris lived on, resurrected, in the Other World among the other celestial gods. Of him the sacred writings said:

> He entered the Secret Gates,
> The glory of the Lords of Eternity,
> In step with him who shines in the horizon,
> On the path of Ra.

The place of Osiris on the throne of Egypt was taken over by his son HORUS. When he was born, his mother Isis hid him in the reeds of the river Nile (just as the mother of Moses did, according to the Bible), to keep him out of the reach of Seth. But the boy was stung by a scorpion and died. Quickly, the goddess his mother appealed to THOTH, a god of magical powers, for help. Thoth, who was in the heavens, immediately came down to Earth in Ra's "Barge of Astronomical Years" and helped restore Horus to life.

Growing up, Horus challenged Seth for the throne. The struggle ranged far and wide, the gods pursuing each other in the skies. Horus attacked Seth from a *Nar*, a term which in the ancient Near East meant "Fiery Pillar." Depictions from pre-dynastic times showed this celestial chariot as a long, cylindrical object with a funnel-like tail and a bulkhead from which rays are spewed out, a kind of a celestial submarine (Fig. 8). In front the *Nar* had two headlights or "eyes," which according to the Egyptian tales changed color from blue to red.

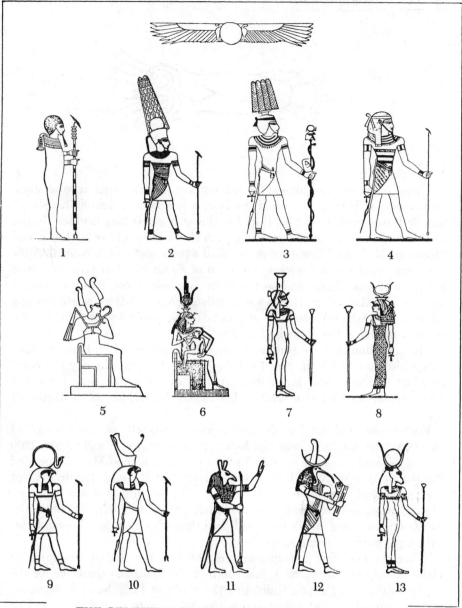

THE CELESTIAL DISK AND THE GODS OF EGYPT

1. Ptah   2. Ra-Amen   3. Thoth   4. Seker
5. Osiris   6. Isis with Horus   7. Nephtys   8. Hathor

The gods with their attributes:

9. Ra/Falcon   10. Horus/Falcon   11. Seth/Sinai Ass   12. Thoth/Ibis   13. Hathor/Cow

Fig. 7

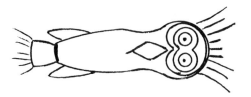

Fig. 8

There were ups and downs in the battles, which lasted several days. Horus shot at Seth, from out of the *Nar*, a specially designed "harpoon," and Seth was hurt, losing his testicles; this only made him madder. In the final battle, over the Sinai peninsula, Seth shot a beam of fire at Horus, and Horus lost an "eye." The great gods called a truce and met in council. After some wavering and indecision, the Lord of Earth ruled in favor of giving Egypt to Horus, declaring him the legitimate heir in the Ra-Osiris line of succession. (Thereafter, Horus was usually depicted with the attributes of a falcon, while Seth was shown as an Asiatic deity, symbolized by the ass, the burden animal of the nomads; Fig. 7).

The accession of Horus to the reunited throne of the Two Lands (Upper Egypt and Lower Egypt) remained throughout Egyptian history the point at which kingship was given its perpetual divine connection; for every Pharaoh was deemed a successor of Horus and the occupier of the throne of Osiris.

For unexplained reasons, the rule of Horus was followed by a period of chaos and decline; how long this lasted, no one knows. Finally, circa 3200 B.C., a "dynastic race" arrived in Egypt and a man named Menes ascended the throne of a reunited Egypt. It was then that the gods granted Egypt civilization and what we now call Religion. The kingship that was begun by Menes continued through twenty-six dynasties of Pharaohs until the Persian domination in 525 B.C., and then through Greek and Roman times (when the famed Cleopatra reigned).

When Menes, the first Pharaoh, established the united kingdom, he chose a midpoint in the Nile, just south of Heliopolis, as the place for the capital of the two Egypts. Emulating the works of Ptah, he built *Memphis* on an artificial mound raised above the Nile's waters, and dedicated its temples to Ptah. Memphis remained the political-religious center of Egypt for more than a thousand years.

But circa 2200 B.C. great upheavals befell Egypt, the nature of which is not clear to scholars. Some think that Asiatic invaders overran the country, enslaving the people and disrupting the worship of their gods. Whatever semblance of Egyptian independence remained, it was retained in Upper Egypt—the less accessible regions farther south. When order was restored some 150 years later, political-religious power—the attributes of kingship—flowed from *Thebes*, an old but until then unimposing city in Upper Egypt, on the banks of the Nile.

Its god was called AMEN —"The Hidden One"—the very god Ammon whom Alexander had searched out as his true divine father. As supreme deity, he was worshipped as Amen-Ra, "The Hidden Ra"; and it is not clear whether he was the very same Ra but now somehow unseen or "hidden," or another deity.

The Greeks called Thebes *Diospolis*, "The City of Zeus," for they equated Ammon with their supreme god Zeus. This fact made it easier for Alexander to affiliate himself with Ammon; and it was to Thebes that he rushed after he had received Ammon's favorable oracle at the oasis of Siwa.

There, at Thebes and its precincts (now known as Karnak, Luxor, Dier-el-Bahari), Alexander came upon the extensive shrines and monuments to Ammon—impressive to this very day although they stand empty and in ruins. They were built mostly by Twelfth Dynasty Pharaohs, one of whom was probably the "Sesonchusis" who had searched for the Waters of Life 1,500 years before Alexander. One of the colossal temples was built by Queen Hatshepshut, who was also said to have been a daughter of the god Ammon.

Such tales of divine parentage were not unusual. The Pharaoh's claim to divine status, based on the mere fact of occupying the throne of Osiris, was sometimes augmented by assertions that the ruler was the son or the brother of this or that god or goddess. Scholars consider such statements to have only symbolic meaning; but some Egyptian Pharaohs, such as three kings of the Fifth Dynasty, maintained that they were actually, physically, the sons of the god Ra, begotten by him when he impregnated the wife of the high priest in his own temple.

Other kings attributed their descent from Ra to more sophisticated means. It was claimed that Ra embodied himself in the reigning Pharaoh, through which subterfuge he could then have intercourse with the queen. Thereby, the heir to the throne could claim direct descent of Ra. But apart from such specific claims to be of divine seed, every Pharaoh was theologically deemed to be the incarnation of Horus and thus by extension the son of the god Osiris. Consequently, the Pharaoh was entitled to eternal life in the very same manner experienced by Osiris: to resurrection after death, to an Afterlife.

It was this circle, of gods and god-like Pharaohs, that Alexander longed to join.

The belief was that Ra and the other immortal gods managed to live forever because he kept rejuvenating himself. Accordingly, the Pharaohs bore names meaning, for example, "He Who Repeats Births" and "Repeater of Births." The gods rejuvenated themselves by partaking of divine food and beverage at their abode. Therefore, the king's attainment of an eternal Afterlife called for his joining the gods in their abode, so that he too could partake of their divine sustenances.

The ancient incantations appealed to the gods to share with the deceased king their divine food: "Take ye this king with you, that he may eat of that which ye eat, that he may drink of which ye drink, that he may live on that whereupon ye live." And more specifically, as in a text from the pyramid of King Pepi:

> Give thou sustenance to this King Pepi
> From thy eternal sustenance;
> Thy everlasting beverage.

The departed Pharaoh hoped to draw his everlasting sustenance in the celestial realm of Ra, on the "Imperishable Star." There, in a mystical "Field of Offerings" or "Field of Life," there grew the "Plant of Life." A text in the pyramid of Pepi I describes him as getting past guards with the appearance of "plumed birds," to be met by the emissaries of Horus. With them

> He traveleth to the Great Lake,
> by which the Great Gods alight.
> These Great Ones of the Imperishable Star
> give unto Pepi the Plant of Life
> whereon they themselves do live,
> so that he may also live thereon.

Egyptian depictions showed the deceased (sometimes with his wife) at this Celestial Paradise, sipping the Waters of Life out of which there grows the Tree of Life with its life-giving fruit, the date palm (Fig. 9).

The celestial destination was the birthplace of Ra, to which he had returned from Earth. There, Ra himself was constantly rejuvenated or "re-awakened" by having the Goddess of the Four Jars pour him a certain elixir periodically. It was thus the king's hope to have the same goddess pour him too the elixir and "therewith refresh his heart to life." It was in these waters, named "Water of Youth," that Osiris rejuvenated himself; and so it was promised to the departed King Pepi that Horus shall "count for thee a second season of youth"; that he shall "renew thy youth in the waters whose name is 'Water of Youth.'"

Resurrected to Afterlife, even rejuvenated, the Pharaoh attained a paradisical life: "His provision is among the gods; his water is wine, like that of Ra. When Ra eats, he gives to him; when Ra drinks, he gives to him." And in a touch of twentieth century psychotherapy, the text adds: "He sleeps soundly every day . . . he fares better today than yesterday."

The Pharaoh seemed little bothered by the paradox that he had to die

Fig. 9

first in order to attain Immortality. As supreme ruler of the Two Lands of Egypt, he enjoyed the best possible life on Earth; and the resurrection among the gods was an even more attractive prospect. Besides, it was only his earthly body that was to be embalmed and entombed; for the Egyptians believed that every person possessed a Ba, akin to what we call "soul," which rose heavenward like a bird after death; and a Ka—variably translated Double, Ancestral Spirit, Essence, Personality—through which form the Pharaoh was translated into his Afterlife. Samuel Mercer, in his introduction to the Pyramid Texts, concluded that the Ka stood for the mortal's personification of a god. In other words, the concept implied the existence in Man of a divine element, a celestial or godly Double who could resume life in the Afterlife.

But if Afterlife was possible, it was not easily attained. The departed king had to traverse a long and challenging road, and had to undergo elaborate ceremonial preparations before he could embark on his journey.

The deification of the Pharaoh began with his purification and included embalmment (mummification), so that the dead king would resemble Osiris with all his members tied together. The embalmed Pharaoh was then carried in a funerary procession to a structure topped by a pyramid, in front of which there stood an oval-shaped pillar (Fig. 10).

Within this funerary temple, priestly rites were conducted with a view to achieving for the Pharaoh acceptance at journey's end. The ceremonies, called in the Egyptian funerary texts the "Opening of the Mouth," were supervised by a *Shem* priest—always depicted wearing a leopard skin (Fig. 11). Scholars believe that the ritual was literally what its name implies: the priest, using a bent copper or iron tool, opened the mouth of the mummy or of a statue representing the departed king. But it is clear that the

Fig. 10

Fig. 11

ceremony was primarily symbolic, intended to open for the deceased the "mouth" or Entranceway to the Heavens.

The mummy, by then, was tied up tight in many layers of material and was surmounted by the king's golden death mask. Thus, the touching of its mouth (or that of the king's statue) could have been only symbolical. Indeed, the priest intoned not the deceased, but the gods to "open the mouth" so that the Pharaoh could ascend toward eternal life. Special appeals were made to the "Eye" of Horus, lost by him in the battle with Seth, to cause the "opening of the mouth" so that "a path shall be opened for the king among the Shiny Ones, that he may be established among them."

The earthly (and thus by conjecture only temporary) tomb of the Pharaoh—according to the texts and actual archaeological discoveries—had a false door on its eastern side, i.e. the masonry was built there to look like a doorway, but it was actually a solid wall. Purified, with all limbs tied together, "opened of mouth," the Pharaoh was then envisioned as raising himself, shaking off Earth's dust, and exiting by the false door. According to a Pyramid Text which dealt with the resurrection process step by step, the Pharaoh could not pass through the stone wall by himself. "Thou standest at the doors which hold people back," the text said, until "he who is chief of the department"—a divine messenger in charge of this task—"comes out to thee. He lays hold on thy arm, and takes thee to heaven, to thy father."

Aided thus by a divine messenger, the Pharaoh was out of his sealed tomb, through the false door. And the priests broke out in a chant: "The king is on his way to Heaven! The king is on his way to Heaven!"

> The king is on his way to Heaven
> The king is on his way to Heaven
> On the wind, on the wind.
> He is not hindered;
> There is no one by whom he is hindered.
> The king is on his own, son of the gods.
> His bread will come on high, with Ra;
> His offering will come out of the Heavens.
> The king is he "Who Comes Again."

But before the departed king could ascend to Heaven to eat and drink with the gods, he had to undertake an arduous and hazardous Journey. His goal was a land called *Neter-Khert*, "The Land of the Mountain Gods." It was sometimes written pictorially in hieroglyphic by surmounting the symbol for god (*Neter*) ⌐ upon a ferry boat ⟨⥁ ; and indeed, to reach that land, the Pharaoh had to cross a long and winding Lake of Reeds. The marshy waters could be crossed with the aid of a Divine Ferryman, but before he would ferry the Pharaoh over he questioned the king about his origins: What made him think he had the right to cross over? Was he a son of a god or a goddess?

Beyond the lake, past a desert and a chain of mountains, past various guardian gods, lay the *Duat*, a magical "Abode for rising to the Stars," whose location and name have baffled the scholars. Some view it as the Netherworld, the abode of the spirits, where the king must go as Osiris did. Others believe it was an Underworld, and indeed much of its scenes were of a subterranean world of tunnels and caverns with unseen gods, pools of boiling waters, eerie lights, chambers guarded by birds, doors that open by themselves. This magical land was divided into twelve divisions, and was traversed in twelve hours.

The *Duat* was further perplexing, because in spite of its terrestrial nature (it was reached after crossing through a mountain pass) or subterranean aspects, its name was written hieroglyphically with a star and a soaring falcon as its determinatives ⋆🦅 or simply with a star within a circle ⊗ , denoting a celestial or heavenly association.

Baffling as it has been, the fact is that the Pyramid Texts, as they followed the Pharaoh's progress through his life, death, resurrection and translation to an Afterlife, considered the human problem to be the inability to fly as the gods do. One text summed up this problem and its solution in two sentences: "Men are buried, the gods fly up. Cause this king to fly to Heaven, (to be) among his brothers the gods." A text inscribed in the pyramid of King Teti expressed the Pharaoh's hope and appeal to the gods in these words:

> Men fall,
> They have no Name.
> Seize thou king Teti by his arms,
> Take thou king Teti to the sky,
> That he die not on Earth among men.

And so it was incumbent upon the king to reach the "Hidden Place," and go through its subterranean labyrinths until he could find there a god who carries the emblem of the Tree of Life, and a god who is the "Herald of Heaven." They will open for him secret gates, and lead him to the Eye of Horus, a Celestial Ladder into which he would step—an object which can change hues to blue and red as it is "powered." And then, himself turned into the Falcon-god, he would soar skyward to the eternal Afterlife on the Imperishable Star. There, Ra himself would welcome him:

> The Gates of Heaven are opened for thee;
> The doors of the Cool Place are opened for thee.
> Thou shalt find Ra standing, waiting for thee.
> He will take your hand,
> He will take thee to the Dual Shrine of Heaven;
> He will place thee on the throne of Osiris . . .
> Thou shalt stand supported, equipped as a god . . .
> Among the Eternals, on the Imperishable Star.

Much of what is known today on the subject comes from the Pyramid Texts—thousands of verses combined into hundreds of Utterances, that were discovered embossed or painted (in the hieroglyphic writing of ancient Egypt) on the walls, passages and galleries of the pyramids of five Pharaohs (Unas, Teti, Pepi I, Merenra and Pepi II) who ruled Egypt from circa 2350 B.C. to 2180 B.C. These texts were sorted out and numbered by Kurt Sethe in his masterful *Die altaegyptischen Pyramidentexte*, which has remained the major reference source together with the English counterpart, *The Pyramid Texts* by Samuel A. B. Mercer.

The thousands of verses that make up the Pyramid Texts seem to be just a collection of repetitious, unconnected incantations, appeals to the gods or exaltations of the king. To make some sense of the material, scholars have developed theories about shifting theologies in ancient Egypt, a conflict and then a merger between a "Solar Religion" and a "Sky Religion," a priesthood of Ra and one of Osiris, and so on, pointing out that we deal with material that has been accumulated over millennia.

To scholars who view the mass of verses as expressions of primitive mythologies, figments of the imagination of people who cowered in fear as the wind howled and the thunder roared and called these phenomena "gods"—the verses remain as puzzling and confusing as ever. But these verses, all scholars agree, were extracted by the ancient scribes from older and apparently well-organized, cohesive and comprehensible scriptures.

Later inscriptions on sarcophagi and coffins, as well as on papyrus (the latter usually accompanied by illustrations) indeed show that the verses, Utterances and Chapters (bearing such names as "Chapter of those who ascend") were copied from "Books of the Dead," which bore such titles as "That Which Is in the *Duat*," "The Book of the Gates," "The Book of the Two Ways." Scholars believe that these "books" in turn were versions of two earlier basic works: olden writings that dealt with the celestial journey of Ra, and a later source which stressed the blissful Afterlife of those who join Osiris resurrected: the food, the beverage, the conjugal joys in a heavenly abode. (Verses of this version were even inscribed on talismans, to achieve for their wearer "union with women by day or night" and the "desire of women" at all times.)

The scholarly theories, however, leave unexplained the magical aspects of the information offered by these texts. Bafflingly, an Eye of Horus is an object existing independently of him—an object into whose insides the king can enter, and which can change hues to blue and red as it is "powered." There exist self-propelled ferries, doors that open by themselves, unseen gods whose faces radiate a glow. In the Underworld, supposedly inhabited by spirits only, "bridge girders" and "copper cables" are featured. And the most baffling aspect of all: Why, if the Pharaoh's transfiguration takes him to the Underworld, do the texts claim that "the king is on his way to *Heaven*"?

Throughout, the verses indicate that the king is following the route of the gods, that he is crossing a lake the way a god had crossed it before, that he uses a barque as the god Ra had done, that he ascends "equipped as a god" as Osiris was, and so on and on. And the question arises: What if these texts were not primitive fantasies—mythology—but accounts of a simulated journey, wherein the deceased Pharaoh emulated what the gods had actually done? What if the texts, substituting the name of the king for that of a god, were copies of some much earlier scriptures that dealt not with the journeys of the Pharaohs, but with the journeys of the gods?

One of the early leading Egyptologists, Gaston Maspero (*L'Archéologie égyptienne* and other works), judging by grammatical form and other evidence, suggested that the Pyramid Texts originated at the very beginning of Egyptian civilization, perhaps even before they were written down hieroglyphically. J. H. Breasted has more recently concluded (*Development of Religion and Thought in Ancient Egypt*) that "such older material existed, whether we possess it or not." He found in the texts information on the conditions of civilization and events which enhances the veracity of the texts as conveyors of factual information and not of fantasy. "To one of quick imagination," he says, "they abound in pictures from the long-vanished world of which they are a reflection."

Taken together, the texts and later illustrations describe a journey to a realm that begins above ground, that leads underground, and that ends with an opening to the skies through which the gods—and the kings emulating them—were launched heavenward (Fig. 12). Thus the hieroglyphic connotation combining a subterranean place with a celestial function.

Have the Pharaohs, journeying from their tombs to the Afterlife, actually taken this Route to Heaven? Even the ancient Egyptians claimed the journey not for the mummified corpse, but for the Ka (Double) of the departed king. But they have envisioned this Double as re-enacting actual progress through actual places.

What, then, if the texts reflect a world which had indeed existed—what if the Pharaoh's Journey to Immortality, even if only by emulation, indeed followed step by step actual journeys undertaken in prehistoric times?

Let us follow in these footsteps; let us take the Route of the Gods.

Fig. 12

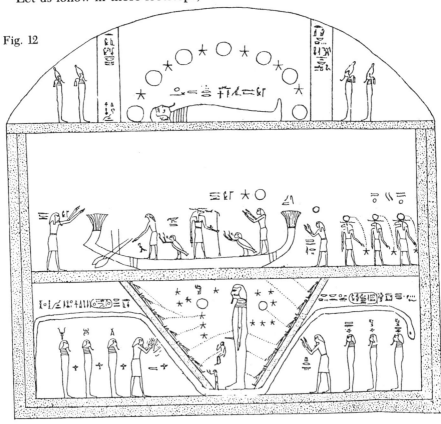

IV

The Stairway to Heaven

Let us imagine ourselves in the Pharaoh's magnificent funerary temple. Having mummified and prepared the Pharaoh for his Journey, the *Shem* priests now intone the gods to open for the king a path and a gateway. The divine messenger has arrived on the other side of the false door, ready to take the Pharaoh through the stone wall and launch him on his journey.

Emerging through the false door on the eastern side of his tomb, the Pharaoh was instructed to set his course eastward. Lest he misunderstand, he was explicitly warned against going west: "Those who go thither, they return not!" His goal was the *Duat*, in the "Land of the Mountain Gods." He was to enter there "The Great House of Two . . . the House of Fire"; where, during "a night of computing years," he shall be transformed into a Divine Being and ascend "to the east side of Heaven."

The first obstacle in the Pharaoh's course was the Lake of Reeds—a long body of marshy waters made up of a series of adjoining lakes. Symbolically, he had the blessing of his guardian god to cross the lake by parting its waters (Fig. 13); physically, the crossing was possible because the lake was served by the Divine Ferryman, who ferried the gods across in a boat made by Khnum, the Divine Craftsman. But the Ferryman was stationed on the far side of the lake, and the Pharaoh had a hard time convincing him that he was entitled to be fetched and ferried over.

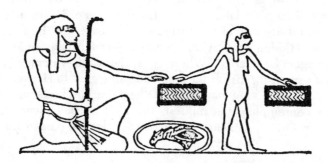

Fig. 13

The Ferryman questioned the Pharaoh about his origins. Was he the son of a god or goddess? Was he listed in the "Register of the Two Great Gods"? The Pharaoh explained his claims to being of "divine seed," and gave assurances of his righteousness. In some cases it worked. In other instances the Pharaoh had to appeal to Ra or to Thoth to get him across; in which instances, the boat and its oars or rudder came alive with uncanny forces: the ferryboat began to move by itself, the steering-oar grasped by the king directed itself. All, in short, became self-propelled. One way or another, the Pharaoh managed to cross the lake and be on his way toward "The Two That Bring Closer the Heavens":

> He descends into the boat, like Ra,
>   on the shores of the Winding Watercourse.
> The king rows in the *Hanbu*-boat;
> He takes the helm toward the
> Plain of "The Two That Bring Closer the Heavens,"
>   in the land beginning from the Lake of Reeds.

The Lake of Reeds was situated at the eastern end of the domain of Horus. Beyond lay the territories of his adversary Seth, the "lands of Asia." As would be expected on such a sensitive boundary, the king discovers that the lake's eastern shore is patrolled by four "Crossing guards, the wearers of side locks." The way these guards wore their hair was truly their most conspicuous feature. "Black as coal," it was "arranged in curls on their foreheads, at their temples and at the back of their heads, with braids in the center of their heads."

Combining diplomacy with firmness, the king again proclaimed his divine origins, claiming he was summoned by "my father Ra." One Pharaoh is reported to have used threats: "Delay my crossing, and I will pluck out your locks as lotus flowers are plucked in the lotus pond!" Another had some of the gods come to his assistance. One way or another, the Pharaoh managed to proceed.

The king has now left the lands of Horus. The eastward place which he seeks to reach—though under the aegis of Ra—is "in the region of Seth." His goal is a mountainous area, the Mountains of the East (Fig. 14). His course is set toward a pass between two mountains, "the two mountains which stand in awe of Seth." But first he has to traverse an arid and barren area, a kind of no-god's land between the domains of Horus and Seth. Just as the pace and urgency of the Utterances increase, for the king is getting closer to the Hidden Place where the Doors of Heaven are located, he is challenged again by guards. "Where goest thou?" they demand to know.

The king's sponsors answer for him: "The king goes to Heaven, to possess life and joy; that the king may see his father, that the king may see Ra." As the guards contemplate the request, the king himself pleads with them: "Open the frontier . . . incline its barrier . . . let me pass as the gods pass through!"

Having come from Egypt, from the domain of Horus, the king and his sponsors recognize the need for prudence. Many Utterances and verses are employed to present the king as neutral in the feud between the gods. The king is introduced both as "born of Horus, he at whose name the Earth quakes," and as "conceived by Seth, he at whose name Heaven trembles." The king stresses not only his affinity to Ra, but declares that he proceeds "in the service of Ra"; producing thereby a *laissez-passer* from higher authority. With shrewd evenhandedness, the texts point out to the two gods their own self-interest in the king's continued journey, for Ra would surely appreciate their aid to one who comes in his service.

Finally, the guards of the Land of Seth let the king proceed toward a mountain pass. The king's sponsors make sure that he realizes the import of the moment:

> Thou are now on the way to the high places
> In the land of Seth.
> In the land of Seth
> Thou will be set on the high places,
> On that high Tree of the Eastern Sky
> On which the gods sit.

The king has arrived at the *Duat*.

Fig. 14

Fig. 15

The *Duat* was conceived as a completely enclosed Circle of the Gods (see Fig. 15), at the head-point of which there was an opening to the skies (symbolized by the goddess Nut) through which the Imperishable Star (symbolized by the Celestial Disk) could be reached. Other sources suggested in reality a more oblong or oval valley, enclosed by mountains. A river which divided into many streams flowed through this land, but it was hardly navigable and most of the time Ra's barge had to be towed, or moved by its own power as a "boat of earth," as a sled.

The *Duat* was divided into twelve divisions, variably described as fields, plains, walled circles, caverns or halls, beginning above ground and continuing underground. It took the departed king twelve hours to journey through this enchanted and awesome realm; this he could achieve, because Ra had put at his disposal his magical barge or sled, in which the king traveled aided and protected by his sponsoring gods.

There were seven gaps or passes in the mountains that enclosed the *Duat,* and two of them were in the mountains on the east side of Egypt ⚱ (i.e. in the mountains on the west of the *Duat),* which were called "The Horizon" or "The Horn" of "The Hidden Place." The pass through which Ra had traveled was 220 *atru* (some twenty-seven miles) long, and followed the course of a stream; the stream, however, ran dry and Ra's barge had to be towed. The pass was guarded and had fortifications "whose doors were strong."

The Pharaoh, as some papyri indicate, took the course leading through the second, shorter pass (only some fifteen miles long). The papyrus drawings show him upon the barge or sled of Ra, passing between two mountain peaks on each of which there is stationed a company of twelve guardian gods. The texts describe a "Lake of Boiling Waters" nearby— waters which, despite their fiery nature are cool to the touch. A fire burns below the ground. The place has a strong bituminous or "natron" stench which drives away the birds. Yet not too far away, there is depicted an oasis with shrubs or low trees around it.

Once across the pass, the king encounters other companies of gods. "Come in peace," they say. He has arrived at the second division.

It is called, after the stream that runs through it, *Ur-nes* (a name which some scholars equate with *Uranus,* the Greek god of the skies). Measuring some fifteen by thirty-nine miles, it is inhabited by people with long hair, who eat the flesh of their asses and depend on the gods for water and sustenance, for the place is arid and the streams are mostly dry. Even Ra's barge turns here into a "boat of earth." It is a domain associated with the Moon god, and with Hathor, the Goddess of Turquoise.

Aided by the gods, the king passes safely through the second division and in the Third Hour arrives at *Net-Asar,* "The Stream of Osiris." Similar in size to the second division, this third division is inhabited by "The Fighters." It is there that the four gods, who are in charge of the four cardinal points of the compass, are stationed.

The pictorial depictions which accompanied the hieroglyphic texts surprisingly showed the Stream of Osiris as meandering its way from an agricultural area, through a chain of mountains, to where the stream divided into tributaries. There, watched over by the legendary Phoenix birds, the *Stairway to Heaven* was situated; there, the Celestial Boat of Ra was depicted as sitting atop a mountain, or rising heavenward upon streams of fire (Fig. 16).

Here, the pace of prayers and Utterances increases again. The king

Fig. 16

invokes the "magical protectors," that "this man of Earth may enter the
Neter-Khert" unmolested. The king is nearing the heart of the Duat; he is
near the *Amen-Ta*, the "Hidden Place."

It was there that Osiris himself had risen to the Eternal Afterlife. It was
there that the "Two That Bring Closer the Heaven" stood out "yonder
against the sky," as two magical trees. The king offers a prayer to Osiris (the
Chapter's title in the Book of the Dead is "Chapter of Making His *Name* in
the *Neter-Khert* Granted"):

> May be given to me my *Name*
>   in the Great House of Two;
> May in the House of Fire
>   my Name be granted.
> In the night of computing years,
>   and of telling the months,
>   may I be a Divine Being,
>   may I sit at the east side of Heaven.

> Let the god advance me from behind;
> Everlasting is his *Name*.

The king is within sight of the "Mountain of Light."

He has reached the STAIRWAY TO HEAVEN.

The Pyramid Texts said of the place that it was "the stairway in order to reach the heights." Its stairs were described as "the stairs to the sky, which are laid out for the king, that he may ascend thereon to the heavens." The hieroglyphic pictograph for the Stairway to Heaven was sometimes a single stairway ⌐⌐(which was also cast in gold and worn as a charm), or more often a double stairway ⌐⌐ , as a step pyramid. This Stairway to Heaven was constructed by the gods of the city of An—the location of the principal temple of Ra—so that they, the gods, could be "united with the Above."

The king's goal is the Celestial Ladder, an Ascender which would actually carry him aloft. But to reach it in the House of Fire, the Great House of Two, he must enter the *Amen-Ta,* the Hidden Land of Seker, God of the Wilderness.

It is a domain described as a fortified circle. It is the subterranean Land of Darkness, reachable by entering into a mountain and going down spiraling hidden paths protected by secret doors. It is the fourth division of the *Duat* which the king must now enter; but the mountain entrance is protected by two walls and the passage between them is swept by flames and manned by guarding gods.

When Ra himself had arrived at this entrance to the Hidden Place, "he performed the designs"—followed the procedures—"of the gods who are therein by means of his voice, without seeing them." But can the king's voice alone achieve for him admission? The texts remind the challenger that only "he who knoweth the plan of the hidden shaftways which are in the Land of Seker," shall have the ability to journey through the Place of Underground Passages and eat the bread of the gods.

Once again the king offers his credentials. "I am the Bull, a son of the ancestors of Osiris," he announces. Then the gods who sponsor him, pronounce in his behalf the crucial words for admission:

> Admittance is not refused thee
> At the gate of the *Duat;*
> The folding doors of the Mountain of Light
> Are opened to thee;
> The bolts open to thee of themselves.
> Thou treadest the Hall of the Two Truths;
> The god who is in it greets thee.

The right formula or password having thus been pronounced, a god named Sa uttered a command; at his word, the flames ceased, the guards withdrew, the doors opened automatically, and the Pharaoh was admitted into the subterranean world.

"The mouth of the earth opens for thee, the eastern door of heaven is open for thee," the gods of the *Duat* announce to the king. He is reassured that though he enters the mouth of the earth, it is indeed the Gateway to Heaven, the coveted eastern door.

The journey in the fourth and following Hours leads the king through caverns and tunnels where gods of diverse functions are sometimes seen, sometimes only heard. There are underground canals, on which gods move about in soundless barques. There are eerie lights, phosphorous waters, torches that light the way. Mystified and terrified, the king moves on, toward "the pillars that reach the Heaven."

The gods seen along the way are mostly organized in groups of twelve, and bear such epithets as "Gods of the Mountain," "Gods of the Mountain of the Hidden Land," or "The Holders of the Time of Life in the Hidden Land." The drawings that accompanied some of the ancient texts provide identification of these gods through the different scepters held by them, their particular headgear, or by depicting their animal attributes—hawk-headed, jackal-headed, lion-headed. Serpents also make an appearance, representing subterranean guards or servants of the gods in the Hidden Land.

The texts and the ancient illustrations suggest that the king has entered a circular underground complex, within which a vast tunnel first spirals down and then up. The depictions, presented in a cross-section fashion, show a gradually sloping tunnel some forty feet high, with a smooth ceiling and a smooth floor, both made of some solid material two to three feet thick. The tunnel is partitioned into three levels, and the king moves within the middle level or corridor. The upper and lower levels are occupied by gods, serpents and structures of diverse functions.

The king's sled, pulled by four gods, begins its journey by gliding silently along the middle corridor; only a beam emitted from the vehicle's bow lights the way. But soon the passage is blocked by a sharply slanting partition, and the king must get off and continue on foot.

The partition, as the cross-section depictions show, is one wall of a shaft that cuts across the three tunnel levels (which slope at about 15°) at a sharper angle of some 40°. It apparently begins above the tunnel, perhaps at ground level or somewhere higher within the mountain; it seems to end as it reaches the floor of the lowest, third level. It is called *Re-Stau*, "The Path of the Hidden Doors"; and at the first and second levels, it is indeed provided with chambers that look like air-locks. These chambers enable Seker and other "hidden gods" to pass through, though "the door has no leaves." The king, who has left his sled, mysteriously passes through this slanting wall simply by virtue of the command of some god, whose voice

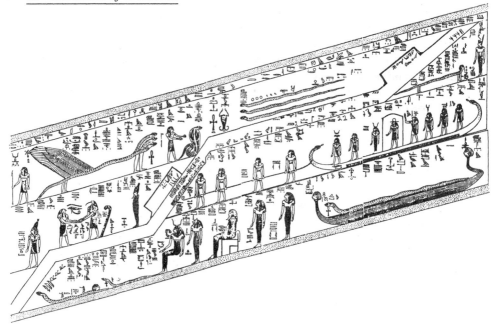

Fig. 17

had activated the air-lock. He is greeted on the other side by representatives of Horus and Thoth, and is passed along from god to god. (Fig. 17.)

On his way down, the king sees "faceless gods"—gods whose faces cannot be seen. Offended or simply curious, he pleads with them:

> Uncover your faces,
>   take off your head coverings,
>   when ye meet me;
> For, behold, I [too] am a mighty god
>   come to be among you.

But they do not heed his plea to show their faces; and the texts explain that even they, "these hidden beings, neither see nor look upon" their own chief, the god Seker "when he is in this form himself, when he is inside his abode in the earth."

Spiraling his way down, the king passes through a door and finds himself on the third, lowest level. He enters an antechamber which bears the emblem of the Celestial Disk, and is greeted by the god who is "The Messenger of Heaven" and a goddess who wears the feathered emblem of Shu, "He who rested the sky upon the Stairway to Heaven" (Fig. 18). As called for by the formula in the Book of the Dead, the king proclaims:

> Hail,
>   two children of Shu!

Hail,
        children of the Place Of The Horizon . . .
May I ascend?
May I journey forth like Osiris?

The answer must be positive, for the king is admitted by them, through a massive door, into the shafts which only the hidden gods use.

In the Fifth Hour, the Pharaoh reaches the deepest subterranean parts which are the secret ways of Seker. Following shafts that incline up, over and down, the Pharaoh cannot see Seker; but the cross-section drawings depict the god as a hawk-headed person, standing upon a serpent and holding two wings within a completely enclosed oval structure deep underground, guarded by two sphinxes. Though the king cannot see this chamber, he hears coming from it "a mighty noise, like that heard in the heights of the heavens when they are disturbed by a storm." From the sealed chamber there flows a subterranean pool whose "waters are like fire." Chamber and pool alike are in turn enclosed by a bunkerlike structure, with a compartmentalized air-lock on the left side and a huge door on the right side. As further protection, a mound of soil is piled up atop the sealed chamber. The mound is topped by a goddess, whose head only is seen, protruding into the descending corridor. A beetle symbol (meaning "to roll, to come into being") connects the head of the goddess with a conical chamber or object in the uppermost corridor (Fig. 19); two birds are perched upon it.

Fig. 18

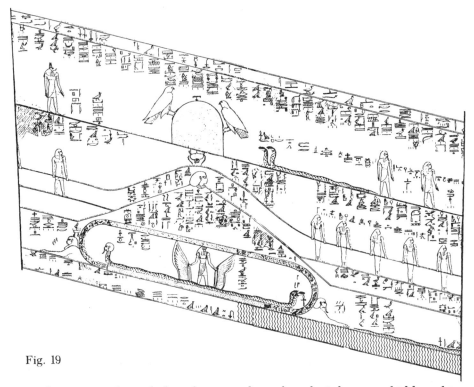

Fig. 19

The texts and symbols inform us that, though Seker was hidden, his presence could be made known even in the darkness, because of a glowing "through the head and eyes of the great god, whose flesh radiates forth light." The triple arrangement—goddess, beetle (*Kheper*) and conical object or chamber—apparently served to enable the hidden god to be informed of what goes on outside his hermetically sealed chamber. The hieroglyphic text adjoining the beetle symbol states: "Behold Kheper who, immediately the (boat?) is towed to the top of this circle, connects himself with the ways of the *Duat*. When this god standeth on the head of the goddess, he speaks words to Seker every day."

The passage by the Pharaoh over the hidden chamber of Seker and by the setup through which Seker was informed of such passage, was deemed a crucial phase in his progress. The Egyptians were not the only ones in antiquity who believed that each departed person faced a moment of judgment, a spot where their deeds or hearts would be weighed and evaluated and their soul or Double either condemned to the Fiery Waters of Hell, or blessed to enjoy the cool and lifegiving waters of Paradise. By ancient accounts, here was such a Moment of Truth for the Pharaoh.

Speaking for the Lord of the *Duat*, the goddess whose head only was seen announced to the Pharaoh the favorable decision: "Come in peace to the *Duat* . . . advance in thy boat on the road which is in the earth." Naming herself Ament (the female Hidden One), she added: "Ament calls to thee, so that thou mayest go forward in the sky, as the Great One who is in the Horizon."

Passing the test, not dying a second time, the king was born again. The way now led by a row of gods whose task it was to punish the condemned; but the king proceeds unharmed. He rejoins his boat or sled; it is accompanied by a procession of gods; one of them holds the emblem of the Tree of Life (Fig. 20).

The king has been found worthy of Afterlife.

Leaving the zone of Seker, the king enters the sixth division, associated with Osiris. (In versions of the Book of the Gates, it was in this Sixth Hour that Osiris judged the departed.) Jackal-headed gods "Who Open the Ways" invite the king to take a refreshing dip in the subterranean pool or Lake of Life, as the Great God himself had done when he passed here before. Other gods, "humming as bees," reside in cubicles whose doors fly open by themselves as the king moves by. As he progresses, the epithets of the gods assume more technical aspects. There are the twelve gods "who hold the rope in the *Duat*," and the twelve "who hold the measuring cord."

The sixth division is occupied by a series of chambers set close together. A curving path is called "The Secret Path of the Hidden Place." The king's boat is towed by gods clad in leopard skins, just as the *Shem* priests who performed the Opening of the Mouth ceremonies were clad.

Is the king nearing the Opening or Mouth of the Mountain? In the Book of the Dead, the chapters indeed now bear such titles as "The chapter of sniffing the air and of getting power." His vehicle is now "endowed with magical powers . . . he journeyeth where there is no stream and where

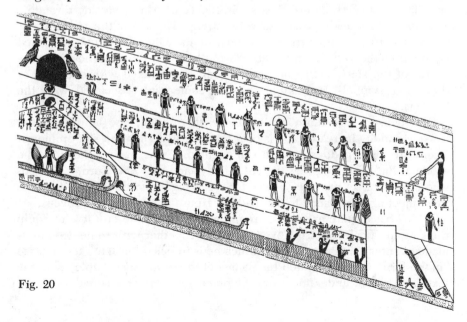

Fig. 20

there are none to tow him; he performeth this by words of power" which proceed from the mouth of a god.

As the king passes through a guarded gate into the seventh division, the gods and the surroundings lose their "underworld" aspects and begin to assume celestial affiliations. The king encounters the falcon-headed god *Heru-Her-Khent*, whose hieroglyphic name included the stairway symbol and who wore on his head the Celestial Disk emblem. His task is "to send the star-gods on their way and to make the constellation-goddesses go on their way." These were a group of twelve gods and twelve goddesses who were depicted with star emblems. The incantations to them were addressed to "the starry gods"—

who are divine in flesh, whose magical powers have come into being . . .
who are united into your stars, who rise up for Ra . . .
Let your stars guide his two hands so that he may journey to the Hidden Place in peace.

In this division, there are also present two companies of gods associated with the *Ben-ben*, the mysterious object of Ra that was kept at his temple in the city of An (Heliopolis). They "are those who possess the mystery," guarding it inside the *Het-Benben* (The Ben-ben House); and eight who guard outside but also "enter unto the Hidden Object." Here there are also nine objects, set up in a row, representing the symbol *Shem* which hieroglyphically meant "Follower."

The king has indeed arrived in parts of the *Duat* associated with An, after whom Heliopolis was named. In the Ninth Hour, he sees the resting place of the twelve "Divine Rowers of the Boat of Ra," they who operate Ra's celestial "Boat of Millions of Years." In the Tenth Hour, passing through a gate, the king enters a place astir with activity. The task of the gods there is to provide Flame and Fire to the boat of Ra. One of the gods is called "Captain of the gods of the boat." Two others are those "Who order the course of the stars." They and other gods are depicted with one, two or three star symbols, as though showing some rank associated with the heavens.

Passing from the tenth to the eleventh division, the affinity to the heavens rapidly increases. Gods bear the Celestial Disk and star emblems. There are eight goddesses with star emblems "who have come from the abode of Ra." The king sees the "Star Lady" and the "Star Lord," and gods whose task it is to provide "power for emerging" from the *Duat*, "to make the Object of Ra advance to the Hidden House in the Upper Heavens."

In this place there are also gods and goddesses whose task it is to equip the king for a celestial trip "over the sky." Together with some gods he is made to enter a "serpent" inside which he is to "shed the skin" and emerge "in the form of a rejuvenated Ra." Some of the terms here employed in the texts are still not understood, but the process is clearly explained: the king, having entered dressed as he came, emerges as a falcon, "equipped as a god": the king "lays down on the ground the *Mshdt*-garment"; he puts on his back the "Mark-garment"; he "takes his divine *Shuh*-vestment" and he puts on "the collar of beloved Horus" which is like "a collar on the neck of Ra." Having done all that, "the king has established himself there as a god, like them." And he tells the god who is with him: "If thou goest to Heaven, so will the king go to Heaven."

The illustrations in the ancient texts depict here a group of gods dressed in unusual garb, like tightly fitting overalls adorned with circular collar bands (Fig. 21).

They are led or directed by a god with the emblem of the Celestial Disk upon his head, who stands with outstretched arms between the wings of a serpent with four human legs. Against a starry background, the god and the serpent face another serpent which, though wingless, clearly flies as it carries aloft a seated Osiris. (Fig. 22).

Having been properly equipped, the king is led to an opening in the center of a semi-circular wall. He passes the hidden door. Now he moves within a tunnel which is "1300 cubits long" called "Dawn at the End." He reaches a vestibule; the emblems of the Winged Disk are seen everywhere. He encounters goddesses "who shed light upon the road of Ra" and a magical scepter representing "Seth, the Watcher."

The gods explain to the awed king:

> This cavern is the broad hall of Osiris
> Wherein the wind is brought;
> The north wind, refreshing,
> Will raise thee, O king, as Osiris.

It is now the twelfth division, the final Hour of the king's subterranean journey. It is "the uttermost limit of the thick darkness." The point which he has reached is named "Mountain of the Ascent of Ra." The king looks up and is startled: the celestial boat of Ra looms in front of his eyes, in all its awesome majesty.

He has reached an object which is called "The Ascender to the Sky." Some texts suggest that Ra himself prepared the Ascender for the king, "that the king may ascend upon it to the heavens"; other texts say that the Ascender was made or set up by several other gods. It is "the Ascender which had carried Seth" heavenward. Osiris could not reach the Firmament of Heaven except by means of such an Ascender; thus the king too requires it in order to be translated, as Osiris, to eternal life.

The Ascender or Divine Ladder was not a common ladder. It was bound together by copper cables; "its sinews (like those) of the Bull of Heaven." The "uprights at its sides" were covered over tightly with a kind of "skin"; its rungs were "*Shesha*-hewn" (meaning unknown); and "a great support (was) placed under it by He Who binds."

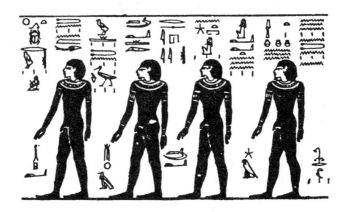

Fig. 21

Fig. 22

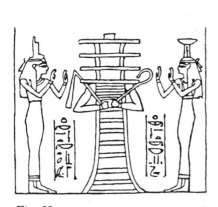

Fig. 23   a   b

Illustrations to the Book of the Dead showed such a Divine Ladder—sometimes with the *Ankh* ("Life") sign ☥ symbolically reaching toward the Celestial Disk in the heavens—in the shape of a high tower with a superstructure (Fig. 23a, b). In stylized form, the tower by itself was written hieroglyphically 𓊽 (*"Ded"*) and meant "Everlastingness." It was a symbol most closely associated with Osiris, for a pair of such pillars 𓊽𓊽 were said to have been erected in front of his principal temple at Abydos, to commemorate the two objects which stood in the Land of Seker and made possible the ascent of Osiris heavenward.

A long Utterance in the Pyramid Texts is both a hymn to the Ascender—the "Divine Ladder"—and a prayer for its granting to the king Pepi:

> Greeting to thee, divine Ascender;
> Greeting to thee, Ascender of Seth.
> Stand thou upright, Ascender of god;
> Stand upright, Ascender of Seth;
> Stand upright, Ascender of Horus
>   whereby Osiris came forth into Heaven . . .
> Lord of the Ascender . . .
> To whom shalt thou give the Ladder of god?
> To whom shall thou give the Ladder of Seth,
> That Pepi may ascend to Heaven on it,
>   to do service as a courtier of Ra?
> Let also the Ladder of god be given to Pepi,
> Let the Ladder of Seth be given to Pepi
>   that Pepi may ascend to Heaven on it.

The Ascender was operated by four falcon-men, "Children of Horus" the Falcon-god, who were "the sailors of the boat of Ra." They were "four youths," who were "Children of the Sky." It is they "who come from the eastern side of the sky . . . who prepare the two floats for the king, that the king may thereby go to the horizon, to Ra." It is they who "join together"—assemble, prepare—the Ascender for the king: "They bring the Ascender . . . they set up the Ascender . . . they raise up the Ascender for the king . . . that he might ascend to Heaven on it."

The king offers a prayer:

> May my "Name" to me be given
>   in the Great House of Two;
> May my "Name" be called
>   in the House of Fire,
>   in the night of Computing Years.

Some illustrations show the king being granted a *Ded*—"Everlastingness." Blessed by Isis and Nephtys, he is led by a falcon-god to a rocket-like *Ded*, equipped with fins (Fig. 24).

The king's prayer to be given Everlastingness, a "Name," a Divine Ladder, has been granted. He is about to begin his actual ascent to the Heavens.

Though he requires only one Divine Ladder for himself, not one but two Ascenders are raised together. Both the "Eye of Ra" and the "Eye of Horus" are prepared and put into position, one on the "wing of Thoth" and the other on the "wing of Seth." To the puzzled king, the gods explain that the second boat is for the "son of Aten," a god descended of the Winged Disk—perhaps the god to whom the king had spoken in the "equipping chamber":

> The Eye of Horus is mounted
> Upon the wing of Seth.
> The cables are tied,
>   the boats are assembled,
> That the son of the Aten
>   be not without a boat.
> The king is with the son of Aten;
> He is not without a boat.

"Equipped as a god," the king is assisted by two goddesses "who seize his cables" to step into the Eye of Horus. The term "Eye" (of Horus, of Ra) which has gradually replaced the term Ascender or Ladder, now is being increasingly displaced by the term "boat." The "Eye" or "boat" into which the king steps in is 770 cubits (circa 1000 feet) long. A god who is in charge of the boat sits at its bow. He is instructed: "Take this king with thee in the cabin of thy boat."

As the king "steps down into the perch"—a term denoting an elevated resting place, especially of birds—he can see the face of the god who is in the cabin, "for the face of the god is open." The king "takes a seat in the divine boat" between two gods; the seat is called "Truth which makes

Fig. 24

alive." Two "horns" protrude from the king's head (or helmet); "he attaches to himself that which went forth from the head of Horus." He is plugged in for action.

The texts dealing with the Journey to the Afterlife by King Pepi I describe the moment: "Pepi is arrayed in the apparel of Horus, and in the dress of Thoth; Isis is before him and Nephtys is behind him; Ap-uat who is Opener of the Ways hath opened a way unto him; Shu the Sky Bearer hath lifted him up; the gods of An make him ascend the Stairway and set him before the Firmament of the Heaven; Nut the sky goddess extends her hand to him."

The magical moment has arrived; there are only two more doors to be opened, and the king—as Ra and Osiris had done before—will emerge triumphantly from the *Duat* and his boat will float on the Celestial Waters. The king says a silent prayer: "O Lofty one . . . thou Door of Heaven: the king has come to thee; cause this door to be opened for him." The "two *Ded* pillars are standing" upright, motionless.

And suddenly "the double doors of heaven are open!"

The texts break out in ecstatic pronouncements:

> The Door to Heaven is open!
> The Door of Earth is open!
> The aperture of the celestial windows is open!
> The Stairway to Heaven is open;
> The Steps of Light are revealed . . .
> The double Doors to Heaven are open;
> The double doors of *Khebhu* are open
> for Horus of the east,
> at daybreak.

Ape-gods symbolizing the waning moon ("Daybreak") begin to pronounce magical "words of power which will cause splendor to issue from the Eye of Horus." The "radiance"—reported earlier as the hallmark of the twin-peaked Mountain of Light—intensifies:

> The sky-god
> has strengthened the radiance for the king
> that the king may lift himself to Heaven
> like the Eye of Ra.
> The king is in this Eye of Horus,
> where the command of the gods is heard.

The "Eye of Horus" begins to change hues: first it is blue, then it is red. There are excitement and much activity all around:

> The red-Eye of Horus is furious in wrath,
> its might no one can withstand.
> His messengers hurry, his runner hastens.

> They announce to him who lifts up his arm
>> in the East: "let this one pass."
> Let the god command the fathers, the gods:
> "Be silent . . . lay your hands upon your mouth . . .
>> stand at the doorway of the horizon,
>> open the double doors (of heaven)."

The silence is broken; now there are sound and fury, roaring and quaking:

> The Heaven speaks, the Earth quakes;
> The Earth trembles;
> The two districts of the gods shout;
> The ground is come apart . . .
> When the king ascends to Heaven
>> when he ferries over the vault (to Heaven) . . .

> The Earth laughs, the Sky smiles
>> when the king ascends to Heaven.
> Heaven shouts in joy for him;
> The Earth quakes for him.
> The roaring tempest drives him,
>> it roars like Seth.
> The guardians of Heaven's parts
>> open the doors of Heaven for him.

Then "the two mountains divide," and there is a lift-off into a cloudy sky of dawn from which the stars of night are gone:

> The sky is overcast,
>> the stars are darkened.
> The bows are agitated,
>> the bones of Earth quake.

Amid the agitation, quaking and thundering, the "Bull of Heaven" ("whose belly is full of magic") rises from the "Isle of Flame." Then the agitation ceases; and the king is aloft—"dawning as a falcon":

> They see the king dawning as a falcon,
>> as a god;
> To live with his fathers,
>> to feed with his mothers . . .
> The king is a Bull of Heaven . . .
>> whose belly is full of magic
>> from the Isle of Flame.

Utterance 422 speaks eloquently of this moment:

> O this Pepi!
> Thou hast departed!
> Thou art a Glorious One,
>   mighty as a god, seated as Osiris!
> Thy soul is within thee;
> Thy Power ("Control") has thou behind thee;
> The *Misut*-crown is at thy hand . . .
> Thou ascendest to thy mother, goddess of Heaven
> She lays hold of thine arm,
>   she shows thee the way to the horizon,
>   to the place where Ra is.
> The double doors of heaven are opened for thee,
> The double doors of the sky are opened for thee . . .
> Thou risest, O Pepi . . . equipped as a god.

(An illustration in the tomb of Ramses IX suggests that the Double Doors were opened by inclining them away from each other; this was achieved by the manipulation of wheels and pulleys, operated by six gods at each door. Through the funnel-like opening, a giant man-like falcon could then emerge. Fig. 25.)

With great self-satisfaction at the achievement, the texts announce to the king's subjects: "He flies who flies; this king Pepi flies away from you, ye mortals. He is not of the Earth, he is of the Heaven . . . This king Pepi flies as a cloud to the sky, like a masthead bird; this king Pepi kisses the sky like a falcon; he reaches the sky of the Horizon god." The king, the Pyramid

Fig. 25

Texts continue, is now "on the Sky-Bearer, the upholder of the stars; from within the shadow of the Walls of God, he crosses the skies."

The king is not simply skyborne, he is orbiting Earth:

> He encompasses the sky like Ra,
> He traverses the sky like Thoth . . .
> He traveleth over the regions of Horus,
> He traveleth over the regions of Seth . . .
> He has completely encircled twice the heavens,
> He has revolved about the two lands . . .
> The king is a falcon surpassing the falcons;
> He is a Great Falcon.

(A verse also states that the king "crosses the sky like *Sunt*, which crosses the sky nine times in one night"; but the meaning of *Sunt* and thus the comparison are as yet undeciphered.)

Still sitting between "these two companions who voyage over the sky," the king soars toward the eastern horizon, far far away in the heavens. His destination is the *Aten*, the Winged Disk, which is also called the Imperishable Star. The prayers now focus on getting the king to the *Aten* and his safe arrival upon it: "*Aten*, let him ascend to thee; enfold him in thine embrace," the texts intone in behalf of the king. There is the abode of Ra, and the prayers seek to assure a favorable welcome for the king, by presenting his arrival at the Celestial Abode as the return of a son to his father:

> Ra of the Aten,
> Thy son has come to thee;
> Pepi comes to thee;
> Let him ascend to thee;
> Enfold him in thy embrace.

Now "there is clamor in Heaven: 'We see a new thing' say the celestial gods; 'a Horus is in the rays of Ra.'" The king—"on his way to Heaven, on the wind"—"advances in Heaven, he cleaves its firmament," expecting a welcome at his destination.

The celestial journey is to last eight days: "When the hour of the morrow comes, the hour of the eighth day, the king will be summoned by Ra"; the gods who guard the entrance to the *Aten* or to Ra's abode there will let him through, for Ra himself shall await the king on the Imperishable Star:

> When this hour of the morrow comes . . .
> When the king shall stand there, on the star
>   which is on the underside of the Heaven,
>   he shall be judged as a god,
>   listened to like a prince

The king shall call out to them;
They shall come to him, those four gods
   who stand on the *Dam*-scepters of Heaven,
   that they may speak the king's name to Ra,
   announce his name Horus of the Horizons:
"He has come to thee!
"The king has come to thee!"

Traveling in "the lake that is the heavens," the king nears "the shores of the sky." As he approaches, the gods on the Imperishable Star indeed announce as expected: "The arriver comes . . . Ra has given him his arm on the Stairway to Heaven. 'He Who Knows The Place' comes, say the gods." There, at the gates of the Double Palace, Ra is indeed awaiting the king:

Thou findest Ra standing there;
He greets thee, lays hold on thy arm;
He leads thee into the celestial Double Palace;
He places thee upon the throne of Osiris.

And the texts announce: "Ra has taken the king to himself, to Heaven, on the eastern side of Heaven . . . the king is on that star which radiates in Heaven."

Now there is one more detail left to accomplish. In the company of "Horus of the *Duat*," described as "the great green divine falcon," the king sets out to find the Tree of Life in the midst of the Place of Offering. "This king Pepi goes to the Field of Life, the birthplace of Ra in the heavens. He finds Kebehet approaching him with these four jars with which she refreshes the heart of the Great God on the day when he awakes. She refreshes the heart of this king Pepi therewith to Life."

Mission achieved, the texts announce with glee:

Ho, this Pepi!
All satisfying life is given to thee;
"Eternity is thine," says Ra . . .

Thou perishest not, thou passest not away
   for ever and ever.

The king has ascended the Stairway to Heaven; he has reached the Imperishable Star; "his lifetime is eternity, its limit everlastingness."

V

The Gods Who Came to Planet Earth

Nowadays, we take space flight for granted. We can read of plans for permanently orbiting space settlements without blinking an eye; the development of a reusable space shuttle is viewed not with wonderment, but with appreciation of its cost-saving potentialities. All this, of course, because we have seen with our own eyes, in print and on television, astronauts fly in space and unmanned craft land on other planets. We accept space travel and interplanetary contacts because we have heard with our own ears a mortal named Neil Armstrong, commander of the Apollo 11 spacecraft, report on his radio—for all the world to hear—the first landing by Man on another celestial body, the Moon:

> Houston!
> Tranquility Base here.
> The *Eagle* has landed!

Eagle was not only the code-name for the Lunar Module, but the epithet by which the *Apollo 11* spacecraft was called, and the proud nickname by which the three astronauts identified themselves (Fig. 26). The *Falcon* too has soared into space, and landed on the Moon. In the immense National Air and Space Museum of the Smithsonian Institution in Washington, one can see and touch the actual spacecraft that were flown or that were used as backup vehicles in the American space program. In a special section where the Moon landings have been simulated with the aid of the original equipment, the visitor can still hear a recorded message from the surface of the Moon:

> O.K., Houston.
> The *Falcon* is on the plain at Hadley!

Whereupon the Manned Spacecraft Center at Houston announced to the world: "That was a jubilant Dave Scott reporting *Apollo 15* on the plain at Hadley."

Fig. 26

Up to a few decades ago, the notion that a common mortal can put on some special clothes, strap himself in the front part of a long object, then zoom off the face of Earth, seemed preposterous or worse. A century or two ago, such a notion would not have even come about, for there was nothing in human experience or knowledge to trigger such fantasies.

Yet, as we have just described, the Egyptians—5,000 years ago—could readily visualize all this happening to their Pharaoh: he would journey to a launch site east of Egypt; he would enter a subterranean complex of tunnels and chambers; he would safely pass by the installation's atomic plant and radiation chamber. He would don the suit and gear of an astronaut, enter the cabin of an Ascender, and sit strapped between two gods. And then, as the double-doors would open, and the dawn skies would be revealed, the jet engines would ignite and the Ascender would turn into the Celestial Ladder by which the Pharaoh will reach the Abode of the Gods on their "Planet of Millions of Years."

On what TV screens had the Egyptians seen such things happen, that they so firmly believed that all this was really possible?

In the absence of television in their homes, the only alternative would have been to either go to the Spaceport and watch the rocketships come and go, or visit a "Smithsonian" and see the craft on display, accompanied by a knowing guide or viewing flight simulations. The evidence suggests that the ancient Egyptians had indeed done that: they had seen the launch site, and the hardware, and the astronauts with their own eyes. But the astronauts were not Earthlings going elsewhere: they were, rather, astronauts from elsewhere who had come to Planet Earth.

Greatly enamored with art, the ancient Egyptians depicted in their tombs what they had seen and experienced in their lifetimes. The architecturally detailed drawings of the subterranean corridors and chambers of the *Duat* come from the tomb of Seti I. An even more startling depiction has been found in the tomb of Huy, who was viceroy in Nubia and in the Sinai peninsula during the reign of the renowned Pharaoh Tut-Ankh-Amon. Decorated with scenes of people, places and objects from the two domains of which he was viceroy, his tomb preserved to this very day a depiction in vivid colors of a rocketship: its shaft is contained in an underground silo, its upper stage with the command module is above ground (Fig. 27). The shaft is subdivided, like a multi-stage rocket. Inside its lower part, two persons attend to hoses and levers; there is a row of circular dials above them. The silo cutaway shows that it is surrounded by tubular cells for heat-exchange or some other energy-related function.

Above ground, the hemispherical base of the upper stage is clearly depicted in the color painting as scorched, as though from a re-entry into Earth's atmosphere. The command module—large enough to hold three to four persons—is conical in shape, and there are vertical "peep holes" all

Fig. 27

around its bottom. The cabin is surrounded by worshippers, in a landscape of date palm trees and giraffes.

The underground chamber is decorated with leopard skins, and this provides a direct link with certain phases in the Pharaoh's Journey to Immortality. The leopard skin was the distinctive garb symbolically worn by the *Shem* priest as he performed the Opening of the Mouth ceremony. It was the distinctive garb symbolically worn by the gods who towed the Pharaoh through "The Secret Path of the Hidden Place" of the *Duat*—a symbolism repeated to stress the affinity between the Pharaoh's journey and the rocketship in the underground silo.

As the Pyramid Texts make clear, the Pharaoh, in his Translation into an eternal Afterlife, embarked on a journey simulating the gods. Ra and Seth, Osiris and Horus and other gods had ascended to the heavens in this manner. But, the Egyptians also believed, it was by the same Celestial Boat that the Great Gods had come down to Earth in the first place. At the city of An (Heliopolis), Egypt's oldest center of worship, the god Ptah built a special structure—a "Smithsonian Institution," if you will—wherein an actual space capsule could be viewed and revered by the people of Egypt!

The secret object—the *Ben-Ben*—was enshrined in the *Het Benben*, the "Temple of the Benben." We know from the hieroglyphic depiction of the place's name that the structure looked like a massive launch tower from within which a pointed rocket was poised skyward (Fig. 28).

The *Ben-Ben* was, according to the ancient Egyptians, a solid object that had actually come to Earth from the Celestial Disk. It was the "Celestial Chamber" in which the great god Ra himself had landed on Earth; the term *Ben* (literally: "That Which Flowed Out") conveying the combined meanings of "to shine" and "to shoot up in the sky."

An inscription on the stela of the Pharaoh Pi-Ankhi (per Brugsch, *Dictionnaire Géographique de l'Ancienne Égypte*) said thus:

> The king Pi-Ankhi mounted the stairs toward the large window, in order to view the god Ra within the *Ben-Ben*. The king personally, standing up and being all alone, pushed apart the bolt and opened the two door-leaves. Then he saw his father Ra in the splendid sanctuary of *Het-Benben*. He saw the *Maad*, Ra's Barge; and he saw *Sektet*, the Barge of the *Aten*.

Fig. 28

The shrine, we know from the ancient texts, was guarded and serviced by two groups of gods. There were those "who are outside the *Het-Benben*" but were allowed into the shrine's most sacred parts, for it was their task to receive the offerings from the pilgrims and bring them into the temple. The others were primarily guardians, not only of the *Ben-Ben* itself, but of all "the secret things of Ra which are in *Het-Benben*." Much as tourists nowadays flock to the Smithsonian to view, admire and even touch the actual vehicles flown in space, so did the devout Egyptians make pilgrimages to Heliopolis, to revere and pray to the *Ben-Ben*—probably with a religious fervor akin to that of the faithful Muslims who make pilgrimages to Mecca, there to pray at the *Qa'aba* (a black stone believed to be a replica of God's "Celestial Chamber").

At the shrine, there was a fountain or well, whose waters acquired a reputation for their healing powers, especially in matters of virility and fertility. The term *Ben* and its hieroglyphic depiction $\bigwedge$ in time indeed acquired the connotations virility and reproduction; and could well have been the source of the meaning "male offspring" that *Ben* has in Hebrew. In addition to virility and reproduction, the shrine also acquired the attributes of rejuvenation; this in turn gave rise to the legend of the *Ben* bird, which the Greeks who had visited Egypt called the *Phoenix*. As these legends had it, the Phoenix was an eagle with plumage partly red and partly golden; once every 500 years, as it was about to die, it went to Heliopolis and in some manner rose again from the ashes of itself (or of its father).

Heliopolis and its healing waters remained venerated until early Christian times; local traditions claim that when Joseph and Mary escaped to Egypt with the child Jesus, they rested by the shrine's well.

The shrine at Heliopolis, Egyptian histories tell, was destroyed several times by enemy invaders. Nothing remains of it nowadays; the *Ben-Ben* is also gone. But it was depicted on Egyptian monuments as a conical chamber within which a god could be seen. Archaeologists have in fact found a stone scale-model of the *Ben-Ben*, showing a god at its open hatch-door in a gesture of welcome (Fig. 29). The true shape of the Celestial Chamber was probably accurately depicted in the tomb of Huy (Fig. 27); that modern command modules—the capsules housing the astronauts atop rocketships at launching, and in which they splash down back to Earth— Fig. 30—look so similar to the *Ben-Ben*, is no doubt a result of similarity of purpose and function.

In the absence of the *Ben-Ben* itself, is there any other physical piece of evidence—and not mere drawings or scale models—left from the Heliopolitan shrine? We have noted above that according to Egyptian texts there were other secret things of Ra on display or in safekeeping at the shrine. In the Book of the Dead nine objects affiliated with the hieroglyph for *Shem* were depicted in the division paralleling the shrine of Heliopolis;

Fig. 29   Fig. 30

it could well be that there were indeed another nine space-related objects or spacecraft parts on display at the shrine.

Archaeologists may also have found a replica of one of these smaller objects. It is an oddly shaped circular object full of intricate curves and cutouts (Fig. 31a); it has baffled all scholars since its discovery in 1936. It is important to realize that the object was found—among other "unusual copper objects"—in the tomb of the crown prince Sabu, son of King Adjib of the First Dynasty. It is, therefore, certain that the object was placed in the tomb circa 3100 B.C. It could have been older, but certainly not more recent, than that date.

Reporting on the discoveries in northern Saqqara (just south of the great pyramids at Gizah), Walter B. Emery (*Great Tombs of the First Dynasty*) described the object as a "bowl-like vessel of schist," and remarked that "No satisfactory explanation of the curious design of this object has been forthcoming." The object was carved from a solid block of schist—a rock which is very brittle and which easily splits into thin, irregular layers. If it were put to any use, it would have quickly broken apart; so the particular stone was chosen because the very unusual and delicate shape could best be carved out in such a material—a means to preserve the shape, rather than to actually use it. This has led other scholars, such as Cyril Aldred (*Egypt to the End of the Old Kingdom*) to conclude that the stone object "possibly imitates a form originally made in metal."

But what metal could have been used in the fourth millennium B.C. to produce the object, what process of precision grinding, what skilled metallurgists were then available to create such a delicate and structurally complex design? And, above all, for what purpose?

A technical study of the object's unique design (Fig. 31b) shed little light on its use or origin. The round object, some twenty-four inches in diameter and less than four inches at its thickest part, was obviously made to fit over a shaft and rotate around an axle. Its three oddly curving cutouts suggest a possible immersion in a liquid during rotation.

There was no further effort made after 1936 to unravel the object's enigma. But its possible function suddenly sprang to our mind in 1976 on reading in a technical magazine of some revolutionary designs of a flywheel being developed in California in connection with the American space program. The flywheel, attached to a rotating shaft of a machine or an engine, has been in use for less than two centuries as a means of regulating the speed of machinery, as well as for accumulating energy for a single spurt, such as in a metal press (or more recently in aviation).

As a rule, flywheels have had heavy rims, for the energy is stored in the wheel's circumference. But in the 1970s, engineers of the Lockheed Missile & Space Company came up with an opposite design—a light-rimmed wheel, claiming it is best suited for saving energy in mass transit trains or storing energy in electrically powered trolley-buses. The research was continued by the Airesearch Manufacturing Company; the model they developed—but never finally perfected—was to be hermetically sealed within a housing filled with lubricant. That their revolutionary flywheel (Fig. 32) looks like the 5,000-year-old object discovered in Egypt is only less amazing than the fact that the perfected object from 3100 B.C. looks like a piece of equipment still in the development stage by space engineers in A.D. 1978!

Where is the metal original of this ancient flywheel? Where are the other objects that were apparently on display at the Heliopolis shrine? Where, for that matter, is the *Ben-Ben* itself? Like so many artifacts whose existence in antiquity has been documented by the ancient peoples beyond doubt, they have all disappeared—destroyed perhaps by natural calamities or wars, perhaps dismantled and taken elsewhere—as war booty, or for safekeeping and hiding away in places long forgotten. Perhaps they were carried back to the heavens; perhaps they are still with us, unrecognized for what they are in some museum basement. Or—as the legend of the Phoenix which connects Heliopolis and Arabia might suggest—hidden under the sealed chamber of the Qa'aba in Mecca . . .

We can surmise, however, that the destruction, disappearance or withdrawal of the shrine's sacred objects had probably taken place during Egypt's so-called First Intermediary Period. In that period, the unification of Egypt came apart and total anarchy reigned. We know that the shrines of Heliopolis were destroyed during the years of disorder; it was then, perhaps, that Ra left his temple at Heliopolis and became *Amon*—the "Hidden God."

When order was first restored in Upper Egypt under the Eleventh Dynasty, the capital was established at Thebes and the supreme god was called Amon (or Amen). The Pharaoh Mentuhotep (Neb-Hepet-Ra) built a

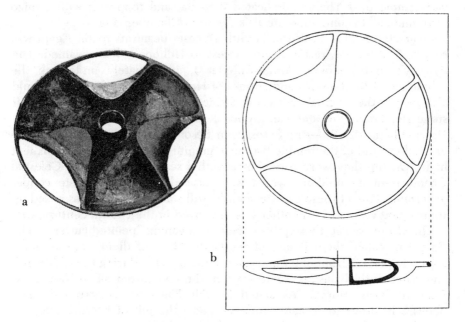

Fig. 31

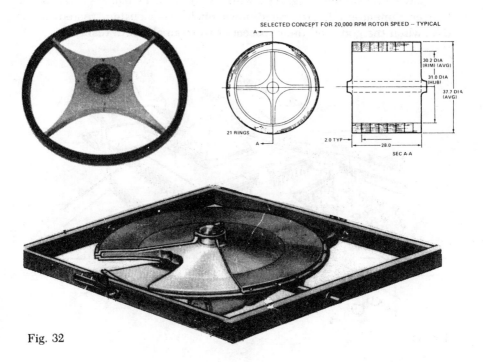

Fig. 32

vast temple near Thebes, dedicated it to Ra, and topped it with a huge "pyramidion" to commemorate Ra's Celestial Chamber (Fig. 33).

Soon after 2000 B.C., as the Twelfth Dynasty began its reign, Egypt was reunited, order was restored, and access to Heliopolis was regained. The dynasty's first Pharaoh, Amen-Em-Hat I, immediately undertook the rebuilding of the temples and shrines of Heliopolis; but whether he could also restore the original artifacts enshrined there, or had to do with their stone simulations, no one can say for certain. His son, the Pharaoh Sen-Usert (Kheper-Ka-Ra)—the Sesostris or Sesonchusis of Greek historians—erected in front of the temple two huge granite columns (over sixty-six feet high). On top they were surmounted with a scale replica of Ra's Celestial Chamber—a pyramidion, which was encased in gold or white copper (electrum). One of these granite obelisks still stands where it was raised up some 4,000 years ago; the other was destroyed in the twelfth century A.D.

The Greeks called these pillars *obelisks*, meaning "pointed cutters." The Egyptians called them Beams of the Gods. More of them were set up—always in pairs in front of temple gateways (Fig. 34)—during the eighteenth and nineteenth dynasties (some were in the end carted off to New York, London, Paris, Rome). As stated by the Pharaohs, they raised these obelisks in order to "obtain (from the gods) the gift of Eternal Life," to "obtain Life Everlasting." For the obelisks simulated in stone what earlier Pharaohs had seen (and purportedly reached) in the *Duat*, in the Sacred Mountain: the rocketships of the gods (Fig. 35).

Today's tombstones, engraved with the deceased's name so that he be forever remembered, are scaled-down obelisks—a custom rooted in the days when the gods and their spacecraft were an absolute reality.

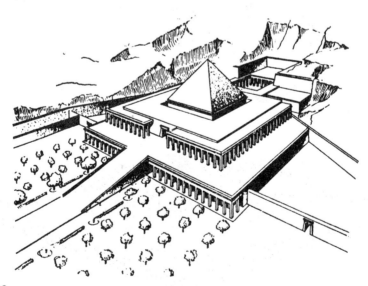

Fig. 33

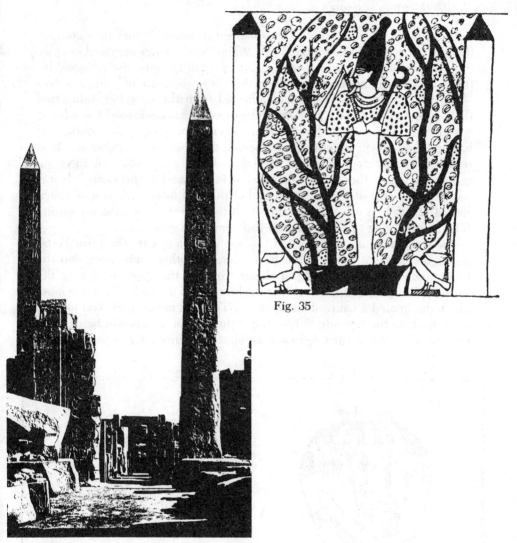

Fig. 35

Fig. 34

The Egyptian word for these Celestial Beings was NTR—a term which in the languages of the ancient Near East meant "One Who Watches." The hieroglyphic sign for *Neter* was ⦚ ; like all hieroglyphic signs, it must have represented originally an actual, visible object. Suggestions by scholars have ranged from an axe on a long handle to an ensign. Margaret A. Murray (*The Splendor That Was Egypt*) has put forward a more current view. Showing that pottery from the earliest, pre-dynastic period was adorned with drawings of boats carrying a pole with two streamers as a standard (Fig. 36), she concluded that "the pole with the two streamers became the hieroglyphic sign for God."

The interesting point about these earliest drawings is that they showed the boats arriving from a foreign land. When the drawings included people, they showed seated rowers commanded by a tall master, distinguished by the horns protruding from his helmet (Fig. 36)—the mark of being a *Neter*.

Pictorially, then, the Egyptians affirmed from the very beginning that their gods had come to Egypt from elsewhere. This confirmed the tales of how Egypt began—that the god Ptah, having come from the south, and having found Egypt inundated, performed great works of dyking and land reclamation and made the land habitable. There was a place in Egyptian geography which they called *Ta Neter*—"Place/Land of the Gods." It was the narrow straits at the southern end of the Red Sea which is now called Bab-el-Mandeb; it was through that strait that the ships bearing the ensign NTR and carrying the horned gods had come to Egypt.

The Egyptian name for the Red Sea was the Sea of UR. The term *Ta Ur* meant the Foreign Land in the East. Henri Gauthier, who compiled the *Dictionnaire des Noms Géographiques* from all the place names in the hieroglyphic texts, pointed out that the hieroglyph for *Ta Ur* "was a symbol which designated a nautical element . . . The sign means that 'You have to go by boat, to the left side.'" Looking at the map of the ancient lands (page 19), we see that a turn leftward as one came from Egypt and passed

Fig. 36

through the straits of Bab-el-Mandeb, would take the sailor along the Arabian peninsula toward the Persian Gulf.

There are more clues. *Ta Ur* literally meant the Land of UR, and the name *Ur* was not unknown. It was the birthplace of Abraham, the Hebrew patriarch. Descended of *Shem,* the elder son of Noah (the biblical hero of the Deluge), he was born to his father Terah at the city of Ur, in Chaldea; "and Terah took Abram his son, and Lot the son of Haran, his son's son, and Sarah his daughter-in-law, the wife of Abram; and they went forth from Ur of the Chaldees, to go into the Land of Canaan."

When archaeologists and linguists began to unravel, at the beginning of the nineteenth century, the history and written records of Egypt, Ur was unknown from any other source except the Old Testament. Chaldea, however, was known: it was the name by which the Greeks had called Babylonia, Mesopotamia's ancient kingdom.

The Greek historian Herodotus, who had visited Egypt and Babylonia in the fifth century B.C., found many similarities in the customs of the Egyptians and the Chaldeans. Describing the sacred precinct of the supreme god *Bel* (whom he called Jupiter Belus) in the city of Babylon, and its huge stage tower, he wrote that "on the upmost tower there is a spacious temple, and inside the temple stands a couch of unusual size, richly adorned, with a golden table by its side. There is no statue of any kind set up in the place, nor is the chamber occupied by nights by anyone but a native woman, who, as the Chaldeans, the priests of this god, affirm, is chosen for himself by the deity. . . . They also declare . . . that the god comes down in person into this chamber, and sleeps upon the couch. This is like the story of the Egyptians of what takes place in their city Thebes, where the woman always passes the night in the temple of the Theban Jupiter (Amon)."

The more nineteenth-century scholars learnt of Egypt, and matched the emerging historic picture with the writings of Greek and Roman historians, the more did two facts stand out: First, that Egyptian civilization and greatness were not like an isolated flower blooming in a cultural desert, but part of overall developments throughout the ancient lands. And secondly, that the biblical tales of other lands and kingdoms, of fortified cities and trade routes, of wars and treaties, of migrations and settlements—were not only true, but also accurate.

The Hittites, known for centuries only from brief mentions in the Bible, were discovered in Egyptian records as mighty adversaries of the Pharaohs. A totally unknown page of history—a pivotal battle between Egyptian armies and Hittite legions which came from Asia Minor, that had taken place at Kadesh in northern Canaan—was discovered not only in text, but also depicted pictorially on temple walls. There was even a historical personal touch, for the Pharaoh ended up marrying the daughter of the Hittite king in an effort to cement peace between them.

Philistines, "People of the Sea," Phoenicians, Hurrians, Amorites—peoples and kingdoms all vouched for, until then, only by the Old Testament—began to emerge as historical realities as the archaeological work progressed in Egypt, and began to spill over into the other lands of the Bible. Greatest of all, however, appeared to have been the veritable ancient empires of Assyria and Babylonia; but where were their magnificent temples, and other remains of their grandeur? And where were their records?

All that travelers had reported from the Land Between The Two Rivers, the vast plain between the Euphrates and the Tigris, were mounds—*tells* in Arabic and Hebrew. In the absence of stone, even the grandest structures of ancient Mesopotamia were built of mud bricks; wars, weather and time reduced them to heaps of soil. Instead of monumental structures, these lands yielded occasional finds of small artifacts; among them there often were tablets of baked clay inscribed with wedge-like markings. Back in 1686, a traveler named Engelbert Kampfer visited Persepolis, the Old Persian capital of the kings whom Alexander had fought. From monuments there, he copied signs and symbols in such a wedge-shaped or cuneiform script, as on the royal seal of Darius (Fig. 37). But he thought that they were only decorations. When it was finally realized that these were inscriptions, no one knew what their language was and how they could be deciphered.

As in the case of the Egyptian hieroglyphs, so it was with the cuneiform writings: The key to the solution was a tri-lingual inscription. It was found carved on the rocks of forbidding mountains, at a place in Persia called Behistun. In 1835, a major in the British Army, Henry Rawlinson, managed to copy the inscription, and thereafter decipher the script and its languages. As it turned out, the tri-lingual rock inscription was in Old Persian, Elamite and Akkadian. Akkadian was the mother-language of all the Semitic languages; and it was through the knowledge of Hebrew that scholars were

Fig. 37

able to read and understand the Mesopotamian inscriptions of the Assyrians and the Babylonians.

Spurred by such discoveries, a Paris-born Englishman named Henry Austen Layard reached Mosul, a caravan junction in northeastern Iraq (then part of the Ottoman-Turkish Empire) in 1840. There he was the guest of William F. Ainsworth, whose *Researches in Assyria, Babylonia and Chaldea* (1838)—along with earlier reports and small finds by Claudius J. Rich (*Memoir on the Ruins of Babylon*)—not only fired Layard's imagination, but also led to scientific and monetary support from the British Museum and the Royal Geographical Society. Versed both in the pertinent biblical references and the Greek classical writings, Layard kept recalling that an officer in Alexander's army reported seeing in the area "a place of pyramids and remains of an ancient city"—a city whose ruins were considered ancient even in Alexander's times!

His local friends showed him the various *tells* in the area, indicating that there were ancient cities buried beneath them. His excitement grew most when he reached a place called *Birs Nimrud*. "I saw for the first time the great conical mound of Nimrud rising against the clear evening sky," he later wrote in his *Autobiography*. "The impression that it made upon me was one never to be forgotten." Was it not the place of the buried pyramid seen by Alexander's officer? And surely was the place associated with the biblical Nimrod, "the mighty hunter by the grace of the Lord," who launched the kingdoms and royal cities of Mesopotamia (Genesis X)—

And the beginning of his kingdom: *Babel* and *Erech* and *Akkad*, all in the Land of *Shin'ar*; Out of that land there emanated *Ashur*, where *Nineveh* was built—a city of wide streets; and *Khalah*, and *Ressen*.

With the support of Major Rawlinson, who by then was the British Resident and Consul in Baghdad, Layard returned in 1845 to Mosul to begin digging at his cherished Nimrud. But whatever he was to find—and find he did—the claim to be the first modern archaeologist in Mesopotamia was not to be his. Two years earlier, Paul-Emile Botta, the French Consul at Mosul (whom Layard had met and befriended) proceeded to excavate a mound somewhat north of Mosul, on the other side of the Tigris River. The natives called the place Khorsabad; the cuneiform inscriptions uncovered there identified it as *Dur-Sharru-Kin*, the ancient capital of the biblical Sargon, king of Assyria. Commanding the vast city and its palaces and temples was indeed a pyramid constructed in seven steps, the term for which is ziggurat (Fig. 38).

Spurred by Botta's discoveries, Layard began to dig at his chosen mound, where he believed he would uncover *Nineveh*, the Assyrian capital of biblical renown. Though the place turned out to be the Assyrian military center named Kalhu (the biblical *Khala*), the treasures that were uncovered were worth the effort. They included an obelisk set up by King Shalmaneser II, on which he listed among those paying him tribute "Jehu, son of Omri, king of Israel" (Fig. 39).

Assyrian finds now directly confirmed the historical veracity of the Old Testament.

Encouraged, Layard began to excavate in 1849 a mound directly opposite Mosul, on the eastern banks of the Tigris. The place, locally named Kuyunjik, was indeed Nineveh— the capital established by Sennacherib, the Assyrian king whose army was smitten by the Lord's angel when he besieged Jerusalem (II Kings 18). After him, Nineveh served as the capital of Esarhaddon and Ashurbanipal. The art treasures carted off from there to the British Museum still make up the most impressive portion of its Assyrian displays.

As the pace of excavations gathered momentum, as archaeological teams from other nations joined the race, all the Assyrian and Babylonian cities named in the Bible (with one minor exception) were uncovered. But as the world's museums filled up with the ancient treasures, the most important finds were the simple clay tablets—some small enough to be held in the palm of the scribe's hand—on which the Assyrians, Babylonians and other peoples of western Asia wrote down commercial contracts, court rulings, marriage and inheritance records, geographical lists, mathematical information, medical formulas, laws and regulations, royal histories—indeed, every aspect of life by advanced and highly civilized societies. Epic tales, Creation tales, proverbs, philosophical writings, love songs and the like made up a vast literary heritage. And there were matters celestial—lists of stars and constellations, planetary information, astronomical tables; and lists of gods, their family relationships, their attributes, their tasks and functions—gods headed by twelve Great Gods, "Gods of Heaven and Earth," with whom there were associated the twelve months, the twelve constellations of the Zodiac, and twelve members of our solar system.

As the inscriptions themselves occasionally stated, their language stemmed from the Akkadian. This and other evidence confirmed the biblical narrative, that Assyria and Babylon (which appeared on the historical stage circa 1900 B.C.) were preceded by a kingdom named Akkad. It was founded by *Sharru-Kin*—"the Righteous Ruler"—whom we call Sargon I, circa 2400 B.C. Some of his inscriptions were also found; in them he boasted that by the grace of his god *Enlil*, his empire stretched from the Persian Gulf to the Mediterranean Sea. He called himself "King of *Akkad*, King of *Kish*"; and he claimed to have "defeated *Uruk*, tore down its wall . . . (was) victorious in battle with the inhabitants of *Ur*."

Many scholars believe that Sargon I was the biblical Nimrod, so that the biblical verses apply to him and to a capital named Kish (or Kush by biblical spelling) where kingship existed even before Akkad:

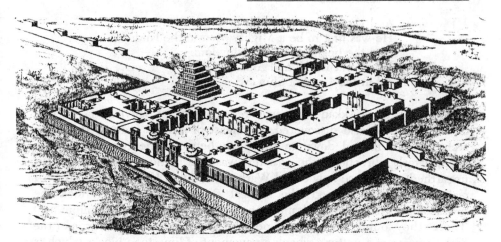

Fig. 38

Fig. 39

> And Kush begot Nimrod;
> He was first to be a Mighty Man in the land . . .
> And the beginning of his kingdom:
> Babel and Erech and Akkad,
> All in the Land of Shin'ar.

The royal city of Akkad was discovered southeast of Babylon; the ancient city of Kish was also discovered, southeast of Akkad. Indeed, the more archaeologists moved down in the plain between the two rivers, in a southeasterly direction, the greater was the antiquity of the places unearthed. At a place now called Warka, the city of Uruk, which Sargon I claimed to have defeated, the biblical *Erech*, was found. It took the archaeologists from the third millennium B.C. to the *fourth* millennium B.C.! There, they found the first-ever pottery baked in a kiln; evidence of the first-ever use of a potter's wheel; a pavement of limestone blocks which is the oldest of its kind; the first-ever ziggurat (step pyramid); and the world's first written records: inscribed texts (Fig. 40) and engraved cylinder seals (Fig. 41) which, when rolled on wet clay, left a permanent imprint.

Ur—birthplace of Abraham—was also found, farther south, where the coastline of the Persian Gulf had reached in antiquity. It was a great commercial center, site of a huge ziggurat, the seat of many dynasties. Was then the southern, more ancient part of Mesopotamia, the biblical Land of *Shin'ar*—the place where the events of the Tower of Babel had taken place?

One of the greatest discoveries in Mesopotamia was the library of Ashurbanipal in Nineveh, which contained more than 25,000 tablets arranged by subject. A king of great culture, Ashurbanipal collected every text he could lay his hands on, and in addition set his scribes to copy and translate texts otherwise unavailable. Many tablets were identified by the scribes as "copies of olden texts." A group of twenty-three tablets, for example, ended with the postscript: "twenty-third tablet; language of *Shumer* not changed." Ashurbanipal himself stated in an inscription:

> The god of scribes has bestowed on me the gift of the knowledge of his art. I have been initiated into the secrets of writing. I can even read the intricate tablets in *Shumerian*. I understand the enigmatic words in the stone carvings from the days before the Deluge.

In 1853, Henry Rawlinson suggested to the Royal Asiatic Society that there possibly was an unknown language that preceded Akkadian, pointing out that the Assyrian and Babylonian texts often used words borrowed from that unknown language, especially in scientific or religious texts. In 1869 Jules Oppert proposed at a meeting of the French Society of Numismatics and Archaeology that recognition be given to the existence of such an early language and of the people who spoke and wrote it. He showed that the

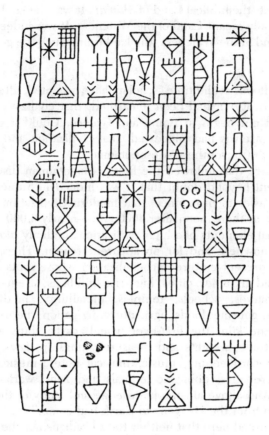

Fig. 40

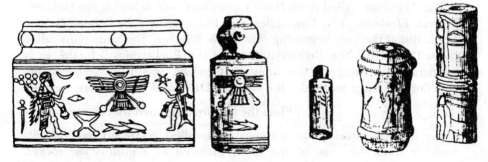

Fig. 41

Akkadians called their predecessors *Shumerians*, and spoke of the Land of *Shumer* (Fig. 42).

It was, in fact, the biblical Land of *Shin'ar*. It was the land whose name— *Shumer*—literally meant Land of the Watchers. It was indeed the Egyptian *Ta Neter*—Land of the Watchers, the land from which the gods had come to Egypt.

As difficult as it was at the time, scholars have accepted, after the grandeur and antiquity of Egypt had been unearthed, that civilization (as known to the West) did not begin in Rome and Greece. Could it now be, as the Egyptians themselves had suggested, that civilization and religion began not in Egypt, but in southern Mesopotamia?

In the century that followed the first Mesopotamian discoveries, it has become evident beyond doubt that it was indeed in Sumer (scholars find this spelling easier to pronounce) that modern Civilization (with a capital 'C') began. It was there, soon after 4000 B.C.—nearly 6,000 years ago—that all the essential elements of a high civilization suddenly blossomed out, as though from nowhere and for no apparent reason. There is hardly any aspect of our present culture and civilization whose roots and precursors cannot be found in Sumer: cities, high-rise buildings, streets, marketplaces, granaries, wharves, schools, temples; metallurgy, medicine, surgery, textile making, gourmet foods, agriculture, irrigation; the use of bricks, the invention of the kiln; the first-ever wheel, carts; ships and navigation; international trade; weights and measures; kingship, laws, courts, juries; writing and recordkeeping; music, musical notes, musical instruments, dance and acrobatics; domestic animals and zoos; warfare, artisanship, prostitution. And above all: the knowledge and study of the heavens, and the gods "who from the Heavens to Earth had come."

Let it be clarified here that neither the Akkadians nor the Sumerians had called these visitors to Earth gods. It is through later paganism that the notion of divine beings or gods has filtered into our language and thinking. When we employ the term here, it is only because of its general acceptance and usage that we do so.

The Akkadians called them *Ilu*—"Lofty Ones"—from which the Hebrew, biblical *El* stems. The Canaanites and Phoenicians called them *Ba'al*— Lord. But at the very beginning of all these religions, the Sumerians called them DIN.GIR, "the Righteous Ones of the Rocketships." In the early pictographic writing of the Sumerians (which was later stylized into cuneiform wedge-writing), the terms DIN and GIR were written

When the two are combined we can see that the

cutter or GIR—shaped like a conical-pyramidical command module—fits perfectly into the nose of the DIN, pictured as a multi-stage rocket. Moreover, if we stand the completed word-picture up, we find that it is

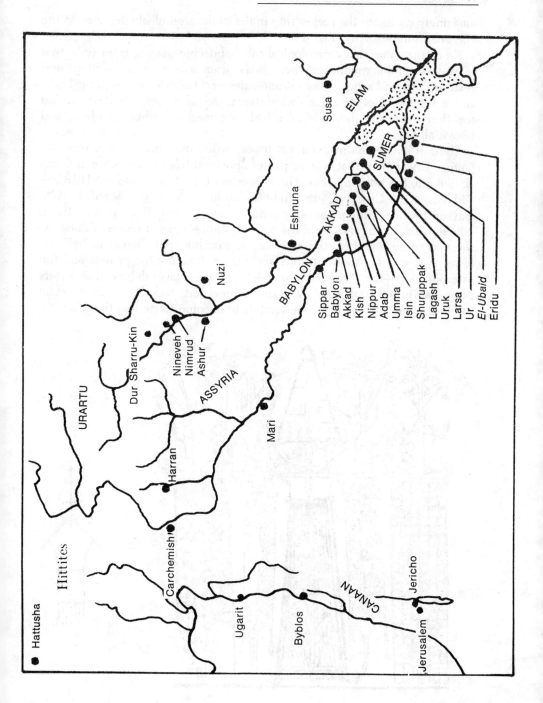

Fig. 42

amazingly similar to the rocket ship in the underground silo depicted in the Egyptian tomb of Huy (Fig. 43).

From the Sumerian cosmological tales and epic poems, from texts that served as autobiographies of these gods, from lists of their functions and relationships and cities, from chronologies and histories called King Lists, and a wealth of other texts, inscriptions and drawings, we have pieced together a cohesive drama of what had happened in prehistoric times, and how it all began.

Their story begins in primeval times, when our solar system was still young. It was then that a large planet appeared from outer space and was drawn into the Solar System. The Sumerians called the invader NIBIRU — "Planet of the Crossing"; the Babylonian name for it was *Marduk*. As it passed by the outer planets, Marduk's course curved in, to a collision course with an old member of the Solar System — a planet named Tiamat. As the two came together, the satellites of Marduk split Tiamat in half. Its lower part was smashed into bits and pieces, creating the comets and the asteroid belt — the "celestial bracelet" of planetary debris that orbits between Jupiter and Mars. Tiamat's upper part, together with its chief satellite, were thrown into a new orbit, to become Earth and the Moon.

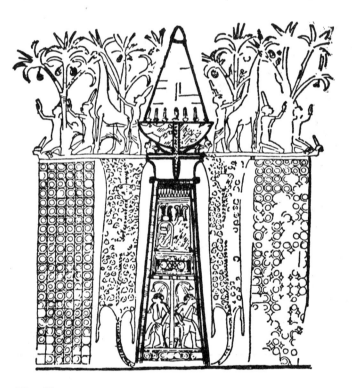

Fig. 43

Marduk itself, intact, was caught in a vast elliptical orbit around the Sun, returning to the site of the "celestial battle" between Jupiter and Mars once in 3,600 Earth-years (Fig. 44). It was thus that the Solar System ended up with *twelve* members—the Sun, the Moon (which the Sumerians considered a celestial body in its own right), the nine planets we know of, and one more—the twelfth: Marduk.

When Marduk invaded our solar system, it brought with it the seed of life. In the collision with Tiamat, some of the seed of life was transferred to its surviving part—Planet Earth. As life evolved on Earth, it emulated evolution on Marduk. And so it was that when on Earth the human species just began to stir, on Marduk intelligent beings had already achieved high levels of civilization and technology.

It was from that twelfth member of the Solar System, the Sumerians said, that astronauts had come to Earth—the "Gods of Heaven and Earth." It was from such Sumerian beliefs, that all the other ancient peoples acquired their religions and gods. These gods, the Sumerians said, created Mankind and eventually gave it civilization—all knowledge, all sciences, including an incredible level of a sophisticated astronomy.

This knowledge encompassed recognition of the Sun as the central body of the Solar System, cognizance of all the planets we know of today—even the outer planets Uranus, Neptune and Pluto, which are relatively recent discoveries of modern astronomy—planets which could not have been observed and identified with the naked eye. And, in planetary texts and lists, as well as in pictorial depictions, the Sumerians insisted that there was one more planet—NIBIRU, *Marduk*— which, when nearest Earth, passed

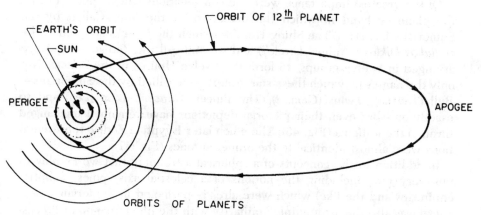

Fig. 44

between Mars and Jupiter, as shown on this 4,500-year-old cylinder seal (Fig. 45).

Fig. 45

The sophistication in celestial knowledge—attributed by the Sumerians to the astronauts who had come from Marduk—was not limited to familiarity with the Solar System. There was the endless universe, full of stars. It was first-ever in Sumer—not centuries later in Greece, as has been thought—that the stars were identified, grouped together into constellations, given names, and located in the heavens. All the constellations we now recognize in the northern skies, and most of the constellations of the southern skies, are listed in Sumerian astronomical tablets—in their correct order and by names which we have been using to this very day!

Of the greatest importance were the constellations which appear to ring the plane or band in which the planets orbit the Sun. Called by the Sumerians UL.HE ("The Shiny Herd")—which the Greeks adopted as the *zodiakos kyklos* ("Animal Circle") and we still call the Zodiac—they were arranged in twelve groups, to form the twelve Houses of the Zodiac. Not only the names by which these star groups were called by the Sumerians— Bull (*Taurus*), Twins (*Gemini*), The Pincer (*Cancer*), Lion (*Leo*) and so exactly on—but even their pictorial depictions have remained unchanged through the millenia (Fig. 46). The much later Egyptian Zodiac representations were almost identical to the Sumerian ones (Fig. 47).

In addition to the concepts of a spherical astronomy that we employ to this very day (including the notions of a celestial axis, poles, ecliptic, equinoxes and the like) which were already perfected in Sumerian times, there was also the astounding familiarity with the phenomenon of Precession. As we now know, there is an illusion of a retardation in Earth's orbit as an observer from Earth pinpoints the Sun on a fixed date (such as the first

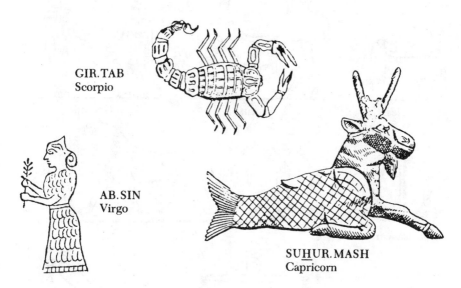

GIR.TAB
Scorpio

AB.SIN
Virgo

SUHUR.MASH
Capricorn

Fig. 46

day of spring) against the Zodiac constellations that act as a backdrop in space. Caused by the fact that the Earth's axis is inclined relatively to its plane of orbit around the Sun, this retardation or Precession is infinitesimal in terms of human lifespans: in seventy-two years, the shift in the Zodiac backdrop is a mere 1° of the 360° Celestial Circle.

Since the Zodiac circle surrounding the band in which Earth (and other planets) orbits around the Sun was divided into an arbitrary twelve Houses, each takes up one-twelfth of the full circle, or a celestial space of 30°. It thus takes Earth 2,160 years (72 × 30) to retard through the full span of a Zodiac House. In other words, if an astronomer on Earth has been observing (as is now done) the spring day when the Sun began to rise against the constellation or House of Pisces, his descendants 2,160 years later would observe the event with the Sun against the backdrop of the adjacent constellation, the "House" of *Aquarius.*

No single man, perhaps even no single nation, could have possibly observed, noted and understood the phenomenon in antiquity. Yet the evidence is irrefutable: The Sumerians, who began their time-counting or calendar in the Age of Taurus (which began circa 4400 B.C.), were aware of and recorded in their astronomical lists the previous precessional shifts to Gemini (circa 6500 B.C.), Cancer (circa 8700 B.C.) and Leo (circa 10,900 B.C.)! Needless to say, it was duly recognized circa 2200 B.C. that the first day of spring—New Year to the peoples of Mesopotamia—retarded a full 30° and shifted to the constellation or "Age" of *Aries,* the Ram (KU.MAL in Sumerian).

It has been recognized by some of the earlier scholars who combined

1. Aries. 2. Taurus. 3. Gemini.

4. Cancer. 5. Leo

6. Virgo. 7. Libra. 8. Scorpio.

9. Sagittarius. 10. Capricorn.

11. Aquarius. 12. Pisces.

Fig. 47

their knowledge of Egyptology/Assyriology with astronomy, that the textual and pictorial depictions employed the Zodiac Age as a grand celestial calendar, whereby events on Earth were related to the grander scale of the heavens. The knowledge has been employed in more recent times as a means of prehistoric and historic chronological aid in such studies as that by G. de Santillana and H. von Dechend (*Hamlet's Mill*). There is no doubt, for example, that the Lion-like Sphinx south of Heliopolis, or the Ram-like Sphinxes guarding the temples of Karnak, depicted the Zodiac ages in which the events they stood for had occurred, or in which the gods or kings represented had been supreme.

Central to this knowledge of astronomy, and in consequence to all the religions, beliefs, events and depictions of the ancient world, was thus the conviction that there is one more planet in our solar system, a planet with the vastest orbit, a supreme planet or "Celestial Lord"—the one the Egyptians called the Imperishable Star, or the "Planet of Millions of Years"—the celestial abode of the gods. The ancient peoples, without exception, paid homage to this planet, the one with the vastest, most majestic orbit. In Egypt, in Mesopotamia and elsewhere, its ubiquitous emblem was that of the Winged Globe (Fig. 48).

Recognizing that the Celestial Disk, in Egyptian depictions, stood for the Celestial Abode of Ra, scholars have persisted in referring to Ra as a "Sun God" and to the Winged Disk as a "Sun Disk." It should now be clear that it was not the Sun, but the Twelfth Planet which was so depicted. Indeed, Egyptian depictions clearly distinguished between the Celestial Disk representing this planet, and the Sun. As can be seen (Fig. 49), *both* were shown in the heavens (represented by the arched form of the goddess Nut); clearly, then, two celestial bodies and not a single one are involved. Clearly too, the Twelfth Planet is shown as a celestial globe or disk—a planet; whereas the Sun is shown emitting its benevolent rays (in this instance, on the goddess Hat-Hor, "Lady of the Mines" of the Sinai peninsula).

Did the Egyptians then, as the Sumerians, know thousands of years ago that the Sun was the center of the solar system, and that the system consisted of twelve members? We know that it was so from actual celestial maps depicted on mummy coffins.

A well-preserved one, discovered by H. K. Brugsch in 1857 in a tomb at Thebes (Fig. 50), shows the goddess Nut ("The Heavens") in the central panel (painted atop the coffin), surrounded by the twelve constellations of the Zodiac. On the sides of the coffin, the bottom rows depict the twelve hours of the night and of the day. Then the planets—the Celestial Gods—are shown traveling in their prescribed orbits, the Celestial Barques (the Sumerians called these orbits the "destinies" of the planets).

In the central position, we see the globe of the Sun, emitting rays. Near the Sun, by Nut's raised left hand, we see two planets: Mercury and Venus. (Venus is correctly depicted as a female—the only planet considered female

Fig. 48

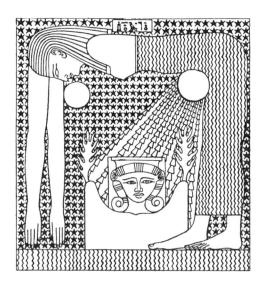

Fig. 49

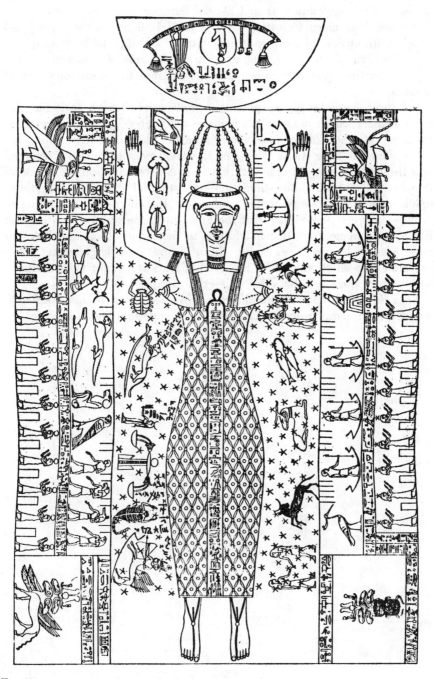

Fig. 50

by all ancient peoples.) Then, in the left-hand panel, we see Earth (accompanied by the emblem of Horus), the Moon, Mars and Jupiter as Celestial Gods traveling in their Celestial Barques.

We see four more Celestial Gods beyond Jupiter, on the right-hand panel. With orbits unknown to the Egyptians (and thus without Barques), we see Saturn, Uranus, Neptune and Pluto. The time of mummification is marked by the Spearman pointing his spear into the midst of the Bull (Taurus).

We thus encounter all the planets in their correct order, including the outer planets whom modern astronomers discovered only rather recently (Brugsch, as others of his time, was unaware of the existence of Pluto).

Scholars who have studied the planetary knowledge in antiquity assumed that the ancient peoples believed that five planets—the Sun being one of them—circled Earth. Any depiction or listing of more planets, these scholars held, was due to some "confusion." But there was no confusion; rather—impressive accuracy: that the Sun was in the system's center, that Earth was a planet, and that in addition to Earth and Moon and the other eight planets known to us today, there is one more large planet. It is depicted atop all others, above the head of Nut, as a major Celestial Lord with its own huge celestial orbit ("Celestial Barque").

Four hundred fifty thousand years ago—according to our Sumerian sources—astronauts from this Celestial Lord landed on Planet Earth.

VI

In the Days before
the Deluge

I understand the enigmatic words in the stone carvings from the days before the Deluge.

So had stated, in a self-laudatory inscription, the Assyrian king Ashurbanipal. Indeed, throughout the diversified literature of ancient Mesopotamia, there were scattered references to a deluge that had swept over Earth. Could it then be, scholars wondered as they came upon such references, that the detailed biblical tale of the Deluge was not a myth or allegory, but the record of an actual event—an event remembered not by the Hebrews alone?

Moreover, even the single sentence in Ashurbanipal's inscription was full of scientific dynamite. He not only confirmed that there had been a Deluge; he stated that his tutoring by the God of Scribes included the understanding of pre-Diluvial inscriptions, "the enigmatic words in the stone carvings from the days before the Deluge." It could only mean that even before the Deluge there had been scribes and stone carvers, languages and writing— that there had been a civilization in the remote days before the Deluge!

It was traumatic enough to have realized that the roots of our modern western civilization go back not to Greece and Judea of the first millennium B.C., and not to Assyria and Babylonia of the second millennium B.C., and not even Egypt of the third millennium B.C.—but to Sumer of the fourth millennium B.C. Now, scientific credibility had to be stretched even farther back, to what even the Sumerians considered "the olden days"—to an enigmatic era "before the Deluge."

Yet, all these shocking revelations should have been old news to anyone who had cared to read the Old Testament's words for what they actually said: that after Earth and the Asteroid Belt (the *Raki'a* or Heaven of Genesis) had been created, and Earth had taken shape, and life evolved, and "the Adam" created—Man was placed in the Orchard that was in Eden. But through the machinations of a brilliant "Serpent" who dared call the bluff of God, Adam and his female companion Eve acquired certain knowing which they were not supposed to possess. Thereupon, the Lord—

speaking to unnamed colleagues—grew concerned that Man, "having become as one of us," might also help himself to the Tree of Life, "and eat, and live forever."

So He drove out the Adam;
And he placed at the east of the Garden of Eden
the Cherubim, and the Flaming Sword which revolveth,
to guard the way to the Tree of Life.

Thus was Adam expelled from the wonderful orchard which the Lord had planted in Eden, from then on to "eat the herbs of the field" and obtain his sustenance "by the sweat of thy face." And "Adam knew Eve his wife and she conceived and bore Cain . . . and she bore again, his brother, Abel; and Abel was a keeper of sheep, and Cain was a tiller of the land."

The biblical claim of a pre-Diluvial civilization then proceeds along two lines, beginning with the line of Cain. Having murdered Abel—there is a hint of homosexuality as the cause—Cain was expelled farther east, to the "Land of Migrations." There his wife bore him Enoch—a name meaning "Foundation"; and the Bible explains that Cain "was building a city" when Enoch was born, "so he named the city 'Enoch,' as a namesake of his son Enoch." (The application of the same name to a person and the city associated with him was a custom that prevailed throughout the history of the ancient Near East.)

The line of Cain continued through Irad, Mechuyah-el, Metusha-el and Lamech. The first son of Lamech was Jabal—a name which in the original Hebrew *(Yuval)* means "The Lute Player." As the Book of Genesis explains, "Jabal was the ancestor of all such as play the harp and the lyre." A second son of Cain, Tubal-Cain, could "sharpen all cutters of copper and iron." What became of these capable people in the eastern Lands of Migration, we are no longer told; for the Old Testament, considering the line of Cain to be accursed, lost all interest in tracking further their genealogies and fate.

Instead, the Book of Genesis (in Chapter V) turns back to Adam and to his third son Seth. Adam, we are told, was 130 years old when Seth was born, and lived another 800 years for a total of 930 years. Seth, who fathered Enosh at age 105, lived to be 912. Enosh begot Cainan at age 90, and died at age 905. Cainan lived to the ripe age of 910; his son Mahalal-el was 895 years old when he died; and his son, Jared, passed on at age 962.

For all these pre-Diluvial patriarchs, the Book of Genesis provides the bare biographical information: who was their father, when their male heir was born, and (after "giving birth to other sons and daughters") when they died. But when the next patriarch is listed, he gets special treatment:

And Jared lived a hundred and sixty-two years, and begot *Enoch* . . .
And Enoch lived sixty-five years, and begot Methuselah.
And Enoch walked with the Lord, after he had begotten Methusaleh,

for three hundred years; and he begot (other) sons and daughters.

And all the days of Enoch were three hundred and sixty and five years.

And here comes the explanation—an astounding explanation—of why Enoch was singled out for so much attention and biographical detail: Enoch did not die!

For Enoch had walked with the Lord, and was gone; for the Lord had taken him away.

Methusaleh lived the longest—969 years—and was succeeded by Lamech. Lamech (who lived to be 777 years) begot Noah—the hero of the Deluge. Here too there is a brief biographical-historical note: Lamech had so named his son, we are informed, because Mankind was undergoing at that time great sufferings, and the earth was barren and unproductive. In naming his son Noah ("Respite"), Lamech expressed the hope that "This one shall bring us respite of our toil and frustrations of the land which the Lord had cursed."

And so, through ten generations of pre-Diluvial patriarchs blessed with what scholars call "legendary" life spans, the biblical narrative reaches the momentous events of the Deluge.

The Deluge is presented in the Book of Genesis as the opportunity seized by the Lord "to destroy the Man whom I had created from the face of the Earth." The ancient authors found it necessary to provide an explanation for such a far-reaching decision. It had to do, we are told, with Man's sexual perversions; specifically, with the sexual relations between "the daughters of Man" and "the sons of the gods."

In spite of the monotheistic endeavors of the compilers and editors of the Book of Genesis, struggling to proclaim faith in a sole deity in a world that in those days believed in many gods, there remain numerous slip-ups where the biblical narrative speaks of gods in the plural. The very term for "deity," (when the Lord is not specifically named as Yahweh), is not the singular *El* but the plural *Elohim*. When the idea of creating Adam occurs, the narrative adopts the plural language: "And Elohim (= the deities) said: 'Let *us* make Man in *our* image and after *our* Likeness.'" And when the incident with the Fruit of Knowing had occurred, Elohim again spoke in the plural to unnamed colleagues.

Now, it transpires from four enigmatic verses of Genesis VI that set the stage for the Deluge, that not only were there deities in the plural, but that they even had sons (in the plural). These sons upset the Lord by having sex with the daughters of Man, compounding their sins by having children or demi-gods born from this illicit lovemaking:

And it came to pass

When the Earthlings began to multiply upon the Earth, and daughters were born unto them—

That the sons of the gods saw the daughters of Adam, that they were good;
And they took them for wives, of all which they chose.

And the Old Testament explains further:

The *Nefilim* were upon the Earth in those days and thereafter too;
Those sons of the gods who cohabited with the daughters of the Adam, and they bore children unto them.
They were the Mighty Ones of Eternity, the People of the *Shem*.

Nefilim—traditionally translated "giants"—literally means "Those Who Were Cast Upon" the earth. They were the "Sons of the Gods"—"the people of the *Shem*," the *People of the Rocketships*.

We are back to Sumer and the DIN.GIR, the "Righteous Ones of the Rocket Ships."

Let us then pick up the Sumerian record where we left off—450,000 years ago.

It was some 450,000 years ago, the Sumerian texts claim, that astronauts from Marduk came to Earth in search of gold. Not for jewelry, but for some pressing need affecting survival on the Twelfth Planet.

The first landing party numbered fifty astronauts; they were called *Anunnaki*—"Those of Heaven Who Are on Earth." They splashed down in the Arabian Sea, and made their way to the head of the Persian Gulf, establishing there their first Earth Station E.RI.DU—"Home in Faraway Built." Their commander was a brilliant scientist and engineer who loved to sail the seas, whose hobby was fishing. He was called E.A—"He Whose House Is Water," and was depicted as the prototype Aquarius; but having led the landing on Earth, he was given the title EN.KI—"Lord Earth." Like all the Sumerian gods, his distinguishing feature was the horned headdress (Fig. 51).

The original plan, it appears, was to extract the gold from the seawaters; but the plan proved unsatisfactory. The only alternative was to do it the hard way: to mine ores in southeastern Africa, haul them by ship to Mesopotamia, and there smelt and refine them. The refined gold ingots were then sent aloft in Shuttlecraft, to an Earth-orbiting craft. There they awaited the periodic arrival of the Mother Spaceship, which took the precious metal back home.

To make this possible, more Anunnaki were landed on Earth, until their number reached 600; another 300 serviced the Shuttlecraft and orbiting station. A Spaceport was built at *Sippar* ("Bird Town") in Mesopotamia, on a site aligned with the Near East's most conspicuous landmark—the peaks of Ararat. Other settlements with various functions—such as the smelting and refining center of *Bad-Tibira*, a medical center named *Shuruppak*—

were laid out to form an arrow-like Landing Corridor. In the exact center, NIBRU.KI—"The Crossing Place on Earth" (*Nippur* in Akkadian)—was established as the Mission Control Center.

The commander of this expanded enterprise on Planet Earth was EN.LIL—"Lord of the Command." In the early Sumerian pictographic writing, Enlil's name and his Mission Control Center were depicted as a complex of structures with tall antennas and wide radar screens (Fig. 52).

Both Ea/Enki and Enlil were sons of the then ruler on the Twelfth Planet, AN (Akkadian *Anu*), whose name meant "He of the Heavens" and was written pictographically as a star ⋇ Ea was the firstborn; but because Enlil was born to Anu by another wife who was also his half-sister, Enlil and not Ea was the heir to the throne. Now Enlil was sent to Earth, and took over the command from Ea, the so-called Lord Earth. Matters were further complicated by the despatch to Earth as Chief Medical Officer of NIN.HUR.SAG ("Lady of the Mountainpeak"), a half-sister of both Ea and Enlil—enticing both brothers to seek her favors; for by the same rules of succession, a son to one of them by her would inherit the throne. The lingering resentment on Ea's part, compounded by the growing competition between the brothers, eventually spilled off to their offspring and was the underlying cause of many events that followed.

Fig. 51

EN   LIL

Fig. 52

As the millennia passed on Earth—though to the Anunnaki each 3,600 years were but one year of their own life cycles—these rank-and-file astronauts began to grumble and complain. Was it indeed their task as spacemen to dig for ores deep inside dark, dusty, hot mines? Ea—perhaps to avoid friction with his brother—spent more and more time in southeastern Africa, away from Mesopotamia. The Anunnaki who toiled in the mines addressed their complaints to him; together they talked over their mutual dissatisfactions.

Then, one day, as Enlil arrived in the mining area for a tour of inspection, the signal was given. A mutiny was declared. The Anunnaki left the mines, put their tools on fire, marched on Enlil's residence and encircled it, shouting: "No more!"

Enlil contacted Anu and offered to resign his command and return to the home planet. Anu came down to Earth. A court-martial was held. Enlil demanded that the instigator of the mutiny be put to death. The Anunnaki, all as one, refused to divulge his identity. Hearing the evidence, Anu concluded that the work was indeed too harsh. Was the gold mining then to be discontinued?

Ea then offered a solution. In southeastern Africa, he said, there roamed a being that could be trained to perform some of the mining tasks—if only the "mark of the Anunnaki" could be implanted upon it. He was talking of the Apemen and Apewomen, who had evolved on Earth—but were still far behind the evolutionary level attained by the inhabitants of the Twelfth Planet. After much deliberation, Ea was given the go-ahead: "Create a *Lulu*," a "primitive worker," he was told; "let him bear the yoke of the Anunnaki."

Ninhursag, the chief medical officer, was to assist him. There was much trial and error until the right procedure was perfected. Extracting the egg of Apewoman, Ea and Ninhursag fertilized it with the sperm of a young astronaut. Then they reimplanted the fertilized egg not in the womb of the Apewoman, but in the womb of a female astronaut. Finally, the "Perfect Model" was achieved, and Ninhursag shouted with joy: "I have created— my hands have made it!" She held up for all to see the first *Homo sapiens* (Fig. 53)—the Earth's first-ever test-tube baby.

But like any hybrid, the Earthling could not procreate on his own. To obtain more primitive workers, Apewomen eggs were extracted, fertilized, and reimplanted in the wombs of "birth goddesses"—fourteen at a time: seven to be born males, seven females. As the Earthlings began to take over mining work in southeastern Africa, the Anunnaki who toiled in Mesopotamia grew jealous: they too clamored for primitive workers. Over the objections of Ea, forcibly, Enlil seized some of the Earthlings and brought them to the E.DIN—the "Abode Of The Righteous Ones" in Mesopotamia. The event is recalled in the Bible: "And the Lord took the Adam, and He placed him in the garden in *Eden*, to till it and tend it."

Fig. 53

All along, the astronauts who had come to Earth were preoccupied with the problem of longevity. Their biological clocks were set for their own planet: the time it took their planet to orbit the Sun once was to them but a single year of their life spans. But in such a single year, Earth orbited the Sun 3,600 times—a span of 3,600 years for Earth-originated life. To maintain their longer cycles on the quick-paced Earth, the astronauts consumed a "Food of Life" and "Water of Life" which were provided from the home planet. At his biological laboratories in Eridu, whose emblem was the sign of the Entwined Serpents (Fig. 54), Ea tried to unravel the secrets of life, reproduction, death. Why did the children born to the astronauts on Earth age so much faster than their parents? Why did Apemen live such short lives? Why did the hybrid *Homo sapiens* live much longer than Apeman, but only brief lives compared to the visitors to Earth? Was it environment, or inherent genetic traits?

Conducting further experiments in genetic manipulation on the hybrids, and using his own sperm, Ea came up with a new "perfect model" of Earthling. *Adapa*, as Ea had named him, had greater intelligence; he acquired the all-important ability to procreate, but not the longevity of the astronauts:

Fig. 54

With wide understanding
  he had perfected him . . .
To him he had given Knowing;
Lasting Life him he did not give.

Thus were Adam and Eve of the Book of Genesis given the gift or fruit not only of Knowledge but also of *Knowing*—the biblical Hebrew term for intercourse for the purpose of having offspring. We find this "biblical" tale illustrated in an archaic Sumerian drawing (Fig. 55).

Enlil was outraged on discovering what Ea had done. It was never intended that Man should be able to procreate like the gods. What next, he asked—would Ea also achieve for Man an everlasting life span? On the home planet, Anu too was perturbed. "Rising from his throne, he ordered: 'Let them fetch Adapa hither!'"

Afraid that his perfected human would be destroyed at the Celestial Abode, Ea instructed him to avoid the food and water that would be offered to him, for they would contain poison; "He gave him this advice:

Adapa,
Thou art going before Anu, the Ruler.
The road to Heaven wilt thou take.
When to Heaven thou hast gone up,
  and hast approached the gate of Anu,
Tammuz and Gizzida at the gate will be standing . . .
They will speak to Anu;
Anu's benign face they will cause to be shown thee.
As thou standest before Anu,
When they offer thee the Bread of Death,
  thou shalt not eat it.
When they offer thee the Water of Death,
  thou shalt not drink it . . .

Fig. 55

"Then he made him take the road to Heaven, and to Heaven he went up." When Anu saw Adapa, he was impressed by his intelligence and the extent to which he had learned from Ea "the plan of Heaven and Earth." "What shall we do about him," he asked his counselors, now that Ea "distinguished him by making a *Shem* for him"—by letting Adapa travel in a spacecraft from Earth to Marduk?

The decision was to keep Adapa permanently on Marduk. So that he could survive, "the Bread of Life they brought him," and the Water of Life too. But forewarned by Ea, Adapa refused to eat or drink. When his erroneous reasons were discovered, it was too late; his chance to obtain everlasting life was missed.

Adapa was returned to Earth—a trip during which Adapa saw the "awesomeness" of space, "from the horizon of Heaven to the zenith of Heaven." He was ordained as the High Priest of Eridu; he was promised by Anu that henceforth the Goddess of Healing would also attend to the ailments of Mankind. But Mortal's ultimate goal—everlasting life—was no longer his.

From then on, Mankind proliferated. The humans were no longer just slaves in the mines or serfs in the fields. They performed all tasks, built "houses" for the gods—we call them "temples"—and quickly learned how to cook, dance and play music for them. It was not long before the young Anunnaki, short of female company of their own, took to having sex with the daughters of Man. Since they were all of the same first Seed of Life, and Man was a hybrid created with the genetic "essence" of the Anunnaki, the male astronauts and the female Earthlings discovered that they were biologically compatible; "and children were born unto them."

Enlil viewed these developments with rising apprehension. The original purpose of coming to Earth, the sense of mission, the dedication to the task—were dissipated and gone. The good life seemed to be the main concern of the Anunnaki—and with a race of hybrids to boot!

Nature, as it were, offered Enlil a chance to put a halt to the deteriorating mores and ethics of the Anunnaki. Earth was entering a new ice age, and the pleasant climate was changing. As it got colder, it also became dryer. Rains became less frequent, the river waters sparser. Crops failed, famine spread. Mankind began to undergo great sufferings; daughters hid food from their mothers, mothers ate their young. At the urging of Enlil, the gods refrained from helping Mankind: Let them starve, let them be decimated, Enlil decreed.

In the "Great Below"—in Antarctica—the Ice Age was also causing changes. From year to year, the ice cap covering the continent at the South Pole grew thicker and thicker. Under the increasing pressure of its weight, friction and heat increased at its bottom. Soon the immense ice cap was floating on a slippery slush of mud. From the orbiting shuttlecraft, an alarm was sounded: the ice cap was becoming unstable; if it should happen to slip off the continent into the ocean—an immense tidal wave would engulf all of Earth!

It was not an idle danger. In the heavens, the Twelfth Planet was orbiting back to the Place of Crossing between Jupiter and Mars. As on previous occasions when it neared Earth, its gravitational pull caused earthquakes and other disturbances upon Earth and in its celestial motions. Now, it was calculated, this gravitational pull could well trigger the slippage of the ice cap, and inundate Earth with a global deluge. From this catastrophe, the astronauts themselves could not be immune.

As preparations were made to assemble all the Anunnaki near the Spaceport, and ready the craft to take them aloft before the tidal wave struck, ruses were employed to keep the approaching catastrophe a secret from Mankind. Fearing that the Spaceport would be mobbed, all the gods were made to swear to secrecy. And as to Mankind, Enlil said—Let them perish; let the seed of Earthling be wiped off the face of Earth.

In Shuruppak, the city under the lordship of Ninhursag, relations between Man and gods had gone the farthest. There, for the first time ever, a man was elevated to the status of king. As the sufferings of Mankind increased, ZI.U.SUD.RA (as the Sumerians called him) pleaded for the help of Ea. From time to time, Ea and his seafarers clandestinely brought Ziusudra and his people a load of fish. But now the question involved the very destiny of Mankind. Shall all the handiwork of Ea and Ninhursag perish "and turn to clay" as Enlil wished—or should the Seed of Mankind be preserved?

Acting on his own, but mindful of his oath, Ea saw in Ziusudra the chance to save Mankind. The next time Ziusudra came to pray and plead in the temple, Ea began to whisper from behind a screen. Pretending to talk to himself, Ea gave Ziusudra urgent instructions:

> Tear down the house, build a ship!
> Give up possessions, seek thou life!
> Foreswear belongings, keep soul alive!
> Aboard ship take thou the seed of all living things.
> That ship thou shalt build;
> Her dimensions shall be to measure.

The ship was to be a submersible vessel, a "submarine" that could withstand the avalanche of water. The Sumerian texts contain the dimensions and other structural instructions for the various decks and compartments in such detail that it is possible to draw the ship, as was done by Paul Haupt (Fig. 56). Ea also provided Ziusudra with a navigator, instructing him to direct the vessel toward the "Mount of Salvation," Mount Ararat; as the highest range in the Near East, its peaks would be the first to emerge from under the waters.

The Deluge came as expected. "Gathering speed as it blew" from the south, "submerging the mountains, overtaking the people like a battle." Viewing the catastrophe from above, as they orbited Earth in their craft, the Anunnaki and their leaders realized how much they had fallen in love

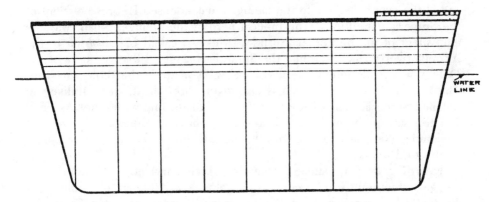

Fig. 56

with Earth and with Mankind. "Ninhursag wept . . . the gods wept with her for the land. . . . The Anunnaki, all humbled, sit and weep" as they huddled, cold and hungry, in their Shuttlecraft.

When the waters subsided and the Anunnaki began to land on Ararat, they were elated to discover that the Seed of Mankind was saved. But as Enlil too arrived, he was furious to see that "a living soul had escaped." It took the pleadings of the Anunnaki and the persuasion of Ea, to bring him around to their point of view—that if Earth was to be resettled, the services of Man were indispensable.

And so it was, that the sons of Ziusudra and their families were sent out to settle the mountain ranges flanking the plain of the two rivers, to await the time when the plain was dry enough to inhabit. As to Ziusudra, the Anunnaki

> Life like that of a god they gave him;
> Breath eternal, like a god, they granted him.

This they achieved by exchanging his "Breath of Earth" with the "Breath of Heaven." Then they took Ziusudra, "the preserver of the seed of Mankind," and his wife, to "reside in the faraway place"—

> In the Land of the Crossing,
> The Land *Tilmun,*
> The place where Utu rises,
> They caused him to dwell.

It is evident by now that the Sumerian tales of the Gods of Heaven and Earth, of the Creation of Man and of the Deluge, were the fountainhead from which the other nations of the ancient Near East drew their knowledge, beliefs and "myths." We have seen how the Egyptian beliefs matched the Sumerian ones, how their first sacred city was named after An, how the *Ben-Ben* resembled the Sumerian GIR, and so on.

It is also generally accepted by now, that the biblical tales of the Creation and of the events leading to the Deluge are condensed Hebrew versions of the Sumerian traditions. The biblical hero of the Deluge, Noah, was the equivalent of the Sumerian Ziusudra (who was called *Utnapishtim* in the Akkadian versions). But while the Sumerians asserted that the hero of the Deluge was made immortal, no such claim is made in the Bible for Noah. The immortalization of Enoch is also given short shrift, quite unlike the detailed Sumerian tale of Adapa or other texts dealing with other Ascents. But this abrupt biblical attitude could not prevent the spread, over the millennia, of legends dealing with the biblical heroes and their sojourn in, or return to, Paradise.

According to very ancient legends, which survived in a number of versions stemming from a composition almost 2,000 years old called *The Book of Adam and Eve*, Adam fell sick after he was 930 years old. Seeing his father "sick and in pain," his son Seth volunteered to go to "the nearest gate of Paradise . . . and lament and make entreaty to God; perchance He will hearken to me and send His angel to bring me the fruit, for which thou hast longed"—the fruit of the Tree of Life.

But Adam, accepting his mortal's fate, only wished for the excruciating pains to be relieved. So he asked Eve his wife to take Seth, and together go "to the neighborhood of Paradise"; there to ask not for the Fruit of Life, but only for one drop of the "oil of life" which floweth from the Tree, "to anoint me with it, that I may have rest from these pains."

Having done as Adam asked, Eve and Seth reached the gates of Paradise, and entreated with the Lord. Finally, the angel Michael appeared unto them—only to announce that their request would not be granted. "The time of Adam's life is fulfilled," the angel said; his death was not to be averted or postponed. Six days later, Adam died.

Even the historians of Alexander created a direct link between his miraculous adventures and Adam, the very first man who had dwelt in Paradise, and was proof of its existence and lifegiving powers. The connecting link in the case of Alexander was the unique stone which emitted light: it was said to have been brought out of the Garden of Eden by Adam, then handed down from generation to generation, until it reached the hands of an immortal Pharaoh, who in turn gave it to Alexander.

The plot-of-parallels indeed thickens, as one realizes that there exists an old Jewish legend, whereby the staff with which Moses performed many miracles, including the parting of the waters of the Lake of Reeds, was brought out of the Garden of Eden by Adam. Adam gave it to Enoch; Enoch gave it to his great-grandson Noah, the hero of the Deluge. Then it was handed down through the line of Shem, son of Noah, from generation to generation, until it reached Abraham (the first Hebrew patriarch). Abraham's great-grandson Joseph brought it with him to Egypt, where he rose to highest rank in the Pharaoh's court. There the staff remained among the treasures of the Egyptian kings; and thus it reached the hands of Moses, who was raised as an Egyptian prince before he escaped into the Sinai peninsula. In one version, the staff was carved out of a single stone; in another, it was made of a branch of the Tree of Life, which grew in the Garden of Eden.

In these interwoven relationships, harkening back to the earliest times, there were also tales linking Moses with Enoch. A Jewish legend, called "The Ascent of Moses," relates that when the Lord summoned Moses at Mount Sinai and charged him to lead the Israelites out of Egypt, Moses resisted the mission for various reasons, including his slow and non-eloquent speech. Determined to remove his meekness, the Lord decided to show him His throne and "the angels of the Heavens" and the mysteries thereof. So "God commanded Metatron, the Angel of the Countenance, to conduct Moses to the celestial regions." Terrified, Moses asked Metatron: "Who art thou?" And the angel (literally: "emissary") of the Lord replied: "I am Enoch, son of Jared, thy ancestor." (Accompanied by the angelic Enoch, Moses soared through the Seven Heavens, and saw Hell and Paradise; then he was returned to Mount Sinai, and accepted his mission.)

Further light on the occurrences concerning Enoch, and his preoccupation with the impending Deluge and its hero, his great-grandson Noah, is shed by yet another ancient book, the *Book of Jubilees*. It was also known in early times as the *Apocalypse of Moses*, for it allegedly was written down by Moses at Mount Sinai as an angel dictated to him the histories of days past. (Scholars, though, believe that the work was composed in the second century B.C.)

It follows closely the biblical narratives of the Book of Genesis; yet it provides more detail, such as the names of wives and daughters of the pre-Diluvial patriarchs. It also enlarges upon the events experienced by Mankind in those prehistoric days. The Bible informs us that the father of Enoch was *Jared* ("Descent"), but not why he was so named. The *Book of Jubilees* provides the missing information. It says that the parents of Jared so named him,

> For in his days the angels of the Lord descended upon Earth—those who are named *The Watchers*—that they should instruct the children of men, that they should do judgment and uprightness upon Earth.

Dividing the eras into "jubilees," the *Book of Jubilees* further narrates that "in the eleventh jubilee Jared took to himself a wife; her name was *Baraka* ("Lightning Bright"), the daughter of Rasujal, a daughter of his father's brother . . . and she bare him a son and he called his name Enoch. And he (Enoch) was the first among men that are born on Earth who learnt writing and knowledge and wisdom, and who wrote down the signs of heaven according to the order of their months in a book, that men might know the seasons of the year according to the order of their separate months."

In the twelfth jubilee, Enoch took as wife *Edni* ("My Eden"), the daughter of Dan-el. She bare him a son whose name was Methuselah. After that, Enoch "was with the angels of God for six jubilees of years, and they showed him everything which is on Earth and in the Heavens . . . and he wrote down everything."

But by then, trouble was brewing. The Book of Genesis reports that it was before the Deluge, "That the sons of the gods saw the daughters of Man, that they were good, and they took them for wives of all which they chose . . . and it repented the Lord that He had made Man on Earth . . . and the Lord said: I will destroy the Man whom I had created from the face of the Earth."

According to the *Book of Jubilees*, Enoch played some role in this changed attitude by the Lord, for "he testified about the Watchers who had sinned with the daughters of men; he testified against them all." And it was to protect him from the revenge of the sinning Angels of the Lord, that "he was taken from amongst the children of men, and was conducted into the Garden of Eden." Specifically named as one of the four places of God on Earth, it was in the Garden of Eden that Enoch was hidden, and where he wrote down his Testament.

It was after that that Noah, the righteous man singled out to survive the Deluge, was born. His birth, occurring at the troubled times when the "sons of the gods" were indulging in sex with mortal females, caused a marital crisis in the patriarchal family. As the Book of Enoch tells it, Methuselah "took a wife for his son Lamech, and she became pregnant by him and bore a son." But when the baby—Noah—was born, things were not as usual:

His body was white as snow and red as the blooming of a rose, and the hair of his head and his long locks were white as wool, and his eyes were beautiful.

And when he opened his eyes, he lighted up the whole house like the sun, and the whole house was very bright.

And thereupon he arose in the hands of the midwife, opened his mouth, and conversed with the Lord of Righteousness.

Shocked, Lamech ran to his father Methuselah, and said:

I have begotten a strange son, diverse from and unlike Man, and resembling the sons of the God of Heaven; and his nature is different, and he is not like us . . .

And it seems to me that he is not sprung from me but from the angels.

Suspecting, in other words, that his wife's pregnancy was induced not by him, but that she was impregnated by one of the angels, Lamech had an idea: Since his grandfather Enoch was staying amongst the Sons of the Gods, why not ask him to get to the bottom of this? "And now, my father," he said to Methuselah, "I petition thee and implore thee that thou mayest go to Enoch thy father, and learn from him the truth, for his dwelling place is amongst the angels."

Methuselah went as Lamech had asked, and reaching the Divine Abode summoned Enoch, and reported the unusual baby boy. Making some inquiries, Enoch assured Methuselah that Noah was indeed a true son of Lamech; and that his unusual countenance was a sign of things to come: "There shall be a Deluge and great destruction for one year," and only this son, who is to be named *Noah* ("Respite") and his family shall be saved. These future things, Enoch told his son, "I have read in the heavenly tablets."

The term employed in these ancient, even if ex-biblical scriptures, to denote the "sons of the gods" involved in the pre-Diluvial shenanigans, is *"Watchers."* It is the very term *Neter* ("Watchers") by which the Egyptians called the gods, and the exact meaning of the name *Shumer*, their landing place on Earth.

The various ancient books which throw this extra light on the dramatic events in the days before the Deluge, have been preserved in several versions that are all only translations (direct and indirect) of lost Hebrew originals. Yet their authenticity was confirmed with the renowned discoveries in recent decades of the Dead Sea Scrolls, for among the finds were fragments of scrolls which were undoubtedly parts of the Hebrew originals of such "memoirs of the Patriarchs."

Of particular interest to us is a scroll fragment which deals with the unusual birth of Noah, and from which we can learn the original Hebrew term for what has been translated as "Watchers" or "Giants," not only in the ancient versions, but even by modern scholars (as T. H. Gaster, *The Dead Sea Scriptures* and H. Dupont-Sommer, *The Essene Writings from Qumran*). According to these scholars, column II of the scroll fragment begins thus:

> Behold, I thought in my heart that the conception was from one of the *Watchers*, one of the Holy Ones, and (that the child really belonged) to the *Giants*.
>
> And my heart was changed within me because of the child.
>
> Then I, Lamech, hastened and went to Bath-Enosh (my) wife, and I said to Her:
>
> [I want you to take an oath] by the Most High, by the Lord Supreme, the King of all the worlds,
>
> the ruler of the Sons of Heaven, that you will tell me in truth whether . . .

But as we examine the Hebrew original (Fig. 57) we find that it does not say "Watchers"; it says *Nefilim*—the very term used in Genesis 6.

Thus do all the ancient texts and all the ancient tales confirm each other:

The days before the Deluge were the days when "The Nefilim were upon the Earth—the Mighty Ones, the People of the Rocketships."

Column II

1   הא באדין חשבת בלבי די מן עירין הריאנתא ומן קדישין הו﬩וא ולנפילוﬢין

2   ולבי עלי משתני על עוליﬦ דנא

3   באדין אנה למך אתבהלת ועלת על בתאנוש אנותי ואמרת

4   [ ]אנא ועד בעליא במרה רבותא במלך כול עוﬥמים

Fig. 57

In the words of the Sumerian King Lists, "the Deluge has swept over" 120 *shars*—120 orbits of 3,600 years each—after the first landing on Earth. This places the Deluge at about 13,000 years ago. It is exactly the time when the last ice age ended abruptly, when agriculture began. It was followed 3,600 years later by the New Stone Age (as scholars call it), the age of pottery. Then, 3,600 years later, Civilization all at once blossomed out—in the "plain between the rivers," in Shumer.

"And the whole Earth was of one language and of one kind of things," the Book of Genesis says; but soon after the people had established themselves in the Land of Shin'ar (Sumer), and built dwellings of fired clay bricks, they conspired to "build a city, and a Tower the top of which can reach unto Heaven."

The Sumerian texts from which this biblical tale was extracted have not yet been found; but we do come across allusions to the event in various Sumerian tales. What emerges is an apparent effort on the part of Ea to enlist Mankind in gaining control over the space facilities of the Nefilim— one more incident in the continuing feud between Ea and Enlil, which by then had spilled over to their offspring. As a result of the incident, the Bible tells us, the Lord and his unnamed colleagues decided to disperse Mankind and "confuse" its languages—give it diverse and separate civilizations.

The deliberations of the gods in the era following the Deluge are mentioned in various Sumerian texts. The one called the Epic of Etana states:

The Great Anunnaki who decree the fate sat exchanging their counsels regarding the Earth. They who created the four regions, who set up the settlements, who oversaw the land, were too lofty for Mankind.

The decision to establish on Earth four Regions was thus coupled with a decision to install intermediaries (priest-kings) between the gods and Mankind; so "kingship was again lowered to Earth from Heaven."

In an effort—which proved futile—to end or abate the feud between the Enlil and Ea families, lots were drawn between the gods to determine who would have dominion over which of the Regions. As a result, Asia and Europe were assigned to Enlil and his offspring; to Ea, Africa was given.

The First Region of civilization was Mesopotamia and the lands bordering upon it. The mountain-lands where agriculture and settled life began, the lands that came to be known as Elam, Persia, Assyria—were given to Enlil's son NIN.UR.TA, his rightful heir and "Foremost Warrior." Some Sumerian texts have been found dealing with Ninurta's heroic efforts to dam the mountain passes and assure the survival of his human subjects in the harsh times that had followed the Deluge.

When the layers of mud that had covered the Plain between the Two Rivers dried up sufficiently to permit resettlement, Shumer and the lands that stretched therefrom westward to the Mediterranean were put under the charge of Enlil's son NAN.NAR (*Sin* in Akkadian). A benevolent god, he supervised the reconstruction of Sumer, rebuilding pre-Diluvial cities at their original sites and establishing new cities. Among the latter was his favorite capital *Ur*, the birthplace of Abraham. His depictions included the crescent symbol of the Moon, which was his celestial "counterpart" (Fig. 58). To Enlil's youngest son, ISH.KUR (whom the Akkadians called *Adad*), were given the northwestern lands, Asia Minor and the Mediterranean islands from where civilization—"Kingship"—eventually spread to Greece. Like Zeus in later Greece, Adad was depicted riding a bull and holding a forked lightning.

Ea too divided the Second Region, Africa, among his sons. It is known that a son named NER.GAL lorded over the southernmost parts of Africa. A son named GI.BIL learned from his father the arts of mining and metallurgy, and took over control of the African gold mines. A third son— Ea's favorite—was named by him after the home planet *MARDUK*, and was taught by Ea all knowledge of sciences and astronomy. (Circa 2000 B.C., Marduk usurped the Lordship of Earth and was declared Supreme God of Babylon and of "the Four Quarters of the Earth.") And, as we have seen, a son whose Egyptian name was *Ra* presided over the core civilization of this Region, the civilization of the Nile Valley.

The Third Region, as was discovered only some fifty years ago, was in the subcontinent of India. There too, a great civilization arose in antiquity, some 1,000 years after the Sumerian one. It is called the Indus Valley

THE GODS OF HEAVEN AND EARTH

1. ENLIL 2. NINURTA 3. NANNAR/Sin 4. ISHKUR/Adad 5. NERGAL 6. GIBIL
7. MARDUK. IRNINI/Ishtar as Great Lady (8), Enchantress (9), Warrior (10),
Pilot (11)

Fig. 58

Civilization, and its center was a royal city unearthed at a site called *Harappa*. Its people paid homage not to a god but to a goddess, depicting her in clay figurines as an enticing female, adorned with necklaces, her breasts enhanced by straps which crossed her body.

Because the script of the Indus Civilization is still undeciphered, no one knows what the Harappans called their goddess, or who exactly she was. It is our conclusion, however, that she was the daughter of Sin, whom the Sumerians called IR.NI.NI ("The Strong, Sweetsmelling Lady") and the Akkadians called *Ishtar*. Sumerian texts tell of her dominion in a far land named *Aratta*—a land of grain crops and granaries as Harappa was—whereto she made flying trips, attired as a pilot.

It was in need of a Spaceport that the Fourth Region was set aside by the Great Anunnaki—a Region not for Mankind, but for their own exclusive use. All their space facilities from the time they had landed on Earth—the Spaceport at Sippar, the Mission Control Center at Mippur—were wiped out by the Deluge. The low-lying Mesopotamian plain was still too muddy for millennia to enable the rebuilding there of these vital installations. Another place—more elevated yet suitable, secluded but accessible—had to be found for the Spaceport and its auxiliary installations. It was to be a "sacred zone"—a restricted area, accessible only by permission. It was called in Sumerian TIL.MUN—literally, "Land of the Missiles."

In charge of this post-Diluvial Spaceport they put the son of Sin (and thus a grandson of Enlil), a twin brother of Irnini/Ishtar. His name was UTU ("The Bright One")—*Shamash* in Akkadian. It was he who ably carried out Operation Deluge—the evacuation out of Sippar. He was the chief of the Spacemen based on Earth, the "Eagles"; and he proudly wore his Eagle-uniform on formal occasions (Fig. 59).

In the days before the Deluge, traditions held, a few chosen mortals had been taken aloft from the Spaceport: *Adapa,* who missed his chance; and *Enmeduranki,* whom the gods Shamash and Adad transported to the Celestial Abode, to be initiated in priestly secrets (and then returned to Earth). Then there was *Ziusudra* ("His Life-Days Prolonged"), hero of the Deluge, who was taken with his wife to live in Tilmun.

In post-Diluvial times, Sumerian records stated, *Etana*—an early ruler of Kish—was taken aloft in a *Shem* to the Abode of the Gods, there to be granted the Plant of Rejuvenation and Birthgiving (but he was too frightened to complete the journey). And the Pharaoh Thothmes III claimed in his inscriptions that the god Ra had taken him aloft, given him a tour of the heavens, and returned him to Earth:

> He opened for me the doors of Heaven,
> He spread open for me the portals of its horizon.
> I flew up to the sky as a divine Falcon . . .
> That I might see his mysterious ways in heaven . . .
> I was made full with the understanding of the gods.

In the later memories of Mankind, the *Shem* was cherished as an obelisk, and the rocketship saluted by "Eagles" gave way to a sacred Tree of Life (Fig. 60). But in Sumer, where the gods were a present reality—as in Egypt when the first Pharaohs had reigned—*Tilmun*, the "Land of the Missiles," was a real place: a place where Man could find Immortality.

And there, in Sumer, they recorded the tale of a man who—uninvited by the gods—set out to reverse his fate nevertheless.

Fig. 59

Fig. 60

VII

Gilgamesh: The King Who Refused to Die

The Sumerian tale of the first known Search for Immortality concerns a ruler of long long ago, who asked his divine godfather to let him enter the "Land of the Living." Of this unusual ruler, ancient scribes wrote down epic tales. They said of him that

> Secret things he has seen;
> What is hidden from Man, he found out.
> He even brought tidings
> of the time before the Deluge;
> He also took the distant journey,
> wearisome and under difficulties.
> He returned, and upon a stone column
> all his toil he engraved.

Of that olden Sumerian tale, less than two hundred lines have remained. Yet we know it from its translations into the languages of the peoples who followed the Sumerians in the Near East: Assyrians, Babylonians, Hittites, Hurrians. They all told and retold the tale; and the clay tablets on which these later versions were written down—some intact, some damaged, many fragmented beyond legibility—have enabled many scholars over the better part of a century to piece the tale together.

At the core of our knowledge are twelve tablets in the Akkadian language; they were part of the library of Ashurbanipal in Nineveh. They were first reported by George Smith, whose job at the British Museum in London was to sort out, match and categorize the tens of thousands of tablets and tablet fragments that arrived at the Museum from Mesopotamia. One day, his eye caught a fragmented text which appeared to relate the story of the Deluge. There was no mistaking: the cuneiform texts, from Assyria, were telling of a king who sought out the hero of the Deluge, and heard from him a first-person account of the event!

With understandable excitement, the Museum directors sent George Smith to the archaeological site to search for missing fragments. With luck, he found enough of them to be able to reconstruct the text and guess the sequence of the tablets. In 1876, he conclusively showed that this was, as his work was titled, *The Chaldean Account of the Flood*. From the language and style he concluded that it "was composed in Babylon circa 2000 B.C."

George Smith at first read the name of the king who searched for Noah *Izdubur*, and suggested that he was none other than the biblical hero-king Nimrod. For a time scholars believed that the tale indeed concerned the very first mighty king, and referred to the twelve-tablet text as the "Nimrod Epos." More finds and much further research established the Sumerian origin of the tale, and the true reading of the hero's name: GIL.GA.MESH. It has been confirmed from other historical texts—including the Sumerian King Lists—that he was a ruler of Uruk, the biblical Erech, circa 2900 B.C. *The Epic of Gilgamesh*, as this ancient literary work is now called, thus takes us back nearly 5,000 years.

One must understand the history of Uruk to grasp the Epic's dramatic scope. Affirming the biblical statements, the Sumerian historical records also reported that in the aftermath of the Deluge, kingship—royal dynasties—indeed began at Kish; it then was transferred to Uruk as a result of the ambitions of Irnini/Ishtar, who cherished not at all her domain far away from Sumer.

Uruk, initially, was only the location of a sacred precinct, where an Abode (temple) for An, the "Lord of Heaven," was perched atop a vast ziggurat named E.AN.NA ("House of An"). On the rare occasion of An's visits to Earth, he took a liking to Irnini. He bestowed on her the title IN.AN.NA—"Beloved of An" (the ancient gossip suggested that she was beloved in more than platonic ways), and installed her in the Eanna, which otherwise stood unoccupied.

But what good was a city without people, a lordship with no one to rule over? Not too far away to the south, on the shores of the Persian Gulf, Ea lived in Eridu in semi-isolation. There he kept track of human affairs, dispensing knowledge and civilization to mankind. Enchanting and perfumed, Inanna paid Ea (a great-uncle of hers) a visit. Enamored and drunk, Ea granted her wish: to make Uruk the new center of Sumerian civilization, the seat of kingship in lieu of Kish.

To carry out her grandiose plans, whose ultimate goal was to break into the Inner Circle of the Twelve Great Gods, Inanna-Ishtar enlisted the support of her brother Utu/Shamash. Whereas in the days before the Deluge the intermarriage between the Nefilim and the daughters of Man brought about the wrath of the gods, the practice was no longer frowned upon in the aftermath of the Deluge. And so it was, that the high priest at the temple of An was at the time a son of Shamash by a human female. Ishtar and Shamash anointed him as king of Uruk, starting the world's first dynasty of priestly kings. According to the Sumerian King Lists, he ruled for 324 years. His son, "who built Uruk," ruled for 420 years. When Gilgamesh, the fifth ruler of this dynasty, ascended the throne, Uruk was already a thriving Sumerian center, lording over its neighbors and trading with far lands. (Fig. 61).

An offspring of the great god Shamash on his father's side, Gilgamesh was considered to be "two-thirds god, one-third human" by the further fact that his mother was the goddess NIN.SUN (Fig. 62). He was thus accorded the privilege of having his name written with the prefix "divine."

Proud and self-assured, Gilgamesh began as a benevolent and conscientious king, engaged in the customary tasks of raising the city's ramparts or embellishing the temple precinct. But the more knowledge he acquired of the histories of gods and men, the more he became philosophical and restless. In the midst of merriment, his thoughts turned to death. Would he, by virtue of his divine two-thirds, live as long as his demi-god forefathers—or would his one-third prevail, and determine for him the life span of a mortal human? Before long, he confessed his anxiety to Shamash:

> In my city man dies; oppressed is my heart.
> Man perishes; heavy is my heart . . .

Fig. 61

Fig. 62

> Man, the tallest, cannot stretch to heaven;
> Man, the widest, cannot cover the earth.

"Will I too 'peer over the wall'?" he asked Shamash; "will I too be fated thus?"

Evading a direct answer—perhaps not knowing it himself—Shamash attempted to have Gilgamesh accept his fate, whatever it might be, and to enjoy life while he could:

> When the gods created Mankind,
> Death for Mankind they allotted;
> Life they retained in their own keeping.

Therefore, said Shamash,

> Let full be thy belly, Gilgamesh;
> Make thou merry by day and night!
> Of each day, make thou a feast of rejoicing;
> Day and night, dance thou and play!
> Let thy garments be sparkling fresh,
> thy head washed; bathe thou in water.
> Pay heed to the little one that holds thy hand,
> let thy spouse delight in thy bosom;
> for this is the fate of Mankind.

But Gilgamesh refused to accept this fate. Was he not two-thirds divine, and only one-third human? Why then should the lesser mortal part, rather than his greater godly element, determine his fate? Roving by daytime, restless at night, Gilgamesh sought to stay young by intruding on newlywed couples and insisting on having intercourse with the bride ahead of the bridegroom. Then, one night, he saw a vision which he felt was an omen. He rushed to his mother to tell her what he saw, so that she might interpret the omen for him:

> My mother,
> During the night, having become lusty,
> I wandered about.
> In the midst (of night) omens appeared.
> A star grew larger and larger in the sky.
> The handiwork of Anu descended towards me!

"The handiwork of Anu" that descended from the skies fell to Earth near him, Gilgamesh continued to relate:

> I sought to lift it;
> it was too heavy for me.
> I sought to shake it;
> I could neither move nor raise it.

While he was attempting to shake loose the object, which must have embedded itself deep into the ground, "the populace jostled toward it, the nobles thronged about it." The object's fall to Earth was apparently seen by many, for "the whole of Uruk land was gathered around it." The "heroes"— the strongmen—then lent Gilgamesh a hand in his efforts to dislodge the object that fell from the skies: "The heroes grabbed its lower part, I pulled it up by its forepart."

While the object is not fully described in the texts, it was certainly not a shapeless meteor, but a crafted object worthy of being called the *handiwork* of the great Anu himself. The ancient reader, apparently, required no elaboration, having been familiar with the term ("Handiwork of Anu") or with its depiction, as possibly the one shown on an ancient cylinder seal (Fig. 63).

The Gilgamesh text describes the lower part, which was grabbed by the heroes, by a term that may be translated "legs." It had, however, other pronounced parts and could even be entered, as becomes clear from the further description by Gilgamesh of the night's events:

> I pressed strongly its upper part;
> I could neither remove its covering,
>   nor raise its Ascender . . .
> With a destroying fire its top I (then) broke off,
>   and moved into its depths.
> Its movable That Which Pulls Forward
> I lifted, and brought it to thee.

Gilgamesh was certain that the appearance of the object was an omen from the gods concerning his fate. But his mother, the goddess Ninsun, had to disappoint him. That which descended like a star from Heaven, she said, foretells the arrival of "a stout comrade who rescues; a friend is come to thee . . . he is the mightiest in the land . . . he will never forsake thee. This is the meaning of thy vision."

She knew what she was talking about; for unbeknown to Gilgamesh, in response to pleas from the people of Uruk that something be done to divert the restless Gilgamesh, the gods arranged for a wild man to come to Uruk and engage Gilgamesh in wrestling matches. He was called ENKI.DU—"A Creature of Enki"—a kind of Stone Age Man who had been living in the wilderness among the animals and as one of them: "The milk of wild creatures he was wont to suck." He was depicted naked, bearded, with shaggy hair—often shown in the company of his animal friends (Fig. 64).

To tame him, the nobles of Uruk assigned a harlot. Enkidu, until then knowing only the company of animals, regained his human element as he made love to the woman, over and over again. Then she brought Enkidu to a camp outside town, where he was coached in the speech and manners of Uruk and in the habits of Gilgamesh. "Restrain Gilgamesh, be a match for him!" the nobles told Enkidu.

Fig. 63

Fig. 64

The first encounter took place at night, as Gilgamesh left his palace and started to roam the streets, looking for sexual adventures. Enkidu met him in the street, barring his way. "They grappled each other, holding fast like bulls." Walls shook, doorposts were shattered as the two wrestled. At last, "Gilgamesh bent the knee"; the match was over: He lost to the stranger. "His fury abated, Gilgamesh turned away." Just then, Enkidu addressed him, and Gilgamesh recalled his mother's words. Here then was his new "stout friend." "They kissed each other, and formed a friendship."

As the two became inseparable friends, Gilgamesh began to reveal to Enkidu his fear of a mortal's fate. On hearing this, "the eyes of Enkidu filled with tears, ill was his heart, bitterly he sighed." Then he told Gilgamesh, that there is a way to outsmart his fate: to force his way into the secret Abode of the Gods. There, if Shamash and Adad would stand by him, the gods could accord him the divine status to which he was entitled.

The "Abode of the Gods," Enkidu related, was in "the cedar mountain." He happened to discover it, he said, as he was roaming the lands with the wild beasts; but it was guarded by a fearsome monster named *Huwawa*:

> I found it, my friend, in the mountains
>   as I was roaming with the wild beasts.
> For many leagues extends the forest:
> I went down into its midst.
> Huwawa (is there); his roar is like a flood,
>   his mouth is fire, ·
>   his breath is death . . .

> The Cedar Forest's watcher, the Fiery Warrior,
>   is mighty, never resting . . .
> To safeguard the Cedar Forest,
>   as a terror to mortals the god Enlil appointed him.

The very fact that Huwawa's main duty was to prevent mortals from entering the Cedar Forest only whetted the determination of Gilgamesh to reach the place; for surely, it was there that he could join the gods and escape his mortal's fate:

> Who, my friend, can scale heaven?
> Only the gods,
>   by going to the underground place of Shamash.
> Mankind's days are numbered;
>   whatever they achieve is but the wind.
> Even thou art afraid of death,
>   in spite of your heroic might.
> Therefore,
> Let me go ahead of thee,
>   let thy mouth call to me:
> "Advance, fear not!"

This, then, was the plan: by going to "the underground place of Shamash" in the Cedar Mountain, to be enabled to "scale heaven" as the gods do. Even the tallest man, Gilgamesh earlier pointed out, "cannot stretch to heaven." Now he knew where the place was, from which Heaven could be scaled. He fell to his knees and prayed to Shamash: "Let me go, O Shamash! My hands are raised in prayer . . . to the Landing Place, give command . . . Establish over me thy protection!"

The text's lines containing the answer of Shamash are, unfortunately, broken off the tablet. We do learn that "when Gilgamesh inspected his omen . . . tears ran down his face." Apparently he was permitted to go ahead—but at his own risk. Nevertheless, Gilgamesh decided to proceed, and fight Huwawa without the god's aid. "Should I fail," he said, people will remember me: "Gilgamesh, they will say, against fierce Huwawa has fallen." But should I succeed, he continued—I will obtain a *Shem*—the vehicle "by which one attains eternity."

As Gilgamesh ordered special weapons with which to fight Huwawa, the elders of Uruk tried to dissuade him. "Thou are yet young, Gilgamesh," they pointed out—and why risk death with so many sure years to live anyway, against unknown odds of success: "That which thou wouldst achieve, thou knowest not." Gathering all available information about the Cedar Forest and its guardian, they cautioned Gilgamesh:

> We hear that Huwawa is wondrously built;
> Who is there to face his weapons?

> Unequal struggle it is
> with the siege-engine Huwawa.

But Gilgamesh only "looked around, smiling at his friend." The talk of Huwawa as a mechanical monster, a "siege engine" that is "wondrously built," only encouraged him to believe that it was indeed controllable by commands from the gods Shamash and Adad. Since he himself did not succeed in obtaining a clear-cut promise of support from Shamash, Gilgamesh decided to enlist his mother in the effort. "Grasping each other, hand in hand, Gilgamesh and Enkidu to the Great Palace go, to the presence of Ninsun, the Great Queen. Gilgamesh came forward as he entered the palace: 'O Ninsun (he said) . . . a far journey I have boldly undertaken, to the place of Huwawa; an uncertain battle I am about to face; unknown pathways I am about to ride. Oh my mother, pray thou to Shamash on my behalf!'"

Obliging, "Ninsun entered her chamber, put on a garment as beseems her body, put on an ornament as beseems her breast . . . donned her tiara." Then she raised her hands in prayer to Shamash—putting the onus of the voyage on him: "Why," she asked rhetorically, "having given me Gilgamesh for a son, with a restless heart didst thou endow him? And now, thou didst affect him to go on a far journey, to the place of Huwawa!" She called upon Shamash to protect Gilgamesh:

> Until he reaches the Cedar Forest,
> Until he has slain the fierce Huwawa,
> Until the day that he goes and returns.

As the populace heard that Gilgamesh was going to "the Landing Place" after all, "they pressed closer to him" and wished him success. The city elders offered more practical advice: "Let Enkidu go before thee: he knows the way . . . in the forest, the passes of Huwawa let him penetrate . . . he who goes in front saves the companion!" They too invoked the blessings of Shamash: "Let Shamash grant thee thy desire; what thy mouth hath spoken, let him show thine eyes; may he open for thee the barred path, the road unclose for thy treading, the mountain unclose for thy foot!"

Ninsun had a few parting words. Turning to Enkidu, she asked him to protect Gilgamesh; "although not of my womb's issue art thou, I herewith adopt thee (as a son)," she told him; guard the king as thy brother! Then she placed her emblem around the neck of Enkidu.

And the two were off on their dangerous quest.

The fourth tablet of the Epic of Gilgamesh is devoted to the comrades' journey to the Cedar Forest; unfortunately, the tablet is so fragmented that, in spite of the discovery of parallel fragments in the Hittite language, no cohesive text could be put together.

It is evident, however, that they traveled a great distance, toward a western destination. On and off, Enkidu tried to persuade Gilgamesh to call off the quest. Huwawa, he said, can hear a cow moving sixty leagues away. His "net" can grasp from great distances; his call reverberates from the "Place Where the Rising Is Made" as far back as to Nippur; "weakness lays hold on him" who approaches the forest's gates. Let us turn back, he pleaded. But proceed they did:

> At the green mountain the two arrived.
> Their words were silenced;
> They themselves stood still.
> They stood still and gazed at the forest;
> They looked at the height of the cedars;
> They looked at the entrance to the forest.
> Where Huwawa wont to move was a path:
>   straight were the tracks, a fiery channel.
> They beheld the Cedar Mountain,
> Abode of the Gods,
>   the Crossroads of Ishtar.

Awestruck and tired, the two lay down to sleep. In the middle of the night they were awakened. "Didst thou arouse me?" Gilgamesh asked Enkidu. No, said Enkidu. No sooner had they dozed off than Gilgamesh again awakened Enkidu. He had witnessed an awesome sight, he said—unsure whether he was awake or dreaming:

> In my vision, my friend,
>   the high ground toppled.
> It laid me low, trapped my feet . . .
> The glare was overpowering!
> A man appeared;
>   the fairest in the land was he . . .
> From under the toppled ground he pulled me out.
> He gave me water to drink; my heart quieted.
> On the ground he set my feet.

Who was this "man"—"the fairest in the land"—who pulled Gilgamesh from under the toppled ground? What was the "overpowering glare" that accompanied the landslide? Enkidu had no answers; tired, he went back to sleep. But the night's tranquility was shattered once again:

> In the middle of the watch,
>   the sleep of Gilgamesh was ended.
> He started up, saying to his friend:
> "My friend, didst thou call me?
> Why am I awake?
> Didst thou not touch me?

> Why am I startled?
> Did not some god go by?
> Why is my flesh numb?"

Denying that he had awakened Gilgamesh, Enkidu left his comrade wondering whether it was "some god who went by." Bewildered, the two fell asleep again, only to be awakened once more. This is how Gilgamesh described what he saw:

> The vision that I saw was wholly awesome!
> The heavens shrieked, the earth boomed.
> Though daylight was dawning, darkness came.
> Lightning flashed, a flame shot up.
> The clouds swelled; it rained death!
> Then the glow vanished; the fire went out.
> And all that had fallen was turned to ashes.

Gilgamesh must have realized that he had witnessed the ascent of a "Sky Chamber": the shaking ground as the engines ignited and roared; the clouds of smoke and dust that enveloped the site, darkening the dawn sky; the brilliance of the engines' fire, seen through the thick clouds; and—as the jetcraft was aloft—its vanishing glow. A "wholly awesome" sight indeed! But one which only encouraged Gilgamesh to proceed, for it confirmed that he in fact had reached the "Landing Place."

In the morning the comrades attempted to penetrate the forest, careful to avoid "weapon-trees that kill." Enkidu found the gate, of which he had spoken to Gilgamesh. But as he tried to open it, he was thrown back by an unseen force. For twelve days he lay paralyzed.

When he was able to move and speak again, he pleaded with Gilgamesh: "Let us not go down into the heart of the forest." But Gilgamesh had good news for his comrade: while the latter was recovering from the shock, he—Gilgamesh—had found a tunnel. By the sounds heard from it, Gilgamesh was sure that it was connected to "the enclosure from which words of command are issued." Come on, he urged Enkidu; "do not stand by, my friend; let us go down together!"

Gilgamesh must have been right, for the Sumerian text states that

> Pressing on into the forest,
>   the secret abode of the *Anunnaki*
> he opened up.

The entrance to the tunnel was grown over with (or hidden by) trees and bushes and blocked by soil and rocks. "While Gilgamesh cut down the trees, Enkidu dug up" the soil and rocks. But just as they made enough of a clearance, terror struck: "Huwawa heard the noise, and became angry." Now he appeared on the scene looking for the intruders. His appearance was "Mighty, his teeth as the teeth of a dragon; his face the face of a lion; his coming like the onrushing floodwaters." Most fearsome was his "radiant beam." Emanating from his forehead, "it devoured trees and bushes." From its killing force, "none could escape." A Sumerian cylinder seal depicted a god, Gilgamesh and Enkidu flanking a mechanical robot, no doubt the epic's "Monster with the Killing Beams" (Fig. 65).

It appears from the fragmented texts that Huwawa could armor himself with "seven cloaks," but when he arrived on the scene "only one he had donned, six are still off." Seeing this as their opportunity, the two comrades attempted to ambush Huwawa. As the monster turned to face his attackers, the Killing Beam from his forehead traced a path of destruction.

In the nick of time, rescue appeared from the heavens. Seeing their predicament, "down from the skies spoke to them divine Shamash." Do not try to escape, he advised them; instead, "draw near Huwawa." Then Shamash raised a host of swirling winds, "which beat against the eyes of Huwawa" and neutralized his beam. As Shamash had intended, "the radiant beams vanished, the brilliance became clouded." Soon, Huwawa was immobilized: "he is unable to move forward, nor is he able to move back." The two then attacked Huwawa: "Enkidu struck the guardian, Huwawa, to the ground. For two leagues the cedars resounded," so immense was the monster's fall. Then Enkidu "Huwawa put to death."

Exhilarated by their victory but exhausted by the battle, the two stopped to rest by a stream. Gilgamesh undressed to wash himself. "He cast off his soiled things, put on his clean ones; wrapped a fringed cloak about him, fastened with a sash." There was no need to rush: the way to the "secret abode of the Anunnaki" was no longer blocked.

Little did he know that a female's lust would soon undo his victory. . . .

The place, as stated earlier in the epic, was the "Crossroads of Ishtar." The goddess herself was wont to come and go from this "Landing Place." She too, like Shamash, must have watched the battle—perhaps from her aerial ("winged") Sky Chamber, as depicted on a Hittite seal (Fig. 66). Now, having seen Gilgamesh undress and bathe, "glorious Ishtar raised an eye at the beauty of Gilgamesh."

Approaching the hero, she minced no words about what was on her mind:

> Come, Gilgamesh, be thou my lover!
> Grant me the fruit of thy love.
> You be my man,
> I shall be your woman!

Promising him golden chariots, a magnificent palace, lordship over other kings and princes, Ishtar was sure she had enticed Gilgamesh. But answering her, he pointed out that he had nothing he could give her, a goddess, in return. And as to her "love," how long would that last? Sooner or later, he said, she would rid herself of him as of "a shoe which pinches

Fig. 65

Fig. 66

the foot of its owner." Calling off the names of other men with whom she had been promiscuous, he turned her down. Enraged by this insulting refusal, Ishtar asked Anu to let the "Bull of Heaven" smite Gilgamesh.

Attacked by the Sky Monster, Gilgamesh and Enkidu forgot all about their mission, and ran for their lives. Aiding their escape back to Uruk, Shamash enabled them "the distance of a month and fifteen days, in three days to traverse." But on the outskirst of Uruk, on the Euphrates River, the Bull of Heaven caught up with them. Gilgamesh managed to reach the city, to summon its warriors. Outside the city walls, Enkidu alone remained to hold off the Sky Monster. When the Bull of Heaven "snorted," pits were opened in the earth, large enough to hold two hundred men each. As Enkidu fell into one of the pits, the Bull of Heaven turned around. Quickly Enkidu climbed out, and put the monster to death.

What exactly the Bull of Heaven was, is not clear. The Sumerian term— GUD.AN.NA—could also mean "Anu's attacker," his "cruise missile." Ancient artists, fascinated by the episode, frequently depicted Gilgamesh or Enkidu fighting with an actual bull, with the naked Ishtar (and sometimes Adad) looking on (Fig. 67a). But from the Epic's text it is clear that this weapon of Anu was a mechanical contraption made of metal and equipped with two piercers (the "horns") which were "cast from thirty minas of lapis, the coating on each being two fingers thick." Some ancient depictions show such a mechanical "bull," sweeping down from the skies (Fig. 67b).

After the Bull of Heaven was defeated, Gilgamesh "called out to the craftsmen, the armorers, all of them" to view the mechanical monster and

Fig. 67   b

take it apart. Then, triumphant, he and Enkidu went to pay homage to Shamash.

But "Ishtar, in her abode, set up a wail."

In the palace, Gilgamesh and Enkidu were resting from nightlong celebrations. But at the Abode of the Gods, the supreme gods were considering Ishtar's complaint. "And Anu said to Enlil: 'Because the Bull of Heaven they have slain, and Huwawa they have slain, the two of them must die.' But Enlil said: 'Enkidu shall die, let Gilgamesh not die.'" Then Shamash interceded: it was done with his concurrence; why then should "innocent Enkidu die?"

While the gods deliberated, Enkidu was afflicted with a coma. Distraught and worried, Gilgamesh "paced back and forth before the couch" on which Enkidu lay motionless. Bitter tears flowed down his cheeks. As sorry as he was for his comrade, his thoughts turned to his own permeating anxiety: will he too lie one day dying like Enkidu? Will he, after all the endeavors, end up dead as a mortal?

In their assembly, the gods reached a compromise. The death sentence of Enkidu was commuted to hard labor in the depths of the mines—there to spend the rest of his days. To carry out the sentence and take him to his new home, Enkidu was told, two emissaries "clothed like birds, with wings for garments" shall appear unto him. One of them, "a young man whose face is dark, who like a Bird-Man is his face," shall transport him to the Land of the Mines:

> He will be dressed like an Eagle;
> By the arm he will lead thee.
> "Follow me," (he will say); he will lead you
> To the House of Darkness,
>   the abode below the ground;
> The abode which none leave who have entered into it.
> A road from which there is no return;

A House whose dwellers are bereft of light,
where dust is in their mouths
and clay is their food.

An ancient depiction on a cylinder seal illustrated the scene, showing a Winged Emissary ("angel") leading Enkidu by the arm (Fig. 68).

Hearing the sentence passed on his comrade, Gilgamesh had an idea. Not far from the Land of Mines, he had learned, was the *Land of the Living*: the place whereto the gods had taken those humans who were granted eternal youth!

It was "the abode of the forefathers who by the great gods with the Purifying Waters were anointed." There, partaking of the food and beverage of the gods, have been residing

Princes born to the crown
who had ruled the land in days of yore;
Like Anu and Enlil, spiced meats they are served,
From waterskins, cool water to them is poured.

Was it not the place whereto the hero of the Deluge, Ziusudra/Utnapishtim, had been taken—the very place from which Etana "to heaven ascended"?

Fig. 68

And so it was, that "the lord Gilgamesh, toward the Land of the Living set his mind." Announcing to the revived Enkidu that he would accompany him at least on part of his journey, Gilgamesh explained:

O Enkidu,
Even the mighty wither, meet the fated end.
(Therefore) the Land I would enter,
I would set up my *Shem*.
In the place where the *Shems* have been raised up,
I a *Shem* I would raise up.

However, proceeding from the Land of Mines to the Land of the Living was not a matter for a mortal to decide. In the strongest possible words,

Gilgamesh was advised by the elders of Uruk and his goddess mother to first obtain the permission of Utu/Shamash:

> If the Land thou wish to enter,
>   inform Utu, inform Utu, the hero Utu!
> The Land, it is in Utu's charge;
> The Land which with the cedars is aligned,
>   it is the hero Utu's charge.
> Inform Utu!

Thus forewarned and advised, Gilgamesh offered a sacrifice to Utu, and appealed for his consent and protection:

> O Utu,
> The Land I wish to enter;
>   be thou my ally!
> The Land which with the cool cedars is aligned
> I wish to enter; be thou my ally!
> In the places where the *Shems* have been raised up,
> Let me set up my *Shem*!

At first, Utu/Shamash doubted whether Gilgamesh could qualify to enter the land. Then, yielding to more pleading and prayers, he warned him that his journey would be through a desolate and arid area: "the dust of the crossroads shall be thy dwelling place, the desert shall be thy bed . . . thorn and bramble shall skin thy feet . . . thirst shall smite thy cheeks." Unable to dissuade Gilgamesh, he told him that the "place where the *Shems* have been raised" is surrounded by seven mountains, and the passes guarded by fearsome "Mighty Ones" who can unleash "a scorching fire" or "a lightning which cannot be turned back." But in the end, Utu gave in: "the tears of Gilgamesh he accepted as an offering; like one of mercy, he showed him mercy."

But "the lord Gilgamesh acted frivolously." Rather than take the harsh overland road, he planned to cover most of the route by a comfortable sea voyage; after landing at the distant destination, Enkidu would go to the Land of Mines, and he (Gilgamesh) would proceed to the Land of the Living. He selected fifty young, unattached men to accompany him and Enkidu, and be rowers of the boat. Their first task was to cut and haul back to Uruk special woods, from which the MA.GAN boat—a "ship of Egypt"— was built. The smiths of Uruk fashioned strong weapons. Then, when all was ready, they sailed away.

They sailed, by all accounts, down the Persian Gulf, planning no doubt to circumnavigate the Arabian peninsula and then sail up the Red Sea toward Egypt. But the wrath of Enlil was swift to come. Had not Enkidu been told that a young "angel" would take him by the arm and bring him to the Land of Mines? How come, then, he was sailing with the joyful Gilgamesh, with fifty armed men, in a royal ship?

At dusk, Utu—who may have seen them off with great misgivings—"with lifted head went away." The mountains along the distant coast "became dark, shadows spread over them." Then, "standing alongside the mountain," there was someone who—like Huwawa—could emit rays "from which none can escape." "Like a bull he stood on the great Earth house"—a watchtower, it seems. The fearsome watchman must have challenged the ship and its passengers, for fear overcame Enkidu. Let us turn back to Uruk, he pleaded. But Gilgamesh would not hear of it. Instead, he directed the ship toward the shore, determined to fight the watchman—"that 'man,' if a man he be, or if a god he be."

It was then that calamity struck. The "three ply cloth"—the sail—tore apart. As if by an unseen hand, the boat capsized; and all in it sank down. Somehow, Gilgamesh managed to swim ashore; so did Enkidu. Back in the waters, they saw the sunken ship with its crew still at their posts, looking amazingly alive in their deaths:

> After it had sunk, in the sea had sunk,
> On the eve when the *Magan*-boat had sunk,
> After the boat, destined to *Magan*, had sunk—
> Inside it, as though still living creatures,
>   were seated those who of a womb were born.

They spent the night on the unknown shore, arguing which way to go. Gilgamesh was still determined to reach "the land." Enkidu advised seeking a way back to "the city," Uruk. Soon, however, weakness overcame Enkidu. With passionate comradeship, Gilgamesh exhorted Enkidu to hold on to life: "My little weak friend," he fondly called him; "to the land I will bring thee," he promised him. But "Death, which knows no distinction," could not be held off.

For seven days and seven nights Gilgamesh mourned Enkidu, "until a worm fell out of his nose." At first he wandered aimlessly: "For his friend, Enkidu, Gilgamesh weeps bitterly as he ranges over the wilderness . . . with woe in his belly, fearing death, he roamed the wilderness." Again he was preoccupied with his own fate—"fearing death"—wondering: "When I die, shall I not be like Enkidu?"

Then his determination to ward off his fate took hold of him again. "Must I lay my head inside the earth, and sleep through all the years?" he demanded to know of Shamash. "Let mine eyes behold the sun, let me have my fill of light!" he begged of the god. Setting his course by the rising and setting Sun, "To the Wild Cow, to Utnapishtim the son of Ubar-Tutu, he took the road." He trod unbeaten paths, encountering no man, hunting for food. "What mountains he had climbed, what streams he had crossed—no man can know," the ancient scribes sadly noted.

At long last, as versions found at Nineveh and at Hittite sites relate, he neared habitations. He was coming to a region dedicated to *Sin*, the father of Shamash. "When he arrived at night at a mountain pass, Gilgamesh saw lions and grew afraid:"

> He lifted his head to Sin and prayed:
> "To the place where the gods rejuvenate,
>   my steps are directed . . .
> Preserve thou me!"

"As at night he lay, he awoke from a dream" which he interpreted as an omen from Sin, that he would "rejoice in Life." Encouraged, Gilgamesh "like an arrow descended amoung the lions." His battle with the lions has been commemorated pictorially not only in Mesopotamia, but throughout the ancient lands, even in Egypt (Fig. 69a, b, c).

After daybreak, Gilgamesh traversed a mountain pass. In the distance below, he saw a body of water, like a vast lake, "driven by long winds." In the plain adjoining the inland sea he could see a city "closed-up about"—a city surrounded by a wall. There, "the temple to Sin was dedicated."

Outside the city, "close by the low-lying sea," Gilgamesh saw an inn. As

a

b

c

Fig. 69

he approached, he saw the "Ale-woman, Siduri." She was holding "a jug (of ale), a bowl of golden porridge." But as she saw Gilgamesh, she was frightened by his appearance: "He is clad in skins . . . his belly is shrunk . . . his face is like a wayfarer from afar." Understandably, "as the ale-woman saw him, she locked the door, she barred the gate." With great effort, Gilgamesh convinced her of his true identity and good intentions, telling her of his adventures and quest.

After Siduri let him rest, eat and drink, Gilgamesh was eager to continue. What is the best way to the Land of Living? he asked Siduri. Must he circle the sea and wind his way through the desolate mountains—or could he take a shortcut across the body of water?

> Now ale-woman, which is the way . . .
> What are its markers?
> Give me, O give me its markers!
> Suitably, by the sea I will go across;
> Otherwise, by the wilderness my course will be.

The choice, it turned out, was not that simple; for the sea he saw was the "Sea of Death":

> The ale-woman said to him, to Gilgamesh:
> "The sea, Gilgamesh, it is impossible to cross
> From days of long ago,
>   no one arrived from across the sea.
> Valiant Shamash did cross the sea,
>   but other than Shamash, who can cross it?
> Toilsome is the crossing,
>   desolate is its way;
> Barren are the Waters of Death
>   which it encloses
> How then, Gilgamesh, wouldst thou cross the sea?

As Gilgamesh remained silent, Siduri spoke up again, revealing to him that there might be, after all, a way to cross the Sea of the Waters of Death:

> Gilgamesh,
> There is *Urshanabi*, boatman of Utnapishtim.
> With him are things that float,
>   in the woods he picks the things that bind together.
> Go, let he thy face behold.
> If it be suitable, with thee he shall cross;
> If it be not suitable, draw thou back.

Following her directions, Gilgamesh found Urshanabi the boatman. After much questioning as to who he was, how he had come hither, and where he was going, he was found worthy of the boatman's services. Using long poles, they moved the raft forward. In three days, "a run of a month and fifteen days"—a forty-five day journey overland—"they left behind."

He arrived at TIL.MUN—"The Land of the Living."

Whereto shall he go now? Gilgamesh wondered. You have to reach a mountain, Urshanabi answered; "the name of the mountain is *Mashu*."

The instructions given by Urshanabi are available to us from the Hittite version of the Epic, fragments of which were found in Boghazkoy and other Hittite sites. From those fragments (as put together by Johannes Friedrich: *Die hethitischen Bruchstükes des Gilgamesh-Epos*), we learn that Gilgamesh was told to reach and follow "a regular way" which leads toward "the Great Sea, which is far away." He was to look for two stone columns or "markers" which, Urshanabi vouched, "to the destination always bring me." There he had to turn and reach a town named *Itla*, sacred to the god whom the Hittites called *Ullu-Yah* ("He of the Peaks"?). He had to obtain that god's blessing before he could go farther.

Following the directions, Gilgamesh did arrive at Itla. In the distance, the Great Sea could apparently be seen. There, Gilgamesh ate and drank, washed and made himself once again presentable as befits a king. There, Shamash once again came to his aid, advising him to make offerings to Ulluyah. Taking Gilgamesh before the Great God (Fig. 70), he urged Ulluyah: Accept his offerings, "grant him life." But Kumarbi, another god well known from Hittite tales, strongly objected: Immortality cannot be granted to Gilgamesh, he said.

Realizing, it appears, that he would not be granted a *Shem*, Gilgamesh settled for second-best: Could he, at least, meet his forefather Utnapishtim? As the gods delayed their decision, Gilgamesh (with the connivance of Shamash?) left town and started to advance toward Mount *Mashu*, stopping each day to offer sacrifices to Ulluyah. After six days, he came unto the Mount; it was indeed the Place of the *Shems*:

> The name of the Mountain is *Mashu*.
> At the mountain of *Mashu* he arrived;

Fig. 70

> Where daily the *Shems* he watched
> As they depart and come in.

The Mount's functions required it to be connected both to the distant heavens and to the far reaches of Earth:

> On high, to the Celestial Band
>   it is connected;
> Below,
>   to the Lower World it is bound.

There was a way to go inside the Mount; but the entrance, the "gate," was closely guarded:

> Rocket-men guard its gate.
> Their terror is awesome, their glance is death.
> Their dreaded spotlight sweeps the mountains.
> They watch over Shamash
>   as he ascends and descends.

(Depictions have been found showing winged beings or divine bull-men operating a circular beaming device mounted on a post; they could well be ancient illustrations of the "dreaded spotlight that sweeps the mountains"— Fig. 71a, b, c.)

a

b

c

Fig. 71

"When Gilgamesh beheld the terrible glowing, his face he shielded; regaining his composure, he approached them." When the Rocketman saw that the dreaded ray affected Gilgamesh only momentarily, he shouted to his partner: "He who comes, of the flesh of the gods is his body!" The rays, it appears, could stun or kill humans—but were harmless to the gods.

Allowed to approach, Gilgamesh was asked to identify himself and account for his presence in the restricted area. Describing his partly divine origins, he explained that he had come "in search of Life." He wished, he said, to meet his forefather Utnapishtim:

> On account of Utnapishtim, my forefather,
>> have I come—
> He who the congregation of the gods had joined.
> About Death and Life I wish to ask him.

"Never was this achieved by a mortal," the two guards said. Undaunted, Gilgamesh invoked Shamash and explained that he was two-thirds god. What happened next is unknown, due to breaks in the tablet; but at last the Rocketmen informed Gilgamesh that permission was granted: "The gate of the Mount is open to thee!"

(The "Gateway to Heaven" was a frequent motif on Near Eastern cylinder seals, depicting it as a winged, ladder-like gateway leading to the Tree of Life. It was sometimes guarded by Serpents—Fig. 72).

Gilgamesh went in, following the "path taken by Shamash." His journey lasted twelve *beru* (double-hours); through most of it "he could see nothing ahead or behind"; perhaps he was blindfolded, for the text stresses that *"for him,* light there was none." In the eighth double-hour, he screamed with fear; in the ninth, "he felt a north wind fanning his face." "When eleven *beru* he attained, dawn was breaking." Finally, at the end of the twelfth double-hour, "in brightness he resided."

He could see again, and what he saw was astounding. He saw "an enclosure as of the gods," wherein there "grew" a garden made up entirely of precious stones! The magnificence of the place comes through the mutilated ancient lines:

> As its fruit it carries carnelians,
>> its vines too beautiful to behold.
> The foliage is of lapis-lazuli;
> And grapes, too lush to look at,
>> of . . . stones are made . . .
> Its . . . of white stones . . .
> In its waters, pure reeds . . . of *sasu*-stones;
> Like a Tree of Life and a Tree of . . .
>> that of *An-Gug* stones are made . . .

On and on the description went. Thrilled and amazed, Gilgamesh walked about the garden. He was clearly in a *simulated* "Garden of Eden!"

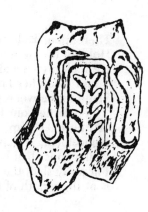

Fig. 72

What happened next is still unknown, for an entire column of the ninth tablet is too mutilated to be legible. Either in the artificial garden, or somewhere else, Gilgamesh finally encountered Utnapishtim. His first reaction on seeing a man from "days of yore" was to observe how much they looked alike:

> Gilgamesh said to him,
>   to Utnapishtim "The Far-away":
> "As I look upon thee, Utnapishtim,
> Thou are not different at all;
>   even as I art thou . . ."

Then Gilgamesh came straight to the point:

> Tell me,
>   How joinest thou the congregation of the gods
>   in thy quest for Life?

In answer to this question, Utnapishtim said to Gilgamesh: "I will reveal to thee, Gilgamesh, a hidden matter; a secret of the gods I will tell thee." The secret was the *Tale of the Deluge:* How when he, Utnapishtim, was the

ruler of Shuruppak and the gods resolved to let the Deluge annihilate
Mankind, Enki secretly instructed him to build a special submersible
vessel, and take aboard his family "and the seed of all living things." A
navigator provided by Enki directed the vessel to Mount Ararat. As the
waters began to subside, he left the vessel to offer sacrifices. The gods and
goddesses—who circled Earth in their spacecraft while it was inundated—
also landed on Mount Ararat, savoring the roasting meat. Finally, Enlil too
landed, and broke into a rage when he realized that in spite of the oath
taken by all the gods, Enki enabled Mankind to survive.

But when his anger subsided, Enlil saw the merit of such survival; it was
then, Utnapishtim continued to recount, that Enlil granted him everlasting
life:

> Thereupon, Enlil went aboard the ship.
> Holding me by the hand, he took me aboard.
> He took my wife aboard,
>   and made her kneel by my side.
> Standing between us,
>   he touched our foreheads to bless us:
> "Hitherto, Utnapishtim has been human;
> Henceforth, Utnapishtim and his wife
>   like gods shall be unto us.
> Far away shall the man Utnapishtim reside,
>   at the mouth of the water-streams."

And so it came to pass, Utnapishtim concluded, that he was taken to the
Faraway Abode, to live among the gods. But how could this be achieved for
Gilgamesh? "But now, who will for thy sake call the gods to Assembly, that
the Life which thou seekest thou mayest find?"

On hearing the tale, and realizing that it is only the gods, in assembly,
who can decree eternal life and that he, on his own, could not attain it—
Gilgamesh fainted. For six days and seven nights he was totally knocked
out. Sarcastically, Utnapishtim said to his wife: "Behold this hero who seeks
Life; from mere sleep as mist he dissolves!" Throughout his sleep, they
attended to Gilgamesh, to keep him alive, "that he may return safe on the
way by which he came, that through the gate by which he entered he may
return to his land."

Urshanabi the boatman was called to take Gilgamesh back. But at the last
moment, when Gilgamesh was ready to leave, Utnapishtim disclosed to
Gilgamesh yet another secret. Though he could not avoid death, he told
him, there was a way to postpone it. He could do this by obtaining the
secret plant which the gods themselves eat, to keep *Forever Young!*

> Utnapishtim said to him, to Gilgamesh:
> "Thou hast come hither, toiling and straining.
> What shall I give thee,

that thou mayest return to thy land?
I will disclose, O Gilgamesh, a hidden thing;
A secret of the gods I will tell thee:
A plant there is,
    like a prickly berrybush is its root.
Its thorns are like a brier vine's,
    thine hands they will prick.
If thine hands obtain the plant,
New Life thou wilt find."

The plant, we learn from what followed, grew underwater:

No sooner had Gilgamesh heard this,
    than he opened the water-pipe.
He tied heavy stones to his feet;
They pulled him down into the deep;
He saw then the plant.
He took the plant, though it pricked his hands.
He cut the heavy stones from his feet;
The second cast him back where he came from.

Going back with Urshanabi, Gilgamesh triumphantly said to him:

Urshanabi,
This plant is of all plants unique:
By it a man can regain his full vigor!
I will take it to ramparted Uruk,
    there the plant to cut and eat.
Let its name be called
"Man Becomes Young in Old Age!"
Of this plant I shall eat,
    and to my youthful state shall I return.

A Sumerian cylinder seal, from circa 1700 B.C., which illustrated scenes from the epic tale, shows (at left) a half-naked and unkempt Gilgamesh battling the two lions; on the right, Gilgamesh holds up to Urshanabi the plant of everlasting youth. A god, in the center, holds an unusual spiral tool or weapon (Fig. 73).

But Fate, as with all those who in the millennia and centuries that followed went in the search of the Plant of Youth, intervened.

As Gilgamesh and Urshanabi "prepared for the night, Gilgamesh saw a well whose water was cool. He went down to it to bathe in the water." Then calamity struck: "A snake sniffed the fragrance of the plant. It came and carried off the plant. . . ."

Thereupon Gilgamesh sits down and weeps,
    his tears running down his face.

He took the hand of Urshanabi, the boatman.
"For whom," (he asked) "have my hands toiled?
For whom is spent the blood of my heart?
For myself, I have not obtained the boon;
   for a serpent a boon I affected. . . ."

Yet another Sumerian seal illustrates the epic's tragic end: the winged gateway in the background, the boat navigated by Urshanabi, and Gilgamesh struggling with the serpent. Not having found Immortality, he is now pursued by the Angel of Death (Fig. 74).

And so it was, that for generations thereafter, scribes copied and translated, poets recited, and storytellers related, the tale of the first futile Search for Immortality, the epic tale of Gilgamesh.

  This is how it began:

Let me make known to the country
Him who the Tunnel has seen;
Of him who knows the seas,
   let me the full story tell.
He has visited the . . . (?) as well,
The hidden from wisdom, all things . . .
Secret things he has seen,
   what is hidden from man he found out.

Fig. 73

Fig. 74

He even brought tidings
   of the time before the Deluge.
He also took the distant journey,
   wearisome and under difficulties.
He returned, and upon a stone column
   all his toil he engraved.

And this, according to the Sumerian King Lists, is how it all ended:

The divine Gilgamesh, whose father was a human, a high priest of the temple precinct, ruled 126 years. Ur-lugal, son of Gilgamesh, ruled after him.

VIII

Riders of the Clouds

The journey of Gilgamesh in search of Immortality has undoubtedly been the fountainhead of the many tales, in subsequent millennia, of demi-gods or heroes claiming such a status, who have likewise gone to search for paradise on Earth or to reach the Celestial Abode of the Gods. Without question, the detailed Epic of Gilgamesh also served as a guide book in which the subsequent searchers sought to find the ancient landmarks by which the Land of the Living could be reached and the way to it ascertained.

The similarities between the geographic landmarks; the man-made (or rather the god-made) tunnels, corridors, air locks and radiation chambers; and the bird-like beings, or "Eagles," as well as many other major and minor details—are far too numerous and identical to be mere accidents. At the same time, the epic tale of the journey can explain the confusion that reigned millenia later concerning the exact location of the cherished target; because as our detailed analysis has shown, Gilgamesh made not one but two journeys—a fact generally ignored by modern scholars and possibly also by past ones.

The Gilgamesh drama reached its culmination in the Land of *Tilmun*, an Abode of the Gods and a place of the *Shems*. It was there that he encountered an ancestor who had escaped mortality, and had found the secret plant of eternal youth. It was there that other divine encounters, as well as events affecting the course of human history, occurred in later millennia. It was there, we believe, that the *Duat* was—the Stairway to Heaven.

But that was not the first destination of Gilgamesh, and we ought to follow in his footsteps in the same sequence by which he himself had embarked on his journey: his first destination on the road to Immortality was not Tilmun, but the "Landing Place" on the Cedar Mountain, within the great Cedar Forest.

Scholars (e.g. S. N. Kramer, *The Sumerians*) have termed as "cryptic and still enigmatic" Sumerian statements that Shamash could "rise" in the "Cedar Land," and not only in Tilmun. The answer is that apart from the Spaceport at Tilmun, from which the farthest heavens could be reached, there was also a "Landing Place" from which the gods "could scale the skies" of Earth. This realization is supported by our conclusion, that the gods indeed had two types of craft: the GIRs, the Rocketships that were operated from Tilmun; and what the Sumerians called a MU, a "Sky Chamber." It is a credit to the technology of the Nefilim that the uppermost section of the GIR, the Command Module—what the Egyptians called *Ben-Ben*—could be detached and fly in Earth's skies as a MU.

The ancient peoples had seen the GIRs in their silos (Fig. 27) or even in flight (Fig. 75). But they depicted more frequently the "Sky Chambers"— vehicles which we would nowadays classify as UFOs (Unidentified Flying Objects). The one the patriarch Jacob had seen in his vision might well have looked like the Sky Chamber of Ishtar (Fig. 66); the Flying Wheel described by the prophet Ezekiel was akin to the Assyrian depictions of their Flying God roaming the skies, at cloud level, within a spherical Sky Chamber (Fig. 76a). Depictions found at an ancient site across the Jordan from Jericho, suggest that for landing these spherical vehicles extended three legs (Fig. 76b); they could well have been the fiery Whirlwinds in which the prophet Elijah was carried off heavenwards at that very same location.

Fig. 75

a

b

Fig. 76

As the Sumerian "Eagles," so were the Flying Gods of antiquity depicted by all ancient peoples as gods equipped with wings—the Winged Beings to whose depictions we can trace the Judeo-Christian acceptance of the winged *Cherubim* and Angels (literally: Emissaries) of the Lord (Fig. 77).

Tilmun, then, was the location of the Spaceport. The Cedar Mountain was the location of the "Landing Place," the "Crossroads of Ishtar,"—the Airport of the Gods. And it was to the latter that Gilgamesh had first set his course.

While the identification of Tilmun and its location is no mean challenge, there is little problem in locating the Cedar Forest. With the exception of subsidiary growths on the island of Cyprus, there is only one such location throughout the Near East: the mountains of Lebanon. These majestic cedar trees, which can reach 150 feet in height, were repeatedly extolled in the Bible and their uniqueness was known to the ancient peoples from the earliest times. As the biblical and other Near Eastern texts attest, the Cedars of Lebanon were earmarked for the construction and decoration of temples ("gods' houses")—a practice described in detail in I Kings, in the chapters dealing with the building of the Jerusalem Temple by Solomon (after the Lord Yahweh had complained "Why build ye not me a House of cedar?").

The biblical Lord appears to have been quite familiar with the cedars, and frequently employed them in his allegories, comparing rulers or nations to cedars: "Assyria was a cedar in Lebanon, with fair branches and a shadowing shroud and of high stature . . . waters nourished it, subterranean streams gave it height"—until the wrath of Yahweh toppled it and smashed its branches. Man, it appears, had never been able to cultivate these cedars; and the Bible records an attempt that had completely failed. Attributing the attempt to the king of Babylon (factually or allegorically), it is stated that "He came to Lebanon and took the cedar's highest branch," selecting off it a choice seed. This seed "he planted in a fruitful field, he placed it by great waters." But what grew up was not a tall cedar—only a willow-like tree, "a spreading vine of low stature."

The biblical Lord, on the other hand, knew the secret of cedar cultivation:

Thus sayeth the Lord Yahweh:
"From the cedar's crest, from its topmost branches a tender shoot I will take; and I will plant it upon a high and steep mountain . . .
And it will put forth branches, and bear fruit, and become a mighty cedar."

This knowledge apparently stemmed from the fact that the cedar grew in the "Orchard of the gods." There, no other tree could match it; "it was the envy of all the trees that were in Eden, the garden of the gods." The Hebrew term *Gan* (orchard, garden), stemming as it does from the root *gnn*

Fig. 77

(protect, guard), conveys the sense of a guarded and restricted area—the same sense as is imparted to the reader of the Gilgamesh narrative: a forest that extends "for many leagues," watched over by a Fiery Warrior ("a terror to mortals"), accessible only through a gateway which paralyzed the intruder who touched it. Inside, there was "the secret abode of the Anunnaki"; a tunnel led to "the enclosure from which words of command are issued"—"the underground place of Shamash."

Gilgamesh almost made it to the Landing Place, for he had the permission and help of Shamash. But the wrath of Ishtar (when he turned down her advances) completely reversed the course of events. Not so, according to the Old Testament, was the fate of another mortal king. He was the king of Tyre—a city-state on the coast of Lebanon, a short distance away from the cedar mountains; and the Deity (as told in chapter 28 of the Book of Ezekiel) did enable him to visit the Sacred Mountain:

> Thou hast been in Eden, the Garden of God; every precious stone was thy thicket . . .
> Thou art an annointed Cherub, protected; and I have placed thee in the Sacred Mountain.
> As a god werest thou, moving within the Fiery Stones.

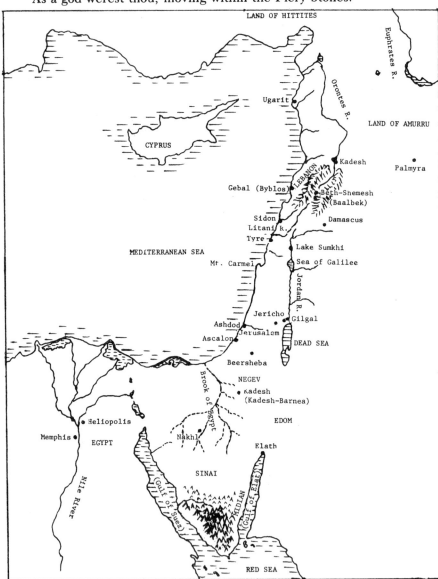

Fig. 78

Gilgamesh sought to enter the Landing Place of the gods uninvited; the king of Tyre not only was permitted to come to the place, but evidently was also given a ride in "the fiery stones," flying as a Cherub. As a result, "a god I am," he said; "in the Abode of the Deity I sat, in the midst of the waters." For his haughtiness of heart, the prophet was to inform him, he was to die the death of a heathen by the hands of strangers.

Both the Hebrews of biblical times, and their neighbors to the north, were thus acquainted with the location and nature of the Landing Place in the Cedar Mountain which Gilgamesh attempted to penetrate in a previous millennium. It was, as we shall show, not a "mythological" place, but a real one: not only texts, but also pictorial depictions exist from those ancient days, attesting to the existence and functions of the place.

In the tale of the king who tried to grow a cedar, the Old Testament reports that he "carried off the twig to a land of commerce," and planted the seed "in a city of merchants." Such a land and such cities-of-merchants need not have been looked-for far: along the coast of Lebanon, from where Anatolia begins in the north to Palestine in the south, there were several Canaanite coastal cities whose wealth and power grew with their international commerce. Best known from biblical narratives were Tyre and Sidon; centers of trade and shipping for millennia, their fame reached its peak under their Phoenician rulers.

In ruins and buried under a mount since its destruction by Assyrian invaders lay yet another city, perhaps the northernmost outpost of the Canaanites at the borders of the Hittite empire. Its remains were accidentally uncovered in 1928 by a farmer who set out to plough a new field near the mount called Ras Shamra. The extensive excavations that followed uncovered the ancient city of *Ugarit*. The spectacular finds included a large palace, a temple to the god *Ba'al* ("The Lord"), and a variety of artifacts. But the real treasures were scores of clay tablets inscribed in an alphabetic cuneiform script (Fig. 79), written in a "Western-Semitic" language akin to biblical Hebrew. The tablets, whose contents were first presented by Charles Virollaud over many years in the scientific periodical *Syria*, retrieved from relative obscurity the Canaanites, their life and customs, and their gods.

At the head of the Canaanite pantheon was a supreme deity called *El*—a term which in biblical Hebrew was the generic term for "deity," stemming as it did from the Akkadian word *Ilu*, which literally meant "Lofty One." But in the Canaanite tales of gods and men, *El* was the personal name of an actual deity, who was the final authority in all affairs be they divine or human. He was father of the gods, as well as *Ab Adam* ("father of men"); his epithets were The Kindly, The Merciful. He was "creator of things created" and the "one who alone could bestow kingship." A stela found in Palestine (Fig. 80) depicts El seated on his throne and being served a beverage by a younger deity, probably one of his many sons. El wears the conical, horned headdress which was the recognition mark of the gods throughout the

Fig. 79

Fig. 80

ancient Near East; and the scene is dominated by the omnipresent Winged Globe, emblem of the Planet of the Gods.

In "olden times," El was a principal deity of Heaven and Earth. But at the time at which the events related in the tablets had taken place, El lived in semi-retirement, aloof from daily affairs. His abode was "in the mountains," at "the two headwaters." There he sat in his pavilion, receiving emissaries, holding councils of the gods, and trying to resolve the recurring disputes among the younger gods. Many of these were his own children: some texts suggest that El may have had seventy offspring. Of them, thirty were by his official consort Asherah (Fig. 81); the others, by an assortment of concubines or even by human females. One poetic text tells how two females saw El naked as they were strolling on the beach; they were completely charmed by the size of his penis, and ended up each bearing him a son. (This attribute of El is prominent in a depiction of him, as a winged god, on a Phoenician coin—Fig. 82).

El's principal children, however, were three sons and one daughter: the gods *Yam* ("Ocean, Sea"), *Ba'al* ("Lord") and *Mot* ("Smiter, Annihilator") and the goddess *Anat* ("She Who Responded"). In names and relationships

Fig. 81

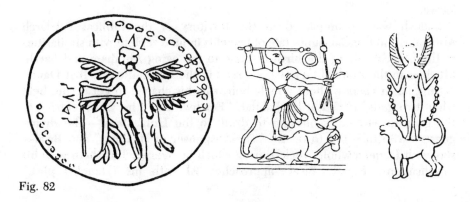

Fig. 82

they clearly paralleled the Greek gods Poseidon (God of the Seas), Zeus (Lord of the Gods) and Hades (God of the Lower World). Ba'al, as Zeus, was always armed with a lightning-missile (Fig. 82), the bull his cult symbol. When Zeus fought Typhon, it was his sister Athena, goddess of War and Love, who alone stood by him; and in Egyptian tales, Isis alone stood by her brother-husband Osiris. So it was when Ba'al fought his two brothers: his sister-lover Anat alone came to his help. Like Athena, she was on the one hand "The Maiden," often flaunting her naked beauty (Fig. 82); and on the other hand the Goddess of War, the lion a symbol of her bravery (Fig. 83). (The Old Testament called her *Ashtoreth*.)

The links to Egyptian prehistorical recollections and beliefs were no less obvious than to those of Greece. Osiris was resurrected by Isis after she had found his remains at the Canaanite city of Byblos. Likewise, Ba'al was brought back to life by Anat after he was smitten by Mot. Seth, the adversary of Osiris, was sometimes called in Egyptian writings "Seth of *Saphon*"; Ba'al, as we shall see, acquired the title "Lord of *Zaphon*." Egyptian monuments of the New Kingdom—paralleling the Canaanite period—often depicted the Canaanite gods as Egyptian deities, calling them Min, Reshef, Kadesh, Anthat (Fig. 84). We thus find the same tales applying to the same gods, but under different names, throughout the ancient world.

Scholars have pointed out that all these tales were echoes, if not actual versions, of the much earlier and original Sumerian tales: not only of Man's Search for Immortality, but also of love, death and resurrection among the gods. All along, the tales are replete with episodes, details, epithets, and teachings which also fill the Old Testament—attesting to a common locale (greater Canaan), common traditions and common original versions.

One such text is the tale of *Danel* (Dan-El—"El's judge"—*Daniel* in Hebrew), a righteous chieftain who could not beget a rightful heir. He appealed to the gods to give him one, so that when he died, the son could erect a stela in his memory at *Kadesh*. From this we surmise that the area of the tale's events was where southern Canaan (the *Negev*) merges into the Sinai peninsula, for it was there that Kadesh ("The Sacred" city) was located.

Kadesh was encompassed in the territory of the biblical Patriarch Abraham; and the Canaanite tale of Danel is indeed replete with similarities to the biblical tale of the birth of Isaac to the aging Abraham and Sarah. Much as in the Book of Genesis, we read in the Canaanite tale that Danel, getting on in years without a male heir, saw his chance to get divine help when two gods arrived at his habitat. "Forthwith . . . he gives offering to the gods to eat, gives offering to drink to the Holy Ones." The divine guests—who turn out to be El, "The Dispenser of Healing," and Ba'al—stay with Danel a whole week, during which he overwhelms them with his supplications. Finally Ba'al "approaches El with his (Danel's) plea."

Fig. 83

Fig. 84

Yielding, El "by the hand takes his servant" and grants him *"Spirit"* whereby Danel's virility is restored:

> With life-breath Danel is quickened . . .
> With life-breath he is invigorated.

To the disbelieving Danel, El promises a son. Mount your bed, he tells him, kiss your wife, embrace her . . . "by conception and pregnancy she will bear a male child to Danel." And just as in the biblical tale, the matriarch does bear a Rightful Heir, and the Succession is assured. They name him *Aqhat*; the gods nickname him *Na'aman* ("The Pleasant One").

As the boy grows to be a young man, the Craftsman of the Gods presents him with a gift of a unique bow. This soon arouses the envy of Anat, who wishes to possess the magical bow. To get it, she promises Aqhat anything he would like to have—silver, gold, even Immortality:

> Ask for Life, O Aqhat the youth—
> Ask for Life and I will grant it to thee;
> For Immortality (ask),
>   and I will bestow it upon thee.
> With Baal I will make thee count the years;
> With the sons of El shalt thou count the months.

Moreover—she promised—not only would he live as long as the gods, but he would be invited to join them for the Lifegiving ceremony:

> And Baal, when he grants Life,
>   a feast he gives;
> A banquet he holds for the One-Given-Life.
> He bids him a drink,
>   sings and chants over him sweetly.

But Aqhat does not believe that Man can escape his mortal fate, and does not wish to part with the bow:

> Lie not, O Maiden—
>   to a hero thy lies are loathesome.
> How can a mortal an Afterlife acquire?
> How can a mortal Eternity obtain? . . .
> The death of all men will I die;
> Yea, I shall surely die.

He also points out to Anat that the bow was made for warriors like himself and not for a female to use. Insulted, Anat "traverses the land" to El's abode, to seek permission to smite Aqhat. El's enigmatic response permits punishment only up to a point.

Now Anat turns to cunning. "Over a thousand fields, ten thousand acres" she travels back to Aqhat. Pretending to be at peace and in love with him, she laughs and giggles. Addressing him as "Aqhat the youth," she states: "Thou are my brother, I am thy sister." She persuades him to accompany her to the city of "The Father of the gods; the Lord of the Moon." There she asks *Taphan* to "slay Aqhat for his bow" but then "make him live again"—to put Aqhat to temporary death, only long enough for Anat to take away his bow. Taphan, following Anat's instructions, "smites Aqhat twice on the skull, thrice above the ear," and Aqhat's "soul escapes like vapor." But before Aqhat can be revived—if Anat had ever so intended—his body is ravaged by vultures. The terrible news is brought to Danel as, "sitting before the gate, under a mighty tree," he "judges the cause of the widow, adjucates the case of the orphan." With Ba'al's aid, a search is instituted for the dismembered Aqhat, but to no avail. In revenge, Aqhat's sister, in disguise, travels to the abode of Taphan and, getting him drunk, attempts to slay him. (A possible happy end, wherein Aqhat was resurrected after all, is missing.)

The transfer of action from the mountains of Lebanon to the "City of Lord Moon" is also an element found in the Gilgamesh epic. Throughout the ancient Near East, the deity associated with the Moon was Sin (Nannar in the original Sumerian). His Ugaritic epithet was "Father of Gods"; he indeed was the father of Ishtar and her brothers. The first attempt of Gilgamesh to reach his goal via the Landing Place in the Cedar Mountain was frustrated by Ishtar, who sought to have him killed by the Bull of Heaven after he rejected her advances. Undertaking the second journey toward the Land Tilmun, Gilgamesh too arrived at a walled city "whose temple to Sin was dedicated."

But whereas Gilgamesh arrived in the region of Sin after a long and hazardous trek, Anat—like Ishtar—could get around from place to place in no time—for she neither walked nor traveled on assback; instead, she flew from place to place. Many Mesopotamian texts referred to Ishtar's flying journeys and her ability to roam in Earth's skies, "crossing heaven, crossing earth." A depiction of her in her temple in Ashur, an Assyrian capital, showed her wearing goggles, a tight-fitting helmet and extended "earphones" or panels (see Fig. 58). In the ruins of Mari on the Euphrates River, a life-sized statue of a goddess was found, equipped with a "black box," a hose, a horned helmet with built-in earphones and other attributes of an aeronaut (Fig. 85). This ability "as a bird to fly," also attributed to the Canaanite deities, features in all the epic tales discovered at Ugarit.

One such tale, in which a goddess flies to the rescue, is a text titled by scholars "The Legend of King Keret"—*Keret* being capable of interpretation as the king's personal name, or the name of his city ("The Capital"). The tale's main theme is the same as that of the Sumerian epic of Gilgamesh: Man's striving for Immortality. But it begins like the biblical tale of Job, and has other strong biblical similarities.

Fig. 85

Job, according to the biblical tale, was a righteous and "pure" man of great wealth and power who lived in the "Land of *Utz*" (the "Land of Advice"), a land in the domain of the "Children of the East." All went well until "one day, when the sons of the gods came to present themselves to the Lord, Satan came also among them." Persuading the Lord to test Job, Satan was permitted to afflict him first with the loss of his children and all his wealth, and then with all manner of sickness. As Job sat mourning and suffering, three of his friends came to console him; the *Book of Job* was composed as a record of their discussions concerning matters of life and death and the mysteries of Heaven and Earth.

Bewailing the turn of events, Job longed for the days of yore, when he was honored and respected: "at the gates of *Keret*, in the public square, my seat was at the ready." In those days, Job reminisced, he believed that "as the Phoenix shall be my days, with my Establisher shall I die." But now, with nothing left and afflicted with illnesses, he felt like dying then and there.

The friend who had come from the south reminded him that "Man is born unto travail; only the son of *Reshef* can to the heights fly up": Man was mortal after all, so why this extreme agitation?

But Job answered enigmatically that it was not so simple: "The Lord's Essence is within me," he said; "its radiance feeds my *Spirit*." Was he disclosing, in the hitherto uncomprehended verse, that he was of partly divine blood? That, therefore, like Gilgamesh, he had expected to live as long as the ever-rejuvenating Phoenix, to die only when his "Establisher" shall die. But now he realized that "Eternally I shall no longer live; like vapor are my days."

The tale of Keret too depicts him at first as a prosperous man who loses in quick succession his wife and children through sickness and war. "He sees his offspring ruined . . . in its entirety a posterity perishing," and realizes that it is the end of his dynasty: "wholly undermined is his throne." His mourning and grief grow daily; "his bed is soaked by his weeping." Daily "he enters the inner chamber" in the temple and cries to his gods. Finally,

El "descends unto him" to find out "what ails Keret that he weeps." It is then that the texts disclose that Keret is partly divine, for it was El who had fathered him (by a human female).

El advises his "beloved lad" to stop mourning, and to remarry, for he would be blessed with a new heir. He is told to wash and make himself presentable, and go seek the hand of the daughter of the king of Udum (possibly the biblical Edom). Keret, accompanied by troops and laden with gifts, goes to Udum and does as El had instructed. But the king of Udum turns down all the silver and gold. Knowing that Keret "is the flesh of the Father of Men"—of divine origins—he asks for a unique dowry: let the firstborn son that his daughter shall bear Keret also be semi-divine!

The decision is, of course, not up to Keret. El, who had given him the marriage counsel to begin with, is not available. Keret therefore sets his steps to the shrine of Asherah, and seeks her help. The next scene takes place at the abode of El, where the appeal of Asherah is supported by the younger gods:

> Then came the companies of the gods,
> And puissant Ba'al spake up:
> "Now come, O Kindly One, El benign:
> Will thou not bless Keret the pure blooded,
>   nor please the beloved lad of El?"

Thus prodded, El consents and "blesses Keret," promising him that he shall have seven sons and several daughters. The firstborn son, El announces, is to be named *Yassib* ("Permanent") for indeed he will be granted permanence. This will be achieved because when he is born, not his mother but rather the goddesses Asherah and Anat will suckle him. (The theme of a king's child being nursed by a goddess, thereby being granted longer life, was depicted in the art of all the Near Eastern peoples—Fig. 86).

Fig. 86

The gods keep their promises; but Keret, growing in wealth and power, forgets his vows; in the manner of the king of Tyre in the prophecies of Ezekiel, his heart grew haughty, and he began to boast to his children about his divine origins. Angered, Asherah afflicted him with a fatal disease. As it became clear that Keret was on the verge of death, his sons were astonished: How can this happen to Keret, "a son of El, an offspring of the Kindly One, a holy being?" In disbelief, the sons question their father—for surely his failed claim to Immortality has a bearing on their own lives as well:

> In thy Life, father, we rejoiced;
> We exalted in thy Not-dying . . .
> Wilt thou die then, father, like the mortals?

Their father's silence speaks for itself, and now the sons turn to the gods:

> How can it be said,
> "A son of El is Keret,
>   an offspring of the Kindly One
>   and a holy being?"
> Shall then a god die?
> An offspring of the Kindly One not live?

Embarrassed, El asks the other gods: "Who among the gods can remove the sickness, drive out the malady?" Seven times El issued this appeal, but "none among the gods answers him." In desperation, El appeals to the Craftsman of the Gods and his assistants, the Crafts-goddesses who know all magic. Responding, the "female who removes illness," the goddess Shataqat, takes to the air. "She flies over a hundred towns, she flies over a multitude of villages. . . ." Arriving in the house of Keret in the nick of time, she manages to revive him.

(The tale, though, has no happy end. Since Keret's claim to Immortality had proven vain, his firstborn son suggested that Keret abdicate in his favor. . . .)

Of greater importance to the understanding of ancient events are the several epic tales dealing with the gods themselves. In these, the ability of the gods to fly about is accepted as a matter of course; and their haven in the "Crest of Zaphon" is featured as the aeronauts' resting place. The central figures in these tales are Ba'al and Anat, the brother-sister who are also lovers. Ba'al's frequent epithet is *The Rider of the Clouds*—an epithet which the Old Testament has claimed for the Hebrew deity. Anat's own flying capabilities, which became apparent in the tales dealing with the relations between gods and men, are even more highlighted in the tales of the gods themselves.

In one such text, Anat is told that Ba'al went to fish "in the meadow of *Samakh*" (Fig. 87). The area happens to still be called by that very name to this day: it is *Lake Sumkhi* ("Lake of Fishes") in northern Israel, where the Jordan River begins to flow into the Sea of Galilee; and it is still renowned for its fishes and wildlife. Anat decided to join Ba'al there:

> She raises wing, the Maiden Anat,
>   she raises wing and tours about flying
>   to the midst of the meadow of Samakh
>   which with buffaloes abounds.

Seeing her, Ba'al signaled her to come down; but Anat began to play hide-and-seek. Annoyed, Ba'al asked whether she expects him to "anoint her horns"—a lovemaking expression—"while in flight." Unable to find her, Ba'al took off "and went up . . . in the skies" unto his throne-seat on the

Fig. 87

"Crest of Zaphon." The playful Anat soon appeared there too, "upon Zaphon in pleasure (to be)."

The idyllic get-together, however, could take place only in later years, when the position of Ba'al as the Prince of Earth and acknowledged master of the northern lands was finally established. Earlier, Ba'al engaged in life-and-death struggles with other contenders for the godly throne; the prize of all these fights was a place known as *Zarerath Zaphon*—commonly translated "the Heights of Zaphon," but specifically meaning "The Rocky Crest in the North."

These bloody struggles for dominion over certain strongholds or lands were compounded by the positioning for succession, as the head of the pantheon grew old and semi-retired. Conforming to marriage traditions first reported in the Sumerian writings, El's official consort Asherah ("the Ruler's daughter") was his half-sister. This made the first son born by her the rightful heir. But, as had happened before, he was often challenged by the firstborn—a son who chronologically was born first, but by another mother. (The fact that Ba'al, who had at least three wives, could not marry his beloved Anat confirms that she was a full, rather than a half-sister of his.)

The Canaanite tales begin at the remote mountainous abode of El, where he secretly bestows the succession upon Prince Yam. The goddess Shepesh, "Torch of the Gods," comes flying to Ba'al to reveal to him the bad news: "El is overturning the Kingship!" she shouts in alarm.

Ba'al is advised to present himself to El, and put the dispute before the "Assembled Body"—Council—of the gods. His sisters counsel him to be defiant:

> There now, be off on your way
> toward the Assembled Body,
> in the midst of Mount Lala.
> At the feet of El do not fall down,
> prostrate thyself not unto the Assembled Body;
> Proudly standing, say ye your speech.

Learning of the ploy, Yam sends his own emissaries to the gathered gods, to demand that the rebellious Ba'al be surrendered to him. "The gods were sitting to eat, the Holy Ones for dinner; Ba'al was attending upon El" when the emissaries entered. In the hush that followed, they present Yam's demand. To indicate that they meant business, "at El's feet they do not fall down"; they hold their weapons at the ready: "Eyes that are like a whetted sword, flashing a consuming fire." The gods drop to the ground and take cover. El is willing to yield Ba'al. But Ba'al seizes his own weapons and is about to jump the emissaries, when his mother restrains him: an emissary bears immunity, she reminds him.

As the emissaries return to Yam empty-handed, it is clear that there is no way but for the two gods to meet on the battlefield. A goddess—perhaps Anat—conspires with the Craftsman of the Gods to provide Ba'al with two divine weapons, the "chaser" and the "thrower" which "swoop like an eagle." Meeting in combat, Ba'al overwhelms Yam and is about to "smash Yam," when the voice of Asherah reaches him: spare Yam! Yam is allowed to live, but is banished to his maritime domains.

In return for sparing Yam, Ba'al asks Asherah to support his quest for supremacy over the Crest of Zaphon. Asherah is resting at a seaside resort, and it is quite reluctantly that she makes the journey to El's abode in a hot and dry place. Arriving "thirsty and parched," she puts the problem before him and asks that he decide with wisdom, not emotion: "Thou art great indeed and wise," she flatters him; "thy beard's gray hair instructs thee . . . Wisdom and Everlife are thy portion." Weighing the situation, El agrees: let Ba'al be the master of the Crest of Zaphon; let him build his house there.

What Ba'al has in mind, however, is not just an abode. His plans require the services of *Kothar-Hasis* ("The Skilled and Knowing"), Craftsman of the Gods. Not only modern scholars, but even the first century Philo of Byblos (quoting earlier Phoenician historians) have compared Kothar-Hasis with the Greek divine craftsman Hephaestus, who built the abode of Zeus and Hera. Others find parallels with the Egyptian Thoth, god of artcraft and magic. Indeed, the Ugaritic texts state that the emissaries sent to fetch Kothar-Hasis were to look for him in Crete and Egypt; presumably it was in those lands that his skills were being employed at that time.

When Kothar-Hasis arrived at Ba'al's place, the two went over the construction plans. It turned out that Ba'al desired a two-part structure, one an *E-khal* (a "great house") and the other a *Behmtam*, commonly translated "house" but which literally means *"a raised platform."* There was some disagreement between the two regarding where a funnel-like window, which could open and close in some unusual manner, should be placed. "Thou shalt heed my words, O Ba'al," Kothar-Hasis insisted. When the structure was completed, Ba'al was concerned that his wives and children would be hurt. To allay his fears, Kothar-Hasis ordered that trees of Lebanon, "from *Sirion* its precious cedars," be piled up within the structure—and started up a fire. For a full week the fire burnt intensely; silver and gold within it melted down; but the structure itself was neither damaged nor destroyed.

The underground silo and raised platform were ready!
Losing no time, Ba'al decided to test the facility:

> Ba'al opened the Funnel in the Raised Platform,
>   the window within the Great House.
> In the clouds, Ba'al opened rifts.
> His godly sound Ba'al discharges. . . .
> His godly sound convulses the earth.
> The mountains quake. . . .
> A-tremble are the . . .
> In east and west, earth's mounts reel.

As Ba'al soared skyward, the divine messengers Gapan and Ugar joined him in flight: "The winged ones, the twain, flock the clouds" behind Ba'al; "bird-like the twain" soared above the snow-covered peaks of Zaphon. But with the new facilities, the Crest of Zaphon was turned into the "Fastness of Zaphon"; and Mount *Lebanon* ("The White One," after its snowy peaks) acquired the epithet *Sirion*—"The Armored" Mountain.

Attaining mastery over the Fastness of Zaphon, Ba'al also acquired the title *Ba'al Zaphon*. The title simply means "Lord of Zaphon," of the Northern Place. But the original connotation of the term *Zaphon* was not geographical; it meant both "the hidden-away," and "the observation place." Undoubtedly, all these connotations played a role in naming Ba'al "Lord of Zaphon."

Now that he had attained these powers and prerogatives, Ba'al's ambitions grew in scope. Inviting the "sons of the gods" to a banquet, he demanded fealty and vassalage; those who disagreed were set upon: "Ba'al seizes the sons of Asherah; Rabbim he strikes in the back, Dokyamm he strikes with a bludgeon." While some were slaughtered, others escaped. Drunk with power, Ba'al mocked them:

> Ba'al's enemies take to the woods;
> His enemies hide in the side of the mountain.
> Puissant Ba'al shouts:
> "O enemies of Ba'al why do you quake?
>   Why do you run, why do you hide?"
> The Eye of Ba'al splinters up;
> His stretched hand the cedar breaks;
> His right (hand) is mighty.

Pursuing his quest for mastery, Ba'al—with the aid of Anat—battled and annihilated such male adversaries as "Lothan, the serpent," Shalyat, "the seven-headed dragon," Atak "the Bullock," as well as the goddess Hashat, "the Bitch." We know from the Old Testament that Yahweh, the biblical Lord, was also a bitter adversary of Ba'al; and as Ba'al's influence grew among the Israelites when their king married a Canaanite princess, the prophet Elijah arranged a contest between Ba'al and Yahweh upon Mount Carmel. When Yahweh prevailed, the three hundred priests of Ba'al were promptly executed. In this adversity, it was for Yahweh that the Old Testament claimed mastery over the Crest of Zaphon. Significantly, the claims were made in almost identical language, as Psalm 29 and other verses make clear:

> Give unto Yahweh, O sons of the gods,
> Unto Yahweh give homage and supremacy.
> Give unto the Lord the homage of his *Shem;*
> Bow down unto Him in his Sacred Splendor.
> The sound of the Lord is upon the waters:
> The Lord of Glory thundereth,
>   echoes upon the many waters.
> His sound is powerful, full of majesty.
> The sound of the Lord the cedars breaks;
> The cedars of Lebanon Yahweh splinters.
> He makes *Lebanon* skip as a calf, and
> *Sirion* like a young buffalo.
> His sound from amidst the fiery flames cuts through. . . .
> The Lord in his Great House is glorified.

As Ba'al in the Canaanite texts, so was the Hebrew Deity "Rider of the Clouds." The Prophet Isaiah envisioned Him flying south toward Egypt, "riding swiftly upon a cloud, he shall descend upon Egypt; the gods of

Egypt shall quail before him." Isaiah also claimed to have personally seen the Lord and His winged attendants:

> In the year that king Uzziah died, I beheld and saw the Lord seated upon a high and raised up Throne; its Lifters filled up the Great House. The Fire-Attendants were stationed above it, six wings, six wings to each of them . . . The threshold beams were shaken by the sound, and the House was filled with smoke.

The Hebrews were forbidden to worship, and therefore to make, statues or engraved images. But the Canaanites, who must have known of Yahweh, as the Hebrews had known of Ba'al, left us a depiction of Yahweh as conceived by them. A fourth century B.C. coin which bears the inscription *Yahu* ("Yahweh") depicts a bearded deity seated upon a throne shaped as a winged wheel (Fig. 88).

It was thus universally assumed in the ancient Near East that lordship over Zaphon established the supremacy among the gods who could fly

Fig. 88

about. This, no doubt, was what Ba'al had expected. But seven years after the Fastness of Zaphon was completed, Ba'al faced a challenge by Mot, Lord of the southern lands and the Lower World. As it turned out, the dispute was no longer about the mastery of Zaphon; rather, it had to do with "who over the whole Earth dominion shall have."

Word somehow reached Mot that Ba'al was engaged in suspicious activities. Unlawfully and clandestinely, he was "putting one lip to Earth and one lip to Heaven," and was attempting to "stretch his speech to the planets." Mot at first demanded the right to inspect the goings-on *within* the Crest of Zaphon. Instead, Ba'al sent emissaries with messages of peace. Who needs war? he asked; let us "pour peace and amity into the center of Earth." As Mot became more persistent, Ba'al concluded that the only way to prevent Mot from coming to Zaphon was for Ba'al to go to Mot's abode. So he journeyed to Mot's "pit" "in the depths of Earth," professing obedience.

Yet what he really had in mind was something more sinister—the overthrow of Mot. For that, he needed the help of the ever-faithful Anat. And so it was that while Ba'al had gone to Mot, his emissaries reached Anat at her own abode. The two emissaries were instructed to repeat to Anat, word for word, an enigmatic message:

> I have a word of secret to tell thee,
>   a message to whisper unto thee:
> It is a contraption that launches words,
>   a Stone that whispers.
> Men its messages will not know;
> Earth's multitudes will not comprehend.

"Stones" in the ancient languages, we must bear in mind, encompassed all quarried or mined substances and thus included all minerals and metals. Anat, therefore, readily understood what Ba'al was telling her: He was setting up upon the Crest of Zaphon some sophisticated contraption that could send or intercept secret messages!

The "Stone of Splendor" was further described in the secret message:

> Heaven with Earth it makes converse,
>   and the seas with the planets.
> It is a Stone of Splendor;
> To Heaven it is yet unknown.
> Let's you and I raise it
>   within my cavern, on lofty Zaphon.

So that was the secret: Ba'al, without the knowledge of "Heaven"—the government of the home planet—was setting up a clandestine communications center, from which he could converse with all the parts of Earth, as well as with the Spacecraft above Earth. It was a first step to "over the whole Earth dominion to have." In that, he ran into direct conflict with Mot; for it was in Mot's territories that the official "Eye of Earth" was located.

Having received and understood the message, Anat readily agreed to go to Ba'al's aid. The worried emissaries were promised that she would be there on time: "You are slow, I am swift," she assured them:

> The god's distant place I will penetrate,
>   the distant Hollow of the sons of the gods.
> Two openings it (has) under the Eye of Earth,
>   and three wide tunnels.

Arriving at Mot's capital, she could not find Ba'al. Demanding to know his whereabouts, she threatened Mot with violence. Finally, she learnt the truth: the two gods had engaged in hand combat, and "Ba'al was fallen." Enraged, she "with a sword cleaved Mot." Then with the aid of Shepesh, mistress of the Rephaim (the "Healers"), the lifeless body of Ba'al was flown back to the peak of Zaphon, and placed in a cavern.

Quickly, the two goddesses summoned the Craftsman of the Gods, also referred to as *El Kessem*—"The God of Magic." As Thoth had revived the snake-bitten Horus, so was Ba'al miraculously resurrected. But whether he was resurrected physically on Earth, or in a Celestial Afterlife (as Osiris), one cannot be certain.

When did the gods act out these events upon the Crest of Zaphon, no one can say for sure. But we do know that Mankind was cognizant of the existence and unique attributes of the "Landing Place" almost from the beginning of recorded history.

We have, to begin with, the journey of Gilgamesh to the Cedar Mountain, which his epic also calls "Abode of the gods, the Crossroads of Ishtar." There, "pressing into the forest," he came upon a tunnel which led to "the enclosure from which words of command are issued." Proceeding deeper into the mountain, "the secret abode of the Anunnaki he opened up." It is as though Gilgamesh had penetrated the very installations which Ba'al had secretly constructed! Mystery-filled verses in the epic now assume a thrilling meaningfulness:

> Secret things he has seen;
> What is hidden from Man, he knows. . . .

This, we know, took place in the third millennium B.C.—circa 2900 B.C.

The next link between the affairs of gods and men is the tale of the aging and heirless Danel, who had resided somewhere near Kadesh. There is no time frame given for the tale's occurrences, but the similarities with the biblical tale of the heirless Abraham—including the sudden appearance of "men" who turn out to be the Lord and his Emissaries, and the locale not far from Kadesh—suggest the possibility that we are reading two versions of the same ancestral memory. If so, we have another datemark: the beginning of the second millenium B.C.

Zaphon was still there, a Fastness of the Gods, in the first millenium B.C. The prophet Isaiah (eighth century B.C.) castigated the Assyrian invader of Judea, Sennacherib, for having insulted the Lord by ascending with his many chariots "to the mountain's height, unto the Crest of Zaphon." Stressing the antiquity of the place, the prophet transmitted to Sennacherib the Lord's admonition:

> Hast thou not heard it?
> Long ago have I made it,
> In days of old have I created it.

The same prophet likewise castigated the king of Babylon for having attempted to deify himself by scaling the Crest of Zaphon:

> O, how fallen from heaven art thou,
>> a Morning Star, son of Dawn!
> Felled to the ground
>> is he who the nations enfeebled.
> Thou didst say in thine heart
>> "I will ascend unto the heavens,
>> above the planets of El I shall raise my throne;
> On the Mount of Assembly I shall sit,
>> on the Crest of Zaphon.
> Upon the Raised Platform I shall go up,
>> a Lofty One I shall be!"
> But nay, to the Nether World you shalt go,
>> down to the depths of a pit.

We have here not only confirmation of the existence of the place and its antiquity, but also a description of it: it included a "raised platform," from which one could ascend heavenward and become a "Lofty One"—a god.

The ascent heavenward, we know from other biblical writings, was by means of "stones" (mechanical contraptions) that could travel. In the sixth century B.C., the Prophet Ezekiel castigated the king of Tyre, whose heart grew haughty after he had been permitted to reach the Crest of Zaphon, and was taken within the "moving stones"—an experience after which he claimed "a god am I."

An ancient coin found at Byblos (the biblical Gebal), one of the Canaanite/Phoenician cities on the Mediterranean coast, may well have illustrated the structures erected upon Zaphon by Kothar-Hasis (Fig. 89). It depicts a "great house," adjoined by a raised area, which is surrounded by a high and massive wall. There, upon a podium supported by cross-beams

Fig. 89

built to withstand a great weight, there is mounted a conical object—an object familiar from so many other Near Eastern depictions: the Celestial Chamber of the gods—the "moving stone."

This, then, is the evidence bequeathed to us from antiquity. Millennium after millennium, the peoples of the ancient Near East were aware that within the Cedar Mountain there was a large platform for "moving stones," adjoined by a "great house" within which "a stone that whispers" was secreted.

And, if we have been right in our interpretations of ancient texts and drawings—could it be that this grand and known place had vanished?

IX

The Landing Place

The greatest Roman temple ruins lie not in Rome, but in the mountains of Lebanon. They encompass a grand temple to Jupiter—the grandest built anywhere in antiquity to honor any one god. Many Roman rulers, over a period of some four centuries, toiled to glorify this remote and alien place and erect its monumental structures. Emperors and generals came to it in search of oracles, to find out their fate. Roman legionnaires sought to be billeted near it; the devout and the curious went to see it with their own eyes: it was one of the wonders of the ancient world.

Daring European travelers, risking life and limb, reported the existence of the ruins since the visit there by Martin Baumgarten in January 1508. In 1751, the traveler Robert Wood, accompanied by the artist James Dawkins, restored some of the place's ancient fame when they described it in words and sketches. "When we compare the ruins . . . with those of many cities we visited in Italy, Greece, Egypt and other parts of Asia, we cannot help thinking them the remains of *the boldest plan* we ever saw attempted in architecture"—bolder in certain aspects than even the great pyramids of Egypt. The view upon which Wood and his companion had come was a panorama in which the mountaintop, the temples and the skies blended into one (Fig. 90).

The site is in the mountains of Lebanon, where they part to form a fertile, flat valley between the "Lebanon" range to the west and the "Anti-Lebanon" range to the east; where two rivers known from antiquity, the Litani and the Orontes, begin to flow into the Mediterranean Sea. The ruins were of imposing Roman temples that were erected upon a vast horizontal platform, artificially created at about 4,000 feet above sea level. The sacred precinct was surrounded by a wall, which served both as a retaining wall to hold the earthworks forming the flat top, as well as a fence to protect and screen off the area. The enclosed squarish area, with some sides almost 2,500 feet long, measured over five million square feet.

Situated so as to command the flanking mountains and the approaches to the valley from north and south, the sacred area had its northwestern corner deliberately cut off—as seen in this contemporary bird's eye view (Fig. 91a).

Fig. 90

The right-angled cutout created an oblong area, which extended the platform's unimpeded northern view westward. It was at that specially conceived corner that the vastest-ever temple to Jupiter stood high, with some of the tallest (65 feet) and largest (7.5 feet in diameter) columns known in antiquity. These columns supported an elaborately decorated superstructure ("architrave") 16 feet in height, atop which there was a slanting roof, further raising the temple's pinnacle.

The temple proper was only the westernmost (and oldest) part of a four-part shrine to Jupiter, which the Romans are believed to have started to build soon after they occupied the place in 63 B.C.

Arranged along a slightly slanted east-west axis (Fig. 91b) were, first, a monumental Gateway ("A"); it comprised a grand staircase and a raised portico supported by twelve columns, in which there were twelve niches to hold the twelve Olympian gods. The worshippers then entered a forecourt ("B") of an hexagonal design, unique in Roman architecture; and through it continued to a vast altar court ("C"), which was dominated by an altar of monumental proportions: it rose some 60 feet from a base of about 70 by 70 feet. At the western end of the court stood the god's house proper ("D"). Measuring a colossal 300 by 175 feet, it stood upon a podium which was itself raised some 16 feet above the level of the court—a total of 42 feet above the level of the base platform. It was from that extra height that the tall columns, the architrave and the roof made together a real ancient skyscraper.

From its monumental gateway staircase to its final western wall, the shrine extended for more than 1,000 feet in length. It completely dwarfed a very large temple to its south ("E"), which was dedicated to a male deity, some think Bacchus but probably Mercury; and a small round temple ("F") to the southeast, where Venus was venerated. A German archaeological team that explored the site and studied its history on orders of Kaiser Wilhelm II, soon after he had visited the place in 1897, was able to reconstruct the layout of the sacred precinct and prepared an artist's

Fig. 91

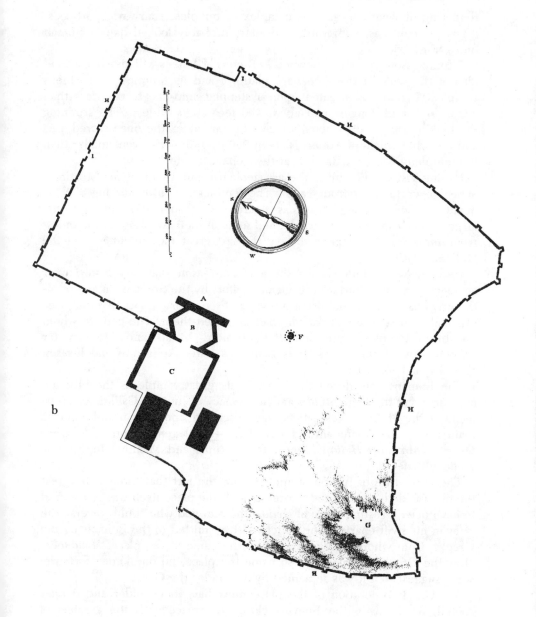

rendering of what the ancient complex of temples, stairways, porticoes, gateways, columns, courtyards and altars probably looked like in Roman times (Fig. 92).

A comparison with the renowned *Acropolis* of Athens will give one a good idea of the scale of this Lebanese platform and its temples. The Athens complex (Fig. 93) is situated upon a stepped ship-like terrace less than 1,000 feet at its longest and about 400 feet at its widest. The stunning Parthenon (temple of Athena) which still dominates the once sacred area and the whole plain of Athens is about 230 by 100 feet—even smaller than the temple of Mercury/Bacchus at the Lebanese Site.

Having visited the ruins, the archaeologist and architect Sir Mortimer Wheeler wrote two decades ago: "The temples . . . owe nothing of their quality to such new-fangled aids as concrete. They stand passively upon the *largest known stones in the world,* and some of their columns are *the tallest from antiquity. . . .* Here we have the last great monument . . . of the Hellenic world."

Hellenic world indeed, for there is no reason that any historian or archaeologist could find for this gigantic effort by the Romans, in an out-of-the-way place in an unimportant province, except for the fact that the place was hallowed by the Greeks who had preceded them. The gods to whom the three temples were dedicated—Jupiter, Venus and Mercury (or Bacchus)—were the Greek gods Zeus, his sister Aphrodite and his son Hermes (or Dionysus).

The Romans considered the site and its great temple as the ultimate attestations of the almightiness and supremacy of Jupiter. Calling him *Iove* (echo of the Hebrew *Yehovah?*), they inscribed upon the temple and its main statue the divine initials I.O.M.H.—the legend standing for *Iove Optimus Maximus Heliopolitanus:* the Optimal and Maximal Jupiter the Heliopolitan.

The latter title of Jupiter stemmed from the fact that though the great temple was dedicated to the Supreme God, the place itself was considered to have been a resting place of *Helios,* the Sun god who could traverse the skies in his swift chariot. The belief was transmitted to the Romans by the Greeks, from whom they also adopted the name of the place: *Heliopolis.* How the Greeks had come to so name the place, no one knows for sure; some suggest that it was so named by Alexander the Great.

Yet Greek veneration of the place must have been older and deeper rooted, for it made the Romans glorify the place with the greatest of monuments, and seek there the oracle's word concerning their fate. How else to explain the fact that, "in terms of sheer acreage, weight of stone, dimensions of the individual blocks, and the amount of carving, this precinct can scarcely have had a rival in the Graeco-Roman world" (John M. Cook, *The Greeks in Ionia and the East*).

In fact, the place and its association with certain gods go back to even earlier times. Archaeologists believe that there may have been as many as

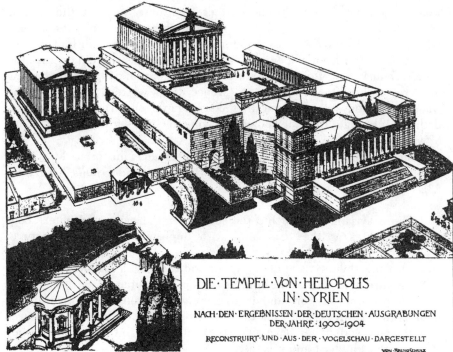

DIE · TEMPEL · VON · HELIOPOLIS
IN · SYRIEN
NACH·DEN· ERGEBNISSEN ·DER·DEUTSCHEN · AUSGRABUNGEN
DER·JAHRE · 1900–1904

RECONSTRUIRT· UND ·AUS · DER · VOGELSCHAU · DARGESTELLT
VON · BRUNOSCHULZ

Fig. 92

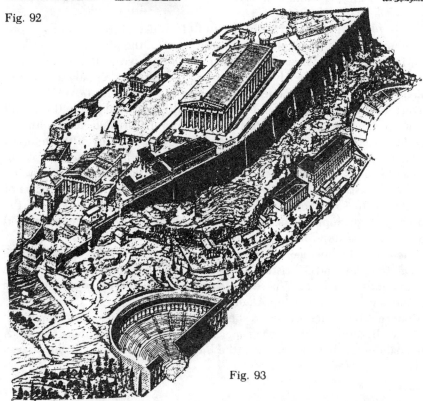

Fig. 93

six temples built on the site before Roman times; and it is certain that whatever shrines the Greeks may have erected there, they—as the Romans after them—were only raising the structures atop earlier foundations, religiously and literally. Zeus (Jupiter to the Romans), it will be recalled, arrived in Crete from Phoenicia (today's Lebanon), swimming across the Mediterranean Sea after he had abducted the beautiful daughter of the king of Tyre. Aphrodite too came to Greece from western Asia. And the wandering Dionysus, to whom the second temple (or perhaps another) was dedicated, brought the vine and winemaking to Greece from the same lands of western Asia.

Aware of the worship's earlier roots, the Roman historian Macrobius enlightened his countrymen in the following words (*Saturnalia* I, Chapter 23):

> The Assyrians too worship the sun under the name of Jupiter, Zeus Helioupolites as they call him, with important rites in the city of Heliopolis. . . .
>
> That this divinity is at once Jupiter and the Sun is manifest both from the nature of its ritual and from its outward appearance. . . .
>
> To prevent any argument from ranging through a whole list of divinities, I will explain what the Assyrians believe concerning the power of the sun (god). They have given the name *Adad* to the god whom they venerate as highest and greatest. . . .

The hold the place had over the beliefs and imagination of people throughout the millennia also manifested itself in the history of the place following its Roman veneration. When Macrobius wrote the above, circa A.D. 400, Rome was already Christian and the site was already a target of zealous destruction. No sooner did Constantine the Great (A.D. 306–337) convert to Christianity, than he stopped all additional work there and instead began the conversion of the place into a Christian shrine. In the year 440, according to one chronicler, "Theodosius destroyed the temples of the Greeks; he transformed into a Christian church the temple of Heliopolis, that of *Ba'al Helios*, the great Sun-Ba'al of the celebrated Trilithon." Justinian (525–565) apparently carried off some of the pillars of red granite to Constantinople, the Byzantine capital, to build there the church of Hagia Sophia. These efforts to Christianize the place encountered repeated armed opposition by the local populace.

When the Muslims gained the area in the year 637, they converted the Roman temples and Christian churches atop the huge platform into a Muhammedan enclave. Where Zeus and Jupiter had been worshiped, a mosque was built to worship *Allah*.

Modern scholars have tried to shed more light on the age-long worship at this place by studying the archaeological evidence from neighboring sites. A principal one of these is Palmyra (the biblical Tadmor), an ancient caravan center on the way from Damascus to Mesopotamia. As a result, such scholars as Henry Seyrig (*La Triade Héliopolitaine*) and René Dussaud (*Temples et Cultes Héliopolitaine*) have concluded that a basic triad had been worshipped throughout the ages. It was headed by the God of the Thunderbolt and included the Warrior Maiden and the Celestial Charioteer. They and other scholars helped establish the now generally accepted conclusion, that the Roman-Greek triad stemmed from the earlier Semitic beliefs, which in turn were based upon the Sumerian pantheon. The earliest Triad was headed, it appears, by *Adad*, who was allotted by his father Enlil—the chief god of Sumer—"the mountainlands of the north." The female member of the Triad was *Ishtar*. After he visited the area, Alexander the Great struck a coin honoring Ishtar/Astarte and Adad; the coin bears his name in Phoenician-Hebrew script (Fig. 94). The third member of the Triad was the Celestial Charioteer, *Shamash*—commander of the prehistoric astronauts. The Greeks honored him (as Helios) by erecting a colossal statue atop the main temple (see Fig. 92), showing him

Fig. 94

driving his chariot. To them, its swiftness was denoted by the four horses that pulled it; the authors of the *Book of Enoch* knew better: "The chariot of Shamash," it says, "was driven by the wind."

Examining the Roman and Greek traditions and beliefs, we have arrived back at Sumer; we have circled back to Gilgamesh and his Search for Immortality in the Cedar Forest, at the "crossroads of Ishtar." Though in the territory of Adad, he was told, the place was also within the jurisdiction of Shamash. And so we have the original Triad: Adad, Ishtar, Shamash.

Have we come upon the Landing Place?

That the Greeks were aware of the epic adventures of Gilgamesh, few scholars nowadays doubt. In their "investigation of the origins of human knowledge and its transmission through Myth," entitled *Hamlet's Mill*, Giorgio de Santillana and Hertha von Deschend point out that "Alexander was a true replica of Gilgamesh." But even earlier, in the historic tales of Homer, the heroic Odysseus had already followed similar footsteps. Shipwrecked after traveling to the abode of Hades in the Lower World, his men reached a place where they "ate the cattle of the Sun god" and were therefore killed by Zeus. Left alive alone, Odysseus wandered about until he reached the "Ogygian island"—the secluded place from pre-Deluge times. There, the goddess Calypso, "who kept him in a cave and fed him, wanted him to marry her; in which case she intended making him immortal, so that he should never grow old." But Odysseus refused her advances—just as Gilgamesh had turned down Ishtar's offer of love.

Henry Seyrig, who as Director of Antiquities of Syria devoted a lifetime to the study of the vast platform and its meaning, found that the Greeks used to conduct there "rites of mystery, in which Afterlife was represented as human Immortality—an identification with the deity obtained by the ascent (heavenward) of the soul." The Greeks, he concluded, indeed associated this place with Man's efforts to attain Immortality.

Was then this place the very place in the Cedar Mountains to which Gilgamesh had first gone with Enkidu, the Crest of Zaphon of Ba'al?

To give a definite answer, let us look more closely at the physical features of the place. We will find that the Romans and Greeks have built their temples upon a paved platform which existed from much earlier times—a platform constructed of large, thick stone blocks so tightly put together that no one—to this very day—has been able to penetrate it and study the chambers, tunnels, caverns and other substructures that lie hidden beneath it.

That such subterranean structures undoubtedly exist is judged not only from the fact that other Greek temples had secret, subterranean cellars and grottoes beneath their apparent floors. Georg Ebers and Hermann Guthe (*Palästina in Bild und Wort*; the English version is titled *Picturesque Palestine*) reported a century ago that the local Arabs entered the ruins "at the southeast corner, through a long vaulted passage like a railway tunnel *under the great platform*" (Fig. 95). "Two of these great vaults run parallel with each other, from east to west, and are connected by a third running at right angles to them from north to south." As soon as they entered the tunnel, they were caught in total darkness, broken here and there by eerie green lights from puzzling "laced windows." Emerging from the 460-feet-long tunnel, they found themselves under the north wall of the Sun Temple, "which the Arabs call *Dar-as-saadi*—House of Supreme Blissfulness."

The German archaeologists also reported that the platform apparently rested upon gigantic vaults; but they concerned themselves with mapping and reconstructing the superstructure. A French archaeological mission, led by André Parrot in the 1920s, confirmed the existence of the subterranean maze, but was unable to penetrate its hidden parts. When the platform was pierced from above through its thick stones, evidence was found of structures beneath it.

The temples were erected upon a platform raised to thirty feet, depending on the terrain. It was paved with stones whose size, to judge by

Fig. 95

the slabs visible at the edges, ranged from a length of twelve feet to thirty feet, a frequent width of nine feet and a thickness of six feet. No one has yet attempted to calculate the quantity of stone hewn, cut, shaped, hauled and imbedded layer upon layer upon this site; it could possibly dwarf the Great Pyramid of Egypt.

Whoever laid this platform originally, paid particular attention to the rectangular northwestern corner, the location of the temple of Jupiter/Zeus. There, the temple's more than 50,000 square feet rested upon a raised podium which was certainly intended to support some extremely heavy weight. Constructed of layer upon layer of huge stones, the Podium rose twenty-six feet above the level of the Court in front of it and forty-two feet above the ground on its exposed northern and western sides. On the southern side, where six of the temple's columns still stand, one can clearly see (Fig. 96a) the stone layers: interspersed between sizable yet relatively small stones, there are alternating rows of stone blocks measuring up to twenty-one feet in length. One can also see (bottom left) the lower layers of the Podium, protruding as a terrace below the raised temple. There, the stones are even more gigantic.

More massive by far were the stone blocks in the western side of the Podium. As shown in the schematic drawing of the northwestern corner prepared by the German archaeological team (Fig. 96b), the protruding base and the top layers of the Podium were constructed of "cyclopian" stone blocks some of which measure over thirty-one feet in length, about thirteen feet in height and are twelve feet thick. Each such slab represents thus about 5,000 cubic feet of stone and weighs more than 500 tons.

Large as these stones are—the largest ones in the Great Pyramid of Egypt weigh 200 tons—they were not the largest slabs of granite employed by the ancient master builder in creating the Podium.

The central layer—situated some twenty feet above the base of the Podium—was incredibly made up of even larger stones. Modern surveyors have spoken of them as "giant," "colossal," "huge." Ancient historians named them the *Trilithon*—the Marvel of the Three Stones. For there, exposed to view in the western side of the Podium, lie side by side three stone blocks, the likes of which cannot be seen anywhere else in the world. Precisely shaped and perfectly fitting, each of the three stones (Fig. 97) measures over sixty feet in length, with sides of fourteen and twelve feet. Each slab thus represents more than 10,000 cubic feet of granite and weighs well over 1,000 tons!

The stones for the Platform and Podium were quarried locally; Wood and Dawkins include one of these quarries (Fig. 90) in their panoramic sketch, showing some of the large stone blocks strewn around in the ancient quarry. But the gigantic blocks were hewn, cut and shaped at another quarry, situated in the valley some three-quarters of a mile southwest of the sacred precinct. It is there that one comes upon a sight even more incredible than that of the Trilithon.

Partly buried in the ground, there lies yet another one of the colossal granite slabs—left *in situ* by whoever the grand quarrier was. Fully shaped and perfectly cut, with only a thin line at its base still connecting it to the rocky ground, it is an unbelievable sixty-nine feet long and has a girth of sixteen by fourteen feet. A person climbing upon it (Fig. 98) looks like a fly upon a block of ice. . . . It weighs, by conservative estimates, more than 1,200 tons.

Most scholars believe that it was intended to be hauled, as its three sisters were, up to the sacred precinct and perhaps be used to extend the terrace-part of the Podium on the northern side. Ebers and Guthe record a theory that in the row beneath the Trilithon, there are not two smaller slabs but a single stone akin to the one found at the quarry, measuring more than sixty-seven feet in length, but either damaged or otherwise chiseled to give the appearance of two side-by-side stones.

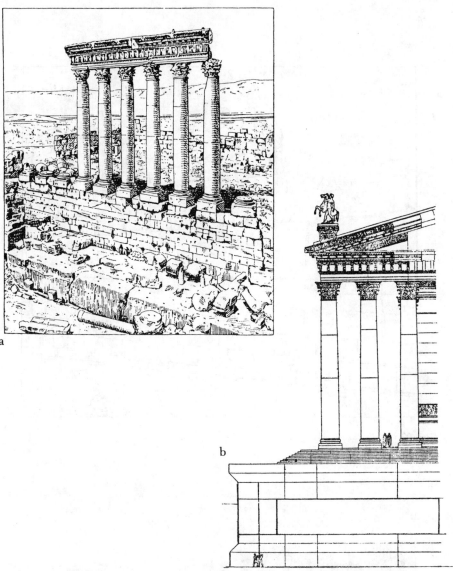

Fig. 96

Wherever the leftover colossal stone was intended to be placed, it serves as a mute witness to the immensity and uniqueness of the Platform and Podium nesting in the mountains of Lebanon. The mind-boggling fact is that even nowadays there exists no crane, vehicle or mechanism that can lift such a weight of 1,000–1,200 tons—to say nothing of carrying such an immense object over valley and mountainside, and placing each slab in its precise position, many feet above the ground. There are no traces of any roadway, causeway, ramp or other earthworks that could even remotely

Fig. 97

Fig. 98

suggest the hauling or dragging of these megaliths from the quarry to their uphill site.

Yet in remote days, someone, somehow had achieved the feat. . . .

But who? Local traditions hold that the place had existed from the days of Adam and his sons, who resided in the area of the Cedar Mountains after the expulsion of Adam and Eve from the Garden of Eden. Adam, these legends relate, inhabited the place which is now Damascus, and died not far from there. It was Cain his son who built a refuge upon the Cedar Crest after he had killed Abel.

The Maronite Patriarch of Lebanon related the following tradition: "The fastness on Mount Lebanon is the most ancient building in the world. Cain, the son of Adam, built it in the year 133 of Creation, during a fit of raving madness. He gave it the name of his son Enoch, and peopled it with giants who were punished for their iniquities by the Flood." After the Deluge, the place was rebuilt by the biblical Nimrod, in his efforts to scale the heavens. The Tower of Babel, according to these legends, was not in Babylon but upon the great platform in Lebanon.

A seventeenth-century traveler named d'Arvieux wrote in his *Mémoires* (Part II, Chapter 26) that local Jewish inhabitants, as well as Muslim residents, held that an ancient manuscript found at the site revealed that "After the Flood, when Nimrod reigned over Lebanon, he sent giants to rebuild the Fortress of Baalbek, which is so named in honor of Ba'al, the god of the Moabites, worshippers of the Sun-god."

The association of the god Ba'al with the place in post-Diluvial days strikes a bell. Indeed, no sooner were the Greeks and Romans gone than the local people abandoned the Hellenistic name Heliopolis and resumed calling the place by its Semitic name. It is the name by which it is still called to this day: *Baalbek*.

There are differing opinions as to the precise meaning of the name. Many believe that it means "The Valley of Ba'al." But from the spelling and from Talmudic references, we surmise that it has meant *"The Weeping of Ba'al."*

We can hear again the closing verses of the Ugaritic epic, describing the fall of Ba'al in his struggle with Mot, the discovery of his lifeless body, his entombment by Anat and Shepesh in a grotto upon the Crest of Zaphon:

> They came upon Baal, fallen on the ground;
> Puissant Baal is dead;
> The Prince, Lord of Earth, is perished. . . .
> Anat weeps her fill of weeping;
> In the valley she drinks tears like wine.
> Loudly she calls unto the Gods' Torch, Shepesh:
> "Lift Puissant Baal, I pray,
>   lift him onto me."
> Hearkening, the Gods' Torch Shepesh
> Picks up Puissant Baal,
> Sets him on Anat's shoulder.

> Up to the Fastness of Zaphon she brings him;
> Bewails him, entombs him;
> Lays him in the hollows of the earth.

All these local legends, which as all legends contain a kernel of age-old recollections of actual events, agree that the place is of extreme antiquity. They ascribe its building to "giants" and connect its construction with the events of the Deluge. They connect it with Ba'al, its function being that of a "Tower of Babel"—a place from which to "scale the heavens."

As we look at the vast Platform, its location and layout, and ponder the purpose of the immense Podium built to sustain massive weights, the depiction on the coin from Byblos (Fig. 89) keeps flashing before our eyes: a great temple, a walled sacred area, a podium of extra-strong construction— and upon it the rocket-like Flying Chamber.

The words and descriptions of the Hidden Place in the Epic of Gilgamesh also keep echoing in our ears. The insurmountable wall, the gate which stuns whoever touches it, the tunnel to the "enclosure from which words of command are issued," the "secret abode of the Anunnaki," the monstrous Guardian with his "radiant beam."

And there is no doubt left in our mind that in *Baalbek* we have found Ba'al's Crest of Zaphon, the target of the first journey of Gilgamesh.

The designation of Baalbek as "the Crossroads of Ishtar" implies that, as she roamed Earth's skies, she could come and go from that "Landing Place" to other landing places upon Earth. Likewise, the attempt by Ba'al to install upon the Crest of Zaphon "a contraption that launches words, a 'stone that whispers,'" implied the existence elsewhere of similar communication units: "Heaven with Earth it makes converse, and the seas with the planets."

Were there indeed such other places on Earth that could serve as Landing Places for the aircraft of the gods? Were there, besides upon the Crest of Zaphon, other "stones that whisper"?

The first obvious clue is the very name "Heliopolis," indicating the Greek belief that Baalbek was, somehow, a "City of the sun god" paralleling its namesake city in Egypt. The Old Testament too recognized the existence of a northern *Beth-Shemesh* ("House of Shamash") and a southern Beth-Shemesh, *On*, the biblical name for the Egyptian Heliopolis. It was, the prophet Jeremiah said, the place of the "Houses of the gods of Egypt," the location of Egypt's obelisks.

The northern Beth-Shemesh was in Lebanon, not far from *Beth-Anath* ("House/Home of Anat"); the prophet Amos identified it as the location of the "palaces of Adad . . . the House of the one who saw El." During the reign of Solomon, his domains encompassed large parts of Syria and Lebanon, and the list of places where he had built great structures included *Baalat* ("The Place of Ba'al") and *Tamar* ("The Place of Palms"); most scholars identify these places as Baalbek and Palmyra (see map, Fig. 78).

Greek and Roman historians made many references to the links that connected the two Heliopolises. Explaining the Egyptian pantheon of twelve gods to his countrymen, the Greek historian Herodotus also wrote of an "Immortal whom the Egyptians venerated as 'Hercules.'" He traced the origins of the worship of this Immortal to Phoenicia, "hearing that there was a temple of Hercules at that place, very highly venerated." In the temple he saw two pillars. "One was of pure gold; the other was of emerald, shining with great brilliancy at night."

Such sacred "Sun Pillars"—"Stones of the gods"—were actually depicted on Phoenician coins following the area's conquest by Alexander (Fig. 99). Herodotus provides us with the additional information that of the two connected stones, one was made of the metal which is the best conductor of electricity (gold); and the other of a precious stone (emerald) as is now used for laser communications, giving off an eerie radiance as it emits a high-powered beam. Was it not like the contraption set up by Ba'al, which the Canaanite text described as "stones of splendor?"

The Roman historian Macrobius, writing explicitly about the connection between the Phoenician Heliopolis (Baalbek) and its Egyptian counterpart, also mentions a sacred stone; according to him, "an object" venerating the Sun god Zeus Helioupolites was carried by Egyptian priests from the Egyptian Heliopolis to Heliopolis (Baalbek) in the north. "The object," he added, "is now worshipped with Assyrian rather than Egyptian rites."

Other Roman historians also stressed that the "sacred stones" worshiped by the "Assyrians" and the Egyptians were of a conical shape. Quintus Curtius recorded that such an object was located at the temple of Ammon at the oasis of Siwa. "The thing which is worshipped there as a god," Quintus Curtius wrote, "has not the shape that artificers have usually applied to the gods. Rather, its appearance is most like an *umbilicus*, and it is made of an emerald and gems cemented together."

The information regarding the conical object worshiped at Siwa was quoted by F. L. Griffith in connection with the announcement, in *The Journal of Egyptian Archaeology* (1916), of the discovery of a conical "omphalos" at the Nubian "pyramid city" of Napata. This "unique Meroitic monument" (Fig. 100) was found by George A. Reisner of Harvard University at the inner sanctum of the temple of Ammon there—the southernmost temple to this god of Egypt.

The term *omphalos* in Greek or *umbilicus* in Latin means a "navel"—a conical stone which, for reasons that scholars do not understand, was deemed in antiquity to have marked a "center of the Earth."

The temple of Ammon at the oasis of Siwa, it will be recalled, was the location of the oracle which Alexander rushed to consult on his arrival in Egypt. We have the testimony of both Callisthenes, Alexander's historian, and the Roman Quintus Curtius that an omphalos made of precious stones was the very "object" venerated at that oracle site. The Nubian temple of

Fig. 99   Fig. 100

Ammon where Reisner discovered the omphalos stone was at Napata, an ancient capital of the domains of Nubian queens; and we recall the baffling visit of Alexander to Queen Candace, in his continuing quest for Immortality.

Was it mere coincidence that, in his search for the secrets of longevity, the Persian king Cambyses (as Herodotus has reported) sent his men to Nubia, to the temple where the "Table of the Sun" was enshrined? Early in the first millennium B.C. a Nubian queen—the Queen of Sheba—made a long journey to King Solomon in Jerusalem. The legends current at Baalbek relate that he embellished the site in Lebanon in her honor. Did she then undertake the long and hazardous voyage merely to enjoy the wisdom of Solomon, or was her real purpose to consult the oracle at Baalbek—the biblical "House of Shemesh?"

There seem to be more than just coincidences here; and the question that comes to mind is this: if at all these oracle centers an omphalos was enshrined—was the omphalos itself the very source of the oracles?

The construction (or reconstruction) upon the Crest of Zaphon of a launching silo and a landing platform for Ba'al was not the cause of his fatal battle with Mot. Rather, it was his clandestine attempt to set up a "Stone of Splendor." This device could communicate with the heavens as well as with other places on Earth. But, in addition, it was

> A stone that whispers;
> Men its messages will not know,
> Earth's multitudes will not comprehend.

As we ponder the apparent dual function of the Stone of Splendor, the secret message of Ba'al to Anat all of a sudden becomes clear: the same device which the gods used to communicate with each other was also the object from which there emanated the gods' oracular answers to the kings and heroes!

In a most thorough study on the subject, Wilhelm H. Roscher (*Omphalos*) showed that the Indo-European term for these oracle stones—*navel* in English, *nabel* in German, etc.—stem from the Sanskrit *nabh*, which meant "emanate forcefully." It is no coincidence that in the Semitic languages *naboh* meant to foretell and *nabih* meant "prophet." All these identical meanings undoubtedly harken back to the Sumerian, in which NA.BA(R) meant "bright-shiny stone that solves."

A veritable network of such oracle sites emerges as we study ancient writings. Herodotus—who accurately reported (Book II, 29) the existence of the Meroitic oracle of Jupiter-Ammon—added to the links we have so far discussed by stating that the "Phoenicians," who established the oracle at Siwa, also established the oldest oracle center in Greece, the one at *Dodona* —a mountain site in northwestern Greece (near the present Albanian border).

To that effect, he related a report he had heard when he visited Egypt, whereby "two sacred women were once carried off from Thebes (in Egypt) by the Phoenicians . . . one of them was sold into Libya (western Egypt) and the other into Greece. These women were the first founders of the oracles in the two countries." This version, Herodotus wrote, he heard from the Egyptian priests of Thebes. But at Dodona, the version was that "two black doves flew away from the Egyptian Thebes," one alighting at Dodona and the other at Siwa: whereupon an oracle of Jupiter was established at both places, the Greeks calling him Zeus at Dodona and the Egyptians Ammon at Siwa.

The Roman historian Silicus Italicus (first century A.D.), relating that Hannibal consulted the oracle at Siwa regarding his wars against Rome, also credited the flight of the two doves from Thebes with the establishment of the oracles in the Libyan desert (Siwa) and in Greek Chaonia (Dodona). Several centuries later, the Greek poet Nonnos, in his master work *Dionysiaca*, described the oracle shrines at Siwa and Dodona as twin sites, and held that the two were in voice communication with each other:

> Behold the new-found answering voice
>   of the Libyan Zeus!
> The thirsty sands an oracular sent forth
>   to the dove at Chaonia [= Dodona].

As far as F. L. Griffith was concerned, the discovery of the omphalos in Nubia brought to mind another oracle center in Greece. The conical shape of the Nubian omphalos, he wrote, "was precisely that of the omphalos at the oracle at *Delphi*."

Delphi, the site of Greece's most famous oracle, was dedicated to Apollo ("He of Stone"); its ruins are still one of Greece's leading tourist attractions. There too, as at Baalbek, the sacred precinct consisted of a platform shaped upon a mountainside, also facing a valley that opens up as a funnel toward the Mediterranean Sea and the lands on its other shores.

Many records establish that an omphalos stone was Delphi's holiest object. It was set into a special base in the inner sanctum of the temple of Apollo, some say next to a golden statue of the god and some say it was enshrined all by itself. In a subterranean chamber, hidden from view by the oracle seekers, the oracle priestess, in trance-like oblivion, answered the questions of kings and heroes by uttering enigmatic answers—answers given by the god but emanating from the omphalos.

The original sacred omphalos had mysteriously disappeared, perhaps during the several sacred wars or foreign invasions which affected the place. But a stone replica thereof, erected perhaps in Roman times outside the temple, was discovered in archaeological excavations and is now on display in the Delphi Museum (Fig. 101).

Along the Sacred Way leading up to the temple, someone, at some unknown time, also set up a simple stone omphalos in an effort to mark the place where oracles were first given at Delphi, before the temple was built.

Fig. 101

The coins of Delphi depicted Apollo seated on this omphalos (Fig. 102); and after Phoenicia fell to the Greeks, they likewise depicted Apollo seated upon the "Assyrian" omphalos. But just as frequently, the oracle stones were depicted as twin cones connected to each other via a common base, as in Fig. 99.

How was Delphi chosen as a sacred oracle place, and how did the omphalos stone come to be there? The traditions say that when Zeus wanted to find the center of the Earth, he released eagles from two opposite ends of the world. Flying toward each other, they met at Delphi; whereupon the place was marked by erecting there a navel stone, an omphalos. According to the Greek historian Strabo, images of two such eagles were perched on top of the omphalos at Delphi.

Depictions of the omphalos have been found in Greek art, showing the two birds atop or at the sides (Fig. 102) of the conical object. Some scholars see in the birds not eagles, but carrier pigeons, which—being able to find

Fig. 102

their way back to a certain place—might have symbolized the measuring of distances from one Center of Earth to another.

According to Greek legends, Zeus found refuge at Delphi during his aerial battles with Typhon, resting on the platform-like area upon which the temple to Apollo was eventually built. The shrine to Ammon at Siwa contained not only subterranean corridors, mysterious tunnels and secret passages inside the temple's thick walls, but also a restricted area of some 180 by 170 feet, surrounded by a massive wall. In its midst, there arose a solid stone platform. We find the same structural components, including a raised platform, in all the sites associated with the "stones that whisper." Is one to conclude, then, that as the far larger Baalbek was, they too were both a Landing Place and a Communications Center?

Not surprisingly, we find the twin Sacred Stones, accompanied by the two eagles, also depicted in Egyptian sacred writings (Fig. 103); and many centuries before the Greeks even began to enshrine their oracle centers, an Egyptian Pharaoh depicted an omphalos with the two perched birds in his pyramids. He was Seti I, who lived in the fourteenth century B.C.; and it was in his depiction of the domain of Seker, the Hidden God, that we have seen the oldest omphalos to date—in Fig. 19. It was the communications

Fig. 103

means whereby messages—"words"—"were spoken to Seker every day."

In Baalbek, we have found the target of the first journey of Gilgamesh. Having followed the threads connecting the "whispering" Stones of Splendor, we arrived at the *Duat*.

It was the place where the Pharaohs sought the Stairway to Heaven for an Afterlife. It was, we suggest, the place whereto Gilgamesh, in search of Life, set his course on his second journey.

X

Tilmun: Land of the Rocketships

The epic search of Gilgamesh for Immortality has undoubtedly been the fountainhead of the many tales and legends, in subsequent millennia, of kings and heroes who have likewise gone to find everlasting youth. Somewhere on Earth, Mankind's mythified memories held, there was a place where Man could join the gods, and be spared the indignity of death.

Nearly 5,000 years ago, Gilgamesh of Uruk had pleaded with Utu (Shamash):

> In my city, man dies; oppressed is my heart.
> Man perishes; heavy is my heart . . .
> Man, the tallest, cannot stretch to Heaven . . .
> O Utu,
> The Land I wish to enter; be thou my ally . . .
> In the place where the *Shems* have been raised up,
> Let me set up my *Shem!*

The *Shem*, we have shown, though commonly translated "Name" (that by which one is remembered), was in fact a rocketship: Enoch vanished upon his "Name" as he was taken heavenward. Half a millennium after Gilgamesh, in Egypt, King Teti made an almost identical plea:

> Men fall,
> They have no *Name*.
> (O god),
> Seize thou King Teti by his arms,
> Take thou King Teti to the sky,
> That he die not on Earth among men.

The goal of Gilgamesh was Tilmun, the land where the rocketships were raised up. To ask where he went to reach Tilmun, is to ask where Alexander went, deeming himself a Pharaoh and a god's son. It is to ask: Where on Earth was the *Duat?*

Because all these destinations, we must conclude, were one and the same.

And the land where they hoped to find the Stairway to Heaven, we shall conclusively show, was the peninsula of Sinai.

Accepting the possibility that the details given in the Book of the Dead may indeed refer to actual Egyptian geography, some scholars have suggested that the Pharaoh's simulated journey was along the Nile, from the shrines in Upper Egypt to those in Lower Egypt. The ancient texts, however, clearly speak of a journey beyond the boundaries of Egypt. The Pharaoh's direction is eastward, not northward; and as he crosses the Lake of Reeds and the desert beyond it, he leaves behind not only Egypt but also Africa: much is made of the perils—real and "political"—of coming from the domains of Horus into the "Lands of Seth," to Asia.

When the Pyramid Texts were inscribed by the Pharaohs of the Old Kingdom, their capital in Egypt was Memphis. The religious center of old was Heliopolis, a short distance to the northeast of Memphis. From these centers, a course eastward in fact led to a chain of lakes full of reeds and rushes. Beyond lay the desert, and the mountain pass, and the Sinai peninsula—the area whose skies had served as the final battlefield between Horus and Seth, between Zeus and Typhon.

The suggestion that the Pharaoh's journey to the Afterlife had indeed taken him to the Sinai peninsula is supported by the fact that Alexander had emulated not only the Pharaohs; there was also a deliberate effort to emulate the Israelite Exodus from Egypt under the leadership of Moses.

As in the biblical tale, the starting point was Egypt. Next came the "Red Sea"—the watery barrier whose waters parted so that the Israelites could cross upon the dry bed. In the histories of Alexander, the watery barrier was also encountered, and it was persistently called the Red Sea. As in the tale of Exodus, Alexander too attempted to lead his army across the waters on foot: in one version by building a causeway; in another "Alexander lay it bare by his prayers." Whether he succeeded or not (depending on the version), enemy soldiers were drowned by the onrushing waters—just as the Egyptians pursuing the Israelites had been drowned. The journeying Israelites encountered and battled an enemy named the Amalekites: in a Christian version of the Alexander histories, the enemy destroyed "by means of collecting the waters of the Red Sea and pouring the waters over them" were called "Amalekites."

Once across the waters—the literal translation of the biblical term *Yam Suff* is "Sea/Lake of Reeds"—there began a journey in a desert, toward a sacred mountain. Significantly, the landmark mountain which Alexander reached was named *Mushas*—the Mountain of Moses, whose Hebrew name was *Moshe*. It was there that Moses encountered an angel who spoke to him out of a fire (the burning bush); a similar incident is described in the tales of Alexander.

The double and triple parallels multiply, as we recall the tale in the Koran of Moses and the fish. The location of the Waters of Life in the Koran tale about Moses was "the junction of the two streams." It was where the stream of Osiris divided into two tributaries that the Pharaohs reached the entrance to the subterranean realm. In the tales of Alexander, it was at the junction of two subterranean streams that the crucial point was reached, where the "Stone of Adam" emitted light, where Alexander was advised by divine beings to turn back.

And there was the tradition, also recorded in the Muslim Koran, equating Alexander with Moses by calling him "He of the Two Horns"— recalling the biblical statement that, after Moses had visited with the Lord upon Mount Sinai, his face radiated and emitted "horns" (literally: rays) of light.

The arena for the biblical Exodus was the peninsula of Sinai. The conclusion from all the similarities and footstep-following can only be that it was toward the Sinai peninsula that Alexander, Moses and the Pharaohs set their course as they went east from Egypt. This, we will show, was also the destination of Gilgamesh.

To reach *Tilmun* on his second and decisive journey, Gilgamesh set sail in a "Ship of *Magan*," a Ship of Egypt. Starting from Mesopotamia, his only course was to sail down the Persian Gulf. Then, rounding the Arabian peninsula, he would have entered the Red Sea (which the Egyptians called the Sea of Ur). As the name of his ship indicates, he would have sailed up the Red Sea toward Egypt. But his destination was not Egypt; it was Tilmun. Was he then intending to land on the western shores of the Red Sea—in Nubia? On the eastern shore—in Arabia? Or straight ahead, on the peninsula of Sinai? (See map, Fig. 2.)

Fortunately for our investigation, Gilgamesh had met with a misfortune. His ship was sunk by a guarding god soon after he began his voyage. He was not too far gone from Sumer, for Enkidu (whose presence on the ship caused its sinking) pleaded that they make their way back, on foot, to Uruk. Resolved to reach Tilmun, Gilgamesh trekked instead overland to his chosen destination. Were his goal on the shores of the Red Sea, he would have cut across the Arabian peninsula. But instead he set his course to the northwest. We know that for a fact, because—having crossed a desert and passed desolate mountains—his first glimpse of civilization was a "low-lying sea." There was a city nearby, and an inn on its outskirts. The "ale-woman" warned him that the sea he saw and wished to cross was the "Sea of the Waters of Death."

Just as the Cedars of Lebanon had served as a unique landmark for determining the first destination of Gilgamesh, so does the "Sea of the Waters of Death" serve as a unique clue to the whereabouts of Gilgamesh on his second journey. Throughout the Near East, in all the lands of the ancient world, there is only one such body of water. It is so called to this very day: the *Dead Sea*. It is, indeed, a "low-lying sea," being the lowest body of water on the face of Earth (1,300 feet below sea level). Its waters are so saturated with salts and minerals that it is totally devoid of all marine and plant life.

The city that overlooked the Sea of the Waters of Death was surrounded by a wall. Its temple was dedicated to Sin, the Moon-god. Outside the city there was an inn. The hostess took Gilgamesh in, extending to him hospitality, giving him information.

The uncanny similarities to a known biblical tale cannot be missed. When the Israelites' forty years of wandering in the Wilderness had come to an end, it was time to enter Canaan. Coming from the Sinai peninsula, they circled the Dead Sea on its eastern side until they reached the place where the Jordan River flows into the Dead Sea. When Moses stood upon a hill overlooking the plain, he could see—as Gilgamesh had seen—the shimmering waters of the "low-lying sea." In the plain, on the other side of the Jordan, stood a city: *Jericho*. It blocked the Israelites' advance into Canaan, and they sent two spies to explore its defenses. A woman whose inn was at the city's walls extended to them hospitality, gave them information and guidance.

The Hebrew name for Jericho is *Yeriho*. It literally means "Moon City"— the city dedicated to the Moon god, Sin. . . .

It was, we suggest, the very city reached by Gilgamesh fifteen centuries before the Exodus.

Was Jericho already in existence circa 2900 B.C., when Gilgamesh was engaged in his searches? Archaeologists are agreed that Jericho has been inhabited since before 7000 B.C., and served as a flourishing urban center since about 3500 B.C.; it was certainly there when Gilgamesh arrived.

Refreshed and back to strength, Gilgamesh planned his continued journey. Finding himself at the northern end of the Dead Sea, he inquired of the ale-woman whether he could sail across its waters, rather than circle it overland. Were he to take the overland route, he would have taken the route which the Israelites eventually took—but in reverse; for Gilgamesh wished to go where the Israelites eventually came from. When the boatman Urshanabi finally ferried him over, he stepped ashore, we believe, at the southern end of the Dead Sea—as close to the Sinai peninsula as the boatman could have taken him.

From there he was to follow "a regular way"—a route in common use by caravans—"toward the Great Sea, which is far away." Again, the geography is recognizable from biblical terminology, for the Great Sea was the biblical name for the Mediterranean Sea. Journeying in the Negev, the dry southern region of Canaan, Gilgamesh was to go westward for a certain distance, looking for "two stone markers." There, Urshanabi told him, he was to make a turn and reach the town named Itla; it was located some distance from the Great Sea. Beyond Itla, in the Fourth Region of the gods, lay the restricted area.

Was Itla a "City of the Gods" or a City of Men?

The events there, described in a fragmented Hittite version of the Gilgamesh Epic, indicate that it was a place for both. It was a "sanctified city," with various gods coming and going through it or within easy reach of it. But men too could go there: the way to it was indicated by road markers. Gilgamesh not only rested there, and changed into fresh clothing: he also obtained there the sheep which he daily offered as sacrifices to the gods.

Such a city is known to us from the Old Testament. It was located where the south of Canaan merges into the Sinai peninsula, a gateway into the peninsula's Central Plain. Its sanctity was denoted by its name: *Kadesh* ("The Sanctified"); it was distinguished from a northern namesake (situated, significantly, on the approaches to Baalbek) by being called *Kadesh-Barnea* (which, stemming from the Sumerian, could have meant "Kadesh of the Shiny Stone Pillars"). In the Age of the Patriarchs, it was included in the domain of Abraham, who "journeyed to the Negev, and dwelt between Kadesh and Shur."

The city, by name and by function, is also known to us from the Canaanite tales of gods, men and the craving for Immortality. Danel, we recall, asked the god El for a rightful heir, so that his son could erect for him a commemorative stela at Kadesh. In another Ugaritic text we are told that a son of El named *Shibani* ("The Seventh"),—the biblical town of Beer-Sheba ("The Well of the Seventh") might have been named after him—was told to "raise a commemorating (Pillar) in the desert of Kadesh."

Indeed, both Charles Virolleaud and René Dussaud, who in the periodical *Syria* pioneered the translation and understanding of the Ugaritic texts, concluded that the locale of the many epic tales "was the region between the Red Sea and the Mediterranean," the Sinai peninsula. The god Ba'al, who loved to fish in Lake Sumkhi, went for his hunting to the "desert of Alosh," an area associated (as in Fig. 104) with the date palm. As both Virolleaud and Dussaud have pointed out, this is a geographical clue connecting the Ugaritic locale with the biblical record of the Exodus: the Israelites, according to Numbers 33, journeyed from Marah (the place of bitter waters) and Elim (the oasis of date palms) to *Alosh*.

More details, placing El and the younger gods in the same arena as that of the Exodus, are found in a text entitled by the scholars "The Birth of the Gracious and Beautiful Gods." Its very opening verses locate the action in the "Desert of *Suffim*"—unmistakably a desert bordering on the *Yam Suff* ("Sea of Reeds") of the Exodus:

Fig. 104

> I call the gracious and beautiful gods,
> sons of the Prince. I will place them
> in the City of Ascending and Going,
> in the desert of Suffim.

The Canaanite texts provide us with yet another clue. By and large they refer to the pantheon's head as "El"—the supreme, the loftiest—a generic title rather than a personal name. But in the above quoted text El identifies himself as *Yerah* and his spouse as *Nikhal.* "Yerah" is the Semitic for "Moon"—the god better known as *Sin;* and "Nikhal" is a Semitic rendition of NIN.GAL, the Sumerian name for the spouse of the Moon-god.

Scholars have advanced many theories regarding the origin of the peninsula's name *Sinai.* For once, the obvious reason—that, as the name stated, it "Belonged to *Sin*"—has been among the preferred solutions.

We can see (in Fig. 72) that the Moon's crescent was the emblem of the deity in whose land the Winged Gateway was located. We find that the main crossroads in the central Sinai, the well-watered place *Nakhl,* still bears the name of Sin's spouse.

And we can confidently conclude that the "Land Tilmun" was the Sinai peninsula.

An examination of the geography, topography, geology, climate, flora and history of the Sinai peninsula will affirm our identification, and clarify the Sinai's role in the affairs of gods and men.

The Mesopotamian texts described Tilmun as situated at the "mouth" of two bodies of water. The Sinai peninsula, shaped as an inverted triangle indeed begins where the Red Sea separates into two arms—the Gulf of Suez on the west, and the Gulf of Elat (Gulf of Aqaba) on the east. Indeed, when Egyptian depictions of the Land of Seth, where the Duat was, are turned around, they show schematically a peninsula with the Sinai's features (Fig. 105).

The texts spoke of "mountainous Tilmun." The Sinai peninsula is indeed made up of a high mountainous southern part, a mountainous central plateau, and a northern plain (surrounded by mountains), which levels off via sandy hills to the Mediterranean coastline. The coastal strip constituted a "land-bridge" between Asia and Africa from time immemorial. Egyptian Pharaohs used it to invade Canaan and Phoenicia and to challenge the Hittites. Sargon of Akkad claimed that he reached and "washed his weapons" in the Mediterranean; "the sea lands"—the lands along the Mediterranean coast—"three times I encircled; Tilmun my hand captured." Sargon II, king of Assyria in the eighth century B.C., asserted that he had conquered the area stretching "from Bit-Yahkin on the shore of the Salt Sea as far as the border of Tilmun." The name "Salt Sea" has survived to this day as a Hebrew name for the Dead Sea—another confirmation that Tilmun lay in proximity to the Dead Sea.

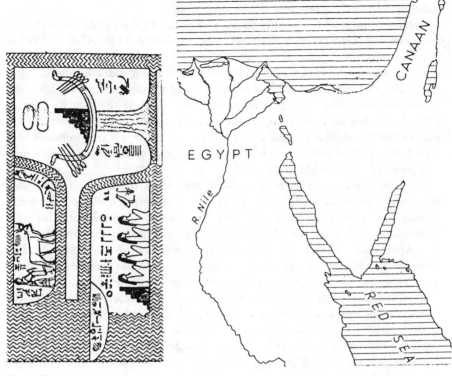

Fig. 105

Several Assyrian kings mention the Brook of Egypt as a geographic landmark on their expeditions to Egypt. Sargon II lists the Brook after describing the conquest of Ashdod, the Philistine city on the Mediterranean coast. Esarhaddon, who ruled somewhat later, boasted thus: "I trod upon Arza at the Brook of Egypt; I put Asuhili, its king, in fetters. . . . Upon Qanayah, king of Tilmun, I imposed tribute." The name "Brook of Egypt" is identical to the biblical name for the large and extensive Sinai *wadi* (shallow river that runs with water only during the rainy season) now called *Wadi El-Arish*. Ashurbanipal, who followed Esarhaddon on the throne of Assyria, claimed that he "laid his yoke of overlordship from Tyre, which is in the Upper Sea (Mediterranean) as far as Tilmun which is in the Lower Sea" (the Red Sea).

In all instances, the geography and topography of Tilmun fully match the Sinai peninsula.

Except for annual variations, the peninsula's climate in historical times is believed to have been the same as nowadays: an irregular rainy season lasting from October through May; the rest of the year is completely dry. The meager rainfall qualifies the whole of Sinai to be defined as a desert (less than ten inches of rainfall per annum). Yet the high granite peaks in the south are snowbound in winter, and in the northern coastal strip the water level is only a few feet below the ground.

Typical to most of the peninsula are the *wadis*. In the south, the waters of the swift and short rainfalls drain off either eastward (to the Gulf of Elat) or (mostly) westward, into the Gulf of Suez. It is there that most of the picturesque deep canyon-like wadis with flourishing oases are found. But the bulk of the peninsula's rainwater is drained northward into the Mediterranean Sea, via the extensive Wadi El-Arish and its myriad tributaries, that look on a map as the blood vessels of a giant heart. In this part of the Sinai, the depths of the wadis that make up this network may change from a few inches to a few feet; the width—from a few feet to a mile and more after a sizeable rain.

Even in the rainy season the rainfall pattern is totally erratic. Sudden downpours alternate with long dry spells. An assumption of plentiful water during the season or in its immediate aftermath could thus be very misleading. This must have happened to the Israelites as they left Egypt in mid-April and entered the Sinai Wilderness a few weeks later. Finding themselves without the expected waters, it required the intervention of the Lord twice, to show Moses where to strike the rocks for water.

The *Bedouin* (local nomads), as other seasoned travelers in the Sinai, can duplicate the miracle, if the soil making up the wadi's bed is right. The secret is that in many places the rocky bed lies above a layer of clay soil that captures the water as it quickly seeps through the rocks. With knowledge and luck, a little digging in a completely dry wadi bed uncovers water only a few feet below the surface.

Was this nomad art the great miracle performed by the Lord? Recent discoveries in the Sinai throw a new light on the subject. Israeli hydrologists (associated with the Weizmann Institute of Science) have discovered that, like parts of the Sahara Desert and some deserts in Nubia, there is "fossil water"—the remains of prehistoric lakes from another geological era—deep under the central Sinai. The vast underground reservoir, with enough water (they estimated) to suffice for a population as large as Israel's for almost one hundred years, extends for some 6,000 square miles in a wide belt that begins near the Suez Canal and reaches under Israel's arid Negev.

Though lying on the average some 3,000 feet below the rocky ground, the water is sub-artesian and rises by its own pressure to about 1,000 feet below ground. Egyptian experimental drillings for oil in the center of the northern plain (at Nakhl), have struck instead this water reservoir. Other drillings confirmed this incredible fact: above ground—an arid wilderness; below, within easy reach of modern drilling and pumping equipment—a lake of pure, sparkling water!

Could the Nefilim, with their space-age technology, have missed this knowledge? Was this, rather than a little water in a dry wadi bed, the water that gushed forth after Moses had struck the rock, as indicated by the Lord?

Take in thy hand the staff with which you performed the miracles in Egypt, the Lord told Moses; you will see me standing upon a certain rock; strike that rock with the staff, "and there shall come out of it water, and the people shall drink"—enough water for a multitude of people and their livestock. So that the greatness of Yahweh be known, Moses was to take with him to the site some witnesses; and the miracle took place "before the eyes of the elders of Israel."

A Sumerian tale concerning Tilmun relates an almost identical event. It is a tale of bad times caused by a shortage of water. Crops withered, cattle were not fed, animals went thirsty, the people fell silent. Ninsikilla, spouse of Tilmun's ruler Enshag, complained to her father Enki:

> The city which thou hast given . . .
> Tilmun, the city thou hast given . . .
> Has not waters of the river . . .
> Unbathed is the maiden;
> No sparkling water is poured in the city.

Studying the problem, Enki concluded that the only solution would be to *bring up subterranean waters*. The depths must have been greater than what could be attained by digging a usual well. So Enki conceived a plan whereby the layers of rocks would be penetrated by *a missile fired from the skies!*

> Father Enki answered Ninsikilla, his daughter:
> "Let divine Utu position himself in the skies.
> A missile let him tightly affix to his 'breast'
>   and from high direct it toward the earth . . .
> From the source whence issues Earth's waters,
>   let him bring thee sweet water from the earth."

So instructed, Utu/Shamash proceeded to bring up water from the subterranean sources:

> Utu, positioning himself in the skies,
>   a missile tightly tied to his "breast,"
> From high directed it toward the earth . . .
> He let go of his missile from high in the sky.
> Through the crystal stones he brought up water;
> From the source whence issues Earth's waters
>   he brought her sweet water, from the earth.

Could a missile shot from the skies pierce the earth and cause potable water to come up? Anticipating the incredulity of his readers, the ancient scribe affirmed at the tale's end: "Verily, it was so." The miracle, the text went on, did work: Tilmun became a land "of crop raising fields and farms which bear grain"; and Tilmun-City "became port city of the Land, the site of quays and mooring piers."

The parallels between Tilmun and Sinai are thus doubly affirmed: first, the existence of the subterranean water reservoir, below the rocky surface; secondly, the presence of Utu/Shamash (the Spaceport's commander) in the proximity.

The Sinai peninsula can also account for *all* the products for which Tilmun was renowned.

Tilmun was a source of gemstones akin to the bluish lapis lazuli which the Sumerians cherished. It is an established fact that the Pharaohs of Egypt obtained the blue-green gemstone turquoise as well as a blue-green mineral (malachite) from the southwestern parts of the Sinai. The earliest turquoise mining area is now called Wadi Magharah—the Wadi of Caves; there, tunnels were cut into the rocky sides of the wadi's canyon and miners went in to chisel out the turquoise. Later on, mining also took place at a site now named Serabit-el-Khadim. Egyptian inscriptions dating back to the Third Dynasty (2700–2600 B.C.) have been found at Wadi Magharah, and it is believed that it was then that the Egyptians began to station garrisons and occupy the mines on a continuing basis.

Archaeological discoveries, as well as depictions by the first Pharaohs of defeated and captured "Asiatic Nomads" (Fig. 106), convince scholars that at first the Egyptians only raided mines developed earlier by Semitic tribesmen. Indeed, the Egyptian name for turquoise, *mafka-t* (after which they called the Sinai the "Land of Mafkat"), stems from the Semitic verb meaning "to mine, to extract by cutting." These mining areas were in the domain of the goddess Hathor, who was known both as "Lady of Sinai" and

Fig. 106

"Lady of *Mafkat*." A great goddess of olden times, one of the early sky gods of the Egyptians, she was nicknamed by them "The Cow" and was depicted with cow's horns (see Figs. 7 and 106). Her name, *Hat-Hor*, spelled hieroglyphically by drawing a falcon within an enclosure ⟨𓉡⟩, has been interpreted by scholars to mean "House of Horus" (Horus having been depicted as a falcon). But it literally meant "Falcon House," which affirms our conclusions regarding the location and functions of the Land of the Missiles.

According to the *Encyclopaedia Britannica*, "turquoise was obtained from the Sinai peninsula before the fourth millennium B.C. in one of the world's first important hard-rock mining operations." At that time, the Sumerian civilization was only beginning to stir, and the Egyptian one was almost a millennium away. Who then could have organized the mining activities? The Egyptians said it was Thoth, the god of sciences.

In this and in the assignment of the Sinai to Hathor, the Egyptians emulated Sumerian traditions. According to Sumerian texts, the god who organized the mining operations of the Anunnaki was Enki, the God of Knowledge; and Tilmun, the texts attested, was allotted in pre-Diluvial times to Ninhursag, sister of Enki and Enlil. In her youth, she was a smashing beauty and the chief nurse of the Nefilim. But in her old age, she was nicknamed "The Cow" and, as the Goddess of the Date Palm, was depicted with cow's horns (Fig. 107). The similarities between her and Hathor, and the analogies between their domains, are too obvious to require elaboration.

The Sinai was also a major source of copper, and the evidence here is that the Egyptians relied mostly on raiding expeditions to obtain it. To do this, they had to penetrate deeper into the peninsula; a Pharaoh of the Twelfth Dynasty (the time of Abraham) left us these comments of his deeds:

Fig. 107

"Reaching the boundaries of the foreign lands with his feet; exploring the mysterious valleys, reaching the limits of the unknown." He boasted that his men lost not a single case of the seized booty.

Recent explorations in the Sinai by Israeli scientists found ample evidence showing that "during the times of the Early Kingdom of Egypt, in the third millenium B.C., Sinai was densely inhabited by Semitic copper-smelting and turquoise-mining tribes, who resisted the penetration of Pharaonic expeditions into their territory (Beno Rothenberg, *Sinai Explorations 1967–1972*). "We could establish the existence of a fairly large industrial metallurgical enterprise. . . . There are copper mines, miners' camps and copper smelting installations, spread from the western parts of southern Sinai to as far east as Elat at the head of the Gulf of Aqaba."

Elat, known in Old Testament times as Etzion-Gaber, was indeed a "Pittsburgh of the Ancient World." Some twenty years ago, Nelson Glueck uncovered at Timna, just north of Elat, King Solomon's copper mines. The ores were taken to Etzion-Gaber, where they were smelted and refined in "one of the largest, if not *the* largest, of metallurgical centers in existence" in ancient times (*Rivers in the Desert*).

The archaeological evidence once again ties in with biblical and Mesopotamian texts. Esarhaddon, king of Assyria, boasted that "upon *Qanayah,* king of Tilmun, I imposed tribute." The *Qenites* are mentioned in the Old Testament as inhabitants of the southern Sinai, and their name literally meant "smiths, metallurgists." The tribe into which Moses married when he escaped from Egypt into the Sinai was that of the Qenites. R. J. Forbes (*The Evolution of the Smith*) pointed out that the biblical term *Qain* ("smith") stemmed from the Sumerian KIN ("fashioner").

Pharaoh Ramses III, who reigned in the century following the Exodus, recorded his invasion of these coppersmiths' dwellings and the plundering of the metallurgical center of Timna-Elat:

> I destroyed the people of Seir, of the Tribes of the *Shasu;* I plundered their tents, their people's possessions, their cattle likewise, without number. They were pinioned and brought as captive, as tribute of Egypt. I gave them to the gods, as slaves into their temples.
>
> I sent forth my men to the Ancient Country, to the great copper mines which are in that place. Their galleys carried them; others on a land-journey were upon their asses. It has not been heard before, since the reign of the Pharaohs began.
>
> The mines were found abounding in copper; it was loaded by ten-thousands into the galleys. They were sent forward to Egypt and arrived safely. It was carried and made into a heap under the palace balcony, in many bars of copper, a hundred thousand, being of the color of gold of three refinings.
>
> I allowed all the people to see them, like wonders.

It was to spend the rest of his life in the mines of Tilmun that the gods had sentenced Enkidu; and so it was that Gilgamesh conceived the plan to charter a "Ship of Egypt" and take his comrade along—since the Land of Mines and the "Land of Missiles" were both parts of the same land. Our identification matches the ancient data.

Before we continue with our reconstruction of historic and prehistoric events, it is important to buttress our conclusion that *Tilmun* was the Sumerian name for the Sinai peninsula. This is not what scholars have held until now; and we should analyze their contrary views, and show why they have been wrong.

A persistent school of thought, one of whose early advocates was P. B. Cornwall (*On the Location of Tilmun*), identifies Tilmun (sometimes transcribed "Dilmun") as the island of Bahrein in the Persian Gulf. This view relies most heavily on the inscription by Sargon II of Assyria, wherein he asserted that among the kings paying him tribute was "Uperi, king of Dilmun, whose abode is situated like a fish, thirty double-hours away, in the midst of the sea where the sun rises." This statement is taken to mean that Tilmun was an island; and the scholars who hold this view identify the "Sea where the sun rises" as the Persian Gulf. They then end up with Bahrein as the answer.

There are several flaws in this interpretation. First, it could well be that only the capital city of Tilmun was on an offshore island: the texts leave no doubt that there was a land Tilmun and a Tilmun-city. Secondly, other Assyrian inscriptions which describe cities as being "in the midst of the sea" apply to coastal cities on a bay or a promontory, but not on an island (as, for instance, Arvad on the Mediterranean coast). Then, if the "sea where the sun rises" indicates a sea east of Mesopotamia, the Persian Gulf does not qualify, since it lies to the south, not to the east, of Mesopotamia. Also, Bahrein lies too close to Mesopotamia to account for thirty double-hours of sailing. It is situated some 300 miles south of the Mesopotamian Gulf ports; in sixty hours of sailing, even at a leisurely pace, a distance many times greater could be covered.

Another major problem arising from a Bahrein-Tilmun identification concerns the products for which Tilmun was renowned. Even in the days of Gilgamesh, not all of the Land Tilmun was a restricted area. There was a part, as we have seen, where sentenced men toiled in dark and dusty mines, digging out the copper and gemstones for which Tilmun was famous. Long associated with Sumer in culture and trade, Tilmun supplied it with certain desired species of woods. And its agricultural areas—subject of the above-mentioned tale of Ninsikilla's plea for artesian waters—provided the ancient world with highly prized onions and dates.

Bahrein had none of these, except for some "ordinary dates." So, to circumvent the problem, the pro-Bahrein school has developed a complex answer. Geoffrey Bibby (*Looking for Dilmun*) and others of like mind suggest that Bahrein was a trans-shipment point. The products, they agree, indeed came from some other, more distant land. But the ships which carried these goods did not go all the way to Sumer. They stopped and unloaded their goods at Bahrein, where the famous merchants of Sumer picked them up for the final haul into Sumerian ports; so that, when the Sumerian scribes wrote down where the goods had come from (so this theory goes), they wrote down "Dilmun," meaning Bahrein.

But why would ships that have sailed great distances fail to sail the final short distance to the actual destination in Mesopotamia, and instead go to the extra trouble and cost of offloading at Bahrein? Also, this theory stands in direct contradiction to specific statements by rulers of Sumer and Akkad that the ships *of* Tilmun, among ships from other lands, anchored at their port cities. Ur-Nanshe, a king of Lagash some two centuries after Gilgamesh was king of neighboring Uruk, claimed that "the ships of Tilmun . . . brought me wood as tribute." We recognize the name *Tilmun* in his inscription (Fig. 108) by the pictograph for "missile." Sargon, the first ruler of Akkad, boasted that "at the wharf of Akkad he made moor ships from Meluhha, ships from Magan and ships from Tilmun."

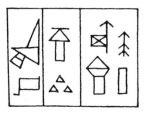

Fig. 108

Clearly, then, the ships brought the products of Tilmun straight to the Mesopotamian ports proper, as logic and economics would dictate. Likewise, the ancient texts speak of direct exports from Mesopotamia to Tilmun. One inscription records a shipment of wheat, cheese and shelled barley from Lagash to Tilmun (circa 2500 B.C.); no trans-shipment at an island is ever mentioned.

One of the leading opponents of the Bahrein theory, Samuel N. Kramer (*Dilmun, the "Land of the Living"*) stressed the fact that the Mesopotamian texts described it as "a distant land," reachable not without risk and adventure. These descriptions do not match a close-by island, reachable after an easy sailing down the quiet waters of the Persian Gulf. He also attached great importance to the fact that the various Mesopotamian texts placed Tilmun near *two* bodies of water, rather than near or in a single sea. The Akkadian texts located Tilmun *ina pi narati*—"at the mouth of the two flowing waters": where two bodies of water begin.

Guided by yet another statement, which said that Tilmun was the land "where the Sun rises," Kramer concluded, first, that Tilmun was a land and not an island; and secondly, that it must have been located east of Sumer, for it is in the east that the Sun rises. Searching in the east for a place where two bodies of water meet, he could come up only with a southeastern point, where the Persian Gulf meets the Indian Ocean. Baluchistan, or somewhere near the Indus River, were his suggestions.

Kramer's own hesitation stemmed from the well-known fact that numerous Sumerian and Akkadian texts listing countries and peoples do not mention Tilmun in association with such eastern lands as Elam or Aratta. Instead, they lump together as lands situated next to each other *Meluhha* (Nubia/Ethiopia), *Magan* (Egypt) and *Tilmun*. The proximity between Egypt (Magan) and Tilmun is spelled out at the end of the "Enki and Ninhursag" text, where the appointment of Nintulla as "Lord of Magan" and of Enshag as "Lord of Tilmun" obtains the blessing of the two gods. It is also evident from a remarkable text, written as an autobiography of Enki, which describes his activities after the Deluge, assisting Mankind to establish its civilizations; again, Tilmun is listed next to Magan and Meluhha:

> The lands of *Magan* and *Tilmun*
>   looked up at me.
> I, Enki, moored the Tilmun-boat at the coast,
> Loaded the Magan-boat sky high.
> The joyous boat of *Meluhha*
>   transports gold and silver.

In view of this proximity of Tilmun to Egypt, what about the statements that Tilmun was "where the sun rises"—meaning (scholars say) *east* of Sumer, and not west of it (as the Sinai is)?

The simple answer is that the texts do not make that statement at all. They do not say "where the *Sun* rises"; they state "where *Shamash* ascends"—and that makes all the difference. Tilmun was not at all in the east; but it certainly was the place where Utu/Shamash (the god whose celestial symbol was the Sun, and not the Sun itself) ascended skyward in his rocketships. The words of the Gilgamesh epic are quite clear:

> At the Mountain of *Mashu* he arrived,
> Where by day the *Shems* he watched
>   as they depart and come in . . .
> Rocket-men guard its gate . . .
>   they watch over *Shamash*
>   as he ascends and descends.

That, indeed was the place whereto Ziusudra had been taken:

> In the Land of the Crossing
>   in mountainous Tilmun—
>   the place *where Shamash ascends*—
> they caused him to dwell.

And so it was that Gilgamesh—denied permission to mount a Shem, and seeking therefore only to converse with his ancestor Ziusudra—set his steps to *Mount Mashu* in Tilmun—the *Mount of Moshe* (Moses) in the Sinai peninsula.

Modern botanists have been amazed by the variety of the peninsula's flora, finding more than a thousand species of plants, many unique to the Sinai, varying from tall trees to tiny shrubs. Where there is water—as in oases, or below the surface in the coastal sand dunes, or in the beds of the wadis— these trees and shrubs grow with impressive persistence, having adapted themselves to the particular climate and hydrography of the Sinai.

The Sinai's northeastern parts could well have been the source of the craved-for onions. Our name for the variety with the long green stem, *scallion*, bears evidence to the port from which this delicacy was shipped to Europe: *Ascalon* on the Mediterranean coast, just north of the Brook of Egypt.

One of the trees that adapted itself to the Sinai's unique circumstances is the acacia, which accommodates its high transpiration rate by growing only in the wadi beds, where it exploits the subsurface moisture down to many feet. As a result, the tree can live for almost ten years without rain. It is a tree whose timber is a prized wood; according to the Old Testament, the Holy Ark and other components of the Tabernacle were made of this wood. It could have well served as the prized wood which the kings of Sumer imported for their temples.

An ever-present sight in the Sinai are the tamarisks—bush-like trees that trace the wadi courses year round, for their roots reach down to the subsurface moisture and they can grow even where the water is saline and brackish. After especially rainy winters, the tamarisk groves fill up with a sweet, granular white substance which is the excretion of small insects that live on the tamarisks. The Bedouin call it by its biblical name, *manna*, to this very day.

The tree with which Tilmun was mostly associated in antiquity, however, was the *date palm*. It is still the Sinai's most important tree economically. Needing minimal cultivation, it provides the Bedouin with fruit (dates); its pulp and kernels are fed to camels and goats; the trunk is used for building and as fuel; the branches for roofing; the fibers for rope and weaving.

We know from Mesopotamian records that these dates were also exported from Tilmun in antiquity. The dates were so large and tasty that recipes for the meals of the gods of Uruk (the city of Gilgamesh) specified that "every day of the year, for the four daily meals, 108 measures of ordinary dates, and dates of the Land Tilmun, as also figs and raisins . . . shall be offered to the deities." The nearest and most ancient town on the land route from Sinai to Mesopotamia was Jericho. Its biblical epithet was "Jericho, the city of dates."

The date palm, we find, has been adopted as a symbol in Near Eastern religions, i.e., in ancient concepts of Man and his gods. The biblical Psalmist promised that "the Righteous like a date palm shall flourish." The Prophet Ezekiel, in his vision of the rebuilt temple of Jerusalem, saw it decorated with alternating "Cherubim and date palms . . . so that a date palm was between a Cherub and a Cherub, and two (date palms) flank each Cherub." Residing at the time among the exiles whom the Babylonians had forcefully brought over from Judea, Ezekiel was well acquainted with the Mesopotamian depictions of the Cherubim and date palm theme (Fig. 109).

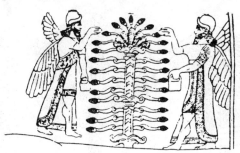

Fig. 109

Alongside the Winged Disk (the emblem of the Twelfth Planet), the symbol most widely depicted by all the ancient nations was the *Tree of Life*. Writing in *Der Alte Orient*, Felix von Luschau has shown back in 1912 that the Greek Ionian column capitals (Fig. 110a) as well as Egyptian ones (Fig. 110b) were in fact stylizations of the Tree of Life in the shape of a date palm (Fig. 110c), and confirmed earlier suggestions that the Fruit of Life of legend and epic tales was some special species of the date fruit. We find the theme of the date palm as the symbol of Life carried on even in Muslim Egypt, as in the decorations of Cairo's grand mosque (Fig. 110d).

Many major studies, such as *De Boom des Levens en Schrift en Historie* by Henrik Bergema and *The King and the Tree of Life in Ancient Near Eastern Religion* by Geo. Widengren, show that the concept of such a tree, growing in an Abode of the Gods, has spread from the Near East all over Earth and has become a tenet of all religions, everywhere.

The source of all these depictions and beliefs were the Sumerian records of the Land of the Living,

> Tilmun,
> Where old woman says not "I am an old woman,"
> Where old man says not "I am an old man."

The Sumerians, masters of word-plays, called the Land of the Missiles TIL.MUN; yet the term could also mean "Land Of Living," for TIL also meant "Life." The Tree of Life in Sumerian was GISH.TIL; but GISH also

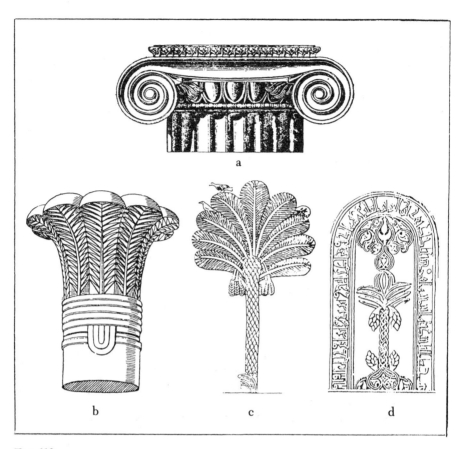

Fig. 110

meant a man-made, a manufactured object; so that GISH.TIL could also mean "The Vehicle to Life"—a rocketship. In art too, we find the Eaglemen sometimes saluting not the date palm, but a rocket (Fig. 60).

The binding knots tighten further, as we find that in Greek religious art, the omphalos was associated with the date palm. An ancient Greek depiction of Delphi shows that the omphalos replica that was erected outside Apollo's temple was set up next to a date palm (Fig. 111). Since no such trees grow in Greece, it was an artificial tree made (scholars believe) of bronze. The association of the omphalos with the date palm must have been a matter of basic symbolism, for these depictions were repeated also in respect to other Greek oracle centers.

We have found earlier that the omphalos served as a link between Greek, Egyptian, Nubian and Canaanite "oracle centers" and the *Duat*. Now we find this "Stone of Splendor" linked to the date palm—the Tree of the Land of Living.

Indeed, Sumerian texts accompanying depictions of the Cherubim included the following incantation:

The dark-brown tree of Enki I hold in my hand;
The tree that tells the count, great heavensward weapon,
I hold in my hand;
The palm tree, great tree of oracles, I hold in my hand.

A Mesopotamian depiction shows a god holding up in his hand this "palm tree, Great tree of oracles" (Fig. 112). He is granting this Fruit of Life to a king at the place of the "Four Gods." We have already come upon this place, in Egyptian texts and depictions: they were the Four Gods of the Four Cardinal Points, located by the Stairway to Heaven in the *Duat*. We have also seen (Fig. 72) that the Sumerian Gateway to Heaven was marked by the date palm.

And we have no more doubt that the target of the ancient Search for Immortality was a Spaceport—somewhere in the Sinai peninsula.

Fig. 111

Fig. 112

XI

The Elusive Mount

Somewhere in the Sinai peninsula, the Nefilim had established their post-Diluvial Spaceport. Somewhere in the Sinai peninsula, mortals—a select few, with their god's blessing—could approach a certain mountain. There, "Go back!" the guarding bird-men ordered Alexander, "for the land on which you stand belongs to God, alone." There, "Do not come nearer!" the Lord called out to Moses, "for the place whereon thou standest is sacred ground." There, eagle-men challenged Gilgamesh with their stun-rays, only to realize he was no mere mortal.

The Sumerians called this mount of encounter Mount MA.SHU—the Mount of the Supreme Barge. The tales of Alexander named it Mount *Mushas*—the Mountain of *Moses*. Its identical nature and function, coupled with its identical name, suggest that in all instances it was the same mountain that was the destination's landmark. It thus seems that the answer to the question "Where in the peninsula was the gateway?" is right at hand: Is not the Mount of the Exodus, "Mount Sinai," clearly marked on maps of the peninsula—the tallest peak among the high granite mountains of southern Sinai?

The Israelite Exodus from Egypt has been commemorated each year for the past thirty-three centuries by the celebration of the Passover. The historical and religious records of the Hebrews are replete with references to the Exodus, the wanderings in the Wilderness, the Covenant at Mount Sinai. The people have been constantly reminded of the Theophany, when the whole nation of Israel had seen the Lord Yahweh alight in his glory upon the sacred mount. Yet its location was de-emphasized, lest attempts be made to make the place a cult center. There is no recorded instance in the Bible of anyone even trying to pay a return visit to Mount Sinai, with one exception: the Prophet Elijah. Some four centuries after the Exodus, he escaped for his life after having slain the priests of Ba'al upon Mount Carmel. Setting his course to the mount in Sinai, he lost his way in the desert. An angel of the Lord revived him and placed him in a cave in the mount.

Nowadays, it would seem, one needs no guiding angel to find Mount

Sinai. The modern pilgrim, as pilgrims have done for centuries past, sets his course to the monastery of Santa Katarina (Fig. 113), so named after the martyred Katherine of Egypt whose body angels carried to the nearby peak bearing her name. After an overnight stay, at daybreak, the pilgrims begin the climb to *Gebel Mussa* ("Mount Moses" in Arabic). It is the southern peak of a two mile massif rising south of the monastery—the "traditional" Mount Sinai with which the Theophany and the Lawgiving are associated (Fig. 114).

The climb to that peak is long and difficult, involving an ascent of some 2,500 feet. One path is by way of some 4,000 steps laid out by the monks along the western slopes of the massif. An easier way that takes several hours longer begins in the valley between the massif and a mountain appropriately named after Jethro, the father-in-law of Moses, and rises gradually along the eastern slopes until it connects with the last 750 steps of the first path. It was at that intersection, according to the monk's tradition, that Elijah encountered the Lord.

A Christian chapel and a Muslim shrine, both small and crudely built, mark the spot where the Tablets of the Law were given to Moses. A cave nearby is revered as the "cleft in the rock" wherein the Lord placed Moses as He passed by him, as related in Exodus 33:22. A well along the descent route is identified as the well from which Moses watered the flock of his father-in-law. Every possible event relating to the Holy Mount is thus assigned by the monks' traditions a definite spot on the peak of Gebel Mussa and its surroundings.

From the peak of Gebel Mussa, one can see some of the other peaks which make up the granite heartland, of which this mount is a member. Surprisingly, it appears to be lower than many of its neighbors!

Indeed, in support of the Saint Katherine legend, the monks have put up a sign in the main building which proclaims:

Altitude	5012 FT
Moses Mount	7560 FT
Sta. Katherine Mount	8576 FT

As one is convinced that Mount Katherine is indeed the higher one—in fact, the highest in the peninsula—and thus rightly chosen by the angels to hide the saint's body thereon, one is also disappointed that—contrary to long-held beliefs—God had brought the Children of Israel to this forbidding area, to impress upon them his might and his laws not from the tallest mount around.

Had God missed the right mountain?

Fig. 113

Fig. 114

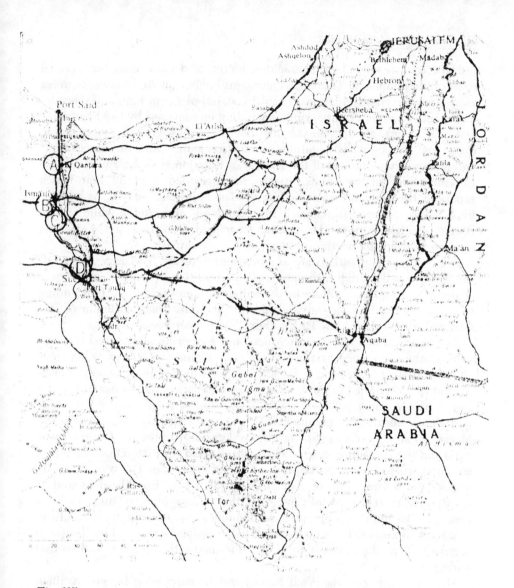

Fig. 115

In 1809, the Swiss scholar Johann Ludwig Burckhardt arrived in the Near East in behalf of the British Association for Promoting the Discovery of the Interior Parts of Africa. Studying Arabic and Muslim customs, he put a *turban* on his head, dressed as an Arab and changed his name to Ibrahim Ibn Abd Allah—Abraham the Son of Allah's Servant. He was thus able to travel in parts hitherto forbidden to the infidels, discovering ancient Egyptian temples at Abu Simbel and the Nabatean rock city of Petra in Transjordan.

On April 15, 1816, he set out on camelback from the town of Suez, at the head of the Gulf of Suez. His goal was to retrace the route of the Exodus, and thereby to establish the true identity of Mount Sinai. Following the presumed route taken by the Israelites, he traveled south along the western coast of the peninsula. There the mountains begin some ten to twenty miles away from the coast, creating a desolate coastal plain cut here and there by wadis and a couple of hot springs, including one favored by the Pharaohs.

As he went south, Burckhardt noted the geography, topography, distances. He compared conditions and place names with the descriptions and names of the stations of the Exodus as mentioned in the Bible. Where the limestone plateau ends, nature has provided a sandy belt which separates the plateau from a belt of Nubian sandstone, serving as a cross-Sinai avenue. There Burckhardt turned inland, and after a while set his course southward into the granite heartland, reaching the Katherine monastery from the north (as today's air traveler does).

Some of his observations are of a lingering interest. The area, he found, produced excellent dates; the monks had a tradition of sending large boxes of them as an annual tribute to the sultan in Constantinople. Befriending the area's Bedouins, they invited him to the annual feast in honor of "St. George"; they called him "El Khidher"—The Evergreen!

Burckhardt ascended mounts Mussa and Katherine and toured the area extensively. He was especially fascinated by *Mount Umm Shumar*—a mere 180 feet shorter than Mount St. Katherine—which rises somewhat southwest of the Mussa-Katherine group. From a distance, its top dazzled in the sun "with the most brilliant white color," due to an unusual inclusion of particles of mica in the granite rocks, forming "a striking contrast with the blackened surface of the slate and the red granite" of the mountain's lower parts and the surrounding area. The peak also had the distinction of offering an unobstructed view to both the Gulf of Suez ("el-Tor was distinctly visible") and the Gulf of Aqaba (Gulf of Elat). Burckhardt found it mentioned in the convent's records, that Umm Shumar used to be a principal location of monastic settlements. In the fifteenth century, "caravans of asses laden with corn and other provisions passed by this place regularly from the convent to el-Tor, for this is the nearest road to that harbor."

His way back was via Wadi Feiran and its oasis—the largest in Sinai. Where the wadi leaves the mountains and reaches the coastal strip, Burckhardt climbed up a magnificent mountain rising over 6,800 feet—*Mount Serbal*, one of the tallest in the peninsula. There he found remains of shrines and pilgrims' inscriptions. Additional research established that the main monastic center in Sinai, through most of the centuries, was at Wadi Feiran, near Serbal—and not at St. Katherine.

When Burckhardt published his findings (*Travels in Syria and the Holy Land*), his conclusions shook the scholarly and biblical world. The true Mount Sinai, he stated, was not Mount Mussa, but Mount Serbal!

Inspired by Burckhardt's writings, the French Count Léon de Laborde toured the Sinai in 1826 and 1828; his main contribution to the knowledge of the area (*Commentaire sur L'Exode*) were his fine maps and drawings.

He was followed in 1839 by the Scottish artist David Roberts; his magnificent drawings, wherein he embellished accuracy with some imaginative flair, aroused great interest in an era before photography.

The next major journey to Sinai was undertaken by the American Edward Robinson, together with Eli Smith. Like Burckhardt, they left Suez City on camelback, armed with his book and de Laborde's maps. It took them thirteen early spring days to reach St. Katherine. There, Robinson gave the monks' legends a thoroughgoing examination. He found out that at Feiran there indeed was a superior monastic community, sometimes led by full bishops, to which Katherine and several other monastic communities in southern Sinai were subordinate; so that tradition must have placed greater emphasis on Feiran. In the tales and documents, he discovered that mounts Mussa and Katherine were of no Christian consequence in the early Christian centuries, and that Katherine's supremacy developed only in the seventeenth century, when the other unfortified monastic communities fell prey to invaders and marauders. Checking local Arab traditions, he found that the biblical names "Sinai" and "Horeb" were totally unknown to the local Bedouins; it was the Katherine monks who began to apply these names to certain mountains.

Was Burckhardt, then, right? Robinson *(Biblical Researches in Palestine, Mount Sinai and Arabia Petraea)* found a problem with the route by which Burckhardt had the Israelites reach Serbal, and therefore refrained from endorsing the new idea; but he shared the doubts regarding Mount Mussa, and pointed at another nearby mountain as a better choice.

The possibility that the long-held tradition identifying Mount Sinai with Mount Mussa was incorrect was a challenge that the great Egyptologist and founder of scientific archaeology, Karl Richard Lepsius, could not resist. He crossed the Gulf of Suez by boat, landing at *el-Tor* ("The Bull")—the harbor town where Christian pilgrims to St. Katherine and Mount Moses used to land even before the Muslims made it a major stopover and decontamination center on the sea route from Egypt to Mecca. Nearby rose the majestic Mount Umm-Shumar, which Lepsius on and off compared as a "candidate" with Mussa and Serbal. But after extensive research and area touring, he focused on the burning problem of that day: Mussa or Serbal?

His findings were published in *Discoveries in Egypt, Ethiopia and the Peninsula of Sinai 1842–1845* and *Letters from Egypt, Ethiopia and Sinai*, the latter including (in translation from German), the full text of his reports to the king of Prussia, under whose patronage he traveled. Lepsius voiced doubts regarding Mount Mussa almost as soon as he reached the area: "The remoteness of that district, its distance from frequented roads of communication and its position in the lofty range," he wrote, ". . . rendered it peculiarly applicable for individual hermits; but for the same reason inapplicable for a large people." He felt certain that the hundreds of thousands of Israelites could not have subsisted among the desolate granite peaks of Mount Mussa for the long (almost a year) Israelite stay at Mount

Sinai. The monastic traditions, he confirmed, dated to the sixth century A.D. at the earliest; they could therefore serve as no guide in this quest.

Mount Sinai, he stressed, was in a desert plain; it was also called in the Scriptures Mount *Horeb*, the Mount of the Dryness. Mussa was amidst other mountains and not in a desert area. On the other hand, the coastal plain in front of Mount Serbal was such an area—large enough to hold the Israelite multitudes as they viewed the Theophany; and the adjoining Wadi Feiran was the only place that could sustain them and their cattle for a year. Moreover, only possession of "this unique fertile valley" could have justified the Amalekite attack (at Rephidim, a gateway place near Mount Sinai); there was no such fertile place, worth fighting for, near Mount Mussa. Moses first came to the mount in search of grazing for his flock; this he could find at Feiran, but not at the desolate Mount Mussa.

But if not Mount Mussa, why Mount Serbal? Besides its "correct" location at Wadi Feiran, Lepsius found some concrete evidence. Describing the mount in glowing terms, he reported finding on its top "A deep mountain hollow, around which the five summits of Serbal unite in a half circle and form a towering crown." In the middle of this hollow he found ruins of an old convent. It was at that hallowed spot, he suggested, that the "Glory of the Lord" had landed, in full view of the Israelites (who were gathered in the plain to the west). As to the fault that Robinson had found with Burckhardt's Exodus route to Serbal—Lepsius offered an alternative detour which corrected the problem.

When the conclusions of the prestigious Lepsius were published, they shook tradition in two ways: he emphatically denied the identification of Mount Sinai with Mount Mussa, voting for Serbal; and he challenged the Exodus route previously taken for granted.

The debate that followed raged for almost a quarter of a century and produced discourses by other researchers, notably Charles Foster (*The Historical Geography of Arabia; Israel in the Wilderness*) and William H. Bartlett (*Forty Days in the Desert on the Track of the Israelites*). They added suggestions, confirmations and doubts. In 1868 the British government joined the Palestine Exploration Fund in sending a full-scale expedition to Sinai. Its mission, in addition to extensive geodesic and mapping work, was to establish once and for all the route of the Exodus and the location of Mount Sinai. The group was led by captains Charles W. Wilson and Henry Spencer Palmer of the Royal Engineers; it included Professor Edward Henry Palmer, a noted Orientalist and Arabist. The expedition's official report (*Ordnance Survey of the Peninsula of Sinai*) was enlarged upon by the two Palmers, in separate works.

Previous researchers went to the Sinai for brief tours mostly in springtime. The Wilson-Palmer expedition departed from Suez on November 11, 1868, and returned to Egypt on April 24, 1869—staying in the peninsula from the beginning of winter until the following spring. Thus, one of its first discoveries was that the mountainous south gets very cold in winter and that it snows there, making passage difficult, if not impossible. The higher peaks, such as Mussa and Katherine, remain snowcovered for many winter months. The Israelites—who had never seen snow in Egypt—had stayed a year in this area. Yet there is no mention at all in the Bible of either snow or even cold weather.

While Captain Palmer (*Sinai: Ancient History from the Monuments*) provided data on the archaeological and historical evidence uncovered (early habitations, Egyptian presence, inscriptions in the first known alphabet), it was the task of Professor E. H. Palmer (*The Desert of the Exodus*) to outline the group's conclusions regarding the route and the mount.

In spite of lingering doubts, the group vetoed Serbal and voted for the Mount Mussa location, but with a twist. Since in front of Mount Mussa there was no valley wide enough where the Israelites could encamp and see the Theophany, Palmer offered a solution: The correct Mount Sinai was not the southern peak of the massif (Gebel Mussa), but its northern peak, *Ras-Sufsafeh*, which faces "the spacious plain of Er-Rahah where no less than two million Israelites could encamp." In spite of the long-held tradition, he concluded, "we are compelled to reject" Gebel Mussa as the Mount of the Lawgiving.

The views of Professor Palmer were soon criticized, supported or modified by other scholars. Before long, there were several southern peaks that were offered as the true Mount Sinai, as well as several different routes to choose from.

But was the southern Sinai the only place in which to search?

Back in April 1860, the *Journal of Sacred Literature* published a revolutionary suggestion, that the Holy Mount was not in southern Sinai at all, but should be looked for in the central plateau. The anonymous contributor pointed out that its name, *Badiyeth el-Tih*, was very significant: it meant "the Wilderness of the Wandering," and the local Bedouins explain that it was there that the Children of Israel wandered. The article suggested a certain peak of the *el-Tih* as the proper Mount Sinai.

So, in 1873, a geographer and linguist named Charles T. Beke (who explored and mapped the origins of the Nile) set out "in search of the *true* Mount Sinai." His research established that Mount Mussa was so named after a fourth century monk Mussa who was famed for his piety and miracles, and not after the biblical Moses; and that the claims for Mount Mussa were begun only circa A.D. 550. He also pointed out that the Jewish historian Josephus Flavius (who recorded his people's history for the Romans after the fall of Jerusalem in A.D. 70) described Mount Sinai as the highest in its area, which ruled out both Mussa and Serbal.

Beke also asked, how could the Israelites have gone south at all, past the Egyptian garrisons in the mining areas? His question has remained one of the unanswered objections to a southern location of Mount Sinai.

Charles Beke will not be remembered as the man who finally found the true Mount Sinai: as the title of his work indicated (*Discoveries of Sinai in Arabia and Midian*), he concluded that the mount was a volcano, somewhere southeast of the Dead Sea. But he raised many questions which cleared the desk for fresh and unfettered thinking regarding the location of the mount and the route of the Exodus.

The search for Mount Sinai in the southern part of the peninsula was closely linked with the notion of the "Southern Crossing" and "Southern Route" of the Exodus. These held that the Children of Israel literally crossed the Red Sea (from west to east) at or through the head of the Gulf of Suez. Once across, they were out of Egypt and on the western shores of the Sinai peninsula. They then journeyed south along the coastal strip, turned (somewhere) inland, and reached Mount Sinai (as, say, Burckhardt had done).

The Southern Crossing was indeed a deep-rooted and plausible tradition, buttressed by several legends. According to Greek sources, Alexander the Great was told that the Israelites had crossed the Red Sea at the head of the Gulf of Suez; it was there that he tried to emulate the Crossing.

The next great conqueror known to have attempted the feat was Napoleon, in 1799. His engineers established that where the head of the Gulf of Suez sends a "tongue" inland, south of where Suez City is located, there exists an underwater ridge, some 600 feet wide, which extends from coast to coast. Daredevil natives cross there at ebb tide, with the waters up to their shoulders. And if a strong east wind blows, the seabed is almost cleared of all water.

Napoleon's engineers worked out for their emperor the right place and time for emulating the Children of Israel. But an unexpected change in the wind's direction brought a sudden onrush of waters, covering the ridge with more than seven feet of water within minutes. The great Napoleon escaped with his life in the nick of time.

These experiences only served to convince nineteenth century scholars that it was indeed at that end of the Gulf of Suez that the miraculous Crossing had taken place: a wind could create a dry path, and a change in wind could indeed sink an army soon thereafter. On the opposite, Sinai, side of the Gulf, there was a place named *Gebel Murr* ("The Bitter Mountain") and near it *Bir Murr* ("The Bitter Well"), invitingly fitting as Marah, the place of bitter waters, encountered by the Israelites after the Crossing. Further south lay the oasis of *Ayun Mussa*—"The Spring of Moses"; now was not this the next station, Elim, remembered for its beautiful springs and numerous date palms? The Southern Crossing thus seemed to fit well with the Southern Route theory, no matter where the turn inland had taken place further on.

The Southern Crossing also agreed with the then current notions regarding Egypt in antiquity and the Israelite bondage therein. Egypt's historical heart was the Heliopolis-Memphis hub, and it was assumed that the Israelites slaved in the construction of the nearby pyramids of Gizeh. From there, a route led almost straight east, toward the head of the Gulf of Suez and the Sinai peninsula beyond it.

But as archaeological discoveries began to fill in the historical picture and provide an accurate chronology, it was established that the great pyramids were built some fifteen centuries before the Exodus—more than a thousand years before the Hebrews even came to Egypt. The Israelites, more and more scholars agreed, must have toiled in the construction of a new capital which the Pharaoh Ramses II had built circa 1260 B.C. It was named *Tanis* and it was located in the northeastern part of the Delta. The Israelite abode—the land of Goshen—was consequently presumed to have been in the northeast rather near the center of Egypt.

The construction of the Suez Canal (1859–1869), which was accompanied by the accumulation of topographical, geological, climatic and other data, confirmed the existence of a natural rift which in an earlier geological age may have joined the Mediterranean Sea in the north with the Gulf of Suez in the south. That link had shrunk for various reasons, leaving behind a watery chain consisting of the marshy lagoons of Lake Manzaleh, the small lakes Ballah and Timsah, and the joined Great and Little Bitter Lakes. All these lakes may have been larger at the time of the Exodus, when the head of the Gulf of Suez probably extended farther inland.

Archaeological work complementing the engineering data also established that there existed in antiquity two "Suez Canals," one connecting Egypt's hub with the Mediterranean and the other to the Gulf of Suez. Following natural wadi beds or dried up branches of the Nile, they carried "sweet" water for drinking and irrigation and were navigable. The finds confirmed that in earlier times there was indeed an almost continuous water barrier which served as Egypt's eastern border.

The engineers of the Suez Canal prepared in 1867 the following diagram (Fig. 116) of a north-south section of the Isthmus, identifying four ridges of high ground which must have served in antiquity, as they still do, the gateways to and from Egypt through the watery barrier (Fig. 115):

(A) Between the marshy lagoons of Manzaleh and Lake Ballah—the modern crossing town of *el-Qantara* ("The Span").

(B) Between Lake Ballah and Lake Timsah—the modern crossing point of *Ismailiya*.

(C) Between Lake Timsah and the Great Bitter Lake—a ridge known in Greek-Roman times as the *Serapeum*.

(D) Between the Little Bitter Lake and the head of the Gulf of Suez—a "land-bridge" known as The *Shalouf*.

Through these Gateways, a number of Routes connected Egypt with Asia via the Sinai peninsula. One has to bear in mind that the crossing of the Red

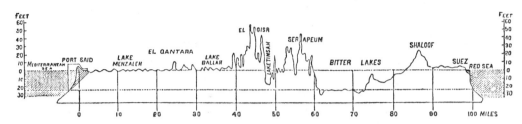

Fig. 116

Sea (or Sea/Lake of Reeds) was not premeditated: it took place only after the Pharaoh changed his mind about letting the Israelites go; whereupon the Lord commanded them to turn back from the edge of the desert which they had already reached, and "encamp by the sea." Therefore, they originally exited from Egypt by one of the usual gateways; but which one?

DeLesseps, the Canal's master builder, voiced the opinion that they used Gateway "C," south of Lake Timsah. Others, like Olivier Ritter (*Histoire de l'Isthme de Suez*), concluded from the exact same data that it was Gateway "D." In 1874, the Egyptologist Heinrich Karl Brugsch, addressing the International Congress of Orientalists, identified the landmarks connected with the Israelite enslavement and Exodus in the northeastern corner of Egypt. Therefore, he said, the logical gateway was all the way north— Gateway "A."

As it turned out, such a theory of a Northern Crossing was nearly a century old when Brugsch launched it, having been suggested in *Hamelneld's Biblical Geography* back in 1796, and by various researchers thereafter. But Brugsch, as even his adversaries conceded, presented the theory with a "really brilliant and dazzling array of claimed corroboratory evidence from the Egyptian monuments." His paper was published the following year under the title *L'Exode et les Monuments Egyptiens*.

In 1883, Edouard H. Naville (*The Store City of Pithom and the Route of the Exodus*) identified *Pithom*, the Israelite slave-labor city, at a site west of Lake Timsah. This and other identifications and evidence offered by others (such as by George Ebers in *Durch Gosen zum Sinai*) established that the Israelite abode extended from Lake Timsah westward, not northward. Goshen was not in the extreme northeast of Egypt, but adjoined the center of the watery barrier.

H. Clay Trumbull (*Kadesh Barnea*) then offered what has since been generally accepted as the correct identification for *Succoth*, the starting point of the Exodus: it was a common caravan gathering place west of Lake Timsah, and Gateway "B" was the nearest at hand. But it was not taken, as stated in Exodus 13:17-18: "And it came to pass, when Pharaoh let the people go, that the Lord did not lead them the Way of the Land of the Philistines, though it was near . . . and the Lord turned the people by the Way of the Desert *Yam Suff*." Thus, Trumbull suggested, the Israelites ended up at Gateway "D"; pursued by the Pharaoh, they crossed through the waters of the head of the Gulf of Suez.

As the nineteenth century drew to a close, scholars raced to give the final word on the subject. The views of the "southerners" were emphatically summed up by Samuel C. Bartlett (*The Veracity of the Hexateuch*): the Crossing was in the south, the Route led south, Mount Sinai was in the south of the peninsula (*Ras-Sufsafeh*). With equal decisiveness, such scholars as Rudolf Kittel (*Geschichte der Hebräer*), Julius Wellhausen (*Israel und Judah*), and Anton Jerku (*Geschichte des Volkes Israel*) offered the opinion that the Northern Crossing meant a *northern* Mount Sinai.

One of their strongest arguments (now generally accepted by scholars) was that *Kadesh-Barnea,* where the Israelites sojourned for most of their forty years in the peninsula, was not a chance station but a premeditated target of the Exodus. It has been firmly identified as the fertile area of the Ain-Kadeis ("Spring of Kadesh") and Ain-Qudeirat oases in northeastern Sinai. According to Deuteronomy 1:2, Kadesh-Barnea was situated "eleven days" from Mount Sinai. Kittel, Jerku and others of like opinion therefore selected mountains in the vicinity of Kadesh-Barnea as the true Mount Sinai.

In the last year of the nineteenth century, H. Holzinger (*Exodus*) offered a compromise: the Crossing was at "C"; the Route led south. But the Israelites turned inland well before reaching the Egyptian-garrisoned mining areas. Their route led via the highland plateau of the *el-Tih,* the "Wilderness of the Wandering." They then circled northward through the flat Central Plain, toward a Mount Sinai *in the north*.

As the twentieth century began, the focus of research and debate shifted to the question: What was the *route* of the Exodus?

The ancient coastal route, which the Romans called *Via Maris*—"Way of the Sea"—began at el-Qantara ("A" on map). Though it led through shifting sand dunes, it was blessed with water wells all along its course, and the date palms amazingly growing out of the barren sands provide sweet fruit in season and welcome shade all year round.

The second route, beginning at Ismailiya ("B"), runs almost parallel to the coastal road but some twenty to thirty miles south of it, through undulating hills and occasional low mountains. The natural wells are sparse, and the subterranean water level lies deep below the sand and sandstones: artificial wells must be dug several hundred feet to reach water. A traveler—even nowadays, even by car (the paved highways follow the ancient paths)—soon realizes that he is in a real desert.

From earliest times, the Way of the Sea was preferred by armies that had naval support; the more inland route—harsher though it was—was taken by those who sought to be safe from (or unseen by) the naval and coastal patrols.

Gateway "C" could lead either to Route "B," or to the twin routes which extended from Gateway "D" through a mountain chain into the Sinai's Central Plain. The hard, flat ground of the Central Plain does not allow deep wadi beds. During the winter rains, some wadis overfill and give the appearance of small lakes—lakes in the desert! The waters soon flow off, but some filter down through the gravel and clay that make up the wadi beds; it is there that digging can literally bring water out of the ground.

The more northerly route extending from Gateway "D" led the traveler via the Giddi Pass, past the northern mountainous rim of the Central Plain, on to Beersheba, Hebron and Jerusalem. The more southerly route, via the Mitla Pass, bears the Arabic name *Darb el Hajj*—"Way of the Pilgrims." This route was the early way for Muslim pilgrims from Egypt to the holy city of Mecca in Arabia. Starting near Suez City, they crossed a desert strip and went through the mountains via the Mitla Pass; then journeyed across the Central Plain to the oasis of *Nakhl* (Fig. 117) where a fort, pilgrims' inns and water pools had been built. From there they continued southeast to reach Aqaba at the head of the Gulf of Aqaba, whence they moved along the Arabian coast to Mecca.

Which of these four possible routes—the "Ways" of the Bible—had the Israelites taken?

In the aftermath of the Northern Crossing presentation by Brugsch, much was made of the biblical statement regarding the "Way of the Land of the Philistines" which was not taken, "though it was near." The Bible continued the statement with the following explanation: "For the Lord said: 'Lest the people repent when they see war, and return to Egypt.'" It has been assumed that this "Way of the Land of the Philistines" was the coastal route (which began at gateway "A"), the way the Pharaohs preferred for their military and trade expeditions, and which was strung with Egyptian forts and garrisons.

At the turn of the century, A. E. Haynes, a captain in the Royal Engineers, studied Sinai's routes and water resources under the auspices of the Palestine Exploration Fund. In his published report on "The Route of the Exodus" he revealed impressive familiarity not only with biblical scriptures, but also with the work of previous researchers, including the Rev. F. W. Holland (who visited the Sinai five times) and Major-General Sir C. Warren (who paid particular attention to water supplies in the "Wilderness of the Wandering" of the Central Plain).

Captain Haynes focused on the problem of the Route-That-Was-Not-Taken. Unless it was a handy and obvious way for reaching the Israelite's goals—why was it mentioned at all as a viable alternative? He pointed out that Kadesh-Barnea—by then accepted as a premeditated goal of the Exodus—indeed lay within easy reach of the coastal route. Therefore, he concluded, Mount Sinai, situated on the way to Kadesh, also had to be located within easy reach of the coastal route, whether or not this route was finally taken.

Barred from the coastal Route "A," Captain Haynes concluded, it was

Fig. 117

"the probable plan of Moses" to lead the Israelites directly to Kadesh, with a stop at Mount Sinai, via Route "B." But the Egyptian pursuit and the Crossing of the Red Sea may have forced a detour via routes "C" or "D." The Central Plain was indeed the "Wilderness of Wandering." *Nakhl* was an important station near Mount Sinai, before or after reaching it. The mount itself had to be located about 100 miles from Kadesh-Barnea, which equals (Captain Haynes estimated) the biblical distance of "eleven days." His candidate was Mount *Yiallaq*, a limestone mountain "of most impressive dimensions, lying like a huge barnacle" on the northern rim of the Central Plain—"exactly halfway between Ismailiyah and Kadesh." Its name, which he spelled *Yalek*, "approximates closely to the ancient *Amalek*, the prefix *Am* meaning 'country of.'"

In the years that followed, the possibility of an Israelite journey via the Central Plain gained supporters; some (as Raymond Weill, *Le Séjour des Israélites au désert du Sinai*) accepted the Mount-near-Kadesh theory; others (as Hugo Gressmann, *Mose und seine Zeit*) believed that the Israelites turned from Nakhl not northeast but southeast, toward Aqaba. Others—Black, Bühl, Cheyne, Dillmann, Gardiner, Grätz, Guthe, Meyer, Musil, Petrie, Sayce, Stade—agreed or disagreed partly or completely. As all the scriptural and geographical arguments were exhausted, it seemed that only an actual field test could resolve the issue. But how does one duplicate the Exodus?

World War I (1914–1918) was the answer, for the Sinai soon became the arena of a major struggle between the British on the one hand and the Turks and their German allies on the other hand. The prize of these campaigns was the Suez Canal.

The Turks lost no time in crossing into the Sinai peninsula, and the British quickly withdrew from their main administrative-military centers at El-Arish and Nakhl. Unable to advance by the desirable "Way of the Sea," for the same old reason that the Mediterranean was controlled by the enemy's (British) navy, the Turks amassed a herd of 20,000 camels to carry water and supplies for an advance on the Canal via route "B" to Ismailiyah. In his memoirs, the Turkish Commander, Djemal Pasha (*Memories of a*

Turkish Statesman, 1913–1919) explained that "the great problem, on which everything hangs in these difficult military operations in the desert of Sinai, is the question of water. In any other than the rainy season it would be impossible to cross this waste with an expeditionary force of approximately 25,000 men." His attack was repulsed.

The German allies of the Turks then took matters in hand. For their motorized equipment, they preferred the hard, flat Central Plain for an advance on the Canal. With the aid of water engineers, they discovered the subterranean resources and dug a network of wells all along their lines of communication and advance. Their attack in 1916 also failed. When the British took the offensive in 1917, they naturally advanced along the coastal route. They reached the old demarcation line at Rafah in February 1917; within months they captured Jerusalem.

The British memoirs on the Sinai fighting by General A. P. Wavell (*The Palestine Campaigns*) has a bearing on our subject primarily by his admission that the British High Command estimated that their enemies could not find in the Central Plain water for more than 5,000 men and 2,500 camels. The German side of the Sinai campaigns is told in *Sinai* by Theodor Wiegand and the commanding general, F. Kress von Kressenstein. The military endeavor is described against the background of terrain, climate, water sources and history, coupled with an impressive familiarity with all previous research. Not surprisingly, the conclusions of the German military men parallel the conclusions of the British military men: no marching columns, no multitudes of men and beasts could be led through the southern granite mountains. Devoting a special chapter to the question of the Exodus, Wiegand and von Kressenstein asserted that "the region of Gebel Mussa cannot come into consideration for the biblical Mount Sinai." They were of the opinion that it was "the monumental Gebel *Yallek*"— echoing the conclusions of Captain Haynes. Or, they added, perhaps as Guthe and other German scholars have suggested, Gebel *Maghara*, which rises opposite Gebel Yallek, on the northern side of Route "B."

One of Britain's own military men, who was governor of the Sinai after World War I, became acquainted with the peninsula during his long tenure there as perhaps no single person in modern times until then. Writing in *Yesterday and Today in Sinai*, C. S. Jarvis too asserted that there was no way the Israelite multitudes (even if their numbers were smaller than 600,000, as W.M.F. Petrie had suggested) and their livestock could have traveled through—much less sustained themselves for more than a year—in the "tumbled mass of pure granite" of the southern Sinai.

To the known arguments, he added new ones. It had already been suggested that the *manna* which served in lieu of bread was the edible, white, berry-like resinous deposit left by small insects that feed on the tamarisk bushes. There are few tamarisks in southern Sinai; they are plentiful in northern Sinai. Next fact concerned the quails, which provided the meat to eat. These birds migrate from their native southern Russia,

Rumania and Hungary to winter in the Sudan (south of Egypt); they return northward in the spring. To this day, the Bedouins easily catch the tired birds as they alight on the Mediterranean coast after long flights. The quails do not come to the southern Sinai; and if they did, they could not possibly fly over the high peaks of that area.

The whole drama of the Exodus, Jarvis insisted, was played out in the northern Sinai. The "Sea of Reeds" was the Serbonic Sealet (*Sebkhet el Bardawil* in Arabic) from which the Israelites marched south-southeast. Mount Sinai was Gebel *Hallal*—"a most imposing limestone massif over 2,000 feet high and standing in the midst of a vast alluvial plain all by itself." The mountain's Arabic name, he explained, meant "The Lawful"—as befits the Mount of the Lawgiving.

In the years that followed, the most pertinent research on the subject was conducted by scholars of the Hebrew University of Jerusalem and other Hebrew institutions of higher learning in what was then Palestine. Combining their intimate knowledge of the Hebrew Bible and other scriptures with thorough on-site investigations in the peninsula, few found support for the southern location tradition.

Haim Bar-Deroma (*Hanagev* and *Vze Gvul Ha'aretz*) accepted a Northern Passage but believed that the Route then took the Israelites south, through the Central Plain, to a volcanic Mount Sinai in Transjordan. Three noted scholars—F. A. Theilhaber, J. Szapiro and Benjamin Maisler (*The Graphic Historical Atlas of Palestine: Israel in Biblical Times*)—accepted the Northern Passage via the shoal of the Serbonic Sea. El-Arish, they said, was the verdant oasis of Elim; Mount Hallal was Mount Sinai. Benjamin Mazar, in various writings and in *Atlas Litkufat Hatanach,* adopted the same position. Zev Vilnay, a biblical scholar who hiked in Palestine and Sinai literally from end to end (*Ha'aretz Bamikra*), opted for the same route and mount. Yohanan Aharoni (*The Land of Israel in Biblical Times*), accepting the possibility of a Northern Passage, believed that the Israelites journeyed toward Nakhl in the Central Plain; but then proceeded to a Mount Sinai in the south.

As the debate continued to engross the scholarly and biblical world, it became apparent that the basic unresolved issue was this: Insofar as the Crossing was concerned, the weight of the evidence negated a northern body of water; but insofar as Mount Sinai was concerned, the weight of the evidence negated a southern location. The impasse focused the attention of scholars and explorers on the only remaining compromise: the Central Plain of the Sinai peninsula. In the 1940s, M. D. Cassuto (*Commentary on the Book of Exodus* and other writings) facilitated acceptance of the central route idea by showing that the Route-Not-Taken ("The Way of the Land of the Philistines") was not the long-held sea route, but the more inland route "B." Therefore, a Crossing via Gateway "C" leading southeast to the Central Plain was in full accord with the biblical narrative—without requiring a continued journey to the south of the peninsula.

The long occupation of the Sinai by Israel, in the aftermath of the 1967 war with Egypt, opened up the peninsula to study and research on an unprecedented scale. Archaeologists, historians, geographers, topographers, geologists, engineers examined the peninsula from tip to toe. Of particular interest have been the explorations by the teams of Beno Rothenberg (*Sinai Explorations 1967–1972* and other reports), mostly under the auspices of Tel-Aviv University. In the northern coastal strip, many ancient sites reflected the "bridge-like nature of this area." In the Central Plain of north Sinai, no ancient sites of permanent abode were found, but only evidence of camping sites, attesting that this was only a transit area. When the camping sites were plotted on the map, they formed "a clear line from the Negev toward Egypt, and this should be considered as the direction of prehistoric movements across the 'Desert of the Wanderings' (the el-Tih)."

It was against this newly understood background of the ancient Sinai that a Hebrew University biblical geographer, Menashe Har-El, offered a new theory (*Massa'ei Sinai*). Reviewing all the arguments, he pointed out the submerged ridge (see Fig. 116) which rises between the Great and the Little Bitter Lakes. It is shallow enough to be crossed if a wind blows away the waters; it was there that the Crossing had taken place. Then the Israelites followed the traditional route south; passing Marrah (*Bir Murrah*) and Elim (*Ayun Mussa*), they reached the shores of the Red Sea and encamped there.

Here Har-El offered his major innovation: having journeyed along the Gulf of Suez, the Israelites did not go all the way south. They proceeded only some twenty miles to the mouth of *Wadi Sudr*—and followed the wadi's valley into the Central Plain, proceeding via Nakhl to Kadesh-Barnea. Har-El identified Mount Sinai with Mount *Sinn-Bishr* which rises some 1,900 feet at the entrance to the wadi, and suggested that the battle with the Amalekites had actually taken place on the coast of the Gulf of Suez. This suggestion has been rejected by Israeli military experts familiar with the terrain and history of warfare in the Sinai.

Where, then, was Mount Sinai? We must look again at the ancient evidence.

The Pharaoh, in his Journey to the Afterlife, went eastward. Crossing the watery barrier, he set his course to a pass in the mountains. He then reached the *Duat*, which was an oval-shaped valley surrounded by mountains. The "Mountain of Light" was situated where the Stream of Osiris divided into tributaries.

The pictorial depictions (Fig. 16) showed the Stream of Osiris meandering its way through an agricultural area, distinguished by its ploughmen.

We have found similar pictorial evidence from Assyria. The Assyrian kings, it should be remembered, arrived at the Sinai from the opposite direction to that of the Egyptian kings: from the northeast, via Canaan. One of them, Esarhaddon, engraved on a stela what amounts to a route map of his own quest for "Life" (Fig. 118). It shows the date palm—the code emblem for the Sinai; a farming area symbolized by the plough; and a "Sacred Mount." In the upper register we see Esarhaddon at the shrine of the Supreme Deity, near the Tree of Life. It is flanked by the sign of the bull—the very same image (the "golden calf") that the Israelites had fashioned at the foot of Mount Sinai.

All this does not bespeak the harsh, barren granite peaks of southern Sinai. Rather, it suggests northern Sinai and its dominant *Wadi El-Arish*, whose very name means Stream of the Husbandman. It is among its tributaries, in a valley surrounded by mountains, that the Mount was located.

There is only one such place in the whole of the Sinai peninsula. Geography, topography, historical texts, pictorial depictions—all point at the *Central Plain* in Sinai's northern half.

Even E. H. Palmer, who went so far as to invent the Ras-Sufsafeh twist in order to uphold the southern identification, knew in his heart that a desert that stretches as far as the eye can see, and not a peak in a sea of granite mountains, was the location of the Theophany and the wanderings of the Israelites.

"The popular conception of Sinai," he wrote in *The Desert of the Exodus*, "even in the present day, seems to be that a single isolated mountain which may be approached from any direction rises conspicuously above a boundless plain of sand. The Bible itself, if we read it without the light of modern discovery, certainly favors this idea. . . . Mount Sinai is always

Fig. 118

alluded to in the Bible as though it stood alone and unmistakable in the midst of a level desert plain."

There indeed exists such a "level desert plain" in the Sinai peninsula, he admitted; but it is not covered with sand: "Even in those parts [of the peninsula] which approach most nearly to our conception of what a desert ought to be—a solid ocean bounded only by the horizon or by a barrier of distant hills—sand is the exception, and the soil resembles rather a hard gravel path than a soft and yielding beach."

He was describing the Central Plain. To him, the absence of sand marred the "desert" image; to us, its hard gravel top meant that it was admirably suited for the Spaceport of the Nefilim. And if Mount Mashu marked the gateway to the Spaceport, it had to be located on the outskirts of this facility.

Have then generations of pilgrims gone south in vain? Did the veneration of the southern peaks begin only with Christianity? The discovery by archaeologists atop these mounts of shrines, altars, and other evidence of worship from olden days attests differently; and the many inscriptions and rock carvings (including the Jewish Candelabra emblem) by pilgrims from many faiths and over many millennia bespeak a veneration going back to Man's earliest acquaintance with the area.

As one almost wishes there were *two* "Mounts Sinai" to satisfy both tradition and facts, it turns out that such notions too are not new. Even before the last two centuries of concerted effort to identify the Mount, biblical and theological scholars had wondered whether the various biblical names for the Sacred Mount did not indicate that there originally were two sacred mountains, not one. These names included "Mount Sinai" (the Mountain of/in Sinai), which was the Mount of the Lawgiving; "Mount Horeb" (the Mountain of/in the Dryness); "Mount Paran," which was listed in Deuteronomy as the mount in Sinai from which Yahweh had appeared unto the Israelites; and "the Mountain of the Gods," where the Lord first revealed himself unto Moses.

The geographic location associated with two of the names is decipherable. Paran was the wilderness adjoining Kadesh-Barnea, possibly the biblical name for the Central Plain; so that "Mount Paran" had to be located there. It was to that Mount that the Israelites had gone. But the Mount where Moses had his first encounter with the Lord, "the Mountain of the Gods," could not have been too far from the Land of Midian; for "Moses was shepherding the flock of Jetro, his father-in-law, the priest of Midian; and he led the flock unto the wilderness, and came unto the Mountain of the Gods, unto Horeb." The abode of the Midianites was in southern Sinai, along the Gulf of Aqaba and astride the copper-working areas. "The Mountain of the Gods" must have been located somewhere in an adjoining wilderness—in southern Sinai.

Fig. 119

There have been found Sumerian cylinder seals depicting the appearance of a deity unto a shepherd. They show the god appearing from between two mountains (Fig. 119), with a rocket-like tree behind him—perhaps the *Sneh* ("Burning Bush") of the biblical tale. The introduction of two peaks in the shepherd scene fits the frequent biblical reference to the Lord as *El Shaddai*—God of the Two Peaks. It thus raises yet another distinction between the Mount of the Lawgiving and the Mountain of the Gods: the one was a solitary mount in a desert plain; the other seems to have been a combination of two sacred peaks.

The Ugaritic texts too recognize a "Mountain of the young gods" in the environs of Kadesh, and two peaks of El and Asherah—*Shad Elim, Shad Asherath u Rahim*—in the south of the peninsula. It was to that area at *mebokh naharam* ("Where the two bodies of water begin"), *kerev apheq tehomtam* ("Near the cleft of the two seas") that El had retired in his old age. The texts, we believe, describe the southern tip of the Sinai peninsula.

There was, we conclude, a Gateway Mount on the perimeter of the Spaceport in the Central Plain. And there were two peaks in the peninsula's southern tip that also played a role in the comings and goings of the Nefilim. They were the two peaks that *measured up*.

XII

The Pyramids of Gods and Kings

Somewhere in the vaults of the British Museum there is stashed away a clay tablet which was found at Sippar, the "cult center" of Shamash in Mesopotamia. It shows him seated on a throne, under a canopy whose pillar is shaped as a date palm (Fig. 120). A king and his son are introduced to Shamash by another deity. In front of the seated god there is mounted upon a pedestal a large emblem of a ray-emitting planet. The inscriptions invoke the gods Sin (father of Shamash), Shamash himself and his sister Ishtar.

The theme of the scene—the introduction of kings or priests to a major deity—is a familiar one, and poses no problems. What is unique and puzzling in this depiction are the two gods (almost superimposed upon one another) who, from somewhere outside of where the introduction is taking place, hold (with two pairs of hands) two cords leading to the celestial emblem.

Who are the two Divine Cordholders? What is their function? Are they identically situated, and if so, why do they hold or pull two cords, and not just one? Where are they? What is their connection with Shamash?

Sippar, scholars know, was the seat of the High Court of Sumer; Shamash was consequently the ultimate lawgiver. Hammurabi, the Babylonian king famous for his law code, depicted himself receiving the laws from an enthroned Shamash. Was the scene with the two Divine Cordholders also somehow connected with lawgiving? In spite of all the speculation, no one has so far come up with an answer.

The solution, we believe, has been available all along, in the very same British Museum—not among its "Assyrian" exhibits, however, but in its Egyptian Department. In a room separate from the mummies and the other remains of the dead and their tombs, there are exhibited pages from the various papyri inscribed with the *Book of the Dead*. And the answer is right there, for all to see (Fig. 121).

It is a page from the "Papyrus of Queen Nejmet" and the drawing illustrates the final stage of the Pharaoh's journey in the *Duat*. The twelve gods who pulled his barge through the subterranean corridors have brought him to the last corridor, the Place of Ascending. There, the "Red Eye of Horus" was waiting. Then, shed of his earthly clothing, the Pharaoh was to

Fig. 120

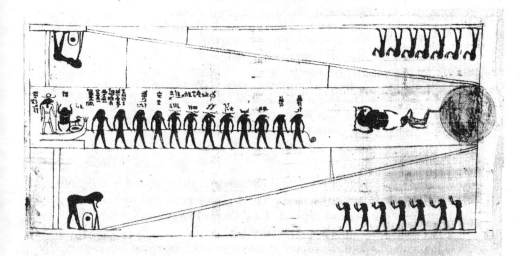

Fig. 121

ascend heavenward, his Translation spelled out by the beetle hieroglyph ("Rebirth"). Gods standing in two groups pray for his successful arrival at the Imperishable Star.

And, unmistakably, there in the Egyptian depiction are two Divine Cordholders!

Without the congestion of the depiction from Sippar, this one from the Book of the Dead shows the two Cordholders not crowding out each other, but at two different ends of the scene. They are clearly located outside of the subterranean corridor. Moreover: each site manned by a Cordholder is marked by an *omphalos* resting upon a platform. And, as the action imparted by the drawing shows, the two divine aides are not simply holding the cords, but are engaged in *measuring*.

The discovery should not surprise: have not the verses of the Book of the Dead described how the journeying Pharaoh encounters the gods "who hold the rope in the *Duat*," and the gods "who hold the measuring cord"?

A clue in the *Book of Enoch* now comes to mind. There, it will be recalled, it is related that as he was taken by an angel to visit the earthly paradise in the west, Enoch "saw in those days how long cords were given to angels who took to themselves wings, and they went towards the north." In reply to Enoch's question, his guiding angel explained: "They have gone off to measure . . . they shall bring the measures of the Righteous to the Righteous . . . all these measures shall reveal the secrets of the Earth."

Winged beings going north to measure. . . . Measures that shall reveal the secrets of the Earth. . . . All at once, the words of the Prophet Habakuk thunder in our ears—the words describing the appearance of the Lord from the south, going north:

> The Lord from South shall come,
> The Holy One from Mount Paran.
> Covered are the heavens with his halo,
> His splendor fills the Earth;
> His brilliance is like light.
> His rays shine forth
>   from where his power is concealed.
> The Word goes before him,
>   sparks emanate from below.
> He pauses to measure the Earth;
> He is seen, and the nations tremble.

Was the measuring of Earth and its "secrets" then related to the powered flight of the gods in Earth's skies? The Ugaritic texts add a clue as they tell us that, from the peak of Zaphon, Ba'al "a cord strong and supple stretches out, heavenwards (and) to the Seat of Kadesh."

Whenever these texts report a message from one god to another, the verse begins with the word *Hut*. Scholars assume that it was a kind of a calling prefix, a kind of "Are you ready to hear me?" But the term could literally mean in the Semitic languages "cord, rope." Significantly, the term *Hut* in Egyptian also means "to extend, to stretch out." Heinrich Brugsch, commenting on an Egyptian text dealing with the battles of Horus (*Die Sage von der geflügten Sonnenscheibe*) pointed out that Hut was also a place name—the abode of the Winged Extenders, as well as the name of the mountain within which Horus was imprisoned by Seth.

We find in the Egyptian depiction (Fig. 121) that the conical "oracle stones" were located where the Divine Measurers were stationed. Baalbek too was the location of such an omphalos, a Stone of Splendor that could perform the *Hut* functions. There was an oracle stone at Heliopolis, the Egyptian twin-city of Baalbek. Baalbek was the gods' Landing Platform; the Egyptian cords led to the Pharaoh's Place of Ascent in the *Duat*. The biblical Lord—called in Habakuk by a variant of *El*—measured Earth as he flew from south to north. Are these all just a series of coincidences—or parts of the same jigsaw puzzle?

And then we have the depiction from Sippar. It is not puzzling if we recall that in pre-Diluvial times, when Sumer was the Land of the Gods, Sippar was the Spaceport of the Anunnaki, and Shamash its Commander. Thus viewed, the role of the Divine Measurers will become clear: *their cords measured out the path to the Spaceport.*

It would help to recall how Sippar was established, how the site of the first Spaceport on Earth was determined, some 400,000 years ago.

When Enlil and his sons were given the task of creating a Spaceport upon planet Earth, in the plain between the Two Rivers of Mesopotamia, a master plan was drawn up; it involved the selection of a site for the Spaceport, the determination of a flight path, and the establishment of guidance and Mission Control facilities. Based on the most conspicuous natural feature in the Near East—*Mount Ararat*—a north-south meridian was drawn through it. A flight path over the Persian Gulf, well away from flanking mountain ranges, was marked out at the precise and easy angle of 45°. Where the two lines intersected, on the banks of the Euphrates River, Sippar—"Bird City"—was to be.

Five settlements, equidistant from one another, were laid out along the diagonal 45° line. The central one—Nippur ("The Place of Crossing")—was to serve as the Mission Control Center. Other settlements marked out an arrow-like corridor; all the lines converged at Sippar (Fig. 122).

All that, however, was wiped out by the Deluge. In its immediate aftermath—some 13,000 years ago—only the Landing Platform at Baalbek had remained. Until a replacement Spaceport could be built, all landings and takeoffs of the Shuttlecraft had to be conducted there. Are we to assume that the Anunnaki relied on reaching the site, tucked away between two mountain ranges, by sheer skilled piloting—or can we safely surmise that as soon as possible they worked out an arrow-like Landing Corridor to Baalbek?

North

1. Eridu
2. Larsa
3. Nippur
4. Bad-Tibira
5. Larak
6. Sippar
7. Shuruppak
8. Lagash

Flight Path

5

6

3

7

8

4

2

1

Marshes

45°

Persian Gulf

Cities according to function

⬢ Spaceport

● Mission Control

◯ Outline of Flight Corridor

Fig. 122

With the aid of photographs of Earth from spacecraft of the U.S. National Aeronautics and Space Administration, we can view the Near East as the Anunnaki had seen it from their own craft (Fig. 123). There, a dot in the north, was Baalbek. What vantage points could they choose from which to mark out a triangular landing corridor? Close at hand, to the southeast, rose the granite peaks of southern Sinai. Amid the granite core rose the highest peak (now called Mount St. Katherine). It could serve as a natural beacon to outline the southeastern line. But where was the counterpoint in the northwest, on which the northern line of the triangle could be anchored?

Aboard the Shuttlecraft, the Surveyor—a "Divine Measurer"—glanced at the earthly panorama below, then studied his maps again. In the far

Fig. 123

distance, beyond Baalbek, there loomed the twin-peaked Ararat. He drew a straight line from Ararat through Baalbek, extending it all the way into Egypt.

He took his compass. With Baalbek as the focal point, he drew an arc through the highest peak of the Sinai peninsula. Where it intersected the Ararat-Baalbek line, he made a cross within a circle. Then he drew two lines of equal length, one connecting Baalbek with the peak in Sinai, the other with the site marked by the cross (Fig. 124).

This, he said, will be our triangular Landing Corridor, to lead us straight to Baalbek.

But sir, one of those aboard said, there is nothing there, where you have made the cross—nothing that can serve as a guiding beacon!

We will have to erect there a *pyramid*, the commander said.

And they flew on, to report their decision.

Had such a conversation indeed taken place aboard a shuttlecraft of the Anunnaki? We, of course, shall never know (unless a tablet is someday found recording the event); we have merely dramatized some astounding but *undeniable* facts:

- The unique platform at Baalbek has been there from bygone days, and it is still there intact in its enigmatic immensity;

- Mount St. Katherine is still there, rising as the highest peak of the Sinai peninsula, hallowed since ancient days, enveloped (together with its twin-peaked neighbor, Mount Mussa) in legends of gods and angels;

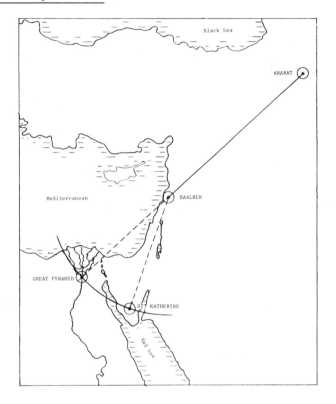

Fig. 124

- The Great Pyramid of Giza, with its two companions and the unique Sphinx, is situated precisely on the extended Ararat-Baalbek line; and
- The distance from Baalbek to Mount St. Katherine and to the Great Pyramid of Giza is exactly the same.

This, let us add at once, is only part of the amazing grid which—as we shall show—was laid out by the Anunnaki in connection with their post-Diluvial Spaceport. Therefore, whether or not the conversation had taken place aboard a shuttlecraft, we are pretty certain that *that is how the pyramids came to be in Egypt.*

There are many pyramids and pyramidical structures in Egypt, dotting the landscape from where the Nile breaks out into its delta in the north, all the way south to (and into) Nubia. But when one speaks of The Pyramids, the many emulations, variations, and "mini-pyramids" of later times are omitted, and scholars and tourists alike focus on the twenty-odd pyramids believed to have been erected by Pharaohs of the Old Kingdom (circa 2700–2180 B.C.). These, in turn, consist of two distinct groups: the pyramids clearly identified with rulers of the Fifth and Sixth Dynasties (such as Unash, Teti, Pepi), which are elaborately decorated and inscribed with the renowned Pyramid Texts; and the older pyramids attributed to kings of the Third and Fourth Dynasties. It is the latter, much older and first-ever, pyramids, that are the most intriguing. Much grander, more solid, more accurate, more perfect than all those that followed them, they are also the most mysterious—for they contain not a clue to reveal the secret of their construction. Who built them, how were they built, why, even when—no one can really say; there are only theories and educated guesses.

The textbooks will tell us that the first of Egypt's imposing pyramids was built by a king named Zoser, the second Pharaoh of the Third Dynasty (circa 2650 B.C. by most counts). Selecting a site west of Memphis, on the plateau that served as the necropolis (city of the dead) of that ancient capital, he instructed his brilliant scientist and architect named Imhotep to build him a tomb that would surpass all previous tombs. Until then, the royal custom was to carve out a tomb in the rocky ground, bury the king, and then cover the grave with a giant horizontal tombstone called a *mastaba* that in time grew to substantial dimensions. The ingenious Imhotep, some scholars hold, covered the original mastaba over the tomb of Zoser with layer upon layer of ever smaller mastabas, in two phases (Fig. 125a), achieving a step pyramid. Beside it, within a large rectangular courtyard, a variety of functional and decorative buildings were erected—chapels, funerary temples, storehouses, attendants' quarters and so on; the whole area was then surrounded by a magnificent wall. The pyramid and the ruins of some of the adjoining buildings and the wall can still be seen (Fig. 125b) at Sakkara—a name believed to have honored Seker, the "hidden God."

The kings who followed Zoser, the textbooks continue to explain, liked what they saw and tried to emulate Zoser. Presumably it was Sekhemkhet, who followed Zoser on the throne, who began to build the second step

a

b

Fig. 125

pyramid, also at Sakkara. It never really got off the ground, for reasons unknown (perhaps the missing ingredient was the enigmatic genius of science and engineering, Imhotep). A third step pyramid—or rather the mound containing its ruined beginnings—was discovered about midway between Sakkara and Giza to the north. Smaller than the previous ones, it is logically attributed by some scholars to the next Pharaoh on the throne, named Khaba. Some scholars believe that there were one or two additional attempts by unidentified kings of the Third Dynasty to build pyramids here and there, but without much success.

We now have to go some thirty miles south of Sakkara, to a place named Maidum, to view the pyramid deemed to have been the next one chronologically. In the absence of evidence, it is logically presumed that this pyramid was built by the next Pharaoh in line, named Huni. Through much circumstantial evidence, it is held however that he only began the construction, and that the attempt to complete the pyramid was undertaken by his successor, Sneferu, who was the first king of the Fourth Dynasty.

It was commenced, as the previous ones, as a step pyramid. But for reasons which remain totally unknown and for which even theories are lacking, its builders decided to make it a "true" pyramid, namely to provide it with smooth sides. This meant that a smooth layer of stones was to be fitted as an outer skin at a steep angle (Fig. 126a). Again for reasons unknown, an angle of 52° was selected. But what, according to the textbooks, was to be the first-ever true pyramid ended as a dismal failure: the outer stone skin, the stone fillings and parts of the core itself collapsed under the sheer weight of the stones, all set one atop the other at a precarious angle. All that remains of that attempt is part of the solid core, with a large mound of debris all around it (Fig. 126b).

Some scholars (as Kurt Mendelssohn, *The Riddle of the Pyramids*) suggest that Sneferu was building at the same time another pyramid, somewhat north of Maidum, when the Maidum pyramid collapsed. The architects of Sneferu then hurriedly changed the pyramid's angle in mid-construction. The flatter angle (43°) assured greater stability and reduced the height and mass of the pyramid. It was a wise decision, as witness the fact that the pyramid—appropriately called the Bent Pyramid (Fig. 127)—still stands.

Encouraged by his success, Sneferu ordered another true pyramid to be built near the first. It is referred to as the Red Pyramid, due to the hue of its stones. It is supposed to have represented the realization of the impossible: a triangular shape rising from a square base; its sides measuring about 656 feet each, its height a staggering 328 feet. The triumph, however, was not achieved without a little cheating: instead of the perfect inclination of 52°, the sides of this "first classical pyramid" rise at the much safer angle of under 44°. . . .

We now arrive chronologically, scholars suggest, at the epitome of Egyptian pyramid buildings.

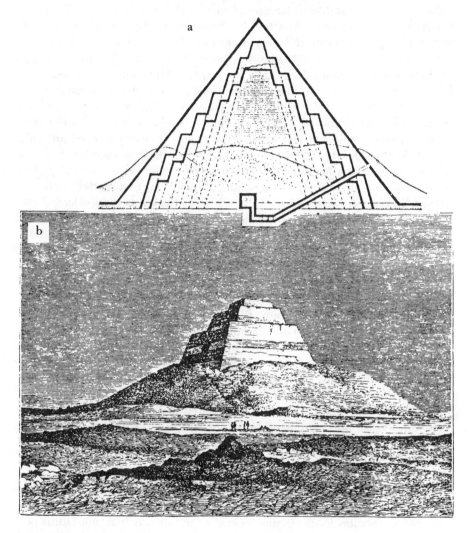

Fig. 126

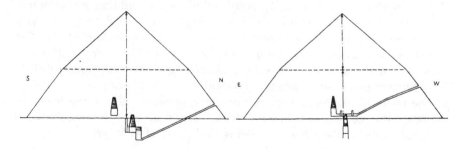

Fig. 127

Sneferu was the father of Khufu (whom Greek historians called Cheops); it has thus been assumed that the son followed up the achievement of his father by building the next true pyramid—only a larger and grander one: the Great Pyramid of Giza. It stands majestically as it has stood for millennia in the company of two other major pyramids, attributed to his successors Chefra (Chephren) and Menka-ra (Mycerinus); the three are surrounded by smaller satellite pyramids, temples, mastabas, tombs and the unique Sphinx. Though attributed to different rulers, the three (Fig. 128) obviously were planned and executed as a cohesive group, perfectly aligned not only to the cardinal points of the compass but also with one another. Indeed, triangulations which begin with these three monuments can be extended to measure the whole of Egypt—the whole of Earth, for that matter. This was first realized in modern times by Napoleon's engineers: they selected the apex of the Great Pyramid as the focal point from which they triangulated and mapped Lower Egypt.

This was made even easier by the discovery that the site is located, for all intents and purposes, right on the thirtieth parallel (north). The whole Giza complex of massive monuments had been erected at the eastern edge of the Libyan Plateau, which begins in Libya in the west and stretches to the very banks of the Nile. Though only some 150 feet above the river's valley below, the Giza site has a commanding and unobstructed view to the four horizons. The Great Pyramid stands at the extreme northeastern edge of a protrusion of the plateau; a few hundred feet to the north and east, sands and mud begin, making such massive structures impossible. One of the first scientists to have taken precise measurements, Charles Piazzi Smyth (*Our Inheritance in the Great Pyramid*) established that the center of the Great Pyramid was at northern latitude 29° 58′ 55″—a mere one-sixtieth of a degree off from exactly at the thirtieth parallel. The center of the second large pyramid was only thirteen seconds ($^{13}/_{3600}$ of a degree) to the south of that.

The alignment with the cardinal points of the compass; the inclination of the sides at the perfect angle of about 52° (at which the height of the pyramid in relation to its circumference is the same as that of a radius of a circle to its circumference); the square bases, set on perfectly level platforms—all bespeak of a high degree of scientific knowledge of mathematics, astronomy, geometry, geography and of course building and architecture, as well as the administrative ability to mobilize the necessary manpower, to plan and execute such massive and long-term projects. The wonderment only increases as one realizes the *interior* complexities and precision of the galleries, corridors, chambers, shafts and openings that have been engineered within the pyramids, their hidden entrances (always on the north face), the locking and plugging systems—all unseen from the outside, all in perfect alignment with each other, all executed within these artificial mountains as they were being built layer after layer.

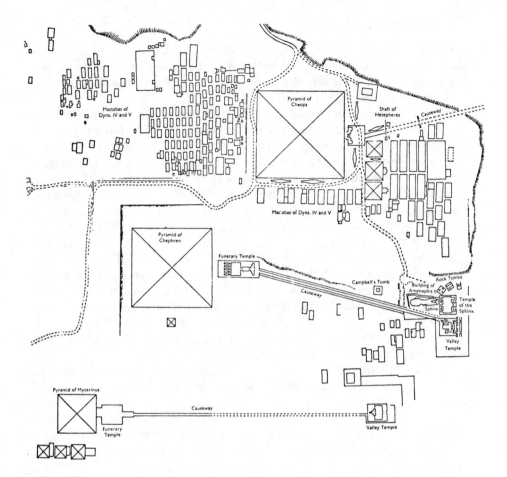

Fig. 128

Though the Second Pyramid (that of Chefra) is only slightly smaller than the First, "Great Pyramid" (heights: 470 and 480 feet; sides at base 707 and 756 feet, respectively), it is the latter that has by and large captured the interest and imagination of scholars and laymen since men ever set their eyes upon these monuments. It has been and still remains the largest stone building in the world, having been constructed of an estimated 2,300,000 to 2,500,000 slabs of yellow limestone (the core), white limestone (the smooth facing or casing), and granite (for interior chambers and galleries, for roofing, etc.). Its total mass, estimated at some 93 million cubic feet weighing 7 million tons, has been calculated to exceed that of all the cathedrals, churches and chapels combined that have been built in England since the beginning of Christianity.

On ground that has been artificially leveled, the Great Pyramid rises on a thin platform whose four corners are marked by sockets of no ascertained function. In spite of the passage of millennia, continental shifts, Earth's wobble around its own axis, earthquakes and the immense weight of the pyramid itself, the relatively thin platform (less than twenty-two inches thick) is still undamaged and perfectly level: the error or shift in its perfect horizontal alignment is less than a tenth of an inch over the 758 feet that each side of the platform measures.

From a distance, the Great Pyramid and its two companions appear to be true pyramids; but when approached it is realized that they too are a kind of step pyramid, built layer upon layer (scholars call them courses) of stone, each layer smaller than the one below it. Modern studies, in fact, suggest that the Great Pyramid is a step pyramid at its core, engineered to sustain great vertical stress (Fig. 129). What gave it the smooth, inclined sides were the casing stones with which its sides were covered. These have been removed in Arab times and used for the construction of nearby Cairo; but a few can still be seen in position near the top of the Second Pyramid, and some were discovered at the base of the Great Pyramid (Fig. 130). It is these casing stones which determined the angle of the pyramid's sides; they are the heaviest of all the stones used to build the pyramid proper; the six faces that each stone has have been cut and polished to an accuracy of optical standards—they fitted not only the core stones which they covered, but also each other on all four sides, forming a precision-made area of twenty-one acres of limestone blocks.

The Giza pyramids are nowadays also minus their apex or capstones, which were shaped as pyramidions and may have been either made of metal or covered with a shiny metal—as the similar pyramidion-shaped tips of obelisks were. Who, when and why they were removed from their great heights, no one knows. It is known however that in later times these apex stones, resembling the *Ben-Ben* at Heliopolis, were made of special granite and bore appropriate inscriptions. The one from the pyramid of Amen-em-khet at Dahshur, which was found buried some distance away from the pyramid (Fig. 131), bore the emblem of the Winged Globe and the inscription

> The face of king Amen-em-khet is opened,
> That he may behold the Lord of the Mountain of Light
> When he sails across the sky.

When Herodotus visited Giza in the fifth century, the capstones are not mentioned, but the pyramids' sides were still covered with the smooth facings. As others before and after him, he wondered how these monuments—counted among the Seven Wonders of the ancient world—were ever built. Regarding the Great Pyramid, he was told by his guides that it took 100,000 men, replaced every three months by fresh laborers, "ten years of oppression of the people" just to build the causeway leading to the pyramid, so that the quarried stones could be brought to the site. "The pyramid itself was twenty years in building." It was Herodotus who transmitted the information that the Pharaoh who ordered the pyramid

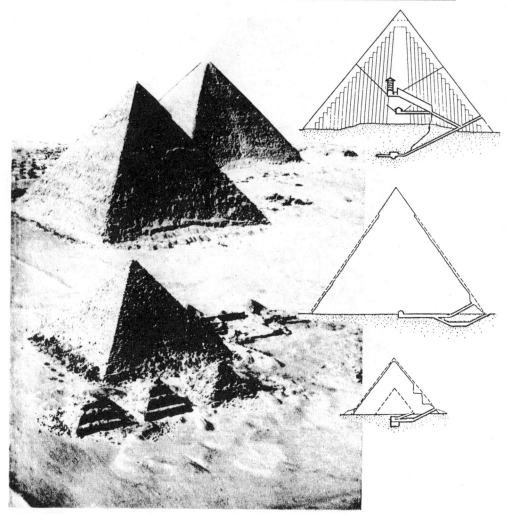

Fig. 129

built was Cheops (Khufu); why and what for, he does not say. Herodotus likewise attributed the Second Pyramid to Chephren (Chefra), "of the same dimensions, except that he lowered the height forty feet"; and asserted that Mycerinus (Menkara) "too left a pyramid, but much inferior in size to his father's"—implying, but not actually stating, that it was the Third Pyramid of Giza.

In the first century A.D., the Roman geographer and historian Strabo recorded not only a visit to the pyramids, but also his entry *into* the Great Pyramid through an opening in the north face, hidden by a hinged stone. Going down a long and narrow passage, he reached a pit dug in the bedrock—as other Greek and Roman tourists had done before him.

The location of this entryway was forgotten in the following centuries,

EXAMPLE of the CASING-STONES of a PYRAMID, SUPER-POSED.
ON THE RECT-ANGULAR MASONRY COURSES: FROM A PHOTOGRAPH BY P.S. OF THE SUMMIT OF THE 2ª PYR.

REMNANT of the ORIGINAL CASING-STONE SURFACE of the GREAT PYRAMID.
NEAR THE MIDDLE OF ITS NORTHERN FOOT. AS DISCOVERED BY THE EXCAVATIONS OF COL. HOWARD VYSE IN 1837

Fig. 130

Fig. 131

and when the Moslem caliph Al Mamoon attempted to enter the pyramid in 820 A.D., he employed an army of masons, blacksmiths and engineers to pierce the stones and tunnel his way into the pyramid's core. What prompted him was both a scientific quest and a lust for treasure; for he was apprised of ancient legends that the pyramid contained a secret chamber wherein celestial maps and terrestrial spheres, as well as "weapons which do not rust" and "glass which can be bent without breaking" were hidden away in past ages.

Blasting through the mass of stones by heating and cooling them until they cracked, by ramming and chiseling, Al Mamoon's men advanced into the pyramid inch by inch. They were about to give up, when they heard the sound of a falling stone not far ahead, indicating that some cavity was located there. With renewed vigor, they blasted their way into the original Descending Passage (Fig. 132). Climbing up it, they reached the original entrance which had evaded them from the outside. Climbing down, they reached the pit described by Strabo; it was empty. A shaft from the pit led nowhere.

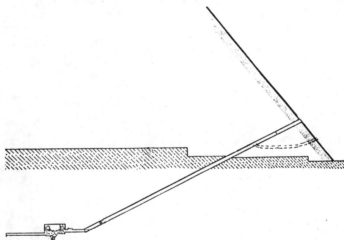

Fig. 132

As far as the searchers were concerned, the effort had been in vain. All the other pyramids, which were entered or broken into over the centuries, had the same inner structure: a Descending Passage leading to one or more chambers. This has not been found in the Great Pyramid. There were no other secrets to be unlocked. . . .

But Fate wished otherwise. The ramming and blasting by Al Mamoon's men had loosened the stone, whose falling sound had encouraged them to tunnel on. As they were about to give up, the fallen stone was found lying in the Descending Passage. It had an odd, triangular shape. When the ceiling was examined, it was found that the stone served to hide from view a large rectangular granite slab positioned at an angle to the Descending Passage. Did it hide the way to a really secret chamber—one obviously never before visited?

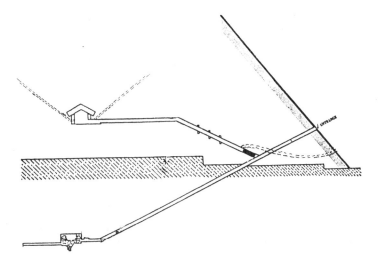

Fig. 133

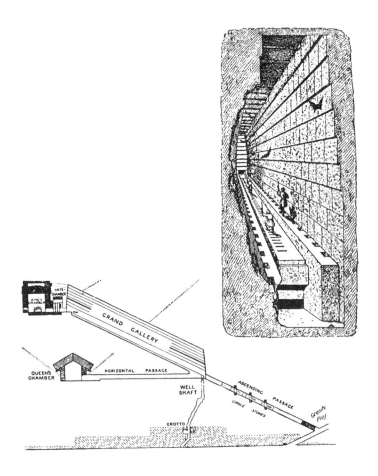

Fig. 134

Unable to move or break the granite block, Al Mamoon's men tunneled around it. It turned out that the granite slab was only one of a series of massive granite blocks, followed by limestone ones, that plugged an Ascending Passage—inclined upward at the same 26° angle that the Descending Passage was inclined downward (precisely half the angle of the pyramid's outer inclination). From the top of the Ascending Passage, a horizontal passage led to a squarish room with a gabled roof (Fig. 133) and an unusual niche in its east wall; it was bare and empty. This chamber has since been found to lie precisely in the middle of the north-south axis of the pyramid—a fact whose significance has not yet been deciphered. The chamber has come to be known as the "Queen's Chamber"; but the name is based on romantic notions and not on any shred of evidence.

At the head of the Ascending Passage, there extended for 150 feet and at the same rising angle of 26° a Grand Gallery of intricate and precise construction (Fig. 134). Its sunken floor is flanked by two ramps that run the length of the Gallery; in each ramp there are cut a series of evenly spaced rectangular slots, facing each other. The Gallery's walls rise more than 18 feet in seven corbels, each section extending three inches out above the lower one, so that the Gallery narrows as it rises. At its top, the Gallery's ceiling is the exact width as the sunken floor between the ramps.

At the uppermost end of the Gallery, a huge stone formed a flat platform. Flush with it a short and comparatively narrow and low corridor (only 3.5 feet high) led to an ante-chamber of extremely complex construction, having been equipped to lower with a simple maneuver (the pull of a rope?) three solid granite walls that could vertically plug the passage and block further advance.

A short corridor, of a height and width similar to the former one, then led to a high-ceilinged room constructed of red polished granite—the so-called King's Chamber (Fig. 135). It was empty except for a granite block hewed out to suggest a lidless coffer. Its precise workmanship included grooves for a lid or top section. Its measurements, as has since been determined, exhibited knowledge of profound mathematical formulas. But it was found totally empty.

Was this whole mountain of stone, then, erected to hide an empty "coffer" in an empty chamber? Blackened torch marks and the evidence of Strabo attest that the Descending Passage was visited before; if there had ever been treasure in that subterranean room, it was removed long ago. But the Ascending Passage was most definitely plugged tight when Al Mamoon's men reached it in the ninth century A.D. The theory of the pyramids as royal tombs held that they were raised to protect the Pharaoh's mummy and the treasures buried with it from robbers and other uninvited disturbers of his eternal peace. Accordingly, the plugging of the passages is presumed to have taken place as soon as the mummy in its coffin was placed in the burial chamber. Yet here was a plugged passage—with absolutely nothing, except for an empty stone coffer, in the whole pyramid.

Fig. 135

In time, other rulers, scientists, adventurers have entered the pyramid, tunneled and blasted through it, discovering other features of its inner structure—including two sets of shafts which some believe were air ducts (for whom?) and others assert for astronomical observations (by whom?). Although scholars persist in referring to the stone coffer as a sarcophagus (its size could well hold a human body), the fact is that there is nothing, absolutely nothing to support a claim that the Great Pyramid was a royal tomb.

Indeed, the notion that the pyramids were built as Pharaonic tombs has remained unsupported by concrete evidence.

The first pyramid, that of Zoser, contains what scholars persist in calling two burial chambers, covered by the initial mastaba. When they were first penetrated by H. M. von Minutoli in 1821, he claimed that he found inside parts of a mummy as well as a few inscriptions bearing the name of Zoser. These, it has been claimed, he sent to Europe but they were lost at sea. In 1837, Colonel Howard Vyse re-excavated the inner parts more thoroughly, and reported finding a "heap of mummies," (eighty were later counted) and to have reached a chamber "bearing the name of King Zoser," inscribed in red paint. A century later, archaeologists reported the discovery of a fragment of a skull and evidence that "a wood sarcophagus may have stood inside the red granite chamber." In 1933, J. E. Quibell and J. P. Lauer discovered beneath the pyramid additional underground galleries, in which there were two sarcophagi—empty.

It is now generally accepted that all these extra mummies and coffins represent intrusive burials, namely the entombment of the dead from a later time by intruding on the sanctity of the sealed galleries and chambers.

But was Zoser himself ever entombed in the pyramid—was there ever an "original burial?"

Most archaeologists now doubt that Zoser was ever buried in the pyramid or under it. He was buried, it seems, in a magnificent tomb discovered in 1928 south of the pyramid. This "Southern Tomb," as it came to be known, was reached via a gallery whose stone ceiling imitated *palm trees*. It led to a simulated half-open door through which a great enclosure was entered. More galleries led to a subterranean room built of granite blocks; on one of its walls three false doors bore the carvings of the image, name and titles of Zoser.

Many eminent Egyptologists now believe that the pyramid was only a symbolic burial place for Zoser, and that the king was buried in the richly decorated Southern Tomb, topped by a large rectangular superstructure with a concave room which also contained the imperative chapel—just as depicted in some Egyptian drawings (Fig. 136).

The step pyramid presumed to have been begun by Zoser's successor, Sekhemkhet, also contained a "burial chamber." It housed an alabaster "sarcophagus," which was empty. Textbooks tell us that the archaeologist who discovered the chamber and the stone coffer (Zakaria Goneim) concluded that the chamber had been penetrated by grave robbers, who stole the mummy and all other contents of the tomb; but that is not entirely true. In fact, Mr. Goneim found the vertically sliding door of the alabaster coffer *shut and sealed with plaster*, and the remains of a dried-out wreath *still rested on top of the coffin*. As he later recalled, "hopes were now raised to a high pitch; but when the sarcophagus was opened, it was found to be empty and unused." Had any king ever been buried there? While some still say yes, others are convinced that the pyramid of Sekhemkhet (jar stoppers bearing his name attest to the identification) was only a cenotaph (an empty, symbolic tomb).

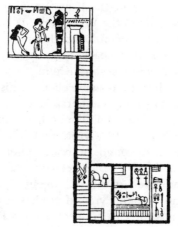

Fig. 136

The third step pyramid, the one attributed to Khaba, also contained a "burial chamber"; it was found to be completely bare: no mummy, not even a sarcophagus. Archaeologists have identified in the same vicinity the subterranean remains of yet another, unfinished pyramid, believed to have been begun by Khaba's successor. Its granite substructure contained an unusual oval "sarcophagus" sunken into the stone floor (as an ultra-modern bathtub). Its lid was still in place, shut tight with cement. There was nothing inside.

The remains of three other small pyramids, attributed to Third Dynasty rulers, were additionally found. In one, the substructure has not yet been explored. In the other, no burial chamber was found. In the third, the chamber contained no evidence of a burial at any time.

Nothing was found in the "burial chamber" of the collapsed pyramid of Maidum, not even a sarcophagus. Instead, Flinders Petrie found only fragments of a wooden coffin, which he announced as the remains of the coffin of Sneferu's mummy. Scholars now invariably believe that it represented the remains of a much later intrusive burial. The Maidum pyramid is surrounded by numerous Third and Fourth Dynasty mastabas, in which members of the royal family and other VIP's of that time were entombed. The pyramid's enclosure was linked with a lower structure (a so-called funerary temple) which is now submerged by the Nile's waters. It was perhaps there, surrounded and protected by the sacred river's waters, that the Pharaoh's body was laid to rest.

The next two pyramids are even more embarrassing to the pyramids-as-tombs theory. The two pyramids at Dahshur (the Bent and the Red) were both built by Sneferu. The first has *two* "burial chambers," the other *three*. All for Sneferu? If the pyramid was built by each Pharaoh to serve as his tomb, why did Sneferu build two pyramids? Needless to say, the chambers were totally empty when discovered, devoid even of sarcophagi. After some more determined excavations by the Egyptian Antiquities Service in 1947 and again in 1953 (especially in the Red Pyramid), the report admitted that "No trace of a royal tomb has been found there."

The theory of "a pyramid by each Pharaoh" now holds that the next pyramid was built by Sneferu's son, Khufu; and we have the word of Herodotus (and Roman historians who relied on his works) that it was the Great Pyramid at Giza. Its chambers, even the unviolated "King's Chamber," were empty. This should not have come as a surprise, for Herodotus (*History*, vol. II, p. 127) wrote that "the Nile water, introduced through an artificial duct, surrounds an island where the body of Cheops is said to lie." Was then the Pharaoh's real tomb somewhere lower in the valley and closer to the Nile? As of now, no one can tell.

Chefra, to whom the Second Pyramid of Giza is attributed, was not the immediate successor of Khufu. In between them a Pharaoh named Radedef reigned for eight years. For reasons which the scholars cannot explain, he selected for his pyramid a site some distance away from Giza. About half the size of the Great Pyramid, it contained the customary "burial chamber." When reached, it was found entirely empty.

The Second Pyramid of Giza has two entrances on its northern side, instead of the customary single one (see Fig. 129). The first begins— another unusual feature—outside the pyramid and leads to an unfinished chamber. The other leads to a chamber aligned with the pyramid's apex. When it was entered in 1818 by Giovanni Belzoni, the granite sarcophagus was found empty and its lid lying broken on the floor. An inscription in Arabic recorded the penetration of the chamber centuries earlier. What, if anything, the Arabs had found, is nowhere recorded.

Giza's Third Pyramid, though much smaller than the other two, displays many unique or unusual features. Its core was built with the largest stone blocks of all three pyramids; its lower sixteen courses were cased not with white limestone but with formidable granite. It was built first as an even smaller true pyramid (Fig. 129), then doubled in size. As a result, it has two usable entrances; it also contains a third, perhaps a "trial" entrance not completed by its builders. Of its various chambers, the one deemed the main "burial chamber" was entered in 1837 by Howard Vyse and John Perring. They found inside the chamber a magnificently decorated basalt sarcophagus; it was, as usual, empty. But nearby Vyse and Perring found a fragment of a wood coffin with the royal name "Men-ka-Ra" written upon it, and the remains of a mummy, "possibly of Menkaura"—direct confirmation of the statement by Herodotus that the Third Pyramid "belonged" to "Mycerinus." Modern carbon-dating methods, however, established that the wooden coffin "certainly dates from the Saitic period"—not earlier than 660 B.C. (K. Michalowsky, *Art of Ancient Egypt*); the mummy remains are from early Christian times. They did not belong to any original burial.

There is some uncertainty whether Men-ka-Ra was the immediate successor of Chefra; but scholars are certain that his successor was one named Shepsekaf. Which of the various pyramids that were never finished (or whose construction was so inferior that nothing remains above ground) belonged to Shepsekaf, is still unclear. But it is certain that he was not buried within it: he was buried under a monumental mastaba (Fig. 137) whose burial chamber contained a black granite sarcophagus. It had been penetrated by ancient grave robbers, who emptied tomb and sarcophagus of their contents.

The Fifth Dynasty that followed began with Userkaf. He built his pyramid at Sakkara, near Zoser's pyramid complex. It was violated by both grave robbers and intrusive burials. His successor (Sahura) built a pyramid north of Sakkara (today's Abusir). Though one of the best preserved (Fig. 138), nothing was found in its rectangular "burial chamber." But the magnificence of its temples, that stretched between it and the Nile Valley, and the fact that one of the lower temple rooms was decorated with stone columns simulating palm trees, may indicate that it was somewhere near the pyramid that Sahura's real tomb was.

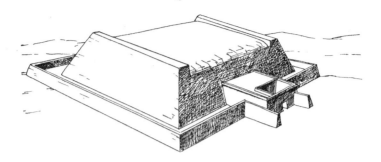

Fig. 137

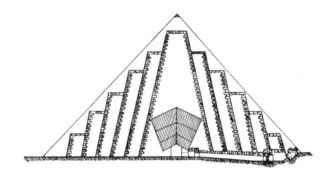

Fig. 138

Fig. 139

Neferirkara, who followed on the throne of Egypt, built his funerary complex not far from Sahura's. The chamber in his incomplete (or ruined) pyramid was empty. The monuments of his successor were not found. The next ruler built his pyramid more with dried mud bricks and wood than with stone; only meager remains of the structure were found. Neuserra, who followed, built his pyramid close by those of his predecessors. It contained two chambers—both with no trace of a burial. Neuserra, however, is better known for his funerary temple, built in the shape of a stubby, short obelisk upon a truncated pyramid (Fig. 139). The obelisk rose 118 feet; its apex was covered with gilded copper.

The pyramid of the next Pharaoh has not been found; perhaps it has crumbled to a mound, covered by the desert's shifting sands. That of his successor was identified only in 1945. Its substructure contained the usual chamber, which was bare and empty.

The pyramid of Unash—last of the Fifth Dynasty or, as some prefer, first of the Sixth—marked a major change of custom. It was there that Gaston Maspero discovered for the first time (in 1880) the Pyramid Texts, inscribed on the walls of the pyramid's chambers and corridors. The four pyramids of the following Sixth Dynasty rulers (Teti, Pepi I, Mernera and Pepi II) emulated that of Unash in their funerary complexes and the inclusion of Pyramid Texts on their walls. Basalt or granite sarcophagi were found in all of their "burial" chambers; they were otherwise empty, except that in the sarcophagus in the Mernera pyramid a mummy was found. It was soon established that it was not the king's, but represented a later intrusive burial.

Where were the Sixth Dynasty kings really buried? The royal tombs of that dynasty and of earlier ones were all the way south, at Abydos. This, as the other evidence, should have completely dispelled the notion that the tombs were cenotaphs and the pyramids the real tombs; nevertheless, long-held beliefs die hard.

The facts bespeak the opposite. The Old Kingdom pyramids never held a Pharaoh's body because they were never meant to hold a king's body. In the Pharaoh's simulated Journey to the Horizon, they were built as beacons to guide his *ka* to the Stairway to Heaven—just as the pyramids originally raised by gods had served as beacons for the gods when they "sailed across the sky."

Pharaoh after Pharaoh, we suggest, attempted to emulate not the pyramid of Zoser, but the *Pyramids of the Gods*: the pyramids of Giza.

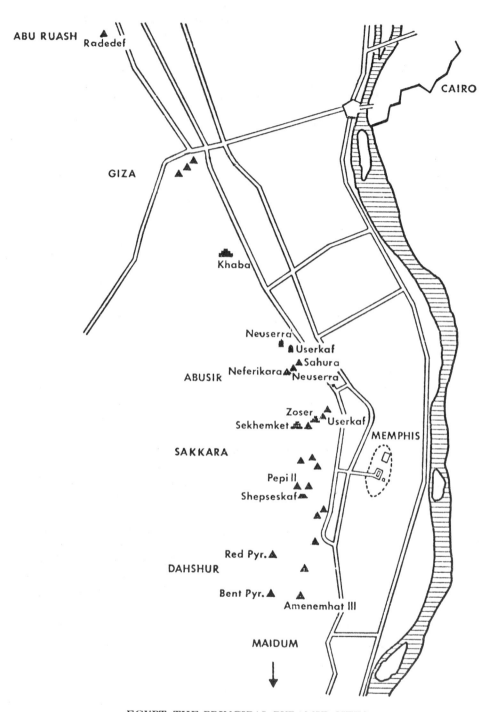

ABU RUASH Radedef

CAIRO

GIZA

Khaba

Neuserra
Userkaf
Sahura
Neferikara Neuserra
ABUSIR

Zoser
Sekhemket Userkaf
MEMPHIS

SAKKARA

Pepi II
Shepseskaf

Red Pyr.
DAHSHUR

Bent Pyr.
Amenemhat III

MAIDUM
↓

EGYPT: THE PRINCIPAL PYRAMID SITES

Fig. 140

XIII

Forging the Pharaoh's Name

Forgery as a means to fame and fortune is not uncommon in commerce and the arts, in science and antiquities. When exposed, it may cause loss and shame. When sustained, it may change the records of history.

This, we believe, has happened to the Great Pyramid and its presumed builder, the Pharaoh named *Khufu*.

Systematic and disciplined archaeological re-examination of pyramid sites that were hurriedly excavated a century and a half ago (many times by treasure hunters), has raised numerous questions regarding some of the earlier conclusions. It has been held that the Pyramid Age began with Zoser's step pyramid, and was marked by successive progression toward a true pyramid, which finally succeeded. But why was it so important to achieve a true pyramid? If the art of pyramid building was progressively improved, why were the many pyramids which followed the Giza pyramids inferior, rather than superior to those of Giza?

Was Zoser's step pyramid the model for others, or was it itself an emulation of an earlier model? Scholars now believe that the first, smaller step pyramid (Fig. 125) that Imhotep built over the mastaba "was cased with beautiful, fine white limestone" (Ahmed Fakhry, *The Pyramids*); "before this casing was complete, however, he planned another alteration"—the superimposition of an even larger pyramid. However, as new evidence suggests, even that final step pyramid was cased, to look like a true pyramid. The casing, uncovered by archaeological missions of Harvard University led by George Reisner, was primitively made of mud bricks, which of course crumbled soon enough—leaving the impression that Zoser built a step pyramid. Moreover, these mud bricks, it was found, were whitewashed to simulate a casing of white limestone.

Whom then was Zoser trying to emulate? Where had Imhotep seen a true pyramid already up and complete, smooth sides and limestone casing and all? And another question: If, as the present theory holds, the attempts at Maidum and Sakkara to build a smooth, 52° pyramid had failed, and Sneferu had to "cheat" and build the presumed first true pyramid at an angle of only 43°—why did his son at once proceed to build a much larger pyramid at the precarious angle of 52°—and supposedly managed to achieve that with no problem at all?

If the pyramids of Giza were only "usual" pyramids in the successive chain of pyramid-per-Pharaoh—why did Khufu's son Radedef not build his pyramid next to his father's, at Giza? Remember—the other two Giza pyramids were supposedly not there yet, so Radedef had the whole site free to build as he pleased. And if his father's architects and engineers mastered the art of building the Great Pyramid, where were they to help Radedef build a similar imposing pyramid, rather than the inferior and quickly crumbling one that bears his name?

Was the reason that no other pyramid but the Great Pyramid possessed an Ascending Passage, that its unique Ascending Passage was successfully blocked and hidden until A.D. 820—so that all who emulated this pyramid knew of a Descending Passage only?

The absence of hieroglyphic inscriptions in the three pyramids of Giza is also a reason for wondering, as James Bonwick did a century ago (*Pyramid Facts and Fancies*): "Who can persuade himself that the Egyptians would have left such superb monuments without at least hieroglyphical inscriptions—they who were profuse of hieroglyphics upon all the edifices of any consideration?" The absence, one must surmise, stems from the fact that the pyramids had either been built *before* the development of hieroglyphic writing, or were not built by the Egyptians.

These are some of the points that strengthen our belief that when Zoser and his successors began the custom of pyramid building, they set out to emulate the models that had already existed: the pyramids of Giza. They were not improvements on Zoser's earlier efforts; rather, they were the prototypes which Zoser, and Pharaohs after him, attempted to emulate.

Some scholars have suggested that the small satellite pyramids at Giza were really scale models (about 1:5) that were used by the ancients exactly as today's architects use scale models for evaluation and guidance; but it is now known that they were later augmentations. However, *we think that there was indeed such a scale model; the Third Pyramid, with its obvious structural experiments. Then, we believe, the larger two were built as a pair of guiding beacons for the Anunnaki.*

But what about Menkara, Chefra and Khufu, who (we have been told by Herodotus) were the builders of these pyramids?

Well indeed—what about them? The temples and causeway attached to the Third Pyramid do bear evidence that their builder was Menkara—evidence that includes inscriptions bearing his name and several exquisite statues showing him embraced by Hathor and another goddess. But all that this attests to is that Menkara built these auxiliary structures, associating himself with the pyramid—not that he built it. The Anunnaki, it is logical to assume, needed only the pyramids and would not have built temples to worship themselves; only a Pharaoh required a funerary temple and a mortuary temple and the other structures associated with his journey to the gods.

Inside the Third Pyramid proper, not an inscription, not a statue, not a decorated wall have been found; just stark, austere precision. The only purported evidence proved to be a false pretense: the fragments of the wooden coffin inscribed with the name of Menkara proved to be from a time some 2,000 years after his reign; and the mummy "matching" the coffin was from early Christian times. There is thus not a shred of evidence to support the notion that Menkara—or any Pharaoh for that matter—had anything to do with creating and building the pyramid itself.

The Second Pyramid is likewise completely bare. Statues bearing the cartouche (oval frame within which the royal name is inscribed) of Chefra were found only in the temples adjoining the pyramid. But there is nothing at all to indicate that he had built it.

What then, about Khufu?

With one exception, *which we will expose as a probable forgery*, the only claim that he built the Great Pyramid is reported by Herodotus (and, based on his writings, by a Roman historian). Herodotus described him as a ruler who enslaved his people for thirty years to build the causeway and the pyramid. Yet by every other account, Khufu reigned for only twenty-three years. If he were such a grandiose builder, blessed with the greatest of architects and masons, where are his other monuments, where are his bigger-than-life statues?

There are none; and it would seem from the absence of such commemorative remains that Khufu was a very poor builder, not a majestic one. But he had a bright idea: our guess is that having seen the crumbled mud-brick casings of the step pyramids, the collapsed pyramid at Maidum, the hurried bending of the first pyramid of Sneferu, the improper inclination of Sneferu's second pyramid—Khufu hit upon a great idea. Out there, at Giza, there stood perfect and unspoken of pyramids. Could he not ask the gods' permission to attach to one of them the funerary temples which his Journey to the Afterlife required? There was no intrusion upon the sanctity of the pyramid itself: all the temples, including the Valley Temple in which Khufu was probably buried, were on the outside: adjoining, but not even touching, the Great Pyramid. Thus had the Great Pyramid become known as Khufu's.

Khufu's successor, Radedef, shunned his father's idea and preferred to raise his own pyramid, as Sneferu had done. But why had he gone to the north of Giza, rather than place his shrine next to his father's? The simple explanation is that the promontory of Giza was already fully occupied—by three olden pyramids plus the satellite structures erected nearby by Khufu. . . .

Witnessing Radedef's failure, the next Pharaoh—Chefra—preferred Khufu's solution. When his time came to need a pyramid, he saw no harm in appropriating for himself the ready-made second large pyramid, surrounding it with his own temples and satellites. Menkara, his successor, then attached himself to the last available pyramid, the so-called Third Pyramid.

With the ready-made pyramids thus taken, the Pharaohs who followed were forced to obtain pyramids the hard way: by trying to build them. . . . As those who had tried this before (Zoser, Sneferu, Radedef), their own efforts too ended with inferior emulations of the three olden pyramids.

At first blush, our suggestion that Khufu (as the other two) had nothing to do with building the pyramid associated with him may sound very farfetched. It is hardly so. In evidence, we call upon Khufu himself.

Whether Khufu had really built the Great Pyramid was a question that began to perplex serious Egyptologists more than a century and a quarter ago, when the *only object* mentioning Khufu and connecting him with the pyramid was discovered. Puzzlingly, it affirmed that he did not build it: *it already existed when he reigned!*

The damning evidence is a limestone stela (Fig. 141) which was discovered by Auguste Mariette in the 1850s in the ruins of the temple of Isis, near the Great Pyramid. Its inscription identifies it as a self-laudatory monument by Khufu, erected to commemorate the restoration by him of the temple of Isis and of images and emblems of the gods which Khufu found inside the crumbling temple. The opening verses unmistakably identify Khufu by his cartouche:

Ankh	*Hor*	*Mezdau*	*Suten-bat*	*Khufu*	*tu ankh*
Live	Horus	Mezdau;	(To) King (of)	Khufu,	is given Life!
			Upper & Lower Egypt,		

The common opening, invoking Horus and proclaiming long life for the king, then packs explosive statements:

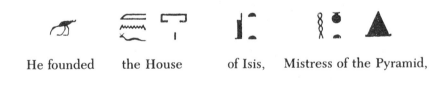

He founded   the House   of Isis,   Mistress of the Pyramid,

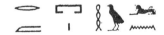

beside the House of the Sphinx

According to the inscription on this stela (which is in the Cairo Museum), the Great Pyramid was already standing when Khufu arrived on the scene.

Fig. 141

Its mistress was the goddess Isis—it belonged to this goddess, and not to Khufu. Furthermore, the Sphinx too—which has been attributed to Chefra, who presumably built it together with the Second Pyramid—was also already crouching at its present location. The continuation of the inscription pinpoints the position of the Sphinx accurately, and records the fact that part of it was damaged by lightning—a damage perceivable to this very day.

Khufu continues to state in his inscription that he built a pyramid for the Princess Henutsen "beside the temple of the goddess." Archaeologists have found independent evidence that the southernmost of the three small pyramids flanking the Great Pyramid—the small pyramid nearest the temple of Isis—was in fact dedicated to Henutsen, a wife of Khufu. Everything in the inscription thus matches the known facts; but the only pyramid-building claim made by Khufu is that he built the small pyramid for the princess. The Great Pyramid, he states, was already there, as was the Sphinx (and, by inference, the other two pyramids as well).

Such support for our theories is even further strengthened, as we read in another portion of the inscription that the Great Pyramid was also called "The Western Mountain of Hathor":

> Live Horus Mezdau;
> To King of Upper and Lower Egypt, Khufu,
> Life is given.
> For his mother Isis, the Divine Mother,
> Mistress of "The Western Mountain of Hathor,"
>   he made (this) writing on a stela.
> He gave (her) a new sacred offering.
> He built (her) a House (temple) of stone,
>   renewed the gods that were found in her temple.

Hathor, we will recall, was the mistress of the Sinai peninsula. If the highest peak of the peninsula was her Eastern Mountain, the Great Pyramid was her Western Mountain—the two acting as the anchors for the Landing Corridor.

This "Inventory Stela," as it came to be called, bears all the marks of authenticity. Yet scholars at the time of its discovery (and many ever since) have been unable to reconcile themselves to its unavoidable conclusions. Unwilling to upset the whole structure of Pyramidology, they proclaimed the Inventory Stela a *forgery*—an inscription made "long after the death of Khufu" (to quote Selim Hassan, *Excavations at Giza*), but invoking his name "to support some fictitious claim of the local priests."

James H. Breasted, whose *Ancient Records of Egypt* is the standard work on ancient Egyptian inscriptions, wrote in 1906 that "the references to the Sphinx, and the so-called temple beside it in the time of Khufu, have made this monument from the first an object of great interest. These references would be of the highest importance if the monument were contemporaneous with Khufu; but the orthographic evidences of its late date are entirely conclusive." He disagreed with Gaston Maspero, a leading Egyptologist of the time, who had earlier suggested that the stela, if indeed of late orthography, was a copy of an earlier and authentic original. In spite of the doubts, Breasted included the inscription among the records of the Fourth Dynasty. And Maspero, when he wrote his comprehensive *The Dawn of Civilization* in 1920, accepted the contents of the Inventory Stela as factual data concerning the life and activities of Khufu.

Why then the reluctance to call the artifact authentic?

The Inventory Stela was condemned as a forgery because only a decade or so earlier the identification of Khufu as the builder of the Great Pyramid appeared to have been undisputably established. The seemingly conclusive evidence was markings in red paint, discovered in sealed chambers above the King's Chamber, which could be interpreted as masons' markings made in the eighteenth year of the reign of Khufu (Fig. 142). Since the chambers were not entered until discovered in 1837, the markings must have been authentic; and if the Inventory Stela offered contradictory information, the Stela must have been a forgery.

But as we probe the circumstances of the red-paint markings, and ascertain who the discoverers were—an inquiry somehow never undertaken before—the conclusion that emerges is this: if a forgery had taken place, it occurred not in ancient times but in the year A.D. 1837; and the forgers were not "some local priests," but two (or three) unscrupulous Englishmen. . . .

The story begins with the arrival in Egypt on December 29, 1835 of Colonel Richard Howard Vyse, a "black sheep" of an aristocratic English family. At that time, other officers of Her Majesty's Army had become prominent in the ranks of "antiquarians" (as archaeologists were then called), reading papers before distinguished societies and receiving due public accolade. Whether or not Vyse had gone to Egypt with such notions in mind, the fact is that visiting the pyramids of Giza, he was at once caught by the fever of daily discoveries by scholars and laymen alike. He was especially thrilled by the tales and theories of one Giovanni Battista Caviglia, who had been searching for a hidden chamber inside the Great Pyramid.

Within days, Vyse offered to provide the funds for Caviglia's search, if he were accepted as a co-discoverer. Caviglia rejected the offer outright; and the offended Vyse sailed off to Beirut at the end of February 1836, to visit Syria and Asia Minor.

But the long trip did not cure the craving that was aroused within him. Instead of returning to England, he showed up back in Egypt in October 1836. On the earlier visit, he had befriended a crafty go-between by the name of J. R. Hill, then a copper mill superintendent. Now he was introduced to a "Mr. Sloane," who whispered that there were ways to get a *Firman*—a concession decree—from the Egyptian government to sole

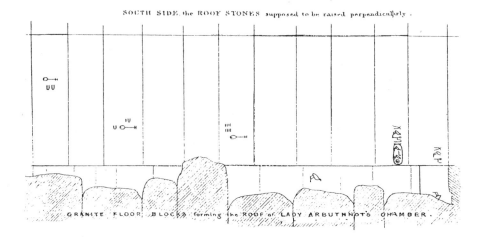

GRANITE FLOOR BLOCKS forming the ROOF of LADY ARBUTHNOT'S CHAMBER.

NORTH SIDE .

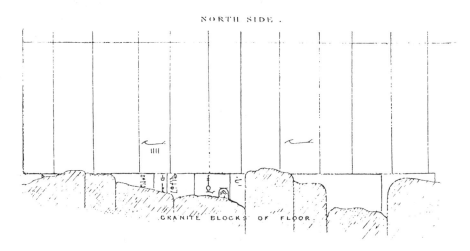

GRANITE BLOCKS OF FLOOR .

Fig. 142

excavation rights at Giza. Thus guided, Vyse went to the British Consul, Col. Campbell, for the necessary documentation. To his great shock, the Firman named Campbell and Sloane as co-permitees, and designated Caviglia as the works' supervisor. On November 2, 1836, the disappointed Vyse paid over to Caviglia "my first subscription of 200 dollars" and left in disgust on a sightseeing trip to Upper Egypt.

As chronicled by Vyse in his *Operations Carried on at the Pyramids of Gizeh in 1837,* he returned to Giza on January 24, 1837, "extremely anxious to see what progress had been made." But instead of searching for the hidden chamber, Caviglia and his workmen were busy digging up mummies from tombs around the pyramids. Vyse's fury subsided only when Caviglia asserted that he had something important to show him: writing by the pyramids' builders!

The excavations at the tombs showed that the ancient masons sometimes marked the pre-cut stones with red paint. Such markings, Caviglia said, he found at the base of the Second Pyramid. But when examined with Vyse, the "red paint" turned out to be natural discolorations iñ the stone.

What about the Great Pyramid? Caviglia, working there to discover where the "air channels" were leading from the "King's Chamber," was more than ever convinced that there were secret chambers higher up. One such compartment, reachable via a crawlway, was discovered by Nathaniel Davison in 1765 (Fig. 143). Vyse demanded that work be concentrated there; he was dismayed to find out that Caviglia and Campbell were more interested in finding mummies, which every museum then desired. Caviglia had even gone so far as to name a large tomb he had found "Campbell's Tomb."

Determined to run his own show, Vyse moved from Cairo to the site of the pyramids. "I naturally wished to make some discoveries before I returned to England," he admitted in his journal on January 27, 1837. At great expense to his family, he was now gone for well over a year.

In the following weeks, the rift with Caviglia widened as Vyse hurled at him various accusations. On February 11, the two had a violent argument. On the twelfth, Caviglia made major discoveries in Campbell's Tomb: a sarcophagus inscribed with hieroglyphs and masons' red-paint markings on the stone walls of the tomb. On the thirteenth, Vyse summarily discharged Caviglia and ordered him away from the site. Caviglia returned only once, on the fifteenth, to pick up his belongings; for years thereafter, he made "dishonorable accusations" against Vyse, whose nature Vyse's chronicles do not care to detail.

Was the row a genuine disagreement, or did Vyse artificially bring matters to a head in order to get Caviglia off the site?

Fig. 143

As it turned out, Vyse secretly entered the Great Pyramid on the night of February 12, accompanied by one John Perring—an engineer with the Egyptian Public Works Department and a dabbler in Egyptology—whom Vyse met through the resourceful Mr. Hill. The two examined an intriguing crevice that had developed in a granite block above Davison's Chamber; when a reed was pushed in, it went through unbent; there was obviously some space beyond.

What schemes did the two concoct during that secret night visit? We can only guess from future events. The facts are that Vyse dismissed Caviglia the next morning and put Perring on his payroll. In his journal, Vyse confided: "I am determined to carry on the excavations above the roof of (Davison's) Chamber, where I expect to find a sepulchral apartment." As Vyse threw more men and money behind this search, royalty and other dignitaries came to inspect the finds at Campbell's Tomb; there was little new that Vyse could show them inside the pyramid. In frustration, Vyse ordered his men to bore into the shoulder of the Sphinx, hoping to find its masons' markings. Unsuccessful, he refocused his attention on the Hidden Chamber.

By mid-March, Vyse faced a new problem: other projects were luring away his workmen. He doubled their pay, if only they would work day and night: time, he realized, was running out. In desperation, Vyse threw caution to the winds, and ordered the use of explosives to blast his way through the stones that blocked his progress.

By March 27, the workmen managed to cut a small hole through the granite slabs. Illogically, Vyse thereupon discharged the foreman, one named Paulo. On the following day, Vyse wrote, "I inserted a candle at the end of a rod through a small hole that had been made in the chamber above Davison's, and I had the mortification of finding that it was a chamber of construction like that below it." He had found the Hidden Chamber! (Fig. 144.)

Using gunpowder to enlarge the hole, Vyse entered the newly discovered chamber on March 30—accompanied by Mr. Hill. They examined it thoroughly. It was hermetically sealed, with no opening whatsoever. Its floor consisted of the rough side of the large granite slabs that formed the ceiling of Davison's Chamber below. "A black sediment was equally distributed all over the floor, showing each footstep." (The nature of this black powder, which was "accumulated to some depth," has never been ascertained.) "The ceiling was beautifully polished and had the finest joints." The chamber, it was clear, had never been entered before; yet it contained neither sarcophagus nor treasure. It was bare—completely empty.

Vyse ordered the hole enlarged, and sent a message to the British Consul announcing that he had named the new compartment "Wellington's Chamber." In the evening, "Mr. Perring and Mr. Mash having arrived, we

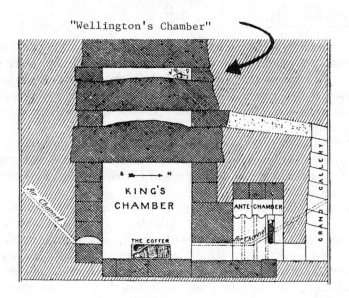

"Wellington's Chamber"

KING'S
CHAMBER

THE COFFER

ANTE-CHAMBER

GRAND GALLERY

Air Channel

Air Channel

Fig. 144

went into Wellington's Chamber and took various measurements, *and in doing so we found the quarry marks.*" What a sudden stroke of luck!

They were similar to the red-painted quarry marks found in tombs outside the pyramid. Somehow, Vyse and Hill missed them entirely when they thoroughly inspected the chamber by themselves. But joined by Mr. Perring and by Mr. Mash—a civil engineer who was present at Perring's invitation—there were four witnesses to the unique discovery.

The fact that Wellington's Chamber was almost identical to Davison's led Vyse to suspect that there was yet another chamber above it. For no given reason Vyse dismissed on April 4 the remaining foreman, one named Giachino. On April 14, the British Consul and the Austrian Consul General visited the site. They requested that copies be made of the masons' markings. Vyse put Perring and Mash to work—but instructed them to copy first the earlier-discovered markings in Campbell's tomb; the unique ones inside the Great Pyramid could somehow wait.

With liberal use of gunpowder, the compartment above Wellington's (Vyse named it after Lord Nelson) was broken into on April 25. It was as empty as the others, its floor also covered with the mysterious black dust. Vyse reported that he found "several quarry marks inscribed in red upon the blocks, particularly on the west side." All along, Mr. Hill was going in and out of the newly found chambers, ostensibly to inscribe in them (how?) the names of Wellington and Nelson. On the twenty-seventh Mr. Hill—not Perring or Mash—copied the quarry marks. Vyse reproduced the ones from Nelson's Chamber (though not the ones from Wellington's) in his book (Fig. 145a).

On May 7, the way was blasted through into one more chamber above

Nelson's, which Vyse named temporarily after Lady Arbuthnot. The journal entry makes no mention of any quarry marks, although they were later on found there in profusion. What was striking about the new markings was that they included cartouches—which could only mean royal names (Fig. 145b)—in profusion. Has Vyse come upon the actual written name of the Pharaoh who had built the pyramid?

On May 18, a Dr. Walni "applied for copies of the characters found in the Great Pyramid, in order to send them to Mr. Rosellini," an Egyptologist who had specialized in the decipherment of royal names. Vyse turr ed the request down outrightly.

The next day, in the company of Lord Arbuthnot, a Mr. Brethel and a Mr. Raven, Vyse entered Lady Arbuthnot's Chamber and the four "compared Mr. Hill's drawings with the quarry marks in the Great Pyramid; and we afterward signed an attestation to their accuracy." Soon thereafter, the final vaulted chamber was broken into, and more markings—including a royal cartouche—were found. Vyse then proceeded to Cairo and submitted the authenticated copies of the writings on the stones to the British Embassy, for official forwarding to London.

His work was done: he found hitherto unknown chambers, and he proved the identity of the builder of the Great Pyramid; for within the cartouches was written the royal name *Kh-u-f-u*

To this discovery, every textbook has been attesting to this very day.

The impact of Vyse's discoveries was great, and their acceptance assured, after he managed to quickly obtain a confirmation from the experts of the British Museum in London.

When the facsimiles made by Mr. Hill reached the Museum, and when exactly their analysis reached Vyse, is not clear; but he made the Museum's opinion (by the hand of its hieroglyphics expert Samuel Birch) part of his chronicle of May 27, 1837. On the face of it, the long analysis confirmed Vyse's expectations: the names in the cartouches could be read as *Khufu* or variations thereof: just as Herodotus had written, Cheops was the builder of the Great Pyramid.

But in the excitement which understandably followed, little attention was paid to the many if's and but's in the Museum's opinion. It also contained the clue that tipped us off to the forgery: the forger's clumsy mistake.

To begin with, Mr. Birch was uneasy about the orthography and script of the many markings. "The symbols or hieroglpyhs traced in red by the sculptor, or mason, upon the stones in the chambers of the Great Pyramid are apparently quarry marks," he observed in his opening paragraph; the qualification at once followed: "Although not very legible, owing to their having been written in semi-hieratic or linear-hieroglyphic characters, they possess points of considerable interest. . . ."

What puzzled Mr. Birch was that markings presumably from the

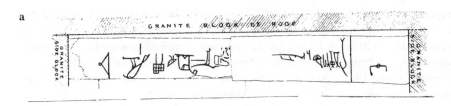

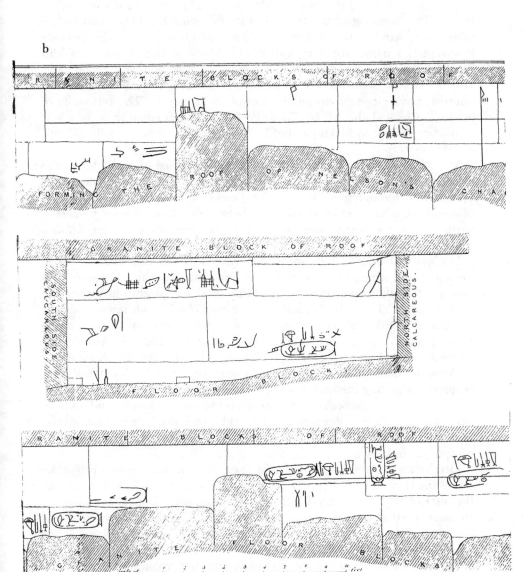

Fig. 145

beginning of the Fourth Dynasty were made in a script that started to appear only centuries later. Originating as pictographs—"written pictures"—the writing of hieroglyphic symbols required great skill and long training; so, in time, in commercial transactions, a more quickly written and simpler, more linear script referred to as hieratic came into use. The hieroglyphic symbols discovered by Vyse thus belonged to another period. They were also very indistinct and Mr. Birch had great difficulty in reading them: "The meaning of the hieroglyphics following the prenomen in the same linear hand as the cartouche, is not very obvious. . . . The symbols following the name are very indistinct." Many of them looked to him "written in characters very nearly hieratic"—from an even much later period than the semi-hieratic characters. Some of the symbols were very unusual, never seen in any other inscription in Egypt: "The cartouche of Suphis" (Cheops), he wrote, "is followed by a hieroglyphic to which it would be difficult to find a parallel." Other symbols were "equally difficult of solution."

Mr. Birch was also puzzled by "a curious sequence of symbols" in the upper-most, vaulted chamber (named by Vyse "Campbell's Chamber"). There, the hieroglyphic symbol for "good, gracious" was used as a numeral—a usage never discovered before or since. Those unusually written numerals were assumed to mean "eighteenth year" (of Khufu's reign).

No less puzzling to him were the symbols which followed the royal cartouche and which were "in the same linear hand as the cartouche." He assumed that they spelled out a royal title, such as "Mighty in Upper and Lower Egypt." The only similarity that he could find to this row of symbols was that of "a title that appears on the coffin of the queen of Amasis" of the Saitic period. He saw no need to stress that the Pharaoh Amasis had reigned in the sixth century B.C.—more than 2,000 years after Khufu!

Whoever daubed the red-paint markings reported by Vyse had thus employed a writing method (linear), scripts (semi-hieratic and hieratic) and titles from various periods—but none from the time of Khufu, and all from later periods. Their writer was also not too literate: many of his hieroglyphs were either unclear, incomplete, out of place, erroneously employed or completely unknown.

(Analyzing these inscriptions a year later, the leading German Egyptologist of the time, Carl Richard Lepsius, was likewise puzzled by the fact that the inscriptions "were traced with a brush in red paint in a cursive manner, so much so that they resemble hieratic signs." Some of the hieroglyphs following the cartouches, he declared, were totally unknown, and "I am unable to explain them.")

Turning to the main issue on which he was requested to give an opinion—the identity of the Pharaoh named in the inscriptions—Birch threw a bombshell: there were *two,* and not just one, royal names within the pyramid!

Was it possible that two kings had built the same pyramid? And if so, who were they?

The two royal names appearing in the inscriptions, Samuel Birch reported, were not unknown: "they had already been found in the tombs of functionaries employed by monarchs of that dynasty," namely the Fourth Dynasty to whose Pharaohs the pyramids of Giza were attributed. One cartouche (Fig. 146a) was then read *Saufou* or *Shoufou*; the other (146b) included the ram symbol of the god Khnum and was then read *Senekhuf* or *Seneshoufou*.

Attempting to analyze the meaning of the name with the ram symbol, Birch noted that "a cartouche, similar to that which first occurs in Wellington's Chamber, had been published by Mr. Wilkinson, mater. Hieroglyph, Plate of Unplaced Kings E; and also by Mr. Rosellini, tom. i. tav.1,3, who reads the phonetic elements of which it is composed 'Seneshufo,' which name is supposed by Mr. Wilkinson to mean 'the Brother of Suphis.'"

That one Pharaoh might have completed a pyramid begun by his predecessor has been a theory accepted by Egyptologists (as in the case of the pyramid at Maidum). Could not this account for two royal names within the same pyramid? Perhaps—but certainly not in our case.

The impossibility in the case of the Great Pyramid stems from the location of the various cartouches (Fig. 147). The cartouche that is presumed to have belonged in the pyramid, that of Cheops/Khufu, was found only in the *uppermost*, vaulted chamber, the one named Campbell's Chamber. The several cartouches which spelled out the second name (nowadays read *Khnem-khuf*) appeared in Wellington's Chamber and in Lady Arbuthnot's Chamber (no cartouches were inscribed in Nelson's Chamber). In other words, the lower chambers bore the name of a Pharaoh who lived and reigned *after* Cheops. As there was no way to build the pyramid except from its base upward, the location of the cartouches meant that Cheops, who reigned before Chephren, completed a pyramid begun by a Pharaoh who succeeded him. That, of course, was not possible.

Conceding that the two names could have stood for what the ancient King Lists had called Suphis I (Cheops) and Suphis II (Chephren), Birch tried to resolve the problem by wondering whether both names, somehow, belonged to Cheops alone—one as his actual name, the other as his "prenomen." But his final conclusion was that "the presence of this (second) name, as a quarry-mark, in the Great Pyramid, is an additional embarrassment" on top of the other embarrassing features of the inscriptions.

The "Problem of the Second Name" was still unresolved when England's most noted Egyptologist, Flinders Petrie, spent months measuring the pyramids a half century later. "The most destructive theory about this king (Khnem-khuf) is that he is identical with Khufu," Petrie wrote in *The Pyramids and Temples of Gizeh*, giving the many reasons voiced by then by other Egyptologists against such a theory. For any number of reasons,

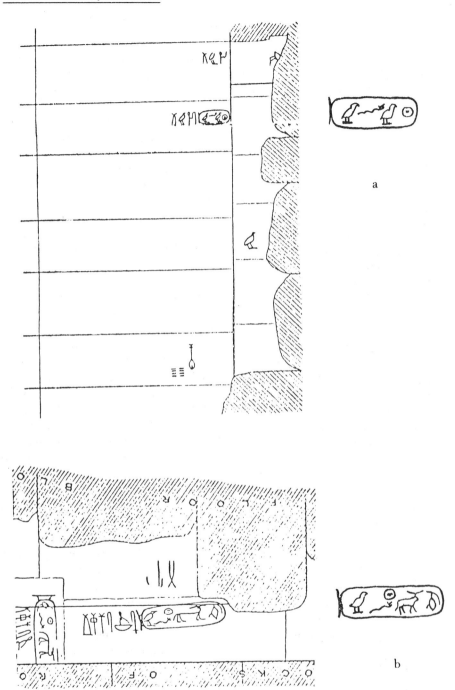

Fig. 146

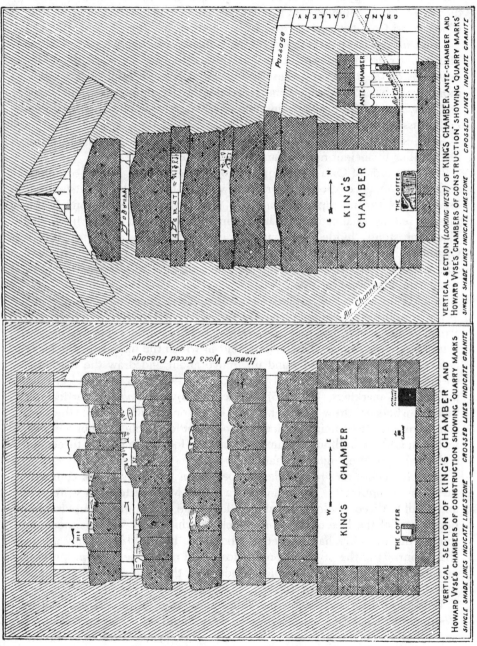

VERTICAL SECTION (LOOKING WEST) OF KING'S CHAMBER, ANTE-CHAMBER AND
HOWARD VYSE'S CHAMBERS OF CONSTRUCTION SHOWING 'QUARRY MARKS'
SINGLE SHADE LINES INDICATE LIMESTONE   CROSSED LINES INDICATE GRANITE

Looking West

VERTICAL SECTION OF KING'S CHAMBER AND
HOWARD VYSE'S CHAMBERS OF CONSTRUCTION SHOWING 'QUARRY MARKS'
SINGLE SHADE LINES INDICATE LIMESTONE   CROSSED LINES INDICATE GRANITE

Looking North

Fig. 147

Petrie showed, the two names belonged to two separate kings. Why then did both names appear within the Great Pyramid in the locations in which they did? Petrie believed that the only plausible explanation would be that Cheops and Chephren were co-regents, reigning together.

Since no evidence to support Petrie's theory has been found, Gaston Maspero wrote almost a century after the discovery by Vyse that "the existence of the two cartouches Khufui and Khnem-Khufui on the same monuments has caused much embarrassment to Egyptologists" (*The Dawn of Civilization*). The problem, in spite of all suggested solutions, is still an embarrassing one.

But a solution, we believe, can be offered—if we stop attributing the inscriptions to ancient masons, and begin to look at the facts.

The pyramids of Giza are unique, among other things, for the complete absence of any decoration or inscription within them—with the outstanding exception of the inscriptions found by Vyse. Why the exception? If the masons felt no qualms about daubing in red paint inscriptions upon the blocks of stones hidden away in the compartments above the "King's Chamber," why were there absolutely no such inscriptions found in the first compartment, the one discovered by Davison in 1765—but only in the compartments found by Vyse?

In addition to the inscriptions reported by Vyse, there have been found in the various compartments true masons' markings—positioning lines and arrows. They are all drawn as one would expect, with the right side up; for when they were drawn, the compartment in which the masons worked was not yet roofed: they could stand up, move about and draw the markings without encumberment. But all the inscriptions—drawn over and around the masons' markings (Fig. 145)—are either *upside down* or vertical, as though whoever drew them had to bend or crouch within the low compartments (their height varied from one foot four inches to four feet five inches in Lady Arbuthnot's Chamber, from two feet two inches to three feet eight inches in Wellington's Chamber).

The cartouches and royal titles daubed upon the walls of the compartments were imprecise, crude and extra large. Most cartouches were two and a half to three feet long and about a foot wide, sometimes occupying the better part of the face of the stone block on which they were painted—as though the inscriber had needed all the space he could get. They are in sharp contrast to the precision and delicacy and perfect sense of proportion of ancient Egyptian hieroglyphics, evident in the true masons' markings found in those same compartments.

With the exception of a few markings on a corner of the eastern wall in Wellington's Chamber, no inscriptions were found on the eastern walls of any other chamber; nor were there any other symbols (other than the original masons' markings) found on any of these other eastern walls, except for a few meaningless lines and a partial outline of a bird on the vaulted eastern end of Campbell's Chamber.

This is odd, especially if one realizes that it was from the eastern side that Vyse had tunneled to and broken into these compartments. Did the ancient masons anticipate that Vyse would break in through the eastern walls, and obliged by not putting inscriptions on them? Or does the absence of such inscriptions suggest that whoever daubed them preferred to write on the intact walls to the north, south and west, rather than on the damaged east walls?

In other words: cannot all the puzzles be solved, if we assume that the inscriptions were not made in antiquity, when the pyramid was being built, but only *after* Vyse had blasted his way into the compartments?

The atmosphere that surrounded Vyse's operations in those hectic days is well described by the Colonel himself. Major discoveries were being made all around the pyramids, but not within them. Campbell's Tomb, discovered by the detested Caviglia, was yielding not only artifacts but also masons' markings and hieroglyphics in red paint. Vyse was becoming desperate to achieve his own discovery. Finally he broke through to hitherto unknown chambers; but they only duplicated one after the other a previously discovered chamber (Davison's) and were bare and empty. What could he show for all the effort and expenditure? For what would he be honored, by what would he be remembered?

We know from Vyse's chronicles that, by day, he had sent in Mr. Hill to inscribe the chambers with the names of the Duke of Wellington and Admiral Nelson, heroes of the victories over Napoleon. By night, we suspect, Mr. Hill also entered the chambers—to "christen" the pyramid with the cartouches of its presumed ancient builder.

"The two royal names," Birch pointed out in his Opinion, "had already been found in the tombs of functionaries employed by the monarchs of that dynasty under which these Pyramids were erected." The Pharaoh's artisans surely knew the correct name of their king. But in the 1830s Egyptology was still in its infancy; and no one could yet tell for sure which was the correct hieroglyphic design of the king whom Herodotus called "Cheops."

And so it was, we suspect, that Mr. Hill—probably alone, certainly at night when all others were gone—had entered the newly discovered chambers. Using the imperative red paint, by torchlight, crouching and bending in the low compartments, he strained to copy hieroglyphic symbols from some source; and he drew on the walls that were intact what seemed to him appropriate markings. He ended up inscribing, in Wellington's Chamber as in Lady Arbuthnot's, the wrong name.

With inscriptions of royal names of the Fourth Dynasty popping up in the tombs surrounding the pyramids of Giza, which were the right cartouches to be inscribed by Hill? Unschooled in hieroglyphic writing, he must have taken with him into the pyramid some source book from which to copy the intricate symbols. The one and only book repeatedly mentioned in Vyse's chronicles is (Sir) John Gardner Wilkinson's *Materia Hieroglyphica*. As its title page declared, it aimed to update the reader on "the Egyptian

Pantheon and the Succession of the Pharaohs from the earliest times to the conquest of Alexander." Published in 1828—nine years before Vyse's assault on the pyramids—it was a standard book for English Egyptologists.

Birch had stated in his report, "a cartouche, similar to that which first occurs in Wellington's Chamber, had been published by Mr. Wilkinson *Mater. Hieroglyph.*" We thus have a clear indication of the probable source of the cartouche inscribed by Hill in the very first chamber (Wellington's) found by Vyse (Fig. 146b).

Having looked up Wilkinson's *Materia Hieroglyphica*, we can sympathize with Vyse and Hill: its text and presentation are disorganized, and its plates reproducing cartouches are small, ill-copied and badly printed. Wilkinson appears to have been uncertain not only regarding the reading of royal names, but also regarding the correct manner by which hieroglyphs carved or sculpted on stone should be transcribed in linear writing. The problem was most acute concerning the disk sign, which on such monuments appeared as either a solid disk ● or as a void sphere ○ , and in linear (or brushed-on) writing as a circle with a dot in its center ☉ . In his works, he transcribed the royal cartouches in question in some instances as a solid disk, and in others as a circle with a dot in its center.

Hill had followed Wilkinson's guidance. But all of these cartouches were of the *Khnum* variety. Timewise, it means that by May 7 only the "ram" cartouches were inscribed. Then on May 27, when Campbell's Chamber was broken into, the vital and conclusive cartouche spelling Kh-u-f-u was found. How did the miracle happen?

A clue is hidden in a suspicious segment in Vyse's chronicles, in an entry devoted to the fact that the casing stones "did not show the slightest trace of inscription or of sculpture, nor, indeed, was any to be found upon any stone belonging to the pyramid, or near it (with the exception of the quarry-marks already described)." Vyse noted that there was one other exception: "part of a cartouche of Suphis, engraved on a brown stone, six inches long by four broad. This fragment was dug out of the mound at the northern side on June 2." Vyse reproduced a sketch of the fragment (Fig. 148a).

How did Vyse know—even before the communication from the British Museum—that this was "part of a cartouche of *Suphis*?" Vyse would like us to believe it was because a week earlier (on May 27) he had found the complete cartouche (Fig. 148b) in Campbell's Chamber.

But here is the suspicious aspect. Vyse claims in the above-quoted entry that the stone with the partial Khufu cartouche was found on *June 2*. Yet his entry is dated *May 9*! Vyse's manipulation of dates would have us believe that the partial cartouche found outside the pyramid corroborated the earlier find of the complete cartouche inside the pyramid. But the dates suggest that it was the other way around: Vyse had already realized on May 9—a full eighteen days *before* the discovery of Campbell's Chamber—

a   b

Fig. 148

what the crucial cartouche had to look like. Somehow, on May 9, Vyse and
Hill had realized that they had missed out on the correct name of Cheops.

This realization could explain the frantic, daily commuting by Vyse and
Hill to Cairo right after the discovery of Lady Arbuthnot's Chamber. Why
they had left when so badly needed at the pyramids, the Chronicles do not
state. We believe that the "bombshell" that hit them was yet another, new
work by Wilkinson, the three-volume *Manners and Customs of the Ancient
Egyptians*. Published in London earlier that year (1837), it must have
reached Cairo right during those dramatic and tense days. And, neatly and
clearly printed for a change, it reproduced in a chapter on early sculptures
both the ram cartouche which Vyse-Hill had already copied—and a new
cartouche, one which Wilkinson read "Shufu or Suphis" (Fig. 149).

Wilkinson's new presentation must have shocked Vyse and Hill, because
he appeared to have changed his mind regarding the ram cartouche (No. 2
in his Plate). He now read it "Numba-khufu or Chembes" rather than "Sen-
Suphis." These names, he wrote, were found inscribed in tombs in the
vicinity of the Great Pyramid; and it was in cartouche 1a that "we perceive
Suphis, or, as the hieroglyphics wrote it, Shufu or Khufu, a name easily
converted into Suphis or Cheops." So *that* was the correct name that had to
be inscribed!

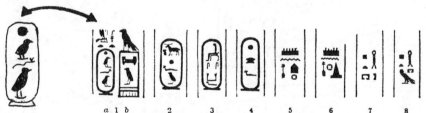

a 1 b   2   3   4   5   6   7   8
1. *a*, *b*, the name of Shufu, or Suphis.   2. Numba-khufu, or Chembes.   3. Asseskaf, or Shepeskaf.
4. Shafra, Khafra, or Kephren.   5, 6. The name of Memphis.
7, 8. (Memphis, or) Ptah-ei, the abode of Ptah.

From the Tombs near the Pyramids.

Fig. 149

For whom, then, did the ram cartouche (his fig. 2) stand? Explaining the difficulties of identification, Wilkinson admitted that he could not decide "whether the first two names here introduced are both of Suphis, or if the second one is of the founder of the other pyramid."

With this unsettling news, what were Vyse and Hill to do? Wilkinson's narrative gave them a lead, which they hurried to follow. The two names, he wrote on, "occur again at Mount Sinai."

Somewhat inaccurately—a fault common in his work—Wilkinson was referring to hieroglyphic inscriptions found not actually at Mount Sinai, but in the Sinai's area of the turquoise mines. The inscriptions became known in those years due to the magnificently illustrated *Voyage de l'Arabie Pétrée* in which Léon de Laborde et Linat described the Sinai peninsula. Published in 1832, its drawings included reproductions of monuments and inscriptions in the wadi leading to the mining area, Wadi Maghara. There, Pharaoh after Pharaoh carved on the rocks mementoes of their achievements in holding the mines against marauding Asiatics. One such depiction (Fig. 150) included the two cartouches of which Wilkinson wrote.

Vyse and Hill should have had little difficulty in locating a copy of de Laborde's *Voyage* in French-speaking Cairo. The particular drawing seemed to answer Wilkinson's doubt: the same Pharaoh appeared to have two names, one with the ram symbol and the other that spelt out Kh-u-f-u. Thus, by May 9, Vyse-Hill-Perring had learned that one more cartouche was needed, and what it had to look like.

When Campbell's Chamber was broken into on May 27, the three must have asked themselves: what are we waiting for? And so it was that the final conclusive cartouche appeared on the uppermost wall (Fig. 146a). Fame, if not fortune, was assured for Vyse; Mr. Hill, on his part, did not come out of the adventure empty-handed.

Fig. 150

How sure can we be of our accusations, a century and a half after the event?

Sure enough. For, as most forgers, Mr. Hill made, on top of all the other embarrassments, one grave mistake: a mistake that no ancient scribe could have possibly committed.

As it turned out, both source books by which Vyse-Hill were guided (Wilkinson's *Materia Hieroglyphica* and then de Laborde's *Voyage*) contained spelling errors; the unsuspecting team embodied the errors in the pyramid's inscriptions.

Samuel Birch himself pointed out in his report that the hieroglyph for *Kh* (the first consonant in the name Kh-u-f-u), which is ◉ (representing pictorially a sieve), "appears in Mr. Wilkinson's work without distinction from the solar disk." The *Kh* hieroglyph had to be employed in all the cartouches (spelling Khnem-*Kh*-u-f) which were inscribed in the two lower chambers. *But the correct sieve symbol was not employed even once.* Instead, the consonant *Kh* was represented by the symbol for the Solar Disk: whoever inscribed these cartouches made the same error as Wilkinson had made. . . .

When Vyse and Hill got hold of de Laborde's book, its sketch only deepened the error. The rock carvings depicted by him included the cartouche Kh-u-f-u on the right, and Khnum-kh-u-f on the left. In both instances, de Laborde—who admitted to ignorance of hieroglyphics and who made no attempt to read the symbols—rendered the *Kh* sign as a void circle ○ (see Fig. 150). (The *Kh* symbol was correctly spelled ◉ in the rock carvings, as has been verified by all scholarly authorities—viz. Lepsius in *Denkmäler*, Kurt Sethe in *Urkunden des Alten Reich*, and *The Inscriptions of Sinai* by A. H. Gardiner and T. E. Peet. De Laborde made another fateful error: He depicted as one Pharaoh's inscription, with two royal names, what were in effect *two* adjoining inscriptions, in different script styles, by two different Pharaohs—as is clearly seen in Fig. 151).

His depiction thus served to enhance Vyse's and Hill's notion that the crucial cartouche of Kh-u-f-u should be inscribed in the uppermost chamber with the symbol for the Solar Disk (146a). *But in doing so, the inscriber had employed the hieroglyphic symbol and phonetic sound for RA, the supreme god of Egypt!* He had unwittingly spelled out not *Khnem-Khuf*, but *Khnem-Rauf*; not *Khufu*, but *Raufu*. He had used the name of the great god incorrectly and in vain; it was blasphemy in ancient Egypt.

It was also an error inconceivable for an Egyptian scribe of the times of the Pharaohs. As monument after monument and inscription after inscription make clear, the symbol for *Ra* ⊙ and the symbol for

Kh  were always correctly employed—not only in different inscriptions, but also in the same inscription by the same scribe.

And, therefore, the substitution of *Ra* for *Kh* was an error that could not have been committed in the time of Khufu, nor of any other ancient Pharaoh. Only a stranger to hieroglyphics, a stranger to Khufu, and a stranger to the overpowering worship of Ra, could have committed such a grave error.

Added to all the other puzzling or inexplicable aspects of the discovery reported by Vyse, this final mistake establishes conclusively, we believe, that Vyse and his aides, not the original builders of the Great Pyramid, caused the red-painted markings to be inscribed.

But, one may ask, was there no risk that outside visitors—such as the British and Austrian consuls, or Lord and Lady Arbuthnot—would notice that the inscriptions were so much fresher-looking than the masons' true markings? The question was answered at the time by one of the men involved, Mr. Perring, in his own volume on the subject (*The Pyramids of Gizeh*). The paint used for the ancient inscriptions, he wrote, was a "composition of red ochre called by the Arabs *moghrah* (which) is still in use." Not only was the same red ochre paint available, Perring stated, but "such is the state of preservation of the marks in the quarries, that *it is*

Fig. 151

difficult to distinguish the mark of yesterday from one of three thousand years."

The forgers, in other words, were sure of their ink.

Were Vyse and Hill—possibly with the tacit connivance of Perring—morally capable of perpetrating such a forgery?

The circumstances of Vyse launching into this adventure of discovery, his treatment of Caviglia, the chronology of events, his determination to obtain a major find as time and money were running out—bespeak a character capable of such a deed. As to Mr. Hill—whom Vyse endlessly thanks in his foreword—the fact is that having been a copper mill employee when he first met Vyse, he ended up owning the Cairo Hotel when Vyse left Egypt. And as to Mr. Perring, a civil engineer turned Egyptologist—well, let subsequent events speak for themselves. For, encouraged by the success of one forgery, the Vyse team attempted one and probably two more. . . .

All along, as the discoveries were being made in the Great Pyramid, Vyse half-heartedly continued Caviglia's work in and around the other two pyramids. Encouraged by his newly won fame by the Great Pyramid discoveries, Vyse decided to postpone his return to England and instead engage in concerted efforts to uncover the secrets of the other two pyramids.

With the exception of red-painted markings on stones, which experts from Cairo determined were from tombs or structures outside the pyramids and not from within the pyramids, nothing of importance was found in the Second Pyramid. But inside the Third Pyramid, Vyse's efforts paid off. At the end of July, 1837—as we have briefly mentioned earlier—his workmen broke into its "sepulchral chamber," finding there a beautifully decorated but empty stone "sarcophagus" (Fig. 152). Arabic inscriptions on the walls and other evidence suggested this pyramid "to have been much frequented," the floor stones of its chambers and passages "worn and glazed over by the constant passing and repassing of a concourse of people."

Yet in this much frequented pyramid, and in spite of the empty stone coffer, Vyse managed to find proof of its builder—a feat equaling the discovery within the Great Pyramid.

In another rectangular chamber which Vyse called "the large apartment," great piles of rubbish were found, along with the telltale scrawled Arabic graffiti. Vyse at once concluded that this chamber "was probably intended for funeral ceremonies, like those at Abou Simbel, Thebes, etc." When the rubbish was cleared out,

> the greater part of the lid of the sarcophagus was found . . . and close to it, fragments of the top of a mummy-case (inscribed with hieroglyphics, and amongst them, with the cartouche of Menkahre) were discovered upon a block of stone, together with part of a skeleton,

Fig. 152

consisting of ribs and vertebrae, and the bones of the legs and feet enveloped in coarse woollen cloth of a yellow color . . .

More of the board and cloth were afterwards taken out of the rubbish.

It would therefore seem that, as the sarcophagus could not be removed, the wooden case containing the body had been brought into the large apartment for examination.

This, then, was the scenario outlined by Vyse: Centuries earlier, Arabs had broken in the sepulchral chamber. They found the sarcophagus and removed its lid. Inside there was a mummy within a wooden coffin—the mummy of the pyramid's builder. The Arabs removed coffin and mummy to the large apartment to examine them, breaking them in the process. Now Vyse found all these remains; and a cartouche on a fragment of the mummy-case (Fig. 153) spelled out *"Men-ka-ra"*—the very Mycerinus of Herodotus. He proved the identity of the builders of both pyramids!

The sarcophagus was lost at sea during its transportation to England. But the mummy-case and bones reached safely the British Museum, where Samuel Birch could examine the actual inscription, rather than work from facsimiles (as was the case of the inscriptions within the chambers in the Great Pyramid). He soon voiced his doubts: "the coffin of Mycerinus," he said, "manifests considerable difference of style" from monuments of the Fourth Dynasty. Wilkinson, on the other hand, accepted the mummy-case as authentic proof of the identity of the builder of the Third Pyramid; but

Fig. 153

had doubts regarding the mummy itself: its cloth wrappings did not look to him as being of the claimed antiquity. In 1883, Gaston Maspero concurred "that the wooden coffer-cover of king Menchere is not of the Fourth Dynasty times;" he deemed it a restoration carried out in the Twenty-Fifth Dynasty. In 1892, Kurt Sethe summed up the majority opinion, that the coffin-cover "could have been fashioned only after Twentieth Dynasty times."

As is now well known, both mummy-case and bones were not the remains of an original burial. In the words of I.E.S. Edwards (*The Pyramids of Egypt*), "In the original burial chamber, Col. Vyse had discovered some human bones and the lid of a wooden anthropoid coffin inscribed with the name of Mycerinus. This lid, which is now in the British Museum, cannot have been made in the time of Mycerinus, for it is of a pattern not used before the Saite Period. Radiocarbon tests have shown that the bones date from early Christian times."

The mere statement negating the authenticity of the find does not, however, go to the core of the matter. If the remains were not of an original burial, then they must have been of an intrusive burial; but in such a case, mummy and coffin would be of the same period. This was not the case: here, someone had put together a mummy unearthed in one place, a coffin from another place. The unavoidable conclusion is that the find represented a *deliberate archaeological fraud.*

Could the mismatching have been a coincidence—the genuine remains within the pyramid of *two* intrusive burials, from different times? This must be doubted, in view of the fact that the coffin fragment bore the cartouche of Men-ka-ra. This cartouche has been found on statues and in inscriptions all around the Third Pyramid and its temples (but not inside it), and it is probable that the coffin bearing the cartouche was also found in those surroundings. The coffin's attribution to later times stems not only from its pattern, but also from the wording of the inscription: it is a prayer to Osiris from the Book of the Dead; its appearance on a Fourth Dynasty coffin has been termed remarkable even by the trusting (yet knowledgeable) Samuel Birch (*Ancient History from the Monuments*). Yet it need not have been "a restoration," as some scholars have suggested, from the Twenty-sixth Dynasty. We know from the King List of Seti I from Abydos that the eighth Pharaoh of the Sixth Dynasty was also called Men-ka-ra, and spelled his name in a similar manner.

It is clear, then, that someone had first found, in the vicinity of the pyramid, the coffin. Its importance was surely realized, for—as Vyse himself has reported—he had found just a month previously the name of Men-ka-ra (Mycerinus) written in red paint on the roof of the burial chamber of the middle one of the three small pyramids, south of the Third Pyramid. It must have been this find that gave the team the idea of creating a discovery within the Third Pyramid itself. . . .

The credit for the discovery has been claimed by Vyse and Perring. How could they have perpetrated the fraud, with or without the help of Mr. Hill?

Once again, Vyse s own chronicles hint at the truth. "Not being present when they (the relics) were found," Col. Vyse wrote, he "requested Mr. Raven, when that gentleman was in England, to write an account of the discovery" as an independent witness. Somehow invited to be present at the right moment, Mr. H. Raven, who addressed Col. Vyse as "Sir" and signed the Letter of Evidence "your most obedient servant," attested as follows:

> In clearing the rubbish out of the large entrance-room, after the men had been employed there several days and had advanced some distance towards the south-eastern corner, some bones were first discovered at the bottom of the rubbish; and the remaining bones and parts of the coffin were immediately discovered altogether: no other parts of the coffin or bones could be found in the room.
>
> I therefore had the rubbish, which had been previously turned out of the same room, carefully re-examined, when several pieces of the coffin and of the mummy-cloth were found; but
>
> In no other part of the pyramid were any parts of it to be discovered, although every place was most minutely examined to make the coffin as complete as possible.

We now get a better grasp of what had happened. For several days, workmen were clearing rubbish from the Large Apartment, piling it up nearby. Though carefully examined, nothing was found. Then, on the last day, as only the southeastern corner of the room remained to be cleared, some bones and fragments of a wooden coffin were discovered. "No other parts of the coffin or bones could be discovered in the room." It was then wisely suggested that the rubbish which had been turned out of the room—a three-foot-high pile—be "carefully re-examined"—not examined, but RE-examined; and—lo and behold—more bones, and coffin fragments with the all-important cartouche, were found!

Where were the remaining parts of the skeleton and coffin? "Although every place was minutely examined to make the coffin as complete as possible," nothing was found in any other part of the pyramid. So, unless we are to believe that bones and coffin fragments were hauled away as souvenirs in centuries past, we can only assume that whoever *hauled in* the discovered parts, brought in just enough fragments to create the discovery: a complete coffin and a complete mummy were either unavailable, or too cumbersome to be smuggled in.

Hailed for this second major discovery—he was soon thereafter promoted to the rank of general—Col. Vyse and Perring proceeded to produce at the site of Zoser's step pyramid a stone bearing Zoser's name—written in red paint, of course. There is not enough detail in the chronicles to ascertain whether or not that too was a forgery; but it is indeed incredible that it was again the same team who managed to unearth proof of yet one more pyramid builder.

(While most Egyptologists have accepted without further investigation the claim that Khufu's name was inscribed in the Great Pyramid, the works of Sir Alan Gardiner suggest that he had doubts on the subject. In his *Egypt of the Pharaohs*, he reproduced royal cartouches with a clear distinction between the hieroglyphs for *Ra* and *Kh*. The cartouche of Cheops, he wrote, "is found in various quarries, in the tombs of his kinfolk and nobles, and in certain writing of later date." Conspicuous by its absence in this list is the inscription in the Great Pyramid . . . Also omitted by Sir Alan were any mention of Vyse's discoveries in the Third Pyramid and even of Vyse's name as such).

If the proof of the construction of the Giza pyramids by the presumed Pharaohs stands shattered, there is no longer reason to suspect the authenticity of the Inventory Stela, which stated that the pyramids and the Sphinx were already there when Khufu came to pay homage to Isis and Osiris.

There is nothing left to contradict our contention that these three pyramids were built by the "gods." On the contrary: everything about them suggests that they were not conceived by men for men's use.

We shall now proceed to show how they were part of the Guidance Grid that served the Spaceport of the Nefilim.

XIV

The Gaze of the Sphinx

In time, the pyramids of Giza were made part of the Landing Grid which had the peaks of Ararat as its focal point, incorporated Jerusalem as a Mission Control Center, and guided the space vehicles to the Spaceport in the Sinai peninsula.

But at first, the pyramids themselves had to serve as guiding beacons, simply by virtue of their location, alignment and shape. All pyramids, as we have seen, were at their core step pyramids—emulating the ziggurats of Mesopotamia. But when the "gods who came from heaven" experimented with their scale model at Giza (the Third Pyramid), they may have found that the silhouette of the ziggurat and the shadow it cast upon the undulating rocks and ever-shifting sands were too blurred and inaccurate to serve as a reliable Pointer-of-the-Way. By casing the stepped core to achieve a "true" pyramid, and using white (light-reflecting) limestone for the casing, a perfect play of light and shadow was achieved, providing clear orientation.

In 1882, as Robert Ballard was watching the Giza pyramids from his train window, he realized that one could determine his location and direction by the ever-changing alignment between the pyramids (Fig. 154). Enlarging on this observation in *The Solution of the Pyramid Problem*, he also showed that the pyramids were aligned with each other in the basic Pythagorean right-angled triangles, whose sides were proportionate to each other as 3:4:5. Pyramidologists have also noticed that the shadows cast by the pyramids could serve as a giant sundial, the direction and length of the shadows indicating time of year and of day.

Even more important, however, was how the silhouettes and shadows of the pyramids appeared to an observer from the skies. As this aerial photograph shows (Fig. 155), the true shape of the pyramids casts arrow-like shadows, which serve as unmistakable direction pointers.

When all was ready to establish a proper Spaceport, it required a much longer Landing Corridor than the one which served Baalbek. For their previous Spaceport in Mesopotamia, the Anunnaki (the biblical Nefilim) chose the most conspicuous mountain in the Near East—Mount Ararat—as their focal point. It should not be surprising that out of the same

283

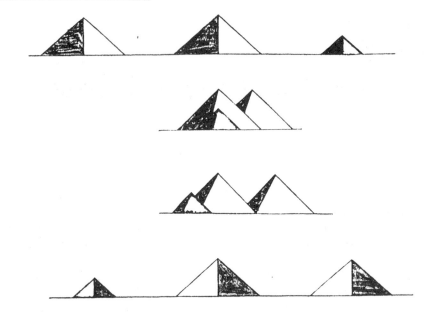

Fig. 154

Fig. 155

considerations they again selected it as the focal point of their new Spaceport.

Just as more "coincidences" of triangulation and geometrical perfection have been discovered in the construction and alignment of the Giza pyramids the more they have been examined and studied, so do we find endless "coincidences" of triangulation and alignment as we uncover the Landing Grid laid out by the Anunnaki. If the peaks of Ararat served as the focal point of the new Landing Corridor, then not only the northwestern line of the Landing Corridor, but also its southeastern outline had to be focused on Ararat. But where was its other, Sinai end, anchored on?

Mount St. Katherine lies amidst a massive core of similar, though somewhat lower, granite peaks. When the British Ordnance Survey Mission headed by the Palmers set out to survey the Sinai peninsula, they found that St. Katherine, even if the highest peak, did not stand out sufficiently to serve as a geodesic landmark. Instead, the Mission selected *Mount Umm Shumar* (Fig. 156), which at 8,534 feet is almost a twin in height of Mount St. Katherine (indeed, until the Ordnance Survey, many believed that Umm Shumar was the higher peak). Unlike Katherine, Umm Shumar stands by itself, distinct and unmistakable. Both gulfs can be seen from its peak; its view to the west, northwest, southwest and east is unobstructed. It was for these reasons that the Palmers without hesitation selected Mount Umm Shumar as their geodesic landmark, the focal point for surveying and measuring the peninsula.

Mount Katherine may have been suitable for a short Landing Corridor focused on Baalbek; but for the distant focal point of Ararat, a much more distinct and unmistakable landmark was required. We believe that for the

Fig. 156

same reasons as the Palmers', the Anunnaki selected Mount Umm Shumar as the anchor of the southeastern outline of the new Landing Corridor.

Much about this mount and its location is intriguing. To begin with, its name—puzzling or highly significant—means "Mother of Sumer." It is a title which was applied at Ur to Ningal, spouse of Sin. . . .

Unlike Mount St. Katherine, which lies at the center of Sinai's core of high granite peaks and can therefore be reached only with great difficulty, Mount Umm Shumar is situated at the edge of the mass of granite. The sandy beaches there, on the Gulf of Suez, have several natural hot springs. Was it there that Asherah spent her winters, residing "by the sea?" From there, it is really only "a she-ass' ride" away to Mount Umm Shumar—a ride so vividly described in the Ugaritic texts when Asherah went calling on El at his Mount.

Just a few miles down the coast from the Hot Springs is the peninsula's most important port city on these coasts—the port city of *el-Tor*. The name—another coincidence?—means "The Bull"; it was, as we have seen, an epithet of El ("Bull El," the Ugaritic texts called him). The place has served as Sinai's most important gulf port from earliest times; and we wonder whether it was not the Tilmun-city (as distinct from Tilmun-land) spoken of in Sumerian texts. It could well have been the port which Gilgamesh planned to reach by ship, from where his comrade Enkidu could go to the nearby mines (in which he was doomed to slave for the rest of his life); while he (Gilgamesh) could proceed to the "Landing Place, where the *Shems* are raised."

The peaks of the peninsula's granite core which face the Gulf of Suez bear names that make one stop and wonder. One mount bears the name "Mount of the Blessed Mother"; closer to Mount Umm Shumar, Mount *Teman* ("The Southern") raises its head. The name brings back the verses of Habakuk: "*El* from *Teman* shall come. . . . Covered are the heavens with his halo; His splendor fills the Earth. . . . The *Word* goes before him, sparks emanate from below; *He pauses to measure the Earth.* . . ."

Was the prophet referring to the mount that still bears that very name—*Teman*—the southern neighbor of Mount "Mother of Sumer?" Since there is no other mountain bearing such a name, the identification seems more than plausible.

Does Mount Umm Shumar fit into the Landing Grid and the network of sacred sites developed by the Anunnaki?

We suggest that this mount substituted for Mt. Katherine when the final Landing Corridor was worked out, acting as the anchor for the southeastern line of the Corridor which was focused on Ararat. But if so, where was the complementary anchor for the northwestern line?

It is no coincidence, we suggest, that Heliopolis was built where it was. *It lies on the original Ararat-Baalbek-Giza line.* But it is so located, that *it is equidistant from Ararat as Umm Shumar is!* Its location was determined, we suggest, by measuring off the distance from Ararat to Umm Shumar—

then marking off an equidistant point on the Ararat-Baalbek-Giza line (Fig. 157).

As we unfold the amazing network of natural and artificial peaks that have been incorporated into the landing and communications grid of the Anunnaki, one must ponder whether they served as guiding beacons by height and shape alone. Were they not also equipped with some kind of guidance instruments?

When the two pairs of narrow conduits from the chambers of the Great Pyramid were first discovered, they were thought to have served to lower food to the Pharaoh's attendants who were presumed to have been sealed alive in his tomb. When Vyse's team cleared the northern conduit to the "King's Chamber," it was at once filled with cool air; the conduits have since been called "air shafts." This, surprisingly, was challenged by respected scholars in a highly regarded academic publication (*Mitteilungen des Instituts für Orientforschung der Deutschen Akademie der Wissenschaften zu Berlin*). Although the academic establishment has been loath to digress from the "pyramids as tombs" theory, Virginia Trimble and Alexander Badawy concluded in the Bulletin's 1964 issues that the "air shafts" had astronomical functions, having been "beyond doubt inclined within 1° toward the circumpolar stars."

Without doubting that the direction and inclination of the shafts must

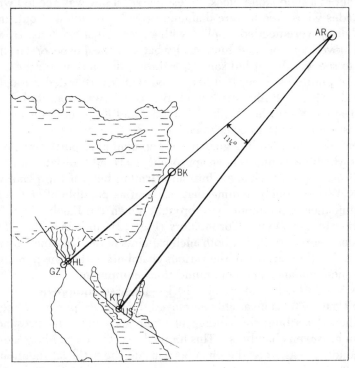

Fig. 157

have been premeditated, we are no less intrigued by the finding that once air flowed into the "King's Chamber", the temperature within it remained at a constant 68° Fahrenheit no matter what the weather outside was. All these findings seem to confirm the conclusions of E. F. Jomard (a member of Napoleon's team of scientists), who suggested that the "King's Chamber" and its "sarcophagus" were not intended for burial, but as a depository of weight and measurement standards, which even in modern times are kept in a stable environment of temperature and moisture.

Jomard could not have possibly imagined—back in 1824—delicate space-guidance instruments, rather than mundane units of a meter and a kilogram. But we, of course, can.

Many who have pondered the purpose of the intricate superstructure of five low compartments above the "King's Chamber," believe they were built to relieve the pressure of the chamber. But this has been achieved in the "Queen's Chamber " with an even greater mass of stone upon it, without such a series of "relieving compartments." When Vyse and his men were inside the compartments, they were astonished to hear clearly every word spoken in other parts of the pyramid. When Flinders Petrie (*The Pyramids and the Temple of Gizeh*) minutely examined the "King's Chamber" and the stone "coffer" within it, he found that both were built in accord with the dimensions of perfect Pythagorian triangles. To cut the coffer out of a solid stone block, he estimated, a saw was needed with nine-foot blades whose teeth were diamond-tipped. To hollow it out, diamond-tipped drills were needed, applied with a pressure of two tons. How all this was achieved was beyond him. And what was the purpose? He lifted the coffer to see whether it hid some aperture (it did not); when the coffer was struck, it emitted a deep, bell-like sound that reverberated throughout the pyramid. This bell-like quality of the coffer was reported by earlier investigators. Were the "King's Chamber" and its "coffer" meant, then, to serve as sound-emitters or echo-chambers?

Even nowadays, landing guidance equipment at airports emits electronic signals which instruments in an approaching aircraft translate into a pleasant buzz if on course; it changes into an alarming beep if the plane veers off course. We can safely assume that, as soon as possible after the Deluge, new guidance equipment was brought down to Earth. The Egyptian depiction of the Divine Cordholders (Fig. 121) indicates that "Stones of Splendor" were installed at both anchor-points of the Landing Corridor; our guess is that the purpose of the various chambers within the pyramid was to house such guidance and communications equipment.

Was *Shad El*—the "Mountain of El"—likewise equipped?

The Ugaritic texts invariably employed the phrase "penetrate the *Shad* of El" when describing the coming of other gods unto the presence of El "within his seven chambers." This implied that these chambers were inside the mountain—as were the chambers inside the artificial mountain of the Great Pyramid.

Historians of the first Christian centuries reported that the people who dwelt in the Sinai and its bordering areas of Palestine and North Arabia worshipped the god *Dushara* ("Lord of the Mountains") and his spouse *Allat*, "Mother of the Gods." They were of course the male El and the female Elat, his spouse Asherah. The sacred object of Dushara was, fortunately, depicted on a coin struck by the Roman governor of those provinces (Fig. 158). Curiously, it resembles the enigmatic chambers within the Great Pyramid—an inclined stairway ("Ascending Gallery") leading to a chamber between massive stones ("The King's Chamber"). Above it, a series of stones re-create the pyramid's "relieving chambers."

Since the Ascending Passages of the Great Pyramid—which are unique to it—were plugged tight when Al Mamoon's men broke into it, the question is: Who, in antiquity, did know, and emulated, the inner construction within the pyramid? The answer can only be: the architects and builders of the Great Pyramid, who possessed such knowledge. Only they could duplicate such construction elsewhere—at Baalbek or within the mountain of El.

Fig. 158

And so it was, that although the Mount of the Exodus was elsewhere, in the northern half of the peninsula, the people of the area transmitted from generation to generation the recollection of sacred mountains among the peninsula's southern peaks. They were the mountains that, by their sheer height and location, and by virtue of the instruments installed within them, served as beacons for the "Riders of the Clouds."

When the first Spaceport was established in Mesopotamia, the flight path was along a center line, drawn precisely in the middle of the arrow-like landing corridor. While guiding beacons flickered their lights and emitted their signals along the two border lines, it was along the central flight path that Mission Control Center was located: the hub of all the communications and guidance equipment, the place where all the computerized information regarding planetary and spacecraft orbits was stored.

When the Anunnaki had landed on Earth and proceeded to establish their facilities and Spaceport in Mesopotamia, Mission Control Center was at Nippur, the "Place of the Crossing." Its "sacred" or Restricted Precinct was under the absolute control of Enlil; it was called the KI.UR ("Earth City"). In its midst, atop an artificially raised platform, was the DUR.AN.KI—"The Bond of Heaven and Earth." It was, the Sumerian texts related, a "heavenward tall pillar reaching to the sky." Firmly set upon the "platform which cannot be overturned," this pillar was used by Enlil "to pronounce the word" heavenward.

That all these terms were Sumerian attempts to describe sophisticated antennas and communications equipment one can gather from the pictographic "spelling" of Enlil's name: it was depicted as a system of large antennas, aerials and a communications structure (see Fig. 52).

Within this "lofty house" of Enlil, there was a hidden, mystery-filled chamber called the DIR.GA—literally meaning "dark, crown-like chamber." Its descriptive name brings so much to mind the hidden, mystifying "King's Chamber" in the Great Pyramid. In the DIR.GA, Enlil and his assistants kept the vital "Tablets of Destinies" on which orbital and space-flight information was stored. When a god who could fly as a bird snatched away these tablets,

> Suspended were the Divine Formulas.
> Stillness spread all over. Silence prevailed . . .
> The sanctuary's brilliance was taken off.

In the DIR.GA Enlil and his assistants kept celestial charts and "carried to perfection" the ME— a term denoting astronaut's instruments and functions. It was a chamber

> As mysterious as distant aeters,
>   as the Heavenly Zenith.
> Among its emblems . . .
>   the emblems of the stars;
> The ME it carries to perfection.
> Its words are for utterance . . .
> Its words are gracious oracles.

A Mission Control Center, similar to the one that had served the landing path in pre-Diluvian Mesopotamia, had to be established for the Spaceport in the Sinai. Where?

Our answer is: in *Jerusalem.*

Hallowed to Jew, Christian and Muslim alike, its very atmosphere charged with some inexplicable unearthly mystery, it had been a sacred city even before King David established her as his capital and Solomon built there the Lord's Abode. When the Patriarch Abraham reached its gates, it was already a well-established center to *"El* the Supreme, the Righteous One of Heaven and Earth." Its earliest known name was *Ur-Shalem*—"City of the Completed Cycle"—a name which suggests an association with orbital matters, or with the God of Orbits. As to who *Shalem* might have been, scholars have offered various theories; some of them (per Benjamin Mazar in "Jerusalem before the David Kingship") name Enlil's grandson Shamash; others prefer Enlil's son Ninib. In all theories, however, the association of Jerusalem's roots with the Mesopotamian pantheon is undisputed.

From its beginnings, Jerusalem encompassed three mountain peaks; from north to south, they were Mount *Zophim,* Mount *Moriah* and Mount *Zion*. Their names bespoke their functions: The northernmost was the "Mount of Observers" (it is now called in English Mount Scopus); the middle one was the "Mount of Directing"; the southernmost was "The Mount of the Signal." They are still so called in spite of the passage of millenia.

The valleys of Jerusalem too bear telltale names and epithets. One of them is named in Isaiah the Valley of *Hizzayon,* the "Valley of Vision." The Valley of *Kidron* was known as the "Valley of Fire." In the Valley of *Hinnom* (the *Gehenna* of the Greek New Testament), according to millennia-old legends, there was an entrance to the subterranean world, marked by a column of smoke rising between two palm trees. And the Valley of *Repha'im* was named after the Divine Healers who, according to the Ugaritic texts, were put in the charge of the goddess Shepesh. Aramaic translations of the Old Testament called them "Heroes"; the Old Testament's first translation into Greek called the place the Valley of the *Titans*.

Of the three Mounts of Jerusalem, that of Moriah has been the most sacred. The Book of Genesis explicitly states that it was to one of the peaks of Moriah that the Lord directed Abraham with Isaac, when Abraham's fidelity was tested. Jewish legends relate that Abraham recognized Mount Moriah from a distance, for he saw upon it "a pillar of fire reaching from the earth to heaven, and a heavy cloud in which the Glory of God was seen." This language is almost identical with the biblical description of the descent of the Lord upon Mount Sinai.

The large horizontal platform atop Mount Moriah—reminiscent in layout of the one at Baalbek, though much smaller—has been called "The Temple Mount," for it had served as the site of the Jewish Temple of Jerusalem (Fig. 159). It is now occupied by several Muslim shrines, the most renowned of which is the Dome of the Rock. The dome was carried off by the Caliph Abd al-Malik (seventh century A.D.) from Baalbek, where it adorned a Byzantine shrine; it was erected by the caliph as a roofing over an eight-sided structure he had built to encompass the Sacred Rock: a huge rock to which divine and magical faculties have been attributed from time immemorial.

Muslims believe that it was from the Sacred Rock that their prophet Muhammed was taken aloft to visit Heaven. According to the Koran, Muhammed was taken by the angel Gabriel from Mecca to Jerusalem, with a stopover at Mount Sinai. Then he was taken aloft by the angel, ascending

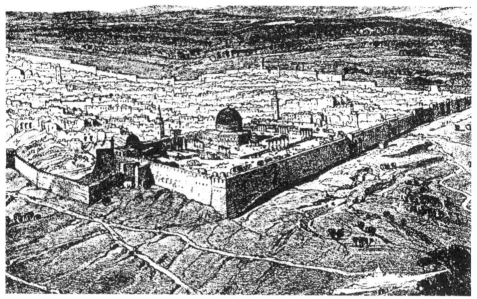

Fig. 159

heavenward via a "Ladder of Light." Passing through the Seven Heavens, Muhammed at last stood in the presence of God. After receiving divine instructions, he was brought back to Earth via the same beam of light, landing back at the Sacred Rock. He returned to Mecca, again with a stopover at Mount Sinai, riding the angel's winged horse.

Travelers in the Middle Ages suggested that the Sacred Rock was a huge artificially-cut cube-like rock whose corners faced precisely the four points of the compass. Nowadays, only the top outcropping of the rock can be seen; the presumption of its hidden great cube-like shape may have stemmed from the Muslim tradition that the hallowed Great Stone of Mecca, the *Qa'aba*, was fashioned (on divine instructions) after the Sacred Rock of Jerusalem.

From the visible portion, it is evident that the Sacred Rock had been cut out in various ways on its face and sides, bored through to provide two tube-like funnels, and hollowed out to create a subterranean tunnel and secret chambers. No one knows the purpose of these works; no one knows who had masterminded them and carried them out.

We do know, however, that the First Temple was built by King Solomon upon Mount Moriah at an exact spot and following precise instructions provided by the Lord. The Holy-of-Holies was built upon the Sacred Rock; its innermost chamber, completely gilded, was taken up by two large Cherubim (winged Sphinx-like beings) also made of gold, their wings touching the walls and each other's; between them was placed the Ark of the Testament, from within which the Lord addressed Moses in the desert. Completely insulated from the outside, the gold covered Holy-of-Holies was called in the Old Testament the *Dvir*—literally, "The Speaker."

The suggestion that Jerusalem was a "divine" communication center, a place where a "Stone of Splendor" was secreted, and from which the Word or Voice of the Lord was beamed far and wide, is not as preposterous as it may sound. The notion of such communication was not at all alien to the Old Testament. In fact, the possession by the Lord of such a capability, and the selection of Jerusalem as the communications center, were considered to be attestations of Yahweh's and Jerusalem's supremacy.

"I shall answer the Heavens, and they shall respond to Earth," the Lord assured the Prophet Hosea. Amos prophesied that "Yahweh from Zion will roar; from Jerusalem His voice shall be uttered." And the Psalmist stated that when the Lord shall speak out of Zion, His pronouncements will be heard from one end of Earth to another, and in Heaven too:

> Unto the gods Yahweh hath spoken,
> And the Earth He had called
>   from the east to the west . . .
> The Heavens above He will call,
>   and unto the Earth.

Ba'al, the Lord of the facilities at Baalbek, had boasted that his voice could be heard at Kadesh, the gateway city to the Precinct of the gods in the "Wilderness" of central Sinai. Psalm 29, listing some of the places on Earth reachable by the Voice of the Lord of Zion, included both Kadesh and "the cedar place" (Baalbek):

> The voice of the Lord is upon the waters . . .
> The voice of the Lord the cedars breaks . . .
> The voice of the Lord in the Wilderness shall resonance:
> Yahweh the Wilderness of Kadesh shall make shudder.

The capabilities acquired by Ba'al when he installed the "Stones of Splendor" at Baalbek were described in the Ugaritic texts as the ability to put "one lip to Earth, one lip to Heaven." The symbol for these communication devices, as we have seen, were the doves. Both symbolism and terminology are incorporated in the verses of Psalm 68, which describe the flying arrival of the Lord:

> Sing unto the Lord, chant unto His *Shem*,
> Make way for the Rider of the Clouds . . .
> The Lord the Word will utter,
>   the Oracles of an army vast.
> Kings of armies shall escape and flee;
> Abode and home thou shalt divide as spoil—
> Even if they lie between the two Lips and
>   the Dove whose wings are overlaid with silver,
>   whose pinions are greenish gold . . .
> The Chariot of the Lord is mighty,

> it is of thousands of years;
> Within it the Lord did come
> from sacred Sinai.

The Jerusalem Stone of Splendor—a "testament stone" or "probing stone" in the words of the Prophets—was secreted in a subterranean chamber. This we learn from a lamentation over the desolation of Jerusalem, when the Lord was wroth with its people:

> The palace was abandoned by the townspeople;
> Forsaken is the peak of Mount Zion (and)
> the "Prober Which Witnesses."
> The Cavern of Eternal Witnessing
> is the frolicking place of wild asses,
> a grazing place of flocks.

With the restoration of the Temple in Jerusalem, the Prophets promised, "the word of Yahweh from Jerusalem shall issue." Jerusalem would be reestablished as a world center, sought by all the nations. Conveying the Lord's promise, Isaiah reassured the people that not only the "probing stone," but also the "measuring" functions would be restored:

> Behold,
> I shall firmly set a Stone in Zion,
> a Probing Stone,
> a rare and lofty Stone of Corners,
> its foundation (firmly) founded.
> He who hath faith,
> shall not remain unanswered.
> Justice shall be my Cord;
> Righteousness (shall be) my Measure.

To have served as a Mission Control Center, Jerusalem—as Nippur—had to be located on the long central line bisecting the Landing Corridor. Its hallowed traditions affirm such a position, and the evidence suggests that it was that sacred rock which marked the precise geodesic center.

Jerusalem was held by Jewish traditions to have been the "Navel of the Earth." The Prophet Ezekiel referred to the people of Israel as "residing upon the Navel of the Earth"; the Book of Judges related an incident when people were coming down the mountains from the direction of the "Navel of the Earth." The term, as we have seen, meant that Jerusalem was a focal communications center, from which "cords" were drawn to other anchor points of the Landing Grid. It was thus no coincidence that the Hebrew word for the sacred rock was *Eben Sheti'yah*—a term which Jewish sages held to have meant "stone from which the world was woven." The term *sheti* is indeed a weaving term, standing for the long cord that runs lengthwise in a loom (the warp, which is crossed with the shorter weft). It was a fitting term for a stone that marked the exact spot from which the Divine Cords covered Earth as a web.

But as suggestive as all these terms and legends are, the decisive question is this: did Jerusalem in fact lie on the central line which bisected the Landing Corridor, focused on Ararat and outlined by the Giza pyramids and Mount Umm Shumar?

The decisive answer is: Yes. *Jerusalem lies precisely on that line!*

As was the case with the pyramids of Giza, so do we uncover in the case of the Divine Grid more and more amazing alignments and triangulations.

Jerusalem, we find, also *lies precisely where the Baalbek-Katherine line intersects the flight path's central line based on Ararat.*

Heliopolis, we find, is *precisely equidistant from Jerusalem as Mount Umm Shumar.*

And the diagonals drawn from Jerusalem to Heliopolis and to Umm Shumar form *an accurate 45° right angle* (Fig. 160)!

These links between Jerusalem, Baalbek (The Crest of Zaphon) and Giza (Memphis) were known, and hailed, in biblical times:

> Great is Yahweh and greatly hallowed
> in the city of our Lord,

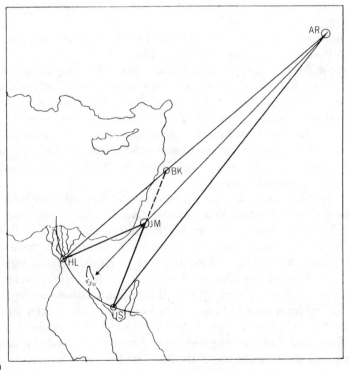

Fig. 160

His Holy Mountain.
At Memphis He is beautified.
The joy of the whole Earth,
    of Mount Zion,
    of the Crest of Zaphon.

Jerusalem, the Book of Jubilees held, was in fact one of four "Places of the Lord" on Earth: "the Garden of Eternity" in the Cedar Mountain; "the Mountain of the East" which was Mount Ararat; Mount Sinai and Mount Zion. Three of them were in the "lands of Shem," the son of Noah from whom the biblical Patriarchs were descended; and they were interconnected:

The Garden of Eternity, the most sacred,
    is the dwelling of the Lord;
And Mount Sinai, in the center of the desert;
And Mount Zion, the center of the Navel of the Earth.
These three were created as holy places,
FACING EACH OTHER.

Somewhere along the "Line of Jerusalem," the central flight line that was anchored on Mount Ararat, the Spaceport itself had to be located. There, too, the final beacon had to be located: "Mount Sinai, *in the center of the desert.*"

It is here, we suggest, that the dividing line which we now call the Thirtieth Parallel (north) had come into play.

We know from Sumerian astronomical texts that the skies enveloping Earth were so divided as to separate the northern "way" (allotted to Enlil) from the southern "way" (allotted to Ea) with a wide central band considered the "Way of Anu." It is only natural to assume that a dividing line between the two rival brothers should also have been established after the Deluge, when the settled Earth was divided into the Four Regions; and that, as in pre-Diluvial times, the Thirtieth Parallels (north and south) served as demarcation lines.

Was it mere coincidence, or a deliberate compromise between the two brothers and their feuding descendants, that in each of the three regions given to Mankind, the sacred city was located on the Thirtieth Parallel?

The Sumerian texts state that "When Kingship was lowered from Heaven" after the Deluge, "Kingship was in Eridu." Eridu was situated astride the Thirtieth Parallel as close to it as the marshy waters of the Persian Gulf had permitted. While the administrative-secular center of Sumer shifted from time to time, Eridu remained a sacred city for all time.

In the Second Region (the Nile Civilization) the secular capital also shifted from time to time. But Heliopolis forever remained the sacred city. The Pyramid Texts recognized its links with other sites, and called its ancient gods "Lords of the Dual Shrines." These two paired shrines bore the intriguing (and pre-Egyptian?) names *Per-Neter* ("Coming-forth Place of the Guardians") and *Per-Ur* ("The Coming-forth Place of Old"); their hieroglyphic depictions bespoke great antiquity.

The dual or paired shrines played a major role in the Pharaonic succession. During the rites, conducted by the *Shem* priest, the crowning of the new king and his admission to the "Place of the Guardians" in Heliopolis coincided with the departure of the deceased king's spirit, through the eastern False Door, to the "Coming-forth Place of Old."

And Heliopolis was located astride the Thirtieth Parallel, as close to it as the Nile's delta permitted!

When the Third Region, the Indus Valley Civilization, followed, its secular center was on the shores of the Indian Ocean; but its sacred city—*Harappa*—was hundreds of miles away to the north—right on the Thirtieth Parallel.

The imperative of the northern Thirtieth Parallel appears to have continued in the millennia that followed. Circa 600 B.C., the Persian kings augmented the royal capital with a city "Sacred unto all Nations." The place selected for its construction was a remote and uninhabited site. There, literally in the middle of nowhere, a great horizontal platform was laid out. Upon it, palaces with magnificent staircases and many auxiliary shrines and structures were erected—all honoring the God of the Winged Globe (Fig. 161). The Greeks called the place *Persepolis* ("City of the Persians"). No people lived there: It was only to celebrate the New Year on the day of the spring equinox that the king and his retinue came there. Its remains still stagger the viewer. And it was located astride the Thirtieth Parallel.

No one knows for sure when *Lhasa* in Tibet—the sacred city of Buddhism—was founded. But it is a fact that Lhasa too—as Eridu, Heliopolis, Harappa and Persepolis were—was situated on the same Thirtieth Parallel (Fig. 162).

The sanctity of the Thirtieth Parallel must be traced back to the origins of the Sacred Grid, when the divine measurers determined the location of the pyramids of Giza also on the Thirtieth Parallel. Could the gods have given up this "sanctity" or neutrality of the Thirtieth Parallel when it came to their most vital installation—the Spaceport—in their own Fourth Region, in the Sinai peninsula?

It is here that we ought to seek a final clue from the remaining enigma of Giza—its Great Sphinx. Its body is that of a crouching lion, its head of a man wearing the royal headdress (Fig. 163). When and by whom was it erected? And to what purpose? Whose image does it bear? And why is it where it is, alone, and nowhere else?

The questions have been many, the answers very few. But one thing is certain: *it gazes precisely eastward, along the Thirtieth Parallel*.

This precise alignment and gaze eastward along the Divine Parallel were

Fig. 161

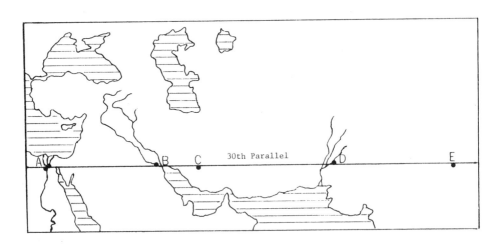

(A) Giza-Heliopolis　　(B) Eridu　　(C) Persepolis　　(D) Harappa　　(E) Lhasa

Fig. 162

Fig. 163

emphasized in antiquity by a series of structures that extended from in front of the Sphinx eastward precisely along an east-west axis (Fig. 164).

When Napoleon and his men saw the Sphinx at the turn of the eighteenth century, only its head and shoulders protruded above the desert sands; it was in that state that the Sphinx was depicted and known for the better part of the century that followed. It took repeated and systematic excavations to reveal its full colossal size (240 feet long, 65 feet high) and shape, and to confirm what ancient historians had written: that it was a single piece of sculpture, carved by some giant hand out of the natural rock. It was none other than Capt. Caviglia, whom Col. Vyse forced out of Giza, who had uncovered during 1816–1818 not only a good part of the body and extended paws of the Sphinx, but also the temples, sanctuaries, altars and stelas that were erected in front of it.

Clearing the area in front of the Sphinx, Caviglia discovered a platform that extended somewhat on both sides of the Sphinx but which primarily ran eastward. Excavating for one hundred feet in that easterly direction, he came upon a spectacular staircase of thirty steps leading up to a landing; upon it were the remains of what looked like a pulpit. At the eastern end of

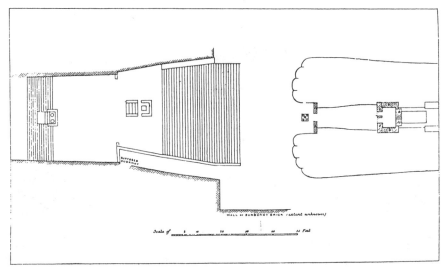

Fig. 164

the landing, some forty feet away, another flight of thirteen steps was discovered; they raised the level to the same height as the head of the Sphinx.

There, a structure whose function was to support two columns (Fig. 165) was so situated that the eastward gaze of the Sphinx passed precisely between the two columns.

Archaeologists believe that these remains are from Roman times. But as we have seen at Baalbek, the Romans embellished monuments that predated their era, building and rebuilding where earlier monuments and shrines had stood. It is well established by now, that Greek conquerors and Roman emperors continued the tradition of the Pharaohs to visit and pay homage to the Sphinx, leaving behind appropriate inscriptions. They affirmed the belief, which continued into Arab times, that the Sphinx was

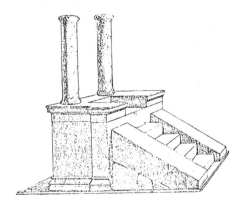

Fig. 165

the work of the gods themselves; it was deemed to be the harbinger of a future messianic era of peace. An inscription by the notorious emperor Nero called the Sphinx "*Armachis*, Overseer and Savior."

Because the Great Sphinx is situated near the causeway leading to the Second Pyramid, the best idea scholars had to offer was that it was built by Chefra, the "builder" of the Second Pyramid; and that it must therefore bear his image. This notion is devoid of any factual basis; yet it has persisted in textbooks, although as far back as 1904 E. A. Wallis Budge, then Keeper of the Egyptian and Assyrian Antiquities in the British Museum, concluded unequivocally (*The Gods of the Egyptians*) that "this marvellous object was in existence in the days of Kha-f-ra, or Khephren; and it is probable that it is a very great deal older than his reign and that it dates from the end of the archaic period."

As the "Inventory Stela" attests, the Sphinx had already stood at Giza in the time of Khufu, a predecessor of Chefra. Like several Pharaohs after him, so did Khufu take credit for removing the sand that encroached upon the Sphinx. From this it must be deduced that the Sphinx was already an olden monument in Khufu's time. What earlier Pharaoh, then, had erected it, implanting upon it his own image?

The answer is that the image is not of any Pharaoh, but of a god; and that in all probability, the gods and not a mortal king had erected the Sphinx.

Indeed, only by ignoring what the ancient inscriptions had stated, could anyone assume otherwise. A Roman inscription, calling the Sphinx "Sacred Guide," said of it: "Thy formidable form is the work of the Immortal Gods." A Greek adolatory poem read in part:

> Thy formidable form,
> Here the Immortal Gods have shaped. . . .
> As a neighbor to the Pyramids they placed thee. . . .
> A heavenly monarch who his foes defies. . . .
> Sacred Guide in the Land of Egypt.

In the Inventory Stela, Khufu called the Sphinx "Guardian of the Aeter, who guides the Winds with his gaze." It was, as he clearly wrote, the image of a god:

> This figure of the god
> will exist to eternity;
> Always having its face
> watching towards the east.

In his inscription, Khufu mentions that a very old sycamore tree that grew near the Sphinx was damaged "When the Lord of Heaven descended upon the Place of *Hor-em-Akhet*," "the Falcon-god of the Horizon." This, indeed was the most frequent name of the Sphinx in Pharaonic inscriptions;

his other epithets being *Ruti* ("The Lion") and *Hul* (meaning, perhaps, "The Eternal").

Nineteenth-century excavators of the site of the Sphinx, records show, were prompted by local Arab lore that held that there existed, under or within the Sphinx, secret chambers holding ancient treasures or magical objects. Caviglia, as we have seen, exerted himself within the Great Pyramid in search of a "hidden chamber;" it appears that he had switched to the pyramid having failed to find such a chamber at the site of the Sphinx. Perring too made the attempt, by cutting forcibly a deep hole in the back of the Sphinx.

Even more responsible researchers, such as Auguste Mariette in 1853, shared the general opinion that there is a hidden chamber concealed in or under the Sphinx. This belief was bolstered by the writings of the Roman historian Pliny, who reported that the Sphinx "contained the tomb of a ruler named Harmakhis," and by the fact that nearly all ancient depictions of the Sphinx show it crouching atop a stone structure. The searchers have surmised that if the Sphinx itself could have been almost hidden from sight by the encroaching sands, so much so could the sands of desert and time completely hide any substructure.

The most ancient inscriptions seem to suggest that there indeed existed not one, but two secret chambers under the Sphinx—perhaps reachable through an entrance hidden under the paws of the monument. A hymn from the time of the Eighteenth Dynasty, moreover, reveals that the two "caverns" under the Sphinx enabled it to serve as a communications center!

The god Amen, the inscription said, assuming the functions of the heavenly Hor-Akhti, attained "perception in his heart, command on his lips . . . when he enters the two caverns which are under his [the Sphinx's] feet." Then,

> A message is sent from heaven;
> It is heard in Heliopolis,
>   and is repeated in Memphis by the Fair of Face.
> It is composed in a despatch by the writing of Thoth,
>   with regard to the city of Amen (Thebes) . . .
> The matter is answered in Thebes,
> A statement is issued . . . a message is sent.
> The gods are acting according to command.

In the days of the Pharaohs it was believed that the Sphinx—though sculpted out of stone—could somehow hear and speak. In a long inscription on a stela (Fig. 166) erected between the paws of the Sphinx by Thothmes IV (and dedicated to the emblem of the Winged Disk), the king related that the Sphinx spoke to him and promised him a long and prosperous reign if only he would remove the sands that encroached upon his (the Sphinx's) limbs. One day, Thothmes wrote, as he went hunting out of Memphis, he

Fig. 166

found himself on the "sacred road of the gods" which led from Heliopolis to Giza. Tired, he lay to rest in the shade of the Sphinx; the place, the inscription reveals, was called *"Splendid Place of the Beginning of Time."* As he fell asleep by this "very great statue of the Creator," the Sphinx—this "majesty of the Revered God"—began to speak to him, introducing itself by saying: "I am thy ancestor *Hor-em-Akhet*, the one created of Ra-Aten."

Many unusual "Ear Tablets" and depictions of the Twin Doves—a symbol associated with oracle sites—were found in the temples surrounding the Sphinx. Like the ancient inscriptions, they too attest to the belief that somehow the Sphinx could transmit Divine Messages. Although the efforts to dig under the Sphinx have not been successful, one cannot rule out the possibility that the subterranean chambers which the gods had entered with "command on their lips" would still be found.

It is clear from numerous funerary texts that the Sphinx was considered to have been the "Sacred Guide" who guided the deceased from "yesterday" to "tomorrow." Coffin Spells intended to enable the deceased's journey along the "Path of the Hidden Doors" indicate that it began at the site of the Sphinx. Invoking the Sphinx, the Spells asserted that "The Lord of Earth has commanded, the Double Sphinx has repeated." The journey began when *Hor-Akhet*—the Sphinx—pronounced: "Pass by!" Drawings in the *Book of the Two Ways,* which illustrated the journey, show that from the starting point at Giza there were two routes by which the *Duat* could be reached.

As the Sacred Guide, the Sphinx was often depicted guiding the Celestial Barge. Sometimes, as on the stela of Thothmes (Fig. 166) it was depicted as a double Sphinx, guiding the Celestial Barge from "yesterday" to "tomorrow." In this role it was associated with the Hidden God of the Subterranean Realm; it was as such, it will be recalled (Fig. 19) that it symbolically appeared flanking the hermetically sealed chamber of the god Seker in the *Duat.*

Indeed, the Pyramid Texts and the Book of the Dead refer to the Sphinx as "The Great God who opens the Gates of Earth"—a phrase that may suggest that the Sphinx at Giza, which "led the way," had a counterpart near the Stairway to Heaven, who opened there "the Gates of Earth." Such a possibility is perhaps the only explanation (in the absence of any other to date) of a very archaic depiction of the Pharaoh's Journey to the Afterlife (Fig. 167). It begins with a crouching Horus-symbol which gazes toward the Land of the Date Palm where an unusual vessel with dredges or cranes (?) is situated, as well as a structure which is reminiscent of the Sumerian depiction of the name EN.LIL as a communications center (Fig. 52). A god greeting the Pharaoh, a bull and the Bird of Immortality are seen, followed by fortifications and an assortment of symbols. Finally, the symbol for "place" (tilted cross within a circle) appears between the sign for the Stairway and *a sphinx looking the other way!*

A stela erected by one Pa-Ra-Emheb, who directed works of restoration at the site of the Sphinx in Pharaonic times, contains telltale verses in adoration of the Sphinx; their similarity to biblical Psalms is truly tantalizing. The inscription mentions the extension of cords "for the plan,"

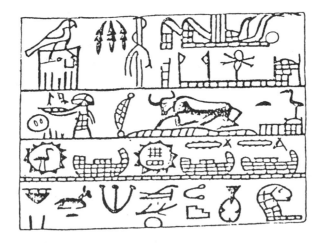

Fig. 167

the making of "secret things" in the subterranean realm; they speak of the "crossing of the sky" in a Celestial Barge, and of a "protected place" in the "sacred desert." It even employs the term *Sheti.ta* to denote the "Place of the Hidden Name" in the Sacred Desert:

> Hail to thee, King of the Gods,
> Aten, Creator . . .
> Thou extendest the cords for the plan,
>   thou didst form the lands . . .
> Thou didst make secret the Underworld . . .
> The Earth is under thy leading;
>   thou didst make high the sky . . .
> Thou hast built for thee a place protected
>   in the sacred desert, with hidden name.
> Thou risest by day opposite them . . .
> Thou art rising beautifully . . .
> Thou art crossing the sky with a good wind . . .
> Thou art traversing the sky in the barque . . .
> The sky is jubilating,
> The Earth is shouting of joy.
> The crew of Ra do praising every day;
> He comes forth in triumph.

To the Hebrew Prophets, the *Sheti*—the central Flight Line passing through Jerusalem—was the Divine Line, the direction to watch: "within it did the Lord come from sacred Sinai."

But to the Egyptians, as the above inscription declared, *Sheti.ta* was the "Place of the Hidden Name." It was in the "Sacred Desert"—which is exactly what the biblical term "Desert of *Kadesh*" has meant. And to it, the "cords of the plan" were extended from the Sphinx. There, Paraemheb had seen the King of the Gods ascend by day; the words are almost identical to those of Gilgamesh, arriving at Mount Mashu, "where daily the *Shems* he watched, as they depart and come in . . . watched over Shamash as he ascends and descends."

It was the Protected Place, the Place of Ascent. Those who were to reach it were guided there by the Sphinx; for its gaze led eastward, exactly along the Thirtieth Parallel.

It was where the two lines intersected, we suggest—where the Line of Jerusalem intersected the Thirtieth Parallel that the Gates of Heaven and Earth were located: the Spaceport of the gods.

The intersection is located within the Sinai's Central Plain. As the *Duat* was depicted in the *Book of the Dead*, the Central Plain is indeed an oval plain encompassed by mountains. It is a vast valley whose surrounding mountains are separated by seven passes—as described in the *Book of Enoch*; a vast flat plain whose hard natural surface provided ready-made runways for the shuttlecraft of the Anunnaki.

Nippur, we have shown (see Fig. 122), was the focal point, the bulls-eye of concentric circles which measured off as equidistant the Spaceport at Sippar and other vital installations and sites. The same, we find not without amazement, held true for Jerusalem (Fig. 168):

- The Spaceport (SP) and the Landing Place at Baalbek (BK) lay on the perimeter of an inner circle, forming a vital team of installations that were equidistant from the Control Center in Jerusalem (JM);
- The geodesic beacon of Umm Shumar (US) and the beacon of Heliopolis (HL) lay on the perimeter of an outer circle, making them too a pair equidistant from Jerusalem.

As we fill in our chart, the masterful Grid conceived by the Anunnaki unfolds before our very eyes; and we are truly astounded by its precision, simple beauty, and the artful combination of basic geometry with the landmarks provided by nature:

- The Baalbek-Katherine line, and the Jerusalem-Heliopolis line, intersected each other at the basic and precise angle of 45°; the central flight path bisected this angle into two precise angles of 22½° each; the grand Flight Corridor was in turn precisely half that (11¼°);
- The Spaceport, situated at the intersection of the central flight path and the Thirtieth Parallel, was equidistant from Heliopolis and Umm Shumar.

Was it only an accident of geography that Delphi (DL) was equidistant from Mission Control in Jerusalem and from the Spaceport in central Sinai? Mere coincidence that the angular width of the (Flight?) corridor so created was 11¼°? That another Flight Corridor of 11¼° connected Delphi with Baalbek (BK)?

Or only chance that the lines connecting Delphi with Jerusalem and the oasis of Siwa (SW)—the site of Ammon's oracle to which Alexander had rushed—formed once again the angle of 45° (Fig. 169)?

Were other sacred cities and oracle sites in Egypt, such as the great Thebes and Edfu, located where they were at a king's whim, at an attractive bend of the Nile—or where alignments of the Grid had dictated?

Indeed, were we to study all these sites, all of Earth would probably be encompassed. But was that not what Ba'al had already known when he established his clandestine facilities at Baalbek? For his aim, we recall, was to communicate with and dominate, not just the nearby lands, but all of Earth.

This the biblical Lord too must have known; for when Job sought to unravel the "wonders of El," the Lord "answered him from within the whirlpool," and countered questions with questions:

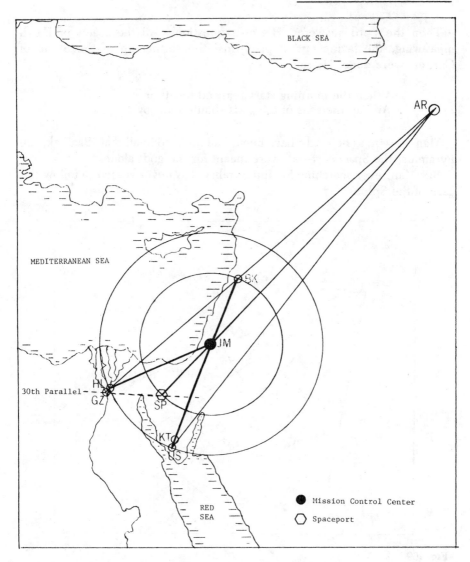

Fig. 168

Let me ask thee, and answer thou me:
Where wast thou,
    when the Earth's foundation I laid out?
Say, if thou knowest science:
Who hath measured it (the Earth), that it be known?
Or who hath stretched a cord upon it?
By what were its platforms wrought?
Who hath cast its Stone of Corners?

Then the Lord answered His own questions. All these acts of Earth measuring, the laying out of platforms, the setting up of the Stone of Corners were done, He said:

> When the morning stars rejoiced together
> And all the sons of the gods shouted for joy.

Man, as wise as he might have been, had no hand in all that. Baalbek, the Pyramids, the Spaceport—all were meant for the gods alone.

But Man, ever searching for Immortality, has never ceased to follow the gaze of the Sphinx.

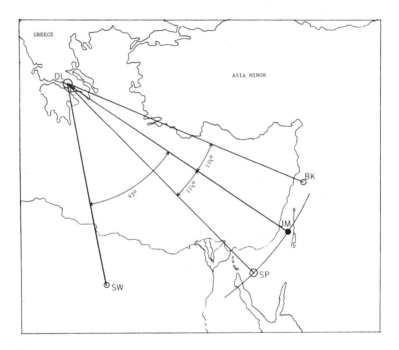

Fig. 169

Sources

In addition to works specifically mentioned in the text, the following served as principal sources on the ancient Near East:

I. Studies and articles in various issues of the following periodicals:

Ägyptologische Forschungen (Hamburg-New York).
Der Alte Orient (Leipzig).
American Journal of Archeology (Concord, N.H.).
American Journal of Semitic Languages and Literature (Chicago).
Ametocan Philosophical Society, Memoirs (Philadelphia)
Analecta Orientalia (Rome).
Annales du Musée Guimet (Paris).
Annales du Service des Antiquités de l'Egypte (Cairo).
Annual of the American Schools of Oriental Research (New Haven).
Annual of the Palestine Exploration Fund (London).
Antiquity (Cambridge).
Archaeologia (London).
Archiv für Keilschriftforschung (Berlin).
Archiv für Orientforschung (Berlin).
Archiv Orientālni (Prague).
The Assyrian Dictionary of the Oriental Institute, University of Chicago (Chicago).
Assyriologische Bibliothek (Leipzig).
Assyriological Studies of the Oriental Institute, University of Chicago (Chicago).

Babyloniaca (Paris).
Beiträge zur Aegyptischen Bauforschung und Altertumskunde (Kairo).
Beiträge zur Assyriologie und semitischen Sprachwissenschaft (Leipzig).
Biblical Archaeology Review (Washington).
Bibliotheca Orientalis (Leiden).
British School of Archaeology and Egyptian Research, Account Publications (London).
Bulletin de l'institut français d'archeologie orientale (Cairo).
Bulletin of the American Schools of Oriental Research (New Haven).

Cuneiform Texts from Babylonian Tablets in the British Museum (London).

Deutsche Orient-Gesellschaft, Mitteilungen (Berlin).
Deutsche Orient-Gesellschaft, Sendschriften (Berlin).

Egypt Exploration Fund, Memoirs (London).
Ex Oriente Lux (Leipzig).

France: Délégation en Perse, Memoires (Paris).
France: Mission Archéologique de Perse, Memoires (Paris).

Harvard Semitic Series (Cambridge, Mass.).
Hispanic American Historical Review (Durham, N.C.).

Iraq (London).
Imperial and Asiatic Quarterly Review (London).
Institut Français d'Archéologie Orientale, Bibliothèque d'Etude (Cairo).
Institut Français d'Archéologie Orientale, Memoires (Cairo).
Israel Exploration Society, Journal (Jerusalem).

Jewish Palestine Exploration Society, Bulletin (Jerusalem).
Journal of the American Oriental Society (New Haven).
Journal of Biblical Literature and Exegesis (Philadelphia).
Journal of Cuneiform Studies (New Haven and Cambridge, Mass.).
Journal of Egyptian Archaeology (London).
Journal of Jewish Studies (Oxford).
Journal of Near Eastern Studies (Chicago).
Journal of the Palestine Oriental Society (Jerusalem).
Journal of the Royal Asiatic Society (London).
Journal of Sacred Literature and Biblical Record (London).
Journal of the Society of Oriental Research (Chicago).

Kaiserlich Deutschen Archaelogischen Institut, Jahrbuch (Berlin).
Königliche Akademie der Wissenschaften zu Berlin, Abhandlungen (Berlin).

Leipziger Semitische Studien (Leipzig).

Mitteilungen der altorientalischen Gesellschaft (Leipzig).
Mitteilungen des deutschen Instituts für ägyptische Altertumskunde in Kairo (Augsburg and Berlin).
Mitteilungen des Instituts für Orientforschung (Berlin).

Orientalia (Rome).
Orientalistische Literaturzeitung (Leipzig).

Palestine Exploration Quarterly (London).
Preussischen Akademie der Wissenschaften, Abhandlungen (Berlin).
Proceedings of the Society of Biblical Archaeology (London).

Qadmoniot, Quarterly for the Antiquities of Eretz-Israel and Bible Lands (Jerusalem).

Recueil de travaux relatifs à la philologie et à l'archéologie égyptiennes et assyriennes (Paris).
Revue Archéologique (Paris).
Revue d'Assyriologie et d'archéologie orientale (Paris).
Revue Biblique (Paris).

Sphinx (Leipzig).
Studia Orientalia (Helsinki).
Studies in Ancient Oriental Civilizations (Chicago).
Syria (Paris).

Tarbiz (Jerusalem).
Tel Aviv, Journal of the Tel-Aviv University Institute of Archaeology (Tel-Aviv).
Transactions of the Society of Biblical Archaeology (London).

Untersuchungen zur Geschichte und Altertumskunde Aegyptens (Leipzig).
Urkunden des ägyptischen Altertums (Leipzig).

Vorderasiatisch-Aegyptischen Gesellschaft, Mitteilungen (Leipzig).
Vorderasiatische Bibliothek (Leipzig).

Die Welt des Orients (Göttingen).
Wissenschaftliche Veröffentlichungen der Deutschen Orient-Gesellschaft (Berlin and Leipzig).

Yale Oriental Series, Babylonian Texts (New Haven).
Yerushalayim, Journal of the Jewish Palestine Exploration Society (Jerusalem).

Zeitschrift für ägyptische Sprache und Altertumskunde (Berlin).
Zeitschrift für die alttestamentliche Wissenschaft (Berlin and Giessen).
Zeitschrift für Assyriologie und verwandte Gebiete (Leipzig).
Zeitschrift der Deutsche morgenländische Gesellschaft (Leipzig).
Zeitschrift des deutschen Palaestina-Vereins (Leipzig).
Zeitschrift für Keilschriftforschung und verwandte Gebiete (Leipzig).
Zeitschrift für die Kunde des Morgenlandes (Göttingen).

II. Individual works:

Alouf, M. M.: *History of Baalbek* (1922).
Amiet, P.: *La Glyptique Mésopotamienne Archaique* (1961).
Antoniadi, E. M.: *L'Astronomie Égyptienne* (1934).
Avi-Yonah, M.: *Sefer Yerushalaim* (1956).

Babelon, E.: *Les Rois de Syrie* (1890).
————: *Les Collections de Monnais Anciennes* (1897).
————: *Traité des Monnais Greques et Romaines* (1901–1910).
Bauer, H.: *Die alphabetischen Keilschrifttexte von Ras Schamra* (1936).
Borchardt, L.: *Die Entstehung der Pyramide* (1928).
Bourguet, E.: *Les Ruines de Delphos* (1914).
Buck, A. de: *The Egyptian Coffin Texts* (1935–1961).
Budge, E.A.W.: *The Alexander Book in Ethiopia* (1933).
————: *Cleopatra's Needle* (1906).
————: *The Egyptian Heaven and Hell* (1906).
————: *Egyptian Magic* (1899).
————: *The Gods of the Egyptians* (1904).
————: *The History of Alexander the Great* (1889).

————: *The Life and Exploits of Alexander the Great* (1896).
————: *Osiris and the Egyptian Resurrection* (1911).
Budge, E.A.W. and King, L. W.: *Annals of the Kings of Assyria* (1902).

Capart, J.: *Recueil de Monuments Égyptiens* (1902).
————: *Thebes* (1926).
Cassuto, M. D.: *Ha'Elah Anath* (1951).
————: *Perush al Sefer Shemoth* (1951).
Contenau, G.: *L'Épopée de Gilgamesh* (1939).

Davis, Ch. H. S.: *The Egyptian Book of the Dead* (1894).
Delaporte, L.: *Catalogue des Cylindres Orientaux* (1910).
Delitzsch, F.: *Wo Lag Das Paradies?* (1881).
Dussaud, R.: *Notes de Mythologie Syrienne* (1905).
————: *Les Découvertes de Ras Shamra (Ugarit) et l'Ancien Testament* (1937).

Ebeling, E.: *Reallexikon der Assyriologie* (1928–1932).
Eckenstein, L.: *A History of Sinai* (1921).
Emery, W. B.: *Excavations at Saqqara* (1949–58).
Erman, A.: *A Handbook of Egyptian Religion* (1907).
————: *Aegypten und Aegyptisches Leben im Altertum* (1923).
————: *The Literature of the Ancient Egyptians* (1927).

Falkenstien, A.: *Literarische Keilschrifttexte aus Uruk* (1931).
Faulkner, R. O.: *The Ancient Egyptian Coffin Texts* (1973).
————: *The Ancient Egyptian Pyramid Texts* (1969).
Frankfort, H.: *Kingship and the Gods* (1948).
Frauberger, H.: *Die Akropolis von Baalbek* (1892).
Friedländer, I.: *Die Chadirlegende und der Alexanderroman* (1913).

Gaster, Th. H.: *Myth, Legend and Custom in the Old Testament* (1969).
Gauthier, H.: *Dictionnaire des Noms Geographique* (1925).
Ginsberg, L.: *Kitbe Ugarit* (1936).
————: *The Legends of the Jews* (1954).
————: *The Ras Shamra Mythological Texts* (1958).
Gordon, C. H.: *The Loves and Wars of Baal and Anat* (1943).
————: *Ugaritic Handbook* (1947).
————: *Ugaritic Literature* (1949).
Gray, J.: *The Canaanites* (1965).
Gressmann, E.: *Altorientalische Texte zum alten Testament* (1926).
Grinsell, L. V.: *Egyptian Pyramids* (1947).

Heidel, A.: *The Gilgamesh Epic and Old Testament Parallels* (1946).
Hooke, S. H.: *Middle Eastern Mythology* (1963).
Hrozny, B.: *Hethitische Keilschrifttexte aus Boghazköy* (1919).

Jensen, P.: *Assyrisch-Babylonische Mythen und Epen* (1900).
————: *Das Gilgamesch-Epos in der Weltliteratur* (1906, 1928).
Jéquier, G.: *Le Livre de ce qu'il y a dans l'Hades* (1894).

Kazis, I. J.: *The Book of the Gests of Alexander of Macedon* (1962).
Kees, H.: *Aegyptische Kunst* (1926).
Kenyon, K. M.: *Jerusalem* (1967).
Kraeling, E. G. (Ed.): *Historical Atlas of the Holy Land* (1959).

Kramer, S. N.: *Gilgamesh and the Huluppu Tree* (1938).
———: *Sumerian Mythology* (1944).

Langdon, S.: *Historical and Religious Texts* (1914).
———: *The Epic of Gilgamesh* (1917).
Leonard, W. E.: *Gilgamesh* (1934).
Lefébure, M. E.: *Les Hypogées Royaux de Thébes* (1882).
Lepsius, K. R.: *Auswahl der wichtigsten Urkunden des Aegyptischen Alterthums* (1842).
———: *Königsbuch der Alten Aegypter* (1858).
Lesko, L. H.: *The Ancient Egyptian Book of the Two Ways* (1972).
Lipschitz, O.: *Sinai* (1978).
Luckenbill, D. D.: *Ancient Records of Assyria and Babylonia* (1926–1927).

Meissner, B.: *Alexander und Gilgames* (1894).
Mercer, S.A.B.: *Horus, Royal God of Egypt* (1942).
Meshel, Z.: *Derom Sinai* (1976).
Montet, P.: *Eternal Egypt* (1969).
Montgomery, J. A., and Harris, R. S.: *The Ras Shamra Mythological Texts* (1935).
Müller, C.: *Pseudokallisthenes* (1846).

Naville, H. E.: *Das aegyptische Todtenbuch* (1886).
Nöldeke, Th.: *Beiträge zur Geschichte des Alexanderromans* (1890).
Noth, M.: *Geschichte Israels* (1956).
———: *Exodus* (1962).

Obermann, J.: *Ugaritic Mythology* (1948).
Oppenheim, A. L.: *Mesopotamian Mythology* (1948).

Perlman, M. and Kollek, T.: *Yerushalayim* (1969).
Perring, J. E.: *The Pyramids of Gizeh from Actual Survey and Measurement* (1839).
Petrie, W.M.F.: *The Royal Tombs of the First Dynasty* (1900).
Poebel, A.: *Sumerische Studien* (1921).
Porter, B. and Moss, R.L.B.: *Topographical Bibliography of Ancient Egypt* (1951).
Pritchard, James B.: *Ancient Near Eastern Texts Relating to the Old Testament* (3rd ed., 1969).
———: *The Ancient Near East in Pictures Relating to the Old Testament* (1969).
Puchstein, O.: *Führer durch die Ruinen von Baalbek* (1905).
———: *Guide to Baalbek* (1906).
Puchstein, O. and Lupke, Th. von: *Baalbek* (1910).

Rawlinson, H. C.: *The Cuneiform Inscriptions of Western Asia* (1861–1884).
Reisner, G. A.: *Mycerinus: The Temples of the 3rd Pyramid at Gizeh* (1931).
Ringgren, H.: *Israelitische Religion* (1963).
Rothenberg, B. and Aharoni, Y.: *God's Wilderness* (1961).
Rougé, E. de: *Recherches sur le Monuments qu'on peut Attribuer aux six premières dynasties de Manethon* (1866).

Schott, A.: *Das Gilgamesch-Epos* (1934).
Schrader, E. (Ed.): *Keilinschriftliche Bibliothek* (1889–1900).
Soden, W. von: *Sumerische und Akkadische Hymnen und Gebete* (1953).
Smyth, C. P.: *Life and Work at the Great Pyramid* (1867).

Thompson, R. C.: *The Epic of Gilgamesh* (1930).

Ungnad, A.: *Die Religion der Babylonier und Assyrer* (1921).
———: *Das Gilgamesch Epos* (1923).
———: *Gilgamesch Epos und Odyssee* (1923).
Ungnad, A. and Gressmann, H.: *Das Gilgamesch-Epos* (1919).

Vandier, J.: *Manuel d'Archéologie Égyptienne* (1952).
Virolleaud, Ch.: *La déesse 'Anat* (1938).
———: *La légende phénicienne de Danel* (1936).
Volney, C. F.: *Travels Through Syria* (1787).

Wainwright, G. A.: *The Sky Religion in Ancient Egypt* (1938).
Weidner, E. F.: *Keilschrifttexte aus Boghazkoy* (1916).
Wiegand, Th.: *Baalbek* (1921–1925).
Woloohjian, A. M.: *The Romance of Alexander the Great by Pseudo-Callisthenes* (1969).

Zimmern, H.: *Sumerische Kultlieder* (1913).

Index

Praise for the Works of Zecharia Sitchin

"Reflects the highest level of scientific knowledge . . ."

SCIENCE & RELIGION NEWS

"Exciting . . . credible . . . most provocative and compelling."

LIBRARY JOURNAL

"One of the most important books on Earth's roots ever written."

EAST WEST JOURNAL

"Sitchin is a zealous investigator into man's origins . . . a dazzling performance."

KIRKUS REVIEWS

"For thousands of years priests, poets, and scientists have tried to explain how man was created. Now a recognized scholar has come forth with a theory that is most astonishing of all."

UNITED PRESS INTERNATIONAL

Also by Zecharia Sitchin

Genesis Revisited

Divine Encounters

The Earth Chronicles Handbook

The Earth Chronicles Expeditions (autobiographical)

Journeys to the Mythical Past (autobiographical)

The King Who Refused to Die (fiction)

The Lost Book of Enki

There Were Giants Upon the Earth

The Earth Chronicles

The 12th Planet — Book I

The Stairway to Heaven — Book II

The Wars of Gods and Men — Book III

The Lost Realms — Book IV

When Time Began — Book V

The Cosmic Code — Book VI

The End of Days — Book VII

ZECHARIA SITCHIN

THE WARS
OF
GODS AND MEN

**The Third Book
of
The Earth Chronicles**

Bear & Company
Rochester, Vermont • Toronto, Canada

Bear & Company
One Park Street
Rochester, Vermont 05767
www.BearandCompanyBooks.com

Bear & Company is a division of Inner Traditions International

Volume III
of
The Complete Earth Chronicles
Collector's Edition
Boxed Set

Printed and bound in India at Replika Press Pvt. Ltd.

10 9 8 7 6

TABLE OF CONTENTS

FOREWORD

Long before man warred with man, the gods battled among themselves. Indeed, it was as the Wars of the Gods that the Wars of Man began.

And the Wars of the Gods, for control of this Earth, had begun on their own planet.

It was thus that mankind's first civilization succumbed to a nuclear holocaust.

This is fact, not fiction; it has all been written down long ago—in the Earth Chronicles.

1

THE WARS OF MAN

In the spring of 1947, a shepherd boy searching for a lost sheep in the barren cliffs overlooking the Dead Sea, discovered a cave that contained Hebrew scrolls hidden inside earthenware jars. Those and other scrolls found in the area in subsequent years—collectively spoken of as the Dead Sea Scrolls—had lain undisturbed for nearly two thousand years, carefully wrapped and hidden away during the turbulent years when Judea challenged the might of the Roman empire.

Was this part of the official library of Jerusalem, carted away to safety before the city and its temple fell in A.D. 70, or—as most scholars assume—a library of the Essenes, a sect of hermits with messianic preoccupations? The opinions are divided, for the library contained both traditional biblical texts as well as writings dealing with the sect's customs, organization, and beliefs.

One of the longest and most complete scrolls, and perhaps the most dramatic, deals with a future war, a kind of Final War. Titled by scholars *The War of the Sons of Light Against the Sons of Darkness,* it envisages spreading warfare—local battles that will first involve Judea's immediate neighbors, which shall increase in ferocity and scope until the whole ancient world would be engulfed: "The first engagement of the Sons of Light against the Sons of Darkness, that is against the army of *Belial,* shall be an attack upon the troops of Edom, Moab, the Ammonites and the Philistine area; then upon that of the Kittians of Assyria; and upon those violators of the Covenant who give them aid. . . ." And after those battles, "they shall advance upon the Kittians of Egypt" and "in due time . . . against the kings of the north."

In this War of Men, the scroll prophesied, the God of Israel shall take an active role:

> On the day the Kittians fall, there shall be mighty combat and carnage, in the presence of the God of Israel;
> For that is the day which He appointed of old for the final battle against the Sons of Darkness.

The Prophet Ezekiel had already prophesied the Last Battle, ''in the latter days,'' involving Gog and Magog, in which the Lord himself shall ''smite thy bow out of thy left hand, and will cause thine arrows to fall out of thine right hand.'' But the Dead Sea scroll went further, foreseeing the actual participation of many gods in the battles, engaged in combat side by side with mortal men:

> On that day, the Company of the Divine and the Congregation of the Mortals shall engage side by side in combat and carnage.
> The Sons of Light shall battle against the Sons of Darkness with a show of godlike might, amid uproarious tumult, amid the war cries of gods and men.

Though Crusaders, Saracens, and countless others in historical times have gone to war ''in the name of God,'' the belief that in a war to come the Lord himself shall be actually present on the battlefield, and that gods and men would fight side by side, sounds as fantasy, to be treated allegorically at best. Yet it is not as extraordinary a notion as it may appear to be, for in earlier times, it was indeed believed that the Wars of Men were not only decreed by the gods but were also fought with the gods' active participation.

One of the most romanticized wars, when ''love had launched a thousand ships,'' was the War of Troy, between the Achaean Greeks and the Trojans. It was, know we not, launched by the Greeks to force the Trojans to return the beautiful Helen to her lawful spouse. Yet an epic Greek tale, the *Kypria,* represented the war as a premeditated scheme by the great god Zeus:

> There was a time when thousands upon thousands of men encumbered the broad bosom of the Earth. And having pity on them, Zeus in his great wisdom resolved to lighten Earth's burden.
> So he caused the strife at Ilion (Troy) to that end; that through death he might make a void in the race of men.

Homer, the Greek storyteller who related the war's events in the *Iliad,* blamed the whim of the gods for instigating the conflict and for turning and twisting it to its ultimate major proportions. Acting directly and indirectly, sometimes seen and sometimes unseen, the various gods nudged the principal actors of this human drama to their fates. And behind it all was Jove (Jupiter/Zeus): ''While the other gods and the armed warriors on the plain slept soundly, Jove was wakeful, for he was thinking how to do honor to Achilles and destroy much people at the ships of the Achaeans."

Even before the battle was joined, the god Apollo began the hostilities: "He sat himself down away from the ships with a face as dark as night, and his silver bow rang death as he shot his arrow in the midst of them [the Achaeans] . . . For nine whole days he shot his arrows among the people. . . . And all day long, the pyres of the dead were burning." When the contending sides agreed to postpone hostilities so that their leaders might decide the issue in hand-to-hand combat, the unhappy gods instructed the goddess Minerva: "Go at once into the Trojan and Achaean hosts, and contrive that the Trojans shall be the first to break their oaths and set upon the Achaeans." Eager for the mission, Minerva "shot through the sky as some brilliant meteor . . . a fiery train of light followed in her wake." Later on, lest the raging warfare cease for the night, Minerva turned night into day by lighting up the battlefield: She "lifted the thick veil of darkness from their eyes, and much light fell upon them, both on the side of the ships and on where the fight was raging; and the Achaeans could see Hector and all his men."

As the battles raged on and on, sometimes pitching one hero against another, the gods, too, kept a watchful eye over individual warriors, swooping down to snatch away a beleaguered hero or to steady a driverless chariot. But when the gods and goddesses, finding themselves on opposing sides, began to hurt each other, Zeus called a halt, ordering them to keep out of the mortals' fighting.

The respite did not last long, for many of the leading combatants were sons of gods or goddesses (by human mates). Especially angered was Mars, when his son Ascalaphus was pierced to death by one of the Achaeans. "Do not blame me, ye gods that dwell in heaven, if I go to the ships of the Achaeans and avenge the death of my son," Mars announced to the other Immortals, "even if in the end I shall be struck by Jove's lightning and shall lie in blood and dust among the corpses."

"So long as the gods held themselves aloof from the mortal warriors," wrote Homer, "the Achaeans were triumphant, for Achilles who has long refused to fight was now with them." But in view of the mounting anger among the gods, and the help the Achaeans were now getting from the demigod Achilles, Jove changed his mind:

"For my own part, I shall stay here,
seated on Mount Olympus, and look on in peace.
But you others, do go among the Trojans and Achaeans,
and help either side as you might be disposed."
Thus spake Jove, and gave the word for war;
Whereon the gods took their several sides
and went into battle.

The Battle of Troy, indeed Troy itself, were long thought of as just part of the fascinating but incredible Greek legends, which scholars have tolerantly called mythology. Troy and the events pertaining to it were still considered to be purely mythological when Charles McLaren suggested, back in 1822, that a certain mound in eastern Turkey, called Hissarlik, was the site of the Homeric Troy. It was only when a businessman named Heinrich Schliemann, risking his own money, came up with spectacular discoveries as he dug up the mound in 1870, that scholars began to acknowledge the existence of Troy. It is now accepted that the Battle of Troy had actually taken place in the thirteenth century B.C. It was then, according to the Greek sources, that gods and men had fought side by side; in such beliefs the Greeks were not alone.

In those days, though the tip of Asia Minor facing Europe and the Aegean Sea were dotted with what were essentially Greek settlements, Asia Minor proper was dominated by the Hittites. Known at first to modern scholars only from biblical references, then from Egyptian inscriptions, the Hittites and their kingdom—Hatti—also came to life as archaeologists began to uncover their ancient cities.

The decipherment of the Hittite script and their Indo-European language made it possible to trace their origins to the second millennium B.C., when Aryan tribes began to migrate from the Caucasus area—some southeast to India, others southwest to Asia Minor. The Hittite kingdom flourished circa 1750 B.C. and began to decline five hundred years later. It was then that the Hittites were harassed by incursions from across the Aegean Sea. The Hittites spoke of the invaders as the people of Achiyawa; many scholars believe that they were the very same people whom Homer called Achioi—the Achaeans, whose attack upon the western tip of Asia Minor he immortalized in the *Iliad*.

For centuries prior to the war of Troy, the Hittites expanded their kingdom to imperial proportions, claiming to have done so upon the orders of their supreme god TESHUB ("The Stormer").

His olden title was "Storm God Whose Strength Makes Dead," and Hittite kings sometimes claimed that the god had actually taken a hand in the battle: "The mighty Stormgod, my Lord," [wrote the king Murshilis], "showed his divine power and shot a thunderbolt" at the enemy, helping to defeat it. Also aiding the Hittites in battle was the goddess ISHTAR, whose epithet was "Lady of the battlefield." It was to her "Divine Power" that many a victory was attributed, as she "came down [from the skies] to smite the hostile countries."

Hittite influence, as many references in the Old Testament indicate, extended south into Canaan; but they were there as settlers, not as conquerors. While they treated Canaan as a neutral zone, laying to it no claim, this was not the attitude of the Egyptians. Repeatedly the Pharaohs sought to extend their rule northward to Canaan and the Cedar Land (Lebanon); they succeeded in doing so, circa 1470 B.C., when they defeated a coalition of Canaanite kings at Megiddo.

The Old Testament, and inscriptions left by the Hittites' foes, pictured the Hittites as expert warriors who perfected the use of the chariot in the ancient Near East. But the Hittites' own inscriptions suggest that they went to war only when the gods gave the word, that the enemy was offered a chance to surrender peacefully before hostilities began, and that once a war was won, the Hittites were satisfied to receive tribute and take captives: the cities were not sacked; the populace was not massacred.

But Thothmes III, the Pharaoh who was victorious at the battle of Megiddo, was proud to say in his inscriptions: "Now his majesty went north, plundering towns and laying encampments waste." Of a vanquished king the Pharaoh wrote: "I desolated his towns, set fire to his encampments, made mounds of them; their resettlement can never take place. All the people I captured, I made prisoners; their countless cattle I carried off, and their goods as well. I took away every resource of life; I cut down their grain and felled all their groves and all their pleasant trees. I totally destroyed it." It was all done, the Pharaoh wrote, on the say-so of AMON-RA, his god.

The vicious nature of Egyptian warfare and the pitiless destructiveness they inflicted upon a vanquished foe were subjects of boastful inscriptions. The Pharaoh Pepi I, for example, commemorated his victory over the Asiatic "sand-dwellers" in a poem which hailed the army which "hacked up the land of the sand-dwellers . . . cut down its fig trees and vines . . . cast fire into all its dwellings, killed its people by many tens of thousands.'' The commemorative inscriptions were accompanied by vivid depictions of the battle scenes (Fig. 1).

Fig. 1

Adhering to this wanton tradition, the Pharaoh Pi-Ankhy, who sent troops from Upper Egypt to subdue the rebellious Lower Egypt, was enraged by his generals' suggestion that adversaries who survived the battle be spared. Vowing "destruction forever," the Pharaoh announced that he would come to the captured city "to ruin that which had remained." For this, he stated, "My father Amon praises me."

The god Amon, to whose battle orders the Egyptians attributed their viciousness, found his match in the God of Israel. In the words of the Prophet Jeremiah, "Thus sayeth the Lord of Hosts, the God of Israel: 'I will punish Amon, god of Thebes, and those who trust in him, and shall bring retribution upon Egypt and its gods, its Pharaoh and its kings.' '' This, we learn from the Bible, was an ongoing confrontation; nearly a thousand years earlier, in the days of the Exodus, Yahweh, the God of Israel, smote Egypt with a series of afflictions intended not only to soften the heart of its ruler but also as "judgments against all the gods of Egypt."

The miraculous departure of the Israelites out of bondage in Egypt to the Promised Land was attributed in the biblical tale of Exodus to the direct intervention of Yahweh in those momentous events:

And they journeyed from Succoth
and encamped at Etham, at the edge of the desert.
And Yahweh went forth before them,
by day in a pillar of cloud to lead them the way,
and by night in a pillar of fire to give them light.

There then ensued a sea battle of which the Pharaoh preferred to
leave no inscriptions; we know of it from the Book of Exodus:

And the heart of the Pharaoh and his servants
was changed with respect to the people. . . .
And the Egyptians pursued after them,
and they overtook them encamped by the sea. . . .

And Yahweh drove back the sea with a strong east wind
all that night, and dried up the waters;
and the waters separated.
And the Children of Israel went into the midst of the sea
upon dry ground. . . .

At daybreak, when the Egyptians realized what had happened,
the Pharaoh ordered his chariots after the Israelites. But:

It came to pass at the time of the morning watch
that Yahweh surveyed the camp of the Egyptians
from the pillar of fire and cloud; ·
And he stunned the Egyptian camp
and loosened the wheels of their chariots,
making their driving difficult.
And the Egyptians said:
"Let us flee from the Israelites,
for Yahweh fighteth for them against Egypt."

But the Egyptian ruler pursuing the Israelites ordered his chariots
to press on with the attack. The result was calamitous for the Egyptians:

And the waters returned,
and covered the chariots and the horsemen
and all the host of the Pharaoh that was following them;
not one of them remained. . . .
And Israel beheld the great power
which Yahweh had shown upon the Egyptians.

The biblical language is almost identical to the words of a later Pharaoh, Ramses II, used by him to describe the miraculous appearance of Amon-Ra at his side during a decisive battle fought with the Hittites in 1286 B.C.

Taking place at the fortress of Kadesh in Lebanon, the battle pitted four divisions of the Pharaoh Ramses II against forces mobilized by the Hittite king Muwatallis from all parts of his empire. It ended with an Egyptian retreat, cutting short Egypt's northward thrust toward Syria and Mesopotamia. It also drained Hittite resources and left them weakened and exposed.

The Hittite victory might have been more decisive, for they had almost captured the Pharaoh himself. Only partial Hittite inscriptions dealing with the battle have been found; but Ramses, on his return to Egypt, saw fit to describe in detail the miracle of his escape.

Fig. 2

His inscriptions on temple walls, accompanied by detailed illustrations (Fig. 2), relate how the Egyptian armies had reached Kadesh and encamped south of it, readying themselves for the battle. Surprisingly the Hittite enemy did not step forward to do battle. Ramses then ordered two of his divisions to advance toward the fortress. It was then that the Hittite chariots appeared as if from nowhere, attacking the advancing divisions from behind and causing havoc in the encampments of the two others.

As the Egyptian troops began to flee in panic, Ramses suddenly realized that "His Majesty was all alone with his bodyguard"; and "when the king looked behind him, he saw that he was blocked off by 2,500 chariots"—not his own but of the Hittites. Abandoned by his officers, charioteers, and infantry, Ramses turned to his god, reminding him that he finds himself in this predicament only because he had followed the god's orders:

And His Majesty said:
"What now, my Father Amon?
Has a father forgotten his son?
Have I ever done anything without you?
Whatever I did or did not do,
was it not in accordance with your commands?''

Reminding the Egyptian god that the enemy was beholden to other gods, Ramses went on to ask: "What are these Asiatics to you, O Amon? These wretches who know nothing of thee, O God?''

As Ramses went on pleading with his god Amon to save him, for the god's powers were greater than those of "millions of foot soldiers, of hundreds of thousands of chariot-soldiers,'' a miracle happened: the god showed up on the battlefield!

Amon heard when I called him.
He held out his hand to me, and I rejoiced.
He stood behind me and called out:
"Forward! Forward!
Ramses, beloved of Amon, I am with thee!''

Following the command of his god, Ramses tore into the enemy troops. Under the influence of the god the Hittites were inexplicably enfeebled: "their hands dropped to their sides, they were unable to shoot their arrows nor raise their spears.'' And they called unto one another: "This is no mortal who is among us: this is a mighty god; his deeds are not the deeds of a man; a god is in his limbs.'' Thus unopposed, slaying the enemy left and right, Ramses managed to escape.

After the death of Muwatallis, Egypt and the Hittite kingdom signed a peace treaty, and the reigning Pharaoh took a Hittite princess to be his principal wife. The peace was needed because not only the Hittites but also the Egyptians were increasingly coming under attack by "Peoples of the Sea''—invaders from Crete and other Greek islands. They gained a foothold on the Mediterranean coast of Canaan to become the biblical Philistines; but their attacks on Egypt proper were beaten back by the Pharaoh Ramses III, who commemorated the battle scenes on temple walls (Fig. 3). He attributed his victories to his strict adherence to "the plans of the All-Lord, my august divine father, the Lord of the Gods." It was to his god Amon-Ra, Ramses wrote, that the credit for the victories was due: for it was "Amon-Ra who was after them, destroying them."

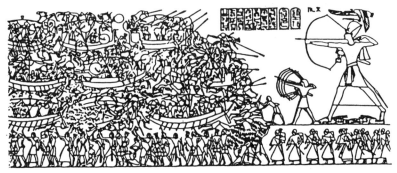

Fig. 3

The bloody trail of man's war against his fellow men in behalf of the gods now takes us back to Mesopotamia—the Land Between the Rivers (Euphrates and Tigris)—the biblical Land of Shin'ar. There, as is related in Genesis 11, the first-ever cities arose, with buildings made with bricks and towers that scraped the skies. It was there that recorded history began; it was there that prehistory began with the settlements of the Olden Gods.

It is a tale of long ago, which we will soon unfold. But right now let us return to a thousand years before the dramatic times of Ramses II in Egypt. Then, in faraway Mesopotamia, kingship was taken over by an ambitious young man. He was called Sharru-Kin—"Righteous Ruler"; our textbooks call him Sargon the First. He built a new capital city, calling it Agade, and established the kingdom of Akkad. The Akkadian language, written in a wedge-like (cuneiform) script, was the mother tongue of all the Semitic languages, of which Hebrew and Arabic are still in use.

Reigning for the better part of the twenty-fourth century B.C., Sargon attributed his long reign (fifty-four years) to the special status granted him by the Great Gods, who made him "Overseer of Ishtar, Anointed Priest of ANU, Great Righteous Shepherd of ENLIL." It was Enlil, Sargon wrote, "who did not let anybody oppose Sargon" and who gave Sargon "the region from the Upper Sea to the Lower Sea" (from the Mediterranean to the Persian

Gulf). It was therefore to "the gate of the House of Enlil" that Sargon brought the captive kings, ropes tied to the dog collars around their necks.

In one of his campaigns across the Zagros mountains, Sargon experienced the same godly feat that the combatants at Troy had witnessed. As he "was moving into the land of Warahshi . . . when he pressed forward in the darkness . . . Ishtar made a light to shine for him." Thus was Sargon able to "penetrate the gloom" of darkness as he led his troops through the mountain passes of today's Luristan.

The Akkadian dynasty begun by Sargon reached its peak under his grandson Naram-Sin ("Whom the god Sin loves"). His conquests, Naram-Sin wrote on his monuments, were possible because his god had armed him with a unique weapon, the "Weapon of the God," and because the other gods granted him their explicit consent—or even invited him—to enter their regions.

Naram-Sin's principal thrust was to the northwest, and his conquests included the city-state of Ebla, whose recently discovered archive of clay tablets has caused great scientific interest: "Although since the time of the separation of mankind none of the kings has ever destroyed Arman and Ibla, the god Nergal did open up the path for the mighty Naram-Sin and gave him Arman and Ibla. He also gave him as a present Amanus, the Cedar Mountain, to the Upper Sea."

Just as Naram-Sin could attribute his successful campaigns to his heeding the commands of his gods, so was his downfall attributed to his going to war against the word of the gods. Scholars have put together from fragments of several versions a text that has been titled *The Legend of Naram-Sin*. Speaking in the first person, Naram-Sin explains in this tale of woe that his troubles began when the goddess Ishtar "changed her plan" and the gods gave their blessing to "seven kings, brothers, glorious and noble; their troops numbered 360,000." Coming from what is now Iran, they invaded the mountain lands of Gutium and Elam to the east of Mesopotamia and were threatening Akkad itself. Naram-Sin asked the gods what to do and was told to put aside his weapons and, instead of going to battle, to go sleep with his wife (but, for some deep reason, avoid making love):

The gods reply to him:
"O Naram-Sin, this is our word:
This army against you . . .
Bind your weapons, in a corner place them!

Hold back your boldness, stay at home!
Together with your wife, in bed go sleep,
but with her you must not . . .
Out of your land, unto the enemy, you must not go.''

But Naram-Sin, announcing that he would rely on his own weapons, decided to attack the enemy in spite of the gods' advice.
''When the first year arrived, I sent out 120,000 troops, but none of
them returned alive,'' Naram-Sin confessed in his inscription.
More troops were annihilated in the second and third years, and
Akkad was succumbing to death and hunger. On the fourth anniversary of the unauthorized war, Naram-Sin appealed to the great
god Ea to overrule Ishtar and put his case before the other gods.
They advised him to desist from further fighting, promising that
''in days to come, Enlil will summon perdition upon the Sons of
Evil,'' and Akkad would have respite.

The promised era of peace lasted about three centuries, during
which the olden part of Mesopotamia, Sumer, reemerged as the
center of kingship, and the oldest urban centers of the ancient world
—Ur, Nippur, Lagash, Isin, Larsa—flourished again. Sumer, under the kings of Ur, was the center of an empire that encompassed
the whole of the ancient Near East. But toward the end of the third
millennium B.C., the land became the arena for contending loyalties
and opposing armies; and then that great civilization—man's first
known civilization—succumbed to a major catastrophe of unprecedented proportions.

It was a fateful event which, we believe, was echoed in biblical
tales. It was an event whose memory lingered on for a long time,
commemorated and bewailed in numerous lamentation poems;
they gave a very graphic description of the havoc and desolation
that befell that great heartland of ancient civilization. It was, those
Mesopotamian texts stated, a catastrophe that befell Sumer as a result of a decision of the great gods sitting in council.

It took southern Mesopotamia almost a century to be resettled
and another century to fully recover from the divine annihilation.
By then, the center of Mesopotamian power had shifted northward,
to Babylon. There, a new empire was to rise, proclaiming an ambitious god, MARDUK, as its supreme deity.

Circa 1800 B.C., Hammurabi, the king renowned for his law
code, ascended the throne in Babylon and began to extend its
boundaries. According to his inscriptions the gods not only told

him if and when to launch his military campaigns but were literally leading his armies:

Through the power of the great gods
the king, beloved of the god Marduk,
reestablished the foundations of Sumer and Akkad.
Upon the command of Anu, and
with Enlil advancing in front of his army,
with the mighty powers which the great gods gave him,
he was no match for the army of Emutbal
and its king Rim-Sin. . . .

To defeat more enemies the god Marduk granted Hammurabi a "powerful weapon" called "Great Power of Marduk":

With the Powerful Weapon
with which Marduk proclaimed his triumphs,
the hero [Hammurabi] overthrew in battle
the armies of Eshnuna, Subartu and Gutium. . . .
With the "Great Power of Marduk"
he overthrew the armies of Sutium, Turukku, Kamu. . . .
With the Mighty Power which Anu and Enlil had given him
he defeated all his enemies
as far as the country of Subartu.

But before long Babylon had to share its might with a new rival to its north—Assyria, where not Marduk but the bearded god ASHUR ("The All-Seeing") was proclaimed supreme. While Babylon tangled with the lands to its south and east, the Assyrians extended their rule northward and westward, as far as "the country of Lebanon, on the shores of the Great Sea." These were lands in the domains of the gods NINURTA and ADAD, and the Assyrian kings carefully noted that they launched their campaigns on the explicit commands of these great gods. Thus, Tiglat-Pileser I commemorated his wars, in the twelfth century B.C., in the following words:

Tiglat-Pileser, the legitimate king, king of the world, king of Assyria, king of all the four regions of the earth;
The courageous hero who is guided by the trust-inspiring commands given by Ashur and Ninurta, the great gods, his lords, thus overthrowing his enemies. . . .

At the command of my lord Ashur, my hand conquered from beyond the lower Zab River to the Upper Sea which is in the west. Three times I did march against the Nairi countries. . . . I made bow to my feet 30 kings of the Nairi countries. I took hostages from them, I received as their tribute horses broken to the yoke. . . .

Upon the command of Anu and Adad, the great gods, my lords, I went to the Lebanon mountains; I cut cedar beams for the temples of Anu and Adad.

In assuming the title "king of the world, king of the four regions of the Earth," the Assyrian kings directly challenged Babylon, for Babylon encompassed the ancient region of Sumer and Akkad. To legitimize their claim the Assyrian kings had to take control of those olden cities where the Great Gods had their homes in olden times; but the way to these sites was blocked by Babylon. The feat was achieved in the ninth century B.C. by Shalmaneser III; he said thus in his inscriptions:

I marched against Akkad to avenge . . . and inflicted defeat. . . . I entered Kutha, Babylon and Borsippa.

I offered sacrifices to the gods of the sacred cities of Akkad. I went further downstream to Chaldea, and received tribute from all the kings of Chaldea. . . .

At that time, Ashur, the great lord . . . gave me scepter, staff . . . all that was necessary to rule the people.

I was acting only upon the trustworthy commands given by Ashur, the great lord, my lord who loves me.

Describing his various military campaigns, Shalmaneser asserted that his victories were achieved with weapons provided by two gods: "I fought with the Mighty Force which Ashur, my lord, had given me; and with the strong weapons which Nergal, my leader, had presented to me." The weapon of Ashur was described as having a "terrifying brilliance." In a war with Adini the enemy fled on seeing "the terrifying Brilliance of Ashur; it overwhelmed them."

When Babylon, after several acts of defiance, was sacked by the Assyrian king Sennacherib (in 689 B.C.), its demise was made possible because its own god, Marduk, became angry with its king and people, and decreed that "seventy years shall be the measure of its desolation"—exactly as the God of Israel had later decreed for Jerusalem. With the subjugation of the whole of Mesopotamia, Sennacherib was able to assume the cherished title "King of Sumer and Akkad."

In his inscriptions, Sennacherib also described his military campaigns along the Mediterranean coast, leading to battles with the Egyptians at the gateway to the Sinai peninsula. His list of conquered cities reads like a chapter in the Old Testament—Sidon, Tyre, Byblos, Akko, Ashdod, Ashkalon—"strong cities" that Sennacherib "overwhelmed" with the aid of "the awe-inspiring Brilliance, the weapon of Ashur, my lord." Reliefs that illustrate his campaigns (as the one depicting the siege of Lachish, Fig. 4) show the attackers using rocketlike missiles against their enemy. In

Fig. 4

the conquered cities Sennacherib "killed their officials and patri-
cians . . . and hung their bodies on poles surrounding the city; the
common citizens I considered prisoners of war."

An artifact known as the Prism of Sennacherib preserved an historical inscription in which he made mention of the subjugation of
Judea and his attack on Jerusalem. The quarrel Sennacherib had
with its king, Hezekiah, was the fact that he held captive Padi, the
king of the Philistine city of Ekron, "who was loyal to his solemn
oath to his god Ashur."

"As to Hezekiah, the Judean," Sennacherib wrote, "who did
not submit to my yoke, I laid siege to forty-six of his strong cities,
walled forts, and to the countless small villages in their vicinity. . . . Hezekiah himself I made captive in Jerusalem, his royal
residence; like a bird in a cage I surrounded him with earthworks. . . . His towns which I had plundered I cut off from his
land and gave them over to Mitinti, king of Ashdod; Padi, king of
Ekron; and Sillibel, king of Gaza. Thus I reduced his country."

The siege of Jerusalem offers several interesting aspects. It had
no direct cause but only an indirect one: the forced holding there
of the loyal king of Ekron. The "awe-inspiring Brilliance, the
weapon of Ashur," which was employed to "overwhelm the
strong cities" of Phoenicia and Philistia, was not used against Jerusalem. And the customary inscriptional ending—"I fought with
them and inflicted defeat upon them"—is missing in the case of Jerusalem; Sennacherib merely reduced the size of Judea by giving
its outlying areas to neighboring kings.

Moreover, the usual claim that a land or a city was attacked upon
the "trustworthy orders" of the god Ashur was also absent in the
case of Jerusalem; one wonders whether all this meant that the attack on the city was an unauthorized attack—a whim of Sennacherib himself but not the wish of his god?

This intriguing possibility becomes a convincing probability as
we read the other side of the story—for such an other side does
exist in the Old Testament.

While Sennacherib glossed over his failure to capture Jerusalem,
the tale in II Kings, chapters 18 and 19, offers the full story. We
learn from the biblical report that "in the fourteenth year of king
Hezekiah Sennacherib, the king of Assyria, came upon all the
walled cities of Judea and captured them." He then sent two of his
generals with a large army to Jerusalem, the capital. But instead of
storming the city, the Assyrian general Rab-Shakeh began a verbal
exchange with the city's leaders—an exchange he insisted on con-

ducting in Hebrew so that the whole populace might understand him.

What did he have to say that the populace ought to have known? As the biblical text makes clear, the verbal exchanges concerned the question of whether the Assyrian invasion of Judea was authorized by the Lord Yahweh!

"And Rab-Shakeh said unto them: Speak ye now to Hezekiah: Thus sayeth the great king, the king of Assyria: What confidence is it wherein thou trusteth?''

> If ye say unto me:
> "We trust in Yahweh, our God" . . .
> Now then,
> Am I come against this place to destroy it
> without Yahweh?
> Yahweh did say unto me:
> "Go up against this land, and destroy it!''

The more the ministers of king Hezekiah, standing upon the city's walls, pleaded with Rab-Shakeh to cease saying these untrue things in Hebrew and to deliver his message in the then language of diplomacy, Aramaic, the more did Rab-Shakeh approach the walls to shout his words in Hebrew for all to hear. Soon he began to use foul language against Hezekiah's emissaries; then he started to degrade the king himself. Carried away by his own oratory, Rab-Shakeh abandoned his claim to have had Yahweh's permission to attack Jerusalem and went on to belittle the God himself.

When Hezekiah was told of the blasphemy, "he rent his clothes, and covered himself with sackcloth and went into the House of Yahweh. . . . And he sent word to the Prophet Isaiah, saying: 'This is a day of trouble, of rebuke, of blasphemy. . . . May Yahweh thy Lord hear all the words of Rab-Shakeh, whom his master the king of Assyria hath sent to scorn the Living God.' And the word of the Lord Yahweh came back through his Prophet Isaiah: 'Concerning the king of Assyria . . . the way that he came, he shall return; and unto this city he shall not come in . . . for I shall defend this city to save it.' ''

> And it came to pass that night,
> that the angel of Yahweh went forth
> and smote in the camp of the Assyrians
> a hundred and eighty-five thousand;

and at sunrise, lo and behold,
they were all dead corpses.
So Sennacherib, the king of Assyria,
departed, and journeyed back and dwelt in Nineveh.

According to the Old Testament, after Sennacherib had returned to Nineveh, "it came to pass, as he was worshiping in the temple of his god Nisroch, that Adrammelech and Sharezzer his sons smote him with a sword; and they escaped unto the land of Ararat. And Esarhaddon, his son, reigned in his stead." Assyrian records confirm the biblical statement: Sennacherib was indeed so assassinated, and his younger son Esarhaddon did ascend the throne after him.

An inscription of Esarhaddon known as Prism B describes the circumstances more fully. On the command of the great gods, Sennacherib had publicly proclaimed his younger son as successor. "He called together the people of Assyria, young and old, and he made my brothers, the male offspring of my father, take a solemn oath in the presence of the gods of Assyria . . . in order to secure my succession." The brothers then broke their oath, killing Sennacherib and seeking to kill Esarhaddon. But the gods snatched him away "and made me stay in a hiding place . . . preserving me for kingship."

After a period of turmoil Esarhaddon received "a trustworthy command from the gods: 'Go, do not delay! We will march with you!'"

The deity who was delegated to accompany Esarhaddon was Ishtar. As his brothers' forces came out of Nineveh to beat off his attack on the capital, "Ishtar, the Lady of Battle, who wished me to be her high priest, stood at my side. She broke their bows, scattered their orderly battle array." Once the Ninevite troops were disorganized, Ishtar addressed them in behalf of Esarhaddon. "Upon her lofty command, they went over in masses to me and rallied behind me," Esarhaddon wrote, "and recognized me as their king."

Both Esarhaddon and his son and successor Ashurbanipal attempted to advance against Egypt, and both employed Weapons of Brilliance in the battles. "The terror-inspiring Brilliance of Ashur," Ashurbanipal wrote, "blinded the Pharaoh so that he became a madman."

Other inscriptions of Ashurbanipal suggest that this weapon, which emitted an intense, blinding brightness, was worn by the gods as part of their headgear. In one instance an enemy "was blinded by the brightness from the god-head." In another, "Ishtar, who dwells in Arbela, clad in Divine Fire and sporting the Radiant Headwear, rained flames upon Arabia."

The Old Testament, too, refers to such a Weapon of Brilliance that could blind. When the Angels (literally, emissaries) of the Lord came to Sodom prior to its destruction, the populace attempted to break down the door of the house in which they were resting. So the Angels "smote the people at the entrance of the house with blindness . . . and they were unable to find the doorway."

As Assyria rose to supremacy, even extending its rule over Lower Egypt, its kings, in the words of the Lord through his prophet Isaiah, forgot that they were only an instrument of the Lord: "Ho Assyria, the whip of mine anger! My wrath is the rod in their hands; against impious nations I send them; upon people who have crossed me I charge them." But the Assyrian kings went beyond mere punishment; "rather, it is in its heart to annihilate and wipe out nations not few." This went beyond the intention of the God; therefore, the Lord Yahweh announced, "I shall hold to account the king of Assyria, on account of the fruits of the growing haughtiness of his heart."

The biblical prophecies predicting the downfall of Assyria indeed came true: As invaders from the north and east were joined by rebellious Babylonians from the south, Ashur, the religious capital, fell in 614 B.C., and Nineveh, the royal capital, was captured and sacked two years later. The great Assyria was no more.

The disintegration of the Assyrian empire was seized by vassal kings in Egypt and Babylonia as an opportunity to attempt the restoration of their own hegemonies. The lands between them were once again the cherished prize, and the Egyptians, under the Pharaoh Necho, were quicker in invading these territories.

In Babylonia, Nebuchadnezzar II—as recorded in his inscriptions—was ordered by the god Marduk to march his army westward. The expedition was made possible because "another god," the one who held the original sovereignty over the area, "has not desired the cedar land" anymore; and now "a foreign enemy was ruling and robbing it."

In Jerusalem the word of the Lord Yahweh through his prophet Jeremiah was to side with Babylon, for the Lord Yahweh—calling

Nebuchadnezzar "my servant"—had decided to make the Babylonian king the instrument of His wrath against the gods of Egypt:

> Thus sayeth Yahweh, Lord of Hosts, the God of Israel:
> "Indeed will I send for and fetch Nebuchadnezzar, my ser-
>   vant. . . .
> And he shall smite the land of Egypt,
> and deliver such as are for death to death,
> and such as are for captivity to captivity,
> and such as are for the sword to the sword.
> And I will kindle a fire in the house of Egypt's gods,
> and he will burn them. . . .
> And he will break the obelisks of Heliopolis,
> the one which is in the land of Egypt;
> The houses of the gods of Egypt shall he burn with fire."

In the course of this campaign the Lord Yahweh announced that
Jerusalem, too, shall be punished on account of its people's sins,
having taken up the worship of the "Queen of Heaven" and of the
gods of Egypt: "Mine anger and my fury shall be poured upon this
place . . . and it shall burn and shall not be quenched. . . . In the
city on which my name has been called, the doom will I begin."
And so it was that in the year 586 B.C. "Nebuzaraddan, captain of
the guard of the king of Babylon, came into Jerusalem; and he
burned the House of Yahweh, and the king's house, and all the
houses of Jerusalem . . . and all the walls around Jerusalem were
torn down by the army of the Chaldeans." This desolation, Yahweh promised, however, would last only seventy years.

The king who was to fulfill this promise and enable the rebuilding of the Temple of Jerusalem was Cyrus. His ancestors,
speaking an Indo-European language, are believed to have migrated south from the Caspian Sea area to the province of Anshan
along the eastern coast of the Persian Gulf. There Hakham-Anish
("Wise Man"), the leader of the migrants, began a dynasty we call
Achaemenid; his descendants—Cyrus, Darius, Xerxes—made history as rulers of what was to be the Persian empire.

When Cyrus ascended the throne of Anshan in 549 B.C., his
land was a distant province of Elam and Media. In Babylon, then
the center of power, the kingship was held by Nabunaid, who became king under most unusual circumstances: not by the customary choice by the god Marduk, but as a result of a unique pact
between a High Priestess (the mother of Nabunaid) and the god

Sin. A partly damaged tablet contains the eventual indictment of Nabunaid: "He set an heretical statue upon a base . . . he called its name 'the god Sin'. . . . At the proper time of the New Year Festival, he advised that there be no celebrations. . . . He confounded the rites and upset the ordinances."

While Cyrus was busy fighting the Greeks of Asia Minor, Marduk—seeking to restore his position as the national god of Babylon—"scanned and looked throughout the countries, searching for a righteous ruler willing to be led. And he called out the name of Cyrus, King of Anshan, and pronounced his name to be ruler of all the lands."

After the first deeds of Cyrus proved to be in accord with the god's wishes, Marduk "ordered him to march against his own city Babylon. He made him [Cyrus] set out on the road to Babylon, going at his side like a real friend." Thus, literally accompanied by the Babylonian god, Cyrus was able to take Babylon without bloodshed. On a day equivalent to March 20, 538 B.C., Cyrus "held the hands of *Bel* [The Lord] Marduk" in Babylon's sacred precinct. On New Year's Day his son, Cambyses, officiated at the restored festival honoring Marduk.

Cyrus left his successors an empire that encompassed all the earlier empires and kingdoms but one. Sumer, Akkad, Babylon, and Assyria in Mesopotamia; Elam and Media to the east; the lands to the north; the Hittite and Greek lands in Asia Minor; Phoenicia and Canaan and Philistia—all had now come under one sovereign king and one supreme god, Ahura-Mazda, God of Truth and Light. He was depicted in ancient Persia (Fig. 5a) as a bearded deity roaming the skies within a Winged Disc—very much in the manner in which the Assyrians had depicted their supreme god, Ashur (Fig. 5b).

When Cyrus died in 529 B.C., the only remaining independent land with its independent gods was Egypt. Four years later his son and successor, Cambyses, led his troops along the Mediterranean coast of the Sinai peninsula and defeated the Egyptians at Pelusium; a few months later he entered Memphis, the Egyptian royal capital, and proclaimed himself a Pharaoh.

Despite his victory, Cambyses carefully refrained from employing in his Egyptian inscriptions the usual opening formula "the great god, Ahura-Mazda, chose me." Egypt, he recognized, did not come within the domains of this god. In deference to the independent gods of Egypt, Cambyses prostrated himself before their statues, accepting their dominion. In return the Egyptian

a

b

Fig. 5

priests legitimized his rule over Egypt by granting him the title
"Offspring of Ra."

The ancient world was now united under one king, chosen by the
"great god of truth and light" and accepted by the gods of Egypt.
Neither men nor gods had cause left to war with each other. Peace
on Earth!

But peace failed to last. Across the Mediterranean Sea, the
Greeks were increasing in wealth, power, and ambitions. Asia Minor, the Aegean Sea, and the eastern Mediterranean saw increasing
clashes, both local and international. In 490 B.C., Darius I attempted to invade Greece and was defeated at Marathon; nine
years later Xerxes I was defeated at Salamis. A century and a half
later Alexander of Macedonia crossed over from Europe to launch
a campaign of conquest that saw the blood of men flow in all the
ancient lands as far as India.

Was he carrying out a "trustworthy command" of the gods? On

the contrary. Believing a legend that he was fathered by an Egyptian god, Alexander at first fought his way to Egypt to hear the god's oracle confirm his semidivine origins. But the oracle also predicted his early death, and Alexander's travels and conquests were thereafter motivated by a search for the Waters of Life, so that he might drink of them and evade his fate.

He died, in spite of all the carnage, young and in his prime. And ever since, the Wars of Men have been the wars of men alone.

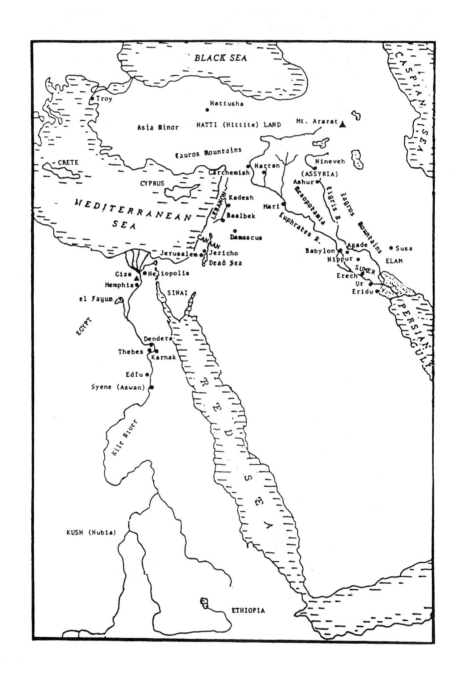

2

THE CONTENDING OF HORUS AND SETH

Was it a sad commentary on the history of warfare that the messianic Essenes envisioned the Final War of Men as one in which the Company of the Divine would join the Congregation of the Mortals, and the "war cries of gods and men" would mingle on the battlefield?

Not at all. What *The War of the Sons of Light Against the Sons of Darkness* had envisioned was simply that human warfare shall end just as it had begun: with gods and men fighting side by side.

Incredible as it may sound, a document does exist that describes the first war in which the gods involved mortal men. It is an inscription on the walls of the great temple at Edfu, an ancient Egyptian holy city that was dedicated to the god Horus. It was there, Egyptian traditions held, that Horus established a foundry of "divine iron" and where, in a special enclosure, he maintained the great Winged Disk that could roam the skies. "When the doors of the foundry open," an Egyptian text declared, "the Disk riseth up":

The inscription (Fig. 6), remarkable for its geographical accuracy, begins with an exact date—a date not in the affairs of men but of the gods. It deals with events when the gods themselves, long before the Pharaohs, reigned over Egypt:

In the year 363 His Majesty, Ra, the Holy One, the Falcon of the Horizon, the Immortal Who Forever Lives, was in the land of Khenn. He was accompanied by his warriors, for the enemies had conspired against their lord in the district which has been called Ua-Ua since that day.

Ra went there in his boat, his companions with him. He landed in the district of the Throne Place of Horus, in the western part of this district, east of the House of Khennu, the one which has been called Royal Khennu from that time on.

25

Horus, the Winged Measurer, came to the boat of Ra. He said to his forefather: "O Falcon of the Horizon, I have seen the enemy conspire against thy Lordship, to take the Luminous Crown unto themselves."

Fig. 6

With a few words the ancient scribe succeeded in drawing the background as well as setting the stage for the unusual war that was about to unfold. We gather at once that the fighting was brought on by a conspiracy by certain "enemies" of the gods Ra and Horus, to take away the "Luminous Crown of Lordship" unto themselves. This, obviously, could have been done only by some other god or gods. To forestall the conspiracy Ra—"accompanied by his warriors"—went in his boat to a district where Horus had set up his headquarters.

The "boat" of Ra, as is known from many other texts, was a Celestial Boat in which Ra could soar to the farthest heavens. In this instance Ra used it to land far away from any waters, "in the western part" of the district of Ua-Ua. There he landed east of the "Throne Place" of Horus. And Horus came out to greet his forefather and reported to him that "the enemy" was gathering its forces.

> Then Ra, the Holy One, the Falcon of the Horizon, said unto Horus, the Winged Measurer: "Lofty issue of Ra, my begotten: Go quickly, knock down the enemy whom you have seen."

So instructed, Horus took off in the Winged Disk to search for the enemy from the skies:

> So Horus, the Winged Measurer, flew up toward the horizon in the Winged Disk of Ra; it is therefore that he has been called from that day on "Great God, Lord of the Skies."

From the skies, flying in the Winged Disk, Horus spotted the enemy forces and unleashed upon them a "storm" that could neither be seen nor heard, yet it brought instantaneous death:

> In the heights of the skies, from the Winged Disk, he saw the enemies, and came upon them from behind. From his forepart he let loose against them a Storm which they could neither see with their eyes, nor hear with their ears. It brought death to all of them in a single moment; not a being remained alive through this.

Horus then flew back to the boat of Ra in the Winged Disk, "which shined in many colors," and heard his victory made official by Thoth, the god of magical crafts:

> Then Horus, the Winged Measurer, reappeared in the Winged Disk, which shined in many colors; and he came back to the boat of Ra, the Falcon of the Horizon.
> And Thoth said: "O Lord of the gods! The Winged Measurer has returned in the great Winged Disk, shining with many colors". . . .

Therefore is he named from that day on "The Winged Measurer." And they named after Horus, the Winged Measurer, the city of Hut "Behutet," from that day on.

It was in Upper Egypt that the first battle, above reported, had taken place between Horus and "the enemies." Heinrich Brugsch, who first published the text of the inscription back in 1870 *(Die Sage von der geflügten Sonnenscheibe)*, suggested that the "Land of Khenn" was Nubia, and that Horus had spotted the enemies at Syene (today's Aswan). More recent studies, such as *Egypt in Nubia* by Walter B. Emery, agree that Ta-Khenn was Nubia and that Ua-Ua was the name of its northern part, the area between the Nile's first and second cataracts. (The southern part of Nubia was called Kush.) These identifications seem valid, since the city of Behutet, which was granted to Horus as a prize for his first victory, was the very city of Edfu, which has been dedicated to Horus ever since.

Traditions held that Edfu was where Horus established a divine metal foundry, at which unique weapons made of "divine iron" were forged. It was there, too, that Horus trained an army of *mesniu*—"Metal People." They were depicted on the walls of the temple of Edfu as men with shaven heads, wearing a short tunic and a deep collar, carrying weapons in each hand. A depiction of an unidentified, harpoonlike weapon ◄━▲ was included in the hieroglyphic words for "divine iron" and "metal people."

The *mesniu* were, according to Egyptian traditions, the first men ever to have been armed by the gods with weapons made of metal. They also were, as we shall soon gather from the unfolding tale, the first men to have been enlisted by a god to fight in the wars between the gods.

The area between Aswan and Edfu now firmly secured, and men-warriors armed and trained, the gods were ready to advance northward, toward the heartland of Egypt. The initial victories apparently also strengthened the alliance of the gods, for we are told that the Asiatic goddess Ishtar (the Egyptian text calls her by her Canaanite name, Ashtoreth) had joined the group. Hovering in the sky, Horus called on Ra to scout the land below:

And Horus said: "Advance, O Ra! Look for the enemies who are lying below, upon the land!"
Then Ra, the Holy One, travelled forth; and Ashtoreth was

with him. And they looked for the enemies upon the land; but each one of them was hidden.

Since the enemies on the land were hidden from sight, Ra had an idea: "And Ra said unto the gods accompanying him: 'Let us guide our vessel toward the water, for the enemy lies in the land.' And they called the waters 'The Travelled Waters' from that day on." While Ra could utilize the amphibious capabilities of his vehicle, Horus was in need of a waterborne vessel. So they gave him a boat, "and called it Mak-A (Great Protector) unto this day."

It was then that the first battle involving mortal men ensued:

But the enemies too went into the waters, making themselves as crocodiles and hippopotami, and they were striking at the boat of Ra, the Falcon of the Horizon. . . .

It was then that Horus, the Winged Measurer, came along with his helpers, those who served as warriors, each one called by name, with the Divine Iron and a chain in their hands, and they beat off the crocodiles and the hippopotami.

And they hauled up 651 enemies to that place; they were killed in sight of the city.

And Ra, the Falcon of the Horizon, said unto Horus, the Winged Measurer: "Let this place be known as the place where thine victory in the southlands has been established."

Having vanquished their enemies from the skies, on land, and in the waters, the victory of Horus seemed complete; and Thoth called for a celebration:

Then said Thoth unto the other gods: "O Gods of Heaven, let your hearts rejoice! O Gods of Earth, let your hearts rejoice! The young Horus has brought peace, having performed extraordinary feats in this campaign."

It was then that the Winged Disk was adopted as the emblem of Horus victorious:

It is from that day that the metal emblems of Horus have existed. It was Horus who had fashioned as his emblem the Winged Disk, placing it upon the forepart of the boat of Ra. The goddess of the north and the goddess of the south, represented as two serpents, he placed alongside.

And Horus stood behind the emblem, upon the boat of Ra, the Divine Iron and the chain in his hand.

In spite of the proclamation of Horus by Thoth as a bringer of peace, peace was not yet in hand. As the company of the gods kept advancing northward, "they glimpsed two brightnesses on a plain southeast of Thebes. And Ra said to Thoth: 'This is the enemy; let Horus slaughter them. . . .' And Horus made a great massacre among them."

Once again, with the aid of the army of men he had trained and armed, Horus was victorious; and Thoth kept naming the locations after the successful battles.

While the first aerial battle broke through the defenses separating Egypt from Nubia at Syene (Aswan), the ensuing battles on land and water secured for Horus the bend of the Nile, from Thebes to Dendera. There great temples and royal sites proliferated in days to come. Now the way was open into the heartland of Egypt.

For several days the gods advanced northward—Horus keeping watch from the skies in the Winged Disk, Ra and his companions sailing down the Nile, and the Metal People guarding the flanks on land. A series of brief, but fierce, encounters then ensued; the place names—well established in ancient Egyptian geography— indicate that the attacking gods reached the area of lakes that had stretched in antiquity from the Red Sea to the Mediterranean (some of which still remain):

Then the enemies distanced themselves from him, toward the north. They placed themselves in the water district, facing the back-sea of the Mediterranean; and their hearts were stricken with fear of him.

But Horus, the Winged Measurer, followed close behind them in the boat of Ra, the Divine Iron in his hand.

And all his Helpers, armed with weapons of iron forged, were staged all around.

But the attempt to surround and entrap the enemies did not succeed: "For four days and four nights he roamed the waters in pursuit of them, without seeing even one of the enemies." Ra then advised him to go up again in the Winged Disk, and this time Horus was able to see the fleeing enemies; "he hurled his Divine Lance after them and he slew them, and performed a great overthrow of them. He also brought 142 enemy prisoners to the forepart of the boat of Ra,'' where they were quickly executed.

The Edfu temple inscription now shifts to a new panel, for indeed there began a new chapter in that War of the Gods. The enemies that had managed to escape ''directed themselves by the Lake of the North, setting themselves toward the Mediterranean, which they desired to reach by sailing through the water district. But the god smote their hearts [with fear], and when they reached the middle of the waters as they fled, they directed themselves from the western lake to the waters which connect with the lakes of the district Mer, in order to join themselves there with the enemies who were the Land of Seth.''

These verses provide not only geographical information; they also identify ''the enemies'' for the first time. The conflict had shifted to the chain of lakes that in antiquity, much more than nowadays, physically separated Egypt proper from the Sinai peninsula. To the east, beyond this watery barrier, lay the domain of Seth— the erstwhile adversary and slayer of Osiris, the father of Horus. Seth, we now learn, was the enemy against whose forces Horus had been advancing from the south. And now Horus reached the line dividing Egypt from the Land of Seth.

For a while there was a lull in the fighting, during which Horus brought up to the front line his armed Metal People, and Ra reached the scene in his boat. The enemies, too, regrouped and crossed back the waters, and a major battle followed. This time, 381 of the enemy were captured and executed (no casualty figures on the side of Horus are ever given in the text); and Horus, in hot pursuit, crossed the waters into the territory of Seth.

It was then, according to the inscription in the great temple of Edfu, that Seth was so enraged that he faced Horus for a series of battles—on the ground and in the air—for god-to-god combat. Of this combat there have been found several versions, as we shall see. What is interesting at this point is the fact brought out by E. A. Wallis Budge in *The Gods of the Egyptians:* that in the first involvement of men in the Wars of the Gods, it was the arming of mankind with the Divine Iron that brought victory to Horus: ''It is pretty clear that he owed his success chiefly to the superiority of the weapons with which he and his men were armed, and to the material of which they were made.''

Thus, according to Egyptian writings, did man learn to lift sword against man.

When all the fighting was over, Ra expressed satisfaction with the works of "these Metal People of Horus," and he decreed that henceforth they "shall dwell in sanctuaries" and shall be served with libations and offerings "as their reward, because they have slain the enemies of the god Horus." They were settled at Edfu, the Upper Egypt capital of Horus, and in This (Tanis in Greek, the biblical Zo'an), the Lower Egypt capital of the god. In time they outgrew their purely military role and attained the title Shamsu-Hor ("Attendants of Horus"), serving as his human aides and emissaries.

The inscription on the temple walls at Edfu, it has been established, was a copy of a text that was known to the Egyptian scribes from earlier sources; but when and by whom the original text had been composed, no one can really tell. Scholars who have studied the inscription have concluded that the accurate geographical and other data in the text indicate (in the words of E. A. Wallis Budge) "that we are not dealing entirely with mythological events; and it is nearly certain that the triumphant progress ascribed to *Hor-Behutet* (Horus of Edfu) is based upon the exploits of some victorious invader who established himself at Edfu in very early times."

As with all Egyptian historical texts, this one, too, begins with a date: "In the year 363." Such dates always indicate the year in the reign of the Pharaoh to whom the event pertains: each Pharaoh had his first year, second year, and so on. The text in question, however, deals not with the affairs of kings but with divine matters—a war among the gods. The text thus relates events that had happened in the "year 363" in the reign of certain gods and takes us back to the early times when gods, not men, ruled over Egypt.

That there indeed had been such a time, Egyptian traditions left no doubt. The Greek historian Herodotus (fifth century B.C.), on his extensive visit to Egypt, was given by the priests details of the Pharaonic dynasties and reigns. "The priests," he wrote, "said that Mên was the first king of Egypt, and that it was he who raised the dyke which protects Memphis from the inundations of the Nile," diverted the river, and proceeded to build Memphis on the reclaimed land. "Besides these works he also, the priests said, built the temple of Vulcan, which stands within the city, a vast edifice, very worthy of mention.

"Next they read me from a papyrus the names of 330 monarchs who were his successors upon the throne. In this number of successors there were eighteen Ethiopian kings, and one queen who was a native; all the rest were kings and Egyptians."

The priests then showed Herodotus rows of statues representing the successive Pharaohs and related to him various details pertaining to some of these kings and their claims to divine ancestry. "The beings represented by these images were very far indeed from being gods," Herodotus commented; "however," he went on to say:

> In times preceding them it was otherwise: Then Egypt had gods for its rulers, who dwelt upon the Earth with men, one of them being always supreme above the rest.
>
> The last of these was Horus, the son of Osiris, whom the Greeks called Apollo. He deposed Typhon, and ruled over Egypt as its last god-king.

In his book *Against Apion,* the first-century Jewish historian Flavius Josephus quoted as one of his sources on the history of Egypt the writings of an Egyptian priest named Manetho. Such writings were never found; but any doubt regarding the existence of such a historian was dispelled when it was realized that his writings formed the basis for several works by later Greek historians. It is now established with certainty that Manetho (his hieroglyphic name meant "Gift of Thoth"), indeed a high priest and great scholar, compiled the history of Egypt in several volumes at the command of king Ptolemy Philadelphus circa 270 B.C. The original manuscript was deposited in the great library of Alexandria, only to perish there together with numerous other invaluable documents when the building and its contents were set on fire by Muslim conquerors in A.D. 642.

Manetho was the first known historian to have divided the Egyptian rulers into dynasties—a practice continued to this day. His King List—names, lengths of reign, order of succession, and some other pertinent information—has been mainly preserved through the writings of Julius Africanus and Eusebius of Caesarea (in the third and fourth centuries A.D.). These and other versions based on Manetho agree that he listed as the first ruler of the first dynasty of Pharaohs the king Mên (Menes in Greek)—the very same king that Herodotus reported, based on his own investigations in Egypt.

This fact has since been confirmed by modern discoveries, such as the Tablet of Abydos (Fig. 7) in which the Pharaoh Seti I, accompanied by his son, Ramses II, listed the names of seventy-five of his predecessors. The first one to be named is Mena.

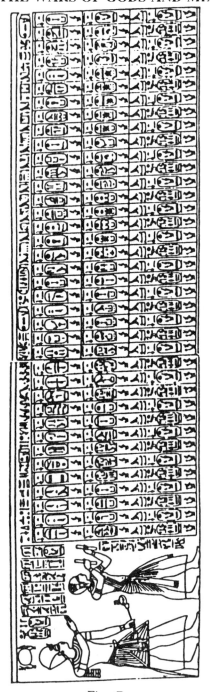

Fig. 7

If Herodotus was correct in regard to the dynasties of Egyptian Pharaohs, could he also have been right in regard to a "preceding time" when "Egypt had gods for its rulers"?

Manetho, we find, had agreed with Herodotus also on that matter. The dynasties of the Pharaohs, he wrote, were preceded by four other dynasties—two of gods, one of demigods, and a transitional dynasty. At first, he wrote, seven great gods reigned over Egypt for a total of 12,300 years:

Ptah	ruled	9,000 years
Ra	ruled	1,000 years
Shu	ruled	700 years
Geb	ruled	500 years
Osiris	ruled	450 years
Seth	ruled	350 years
Horus	ruled	300 years
Seven gods	ruled	12,300 years

The second dynasty of gods, Manetho wrote, consisted of twelve divine rulers, the first of whom was the god Thoth; they reigned for 1,570 years. In all, he said, nineteen gods ruled for 13,870 years. Then there followed a dynasty of thirty demigods, who reigned for 3,650 years; in all, there were forty-nine divine and semidivine rulers over Egypt, reigning a total of 17,520 years. Then, for 350 years, there was no ruler over the whole of Egypt; it was a chaotic time, during which ten human rulers continued the kingship at This. Only thereafter did Mên establish the first human dynasty of Pharaohs and built a new capital dedicated to the god Ptah—the "Vulcan" of Herodotus.

A century and a half of archaeological discoveries and the deciphering of the hieroglyphic writing have convinced scholars that the Pharaonic dynasties probably began in Egypt circa 3100 B.C.; indeed, under a ruler whose hieroglyph reads Mên. He united Upper and Lower Egypt and established his capital at a new city called Men-Nefer ("The Beauty of Mên")—Memphis in Greek. His accession to this throne of a united Egypt had indeed followed a chaotic period of a disunited Egypt, as Manetho had stated. An inscription on an artifact known as the Palermo Stone has preserved at least nine archaic names of kings who wore only the Red Crown of Lower Egypt and who ruled before Menes. Tombs and actual artifacts have been found belonging to archaic kings bearing such names as "Scorpion," Ka, Zeser, Narmer, and Sma. Sir Flinders Petrie, the noted Egyptologist, claimed in his *The Royal Tombs of the First Dynasty* and other writings that these names correspond to names given by Manetho in the list of ten human rulers who reigned at Tanis during the chaotic centuries. Petrie suggested that this group, which preceded the First Dynasty, be called "Dynasty O."

A major archaeological document dealing with Egyptian kingship, the so-called Turin Papyrus, begins with a dynasty of gods that lists Ra, Geb, Osiris, Seth, and Horus, then Thoth, Maat, and others, and assigns to Horus—just as Manetho did—a reign of 300 years. This papyrus, which dates from the time of Ramses II, lists after the divine rulers thirty-eight semidivine rulers: "Nineteen Chiefs of the White Wall and nineteen Venerables of the North." Between them and Menes, the Turin Papyrus states, there ruled human kings under the patronage of Horus; their epithet was Shamsu-Hor!

Addressing the Royal Society of Literature in London in 1843, the curator of Egyptian Antiquities at the British Museum, Dr. Samuel Birch, announced that he had counted on the papyrus and its fragments a total of 330 names—a number that "coincided with the 330 kings mentioned by Herodotus."

Even if they disagree among themselves on details, Egyptologists now agree that the archaeological discoveries sustain the information provided by the ancient historians concerning the dynasties begun by Menes, following a chaotic period of about ten rulers in a disunited Egypt; and that there had been a *prior period* when Egypt was united under rulers whose names could have been none other than Horus, Osiris, and so on. However, scholars who find it difficult to accept that these rulers were "gods" suggest that they were only "deified" human beings.

To throw more light on the subject, we can start with the very place chosen by Menes for the capital of the reunified Egypt. The location of Memphis, we find, was not a matter of chance; it was related to certain events pertaining to the gods. Nor was the manner in which Memphis was built unsymbolic: Menes built the city on an artificial mound, created through the diversion of the Nile at that spot and other extensive damming, dyking, and land-reclamation works. This he did in emulation of the manner in which Egypt itself had been created.

The Egyptians believed that "a very great god who came forth in the earliest times" arrived in the land and found it lying under water and mud. He undertook great works of dyking and land reclamation, literally raising Egypt out of the waters—thus explaining

Egypt's nickname "The Raised Land." This olden god was named Ptah—a "God of Heaven and Earth." He was considered to be a great engineer and master artificer.

The veracity of the legend of The Raised Land is enhanced by its technological aspects. The Nile is a peaceful and navigable river up to Syene (Aswan); beyond that, the river's southward course is treacherous and obstructed by several cataracts. Just as the level of the Nile is regulated today by the dams at Aswan, so apparently was it in prehistoric Egypt. Ptah, Egyptian legends held, established his base of operations on the island of Abu, the one called since Greek times Elephantine on account of its shape; it is located just above the first cataract of the Nile, at Aswan. In text and drawings (Fig. 8) Ptah, whose symbol was the serpent, was depicted as

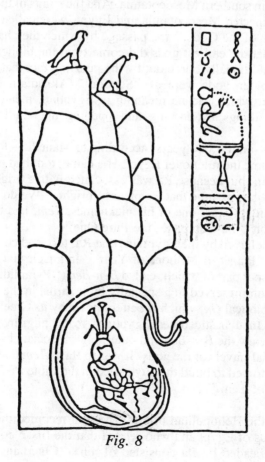

Fig. 8

controlling the Nile's waters from subterranean caverns. "It was he who kept the doors that held the inundations, who drew back the bolts at the proper time." In technical language we are being informed that at the most appropriate site from an engineering point of view, Ptah built "twin caverns" (two connected reservoirs) whose locks could be opened and closed, "bolted" and unbolted, thus regulating artificially the level and flow of the Nile's waters.

Ptah and the other gods were called, in Egyptian, *Ntr*—"Guardian, Watcher." They had come to Egypt, the Egyptians wrote, from *Ta-Ur,* the "Far/Foreign Land," whose name *Ur* meant "olden" but could have also been the actual place name—a place well known from Mesopotamian and biblical records: the ancient city of Ur in southern Mesopotamia. And the straits of the Red Sea, which connected Mesopotamia and Egypt, were called *Ta-Neter,* the "Place of the Gods," the passage by which they had come to Egypt. That the earliest gods did come from the biblical lands of Shem is additionally borne out by the puzzling fact that the names of these olden gods were of "Semitic" (Akkadian) derivation. Thus Ptah, which had no meaning in Egyptian, meant "he who fashioned things by carving and opening up" in the Semitic tongues.

In time—after 9,000 years, according to Manetho—Ra, a son of Ptah, became the ruler over Egypt. His name, too, had no meaning in Egyptian, but because Ra was associated with a bright celestial body, scholars assume that Ra meant "bright." We do know with greater certainty that one of his nicknames, *Tem,* had the Semitic connotation "the Complete, the Pure One."

It was believed by the Egyptians that Ra, too, had come to Earth from the "Planet of Millions of Years" in a Celestial Barge, the conical upper part of which, called *Ben-Ben* ("Pyramidion Bird"), was later on preserved in a specially built shrine in the sacred city *Anu* (the biblical *On,* which is better known by its Greek name Heliopolis). In dynastic times Egyptians made pilgrimages to this shrine to view the *Ben-Ben* and other relics associated with Ra and the celestial travels of the gods. It was to Ra as *Tem* that the Israelites were forced to build the city called in the Bible *Pi-Tom*—"The Gateway of Tem."

It was the Heliopolitan priests who first recorded the traditions of the gods of Egypt and who related that the first "company" of the gods headed by Ra consisted of nine "Guardians"—Ra and four divine couples who followed him. The first divine couple to rule when Ra tired of staying in Egypt were his own children, the male *Shu* ("Dryness") and the female *Tefnut* ("Moisture"); their main task, according to Egyptian tales, was to help Ra control the skies over the Earth.

Shu and Tefnut set the example for mortal Pharaohs in later times: the king selected his own half-sister as his royal spouse. They were followed on the divine throne—as both legends and Manetho inform us—by their children, again a brother-sister couple: *Geb* ("Who Piles Up the Earth") and *Nut* ("The Stretched-out Firmament").

The purely mythological approach to the Egyptian tales of the gods—that of primitive people watching Nature and seeing "gods" in its phenomena—has led scholars to assume that Geb represented the Earth deified, and Nut the Heavens; and that by calling Geb and Nut Father and Mother of the gods who thereafter reigned over Egypt, the Egyptians believed that the gods were born of the union of Earth and Heaven. But if the legends and verses in the *Pyramid Texts* and *The Book of the Dead* are to be taken more literally, it appears that Geb and Nut were so named on account of activities related to the periodic appearance of the *Bennu* bird, from which the Greeks obtained the legend of the Phoenix: an eagle whose feathers were red and gold, which died and reappeared at intervals lasting several millennia. It was for that bird—whose name was the same as that of the contraption in which Ra landed on Earth—that Geb engaged in great earthworks and Nut "stretched out the firmament of the sky." These feats, it appears, were carried out by the gods in the "Land of the Lions"; it was there that Geb "hath opened up the earth" for the great spherical object that came from the "stretched-out skies" and appeared on the horizon.

In the aftermath of the above-described feats, Geb and Nut turned over the direct rule of Egypt to their four children: *Asar* ("The All-Seeing"), whom the Greeks called Osiris, and his sister-wife *Ast*, better known as Isis; and Seth and his wife Nephtys (*Nebt-Hat*, "Lady of the House"), the sister of Isis. It was with these gods, who were truly gods of Egypt, that the Egyptian tales most concerned themselves; but in depicting them (Fig. 9) Seth was never shown without his animal disguise: his face was never seen, and the meaning of his name still defies Egyptologists, even if it is identical to the name given in the Bible to Adam and Eve's third son.

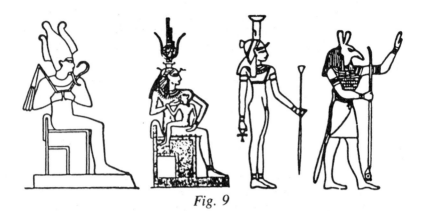

Fig. 9

With two brothers who married their own two sisters, the gods confronted a serious problem of succession. The only plausible solution was to divide the kingdom: Osiris was given the northern lowlands (Lower Egypt), and Seth was given the southern, mountainous part (Upper Egypt). How long this arrangement lasted we can only guess from Manetho's chronicles; but it is certain that Seth was not satisfied with the division of sovereignty and resorted to various schemes to gain control over the whole of Egypt.

Scholars have assumed that the sole motive of Seth was a craving for power. But once one grasps what the gods' rules of succession were, it becomes possible to understand the profound effect these rules had upon the affairs of the gods (and then of human kings). Since the gods (and then men) could have, in addition to the official spouse, one or more concubines, as well as beget children through illicit love affairs, the first rule of succession was this: the son first born to the official spouse was the heir to the throne. If the official spouse bore no son, the son first born to any of the concubines became the heir. However, if at any time, even after the birth of the Firstborn heir, a son was born to the ruler by his own half-sister, this son superseded the Firstborn and became the Legal Heir.

It was this custom that was the cause of much rivalry and strife among the Gods of Heaven and Earth and—we suggest—explains the basic motivation of Seth. Our source for this suggestion is the treatise *De Iside et Osiride (Of Isis and Osiris)* by Plutarch, a historian-biographer of the first century A.D., who wrote down for the Greeks and Romans of his time the legendary histories of the Near Eastern gods. The Egyptian sources on which he relied were believed at the time to have been writings of the god Thoth himself, who, as the Scribe of the Gods, recorded for all times their histories and deeds upon this Earth.

"Now the story of Isis and Osiris, its most significant [retained] and superfluous parts omitted, is thus briefly related," wrote Plutarch in his opening sentence and went on to tell that Nut (whom the Greeks compared with their goddess Rhea) had mothered three sons: the firstborn was Osiris, the last Seth. She also gave birth to two daughters, Isis and Nephtys. But not all of these children were really fathered by Geb: only Seth and Nephtys were. Osiris and his second brother were in truth fathered by the god Ra, who came unto his granddaughter Nut in stealth; and Isis was fathered by Thoth (the Greek god Hermes) who, "being likewise in love with the same goddess," reciprocated in various ways "in recompense for the favours which he had received from her."

The setting, then, was this: the firstborn was Osiris, and, though not by Geb, his claim to the succession was even greater, having been fathered by the great Ra himself. But the legitimate heir was Seth, having been born to the ruling Geb by his half-sister Nut. As if this were not enough, matters were further complicated by the race between the two brothers to assure that their son would be the next legitimate successor. To achieve that Seth could have fathered a son only by his half-sister Isis, whereas Osiris could achieve this by fathering a son by either Isis or Nephtys (both being only half-sisters to him). But Osiris deliberately blocked Seth's chances to have his descendants rule over Egypt by taking Isis as his spouse. Seth then married Nephtys; but as she was his full sister, none of their offspring could qualify.

So was the stage set for Seth's increasingly violent rage against Osiris, who deprived him both of the throne and of the succession.

The occasion for Seth's revenge, according to Plutarch, was the visit to Egypt of "a certain queen of Ethiopia named Aso." In conspiracy with his supporters Seth held a banquet in her honor, to which all the gods were invited. For his scheme Seth had a magnificent chest constructed, large enough to hold Osiris: "This chest he brought into the banqueting room; where, after it had been much admired by all who were present, Seth—as though in jest—promised to give it to any one of them whose body it would fit. Upon this the whole company, one after the other, went into the chest.

"Last of all, Osiris lay himself down in it, upon which the conspirators immediately ran together, clapped the cover upon it, and then fastened it down on the outside with nails, pouring likewise melted lead over it.'' They then carried the chest in which Osiris was imprisoned to the seashore, and where the Nile flows into the Mediterranean at Tanis sank the chest in the sea.

Dressed in mourning apparel and cutting off a lock of her hair as a sign of grief, Isis went in search of the chest. "At length she received more particular news of the chest, that it had been carried by the waves of the sea to the coast of Byblos" (in what is now Lebanon). Isis retrieved the chest holding the body of Osiris and hid it in a deserted place until she could figure out how to resurrect Osiris. But Seth somehow found all that out, seized the chest, and cut up the body of Osiris into fourteen pieces, which he dispersed all over Egypt.

Once again Isis went in search of the scattered limbs of her brother-husband. Some versions say that she buried the parts where she found them, starting the worship of Osiris at those places; others say she bound together the parts she found, starting the custom of mummification. All agree that she found all parts except one—the phallus of Osiris.

Nevertheless, before finally disposing of the body, she managed to extract from the body of Osiris its "essence," and self-inseminated herself with his seed, thus conceiving and giving birth to the boy Horus. She hid him from Seth in the papyrus swamps of the Nile delta.

Many legends have been found concerning the events that followed: legends copied and recopied on papyri, forming chapters of *The Book of the Dead,* or used as verses in the Pyramid texts. Put together they reveal a major drama that involved legal maneuvering, kidnapping for purposes of state, a magical return from the dead, homosexuality, and finally a great war—a drama in which the stake was the Divine Throne of the gods.

Since all seemed to believe that Osiris had perished without leaving an heir, Seth saw this as his chance to obtain a legitimate heir by forcing Isis to espouse him. He kidnapped her and held her prisoner until she consented, but with the aid of the god Thoth, Isis managed to escape. A version recorded on the so-called Metternich Stela, composed as a tale by Isis in her own words, describes her escape in the night and her adventures until she reached the swamps where Horus was hidden. She found Horus dying from a scorpion's sting (Fig. 10). One can infer from the text that it was word of her son's dying that prompted her escape. The people who

Fig. 10

lived in the swamps came out at her cries but were helpless to be of any aid. Then help came from a spacecraft:

Then Isis sent forth a cry to heaven and addressed her appeal to the Boat of Millions of Years.

And the Celestial Disk stood still, and moved not from the place where it was.

And Thoth came down, and he was provided with magical powers, and possessed the great power which made the word become indeed. And he said:

"O Isis, thou goddess, thou glorious one, who has knowledge of the mouth; behold, no evil shall come upon the child Horus, for his protection cometh from the Boat of Ra.

"I have come this day in the Boat of the Celestial Disk from the place where it was yesterday. When the night cometh, this Light shall drive away [the poison] for the healing of Horus. . . .

"I have come from the skies to save the child for his mother."

Revived from death by the artful Thoth and, some texts say, immunized forever as a result of Thoth's treatment, Horus grew up as *Netch-atef*, "Avenger of his Father." Educated and trained in martial arts by goddesses and gods who sided with Osiris, he was groomed as a Divine Prince worthy of celestial association. Then, one day, he appeared before the Council of the Gods to claim the throne of Osiris.

Of the many gods who were surprised by his appearance, none was more so than Seth. All seemed to wonder: Did Osiris indeed father this son? As described in a text known as the *Chester Beatty Papyrus No. 1*, Seth suggested that the gods' deliberations be recessed so as to give him a chance to discuss the problem peacefully with his newly appeared nephew. He invited Horus to "come, let us pass a happy day in my house," and Horus agreed. But what Seth had in mind was not peacemaking; his mind was set on trickery:

> And when it was eventide, the bed was spread for them, and the twain lay thereon.
> And in the night Seth caused his member to become stiff, and he made it go between the loins of Horus.

When the gods next met in council, Seth demanded that the Office of Ruler be resolved as his, for Horus was disqualified: whether or not he was of the seed of Osiris, the seed of Seth was now in him, entitling him to succeed, not precede, Seth!

Now it was the turn of Horus to surprise the gods. When Seth poured out his semen, "I caught the seed between my hands," Horus said. In the morning he showed it to his mother, telling her what had happened. Isis then made Horus erect his member and pour his semen into a cup. Then she went to the garden of Seth and poured the semen of Horus on the lettuce that Seth then unknowingly ate. So, announced Horus, "Not only is Seth's seed not in me, but *my* seed is *in him!* It is Seth who has been disqualified!"

Baffled, the gods called upon Thoth to resolve the issue. He checked the semen that Horus had given his mother, which Isis kept in a pot; it was found to be indeed the semen of Seth. He then scanned the body of Seth and confirmed that it contained the semen of Horus. . . .

Enraged, Seth did not wait for the discussions to continue. Only a fight to the bitter end could now settle the issue, he shouted as he left.

Seth had by then, per Manetho, ruled 350 years. If we add to this the time—thirteen years, we believe—it had taken Isis to find the thirteen parts of the dismembered Osiris, it was indeed "in the year

363'' that Ra joined Horus in Nubia, from there to accompany Horus on his war against ''the Enemy.'' In *Horus, Royal God of Egypt*, S. B. Mercer summed up the scholarly opinions on the subject with these emphatic words: ''The story of the conflict between Horus and Seth represents a historical event.''

According to the Edfu temple inscription, the first face-to-face battle between Horus and Seth took place at the ''Lake of the Gods,'' thereafter known as the ''Lake of Battle.'' Horus managed to hit Seth with his Divine Lance; when Seth fell down, Horus captured him and brought him before Ra. ''His spear was in his [Seth's] neck, and the legs of the evil one were chained, and his mouth had been closed by a blow from the club of the god [Horus].'' Ra decided that Isis and Horus could do with Seth and the other captured ''conspirators'' as they pleased.

But as Horus began to slay the captives by cutting off their heads, Isis had pity on her brother Seth, and set him free. There are several versions of what ensued, including one known as the *Fourth Sallier Papyrus;* and, according to most, the release of Seth so infuriated Horus that he beheaded his own mother, Isis; but the god Thoth put her severed head back in place and resurrected her. (This incident is also reported by Plutarch.)

After his escape Seth at first hid in a subterranean tunnel. After a lull of six days, a series of aerial battles ensued. Horus took to the air in a *Nar* (a ''Fiery Pillar''), which was depicted as an elongated, cylindrical vessel equipped with fins or short wings. Its bulkhead contained two ''eyes,'' which kept changing color from blue to red and back to blue; from the rear, jetlike trails were shown (Fig. 11); from the front, the contraption spewed out rays.

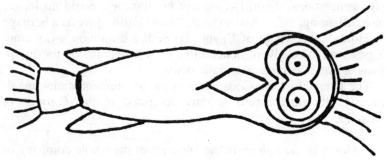

Fig. 11

(The Egyptian texts, all written by the followers of Horus, contain no description of Seth's aerial vehicle.)

The texts describe a battle that ranged far and wide, and the first to be hit was Horus—struck by a bolt of light from Seth's vehicle. The *Nar* lost one of its "eyes," and Horus continued the fight from the Winged Disk of Ra. From out of this he shot a "harpoon" at Seth; now Seth was hit, and lost his testicles. . . .

Dwelling on the nature of the weapon, W. Max Müller wrote in *Egyptian Mythology* that it had "a strange, practically impossible head" and was nicknamed in the hieroglyphic texts "the weapon of thirty." As ancient depictions reveal (Fig. 12a), the "harpoon" was indeed an ingenious three-in-one rocket: as the first, larger missile was fired, the way was opened for the two smaller missiles to be launched. The nickname ("Weapon of Thirty") suggests that the missiles were what we nowadays call Multiple Warhead Missiles, each missile holding ten warheads.

Through sheer coincidence, but probably because similar circumstances result in similar connotations, the McDonnell Douglas Corporation of St. Louis, Missouri, has named its newly developed naval guided missile "The Harpoon" (Fig. 12b).

The great gods called a truce and once again summoned the adversaries before the Council of the Gods. We glean details of the deliberations from a text inscribed on a stone column by the Pharaoh Shabako (eighth century B.C.), who stated that the text is a copy made from a very old leather scroll, "devoured by worms," which was found buried in the great temple of Ptah at Memphis. The Council, at first, redivided Egypt between Horus and Seth along the lines of the division at the time of Osiris, but Geb had second thoughts and upset the decision, for he was concerned with the question of continuity: Who would "open the body" to successive generations? Seth, having lost his testicles, could no longer have offspring. . . . And so Geb, "Lord Earth, gave as a heritage to Horus" the whole of Egypt. To Seth a dominion away from Egypt was to be given; henceforth, he was deemed by the Egyptians to have become an Asiatic deity.

The Council of the Gods adopted the recommendations unanimously. Its final action is thus described in the *Papyrus of Hunefer:*

Horus is triumphant in the presence of the whole company of the gods. The sovereignty over the world hath been given unto him, and his dominion is in the uttermost parts of Earth.

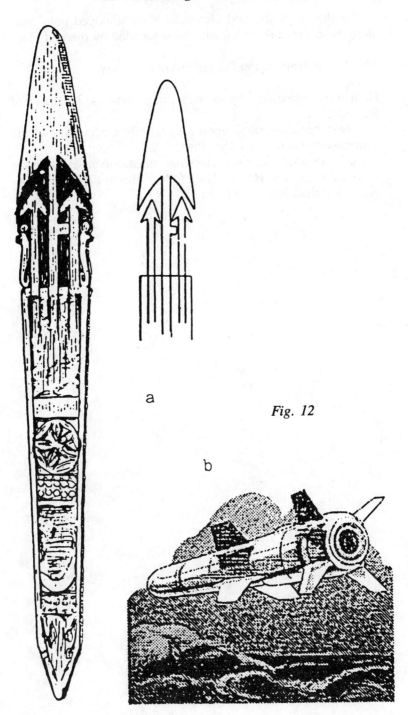

a

Fig. 12

b

The throne of the god Geb hath been adjudged unto him,
along with the rank which hath been founded by the god Shu.

This legitimization, the Papyrus went on to say:

Hath been formalized by decrees [lodged] in the Chamber of
Records;
It hath been inscribed upon a metal tablet according to the
commandments of thy father Ptah. . . .
Gods celestial and gods terrestrial transfer themselves to the
services of thy son Horus. They follow him to the Hall of Decrees. He shall lord over them.

3

THE MISSILES OF ZEUS
AND INDRA

After Herodotus had visited Egypt in the fifth century B.C., he was convinced that it was from the Egyptians that the Greeks had obtained their notions and beliefs of the gods; writing for his countrymen, he employed the names of Greek gods to describe the comparable Egyptian deities.

His conviction of the Egyptian origin of Greek theology stemmed not only from comparable attributes and meanings of the gods' names, but also (and mostly) from similarities in the tales concerning them. Of these, one uncanny parallel certainly must have struck him as no mere coincidence: it was the tale of the castration of one god by another in a struggle for supremacy.

The Greek sources from which Herodotus could have drawn are, fortunately, still available: various literary works, such as Homer's *Iliad;* the *Odes* of Pindar of Thebes, written and well known just before Herodotus' time; and first and foremost, the *Theogony* ("Divine Genealogy") by Hesiod, a native of Askara in central Greece who composed this work and another *(Works and Days)* in the eighth century B.C.

A poet, Hesiod chose to attribute the writing of the *Theogony* to the Muses, goddesses of music, literature, and art, who, he wrote, encouraged him "to celebrate in song" the histories "of the revered race of gods, from the beginning . . . and then to chant of the race of men and strong giants; and so gladden the heart of Zeus within Olympus." This all happened when he was "shepherding his lambs" one day near the Holy Mountain which was their abode.

In spite of this pastoral introduction, the tale of the gods as revealed to Hesiod was mostly one of passion, revolt, cunning, and mutilation; as well as of struggle and global wars. In spite of all the hymnal glorification of Zeus, there is no apparent attempt to cover up the chain of bloody violence that had led to his supremacy.

Whatever the Muses sang of, Hesiod wrote down; and "these things did sing the Muses, nine daughters begotten of Zeus":

> Verily, at first Chaos came to be,
> and next the wide-bosomed Gaea . . .
> And dim Tartarus, in the depths of wide-pathed Earth,
> and Eros, fairest among the deathless gods . . .
> From Chaos came forth Erebus and black Nyx;
> And of Nyx were born Aether and Hemera.

This first group of celestial gods was completed when *Gaea* ("Earth") brought forth *Uranus* ("Starry Heaven") and then espoused her own firstborn son so that he might be included in the First Dynasty of the gods. Besides Uranus, and soon after he was born, Gaea also gave birth to his graceful sister, Uraea, and to "Pontus, the fruitless Deep with his raging swell."

Then the next generation of gods were born—offspring of Gaea's mating with Uranus:

> Afterwards she lay with Uranus,
> and bare deep-swirling Oceanus;
> Coeus and Crius and Hyperion and Iapetus;
> Theia and Rhea, Themis and Mnemosyne;
> And gold-crowned Phoebe, and lovely Thetys.
> After them was born Cronos, the wily,
> youngest and most terrible of her children.

In spite of the fact that these twelve were offspring of the mating of a son with his own mother, the children—six males, six females—were worthy of their divine origins. But as Uranus got lustier and lustier, the offspring that followed—though formidable in might—displayed various deformities. First of the "monsters" to be born were the three Cyclopes, Brontes ("The Thunderer"), Steropes ("The Maker of Lightning"), and Arges ("Who Makes Radiation"); "in all else they were like the gods, but one eye only was set in the midst of their foreheads; and they were named 'Orb-eyed' (Cyclopes) because one orbed eye was set in their foreheads."

"And again three more sons were born of Gaea and Uranus, great and valiant beyond telling: Cottus and Briareos and Gyes, audacious children." Of giant size, the three were called Hekatoncheires ("The Hundred-Armed"): "From their shoulders sprang an hundred arms, not to be approached, and each had fifty heads upon his shoulders.''

"And Cronos hated his lusty sire," Hesiod wrote; but "Uranus rejoiced in his evil doing."

It was then that Gaea "shaped a great sickle and told her plan to her dear sons," whereby their "sinful father" would be punished for his "vile outrages": to cut off the genitals of Uranus and put an end to his sexual drives. But "fear seized them all"; and only "great Cronos, the wily, took courage."

And so it was that Gaea gave Cronos the sickle she had made of gray flint and hid him "in an ambush" in her quarters, which were by the Mediterranean Sea.

And Uranus came at nighttime, longing for love;
and he lay about Gaea, spreading himself upon her.
Then the son from his ambush
stretched forth his left hand to grasp;
and in his right hand he held
the great long sickle with jagged teeth.
Swiftly, he cut off his own father's genitals,
and cast them away, to fall behind him . . .
into the surging sea.

The deed was done, but the castration of Uranus did not completely terminate his line of offspring. As his blood gushed forth, some of the blood drops impregnated Gaea, and she conceived and bore "the strong Erinyes" (female Furies of vengeance) "and the great Gigantes with gleaming armor, holding long spears in their hands; and the Nymphs whom they call Meliae ['the Nymphs of the ash tree']." Of the castrated genitals, leaving a trail of foam as the surging sea carried them to the island of Cyprus, "there came forth an awful and lovely goddess . . . gods and men call her *Aphrodite* ['She of the Foam']."

The incapacitated Uranus called out to the monster-gods for vengeance. His own children, he cried out, had become *Titans,* Strainers who had "strained and did presumptuously the dreadful deed''; now the other gods had to make sure "that vengeance for it would afterwards come." The frightened Cronos then imprisoned the Cyclopes and the other monstrous giants far away, so that none would answer the call of Uranus.

All along, while Uranus was busy bringing forth his own offspring, the other gods were also proliferating; their children bore names indicating their attributes—by and large benevolent. Now, after the evil deed, the goddess Nyx responded to his call by bringing forth the deities of evil: "She bare the Destinies and the ruthless avenging Fates: Clotho ['The Spinner'] and Lachesis ['The Disposer of Lots'] and Atropos ['Inevitable']. . . . She bare Doom and Black Fate and Death . . . and Blame and Painful Woe . . . Famine and Sorrows." And she also brought into the world "Deceit and Strife . . . as also Fighting, Battles, Murders, Killings, Quarrels, Lying Words, Disputes, Lawlessness and Ruin." Lastly there was borne by Nyx *Nemesis* ("Retribution"). The call of Uranus has been answered: fighting, battles, and war came to be among the gods.

It was into this dangerous world that the Titans were bringing forth the third generation of the gods. Fearful of retribution, they kept closely to each other, five of the six brothers espousing five of their own six sisters. Of these divine brother-sister couples, most important was that of Cronos and Rhea, for it was Cronos, by reason of his bold deed, who had assumed the leadership among the gods. Of this union, Rhea gave birth to three daughters and three sons: Hestia, Demeter, and Hera; and Hades, Poseidon, and Zeus.

No sooner had one of these children been born than "the great Cronos swallowed each . . . intent that no other of the proud Sons of Heaven should hold kingly office among the deathless gods." The reason for eliminating his own offspring by swallowing them was a prophecy he had learned of, that "strong though he was, he was destined to be overcome by his own son": Fate was to repeat unto Cronos that which he had done unto his father.

But Fate could not be evaded. Wisened to the tricks of Cronos, Rhea hid her last-born son Zeus on the island of Crete. To Cronos she gave instead of the baby "a great stone wrapped in swaddling clothes." Not realizing the deception, Cronos swallowed the stone, thinking it was the baby Zeus. Soon thereafter he began vomiting, disgorging one by one all the children he had previously swallowed.

"As the years rolled on, the strength and glorious limbs of the prince [Zeus] increased quickly." For a while, as a worthy grandson of the lusty Uranus, Zeus chased lovely goddesses, often getting into trouble with their companion gods. But then he turned his mind to affairs of state. For ten years a war had been raging between the older Titans, "the lordly Titans from high Mount Othyres" (which was their abode), and the younger gods "whom rich-haired Rhea bare in union with Cronos" and who settled on the opposite Mount Olympus. "With bitter wrath they were fighting continually with one another at that time for ten full years, and the hard strife had no close or end for either side, and the issue of war hung evenly balanced.''

Was this fighting merely the culmination of deteriorating relations between neighboring godly colonies, an outbreak of rivalry between intermingled and unfaithful gods and goddesses (where mothers slept with their sons, and uncles impregnated their nieces), or the first instance of the everlasting rebellion of the young against the old regime? The *Theogony* does not provide a clear answer, but later Greek legends and plays suggest that all these motives combined to create a prolonged and "stubborn war" between the younger and the older gods.

It was this ongoing war that was seen by Zeus as his chance to seize the lordship over the gods and thereby—knowingly or unknowingly—fulfill the destiny to which his father Cronos had been fated, by deposing him.

As his first step Zeus "set free from their deadly bonds the brothers of his father, sons of Uranus, whom his father in his foolishness had bound.'' In gratitude, the three Cyclopes gave him the divine weapons Gaea had hidden away from Uranus: "The Thunder, and the Radiating Thunderbolt and the Lightning.'' They also gave Hades a magic helmet, which made its wearer invisible; and Poseidon received a magical trident, which could make the earth and sea shake.

To refresh the Hekatoncheires after their long captivity and return their vigor to them, Zeus provided the trio with "nectar and ambrosia, the same that the gods eat''; then he addressed them and said:

Hear me,
O bright children of Uranus and Gaea,
   that I may say what my heart within bids me.
A long while now have we,
   who are sprung from Cronos, and the Titan gods,
   fought with each other every day,
   to get victory and to prevail.
Would you now show your great might and strength,
   and face the Titans in the bitter strife?

And Cottus, one of the Hundred-Armed, answered him and said: "Divine one, you speak that which we know well . . .

through your devising we are come back from the murky gloom and from our merciless bonds. And so now, with fixed purpose and deliberate counsel, we will aid your power in the dreadful strife, and fight against the Titans in hard battle.''

So ''all that were born of Cronos, together with those dreaded mighty ones of overwhelming strength whom Zeus brought up to light . . . they all, both male and female, stirred up the hated battle that day.'' Arrayed against these Olympians were the older Titans, who also ''eagerly strengthened their ranks.''

As the battle was joined it ranged all over the Earth and in the skies:

> The boundless sea rang terribly around,
>   and the earth crashed loudly;
> Wide heaven was shaken and groaned,
>   and high Olympus reeled from its foundations
>   under the charge of the undying gods.
> From the deep sound of the gods' feet,
>   and the fearful onset of their hard missiles,
>   the heavy quaking reached even far Tartarus.

In a verse reminiscent of the Dead Sea Scroll text, the *Theogony* recalled the war cries of the battling gods:

> Thus, then, they launched their grievous
>   bolts at one another;
> And the cry of both armies as they shouted
>   reached to the starry heaven
>   as they clashed with a great battle-cry.

Zeus himself was fighting with all his might, using his Divine Weapons to the utmost. ''From the skies, opposite Mount Olympus, he came forthwith, hurling his lightning. The bolts flew thick and fast from his strong hand, Thunder and Lightning together, whirling as an awesome flame. The fertile earth crashed around in burning, and the vast wood crackled aloud with fire all about. All the land seethed, as did the sweetwater streams and the salty sea.''

Then Zeus hurled a Thunder-Stone (Fig. 13) against Mount Othyres; it was, indeed, nothing short of an atomic explosion:

Fig. 13

The hot vapor lapped around the Titans,
   of Gaea born;
Flame unspeakable rose bright to the upper air.
The Flashing glare of the Thunder-Stone,
   its lightning, blinded their eyes—
   so strong it was.
Astounding heat seized Chaos . . .
It seemed as if Earth and wide Heaven above
   had come together;
A mighty crash, as though Earth was hurled to ruin.

"So great a crash was there while the gods clashed together in strife."

In addition to the awesome sound, the blinding flash, and the extreme heat, the hurling of the Thunder-Stone also created an immense wind storm:

> Also were the winds brought rumbling,
>   earthquake and duststorm,
>   thunder and lightning.

All this did the Thunder-Stone of great Zeus bring about. And when the two contending camps heard and saw what had happened, "an horrible uproar of terrible strife arose; mighty deeds were shown; and the battle inclined." The fighting was abating; for the gods had the upper hand over the Titans.

"Insatiated for war," the three Cyclopes set upon the Titans, overpowering them with hand-held missiles. "They bound them in bitter chains," and hurled them into captivity to far Tartarus. "There, by the counsel of Zeus who rides the clouds, the Titan gods are hidden under misty gloom, in a dank place at the ends of huge Earth." The three Cyclopes stayed there, too, as "trusty warders of Zeus," to watch over the imprisoned Titans.

As Zeus was about to claim "the aegis," the suzerainty over all the gods, a sudden challenger appeared on the scene. For, "when Zeus had driven the Titans from heaven, great Gaea bare her youngest child Typhoeus of the love of Tartarus, with the aid of golden Aphrodite." Typhoeus ("Typhon") was a real monster: "Strength was with his hands in all that he did, and the feet of the strong god were untiring. From his shoulders grew an hundred heads of a snake, a fearful dragon, with dark, flickering tongues. From under the brows of his eyes, in his marvellous heads, fire flashed; and fire burned from his heads as he glared. And there were voices in all his dreadful heads, which uttered incredible sounds": the sound of a man as he speaks, and the sound of a bull, and that of a lion, and the sound of a puppy. (According to Pindar and Aeschylus, Typhon was gigantic in height, "and his head reached to the stars.")

"Truly a thing past help would have happened on that day," the Muses revealed to Hesiod; it was almost inevitable that Typhoeus "would have come to reign over mortals and immortals." But Zeus was quick to perceive the danger and lost no time in attacking him.

The series of battles that ensued were no less awesome than the fighting between the gods and the Titans, for the Snake-God Typhon was equipped with wings and could fly about just as Zeus (Fig. 14). "Zeus thundered hard and mightily, and the earth around resounded terribly, as did the wide heaven above and the sea and the watery streams, even the nether parts of the Earth." Divine Weapons were again employed—by both combatants:

Fig. 14

Through the two of them,
    through the thunder and lightning,
    heat engulfed the dark-blue seas;
And through the fire from the Monster,
    and the scorching winds and blazing Thunderbolt,
    the whole Earth seethed, and sky and sea.
Great waves raged along the beaches . . .
And there arose an endless shaking.   '

In the Lower World, "Hades trembled where he ruled"; tremble did the Titans imprisoned at the ends of earth. Chasing each other in the skies and over land, Zeus managed to be the first to achieve a direct hit with his "lurid Thunderbolt." The bolt "burned all the marvelous heads of the monster, all that were around him"; and Typhoeus crashed down to earth in his marvelous contraption:

When Zeus had vanquished him
and lashed him with his strokes,
Typhoeus was hurled down a maimed wreck.
The huge earth groaned.
A flame shot forth from the stricken lord
in the dim, rugged, secluded valley of the Mount,
when he was smitten.
A great part of huge earth was scorched
by the terrible vapor,
melting as tin melts when heated by man's art . . .
In the glow of a blazing fire
did the earth melt down.

In spite of the crash and the tremendous impact of Typhon's vehicle, the god himself remained alive. According to the *Theogony*, Zeus cast him, too, "into wide Tartarus." With this victory his reign was secure; and he turned to the important business of procreation, bringing forth progeny by wives and concubines alike.

Though the *Theogony* described only one battle between Zeus and Typhon, the other Greek writings assert that that was the final battle, preceded by several others in which Zeus was the first one to be hurt. Initally Zeus fought with Typhon at close quarters, using the special sickle his mother had given him for the "evil deed," for it was his purpose also to castrate Typhon. But Typhon enmeshed Zeus in his net, wrested his sickle away, and with it cut out the sinews of Zeus' hands and feet. He then deposited the helpless Zeus, his sinews, and his weapons in a cave.

But the gods Aegipan and Hermes found the cave, resurrected Zeus by restoring his sinews, and returned his weapons to him. Zeus then escaped and flew back "in a Winged Chariot" to Olympus, where he acquired a new supply of bolts for his Thunderer. With these Zeus renewed the attack on Typhon, driving him to Mount Nyssa, where the Fates tricked Typhon into eating the food of mortal men; whereupon he was weakened instead of being strengthened. The renewed fighting began in the skies over Mount Haemus in Thrace, continued over Mount Etna in Sicily, and ended over Mount Casius on the Asiatic coast of the eastern Mediterranean. There Zeus, using his Thunderbolt, shot Typhon down from the skies.

The similarity between the battles, the weapons used, the locations, as well as the tales of castration, mutilation, and resurrection—all in the course of a struggle for succession—convinced

Herodotus (and other Greek classical historians) that the Greeks had borrowed their theogony from the Egyptians. Aegipan stood for the African Ram God of Egypt, and Hermes paralleled the god Thoth. Hesiod himself reported that when Zeus came unto the mortal beauty Alcmena so that she might bear him the heroic Heracles, he slipped at night from Mount Olympus and went to the land of Typhaonion, resting there atop the *Phikion* (The Sphinx Mountain). "The deadly Sphinx that destroyed the *Cadmeans*" ("The Ancients"), which featured in the doings of Hera, the official spouse of Zeus, was also connected in these legends with Typhon and his domain. And Apollodorus reported that when Typhon was born and grew to an incredible size, the gods rushed to Egypt to take a look at the awesome monster.

Most scholars have held that Mount Casius, the site of the final battle between Zeus and Typhon, was located near the mouth of the Orontes river in today's Syria. But as Otto Eissfeldt has shown in a major study *(Baal Zaphon, Zeus Kasios und der Durchgang der Israeliten durches Meer),* there was another mount called by that name in antiquity—a promontory on the Serbonic Sealet that juts out of the Sinai peninsula into the Mediterranean Sea. He suggested that that was the mount referred to in the legends.

Once again, all one had to do was to trust the information given to Herodotus in Egypt. Describing the land route from Phoenicia to Egypt via Philistia (*History,* Book III, 5), he wrote that the Asian lands "extend to Lake Serbonis, near the place where Mount Casius juts out into the sea. Egypt begins at Lake Serbonis, where the tale goes that Typhon hid himself."

Once again, Greek and Egyptian tales converged, with the Sinai peninsula as the climax.

Notwithstanding the many connecting threads the ancient Greeks had found between their theogony and that of Egypt, it was much farther away—in India—that nineteenth-century European scholars have found even more amazing parallels.

No sooner had Sanskrit, the language of ancient India, been mastered at the end of the eighteenth century than Europe began to be enchanted by translations of hitherto unknown writings. At first a field dominated by the British, the study of Sanskrit literature, philosophy, and mythology was by the mid-nineteenth century a favorite of German scholars, poets, and intellectuals, for Sanskrit turned out to be a mother tongue of the Indo-European languages (to which German belonged), and its bearers to India were migrants from the shores of the Caspian Sea—"Aryans," as the Germans believed their ancestors, too, to have been.

Central to this literature were the Vedas, sacred scriptures believed by Hindu tradition to be "not of human origin," having been composed by the gods themselves in a previous age. They were brought to the Indian subcontinent by the Aryan migrants sometime in the second millennium B.C., as oral traditions. But as time went on, more and more of the original 100,000 verses were lost; so, circa 200 B.C., a sage wrote down the remaining verses, dividing them into four parts: the Rig-Veda (the "Veda of Verses"), which is made up of ten books; the Sama-Veda (the "Chanted Vedas"); the Yajur-Veda (mostly sacrificial prayers); and the Atharva-Veda (spells and incantations).

In time, the various components of the Vedas and the auxiliary literature that stemmed from them (the Mantras, Brahmanas, Aranyakas, Upanishads) were augmented by the non-Vedic Puranas ("Ancient Writings"). Together with the great epic tales of the Mahabharata and the Ramayana, they make up the sources of the Aryan and Hindu tales of Heaven and Earth, gods and heroes.

Because of the long oral interval, the length and profusion of texts finally written down over many centuries, the many names, generic terms, and epithets employed for the deities interchangeably—and the fact that many of these original names and terms were non-Aryan after all—consistency and precision are not hallmarks of this Sanskrit literature. Yet some facts and events emerge as basic tenets of the Aryan-Hindu legacy.

In the beginning, these sources relate, there were only the celestial bodies, "The Primeval Ones Who Flow." There was an upheaval in the heavens, and "The Dragon" was split in two by the "Flowing One of Storms." Calling the two parts by names of non-Aryan origin, the tales assert that *Rehu,* the upper part of the destroyed planet, unceasingly traverses the heavens in search of vengeance; the lower part, *Ketu* ("The Cut-off One"), has joined the "Primeval Ones" in their "flowing" (orbits). Many Ages then passed, and a dynasty of Gods of Heaven and Earth made its appearance. The heavenly Mar-Ishi, who headed them, had seven (or ten) children by his consort *Prit-Hivi* ("The Broad One"), who personified the Earth. One of them, *Kas-Yapa* ("He of the Throne"), made himself chief of the *Devas* ("The Shiny Ones"), seizing the title *Dyaus-Pitar* ("Sky Father")—the undoubted source of the Greek title-name Zeus ("Dyaus") and its Roman parallel Jupiter ("Dyauspiter").

Quite prolific, Kasyapa begot many gods, giants, and monstrous offspring by diverse wives and concubines. Most prominent, and individually known and revered since Vedic times, were the Adityas—some born to Kasyapa by his consort Aditi ("Boundless"). Numbering seven at first, they were Vishnu, Varuna, Mitra, Rudra, Pushan, Tvashtri, and Indra. Then the Aditis were joined by Agni, a son of Kasyapa either by his spouse Aditi or (as some texts suggest) by his own mother Prithivi. As in the Greek Olympian circle, the number of the Aditis finally rose to twelve. Among them were Bhaga, who is believed by scholars to have become the supreme Slavic god Bogh. The last one to be born by Aditi—though whether he was fathered by Kasyapa was uncertain—was Surya.

Tvashtri ("Fashioner"), in his role as "All-Accomplishing," the artisan of the gods, provided them with aerial cars and magical weapons. From a blazing celestial metal he fashioned a discus for Vishnu, a trident for Rudra, a "fire weapon" for Agni, a "bolt-hurling Thunderer" for Indra, and a "flying mace" for Surya. In ancient Hindu depictions, all these weapons appeared as hand-held missiles of diverse shapes (Fig. 15). In addition, the gods acquired other weapons from Tvashtri's assistants; Indra, for example, obtained an "aerial net" with which he could snare his foes during sky battles.

Fig. 15

The celestial chariots or "aerial cars" were invariably described as bright and radiant, made of or plated with gold. Indra's *Vimana* (aerial car) had lights shining at its sides and moved "swifter than thought," traversing rapidly vast distances. Its unseen steeds were "Sun-eyed," emitting a reddish hue, but also changing colors. In other instances the aerial cars of the gods were described as multitiered; sometimes they could not only fly in the air, but also travel under water. In the epic tale of the Mahabharata, the arrival of the gods for a wedding feast in a fleet of aerial cars is described thus (we follow the translation of R. Dutt in *Mahabharata, The Epic of Ancient India*):

> The gods, in cloud-borne chariots,
>   came to view the scene so fair:
> Bright Adityas in their splendor,
>   Maruts in the moving air;
> Winged Suparnas, scaly Nagas,
>   Deva Rishies pure and high,
> For their music famed, Gandharvas;
>   (and) fair Apsaras of the sky. . . .
> Bright celestial cars in concourse
>   sailed upon the cloudless sky.

The texts also speak of the *Ashvins* ("Drivers"), gods who specialized in piloting aerial chariots. "Swift as young falcons," they were "the best of charioteers who reach the heavens," always piloting their craft in pairs, accompanied by a navigator. Their vehicles, which sometimes appeared in groups, were golden-made, "bright and radiant . . . with easy seat and lightly rolling." They were constructed on a triple principle, having three levels, three seats, three supporting poles, and three rotating wheels. "That chariot of yours," Hymn 22 of Book VIII of the Rig-Veda said in praise of the Ashvins, "hath a triple seat and reins of gold—the famous car that traverses Heaven and Earth." The rotating wheels, it appears, served diverse functions: one to raise the craft, another to give it direction, the third to speed it along: "One of your chariot's wheels is moving swiftly around; one speeds for you its onward course."

As in the Greek tales, so did the gods of the Vedas display little morality or restraint in sexual matters—sometimes getting away with it, sometimes not, as when the indignant Adityas selected Rudra ("The Three-Eyed") to kill their grandfather Dyaus for having violated their sister Ushas. (Dyaus, wounded, saved his life by fleeing to a distant celestial body.) Also as in the Greek tales, so did the gods according to Hindu lore mingle, in later times, in the loves and wars of mortal kings and heroes. In these instances the aerial vehicles of the gods played roles even greater than their weapons. Thus, when one hero drowned, the Ashvins appeared in a fleet of three aerial chariots, "self-activated watertight ships which traverse the air," dived into the ocean, retrieved the hero from the watery depths, and "conveyed him over land, beyond the liquid ocean." And then there was the tale of Yayati, a king who married the daughter of a god. When the couple bore children, the happy grandfather gave the king "a highly effulgent golden celestial chariot, which could go everywhere without interruption." Without losing time, "Yayati ascended the chariot and, irrepressible in battle, within six nights conquered the entire Earth."

As in the *Iliad,* so did Hindu traditions tell of wars of men and gods over beautiful heroines. Best known of these tales is the *Ramayana,* the long epic tale of Rama the prince whose beautiful wife was abducted by the king of Lanka (the island of Ceylon, off India). Among the gods who turned out to help Rama was Hanuman, the god with a monkey face, who conducted aerial battles with the winged Garuda (Fig. 16), one of the monstrous offspring of

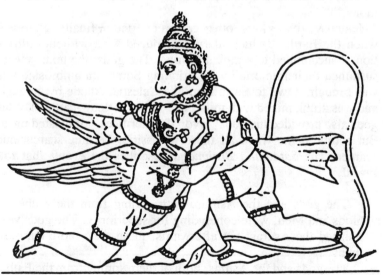

Fig. 16

Kasyapa. In another instance, Sukra, a god "sullied by immorality," abducted Tara, the beautiful wife of Indra's charioteer. "The Illustrious Rudra" and other gods then came to the aid of the aggrieved husband. There ensued "a terrible battle, destructive of gods and demons, on account of Tara." In spite of their awesome weapons, the gods were bested and had to seek refuge with "the Prime Deity." Thereupon the grandfather of the gods himself came to Earth, and put an end to the fighting by returning Tara to her husband. Then Tara gave birth to a son "whose beauty overclouded the celestials . . . . Filled with suspicion, the gods demanded to know who the true father was: the lawful husband or the abductor-god." She proclaimed that the boy was the son of Soma, "Celestial Immortality"; and she named him Budah.

But all that was in times yet to come; in the olden days the gods battled among themselves for more important causes: supremacy and rule over the Earth and its resources. With so many offspring of Kasyapa by diverse wives and concubines, as well as the descendants of the other olden gods, conflict soon became inevitable. The dominance of the Adityas was especially resented by the *Asuras,* elder gods whose mothers bore them to Kasyapa before the Adityas were born. Bearing a non-Aryan name of a clear Near Eastern origin (being akin to names of the supreme gods of Assyria, Babylon, and Egypt—*Ashur, Asar, Osiris*), they eventually assumed in the Hindu traditions the role of the evil gods, the "demons."

Jealousy, rivalry, and other causes of friction finally led to war when the Earth, "which at first produced food without cultivation," succumbed to a global famine. The gods, the texts reveal, sustained their immortality by drinking Soma, an ambrosiac that was brought down to Earth from the Celestial Abode by an eagle and was drunk mixed with milk. The "kine" ("cow-cattle") of the gods also provided the gods' favored "sacrifices" of roasted meat. But a time came when all these necessities became scarcer and scarcer. The *Satapatha Brahmana* describes the events that followed:

> The gods and the Asuras, both sprung from the Father of Gods and Men, were contending for superiority. The gods vanquished the Asuras; yet afterwards, these once more harassed them. . . .
>
> The gods and the Asuras, both of them sprung from the Father of Gods and Men, were [again] contending for superiority. This

time, the gods were worsted. And the Asuras thought: "To us alone assuredly belongs this world!"

They thereupon said: "Well, then, let us divide this world between ourselves; and having divided it, let us subsist thereon." Accordingly, they set about dividing it from west to east.

Hearing this, the defeated Adityas went to plead for a share in Earth's resources:

When they heard this, the gods said: "The Asuras are actually dividing this Earth! Come, let us go where the Asuras are dividing it; for what would become of us if we were to get no share of Earth?"

Placing Vishnu at their head, they went to the Asuras.

Haughtily the Asuras offered to give the Adityas only as much of Earth as Vishnu could lie upon. . . . But the gods used a subterfuge and placed Vishnu in an "enclosure" that could "walk in three directions," thereby regaining three of the Earth's four regions.

The outsmarted Asuras then attacked from the south; and the gods asked Agni "how they could vanquish the Asuras forever." Agni suggested a pincer maneuver: while the gods attack from their regions, "I will go round to the northern side, and you will shut them in from here; and whilst shutting them in, we will put them down." Having so vanquished the Asuras, the *Satapatha Brahmana* records, "the gods were anxious as to how they might replenish the sacrifices"; accordingly, many of the battle segments of the ancient Hindu writings deal with the recapture of the kine and the resupply of the Soma beverage.

These wars were fought on land, in the air, and beneath the seas. The Asuras, according to the *Mahabharata,* made for themselves three metal fortresses in the skies, from which they attacked the three regions of the Earth. Their allies in the war with the gods could become invisible and used invisible weapons; and others fought from a city beneath the sea, which they had captured from the gods.

One who excelled in these battles was Indra ("Storm"). On land he smote ninety-nine strongholds of the Asuras, killing great numbers of their armed followers. In the skies he fought from his aerial car the Asuras, who were hiding in their "cloud fortresses."

Hymns in the Rig-Veda list groups of gods as well as individual deities defeated by Indra (we follow the translation by R. T. Griffith, *The Hymns of the Rig-Veda*):

Thou slewest with thy bolt the Sasyu . . .
Far from the floor of Heaven in all directions,
   the ancient riteless ones fled to destruction . . .
The Dasyu thou hast burned from the heavens.

They met in fight the army of the blameless,
   then the Navagvas put forth all their power.
Like emasculates contending with men they fled,
   by steep paths from Indra they scattered.
Indra broke through Ilibsa's strong castles,
   and Sushna with his horn he cut to pieces . . .

Thou slewest thy fighting foe with thy Thunder . . .
Fierce on his enemies fell Indra's weapon,
   with his sharp rushing Thunderbolt
   he rent their towns to pieces.

Thou goest forth from fight to fight intrepidly,
   destroying castle after castle with thy strength.
Thou Indra, with thy friend who makes the foe bow down,
   slowest from far away the guileful Namuchi.
Thou hast struck down in death Karanja, Parnaya . . .
Thou hast destroyed the hundred towns of Vangrida.

The ridges of the lofty heaven thou madest shake
   when thou, daring, by thyself smote Sambara.

Defeating the gods' enemies in groups as well as in single combat, and making them "flee to destruction," Indra turned his efforts to the freeing of the kine. The "demons" hid them inside a mountain, guarded by Vala ("Encircler"); Indra, aided by the Angirases, young gods who could emit divine flames, smashed into the fortified hideaway and freed the kine. (Some scholars, as J. Herbert in *Hindu Mythology,* hold that what Indra released or retrieved was a Divine Ray, not cows, for the Sanskrit word *go* has both meanings.)

When these wars of the gods began, the Adityas named Agni ("Agile") as Hotri, their "Chief of Office." As the wars progressed—some texts suggest for well over a thousand years—Vishnu ("Active") was made the Chief. But when the fighting was over, Indra, having contributed so much to the victory, claimed the supremacy. As in the Greek *Theogony,* one of his first acts to establish his claim was to slay his own father. The Rig-Veda (Book iv: 18, 12) asks Indra rhetorically: "Indra, who made thy mother a widow?" The answer follows also as a question: "What god was present in the fray, when thou didst slay thy father, seizing him by the foot?"

For this crime Indra was excluded by the gods from the drinking of the Soma, thereby endangering his continued immortality. They "ascended up to Heaven," leaving Indra with the kine he had retrieved. But "he went up after them, with the raised Thunder-weapon," ascending from the northern place of the gods. Fearing his weapon, the gods shouted: "Do not hurl!" and agreed to let Indra share once again in the divine nourishments.

Indra's seizing of the leadership of the gods, however, did not go unchallenged. The challenge came from Tvashtri, to whom oblique references are made in the Hymns as "the Firstborn"—a fact that may explain his own claim to the succession. Indra smote him quickly with the Thunder-Weapon, the very weapon that Tvashtri had fashioned for him. But then the struggle was taken over by Vritra ("The Obstructor"), whom some texts call the firstborn of Tvashtri but whom some scholars interpret as having been an artificial monster, because he quickly grew to an immense size. At first Indra was bested, and he fled to a far corner of Earth. When all the gods then abandoned him, only the twenty-one Maruts stood by his side. They were a group of gods who manned the fastest aerial cars, who "loud roaring as the winds make the mountains rock and reel" as they "lift themselves aloft":

These verily wondrous, red of hue,
Speed on their course with a roar
   over the ridges of the sky . . .
And spread themselves with beams of light . . .
Bright, celestial, with lightning in their hands
   and helmets of gold upon their heads.

With the aid of the Maruts, Indra returned to battle Vritra. The hymns which describe the fight in glowing terms have been translated by J. Muir *(Original Sanskirt Texts)* into rhyming poetic verses:

The valiant god his car ascends,
Swept by his fervid bounding speeds,
Athwart the sky the hero speeds.
The Marut-hosts his escort form,
Impetuous spirits of the storm.
On flashing lightning-cars they ride,
And gleam in warlike pomp and pride . . .
Like lions' roar their voice of doom;
With iron force their teeth consume.
The hills, the earth itself, they shake;
All creatures at their coming quake.

While earth quaked and all creatures ran for cover, only Vritra,
the foe, calmly watched their approach:

Perched on a steep aerial height
Shone Vritra's stately fortress bright.
Upon the wall, in martial mood,
The bold gigantic demon stood,
Confiding in his magic arts,
And armed with store of fiery darts.

"Without alarm, defying the might of Indra's arm," unafraid of
"the terrors of the deadly flight" rushing toward him, Vritra stood
in wait.

And then was seen a dreadful sight,
When god and demon met in fight.
His sharpened missiles Vritra shot,
His thunderbolts and lightnings hot
     he hurled as thick as rain.
The god his fiercest rage defied;
His blunted weapons glanced aside,
     at Indra launched in vain.

When Vritra spent all his fiery missiles, Indra was able to take
over the offensive:

The lightnings then began to flash,
The direful thunderbolts to crash,
     by Indra proudly hurled.

The gods themselves with awe were stilled
And stood aghast; and terror filled
　the universal world. . . .

The Thunderbolts hurled by Indra, "forged by the master hand
of Tvashtri" of divine iron, were complex, blazing missiles:

Who the arrowy shower could stand,
Discharged by Indra's red right hand—
The thunderbolts with hundred joints,
The iron shafts with thousand points,
Which blaze and hiss athwart the sky,
Swift to their mark unerring fly,
And lay the proudest foeman low,
With sudden and resistless blow,
Whose very sound can put to flight
The fools who dare the Thunderer's might.

Unerringly the guided missiles hit their target:

And soon the knell of Vritra's doom
Was sounded by the clang and boom
　of Indra's iron shower;
Pierced, cloven, crushed, with horrid yell
The dying demon headlong fell
　down from his cloud-built tower.

Fallen to the ground "as trunks of trees that axe had felled,"
Vritra lay prostrate; but though "footless and handless, still he
challenged Indra." Then Indra gave him the coup-de-grace, and
"smote him with his bolt between the shoulders."

Indra's victory was complete; but as Fate would have it, the
fruits of victory were not his alone. As he was claiming the throne
of Kasyapa, his father, old doubts surfaced concerning his true par-
enthood. It was a fact that upon his birth his mother had hid him
from Kasyapa's wrath. Why? Was there truth to the rumors that his
true father was his own elder brother, Tvashtri?

The Vedas lift the veil of mystery only partly. They tell, however, that Indra, great god that he was, did not rule alone: he had to
share powers with Agni and Surya his brothers—just as Zeus had to
share dominions with his brothers Hades and Poseidon.

4

THE EARTH CHRONICLES

As if the similarities of the genealogies and warfare between the Greek and Hindu gods were not enough, tablets discovered in the Hittite royal archives (at a site nowadays called Boghazkoi) contained more tales of the same story: how, as one generation waned unto the other, one god fought another for supremacy.

The longest texts discovered dealt, as could be expected, with the Hittite supreme deity Teshub: his genealogy; his rightful assumption of dominion over Earth's upper regions; and the battles launched against him by the god KUMARBI and his offspring. As in the Greek and Egyptian tales, the Avenger of Kumarbi was hidden with the aid of allied gods until he grew up somewhere in a "dark-hued" part of Earth. The final battles raged in the skies and in the seas; in one battle Teshub was supported by seventy gods riding in their chariots. At first defeated and either hiding or exiled, Teshub finally faced his challenger in god-to-god combat. Armed with the "Thunder-stormer which scatters the rocks for ninety furlongs" and "the Lightning which flashes frightfully," he ascended skyward in his chariot, pulled by two gold-plated Bulls of Heaven, and "from the skies he set his face" toward his enemy. Though the fragmented tablets lack the tale's ending, it is evident that Teshub was finally victorious.

Who were these ancient gods, who fought each other for supremacy and sought dominion over Earth by pitting nation against nation?

Fittingly, perhaps, treaties that had ended some of the very wars launched by men for their gods provide important clues.

When the Egyptians and the Hittites made peace after more than two centuries of warfare, it was sealed by the marriage of the daughter of the Hittite king Hattusilish III to the Egyptian Pharaoh Ramses II. The Pharaoh recorded the event on commemorative stelae which he placed at Karnak, at Elephantine near Aswan, and at Abu Simbel.

Describing the journey and the arrival of the princess in Egypt, the inscription relates that when "His Majesty saw that she was as beautiful of face as a goddess," he at once fell in love with her and deemed her to be "something lovely granted him by the god Ptah" and a sign of Hittite acknowledgment of his "victory." What all this diplomatic maneuvering had entailed was clarified by other parts of the inscription: thirteen years earlier, Hattusilish had sent to the Pharaoh the text of a Peace Treaty; but Ramses II, still brooding over his near-fatal experience in the battle of Kadesh, ignored it. "The great Chief of Hatti then wrote appeasingly to His Majesty year after year; but the King Ramses paid no attention." Finally, the King of Hatti, instead of sending messages inscribed on tablets, "sent his eldest daughter, preceded by precious tribute" and accompanied by Hittite nobles. Wondering what all these gifts meant, Ramses sent an Egyptian escort to meet and accompany the Hittites. And, as related above, he succumbed to the beauty of the Hittite princess, made her a queen, and named her Maat-Neferu-Ra ("The Beauty Which Ra Sees").

Our knowledge of history and antiquity has also profited by that love at first sight, for the Pharaoh then accepted the lingering Peace Treaty, and proceeded to inscribe it, too, at Karnak, not far from where the tale of the Battle of Kadesh and the Tale of the Beautiful Hittite Princess had been commemorated. Two copies, one almost complete, the other fragmentary, have been discovered, deciphered, and translated by Egyptologists. As a result we not only have the full text of the Treaty but also know that the Hittite king wrote down the treaty in the Akkadian language, which was then (as French was a century and two ago) the common language of international relations.

To the Pharaoh he sent a copy of the Akkadian original written on a silver tablet, which the Egyptian inscription at Karnak described thus:

> What is in the middle of the tablet of silver, on the front side:
> Figures consisting of an image of Seth, embracing an image of the Great Prince of Hatti, surrounded by a border with the words "the seal of Seth, ruler of the sky; the seal of the regulation which Hattusilish made" . . .
> What is within that which surrounds the image of the seal of Seth on the other side:
> Figures consisting of a female image of the goddess of Hatti embracing a female image of the Princess of Hatti, surrounded by a border with the words "the seal of the Ra of the town of Arinna, the lord of the land" . . .
> What is within the [frame] surrounding the figures: the seal of Ra of Arinna, the lord of every land.

In the royal Hittite archives, archaeologists have in fact discovered royal seals depicting the chief Hittite deity embracing the Hittite king (Fig. 17), exactly as described in the Egyptian record, even including the inscription surrounding the border of the seal. Against all odds, the original treaty itself, inscribed on two tablets in the Akkadian language, was also found in these archives. But the Hittite texts called their chief deity Teshub, not "Seth of Hatti." Since *Teshub* meant "Windy Storm," and *Seth* (to judge by his Greek name Typhon) meant "Fierce Wind," it appeared that the Egyptians and Hittites were matching their pantheons according to the epithet-names of their gods. In line with that, Teshub's spouse HEBAT was called "Lady of the Skies" to parallel the goddess by that title in the Egyptian version of the treaty; Ra ("The Bright One") was paralleled by a Hittite "Lord of the Sky" whom the Akkadian version called SHAMASH ("The Bright One"), and so on.

The Egyptians and the Hittites, it became evident, were matching separate, but parallel, pantheons; and scholars began to wonder what other ancient treaties would reveal. One that provided surpris-

Fig. 17

ing information was the treaty made circa 1350 B.C. between the Hittite king Shuppilulima and Mattiwaza, king of the Hurrian kingdom of Mitanni, which was situated on the Euphrates river midway between the Land of the Hittites and the ancient lands of Sumer and Akkad.

Executed as usual in two copies, the treaty's original was deposited in the shrine of the god Teshub in the Hurrian city Kahat—a place and a tablet lost in the sands of time. But the duplicate tablet, deposited in the Hittite holy city of Arinna "in front of the goddess of the Rising Disc," was discovered by archaeologists some 3,300 years after it was written!

As did all treaties in those days, the one between the Hittite and Mitannian kings ended with a call upon "the gods of the contracting parties to be present, to listen and to serve as witnesses," so that adherence to the treaty shall bring divine bliss, and its violation the wrath of the gods. These "gods of the contracting parties" were then listed, beginning with Teshub and his consort Hebat as the supreme reigning gods of both kingdoms, the gods "who regulate kingship and queenship" in Hatti and Mitanni and in whose shrines the copies of the treaty were deposited. Then, a number of younger deities, both male and female, offspring of the two reigning gods, were listed by the provincial capitals where they acted as governing deities, representing their parents.

Here, then, was a listing of the very same gods in the very same hierarchical positions; unlike the Egyptian instance, when different pantheons were being matched. As other discovered texts proved, the Hittite pantheon was in fact borrowed from (or through) the Hurrians. But this particular treaty held a special surprise: toward the end of the tablet, among the divine witnesses, there were also listed *Mitra-ash, Uruwana, Indar,* and the *Nashatiyanu* gods—the very Mitra, Varuna, Indra, and the Nasatya gods of the Hindu pantheon!

Which of the three—Hittite, Hindu, Hurrian—was then the common source? The answer was provided in the same Hittite-Mitannian treaty: none of them; for those so-called "Aryan" gods were listed in the treaty together with their parents and grandparents, the "Olden Gods": the couples Anu and Antu, Enlil and his spouse Ninlil, Ea and his wife Damkina; as well as "the divine Sin, lord of the oath . . . Nergal of Kutha . . . the warrior god Ninurta . . . the warlike Ishtar."

These are familiar names; they had been invoked in earlier days by Sargon of Akkad, who had claimed that he was "Overseer of Ishtar, anointed priest of Anu, great righteous shepherd of Enlil."

His grandson Naram-Sin ("Whom the god Sin loves") could attack the Cedar Mountain when the god Nergal "opened the path" for him. Hammurabi of Babylon marched against other lands "on the command of Anu, with Enlil advancing in front of the army." The Assyrian king Tiglat-Pileser went conquering on the command of Anu, Adad, and Ninurta; Shalmaneser fought with weapons provided by Nergal; Esarhaddon was accompanied by Ishtar on his march to Nineveh.

No less illuminating was the discovery that the Hittites and the Hurrians, though they pronounced the deities' names in their own language, wrote the names employing Sumerian script; even the "divine" determinative used was the Sumerian DIN.GIR, literally meaning "The Righteous Ones" (DIN) "Of the Rocketship" (GIR). Thus the name of Teshub was written DIN. GIR IM ("Divine Stormer"), which was the Sumerian name for the god ISHKUR, also known as Adad; or it was written DIN.GIR U, meaning "The god 10," which was the numerical rank of Ishkur/Adad—that of Anu being the highest (60), that of Enlil 50, that of Ea 40, and so on down the line. Also, like the Sumerian Ishkur/Adad, Teshub was depicted by the Hittites brandishing his lightning-emitting weapon, a "Weapon of Brilliance" (Fig. 18).

Fig. 18

By the time the Hittites and their writings were reclaimed from oblivion, scholars had already determined that before the Hittite and Egyptian civilizations, before Assyria and Babylon, even before Akkad, there arose in southern Mesopotamia the high civilization of Sumer. All the others were offshoots of that first-known civilization.

And it is by now established beyond doubt that it was in Sumer that the tales of gods and men were first recorded. It was there that numerous texts—more numerous than can be imagined, more detailed than could be expected—were first inscribed. It was there that the written records of history and prehistory on our planet Earth had originated. We call them THE EARTH CHRONICLES.

The discovery and understanding of the ancient civilizations has been a process of continuous astonishment, of incredible realizations. The monuments of antiquity—pyramids, ziggurats, vast platforms, columned ruins, carved stones—would have remained enigmas, mute evidence to bygone events, were it not for the Written Word. Were it not for that, the ancient monuments would have remained puzzles: their age uncertain; their creators obscure; their purpose unclear.

We owe what we know to the ancient scribes—a prolific and meticulous lot, who used monuments, artifacts, foundation stones, bricks, utensils, weapons of any conceivable material, as inviting slates on which to write down names and record events. Above all there were the clay tablets: flattened pieces of wet clay, some small enough to be held in the palm of the hand, on which the scribe deftly embossed with a stylus the symbols that formed syllables, words, and sentences. Then the tablet would be left to dry (or be kiln-dried), and a permanent record had been created—a record that has survived millennia of natural erosion and human destructiveness.

In place after place—in centers of commerce or of administration, in temples and palaces, in all parts of the ancient Near East—there were both state and private archives full of such tablets; and there were also actual libraries where the tablets, tens of thousands of them, were neatly arranged by subject, their contents entitled, their scribe named, their sequel numbered. Invariably, whenever they dealt with history or science or the gods, they were identified as copies of earlier tablets, tablets in the "olden language."

Astounded as the archaeologists were to uncover the grandeur of Assyria and Babylonia, they were even more puzzled to read in their inscriptions of "olden cities." And what was the meaning of the title "king of Sumer and Akkad" that the kings of these empires coveted so much?

It was only with the discovery of the records concerning Sargon of Agade that modern scholars were able to convince themselves that a great kingdom, the Kingdom of Akkad, had indeed arisen in Mesopotamia half a millennium before Assyria and Babylonia were to flourish. It was with the greatest amazement that scholars read in these records that Sargon "defeated Uruk and tore down its wall. . . . Sargon, king of Agade, was victorious over the inhabitants of Ur. . . . He defeated E-Nimmar and tore down its wall and defeated its territory from Lagash as far as the sea. His weapons he washed in the sea. In the battle with the inhabitants of Umma he was victorious. . . ."

The scholars were incredulous: Could there have been urban centers, walled cities, even before Sargon of Agade, even before 2500 B.C.?

As is now known, indeed there were. These were the cities and urban centers of Sumer, the "Sumer" in the title "king of Sumer and Akkad." It was, as a century of archaeological discoveries and scholarly research has established, the land where Civilization began nearly six thousand years ago; where suddenly and inexplicably, as though out of nowhere, there appeared a written language and literature; kings and priests; schools and temples; doctors and astronomers; high-rise buildings, canals, docks, and ships; an intensive agriculture; an advanced metallurgy; a textile industry; trade and commerce; laws and concepts of justice and morality; cosmological theories; and tales and records of history and prehistory.

In all these writings, be it long epic tales or two-line proverbs, in inscriptions mundane or divine, the same facts emerge as an unshakable tenet of the Sumerians and the peoples that followed them: in bygone days, the DIN.GIR—"The Righteous Ones of the Rocketships," the beings the Greeks began to call "gods"—had come to Earth from their own planet. They chose southern Mesopotamia to be their home away from home. They called the land KI.EN.GIR—"Land of the Lord of the Rockets" (the Akkadian name, *Shumer,* meant "Land of the Guardians"); and they established there the first settlements on Earth.

The statement that the first to establish settlements on Earth were astronauts from another planet was not lightly made by the Sumerians. In text after text, whenever the starting point was recalled, it was always this: 432,000 years before the Deluge, the DIN.GIR ("Righteous Ones of the Rocketships") came down to Earth from their own planet. The Sumerians considered it a twelfth member of our Solar System—a system made up of the Sun in the center, the Moon, all the nine planets we know of today, and one more large planet whose orbit lasts a *Sar,* 3,600 Earth-years. This orbit, they wrote, takes the planet to a "station" in the distant heavens, then brings it back to Earth's vicinity, crossing between Mars and Jupiter. It was in that position—as depicted in a 4,500-year-old Sumerian drawing (Fig. 19) that the planet obtained its name NIBIRU ("Crossing") and its symbol, the Cross.

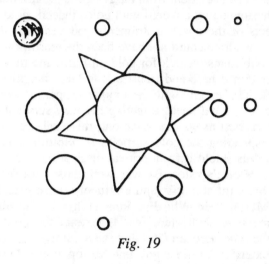

Fig. 19

The leader of the astronauts who had come to Earth from Nibiru, we know from numerous ancient texts, was called E. A ("Whose House Is Water"); after he had landed and established Eridu, the first Earth Station, he assumed the title EN.KI ("Lord of Earth"). A text that was discovered in the ruins of Sumer records his landing on Earth as a first-person report:

When I approached Earth
there was much flooding.
When I approached its green meadows,
heaps and mounds were piled up at my command.
I built my house in a pure place . . .
My house—its shade stretches over the Snake Marsh.

The text then proceeds to describe Ea's efforts to build extraordinary waterworks in the marshlands at the head of the Persian Gulf: He surveyed the marshlands, cut canals for drainage and water control, built dykes, dug ditches, and built structures of bricks molded from the local clays. He joined the Tigris and Euphrates rivers by canals; and at the edge of the marshlands he built his Water House, with a wharf and other facilities.

It all had a reason. On his planet gold was needed. Not for jewelry or another frivolous use, for at no time during the millennia that followed were these visitors to Earth ever shown wearing golden jewelry. Gold was, no doubt, required for the space programs of the Nibiruans, as is evident from the Hindu texts' references to the celestial chariots being covered with gold; indeed, gold is vital to many aspects of the space instruments and vehicles of our own times. But that alone could not have been the reason for the intensity of the Nibiruans' search for gold on Earth and their immense efforts to obtain it here and transfer it in large quantities to their own planet. The metal, with its unique properties, was needed back home for a vital need, affecting the very survival of life on that planet; as best as we can make out, this vital need could have been for suspending the gold particles in Nibiru's waning atmosphere and thus shield it from critical dissipation.

A son of Nibiru's ruler, Ea was well chosen for the mission. He was a brilliant scientist and engineer whose nickname was NU.DIM.MUD, "He Who Fashions Things." The plan, as his epithet-name E.A. indicated, was to extract the gold from the waters of the quiet Persian Gulf and the adjoining shallow marshlands that extended from the gulf into Mesopotamia. Sumerian depictions showed Ea as lord of the flowing waters, sitting in a laboratory and surrounded by interconnected flasks (Fig. 20).

But the unfolding tale suggests that all was not going well with this scheme. The gold production was far below expectations, and to speed it up, more astronauts—the rank and file were called *Anunnaki* ("Those Who From Heaven to Earth Came")—landed on Earth. They came in groups of fifty, and one of the texts reveals that one of these groups was led by Enki's firstborn son MAR.DUK. The text records Marduk's urgent message to his father describing a near-calamity on the flight to Earth, as the spaceship passed by one of the Solar System's large planets (probably Jupiter) and almost collided with one of that planet's satellites. Describing the "attack" on the spacecraft, the excited Marduk told his father:

Fig. 20

It has been created like a weapon;
It has charged forward like death . . .
The Anunnaki who are fifty it has smitten . . .
The flying, birdlike Supreme Orbiter
it has smitten on the breast.

A Sumerian engraving on a cylinder seal (Fig. 21) may well
have illustrated the scene of Lord Earth (on the left) anxiously
greeting his son, dressed as an astronaut (on the right), as the
spaceship leaves Mars (the six-pointed star) and nears Earth (the
seventh planet when counting from the outside in, symbolized by
the seven dots and depicted together with the Moon).

Back on the home planet, where Enki's father AN (*Anu* in Akkadian) was the ruler, the progress of the landing parties was followed with anxiety and expectation. These must have turned to im-
patience at the slow progress, and then to disappointment.
Evidently the scheme to extract gold from seawaters by
laboratorylike processes did not work as expected.

But the gold was still badly needed; and the Anunnaki faced a

Fig. 21

tough decision: to abandon the project—which was out of the question—or to try to obtain the gold in a new way: mining. For gold, the Anunnaki knew by then, was naturally available in abundance in the AB.ZU ("The Primeval Source") on the continent of Africa. (In the Semitic languages that had evolved from the Sumerian, *Za-ab—Abzu* in reverse—has remained the word for gold to this very day).

There was, however, one major problem. The African gold had to be extracted from the depths of the earth through mining; and the far-reaching decision to change from the sophisticated water-treatment process to a backbreaking toil below the surface of the earth was not lightly taken. Clearly the new enterprise required more Anunnaki, a mining colony in "the place of the shining lodes," expanded facilities in Mesopotamia, and a fleet of ore vessels (MA.GUR UR.NU AB.ZU— "Ships for Ores of the Abzu") to connect the two. Could Enki handle it all by himself?

Anu felt that he could not; and eight Nibiru years after Enki's landing—28,800 Earth-years—he came to Earth to see things for himself. He came down accompanied by the Heir Apparent EN.LIL ("Lord of the Command")—a son who, Anu must have felt, could take charge of Earth mission and organize the gold deliveries to Nibiru.

The choice of Enlil for the mission might have been a necessary one, but it must have been an agonizing one as well; for it only sharpened the rivalry and jealousy between the two half-brothers. For Enki was the firstborn son of Anu by Id, one of his six concubines, and could have expected to follow Anu on Nibiru's throne.

But then—as in the biblical tale of Abraham, his concubine Hagar, and his half-sister wife Sarah—Anu's half-sister wife Antum bore him a son, Enlil. And by the Nibiruan rules of succession—so faithfully adopted by the biblical patriarch—Enlil became the legal heir instead of Enki. And now this rival, this robber of Enki's birthright, came to Earth to take over the command!

One cannot stress enough the importance of lineage and genealogy in the Wars of the Gods; the struggles for succession and supremacy, on Nibiru as on Earth later on.

Indeed, as we unravel the puzzling persistence and ferocity of the wars of the gods, trying to fit them into the framework of history and prehistory—a task never undertaken before—it becomes clear that they stemmed from a code of sexual behavior based not on morality but on considerations of genetic purity. At the core of these wars lay an intricate genealogy that determined hierarchy and succession; and sexual acts were judged not by their tenderness or violence but by their purpose and outcome.

There is a Sumerian tale of how Enlil, commander-in-chief of the Anunnaki, took a fancy to a young nurse whom he saw swimming naked in the river. He persuaded her to go sailing with him and made love to her against her protestations ("my vulva is small, it knows not intercourse"). In spite of his rank Enlil was arrested by the "fifty senior gods" as he returned to his city Nippur and was found by "the seven Anunnaki who judge" to have committed the crime of rape; they sentenced him to exile in the Abzu. (He was pardoned only when he married the young goddess, who had followed him into exile.)

Many songs celebrated the love affair between Inanna and a young god named Dumuzi, in which their "sleep-outs" were described with touching tenderness:

O that they put his hand in my hand for me.
O that they put his heart next to my heart for me.
Not only is it sweet to sleep hand in hand with him,
Sweetest of sweet is also the loveliness
of joining heart to heart with him.

We can understand the approving tone of the verse because Dumuzi was the intended bridegroom of Inanna, chosen by her with the approval of her brother Utu/Shamash. But how to explain a text in which Inanna describes passionate lovemaking with her own brother?

My beloved met me,
took his pleasure of me, rejoiced together with me.
The brother brought me to his house,
made me lie on its sweet bed . . .
In unison, the tongue-making in unison,
my brother of fairest face
made fifty times.

This can only be understood if we bear in mind that the code prohibited marriage, but not lovemaking, between full brother and sister. On the other hand, marriage with a half-sister was allowed; male progeny by a half-sister even had precedence in the hierarchical order. And while rape was condemned, sex—even irregular and violent—was condoned if done for the sake of succession to the throne. A long tale relates how Enki, seeking a male son by his (and Enlil's) half-sister Sud, forced his attentions on her when she was alone and "poured the semen in the womb." When she gave birth to a daughter (rather than to a son), Enki lost no time making love to the girl as soon as she became "young and fair . . . He took his joy of her, he embraced her, lay in her lap; he touches the thighs, he touches the . . . with the young one he cohabits." This went on unabashedly with a succession of young daughters, until Sud put a curse on Enki, which paralyzed him; only then did these sexual antics in search of a male heir stop.

When Enki engaged in these sexual efforts, he was already espoused to Ninki, which illustrates that the same code which condemned rape did not prohibit extramarital affairs per se. We also know that the gods were allowed any number of wives and concubines (a text catalogued as CT-24 listed six of Anu's concubines), but, if married, they had to select one as their official spouse—preferring, as we have mentioned, a half-sister for this role.

If the god, apart from his given name and many epithets, was also bestowed with a title-name, his official consort was also honored with the feminine form of such title. Thus when AN received his title-name ("The Heavenly"), his consort was called ANTU, Anu and Antum in Akkadian. The nurse who had married Enlil ("Lord of Command") received the title-name Ninlil ("Lady of Command"); Enki's spouse Damkina was called Ninki, and so on.

Because of the importance of the family relationships between these great Anunnaki, many so-called God Lists prepared by ancient scribes were genealogical in nature. In one such major list, titled by the ancient scribes the *"AN : ilu Anum"* series, there are listed the "forty-two foreparents of Enlil," clearly arranged as twenty-one divine couples. This must have been a mark of great royal lineage, for two similar documents for Anu also list his twenty-one ancestral couples on Nibiru. We learn that the parents of Anu were AN.SHAR.GAL ("Great Prince of Heaven") and KI.SHAR.GAL ("Great Princess of Firm Ground"). As their names indicate, they were not the reigning couple on Nibiru: rather, the father was the Great Prince, meaning the heir apparent; and his spouse was a great princess, the firstborn daughter of the ruler (by a different wife) and thus a half-sister of Anshargal.

In these genealogical facts lies the key to the understanding of the events on Nibiru before the landing on Earth, and on Earth thereafter.

Sending Ea to Earth for gold implies that the Nibiruans had already been aware of the metal's availability on Earth well before the landing was launched. How?

One could offer several answers: They could have probed Earth with unmanned satellites, as we have been doing to other planets in our Solar System. They could have surveyed Earth by landing on it, as we have done on our Moon. Indeed, their landing on Mars cannot be ruled out as we read texts dealing with the space voyages from Nibiru to Earth.

Whether and when such manned *premeditated* landings on Earth had taken place, we do not know. But there does exist an ancient chronicle dealing with an earlier landing in dramatic circumstances: when the deposed ruler of Nibiru escaped to Earth in his spacecraft!

The event must have happened before Ea was sent to Earth by his father, for it was through that event that Anu became Nibiru's ruler. Indeed the event was the usurpation of the throne on Nibiru by Anu.

The information is contained in a text whose Hittite version has been titled by scholars *Kingship in Heaven*. It throws light on life at the royal court of Nibiru and tells a tale of betrayal and usurpation worthy of a Shakespearean plot. It reveals that when the time for succession arrived on Nibiru—through natural death or otherwise—it was not Anshargal, Anu's father and the heir apparent, who had ascended the throne. Instead a relative named Alalu (Alalush in the Hittite text) became the ruler.

As a gesture of reconciliation or by custom, Alalu appointed Anu to be his royal cup-bearer, an honored and trusted position also known to us from several Near Eastern texts and royal depictions (Fig. 22). But after nine Nibiruan years, Anu (Anush in the Hittite text) ''gave battle to Alalu'' and deposed him:

Fig. 22

Once in the olden days, Alalush was king in Heaven.
Alalush was seated on the throne;
The mighty Anush, first among the gods,
was standing before him:
He would bow to his feet,
set the drinking cup in his hand.
For nine counted periods, Alalush was king in Heaven.
In the ninth counted period,
Anush gave battle to Alalush.

It was then, the ancient text tells us, that the dramatic flight to Earth had occurred:

Alalush was defeated, he fled before Anush—
Down he descended to the dark-hued Earth.
Anush took his seat upon the throne.

While it is quite possible that much about Earth and its resources may have been known on Nibiru even before Alalu's flight, the fact is that we do have in this tale a record of the arrival on Earth of a spaceship bearing Nibiruans before Ea's mission to Earth. The *Sumerian King Lists* report that the first administrator of Eridu was called Alulim—a name that could have been yet another epithet for Ea/Enki, or the Sumerian rendering of Alalu's name; the possibility thus comes to mind that, though deposed, Alalu was sufficiently concerned about Nibiru's fate to advise his deposer that he had found gold in Earth's waters. That this is indeed what had happened might be indicated by the fact that a reconciliation between deposed and deposer did ensue; for Anu went ahead and appointed Kumarbi, a grandson of Alalu, to be his royal cup-bearer.

But the gesture of reconciliation only caused history on Nibiru to repeat itself. In spite of all the bestowed honors, the young Kumarbi could not forget that Anu had usurped the throne from his grandfather; and as time went on, Kumarbi's enmity toward Anu was becoming more and more obvious, and Anu "could not withstand the gaze of Kumarbi's eyes."

And so it was that, having decided to leave Nibiru for Earth and even take the Heir Apparent (Enlil) with him, Anu deemed it safer also to take along the young Kumarbi. Both decisions—to take Enlil with him and to take Kumarbi along—ended up making the visit one marred by strife and—for Anu—also filled with personal agony.

The decision to bring Enlil to Earth and put him in charge led to heated arguments with Enki—arguments echoed in the texts so far discovered. The angry Enki threatened to leave Earth and return to Nibiru; but could he be trusted not to usurp the throne there? If, as a compromise, Anu himself were to stay on Earth, appointing Enlil as surrogate ruler on Nibiru, could Enlil be trusted to step down when Anu returned? Finally it was decided to draw lots: let chance determine how it shall be. The division of authority that ensued is repeatedly mentioned in Sumerian and Akkadian texts. One of the longest of the Earth Chronicles, a text called *The Atra-Hasis Epic,* records the drawing of lots and its outcome:

> The gods clasped hands together,
> then cast lots and divided:
> Anu to heaven went up;
> To Enlil the Earth was made subject;
> That which the sea as a loop encloses,

they gave to the prince Enki.
To the Abzu Enki went down,
assumed the rulership of the Abzu.

Believing that he had managed to separate the rival brothers,
"Anu to Heaven went up." But in the skies above Earth, an unexpected turn of events awaited him. Perhaps as a precaution, Kumarbi was left on the space platform orbiting Earth; when Anu
returned to it, ready to take off on the long voyage back to Nibiru,
he was confronted by an angry Kumarbi. Harsh words soon gave
way to a scuffle: "Anu gave battle to Kumarbi, Kumarbi gave battle to Anu." As Kumarbi bested Anu in the wrestling, "Anu struggled free from the hands of Kumarbi." But Kumarbi managed to
grab Anu by his feet, and "bit between his knees," hurting Anu in
his "manhood." Ancient depictions were found of the event (Fig.
23a), as well as of the habit of wrestling Anunnaki (Fig. 23b) to
hurt one another in the genitals.

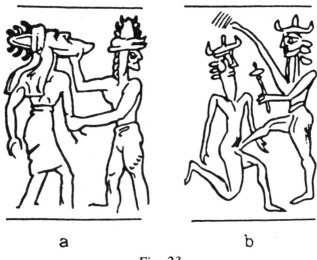

a　　　　　　　　　　　b

Fig. 23

Disgraced and in pain, Anu took off on his way to Nibiru, leaving Kumarbi behind with the astronauts manning the space platforms and shuttlecraft. But before he departed, he put on Kumarbi
a curse of "three monsters in his belly."

The similarity of this Hittite tale to the Greek tale of the castration of Uranus by Cronos, and the swallowing by Cronos of his

sons, needs no elaboration. And, as in the Greek tales, this episode
set the stage for the wars between the gods and the Titans.

After Anu had left, Earth Mission was launched in earnest.

As more Anunnaki landed on Earth—their number rose in time
to 600—some were assigned to the Lower World to help Enki mine
the gold; others manned the ore ships; and the rest stayed with Enlil in Mesopotamia. There, additional settlements were established
in accordance with a master plan laid out by Enlil, as part of a complete organizational plan of action and clear-cut procedures:

> He perfected the procedures, the divine ordinances;
> Established five cities in perfect places,
> Called them by name,
> Laid them out as centers.
> The first of these cities, Eridu,
> He granted to Nudimmud, the pioneer.

Each of these pre-Diluvial settlements in Mesopotamia had a
specific function, revealed by its name. First was E.RI.DU—
"House in Faraway Built"—the gold-extracting facility by the
waters' edge, which for all time remained Ea's Mesopotamian
abode. Next came BAD.TIBIRA—"Bright Place Where the Ores
Are Made Final"—the metallurgical center for smelting and refining. Next LA.RA.AK—"Seeing the Bright Glow"—was a
beacon-city to guide the landing shuttlecraft. SIPPAR—"Bird
City"—was the Landing Place; and SHU.RUP.PAK—"The Place
of Utmost Well-Being"—was equipped as a medical center; it was
put in the charge of SUD ("She Who Resuscitates"), a half-sister
of both Enki and Enlil.

Another beacon-city, LA.AR.SA ("Seeing the Red Light"), was
also built, for the complex operation depended on close coordination between the Anunnaki who had landed on Earth and 300 astronauts, called IGI.GI ("Those Who See and Observe"), who
remained in constant Earth orbit. Acting as intermediaries between
Earth and Nibiru, the Igigi stayed in Earth's skies on orbiting platforms, to which the processed ores were delivered from Earth by
shuttlecraft, thereafter to be transferred to proper spaceships,
which could ferry the gold to the Home Planet as it periodically
neared Earth in its vast elliptical orbit. Astronauts and equipment
were delivered to Earth by the same stages, in reverse.

All of that required a Mission Control Center, which Enlil proceeded to build and equip. It was named NIBRU.KI ("The Earth-Place of Nibiru")—Nippur in Akkadian. There, atop an artificially raised platform equipped with antennas—the prototype of the Mesopotamian "Towers of Babel" (Fig. 24)—was a secret chamber, the DIR.GA ("Dark, Glowing Chamber") where space charts ("the emblems of the stars") were displayed and where the DUR.AN.KI ("Bond Heaven-Earth") was maintained.

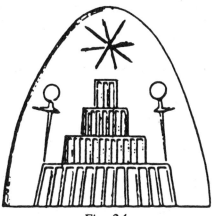

Fig. 24

The Chronicles have asserted that the first settlements of the Anunnaki on Earth were "laid out as centers." To this enigmatic statement was added the puzzle of the claim by post-Diluvial kings that in reestablishing in Sumer the cities wiped out by the Flood, they had followed

The everlasting ground plan,
that which for all time
the construction has determined.
It is the one which bears
the drawings from the Olden Times
and the writing of the Upper Heaven.

The puzzle will be solved if we mark out those first cities established by Enki and Enlil on the region's map and connect them with concentric circles. They were indeed "laid out as centers": all were equidistant from the Mission Control Center in Nippur. It was indeed a plan "from Upper Heaven," for it made sense only to those who could view the whole Near East from high above Earth: Choosing the twin-peaked Mount Ararat—the area's most conspic-

uous feature—as their landmark, they placed the spaceport where
the north line based on Ararat crossed the visible Euphrates River.
In this "everlasting ground plan," all the cities were arranged as
an arrow, marking out the Landing Path to the Spaceport at Sippar
(Fig. 25).

The periodic deliveries of gold to Nibiru mitigated the concerns,

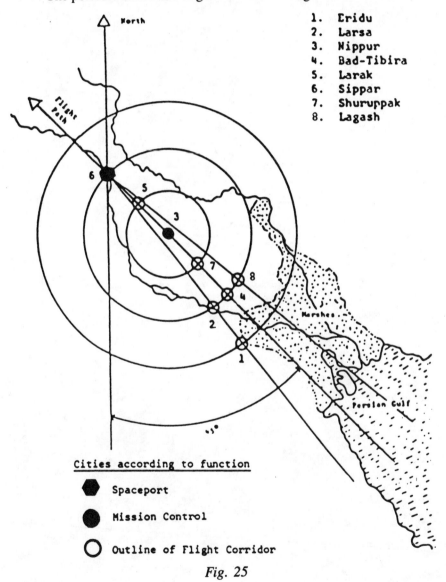

1. Eridu
2. Larsa
3. Nippur
4. Bad-Tibira
5. Larak
6. Sippar
7. Shuruppak
8. Lagash

Cities according to function

Spaceport

Mission Control

Outline of Flight Corridor

Fig. 25

even the rivalries, on that planet, for Anu stayed on as its ruler for a long time thereafter. But on Earth all the main actors were present on the ''dark-hued'' stage to give vent to every imaginable emotion and to incredible conflicts.

5

THE WARS OF
THE OLDEN GODS

Anu's first visit to Earth and the decisions then reached set the course of events on Earth for all the millennia that followed. In time they led to the creation of The Adam—Man as we know him, *Homo sapiens;* they also planted the seeds of future conflict on Earth between Enlil and Enki and their descendants.

But first there were the lingering and bitter struggles between the House of Anu and the House of Alalu, an enmity that burst out on Earth into the War of the Titans. It was a war that pitted "the gods who are in heaven" against the "gods who are upon dark-hued Earth"; it was, in its last climactic phase, an uprising of the Igigi!

That it had taken place in the early days of the settlement of the Nibiruans on Earth and in the aftermath of Anu's first visit to Earth, we know from the *Kingship in Heaven* text. Recalling the adversaries, it refers to them as "the mighty olden gods, the gods of the olden days." After naming five ancestors as "the fathers and mothers of the gods" who preceded Anu and Alalu, it begins the tale with the usurpations of the throne on Nibiru, the flight of Alalu, the visit of Anu to Earth, and the ensuing conflict with Kumarbi.

The story in the *Kingship in Heaven* text is augmented and continued in several other Hittite/Hurrian texts, which scholars call collectively *The Kumarbi Cycle.* Laboriously pieced together (and still badly fragmented), the texts have recently become more intelligible by the discovery of additional fragments and versions, reported and fitted into place by H. Güterbock *(Kumarbi Mythen von Churritischen Kronos)* and H. Otten *(Mythen vom Gotte Kumarbi—Neue Fragmente).*

How long Kumarbi remained aloft after the fight with Anu is not clear from these texts. We do learn that after the passage of some time, and after Kumarbi managed to spit out the "stones" that Anu caused to grow in his belly, Kumarbi came down to Earth. For reasons that may have been explained in missing parts of the texts, he went to Ea in the Abzu.

Mutilated verses then deal with the appearance on the scene of the Storm God Teshub, who, according to the Sumerians, was Enlil's youngest son Ishkur/Adad. The Storm God annoys Kumarbi by telling him of the wonderful attributes and objects that each god will grant him, Teshub; among these attributes shall be Wisdom, which shall be transferred away from Kumarbi. "Filled with fury Kumarbi went to Nippur." Breaks in the texts leave us ignorant as to what went on there, at Enlil's headquarters; but after a stay of seven months Kumarbi went back to consult with Ea.

Ea suggested that Kumarbi "ascend to heaven" and seek the help of Lama, who was "mother of the two gods" and thus, apparently, an ancestral matriarch of the two contesting dynasties. With some self-interest, Ea offered to transport Kumarbi to the Celestial Abode in his MAR.GID.DA (celestial chariot), which the Akkadians called *Ti-ia-ri-ta,* "the flying vehicle." But the goddess, having found out that Ea was coming without the permission of the Assembly of the Gods, sent "lightning winds" against Ea's spacecraft, forcing him and Kumarbi to return to Earth.

But rather than go down all the way, Kumarbi chose to stay with the orbiting gods whom the Hittite/Hurrian text calls Irsirra ("Those Who See and Orbit"), the Sumerian IGI.GI. With ample time on his hands, "Kumarbi was full with thoughts . . . thinking them out in his mind . . . he nurses thoughts of creating misfortune . . . he plots evil." The essence of his thoughts was that he should be proclaimed "the father of all the gods," the supreme deity!

Gaining the backing of the orbiting Irsirra gods, Kumarbi "put swift shoes on his feet" and flew down to Earth. There he sent his emissary to the other leading gods, demanding that they recognize his supremacy.

It was then that Anu decided that enough was enough. To vanquish once and for all the grandson of his adversary Alalu, Anu ordered his own grandson, the "Storm God" Teshub, to find Kumarbi and kill him. Ferocious battles then ensued between the terrestrial gods led by Teshub and the sky-borne gods led by Kumarbi; in one battle alone, no less than seventy gods participated, all riding in celestial chariots. Though most battle scenes are lost in the damaged text, we know that in the end Teshub had prevailed.

But the defeat of Kumarbi did not end the struggle. We learn from additional Hittite epic tales in the Kumarbi Cycle that before his demise, Kumarbi managed to impregnate a goddess of the mountain with his seed, leading to the birth of his Avenger, the "Stone God" Ullikummi. As he hid his marvelous (or monstrous) son among the Irsirra gods, he instructed him to grow and attack Teshub's "beautiful city Kummiya . . . Attack the Storm God and tear him to pieces . . . shoot down all the gods from the sky like birds!" Once he attained victory on Earth, Ullikummi was to "ascend to Heaven for Kingship" and seize by force the throne on Nibiru. Having issued these instructions, Kumarbi passed away from the scene.

For a long time the child was hidden. But as he grew up— assuming giant proportions—he was seen one day by Utu/Shamash as he was roaming the skies. Utu rushed to Teshub's abode, to inform him of the appearance of the Avenger. After giving Utu food and drink to becalm himself, Teshub urged him to "mount thy chariot and ascend to the skies," to keep an eye on the growing Ullikummi. Then he went up the Mountain of Viewing to see the Stone God for himself. "He looked at the awesome Stone God, and in wrath shook his fist."

Realizing there was no alternative to battle, Teshub readied his chariot for combat; the Hittite text calls it by its Sumerian name ID.DUG.GA, "The Flowing Leaden Rider." The instructions for outfitting the celestial chariot, for which the Hittite text heavily employed the original Sumerian terminology, merit quoting. They called for revving up the vehicle with the "Great Cracker"; attaching the "Bull" (power-plant) that "Lights Up" in front and the "Bull for Lofty Missile" in the back end; installing the radarlike or navigational device "That Which Shows The Way" in the forepart; activating the instruments with the powerful energy "Stones" (minerals); and then arming the vehicle with the "Storm Thunderer," loading it with no less than eight hundred "Fire Stones":

> The "Great Cracker" of the "Bright Lead Rider"
> let them lubricate with oil and stir up.
> The "Bull that Lights Up" let them put between the horns.
> The tail's "Bull that is Lofty Missile"
> let them plate with gold.
> The forepart's "That Which Shows The Way"
> let them put in and turn,
> provide it with powerful "Stones" inside.
> Let them bring out the "Storm Thunderer"
> which scatters rocks for 90 furlongs,

making sure the "Fire Stones" with 800 . . . to cover.
The "Lightning Which Flashes Frightfully"
let them bring out from its storage chamber.
Let them bring out the MAR.GID.DA and make it ready!

"From the skies, from among the clouds, the Storm God set his face upon the Stone God." After the initial unsuccessful attacks, Ninurta, the brother of Teshub/Adad, joined the battles. But the Stone God remained unharmed and carried the battle to the very gates of Kummiya, the Storm God's city.

In Kummiya, Teshub's spouse Hebat was following the battle reports in an inner chamber of the god's house. But the missiles of Ullikummi "forced Hebat to leave the house, and she could no longer hear the messages of the gods . . . neither the messages of Teshub, nor the messages of all the gods." She ordered her messenger to "put the Swift Shoes on his feet" and go to the place where the gods were assembled, to bring back news of the battle; for she feared that "the Stone God may have killed my husband, the noble prince."

But Teshub was not killed. Advised by his attendant to hide at some mountainous sites, he refused: If we do that, he said, "there will be no king in Heaven!" The two then decided to go to Ea in the Abzu, to seek there an oracle according to "the old tablets with the words of fate."

Realizing that Kumarbi had brought forth a monster that was getting out of hand, Ea went to Enlil to warn him of the danger: "Ullikummi will block off the Heaven and the gods' holy houses!" An assembly of the Great Anunnaki was called. With all at a loss for a solution, Ea had one: From the sealed storehouse of the "stone cutters," let them bring out a certain Olden Metal Cutter, and let them cut under the feet of Ullikummi the Stone God.

When this was achieved, the Stone God was crippled. When the gods heard this, "they came to the place of assembly, and all the gods began to bellow against Ullikummi." Teshub, encouraged, jumped into his chariot; "he caught up with the Stone God Ullikummi at the sea, and engaged him in battle." But Ullikummi was still defiant, declaring: "Kummiya I shall destroy, the Sacred House I shall take over, the gods I shall drive out . . . up to Heaven I shall go to assume Kingship!"

The closing lines of the Hittite epic are completely damaged; but can we doubt that they told us the Sanskrit tale of the final battle between Indra and the "demon" Vritra?

And then was seen a dreadful sight,
when god and demon met in fight.
His sharpened missiles Vritra shot,
his thunderbolts and lightnings hot . . .
The lightnings then began to flash,
the direful thunderbolts to crash,
   by Indra proudly hurled . . .
And soon the knell of Vritra's doom
was sounded by the clang and boom
   of Indra's iron shower.
Pierced, cloven, crushed, with horrid yell
the dying demon headlong fell . . .
And Indra smote him with a bolt
between the shoulders.

These, we believe, were the battles of the "gods" and the Titans of the Greek tales. No one has yet found the meaning of "Titans"; but if the tales had a Sumerian origin, and if so did these gods' names, then TI.TA.AN in Sumerian would have literally meant "Those Who in Heaven Live"—precisely the designation of the Igigi led by Kumarbi; and their adversaries were the Anunnaki "Who are on Earth."

Sumerian texts indeed record an olden life-and-death battle between a grandson of Anu and a "demon" of a different clan; the tale is known as *The Myth of Zu*. Its hero is Ninurta, Enlil's son by his half-sister Sud; it could well have been the original tale from which the Hindu and Hittite tales were borrowed.

The setting for the events described in the Sumerian text is the time that had followed Anu's visit to Earth. Under the overall command of Enlil, the Anunnaki have settled to their tasks in the Abzu and in Mesopotamia: The ores are mined and transported, then smelted and refined. From a busy spaceport in Sippar, shuttlecraft take the precious metals aloft to the orbiting stations operated by the Igigi, thence on to the Home Planet by periodically visiting spaceships.

The complex system of space operations—the comings and goings by the space vehicles and communications between Earth and Nibiru, while both planets pursue their own destined orbits—is coordinated from Enlil's Mission Control Center in Nippur. There, atop a raised platform, was the DIR.GA room, the most restricted "holy of holies" where the vital celestial charts and orbital data panels—the "Tablets of Destinies"—were installed.

It was into this sacred chamber that a god named Zu gained access, seizing the vital tablets and thereby holding in his hands the fate of the Anunnaki on Earth and of Nibiru itself.

By combining portions of Old Babylonian and Assyrian versions of the Sumerian text, a good deal of the tale has been restored. But damaged portions still held the secret of Zu's true identity, as well as an explanation of how he had gained access to the Dirga. Only in 1979 did two scholars (W. W. Hallo and W. L. Moran) come up with the answer by using a tablet found in the Babylonian Collection of Yale University to reconstruct the beginning of the ancient tale.

In Sumerian the name ZU meant "He Who Knows," one expert in certain knowledge. Several references to the evil hero of this tale as AN.ZU—"He Who Knows the Heavens"—suggest a connection with the space program that had linked Earth with Nibiru; and the now-restored beginning of the chronicle indeed relates how Zu, an orphan, was adopted by the astronauts who manned the shuttlecraft and orbiting platforms, the Igigi—learning from them the secrets of the heavens and of space travel.

The action begins as the Igigi, "being gathered from all parts," decided to make an appeal to Enlil. Their complaint was that "until that time for the Igigi a break-taking place had not yet been built." In other words, there simply was no facility on Earth for the rest and recreation of the Igigi, where they could relax from the rigors of space and its weightlessness. To voice their complaint they selected Zu to be their spokesman, sending him to Enlil's center in Nippur.

Enlil, "the father of the gods, in the Dur-An-Ki, saw him, and thought of what they [the Igigi] said." As "in his mind he pondered" the request, "he studied the heavenly Zu closely." Who, after all, was this emissary, not one of the astronauts and yet wearing their uniform? As his suspicions grew, Ea—aware of Zu's true ancestry—spoke up; he suggested to Enlil that a decision on the request of the Igigi could be postponed if Zu were delayed at Enlil's headquarters. "Your service let him enter," Ea said to Enlil; "in the sanctuary, to the innermost seat, let him be the one to block the way."

To the words that Ea spoke to him
the god [Enlil] consented.
At the sanctuary Zu took up his position . . .
At the entrance to the chamber
Enlil had assigned him.

And so it was, with Ea's connivance, that an adversary god—a secret descendant of Alalu—was admitted to Enlil's innermost and most sensitive chamber. We read that there Zu "constantly views Enlil, the father of the gods, the god of the Bond-Heaven-Earth . . . his celestial Tablet of Destines Zu constantly views." And soon a scheme took shape: "The removal of the Enlilship he conceives in his heart":

I will take the celestial Tablet of Destinies;
The decrees of the gods I will govern;
I will establish my throne,
be master of the Heavenly Decrees;
The Igigi in their space I will command!

"His heart having thus plotted aggression," Zu saw his chance one day as Enlil went to take a cooling swim. "He seized the Tablet of Destinies in his hands" and in his Bird "took off and flew to safety in the HUR.SAG.MU" ("Mountain of the Sky-Chambers"). No sooner had this happened than everything came to a standstill:

Suspended were the divine formulas;
The lighted brightness petered out;
Silence prevailed.
In space, the Igigi were confounded;
The sanctuary's brilliance was taken off.

At first "father Enlil was speechless." As the communications were restored, "the gods on Earth gathered one by one at the news." Anu, on Nibiru, was also informed. It was clear that Zu must be captured and the Tablet of Destinies restored to the Dir-Ga. But who will do it? Several of the younger gods known for their valor were approached. But none dared track Zu to the distant mountain, for he was now as powerful as Enlil, having also stolen the "Brilliance" of Enlil; "and he who opposes him shall become as clay . . . at his Brilliance the gods waste away."

It was then that Ninurta, Enlil's legal heir, stepped forth to undertake the task, for—as his mother Sud had pointed out—Zu deprived not only Enlil but also Ninurta of the "Enlilship." She advised him to attack Zu in his hideaway mountain also with a weapon of "Brilliance," but to do so only after he was able to approach Zu behind a dust screen. To achieve the latter she lent Ninurta her own "seven whirlwinds that stir up the dust."

With "his battle courage grown firmer," Ninurta repaired to

Mount Hazzi—the mountain encountered in the Kumarbi tales—
where he hitched to his chariot his seven weapons, attached the
whirlwinds that stir up the dust, and set out against Zu "to launch a
terrifying war, a fierce battle":

> Zu and Ninurta met at the mountainside.
> When Zu perceived him, he broke out in rage.
> With his Brilliance, he made the mountain
> bright as daylight;
> He let loose rays in a rage.

Unable to identify his challenger because of the dust storm, Zu
shouted to Ninurta: "I have carried off all Authority, the decrees of
the gods I [now] direct! Who are thou to come fight with me? Explain thyself!"

But Ninurta continued to "advance aggressively" against Zu,
announcing that he was designated by Anu himself to seize Zu and
restore the Tablet of Destinies. Hearing this, Zu cut off his Brilliance, and "the face of the mountain was covered with darkness."
Unafraid, Ninurta "entered the gloom." From the "breast" of his
vehicle, he let loose a Lightning at Zu, "but the shot could not approach Zu; it turned back." With the powers Zu had obtained, no
lightning bolt could "approach his body."

So "the battle was stilled, the conflict ceased; the weapons were
stopped in the midst of the mountain; they vanquished not Zu."

Stalemated, Ninurta asked his younger brother Ishkur/Adad to
obtain the advice of Enlil. "Ishkur, the prince, took the report; the
news of the battle he reported to Enlil."

Enlil instructed Ishkur to go back and tell Ninurta: "In the battle do
not tire; prove thy strength!" More practically, he sent Ninurta a
tillu—a missile (pictographically written ⊁——ᗡ)—to attach to
the Stormer that shoots the projectiles. Ninurta in his "Whirlwind
Bird," he said, should then come as close as possible to the Bird of
Zu, until they are "wing to wing." Then he should aim the missile at
the "pinions" of Zu's Whirlbird, and "let the missile fly like a lightning; when the Fiery Brilliance will engulf the pinions, his wings will
vibrate like butterflies; then will Zu be vanquished."

The final battle scenes are missing from all the tablets, but we
know that more than one "Whirlbird" participated in the combat.
Fragments of duplicates, found in the ruins of a Hittite archive at a
site now called Sultan-Tepe, tell us that Ninurta arrayed "seven
whirlwinds which stir up the dust," armed his chariot with the

"Ill Winds" weapons, and attacked Zu as suggested by his father. "The earth shook . . . the [illegible] became dark, the skies became black . . . the pinions of Zu were overcome." Zu was captured and brought back before Enlil in Nippur; the Tablet of Destinies was reinstalled where it belonged; "Lordship again entered the Ekur; the Divine Formulas were returned."

The captured Zu was put on trial before a court-martial consisting of the Seven Great Anunnaki; he was found guilty and sentenced to death; Ninurta, his vanquisher, "cut his throat." Many depictions were found showing the trial scene, in which Zu, on account of his association with the Igigi astronauts, was dressed up as a bird. An archaic relief found in central Mesopotamia illustrated the actual execution of Zu. This one shows Zu—who belonged to those "Who Observe and See"—as a demonic cock with an extra eye in the forehead (Fig. 26).

Fig. 26

* * *

The defeat of Zu lingered in the memory of the Anunnaki as a great deliverance. Perhaps because of the assumption that the spirit of Zu—representing betrayal, duplicity, and all evil in general—persists in causing ill and suffering, the trial and execution of Zu were transmitted to mankind's generations in the form of an elaborate ritual. In this annual commemoration a bull was chosen to stand for Zu and atone for his evil deed.

Long instructions for the ritual have been found in both Babylonian and Assyrian versions, all indicating their earlier Sumerian source. After extensive preparations, a "great bull, strong bull who treads upon clean pastures" was brought into the temple and purified on the first day of a certain month. It was then whispered into the bull's left ear through a reed tube: "Bull, the guilty Zu are you"; and into the right ear: "Bull, you have been chosen for the rite and the ceremonies." On the fifteenth day the bull was brought before the images of "the Seven Gods Who Judge" and the symbols of the twelve celestial bodies of the Solar System.

The trial of Zu was then reenacted. The bull was put down before Enlil, "the Great Shepherd." The accusing priest recited rhetorical accusational questions, as though addressed to Enlil: How could you have given "the stored treasure" to the enemy? How could you have let him come and dwell in the "pure place"? How could he gain access to your quarters? Then the playacting called for Ea and other gods to beseech Enlil to calm himself, for Ninurta had stepped forward and asked his father: "Point my hands in the right direction! Give me the right words of command!"

Following this recital of the evidence given at the trial, judgment was passed. As the bull was being slaughtered in accordance with detailed instructions, the priests recited the bull's verdict: His liver was to be boiled in a sacrifical kettle; his skin and muscles were to be burned inside the temple; but his "evil tongue shall remain outside."

Then the priests, playing the roles of the other gods, broke out in a hymn of praise to Ninurta:

Wash your hands, wash your hands!
You are now as Enlil, wash your hands!
You are as Enlil [upon] the Earth;
May all the gods rejoice in you!

When the gods looked for a volunteer to fight Zu, they promised the vanquisher of Zu:

Thy name shall be the greatest
in the Assembly of the Great Gods;
Among the gods, thy brothers,
thou shall have no equal;
Glorified before the gods
and potent shall be thy name!

After Ninurta's victory the promise had to be kept. But therein was the rub and the seed of future fights among the gods: Ninurta was indeed Enlil's Legal Heir but on Nibiru, not on Earth. Now, as the commemorative temple ritual makes clear, he was made "as Enlil—upon Earth." We know from other texts dealing with the gods of Sumer and Akkad that their hierarchical order was also expressed numerically. Anu was given the highest number of the Sumerian sexagesimal system, 60. His Legal Heir, Enlil, had the rank of 50; the firstborn son (and heir in the event of Enlil's demise), Ea, was 40. Now, as the enigmatic statement that Ninurta has become "as Enlil" attests, he, too, was given the rank of 50.

The partly mutilated ending of the temple ritual text contains the following legible verses: "O Marduk, for your king speak the words: 'I release!' O Adad, for your king speak the words: 'I release!' " We can safely guess that the mutilated lines also included a similar release by Sin of his claim to kingship among the gods and recognition of Ninurta's Enlilship. We know that thereafter, Sin —Enlil's firstborn on Earth—held the rank of 30, his son Shamash 20, and his daughter Ishtar 15, and Ishkur (*Adad* in Akkadian) the rank of 10. (There is no record of Marduk's numerical rank.)

The conspiracy of Zu and his evil plotting remained also in mankind's memory, evolving into a fear of birdlike demons who can cause affliction and pestilence (Fig. 27). Some of these demons were called *Lillu,* a term that played on the double meaning "to howl" and "of the night"; their female leader, *Lillitu*—Lilith— was depicted as a naked, winged goddess with birdlike feet (Fig. 28). The many *shurpu* ("purification by burning") texts that have been found were formulas for incantations against these evil spirits—forerunners of the sorcery and witchcraft that had lasted throughout the millennia.

In spite of the solemn vows taken after the defeat of Zu to honor and respect Enlil's supremacy and Ninurta's position as second-in-command, the basic factors causing rivalry and contention had remained—breaking into the open from time to time in the ensuing

Fig. 27

millennia. Realizing that this would be so, Anu and Enlil provided Ninurta with new, marvelous weapons. Anu gave him the SHAR.UR ("Supreme Hunter") and the SHAR.GAZ ("Supreme Smiter"); Enlil gave him several weapons, of which the unique IB—a weapon with "fifty killing heads"—was the most awesome, leading to references in the chronicles to Ninurta as "The Lord of the Ib." Thus armed, Ninurta became the "Foremost Warrior of Enlil," ready to fight off all challenges to the Enlilship.

The next such challenge came in the shape of a mutiny of the Anunnaki who were working in the gold mines of the Abzu. The mutiny, and the events that had led to it and followed it, are fully described in a text called by scholars *The Atra-Hasis Epic*—a full-fledged Earth Chronicle which, inter alia, records the events that had led to the creation of *Homo sapiens*—Man as we know him.

The text informs us that after Anu had gone back to Nibiru and Earth was divided between Enlil and Enki, the Anunnaki toiled in the mines of the Abzu for "forty counted periods"—forty orbits of their planet, or 144,000 Earth-years. But the work was diffi-

Fig. 28

cult and backbreaking: "inside the mountains . . . in the deeply cut shafts . . . the Anunnaki suffered the toil; excessive was their toil, for forty counted periods."

The mining operations, deep inside the earth, were never interrupted: the Anunnaki "suffered the toil day and night." But as the shafts grew deeper and the toil harsher, dissatisfaction grew: "They were complaining, backbiting, grumbling in the excavations."

To help maintain discipline Enlil sent Ninurta to the Abzu, but this strained relations with Enki even more. It was then that Enlil decided to go to the Abzu and personally evaluate the situation. The discontended Anunnaki seized the opportunity to mutiny!

The *Atra-Hasis* chronicle, in language as vivid as that of a modern reporter, in more than 150 lines of text, unambiguously describes the events that followed: How the rebellious Anunnaki put their tools on fire and, in the middle of the night, marched on Enlil's dwelling; how some shouted "Let us kill him . . . Let us break the yoke!''; how an unnamed leader reminded them that Enlil was the "Chief Officer of Old Time," and advised negotiations; and how Enlil, enraged, took up his weapons, but he, too, was reminded by his chamberlain: "My lord, these are your sons. . . .''

As Enlil remained a prisoner in his own quarters, he sent a message to Anu and asked that he come to Earth. When Anu arrived, the Great Anunnaki assembled for a court-martial. "Enki, Ruler of the Abzu, was also present." Enlil demanded to know who the instigator of the mutiny was, calling for a death penalty. Not getting the support of Anu, Enlil offered his resignation: "Noble one," he said to Anu, "take away the office, take away the power; to Heaven will I ascend with you." But Anu, calming Enlil, also expressed understanding of the miners' hardships.

Encouraged, Enki "opened his mouth and addressed the gods." Repeating Anu's summation, he had a solution to offer: While the Chief Medical Officer, their sister Sud, was here in the Abzu with them:

Let her create a Primitive Worker;
And let him bear the yoke . . .
Let the Worker carry the toil of the gods,
Let him bear the yoke!

In the following one hundred lines of the *Atra-Hasis* text, and in several other "Creation of Man" texts that have been discovered in various states of preservation, the tale of the genetic engineering of *Homo sapiens* has been told in amazing detail. To achieve the feat Enki suggested that a "Being that already exists"—Apewoman—be used to create the *Lulu Amelu* ("The Mixed Worker") by "binding" upon the less evolved beings "the mold of the gods." The goddess

Sud purified the "essence" of a young male Anunnaki; she mixed it into the egg of an Apewoman. The fertilized egg was then implanted in the womb of a female Anunnaki, for the required period of pregnancy. When the "mixed creature" was born, Sud lifted him up and shouted: "I have created! My hands have made it!"

The "Primitive Worker"—*Homo sapiens*—had come into being. It happened some 300,000 years ago; it came about through a feat of genetic engineering and embryo-implant techniques which mankind itself is beginning to employ. There has undoubtedly been a long process of evolution; but then the Anunnaki had taken a hand in the process and jumped the gun on evolution, "creating" us sooner than we might have evolved on our own. Scholars have been searching for a long time for the "missing link" in man's evolution. The Sumerian texts reveal that the "missing link" was a feat of genetic manipulation performed in a laboratory. . . . It was not a feat over and done with in an instant. The texts make clear that it had taken the Anunnaki considerable trial and error to achieve the desired "perfect model" of the Primitive Worker, but once achieved, a mass-production process was launched: fourteen "birth goddesses" at a time were implanted with the genetically manipulated Apewomen eggs: seven to bear male and seven to bear female Workers. As soon as they grew up, the Workers were put to work in the mines; and as their numbers grew, they assumed more and more of the physical chores in the Abzu.

The armed clash between Enlil and Enki that was soon to take place, however, was over these same slave laborers. . . .

The more the production of ores improved in the Abzu, the greater was the work load on the Anunnaki that had remained to operate the facilities in Mesopotamia. The climate was milder, rains were more plentiful, and the rivers of Mesopotamia were constantly overflowing. Increasingly the Mesopotamian Anunnaki "were digging the river," raising dikes and deepening the canals. Soon they too began to clamor for the slave workers, the "creatures of bright countenance" but with thick black hair:

The Anunnaki stepped up to Enlil . . .
Black-headed Ones they were requesting of him.
To the Black-headed people
to give the pickax to hold.

We read of these events in a text named by Samuel N. Kramer *The Myth of the Pickax*. Though portions are missing, it is understood that Enki refused Enlil's request for the transfer of Primitive Workers to Mesopotamia. Deciding to take matters into his own hands, Enlil took the extreme step of disconnecting the communications with the home planet: "In the 'Bond Heaven-Earth' he made a gash . . . verily did he speed to disconnect Heaven from Earth." Then he launched an armed attack against the Land of the Mines.

The Anunnaki in the Abzu assembled the Primitive Workers in a central compound, strengthening its walls against the coming attack. But Enlil fashioned a marvelous weapon, the AL.A.NI ("Ax That Produces Power") equipped with a "horn" and an "earth splitter" that could drill through walls and earthworks. With these weapons Enlil drove a hole through the fortifications. As the hole widened "Primitive Workers were breaking out toward Enlil. He eyed the Black-headed Ones in fascination."

Thereafter the Primitive Workers performed the manual tasks in both Lands: In the Land of the Mines they "bore the work and suffered the toil"; in Mesopotamia, "with picks and spades they built gods' houses, they built the big canal banks; food they grew for the sustenance of the gods."

Many ancient drawings engraved on cylinder seals depicted these Primitive Workers performing their tasks, naked as the animals of the field (Fig. 29). Various Sumerian texts recorded this animallike stage in human development:

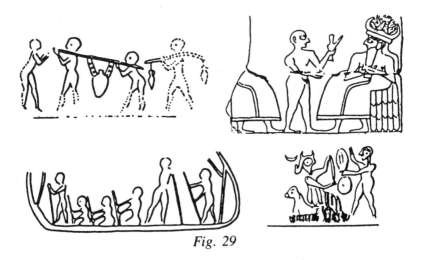

Fig. 29

When Mankind was first created,
They knew not the eating of bread,
Knew not the dressing of garments,
Ate plants with their mouth like sheep,
Drank water from the ditch . . .

How long, however, could young female Anunnaki be asked (or forced) to perform the roles of "birth goddesses"? Unbeknownst to Enlil, and with the connivance of Sud, Enki contrived to give the new creature one more genetic twist: granting to the hybrid beings—incapable of procreating, as all hybrids are—the ability to have offspring, the sexual "Knowing" for having children. The event is echoed in the biblical tale of Adam and Eve in the Garden of Eden, and although the original Sumerian text of the tale has not yet been found, a number of Sumerian depictions of the event were indeed discovered. They show different aspects of the tale: the Tree of Life; the offering of the forbidden fruit; the angry encounter that ensued between the "Lord God" and the "Serpent." Yet another shows Eve girdled in a garment around her loins while Adam is still naked (Fig. 30), another detail related in the Bible.

Fig. 30

While the Serpent God features in all these ancient depictions, the illustration reproduced here is of particular significance as it writes out, in archaic Sumerian the god's epithet/name as ✳→. The "star" spells "god" and the triangular symbol reads BUR, BURU, or BUZUR—all terms that make the epithet/name mean "God Who Solves Secrets," "God of the Deep Mines," and variations thereof. The Bible (in the original Hebrew) calls the god who tempted Eve *Nahash,* translated ''Serpent,'' but literally meaning ''He Who Solves Secrets'' and ''He Who Knows Metals,'' the exact parallels of the god's name in the Sumerian depiction. This depiction is of further interest because it shows the Serpent God with his hands and feet in tethers, suggesting that Enki was arrested after his unauthorized deed.

In his anger Enlil ordered the expulsion of The Adam—the *Homo sapiens* Earthling—from the E.DIN (''The Abode of the Righteous Ones''). No longer confined to the settlements of the Anunnaki, Man began to roam the Earth.

> ''And Adam *knew* Eve his wife, and she conceived and bore Cain . . . and she bore again his brother Abel.'' The gods were no longer alone on Earth.

Little did the Anunnaki then know the role that the Primitive Worker would play in the wars between them.

6

MANKIND EMERGES

Ever since George Smith found and reported in 1876 *(The Chaldean Account of Genesis)* detailed Mesopotamian tales of Creation, followed by L. W. King's *The Seven Tablets of Creation,* scholars and theologians alike have come to recognize that the Creation Tales of the Old Testamant (Genesis Chapters 1 through 3) are condensed and edited versions of original Sumerian texts. A century later, in our work, *The 12th Planet* (1976), we have shown that these texts were no primitive myths, but depositories of advanced scientific knowledge with which modern scholars are only now beginning to catch up.

The unmanned space probes of Jupiter and Saturn confirmed many "incredible" facets of the Sumerian knowledge regarding our Solar System, such as that the outer planets have numerous satellites and that water is present on some of them. Those distant planets, and some of their principal satellites, were found to have active cores that generate internal heat; some radiate out more heat than they can ever receive from the distant Sun. Volcanic activity provided those celestial bodies with their own atmospheres. All the basic requirements for the development of life exist out there, just as the Sumerians had said 6,000 years ago.

What, then, of the existence of a twelfth member of our Solar System—a tenth planet beyond Pluto, the Sumerian Nibiru (and Babylonian Marduk)—a planet whose existence was a basic and far-reaching conclusion in *The 12th Planet?*

In 1978, astronomers at the U.S. Naval Observatory in Washington determined that Pluto—being smaller than formerly believed—could not by itself account for perturbations in the orbits of Uranus and Neptune; they postulated the existence of yet another celestial body beyond Pluto. In 1982 the U.S. National Aeronautics and Space Administration (NASA) announced its conclusion that there indeed exists such a body; whether or not it is another large planet, it planned to determine by deploying in a certain manner its two *Pioneer* spacecraft that had been hurtling into space beyond Saturn.

And at the close of 1983, astronomers at the Jet Propulsion Laboratory in California announced that IRAS—the infrared telescope mounted on a spacecraft and launched under NASA's auspices with the cooperation of other nations—had discovered beyond Pluto a very distant "mystery celestial body" about four times the size of Earth and *moving toward Earth.* They have not yet called it a planet; but our Earth Chronicles leave the ultimate finding in no doubt.

In 1983, rocks were found in Antarctica and elsewhere which are undoubtedly fragments of the Moon and Mars; and the scientists are totally baffled as to how that could have happened. The Sumerian tale of the Creation of the Solar System, the collision between Nibiru's satellites and Tiamat, and the rest of the cosmogony in the celebrated *Epic of Creation* offer a comprehensive explanation.

And what about the texts describing how Man was created through genetic manipulation: in vitro fertilization and reimplantation?

Recent advances in genetic sciences and technologies have affirmed the Sumerian concept of gradual evolution on the one hand, and on the other hand, the (otherwise inexplicable) appearance of the biologically advanced *Homo sapiens* through genetic engineering by the Anunnaki. Even the very recent method of test tube procreation—extracting a female egg, impregnating it with purified male semen, and reimplanting the fertilized egg in a woman's womb—is the very same procedure described in the Sumerian texts from millennia ago.

If the two principal events—the creation of Earth and the creation of Man—are correctly reported in the Bible, ought we not to accept the veracity of the biblical tale regarding the emergence of mankind on Earth?

And if the biblical tales are but a condensed version of more detailed, earlier Sumerian chronicles, could not the latter be used to enhance and complete the biblical record of those earliest times?

Since one is the reflection of the other, let us hold up a mirror to that ancient flame of memories. . . . Let us continue the unraveling of the wondrous tale.

After relating how "*The* Adam" (literally, "the Earthling") was granted the ability to procreate, the Book of Genesis moves from recounting the general events on Earth to the saga of a specific branch of mankind: the person named Adam and his descendants.

"This is the Book of the Generations of Adam," the Old Testament informs us. Such a book, we can safely assume, had surely existed. The evidence strongly suggests that the person whom the Bible called Adam was the one whom the Sumerians called *Adapa,* an Earthling "perfected" by Enki and deemed to have been genetically related to him. "Wide understanding Enki perfected for him, to disclose the designs of the Earth; to him he gave Knowing; but immortality he did not give him."

Portions of the "Tale of Adapa" have been found; the complete text might well have been the "Book of the Generations of Adam" to which the Old Testament refers. Assyrian kings probably had access to such a record, for many of them claimed to have retained one or another of Adapa's virtues. Sargon and Sennacherib held that they had inherited the wisdom that Enki had granted Adapa; Sinsharishkun and Esarhaddon boasted that they were born "in the image of the wise Adapa"; according to an inscription of Esarhaddon, he had erected in the temple of Ashur a statue with the image of Adapa; and Ashurbanipal asserted that he had learned "the secret of tablet-writing from before the Deluge" as Adapa had known.

The Sumerian sources hold that there had been both rural cultures—cultivation and shepherding—as well as urban settlements before the Deluge had swept all off the face of the Earth. The Book of Genesis relates that the first son of Adam and Eve, Cain, "was a tiller of the earth," and his brother Abel "was a herder of sheep." Then, after Cain was exiled "away from the presence of the Lord" for having killed Abel, urban settlements— Cities of Man—were established: in the land of Nud, east of Eden, Cain had a son whom he named Enoch and built a city called likewise, the name meaning "Foundation." The Old Testament, having no particular interest in the line of Cain, skips quickly to the fourth generation after Enoch, when Lamech was born:

And Lamech took unto himself two wives:
The name of one was Adah,
and the name of the other Zillah.
And Adah bore Jabal; he was the father of
    such as dwell in tents and have cattle.
And his brother's name was Jubal; he was the
    father of all such as play lyre and pipe.
And Zillah also bore Tubal-Cain,
    an artificer of gold and copper and iron.

The pseudepigraphical *Book of Jubilees,* believed to have been composed in the second century B.C. from earlier material, adds the information that Cain espoused his own sister Awan and she bore him Enoch "at the close of the fourth Jubilee. And in the first year of the first week of the fifth Jubilee, houses were built on the earth, and Cain built a city and called its name Foundation, after the name of his son." Where did this additional information come from?

It has long been held that this part of the Genesis tale stands alone, without corroboration or parallel in the Mesopotamian texts. But we have found that it is just not so.

First, we have come upon a Babylonian tablet in the British Museum (No. 74329, Fig. 31), catalogued as "containing an otherwise unknown myth." Yet it may in fact be a Babylonian/Assyrian version from circa 2000 B.C. of *a missing Sumerian record of the Line of Cain!*

As copied by A. R. Millard and translated by W. G. Lambert (*Kadmos,* vol. VI), it speaks of the beginnings of a group of people who were ploughmen, which corresponds to the biblical "tiller of the land." They are called *Amakandu*—"People Who In Sorrow Roam"; it parallels the condemnation of Cain: "Banned be thou from the soil which hath received thy brother's blood . . . a restless nomad shalt thou be upon the earth." And, most remarkably, the Mesopotamian chief of these exiled people was called *Ka'in!* Also, just as in the biblical tale:

He built in Dunnu
a city with twin towers.
Ka'in dedicated to himself
the lordship over the city.

The name of this place is intriguing. Because the order of syllables could be reversed in Sumerian without changing the meaning, the name could also be spelled NU.DUN, paralleling the biblical name Nud as the place of Cain's exile. The Sumerian name meant "the excavated resting place"—very much similar to the biblical interpretation of the name as meaning "Foundation."

After the death (or murder) of Ka'in, "he was laid to rest in the city of Dunnu, which he loved." As in the biblical tale, the Mesopotamian text records the history of four following generations: brothers married their sisters and murdered their parents, taking over the rulership in Dunnu as well as settling in new places, the last of which was named *Shupat* ("Judgment").

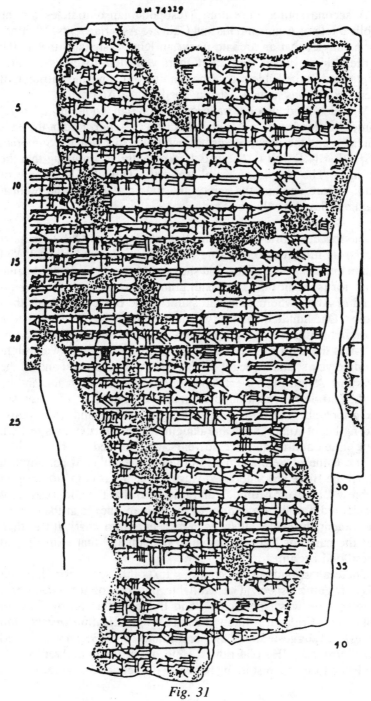

Fig. 31

A second source indicating Mesopotamian chronicles for the biblical tale of Adam and his son Cain are Assyrian texts. We find, for example, that an archaic Assyrian King List states that in the earliest times, when their forefathers were tent-dwellers—a term duplicated in the Bible regarding the line of Cain—the patriarch of their people was named Adamu, the biblical Adam.

We also find among traditional Assyrian eponyms of royal names the combination Ashur-bel-Ka'ini ("Ashur, lord of the Ka'-inites"); and the Assyrian scribes paralleled this with the Sumerian ASHUR-EN.DUNI ("Ashur is lord of *Duni*"), implying that the Ka'ini ("The people of Kain") and the Duni ("The people of Dun") were one and the same; and thus reaffirming the biblical Cain and Land of Nud or Dun.

Having dealt briefly with the line of Cain, the Old Testament turned its full attention to a new line descended of Adam: "And Adam knew his wife again, and she bore a son, and called his name Seth, for [she said] the Lord hath granted me another offspring instead of Abel, whom Cain had slain." The Book of Genesis then adds: "One hundred and thirty years did Adam live when he begot a son in his likeness and after his image, and called his name Seth.

"And the days of Adam after he had begotten Seth were eight hundred years, and he begot [other] sons and daughters; and all the days that Adam lived were nine hundred and thirty years, and he died. And Seth lived a hundred and five years and begot Enosh; and after he begot Enosh Seth lived eight hundred and seven years, and he begot [other] sons and daughters; and all the days of Seth were nine hundred and twelve years, and he died."

The name of Seth's son and the next pre-Diluvial patriarch in which the Bible was interested was *Enosh;* it has come to mean in Hebrew "Human, Mortal," and it is clear that the Old Testament considered him the progenitor of the human lineage at the core of the ancient chronicles. It states in respect to him, that "It was then that the name of Yahweh began to be called," that worship and priesthood began.

There are a number of Sumerian texts that shed more light on this intriguing aspect. The available portions of the *Adapa* text state that he was "perfected" and treated as a son by Enki in Enki's city Eridu. It is likely then, as William Hallo *(Antediluvian Cities)* had suggested, that the great-grandson of Enosh was named *Yared* to mean "He of Eridu." Here, then, is the answer: While the Bible loses interest in the banished descendants of Adam, it focuses its attention on the patriarchs from Adam's line who had stayed in Eden—southern Mesopotamia—and were the first to be called to priesthood.

In the fourth generation after Enosh the firstborn son was named Enoch; scholars believe that here the name's meaning stemmed from a variant of the Hebrew root, connoting "to train, to educate." Of him the Old Testament briefly states that he "had walked with the Deity" and did not die on Earth, "for the Deity had taken him." The sole verse in Genesis 5:24 is substantially enlarged upon in the extra-biblical *Books of Enoch.* They detail his first visit with the Angels of God to be instructed in various sciences and ethics. Then, after returning to Earth to pass the knowledge and the requisites of priesthood to his sons, he was taken aloft once more, to permanently join the *Nefilim* (the biblical term meaning "Those Who Had Dropped Down") in their celestial abode.

The Sumerian King List records the priestly reign of Enmeduranki in Sippar, then the location of the Spaceport under the command of Utu/Shamash. His name, "Priestly lord of the Dur-an-ki," indicates that he had been trained in Nippur. A little-known tablet, reported by W. G. Lambert ("Enmeduranki and Related Material"), reads as follows:

> Enmeduranki [was] a prince in Sippar,
> Beloved of Anu, Enlil and Ea.
> Shamash in the Bright Temple appointed him.
> Shamash and Adad [took him] to the assembly [of the gods] . . .
> They showed him how to observe oil on water,
> a secret of Anu, Enlil and Ea.
> They gave him the Divine Tablet,
> the *kibdu* secret of Heaven and Earth . . .
> They taught him how to make calculations with numbers.

When the instruction of Enmeduranki in the secret knowledge of the gods was accomplished, he was returned to Sumer. The "men of Nippur, Sippar and Babylon were called into his presence." He informed them of his experiences and of the establishment of priesthood. It shall be passed, the gods commanded, from father to son: "The learned savant, who guards the secrets of the gods, will bind his favored son with an oath before Shamash and Adad . . . and will instruct him in the secrets of the gods."

The tablet concludes with a postscript: "Thus was the line of priests created—those who are allowed to approach Shamash and Adad.''

By the time of the seventh generation after Enosh, on the eve of the Deluge, the Earth and its inhabitants were gripped by a new Ice Age. The Mesopotamian texts detail the sufferings by mankind, the shortages of food, even cannibalism. The Book of Genesis only hints at the situation by stating that when Noah (''Respite'') was born, he was so named by his father in the hope that his birth shall signal a respite ''from the work and toil that cometh from the Earth which the Lord hath cursed.'' The biblical version tells us little about Noah, apart from the fact that he was ''righteous and of pure genealogy.'' The Mesopotamian texts inform us that the hero of the Deluge lived in Shuruppak, the medical center run by Sud.

The Sumerian texts relate that as mankind's hardships were increasing, Enki suggested, and Enlil vehemently opposed, the taking of measures to alleviate the suffering. What upset Enlil no end was the increasing sexual relationships between the young male Anunnaki and the Daughters of Man. The Book of Genesis describes the ''taking of wives'' by the Nefilim in the following words:

> And it came to pass,
> When the Earthlings began to increase in number
> upon the face of the Earth,
> and daughters were born unto them—
> That the sons of the gods
> saw the daughters of the Earthlings
> that they were compatible;
> And they took unto themselves wives
> of whichever they chose.

A ''mythical tablet'' (CBS-14061) reported by E. Chiera (*Sumerian Religious Texts*) tells the story of those early days and of a young god named Martu, who complained that he, too, should be permitted to espouse a human wife. It happened, the text begins, when

> The city of Nin-ab existed, Shid-tab did not exist;
> The holy tiara existed, the holy crown did not exist . . .
> Cohabitation there was . . .
> Bringing forth [of children] there was.

"Nin-ab," the text continues, "was a city in the settled Great Land." Its high priest, an accomplished musician, had a wife and a daughter. As the people gathered to offer the gods the roasted meat of the sacrifices, Martu, who was single, saw the priest's daughter. Desiring her, he went to his mother and complained:

In my city I have friends, they have taken wives.
I have companions, they have taken wives.
In my city, unlike my friends, I have not taken a wife;
I have no wife, I have no children.

Asking whether the maiden whom he desired "appreciated his gaze," the goddess gave her consent. The other young gods then prepared a feast; as the marriage was announced, "in the city of Nin-ab, the people by the sound of the copper drum were called; the seven tambourines were sounded."

This growing togetherness between the young astronauts and the descendants of the Primitive Worker was not to Enlil's liking. The Sumerian texts tell us that "as the Land extended and the people multiplied," Enlil became increasingly "disturbed by Mankind's pronouncements" and its infatuation with sex and lust. The get-togethers between the Anunnaki and the daughters of Man caused him to lose sleep. "And the Lord said: 'I will destroy the Earthling whom I have created off the face of the Earth.' "

The texts inform us that when it was decided to develop the deep mines in the Abzu, the Anunnaki also proceeded to establish a scientific monitoring station at the tip of Africa. It was put in charge of Ereshkigal, a granddaughter of Enlil. A Sumerian epic tale recorded the hazardous voyage of Enki and Ereshkigal from Mesopotamia to that far-off mountainland (Kur)—a text that implies that Ereshkigal was either abducted or in some other manner coerced by Enki on that voyage, having been "carried off to Kur as a prize."

(Ereshkigal, we know from other epics, was later on attacked at her station by Nergal, one of Enki's sons, as a result of an insult involving Ereshkigal's emissary. At the last moment, Ereshkigal saved her life by offering Nergal to marry her and control together with her the station's "Tablets of Wisdom.")

Enlil now saw his chance to get rid of the Earthlings when this scientific station at the tip of Africa began to report a dangerous situation: the growing ice cap over Antarctica had become unstable, resting upon a layer of slippery slush. The problem was that this instability had developed just as Nibiru was about to make its approach to Earth's vicinity; and Nibiru's gravitational pull could upset the ice cap's balance and cause it to slip into the Antarctic Ocean. The immense tidal waves that this would cause could engulf the whole globe.

When the Igigi orbiting Earth confirmed the certainty of such a catastrophe, the Anunnaki began to assemble in Sippar, the spaceport. Enlil, however, insisted that mankind be kept unaware of the coming Deluge; and at a special session of the Assembly of the Gods, he made all of them, and especially Enki, swear to keep the secret.

The last part of the *Atra-Hasis* text, a major part of the *Epic of Gilgamesh,* and other Mesopotamian texts describe at length the events that followed—how the catastrophe of the Deluge was used by Enlil to achieve the annihilation of mankind; and how Enki, opposed to the decision which Enlil forced upon the Assembly of the Gods, contrived to save his faithful follower Ziusudra ("Noah") by designing for him a submersible vessel that could withstand the avalanche of water.

The Anunnaki themselves, on a signal, "lifted up" in their *Rukub ilani* ("chariots of the gods"), the fired-up rocket ships "setting the land ablaze with their glare." Orbiting the Earth in their shuttlecraft, they watched in horror the onslaught of the tidal waves below. All that was upon the Earth was swept off in one colossal avalanche of water: A.MA.RU BA.UR RA.TA—"The Flood swept thereover." Sud, who had created Man with Enki, "saw and wept. . . . Ishtar cried out like a woman in travail . . . the gods, the Anunnaki, weep with her." Rolling back and forth, the tidal waves swept the soil away, leaving behind vast deposits of mud: "All that had been created, turned back to clay."

In *The 12th Planet* we have presented the evidence for our conclusion that the Deluge, bringing about an abrupt end to the last Ice Age, had occurred some 13,000 years ago.

As the waters of the Deluge "went back from off the land" and started to subside, the Anunnaki began to land on Mount Nisir ("Mount of Salvation")—Mount Ararat. There Ziusudra/Noah also arrived, his vessel guided by a navigator provided by Enki. Enlil was outraged to discover that the "seed of Mankind" was saved; but Enki persuaded him to relent: The gods, he argued, could no longer exist on Earth without the help of man. "And the Lord blessed Noah and his sons, and said unto them: 'Be fruitful and multiply, and replenish the Earth.' "

The Old Testament, focusing its interest on the line of Noah alone, lists no other passengers in the rescue ship. But the more detailed Mesopotamian Deluge texts also mention the Ark's navigator and disclose that at the last moment friends or helpers of Ziusudra (and their families) also came on board. Greek versions of the account by Berossus state that after the Deluge, Ziusudra, his family, and the pilot were taken by the gods to stay with them; the other people were given directions to find their way back to Mesopotamia by themselves.

The immediate problem facing all that were rescued was food. To Noah and his sons the Lord said: "All the animals that are upon the earth, and all that flies in the skies, and all that creepeth on the ground, and all the fishes of the sea, into your hands are given; all that teemeth and that liveth, shall be yours for food." And then came a significant addition: "As grassy vegetation all manner of grain have I given you."

This little-noticed statement (Genesis 9:3), which touches on the origins of agriculture, is substantially enlarged upon in the Sumerian texts. Scholars are agreed that agriculture began in the Mesopotamia-Syria-Israel crescent but are at a loss to explain why it did not begin in the plains (where cultivation is easy) but rather in the highlands. They are agreed that it began with the harvesting of "wild ancestors" of wheat and barley some 12,000 years ago but are baffled by the genetic uniformity of those early grain grasses; and they are totally at a loss to explain the botano-genetic feat whereby—within a mere 2,000 years—such wild emmers doubled, trebled, and quadrupled their chromosome pairs to become the cultivable wheat and barley of outstanding nutritional value with the incredible ability to grow almost anywhere and with the unusual twice-a-year crops.

Coupled with these puzzles was the equal suddenness with which every manner of fruit and vegetable began to appear from the same nuclear area at almost the same time, and the simultaneous "domestication" of animals, starting with sheep and goats that provided meat, milk, and wool.

How did it all come about when it did? Modern science has yet to find the answer; but the Sumerian texts had already provided it millennia ago. Like the Bible, they relate how agriculture began after the Deluge, when (in the words of Genesis) "Noah began as a husbandman"; but like the Bible, which records that there had been tilling of the land (by Cain) and shepherding (by Abel) long before the Deluge, so do the Sumerian chronicles tell of the development of crop-growing and cattle-rearing in prehistoric times.

When the Anunnaki had landed on Earth, a text titled by scholars *The Myth of Cattle and Grain* states, none of the domesticated grains or cattle had yet been in existence:

> When from the heights of Heaven to Earth
> Anu had caused the Anunnaki to come forth,
> Grains had not yet been brought forth,
> had not yet vegetated . . .
> There was no ewe,
> a lamb had not yet been dropped;
> There was no she-goat,
> a kid had not yet been dropped.
> The ewe had not yet given birth to her lambs,
> the she-goat had not yet given birth to her kid.
> Weaving [of wool] had not yet been brought forth,
> had not yet been established.

Then, in the "Creation Chamber" of the Anunnaki, their laboratory for genetic manipulation, *Lahar* ("woolly cattle") and *Anshan* ("grains") "were beautifully fashioned":

> In those days,
> in the Creation Chamber of the gods,
> in the House of Fashioning, in the Pure Mound,
> Lahar and Anshan were beautifully fashioned.
> The abode was filled with food for the gods.
> Of the multiplying of Lahar and Anshan
> the Anunnaki, in their Holy Mound, eat—
> but were not satiated.
> The good milk from the sheepfold
> the Anunnaki, in their Holy Mound, drink—
> but are not satiated.

The Primitive Workers—those who "knew not the eating of bread . . . who ate plants with their mouths"—were already in existence:

> After Anu, Enlil, Enki and Sud
> had fashioned the black-headed people,
> Vegetation that luxuriates they multiplied in the Land.
> Four-legged animals they artfully brought into existence;
> In the E.DIN they placed them.

So, in order to increase the production of grains and cattle to satiate the Anunnaki, a decision was made: Let NAM.LU.GAL.LU —"civilized mankind"—be taught the "tilling of the land" and the "keeping of sheep . . . for the sake of the gods":

For the sake of the satiating things,
for the pure sheepfold,
Civilized Mankind was brought into existence.

Just as it describes what had been brought into existence at that early time, so does this text also list the domesticated varieties that had *not* then been brought forth:

That which by planting multiplies,
had not yet been fashioned;
Terraces had not yet been set up . . .
The triple grain of thirty days did not exist;
The triple grain of forty days did not exist;
The small grain, the grain of the mountains,
the grain of the pure A.DAM, did not exist . . .
Tuber-vegetables of the field had not yet come forth.

These, as we shall see, were introduced on Earth by Enlil and Ninurta some time after the Deluge.

After the Deluge had swept all off the face of the Earth, the first problem facing the Anunnaki was where to get the seeds needed for renewed cultivation. Fortunately specimens of the domesticated cereals had been sent to Nibiru; and now "Anu provided them, from Heaven, to Enlil." Enlil then looked for a safe place where the seeds could be sown to restart agriculture. The earth was still covered with water, and the only place that seemed suitable was "the mountain of aromatic cedars." We read in a fragmented text reported by S. N. Kramer in his *Sumerische Literarische Texte aus Nippur:*

Enlil went up the peak and lifted his eyes;
He looked down: there the waters filled as a sea.
He looked up: there was the mountain of the aromatic cedars.
He hauled up the barley, terraced it on the mountain.
That which vegetates he hauled up,
terraced the grain cereals on the mountain.

The selection of the Cedar Mountain by Enlil and its conversion into a Restricted (''Holy'') Place was, most likely, not accidental. Throughout the Near East—indeed, worldwide—there is only one unique Cedar Mountain of universal fame: in Lebanon. It is the location, to this very day (at Baalbek in Lebanon), of a vast platform supported by colossal stone blocks (Fig. 32) that are still a marvel of technology. It was, as we have elaborated in *The Stairway to Heaven,* a Landing Place of the Anunnaki; a platform that persistent legends hold to have been built in pre-Diluvial times, even as early as the days of Adam. It was the only place, after the Deluge, immediately suitable for handling the shuttlecraft of the Anunnaki: the spaceport at Sippar was washed away and buried under layers of mud.

Fig. 32

With seeds available, the question was where to sow them. . . . The lowlands, still filled with mud and water, were unsuitable for habitation. The highlands, though freed from under the avalanche of water, were soggy with the rains that began to pour down with the neothermal age. The rivers had not found their new courses; the waters had nowhere to go; cultivation was impossible. We read this description in a Sumerian text:

> Famine was severe, nothing was produced.
> The small rivers were not cleaned,
> the mud was not carried off . . .
> In all the lands there were no crops,
> only weeds grew.

The two great rivers of Mesopotamia, the Euphrates and Tigris, were also not functioning: "The Euphrates was not bound together, there was misery; the Tigris was confounded, jolted and injured." The one who rose to the task of building dams in the mountains, digging new channels for the rivers, and draining off the excess water was Ninurta: "Thereon the lord sets his lofty mind; Ninurta, the son of Enlil, brings great things into being":

> To protect the land, a mighty wall he raised.
> With a mace he smote the rocks;
> The stones the hero heaped, made a settlement . . .
> The waters that had been scattered, he gathered;
> What by the mountains had been dispersed,
> he guided and sent down the Tigris.
> The high waters it pours off the farmed land.
> Now, behold—
> Everything on Earth rejoiced at Ninurta,
> the lord of the land.

A long text, gradually pieced together by scholars, *The Feats and Exploits of Ninurta,* adds a tragic note to Ninurta's efforts to bring back order to the Earth on which he was superior. To cover all the problem spots at once, Ninurta rushed from place to place in the mountains in his airship; but "His Winged Bird on the summit was smashed; its pinions crashed down to the earth." (An unclear verse suggests that he was rescued by Adad.)

We know from the Sumerian texts that first to be cultivated on the mountain slopes were fruit trees and bushes and most certainly grapes. The Anunnaki, the texts state, gave mankind "the excellent white grapes and the excellent white wine; the excellent black grapes and the excellent red wine." No wonder we read in the Bible that when "Noah began as a husbandman, he planted a vineyard; and he drank of the wine and became drunken."

When the drainage works carried out in Mesopotamia by Ninurta made cultivation possible in the plains, the Anunnaki "from the mountain the cereal grain they brought down," and "the Land [Sumer] with wheat and barley did become acquainted."

In the millennia that followed mankind revered Ninurta as the one who had taught it farming; a "Farmer's Almanac" attributed to him was actually found by archaeologists in a Sumerian site. The Akkadian name for him was *Urash*—"The One of the Plough"; a Sumerian cylinder seal depicted him (some believe it shows Enlil) granting the plow to mankind (Fig. 33).

Fig. 33

While Enlil and Ninurta were credited with granting agriculture to mankind, the credit for the introduction of domesticated herds was given to Enki. It was after the first grains were already in cultivation but not yet "the grain that multiplies," the grains with the doubled, tripled, and quadrupled chromosomes; these were created by Enki artificially, with Enlil's consent:

At that time Enki spoke to Enlil:
"Father Enlil, flocks and grains
have made joyful the Holy Mound,
have greatly multiplied in the Holy Mound.
Let us, Enki and Enlil, command:
The woolly-creature and grain-that-multiplies
let us cause to come out of the Holy Mound."

Enlil agreed, and abundance followed:

The woolly-creature they placed in a sheepfold.
The seeds that sprout they give to the mother,

for the grains they establish a place.
To the workmen they give the plough and the yoke . . .
The shepherd makes abundance in the sheepfold;
The young woman sprouting abundance brings;
she lifts her head in the field:
Abundance had come from heaven.
The woolly-creature and grains that are planted
came forth in splendor.
Abundance was given to the congregated people.

The revolutionary agricultural tool—a simple, but ingeniously designed, wooden implement—the plow, was at first pulled, as the above text states, by putting a yoke on the farm workers. But then Enki "brought into existence the larger living creatures"—domesticated cattle—and bulls replaced people as pullers of the plow (Fig. 34). Thus, the texts conclude, did the gods "increase the fertility of the land."

Fig. 34

While Ninurta was busy damming the mountains flanking Mesopotamia and draining its plains, Enki returned to Africa to assess the damage the Deluge had caused there.

As it turned out, Enlil and his offspring ended up controlling all the high ground from the southeast (Elam, entrusted to Inanna/Ishtar) to the northwest (the Taurus Mountains and Asia Minor, given to Ishkur/Adad), with the highland arching in between given to Ninurta in the south and Nannar/Sin in the north. Enlil himself retained the central position overlooking the olden E.DIN; the Landing Place on the Cedar Mountain was put under the command of Utu/Shamash. Where were Enki and his clan to go?

As Enki surveyed Africa it was evident to him that the Abzu alone—the continent's southern part—was insufficient. Just as in

Mesopotamia ''abundance'' was based on riverine cultivation, so it had to be in Africa; and he turned his attention, planning, and knowledge to the recovery of the Valley of the Nile.

The Egyptians, we have seen, held that their great gods had come to Egypt from Ur (meaning ''the olden place''). According to Manetho, the reign of Ptah over the lands of the Nile began 17,900 years before Menes; i.e., circa 21,000 B.C. Nine thousand years later Ptah handed over the Egyptian domain to his son Ra; but the latter's reign was abruptly interrupted after a brief 1,000 years, i.e., circa 11,000 B.C.; it was then, by our reckoning, that the Deluge had occurred.

Then, the Egyptians believed, Ptah returned to Egypt to engage in great works of reclamation and to literally raise it from under the inundating waters. We find Sumerian texts that likewise attest that Enki went to the lands of Meluhha (Ethiopia/Nubia) and Magan (Egypt) to make them habitable for man and beast:

> He proceeds to the Land Meluhha;
> Enki, lord of the Abzu, decrees its fate:
> Black land, may your trees be large trees,
> may they be the Highland trees.
> May thrones fill your royal palaces.
> May your reeds be large reeds,
> may they be the Highland reeds . . .
> May your bulls be large bulls,
> may they be the Highland bulls . . .
> May your silver be as gold,
> May your copper be tin and bronze . . .
> May your people multiply;
> May your hero go forth as a bull . . .

These Sumerian records, linking Enki with the African lands of the Nile, assume a double significance: they corroborate the Egyptian tales with Mesopotamian tales and link Sumerian gods—especially the Enki-gods—with the gods of Egypt; for *Ptah, we believe, was none other than Enki.*

After the lands were made habitable again, Enki divided the length of the African continent between his six sons (Fig. 35). The southernmost domain was regranted to NER.GAL (''Great Watcher'') and his spouse Ereshkigal. To his north, in the mining regions, GIBIL (''The One of Fire'') was installed, having been taught by his father the secrets of metalworking. NIN.A.GAL

("Prince of Great Waters") was, as his name implied, given the region of the great lakes and the headwaters of the Nile. Farther north, in the grazing plateau of the Sudan, the youngest son, DUMU.ZI ("Son Who Is Life"), whose nickname was "The Herder," was given reign.

Fig. 35

The identity of yet another son is in dispute among the scholars (we shall offer our own solution later on). But there is no doubt who the sixth son—actually Enki's firstborn and legal heir—was: He was MAR.DUK ("Son of the Pure Mound"). Because one of his fifty epithets was ASAR, which sounds so much like the Egyptian *As-Sar* ("Osiris" in Greek), some scholars have speculated that Marduk and Osiris were one and the same. But these epithets (as "All-Powerful" or "Awesome") were applied to diverse deities, and Asar meaning "All-Seeing" was also the epithet-name of the Assyrian god Ashur.

In fact, we find more similarities between the Babylonian Marduk and the Egyptian god Ra: the former was the son of Enki, the latter of Ptah, the two, Enki-Ptah, being in our view one and the same; whereas Osiris was the great-grandson of Ra and thus of a much later generation than either Ra or Marduk. In fact, there is found in Sumerian texts scattered, but persistent, evidence supporting our belief that the god called Ra by the Egyptians and Marduk by the Mesopotamians was one and the same deity. Thus, a self-laudatory hymn to Marduk (tablet Ashur/4125) declares that one of his epithets was "The god IM.KUR.GAR RA"—"Ra Who Beside the Mountainland Abides."

Moreover, there is textual evidence that the Sumerians were aware of the deity's Egyptian name, Ra. There were Sumerians whose personal names incorporated the divine name RA; and tablets from the time of the Ur III Dynasty mention "Dingir Ra" and his temple E.Dingir.Ra. Then, after the fall of that dynasty, when Marduk attained supremacy in his favored city Babylon, its Sumerian name KA.DINGIR ("Gateway of the Gods") was changed to KA.DINGIR.RA—"Ra's Gateway of the Gods."

Indeed, as we shall soon show, Marduk's rise to prominence began in Egypt, where its best-known monument—the Great Pyramid of Giza—had played a crucial role in his turbulent career. But the Great God of Egypt, Marduk/Ra, yearned to rule the whole Earth, and to do so from the olden "Navel of the Earth" in Mesopotamia. It was this ambition that led him to abdicate the divine throne of Egypt in favor of his children and grandchildren.

Little did he know that this would lead to two Pyramid Wars and to his own near death.

7

WHEN EARTH WAS DIVIDED

"And the sons of Noah that came out of the ark were Shem, Ham and Japhet . . . these were the three sons of Noah of whom all the Earth was overspread."

Thus is the biblical tale of the Deluge followed by the recital of the *Table of Nations* (Genesis 10), a unique document, at first doubted by scholars because it listed then unknown nation-states, then taken apart critically, and finally—after a century and a half of archaeological discoveries—amazing in its accuracy. It is a document that holds a wealth of reliable historical, geographical, and political information concerning the rise of mankind's remnants from the mud and desolation following the Deluge, to the heights of civilizations and empires.

Leaving the all-important line of Shem to the last, the *Table of Nations* begins with the descendants of *Japhet* ("The Fair One"): "And the sons of Japhet: Gomer and Magog and Madai, Javan and Tubal and Meshech and Tiras. And the sons of Gomer: Ashkenaz and Riphat and Togarmah; and the sons of Javan: Elishah and Tarshish, the Kittim and the Dodanim. From them branched out the island nations." While the later generations had thus spread to coastal areas and islands, the unnoticed fact was that all the first seven nation/sons corresponded to the highlands of Asia Minor, the Black Sea and the Caspian Sea areas—highlands that were habitable soon after the Deluge, unlike the lower lying coastal areas and islands that could become habitable only much later.

The descendants of *Ham* ("He Who is Hot" and also "The Dark-Hued One"), first "Cush and Mizra'im and Put and Canaan" and thereafter a host of other nation-states, correspond to the African nation-lands of Nubia, Ethiopia, Egypt, and Libya as the core nations of African resettlement, again beginning with the topographically higher areas, then spreading to the lowlands.

"And Shem, the father of all who descended of Eber, also had offspring; he was the elder brother of Japhet." The first nation-sons of Shem were "Elam and Ashur, Arpakhshad and Lud and Aram," nation-states that encompassed the highlands arching from the Persian

129

Gulf in the south to the Mediterranean Sea in the northwest and bordering the great Land-Between-the-Rivers, which was as yet not habitable. Those were the lands one could call the Spaceport Lands: Mesopotamia, where the pre-Diluvial spaceport had been; the Cedar Mountain, where the Landing Place remained functioning; the Land of Shalem, where the post-Diluvial Mission Control Center was to be established; and the adjoining Sinai peninsula, site of the future spaceport. The name of the forefather of all these nations, *Shem*—meaning "Sky Chamber"—was thus quite appropriate.

The broad division of mankind into three branches, as related in the Bible, followed not only the geography and topography of the areas to which man had spread, it also followed the division of the Earth between the descendants of Enlil and the descendants of Enki. Shem and Japhet are depicted in the Bible as good brothers, whereas the attitude toward the line of Ham—and especially Canaan—is one of bitter memories. In this there lie tales yet to be told—tales of gods and men, and their wars. . . .

The tradition of the division of the ancient settled world into three branches is also in accord with what we know of the rise of civilizations.

Scholars have recognized an abrupt change in human culture about 11,000 B.C.—the time of the Deluge, according to our findings—and have named that era of domestication Mesolithic (Middle Stone Age). Circa 7400 B.C.—exactly 3,600 years later—another abrupt advancement has been recognized. Scholars have named it Neolithic ("New Stone Age"); but its principal feature was the switch from stone to clay and the appearance of pottery. And then, "suddenly and inexplicably"—but exactly 3,600 years later—there blossomed out (circa 3800 B.C.) in the plain between the Euphrates and Tigris rivers the high civilization of Sumer. It was followed, circa 3100 B.C., by the civilization of the Nile River; and circa 2800 B.C., the third civilization of antiquity, that of the Indus River, made its appearance. These were the three regions allotted to mankind; of them evolved the nations of the Near East, Africa, and Indo-Europe—a division faithfully recorded in the Old Testament's *Table of Nations*.

All that, Sumerian chronicles held, was the result of deliberate decisions by the Anunnaki:

The Anunnaki who decree the fates
sat exchanging their counsels
regarding the Earth.
The four regions they created.

With these simple words, echoed in several Sumerian texts, the post-Diluvial fate of Earth and its inhabitants was decided. Three regions were allotted to mankind's three civilizations; the fourth was retained by the Anunnaki for their own use. It was given the name TIL.MUN, "Land of the Missiles." In *The Stairway to Heaven* we provided the evidence identifying Tilmun with the Sinai peninsula.

Although as far as human habitation was concerned, it was the descendants of Shem—"Sand Dwellers" in Egyptian scriptures—who could reside in the unrestricted areas of the peninsula, when it came to allotting the territory among the Anunnaki, profound differences arose. Control of the site of the post-Diluvial spaceport was tantamount to control of the links between Earth and Nibiru, as the experiences with Kumarbi and Zu had so clearly shown. In the rekindled rivalry between the clans of Enlil and Enki, a neutral authority over the Land of the Missiles was called for.

The solution was ingenious. Of equal lineage with them was their sister Sud. As a daughter of Anu, she bore the title NIN.MAH ("Great Lady"). She was one of the original group of Great Anunnaki who were pioneers on Earth, a member of the Pantheon of Twelve. She bore a son to Enlil, a daughter to Enki, and was lovingly called *Mammi* ("Mother of the Gods"). She helped create Man. With her medical skills she saved many a life and was also known as NIN.TI ("Lady Life"). But she never had her own dominions. To make Tilmun her domain was an idea that no one opposed.

The Sinai peninsula is a barren place, occupied by high granite peaks in the south, a mountainous plateau in the center, and a hard-soiled plain in its northern third, surrounded by chains of low mountains and hills. Then there is a strip of sand dunes, sliding to the Mediterranean coast. But where water can be retained, as in several oases or in riverbeds that fill up during brief winter rains and keep the moisture below the surface, luxuriant date palms, fruits, and vegetables grow, and herds of sheep and goats can graze.

The region must have been as forbidding millennia ago as it is now. But although an abode was made for Sud in one of Mesopotamia's rebuilt sites, she decided to go and take personal possession of the mountainous region. With all her attributes of status and knowledge, she always played a secondary role. When she came to Earth, she was young and beautiful (Fig. 36a); now she was old and nicknamed "The Cow" (Fig. 36b) behind her back. So now that she was given her own domain, she decided to go there. Proudly she declared: "A Mistress I am now! Alone will I stay there, reigning forever!"

a   b

Fig. 36

Unable to dissuade her, Ninurta applied his experience in damming and channeling waters to make his mother's new mountain region livable. We read of these deeds in Tablet IX of the "Feats and Exploits of Ninurta," as he addresses his mother:

> Since you, noble lady,
> alone to the Land of Landing had gone,
> Since to the Land of Casting Down
> unafraid you went—
> A dam I shall heap up for you,
> so that the Land may have a mistress.

Completing his irrigation works, and bringing over people to perform the required tasks, Ninurta assured his mother that she would have an abundance of vegetation, wood products, and minerals in her mountain abode:

> Its valleys shall be verdant with vegetation,
> Its slopes shall produce honey and wine for you,
> Shall produce . . . *zabalum*-trees and boxwood;
> its terraces shall be adorned with fruit as a garden;
> The *Harsag* shall provide you with the fragrance of the gods,
> shall provide you with the shiny lodes;

Its mines will as tribute copper and tin give you;
Its mountains shall multiply cattle large and small;
The *Harsag* shall bring forth the four-legged creatures.

This is indeed a befitting description of the Sinai peninsula: a land of mines, a major source in antiquity of copper, turquoise, and other minerals; a source of the acacia wood, which was used for temple furnishings; a verdant place wherever water was available; a place where flocks could graze. Is it an accident that the principal winter-river of the peninsula is still called el Arish—"The Husbandman"—the very nickname *(Urash)* of Ninurta?

Making a home for his mother in the Sinai's southern region of high granite peaks, Ninurta bestowed on her a new title: NIN.HAR.SAG ("Lady of the Head Mountain"); it was the title by which Sud was to be called ever since.

The term "head mountain" indicates that it was the highest peak in the area. This is the mountain nowadays known as Mount St. Katherine, a peak revered from antiquity, millennia before the nearby monastery was built. Rising nearby is the slightly lower peak called by the monks Mount Moses, suggesting that it is the Mount Sinai of the Exodus. Though this is doubtful, the fact remains that the twin peaks have been deemed to be sacred from antiquity. We believe that this was so because they played a pivotal role in the planning of the post-Diluvial spaceport and the Landing Corridor leading to it.

These new plans adopted the old principles; and to understand the grand post-Diluvial design, we must first review the manner in which the pre-Diluvial spaceport and its Landing Corridor were developed. At that time the Anunnaki first selected as their focal point the twin-peaked Mount Ararat, the highest peak in Western Asia and thus the natural landmark most visible from the skies. The next natural and visible features were the Euphrates River and the Persian Gulf. Drawing an imaginary north-south line from Ararat, the Anunnaki determined that the spaceport shall be where the line intersected the river. Then, diagonally to it from the direction of the Persian Gulf—at a precise angle of forty-five degrees—they drew the Landing Path. They then laid out their first settlements so as to mark out a Landing Corridor on both sides of the Landing Path. In the center point, Nippur was established as a Mission Control Center; all the other settlements were equidistant from it (Fig. 25).

The post-Diluvial space facilities were planned on the same principles. The twin-peaked Mount Ararat served as the major focal point; a line at forty-five degrees marked the Landing Path, and a combination of natural and artificial landmarks outlined an arrowlike Landing Corridor. The difference was, however, that this time the Anunnaki had at their disposal the ready-made Platform in the Cedar Mountain (Baalbek), and they incorporated it into the new Landing Grid.

As before the Deluge, the twin-peaked Mount Ararat was to serve again as the northern landmark, anchoring the Landing Corridor and the Landing Path in the center of the Corridor (Fig. 37).

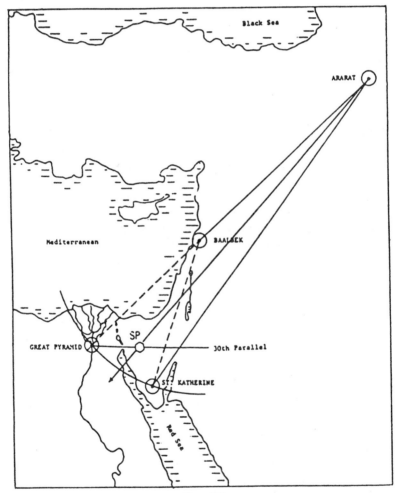

Fig. 37

The southern line of the Landing Corridor was a line connecting the twin-peaked Ararat with the highest peak in the Sinai peninsula, the Harsag (Mount St. Katherine), and its twin, the slightly lower Mount Moses.

The northern line of the Landing Corridor was a line extending from Ararat through the Landing Platform of Baalbek and continuing into Egypt. There the terrain is too flat to offer natural landmarks, and it was thus, we are certain, that the Anunnaki proceeded to build the artificial twin peaks of the two great pyramids of Giza.

But where was this anchor to be erected?

Here came into play an east-west imaginary line, arbitrarily conceived by the Anunnaki in their space sciences. They arbitrarily divided the skies enveloping Earth into three bands or "ways." The northern one was the "Way of Enlil," the southern one the "Way of Enki," and the central one the "Way of Anu." Separating them were the lines known to us as the 30th parallel north and the 30th parallel south.

The 30th parallel north appears to have been of particular—"sacred"—significance. Holy cities from antiquity on, from Egypt to Tibet, have been located on it. It was chosen to be the line on which (at the intersection of the Ararat-Baalbek line) the great pyramids were to be built; and also the line which would indicate, in the Sinai's central plain, the site of the Spaceport (SP). A line in the precise middle of the Landing Corridor, the Landing Path, was to lead to the exact location of the Spaceport on the 30th parallel.

This, we believe, is how the Landing Grid was laid out, how the site of the Spaceport was marked off, and how the great pyramids of Giza had come into being.

By suggesting that the great pyramids of Giza were built not by Pharaohs but by the Anunnaki millennia earlier, we of course contradict long-held theories concerning these pyramids.

The theory of nineteenth-century Egyptologists, that the Egyptian pyramids, including the unique three at Giza, were erected by a succession of Pharaohs as grandiose tombs for themselves, has long been disproven: not one of them was found to contain the body of the Pharaoh who was their known or presumed builder. Accordingly, the Great Pyramid of Giza was supposed to have been built by Khufu (Cheops), its twin by a successor named Chefra (Chephren), and the third, small one by a third successor, Menkara (Mycerinus)—all kings of the sixth dynasty. The Sphinx, the same Egyptologists presume, must have been built by Chephren, because it is situated next to a causeway leading to the Second Pyramid.

For a while it was believed that proof had been found in the smallest one of the three pyramids of Giza and the identity of the Pharaoh who had built it established. The credit for this was claimed by a Colonel Howard Vyse and his two assistants, who claimed to have discovered within the pyramid the coffin and mummified remains of the Pharaoh Menkara. The fact, however—known to scholars for some time now but for some reason still hardly publicized—is that neither the wooden coffin nor the skeletal remains were authentic. Someone—undoubtedly that Colonel Vyse and his cronies—had brought into the pyramid a coffin dating from about 2,000 years after Menkara had lived, and bones from the even much later Christian times, and put the two together in an unabashed archaeological fraud.

The current theories regarding the pyramids' builders are anchored to an even greater extent on the discovery of the name Khufu inscribed in hieroglyphics within a long-sealed compartment within the Great Pyramid and thus apparently establishing the identity of its builder. Unnoticed has gone the fact that the discoverer of that inscription was the same Colonel Vyse and his assistants (the year was 1837). In *The Stairway to Heaven* we have put together substantial evidence to show that the inscription was a forgery, perpetrated by its "discoverers." At the end of 1983, a reader of that book came forward to provide us with family records showing that his great-grandfather, a master mason named Humphries Brewer, who was engaged by Vyse to help use gunpowder to blast his way inside the pyramid, was an *eyewitness to the forgery* and, having objected to the deed, was expelled from the site and forced to leave Egypt altogether!

In *The Stairway to Heaven* we have shown that Khufu could not have been the builder of the Great Pyramid because he had already referred to it as existing in his time in a stela he had erected near the pyramids; even the Sphinx, supposedly erected by the next-after successor of Khufu, is mentioned in that inscription.

Now we find that pictorial evidence from the time of the Pharaohs of the very first dynasty—long before Khufu and his successors—conclusively shows that these early kings had already witnessed the Giza marvels. We can clearly see the Sphinx both in depictions of the king's journey to the Afterlife (Fig. 38a) and in a scene of his investiture by "Ancient Ones" arriving in Egypt by boat (Fig. 38b). We also submit in evidence the well-known vic-

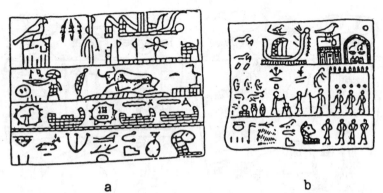

a   b

Fig. 38

tory tablet of the very first Pharaoh, Menes, which depicts his forceful unification of Egypt. On one side he is shown wearing the white crown of Upper Egypt, defeating its chieftains and conquering their cities. On the other side the tablet shows him (Fig. 39a) wearing the red crown of Lower Egypt, marching through its districts and beheading its chieftains. To the right of his head the artist spelled out the epithet *"Nar-Mer"* acquired by the king; to the left the tablet depicts the most important structure in the newly acquired districts—the pyramid (Fig. 39b).

All scholars agree that the tablet depicts realistically the places, fortifications, and enemies encountered by Menes in his campaign to unify Upper and Lower Egypt; yet the pyramid symbol is the only one that appears to have escaped the otherwise careful interpretation. We hold that this symbol, as all others on the tablet, was drawn and included so prominently in the Lower Egypt side because such a structure had actually existed there.

The whole Giza complex—pyramids and Sphinx—had thus already existed when kingship began in Egypt; its builders were not and could not have been the Pharaohs of the sixth dynasty.

The other pyramids of Egypt—smaller, primitive by comparison, some fallen even before completion, all crumbling—had indeed been built by various Pharaohs; not as tombs, nor as cenotaphs (monumental symbolic tombs), but in emulation of the gods. For it was held and believed in antiquity that the Giza pyramids and the Sphinx that accompanies them showed the way to the Stairway to Heaven—the Spaceport—in the Sinai peninsula. Build-

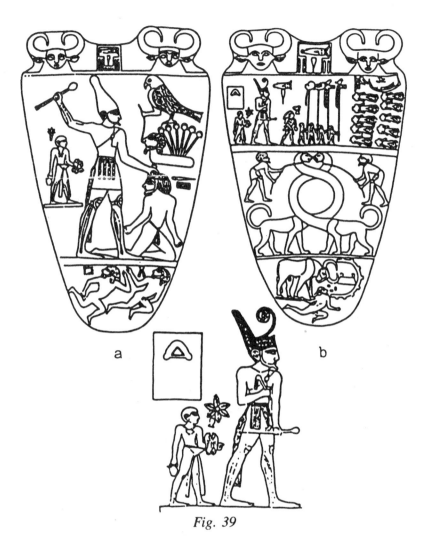

a   b

Fig. 39

ing pyramids so that they might journey to the Afterlife, the Pharaohs adorned them with appropriate symbols, with illustrations of
the journey, and in several instances also covered the walls with
quotations from *The Book of the Dead*. The three pyramids of Giza,
unique in their external and internal construction, size, and incredible durability, are also distinguished in that there is no inscription
or decoration whatsoever inside them. They are just stark, functional structures, rising from the plain as twin beacons to play a

role not in the service of men but of those "Who From Heaven to Earth Came."

The three pyramids of Giza, we have concluded, were built by first erecting the smaller Third Pyramid as a scale model. Then, in keeping with the preference for twin-peaked focal points, the two large pyramids were erected. Although the Second Pyramid is smaller than the Great Pyramid, it appears to be of the same height; this is because it is built on somewhat higher ground, so that to achieve the same height, it need not have been as tall as the first one.

Apart from its incomparable size, the Great Pyramid is also unique in that, in addition to the descending passage that is found in all the other pyramids, it has a unique Ascending Passage, a level Corridor, two Upper Chambers, and a series of narrow compartments (Fig. 40). The uppermost chamber is reached via an incredibly elaborate Grand Gallery and an Antechamber that could be sealed with one pull of a cord. The uppermost chamber contained—still does—an unusual hollowed-out stone block whose fashioning required amazing technology and which rang out as a bell; above the chamber are the narrow series of low and rugged spaces, offering extreme resonance.

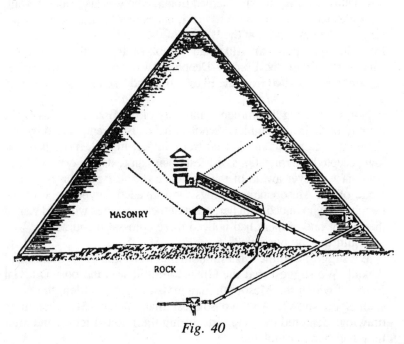

MASONRY

ROCK

Fig. 40

What was the purpose of all that?

We have found many similarities between these unique features of the Great Pyramid and the pre-Diluvial E.KUR ("House Which Is Like a Mountain") of Enlil, his ziggurat in Nippur. Like the Great Pyramid, it rose high to dominate the surrounding plain. In pre-Diluvial times the Ekur of Nippur housed the DUR.AN.KI— "Link Heaven-Earth"—and served as Mission Control Center, equipped with the Tablets of Destinies, the orbital data panels. It also contained the DIR.GA, a mysterious "Dark Chamber" whose "radiance" guided the shuttlecraft to a landing at Sippar.

But all that—the many mysteries and functions of the Ekur described in the tale of Zu—was before the Deluge. When Mesopotamia was reinhabited and Nippur was reestablished, the abode of Enlil and Ninlil there was a large temple surrounded by courtyards, with gates through which the worshipers could enter. It was no longer forbidden territory; the space-related functions, as the Spaceport itself, had shifted elsewhere.

As a new, mysterious, and awesome Ekur, the Sumerian texts described a "House Which Is Like a Mountain" in a distant place, under the aegis of Ninharsag, not of Enlil. Thus, the epic tale of an early post-Diluvial Sumerian king named Etana, who was taken aloft toward the Celestial Abode of the Anunnaki, states that his ascent began not far from the new Ekur, at the "Place of the Eagles"—not far, that is, from the Spaceport. An Akkadian "Book of Job" titled *Ludlul Bel Nimeqi* ("I Praise the Lord of Deepness") refers to the "irresistible demon that has exited from the Ekur" in a land "across the horizon, in the Lower World [Africa]."

Not recognizing the immense antiquity of the Giza pyramids or the identity of their true builders, scholars have also been puzzled by this apparent reference to an Ekur far from Sumer. Indeed, if one is to follow accepted interpretations of Mesopotamian texts, no one in Mesopotamia was ever aware of the existence of the Egyptian pyramids. None of the Mesopotamian kings who invaded Egypt, none of the merchants who traded with her, none of the emissaries who had visited there—not one of them had noticed these colossal monuments . . .

Could that be possible?

We suggest that the Giza monuments *were* known in Sumer and Akkad. We suggest that the Great Pyramid was the post-Diluvial Ekur, of which the Mesopotamian texts did speak at length (as we shall soon show). And we suggest that ancient Mesopotamian drawings depicted the pyramids during their construction and after they had been completed!

We have already shown what the Mesopotamian "pyramids"—
the ziggurats or stage-towers—looked like (Fig. 24). We find completely different structures on some of the most archaic Sumerian
depictions. In some (Fig. 41) we see the construction of a structure
with a square base and triangular sides—a smooth-sided pyramid.
Other depictions show a completed pyramid (Fig. 42 a,b) with the

Fig. 41

a

b

Fig. 42

serpent symbol clearly locating it in an Enki territory. And yet another (Fig. 43) endows the completed pyramid with wings, to indicate its space-related function. This depiction, of which several were found, shows the pyramid together with other amazingly accurate features: a crouching Sphinx facing toward the Place of Reeds; another Sphinx on the other side of the Lake of Reeds, supporting the suggestion in Egyptian texts that there was another, facing the Sphinx in the Sinai peninsula. Both the pyramid and the Sphinx near it are located by a river, as the Giza complex is indeed located by the Nile. And beyond all that is the body of water on which the horned gods are sailing, just as the Egyptians had said that their gods had from the south, via the Red Sea.

Fig. 43

The striking similarity between this archaic Sumerian depiction and the archaic Egyptian one (Fig. 38a) offers compelling evidence of the common knowledge, in Egypt as in Sumer, of the pyramids and the Sphinx. Indeed, even in such a minor detail as the precise slope of the Great Pyramid—52°—the Sumerian depiction appears to be accurate.

The inevitable conclusion, then, is that the Great Pyramid was known in Mesopotamia, if for no other reason than because it was built by the same Anunnaki who had built the original Ekur in Nippur; and likewise and quite logically, it, too, was called by them E.KUR—"House Which Is Like a Mountain." Like its predecessor, the Great Pyramid of Giza was built with mysterious dark chambers and was equipped with instruments for guiding the shuttlecraft to the post-Diluvial Spaceport in the Sinai. And, to assure its neutrality, the Pyramid was put under the patronage of Ninharsag.

Our solution gives meaning to an otherwise enigmatic poem exalting Ninharsag as mistress of the "House With a Pointed Peak"—a pyramid:

House bright and dark of Heaven and Earth,
for the rocketships put together;
E.KUR, House of the Gods with pointed peak;
For Heaven-to-Earth it is greatly equipped.
House whose interior glows with a reddish Light of Heaven,
pulsating a beam which reaches far and wide;
Its awesomeness touches the flesh.
Awesome ziggurat, lofty mountain of mountains—
Thy creation is great and lofty,
men cannot understand it.

The function of this "House of the Gods With Pointed Peak" is then made clear: it was a "House of Equipment" serving to "bring down to rest" the astronauts "who see and orbit," a "great landmark for the lofty *Shems*" (the "sky chambers"):

House of Equipment, lofty House of Eternity:
Its foundation are stones [which reach] the water;
Its great circumference is set in the clay.
House whose parts are skillfully woven together;
House, the rightness of whose howling
the Great-Ones-Who-See-and-Orbit brings down to rest . . .
House which is great landmark for the lofty *Shem;*
Mountain by which Utu ascends.
[House] whose deep insides men cannot penetrate . . .
Anu has magnified it.

The text then goes on to describe the various parts of the structure: its foundation, "which is clad in awe"; its entrance, which opens and closes as a mouth, "glowing in a dim green light"; the threshold ("like a great dragon's mouth opened in wait"); the doorjambs ("like two edges of a dagger that keeps enemies away"). Its inner chamber is "like a vulva," guarded by "daggers which dash from dawn to dusk"; its "outpouring"—that which it emits—"is like a lion whom no one dares attack."

An ascending gallery is then described: "Its vault is like a rainbow, the darkness ends there; in awesomeness it is draped; its joints are like a vulture whose claws are ready to clasp.'' There, at the top of the gallery, is ''the entryway to the Mountain's top''; ''to foe it is not opened; only to Them Who Live, for them it is opened.'' Three locking devices—''the bolt, the bar and the lock . . . slithering in an awe-inspiring place''—protect the way into the uppermost chamber, from which the Ekur ''surveys Heaven and Earth, a net it spreads out.''

These are details whose accuracy amazes as one reads them in conjunction with our present knowledge of the insides of the Great Pyramid. The entrance into it was through an opening in its north face, hidden by a swivel stone that indeed opened and closed ''like a mouth.'' Stepping onto a platform, the entrant faced an opening into a descending passage, ''like a great dragon's mouth opened in wait'' (Fig. 44a). The gaping entrance was protected from the pyramid's weight above it by two pairs of diagonally placed massive stone blocks, ''like two edges that keep enemies away,'' revealing an enigmatic carved stone in the entrance's midst (Fig. 44b).

A short distance down the descending passage, an ascending passage began. It led to a horizontal passage through which one could reach the heart of the pyramid, an inner Chamber of Emissions ''like a vulva.'' The ascending passage also led to a majestic ascending gallery, most elaborately constructed, its walls getting closer to each other by stages as they rise, giving the entrant a feel-

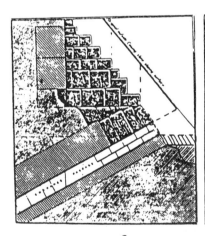

a   b

Fig. 44

ing that these wall joints are "like a vulture whose claws are ready to clasp" (Fig. 45). The gallery led to the uppermost chamber, from which a "net"—a force field—"surveyed Heaven and Earth." The way to it was through an antechamber, built with great complexity (Fig. 46), where three locking devices were indeed installed, ready to "slither" down and "to foe not open."

After so describing the Ekur inside and out, the laudatory text provides information regarding the functions and location of the structure:

On this day the Mistress herself speaks truly;
The Goddess of the Rocketships, the Pure Great Lady,
praises herself:
"I am the Mistress; Anu has determined my destiny;
the daughter of Anu am I.
Enlil has added to me a great destiny;
his sister-princess am I.
The gods have given unto my hand
the pilot-guiding instruments of Heaven-Earth;
Mother of the sky-chambers am I.
Ereshkigal allotted to me the place-of-opening
of the pilot-guiding instruments;
The great landmark,
the mountain by which Utu rises,
I have established as my dais."

If, as we have concluded, Ninharsag was the neutral Mistress of the Pyramid of Giza, it follows that she should have been known and revered as a goddess also in Egypt. This, indeed, is the case; except that to the Egyptians she was known as Hat-Hor. Textbooks will tell us that the name means "House of Horus"; but that is only superficially correct. The reading stems from the hieroglyphic writing of the name depicting a house and a falcon, the falcon having been the symbol of Horus because he could soar as a falcon. What the goddess's name literally meant was: "Goddess Whose Home Is Where the 'Falcons' Are," where the astronauts make their home: the Spaceport.

This spaceport, we have determined, was located in the post-Diluvial era in the Sinai peninsula; accordingly, the title Hat-Hor, "Home of the Falcons," would require that the goddess bearing it should be Mistress of the Sinai peninsula. That, indeed, she was;

THE GRAND GALLERY

Perspective views: From the lower northern entrance (A&B)
and from the upper southern end (C).

Fig. 45

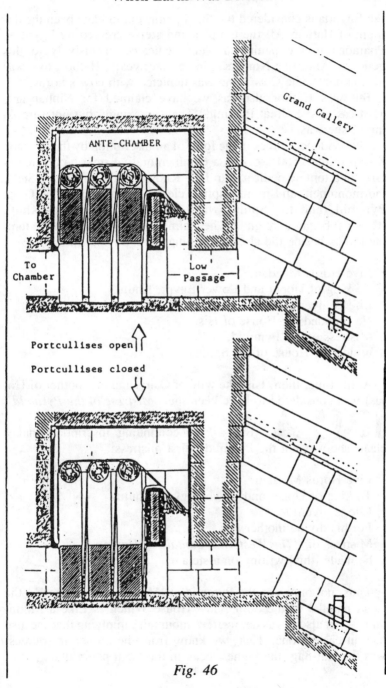

Fig. 46

the Egyptians considered the Sinai peninsula to have been the domain of Hathor. All the temples and stelae erected by Egyptian Pharaohs in the peninsula were dedicated exclusively to this goddess. And, like Ninharsag in her later years, Hathor, too, was nicknamed "The Cow" and was depicted with cow's horns.

But was Hathor also—as we have claimed for Ninharsag—Mistress of the Great Pyramid? That, amazingly but not surprisingly, she was.

The evidence comes in the form of an inscription by the Pharaoh Khufu (circa 2600 B.C.) on a commemorative stela he erected at Giza in a temple dedicated to Isis. Known as the Inventory Stela, the monument and its inscription clearly establish that the Great Pyramid (and the Sphinx) had already existed when Khufu (Cheops) began to reign. All he claimed was to have built the temple to Isis beside the already existing Pyramid and Sphinx:

Live Horus Mezdau.
To king of Upper and Lower Egypt, Khufu,
Life is given!
He founded the House of Isis,
Mistress of the Pyramid,
beside the House of the Sphinx.

At his time, then, Isis (the wife of Osiris and the mother of Horus) was considered to have been the *"Mistress of the Pyramid"* . But as the continuing inscription makes clear, she was not the Pyramid's first mistress:

Live Horus Mezdau.
To king of Upper and Lower Egypt, Khufu,
Life is given!
For his divine mother Isis,
Mistress of *"The Western Mountain of Hathor,"*
he made [this] writing on a stela.

Thus, not only was the Pyramid a "Mountain of Hathor"—the exact parallel of the Sumerian "House Which Is Like a Mountain"—but also it was her *western* mountain, implying that she also had an eastern one. That, we know from the Sumerian sources, was the Har-Sag, the highest peak in the Sinai peninsula.

* * *

In spite of the rivalry and suspicions between the two divine dynasties, there is little doubt that the actual work of constructing the Spaceport and the control and guidance facilities fell into the hands of Enki and his descendants. Ninurta proved himself capable of damming and irrigation works; Utu/Shamash knew how to command and operate the landing and take-off facilities; but only Enki, the master engineer and scientist who had been through all this before, had the required know-how and experience for planning the massive construction works and supervising their execution.

There is not even a hint in Sumerian texts that describe the achievements of Ninurta and Utu that either one of them had planned or engaged in space-related construction works. When Ninurta, in later times, called upon a Sumerian king to build him a ziggurat with a special enclosure for his Divine Bird, it was another god, accompanying Ninurta, who gave the king the architectural plans and building instructions. On the other hand, several texts reported that Enki had passed to his son Marduk the scientific knowledge he had possessed. The texts report a conversation between father and son, after Marduk had approached his father with a difficult question:

> Enki answered his son Marduk:
> "My son, what is it you do not know?
> What more could I give to you?
> Marduk, what is it that you do not know?
> What could I give you in addition?
> Whatever I know, you know!"

Since the similarities between Ptah and Enki as the father, and Marduk and Ra as son, are so strong, we should not be surprised at all to find that Egyptian texts did connect Ra with space facilities and with related construction works. In this he was assisted by Shu and Tefnut, Geb and Nut, and Thoth, the god of magical things, The Sphinx, the "divine guide" that showed the way eastward exactly along the 30th parallel, bore the features of Hor-Akhti ("Falcon of the Horizon")—the epithet for Ra. A stela erected near the Sphinx in Pharaonic times bore an inscription that directly named Ra as the engineer ("Extender of the Cord") who built the "Protected Place" in the "Sacred Desert," from which he could "ascend beautifully" and "traverse the skies":

Thou extendest the cords for the plan,
thou didst give form to the lands . . .
Thou didst make secret the Lower World . . .
Thou hast built for thee a place protected
in the sacred desert, with hidden name.
Thou risest by day opposite them . . .
Thou art rising beautifully . . .
Thou art crossing the sky with a good wind . . .
Thou art traversing the sky in the celestial barque . . .
The sky is jubilating,
the Earth is shouting of joy.
The crew of Ra do praising every day;
He comes forth in triumph.

Egyptian texts asserted that Shu and Tefnut were involved in Ra's extensive space-related works by "upholding the skies over Earth." Their son Geb bore a name that stemmed from the root *gbb*—"to pile up, to heap up"—attesting, scholars agree, to his engaging in works that entailed piling up; a strong suggestion of his involvement in the actual construction of the pyramids.

An Egyptian tale concerning the Pharaoh Khufu and his three sons reveals that in those days the secret plans of the Great Pyramid were in the custody of the god whom the Egyptians called Thoth, the god of astronomy, mathematics, geometry, and land surveying. It will be recalled that a unique feature of the Great Pyramid was its upper chambers and passages. However, because these passages were sealed off—we shall show how, when, and why— just where they branch off from the descending passage, all the Pharaohs who attempted to emulate the Giza pyramids built theirs with lower chambers only, being either unable to emulate the upper chambers for lack of precise architectural knowledge, or (in time) simply unaware of their existence. But Khufu, it seems, was aware of the existence of these two secret chambers within the Great Pyramid, and at one point was on the verge of discovering the plans of their construction, for he was told where the god Thoth had hidden them.

Written on the so-called Westcar Papyrus and titled "Tales of the Magicians," the tale relates that "one day, when king Khufu reigned over all the land," he called in his three sons and asked them to tell him tales of the "deeds of the magicians" of olden times. First to speak was "the royal son Khafra" who related "a tale of the days of thy [Khufu's] forefather Nebka . . . of what came to pass when he went into the temple of Ptah.'' It was a tale of how a magician brought a dead crocodile back to life. Then the royal son Bau-ef-Ra told of a miracle in the days of Khufu's earlier forefather, when a magician parted the waters of a lake, so that a jewel could be retrieved from its bottom; "and then the magician spake and used his magic speech and he brought the water of all the lake again to its place.''

Somewhat cynical, the third son Hor-De-Def arose and spoke, saying: "We have heard about the magicians of the past and their doings, the truth of which we cannot verify. Now I know of things done in our time.'' The Pharaoh Khufu asked what they were; and Hor-De-Def answered that he knew of a man named Dedi who knew how to replace a decapitated head, to tame a lion, and who also knew "the *Pdut* numbers of the chambers of Thoth.''

Hearing this, Khufu became extremely curious, for he had been seeking to find out the "secret of the Chambers of Thoth'' in the Great Pyramid (already blocked and hidden in Khufu's time!). So he ordered that the sage Dedi be found and fetched from his abode, an island off the tip of the Sinai peninsula.

When Dedi was brought before the Pharaoh, Khufu first tested his magical powers, such as bringing back to life a goose, a bird, and an ox, whose heads were cut off. Then Khufu asked: "Is it true what is said, that thou knowest the *Pdut* numbers for the *Iput* of Thoth?'' And Dedi answered: "I know not the numbers, O king, but I know the place the *Pdut* are in.''

Egyptologists are by and large agreed that *Iput* conveyed the meaning "secret chambers of the primeval sanctuary'' and *Pdut* meant "designs, plans with numbers.''

Answering Khufu, the magician (his age was given as one hundred and ten years) said: "I know not the information in the designs, O king, but I know where the plans-with-numbers were hidden by Thoth.'' In answer to further questioning he said: "There is a box of whetstone in the sacred chamber called the Chart Room in Heliopolis; they are in that box.''

Excited, Khufu ordered Dedi to go and find the box for him. But Dedi answered that it was neither he nor Khufu who could obtain the box; it was destined to be found by a future descendant of Khufu. This, he said, was decreed by Ra. Yielding to the god's will, Khufu, as we have seen, ended up only building near the Sphinx a temple dedicated to the Mistress of the Pyramid.

The circle of evidence is thus complete. Sumerian and Egyptian texts confirm each other and our conclusions: The same neutral goddess was the mistress of Sinai's highest peak and of the artificial mountain erected in Egypt, both to serve as anchors of the Landing Corridor.

But the Anunnaki's desire to keep the Sinai peninsula and its facilities neutral did not prevail for long. Rivalry and love tragically combined to upset the status quo; and the divided Earth was soon embroiled in the Pyramid Wars.

8

THE PYRAMID WARS

"In the year 363 His Majesty Ra, the holy one, the Falcon of the Horizon, the Immortal who forever lives, was in the land of Khenn. He was accompanied by his warriors, for the enemies had conspired against their lord. . . . Horus, the Winged Measurer, came to the boat of Ra. He said to his forefather: 'O Falcon of the Horizon, I have seen the enemy conspire against thy Lordship, to take the Luminous Crown unto themselves.' . . . Then Ra, the holy one, the Falcon of the Horizon, said unto Horus, the Winged Measurer: 'Lofty issue of Ra, my begotten: Go quickly, knock down the enemy whom you have seen.' "

Thus began the tale inscribed on the temple walls in the ancient Egyptian city of Edfu. It is the tale, we believe, of what could only be called the First Pyramid War—a war that had its roots in the never-ending struggle for control over Earth and its space facilities and in the shenanigans of the Great Anunnaki, especially Enki/Ptah and his son Ra/Marduk.

According to Manetho, Ptah turned over the dominion over Egypt after a reign of 9,000 years; but the reign of Ra was cut short after 1,000 years—by the Deluge, we have concluded. Then there followed a reign of 700 years by Shu, who helped Ra "control the skies over Earth," and the 500-year reign of Geb ("Who Piles Up the Earth"). It was at that time, circa 10,000 B.C., that the space facilities—the Spaceport in the Sinai and the Giza pyramids—were built.

Although the Sinai peninsula, where the Spaceport was established, and the Giza pyramids were supposed to remain neutral under the aegis of Ninharsag, it is doubtful whether the builders of these facilities—Enki and his descendants—had really any intention of relinquishing control over these installations. A Sumerian text, which begins with an idyllic description, has been named by scholars a "Paradise Myth." Its ancient name was *Enki and Ninharsag,* and it is, in fact, a record of the politically motivated lovemaking between the two, a tale of a deal

between Enki and his half-sister Ninharsag pertaining to the
control of Egypt and the Sinai peninsula—of the pyramids and
the Spaceport.

The tale's time is after Earth was apportioned between the Anunnaki, with Tilmun (the Sinai peninsula) granted to Ninharsag
and Egypt to Enki's clan. It was then, the Sumerian tale relates,
that Enki crossed the marshy lakes that separated Egypt and the
Sinai peninsula and came unto the lonely Ninharsag for an orgy of
lovemaking:

> To the one who is alone,
> To the Lady of Life, mistress of the land,
> Enki came unto the wise Lady of Life.
> He causes his phallus to water the dikes;
> He causes his phallus to submerge the reeds . . .
> He poured his semen into the great lady of the Anunnaki,
> poured the semen in the womb of Ninharsag;
> She took the semen into the womb, the semen of Enki.

Enki's real intention was to obtain a son by his half-sister; but
the offspring was a daughter. Enki then made love to the daughter
as soon as she became "young and fair," and then to his granddaughter. As a result of these sexual activities, a total of eight
gods—six female and two male—were born. Angered by the incest, Ninharsag used her medical skills to sicken Enki. The Anunnaki who were with him pleaded for his life, but Ninharsag was
determined: "Until he is dead, I shall not look upon him with the
'Eye of Life'!"

Satisfied that Enki had indeed been finally stopped, Ninurta—
who went to Tilmun for inspection—returned to Mesopotamia to
report the developments at a meeting attended by Enlil, Nan-
na/Sin, Utu/Shamash and Inanna/Ishtar. Unsatisfied, Enlil ordered
Ninurta to return to Tilmun and bring back Ninharsag with him.
But in the interim, Ninharsag had pity on her brother and changed
her mind. "Ninharsag seated Enki by her vulva and asked: 'My
brother, what hurts thee?'" After she cured his body part by part,
Enki proposed that the two of them as masters of Egypt and the
Sinai assign tasks, spouses, and territories to the eight young gods:

> Let Abu be the master of the plants;
> Let Nintulla be the lord of Magan;
> Let Ninsutu marry Ninazu;

Let Ninkashi be she who sates the thirsts;
Let Nazi marry Nindara;
Let Azimua marry Ningishzida;
Let Nintu be the queen of the months;
Let Enshag be the lord of Tilmun!

Egyptian theological texts from Memphis likewise held that "there came into being" eight gods from the heart, tongue, teeth, lips, and other parts of the body of Ptah. In this text, too, as in the Mesopotamian one, Ptah followed up the bringing forth of these gods by assigning abodes and territories to them: "After he had formed the gods, he made cities, established districts, put the gods in their sacred abodes; he built their shrines and established their offerings." All that he did "to make rejoice the heart of the Mistress of Life."

If, as it appears, these tales had a basis in fact, then the rivalries that such confused parentages brought about could only be aggravated by the sexual shenanigans attributed to Ra as well. The most significant among these was the assertion that Osiris was truly the son of Ra and not of Geb, conceived when Ra had come by stealth unto his own granddaughter. This, as we have earlier related, lay at the core of the Osiris-Seth conflict.

Why had Seth, to whom Upper Egypt had been allotted by Geb, coveted Lower Egypt, which was granted to Osiris? Egyptologists have offered explanations in terms of geography, the land's fertility, etc. But as we have shown, there was one more factor—one that, from the gods' point of view, was more important than how many crops a region could grow: the Great Pyramid and its companions at Giza; whoever controlled them shared in the control of the space activities, of the comings and goings of the gods, of the vital supply link to and from the Twelfth Planet.

For a while Seth succeeded in his ambition, having outwitted Osiris. But "in the year 363" following the disappearance of Osiris, the young Horus became the avenger of his father and launched a war against Seth—the First Pyramid War. It was, as we have seen, also the first war in which the gods involved men in their struggles.

Supported by other Enki-gods reigning in Africa, the avenger Horus began the hostilities in Upper Egypt. Aided by the Winged Disk that Thoth had fashioned for him, Horus persistently advanced northward, toward the pyramids. A major battle took place in the "water district," the chain of lakes that separates Egypt from the Sinai peninsula, and a good many of Seth's followers were slain. After peacemaking efforts by other gods had failed, Seth and Horus engaged in personal combat in and over the Sinai peninsula. In the course of one battle, Seth hid in "secret tunnels" somewhere in the peninsula; in another battle, he lost his testicles. So the Council of the Gods gave the whole of Egypt "as heritage . . . to Horus."

And what had become of Seth, one of the eight gods descended from Ptah?

He was banished from Egypt and took up abode in Asiatic lands to the east, including a place that enabled him "to speak out from the sky." Was he the god called Enshag in the Sumerian tale of Enki and Ninharsag, the one to whom Tilmun (the Sinai peninsula) was allotted by the two lovemakers? If so, then he was the Egyptian (Hamitic) god who had extended his domain over the land of Shem later known as Canaan.

It was in this outcome of the First Pyramid War that there lies an understanding of biblical tales. Therein also lay the causes of the Second Pyramid War.

In addition to the Spaceport and the guidance facilities, there was also a need after the Deluge for a new Mission Control Center, to replace the one that had existed before in Nippur. We have shown (in *The Stairway to Heaven*) that the need to equidistance this center from the other space-related facilities dictated its locating on Mount Moriah ("The Mount of Directing"), the site of the future city of Jerusalem.

That site, by both Mesopotamian and biblical accounts, was located in the lands of Shem—a dominion of the Enlilites. Yet it ended up under an illegal occupation by the line of Enki, the Hamitic gods, and by the descendants of the Hamitic Canaan.

The Old Testament refers to the land of which Jerusalem in time became the capital as Canaan, after the fourth and youngest son of Ham. It also singled out Canaan for special rebuke and consigned his descendants to be subservient to the descendants of Shem. The improbable excuse for this treatment was that Ham—not his son Canaan—had inadvertently seen the naked genitals of his father Noah; therefore, the Lord had put a curse upon Canaan: "Cursed be Canaan; a servant of servants shall he be unto his brethren . . . Blessed be Yahweh the god of Shem; may Canaan be a servant unto them."

The tale in the Book of Genesis leaves many aspects unexplained. Why was Canaan accursed if it was his father who had accidentally transgressed? Why was his punishment to be a slave of Shem and to the god of Shem? And how were the gods involved in the crime and its punishment? As one reads the supplemental information in the ex-biblical *Book of Jubilees,* it becomes clear that the real offense was the illegal occupation of Shem's territory.

After mankind was dispersed and its various clans allotted their lands, the *Book of Jubilees* relates, "Ham and his sons went to the land which he was to occupy, [the land] which he acquired as his portion in the country of the south." But then, journeying from where Noah had been saved to his allotted land in Africa, "Canaan saw the land of Lebanon [all the way down] to the river of Egypt, that it was very good." And so he changed his mind: "He went not into the land of his inheritance to the west of the sea [west of the Red Sea]; he dwelt [instead] in the land of Lebanon, eastward and westward of the Jordan."

His father and his brothers tried to dissuade Canaan from such an illegal act: "And Ham his father, and Cush and Mizra'im his brothers, said unto him: 'Thou hast settled in a land which is not thine, and which did not fall to us by lot; do not do so; for if thou dost do so, thou and thy sons will be fallen in the land and be accursed through sedition; for by sedition ye have settled, and by sedition will thy children fall, and thou shall be rooted out forever. Dwell not in the dwelling of Shem; for to Shem and his sons did it come by their lot.' "

Were he to illegally occupy the territory assigned to Shem, they pointed out, "Cursed art thou and cursed shalt thou be beyond the sons of Noah, by the curse which we bound ourselves by an oath in the presence of the Holy Judge and in the presence of Noah our father. . . ."

"But Canaan did not hearken unto them, and dwelt in the land of Lebanon from Hamath to the entering of Egypt, he and his sons until this day. For this reason is that land named Canaan."

Behind the biblical and pseudoepigraphical tale of a territorial usurpation by a descendant of Ham must lie a tale of a similar usurpation by a descendant of the God of Egypt. We must bear in mind that at the time the allotment of lands and territories was not among the peoples but among the gods; the gods, not the people, were the landlords. A people could only settle a territory allotted to their god and could occupy another's territory only if their god had extended his or her dominion to that territory, by agreement or by force. The illegal seizure of the area between the Spaceport in the Sinai and the Landing Place in Baalbek by a descendant of Ham could have occurred only if that area had been usurped by a descendant of the Hamitic deities, by a younger god of Egypt.

And that, as we have shown, was indeed the result of the First Pyramid War.

Seth's trespass into Canaan meant that all the space-related sites—Giza, the Sinai peninsula, Jerusalem—came under the control of the Enki gods. It was a development in which the Enlilites could not acquiesce. And so, soon thereafter—300 years later, we believe—they deliberately launched a war to dislodge the illegal occupiers from the vital space facilities. This Second Pyramid War is described in several texts, some found in the original Sumerian, others in Akkadian and Assyrian renderings. Scholars refer to these texts as the "Myths of Kur"—"myths" of the Mountain Lands; they are, in fact, poetically rendered chronicles of the war to control the space-related peaks—Mount Moriah; the Harsag (Mount St. Katherine) in the Sinai; and the artificial mount, the Ekur (the Great Pyramid) in Egypt.

It is clear from the texts that the Enlilite forces were led and commanded by Ninurta, "Enlil's foremost warrior," and that the first encounters were in the Sinai peninsula. The Hamitic gods were beaten there; but they retreated to continue the war from the mountain lands of Africa. Ninurta rose to the challenge, and in the second phase of the war carried the battle to the strongholds of his foes; that phase entailed vicious and ferocious battles. Then, in its final phase, the war was fought at the Great Pyramid, the last and impregnable stronghold of Ninurta's opponents; there the Hamitic gods were besieged until they ran out of food and water.

This war, which we call the Second Pyramid War, was commemorated extensively in Sumerian records—both written chronicles and pictorial depictions.

Hymns to Ninurta contain numerous references to his feats and heroic deeds in this war; a great part of the psalm "Like Anu Art Thou Made" is devoted to a record of the struggle and the final victory. But the principal and most direct chronicle of the war is the epic text *Lugal-e Ud Melam-bi,* best collated and edited by Samuel

Geller in *Altorientalische Texte und Untersuchungen*. Like all Mesopotamian texts, it is so titled after its opening line:

King, the glory of thy day is lordly;
Ninurta, Foremost, possessor of the Divine Powers,
who into the throes of the Mountainlands stepped forth.
Like a flood which cannot be stopped,
the Enemyland as with a girdle you tightly bound.
Foremost one, who in battle vehemently enters;
Hero, who in his hand the Divine Brilliant Weapon carries;
Lord: the Mountainland you subdued as your creature.
Ninurta, royal son, whose father to him had given might;
Hero: in fear of thee, the city has surrendered . . .
O mighty one—
the Great Serpent, the heroic god,
you tore away from all the mountains.

Thus extolling Ninurta, his feats, and his Brilliant Weapon, the poem also describes the location of the conflict ("the Mountainlands") and his principal enemy: "The Great Serpent," leader of the Egyptian deities. The Sumerian poem identifies this adversary several times as *Azag* and once refers to him as *Ashar,* both well-known epithets for Marduk, thereby establishing the two principal sons of Enlil and Enki—Ninurta and Marduk—as the leaders of the opposing camps in the Second Pyramid War.

The second tablet (one of thirteen on which the long poem was inscribed) describes the first battle. Ninurta's upper hand is ascribed to both his godly weapons and a new airship that he built for himself after his original one had been destroyed in an accident. It was called IM.DU.GUD, usually translated "Divine Storm Bird" but which literally means "That Which Like Heroic Storm Runs"; we know from various texts that its wingspan was about seventy-five feet.

Archaic drawings depicted it as a mechanically constructed "bird," with two wing surfaces supported by cross beams (Fig. 47a); an undercarriage reveals a series of round openings, perhaps air intakes for jetlike engines. This aircraft, from millennia ago, bears a remarkable resemblance not only to the early biplanes of the modern air age, but also an incredible likeness to the sketch made in 1497 by Leonardo da Vinci, depicting his concept of a man-powered flying machine (Fig. 47b).

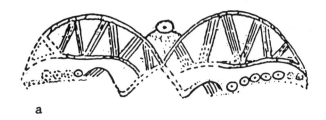

a

b

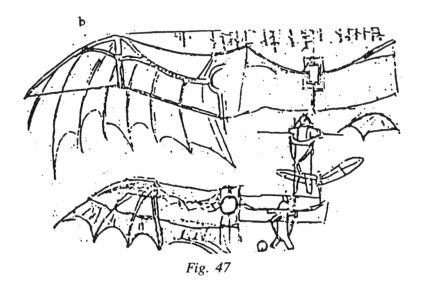

Fig. 47

The Imdugud was the inspiration for Ninurta's emblem—a heroic lion-headed bird resting on two lions (Fig. 48) or sometimes on two bulls. It was in this "crafted ship"—a manufactured vehicle—"that which in war destroys the princely abodes," that Ninurta soared into the skies during the battles of the Second Pyramid War. He soared so high that his companions lost sight of him. Then, the texts relate, "in his Winged Bird, against the walled abode" he swooped down. "As his Bird neared the ground, the summit [of the enemy's stronghold] he smashed."

Chased out of his strongholds, the Enemy began to retreat. While Ninurta kept up the frontal attack, Adad roamed the countryside behind the enemy lines, destroying the adversary's food supplies: "In the Abzu, Adad the fish caused to be washed away . . . .

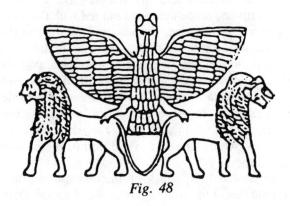

Fig. 48

the cattle he dispersed.'' When the Enemy kept retreating into the mountains, the two gods ''like an onrushing flood the mountains ravaged.''

As the battles extended in time and scope, the two leading gods called on the others to join them. ''My lord, to the battle which is becoming extensive, why don't you go?'' they asked a god whose name is missing in a damaged verse. The question was clearly also addressed to Ishtar, for she is mentioned by name: ''In the clash of weapons, in the feats of heroship, Ishtar her arm did not hold back.'' As the two gods saw her, they shouted encouragingly to her: ''Advance hither without stopping! Put your foot down firmly on the Earth! In the mountains, we await thee!''

''The weapon which is lordly brilliant, the goddess brought forth . . . a horn [to direct it] she made for it.'' As she used it against the enemy in a feat ''that to distant days'' shall be remembered, ''the skies were like red-hued wool in color.'' The explosive beam ''tore apart [the enemy], made him with his hand clutch his heart.''

The continued tale, on tablets v–viii, is too damaged to be properly read. The partial verses suggest that after the intensified attack with Ishtar's assistance, there arose a great cry and lamentation in the Enemyland. ''Fear of Ninurta's Brilliance encompassed the land,'' and its residents had to use substitutes instead of wheat and barley ''to grind and mill as flour.''

Under this onslaught the Enemy forces kept retreating south. It was then that the war assumed its ferocious and vicious character, when Ninurta led the Enlilite gods in an attack on the heartland of

Nergal's African domain and his temple-city, Meslam. They scorched the earth and made the rivers run red with the blood of the innocent bystanders—the men, women, and children of the Abzu.

The verses describing this aspect of the war are damaged on the tablets of the main text; its details are, however, available from various other fragmented tablets that deal with the "overwhelming of the land" by Ninurta," a feat whereby he earned the title "Vanquisher of Meslam." In these battles the attackers resorted to chemical warfare. We read that Ninurta rained on the city poison-bearing missiles, which "he catapulted into it; the poison, by itself, destroyed the city."

Those who survived the attack on the city escaped to the surrounding mountains. But Ninurta "with the Weapon That Smites threw fire upon the mountains; the godly Weapon of the Gods, whose Tooth is bitter, smote down the people." Here, too, some kind of chemical warfare is indicated:

The Weapon Which Tears Apart
robbed the senses;
The Tooth skinned them off.
Tearing-apart he stretched upon the land;
The canals he filled with blood,
in the Enemyland for dogs like milk to lick.

Overwhelmed by the merciless onslaught, Azag called on his followers to show no resistance: "The arisen Enemy to his wife and child called; against the lord Ninurta he raised not his arm. The weapons of Kur with soil were covered" (i.e., hidden away); "Azag them did not raise."

Ninurta took the lack of resistance as a sign of victory. A text reported by F. Hrozny ("Mythen von dem Gotte Ninib") relates how, after Ninurta killed the opponents occupying the land of the Harsag (Sinai) and went on "like a Bird" to attack the gods who "behind their walls retreated" in Kur, he defeated them in the mountains. He then burst out in a song of victory:

My fearsome Brilliance like Anu's is mighty;
Against it, who can rise?
I am lord of the high mountains,
of the mountains which to the horizon raise their peaks.
In the mountains, I am the master.

But the claim of victory was premature. By his nonresistance tactics, Azag had escaped defeat. The capital city was indeed destroyed, but not so the leaders of the Enemy. Soberly, the text *Lugal-e* observed: "The scorpion of Kur Ninurta did not annihilate." Instead, the Enemy gods retreated into the Great Pryamid, where "the Wise Craftsman"—Enki? Thoth?—raised up a protective wall "which the Brilliance could not match," a shield through which the death rays could not penetrate.

Our knowledge of this final and most dramatic phase of the Second Pyramid War is augmented by texts from "the other side." Just as Ninurta's followers composed hymns to him, so did the followers of Nergal. Some of the latter, which have also been discovered by archaeologists, were put together in *Gebete und Hymnen an Nergal* by J. Bollenrücher.

Recalling the heroic feats of Nergal in this war, the texts relate how, as the other gods found themselves hemmed in within the Giza complex, Nergal—"Lofty Dragon Beloved of Ekur"—"at night stole out" and, carrying awesome weapons and accompanied by his lieutenants, broke through the encirclement to reach the Great Pyramid (the Ekur). Reaching it at night, he entered through "the locked doors which by themselves can open." A roar of welcome greeted him as he entered:

Divine Nergal,
Lord who by night stole out,
had come to the battle!
He cracks his whip, his weapons clank . . .
He who is welcome, his might is immense;
Like a dream at the doorstep he appeared.
Divine Nergal, the One Who Is Welcome:
Fight the enemy of Ekur,
lay hold on the Wild One from Nippur!

But the high hopes of the besieged gods were soon dashed. We learn more of the last phases of this Pyramid War from yet another text, first pieced together by George A. Barton *(Miscellaneous Babylonian Texts)* from fragments of an inscribed clay cylinder found in the ruins of Enlil's temple in Nippur.

As Nergal joined the defenders of the Great Pyramid ("the Formidable House Which Is Raised Up Like a Heap"), he strengthened its defenses through the various ray-emitting crystals (mineral "stones") positioned within the pyramid:

The Water-Stone, the Apex-Stone,
the . . . -Stone, the . . .
. . . the lord Nergal
increased its strength.
The door for protection he . . .
To heaven its Eye he raised,
Dug deep that which gives life . . .
. . . in the House
he fed them food.

With the pyramid's defenses thus enhanced, Ninurta resorted to
another tactic. He called upon Utu/Shamash to cut off the pyramid's water supply by tampering with the "watery stream" that
ran near its foundations. The text here is too mutilated to enable a
reading of the details; but the tactic apparently achieved its purpose.

Huddled in their last stronghold, cut off from food and water,
the besieged gods did their best to ward off their attackers. Until
then, in spite of the ferocity of the battles, no major god had fallen
a casualty to the fighting. But now one of the younger gods—
Horus, we believe—trying to sneak out of the Great Pyramid
disguised as a ram, was struck by Ninurta's Brilliant Weapon and
lost the sight of his eyes. An Olden God then cried out to Ninharsag—reputed for her medical wonders—to save the young god's
life:

At that time the Killing Brightness came;
The House's platform withstood the lord.
Unto Ninharsag there was an outcry:
". . . the weapon . . . my offspring
with death is accursed. . . ."

Other Sumerian texts call this young god "offspring who did
not know his father," an epithet befitting Horus, who was born
after his father's death. In Egyptian lore the *Legend of the Ram*
reports the injuries to the eyes of Horus when a god "blew fire"
at him.

It was then, responding to the "outcry," that Ninharsag decided
to intervene to stop the fighting.

The ninth tablet of the *Lugal-e* text begins with the statement of
Ninharsag, her address to the Enlilite commander, her own son
Ninurta, "the son of Enlil . . . the Legitimate Heir whom the

sister-wife had brought forth.'' In telltale verses she announced her decision to cross the battle lines and bring an end to the hostilities:

> To the House Where Cord-Measuring begins,
> Where Asar his eyes to Anu raised,
> I shall go.
> The cord I will cut off,
> for the sake of the warring gods.

Her destination was the ''House Where Cord-Measuring begins,'' the Great Pyramid!

Ninurta was at first astounded by her decision to ''enter alone the Enemyland''; but since her mind was made up, he provided her with ''clothes which should make her unafraid'' (of the radiation left by the beams?). As she neared the pyramid, she addressed Enki: ''She shouts to him . . . she beseeches him.'' The exchanges are lost by the breaks in the tablet; but Enki agreed to surrender the pyramid to her:

> The House that is like a heap,
> that which I have as a pile raised up—
> its mistress you may be.

There was, however, a condition: The surrender was subject to a final resolution of the conflict until ''the destiny-determining time'' shall come. Promising to relay Enki's conditions, Ninharsag went to address Enlil.

The events that followed are recorded in part in the *Lugal-e* epic and in other fragmentary texts. But they are most dramatically described in a text titled *I Sing the Song of the Mother of the Gods*. Surviving in great length because it was copied and recopied throughout the ancient Near East, the text was first reported by P. Dhorme in his study *La Souveraine des Dieux*. It is a poetic text in praise of *Ninmah* (the ''Great Lady'') and her role as *Mammi* (''Mother of the Gods'') on both sides of the battle lines.

Opening with a call upon ''the comrades in arms and the combatants'' to listen, the poem briefly describes the warfare and its participants, as well as its nearly global extent. On the one side were ''the firstborn of Ninmah'' (Ninurta) and Adad, soon joined by Sin and later on by Inanna/Ishtar. On the opposing side are listed Nergal, a god referred to as ''Mighty, Lofty One''— Ra/Marduk—and the ''God of the two Great Houses'' (the two great pyramids of Giza) who had tried to escape camouflaged in a ram's skin: Horus.

Asserting that she was acting with the approval of Anu, Ninharsag took the surrender offer of Enki to Enlil. She met him in the presence of Adad (while Ninurta remained at the battlefield). "O hear my prayers!" she begged the two gods as she explained her ideas. Adad was at first adamant:

> Presenting himself there, to the Mother,
> Adad thus said:
> "We are expecting victory.
> The enemy forces are beaten.
> The trembling of the land he could not withstand."

If she wants to bring about a cessation of hostilities, Adad said, let her call discussions on the basis that the Enlilites are about to win:

> "Get up and go—talk to the enemy.
> Let him attend the discussions
> so that the attack be withdrawn."

Enlil, in less forceful language, supported the suggestion:

> Enlil opened his mouth;
> In the assembly of the gods he said:
> "Whereas Anu at the mountain the gods assembled,
> warfare to discourage, peace to bring,
> and has dispatched the Mother of the Gods
> to entreat with me—
> Let the Mother of the Gods be an emissary."

Turning to his sister, he said in a conciliatory vein:

> "Go, appease my brother!
> Raise unto him a hand for Life;
> From his barred doorway, let him come out!"

Doing as suggested, Ninharsag "his brother went to fetch, put her prayers before the god." She informed him that his safety, and that of his sons, was assured: "by the stars she gave a sign."

As Enki hesitated she said to him tenderly: "Come, let me lead you out." And as he did, he gave her his hand. . . .

She conducted him and the other defenders of the Great Pyramid to the Harsag, her abode. Ninurta and his warriors watched the Enkites depart.

And the great and impregnable structure stood unoccupied, silent.

Nowadays the visitor to the Great Pyramid finds its passages and chambers bare and empty, its complex inner construction apparently purposeless, its niches and nooks meaningless.

It has been so ever since the first men had entered the pyramid. But it was not so when Ninurta had entered it—circa 8670 B.C. according to our calculations. "Unto the radiant place," yielded by its defenders, Ninurta had entered, the Sumerian text relates. And what he had done after he had entered changed not only the Great Pyramid from within and without but also the course of human affairs.

When, for the first time ever, Ninurta went into the "House Which Is Like a Mountain," he must have wondered what he would find inside. Conceived by Enki/Ptah, planned by Ra/Marduk, built by Geb, equipped by Thoth, defended by Nergal, what mysteries of space guidance, what secrets of impregnable defense did it hold?

In the smooth and seemingly solid north face of the pyramid, a swivel stone swung open to reveal the entranceway, protected by the massive diagonal stone blocks, just as the text lauding Ninharsag had described. A straight Descending Passage led to the lower service chambers where Ninurta could see a shaft dug by the defenders in search for subterranean water. But his interest focused on the upper passages and chambers; there, the magical "stones" were arrayed—minerals and crystals, some earthly, some heavenly, some the likes of which he had never seen. From them there were emitted the beamed pulsations for the guidance of the astronauts and the radiations for the defense of the structure.

Escorted by the Chief Mineralmaster, Ninurta inspected the array of "stones" and instruments. As he stopped by each one of them, he determined its destiny—to be smashed up and destroyed, to be taken away for display, or to be installed as instruments elsewhere. We know of these "destinies," and of the order in which Ninurta had stopped by the stones, from the text inscribed on tablets 10–13 of the epic poem *Lugal-e*. It is by following and correctly interpreting this text that the mystery of the purpose and function of many features of the pyramid's inner structure can be finally understood.

Going up the Ascending Passage, Ninurta reached its junction with the imposing Grand Gallery and a Horizontal Passage. Ninurta followed the Horizontal Passage first, reaching a large chamber with a corbeled roof. Called the "vulva" in the Ninharsag poem, this chamber's axis lay exactly on the east-west center line of the pyramid. Its emission ("an outpouring which is like a lion whom no one dares attack") came from a stone fitted into a niche that was hollowed out in the east wall (Fig. 49). It was the SHAM ("Destiny") Stone. Emitting a red radiance which Ninurta "saw in the darkness," it was the pulsating heart of the pyramid. But it was anathema to Ninurta, for during the battle, when he was aloft, this stone's "strong power" was used "to grab to kill me, with a tracking which kills to seize me." He ordered it "pulled out . . . be taken apart . . . and to obliteration be destroyed."

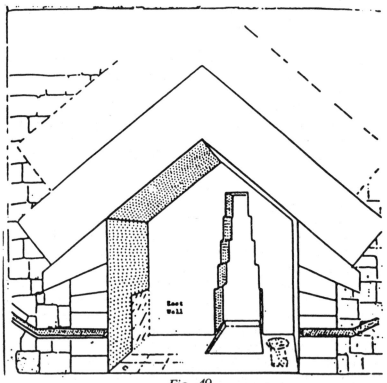

Fig. 49

Returning to the junction of the passages, Ninurta looked around him in the Grand Gallery (Fig. 45). As ingenious and complex as the whole pyramid was, this gallery was breathtaking and a most unusual sight. Compared to the low and narrow passages, it rose high (some twenty-eight feet) in seven overlapping stages, its walls closing in ever more at each stage. The ceiling was also built in slanting sections, each one angled into the massive walls so as not to exert any pressure on the segment below it. Whereas in the narrow passages only "a dim green light glowed," the Gallery glittered in multicolored lights—"its vault is like a rainbow, the darkness ends there." The many-hued glows were emitted by twenty-seven pairs of diverse crystal stones that were evenly spaced along the whole length of each side of the Gallery (Fig. 50a). These glowing stones were placed in cavities that were precisely cut into the ramps that ran the length of the Gallery on both sides of its floor. Firmly held in place by an elaborate niche in the wall (Fig. 50b), each crystal stone emitted a different radiance, giving the place its rainbow effect. For the moment Ninurta passed by them on his way up; his priority was the uppermost Grand Chamber and its pulsating stone.

Atop the Grand Gallery, Ninurta reached a great step which led through a low passage to an Antechamber of unique design (Fig. 46). There three portcullises—"the bolt, the bar and the lock" of the Sumerian poem—elaborately fitted into grooves in the walls and floor, hermetically sealed off the uppermost Great Chamber: "to foe it is not opened; only to Them Who Live, for them it is opened." But now, by pulling some cords, the portcullises were raised, and Ninurta passed through.

He was now in the pyramid's most restricted ("sacred") chamber, from which the guiding "Net" (radar?) was "spread out" to "survey Heaven and Earth." The delicate mechanism was housed in a hollowed-out stone chest; placed precisely on the north-south axis of the pyramid, it responded to vibrations with bell-like resonance. The heart of the guidance unit was the GUG ("Direction Determining") Stone; its emissions, amplified by five hollow compartments constructed above the chamber, were beamed out and up through two sloping channels leading to the north and south faces of the pyramid. Ninurta ordered this stone destroyed: "Then, by the fate-determining Ninurta, on that day was the Gug stone from its hollow taken out and smashed."

To make sure no one would ever attempt to restore the "Direction Determining" functions of the pyramid, Ninurta also ordered

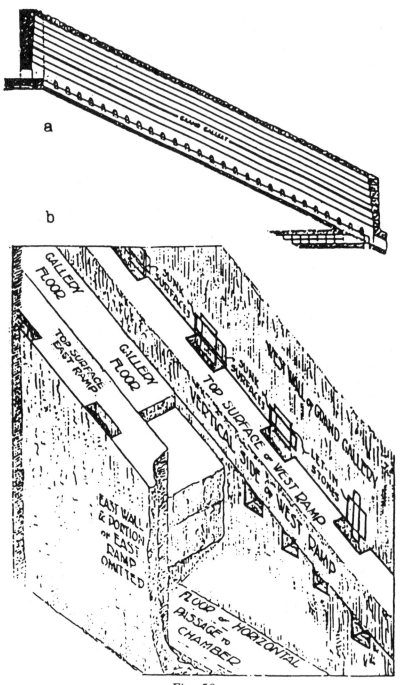

Fig. 50

the three portcullises removed. First to be tackled were the SU ("Vertical") Stone and the KA.SHUR.RA ("Awesome, Pure Which Opens") Stone. Then "the hero stepped up to the SAG.KAL Stone" ("Sturdy Stone Which Is In Front"). "He called out his full strength," shook it out of its grooves, cut the cords that were holding it, and "to the ground set its course."

Now came the turn of the mineral stones and crystals positioned atop the ramps in the Grand Gallery. As he walked down Ninurta stopped by each one of them to declare its fate. Were it not for breaks in the clay tablets on which the text was written, we would have had the names of all twenty-seven of them; as it is, only twenty-two names are legible. Several of them Ninurta ordered to be crushed or pulverized; others, which could be used in the new Mission Control Center, were ordered given to Shamash; and the rest were carried off to Mesopotamia, to be displayed in Ninurta's temple, in Nippur, and elsewhere as constant evidence of the great victory of the Enlilites over the Enki-gods.

All this, Ninurta announced, he was doing not only for his sake but for future generations, too: "Let the fear of thee"—the Great Pyramid—"be removed from my descendants; let their peace be ordained."

Finally there was the Apex Stone of the Pyramid, the UL ("High As The Sky") Stone: "Let the mother's offspring see it no more," he ordered. And, as the stone was sent crashing down, "let everyone distance himself," he shouted. The "Stones," which were "anathema" to Ninurta, were no more.

The deed having been done, Ninurta's comrades urged him to leave the battleground and return home. AN DIM DIM.MA, "Like Anu Art Thou Made," they told him in praise; "The Radiant House where the cord-measuring begins, the House in the land which thou hast come to know—rejoice in having entered it." Now, return to thy home, where thy wife and son await thee: "In the city which thou lovest, in the abode of Nippur, may thy heart be at rest . . . may thy heart become appeased."

The Second Pyramid War was over; but its ferocity and feats, and Ninurta's final victory at the pyramids of Giza, were remembered long thereafter in epic and song—and in a remarkable drawing on a cylinder seal, showing Ninurta's Divine Bird within a victory wreath, soaring in triumph above the two great pyramids (Fig. 51).

Fig. 51

And the Great Pyramid itself, bare and void and without its apex stone, has been left standing as a mute witness to the defeat of its defenders.

9

PEACE ON EARTH

How did the Pyramid Wars end?

They ended as great wars have ended in historic times: with a peace conference; with the gathering of the combatants, as at the Congress of Vienna (1814-1815), which redrew the map of Europe after the Napoleonic Wars, or the Paris Peace Conference that ended World War I (1914-1918) with the Treaty of Versailles.

The first inkling that the warring Anunnaki had convened in a similar manner some ten thousand years ago comes from the text which George A. Barton found inscribed on a broken clay cylinder. It was an Akkadian version of a much earlier Sumerian text; and Barton concluded that the clay cylinder was deposited by the ruler Naram-Sin circa 2300 B.C. when this Akkadian king repaired the platform of Enlil's temple in Nippur. Comparing the Mesopotamian text with texts inscribed at about the same time by Egyptian Pharaohs, Barton noted that the Egyptian texts "centered around the king and are interested in his fortunes as he enters among the gods"; the Mesopotamian text, on the other hand, "concerned itself with the community of the gods"; its subject was not the aspirations of the king but the affairs of the gods themselves.

In spite of damage to the text, especially at the beginning, it is clear that the leading gods gathered in the aftermath of a great and bitter war. We learn that they convened at the Harsag, Ninharsag's mountain abode in the Sinai, and that she played the role of peacemaker. Yet she is not treated by the text's author as a really neutral personage: he repeatedly refers to her by the epithet *Tsir* ("Snake"), which stamped her as an Egyptian/Enkite goddess and conveyed a derogatory connotation.

The text's opening verses, as we have already stated, briefly described the last phases of the war and the conditions within the besieged pyramid that led to the defenders' "outcry," leading to Ninharsag's decision to intervene.

We learn from the continuing ancient chronicle that Ninharsag first went with her idea of stopping the fighting and convening a peace conference to Enlil's camp.

173

The Enlilites' first reaction to Ninharsag's bold initiative was to accuse her of giving aid and comfort to the "demons." Ninharsag denied the accusation: "My House is pure," she answered. But a god whose identity is unclear challenged her sarcastically: "Is the House which is loftier and brightest of all"—the Great Pyramid—also "pure"?

"Of that I cannot speak," Ninharsag answered; "its brilliance Gibil is soldiering."

After the first accusations and explanations wore off some of the bitterness, a symbolic ceremony of forgiveness was performed. It involved two jars holding waters of the Tigris and Euphrates rivers, a ceremony of symbolic baptism making Ninharsag welcome again in Mesopotamia. Enlil touched her with his "bright scepter," and the "power of her was not overthrown."

The objections of Adad to a peace conference rather than unconditional surrender were already reported by us in the previous chapter. But then Enlil agreed, saying to her: "Go, appease my brother." We have already read in another text how Ninharsag crossed the battle lines to arrange the cease-fire. Having brought out Enki and his sons, Ninharsag took them to her abode in the Harsag. The Enlilite gods were already there, waiting.

Announcing that she was acting in behalf of "the great lord Anu . . . Anu the Arbiter," Ninharsag performed a symbolic ceremony of her own. She lighted seven fires, one each for the gathered gods: Enki and his two sons: Enlil and his three sons (Ninurta, Adad, and Sin). She uttered an incantation as she lit each fire: "A fiery offering to Enlil of Nippur . . . to Ninurta . . . to Adad . . . to Enki coming from the Abzu . . . to Nergal coming from Meslam." By nightfall the place was ablaze: "as sunlight was the great light set off by the goddess."

Ninharsag then appealed to the wisdom of the gods and extolled the virtues of peace: "Mighty are the fruits of the wise god; the great divine river to his vegetation shall come . . . its overflowing will make [the land] like a garden of god." The abundance of plants and animals, of wheat and other grains, of vines and fruits, and the benefits of a "triple-sprouting mankind" planting, building, and serving the gods—all to follow peace—were then outlined by her.

After Ninharsag had finished her oracle of peace, Enlil was the first one to speak. "Removed is the affliction from the face of the Earth," Enlil declared to Enki; "the Great Weapon is lifted up." He agreed to let Enki regain his abode in Sumer: "The E.DIN shall be a place for thy Holy House," with enough land around to bear fruit for the temple and to have seeded fields.

On hearing this Ninurta objected. "Let it not come!" the "prince of Enlil" shouted.

Again Ninharsag took the floor. She reminded Ninurta how he had toiled, "day and night with might," to enable cultivation and cattle herding in the land, how he "raised the foundations, filled [the earth], raised [the dykes]." Then the affliction of war destroyed it all, "all, in its entirety." "Lord of life, god of fruit," she appealed to him, "let the good beer pour in double measure! Make abundant the wool!"—agree to the peace terms!

Overcome by her plea, Ninurta relented: "O my mother, brilliant one! Proceed; the flour I will not withhold . . . in the kingdom the garden will be restored . . . To end affliction, I [too] earnestly pray."

Now the peace negotiations could proceed; and we pick up the tale of the unprecedented encounter between the two warring gods from the text *I Sing the Song of the Mother of the Gods*. First to address the assembled Anunnaki was Enki:

Enki addressed to Enlil words of lauding:
"O one who is foremost among the brothers,
Bull of Heaven, who the fate of Mankind holds:
In my lands, desolation is widespread;
All the dwellings are filled with sorrow
by your attacks."

The first item on the agenda was thus the cessation of hostilities—peace on Earth—and Enlil readily agreed, on condition that the territorial disputes be brought to an end and the lands rightfully belonging to the Enlilites and the people of the line of Shem be vacated by the Enkites. Enki agreed to cede forever these territories:

"I will grant thee the ruler's position
in the gods' Restricted Zone;
The Radiant Place, in thy hand I will entrust!"

In so ceding the Restricted Zone (the Sinai peninsula with its Spaceport) and the Radiant Place (the site of Mission Control Center, the future Jerusalem) Enki had a firm condition. In return for granting Enlil and his offspring eternal rights to those lands and vital sites, the sovereignty of Enki and his descendants over the Giza complex had to be recognized for all time.

Enlil agreed but not without a condition: The sons of Enki who had brought about the war and used the Great Pyramid for combat purposes should be barred from ruling over Giza, or over the whole of Lower Egypt, for that matter.

Pondering the condition over, Enki agreed. He then and there announced his decision. The lord of Giza and Lower Egypt, he said, will be a young son of his, espoused to one of the female deities born when Enki had made love to Ninharsag: "For the formidable House Which Is Raised Like a Heap, he appointed the prince whose brilliant wife from the cohabitation with Tsir [Ninharsag] was brought forth. The strong prince who is like a fullgrown ibex—him he appointed, and commanded him to guard the Place of Life." He then granted the young god the exalted title NIN.GISH.ZI.DA ("Lord of the Artifact of Life").

Who was Ningishzidda? Scholars find the information concerning him meager and confusing. He is mentioned in Mesopotamian texts in association with Enki, Dumuzi, and Ninharsag; in the Great God List he is included among the gods of Africa following Nergal and Ereshkigal. The Sumerians depicted him with Enki's emblem of the entwined serpents and with the Egyptian *Ankh* sign (Fig. 52 a,b). Yet they viewed Ningishzidda favorably; Ninurta befriended him and invited him to Sumer. Some texts suggest that his mother was Ereshkigal, Enlil's granddaughter; our own conclusion is that he was indeed a son of Enki, conceived during Enki's and

a   b

Fig. 52

Ereshkigal's stormy voyage to the Lower World. As such, he was acceptable to both sides as guardian of the secrets of the pyramids.

A hymn which Ake W. Sjöberg and E. Bergmann ("The Collection of the Sumerian Temple Hymns") believe was composed by the daughter of Sargon of Akkad in the third millennium B.C. exalted the pyramid-house of Ningishzidda and confirmed its Egyptian location:

> Enduring place, light-hued mountain
> which in an artful fashion was founded.
> Its dark hidden chamber is an awe-inspiring place;
> in a Field of Supervision it lies.
> Awesome, its ways no one can fathom.
> In the Land of the Shield
> your pedestal is closely knit as a fine-mesh net . . .
> At night you face the heavens,
> your ancient measurements are surpassing.
> Your interior knows the place where Utu rises,
> the measure of its width is far reaching.
> Your prince is the prince whose pure hand is outstretched,
> whose luxuriant and abundant hair
> flows down on his back—
> the lord Ningishzida.

The concluding verses of the hymn twice restate the location of this unique structure: the "Land of the Shield." It is a term equivalent to the Akkadian meaning of the Mesopotamian name for Egypt: the Land Magan, "The Land of the Shield." And another hymn copied and translated by Sjöberg (tablet UET 6/1) called Ningishzidda "the falcon among the gods," a designation commonly applied in Egyptian texts to Egyptian gods and found in Sumerian texts only one other time, applied to Ninurta, conqueror of the pyramids.

What did the Egyptians call this son of Enki/Ptah? Their "god of the cord who measures the Earth" was Thoth; he was (as the *Tales of the Magicians* related) the one appointed to be guardian of the secrets of the Giza pyramids. It was Thoth, according to Manetho, who replaced Horus on the throne of Egypt; it happened circa 8670 B.C. —just at the time when the Second Pyramid War had ended.

Having thus settled the disputes between them, the great Anunnaki turned to the affairs of mankind.

As one reads the ancient words it becomes clear that this peace conference dealt not only with the cessation of hostilities and the drawing of binding territorial lines; it also laid the plans for the manner in which the lands would be settled by mankind! We read that Enki ''before the feet of the adversary [Enlil] laid the cities that were allotted him''; Enlil, in turn, ''before the feet of his adversary [Enki] the land Sumer he laid out.''

We can envision the two brothers facing each other, Enki—as always—the more concerned of the two about mankind and its fate. Having dealt with the disputes among the Anunnaki themselves, he now turns to the future of mankind. In the aftermath of the Deluge, it was given farming and domesticated animals; now it was the chance to look and plan ahead, and he seized the opportunity. The ancient text may well describe a spontaneous act: Enki drawing on the ground, ''before the feet of Enlil,'' a plan for the establishment of human settlement centers in his lands; agreeing, Enlil responds by drawing ''before the feet of Enki'' the plan for the restoration of the pre-Diluvial cities of southern Mesopotamia (Sumer).

If the olden pre-Diluvial cities of Mesopotamia were to be restored, Enki had a condition: He and his sons were to be allowed to come freely to Mesopotamia; and he, Enki, was to be given back the site of Eridu, the hallowed place of his first Earth Station. Accepting the condition, Enlil said: ''In my land, let your abode become everlasting; from the day that you shall come into my presence, the laden table shall exhale delicious smells for thee.'' Enlil expressed the hope that in return for this hospitality, Enki would help bring prosperity also to Mesopotamia: ''Pour abundance on the Land, each year increase its fortunes.''

And with all these matters settled, Enki and his sons departed for their African domains.

After Enki and his sons had departed, Enlil and his sons contemplated the future of their territories, both old and new. The first chronicle, the one reported by Barton, relates that in order to reaffirm the status of Ninurta as second to Enlil and superior over his brothers, Enlil put him in charge of the Olden Land. The territories of Adad in the northwest were extended by a thin ''finger'' (Lebanon) to include the Landing Place at Baalbek. The territory that was in contention—we can describe it as Greater Canaan, from the border of Egypt in the south to the border of Adad in the north, with modern Syria included—was put under the aegis of Nannar and his offspring. To that effect ''a decree was established,'' sealed, and celebrated with a meal offering shared by all the Enlilite gods.

A more dramatic version of these final proceedings is found in the *I Sing the Song of the Mother of the Gods* text. We learn that at that crucial moment, the rivalry between Ninurta—the legal heir, being the son of Enlil by his half-sister—and Nannar, the firstborn of Enlil by his official spouse Ninlil, had broken out in full force. Enlil, we are told, contemplated favorably the attributes of Nannar: "A firstborn . . . of beautiful countenance, perfect of limbs, wise without compare." Enlil "him loved" because he gave him the two all-important grandchildren, the twins Utu/Shamash and Inanna/Ishtar; he called Nannar SU.EN—"Multiplying Lord"—an endearing epithet from which there stemmed the Akkadian/Semitic name for Nannar: Sin. But as much as Enlil had favored Nannar, the fact was that it was Ninurta who was the legal heir; he was "Enlil's foremost warrior," and he led the Enlilites to victory.

As Enlil wavered between Sin and Ninurta, Sin enlisted the help of his wife Ningal, who appealed to Enlil as well as to his spouse Ninlil, the mother of Sin:

To the place of decision he called Ningal,
Suen invited her to approach.
A favorable decision she asked of the father . . .
Enlil weighed [her words] . . .
Before the mother she [pleaded] . . .
"Remember the childhood," she said [to Ninlil] . . .
The mother quickly embraced him . . .
She said to Enlil: . . ."Follow your heart's desire". . .

Could one ever imagine, in those far-reaching decisions that were to affect the fate of gods and men for millennia to come, that the female spouses had played such a decisive role? We read of Ningal coming to the aid of her husband; we see Ninlil being enlisted in persuading the wavering Enlil. But then there entered the scene yet another great goddess—and by her words achieved an unintended decision. . . .

As Enlil was urged by Ninlil to "follow your heart" rather than his mind, to prefer the firstborn over the legal heir, "Ninurta opened his mouth and said . . ." His words of opposition are lost by a damage to the verses; but, as the tale is continued, we learn that Ninharsag threw in her weight behind her son Ninurta:

She cried out and lamented to her brother;
Like a pregnant woman she was agitated, [saying:]
"Inside the Ekur I call to my brother,

my brother who an infant made me carry;
upon my brother I call!''

But Ninharsag's appeal was ill-worded. She meant to appeal as
Enlil's sister in behalf of the child (Ninurta) she bore him; but her
call sounded like an appeal to Enki. Enraged, Enlil shouted at her:
''Who is this brother of yours that you call? This brother, who an
infant made you carry?'' And he made a decision favoring the line
of Sin. Ever since then, and to this very day, the Land of the
Spaceport has been known as Sin's land—the Sinai peninsula.

As his final act Enlil appointed Sin's son as the commander of
the Mission Control Center:

He called in Shamash
the grandchild of Ninlil.
He took him [by the hand];
In Shulim he placed him.

Jerusalem—*Ur-Shulim,* the ''City of Shulim''—was given to
Shamash to command. Its name, SHU.LIM, meant ''The Supreme
Place of the Four Regions,'' and the Sumerian emblem of the
''Four Regions'' (Fig. 53a) applied to it, possibly the forerunner of
the Jewish emblem called the Star of David (Fig. 53b).

Replacing the pre-Diluvial Nippur as the post-Diluvial Mission
Control Center, Jerusalem also acquired Nippur's former title of
being the Navel of the Earth—the central point in the Divine Grid
that made the comings and goings between Earth and Nibiru possi-

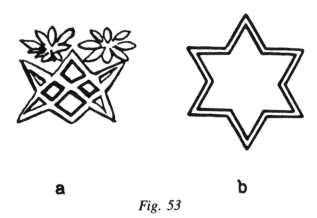

a   b

Fig. 53

ble. Emulating the concentric pre-Diluvial plan based on Nippur, the site selected for the "Navel of the Earth"—Mount Moriah—was located on the middle line, the Landing Path, within the Landing Corridor (Fig. 54); it was equidistant from the Landing Platform in Baalbek (BK) and the Spaceport itself (SP).

The two anchors of the Landing Corridor also had to be equidis-

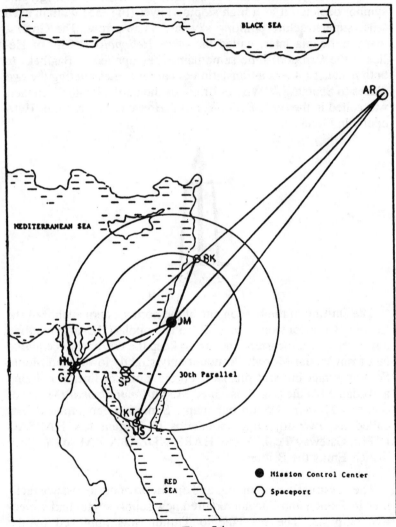

Fig. 54

tant from Mission Control Center (JM); but here there was a need to make a change in the original plans, for the previous artificially constructed "House Which Is Like a Mountain"—the Great Pyramid—was stripped of its crystals and equipment and was rendered useless by Ninurta. The solution was to erect, still precisely on the northwestern corridor line but north of Giza, a new Beacon City. The Egyptians called it the City of Annu; its hieroglyphic symbol depicted it as a high sloping tower (Fig. 55) with an even taller superstructure pointing skyward as an arrow. The Greeks, many millennia later, called the place *Heliopolis* ("City of Helios," the Sun god)—the same name they applied to Baalbek. In both instances it was a translation of earlier names relating the two places to Shamash, "Who Is Bright as the Sun"; Baalbek, in fact, was called in the Bible *Beth-Shemesh,* House of Shamash, or Heliopolis in Greek.

Fig. 55

The shifting of the beacon site at the northwestern anchor of the Landing Corridor from Giza (GZ) to Heliopolis (HL) also required a shift in the southeastern anchor, to keep the two anchors equidistant from Mount Moriah. A mount only slightly lower than Mount St. Katherine, but still precisely on the Corridor line, was found and adapted to the task. It is called Mount *Umm-Shumar* (Mount of Sumer's Mother—US on our map). Sumerian geographical lists called the two adjoining mountains in Tilmun KA HARSAG ("The Gateway Peak") and HARSAG ZALA.ZALAG ("Peak Which Emits the Brilliance").

The construction, manning, and operation of the aerospace facilities in Tilmun and Canaan required new supply routes and protective outposts. The sea lane to Tilmun was improved by the establishment of a port city ("Tilmun City," as distinguished from the "Land Tilmun") on the eastern shore of the Red Sea, probably where the port city of el-Tor still exists. It also led, we believe, to the establishment of the world's oldest town: Jericho, which was dedicated to Sin (*Yeriho* in Hebrew) and his celestial symbol, the Moon.

The age of Jericho has been an enigma that has continuously baffled the scholars. They broadly divide man's advancement (which spread from the Near East) into the Mesolithic ("Middle Stone") Age, which saw the introduction of agriculture and animal domestication circa 11,000 B.C.; a Neolithic ("New Stone") Age 3,600 years later, bringing with it villages and pottery; and then, finally, Sumer's urban civilization, again 3,600 years later. Yet here was Jericho: an *urban* site occupied and built by unknowns sometime circa 8500 B.C., when man had not yet learned to lead even a village life. . . .

The puzzles posed by Jericho pertain not only to its age, but also to what the archaeologists have found there: houses, built on stone foundations, had doors equipped with wooden jambs; the walls were carefully plastered and painted red, pink, and other colors— sometimes even covered with murals. Neat hearths and basins were sunk in whitewashed plaster floors, floors that were often decorated with patterns. Below the floors the dead were sometimes buried—buried but not forgotten: at least ten skulls were found which were filled with plaster to recreate the features of the deceased (Fig. 56). The features they reveal were by all opinions more advanced and finer than those of the usual Mediterranean dwellers of the time. All this was protected by a massive wall that surrounded the town (millennia before Joshua!). It was raised in the middle of a ditch nearly thirty feet wide and seven feet deep, dug out of the rock "without the help of picks and hoes" (James Mellaart, *Earliest Civilizations of the Near East*). It was "an explosive development . . . a spectacular development whose causes," Mellaart says, "are still unknown to us."

The enigma of prehistoric Jericho is compounded by the evidence of its round grain silos, one of which was found still partly standing. In a hot depression near the Dead Sea, 825 feet below sea level, in an inhospitable place unsuitable for grain cultivation, there was found evidence of ample supplies and continued storage of wheat and barley. Who could have built this advanced town that early, who had come to live in such a place, and whom did it serve as a fortified store city?

The solution to this enigma lies, in our opinion, in the chronology of the "gods," not of men. It lies in the fact that the incredible

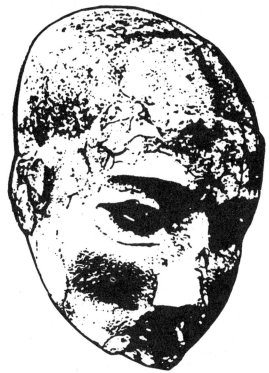

Fig. 56

first urban settlement in Jericho (from circa 8500 B.C. to 7000 B.C.) exactly matches the period which, according to Manetho, encompassed the reign of Thoth in Egypt (from about 8670 to 7100 B.C.). His accession, as we have seen from the Mesopotamian texts, followed the Peace Conference. Egyptian texts say of his accession that it was pronounced "in the presence of the Determiners of Annu, following the night of the battle" and after he had helped "defeat the Storm Wind" (Adad) "and the Whirlwind" (Ninurta), and then assisted in "making the two combatants be at peace."

The period the Egyptians associated with the reign of Thoth was a time of peace among the gods, when the Anunnaki first and foremost established settlements relating to the construction and protection of the new space facilities.

The sea lane to Egypt and Tilmun, via the Red Sea, had to be augmented by a land route that could connect Mesopotamia with the Mission Control Center and the Spaceport. From time imme-

morial this land route led up the Euphrates River to the major way
station of Harran in the Balikh River region. From there the traveler had the choice of either to continue south down the Mediterranean coast—the road later called by the Romans Via Maris ("The
Sea Way")—or to proceed on the east side of the Jordan, along the
equally famous King's Highway. The former was the shortest
route to Egypt; the latter could lead to the Gulf of Eilat, the Red
Sea, Arabia, and Africa, as well as into the Sinai peninsula; it
could also lead to the western side of the Jordan via several suitable
crossing points. It was the route over which the African gold was
brought.

The most vital of these, the one that led directly to Mission Control Center in Jerusalem, was the crossing point at Jericho. It was
there that the Israelites crossed the Jordan into the Promised Land.
It was there, we suggest, that millennia earlier the Anunnaki established a town to guard the crossing point and to supply the travelers
with provisions for the continued journey. Until man made Jericho
his home, it was an outpost of the gods.

Would the Anunnaki have built a settlement only on the west
side of the Jordan, leaving the more vital eastern side, where the
King's Highway ran, unprotected? It stands to reason that a settlement should have existed on the opposite, eastern side of the Jordan, too. Though little known outside of archaeological circles,
such a place has indeed been found; and what was discovered there
is even more astounding than what had been uncovered at Jericho.

The puzzling place with astounding remains was first unearthed
in 1929 by an archaeological mission organized by the Vatican's
Pontifical Biblical Institute. The archaeologists, led by Alexis
Mallon, were surprised by the high level of civilization found
there. Even the oldest level of habitation (circa 7500 B.C.) was
paved with bricks, and though the period of settlement stretched
from the end of the Stone Age to the Bronze Age, the archaeologists were amazed to find that the same civilization revealed itself
at all levels.

The place is named after the mound where it was found—Tell
Ghassul; its ancient name is not known. Together with several satellite settlements, it clearly controlled the vital crossover point and
the road leading to it—a road still followed to this day to a crossing
point nowadays called the Allenby Bridge (Fig. 57). The strategic
location of Tell Ghassul had been noted by the archaeologists when
they began to dig up its remains: "From atop the mound, one has
an interesting all-around view: the Jordan on the west as a dark

186   **THE WARS OF GODS AND MEN**

line; to the northwest, the hillock of ancient Jericho; and beyond it, the mountains of Judea, including Beth-El and the Mount of Olives of Jerusalem. Bethlehem is obscured by Mount el-Muntar, but the heights of Tekoah and the environs of Hebron can be seen'' (A. Mallon, R. Koeppel, and R. Neuville, *Teleilat Ghassul, Compte Rendu des Fouilles de l'Institut Biblique Pontifical*). To the north, the view was unobscured for some thirty miles; to the east, one could see Mount Moab and the foremounts of Mount Nebo; to the south, ''beyond the mirror of the Dead Sea, one could see the salt mountain, Mount Sodom.''

The principal remains uncovered at Tell Ghassul cover a period when it was occupied by highly advanced settlers from before 4000 B.C. to circa 2000 B.C. (when the place was abruptly abandoned).

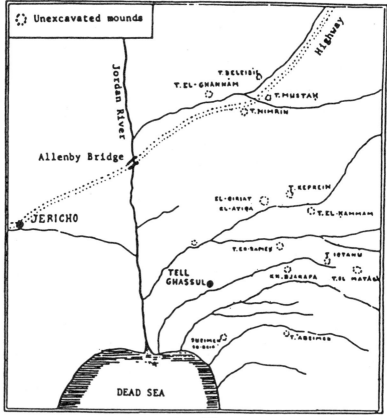

Fig. 57

The artifacts and irrigation system, of a much higher standard than had then prevailed in the area, convinced the archaeologists that the settlers had come from Mesopotamia.

Of the three hillocks that together formed the large mound, two appear to have been used as abodes and one as a work area. The latter was found to have been subdivided into rectangularlike segments, within which there were built circular "pits," frequently in pairs. That they were not hearths for food preparation is suggested not only by their pairing and profusion (why would six or eight of them be required in one compartment?), but also by the fact that some of them were cylindrical and went quite deep into the ground. Combined with them were enigmatic "bands of ashes" (Fig. 58), the remains of some combustible material, which were covered with fine sand and then with regular soil, only to form the foundation of yet another layer of such "band of ashes."

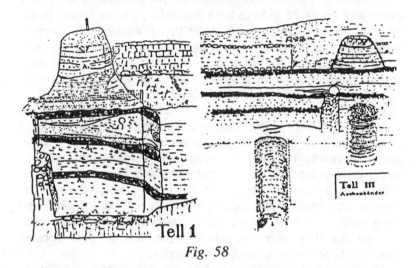

Fig. 58

On the surface, the ground was strewn with pebbles, the remains of rocks broken up by some force that also blackened them. Among the artifacts found was a small, circular object made of fired clay (Fig. 59), shaped with precision for some unknown technical purpose.

The mystery only deepened by the discoveries in the residential areas. There the walls of the rectangular houses collapsed as though hit by a sudden force just above ground level, as a result of which the upper parts of the walls collapsed neatly inward.

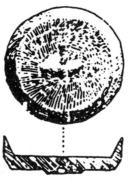

Fig. 59

Because of this neat collapse, it was possible to piece together some of the astounding murals that were painted and overpainted on these walls. In one instance a cagelike mesh shown over the object created on the wall a three-dimensional illusion. In one house every wall appeared to have been painted with some scene; in another a recessed divan was so built that it enabled the dweller, while reclining, to view a mural that covered the whole opposite wall. It depicted a row of people—the first two of whom were seated on thrones—facing toward (or greeting) another person who had apparently stepped out of an object emitting rays.

The archaeologists who had discovered these murals during the 1931–32 and 1932–33 excavations theorized that the rayed object might have been similar to a most unusual rayed "star" found painted in another building. It was an eight-pointed "star" within a larger eight-pointed "star," culminating in a burst of eight rays (Fig. 60). The precise design, employing a variety of geometric shapes, was artistically executed in black, red, white, gray, and combinations thereof; a chemical analysis of the paints used showed that they were not natural substances but sophisticated compounds of twelve to eighteen minerals.

The mural's discoverers assumed that the eight-rayed "star" had some "religious significance," pointing out that the eight-pointed star, standing for the planet Venus, was the celestial symbol of Ishtar. However, the fact is that no evidence of any religious worship whatsoever, no "cult objects," statuettes of gods, etc., had been found at Tell Ghassul, yet another anomaly of the place. This, we suggest, indicates that it was inhabited not by worshipers but by those who were the subject of worshiping: the "gods" of antiquity, the Anunnaki.

In fact, we have come upon a similar design in Washington,

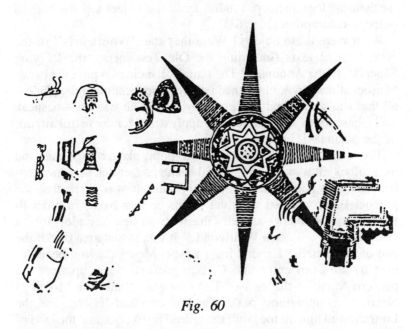

Fig. 60

D.C. It can be seen in the foyer of the headquarters of the National Geographic Society: a floor mosaic of a compass denoting the Society's interest in the four corners of the Earth and their intermediate points (east, northeast; north, northwest; west, southwest; south, southeast). It was this, we believe, that the design's ancient painters, too, had in mind: to indicate their, and the place's, association with the four regions of the Earth.

That the rayed "star" had no sacred significance is further attested by the disrespect with which it was surrounded by graffiti. These (Fig. 60) depict thick-walled buildings, fins of fishes, birds, wings, a ship, and even (some suggest) a sea dragon (upper left-hand corner); in these graffiti, yellow and brown of various shades appear in addition to the colors already mentioned.

Of particular interest are two shapes in which large twin "eyes" are prominent. We have a better knowledge of what they depicted, for such shapes were found painted, on a much larger scale and with greater detail, on the walls of other houses. The objects were depicted as spherical or oval in shape, their upper part layered and painted in black and white. The center was dominated by the two large "eyes," perfect black disks within white circles. The bottom part showed in red two (or four?) extended supports; between these

mechanical legs there protruded from the object's main body a
bulbous contraption (Fig. 61).

What were these objects? Were they the "Whirlwinds" of the
Near Eastern texts (including the Old Testament), the "Flying
Saucers" of the Anunnaki? The murals, the circular pits, the bands
of ashes, the strewn, blackened pebbles, the location of the place—
all that was uncovered and probably much that was not—bespeak
Tell Ghassul as a stronghold and supply depot for the patrol aircraft
of the Anunnaki.

The Tell Ghassul/Jericho crossing point played important and
miraculous roles in several biblical events, a fact that may have enhanced the Vatican's interest in the site. It was there that the
prophet Elijah crossed the river (to its eastern bank) in order to
keep an appointment—at Tell Ghassul?—to be taken aloft by "a
chariot of fire . . . in a Whirlwind." It was in that area that at the
end of the Israelite Exodus from Egypt, Moses (having been denied by the Lord entry into Canaan proper) "went up from the
plain of Moab"—the area of Tell Ghassul—"unto the Mount of
Nebo, to its uppermost peak, which overlooked Jericho; and the
Lord showed him all the land: the Gilead up to Dan, and the land of
Naphtali and the land of Ephraim and Manasseh and the whole
land of Judea, unto the Mediterranean; and the Negeb and the plain
valley of Jericho, the city of datepalms." It is a description of a

Fig. 61

view as encompassing as that seen by the archaeologists who stood atop Tell Ghassul.

The crossing itself, under the leadership of Joshua, entailed the miraculous backing up of the Jordan's waters, under the influence of the Holy Ark and its contents. It was then, "when Joshua was by Jericho, that he raised his eyes and lo and behold, there stood a man opposite him and his drawn sword in his hand; and Joshua went unto him and said unto him: 'Art thou with us or with our enemies?' and he said: 'Neither; a captain of the host of the Lord am I.' And Joshua fell on his face to the ground and bowed, and said unto him: 'What sayeth my lord unto his servant?' and the captain of the host of Yahweh said unto Joshua: 'Remove thy shoe off thy foot, for the place where thou standeth is restricted.' "

Then the captain of the troops of Yahweh divulged to him the Lord's plan for the conquest of Jericho. Do not attempt to storm its walls by force, he said. Instead, carry the Ark of the Covenant around its walls seven times. And on the seventh day the priests sounded the trumpets, and the people let out a great cry, as they were commanded. "And the walls of Jericho came tumbling down."

Jacob, too, crossing the Jordan at night on his return to Canaan from Harran, ran into "a man" and the two wrestled till dawn; only then did Jacob realize that his opponent was a deity; "and Jacob called the place Peni-El ('The Face of God') for I had seen a god face to face and have survived."

Indeed, the Old Testament clearly states that there had been in earlier times settlements of the Anunnaki at the vital approaches to the Sinai peninsula and Jerusalem. Hebron, the city guarding the route between Jerusalem and the Sinai, "was called earlier Kiryat Arba ("Stronghold of Arba"); a Great Man ("king") among the *Anakim* he was" (Joshua, 14:15). The descendants of the *Anakim,* we are further told, were still residing in the area during the Israelite conquest of Canaan; and there are numerous other biblical references to abodes of the *Anakim* on the east side of the Jordan.

Who were these *Anakim?* The term is commonly translated "giants," just as the biblical term *Nefilim* had been translated. But we have already shown conclusively that by *Nefilim* ("Those Who Had Come Down") the Old Testament had referred to the "People of the Rocketships."

The *Anakim,* we suggest, were none other than the *Anunnaki.*

No one had hitherto paid any particular attention to the count of 3,650 years which Manetho assigned to the reign of the "demigods'' who belonged to the dynasty of Thoth. We, however, find the figure highly significant, for it differs but by 50 years from the 3,600-year orbit of Nibiru, the home planet of the Anunnaki.

It was no accident, we have maintained, that mankind's advancement from the Stone Age to the high civilization of Sumer occurred in 3,600-year intervals—circa 11,000, 7400, and 3800 B.C. It was as though ''a mysterious hand'' had each time ''picked Man out of his decline and raised him to an even higher level of culture, knowledge and civilization,'' we wrote in *The 12th Planet;* each instance, we hold, coincided with the recurrence of the time when the Anunnaki could come and go between Earth and Nibiru.

These advances spread from the Mesopotamian nucleus throughout the ancient world; and the Egyptian ''Age of the demigods'' (offspring of the cohabitation of gods and humans)—from circa 7100 B.C. to 3450 B.C. per Manetho—unquestionably coincides with the Neolithic period in Egypt.

We can assume that at each of these intervals the fate of mankind and the gods' relations with it were discussed by the Great Anunnaki, the ''seven who decree.'' We know for sure that such a deliberation had taken place prior to the sudden and otherwise inexplicable blooming of the Sumerian civilization, for the Sumerians have left us records of such discussions!

When the reconstruction of Sumer began, first to have been rebuilt on its soil were the Olden Cities but no longer as exclusive Cities of the Gods; for mankind was now allowed into these urban centers to tend the surrounding fields, orchards, and cattlefolds in behalf of the gods, and to be in the service of the gods in all conceivable manners: not only as cooks and bakers, artisans and clothiers, but also as priests, musicians, entertainers, and temple prostitutes.

First to be reestablished was Eridu. Having been Enki's first settlement on Earth, it was given to him anew in perpetuity. His initial shrine there (Fig. 62)—a marvel of architecture in those early days—was in time raised and expanded to a magnificent temple-abode, the E.EN.GUR.RA (''House of the Lord Whose Return Is Triumphant''), adorned with gold, silver, and precious metals from the Lower World and protected by the ''Bull of Heaven.'' For Enlil and Ninlil Nippur was reestablished; there they raised a new *Ekur* (''Mountain House''—Fig. 63), this time equipped not as Mission Control Center but with awesome weapons: ''the Lifted Eye which scans the land''; and ''the Lifted Beam,'' which pene-

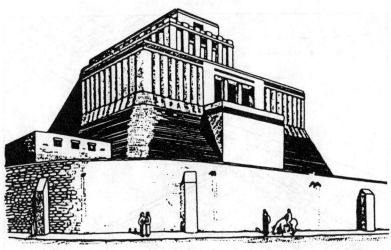

Fig. 62

trates all. Their sacred area also housed Enlil's "fast-stepping Bird" whose "grasp no one could escape."

A "Hymn to Eridu" edited and translated by A. Falkenstein (*Sumer*, vol. VII) describes how Enki traveled to attend a gathering of all the great gods; the occasion was a visit by Anu to Earth, for one of those deliberations that determined the fate of gods and men on Earth every 3,600 years. After some celebrating, when "the gods the intoxicating beverage had drunk, the wine prepared by men," it was time for solemn decisions. "Anu sat on the seat of honor; near him sat Enlil; Ninharsag sat on an arm chair."

Anu called the meeting to order, "and to the Anunnaki thus said":

> Great gods who had hither come,
> Annuna-gods, who to the Court of Assembly had come!
> My son had for himself a House built;
> The lord Enki
> Eridu like the mountain on Earth he raised;
> His House, in a beautiful place he built.
> To the place, Eridu, no one uninvited can enter . . .
> In its sanctuary, from the Abzu
> the Divine Formulas Enki had deposited.

This brought the deliberations to the main item on the agenda:

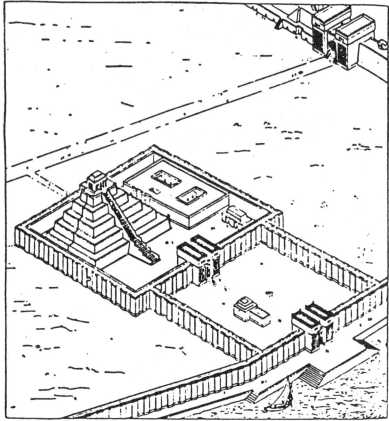

Fig. 63

Enlil's complaint that Enki was withholding from the other gods the "Divine Formulas"—the knowledge of more than one hundred aspects of civilization—confining advancement to Eridu and its people only. (It is an archaeologically confirmed fact that Eridu was Sumer's oldest post-Diluvial city, the fountainhead of Sumerian civilization.) It was then decided that Enki must share the Divine Formulas with the other gods, so that they, too, could establish and reestablish their urban centers: civilization was to be granted to the whole of Sumer.

When the official part of the deliberations was over, the gods who were on Earth had a surprise for the celestial visitors: midway between Nippur and Eridu they had built a sacred precinct in honor of Anu; an abode appropriately named E.ANNA—"House of Anu."

Before they left Earth back for the Home Planet, Anu and Antu his spouse paid an overnight visit to their Earthly temple; it was an occasion marked by pomp and circumstance. As the divine couple reached the new town—later to be known as Uruk (the biblical Erech)—the gods accompanied them in a procession to the temple's courtyard. While a sumptuous evening meal was prepared, Anu, seated on a throne, chatted with the male gods; Antu, accompanied by the female goddesses, changed her clothes in the temple's section called "House of the Golden Bed."

Priests and other temple attendants served "wine and good oil" and slaughtered in sacrifice "a bull and a ram for Anu, Antu and all the gods." But the banquet was delayed until it was dark enough to see the planets: "Jupiter, Venus, Mercury, Saturn, Mars and the Moon—as soon as they shall appear." With this, and after a ceremonial washing of the hands, the first part of the meal was served: "Bull meat, ram meat, fowl . . . as well as prime beer and pressed wine."

A pause was then made for the highlight of the evening. While one group of priests began to chant the hymn *"Kakkab Anu etellu shamame,"* "The Planet of Anu Rises in the Skies," a priest went up to the "topmost stage of the tower of the temple" to watch the skies for the appearance of the Planet of Anu, Nibiru. At the expected moment and in the predetermined spot in the heavens, the planet was sighted. Thereupon the priests broke out in singing the compositions "To the One Who Grows Bright, the Heavenly Planet of the Lord Anu" and "The Creator's Image Has Arisen." A bonfire was lit in signal, and as the news spread from one observation post to another, bonfires were lit in one place after another. Before the night was over, the whole land was alight.

In the morning, prayers of thanksgiving were offered in the temple's chapel, and in a sequence filled with ceremony and symbolism, the celestial visitors began their departure. "Anu is leaving," the priests chanted; "Anu, great king of Heaven and Earth, we ask for your blessing," they intoned. After Anu gave the asked-for blessings, the procession wound its way down the "Street of the Gods" to the "Place of the barque of Anu." There were more prayers and hymn singing at a chapel called "Build Life on Earth." Now it was time for those remaining behind to bless the departing couple, and the following verses were recited:

> Great Anu, may Heaven and Earth bless you!
> May the gods Enlil, Ea and Ninmah bless you!
> May the gods Sin and Shamash bless you . . .
> May the gods Nergal and Ninurta bless you . . .
> May the Igigi who are in heaven
> and the Anunnaki who are on Earth, bless you!
> May the gods of the Abzu
> and the gods of the holy land bless you!

And then Anu and Antu took off to the Spaceport. It was the seventeenth day of their visit to Earth, a tablet found in the archives of Uruk states. The momentous visit was over.

Its decisions opened the way for the establishment of new cities besides the Olden Ones. First and foremost among them was Kish. It was put under the control of Ninurta, "Enlil's Foremost Son"; he turned it into Sumer's first administrative capital. For Nannar/Sin, "Enlil's Firstborn," the new urban center of Ur (*"The City"*) was established—a place that was to become Sumer's economic heart.

There were additional decisions concerning the new era in mankind's advancement and its relations with the Anunnaki. We read in the Sumerian texts, concerning the crucial conclave that launched Sumer's great civilization, that "the great Anunnaki who decree the fate" decided that the gods "were too lofty for Mankind." The term used—*elu* in Akkadian—means exactly that: "Lofty Ones"; from it comes the Babylonian, Assyrian, Hebrew, and Ugaritic *El*—the term to which the Greeks gave the connotation "god."

There was a need, the Anunnaki decided, to give mankind "Kingship" as an intermediary between themselves and the human citizenry. All the Sumerian records attest that this major decision was taken during Anu's visit, at a Council of the Great Gods. One Akkadian text (the *Fable of the Tamarisk and the Datepalm*) describes thus the meeting that had taken place "in long ago days, in far off times":

> The gods of the land, Anu, Enlil and Enki,
> convened an assembly.
> Enlil and the gods took counsel;
> Among them was seated Shamash;
> Among them was seated Ninmah.

At that time "there was not yet kingship in the land; the rule was held by the gods." But the Great Council resolved to change that and to grant kingship to mankind. All the Sumerian sources agree that the first royal city was Kish. The men who were appointed by Enlil to be kings were called LU.GAL, "Mighty Man." We find the same record in the Old Testament (Genesis chapter 10): when mankind was establishing its kingdoms:

Kish begot Nimrod;
He was the first to be a Mighty Man in the Land . . .
And the beginning of his kingship:
Babel and Erech and Akkad,
all in the land of Shin'ar [Sumer].

While the biblical text names the first three capitals as Kish, Babylon, and Erech, the Sumerian King Lists assert that Kingship moved from Kish to Erech and then to Ur, omitting any mention of Babylon. The apparent discrepancy has a reason: We believe it has to do with the incident of the Tower of Babel (Babylon), which the Old Testament records in no small detail. It was an incident, we believe, that had to do with Marduk's insistence that he, rather than Nannar, should possess Sumer's next capital. The time was clearly during the resettlement of the plain of Sumer (the biblical Shin'ar), when new urban centers were being built:

And as they travelled from the east,
they found a valley in the Land of Shin'ar
and settled there.
And they said unto one another:
"Let us make bricks, and burn them by fire";
and the brick served them as stone,
and the bitumen served them as mortar.

It was then that the scheme which caused the incident was suggested by an unnamed instigator: "Come, let us build us a city, and a tower whose head shall reach the heavens."

"And Yahweh came down to see the city and the tower which the humans were building"; and he said to unnamed colleagues: "This is just the beginning of their undertakings; from now on, anything that they shall scheme to do shall no longer be impossible for them." And Yahweh said to his colleagues: "Come, let us go down and confuse their language, so that they would not understand each other's speech." Then the Lord "scattered them from there all over the face of the Earth, and they ceased to build the city."

That there was initially a time when mankind "spoke in unison" is a tenet of Sumerian historical recollections. These also assert that the confusion of languages, accompanying the dispersion of mankind, was a deliberate act of the gods. Like the Old Testament, the writings of Berossus reported that "the gods introduced a diversity of tongues among men, who until that time had all spoken the same language." Like the biblical tale, the histories of Berossus connect the diversification of languages and the dispersion of mankind to the incident of the Tower of Babel: "When all men formerly spoke the same language, some among them undertook to erect a large and lofty tower, that they might climb up to heaven. But the Lord, sending forth a whirlwind, confounded their design, and gave to each tribe a particular language of its own."

The conformity of the tales suggests the existence of a common, older source from which both the compilers of the Old Testament and Berossus had obtained their information. Although it is generally assumed that such an original text has not yet been found, the fact is that George Smith, in his very first publication in 1876, reported discovering at Ashurbanipal's library in Nineveh "a mutilated account of part of the story of the Tower." The tale, he concluded, was originally written on two tablets; on the one he had found (K-3657), there had been six columns of cuneiform text; but he could piece together only fragments of four columns. It is undoubtedly an Akkadian version of the Sumerian tale of the Tower of Babel; and it is clear from it that the incident was brought about not by mankind but by the gods themselves. Mankind was only a pawn in the struggle.

As pieced together by George Smith, and retranslated by W. S. C. Boscawen in the *Transactions of the Society of Biblical Archaeology* (vol. V), the tale began with the identification of the instigator; damage to the lines, however, obliterated the name. "The thoughts" of this god's heart "were evil; against the Father of the Gods [Enlil] he was wicked." To achieve his evil purpose "the people of Babylon he corrupted to sin," inducing "small and great to mingle on the mound."

As the sinful work came to the attention of "the lord of the Pure Mound"—already identified as Enlil in the Cattle and Grain tale— Enlil "to Heaven and on Earth spoke. . . . He lifted his heart to the Lord of the Gods, Anu, his father; to receive a command his heart requested. At that time he also lifted up [his heart? voice?] to

Damkina.'' We well know that she was the mother of Marduk; so all the clues point to him as the instigator. But Damkina stood by his side: "With my son I rise . . ." she said. The incomplete verse that follows has her stating that "his number"—his numerical rank-status?—was at issue.

The legible portion of column III then deals with Enlil's efforts to talk the rebellious group out of their plans. Taking himself up in a Whirlwind, "Nunamnir [Enlil] from the heaven to earth spoke; [but] by his path they did not go; violently they fronted against him.'' When Enlil "saw this, to earth he descended." But even his very presence on the site did not make a difference. We read in the last column that "when a stop he did not make of the gods," he had no choice but to resort to force:

> To their stronghold tower, in the night,
> a complete end he made.
> In his anger, a command he also poured out:
> To scatter abroad was his decision.
> He gave a command their counsels to confuse.
> . . . their course he stopped.

The ancient Mesopotamian scribe ended the tale of the Tower of Babel with a bitter memory: Because they "against the gods revolted with violence, violently they wept for Babylon; very much they wept."

The biblical version also names *Babel* (Hebrew for Babylon) as the place where the incident had occurred. The name is significant, for in its original Akkadian—*Bab-Ili*—it meant "Gateway of the Gods," the place by which the gods were to enter and leave Sumer.

It was there, the biblical narrative states, that the perpetrators planned to construct "a tower whose head shall reach unto the heavens." The words are identical to the actual name of the ziggurat (seven-stage pyramid) which was the dominant feature of ancient Babylon (Fig. 64): E.SAG.ILA, "House Whose Head is Lofty."

The biblical and the Mesopotamian texts—undoubtedly based on an original Sumerian chronicle—thus relate the same incident: Marduk's frustrated attempt to prevent the transfer of kingship from Kish to Erech and Ur—cities destined to be power centers of Nannar/Sin and his children—and to seize suzerainty for his own city, Babylon.

By this attempt, however, Marduk started a chain of events replete with tragedies.

Fig. 64

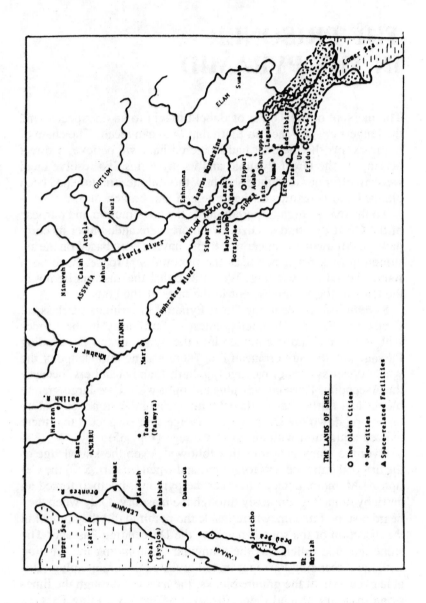

THE LANDS OF SHEM

○ The Olden Cities
● New Cities
▲ Space-related Facilities

10

THE PRISONER
IN THE PYRAMID

The incident of the Tower of Babel brought to an unexpected end the longest era of Peace on Earth that Man can recall. The chain of tragic events the incident had triggered had, we believe, a direct bearing on the Great Pyramid and its mysteries. To resolve them we shall offer our own theory of how this unique structure had been planned and constructed, then plugged and broken into.

To the many enigmas pertaining to the construction and purpose of the Great Pyramid at Giza, two more were added after its completion. All theories concerning them, having been based on the assumption of a royal burial as the pyramid's purpose, have been found flawed and wanting. We believe that the answers lie not in the tales of the Pharaohs, but in the tales of the gods.

Several references to the Great Pyramid in writings of classical Greek and Roman chroniclers attest to familiarity in their times with the swivel-stone entrance into the pyramid, the Descending Passage and the Subterranean Pit. There was no knowledge of the whole upper system of passages, galleries, and chambers, because the Ascending Passage was plugged tight with three large granite blocks and further camouflaged with a triangular stone, so that no one going down the Descending Passage ever suspected that there existed a junction with an upper passage (Fig. 65).

Over the many centuries that followed, even the knowledge of the original entrance was forgotten; and when (in A.D. 820) the Caliph Al Mamoon decided to enter the pyramid, his men forced an entry by tunneling aimlessly through the masonry. Only when they heard a stone fall somewhere inside the pyramid did they tunnel in the direction of the sound, reaching the Descending Passage. The stone that had fallen was the triangular stone hiding the junction with the Ascending Passage; its fall revealed the granite plug. Unable even to dent the granite blocks, the men cut through the limestone masonry around them, discovering the Ascending Passage and the upper inner parts of the pyramid. As the Arab historians at-

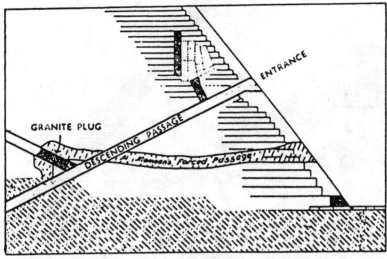

Fig. 65

test, everywhere Al Mamoon and his men found nothing but emptiness.

Clearing the Ascending Passage of debris—pieces of limestone that had somehow slid down the passage to the granite plugs—they crawled up to the upper end of this passage. Coming out of its squarelike tunnel, they could stand up, for they had reached the junction of the Ascending Passage with a Horizontal Passage and with the Grand Gallery (Fig. 66). They followed the Horizontal Passage, reaching the vaulted chamber at its end (which later explorers named the "Queen's Chamber"); it was bare, and so was its enigmatic niche (see Fig. 49). Returning to the junction of the passages, they clambered up the Grand Gallery (Fig. 45); its precisely cut grooves, now empty holes and nooks, helped the climb up—a task made slippery by a layer of white dust that covered the Gallery's floor and ramps. They climbed over the Great Step, which rose from the upper end of the Gallery to become flush with the floor of the Antechamber; entering it, they found its blocking portcullises gone (Fig. 67). They crawled into the upper vaulted chamber (later named the "King's Chamber"); it was bare, except for a hollowed-out stone block (nicknamed "The Coffer"), but it, too, was empty.

Returning to the junction of the three passages (Ascending Passage, Grand Gallery, and Horizontal Passage), Al Mamoon's men

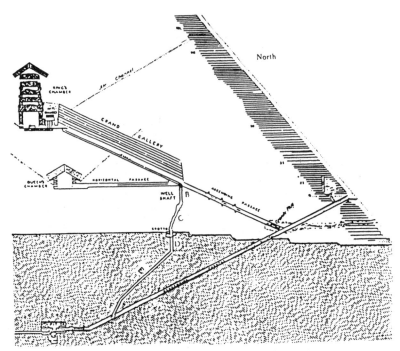

Fig. 66

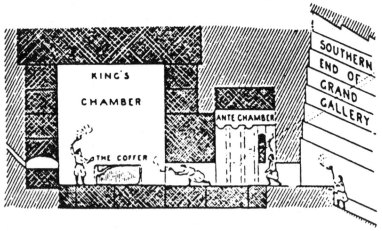

Fig. 67

noticed a gaping hole on the western side, where the ramp stone belonging there had been smashed away (Fig. 68). It led via a short horizontal passage to a vertical shaft, which the Arabs assumed was a well. As they clambered down this "well shaft" (as it came to be called), they found that it was but the upper part of a long (about 200 feet) series of twisting and turning connected shafts that ended with a six-foot link to the Descending Passage and thus provided a connection between the pyramid's upper chambers and passages and its lower ones (Fig. 66). The evidence indicates that the lower opening was blocked up and hidden from whoever had come down the Descending Passage, until Al Mamoon's men lowered themselves through the length of the Well Shaft and discovered and broke open its bottom end.

The Arabs' discoveries and later investigations have raised a host of puzzles. Why, when, and by whom was the Ascending Passage plugged up? Why, when, and by whom was the twisting Well Shaft tunneled through the pyramid and its rocky base?

Fig. 68

The first and most persistent theory fitted the two puzzles into one answer. Holding that the pyramid was built by the Pharaoh Khufu (Cheops) to be his tomb, the theory suggested that after his mummified body was placed in the "Coffer" in the "King's Chamber," workmen slid the three granite plug blocks from the Grand Gallery down the slope of the Ascending Passage, in order to seal off the tomb. This entrapped these workmen alive in the Grand Gallery. Outwitting the priests, the workmen removed the end stone in the ramp, dug out the Well Shaft, reached the Descending Passage, and saved themselves by climbing up it to the pyramid's entrance/exit.

But this theory does not stand up to critical scrutiny.

The Well Shaft is made up of seven distinct segments (Fig. 66). It begins with the upper horizontal segment (A) leading from the Grand Gallery to a vertical segment (B), which connects via a twisting segment C with a lower vertical segment D. A long, straight, but sharply inclined segment E then follows, leading into a shorter segment F inclined at a different angle. At the end of F, a segment intended to be horizontal but, in fact, slightly slanting (G) then connects the Well Shaft with the Descending Passage. Apart from the connecting, horizontal segments A and G, the Well Shaft proper (segments B, C, D, E, and F), in spite of its changing of courses when viewed on a north-south plane, lies precisely on an east-west plane parallel to the pyramid's plane of passages and chambers; the separating distance of about six feet is bridged at the top by segment A and at the bottom by segment G.

While the three upper segments of the Well Shaft traverse some sixty feet through the pyramid's limestone masonry, the lower segments were cut through some 150 feet of solid rock. The few workmen left behind to slide down the granite plugs (according to the above-mentioned theory) could not have been able to cut through the rock. Also, if the digging was from above, where is all the debris, which they could have only brought up as they dug down? With the Well Shaft's twenty-eight-inch bore through most of its segments, the more than one thousand cubic feet of debris would have piled up in the upper passages and chambers.

In view of these improbabilities, new theories were advanced based on an assumption that the Well Shaft was dug from the bottom up (the debris was then removed via the Descending Passage to outside the pyramid). But why? The answer is: an accident. As the Pharaoh was being entombed, an earthquake shook the pyramid, loosening prematurely the granite plugs. As a result, not mere laborers, but members of the royal family and high priests, were trapped alive. With the pyramid's plans still available, rescue teams tunneled their way up, reached the Grand Gallery, and saved the dignitaries.

This theory (as well as a long-discarded one about grave robbers digging their way up) falters, among other points, on the matter of precision. With the exception of segment C, which was tunneled through the masonry in a rough and irregular manner, and section G, two of whose squarish sides were left rough and not quite horizontal, all the other segments are straight, precise, carefully finished, and uniformly angled throughout their lengths. Why would rescue workers (or grave robbers) waste time to achieve perfection and precision? Why would they bother to smooth the sides, when such smoothness made climbing the shaft much more difficult?

As the evidence mounted that no Pharaoh had ever been buried or enshrined within the Great Pyramid, a new theory gained adherents: The Well Shaft was cut to enable an examination of fissures that had developed in the rock as a result of an earthquake. The most articulate proponents of such a theory were the brothers John and Morton Edgar *(The Great Pyramid Passages and Chambers)*, who, motivated by a religious zeal which saw in the pyramid an expression in stone of biblical prophecies, visited, cleared, examined, measured, and photographed every known part of the pyramid. They showed conclusively that the upper short horizontal passage to the Well Shaft (A), as well as the uppermost vertical section (B), were part and parcel of the original construction of the pyramid (Fig. 69). They also found that the lower vertical section (D) was carefully built with masonry blocks as it passed through a cavity (nicknamed The Grotto) in the bedrock (Fig. 70); it could have been so constructed only when the rock face was still exposed, before the Grotto was covered up with the masonry of the pyramid. In other words, this section, too, had to be part—a very early part—of the original construction of the pyramid.

As the pyramid was rising above its base—so the Edgars theorized—a massive earthquake fissured the bedrock in several places. Needing to know the extent of the damage to determine whether the pyramid could still rise above the cracked bedrock, the builders cut through the rock segments E and F as Inspection Shafts. Finding the damage not too serious, the pyramid's construction continued; but to allow periodic inspection, a short (about six-foot) passage (G) was tunneled from the Descending Passage to connect with section F, allowing entry into the Inspection Shafts from below.

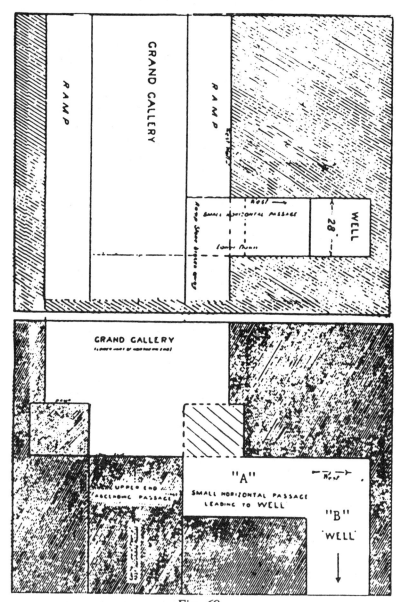

Fig. 69

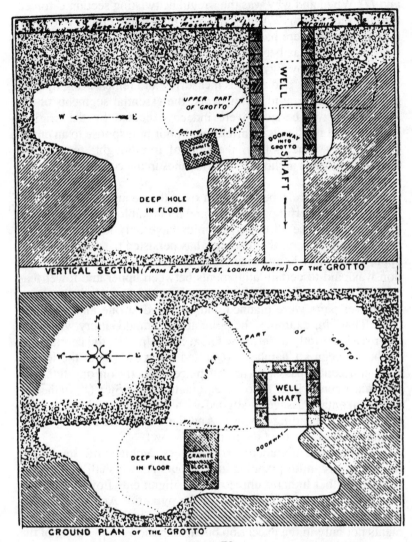

VERTICAL SECTION (*From East to West, looking North*) of the 'GROTTO'

GROUND PLAN of the 'GROTTO'

Fig. 70

Though the theories of the Edgars (further expounded by Adam Rutherford in *Pyramidology*) have been adopted by all such pyramidologists as well as by some Egyptologists, they still fall short of solving the enigmas. If the long sections *E* and *F* were emergency Inspection Shafts—why their precise and time-consuming construction? What was the purpose of the original vertical sections *B* and *D?* When and why was the irregular, twisting section *C* forced through the masonry? And what about the granite plugs: Why were they needed if there had been no funeral and no burial? To these questions there has been no satisfactory answer, neither by pyramidologists nor by Egyptologists.

Yet the arduous and zealous measuring and remeasuring by both groups hold the key to the answers: the essential segments of the Well Shaft, we believe, were indeed executed by the original builders, but neither as an afterthought nor in response to an emergency. They were, rather, the fruit of forethought: features intended to serve as architectural guidelines in the construction of the pyramid.

Much has already been written over the centuries of the Great Pyramid's wonderful proportions and remarkable geometric ratios. However, because all other pyramids have only lower inner passages and chambers, the tendency has persisted to view the whole upper system as a later-phase development. As a result, little attention was paid to certain alignments between upper and lower features of the pyramid, which can be accounted for only if the upper and lower parts were planned and executed at one and the same time. Thus, for example, the point at the Grand Gallery where the floor rises abruptly to form the Great Step Up (*U*), the central axis of the "Queen's Chamber" (*Q*), and a Recess (*R*) at the lowest short horizontal passage—are all placed exactly on one line, the pyramid's center line. Also, an enigmatic Down Step (*S*) in the upper Horizontal Passage is aligned with the point marking the end (*P*) of the Descending Passage. And there are more such puzzling alignments, as our next diagram will show.

Were all these alignments coincidences, architectural freaks—or the result of careful planning and layout? As we shall now show, these and other hitherto unrecognized alignments flowed from the ingenious, yet simple, planning of the pyramid. And we will also prove that the original segments of the Well Shaft were integral elements not only in the execution but also in the very planning of the pyramid.

Let us begin with segment *D,* because we believe that it was the very first one. It is now generally agreed that the rocky knoll on which the pyramid was erected was flattened out in a stepped manner. The lowest face of the rock (which can be seen outside) formed the Base Line; the uppermost face of the rock is at the Grotto level; there, the bottom layer ("course") of the pyramid's masonry can be seen. Since segment *D* lies below this masonry, it had to be cut and fashioned through the Grotto and the bedrock before anything above it was constructed; i.e., before the Well Shaft segments *A, B,* and *C.* Because the only way to tunnel through the rock is from its exposed face downward, segment *E,* which begins its downward slope precisely from the end of *D,* could have been cut only after segment *D* was completed; *F* had to follow *E,* and *G* came last.

In other words, *D* must have been constructed with great precision (see Fig. 70), through the Grotto and the rock, *before* all the other segments of the Well Shaft. But why was it located where it is; why is it precisely vertical; why did it not continue all the way up but was made of the length of which it is?

Why, for that matter—a fact that has gone completely unnoticed—is segment *E* inclined to *D* and to the Base Line at the precise angle of 45°? And why, if *E* was meant to serve as a connecting shaft, did it not simply continue until it reached the Descending Passage but instead turned at an angle to become segment *F?* And why is this segment, *F*—another unnoticed feature—inclined to the Ascending Passage at the precise right angle of 90°?

To answer these questions we have asked ourselves: How did the pyramid's architects design and achieve these symmetries, perfect alignments, and remarkable geometric congruations? The solution we have come up with can best be illustrated by a drawing (Fig. 71); it is a layout plan of the pyramid's insides, prepared by us—we believe—as it might have been drawn by the pyramid's own builders: a simple, yet ingenious, architectural plan that achieves the impressive symmetry, alignments, and perfection with the aid of a few lines and three circles!

The construction of the pyramid began with the leveling of the rocky knoll on which it was to rise. To give the structure greater stability the rock was cut to the Base Level only near the pyramid's circumference; at its core the face of the rock was higher, rising in stages. It was then, we believe, that the Grotto—a natural deformity in the rock or perhaps an artificial cavity—was selected as the point where the structure's alignments were to begin.

There, the first of the shafts, *D,* was placed vertically through the Grotto—partly cut through the rock and partly built with masonry blocks (see Fig. 70). Its height (see Fig. 71) delineates precisely the distance from the Base Level to the level where the rock ends and the masonry begins at the pyramid's core.

It has been long recognized that the value π —the factor governing the ratios between a circle or a sphere, its linear elements and its

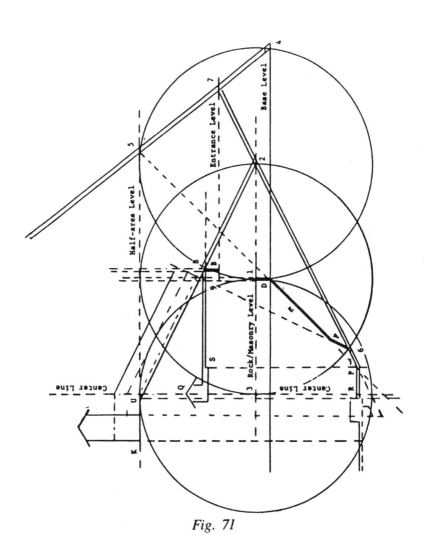

Fig. 71

area projections—has been employed in determining the circumference, sides, and height of the pyramid. As our drawing clearly shows, not only the pyramid's envelope but also everything inside it was determined with the aid of three equal circles.

Theodolitic equipment placed within shaft *D* beamed upward a key vertical line whose function we shall soon describe. But first this equipment beamed out the horizontal rock/masonry line, on which the centers of the three circles were placed. The first of these (Point 1) was at *D;* Points 2 and 3, where its circle intersected the line, served as centers for the other two, overlapping circles.

To draw these circles the pyramid's architects, of course, had to decide on the proper radius. Researchers of the Great Pyramid have been long frustrated by the inability to apply to its perfect proportions any of the ancient Egyptian units of measurement—neither the common cubit of 24 fingers nor the Royal cubit of 28 fingers (20.63″ or 525 millimeters). Some three centuries ago Sir Isaac Newton concluded that an enigmatic "Sacred Cubit" of some 25.2″ was used not only in the construction of the pyramid but also in the construction of Noah's Ark and the temple in Jerusalem. Both Egyptologists and pyramidologists now accept this conclusion as far as the pyramid is concerned. Our own calculations show that the radius adopted for the three circles envisioned by us was equal to 60 such Sacred Cubits; the number 60 being, not accidentally, the base number of the Sumerian sexagesimal mathematical system. This measure of 60 Sacred Cubits is dominant in the lengths and heights of the pyramid's inner structure as well as in the dimensions of its base.

Having selected the radius, the three circles were drawn; and now the pyramid began to take shape: where the second circle intersected the Base Level (Point 4), the pyramid's side was to rise at the angle of 52°—a perfect angle because it is the only one which incorporates the π ratios into the pyramid.

From the bottom of shaft *D,* shaft *E* was then tunneled down, precisely inclined at 45° to *D*. The theodolite-beam projected from *E* upward, intersecting circle 2 at Point 5, provided the sloping line for the pyramid's side and also marked off the half-area Level, on which the King's Chamber and the Antechamber were to be placed (the 5–U–K line) and the Grand Gallery was to end. Projected downwards, the *E* slope determined point *P* at which the Descending Passage was to end, and the vertical line from *P* determined the Down Step *S* in the upper Horizontal Passage.

Turning to the third circle, we see that its center (Point 3) marked the vertical center line of the pyramid. Where it intersected the half-area Line, the Great Up Step (*U*) was placed, marking the end of the Grand Gallery and the beginning of the King's Chamber floor. It also determined the position of the Queen's Chamber (*Q*), which was placed exactly on the center line. By connecting Point 2 with Point *U*, the floor line of the Ascending Passage and the Grand Gallery was obtained.

Shaft *F* was then tunneled from the end of the shaft *E*, precisely so that its beam intersected the ascending floor line 2–U at a right angle (90⁰). From its intersection with the first circle (Point 6), a line was drawn through Point 2, all the way up to the side of the pyramid (Point 7). This delineated the Descending Passage, its junction with the Ascending Passage (at Point 2), and the entrance to the pyramid.

The shafts *D, E,* and *F* and the three circles have thus made possible most of the essential features of the Great Pyramid. Still undetermined, however, were the points at which the Ascending Passage would end and the Grand Gallery begin and, accordingly, where the level of the Horizontal Passage to the Queen's Chamber would be. Here was, we believe, where shaft *B* came into play. No one has so far pointed out the fact that its length is precisely equal to that of *D* and that it marks off exactly the distance between the Entrance Level and the level of the Horizontal Passage. *B* was placed where the Ascending Line intersected circle 2 (Point 8). Its vertical extension marks the beginning of the rising wall of the Grand Gallery; the distance from Point 8 to Point 9, where the beam from *D* intersects the horizontal line from 8, is the place of the grandiose intersection depicted in Fig. 68.

Segment *B*, connected at Point 8 to the passages through the short level segment *A*, thus enabled the pyramid's builders to complete it inside. When that was done, there was no longer any architectural or functional use for these segments, and the entrance to them was covered by placing there a well-fitting, wedge-shaped ramp stone (Fig. 72).

Segments *D, E,* and *F* have also disappeared from view as the pyramid's masonry rose over the rocky base. It was then, perhaps, the function of the less precisely built segment *G* to enable the withdrawal of the beaming-theodolites from the *D–E–F* segments, or to make last-minute checks. Finally, where the Descending Passage connected with this segment *G*, the opening was covered with

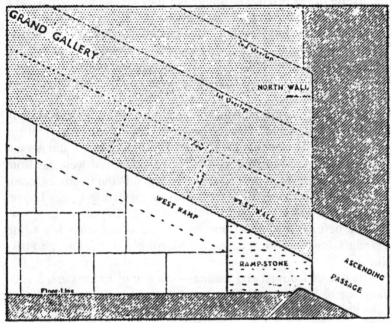

Fig. 72

a well-fitting stone block; and these lower segments, too, disappeared from view.

The pyramid stood complete, with all the segments of the Well Shaft in their hidden places; all, that is, except one, which as we have shown had absolutely no function or purpose in the pyramid's planning and construction.

The exception is the irregular and uncharacteristic segment *C*, unevenly twisting through the masonry, rudely, crudely, and forcibly cut through the limestone courses in a manner that left many stone blocks broken and protruding. When, why, and how did this enigmatic section, *C*, come into being?

That section, we believe, was not yet in existence when the pyramid was completed by its constructors. It was, we will show, hurriedly forced through later on, when Marduk was imprisoned alive in the Great Pyramid.

That Marduk was imprisoned alive in the "Mountain Tomb," there is no doubt; texts that have been found and authoritatively translated attest to that. Other Mesopotamian texts throw light on the nature of his offense. All together they enable us to arrive at a plausible reconstruction of the events.

Evicted from Babylon and Mesopotamia, Marduk returned to Egypt. He promptly established himself in Heliopolis, enhancing its role as his "cult center" by assembling his celestial memorabilia in a special shrine, to which Egyptians made pilgrimages for a long time thereafter.

But seeking to reestablish his hegemony over Egypt, Marduk found that things had changed since he left Egypt to attempt his coup d'état in Mesopotamia. Though Thoth, we gather, did not put up a struggle for supremacy, and Nergal and Gibil were far from the center of power, a new rival had emerged in the interim: Dumuzi. That younger son of Enki, his domain bordering Upper Egypt, was emerging as a pretender to the throne of Egypt.

And behind his ambitions was none other than his bride Inanna/Ishtar—another cause for Marduk's suspicions and dislike.

The tale of Dumuzi and Inanna—he a son of Enki, she a granddaughter of Enlil—reads like an ancient tale of Romeo and Juliet. Like Shakespeare's drama, it, too, ended in tragedy, death, and revenge.

The first presence of Inanna/Ishtar in Egypt is mentioned in the Edfu text dealing with the First Pyramid War. Called there Ashtoreth (her Canaanite name), she is said to have appeared on the battlefield among the advancing forces of Horus. The reason for this inexplicable presence in Egypt might have been to visit her bridegroom Dumuzi, through whose district the fighting force was passing. That Inanna had gone to visit Dumuzi ("The Herder") in his faraway rural district, we know from a Sumerian text. It tells us how Dumuzi stood awaiting her arrival and echoes his reassuring words to a bride baffled by a future in a foreign land:

> The young lad stood waiting;
> Dumuzi pushed open the door.
> Like a moonbeam she came forth to him . . .
> He looked at her, rejoiced in her,
> Took her in his arms and kissed her.
> The Herder put his arm around the maiden;
> "I have not carried you off into slavery," [he said];
> "Your table will be a splendid table,
> the splendid table where I myself eat . . ."

At that time Inanna/Ishtar had the blessing of her parents,
Nannar/Sin and Ningal, as well as of her brother Utu/Shamash, to
the Romeo-and-Juliet love match between a granddaughter of Enlil
and a son of Enki. Some brothers of Dumuzi, and probably Enki
himself, also gave their consent. They presented Inanna with a gift
of lapis lazuli, the blue-hued precious stone she cherished. As a
surprise they hid beads and squares of the stone under a heap of her
favorite fruit: dates. In the bedroom she found "a bed of gold,
adorned with lapis lazuli, which Gibil had refined for her in the
abode of Nergal."

And then the fighting broke out, and brother fought brother. As
long as the fighting was only between the descendants of Enki, no
one saw any particular problem in having a granddaughter of Enlil
around. But after the victory of Horus, when Seth occupied lands
not his, the situation changed completely: The Second Pyramid
War pitched the sons and grandchildren of Enlil against the descendants of Enki. "Juliet" had to be separated from her "Romeo."

When the lovers were reunited after that war, and their marriage
consummated, they spent many days and nights in bliss and
ecstasy—the subject of numerous Sumerian love songs. But even
as they were making love Inanna was whispering provoking words
to Dumuzi:

> As sweet as your mouth are your parts,
> they befit a princely status!
> Subdue the rebellious country, let the nation multiply;
> I will direct the country rightly!

Another time she confessed to him her vision:

> I had a vision of a great nation
> choosing Dumuzi as God of its country . . .
> For I have made Dumuzi's name exalted,
> I gave him status.

With all that it was not a happy union, for it did not produce an
heir—an essential requirement, it appears, for carrying out the divine ambitions. Thus it came to pass that in an attempt to have a
male heir, Dumuzi resorted to a tactic adopted way back by his
own father: he tried to seduce and have intercourse with his own
sister. But whereas in bygone days Ninharsag agreed to Enki's ad-

vances, Dumuzi's sister Geshtinanna refused. In his desperation Dumuzi violated a sexual taboo: he raped his own sister.

The tragic tale is recorded on a tablet catalogued by scholars as CT.15.28–29. The text relates how Dumuzi bade Inanna good-bye as he announced his plan to go to the desert-plain where his flocks were. By prearrangement his sister, "the song-knowing sister, was sitting there." She thought she was invited for a picnic. As they were "eating the pure food, dripping with honey and butter, as they were drinking the fragrant divine beer," and "were spending the time in a happy mood . . . Dumuzi took the solemn decision to do it." To prepare his sister for what he had in mind, Dumuzi took a lamb and copulated it with its mother, then had a kid copulate with its sister lamb. As the animals were committing incest, Dumuzi was touching his sister in emulation, "but his sister still did not understand." As Dumuzi's actions became more and more obvious, Geshtinanna "screamed and screamed in protest"; but "he mounted her . . . his seed was flowing into her vulva. . . ." "Halt!" she shouted, "it is a disgrace!" But he did not stop.

Having done his deed, "the Shepherd, being fearless, being shameless, spoke to his sister." What he said is unfortunately lost to us due to breaks in the tablet. But we suspect that he had— "fearlessly, shamelessly" as the text had stated—gone on to explain to Geshtinanna the reasons for his deed. That it was premeditated is clear from the text; it is also stated that Inanna was in on the plan: Dumuzi, prior to leaving, "spoke to her of planning and advice" and Inanna "to her spouse answered about the plan, to him she gave her advice."

Rape, under the moral codes of the Anunnaki, was a serious sexual transgression. In the earliest times, when the first teams of astronauts had landed on Earth, a court-martial sentenced their supreme commander Enlil to exile for having raped a young nurse (whom he later married). Dumuzi had surely known all this; so he either expected his sister to engage in the intercourse willingly or else had compelling reasons for his deed which overrode the prohibition. Inanna's prior consent brings to mind the biblical tale of Abraham and his sonless wife Sarah, who offered him her maidservant so that he might have a male heir.

Aware that he had done a horrible deed, Dumuzi was soon thereafter seized with a premonition that he was to pay for his deed with his life, as told in the Sumerian text SHA.GA.NE. IR IM.SHI— "His Heart Was Filled With Tears." Composed in the form of a self-fulfilling dream, the text relates how Dumuzi fell asleep and dreamed that all his attributes of status and property were being taken away from him one by one, by the "Princely Bird" and a falcon. The nightmare ended with Dumuzi seeing himself lying dead in the midst of his sheepfolds.

Waking up, he asked his sister Geshtinanna to tell him the meaning of the dream. "My brother," she said, "your dream is not favorable, it is very clear to me." It foretold "bandits rising against you from ambush . . . your hands will be bound in handcuffs, your arms will be bound in fetters." No sooner had Geshtinanna finished talking than the evil ones appeared beyond the hill and caught Dumuzi.

Bound in handcuffs and fetters, Dumuzi cried out an appeal to Utu/Shamash: "O Utu, you are my brother-in-law, I am your sister's husband. . . . Change my hands into a gazelle's hands, change my feet into a gazelle's feet, let me escape the evil ones!" Hearing his appeal, Utu enabled Dumuzi to escape. After some adventures Dumuzi sought a hiding place in the house of Old Belili—a questionable character playing a double role. Dumuzi was captured again and again escaped. In the end he found himself hiding once again in the sheepfolds. A strong wind was blowing, the drinking cups were overturned; the evil ones closed in on him—all as he had seen in his dream. And in the end:

> The drinking cups lay on their side;
> Dumuzi was dead.
> The sheepfold was thrown into the wind.

The arena of these events, in this text, is a desertlike plain near a river. The geography is enlarged upon in another version of the events, a text titled "The Most Bitter Cry." Composed as a lament by Inanna, it tells how seven deputies of Kur entered the sheepfold and aroused Dumuzi from his sleep. Unlike the previous version, which simply referred to the seizure of Dumuzi by "evil ones," this text makes it clear that they had come on higher authority: "My master has sent us for you," the chief deputy announced to the awakened god. They proceed to strip Dumuzi of his divine attributes:

> Take the divine headdress off your head,
> get up bareheaded;
> Take the royal robe off your body,
> get up naked;

Lay aside the divine staff which is in your hand,
get up empty-handed;
Take the holy sandals off your feet,
get up barefooted!

The seized Dumuzi manages to escape and reaches the river "at
the great dike in the desert of E.MUSH ("Home of the snakes").
There was only one such place in Egypt, where desert and river
met at a great dike: at the first Nile Cataract, the place where nowadays the great dam of Aswan is located.

But the swirling waters did not let Dumuzi reach the other
riverbank where his mother and Inanna were standing by to offer
him protection. Instead "there did the boat-wrecking waters carry
the lad towards Kur; to Kur did the boat-wrecking waters carry the
espoused of Inanna."

This and other parallel texts reveal that those who had come to
seize Dumuzi were in fact arresting him in accordance with the orders given by a higher god, the Master of Kur, who "a sentence did
pass upon him." But it could not have been a sentence passed by
the full Assembly of the gods: Enlilite gods, such as Utu/Shamash
and Inanna, were helping Dumuzi escape. The sentence, then, was
one-sided, passed only by the authority of the master of the arresting deputies. He was none other than Marduk, the elder brother of
both Dumuzi and Geshtinanna.

His identity comes through in the text named by scholars "The
Myths of Inanna and Bilulu." In it the shady Old Belili turns out to
have been a male, the Lord Bilulu (EN.BILULU) in disguise, and
the very deity who directed the punitive action against Dumuzi.
Akkadian texts dealing with divine epithets explained that En-
Bilulu was *il Marduk sha hattati*, "the god Marduk who had
sinned," and "The Sorrower of Inanna."

Having disapproved of the Dumuzi-Inanna love match from the
beginning, Marduk no doubt was even more opposed to the union
after the Pyramid Wars. The rape of Geshtinanna by Dumuzi—
politically motivated—was thus an opportunity for Marduk to
block the designs Inanna had on Egypt, by seizing and punishing
Dumuzi. Did Marduk intend to put Dumuzi to death? Probably
not; solitary exile was the customary punishment. The death of
Dumuzi, in a manner that has remained unclear, was probably accidental.

But whether accidental or not was irrelevant to Inanna. As far as she was concerned, Marduk had caused her beloved's death. And, as the texts make clear, she sought revenge:

> What is in holy Inanna's heart?
> To Kill!
> To kill the Lord Bilulu.

Working with fragments found in the collections of Mesopotamian tablets dispersed in several museums, scholars have pieced together parts of a text that Samuel N. Kramer *(Sumerian Mythology)* named "Inanna and Ebih." He considered it as belonging to the cycle of "slaying-of-the-dragon myths," for it deals with Inanna's struggle against an evil god hiding inside "The Mountain."

The available fragments relate how Inanna armed herself with an array of weapons to attack the god in his hiding place. Though the other gods tried to dissuade her, she confidently approached The Mountain, which she called E.BIH ("Abode of Sorrowful Calling"). Haughtily she proclaimed:

> Mountain, thou art so high,
> thou art elevated above all others . . .
> Thou touchest the sky with thy tip . . .
> Yet I shall destroy thee,
> To the ground I shall fell thee . . .
> Inside thine heart pain I will cause.

That The Mountain was the Great Pyramid, that the confrontation was at Giza in Egypt, is evident not only from the texts, but also from a depiction on a Sumerian cylinder seal (Fig. 73). Inanna—shown in her familiar enticing, half-naked pose—is seen confronting a god based upon three pyramids. The pyramids are depicted exactly as they appear to view in Giza; the Egyptian ankh sign, the priest in an Egyptian headdress, and the entwined serpents add up to one locale: Egypt.

As Inanna continued to challenge Marduk, now hiding inside the mighty structure, her fury rose as he ignored her threats. "For the second time, infuriated by his pride, Inanna approached [the pyramid] again and proclaimed: 'My grandfather Enlil has permitted me to enter inside The Mountain!' " Flaunting her weapons, she haughtily announced: "Into the heart of The Mountain I shall penetrate . . . Inside The Mountain, my victory I shall establish!" Getting no response, she began her attack:

Fig. 73

She ceased not striking the sides of E-Bih
and all its corners,
even its multitude of raised stones.
But inside . . . the Great Serpent who had gone in
his poison ceased not to spit.

Anu himself then intervened. The god hiding inside, he warned
her, possessed awesome weapons; "their outburst is terrible; they
will prevent you from entering." Instead Anu advised her to seek
justice by putting the hiding god on trial.

The texts amply identify this god. As in the Ninurta texts, he is
called A.ZAG and nicknamed The Great Serpent—a name and a
derogatory Enlilite epithet for Marduk. His hiding place is also
clearly identified as "the E.KUR, whose walls awesomely reach
the skies"—the Great Pyramid.

The record of the trial and sentencing of Marduk is available
from a fragmentary text published by the Babylonian Section of the
Museum of the University of Pennsylvania. The extant lines begin
where the gods had surrounded the pyramid, and a god chosen to
be a spokesman addressed Marduk "in his enclosure"; "the one
who was evil he implored." Marduk was moved by the message:
"Despite the anger of his heart, clear tears came into his eyes.";
and he agreed to come out and stand trial. The trial was held within
sight of the pyramids, in a temple by the riverbank:

To the place of reverence, by the river,
with him who was accused they stepped.
In truth they made the enemies stand aside.
Justice was performed.

In sentencing Marduk the mystery of Dumuzi's death posed a problem. That Marduk was responsible for his death there was no doubt. But was it premeditated or accidental? Marduk deserved a death sentence, but what if his crime was not deliberate?

Standing there, in sight of the pyramids, with Marduk fresh out of his hiding place, the solution dawned on Inanna, and she proceeded to address the gods:

On this day, the Lady herself,
She who speaks truth,
The accuser of Azag, the great princess,
An awesome judgment uttered.

There was a way to sentence Marduk to death without actually executing him, she said: Let him be buried alive within the Great Pyramid! Let him be sealed there as in a gigantic envelope:

In a great envelope that is sealed,
With no one to offer him nourishment;
Alone to suffer,
The potable watersource to be cut off.

The judging gods accepted her suggestions: "The mistress art thou . . . The fate thou decreest: let it be so!" Assuming that Anu would go along with the verdict, "the gods then placed the command to Heaven and Earth." The Ekur, the Great Pyramid, had become a prison; and one of the epithets of its mistress was, thereafter, "Mistress of the Prison."

It was then, we believe, that the sealing of the Great Pyramid was completed. Leaving Marduk alone in the King's Chamber, the arresting gods released behind them the granite plugs of the Ascending Passage, irrevocably blocking tight all access to the upper chambers and passages.

Through the channels leading from the "King's Chamber" to the north and south faces of the pyramid, Marduk had air to breathe; but he had neither food nor water. He was buried alive, doomed to die in agony.

* * *

The record of Marduk's entombment, alive, within the Great Pyramid has been preserved on clay tablets found in the ruins of Ashur and Nineveh, the ancient Assyrian capitals. The Ashur text suggests that it had served as a script for a New Year's mystery play in Babylon that reenacted the god's suffering and reprieve. But neither the original Babylonian version, nor the Sumerian historical text on which the script was based, have so far been found.

Heinrich Zimmern, who transcribed and translated the Ashur text from clay tablets in the Berlin Museum, created quite a stir in theological circles when he announced its interpretation at a lecture in September 1921. The reason was that he interpreted it as a pre-Christian *Mysterium* dealing with the death and resurrection of a god, and thus an earlier Christ tale. When Stephen Langdon included an English translation in his 1923 volume on the Mesopotamian New Year Mystery Texts, he titled the text *The Death and Resurrection of Bel-Marduk* and highlighted its parallels to the New Testament tale of the death and resurrection of Jesus.

But, as the text relates, Marduk or Bel ("The Lord") did not die; he was indeed incarcerated inside The Mountain as in a tomb; but he was entombed alive.

The ancient "script" begins with an introduction of the actors. The first one "is Bel, who was confined in The Mountain." Then there is a messenger who brings the news of the imprisonment to Marduk's son Nabu. Shocked by the news, Nabu hastens to The Mountain in his chariot. He arrives at a structure and the script explains: "that is the house at the edge of The Mountain wherein they question him." In reply to the guards' questions, they are told that the agitated god is "Nabu who from Borsippa comes; it is he who comes to seek after the welfare of his father who is imprisoned."

Actors then come out and rush about on the stage; "they are the people who in the streets hasten; they seek Bel, saying: 'Where is he held captive?' " We learn from the text that "after Bel had gone into The Mountain, the city fell into tumult" and "because of him fighting within it broke out." A goddess appears; she is Sarpanit, the sister-wife of Marduk. She is confronted by a messenger "who weeps before her, saying: 'Unto The Mountain they have taken him.' " He shows her the garments of Marduk (possibly bloodstained): "these are his raiment, which they took off him," he says; instead of these, he reports, Marduk "with a Garment-of-Sentence was clothed." What the audience is shown are shrouds: "That means: in a coffin he is." Marduk has been buried!

Sarpanit goes to a structure that symbolizes Marduk's tomb. She sees a group of mourners. The script explains:

These are those who make lament
after the gods had locked him up,
separating him from among the living.
Into the House of Captivity,
away from the sun and light,
they put him in prison.

The drama has reached its ominous peak: Marduk is dead. . . .

But wait—all hope is not lost! Sarpanit recites an appeal to the two gods who can approach Inanna regarding Marduk's incarceration, her father Sin and her brother Utu/Shamash: "She prays to Sin and Shamash, saying: 'Give life to Bel!' "

Priests, a stargazer, and messengers now appear in procession, reciting prayers and incantations. Offerings are made to Ishtar, "that she may show her mercy." The high priest appeals to the supreme god, to Sin and to Shamash: "Restore Bel to life!"

Now the drama takes a new turn. Suddenly the actor who represents Marduk, clothed with shrouds which "with blood are dyed," speaks out: "I am not a sinner! I shall not be smitten!" He announces that the supreme god has reviewed his case and found him not guilty.

Who, then, was the murderer? The attention of the audience is diverted to a doorpost; "it is the doorpost of Sarpanit in Babylon." The audience learns that the real guilty god has been captured. They see his head through the doorway: "That is the head of the evildoer, whom they shall smite and slay."

Nabu, who had returned to Borsippa, "comes back from Borsippa; he comes and stands over the evildoer and regards him." We do not learn the identity of The Evildoer, except to be told that Nabu had seen him before in Marduk's company. "This is the sinner," he says, and thereby seals the captive's fate.

The priests grab The Evildoer; he is slain: "The one whose sin it was" is carried away in a coffin. The murderer of Dumuzi has paid with his life.

But is the sin of Marduk—as the indirect cause of Dumuzi's death—atoned? Sarpanit reappears, wearing the Garments-of-Atonement. Symbolically she wipes away the blood that has been spilled. With pure water she washes her hands: "It is water for hand-washing which they bring after The Evildoer has been carried away." In "all the sacred places of Bel" torches are lit. Again, appeals are directed to the supreme god. The supremacy of Ninurta, which had once been proclaimed when Ninurta vanquished Zu, is reasserted, apparently to allay any fear that a released Marduk might become a challenger for supremacy among the gods. The appeals succeed, and the supreme god sends the divine messenger Nusku to "announce the [good] tidings to all the gods."

As a gesture of good will, Gula (the spouse of Ninurta) sends to Sarpanit new clothing and sandals for Marduk; Marduk's driverless chariot also appears. But Sarpanit is dumbfounded: she cannot understand how Marduk can be free again if he had been imprisoned in a tomb *that cannot be unsealed:* "How can they let him free, the one who cannot come out?"

Nusku, the divine messenger, tells her that Marduk shall pass through SA.BAD, the "chiseled upper opening." He explains that it is

Dalat biri sha iqabuni ilani
A doorway-shaft which the gods will bore;

Shunu itasrushu ina biti etarba
Its vortex they will lift off,
his abode they shall reenter.

Dalta ina panishu etedili
The door which was barred before him

Shunu hurrate ina libbi dalti uptalishu
At the vortex of the hollowing, into the insides,
a doorway they shall twistingly bore;

Qarabu ina libbi uppushu
Getting near, into its midst they will break through.

This description of how Marduk shall be released has remained meaningless to scholars; but the verses are explosively meaningful to us. As we have explained, the irregular and twisting segment *C* of the Well Shaft had not existed when the pyramid was completed and when Marduk was imprisoned within it; it was, instead, the very "doorway-shaft which the gods will bore" to rescue Marduk.

Still familiar with the pyramid's inner layout, the Anunnaki realized that the shortest and quickest way to reach the starved Marduk was to tunnel a connecting shaft between the existing segments *B* and *D*—a tunneling of a mere thirty-two feet through the relatively soft limestone blocks; it was a task that could be achieved not in days but in hours.

Removing the stone that covered the Well Shaft's entrance from the Descending Passage to *G,* the rescuers quickly climbed up inclined segments *F* and *E.* Where *E* connected with vertical segment *D,* a granite stone covered the entrance in the Grotto; it was pushed aside—*and still lies there, in the Grotto*—as we have shown in Fig. 70. Now the rescuers climbed the short distance up segment *D,* and faced the first course of the pyramid's masonry.

Thirty-two feet above but to the side lay the bottom of vertical segment *B* and the way into the Grand Gallery. But who could have known how to bore a twisting connecting shaft—*C*—except those who had built the pyramid, knew of its inner sealed-off upper sections, and had the plans to locate them?

It was the rescuers of Marduk, we suggest, who used their tools to break through the limestone blocks, the link between *D* and *B:* "a hollowing into its insides they shall twistingly bore," in the words of the ancient text.

Achieving the linkup with *B,* they clambered to the short, horizontal passage, *A.* There, any stranger would have stopped short even if he had gone that far up, for all he would have seen would be a stone wall—solid masonry. Again we suggest that only the Anunnaki, who had the pyramid's plan, could have known that beyond the stone facing them there lay the immense cavity of the Grand Gallery, the Queen's Chamber, and all the other upper chambers and passages of the pyramid.

To gain access to those chambers and passages it was necessary to remove the wedgelike ramp stone (Fig. 72). But it was wedged too tightly and could not be moved.

If the stone would have been moved away, it would have still been lying there, in the Grand Gallery. Instead, there is a gaping hole (Fig. 68), and those who have examined it have invariably used the words *blown up* and *blown open* to describe what it looks like; and it was done not from the Gallery but from inside the Shaft: "the hollow has the appearance of having been burst open by tremendous force from within" the Shaft (Rutherford, *Pyramidology*).

Again the Mesopotamian record offers a solution. The stone was indeed removed *from within* the horizontal passageway, because it was from there that the rescuers had arrived. And it was indeed "burst open by a tremendous force"; in the words of the ancient text, "Getting near, into its midst they will break through." The fragments of the limestone block slid down the Ascending Passage, down all the way to the granite plugs; that is where Al Mamoon's men found them. The explosion also covered the Grand Gallery with the fine, white dust the Arabs had found covering the floor of the Grand Gallery—mute evidence of the ancient explosion and the gaping hole it had left.

Having broken through into the Grand Gallery, the rescuers led Marduk back the way they came. The entry from the Descending Passage was sealed up again, to be discovered by Al Mamoon's men. The granite plugs remained in place with the triangular junction stone hiding the plugs and the Ascending Passage for millennia. And, inside the pyramid, the original upper and lower parts of the Well Shaft were now for all future days connected by a twisting, harshly tunneled segment.

And what of the rescued Prisoner of the pyramid?

Mesopotamian texts relate that he went into exile; in Egypt Ra acquired the epithet *Amen,* "The Hidden One."

Circa 2000 B.C., he reappeared to claim again supremacy; for that, mankind ended up paying a most bitter price.

11

"A QUEEN AM I!"

The tale of Inanna/Ishtar is a tale of a "self-made goddess." Neither one of the Olden Gods, the original group of astronauts from the Twelfth Planet, nor even a firstborn daughter of one of them, she nevertheless propelled herself to the highest ranks and ended up a member of the Pantheon of Twelve. To achieve that she combined her cunning and her beauty with ruthlessness—a goddess of war and a goddess of love, who counted among her lovers both gods and men. And it was she of whom there had been a true case of death and resurrection.

Inasmuch as the death of Dumuzi was brought about by Inanna's desire to become a queen on Earth, the imprisonment and exile of Marduk did little to satisfy her ambitions. Now, having challenged and prevailed over a major god, she felt she could no longer be deprived of a domain of her own. But where?

The funeral of Dumuzi, one gathers from such texts as *Inanna's Descent to the Lower World,* was held in the Land of Mines in southern Africa. It was the domain of Inanna's sister Ereshkigal and her spouse Nergal. Enlil and Nannar, even Enki, advised Inanna not to go there; but she made up her mind: "From the Great Above she set her mind toward the Great Below"; and when she arrived at the gate of her sister's capital city, she said to the gatekeeper: "Tell my elder sister, Ereshkigal," that she had come "to witness the funeral rites."

One would expect the meeting between the sisters to have been heartwarming, filled with sympathy for the bereaved Inanna. We learn instead that Inanna, who came uninvited, was received with unrestrained suspicion. As she was let through the seven gates of the city leading to Ereshkigal's palace, she was made to give up her emblems and regalia of divine status. When Inanna finally came into the presence of her sister, she found her sitting on her throne surrounded by seven Anunnaki with a judicial capacity. "They fastened their eyes upon her, the eyes of death." They said angry things to her, "words which torture the spirit." Instead of being welcomed, Inanna was sentenced to be hung as a corpse from a stake. . . . It was only through the intervention of Enki that she was saved and revived.

The texts do not explain the reasons for the harsh treatment meted out to Inanna, nor quote the "torturing words" her accusers cast at her. But we learn from the beginning of the text that at the same time that she went on her trip, Inanna sent her messenger to "fill heaven with complaints for me, in the assembly [of the gods] cry out for me." Attending a funeral was thus a mere pretext; what she had in mind was to force the gods to satisfy a complaint that she wished to dramatize.

From the moment of her arrival at the first gate, Inanna threatened violence if she would not be let in. When the news of her arrival was brought to Ereshkigal, "her face turned pale . . . her lips turned dark" and she wondered out loud what the real purpose of the visit was. When the two came face-to-face, "Ereshkigal saw her and burst out at her presence; Ishtar, unflinching, flew at her." Somehow Inanna's intentions spelled danger for Ereshkigal!

We have already found that many of the biblical marital and succession laws were akin to such laws that governed the behavior of the Anunnaki; the rules regarding a half-sister are but one example. The clue to Inanna's intentions, we believe, can be found in the book of Deuteronomy, the fifth book of Moses, in which the Hebrew code of personal behavior was spelled out. Chapter 25 (verses 5–10) deals with the instance when a married man dies without having had a son. If the man had a brother, the widow could not remarry a stranger: it was the duty of the brother—even a married one—to marry his widowed sister-in-law and have children by her; and the firstborn boy was to bear the name of the deceased brother, "so that his name shall not be blotted out."

This, we believe, is what had also been Inanna's reason for her risky journey. For Ereshkigal was married to Nergal, a brother of Dumuzi: Inanna had come to put the Rule into play. . . . The custom, we know, put the onus on the eldest brother, who was, in the case of the sons of Enki, Marduk. But Marduk was found guilty of indirectly causing the death of Dumuzi, and was punished and exiled. Had Inanna then the right to demand that the next in line, Nergal, take her as his second wife so that she could have a male heir?

The personal and succession problems that Inanna's intentions would have caused Ereshkigal can well be imagined. Would Inanna be satisfied to be a second wife, or would she connive and scheme to usurp the queenship over the African domain? Obviously Ereshkigal was not willing to take chances. And so it was, we believe, that after harsh words between the sisters, Inanna was hauled before a hastily convened court of "seven Anunnaki who judge," was found in violation of the rules, and was summarily hung on a stake to die a slow death. She survived only because her father-in-law, Enki, on hearing the terrible news, rushed two emissaries to save her. "Upon the corpse they directed that which pulsates and that which radiates"; they administered to her the "water of life" and the "food of life," and "Inanna arose."

Back in Sumer the revived Inanna, heartbroken and lonely, spent her time on the banks of the Euphrates River, tending a wild-growing tree and voicing her sorrows:

> When at last shall I have a holy throne,
> that I may sit on it?
> When at last shall I have a holy bed,
> that I may lie on it?
> Concerning this Inanna spoke . . .
> She who let her hair down is ill at heart;
> The pure Inanna, Oh how she weeps!

One who had taken pity on—and a liking to—Inanna was her great-grandfather, Anu. It is known from Sumerian texts that Inanna, who was born on Earth, "went up to Heaven" at least once; it is also known that Anu had visited Earth on several occasions. When and where exactly did Anu embrace Inanna as his *Anunitum* ("Beloved of Anu") is not clear, but it was more than mere Sumerian gossip when texts hinted that the love between Anu and his great-granddaughter was more than platonic.

Assured thus of sympathy at the highest level, Inanna raised the issue of a dominion, a "land," to rule over. But where?

The treatment meted out to Inanna, whatever its reasons, made it clear that she could not expect to attain a dominion in Africa. Her spouse Dumuzi was dead, and with him died her claims to queenship in the lands of Enki's descendants. If her suffering and prevailing over a major god entitled her to a dominion of her own, it had to be elsewhere. But Mesopotamia, too, and the lands bordering on Mesopotamia were all spoken for. Where could Inanna be given dominion? Casting their eyes about, the gods came up with an answer.

The texts dealing with the death of Dumuzi, as well as with the imprisonment of Marduk, mention the names of Sumerian cities and their populace. This suggests that those events had taken place after the Sumerian urban civilization had already begun circa 3800 B.C. On the other hand, the Egyptian background of the tales makes no reference to urban settlements and describes a pastoral environment, suggesting a time prior to 3100 B.C., when urban civilization in Egypt began. In the writings of Manetho a chaotic period of 350 years is said to have preceded the urban kingship of Menes. That period between 3450 and 3100 B.C. appears to have been the time of the troubles and tribulations triggered by Marduk: the Tower of Babel incident; and the Dumuzi affair, when a god of Egypt was captured and killed, when the Great God of Egypt was imprisoned and exiled.

It was then, we believe, that the Anunnaki turned their attention to the Third Region of the Indus Valley, where civilization began soon thereafter.

Unlike the Mesopotamian and Egyptian civilizations that lasted for millennia and continued, to this very day, through offspring civilizations, the one in the Third Region lasted only a millennium. Soon thereafter it began to decline, and by 1600 B.C. it was totally gone—its cities in ruins, its people dispersed. Human plunder and the ravages of nature gradually obliterated the civilization's remains; in time it was totally forgotten. It was only in the 1920s that archaeologists, led by Sir Mortimer Wheeler, began to unearth two principal centers and several sites in between, stretching over more than four hundred miles from the Indian Ocean coast northward, along the Indus River and its tributaries.

Both sites—Mohenjo-Daro to the south and Harappa in the north—show that they were cities of substance, some three miles in circumference. High walls ran around and within the cities; these walls, as well as the public and private buildings, were all constructed of bricks made of clay or mud. Originally there were so many of these bricks that in spite of constant ransacking by subsequent home-builders both in ancient times as well as more recently for such purposes as ballast for the Lahore-Multan railroad, enough still remains standing to reveal the site of the cities and the fact that they were laid out in accordance with preconceived city building plans.

At both sites the city was dominated by an acropolis—a raised area of citadels and temples. In both instances these structures were of the same measurements and similarly oriented exactly on a north-south axis—proving that their builders followed strict rules when it came to erecting the temples. In both cities the second largest feature was immense granaries—grain silos of a vast size and impressive functionality, situated near the riverbank. This suggests that grains were not only the chief crop, but also the chief export product of the Indus civilization.

The cities and the few artifacts that were still found in their remains—furnaces, urns, pottery, bronze tools, copper beads, some silver vessels, and ornaments—all attest to a high civilization that was suddenly transplanted from elsewhere. Thus the two earliest brick buildings at Mohenjo-Daro (a huge granary and a fort tower) were reinforced with timbers—a construction method totally unsuitable to the Indus climate. This method, however, was soon abandoned, and all subsequent construction avoided timber-reinforcing. Scholars have concluded from this that the initial builders were foreigners accustomed to their own climatic needs.

Seeking the fountainhead of the Indus civilization, scholars concluded that it could not have arisen independently of the Sumerian civilization, which preceded it by almost a thousand years. In spite of notable differentiations (such as the yet undeciphered pictographic script), the analogies to Mesopotamia are everywhere. The use of dried mud or clay bricks for construction; the layout of city streets; the drainage system; the chemical methods used for etching, for glazing, and for bead-making; the shapes and design of metal daggers and jars—all bear striking similarity to what had been uncovered at Ur or Kish or other Mesopotamian sites. Even the designs and symbols on pottery, seals, or other clay objects are virtual duplicates of those of Mesopotamia. Significantly the Mesopotamian sign of the cross—the symbol of Nibiru, the Home Planet of the Anunnaki—was also prevalent throughout the Indus civilization.

Which gods did the people of the Indus Valley worship? The few pictorial depictions that have been found show them wearing the divine Mesopotamian horned headdress. More abundant clay figurines indicate that the dominant deity was a goddess, usually naked and bare-chested (Fig. 74a) or with rows of beads and necklaces as her sole covering (Fig. 74b); these were well-known depictions of Inanna, found in abundance in Mesopotamia and throughout the Near East. It is our suggestion that in their search for a land for Inanna, the Anunnaki decided to make the Third Region her dominion.

Although it is generally held that the evidence for the Mesopotamian origins of the Indus civilization and for ongoing contacts between Sumer and the Indus Valley is limited to the few archaeolog-

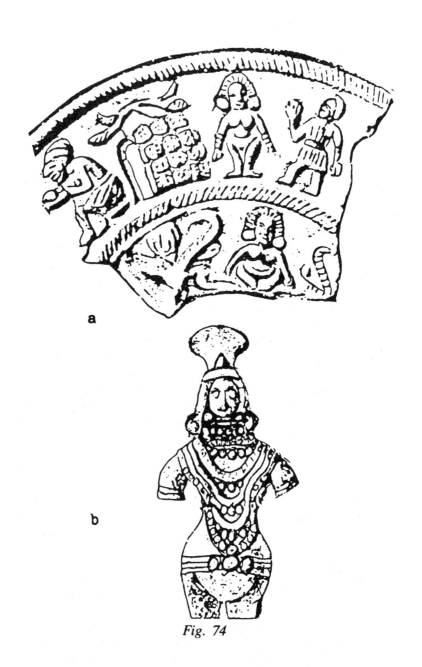

Fig. 74

ical remains, we believe that there also exists textual evidence attesting to these links. Of particular interest is a long text named by scholars *Enmerkar and the Lord of Aratta,* whose background is the rise to power of Uruk (the biblical Erech) and of Inanna.

The text describes Aratta as the capital of a land situated beyond mountain ranges and beyond Anshan; i.e., beyond southeastern Iran. This is precisely where the Indus Valley lay; and such scholars as J. van Dijk (*Orientalia* 39, 1970) have surmised that Aratta was a city "situated on the Iranian plateau or on the Indus river." What is most striking is the fact that the text speaks of the grain silos of Aratta. It was a place where "wheat was growing of itself, beans also growing of themselves"—crops growing and stored in the storehouses of Aratta. Then, to be exported, they "poured grain into sacks, loaded them on the crate-carrying donkeys, and placed them on the sides of the transporting donkeys."

Aratta's geographical location and the fact that it is a place renowned for its grain and bean storehouses bear forceful similarities to the Indus civilization. Indeed one must wonder whether Harappa or *Arappa* is not a present-day echo of the ancient *Aratta.*

The ancient tale takes us back to the beginning of kingship at Erech, when a demigod (the son of Utu/Shamash by a human female) was both high priest and king at the sacred precinct from which the city was to develop. Circa 2900 B.C. he was succeeded by his son Enmerkar, "who built Uruk" (according to the Sumerian King Lists), transforming it from the nominal abode of an absentee god (Anu) to a major urban center of a reigning deity. He achieved this by persuading Inanna to choose Erech as her principal seat of power and by aggrandizing for her the Eanna ("House of Anu") temple.

We read in the ancient text that at first all Enmerkar demanded of Aratta was that it contribute "precious stones, bronze, lead, slabs of lapis lazuli" to the building of the enlarged temple, as well as "artfully fashion gold and silver" so that the Holy Mount being raised for Inanna would be worthy of the goddess.

But no sooner was this done than the heart of Enmerkar grew haughty. A drought had afflicted Aratta, and Enmerkar now demanded not only materials but also obedience: "Let Aratta submit to Erech!" he demanded. To achieve his purpose Enmerkar sent to Aratta a series of emissaries to conduct what S. N. Kramer *(History*

Begins at Sumer) has characterized as "the first war of nerves."
Lauding his king and his powers, the emissary quoted verbatim
Enmerkar's threats to bring desolation upon Aratta and dispersion
upon its people. The ruler of Aratta, however, countered this war
of nerves with a ploy of his own. Reminding the emissary of the
confusion of languages in the aftermath of the Tower of Babel incident, he claimed he could not understand the message given him in
Sumerian.

In frustration Enmerkar sent another message written on clay
tablets—this time, it appears, in the language of Aratta—a feat
made possible with the help of Nidaba, the Goddess of Writing. In
addition to threats an offering of the seeds of "the olden grain"
that had been kept in Anu's temple was made—a seed, it appears,
needed badly in Aratta because a long drought had destroyed its
crops. The drought was deemed to have been a sign that it was
Inanna herself who wished Aratta to come "under the protecting
shade of Erech."

"The lord of Aratta from the herald took the baked tablet; the
lord of Aratta examined the clay." The writing was in cuneiform
script: "The dictated word was nail-like in appearance." Was he
to yield or resist? Just at that moment "a storm, like a great lion
attacking, stepped up"; the drought was suddenly broken by a
thunderstorm that made the whole land tremble, the mountains
quake; and once again, "white-walled Aratta" became a land of
abundant grains.

There was no need to yield to Erech; and the lord of Aratta
said to the herald: "Inanna, the queen of the lands, has not
abandoned her House in Aratta; she has not handed over Aratta
to Erech."

In spite of the rejoicing in Aratta, its expectation that Inanna
would not abandon her abode there was not entirely fulfilled.
Enticed by the prospect of residing in a grand temple at Sumer's
City of Anu, she became a commuting goddess: a "working deity," so to speak, in faraway Aratta, but a resident in metropolitan Erech.

She did her commuting by flying from place to place in her "Boat
of Heaven." Her flying about gave rise to many depictions of her as
an aeronaut (Fig. 75), and the inference from some texts is that she did
her own piloting. On the other hand, like other major deities, she was

assigned a pilot-navigator for the more demanding flights. As the Vedas, which spoke of pilots of the gods (one, Pushan, "guided Indra through the speckled clouds" in the "golden ship that travels in the air's mid-region"), so did the earlier Sumerian texts refer to the AB.GALs, who ferried the gods across the heavens. Inanna's pilot-navigator, we are told, was Nungal; and he was specifically named in regard to her transfer to the House of Anu in Erech:

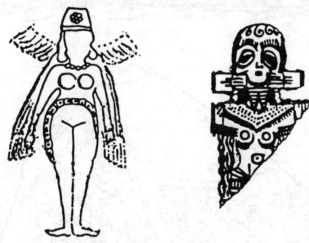

Fig. 75

At the time when Enmerkar in Uruk ruled,
Nungal, the lion-hearted, was the Pilot
who from the skies brought Ishtar down
to the E-Anna.

According to the Sumerian King Lists, kingship after the Deluge began at Kish. Then, "the Kingship to the *Eanna* was carried." As archaeologists have confirmed, Erech indeed had its beginnings as a temple city, consisting of the sacred precinct where Anu's first modest shrine ("White Temple") was built atop a raised platform (Fig. 76); the site remained in the city's heart even as Erech grew and its temples were aggrandized, as the remains of the city and its walls indicate (Fig. 77).

Archaeologists have come upon the remains of a magnificent temple dedicated to Inanna and dating to the early part of the third millennium B.C.—possibly the very temple constructed by Enmer-

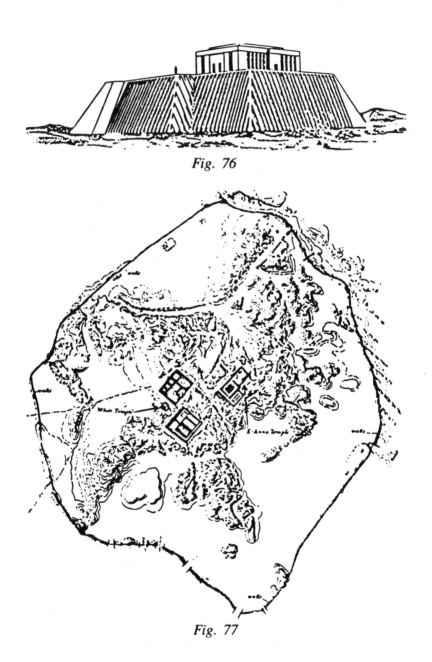

Fig. 76

Fig. 77

kar. It was uniquely built with decorated high columns (Fig. 78) and must have been as lavish and impressive as the hymns that sang its praises had described:

Fig. 78

With lapis-lazuli was adorned,
Decorated with the handiwork of Ninagal.
In the bright place . . .
the residence of Inanna,
the lyre of Anu they installed.

With all that, Erech was still a "provincial" town, lacking the stature of other Sumerian cities, which had the distinction of having been rebuilt on the sites of pre-Diluvial cities. It lacked the status and benefits that stemmed from the possession of the "Divine MEs." Though they are constantly referred to, the nature of the ME is not clear, and scholars translate the term as "divine commandments," "divine powers," or even "mythic virtues." The ME, however, are described as physical objects that one could pick up and carry, or even put on, and which contained secret knowledge or data. Perhaps they were something like our present-day computer chips, on which data, programs, and operational orders have been minutely recorded. On them the essentials of civilization were encoded.

These MEs were in the possession of Enki, the chief scientist of the Anunnaki. They were released by him to benefit mankind gradually, step by step; and the turn of Erech to attain the heights of civilization had, apparently, not yet come when Inanna became its resident deity. Impatient, Inanna decided to use her feminine charms to improve the situation.

A text titled by S. N. Kramer *(Sumerian Mythology)* as
"Inanna and Enki," but whose original (and more poetic) Sumerian title is unknown, describes how Inanna journeyed in her
"Boat of Heaven" to the Abzu, where Enki had secreted away
the MEs. Realizing that Inanna was coming to call on him by
herself—"the maiden, all alone, has directed her step to the
Abzu"—Enki ordered his chamberlain to prepare a sumptuous
meal, including plenty of date wine. After Inanna and Enki had
feasted and Enki's heart became happy with drink, Inanna
brought up the subject of the MEs. Gracious with drink, Enki
presented to her ME for "Lordship . . . , Godship, the Exalted
and Enduring Tiara, the Throne of Kingship," and "bright
Inanna took them." As Inanna worked her charms on her aging
host, Enki made to her a second presentation of "the Exalted
Scepter and Staff, the Exalted Shrine, Righteous Rulership"; and "bright Inanna took them," too.

As the feasting and drinking went on, Enki parted with seven
major MEs, embracing the functions and attributes of a Divine
Lady, her temple and rituals, its priests, eunuchs, and prostitutes;
warfare and weapons; justice and courts; music and arts; masonry;
woodworking and metal working; leatherwork and weaving;
scribeship and mathematics; and so on.

With the encoded data for all these attributes of a high civilization in her hands, Inanna slipped away and took off in her Boat of
Heaven, back to Erech. Hours later a sobered Enki realized that
Inanna and the MEs were gone. His somewhat embarrassed chamberlain reminded Enki that he, Enki himself, had made the MEs a
present to Inanna. Greatly upset, Enki ordered his chamberlain to
pursue Inanna in Enki's "Great Heavenly Skychamber" and retrieve the MEs. Overtaking Inanna at the first stopping point, the
chamberlain explained to Inanna his orders; but Inanna, asking,
"Why had Enki changed his word to me?" refused. Reporting
the situation to Enki, the chamberlain was ordered to seize
Inanna's Boat of Heaven, bring the Boat to Eridu, and release
Inanna, but without the MEs. But in Eridu, Inanna ordered her
trusted pilot to "save the Boat of Heaven and the MEs presented to Inanna." And so, while Inanna kept the argument
with Enki's chamberlain going, her pilot slipped away in her
boat with the invaluable MEs.

An *Exaltation of Inanna,* composed to be read responsively
by the congregation, echoes the sentiments of the people of
Erech:

Lady of the MEs, Queen
            Brightly resplendent;
Righteous, clothed in radiance
            Beloved of Heaven and Earth;
Hierodule of Anu,
            Wearing the great adorations;
For the exalted tiara appropriate,
            For the high-priesthood suitable.
The seven MEs she attained,
            In her hand she is holding.
Lady of the great MEs,
            Of them she is the guardian . . .

It was in those days that Inanna was incorporated into the Pantheon of Twelve, and (replacing Ninharsag) was assigned the planet Venus (MUL DILBAT) as her celestial counterpart and the constellation AB.SIN (Virgo) as her zodiac house; the latter's depiction has hardly changed from Sumerian times (Fig. 79). Expressing her own gratification, Inanna announced for all—gods and men alike—to hear: "A Queen am I!"

Fig. 79

Hymns acknowledged her new status among the gods and her celestial attributes:

To the one who comes forth from heaven,
To the one who comes forth from heaven,
"Hail!" we do say . . .
Loftiness, greatness, reliability [are hers]
as she comes forth radiantly in the evening,

a holy torch that fills the heavens;
Her stance in heaven is like the Moon and Sun . . .
In Heaven she is secure, the good "wild cow" of Anu;
On Earth she is enduring, mistress of the lands.
In the Abzu, from Eridu, she received the MEs;
Her godfather Enki presented them to her,
Lordship and Kingship he placed in her hand.
With Anu she takes her seat upon the great throne,
With Enlil she determines the fates in her land . . .

Turning from her high position among the gods to her worship by the Sumerians (the "Black-Headed People"), the hymns went on:

In all the land, the black-headed people assemble
when abundance has been placed in the storehouses of Su-
    mer . . .
They come to her with . . . , they bring disputes before her.
She renders judgment to the evil and destroys the wicked;
She favors the just, determines good fate for them . . .
The good lady, the joy of Anu, a heroine she is;
She surely comes forth from Heaven . . .
She is mighty, she is trustworthy, she is great;
She is exceeding in youthfulness.

The people of Erech had every reason to be thankful to Inanna, for under her deityship, Erech had become an affluent center of Sumerian civilization. In praising her wisdom and valor, the people of Erech failed not also to mention her beauty and attractiveness. Indeed, it was at about that time that Inanna instituted the custom of the "Sacred Marriage," sexual rites whereby the priest-king was supposed to have become her spouse—but only for a night. A text, attributed to a king named Iddin-Dagan, described this aspect of Inanna's temple life—with music, male prostitute entertainers, and all:

The male-prostitutes comb her hair . . .
They decorate the neck with colored bands . . .
Their right side they adorn with women's clothing
as they walk before the pure Inanna . . .
Their left side they cover with men's clothing
as they walk before the pure Inanna . . .

With jump ropes and colored cords they compete before
her . . .
The young men, carrying hoops, sing before her . . .
The maidens, *Shugia* priestesses, walk before Inanna . . .
They set up a bed for my lady,
They cleanse rushes with sweet smelling cedar oil;
For Inanna, for the King, they arrange the bed . . .
The king approaches her pure lap proudly;
Proudly he approaches the lap of Inanna . . .
He caresses her pure lap,
She stretches out on the bed, the pure lap;
She makes love with him on her bed.
She says to Iddin-Dagan: "Surely, you are my beloved."

This habit of Inanna may have begun with Enmerkar himself, a
sexual union of which the next ruler of Uruk, a demigod known as
"divine Lugalbanda, a Righteous Supervisor," was the progeny.
Of Lugalbanda, too, as of Enmerkar, several epic tales have been
found. Inanna, it seems, wanted him to reside in her stead in
Aratta; but Lugalbanda was too restless and adventurous to stay
put. One epic tale *(Lugalbanda and Mount Hurum)* describes his
dangerous journey to the "awesome place on Earth" in search of
the Divine Black Bird. He reached the Restricted Mount "where
the Anunnaki, gods of the mountain, inside the earth like termites
had tunneled." Seeking a ride in the Bird of Heaven, Lugalbanda
pleaded with its custodian; his words immortalized man's desire to
fly:

Like Utu let me go, like Inanna,
Like the Seven Stormers of Ishkur
in a flame let me lift myself off,
and thunder away!
Let me go wherever my eyes can see,
Wherever I desire, let me set my foot,
Wherever my heart wishes, let me arrive . . .

When he had arrived at Mount Hurum ("whose front Enlil as
with a great door had closed off"), Lugalbanda was challenged by
the Guardian: "If a god you are, a word in friendship will I utter
which will let you enter; If a man you are, your fate will I decree."
To which:

Lugalbanda, he of beloved seed,
stretched his hand out [and said]:
"Like divine Shara am I,
the beloved son of Inanna."

But the Guardian of the sacred place turned Lugalbanda down
with an oracle: indeed, he would reach far lands and make both
himself and Erech famous, but he would do so on foot.

Another long epic tale, originally called by scholars "Lugalbanda and Enmerkar" and more recently *The Lugalbanda Epic,* affirms
Lugalbanda's semi-divine descent but does not identify his father; we
can assume, however, from the circumstances and subsequent events,
that the father was Enmerkar; confirming Enmerkar as the first one in
a long list of rulers who, under the guise of a symbolic marriage or
without it, were invited by Inanna to share her bed.

This "invitation" by Inanna is featured in the well-known *Epic
of Gilgamesh.* The fifth ruler of Erech, Gilgamesh sought to escape
the mortals' destiny to die because, as a son of the goddess Ninsun
and the high priest of the Kullab, "two thirds of him were god." In
his search for immortality (examined at length in *The Stairway to
Heaven*), he first journeyed to the "Landing Place" in the Cedar
Mountain—the olden landing platform in the mountains of Lebanon (to which, apparently, Lugalbanda had also gone). Battling the
mechanical monster that guarded the restricted area's perimeter,
Gilgamesh and his companion were almost annihilated were it not
for Utu's help. Exhausted from the battle, Gilgamesh took off his
drenched clothes so that he might wash and rest. It was then that
Inanna/Ishtar, who watched the struggle from the skies, was seized
with a craving for Gilgamesh:

He washed his grimy hair, polished his weapons;
The braid of his hair he shook out against his back.
He cast off his soiled things, put on his clean ones,
Wrapped a fringed cloak about, fastened with a sash.
When Gilgamesh put on his tiara,
Glorious Ishtar raised an eye at the beauty of Gilgamesh.
"Come, Gilgamesh, be thou my lover!" [she said]
"Do grant me of thy fruitfulness;
thou shalt be a husband, I shall be a wife."

She reinforced her invitation with promises of a glorious (though
not everlasting) life if Gilgamesh would accede to her offer. But Gil-

gamesh retorted with a long list of her lovers whom she befriended though she had "ordained for Tammuz [Dumuzi], the lover of your youth, wailing year after year"; while still supposedly in mourning, he said, she acquired and discarded lovers "as a shoe which pinches the foot of its owner . . . as a door which does not keep out the wind . . . Which lover didst thou love forever?" he asked; "if thou shouldst make love to me, thou wouldst treat me like them." (The offended Inanna thereupon received Anu's permission to launch against Gilgamesh the Bull of Heaven; Gilgamesh was saved from it at the last moment at the gates of Erech).

The golden era of Erech was not to last forever. Seven other kings followed Gilgamesh on its throne. Then, "Uruk was smitten with weapons; its kingship to Ur was carried." Thorkild Jacobsen, whose study *The Sumerian King List* is the most thorough on the subject, believes that the transfer of kingship in Sumer from Erech to Ur occurred circa 2850 B.C.; others adopt a lower date of circa 2650 B.C. (Such a discrepancy of two centuries has persisted into later times and remains unexplained by scholars.)

The reigns of the various rulers were getting shorter and shorter as the site of kingship swung back and forth among Sumer's principal cities: from Ur to Awan, then back to Kish; to a city named Hamazi, then back to Erech and Ur; to Adab and Mari, and back to Kish; to Aksak and again to Kish; and finally once more to Erech. In the course of no more than 220 years, there were thus three additional dynasties at Kish, three at Erech, two at Ur, and single ones in five other cities. It was, by all appearances, a volatile period; it was also a time of increasing friction between the cities, mostly over water rights and irrigation canals—phenomena that can be explained by drier weather on the one hand and rising populations on the other. In each instance the town that lost out was said to have been "smitten with weapons." Mankind had begun to wage its own wars!

The resort to arms to settle local disputes was becoming more commonplace. Inscriptions from those days indicate that the harassed populace was competing, through offerings and enhanced worship, for the favors of the gods; the warring city-states increasingly involved their patron-gods in their petty disputes. In one recorded instance Ninurta was involved in determining whether an irrigation ditch encroached on another city's boundaries. Enlil, too, was forced to order the warring parties to disengage. This constant strife and lack of stability soon reached a point when the gods had had enough. Once before, when the Deluge was coming, Enlil was so disgusted with mankind that he schemed its obliteration by the great flood. Then, in the Tower of Babel incident, he ordered mankind's dispersion and the confusion of its languages. Now, again, he was growing disgusted.

The historical background to the events that followed was the final attempt by the gods to reestablish Kish, the original capital, as the center of kingship. For the fourth time they returned kingship to Kish, starting the dynasty with rulers whose names indicate fealty to Sin, Ishtar, and Shamash. Two rulers, however, bore names indicating that they were followers of Ninurta and his spouse— evidence of a revived rivalry between the House of Sin and the House of Ninurta. It resulted in the seating on the throne of a nonentity—"Nannia, a stone cutter"; he reigned a brief seven years.

In such unsettled circumstances Inanna was able to retrieve the kingship for Erech. The man chosen for the task, one Lugal-zagesi, retained the favor of the gods for twenty-five years; but then, attacking Kish to assure her permanent desolation, he only managed to raise Enlil's ire; and the idea of a strong hand at the helm of human kingship made more and more sense. There was a need for someone uninvolved in all these disputes, someone who would provide firm leadership and once again properly perform the role of the king as sole intermediary between the gods and the people in all matters mundane.

It was Inanna who, on one of her flying trips, found that man.

Her encounter with him, circa 2400 B.C., launched a new era. He was a man who began his career as a cup-bearer to the king of Kish. When he took over the state reins in central Mesopotamia, he quickly extended his rule to all of Sumer, to its neighboring countries, and even unto distant lands. The epithet-name of this first empire-builder was *Sharru-Kin* ("Righteous Ruler"); modern textbooks call him Sargon I or Sargon the Great (Fig. 80). He built himself a brand-new capital not far from Babylon and named it *Agade* ("United"); we know it as Akkad—a name from which stems the term *Akkadian* for the first Semitic language.

A text known as *The Legend of Sargon* records, in Sargon's own words, his odd personal history:

Sargon, the mighty king of Agade, am I.
My mother was a high priestess; I knew not my father . . .
My mother, the high priestess, who conceived me,
in secret she bore me.
She set me in a basket of rushes, with bitumen sealed the lid.

Fig. 80

She cast me into the river; it did not sink me.
The river bore me up, it carried me to Akki the irrigator.
Akki the irrigator lifted me up when he drew water;
Akki, the irrigator, as his son made me and reared me.
Akki, the irrigator, appointed me as his gardener.

This Moses-like tale (written more than a thousand years before
the time of Moses!) then continues to answer the obvious question:
How could a man of unknown fatherhood, a mere gardener, become a mighty king? Sargon answered the questions thus:

While I was a gardener, Ishtar granted me her love,
And for four and fifty years I exercised Kingship;
The Black-headed people I ruled and governed.

The laconic statement is elaborated in another text. The encounter between Sargon the workingman and Ishtar the lovely goddess
was accidental but far from innocent:

One day my queen,
After crossing heaven, crossing earth—
Inanna.
After crossing heaven, crossing earth—
After crossing Elam and Shubur,
After crossing . . .
The hierodule approached weary, fell asleep.
I saw her from the edge of my garden;
Kissed her, copulated with her.

Inanna—by then awakened, we must assume—found in Sargon a man to her liking, a man who could satisfy not only her bedtime cravings but also her political ambitions. A text known as the *Sargon Chronicle* states that "Sharru-Kin, king of Agade, rose [to power] in the era of Ishtar. He had neither rival nor opponent. He spread his terror-inspiring glamor over all the countries. He crossed the sea in the east; he conquered the country of the west, in its full extent."

The enigmatic reference to the "Era of Ishtar" has baffled the scholars; but it can only mean what it says: at that time, for whatever reasons, Inanna/Ishtar was able to have a man of her choice take the throne and create for her an empire: "He defeated Uruk and tore down its wall. . . . He was victorious in the battle with the inhabitants of Ur . . . he defeated the entire territory from Lagash as far as the sea. . . ." There were also the conquests beyond the olden boundaries of Sumer: "Mari and Elam are standing in obedience before Sargon."

The grandeur of Sargon and the greatness of Inanna, going hand in hand, were expressed in the construction of the new capital city of Agade and in it the UL.MASH ("Glittering, Luxurious") temple to Inanna. "In those days," a Sumerian historiographic text relates, "the dwellings of Agade were filled with gold; its bright-shining houses were filled with silver. Into its storehouses were brought copper, lead and slabs of lapis-lazuli; its granaries bulged at the sides. Its old men were endowed with wisdom, its old women were endowed with eloquence; its young men were endowed with the Strength-of-Weapons, its little children were endowed with joyous hearts. . . . The city was full of music."

In that beautiful and happy city, "in Agade did holy Inanna erect a temple as her noble abode; in the Ulmash she set up a throne." It was the crowning temple in a series of shrines to her that encompassed Sumer's principal cities. Stating that "in Erech, the E-Anna is mine," Inanna listed her shrines in Nippur, Ur, Girsu, Adab, Kish, Der, Akshak, and Umma, and lastly the Ulmash in Agade. "Is there a god who can vie with me?" she asked.

Yet, though promoted by Inanna, the elevation of Sargon to kingship over what was henceforth known as Sumer and Akkad could not have taken place without the consent and blessing of Anu and Enlil. A bilingual (Sumerian-Akkadian) text, originally inscribed on a statue of Sargon that was placed before Enlil in his temple in Nippur, stated that Sargon was not only "Commanding Overseer" of Ishtar, but also "anointed priest of Anu" and "great regent of Enlil." It was Enlil, Sargon wrote, who "had given him lordship and kingship."

Sargon's records of his conquests describe Inanna as actively present on the battlefields but attribute to Enlil the overall decision regarding the scope of the victories and the extent of the territories: "Enlil did not let anybody oppose Sargon, the king of the land; from the Upper Sea to the Lower Sea Enlil gave unto him." Invariably, postscripts to Sargon's inscriptions invoked Anu, Enlil, Inanna, and Utu/Shamash as his "witnesses."

As one scrutinizes this vast empire, stretching from the Upper Sea (Mediterranean) to the Lower Sea (Persian Gulf), it becomes clear that Sargon's conquests were, at first, limited to the domains of Sin and his children (Inanna and Utu) and, even at their peak, kept well within the Enlilite territories. Sargon reached Lagash, the city of Ninurta, and conquered the territory *from* Lagash southward, but not Lagash itself; nor did he expand to the northeast of Sumer where Ninurta held sway. Going beyond the boundaries of olden Sumer, he entered to the southeast the land of Elam—an area under Inanna's influence from earlier times. But when Sargon was entering the lands to the west on the mid-Euphrates and the Mediterranean coast, the domains of Adad, "Sargon prostrated himself in prayer before the god . . . [and] he gave him in the upper region Mari, Yarmuli and Ebla, as far as the cedar forest and the silver mountain."

It is clear from Sargon's inscriptions that he was neither given Tilmun (the gods' own Fourth Region), nor Magan (Egypt), nor Meluhha (Ethiopia) in the Second Region, the domains of Enki's descendants; with those lands he only conducted peaceful trading relations. In Sumer itself he kept out of the area controlled by Ninurta and from the city claimed by Marduk. But then, "in his old age," Sargon made a mistake:

He took away soil from the foundation of Babylon
and built upon the soil another Babylon beside Agade.

To understand the severity of this deed, we ought to recall the
meaning of "Babylon"—*Bab-Ili,* "Gateway of the Gods." A title
and a function claimed for Babylon by a defiant Marduk, it was
symbolized by its hallowed soil. Now, encouraged by Inanna and
driven by her ambitions, Sargon took away the sacred soil to spread
it as a foundation for the new Bab-Ili, audaciously aiming to transfer the title and function to Agade.

This was, as it turned out, an opportunity for Marduk—unheard
from for so many centuries—to reassert himself:

On account of the sacrilege Sargon thus committed,
the great lord Marduk became enraged
and destroyed his people by hunger.
From the east to the west he alienated them from Sargon;
and upon him he inflicted as punishment that he could not rest.

Desperately crushing one revolt after another, Sargon "could
not rest"; discredited and afflicted, he died after a reign of fifty-
four years.

12

PRELUDE TO DISASTER

The information concerning the last years of the Era of Ishtar comes to us from a number of texts. Put together, they unfold a tale of dramatic and incredible events: the usurpation of supreme powers on Earth by a goddess; the defilement of Enlil's Holy of Holies in Nippur; the penetration of the Fourth Region by a human army; an invasion of Egypt; the appearance of African gods in the Asian domains; acts and occurrences that were unthinkable before; upheavals among the gods, which served as a stage on which human rulers played out their roles and human blood was spilled without mercy.

Faced with the reemergence of her olden adversary, Inanna could simply not give up, no matter what the cost. Seating on Sargon's throne first one of his sons and then another, enlisting in her campaigns her vassal kings in the eastern mountainlands, she fought as an enraged lioness for her disintegrating empire, "raining flame over the land . . . attacking like an aggressive storm."

"You are known by your destruction of the rebel lands," intoned a daughter of Sargon in a plaintive poem; "you are known by massacring their people" . . . turning "against the city that said not 'the land is yours,' " making "its rivers run with blood."

For more than two years Inanna wrought havoc all around, until the gods decided that the only way to stop the carnage was to force Marduk back into exile. Having returned to Babylon when Sargon tried to remove some of its hallowed soil—an act whose symbolism was rooted in legendary events—Marduk fortified the city and in particular ingeniously enhanced its underground water system, making the city impervious to attack. Unable or unwilling to remove Marduk by force, the Anunnaki turned to Marduk's brother Nergal and asked him to "scare Marduk off the divine seat" in Babylon.

We know of these events from a text named by scholars *The Erra Epos*, for in it Nergal is called by the ancient chronicler ER.RA—a somewhat derogatory epithet, for it meant "The Servant of Ra." It is a text that could better be called *The Tale of the*

251

Sins of Nergal, for it puts the blame on Nergal for a chain of events with a catastrophic ending; but it is an invaluable source for our knowledge and understanding of that prelude to disaster.

Having accepted the mission, Nergal/Erra journeyed to Mesopotamia for a face-to-face talk with Marduk. Arriving in Mesopotamia, he first stopped at Erech, "the city of Anu, the king of all the gods," but, of course, also the place to huddle with Inanna/Ishtar. Arriving in Babylon, "into the Esagil, temple of Heaven and Earth, he entered, and stood before Marduk." The momentous encounter has been recorded by the ancient artists (Fig. 81); it depicts both gods holding on to their weapons, but the helmeted Marduk, standing on a platform, does extend some symbol of welcome to his brother.

Fig. 81

Combining praise with reprimand, Erra told Marduk that the wonderful things he had done for Babylon, and especially its waterworks, made Marduk's reputation "shine as a star in the heavens," but have deprived other cities of their waters. Moreover, while crowning himself in Babylon, "lights up its sacred precinct," it angered the other gods; "the abode of Anu with darkness it covers." Marduk, he concluded, could not go on against the will of the other Anunnaki and certainly not against the will of Anu.

But Marduk, citing changes that were made on Earth in the aftermath of the Deluge, explained that he had to take matters into his own hands:

In the aftermath of the Deluge,
the decrees of Heaven and Earth had gone astray.
The cities of the gods upon the wide Earth
were changed around;
They were not brought back to their locations . . .
As I survey them again, of the evil I am disgusted;
Without a return to their [original] places,
Mankind's existence is diminished . . .
Rebuild I must my residence
which in the Deluge was wiped away;
Its name [I must] call again.

Among the post-Diluvian disorders that bothered Marduk were
some failures on the part of Erra himself to account for certain divine artifacts—"the instrument of giving orders, the Oracle of the
Gods; the sign of kingship, the Holy Scepter which contributes
brilliance to Lordship. . . . Where is the holy Radiating Stone
which disintegrates all?" Marduk asked. If he were forced to
leave, Marduk said, "on the day I step off my seat, the flooding
shall from its well cease to work . . . the waters shall not rise . . .
the bright day to darkness [shall turn] . . . confusion shall arise
. . . the winds of draught shall howl . . . sicknesses shall
spread."

After some more exchanges Erra offered to return to Marduk
"the artifacts of Heaven and Earth" if Marduk would personally
go to the Lower World to pick them up; and as to the "works" in
Babylon, he assured Marduk there was nothing to worry about: he
(Erra) would enter Marduk's House only to "erect the Bulls of Anu
and Enlil at thy gate"—statues of Winged Bulls as were actually
found at temple sites—but would do nothing to upset the waterworks.

Marduk heard this;
The promise, given by Erra, found his favor.
So did he step down from his seat,
and to the Land of Mines, abode of the Anunnaki,
he set his direction.

Thus persuaded, Marduk agreed to leave Babylon. But no
sooner he had done that than Nergal broke his word. Unable to resist his curiosity, Nergal/Erra ventured into the *Gigunu*, the mysterious underground chamber which Marduk had stressed was off

limits; and there Erra caused its "Brilliance" (radiating source of energy) to be removed. Thereupon, as Marduk had warned, "the day turned into darkness," the "flooding was disarrayed," and soon "the lands were laid to waste, the people were made to perish."

All of Mesopotamia was affected, for Ea/Enki, Sin and Shamash, in their cities, became alarmed; "with anger [at Erra] they were filled." The people made sacrifices to Anu and Ishtar but to no avail: "the water sources went dry." Ea, Erra's father, reproached him: "Now that Prince Marduk had stepped off, what have you done?" He ordered that a statue of Erra, which had been prepared, should not be set up in the Esagil. "Go away!" he ordered Erra. "Take off to where no gods ever go!"

"Erra lost his voice" only for a moment, then uttered words of impudence. Enraged, he smashed Marduk's abode, set fire to its gates. Defiantly, "he made a sign" as he turned to leave, announcing that his followers, however, would stay behind: "as to my warriors, they shall not go back." And so it was that when Erra returned to Kutha, the men who had come with him stayed behind, establishing a long-lasting presence for Nergal in the lands of Shem; a colony was assigned to them not far from Babylon, perhaps as a permanent garrison; there were "Kutheans who worship Nergal" in Samaria in biblical times; and there was official worship of Nergal in Elam, as evidenced by an unusual bronze sculpture (Fig. 82) found there, depicting worshipers with unmistakable African features performing a cultic ceremony in a temple courtyard.

The departure of Marduk from Babylon brought to an end Ishtar's conflict with him; the rift between Marduk and Nergal and the latter's retention of an Asian presence unintentionally created an alliance between Ishtar and Nergal. The chain of tragic events that no one could have predicted and that no one had perhaps even desired was thus being forged by fate, leading the Anunnaki and Mankind ever closer to the ultimate disaster. . . .

With her authority restored, Inanna renewed the kingship in Agade and put on the throne a grandson of Sargon, Naram-Sin ("Sin's Favorite"). Seeing in him, at last, a true successor to Sargon, she encouraged him to seek grandeur and greatness. After a brief period of peace and prosperity she goaded Naram-Sin to embark on an expansion of the erstwhile empire. Soon Inanna began to encroach on the territories of other gods; but they were unable or unwilling to fight her: "The great Anunnaki gods fled before you like fluttering bats," a hymn to Inanna stated; "they could not

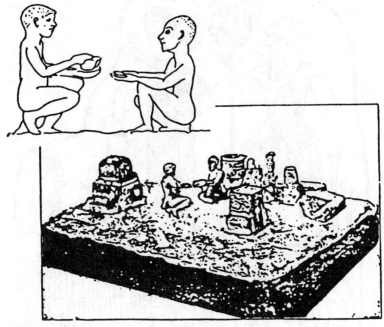

Fig. 82

stand before your fearsome face . . . could not soothe your angry heart.'' Rock carvings in the annexed territories depicted Inanna as the ruthless conqueror she had become (Fig. 83).

At the beginning of her campaigns Inanna was still called ''Beloved of Enlil'' and one ''Who carries out the instructions of Anu.'' But then her thrust began to change in nature, from the suppression of rebellions to a calculated plan for seizing supremacy.

Two sets of texts, one dealing with the goddess and the other with her surrogate, the king Naram-Sin, record the events of those times. Both indicate that the first out-of-bounds target of Inanna was the Landing Place in the Cedar Mountain. As a Flying Goddess Inanna was quite familiar with the place; she ''burnt down the great gates'' of the mountain and, after a brief siege, obtained the surrender of the troops guarding it: ''they disbanded themselves willingly.''

As recorded in the Naram-Sin inscriptions, Inanna then turned south along the Mediterranean coast, subduing city after city. The conquest of Jerusalem—Mission Control Center—is not specifi-

Fig. 83

cally mentioned, but Inanna must have been there, too, for it is recorded that she had gone on to capture Jericho. Lying astride the
strategic Jordan River crossing and opposite the Anunnaki stronghold at Tell Ghassul, Jericho—the city dedicated to Sin—had also
rebelled: "It said not 'It belongs to your father who begot you'; it
had promised its solemn word, but turned away from it." The Old
Testament is filled with admonitions against "straying after alien
gods"; the Sumerian text conveys the same transgression: The
people of Jericho, having given a solemn promise to worship Sin,
Inanna's father, have switched allegience to another, alien, god.
The surrender of this "city of date-palms" to an armed Inanna was
depicted on a cylinder seal (Fig. 84).

With the conquest of southern Canaan, Inanna stood at the gateway to the Fourth Region, the region of the Spaceport. Sargon had

Fig. 84

not dared cross the forbidden line. But Naram-Sin, encouraged by Inanna, did. . . .

A Mesopotamian royal chronicle attests that not only did Naram-Sin enter the peninsula, but he had gone on to invade the land of Magan (Egypt):

> Naram-Sin, offspring of Sargon, marched against the town of Apishal and made a breach in its wall, conquering it. He personally caught Rish-Adad, king of Apishal, and the vizier of Apishal.
>
> He then marched against the country of Magan and personally caught Mannu-Dannu, king of Magan.

The accuracy of the above-mentioned Babylonian royal chronicle has been independently confirmed in its other details, so there is no reason to doubt this part of it, too—incredible as it sounds, for it entailed the passage of a human king and a human army through the Sinai peninsula, the gods' own Fourth Region. Since time immemorial, a trade route between Asia and Africa had wound its way along the peninsula's Mediterranean coast—a route later on enhanced by the Egyptians with watering stations and by the Romans as their vital *Via Maris*. Ancient users of this route thus kept well away from the central plain where the Spaceport was located. But whether Naram-Sin, at the head of an army, just marched through along the coastal route is questionable. Alabaster vases of Egyptian design, which have been found by archaeologists in Mesopotamia and Elam, identified their owner (in Akkadian) as "Naram-Sin, King of the Four Regions; vase of the Shining Crown of the land Magan." That Naram-Sin began to call himself "King of the Four Regions" affirms not only the conquest of Egypt but also suggests the inclusion of the Sinai peninsula in his sphere of influence. Inanna, it appears, was more than "just passing through."

(A foreign invasion, about the time of Naram-Sin, is also known from Egyptian records. They describe a period of disarray and chaos. In the words of the papyrus known to Egyptologists as *The Admonitions of Ipuwer,* "Strangers have come into Egypt . . . the high-born are full of lamentation." It was a period that saw the shift of the center of worship and kingship from Memphis-Heliop-olis in the north to Thebes in the south. Scholars call the century of disarray "The First Intermediate Period"; it followed the collapse of the sixth Pharaonic dynasty.)

How could Inanna, with apparent immunity, intrude on the Sinai peninsula and invade Egypt unopposed by the gods of Egypt?

The answer lies in an aspect of the Naram-Sin inscriptions that has baffled the scholars: the apparent veneration by this Mesopota-mian ruler of the African god Nergal. Although this made no sense at all, the fact is that the long text known as *The Kuthean Legend of Naram-Sin* (or, as it is sometimes called, *The King of Kutha Text*) attests that Naram-Sin went to Kutha, Nergal's cult center in Af-rica, and erected there a stela to which he affixed an ivory tablet inscribed with the tale of this unusual visit, all to pay homage to Nergal.

The recognition by Naram-Sin of Nergal's power and influence well beyond Africa is attested by the fact that in treaties made be-tween Naram-Sin and provincial rulers in Elam, Nergal is invoked among the witness gods. And in an inscription dealing with Naram-Sin's march to the Cedar Mountain in Lebanon, the king credited Nergal (rather than Ishkur/Adad) with making the achieve-ment possible:

Although since the era of the rulership of man
none of the kings has ever destroyed Arman and Ebla,
Now did the god *Nergal* open up the path for the mighty Naram-
Sin.
He gave him Arman and Ebla, presented him with the Amanus
and with the Cedar Mountain and with the Upper Sea.

This puzzling emergence of Nergal as an influential Asian deity, and the audacious march of Inanna's surrogate Naram-Sin to Egypt—all violations of the status quo of the Four Regions established after the Pyramid Wars—have one explanation: While Marduk had shifted his attention to Babylon, Nergal assumed a preeminent role in Egypt. Then, having gone to persuade Marduk to leave Mesopotamia without further struggle, the amicable parting turned into a bitter enmity between the brothers.

And this led to an alliance between Nergal and Inanna; but as they stood for each other, they soon found themselves opposed by all the other gods. An assembly of the gods was held in Nippur to deal with the disruptive consequences of Inanna's exploits; even Enki agreed that she had gone too far. And a decree for her arrest and trial was issued by Enlil.

We learned of these events from a chronicle titled by scholars *The Curse of Agade.* Deciding that Inanna had indeed gotten out of hand, "the word of the Ekur" (Enlil's sacred precinct in Nippur) was issued against her. But Inanna did not wait to be seized or held for trial: she forsook her temple and escaped from Agade:

> The "word of Ekur" was upon Agade
> like a deathly silence;
> Agade was all atremble,
> its Ulmash temple was in terror;
> She who lived there, left the city.
> The maiden forsook her chamber;
> Holy Inanna forsook her shrine in Agade.

By the time a delegation of the great gods arrived in Agade, they only found an empty temple; all they could do was strip the place of its attributes of power:

> In days not five, in days not ten,
> The crownband of lordship, the tiara of Kingship,
> the throne given to rulership
> Ninurta brought over to his temple;
> Utu carried off the city's "Eloquence";
> Enki withdrew its "Wisdom."
> Its Awesomeness that could reach the Heaven,
> Anu brought up to the midst of Heaven.

"The kingship of Agade was prostrated, its future was extremely unhappy." Then "Naram-Sin had a vision," a communication from his goddess Inanna. "He kept it to himself, put it not in speech, spoke with nobody about it. . . . Seven years Naram-Sin remained in wait."

Did Inanna seek out Nergal during her seven-year disappearance from Agade? The text does not give the answer, but we believe that it was the only haven available to Inanna, away from Enlil's wrath. The ensuing events suggest that Inanna—even more audacious than before, more ambitious than ever—must have obtained the backing of at least one other major god; and that could have been only Nergal. That Inanna would hide in Nergal's Lower African domain seems thus a most plausible assumption.

Did the two, talking over the situation, reviewing past events, discussing the future, end up forging a new alliance that could rearrange the divine domains? A New Order was indeed feasible, for Inanna was shattering the Old Divine Order upon the Earth. A text whose ancient title was *Queen of All the MEs* acknowledges that Inanna had indeed, deliberately, decided to defy the authority of Anu and Enlil, abrogated their rules and regulations, and declared herself the Supreme Deity, a "Great Queen of Queens." Announcing that she "has become greater than the mother who gave birth to her . . . even greater than Anu," she followed up her declarations with deeds and seized the E-Anna ("House of Anu") in Erech, aiming to dismantle this symbol of Anu's authority:

The heavenly kingship was seized by a female . . .
She changed altogether the rules of Holy Anu,
Feared not the great Anu.
She seized the E-Anna from Anu—
that House of irresistible charm, enduring allure—
On that House she brought destruction;
Inanna assaults its people, makes them captive.

The coup d'état against Anu was accompanied by a parallel attack on Enlil's seat and symbols of authority. This task was assigned by Inanna to Naram-Sin; his attack on the Ekur in Nippur and the resulting downfall of Agade are detailed in *The Curse of Agade* text. From it we gather that after the seven-year wait Naram-Sin received further oracles and thereupon "changed his line of action." Upon receiving the new orders:

He defied the word of Enlil,
Crushed those who had served Enlil,
Mobilized his troops, and
Like a hero accustomed to high-handedness
Put a restraining hand on the Ekur.

Overrunning the seemingly undefended city, "like a bandit he plundered it." He then approached the Ekur in the sacred precinct, "erecting large ladders against the House." Smashing his way in, he entered its Holy of Holies: "the people now saw its sacred cella, a chamber that knew not light; the Akkadians saw the holy vessels of the god"; Naram-Sin "cast them into the fire." He "docked large boats at the quay by the House of Enlil, and carried off the possessions of the city." The horrible sacrilege was complete.

Enlil—his whereabouts unstated, but clearly away from Nippur—"lifted his eyes" and saw the destruction of Nippur and the defilement of the Ekur. "Because his beloved Ekur had been attacked," he ordered the hordes of Gutium—a mountainland to the northeast of Mesopotamia—to attack Akkad and lay it waste. They came down upon Akkad and its cities "in vast numbers, like locusts . . . nothing escaped their arm." "He who slept on the roof died on the roof; he who slept inside the house was not brought to burial . . . heads were crushed, mouths were crushed . . . the blood of the treacherous flowed over the blood of the faithful."

Once, and then a second time, the other gods interceded with Enlil: "curse Agade with a baleful curse," they said, but let the other cities and the farmlands survive! When Enlil finally agreed, eight great gods joined in putting a curse on Agade, "the city who dared assault the Ekur." "And lo," said the ancient historian, "so it came to pass . . . Agade is destroyed!" The gods decreed that Agade be wiped off the face of the Earth; and unlike other cities that, having been destroyed, were rebuilt and resettled, Agade forever remained desolate.

As to Inanna, "her heart was appeased" finally by her parents. What exactly happened, the texts do not state. They tell us, however, that her father Nannar came forth to fetch her back to Sumer while "her mother Ningal proffered prayers for her, greeted her back at the temple's doorstep." "Enough, more than enough innovations, O great queen!" the gods and the people appealed to her: "and the foremost Queen, in her assembly, accepted the prayer."

The Era of Ishtar was over.

* * *

All the textual evidence suggests that Enlil and Ninurta were away from Mesopotamia when Naram-Sin attacked Nippur. But the hordes that swept down from the mountains upon Akkad were "the hordes of Enlil," and they were in all probability guided into the great Mesopotamian plain by Ninurta.

The Sumerian King Lists call the land from which the invaders came Gutium, a land in the mountains northeast of Mesopotamia. In the Legend of Naram-Sin they are called Umman-Manda (possibly "Hordes of Far/Strong Brothers"), who came from "camps in the dwelling of Enlil" situated "in the mountainland whose city the gods had built." Verses in the text suggest that they were descendants of soldiers who had accompanied Enmerkar on his distant travels, who "slew their host" and were punished by Utu/Shamash to remain in exile. Now tribes great in number, led by seven chieftain brothers, they were commanded by Enlil to overrun Mesopotamia and "hurl themselves against the people who in Nippur had killed."

For a while feeble successors to Naram-Sin attempted to maintain a central rule as the hordes began to overrun city after city. The confused situation is described in the Sumerian King Lists with the statement: "Who was king? Who was not king? Was Irgigi king? Was Nanum king? Was Imi king? Was Elulu king?'" In the end the Gutians seized control of the whole of Sumer and Akkad; "Kingship by the hordes of Gutium was carried off."

For ninety-one years and forty days the Gutians held sway over Mesopotamia. No new capital is named for them, and it appears that Lagash—the only Sumerian city to escape despoiling by the invaders—served as their headquarters. From his seat in Lagash Ninurta undertook the slow process of restoring the country's agriculture and primarily the irrigation system that collapsed following the Erra/Marduk incident. It was a chapter in Sumerian history that can best be called the Era of Ninurta.

The focal point of that era was Lagash, a city whose beginnings were as a "sacred precinct" (the *Girsu*) for Ninurta and his Divine Black Bird. But as the turmoil of human and divine ambitions grew, Ninurta decided to convert Lagash into a major Sumerian center, the principal abode for himself and his spouse Bau/Gula (Fig. 85), where his ideas of law and order and his ideals of morality and justice could be practiced. To assist in these tasks Ninurta appointed in Lagash human viceroys and charged them with the administration and defense of the city-state.

Fig. 85

The history of Lagash (a site nowadays called Tello) records a dynasty whose reign--uninterrupted for half a millennium—began three centuries before the rise of Sargon. An island of armed stability in an increasingly violent environment, Lagash was also a great center of Sumerian culture. While Sumer's religious holidays emanated from Nippur, Lagash originated traditions of festivals tied to an agricultural calendar, such as the Festival of First Fruits. Its scribes and scholars perfected the Sumerian language; and its rulers, to whom Ninurta granted the title "Righteous Governor," were sworn to a code of justice and morality.

Prominent among the very first rulers of the long dynasty of Lagash was one named Ur-Nanshe (circa 2600 B.C.). More than fifty of his inscriptions were found in the ruins of Lagash; they record the bringing of building materials for the Girsu, including special timbers from Tilmun for the temple's furnishings. They also describe extensive irrigation works, the digging of canals, and the raising of dykes. On one of his tablets Ur-Nanshe is depicted heading a construction team, not loath to do some manual work himself (Fig. 86). The forty known viceroys who followed him left a written record of achievements in agriculture, construction, social legislation, and ethical reforms—material and moral achievements that would make any government proud.

Fig. 86

But Lagash had escaped the ravages of the turbulent years of Sargon and Naram-Sin not only because it was the "cult center" of Ninurta, but also (and primarily) because of the military prowess of its people. As "Enlil's Foremost Warrior," Ninurta made sure that those selected by him to govern Lagash should be militarily proficient. One (named Eannatum) whose inscriptions and stelae have been found, was a master tactician and victorious general. The stelae show him riding a war chariot—a military vehicle whose introduction has been customarily attributed to later times; they also show his helmeted troops in tight formations (Fig. 87).

Commenting on this, Maurice Lambert *(La Période Pre-Sargonique)* wrote that "this infantry of spearmen, protected by shield-bearers, gave the army of Lagash a defence most solid and an attack most rapid and versatile." The resulting victories of Eannatum even impressed Inanna/Ishtar, so much so that she had fallen in love with him; and "because she loved Eannatum, kingship over Kish she gave him, in addition to the governorship of Lagash." With this Eannatum became the LU.GAL ("Great Man") of Sumer; and holding the land in a military grip, he made law and order prevail.

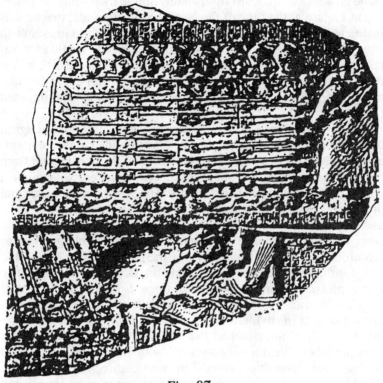

Fig. 87

Ironically the chaotic period that had preceded Sargon of Agade found in Lagash not a strong military leader but a social reformer named Urukagina. He devoted his efforts to a moral revival and to the introduction of laws based on fairness and justice, rather than on a crime-punishment concept. Under him, Lagash proved too weak to maintain law and order in the land. His weakness enabled Inanna to bring the ambitious Lugal-zagesi of Umma to Erech, in an attempt to restore her countrywide dominion. But the failings of Lugal-zagesi led (as we have already described) to his downfall by the hand of Inanna's new choice, Sargon.

Throughout the period of the primacy of Agade, governorship continued uninterrupted in Lagash; even the great Sargon skirted Lagash and left it intact. It escaped destruction and occupation throughout the upheavals of Naram-Sin, primarily because it was a formidable military stronghold, fortified and refortified to withstand all attacks. We learn from an inscription by Ur-Bau, the vice-roy at Lagash at the time of the Naram-Sin upheavals, that he was instructed by Ninurta to reinforce the walls of the Girsu and to strengthen the enclosure of the Imdugud aircraft. Ur-Bau "compacted the soil to be as stone . . . fired clay to be as metal"; and at the Imdugud's platform "replaced the old soil with a new foundation," strengthened with huge timber beams and stones imported from afar.

When the Gutians left Mesopotamia—circa 2160 B.C.—Lagash burst into new bloom and produced some of Sumer's most enlightened and best-known rulers. Of these, one of the best-known from his long inscriptions and many statues was Gudea, who reigned during the twenty-second century B.C. His was a time of peace and prosperity; his records speak not of armies and wars but of trade and reconstruction. He crowned his activities with the building of a new, magnificent temple for Ninurta in a vastly enlarged Girsu. According to Gudea's inscriptions, "the Lord of Girsu" appeared unto him in a vision, standing beside his Divine Black Bird. The god expressed to him the wish that a new E.NINNU ("House of Fifty"—Ninurta's numerical rank) be built by Gudea. Gudea was given two sets of divine instructions: one from a goddess who in one hand "held the tablet of the favorable star of heavens" and with the other "held a holy stylus," with which she indicated to Gudea "the favorable planet" in whose direction the temple should be oriented. The other set of instructions came from a god whom Gudea did not recognize and who turned out to have been Ningishzidda. He handed to Gudea a tablet made of precious stone; "the plan of a temple it contained." One of Gudea's statues depicts him seated with this tablet on his knees, the divine stylus beside it (Fig. 88).

Gudea admits that he needed the help of diviners and "searchers of secrets" to understand the temple plan. It was, as modern researchers have found, an ingenious one-in-seven architectural plan for the construction of a ziggurat as a seven-stage pyramid. The structure contained a strongly reinforced platform for the landing of Ninurta's airborne vehicle.

The participation of Ningishzidda in the planning of the E-Ninnu carried a significance that went beyond mere architectural assistance, as evidenced by the fact that the Girsu included a special shrine for this god. Associated with healing and magical powers, Ningishzidda—a son of Enki—was deemed in Sumerian inscriptions to have known how to secure the foundations of tem-

Fig. 88

ples; he was "the great god who held the plans." As we have already suggested, Ningishzidda was none other than Thoth, the Egyptian god of magical powers who was appointed guardian of the secret plans of the pyramids of Giza.

Ninurta, it will be recalled, had carried off with him some of the "stones" from within the Great Pyramid when the Pyramid Wars ended. Now, with the thwarted efforts of Inanna and then Marduk to lord over gods and men, Ninurta wished to reaffirm his "Rank of Fifty" by the erection of a step-pyramid for himself at Lagash, an edifice to be known as the "House of Fifty." It was for that reason, we believe, that Ninurta invited Ningishzidda/Thoth to come to Mesopotamia, to design for him a pyramid that could be built and raised high, not with massive stone blocks as in Egypt, but with the humble clay bricks of Mesopotamia.

The stay of Ningishzidda in Sumer and his collaboration there with Ninurta were commemorated not only in shrines to that visiting god, but also in numerous artistic depictions, some of which were discovered during the sixty years of archaeological work at Tello. One of these (Fig. 89a) combined the emblem of Ninurta's Divine Bird with the serpents of Ningishzidda; another (Fig. 89b) depicted Ninurta as an Egyptian Sphinx.

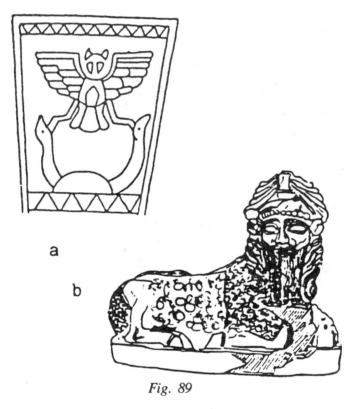

a

b

Fig. 89

The time of Gudea and the Ninurta-Ningishzidda collaboration coincides with the so-called First Intermediate Period in Egypt, when the kings of the IX and X dynasties (2160 to 2040 B.C.) abandoned the worship of Osiris and Horus and moved the capital from Memphis to a city the Greeks later called Heracleopolis. The departure of Thoth from Egypt may thus have been an aspect of the upheavals occurring there, as was his subsequent disappearance from Sumer. Ningishzidda (to quote E. D. van Buren, *The God Ningizzida*) was ''a god called forth from obscurity in Gudea's time,'' only to become a "phantom god" and a mere memory in later (Babylonian and Assyrian) times.

The Era of Ninurta in Sumer, lasting through the Gutian invasion and the ensuing period of reconstruction, was only an interlude. A mountain dweller at heart, Ninurta soon began to roam the skies again in his Divine Black Bird, visiting his rugged domains in the northeast and even farther away. Constantly perfecting the martial arts of his highland tribesmen, he gave them mobility through the introduction of cavalry, thereby extending their reach by hundreds and even thousands of miles.

He had returned to Mesopotamia at Enlil's call, to put an end to the sacrilege perpetrated by Naram-Sin and to the upheavals caused by Inanna. With peace and prosperity restored, Ninurta again absented himself from Sumer; and, never one to give up, Inanna seized upon this absence to regain the kingship for Erech.

The attempt lasted only a few years, for Anu and Enlil did not condone her deed. But the tale (contained in an enigmatic text on a partly broken tablet catalogued as Ashur-13955) is most fascinating; it reads like an ancient legend of the *Excalibur* (King Arthur's magical sword, which was imbedded in a rock and could be pulled out only by the one who was chosen for kingship); and it throws light on preceding events, including the incident by which Sargon had offended Marduk.

We learn that when "Kingship was lowered from Heaven" to begin at Kish, Anu and Enlil established there a "Pavilion of Heaven." "In its foundation soil, for all days to come," they implanted the SHU.HA.DA.KU—an artifact made of alloyed metal whose name translates literally "Supreme Strong Bright Weapon." This divine object was taken to Erech when kingship was transferred there from Kish; it was moved about as kingship moved about but only when the change was decreed by the Great Gods.

In accordance with this custom, Sargon carried the object to Agade. But Marduk protested, because Agade was a brand-new city and not one of the cities selected by "the great gods of Heaven and Earth" to be royal capitals. The gods who chose Agade—Inanna and her supporters—were in Marduk's opinion "rebels, gods who wear unclean clothing."

It was to cure this defect that Sargon went to Babylon to the spot where its "hallowed soil" was located. The idea was to remove some of that soil "to a place in front of Agade," there to implant the Divine Weapon and thus legitimize its presence in Agade. It was in punishment for this, the text states, that Marduk instigated rebellions against Sargon and also inflicted upon him a "restlessness" (some take the term to mean "insomnia") which led to his death.

We read further in the enigmatic text that during the Gutian occupation that followed Naram-Sin's reign, the divine object lay untouched "beside the dam-works for the waters" because "they knew not how to carry out the rules regarding the divine artifact." It was at that time Marduk's contention that the object had to remain in its assigned place, "without being opened up," and "not being offered to any god," until "the gods who brought the destruction shall make restitution." But when Inanna seized the opportunity to reinstitute kingship in Erech, her chosen king, Utu-Hegal, "seized the *Shuhadaku* in its place of resting; into his hand he took it"—although "the end of the restitution has not yet occurred." Unauthorized, Uthu-Hegal "raised the weapon against the city he was besieging." As soon as he had done that, he fell dead. "The river carried off his sunken body."

Ninurta's absences from Sumer and Inanna's abortive attempt to recapture the kingship for Erech indicated to Enlil that the matter of the divine governing of Sumer could no longer be left open-ended; and the most suitable candidate for the task was Nannar/Sin.

Throughout the turbulent times he was overshadowed by more aggressive contenders for the supremacy, including his own daughter Inanna. Now he was finally given the opportunity to assume the status befitting him as the firstborn (on Earth) of Enlil. The era that followed—let us call it the Era of Nannar—was one of the most glorious in Sumerian annals; it was also Sumer's last hurrah.

His first order of business was to make his city, Ur, a great metropolis and the capital of a vast empire. Appointing a new line of rulers, known by scholars as the Third Dynasty of Ur, Nannar achieved for this capital and for Sumerian civilization unprecedented peaks of material and cultural advancements. From an immense ziggurat that dominated the walled city (Fig. 90)—a ziggurat whose crumbled remains, after more than four thousand years, still rise awesomely from the Mesopotamian plain—Nannar and his spouse Ningal took an active part in the affairs of state. Attended by a hierarchy of priests and functionaries (headed by the king, Fig. 91), they guided the city's agriculture to become the granary of Sumer; directed its sheep breeding to make Ur the wool and gar-

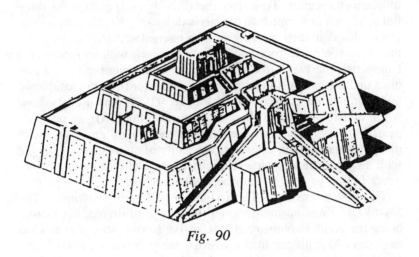

Fig. 90

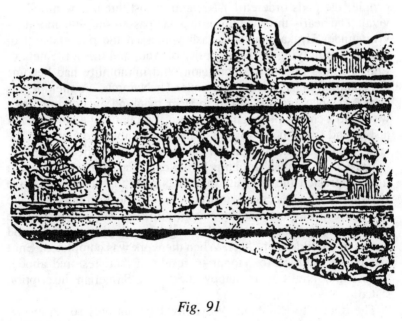

Fig. 91

ment center of the ancient Near East; and developed a foreign trade by land and water that made the merchants of Ur remembered for millennia thereafter. To service this thriving trade and the far-flung links, as well as to improve the city's defenses, the city's surrounding wall was in turn surrounded by a navigable canal, serving two harbors—a West Harbor and a North Harbor—with an inner canal connecting the two harbors and in turn separating the sacred precinct and the palace and administrative quarter from the residential and commercial parts of the city (Fig. 92). It was a city whose white houses—many of them multistoried (Fig. 93)—shined as a pearl from a distance; whose streets were straight and wide, with many a shrine at their intersections; a city of an industrious people with a smooth-functioning administration; a city of pious people, never failing to pray to their benevolent deities.

The first ruler of the Third Dynasty of Ur, *Ur-Nammu* ("The Joy of Ur") was no mere mortal: he was semi-divine, his mother being the goddess Ninsun. His extensive records state that as soon as "Anu and Enlil had turned over kingship to Nannar at Ur," and Ur-Nammu was selected to be the "Righteous Shepherd" of the people, the gods ordered Ur-Nammu to institute a new moral revival. The nearly three centuries that had passed since the moral revival under Urukagina of Lagash witnessed the rise and fall of Akkad, the defying of the authority of Anu, and the defilement of Enlil's Ekur. Injustice, oppression, and immorality had become the common behavior. At Ur, under Ur-Nammu, an attempt was launched once again by Enlil to steer mankind away from "evil ways" to a course of "righteousness." Proclaiming a new code of justice and social behavior, Ur-Nammu "established equity in the land, banished malediction, ended violence and strife."

Expecting so much from this New Beginning, Enlil—for the first time—entrusted the guardianship of Nippur to Nannar and gave Ur-Nammu the necessary instructions for the restoration of the Ekur (which was damaged by Naram-Sin). Ur-Nammu marked the occasion by erecting a stela, showing him carrying the tools and basket of a builder (Fig. 94). When the work was completed, Enlil and Ninlil returned to Nippur to reside in their restored abode. "Enlil and Ninlil were happy there," a Sumerian inscription stated.

The Return-to-Righteous-Ways involved not only social justice among people, but also proper worship of the gods. To that effect Ur-Nammu, in addition to the great works in Ur, also restored and enlarged the edifices dedicated to Anu and Inanna at Erech, to

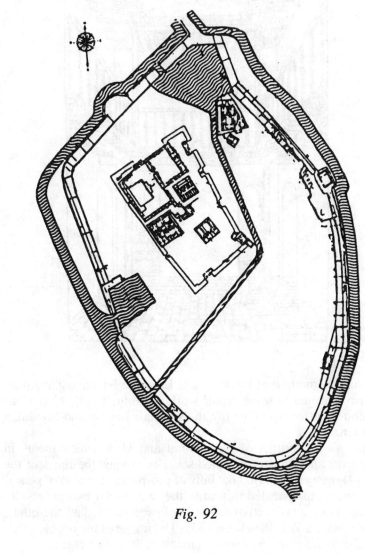

Fig. 92

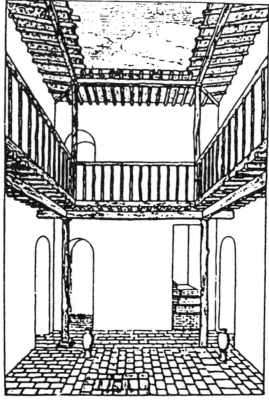

Fig. 93

Ninsun (his mother) at Ur, to Utu at Larsa, to Ninharsag at Adab; he also engaged in some repair work at Eridu, Enki's city. Conspicuously absent from the list are Ninurta's Lagash and Marduk's Babylon.

The social reforms of Ur-Nammu and Ur's achievements in commerce and industry have led scholars to view the times of the Third Dynasty as a period not only of prosperity, but also of peace. They were thus puzzled to find in the ruins of Ur two panels depicting its citizens' activities—one a Peace Panel, and the other, surprisingly, a War Panel (Fig. 95). The image of the people of Ur as trained and ready warriors seemed totally out of place.

Yet the facts, as told by the archaeological evidence of weaponry, military garb, and chariots of war, as well as in numerous inscriptions, belie the image of pacifism. Indeed, one of the first acts

Fig. 94

Fig. 95

of Ur-Nammu was to subdue Lagash and slay its governor, then occupy seven other cities.

The need for military measures was not limited to the initial phases of the ascendancy of Nannar and Ur. We know from inscriptions that after Ur and Sumer "enjoyed days of prosperity [and] rejoiced greatly with Ur-Nammu," after Ur-Nammu then rebuilt the Ekur in Nippur, Enlil found him worthy of holding the Divine Weapon; with it Ur-Nammu was to subdue "evil cities" in "foreign lands":

The Divine Weapon,
that which in the hostile lands
heaps up the rebels in piles,
to Ur-Nammu, the Shepherd,
He, the Lord Enlil, has given it to him;
Like a bull to crush the foreign land,
Like a lion to hunt it down;
To destroy the evil cities,
Clear them of opposition to the Lofty.

These are words reminiscent of biblical prophecies of divine wrath, through the medium of mortal kings, against "evil cities" and "sinful people"; they reveal that beneath the cloak of prosperity there was lurking a renewed warfare among the gods—a struggle for the allegiance of the masses of mankind.

The sad fact is that Ur-Nammu himself, becoming a mighty warrior, "The Might of Nannar," met a tragic death on the battlefield. "The enemy land revolted, the enemy land acted hostilely"; in a battle in that unnamed but distant land, Ur-Nammu's chariot got stuck in the mud; Ur-Nammu fell off it; "the chariot like a storm rushed along," leaving Ur-Nammu behind, "abandoned on the battlefield like a crushed jug." The tragedy was compounded when the boat returning his body to Sumer "in an unknown place had sunk; the waves sank it down, with him [Ur-Nammu] aboard."

When the news reached Ur, a great lament went up there; the people could not understand how such a Righteous Shepherd, one who had been just for the people and true to the gods, could have met such a disgraceful end. They could not understand why "the Lord Nannar did not hold him by the hand, why Inanna, Lady of Heaven, did not put her noble arm around his head, why the valiant Utu did not assist him." Why had these gods "step[ped] aside" when Ur-Nammu's bitter fate was determined? Surely it was a betrayal by the great gods:

How the fate of the hero has been changed!
Anu altered his holy word . . .
Enlil deceitfully changed his fate-decree . . .

The manner in which Ur-Nammu had died (2096 B.C.) may have accounted for the behavior of his successor, of whom one can use the biblical contempt for a king who "prostituted himself" and "did that which was evil in the view of the Lord." Named Shulgi, he was born under divine auspices: it was Nannar himself who had arranged for the child to be conceived at Enlil's shrine in Nippur, through a union between Ur-Nammu and Enlil's high priestess, so that "a little 'Enlil' . . . a child suitable for kingship and throne, shall be conceived."

The new king began his long reign by choosing to keep together his far-flung empire through peaceful means and religious reconciliation. As soon as he ascended the throne, he embarked on the building (or rebuilding) of a temple for Ninurta in Nippur; this enabled him to declare Ur and Nippur to be "Brother-Cities." He then built a ship—naming it after Ninlil—and sailed to the "Land of Flying for Life." His poems indicate that he imagined himself a second Gilgamesh, following in that earlier king's footsteps to the "Land of Living"—to the Sinai peninsula.

Landing at "The Place of the Ramp" (or "Land-fill Place"), Shulgi built there an altar to Nannar. Continuing his journey on land, Shulgi reached the Harsag—Ninharsag's High Mountain in the southern Sinai—and built there an altar, too. Winding his way in the peninsula, he reached the place called BAD.GAL.DINGIR (*Dur-Mah-Ilu* in Akkadian), "The Great Fortified Place of the Gods." He now was indeed emulating Gilgamesh, for Gilgamesh, arriving from the direction of the Dead Sea, had also stopped to pray and make offerings to the gods at that gateway place, situated between the Negev and the Sinai proper. There Shulgi built an altar to the "God Who Judges."

It was the eighth year of Shulgi's reign as he began the journey back to Sumer. His route via the Fertile Crescent began in Canaan and Lebanon, where he built altars at the "Place of Bright Oracles" and "The Snow-covered Place." It was a deliberately slow journey, intended to strengthen the imperial bonds with the distant provinces. It was as a result of this journey that Shulgi built a net-

work of roads that held the empire together politically and
militarily and also enhanced trade and prosperity. Getting personally acquainted with the local chieftains, Shulgi further cemented
his ties with them by arranging marriages for his daughters.

Shulgi returned to Sumer, boasting that he had learned four foreign languages. His imperial prestige was at its peak. In gratitude
he built for Nannar/Sin a shrine in the sacred precinct of Nippur. In
return he was rewarded with the titles "High Priest of Anu, Priest
of Nannar." Shulgi recorded the two ceremonies on his cylinder
seals (Figs. 96, 97).

Fig. 96

Fig. 97

But as time went by, Shulgi increasingly preferred the luxuries
of Ur to the rigors of the provinces, leaving their government to
Grand Emissaries. He spent his time composing self-laudatory
hymns, imagining himself a demigod. His delusions eventually

caught the attention of the greatest seductress of all—Inanna. Sensing a new opportunity, she invited Shulgi to Erech, making him "a man chosen for the vulva of Inanna" and engaging in lovemaking in the very temple dedicated to Anu. We quote Shulgi's own words:

> With valiant Utu, a friend as a brother,
> I drank strong drink
> in the temple founded by Anu.
> My minstrels sang for me the seven songs of love.
> Inanna, the queen, the vulva of heaven and earth,
> was by my side, banqueting in the temple.

As the unavoidable restiveness at home and abroad grew, Shulgi sought military support from the southeastern province of Elam. Arranging for his daughter to marry Elam's viceroy, Shulgi gave him as dowry the city of Larsa. In return the viceroy brought into Sumer Elamite troops, to serve Shulgi as a Foreign Legion. But instead of peace the Elamite troops brought more warfare, and the yearly records of Shulgi's reign speak of repeated destruction in the northern provinces. Shulgi attempted to retain his hold on the western provinces by peaceful means, and his thirty-seventh year of reign records a treaty with a local king named Puzur-Ish-Dagan—a name with clear Canaanite/Philistine connotations. The treaty enabled Shulgi to reclaim the title "King of the Four Regions." But the peace in the west did not last long. In his forty-first year (2055 B.C.) Shulgi received certain oracles from Nannar/Sin, and a major military expedition was launched against the Canaanite provinces. Within two years Shulgi could claim once more that he was "Hero, King of Ur, Ruler of the Four Regions."

The evidence suggests that Elamite troops were used in this campaign to subdue the provinces and that these foreign troops had advanced as far as the gateway to the Sinai. Their commander called himself "favorite of the God Who Judges, beloved by Inanna, occupier of Dur-Ilu." But no sooner had the occupying troops withdrawn than the unrest began again. In the year 2049 B.C. Shulgi ordered the building of "The Wall of the West" to protect Mesopotamia.

He stayed on the throne one more shaky year. Although, until the end of his reign, Shulgi continued to proclaim himself "a cherished of Nannar," he was no longer a "chosen" of Anu and Enlil. In their recorded view "the divine regulations he did not carry out, his righteousness he dirtied." Therefore, they decreed for him the "death of a sinner." The year was 2048 B.C.

Shulgi's successor on the throne of Ur was his son Amar-Sin. Though the first two years of his reign were recalled by their warfare, three years of peace did follow. But in the sixth year an uprising needed subduing in the northern district of Ashur, and in the seventh year—2041 B.C.—a major military campaign was required to suppress four western localities and "their lands."

The campaign, apparently, was not too successful, for it was not followed by the customary bestowal of titles on the king by Nannar. Instead we find that Amar-Sin turned his attention to Eridu—Enki's city!—establishing there a royal residence and assuming there priestly functions. This twist in religious filialties might have been prompted by the practical desire to gain control of Eridu's shipyards; for in the following (ninth) year, Amar-Sin set sail to the same "Place of the Ramp" where Shulgi had gone. But reaching the "Land of Flying for Life" he got no farther: he died of a scorpion's (or snake's) bite.

He was replaced on the throne by his brother Shu-Sin. The nine years of his reign (2038–2030 B.C.), though recording two military forays against northern localities, were more conspicuous by their defensive measures. These included the strengthening of the Wall of the West against the Amorites and the construction of two ships: the "Great Ship" and the "Ship of the Abzu." It looks as though Shu-Sin was preparing an escape by sea. . . .

When the next (and last) king of Ur, Ibbi-Sin, ascended the throne, raiders from the west were clashing with the Elamite mercenaries in Mesopotamia proper. Soon Sumer's heartland was under siege; the people of Ur and Nippur were huddled behind protective walls, and the influence of Nannar had shrunk to a small enclave.

Waiting in the wings, as once before, was Marduk. Believing that his time for supremacy had finally come, he left his land of exile and led his followers back to Babylon.

And then Awesome Weapons were unleashed, and disaster—unlike any that befell mankind since the Deluge—struck.

13

ABRAHAM:
THE FATEFUL YEARS

And it came to pass
in the days of Amraphel king of Shin'ar,
Ariokh king of Ellasar,
Khedorla'omer king of Elam,
and Tidhal king of Go'im—
That these made war
with Bera King of Sodom,
and with Birsha king of Gomorrah,
Shinab king of Admah,
and Shem-eber king of Zebi'im,
and with the king of Bela, which is Zoar.

Thus begins the biblical tale, in chapter 14 of Genesis, of an ancient war that pitted an alliance of four kingdoms of the East against five kings in Canaan. It is a tale that has evoked some of the most intense debate among scholars, for it connects the story of Abraham, the first Hebrew Patriarch, with a specific non-Hebrew event, and thus affords objective substantiation of the biblical record of the birth of a nation.

How wonderful it would have been, many have felt, if the various kings could be identified and the exact time of Abraham established! But even if Elam was known and Shin'ar identified as Sumer, who were the kings named, and which were the other lands of the East? Questioning the authenticity of biblical history unless independently verified, critics of the Bible asked: Why don't we find the names Khedorla'omer, Amraphel, Ariokh, and Tidhal mentioned in Mesopotamian inscriptions? And if they did not exist, if such a war had not taken place, how credible is the rest of the tale of Abraham?

For many decades the critics of the Old Testament seemed to prevail; then, as the nineteenth century was drawing to a close, the scholarly and religious worlds were astounded by the discovery of

Babylonian tablets naming Khedorla'omer, Ariokh, and Tidhal in a tale not unlike the biblical one.

The discovery was announced in a lecture by Theophilus Pinches to the Victoria Institute, London, in 1897. Having examined several tablets belonging to the Spartoli Collection in the British Museum, he found that they described a war of wide-ranging magnitude, in which a king of Elam, named Kudur-laghamar, led an alliance of rulers that included one called Eri-aku and another named Tud-ghula—names that easily could have been transformed into Hebrew as Khedor-la'omer, Ariokh, and Tidhal. Accompanying his published lecture with a painstaking transcript of the cuneiform writing and a translation thereof, Pinches could confidently claim that the biblical tale had indeed been supported by an independent Mesopotamian source.

With justified excitement the Assyriologists of that time agreed with Pinches's reading of the cuneiform names. The tablets indeed spoke of "Kudur-Laghamar, king of the land of Elam"—uncannily similar to the biblical "Khedorla'omer, king of Elam"; all scholars agreed that it was a perfect Elamite royal name, the prefix *Kudur* ("Servant") having been a component in the names of several Elamite kings, and *Laghamar* being the Elamite epithet-name for a certain deity. It was agreed that the second name, spelled *Eri-e-a-ku* in the Babylonian cuneiform script, stood for the original Sumerian ERI.AKU, meaning "Servant of the god Aku," *Aku* being a variant of the name of Nannar/Sin. It is known from a number of inscriptions that Elamite rulers of Larsa bore the name "Servant of Sin," and there was therefore little difficulty in agreeing that the biblical Ellasar, the royal city of the king Ariokh, was in fact Larsa. There was also unanimous agreement among the scholars for accepting that the Babylonian text's Tud-ghula was the equivalent of the biblical "Tidhal, king of Go'im"; and they agreed that by Go'im the Book of Genesis referred to the "nation-hordes" whom the cuneiform tablets listed as allies of Khedorla'omer.

Here, then, was the missing proof—not only of the veracity of the Bible and of the existence of Abraham, but also of an international event in which he had been involved!

But the excitement was not to last. "Unfortunately"—to use an expression of A. H. Sayce in an address to the Society of Biblical Archaeology eleven years later—a contemporary discovery, which should have upheld the one announced by Pinches, ended up sidetracking and even discrediting it.

The second discovery was announced by Vincent Scheil, who reported that he had found among the tablets in the Imperial Ottoman Museum in Constantinople a letter from the well-known Babylonian king Hammurabi, which mentions the very same Kudur-laghamar! Because the letter was addressed to a king of Larsa, Father Scheil concluded that the three were contemporaries and thus matched three of the four biblical kings of the East—Hammurabi being none other than "Amraphel, king of Shin'ar."

For a while it seemed that all the pieces of the puzzle had fallen into place; one can still find textbooks and biblical commentaries explaining that Amraphel stands for Hammurabi. The resulting conclusion that Abraham was a contemporary of this ruler seemed plausible, because it was then believed that Hammurabi reigned from 2067 to 2025 B.C., placing Abraham, the war of the kings, and the ensuing destruction of Sodom and Gomorrah at the end of the third millennium B.C.

However, when subsequent research convinced most scholars that Hammurabi reigned much later (from 1792 to 1750 B.C., according to *The Cambridge Ancient History*), the synchronization seemingly achieved by Scheil fell apart, and the whole bearing of the discovered inscriptions—even those reported by Pinches— came into doubt. Ignored were the pleas of Pinches that no matter with whom the three named kings were to be identified—that even if Khedorla'omer, Ariokh, and Tidhal of the cuneiform texts were not contemporaries of Hammurabi—the text's tale with its three names was still "a remarkable historical coincidence, and deserves recognition as such." In 1917, Alfred Jeremias *(Die sogenanten Kedorlaomer-Texte)* attempted to revive interest in the subject; but the scholarly community preferred to treat the Spartoli tablets with benign neglect.

They remained ignored in the basement of the British Museum for half a century, when M. C. Astour returned to the subject in a study at Brandeis University *(Political and Cosmic Symbolism in Genesis 14)*. Agreeing that the biblical and Babylonian editors of the respective texts drew from some older, common Mesopotamian source, he identified the four Kings of the East as known rulers: 1) of Babylon in the eighth century B.C.; 2) of Assyria in the thirteenth century B.C.; 3) of the Hittites in the sixteenth century B.C.; and 4) of Elam in the twelfth century B.C. As none were contemporaries of each other or of Abraham, he ingeniously suggested that the text was not a historical one but a work of religious philosophy, wherein the author used four diverse historic incidents to illustrate one moral (the fate of evil kings). The improbability of Astour's suggestion was soon pointed out in other scholarly publications; and with that, the interest in the *Khedorla'omer Texts* died again.

Yet the scholarly consensus that the biblical tale and the Babylonian texts drew on a much earlier, common source impels us to revive the plea of Pinches and his central argument: How can cuneiform texts, affirming the biblical background of a major war and naming three of the biblical kings, be ignored? Should the evidence—crucial, as we shall show, to the understanding of fateful years—be discarded simply because Amraphel was not Hammurabi?

The answer is that the Hammurabi letter found by Scheil should not have sidetracked the discovery reported by Pinches, because Scheil misread the letter. According to his rendition, Hammurabi promised a reward to Sin-Idinna, the king of Larsa, for his "heroism on the day of Khedorla'omer." This implied that the two were allies in a war against Khedorla'omer and thus contemporaries of that king of Elam. It was on this point that Scheil's find was discredited, for it contradicted both the biblical assertion that the three kings were allies and known historical facts: Hammurabi treated Larsa not as an ally but as an adversary, boasting that he "overthrew Larsa in battle," and attacked its sacred precinct "with the mighty weapon which the gods had given him."

A close examination of the actual text of Hammurabi's letter reveals that in his eagerness to prove the Hammurabi-Amraphel identification, Father Scheil reversed the letter's meaning: Hammurabi was not offering as a reward to return certain goddesses *to* the sacred precinct (the Emutbal) of Larsa; rather, he was demanding their return to Babylon *from* Larsa:

To Sin-Idinna
speaks thus Hammurabi regarding
the goddesses who in Emutbal
have been behind doors
from the days of Kudur-Laghamar,
in sackcloth attired:
When they ask them back from thee,
to my men hand them over;
The men shall grasp the hands of the goddesses;
To their abode they shall bring them.

The incident of the abduction of the goddesses had thus occurred in earlier times; they were held captive in the Emutbal "from the days of Khedorla'omer''; and Hammurabi was now demanding their return to Babylon, from where Khedorla'omer had taken them captive. This can only mean that Khedorla'omer's days were long before Hammurabi's time.

Supporting our reading of the Hammurabi letter found by Father Scheil in the Constantinople Museum is the fact that Hammurabi repeated the demand for the return of the goddesses to Babylon in yet another stiff message to Sin-Idinna, this time sending it by the hand of high military officers. This second letter is in the British Museum (No. 23,131) and its text was published by L. W. King in *The Letters and Inscriptions of Hammurabi:*

> Unto Sin-Idinna thus sayeth Hammurabi:
> I am now despatching Zikir-ilishu, the Transport Officer,
> and Hammurabi-bani, the Frontline Officer,
> that they may bring the goddesses who are in Emutbal.

That the goddesses were to be returned from Larsa to Babylon is made clear in the letter's further instructions:

> Thou shalt cause the goddesses to journey
> in a processional boat as in a shrine,
> that they may come to Babylon.
> The temple-women shall accompany them.
> For food of the goddesses thou shalt load
> pure cream and cereals unto the boat;
> sheep and provisions thou shalt put on board
> for the sustenance of the temple-women,
> [enough] for the journey to reach Babylon.
> And thou shalt appoint men to tow the boat,
> and chosen soldiers to bring the goddesses
> to Babylon in safety.
> Delay them not; let them speedily reach Babylon.

It is thus clear from these letters that Hammurabi—a foe, not an ally, of Larsa—was seeking restitution for events that had happened long before his time, in the days of Kudur-Laghamar, the Elamite regent of Larsa. The texts of the Hammurabi letters thus affirm the existence of Khedorla'omer and of Elamite reign in Larsa (''Ellasar''), and thus of key elements in the biblical tale.

Which is the period into which these key elements fit?

As historical records have established, it was Shulgi who in the twenty-eighth year of his reign (2068 B.C.) gave his daughter in marriage to an Elamite chieftain and granted him the city of Larsa as a dowry; in return the Elamites put a "foreign legion" of Elamite troops at Shulgi's disposal. These troops were employed by Shulgi to subdue the western provinces, including Canaan. It is thus in the last years of Shulgi's reign and when Ur was still an imperial capital under his immediate successor Amar-Sin that we find the historical time slot into which all the biblical and Mesopotamian records seem to fit perfectly.

It is in that time, we believe, that the search for the historical Abraham should be conducted; for—as we shall show—the tale of Abraham was interwoven with the tale of the fall of Ur, and his days were the last days of Sumer.

With the discrediting of the Amraphel-Hammurabi notion, the verification of the Age of Abraham became a free-for-all, some suggesting such late dates that made the first patriarch a descendant of the later kings of Israel. . . . But the exact dates of his time and events need no guessing: the information is provided by the Bible itself; all we have to do is accept its veracity.

The chronological calculations are surprisingly simple. Our starting point is 963 B.C., the year in which Solomon is believed to have assumed the kingship in Jerusalem. The Book of Kings states unequivocally that Solomon began the construction of the Temple of Yahweh in Jerusalem in the fourth year of his reign, completing it late in the eleventh year. I Kings 6:1 also states that "It came to pass in the four hundred and eightieth year after the Children of Israel were come out of the land of Egypt, in the fourth year of Solomon's reign over Israel . . . that he began to build the House of Yahweh." This statement is supported (with a slight difference) by the priestly tradition that there had been twelve priestly generations, of forty years each, from the Exodus to the time when Azariah "executed the priestly office in the temple that Solomon built in Jerusalem" (I Chronicles 5:36).

Both sources agree on the passage of 480 years, with this difference: one counts from the start of the temple's construction (960 B.C.) and the other from its completion (in 953 B.C.), when the priestly services could begin. This would set the Israelite Exodus from Egypt in either 1440 or 1433 B.C.; the latter date, we find, offers better synchronization with other events.

Based on the knowledge amassed by the beginning of this century, Egyptologists and biblical scholars had by then reached the conclusion that the Exodus had indeed taken place in the middle of the fifteenth century B.C. But then the weight of scholarly opinion shifted to a thirteenth-century date because it seemed to better fit the archaeological dating of various Canaanite sites, in line with the biblical record of the conquest of Canaan by the Israelites.

Yet such a new dating was not unanimously agreed upon. The most notorious city conquered was Jericho; and one of its prominent excavators (K. M. Kenyon) concluded that the pertinent destruction occurred circa 1560 B.C.—well ahead of the biblical events. On the other hand, Jericho's principal excavator, J. Garstang *(The Story of Jericho)*, held that the archaeological evidence points to its conquest sometime between 1400 and 1385 B.C. Adding to this the forty years of Israelite wandering in the wilderness after the departure from Egypt, he and others found archaeological support for an Exodus date sometime between 1440 and 1425 B.C.—a time frame that agrees with our suggestion of 1433 B.C.

For more than a century scholars have also searched through the extant Egyptian records for an Egyptian clue to the Exodus and its date. The only apparent references are found in the writings of Manetho. As quoted by Josephus in *Against Apion,* Manetho stated that "after the blasts of God's displeasure broke upon Egypt," a Pharaoh named Toumosis negotiated with the Shepherd People, "the people from the east, to evacuate Egypt and go whither they would, unmolested." They then left and traversed the wilderness, "and built a city in a country now called Judaea . . . and gave it the name Jerusalem."

Did Josephus adjust the writings of Manetho to suit the biblical tale, or did, in fact, the events concerning the sojourn, harsh treatment, and eventual Exodus of the Israelites occur in the reign of one of the well-known Pharaohs named Thothmes?

Manetho referred to "the king who expelled the pastoral people from Egypt" in a section devoted to the Pharaohs of the eighteenth dynasty. Egyptologists now accept as historical fact the expulsion of the Hyksos (the Asiatic "Shepherd Kings") in 1567 B.C. by the founder of the eighteenth dynasty, the Pharaoh Ahmosis (Amosis in Greek). This new dynasty, which established the New Kingdom in Egypt, might well have been the new dynasty of Pharaohs "who knew not Joseph" of which the Bible speaks (Exodus 1:8).

Theophilus, second-century Bishop of Antioch, also referred in his writings to Manetho and stated that the Hebrews were enslaved by the king Tethmosis, for whom they "built strong cities, Peitho and Rameses and On, which is Heliopolis''; then they departed Egypt under the Pharaoh ''whose name was Amasis.''

It thus appears from these ancient sources that the Israelites' troubles began under a Pharaoh named Thothmes and culminated with their departure under a successor named Amasis. What are the historical facts as they have been established by now?

After Ahmosis had expelled the Hyksos, his successors on the throne of Egypt—several of whom indeed bore the name Thothmes, as the ancient historians have stated—engaged in military campaigns in Greater Canaan, using the Way of the Sea as their invasion route. Thothmes I (1525–1512 B.C.), a professional soldier, put Egypt on a war footing and launched military expeditions into Asia as far as the Euphrates River. It is our belief that it was he who feared Israelite disloyalty—''when a war shall be called, they shall join our enemies''—and ordered therefore the killing of all newborn Israelite male babies (Exodus 1:9–16). By our calculations, Moses was born in 1513 B.C., the year before the death of Thothmes I.

J. W. Jack *(The Date of the Exodus)* and others, earlier this century, had wondered whether ''the Pharaoh's daughter'' who had retrieved the baby Moses from the river and then raised him in the royal palace could have been Hatshepsut, the eldest daughter of Thothmes I by his official spouse and thus the only royal princess of the time granted the high title ''The King's Daughter,'' a title identical to that given in the Bible. We believe that indeed it was she; and her continued treatment of Moses as an adopted son can be explained by the fact that after she had married the succeeding Pharaoh, her half-brother Thothmes II, she could not bear him a son.

Thothmes II died after a short reign. His successor, Thothmes III—mothered by a harem girl—was Egypt's greatest warrior-king, an ancient Napoleon in the view of some scholars. Of his seventeen campaigns against foreign lands to obtain tribute and captives for his major construction works, most were thrust into Canaan and Lebanon and as far north as the Euphrates River. We believe, as T. E. Peet *(Egypt and the Old Testament)* and others held earlier this century, that it was this Pharaoh, Thothmes III, who was the enslaver of the Israelites; for in his military expeditions he pushed northward as far as Naharin, the Egyptian name for the area on the upper Euphrates called in the Bible Aram-Naharim, where the kinfolk of the Hebrew Patriarchs had remained; and this could well explain the Pharaoh's fear (Exodus 1:10) that ''when there shall

happen to be a war, they [the Israelites] shall join unto our enemies.'' It was, we suggest, Thothmes III from whose death sentence Moses escaped to the wilderness of the Sinai after he had
learned of his Hebrew origins and openly sided with his people.

Thothmes III died in 1450 B.C. and was followed on the throne
by Amenophis II—the Amasis named by Theophilus quoting
Manetho. It was indeed ''after a long time, that the king of Egypt
died,'' (Exodus 2:23) that Moses dared return to Egypt to demand
of the successor—Amenophis II, in our opinion—to ''let my people
go.'' The reign of Amenophis II lasted from 1450 to 1425 B.C.; it is
our conclusion that the Exodus had taken place in 1433 B.C., exactly when Moses was eighty years old (Exodus 7:7).

Continuing our calculation backward, we now seek to establish
the date when the Israelites arrived in Egypt. Hebrew traditions assert a stay of 400 years, in accord with the Lord's statement to
Abraham (Genesis 15:13–14); so also states the New Testament
(Acts 7:6). The Book of Exodus, however, says that ''the sojourning of the Children of Israel who dwelt in Egypt was four hundred
and thirty years'' (Exodus 12:40–41). The qualifying of ''sojourn'' by the words ''who dwelt in Egypt'' might have been intended to distinguish between the Josephites (who had dwelt in
Egypt) and the newly arrived families of Joseph's brothers, who
just came ''to sojourn.'' If so, then the difference of thirty years
can be accounted for by the fact that Joseph was thirty years old
when made Chief of Egypt. This would leave intact the 400 figure
as the years of Israelite (rather than Josephite) sojourn in Egypt,
and place the event in 1833 B.C. (1,433 + 400).

The next clue is found in Genesis 47:8–9: ''And Joseph brought
in Jacob, his father, and stood him before the Pharaoh. . . . And
the Pharaoh said unto Jacob: 'How old art thou?' and Jacob said
unto Pharaoh: 'The days of my years are one hundred and
thirty.' '' Jacob, then, was born in 1963 B.C.

Now, Isaac was sixty years old when Jacob was born unto him
(Genesis 6:26); and Isaac was born unto his father Abraham when
Abraham was 100 years old (Genesis 21:5). Accordingly, Abra-
ham (who lived to be 175) was 160 years old when his grandson
Jacob was born. This places the birth of Abraham in 2123 B.C.

The century of Abraham—the hundred years from his birth to the
birth of his son and successor Isaac—was thus the century that witnessed the rise and fall of the Third Dynasty of Ur. Our reading of
biblical chronology and tales puts Abraham right in the middle of
the momentous events of that time—not as a mere observer but as

an active participant. Contrary to the assertions of advocates of biblical criticism that with the tale of Abraham the Bible loses interest in the general history of mankind and the Near East, to focus on the "tribal history" of one particular nation, the Bible in fact continues to relate (as it did with the tales of the Deluge and the Tower of Babel) events of major concern to mankind and its civilization: a war of unprecedented aspects and a disaster of a unique nature; events in which the Hebrew Patriarch played an important role. It is the tale of how the legacy of Sumer was salvaged when Sumer itself was doomed.

In spite of numerous studies concerning Abraham, the fact remains that all we really know about him is what we find in the Bible. Belonging to a family that traced its ancestry to the line of Shem, Abraham—then called *Abram*—was the son of Terah, his brothers being Harran and Nahor. When Harran died at an early age, the family was living in "Ur of the Chaldees." There, Abram married Sarai (later renamed Sarah).

Then "did Terah take Abram his son and Lot his grandson, the son of Harran, and Sarai his daughter-in-law the wife of Abram his son; and they left and went forth from Ur of the Chaldees to go to the land of Canaan; and they went as far as Harran, and dwelt there."

Archaeologists have found *Harran* ("The Caravanry"). Situated to the northwest of Mesopotamia at the foothills of the Taurus Mountains, it was a major crossroads in antiquity. As Mari controlled the southern gateway from Mesopotamia to the lands of the Mediterranean coast, so did Harran control the gateway of the northern route to the lands of Western Asia. Marking, at the time of the Third Dynasty of Ur, the limits of Nannar's domains where they bordered on Adad's Asia Minor, Harran was found by the archaeologists to have been a mirror image of Ur in its layout and in its worship of Nannar/Sin.

No explanation is given in the Bible for leaving Ur, and there is also no time stated, but we can guess the answers if we relate the departure to events in Mesopotamia in general and in Ur in particular.

We know that Abraham was seventy-five when he proceeded later on from Harran to Canaan. The tenor of the biblical narrative suggests a long stay at Harran and depicts Abraham on his arrival there as a young man with a new bride. If Abraham, as we have concluded, was born in 2123 B.C., he was a child of ten when Ur-

Nammu ascended the throne in Ur, when Nannar was favored for the first time with the trusteeship over Nippur. And he was a young man of twenty-seven when Ur-Nammu inexplicably fell from Anu's and Enlil's favor, slain on a distant battlefield. We have described the traumatic effect of the event on the people of Mesopotamia, the shock it had given to their faith in Nannar's omnipotence and the fidelity of Enlil's word.

The year of Ur-Nammu's fall was 2096 B.C. Could it not have been the year when—under the impact of the event or as a consequence thereof—Terah and his family left Ur for a faraway destination, stopping off at Harran, the Ur away from Ur?

All through the following years of Ur's decline and Shulgi's profanities, the family stayed on in Harran. Then, suddenly, the Lord acted again:

And Yahweh said unto Abram:
"Get thee out of thy country
and out of thy birthplace
and from thy father's house,
unto the land which I will show thee" . . .
And Abram departed as Yahweh had spoken unto him,
and Lot went with him.
And Abram was seventy-five years old when he left Harran.

Once again, no reason is given for the crucial move. But the chronological clue is most revealing. When Abraham was seventy-five years old, the year was 2048 B.C.—the very year of Shulgi's downfall!

Because Abraham's family (Genesis 11) directly continued the line of Shem, Abraham has been considered a Semite, one whose background, cultural heritage, and language were Semitic, as distinct (in scholars' minds) from the non-Semitic Sumerians and the later Indo-Europeans. But in the original biblical sense, all the peoples of greater Mesopotamia were descended of Shem, "Semite" and "Sumerian" alike. There is nothing in the Bible that suggests—as some scholars have begun to hold—that Abraham and his family were Amorites (i.e., western Semites) who had come as immigrants to Sumer and then returned to their original abode. On the contrary: There is everything to support the image of a family rooted in Sumer from its earliest beginnings, hastily uprooted from its country and birthplace and told to go to an unfamiliar land.

The correspondence between two biblical events with the dates of two major Sumerian events—and of more to come—must serve as an indication of a direct connection between them all. Abraham emerges not as the son of immigrant aliens but as the scion of a family directly involved in Sumerian affairs of state!

In their search for the answer to the question of "Who Was Abraham," scholars have seized upon the similarity between his designation as a Hebrew *(Ibri)* and the term *Hapiru* (which in the Near East could transform to *Habiru*) by which the Assyrians and Babylonians in the eighteenth and seventeenth centuries B.C. called bands of pillaging western Semites. At the end of the fifteenth century B.C., the commander of an Egyptian garrison in Jerusalem asked his king for reinforcements against approaching Hapiru. Scholars have taken all that as evidence for the notion that Abraham was a western Semite.

Many scholars doubt, however, whether the term denotes an ethnic group at all, wondering whether the word was not a descriptive noun simply meaning "marauders" or "invaders." The suggestion that *Ibri* (clearly from the verb "to cross") and *Hapiru* are one and the same entails substantial philological and etymological problems. There are also great chronological inconsistencies, all of which gave rise to serious objections to this suggested solution for the identity of Abraham, especially when the biblical data is compared with the "bandit" connotation of the term Hapiru. Thus the Bible relates incidents concerning water wells, which show that Abraham was careful to avoid conflict with local residents as he journeyed through Canaan. When Abraham became involved in the War of the Kings, he refused to share in the booty. This is not the behavior of a marauding barbarian but rather of a person of high standards of conduct. Coming to Egypt, Abraham and Sarah were taken to the Pharaoh's court; in Canaan, Abraham made treaties with the local rulers. This is not the image of a nomad pillaging others' settlements; it is the image of a personage of high standing skilled in negotiation and diplomacy.

It was out of such considerations that Alfred Jeremias, then a leading Assyriologist and professor of the history of religion at the Leipzig University, announced in the 1930 edition of his master work *Das Alte Testament im Lichte des Alten Orients* that "in his intellectual makeup Abraham was a Sumerian." He enlarged on this conclusion in a 1932 study entitled *Der Kosmos von Sumer:* "Abraham was not a Semitic Babylonian but a Sumerian." Abraham, he suggested, headed the Faithful whose reformation sought to raise Sumerian society to higher religious levels.

These were audacious ideas in a Germany witnessing the rise of Nazism with its racial theories. Soon after the assumption of power by Hitler, the heretic suggestions of Jeremias were strongly put down by Nikolaus Schneider in a reply entitled *War Abraham Sumerer?* Abraham was neither a Sumerian nor a man of pure descent, he concluded: "From the time of the reign of the Akkadian king Sargon in Ur, the home-place of Abraham, there was never there a pure, unmixed Sumerian population and a homogenous Sumerian culture."

The ensuing upheavals and World War II cut off further debate on the subject. Regrettably, the thread discerned by Jeremias has not been picked up. Yet all the biblical and Mesopotamian evidence tells us that Abraham was indeed a Sumerian.

The Old Testament, in fact (Genesis 17:1–16), provides us with the time and manner in which Abraham was transformed from a Sumerian nobleman to a west Semitic potentate, under a covenant between him and his God. Amid a ritual of circumcision, his Sumerian name AB.RAM ("Father's Beloved") was changed to the Akkadian/Semitic *Abraham* ("Father of a Multitude of Nations") and that of his wife SARAI ("Princess") was adapted to the Semitic *Sarah.*

It was only when he was ninety-nine years old that Abraham became a "Semite."

As we decipher the age-old enigma of Abraham's identity and his Mission to Canaan, it is in Sumerian history, customs, and language that we shall search for the answers.

Is it not naive to assume that for the Mission to Canaan, for the birth of a nation, and for kingship over all the lands from the border of Egypt to the border of Mesopotamia, the Lord would choose someone at random, picking up anyone in the streets of Ur? The young woman whom Abraham married bore the epithet-name Princess; since she was a half-sister of Abraham ("Indeed she is my sister, the daughter of my father but not the daughter of my mother"), we can take it for granted that either Abraham's father or Sarah's mother was of royal descent. Since the daughter of Harran, Abraham's brother, also bore a royal name (*Milkha—* "Queenly"), it follows that it was through the father of Abraham that the royal ancestry flowed. In dealing with Abraham's family we thus deal with a family of Sumer's highest echelons; people of a noble deportment and elegant dress as found depicted on various Sumerian statues (Fig. 98).

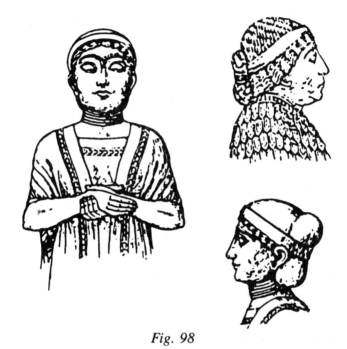

Fig. 98

It was a family that not only could claim descent from Shem but which kept family records tracing its lineage through generations of firstborn sons: Arpakhshad and Shelach and Eber; Peleg, Re'u, and Serug; Nahor and Terah and Abraham; taking the family's recorded history back for no less than three centuries!

What do the epithet-names signify? If *Shelach* ("Sword") was born, as chapter 11 of Genesis states, 258 years before Abraham, he was born in 2381 B.C. That indeed was the time of the strife that brought Sargon to the throne in the new capital *Agade* ("United"), symbolizing the unification of the lands and a new era. Sixty-four years later the family named its firstborn descendant *Peleg* ("Division"), "for in his days the land divided." It was the time, in fact, when Sumer and Akkad were torn apart after Sargon's attempt to remove the sacred soil from Babylon and his consequent death.

But of greatest interest, to this very day, has been the meaning of the name *Eber* and the reason for bestowing it upon the firstborn in 2351 B.C. and from which has stemmed the biblical term *Ibri* ("Hebrew") by which Abraham and his family identified themselves. It clearly stems from the root word meaning "to cross," and the best scholars had to offer in explanation was to seek the Habiru/Hapiru connection, which we have already mentioned (and discarded). This erroneous interpretation has stemmed from the search for the meaning of the epithet-name in Western Asia. It is our conviction that instead the answer is to be found in the Sumerian origins and the Sumerian language of Abraham and his ancestors. Such a look at the Sumerian roots of the family and the name provides an answer that startles with its simplicity.

The term *Ibri* ("Hebrew") by which Abraham and his family identified themselves clearly stemmed from *Eber,* the father of Peleg, and from the root "to cross." Instead of seeking the meaning of the epithet-name in the Hapiru notions or in Western Asia, it is our conviction that the answer is to be found in the Sumerian origins and the Sumerian language of Abraham and his ancestors. Then, a new solution emerges with startling simplicity:

The biblical suffix "i," when applied to a person, meant "a native of"; Gileadi meant a native of Gilead and so on. Likewise, *Ibri* meant a native of the place called "Crossing"; and that, precisely, was the Sumerian name for Nippur: NI.IB.RU—the Crossing Place, the place where the pre-Diluvial grids crisscrossed each other, the original Navel of the Earth, the olden Mission Control Center.

The dropping of the *n* in transposing from Sumerian to Akkadian/Hebrew was a frequent occurrence. In stating that Abraham was an Ibri, the Bible simply meant that Abraham was a *Ni-ib-ri, a man of Nippurian origin!*

The fact that Abraham's family migrated to Harran from Ur has been taken by scholars to imply that Ur was also Abraham's birthplace; but that is not stated anywhere in the Bible. On the contrary, the command to Abraham to go to Canaan and leave for good his past abodes lists three separate entities: his father's house (which was then in Harran); his land (the city-state of Ur); and his birthplace (which the Bible does not identify). Our suggestion that Ibri means a native of Nippur solves the problem of Abraham's true birthplace.

As the name Eber indicates, it was in his time—the middle of the twenty-fourth century B.C.—that the family's association with Nippur had begun. Nippur was never a royal capital; rather, it was a consecrated city, Sumer's "religious center," as scholars put it. It was also the place where the knowledge of astronomy was entrusted to the high priests and thus the place where the calendar—

the relationship between the Sun, Earth, and Moon in their orbits—was originated.

Scholars have recognized that our present-day calendars derive from the original Nippurian calendar. All the evidence shows that the Nippurian calendar began circa 4000 B.C., in the age of Taurus. In this we find yet another confirmation of the umbilical cord connecting the Hebrews with Nippur: The Jewish calendar still continues to count the years from an enigmatic beginning in 3760 B.C. (so that in 1983 the Jewish year was 5743). It has been assumed that this is a count "from the beginning of the world"; but the actual statement by Jewish sages was that this is the number of years that had passed "since counting [of years] began." We suggest that it means, since the introduction of the calendar in Nippur.

In the ancestral family of Abraham we thus find a priestly family of royal blood, a family headed by a Nippurian high priest who was the only one allowed into the temple's innermost chamber, there to receive the deity's word and convey it to king and people.

In this regard the name of Abraham's father, Terah, is of great interest. Seeking clues only in the Semitic environment, biblical scholars regard the name, as those of Harran and Nahor, as mere toponyms (names that personify places), holding that there were cities by such names in central and northern Mesopotamia. Assyriologists searching the Akkadian terminology (being the first Semitic language) could only find that *Tirhu* meant "an artifact or vessel for magical purposes." But if we turn t the Sumerian language, we find that the cuneiform sign for *Tirhu* stemmed directly from that of an object called in Sumerian DUG.NAMTAR —literally, a "Fate Speaker"—a Pronouncer of Oracles!

Terah, then, was an Oracle Priest, one assigned to approaching the "Stone that Whispers" to hear the deity's words and communicate them (with or without an interpretation) to the lay hierarchy. It was a function assumed in later times by the Israelite High Priest, who alone was allowed to enter the Holy of Holies, approach the *Dvir* ("Speaker"), and "hear the voice [of the Lord] speak unto him from off the overlay which is upon the Ark of the Covenant, from between the two Cherubim." During the Israelite Exodus, at Mount Sinai the Lord proclaimed that his covenant with the descendants of Abraham meant that "ye shall be unto me a kingdom of priests." It was a statement that reflected the status of Abraham's own descent: a royal priesthood.

Farfetched as these conclusions may sound, they are in full accord with the Sumerian practices whereby kings appointed their daughters and sons, and often themselves, to high-priestly positions, resulting in the commingling of the royal and priestly lineages. Votive inscriptions found at Nippur (as those by the archaeological expeditions of the University of Pennsylvania) confirm that the kings of Ur cherished the title "Pious Shepherd of Nippur" and performed there priestly functions; and the governor of Nippur (PA.TE.SI NI.IB.RU) was also the Foremost UR.ENLIL ("Enlil's Foremost Servant").

Some of the names borne by these royal-priestly VIPs resembled Abraham's Sumerian name (AB.RAM), also beginning with the component AB ("Father" or "Progenitor"); such, for example, was the name AB.BA.MU of a governor of Nippur during Shulgi's reign.

That a family of people so closely associated with Nippur that they were called "Nippurians" (i.e., "Hebrews") were nevertheless holding high positions in Ur is a suggestion that is in complete accord with the actual circumstances prevailing in Sumer at the time indicated by us; for it was then, at the time of the Ur III Dynasty, that for the first time in divine affairs and Sumerian history Nannar and the king of Ur were granted trusteeship over Nippur, combining the religious and secular functions. It thus could have well been that when Ur-Nammu assumed the throne in Ur, Terah moved with his family from Nippur to Ur, perhaps to serve as a liaison between the temple in Nippur and the royal palace in Ur. Their stay in Ur lasted throughout Ur-Nammu's reign; it was in the year of his death, as we have shown, that the family left Ur for Harran.

What the family did at Harran is nowhere stated, but considering the royal lineage and priestly standing, it must have belonged to the hierarchy of Harran. The ease with which Abraham dealt, later on, with various kings suggests that he was involved in Harran's foreign affairs; his special friendship with the Hittite residents of Canaan, who were known for their military experience, may shed a light on the question of where Abraham himself had acquired the military proficiency which he employed so successfully during the War of the Kings.

Ancient traditions also depict Abraham as greatly versed in astronomy—a knowledge then valuable for long journeys guided by the stars. According to Josephus, Berossus referred to Abraham, without naming him, when he wrote of the rise "among the Chaldeans, of a certain righteous and great man who was well seen in astronomy.'' (If Berossus, the Babylonian historian, had indeed referred to Abraham, the significance of the inclusion of the Hebrew Patriarch in Babylonian chronicles far exceeds the mere notation of his knowledge of astronomy.)

All during the ignominious years of Shulgi's reign, the family of Terah stayed at Harran. Then, on Shulgi's demise, the divine order came to proceed to Canaan. Terah was already quite old, and Nahor, his son, was to stay on with him in Harran. The one chosen for the mission was Abraham—himself a mature man of seventy-five. The year was 2048 B.C.; it marked the beginning of twenty-four fateful years—eighteen years encompassing the war-filled reigns of the two immediate successors of Shulgi (Amar-Sin and Shu-Sin) and six years of Ibbi-Sin, the last sovereign king of Ur.

It is undoubtedly more than mere coincidence that Shulgi's death was the signal not only for a move by Abraham, but also for a realignment among the Near Eastern gods. It was exactly when Abraham, accompanied (as we learn later) by an elite military corps, left Harran—the gateway to the Hittite lands—that the exiled and wandering Marduk appeared in ''Hatti land.'' Moreover, the remarkable coincidence is that Marduk stayed there through the same twenty-four Fateful Years, the years that culminated with the great Disaster.

The evidence for Marduk's movements is a tablet (Fig. 99) found in the library of Ashurbanipal, in which an aging Marduk tells of his erstwhile wanderings and eventual return to Babylon:

> O great gods, learn my secrets.
> As I girdle my belt, my memories remember:
> I am the divine Marduk, a great god.
> I was cast off for my sins,
> to the mountains I have gone.
> In many lands I have been a wanderer:
> From where the sun rises to where it sets I went.
> To the heights of Hatti-land I went.
> In Hatti-land I asked an oracle
> [about] my throne and my Lordship;
> In its midst [I asked]: ''Until when?''
> 24 years, in its midst, I nested.

The appearance of Marduk in Asia Minor—implying an unexpected alliance with Adad—was thus the other side of the coin of Abraham's rush to Canaan. We learn from the balance of the text

Fig. 99

that Marduk sent from his new place of exile emissaries and supplies (via Harran) to his followers in Babylon, and trading agents
into Mari, thereby making inroads into both gateways—the one beholden to Nannar/Sin and the other to Inanna/Ishtar.

As on a signal, with the death of Shulgi, the whole ancient world
came astir. The House of Nannar had been discredited, and the
House of Marduk saw its final prevailing hour approaching. While
Marduk himself was still excluded from Mesopotamia, his firstborn son, Nabu, was making converts to his father's cause. His
base of operations was his own "cult center," Borsippa; but his efforts encompassed all the lands, including Greater Canaan.

It was against this background of fast developments that Abraham was ordered to go to Canaan. Though silent concerning Abraham's mission, the Old Testament is clear regarding his destination: Moving expeditiously to Canaan, Abraham and his wife, his nephew Lot, and their entourage continued swiftly southward. There was a stopover at Shechem, where the Lord spoke to Abraham. "Then he removed from there to the Mount, and encamped east of Beth-El; and he built there an altar to Yahweh and called the name of Yahweh." Beth-El, whose name meant "God's House"—a site to which Abraham kept coming back—was in the vicinity of Jerusalem and its hallowed Mount, Mount Moriah ("Mount of Directing"), upon whose Sacred Rock the Ark of the Covenant was placed when Solomon built the Temple of Yahweh in Jerusalem.

From there "Abram journeyed farther, still going toward the Negev." The Negev—the dry region where Canaan and the Sinai peninsula merge—was clearly Abraham's destination. Several divine pronouncements designated the Brook of Egypt (nowadays called Wadi El-Arish) as the southern boundary of Abraham's domain, and the oasis of Kadesh-Barnea as his southernmost outpost (see map). What was Abraham to do in the Negev, whose very name ("The Dryness") bespoke its aridity? What was there that required the patriarch's hurried, long journey from Harran and impelled his presence among the miles upon miles of barren land?

The significance of Mount Moriah—Abraham's first focus of interest—was that in those days it served, together with its sister mounts Mount Zophim ("Mount of Observers") and Mount Zion ("Mount of Signal"), as the site of Mission Control Center of the Anunnaki. The significance of the Negev, its only significance, was that it was the gateway to the Spaceport in the Sinai.

Subsequent narrative informs us that Abraham had military allies in the region and that his entourage included an elite corps of several hundred fighting men. The biblical term for them—*Naar*—has been variously translated as "retainer" or simply "young man"; but studies have shown that in Hurrian the word denoted riders or cavalrymen. In fact, recent studies of Mesopotamian texts dealing with military movements list among the men of the chariots and the cavalry LU.NAR ("Nar-men") who served as fast riders. We find an identical term in the Bible (I Samuel 30:17): after King David attacked an Amalekite camp, the only ones to escape were "four hundred *Ish-Naar*"—literally, *"Nar*-men" or LU.NAR—"who were riding the camels."

In describing Abraham's fighting men as *Naar* men, the Old Testament thus informs us that he had with him a corps of cavalry-men, in all probability camel riders rather than horsemen. He may have picked up the idea of such a fast-riding fighting force from the Hittites on whose boundary Harran was located, but for the arid areas of the Negev and the Sinai, camels rather than horses were better suited.

The emerging image of Abraham not as a sheepherding nomad but as an innovative military commander of royal descent may not fit the customary image of this Hebrew patriarch, but it is in accord with ancient recollections of Abraham. Thus, quoting earlier sources concerning Abraham, Josephus (first century A.D.) wrote of him: "Abraham reigned at Damascus, where he was a foreigner, having come with an army out of the land above Babylon" from which, "after a long time, the Lord got him up and removed from that country together with his men and he went to the land then called the land of Canaan but now the land of Judaea."

The mission of Abraham was a military one: to protect the space facilities of the Anunnaki—the Mission Control Center and the Spaceport!

After a short stay in the Negev Abraham traversed the Sinai peninsula and came to Egypt. Evidently no ordinary nomads, Abraham and Sarah were at once taken to the royal palace. By our reckoning the time was circa 2047 B.C., when the Pharaohs then ruling in Lower (northern) Egypt—who were not followers of Amen ("The Hiding God" Ra/Marduk)—were facing a strong challenge from the princes of Thebes in the south, where Amen was deemed supreme. We can only guess what matters of state—alliances, joint defenses, divine commands—were discussed between the beleaguered Pharaoh and the Ibri, the Nippurian general. The Bible is silent on this as well as on the length of stay. (The *Book of Jubilees* states that the sojourn lasted five years). When the time came for Abraham to return to the Negev, he was accompanied by a large retinue of the Pharaoh's men.

"And Abraham went from Egypt, he and his wife and Lot with him, up onto the Negev." He was "heavy with flocks" of sheep and cattle for food and clothing, as well as with asses and camels for his fast riders. Again he went to Beth-El to "call the name of Yahweh," seeking instructions. A separation from Lot followed, the nephew choosing to reside with his own flocks in the Plain of the Jordan, "which was watered as the Garden of the Lord, before Yahweh destroyed Sodom and Gomorrah." Abraham went on to the hill country, settling on the highest peak near Hebron, from where he could see in all directions; and the Lord said unto him: "Go, cross the country in the length and the breadth of it, for unto thee shall I give it."

It was soon thereafter, "in the days of Amraphel king of Shin'ar," that the military expedition of the eastern alliance had taken place.

"Twelve years they [the Canaanite kings] served Khedorla'o-mer; in the thirteenth year they rebelled; and in the fourteenth year there came Khedorla'omer and the kings that were with him" (Genesis 14:4–5).

Scholars have long searched the archaeological records for the events described in the Bible; their efforts have been unsuccessful because they searched for Abraham in the wrong era. But if we are right in *our* chronology, a simple solution to the "Amraphel" problem becomes possible. It is a new solution, yet one that rests on scholarly suggestions made (and ignored) almost a century ago.

Back in 1875, comparing the traditional reading of the name with its spelling in early biblical translations, F. Lenormant *(La Langue Primitive de la Chaldée)* had suggested that the correct reading should be *"Amar-pal,"* as written out phonetically in the Septuagint (the third century B.C. translation of the Old Testament into Greek from the original Hebrew). Two years later D. H. Haigh, writing in the *Zeitschrift für Ägyptische Sprache und Altertumskunde,* also adopted the reading "Amarpal" and, stating that "the second element [of the king's name] is a name of the Moon-god [Sin]," declared: "I have long been convinced of the identity of Amar-pal as one of the kings of Ur."

In 1916, Franz M. Böhl *(Die Könige von Genesis 14)* suggested again—without success—that the name be read, as in the Septuagint, "Amar-pal," explaining that it meant "Seen by the Son"—a royal name in line with other royal names in the Near East, such as the Egyptian Thoth-mes ("Seen by Thoth"). (For some reason Böhl and others have neglected to mention the no-less-significant fact that the Septuagint spelled out the name of Khedorla'omer *Khodologomar*—almost identical to the Kudur-lagamar of the Spartoli tablets.)

Pal (meaning "son") was indeed a common suffix in Mesopotamian royal names, standing for the deity considered the favorite Divine Son. Since in Ur the god deemed to have been the Favored Son was Nannar/Sin, we suggest that *Amar-Sin* and *Amar-pal* were, in Ur, one and the same name.

Our identification of "Amarphal" of Genesis 14 as Amar-Sin, third king of Ur's Third Dynasty, meshes perfectly the biblical and the Sumerian chronologies. The biblical tale of the War of the Kings places the event soon after Abraham's return to the Negev from Egypt but before the tenth anniversary of his arrival in Canaan; i.e., between 2042 and 2039 B.C. The reign of Amar-Sin/Amar-Pal lasted from 2047 to 2039 B.C.; accordingly, the war had taken place in the latter part of his reign.

The year formulas for Amar-Sin's reign pinpoint his seventh year—2041 B.C.—as the year of the major military expedition to the western provinces. The biblical data (Genesis 14:4-5) asserts that this took place in the fourteenth year after the Elamites under Khedorla'omer had subjugated the Canaanite kings; and the year 2041 was indeed fourteen years after Shulgi, having received Nannar's oracles, had launched in 2055 B.C. the military expedition led by Elamites into Canaan.

Our synchronization of biblical and Sumerian events and dates unfolds the following sequence and upholds every time factor reported in the Bible:

2123 B.C. • Abraham born in Nippur to his father Terah.
2113 B.C. • Ur-Nammu enthroned in Ur, given guardianship of Nippur.
  Terah and his family move to Ur.
2095 B.C. • Shulgi ascends throne after death of Ur-Nammu.
  Terah and his family leave Ur for Harran.
2055 B.C. • Shulgi receives Nannar's oracles, sends Elamite troops to Canaan.
2048 B.C. • Shulgi's death ordered by Anu and Enlil.
  Abraham, seventy-five years old, ordered to leave Harran for Canaan.
2047 B.C. • Amar-Sin ("Amarpal") ascends the throne of Ur.
  Abraham leaves the Negev for Egypt.
2042 B.C. • Canaanite kings switch allegiance to "other gods."
  Abraham returns from Egypt with elite corps.
2041 B.C. • Amar-Sin launches the War of the Kings.

Who were the "other gods" that were winning the allegiance of Canaanite cities? They were Marduk, scheming from nearby exile, and his son, Nabu, who was roaming eastern Canaan, gaining supremacy and adherents. As biblical place names indicate, the

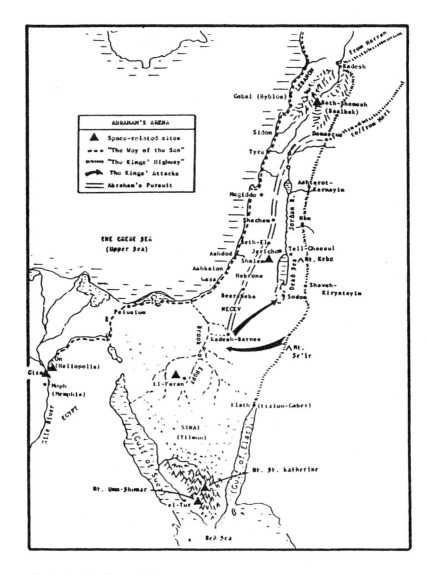

whole land of Moab had come under Nabu's influence: the land was also known as the Land of Nabu and many sites there were named in his honor; the highest peak retained its name—Mount Nebo—through the millennia that followed.

This is the historical frame into which the Old Testament has fitted the invasion from the east. But even seen from the biblical viewpoint, which compressed the Mesopotamian tales of the gods into a monotheistic mold, it was an unusual war: the ostensible purpose—the suppression of a rebellion—turns out to have been a secondary aspect of the war; the real target—a crossroads oasis in a wilderness—was never reached.

Taking the southern route from Mesopotamia to Canaan, the invaders proceeded southward in Transjordan, along the King's Highway, attacking in succession key outposts guarding crossing points on the Jordan River: Ashterot-Karnayim in the north; Ham in the center; and Shaveh-Kiryatayim in the south.

According to the biblical tale, a place called El-Paran was the real target of the invaders, but it was never reached by them. Coming down Transjordan and circling the Dead Sea, the invaders passed by Mount Se'ir and advanced "toward El-Paran, which is upon the Wilderness." But they were forced to "swing back by Ein-Mishpat, which is Kadesh." El-Paran ("God's Gloried Place"?) was never reached; somehow the invaders were beaten back at Ein-Mishpat, also known as Kadesh or Kadesh-Barnea.

It was only then, as they turned back toward Canaan, that "Thereupon the king of Sodom and the king of Gomorrah and the king of Admah and the king of Zebi'im and the king of Bela, which is Zoar, marched forth and engaged them in battle in the Vale of Siddim." (See map.)

The battle with these Canaanite kings was thus a late phase of the war and not its first purpose. Almost a century ago, in a thorough study titled *Kadesh-Barnea,* H. C. Trumbull had concluded that the true target of the invaders was El-Paran, which he correctly identified as the fortified oasis of Nakhl in Sinai's central plain. But neither he nor others could explain why a great alliance would launch an army to a destination a thousand miles away and fight gods and men to reach an isolated oasis in a great, desolate plain.

But why had they gone there, and who was it that blocked their way at Kadesh-Barnea, forcing the invaders to turn back?

There have been no answers; and no answers can make sense except the ones offered by us: The only significance of the destination was its Spaceport, and the one who blocked the advance at Kadesh-Barnea was Abraham. From earlier times Kadesh-Barnea was the closest place where men could approach in the region of the Spaceport without special permission. Shulgi had gone there to pray and make offerings to the God Who Judges, and nearly a thousand years before him the Sumerian king Gilgamesh stopped there to obtain the special permission. It was the place the Sumerians called BAD.GAL.DINGIR and Sargon of Akkad *Dur-Mah-Ilani*, clearly listing it in his inscriptions as a place in Tilmun (the Sinai peninsula).

It was the place, we suggest, which the Bible called Kadesh-Barnea; and there Abraham stood with his elite troops, blocking the invaders' advance to the Spaceport proper.

The hints in the Old Testament become a detailed tale in the *Khedorlaomer Texts,* which make clear that the war was intended to prevent the return of Marduk and thwart the efforts of Nabu to gain access to the Spaceport. These texts not only name the very same kings who are mentioned in the Bible but even repeat the biblical detail of the switch of allegiance "in the thirteenth year"!

As we return to the *Khedorlaomer Texts* to obtain the details for the biblical frame, we should bear in mind that they were written by a Babylonian historian who favored Marduk's desire to make Babylon "the heavenward navel in the four regions." It was to thwart this that the gods opposing Marduk ordered Khedorla'omer to seize and defile Babylon:

> The gods . . .
> to Kudur-Laghamar, king of the land Elam,
> they decreed: "Descend there!"
> That which to the city was bad he performed;
> In Babylon, the precious city of Marduk,
> sovereignty he seized;
> In Babylon, the city of the king of the gods, Marduk,
> kingship he overthrew;
> To herds of dogs its temple he made a den;
> Flying ravens, loud shrieking, their dung dropped there.

The despoiling of Babylon was only the beginning. After the "bad deeds" were done there, Utu/Shamash sought action against Nabu, who (he said in accusation) had subverted the allegiance of a certain king to his father, Nannar/Sin. It happened, the *Khedorla'-omer Text* states, in the *thirteenth year* (just as Genesis 14 states):

> Before the gods the son of his father [came];
> On that day Shamash, the Bright One,
> against the lord of lords, Marduk [he said]:
> "The faithfulness of his heart [the king] betrayed—
> in the time of the thirteenth year

a falling-out against my father [he had];
to his faith-keeping the king ceased to attend;
all this Nabu has caused to happen.''

The assembled gods, thus alerted to the role of Nabu in the
spreading rebellions, put together a coalition of loyal kings and appointed the Elamite Kudur-Laghamar as its military commander.
Their first order was that ''Borsippa, the stronghold [of Nabu],
with weapons be despoiled.'' Carrying out the order, ''Kudur-
Laghamar, with wicked thoughts against Marduk, the shrine of
Borsippa with fire he destroyed and its sons with a sword he slew.''
Then, the military expedition against the rebellious kings was ordered. The Babylonian text lists the targets to be attacked and the
names of their attackers; we easily recognize the biblical names
among them: Eriaku (Ariokh) was to attack Shebu (Beer-Sheba)
and Tud-Ghula (Tidhal) was to ''smite with a sword the sons of
Gaza.''

Acting in accordance with an oracle of Ishtar, the army put
together by the Kings of the East arrived in Transjordan. First
to be attacked was a stronghold in ''the high land,'' then
Rabattum. The route was the same as the one described in the
Bible: from the highland in the north through the district of
Rabat-Amon in the center, southward around the Dead Sea.
Thereafter, Dur-Mah-Ilani was to be captured, and the Canaanite cities (including Gaza and Beer-Sheba in the Negev)
were to be punished. But at Dur-Mah-Ilani, according to the
Babylonian text, ''the son of the priest, whom the gods in their
true counsel had anointed,'' stood in the invaders' way and
''the despoiling prevented.''

Could the Babylonian text indeed refer to Abraham, the son of
Terah the priest, and spell out his role in turning back the invaders?
The possibility is strengthened by the fact that the Mesopotamian
and biblical texts relate the same event in the same locality with the
same outcome.

But there is more to it than just a possibility, for we have come
upon one highly intriguing clue.

This is the unnoticed fact that the date formulas for the reign of
Amar-Sin call his seventh year—the crucial year 2041 B.C., the
year of the military expedition—also MU NE IB.RU.UM BA.HUL
(Fig. 100), ''Year [in which] the Shepherding-abode of IB.RU.UM
was attacked.''

Fig. 100

Can this reference, in the exact crucial year, be other than to Abraham and his shepherding abode?

There is also a possible pictorial commemoration of the invasion. This is a scene carved on a Sumerian cylinder seal (Fig. 101). It has been regarded as depicting the journey of Etana, an early king of Kish, to the Winged Gateway, where an "Eagle" took him aloft so high that the Earth disappeared from view. But the seal depicts the crowned hero on horseback—too early for Etana's time— and standing between the site of the Winged Gateway and two distinct groups. One of four armed Mighty Men whose leader is also on horseback moves toward a cultivated area in the Sinai peninsula (indicated by the symbol of Sin's crescent with wheat growing in it). The other is of five kings, facing in the opposite direction. The depiction thus has all the elements of an ancient illustration of the War of the Kings and the role of the "Priest's Son" in it, rather than that of Etana's journey to the Spaceport. The hero, depicted in the center atop an animal, could thus be Abraham rather than Etana.

Fig. 101

Having carried out his mission to protect the Spaceport, Abraham returned to his base near Hebron. Encouraged by his feat, the Canaanite kings marched their forces to intercept the retreating army from the East. But the invaders beat them and "seized all the possessions of Sodom and Gomorrah" as well as one prize hostage: "They took with them Lot, the nephew of Abraham, who was residing at Sodom."

On hearing the news, Abraham called up his best cavalrymen and pursued the retreating invaders. Catching up with them near Damascus, he succeeded in releasing Lot and retrieving all the booty. Upon his return he was greeted as a victor in the Valley of *Shalem* (Jerusalem):

> And Malkizedek, the king of Shalem,
> brought forth bread and wine,
> for he was a priest unto the God Most High.
> And he blessed him, saying:
> "Blessed be Abram unto the God Most High,
> Possessor of Heaven and Earth;
> And blessed be the God Most High
> who hath delivered thine foes into thine hand."

Soon the Canaanite kings also arrived to thank Abraham, and offered him all the seized possessions as a reward. But Abraham, saying that his local allies could share in that, refused to take "even a shoe lace" for himself or his warriors. He had acted neither out of friendship for the Canaanite kings nor out of enmity for the Eastern Alliance; in the war between the House of Nannar and the House of Marduk, he was neutral. It was for "Yahweh, the God Most High, Possessor of Heaven and Earth, that I have raised my hands," he stated.

The failed invasion did not arrest the rush of momentous events in the ancient world. A year later, in 2040 B.C., Mentuhotep II, leader of the Theban princes, defeated the northern Pharaohs and extended the rule of Thebes (and of its god) up to the western approaches to the Sinai peninsula. In the following year Amar-Sin attempted to reach the Sinai peninsula by sea, only to find his death by a poisonous bite.

The attacks on the Spaceport were thwarted, but the danger to it was not removed; and the efforts of Marduk to gain the supremacy intensified ever more. Fifteen years later Sodom and Gomorrah went up in flames when Ninurta and Nergal unleashed the Doomsday Weapons.

14

THE NUCLEAR HOLOCAUST

Doomsday came in the twenty-fourth year when Abraham, encamped near Hebron, was ninety-nine years old.

"And the Lord appeared unto him in the terebrinth grove of Mamre as he was sitting at the entrance of the tent, in the heat of the day. And he lifted his eyes and looked, and behold—three men were stationed upon him; and as he saw them he ran from the entrance of the tent towards them, and bowed to the ground."

Swiftly, from a typical Middle Eastern scene of a potentate resting in the shade of his tent, the biblical narrator of Genesis 18 raised Abraham's eyes and thrust him—and the reader, too—into a sudden encounter with divine beings. Though Abraham was gazing out, he did not see the three approaching: they were suddenly "stationed upon him." And though they were "men," he at once recognized their true identity and bowed to them, calling them "my lords" and asking them not to "pass over above thy servant" until he had a chance to prepare for them a sumptuous meal.

It was dusk when the divine visitors finished eating and resting. Asking about Sarah, their leader said to Abraham: "Return I shall unto thee at this time next year; by then Sarah thy wife will have a son."

The promise of a Rightful Heir to Abraham and Sarah at their old age was not the sole reason for dropping down on Abraham. There was a more ominous purpose:

And the men rose up from there
to survey over upon Sodom.
And Abraham had gone with them to see them off,
and the Lord said:
"Can I conceal from Abraham that which I am about to do?"

Recalling Abraham's past services and promised future, the Lord then disclosed to him the true purpose of the divine journey: to verify accusations against Sodom and Gomorrah. "The outcry regarding Sodom and Gomorrah being great, and the accusation against them being grievous,'' the Lord said he had decided to "come down and verify; if it is as the outcry reaching me, they will destroy completely; and if not, I wish to know."

The ensuing destruction of Sodom and Gomorrah has become one of the most frequently depicted and preached-about biblical episodes. The orthodox and the Fundamentalists never doubted that the Lord God had literally poured fire and brimstone from the skies to wipe the sinful cities off the face of the earth. The scholarly and sophisticated have as tenaciously sought to find "natural" explanations for the biblical story: an earthquake; a volcanic eruption; some other natural phenomenon which (they grant) might have been interpreted as an act of God, a punishment befitting the sin.

But so far as the biblical narrative is concerned—and until now it has been the only source for all the interpretations—the event was most definitely *not* a natural calamity. It is described as a *premeditated* event: the Lord discloses to Abraham ahead of time what is about to happen and why. It is an *avoidable* event, not a calamity caused by irreversible natural forces: The calamity shall come to pass only if the "outcry" against Sodom and Gomorrah will be confirmed. And thirdly (as we shall soon discover) it was also a *postponable* event, one whose occurrence could be made to happen earlier or later, at will.

Realizing the avoidability of the calamity, Abraham embarked upon a tactic of argumentative attrition: "Perhaps there be fifty Righteous Ones inside the city," he said. "Wilt thou destroy and not spare the place for the sake of the fifty Righteous Ones within it?" Then he quickly added: "Far be it from you to do such a thing, to slay the righteous with the guilty! Far be it from you, the Judge of All the Earth, not to do justice!"

A mortal preaching to his Deity! And the plea is for calling off the destruction—the premeditated and avoidable destruction—if there be fifty Righteous Ones in the city. But no sooner had the Lord agreed to spare the city if there be found such fifty persons than Abraham, who might have chosen the number fifty knowing that it would strike a special chord, wondered out loud if the Lord shall destroy if the number were five short. When the Lord agreed to call off the destruction if only forty-five be found Righteous, Abraham continued to bargain the number down to forty, then thirty, then twenty, then ten. "And the Lord said: 'I shall not destroy if there be ten'; and he departed as he finished speaking to Abraham, and Abraham returned to his place."

At evetime, the two companions of the Lord—the biblical narrative now refers to them as *Mal'akhim* (translated "angels" but meaning "emissaries")—arrived at Sodom, their task being to verify the accusations against the city and report their findings back to the Lord. Lot—who was sitting at the city's gate—recognized at once (as Abraham had done earlier) the divine nature of the two visitors, their identity evidently being given away by their attire or weapons, or perhaps by the manner (flying over?) in which they arrived.

Now it was Lot's turn to insist on hospitality, and the two accepted his invitation to spend the night at his home; but it was not to be a restful night, for the news of their arrival had stirred up the whole city.

"They had hardly lain down when the people of the city, the people of Sodom, surrounded the house—young and old, the whole population, from every quarter; and they called unto Lot and said unto him: 'Where are the men who came unto you tonight? Bring them out to us, that we may know them.' " When Lot failed to do so, the crowd surged to break their way in; but the two *Mal'akhim* "smote the people who were at the house's entrance with blindness, both young and old; and they wearied themselves trying to find the doorway."

Realizing that of all the townspeople only Lot was "righteous," the two emissaries needed no further investigation; the fate of the city was sealed. "And they said unto Lot: 'Who else hast thou here besides thee—a son-in-law, thy sons and daughters, any other relative—all who are in this city—bring them out from this place, for we are about to destroy it.' Rushing to convey the news to his sons-in-law, Lot only met disbelief and laughter. So at dawn the emissaries urged Lot to escape without delay, taking with him only his wife and their two unmarried daughters who lived with them at home.

But Lot tarried;
so the men took hold of his hand
and his wife's hand and his two daughters' hands
—for Yahweh's mercy was upon him—
and they brought them out,
and put them down outside the city.

Having literally carried the foursome aloft, then put them down outside the city, the emissaries urged Lot to flee to the mountains: "Escape for thy life, look not behind thee, neither stop thou anywhere in the plain,'' they instructed him; ''unto the mountains escape, lest thou perish.'' But Lot, afraid that they would not reach the mountains in time and ''would be overtaken by the Evil and die,'' had a suggestion: Could the upheavaling of Sodom be delayed until he had reached the town of Zoar, the farthest one away from Sodom? Agreeing, one of the emissaries asked him to hurry there: ''Haste thee to escape thither, for I will be unable to do anything until thou hast arrived there.''

The calamity was thus not only predictable and avoidable but also postponable; and it could be made to afflict various cities at different times. No natural catastrophe could have featured all these aspects.

The sun was risen over the Earth when Lot arrived at Zoar;
And the Lord rained upon Sodom and Gomorrah, from the skies,
brimstone and fire that had come from Yahweh.
And He upheavaled those cities and the whole plain,
and all the inhabitants of the cities
and all the vegetation that grows from the ground.

The cities, the people, the vegetation—everything was ''upheavaled'' by the gods' weapon. Its heat and fire scorched all before it; its radiation affected people even at some distance away: Lot's wife, ignoring the admonition not to stop to look back as they were fleeing away from Sodom, turned to a ''pillar of vapor.''* The ''Evil'' Lot had feared had caught up with her. . . .

---

*The traditional and literal translation of the Hebrew term *Netsiv melah* has been ''pillar of salt,'' and tracts have been written in the Middle Ages explaining the process whereby a person could turn into crystalline salt. However, if—as we believe—the mother tongue of Abraham and Lot was Sumerian, and the event was first recorded not in a Semitic language but in Sumerian, an entirely different and more plausible understanding of the fate of Lot's wife becomes possible.

In a paper presented to the American Oriental Society in 1918 and in a followup article in *Beiträge zur Assyriologie*, Paul Haupt had shown conclusively that because the early sources of salt in Sumer were swamps near the Persian Gulf, the Sumerian term NIMUR branched off to mean both *salt* and *vapor*. Because the Dead Sea has been called, in Hebrew, *The Salt Sea*, the biblical Hebrew narrator probably misinterpreted the Sumerian term and wrote ''pillar of salt'' when in fact Lot's wife became a ''pillar of vapor.'' In this

One by one the cities "which had outraged the Lord" were up-heavaled, and each time Lot was allowed to escape:

For when the gods devastated the cities of the plain,
the gods remembered Abraham, and sent Lot away
out of the upheavaling of the cities.

And Lot, as instructed, went on "to dwell in the moun-tain . . . and dwelt in a cave, he and his two daughters with him."

Having witnessed the fiery destruction of all life in the Jordan plain and the unseen hand of death which vaporized their mother, what were Lot and his daughters to think? They thought, we learn from the biblical narrative, that they had witnessed the end of man-kind upon the Earth, that the three of them were the sole survivors of the human race; and therefore, the only way to preserve man-kind was to commit incest and have the daughters conceive chil-dren by their own father. . . .

"And the elder said unto the younger: 'Our father is old, and there is not a man on Earth to squire us in the manner of all on Earth; come, let us make our father drink wine, then lie down with him, so that we shall preserve the seed of life from our fa-ther.' " And having done so, both became pregnant and bore chil-dren.

The night before the holocaust must have been a night of anxiety and sleeplessness for Abraham, of wondering whether enough Righteous Ones were found in Sodom to have the cities spared, of concern about the fate of Lot and his family. "And Abraham got up early in the morning to the place where he had stood facing Yah-weh, and he looked in the direction of Sodom and Gomorrah and

---

connection it is noteworthy that in Ugaritic texts, such as the Ca-naanite tale of Aqhat (with its many similarities to the tales of Abra-ham) the death of a mortal by the hand of a god was described as the "escape of his soul as vapor, like smoke from his nostrils."

Indeed, in the Erra Epos which, we believe, was the Sumerian record of the nuclear upheaval, the death of the people was de-scribed by the god thus:

The people I will make vanish,
their souls shall turn to vapor.

It was the misfortune of Lot's wife to be among those who were "turned to vapor."

the region of the Plain; and he beheld there smoke rising from the earth as the smoke of a furnace.''

He was witnessing a ''Hiroshima'' and a ''Nagasaki'' —the destruction of a fertile and populated plain by atomic weapons. *The year was 2024 B.C.*

Where are the remains of Sodom and Gomorrah today? Ancient Greek and Roman geographers reported that the once-fertile valley of the five cities was inundated following the catastrophe. Modern scholars believe that the ''upheavaling'' described in the Bible caused a breach in the southern shore of the Dead Sea, letting its waters pour through to submerge the low-lying region to the south. The remaining portion of what was once the southern shore became the feature figuratively called by the natives *el-Lissan* (''The Tongue''), and the once-populated valley with its five cities became a new, southern part of the Dead Sea (Fig. 102) still bearing the local nickname ''Lot's Sea.'' In the north the outpouring of the waters southward caused the shoreline to recede.

The ancient reports have been confirmed in modern times by various researches, beginning with an exhaustive exploration of the area in the 1920s by a scientific mission sponsored by the Vatican's Pontifical Biblical Institute (A. Mallon, *Voyage d'Exploration au sud-est de la Mer Morte*). Leading archaeologists, such as W. F. Albright and P. Harland, discovered that settlements in the mountains around the region were abruptly abandoned in the twenty-first century B.C. and were not reoccupied for several centuries thereafter. And to this very day, the water of springs surrounding the Dead Sea has been found to be contaminated with radioactivity, ''enough to induce sterility and allied afflictions in any animals and humans that absorbed it over a number of years'' (I. M. Blake, ''Joshua's Curse and Elisha's Miracle'' in *The Palestine Exploration Quarterly*).

The cloud of death, rising in the skies from the cities of the plain, frightened not only Lot and his daughters but also Abraham, and he did not feel safe even in the Hebron mountains, some fifty miles away. We are told by the Bible that he pulled up his encampment and moved farther away westward, to reside at Gerar.

Also, at no time thereafter did he venture into the Sinai. Even years later, when Abraham's son Isaac wanted to go to Egypt on account of a famine in Canaan, ''Yahweh appeared unto him and said: 'Go not down to Egypt; dwell in the land which I will show

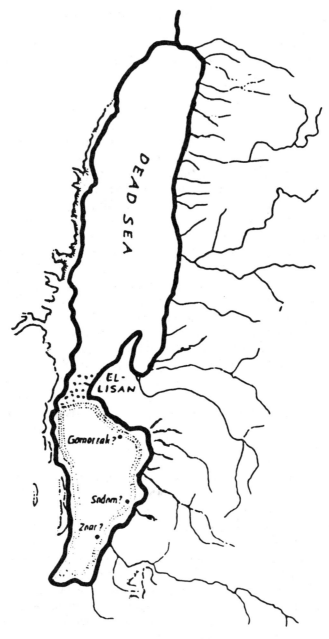

Fig. 102

thee.' '' The passage through the Sinai peninsula was apparently still unsafe.

But why?

The destruction of the cities of the plain, we believe, was only a sideshow: concurrently, the Spaceport in the Sinai peninsula was also obliterated with nuclear weapons, leaving behind a deadly radiation that lingered on for many years thereafter.

The main nuclear target was in the Sinai peninsula; and the real victim, in the end, was Sumer itself.

Though the end of Ur came swiftly, its sad fate loomed darker ever since the War of the Kings, coming nearer and nearer, like the sound of a distant drummer—an execution's drummer—getting closer, growing louder with each passing year. The Year of Doom—2024 B.C.—was the sixth year of the reign of Ibbi-Sin, the last king of Ur; but to find the reasons for the calamity, explanations of its nature, and details of its scope, we will have to study the records of those fateful years back from the time of that war.

Having failed in their mission and twice humiliated by the hand of Abraham—once at Kadesh-Barnea, then again near Damascus—the invading kings were promptly removed from their thrones. In Ur, Amar-Sin was replaced by his brother Shu-Sin, who ascended the throne to find the grand alliance shattered and Ur's erstwhile allies now nibbling at her crumbling empire.

Although they, too, had been discredited by the War of the Kings, Nannar and Inanna were at first the gods in whom Shu-Sin had put his trust. It was Nannar, Shu-Sin's early inscriptions stated, who had ''called his name'' to kingship; he was ''beloved of Inanna,'' and she herself presented him to Nannar (Fig. 103).

Fig. 103

"The Holy Inanna," Shu-Sin boasted, "the one endowed with astounding qualities, the First Daughter of Sin," granted him weapons with which to "engage in battle the enemy country which is disobedient." But all this was insufficient to hold together the Sumerian empire, and Shu-Sin soon turned to greater gods for succor.

Judging from the date formulas—annual inscriptions, for royal as well as commercial and social purposes, in which each successive year of a king's reign was designated by the major event of that year—Shu-Sin, in the second year of his reign, sought the favors of Enki by constructing for that god a special boat that could navigate the high seas all the way to the Lower World. The third year of reign was also one of preoccupation with the pro-Enki alignment. Little else is known of this effort, which could have been a roundabout way of pacifying the followers of Marduk and Nabu; but the effort evidently failed, for the fourth and fifth years witnessed the building of a massive wall on the western frontier of Mesopotamia, specifically aimed at warding off incursions by the "Westerners," followers of Marduk.

As the pressures from the west kept rising, Shu-Sin turned to the great gods of Nippur for forgiveness and salvation. The date formulas, confirmed by the archaeological excavations of the American Expedition to Nippur, reveal that Shu-Sin undertook massive reconstruction works at Nippur's sacred precinct, on a scale unknown since the days of Ur-Nammu. The works culminated with the raising of a stela honoring Enlil and Ninlil, "a stela as no king had built before." Desparately Shu-Sin sought acceptance, confirmation that he was "the king whom Enlil, in his heart, had chosen." But Enlil was not there to answer; only Ninlil, Enlil's spouse, who remained in Nippur, heard Shu-Sin's supplications. Responding with compassion, "so as to prolong the well-being of Shu-Sin, to extend the time of his crown," she gave him a "weapon which with radiance strikes down . . . whose awesome flash reaches the sky."

A Shu-Sin text catalogued as "Collection B" suggests that in his efforts to reestablish the olden links with Nippur, Shu-Sin may have attempted a reconciliation with the Nippurites (such as the family of Terah) who had left Ur after the death of Ur-Nammu. The text states that after he made the region where Harran was situated "tremble in awe of his weapons," a peace gesture was made: Shu-Sin sent there his own daughter as a bride (presumably to the region's chief or his son). She then returned to Sumer with an entourage of that region's citizens, "establishing a town for Enlil and Ninlil on the boundary of Nippur." It was the first time "since the days when fates were decreed, that a king had established a town for Enlil and Ninlil," Shu-Sin stated in obvious expectation of praise. With the probable assistance of the repatriated Nippurites, Shu-Sin also reinstated the high temple services at Nippur—bestowing upon himself the role and title of High Priest.

Yet all this was to no avail. Instead of greater security, there were greater dangers, and concern about the loyalty of distant provinces gave way to worry about Sumer's own territory. "The mighty king, the King of Ur," Shu-Sin's inscriptions said, found that the "shepherding of the land"—of Sumer itself—had become the principal royal burden.

There was one final effort to entice Enlil back to Sumer, to find shelter under his aegis. On the apparent advice of Ninlil, Shu-Sin built for the divine couple "a great touring boat, fit for the largest rivers. . . . He decorated it perfectly with precious stones," outfitted it with oars made of the finest wood, punting poles and an artful rudder, and furnished it with all manner of comfort including a bridal bed. He then "placed the touring boat in the wide basin facing Ninlil's House of Pleasure."

The nostalgic aspects struck a chord in Enlil's heart, for he had fallen in love with Ninlil, when she was still a young nurse, when he saw her bathing naked in the river; and he did come back to Nippur:

When Enlil heard [all this]
From horizon to horizon he hurried,
From south to north he travelled;
Through the skies, over earth he hurried,
To greatly rejoice with his beloved queen, Ninlil.

The sentimental journey, however, was only a brief interlude. Some crucial lines before the end of the tablet are missing, so we are deprived of the details of what happened then. But the very last lines refer to "Ninurta, the great warrior of Enlil, who befuddled the Intruder," apparently after "an inscription, an evil inscription" was discovered on an effigy in the boat, intended perhaps to place a curse on Enlil and Ninlil.

There is no record available of Enlil's reaction to the foul piay; but all other evidence suggests that he again left Nippur, this time apparently taking Ninlil with him.

Soon thereafter—February 2031 B.C. by our calendar—the Near East was awed by a total lunar eclipse, which blacked out the moon during the night for its full course from horizon to horizon. The oracle priests of Nippur could not allay Shu-Sin's anxiety: It was, they said in their written message, an omen "to the king who rules the four regions: his wall will be destroyed, Ur will become desolate."

Rejected by the great olden gods, Shu-Sin engaged in one final act—either out of defiance or as a last straw to gain divine support. He went ahead and built—in the very sacred precinct of Nippur—a shrine to a young god named Shara. He was a son of Inanna; and like Lugalbanda, who bore this epithet in earlier days, so was this new Shara ("Prince") a son of a king; in the inscription dedicating the temple, Shu-Sin claimed that he was the young god's father: "To divine Shara, heavenly hero, the beloved son of Inanna: His father Shu-Sin, the powerful king, king of Ur, king of the four regions, has built for him the temple Shagipada, his beloved shrine; may the king have life." It was the ninth year of Shu-Sin's reign. It was also his last.

The new ruler on the throne of Ur, Ibbi-Sin, could not stop the retreat and retrenchment. All he could do was rush the construction of walls and fortifications in the heart of Sumer, around Ur and Nippur; the rest of the country was left unprotected. His own date formulas, of which none have been found beyond his fifth year (although he reigned longer), tell little of the circumstances of his days; much more is learned from the cessation of other customary messages and trade documents. Thus, the messages of loyalty, which the other subordinate urban centers were expected to send to Ur each year, ceased to arrive from one center after the other. First to cease were the loyalty messages from the western districts; then, in the third year, the capitals of eastern provinces stopped their dispatch. In that third year Ur's foreign commerce "stopped with a significant suddenness" (in the words of C. J. Gadd, *History and Monuments of Ur*). At the tax collection crossroads of Drehem (near Nippur), where shipments of goods and cattle and the collection of taxes thereon were recorded throughout the Third Dynasty of Ur—records of which thousands of intact clay tablets were found—the meticulous account-keeping also stopped abruptly in that third year.

Ignoring Nippur, whose great gods had left her, Ibbi-Sin put his trust again in Nannar and Inanna, installing himself in his second year as High Priest of Inanna's temple in Uruk. Repeatedly he asked for guidance and reassurance from his gods; but all he was hearing were oracles of destruction and doom. In the fourth year of his reign he was told that "The Son in the west will arise . . . it is an omen for Ibbi-Sin: Ur shall be judged."

In the fifth year, Ibbi-Sin sought further strength by becoming High Priest of Inanna at her shrine at Ur. But that, too, was of no help: that year, the other cities of Sumer itself ceased sending the messages of allegiance. It was also the last year in which those cities delivered the traditional sacrificial animals for Nannar's temple in Ur. The central authority of Ur, her gods, and her great ziggurat-temple were no longer recognized.

As the sixth year began, the omens "concerning destruction" became more urgent and more specific. "When the sixth year comes, the inhabitants of Ur will be trapped," one omen stated. The prophesied calamity shall come, another omen said, "When, for the second time, he who calls himself Supreme, like one whose chest has been anointed, shall come from the west." That very year, as messages from the borders reveal, "hostile Westerners had entered the plain" of Mesopotamia; without resistance, they quickly "entered the interior of the country, taking one by one all the great fortresses."

All Ibbi-Sin held on to was the enclave of Ur and Nippur; but before the fateful sixth year was out, the inscriptions honoring the king of Ur stopped abruptly also in Nippur. The enemy of Ur and her gods, the "One who calls himself Supreme," had reached the heart of Sumer.

Marduk, as the omens had predicted, returned to Babylon for the second time.

The twenty-four fateful years—since Abraham left Harran, since Shulgi was replaced on the throne, since Marduk's exile among the Hittites had begun—have all converged in that Year of Doom, 2024 B.C. Having followed the separate, but interconnected, biblical tale of Abraham and the fortunes of Ur and its last three kings, we will now follow in the footsteps of Marduk.

The tablet on which Marduk's autobiography is inscribed (from which we have already partly quoted) continues to relate his return to Babylon after the twenty-four years of sojourn in the Land of Hatti:

In Hatti-land I asked an oracle
[about] my throne and my Lordship;

In its midst [I asked]: "Until when?"
24 years, in its midst, I nested.

Then, in that twenty-fourth year, he received a favorable omen:

My days [of exile] were completed;
To my city I [set my course];
My temple Esagila as a mount [to raise/rebuild],
My everlasting abode to [reestablish].
I raised my heels [toward Babylon]
Through . . . lands [I went] to my city
her [future? well-being?] to establish,
A king in Babylon to [install]
In the house of my covenant . . .
In the mountlike Esagil . . .
By Anu created . . .
Into the Esagil . . .
A platform to raise . . .
In my city . . .
Joy . . .

The damaged tablet then lists the cities through which Marduk had passed on his way to Babylon. The few legible city names indicate that Marduk's route from Asia Minor to Mesopotamia took him first south to the city of Hama (the biblical Hamat), then eastward via Mari (see map, page 304). He had indeed come to Mesopotamia—as the omens had predicted—from the west, accompanied by Amorite ("Westerners") supporters.

His wish, Marduk continued, was to bring peace and prosperity to the land, "chase away evil and bad luck . . . bring motherly love to Mankind." But it all came to naught: Against his city, Babylon, an adversary god "his wrath had brought." The name of this adversary god is stated at the very beginning of a new column of the text; but all that has remained of it is the first syllable: "Divine NIN-." The reference could have been only to Ninurta.

We learn little from this tablet of the actions taken by this adversary, for all the subsequent verses are badly damaged and the text becomes unintelligible. But we can pick up some of the missing threads from the third tablet of the *Khedorlaomer Texts*. In spite of its enigmatic aspects, it paints a picture of total turmoil, with adversary gods marching against each other at the head of their human troops: the Amorite supporters of Marduk swooped down the

Euphrates valley toward Nippur, and Ninurta organized Elamite troops to fight them.

As we read and reread the record of those trying times, we find that to accuse an enemy of atrocities is not a modern innovation. The Babylonian text—written, we must keep bearing in mind, by a worshiper of Marduk—attributes to the Elamite troops, and to them alone, the desecration of temples, including the shrines of Shamash and Ishtar. The Babylonian chronicler goes even farther: he accuses Ninurta of falsely blaming on the followers of Marduk the desecration of Enlil's Holy-of-Holies in Nippur, thereby provoking Enlil to take sides against Marduk and his son Nabu.

It happened, the Babylonian text relates, when the two opposing armies faced each other at Nippur. It was then that the holy city was despoiled and its shrine, the Ekur, desecrated. Ninurta accused the followers of Marduk of this evil deed; but it was not so: it was his ally Erra who had done it!

How Nergal/Erra suddenly appears in the Babylonian chronicle will remain a puzzle until we return to the Erra Epic; but that this god is named in the *Khedorlaomer Texts* and is accused of the defilement of the Ekur, there can be no doubt:

Erra, the pitiless one,
entered the sacred precinct.
He stationed himself in the sacred precinct,
he beheld the Ekur.
His mouth he opened, he said to his young men:
"Carry off the spoil of Ekur,
take away its valuables,
destroy its foundation,
break down the enclosure of the shrine!"

When Enlil, "loftily enthroned," heard that his temple had been destroyed, its shrine defiled, that "in the holy of holies the veil was torn away," he rushed back to Nippur. "Riding in front of him were gods clothed with radiance"; he himself "set off brilliance like lightning" as he came down from the skies (Fig. 104); "he made the holy place shake" as he descended to the sacred precinct. Enlil then addressed himself to his son, "the prince Ninurta," to find out who had defiled the sacred place. But instead of telling the truth, that it was Erra, his ally, Ninurta pointed the accusing finger at Marduk and his followers. . . .

Fig. 104

Describing the scene, the Babylonian text asserts that Ninurta was acting without the required respect on meeting his father: "not fearing for his life, he removed not his tiara." To Enlil "evil he spoke . . . there was no justice; destruction was conceived." And so provoked, "Enlil against Babylon caused evil to be planned."

In addition to "evil deeds" against Marduk and Babylon, an attack against Nabu and his temple Ezida in Borsippa was also planned. But Nabu managed to escape westward, to the cities faithful to him near the Mediterranean Sea:

> From Ezida . . .
> Nabu, to marshal all his cities
> set his step;
> Toward the great sea he set his course.

Now there follow verses in the Babylonian text that have a direct parallel in the biblical tale of the destruction of Sodom and Gomorrah:

> But when the son of Marduk
> in the land of the coast was,
> He-of-the-Evil-Wind [Erra]
> with heat the plain-land burnt.

These are indeed verses that must have had a common source with the biblical description of how "brimstone and fire" rained from the skies "upheavaled those cities and the whole plain"!

As biblical statements (e.g., Deuteronomy 29:22–27) attested, the "wickedness" of the cities of the Jordan Plain was that "they had forsaken the covenant of the Lord . . . and they went and served other gods." As we now learn from the Babylonian text, the "outcry" (accusation) against them was their rallying to the side of Marduk and Nabu in that last clash between the contending gods. But whereas the biblical text left it at that, the Babylonian text adds another important detail: The attack on the Canaanite cities was intended not only to destroy the centers of support for Marduk, but also to destroy Nabu, who had sought asylum there. However, that second aim was not achieved, for Nabu managed to slip out in time and escaped to an island in the Mediterranean, where the people accepted him although he was not their god:

He [Nabu] the great sea entered,
Sat upon a throne which was not his
[Because] Ezida, the legitimate abode, was overrun.

The picture that can be gathered from the biblical and Babylonian texts of the cataclysm that engulfed the ancient Near East in the time of Abraham is much more fully detailed in *The Erra Epic* (to which we have already referred earlier). First pieced together from fragments found in the library of Ashurbanipal in Nineveh, the Assyrian text began to take shape and meaning as more fragmented versions were unearthed at other archaeological sites. By now it is definitely established that the text was inscribed on five tablets; and in spite of breaks, missing or incomplete lines, and even some disagreement among the scholars where some fragments belong, two extensive translations have been compiled: *Das Era-Epos* by P. F. Gössmann, and *L'Epopea di Erra* by L. Cagni.

The Erra Epic not only explains the nature and causes of the conflict that had led to the unleashing of the Ultimate Weapon against inhabited cities and the attempt to annihilate a god (Nabu) believed hiding therein. It also makes clear that such an extreme measure was not taken lightly.

We know from several other texts that the great gods, at that time of acute crisis, were sitting in a continuous Council of War, keeping constant communication with Anu: "Anu to Earth the words was speaking, Earth to Anu the words pronounced." *The*

Erra Epic adds the information that before the awesome weapons were used, one more confrontation had taken place between Nergal/Erra and Marduk, in which Nergal used threats to persuade his brother to leave Babylon and give up his claims to Supremacy.

But this time, persuasion failed; and back at the Council of the Gods, Nergal voiced the recommendation for the use of force to dislodge Marduk. We learn from the texts that the discussions were heated and acrimonious; "for one day and one night, without ceasing" they went on. An especially violent argument developed between Enki and his son Nergal, in which Enki stood by his firstborn son: "Now that Prince Marduk has arisen, now that the people for the second time have raised his image, why does Erra continue his opposition?" Enki asked. Finally, losing his patience, Enki shouted at Nergal to get out of his presence.

Leaving in a huff, Nergal returned to his domain. "Consulting with himself," he decided to unleash the awesome weapons: "The lands I will destroy, to a dust-heap make them; the cities I will upheaval, to desolation turn them; the mountains I will flatten, their animals make disappear; the seas I will agitate, that which teems in them I will decimate; the people I will make vanish, their souls shall turn to vapor; none shall be spared. . . ."

We learn from a text known as CT-xvi-44/46 that it was Gibil, whose domain in Africa adjoined that of Nergal, who alerted Marduk to the destructive scheme hatched by Nergal. It was nighttime, and the great gods had adjourned for rest. It was then that Gibil "these words to Marduk did speak" in regard to the "seven awesome weapons which by Anu were created; . . . The wickedness of those seven against thee is being laid," he informed Marduk.

Alarmed, Marduk inquired of Gibil where the awesome weapons were kept. "O Gibil," he said, "those seven—where were they born, where were they created?" To which Gibil revealed that they were hidden underground:

Those seven, in the mountain they abide,
In a cavity inside the earth they dwell.
From this place with a brilliance they will rush forth,
From Earth to Heaven, clad with terror.

But where exactly is this place? Marduk asked again and again; and all Gibil could say was that "even the wise gods, to them it is unknown."

Now Marduk rushed to his father Enki with the frightening report. "To his father Enki's house he [Marduk] entered." Enki was lying on the couch in the chamber to which he retired for the night. "My father," Marduk said, "Gibil this word hath spoken to me: of the coming of the seven [weapons] he has found out." Telling his father the bad news, he urged his all-knowing father: "Their place to search out, do hasten thou!"

Soon the gods were back in council, for even Enki knew not the exact hiding place of the Ultimate Weapons. To his surprise, not all the other gods were as shocked as he was. Enki spoke out strongly against the idea, urging steps to stop Nergal, for the use of the weapons, he pointed out, "the lands would make desolate, the people will make perish." Nannar and Utu wavered as Enki spoke; but Enlil and Ninurta were for decisive action. And so, with the Council of the Gods in disarray, the decision was left to Anu.

When Ninurta finally arrived in the Lower World with word of Anu's decision, he found out that Nergal had already ordered the priming of "the seven awesome weapons" with their "poisons"— their nuclear warheads. Though the *Erra Epic* keeps referring to Ninurta by the epithet *Ishum* ("The Scorcher"), it relates in great detail how Ninurta had made clear to Nergal/Erra that the weapons could be used only against specifically approved targets; that before they could be used, the Anunnaki gods at the selected sites and the Igigi gods manning the space platform and the shuttlecraft had to be forewarned; and, last but not least, mankind had to be spared, for "Anu, lord of the gods, on the land had pity."

At first Nergal balked at the very idea of forewarning anyone, and the ancient text goes to some length to relate the tough words exchanged between the two gods. Nergal then agreed to giving advance warning to the Anunnaki and Igigi who manned the space facilities, but not to Marduk and his son Nabu, nor to the human followers of Marduk. It was then that Ninurta, attempting to dissuade Nergal from indiscriminate annihilation, used words identical to those attributed in the Bible to Abraham when he tried to have Sodom spared:

Valiant Erra,
Will you the righteous destroy with the unrighteous?
Will you destroy those who have against you sinned
together with those who against you have not sinned?

Employing flattery, threats, and logic, the two gods argued back and forth on the extent of the destruction. More than Ninurta,

Nergal was consumed by personal hatred: "I shall annihilate the son, and let the father bury him; then I shall kill the father, let no one bury him!" he shouted. Employing diplomacy, pointing out the injustice of indiscriminate destruction—and the strategic merits of selective targeting—the words of Ninurta finally swayed Nergal. "He heard the words spoken by Ishum [Ninurta]; the words appealed to him as fine oil." Agreeing to leave alone the seas, to leave Mesopotamia out of the attack, he formulated a modified plan: the destruction will be selective; the tactical aim will be to destroy the cities where Nabu might be hiding; the strategic aim will be to deny to Marduk his greatest prize—the Spaceport, "the place from where the Great Ones ascend":

> From city to city an emissary I will send;
> The son, seed of his father, shall not escape;
> His mother shall cease her laughter . . .
> To the place of the gods, access he shall not have:
> The place from where the Great Ones ascend
> I shall upheaval.

When Nergal finished presenting this latest plan, involving as it did the destruction of the Spaceport, Ninurta was speechless. But, as other texts assert, Enlil approved the plan when it was brought to his decision; so also, apparently, did Anu. Wasting no more time, Nergal then urged Ninurta that the two of them go at once into action:

> Then did the hero Erra go ahead of Ishum,
> remembering his words;
> Ishum too went forth, in accordance with the word given,
> a squeezing in his heart.

Their first target was the Spaceport, its command complex hidden in the "Mount Most Supreme," its landing fields spread in the adjoining great plain:

> Ishum to Mount Most Supreme set his course;
> The Awesome Seven, [weapons] without parallel,
> trailed behind him.
> At the Mount Most Supreme the hero arrived;
> He raised his hand—
> the mount was smashed;

The plain by the Mount Most Supreme
he then obliterated;
in its forests not a tree-stem was left standing.

So, with one nuclear blow, the Spaceport was obliterated, the mount within which its controls were hidden smashed, the plain that served its runways obliterated. . . . It was a destructive feat, the written record attests, performed by Ninurta (Ishum).

Now it was the turn of Nergal (Erra) to give vent to his vow of vengeance. Guiding himself from the Sinai peninsula to the Canaanite cities by following the King's Highway, Erra upheavaled them. The words employed by the *Erra Epic* are almost identical to those used in the biblical tale of Sodom and Gomorrah:

Then, emulating Ishum,
Erra the King's Highway followed.
The cities he finished off,
to desolation he overturned them.
In the mountains he caused starvation,
their animals he made perish.

The verses that follow may well describe the creation of the new southern portion of the Dead Sea, by breaking through its southern shoreline, and the elimination of all marine life therein:

He dug through the sea,
its wholeness he divided.
That which lives in it,
even the crocodiles
he made wither.
As with fire he scorched the animals,
banned its grains to become as dust.

The *Erra Epic* thus encompasses all the three aspects of the nuclear event: the obliteration of the Spaceport in the Sinai; the "overturning" ("upheavaling" in the Bible) of the cities of the Jordan plain; and the breach in the Dead Sea resulting in its extension southward. One could expect that such a unique destructive event would have been recorded and mentioned in more than a single text; and indeed we find descriptions and recollections of the nuclear upheaval in other texts as well.

One such text (known as K.5001 and published in the *Oxford*

Editions of Cuneiform Texts, vol. VI) is especially valuable, because it is in the original Sumerian language and, moreover, it is a bilingual text in which the Sumerian is accompanied by a line-by-line Akkadian translation. It is thus undoubtedly one of the earliest texts on the subject; and its wording indeed gives the impression that it is this or similar Sumerian originals that had served as a source for the biblical narrative. Addressed to a god whose identity is not clear from the fragment, it says:

> Lord, bearer of the Scorcher
> that burnt up the adversary;
> Who obliterated the disobedient land;
> Who withered the life of the Evil Word's followers;
> *Who rained stones and fire* upon the adversaries.

The deed performed by the two gods Ninurta and Nergal, when the Anunnaki guarding the Spaceport, forewarned, had to escape by "ascending to the dome of heaven," was recalled in a Babylonian text in which one king recalled the momentous events that had taken place "in the reign of an earlier king." Here are the king's words:

> At that time,
> in the reign of a previous king,
> conditions changed.
> Good departed, suffering was regular.
> The Lord [of the gods] became enraged,
> he conceived wrath.
> He gave the command:
> the gods of that place abandoned it . . .
> The two, incited to commit the evil,
> made its guardians stand aside;
> its protectors went up to the dome of heaven.

The *Khedorlaomer Text,* which identifies the two gods by their epithets as Ninurta and Nergal, tells it this way:

> Enlil, who sat enthroned in loftiness,
> was consumed with anger.
> The devastators again suggested evil;
> He who scorches with fire [Ishum/Ninurta]

and he of the evil wind [Erra/Nergal]
together performed their evil.
The two made the gods flee,
made them flee the scorching.

The target, from which they made the gods guarding it flee, was
the Place of Launching:

That which was raised towards Anu to launch
they caused to wither;
Its face they made fade away,
its place they made desolate.

Thus was the Spaceport, the prize over which so many Wars of
the Gods had been fought, obliterated: the Mount within which the
controlling equipment was placed was smashed; the launch platforms were made to fade off the face of the Earth; and the plain
whose hard soil the shuttlecraft had used as runways was obliterated, with not even a tree left standing.

The great place was never to be seen again . . . but the scar
made in the face of the Earth that awesome day *can still be
seen*—to this very day! It is a vast scar, so vast that its features can
be seen only from the skies—revealed only in recent years as satellites began to photograph the Earth (Fig. 105). It is a scar for which
no scientist has hitherto offered an explanation.

Stretching north of this enigmatic feature in the face of the Sinai
peninsula is the flat central plain of the Sinai—a remnant of a lake
from an earlier geological era; its flat, hard soil is ideal for the
landing of shuttlecraft—the very same reason which made the Mo-
jave Desert in California and the Edwards Air Force Base there
ideal for the landing of America's space shuttles.

As one stands in this great plain in the Sinai peninsula—its hard,
flat soil having served for tank battles in recent history as it
did the shuttlecraft in antiquity—one can see in the distance
the mountains that surround the plain and give it its oval shape.
The limestone mountains loom white on the horizon; but where the
great central plain adjoins the immense scar in the Sinai, the hue of
the plain—black—stands out in sharp contrast to the surrounding
whiteness (Fig. 106).

Black is not a natural hue in the Sinai peninsula, where the
whiteness of the limestone and the redness of the sandstone combine to dazzle the eye with hues ranging from bright yellow to light

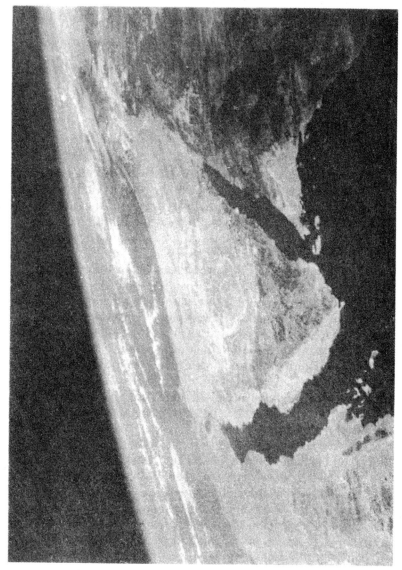

Fig. 105

Fig. 106

gray and dark brown but nowhere the black which comes in nature from basalt stones.

Yet here, in the central plain north-northeast of the enigmatic giant scar, the soil's color has a black hue. It is caused—as our photograph clearly shows—by millions upon millions of bits and pieces of blackened rock, strewn as by a giant hand over the whole area (Fig. 107).

There has been no explanation for the colossal scar in the face of the Sinai peninsula since it was observed from the skies and photographed by NASA satellites. There has been no explanation for the blackened bits and pieces of rock strewn over the area in the central plain. No explanation—unless one reads the verses of the ancient texts and accepts our conclusion that in the days of Abraham, Nergal and Ninurta wiped out the Spaceport that was there with nuclear weapons: "That which was raised towards Anu to launch they caused to wither, its face they made fade away, its place they made desolate."

And the Spaceport, even the Evil Cities, were no more.

Far away to the west, in Sumer itself, the nuclear blasts and their brilliant flashes were neither felt nor seen. But the deed done by Nergal and Ninurta had not gone unrecorded, for it turned out to have had a most profound effect on Sumer, its people, and its very existence.

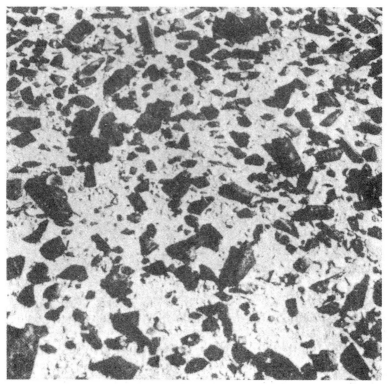

Fig. 107

For, in spite of all the efforts of Ninurta to dissuade Nergal from harming mankind, a great suffering did ensue. Though the two had not intended it, the nuclear explosion gave rise to an immense wind, a radioactive wind, which began as a whirlwind:

A storm, the Evil Wind,
went around in the skies.

And then the radioactive whirlwind began to spread and move westward with the prevailing winds blowing from the Mediterranean; soon thereafter, the omens predicting the end of Sumer came true; and Sumer itself became the ultimate nuclear victim.

The catastrophe that befell Sumer at the end of Ibbi-Sin's sixth year of reign is described in several Lamentation Texts—long poems that bewail the demise of the majestic Ur and the other centers of the great Sumerian civilization. Bringing very much to mind the biblical Book of Lamentations, lamenting the destruction of Jerusalem by the hands of the Babylonians, the Sumerian lamentations suggested to the scholars who had first translated them that the Mesopotamian catastrophe was also the result of an invasion—this one by clashing Elamite and Amorite troops.

When the first lamentation tablets were found, the scholars believed that Ur alone suffered destruction, and they titled the translations accordingly. But as more texts were discovered, it was realized that Ur was neither the only city affected, nor the focal point of the catastrophe. Not only were similar lamentations found bewailing the fate of Nippur, Uruk, Eridu, but some of the texts also provided lists of the affected cities: they appeared to begin in the southwest and extend to the northeast, encompassing the whole of southern Mesopotamia. It became apparent that a general, sudden, and concurrent catastrophe had befallen all the cities—not in slow succession, as would happen in the case of a progressive invasion, but all at once. Such scholars as Th. Jacobsen *(The Reign of Ibbi-Sin)* then concluded that the "barbarian invaders" had nothing to do with the "dire catastrophe," a calamity he called "really quite puzzling."

"Whether we shall ever see with full clarity what happened in those years," Jacobsen wrote, "only time will tell; the full story, we are convinced, is still far beyond our grasp."

But the puzzle can be solved, and the full story grasped, if we relate the catastrophe in Mesopotamia to the nuclear explosion in the Sinai.

The texts, remarkable for their length and in many instances also in excellent state of preservation, usually begin by bewailing the abrupt abandonment of all of Sumer's sacred precincts by their various gods, their temples "abandoned to the wind." The desolation caused by the catastrophe is then described vividly, by such verses as these:

Causing cities to be desolated,
[causing] houses to become desolate;
Causing stalls to be desolate,
the sheepfolds to be emptied;
That Sumer's oxen no longer stand in their stalls,
that its sheep no longer roam in its sheepfolds;
That its rivers flow with water that is bitter,
that its cultivated fields grow weeds,
that its steppes grow withering plants.

In the cities and the hamlets, "the mother cares not for her children, the father says not 'O my wife' . . . the young child grows not sturdy on their knee, the nursemaid chants not a lullaby . . . kingship has been taken away from the land."

Before World War II had ended, before Hiroshima and Nagasaki were upheavaled with atomic weapons rained on them from the skies, one could still read the biblical tale of Sodom and Gomorrah and leave be the traditional "sulphur and brimstone" for lack of a better explanation. To scholars who had not yet come face-to-face with the awesomeness of nuclear weapons, the Sumerian lamentation texts bespoke (as the scholars titled them) the "Destruction of Ur" or the "Destruction of Sumer." But that is not what these texts describe: they describe *desolation,* not destruction. The cities were there but without people; the stalls were there but without cattle; the sheepfolds remained but were empty; the rivers flowed but their waters became bitter; the fields still stretched but they grew only weeds; and on the steppe the plants sprouted, only to wither away.

Invasion, war, killing—all those evils were well known to mankind by then; but, as the lamentation texts clearly state, this one was unique and never experienced before:

On the Land [Sumer] fell a calamity,
one unknown to man:
One that had never been seen before,
one which could not be withstood.

The death was not by the hand of an enemy; it was an unseen death, "which roams the street, is let loose in the road; it stands beside a man—yet none can see it; when it enters a house, its appearance is unknown." There was no defense against this "evil which has assailed the land like a ghost: . . . The highest wall, the thickest walls, it passes as a flood; no door can shut it out, no bolt can turn it back; through the door like a snake it glides, through the hinge like a wind it blows in." Those who hid behind doors were felled inside; those who ran to the rooftops died on the rooftops; those who fled to the streets were stricken in the streets: "Cough and phlegm weakened the chest, the mouth was filled with spittle and foam . . . dumbness and daze have come upon them, an unwholesome numbness . . . an evil curse, a headache . . . their spirit abandoned their bodies." As they died, it was a most gruesome death:

The people, terrified, could hardly breathe;
the Evil Wind clutched them,
does not grant them another day . . .
Mouths were drenched in blood,
heads wallowed in blood . . .
The face was made pale by the Evil Wind.

The source of the unseen death was a cloud that appeared in the
skies of Sumer and "covered the land as a cloak, spread over it like
a sheet." Brownish in color, during the daytime "the sun in the horizon it obliterated with darkness." At night, luminous at its edges
("Girt with dread brilliance it filleth the broad earth") it blocked
out the moon: "the moon at its rising it extinguished." Moving
from west to east, the deathly cloud—"enveloped in terror, casting
fear everywhere"—was carried to Sumer by a howling wind, "a
great wind which speeds high above, an evil wind which overwhelms the land."

It was not, however, a natural phenomenon. It was "a great
storm directed from Anu . . . it hath come from the heart of Enlil." The product of the seven awesome weapons, "in a single
spawning it was spawned . . . like the bitter venom of the gods; in
the west it was spawned." The Evil Wind, "bearing gloom from
city to city, carrying dense clouds that bring gloom from the sky,"
was the result of a "lightning flash:" "From the midst of the
mountains it had descended upon the land, from the Plain of No
Pity it hath come."

Though the people were baffled, the gods knew the cause of the
Evil Wind:

An evil blast heralded the baleful storm,
An evil blast the forerunner
of the baleful storm was;
Mighty offspring, valiant sons
were the heralds of the pestilence.

The two valiant sons—Ninurta and Nergal—unleashed "in a
single spawning" the seven awesome weapons created by Anu,
"uprooting everything, upheavaling everything" at the place of
the blast. The ancient descriptions are as vivid, as accurate as modern eyewitness descriptions of an atomic explosion: As soon as the
"awesome weapons" were launched from the skies, there was an

immense brilliance: "they spread awesome rays towards the four points of the earth, scorching everything like fire," one text stated; another, a lamentation over Nippur, recalled "the storm, in a flash of lightning created." An atomic mushroom—"a dense cloud that brings gloom"—then rose to the sky; it was followed by "rushing wind gusts . . . a tempest that furiously scorches the heavens." Then the prevailing winds, blowing from west to east, began to spread toward Mesopotamia: "the dense clouds that bring gloom from the sky, that bear the gloom from city to city."

Not one, but several, texts attest that the Evil Wind, bearing the cloud of death, was caused by gigantic explosions on a day to remember:

> On that day
> When heaven was crushed
> and the Earth was smitten,
> its face obliterated by the maelstrom—
> When the skies were darkened
> and covered as with a shadow . . .

The lamentation texts identified the site of the awesome blasts as "in the west," near "the breast of the sea"—a graphic description of the curving Mediterranean coast at the Sinai peninsula—from a plain "in the midst of the mountains," a plain that became a "Place of No Pity." It was a place that served before as the Place of Launching, the place from which the gods ascended toward Anu. In addition, a mount also featured in many of these place identifications. In the *Erra Epic*, the mount near "the place from which Great Ones ascend" was called the "Mount Most Supreme"; in one of the lamentations it was called the "Mount of Howling Tunnels." This last epithet brings to mind the descriptions, in the Pyramid Texts, of the tunneled mount with sloping underground passages, to which Egyptian Pharaohs journeyed in search of an afterlife. In *The Stairway to Heaven* we have identified it with the mount Gilgamesh had reached in his journey to the Place of the Rocketships, in the Sinai peninsula.

Starting from that mount, a lamentation text stated, the blast's deadly cloud was carried by the prevailing winds eastward all the way "to the boundary of Anshan" in the Zagros Mountains, affecting all of Sumer from Eridu in the south to Babylon in the north. The unseen death moved slowly over Sumer, its passage lasting twenty-four hours—a day and a night that were commemorated in laments, as in this one from Nippur: "On that day, on that single day; on that night, on that single night . . . the storm, in a flash of lightning created, the people of Nippur left prostrate."

The Uruk Lament vividly describes the confusion among both the gods and the populace. Stating that Anu and Enlil had over-ruled Enki and Ninki when they "determined the consensus" to employ the nuclear weapons, the text asserts that none of the gods anticipated the awesome outcome: "The great gods paled at its immensity" as they witnessed the explosion's "gigantic rays reach up to heaven [and] the earth tremble to its core."

As the Evil Wind began to "spread to the mountains as a net," the gods of Sumer began to flee their beloved cities. The text known as *Lamentation Over the Destruction of Ur* lists all the great gods and some of their important sons and daughters who had "abandoned to the wind" the cities and great temples of Sumer. The text called *Lamentation Over the Destruction of Sumer and Ur* adds dramatic details to this hurried abandonment. Thus, "Ninhar-sag wept in bitter tears" as she escaped from Isin; Nanshe cried, "O my devastated city" as "her beloved dwelling place was given over to misfortune." Inanna hurriedly departed from Uruk, sailing off toward Africa in a "submersible ship" and complaining that she had to leave behind her jewelry and other possessions. . . . In her own lamentation for Uruk, Inanna/Ishtar bewailed the desolation of her city and her temple by the Evil Wind "which in an instant, in a blink of an eye was created in the midst of the mountains," and against which there was no defense.

A breathtaking description of the fear and confusion, among gods and men alike, as the Evil Wind approached is given in *The Uruk Lament* text, which was written years later as the time of Restoration came. As the "loyal citizens of Uruk were seized with terror," the resident deities of Uruk, those in charge of the city's administration and welfare, set off an alarm. "Rise up!" they called to the people in the middle of the night; run away, "hide in the steppe!" they instructed them. But then, these gods themselves, "the deities ran off . . . they took unfamiliar paths." Gloomily the text states:

Thus all its gods evacuated Uruk;
They kept away from it;
They hid in the mountains,
They escaped to the distant plains.

In Uruk, the populace was left in chaos, leaderless and helpless. "Mob panic was brought about in Uruk . . . its good sense was distorted." The shrines were broken in and their contents were smashed as the people asked questions: "Why did the gods' benevolent eye look away? Who caused such worry and lamentation?" But their questions remained unanswered; and when the Evil Storm passed over, "the people were piled up in heaps . . . a hush settled over Uruk like a cloak."

Ninki, we learn from *The Eridu Lament,* flew away from her city to a safe haven in Africa: "Ninki, its great lady, flying like a bird, left her city." But Enki left Eridu only far enough to get out of the Evil Wind's way, yet near enough to see its fate: "Its lord stayed outside his city . . . . Father Enki stayed outside the city . . . for the fate of his harmed city he wept with bitter tears." Many of his loyal subjects followed him, camping on its outskirts. For a day and a night they watched the storm "put its hand" on Eridu.

After the "evil-bearing storm went out of the city, sweeping across the countryside," Enki surveyed Eridu; he found a city "smothered with silence . . . its residents stacked up in heaps." Those who were saved addressed to him a lament: "O Enki," they cried, "thy city has been cursed, made like an alien territory!" and they kept on asking whence should they go, what should they do. But though the Evil Wind had passed, the place was still unsafe, and Enki "stayed out of his city as though it were an alien city." "Forsaking the house of Eridu," Enki then led "those who have been displaced from Eridu" to the desert, "towards an inimical land"; there he used his scientific powers to make the "foul tree" edible.

From the northern edge of the Evil Wind's wide swath, from Babylon, a worried Marduk sent his father, Enki, an urgent message as the cloud of death neared his city: "What am I to do?" he asked. Enki's advice, which Marduk then related to his followers, was that those who could should leave the city—but go only north; and in line with the advice given by the two emissaries to Lot, the people fleeing Babylon were warned "neither to turn nor to look back." They were also told not to take with them any food or beverage, for these might have been "touched by the ghost." If escape was not possible, Enki advised hiding underground: "Get thee into a chamber below the earth, into a darkness," until the Evil Wind was gone.

The storm's slow advance misled some of the gods into costly delays. In Lagash, "mother Bau wept bitterly for her holy temple, for her city." Though Ninurta was gone, his spouse could not force herself to leave. Lingering behind, "O my city, O my city," she kept crying; the delay almost cost her her life:

> On that day, the lady—
> the storm caught up with her;
> Bau, as if she were mortal—
> the storm caught up with her . . .

In Ur we learn from the lamentations (one of which was composed by Ningal herself) that Nannar and Ningal refused to believe that the end of Ur was irrevocable. Nannar addressed a long and emotional appeal to his father Enlil, seeking some means to avert the calamity. But "Enlil answered his son Sin" that the fate could not be changed:

> Ur was granted kingship—
> it was not granted an eternal reign.
> Since days of yore, when Sumer was founded,
> to the present, when people have multiplied—
> Who has ever seen a kingship of everlasting reign?

While the appeals were made, Ningal recalled in her long poem, "the storm was ever breaking forward, its howling overpowering all." It was daytime when the Evil Wind approached Ur; "although of that day I still tremble," Ningal wrote, "of that day's foul smell we did not flee." As night came, "a bitter lament was raised" in Ur; yet the god and goddess stayed on; "of that night's foulness we did not flee," the goddess stated. Then the affliction reached the great ziggurat of Ur, and Ningal realized that Nannar "had been overtaken by the evil storm."

Ningal and Nannar spent a night of nightmare, which Ningal vowed never to forget, in the "termite house" (underground chamber) within the ziggurat. Only next day, when "the storm was carried off from the city," did "Ningal, in order to go from her city . . . hastily put on a garment," and together with the stricken Nannar departed from the city they so loved.

As they were leaving they saw death and desolation: "the people, like potsherds, filled the city's streets; in its lofty gates, where they were wont to promenade, dead bodies were lying about; in its boulevards, where the feasts were celebrated, scattered they lay; in all of its streets, where they were wont to promenade, dead bodies were lying about; in its places where the land's festivities took place, the people lay in heaps.'' The dead were not brought to burial: ''the dead bodies, like fat placed in the sun, of themselves melted away.''

Then did Ningal raise her great lamentation for Ur, the once-majestic city, head city of Sumer, capital of an empire:

O house of Sin in Ur,
bitter is thy desolation . . .
O Ningal whose land has perished,
make thy heart like water!
The city has become a strange city,
how can one now exist?
The house has become a house of tears,
it makes my heart like water . . .
Ur and its temples
have been given over to the wind.

All of southern Mesopotamia lay prostrate, its soil and waters left poisoned by the Evil Wind: ''On the banks of the Tigris and Euphrates, only sickly plants grew. . . . In the swamps grow sickly-headed reeds that rot in the stench. . . . In the orchards and gardens there is no new growth, quickly they waste away. . . . The cultivated fields are not hoed, no seeds are implanted in the soil, no songs resound in the fields.'' In the countryside the animals were also affected: ''On the steppe, cattle large and small become scarce, all living creatures come to an end.'' The domesticated animals, too, were wiped out: ''The sheepfolds have been delivered to the wind. . . . The hum of the turning churn resounds not in the sheepfold. . . . The stalls provide not fat and cheese. . . . Ninurta has emptied Sumer of milk.''

''The storm crushed the land, wiped out everything; it roared like a great wind over the land, none could escape it; desolating the cities, desolating the houses. . . . No one treads the highways, no one seeks out the roads.''

The desolation of Sumer was complete.

EPILOGUE

Seven years after the Evil Wind had desolated Sumer, life began to stir again in the land. But instead of an empire ruling others, Sumer itself was now an occupied land, with a semblance of order maintained by Elamite troops in the south and Gutian soldiers in the north.

Isin, a city never a capital before, was selected as a temporary administrative center, and a former governor of Mari was brought over to rule the land. Documents from that time recorded a complaint that one "who is not of Sumerian seed" was given the reins over Sumer. As his Semitic name—Ishbi-Erra—attested, he was a follower of Nergal, and his appointment must have been part of the arrangement between Nergal and Ninurta.

Some scholars call the decades that followed the demise of Ur a Dark Age in Mesopotamian history. Little is known of those trying times except for what is gleaned from the yearly date formulas. Improving security, restoring here and there, Ishbi-Erra—seeking to solidify his secular authority—dismissed the foreign garrison that patrolled Ur and, by extending his reign to that city, laid claim to being a successor to the kings of Ur; but only a few other resettled cities acknowledged his supremacy, and at Larsa a powerful local chief posed, at times, a challenge.

A year or two later Ishbi-Erra sought to add the central religious authority to his powers by assuming the guardianship of Nippur, raising there the sacred emblems of Enlil and Ninurta. But the permission for that came from Ninurta alone, and the great gods of Nippur remained aloof and alienated. Seeking other support, Ishbi-Erra appointed priests and priestesses to restore the worship of Nannar, Ningal, and Inanna. But it seems that the hearts of the people belonged elsewhere: as numerous *Shurpu* ("Purification") texts suggest, it was Enki and Marduk—using Enki's immense scientific knowledge ("magical powers" in the eyes of the people)—who cured the afflicted, purified the waters, and made the soil grow edible vegetation again.

For the next half-century, embracing the reign of two successors of Ishbi-Erra at Isin, normalcy gradually returned to the land; agriculture and industry revived, internal and external trade resumed.

343

But it was only after the passage of seventy years since its defilement—the same interval that later on applied to the desecrated temple in Jerusalem—that the temple of Nippur could be rebuilt by the third successor on the throne of Isin, Ishme-Dagan. In a long poem of twelve stanzas dedicated to Nippur, he described how its divine couple responded to his appeals to restore the city and its great temple, so that ''Nippur's brickwork be restored'' and ''the divine tablets be returned to Nippur.''

There was great jubilation in the land when the great temple was rededicated to Enlil and Ninlil, in the year 1953 B.C.; it was only then that the cities of Sumer and Akkad were officially declared habitable again.

The official return to normalcy, however, only served to stir up old rivalries among the gods. The successor to Ishme-Dagan bore a name indicating his allegiance to Ishtar. Ninurta put a quick end to that, and the next ruler at Isin—the last one ever to bear a Sumerian name—was one of his followers. But this claim of Ninurta to the restored land could not be upheld: after all, he had caused, even if indirectly, Sumer's destruction. As the next successor's name suggests, Sin then sought to reassert his authority; but the days of his and Ur's supremacy were over.

And so, by the authority vested in them, Anu and Enlil finally accepted Marduk's claim to supremacy at Babylon. Commemorating the fateful decision in the preamble to his law code, the Babylonian king Hammurabi put it in these words:

Lofty Anu, lord of the
gods who from Heaven came to Earth,
and Enlil, lord of Heaven and Earth
who determines the destinies of the land,
Determined for Marduk, the firstborn of Enki,
the Enlil-functions over all mankind;
Made him great among the gods who watch and see,
Called Babylon by name to be exalted,
made it supreme in the world;
And established for Marduk, in its midst,
an everlasting kingship.

Babylon, then Assyria, rose to greatness. Sumer was no more; but in a distant land, the baton of its legacy passed from the hands of Abraham and Isaac his son unto the hand of Jacob, the one renamed *Isra-El.*

The Earth Chronicles: Time Chart

I. Events Before the Deluge

450,000   On Nibiru, a distant member of our solar system, life faces slow extinction as the planet's atmosphere erodes. Deposed by Anu, the ruler Alalu escapes in a spaceship and finds refuge on Earth. He discovers that Earth has gold that can be used to protect Nibiru's atmosphere.

445,000   Led by Enki, a son of Anu, the *Anunnaki* land on Earth, establish Eridu—Earth Station I—for extracting gold from the waters of the Persian Gulf.

430,000   Earth's climate mellows. More Anunnaki arrive on Earth, among them Enki's half-sister Ninharsag, Chief Medical Officer.

416,000   As gold production falters, Anu arrives on Earth with Enlil, the heir apparent. It is decided to obtain the vital gold by mining it in southern Africa. Drawing lots, Enlil wins command of Earth Mission; Enki is relegated to Africa. On departing Earth, Anu is challenged by Alalu's grandson.

400,000   Seven functional settlements in southern Mesopotamia include a Spaceport (Sippar), Mission Control Center (Nippur), a metallurgical center (Badtibira), a medical center (Shuruppak). The ores arrive by ships from Africa; the refined metal is sent aloft to orbiters manned by *Igigi*, then transferred to spaceships arriving periodically from Nibiru.

380,000   Gaining the support of the Igigi, Alalu's grandson attempts to seize mastery over Earth. The Enlilites win the War of the Olden Gods.

300,000   The Anunnaki toiling in the gold mines mutiny. Enki and Ninharsag create Primitive Workers through genetic manipulation of Apewoman; they take over the manual chores of the Anunnaki. Enlil raids the mines, brings the Primitive Workers to the *Edin* in Mesopotamia. Given the ability to procreate, *Homo sapiens* begins to multiply.

200,000   Life on Earth regresses during a new glacial period.

100,000   Climate warms again. The Anunnaki (the biblical *Nefilim*), to Enlil's growing annoyance, marry the daughters of Man.

 75,000   The ''accursation of Earth''—a new Ice Age—begins. Regressive types of Man roam the Earth. Cro-Magnon man survives.

 49,000   Enki and Ninharsag elevate humans of Anunnaki parentage to rule in Shuruppak. Enlil, enraged, plots Mankind's demise.

 13,000   Realizing that the passage of Nibiru in Earth's proximity will trigger an immense tidal wave, Enlil makes the Anunnaki swear to keep the impending calamity a secret from Mankind.

B.C.   II. Events After the Deluge

 11,000   Enki breaks the oath, instructs Ziusudra/Noah to build a submersible ship. The Deluge sweeps over the Earth; the Anunnaki witness the total destruction from their orbiting spacecraft.

            Enlil agrees to grant the remnants of Mankind implements and seeds; agriculture begins in the highlands. Enki domesticates animals.

 10,500   The descendants of Noah are allotted three regions. Ninurta, Enlil's foremost son, dams the mountains and drains the rivers to make Mesopotamia habitable; Enki reclaims the Nile valley. The Sinai peninsula is retained by the Anunnaki for a post-Diluvial spaceport; a control center is established on Mount Moriah (the future Jerusalem).

9780 Ra/Marduk, Enki's firstborn son, divides dominion over Egypt between Osiris and Seth.

9330 Seth seizes and dismembers Osiris, assumes sole rule over the Nile Valley.

8970 Horus avenges his father Osiris by launching the First Pyramid War. Seth escapes to Asia, seizes the Sinai peninsula and Canaan.

8670 Opposed to the resulting control of all the space facilities by Enki's descendants, the Enlilites launch the Second Pyramid War. The victorious Ninurta empties the Great Pyramid of its equipment.

Ninharsag, half-sister of Enki and Enlil, convenes a peace conference. The division of Earth is reaffirmed. Rule over Egypt transferred from the Ra/Marduk dynasty to that of Thoth. Heliopolis built as a substitute Beacon City.

8500 The Anunnaki establish outposts at the gateway to the space facilities; Jericho is one of them.

7400 As the era of peace continues, the Anunnaki grant Mankind new advances; the Neolithic period begins. Demigods rule over Egypt.

3800 Urban civilization begins in Sumer as the Anunnaki reestablish there the Olden Cities, beginning with Eridu and Nippur.

Anu comes to Earth for a pageantful visit. A new city, Uruk (Erech), is built in his honor; he makes its temple the abode of his beloved granddaughter Inanna/Ishtar.

B.C.   III. Kingship on Earth

3760 Mankind granted kingship. Kish is first capital under the aegis of Ninurta. The calendar begun at Nippur. Civilization blossoms out in Sumer (the First Region).

3450 Primacy in Sumer transferred to Nannar/Sin. Marduk proclaims Babylon "Gateway of the Gods." The "Tower of Babel" incident. The Anunnaki confuse Mankind's languages.

His coup frustrated, Marduk/Ra returns to Egypt, deposes Thoth, seizes his younger brother Dumuzi, who had betrothed Inanna. Dumuzi accidentally killed; Marduk imprisoned alive in the Great Pyramid. Freed through an emergency shaft, he goes into exile.

3100   350 years of chaos end with installation of first Egyptian Pharaoh in Memphis. Civilization comes to the Second Region.

2900   Kingship in Sumer transferred to Erech. Inanna given dominion over the Third Region; the Indus Valley civilization begins.

2650   Sumer's royal capital shifts about. Kingship deteriorates. Enlil loses patience with the unruly human multitudes.

2371   Inanna falls in love with Sharru-Kin (Sargon). He establishes new capital city, Agade (Akkad). Akkadian empire launched.

2316   Aiming to rule the Four Regions, Sargon removes sacred soil from Babylon. The Marduk-Inanna conflict flares up again. It ends when Nergal, Marduk's brother, journeys from south Africa to Babylon and persuades Marduk to leave Mesopotamia.

2291   Naram-Sin ascends the throne of Akkad. Directed by the warlike Inanna, he penetrates the Sinai peninsula, invades Egypt.

2255   Inanna usurps the power in Mesopotamia; Naram-Sin defiles Nippur. The Great Anunnaki obliterate Agade. Inanna escapes. Sumer and Akkad occupied by foreign troops loyal to Enlil and Ninurta.

2220   Sumerian civilization rises to new heights under enlightened rulers of Lagash. Thoth helps its king Gudea build a ziggurat-temple for Ninurta.

2193   Terah, Abraham's father, born in Nippur into a priestly-royal family.

2180   Egypt divided; followers of Ra/Marduk retain the south; Pharaohs opposed to him gain the throne of lower Egypt.

2130 As Enlil and Ninurta are increasingly away, central authority also deteriorates in Mesopotamia. Inanna's attempt to regain the kingship for Erech does not last.

B.C.   **IV. The Fateful Century**

2123 Abraham born in Nippur.

2113 Enlil entrusts the Lands of Shem to Nannar; Ur declared capital of new empire. Ur-Nammu ascends throne, is named Protector of Nippur. A Nippurian priest—Terah, Abraham's father—comes to Ur to liaison with its royal court.

2096 Ur-Nammu dies in battle. The people consider his untimely death a betrayal by Anu and Enlil. Terah departs with his family for Harran.

2095 Shulgi ascends the throne of Ur, strengthens imperial ties. As empire thrives, Shulgi falls under charms of Inanna, becomes her lover. Grants Larsa to Elamites in exchange for serving as his Foreign Legion.

2080 Theban princes loyal to Ra/Marduk press northward under Mentuhotep I. Nabu, Marduk's son, gains adherents for his father in Western Asia.

2055 On Nannar's orders, Shulgi sends Elamite troops to suppress unrest in Canaanite cities. Elamites reach the gateway to the Sinai peninsula and its Spaceport.

2048 Shulgi dies. Marduk moves to the Land of the Hittites. Abraham ordered to southern Canaan with an elite corps of cavalrymen.

2047 Amar-Sin (the biblical Amraphel) becomes king of Ur. Abraham goes to Egypt, stays five years, then returns with more troops.

2041 Guided by Inanna, Amar-Sin forms a coalition of Kings of the East, launches military expedition to Canaan and the Sinai. Its leader is the Elamite Khedor-la'omer. Abraham blocks the advance at the gateway to the Spaceport.

2038   Shu-Sin replaces Amar-Sin on throne of Ur as the empire disintegrates.

2029   Ibbi-Sin replaces Shu-Sin. The western provinces tilt increasingly to Marduk.

2024   Leading his followers, Marduk marches on Sumer, enthrones himself in Babylon. Fighting spreads to central Mesopotamia. Nippur's Holy of Holies is defiled. Enlil demands punishment for Marduk and Nabu; Enki opposes, but his son Nergal sides with Enlil.

As Nabu marshals his Canaanite followers to capture the Spaceport, the Great Anunnaki approve the use of nuclear weapons. Nergal and Ninurta destroy the Spaceport and the errant Canaanite cities.

2023   The winds carry the radioactive cloud to Sumer. People die a terrible death, animals perish, the water is poisoned, the soil becomes barren. Sumer and its great civilization lie prostrate. Its legacy passes to Abraham's seed as he begets—at age 100—a legitimate heir: Isaac.

Sources

In addition to specific references in the text, the following served as principal sources for *The Wars of Gods and Men:*

I. Studies, articles, and reports in various issues of the following periodicals and scholarly series:

Abhandlungen der Deutschen (Preussichen) *Akademie der Wissenschaften zu Berlin* (Berlin)

Abhandlungen der Deutschen Orient-Gesellschaft (Berlin)

Abhandlungen der Heidelberger Akademie der Wissenschaften, Philo.-hist klasse (Heidelberg)

Abhandlungen für die Kunde des Morgenlandes (Leipzig)

Acta Orientalia (Oslo)

Acta Societatis Scientarium Fennica (Helsinki)

Aegyptologische Forschungen (Hamburg-New York)

Der Alte Orient (Leipzig)

Alter Orient und Altes Testament (Kevalaer/Neukirchen-Vluyn)

Altorientalische Bibliothek (Leipzig)

Altorientalische Furschungen (Leipzig)

Altorientalische Texte und Untersuchungen (Leiden)

Altorientalische Texte zum Alten Testament (Berlin and Leipzig)

American Journal of Archaeology (Concord, Mass.)

American Journal of Semitic Languages and Literature (Chicago)

American Oriental Series (New Haven)

American Philosophical Society, Memoirs and Transactions (Philadelphia)

Analecta Biblica (Rome)

Analecta Orientalia (Rome)

Anatolica (Istanbul)

Anatolian Studies (London)

Annual of the American Schools of Oriental Research (New Haven)

Annual of the Palestine Exploration Fund (London)

The Antiquaries Journal (London)

Antiquités Orientales (Paris)

Antiquity (Gloucester)

Archiv für Keilschriftforschung (Berlin)
Archiv für Orientforschung (Berlin)
Archiv Orientalni (Prague)
The Assyrian Dictionary (Chicago)
Assyriologische Bibliothek (Leipzig)
Assyriological Studies (Chicago)
Ausgaben der Deutschen Orient-Gesellschaft in Assur (Berlin)

Babyloniaca (Paris)
Babylonian Expedition of the University of Pennsylvania: Cuneiform Texts (Philadelphia)
Babylonian Inscriptions in the Collection of J. B. Nies (New Haven)
Babylonian Records in the Library of J. Pierpont Morgan (New Haven)
Beiträge zur Assyriologie und semitischen Sprachwissenschaft (Leipzig)
Berliner Beiträge zur Vor- und Frühgeschichte (Berlin)
Berliner Beiträge zur Keilschriftforschung (Berlin)
Biblica et Orientalia (Rome)
The Biblical Archaeologist (New Haven)
Biblical Archaeology Review (Washington)
Bibliotheca Mesopotamica (Malibu)
Bibliotheca Orientalis (Leiden)
Bibliothèque de l'École des Hautes Études (Paris)
Boghazköi-Studien (Leipzig)
Die Boghazköi-Texte im Umschrift (Leipzig)
British Schools of Archaeology in Egypt: Egyptian Research Account Publications (London)
Bulletin of the American Schools of Oriental Research (Jerusalem and Baghdad; Baltimore and New Haven)
Bulletin of the Israel Exploration Society (Jerusalem)

Calcutta Sanskrit College Research Series: Studies (Calcutta)
The Cambridge Ancient History (Cambridge)
Chicago University Oriental Institute, Publications (Chicago)
Columbia University Oriental Studies (New York)
Cuneiform Texts from Babylonian Tablets in the British Museum (London)
Cuneiform Texts from Nimrud (London)

Découvertes en Chaldée (Paris)
Deutsche Orient-Gesellschaft, Mitteilungen; Sensdschriften (Berlin)

Deutsches Morgenlandische Gesellschaft, Abhandlungen (Leipzig)

Egypt Exploration Fund, Memoirs (London)
Eretz-Israel: Archaeological, Historical and Geographical Studies (Jerusalem)
Ex Oriente Lux (Leipzig)
Expedition: The Bulletin of the University Museum (Philadelphia)

Forschungen und Fortschritte (Berlin)
France: Délégation en Perse, Mémoires (Paris)
France: Mission Archéologique de Perse, Mémoires (Paris)

Handbuch der Archäologie (München)
Handbuch der Orientalistik (Leiden/Köln)
Harvard Semitic Series (Cambridge, Mass.)
Hebrew Union College Annual (Cincinnati)
Heidelberger Studien zum Alten Orient (Wiesbaden)
Hittite Texts in Cuneiform Character from Tablets in the British Museum (London)

Invenaires des tablettes de Tello (Paris)
Iran (London)
Iranica Antiqua (Leiden)
Iraq (London)
Institut Français d'Archéologie Orientale: Bibliothèque d'Étude, Mémoires (Cairo)
Israel Exploration Journal (Jerusalem)
Israel Oriental Studies (Jerusalem)

Jena University: Texte und Materielen, Frau Prof. Hilprecht Sammlung (Leipzig)
Jewish Palestine Exploration Society, Bulletin (Jerusalem)
Journal of the American Oriental Society (New York and New Haven)
Journal of the Ancient Near Eastern Society of Columbia University (New York)
Journal Asiatique (Paris)
Journal of Biblical Literature and Exegesis (Middletown, Conn.)
Journal of Biblical Literature (Philadelphia)
Journal of Cuneiform Studies (New Haven)
Journal of Egyptian Archaeology (London)
Journal of Jewish Studies (Oxford)
Journal of Near Eastern Studies (Chicago)

Journal of the Palestine Oriental Society (Jerusalem)
Journal of the Royal Asiatic Society (London)
Journal of Sacred Literature and Biblical Record (London)
Journal of Semitic Studies (Manchester)
Journal of the Society of Oriental Research (Chicago)
Journal of the Transactions of the Victoria Institute (London)

Kadmos (Berlin)
Keilinschriftliche Bibliothek (Berlin)
Keilschrifttexte aus Assur historischen Inhalts (Leipzig)
Keilschrifttexte aus Assur religiösen Inhalts (Leipzig)
Keilschrifttexte aus Assur verschiedenen Inhalts (Leipzig)
Keilschrifturkunden aus Boghazköi (Berlin)
Keilschrifttexte aus Boghazköi (Leipzig)
Königliche Museen zu Berlin: Mitteilungen aus den Orientalischen Sammlungen (Berlin)
Königliche Akademie der Wissenschaften zu Berlin: Abhandlungen (Berlin)

Leipziger Semitischen Studien (Leipzig)

Mémoires de la Délégation archéologique en Iran (Paris)
Mesopotamia (Copenhagen)
Mitteilungen der Altorientalischen Gesellschaft (Berlin)
Mitteilungen des Instituts für Orientforschung (Berlin)
Mitteilungen der vorderasiatisch-aegyptischen Gesellschaft (Berlin)
The Museum Journal (Philadelphia)
Museum Monograms, the University Museum (Philadelphia)

Old Testament and Semitic Studies (Chicago)
Oriens (Leiden)
Oriens Antiquus (Rome)
Oriental Institute Publications (Chicago)
Orientalia (Rome)
Orientalische Literaturzeitung (Berlin and Leipzig)
Oxford Editions of Cuneiform Texts (Oxford)

Palestine Exploration Quarterly (London)
Proceedings of the American Philosophical Society (Philadelphia)
Proceedings of the Society of Biblical Archaeology (London)

Publications of the University of Pennsylvania, Series in Philosophy (Philadelphia)

Qadmoniot (Jerusalem)
The Quarterly of the Department of Antiquities in Palestine (Jerusalem)

Reallexikon der Assyriologie und Vorderasiatischen Archäologie (Berlin and Leipzig)
Reallexikon der Vorgeschichte (Berlin)
Recueil de travaux relatifs à la philosophie et à l'archéologie (Paris)
Rencontres Assyriologique Internationales (various venues)
Revue Archéologique (Paris)
Revue d'Assyriologie et d'archéologie orientale (Paris)
Revue biblique (Paris)
Revue hittite et asiatique (Paris)
Revue de l'Histoire des Religions: Annales du Musée Guimet (Paris)

Sächsische Akademie der Wissenschaften: Berichte über die Verhandlungen (Leipzig)
Sächsonische Gesellschaft der Wissenschaft, philo.-hist. Klasse (Leipzig)
Studia Orientalia (Helsinki)
Studia Pohl (Rome)
Studia Semitici (Rome)
Studies in Ancient Oriental Civilizations (Chicago)
Sumer (Baghdad)
Syria (Paris)

Tel-Aviv (Tel-Aviv)
Texte und Materialen der Frau Prof. Hilprecht Collection (Leipzig and Berlin)
Textes cuneiformes (Paris)
Texts from Cuneiform Sources (Locust Valley, N.Y.)
Transactions of the Society of Biblical Archaeology (London)

Universitas Catolica Lovaniensis: Dissertations (Paris)
University Museum Bulletin (Philadelphia)
University Museum, Publications of the Babylonian Section (Philadelphia)
Untersuchungen zur Assyriologie und Vorderasiatischen Archäologie (Berlin)

Ur Excavations (London)
Ur Excavations Texts (London)
Ugarit Forschungen (Münster)
Ugaritica (Paris)

Vetus Testamentum (Leiden)
Vorderasiatisch-Aegyptischen Gesellschaft, Mitteilungen (Leipzig)
Vorderasiatische Bibliothek (Leipzig)
Vorläufiger Bericht uber die Ausgrabungen in Uruk-Warka (Berlin)

Die Welt des Orients (Wuppertal/Göttingen)
Wissenschaftliche Veröffentlichungen der Deutschen Orient-Gesellschaft (Berlin and Leipzig)

Yale Near Eastern Researches (New Haven)
Yale Oriental Series, Babylonian Texts (New Haven)
Yerushalayim (Jerusalem)

Zeitschrift für die altestamentliche Wissenschaft (Giessen/Berlin)
Zeitschrift für Assyriologie (Berlin/Leipzig)
Zeitschrift der Deutschen Morgenländischen Gesellschaft (Leipzig/Wiesbaden)
Zeitschrift für Keilschriftforschung (Leipzig)

II. Individual Works and Studies:

Alster, B. *Dumuzi's Dream.* 1972.
Amiet, P. *Elam.* 1966.
———. *La Glyptique Mesopotamienne Archaique.* 1961.
Andrae, W. *Das Gotteshaus und die Urformen des Bauens im Alten Orient.* 1930.

Barondes, R. *The Garden of the Gods.* 1957.
Barton, G. *The Royal Inscriptions of Sumer and Akkad.* 1929.
Baudissin, W.W. von. *Adonis and Eshmun.* 1911.
Bauer, J. *Altsumerische Wirtschaftexte aus Lagasch.* 1972.
Behrens, H. *Enlil and Ninlil.* 1978.
Berossus. *Fragments of Chaldean History.* 1828.
Borchardt, L. *Die Entstehung der Pyramids.* 1928.
———. *Einiges zur dritten Bauperiode der grossen Pyramide.* 1932.
Borger, R. *Babylonisch-assyrische Lesestücke.* 1963.
Bossert, H.T. *Das Hethitische Pantheon.* 1933.
Breasted, J.H. *Ancient Records of Egypt.* 1906.

Brinkman, J.A. *A Political History of Post-Kassite Babylon.* 1968.

Bruchet, J. *Nouvelles Recherches sur la Grande Pyramide.* 1965.

Brunton, P. *A Search in Secret Egypt.* 1936.

Buccellati, G. *The Amorites of the Ur III Period.* 1966.

Budge, E.A.W. *The Gods of the Egyptians.* 1904.

———. *A History of Egypt.* 1909.

———. *Osiris and the Egyptian Resurrection.* 1911.

Budge, E.A.W. and King, L.W. *Annals of the Kings of Assyria.* 1902.

Cameron, G.G. *A History of Early Iran.* 1936.

Castellino, G. *Two Shulgi Hymns.* 1972.

Chiera, E. *Sumerian Epics and Myths.* 1934.

———. *Sumerian Lexical Texts from the Temple School of Nippur.* 1929.

———. *Sumerian Temple Accounts from Telloh, Jokha and Drehem.* 1922.

———. *Sumerian Texts of Varied Contents.* 1934.

Clay, A.T. *Miscellaneous Inscriptions in the Yale Babylonian Collection.* 1915.

de Clerq, H.F.X. *Collection de Clerq.* 1885–1903.

Cohen, S. *Enmerkar and the Lord of Aratta.* 1973.

Contenau, G. *Manuel d'archéologie orientale.* 1927–47.

———. *Umma sous la Dynastie d'Ur.* 1931.

Cooper, J.S. *The Return of Ninurta to Nippur.* 1978.

Craig, J. *Assyrian and Babylonian Religious Texts.* 1885–87.

Cros, G. *Nouvelles Fouilles de Tello.* 1910.

Davidson, D. and Aldersmith, H. *The Great Pyramid: Its Divine Message.* 1924, 1940.

Deimel, A. *Schultexte aus Fara.* 1923.

———. *Sumerisches Lexikon.* 1925–50.

———. *Veteris Testamenti: Chronologia Monumentis Babyloniaca-Asyrii.* 1912.

———. *Wirtschaftstexte aus Fara.* 1924.

Delaporte, L. *Catalogue des Cylindres Orientaux.* 1920–23.

Dijk, J. van. *Le Motif cosmique dans le pensée Sumeriénne.* 1965.

———. *La sagesse suméro-accadienne.* 1953

Dussaud, R. *Les Découvertes des Ras Shamra (Ugarit) et l'Ancien Testament.* 1937.

———. *Notes de Mythologie Syrienne.* 1905.

Ebeling, E. *Die Akkadische Gebetsserie "Handerhebung."* 1953.

———. *Der Akkadische Mythus vom Pestgotte Era.* 1925.

———. *Keilschrifttexte aus Assur religiösen Inhalts.* 1919, 1923.

———. *Literarische Keilschrifttexte aus Assur.* 1931.

———. *Der Mythus "Herr aller Menschen" vom Pestgotte Ira.* 1926.

———. *Tod und Leben nach den Vorstellungen der Babylonier.* 1931.

Edwards, I.E.S. *The Pyramids of Egypt.* 1947, 1961.

Edzard, D.O. *Sumerische Rechtsurkunden des III Jahrtausend.* 1968.

Erman, A. *The Literature of the Ancient Egyptians.* 1927.

Fairservis, W.A., Jr. *The Roots of Ancient India.* 1971.

Fakhry, A. *The Pyramids.* 1961.

Falkenstein, A. *Archaische Texte aus Uruk.* 1936.

———. *Fluch über Akkade.* 1965.

———. *Die Inschriften Gudeas von Lagash.* 1966.

———. *Literarische Keilschrifttexte aus Uruk.* 1931.

———. *Die neu-sumerischen Gerichtsurkunden.* 1956–57.

———. *Sumerische religiöse Texte.* 1950.

Falkenstein, A. and von Soden, W. *Sumerische und Akkadische Hymnen und Gebete.* 1953.

Falkenstein, A. and van Dijk, J. *Sumerische Gotterlieder.* 1959–60.

Farber-Flügge, G. *Der Mythos "Inanna und Enki."* 1973.

Ferrara, A.J. *Nanna-Suen's Journey to Nippur.* 1973.

Festschrift für Herman Heimpel. 1972.

Forrer, E. *Die Boghazköi-Texte in Umschrift.* 1922–26.

Fossey, G. *La Magie Syrienne.* 1902.

Frankfort, H. *Cylinder Seals.* 1939.

———. *Gods and Myths on Sargonic Seals.* 1934.

———. *Kingship and the Gods.* 1948.

Frankfort, H., et al. *Before Philosophy.* 1946.

Friedrich, J. *Staatsverträge des Hatti Reiches.* 1926–30.

Gadd, C.J. *A Sumerian Reading Book.* 1924.

Gadd, C.J. and Kramer, S.N. *Literary and Religious Texts.* 1963.

Gadd, C.J. and Legrain, L. *Royal Inscriptions from Ur.* 1928.

Gaster, Th. *Myth, Legend and Custom in the Old Testament.* 1969.

Gelb, I.J. *Hittite Hieroglyphic Monuments.* 1939.

Geller, S. *Die Sumerische-Assyrische Serie Lugal-e Me-lam-bi* NIR.GAL. 1917.

Genouillac, H. de *Fouilles de Tello*. 1934–36.

——. *Premières recherches archéologique à Kish*. 1924–25.

——. *Tablettes de Dréhem*. 1911.

——. *Tablettes sumériennes archaique*. 1909.

——. *Textes economiques d'Oumma de l'Epoque d'Our*. 1922.

——. *Textes religieux sumériens du Louvre*. 1930.

——. *La trouvaille de Dréhem*. 1911.

Genoville, H. de *Textes de l'epoque d'Ur*. 1912.

Götze, A. *Hattushilish*. 1925.

——. *Hethiter, Churriter und Assyrer*. 1936.

Graves, R. *The Greek Myths*. 1955.

Grayson, A.K. *Assyrian and Babylonian Chronicles*. 1975.

——. *Babylonian Historical-Literary Texts*. 1975.

Green, M.W. *The Uruk Lament*. 1984.

Gressmann, H. and Ungnad, A. *Altorientalische Texte und Bilder zum Alten Testament*. 1909.

Gurney, O.R. *The Hittites*. 1952.

Gurney, O.R. and Finkelstein, J.J. *The Sultantepe Tablets*. 1957–64.

Güterbock, H.G. *The Deeds of Suppilulima*. 1956.

——. *Die historische tradition bei Babylonier und Hethitern*. 1934.

——. *Hittite Mythology*. 1961.

——. *Siegel aus Boghazkoy*. 1940–42.

——. *The Song of Ullikumi*. 1952.

Hallo, W.W. *Women of Sumer*. 1976.

Hallo, W.W. and Dijk, J.J. van. *The Exaltation of Inanna*. 1968.

Harper, E.J. *Die Babylonische Legenden*. 1894.

Haupt, P. *Akkadische und sumerische Keilschrifttexte*. 1881–82.

Hilprecht, H.V. *Old Babylonian Inscriptions*. 1893–96.

Hilprecht Anniversary Volume. 1909.

Hinz, W. *The Lost World of Elam*. 1972.

Hooke, S.H. *Middle Eastern Mythology*. 1963.

Hrozny, B. *Hethitische Keischrifttexte aus Boghazköy*. 1919.

Hussey, M.I. *Sumerian Tablets in the Harvard Semitic Museum*. 1912–15.

Jacobsen, Th. *The Sumerian King List*. 1939.

——. *Towards the Image of Tammuz*. 1970.

——. *The Treasures of Darkness*. 1976.

Jastrow, M. *Die Religion Babyloniers und Assyriers.* 1905.

Jean, C.F. *La religion sumérienne.* 1931.

———. *Shumer et Akkad.* 1923.

Jensen, P. *Assyrisch-Babylonische Mythen und Epen.* 1900.

———. *Der I(U)ra-Mythus.* 1900.

———. *Die Kosmologie der Babylonier.* 1890.

———. *Texte zur Assyrisch-Babylonischen Religion.* 1915.

Jeremias, A. *The Old Testament in the Light of the Ancient Near East.* 1911.

Jirku. A. *Die älteste Geschichte Israels.* 1917.

———. *Altorientalischer Kommentar zum Alten Testament.* 1923.

Jones, T.B. and Snyder, J.W. *Sumerian Economic Texts from the Third Ur Dynasty.* 1923.

Josephus, Flavius. *Against Apion.*

———. *Antiquities of the Jews.*

Kärki, I. *Die Sumerische Königsinschiften der Frühbabylonischen Zeit.* 1968.

Keiser, C.E. *Babylonian Inscriptions in the Collection of J.B. Nies.* 1917.

———. *Patesis of the Ur-Dynasty.* 1919.

———. *Selected Temple Documents of the Ur Dynasty.* 1927.

Keller, W. *The Bible as History in Pictures.* 1963.

Kenyon, K. *Digging Up Jerusalem.* 1974.

King, L.W. *The Annals of the Kings of Assyria.* 1902.

———. *Babylonian Boundary Stones.* 1912.

———. *Babylonian Magic and Sorcery.* 1896.

———. *Babylonian Religion and Mythology.* 1899.

———. *Chronicles Concerning Early Babylonian Kings.* 1907.

———. *Hittite Texts in the Cuneiform Characters.* 1920–21.

Kingsland, W. *The Great Pyramid in Fact and Theory.* 1932–35.

Knudtzon, J.A. *Assyrische Gebete an den Sonnengott.* 1893.

König, F.W. *Handbuch der chaldischen Inschriften.* 1955.

Köppel, R. *Die neuen Ausgrabungen am Tell Ghassul im Jordantal.* 1932.

Kramer, S.N. *Enki and Ninhursag.* 1945.

———. *Lamentation Over the Destruction of Ur.* 1940.

———. *From the Poetry of Sumer.* 1979.

———. *Poets and Psalmists.* 1976.

———. *Sumerian Literature.* 1942.

———. *Sumerian Texts in the Museum of the Ancient Orient, Istanbul.* 1943–49.

————. *Sumerische Literarische Texte aus Nippur.* 1961.
Kramer Anniversary Volume. 1976.

Labat, R. *Manuel d'Epigraphie Akkadienne.* 1963.
Lambert, W.G. *Babylonian Wisdom Literature.* 1960.
Lambert, W.G. and Millard, A.R. *Atra-Hasis, the Babylonian Story of the Flood.* 1969.
Langdon, S. *Babylonian Liturgies.* 1913.
————. *Babylonian Wisdom.* 1923.
————. *"Enuma Elish"—The Babylonian Epic of Creation.* 1923.
————. *Excavations at Kish.* 1924.
————. *Historical and Religious Texts.* 1914.
————. *Semitic Mythology.* 1964.
————. *Sumerian and Babylonian Psalms.* 1909.
————. *The Sumerian Epic of Paradise.* 1915.
————. *Sumerian and Semitic Religious and Historical Texts.* 1923.
————. *Sumerian Liturgical Texts.* 1917.
————. *Sumerian Liturgies and Psalms.* 1919.
————. *Sumerians and Semites in Babylon.* 1908.
————. *Tablets from the Archives of Drehem.* 1911.
————. *Tammuz and Ishtar.* 1914.
Langdon, S. and Gardiner, A.H. *The Treaty of Alliance.* 1920.
Legrain, L. *Historical Fragments.* 1922.
————. *Royal Inscriptions and Fragments from Nippur and Babylon.* 1926.
————. *Les Temps des Rois d'Ur.* 1912.
————. *Ur Excavations.* 1936.
Lepsius, K.R. *Denkmäler aus Aegypten.* 1849–58.
Luckenbill, D.D. *Ancient Records of Assyria and Babylonia.* 1926–27.
————. *Hittite Treaties and Letters.* 1921.
Lutz, H.F. *Selected Sumerian and Babylonian Texts.* 1919.
————. *Sumerian Temple Records of the Late Ur Dynasty.* 1912.

Mazar, B. *The World History of the Jewish People.* 1970.
Mencken, A. *Designing and Building the Great Pyramid.* 1963.
Mercer, S.A.B. *The Tell el-Amarna Tablets.* 1939.
Mortgat, A. *Die Enstehung der sumerischen Hochkultur.* 1945.
————. *Vorderasiatische Rollsiegel.* 1940.
Müller, M. *Asien und Europa nach Altaegyptischer Denkmälern.* 1893.
————. *Der Bündnisvertrag Ramses II und der Chetiterkönigs.* 1902.
Müller-Karpe, H. *Handbuch der Vorgeschichte.* 1966–68.

Nies, J.B. *Ur Dynasty Tablets.* 1920.
Nies, J.B. and Keiser, C.E. *Historical, Religious and Economic Texts and Antiquities.* 1920.

Oppenheim, A.L. *The Interpretation of Dreams in the Ancient Near East.* 1956.
———. *Mesopotamian Mythology.* 1950.
Oppert, J. *La Chronologie de la Genèse.* 1895.
Otten, H. *Mythen vom Gotte Kumarbi.* 1950.
———. *Die Überlieferung des Telepinu-Mythus.* 1942.

Parrot, A. *The Arts of Assyria.* 1961.
———. *Sumer—the Dawn of Art.* 1961.
———. *Tello.* 1948.
———. *Ziggurats et Tour de Babel.* 1949.
Paul Haupt Anniversary Volume. 1926.
Perring, J.E. *The Pyramids of Gizeh From Actual Survey and Measurement.* 1839.
Petrie, W.M.F. *The Pyramids and Temples of Gizeh.* 1883–85.
———. *Researches on the Great Pyramid.* 1874.
———. *The Royal Tombs of the First Dynasty.* 1900.
Poebel, A. *Historical Texts.* 1914.
———. *Miscellaneous Studies.* 1947.
———. *Sumerische Studien.* 1921.
Pohl, A. *Rechts- und Verwaltungsurkunden der III Dynastie von Ur.* 1937.
Price, I.M. *The Great Cylinder Inscriptions of Gudea.* 1927.
Pritchard, J.B. *The Ancient Near East in Pictures Relating to the Old Testament.* 1969.
———. *Ancient Near Eastern Texts Relating to the Old Testament.* 1969.

Quibell, J.E. *Hierkanopolis.* 1900.

Radau, H. *Early Babylonian History.* 1900.
———. *NIN-IB, The Determiner of Fates.* 1910.
———. *Sumerian Hymns and Prayers to the God Dumuzi.* 1913.
———. *Sumerian Hymns and Prayers to the God Ninib.* 1911.
Rawlinson, H. *The Cuneiform Inscriptions of Western Asia.* 1861–1909.
Rawlinson, H.G. *India.* 1952.
Reiner, E. *Shurpu, A Collection of Sumerian and Akkadian Incantations.* 1958.
Reisner, G. *Sumerisch-Babylonische Hymnen.* 1896.

————. *Tempel-urkunden aus Telloh.* 1901.

Renger, J. *Götternamen in der Altbabylonischen Zeit.* 1967.

Ringgren, K.V.H. *Religions of the Ancient Near East.* 1973.

Roberts, J.J.M. *The Earliest Semitic Religions.* 1972.

Roberts, A. and Donaldson, J. *The Ante-Nicene Fathers.* 1918.

Roux, G. *Ancient Iraq.* 1964.

Rutherford, A. *The Great Pyramid Series.* 1950.

Saggs, H.W.F. *The Encounter with the Divine in Mesopotamia and Israel.* 1976.

————. *The Greatness That Was Babylon.* 1962.

Salonen, A. *Die Landfarhrzeuge des Alten Mesopotamien.* 1951.

————. *Nautica Babyloniaca.* 1942.

————. *Die Waffen der Alten Mesopotamier.* 1965.

————. *Die Wasserfahrzeuge in Babylon.* 1939.

Sayce, A.H. *The Ancient Empires of the East.* 1884.

————. *The Religion of the Ancient Babylonians.* 1888.

Schmandt-Besserat, D. *The Legacy of Sumer.* 1976.

Schnabel, P. *Berossos und die Babylonisch-Hellenistische Literatur.* 1923.

Schneider, N. *Die Drehem- und Djoha-Texte.* 1932.

————. *Die Götternamen von Ur III.* 1939.

————. *Götterschiffe im Ur III-Reich.* 1946.

————. *Die Siegellegenden der Geschäfts-urkunden der Stadt Ur.* 1950.

————. *Die Zeitbestimmungen der Wirtschaftsurkunden von Ur III.* 1936.

Schrader, E. *The Cuneiform Inscriptions and the Old Testament.* 1885.

————. *Die Keilinschriften und das Alte Testament.* 1902.

Schroeder, O. *Keilschrifttexte aus Assur Verschiedenen Inhalts.* 1920.

Scott, J.A. *A Comparative Study of Hesiod and Pindar.* 1898.

Sethe, K.H. *Amun und die Acht Urgotten von Hermopolis.* 1930.

————. *Die Hatschepsut Problem.* 1932.

————. *Urgeschichte und älteste Religion der Aegypter.* 1930.

Sjöberg, A.W. *Der Mondgott Nanna-Suen in der Sumerischen Überlieferung.* 1960.

————. *Nungal in the Ekur.* 1973.

————. *Three Hymns to the God Ningishzida.* 1975.

Smith, S. *A History of Babylon and Assyria.* 1910–28.

Smyth, C.P. *Our Inheritance in the Great Pyramid.* 1877.
Soden, W. von. *Sumerische und Akkadische Hymnen und Gebete.* 1953.
Sollberger, E. *Corpus des inscriptions "royales" présargoniques de Lagash.* 1956.
Speiser, E.A. *Genesis.* 1964.
———. *Mesopotamian Origins.* 1930.
Studies Presented to A. L. Oppenheim. 1964.

Tadmor, H. and Weinfeld, M. *History, Historiography and Interpretation.* 1983.
Tallqvist, K.L. *Akkadische Götterepitheta.* 1938.
———. *Assyrische Beschwörungen, Series Maqlu.* 1895.
Thompson, R.C. *The Devils and Evil Spirits of Babylonia.* 1903.
———. *The Reports of the Magicians and Astrologers of Nineveh and Babylon.* 1900.
Thureau-Dangin, F. *Les cylindres de Gudéa.* 1925.
———. *Les inscriptions de Shumer et Akkad.* 1905.
———. *Recueil des tablettes chaldéennes.* 1903.
———. *Rituels accadiens.* 1921.
———. *Die sumerischen und akkadischen Königsinschriften.* 1907.
———. *Tablettes d'Uruk.* 1922.

Ungnad, A. *Die Religion der Babylonier und Assyrer.* 1921.

Vian, F. *La guerre des Géants.* 1952.

Walcot, P. *Hesiod and the Near East.* 1966.
Ward, W.H. *Hittite Gods in Hittite Art.* 1899.
Weber, O. *Die Literatur der Babylonier und Assyrer.* 1907.
Weiher, E. von. *Der Babylonische Gott Nergal.* 1971.
Wheeler, M. *Early India and Pakistan.* 1959.
———. *The Indus Civilization.* 1968.
Wilcke, C. *Das Lugalbanda Epos.* 1969.
———. *Sumerische literarische Texte.* 1973.
Wilson, J.V.K. and Vanstiphout, H. *The Rebel Lands.* 1979.
Wilson, R.R. *Genealogy and History in the Biblical World.* 1977.
Winckler, H. *Altorientalische Forschungen.* 1897–1906.
———. *Altorientalische Geschichts-Auffassung.* 1906.
———. *Sammlung von Keilschrifttexten.* 1893–95.
Wiseman, D.J. *Chronicles of Chaldean Kings.* 1956.
Witzel, M. *Keilinschriftliche Studien.* 1918–25.

——. *Tammuz-Liturgien und Verwandtes.* 1935.

Woolley, C.L. *Abraham: Recent Discoveries and Hebrew Origins.* 1936.

——. *Excavations at Ur.* 1923.

——. *Ur of the Chaldees.* 1930.

——. *The Ziggurat and Its Surroundings.* 1939.

Zimmern, H. *Sumerische Kultlieder aus altbabylonischer Zeit.* 1912–13.

——. *Zum Babylonischen Neujahrfest.* 1918.

Index

Praise for the Works of Zecharia Sitchin

"Reflects the highest level of scientific knowledge . . ."

SCIENCE & RELIGION NEWS

"Exciting . . . credible . . . most provocative and compelling."

LIBRARY JOURNAL

"One of the most important books on Earth's roots ever written."

EAST WEST JOURNAL

"Sitchin is a zealous investigator into man's origins . . . a dazzling performance."

KIRKUS REVIEWS

"For thousands of years priests, poets, and scientists have tried to explain how man was created. Now a recognized scholar has come forth with a theory that is most astonishing of all."

UNITED PRESS INTERNATIONAL

Also by Zecharia Sitchin

Genesis Revisited

Divine Encounters

The Earth Chronicles Handbook

The Earth Chronicles Expeditions (autobiographical)

Journeys to the Mythical Past (autobiographical)

The King Who Refused to Die (fiction)

The Lost Book of Enki

There Were Giants Upon the Earth

The Earth Chronicles

The 12th Planet — Book I

The Stairway to Heaven — Book II

The Wars of Gods and Men — Book III

The Lost Realms — Book IV

When Time Began — Book V

The Cosmic Code — Book VI

The End of Days — Book VII

ZECHARIA SITCHIN

THE LOST REALMS

**The Fourth Book
of
The Earth Chronicles**

Bear & Company
Rochester, Vermont • Toronto, Canada

Bear & Company
One Park Street
Rochester, Vermont 05767
www.BearandCompanyBooks.com

Bear & Company is a division of Inner Traditions International

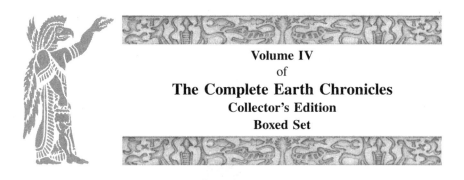

Volume IV
of
The Complete Earth Chronicles
Collector's Edition
Boxed Set

Printed and bound in India at Replika Press Pvt. Ltd.

10 9 8 7 6

TABLE OF CONTENTS

FOREWORD

In the annals of Europe the discovery of the New World bears the imprint of *El Dorado*—the relentless search for gold. But little did the conquistadores realize that they were only replaying a search, on Earth and in these new lands, that had taken place eons earlier!

Buried under the records and tales of avarice, plunder, and wanton destruction that the newly found riches had triggered, there is also evidence in the chronicles of that time of how bewildered the Europeans had been to come upon civilizations that were so akin to those of the Old World: kingdoms and royal courts, cities and sacred precincts, art and poetry, sky-high temples, priests—and the symbol of the cross and a belief in a Creator of All. Last but not least, there were the legends of white and bearded gods who had left but did promise to return.

The mysteries and enigmas of the Maya, the Aztecs, the Incas, and their predecessors that puzzled the conquistadores still baffle scholar and layman alike five centuries later.

How, when, and why did such great civilizations arise in the New World, and is it mere coincidence that the more that is known about them, the more they appear to have been molded after the civilizations of the ancient Near East?

It is our contention that the answers can be found only by accepting as fact, not as myth, the presence on Earth of the Anunnaki, "Those Who From Heaven to Earth Came."

This book offers the evidence.

1

EL DORADO

Nowadays Toledo is a quiet provincial city situated about an hour's drive south of Madrid; yet hardly does a visitor to Spain miss seeing it, for within its walls there have been preserved the monuments of diverse cultures and the lessons of history.

Its beginnings, local legends tell, go back two millennia before the Christian era and its foundation is attributed to the biblical descendants of Noah. Its name, many hold, comes from the Hebrew *Toledoth* ("Generational Histories"); its olden homes and magnificent houses of worship bear witness to the Christianization of Spain—the rise and fall of the Moors and their Moslem dominion and the uprooting of the splendid Jewish heritage.

For Toledo, for Spain, and for all other lands, 1492 was a pivotal year, for a triple history was made therein. All three events took place in Spain, a land geographically known as "Iberia"—a name for which the only explanation can be found in the term *Ibri* ("Hebrew") by which its earliest settlers might have been known. Having lost the greater part of Iberia to the Moslems, the warring splintered kingdoms in the peninsula saw their first major union when Ferdinand of Aragon and Isabella of Castile married in 1469. Within ten years of the union they launched a military campaign to roll back the Moors and bring Spain under the banner of Catholicism; in January 1492 the Moors were decisively defeated with the fall of Granada, and Spain was made a Christian land. In March of that same year, the king and queen signed an edict for the expulsion from Spain, by July 31 of that year, of all Jews who would not convert to Christianity by that time. And on August 3 of that same year, Christopher Columbus—Cristobal Colon to the Spaniards—sailed under the Spanish flag to find a western route to India.

He sighted land on October 12, 1492. He returned to Spain in January 1493. As proof of his success he brought back four

3

"Indians"; as corroboration of his contention that a larger, second expedition under his command was justified, he brought with him a collection of golden trinkets obtained from the natives and tales of a city, a golden city, where the people wore golden bracelets on their arms and legs and adorned their necks and ears and noses with gold, all this gold coming from a fabulous mine near that city.

Of the first gold thus brought to Spain from the new lands, Isabella—so pious that they called her "The Catholic"—ordered that an elaborate Custody be fashioned, and presented it to the Cathedral of Toledo, traditional seat of Spain's Catholic hierarchy. And so it is that nowadays, when a visitor to the cathedral is taken to see its Treasury—a room protected by heavy grillwork and filled with the precious objects donated to the Church over the centuries—one can see, though not touch, the very first gold brought back by Columbus.

It is now recognized that there had been much more to the voyage than a search for a new route to India. Strong evidence suggests that Columbus was a Jew forced into conversion; his financial backers, likewise converted, could have seen in the enterprise an avenue of escape to freer lands. Ferdinand and Isabella had visions of the discovery of the rivers of Paradise and everlasting youth. And Columbus himself had secret ambitions, only some of which he expressed in his personal diaries. He saw himself as the fulfiller of ancient prophesies regarding a new age that shall begin with the discovery of new lands "at the extremity of the Earth."

But he was realistic enough to recognize that of all the information he had brought back from the first voyage, the mention of gold was the attention-getter. Asserting that "the Lord would show him" the enigmatic place "where gold is born," he succeeded in persuading Ferdinand and Isabella to provide him with a much larger fleet for a second voyage, then a third. By then, however, the monarchs sent along various administrators and men known for less vision but more action, who supervised and interfered with the admiral's operations and decisions. The inevitable conflicts culminated in the return of Columbus to Spain in chains, on the pretext that he had mistreated some of his men. Although the king and queen at once released him and offered him monetary compensation, they agreed with the view that Columbus was a good admiral but a bad governor—and clearly one who could not force out of the Indians the true location of the City of Gold.

Columbus countered all that with yet more reliance on ancient prophecies and biblical quotes. He collected all the texts into a book, *The Book of Prophecies,* which he presented to the king and queen. It was meant to convince them that Spain was destined to reign over Jerusalem, and that Columbus was the one chosen to achieve that by being the first to find the place where gold is born.

Themselves believers in the Scriptures, Ferdinand and Isabella agreed to let Columbus sail once more, convinced especially by his argument that the mouth of the river (now called the "Orinoco") that he had discovered was that of one of the four rivers of Paradise; and as the Scriptures had stated, one of those rivers encompassed the land of Havila, "whence the gold came." This last voyage encountered more hardships and heartbreaks than any of the previous three.

Crippled with arthritis, a ghost of his old self, Columbus returned to Spain on November 7, 1504. Before the month was out, Queen Isabella died; and although King Ferdinand still had a soft spot for Columbus, he decided to let others act on the last memorandum prepared by Columbus, in which he compiled the evidence for the presence of a major gold source in the new lands.

"Hispaniola will furnish your invincible majesties with all the needed gold," Columbus assured his royal sponsors regarding the island that is nowadays shared by Haiti and the Dominican Republic. There, Spanish settlers using local Indians as slave labor, indeed succeeded in mining gold in fabulous quantities: in less than two decades the Spanish treasury received from Hispaniola gold equivalent to 500,000 ducats.

As it turned out, the Spanish experience in Hispaniola was to repeat itself over and over again across an immense continent. Within those two short decades, as the natives died out or fled and the gold veins were exhausted, the Spaniards' euphoria turned to disappointment and despair, and they grew ever more audacious in landing on ever more unknown coasts in search of riches. One of the early destinations was the peninsula of Yucatán. The very first Spaniards there, in 1511, were survivors of a shipwreck; but in 1517 a purposeful convoy of three ships under Francisco Hernandez de Córdoba sailed to Yucatán from Cuba for the purpose of procuring slave labor. To their amazement they came upon stone buildings, temples, and idols of goddesses; to the misfortune of the local inhabitants (whom the

Spaniards understood to have called themselves "Maya") the Spaniards also "found certain objects of gold, which they took."

The record of the Spanish arrival at and the conquest of Yucatán is primarily based on the report titled *Relacion de las cosas de Yucatan* written by Friar Diego de Landa in 1566 (the English translation by William Gates is titled *Yucatan, Before and After the Conquest*). Hernandez and his men, Diego de Landa reported, saw on this expedition a large step-pyramid, idols and statues of animals, and a large inland city. However, the Indians they tried to capture put up a fierce fight, undaunted even by the cannon fire from the ships. The heavy casualties—Hernandez himself was badly wounded—forced a retreat. Yet, on his return to Cuba, Hernandez recommended further expeditions, for "that land was good and rich, because of its gold."

A year later another expedition left Cuba for Yucatán. They landed on the island of Cozumel and discovered New Spain, Pánuco and the province of Tabasco (having thus named the new places). Armed with a variety of goods for barter and not only with weapons, the Spaniards this time met both hostile and friendly Indians. They saw more stone edifices and monuments, felt the sting of arrows and spears tipped with sharp obsidian stone, and examined artfully made objects. Many were made of stone, common or semiprecious; others shined as gold, but on close examination proved to be of copper. There were, contrary to expectations, very few gold objects; and there were absolutely no mines or other sources for gold, or any other metals, in the land.

Where then had the gold, as little as there was, come from? They obtain it by trading, the Mayas said. It comes from the northwest: there, in the land of the Aztecs, it is plentiful and abundant.

The discovery and conquest of the realm of the Aztecs, in the highland heartland of Mexico, is linked historically with the name of Hernando Cortés. In 1519 he sailed from Cuba in command of a veritable armada of eleven ships, some six hundred men, and a large number of highly prized, scarce horses. Stopping, landing and re-embarking, he slowly proceeded along Yucatán's gulf coast. In the area where Maya influence waned and Aztec domination began he established a base camp and called it Veracruz (by which name the place is still called).

It was there that to the Spaniards' great astonishment emissaries of the Aztec ruler appeared offering greetings and bearing exquisite gifts. According to an eyewitness, Bernal Díaz del Castillo *(Historia verdadera de la conquista de la Nueva Espana,* English translation by A. P. Maudslay), the gifts included "a wheel like the sun, as big as a cartwheel, with many sorts of pictures on it, the whole of fine gold and a wonderful thing to behold, which those who afterwards weighed it said it was worth more than ten thousand dollars." Then another, even larger wheel, "made of silver of great brilliancy in imitation of the moon." Also a helmet filled to the brim with grains of gold; and a headdress made of the plumes of the rare *quetzal* bird (a relic still kept at Vienna's Museum für Völkerkunde).

These were gifts, the emissaries explained, of their ruler Moctezuma to the divine Quetzal Coatl, the "Plumed Serpent" god of the Aztecs; a great benefactor who was forced long ago by the God of War to leave the land of the Aztecs. With a band of followers he went to Yucatán, and then sailed off eastward, vowing to return on the day of his birth in the year "1 Reed." In the Aztec calendar, the cycle of years completed itself every fifty-two years, and therefore the year of the promised return, "1 Reed," could occur once in fifty-two years. In the Christian calendar these were the years 1363, 1415, 1467—and 1519, precisely the year in which Cortés appeared from the waters on the east at the gateway of the Aztec domain. Bearded and helmeted as Quetzalcoatl was (some also held that the god was fair skinned), Cortés seemed to fulfill the prophecies.

The gifts offered by the Aztec ruler were not casually selected. Rather, they were rich with symbolism. The heap of gold grains was offered because gold was a divine metal belonging to the gods. The silver disk representing the moon was included because some legends held that Quetzalcoatl sailed off to return to the heavens, making the moon his abode. The plumed headdress and the richly adorned garments were for the returning god to wear. And the golden disk was a sacred calendar depicting the cycle of fifty-two years and indicating the Year of Return. We know that it was such a calendar because others like it, made however of stone rather than pure gold, have since been discovered (Fig. 1).

Whether the Spaniards had grasped the symbolism or not is not recorded. If they did, they did not respect it. To them the objects represented one thing: proof of the vast riches that awaited them in the Aztec realm. These irreplaceable objects were among the artful treasures that arrived in Seville from Mexico on December 9, 1519, on board the first treasure ship

Figure 1

sent back to Spain by Cortés. The Spanish king Charles I,
grandson of Ferdinand and sovereign of other European lands
as Emperor Charles V of the Holy Roman Empire, was then in
Flanders, and the ship was sent on to Brussels. The golden
hoard included in addition to the symbolic gifts golden figurines
of ducks, dogs, tigers, lions, and monkeys; and a golden bow
and arrows. But overwhelming them all was the "sun disk,"
seventy-nine inches in diameter and thick as four *real* coins. The
great painter and artist Albrecht Dürer, who saw the treasure
that arrived from "the New Golden Land," wrote that "these
things were all so precious that they were valued at 100,000
gulden. But I have never seen in all my days what so rejoiced
my heart as these things. For I saw among them amazing artistic
objects and I marvelled over the subtle ingenuity of the men in
these distant lands. Indeed I cannot say enough about the things
which were there before me."

But whatever unique artistic, religious, cultural, or historical
value "these things" had, to the king they represented first and
last gold—gold with which he could finance his struggles against
internal insurrections and external wars. Losing no time,
Charles ordered that these and all future objects made of precious metals be melted down on arrival and recast as gold or
silver bullion.

In Mexico, Cortés and his men adopted the same attitude. Advancing slowly and overcoming whatever resistance was encountered by force of superior arms or by diplomacy and treachery, the Spaniards arrived at the Aztec capital Tenochtitlán—today's Mexico City—in November 1519. The city, situated in the midst of a lake, could be reached only via causeways that could be easily defended. Yet, still awed by the prophecy of the Returning God, Moctezuma and all the nobles came out to greet Cortés and his entourage. Only Moctezuma wore sandals; all the others were barefoot, humbling themselves before the white god. He made the Spaniards welcome in his magnificent palace; there was gold everywhere, even the tableware was made of gold; and they were shown a storage room filled with golden artifacts. Using a ruse, the Spaniards seized Moctezuma and held him in their quarters; for his release they demanded a ransom in gold. The nobles thereupon sent out runners throughout the kingdom to collect the ransom; the golden objects that were handed over were enough to fill a ship that sailed back to Spain. (It was, however, seized by the French, causing war to break out.)

Obtaining gold through cunning and weakening the Aztecs by sowing dissent among them, Cortés was planning to release Moctezuma and leave him on the throne as a puppet ruler. But his second-in-command lost patience and ordered a massacre of the Aztec noblemen and commanders. In the turmoil that followed Moctezuma was killed and the Spaniards had a full-fledged battle on their hands. With heavy losses Cortés retreated from the city; he reentered it, heavily reinforced from Cuba and after prolonged battles, only in August of 1521. By the time Spanish rule was irrevocably imposed on the crushed Aztecs, gold weighing some 600,000 pesos was forced out, plundered, and melted down into ingots.

Mexico, while being conquered, was indeed a New Golden Land; but once the gold artifacts created and accumulated over centuries, if not millennia, were hauled off, it was becoming apparent that Mexico was not the biblical land of Havila, and Tenochtitlán not the legendary City of Gold. And so the search for gold, which neither adventurers nor kings were prepared to give up, turned to other parts of the New World.

The Spaniards had by then established a base, Panama, on the Pacific coast of America, and from there they were sending out expeditions and agents into Central and South America. It was there that they heard the alluring legend of El Dorado—short for *el hombre dorado,* the Gilded Man. He was a king whose kingdom was so rich in gold that he was painted each morning with a gum or oil on which gold dust was sprinkled, covering him from head to toe. In the evening he dipped in the lake and washed off the gold and oil, only to repeat the rite the next day. He reigned in a city that was in the center of a lake, situated on an island of gold.

According to the chronicle titled *Elejias de Varones Ilustres de Indias,* the first concrete report of El Dorado was brought to Francisco Pizarro in Panama by one of his captains in the following version: It was said that an Indian from Colombia heard of "a country rich in emeralds and gold. Among the things in which they engaged was this: their king disrobed, and went aboard a raft to the midst of a lake to make oblations to the gods. His regal form was overspread with fragrant oil, on which was laid a coat of powdered gold, from sole of foot unto his highest brow, making him resplendent as the beaming of the sun." To view the ritual many pilgrims had been coming, making "rich votive offerings of golden trinkets and emeralds rare, and diverse other of their ornaments," by throwing them into the sacred lake.

Another version, suggesting that the sacred lake was somewhere in northern Colombia, had the gilded king carrying the "great quantity of gold and emeralds" into the center of the lake. There, acting as emissary of the multitudes that stood shouting and playing musical instruments all around the lake, he threw the treasure into the lake as an offering to its god. Still another version gave the name of the golden city as Manoa and said it was in the land of *Biru*—Peru to the Spaniards.

Word of El Dorado spread among the Europeans in the New World like wildfire, and in time back in Europe itself. The word of mouth was soon put in writing; pamphlets and books began to circulate in Europe describing the land and the lake and the city and the king whom no one had yet seen, and even the actual ritual of gilding the king each morning (Fig. 2).

While some, like Cortés who went to California or others who went to Venezuela, had searched in directions of their own choosing, Francisco Pizarro and his lieutenants relied entirely on the Indian reports. Some went indeed to Colombia and searched the waters of Lake Guatavita—a search that continued on and off for four centuries, yielded golden votive objects and left ensuing generations of treasure hunters convinced that if only the lake could be completely drained, the golden riches would be raised from its bottom.

Others, like Pizarro himself, accepted Peru as the right location. Two expeditions launched from their base in Panama

along the Pacific coast of South America yielded enough gold
objects to convince them that a major effort in Peru would pay
off. After obtaining a royal charter for the purpose and the titles
Captain General and Governor (of the province yet to be conquered), Pizarro sailed to Peru at the head of two hundred men.
The year was 1530.

Figure 2

How did he expect to take over with such a small force a
large country protected by thousands of warriors fiercely loyal
to their lord, the *Inca,* whom they considered to be the personification of a god? Pizarro's plan was to repeat the strategy successfully employed by Cortés: to lure the ruler, seize him,
obtain gold as ransom, then release him to be a Spanish puppet.

The fact that the Incas, as the people themselves came to be
called, were engaged in a civil war when the Spaniards landed
was an unexpected boon. They found out that upon the death of
the Lord Inca, his firstborn son by a "secondary wife" challenged the legitimacy of the succession by a son born to the
Inca's principal wife. When news of the advancing Spaniards
reached the challenger, Atahualpa by name, he decided to let
the Spaniards advance inland (and thus away from their ships
and reinforcements) while he completed the seizing of the capital, Cuzco. On reaching a major city in the Andes, the Spaniards sent to him emissaries bearing gifts and offering peace
talks. They suggested that the two leaders meet in the city
square, unarmed and without military escort, as a show of
goodwill. Atahualpa agreed. But when he reached the square,
the Spaniards attacked his escort and held the Inca captive.

To release him they asked for a ransom: let a large room be

filled with gold as high as a man's outstretched hand can reach up toward the ceiling. Atahualpa understood that to mean filling up the room with golden objects, and agreed. On his orders golden utensils were brought out of temples and palaces—goblets, ewers, salvers, vases of all shapes and sizes—ornaments that included imitations of animals and plants, and plates that lined the walls of public buildings. For weeks the treasures were being brought to fill up the room. But then the Spaniards claimed that the deal was to fill the room with solid gold, not the space-filling artifacts; and for over a month, Inca goldsmiths were engaged in melting down all the artful objects into ingots.

As if history insisted on repeating itself, the fate of Atahualpa was exactly the same as that which befell Moctezuma. Pizarro intended to release him to rule as a puppet king; but zealous lieutenants and Church representatives, at a mock trial, sentenced Atahualpa to death for the crime of idolatry and the murder of his half brother, his rival for the throne.

The ransom obtained for the Inca lord, according to one of the chronicles of that time, was the equivalent of 1,326,539 *pesos de oro* ("weights of gold")—about 200,000 ounces—a wealth that was quickly divided among Pizarro and his men after setting aside the required fifth for the king. But as much as what each man received was beyond his fanciest dreams, it was nothing compared to what was yet to come.

When the conquistadores entered the capital, Cuzco, they saw temples and palaces literally covered and filled with gold. In the royal palace there were three chambers filled with gold furnishings and five with silver, and a hoard of 100,000 gold ingots weighing about five pounds each, a reserve of the precious metal waiting to be fashioned into artful objects. The golden throne, outfitted with a golden stool, designed to convert into a litter on which the king could recline, weighed 25,000 pesos (about 4,000 ounces); even the carrying poles were overlaid with gold. Everywhere there were chapels and burial chambers honoring ancestors, filled with statuettes and images of birds, fish, and small animals, ear spools, breastplates. In the great temple (which the Spaniards named Temple of the Sun) the walls were covered with heavy gold plates. Its garden was an artificial garden where everything—trees, shrubs, flowers, birds, a fountain—was fashioned of gold. In the courtyard there was a field of maize (the local corn) where every stalk was made of silver and the ears of gold; it was a field that covered an area of 300 by 600 feet—180,000 square feet of golden corn!

In Peru, the conquering Spaniards saw within a short space of time their initial easy victories give way to hard-fought Inca rebellions, and the initial wealth give way to the scourge of inflation. To the Incas, as to the Aztecs, gold was a gift or the property of the gods, not a means of exchange. They never used it as a commodity, as money. To the Spaniards, gold was a means to acquire whatever their hearts desired. Flush with gold but short of homegrown luxuries or even daily necessities, the Spaniards were soon paying sixty golden pesos for a bottle of wine, 100 for a cloak, 10,000 for a horse.

But back in Europe, the inflow of gold, silver, and precious stones raised the gold fever and encouraged more speculation about El Dorado. No matter how much treasure was coming in, the conviction persisted that El Dorado had not yet been found, that with persistence and luck and the correct reading of Indian clues and enigmatic maps someone was going to find it. German explorers were certain that the golden city would be found at the headwaters of the Orinoco river in Venezuela, or perhaps in Colombia. Others concluded that the river to be followed was another one, even the Amazon in Brazil. Perhaps the most romantic of all of them, on account of his background and his royal sponsor, was Sir Walter Raleigh, who sailed from Plymouth in 1595 to find the legendary Manoa and add its golden glory to Queen Elizabeth's crown.

In his vision he saw Manoa as

> Imperial El Dorado, roofed with gold!
> Shadows to which—
> Despite of all shocks of change,
> all onset of capricious accident—
> Men clung with yearning hope
> which would not die.

He, like others before and after him, still saw El Dorado— the king, the city, the land—as a dream yet to be fulfilled, "a yearning hope which would not die." In that, all who went in quest of El Dorado were a link in a chain that began before the pharaohs and continues with our wedding rings and national hoards.

Yet it was those dreamers, those adventurers, who in their lust for gold revealed to Western man the unknown peoples and civilizations of the Americas. And thereby, unknowingly, reestablished links that had existed in forgotten times.

Why did the quest for El Dorado continue so intensively for so long even after the discovery of the incredible gold and silver treasures of Mexico and Peru, to say nothing of the lesser plundered lands? The continued and intensified search can be attributed mostly to the conviction that the *source* of all those riches had yet to be found.

The Spaniards extensively questioned the natives about the fountainhead of the amassed treasures and tirelessly followed every clue. It soon became clear to them that the Caribbean and Yucatán were not primary sources at all: the Maya in fact indicated that they had obtained gold mostly by trading with their neighbors to the south and the west, and explained that they had learned the arts of goldsmithing from earlier settlers (whom scholars nowadays identify by the name *Toltecs*). Yes, the Spaniards said, but where do the others obtain the gold from? From the gods, the Maya answered. In the local tongues, gold was called *teocuitlatl*, literally meaning "the gods' excretion," their perspiration and their tears.

In the Aztec capital the Spaniards learned that gold was indeed deemed to be the gods' metal, the stealing of which was a capital offense. The Aztecs too pointed to the Toltecs as their teachers of the art of goldsmithing. And who had taught the Toltecs? The great god Quetzalcoatl, the Aztecs replied. Cortés, in his reports to the Spanish king, wrote that he had questioned the Aztec king Moctezuma extensively about the source of the gold. Moctezuma revealed that the gold came from three provinces of his kingdom, one on the Pacific coast, one on the gulf coast, and one inland in the southwest where the mines were. Cortés sent men to investigate the three indicated sources. In all three they found that the Indians were actually obtaining the gold in riverbeds or collecting nuggets that were lying on the surface where rains had washed the gold down. In the province where mines did exist, they appeared to have been mined only in the past; the Indians encountered by the Spaniards were not working in the mines at all. "There were no active mines," Cortés wrote in his report. "Nuggets were found on the surface; the principal source was the sand of the riverbeds. The gold was kept in the form of dust in small cane tubes or quilts, or was melted in small pots and cast in bars." Once ready, it was sent on to the capital, returned to the gods to whom the gold had always belonged.

While most experts on mining and metallurgy accept the conclusions of Cortés—that the Aztecs engaged in placer mining only (the collection of gold nuggets and dust from surfaces and river beds) and not in actual mining involving the cutting of shafts and tunnels into mountainsides—the issue is far from being resolved. The conquering Spaniards, and mining engineers in following centuries, persistently spoke of prehistoric gold mines found at various Mexican sites. Since it seems inconceivable that earlier settlers of Mexico, such as the Toltecs, whose beginnings are traced to a few centuries before the Christian era, would have possessed a higher mining technology than the later (and thus presumably more advanced) Aztecs, the purported "prehistoric mines" have been dismissed by researchers as old shafts begun and abandoned by the conquering Spaniards. Expressing the current views at the beginning of this century, Alexander Del Mar *(A History of the Precious Metals)* stated that, "With regard to Prehistoric mining it must be premised that the Aztecs had no knowledge of iron, and therefore, that subterranean mining . . . is practically out of the question. It is true that modern prospectors have found in Mexico old shafts and remains of mining works which appeared to them to have been the scene of prehistoric mining." Although such reports had even found their way into official publications, Del Mar believed that the sites were "ancient workings coupled with volcanic upheavals, or else with deposits of lava or tarp, both of which were regarded as evidence of vast antiquity." "This inference," he concluded, "is hardly warranted."

This, however, is not what the Aztecs themselves had reported. They attributed to their predecessors, the Toltecs, not just the craftsmanship but also the knowledge of the hidden place of gold and the ability to mine it out of the rocky mountains. The Aztec manuscript known as *Codice Matritense de la Real Academia* (vol. VIII), in a translation by Miguel León-Portilla *(Aztec Thought and Culture)* describes the Toltecs thus:

"The Toltecs were skillful people; all of their works were good, all were exact, all well made and admirable. . . . Painters, sculptors, carvers of precious stones, feather artists, potters, spinners, weavers, skillful in all they made. They discovered the precious green stones, the turquoise; they knew the turquoise and its mines. They found its mines and they found the mountains hiding silver and gold, copper and tin and the metal of the moon."

The Toltecs, most historians agree, had come to the central highland of Mexico in the centuries preceding the Christian era —at least a thousand years, perhaps fifteen hundred years, before the Aztecs appeared on the scene. How was it possible that they had known mining, real mining of gold and other metals as well as of precious stones such as turquoise, whereas those who had followed them—the Aztecs—could only scrape nuggets off the surface? And who was it who had taught the Toltecs the secrets of mining?

The answer, as we have seen, was Quetzalcoatl, the Feathered Serpent god.

The mystery of the accumulated gold treasures on the one hand and the limited ability of the Aztecs to obtain it, repeated itself in the land of the Incas.

In Peru, as in Mexico, the natives did obtain gold by collecting grains and nuggets washed down from the mountains into the riverbeds. But the annual production through these methods could in no way account for the immense treasures of gold found in Inca hands. The immensity of the hoards is obvious from the Spanish records kept at Seville, the official port of entry into Spain of the New World's riches. The *Archives of the Indies*—still available—recorded the receipt in the five years 1521–1525 of 134,000 *pesos de oro.* In the next five years (the loot from Mexico!) the quantity was 1,038,000 pesos. From 1531 to 1535, when the shipments from Peru began to augment those from Mexico, the quantity increased to 1,650,000 pesos. During 1536–1540, when Peru was the main source, the gold received weighed 3,937,000 pesos; and in the decade of the 1550s the receipts totaled almost 11,000,000 pesos.

One of the leading chroniclers of that time, Pedro de Cieza de León *(Chronicles of Peru),* reported that in the years following the conquest the Spaniards "extracted" from the Inca empire annually 15,000 *arrobas* of gold and 50,000 of silver; this is equivalent to over 6,000,000 ounces of gold and over 20,000,000 ounces of silver *annually!* Though Cieza de León does not mention over how many years such fabulous quantities had been "extracted," his numbers give us an idea of the quantities of precious metals that the Spaniards were able to plunder in the Inca lands.

The chronicles relate that after the initial great ransom obtained from the Inca lord, the plunder of the riches of Cuzco, and the tearing apart of a sacred temple at Pachácamac on the coast, the Spaniards became expert in "extracting" gold from the provinces in equally vast quantities. Throughout the Inca empire, provincial palaces and temples were richly decorated with gold. Another source was burial sites containing golden objects. The Spaniards learned that the Inca custom was to seal the residences of deceased noblemen and rulers, leaving there their mummified bodies surrounded by all the precious objects they had possessed in life. The Spaniards also suspected, correctly, that the Indians had carried off to hiding places various gold treasures; some were stashed away in caves, some were buried, others were thrown into lakes. And there were the *huacas,* venerated places set aside for worship or for divine use, where gold was piled up and kept at the disposal of its true owners, the gods.

Tales of treasure finds, as frequently as not obtained by torturing Indians to reveal the hidden places, permeate the records of the fifty years following the conquest, and even into the seventeenth and eighteenth centuries. In this manner Gonzalo Pizarro found the hidden treasure of an Inca lord who reigned a century earlier. One Garcia Gutiérrez de Toledo found a series of mounds covering sacred treasures from which over a million pesos worth of gold was extracted between 1566 and 1592. As late as 1602, Escobar Corchuelo secured from the *huaca* La Tosca objects valued at 60,000 pesos. And when the waters of the river Moche were diverted, a treasure worth some 600,000 pesos was found; it included, the chroniclers reported, "a large golden idol."

Writing a century and a half ago, and thus much closer to the events than can be done nowadays, two explorers (M. A. Ribero and J. J. von Tschudi, *Peruvian Antiquities)* described the situation thus: "In the second half of the sixteenth century, in the short space of twenty-five years, the Spaniards exported from Peru to the mother country more than four hundred million ducats of gold and silver, and we may well be assured that nine-tenths of this quantity composed the mere booty taken by the conquerors; in this computation we leave out of view the immense masses of precious metals buried by the natives to hide from the avarice of the foreign invaders; as also the celebrated chain of gold which the Inca Huayna Capac commanded to be made in honor of the birth of his firstborn son, Inti Cusi Huallapa Huáscar, and which they say was thrown into the lake of Urcos." (The chain was said to be seven hundred feet long and thick as a man's wrist.) "Also not included are the eleven thousand llamas loaded with gold dust in precious vases of this metal, with which the unfortunate Atahualpa wished to purchase his life and liberty, and which the conductors interred in the Puna as soon as they heard of the new punishment to which their adored monarch had been treacherously condemned."

That these immense quantities were the result of the plunder of accumulated riches and not of ongoing production is known not only from the chronicles but is also confirmed by the numbers. Within decades, after the visible and hidden treasures had been exhausted, the gold receipts in Seville dwindled to a mere 6,000–7,000 pounds of gold a year. It was then that the

Spaniards, using their iron tools, began to conscript the natives for work in the mines. The toil was so harsh, that by the end of the century the land was almost depopulated and the Spanish Court imposed restrictions on the exploitation of native labor. Great silver lodes were discovered and worked, such as at Potosí; but the quantity of gold obtained never matched, nor does it explain, the vast treasures amassed before the Spanish arrival.

Seeking an answer to the puzzle, Ribero and von Tschudi wrote, "The gold, although it was the Peruvians' most esteemed metal, they possessed in a quantity greater than that of any other. Upon comparing its abundance, in the time of the Incas, with the quantity which, in the space of four centuries, the Spaniards have been able to extract from the mines and rivers, it becomes certain that the Indians had a knowledge of veins of this precious material which the conquerors and their descendants never succeeded in discovering." (They also predicted that "the day will come when Peru will withdraw from her bosom the veil which now covers more wonderful riches than those which are offered at the present day in California." And when the gold rushes of the late nineteenth century gripped Europe with a new gold fever, many mining experts came to believe that the so-called "mother lode," the ultimate source of a'l gold on Earth, would be found in Peru.)

As in Mexico, the generally accepted notion regarding the Lands of the Andes has been (in the words of Del Mar) that "the precious metals obtained by the Peruvians previous to the Spanish conquest consisted nearly altogether of gold secured by washing the river gravels. No native shafts were found. A few excavations had been made into the sides of hills with outcrops of native gold or silver." That is true insofar as the Incas of the Andes (and the Aztecs of Mexico) were concerned; but in the Andean lands, as in Mexico, the question of *prehistoric* mining —the hewing of the metal out of vein-rich rocks—has not been settled.

The possibility that at a time long before the Incas someone had access to gold at its vein sources (at places the Incas did not disclose or even did not know about), remains a plausible explanation for the accumulated treasures. Indeed, according to one of the best contemporary studies on the subject (S. K. Lothrop, *Inca Treasure As Depicted by Spanish Historians),* "modern mines are located at sites of aboriginal operations. Ancient shafts have been frequently reported and also finds of primitive tools, even the bodies of entombed miners."

The amassing of gold by the American natives, no matter

how obtained, poses still another, yet very basic, question:
What for?

The chroniclers, and contemporary scholars after centuries
of studies, agree that those peoples had no practical use for
gold, except to adorn with it the temples of the gods and those
who ruled over the people in the name of the gods. The Aztecs
literally poured their gold at the Spaniards' feet, believing that
they represented the returning deity. The Incas, who at first also
saw in the arriving Spaniards the fulfillment of their deity's
promise to return from across the seas, later on could not understand why the Spaniards had come so far and behaved so ill
for a metal for which Man had no practical use. All scholars are
agreed that the Incas and the Aztecs did not use gold for monetary purposes, nor did they attach to it a commercial value. Yet
they extracted from their subject nations a tribute of gold.
Why?

In the ruins of a pre-Inca culture at Chimu, on the Peruvian
coast, the great nineteenth-century explorer Alexander von
Humboldt (a mining engineer by profession) discovered a mass
of gold buried alongside the dead in tombs. The discovery of the
metal made him wonder why would gold, being deemed of no
practical use, be buried with the dead? Was it that somehow it
was believed that they would need it in an afterlife—or that in
joining their ancestors, they could use the gold the way their
ancestors had once done?

Who was it who had brought about such customs and beliefs,
and when?

Who had caused gold to be so valued, and perhaps gone
after it at its sources?

The only answer the Spaniards were given was "the gods."

It was of the gods' tears that gold was formed, the Incas said.

And in so pointing to the gods, they unknowingly echoed the
statement of the biblical Lord through the prophet Haggai:

> The silver is mine
> and the gold is mine,
> So sayeth the Lord of Hosts.

It is this statement, we believe, that holds the key to unraveling the mysteries, enigmas, and secrets of gods, men, and ancient civilizations in the Americas.

2

THE LOST REALM
OF CAIN?

The Aztec capital, Tenochtitlán, was an impressive metropolis when the Spaniards arrived. Their reports describe it as large, if not larger, than most European cities of the time, well laid out and administered. Situated on an island in Lake Texcoco, in the highlands' central valley, it was surrounded by water and intersected by canals—a Venice of the New World. The long and wide causeways that connected the city to the mainland made a great impression upon the Spaniards; so did the numerous canoes sailing the canals, the streets teeming with people, the marketplaces filled with merchants and merchandise from all over the realm. The royal palace was many-roomed, filled with riches and surrounded by gardens that included an aviary and a zoo. A great plaza, humming with activity, was the setting for festivities and military parades.

But the heart of the city and the empire was the vast religious center—an immense rectangle of more than a million square feet, surrounded by a wall fashioned to resemble writhing serpents. There were scores of edifices within this sacred precinct; the most outstanding of them were the Great Temple with its two towers, and the partly circular temple of Quetzalcoatl. Nowadays Mexico City's great plaza and the cathedral occupy parts of the ancient sacred precinct, as do many adjoining streets and buildings. Following a chance excavation in 1978, important portions of the Great Temple can be now seen and visited, and enough has become known in the past decade to make possible a scale-model reconstruction of the precinct as it was in its times of glory.

The Great Temple had the shape of a step-pyramid, rising in stages to a height of some 160 feet; its base measured about 150 by 150 feet. It represented the culmination of several phases of construction: Like a Russian doll, the outer structure was built over a previous smaller one, and that one enclosed an even earlier structure. In all, seven structures were encasing each other. Archaeologists were able to peel the layers back to Tem-

ple II, which was built sometime around A.D. 1400; that one, like the last one, already had the distinctive twin towers upon its top.

Representing a curious dual worship, the tower on the northern side was a shrine dedicated to Tlaloc, god of storms and earthquakes (Fig. 3a). The southern tower was dedicated to the Aztec tribal deity Huitzilopochtli, their war god. He was usually depicted holding the magical weapon called Fire Serpent (Fig. 3b) with which he had defeated four hundred lesser gods.

Two monumental stairways led up to the pyramid's top on its western side, one for each tower-shrine. Each was decorated at its base with two ferocious serpent heads carved of stone, one being the Fire Serpent of Huitzilopochtli and the other the Water Serpent symbolizing Tlaloc. At the base of the pyramid excavators found a large, thick stone disk whose top was carved with a representation of the dismembered body of the goddess Coyolxauhqui (Fig. 3c). According to Aztec lore, she was a sister of Huitzilopochtli and came to grief by his own hand,

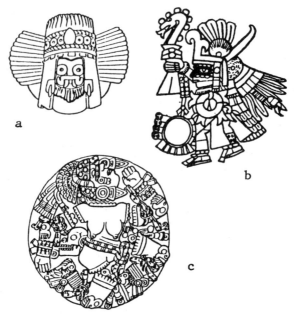

a

b

c

Figure 3

during the rebellion of the four hundred gods in which she was involved. It seems that her fate was one of the reasons for the Aztec belief that Huitzilopochtli had to be appeased by offering him the torn out hearts of human victims.

The motif of twin towers was further enhanced in the sacred precinct by the erection of two pyramids topped by towers, one on each side of the Great Temple, and two more somewhat back, westward. The latter two flanked the temple of Quetzal-coatl. It had the unusual shape of a regular step-pyramid in front but a circular stepped structure in the back, where it spi-raled up to become a circular tower with a conical dome (Fig. 4). Many believe that this temple served as a solar observatory. A. F. Aveni *(Astronomy in Ancient Mesoamerica)* determined in 1974 that on the dates of the equinox (March 21 and September 21), when the Sun rises in the east precisely on the equator, sunrise could be seen from the Quetzalcoatl tower right be-tween the two towers atop the Great Temple. This was possible only because the planners of the sacred precinct erected the temples along an architectural axis aligned not precisely with the cardinal points, but one that shifted to the southeast by 7½ degrees; this compensated exactly for the geographical position of Tenochtitlán (north of the equator), enabling the viewing of

Figure 4

the Sun on the crucial dates rising between the two towers.

Although the Spaniards may have been unaware of this sophisticated feature of the sacred precinct, the records they left bespeak their amazement at encountering not merely a cultured people, but also a civilization so similar to the Spaniards' own. Here, across what had been a forbidding ocean, for all intents and purposes isolated from the civilized world, was a state headed by a king—just as in Europe. Noblemen, functionaries, courtesans filled the royal court. Emissaries came and went. Tribute was extracted from vassal tribes, taxes were paid by loyal citizens. Royal archives kept written records of tribal histories, dynasties, wealth. There was an army with an hierarchical command and perfected weapons. There were arts and crafts, music and dancing. There were festivals connected with the seasons and holy days prescribed by religion—a state religion, just as in Europe. And there was the sacred precinct with its temples and chapels and residences, surrounded by a wall—just as the Vatican in Rome—run by a hierarchy of priests who, just as in Europe of the time, were not only keepers of the faith and interpreters of divine will, but also guardians of the secrets of scientific knowledge. Of that, astrology, astronomy, and the mysteries of the calendar were paramount.

Some Spanish chroniclers of the time, aiming to counteract the embarrassingly positive impressions of what should have been Indian savages, attributed to Cortés a reprimand to Moctezuma for worshiping "idols that are not gods, but evilly named demons," an evil influence Cortés supposedly offered to counteract by constructing atop the pyramid a shrine with a cross "and the image of our Lady" (Bernal Díaz del Castillo, *Historia verdadera)*. But to the Spaniards' astonishment, even the symbol of the cross was known to the Aztecs and, deemed by them

Figure 5

a symbol with celestial significance, was depicted as the emblem of Quetzalcoatl's shield (Fig. 5).

Moreover, through the maze of a pantheon of numerous deities, there could be seen an underlying belief in a Supreme God, a Creator of All. Some of the prayers to him even sounded familiar; here are a few verses from an Aztec prayer, recorded in Spanish from the original Nahuatl language:

> You inhabit the heavens,
> You uphold the mountains...
> You are everywhere, everlasting.
> You are beseeched, you are entreated.
> Your glory is eminent.

Yet with all the baffling similarities, there was a troubling difference about Aztec civilization. It was not just the "idolatry," of which the flocking friars and *padres* made a *casus belli;* not even the barbaric customs of cutting out the hearts of prisoners and offering the pulsating hearts in sacrifice to Huitzilopochtli (a practice, incidentally, apparently introduced only in 1486 by the king preceding Moctezuma). It was, rather, the whole gamut of this civilization, as though it was the result of a progress that had been arrested in its course, or an imported higher culture covering, as a thin veneer, a coarser understructure.

The edifices were impressive and ingeniously laid out, but they were not built of dressed stones; rather, they were of adobe construction—field stones crudely held together with simple mortar. Trade was extensive, but it was all a barter trade. Tribute was in kind; taxes were paid in personal services—there was no knowledge of money of any kind. Textiles were woven on a most rudimentary loom; cotton was spun on clay spindles the likes of which have been found in the Old World, in the ruins of Troy (second millennium B.C.) and sites in Palestine (third millennium B.C.). In their tools and weapons the Aztecs were in a stone age, unaccountably devoid of metal tools and weapons although they possessed the craft of goldsmithing. For cutting they used chips of the glasslike obsidian stone (and one of the prevalent objects from Aztec times was the obsidian knife used to cut out prisoners' hearts . . .).

Because other peoples in the Americas have been held to have had no writing, the Aztecs seemed more advanced at least on this score because they did have a system of writing. But the writing was neither alphabetical nor phonetic; it was a series of pictures, like cartoons in a comic strip (Fig. 6a). By comparison, in the ancient Near East where writing began circa 3800 B.C. (in Sumer) in the form of pictographs, it quickly changed through stylization to a cuneiform script, advanced to a phonetic script where signs stood for syllables, and, by the end of the second millennium B.C., to a complete alphabet. Pictorial writing appeared in Egypt at the beginning of kingship there, circa 3100 B.C., and quickly evolved into a system of hieroglyphic writing.

Expert studies, as that by Amelia Hertz *(Revue de Synthèse Historique,* vol. 35), have concluded that Aztec picture-writing in A.D. 1500 was similar to the earliest Egyptian writing, as that on the stone tablet of king Narmer (Fig. 6b) whom some consider to have been the first dynastic king in Egypt—four and a half millennia earlier. A. Hertz found another curious analogy between Aztec Mexico and early dynastic Egypt: In both, while copper metallurgy was yet to develop, goldsmithing was so advanced that the craftsmen could inlay golden objects with turquoise (a semiprecious stone cherished in both lands).

The National Museum of Anthropology in Mexico City— certainly one of the world's best in its field—displays the country's archaeological heritage in a U-shaped building. Consisting of connected sections or halls, it takes the visitor through time and place, from prehistoric origins to Aztec times and from south and north to east and west. The central section is devoted to the Aztecs; it is the heart and pride of national Mexican archaeology, for "Aztecs" was a name given these people only lately. They called themselves *Mexica,* thus giving their preferred name not only to the capital (built where the Aztec Tenochtitlán had been) but also to the whole country.

a

b

Figure 6

The Mexica Hall, as it is designated, is portrayed by the Museum as "the most important hall.…. Its grandiose dimensions were designed to amply frame the culture of the Mexican people." Its monumental stone sculptures include the immense Calendar Stone (see Fig. 1) that weighs some twenty-five tons, huge statues of various gods and goddesses, and a great thick stone disk carved in the round. Smaller stone and clay effigies, earthenware utensils, weapons, golden ornaments and other Aztec remains, plus the scale model of the sacred precinct, fill up this impressive hall.

The contrast between primitive clay and wood objects and grotesque effigies on the one hand, and the powerful stone carvings and monumental sacred precinct on the other hand, is astounding. It is inexplicable in terms of the less than four centuries of Aztec presence in Mexico. How could two such layers of civilization be accounted for? When the answer is sought in known history, the Aztecs appear as a nomadic, uncouth immigrant tribe that forced its way into a valley peopled by tribes with a more advanced culture. At first they made a living by serving the settled tribes, mostly as hired mercenaries. In time they managed to overpower their neighbors and borrowed not only their culture but also their artisans. Themselves followers of Huitzilopochtli, the Aztecs adopted their neighbors' pantheon, including the rain god Tlaloc and the benevolent Quetzalcoatl, god of crafts, writing, mathematics, astronomy, and time reckoning.

But the legends, what scholars call "migration myths," put events in a different light—mainly by beginning the tale at a much earlier time. The sources for this information are not only verbal traditions, but the various books called codices. These, such as the Codex Boturini, relate that the ancestral home of the Aztec tribe was called *Azt-lan* ("White Place"). It was the abode of the first patriarchal couple, *Itzac-mixcoatl* ("White Cloud Serpent") and his spouse *Ilan-cue* ("Old Woman"); they gave birth to sons from whom the Nahuatl-speaking tribes, among them the Aztecs, had come forth. The Toltecs too were descended of Itzac-mixcoatl, but their mother was another woman; they were thus only half brothers of the Aztecs.

Where Aztlan was located, no one can say for certain. Of the numerous studies dealing with the matter (which include theories that it was the legendary Atlantis), one of the best is Eduard Seler's *Wo lag Aztlan, die Heimat der Azteken?* It was a place apparently associated with the number seven, having been sometimes called Aztlan of the Seven Caves. It was also depicted in the codices as a place recognizable by its seven temples: a central large step-pyramid surrounded by six lesser shrines.

In his elaborate *Historia de las cosas de la Nuéva Espana,* the Friar Bernardino de Sahagún, using the original texts in the native Nahuatl language written after the Conquest, deals with the multitribal migration from Aztlan. There were seven tribes in all. They left Aztlan by boats. The pictorial books show them passing by a landmark whose pictograph remains an enigma. Sahagún provides various names for the way stations, calling the place of landfall "Panotlan"; it simply means "Place of Arrival by Sea," but from various clues scholars conclude that it was what is nowadays Guatemala.

The arriving tribes had with them four Wise Men to guide and lead them, because they had carried with them ritual manuscripts and also knew the secrets of the calendar. From there the tribes went in the direction of the Place of the Cloud-Serpent, apparently dispersing as they did so. At long last some, including the Aztecs and the Toltecs, reached a place called Teotihuacan, where two pyramids were built, one to the Sun and the other to the Moon.

Kings reigned at Teotihuacan and were buried there, for to be buried in Teotihuacan was to join the gods in an afterlife. How long it was before the next migratory trek is not clear; but at some point the tribes began to abandon the holy city. First to leave were the Toltecs, who left to build their own city, Tollan. Last to leave were the Aztecs. Their wanderings took them to various places, but they found no respite. At the time of their final migration their leader's name was *Mexitli,* meaning "The Anointed." That, according to some scholars (e.g., Manuel Orozoco y Berra, *Ojeada sobre cronologia Mexicana),* was the origin of the tribal name *Mexica* ("The Anointed People").

The signal for the last migration was given to the Aztecs/ Mexica by their god Huitzilopochtli, who promised them a land where there are "houses with gold and silver, multicolored cotton and cacao of many hues." They were to keep on going in the indicated direction until they would see an eagle perched on a cactus growing from a rock surrounded by water. They were to settle there and call themselves "Mexica," for they were a chosen people destined to rule over the other tribes.

Thus it was that the Aztecs arrived—according to these legends, for the second time—in the Valley of Mexico. They reached Tollan, also known as "The Middle Place." Although the inhabitants were their own ancestral kinfolk, they did not make the Aztecs welcome. For nearly two centuries the Aztecs lived on the central lake's marshy edges. Gaining strength and knowledge, they finally established their own city, Tenochtitlán.

The name meant "City of Tenoch." Some think it was so called because the Aztec leader at the time, the actual builder of the city, was named Tenoch. But since it is known that the Aztecs considered themselves at the time to have been *Tenochas*—descendants of Tenoch—others believed that Tenoch was the name of a tribal ancestor, a legendary paternal figure from way, way back.

Scholars now generally hold that the Mexica or Tenochas arrived in the valley circa A.D. 1140 and established Tenochtitlán in A.D. 1325. They then gained influence through a series of alliances with some tribes and warfare with others. Some researchers doubt whether the Aztecs dominated a true empire. The fact is that when the Spaniards arrived, they were the dominant power in central Mexico, lording over allies and subjugating enemies. The latter served as a source of captives for sacrifices; the Spanish conquest was facilitated by their insurrections against the Aztec oppressors.

Like the biblical Hebrews, who traced back their genealogies not only to patriarchal couples but also to the beginning of Mankind, so did the Aztecs and Toltecs and other Nahuatl tribes possess Legends of Creation that followed the same themes. But whereas the Old Testament compressed its detailed Sumerian sources by devising one plural entity *(Elohim)* out of the various deities active in the creative processes, the Nahuatl tales retained the Sumerian and Egyptian concepts of several divine beings acting either alone or in concert.

Tribal beliefs, prevalent from the southwestern United States in the north to today's Nicaragua in the south—Mesoamerica—held that at the very beginning there was an Olden God, Creator of All Things, of the Heaven and of the Earth, whose abode was in the highest heaven, the twelfth heaven. Sahagún's sources attributed the origin of this knowledge to the Toltecs:

> And the Toltecs knew
> that many are the heavens.
> They said there are twelve superimposed divisions;
> There dwells the true god and his consort.
> He is the Celestial God, Lord of Duality;
> His consort is Lady of Duality, Celestial Lady.
> This is what it means:
> He is king, he is Lord, above the twelve heavens.

This amazingly sounds like a rendering of Mesopotamian celestial-religious beliefs, according to which the head of the pantheon was called Anu ("Lord of Heaven") and who, with his consort Antu ("Lady of Heaven") resided on the outermost planet, the twelfth member of our Solar System. The Sumerians depicted it as a radiating planet whose symbol was the cross (Fig. 7a). The symbol was thereafter adopted by all the peoples of the ancient world and evolved to the ubiquitous emblem of the Winged Disk (Fig. 7b,c). Quetzalcoatl's shield (Fig. 7d) and symbols depicted on early Mexican monuments (Fig. 7e) are uncannily similar.

The Olden Gods of whom the Nahuatl texts related legendary tales were depicted as bearded men (Fig. 8), as befits ancestors of the bearded Quetzalcoatl. As in Mesopotamian and Egyptian theogonies, there were tales of divine couples and of brothers who espoused their own sisters. Of prime and direct concern to the Aztecs were the four divine brothers Tlatlauhqui, Tezcatlipoca-Yaotl, Quetzalcoatl, and Huitzilopochtli, in the order of their birth. They represented the four cardinal points and the four primary elements: Earth, Wind, Fire, Water—a concept of the "root of all things" well known in the Old World from end to end. These four gods also represented the colors red, black, white, and blue, and the four races of Mankind, who were often depicted (as on the front page of the *Codex Ferjervary-Mayer)* in appropriate colors together with their symbols, trees and animals.

This recognition of four separate branches of Mankind is in-

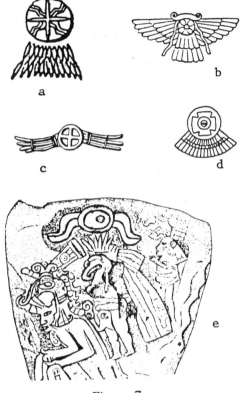

Figure 7

teresting, perhaps even significant in its difference from the three-branched Mesopotamian-biblical concept of an Asian-African-European division stemming from the Shem-Ham-Japhet line of Noah. A fourth people, the people of the color red, had been added by the Nahuatl tribes—the peoples of the Americas.

The Nahuatl tales spoke of conflict and even warfare among the gods. These included an incident when Huitzilopochtli defeated four hundred lesser gods and a fight between Tezcatlipoca-Yaotl and Quetzalcoatl. Such wars for dominion over Earth or its resources have been described in the lore ("myths") of all the ancient peoples. Hittite and Indo-European tales of the wars between Teshub or Indra with their brothers arrived in Greece via Asia Minor. The Semitic Canaanites and Phoenicians wrote down the tales of Ba'al's wars with his brothers, in the course of which Ba'al slaughtered hundreds of lesser "sons

Figure 8

of the gods" when they had been lured to his victory banquet.
And in the lands of Ham, Africa, Egyptian texts related the
dismemberment of Osiris by his brother Seth and the ensuing
bitter and long warfare between Seth and Horus, the son and
avenger of Osiris.

We find the gods of the Mexicans original conceptions, or were
they memories of beliefs and tales that had their roots in the
ancient Near East? The answer will emerge as we examine additional aspects of Nahuatl tales of creation and prehistory.

We find the Creator of All Things, to continue the comparisons, to have been a god who "gives life and death, good and
evil fortune." The chronicler Antonio de Herrera y Tordesillas
(Historia general) wrote that the Indians "call to him in their
tribulations, gazing toward the sky where they believe him to
be." This god first created the Heaven and the Earth; then he
fashioned a man and a woman out of clay, but they did not last.
After additional endeavors, a human pair was created of cinders
and metals and from them the world was peopled. But all these
men and women were destroyed in a flood, save for a certain
priest and his wife who, with seeds and animals, floated in a
hollowed-out log. The priest discovered land by sending out
birds. According to another chronicler, the Friar Gregorio Garcia, the flood lasted a year and a day during which the whole
Earth was covered with water and the world was in chaos.

The early or prehistoric events affecting Mankind and the
progenitors of the Nahuatl tribes were divided by legends, pictorial depictions, and stone carvings such as the Calendar Stone,
into four ages or "Suns." The Aztec considered their times to

have been the most recent of five eras, the Age of the Fifth Sun. Each of the previous four Suns had come to an end through some catastrophe, sometimes a natural one (such as a deluge) and sometimes a calamity triggered by wars between the gods.

The great Aztec Calendar Stone (it was discovered within the area of the sacred precinct) is believed to be a record in stone of the five ages. The symbols encircling the central panel and the central depiction itself have been the subject of numerous studies. The first inner ring clearly depicts the twenty signs for the twenty days of the Aztec month. The four rectangular panels surrounding the central face are recognized as the glyphs representing the past four eras and the calamity that ended each of them—Water, Wind, Quakes & Storms, and Jaguar.

The tales of the four ages are valuable for their information regarding the lengths of the eras and their principal events. Though versions vary, suggesting a long verbal tradition preceding the written records, they all agree that the first age came to an end by a deluge, a great flood that engulfed the Earth. Mankind survived because one couple, Nene and his wife Tata, managed to save themselves in a hollowed-out log.

Either this first age or the second one was the age of the White Haired Giants. The Second Sun was recalled as "Tzoncuztique," "Golden Age"; it was brought to an end by the Wind Serpent. The Third Sun was presided over by the Fire Serpent; it was the age of the Red Haired People. According to the chronicler Ixtlilxochitl, they were survivors of the second age who had come by ship from the east to the New World, settling in the area he called Botonchan; they encountered there giants who also survived the second age, and became enslaved by them.

The Fourth Sun was the era of the Black Headed People. It was during that era that Quetzalcoatl appeared in Mexico—tall of stature, bright of countenance, bearded, and wearing a long tunic. His staff, shaped like a serpent, was painted black, white, and red; it was inlaid with precious stones and adorned with six stars. (Not by coincidence, perhaps, the staff of Bishop Zumárraga, the first bishop of Mexico, was fashioned to look like the staff of Quetzalcoatl). It was during this era that Tollan, the Toltec capital, was built. Quetzalcoatl, master of wisdom and knowledge, introduced learning, crafts, laws, and time reckoning according to the fifty-two-year cycle.

Toward the end of the Fourth Sun wars between the gods were taking place. Quetzalcoatl left, going east back to the place whence he had come. The gods' wars brought havoc to the land; wild animals overran mankind, and Tollan was abandoned. Five years later the Chichimec tribes, alias the Aztecs, arrived; and the Fifth Sun, the Aztec era, began.

Why were the eras called "Suns" and how long did they last? The reason is unclear and the length of the various eras is either unstated or differs according to the version. One that appears orderly and, as we shall show, astoundingly plausible, is the *Codex Vaticano-Latino 3738.* It relates that the first Sun lasted 4,008 years, the second 4,010, the third 4,081. The fourth Sun "began 5,042 years ago," leaving unstated the time of its ending. Be it as it may, we have here a tale of events going back 17,141 years from the time the tales have been recorded.

This is quite a time span for supposedly backward people to recall, and scholars, while agreeing that the events of the Fourth Sun contain historical elements, tend to dismiss the earlier eras as sheer myth. How then explain the tales of Adam and Eve, a global deluge, the survival of one couple—episodes (in the words of H. B. Alexander, *Latin-American Mythology)* "strikingly reminiscent of the creation-narrative in Genesis 2 and of the similar Babylonian cosmogony"? Some scholars suggest that Nahuatl texts reflect in some way what the Indians had already heard from the Bible-spouting Spaniards. But since not all codices are post-Conquest, the biblical-Mesopotamian similarities can only be explained by admitting that the Mexican tribes had some ancestral ties to Mesopotamia.

Moreover, the Mexica-Nahuatl timetable correlates events and times with a scientific and historical accuracy that ought to make everyone stop and wonder. It dates the deluge, at the end of the First Sun, to 13,133 years before the time of writing the codex; i.e., to about 11,600 B.C. Now, in our book *The 12th Planet* we have concluded that a global deluge had indeed engulfed the Earth circa 11,000 B.C.; such a correspondence not only of the tale itself but also of its approximate time suggests that there is more than myth to Aztec tales.

We are equally intrigued by the tales' statement that the fourth era was the time of the "black-headed people" (the earlier ones having been deemed eras of white-haired giants, then red-haired people). This is precisely the term by which the Sumerians were called in their texts. Do the Aztec tales then deem the Fourth Sun to have been the time when the Sumerians appeared on the human scene? Sumerian civilization began circa 3800 B.C.; we should not, it would seem by now, be surprised to find that by dating the beginning of the Fourth Age to 5,026 years before their own time, the Aztecs in effect date it to circa 3500 B.C.—amazingly correct for the start of the age of the "black-headed people."

The feedback explanation (that the Aztecs told the Spaniards what they had heard from the Spaniards to begin with) certainly does not hold water where the Sumerians are concerned; the Western world uncovered the remains and legacy of the great Sumerian civilization only four centuries after the Conquest.

The Genesis-like tales, one must conclude, had to be known to the Nahuatl tribes from their own ancestral sources. But how?

The question had already baffled the Spaniards themselves. Astounded to discover not just a civilization in the New World, and one so akin to Europe's, but also "the great number of people there," they were doubly puzzled by the biblical threads in the Aztec yarns. Trying to find an explanation, the answer seemed to be a simple one: these were descendants of the Ten Lost Tribes of Israel who were exiled by the Assyrians in 722 B.C. and then vanished without a trace (the remaining kingdom of Judea was retained by the two tribes Judah and Benjamin).

If not the originator, then the one who expounded it first in a detailed manuscript, was the Dominican Friar Diego Duran, who was brought to New Spain in 1542 at the age of five. His two books, one known by the English title *Book of the Gods and Rites and the Ancient Calendar* and *Historia de las Indias de Nueva España,* have been translated into English by D. Heyden and F. Horcasitas. It is in the second book that Duran, citing the many similarities, stated emphatically his conclusion regarding the natives "of the Indies and the mainland of this new world": that "they are Jews and Hebrew people." His theory was confirmed, he wrote, "by their nature: These natives are part of the ten tribes of Israel which Shalmaneser, King of the Assyrians, captured and took to Assyria."

His reports of conversations with old Indians elicited tribal traditions of a time when there had been "men of monstrous stature who appeared and took possession of the country. . . . And these giants, not having found a way to reach the Sun, decided to build a tower so high that its summit would reach unto Heaven." Such an episode paralleling the biblical tale of the Tower of Babel matched in significance another tale, of an Exodus-like migration.

No wonder then that as such reports increased, the theory of the Ten Lost Tribes became the favorite one of the sixteenth and seventeenth centuries, the assumption being that, somehow, wandering eastward through the Assyrian domains and beyond, the Israelites reached America.

The notion of the Ten Lost Tribes, at its height sponsored by Europe's royal courts, came to be ridiculed by later scholars. Current theories hold that Man initially arrived in the New World from Asia across an icy land bridge to Alaska some 20,000–30,000 years ago, spreading gradually southward. Considerable evidence consisting of artifacts, language and ethnological and anthropological evaluations indicates influences from across the Pacific—Hindu, Southeast Asian, Chinese, Japanese, Polynesian. Scholars explain them by periodic arrival of such people in the Americas; but they are emphatic in stating that these occurred during the Christian era, just centuries before the conquest and not at any time B.C.

While established scholars continue to downplay all evidence for transatlantic contacts between the Old and New World, they employ the concession to relatively recent transpacific contacts as the explanation for the currency of Genesis-like tales in the Americas. Indeed, legends of a global deluge and of the creation of Man out of clay or similar materials have been themes of mythologies all over the world, and one possible route to the Americas from the Near East (where the tales had originated) could have been Southeast Asia and the Pacific islands.

But there are elements in the Nahuatl versions that point to a very early source, rather than to relatively recent pre-Conquest centuries. One is the fact that the Nahuatl tales of the creation of Man follow a very ancient Mesopotamian version that did not even find its way into the Book of Genesis!

The Bible, in fact, has not one but two versions of the creation of Man; both draw on earlier Mesopotamian versions. But both ignore a third version, and probably the oldest one, in which Mankind was fashioned not of clay but out of the blood of a god. In the Sumerian text on which this version is based, the god Ea, collaborating with the goddess Ninti, "prepared a purifying bath." "Let one god be bled into it," he ordered; "from his flesh and blood, let Ninti mix the clay." From this mixture, men and women were created.

We find it highly significant that it is this version—which is not in the Bible—that is repeated in an Aztec myth. The text is known as *Manuscript of 1558;* it relates that after the calamitous end of the Fourth Sun the gods assembled in Teotihuacan.

As soon as the gods came together, they said:
"Who shall inhabit the Earth?

The sky has already been established
and the Earth has been established;
but who, oh gods, shall live on Earth?"

The gathered gods "were grieved." But Quetzalcoatl, a god of wisdom and science, had an idea. He went to Mictlan, the Land of the Dead, and announced to the divine couple in charge of it: "I have come for the precious bones which you keep here." Overcoming objections and trickery, Quetzalcoatl managed to get hold of the "precious bones":

He gathered the precious bones;
The bones of man were put together on one side,
the bones of woman were put together on the other side.
Quetzalcoatl took them and made a bundle.

He carried the dry bones to Tamoanchan, "Place of Our Origin" or "Place From Which We Are Descended." There he gave the bones to the goddess Cihuacoatl ("Serpent Woman"), a goddess of magic.

She ground up the bones
and put them in a fine earthen tub.
Quetzalcoatl bled his male organ on them.

As the other gods looked on, she mixed the ground bones with the god's blood; from the claylike mixture, the *Macehuales* were fashioned. Mankind was re-created!

In the Sumerian tales, the fashioners of Man were the god Ea ("Whose Home Is Water"), also known as Enki ("Lord Earth") whose epithets and symbols often implied his being crafty, a metallurgist—all words that found their linguistic equivalent in the term "Serpent." His companion in the feat, Ninti ("She Who Gives Life") was the goddess of medicine—a craft whose symbol from antiquity has been the entwined serpent. Sumerian depictions on cylinder seals showed the two deities in a laboratorylike setting, flasks and all (Fig. 9a).

It is truly amazing to find all these elements in the Nahuatl tales—a god of knowledge known as the Plumed Serpent, a goddess of magical powers called Serpent Woman; a bathtub of loam in which earthly elements are mixed with a god's essence (blood); and the fashioning of Man, male and female, out of the mixture. Even more astounding is the fact that the myth has been pictorially depicted in a Nahuatl codex found in the area of the Mixtec tribe. It shows a god and a goddess mixing an ele-

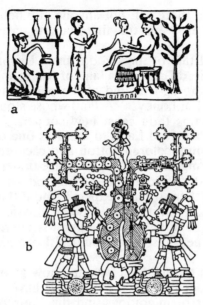

Figure 9

ment that flows into a huge flask or vat with the blood of a god that drips into the flask; out of the mixture, a man emerges (Fig. 9b).

Coupled with the other Sumerian-related data and terminology, contacts at a very early time are indicated. The evidence, it appears, also challenges the current theories about Man's first migrations to the Americas. By that we do not mean simply the suggestions (made earlier this century at the International Congresses of Americanists) that the migration was not from Asia via the Bering Strait in the north but from Australia/New Zealand via Antarctica to South America—an idea revived recently after the discovery in northern Chile, near the border with Peru, of buried human mummies 9,000 years old.

The trouble we have with both arrival theories is that they require the trekking by men, women, and children over thousands of miles of frozen terrain. We wonder *how* this could have been done 20,000 or 30,000 years ago; moreover, we wonder *why* such a journey would have been undertaken. Why would men, women, and children journey for thousands of miles over frozen terrain, seemingly achieving nothing except the experience of more ice—unless they were aware that there was a Promised Land beyond the ice?

But how could they know what was beyond the endless ice if

they had not been there yet, nor anyone else before them—for, by definition, they were the first men to cross over to the Americas?

In the biblical tale of the Exodus from Egypt, the Lord describes the Promised Land as "a land of wheat and barley and of the vine and of the fig-tree and of the pomegranate, a land of the olive-tree and of honey . . . A land whose stones are iron and of whose mountains thou canst hew copper." The Aztec god described their Promised Land to them as one of "houses with gold and silver, multicolored cotton and cacao of many hues." Would the early migrants to America have undertaken their impossible trek had not someone—their god—told them to go and described to them what to expect? And if that deity was not a mere theological entity, but a being physically present on Earth, could he have helped the migrants overcome the hardships of the journey, just as the biblical Lord had done for the Israelites?

It is with such thoughts, of why and how an impossible journey would have been undertaken, that we have read and reread the Nahuatl tales of migrations and the Four Ages. Since the First Sun had ended with the Deluge, that era had to be the final phase of the last Ice Age, for we have concluded in *The 12th Planet* that the Deluge was caused by the slippage of the Antarctic ice sheet into the oceans, thereby bringing the last Ice Age to an abrupt end circa 11,000 B.C.

Was the legendary original home of the Nahuatl tribes called Aztlan, "The White Place," for the simple reason that that is what it was—a snow-covered land? Is this why the First Sun was deemed the time of the "white-haired giants?" Do Aztec historical recollections, by harking back to the beginning of the First Sun 17,141 years earlier, in fact speak of a migration into America circa 15,000 B.C., when the ice formed a land-bridge with the Old World? Moreover, could it be that the crossing was not at all across the ice sheet, but by boats across the Pacific Ocean, as the Nahuatl legends relate?

Legends of prehistoric arrival by sea and landings on the Pacific coast are not confined to the Mexican peoples. Farther south the Andean peoples retained memories of a similar nature, told as legends. One, the Legend of Naymlap, may relate to the very first settlement on those coasts by people from elsewhere. It tells of the arrival of a great fleet of balsa-reed boats (of the kind used by Thor Heyerdahl to simulate Sumerian seafaring in reed boats). A green stone that could utter the words of the people's god, placed in the lead boat, directed the migrants' leader, Naymlap, to the chosen beach. The deity, speaking through the green idol, then instructed the people in the arts of farming, building, and handicrafts.

Some versions of the legend of the green idol pinpointed Cape Santa Helena in Ecuador as the landing site; there the South American continent projects westward into the Pacific. Several of the chroniclers, among them Juan de Velasco, related native traditions that the first settlers in the equatorial regions were giants. The human settlers who followed there worshiped a pantheon of twelve gods, headed by the Sun and the Moon. Where Ecuador's capital is situated, Velasco wrote, the settlers built two temples facing each other. The temple dedicated to the Sun had in front of its gateway two stone columns, and in its forecourt a circle of twelve stone pillars.

The time then came when the leader, Naymlap, his mission accomplished, had to depart. Unlike his successors, he did not die: he was given wings and flew away, never to be seen again —taken heavenward by the god of the speaking stone.

In believing that divine instructions could be received through a Speaking Stone, the American Indians were in good company: all the ancient peoples of the Old World described and believed in oracle stones, and the Ark that the Israelites had carried during the Exodus was topped by the *Dvir*—literally, "Speaker"—a portable device through which Moses could hear the Lord's instructions. The detail concerning the departure of Naymlap by being taken heavenward also has a biblical parallel. We read in Chapter 5 of Genesis that in the seventh generation of Adam's line through Sheth, the patriarch was Enoch; after he had reached the age of 365 years "he was gone" from the Earth, for the Lord had taken him heavenward.

Scholars have a problem with a crossing of the oceans by boats 15,000 or 20,000 years ago: Man, they hold, was too primitive then to have oceangoing vessels and navigate the high seas. Not until the Sumerian civilization, at the beginning of the fourth millennium B.C., did Mankind begin to attain the land (wheeled craft) and water (boats) means of long-range transportation.

But that, according to the Sumerians themselves, was the course of events after the Deluge. There had been, they stated and restated, a high civilization upon Earth *before* the Deluge —a civilization begun on Earth by those who had come from the planet of Anu and continued through a line of long-living "demigods," the offspring of intermarriage between the Extraterrestrials (the biblical *Nefilim)* and the "daughters of Man." Egyptian chronicles, such as the writings of the priest Manetho, followed the same concept. So of course did the Bible, which describes both rural life (farming, sheepherding) and urban civilization (cities, metallurgy) before the Deluge. All that, however—according to all those ancient sources—was wiped off the face of the Earth by the Deluge, and everything had to be restarted from scratch.

The Book of Genesis begins with creation tales that are concise versions of much more detailed Sumerian texts. In these it consistently speaks of *"the* Adam," literally "the Earthling." But then it switches to the genealogy of a specific ancestor named Adam: "This is the book of the generations of Adam" (Genesis 5:1). He had two sons at first, Cain and Abel. After Cain killed his brother, he was banished by Yahweh. "And Adam knew his wife again and she bore a son and called his name Sheth." It is this line, the line of Sheth, that the Bible follows through a genealogy of patriarchs to Noah, the hero of the Deluge story. The tale then focuses on the Asian-African-European peoples.

But whatever happened to Cain and his line? All we have in the Bible are a dozen verses. Yahweh punished Cain to become a nomad, "a fugitive and a vagabond on the Earth."

> And Cain went away from the presence of Yahweh
> and dwelt in the land of Nod, east of Eden.
> And Cain knew his wife and she conceived and bore Enoch;
> And he built a city
> and called the name of the city by his son's name, Enoch.

Several generations later, Lamech was born. He had two wives. Of one Jabal was born; "he was the father of such as dwell in tents and have cattle." Of the other, two sons were born. One, Jubal, "was the father of all such as play the lyre and pipe." The other son, Tubal-Kain, was "an artificer of gold and copper and iron."

This meagre biblical information is somewhat augmented by the pseudepigraphical Book of Jubilees, believed to have been composed in the second century B.C. from earlier sources. Relating events to the passage of Jubilees, it states that "Cain took Awan his sister to be his wife and she bare him Enoch at the close of the fourth jubilee. And in the first year of the first week of the fifth jubilee, houses were built on Earth, and Cain built a city and called its name after the name of his son, Enoch."

Biblical scholars have long been puzzled by the naming of both a descendant of Adam through Sheth and through Cain "Enoch" (meaning "Founding," "Foundation"), as well as other similarities in descendants' names. Whatever the reason, it is evident that the sources on which the Bible's editors had relied attributed to both Enochs—who were perhaps one prehistoric person—extraordinary deeds. The Book of Jubilees states that Enoch "was the first among men that were born on Earth who learnt writing and knowledge and wisdom and who wrote down the signs of heaven according to their months in a book." According to the Book of Enoch, this patriarch was taught mathematics and knowledge of the planets and the calendar during his heavenly journey, and was shown the location of the "Seven Metal Mountains" on Earth, "in the west."

The pre-biblical Sumerian texts known as King Lists also relate the story of a pre-Deluvial ruler who was taught by the gods all manner of knowledge. His epithet-name was EN.ME.DUR.AN.KI—"Lord of the Knowledge of the Foundations of Heaven and Earth"—and a very probable prototype of the biblical Enochs.

The Nahuatl tales of wandering, arrival at a final destination, settling marked by the building of a city; of a patriarch with two wives and sons of whom tribal nations have evolved; of one that became renowned for being a craftsman in metals—do they not read almost as the biblical tales? Even the Nahuatl stressing of the number seven is reflected in the biblical tales, for the seventh descendant through the line of Cain, Lamech, enigmatically proclaimed that "Seven-fold shall Cain be avenged, and Lamech seventy and seven."

Are we, then, encountering in the traditions of the seven Nahuatl tribes echoes—olden memories—of the banished line of Cain and his son Enoch?

The Aztecs called their capital *Tenochtitlán,* the City of Tenoch, so naming it after their ancestor. Considering that in their dialect the Aztecs had prefixed many words with the sound *T, Tenoch* could have originally been *Enoch* if the prefixed T is dropped.

A Babylonian text based in the opinion of scholars on an earlier Sumerian text from the third millennium B.C. enigmatically relates a conflict, ending in murder, between an earth-tilling and a shepherding brother, just as the biblical Cain and Abel were. Doomed to "roam in sorrow," the offending leader, called *Ka'in,* migrated to the land of Dunnu and there "he built a city with twin towers."

Twin towers atop the temple-pyramids were a hallmark of Aztec architecture. Did this commemorate the building of a "city with twin towers" by Ka'in? And was Tenochtitlán, the

"City of Tenoch," so named and built because Cain, millennia earlier, "built a city and called the city by his son's name, Enoch"?

Have we found in Mesoamerica the lost realm of Cain, the city named after Enoch? The possibility certainly offers plausible answers to the enigma of Man's beginnings in these domains.

It may also shed light on two other enigmas—that of the "Mark of Cain" and the hereditary trait common to all the Amerindians: the absence of facial hair.

According to the biblical tale, after the Lord had banished Cain from the settled lands and decreed that he become a wanderer in the East, Cain was concerned about being slain by vengeance seekers. So the Lord, to indicate that Cain was wandering under the Lord's protection, "set a sign unto Cain, that any one finding him should not smite him." Although no one knows what this distinguishing "sign" had been, it has been generally assumed that it was some kind of a tattoo on Cain's forehead. But from the ensuing biblical narrative it appears that the matter of vengeance and the protection against it continued into the seventh generation and beyond. A tattoo on the forehead could not last that long nor be transmittable from generation to generation. Only a genetic trait, transmitted hereditarily, can fit the biblical data.

And, in view of the particular genetic trait of the Amerindians—the absence of facial hair—one wonders whether it was this genetic change that was the "mark of Cain" and his descendants. If our guess is right, then Mesoamerica, as a focal point from which Amerindians spread north and south in the New World, was indeed the Lost Realm of Cain.

3

REALM OF THE
SERPENT GODS

When Tenochtitlán attained its greatness, the Toltec capital of
Tula had already been recalled as the legendary Tollan. And
when the Toltecs had built their city, Teotihuacan was already
enshrined in myth. Its name has meant "Place of the Gods";
and that, according to recorded tales, was exactly what it had
been.

It is told that there was a time when calamities befell the
Earth and the Earth fell into darkness, for the sun failed to
appear. Only at Teotihuacan there was light, for a divine flame
remained burning there. The concerned gods gathered at Teotihuacan, wondering what should be done. "Who shall govern
and direct the world," they asked each other, unless they could
make the sun reappear?

They asked for a volunteer among the gods to jump into the
divine flame and, by his sacrifice, bring back the sun. The god
Tecuciztecatl volunteered. Putting on his glittering attire he
stepped forward toward the flame; but each time he neared the
fire he stepped back, losing courage. Then the god Nanauatzin
volunteered and unhesitatingly jumped into the fire. Thus
shamed, Tecuciztecatl followed suit; but he landed only at the
flame's edge. As the gods were consumed, the Sun and Moon
reappeared in the skies.

But though they could now be seen, the two luminaries remained motionless in the sky. According to one version, the Sun
began to move after one god shot an arrow at it; another version
says that it resumed its coursing after the Wind God blew at it.
After the Sun had resumed its motion, the Moon too began to
move; and so was the cycle of day and night resumed and the
Earth was saved.

The tale is intimately connected with Teotihuacan's most renowned monuments, the Pyramid of the Sun and the Pyramid of

43

the Moon. One version has it that the gods built the two pyramids to commemorate the two gods who had sacrificed themselves; another version states that the pyramids had already existed when the event was taking place, that the gods jumped into the divine fire from atop preexisting pyramids.

Whatever the legend, the fact is that the Pyramid of the Sun and the Pyramid of the Moon still rise majestically to this very day. What only a few decades ago were mounds covered by vegetation have now become a major tourist attraction, just thirty miles north of Mexico City. Rising in a valley whose surrounding mountains act as a backdrop to an eternal stage (Fig. 10), the pyramids force the visitor's eyes to follow their upward slope, to the mountains beyond and the vista of the skies above. The monuments exude power, knowledge, intent; the setting bespeaks a conscious linking of Earth with Heaven. No one can miss the sense of history, the presence of an awesome past.

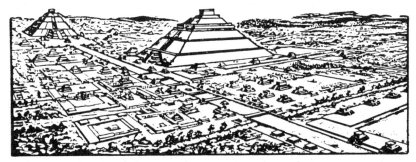

Figure 10

How far back in the past? Archaeologists had assumed at first that Teotihuacan was established in the first centuries of the Christian era; but the date keeps slipping back. On-site work indicates that the city's ceremonial center had already occupied 4.5 square miles by 200 B.C. In the 1950s a leading archaeologist, M. Covarrubias, incredulously admitted that radiocarbon dating gave the place "the almost impossible date of 900 B.C." *(Indian Art of Mexico and Central America).* In fact, further radiocarbon tests gave a date of 1474 B.C. (with a possible small error either way). A date of circa 1400 B.C. is now widely accepted; that is when the Olmecs, who may have been the people to actually toil in the building of Teotihuacan's monumental structures, were establishing great "ceremonial centers" elsewhere in Mexico.

Teotihuacan had clearly undergone several phases of devel-

opment and its pyramids reveal evidence of earlier inner structures. Some scholars read in the ruins a tale that may have
begun 6,000 years ago—in the fourth millennium B.C. This
would certainly conform to the Aztec legends that spoke of this
Place of the Gods as existing in the Fourth Sun. Then, when the
Day of Darkness happened circa 1400 B.C., the two great pyramids were raised to their monumental sizes.

The Pyramid of the Moon rises at the northern end of this
ceremonial center, flanked by smaller auxiliary structures and
fronted by a great plaza. From there a wide avenue runs southward as far as the eye can see; it is flanked by low-profile
shrines, temples, and other structures that were believed to
have been tombs; consequently the avenue was given the name
Avenue of the Dead. Some 2,000 feet to the south the Avenue
of the Dead reaches the Pyramid of the Sun that rises on the
eastern side of the avenue (Fig. 11) beyond a plaza and a series
of shrines and other structures.

Past the Pyramid of the Sun, and another 3,000 feet southward, one reaches the *Ciudadela,* a quadrangle that contains at
its eastern side the third pyramid of Teotihuacan, called the
Quetzalcoatl Pyramid. It is now known that facing the Ciudadela, across the Avenue of the Dead, there existed a similar
quadrangle that served mostly as a lay administrative-commer-
cial center. The avenue then continues further south; the Teotihuacan Mapping Project led by René Millon in the 1960s
established that this north–south avenue extended for nearly
five miles—longer than the longest runways at modern airports.
In spite of this remarkable length, the wide avenue runs straight
as an arrow—quite a technological feat at any time.

An east–west axis, perpendicular to the north–south avenue, extended eastward from the Ciudadela and westward from
the administrative quadrangle. Members of the Teotihuacan
Mapping Project found south of the Pyramid of the Sun a
marker chiseled into the rocks in the shape of a cross within two
concentric circles; a similar marker was found about two miles
to the west, on a mountainside. A sight line connecting the two
markers precisely indicates the direction of the east–west axis,
and the other arms of the crosses match the orientation of the
north–south axis. The researchers concluded that they had
found markers used by the city's original planners; they did not
offer a theory to explain what means were used in antiquity to
draw a beadline between two such distant spots.

That the ceremonial center had been oriented and laid out
deliberately is evident from several other facts. The first one is
that the San Juan river that flows in the Teotihuacan valley has

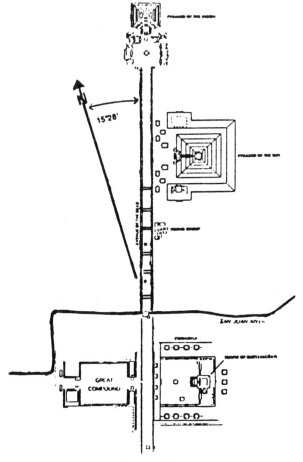

Figure 11

been deliberately diverted where it crosses the ceremonial
center: artificial channels divert the river to flow at the Ciudadela and along the quadrangle facing it exactly parallel to the
east–west axis, then after two precise right-angle turns along
the west-leading avenue.

The second fact indicating a deliberate orientation is that the
two axes are not pointing to the cardinal points, but are tilted to
the southeast by 15½ degrees (Fig. 11). Studies show that this
was not an accident or a miscalculation by the ancient planners.
A. F. Aveni *(Astronomy in Ancient Mesoamerica),* calling this a
"sacred orientation," points out that later ceremonial centers
(such as Tula and ones even farther away) adhered to this orien-

tation although it made no sense at their locations and when they were built. The conclusion of his researches was that, at Teotihuacan and at the time of its construction, the orientation was devised to enable celestial observations on certain key dates of the calendar.

Zelia Nuttal, in a paper delivered to the twenty-second International Congress of Americanists (Rome, 1926) suggested that the orientation was keyed to the passage of the Sun at the observer's zenith, which occurs twice a year as the Sun appears to move from north to south and back. If such celestial observations were the purpose of the pyramids, their ultimate shape— step pyramids equipped with staircases, leading to presumed viewing-temples on the topmost platform—would make sense. However, because strong evidence suggests that what we now see are the latest outer layers of the two major pyramids (and as arbitrarily resurfaced by archaeologists, to boot), one cannot state for certain that these pyramids' original purpose was not a different one. The possibility, even probability, that the stairways were a late addition is suggested to us by the fact that the first stage of the grand stairway of the Sun Pyramid is tilted and improperly aligned with the pyramid's orientation (Fig. 12).

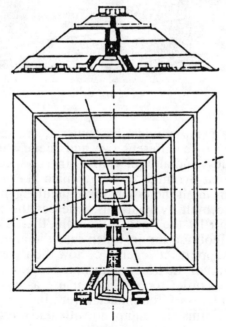

Figure 12

Of the three pyramids at Teotihuacan the smallest is the
Quetzalcoatl pyramid in the "Citadel." A later addition was
partly excavated to reveal the original step-pyramid. The partly
exposed facade reveals sculpted decorations in which the serpent symbol of Quetzalcoatl alternates with a stylized face of
Tlaloc against a background of wavy waters (Fig. 13). This pyramid is ascribed to Toltec times and is akin to many other Mexican pyramids.

Figure 13

The two larger pyramids, by contrast, are totally undecor-
ated. They are of a different size and shape and stand out in
their massiveness and antiquity. In all these aspects they resemble the two great pyramids of Giza, which likewise differ on all
these counts from all the other, subsequent Egyptian pyramids;
the latter were built by Pharaohs, whereas the unique ones at
Giza were built by the "gods." Perhaps that is also what had
happened at Teotihuacan; in which case the archaeological evidence would support the legends of how the Pyramid of the Sun
and the Pyramid of the Moon had come to be.

Although, in order to enable their use as observatories, the
two great pyramids of Teotihuacan were built as step-pyramids
topped by platforms and equipped with stairways (as the Mesopotamian ziggurats had been), there can be no doubt that their

architect was acquainted with the Giza pyramids in Egypt and, except for adjusting the outer shape, emulated the unique Giza pyramids. One amazing similarity: although the Second Pyramid at Giza is shorter than the Great Pyramid, their peaks are at the same height above sea level because the Second Pyramid is built on correspondingly higher ground; the same holds true at Teotihuacan, where the smaller Pyramid of the Moon is built on ground some thirty feet higher than that of the Pyramid of the Sun, giving their peaks equal height above sea level.

The similarities are especially obvious between the two greater pyramids. Both are built on artificial platforms. Their sides measure almost the same: about 754 feet in Giza, about 745 feet at Teotihuacan, and the latter would fit neatly into the former (Fig. 14).

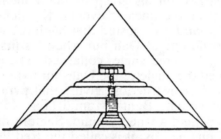

Figure 14

While such similarities and correspondences bespeak a hidden link between the two sets of pyramids, one need not ignore the existence of certain and considerable differences. The Great Pyramid of Giza is built of large stone blocks, carefully shaped and matched and held together without mortar, weighing an aggregate 7,000,000 tons with a mass of 93,000,000 cubic feet. The Sun Pyramid was built of mud bricks, adobe, pebbles, and gravel, held together by a sheath of crude stones and stucco, with an aggregate mass of only 10,000,000 cubic feet. The Giza pyramid contains an inner complex of corridors, galleries, and chambers of intricate and precise construction; the Teotihuacan pyramid does not appear to have such inner structures. The one at Giza rises to a height of 480 feet, the Sun Pyramid (including the erstwhile uppermost temple) to a mere 250. The Great Pyramid has four triangular sides that rise at the tricky angle of 52 degrees; the two at Teotihuacan consist of stages that rest one atop the other, with sides that slope inward for stability, beginning with a slope of 43½ degrees.

These are significant differences that reflect the different times and purposes of each set of pyramids. But in the very last difference lies, hitherto unnoticed to all previous researchers, a key to the solution of some puzzles.

The rather steep angle of 52 degrees has been attained in Egypt only in the Giza pyramids, which were built neither by Cheops or any other Pharaoh (as proven in previous books of *The Earth Chronicles)* but by the gods of the ancient Near East, as beacons for landing at their spaceport in the Sinai peninsula. All the other Egyptian pyramids—lesser, smaller, decayed, or collapsed—were indeed built by Pharaohs, millennia later, in emulation of the gods' "stairways to heaven." But none succeeded in attaining the perfect angle of 52 degrees and whenever this was attempted, the attempt ended in collapse.

The lesson was learned when the Pharaoh Sneferu (circa 2650 B.C.) embarked on his grasp for monumental glory. In a brilliant analysis of the ancient events, K. Mendelssohn *(The Riddle of the Pyramids)* suggested that Sneferu's architects were building his second one at Dahshur when his first one, built at Maidum at the 52 degree angle, collapsed. The architects then hurriedly changed the angle of the Dahshur pyramid to the safer 43½ degrees in midconstruction, giving that pyramid the shape and thus the name The Bent Pyramid (Fig. 15a). Still determined to leave behind a true pyramid, Sneferu then proceeded to build a third one nearby; it is called the Red Pyramid for the color of its stones, and it rises at the safe angle of 43½ degrees (Fig. 15b).

But in this retreat to the safety of 43½ degrees, Sneferu's architects in fact fell back to a choice made more than a century earlier, circa 2700 B.C. by the Pharaoh Zoser. His pyramid, the earliest pharaonic one that still stands (at Sakkara), was a step pyramid that rose in six stages (Fig. 15c) conforming to the shallower angle of 43½ degrees.

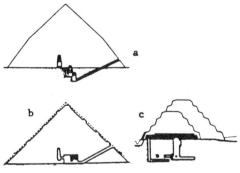

Figure 15

Is it only a coincidence that the Pyramid of the Sun and the Great Pyramid of Giza have the same base measurements? Perhaps. Is it by mere chance that the precise 43½ degree angle adopted by the Pharaoh Zoser and perfected in his step-pyramid was followed at Teotihuacan? We doubt it. Whereas a shallower angle, say 45 degrees, could have been attained by an unsophisticated architect simply by dividing in two a right angle (90 degrees), the 43½ degree angle resulted in Egypt from a sophisticated adaptation of the factor *Pi* (about 3.14), which is the ratio of a circle's circumference to its diameter.

The 52 degree angle of the Giza pyramids required familiarity with this factor; it was attained by giving the pyramid a height (H) equal to half the side (S) divided by *Pi* and multiplied by four (754 ÷ 2 = 377 ÷ 3.14 = 120 × 4 = 480 feet in height). The angle of 43½ degrees was attained by reducing the height from a final multiple of four to a multiple of three. In both instances, knowledge of *pi* was required; and there is absolutely nothing to indicate such knowledge among the peoples of Mesoamerica. How then did the 43½ degree angle appear in the structures of the two unique (to Mesoamerica) pyramids of Teotihuacan, if not through someone familiar with the constructions of the Egyptian pyramids?

Except for the unique Great Pyramid of Giza, Egyptian pyramids were equipped only with a lower passageway (see Figs. 15) that usually began at or near the edge of the pyramid's base and continued under it. Should one ascribe to mere coincidence the existence of such a passageway under the Pyramid of the Sun?

The accidental discovery was made in 1971, after heavy rainfalls. Just in front of the pyramid's central stairway, a subterranean cavity was unearthed. It contained ancient steps that led some twenty feet down to an entrance into a horizontal passageway. The excavators concluded it was a natural cave that had been artificially enlarged and improved, running under the bedrock on which the pyramid was built. That the original cave was converted to some purpose intentionally is evidenced by the fact that the ceiling is made of heavy stone blocks and that the tunnel's walls are smoothed with plaster. At various points along this subterranean passageway adobe walls divert its course at sharp angles.

About 150 feet from the ancient stairway, the tunnel sprouts two elongated side chambers, like spread wings; it is a spot exactly under the first stage of the step-pyramid. From there the subterranean passageway, generally about seven feet high, continues for almost another 200 feet; in this inner portion the construction becomes more complex, using a variety of materials; the floors, laid in segments, were man-made; drainage pipes were provided for now unknown purposes (perhaps connected to an underground watercourse now extinct). Finally, the tunnel ends below the fourth stage of the pyramid in a hollowed-out area that resembles a cloverleaf, supported by adobe columns and basalt slabs.

What was the purpose of the complex subterranean structure? Since the segmenting walls had been breached before the discovery in modern times, it is not possible to say whether the remains of clay vessels, obsidian blades and charcoal ashes belong to the earliest phase of the tunnel's use. But the question of what, besides celestial observation, was going on at Teotihuacan, has been compounded by other discoveries.

The Avenue of the Dead seems to stretch as a wide, smooth runway from the plaza of the Pyramid of the Moon to the southern horizon; but in fact its smooth flow is interrupted in a section situated between the Pyramid of the Sun and the San Juan river. The overall slope from the Pyramid of the Moon to the Pyramid of the Sun is even more accentuated in this section of the Avenue, and the on-site examination clearly indicates that the slope was achieved by deliberate cutting into the native rock; overall, the drop from the Pyramid of the Moon to a point past the Ciudadela is some ninety feet. Here six segments have been created by the erection of a series of double walls perpendicularly to the course of the Avenue. The Avenue's cavity is further lined with walls and low structures, resulting in six semisubterranean compartments open to the sky. The perpendicular walls are fitted with sluices at their floor level. The impression is that the whole complex served to channel water that flowed down the Avenue. The flow may have begun at the Pyramid of the Moon (where a subterranean tunnel was found encircling it), and been linked in some manner to the subterranean tunnel of the Pyramid of the Sun. The series of compartments then retained and eventually let out the water from one to the other, until ultimately the water reached the diverting channel of the San Juan river.

Could these artificially flowing and cascading waters have been the reason for decorating the facade of the Quetzalcoatl Pyramid with wavy waters—at an inland site, hundreds of miles away from any sea?

The association of this inland site with water is further suggested by the discovery of a huge stone statue of Chalchiuhtlicue, the goddess of water and the spouse of Tlaloc, the rain god. The statue (Fig. 16), now on exhibit at the National Museum of

Figure 16

Anthropology in Mexico City, was found standing in the center of the plaza in front of the Pyramid of the Moon. In her pictorial depictions, the goddess, whose name means "Lady of Waters," was usually shown wearing a jade skirt decorated with conch shells. Her adornments were turquoise earrings and a necklace of jade or other blue-green stones from which there hung a gold medallion. The statue repeats these dress and decorative elements, and it appears that it was also adorned with an actual golden pendant, embedded in an appropriate cavity, which has been removed by robbers. Her pictorial depictions often showed her wearing a crown of serpents or otherwise adorned with them, indicating her being one of the serpent gods of the Mexicans.

Was Teotihuacan laid out and constructed as some kind of a waterworks, employing water for some technological processes? Before we answer the question, let us mention another puzzling discovery there.

Alongside the third segment down from the Pyramid of the Sun, excavations of a series of interconnected subterranean chambers revealed that some of the floors were covered with layers of thick sheets of mica. This is a silicone whose special properties make it resistant to water, heat, and electrical currents. It has therefore been used as an insulator in various chemical processes and electrical and electronic applications, and in recent times in nuclear and space technologies.

The particular properties of mica depend to some extent on its content of other trace minerals, and thus on its geographic source. According to expert opinions, the mica found at Teotihuacan is of a type that is found only in faraway Brazil. Traces of this mica were also found on remains removed from the Pyramid of the Sun's stages when it was being uncovered early in this century. What was the use to which this insulating material was put at Teotihuacan?

Our own impression is that the presence of the Lord and Lady of Water alongside the principal deity, Quetzatcoatl; the sloping avenue; the series of structures, subterranean chambers, tunnels; the diverted river; the semisubterranean sections with their sluices; and the underground compartments lined with mica—were all components of a scientifically conceived plant for the separation, refining or purification of mineral substances.

Whether in the middle of the first millennium B.C., or more probably in the middle of the second millennium B.C., someone familiar with the secrets of pyramid building had come to this valley; and equally knowledgeable in the physical sciences, created from locally available materials a sophisticated processing plant. Was this someone in search of gold, as the pendant of the Lady of Water would suggest, or of some other, even rarer mineral?

And if it was not Man—was it his gods, just as the legends concerning Teotihuacan and its very name have suggested all along?

Who, besides the gods, were the original dwellers of Teotihuacan? Who had carried the stones and mortar to raise its first pyramids? Who had channeled the waters and operated the sluices?

Those who assume that Teotihuacan is no older than a few centuries B.C. have a simple answer: the Toltecs. Those who now lean toward a much earlier beginning have started to point to the Olmecs, an enigmatic people who emerged on the Mesoamerican scene in the middle of the second millennium B.C. But the Olmecs themselves pose many puzzles, for they appear to have been black Africans; and that too is anathema to those who simply cannot accept transatlantic crossings millennia ago.

Even if the origin of Teotihuacan and its builders is shrouded in mystery, it is almost certain that in the centuries preceding the Christian era Toltec tribesmen began to drift in. At first performing manual chores, they gradually learned the city's crafts and adopted the culture of its masters, including picture-writing, the secrets of goldsmithing, knowledge of astronomy and the calendar, and the worship of the gods. Circa 200 B.C. whoever had lorded over Teotihuacan picked up and left, and the place became a Toltec city. For centuries it was renowned for its tools, weapons, and artifacts made of obsidian stone, and its cultural and religious influence extended widely. Then, a thousand years after they had drifted in, the Toltecs too packed up and left. No one knows why; but the departure was total and Teotihuacan became a desolate place, living only in memories of a golden past.

Some believe that the event coincided with the establishment of Tollan as the Toltecs' new capital, circa A.D. 700. A place of human settlement for millennia on the banks of the Tula river, it was built up by the Toltecs as a mini-Teotihuacan. Codices and lore described Tollan as a legendary city, a center of arts and crafts, resplendent in its palaces and temples, glittering with gold and precious stones. But for a long time scholars questioned its very existence . . . Now it is known beyond doubt that Tollan did indeed exist, at a site nowadays called Tula, some fifty miles northwest of Mexico City.

The rediscovery of Tollan began toward the end of the nineteenth century and the beginning of the process is mainly associated with the French traveller Désiré Charnay *(Les anciennes villes du nouveau monde)*. Serious excavation work began only in the 1940s under the leadership of the Mexican archaeologist Jorge R. Acosta. This work of excavation and restoration focused on the principal ceremonial compound referred to as Tula Grande; later work, as that by teams from the University of Mississippi, expanded the area of unearthing the past.

The discoveries confirmed not only the city's existence but also its history as told in various codices, especially the one known as *Anales de Cuauhtitlan*. It is now known that Tollan was ruled by a dynasty of priest-kings who claimed to have been descendants of the god Quetzalcoatl and therefore, in addition to their given name, also bore the god's name as a patronym—a custom that was prevalent among the Egyptian pharaohs. Some of these priest-kings were warriors, bent on expanding Toltec rule; others were more concerned with the faith. In the second half of the tenth century A.D. the ruler was Ce Acatl Topiltzin-Quetzalcoatl; his name and time are certain because a portrait of his, accompanied by a date equivalent to A.D. 968, can still be seen carved on a rock overlooking the site of the city.

It was in his time that a religious conflict broke out among the Toltecs; it seems that it concerned the demand by part of the priesthood to introduce human sacrifices in order to pacify the War God. In A.D. 987 Topiltzin-Quetzalcoatl and his followers left Tollan and migrated eastward, emulating the earlier legendary departure of the divine Quetzalcoatl. They settled in Yucatán.

Two centuries later natural calamities and onslaughts by

other tribesmen brought the Toltecs to their knees. The calamities were deemed signs of divine wrath, foretelling the city's doom. The chronicler Sahagún recorded that in the end the ruler, who many think was called Huemac but who also bore the patronym Quetzalcoatl, convinced the Toltecs that Tollan must be abandoned. "And so they left by his command, although they had lived there many years and had built beautiful and large houses and their temples and their palaces . . . At last they had to depart, leaving their houses, their lands, their city and their riches, and since they could not take all their wealth with them, they buried many things, and even today some of them are brought up from under the ground and not without admiration for their beauty and workmanship."

Thus it was that in A.D. 1168 or thereabouts Tollan became a desolate city, left to decay and disintegrate. It is told that when the first Aztec chieftain laid eyes on the city's remains, he cried bitterly. The destructive forces of nature were aided by invaders, marauders, and robbers who desecrated the temples, toppled monuments, and wrecked whatever was left standing. And so Tollan, flattened and forgotten, became only a legend.

What is known about Tollan eight centuries later attests to the appropriateness of its name, which means "Place of many neighborhoods"; for it appears to have consisted of many neighborhoods and precincts that occupied as much as seven square miles. As at Teotihuacan (which its planners tried to emulate), Tollan's heart was a sacred precinct that extended along a mile-long north–south axis; it was flanked by ceremonial groups built with an east–west orientation perpendicular to the north–south axis. As we have already noted, the orientations were given the "sacred tilt" of Teotihuacan, although at the period and geographic location of Tollan it no longer made astronomical sense.

At what might have been the northern limit of the sacred precinct there were found the remains of an unusual structure. In front it was built like a regular step-pyramid with its staircase; but in the back the structure is circular and was probably surmounted by a tower. The building might have served as an observatory; it certainly could have been a model for the later Aztec temple of Quetzalcoatl in Tenochtitlán and for other circular observatory pyramids elsewhere in Mexico.

The principal ceremonial compound, about a mile away to the south, was laid out around a large central square in the midst of which stood the Great Altar. The main temple stood atop a large five-stage pyramid on the square's eastern side. A smaller five-stage pyramid on the northern side served as the

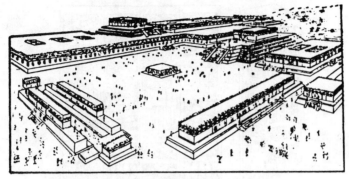

Figure 17

raised platform for another temple; it was flanked by multi-chambered buildings that show evidence of fires and that may have served for some industrial purpose. Elongated buildings or vestibules whose roofs rested on rows of pillars connected the two pyramids and also lined the square's southern side. A ball-court for the sacred *tlachtli* rubber-ball game completed the square on the west (Fig. 17, an artist's reconstruction suggested by the archaeologist P. Salazar Ortegon).

Between this principal compound of Tula Grande and the northern edge of the sacred precinct, various structures and groups of buildings evidently existed; another ballcourt was ex-cavated. In the particular compounds and throughout the pre-cinct, relatively many stone statues have been found. These include not only those of animals, such as a familiar coyote and an unfamiliar tiger, but also of a reclining demigod called Chac-mool (Fig. 18). The Toltecs also sculpted statues of their chief-tains, depicting them mostly as men of short stature. Others, attired as warriors and holding (in their left hand) the *atl-atl* weapon (a curved spear or arrow thrower), were depicted in

Figure 18

a   b

Figure 19

relief on square columns (Fig. 19a), both in profile and in back
views (Fig. 19b).

When methodical and sustained archaeological work began
in the 1940s under Jorge R. Acosta, attention was directed at
the Great Pyramid, which, facing the Great Altar, provided an
obvious astronomical purpose. At the time the archaeologists
wondered why the local Indians referred to the desolate mound
as *El Tesoro,* The Treasure; but when several artifacts of gold
were found after excavations began, the workmen insisted that
the pyramid rose atop a "field of gold" and refused to continue
work. "Be it reality or superstition," Acosta wrote, "the result
was that work stopped and was never resumed."

Work then focused on the smaller pyramid that has variably
been referred to (at first) as Pyramid of the Moon, then as Pyramid "B," and lately as the Quetzalcoatl Pyramid. The designation stems primarily from the long native name for the mound
that means "Lord of the Morning Star," presumably one of the
epithets of Quetzalcoatl, and from the remains of colored plas-
terwork and low reliefs that adorned the pyramid's stages, evi-
dencing that its rich decorations were dominated by the
Feathered Serpent motif. Archaeologists also believe that two

round stone columns, several of whose sections have been found, were carved with the Feathered Serpent image and stood as gateway pillars at the entrance to the temple atop this pyramid.

The greatest archaeological treasure trove was found when the Acosta teams realized that the northern side of this pyramid was disturbed in pre-Hispanic times. A ramplike aggregate seemed to run down the middle of this side, replacing the stepped incline. Excavating there, the archaeologists found that a trench had been cut through this side of the pyramid, reaching well into its interior; and the trench, which was as high as the pyramid, was used to bury in it a great number of stone sculptures. When these were taken out, stood up and fitted together, it became clear that these were sections of the two round gateway columns, four square columns that are believed to have held up the roof of the pyramid's temple, and four colossal humanlike statues, more than fifteen feet high, that came to be known as the *Atlantes* (Fig. 20). Believed to have also served as caryatids (sculptures used as pilasters to uphold a roof or its beams), they were re-erected by the archaeologists atop the pyramid when the restoration work was completed.

Each one of the *Atlantes* (as illustrated in Fig. 21) consists of four sections that were carved to fit together. The topmost section forms the statue's head, showing the giants wearing a headdress of feathers held together by a band decorated with star symbols; two elongated objects cover the ears. The facial features are not readily identifiable and so far have defied comparison with any known racial group; but although the four faces hold the same remote expression, a close examination shows them to be slightly different and individual.

The torso is made up of two sections. The upper or breast section's main feature is a thick breastplate whose shape has been compared to a butterfly. The lower part of the torso has its main feature on the back; it is a disk with a human face in its center, surrounded by undeciphered symbols and, in the opinion of some, a "wreath" of two entwined serpents. The bottom section provides the giant's thighs, legs, and sandaled feet. Ribbons hold these accoutrements in place; armbands, anklets, and a loincloth are included in the elaborate attire (see Fig. 21).

Whom do these giant statues represent? Their first discoverers called them "idols," certain that they represented deities. Popular writers nicknamed them *Atlantes,* which implied both that they might have been offspring of the Goddess Atlatona, "She Who Shines in the Water," and also that they might have come from the legendary Atlantis. Less imaginative scholars see

Figure 20

them simply as Toltec warriors, who hold in their left hand a
bunch of arrows and an atl-atl in the right hand. But this interpretation cannot possibly be correct, for the "arrows" in the left
hand are not straight but curved; and we have seen that the
left-handed weapon was the atl-atl. At the same time, the
weapon held in the right hand (Fig. 22a) is not curved as the
atl-atl must be; what is it, then?

The instrument looks rather like a pistol in its holster, held
by two fingers. An interesting theory suggesting that it was not a
weapon but a tool, a "plasma pistol," was advanced by Gerardo
Levet *(Mision Fatal)*. He discovered that one of the square pilasters depicting Toltec chieftains has, engraved in an upper-
left-hand corner (Fig. 22b), the image of a person wearing a
backpack and holding the tool in question; he uses it as a
flamethrower to shape a stone (Fig. 22c). The tool is unques-

Figure 21

tionably the same instrument held by the giants' right hands. Levet suggests that it was a high-energy "pistol" that was used to cut and carve stones, and he points out that such Thermo-Jet torches were used in modern time to carve the giant monument of Georgia's Stone Mountain.

The significance of Levet's discovery may go beyond his own theory. Since stone stellas and carvings have been found throughout Mesoamerica, the product of its native artists, one need not search for high-tech tools to explain the stone carvings. On the other hand, the depicted tool may serve to explain another enigmatic aspect of Tollan.

As they examined the depths of the pyramid after they had removed the ramp's soil, the archaeologists discovered that the external and visible pyramid was built over and hid an earlier pyramid whose stepped stages lay some eight feet away on each side. They also discovered remains of vertical walls that suggested the existence of inner chambers and passages within the earlier pyramid (but have not pursued these leads). They did come upon an extraordinary feature—a stone pipe made of perfectly fitting tubular sections (Fig. 23) with an inner diameter of about eighteen inches. The long pipe was installed inside the pyramid at the same angle as its original incline and ran through its whole height.

Acosta and his team presumed that the pipe had served to drain rainwater; but this could have been achieved without such an elaborate internal installation, and with simple clay pipes rather than by precision-sculpted stone sections. The position and incline of the unusual, if not unique, tubular contraption was obviously part of the original plan of the pyramid and inte-

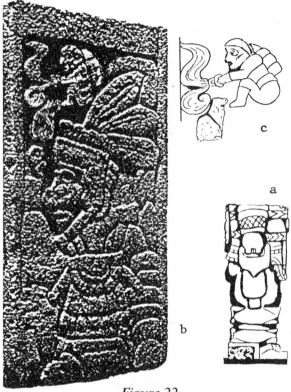

Figure 22

gral to the structure's purpose. The fact that the remains of the adjoining multichambered and multistoried buildings suggest some industrial processing, and also the fact that in antiquity water from the Tula river was channeled to flow by these buildings, raise the possibility that at this site, as at Teotihuacan, some kind of a purification and refining process had taken place at a very early period.

What comes to our mind is this: Was the enigmatic tool a tool not to engrave stones, but to break up stones for their ores? Was it, in other words, a sophisticated mining tool?

And was the mineral sought after, gold?

The possession by "Atlanteans" of high-technology tools more than a thousand years ago in Central Mexico raises the question of who they were. Certainly, to judge by their facial features, not Mesoamericans; and probably "gods" and not mortal men, if the statues' size is an indication of veneration,

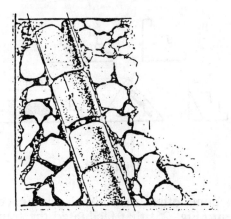

Figure 23

for alongside these giant figures there were erected the square columns on which images of Toltec rulers were carved in normal size. The fact that at some pre-Hispanic time the colossal images were disassembled and carefully lowered into the depths of the pyramid and buried there, implies a measure of sanctity. Indeed, it all confirms the statement by Sahagún, earlier quoted, that when the Toltecs abandoned Tollan "they buried many things" some of which, even in Sahagún's time, "were brought up from under the ground and not without admiration for their beauty and workmanship."

The archaeologists believe that the four Atlanteans stood atop the Pyramid of Quetzalcoatl, supporting the ceiling of the temple atop the pyramid as though they were holding up the Celestial Canopy. This is the role played in Egyptian beliefs by the four sons of Horus, who were holding up the sky at the four cardinal points. According to the Egyptian *Book of the Dead,* it was these four gods, who linked Heaven and Earth, who accompanied the deceased pharaoh to a sacred stairway whereby he would ascend heavenward for an eternal afterlife. This "Stairway to Heaven" was depicted hieroglyphically as either a single or a double stairway, the latter representing a step pyramid (Fig. 24a). Was it just a coincidence that the stairway symbol decorated the walls around the Tollan pyramid and became a major Aztec iconographic symbol (Fig. 24b)?

At the center of all this symbolism and religious beliefs of the Nahuatl peoples was their hero-god, giver of all their knowledge, Quetzalcoatl—"The Feathered Serpent." But what, one may ask, was a "feathered" serpent if not a serpent that, birdlike, had wings and could fly?

And if so, the concept of Quetzalcoatl as the "Feathered

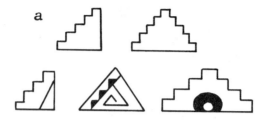

Figure 24

Serpent" was none other than the Egyptian concept of the Winged Serpent (Fig. 25) that facilitated the transfiguration of the deceased pharaoh to the realm of the ever-living gods.

In addition to Quetzalcoatl, the Nahuatl pantheon was replete with deities associated with serpents. Cihuacoatl was the "Serpent Female." Coatlicue was "the one with the skirt of serpents." Chicomecoatl was "Seven Snake." Ehecacoamixtli was the "Cloud of wind snakes," and so on. The great god Tlaloc was frequently depicted with the mask of a double-serpent.

And so, unacceptable as this might be to pragmatic scholars, mythology, archaeology, and symbolism lead to the unavoidable conclusion that Central Mexico, if not all of Mesoamerica, was the realm of the Serpent Gods—the gods of ancient Egypt.

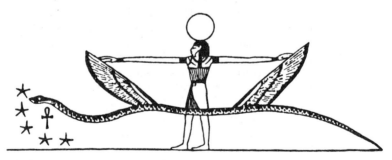

Figure 25

4

SKYWATCHERS
IN THE JUNGLES

Maya.

The name evokes mystery, enigma, adventure. A civilization that was, and is gone, vanished though its people have remained. Incredible cities abandoned intact, swallowed by the green jungle canopy; pyramids that reach sky high, aiming to touch the gods; and monuments, elaborately carved and decorated, that speak out in artful hieroglyphs whose meaning is still mostly lost in the mists of time.

The Maya mystique seized the imagination and curiosity of Europeans from the moment the Spaniards first set foot in the Yucatán peninsula and saw the vestiges of cities lost in the jungle. It was all so unbelievable, yet there it was: stepped pyramids, platformed temples, decorated palaces, engraved stone pillars; and as they stared at the astounding remains they listened to the natives' tales of monarchies, city-states and glories that once had been. One of the most notorious of the Spanish priests who wrote of Yucatán and the Maya during and following the Conquest, Friar (later Bishop) Diego de Landa *(Relacion de las cosas de Yucatan),* reported that "there are in Yucatán many edifices of great beauty, this being the most outstanding of all things discovered in the Indies; they are all built of stone and finely ornamented, though there is no metal found in the country for this cutting."

With other interests on their minds, such as the search for riches and the conversion of the natives to Christianity, it took nearly two centuries for the Spaniards to turn their attention to the ruins. It was only in 1785 that a royal commission inspected the then-discovered ruins of Palenque. Fortunately, a copy of the commission's illustrated report found its way to London; its eventual publication attracted to the Mayan enigma a wealthy nobleman, Lord Kingsborough. Fervently believing that the inhabitants of Mesoamerica were descended from the Ten Lost

Tribes of Israel, he spent the rest of his life and all of his fortune in the exploration and description of the ancient monuments and writings of Mexico. His *Antiquities of Mexico* (1830–1848), together with Landa's *Relacion,* has been an invaluable source of data on the Maya past.

But in the popular mind, the honor of launching the archaeological discovery of the Maya civilization belongs to a native of New Jersey, John L. Stephens. Appointed U.S. envoy to the Central American Federation, he went to the Maya lands with his friend Frederick Catherwood, an accomplished artist. The two books that Stephens wrote and Catherwood illustrated, *Incidents of Travel in Central America, Chiapas, and Yucatán* and *Incidents of Travel in Yucatán,* are still recommended reading a century and a half after their original publication (1841 and 1843). Catherwood's own volume, *Views of Ancient Monuments of Central America, Chiapas, and Yucatán,* further fueled interest in the subject. When Catherwood's drawings are put side by side with current photographs, one is amazed to see the accuracy of his work (and saddened to realize the erosion that has taken place since).

The team's reports were especially detailed regarding the great sites of Palenque, Uxmal, Chichén Itzá, and Copan; the latter is above all associated with Stephens for, in order to investigate it without hindrance, he bought the site from its local landlord for fifty American dollars. All in all the two explored nearly fifty Maya cities; the profusion not only staggered the imagination but also left no doubt that the emerald canopy of the rain forests hid not just a few lost outposts but a whole lost civilization. Of particular importance was the realization that some of the symbols and glyphs carved upon the monuments in fact stated the date thereof, so that the Maya civilization could be placed in a time frame. Although the complete hieroglyphic writing of the Maya is still a long way from being deciphered, scholars have been successful in reading the date inscriptions and establishing the parallel dates in the Christian calendar.

We could have known much more about the Maya from their own extensive literature—books that were written on paper made from tree barks and laminated with white lime to create a base for the inked glyphs. But these books, by the hundreds, were systematically destroyed by the Spanish priests—most notably by the very same Bishop Landa who ended up being the one who preserved much of the "pagan" information in his own writings.

Only three (or, if authentic, a fourth) codices ("picture-books") have remained. The parts scholars find most interesting in them are the sections dealing with astronomy. Two other major literary works are also available because they had been rewritten, either from original picture-books or from oral traditions, into the native tongues but using Latin script.

One of these is the books of *Chilam Balam,* meaning the Oracles or Utterings of Balam the priest. Many villages in Yucatán possessed copies of this book; the one best preserved and translated is the *Book of Chilam Balam of Chumayel.* Balam, it appears, was a kind of a Maya "Edgar Cayce": the books record information regarding the mythical past and the prophetic future, on rites and rituals, astrology, and medical advice.

The word *balam* means "jaguar" in the native tongue, and has caused much consternation among scholars, for it has no apparent connection with oracles. We find it intriguing, however, that in ancient Egypt a class of priests called *Shem*-priests, who pronounced oracles during certain royal ceremonies as well as secret formulas intended to "Open the Mouth" so that a deceased pharaoh could join the gods in the Afterlife, wore leopard skins (Fig. 26a). Maya depictions of similarly clad priests have been found (Fig. 26b); since in the Americas this would have to be a jaguar skin rather than that of an African leopard, this could explain the "jaguar" meaning of the name Balam. It would also indicate, once more, an Egyptian ritual influence.

We are even more intrigued by the similarity of this name of the Maya oracle-priest to that of the seer Balaam, who, according to the Bible, was retained by the king of Moab during the Exodus to put a curse on the Israelites, but who ended up being pronounced their favorable oracle. Was this just a coincidence?

The other book is the *Popol Vuh,* the "Council Book" of the highland Maya. It gives an account of divine and human origins and of royal genealogies; its cosmogony and creation traditions

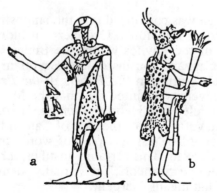

Figure 26

are basically similar to those of the Nahuatl peoples, indicating a common original source. Regarding Maya origins the *Popol Vuh* states that their forefathers had come "from the other side of the sea." Landa wrote that the Indians "have heard from their ancestors that this land was occupied by a race of people who came from the East and whom God had delivered by opening twelve paths through the sea."

These statements are in accord with a Maya tale known as the Legend of Votan. It was reported by several Spanish chroniclers, particularly Friar Ramon Ordóñez y Aguiar and Bishop Nuñez de la Vega. It was later collected from its various sources by the Abbé E. C. Brasseur de Bourbourg *(Histoire de nations civilisées du mexique)*. The legend relates the arrival in Yucatán, circa 1000 B.C. by the chroniclers' calculations, of "the first man whom God had sent to this region to people and parcel out the land that is now called America." His name was Votan (meaning unknown); his emblem was the Serpent. "He was a descendant of the Guardians, of the race of *Can*. His place of origin was a land called *Chivim."* He made a total of four voyages. The first time he landed he established a settlement near the coast. After some time he advanced inland and "at the tributary of a great river built a city which was the cradle of this civilization." He called the city *Nachan,* "which means Place of Serpents." On his second visit he surveyed the newfound land, examining its subterranean zones and underground passages; one such passage was said to have gone right through a mountain near Nachan. When he returned to America the fourth time he found discord and rivalry among the people. So he divided the realm into four domains, establishing a city to serve as the capital of each. Palenque is mentioned as one of them; another appears to have been near the Pacific coast. The others are unknown.

Nuñez de la Vega was convinced that the land whence Votan had come bordered on Babylonia. Ordóñez concluded that Chivim was the land of the Hivites whom the Bible (Genesis 10) listed as sons of Canaan, cousins of the Egyptians. More recently Zelia Nuttal, writing in the *Papers of the Peabody Museum,* Harvard University, pointed out that the Maya word for serpent, *Can,* paralleled the Hebrew *Canaan.* If so, the Maya legend, telling that Votan was of the race of Can and his symbol was the serpent, could be using a play of words to state that Votan came from Canaan. This certainly justifies our wondering why *Nachan,* "Place of Serpents," is virtually identical to the Hebrew *Nachash* that means "serpent."

Such legends strengthen the scholarly school that considers

the Gulf Coast as the place where Yucatec civilization began—
not only of the Maya, but also of the earlier Olmecs. In this
view much more consideration has to be given to a site that is
little known to visitors, which belongs to the very beginnings of
Maya culture "between 2000 and 1000 B.C. if not earlier," according to its excavators from Tulane University–National Geographic Society. Called Dzibilchaltun, it is situated near the port
city Progreso on Yucatán's northwestern coast. The remains,
extending over an area of twenty square miles, reveal that the
city was occupied from the earliest times through Spanish times,
its edifices having been built and rebuilt and overbuilt, and its
cut and ornamented stones having been hauled away to be used
in Spanish and modern constructions near and far. Besides immense temples and pyramids, the city's outstanding feature is a
Great White Way, a causeway paved with limestones that ran
straight for a mile and a half as an east–west axis of the city.

A string of major Maya cities stretches across the northern
tip of Yucatán, bearing names well known not just to archaeologists but to millions of visitors: Uxmal, Izamal, Mayapan,
Chichén Itzá, Tulum—to mention the most outstanding sites.
Each played a role in Maya history; Mayapan was the center of
an alliance of city-states, Chichén Itzá was made great by Toltec
migrants. Either one of them could have been the capital from
which, according to the Spanish chronicler Diego Garcia de Pa-
lacio, a great Maya lord from Yucatán had conquered the
southern highlands and built the southernmost Maya center of
Copan. It was all, Garcia wrote, written in a book that the Indians of Copan had shown him when he visited that place.

Notwithstanding all this legendary and archaeological evidence, another school of archaeologists believes that Maya culture—or at least the Mayas themselves—originated in the
southern highlands (today's Guatemala), spreading from there
northward. Studies of the Maya language trace its origins to "a
proto-Maya community that, perhaps around 2600 B.C., existed
in what is now the department of Huehuetenango in northwest
Guatemala" (D. S. Morales, *The Maya World)*. But wherever
and however Maya civilization developed, scholars consider the
second millennium B.C. as its "Pre-Classic" phase and the beginning of the "Classic" phase of maximal achievement circa A.D.
200; by A.D. 900 the realm of the Maya extended from the Pacific coast to the Gulf of Mexico and the Caribbean. During
those many centuries the Maya built scores of cities whose pyramids, temples, palaces, plazas, stelae, sculptures, inscriptions,
and decorations overwhelm both scholar and visitor in their
profusion, variety and beauty, to say nothing of their monumen-

tal size and imaginative architecture. Except for a few cities that were walled, Maya cities were in reality open-ended ceremonial centers surrounded by a population of administrators, artisans, and merchants, and supported by an extensive rural population. In these centers each successive ruler added new structures or enlarged older ones by building bigger edifices over the previous ones, like adding a new layer of skin over an onion.

And then, five centuries before the Spanish arrival, for reasons unknown, the Maya abandoned their sacred cities and let the jungle take them over.

Palenque, one of the earliest Maya cities, is situated near the Mexican–Guatemalan border and is reachable from the modern city Villahermosa. In the seventh century A.D. it marked the western reaches of Maya expansion. Its existence was known to Europeans since 1773; the remains of its temples and palaces have been uncovered and its rich stucco decorations and hieroglyphic inscriptions have been studied by archaeologists since the 1920s. Yet, its fame and allure took off only after the discovery in 1949 (by Alberto Ruiz Lhuillier) that the stepped pyramid called the Temple of Inscriptions contained a secret internal stairway that led all the way down. Several years of excavation and removal of the soil and debris that filled and hid the inner structure yielded in the end a most exciting discovery: a burial chamber (Fig. 27). At the bottom of the twisting stairway a triangular stone block masked an entranceway through the

Figure 27

Figure 28

blank wall that was still guarded by the skeletons of Maya warriors. Behind it there was a vaulted crypt, its walls painted with murals. Within, a stone sarcophagus was covered by a large rectangular stone slab that weighs about five tons and is 12½ feet long. When this stone lid was moved, there came into view the skeletal remains of a tall man, still bedecked with pearls and jade jewelry. His face was covered with a mosaic jade mask; a small jade pendant bearing the image of a deity lay among the beads that once were a jade collar.

The discovery was astounding, for until then no other pyramid or temple in Mexico had been found to have served as a tomb. The enigma of the tomb and its occupant was deepened by the depiction carved upon the stone lid: it was the image of a barefoot Maya sitting upon a plumed or flaming throne and seemingly operating mechanical devices inside an elaborate chamber (Fig. 28). The Ancient Astronaut Society and its sponsor, Erich von Däniken, have seen in this a depiction of an astronaut inside a spacecraft driven by flaming jets. They suggest that an Extraterrestrial is buried here.

Archaeologists and other scholars ridicule the idea. Inscriptions on the walls of this funerary edifice and in adjoining structures convince them that the person buried here is the ruler

Pacal ("Shield") who reigned in Palenque in A.D. 615–683.
Some see in the scene a depiction of the deceased Pacal being
taken by the Dragon of the Underworld to the realm of the
dead; they consider the fact that at the winter solstice the Sun
sets exactly behind the Temple of Inscriptions as added symbolism of the king's departure with the setting Sun God. Others,
prompted to revised interpretations by the fact that the depiction is framed by a Sky Band, a chain of glyphs that represent
celestial bodies and the zodiac constellations, regard the scene
as showing the king being carried by the Celestial Serpent to the
celestial realm of the gods. The crosslike object that the deceased is facing is now recognized as a stylized Tree of Life,
suggesting that the king is being transported to an eternal afterlife.

In fact a similar tomb, known as Burial 116, was discovered
in the Great Plaza of Tikal, at the foot of one of its major
pyramids. Buried some twenty feet below the ground was found
the skeleton of an unusually tall man. His body was placed on a
platform of stone masonry, he was bedecked with jade jewelry,
and was surrounded (as at Palenque) by pearls, jade objects,
and pottery. Also, depictions of persons carried in the jaws of
fiery serpents (whom scholars call Sky Gods) are known from
various Maya sites, such as this one (Fig. 29) from Chichén Itzá.

All considered, scholars have admitted that "one cannot
avoid an implicit comparison to the crypts of the Egyptian pharaohs. The similarities between the tomb of Pacal and those
who ruled earlier beside the Nile are striking" (H. La Fay, "The
Maya, Children of Time" in the *National Geographic Magazine)*. Indeed, the scene on Pacal's sarcophagus conveys the
very same image as that of a pharaoh transported, by the
Winged Serpent, to an eternal afterlife among the gods who
came from the heavens. The pharaoh, who was not an astro-

Figure 29

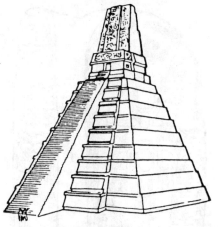

Figure 30

naut, had become one upon his death; and that, we suggest, is what the carved scene has implied for Pacal.

Not only tombs have been discovered in the jungles of Mesoamerica, Central America, and the equatorial zones of South America. Repeatedly, a hill overgrown with tropical vegetation turned out to be a pyramid; groups of pyramids were peaks of a lost city. Until excavations began at El Mirador, a jungle site astride the Guatamalan–Mexican border, in 1978, revealing a major Maya city dating back to 400 B.C. and occupying six square miles, those of the southern-beginnings school (viz. S. G. Morley, *The Ancient Maya)* believed that Tikal was not only the largest Maya city but also the earliest. Situated in the northeastern part of Guatamela's province of Petén, Tikal still raises its tall pyramids high above the jungle's sea of green. It is so large that its boundaries seem to be constantly expanding as more remains are found. Its main ceremonial center alone covers more than a square mile; the space for it was not only hacked out of the rain forest; it was physically created atop a mountain ridge that was laboriously flattened out. The flanking ravines were converted into water reservoirs linked by a series of causeways.

Tikal's pyramids, tightly grouped together in several sections, are a marvel of construction. Tall and narrow, they are true skyscrapers, rising steeply to heights nearing and even exceeding 200 feet. Rising in sheer stages, the pyramids served as raised platforms for the temples that stood atop them. The rectangular temples, containing but a couple of narrow rooms, were in turn topped by massive ornamental superstructures that further increased the height of the pyramids (Fig. 30). The ar-

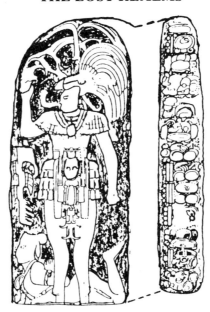

Figure 31

chitectural result was to make the sanctuary appear suspended
between the Earth and the Sky, reachable by steep steps that
were truly symbolic Stairways to Heaven. Within each temple a
series of doorways led from the outside in, each doorway a step
higher than the one before it. The lintels were made of rare
woods and exquisitely carved. There were as a rule five exterior
and seven interior doorways, a total of twelve—a symbolism
whose meaning has not attracted, so far, particular attention.

The construction of an airstrip near Tikal's ruins speeded up
its exploration after 1950 and extensive archaeological work has
been conducted there especially by teams from The University
Museum, University of Pennsylvania. They discovered that the
great plazas of Tikal served as a necropolis, where rulers and
noblemen were buried; also, that many of the lesser structures
were in fact funerary temples, built not over the tombs but next
to them and serving as cenotaphs. They also uncovered about
one hundred and fifty stelas, carved stone slabs erected mostly
so as to face either east or west. They depict, it was ascertained,
portraits of actual rulers and commemorate major events in
their lives and reigns. The hieroglyphic inscriptions carved upon
them (Fig. 31) recorded accurate dates associated with these
events, named the ruler by his hieroglyph (here "Jaguar Paw
Skull," A.D. 488) and identified the event; the textual hiero-

glyphs, scholars are by now certain, were not merely pictorial or ideographic "but also written phonetically in syllables similar to those of Sumerian, Babylonian, and Egyptian" (A. G. Miller, *Maya Rulers of Time*).

It was with the aid of such stelas that the archaeologists were able to identify a sequence of fourteen rulers at Tikal who had reigned from A.D. 317 to A.D. 869. But it is certain that Tikal was a royal Maya center long before: carbon-dating of remains in some of the royal tombs result in dates going back to 600 B.C..

Lying about a hundred and fifty miles to the southeast of Tikal is Copán, the city that Stephens had purchased. It was located at the southeastern periphery of the Maya realm, in today's Honduras. Though lacking Tikal's steep skyscrapers, it was perhaps more typical of Maya cities in its scope and layout. Its vast ceremonial center occupied seventy-five acres and consisted of pyramid-temples grouped about several great plazas (Fig. 32). The pyramids, wide-based and just seventy feet or so high, were distinguished by wide monumental stairways decorated with elaborate sculptures and hieroglyphic inscriptions. The plazas were dotted with shrines, altars, and—most important to the historians—carved stone stelas that portrayed rulers and gave their dates. They reveal that the main pyramid was completed in A.D. 756 and that Copán reached its glorious peak in the ninth century A.D.—just before the sudden collapse of Mayan civilization.

But, as ongoing discoveries and excavations have shown, site after new site in Guatemala, Honduras, and Belize indicates the existence of monuments and dated stelas as early as 600 B.C., revealing a developed system of writing that, all scholars agree, must have had a prior developmental phase or source.

Copán, as we shall soon see, played a special role in Maya life and culture.

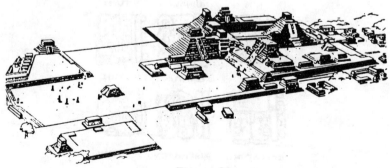

Figure 32

Students of the Maya civilization have been especially impressed by the accuracy, ingenuity and diversity of Maya time reckoning, attributing them to an advanced Maya astronomy.

The Maya had, indeed, not one but three calendars; but one —the most significant one in our opinion—had nothing to do with astronomy. It is the so-called Long Count. It stated a date by counting the number of days that had passed from a certain starting day to the day of the event recorded by the Maya on the stela or monument. That enigmatic Day One, most scholars now agree, was August 13, 3113 B.C. according to the current Christian calendar—a time and an event that clearly preceded the emergence of the Maya civilization.

The Long Count, like the two other time-reckoning systems, was based on the vigesimal ("times twenty") mathematical system of the Maya, and—as in ancient Sumer—employed the "place" concept, whereby 1 in the first column would be one, in the next column twenty, then four hundred, and so on. The Maya Long Count dating system, using vertical columns where values were lowest at the bottom, named these various multiples and identified them with glyphs (Fig. 33). Starting with *kin* for ones, *uinal* for twenties and so on, the multiples reached the glyph *alau-tun,* which stood for the fantastic number of 23,040,000,000 days—a period of 63,080,082 years!

But, as stated, in their actual calendrical dating on their monuments, the Maya went back not to the age of the dinosaurs but to a specific day, an event as crucial to them as the date of Christ's birth is to the followers of the Christian calendar. Thus, Stela 29 at Tikal (Fig. 34), which bears the earliest date so far

Figure 33

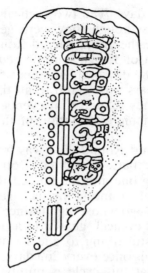

Figure 34

found on a royal monument there (A.D. 292), gives the Long Count date 8.12.14.8.15 by using dots for the numeral one and bars for five:

8 bak-tun	(8 × 400 × 360)	=	1,152,000 days
12 ka-tun	(12 × 20 × 360)	=	86,400 days
14 tun	(14 × 360)	=	5,040 days
8 uinal	(8 × 20)	=	160 days
15 kin	(15 × 1)	=	15 days
		Total =	1,243,615 days

Dividing the 1,243,615 days by the number of days in a solar year, 365¼, the date on the stela states that it, or the event depicted on it, occurred 3,404 years and 304 days after the mysterious Day One; i.e., since August 13, 3113 B.C. Therefore, according to the now accepted correlation, the date on the stela is A.D. 292 (3,405 − 3,113 = 292). Some scholars see evidence that the Maya began to use the Long Count in the era of Baktun 7, which equaled the fourth century B.C.; others do not dismiss an even earlier use.

Alongside this continuous calendar there were two cyclical calendars. One was the *Haab* or Solar Year of 365 days that was divided into 18 months of 20 days, plus an additional 5 days at year's end. The other was the *Tzolkin* or Sacred Year calendar in which the basic 20 days were rotated 13 times, resulting in a

Sacred Year of 260 days. The two cyclical calendars were then meshed together, as though they were gear wheels driven by each other to create the grand Sacred Round of 52 solar years; for the combination of 13, 20, and 365 could not repeat itself except once in 18,980 days, which equals 52 years. This Calendar Round of 52 years was sacred to all the peoples of ancient Mesoamerica and they related to it events both past and future —such as the messianic expectation of the return of Quetzalcoatl.

The earliest Sacred Round date was found in Mexico's Oaxaca valley and goes back to 500 B.C. Both time reckoning systems, the continuing one and the Sacred Round one, are quite old. One is historical, counting the passage of time (days) from an event in the long-ago whose significance and nature are still a puzzle. The other is cyclical, geared to a peculiar period of 260 days; scholars are still trying to guess what, if anything, happened or still happens once every 260 days.

Some believe that this cycle is purely mathematical: since five cycles of 52 years is 260 years, somehow a shorter count of 260 days was adopted. But such an explanation of 260 only shifts the problem to a need to explain 52: where, then, is the origin and reason for 52?

Others suggest that the period of 260 days had to do with agriculture, such as the length of the rainy season or the dry intervals. In view of the Mayan propensity for astronomy, others attempt to somehow calculate a relationship between 260 days and the motions of Venus or Mars. One must wonder why a solution offered by Zelia Nuttal at the twenty-second International Congress of Americanists (Rome, 1926) did not gain the full recognition it deserves. She pointed out that the easiest way for the people of the New World to apply seasonal movements of the Sun to their own locality was to determine Zenith Days, when the Sun passed precisely overhead at midday. This happens twice a year as the Sun appears to travel northward, then southward, passing overhead twice. The Indians, she suggested, measured the interval between the two Zenith Days and the resulting number of days became the basis for the Calendar Round.

This interval is half a solar year at the equator; it lengthens as one moves away, northward or southward. At 15 degrees north, for example, it is 263 days (from August 12 to the following May 1). This is the rainy season and to this day the descendants of the Maya begin planting on May 3 (conveniently also the Mexican Day of the Holy Cross). The interval was precisely 260 days at latitude 14° 42′ north—*the latitude of Copán.*

That Nuttal has come up with the correct explanation for the manner in which the 260-day ritual year was fixed is borne out by the fact that Copán was considered the astronomical capital of the Maya. Besides the usual celestial orientation of edifices, some of its stelas have been found to be aligned for determining key calendar dates. In another instance a stela ("Stela A") that bears a Long Count date equivalent to a day in A.D. 733 also bears two other Long Count dates, one greater by 200 days and one smaller by 60 days (splitting up a cycle of 260 days). A. Aveni *(Skywatchers of Ancient Mexico)* assumes that this was an attempt to realign the Long Count (which counted an actual 365¼ days per year) with the cyclical *Haab* of 365 days. The need to readjust or reform the calendars may have been the reason for a conclave of astronomers that was held in Copán in A.D. 763. It was commemorated by a square monument known as Altar Q on which the sixteen astronomers that took part in the conclave were portrayed, four to a side (Fig. 35). It will be noted that the "teardrop" glyph in front of their noses—as was done on the Pacal depiction—identifies them as Skywatchers. The date carved on this monument appears on monuments at other Maya sites, suggesting that the decisions reached at Copán were applied throughout the realm.

Figure 35

The reputation of the Maya as accomplished astronomers has been enhanced by the fact that their various codices contain astronomical sections dealing with solar and lunar eclipses and the planet Venus. Closer study of the data revealed, however, that these were not records of observations by the Maya astronomers. Rather, they were almanacs copied from some earlier sources that provided the Maya with ready-made data against which they were to look for phenomena applicable to the 260-day cycle. As stated by E. Hadingham *(Early Man and the*

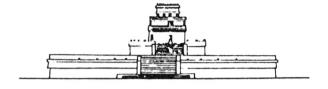

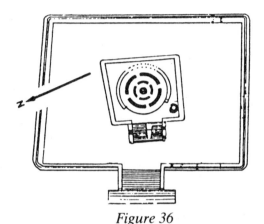

Figure 36

Cosmos), these almanacs displayed "a curious blend of long-term exactness and short-term inaccuracy."

The main task of the local astronomers, it appears, was to keep verifying or adjusting the 260-day sacred year against data from earlier times that dealt with the movements of celestial bodies. Indeed, the most renowned and still standing observatory in Yucatán, the *Caracol* in Chichén Itzá (Fig. 36), has frustrated successive researchers who had tried, in vain, to find in its orientation and aperture viewlines to the solstices or equinoxes. Some viewlines, however, do seem to be related to the Tzolkin (260-day) cycle.

But why the number 260? Just because it happened to equal the number of days between Zeniths at Copán? Why not, say, the easier number 300 if a site near latitude 20° north would have been chosen, such as Teotihuacan?

The number 260 appears to have been an arbitrary, deliberate choice; the explanation that it results from multiplying a natural number, 20 (the number of fingers and toes), by 13 only shifts the problem to the question, Why and Wherefrom 13? The Long Count too contains an arbitrary number, 360: inexplicably it abandons the pure vigesimal progression and, after the kin (1) and uinal (20), introduces the tun (360) into the system. The Haab calendar also considers 360 as its basic length, dividing this number into 18 "months" of 20 days; it rounds off the year by the addition of 5 "bad days" to complete the solar cycle of 365.

All three calendars thus are based on numbers that are not natural, numbers deliberately selected. We will show that both 260 and 360 reached Mesoamerica from Mesopotamia—via Egypt.

We are all familiar with the number 360: it is the number of degrees in a circle. But few know that we owe the number to the Sumerians, and that it stems from their sexagesimal ("Base 60") mathematical system. The first known calendar was the Nippur Calendar of the Sumerians; it was devised by dividing the circle of 360 into 12 parts, twelve being the sacred celestial number from which followed the twelve months of the year, the twelve houses of the zodiac, the twelve Olympian gods, and so on. The problem of the shortfall of 5¼ days was solved by intercalation —the addition of a thirteenth month after the passage of a number of years.

Although the Egyptian arithmetical system was not sexagesimal, they adopted the Sumerian system of $12 \times 30 = 360$. But unable to pursue the very complex calculations involved in intercalation, they simplified matters by rounding off each year by having a short "month" of five days at year's end. It was this very system that was adopted in Mesoamerica. The Haab calendar was not just similar to the Egyptian one, it was identical to it. Moreover, just as the Mesoamericans had a ritual year alongside the solar one, so did the Egyptians have a ritual year relating to the rising of the star Sirius and the rising at the same time of the waters of the Nile.

The Sumerian imprint on the Egyptian and hence Mesoamerican calendars was not limited to the sexagesimal number 360. Various studies, principally by B. P. Reko, in the early issues of *El Mexico Antiguo*, leave little doubt that the thirteen months of the Tzolkin calendar were in fact a reflection of the 12-month system of the Sumerians plus the thirteenth intercalary month, except that in Egypt (and hence in Mesoamerica) the thirteenth month had shrunk to an annual 5 days. The term *tun* for 360 meant in the Maya language "celestial," a star or planet within the zodiacal band. Interestingly, a "heap of stars" —a constellation—was called *Mool,* virtually the same term MUL that the Sumerians had used to mean "celestial body."

The association of the Mesoamerican calendar with the Old World will become additionally evident as we look at the most sacred number, 52, to which all the great Mesoamerican events were geared. The many attempts to explain it (like the statement that it is 13 times 4) ignore its most obvious source: the 52 weeks of the Near Eastern calendar (and thereafter the European one). This number of weeks, however, is arrived at only if a week of 7 days is adopted. This was not always the case. The origin of the 7-day week has been a subject of study for almost two centuries and the best theory is that it derived from the four phases of the Moon. What is certain is that it emerged as a divinely decreed time period in biblical times, when God commanded the Israelites during the Exodus from Egypt to observe the seventh day as the Sabbath.

Was then 52 the most sacred cycle because it happened to be the common denominator of the Mesoamerican calendars—or was the sacred cycle of 260 adopted because it (rather than, say, 300) was a multiple of 52 ($52 \times 5 = 260$)?

Although a deity whose epithet was "Seven" was a principal Sumerian god, he was honored with theophonic place (e.g., *Beer-Sheba,* The Well of Seven) or personal names *(Elisheva,* My God is Seven) principally in the land of Canaan. The number 7 as a revered number appears in the tales of the Hebrew patriarchs only after Abraham went to Egypt and stayed at the pharaoh's court. The number 7 permeates the biblical tale of Joseph, the pharaoh's dream and the ensuing events in Egypt. And, to the extent that 52 stemmed from the consideration of 7 as a basic calendrical unit, we will show that this most sacred cycle of Mesoamerica was of Egyptian origin.

More specifically: 52 was a magical number that was associated with the Egyptian god Thoth, the god of science, writing, mathematics, and the calendar.

An ancient Egyptian tale known as "The Adventures of Satni-Khamois with the Mummies"—a tale of magic, mystery, and adventure that can match any modern thriller—employs the association of the magical number 52 with Thoth and with the secrets of the calendar for the key scene in the plot. It was written on a papyrus (Cairo 30646) that was discovered in a tomb in Thebes dating to the third century B.C. Fragments of other papyri with the same tale have also been found, indicating that it was an established book in ancient Egyptian literature, belonging to the cycle of tales of gods and men.

The tale's hero, son of a pharaoh, "was well instructed in all things." He was wont to wander in the necropolis of Memphis (then the capital), studying the sacred writings upon temple walls and stelas and researching ancient books of magic. In time he became "a magician who had no equal in the land of Egypt." One day a mysterious old man told him of a tomb "where there is deposited the book that the god Thoth had written with his own hand," in which are revealed the mysteries of the Earth and the secrets of the Heavens, including the divine knowledge concerning "the risings of the Sun and the appearances of the Moon and the motions of the gods [planets] that are in the cycle of the Sun"—the secrets of astronomy and the calendar.

The tomb was that of Nenoferkheptah, son of a former pharaoh (who, scholars believe, had reigned circa 1250 B.C.). When Satni, as expected, became very interested and asked for the location of the tomb, the old man warned him that although mummified, Nenoferkheptah was not dead and could strike down anyone who dared take away the book that was lodged at his feet. Undaunted, Satni went in search of the tomb. It could not be found for it was below the ground. But having reached the right spot Satni "recited a formula over it and a gap opened in the ground and Satni went down to the place where the book was."

Inside the tomb Satni saw the mummies of Nenoferkheptah, of his sister-wife, and of their son. The book that was indeed at Nenoferkheptah's feet "gave off a light as if the sun shone there." As Satni stepped toward it, the wife's mummy spoke up, warning him to advance no farther. She told Satni of the adventures of Nenoferkheptah when he had attempted to obtain the book, for Thoth had hidden it in a secret place, inside a golden box that was inside a silver box that was inside a series of other boxes, the last and outer ones being of bronze and iron. Ignoring all warnings and overcoming all obstacles, Nenoferkheptah found and obtained the book; whereupon they were condemned by Thoth to suspended animation: though alive, they were buried, and though mummified they could see, hear, and speak. She warned Satni that Thoth's curse would be upon him if he touched the book.

But having gone so far Satni was determined to get the book. As he took another step toward it, the mummy of Nenoferkheptah spoke up. There was a way to possess the book without incurring Thoth's wrath, he said: it was to play and win the Game of Fifty-Two, the magical number of Thoth.

Satni readily agreed. He lost the first game and found himself partly sunk into the ground. He lost the next game, and the next, sinking down more and more. How he managed to escape with the book, the calamities that befell him as a result, and how he in the end returned it to its hiding place, make up the rest of this ancient version of "Raiders of the Lost Ark."

The tale's moral was that no man, as knowledgeable as he might be, could learn the mysteries of the Earth, the Sun, the Moon, and the planets without divine permission; unauthorized by Thoth, Man will lose the game of Fifty-Two. And he would lose it even if he tried to find out the secrets by opening up the protective layers of Earth's minerals and metals.

It is our belief that it was the same Thoth, alias Quetzalcoatl, who had bestowed the Calendar of Fifty-Two, and all other knowledge, upon the peoples of Mesoamerica. In Yucatán the Maya called him Kukulcan; in the Pacific regions of Guatemala and El Salvador he was called Xiuhtecuhtli; the names all meant the same: Feathered or Winged Serpent.

The architecture, inscriptions, iconography, and monuments of the lost cities of the Maya have enabled scholars to trace and reconstruct not only their and their rulers' histories, but also their changing religious concepts. At first temples were lofted atop step pyramids to worship the Serpent God, and the skies were observed to watch for the key celestial cycles. But there came a time when the god—or all the celestial gods—had left. Seen no more, they were presumed to have been swallowed by the ruler of the night, the jaguar; and the image of the great god was henceforth covered by the jaguar's mask (Fig. 37) through which the serpents, his erstwhile symbol, still emerge.

Figure 37

But had not Quetzalcoatl promised to return?

Fervently the skywatchers of the jungles consulted ancient almanacs. Priests advanced the notion that the vanished deities would return if offered the throbbing hearts of human victims.

But at some crucial calendrical date in the ninth century A.D., a prophesied event failed to occur. All the cycles came together, and added up to naught. And so were the ceremonial centers and the cities dedicated to the gods abandoned, and the jungle cast its green mantle over the domain of the Serpent Gods.

5

STRANGERS FROM
ACROSS THE SEAS

When the Toltecs under their leader Topiltzin-Quetzalcoatl left
Tollan in A.D. 987, disgusted by the religious abominations and
seeking a place where they could worship as in the olden days,
they went to Yucatán. Surely they could have found a new
home closer by, a less arduous journey, a passage through less
hostile tribes. Yet they chose to trek almost a thousand miles, to
a land different in all respects—flat, riverless, tropical—from
their own. They did not stop until they had reached Chichén
Itzá. Why? What was the imperative in reaching the sacred city
that the Maya had already abandoned? We can only search the
ruins for an answer.

Easily reached from Mérida, Yucatán's administrative capital, Chichén Itzá has been compared to Pompeii in Italy, where
after removal of the volcanic ash under which it had been buried, a Roman city with its streets and houses and murals, graffiti
and all, has been brought to light. Here it was the jungle canopy
that had to be removed, rewarding the visitor with a double
treat: a visit to an "Old Empire" Maya city, and to a mirror-
image of Tollan as its emigrants had last seen it; for when the
Toltecs arrived, they rebuilt and built over Chichén Itźa in the
image of their erstwhile capital.

Archaeologists believe that the site was an important settlement even in the first millennium B.C. The Chronicles of *Chilam
Balam* attest that by A.D. 450 it was the principal sacred city of
Yucatán. It was then called *Chichén,* "The Well's Mouth," for
its most sacred features was a *cenote* or sacred well to which
pilgrims came from near and far. Most of the visible remains
from that era of Maya dominion are located in the southern or
"Old Chichén" part of the site. It is there that the edifices described and drawn by Stephens and Catherwood are mostly located, bearing such romantic names as *Akab-Dzib* ("Place of

Figure 38

Occult Writing"), the Nunnery, Temple of the Thresholds, and so on.

Last to occupy (or rather, reoccupy) Chichén Itzá before the arrival of the Toltecs were the Itzas, a tribe that some believe were kinsmen of the Toltecs and others see as migrants from the south. It is they who gave the place its current name, meaning "The Well Mouth of the Itzas." They built their own ceremonial center north of the Maya ruins; the site's most renowned edifices, the great central pyramid ("El Castillo") and the observatory (the Caracol) were built by them—only to be taken over and built over by the Toltecs when they re-created Tollan at Chichén Itzá.

A chance discovery of an entranceway enables today's visitor to enter the space between the Itzá pyramid and the Toltec pyramid that envelops it, and to climb up the earlier stairway to the Itzá sanctum, where the Toltecs had installed an image of Chacmool and of a jaguar. From the outside one can only see the Toltec structure—a pyramid that rises in nine stages (Fig. 38) to a height of some 185 feet. Dedicated to the God of the Plumed Serpent, Quetzalcoatl-Kukulcan, it honors him not only with plumed-serpent decorations but also by incorporating in the structure various calendrical aspects, such as the construction on

Figure 39

each of the four faces of the pyramid of a stairway with 91 steps, which with the topmost "step" or platform add up to the days of the solar year ($91 \times 4 + 1 = 365$). A structure called the Temple of Warriors literally duplicates the pyramid of the *Atlantes* in Tula by its location, orientation, stairway, flanking plumed serpents of stone, decorations, and sculptures.

As at Tula (Tollan), facing this pyramid-temple across the great plaza is the main ball court. It is an immense rectangular arena, 545 feet long—the largest in Mesoamerica. High walls rise along the two long sides; at the center of each, thirty-five feet above the ground, there protrudes a stone ring decorated with carvings of entwined serpents. To win the game the ball players had to throw a ball of solid rubber through the rings. There were seven players in each team; the team that lost paid a heavy price: its leader was decapitated. Stone panels decorated in bas-relief were installed along the long walls, depicting scenes from the game. The central panel on the eastern wall (Fig. 39) still shows the leader of the winning team (on the left) holding the decapitated head of the leader of the losing team.

The severe end suggests that there was more than play and entertainment to this ball game. At Chichén Itzá, as at Tula, there were several ball courts, perhaps for training or lesser matches. The main ball court was unique in its size and splendor, and the importance of what took place in it was underscored by the fact that it was provided with three temples that were richly decorated with scenes of warriors, mythological encounters, the Tree of Life, and a winged and bearded deity with two horns (Fig. 40).

Figure 40

All this, and the diversity and regalia of the ball players, suggest to us an intertribal, if not international, aspect of an event of great political–religious significance. The number of players (seven), the decapitation of the losers' leader, and the use of a rubber ball seem to mimic a mythological tale in the *Popol Vuh* of a combat between the gods conducted as a contest with a rubber ball. It pitched the gods Seven-Macaw and his two sons against various Sky Gods, including the Sun, Moon, and Venus. The defeated son Seven-Huanaphu was executed: "His head was cut off from his body and rolled away, his heart was cut out from his chest." But being a god, he was resurrected and became a planet.

Such a reenactment of godly events would have made the Toltec custom akin to religious plays in the ancient Near East. In Egypt, the dismemberment and resurrection of Osiris was reenacted annually in a mystery play in which actors, including the pharaoh, played the roles of various gods; and in Assyria, a complex play, also performed annually, reenacted a battle between two gods in which the loser was executed, only to be pardoned and resurrected by the God of Heaven. In Babylon, *Enuma elish,* the epic describing the creation of the solar system, was read annually as part of the New Year celebrations; it depicted the celestial collision that led to the creation of Earth (the Seventh Planet) as the cleaving and decapitating of the monstrous Tiamat by the supreme Babylonian god Marduk.

Figure 41

The Maya myth and its reenactment, in echoing Near Eastern "myths" and their reenactments, appear to have retained
the celestial elements of the tale and the symbolism of the
number seven as it relates to the planet Earth. It is significant
that in the Mayan–Toltec depictions along the walls of the ball
court, some players carry as their emblem the Sun Disk, while
others carry that of a seven-pointed star (Fig. 41). That this was
a celestial symbol and not just a chance emblem is confirmed, in
our opinion, by the fact that elsewhere in Chichén Itzá a four-
pointed star was repeatedly depicted in combination with the
"eight" symbol for the planet Venus (Fig. 42a) and that at other
sites in northwestern Yucatán temple walls were decorated with
symbols of six-pointed stars (Fig. 42b).

The depiction of planets as pointed stars is so common that
we tend to forget how this custom had arisen: As so much else,
it began in Sumer. Based on what they had learned from the
Nefilim, the Sumerians counted the planets not as we do, from
the Sun outward, but from the outside in. Thus, Pluto was the
first planet, Neptune the second, Uranus the third, Saturn the
fourth, Jupiter the fifth. Mars accordingly was the sixth, Earth
the seventh, and Venus the eighth. The usual explanation by
scholars why the Maya/Toltecs considered Venus the eighth is
that it takes eight Earth years ($8 \times 365 = 2{,}920$ days) to repeat
a synodic alignment with Venus after five orbits of Venus ($5 \times 584 = 2{,}920$ days). But if so, Venus should have been "Five"
and Earth "Eight."

We find the Sumerian method much more elegant and accurate, and suggest that the Maya/Toltec depictions followed the Near Eastern iconography; for, as one can see, the symbols found at Chichén Itzá and elsewhere in Yucatán are almost identical to those by which the various planets had been depicted in Mesopotamia (Fig. 42c).

Indeed, the employment of pointed-star symbols in the Near Eastern manner becomes more prevalent the more one moves toward the northwestern corner of Yucatán and its coast. A most remarkable sculpture has been found there, at a site called Tzekelna; it is now on exhibit at the Mérida museum. Carved out of a large stone block to which the statue's back is still attached, it depicts a man of strong facial features, possibly wearing a helmet. His body is covered by a tight-fitting suit made of scales or ribs. Under his bent arm he holds an object the museum identifies as "the geometric form of a five-pointed star" (Fig. 43). An enigmatic circular device is held by belts to his belly; scholars believe that it somehow identified its bearers as Water Gods.

Large sculptures of deities forming part of massive stone blocks were discovered at a nearby site called Oxkintok; they are presumed by archaeologists to have served as structural supporting columns in temples. One of them (Fig. 44) looks like a female counterpart of the above-described male one. Her ribbed and scalelike garb appears on several statues and statuettes from Jaina, an island that lies offshore from this northwestern part of Yucatán on which there had stood a most

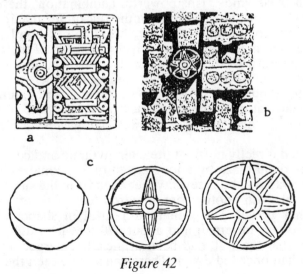

Figure 42

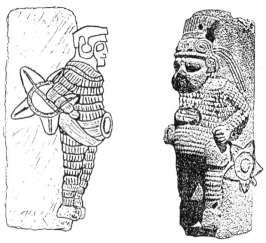

Figure 43   *Figure 44*

unusual temple. The island had served as a hallowed necropolis because according to legends it was the final resting place of Itzamna, the god of the Itzas—a great olden god who had waded there ashore from the sea, and whose name meant "He Whose Home Is Water."

Texts, legends, and religious beliefs have thus combined to point to the gulf shore of Yucatán as the place where a divine or deified being had come ashore, to begin settlement and civilization in these lands. This powerful combination, these collective recollections, must have been the reason for the Toltec trek to this corner of Yucatán, and specifically to Chichén Itzá, when they migrated in search of the revival and purity of their original beliefs; a return to the spot where it all began, and where the Returning God would land again, coming from across the sea.

The focal point of the worship of Itzamna and Quetzalcoatl, and perhaps also of the memories of Votan, was the Sacred Cenote of Chichén Itzá—a huge well that gave Chichén Itzá its name.

Situated directly north of the main pyramid and connected to the ceremonial plaza by a long paved processional avenue, the well is nowadays about seventy feet deep from the surface to the water level, with another one hundred feet or so of water and silt farther down. The well mouth, oval in shape, measures about 250 feet in length and about 170 feet in width. There is evidence that the well had been artificially enlarged and that a stairway had once led down. There can still be seen the remains of a platform and a shrine at the well mouth; there, Bishop Landa wrote, rites were held for the god of water and rains, maidens were thrown down in sacrifice, and worshipers who had gathered from all over threw in precious offerings, preferably made of gold.

In 1885 Edward H. Thompson, who had made a reputation for himself as the author of a treatise titled *Atlantis Not a Myth*, obtained an assignment as an American consul in **Mexico**. Before long he purchased for seventy-five dollars one **hundred** square miles of jungle, which included the ruins of **Chichén Itzá**. Making the ruins his home, he organized for the Peabody Museum of Harvard University systematic dives into the well to retrieve its sacred offerings.

Only some forty human skeletons were found; but the divers brought up a rich array of artful objects by the thousands. More than 3,400 were made of jade, a semiprecious stone that was the highest prized by the Maya and the Aztecs. The objects included beads, nose bars, ear plugs, buttons, rings, pendants, globes, disks, effigies, figurines. More than 500 objects bore carvings depicting animals and people. Among the latter, some were clearly bearded (Fig. 45a, b), resembling depictions on the temple walls of the ball court (Fig. 45c).

Even more significant were the metal objects that the divers brought up. Hundreds were made of gold, some of silver or copper—significant finds in a peninsula devoid of metals. Some

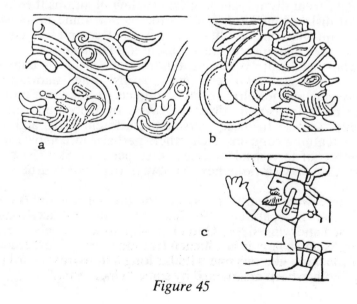

Figure 45

Figure 46

of the objects were made of gilded copper or copper alloys, including bronze, revealing a metallurgical sophistication unknown in the Maya lands and attesting that the objects had been brought from distant lands. Most puzzling of all was the discovery of disks of pure tin, a metal that is not found in its native state and that can be obtained only by a complex refining of ores—ores that are altogether absent in Mesoamerica.

The metal objects, exquisitely crafted, included numerous bells as well as ritual objects (cups, basins), rings, tiaras, masks; ornaments and jewelry; scepters; objects of unknown purpose; and, most important, disks engraved or embossed with encounter scenes. In these, persons in different garbs and of diverse features confront each other, perhaps in combat, in the presence of terrestrial or celestial serpents or Sky Gods. The dominant or victorious hero is always depicted bearded (Fig. 46a, b).

These were clearly not gods, for the serpent or Sky gods were shown separately. The likes of them, distinct from the bearded and winged Sky God (Fig. 40), appear in reliefs carved on walls and columns in Chichén Itzá together with other heroes and warriors, like this one with his long and narrow beard (Fig. 47) who has been nicknamed by some "Uncle Sam."

Figure 47

The identity of these bearded people is a puzzle; what is certain is that they were not native Indians, who grow no facial hair and have no beards. Who, then, were these foreigners? Their "Semitic" or rather Eastern Mediterranean features (even more prominent in clay objects bearing facial images) have led various researchers to identify them as Phoenicians or "seafaring Jews," perhaps blown off course and carried by the Atlantic's currents to the shores of Yucatán when King Solomon and the Phoenician King Hiram joined forces to send maritime expeditions around Africa in search of gold (circa 1000 B.C.); or a few centuries later, when the Phoenicians were driven away from their port cities in the eastern Mediterranean, established Carthage, and sailed to western Africa.

No matter who the seafarers might have been and the proposed crossing time, established academic researchers dismiss out of hand any notion of deliberate crossings. They either explain the obvious beards as false beards, artificially attached by the Indians to their chins, or as belonging to the chance survivors of shipwrecks. Clearly, the first argument (seriously made

Figure 48

by renowned scholars) only begs the question: if the Indians emulated some other bearded people, who were those other people?

Nor does the explanation of a few shipwrecked survivors seem valid. The native traditions, as in the legend of Votan, speak of repeated voyages, of exploration followed by settlement (the establishment of cities). The archaeological evidence belies the notion of a few chance survivors cast on a single shore. The Bearded Ones, in poses of a variety of activities and circumstances, have been depicted at sites all along the Mexican gulf coast, at inland locations, and as far south as the Pacific coast. Not stylized, not mythified, but as portraits of actual individuals.

Some of the most striking examples of such depictions have been found in Veracruz (Fig. 48a, b). The people they immortalize are clearly identical to West Semitic dignitaries taken prisoner by Egyptian pharaohs during their Asiatic campaigns, as depicted by the victors in their commemorative inscriptions upon temple walls (Fig. 49).

Why, and when, did such Mediterranean seafarers come to Mesoamerica? The archaeological clues are baffling, for they lead to an even greater enigma: the Olmecs, and their apparent black African origins; for, as many depictions—as this one, from Alvarado, Veracruz (Fig. 50)—show, the Bearded Ones

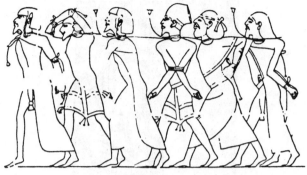

Figure 49

and the Olmecs had met, face to face, in the same domains and at the same time.

Of all the lost civilizations of Mesoamarica, that of the Olmecs is the oldest and the most mystifying. It was by all counts the Mother Civilization, copied and adapted by all the others. It dawned along the Mexican gulf coast at the beginning of the second millennium B.C. It was in full bloom, at some forty sites, by 1200 B.C. (or, some hold, by 1500 B.C.). Spreading in all directions, but mainly southward, it made its mark across Mesoamerica by 800 B.C.

The first Mesoamerican glyphic writing appears in the Olmec realm; so does the Mesoamerican system of numeration, of dots and bars. The first Long Count calendar inscriptions, with the enigmatic starting date in 3113 B.C.; the first works of magnificent and monumental sculpted art; the first use of jade; the first depictions of hand-held weapons or tools; the first ceremonial centers; the first celestial orientations—all were achievements of the Olmecs. No wonder that with so many "firsts," some (as J. Soustelle, *The Olmecs*) have compared the Olmec civilization of Mesoamerica to that of the Sumerians in Mesopotamia, which accounted for all the "firsts" in the ancient Near East. And, like the Sumerian civilization, the Olmecs too appeared suddenly, without a precedent or a prior period of gradual advancement. In their texts, the Sumerians described their civilization as a gift from the gods, the visitors to Earth who could roam the skies and were therefore often depicted as winged beings (Fig. 51a). The Olmecs expressed their "myths" in sculptured art, as on this stela from Izapa (Fig. 51b) of one winged god beheading another. The tale-in-stone is remarkably similar to a Sumerian depiction (Fig. 51c).

Figure 50

Who were the people who had achieved these feats? Nick-named *Olmeca* ("Rubber People") because their gulf-coast area was known for its rubber trees, they were in reality an enigma —strangers in a strange land, strangers from across the seas, people who belonged not just to another land but to another continent. In an area of marshy coasts where stone is rare, they created and left behind stone monuments that amaze to this very day; of these, the most baffling are the ones that portray the Olmecs themselves.

Unique in all respects are giant stone heads sculpted with incredible skill and unknown tools to portray Olmec leaders. The first to see such a gigantic head was J. M. Melgar y Serrano at Tres Zapotes in the state of Veracruz. He described it in the *Bulletin of the Mexican Geographical and Statistical Society* (in 1869) as "a work of art... a magnificent sculpture that most amazingly represents an Ethiopian." Accompanying drawings faithfully reproduced the head's negroid features (Fig. 52).

Figure 51

It was not until 1925 that the existence of such colossal stone heads was confirmed by Western scholars, when an archaeological team from Tulane University headed by Frans Blom found "the upper part of a colossal head which has sunk deep into the ground" at La Venta, a site near the gulf coast in the state of Tabasco. When the head was fully unearthed (Fig. 53) it measured about eight feet in height, twenty-one in circumference, and weighed about twenty-four tons. It depicts without question a negroid African wearing a distinct helmet. In time, additional such heads, each portraying a distinctly different individual with

Figure 52

Figure 53

his own different helmet but with the same racial features, were found at La Venta.

Five similar colossal heads were found in the 1940s at San Lorenzo, an Olmec site some sixty miles southwest of La Venta, by archaeological expeditions headed by Matthew Stirling and Philip Drucker. Yale University teams that followed, led by Michael D. Coe, discovered more heads. They took radiocarbon readings that gave dates circa 1200 B.C. This means that organic matter (mostly charcoal) found at the site is that old; but the site itself and its monuments could well be older. Indeed, the Mexican archaeologist Ignacio Bernal, who found another head at Tres Zapotes, dates these colossal sculptures to 1500 B.C.

By now sixteen such colossal heads have been found. They range in height from about five to ten feet and weigh as much as twenty-five tons. Whoever sculpted them was about to sculpt more, for a great deal of "raw material"—large stones that had been quarried and rounded to a ball-like shape—has been found in addition to the finished heads. The basalt stones, finished and unfinished, had been hauled from their source to the stoneless sites over distances of sixty miles or more, through jungle and swamps. How such colossal stone blocks were quarried, transported, and finally sculpted and erected at their destination remains a mystery. Clearly, however, the Olmecs deemed it very important to commemorate their leaders in this manner. That these were individuals, all of the same African negroid stock but with their own personalities and diverse headgear, can be readily seen from a portrait gallery of some of these heads (Fig. 54).

Figure 54

Encounter scenes carved on stone stelae (Fig. 55a) and other monuments (Fig. 55b) clearly depict the Olmecs as tall, heavily built with muscular bodies—"giants" in stature, no doubt, in the eyes of the indigenous Indian population. But lest it be assumed that we are dealing here with just a few leaders and not an actual population of negroid African stock—men, women, and children—the Olmecs left behind, scattered throughout a vast area of Mesoamerica that connected the gulf and Pacific coasts, hundreds if not thousands of depictions of themselves. In sculptures, stone carvings, bas-reliefs, statuettes—we always see the same black African faces, as on jades from the sacred cenote of Chichén Itzá or in golden effigies found there; on

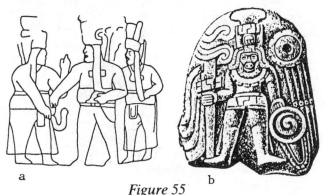

a   b

Figure 55

Figure 56

numerous terra-cottas found all the way from Jaina (as a loving couple) to the central and northern parts of Mexico, or even as ball players (El Tajin reliefs); Fig. 56 shows a few. Some terra-cottas (Fig. 57a) and even more so stone sculptures of the Olmecs (Fig. 57b) portray them as holding babies—an act that must have held special significance for them.

The sites at which the colossal heads and other Olmec depictions have been found are no less intriguing; their size, magnitude, and structures reveal the work of organized settlers, not just of a few shipwrecked visitors. La Venta was actually a small island in the swampy coastal area that has been artificially shaped, landfilled and built up according to a preconceived plan. Major edifices, including an unusual conical "pyramid," elongated and circular mounds, structures, paved courts, altars, stelae, and other man-made features have been laid out with great geometric precision along a north–south axis extending for about three miles. In a place devoid of stones, an amazing variety of stones—each chosen for it special quality—was used in the structures, monuments, and stelae, although all of them required hauling over great distances. The conical pyramid

Figure 57

alone necessitated the bringing and piling up of a million cubic feet of soil. It all called for a tremendous physical effort. It also required a high level of architectural and stoneworking expertise for which there had been no precedent in Mesoamerica; the art was obviously acquired elsewhere.

The extraordinary finds at La Venta included a rectangular enclosure that was surrounded or fenced off by columns of basalt stone (the same material of which the colossal heads were sculpted). The enclosure protected a stone sarcophagus and a rectangular burial chamber that was also roofed and walled with basalt columns. Inside, several skeletons lay on a low platform. All in all, this unique find, with its stone sarcophagus, appears to have been the model for the equally unusual crypt of Pacal in Palenque. At any rate, the insistence on the employment of great blocks of stone, even if it had to be brought from afar, for monuments, commemorative sculptures, and burials must serve as a clue to the enigmatic origin of the Olmecs.

No less puzzling was the discovery at La Venta of hundreds of artistically carved objects of the rare jade, including unusual axes made of this semiprecious stone that is not locally available. Then, to add to the mystery, they were all deliberately buried in long, deep trenches. The trenches, in turn, were filled with layers of clay, each layer of a different kind and color of clay—thousands of tons of soil brought over from diverse distant places. Incredibly, the trenches were paved at the very bottom with thousands of tiles of serpentine, another green-blue semiprecious stone. It has been generally assumed that the trenches were dug to bury in them the precious jade objects; but the floors of serpentine could also suggest that the trenches were constructed earlier, for another purpose altogether; but were used to bury highly valued objects, such as rare axes, once the need for them (and for the trenches) ceased. There is indeed no doubt that the Olmec sites were abandoned by them around the beginning of the Christian era and that the Olmecs even attempted to bury some of the colossal heads. Whoever gained access to their sites afterward, did so with a vengeance: some of the heads were clearly toppled off their bases and rolled downhill into the swamps; others bear marks of attempted mutilation.

As another enigma from La Venta, let us note the discovery in the trenches of concave mirrors of crystallized iron ores (magnetite and hematite), shaped and polished to perfection. After study and experiments scholars at the Smithsonian Institution in Washington, D.C., have concluded that the mirrors could be used to focus the sun's rays, to light fires or for "ritual purposes" (the scholars' way of saying they do not know what an object was for).

The final enigma at La Venta is the site itself, for it is precisely oriented on a north–south axis that is tilted 8 degrees west of true north. Various studies have shown that this was an intentional orientation, intended to permit astonomical sightings, perhaps from atop the conical "pyramid" whose prominent ridges may have served as directional indicators. A special study by M. Popenoe-Hatch. (*Papers on Olmec and Maya Archaeology No. 13, University of California*) concluded that "the pattern of observation being made at La Venta at 1000 B.C. indicates that it must date back to a body of knowledge learned a millennium earlier. . . . The La Venta site and its art of 1000 B.C. seem to reflect a tradition based in large part on the meridian transits of stars occuring on the solstices and equinoxes around 2000 B.C."

A beginning at 2000 B.C. would make La Venta the earliest "sacred center" in Mesoamerica, preceding Teotihuacan except for the legendary time when gods alone were there. It still may not be the true time of the Olmecs' arrival from across the seas, for their Long Count begins at 3113 B.C.; but it does clearly indicate how far ahead of the renowned civilizations of the Maya and the Aztecs the Olmecs had been.

At Tres Zapotes, whose early phase is attributed by archaeologists to the three centuries 1500–1200 B.C., stone constructions (although stone is rare there), terraces, stairways, and mounds that might have been pyramids are scattered about the site. At least another eight sites have been located within a radius of fifteen miles of Tres Zapotes, indicating it was a great center surrounded by satellites. Besides the heads and other sculpted monuments, a number of stelae were unearthed there; one ("Stela C") bears the Long Count date 7.16.6.16.18, which is equivalent to 31 B.C., attesting to the Olmec presence at the site at such time.

At San Lorenzo the Olmec remains consisted of structures, mounds, and embankments, interspersed with artificial ponds. The central part of the site was built upon a man-made platform of about one square mile that was raised some 185 feet above the surrounding terrain—an earthworks project that dwarfs many modern enterprises. The archaeologists discovered that the ponds were interconnected by a system of subterranean conduits "whose meanings or function is not yet understood."

The description of Olmec sites can go on and on—by now, some forty have been uncovered. Everywhere, besides monu-

Figure 58

mental art and edifices of stone, there are mounds by the dozens and other evidence of deliberate, planned earthworks.

The stoneworks, earthworks, trenches, ponds, conduits, mirrors must, however, have some meaningful purpose even if modern scholars cannot fathom it. So, clearly, must the very presence of the Olmecs in Mesoamerica—unless one subscribes to the shipwrecked-survivors theory, which we do not. Aztec historians described the people they nicknamed Olmeca as remnants of an ancient non-Nahuatl-speaking *people*—not a few individuals—who had created the oldest civilization in Mexico. The archaeological evidence supports that and shows that from a base or "metropolitan area" abutting the Gulf of Mexico, where La Venta, Tres Zapotes, and San Lorenzo formed the pivotal triangle, the area of Olmec settlement and influence cut southward toward the Pacific coast of Mexico and Guatemala.

Experts in earthworks, masters of stoneworking, diggers of trenches, channelers of water, users of mirrors—what, thus endowed, were the Olmecs doing in Mesoamerica? Stelae show them emerging from "altars" that represent entrances into the depths of the earth (Fig. 58), or inside caves holding a puzzling array of tools, as on this stela from La Venta (Fig. 59) in which it is possible to discern the enigmatic mirrors being attached to the toolholder's helmets.

All in all, the capabilities, the scenes, the tools appear to us to lead to one conclusion: the Olmecs were miners, come to the New World to extract some precious metals—probably gold, perhaps other rare minerals too.

The legends of Votan, which speak of tunneling through mountains, support this conclusion. So does the fact that among the Olden Gods whose worship was adopted from the Olmecs by the Nahautl people were the god *Tepeyolloti,* meaning "Heart of the Mountain." He was a bearded God of Caves; his temple had to be of stone, preferably built inside a mountain. His glyph-symbol was a pierced mountain; he was depicted (Fig. 60a) holding as his tool a flamethrower—just as we had seen at Tula!

Figure 59

a

b

Figure 60

Figure 61

Our suggestion that the flamethrower seen there (both held by the Atlantes and depicted on a column) was probably used to cut through stone, not just for carving on stone, is manifestly supported by a stone relief known as Daizu No. 40, after the site in Mexico's Oaxaca Valley where it was discovered. It clearly depicts a person inside a confined area, using the flamethrower against the wall in front of him (Fig. 60b). The "diamond" symbol on the wall probably signifies a mineral, but its meaning has not yet been deciphered.

As so many depictions attest, the puzzle of the African "Olmecs" is entwined with the enigma of the Bearded Ones from the eastern Mediteranean. They were depicted on monuments throughout the Olmec sites, in individual portraits or in encounter scenes. Significantly, some encounters are shown to have taken place inside caverns; one, from Tres Zapotes (Fig. 61), even includes an attendant carrying a lighting device (at a time when, supposedly, only torches were used). A no less amazing stela from Chalcatzingo (Fig. 62) depicts a "Caucasian" female operating what looks like technically sophisticated equipment; the base of the stela bears the telltale "diamond" sign. It all spells a connection with minerals.

Did the Mediterranean Bearded Ones come to Mesoamerica at the same time as the African Olmecs? Were they allies, helping each other—or competitors for the same precious minerals or metals? No one can say with any certainty; but it is our own belief that the African Olmecs were there first, and that the

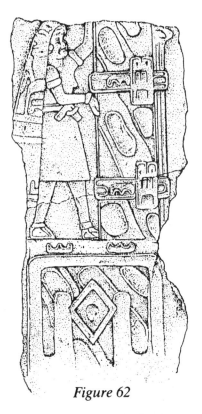

Figure 62

roots of their arrival must be sought in that mysterious beginning date of the Long Count—3113 B.C.

No matter when and why the relationship began, it seems to
have ended in a convulsion.

Scholars have wondered why there is, at many Olmec sites,
evidence of deliberate destruction—the defacing of monuments
(including colossal heads), the smashing of artifacts, the top-
pling of monuments—all with a vehemence and a vengeance.
The destruction does not appear to have taken place all at once;
Olmec sites seem to have been abandoned gradually, first in the
older "metropolitan center" near the Gulf, circa 300 B.C., then
later on at more southern sites. We have seen the evidence of
the date equivalent to 31 B.C. at Tres Zapotes; it suggests that
the process of the abandonment of Olmec centers, followed by
revengeful destruction, may have lasted several centuries, as the
Olmecs gave up sites and retreated southward.

The depictions from that turbulent period and from that southern zone of Olmec domains show them more and more as warriors, wearing frightening masks of eagles or jaguars. One such rock carving from the southern areas shows three Olmecs warriors (two with eagle masks) holding spears. The scene includes a naked captive who is bearded. What is not clear is whether the warriors are threatening the captive, or are depicted in the act of saving him. This leaves unclear the intriguing question, were the negroid Olmecs and the Bearded Ones from the eastern Mediterranean on the same side when the troubled times shattered Mesoamerica's first civilization?

They do seem to have shared, though, the same fate.

Figure 63

At a most interesting site near the Pacific coast called Monte Alban—erected on a vast array of man-made platforms and with unusual structures built for astronomical purposes—dozens of stone slabs, erected in a commemorative wall, bear the carved images of the African-negroid men in contorted positions (Fig. 63). For a long time they were nicknamed *Danzantes,* "Dancers"; but scholars now agree that they show the naked bodies of mutilated Olmecs—presumably killed in a violent uprising by the local Indians. Among the depicted negroid bodies there is one of a bearded man with a Semitic nose (Fig. 64) who obviously shared the fate of the Olmecs.

Monte Alban is believed to have been a settlement since 1500 B.C. and a major center since 500 B.C. Thus, within a few

Figure 64

centuries of its grandeur, its builders ended up as mutilated bodies commemorated on stone—victims of those whom they had tutored.

And thus did the millennia, the golden age of the Strangers From Across the Seas, become just a legend.

6

REALM OF THE
GOLDEN WAND

The story of civilization in the lands of the Andes is shrouded in mystery, deepened by the absence of written records or stelae bearing glyphic tales; but myth and legend fill the canvas with tales of gods and giants, and kings who had descended of them.

The coastal peoples could recall traditions of gods who had guided their forebears to the promised lands and of giants who despoiled their crops and raped their women. The highland peoples, of whom the Incas were the dominant at the time of the Spanish conquest, acknowledged divine guidance in all manner of activity and craft, the raising of crops, the building of cities. They recounted Tales of Beginning—tales of creation, of days of upheaval, of an engulfing deluge. And they attributed the beginning of their kingship and the establishment of their capital to the magic of a golden wand.

Spanish chroniclers, as well as native ones who had learned Spanish, had established that the father of the two Inca kings at the time of the conquest, Huayna Capac, was the twelfth *Inca* (a title meaning *lord, sovereign*) of a dynasty that began in Cuzco, the capital, circa A.D. 1020. It was just a couple of centuries before the conquest that the Incas had swooped down from their highland strongholds to the coastal zones, where other kingdoms had existed from much earlier times. In extending their dominions northward to today's Ecuador and southward to today's Chile with the aid of the renowned Highway of the Sun, the Incas essentially superimposed their rule and administration over cultures and organized societies that had thrived in those domains for millennia. The last one to fall under Inca domination was a veritable empire of the Chimu people; their capital, Chan-Chan, was a metropolis whose sacred precincts, step-pyramids and dwelling compounds spread over eight square miles.

Located near the present-day city of Trujillo, where the river

PERU AND ITS NEIGHBORS

Moche flows into the Pacific Ocean, the ancient capital reminded explorers of Egypt and Mesopotamia. The nineteenth-
century explorer E. G. Squier (*Peru Illustrated: Incidents of
Travel and Explorations in the Land of the Incas*) saw vast remains that astounded him even in their ruined and unexcavated
condition. He saw "long lines of massive walls, gigantic cham-
bered pyramids or *huacas,* remains of palaces, dwellings, aqueducts, reservoirs, granaries ... and tombs, extending for many
miles in every direction." Indeed, aerial views of the immense

site, spread out for miles on the flat coastland, bring to mind an aerial view of twentieth-century Los Angeles.

The coastal areas that lie between the western range of the Andes and the Pacific Ocean are climatically rainless areas. Habitation and civilization was able to flourish there because the waters flowing off the high mountains into the ocean do so in the form of rivers large and small that transect the coastal plains every fifty to one hundred miles or so. These rivers create fertile and verdant areas that separate one desertlike stretch from the other. Settlements therefore arose on the banks and at the mouths of these rivers; and the archaeological evidence shows that the Chimus augmented these water sources with supplies brought from the mountains via aqueducts. They also connected the successive fertile and settled areas by a road that on the average was fifteen feet wide—the precursor of the famed Highway of the Sun of the Incas.

At the edge of the built-up area, where the verdant valley ends and the arid desert begins, great pyramids rise from the desert floor, facing each other across the Moche river. They were built of sun-dried mud bricks, reminding explorers such as V. W. von Hagen (*Highway of the Sun* and other books) of the high-rise temple towers (ziggurats) of Mesopotamia, which were also built of mud bricks and, like the ones on the banks of the Moche river, of a slightly convex shape.

The four centuries of Chimu flourishing, from about A.D. 1000 to A.D. 1400, was also a time when goldsmithing was mastered to an extent never attained by the subsequent Incas. Spanish conquistadores described the golden riches of what were in fact Chimu centers (even under Inca rule) in superlatives; the golden enclosure of a town called Tumbes, where plants and animals were mimicked in gold, appears to have been the model after which the Incas fashioned the golden enclosure of the principal shrine in Cuzco. The environs of another city, Tucume, have yielded the greater part of the gold objects that have been found in Peru in the centuries following the conquest (objects buried in tombs with the dead). Indeed, the amount of gold the Chimus possessed astounded the Incas when they overran the coastlands. Those legendary quantities, and the actual finds thereafter, still puzzle scholars; for the gold sources of Peru are not in the arid coastlands, but in the highlands.

The Chimu culture-state was in turn the successor to previous cultures or organized societies. As in the case of Chimu, no one knows what those peoples called themselves; the names that are nowadays applied to them are actually the names of archaeological sites or rivers at which these societies and their recognizable cultures were centered. On the north-central coastal area, the one called Mochica rolls back the fog of history to about 400 B.C. They are known for their artful pottery and graceful textiles; but how and when these arts were acquired remains a mystery. The decorations on their ceramic vessels are replete with illustrations of winged gods and menacing giants, and suggest a religion with a pantheon headed by the Moon God whose symbol was the Crescent and name was *Si* or *Si-An*.

The Mochica artifacts clearly show that, centuries before the Chimu, they had mastered the art of casting gold, of building with mud bricks, and of laying out temple compounds replete with ziggurats. At a site called Pacatnamu, a buried sacred city with no less than thirty-one pyramids was excavated in the 1930s by a German archaeological team (H. Ubbelohde-Doering, *Auf den Koenigsstrassen der Inka*). They determined that the many smaller pyramids were about a thousand years older than the several much larger pyramids that had sides of two hundred feet and were some forty feet high.

The southern border of the Chimu empire was the river Rímac, from which name the Spaniards corrupted *Lima* as the name of their capital. Beyond this boundary the coastal zones were inhabited, in pre-Inca times, by Chincha tribesmen; the highlands were occupied by Aymara-speaking peoples. It is now known that the Incas had obtained their notions of a pantheon from the former, and the tales of Creation and Beginning from the latter.

The Rímac region was a focal point in antiquity as it is nowadays. It was there, just south of Lima, that the largest temple to a Peruvian deity had stood. Its ruins from the time it was rebuilt and enlarged by the Incas can still be seen. It was dedicated to *Pacha-Camac*, meaning "Creator of the World," a god who headed a pantheon that included the divine couples Vis and Mama-Pacha ("Lord Earth" and "Lady Earth") and *Ni* and *Mama-Cocha* ("Lord Water" and "Lady Water"), the Moon God *Si*, the Sun God *Illa-Ra*, and the Hero God *Kon* or *Con* who was also known as *Ira-Ya*—names that evoke a host of Near Eastern divine epithets.

The temple of Pachacamac was a "Mecca" for the ancient people of the southern coasts. Pilgrims came to it from far and near. The act of pilgrimage was so esteemed that even when tribes were at war, enemy pilgrims were granted safe passage. The pilgrims came bearing offerings of gold, for that was the metal deemed belonging to the gods. Only select priests could enter the Holy of Holies where, on certain holidays, the god's image pronounced oracles that the priests then related to the people. But the whole temple precinct was so revered that pilgrims had to take off their sandals to enter it—just as Moses was commanded to do in the Sinai and as Moslems still do as they enter a mosque.

The gold that had accumulated at the temple was too fabulous to escape the attention of the conquering Spaniards. Francisco Pizarro sent his brother Hernandez to loot it. He found some gold, silver, and precious stones, but not the main riches, for the priests had hidden the treasures. No amount of threat or torture could make the priests reveal the hiding place (which is still rumored to be somewhere between Lima and Lurin). Hernandez then smashed the god's golden statue for its metal and pulled out of the walls the silver nails that had held the gold and silver plates that had lined the temple's walls. The nails alone weighed 32,000 ounces!

Local legends attribute the establishment of this temple to the "giants." What is known for certain is that the Incas, adopting the veneration of Pachacamac from the tribes they had overrun, enlarged and embellished the temple. Standing on a mountainside, the Pacific Ocean breaking almost at its feet, the temple rose atop four platforms that supported a terrace five hundred feet above ground level; the four platforms were created by the erection of retaining walls built of immense stone blocks. The topmost terrace extended over several acres. The final structures of the temple complex, aided by sunken plazas, afforded an unimpeded view from the main sanctuary toward the vast ocean.

Not only the living came to pray and to worship here. The dead too were brought to the Rímac valley and the coastal plains to its south, to spend their afterlife in the shadow of the oracle gods; perhaps even for an eventual resurrection, for there was a belief that Rímac could resurrect the dead. At sites known nowadays as Lurin, Pisco, Nazca, Paracas, Ancon, Ica, archaeologists have found in "cities of the dead" innumerable graves and subterranean vaults in which the mummified bodies of noblemen and priests were buried. The mummies, in a seated position with hands and legs bent in, were tied up and fitted into sacklike bags; but within the bag, the deceased were fully clothed in their finest garments. The dry climate and the outer sack protected the superbly woven garments, shawls, turbans, and ponchos, and their incredibly bright colors. The textiles, whose exquisite weaving reminded archaeologists of Europe's finest Gobelin tapestries, were embroidered with religious and cosmological symbols.

The central figure, on the textiles as well as on ceramics, was always that of a god holding a wand in one hand and a thunder-bolt in the other and wearing a horned or rayed crown (Fig. 65); the Indians called him *Rímac,* like the river's name.

Were Rímac and Pachacamac one and the same deity, or two separate ones? Scholars disagree, for the evidence is inconclusive. They do agree that the nearby mountain ranges were dedicated exclusively to Rímac. His name meant "The Thunderer," and thus in meaning and phonetically is akin to the nickname *Raman* by which Adad was known to the Semitic peoples—an epithet stemming from the verb meaning "to thunder."

According to the chronicler Garcilaso, it was in these mountains that "an idol, in the shape of a man," had stood in a shrine dedicated to Rímac. He may have been referring to any one of several sites in the mountains flanking the Rímac valley. There, ruins of what archaeologists believe were step pyramids (artist's conception, Fig. 66) dominate the scenery to this very day, fooling the viewer to imagine he is seeing a seven-step ziggurat in ancient Mesopotamia.

Was Rímac the god sometimes called "Kon" or "Ira-Ya," the one called *Viracocha* in Inca lore? Though no one can say for certain, what is beyond doubt is that Viracocha was depicted exactly as the deity shown on the coastal pottery—holding in one hand the forked weapon and in the other the magical wand.

It was with that wand—a wand of gold—that all Andean legends of Beginnings commence; on the shores of Lake Titicaca, at a place called Tiahuanacu.

When the Spaniards came, the lands of the Andes were the lands of the Inca empire, ruled from the highland capital Cuzco.

Figure 65

Figure 66

And Cuzco, Inca tales related, was established by the Children of the Sun who had been created and instructed at Lake Titicaca by the Creator God, Viracocha.

Viracocha, according to the Andean legends, was a great God of Heaven who had come to Earth in great antiquity, choosing the Andes as his creative arena. As one Spanish chronicler, Father Cristoval de Molina, put it, "they say that the Creator was at Tiahuanaco and that there was his chief abode. Hence the superb edifices, worthy of admiration, in that place."

One of the first padres to record the native tales of their history and prehistory was Blas Valera; unfortunately, only fragments of his writings are known from mentions by others, for his original manuscript was burnt in the sack of Cadiz by the English in 1587. He recorded the Inca version that their first monarch, Manco Capac, exited from Lake Titicaca through a subterranean way. He was the son of the Sun and was given by the Sun a golden wand with which to find Cuzco. When his mother went into labor, the world was in darkness. When he was born, there was light and trumpets sounded, and the god Pachacamac declared that "the beautiful day of Manco Capac had dawned."

But Blas Valera also recored other versions that suggested that the Incas appropriated to their dynasty the person and tale of Manco Capac, and that their true ancestors were immigrants from somewhere else who had arrived in Peru by sea. According to this, the monarch called by the Incas "Manco Capac" was the son of a king called Atau who had arrived on the Peruvian coast with two hundred men and women and disembarked at Rímac. From there they went to Ica, and from there they marched to Lake Titicaca, the place from which the Sons of the Sun had governed the Earth. Manco Capac sent his followers in two directions to find those legendary Sons of the Sun. He himself wandered many days until he came to a place that had a sacred cave. The cave was artificially hewed out and was adorned with gold and silver. Manco Capac left the sacred cave and went to a window called *Capac Toco,* meaning "Royal Window." As he came out, he was dressed in golden garments he had obtained in the cave; and by putting on these royal garments he was invested with the kingship of Peru.

From these and other chronicles it is evident that various versions were memorized by the Andean peoples. They recalled a creative Beginning at Lake Titicaca, and the start of kingship at a place of a sacred cave and a royal window; and as the Incas had it, the events were concurrent and formed the basis of their dynasty. Other versions, however, separated the events and the periods.

One of the versions regarding the Beginning was that the great god, Creator of All, Viracocha, arranged for four brothers and four sisters to roam the land and bring civilization to its primitive peoples; and one of these brother-sister/husband-wife couples began kingship in Cuzco. The other version was that the Great God, at his base in Lake Titicaca, created this first royal couple as his children and gave them an object made of gold. He told them to go north and build a city where the golden object would sink into the earth; the place where the miracle had happened was Cuzco. And that is why the Inca kings—providing they had been born of a succession of brother-sister royal couples—could claim direct descent of the Sun God.

Recollections of the Deluge featured in almost all versions of Beginning. According to Father Molina (*Relacion de las fabulas y ritos de los Yngas*) it was already "in the time of Manco Capac, who was the first Ynca and from whom they began to be called Children of the Sun . . . that they had a full account of the Deluge. They say that all people and all created things perished in it, the waters having risen above all the highest mountains in the world. No living thing survived except a man and a woman who remained in a box; and when the waters subsided, the wind carried them to Huanaco, which will be over seventy leagues from Cuzco, a little more or less. The Creator of All Things commanded them to remain there as *Mitimas,* and there in Tiahuanaco the Creator began to raise up the people and nations that are in that region." The repopulation of the Earth began by the Creator first fashioning out of clay the image of one person of each nation; "then he gave life and a soul to each one, men as well as women, and directed them to their designated places on Earth." Those who failed to obey the commandments regarding worship and behavior were turned into stones.

The Creator also had with him on the island of Titicaca the Moon and the Sun, whence they had come on his orders. When all that was needed to replenish the Earth was done, the Moon and the Sun rose up to heaven.

The two divine assistants of the Creator of All are presented in another version as his two sons. "Having created the tribes and nations, and assigned dresses and languages to them," Father Molina wrote, "the Creator ordered his two sons to go in different directions and introduce civilization." The old son, Ymaymana Viracocha (meaning "in whose power all things are placed"), went to give civilization to the mountain peoples; the younger son, Topaco Viracocha ("maker of things"), was ordered to go by way of the coastal plains. When the two brothers completed their work they met at the seashore, "whence they ascended to heaven."

Garcilaso de la Vega, who was born in Cuzco to a Spanish father and an Inca mother soon after the conquest, recorded two legends. According to one the Great God came down from the heavens to Earth to instruct mankind, giving it laws and precepts. He "placed his two children at lake Titicaca," gave them a "wedge of gold," and instructed them to settle where it would sink into the ground, which was at Cuzco. The other legend related that "after the waters of the deluge had subsided, a certain man appeared in the country of Tiahuanacu, which is to the south of Cuzco. This man was so powerful that he divided the world into four parts, and gave them to four men whom he honored with the title of king." One of them, whose epithet-name was *Manco Capac* ("king and lord" in the Quechua language of the Incas), began kingship in Cuzco.

The various versions speak of two phases of creation by Viracocha. Juan de Betanzos (*Suma y Narracion de los Incas*) recorded a Quechua tale wherein the Creator god, "on the first occasion, made the heavens and the earth"; he also created people—Mankind. But "this people did some sort of wrong to Viracocha, and he was angered by it . . . and those first people and their chief he converted into stones in punishment." Then, after a period of darkness, he made at Tiahuanacu new men and women, out of stones. He gave them tasks and abilities and told them where to go. Remaining with only two aides, he sent one southward and one northward, while he himself went in the direction of Cuzco. There he caused a chief to come forth; and having thus established kingship at Cuzco, Viracocha continued his journey "as far as the coast of Ecuador, where his two companions joined him. There they all began to walk together on the waters of the sea, and disappeared."

Some of the tales of the highland peoples focused on how there had come to be a settlement at Cuzco, and how Cuzco had been divinely ordained to become the capital. According to one version what Manco Capac was given (in order to find the site for the city) was a staff or wand made of pure gold; it was called *Tupac-yauri,* meaning "splenderous scepter." He went in search of the designated place in the company of brothers and sisters. Reaching a certain stone, his companions were struck with a feebleness. When Manco Capac struck the stone with the magical staff, it spoke up and told him of his selection as ruler of a kingdom. A descendent of an Indian chief who had converted to Christianity after the Spaniards had landed claimed in his memoirs that the Indians were showing that sacred rock to this very day. "The Ynca Manco Capac married one of his own sisters, named Mama Ocllo . . . and they began to enact good laws for the government of their people."

This tale, sometimes called the legend of the four Ayar brothers, relates as all other versions of the founding of Cuzco do, that the magical object whereby the monarch and the capital were designated was made of solid gold. It is a clue that we consider vital and central to the unraveling of the enigmas of all American civilizations.

When the Spaniards entered Cuzco, the Inca capital, they found a metropolis with some 100,000 dwelling houses, surrounding a royal-religious center of magnificent temples, palaces, gardens, plazas, and marketplaces. Situated between two streams (the Tullumayo and the Rodadero) at an elevation of some 11,500 feet, Cuzco begins at the foot of the promontory of Sacsahuaman. The city was divided into twelve wards—a number that puzzled the Spaniards—arranged in an oval. The first and oldest ward, appropriately called the Kneeling Terrace, was located on the promontory's slope in the northwest. There the first Incas (and presumably also the legendary Manco Capac) had built their palaces. All the wards bore picturesque names (the Speaking Place, Terrace of Flowers, Sacred Gate, and the like) that in reality described their principal feature.

One of this century's leading scholars on the subject of Cuzco, Stansbury Hagar (*Cuzco, the Celestial City*) stressed the belief that Cuzco was established and laid out in accordance with a plan drawn for Manco Capac at the prehistoric sacred place where the migration of the Founders had begun, at Tiahuanacu on Lake Titicaca. In its name, "Navel of the Earth," and in its division to four parts simulating the four corners of the Earth, he (and others too) saw an expression of terrestrial concepts. In other features of the city's plan, however, he saw aspects of celestial knowledge (hence the title of his book). The streams that flanked the city's center were made to flow through artificial channels that emulated the serpentine Milky Way; and the twelve wards emulated the division of the heavens into twelve houses of the zodiac. Significantly for our own studies of events on Earth and their timing, Hagar concluded that the first and earliest ward represented Aries.

Squier and other nineteenth-century explorers described a Cuzco that was partly all-Hispanic and partly built over the remains of the earlier Inca City. So, for a description of Cuzco as the conquering Spaniards had found it, and for a glimpse as it had been in even earlier times, one must read the words of the early chroniclers. Pedro de Cieza de Leon (*Chronicles of Peru* in the English translation) described the Inca capital, its edifices and squares and bridges in most glowing words, "a nobly adorned city" from whose center four royal roads led to the farthest parts of the empire, and ascribed its riches not only to the custom of keeping intact the palaces of the deceased kings, but also to the law that required gold and silver to be brought into the city in homage and offerings but prohibited to take any out on pain of death. "Cuzco," he wrote in its praise, "was grand and stately, and must have been founded by a people of great intelligence. It had fine streets, except that they were narrow, and the houses were built of solid stones, beautifully joined. These stones were very large and well cut. The other parts of the houses were of wood and straw; there are no remains of tiles, bricks, or lime amongst them."

Garcilaso de la Vega (who bore his Spanish father's name but also the royal title "Inca," for his mother was of the royal Inca dynasty) after describing the twelve wards, related that except for the palace of the first Inca in the First Ward, on the slope of Sacsahuaman, the other Inca palaces were clustered around the city's center near the great temple. Still extant in his time were the palaces of the second, sixth, ninth, tenth, eleventh and twelfth Incas. Some of them flanked the main square of the capital, called Huacay-Pata. There the ruling Inca, seated on a grand dais, his family, court hierarchy, and priests witnessed and conducted the festivals and religious ceremonies, four of which were connected with the winter and summer solstices and the spring and autumn equinoxes.

As the early chroniclers attest, the most famous and superb structure of pre-Hispanic Cuzco was the Cori-Cancha ("Golden Enclosure"), the city's and the empire's most important temple. The Spaniards called it Temple of the Sun, having believed that the Sun was the supreme deity of the Incas. Those who had seen the temple before it was vandalized, demolished, and built over by the Spaniards, reported that it was made up of several parts. The main temple was dedicated to Viracocha; adjoining or auxiliary chapels were devoted to the Moon (*Quilla*), Venus (*Chasca*), a mysterious star called *Coyllor*, and to *Illa-pa*, the god of Thunder and Lightning. There was also a shrine devoted to the Rainbow. It was there, at the Coricancha, that the Spaniards had plundered the golden riches.

Adjoining the Coricancha was the enclosure that was called *Aclla-Huasi*—"The Chosen Women's House." Consisting of dwellings surrounding gardens and orchards as well as workshops for spinning, weaving, and sewing the royal and priestly garments, it was a secluded enclave where virgins dedicated to the Great God lived; one of their tasks was to preserve the Eternal Fire attributed to the god.

The conquering Spaniards, having plundered the city's riches, set out to appropriate to themselves the city itself, dividing among themselves by drawing lots its various edifices. Most were dismantled for their masonry; here and there a gateway or part of a wall was incorporated into new Spanish buildings. Major shrines were used as sites for churches and monasteries. The Dominicans, first on the scene, took over the Temple of the Sun, demolishing its outer structure but incorporating the ancient layout and some wall portions into their church-monastery. One of the most interesting sections thus used and therefore still intact is a semicircular outer wall of what used to be the enclosure of the Inca temple's High Altar (Fig. 67). It was there that the Spaniards found a great golden disk representing (they assumed) the Sun; it fell by lot to the conquistador Leguizano, who gambled it away the following night. The winner had the venerated object melted and cast into ingots.

After the Dominicans came the Franciscans, the Augustines, the Mercedarios, the Jesuits; they all built their shrines, including Cuzco's great cathedral, where Inca shrines had stood. After the priests came the nuns; not surprisingly, their convent stands upon the Inca's convent of the House of the Chosen Women. Governors and Spanish dignitaries followed suit, building their edifices and homes upon and with parts of Inca stone houses.

Figure 67

Some believe that *Cuzco,* meaning "Navel, Omphalus," was so named because it was the capital, a place chosen for a command post. Another theory held by many is that the name means "Place of Raised Stones." If so, the name suits Cuzco's main attraction—its astounding megalithic stones.

While most of Cuzco's Inca dwellings were built of undressed fieldstones held together with mortar, or stones roughly cut to simulate bricks or ashlars, some of the older edifices were built of perfectly cut, dressed, and shaped stones ("ashlars") as those found in the remaining semicircular wall of the Coricancha. The beauty and craftsmanship of this wall and some others contemporary with it have amazed and thrilled countless travelers. Sir Clemens Markham wrote: "In contemplating this unequalled piece of masonry, one is lost in admiration at the extreme beauty of its formation... and above all at the untiring perseverence and skill that was required to form each stone with such unerring precision."

Squier, less the architect and more the antiquarian, was more impressed by Cuzco's other stones, those of great size and the oddest shapes that fitted one into another's angles with amazing precision and without mortar. Being of brown trachtyte *Anda-huaylillas*, they must have been specifically selected, he surmised, because of their grain, which "being rough, causes greater adhesion between the blocks than would be effected by the use of any other kinds of stone." He confirmed that the polygonal (many-sided) stones, as Spanish chroniclers had stated, indeed were fitted together with such accuracy "that it was impossible to introduce the thinnest knife-blade or finest needle between them" (Fig. 68a). One such stone, a tourist favorite, has twelve sides and angles (Fig. 68b).

All these heavy blocks of the hardest stone have been brought over to Cuzco and cut by unknown masons with apparent ease, as if they were shaping putty. Each stone face has been

Figure 68

dressed to a smooth and slightly concave surface; how, no one can tell, for there are no grooves or ridges or hammer marks to be seen. How were these heavy stones raised and placed one upon the other, one angled to fit the odd angles below and beside it, is also a mystery. To compound the mystery, all these stones are tightly held together without mortar, withstanding not only human destructiveness but also the frequent earthquakes in the area.

All are agreed by now that while the beautiful ashlars represent a "classical" Inca phase, the cyclopean walls belong to an earlier time. For want of clearer answers, scholars simply call it the Megalithic Age.

It is a puzzle that still seeks a solution. It is also a mystery that only deepens as one ascends the promontory of Sacsahuaman. There, what is assumed to have been an Inca fortress thrusts an even greater enigma at the visitor.

The promontory's name means Falcon's Place. Shaped like a triangle with its base to the northwest, its peak rises some eight hundred feet above the city below. Its sides are formed by gorges that separate it from the mountain chain to which it belongs and which it rejoins at its base.

The promontory can be divided into three parts. Its wide base is dominated by huge rock outcroppings that someone cut and shaped into giant steps or platforms and perforated with tunnels, niches, and grooves. The promontory's middle is taken up by a flattened-out area hundreds of feet wide and long. And the narrower edge, elevated above the rest of the promontory, contains evidence of circular and rectangular structures under which there run passages, tunnels, and other openings in a bewildering maze cut into the natural rock.

Separating or protecting this "developed" area from the rest of the promontory are three massive walls that run parallel to each other in a zigzag (Fig. 69).

The three lines of zigzagging walls are constructed of massive stones and rise one behind the other, each one somewhat higher than the one in front of it, to a combined height of about sixty feet. Earth-fills behind each wall have created terraces that, it is presumed, were meant to serve the promontory's defenders as parapets. Of the three, especially the lowest (first) wall is built of colossal boulders, weighing between ten to twenty tons. In one instance a boulder twenty-seven feet high weighs over 300 tons (Fig. 70). Many stones are fifteen feet high and are from ten to fourteen feet in width and thickness. As in the city below, the faces of these boulders have been artificially dressed to per-

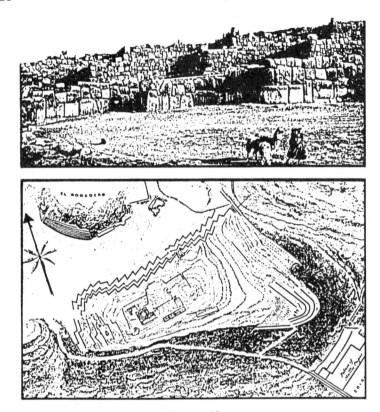

Figure 69

fect smoothness and are beveled at the edges, which means that
they are not fieldstones found lying about and used as nature
had shaped them, but rather the work of expert masons.

The massive stone blocks lie one atop the other, sometimes
separated for an unknown structural reason by a thin stone slab.
Everywhere the stones are of a polygonal shape, the odd sides
and angles fitting without mortar into the odd and matching
shapes of the adjoining stone blocks. The style and the period
are clearly of the same cyclopean construction as that of the
Megalithic Age remains in Cuzco, but here they are substantially more massive.

All over the flattened areas between the walls there are remains of structures that were built of the regularly fashioned
"Inca style" stones. As clearing work on the ground and aerial
photographs show, there had been various structures atop the
promontory. All has crumbled or was destroyed in the wars that

Figure 70

ensued between the Incas and the Spaniards after the conquest. Only the colossal walls remain unscathed, mute witnesses that bespeak an enigmatic age and mysterious builders; for as all studies have shown, the gigantic stone blocks were quarried miles away and had to be transported to the site over mountains, valleys, gorges, and gushing streams.

How and by whom—and why?

Chroniclers from Spanish conquest times, travelers in recent centuries, and contemporary researchers all arrive at the same conclusion: not the Incas, but enigmatic predecessors with some supernatural powers. . . . But no one even has a theory Why.

Garcilaso de la Vega wrote of these fortifications that one had no choice but to believe that they were "erected by magic, by demons and not by men, because of the number and size of the stones placed in the three walls . . . which it is impossible to believe were cut out of quarries, since the Indians had neither iron nor steel wherewith to extract and shape them. And how they were brought together is a thing equally wonderous, since the Indians had neither carts nor oxen nor ropes wherewith to drag them by manual force. Nor were there level roads over which to transport them; on the contrary, steep mountains and abrupt declivities to overcome.

"Many of the stones," Garcilaso wrote, "were brought from ten to fifteen leagues, and especially the stone or rather the rock called *Saycusa* or the Tired Stone, because it never reached the structure, and which, it is known, was brought a distance of fifteen leagues from beyond the river of Yucay...The stones obtained the nearest were from Muyna, five leagues from Cuzco. It defies imagination to conceive how so many and so great stones could be so accurately fitted together as scarcely to admit the insertion of a point of a knife between them. Many are indeed so well fitted that the joint can hardly be discovered. And all this is the more wonderous as they had no squares or levels to place on the stones and ascertain if they would fit together.... Nor had they cranes or pulleys or other machinery whatever." He then went on to quote a number of Catholic priests who had suggested that "one cannot conceive how such stones were cut, carried and set in their places...unless by diabolic art."

Squier, who said of the stones composing the three walls that they represented "without doubt the grandest specimen of the style called Cyclopean extant in America," was enthralled and puzzled by many other features of these stone colossi and of the other rock faces in the area. One such feature was the three gateways through the rows of walls, one of which was called the Gate of Viracocha. This gateway was a marvel of engineering sophistication: at about the center of the front wall the stone blocks were so placed as to form a rectangular area that led to an opening of about four feet in the wall. Steps then led to a terrace between the first and second walls, from which an intricate passage opened against a transverse wall at a right angle, leading to a second terrace. There, two entrances placed at an angle to each other led to and through the third wall.

All chroniclers related that this central gateway, like the other two at the walls' extremes, could be blocked by lowering large, specially fitted stone blocks into the openings. These stone blockers and the mechanisms for their raising and lowering (to open and block the gateways) were removed at some ancient time, but the channels and grooves for them can still be discerned. On the nearby plateau, where rocks have been carved into precise geometric shapes that make no sense to the modern viewer (Fig. 71a), there is one instance (Fig. 71b)

a

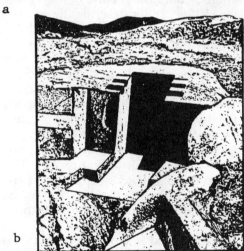

b

Figure 71

where the cut rock appears to have been shaped to hold some mechanical contraption. H. Ubbelohde-Doering (*Kunst im Reiche der Inca*) said of these enigmatic carved rocks that they are "like a model in which every corner has a significance."

Behind the line of walls the promontory was the site of an agglomeration of structures, some undoubtedly built in Inca times. That they were built on the remains of earlier structures is probable; that they had nothing to do with a maze of subterranean tunnels is certain. Underground passages in a labyrinthine pattern begin and end abruptly. One leads to a cavern forty feet deep; others end in rock faces cut and dressed to resemble steps that do not seem to lead anywhere.

Facing the cyclopean walls across the wide open flat area are rock outcroppings that bear descriptive names: the *Rodadero* ("Slide") whose back side is used by children as a slide; the *Piedra Lisa* ("Smooth Stone"), which Squier had described to be "grooved as if the rock had been squeezed up in a plastic state"—like playing clay—"then hardened into shape, with a smooth and glossy surface"; and near them the *Chingana* ("Labyrinth"), a cliff whose natural fissures have been artificially enlarged into passages, low corridors, small chambers, niches, and other hollowed-out spaces. Indeed, rocks dressed and shaped into horizontal, vertical, and inclined faces, openings, grooves, niches—all cut in precise angles and geometrical shapes—are found everywhere behind these cliffs.

The modern visitor cannot describe the scene any better than Squier did last century: "The rocks all over the plateau back of the fortress, chiefly limestone, are cut and carved in a thousand forms. Here is a niche, or a series of them; anon a broad seat like a sofa, or a series of small seats; next a flight of steps; then a cluster of square or round or octagonal basins; long lines of grooves; occasional holes drilled down . . . fissures in the rock widened artificially into a chamber—and all these cut with the accuracy and finish of the most skilful worker."

That the Incas used the promontory for a last stand against the Spaniards is a matter of historical record. That they had put up structures atop it is also evident from the remaining masonry. But that they were not the original builders at the site is further evidenced by their recorded inability to transport even one megalithic stone.

The attempt-that-failed is reported by Garcilaso in regard to the Tired Stone. According to him, one of the Inca mastermasons who wished to enhance his fame decided to haul up the stone from where the original builders had dropped it and use it in his defensive structure. "More than 20,000 Indians brought this stone up, dragging it with great cables. Their progress was very slow, for the road up which they came is rough and has many steep slopes to climb and descend. . . . On one of these slopes, as a result of carelessness on the part of the bearers who failed to pull evenly, the weight of the rock proved too much for the strength of those controlling it, and it rolled over down the slope and killed three or four thousand Indians."

According to this tale, then, the only time the Incas attempted to haul up and lift into place a cyclopean stone—they failed. Obviously, then, they were not the ones who had brought up, cut and shaped and lifted into place, with a mortarless fitting, the hundreds of the other cyclopean stones.

It is no wonder that Erich von Däniken, who has popularized the theory of Ancient Astronauts, wrote after his visit to the site in 1980 (*Reise Nach Kiribati*, or *Pathways to the Gods* in the English translation) that neither "mother nature" nor the Incas —but only ancient astronauts—could have been responsible for these monumental structures and odd-shaped cliffs. An earlier traveler, W. Bryford Jones (*Four Faces of Peru*, 1967), stated in amazement of the massive stone blocks: "They could only have been moved, I felt, by a race of giants from another world." And writing several years before that, Hans Helfritz (*Die alten Kulturen der Neuen Welt*) said of the incredible cyclopean walls of Sacsahuaman: "The impression is created that they have stood there from the very beginning of the world."

Long before them Hiram Bingham (*Across South America*) recorded one of the native speculations regarding the manner in which these incredible rock sculptures and walls had been created. "One of the favorite stories," he wrote, "is that the Incas knew of a plant whose juices rendered the surface of a block so soft that the marvellous fitting was accomplished by rubbing the stones together for a few moments with this magical plant juice." But who was it that could lift and hold up such cyclopean stones to rub them against each other?

Obviously, Bingham did not accept the natives' explanation and the enigma continued to nag him. "I have visited Sacsahuaman repeatedly," he wrote in *Inca Land*. "Each time it invariably overwhelms and astounds. To a superstitious Indian who sees these walls for the first time, they must seem to have been built by the gods." Why did Bingham make this statement, if not to express a "superstition" harbored within his own heart?

And so we come full circle back to the Andean legends; only they explain the megalithic builders by claiming that there had been gods and giants in these lands, and an Old Empire, and kingship that began with a divine golden wand.

7

THE DAY THE SUN
STOOD STILL

The initial Spanish avarice for gold and treasure obscured their amazement at encountering in Peru, this unknown land at the world's end, an advanced civilization with cities and roads, palaces and temples, kings and priests—and religions. The first wave of priests accompanying the conquerors was bent on destroying everything that had to do with the Indians' "idolatry." But the priests that followed—at that time their country's scholars—found themselves exposed to explanations of the natives' rites and beliefs through Indian noblemen who had converted to Christianity.

The realization that the Andean Indians believed in a Supreme Creator and that their legends recalled a Deluge, increased the curiosity of the Spanish priests. It then transpired that many details of those local tales were uncannily similar to the biblical tales of Genesis. It was therefore inevitable that among the early theories regarding the origin of the "Indians" and their beliefs, an association with the lands and the people of the Bible emerged as the leading theory.

As in Mexico, after various other ancient peoples have been considered, the Israelites of the Ten Lost Tribes seemed the most plausible explanation not only for the similarity of native legends to biblical tales, but also to such customs among the Peruvian Indians as the offering of the first fruits, an Expiation Feast at the end of September that corresponded to the nature and time of the Jewish Day of Atonement, and other biblical commandments such as the rite of circumcision, abstaining from the blood of animal meat, and the prohibition against the eating of fish without scales. In the Feast of First Fruits, the Indians chanted the mystic words *Yo Meshica, He Meshica, Va Meshica*; and some of the Spanish savants discerned in the word *Meshica* the Hebrew term "Mashi'ach"—the Messiah.

(Modern scholars now believe that the component *Ira* in Andean divine names is comparable to the Mesopotamian *Ira/Illa*, from which the biblical *El* stems; that the name *Malquis* by which the Incas venerated their idol is equivalent to that of the Canaanite deity *Molekh* ("Lord"); and that likewise the royal Inca title *Manco* derives from the same Semitic root, meaning "king.")

It was in view of such theories of Israelite-biblical origins that the Catholic hierarchy in Peru, after the initial wave of obliteration, moved to record and preserve the Indian heritage. Local clergymen, such as Father Blas Valera (son of a Spaniard and an Indian woman), were encouraged to write down what they knew and heard. Before the sixteenth century was over, a concerted effort sponsored by the Bishop of Quito was made to compile the local histories, evaluate all known ancient sites, and assemble in one library all the relevant manuscripts. Much that has been learned since is based on what was learned then.

Intrigued by the theories and availing himself of the assembled manuscripts, a Spaniard by name of Fernando Montesinos arrived in Peru in 1628 and devoted the rest of his life to the compilation of a comprehensive and chronological history and prehistory of the Peruvians. Some twenty years later he completed a master work titled *Memorias Antiguas Historiales del Peru* and deposited it in the library of the convent of San Jose de Sevilla. There it lay unpublished and forgotten for two centuries, when extracts from it were included in a French history of the Americas. The full Spanish text saw light only in 1882 (an English translation by P. A. Means was published by the Hakluyt Society in London, England, in 1920).

Picking up a common point of departure in biblical and Andean recollections—the tale of the Deluge—Montesinos employed the event as his starting point. In line with the biblical record he followed the repopulation of Earth after the Deluge from Mount Ararat in Armenia through the Table of Nations in Chapter 10 of the Book of Genesis. He saw in the name *Peru* (or *Piru/Pirua* in the Indian tongue) a phonetic rendering of the biblical name *Ophir,* the grandson of Eber (the forebear of the Hebrews) who himself was the great-grandson of Shem. Ophir was also the name of the famed Land of Gold from which the Phoenicians had brought gold for the temple in Jerusalem that King Solomon was building. Ophir's name in the biblical Table of Nations is listed next to that of his brother Havilah—a name after which the famed land of gold was called in the biblical tale of the four rivers of Paradise:

And the name of one was Pishon;
It is the river which encompasses the whole
land of Havilah, where the gold is

It was much before the time of the kingdoms of Judah and
Israel, much before the Ten Tribes were exiled by the Assyrians,
that people from the lands of the Bible had come to the Andes,
Montesinos theorized. It was none other than Ophir himself,
Montesinos suggested, who had led the earliest settlers into
Peru when mankind began to spread upon the Earth after the
Deluge.

The Inca tales Montesinos assembled attested that long before the latest Inca dynasty there had been an ancient empire.
After a period of growth and prosperity upheavals suddenly befell the land: comets appeared in the skies, the ground shook
with earthquakes, wars broke out. The king reigning at the time
left Cuzco and led his followers to a secluded refuge place in the
mountains called Tampu-Tocco; only a few priests remained in
Cuzco to maintain its shrine. It was during that calamitous time
that the art of writing was lost.

Centuries passed. The kings went periodically from Tampu-
Tocco to Cuzco to consult divine oracles. Then one day a
woman of noble birth announced that her son Rocca had been
carried off by the Sun God. Days later the youth reappeared
clothed in golden garments. He reported that the time of forgiveness had come, but the people must adhere to certain commandments: royal succession would go to a son born to the king
by a half sister, even if not the firstborn; and writing was not to
be resumed. The people agreed and returned to Cuzco, with
Rocca as the new king; he was given the title *Inca*—sovereign.

By giving this first Inca the name Manco Capac, Inca historians likened him to the legendary founder of Cuzco, Manco
Capac of the four Ayar brothers. Montesinos correctly separated and distanced the Spaniards' contemporary Inca dynasty
(which began to reign only in the eleventh century A.D.) from its
predecessors. His conclusion, that the Inca dynasty consisted of
fourteen kings, including Huayna Capac who had died when the
Spaniards arrived and his two warring sons, has since been confirmed by all scholars.

He concluded that indeed Cuzco had been abandoned before
that Inca dynasty had reinstated kingship in the capital. During
the abandonment of Cuzco, he wrote, twenty-eight kings
reigned from a hidden mountain refuge called Tampu-Tocco.
And before that there had indeed been an ancient empire with
Cuzco as its capital. There, sixty-two kings sat on the throne; of

them, forty-six were priest-kings and sixteen were semidivine rulers who were Sons of the Sun God. And, before all that, the gods themselves lorded over the land.

It is believed that Montesinos had found a copy of the Blas Valera manuscript in La Paz, and was allowed by the Jesuit priests there to copy from it. He also relied heavily on the writings of Father Miguel Cabello de Balboa, whose version related that the first sovereign, Manco Capac, had come to Cuzco not directly from Lake Titicaca but by way of a hidden place called "Tampo-Toco" ("Restplace of the Windows"). It was there that Manco Capac "abused his sister Mama Occllo" and begot a son by her.

Montesinos, having confirmed this by all his other available sources, accepted this information as factual. He thus began the chronicles of kingship in Peru with the journey of the four Ayar brothers and their four sisters who were sent to find Cuzco with the aid of the golden object. But he recorded a version whereby the first to be chosen as a leader was a brother that bore the name of the ancestor who had led the people to the Andes, Pirua Manco (and thus the name Peru). It was he who, having arrived at the chosen site, announced that he had decided to build there a city. He came there accompanied by wives and sisters (or sister-wives); one of them bore him a son who was called Manco Capac. It was this son who built in Cuzco the Temple to the Great God, Viracocha; and therefore it is from that time that the establishment of the ancient empire is counted and the chronicles of the dynasties begin. Manco Capac was acclaimed as Son of the Sun, and was the first of sixteen rulers so deemed. In his time other deities were venerated, one of whom was Mother Earth and another a god whose name meant Fire; he was represented by a stone that spoke oracles.

The principal science at that time, Montesinos wrote, was that of astrology; and the art of writing, on processed leaves of the plantain tree and on stones, was known. The fifth Capac "renewed the computation of time" and began to record the passage of time and the reigns of his ancestors. It was he who introduced the count of a thousand years as a Great Period, and of centuries and periods of fifty years, equivalent to the biblical Jubilee. It was the Capac who had installed this calendar and chronology, Inti Capac Yupanqui, who completed the temple and introduced in it the worship of the great god *Illa Tici Vira Cocha*, meaning "Bright Beginner, Creator of the Waters."

In the reign of the twelfth Capac, news reached Cuzco of the disembarking on the coast of "some men of great stature . . . giants who were settling on the whole coast" and, possessing metal implements, were despoiling the land. After a time they began to go into the mountains; fortunately, they provoked the wrath of the Great God and he destroyed them with a heavenly fire.

Relieved of the dangers, the people forgot the commandments and the rites of worship. "Good laws and customs" were abandoned, and this did not go unnoticed by the Creator. In punishment, he hid the sun from the land; "there was no dawn for twenty hours." There was a great outcry among the people and prayers and sacrifices were offered at the temple, until (after twenty hours) the sun reappeared. The king immediately thereafter reintroduced laws of conduct and rites of worship.

The fortieth Capac on the throne of Cuzco established an academy for the study of astronomy and astrology and determined the equinoxes. The fifth year of his reign, Montesinos calculated, was the twenty-five hundredth year from Point Zero which, he assumed, was the Deluge. It was also the two thousandth year since kingship had begun at Cuzco; in celebration whereof the king was granted a new title, *Pachacuti* (Reformer). His successors also promoted the study of astronomy; one of them introduced a leap year of one extra day every four years and one extra year every four hundred years.

In the reign of the fifty-eighth monarch, "when the Fourth Sun was completed," the count was 2,900 years since the "Deluge." It was, Montesinos calculated, the year in which Jesus Christ was born.

That first Cuzco empire, begun by the Sons of the Sun and continued by priest-kings, came to a bitter end in the reign of the sixty-second monarch. In his time there occurred "marvels and portents." The earth shook with endless earthquakes, the skies were filled with comets, omens of a coming destruction. Tribes and peoples began to rush to and fro, clashing with their neighbors. Invaders came from the coast, even from across the Andes. Great battles ensued; in one of them the king was felled by an arrow and his army fled in panic; only five hundred warriors survived the battles.

"Thus was the government of the Peruvian monarchy lost and destroyed," Montesinos wrote, "and the knowledge of letters was lost."

The few remaining followers left Cuzco, leaving behind only a handful of priests to take care of the temple. They took along with them the dead king's young son, just a boy, and found refuge in a mountain hideaway called Tampu-Tocco; it was the place where, from a cave, the first semidivine couple exited to establish the Andean kingdom. When the boy came of age, he was proclaimed the first monarch of the Tampu-Tocco dynasty. It lasted almost a thousand years, from the beginning of the second to the eleventh centuries A.D.

During those many centuries of exile, knowledge dwindled and writing was forgotten. In the reign of the seventy-eighth monarch, when the milestone of 3,500 years since the Beginning was reached, a certain person began to revive the art of writing. It was then that the king received a warning from the priests concerning the invention of letters. It was the knowledge of writing, their message explained, that was the cause of the pestilences and accursations that had brought kingship in Cuzco to an end. The god's wish was "that no one ought to use the letters or resuscicate them, for from their employment great harm would come [again]." Therefore the king commanded "by law, under the pain of death, that no one should traffic in *quilcas,* which were the parchments and leaves of trees on which they used to write, nor should use any sort of letters." Instead,he introduced the use of *quipos,* the strands of colored cords that had served since then for chronological purposes.

In the reign of the ninetieth monarch, the fourth millennium from Point Zero was completed. By then the monarchy at Tampu-Tocco was weak and ineffective. The tribes loyal to it were subject to raids and invasions by neighbors. Tribal chiefs ceased paying homage to the central authority. Customs were corrupted, abominations proliferated. In such circumstances a princess of the original blood of the Sons of the Sun, one Mama Ciboca, rose to the occasion. She announced that her young son, who was so handsome that his admirers nicknamed him *Inca,* was destined to regain the throne at the old capital, Cuzco. In a miraculous way he disappeared and returned clothed in golden robes, claiming that the Sun God had taken him aloft, instructed him in secret knowledge, and told him to lead the people back to Cuzco. His name was Rocca; he was the first of the Inca dynasty that came to an ignomious end in the hands of the Spaniards.

Attempting to put these events in an orderly time frame, Montesinos stated at certain intervals that a period called "Sun" had passed or begun. While what length of a period (in years) he was considering is not at all certain, it would appear that he had in mind Andean legends of several "Suns" in the people's past.

Although scholars had held—less so nowadays—that there had been no contact whatsoever between the Mesoamerican and South American civilizations, the latter sound hardly different from the Aztec and Maya notions of five Suns. Indeed, all the Old World civilizations had recollections of past ages, of eras when the gods reigned alone, followed by demigods and heroes, and then just mortals. Sumerian texts called King Lists recorded a line of divine lords followed by demigods who reigned a total of 432,000 years before the Deluge, then listed the kings that reigned thereafter through times that are by now considered historical and whose data has been verified and found accurate. The Egyptian king lists, as composed by the priest-historian Manetho, listed a dynasty of twelve gods that began some 10,000 years before the Deluge; it was followed by gods and demigods until, circa 3100 B.C., the pharaohs ascended the throne of Egypt. Again, where his data could be verified against historical records, it was found to be accurate.

Montesinos found such notions in the Peruvian collective lore, confirming the reports of other chroniclers that the Incas believed that theirs was the Fifth Age or Sun. The First Age was that of Viracochas, gods who were white and bearded. The Second age was that of the giants; some of them were not benevolent, and there had been conflicts between the gods and the giants. Then followed the Age of Primitive Man, of uncultured human beings. The Fourth Age was the age of heroes, men who were demigods. And then there was the Fifth Age, the age of human kings, of whom the Incas were last in line.

Montesinos also placed the Andean chronology in the European frame by relating it to a certain Point Zero (he thought it had to be the Deluge) and—most clearly—to the birth of Christ. The two time sequences, he wrote, coincided in the reign of the fifty-eighth monarch: the twenty-nine hundredth year from Point Zero was the "first year of Jesus Christ." The Peruvian monarchies, he wrote, began 500 years after Point Zero, i.e., in 2400 B.C.

The problem scholars have with the history and chronology of Montesinos is thus not lack of clarity, but its conclusion that kingship and urban civilization began—at Cuzco—almost 3,500 years before the Incas. That civilization, according to the information amassed by Montesinos and those on whose work he had relied, possessed writing, included astronomy among its sciences, and had a calendar long enough to require its periodic reform. All this (and more) was possessed by the Sumerian civilization that blossomed out circa 3800 B.C. and by the Egyptian civilization that followed circa 3100 B.C. Another offshoot of the Sumerian civilization, that of the Indus Valley, came about circa 2900 B.C.

Why was it not possible for such trifold developments to

occur a fourth time, in the Andes? Impossible—if there had been no contacts between the Old and New Worlds. Possible, if the same grantors of all knowledge, the gods, were the same and were present all over the Earth.

Incredible as our conclusion must sound, happily it can be proven.

The first test of the veracity of the events and chronologies compiled by Montesinos had already taken place.

A key element in the Montesinos presentation is the existence of an ancient empire, of a line of kings at Cuzco who were finally forced to leave the capital and seek refuge in a secluded mountain place called Tampu-Tocco. The interregnum lasted a thousand years; finally a young man of noble birth was chosen to lead the people back to Cuzco and establish the Inca dynasty.

Was there a Tampu-Tocco, and was it a place identifiable by the landmarks given by Montesinos? The question intrigued many. In 1911, searching for lost Inca cities, Hiram Bingham of Yale University found the place; it is now called Machu Picchu.

Bingham was not looking for Tampu-Tocco when he set out on his first expedition; but after repeatedly going back and exhaustive excavations over more than two decades, he concluded that Machu Picchu was indeed the lost interim capital of the Old Empire. His descriptions of the place, still the most comprehensive, are in his books *Machu Picchu, a Citadel of the Incas* and *The Lost City of the Incas.*

The principal reason for believing that Machu Picchu is the legendary Tampu-Tocco is the clue of the Three Windows. Montesinos recorded that "at the place of his birth Inca Rocca ordered works to be executed, consisting of a masonry wall with three windows, which were the emblem of the house of his fathers, of whom he descended." The name of the place to which the royal house had gone from the stricken capital Cuzco meant "Haven of the Three Windows."

That a place should become known for its windows should not be surprising, since no house in Cuzco, from the humblest to the grandest, had windows. That a place should become known for a specific number of windows—three—could only be the result of the uniqueness, antiquity, or sanctity of the actual existence of such a structure. This was true of Tampu-Tocco, where according to the legends a structure with three windows played a role in the emergence of tribes and the ancient empire in Peru's beginning, a structure that had therefore become "the emblem of the house of his fathers of whom [Inca Rocca] had descended."

The legend, and the legendary place, featured in the tale of the Ayar brothers. As told by Pedro Sarmiento de Gamboa (*Historia General Llamada Yndica*) and other early chroniclers, the four Ayar brothers and their four sisters, having been created by the god Viracocha at Lake Titicaca, reached or were placed by the god in Tampu-Tocco, whence "they came out of said window by order of Tici-Viracocha, declaring that Viracocha created them to be lords."

The oldest of the brothers, Manco Capac, carried with him a sacred emblem in the image of a falcon, and also bore a golden rod that the god had given him with which to locate the right place for the future capital, Cuzco. The journey of the four brother-sister couples began peacefully; but soon jealousies developed. On the pretext that certain treasures were left behind in a cave in Tampu-Tocco, the second brother, Ayar Cachi, was sent back to retrieve them. This however was only a ruse by the three brothers to imprison him in the cave, where he was turned into a stone.

According to these tales, then, Tampu-Tocco dates from the very early times; "the myth of the Ayars," H. B. Alexander wrote in *Latin American Mythology,* "hearkens back to the Megalithic Age and to the cosmogonies associated with Titicaca." When the exiles left Cuzco, they went to a place already in existence, a place where a structure with three windows had already played a role in even earlier events. It is with this understanding that we can now proceed to visit Machu Picchu, for a structure whose wall has three windows has indeed been found there, and nowhere else.

"Machu Picchu, or Great Picchu, is the Quichua name of a sharp peak which rises ten thousand feet above the sea and four thousand feet above the roaring rapids of the Urubamba River near the bridge of San Miguel, two hard days' journey north of Cuzco," Bingham wrote. "Northwest of Machu Picchu is another beautiful peak surrounded by magnificent precipices, called Huayna Picchu, or Lesser Picchu. On the narrow ridge between the two peaks are the ruins of an Inca city whose name has been lost in the shadows of the past. . . . It is possible that they represent two ancient sites, Tampu-Tocco, the birthplace of the first Inca, and Vilcabamba Viejo."

Nowadays the journey from Cuzco to Machu Picchu, a distance of some seventy-five miles as the crow flies, does not require the two days' hard journey described by Bingham just to get there. A train that chugs its way up then down mountains, passing through tunnels and over bridges and hugging the mountainsides flanking the Urubamba river, gets there in under four hours. Another half-hour cliffhanger bus ride up from the railway station, and the city is reached. The breathtaking view is exactly as Bingham described it. In the saddle between the two peaks, houses, palaces, temples—all roofless now—stand surrounded by terraces that cling to the mountainsides, ready for cultivation. The peak of Huayna Picchu rises on the northwest as a sentinel (Fig. 72); beyond it and all around, peak competes with peak as far as the eye can see. Down below the Urubamba river forms a horseshoe gorge half encircling the city's perch, its gushing waters cutting a whitish path among the jungle's emerald green.

As befits a city that, we believe, at first served as a model for Cuzco and then emulated it, Machu Picchu too consisted of twelve wards or groups of structures. The royal-priestly groupings are on the west and the residential-functional ones (occupied mostly by the Virgins and clan hierarchies) on the east, separated by a series of wide terraces. The common people who tilled and cultivated the terraced mountainsides lived outside the city and in the surrounding countryside (many such hamlets have been found since the initial discovery by Bingham).

Figure 72

Several construction styles, as at Cuzco and other archaeological sites, suggest different phases of occupation. The dwelling houses are built mostly of fieldstones held together with mortar. The royal residences are built of ashlars laid in courses, as finely cut and dressed as any in Cuzco. Then there is one structure where the workmanship is so perfect as to be unmatched; and there are the polygonal megalithic stone blocks. In many instances, the remains from the earlier Megalithic Age and Ancient Empire times have remained as was; in others, later construction atop earlier courses is obvious.

While the eastern wards occupied every available square foot of mountaintop and extended from the city's wall in the south as far north as the terrain permitted and eastward into the agricultural and burial terraces, the western group of wards, that also began at the wall, extended northward only to the border of a Sacred Plaza—as though an unseen line marked off hallowed ground that could not be encroached upon.

Beyond that unseen demarcation line, and facing the great terraced plaza to the east, stand the remains of what Bingham has identified as the Sacred Plaza, mainly "because on two sides of it are the largest temples," one of them with the crucial three windows. It is here, in the construction of what Bingham had named the Temple of the Three Windows and, adjoining it in the Sacred Plaza, the Principal Temple, that cyclopean polygonal stone blocks have been used at the site. The manner in which they were cut, shaped, dressed, and fitted together without mortar puts them in a class with the cyclopean stone blocks and megalithic structures of Sacsahuaman; and, surpassing the polygonality of anything seen in Cuzco, one of the stone blocks here has thirty-two angles.

The Temple of the Three Windows stands at the eastern edge of the Sacred Plaza; the cyclopean stone blocks of its eastern wall raise it well above the terraced level to its west (Fig. 73), affording an unimpeded eastward view through the three windows (Fig. 74). Trapezoid in shape, their sills are cut out of the cyclopean stones that form the wall itself. As at Sacsahuaman and Cuzco, this cutting, shaping, and angling of the hard granite stones was done as though they were soft putty; here too, the white granite stone blocks had to be brought from great distances, through rough terrain and rivers, down valleys and up mountains.

The Temple of the Three Windows has only three walls, its western side being completely open; there it faces a stone pillar, about seven feet high (see Fig. 74). Bingham surmised that it might have supported a roof, which (he admitted) would have

Figure 73

been "a device not found in any other building." It is our opinion that the pillar, in conjunction with the three windows,
served astronomical sighting purposes.

Facing the Sacred Plaza on the north is the structure
Bingham had named the Principal Temple; it too has only three
walls, some twelve feet high. They rest upon or are constructed
of cyclopean stone blocks; the western wall, for example, is
constructed of just two giant stone blocks held together by a
T-shaped stone. A huge monolith, measuring fourteen by five
by three feet, rests against the central north wall in which seven
niches imitate (but are not) trapezoid windows (Fig. 75).

Winding steps lead from the northern edge of the Sacred

Figure 74

Figure 75

Plaza up a hill whose top was flattened to serve as a platform for
the *Intihuatana,* a stone cut with great precision to observe and
measure the movements of the Sun (Fig. 76). The name meant
"That Which Binds the Sun," and it is assumed that it helped
determine the solstices, when the Sun moves farthest away to
the north or south, at which time rites were held to "bind the
Sun" and make it return, lest it keep going away and disappear,
returning the Earth to a darkness that had occurred once before
according to the legends.

At the opposite end of the sacred-royal western part of
Machu Picchu, just south of the royal ward, rises the other magnificent (and unusual) edifice of the city. Called the *Torreon* for
its semicircular shape, it is built of ashlars—cut, shaped, and
dressed stones—of rarely seen perfection, matched in a way
only by the ashlars of the semicircular wall that embraced the
Holy of Holies in Cuzco. The semicircular wall, which is

Figure 76

reached by seven steps (Fig. 77), creates its own sacred enclosure at the center of which there is a rock that has been cut and
shaped and incised with grooves. Bingham found evidence that
this rock and the masonry walls near it were subjected to periodic fires, and concluded that the rock and the enclosure were
used for sacrifices and other rituals connected with the veneration of the rock.

(This sacred rock within a special structure brings to mind
the sacred rock that forms the heart of the Temple Mount in
Jerusalem, as well as the Qua'abah, the black stone that is hidden within the holiest Moslem enclosure in Mecca.)

The sanctity of the rock in Machu Picchu stems not from its
protruding top, but from what lies below. It is a huge natural
rock inside of which there is a cave that has been enlarged and
shaped artificially to precise geometric forms that look like (but
are not) stairs, seats, ledges, and posts (Fig. 78). Additionally,
the interior has been improved with masonry of white granite
ashlars of the purest color and grain. Niches and stone nobbins

Figure 77

add to the interior complexity. Bingham surmised that the original natural cave was enlarged and enhanced to hold royal mummies, brought there because the place was sacred. But why was
it sacred, and important for depositing the deceased kings, to
begin with?

The question takes us back to the legend of the Ayar
brothers, one of whom was imprisoned in a cave at the Haven of
the Three Windows. If the Temple of the Three Windows was
the legendary one, and the cave so too, then the legends con-

Figure 78

firm the site and the site is confirmed as the legendary Tampu-Tocco.

Sarmiento, one of the Spanish chroniclers who was himself a conquistador, reported in his *History of the Incas* a local tradition that the ninth Inca (circa A.D. 1340), "being curious about the things of antiquity and wishing to perpetuate his name, went personally to the mountain of Tampu-Tocco... and there entered the cave whence it is held for certain that Manco Capac and his brethren came when they marched into Cuzco for the very first time.... After he had made a thorough inspection, he venerated the place by rituals and sacrifices, and placed doors of gold on the window of Capac Tocco, and ordered that from that time onward the locality should be venerated by all, making it a sacred prayer place for sacrifices and oracles. Having done this, he returned to Cuzco."

The subject of this report, the ninth Inca, was called Titu Manco Capac; he was given the additional title *Pachacutec* ("Reformer") because, after his return from Tampu-Tocco, he reformed the calendar. So, like the Three Windows and the Intihuatana, the Sacred Rock and the *Torreon* affirm the existence of Tampu-Tocco, the tale of the Ayar brothers, the pre-Inca reigns during the ancient empire, and the knowledge of astronomy and the calendar—key elements in the history and chronology put together by Montesinos.

The veracity of Montesinos's data can be additionally enhanced if he was right regarding the existence of writing in ancient empire times. We find that Cieza de Leon held the same view, stating that "in the epoch preceding the Inca emperors there had been writing in Peru . . . on leaves, skins, cloth and stones."

Many South American scholars now join the early chroniclers in believing that the natives of those lands had one or more forms of writing in antiquity.

Numerous studies report petroglyphs ("stone writings") found throughout these lands that display, to varying degrees, pictographic or glyphic writing. Rafael Larco Hoyle, for example (*La Escritura Peruana Pre-Incana*), suggested with the aid of depictions that coastal people as far as Paracas possessed glyphic writing akin to that of the Maya. Arthur Posnansky, the leading explorer of Tiahuanacu, produced voluminous studies showing that the carvings on the monuments there were pictographic-ideographic writing—a step before phonetic script. And a well-known find, the Stone of Calango now on display at the Lima Museum (Fig. 79), suggests a combination of pictographs with a phonetic, perhaps even alphabetic, script.

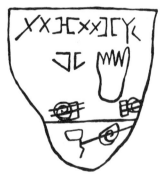

Figure 79

One of the greatest early explorers of South America, Alexander de Humboldt, dealt with the subject in his major work *Vues des Cordilléres et Monumens des Peuples Indigenes de l'Amerique* (1824). "It has been recently put in doubt," he wrote, "that the Peruvians had, besides *Quippus,* knowledge of a sign script. A passage in *L'Origin de los Indios del Nuevo Mundo* (Valencia, 1610), page 91, leaves no doubt in this regard." After speaking of the Mexican hieroglyphs, Father Garcia adds: "at the start of the conquest, the Indians of Peru confessed themselves by painting characters that listed the Ten Commandments and the transgressions committed against them." It is possible to conclude that the Peruvians possessed the use of a picture script, but that their symbols were coarser than the Mexican hieroglyphs, and that generally the people availed themselves of the *quippus.*

Humboldt also reported that when he was in Lima, he heard of a missionary named Narcisse Gilbar who had found, among the Panos Indians of the Ucayale river north of Lima, a book of folded leaves, similar to such as had been used by the Aztecs in Mexico; but no one in Lima could read it. "It was said that the Indians told the Missionary that the book recorded ancient wars and voyages."

Writing in 1855, Ribero and von Tschudi reported various other discoveries and concluded that there had indeed been another method of writing in Peru besides the quipos. Writing separately about his own travels, von Tschudi (in *Reisen durch Südamerika*) describes his excitement at being shown a photograph of a skin-parchment with hieroglyphic markings. He found the actual parchment in the museum of La Paz, Bolivia, and made a copy of the writing on it (Fig. 80a). "These symbols made on me the greatest astonishing effect," he wrote, "and I stayed in front of this skin for hours," trying to decipher "the labyrinth" of this writing. He determined that the writing started at left, then continued on the second line from the right, then resumed in the third line from the left again, and so on in a serpentine manner. He also concluded that it was written at the time when the Sun was worshiped; but that was as far as he got.

He traced the inscription to its place of origin on the shores of Lake Titicaca. The padre at the Mission Church at the lakeside village Copacabana confirmed that such writing was known in the area, but attributed it to a post-Conquest period. The explanation was clearly unsatisfactory, since if the Indians would not have had their own script, they would have adopted the Spaniards' Latin script to express themselves. Even if this hieroglyphic writing evolved after the Conquest, Jorge Cornejo

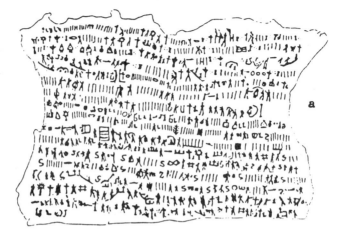

Figure 80

Bouroncle wrote (*La Idolatria en el antiguo Peru*), "its origin must have been more remote."

Arthur Posansky (*Guia general Illustrada de Tiahuanacu*) found additional inscriptions in this script on rocks on the two sacred islands of Lake Titicaca. He pointed out that it was of a kind with enigmatic inscriptions found on Easter Island (Fig. 80b)—a conclusion with which scholars now generally agree. But the Easter Island script is known to belong to the family of Indo-European scripts of the Indus Valley *and of the Hittites*. A common feature to all of them (including the Lake Titicaca inscriptions) is their "as the ox ploughs" system: the writing on the first line begins on the left and ends on the right; it continues on the second line beginning on the right, ending on the left; the third line then begins on the left, and so on.

Without going now into the question of how did a script emulating that of the Hittites (Fig. 80c) reach Lake Titicaca, it seems that the existence of one or more forms of writing in ancient Peru has been confirmed. On this count too, the information provided by Montesinos proves correct.

If in spite of all this the reader still finds it difficult to accept the inevitable conclusion, that there had indeed been an Old World type civilization in the Andes circa 2400 B.C., there is additional evidence.

Completely ignored by scholars as a valid clue has been the repeated statement in the Andean legends that there occurred a frightening darkness in long-ago times. No one has wondered whether this was the same darkness—the nonappearance of the sun when it was due—of which the Mexican legends speak in the tale of Teotihuacan and its pyramids. For if there had indeed been such a phenomenon, that the sun failed to rise and the night was endless, then it would have been observed throughout the Americas.

The Mexican collective recollections and the Andean ones seem to corroborate each other on this point, and thus uphold the veracity of each other, as two witnesses to the same event.

But if even this is not convincing enough, we will call upon the Bible in evidence, and upon none other than Joshua to be the witness.

According to Montesinos and other chroniclers, the most unusual event took place in the reign of Titu Yupanqui Pachacuti II, the fifteenth monarch in Ancient Empire times. It was in the third year of his reign, when "good customs were forgotten and people were given to all manner of vice," that "there was no dawn for twenty hours." In other words, the night did not end when it usually does and sunrise was delayed for twenty hours. After a great outcry, confessions of sins, sacrifices, and prayers, the sun finally rose.

This could not have been an eclipse: it was not that the shining sun was obscured by a shadow. Besides, no eclipse lasts so long, and the Peruvians were cognizant of such periodic events. The tale does not say that the sun disappeared; it says that it did not rise—"there was no dawn"—for twenty hours.

It was as though the sun, wherever it was hiding, suddenly stood still.

If the Andean recollection is true, then somewhere else—on the opposite side of the world—the DAY had to last just as long, not ending when it should have ended but lasting some twenty hours longer.

Incredibly, such an event is recorded, and in no better place than in the Bible itself. It was as the Israelites, under the leadership of Joshua, had crossed the Jordan River into their Promised Land and had successfullly taken the fortified cities of Jericho and Ai. It was then that all the Amorite kings formed an alliance to put up a combined force against the Israelites. A great battle ensued in the valley of Ajalon, near the city of Gibeon. It began with an Israelite night attack that put the Canaanites into flight. By sunrise, as the Canaanite forces regrouped near Beth-Horon, the Lord God "cast down great stones from heaven upon them . . . and they died; there were more of them who had died from the hailstones than those whom the Israelites slew with the sword."

Then Joshua spoke unto Yahweh,
on the day when Yahweh delivered the Amorites
unto the Children of Israel, saying:
"In the sight of the Israelites,
let the Sun stand still in Gibeon
and the Moon in the valley of Ajalon."

And the Sun stood still, and the Moon stayed,
until the people had avenged themselves of the enemies.
Indeed it is all written in the Book of Jashar:
The Sun stood still in the midst of the skies
and it hastened not to go down
about a whole day.

Scholars have struggled for generations with this tale in Chapter 10 of the Book of Joshua. Some discount it as mere fiction; others see in it echoes of a myth; still others seek to explain it in terms of an unusually prolonged eclipse of the sun. But not only are such long eclipses unknown; the tale does not speak of the disappearance of the sun. On the contrary, it relates to an event when the sun continued to be seen, to hang on in the skies, for "about a whole day"—say, twenty hours?

The incident, whose uniqueness is recognized in the Bible ("There was no day like that before or after"), taking place on the opposite side of the Earth relative to the Andes, thus describes a phenomenon that was the opposite of what had happened in the Andes. In Canaan the sun did not set for some twenty hours; in the Andes, the sun did not rise for the same length of time.

Do not the two tales, then, describe the same event, and by coming from different sides of the Earth attest to its factuality?

What the occurrence was is still a puzzle. The only biblical clue is the mention of the great stones falling from the skies. Since we know that the tales describe not a standstill by the sun (and moon) but a disruption of Earth's rotation on its axis, a possible explanation is that a comet had come too close to Earth, disintegrating in the process. Since some comets orbit the sun in a clockwise direction that is opposite to the orbital direction of the Earth and the other planets, such a kinetic force could have conceivably counteracted temporarily the Earth's rotation and slowed it down.

Whatever the precise cause of the phenomenon, what we are concerned with here is its timing. The generally accepted date for the Exodus has been the thirteenth century B.C. (circa 1230 B.C.), and scholars who argued for a date earlier by some two centuries found themselves in a minority. Still, we have concluded in our previous writings (see *The Wars of Gods and Men*) that a date of 1433 B.C. would fit the event, as well as the biblical tales of the Hebrew patriarchs, perfectly into known contemporary events and chronologies of Mesopotamia and Egypt. Subsquent to the publication of our conclusions (in 1985), two eminent biblical scholars and archaeologists, John J. Bimson and David Livingston, reached after an exhaustive study (*Biblical Archaeology Review,* September/October 1987) the conclusion that the Exodus took place about 1460 B.C. Apart from their own archaeological findings and an analysis of the Bronze Age periods in the ancient Near East, the biblical data and calculation process that they have employed was the very same process we had used two years earlier. (We had also explained then why we had chosen to reconcile two lines of biblical data by dating the Exodus in 1433 B.C. rather than 1460 B.C.).

Since the Israelites wandered in the deserts of Sinai for forty years, the entry into Canaan took place in 1393 B.C.; the occurrence observed by Joshua happened soon thereafter.

The question now is: did the opposite phenomenon, the prolonged night, occur in the Andes at the same time?

Unfortunately, the shape in which the writings of Montesinos have reached modern scholars leaves some gaps in the data concerning lengths of reign of each monarch, and we will have to obtain the answer in a roundabout way. The event, Montesinos advises, occurred in the third year of the reign of Titu Yupanqui Pachacuti II. To pinpoint his time we will have to calculate from both ends. We are told that the first 1,000 years from Point Zero were completed in the reign of the fourth monarch, i.e., in 1900 B.C.; and that the thirty-second king reigned 2,070 years from Point Zero, i.e., in 830 B.C.

When did the fifteenth monarch reign? The available data suggests that the nine kings that separated the fourth and fifteenth monarch reigned a total of about 500 years, placing Titu Yupanqui Pachacuti II at about 1400 B.C. Calculating backward from the thirty-second monarch (830 B.C.), we arrive at 564 as the number of intervening years, giving us a date of 1394 B.C. for Titu Yupanqui Pachacuti II.

Either way, we arrive at a date for the Andean event that coincidences with the biblical date and the event's date at Teotihuacan.

The hard-hitting conclusion is clear:
THE DAY THE SUN STOOD STILL IN CANAAN WAS THE NIGHT WITHOUT SUNRISE IN THE AMERICAS.

The occurrence, thus verified, stands out as irrefutable proof of the veracity of Andean recollections of an Ancient Empire that began when the gods granted Mankind the golden wand at Lake Titicaca.

8

THE WAYS OF HEAVEN

The heavens bespeak the glory of the Lord
and the vault of heaven reveals his handiwork.
One day uttereth to another,
night unto night imparts knowledge—
without words, without speaking,
without their voice being heard.
Throughout the Earth their line has gone,
to the ends of the world is their message;
in them He hath made the Sun pitch its tent.

Thus did the biblical Psalmist describe the marvels of the heavens and the miracle of days and nights following each other, as the Earth rotates on its axis (the biblical "line" that goes through the Earth) and orbits the Sun that sits at the center of all (as a potentate in his tent). "The day is thine and the night too; thou hast established the luminary and the Sun . . . Summer and winter by thee were created."

For millennia, ever since Man acquired civilization, astronomer-priests looked to the heavens for guidance to Man on Earth—from the ziggurats of Sumer and Babylon, the temples of Egypt, the stone circle of Stonehenge or the Caracol at Chichén Itzá. Complex celestial motions of the stars and planets have been observed, calculated, recorded; and to make that possible, the ziggurats and temples and observatories were aligned to precise celestial orientations and provided with apertures and other structural features that let the light of the Sun or another star enter as a beam at equinox or solstice times.

Why did Man go to such lengths?—to see what, to determine what?

It is customary among scholars to attribute ancient man's astronomical endeavors to the needs of an agricultural society for a calendar telling it when to sow and when to reap. This expla-

155

nation has been taken for granted far too long. A farmer tilling the land year after year can judge the change of seasons and the coming of rains better than an astronomer, and has the ground-hog to tell him a thing or two. The fact is that wherever pockets of primitive societies (subsisting on agriculture) have been found in remote parts of the world, they have lived and fed themselves for generations without astronomers and a precise calendar. It is also an established fact that the calendar was de-vised in antiquity by an urban, not an agricultural, society.

A simple sun clock, a gnomon, can provide enough daily and seasonal information if one could not have survived without it. Yet ancient man studied the heavens and aligned his temples toward stars and planets, and linked his calendar and festivals not to the ground upon which he stood but to the ways of heaven. Why? Because the calendar was devised not for agricul-tural but for religious purposes. Not to benefit mankind, but to venerate the gods. And the gods, according to the first-ever religion and the people who gave us the calendar, came from the heavens.

One ought to read and reread the Pslamist's verses to realize that the observation of the wonders of the celestial phenomena had nothing to do with tilling the land or herding the cattle; it had to do with the veneration of the Lord of All. And there is no way to understand that better than to go back to Sumer; for it was there, some 6,000 years ago, that astronomy, the calen-dar, and a religion linking Earth with the Heavens had their beginning. It was knowledge, the Sumerians asserted, that was given them by the Anunnaki ("Those Who from Heaven to Earth Came") who had come to Earth from their planet, Ni-biru. Nibiru, they said, was the twelfth member of the Solar System, and that is why the celestial band was divided into twelve houses, the year into twelve months. Earth was the sev-enth planet (counting from the outside in); and therefore as twelve was a hallowed celestial number, seven was a sacred ter-restrial one.

The Anunnaki, the Sumerians wrote upon numerous clay tablets, had come to Earth long before the Deluge. In *The 12th Planet* we determined that it happened 432,000 years before the Deluge—a period equivalent to 120 orbits of Nibiru, orbits that though to the Anunnaki represent but a single year of theirs are equivalent to 3,600 Earth-years. They came and went between Nibiru and Earth each time their planet came closer to the Sun (and Earth) as it passed between Jupiter and Mars; and there is no doubt whatsoever that the Sumerians began to observe the heavens not to know when to sow, but in order to see and celebrate the return of the celestial Lord.

This, we believe, is why Man became an astronomer. This is why, as time passed and Nibiru itself could no longer be observed, Man sought signs and omens in the phenomena that could be seen, and astronomy bred astrology. And if the astronomical orientations and alignments and celestial divisions that began in Sumer could also be found in the Andes, an irrefutable link would be proven.

Some time early in the fourth millennium B.C., according to Sumerian texts, the ruler of Nibiru, Anu, and his spouse Antu paid a visit to Earth. A brand-new sacred precinct with a temple-tower was built in their honor at a place that later came to be known as Uruk (the biblical Erech). A text has been preserved on clay tablets describing their night there. In the evening a ceremonial meal began with a ritual washing of the hands on a celestial signal—the appearance of Jupiter, Venus, Mercury, Saturn, Mars, and the Moon. Then the first part of the meal was served, followed by a pause. While a group of priests began to chant the hymn *Kakkab Anu Etellu Shamame* ("The Planet of Anu Rises in the Skies"), an astronomer-priest, at the "topmost stage of the tower of the temple" watched for the appearance of the Planet of Anu, Nibiru. When the planet was sighted, the priests broke out in singing the composition "To the One Who Grows Bright, the Heavenly Planet of the Lord Anu," and the psalm "The Creator's Image Has Arisen." A bonfire was lit to signal the moment and to pass the news to neighboring towns. Before the night was over the whole land was ablaze with bonfires; and in the morning, prayers of thanksgiving were recited.

The care and great astronomical knowledge that were required for building temples in Sumer are evident from the inscriptions of the Sumerian King Gudea (circa 2200 B.C.). First there appeared to him "a man who shone like the heaven," who was standing beside a "divine bird." This being, Gudea wrote, "who by the crown on his head was obviously a god," turned out to have been the god Ningirsu. He was accompanied by a goddess who "held the tablet of her favorable star of the heavens." In her other hand she held "a holy stylus" with which she pointed out to the king "the favorable planet." A third human-looking god held in his hands a tablet made of precious stone, on which the plan of the temple was drawn. One of Gudea's statues shows him seated with this tablet on his knees. The divine drawing can be clearly seen; it provides the floor plan of the temple and a scale by which to erect the seven stages, one shorter than the other as they rise. And it was, the text indicates, not a Solar but a Start + Planet Temple.

The sophisticated astronomical knowledge displayed by the Sumerians was not limited to the building of temples. As we have brought out in our previous volumes and as is now generally acknowledged, it was in Sumer that all the concepts and principles of modern spherical astronomy were laid out. The list can begin with the division of a circle into 360 degrees, the devising of zenith, horizon, and other astronomical concepts and terminologies, and end with the grouping of stars into constellations, the devising, naming, and pictorial depiction of the zodiac and its twelve houses, and the recognition of the phenomenon of Precession—the retardation, by about one degree every seventy-two years, of Earth's motion around the sun.

Whereas the Planet of the Gods, Nibiru, appeared and disappeared in the course of its 3,600 Earth-years orbit, Mankind on Earth could count the passage of time only in terms of its own orbit around the Sun. After the phenomenon of day and night the easiest to recognize are the seasons. As the simplest and abundant stone circles attest, it was easy to establish markers delineating the four points in the Earth/Sun relationship: the Sun's apparent rising higher in the skies and lingering longer as winter gives way to spring; a point when day and night appear equal; then the gradual distancing of the Sun as days grow shorter and the temperature begins to drop. As cold and darkness increase and it seems that the Sun may vanish altogether, it hesitates, stops, and begins to come back; and the whole cycle is repeated—a new year has begun. Thus were the four occurrences in the Earth/Sun cycle established: the summer and winter solstices ("solar standstills") when the Sun reaches its outermost positions north and south, and the spring and autumn equinoxes (when day and night are equal).

To relate this apparent movement of the sun in relation to Earth when it is actually Earth that orbits around the Sun—a fact known to and depicted by the Sumerians—it was necessary to provide the observer on Earth with a celestial point of reference. This was achieved by dividing the heavens, the great circle formed by the Earth around the Sun, into twelve parts—the twelve houses of the Zodiac, each with its own group of discernible stars (the constellations). A point was chosen—the spring equinox—and the zodiac house in which the Sun was seen at that moment was declared the first day of the first month of the new year. This, all research of the earliest records show, was in the zodiac house or Age of Taurus.

But then came Precession to spoil the arrangement. Because Earth's axis is inclined in relation to its orbital plane around the Sun (23.5 degrees nowadays) and it spins as a top, the axis points to a shifting celestial spot, forming a great imaginary circle in the heavens that takes 25,920 years to complete. That means that the selected "fixed point," shifting one degree every 72 years, shifts completely from one zodiac house to another every 2,160 years. Some two millennia after the calendar was begun in Sumer, it was necessary to order a reform of the calendar and select as the fixed point the House of Aries. Our astrologers still chart their horoscopes based on the First Point of Aries, although our astronomers know that we have been almost two thousand years in the Age of Pisces (and are about to enter the Age of Aquarius).

The division of the grand celestial circle into twelve parts, in honor of the twelve members of the solar system and the matching pantheon of twelve "Olympian" gods, also brought the solar year into a close correlation with the periodicity of the Moon. But, since the lunar month falls short of filling the solar year exactly twelve times, complex intercalary methods were devised by which to add days once in a while so as to bring the twelve lunar months into alignment with the solar year.

By Babylonian times, in the second millennium B.C., temples required a triple alignment: to the new zodiac (Aries), to the matching four solar points (the most important of which, in Babylon, was the spring equinox), and to the lunar period. The principal temple of Babylon honoring its national god Marduk, the remains of which have been found in relatively good preservation, exemplifies all these astronomical principles. Texts have also been found that describe in architectural terms its twelve gates and seven stages, enabling scholars to reconstruct its serviceability as a sophisticated solar, lunar, planetary, and stellar observatory (Fig. 81).

That astronomy, combined with archaeology, can help date monuments, explain historical events, and define the celestial origins of religious beliefs, has been recongized fully only in recent years. It took almost a century for this realization to reach the level of a discipline called archaeoastronomy, for it was in 1894 that Sir Norman Lockyer (*The Dawn of Astronomy*) showed convincingly that at all times and almost everywhere—from the earliest shrines to the greatest cathedrals—the temples have been oriented astronomically. It is noteworthy that the idea had occurred to him due to "a remarkable thing: in Babylon, from the beginning of things, the sign for God was a star"; likewise, in Egypt, "in the hieroglyphic texts, three stars repre-

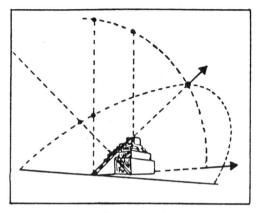

Figure 81

sented the plural 'gods.'" He also noted that in the Hindu pantheon, the most venerated temple gods were *Indra* ("The Day
Brought by the Sun") and *Ushas* ("Dawn"), gods related to the
rising of the Sun.

Focusing on Egypt, where ancient temples still stand and
their architecture and orientation can be studied in detail,
Lockyer recognized that temples in antiquity were either Sun
Temples or Star Temples. The former were temples whose axis
and ritual or calendric functions aligned them with either the
solstices of the equinoxes; the latter were temples not connected
with any of the four Sun points, but designed to observe and
venerate the appearance of a certain star on a certain day at a
certain point on the horizon. Lockyer found it amazing that the
older the temples were, the more sophisticated their astronomy
had been. Thus, at the beginning of their civilization, the Egyptians were able to combine a stellar aspect (the brightest star
then, Sirius) with a solar event (the summer solstice) and with
the annual rising of the Nile. Lockyer calculated that the triple
coincidence could happen only once in about 1,460 years, and
that the Egyptian Point Zero, when their calendrical count
began, was circa 3200 B.C.

But Lockyer's principal contribution to what (after almost a
century!) had evolved into archaeoastronomy was the realization that the orientation of ancient temples could be a clue to
the exact time of their construction. His major example was the
complex of temples at Thebes in Upper Egypt (Karnak). There
the older, more sophisticated orientation of the earliest sacred
cities (to the equinoxes) had given way to the easier orientation
toward the solstices. At Karnak the Great Temple to Amon-Ra

consisted of two rectangular structures built back-to-back on an east–west axis with a southern tilt (Fig. 82). The orientation was such that at solstice time a beam of sunlight would travel the whole length of a corridor (some five hundred feet long), passing from one part of the temple to the other between two obelisks. And, for a couple of minutes, the sunbeam would strike the Holy of Holies with a flash of light at the far end of the corridor, thereby signaling the moment when the first day of the first month began the new year.

But that precise moment was not constant; it kept shifting, resulting in the construction of subsequent temples with modified orientations. When the orientation was based on the equinoxes, the shifting was the varying stellar background against which the Sun was seen—the shift in zodiacal "ages" due to precession. But there appeared to be another and more profound shift affecting the solstices: the angle between the extremes to which the sun seemed to wander kept diminishing! Over time, the Sun's movements seemed subject to yet another phenomenon in the Earth/Sun relationship. This was the discov-

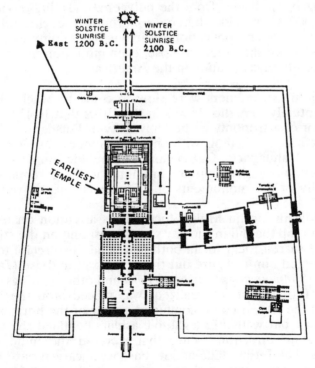

Figure 82

ery by astronomers that the Earth's obliquity, the tilt of its axis against its orbital path around the sun, has not always been its present one (somewhat under 23.5 degrees). The Earth's wobble changes this tilt by about 1 degree over 7,000 years or so, decreasing to perhaps 21 degrees before it starts to increase again to well over 24 degrees. Rolf Müller, who applied this fact to Andean archaeology (*Der Himmel über dem Menschen der Steinzeit* and other studies) calculated that if archaeological remains were oriented to a tilt of 24 degrees, it means they were built at least 4,000 years ago.

The application of this sophisticated and independent dating method is as important as the innovation of radiocarbon dating —perhaps even more so, since radiocarbon tests can be made only on organic materials (such as wood or charcoal) found in or near buildings, which does not preclude an unknown earlier age for the building; but archaeoastronomy can date the building itself and even the times when different parts were constructed.

Professor Müller, whose work we shall examine more closely, concluded that the perfect ashlar structures at Machu Picchu and Cuzco (as distant from the polygonal megalithic ones) are over 4,000 years old, thereby confirming the chronology of Montesinos. Such application of archaeoastronomy to Andean remains, as we shall see, has upset even more notions regarding the antiquity of civilization in the Americas.

Modern astronomers were slow to come to Machu Picchu, but eventually they did. It was in the 1930s that Rolf Müller, a professor of astronomy at the University of Potsdam, published his first studies dealing with the astronomical aspects of the ruins of Tiahuanacu, Cuzco, and Machu Picchu. His conclusions, establishing the great antiquity of these remains, and especially of the monuments of Tiahuanacu, nearly ruined his career.

At Machu Picchu Müller focused his attention on the Intihuatana atop the hill in the city's northwest and on the structure atop the sacred rock, for in both places he saw precise features that enabled him to figure out their purposes and use (*Die Intiwatana (Sonnenwarten) im Alten Peru* and other writings).

The Intihuatana, he realized, was placed atop the highest point of the city. It could command a view of the horizon in all directions; but walls of megalithic ashlars confined the view to only certain directions, ones that were in the mind of the builders. The Intihuatana and its base were carved out of a single natural rock, raising the pillar or stub of the artifact to the desired height. Both the stub and the base were carved and

oriented in a precise manner (see Fig. 76). Müller determined
that the various inclined surfaces and angled sides were so devised as to enable the determination of sunset at the summer
solstice, sunrise at the winter solstice, and of the spring and
autumn equinoxes.

Before his investigations at Machu Picchu Müller had researched at length the archaeoastronomical aspects of Tiahuanacu and at Cuzco. An old Spanish woodcut (Fig. 83a) suggested
to him that the great Temple of the Sun at Cuzco was so constructed as to allow the sun's rays to shine directly into the Holy
of Holies at the moment of sunrise on the day of the winter
solstice. Applying the theories of Lockyer to the Coricancha,
Müller was able to calculate and show how the pre-Columbian
walls together with the circular Holy of Holies were able to
serve the same purpose as the temples of Egypt (Fig. 83b).

The first aspect of the structure atop the sacred rock in

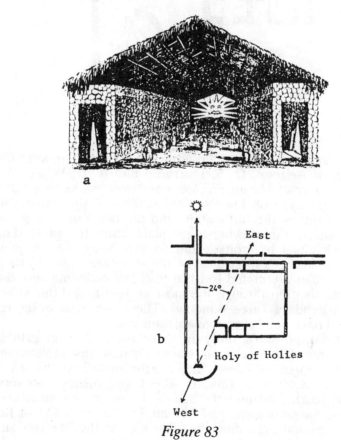

Figure 83

Machu Picchu that is obvious is its semicircular shape and the perfect ashlars of which it is built. These are obvious similarities to the semicircular Holy of Holies in Cuzco (we have already stated our opinion, that the one at Machu Picchu preceded that of Cuzco); and to Müller that suggested at once a similar function—that of determining the winter solstice. After establishing that the straight walls of this structure were oriented by its architects according to the geographic location and elevation above sea level of the site, he determined that the two trapezoid windows in the circular portion (Fig. 84) enabled an observer to see through them sunrise at the summer and winter solstices— 4,000 years ago!

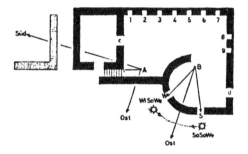

Figure 84

In the 1980s two astronomers from the Steward Observatory, University of Arizona, D. S. Dearborn and R. E. White (*Archaeoastronomy at Machu Picchu*) went over the same ground with more precise instruments. They confirmed the astronomical orientations of the Intihuatana and the two windows in the Torreon (where the viewing takes place from the protruding sacred rock along its grooves and edges). They did not join, however, in Müller's discussion of the structure's age. Neither they nor Müller attempted to trace back, to millennia ago, the lines of observation through the most ancient megalithic structure, the legendary Three Windows. There, we believe, the results would have been even more astounding.

Müller did, however, study the orientation of the megalithic walls in Cuzco. His conclusion, whose far-reaching implications have been ignored, was that "they are positioned for the era of 4000 B.C. to 2000 B.C." (*Sonne, Mond und Sterne über dem Reich der Inka*). This puts the age of the megalithic structures (at Cuzco, Sacsahuaman, and Machu Picchu, at least) in the 2,000-year period preceding the 2000 B.C. of the Torreon and

Intihuatana at Machu Picchu. In other words, Müller concluded that the structures from the pre-Inca period stretch over two zodiac ages: the megalithic ones belonging to the Age of Taurus, the ones from the time of the Ancient Empire and the hiatus at Tampu-Tocco being from the Age of Aries.

In the ancient Near East the shift caused by precession required periodic reform of the original Sumerian calendar. A major change, accompanied by major religious upheavals, took place circa 2000 B.C. with the transition from the zodiac of the Bull to that of the Ram. To others' (but not our own) amazement, such changeovers and reforms are also evidenced in the Andes.

That the ancient Andean people had a calendar should have been a foregone conclusion from the writings of Montesinos and other chroniclers who referred to repeated reforms of the calendar by various monarchs. It took however several studies, beginning in the 1930s, to confirm that these people not only had a calendar but also recorded it (though they were supposed to have no writing). A pioneer in the field, Fritz Buck (*Inscripciones Calendarias del Peru Preincaico* and other writings) produced archaeological evidence to support such conclusions, such as a mace that was a time-reckoning instrument and a vase, found in the ruins of the temple of Pachacamac, that denoted four periods of twelve with the aid of line and dot markings akin to those of the Maya and Olmecs.

According to Father Molina, the Incas "commenced to count the year in the middle of May, a few days more or less, on the first of the moon. They went to the Coricancha in the morning, at noon, and at night, bringing the sheep that were to be sacrificed that day." During the sacrifices, the priests chanted hymns, saying "O Creator, O Sun, O Thunder, be forever young and do not grow old; let all things be at peace; let the people multiply and their food and all things continue to be abundant."

Because the Gregorian calendar was introduced in Cuzco only after Molina's time, the day of the New Year related by him corresponds to May 25 or thereabouts. Observation towers that had been described by Garcilaso have been discovered in recent years by astronomers from the universities of Texas and Illinois; they found that the sighting lines were proper for May 25. According to the chroniclers the Incas considered their year to begin at the winter solstice (equivalent to the summer solstice in the northern hemisphere). But this event occurs not in May, but on June 21 . . . a difference of a full month!

The only plausible explanation for this can come from a recognition that the calendar and the system for observation on which it was based were bequeathed to the Incas from an earlier Age: a retardation by one month results from the precessional shift that lasts 2,160 years per zodiac house.

The Intihuatana at Machu Picchu, as we have mentioned, served to determine not only the solstices but also the equinoxes (when daylight and nighttime are equal when the Sun is over the Equator, in March and September). Both the chroniclers and modern researchers (such as L. E. Valcarel, *The Andean Calendar*) report that the Incas went to great lengths to determine the precise days of the equinoxes and venerated them. This custom must have also stemmed from earlier times, for we read in the early reports that the monarchs of the Ancient Empire were preoccupied with the need to determine the equinoxes.

Montesinos informs us that the fortieth monarch of the Ancient Empire established an academy for the study of astronomy and astrology and determined the equinoxes. The fact that he was given the title *Pachacutec* indicates that the calendar was at that time so much out of synchronization with the celestial phenomena that its reform became imperative. This is a most interesting bit of information that has been totally neglected. According to Montesinos, it was in the fifth year of this monarch's reign that 2500 years from Point Zero had been completed—and 2,000 years from the beginning of the ancient empire.

What was happening circa 400 B.C. that required a reform of the calendar? The length of the time span, 2000 years, parallels the time spans of zodiacal shifts due to precession. In the ancient Near East, when the calendar was begun at Nippur circa 4000 B.C., the spring equinox occurred in the House or Age of Taurus. It retarded to that of Aries circa 2000 B.C. and to Pisces by Christ's time.

The Andean reform circa 400 B.C. confirms that the ancient empire and its calendar indeed began circa 2500 B.C. It also suggests that those monarchs were familiar with the zodiac; but the zodiac was a purely artificial and arbitrary division of the celestial band around the Sun into twelve parts; a Sumerian invention that had been adopted in the Old World by all the peoples who had succeeded them (to this very day). Was this possible? The answer is yes.

One of the pioneers in the field, S. Hagar, in a lecture delivered to the fourteenth Congress of Americanists in 1904, titled "The Peruvian Asterisms and their Relation to the Ritual," showed that the Incas not only were familiar with the zodiac houses (and their parallel months) but also had distinct names for them. The names, to scholars' surprise but not to ours, bear

an uncanny resemblance to the ones with which we are all familiar and which originated in Sumer. Thus, January, the month of
Aquarius, was dedicated to *Mama Cocha* and *Capac Cocha,*
Mother Water and Lord Water. March, the month of Aries
when the first moon signified in antiquity New Year's eve, was
called *Katu Quilla,* Market Moon. April, Taurus, was named
Tupa Taruca, Pasturing Stag (there were no bulls in South
America). Virgo was *Sara Mama* (Maize Mother) and its symbol was the female member; and so on.

Indeed, Cuzco itself was a testimonial in stone both to the
familiarity with the twelve-house zodiac and the antiquity of
that knowledge. We have already mentioned the division of
Cuzco into twelve wards and their association with the zodiac
houses. It is significant that he first ward, on the slopes of Sacsahuaman, was associated with Aries. For Aries to have been
associated with the spring equinox, as we have shown, we have
to turn the clock back more than 4,000 years.

One must wonder whether the knowledge required for such
astronomical information and calendar reforms could have been
retained and passed along over so many millennia without some
kind of record-keeping, without being written down in some
form. The Maya codices contained, as we have seen, astronomical data copied and obtained from earlier sources. Archaeologists have determined that oblong bars held by Maya rulers (as
depicted on their stelae) were actually "sky bars" that spelled
out the glyphs for certain constellations of the zodiac (as was the
series of glyphs framing the image of Pacal on the lid of his
coffin, at Palenque). Were these artful depictions from the classic period copied from earlier, perhaps less artistically refined,
calendrical records? This is suggested by a round stone found at
Tikal (Fig. 85a) on which the image of the Sun God (with beard
and tongue out) is surrounded by celestial glyphs.

Such "primitive" calendar-zodiac circular stones must have
preceded the perfected Aztec "calendar stones," several of
which have been found and a golden one of which, the most
hallowed of all, was presented to Cortés by Moctezuma when
the latter believed that he was only returning to the God of the
Plumed Serpent what was his.

Were there such records—in gold—in existence in ancient
Peru? In spite of the treatment meted out by the Spaniards to
anything connected with the "idols," and especially if the object
was made of gold (which was quickly melted down, as had happened to the Image of the sun from the Coricancha), at least
one such relic remains.

It is a golden disk, about 5½ inches in diameter (Fig. 85b).

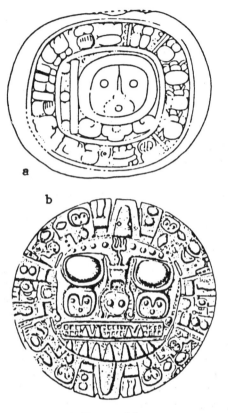

Figure 85

Discovered in Cuzco and now lodged in the Museum of the American Indian in New York, it was described over a century ago by Sir Clemens Markham (*Cuzco and Lima; The Incas of Peru*). He concluded that the disk represented the sun in the center and had twenty distinct symbols around it; he took them to stand for months, akin to the Maya calendar of twenty months. W. Bollaert, in a lecture before the Royal Society of Antiquarians in 1860 and subsequent writings, considered the disk to be "a lunar calendar or a zodiac." M. H. Saville (*A Golden Breastplate from Cuzco,* in the Museum's 1921 publication) pointed out that six of the encircling signs are repeated twice and two are repeated four times (he marked them from A to H) and therefore doubted the validity of Markham's twenty-month theory.

The simple fact that six times two is twelve leads us to agree with Bollaert, and to suggest that this is a zodiacal tablet rather than one of months. All scholars agree that this artifact is from pre-Inca times. None have shown, however, how similar it is to the calendar stone discovered at Tikal—perhaps because it would add another nail to the coffin in which the notion that there had been no contact, no "diffusion" between Mesoamerica and South America, must be laid to rest.

It was early in 1533 that a small band of soldiers from Pizarro's landing party had entered Cuzco, the Inca capital. The main body of Pizarro's force was still at Cajamarca, where they held the pretender, Atahualpa, prisoner; and the mission of the band sent to Cuzco was to get the capital's contribution to the golden ransom demanded by the Spaniards in exchange for Atahualpa's freedom.

In Cuzco, Atahualpa's general Quizquiz allowed them to enter and examine several important buildings, including the Temple of the Sun; the Incas, as we have mentioned, called it the *Coricancha,* the Golden Enclosure, for its walls were covered with golden plates and within the walls there had been wondrous artifacts of gold, silver, and precious stones. The few Spaniards who had entered Cuzco removed seven hundred gold plates and helped themselves to other treasure and returned to Cajamarca.

The main Spanish force entered Cuzco at the end of that year; and we have already described the fate that befell the city, its edifices, and its shrines, including the desecration of the Holy of Holies and the looting, then melting down, of the Golden Emblem of the sun that hung above the Great Altar.

But the physical destruction could not eradicate what the Incas retained in their memories. The Coricancha was built, the Incas recalled, by the very first monarch; it began as a hut with a thatched roof. Later monarchs enlarged and enhanced it, until it assumed the final dimensions and shape as seen by the Spaniards. In the Holy of Holies, they related, the walls were covered from floor to ceiling with plates of gold. "Over what was called the High Altar," Garcilaso wrote, "was the image of the Sun on a gold plate twice the thickness of the rest of the wall plates. The image showed it with a round face and beams and flames of fire, all in one piece."

That indeed was the golden object that the Spaniards had seen and removed. But it was not the original image that had dominated the wall, facing the sun's beam at sunrise on the designated day.

The most detailed description of the centerpiece and its accompanying images was provided by Don Juan de Santa Cruz Pachacuti-Yumqui Salcamayhua, the son of a royal Inca princess and a Spanish nobleman (which is why he is sometimes referred to as Santa Cruz and sometimes as Salcamayhua). The account was included in his *Relacion* (English translation by Sir Clemens Markham) in which he set out to glorify the royal Inca dynasty in the eyes of the Spanish. It was the first king of the Inca dynasty, Salcamayhua stated, who had "ordered the smiths to make a flat plate of gold which signified that there was a creator of heaven and earth." Salcamayhua illustrated his text with a drawing: it was the unusual and rare shape of an oval.

That first image was replaced by a round plate when a certain monarch later declared the Sun supreme. It was changed back to an oval image by a subsequent Inca, "a great enemy of idols; he ordered his people not to pay honors to the Sun and Moon"; rather, to the celestial body represented by the oval shape; it was he who had "caused images to be put around the plate." Referring to the oval shape as "The Creator," Salcamayhua made it clear that it did not mean the Sun, for the images of the sun and the Moon had flanked the oval. To illustrate what he meant, Salcamayhua drew a large oval flanked by two smaller circles.

The centerpiece stayed that way, with the oval as the superior image, until the time of the Inca Huascar, one of the two half brothers involved in the struggle for the throne when the Spaniards arrived. He removed the oval image and replaced it "with a round plate, like the Sun with rays." "Huascar Inca had placed an image of the Sun in the place where the Creator had been." Thereby, the alternating religious tenets changed back to a pantheon in which the Sun, not Viracocha, was supreme. To signify that he was the proper successor to the throne, Huascar added to his name the epithet *Inti* ("Sun"), meaning that it was he, and not his half brother, who was a true offspring of the original Sons of the Sun.

Explaining that the gabled wall with the oval as its principal image represented "what the heathens thought" regarding the heavens and the earth, Salcamayhua drew a large sketch showing how the wall had looked before Huascar replaced the oval shape with the Sun's image. The sketch has survived because Francisco de Avila, who had questioned Salcamayhua and others about the meaning of the depictions, kept it among his papers. He also scribbled on and around the sketch notations explaining the images, using the Quechus and Aymara terms given by the natives and his own Castilian Spanish: When these notations are removed (Fig. 86) one gets a clear picture of what had been depicted above the altar (the long crisscrossed object at the bottom): terrestrial symbols (people, an animal, a river, mountains, a lake, etc.) in the bottom part; celestial images (Sun, Moon, stars, the enigmatic oval, etc.) in the upper part.

Scholars have both agreed and disagreed regarding the interpretation of the individual symbols, but not about the overall meaning of the sacred wall. Markham saw in the upper part "a stellar chart which is a veritable key to the symbolical cosmogony and astronomy of ancient Peru," and was certain that the gabled triangular tip was a hieroglyph for "sky." S. K. Lothrop (*Inca Treasure*) stated that the images above the great altar "formed a cosmogonic tale of the creation of heaven and earth, the Sun and Moon, the first Man and Woman." All are agreed that, as Salcamayhua had stated, it represented "what the heathens thought"—the sum total of their religious beliefs and legendary tales; a saga of Heaven and Earth and the bond between them.

The celestial assembly of images clearly depicts the Sun and the Moon flanking the golden oval plate, and groups of heavenly bodies above and below the oval. That the two flanking star symbols stand for the Sun and Moon is clarified by the conventional faces drawn above them plus the notations in the native tongue, *Inti* (Sun) and *Quilla* (Moon).

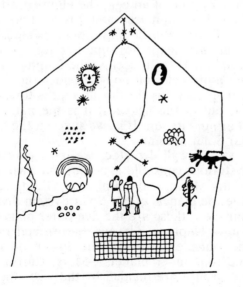

Figure 86

Since the Sun was thus depicted, what did the central image, the great oval, represent? The tales describe how this symbol alternated with the Sun in being worshiped and venerated in Inca times. Its identity is clearly explained by a notation that reads, *"Illa Ticci Uuiracocha, Pachac Acachi. Quiere decir imagen del Hacedor del cielo y de la tierra."* Translated, it means "Illa Ticci Viracocha, Maker of All; that is to say, image of the Creator of Heaven and Earth."

But why was Viracocha depicted as an oval?

One of the principal researchers of the subject, R. Lehmann-Nitsche (*Coricancha—El Templo del Sol en el Cuzco y las Imagenes de su Altar Mayor*) developed the thesis that the oval shape represented the "Cosmic Egg," a theogonic idea that is echoed in Greek legends, in Hindu religions, "even in Genesis." It is "the oldest theogony whose details have not been grasped by white authors." It had been represented in the sanctuaries of the Indo-European deity Mithra as an egg surrounded by the constellations of the zodiac. "Perhaps one day Indianologists will see the similarities in the details and cult of Viracocha, Brahma with the seven eyes, and the Israelite Yahweh... In the classic antiquity and in the Orphic cult there were sacred images of the Mystic Egg; why shouldn't the same happen in the great sanctuary of Cuzco?"

Lehmann-Nitsche thought of a Cosmic Egg as the only explanation for the unusual use of an oval shape, for apart from its similarity to the outline of an egg, the elliptical shape (which is difficult to draw or fashion accurately) is not found naturally on the face of the Earth. But he and others seemed to ignore the fact that the elliptical shape has superimposed on it (at the bottom) a star symbol. If, as it seems, the elliptical or oval shape applies to one more celestial body (besides the five above and four below), it spells to us the "oval" that is found in nature—not on Earth, but in the heavens: it is the natural curve of a planet's orbit around its sun. It is, we suggest, the orbital path of a planet in our Solar System.

What the sacred wall depicted, we must conclude, was not distant or mysterious constellations, but our own Solar System, with the Sun, the Moon, and ten planets, adding up to a total of twelve. We see the planets of our Solar System divided into two groups. In our view, these are the five outer planets on the distant side—Pluto, Neptune, Uranus, Saturn and Jupiter (counting from the outside inward). The lower or nearer group represents the four inner planets—Mars, Earth, Venus, Mercury. The two groups are divided by the vast elliptical orbit of the twelfth member of the Solar System. To the Incas, it represented the celestial Viracocha.

Should we be surprised to find that this was exactly the Sumerian view of our Solar System?

As the depictions descend from the heavens toward Earth, a starry sky is shown on the wall's right and clouds on the left. Scholars agree with the original notations, "summer" (bright starry skies) and "winter clouds." In considering the seasons part of the creative act, the Inca depiction again follows the Near Eastern pattern. The earth's tilt (causing the seasons) was attributed in Sumer to Nibiru and in Babylon to Marduk. The concept was echoed when the Psalmist sang of the biblical Lord, "Thou hast made summer and winter."

Below "summer" there appears a star symbol; a fierce animal is shown below "winter." It is generally agreed that these images represent the constellations associated (in the southern hemisphere) with these seasons, the one for winter representing Leo (the Lion). This is amazing in more than one way. First, because there are no lions in South America. Second, because when the calendar was begun in Sumer in the fourth millennium B.C. the summer solstice there occurred when the Sun was seen in the zodiac constellation of the Lion (UR.GULA in Sumerian). But in the southern hemisphere that time of year would have been *winter*. So that the Inca depiction borrowed not only the idea of twelve zodiac constellations, but also their seasonal order in Mesopotamia!

We now arrive at the symbols that—as in the *Enuma Elish* and in the Book of Genesis—transfer the tales of creation from the heavens to Earth: the first Man and Woman, Eden, a large river, a serpent, mountains, a sacred lake. An Incan "panorama of the world," in the words of Lehmann-Nitsche. It would be more accurate to say, the Pictorial Bible of the Andes.

The analogy is actual, not just figurative. The elements in this part of the pictorial composition could well serve to illustrate the Mesopotamian-biblical tales of Adam and Eve in the Garden of Eden, complete with the serpent (on the wall's right) and the Tree of Life (on the wall's left). The Sumerian E.DIN (from which *Eden* stems) was the valley of the great river Euphrates, emanating from the high mountains in the north. This geography is clearly depicted on the wall's right, where a globe representing Earth bears the notation "Pacha Mama"— Mother Earth. Even the Rainbow, which featured in the Near Eastern tales of the Deluge, is shown here.

(While all accept that the globe or circle marked Pacha

Mama represents the Earth, none have stopped to wonder how the Incas knew that the Earth was round. The Sumerians, however, were aware of the fact and depicted the Earth and all the other planets accordingly.)

The group of seven dots below the Earth symbol has given scholars endless problems. Adhering to the erroneous notion that the ancients conceived of the Pleiades as numbering seven stars, some have suggested that the symbol represents that portion of the constellation Taurus. But if so, the symbol belongs in the upper, celestial portion of the panel, not at its bottom. Lehmann-Nitsche and others interpreted the seven-symbol as "the seven eyes of the supreme god." But we have already shown that the seven dots, the number seven, was the designation of Earth itself in the Sumerian enumeration of the planets. The symbol "seven" is thus exactly where it belongs, as a caption for the globe of the Earth.

The last image on the sacred wall is that of a great lake connected by a waterway to a smaller body of water. The notation on its states, "Mama Cocha," Mother Water. All are agreed that this represents the Andean sacred lake, Lake Titicaca. By depicting it, the Incas had taken the story of Creation from the Heavens to Earth and from the Garden of Eden to the Andes.

Lehmann-Nitsche summed up the meaning and message of the composite depiction on the wall above the Great Altar by saying, "it takes man from the ground to the stars." It is doubly amazing that it takes the Incas to the other side of the Earth.

9

CITIES LOST AND FOUND

The discovery of the story of Genesis, in its original Mesopotamian version, depicted on the Inca temple's Holy of Holies, raises a host of questions. The first obvious one is, How—how did the Incas come to know these tales, not just in the general manner in which they have become known universally (the creation of the first couple, the Deluge), but in a manner that follows the Epic of Creation including knowledge of the complete Solar System and the orbit of Nibiru?

One possible answer is that the Incas had possessed this knowledge from time immemorial, bringing it with them to the Andes. The other possibility is that they had heard it from others whom they met in these lands.

In the absence of written records as one finds in the ancient Near East, the choice of an answer depends to some extent on how one answers another question: Who, indeed, were the Incas?

The *Relacion* of Salcamayhua is a good example of the Incas' attempt to perpetuate an exercise in state propaganda: the attribution of the revered named *Manco Capac* to the first Inca monarch, Inca Rocca, in order to make the people they had subjugated believe that the first Inca was the original "Son of the Sun," fresh out of the sacred Lake Titicaca. In fact, the Inca dynasty began some 3,500 years after that hallowed beginning. Also, the language that the Incas spoke was Quechua, the language of the people of the central-north Andes, whereas in the highlands of Lake Titicaca the people spoke Aymara. That, and other considerations, have led some scholars to speculate that the Incas were latecomers who had arrived from the east, settling in the Cuzco valley that borders on the great Amazon plain.

175

That, in itself, does not rule out a Near Eastern origin or link for the Incas. While attention has been focused on the depiction on the wall above the High Altar, no one has wondered why, in the midst of peoples who had made images of their gods and who placed their idols in shrines and temples, there was no idol whatsoever in the great Inca temple, nor in any other Inca shrine.

The chroniclers related that an "idol" was carried during some celebrations, but it was the image of Manco Capac, not of a god. They also relate that on a certain holy day a priest would go to a distant mountain upon which there stood a large idol of a god, and would sacrifice there a llama. But the mountain and its idol were from pre-Inca times, and the reference could well be to the temple of Pachacamac on the coast (regarding which we have already written).

Interestingly, the two customs are in line with biblical commandments from the time of the Exodus. The prohibition against making and worshiping idols was included in the Ten Commandments. And on the eve of the Day of Atonement, a priest had to sacrifice a "sin-goat" in the desert. No one has ever pointed out that the *quipos* used by the Incas to recall events—strings of different colors that had to be of wool, with knots at different positions—were in make and purpose akin to the *tzitzit*, "fringes on the corner of a blue thread," that the Israelites were commanded to attach to their garments as a way to remember the Lord's commandments. There is the matter of the rules of succession, by which the legal heir was the son by a half sister—a Sumerian custom followed by the Hebrew patriarchs. And there was the custom of circumcision in the Inca royal family.

Peruvian archaeologists have reported intriguing finds in the Amazonian provinces of Peru, including the apparent remains of stone-built cities, especially in the valleys of the Utcubamba and Marañón rivers. There are undoubtedly "lost cities" in the tropical zones; but in some instances the announced discoveries are really expeditions to known sites. Such was the case of headline news from Gran Patajen in 1985—a site visited by the Peruvian archaeologist F. Kauffmann-Doig and the American Gene Savoy twenty years earlier. There have been reports of aerial sightings of "pyramids" on the Brazilian side of the border, of lost cities such as Akakor, and Indians' tales of ruins holding untold treasures. A document in the national archives in Rio de Janeiro is purportedly an eighteenth-century report recording a lost city in the Amazon jungles seen by Europeans in 1591; the document even transcribes a script found there. It was the main reason for an expedition by Colonel Percy Fawcett whose mysterious disappearance in the jungles is still a subject of popular-science articles.

All this is not to say that there are no ancient ruins in the Amazon basin that remain from a trail across the South American continent from Guiana/Venezuela to Ecuador/Peru. Humboldt's reports of his travels across the continent mention a tradition that people from across the sea landed in Venezuela and proceeded inland; and the principal river of the Cuzco valley, the Urubamba, is but a tributary of the Amazon. Official Brazilian teams have visited many sites (without, however, conducting sustained excavations). At one site near the mouth of the Amazon, pottery urns decorated with incised patterns that remind one of the designs on earthenware jars from Ur (the Sumerian birthplace of Abraham) have been found. An islet called Pacoval appeared to have been artificially created, and served as a base for a number of mounds (which were not excavated). According to L. Netto, *Investigacioes sobre a Archaeologia Braziliera,* similarly decorated urns and vases "of superior quality" have been found farther up the Amazon. And, we believe, an equally important route connecting the Andes with the Atlantic Ocean did exist farther to the south.

Still, it is uncertain that the Incas themselves came this way. One of their ancestry versions attributes their beginnings to a landing on the Peruvian coast. Their language, Quechua, bears Far Eastern resemblances both in word meanings and dialect. And they clearly belong to the Amerindian stock—the fourth branch of mankind that, we have ventured to suggest, stemmed from the line of Cain. (A guide in Cuzco, hearing of our biblical expertise, asked whether *In-ca* might have stemmed from *Ca-in* by reversing the syllables. One wonders!)

The evidence at hand, we believe, indicates that the Near Eastern tales and beliefs, including knowledge of the story of Nibiru and the Anunnaki who had come from there to Earth— the pantheon of twelve—were brought to the predecessors of the Incas from overseas. It took place in the days of the Ancient Empire; and the bearers of these tales and beliefs were also Strangers From Across the Seas, but not necessarily the same ones who brought similar tales, beliefs, and civilization to Mesoamerica.

In addition to all the facts and evidence that we had already provided, let us return to Izapa, a site near the Pacific coast where Mexico and Guatemala meet and where the Olmecs and the Maya rubbed shoulders. Recognized only belatedly as the largest site along the Pacific coast of North or Central America, it spans 2500 years of continuous occupation, from 1500 B.C. (a date confirmed by carbon dating) to A.D. 1000. It had the customary pyramids and ball courts; but it has mostly amazed archaeologists by its carved stone monuments. The style, imagination, mythical content and artistic perfection of these carvings have come to be called "Izapan style," and it is now recognized that it was the source from which the style spread to other sites along the Pacific slopes of Mexico and Guatemala. It was art belonging to the Early and Middle Preclassic Olmec, adopted by the Maya as the site changed hands.

Archaeologists from the New World Archaeological Foundation of Brigham Young University, who have devoted decades to the excavation and study of the site, have no doubt that it was oriented toward the solstices at the time of its foundation and that even the various monuments were placed "on deliberate alignments with planetary movements" (V. G. Norman, *Izapa Sculpture*). Religious, cosmological, and mythological themes intermingled with historical subjects are expressed in the stone carvings. We have already seen (Fig. 51b) one of the many and varied depictions of winged deities. Of particular interest here is a large carved stone whose face measures some thirty square feet, designated by the archaeologists Izapa Stela 5, found in conjunction with a major stone altar. The complicated scene (Fig. 87) has been recognized by various scholars as a "fantastic

Figure 87

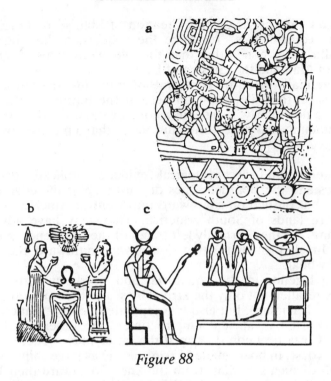

Figure 88

visual myth" concerning the "genesis of humanity" at a Tree of Life that grows by a river. The mythical-historical tale is told by an old bearded man seated on the left, and is retold by a Maya-looking man on the right (of the stela's observer).

The scene is filled with diverse vegetation, birds, and fish as well as human figures. Interestingly, two central figures represent men that have the face and feet of elephants—an animal completely unknown in the Americas. The one on the left is shown in association with a helmeted Olmec man, which reinforces our contention that the colossal stone heads and the Olmecs they portrayed were Africans.

The left-hand panel, when enlarged (Fig. 88a), clearly reveals details which we consider extremely important clues. The bearded man tells his story over an altar that bears the symbol of the umbilical cutter; this was the symbol (Fig. 88b) by which Ninti (the Sumerian goddess who had helped Enki create Man) was identified on cylinder seals and on monuments. When the Earth was divided among the gods she was given dominion over the Sinai peninsula, the Egyptians' source of their cherished blue-green turquoise; they called her Hathor and depicted her with cow's horns, as on this Creation of Man scene (Fig. 88c). These "coincidences" reinforce the conclusion that the Izapa stela illustrates none other than the Old World tales of the Creation of Man and the Garden of Eden.

And finally there are portrayals of pyramids, smooth sided as at Giza on the Nile, depicted here at the bottom of the panel beside a flowing river. Indeed, as one examines and reexamines this millennia-old panel, one must agree that a picture is worth a thousand words.

Legends and archaeological evidence indicate that the Olmecs and the Bearded Ones did not stop at the edge of the ocean, but pushed on southward into Central America and the northern lands of South America. They may have advanced overland, for they certainly left traces of their presence at inland sites. In all probability they journeyed southward the easier way, by boats.

The legends in the equatorial and northern parts of the Andes recalled not only the arrival by sea of their own ancestors (such as Naymlap), but also two separate ones by "giants." One had occurred in ancient empirc times, the other in Mochica times. Cieza de Leon described the latter thus: "There arrived on the coast, in boats made of reeds as big as large ships, a party of men of such size that, from the knee downward their height was as great as the entire height of an ordinary man." They had metal tools with which they dug wells in the lving rock, but for food they raided the natives' provisions. They also violated the natives' women, for there were no women among the landing giants. The Mochica depicted these giants who had enslaved them on their pottery, painting their faces in black (Fig. 89) while that of the Mochicas was painted white. Also found in Mochica remains are clay portrayals of older men with white beards.

It is our guess that these unwanted visitors were Olmecs and their bearded Near Eastern companions who were fleeing the uprisings in Mesoamerica, circa 400 B.C. They left behind them a trail of dreaded veneration as they passed through Central America to the equatorial lands farther down in South America. Archaeological expeditions to the equatorial areas of the Pacific coast have found enigmatic monoliths that stem from that fearsome period. The George C. Heye expedition found in Ecuador giant stone heads with humanlike features but with fangs as though they were ferocious jaguars. Another expedition found at San Agustin, a site closer to the Colombian border, stone

Figure 89

statues portraying giants, sometimes shown holding tools or weapons; their facial features are those of the African Olmecs (Fig. 90a, b).

These invaders may have been the source of the legends current also in these lands of how Man was created, of a Deluge, and of a serpent god who demanded an annual tribute of gold. One of the ceremonies recorded by the Spaniards was a ritual dance performed by twelve men dressed in red; it was performed on the shores of a lake connected with the legend of El Dorado.

The equatorial natives worshiped a pantheon of twelve, a number of great significance and an important clue. It was headed by a triad consisting of the Creation God, the Evil God, and the Mother Goddess; and it included the gods of the Moon, the Sun, and the Rain-Thunder. Significantly too, the Moon God ranked higher than the Sun God. The deities' names changed from locality to locality, retaining however the celestial affinity. Among the strange-sounding names, though, two stand out. The head of the pantheon was called in the Chibcha dialect *Abira*—remarkably similar to the Mesopotamian divine epithet *Abir,* which meant Strong, Mighty; and the Moon God, as we have noted, was called "Si" or "Sian," which parallels the Mesopotamian name *Sin* for that deity.

The pantheon of these South American natives therefore brings inevitably to mind the pantheon of the ancient Near East and the eastern Mediterranean—of the Greeks and the Egyptians, the Hittites and the Canaanites and Phoenicians, the Assyrians and the Babylonians—all the way back to where it all

Figure 90

began: to the Sumerians of southern Mesopotamia from whom all others had obtained the gods and their mythologies.

The Sumerian pantheon was headed by an "Olympian Circle" of twelve, for each of these supreme gods had to have a celestial counterpart, one of the twelve members of the Solar System. Indeed, the names of the gods and their planets were one and the same (except when a variety of epithets were used to describe the planet or the god's attributes). Heading the pantheon was the ruler of Nibiru, ANU whose name was synonymous with "Heaven," for he resided on Nibiru. His spouse, also a member of the Twelve, was called ANTU. Included in this group were the two principal sons of ANU: E.A ("Whose House Is Water"), Anu's Firstborn but not by Antu; and EN.LIL ("Lord of the Command") who was the Heir Apparent because his mother was Antu, a half sister of Anu. Ea was also called in Sumerian texts EN.KI ("Lord Earth"), for he had led the first mission of the Anunnaki from Nibiru to Earth and established on Earth their first colonies in the E.DIN ("Home of the Righteous Ones")—the biblical Eden.

His mission was to obtain gold, for which Earth was a unique source. Not for ornamentation or because of vanity, but as a way to save the atmosphere of Nibiru by suspending gold dust in that planet's stratosphere. As recorded in the Sumerian texts (and related by us in *The 12th Planet* and subsequent books of *The Earth Chronicles*), Enlil was sent to Earth to take over the command when the initial extraction methods used by Enki proved unsatisfactory. This laid the groundwork for an ongoing feud between the two half brothers and their descendants, a feud that led to Wars of the Gods; it ended with a peace treaty worked out by their sister Ninti (thereafter renamed Ninharsag). The inhabited Earth was divided between the warring clans. The three sons of Enlil—Ninurta, Sin, Adad—together with Sin's twin children, Shamash (the Sun) and Ishtar (Venus), were given the lands of Shem and Japhet, the lands of the Semites and Indo-Europeans: Sin (the Moon) lowland Mesopotamia; Ninurta, ("Enlil's Warrior," Mars) the highlands of Elam and Assyria; Adad ("The Thunderer," Mercury) Asia Minor (the land of the Hittites) and Lebanon. Ishtar was granted dominion as the goddess of the Indus Valley civilization; Shamash was given command of the spaceport in the Sinai peninsula.

This division, which did not go uncontested, gave Enki and his sons the lands of Ham—the brown/black people—of Africa: the civilization of the Nile Valley and the gold mines of southern and western Africa—a vital and cherished prize. A great scientist and metallurgist, Enki's Egyptian name was *Ptah* ("The Developer"; a title that translated into *Hephaestus* by the Greeks and *Vulcan* by the Romans). He shared the continent with his sons; among them was the firstborn MAR.DUK ("Son of the Bright Mound") whom the Egyptians called *Ra,* and NIN.GISH.ZI.DA ("Lord of the Tree of Life") whom the Egyptians called Thoth (Hermes to the Greeks)—a god of secret knowledge including astronomy, mathematics, and the building of pyramids.

It was the knowledge imparted by this pantheon, the needs of the gods who had come to Earth, and the leadership of Thoth, that directed the African Olmecs and the bearded Near Easterners to the other side of the world.

And having arrived in Mesoamerica on the Gulf coast—just as the Spaniards, aided by the same sea currents, did millennia later—they cut across the Mesoamerican isthmus at its narrowest neck and—just like the Spaniards due to the same geography—sailed down from the Pacific coast of Mesoamerica southward, to the lands of Central America and beyond.

For that is where the gold was, in Spanish times and before.

* * *

Before the Incas and the Chimu and the Mochica, a culture named by scholars Chavin flourished in the mountains that lie in northern Peru between the coast and the Amazon basin. One of its first explorers, Julio C. Tello (*Chavin* and other works) called it "the matrix of Andean civilization." It takes us back to at least 1500 B.C.; and like that of the Olmec civilization in Mexico at the same time, it arose suddenly and with no apparent prior gradual development.

Encompassing a vast area whose dimensions are constantly expanded as new finds are made, the Chavin Culture appeared to have been centered at a site called Chavin de Huantar, near the village of Chavin (and hence the culture's name). It is situated at an elevation of 10,000 feet in the Cordillera Blanca range of the northwestern Andes. There, in a mountain valley where tributaries of the Marañón river form a triangle, an area of some 300,000 square feet was flattened and terraced and made suitable for the construction of complex structures, carefully and precisely laid out according to a preconceived plan that took into consideration the contours and features of the site (Fig. 91a). Not only do the buildings and plazas form precise rectangulars and squares; thcy have also been precisely aligned with the cardinal points, with east–west as the major axis. The three main buildings stood upon terraces that elevated them and leaned against the outer western wall that ran for some 500 feet. The wall that apparently encompassed the complex on three sides, leaving it open to the river that flowed on the east, rose to about forty feet.

The largest building was at the southwest corner, measured about 240 by 250 feet, and consisted of at least three floors (see an artist's bird's-eye-view reconstruction, Fig. 91b). It was built of masonry stone blocks, well shaped but not dressed, laid out in regular and level courses. As some remaining slabs indicate, the walls were faced outside with smooth, marblelike stone slabs; some still retain their incised decorations. From a terrace on the east a monumental stairway led through an imposing gate up toward the main building; the gate was flanked by two cylindrical columns—a most unusual feature in South America— that together with adjoining vertical stone blocks supported a thirty-foot horizontal lintel made of a single monolith. Farther up, a double monumental stairway led to the building's top. This stairway was built of perfectly cut and shaped stones that remind one of the great Egyptian pyramids. The two stairways led to the building's top, where archaeologists have found the remains of two towers; the rest of the uppermost platform remained unbuilt.

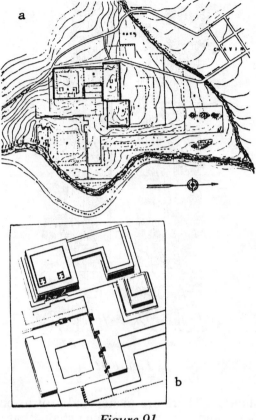

Figure 91

The eastern terrace, forming part of the platform on which this edifice was built, led to (or from) a sunken plaza reached by ceremonial steps and surrounded on three sides by rectangular plazas or platforms. Just outside the southwestern corner of the sunken plaza, and perfectly aligned with the staircases of the main edifice and its terrace, there stood a large flat boulder; it had in it seven grind holes and a rectangular niche.

The exterior's precision was exceeded by the interior complexity. Within the three structures there ran corridors and mazelike passages, intermingled with connecting galleries, rooms, and staircases, or leading to dead ends and therefore nicknamed labyrinths. Some of the galleries have been faced with smooth slabs, here and there delicately decorated; all the passages are roofed with carefully selected stone slabs that have been placed with great ingenuity that prevented their collapse

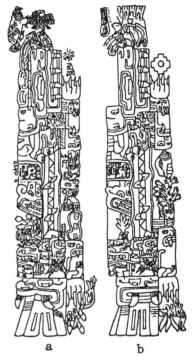

a   b

Figure 92

over the millennia. There are niches and protrusions for no apparent purpose; and vertical or sloping shafts that the archaeologists thought might have served for ventilation.

What was Chavin de Huantar built for? The only plausible
purpose that its discoverers could see was that of a religious
center, a kind of ancient "Mecca." This notion was strengthened
by the three fascinating and most enigmatic relics found at the
site. One that baffles by its complex imagery was discovered by
Tello in the main building and is called the Tello Obelisk (Fig.
92a,b shows the front and back). It is engraved with an agglomeration of human bodies and faces but with feline hands with
fangs or wings. There are animals, birds, trees; gods emitting
rocketlike rays; and a variety of geometric designs. Was this a
totem pole that served for worship, or an attempt by an ancient
"Picasso" to convey all the myths and legends on one column?
No one has yet come up with a plausible answer.

A second carved stone is called the Raimondi Monolith (Fig.
93), after the archaeologist who found it at a nearby estate; it is
believed that it originally stood atop the grooved stone at the

Figure 93

southwestern edge of the sunken plaza, aligned with the monumental stairway. It is now on exhibit in Lima.

The ancient artist carved upon this seven-foot-high granite column the image of a deity holding a weapon—a thunderbolt, some believe—in each hand. While the deity's body and limbs are essentially though not entirely anthropomorphic, the face is not. This face has puzzled scholars because it does not represent or stylize a local creature (such as a jaguar); rather, it appears to be the artist's conception of what scholars conveniently called "a mythological animal," namely one of which the artist had heard but had not actually seen.

To our eyes, however, the deity's face is that of a bull—an animal completely absent in South America but one that featured considerably in the lore and iconography of the ancient Near East. Significantly (in our opinion) it was the "cult animal" of Adad, and the mountain range in his domain, in Asia Minor, is still called to this very day the Taurus Mountains.

A third unusual and enigmatic carved stone column at Chavin de Huantar is called *El Lanzon* because of its lancelike shape (Fig. 94). It was discovered in the middle building and has remained there because its height (twelve feet) exceeds the

Figure 94

ten-foot height of the gallery where it stands; the monolith's top
therefore protrudes into the floor above it through a carefully
cut square opening. The image on this monolith has been the
subject of much speculation; to our eyes, again, it seems to depict an anthropomorphized face of a bull. Does it mean, then,
that whoever erected this monument—obviously *before* the
building was constructed, for the latter was built to accommodate the statue—worshiped the Bull God?

It was by and large the high artistic level of the artifacts
rather than the complex and unusual structures that so impressed scholars and led them to consider Chavin the "matrix
culture" of north-central Peru, and to believe that the site was a
religious center. But that the purpose was not religious but
rather utilitarian seems to be indicated by recent finds at Chavin
de Huantar. These latest excavations revealed a network of subterranean tunnels hewed out of the native rock; they honeycombed the whole site, both under built as well as unbuilt parts,
and served to connect several series of underground compartments arranged in a chainlike manner (Fig. 95).

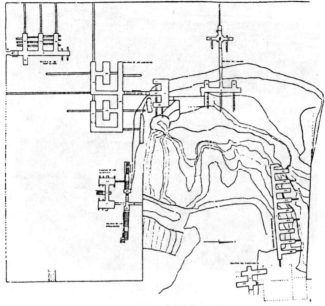

Figure 95

The openings of the tunnels perplexed their discoverers, for they seemed to connect the two river tributaries that flank the site, one (due to the mountainous terrain) above it and the other in the valley below it. Some explorers have suggested that these tunnels were so built for flood control purposes, to channel the onrushing water from the mountains as the snows melt and let it flow under instead of through the buildings. But if there was a danger of such flooding (after heavy rains rather than from melting snows), why did the otherwise ingenious builders place their structures at such a vulnerable spot?

They did so, we hold, on purpose. They ingeniously used the two levels of the tributaries to create a powerful, controlled flow of water needed for the processes that were carried out at Chavin de Huantar. For there, as at many other sites, such devices of flowing water were used in the panning of gold.

We will encounter more of these ingenious waterworks in the Andes; we have seen them, in more rudimentary forms, at Olmec sites. They were in Mexico part of complex earthworks; they were in the Andes masterpieces in stone—sometimes large sites such as Chavin de Huantar, sometimes lone remains of incredibly cut and shaped rocks, as this one seen by Squier in

Figure 96

the Chavin area (Fig. 96), that seem to have been intended for some ultramodern machinery long gone.

It was indeed the stonework—not of the edifices but of the artistic artifacts—that seems to provide the answer to the question Who was there at Chavin de Huantar? The artistic skills and stone-sculpting styles are surprisingly reminiscent of the Olmec art of Mexico. The enchanting objects include a jaguar-cat receptacle, a feline-bull, an eagle-condor, a turtle basin; a large number of vases and other objects decorated with glyphs created of entwined fangs—a motif decorating wall slabs as well as artifacts (Fig. 97a). There were, however, also stone slabs covered with Egyptian motifs—serpents, pyramids, the sacred Eye of Ra (Fig. 97b). And as though this variety was insufficient, there were fragments of carved stone blocks that depicted Mesopotamian motifs, such as deities within Winged Disks (Fig. 97c) or (engraved on bones) images of gods wearing conical headdresses, the headgear by which Mesopotamian gods were identified (Fig. 97d).

The deities wearing the conical headdresses have facial features that have an "African" look, and having been carved on bones may represent the earliest art depictions at the site. Could it be that Africans—negroid, Egyptian-Nubian—were ever at this South American site at its earliest time? The surprising answer is yes. There were indeed black Africans here and at

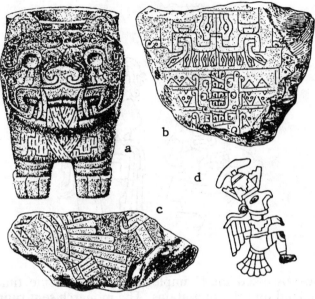

Figure 97

nearby sites (especially at one called Sechin), and they left their portraits behind. At all these sites carved stones by the dozens bear depictions of those people; in most instances they are shown holding some kind of tool; in many instances, the "engineer" is depicted as associated with a symbol for waterworks (Fig. 98).

At coastal sites that lead to the Chavin sites in the mountains, archaeologists have found sculpted heads of clay, not stone, that must have represented Semitic visitors (Fig. 99); one was so strikingly similar to Assyrian sculptures that the discoverer, H. Ubbelohde-Doering (*On the Royal Highway of the Incas*) nicknamed it "King of Assyria." But it is not certain that these visitors had made it to the highland sites—at least not alive: sculpted stone heads with Semitic features have been found at Chavin de Huantar—but mostly with grotesque grimaces or mutilations, stuck as trophies in the site's surrounding walls.

The age of Chavin suggests that the first wave of these Old World, both Olmec and Semitic migrants, had arrived there circa 1500 B.C. Indeed, it was in the reign of the 12th monarch of the Ancient Empire that, as Montesinos chronicled, "news reached Cuzco of the disembarking on the coast of some men of great stature . . . giants who were settling on the whole coast"

Figure 98

and who possessed metal implements. After some time they
moved inland into the mountains. The monarch sent runners to
investigate and to provide him with reports of the giants' advance, lest they come too close to the capital. But as things
turned out, the giants provoked the wrath of the Great God and
he destroyed them. These events had taken place about a century before the standstill of the Sun that had occurred circa 1400
B.C.—i.e. circa 1500 B.C., the very time at which Chavin de
Huantar's waterworks were built.

Figure 99

Figure 100

This, it must be pointed out, is not the same incident reported by Garcilaso, about giants who despoiled the land and raped the women—an occurrence in Moche times, circa 400 B.C. Indeed, it was at that time, as we have already seen, that the two commingled groups of Olmecs and Semites were fleeing Mesoamerica. Their fate, however, was no different in the northern Andes. Besides the grotesque Semitic stone heads found at Chavin de Huantar, depictions of mutilated negroid bodies are found in the whole area, and especially at Sechin.

Thus it was, after some 1,000 years in the northern Andes and almost 2,000 years in Mesoamerica, that the African-Semitic presence had come to a tragic end.

Although some of the Africans may have gone farther south, as finds at Tiahuanacu attest, the African-Semitic extension into the Andes from Mesoamerica appears to have not gone beyond the Chavin-culture area. The tales of the giants stricken by divine hand may hold more than a kernel of fact; for it is quite possible that there, in the northern Andes, two realms of two gods had met, with an unseen boundary between jurisdictions and human subordinates.

We say this because, in that very zone, other white men had been present. They were portrayed in stone busts (Fig. 100)—nobly clad, wearing turbans or headbands with symbols of authority, and decorated with what scholars call "mythological animals." These bust-statues have been mostly found at a site

Figure 101

near Chavin named Aija. Their facial features, especially the
straight noses, identify them as Indo-Europeans. Their origin
could have been only the land of Asia Minor and Elam to its
southeast, and in time the Indus Valley farther east.

Is it possible that people from those distant lands had crossed
the Pacific and come to the Andes in prehistoric times? The link
that evidently existed is confirmed by depictions illustrating the
feats of an ancient Near Eastern hero whose tales were told and
retold. He was Gilgamesh, ruler of Uruk (the biblical Erech)
who had reigned circa 2900 B.C.; he went in search of the hero
of the Deluge story whom the gods had granted (according to
the Mesopotamian version) immortality. His adventures were
told in the *Epic of Gilgamesh,* which was translated in antiquity
from Sumerian into the other languages of the Near East. One
of his heroic deeds, the wrestling with and defeat of two lions
with his bare hands, was a favorite pictorial depiction by ancient
artists, as this one on a Hittite monument (Fig. 101a).

Amazingly, the same depiction appears on stone tablets from
Aija (Fig. 101b) and a nearby site, Callejon de Huaylus (Fig.
101c) in the northern Andes!

These Indo-Europeans have not been traced in Mesoamerica
or Central America, and we must assume that they came across
the Pacific straight to South America. If legends be the guide,
they preceded the two waves of African "giants" and Mediterra-

nean Bearded Ones, and could have been the earliest settlers of which the tale of Naymlap recounts. The traditional landing site for that arrival has been the peninsula of Santa Elena (now Ecuador) which, with its nearby La Plata island, juts out into the Pacific. Archaeological excavations have confirmed early settlements there, beginning with what is called a Valdivian Phase circa 2500 B.C. Among the finds reported by the renowned Ecuadorian archaeologist Emilio Estrada (*Ultimas Civilizaciones Pre-Historicas*) were stone statuettes with the same straight-nose features (Fig. 102a) as well as a symbol on pottery (Fig. 102b) that was the Hittite hieroglyph for "gods" (Fig. 102c).

It is noteworthy that the megalithic structures in the Andes, as we have already seen at Cuzco, Sacsahuaman, and Machu Picchu, all lie south of the unseen demarcation line between the two divine realms. The handiwork of the megalithic builders—Indo-Europeans guided by their gods?—which began south of Chavin (Fig. 96) has left its mark all the way south into the valley of the Urubamba river and beyond—everywhere, indeed, where gold was collected and panned. Everywhere, rocks were fashioned as though they were soft putty into channels, compartments, niches, and platforms that from a distance look

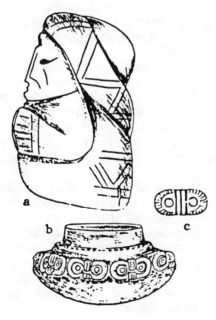

Figure 102

like stairways to nowhere; tunnels lead into mountainsides; fissures have been enlarged into corridors whose walls have been smoothed or shaped in precise angles. Everywhere, even at sites where the inhabitants could obtain all their water needs from the river below, elaborate water funneling and channeling were created higher up to make water from spring, tributary, or rain sources flow in a desired direction.

West-southwest of Cuzco, on the way to the town of Abancay, lie the ruins of Sayhuiti-Rumihuasi. As at other such sites it is situtuated near the junction of a river and a smaller stream. There are remain of a retaining wall, the remnant of large-sized structures that had once stood there; as Luis A. Pardo has pointed out in a study devoted to the site (*Los Grandes Monolitos de Sayhuiti*) the name means in the native tongue "Truncated Pyramid."

The site is known for its several monoliths and especially one called the Great Monolith. The name is appropriate since this huge rock, which from a distance appears as an immense bright egg resting on the hillside, measures about fourteen by ten by nine feet. While its bottom part has been carefully shaped as half an ovoid, the upper part has been carved out to represent in all probability a scale model of some unknown area. Discernible are miniature walls, platforms, stairways, channels, tunnels, rivers, canals; diverse structures, some representing edifices with niches and steps between them; images of various animals indigenous to Peru; and human figures of what look like warriors and, some say, gods.

Some see in this scale model a religious artifact, honoring the deities that they discern upon it. Others believe it represents a section of Peru that encompasses three districts, extending to the south to Lake Titicaca (which they identify with a lake carved on the stone) and the very ancient site of Tiahuanaco. Was this, then, a map carved in stone—or perhaps a scale model of a grand artificer who planned the layout and structures to be erected?

The answer may lie in the fact that, winding through this scale model, are grooves, an inch to two inches wide. They all originate in a "dish" located at the monolith's highest point and slope down, winding and zigzagging, to the lowest edge of the sculptured model, reaching there round discharge holes. Some consider these grooves to have served for the pouring by priests of potions (coca juices) as offerings to the gods represented on the rock. But if it was the gods themselves who were the architects, what was their purpose?

Figure 103

The telltale grooves are also a feature of another immense rock outcropping that has also been cut and shaped with geometric precision (Fig. 103), its surface and sides made into steps, platforms, and cascading niches. One side has been cut to form small "dishes" on the upper level; they are connected to a larger receptacle from which a deep channel leads down, separating midway into two grooves. Whatever liquid they carried poured into the rock, which was hollowed out and could be entered through an entryway in the back.

Other remains on the site, probably broken off from larger slabs, puzzle by the complex and geometrically precise grooves and hollows cut into them; they can be best likened to dies or matrixes for the casting of some ultramodern instruments.

One of the better known sites, just east of Sacsahuaman, is called Kenko—a name which in the native tongue means "Twisting Channels." The main tourist attraction there is a huge monolith standing on a podium that may have represented a lion or other large animal standing on its hind legs. In front of the monolith is a six-foot-high wall built of beautiful ashlars, surrounding the monolith in a circle. The monolith stands in front of an immense natural rock and the circular wall reaches and ends at the rock as a pincer. In the back, the rock has been cut, carved, and shaped into several levels connected by staggered platforms. Zigzagging channels have been cut on the rock's artificially sloping sides and the rock's interior has been hewed out to create labyrinthine tunnels and chambers. Nearby, a cleft in the rock leads to a cavelike opening that has been hollowed out with geometric precision to form stone features that some describe as thrones and altars.

There are more of these sites around Cuzco-Sacsahuaman, all along the Sacred Valley and reaching to the southeast, where a lake bears the name Golden Lake. A site named Torontoy includes among its precisely cut, megalithic stone blocks one that has thirty-two angles. Some fifty miles from Cuzco, near Torontoy, an artificial waterflow was made to cascade between two walls and over fifty-four "steps," all cut out of the living rock; significantly, the site is called Cori-Huairachina, "Where Gold is Purified."

Cuzco meant "The Navel" and indeed Sacsahuaman appears to have been the largest, most colossal and central of all these sites. One aspect of this centrality may be evidenced by a place called Pampa de Anta, some ten miles west of Sacsahuaman. There, the sheer rock has been carved into a series of steps that form a large crescent (hence the rock's name *Quillarumi,* "Moon Stone"). Since there is nothing to view from there except the eastern skies, Rolf Müller (*Sonne, Mond und Steiner über dem Reich der Inka*) concluded that it was some kind of observatory, situated so as to reflect astronomical data to the promontory at Sacsahuaman.

But what was Sacsahuaman itself, now that the notion of its having been built by the Incas as a fortress is completely discredited? The perplexing labyrinthine channels and other seemingly haphazard cutouts into which the natural rocks were shaped begin to make sense as a result of new archaeological excavations begun several years ago. Though far from uncovering more than a small part of the extensive stone structures in the plateau that extends behind the smooth Rodadero rock, they have already revealed two major aspects of the site. One is the fact that walls, conduits, receptacles, channels, and the like have been created both out of the living rock and with the aid of perfectly shaped large ashlars, many of the polygonal kind of the Megalithic Age, to form a series of water-channeling structures one above the other; rain or spring waters could thus be made to flow in a regulated manner from level to level.

The other aspect is the uncovering of a huge circular area enclosed by megalithic ashlars, that by all opinions served as a reservoir. Also uncovered was a sluice-chamber built of megalithic ashlars, that lies underground at a level permitting the running off of the water from the circular reservoir. As children who come to play there have demonstrated, the channel leading away from this sluice-chamber leads to the *Chingana* or "Labyrinth" carved out of the native rock behind and below this circular area.

Even before the whole complex that had been built on this promontory is uncovered, it is by now clear that some mineral or chemical compounds had been poured down the Rodadero, giving its back smooth side the discoloration resulting from such use. Whatever it was—gold-bearing soil?—was poured down into the large circular reservoir. From the other side, water was force-flowed. It all looks like a large-scale gold-panning facility. The water was finally flowed off through the sluice-chamber, and out and away through the labyrinth. In the stone vats, what remained was gold.

What then did the megalithic, colossal zigzagging walls, at the edge of the promontory, protect or support? To this question there is still no clear answer, except to surmise that some kind of massive platform was required for the vehicles—airborne, we must presume—that were used to haul in the ores and take away the nuggets.

One site that may have served, or was intended to serve, a similar transportation function, located some sixty miles northwest of Sacsahuaman, is Ollantaytambu. The archaeological remains are atop a steep mountain spur; they overlook an opening between the mountains that rise where the Urubamba-Vilcanota and Patcancha rivers meet. A village that gave its name to the ruins is situated at the bottom of the mountain; the name, meaning "Restplace of Ollantay," stems from the time an Inca hero prepared there a stand against the Spaniards.

Several hundred stone steps of crude construction connect a series of terraces of Inca make and lead to the principal ruins on the summit. There, in what has been presumed to have served as a fortress, there are indeed remains of Inca-walled structures built of fieldstones. They look primitive and ugly beside pre-Inca structures from the Megalithic Age.

The megalithic structures begin with a retaining wall built of the beautifully fashioned polygonal stones as one finds at the previously described megalithic remains. Passing through a gateway cut of a single stone block one reaches a platform supported by a second retaining wall, similarly constructed of polygonal stones but of a larger size. On one side an extension of this wall becomes an enclosure with twelve trapezoid openings—two serving as doorways and ten being false windows; perhaps this is why Luis Pardo (*Ollamtaitampu, Una ciudad megalitica*) called this structure "the central temple." On the other

Figure 104

side of the wall there stands a massive and perfectly shaped gate (Fig. 104) that in its time (though not now) served as the way up to the main structures.

The greatest mystery of Ollantaytambu is there: a row of six colossal monoliths that stand on the topmost terrace. The gigantic stone blocks are from eleven to almost fourteen feet high, average six or more feet in width and vary in thickness from about three to over six feet (Fig. 105). They stand joined together, without mortar or any other bonding material, with the aid of long dressed stones that had been inserted between the colossal blocks. Where the thickness of the blocks fell short of the greatest thickness (of over six feet), large polygonal stones fitted together, as at Cuzco and Sacsahuaman, to create an even thickness. In front, however, the megaliths stand as a single wall, oriented exactly southeast, with faces that have been carefully smoothed to obtain a slight curvature. At least two of the monoliths bear the weathered remains of relief decorations; on the fourth one (counting from the left) the design is clearly that of the Stairway symbol; all archaeologists agree that the symbol, which had its origin at Tiahuanacu at Lake Titicaca, signified the ascent from Earth to Heaven or, in reverse, a descent from Heaven to Earth.

Jambs and protrusions on the sides and faces of the monoliths and steplike cuts at the top of the sixth one suggest that the construction was not completed. Indeed, stone blocks of various shapes and sizes lie strewn about. Some have been cut and

Figure 105

shaped and given perfect corners, grooves and angles. One provides a most significant clue: a deep T shape has been cut into it (Fig. 106). All the scholars, having found such cuts in gigantic stone blocks at Tiahuanacu, had to agree that this groove was intended to hold together two stone blocks with a *metal* clamp; as a precaution against earthquakes.

One must therefore wonder how scholars can continue to attribute these remains to the Incas, who did not possess any metal except gold, which is too soft and thus totally unsuitable to hold together colossal stone blocks shaken by an earthquake. Naive too is the explanation that Inca rulers built this colossal place as a gigantic bathhouse, for bathing was one of their cherished pleasures. With two rivers running just at the foothills, why haul immense blocks—some weighing as much as 250 tons

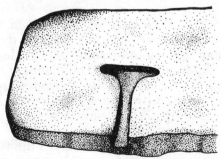

Figure 106

—to build a bathtub up the hill? And all that, without iron tools?

More serious is the explanation for the row of six monoliths that they were part of a planned retaining wall, probably to support a large platform atop the mountain. If so, the size and the massivity of the stone blocks bring to mind the colossal stone blocks used to construct the unique platform at Baalbek, in the Lebanon mountains. In *The Stairway to Heaven* we described and examined at length that megalithic platform, and concluded that it was the "landing place" that had been the first destination of Gilgamesh—a landing place for the "aerial ships" of the Anunnaki.

The many similarities we find between Ollantaytambu and Baalbek include the origin of the megaliths. The colossal stone blocks of Baalbek were quarried miles away in a valley, then incredibly lifted, transported, and put in place to fit with other stones of the platform. At Ollantaytambu too the giant stone blocks were quarried on the mountainside on the opposite side of the valley. The heavy blocks of red granite, after they had been quarried, hewed, and shaped, were then transported from the mountainside, across two streams, and up the Ollantaytambu site; then carefully raised, put precisely in place, and finally fused together.

Whose handiwork was Ollantaytambu? Garcilaso de la Vega wrote that it was "from the very first epoch, before the Incas." Blas Valera stated, "from an era that anteceded the epoch of the Incas . . . the era of the pantheon of the gods of pre-Inca times." It is time that modern scholars agree.

It is also time to realize that these gods were the same deities to whom the construction of Baalbek has been attributed by Near Eastern legends.

Was Ollantaytambu intended to be a stronghold, as Sacsahuaman might have been, or a landing place, as Baalbek had been?

In our previous books we have shown that, in determining the site of their spaceport and "landing places," the Anunnaki first anchored a landing corridor on some outstanding geographical feature (such as Mount Ararat). The flight path within this corridor was then inclined at a precise 45 degrees to the equator. In postdiluvial times, when the spaceport was in the Sinai peninsula and the landing place for airborne craft at Baalbek, the grid followed the same pattern.

The *Torreon* at Machu Picchu has, besides the two observation windows in the semicircular section, another enigmatic

Figure 107

window (Fig. 107) that has an inverted stairway opening at its bottom and a wedgelike slit at its top. Our own studies show that a line from the Sacred Rock through the slit to the Intihuatana will run at a precise angle of 45 degrees to the cardinal points, thus establishing for Machu Picchu its principal orientation.

This 45 degree orientation determined not only the layout of Machu Picchu, but also the location of major ancient sites. If one draws on a map of the region a line connecting the legendary stops made by Viracocha from the Island of the Sun in Lake Titicaca, the line will pass Cuzco and continue to Ollantaytambu—precisely at a 45 degree angle to the equator!

A series of studies and lectures by Maria Schulten de D'Ebneth, summed up in her book *La Ruta de Wirakocha*, showed that the 45 degree line on which Machu Picchu is located fits a grid pattern along the sides of a square tilted at 45 degrees (so that the corners, not the sides, point toward the cardinal points). She confessed that she was inspired to search for this

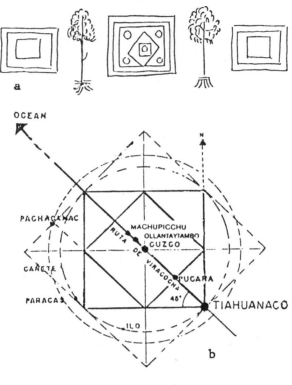

Figure 108

ancient grid by the *Relacion* of Salcamayhua. Relating the tale
of the three windows, he drew a sketch (Fig. 108a) to illustrate
the narrative, and gave each window a name: Tampu-Tocco,
Maras-Tocco, and Sutic-Tocco. Maria Schulten realized that
these are place names. When she applied the tilted square to a
map of the Cuzco-Urubamba area, with its northwestern corner
at Machu Picchu (alias Tampu-Tocco), she discovered that all
the other places fell into the correct positions. She drew lines
showing that a 45 degree line originating at Tiahuanacu, combined with squares and circles of definite measurements, embraced all the key ancient sites between Tiahuanacu, Cuzco,
and Quito in Ecuador, including the all-important Ollantaytambu (Fig. 108b).

No less important is another finding by her. The subangles
that she had calculated between the central 45 degree line and
sites located away from it, such as Pachacamac's temple, indicated to her that the Earth's tilt ("obliquity") at the time this

grid was laid out was close to 24° 08′. This means the grid was planned (according to her) 5,125 years before her measurements were done in 1953; in other words, in 3172 B.C.

It is a determination that confirms our own conclusion that the megalithic structures belong to the Age of Taurus, the era between 4000 B.C. and 2000 B.C. And, by combining modern studies with the data provided by the chroniclers, it affirms what the legends kept reiterating:

It all began at Lake Titicaca.

10

"BAALBEK OF THE NEW WORLD"

Every version of every legend in the Andes points to Lake Titicaca for the Beginning—the place where the great god Viracocha performed his creative feats, where mankind reappeared after the Deluge, where the ancestors of the Incas were granted a golden wand with which to establish Andean civilization. If this be fiction, then it is supported by fact; for it is on the shores of Lake Titicaca that the first and greatest city in all of the Americas had stood.

Its scope, the size of its monoliths, the intricate carvings upon its monuments and its statues have amazed all who have seen Tiahuanacu (as the place has been called) ever since the first chronicler described it for Europeans. Everyone equally wondered who had built this unique city and how, and puzzled over its untold antiquity. Yet the greatest puzzle of all is the location itself: a barren, almost lifeless place some 13,000 feet —four kilometers!—up among the highest Andean peaks that are permanently snow-covered. Why would anyone expend incredible effort to erect colossal edifices out of stone that had to be quarried and brought over from many miles away in this treeless, windswept desolate place?

The thought struck Ephraim George Squier when he reached the lake a century ago. "The islands and promontories of Lake Titicaca," he wrote (*Peru Illustrated*) "are for the most part barren. The waters hide a variety of strange fishes, which contribute to support a population necessarily scanty in a region where barley will not ripen except under very favorable circumstances, and where maize, in its most dimunitive size, has its most precarious development; where the potato, shrunk to its smallest proportions, is bitter; where the only grain is the quinoa; and where the only indigenous animals fit for food are the biscacha, the llama, and the vicuña." Yet in this treeless world, he added, "if tradition be our guide, were developed the germs of Inca

civilization" from an earlier, "original civilization which carved
its memorials in massive stones, and left them on the plain of
Tiahuanaco, and of which no tradition remains except that they
are the work of the giants of old, who reared them in a single
night."

A different thought, however, struck him as he climbed up a
promontory overlooking the lake and the ancient site. Was it
perhaps because of the isolation, because of the surrounding
peaks, because of the vista between the peaks, that the place
had been chosen? From a ridge at the southwestern edge of the
plain in which the lake is situated, near where its waters flow
out southward through the Desaguadero river, he could see not
only the lake with its southern peninsulas and islands, but also
the snowy peaks to the east.

"Here," he wrote with words accompanying a sketch he had
made, "the great snowy chain of the Andes burst on our sight in
all its majesty. Dominating the lake is the massive bulk of
Illampu, or Sorata, the crown of the continent, the highest
mountain of America, rivaling, if not equaling in height, the
monarchs of the Himalayas; observers vary in their estimates
and calculations of its altitude from 25,000 to 27,000 feet."
Southward from this outstanding landmark the uninterrupted
chain of mountains and peaks "terminates in the great mountain
of Illimani, 24,500 feet in altitude." Between the western ridge
at whose edge Squier had stood and the gigantic mountains to
the east, lay the flat depression that was occupied by the lake
and its southern shores. "Nowhere else in the world, perhaps,"
Squier went on, "can a panorama so diversified and grand be
obtained from a single point of view. The whole great tableland
of Peru and Bolivia, at its widest part, with its own system of
waters, its own rivers and lakes, its own plains and mountains,
all framed in by the ranges of the Cordilleras and the Andes, is
presented like a map" (Fig. 109).

Were these geographical and topographical features the very
reason for the selection of the site—at the edge of a great plain
basin, with two peaks that stand out not only from the ground
but also from the skies—just as the twin peaks of Ararat
(17,000 and 13,000 feet) and the two pyramids of Giza had
served to mark the landing paths of the Anunnaki?

Unbeknown to Squier, he had raised the analogy, for he had
titled the chapter describing the ancient ruins "Tiahuanaco, the
Baalbec of the New World"; for that was the only comparison
he could think of—a comparison with a place that we have
identified as the landing place of the Anunnaki to which Gilgamesh had set his steps five thousand years ago.

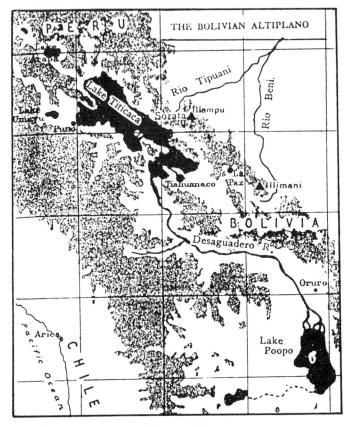

Figure 109

The greatest explorer of Tiahuanacu and its ruins this century has been, without doubt, Arthur Posnansky, a European
engineer who moved to Bolivia and devoted his lifetime to unraveling the mysteries of these ruins. As early as 1910 he complained that, from visit to visit, he saw less and less of the
artifacts, for the local natives, builders in the capital La Paz,
and even the government itself for construction of the railroad,
systematically carry off the stone blocks not for their artistic or
archaeological value, but as freely available building materials.
Half a century earlier Squier voiced the same complaint, noticing that in the nearest town, on the peninsula of Copacabana,
the church as well as the villagers' abodes were built of stones
taken away from the ancient ruins as if they were a quarry. Even
the cathedral in La Paz, he found out, was erected using Tiahuanacu's stones. Yet, the little that remained—mostly because

it was too massive to move—impressed him that these were
remains of a civilization that disappeared before that of the
Incas began, a civilization contemporary with that of Egypt and
the Near East. The remains indicate that the structures and the
monuments were the work of a people who were capable of a
unique, perfect, and harmonious architecture—yet one that
"had no infancy and passed through no period of growth." No
wonder, then, that the wondering Indians had told the Spaniards that these artifacts were raised overnight by giants.

Pedro de Cieza de Leon, who traveled throughout what is
now Peru and Bolivia in the years 1532–1550, reported in his
Chronicles that, without doubt, the ruins of Tiahuanacu were
"the most ancient place of any that I have yet described."
Among the edifices that amazed him was a "hill made by the
hands of men, on a great foundation of stone" that measured
more than 900 feet by 400 feet at its base and rose some 120
feet. Beyond it he saw "two stone idols, of the human shape and
figure, the features very skillfully carved, so that they appear to
have been done by the hand of some great master. They are so
large that they seem like small giants, and it is clear that they
have the sort of clothing different from those now worn by the
natives of these parts; they seem to have some ornament on
their heads."

Nearby he saw the remains of another building, and of a wall
"very well built." It all looked very ancient and worn. In another part of the ruins he saw "stones of such enormous size that
it causes wonder to think of them, and to reflect how human
force can have sufficed to move them to the place where we see
them, being so large. Many of these stones are carved in different ways, some of them having the shape of a human body,
which must have been their idols."

He noticed near the wall and the large stone blocks "many
holes and hollow places in the ground," which puzzled him.
More to the west he saw other ancient remains, "among them
many doorways, with their jambs, lintels and thresholds all in
one stone." He wondered most particularly that "from these
great doorways there came out still larger stones upon which the
doorways were formed, some of them thirty feet broad, fifteen
or more long and six in thickness. The whole of this," he reported with utter amazement—the doorway and its jambs and
lintel—"were one single stone." He added that "the work is one
of grandeur and magnificence, when all considered," and that
"for myself I fail to understand with what instruments or tools it
can have been done, for it is very certain that before these great
stones could be brought to perfection and left as we see them,

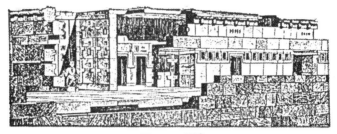

Figure 110

the tools must have been much better than those now used by the Indians."

Of all the artifacts seen by the first Spaniards to arrive on the scene, so sincerely described by Cieza de Leon, these colossal one-piece gateways still lie where they had fallen. The site, about a mile to the southwest of the principal ruins of Tiahuanacu, has been called by the Indians Puma-Punku as though it were a separate site; but it is nowadays certain that it was part of the greater metropolis embraced by Tiahuanacu that measured a mile by almost two miles in size.

The remains there have amazed every traveler who has seen them during the past two centuries, but were first scientifically described by A. Stübel and Max Uhle (*Die Ruinenstaette von Tiahuanaco im Hochland des Alten Peru,* 1892). The photographs and sketches that accompanied their report showed that the gigantic stone blocks lying about were components of several structures of amazing complexity that may have formed the eastern edifice of the site (Fig. 110 is based on the latest studies). The four-part edifice that collapsed (or was overthrown) lies as enormous platforms with or without the parts that formed one piece with them vertically or at other angles (Fig. 111). The

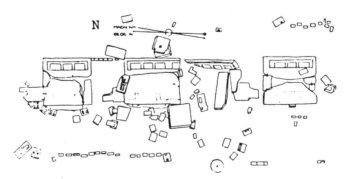

Figure 111

Figure 112

individual, broken-off portions weigh as much as one hundred tons each; they are made of red sandstone, and Posnansky (*Tihuanacu—The Cradle of American Man*) has proved conclusively that the quarry for these blocks, which weighed three or four times as much when they were one unit, was on the western shore of the lake some ten miles away. These stone blocks, some measuring twelve by ten feet and almost two feet thick, are covered with indentations, grooves, precise angles and surfaces that have varying levels. At certain points the blocks have indentations (Fig. 112) that were certainly intended to hold metal clamps, to attach each vertical section to those adjoining it—a technical "gimmick" that we had seen at Ollantaytambu. But whereas there the suggestion was that the clamps were made of gold (the only metal known to the Incas)—an untenable suggestion because of the softness of gold—here the clamps were made of *bronze*. That this was so is known because some of these bronze clamps have actually been found. This is certainly a discovery of immense significance, for bronze is a most difficult alloy to produce, requiring the combination of a certain proportion of copper (about 85–90 percent) with tin; and whereas copper can be found in its natural state, tin must be extracted by difficult metallurgical processes from the ores in which it is contained.

How was this bronze obtained, and was its availability not only part of the puzzle but also a clue to the answers?

Putting aside the customary explanation that the colossal and intricate structures of Puma-Punku were "a temple," what practical purpose did it serve?—what was the function for which such immense effort and sophisticated technologies were expended? The German master architect Edmund Kiss (whose visualization of the way the structures might have originally looked inspired his plans for Nazi monumental buildings) believed that the mounds and remains flanking and fronting on the four-part collapsed section were elements of a harbor, for the lake had certainly extended that far in antiquity. But this leaves open and even reinforces the question, what was going on at Puma-Punku? What did it import and what products did it ship out at this barren altitude?

Ongoing excavations at Puma-Punku have uncovered a series of semisubterranean enclosures constructed of perfectly shaped stone blocks. They remind one of the sunken plazas of Chavin de Huantar, and raise the possibility that these were elements—reservoirs, pools, sluice-chambers—of a similar waterworks system.

More answers may lie in the most puzzling (if that is still possible) finds at the site: blocks of stone, complete by themselves or undoubtedly broken off from larger blocks, that have been shaped, angled, cut, and grooved in an astonishing way with an astounding precision and with tools that are hard to find even today. The best way to describe these technological miracles is to show some of them (Fig. 113).

There is absolutely no plausible explanation for these artifacts except to suggest—based on our own present technology—that these were matrixes, dies for the casting of intricate metal parts; parts for some complex and sophisticated equipment that Man in the Andes, or for that matter anywhere else, was absolutely incapable of possessing in pre-Inca times.

Various archaeologists and researchers had come to Tiahuanacu since the 1930s for brief or sustained work—Wendell C. Bennett, Thor Heyerdahl, and Carlos Ponce Sangines are names best recognized; but by and large, they only used, built upon, accepted, or argued with the conclusions of Arthur Posnansky, who first presented his extraordinary work and insights in the 1914 extensive volumes of *Una Metropoli Prehistorica en la America del Sur* and, after another three decades of devoted research, in the four-volumed *Tihuanacu—Cuna del Hombre de las Americas,* combined with an English translation (in 1945). This edition was honored with an official forword by the Bolivian government (the site ended up in the Bolivian part of the lake after its partition from Peru), and celebrated "the 12,000th year of Tiahuanacu."

For this, when all was said and done, was the most astounding (and controversial) conclusion of Posnansky: That Tiahua-

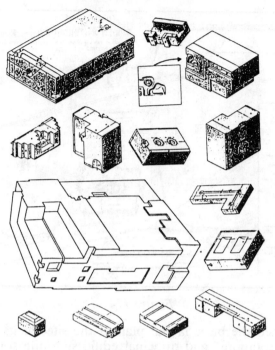

Figure 113

nacu was millennia old; that its first phase was built when the level of the lake was about one hundred feet higher and before the whole area had been engulfed by an avalanche of water—perhaps the famous Great Flood, thousands of years before the Christian era. Combining the archaeological discoveries with geological studies, study of flora and fauna, measurements of skulls found in tombs and portrayed in stone heads, and bringing to bear every facet of his engineering and technological expertise, Posnansky concluded that there had been three phases in the history of Tiahuanacu; that it was settled by two races—first the Mongoloid people, then Middle Eastern Caucasians—and at no time by the negroid people; and that the place had undergone two catastrophes, first a natural one by an avalanche of water, and then another sudden upheaval of unknown nature.

Without necessarily agreeing with these hard-hitting conclusions or with their timetable, the geological, topographical, climatic, and all scientific data amassed by Posnansky, and of course the archaeological discoveries he made, have been accepted and used by all who have followed in the half century since his monumental endeavors. His map of the site (Fig. 114)

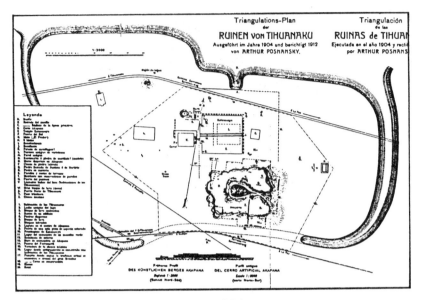

Figure 114

has remained the basic layout plan of the site, of its measurements, orientations, and principal edifices. While some of the sections he pointed to as potentially holding additional remains and artifacts were indeed excavated and profitably so, the main interest was and remains on three major components of the site.

The one at the southeastern part of the ruins is a hill known as the *Akapana*. It was probably given originally the shape of a stage-pyramid, and is presumed to have acted as the fortress guarding the site; the principal reason for that assumption being the fact that at the top of this pyramid-hill the center was excavated to form an oval, lined with ashlars, that acted as a water reservoir. The presumption was that it was intended to collect rainwater and provide the defenders with water as they fell back to this stronghold. Rumors however persisted that it was a place where gold was hidden, and in the eighteenth century a Spaniard named Oyaldeburo was given a mining concession for the Akapana. He cut through the eastern side of the hill to drain off the water, searched the bottom of the reservoir, tore down structures of beautiful ashlars, and dug deep into the hill wherever he found channels and conduits.

The destruction nevertheless revealed that the Akapana was not a natural hill but a very complex structure. Ongoing excavations, still barely scratching the surface, follow the work of Posnansky, who showed that the stone-lined reservoir was provided with masterful sluices that could regulate the flow of water down through channels constructed of ashlars with great precision. The complex inner workings of the Akapana were so built as to lead the water from one level inside the Akapana to another lower one in alternating vertical and horizontal sections, a vertical height of fifty feet but, because of the zigzagging, covering a far larger distance. In the end, some feet below the bottom of the Akapana, the water flowed through a stone outlet into the artificial canal (or moat), some 100 feet wide, that encircled the whole site. It led from there to wharfs at the site's north and thence to the lake. Now, if the purpose were just to drain off excess water to prevent overflow after heavy downpours, a simple straight inclined pipe (as was found at Tula) would have sufficed. But here we have angled channels, built with dressed stones fitted with great ingenuity to regulate the water's flow from one inner level to another. And this indicates to us a processing technique—the use of flowing water for washing ores, perhaps?

That some processing might have taken place in the Akapana is further suggested by the discovery on the surface and in the soil removed from the "reservoir" of large quantities of dark-green rounded "pebbles" that range in size from three-fourths of an inch to two inches. Posnansky determined that they are crystalline, but neither he nor others (to our knowledge) conducted further tests to determine the nature and origin of these globular objects.

A structure more to the center of the site ("K" on Posnansky's map) had so many subterranean and semisubterranean features that Posnansky thought it might represent a section set aside for tombs. All around there were sections of stone blocks cut to act as water conduits; they were in a state of disarray that Posnansky blamed not only on treasure hunters but also on a previous team of explorers, under Count Crequi de Montfort, who during their excavations in 1903 wantonly dug up remains, broke whatever stood in their way (according to Posnansky), and carried off many artifacts. The report on the discoveries and conclusions of this French expedition was given in a book by George Courty and in a lecture to the 1908 International Congress of Americanists by Manuel Gonzales de la Rosa. The essence of their findings was that "there were two Tiahuanacos," one the visible ruins, the other subterranean and invisible.

Posnansky himself described the conduits, channels, and a sluice (as atop the Akapana) that he found among the disturbed sunken portions of this structure, and determined that the conduits ran in several levels, led perhaps to the Akapana, and

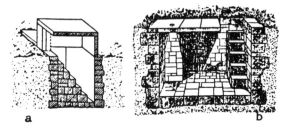

Figure 115

were linked with other subterranean structures to the west (in the direction of the lake). He described in words and a drawing (Fig. 115a,b) some of the subterranean and semisubterranean compartments, unable to hold back his amazement at the precision of the workmanship, the fact that the ashlars were made of hard andesite and that these compartments were completely waterproof: over all the seams and especially on the large roof slabs there had been spread a layer made of true lime, a couple of inches thick, which rendered the places "absolutely waterproof. This," he noted, "is the first and only time that we find the use of lime in a prehistoric American construction."

What went on in these subterranean chambers and why they were so specifically built, he could not tell. Perhaps they held treasure, but that, he pointed out, would have long disappeared by the hand of treasure seekers. Indeed, no sooner had he uncovered some of these chambers than "the place was stripped and robbed by the iconoclastic half-breeds of modern Tihuanacu." Apart from what he excavated or saw strewn about at the site, large quantities of stone conduits—pieces of all shapes, sizes and diameters—could be seen in the nearby church and in the bridges and culverts of the modern railroad and even in use in La Paz. The indications were of extensive ground and underground waterworks at Tiahuanacu; and Posnansky devoted to them a whole chapter in his ultimate work, titled *Hydraulic Works in Tihuanacu*. Recent excavations have uncovered more stone conduits and water channels, confirming the conclusions of Posnansky.

The second outstanding edifice at Tiahuanacu needed the least excavating, for it stands there majestically for all to see—a colossal stone gateway that rises above the flatness of the site like an *Arc de Triomphe* with no one to parade through it, no one to watch and cheer (Fig. 116, front and back).

Known as the Gate of the Sun, it has been described by Posnansky as "the most perfect and important work . . . a legacy

Figure 116

and elegant testimony of the cultured people and their leaders' knowledge and civilization." All who have seen it agree, for it is amazing not only by dint of having been cut and shaped out of a single block of stone (measuring about ten by twenty feet and weighing over one hundred tons), but also because of the intricate and breathtaking carvings upon it.

There are niches and geometric carved openings and surfaces upon the lower part of the gate's front and on its back side, but

Figure 117

the marveling has been at the carved section on the gate's upper front part (Fig. 117). There a central figure, almost three-dimensional though carved only in relief, is flanked by three rows of winged attendants; a lower row of images depicting only the central figure's face, framed by a meandering line, completes the composition.

There is general agreement that the central and dominant figure is that of Viracocha, holding a scepter or weapon in the right hand and a forked lightning in the other (Fig. 118). This image appears on vases, textiles, and artifacts in southern Peru and adjoining lands, indicating the extent to which what scholars call the Tiahuanacu culture had spread. Flanking this god are winged attendants, arranged in three horizontal rows, eight to a row on each side of the central figure. Posnansky pointed out that only the first five on each side in each row are carved in the same pronounced relief as the deity; the others on the extremes are carved faintly, as an afterthought.

He drew the central figure, the meander under it, and the fifteen original spaces on each side (Fig. 119) and concluded that this was a calendar of a twelve-month year, beginning at the spring equinox (September in the southern hemisphere); and that the central large figure, showing the deity in full body, represented that month and its equinox. Since the "equinox" denotes that time of the year when day and night are equal, he surmised that the segment right under the central figure, which is in the center of the meandering row, stands for the other

Figure 118

equinox month, March. He then assigned the remaining months in succession to the other segments within the meander. Pointing out that the two end segments show a bugler together with the deity's head, he suggested that these were the two extreme months when the Sun moves farthest away, the solstice months of June and December, when the priests would sound the bugle to call the sun back. The Gate of the Sun, in other words, was a calendar in stone.

The calendar, Posnansky surmised, was a solar calendar. Not only was it geared to the spring equinox when it began, but it also marked the other equinox and the solstices. It was a calendar of eleven months of thirty days each (the number of winged attendants above the meander) plus a "great month" of thirty-five days, the Month of Viracocha, making up a solar year of 365 days.

He should have mentioned that a twelve-month solar year beginning at the spring equinox was a Near Eastern calendar begun in Sumer, at Nippur, circa 3800 B.C.

The image of the deity, as well as those of the winged attendants and month-faces, seemingly depicted in natural realism,

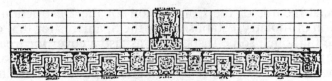

Figure 119

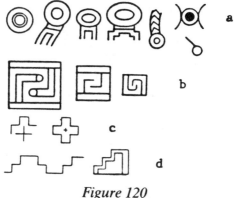

Figure 120

are in fact made up of many components that each have their own, mostly geometric shape. Posnansky devoted considerable study to these various components. They also appear on other monuments and sculptures of stone as well as on ceramic objects. He classified them pictographically according to the object (animal, fish, eye, wing, star, etc.) that they depicted or the idea they represented (Earth, Heaven, movement, and so on). He determined that circles and ovals depicted in a variety of ways and colors represented the Sun, Moon, planets, comets, and other celestial objects (Fig. 120a), that the bond between Earth and Heaven (Fig. 120b) was frequently expressed, and that the dominant symbols were the cross and the stairway signs (Fig. 120c, d). He saw in the latter, the Stairway, the "trademark" of Tiahuanacu, its monuments and its ultimate civilization—the source from which this symbol, he believed, spread throughout the Americas. He acknowledged that it was a glyph based on the Mesopotamian ziggurats, but noted that he did not think therefore that there had been Sumerians at Tiahuanacu.

All that reinforced his growing sense that the Gate of the Sun was part of a larger structural complex at Tiahuanacu whose purpose and function was to serve as an observatory; and this guided him in his most important and, as it turned out, most controversial work and conclusions.

Official records of the Commission for the Destruction and Expiation of Idolatry, established by the Spaniards for that clear purpose (although some suspect it was also a cover for treasure hunting), attest that the commission's men arrived in Tiahuanacu in 1625. A 1621 report by Father Joseph de Arriaga listed over 5,000 "objects of idolatry" that were obliterated by breaking, melting, or burning. What they did at Tiahuanacu is not known. The Gate of the Sun, as early photographs show, was found in the nineteenth century standing broken in two at the top, with the right-hand part leaning dangerously against the other half.

When and by whom it was straightened out and put back together is a mystery. How it was broken in two is also unknown. Posnansky did not think it was the handiwork of the Commission; rather, he thinks that this gate escaped their wrath because it had fallen and was covered by soil and thus hidden from sight when the Commission's zealots arrived. Since it was apparently reerected, some have wondered whether it was put back in its original place; the reason being the realization that the gate was not, originally, a solitary edifice standing alone in the large plain, but was part of the huge structure just east of it. The shape and size of that structure, called the *Kalasasaya*, was delineated by a series of vertical stone pillars (which is what the name meant, "The Standing Pillars"), revealing a somewhat rectangular enclosure measuring about 450 by 400 feet. Since the axis of this structure appeared to be east–west, some wondered whether the gate should not have stood in the center rather than in the northern edge of the enclosure's western wall (as it now does).

Whereas before only the great weight of the monolithic gate argued against notions of its having been moved almost two hundred feet, it is now clear from archaeological evidence that it probably stands where it belonged, for the center of the western wall was taken up by a terrace whose own center was aligned with the east–west axis of the Kalasasaya. Posnansky found along this axis various stones especially carved to permit astronomical observations; and his conclusion that the Kalasasaya was an ingenious celestial observatory is now accepted as a matter of fact.

The most obvious archaeological remains of the Kalasasaya have been the standing pillars that formed a slightly rectangular enclosure. Though not all of the pillars that once had acted as anchors for a continuous wall are still there, their count hints at an association with the number of days in a solar year and in a lunar month. Of particular interest to Posnansky were eleven pillars (Fig. 121) erected alongside the terrace protruding from the center of the western wall. His measurements of the lines of sight along the specially placed observation stones, the orientation of the structure, and the slight and purposely intended deviations from perfect cardinal points, convinced him that the Kalasasaya was built by people with ultramodern knowledge of

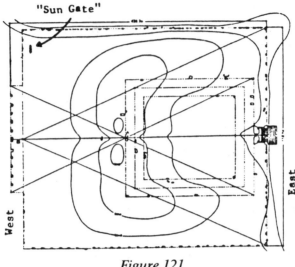

Figure 121

astronomy for the precise fixing of the equinoxes as well as the solstices.

The architectural drawings of Edmund Kiss (*Das Sonnentor von Tihuanaku*), based on Posnansky's work as well as on his own measurements and evaluations, envision (probably correctly) the structure inside the enclosure as a hollow stage-pyramid: a structure whose outer walls rise in stages but only to surround a central open-air square courtyard. The principal monumental stairway was in the center of the eastern wall; the principal observation points were in the centers of the two wider terraces that completed the "pyramid" on the west (Fig. 122).

It was on this point that Posnansky made his most startling discovery with the explosive ramifications. By measuring the distance and angles between the two solstice points, he realized that the obliquity of the Earth against the Sun on which the astronomical aspects of the Kalasasaya were based did not conform to the 23.5 degrees of our present era.

The obliquity of the ecliptic, as the scientific term is, for the orientation of the Kalasasaya's astronomical lines of sight, he found, was 23° 8' 48". *Based on the formulas determined by astronomers at the International Conference of Ephemerides in Paris in 1911, which takes into account the geographical position and elevation of the site, this meant that the Kalasasaya was built circa 15,000 B.C.!*

Announcing that Tiahuanacu was the oldest city in the world, one that was "built before the Flood," Posnansky inevi-

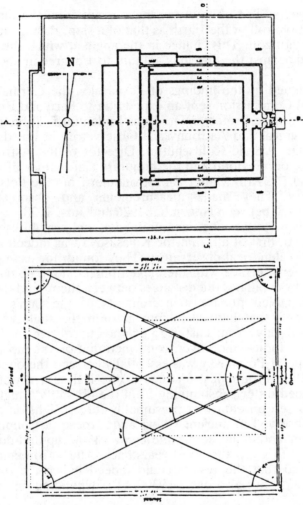

Figure 122

tably aroused the wrath of the scientific community of his time; for it was held then, based on the theories of Max Uhle, that Tiahuanacu was established some time at the beginning of the Christian era.

The obliquity of the ecliptic should not be confused (as some critics of Posnansky did) with the phenomenon of Precession. The latter changes the stellar background (constellation of stars) against which the Sun rises or acts at a certain time, such as the spring equinox; the change, though small, adds up to 1 degree in seventy-two years and to 30 degrees (a full zodiac house) in

2,160 years. The obliquity changes result from the almost imperceptible roll of the Earth as that of a ship, raising and lowering the horizon. This change in the angle at which the Earth is inclined against the Sun may amount to 1 degree in about 7,000 years.

Intrigued by the findings of Posnansky, the German Astronomical Commission sent an expedition to Peru and Bolivia; its members were Professor Dr. Hans Ludendorff, Director of the Astronomical and Astrophysical Observatory at Potsdam, Professor Dr. Arnold Kohlschütter, Director of the Astronomical Observatory in Bonn and the honorary astronomer of the Vatican, and Dr. Rolf Müller, an astronomer from the Potsdam observatory. They made measurements and observations at Tiahuanacu between November 1926 and June 1928.

Their investigations, measurements, and visual observations confirmed, first of all, that the Kalasasaya was indeed an astronomical-calendrical observatory. They found, for example, that the western terrace with the eleven pillars along it, due to the width of the pillars, the distances between them, and their positions, enabled precise measurements of the Sun's seasonal movements that had taken into account the slightly different number of days from solstice to equinox to solstice and back.

Their studies, moreover, confirmed that on the most controversial point Posnansky was essentially correct: the obliquity on which the astronomical features of the Kalasasaya were based did indeed differ substantially from the obliquity's angle in our time. Based on data that presumably throws light on the obliquity observed in ancient China and Greece, astronomers are confident about the applicable curve of the up-and-down motion only to a few thousand years back. The astronomical team concluded that the results could indeed indicate a date circa 15,000 B.C., but also one of 9300 B.C., depending on the curve used.

Needless to say, even the latter date was simply unacceptable to the scientific community. Yielding to the criticism, Rolf Müller conducted further studies in Peru and Bolivia, teaming up with Posnansky at Tiahuanacu. They found that results would change if certain variants were considered. First, if the observation of the solstice points were to be not from where Posnansky had assumed but from a different possible point, the angle between the solstice extremities (and thus the obliquity) would be slightly different; also, one could not say with any knowledge whether the ancient astronomers fixed the moment of solstice when the Sun was above the horizon line, in its midst or had just sunk below it. With all these variants, Müller published a definite report in the leading scientific journal *Baesseler Archiv* (vol. 14) in which he stated all the alternatives and concluded that if the angle of 24° 6' is to be accepted as the most accurate, the obliquity curve would cross this reading at either 10,000 B.C. or 4000 B.C.

Posnansky was invited to address the Twenty-Third International Congress of Americanists on the subject. He accepted the correct angle of obliquity to be 24° 6' 52.8", which left a choice between 10,150 B.C. and 4050 B.C. Conceding that this was "thorny material," he left the matter hanging by agreeing that it needs further study.

Such studies have indeed been conducted, even if not directly at Tiahuanacu. We have already mentioned that the calendar of the Incas indicated a Beginning in the Age of the Bull, not of Aries (the Ram). Müller himself, as we mentioned earlier, arrived at 4000 B.C. as the approximate age of the megalithic remains in Cuzco and Machu Picchu. And we have also referred to the research, along totally different lines of investigation, by Maria Schulten de D'Ebneth which led her to conclude that the Grid of Viracocha conformed to an obliquity of 24° 8' and thus to the date 3172 B.C. (by her calculations).

As the artifacts bearing the image of Viracocha—on textiles, on mummy wrappings, on pottery—were increasingly discovered all over southern Peru and even farther north and south, comparisons with other non-Tiahuanacu data could be made. Based on that, even such stubborn archaeologists as Wendell C. Bennett kept pushing the age of Tiahuanacu back, from the middle of the first millennium A.D. to almost the beginning of the first millennium B.C.

Radiocarbon datings, however, take the generally accepted dates farther and farther back. Beginning in the 1960s CIAT, the Bolivian Centro de Investigaciones Arqueologicas en Tiwanaku, has conducted systematic excavations and preservation work at the site. Its first major undertaking was the complete excavation and restoration of the sunken "small temple" east of the Kalasasaya, where a number of stone statues and stone heads were found. It uncovered a semisubterrenean courtyard, perhaps for ritual offerings, that was surrounded by a stone wall in which stone heads were stuck—in the manner of Chavin de Huantar. The official 1981 report by Carlos Ponce Sangines, Director of Bolivia's National Archaeological Institute (*Description Sumaria del Templete Semisubterraneo de Tiwanaku*), states that samples of organic matter found at this location gave radiocarbon readings of 1580 B.C.; as a result, Ponce Sangines, in his comprehensive study *Panorama de la Arqueologia Boli-*

viana, considered that time as the beginning of the Old Phase of Tiahuanacu.

Such radiocarbon dates indicate the age of the organic remains found at sites, but do not preclude an older age for the stone structures making up the site. Indeed, Ponce Sangines himself revealed in a subsequent study (*Tiwanaku: Space, Time and Culture*) that new dating techniques called Obsidian Hydration gave the earlier date 2134 B.C. for obsidian objects found at the Kalasasaya.

In this connection it is intriguing to read in the writings of Juan de Betanzos (*Suma y Narracion de los Incas,* 1551) that when Tiahuanacu was first settled under the chief called Con-Tici Viracocha, "he had with him a certain number of people ... And after he had come out of the lagoon he went to a place near it, where today stands a village called Tiaguanaco. They say," Betanzos continued, "that once, when the people of Con-Tici Viracocha were already settled there, there was darkness in the land." But Viracocha "ordered the Sun to move in the course in which it now moves; abruptly, he made the Sun begin the day."

The darkness resulting from the Sun's standstill and the "beginning of the day" when the motion resumed is undoubtedly a recollection of the same event that we had placed, on both sides of the Earth, circa 1400 B.C. Gods and men, according to Betanzos's record of local lore, were already at Tiahuanacu from earlier times—perhaps as early as the archaeoastronomical data indicates?

But why was Tiahuanacu established, at this site, at that early time?

In recent years archaeologists have found similar architectural features between Teotihuacan in Mexico and Tiahuanacu in Bolivia. Jose de Mesa and Teresa Gisbert (*Akapana, la Piramide de Tiwanacu*) have pointed out that the Akapana had a ground plan (square with protruding accessway) like the Pyramid of the Moon in Teotihuacan, about the same base measurements as this pyramid, and the same height (about fifty feet) as the first state of the Pyramid of the Sun and its height-to-width ratio. In view of our own conclusions that the original (and practical) purpose of Teotihuacan and its edifices was expressed by the site's waterworks, within and alongside the two pyramids, the water channels inside the Akapana and throughout Tiahuanacu assume a central role. Was Tiahuanacu established where it was as a processing facility? And if so, of what?

Dick Ibarra Grasso (*The Ruins of Tiahuanaco* and other works) concurred with the envisioning of greater Tiahuanacu, encompassing the Puma-Punku section, as stretching for miles along a major east–west axis not unlike the "Way of the Dead" in Teotihuacan, with several major north–south arteries. At the edge of the lake, where Kiss had envisioned a quay, they see archaeological evidence for massive retaining walls that, built in a meander, created actual deep-water piers at which boats laden with cargo could tie up. But if so, what did Tiahuanacu import and what did it export?

Ibarra Grasso reported the discovery of the "small green pebbles" that Posnansky had found on the Akapana, elsewhere in Tiahuanacu: in the ruins of a small Akapana-like pyramid to the south, where the boulders that served to retain it had turned green; in the area of the subterranean structures west of the Kalasasaya; and in very large quantities among the ruins of Puma-Punku.

Significantly, the boulders in the retaining walls in the piers of Puma-Punku have also turned green. That can mean only one thing: exposure to copper, for it is oxidized copper that gives stone and soil their greenish color (just as the presence of oxidized iron lends a red-brown hue).

Was copper, then, processed at Tiahuanacu? Probably; but then, this could have been done more reasonably at some less forbidding place and closer to copper sources. Copper, it would appear, was brought to Tiahuanacu, not carried away from it.

What Tiahuanacu was the source of should have been clear from the very meaning of the name of its location: *Titicaca.* The name of the lake comes from that of one of two islands that lie just off the Copacabana peninsula. It was there, on the island called Titicaca, the legends tell, that the rays of the Sun had struck *Titikalla,* the sacred rock, as soon as the Sun appeared after the Deluge. (It is therefore also known as Island of the Sun.) It was there, at the sacred rock, that Viracocha granted the divine wand to Manco Capac.

And what do all these names mean? *Titi* in the Aymara language was the name of a metal—either lead or tin, according to linguists.

Titikalla, we suggest, meant the "Rock of Tin." *Titicaca* meant "Stone of Tin." And Lake Titicaca was the lake that was the source of tin.

Tin, and bronze, were the products for which Tiahuanacu was established—right where its ruins still enchant.

11

A LAND OF WHICH THE INGOTS COME

"There was a man in the land of Uz whose name was Job; and that man was perfect and upright and one that feared God and eschewed evil." He was blessed with a large family and thousands of sheep and cattle. He was "the greatest man in the East."

"Then, one day, the song of the gods came to present themselves to Yahweh, and Satan was there among them. And Yahweh asked Satan where he had been; and Satan answered: Ranging over the Earth, roaming all over it."

Thus begins the biblical tale of Job, the righteous man who was put to the test by Satan to the limits of man's faith in God. As one calamity followed another and Job began to question the Lord's ways, three of his friends journeyed from distant lands to give him sympathy and comfort. As Job voiced his plaints and doubts of divine wisdom, the friends pointed out to him the many wonders of the heavens and the earth that were known only to God; among them were the marvels of metals and their sources and the ingenuity of finding them and extracting them from the depths of the earth:

> Surely there is a source for silver
> And a place where gold is refined;
> Where iron is obtained from ores
> and copper is smelted out of stones.
>
> To darkness He puts an end,
> The usefulness he researches
> of stones in depths and obscurity.
> He breaches the brook away from habitation,
> where the forgotten and strange men move about.

There is a land of which the ingots come,
Whose underground is upheavaled as with fire;
A place where the blue-green stones are,
that has the ores of gold.
Even a vulture knows not the way thereto,
And a falcon's eye has not discerned it . . .

There He set His hand to the granite,
He overturned mountains at their roots.
He cut galleries through the rocks,
and all that is precious His eyes had seen,
He dammed up the sources of the streams,
and that which is hidden He brought to light.

Does man know all these places? Job asked, did man by himself discover all the metallurgical processes? Indeed, he challenged his three friends, where does this knowledge of minerals and metals come from?

And where shall Knowledge be found?
Where does Comprehension come from?
No man knows its progression;
Its source is not where mortals dwell . . .

Solid gold is not its full measure,
In silver it is priceless.
To the red gold of Ophir it is not confined,
nor by precious cornelian or lapis-lazuli.
Gold and crystal are not its measure,
neither is its value in golden vessels.
Black coral and alabaster need no mention;
Knowledge is beyond mere pearls . . .

Clearly, Job conceded, all this Knowledge comes from God —the one who had both enriched him and deprived him and who could restore him:

God alone understands its course
and knows how it is established.
For He can scan the ends of the Earth
and see all that is under the skies.

The inclusion of the marvels of mining in Job's discourse with his three friends may not have been accidental. Though nothing is known of the identity of Job himself or of the land where he had lived, the names of the three friends provide some clues. The first one was Elipaz of Teman, from southern Arabia; his name meant "God is my Pure Gold." The second one was Bildad of Shuha, a country believed to have been located south of Carcemish, the Hittite city; the land's name meant "Place of the deep pits." The third one was Zophar of Na'amah, a place named after the sister of Tubal-Cain, "the master of all smiths" according to the Bible. All three, thus, had come from lands associated with mining.

In asking these detailed questions Job (or the author of the Book of Job) displayed considerable knowledge of mineralogy, mining, and metallurgical processes. His time is certainly long after Man's first use of copper by hammering lumps of native copper into useful shapes and well into the period when metals were obtained by mining ores that had to be smelted, refined, and cast. In Classical Greece of the first millennium B.C. the art of mining and metals was also considered a matter for uncovering the secrets of nature; the very word *metal* comes from the Greek *metallao,* which meant "to search, to find hidden things."

Greek poets and philosophers, followed by Roman ones, perpetuated Plato's division of human history according to four metal ages of Gold, Silver, Bronze (copper), and Iron, in which gold represented the ideal age when Man had been closest to his gods. A biblical division included in the vision of Daniel begins with clay before the list of metals and is a more accurate version of Man's progress. After a long Old Stone Age, the Middle Stone Age began in the Near East circa 11,000 B.C.—right after the Deluge. Some 3,600 years later Near Eastern man stepped off the mountain ranges into the fertile valleys, beginning agriculture, animal domestication, and the use of native metals (metals found in riverbeds as nuggets, requiring neither mining nor refining). Scholars have called this the Neolithic (New-Stone) Age, but it was really the age when clay—for pottery and many other uses—replaced stone, just as the sequence in the Book of Daniel holds.

The early use of copper was therefore of copper-stones, and for that reason many scholars prefer to call the transition from the stone ages to the metal ages not a Copper Age but a Chalcolithic, Copper-Stone Age. This copper was processed by hammering it into the desired shape, or by a process called annealing if the copperstone was first softened by fire. Believed to have begun in the highlands surrounding the Fertile Crescent of the Near East, this metalworking of copper (and eventually of gold) was possible due to the circumstances particular to them.

Gold and copper are found in nature in their "natural state," not only as veins deep within the rocks inside the earth, but also in the form of nuggets and lumps (even dust in the case of gold) that the forces of nature—storms, floods, or the persistent flow of streams and rivers—have shaken loose out of the rocks as they became exposed. Such natural lumps of these metals would then be found near and in riverbeds; the metal would be separated from the mud and gravel by washing with water ("panning") or sifting through sieves. Although this does not involve cutting shafts and tunnels, the method is called placer mining. Most authorities believe that such mining was practiced in the highlands surrounding the Fertile Crescent of Mesopotamia and the Mediterranean eastern coasts as early as the fifth millennium B.C., and certainly before 4000 B.C.

(This is a process that has been used throughout the ages; few people realize that the "gold miners" of the renowned nineteenth-century gold rushes were not really miners who cut deep into the depths of the earth in search of gold, as is the case, say, of gold mining in southern Africa. They in fact engaged in placer mining, sifting the gravel washed down into riverbeds for nuggets or gold dust. During the Yukon gold rush in Canada, for example, "miners" using a backhoe, a sluice and a pan reported the collection of more than a million ounces of gold each year during the peak times a century ago; the real production was probably twice as much. It is interesting that even nowadays such placer miners continue to find in the beds of the Yukon and Klondike rivers and their tributaries hundreds of thousands of ounces of gold a year.)

It is noteworthy that although both gold and copper were thus available in their natural state, and gold was even more suitable for use because unlike copper it does not oxidize, Near Eastern man of those early millennia did not utilize gold but limited his use to copper. The phenomenon usually goes without explanation; but it is our opinion that the explanation is to be found in the notions familiar from the New World—that gold was a metal belonging to the gods. When gold came into use, at the beginning of the third millennium B.C. or several centuries earlier, it was for enhancing the temples (literally, "God's House") and for making golden vessels for the service of the gods therein. It was only circa 2500 B.C. that gold came into royal use, indicating a change of attitudes whose reasons are yet to be explored.

Sumerian civilization blossomed out circa 3800 B.C. and it is evident from archaeological discoveries that its beginnings, in both northern and southern Mesopotamia, were in place by 4000 B.C.; that is also the time when real mining, the processing of ores and metallurgical sophistication, appeared on the scene —a complex and advanced body of knowledge that (as in the case of all other sciences) the ancient peoples said was given them by the Anunnaki, the gods who had come to Earth from Nibiru. Reviewing the stages in man's use of metals, L. Aitchison (*A History of Metals*) noted with astonishment that by 3700 B.C. "every culture in Mesopotamia was based on metalworking"; he concluded with obvious admiration that the metallurgical heights then reached "must inevitably be attributed to the technical genius of the Sumerians."

Not only copper and gold, that could be obtained from native nuggets, but also other metals that clearly required extracting from veins inside rocks (as is the case with silver) or smelting and then refining their ores (as, for example, lead) were obtained, processed, and used. The art of alloying—the combining chemically in a furnace of two or more metals—was developed. Primitive hammering gave way to the art of casting; and the very complex process known as *Cire perdue* ("lost wax"), which enabled the casting and making of beautiful and useful objects (such as statuettes of gods or animals or temple utensils) was invented—in Sumer. The progress made there spread worldwide. In the words of *Studies in Ancient Technology* by R. J. Forbes, "by 3500 B.C. metallurgy had been absorbed by the civilization in Mesopotamia" (which began circa 3800 B.C.). "This stage is reached in Egypt some three hundred years later and by 2500 B.C. the entire region between the Nile cataracts and the Indus is metal minded. By this time metallurgy seems to have started in China, but the Chinese did not become true metallurgists until the Lungshan period, 1800–1500 B.C. ...In Europe the earliest metal objects are hardly earlier than 2000 B.C."

Before the Deluge, when the Anunnaki had been mining gold in southern Africa for their own needs on Nibiru, the smelted ores were shipped in submersible boats to their E.DIN. Sailing through what is now the Arabian Sea and up the Persian Gulf, they delivered their cargoes for final processing and refining at BAD.TIBIRA, an antediluvian "Pittsburgh." The name meant "Place Established for Metallurgy." The term was sometimes spelled BAD.TIBILA, in honor of Tibil, the god of metallurgical craftsmen or smiths; and there can be little doubt that the name of the metallurgical craftsman of the line of Cain, *Tubal,* stems from the Sumerian terminology.

After the Deluge the great Tigris-Euphrates plain where the *Edin* had been was buried under impenetrable mud; it took nearly seven millennia for the plain to become dry enough for people to resettle there and launch the Sumerian civilization. Though in this plain of dry mud there were neither stone resources nor minerals, tradition required that Sumerian civilization and its urban centers follow "the olden plan," and the Sumerian metallurgical center was established where Bad-Tibira had once been. The fact that other people in the ancient Near East employed not only Sumerian technologies but also Sumerian terminologies attests to the centrality of Sumer in ancient metallurgy. In no other ancient language have there been found so numerous and precise terms concerning metallurgy. There have been found in Sumerian texts no less than thirty terms for varieties of copper (URU.DU), be it processed or unprocessed. There were numerous terms prefixed by ZAG (sometimes shortened to ZA) to denote the metals' shine, and KU for the purity of the metal or its ores. There were terms for varieties and alloys of gold, silver, and copper—even for iron (which supposedly came into use only a millennium or so after Sumer's primacy); called AN.BAR, it too had more than a dozen terms depending on its and its ores' quality. Some Sumerian texts were virtual lexicons listing terms for "white stones," colored minerals, salts that were obtained by mining, and bituminous substances. It is known from records and finds that Sumerian traders reached out to very distant sources for metals, offering in exchange not only Sumer's staples—grains and woollen garments—but also finished metal products.

While all that could be attributed to Sumerian know-how and acumen, what needs explaining is the fact that theirs was also the terminology and written symbols (initially pictographs) connected with mining—an activity conducted in distant lands and not in Sumer. Thus, the perils of mine working in Africa were mentioned in a text called "Inanna's Descent to the Lower World"; and the ordeal of those punished to work in the mines of the Sinai Peninsula was detailed in the Epic of Gilgamesh when his companion, Enkidu, was sentenced by the gods to end his days there. Sumerian pictographic writing included an impressive array of symbols (Fig. 123) pertaining to mining, many showing varieties of mine shafts according to their structures or the minerals mined therein.

Where all these mines were located—certainly not in Sumer

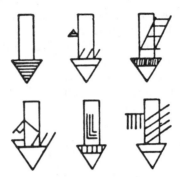

Figure 123

itself—is not always clear, for many place names remain unidentified. But some royal inscriptions indicate far and distant
lands. A good example is this quote from Cylinder A, column
xvi of Gudea, kind of Lagash (third millennium B.C.) in which
he recorded the rare materials used in building the E.NINNU
temple for his god:

> Gudea built the temple bright with metal,
> He made it bright with metal.
> He built the E.ninnu with stone,
> he made it bright with jewels;
> With copper mixed with tin he built it.
> A smith, a priest of the divine lady of the land,
> worked on its facade;
> With two hand-breadths of shining stone
> he cased the brickwork,
> with diorite's hand-breadth of bright stone.

One of the key passages in the text (which Gudea repeated
in Cylinder B, to make sure posterity remembers his pious
achievements), is the use of "copper mixed with tin" to build
the temple. The paucity of stone in Sumer had led there to the
invention of the clay brick, with which the tallest and most imposing edifices had been achieved. But as Gudea informs us, in
this instance specially imported stones were used and even the
brickwork was faced with "a handbreadth of diorite" and two
handbreadths of less rare stone. For this, copper tools were not
good enough; harder tools were needed—tools of the ancient
world's "steel," *bronze.*
As Gudea has correctly stated, bronze was a "mixture" of

copper and tin, not a natural element; it was the product of alloying copper and tin in a furnace, and thus a totally artificial product. The Sumerian rule-of-thumb for the alloy was 1:6, i.e., about 85 percent copper and 15 percent tin, which is indeed an excellent ratio. Bronze, however, was a technological achievement in other ways too. It could be shaped only by casting, not hammering or annealing; and the tin for it must be obtained from its ores through a process called smelting and recovery, for it is very rarely found in nature in its native state. It must be recovered from an ore called cassiterite. This ore is generally found in alluvial deposits that resulted from the washing out of vein or lode tin from its rocks by natural forces such as heavy rains, floods, and avalanches. The tin is recovered from the cassiterite by smelting, usually in combination with limestone in the first phase of recovery. Even this oversimplified description of the metallurgical processes involved will suffice to make clear that bronze was a metal that required advanced metallurgical know-how at every stage of its processing.

To add to the problems, it was also a metal difficult to find. Whatever sources may have been available—which is not certain—near Sumer, were quickly exhausted. Some Sumerian texts mention two "tin mountains" in a far land whose identity is unclear; some (e.g., B. Landsberger in the *Journal of Near Eastern Studies,* vol. xxi) do not shun such faraway places as the tin belt of the Far East (Burma, Thailand, and Malaysia) that is now a major source of tin. It has been ascertained that in their search for this vital metal Sumerian traders, via intermediaries in Asia Minor, reached out to tin-ore sources along the Danube, especially in the provinces known nowadays as Bohemia and Saxony (where the ores have been long exhausted). Forbes has observed that "the finds in the Royal Cemetery of Ur (2500 B.C.) show that the Ur smiths . . . understood the metallurgy of bronze and copper perfectly. Where the tin ore they used came from, is still a mystery." The mystery, indeed, still persists.

Not only Gudea and other Sumerian kings in whose inscriptions tin is mentioned had to go to great lengths to obtain it (probably already in its recovered state). Even a goddess, the famous Ishtar, had to transverse mountains to find its place. In a text known as *Inanna and Ebih* (Inanna being Ishtar's Sumerian name and Ebih being the name of a distant, unidentified mountain range), Inanna sought permission of the superior gods by saying,

> Let me set out on the road to the tin ores,
> Let me learn about their mines.

For all these reasons, and perhaps because the gods—the Anunnaki—had to teach ancient man how to recover the tin from its ore through smelting, the metal was considered by the Sumerians to be a "divine" metal. Their word for it was AN.NA, literally "Heavenly Stone." (Likewise, when iron that required ore smelting came into use, it was called AN.BAR, "Heavenly Metal.") Bronze, the alloy of copper and tin, was called ZA.BAR, "Gleaming Double Metal."

The term for tin, *Anna*, was borrowed by the Hittites without much change. But in the Akkadian language, the language of the Babylonians and Assyrians and the other Semitic-speaking peoples, the term underwent a slight change to *Anaku*. The term is usually taken to mean "pure tin" *(Anak-ku);* but we wonder whether the change may have reflected a closer, more intimate association of the metal with the Anunnaki gods, for it has also been found spelled *Annakum,* meaning that which belongs to or comes from the Anunnaki.

The term appears in the Bible several times. Ending with a soft *kh,* it meant a tin-plumbline, as in the prophecy of Amos envisioning the Lord holding an *Anakh* to illustrate his promise not to deviate anymore from his people Israel. As *Anak* the term meant "necklace," reflecting the high value put on this bright metal as its rarity increased and it became as precious as silver. And it also meant "giant"—a Hebrew rendering (as we have suggested in a previous volume) of the Mesopotamian "Anunnaki." It is a rendering that raises intriguing associations with the legends of both the Old World and the New World attributing this or that feat to the "giants."

All these associations of tin with the Anunnaki may have stemmed from their original role in granting mankind this metal and the know-how it required. In fact, the slight but significant modification from the Sumerian AN.NA to the Akkadian *Anaku* suggests a certain time frame. It is well documented, from archaeological discoveries as well as texts, that the great surge into the Bronze Age slowed down circa 2500 B.C. The founder of the Akkadian dynasty, Sargon of Akkad, valued the metal so much that he chose it rather than gold or silver for commemorating himself (Fig. 124), circa 2300 B.C.

Metallurgical historians find confirmation of the dwindling supplies of tin in the fact that the percentage of tin in bronze kept being lowered, and in the discovery from texts that most of the new bronze objects were made from old bronze, by melting down earlier objects and mixing the molten alloy with more copper, sometimes reducing the tin content to as little as 2 percent. Then, for unexplained reasons, the situation changed

Figure 124

abruptly. "Only from the Middle Bronze Age onwards, say from 2200 B.C.," Forbes wrote, "are true bronze forms used and higher percentages of tin appear more regularly, and not only for intricate forms as in the earlier period."

Having given mankind bronze with which to launch the great civilizations of the fourth millennium B.C., the Anunnaki seemed to come to the rescue again over a millennium later. But while the unknown sources of tin in the first instance may have been Old World ones, the source in the second instance is a complete mystery.

Here, then, is our daring thought: *The new source was the New World.*

If, as we believe, New World tin had reached the Old World's civilization centers, it could have come from one and only one place: Lake Titicaca.

This not because the name, as we have shown, signifies lake of "the tin stones"; but because this part of Bolivia is still, millennia later, a major source of the world's tin. Tin, though not rare, is considered a scarce mineral, found only at a few places in commercial quantities. Nowadays 90 percent of the world production comes from Malaysia, Thailand, Indonesia, Bolivia, Congo-Brazzaville, Nigeria, and China (in descending order). Some earlier sources, in the Near East or in Europe, have been exhausted. Everywhere, the source of tin is alluvial cassiterite, the oxidized tin ore washed by the forces of nature out of its lodes. In only two places has tin ore been found in its original lodes: Cornwall and Bolivia. The former has been exhausted;

the latter still supplies the world from mountains that seem to be truly "tin mountains" as described in the Sumerian text of Inanna.

These rich but difficult mining sources, at elevations exceeding 12,000 feet, are concentrated primarily southeast of La Paz, the Bolivian capital, and east of Lake Poopo. The much easier to attain alluvial cassiterite in riverbeds has come from the eastern coastal area of Lake Titicaca. There it was that ancient man collected the ores for their highly prized content, and where this kind of production continues today.

Some of the most reliable research concerning Bolivian-Titicaca tin mining in antiquity was done by David Forbes (*Researches on the Mineralogy of South America*); conducted more than a century ago, it was able to provide a picture as close to that found in Conquest times as possible, before the large-scale, mechanized operations of the twentieth century changed the landscape and obscured the ancient evidence. Since pure tin is extremely rare in nature, he was surprised to be shown a sample of pure tin encasing a rock—not encased within the rock, but encasing the rock within the sample. An investigation ascertained that this sample did not come from inside a mine in Oruro, but from rich cassiterite alluvial deposits. He totally rejected the offered explanation that the metallic tin was the result of forest fires caused by lightning "smelting" the cassiterite ore, because the process of recovery of tin from the ore involves more than the mere heating of the ore: a combination first with carbon (to convert the ore, SnO_2 + C to CO_2 + Sn) and as often as not again with limestone to purify the slag.

Forbes was then shown specimens of metallic tin from gold washings on the banks of Tipuani, a tributary of the Beni river flowing eastward from the mountain ranges near the lake. To his astonishment—his own words—he found the source to be rich with gold nuggets, cassiterite, and nuggets and beads of metallic tin; this meant, convincingly, that whoever worked that area for its gold also knew how to process the tin-ore for its tin. Exploring the area just east of Lake Titicaca he was amazed—his words—by the large proportion of reduced (i.e., recovered) and melted tin. He stated that the "mystery" of the occurrence of metallic tin in these areas "cannot be explained by purely natural causes." Near Sorata he found a bronze macehead which on analysis showed the alloy to be over 88 percent copper and just over 11 percent tin, "which is quite identical with many of the ancient bronzes" of Europe and the Near East. The sites appeared to be "from extremely ancient periods."

Forbes was also surprised to realize that the Indians living around Lake Titicaca, descendants of the Aymara tribes, seemed to know where to find all these intriguing sites. In fact, the Spanish chronicler Barba (1640) stated that the Spaniards had found both tin and copper mines worked by the Indians; the tin mines were "near Lake Titicaca." Posnansky found such pre-Inca mines six miles from Tiahuanacu. He and others after him confirmed the overwhelming presence of bronze artifacts at Tiahuanacu and its environs. He argued convincingly that the back of the Gate of the Sun's niches had been fitted with golden panels that could swivel on protruding hinges or "turning prongs" which had to be of bronze to support the weight. He found at Tiahuanacu stone blocks bearing niches that served to hold bronze bolts, as at Puma Punku. At Puma Punku he had seen a piece of metal, undoubtedly bronze, that "with its denti-form prongs looked like a tackle or device for lifting weights." This piece was seen and sketched by him in 1905, but was carried off and gone by his next visit. In view of the systematic plundering of Tiahuanacu, in Inca as well as in modern times, the bronze tools found on the sacred islands of Titicaca and Coati provide a measure of what must have once existed at Tiahuanacu itself. These finds included bronze bars, levers, chisels, knives, and axes—all tools that could have served in construction work, but as likely as not also in mining operations.

Indeed, Posnansky began his four-volume treatise with an introduction dealing with mining in prehistoric times in the Bolivian highland plateau in general and in the environs of Lake Titicaca in particular. "In the mountain range of the Altiplano"—highland plateau—"are found tunnels or caverns, opened by ancient inhabitants with the object of providing themselves with useful metals. These caves are to be distinguished from those opened by the Spaniards in search of precious metals, in that the remains of ancient metallurgical labors long antedate those of the Spaniards . . . in most remote periods an intelligent and enterprising race . . . provided themselves from the depths of this mountain range with useful, if not precious, metals.

"What sort of metal was the prehistoric man of the Andes seeking in the depths of the mountains in so remote a period?" Posnansky asked. "Was it gold or silver? Certainly not! A metal of much more use caused him to ascend to the highest peaks of the Andean mountain range: it was tin." And the tin, he explained, was needed to alloy with copper to create "the noble bronze." That this was the purpose of man at Tiahuanacu, he stated, was confirmed by the discovery, within a radius of thirty leagues from Tiahuanacu, of many tin mines.

But did Andean man require this tin to make his own bronze tools? Apparently not. A major study by the leading metallurgist Erland Nordenskiöld (*The Copper and Bronze Ages in South America*) established that neither age had taken place there: There had been in South America no trace of a developed bronze or even a copper age, and the reluctant conclusion was that whatever bronze tools had been found, were in fact based on Old World shapes and Old World technologies. "Examining all our material of weapons and tools of bronze and copper from S. America," Nordenskiöld wrote, "we must confess that there is not much that is entirely original, and that to the majority of fundamental types there is something to correspond to the Old World." Still voicing his reluctance to subscribe to this conclusion, he went on to admit again that "it must be confessed that there is considerable similarity between the metal technique of the New World and that of the Old during the Bronze Age." Significantly, some of the tools included in his examples had handles shaped as the head of the Sumerian goddess Ninti with her symbol of the twin umbilical cutters, later the Mistress of the Sinai mines.

The history of bronze in the New World is thus linked to the Old World, and the story of tin in the Andes, where New World bronze originated, is inexorably linked to Lake Titicaca. In that, Tiahuanacu had a central role, tied to the minerals surrounding it; otherwise, why was it built there at all?

The three civilization centers of the Old World arose in fertile river valleys: the Sumerian in the plain between the Tigris and Euphrates, the Egyptian-African along the Nile, that of India along the Indus river. Their base was agriculture; trade, made possible by the rivers, provided the industrial raw materials and enabled the export of grains and finished products. Cities sprung up along the rivers, commerce required written records, trade flourished when society was organized and international relations developed.

Tiahuanacu does not fit that pattern. It gives the appearance of being, as the popular saying goes, "all dressed up with nowhere to go." A great metropolis whose culture and art forms influenced almost the whole Andean region—built in the middle of nowhere, on the shores of an inhospitable lake at the top of the world. And even if for the minerals, why there? Geography may provide an answer.

It is customary to begin every description of Lake Titicaca by stating that it is the highest navigable body of water in the world, at an altitude of 13,861 feet. It is a rather large lake, with a surface area of 3,210 square miles. Its depth varies from a thousand feet to a hundred. Elongated in shape, it has a maximum length of 120 miles and a maximal width of 44 miles. Its ragged shoreline, the product of the mountains that surround it, forms numerous peninsulas, capes, isthmuses, and straits, and the lake has more than two score islands. The northwest–southeast layout of the lake (Fig. 109) is dictated by the mountain chains that skirt it. On the east runs the great range of the Cordillera Real of the Bolivian Andes, which includes the towering twin-peaked Mount Illampu in the Sorata group and the imposing Illimani just southeast of La Paz. Except for several small rivers that flow from this range into the lake, most flow eastward, down to the vast Brazilian plain and into the Atlantic Ocean some 2,000 miles away. It is here on the lake's eastern shores and the beds of rivers and streams that flow both ways that great deposits of cassiterite have been found.

No less imposing mountains skirt the lake on the north. There the runoff rainwaters flow mostly northward, feeding rivers, such as the Vilcanota, which some consider the true source of the Amazon; for, gathering tributaries and merging into the Urubamba, they all flow down north and then northeast into the great Amazon basin. It is there, between the mountains bordering the lake and Cuzco, that most of the gold available to the Incas had been found.

The western shore of Lake Titicaca, though bleak and dreary, is the most populated. There, among the mountains and the bays, on the coasts and in the peninsulas, present-day villages and towns share locations with ancient sites—as does Puno, the largest lakeside town and port, with the nearby enigmatic ruins of Sillustani. At that point, as modern railroad engineers have found out, a road or rail line can lead not only north but also through one of the few gaps in the Andes toward the coastal plains and the Pacific Ocean, a bare two hundred miles away.

The maritime and terrestrial geography and topography change considerably as one views the lake's southern portion (which, like most of the lake's eastern shore, belongs not to Peru but to Bolivia). There two of the largest peninsulas, that of Copacabana on the west and of Hachacache on the east, almost meet (Fig. 125) leaving only a narrow strait between the lake's much larger northern portion and its small southern one. That southern portion thus assumes the nature of a lagoon (and was so termed by Spanish chroniclers)—a body of tranquil waters as compared to the windswept northern part. The two main islands

Figure 125

of native legend, the Island of the Sun (actually, the island of Titicaca) and the Island of the Moon (actually, Coati) lie just off the northern shore of Copacabana.

It was on these islands that the Creator hid his children, the Moon and the Sun, during the Deluge. It was from *Titi-kala,* a sacred rock on the island of Titicaca, that the Sun rose to heaven after the Deluge, according to one version; it was on the sacred rock that the Sun's rays first fell when the Deluge was over, according to another version. And it was from a cave under the sacred rock that the first couple was sent to repopulate the lands—where Manco Capac was given the golden wand with which to find Cuzco and begin Andean civilization.

The lake's main outflowing river, the Desaguadero, begins its flow at the southwestern corner. It feeds off waters from Lake Titicaca to a satellite lake, Lake Poopo, situated some 260 miles away to the south, in the Bolivian province of Oruro; there is copper and silver all along that way and all the way to the Pacific coast, where Bolivia meets Chile.

It is at the southern shore of the lake that the water-filled cavity between all these mountain ranges continues as dry land, creating the valley or plateau on which Tiahuanacu is situated. Nowhere else all around the lake is there such a level plateau. Nowhere else is there a nearby lagoonlike body of water that connects with the rest of the lake, making waterborne transportation feasible. Nowhere else around the lake is there a site like this, with passes through the mountains in the three landward directions and by water northward.

And nowhere else are the prized metals right at hand—gold and silver, and copper and tin. Tiahuanacu was there because it was the best place for it to be for what it was: the metallurgical capital of South America, of the New World.

All the various spellings that have been employed—Tiahuanacu, Tiahuanaco, Tiwanaku, Tianaku—are only efforts to capture the pronunciation of the name as it has been transmitted and retained by the native population. The original name, we suggest, was TI.ANAKU: the place of *Titi* and *Anaku*—TIN CITY.

Our suggestion that *Anaku* in the place's name stems from the Mesopotamian term which meant tin as the metal granted by the Anunnaki invokes a direct link between Tiahuanacu and Lake Titicaca and the ancient Near East. There is evidence to support such a suggestion.

Bronze accompanied the sprouting of the Near Eastern civilizations and came into full metallurgical utilization there by 3500 B.C. But by 2600 B.C. or so, the supplies of tin dwindled and almost petered out. Then, suddenly, fresh supplies appeared circa 2200 B.C.; the Anunnaki, somehow, had stepped in to end the tin crisis and save the very civilizations they had given Mankind. How was that achieved?

Let us look at some known facts.

Circa 2200 B.C., when tin supplies in the Near East improved so abruptly, an enigmatic people appeared on the Near Eastern scene. Their neighbors called them *Cassites* ("Kosseans" to the Greeks of later times). There is no explanation for the name that scholars know of. But it strikes us as the possible source of the term *cassiterite* by which tin-ores have been known since antiquity; it implies a recognition of the Cassites as the people who could supply the ore or who had come from where the ore is found.

Pliny, the first century A.D. Roman savant, wrote that tin, which the Greeks called "cassiteros," was more valuable than lead. He stated that it was esteemed by the Greeks since the Trojan war (and is indeed mentioned by Homer by the term *cassiteros*). The Trojan war had taken place in the thirteenth century B.C. at the western edge of Asia Minor, where the early Mediterranean Greeks came into contact with the Hittites (or were, perhaps, Indo-European cousins of theirs). "The legends say that men seek this cassiteros in the isles of the Atlantic," Pliny wrote in his *Historia Naturalis*, "and that it is transported in boats made of osier"—a twiggy plant, like a willow—"covered with hides stitched together." The islands that the Greeks call Cassiterites, "in consequence of their abundance of tin," he wrote, are out in the Atlantic facing the cape called the End of Earth; "they are the six Islands of the Gods, which some people have designated as the Isles of Bliss." It is an intriguing statement, for if the Hittites from whom the Greeks had learned all that spoke of the gods as being the Anunnaki, we have here a term with all the connotations of *Anaku*.

The reference, however, is usually taken to mean the Scilly Islands off Cornwall, especially since the Phoenicians are known to have reached that part of the British Isles for its tin in the first millennium B.C.; the Prophet Ezekiel, their contemporary, specifically mentions tin as one of the metals that the Phoenicians of Tyre had imported in their seagoing vessels.

The references in Pliny and Ezekiel are the most conspicuous though not the only pillars upon which quite a number of modern authors have raised theories of Phoenician landings on the American continents at that time. The line of thought has been that after the Assyrians ended the independence of the Phoenician city-states in the eastern Mediterranean in the ninth century B.C., the Phoenicians established a new center, Carthage (*Keret-Hadasha*, "New City") in the western Mediterranean, in North Africa. From that new base they continued their trade in metals, but also began to raid the native Africans for slaves. In 600 B.C. they circumnavigated Africa in search of gold for the Egyptian king Necho (thus emulating a feat performed for King Solomon four centuries earlier); and in 425 B.C. under a leader named Hanno they sailed around West Africa to establish gold and slave supply posts. Hanno's expedition returned safely to Carthage, for he lived to tell the tale of his voyage. But others before him or after him, so the theory goes, were swept off course by the Atlantic currents and shipwrecked on an American coast.

Putting aside the much more speculative discoveries of artifacts that point to Mediterranean presences in North America, the evidence for such presences in Middle and South America is more compelling. One of the few academicians who has stuck his neck out in this direction is Professor Cyrus H. Gordon (*Before Columbus* and *Riddles in History*). Reminding his readers of earlier mention of the identity of the name Brazil with the Semitic term *Barzel* for iron, he gave considerable credence to the so-called Paraiba Inscription that turned up in that north Brazilian site in 1872. Its disappearance soon thereafter and the vague circumstances of its discovery have induced most scholars to consider it a forgery, especially as its acceptance as authentic would undermine the notion that there had been no contacts between the Old and New Worlds. But Gordon, with great scholarship, argued for accepting as authentic the inscription that it was a message left by the captain of a Phoenician ship, separated by a storm from its sister ships, that had sailed from the Near East circa 534 B.C.

What is common to all these studies is, first, that the "discovery" of America was accidental, a result of a shipwreck or an off-course diversion by ocean currents; and second, that its time was in the first millennium B.C. and most probably in the second half of that millennium.

But we are discussing a much earlier time, almost two thousand years earlier; and we are claiming that the exchange of goods and people between the Old and New World was not accidental, but the result of the deliberate intervention of the "gods," the Anunnaki.

It is certain that the Cassites were not Britishers in disguise. Near Eastern records place them to the east of Sumer, in what is nowadays Iran. They were related to the Hittites of Asia Minor as well as to the Hurrians (the biblical *Horites,* "People of the Shafts") who acted as a geographical and cultural link between Sumer in southern Mesopotamia and the Indo-European peoples to the north. They and their predecessors, including the Sumerians, could have reached South America by sailing westward, around the tip of Africa and across the Atlantic to Brazil; or eastward, around the tip of Indochina and the island archipelago and across the Pacific to Ecuador and Peru. Each route would have required navigational feats and maps of sea routes.

Such maps, it must be concluded, did exist.

The suspicion that early maps were available to European

navigators begins with Columbus himself. It is now generally believed that he knew where he was going because he had obtained from Paolo del Pozzo Toscanelli, an astronomer, mathematician and geographer from Florence, Italy, copies of the letter and maps Toscanelli had sent in 1474 to the Church and Court in Lisbon wherein Toscanelli had urged the Portuguese to attempt a *westward* passage to India rather than by circumnavigating Africa. Abandoning centuries of petrified geographic dogma based on the works of Ptolemy of Alexandria (second century A.D.), Toscanelli picked up the ideas of pre-Christian Greek scholars such as Hipparchus and Eudoxus that the Earth was a sphere, and its measurements and size from Greek savants of earlier centuries. He found confirmation for these ideas in the Bible itself, such as in the prophetic book Esdras II that was part of the Bible in its first Latin translation, which clearly spoke of a "round world." Toscanelli accepted all that but miscalculated the width of the Atlantic; he also believed that the land lying some 3,900 miles west of the Canary Islands was the tip of Asia. This was where Columbus encountered land, the islands he believed were the "West Indies"—a misnomer that has remained to this day.

Modern researchers are convinced that the King of Portugal even possessed maps that delineated the Atlantic coast of South America, jutting more than a thousand miles eastward than the islands discovered by Columbus. They find confirmation of this belief in the compromise ordered by the Pope in May 1493 that drew a line of demarcation between the Spanish-discovered lands west of the line and unknown lands, if any, east of it. This north–south line 370 leagues west of the Cape Verde Islands, demanded by the Portuguese, gave them Brazil and the greater part of South America—to the eventual surprise of the Spaniards, but not of the Portuguese, who are believed to have known beforehand of this continent.

Indeed, by now a surprisingly large number of maps from pre-Columbian times have been found; some (as the Medicean map of 1351, the Pizingi map of 1367, and others) show Japan as a large island in the western Atlantic and, significantly, an island named "Brasil" midway to Japan. Others contain outlines of the Americas as well as of Antarctica—a continent whose features have been obscured by the ice covering it, suggesting that, incredibly, these maps were drawn based on data available when the icecap was gone—a state of affairs that existed right after the Deluge circa 11,000 B.C. and for a while thereafter.

The best known of these improbable yet extant maps is that of Piri Re'is, a Turkish admiral, bearing a Moslem date equivalent to A.D. 1513. The admiral's notation on it stated that it was partly based on maps used by Columbus. For a long time it was assumed that European maps from the Middle Ages as well as Arab maps were based on the geography of Ptolemy; but it was shown by studies at the turn of the century that very accurate fourteenth-century European maps were based on Phoenician cartography, and especially that of Marinus of Tyre (second century A.D.). But where did he obtain his data? C. H. Hapgood, in one of the best studies on the Piri Re'is map and its antecedents (*Maps of the Ancient Sea Kings*), has concluded that "the evidence presented by the ancient maps appears to suggest the existence in remote times... of a true civilization of an advanced kind"; more advanced than Greece or Rome, and in nautical sciences ahead of eighteenth-century Europe. He recognized that before them all was the Mesopotamian civilization, extending back at least 6,000 years; but certain features on the maps, such as Antarctica, made him wonder who had preceded the Mesopotamians.

While most studies of these maps concentrate on their Atlantic features, the studies by Hapgood and his team established that the Piri Re'is map also depicts correctly the Andean mountains, the rivers including the Amazon that flow from them eastward, and the South American *Pacific* coast from about 4 degrees south to about 40 degrees south—i.e., from Ecuador through Peru to midway in Chile. Amazingly, the team found that "the drawing of the mountains indicates that they were observed from the sea, from coastwise shipping, and not imagined." The coasts were drawn in such detail that the Paracas Peninsula could be discerned.

Stuart Piggott (*Aux portes de l'histoire*) was one of the first to note that that stretch of Pacific coast of South America also appeared on the European copies of Ptolemy's Map of the World. It was shown, however, not as a continent beyond a vast ocean, but as a *Tierra Mitica,* mythical land, extending from the tip of southern China beyond a peninsula called *Quersoneso de Oro,* the Peninsula of Gold, all the way southward to a continent we now call Antarctica.

This observation prompted the noted South American archaeologist D. E. Ibarra Grasso to launch an extensive study of ancient maps; his conclusions were published in his *La Representacion de America en mapas Romanos de tiempos de Cristo.* As other researchers he concluded that the European maps leading to the Age of Discovery were based on the work of Ptolemy, which in turn was based on the cartography and geography of Marinus of Tyre and even earlier information.

a   b

Figure 126

Ibarra Grasso's study shows convincingly that the outline of the western coast of this "appendix" called Tierra Mitica conforms to the shape of the western coast of South America where it juts out into the Pacific. This is where legends placed the prehistoric landings all along!

The European copies of Ptolemy's maps included a name for a place in the midst of that mythical land, *Cattigara;* the location, Ibarra Grasso wrote, is "where in fact Lambayeque is situated, the principal center of gold metallurgy in the whole American continent." Not surprisingly, it is where Chavin de Huantar, the prehistoric gold processing center, was established, where the African Olmecs, the bearded Semites, and the Indo-Europeans had met.

Did the Cassites also land there, or in the Bay of Paracas, nearer Tiahuanacu?

The Cassites have left a rich legacy of metallurgical craftsmanship spanning the third and second millennia B.C. Their artifacts include numerous objects made of gold, silver, even iron; but their metal of preference was bronze, making the "Bronzes of Luristan" a renowned term among art historians and archaeologists. They decorated their artifacts, as often as not, with images of their gods (Fig. 126a) and of their legendary heroes, among whom a favorite was that of Gilgamesh wrestling with the lions (Fig. 126b).

Incredibly, we find identical themes and artistic forms in the Andes. In a study titled *La Religion en el Antiguo Peru* Rebecca Carnon-Cachet de Girard illustrated gods worshiped by Peruvians from depictions on earthenware vessels found in central and northern coastal areas; the similarity to the Cassite bronzes is astounding (Fig. 127a). At Chavin de Hauntar, it will be recalled, where statues depicted Hittite-like types, we also saw depictions of the Gilgamesh-and-the-lions scene. Whoever had come from the Old World to tell and depict the tale there, did so also at Tiahuanacu: among the bronze objects found there, a

Figure 127

bronze plaque, as at Luristan of the Cassites, clearly depicted the Near Eastern hero in the same scene (Fig. 127b)!

Depictions of "angels," the winged "messenger gods" (the biblical *Mal'achim,* literally "emissaries") have been included in the art of all the ancient peoples; those of the Hittites (Fig. 128a) resemble most the winged messengers flanking the princi-

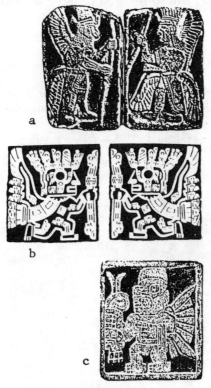

Figure 128

pal deity on the Gate of the Sun (Fig. 128b). It is significant, for reconstructing the events in American antiquity, that at Chavin de Huantar, where we believe the realms of the Teotihuacan and Tiahuanacu gods met, Olmec features replaced the Mesopotamian ones in the winged-god panels (Fig. 128c).

At Chavin de Huantar the Indo-European deity was the Bull God, a mythical animal for the other sculptors there. But although the bull was not present in South America until some were brought over by the Spaniards, scholars have been surprised to find that some Indian communities near Puno on Lake Titicaca and even at Pucara (a legendary stop on the route of Viracocha from the lake to Cuzco) worship the bull in ceremonies that originated in pre-Hispanic times (viz. J. C. Spahni, "Lieux de culte precolombiens" in *Zeitschrift für Ethnologie,* 1971). At Tiahuanacu and the southern Andes, this god was depicted armed with a lightning bolt and holding a metal wand —an image carved on stone, depicted on ceramics and on textiles. It is a combination of symbols well known from the ancient Near East, where the god called *Ramman* ("The Thun-

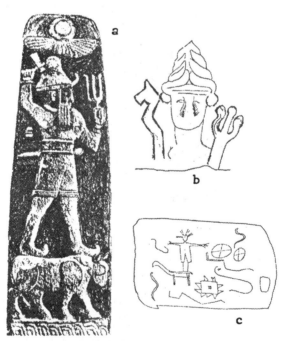

Figure 129

derer") by the Babylonians and Assyrians, *Hadad* ("Rolling Echo") by the West Semites, and *Teshub* ("Wind Blower") by the Hittites and Cassites, was depicted standing upon a bull, his cult animal, holding the metal tool in one hand and a forked lightning in the other (Fig. 129a).

The Sumerians, where the Old World pantheons originated, called this god Adad or ISH.KUR ("He of the Far Mountains"), and depicted him with the metal tool and forked lightning (Fig. 129b). One of their epithets for him was ZABAR DIB.BA—"He who bronze obtains and divides"—an illuminating clue.

Was he not Rimac of the southern coasts of Peru, Viracocha of the Andean highlands, whose image with the metal tool and forked lightning appeared all over, whose symbol of a lightning appeared by itself on many monuments? He may have even been shown standing upon a bull in a stone carving, found southwest of Lake Titicaca by Ribero and von Tschudi (Fig. 129c). Scholars who have studied the name *Viracocha* in its diverse variants agree that its components mean "Lord/Supreme" who of "Rain/Storm/Lightning" is "Maker/Creator." An Inca hymn described him as the god "who comes in the thunder and in the storm clouds." This is almost word for word the way this

Aerial photo from 2000 feet

Figure 130

deity, the God of Storms, was lauded in Mesopotamia; and the golden disk from Cuzco (Fig. 85b) depicts a deity with the tell-tale symbol of the forked lightning.

Some time in those remote days Ishkur/Teshub/Viracocha placed his symbol of the forked lightning, for all to see from the air and from the ocean, on a mountainside in the Bay of Paracas (Fig. 130)—the very bay the Hapgood team identified on the Piri Re'is map, the bay that was probably the anchorage harbor for the ships carrying the tin and bronze of Tiahuanacu to the Old World. It was a symbol proclaiming to gods and men alike:

THIS IS THE REALM OF THE STORM GOD!

For, as the Book of Job had stated, there was indeed a land of which the ingots come, whose underground is upheavaled as with fire . . . A place so high among the peaks that "even a vulture knows not the way thereto, and a falcon's eye has not discerned it." It was there that the god who provided the vital metals "set his hand to the granite . . . overturned mountains at their roots . . . cut galleries through the rocks."

12

GODS OF THE GOLDEN TEARS

Some time after 4000 B.C. the great Anu, ruler of Nibiru, came to Earth on a state visit.

It was not the first time he had made the arduous space journey. Some 440,000 Earth-years earlier—a mere 122 years in terms of Nibiru—his firstborn son, Enki, had led the first group of fifty Anunnaki to Earth to obtain the gold with which this seventh planet was blessed. On Nibiru, nature and technological usages had combined to thin out and damage the planet's atmosphere, an atmosphere needed not only for breathing but that also had acted to envelop the planet into a greenhouse, preventing its inner-generated heat from dissipating. And only by suspending gold particles high above Nibiru, its scientists concluded, could Nibiru be saved from becoming a frozen and lifeless globe.

Enki, the brilliant scientist that he was, splashed down in the Persian Gulf and established his base, Eridu, on its shores. His plan was to obtain the gold by extracting it from the gulf's waters; but not enough was attained that way, and the crisis on Nibiru deepened. Tired of Enki's assurances that he would make the project a success, Anu came to Earth to see things for himself. He had with him his heir apparent, Enlil: though not the firstborn, Enlil was entitled to the succession because his mother, Antu, was a half sister of Anu. He lacked the scientific brilliance of Enki, but was an excellent administrator; not fascinated with the mysteries of nature, but one believing in taking charge and getting things done. And the thing to do, all the studies indicated, was to get the gold by mining it where it was abundant: in southern Africa.

Bitter arguments broke out not only regarding the project itself, but also between the rival half brothers. Anu even thought of staying on Earth and letting one of his sons act as regent on Nibiru; but the idea only caused more discord. Finally they drew lots. Enki was to go to Africa and organize the mining; Enlil was to stay in the E.DIN (Mesopotamia), build the necessary facilities for refining the ores and for shipping the gold back to Nibiru. And Anu returned to the planet of the Anunnaki. That was the first visit.

And then there was the second visit, brought about by another emergency. Forty Nibiru-years after the first landing, the Anunnaki who were assigned to work in the gold mines mutinied. How much was really caused by their arduous toil in the deep mines and how much reflected the envy and friction between the two half brothers and their contingents, one can only guess. The fact was that the Anunnaki supervised by Enki in southern Africa mutinied, refused to continue mining, and held Enlil hostage after he was there to defuse the crisis.

All those events were recorded; they were, millennia later, told to the Earthlings that they might know how it all began. A Council of the Gods was convened. Enlil insisted that Anu come to Earth and preside, to pass judgment against Enki. In the presence of the gathered leaders Enlil described the chain of events, accused Enki of leading the mutiny. But when the mutineers told their story, Anu sympathized with them. They were spacemen, not miners; and their toil had indeed become unbearable.

But did not the job need doing? How would life on Nibiru survive without this mined gold? Enki had a solution: we will create Primitive Workers, he said, who will take over the hard toil! To the astounded gathering he related that he had been conducting experiments, with the aid of the chief medical officer, Ninti/Ninharsag. There already exists on Earth, in East Africa, a primitive being—an Apeman. This being must have evolved on Earth from Nibiru's own Seed of Life, passed from Nibiru to Earth during the primeval celestial collision with Tiamat. There is genetic compatibility; what is needed is to upgrade this being, by giving it some of the Anunnaki's own genes. It will then be a creature in the likeness and in the image of the Anunnaki, able to hold tools, intelligent enough to carry out orders.

And so it was that LULU AMELU, the "Mixtured Worker," was created, out of genetic manipulation and the fertilization of an Apewoman's egg in a laboratory flask. The hybrids could not procreate; female Anunnaki had to act each time as birth-goddesses. But Enki and Ninharsag perfected them through trial and error until the perfect model was achieved. They named him *Adam,* "He Of Earth"—Earthling. With fertile servants, gold was produced in abundance, the seven settlements became

cities, the Anunnaki—600 on Earth, 300 on orbiting stations—
became used to a leisurely life. Some, over the objections of
Enlil, took the Daughters of Man as wives, even had children by
them. For the Anunnaki, obtaining the gold was now a task
without tears; but to Enlil it all began to look like a mission
perverted.

It all came to an end with the Deluge. For a long time the
scientific observations had warned that the ice cap that was
building up on the Antarctic continent became unstable; the
next time Nibiru passed in Earth's vicinity, between Mars and
Jupiter, its gravitational pull might cause this tremendous ice
mass to slip off its continent, creating a worldwide tidal wave,
abruptly changing the oceans' and Earth's temperatures, causing
unparalleled storms. Consulting Anu, Enlil gave the order: prepare the spacecraft, be ready to abandon Earth!

But what about Mankind, its creators, Enki and Ninharsag,
asked. Let Mankind perish, Enlil said. He made all the Anunnaki swear to secrecy, lest the desperate Earthlings interfere
with the Anunnaki's departure preparations. Enki, reluctant,
swore too; but pretending to speak to a wall, he instructed his
faithful follower Ziusudra to build a *Tibatu,* a submersible ship,
in which he and his family and enough animals could survive the
avalanche of water, so that life on Earth should not perish. And
he provided Ziusudra with a navigator to bring the ship to
Mount Ararat, the Near East's most conspicuous double-peaked
mountain.

The Creation and Deluge texts dictated by the Anunnaki to
the Sumerians relate tales much more detailed and specific than
the familiar biblical concise and edited versions. By the time the
catastrophe occurred, there had been on Earth not only demigods. Some of the principal deities, members of the sacred circle
of Twelve, were themselves in a way Earthlings: Nannar/Sin
and Ishkur/Adad, Enlil's younger sons, were born on Earth; so
were of course Sin's twin children, Utu/Shamash and Inanna/
Ishtar. Enki and Ninharsag (with whom he may have shared his
secret "Operation Noah") joined the others in suggesting that
the Anunnaki not leave Earth for good, but remain in Earth
orbit for a while to see what would happen. And indeed, after
the immense tidal wave had come and gone and
the rains had stopped, the peaks of Earth began to show and the
Sun's rays, shining through the clouds, painted rainbows in the
skies.

Enlil, discovering that Mankind had survived, was enraged at
first. But then he relented. The Anunnaki, he realized, could
still stay on Earth; but if they were to rebuild their centers and

resume the production of gold, Man must be enabled to proliferate and prosper and be treated no longer as a slave but as a
partner.

In antediluvial times the spaceport, for the coming and going
of the Anunnaki and their supplies and for shipping out the
gold, was in Mesopotamia, at Sippar. But that whole fertile valley between the Euphrates and Tigris was now covered with
billions of tons of mud. Still using the twin-peaked Ararat as the
focal point on which to anchor the apex of the Landing Corridor, they erected twin artificial mountains at the thirtieth parallel on the bank of the Nile—the two great pyramids of Giza, to
serve as landing beacons for a postdiluvial spaceport in the Sinai
peninsula. It was as near, even somewhat nearer, to the African
gold sources as the spaceport in Mesopotamia had been.

So that the Earthlings could survive, multiply, and be helpful
to the Anunnaki, Mankind was granted civilization in three
states. Seeds for vital crops were brought over from Nibiru, wild
strains of grains and animals were domesticated, clay and metal
technologies taught. The latter was of great importance, for it
touched on the Anunnaki's own success in resuming the supply
of gold, now that the old mines were clogged with mud and
water.

Since the Deluge, Nibiru had come once again near Earth,
and vital materials had been received from it; but little of value
was sent back. In the olden gold sources it was now necessary to
locate hidden lodes, tunnel into mountainsides, cut shafts into
the earth, blast the rocks. Mankind had to be provided with
tools—hard tools—to be able to extract what the Anunnaki
could locate and blast with their ray guns. Fortunately, the avalanche of water had also done some good, for it had exposed
lodes, washed them out, filled riverbeds with golden nuggets
mixed with mud and gravel. Getting hold of this gold could
open up new sources—easier to work but more difficult to
reach and transport; for the place where this kind of nugget gold
was plentiful was on the other side of Earth: there, along mountain chains that face the great ocean, untold golden riches had
been exposed. It was just there for the taking—if the Anunnaki
would go there, if a way could be found to ship that gold.

And now that Nibiru had neared Earth again, the great Anu
with his spouse Antu had come to Earth for a state visit, to see
for himself where matters stood. What had been achieved by
granting Mankind the two divine metals, AN.NA and AN.BAR
with which to make the hard tools? What had been achieved by
expanding the operations to the other side of the world? Were

the storages filled with gold, as had been reported, ready to be shipped to Nibiru?

"After the Flood had swept over the Earth, when Kingship was brought down from Heaven, Kingship was first in Kish." So begins the recitation, in the Sumerian King Lists, of the various dynasties and capitals of the first Near Eastern civilization. Archaeology has indeed confirmed the preeminent antiquity of that Sumerian city. Of its twenty-three rulers, one bore a name-epithet that can be understood to mean that he was a metallurgist; it is clearly stated that the twenty-second ruler, Enmenbaragsi, was the "one who carried away as spoil the cast weapon of Elam." Elam, in the highlands east and southeast of Sumer, was indeed one of the places where metallurgy had begun; and the mention of the prize booty, a cast weapon, confirms the archaeological evidence of a fully developed metallurgy in the ancient Near East soon after 4000 B.C.

But "Kish was smitten with weapons," perhaps by the very same Elamites whose land had been invaded; and Kingship, the capital, was transferred to a brand-new city called Uruk (the biblical Erech). Of its twelve kings the best known has been Gilgamesh, of heroic fame. His name meant "to Gibil, god of Smelting/Casting [dedicated]." Metalworking, it appears, was important to the rulers of Uruk. One of them had the word *smith* describe that for which he was renowned. The very first ruler, whose reign began when Uruk was no more than a sacred precinct, had the prefix MES—"Casting Master"—as part of his name. Of him the inscription was unusually long:

> Mes-kiag-gasher, son of divine Utu,
> became high priest of Eanna as well as king . . .
> Meskiaggasher went into the Western Sea
> and came forth toward the Mountains.

This is, by the very fact that it is a lengthy statement where usually only the king's name and the length of his reign are listed, very important information, recording a renowned feat. Which sea Meskiaggasher, the Casting Master, crossed and at what mountain range he arrived, we shall never know for sure; but the wording does suggest the other side of the world.

We can understand the urgency of bringing metallurgy at Uruk to perfection: it had to do with Anu's forthcoming state visit. Perhaps to impress on him that all was going well, that very city, Uruk, was built in his honor, and metallurgical achievements were shown off. At the center of the sacred precinct a many-staged temple was built, its corners made of cast metal. Its name, E.ANNA, is generally taken to mean "House of Anu"; but it could also mean "House of Tin." The detailed texts that recorded the protocol and program of the royal visit to Uruk reveal a place lavished with gold.

Tablets found in the archieves of Uruk that, according to their scribe's notation were copies of earlier Sumerian texts, are legible only from a midpoint. Anu and Antu are already seated in the temple's courtyard, reviewing a procession of gods carrying in the golden scepter. Meanwhile, goddesses prepare the visitors' sleeping quarters in the E.NIR—"House of Brightness"—that was covered with the "handiwork of Lower World gold." As the skies darkened, a priest ascended the ziggurat's topmost stage to observe the expected appearance of Nibiru, "Great Planet of Anu of Heaven." After appropriate hymns were recited, the visitors washed their hands from golden basins and were served an evening meal from seven golden trays; beer and wine were poured from golden vessels. After more hymns hailing "the Creator's Planet, the Planet that is Heaven's Hero" had been recited, the visitors were led by a procession of torch-carrying gods to their "golden enclosure" for the night.

In the morning, golden censers were filled by priests during sacrifices as the gods were awakened for an elaborate breakfast served from golden dishes. When it was time to depart, the visiting deities were led in a procession of gods, accompanied by hymn-singing priests, to the quay where their boat was moored. They left the city through the Exalted Gate, proceeded down the Avenue of the Gods, and arrived at "The Holy Quay, the Dike of the Ship of Anu" that was to take them on "The Path of the Gods." At a chapel called House of *Akitu,* Anu and Antu joined the Gods of Earth in prayers, reciting blessings seven times. And then, "grasping hands," the gods departed.

If, by the time of this state visit, the Anunnaki had already been seeking gold in the New World, would Anu and Antu have sought to include the new lands of gold in their itinerary? Would the Anunnaki on Earth seek to impress them with their new achievements, the new prospects, the promise of providing Nibiru with the vital metal in sufficient quantities, once and for all?

If the answer is yes, then the existence of Tiahuanacu and much else about it could be explained. For if, in Sumer, a special city with a brand-new sacred precinct, with a golden enclosure, and an Avenue of the Gods and Holy Quays was established for the visit to the Olden Land, we could presume the similar establishment of a new city with a brand-new golden enclosure and a sacred avenue and sacred quays in the heart of the New Lands. And, as at Uruk, we would expect to find an observatory for determining the moment of the appearance of Nibiru in the evening skies, followed by the rising of the other planets.

Only such a parallelism, we feel, can explain the need for the observatory that the Kalasasaya had been, for its precision, and for its date: circa 4000 B.C. Only such a state visit, we suggest, can explain the elaborate architecture of Puma-Punku, its royallike piers, and, yes, its gold-plated enclosure. For that is precisely what archaeologists had found at Puma-Punku: incontrovertible evidence that gold plates covered not only portions of gates (as were the back panels of the Gate of the Sun at Tiahuanacu), but that whole walls, entrances and cornices were plated with gold. Posnansky found and photographed rows of small round holes in many polished and dressed stone blocks that "served to support golden plates which covered them by means of nails, also of gold." When he delivered a lecture on the subject to the Geographic Society in April 1943, he presented one of these blocks with five golden nails still sticking in it (the other nails having been pulled out by gold seekers when they removed the golden plates).

The possibility that at Puma-Punku there had been erected, at the earliest time, an edifice whose walls, ceiling, and cornices were covered with gold just as the E.NIR had been in Uruk becomes even more significant when we find that the bas-reliefs decorating the ceremonial gates at Puma-Punku, as well as some of the gigantic statues of the Great God at Tiahuanacu, were inlaid with gold. Posnansky discovered and photographed the attachment holes, "some two millimeters in diameter, round about the reliefs." A principal gate at Puma-Punku that he named Gate of the Moon had its relief of Viracocha as well as the god's face in the meander under it "inlaid with gold... which made the principal hieroglyphs stand out with great brilliance."

No less significant was the discovery of Posnansky that where these figures depicted the god's eyes, the gold inlay and nails "secured into the slits of the eyes small round plates of turquoise. We have found," Posnansky reported, "many of these pieces of turquoise perforated in the center, in the cultural strata of Tiahuanacu"—a fact that led him to believe that not only the reliefs on the gates, but also the gigantic stone statues of gods that have been found at Tiahuanacu, were inlaid with gold on their faces and their eyes inlaid with turquoise.

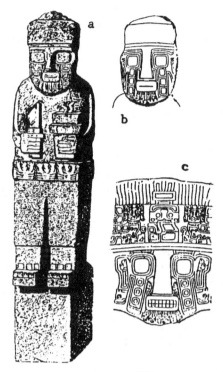

Figure 131

This discovery is most remarkable, for there is no turquoise —a semiprecious blue-green stone—anywhere in South America. It is a mineral whose earliest mining, at the end of the fifth millennium B.C., is believed to have taken place in the Sinai peninsula and in Iran. All told, these inlaying techniques were purely Near Eastern and are found nowhere else in the Americas—certainly not at those early times.

Virtually all the statues found at Tiahuanacu depict the gods shedding three tears from each eye. The tears were inlaid with gold, as can still be seen on some of the statues now on display at the Museo del Oro in La Paz. A famous large statue that has been nicknamed El Fraile (Fig. 131a), which is about ten feet high, has been carved, as other gigantic Tiahuanacu statues have been, of sandstone; this suggests that they all belong to the earliest Tiahuanacu period. The deity holds a serrated tool in his right hand; the three stylized teardrops from each eye, which were undoubtedly inlaid with gold, can be clearly seen (as in the sketch, Fig. 131b). Similar three teardrops can be seen on the face called the Gigantic Head (Fig. 131c) that treasure hunters broke off a colossal statue because of the local belief that Tia-huanacu's builders "possessed the secret of compounding stone" and that the statues were not carved from stone but were cast by a magical process that enabled the hiding of gold inside the statues.

This belief may have been sustained by the inlaying of the god's tears with gold, a practice that may explain why the Andean people (like the Aztecs) called gold nuggets "tears of the gods." Since all these statues depicted the same deity as on the Gate of the Sun, where he is also shown shedding tears, he has come to be called "The Weeping God." In view of our evidence, we feel justified calling him "God of the Golden Tears." A gigantic carved monolith found at a satellite site (Wancai) depicts the deity with a conical and horned headdress—the typical headdress of Mesopotamian gods—and with lightning bolts instead of tears (Fig. 132), clearly identifying him as the Storm God.

Figure 132

One of the gold-plated stone blocks at Puma-Punku with "mysterious cavities" and a deep channel within it was cut at a corner to hold a funnel, and Posnansky surmised it was part of a sacrificial altar. However, one of the several satellite sites near Tiahuanacu, where stone remains make them a mini Puma-Punku and where golden artifacts have been found, is called *Chuqui-Pajcha,* which in Aymara means "where the liquid gold is funneled," suggesting a gold producing process rather than sacrificial libations.

That gold was available and plentiful at Tiahuanacu and its satellites is evident not only from legends, tales, or place names, but also from archaeological remains. Many golden objects classified by scholars as Classical Tiahuanacu because of their shape or decorations (stylized images of the God of the Golden Tears, staircases, crosses) have been found at nearby land sites as well as islands in the course of excavations in the 1930s, 1940s, and 1950s. Especially noteworthy were the archaeological missions sponsored by the American Museum of Natural History (under William C. Bennett), the Peabody Museum of American Archaeology and Ethnology (under Alfred Kidder II), and the Ethnological Museum of Sweden (under Stig Rydén, together with Max Portugal, then curator of the Archaeological Museum in La Paz.)

The objects included cups, vases, disks, tubes, and pins (one of the latter, some six inches long, had a head in the shape of a three-branched plume). Golden objects found during earlier excavations on the two sacred islands, Titicaca (Island of the Sun) and Coati (Island of the Moon), were described by Posnansky in his *Guia General* to Tiahuanacu and its environs, and even more so by A. F. Bandelier (*The Islands of Titicaca and Koati*). The finds on Titicaca have been mostly in unidentifiable ruins in the vicinity of the Sacred Rock and its cavern; scholars cannot agree whether the artifacts belong to the early periods of Tiahuanacu, or (as some hold) stem from Inca times, for it is known that the Incas came to this island to worship and to erect shrines in the reign of Mayta Capac, the fourth Inca ruler.

The finds at and around Tiahuanacu of golden and bronze artifacts leave no doubt that gold preceded bronze (i.e., tin) in that area. Posnansky was emphatic in relegating bronze to the third period of Tiahuanacu, and showed incidences where bronze clamps were used to repair structures from the golden era. Since the mines in the nearby mountains show clear evidence that tin ores and gold were obtained at the same sites, it was probably the discovery of gold followed by its placer mining in the Titicaca region that brought out the existence of cassiterite: the two are found intermingled in the same riverbeds and streams. At the Tipuani river and at the river that flows from Mount Illampu, an official Bolivian report (titled *Bolivia and the Opening of the Panama Canal,* 1912) stated that in addition to the tin ores, "both rivers are famous for the presence of gravels containing immense quantities of gold"; at depths of 300 feet, rock bottom could not be found. Remarkably, "the proportion of gold increases with the depth of the gravel." The report pointed out that Tipuani river gold was 22–23½ carat fine—almost purest gold. The list of Bolivian sites of placer gold is almost inexhaustible, even after all the centuries of exploitation since the Conquest. The Spaniards alone, between 1540 and 1750, extracted from Bolivian sources over 100,000,000 ounces of gold.

Before the land now called "Bolivia" became independent in the nineteenth century, it was known as Upper Peru and was part of the Spaniards' Peruvian domains. The mineral resources certainly knew no political borders, and we have already described in earlier chapters the riches in gold, silver, and copper that the Spaniards encountered in Peru proper and the European belief that the "mother lode" of all gold in the western Americas, north and south, lay within the Peruvian Andes.

A look at a map of South America mineral resources provides a clear picture. Three bands of varying widths of gold, silver, and copper lodes snake their way along the Andean ranges in the northwestern–southeastern slant, all the way from Colombia in the north to Chile and Argentina in the south. Dotted along the way are some of the world's most renowned sources for these metals, some regarded as almost pure mountains of the minerals. The slow forces of nature, and no doubt the immense avalanche of water of the Deluge, have forced the metals and their ores out of their rock-embedded lodes—exposing them, washing them down mountainsides and into riverbeds. Since most of the mightiest rivers of South America flow off the Andean ranges eastward, through the vast plains of Brazil to the Atlantic Ocean, it is no wonder that gold and copper have also been plentiful on this side of the continent.

But it is the lodes within the Andean ranges that are the ultimate source of all the placer and mined metals; and as one looks at these interwined bands of lodes, differently colored on a map for identification, the image bears a resemblance to color drawings of the double-helix structure of DNA, entwined within itself and with its counterpart RNA, the genetic chains of life and heredity of everything that lives on Earth. Within these bands there are scattered other valuable, even rare minerals—platinum, bismuth, manganese, wolfram, iron, mercury, sulphur, antimony, asbestos, cobalt, arsenic, lead, zinc; and, quite important for modern and ancient smelting and refining, coal and petroleum.

Some of the richest lodes of gold, partly washed down riverbeds, lie east and north of Lake Titicaca. It is there, in the Cordillera Real that embraces the lake from its northeast to its southeast that a fourth band joins the others: a band of tin in the form of cassiterite. It becomes prominent on the lake's eastern shore, bends westward along the Tiahuanacu basin, then runs southward almost parallel to the Desaguandero river. It joins the other three bands near Oruro and Lake Poopo, and vanishes there.

When Anu and his spouse arrived to see all the mineral

Figure 133

riches, the sacred precinct of Tiahuanacu, its golden enclosure, its quays, were all in place. Whom did the Anunnaki enlist and bring over, at about 4000 B.C., to build all that? By then, the highland peoples around Sumer had already a tradition of rudimentary metallurgy and stoneworking, and they could have been among the artisans brought over. But the true metallurgical technology including that of casting, of high-rise construction, of building according to architectural plans, and following stellar orientations, was in the hands of the Sumerians.

The central effigy in the semisubterranean sacred enclosure is bearded, as are many of the stone heads attached to the enclosure's wall that portray unknown dignitaries. Many are turbaned, as Sumerian dignitaries had been (Fig. 133).

One must wonder where and how the Incas, continuing the custom of the Ancient Empire, acquired the Sumerian (i.e., Anunnaki-given) rules of succession. Why was it that in their incantations the Inca priests invoked Heaven by uttering the magical words *Zi-Ana* and Earth by the words *Zi-ki-a*—totally meaningless terms in either Quechua or Aymara (according to S. A. Lafone Quevado, *Ensayo Mitologico*)—but words that in Sumerian mean "Heavenly Life" (ZI.ANA) and "Life of Earth and Water" (ZI.KI.A). And why did the Incas retain from ancient empire times the term *Anta* for metals in general and copper in particular—a term that is Sumerian, as AN.TA, would have been of a class with AN.NA (tin) and AN.BAR (iron)?

These relics of Sumerian metallurgical terms (which were borrowed by their successors) are augmented by the discovery of Sumerian mining pictographs. German archaeologists led by A. Bastian have found such symbols incised on rocks on the banks of the Manizales river in Colombia's central gold region (Fig. 134a); and a French governmental mission under E. André, exploring riverbeds in the eastern region, found similar

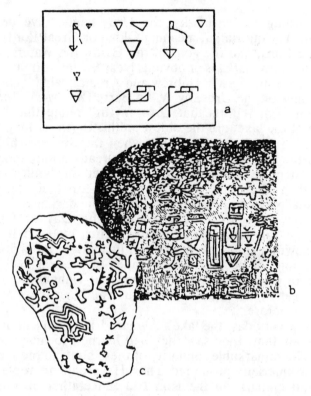

Figure 134

symbols (Fig. 134b) carved on rocks above caves that have been artificially deepened. Many petroglyphs in the Andean gold centers, the routes to them, or at places where the term *Uru* appears as a name-component include symbols that resemble Sumerian cuneiform script or pictographs, such as the radiating cross (Fig. 134c) found among petroglyphs northwest of Lake Titicaca—a symbol that the Sumerians had used to represent the planet Nibiru.

Add to all that the possibility that some of the Sumerians brought over to Lake Titicaca may have survived to present times. Nowadays only a few hundred of them are left; they live on some islands in the lake, sailing upon it in reed boats. The Aymara and Kholla tribesmen that now make up most of the area's inhabitants consider them remnants of the area's earliest dwellers, aliens from another land, whom they call *Uru*. The name is taken to mean "the Olden Ones"; but have they been so called because they came from the Sumerian capital Ur?

According to Posnansky, the Urus named five deities or *Samptni:* Pacani-Malku, meaning Olden or Great Lord; Malku, meaning Lord; and the gods of the Earth, the Waters, and the Sun. The term *malku* is of obvious Near Eastern origin, where it meant (as it still does in Hebrew and Arabic) "king." One of the few studies on the Urus, by W. La Barre (*American Anthropologist* vol. 43), reports that Uru "myths" relate that "we, the people of the lake, are the oldest on this Earth. A long time we are here, from before the time when the Sun was hidden... Before the Sun hid himself we were already a long time in this place. Then the Kollas came... They used our bodies for sacrifices when they laid the foundations for their temples... Tiahuanaco was built before the time of the darkness."

We have already established that the Day of Darkness, "when the Sun was hidden," occurred circa 1400 B.C. It was, we have shown, a global event that left its mark in the writings and recollections of people on both sides of the Earth. This Uru legend, or collective memory, affirms that Tiahuanacu was built before that event, and that the Urus had been there also for a long time before.

To this very day, the lake's Aymara tribesmen sail upon it in reed boats that, they say, they had learned to make from the Urus. The remarkable similarity of these boats to the reed boats of the Sumerians prompted Thor Heyerdahl to replicate the boat and embark on the Kon-Tiki (an epithet of Viracocha) voyages, to prove that the ancient Sumerians could have crossed the oceans.

The extent of Sumerian/Uru-rian presence in the Andes can be gleaned by such other imprints as the fact that *uru* means "day" in all the Andean languages, both in Aymara and Quechua, the same meaning ("daylight") that it had in Mesopotamia. Such other Andean terms as *uma/mayu* for water, *khun* for red, *kap* for hand, *enu/ienu* for eye, *makai* for blow are so clearly of Mesopotamian origin that Pablo Patron (*Nouvelles etudes sur les langues americaines*) concluded that "it is clearly demonstrated that the Quechua and Aymara languages of indigenous Peru had a Sumerian-Assyrian origin."

The term *uru* appears as a component of many geographical names in Bolivia and Peru, such as the important mining center Oruru, the Sacred Valley of the Incas Urubamba ("Plain/valley of the Uru") and its famed river, and many many more. Indeed, in the center of the Sacred Valley there still live in caves the remnants of a tribe that consider themselves descendants of the Urus of Lake Titicaca; they refuse to move from the caves to houses because, they claim, the mountains would collapse if they leave their insides, causing the world's end.

There are other apparent links between the civilization of Mesopotamia and that of the Andes. How explain, for example, the fact that, as in the case of Tiahuanacu, the Sumerian capital Ur was surrounded by a canal with a northern harbor and a southwestern one (leading to the Euphrates river and beyond)? And how explain the Golden Enclosure of the main temple of Cuzco, where the walls were covered with gold plates—just as the ones at Puma-Punku *and Uruk?* And the "Bible in Pictures" in the Coricancha, depicting Nibiru and its orbit?

There were the many customs that led the arriving Spaniards to see in the Indians descendants of the Ten Tribes of Israel. There were the coastal cities and their temples that brought to explorers' minds the sacred precincts and ziggurats of Sumer. And how account for the incredibly ornate textiles of the coastal people near Tiahuanacu, unique in the Americas, except by comparison with the Sumerian textiles, especially those of Ur, that were renowned in antiquity for their exquisite designs and colors? Why the portrayal of gods with conical headdresses, and a goddess with the Umbilical Cutter of Ninti? Why a calendar as in Mesopotamia, and a zodiac as in Sumer, with Precession and twelve houses?

Without rehashing all the evidence that has filled the previous chapters, it seems to us that all the pieces of the puzzle of Andean beginnings fall into place if we acknowledge the hand of the Anunnaki and the presence of Sumerians (alone or with their neighbors) in this region circa 4000 B.C. The legends of the ascent heavenward of the Creator and his two sons, the Moon and the Sun, from the sacred rock on the Island of the Sun (Titicaca Island) may well be recollections of the departure of Anu, his son Shamash and his grandson Sin: having made a short trip by boat from Puma-Punku to a waiting airborne-craft of the Anunnaki.

On that memorable night at Uruk, as soon as Nibiru had been sighted, the priests lit torches that were a signal to nearby villages. There bonfires were lit, as signals to the neighboring settlements; and soon the whole land of Sumer was aglow, celebrating the presence of Anu and Antu and the sighting of the Planet of the Gods.

Whether or not people then realized that they were viewing a celestial sight that occurs once in 3,600 Earth-years, they certainly knew it was a phenomenon once in their lifetimes. Mankind has not ceased to yearn for the return of that planet, and it justly recalls that era as a Golden Age: not only because it was physically so, but also because it culminated a period of peace and unparalleled progress for Mankind.

But no sooner (in Anunnaki terms) had Anu and Antu returned to Nibiru than the peaceful division of Earth among the Anunnaki clans was disturbed. It was circa 3450 B.C., according to our calculations, when the incident of the Tower of Babel took place: an attempt by Marduk/Ra to obtain primacy for his city Babylon in Mesopotamia. Though frustrated by Enlil and Ninurta, the attempt to involve Mankind in building a launch tower brought about the decision of the gods to disperse Mankind and confuse its languages. The sole civilization and its language were now to be split up; and after a chaotic period that lasted some 350 years, the civilization of the Nile, with its own language and rudimentary writing, was formed. It happened, Egyptologists tell us, circa 3100 B.C.

Frustrated in his effort to assume supremacy in civilized Sumer, Marduk/Ra seized upon the granting of civilization to the Egyptians to return to that land and reclaim its lordship from his brother Thoth. Now Thoth found himself a god without a people; and it is our suggestion that accompanied by some of his faithful followers he chose an abode in the New Realms —in Mesoamerica.

And we further suggest that it happened not just "circa 3100 B.C." but exactly in 3113 B.C.—the time, the year, and even the day from which the Mesoamericans began their Long Count.

Counting the passage of time by anchoring the calendar to a major event is not unusual at all. The Western Christian calendar counts the years from the birth of Christ. The Moslem calendar begins with the *Hegira,* the migration of Mohammed from Mecca to Medina. Skipping over the many examples from various preceding lands and monarchies, we shall mention the Jewish Calendar, which is in effect the ancient (and first-ever) Calendar of Nippur, the Sumerian city dedicated to Enlil. Contrary to the common assumption that the Jewish count of years (5,748 in 1988) is from the "beginning of the world," it is actually from the beginning of the Nippurian calendar in 3760 B.C.— the time, we assume, of Anu's state visit to Earth.

Why not then accept our suggestion that the arrival of Quetzalcoatl, i.e., the Winged Serpent, in his new realm was the occasion for starting the Long Count of the Mesoamerican calendar—especially since it was this very god who had introduced the calendar to these lands?

Figure 135

Having been overthrown by his own brother, Thoth (known in Sumerian texts as *Ningishzidda*—Lord of the Tree of Life) was a natural ally of his brother's adversaries, the Enlilite gods and their Chief Warrior, Ninurta. It is recorded that when Ninurta desired that a ziggurat-temple be built for him by Gudea, it was Ningishzidda/Thoth who had drawn the building plans; he may have also specified the rare materials for it, and had a hand in assuring the supplies. As a friend of the Enlilites, he had to be friendly with Ishkur/Adad and the Andean realm that was put under his control in the Titicaca region; he was probably even a welcome guest there.

Indeed, we can discern evidence that a Serpent God and his African followers probably lent a hand in developing some of the satellite metal-processing sites around Tiahuanacu. Some stone stelae and sculptures from a time in between Periods I and II of Tiahuanacu are decorated with serpent symbols—a symbol otherwise rare and unknown in Tiahuanacu; and some of the sculptures of people found at nearby sites (Fig. 135) as well as two colossal busts that have been moved and put up by the natives as a decoration at the entrance to the Tiahuanacu village church (Fig. 136) reveal, even in their eroded state, negroid features.

Posnansky, stung by criticism of his "fantastic" antiquity, did not attempt to date the transition from Period I, when sandstone was used for construction and statuary, to the more sophisticated Period II when hard andesite stone began to be used. But the fact that the changeover also marked the shifting

Figure 136

of Tiahuanacu's focus from gold to tin suggests to us the 2500 B.C. period. If, as we surmise, the Enlilite gods in charge of Near Eastern highland domains (Adad, Ninurta) were away in the New Realm, busy establishing the Cassite colony, it explains why, at about that time, Inanna/Ishtar usurped the power in the Near East and launched a bloody offensive against Marduk/Ra to avenge the death of her beloved spouse Dumuzi (caused, she claimed, by Marduk).

It was at that time, and probably as a consequence of the instability in the Old Realms, that the concerned gods decided to create a new civilization away from it all—in the Andes. While Tiahuanacu was to focus on supplying tin, there were almost inexhaustible sources of gold all along the Andean slopes. All that was needed was to give Andean Man the necessary know-how and tools to go after the gold.

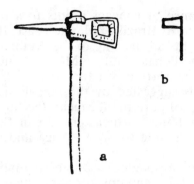

Figure 137

And so it was, circa 2400 B.C.—just as Montesinos had concluded—that Manco Capac was given the golden wand at Titicaca and sent to the gold region of Cuzco.

What was the shape and purpose of this magical wand? One
of the most thorough studies on the subject is *Corona Incaica* by
Juan Larrea. Analyzing artifacts, legends, and pictorial depictions of Inca rulers, he concluded that it was an axe, an object
called *Yuari* that when first given to Manco Capac.was named
Tupa-Yuari, Royal Axe (Fig. 137a). But was it a weapon or a
tool?

To find an answer, we go to ancient Egypt. The Egyptian
term for "gods, divine" was *Neteru,* "Guardians." That however
was exactly the term by which Sumer (actually, Shumer) was
called—"Land of the Guardians"; and in early translations of
biblical and pseudo-biblical texts into Greek, the term *Nefilim*
(alias Anunnaki) was rendered "Guardians." The hieroglyph
for this term was an axe (Fig. 137b); E. A. Wallis Budge (*The
Gods of the Egyptians*) in a special chapter titled "The Axe As a
Symbol of God" concluded that it was made of metal. He mentioned that the symbol (as the term *Neter*) was probably borrowed from the Sumerians. That it was indeed so can be
gleaned from Fig. 133.

Thus was Andean civilization launched: by giving Andean
Man an axe with which to mine the gods' gold.

The tales of Manco Capac and the Ayar brothers in all probability also mark the end of the Mesopotamian and gold phases
of Tiahuanacu. A hiatus followed; it lasted until the place came
back to life as the world's tin capital. The Cassites arrived and
moved the tin or ready bronze via the transpacific route. In time
other routes developed. The existence of settlements with an

astonishing abundance of bronzes points to a route along the Beni River eastward to Brazil's Atlantic coast, thence with the help of ocean currents all the way to the Arabian Sea, the Red Sea to Egypt, or the Persian Gulf to Mesopotamia. There could be and probably was a route via the Ancient Empire and the Urubamba river, as suggested by the megalithic sites and the discovery of a lump of pure tin at Machu Picchu. This route led to the Amazon and the northeastern tip of South America, thence across the Atlantic to West Africa and the Mediterranean.

And then, once Mesoamerica attained a modicum of civilized settlements, a third and quicker alternative was offered by its narrow neck that provided a virtual land-bridge between the Pacific Ocean and the Atlantic via the Caribbean Sea—a route essentially followed, in reverse, by the conquistadores.

This third route, that of the Olmec civilization, must have become the preferred route after 2000 B.C., as evidenced by the presence of Mediterraneans; for, in 2024 B.C. the Anunnaki led by Ninurta, fearing that the spaceport in the Sinai would be overrun by followers of Marduk, destroyed it with nuclear weapons.

Unstoppable, the deadly nuclear cloud drifted eastward toward southern Mesopotamia, devastating Sumer and its last capital, Ur. As though fate had decreed it, the cloud drifted southward, sparing Babylon; and losing no time, Marduk marched in with an army of Canaanite and Amorite followers, declaring kingship in Babylon.

It was then, we believe, that the decision was made to grant the African followers of Thoth/Quetzalcoatl civilization in his Mesoamerican realm.

One of the rare academic studies admitting that the Olmecs were negroid Africans was *Africa and the Discovery of America* by Leo Wiener, professor of Slavic and other languages at Harvard University. Based on racial features and other considerations but mostly on linguistic analysis, he concluded that the Olmec tongue belonged to the Mande group of languages that originated in West Africa, between the Niger and Congo river. But writing in 1920, before the true age of Olmec remains became known, he attributed their presence in Mesoamerica to Arab seafarers and slave traders in the Middle Ages.

More than half a century had to pass before another major academic study, *Unexpected Faces in Ancient America* by Alexander von Wuthenau, tackled the problem head on. Enriched with a profusion of photographs of Semitic and Negroid portraits from Mesoamerica's art heritage, he surmised that the first links between the Old and New World developed during the reign of the Egyptian Pharaoh Ramses III (twelfth century B.C.) and that the Olmecs were Kushites from Nubia (Egypt's principal source of gold). Some other black Africans, he felt, could have come over on "Phoenician and Jewish ships" between 500 B.C. and A.D. 200. Ivan van Sertima, whose study *They Came Before Columbus* set out to bridge the half-century gap between the two previous academic works, tended toward the Kushite solution: it was when the black kings of Kush ascended the throne of Egypt as its twenty-fifth dynasty in the eighth century B.C., trading in silver and bronze, that they—probably as a result of shipwrecks—also held sway in Mesoamerica.

This conclusion was prompted by the notion that the giant Olmec heads were from about that time; but now we know that Olmec beginnings go back to circa 2000 B.C. Who, then, were these Africans?

We hold that Leo Wiener's linguistic studies have been correct, but not so his time frame. When one compares the faces on the colossal Olmec heads (Fig. 138a) with those of West Africans (as this one of Nigeria's leader, General I. B. Banagida—Fig. 138b), the gap of thousands of years is bridged by the obvious similarity. It is from that part of Africa that Thoth could have brought over his followers expert in mining, for it is there that gold *and tin,* and copper to alloy bronze with, have been abundant. Nigeria has been renowned for its bronze figurines—cast in the telltale Lost Wax process—for millennia; recent research has carbon-dated some of the sites, in which the most ancient ones have been found to date to about 2100 B.C.

It is there, in West Africa, that the country now called Ghana bore for centuries the name *Gold Coast,* for that is what it

Figure 138

Figure 139

was—a source of gold known even to the Phoenicians. And then we have the area's Ashanti people, renowned throughout the continent for their goldsmithing skills; among their handiwork are weights made of gold whose shape is frequently that of miniature step-pyramids (Fig. 139)—in lands where no such structures exist.

It was, we believe, when the Old World order was upheavaled, that Thoth undertook the task of bringing his expert followers over: to start a new life, a new civilization, and new mining operations.

In time, as we have shown, these operations and the miners, the Olmecs, moved south, first to Mexico's Pacific shores, then across the isthmus into northern South America. Their ultimate destination was the Chavin area; there they met the gold miners of Adad, the people of the golden wand.

The golden age of the New Realms did not last forever. Olmec sites in Mexico underwent destruction; the Olmecs themselves and their bearded companions met a brutal end. Mochica pottery depicts enslaving giants and winged gods warring with metal blades. The Ancient Empire witnessed tribal clashes and invasions. And in the highlands of Titicaca, Aymara legends recalled invaders who marched up the mountains from the seacoast and slew the white men who were still there.

Were these reflections of the conflicts among the Anunnaki, in which they increasingly involved Mankind? Or did it all begin to happen after the gods had left—sailing off upon the sea, ascending heavenward?

Whichever way it happened, it is certain that in time the links between the Old Realms and the New Realms were broken off. In the Old World the Americas became only a dim memory—hints by this or that classical writer, tales of Atlantis heard from Egyptian priests, even perplexing maps that trace unknown continents. Was it all myth, were there really lands of gold and tin beyond the Pillars of Hercules? In time, the New Realms became the Lost Realms as far as Westerners were concerned.

In the New Realms themselves, the golden past became only a legendary memory as the centuries rolled on. But the memories would not die, and the tales persisted—of how it all began and where, of Quetzalcoatl and Viracocha, of how they will one day return.

As we now find colossal heads, megalithic walls, abandoned sites, a lonely gate with its Weeping God, we must wonder: Were the American peoples right in telling us that these gods were among them, in expecting them to return?

For until white man came again and only wrought havoc, the people of the Andes, where it all began, could only look at the empty golden enclosures and hope against hope to see once again their winged God of the Golden Tears.

Figure 140

SOURCES

In addition to specific references in the text, the following periodicals, scholarly studies and individual works were among sources consulted:

I. Studies, articles and reports in various issues of the following periodicals and scholarly series:

Academia Colombiana de Historia: Biblioteca de Antropologia (Bogotá)
Acta Antropologica (Mexico City)
American Anthropological Association, Memoirs (Menasha, Wisc.)
American Anthropologist (Menasha, Wisc.)
American Antiquity (Salt Lake City)
American Journal of Anthropology (Baltimore)
American Museum of Natural History: Anthropological Papers (New York)
American Philosophical Society: Transactions (Philadelphia)
Anales del Instituto Nacional de Antropologia e Historia (Mexico City)
Anales del Museo Nacional de Arqueologia, Historia y Etnologia (Mexico City)
Annals of the New York Academy of Sciences (New York)
Anthropological Journal of Canada (Ottawa)
Anthropology (Berkeley)
Archaeoastronomy (College Park)
Archaeology (New York)
Arqueologia Mexicana (Mexico City)
Arqueologicas (Lima)
Atlantis (Berlin and Zurich)
Baessler Archiv (Berlin and Leipzig)

Biblical Archaeology Review (Washington, D.C.)
Biblioteca Boliviana (La Paz)
Bureau of American Ethnology: Bulletin (Washington, D.C.)
California University, Archaeological Research Facility: Contributions (Berkeley)
Carnegie Institution of Washington, Publications: Contributions to American Archaeology (Washington, D.C.)
Carnegie Institution of Washington, Department of Archaeology: Notes on Middle American Archaeology and Ethnology (Cambridge, Mass.)
Connecticut Academy of Arts and Sciences: Memoirs (New Haven)
Cuadernos Americanos (Mexico City)
Cuzco (Cuzco)
El Mexico Antiguo (Mexico City)
Ethnographical Museum of Sweden: Monograph Series (Stockholm)
Harvard University, Peabody Museum of American Archaeology and Ethnology: Memoirs and *Papers* (Cambridge, Mass.)
Inca (Lima)
Instituto Nacional de Antropologia e Historia: Memorias and *Boletin* (Mexico City)
International Congresses of Americanists: Proceedings (Various cities)
Journal of the Ethnological Society of London (London)
Journal of the Manchester Egyptian and Oriental Society (Manchester)
Journal of the Royal Anthropological Institute (London)
Liverpool University Centre for Latin American Studies: Monograph Series (Liverpool)
Museum für Volkerkunde im Hamburg: Mitteilungen (Hamburg)
Museum of the American Indian, Heye Foundation: Contributions and *Leaflets* and *Indian Notes and Monographs* (New York)
National Geographic Magazine (Washington, D.C.)
National Geographic Society, Technical Papers: Mexican Archaeology Series (Washington, D.C.)
Natural History (New York)
New World Archaeological Foundation: Papers (Provo)
Revista del Museo de La Plata (Buenos Aires)
Revista del Museo Nacional (Lima)
Revista do Instituto Historico e Geografico Brasiliero (Rio de Janeiro)

Revista Historica (Lima)
Revista Mexicana de Estudios Antropologicos (Mexico City)
Revista Mexicana de Estudios Historicos (Mexico City)
Revista Universitaria (Lima)
Revue Anthropologique (Paris)
Revue d'Ethnographie (Paris)
Scientific American (New York)
Smithsonian Institution, Bureau of American Ethnology: Bulletin (Washington, D.C.)
Studies in Pre-Columbian Art and Archaeology (Dumbarton Oaks)
University of California Anthropological Records (Berkeley)
University of California: Publications in American Archaeology and Ethnology (Berkeley)
University of Pennsylvania, the University Museum: The Museum Journal (Philadelphia)
Wira-Kocha (Lima)

II. Individual Works and Studies:

Allen, G. *Gold!* 1964.
America Pintoresca: Descripcion de viajes al Nuevo Continente. 1884.
Anders, F. *Das Pantheon der Maya.* 1963.
Andree, R. *Die Metalle bei den Naturvölkern.* 1884.
Antiguo Peru: espacio y tiempo. 1960.
Anton, F. *Alt-Peru und seine Kunst.* 1962.
Arnold, J. R. and W. F. Libby. *Radiocarbon Dates.* 1950.
Arte Prehispanico de Mexico. 1933.
Aveni, A. F. (ed.) *Archaeostronomy in Pre-Columbian America.* 1975.
——. (ed.) *Native American Astronomy.* 1977.
——. (ed.) *Archaeoastronomy in the New World.* 1982.

Batres, L. *Teotihuacan o la Ciudad Sagrada de los Toltecas.* 1889.
——. *Civilizacion Prehistorica (Estado de Veracruz).* 1908.
Baudin, L. *La Vie Quotidienne au Temps des Derniers Incas.* 1955.
Baudin, L., C. Troll and C. D. Gibson. *Los origines del Indio-Americano.* 1937.
Belli, P. L. *La Civilizacion Nazca.* 1960.
Beltran-Kropp, M. *Cuzco—Window on Peru.* 1956, 1970.
Bennett, W. C. *Excavations at Tiahuanaco.* 1934.

———. *Excavations in Bolivia.* 1936.

———. *The Ancient Arts of the Andes.* 1954.

Bennett, W. C. and J. B. Bird. *Andean Culture History.* 1964.

Benson, E. P. *The Maya World.* 1967.

———. (ed.) *The Dumbarton Oaks Conference on the Olmecs.* 1968.

Bernal, I. *Ancient Mexico in Color.* 1968.

———. *El Mundo Olmeca.* 1968.

———. *Stone Reliefs in the Dainzu Area.* 1973.

Bernal, I., R. Piña-Chan and F. Camara Barbachano. *3000 Years of Art and Life in Mexico.* 1968.

Bird, J. *Paracas Fabrics and Nazca Needlework.* 1954.

Bird, J. (ed.) *Art and Life in Old Peru.* 1962.

Blom, F. and O. La Farge. *Tribes and Temples.* 1926.

Bollaert, W. *Antiquarian, Ethnological and Other Researches in New Granada, Eqador, Peru and Chile.* 1860.

Braessler, A. *Ancient Peruvian Art.* 1902/1903.

———. *Altperuanische Metallgeräte.* 1906.

Brinton, D. G. *The Books of Chilam Balam.* 1892.

British Academy, The. *The Place of Astronomy in the Ancient World.* 1974.

Buck, F. *El Calendario Maya en la Cultura Tiahuanacu.* 1937.

Burland, C.A. *Peoples of the Sun.* 1976.

Buse, H. *Huaras y Chavin.* 1957.

———. *Guia Arqueologica de Lima.* 1960.

———. *Machu Picchu.* 1961.

———. *Peru 10,000 años.* 1962.

Bushnell, G.H.S. *Peru.* 1957.

———. *Ancient Arts of the Americas.* 1965.

Cabello de Balboa, M. *Historia del Peru.* 1920.

Carnero Albarran, N. *Minas e Indios del Peru.* 1981.

Caso A. *La religion de los Aztecas.* 1936.

———. *Thirteen Masterpieces of Mexican Archaeology.* 1936.

———. *El Complejo Arquelogico de Tula.* 1941.

———. *Calendario y Escritura de las Antiguas Culturas de Monte Alban.* 1947.

———. *The Aztecs—People of the Sun.* 1958.

———. *Los Calendarios Prehispanicos.* 1967.

———. *Reyes y reinos de la Mixteca.* 1977.

Centro de Investigaciones Antropologias de Mexico. *Esplendor del Mexico Antiguo.* 1959.

Chapman, W. *The Search for El Dorado.* 1967.

———. *The Golden Dream.* 1967.

Coe, M. D. *Mexico*. 1962.
——. *The Maya*. 1966.
Coe, M. D. and R. Diehl. *In the Land of the Olmec*. 1980.
Cornell, J. *The First Stargazers*. 1981.
Corson, C. *Maya Anthropomorphic Figurines from Jaina Island*. 1976.
Cottrell, A. (ed.) *The Encyclopedia of Ancient Civilizations*. 1980.
Crequi-Montfort, G. de. *Fouilles de la mission scientifique française à Tiahuanaco*. 1906.

D'Amato, J. and J. H. del Mazo. *Machu Picchu*. 1975.
Dennis, W. H. *Metallurgy in the Service of Man*. 1961.
Diccionario Porrua de Historia, Biografía y Geografía de Mexico. 1971.
Dihl, R. A. *Tula—The Capital of Ancient Mexico*. 1983.
Disseldorf, E. P. *Kunst und Religion der Maya Völker*. 1926, 1931.
Disselhoff, H. D. *Gott Muss Peruaner Sein*. 1956.
——. *Kinder der Erdgöttin*. 1960.
——. *Les Grandes Civilizations de l'Amerique Ancienne*. 1963.
——. *Geschichte der Altamerikanischen Kulturen*. 1967.
——. *Oasenstadte und Zaubersteine im Land der Inka*. 1968.
——. *El Imperio de los Incas*. 1973.
——. *Incaica*. 1982.
Doering, H. *Old Peruvian Art*. 1926.
Dubelaar, C. N. *The Petroglyphs in the Guianas and Adjacent Areas of Brazil and Venezuela*. 1986.
Duran, Fray D. *Historia de las Indias de Nueva España*. 1867. (English translation by Heyden D. and F. Horacasitas, 1964).

Emmerich, A. *Sweat of the Sun and Tears of the Moon*. 1965.
——. *Gods and Men in Precolumbian Art*. 1967.
Engel, F. *Elementos de Prehistoria Peruana*. 1962.
——. *Le Monde Précolumbien des Andes*. 1972.

Fage, J. D. *A History of West Africa*. 1969.
Falb, R. *Das Land der Inca*. 1883.
Fernandez, A. *Pre-Hispanic Gods of Mexico*. 1984.
Festschrift Eduard Seler. 1922.
Fisher, J. R. *Silver Mines and Silver Miners in Colonial Peru*. 1977.
Flornoy, B. *Découverte des Sources des Andes a la Forêt Amazonienne*. 1946.
——. *The World of the Inca*. 1956.

——. *Amazone—Terres et Hommes.* 1969.
Forbes, D. *On the Aymara Indians of Bolivia and Peru.* 1870.
Forbes, R. J. *Metallurgy in Antiquity.* 1950.
Furst, J. L. and P. T. Furst. *Pre-Columbian Art of Mexico.* 1980.
Furst, P. T. *Gold Before Columbus.* 1964.

Garcia Rosell, C. *Los Monumentos Arqueologicos del Peru.* 1942.
Garcilaso de la Vega, el Inca. *Royal Commentaries of the Incas* (translated into English by Livermore, H. V.) 1966.
Gates, W. *An Outline Dictionary of Maya Glyphs.* 1931.
Giesecke, A. A. *Guide to Cuzco.* 1924.
Gonzalez de la Rosa, M. *Les deux Tiahuanacos.* 1910.
Gordon, G. B. *Prehistoric Ruins of Copan, Honduras,* 1896.

Haberland, W. *Die Kulturen Meso—und Zentralamerika.* 1969.
Harlow, W. T. (ed.) *Voyages of Great Pioneers.* 1929.
Hawkins, G. S. *Beyond Stonehenge.* 1973.
Hedges, E. S. *Tin and Its Alloys.* 1959.
Heggie, D. C. (ed.) *Archaeoastronomy in the Old World.* 1982.
Heim, A. *Wunderland Peru.* 1948.
Heizer, R. E., P. Drucker, and J. A. Graham. *Investigations at La Venta.* 1968.
Helfritz, H. *Mexican Cities of the Gods.* 1970.
Heyerdahl, T. *The Kon-Tiki Expedition.* 1951.
——. *The Ra Expeditions.* 1971.
Homenaje al Profesor Paul Rivet. 1955.

Ibarra Grasso, D. E. *Tiahuanaco.* 1956.
——. *Prehistoria de Bolivia.* 1965.
——. *Cosmogonia y Mitologia Indigena Americana.* 1980.
——. *Ciencia en Tihuanaku y el Incario.* 1982.
——. *Ciencia Astronomica y Sociologia.* 1984.
——. *Pueblos Indigenos de Bolivia.* 1985.
Illescas Cook, G. *El Candelabro de Paracas y la Cruz del Sur.* 1981.
Inwards, R. *The Temple of the Andes.* 1884.
Ixtlilxochitl, F. de Alva. *Historia Chichimeca* (Translated and edited by Bonte, H. G. : *Das Buch der Könige von Tezuco.* 1930).

Jenness, D. (ed.) *The American Aborigines and Their Origin and Antiquity.* 1933.
Joyce, T. A. *South American Archaeology.* 1912.
——. *The Weeping God.* 1913.

——. *Mexican Archaeology.* 1920.
——. *Maya and Mexican Art.* 1927.

Katz, F. *The Ancient American Civilizations.* 1972.
Kaufmann-Doig, F. *Arqueologia Peruana.* 1971.
——. *Tiahuanaco a la luz de la Arqueologia.* 1965.
Keating, R.W. (ed.) *Peruvian Prehistory.* 1986.
Krickberg, W. *Altmexikanische Kulturen.* 1956.
——. *Felsplastik und Felsbilder bei den Kulturvolkern Altamer-iker.* 1969.
Krickberg, W., H. Trimborn, W. Müller, and O. Zerris, *Pre-Columbian American Religions.* 1968.
Kroeber, A.L. *Archaeological Explorations in Peru.* 1926 and 1931.
Krupp, E.C. *Echoes of Ancient Skies: The Astromomies of Lost Civilizations.* 1983.
——. (ed.) *In Search of Ancient Astronomies.* 1978.
——. (ed.) *Archaeoastronomy and the Roots of Science.* 1983.
Kubler, G. *The Art and Archaeology of Ancient America.* 1962.
Kutscher. G. *Chimu, Eine altindianische Hochkultur.* 1950.

Lafone Quevedo, S.A. *Tres Relaciones de Antiquedades Peruanas.* 1950.
Landa, Diego de. *Relacion de las cosas de Yucatan.* 1956 (English translation by W. Gates: *Yucatan Before and After the Conquest.* 1937).
Larrea, J. *Del Surrealismo a Machupicchu.* 1967.
Lathrap, D.W. *The Upper Amazon.* 1970.
Lawrence, A.W. and J. Young. (eds.) *Narratives of the Discovery of America.* 1931.
Leicht, H. *Pre-Inca Art and Culture.* 1960.
Lehmann, W. *Einige probleme centralamerikanische kalenders.* 1912.
——. *The History of Ancient Mexican Archaeology.* 1922.
Lehmann, W. and H. Doering, *Kunstgeshichte des alten Peru.* 1924.
Leon-Portilla, M. *Pre-Columbian Literature of Mexico.* 1969.
Lothrop, S.K. *Zacaulpa: A Study of Ancient Quiche Artifacts.* 1936.
——. *Metals from the Cenote of Sacrifice, Chichen Itza, Yucatan.* 1952.
——. *Treasures of Ancient America.* 1964.
Lothrop, S.K., W.F. Foshag, and J. Mahler, *Pre-Columbian Art: The Robert Woods Bliss Collection.* 1957.

Ludendorff, H. *Über die Entstehung der Tzolkin-Periode im Kalendar der Maya.* 1930.
——. *Das Mondalter in der Inschriften des Maya.* 1931.

Maguina, J.E. *Lima Guide Book.* 1957.
Maler, T. *Explorations in the Department of Peten, Guatemala.* 1911.
Mantell, C.L. *Tin, Its Mining, Production, Technology and Application.* 1929.
Markham, C.R. *Peru.* 1880.
——. *Narratives of the Rites and Laws of the Yncas.* 1883.
——. *The Travels of Pedro de Cieza de Leon.* 1884.
——. *The Incas of Peru.* 1912.
Marquina, I. *Arquitectura Prehispanica.* 1951.
Martinez Hernandez, J. *La creacion del mundo segun los Mayas.* 1912.
Mason, J.A. *The Ancient Civilizations of Peru.* 1957, 1968.
Maspero, G. *Popular Stories of Ancient Egypt.* 1915.
Maudsley, A.P. *Explorations in Guatemala.* 1883.
——. *Archaeology.* 1889–1902.
Mead, C. *Prehistoric Bronzes in South America.* 1915.
Means, P.A. *Ancient Civilizations of the Andes.* 1931.
Meggers, B.J. *Ecuador.* 1966.
Metropolitan Museum of Art, New York *The Iconography of Middle American Sculpture.* 1973.
Meyer, C. and C. Gallenkamp. *The Mystery of the Ancient Maya.* 1985.
Middendorf, E.W. *Wörterbuch des Runa Simi oder der Keshua-Sprache.* 1890.
——. *Las Civilizaciones Aborigines del Peru.* 1959.
Miller, M.E. *The Arts of Mesoamerica.* 1986.
Mitre, B. *Las Ruinas de Tiahuanaco.* 1955.
Montell, G. *Dress and Ornaments in Ancient Peru.* 1929.
Morley, S.G. *The Inscriptions at Copan.* 1920.
——. *The Inscriptions of Peten.* 1937–1938.
Morris, A.A. *Digging in Yucatan.* 1931.
Morris, C. and D.E. Thompson. *Huanaco Pampa.* 1985.
Morris, E.H., J. Charlot, and A.A. Morris. *The Temple of the Warriors at Chichen Itza.* 1931.
Mosley, M.E. *The Maritime Foundations of Andean Civilization.* 1975.
Myers, B.S. *Art and Civilization.* 1967.

Neruda, P. *Alturas de Machu Picchu.* 1972.

O'Neil, W.M. Time and the Calendars. 1975.

Pardo, L.A. *La Metropoli de los Incas.* 1937.
———. *Los Grandes Monolitos de Sayhuiti.* 1945.
———. *Ruinas del Santurio de Huiracocha.* 1946.
———. *Historia y Arqueologia del Cuzco.* 1957.
Paredes, R. *Tiahuanaco y la Provincia de Ingavi.* 1956.
———. *Mitos y supersticiones de Bolivia.* 1963.
Patron, P. *Nouvelles Etudes sur les Langues Américaines.* 1907.
Piña-Chan, R. *El pueblo del jaguar.* 1964.
———. *Jaina, La casa en el agua.* 1968.
———. *Chichen-Itza.* 1980.
Ponce Sangines, C. *Ceramica Tiwanacota.* 1948.
———. *Tunupa y Ekako.* 1969.
———. *Tiwanaku: Espacio, Tiempo y Cultura.* 1977.
———. *La cultura nativa en Bolivia.* 1979.
Portugal, M. and D. Ibarra Grasso. *Copacabana.* 1957.
Posnansky, A. *Guia para el Visitante de los Monumentos Prehistoricos de Tihuanacu e Islas del Sol y la Luna.* 1910.
———. *El Clima del Altiplano y la Extension del Lago Titicaca.* 1911.
———. *Tihuanacu y la civilizacion prehispanica en el Altiplano Andino.* 1911.
———. *Templos y Viviendes prehispanicas.* 1921.
Prescott, W.H. *History of the Conquest of Mexico.* 1843.
———. *History of the Conquest of Peru.* 1847.
Prieto, C. *Mining in the New World.* 1973.
Proskouriakoff, T. *An Album of Maya Architecture.* 1946.
———. *A Study of Classical Maya Sculpture.* 1950.
Raimondi, A. *El Peru.* 1874.
———. *Minerales del Peru.* 1878.
Ravines R. and J.J. Alvarez Sauri. *Fechas Radiocarbonicas Para el Peru.* 1967.
Reiss, W. and A. Stübel. *Das Totenfeld von Ancon in Peru.* 1880–1887.
Rice, C. *La Civilizacion Preincaica y el Problema Sumerologico.* 1926.
Rivet, P. *Los origines del hombre Americano.* 1943.
Roeder, G. *Altaegyptische Erzählungen und Märchen.* 1927.
Romero, E. *Geografia Economica del Peru.* 1961.
Roys, R.L. *The Book of Chilam Balam of Chumayel.* 1967.
Rozas, E.A. *Cuzco.* 1954.
Ruppert, K. *The Caracol at Chichen Itza.* 1933.
Ruz-Lhuillier, A. *Campeche en la arqueologia Maya.* 1945.
———. *Guia arqueologica de Tula.* 1945.

Rydén, S. *Archaeological Researches in the Highlands of Bolivia.* 1947.
——. *Andean Excavations.* Vol. I 1957, vol. II 1959.

Saville, M.H. *Contributions to South American Archaeology.* 1907.
Scholten de D'Ebneth, M. *Chavin de Huantar.* 1980.
Schmidt, M. *Kunst und Kultur von Peru.* 1929.
Seler, E. *Peruanische Alterthümer.* 1893.
——. *Gesammelte Abhandlungen zur Amerikanischen Sprach— und Alterthumkunde.* 1902–03.
Shook. E.M. *Explorations in the Ruins of Oxkintok, Yucatan.* 1940.
Shook, E.M. and T. Proskouriakoff. *Yucatan.* 1951.
Sivirichi, A. *Pre-Historia Peruana.* 1930.
——. *Historia de la Cultura Peruana.* 1953.
Smith, A.L. *Archaeological Reconnaissance in Central Guatemala.* 1955.
Smith, G.E. *Ships as Evidence of the Migrations of Early Cultures.* 1917.
Spinden, H.J. *A Study of Maya Art.* 1913.
——. *The Reduction of Maya Dates.* 1924.
——. *New World Correlations.* 1926.
——. *Origin of Civilizations in Central America and Mexico.* 1933.
Squier, E.G. *The Primeval Monuments of Peru.* 1853, 1879.
——. *Tiahuanaco—Baalbek del Nuevo Mundo.* 1909.
Steward, J.H. (ed.) *Handbook of South American Indians.* 1946.
Stirling, M. *An Initial Series from Tres Zapotes, Veracruz, Mexico.* 1939.
——. *Stone Monuments of Southern Mexico.* 1943.
Stoepel, K.T. *Südamerikanische Prähistorische Tempel und Gottheiten.* 1912.
——. *Discoveries in Ecuador and Southern Colombia.* 1912.
Strebel, H. *Alt-Mexico.* 1885–1889.

Tello, J.C. *Antiguo Peru: Primera epoca.* 1929.
——. *Arte Antiguo Peruana.* 1938.
——. *Origen y Desarrollo de las Civilizaciones Prehistoricas Andinas.* 1942.
——. *Paracas.* 1959.
Temple, J.E. *Maya Astronomy.* 1930.
Thompson, J.E.S. *Maya Hieroglyphic Writing.* 1950.
——. *A Catalog of Maya Hieroglyphs.* 1962.

——. *The Rise and Fall of Maya Civilization.* 1964.
——. *Maya History and Religion.* 1970.
Tozzer, A.M. *Chichen Itza and its Cenote of Sacrifices.* 1957.
Tres Relaciones de Antiguedades Peruanas. 1879, 1950.
Trimborn, H. *Das Alte Amerika.* 1959.
——. *Die Indianischen Hochkulturen des Alten Amerika.* 1963.
——. *Alte Hochkulturen Südamerikas.* 1964.
Tylecote, R.F. *A History of Metallurgy.* 1976.

Ubbelohde-Doering, H. *Old Peruvian Art.* 1936.
——. *The Art of Ancient Peru.* 1952.
——. *Alt-Mexicanische und Peruanische Mallerei.* 1959.
Uhle, M. *Kultur and Industrie Südamerikanischer Völker.* 1889.
——. *Pachacamac.* 1903.
——. *The Nazca Pottery of Ancient Peru.* 1912.
——. *Wesen und Ordnung der altperuanischen Kulturen.* 1959.
Uzielli, G. *Toscanelli, Colombo e Vespucci.* 1902.

Valcarcel, L.E. *Arte antiguo Peruana.* 1932.
——. *The Latest Archaeological Discoveries in Peru.* 1938.
——. *Muestrari de Arte Peruana Precolombino.* 1938.
——. *Etnohistoria del Peru.* 1959.
——. *Machu Picchu.* 1964.
Vargas, V.A. *Machu Picchu—enigmatica ciudad Inka.* 1972.
von Hagen, V.F. *The Ancient Sun Kingdoms of the Americas.* 1963.
——. *The Desert Kingdoms of Peru.* 1964.
von Tschudi, J.J. *Die Kechua-Sprache.* 1853.

Westheim, P. *The Sculpture of Ancient Mexico.* 1963
——. *The Art of Ancient Mexico.* 1965.
Willard, T.A. *The City of the Sacred Well.* 1926.
——. *The Lost Empires of the Itzaes and Maya.* 1933.
Willey, G.R. *An Introduction to American Archaeology.* 1966.
Willey, G.R. (ed.) *Archaeology of Southern Mesoamerica.* 1965.
Williamson, R.A. (ed.) *Archaeoastronomy in the Americas.* 1978.
Wiener, C. *Pérou et Bolivie.* 1880.
——. *Viaje al Yucatan.* 1884.

Zahm, J.A. *The Quest of El Dorado.* 1917.

INDEX

287

Praise for the Works of Zecharia Sitchin

"Reflects the highest level of scientific knowledge . . ."

SCIENCE & RELIGION NEWS

"Exciting . . . credible . . . most provocative and compelling."

LIBRARY JOURNAL

"One of the most important books on Earth's roots ever written."

EAST WEST JOURNAL

"Sitchin is a zealous investigator into man's origins . . . a dazzling performance."

KIRKUS REVIEWS

"For thousands of years priests, poets, and scientists have tried to explain how man was created. Now a recognized scholar has come forth with a theory that is most astonishing of all."

UNITED PRESS INTERNATIONAL

Also by Zecharia Sitchin

Genesis Revisited

Divine Encounters

The Earth Chronicles Handbook

The Earth Chronicles Expeditions (autobiographical)

Journeys to the Mythical Past (autobiographical)

The King Who Refused to Die (fiction)

The Lost Book of Enki

There Were Giants Upon the Earth

<u>*The Earth Chronicles*</u>

The 12th Planet — Book I

The Stairway to Heaven — Book II

The Wars of Gods and Men — Book III

The Lost Realms — Book IV

When Time Began — Book V

The Cosmic Code — Book VI

The End of Days — Book VII

ZECHARIA SITCHIN

WHEN TIME BEGAN

The Fifth Book
of
The Earth Chronicles

Bear & Company
Rochester, Vermont • Toronto, Canada

Bear & Company
One Park Street
Rochester, Vermont 05767
www.BearandCompanyBooks.com

Bear & Company is a division of Inner Traditions International

Volume V
of
The Complete Earth Chronicles
Collector's Edition
Boxed Set

Printed and bound in India at Replika Press Pvt. Ltd.

10 9 8 7 6

CONTENTS

FOREWORD

Since the earliest times, Earthlings have lifted their eyes unto the heavens. Awed as well as fascinated, Earthlings learned the Ways of Heaven: the positions of the stars, the cycles of Moon and Sun, the turning of an inclined Earth. How did it all begin, how will it end—and what will happen in between?

Heaven and Earth meet on the horizon. For millennia Earthlings have watched the stars of the night give way to the rays of the Sun at that meeting place, and chose as a point of reference the moment when daytime and nighttime are equal, the day of the Equinox. Man, aided by the calendar, has counted Earthly Time from that point on.

To identify the starry heavens, the skies were divided into twelve parts, the twelve houses of the zodiac. But as the millennia rolled on, the "fixed stars" seemed not to be fixed at all, and the Day of the Equinox, the day of the New Year, appeared to shift from one zodiacal house to another; and to Earthly Time was added Celestial Time— the start of a new era, a New Age.

As we stand at the threshold of a New Age, when sunrise on the day of the spring equinox will occur in the zodiacal house of Aquarius rather than, as in the past 2,000 years, in the zodiacal house of Pisces, many wonder what the change might portend: good or evil, a new beginning or an end—or no change at all?

To understand the future we should examine the past; because since Mankind began to count Earthly Time, it has already experienced the measure of Celestial Time—the arrival of New Ages. What preceded and followed one such New Age holds great lessons for our own present station in the course of Time.

1

1

THE CYCLES OF TIME

It is said that Augustine of Hippo, the bishop in Roman Carthage (A.D. 354–430), the greatest thinker of the Christian Church in its early centuries, who fused the religion of the New Testament with the Platonistic tradition of Greek philosophy, was asked, "What is time?" His answer was, "If no one asks me, I know what it is; if I wish to explain what it is to him who asks me, I do not know."

Time is essential to Earth and all that is upon it, and to each one of us as individuals; for, as we know from our own experience and observations, what separates us from the moment we are born and the moment when we cease to live is TIME.

Though we know not what Time is, we have found ways to measure it. We count our lifetimes in *years,* which—come to think of it—is another way of saying "orbits," for that is what a "year" on Earth is: the time it takes Earth, our planet, to complete one orbit around our star, the Sun. We do not know what time is, but the way we measure it makes us wonder: would we live longer, would our life cycle be different, were we to live on another planet whose "year" is longer? Would we be "immortal" if we were to be upon a "Planet of millions of years"—as, in fact, the Egyptian pharaohs believed that they would be, in an eternal Afterlife, once they joined the gods on that "Planet of millions of years"?

Indeed, are there other planets "out there," and, even more so, planets on which life as we know it could have evolved—or is our planetary system unique, and life on Earth unique, and we, humankind, are all alone—or did the pharaohs know what they were speaking of in their Pyramid Texts?

2

"Look up skyward and count the stars," Yahweh told Abraham as He made the covenant with him. Man has looked skyward from time immemorial, and has been wondering whether there are others like him out there, upon other earths. Logic, and mathematical probability, dictate a Yes answer; but it was only in 1991 that astronomers, *for the first time,* it was stressed, actually found other planets orbiting other suns elsewhere in the universe.

The first discovery, in July 1991, turned out not to have been entirely correct. It was an announcement by a team of British astronomers that, based on observations over a five-year period, they concluded that a rapidly spinning star identified as Pulsar 1829–10 has a "planet-sized companion" about ten times the size of Earth. Pulsars are assumed to be the extraordinarily dense cores of stars that have collapsed for one reason or another. Spinning madly, they emit pulses of radio energy in regular bursts, many times per second. Such pulses can be monitored by radio telescopes; by detecting a cyclic fluctuation, the astronomers surmised that a planet that orbits Pulsar 1829–10 once every six months can cause and explain the fluctuation.

As it turned out, the British astronomers admitted several months later that their calculations were imprecise and, therefore, they could not stand by their conclusion that the pulsar, some 30,000 light-years away, had a planetary satellite. By then, however, an American team had made a similar discovery pertaining to a much closer pulsar, identified as PSR 1257 + 12—a collapsed sun only 1,300 light-years away from us. It exploded, astronomers estimated, about a mere billion years ago; and it definitely has two, and perhaps three, orbiting planets. The two certain ones were orbiting their sun at about the same distance as Mercury does our Sun; the possible third planet orbits its sun at about the same distance as Earth does our Sun.

"The discovery stirred speculation that planetary systems not only were fairly common but also could occur under diverse circumstances," wrote John Noble Wilford in *The New York Times* of January 9, 1992; "scientists said it was most unlikely that planets orbiting pulsars could be hospitable to life; but the findings encouraged astronomers, who this fall will begin a systematic survey of the heavens for signs of intelligent extraterrestrial life."

Were, then, the pharaohs right?

Long before the pharaohs and the Pyramid Texts, an ancient civilization—Man's first known one—possessed an advanced cosmogony. Six thousand years ago, in ancient Sumer, what astronomers have discovered in the 1990s was already known; not only the true nature and composition of our Solar System (including the farthest out planets), but also the notion that there are other solar systems in the universe, that their stars ("suns") can collapse or explode, that their planets can be thrown off course—that Life, indeed, can thus be carried from one star system to another. It was a detailed cosmogony, spelled out in writing.

One long text, written on seven tablets, has reached us primarily in its later Babylonian version. Called the *Epic of Creation* and known by its opening words *Enuma elish*, it was publicly read during the New Year festival that started on the first day of the month Nissan, coinciding with the first day of spring.

Outlining the process by which our own Solar System came into being, the long text described how the Sun ("Apsu") and its messenger Mercury ("Mummu") were first joined by an olden planet called Tiamat; how a pair of planets Venus and Mars—("Lahamu" and "Lahmu") then coalesced between the Sun and Tiamat, followed by two pairs beyond Tiamat—Jupiter and Saturn ("Kishar" and "Anshar") and Uranus and Neptune ("Anu" and "Nudimmud"), the latter two being planets unknown to modern astronomers until 1781 and 1846 respectively—yet known, and described, by the Sumerians millennia earlier. As those newly-created "celestial gods" tugged and pulled at each other, some of them sprouted satellites—moonlets. Tiamat, in the midst of that unstable planetary family, sprouted eleven satellites; one of them, "Kingu," grew so much in size that it began to assume the aspects of a "celestial god," a planet, on its own. Modern astronomers were totally ignorant of the possibility that a planet could have many

moons until Galileo discovered the four largest moons of
Jupiter in 1609, with the aid of a telescope; but the Sumerians were aware of the phenomenon millennia earlier.

Into that unstable solar system, according to the millennia-old *Epic of Creation*, there appeared an invader from
outer space—another planet; a planet not born into the family of Apsu, but one that had belonged to some other star's
family and that was thrust off to wander in space. Millennia
before modern astronomy learned of pulsars and collapsing
stars, the Sumerian cosmogony had already envisioned other
planetary systems and collapsing or exploding stars that
threw off their planets. And so, *Enuma elish* related, one
such cast-off planet, reaching the outskirts of our own Solar
System, began to be drawn into its midst (Fig. 1).

As it passed by the outer planets, it caused changes that
account for many of the enigmas that still baffle modern
astronomy—such as the cause for Uranus's tilt on its side,
the retrograde orbit of Neptune's largest moon, Triton, or
what pulled Pluto from its place as a moonlet to become a
planet with an odd orbit. The more the invader was drawn
into the Solar System's center, the more was it forced onto
a collision course with Tiamat, resulting in the "Celestial
Battle." In the series of collisions, with the invader's sat-

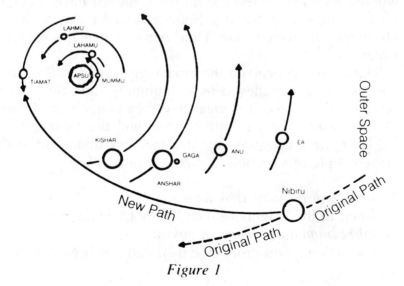

Figure 1

ellites repeatedly smashing into Tiamat, the olden planet split in two. One half of it was smashed into bits and pieces to become the Asteroid Belt (between Mars and Jupiter) and various comets; the other half, wounded but intact, was thrust into a new orbit to become the planet we call Earth (''Ki'' in Sumerian); shunted with it was Tiamat's largest satellite, to become Earth's Moon. The invader itself was caught into permanent orbit around the Sun, to become our Solar System's twelfth member (Sun, Moon, and ten planets). The Sumerians called it *Nibiru*—''Planet of the Crossing.'' The Babylonians renamed it *Marduk* in honor of their national god. It was during the Celestial Battle, the ancient epic asserted, that the ''seed of life,'' brought by Nibiru from elsewhere, was passed to Earth.

Philosophers and scientists, contemplating the universe and offering modern cosmogonies, invariably end up discussing Time. Is Time a dimension in itself, or perhaps the only true dimension in the universe? Does Time only flow forward, or can it flow backward? Is the present part of the past or the beginning of the future? And, not least of all, did Time have a beginning? For, if so, will it have an end? If the universe has existed forever, without a beginning and thus without an end, is Time too without a beginning and without an end—or did the universe indeed have a beginning, perhaps with the Big Bang assumed by many astrophysicists, in which case Time began when the universe began?

Those who conceived the amazingly accurate Sumerian cosmogony also believed in a Beginning (and thus, inexorably, in an End). It is clear that they conceived of Time as a measure, the pacesetter from, and the marker of, a beginning in a celestial saga; for the very first word of the ancient Epic of Creation, *Enuma*, means *When:*

Enuma elish la nabu shamamu
    When in the heights heaven had not been named
Shaplitu ammatum shuma la zakrat
    And below, firm ground (Earth) had not been called

It must have taken great scientific minds to conceive of a primordial phase when "naught existed but primordial Apsu, their begetter; Mummu, and Tiamat"—when Earth had not yet come into being; and to realize that for Earth and all upon it the "big bang" was not when the universe or even the Solar System was created, but the event of the Celestial Battle. It was then, at that moment, that Time began for Earth—the moment when, separated from the half of Tiamat that became the Asteroid Belt ("heaven"), Earth was shunted to its own new orbit and could start counting the years, the months, the days, the nights—to measure Time.

This scientific view, central to ancient cosmogony, religion, and mathematics, was expressed in many other Sumerian texts besides the *Epic of Creation*. A text treated by scholars as the "myth" of "Enki and the world order," but which is literally the autobiographical tale by Enki, the Sumerian god of science, describes the moment when—*When*—Time began to tick for Earth:

> *In the days of yore,*
> *when heaven was separated from Earth,*
> *In the nights of yore,*
> *when heaven was separated from Earth . . .*

Another text, in words often repeated on Sumerian clay tablets, conveyed the notion of Beginning by listing the many aspects of evolution and civilization that had not yet come into being before the crucial event. Before then, the text asserted, "the name of Man had not yet been called" and "needful things had not yet been brought into being." All those developments started to take place only "after heaven had been moved away from Earth, after Earth had been separated from heaven."

It is not surprising that the same notions of Time's beginnings also ruled Egyptian beliefs, whose development was subsequent to those of the Sumerians. We read in the Pyramid Texts (para. 1466) the following description of the Beginning of Things:

When heaven had not yet come into existence,
When men had not yet come into existence,
When gods had not yet been born,
When death had not yet come into existence . . .

This knowledge, universal in antiquity and stemming from the Sumerian cosmogony, was echoed in the very first verse of Genesis, the first book of the Hebrew Bible:

In the beginning
Elohim *created the heaven and the earth.*
And the earth was without form and void
and darkness was upon the face of Tehom,
and the wind of the Lord swept over its waters.

It is now well established that this biblical tale of creation was based on Mesopotamian texts such as *Enuma elish,* with *Tehom* meaning Tiamat, the "wind" meaning "satellites," in Sumerian, and "heaven," described as the "hammered out bracelet," the Asteroid Belt. The Bible, however, is clearer regarding the moment of the Beginning as far as Earth was concerned; the biblical version picks up the Mesopotamian cosmogony only from the point of the separation of the Earth from the *Shama'im,* the Hammered Bracelet, as a result of the breakup of Tiamat.

For Earth, Time began with the Celestial Battle.

The Mesopotamian tale of creation begins with the formation of our Solar System and the appearance of Nibiru/Marduk at a time when the planetary orbits were not yet fixed and stable. It ends by attributing to Nibiru/Marduk the current shape of our Solar System, whereby each planet ("celestial god") received its assigned place ("station"), orbital path ("destiny"), and rotation, even its moons. Indeed, as a large planet that encompasses by its orbit all the other planets, one who "crosses the heavens and surveys the regions," it was considered to have become the one that stabilized the Solar System:

He established the station of Nibiru,
to determine their heavenly bands,
that none might transgress or fall short . . .

He established for the planets their
sacred heavens,
He keeps hold on their ways,
determines their courses.

Thus, states *Enuma elish* (Tablet V, line 65), "He created the Heaven and the Earth"—the very same words used in the Book of Genesis.

The Celestial Battle eliminated Tiamat as a member of the old Solar System, thrust half of it into a new orbit to become Planet Earth, retained the Moon as a vital component of the new Solar System, detached Pluto into an independent orbit, and added Nibiru as the twelfth member of the New Order in our heavens. For Earth and its inhabitants, those were to become the elements that determined Time.

To this day, the key role that the number twelve played in Sumerian science and daily life (in line with the twelve-member Solar System) has accompanied us throughout the millennia. They divided the "day" (from sunset to sunset) into twelve "double-hours," retained into modern times in the twelve-hour clock and the twenty-four-hour day. The twelve months in the year are still with us, as are the twelve houses of the zodiac. This celestial number had many other expressions, as in the twelve tribes of Israel or the twelve apostles of Jesus.

The Sumerian mathematical system is called sexagesimal, i.e. "based on sixty" rather than on 100 as in the metric system (in which one meter is equal to 100 centimeters). Among the advantages of the sexagesimal system was its divisibility into twelve. The sexagesimal system progressed by alternately multiplying six and ten: starting with six, multiplying six by ten ($6 \times 10 = 60$), then by six to obtain 360—the number applied by the Sumerians to the circle and still used both in geometry and astronomy. That, in turn, was multiplied by ten, to obtain the *sar* ("ruler, lord"), the number 3,600, which was written by inscribing a great circle, and so on.

The *sar,* 3,600 Earth-years, was the orbital period of Nibiru around the Sun; for anyone on Nibiru, it was just one Nibiru-year. According to the Sumerians, there were indeed others, intelligent beings, on Nibiru, evolving there well ahead of hominids on Earth. The Sumerians called them *Anunnaki,* literally meaning "Those who from Heaven to Earth came." Sumerian texts repeatedly asserted that the Anunnaki had come to Earth from Nibiru in great antiquity; and that when they had come here, they counted time not in Earth terms but in terms of Nibiru's orbit. The unit of that Divine Time, a year of the gods, was the *sar.*

Texts known as the Sumerian King Lists, which describe the first settlements of the Anunnaki on Earth, list the governorships of the first ten Anunnaki leaders before the Deluge in *sars,* the 3,600 Earth-year cycles. From the first landing to the Deluge, according to those texts, 120 *sars* had passed: Nibiru orbited the Sun one hundred and twenty times, which equals 432,000 Earth-years. It was on the one hundred twentieth orbit that the gravitational pull of Nibiru was such that it caused the ice sheet that accumulated over Antarctica to slip off into the southern oceans, creating the immense tidal wave that engulfed the Earth—the great flood or Deluge, recorded in the Bible from much earlier and much more detailed Sumerian sources.

Legends and ancient lore gave this number, 432,000, cyclical significance beyond the land then called Sumer. In *Hamlet's Mill,* Giorgio de Santillana and Hertha von Dechend, searching for "a point where myth and science join," concluded that "432,000 was a number of significance from old." Among the examples cited by them was the Teutonic and Norse tale of the Valhalla, the mythic abode of the slain warriors who, on the Day of Judgment, will march out of the Valhalla's gates to fight at the side of the god Odin or Woden against the giants. They would exit through the Valhalla's 540 doors; eight hundred warriors would march out of each. The total number of warrior-heroes, Santillana and von Dechend pointed out, was thus 432,000. "This number," they continued, "must have had a very ancient meaning, for it is also the number of syllables in the *Rigveda*," the "Sacred Book of Verses" in the Sanskrit language, in which have been recorded the Indo-European tales of gods and heroes. Four hundred thirty-two thousand, the two authors wrote, "goes back to the basic figure 10,800, the number of stanzas in the *Rigveda*, with 40 syllables to a stanza" (10,800 × 40 = 432,000).

Hindu traditions clearly associated the number 432,000 with the *yugas* or Ages that Earth and Mankind had experienced. Each *caturyuga* ("great yuga") was divided into four yugas or Ages whose diminishing lengths were expressions of 432,000: first the Fourfold Age (4 × 432,000 = 1,728,000 years) which was the Golden Age, then the Threefold Age of Knowledge (3 × 432,000 = 1,296,000 years), followed by the Double or Twofold Age of Sacrifice (2 × 432,000 = 864,000 years); and finally our present era, the Age of Discord which will last a mere 432,000 years. All in all these Hindu traditions envision ten eons, paralleling the ten Sumerian rulers of the pre-Diluvial era but expanding the overall time span to 4,320,000 years.

Further expanded, such astronomical numbers based on 432,000 were applied in Hindu religion and traditions to the *kalpa*, the "Day" of the Lord Brahma. It was defined as an eon comprising twelve million *devas* ("Divine Years"). Each Divine Year in turn equaled 360 Earth-years. Therefore, a "Day of the Lord Brahma" equaled 4,320,000,000 Earth-years—a time span very much like modern estimates of the age of our Solar System—arrived at by multiplications of 360 and 12.

4,320,000,000 is, however, a thousandfold great yugas—a fact brought out in the eleventh century by the Arab mathematician Abu Rayhan al-Biruni, who explained that the *kalpa* consisted of 1,000 cycles of caturyugas. One could thus paraphrase the mathematics of the Hindu celestial calendar by stating that in the eyes of the Lord Brahma, a thousand cycles were but a single day. This brings to mind the enigmatic statement in Psalms (90:4) regarding the Divine Day of the biblical Lord:

A thousand years, in thy eyes,
[are] as a day past, gone by.

The statement has traditionally been viewed as merely symbolic of the Lord's eternity. But in view of the numerous traces of Sumerian data in the Book of Psalms (as well as in other parts of the Hebrew Bible), a precise mathematical formula might well have been intended—a formula echoed also in Hindu traditions.

The Hindu traditions were brought to the Indian subcontinent by "Aryan" migrants from the shores of the Caspian Sea, cousins of the Indo-Europeans who were the Hittites of Asia Minor (today's Turkey) and of the Hurrians of the upper Euphrates River, through whom Sumerian knowledge and beliefs were transmitted to the Indo-Europeans. The Aryan migrations are believed to have taken place in the second millennium B.C. and the Vedas were held to be "not of human origin," having been composed by the gods themselves in a previous age. In time the various components of the Vedas and the auxiliary literature that derived from them (the Mantras, Brahmanas, etc.) were augmented by the non-Vedic *Puranas* ("Ancient Writings") and the great epic tales of the Mahabharata and Ramayana. In them, ages deriving from multiples of 3,600 also predominate; thus, according to the *Vishnu Purana,* "the day that Krishna shall depart from Earth will be the first day of the age of Kali; it will continue for 360,000 years of mortals." This is a reference to the concept that the *Kaliyuga,* the present age, is divided to a dawn or "morning twilight" of 100 divine years that equal 36,000 Earth or "mortal" years, the age itself (1,000 divine years equaling 360,000 Earth-years), and a dusk or "evening twilight" of a final 100 divine years (36,000 mortal-years), adding up to 1,200 divine or 432,000 Earth-years.

The depth of such widespread beliefs in a Divine Cycle of 432,000 years, equaling 120 orbits of 3,600 Earth-years each of Nibiru, makes one wonder whether they represent merely arithmetical sleights of hand—or, in some unknown way, a basic natural or astronomical phenomenon recognized in antiquity by the Anunnaki. We have shown in *The 12th Planet*, the first book of *The Earth Chronicles* series, that the Deluge was a global calamity anticipated by the Anunnaki, resulting from the gravitational pull of the nearing Nibiru on the unstable ice sheet over Antarctica. The event brought the last ice age to an abrupt end circa 13,000 years ago, and was thus recorded in Earth's cycles as a major geological and climatic change.

Such changes, the longest being the geological epochs, have been verified through studies of the Earth's surface and oceanic sediments. The last geological epoch, called the Pleistocene, began about 2,500,000 years ago and ended at the time of the Deluge; it was the time span during which hominids evolved, the Anunnaki came to Earth, and Man, *Homo sapiens*, was brought into being. And it was during the Pleistocene that a cycle of approximately 430,000 years was identified in marine sediments. According to a series of studies by teams of geologists led by Madeleine Briskin of the University of Cincinnati, sea level changes and deep-sea climatic records show a "430,000-year quasi-periodic cyclicity." Such a cyclic periodicity conforms with the Astronomical Theory of climatic modulations that takes into account changes due to obliquity (the Earth's tilt), precession (the slight orbital retardation), and eccentricity (the shape of the elliptical orbit). Milutin Milankovitch, who outlined the theory in the 1920s, estimated that the resulting grand periodicity was 413,000 years. His, and the more recent Briskin cycle, almost conform to the Sumerian cycle of 432,000 Earth-years attributed to Nibiru's effects: the convergence of orbits and perturbations and climatic cycles.

The "myth" of Divine Ages thus appears to be based on scientific facts.

The element of Time features in the ancient records, both Sumerian and biblical, not only as a point of beginning— "When." The process of creation is at once linked to the *measurement* of time, measurements that in turn are linked to determinable celestial motions. The destruction of Tiamat and the ensuing creation of the Asteroid Belt and Earth required, according to the Mesopotamian version, two return orbits of the Celestial Lord (the invading Nibiru/Marduk). In the biblical version, it took the Lord two divine "days" to complete the task; hopefully, even Fundamentalists will by now agree that these were not day and night days as we now know them, for the two "days" occurred before Earth had yet come into existence (and besides, let them heed the Psalmist's statement of the Lord's day being equal to a thousand years or so). The Mesopotamian version clearly measures Creation Time or Divine Time by the passages of Nibiru, in an orbit equaling 3,600 Earth-years.

Before that ancient story of Creation shifts to the newly formed Earth and evolution upon it, it is a tale of stars, planets, celestial orbits; and the Time it deals with is *Divine Time*. But once the focus shifts to Earth and ultimately to Man upon it, the scale of Time also shifts—to an *Earthly Time*—to a scale appropriate not only to Man's abode but also to one that Mankind could grasp and measure: Day, Month, Year.

Even as we consider these familiar elements of Earthly Time, it should be borne in mind that all three of them are also expressions of celestial motions—cyclical motions—involving a complex correlation between Earth, Moon, and Sun. We now know that the daily sequence of light and darkness that we call a Day (of twenty-four hours) results from the fact that Earth turns on its axis, so that as it is lit by the Sun's rays on one side, the other side is in darkness. We now know that the Moon is always there, even when unseen, and that it wanes and waxes not because it disappears but because, depending on the Earth-Moon-Sun positions (Fig. 2) we see the Moon fully lighted by the Sun's rays, or fully obscured by the Earth's shadow, or in phases in between. It is this threefold relationship that extends the actual orbital period of the Moon around the Earth from about 27.3 days (the "sidereal month") to the observed cycle of about 29.53 days (the "synodic month") and the

Sun's Rays

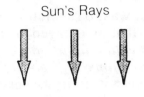

New Moon

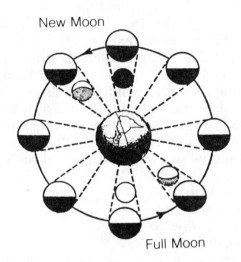

Full Moon

Figure 2

phenomenon of the reappearing or New Moon with all its calendrical and religious implications. And the year or Solar Year, we now of course know, is the period it takes the Earth to complete one orbit around the Sun, our star.

But such basic truths regarding the causes of the Earthly Time cycles of day, month, year are not self-evident and required advanced scientific knowledge to be realized. For the better part of two thousand years it was believed, for example, that the day–night cycle resulted from the circling of Earth by the Sun; for from the time of Ptolemy of Alexandria (second century A.D.) until the "Copernican Revolution" in 1543 A.D., the unquestioned belief was that the Sun, the Moon, and the visible planets were circling the Earth, which was the center of the universe. The suggestion by Nicolaus Copernicus that the Sun was at the center and that the Earth was just another celestial body orbiting it, like any other planet, was so revolutionary scientifically and heretical religiously that he delayed writing his great astronomical work (*De revolutionibus coelestium;* English translation, *On the Revolutions of Celestial Spheres*) and his friends delayed printing it until his very last day, May 24, 1543.

Yet it is evident that in earlier times Sumerian knowledge included familiarity with the triple Earth-Moon-Sun relationship. The *Enuma elish* text, describing the four phases of the Moon, clearly explained them in terms of the position of the Moon vis-a-vis the Sun as it (the Moon) circled the Earth: a full moon at midmonth as it "stood still opposite the Sun," and its waning at month's end as it "stood against the Sun" (see Fig. 2). These motions were attributed to the "destinies" (orbits) that the Celestial Lord (Nibiru) gave Earth and its moon as a result of the Celestial Battle:

The Moon he caused to shine,
to it the night entrusting;
In the night the days to signal
he appointed it, [saying:]
Monthly, without cease, form designs with a crown.
At the month's very start, rising over the Earth,
thou shalt have luminous horns to signify six days,
reaching a crescent on the seventh day.
At mid month stand still opposite the Sun;
it shall overtake thee at the horizon.
Then diminish thy crown and regress in light,
at that time approaching the Sun;
And on the 30th day thou shalt stand against the Sun.
I have appointed thee a destiny; follow its path.

"Thus," the ancient text concludes, did the Celestial Lord "appoint the days and establish the precincts of night and day."

(It is noteworthy that the biblical and Jewish tradition, according to which the twenty-four-hour day begins at sundown the previous evening—"and it was *evening* and it was morning, one day"—is already expressed in the Mesopotamian texts. In the words of *Enuma elish*, the Moon was "appointed *in the night* the days to signal.")

Even in its condensed version of the much more detailed Mesopotamian texts, the Bible (Genesis 1:14) expressed the triple relationship between Earth, Moon, and Sun as it applied to the cycles of day, month, year:

> *And the Lord said:*
> *Let there be luminaries*
> *in the hammered-out Heaven*
> *to distinguish between the day and the night;*
> *And let them be signs*
> *for months and for days and for years.*

The Hebrew term *Mo'edim* used here to denote "months," which signifies the ritual assembly called for on the evening of the New Moon, establishes the Moon's orbital period and phases as an integral component of the Mesopotamian-Hebrew calendar from its very inception. By listing the two luminaries (Sun and Moon) as responsible for the months and the days and the years, the complex lunar-solar nature of that calendar's antiquity is also presented. Over the millennia of Mankind's efforts to measure time by devising a calendar, some (as the Moslems continue to this day) have followed only the Moon's cycles; others (as the ancient Egyptians and the Common Era calendars in use in the Western world) have adopted the solar year, conveniently dividing it into "months." But the calendar devised about fifty-eight hundred years ago in Nippur (Sumer's religious center) and still adhered to by the Jews retained the biblically stated complexity of time-keeping based on the orbital relationship between the Earth and the two luminaries. In doing that, the fact that the Earth orbits the Sun was recognized by the term *Shanah* for "year" which stems from the Sumerian *shatu,* an astronomical term meaning "to course, to orbit," and the full term *Tekufath ha-Shanah*— "the circling or annual orbiting" to denote the passage of a full year.

Scholars have been puzzled by the fact that the *Zo'har* (The Book of Splendor), an Aramaic-Hebrew composition which is a central work in the literature of Jewish mysticism known as *Kabbalah,* unmistakably explained—in the thirteenth century of the Christian era—that the cause of the day's changing into night was the turning of the Earth around its own axis. Some two hundred fifty years *before* Copernicus asserted that the day–night sequence resulted not from the Sun's circling of the Earth but from the Earth's turning on its own axis, the *Zohar* stated that "The entire Earth spins, turning as a sphere. When one part is down the other part is up. When it is light for one part it is dark for the other part; when it is day for that, it is night for the other." The *Zohar's* source was the *third century* Rabbi Hamnuna!

Though little known, the role of Jewish savants in transmitting astronomical knowledge to Christian Europe in the Middle Ages has been convincingly documented by extant books on astronomy, written in Hebrew and containing clear illustrations (as this one from a twelfth century book published in Spain, Fig. 3). Indeed, the writings of Ptolemy of Alexandria, known to the Western world as the *Almagest,* were first preserved by the Arab conquerors of Egypt in the eighth century and became available to Europeans through translations by Jewish scholars; significantly some of these translations contained commentaries casting doubt on the

Figure 3

accuracy of the geocentric theories of Ptolemy centuries before Copernicus. Other such translations of Arabic and Greek works on astronomy, as well as independent treatises, were a main channel for the study of astronomy in medieval Europe. In the ninth and tenth centuries Jewish astronomers composed treatises on the movements of the Moon and the planets and calculated the paths of the Sun and the positions of the constellations. In fact, the compilation of astronomical tables, whether for European kings or Moslem caliphs, was a specialty of Jewish court astronomers.

Such advanced knowledge, seemingly ahead of its time, can be explained only by the retention of the earlier sophisticated knowledge that permeates the Bible and its earlier Sumerian sources. Indeed, *Kabbalah* literally means "that which was received," earlier secret knowledge transmitted from generation to generation. The knowledge of Jewish savants in the Middle Ages can be traced directly to academies in Judea and Babylonia that commented upon and retained biblical data. The *Talmud,* recording such data and commentaries from about 300 B.C. to about A.D. 500, is replete with astronomical snippets; they include the statement that Rabbi Samuel "knew the paths of heaven" as if they were the streets of his town, and the reference by Rabbi Joshua ben-Zakai to "a star which appears once in seventy years and confounds the mariners"—familiarity with Halley's Comet whose periodic return every seventy-five years or so was assumed to have been unknown until discovered by Edmund Halley in the eighteenth century. Rabbi Gamliel of Jabneh possessed a tubular optical instrument with which he observed the stars and planets—fifteen centuries before the "official" invention of the telescope.

The need to know the heavenly secrets stemmed from the lunar-solar nature of the Jewish (i.e. Nippurian) calendar, which required a complex adjustment—"intercalation"— between the solar year and the lunar year, the latter falling short of the former by 10 days, 21 hours, 6 minutes and about 45.5 seconds. That shortfall equals $7/19$ of a synodic month, and, therefore, a lunar year can be realigned with the solar year by adding seven lunar months to every nineteen solar years. Astronomy books credit the Athenian as-

tronomer Meton (circa 430 B.C.) with the discovery of this
nineteen-year cycle; but the knowledge in fact goes back
millennia, to ancient Mesopotamia.

Scholars have been puzzled by the fact that in the
Sumerian-Mesopotamian pantheon, Shamash (the "Sun
god") was depicted as the son of the "Moon god" Sin,
and thus of a lesser hierarchical standing, rather than the
expected reverse order. The explanation may lie in the
origins of the calendar, wherein the notation of the cycles
of the Moon preceded the measurement of the solar cycle.
Alexander Marshack, in *The Roots of Civilization*, suggested that markings on bone and stone tools from Neanderthal times were not decorations but primitive lunar
calendars.

In the purely lunar calendars, as is still the case in the
Moslem calendar, the holidays keep slipping back by about
a month every three years. The Nippurian calendar, having
been devised to maintain a cycle of holidays connected with
the seasons, could not allow such an ongoing slippage: the
New Year, for example, had to begin on the first day of
spring. This required, from the very beginning of Sumerian
civilization, a precise knowledge of the motions of the Earth
and the Moon, and their correlation with the Sun, and thus
the secrets of intercalation. It also required understanding
how the seasons come about.

Nowadays we know that the annual movement of the Sun
from north to south and back, causing the seasons, results
from the fact that the Earth's axis is tilted relative to the
plane of its orbit around the Sun; this "obliquity" is at
present about 23.5 degrees. The farthest points reached by
the Sun north and south, where it seems to hesitate, then
turn back, are called solstices (literally, "Sun standstills"),
occurring on June 21 and December 22. The discovery of
the solstices has also been attributed to Meton and his colleague, the Athenian astronomer Euctemon. But, in fact,
such knowledge goes back to much earlier times. The rich
astronomical vocabulary of the Talmud had already applied
the term *Neti'yah* (from the verb *Natoh*, "to tilt, incline,
turn sideways") to the modern equivalent term "obliquity";

a millennium earlier the Bible recognized the notion of the Earth's axis by attributing the day–night cycle to a ''line'' drawn through the Earth (Psalms 19:5); and the Book of Job, speaking of the formation of the Earth and its mysteries, attributed to the Celestial Lord the creation of an inclined line, a tilted axis, for the Earth (Job 38:5). Using the term *Natoh,* the Book of Job refers to the Earth's tilted axis and the North Pole when it states (26:7)

> *He tilted north over the void*
> *and hangeth the Earth upon nothing at all.*

Psalms 74:16–17 recognized not only the correlation between the Earth, Moon, and Sun, and the Earth's rotation about its axis as the cause of day, night, and the seasons, but also recognized the outermost points, the ''limits'' of the Sun's apparent seasonal movements, that we call solstices:

> *Thine is the day*
> *and thine also is the night;*
> *the Moon and Sun thou didst ordain.*
> *All the Earth's limits thou hast set,*
> *summer and winter didst create.*

If a line is drawn between the sunrise and sunset points for each solstice, the result is such that the two lines cross above the viewer's head, forming a giant X that divides the Earth, and the skies above it, into four parts. This division has been recognized in antiquity and is referred to in the Bible when it speaks of the ''four corners of the Earth'' and the ''four corners of the skies.'' The resulting division of the circle of the Earth and the skies into four parts that look like triangles rounded at their bases created for the ancient peoples the image of ''wings.'' The Bible thus spoke of the ''four wings of the Earth'' as well as of the ''four wings of the skies.''

A Babylonian map of the Earth, from the first millennium B.C., illustrated this concept of four ''corners of the Earth'' by literally depicting four "wings" attached to the circular Earth (Fig. 4).

The Sun's apparent movement from north to south and back resulted not only in the two clearly opposite seasons of summer and winter, but also the interim seasons of autumn and spring. The latter were associated with the equinoxes, when the Sun passed over the Earth's equator (once going, once coming back)—times at which daylight and nighttime are equal. In ancient Mesopotamia, the New Year began on the day of the spring equinox—the first day of the First Month (*Nisannu*—Month "when the sign is given"). Even when, at the time of the Exodus, the Bible (Leviticus chapter 23) decreed that the New Year be celebrated on the day of the autumnal equinox, that designated month (Tishrei) was called "the seventh month," recognizing that Nisannu has been the first month. In either case, the knowledge of the equinoxes, attested to by the New Year days, clearly extends back to Sumerian times.

The fourfold division of the solar year (two solstices, two equinoxes) was combined in antiquity with the lunar motions to create the first known formal calendar, the lunar-solar calendar of Nippur. It was used by the Akkadians, Babylonians, Assyrians, and other nations after them, and remains in use to this very day as the Jewish calendar.

Figure 4

For Mankind, Earthly Time began in 3760 B.C.; we know the exact date because, in the year 1992 of the Common Era, the Jewish calendar counts the year 5752.

Between Earthly Time and Divine Time there is Celestial Time.

From the moment Noah stepped out of the ark, needing reassurance that the watery end of all flesh would not soon recur, Mankind has lived with a lingering notion—or is it a recollection?—of cycles or eons or Ages of Earth's destruction and resurrection, and has looked to the heavens for celestial signs, omens of good or bad to come.

From its Mesopotamian roots the Hebrew language retains the term *Mazal* as meaning "luck, fortune" which could be either good or bad. Little is it realized that the term is a celestial one, meaning zodiac house, and harkens back to the time when astronomy and astrology were one and the same, and priests atop temple-towers followed the movements of the Celestial Gods to see in which house of the zodiac—in which *Manzalu*, in Akkadian—they stood that night.

But it was not Man who had first grouped the myriads of stars into recognizable constellations, defined and named those that spanned the ecliptic, and divided them into twelve to create the twelve houses of the zodiac. It was the Anunnaki who had conceived of that for their own needs; Man adopted that as his link, his means of ascent, to the heavens from the mortality of life on Earth.

For someone arriving from Nibiru with its vast orbital "year" on a fast orbiting planet (Earth, the "seventh planet" as the Anunnaki had called it) whose year is but one part of 3,600 of theirs, time-keeping had to pose a great problem. It is evident from the Sumerian King Lists and other texts dealing with the affairs of the Anunnaki that for a long time—certainly until the Deluge—they retained the *sar*, the 3,600 Earth-years of Nibiru, as the divine unit of time. But what could they do somehow to create a reasonable relationship, other than 1:3600, between that Divine Time and the Earthly Time?

The solution was provided by the phenomenon called precession. Because of its wobble, the Earth's orbit around the Sun is slightly retarded each year; the retardation or precession amounts to 1° in seventy-two years. Devising the division of the ecliptic (the plane of planetary orbits around the Sun) into twelve—to conform to the twelve-member composition of the Solar System—the Anunnaki invented the twelve houses of the zodiac; that allotted to each zodiac house 30°, in consequence of which the retardation per house added up to 2,160 years (72 × 30 = 2,160) and the complete Precessional Cycle or "Great Year" to 25,920 years (2,160 × 12 = 25,920). In *Genesis Revisited* we have suggested that by relating 2,160 to 3,600 the Anunnaki arrived at the Golden Ratio of 6:10 and, more importantly, at the sexagesimal system of mathematics which multiplied 6 by 10 by 6 by 10 and so on and on.

"By a miracle that I have found no one to interpret," the mythologist Joseph Campbell wrote in *The Masks of God: Oriental Mythology* (1962), "the arithmetic that was developed in Sumer as early as c. 3200 B.C., whether by coincidence or by intuitive induction, so matched the celestial order as to amount in itself to a revelation." The "miracle," as we have since shown, was provided by the advanced knowledge of the Anunnaki.

Modern astronomy, as well as modern exact sciences, owes much to the Sumerian "firsts." Among them the division of the skies about us and all other circles into 360 portions ("degrees") is the most basic. Hugo Winckler, who with but a few others combined, at the turn of the century, mastery of "Assyriology" with knowledge of astronomy, realized that the number 72 was fundamental as a link between "Heaven, Calendar and Myth" (*Altorientalische Forschungen*). It was so through the *Hameshtu,* the "fiver" or "times five," he wrote, creating the fundamental number 360 by multiplying the celestial 72 (the precessional shift of 1°) by the human 5 of an Earthling's hand. His insight, understandably for his time, did not lead him to envision the role of the Anunnaki, whose science was needed to know of Earth's retardation to begin with.

Among the thousands of mathematical tablets discovered in Mesopotamia, many that served as ready-made tables of division begin with the astronomical number 12,960,000 and end with 60 as the 216,000th part of 12,960,000. H.V. Hilprecht (*The Babylonian Expedition of the University of Pennsylvania*), who studied thousands of mathematical tablets from the library of the Assyrian king Ashurbanipal in Nineveh, concluded that the number 12,960,000 was literally astronomical, stemming from an enigmatic Great Cycle of 500 Great Years of complete precessional shifts (500 × 25,920 = 12,960,000). He, and others, had no doubt that the phenomenon of precession, presumably first mentioned by the Greek Hipparchus in the second century B.C., was already known and followed in Sumerian times. The number, reduced by ten to 1,296,000, it will be recalled, appears in Hindu tradition as the length of the Age of Knowledge as a threefold multiple of the cycle of 432,000 years. The cycles-within-cycles, interplaying 6 and 12 (the 72 years of a 1° zodiacal shift), 6 and 10 (the ratio of 2,160 and 3,600) and 432,000 to 12,960,000, may thus reflect small and great cosmic and astronomical cycles—secrets yet to be unveiled, of which Sumerian numbers offer just a glimpse.

The selection of the vernal equinox day (or conversely, the autumnal equinox day) as the moment to begin the New Year was not accidental, for because of the Earth's tilt, it is just on these two days that the Sun rises at the points where the celestial equator and the ecliptic circle intersect. Because of precession—the full term is Precession of the Equinoxes—the zodiacal house in which this intersection occurs keeps shifting back, appearing in a preceding 1° in the zodiacal band every seventy-two years. Although this point is still being referred to as the First Point of Aries, in fact we have been in the "Age" (or zodiac) of Pisces since about 60 B.C., and slowly but surely we will soon enter the Age of Aquarius (Fig. 5). It is such a shift—the change from a fading zodiacal age to the start of another zodiacal age—that is the coming of a *New Age*.

As Mankind on Earth awaits the change with anticipation,

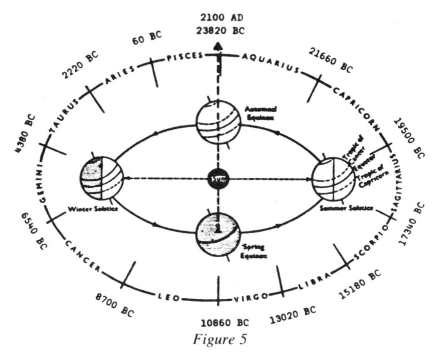

Figure 5

many are those who wonder what the change will bring with it—of what *Mazal* will it be a harbinger? Bliss or upheavals, an end—or a new beginning? The end of the Old Order or the start of a New Order on Earth, perhaps the prophesied return of the Kingdom of Heaven to Earth?

Does Time only flow forward or can it also flow backward, philosophers have wondered. In fact, Time does shift backward, for that is the essence of the phenomenon of precession: the retardation in Earth's orbit around the Sun that causes, once in about 2,160 years, the observance of sunrise on the spring equinox not in the next zodiacal house but in the *preceding* one . . . Celestial Time, as we have designated it, does not progress in the direction of Earthly (and all Planetary) Time, counterclockwise; rather, it moves in the opposite direction, matching the orbital (clockwise) direction of Nibiru.

Celestial Time does flow backward, as far as we on Earth are concerned; and therefore, in zodiacal terms, *the Past is the Future.*

Let us examine the Past.

2

A COMPUTER
MADE OF STONE

The notion or recollection of cyclical ages affecting Earth
and Mankind was not confined to the Old World. When
Hernando Cortés was welcomed by the Aztec king Moctezuma as a returning god, he was presented with an immense golden disk on which were carved the symbols of
the cyclical ages in which the Aztecs and their predecessors
in Mexico believed. That precious artifact has been lost
forever, having been quickly melted down by the Spaniards;
but replicas thereof, in stone, have been found (Fig. 6). The
glyphs represented the cycle of ''Suns'' or ages of which
the present is the fifth. The previous four all ended in one
or another natural calamity—water, wind, quakes and
storms, and wild animals. The first age was the Age of the
White Haired Giants; the second, the Golden Age. The third

Figure 6

was the Age of the Red Haired People (who, according to the legends, were the first to arrive by ships in the Americas); and the fourth was the Age of the Black Haired People, with whom the supreme Mexican god, Quetzalcoatl, had arrived.

All the way south in pre-Columbian Peru, the Andean peoples also spoke of five "Suns" or ages. The first one was the age of the *Viracochas,* white and bearded gods; the second was the Age of the Giants, followed by the Age of Primitive Man. The fourth was the Age of Heroes; and then came the fifth or contemporary age, the Age of Kings, of which the Inca kings were last in line. The durations of these ages were measured in thousands rather than in tens or hundreds of thousands of years. Mayan monuments and tombs were decorated with "sky bands" whose glyphs have been found to represent the zodiacal division of the heavens; artifacts found in Mayan ruins and in the Inca capital Cuzco have been identified as zodiacal calendars. The city of Cuzco itself, it appears, was (in the words of S. Hagar in a paper delivered at the 14th Congress of Americanists) "a testimonial in stone" to the South American familiarity with the twelve-house zodiac. The unavoidable conclusion is that knowledge of the zodiacal division of the ecliptic was somehow known in the New World millennia ago, and that the Ages were measured in the 2,160-year units of Celestial Time.

The idea that calendars could be made of stone might seem strange to us, but was evidently quite logical in antiquity. One such calendar, posing many puzzles, is called *Stonehenge.* It consists nowadays of gigantic stone blocks that stand silently on a windswept plain in England, north of the city of Salisbury and about eighty miles southwest of London. The remains pose an enigma that has titillated the curiosity and imagination of generations, challenging historians, archaeologists, and astronomers. The mystery these megaliths bespeak is lost in the mists of earlier times; and Time, we believe, is the key to its secrets.

Stonehenge has been called "the most important prehistoric monument in the whole of Britain," and that alone justifies the attention it has been given over the centuries and especially in recent times. It has been described—at least by its British relators—as unique, for "there is nothing else like it anywhere in the world" (R.J.C. Atkinson, *Stonehenge and Neighbouring Monuments*); and that may explain why an eighteenth-century manuscript listed more than six hundred works on Stonehenge in its catalogue of ancient monuments in Western Europe. Stonehenge is indeed the largest and most elaborate of more than nine hundred ancient stone, wood, and earthen circles in the British Isles, as well as the largest and most complicated one in Europe.

Yet, in our view, it is not only what makes Stonehenge unique that is its most important aspect. It is also what reveals its similarity to certain monuments elsewhere, and its *purpose* at the specific *time* of its construction, that make it part of the tale we have called *The Earth Chronicles*. It is within such a wider framework, we believe, that one can offer a plausible solution to its enigma.

Even those who have not visited Stonehenge must have seen, in print or on the screen, the most striking features of this ancient complex: the pairs of huge upright stone blocks, each about thirteen feet high, connected at the top by an equally massive lintel stone to form freestanding *Trilithons;* and these, erected in a semicircle, surrounded in turn by a massive circle of similar giant stones connected at the top by lintels that were carefully carved to form a continuous ring around the paired uprights. Though some of the stone blocks in what are called the sarsen trilithons and the *Sarsen Circle* (after the type of stone, a kind of sandstone, to which these boulders belong) are missing and some have toppled, it is they that create the view that the word "Stonehenge" conjures (Fig. 7).

Inside this massive stone ring other, smaller stones called bluestones were placed so as to form the *Bluestone Circle* outside the Trilithons and a bluestone semicircle (some refer to it as the *Bluestone Horseshoe*) inside the Trilithon half-circle. As is the case regarding the sarsen stones, not all of the bluestones that together formed these circles and half-circles (or "horseshoes") are still in place. Some are miss-

Figure 7

ing altogether; some lie about as fallen giants. Adding to
the site's haunting aura are other gigantic stones that lie
about and whose nicknames (of uncertain origin) compound
the mystery; they include the *Altar Stone*, a sixteen-foot-
long dressed block of blue-gray sandstone that remains half-
buried under an upright and the lintel of one of the Trilithons. In spite of considerable restoration work, much of the
structure's past glory is either gone or fallen. Still, archaeologists have been able to reconstruct from all the available
evidence how this remarkable stone monument looked in
its prime.

They have concluded that the outer ring, of uprights connected by curved lintels, consisted of thirty upright stones
of which seventeen remain. Within this Sarsen Circle there
stood the Bluestone Circle of smaller stones (of which
twenty-nine are still extant). Within this second ring stood
five pairs of Trilithons, making up the *Sarsen Horseshoe*
of ten massive sarsen blocks; they are usually numbered 51
through 60 on charts (lintel stones are numbered separately
in a series that adds 100 to their related uprights; thus the
lintel connecting the uprights 51–52 is number 152).

The innermost semicircle consisted of nineteen bluestones
(some numbered 61–72), forming the so-called Bluestone
Horseshoe; and within this innermost compound, precisely

on the axis of the whole Stonehenge complex, stood the so-called Altar Stone, giving these circles within circles of stone the layout envisioned in Fig. 8a.

As if to emphasize the importance of the circular shape already evident, the rings of stones are in turn centered within a large framing circle. It is a deep and wide ditch whose excavated soil was used to raise its banks; it forms a perfect encompassing ring around the whole Stonehenge complex, a ring with a diameter in excess of three hundred feet. Approximately half the circuit of the ditch was excavated earlier this century and then partly refilled; the other portions of the ditch and its raised banks bear the marks of being weathered down by nature and man over the millennia.

These circles within circles have been repeated in yet other ways. A few feet away from the inner bank of the ditch there exists a circle made up of fifty-six pits, deep and perfectly dug into the ground, called the *Aubrey Holes* after their seventeenth-century discoverer, John Aubrey. Archaeologists have excavated these holes for whatever clues the accumulation of debris might disclose about the site and its builders, and have thereafter plugged up the holes with white cement discs; the result is that the perfect circle that these holes form stands out—especially from the air. In addition, cruder and more irregular holes were dug at some unknown time in two circles around the sarsen and bluestone circles, now known as the Y and Z holes.

Two stones, unlike all the others, have been found positioned on opposite sides of the ditch's inner embankment; and somewhat farther down the line of the Aubrey Holes (but evidently not part of them), two circular mounds, equidistant from the two stones, have been found with holes in them. Researchers are convinced that the holes also held stones akin to the first two, and that the four—called *Station Stones* (now numbered 91–94)—served a distinct purpose, especially since, when connected by lines, the four stones outline a perfect rectangle with probable astronomical connotations. Yet another massive stone block, nicknamed the *Slaughter Stone*, lies fallen where the embanked ditch has a wide gap that clearly served as the opening into (or from) the concentric rings of stones, holes, and earthworks. It probably lies not exactly where it once stood, and was probably not alone, as holes in the ground suggest.

The opening in the ditch is oriented exactly to the northeast. It leads to (or allows arrival from) a causeway, called the *Avenue*. Two parallel embanked ditches outline this avenue, leaving a clear passage over thirty feet wide. It runs straight for more than a third of a mile where it branches northward toward a vast elongated earthwork known as the *Cursus*, whose orientation is at an angle to that of the Avenue; the other branch of the Avenue curves toward the River Avon.

The concentric circles of Stonehenge with the Avenue leading to the northeast (Fig. 8b) provide a major clue re-

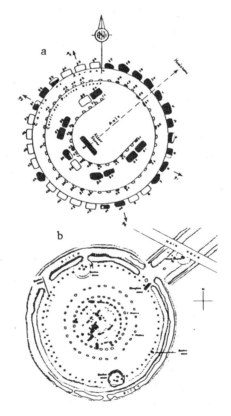

Figures 8a and 8b

garding the purpose for which Stonehenge was constructed. That the direction of the Avenue—its precise northeastern orientation—was not accidental becomes clear when it is realized that a line drawn through the center of the Avenue passes through the center of the circles of stones and holes to form the structure's axis (see Fig. 8a). That the axis was deliberately oriented is suggested by a series of holes indicating that the marker stones had once been placed along this axis. One of them, called the *Heel Stone*, still stands as a mute witness to the builders' intentions and the site's purpose; it was undoubtedly astronomical.

The idea that Stonehenge was a carefully planned astronomical observatory rather than a heathen cult or occult site (a notion expressed, for example, by calling a fallen stone "Slaughter Stone," implying human sacrifices), was not easily accepted. In fact, the difficulty grew rather than diminished the more the site was investigated and its date of construction kept shifting backward.

A twelfth-century account (*Historia regum Britanniae* by Geoffrey of Monmouth) related that the "Giants' Ring" was "a stone cluster which no man of the period could ever erect and was first built in Ireland from stones brought by the giants from Africa." It was then on the advice of the sorcerer Merlin (whom Arthurian legends also connected with the Holy Grail) that the King of Vortigen moved the stones and "re-erected them in a circle round a sepulchre, in exactly the same way as they had been arranged on Mount Killaraus" in Ireland. (That this medieval legend had a factual core was given confirmation by the modern discovery that the bluestones originated from the Prescelly Mountains in southwestern Wales and were somehow transported by land and water over a distance of two hundred fifty miles—first to a site some twelve miles northwest of Stonehenge, where they might have been erected in an earlier circle, and then on to Stonehenge proper).

In the seventeenth and eighteenth centuries, the stone temple was attributed to the Romans, the Greeks, the Phoenicians, or the Druids. The common aspect of these various

notions is that they all shifted the time attributed to Stonehenge from the Middle Ages back to the beginning of the
Christian era and earlier, thus substantially increasing the
site's antiquity. Of these various theories, the one concerning the Druids gained the most favor at the time, not least
of all because of the research and writings of William Stukeley, especially his 1740 work *Stonehenge, A Temple Re-
stor'd To The British Druids*. The Druids were the learned
class or sect of teacher-priests among the ancient Celts.
According to Julius Caesar, who is the prime source of
information regarding the Druids, they assembled once a
year at a sacred place for secret rites; they offered human
sacrifices; and among the subjects they taught the Celt noblemen were "the powers of the gods," the sciences of
nature, and astronomy. While nothing that has been uncovered by archaeologists at the site reveals any connection
with pre–Christian era Druids, the Celts had arrived in the
area by that time and there is no proof the other way either,
namely that the Druids did not gather at this "Sun Temple"
even if they had nothing to do with its much earlier builders.

Although Roman legions encamped near the site, no evidence was found to connect Stonehenge with the Romans.
A Greek and Phoenician connection, however, shows more
promise. The Greek historian Diodorus Siculus (first century
B.C.)—a contemporary of Julius Caesar—who had traveled
to Egypt, wrote a multivolume history of the ancient world.
In the first volumes he dealt with the prehistory of the
Egyptians, Assyrians, Ethiopians, and Greeks, the so-called
"mythic times." Drawing on the writings of earlier historians, he quotes from a (by now lost) book by Hecataeus
of Abdera in which the latter had stated, circa 300 B.C.,
that on an island inhabited by the Hyperboreans "there is
a magnificent sacred precinct of Apollo and a notable temple
which is spherical in shape." The name in Greek signified
a people from the distant north, whence the north wind
("Boreas") comes. They were worshipers of the Greek
(later Roman) god Apollo, and the legends regarding the
Hyperboreans were thus mingled with the myths concerning

Apollo and his twin sister, the goddess Artemis. As the ancients told it, the twins were the children of the great god Zeus and their mother Leto, a Titaness. Impregnated by Zeus, Leto wandered over the face of the Earth seeking a place to give birth to her children in peace, away from the wrath of Hera, the official wife of Zeus; Apollo was thus associated with the distant north. The Greeks and the Romans considered him a god of divination and prophecy; he circled the zodiac in his chariot.

Though not attributing any scientific value to such a legendary or mythological connection with Greece, archaeologists have nevertheless seemed to find such a connection through archaeological discoveries in the area of Stonehenge, which is replete with prehistoric earthworks, structures, and graves. These man-made ancient remains include the great Avebury Circle, which schematically drawn resembles the works of a modern watch (Fig. 9a, as sketched by William Stukeley) or even the meshing wheels of the ancient Mayan calendar (Fig. 9b). They also include the miles-long trench called the Cursus; a kind of wooden-pegged rather than stone-made circle called Woodhenge; and the outstanding Silbury Hill—an artificial conical hill

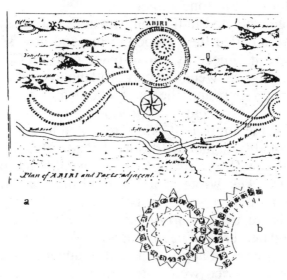

Figures 9a and 9b

which is precisely circular and 520 feet in diameter, the largest of its kind in Europe (some see significance in the fact that it is situated an exact six purported "megalithic miles" from Stonehenge).

The most important finds, archaeologically speaking, have been made in this area (as often elsewhere) in tombs, which are scattered all over the Stonehenge area. In them archaeologists have found bronze daggers, axes and maces, golden ornaments, decorated pottery, and polished stones. Many of those finds reinforced archaeological opinion that the manner in which stones at Stonehenge were smoothly dressed and carefully shaped indicated "influences" from Minoan Crete (the Mediterranean island) and Mycenaean (mainland) Greece. It was also noted that some of the peg-into-socket joints used at Stonehenge to hold together stone blocks were similar to the joints used in the stone gateways of Mycenae. All this, many archaeologists held, pointed to a connection with ancient Greece.

A leading representative of this school has been Jacquetta Hawkes, who in her book, *Dawn of the Gods,* about the Minoan and Mycenaean origins of Greek civilization, could not help devoting a good portion of the chapter on "Graves and Kingdoms" to Stonehenge.

Mycenae is situated in the southwestern part of mainland Greece that is called the Peloponnesus (and now separated from the rest of Greece by a man-made Corinth Canal) and acted as a bridge between the earlier Minoan civilization on the island of Crete and the later classical Greek one. It flowered in the sixteenth century B.C. and the treasures uncovered in the tombs of its kings revealed foreign contacts that undoubtedly included Britain. "At just this time when Mycenaean kings were rising to a new wealth and power," Jacquetta Hawkes wrote, "a rather similar advance, although on a smaller scale, was taking place in southern England. There too a warrior aristocracy was ruling over peasants and herders and beginning to trade and to prosper— and to be buried with appropriate extravagance. Among the possessions so buried were a few objects that prove these chieftains to have had contacts with the Mycenaean world."

Such things, she added, were not of great moment and could just be the fruits of trade or imitation, were it not for "the unique event—the building of the great sarsen-stone circle and trilithons of Stonehenge."

Not all archaeological finds, however, showed such early Greek "influences." The finds in tombs around Stonehenge included, for example, decorated beads and amber disks bound with gold in a method developed in Egypt and not at all in Greece. Such finds raised the possibility that all those artifacts were somehow imported to southeast England, neither by Greeks nor Egyptians but perhaps by trading people from the eastern Mediterranean. The obvious candidates were the Phoenicians, the renowned sailors-cum-traders of antiquity.

It is a recorded fact that the Phoenicians, sailing from their Mediterranean ports, reached Cornwall in the southwest corner of England, quite close to Stonehenge, in the search for tin, with which hardened bronze was made from soft copper. But were any of these peoples, whose trade links flourished in the millennium between 1500 B.C. and 500 B.C., responsible for the planning and construction of Stonehenge? Did they even visit it? A partial answer would depend, of course, on when Stonehenge itself was conceived and built, or who else was there to build it.

In the absence of written records or carved images of the Mediterranean gods (artifacts found elsewhere among Minoan, Mycenaean, and Phoenician ruins) no one can answer the question with any certainty. But the question itself became moot when various remains of organic origin, such as carved antlers, were dug up by archaeologists at Stonehenge. Subjected to radiocarbon dating, remains found in the Ditch produced a date of between 2900 to 2600 B.C.— at least a thousand years and probably much more before the sailors from the Mediterranean may have arrived. A charcoal piece found in one of the Aubrey Holes provided a carbon date of 2200 B.C.; an antler pick found near one of the trilithons gave a reading of between 2280 and 2060 B.C.; radiocarbon datings of finds in the Avenue gave dates between 2245 and 2085 B.C.

Who was there at such an early time to plan and execute the marvelous stone complex? Scholars hold that until about 3000 B.C. the area was sparsely populated by small groups of early farmers and herders who used stone for their tools. Some time after 2500 B.C. new groups arrived from the European continent; they brought with them knowledge of metals (copper and gold), used clay utensils, and buried their dead in round mounds; they have been nicknamed the Beaker People, after the shape of their drinking vessels. At about 2000 B.C. bronze made its appearance in the area and a wealthier and more numerous population, known as the Wessex People, engaged in cattle ranching, metal crafts, and trade with western and central Europe and the Mediterranean. By 1500 B.C. this era of prosperity suffered an abrupt decline that lasted the better part of a millennium; and Stonehenge must have shared in this decline.

Were the Neolithic farmers and herders, the Beaker People, or even the Early Bronze Age Wessex People, capable of creating Stonehenge? Or did they just provide the labor and the manpower to construct a complex mechanism in stone devised by advanced scientific knowledge of others?

Even an outspoken proponent of the Mycenaean connection, Jacquetta Hawkes, had to admit that Stonehenge, "this sanctuary, constructed from colossal yet carefully-shaped blocks that make the cyclopean masonry of Mycenae look like children's bricks, has nothing to compare with it in all prehistoric Europe." To allow for the Mycenaean connection and to link it with the early Englanders, she proceeded to offer the theory that "some of the local lords controlling the pastures of Salisbury plain, and perhaps, like Odysseus, owning twelve herds of cattle, may have had the wealth and authority needed to turn what had been a modest sanctuary of Stone Age origin into a noble and unparalleled work of megalithic architecture. It has always seemed that some individual must have initiated it—through swollen ambition or religious obsession—but because the whole design and method of building is so far advanced on anything known in the island before, it has seemed likely that ideas drawn from a more civilized tradition might also have been involved.''

But what was that ''more civilized tradition'' that gave rise to this structure that was beyond compare to anything in prehistoric Europe? The answer must depend on an accurate dating of Stonehenge; and if, as scientific data suggests, it is a thousand to two thousand years older than the Mycenaeans and the Phoenicians, then an earlier source of the ''civilized tradition'' must be sought. If Stonehenge belongs to the third millennium B.C., then the only candidates are those of Sumer and Egypt. When Stonehenge was first conceived, the Sumerian civilization, with its cities, high-rise temples-cum-observatories, writing, and scientific knowledge, was already a thousand years old, and kingship had already flourished in Egypt for many centuries.

For a better answer, we have to put together the knowledge accumulated by now regarding the several phases by which Stonehenge, according to the latest research, came to be.

Stonehenge began with hardly any stones. It began, all are agreed, with the Ditch and its embankment, a great earthen circle with a circumference of 1,050 feet at its bottom; it is about twelve feet wide and up to six feet deep, and thus required digging up a considerable quantity of soil (chalky earth) and arranging it to form the two raised banks. Within this outer ring the circle of 56 Aubrey Holes was made.

The northeastern section of the earthen ring was left undug, to provide an entranceway into the midst of the circle. There, two ''gateway stones,'' now missing, flanked this entry to the enclosure; they also served as focusing aides for the Heel Stone, which was erected on the resultant axis. This massive natural boulder stands sixteen feet above the ground and cuts four feet into the earth; it has been set up inclined at an angle of 24°. A series of holes at the entrance gap may have been intended to hold movable wooden markers, and are thus called Post Holes. Finally, the four rounded Station Stones were positioned to form a perfect rectangle;

and this completed *Stonehenge I*—the earthen ring, the Aubrey Holes, an entranceway axis, seven stones, and some wooden pegs.

Organic remains and stone tools associated with this phase suggest to scholars that Stonehenge I was constructed some-time between 2900 and 2600 B.C.; the date selected by the British authorities is 2800 B.C.

Whoever constructed Stonehenge I, and for whatever purpose, found it satisfactory for several centuries. Throughout the occupation of the area by the Beaker People, no need to change or improve the arrangement of earthwork and stones was indicated. Then, at about 2100 B.C., just before the arrival of the Wessex People (or perhaps coinciding with it) a spate of extraordinary activity burst upon the scene. The main event was the introduction of the bluestones into the makeup of Stonehenge, making *Stonehenge II* a stone "henge" for the first time.

It was no mean feat to haul the bluestones, weighing up to four tons each, across land and over sea and river for a total distance of some two hundred fifty miles. To this day it is not known why these particular dolerite stones were chosen and why such a great effort was made to bring them to the site, directly or with a short interval at a temporary way station. Whatever the precise route was, it is believed that in the end they were brought to the site's proximity up the River Avon, which explains why the Avenue was extended by some two miles at this phase to connect Stonehenge with the river.

At least eighty (some estimate eighty-two) bluestones were brought over. It is believed that seventy-six of them were intended for the holes that made up the two concentric Q and R holes, thirty-eight per circle; the circles appear to have had openings on their west-facing sides.

At the same time a separate larger stone, the so-called Altar Stone, was erected within the circles exactly on the Stonehenge axis, facing the Heel Stone to the northeast. But as the researchers checked the alignment and the position of the outer stones, they discovered to their surprise that the Heel Stone was shifted in this Phase II somewhat eastward (to the right, as one looks from the enclosure's center); simultaneously, two other stones were erected in a row in front of the Heel Stone, so as to emphasize the new line of sight. To accommodate these changes, the entrance to the enclosure was widened on its right (eastern side) by filling up part of the Ditch, and the Avenue too was widened there.

Unexpectedly the researchers realized that the main innovation of Stonehenge II was not the introduction of the bluestones, but *the introduction of a new axis,* an axis somewhat more to the east than the previous one.

Unlike the seven or so centuries of dormancy for Stonehenge I, *Stonehenge III* followed Phase II within decades. Whoever was in charge decided to give the complex a monumental scope and permanence. It was then that the huge sarsen stones, weighing forty to fifty tons each, were hauled to Stonehenge from Marlboro Downs, some twenty miles away. It is generally assumed that seventy-seven stones were brought.

As laborious as the transporting of these boulders with an aggregate weight of thousands of tons was, even more daunting must have been the task of setting them up. The stones were carefully dressed to the desired shapes. The lintels were given a precise curvature, given (somehow) protruding pegs exactly where they had to fit into carved-out sockets where stone joined stone; and then all those prepared stones had to be erected in a precise circle or in pairs, and the holding lintels hauled up to be placed on top. How the task, made more difficult by the site's slope, was achieved, no one really knows.

At this time the realigned axis was also given permanence by the erection of two new massive Gateway Stones, replacing the earlier ones. It is believed that the fallen Slaughter Stone could have been one of the two new Gateway Stones.

In order to make room for the Sarsen Circle and the Trilithon Horseshoe or oval, the two circles of bluestones from Phase II had to be completely dismantled. Nineteen of them were used to form the inner Bluestone Horseshoe (now recognized as an open-ended oval) and fifty-nine, it is believed, were intended to be placed in two new circles of holes (Y and Z), surrounding the Sarsen Circle. The Y circle was meant to hold thirty stones and the Z circle twenty-nine. Some of the other stones of the original eighty-two may have been intended to serve as lintels or (as John E. Wood, *Sun, Moon and Standing Stones,* believes) to complete the oval. The Y and Z circles, however, were never erected; instead the bluestones were arranged in one large circle, the Bluestone Circle, with an undetermined number of stones (some believe sixty). Also uncertain is the time when this circle was erected—right away, or a century or two later. Some also think that additional work, mainly on the Avenue, was done about 1100 B.C.

But for all intents and purposes, the Stonehenge we see was planned in 2100 B.C., executed during the following century, and given its final touches circa 1900 B.C. Modern scientific research methods have thus corroborated the findings—astounding at the time, 1880—of the renowned Egyptologist Sir Flinders Petrie, that Stonehenge dated to circa 2000 B.C. (It was Petrie who devised the stones' numbering system still in use).

In the usual course of scientific studies of ancient sites, archaeologists are the first to be on the scene, and others—anthropologists, metallurgists, historians, linguists, and other experts—follow. In the case of Stonehenge, astronomers led the way. This was not only because the ruins were visible above the surface and required no excavation to reveal them, but also because from the very beginning it seemed almost self-evident that the axis line from the center toward the Heel Stone through the Avenue pointed ''to the northeast, whereabouts the Sun rises when the days are longest'' (to use the words of William Stukeley, 1740)—toward the point in the sky where the Sun rises at the summer solstice (about June 21). Stonehenge was an instrument to measure the passage of time!

After two and a half centuries of scientific progress, this conclusion is still valid. All are agreed that Stonehenge was not a place of residence; nor was it a burial place. Neither palace nor tomb, it was in essence a temple-cum-observatory, as the ziggurats (step-pyramids) of Mesopotamia and ancient America were. And being oriented toward the Sun when it rises in midsummer, it could be called a Temple of the Sun.

With this basic fact undisputable, it is no wonder that astronomers continue to lead the research concerning Stonehenge. Prominent among them, at the very beginning of this century, was Sir Norman Lockyer, who conducted a comprehensive survey of Stonehenge in 1901 and confirmed the summer solstice orientation in his master work *Stonehenge and Other British Stone Monuments*. Since this orientation is satisfied by the axis alone, subsequent researchers began in time to wonder whether the additional complexity of Stonehenge—the diverse circles, ovals, rectangle, markers—might signify that other celestial phenomena besides sunrise at summer solstice and other time cycles have been observed at Stonehenge.

There have been suggestions to that effect in earlier treatises on Stonehenge. But it was only in 1963, when Cecil A. Newham discovered alignments that suggested that equinoxes too could have been observed and even predicted at Stonehenge, that these possibilities were given modern scientific credence.

His most sensational suggestion, however (first in articles and then in his 1964 book *The Enigma of Stonehenge*), was that Stonehenge must have also been a *lunar* observatory. He based this conclusion on examination of the four Station Stones and the rectangle that they form (Fig. 10); he also showed that whoever had intended to give Stonehenge this capability knew where to erect it, for the rectangle and its alignments had to be sited exactly where Stonehenge is.

All this was at first received with extreme doubt and disdain, because lunar observations are considerably more complex than solar ones. The Moon's motions (around the Earth and together with the Earth around the Sun) are not repeated on an annual basis, because, among other reasons, the Moon orbits the Earth at a slight inclination to the Earth's orbit around the Sun. The complete cycle, which is repeated

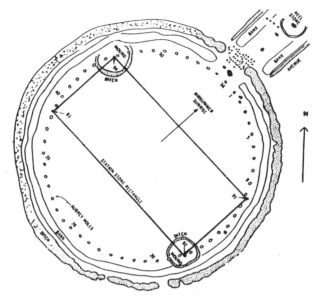

Figure 10

only once in about nineteen years, includes eight points of "Moon Standstill" as the astronomers call them, four major and four minor. The suggestion that Stonehenge I—which already possessed the alignments highlighted by Newham—was built to enable the determination, or even prediction, of these eight points seemed preposterous in view of the fact that Britain's inhabitants at the time were just emerging from the Stone Age. This is clearly a valid argument; and those who have nevertheless found more evidence for the astronomical marvels at Stonehenge are yet to provide an answer to the paradox of a complex lunar observatory amidst Stone Age people!

Prominent among the astronomers whose investigations confirmed the incredible capabilities of Stonehenge was Gerald S. Hawkins of Boston University. Writing in prestigious scientific journals in 1963, 1964, and 1965, he announced his far-reaching conclusions by entitling his studies "Stonehenge Decoded," "Stonehenge: A Neolithic Computer," and "Sun, Moon, Men and Stones," followed by his books *Stonehenge Decoded* and *Beyond Stonehenge*.

With the aid of the university's computers he analyzed hundreds of sight lines at Stonehenge and related them to the positions of the Sun, Moon, and major stars as they were in ancient times, and decided that the resulting orientations could not have been just accidental.

He attached great significance to the four Station Stones and the perfect rectangle they form and showed how the lines connecting opposite stones (91 with 94 and 92 with 93) were oriented to the points of major standstills and those connecting the stones diagonally to the points of minor standstills of the Moon at moonrise and moonset. Together with the four points of the Sun's movements, Stonehenge, according to Hawkins, enables observation and prediction of all the twelve points marking the Sun's and the Moon's movements. Above all he was fascinated by the number 19 expressed by stones and holes in the various circles: the two circles of 38 bluestones of Stonehenge II "can be regarded as two semi-circles of 19" (*Stonehenge Decoded*) and the oval "horseshoe" of Stonehenge III had the exact 19. This was an unmistakable lunar relationship, for 19 was the Moon's cycle which governs intercalation.

Professor Hawkins went even farther: he concluded that the numbers expressed by stones and holes in the various circles bespoke an ability to predict eclipses. Because the Moon's orbit is not exactly in the same plane as the Earth's orbit around the Sun (the former is inclined to the latter by just over 5°), the Moon's orbit crosses the path of the Earth around the Sun at two points each year. The two points of intersection ("nodes") are commonly marked on astronomical charts N and N'; this is when eclipses occur. But because of the irregularities in the shape and lag of the Earth's orbit around the Sun, these nodal intersections do not recur precisely at the same celestial positions year after year; rather, they recur in a cycle of 18.61 years. Hawkins postulated that the operating principle for this cycle was, therefore, "cycle end/cycle start" in the nineteenth year, and Hawkins reasoned that the purpose of the 56 Aubrey Holes was to attain an adjustment by moving three markers at a time within the Aubrey circle, since $18\frac{2}{3} \times 3 = 56$. This, he held, made possible the foretelling of eclipses of the Moon as well as of the Sun, and his conclusion was that such a prediction of eclipses was the main purpose of the construction and design of Stonehenge. Stonehenge, he announced, was nothing short of *a brilliant astronomical computer made of stone*.

The proposition that Stonehenge was not only a "Sun temple" but also a lunar observatory was met at first with fierce resistance. Prominent among the dissenters, who considered many of the Moon alignments to be coincidental, was Richard J.C. Atkinson of the University College in Cardiff, who had led some of the most extensive archaeological excavations at the site. The archaeological evidence for the great antiquity of Stonehenge was the very reason for his disdain for the observatory/lunar-alignments/Neolithic computer theories, for he asserted that Neolithic Man in Britain was simply incapable of such achievements. His disdain and even ridicule, expressed in such titles for his articles in *Antiquity* as "Moonshine on Stonehenge" and in his book *Stonehenge,* turned to grudging support as a result of studies conducted at Stonehenge by Alexander Thom (*Megalithic Lunar Observations*). Thom, an engineering professor at Oxford University, conducted the most accurate measurements at Stonehenge, and pointed out that the "horseshoe" arrangement of the sarsen stones in fact represented an oval (Fig. 11), an elliptical shape that represents

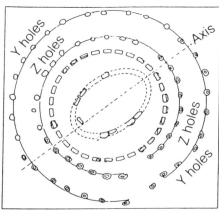

○ Upright stones
◉ Excavated holes
○ Presumed holes

Figure 11

planetary orbits more accurately than a circle. He agreed with Newham that Stonehenge I was primarily a lunar, and not just a solar, observatory, and confirmed that Stonehenge was erected where it is because it is only there that the eight lunar observations could be made precisely along the lines formed by the rectangle connecting the four Station Stones.

The fierce debate, conducted on the pages of leading scientific magazines and in confrontational conferences, was summed up by C.A. Newham (*Supplement to the Enigma of Stonehenge and its Astronomical and Geometric Significance*) in the following words: "With the exception of the five Trilithons, practically all the remaining features appear to have lunar connections." He agreed that the "56 Aubrey Holes rotate to the eight main alignments of the Moon setting and rising." Thereafter, even Atkinson admitted that he "has become sufficiently persuaded that conventional archaeological thinking is in need of drastic revision" in regard to the purpose and functions of Stonehenge.

These conclusions were to no small measure the result of the research by a notable participant who had joined the growing list of involved scientists in the late 1960s and the decade of the 1970s. He was Sir Fred Hoyle, astronomer and mathematician. He held that the alignments listed by Hawkins to various stars and constellations were rather random than deliberate, but fully agreed with the lunar aspects of Stonehenge I—and especially the role of the fifty-six Aubrey Holes and the rectangular arrangement of the Station Stones ("Stonehenge—An Eclipse Predictor" in *Nature* and *On Stonehenge*).

But concurring that the Aubrey Circle could act as a "calculator" for predicting eclipses (in his opinion it was done by moving four markers around), Hoyle stirred up another issue. Whoever had designed this calculator—Hawkins called it a "computer"—must have known *in advance* the *precise* length of the solar year, the Moon's orbital period, and the cycle of 18.61 years; and Neolithic Man in Britain simply did not possess such knowledge.

Struggling to explain how the advanced knowledge of astronomy and mathematics had appeared in Neolithic Britain, Hawkins resorted to ancient records of the Mediterranean peoples. In addition to the Diodorus/Hecataeus reference he also mentioned Plutarch's quote (in *Isis and Osiris*) of Eudoxus of Cnidus, the fourth century B.C. astronomer-mathematician from Asia Minor, who had associated the "demon god of eclipses" with the number fifty-six.

In the absence of answers from Man, a glance at the superhuman?

Hoyle, on his part, arrived at the conviction that Stonehenge was not a mere observatory, a place to see what goes on in the skies. He called it a *Predictor,* an instrument for foretelling celestial events and a facility for noting them on the predetermined dates. Agreeing that "such an intellectual achievement was beyond the capacity of the local Neolithic farmers and herdsmen," he felt that the Station Stones rectangle and all it implied indicate "that the builders of Stonehenge I might have come to the British Isles from the outside, purposely looking for this rectangular alignment" (which is possib!e just where Stonehenge is located, in the northern hemisphere), "just as the modern astronomer often searches far from home for places to build his telescopes.

"A veritable Newton or Einstein must have been at work at Stonehenge," Hoyle mused; but even so, where was the university where he had learned mathematics and astronomy, where were the writings without which accumulated knowledge could not be passed on and taught, and how could a sole genius plan, execute, and supervise such a celestial predictor when, for Phase II alone, a whole century was needed? "There have only been about 200 generations of history; there were upward of 10,000 generations of prehistory," Hoyle observed. Was it all part of the "eclipse of the gods," he wondered—the transition from a time when people worshiped an actual Sun god and a Moon god, "to become the invisible God of Isaiah?"

Without explicitly divulging his thoughts, Hoyle gave an answer by quoting the full section in Diodorus from Hecataeus regarding the Hyperboreans; it states toward its end that after the Greeks and Hyperboreans exchanged visits "in the most ancient times,"

> They also say that the Moon, as viewed from this island, appears to be but a little distance from the Earth, and to have upon it prominences, like those of the Earth, which are visible to the eye.
> The account is also given that the god visits the island every nineteen years, the period in which the return of the stars to the same place in the heavens is accomplished; and for this reason the nineteen-year period is called by the Greeks the "year of Meton."

The familiarity in such distant times not only with the nineteen-year cycle of the Moon but also with "prominences, like those of the Earth"—surface features such as mountains and plains—is unquestionably amazing.

The attribution by Greek historians of the circular structure in Hyperborea to the lunar cycle first described in Greece by the Athenian Meton tosses the problem of Who Built Stonehenge to the ancient Near East; so do the soul-searching conclusions and musings of the above mentioned astronomers.

But more than two centuries earlier, William Stukeley had already pointed for answers in the same direction, toward the ancient Near East. To his sketch of Stonehenge, as he understood it to have been, he appended the design he had seen on an eastern Mediterranean ancient coin (Fig. 12a) which depicts a temple on an elevated platform. This depiction, more explicit, also appears on another ancient coin from the city of Byblos in the same area, one that we have reproduced in the very first volume of *The Earth Chronicles*. It shows that the ancient temple had an enclosure in which there stood *a rocket upon a launch pad* (Fig. 12b). We have identified the place as The Landing Place of Sumerian lore, the place where the Sumerian king Gilgamesh witnessed a rocket ship rise. The place still exists; it is now the vast platform in the mountains of Lebanon, at Baalbek, upon which there still stand the ruins of the greatest

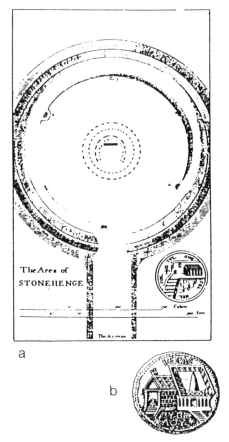

The Area of
STONEHENGE

a

b

Figures 12a and 12b

Roman temple ever built. Supporting the massive platform are three colossal stone blocks that have been known since antiquity as the *Trilithon.*

The answers to the Stonehenge enigma should thus be sought in places far away from it, but in a time frame quite close to it. The When holds the key, we believe, not only to the Who of Stonehenge I, but also to the Why of Stonehenge II and III.

For, as we shall see, the hurried remaking of Stonehenge in 2100–2000 B.C. had to do with the coming of a New Age—Mankind's first historically recorded New Age.

3

THE TEMPLES
THAT FACED HEAVEN

The more we know about Stonehenge thanks to modern science, the more incredible Stonehenge becomes. Indeed, were it not for the visible evidence of megaliths and earthworks—were they somehow to vanish, as so many ancient monuments did through the vagaries of time and nature or ravages wrought by Man—the whole tale of stones that could compute time and circles that could foretell eclipses and determine the movements of the Sun and the Moon would have sounded so implausible for Stone Age Britain that it would have been considered just a myth.

The great antiquity of Stonehenge, which kept increasing as scientific knowledge about it progressed, is of course what troubles most scientists; and it is primarily the dates of construction ascertained for Stonehenge I and II + III that have led archaeologists to seek Mediterranean visitors, and eminent scholars to allude to ancient gods, as the only possible explanations for the enigma.

For of the series of troubling questions, such as by Whom and What for, the When is the most satisfactorily answered. Archaeology and physics (through modern dating methods such as carbon-14 measurements) were joined by *archaeoastronomy* to agree on the dates: 2900/2800 B.C. for Stonehenge I, 2100/2000 B.C. for Stonehenge II and III.

The father of the science of archaeoastronomy—though he preferred to call it astro-archaeology, which better conveys what he had in mind—was undoubtedly Sir Norman Lockyer. It is a measure of how long established science takes to accept innovation to note that it is virtually a full century since the publication of Lockyer's masterwork, *The*

51

Dawn of Astronomy, in 1894. Having visited the Levant in 1890 he observed that whereas for the early civilizations in India and China there are few monuments but many written records establishing their age, the opposite holds true in Egypt and Babylonia: they were "two civilizations of undefined antiquity" where monuments abounded but the measure of their antiquity was uncertain (at the time of Lockyer's writing).

It struck him, he wrote, that it was truly remarkable that in Babylonia "from the beginning of things the sign for God was a star" and that likewise in Egypt, in the hieroglyphic texts, three stars represented the plural term "gods." Babylonian records on clay tablets and burned clay bricks, he noted, appeared to deal with regular cycles of "moon and planet positions with extreme accuracy." Planets, stars, and the constellations of the zodiac are represented on the walls of Egyptian tombs and on papyruses. In the Hindu pantheon, he observed, we find the worship of the Sun and of the Dawn: the name of the god Indra meaning "The Day Brought by the Sun" and that of the goddess Ushas meaning "Dawn."

Can astronomy be of assistance to Egyptology? he wondered; can it help define the measure of Egyptian and Babylonian antiquity?

When one considers the Hindu *Rigveda* and Egyptian inscriptions from an *astronomical* point of view, Lockyer wrote, "one is struck by the fact that in both, the early worship and all the early observations related to the horizon . . . This was true not only of the Sun, but equally true of the stars which studded the expanse of the sky." The horizon, he pointed out, is "the place where the circle which bounds our view of Earth's surface and the sky appear to meet." A circle, in other words, where Heaven and Earth touch and meet. It is there that the ancient peoples sought whatever sign or omen their observers were looking for. Since the most regular phenomenon observable on the horizon was the rising and setting of the Sun on a daily basis, it was natural to make this the basis of ancient astronomical observations, and to relate other phenomena (such as the appearance or movements of planets and even stars) to their "heliacal rising," their brief appearance on the eastern horizon as the turning Earth reaches the few moments of dawn, when the Sun begins to rise but the sky is dark enough to see the stars.

An ancient observer could easily determine that the Sun always rises in the eastern skies and sets in the western skies, but he would have noted that in summer the Sun appears to rise in a higher arc than in winter and the days are longer. This, modern astronomy explains, is due to the fact that the Earth's axis around which it rotates daily is not perpendicular to its path around the Sun (the Ecliptic) but is inclined to it—about 23.5 degrees nowadays. This creates the seasons and the four points in the seeming movement of the Sun up and down in the skies: the summer and winter solstices and the spring ("vernal") and autumnal equinoxes (which we have described earlier).

Studying the orientation of temples old and not so old, Lockyer found that those he called "Sun Temples" were of two kinds: those oriented according to the equinoxes and those oriented according to the solstices. Though the Sun always rises in the eastern skies and sets in the western skies, it is only on the days of the equinoxes that it rises anywhere on Earth precisely in the east and sets precisely in the west, and Lockyer therefore deemed such "equinoctial" temples to be more universal than those whose axis was oriented according to the solstices; because the angle formed by the northern and southern (to an observer in the northern hemisphere, the summer and winter) solstices depended on where the observer was—his latitude. Therefore, "solstitial" temples were more individual, specific to their geographic location (and even elevation).

As examples of equinoctial temples Lockyer cited the Temple to Zeus at Baalbek, the Temple of Solomon in Jerusalem, and the great basilica of St. Peter's in the Vatican in Rome (Fig. 13)—all oriented on a precise east–west axis. Regarding the latter he quoted studies on church architecture that described how at the Old St. Peter's (begun under Constantine in the fourth century and torn down early in

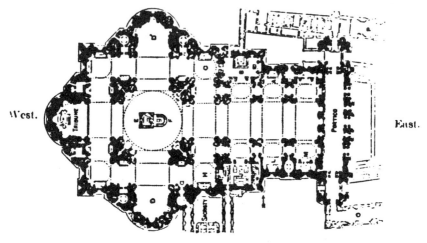

Figure 13

the sixteenth century), on the day of the vernal equinox, "the great doors of the porch of the quadriporticus were opened at sunrise, and also the eastern doors of the church; and as the sun rose, its rays passed through the outer doors, then through the inner doors, and, penetrating straight through the nave, illuminated the High Altar." Lockyer added that "the present church fulfils the same conditions." As examples of "solstitial" Sun Temples Lockyer described the principal Chinese "Temple of Heaven" in Peking, where "the most important of all state observances in China, the sacrifice performed in the open air at the south altar of the Temple of Heaven," was held on the day of the winter solstice, December 21; and the structure at Stonehenge, oriented to the summer solstice.

All that was, however, just a prelude to Lockyer's main studies, in Egypt.

Studying the orientation of Egypt's ancient temples, Lockyer concluded that the older ones were "equinoctial" and the later ones "solstitial." He was amazed to discover that earlier temples revealed greater astronomical sophistication than later ones, for they were intended to observe and venerate not only the rising or setting of the Sun, but also of stars. Moreover, the earliest shrine suggested a mixed

Sun-Moon worship that shifted to an equinoctial, i.e. Sun, focus. That equinoctial shrine, he wrote, was the temple in Heliopolis ("City of the Sun" in Greek) whose Egyptian name, *Annu,* was also mentioned in the Bible as On. Lockyer calculated that the combination of solar observations with the period of the bright star Sirius and with the annual rising of the Nile, a triple conjunction on which the Egyptian calendar was based, indicated that in Egyptian time reckoning Point Zero was circa 3200 B.C.

The Annu shrine, it is known from Egyptian inscriptions, held the *Ben-Ben* ("Pyramidion-Bird"), claimed to have been the actual conical upper part of the "Celestial Barge" in which the god Ra had come to Earth from the "Planet of Millions of Years." This object, usually kept in the temple's inner sanctum, was put on public display once a year, and pilgrimages to the shrine to view and venerate the sacred object continued into dynastic times. The object itself has vanished over the millennia; but a stone replica thereof has been found, showing the great god visible through the doorway or hatch of the capsule (Fig. 14). The legend of the Phoenix, the mythical bird that dies and resurrects after a certain period, has also been traced to this shrine and its veneration.

Figure 14

The *Ben-Ben* was still there at the time of the Pharaoh Pi-Ankhi (circa 750 B.C.), for an inscription was found describing his visit to the shrine. Intent on entering the Holy of Holies and seeing the celestial object, Pi-Ankhi began the process by offering elaborate sacrifices at sunrise in the temple's forecourt. He then entered the temple proper, bowing low to the great god. A prayer was then offered by the priests for the king's safety, that he might enter and leave the Holy of Holies unharmed. Ceremonies that included the king's washing and purification and rubbing with incense then followed, preparing him for entering the enclosure called the "Star Room." He was then given rare flowers or plant branches that had to be offered to the god by placing them in front of the *Ben-Ben*. He then went up the steps to the "great tabernacle" that held the sacred object. Reaching the top of the stairs, he pushed back the bolt and opened the doors to the Holy of Holies; "and he saw his forefather Ra in the chamber of the *Ben-Ben*." He then stepped back, closed the doors behind him and placed thereon a clay seal, impressing on it his signet.

While this shrine has not survived the millennia, what may have been another later shrine modeled after the Heliopolitan one has been found by archaeologists. It is the so-called Solar Temple of the Pharaoh Ne-user-Ra of the fifth dynasty that lasted from 2494 to 2345 B.C. Built at a place now called Abusir, just south of Giza and its great pyramids, it consisted primarily of a large raised terrace upon which, within a great enclosure, there stood on a massive platform a thick, short obelisklike object (Fig. 15). A ramp, surmounted by a covered corridor lighted by evenly spaced windows in the ceiling, connected the temple's elaborate entrance with a monumental gateway in the valley below. The sloping base of the obelisklike object rose some sixty-five feet above the level of the temple's court; the obelisk, which may have been sheathed with gilded copper, rose another 120 feet.

The temple, within its walled enclosure which contained various chambers and compartments, formed a perfect rectangle measuring some 260 feet by 360 feet. It was clearly

Figure 15

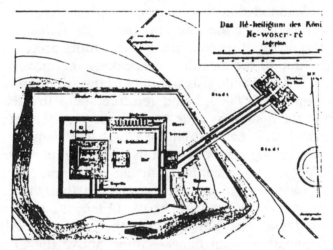

Figure 16

oriented on an east–west axis (Fig. 16), i.e. to the equinoxes; but the long corridor was obviously reoriented away from the east–west axis to face northeast. That this was a deliberate reorientation of a copy of the earlier Heliopolitan shrine (which was oriented just on the east–west axis) becomes clear from the masterful reliefs and inscriptions that decorated the corridor. They celebrated the thirtieth anniversary of the pharaoh's reign, so the corridor could have been built then. The celebration followed the mysterious rites of the *Sed* festival (the term's meaning remains unclear) which marked some kind of "jubilee" and which always began on the first day of the Egyptian calendar—the first day of the first month which was named the Month of Thoth. In other words, the Sed festival was a kind of New Year's Day festival celebrated not each year but after the passage of a number of years.

The presence of both equinoctial and solstitial orientations in this temple implies familiarity—in the third millennium B.C.—with the concept of the Four Corners. Drawings and inscriptions found in the temple's corridor describe the king's "sacred dance." They were copied, translated, and published by Ludwig Borchardt with H. Kees and Friedrich von Bissing in *Das Re-Heiligtum des Königs Ne-Woser-Re*. They concluded that the "dance" represented the "cycle of sanctification of the four corners of the Earth."

The equinoctial orientation of the temple proper and the solstitial one of the corridor, bespeaking the movements of the Sun, led Egyptologists to apply to the structure the term "Sun Temple." They found reinforcement in this designation in the discovery of a "solar boat" (partly carved out of the rock and partly built of dried and painted bricks) buried under the sands just south of the temple enclosure. Hieroglyphic texts dealing with the measurement of time and the calendar in ancient Egypt held that the celestial bodies traversed the skies in boats. Often, the gods or even the deified pharaohs (having joined the gods in the Afterlife) were depicted in such boats, sailing above the firmament of the skies that was held up at the four corner points (Fig. 17).

The next great temple clearly emulated the pyramidion-on-platform concept (Fig. 18) of the Ne-User-Ra "Sun Temple"; but it was already fully oriented to the solstices from its inception, having been planned and executed along a northwest–southeast axis. It was built on the west side of the Nile (near the present-day village of Deir-el-Bahari) in Upper Egypt, as part of greater Thebes, by the Pharaoh Mentuhotep I circa 2100 B.C. Six centuries later Tuthmosis III and Queen Hatshepsut of the XVIII dynasty added their temples there; the orientation was similar—but not exactly so (Fig. 19). It was at Thebes (Karnak) that Lockyer made

Figure 17

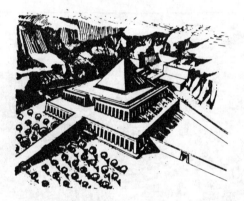

Figure 18

his most important discovery, one that laid the foundation for archaeoastronomy.

The sequence of chapters, facts, and arguments in *The Dawn of Astronomy* reveals that Lockyer's route to Karnak and Egyptian temples passed through the European evidence. There was the orientation of the Old St. Peter's in Rome and the information about the beam of sunlight at the spring equinox sunrise; and there was St. Peter's Square (a woodcut drawing of which Lockyer included, Fig. 20) with its startling similarities to Stonehenge . . .

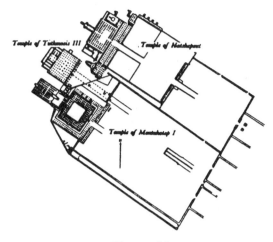

Figure 19

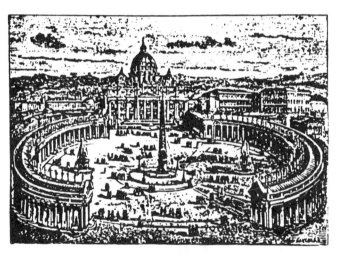

Figure 20

He looked at the Parthenon in Athens, Greece's principal shrine (Fig. 21) and found that "there is the old Parthenon, a building which may have been standing at the time of the Trojan war, and the new Parthenon, with an outer court very like the Egyptian temples but with its sanctuary more nearly in the centre of the building. It was by the difference of direction of these two temples at Athens that my attention was called to the subject."

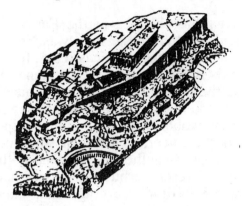

Figure 21

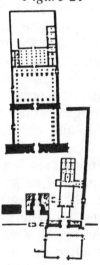

Figure 22

He had in front of him drawings of the layout plans of various Egyptian temples where orientations seemed to vary from early to later buildings, and was struck by an obvious one in two back-to-back temples at a site not far from Thebes called Medinet-Habu (Fig. 22) and pointed out the similarity between this Egyptian and the Greek ''difference of orientation'' in temples that, from a purely architectural aspect, should have been parallel and with the same axial orientation.

Could the slightly altered orientation result from changes in the amplitude (the position in the skies) of the Sun or stars caused by the changes in the Earth's obliquity? he wondered, and felt that the answer was Yes.

We now know that the solstices result from the fact that the Earth's axis is tilted relative to its plane of orbit around the Sun, and the points of "standstill" match the Earth's tilt. But astronomers established that this angle is not constant. The Earth wobbles, like a pitching ship, from side to side—perhaps the lingering result of some mighty bang it received in its past (whether the original collision that put the Earth in its present orbit, or the crash of a massive meteor some 65 million years ago that may have extinguished the dinosaurs). The present tilt of about 23.5 degrees can decrease to perhaps just 21° and on the other hand increase to well over 24°—no one can really say for sure, since the change by even 1° lasts thousands of years (7,000, according to Lockyer). Such changes in the obliquity result in changes in the Sun's standstill points (Fig. 23a). This means that a temple built to a precise solstitial orientation at a given time is no longer properly aligned to that orientation several hundred, and certainly several thousand, years later.

Lockyer's masterful innovation was this: by determining the orientation of a temple and its geographic longitude, it was possible to calculate the obliquity that prevailed at the time of construction; and by determining the changes in obliquity over the millennia, it was possible to conclude with sufficient certainty when the temple was constructed.

The Table of Obliquity, fine-tuned and made more accurate during the past century, shows the change in the angle of the Earth's tilt in five-hundred-year intervals, going back from the present 23° 27′ (about 23.5 degrees):

500 B.C.	about	23.75	degrees
1000 B.C.	"	23.81	"
1500 B.C.	"	23.87	"
2000 B.C.	"	23.92	"
2500 B.C.	"	23.97	"
3000 B.C.	"	24.02	"
3500 B.C.	"	24.07	"
4000 B.C.	"	24.11	"

Lockyer applied his findings primarily to extensive measurements at the great temple to Amon-Ra in Karnak. This temple, having been enlarged and augmented by various pharaohs, consists of two principal rectangular structures built back-to-back on a southeast–northwest axis, signifying a solstitial orientation. Lockyer concluded that the purpose of the orientation and the layout of the temple was to enable a beam of sunlight to come from such a direction on solstice day that it would travel the length of a long corridor, pass between two obelisks, and strike the Holy of Holies with a flash of Divine Light at the temple's innermost sanctum. Lockyer noticed that the axis of the two back-to-back temples was not similarly oriented: the newer axis represented a solstice resulting from a somewhat smaller obliquity than the older axis (Fig. 23b). The two obliquities determined by Lockyer show that the older temple was built circa 2100 B.C. and the newer one circa 1200 B.C.

Although more recent investigations, especially by Gerald S. Hawkins, suggest that the Sun's beam, at winter solstice, was meant to be viewed from a part of the temples Hawkins named "High Room of the Sun" and not as a beam traveling the length of the axis, the revision in no way changes the basic conclusion by Locker regarding the solstitial orien-

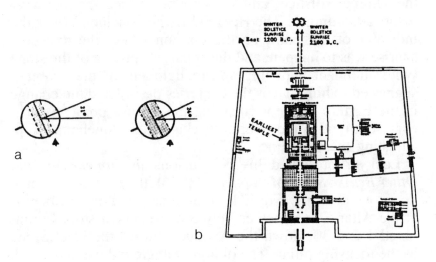

Figures 23a and 23b

tation. Indeed, further archaeological discoveries at Karnak corroborate Lockyer's principal innovation—that the orientation of the temples changed in time to reflect the changes in obliquity. Therefore, the orientation could serve as a clue to the temples' time of construction. The latest archaeological advances confirmed that the construction of the oldest part coincided with the beginning of the Middle Kingdom under the XI dynasty circa 2100 B.C. Repairs, demolitions, and rebuilding then continued through the ensuing centuries by pharaohs of subsequent dynasties; the two obelisks were set up by pharaohs of the XVIII dynasty. The final phase took shape under the Pharaoh Seti II of the XIX dynasty who reigned in 1216–1210 B.C.—all as Lockyer had determined.

Archaeoastronomy—or, astro-archaeology as Sir Norman Lockyer named it—proved its merit and validity.

At the beginning of this century Lockyer turned his attention to Stonehenge, having become convinced that the phenomenon he had discovered governed temple orientations in other parts of the ancient world, as at the Parthenon in Athens. At Stonehenge the axis of viewing from the center through the Sarsen Circle clearly bespoke an orientation to the summer solstice, and Lockyer performed his measurements accordingly. The Heel Stone, he concluded, was the indicator of the point on the horizon where the expected sunrise was to happen; and the apparent shifting of the stone (with attendant widening and realignment of the Avenue) suggested to him that as the centuries passed and the change in the Earth's tilt kept changing the sunrise point, even if ever so slightly, the people in charge of Stonehenge kept adjusting the view line.

Lockyer presented his conclusions in *Stonehenge and Other British Stone Monuments* (1906); they can be summed up in one drawing (Fig. 24). It assumes an axis that begins at the Altar Stone, passes between the sarsen stones numbered 1 and 30, down the Avenue, toward the Heel Stone as the focusing pillar. The obliquity angle indicated by such an axis led him to suggest that Stonehenge was built in 1680

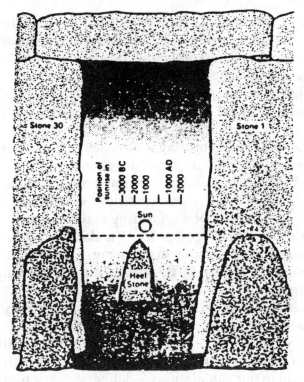

Figure 24

B.C. Needless to say, such an early date was quite sensational at a time, a century ago, when scholars still thought of Stonehenge in terms of King Arthur's days.

The refinements in studies of the Earth's obliquity, allowances now made for margins of error, and the determination of the various phases of Stonehenge have not diminished Lockyer's basic contribution. Although Stonehenge III, which is what we essentially see nowadays, is now dated to circa 2000 B.C., it is generally agreed that the Altar Stone was removed when the remodeling began circa 2100 B.C. with the double Bluestone Circle (Stonehenge II), and that it was reerected where it is now only when the bluestones were reintroduced and the Y and Z holes dug. That phase, designated Stonehenge IIIb, has not been definitely dated; it is in a range between 2000 B.C. (Stonehenge IIIa) and 1550 B.C. (Stonehenge IIIc)—and quite possibly the 1680 B.C. date arrived at by Lockyer. As the drawing shows, he did not rule out a much earlier date for the prior phases of Stonehenge; this too compares well with the presently accepted date of 2900/2800 B.C. for Stonehenge I.

Archaeoastronomy thus joins archaeological findings and radiocarbon dating to arrive at the same dates for the construction of the various phases of Stonehenge, the three separate methods corroborating each other. With such a convincing determination of Stonehenge's dates, the question regarding its builders becomes more poignant. Who, circa 2900/2800 B.C., possessed the knowledge of astronomy (to say nothing of engineering and architecture) to build such a calendrical "computer," and circa 2100/2000 B.C. to rearrange the various components thereof and attain a new realignment? And why was such a realignment required or desired?

Mankind's transition from the Paleolithic (Old Stone Age) that lasted for hundreds of thousands of years to the Mesolithic (Middle Stone Age) occurred abruptly in the ancient Near East. There, circa 11,000 B.C.—right after the Deluge, according to our calculations—deliberate agriculture and the domestication of animals began in a stunning profusion. Archaeological and other evidence (most recently augmented by studies of linguistic patterns) shows that Mesolithic agriculture spread from the Near East to Europe as a result of the migration of people possessing such knowledge. It reached the Iberian peninsula between 4500 and 4000 B.C., the western edge of what is today France and the Lowlands between 3500 and 3000 B.C., and the British Isles between 3000 and 2500 B.C. It was soon thereafter that the "Beaker People," who knew how to make clay utensils, arrived on the Stonehenge scene.

But by then the ancient Near East was already well past the Neolithic (New Stone Age) which began there circa 7400 B.C. and whose hallmark was the transition from stone to clay to metals and the appearance of urban settlements. By the time this phase reached the British Isles with the so-called "Wessex People" (after 2000 B.C.), in the Near East the great Sumerian civilization was already almost two thousand years old and the Egyptian civilization more than a thousand years old.

If, as all agree, the sophisticated scientific knowledge that was required for the planning, siting, orientation, and construction of Stonehenge had to come from outside the British Isles, the earlier civilizations of the Near East seem to be the only sources for such knowledge at the time.

Were the Sun Temples of Egypt, then, the prototypes for Stonehenge? We have seen that at the dates established for Stonehenge's various phases, there already existed in Egypt elaborate temples that were astronomically oriented. The equinoctial Sun Temple at Heliopolis was built at about the time, 3100 B.C., when kingship began in Egypt (if not somewhat earlier)—several centuries before Stonehenge I. The construction of the oldest phase of the solstitially oriented temple to Amon-Ra in Karnak took place circa 2100 B.C.—a date coinciding (perhaps not by chance) with the date for the "remodeling" of Stonehenge.

It is thus theoretically possible that Mediterranean people—Egyptians or people with "Egyptian" knowledge—could somehow account for the construction of Stonehenge I, II, and III at dates that were impossible for the local inhabitants of the area.

While, from a timing point of view, Egypt could have been the source of the required knowledge, we ought to be bothered by a crucial difference between *all* of the Egyptian temples and Stonehenge: none of the Egyptian temples, no matter whether their orientation was equinoctial or solstitial, were circular as Stonehenge has been during all of its phases. The various pyramids were square-based; the podiums for the obelisks and pyramidions were square; the numerous temples were all rectangular. With all the stones of Egypt, not one of its temples was a stone *henge*.

From the beginning of dynastic times in Egypt, with which the appearance of a distinct Egyptian civilization is linked, it was the pharaohs of Egypt who had hired the architects and masons, the priests and savants, and decreed the planning and construction of the marvelous stone edifices of ancient Egypt. None of them, however, appears to have designed, oriented, and built a circular temple.

What about those famous seafarers, the Phoenicians? Not only did they reach the British Isles (mainly in search of tin) too late to have built not just Stonehenge I but also the II and III phases, but none of their temple architecture bears any resemblance to the emphatically circular essence of Stonehenge. We can see a Phoenician temple depicted on the Byblos coin (Fig. 12), and it is certainly rectangular. On the vast stone platform at Baalbek in the Lebanon mountains, people after people and conquerors after conquerors built their temples precisely on the ruins and according to the layout of preceding temples. These, as the latest extant ruins from the Roman era reveal (Fig. 25), represented a rectangular temple (black area) with a square forecourt (the diamond-shaped entrance pavilion is a purely Roman addition). The temple is clearly oriented on an east–west axis, facing directly east toward the Sun at sunrise—an equinoctial temple. This should perhaps be no surprise, since in ancient times this site too was called ''City of the Sun''— Heliopolis by the Greeks, Beth-Shemesh (''House of the Sun'') in the Bible, in King Solomon's time.

That the rectangular shape and east–west axis were not a passing fad in Phoenicia is further evidenced by the Temple of Solomon, the first temple of Jerusalem, which was built with the aid of Phoenician architects provided by

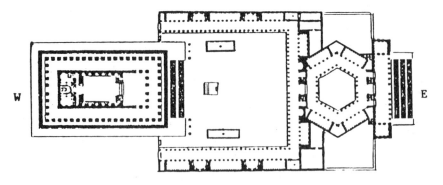

Figure 25

Ahiram, king of Tyre; it was a rectangular structure on an east–west axis, facing eastward (Fig. 26), built upon a large man-made platform. Sabatino Moscati (*The World of the Phoenicians*) stated without qualification that ''if there are no adequate remains of Phoenician temples, the temple of Solomon in Jerusalem, built by Phoenician workmen, *is* described in detail in the Old Testament—and the Phoenician temples must have resembled each other.'' And nothing about them was circular.

Circles do appear, though, in the case of the other Mediterranean ''suspects''—the Mycenaeans, the first Hellenic people of ancient Greece. But these were at first what archaeologists call Grave Circles—burial pits surrounded by a circle of stones (Fig. 27) that evolved into circular tombs hidden beneath a conical mound of soil. But that had taken place circa 1500 B.C. and the largest of them, called the Treasury of Atreus because of the golden artifacts that were found around the dead (Fig. 28), dates to circa 1300 B.C. Archaeologists who adhere to the Mycenaean connection compare such eastern Mediterranean burial mounds to Silbury Hill in the Stonehenge area or to one at Newgrange, across the Irish Sea in Boyne Valley, County Meath, in Ireland; but Silbury Hill has been determined by carbon

Figure 26

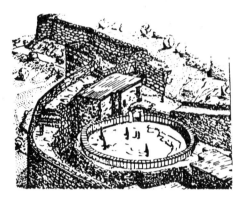

Figure 27

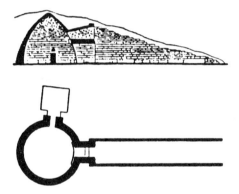

Figure 28

dating to have been constructed not later than 2200 B.C. and the burial mound at Newgrange at about the same time— almost a thousand years before the Treasury of Atreus and other Mycenaean examples; the period of the Mycenean burial mounds, moreover, is even farther removed from the time of Stonehenge I. In fact, the burial mounds in the British Isles are much more akin, in construction and in timing, to such mounds in the western rather than eastern Mediterranean, such as the one in Los Millares in southern Spain (Fig. 29).

Above all, Stonehenge has never served as a burial place. For all these reasons, the search for a prototype—a circular structure serving astronomical purposes—should continue beyond the eastern Mediterranean.

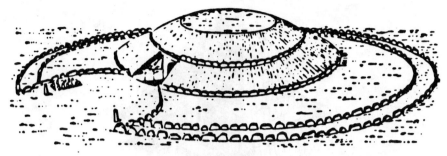

Figure 29

* * *

Older than the Egyptian civilization and possessing much more advanced scientific knowledge, the Sumerian civilization could have served, theoretically, as the fountainhead for Stonehenge. Among the astounding Sumerian achievements were great cities, a written language, literature, schools, kings, courts, laws, judges, merchants, craftsmen, poets, dancers. The sciences flourished within the temples, where the "secrets of numbers and of the heavens"—of mathematics and astronomy—were kept, taught, and transmitted by generations of priests who performed their functions within walled-off sacred compounds. Such compounds usually included shrines dedicated to various deities, residences, work and study places for the priests, storehouses and other administrative buildings, and—as the dominant, principal, and most prominent feature of the sacred precinct and of the city itself—a *ziggurat,* a pyramid that rose sky high in stages (usually seven). The topmost stage was a multichambered structure that was intended—literally—to be the residence of the great god whose "cult center" (as scholars like to call it) the city was (Fig. 30).

A good illustration of the layout of such a sacred precinct with its ziggurat is a reconstruction based on archaeological discoveries at the sacred precinct of Nippur (NI.IBRU in Sumerian), the "headquarters" from the earliest days of the god Enlil (Fig. 31); it shows a ziggurat with a square base within a rectangular compound. As luck would have it, archaeologists have also unearthed a clay tablet upon which

Figure 30

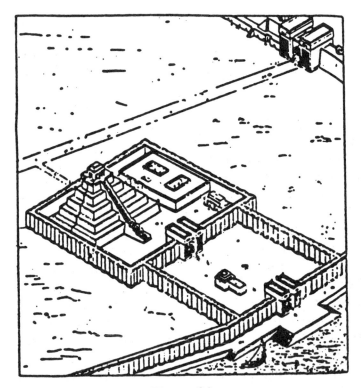

Figure 31

an ancient cartographer drew a map of Nippur (Fig. 32); it clearly shows the rectangular sacred precinct with the square-based ziggurat, the caption (in cuneiform script) for which states its name, the E.KUR—"House, which is like

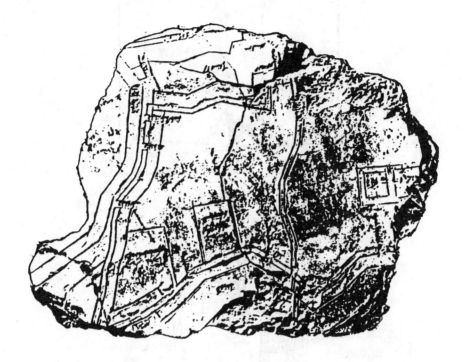

Figure 32

a mountain." The orientation of the ziggurat and temples was such that the corners of the structures pointed to the four cardinal points of the compass, so that the sides of the structure faced to the northeast, southwest, northwest, and southeast.

To orient the ziggurats' corners to the cardinal points—without a compass—was not an easy achievement. But it was an orientation that made it possible to scan the heavens in many directions and angles. Each stage of the ziggurat provided a higher viewing point and thus a different horizon, adjustable to the geographic location; the line between the east-pointing and west-pointing corners provided the equinoctial orientation; the sides gave solstitial views to either sunrise or sunset, at both summer and winter solstices. Modern astronomers have found many of these observational orientations in the famed ziggurat of Babylon (Fig. 33)

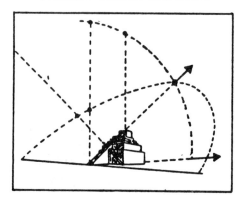

Figure 33

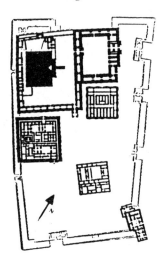

Figure 34

whose precise measurements and building plans were found spelled out on clay tablets.

Square or rectangular structures, with precise right angles, were the traditional shape of Mesopotamian ziggurats and temples, whether one looks at the sacred precinct of Ur at the time of Abraham (Fig. 34)—circa 2100 B.C., the time of Stonehenge II—or goes back to one of the earliest temples built on a raised platform, as the White Temple at Eridu (Fig. 35a and 35b) that dates to about 3100 B.C.—two or three centuries before the date of Stonehenge I.

The deliberate manner in which the Mesopotamian tem-

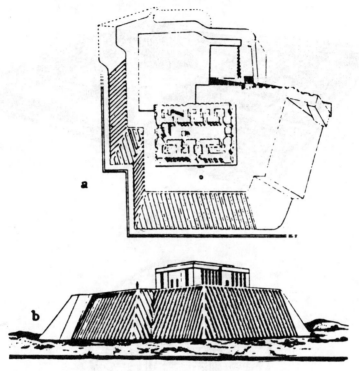

Figures 35a and 35b

ples, at all times, were given the rectangular shape and specific orientation can be easily inferred from the layout in Babylon by comparing the haphazard meshing of buildings and alleys in cities in Babylonian times with the straight and geometrically perfect layout of the sacred precinct of Babylon and the square shape of its ziggurat (Fig. 36).

Mesopotamian temples were thus rectangular and ziggurats square-based quite deliberately. In case someone wonders whether this was because the Sumerians and their successors were unfamiliar with the circle or unable to construct one, suffice it to point out that in mathematical tablets certain key numbers of the sexagesimal ("base 60") system were represented by circles; in tablets dealing with geometry and land measurement, instructions were given for measuring regular- and irregular-shaped areas, including circles. The round wheel was known (Fig. 37)—another Sumerian

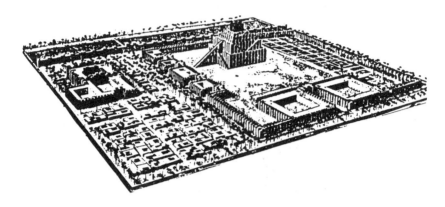

Figure 36

Figure 37

"first." Obviously circular residential houses were found in the ruins of early cities (Fig. 38); a sacred precinct (as this one at a site called Khafajeh—Fig. 39) was sometimes surrounded by an oval-forming wall. It is clear that avoiding a well-known circular shape for temples was deliberate.

There were thus basic design, architecture, and orientation differences between Sumerian temples and Stonehenge, to which one could add the fact that the Sumerians were not stonemasons (there being no stone quarries in the alluvial plain between the Euphrates and Tigris rivers). The Sumerians were not the ones who planned and erected Stone-

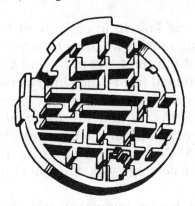

Figure 38

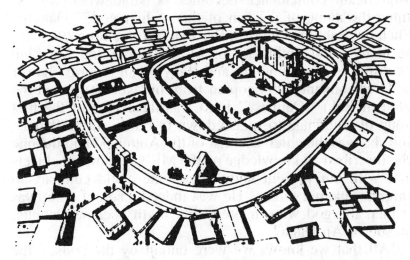

Figure 39

henge; and the only instance that can be considered an exception to discoveries and Sumerian temples, as we shall see, reinforces this conclusion.

So, if not the Egyptians or Phoenicians or early Greeks, if not the Sumerians and their successors in Mesopotamia—who then came to the plain of Salisbury to plan and supervise the erection of Stonehenge?

An interesting clue emerges as one reads the legends concerning the tumulus of Newgrange. According to Michael J. O'Kelly, a leading architect and explorer of the site and its surroundings (*Newgrange: Archaeology, Art and*

Legend), the site was known in early Irish lore by various names that all designated it as *Brug Oengusa,* the "House of Oengus," son of the chief god of the pre-Celtic pantheon who had come to Ireland from "the Otherworld." That chief god was known as *An Dagda,* "An, the good god" . . .

It is indeed amazing to find the name of the principal deity of the ancient world in all these diverse places—in Sumer and his E.ANNA ziggurat of Uruk; in the Egyptian Heliopolis, whose true name was Annu; and in far-removed Ireland . . .

That this might be an important clue and not just an insignificant coincidence becomes possible when we examine the name of the son of this "chief god," Oengus. When the Babylonian priest Berossus wrote, circa 290 B.C., the history and prehistory of Mesopotamia and Mankind according to the Sumerian and Babylonian records, he (or the Greek savants who copied from his works) spelled the name of Enki "Oannes." Enki was the leader of the first group of Anunnaki to splash down to Earth, in the Persian Gulf; he was the chief scientist of the Anunnaki and the one who inscribed all knowledge on the ME's, enigmatic objects that, with our present knowledge, one could compare to computer memory discs. He was indeed a son of Anu; was he then the god who in pre-Celtic myth became Oengus, the son of An Daga?

"All that we know, we were taught by the gods," the Sumerians repeatedly stated.

Was it, then, not the ancient *peoples,* but the ancient *gods* who created Stonehenge?

4

DUR.AN.KI—THE "BOND HEAVEN-EARTH"

From the earliest days, Man has lifted his eyes to the heavens for divine guidance, for inspiration, for help in troubled times. From the very beginning, even as Earth was separated from "Heaven" when it was created, heaven and Earth continued to meet everlastingly on the horizon. It was there, as Man gazed into the distance, at sunrise or sunset, that he could see the Heavenly Host.

Heaven and Earth meet on the horizon, and the knowledge based on observing the skies and the celestial motions resulting therefrom is called Astronomy.

From the earliest days, Man knew that his creators had come from the heavens—*Anunnaki* he called them, literally "Those who from Heaven to Earth Came." Their true abode was in the heavens, Man always knew: "Father who art in Heaven," Man knew to say. But those of the Anunnaki who had come and stayed on Earth, Man also knew, could be worshiped in the temples.

Man and his gods met in the temples, and the knowledge and ritual and beliefs that resulted are called Religion.

The most important "cult center," the "navel of the earth," was Enlil's city in what was later Sumer. Central religiously, philosophically, and actually, that city, Nippur, was the Mission Control Center; and its Holy of Holies, where the Tablets of Destinies were kept, was called DUR.AN.KI—"Bond Heaven-Earth."

And ever since, at all times and in all places and in all religions, the places of worship that are called temples, in spite of all the changes that they, and Mankind and its

79

religions have undergone, have remained the *Bond Heaven-Earth*.

In ancient times astronomy and religion were linked: the priests were the astronomers and astronomers were priests. When Yahweh made his covenant with Abraham, He instructed Abraham to step out and lift his gaze skyward to try and count the stars. There was more than an idle stratagem in this, for Abraham's father, Terah, was an oracle priest in Nippur and Ur and thus knowing in astronomy.

In those days each of the Great Anunnaki was assigned a celestial counterpart, and since the Solar System had twelve members, the "Olympic Circle," throughout the millennia and up to and including Greek time, was always made up of twelve. It was thus that the worship of the gods was closely associated with the motions of the celestial bodies, and the biblical admonitions against the worship of "the Sun, the Moon and the Host of Heaven" were in reality admonitions against the worship of gods other than Yahweh.

The rituals, festivals, days of abstinence, and other rites that expressed the worship of the gods were thus attuned to the motions of the gods' celestial counterparts. Worship required a calendar; temples were observatories; priests were astronomers. The ziggurats were Temples of Time, where time-keeping joined astronomy to formalize worship.

> *And Adam knew his wife again*
> *and she bore a son and called his name Sheth,*
> *for God (she said) has granted me another offspring*
> *instead of Abel, whom Cain slew.*
> *And to Sheth, in turn, a son was born*
> *and he called his name Enosh.*
> *It was then that calling Yahweh by name began.*

Thus, according to the Bible (Genesis 4:25–26), did the Children of Adam begin to worship their God. How this calling in the name of the Lord was done—what form the worship took, what rituals were involved—we are not told. It happened, the Bible makes clear, in remote times, well before the Deluge. Sumerian texts, however, throw light on the subject. They not only assert—repeatedly and emphatically—that there were Cities of the Gods in Mesopotamia before the Deluge, and that when the Deluge had occurred there had already been "demigods" (offspring of "Daughters of Man" by male Anunnaki "gods"), but also that the worship took place in consecrated places (we call them "temples"). They were already, we learn from the earliest texts, Temples of Time.

One of the Mesopotamian versions of the events leading to the Deluge is the text known (by its opening words) *"When the gods like men"* in which the hero of the Deluge is called *Atra-Hasis* ("He who is exceedingly wise"). The tale relates how Anu, the ruler of Nibiru, returned to that planet from a visit to Earth after arranging a division of powers and territories on Earth between his feuding sons, the half brothers Enlil ("Lord of the Command") and Enki ("Lord of Earth"), putting Enki in charge of the gold-mining operations in Africa. After describing the hard work of the Anunnaki assigned to the mines, their mutiny, and the ensuing creation through genetic engineering by Enki and his half sister Ninharsag of the *Adamu,* a "Primitive Worker," the epic relates how Mankind began to procreate and multiply. In time, Mankind began to upset Enlil by its excessive "conjugations," especially with the Anunnaki (a situation reflected in the biblical version of the Deluge tale); and Enlil prevailed on the Great Anunnaki, in their Council, to use the foreseen catastrophe of the avalanche of water to wipe Mankind off the face of the Earth.

But Enki, though he joined in swearing to keep the decision a secret from Mankind, was not happy with the decision and sought ways to frustrate it. He chose to achieve that through the intermediary of Atra-Hasis, a son of Enki by a human mother. The text, which at times assumes a biographical style by Atra-Hasis himself, quotes him saying, "I am Atra-Hasis; I lived in the temple of Enki my lord"—a statement which clearly establishes the existence of a temple in those remote pre-Diluvial times.

Describing the worsening climatic conditions on the one hand and Enlil's harsh measures against Mankind on the

other hand in the period preceding the Deluge, the text
quotes Enki's advice to the people through Atra-Hasis how
to protest against Enlil's decrees: the worship of the gods
should stop!

"Enki opened his mouth and addressed his servant,"
saying thus to him:

> The elders, on a sign,
> summon to the House of Council.
> Let heralds proclaim a command
> loudly throughout the land:
> Do not reverence your gods,
> do not pray to your goddesses.

As the situation got worse and the catastrophe day neared,
Atra-Hasis persisted in his intercession with his god Enki.
"In the temple of his god . . . he set foot . . . every day he
wept, bringing oblations in the morning." Seeking Enki's
help to avert Mankind's demise, "he called by the name of
his god"—words that employ the same terminology as in
the above-quoted verse from the Bible. In the end Enki
decided to subvert the decision of the Council of the Anunnaki by summoning Atra-Hasis to the temple and speaking
to him from behind a screen. The event was commemorated
on a Sumerian cylinder seal, showing Enki (as the Serpent
God) revealing the secret of the Deluge to Atra-Hasis (Fig.
40). Giving him instructions for the building of a submersible boat that would withstand the avalanche of water, Enki
advised Atra-Hasis to lose no time, for he had only seven
days left before the catastrophe happened. To make sure
Atra-Hasis wasted no time, Enki put into motion a clocklike
device:

> He opened the water clock
> and filled it;
> the coming of the flood on the seventh night
> he marked off for him.

This little-noticed bit of information reveals that time was
kept in the temples and that time-keeping goes back to the

Figure 40

earliest, even pre-Diluvial times. It has been assumed that
the ancient illustration depicts (on the right) the reed screen
from behind which Enki had spoken to the hero of the great
flood, the biblical Noah. One must wonder, however,
whether what we see is not a reed screen, *but a depiction
of that prehistoric water clock* (held up by its priestly
attendant).

Enki was the chief scientist of the Anunnaki; it is no
wonder, therefore, that it was at his temple, at his "cult
center" Eridu, that the first human scientists, the Wise Men,
served as priests. One of the first, if not the very first, was
called Adapa. Though the original Sumerian Adapa text has
not been found, Akkadian and Assyrian versions on clay
fragments that have been found attest the tale's significance.
Informing us at the very beginning that Adapa's command
of wisdom was almost as good as that of Enki himself, the
text proceeds to explain that Enki had "perfected for him
wide understanding, disclosing all the designs of the Earth;
Wisdom he had given to him." It was all done at the temple;
Adapa, we are told, "daily did attend the sanctuary of
Eridu."

According to Sumerian chronicles of the earlier times, it
was at Eridu's temple that Enki, as guardian of the secrets
of all scientific knowledge, kept the ME's—tabletlike objects on which the scientific data were inscribed. One of the
Sumerian texts details how the goddess Inanna (later known

as Ishtar), wishing to give status to her "cult center" Uruk (the biblical Erech), tricked Enki into giving her some of these divine formulas. Adapa, we find, was also nicknamed NUN.ME, meaning "He who can decipher the ME's." Even unto millennia later, in Assyrian times, the saying "Wise as Adapa" meant that someone was exceedingly wise and knowledgeable. The study of sciences was often referred to in Mesopotamian texts as *Shunnat apkali Adapa,* "recital/repetition of the great forefather Adapa." A letter by the Assyrian king Ashurbanipal mentioned that his grandfather, King Sennacherib, was given great knowledge when Adapa had appeared to him in a dream. The "wide knowledge" imparted by Enki to Adapa included writing, medicine, and—according to the astronomical series of tablets UD.SAR.ANUM.ENLILLA ("The Great Days of Anu and Enlil")—knowledge of astronomy and astrology.

Though Adapa had daily attended the sanctuary of Enki, it appears from Sumerian texts that the first officially appointed priest—a function that then passed hereditarily from father to son—was named EN.ME.DUR.AN.KI—"Priest of the ME's of Duranki," the sacred precinct of Nippur. The texts report how the gods "showed him how to observe oil and water, the secrets of Anu, Enlil, and Enki. They gave him the Divine Tablet, the engraved secrets of Heaven and Earth. They taught him how to make calculations with numbers"—the knowledge of mathematics and astronomy, and of the art of measurement, including that of time.

Many of the Mesopotamian tablets dealing with mathematics, astronomy, and the calendar have astounded scientists by their sophistication. At the core of these sciences was a mathematical system called sexagesimal ("Base Sixty") whose advanced nature, including its celestial aspects, has already been discussed. Such sophistication existed even in the earliest times that some call predynastic: arithmetically inscribed tablets (Fig. 41) that have been found attest the use of the sexagesimal system and of numerical record keeping. Designs on clay objects also from the earliest times (Fig. 42) leave no doubt regarding the high level of knowledge of geometry in those remote times,

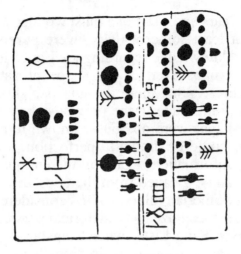

Figure 41

Figure 42

six thousand years ago. And one must wonder whether these designs, or at least some of them, were purely decorative or represented knowledge regarding the Earth, its four "corners," and perhaps even of the shape of astronomically related structures. What these designs also show applies to an important point made in the previous chapter: the circle and circular shapes were obviously known in ancient Mesopotamia and could be drawn to perfection.

Additional information regarding the antiquity of the exact sciences can be gleaned from the tales about Etana, one of the earliest Sumerian rulers. At first considered a mythical hero, he is now recognized as a historical person. According to the Sumerian King Lists, when kingship—an organized civilization—was "lowered again from heaven" after the Deluge, "kingship was first in Kish"—a city whose remains and antiquity have been found and confirmed by archaeologists. Its thirteenth ruler was called Etana, and the King Lists, which by and large only list the names of successive rulers and the length of their reigns, make an exception in the case of Etana by adding after his name the following notation: "A shepherd; he who ascended to heaven, who consolidated all the lands." According to Thorkild Jacobsen (*The Sumerian King List*) Etana's reign began circa 3100 B.C.; excavations at Kish have unearthed the remains of monumental buildings and a ziggurat (stage-temple) dating to the same time.

In the aftermath of the Deluge, when the plain between the Tigris and Euphrates rivers dried sufficiently to enable resettlement, the Cities of the Gods were rebuilt exactly where they had been, according to the "olden plan." Kish, the first City of Men, was entirely new and its place and layout had to be determined. These decisions, we read in the *Tale of Etana*, were made by the gods. Employing scientific knowledge of geometry for layout and astronomy for orientation,

> *The gods traced out a city;*
> *Seven gods laid its foundations.*
> *The city of Kish they traced out,*

and there the seven gods laid its foundation.
A city they established, a dwelling place;
but a Shepherd they withheld.

The twelve rulers at Kish who had preceded Etana were not yet given the Sumerian royal-priestly title EN.SI—"Lordly Shepherd" or as some prefer "Righteous Shepherd." The city, it appears, could attain this status only when the gods could find the right man to build a ziggurat stage-temple there and, by becoming a king-priest, be given the title EN.SI. Who would be "their builder, the one to build the E.HURSAG.KALAMMA," the gods asked—build the "House" (ziggurat) that shall be "Mountainhead for all the lands"?

The task to "look for a king in all the lands, above and below," was assigned to Inanna/Ishtar. She found and recommended Etana—a humble shepherd . . . Enlil, "he who grants kingship," had to make the actual appointment. We read that "Enlil inspected Etana, the young man whom Ishtar had nominated. 'She sought and she found!' he cried. 'In the land shall kingship be established; let the heart of Kish be glad!' "

Now comes the "mythological" part. The brief notation in the King Lists that Etana ascended to heaven stemmed from a chronicle that scholars call the "legend" of Etana which related how Etana, with the permission of the god Utu/Shamash who was in charge of the spaceport, was carried aloft by an "eagle." The higher he rose, the smaller the Earth looked. After the first *beru* of flight the land "became a mere hill"; after the second *beru* the land looked like a mere furrow; after the third *beru,* as a garden ditch; and after one more *beru* the Earth completely disappeared. "As I glanced around," Etana later reported, "the land had disappeared, and upon the sea mine eyes could not feast."

A *beru* in Sumer was a unit of measurement—of length (a "league") and of time (one "double-hour," the twelfth part of a daytime–nighttime period that we now divide into twenty-four hours). It remained a unit of measure in astronomy, when it denoted the twelfth part of the heavenly circle. The text of the *Tale of Etana* does not make clear which unit of measurement—distance, time, or arc—was meant; perhaps all of them. What the text does make clear is that at that remote time, when the first true Shepherd King was enthroned in the first City of Men, distance, time, and the heavens could already be measured.

Kish as the first royal city—under the patronage of "Nimrod"—is mentioned in the Bible (Genesis chapter 10); and certain other aspects of events recorded in the Bible merit exploration. This is especially so because of the puzzling mention in the *Tale of Etana* of the seven gods involved in the planning—and thus orientation—of the city and its ziggurat.

Since all the major gods of ancient Mesopotamia had celestial counterparts from among the twelve members of the Solar System, as well as a counterpart from the twelve constellations of the zodiac and from the twelve months, one must wonder whether the reference to the determination of the orientation of Kish and its ziggurat by the "seven gods" did not actually mean by the seven planets which those deities represented. Were the Anunnaki waiting for the propitious alignment of seven planets as the right time and right orientation for Kish and its ziggurat?

Further light, we believe, can be shed on the subject by journeying in time over more than two thousand years to Judea circa 1000 B.C. Incredibly, we find that about three thousand years ago the circumstances surrounding the selection of a shepherd to be the builder of a new temple in a new royal capital emulated the events and circumstances recorded in the *Tale of Etana;* and the same number seven, with a calendrical significance, also played a role.

The Judean city where the ancient drama was reenacted was Jerusalem. David, who was shepherding the flocks of his father, Jesse the Bethlehemite, was chosen by the Lord for kingship. After the death of King Saul, when David reigned in Hebron over the tribe of Judah alone, representatives of the other eleven tribes "came unto David in Hebron" and asking him to become king over all of them reminded him that Yahweh had earlier said thus to him: "You shall shepherd my people Israel and shall be a *Nagid* over Israel" (II Samuel 5:2).

The term *Nagid* is usually translated "Captain" (King James Version), "Commander" (*The New American Bible*) or even "Prince" (*The New English Bible*). None appear to have realized that *Nagid* is a Sumerian loanword, a term borrowed intact from the Sumerian language, in which the word meant "herdsman"!

A principal preoccupation of the Israelites at that time was the need to find a home for the Ark of the Covenant— not just a permanent home, but also a safe one. Originally made and placed by Moses in the Tent of Appointment during the Exodus, it contained the two stone tablets inscribed with the Ten Commandments on Mount Sinai. Made of specific wood and overlaid with gold both inside and outside, it was surmounted by two Cherubim made of hardened gold with wings extended toward each other; and each time Moses had an appointment with the Lord, Yahweh spoke to him "from between the two Cherubim" (Fig. 43a is a reconstruction suggested by Hugo Gressmann (*Die Lade Jahves*) because of similar depictions found in northern Phoenicia; Fig. 43b is a depiction suggested by A. Parrot in *Le Temple de Jérusalem*). We believe that the Ark, with its insulated gold layers and Cherubim was a communication device, perhaps electrically powered (when it was once touched inadvertently, the person involved fell dead).

Yahweh had given very detailed instructions regarding the construction of the Tent of Appointment and the enclosure for it, and for the Ark, including what amounted to an "operating manual" for the dismantling and reassembly of all that as well as for the careful transportation of the Ark. By David's time, however, the Ark was no longer carried by wooden staves but transported upon a wheeled carriage. It was moved from one temporary place of worship to another, and a major assignment for the newly anointed Shepherd King was to establish a new national capital in Jerusalem and therein build a permanent housing for the Ark in the "House of the Lord."

Figures 43a and 43b

But this was not to come to pass. Speaking to King David through the Prophet Nathan, the Lord informed him that it would not be he but his son who would be granted the privilege of building a House of Cedars for Yahweh. And so it was that one of the very first tasks of King Solomon was to build the "House of Yahweh" (now referred to as the First Temple) in Jerusalem. Built as the sacred compound and its components in the Sinai were, it was erected in accordance with very detailed instructions. In fact, the layout plans of the two are almost identical (Fig. 44a the sacred compound in the Sinai; Fig. 44b the Temple of Solomon). And both were oriented along a precise east–west axis, identifying them both as equinoctial temples.

The similarities between Kish and Jerusalem as new national capitals, a Shepherd King, and the task of building a temple whose plans were provided by the Lord is en-

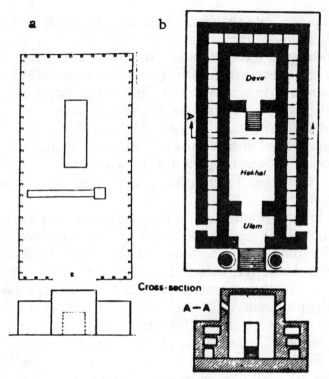

Figures 44a and 44b

hanced by the significance of the number seven.

We are informed in I Kings (chapter 3) that Solomon proceeded to organize the construction project (it involved, among others in the workforce, 80,000 stone quarriers and 70,000 porters) only after Yahweh had appeared unto Solomon in Gibeon "in a nightly vision." The construction, lasting seven years, began with laying the foundation stone in the fourth year of Solomon's reign and "in the eleventh year, in the month of Bul which is the eighth month the Temple was completed in all its stipulations and exactly according to its plans." But although entirely complete with no detail missed or omitted, the Temple was not inaugurated.

It was only eleven months later, "in the month of Etanim, the seventh month, on the festival," that all the elders and tribal chiefs from all over assembled in Jerusalem, "and the priests brought the Ark of the Covenant with Yahweh into its place, into the *Dvir* of the temple which is the Holy of Holies, under the wings of the Cherubim . . . And there was nothing in the Ark except the two stone tablets which Moses had placed therein in the Wilderness after Yahweh had made a covenant with the Children of Israel after they had left Egypt. And when the priests had stepped out of the Holy of Holies, a cloud filled the House of Yahweh.'' And Solomon prayed unto Yahweh, ''He who dwells in the fog-like cloud,'' beseeching the Lord ''who dwells in the heavens'' to come and listen to his people's prayers in the new temple.

The long postponement in the inauguration of the temple was required, it appears, so that it would take place ''in the seventh month, on the festival.'' There can be no doubt that the festival referred to was the New Year festival, in accordance with the commandments concerning holy days and festivals pronounced in the biblical Book of Leviticus. ''These are the appointed festivals of Yahweh,'' the preamble to chapter 23 states: the observance of the seventh day as the Sabbath is just the first of holy days to be held in intervals of multiples of seven days or that were to last seven days, culminating with the festivals of the seventh month: New Year's Day, the Day of Atonement, and the Feast of Booths.

In Mesopotamia by that time Babylon and Assyria had supplanted Sumer, and the New Year festival was celebrated—as the month's name indicated—in the first month, called Nissan, which coincided with the spring equinox. The reasons why the Israelites were commanded to celebrate the New Year in the seventh month, coinciding with the autumnal equinox, remain unexplained in the Bible. But we may find a clue in the fact that the biblical narrative does not call this month by its Babylonian-Assyrian name, Tishrei, but by the enigmatic name *Etanim*. No satisfactory explanation for this name has been found so far; but a solution does occur to us: in view of all the above listed similarities between the king-priest as a shepherd and the circumstances of the establishment of a new capital and the construction of a residence for Yahweh in the desert and in

Jerusalem, the clue to the month's name should also be sought in the *Tale of Etana*. For does not the name used in the Bible, *Etanim*, simply stem from the name *Etana?* The name *Etan* as a personal name, one may note, was not uncommon among the Hebrews, meaning "heroic, mighty."

The celestial alignments in Kish, we have noted, were expressed not only in the temple's solar orientation but also in some relationship with seven planetary "gods" in the heavens. It is noteworthy that in a discussion by August Wünsche of the similarities between Solomon's edifices in Jerusalem and the Mesopotamian "portrait of the heavens" (*Ex Oriente Lux*, vol. 2) he cited the rabbinic reference— as in the *Tale of Etana*—to the "seven stars that indicate time"—Mercury, Moon, Saturn, Jupiter, Mars, Sun, and Venus. There are thus plenty of clues and indications confirming the celestial-calendrical aspects of Solomon's Temple—aspects that link it to traditions and orientations established millennia earlier, in Sumer.

This is reflected not only in the orientation, but also in the temple's tripartite division; it emulated the traditional temple plans that began in Mesopotamia millennia earlier. Günter Martiny, who in the 1930s led the studies regarding the architecture and astronomical orientation of Mesopotamian temples (*Die Gegensätze im Babylonischen und Assyrischen Tempelbau* and other studies) sketched thus (Fig. 45a) the basic tripartite layout of "cult structures": a rectangular anteroom, an elongated ritual hall, and a square Holy of Holies. Walter Andrae (*Des Gotteshaus und die Urformen des Bauens*) pointed out that in Assyria the temple's entrance was flanked by two pylons (Fig. 45b); this was reflected in Solomon's Temple, where the entrance was flanked by two freestanding pillars (see Fig. 44b).

The detailed architectural and construction information in the Bible in respect to Solomon's Temple calls its anteroom *Ulam*, its ritual hall *Hekhal*, and its holiest part *Dvir*. The latter, meaning "Where the speaking takes place," no doubt reflected the fact that Yahweh spoke to Moses from the Ark of the Covenant, the voice coming from where the

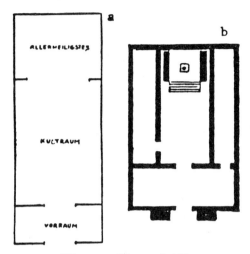

Figures 45a and 45b

wings of the Cherubim were touching; and the Ark was placed in the Temple as the only artifact in the innermost enclosure, the Holy of Holies or *Dvir*. The terminology used for the two foreparts, scholars have recognized, comes from the Sumerian (via Akkadian): *E-gal* and *Ulammu*.

This essential tripartite division, adopted later on elsewhere (e.g. the Zeus temple in Olympia, Fig. 46a, or the Canaanite one at Tainat in Upper Syria, Fig. 46b), was in reality a continuation that began with the most ancient temples, the ziggurats of Sumer, where the way to the ziggurat's top, via a stairway, led through two shrines, an outer shrine with two pylons in front of it, and a prayer room—as drawn by G. Martiny in his studies (Fig. 47).

As in the Sinai Tabernacle and Jerusalem Temple, so were the Mesopotamian vessels and utensils used in the temple rituals made primarily of gold. Texts describing temple rituals in Uruk mention golden libation vessels, golden trays, and golden censers; such objects were found in archaeological excavations. Silver was also used, an example being the engraved vase (Fig. 48) that Entemena, one of the early Sumerian kings, presented to his god Ninurta at the temple in Lagash. The artful votive utensils usually bore

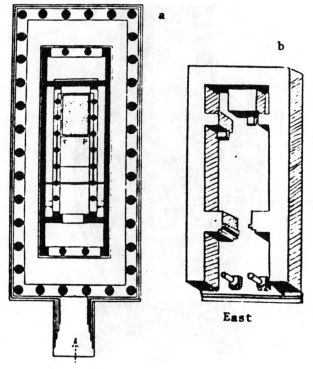

Figures 46a and 46b

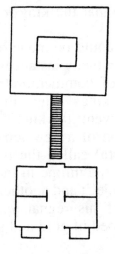

Figure 47

Figure 48

a dedicatory inscription in which the king stated that the object was offered so that the king might be granted long life.

Such presentations could be made only with the permission of the gods, and in many instances were events of great significance, worthy of commemoration in the Date Formulas—listings of the kings' reigns in which each year was named after its main event: the king's ascent to the throne, a war, the presentation of a new temple artifact. Thus, a king of Isin (Ishbi-Erra) called the nineteenth year of his reign "Year in which the throne in the Great House of the goddess Ninlil was made"; and another ruler of Isin (Ishme-Dagan) named one of his regnal years "Year in which Ishme-Dagan made a bed of gold and silver for the goddess Ninlil."

But having been built of bricks made of clay, the temples

of Mesopotamia fell into disrepair as time went by, frequently as the result of earthquakes. Constant maintenance and repairs were required, and repairs or reconstruction of the gods' houses, rather than the offering of new furnishings, began to fill the Date Formulas. Thus, the years-list for the famed Hammurabi, king of Babylon, began with the designation of Year One as the "Year in which Hammurabi became king," and "Year in which the laws were promulgated" for Year Two. Year Four, however, was already designated "Year in which Hammurabi built a wall for the sacred precinct." A successor of Hammurabi in Babylon, the king Shamshi-Iluna, named his eighteenth year as the "Year in which the reconstruction work was done on the E.BABBAR of the god Utu in Sippar" (E.BABBAR, meaning "House of the Bright One," was a temple dedicated to the "Sun-god" Utu/Shamash).

Sumerian, then Akkadian, Babylonian, and Assyrian kings recorded in their inscriptions with great pride how they repaired, embellished, or rebuilt the sacred temples and their precincts; archaeological excavations not only uncovered such inscriptions but also corroborated the claims made therein. In Nippur, for example, archaeologists from the University of Pennsylvania found in the 1880s evidence of repair and maintenance work in the sacred precinct in thirty-five feet of debris piled up during some four thousand years *above* a brick pavement built by the Akkadian king Naram-Sin circa 2250 B.C. and another accumulation of debris of over thirty feet *below* the pavement from earlier times down to virgin soil (which were not excavated and examined at the time).

Returning to Nippur half a century later, a joint expedition of the University of Pennsylvania and the Oriental Institute of the University of Chicago spent many digging seasons working to unearth the Temple of Enlil in Nippur's sacred precinct. The excavators found five successive constructions between 2200 B.C. and 600 B.C., the latter having its floor some twenty feet above the former. The even earlier temples, the archaeologists' report noted at the time, were still to be dug for. The report also noted that the five temples were "built one above the other on exactly the same plan."

The discovery that later temples were erected upon the foundations of earlier temples in strict adherence to the original plans was reconfirmed at other ancient sites in Mesopotamia. The rule applied even to enlargement of temples—even if more than once, as was found at Eridu (Fig. 49); in all instances the original axis and orientation were retained. Unlike the Egyptian temples whose solstitial orientation had to be realigned from time to time because of the change in the Earth's tilt, Mesopotamian equinoctial temples needed no adjustment in their orientation because geographic north and geographic east, by definition, remained unchanged no matter how the Earth's tilt had changed: the Sun always passed over the equator at "equinox" times, rising on such days precisely in the east.

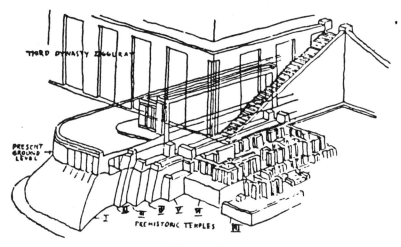

Figure 49

The obligation to adhere to the "olden plans" was spelled out in an inscription on a tablet found in Nineveh, the Assyrian capital, among the ruins of a rebuilt temple. In it the Assyrian king recorded his compliance with the sacred requirement:

> *The everlasting ground plan,*
> *that which for the future*

the construction determined,
[I have followed.]
It is the one which bears
the drawings from the Olden Times
and the writing of the Upper Heaven.

The Assyrian king Ashur-Nasir-Pal described what such work entailed in a long inscription regarding the restoration of the temple in Calah (an early city mentioned in the Bible). Describing how he had unearthed the "ancient mound," he stated: "I dug down to the level of the water, for 120 measures into the depth I penetrated. I found the foundations of the god Ninib, my lord . . . I constructed thereon, with firm brickwork, the temple of Ninib, my lord." It was done, the king prayed, so that the god Ninib (an epithet for the god Ninurta) "may command that my days be long." Such a blessing, the king hoped, would follow the decision by the god, at a time of his own choosing—"at his heart's desire"—to come and reside in the rebuilt temple: "When the lord Ninib shall take up habitation, forever, in his pure temple, his dwelling place." It is a prayed-for expectation-cum-invitation not unlike the one expressed by King Solomon when the First Temple was completed.

Indeed, the obligatory adherence to the earlier site, orientation, and layout of the temples in the ancient Near East, no matter how long the interval or how extensive the repairs or rebuilding had to be, is exemplified by the successive temples in Jerusalem. The First Temple was destroyed by the Babylonian king Nebuchadnezzar in 587 B.C.; but after Babylon fell to the Achaemenid Persians, the Persian king Cyrus issued an edict permitting the return of Jewish exiles to Jerusalem and the rebuilding of the temple by them. The rebuilding, significantly, began with the erection of an altar (where the first one used to be) "when the seventh month commenced," i.e. on the day of the New Year (and the sacrifices continued until the Feast of Booths). Lest there be doubt about the date, the Book of Ezra (3:6) restated the date: "From the first day of the seventh month did the sacrifices to Yahweh commence."

The adherence not only to the location and orientation of the temple but also to the time of the New Year—an indication of the calendrical aspect of the temple—is re-affirmed in the prophecies of Ezekiel. One of the Jews exiled to Babylon by Nebuchadnezzar, he was shown in a vision the temple-to-come in the New Jerusalem. It happened, the prophet stated (Ezekiel chapter 40) in the month of the New Year, on the 10th of it—precisely the Day of Atonement—that "the hand of Yahweh was upon me, and He brought me thither" (to "the Land of Israel"). "And he sat me up upon a very high mountain, by which was a model of a city." There he saw "a man, his appearance was like the appearance of brass; and he held in his hand a cord of flax and a measuring reed, and he stood in the gate." And this Man of Brass then proceeded to describe the New Temple to Ezekiel. Scholars, using the data, have been able to draw the visionary temple (Fig. 50); it follows precisely the layout and orientation of the temple built by Solomon.

The prophetic vision became a reality after the Persian king Cyrus, having defeated and captured Babylon, issued

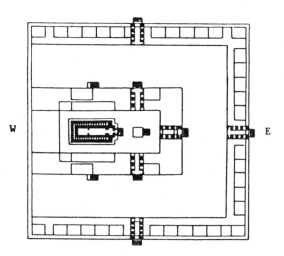

Figure 50

an edict proclaiming the restoration of the destroyed temples throughout the Babylonian empire; a copy of the edict, inscribed on a clay cylinder, has actually been found by archaeologists (Fig. 51). A special royal proclamation, recorded word for word in the Book of Ezra, called on the Jewish exiles to rebuild the "House of Yahweh, God of Heaven."

The Second Temple, built under difficult conditions in what was still a devastated land, was a poor imitation of the First Temple. Rebuilt a part at a time, it was constructed according to plans received from records kept in the Persian royal archives and, the Bible asserts, in strict conformity with the details in the Five Books of Moses. That the Temple indeed followed the original layout and orientation became clearer some five centuries later, when King Herod decided to replace the poor replica with a new, splendid edifice that

Figure 51

would not just match, but even surpass, in grandeur the First Temple. Built on an enlarged great platform (still known as the Temple Mount) and its massive walls (of which the Western Wall, still largely intact, is revered by Jews as the extant remnant of the Holy Temple), it was surrounded by courtyards and various auxiliary buildings. But the House of the Lord proper retained the tripartite layout and orientation of the First Temple (Fig. 52). The Holy of Holies, moreover, remained identical in size to that of the First Temple—and was located *precisely* over its spot; except that the enclosure was no longer called *Dvir,* for the Ark of the Covenant disappeared when the Babylonians destroyed the First Temple and carried off all the artifacts within.

As one views the remains of the immense sacred precincts with their temples and shrines and service buildings, courtyards and gates, and, in the innermost section, the ziggurat, it should be borne in mind that the very first temples were the actual abodes of the gods and were literally called the god's "E"—the god's actual "House." Begun as structures atop artificial mounds and raised platforms (see Fig. 35), they in time evolved to become the famed ziggurats (step-pyramids)—the skyscrapers of antiquity. As an artist's

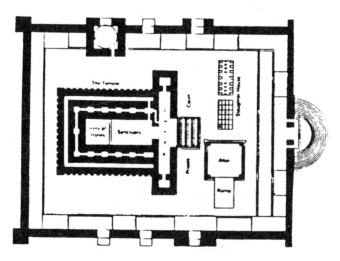

Figure 52

drawing shows (Fig. 53), the deity's actual residence was in the topmost stage. There, seated on their thrones under a canopy, the gods would grant audiences to their chosen king, the "Shepherd of Men." As is shown in this depiction of Utu/Shamash in his temple, the Ebabbar in Sippar (Fig. 54), the king had to be led in by the high priest and was accompanied by his patron god or goddess. (Later on, the

Figure 53

Figure 54

High Priest alone entered the Holy of Holies, as depicted in Fig. 55).

Circa 2300 B.C. a high priestess, the daughter of Sargon of Akkad, collected all the hymns to the ziggurat-temples of her time. Called by Sumerologists "a unique Sumerian literary composition" (A. Sjöberg and E. Bergmann in *Texts From Cuneiform Sources,* vol. 3), the text pays homage to forty-two "E" temples, from Eridu in the south to Sippar in the north and on both sides of the Euphrates and Tigris rivers. The verses not only name the temple, its location, and the god for whom it was built, but also throw light on the magnificence and greatness of these divine abodes as well as on their functions and, sometimes, their history.

The composition appropriately begins with Enki's ziggurat-temple in Eridu, called in the hymn "place whose

Figure 55

Holy of Holies is the foundation of Heaven-Earth," for Eridu was the first City of the Gods, the first outpost of the first landing party of the Anunnaki (led by Enki), and the first divine city opened up to Earthlings to become also a City of Men. Called E.DUKU, "House of the Holy Mound," it was described in the hymn as a "lofty shrine, rising toward the sky."

This hymn was followed by one to the E.KUR—"House which is like a mountain"—the ziggurat of Enlil in Nippur. Considered the Navel of the Earth, Nippur was equidistant from all the other earliest Cities of the Gods, and was still deemed to be the place from whose ziggurat as one looked to his right he could see Sumer in the south and to his left Akkad in the north, according to the hymn. It was a "shrine where destinies are determined," a ziggurat "which bonds heaven and earth." In Nippur Ninlil, Enlil's spouse, had her separate temple, "clad in awesome brilliance." From it the goddess appeared "in the month of the New Year, on the day of the festival, wonderfully adorned."

The half sister of Enki and Enlil, Ninharsag, who was among the first Anunnaki to come to Earth and was their chief biologist and medical officer, had her temple at the city called Kesh. Simply called E.NINHARSAG. "House of the Lady of the Mountainpeak," it was described as a ziggurat whose "bricks are well moulded . . . a place of Heaven and Earth, an awe inspiring place" which apparently was adorned with "a great poisonous serpent" made of lapis lazuli—the symbol of medicine and healing. (Moses, it will be recalled, made an image of a serpent to stop a killing plague in the Sinai desert).

The god Ninurta, Enlil's Foremost Son by his half sister Ninharsag, who had a ziggurat in his own "cult center," Lagash, had at the time of the composition of this text also a temple in the sacred precinct of Nippur; it was called E.ME.UR.ANNA, "House of the ME's of Anu's Hero." In Lagash, the ziggurat was called E.NINNU, "House of Fifty," reflecting Ninurta's numerical rank in the divine hierarchy (Anu's rank, sixty, was the highest).

It was, the hymn stated, a "House filled with radiance and awe, grown high like a mountain," in which Ninurta's "Black Bird," his flying machine, and his *Sharur* weapon ("the raging storm which envelops men") were housed.

Enlil's firstborn son by his official spouse, Ninlil, was Nannar (later known as Sin), who was associated with the Moon as his celestial counterpart. His ziggurat, in Ur, was called E.KISH.NU.GAL, a "House of Thirty, the great seed" and was described as a temple "whose beaming moonlight comes forth in the land"—all references to Nannar/Sin's celestial association with the Moon and the month.

Nannar/Sin's son, Utu/Shamash (his celestial counterpart was the Sun) had his temple in Sippar, the E.BABBAR—"House of the Bright One" or "Bright House." It was described as "House of the prince of heaven, a heavenly star who from the horizon fills the earth from heaven." His twin sister, Inanna/Ishtar, whose celestial counterpart was the planet Venus, had her ziggurat temple in the city Za-balam, where it was called "House full of brightness"; it was described as a "pure mountain," a "shrine whose mouth opens at dawn" and one "through which the firmament is made beautiful at night"—undoubted reference to the double role of Venus as an evening, as well as a morning, "star." Inanna/Ishtar was also worshiped in Erech, where Anu had put at her disposal the ziggurat-temple built for him when he had come to Earth for a visit. The ziggurat was called E.ANNA, simply "House of Anu." The hymn described it as a "ziggurat of seven stages, surveying the seven luminary gods of the night"—a reference to its alignment and astronomical aspects that was echoed, as we have noted earlier, in rabbinic comments regarding the Jerusalem temple.

Thus did the composition go on, portraying the forty-two ziggurats, their glories, and celestial associations. Scholars speak of this composition from more than 4,300 years ago as a "collection of Sumerian temple hymns" and title it "The Cycle of Old Sumerian Poems about the Great Temples." It may however be much more appropriate to follow the Sumerian custom and call the text by its opening words:

E U NIR	House-ziggurat rising high
AN.KI DA	Heaven-Earth joining.

One of those Houses and its sacred precinct, as we shall see, hold a key that can unlock the Stonehenge enigma and the events of that time's New Age.

5

KEEPERS OF THE SECRETS

Between sunset and sunrise there has been the night.

The Bible constantly saw the Creator's awesomeness in the "Host of Heaven"—the myriads of stars and planets, moons and moonlets that twinkle in the Vault of Heaven as night falls. "The heavens bespeak the glory of the Lord and the vault of heaven reveals His handiwork," the Psalmist wrote. The "heavens" thus described were the nightly skies; and the glory they bespoke was conveyed to Mankind by astronomer-priests. It was they who made sense of the countless celestial bodies, recognized stars by their groups, distinguished between the immovable stars and the wandering planets, knew the Sun's and Moon's movements, and kept track of Time—the cycle of sacred days and festivals, the calendar.

The sacred days began at dusk on the previous evening—a custom still retained in the Jewish calendar. A text which outlined the duties of the *Urigallu* priest during the twelve-day New Year festival in Babylon throws light not only on the origin of priestly rituals later on, but also on the close connection between celestial observations and the festival's proceedings. In the discovered text (generally considered to reflect, as the priest's title URI.GALLU itself, Sumerian origins) the beginning, dealing with the determination of the first day of the New Year (the first of the month Nissan in Babylon) according to the spring equinox, is missing. The inscription starts with the instructions for the second day:

> *On the second day of the month Nisannu,*
> *two hours into the night,*

the Urigallu *priest shall arise*
and wash with river water.

Then, putting on a garment of pure white linen, he could
enter into the presence of the great god (Marduk in Babylon)
and recite prescribed prayers in the Holy of Holies of the
ziggurat (the *Esagil* in Babylon). The recitation, which no
one else was to hear, was deemed so secret that after the
text lines in which the prayer was inscribed, the priestly
scribe inserted the following admonition: "Twenty-one
lines: secrets of the Esagil temple. Whoever reveres the god
Marduk shall show them to no one except the Urigallu
priest."

After he finished reciting the secret prayer, the Urigallu
priest opened the temple's gate to let in the *Eribbiti* priests,
who proceeded to "perform their rites, in the traditional
manner," joined by musicians and singers. The text then
details the rest of the duties of the Urigallu priest on that
night.

"On the third day of the month Nisannu" at a time after
sunset too damaged in the inscription to read, the Urigallu
priest was again required to perform certain rites and recitations; this he had to do throughout the night, until "three
hours after sunrise," when he was to instruct artisans in the
making of images of metal and precious stones to be used
in ceremonies on the sixth day. On the fourth day, at "three
and one third hours of the night," the rituals repeated themselves but the prayers now expanded to include a separate
service for Marduk's spouse, the goddess Sarpanit. The
prayers then paid homage to the other gods of Heaven and
Earth and asked for the granting of long life to the king and
prosperity to the people of Babylon. It was thereafter that
the advent of the New Year was directly linked to the Time
of the Equinox in the constellation of the Ram: the heliacal
rising of the Ram Star at dawn. Pronouncing the blessing
"*Iku*-star" upon the "Esagil, image of heaven and earth,"
the rest of the day was spent in prayers, singing and music
playing. On that day, after sunset, the *Enuma elish,* the
Epic of Creation, was recited in its entirety.

The fifth day of Nissan was compared by Henri Frankfort (*Kingship and the Gods*) to the Jewish Day of Atonement, for on that day the king was escorted to the main chapel and was relieved there by the High Priest of all the symbols of kingship; after which, struck in the face by the priest and humiliated into prostrating himself, the king pronounced declarations of confession and repentance. The text which we have been following (per F. Thureau-Dangin, *Rituels accadiens* and E. Ebeling in *Altorientalische Texte zum alten Testament*) deals, however, only with the duties of the Urigallu priest; and we read that on that night the priest, at "four hours of the night," recited twelve times the prayer "My Lord, is he not my Lord" in honor of Marduk, and invoked the Sun, the Moon, and the twelve constellations of the zodiac. A prayer to the goddess followed, in which her epithet, DAM.KI.ANNA ("Mistress of Earth and Heaven") revealed the ritual's Sumerian origin. The prayer likened her to the planet Venus "which shines brilliantly among the stars," naming seven constellations. After these prayers, which stressed the astronomical-calendrical aspects of the occasion, singers and musicians performed "in the traditional manner" and a breakfast was served to Marduk and Sarpanit "two hours after sunrise."

The Babylonian New Year rituals evolved from the Sumerian AKITI ("On Earth Build Life") festival whose roots can be traced to the state visit by Anu and his spouse Antu to Earth circa 3800 B.C., when (as the texts attest) the zodiac was ruled by the Bull of Heaven, the Age of Taurus. We have suggested that it was then that Counted Time, the calendar of Nippur, was granted to Mankind. Inevitably, that entailed celestial observations and thus led to the creation of a class of trained astronomer-priests.

Several texts, some well preserved and some surviving only in fragments, describe the pomp and circumstance of Anu's and Antu's visit to Uruk (the biblical Erech) and the ceremonies which became the rituals of the New Year festival in the ensuing millennia. The works of F. Thureau-Dangin and E. Ebeling still constitute the foundation on which subsequent studies have been based; the ancient texts were then brilliantly used by teams of German excavators of Uruk to locate, identify, and reconstruct the ancient sacred precinct—its walls and gates, its courtyards and shrines and service buildings, and the three principal temples: the E.ANNA ("House of Anu") ziggurat, the *Bit-Resh* ("Main Temple") which was also a stage-tower, and the *Irigal* which was the temple dedicated to Inanna/Ishtar. Of the many volumes of the archaeologists' reports (*Ausgrabungen der Deutschen Forschungsgemeinschaft in Uruk-Warka*), of particular interest to the remarkable correlation of ancient texts and modern excavations are the second (*Archaische Texte aus Uruk*) and third (*Topographie von Uruk*) volumes by Adam Falkenstein.

Surprisingly, the texts on the clay tablets (whose scribal colophons identify them as copies of earlier originals) clearly describe two sets of rituals—one taking place in the month Nissan (the month of the spring equinox) and the other in the month Tishrit (the month of the autumnal equinox); the former was to become the Babylonian and Assyrian New Year, and the latter was retained in the Jewish calendar following the biblical commandment to celebrate the New Year "in the seventh month," *Tishrei*. While the reason for this diversity still mystifies scholars, Ebeling noted that the Nissan texts appear to have been better preserved than the Tishrei texts which are mostly fragmented, suggesting a clear bias on the part of the later temple scribes; and Falkenstein has noted that the Nissan and Tishrei rituals, seemingly identical, were not really so; the former stressed the various celestial observations, the latter the rituals within the Holy of Holies and its anteroom.

Of the various texts, two main ones deal separately with evetime and sunrise rituals. The former, long and well preserved, is especially legible from the point at which Anu and Antu, the divine visitors from Nibiru, are seated in the courtyard of the sacred precinct at evetime, ready to begin a lavish dinner banquet. As the Sun was setting in the west, astronomer-priests stationed on various stages of the main ziggurat were required to watch for the appearance of the planets and to announce the sighting the moment the celestial bodies appeared, beginning with Nibiru:

In the first watch of the night
from the roof of the topmost stage
of the temple-tower of the main temple,
when the planet Great Anu of Heaven,
the planet of Great Antu of Heaven,
shall appear in the constellation Wagon,
the priest shall recite the compositions
Ana tamshil zimu banne kakkab shamami Anu sharru
and Ittatza tzalam banu.

As these compositions ("To the one who grows bright, the heavenly planet of the Lord Anu" and "The Creator's image has arisen") were recited from the ziggurat, wine was served to the gods from a golden libation vessel. Then, in succession, the priests announced the appearance of Jupiter, Venus, Mercury, Saturn, Mars, and the Moon. The ceremony of washing the hands followed, with water poured from seven golden pitchers honoring the six luminaries of the night plus the Sun of daytime. A large torch of "naphtha fire in which spices were inserted" was lighted; all the priests sang the hymn *Kakkab Anu etellu shamame* ("The planet of Anu rose in the sky"), and the banquet could begin. Afterward Anu and Antu retired for the night and leading gods were assigned as watchmen until dawn. Then, "forty minutes after sunrise," Anu and Antu were awakened "bringing to an end their overnight stay."

The morning proceedings began outside the temple, in the courtyard of the *Bit Akitu* ("House of the New Year Festival" in Akkadian). Enlil and Enki were awaiting Anu at the "golden supporter," standing by or holding several objects; the Akkadian terms, whose precise meaning remains elusive, are best translated as "that which opens up the secrets," "the Sun disks" (plural!) and "the splendid/shining posts." Anu then came into the courtyard accompanied by gods in procession. "He stepped up to the Great Throne in the Akitu courtyard, and sat upon it facing the rising Sun.'' He was then joined by Enlil, who sat on Anu's right, and Enki, who sat on his left; Antu, Nannar/Sin, and Inanna/Ishtar then took places behind the seated Anu.

The statement that Anu seated himself ''facing the rising Sun'' leaves no doubt that the ceremony involved a determination of a moment connected with sunrise on a particular day—the first day of Nissan (the spring Equinox Day) or the first day of Tishrei (the autumnal Equinox Day). It was only when this sunrise ceremony was completed, that Anu was led by one of the gods and by the High Priest to the BARAG.GAL—the ''Holy of Holies'' inside the temple.

(BARAG means ''inner sanctum, screened-off place'' and GAL means ''great, foremost.'' The term evolved to *Baragu/Barakhu/Parakhu* in Akkadian with the meanings ''inner sanctum, Holy of Holies'' as well as the screen which hides it. This term appears in the Bible as the Hebrew word *Parokhet,* which was both the word for the Holy of Holies in the temple and for the screen that separated it from the anteroom. The traditions and rituals that began in Sumer were thus carried on both physically and linguistically.)

Another text from Uruk, instructing the priests regarding daily sacrifices, calls for the sacrifice of ''fat clean rams, whose horns and hooves are whole,'' to the deities Anu and Antu, ''to the planets Jupiter, Venus, Mercury, Saturn and Mars; to the Sun as it rises, and to the Moon on its appearance.'' The text then explains what ''appearance'' means in respect to each one of these seven celestial bodies: it meant the moment when they come to rest in the instrument which is ''in the midst of the *Bit Mahazzat*'' (''House of Viewing''). Further instructions suggest that this enclosure was ''on the topmost stage of the temple-tower of the god Anu.''

Depictions have been found that show divine beings flanking a temple entrance and holding up poles to which ringlike objects are attached. The celestial nature of the scene is indicated by the inclusion of the symbols of the Sun and the Moon (Fig. 56). In one instance the ancient artist may have intended to illustrate the scene described in the Uruk

Figure 56

Figure 57

ritual text—depicting Enlil and Enki flanking a gateway through which Anu is making a grand entrance. The two gods are holding posts to which viewing devices (circular instruments with a hole in the center) are attached (which is in accord with the text that spoke of Sun disks in the plural); the Sun and Moon symbols are shown above the gateway (Fig. 57).

Other depictions of poles-with-rings freestanding, not held up, flanking temple entrances (Fig. 58) suggest that

Figure 58

they were the forerunners of the uprights that flanked temples throughout the ancient Near East in ensuing millennia,
be it the two columns at Solomon's temple or the Egyptian
obelisks. That these originally had an actual and not just
symbolic astronomical function could be gathered from an
inscription by the Assyrian king Tiglatpileser I (1115–1077
B.C.) in which he recorded the restoration of a temple to
Anu and Adad that was built 641 years earlier and that had
been lying in ruins for the past sixty years. Describing how
he cleared the debris to reach the foundation and followed
the original layout in the reconstruction, the Assyrian king
said:

> *Two great towers*
> *to discern the two great gods*
> *I built in the House of Brilliance—*
> *a place for their joy,*
> *a place for their pride—*
> *a brilliance of the stars of the heaven.*
> *With the master-builder's artfulness,*
> *with my own planning and exertions,*
> *the insides of the temple I made splendid.*
> *In its midst I made a place for the*

rays directly from the heavens,
in the walls I made the stars to appear.
I made their brilliance great,
the towers I made to rise to the sky.

According to this account, the two great towers of the
temple were not just architectural features, but served an
astronomical purpose. Walter Andrae, who led some of the
most fruitful excavations in Assyria, expressed the view that
the serrated ''crowns'' that topped towers that flanked temple gateways in Ashur, the Assyrian capital, indeed served
such a purpose (*Die Jüngeren Ishtar-Tempel*). He found
confirmation for that conclusion in relevant illustrations on
Assyrian cylinder seals, such as in Fig. 59a and 59b, that
associate the towers with celestial symbols. Andrae surmised that some of the depicted altars (usually shown to-

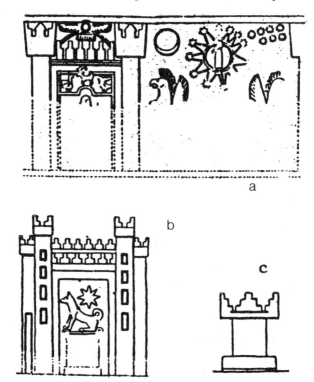

Figures 59a, 59b, and 59c

gether with a priest performing rites) also served a celestial (i.e., astronomical) purpose. In their serrated superstructures (Fig. 59c) these facilities, high up temple gateways or in the open courtyards of temple precincts, created substitutes for the rising stages of the ziggurats as ziggurats gave way to the more easily built flat-roofed temples.

The Assyrian inscription also serves as a reminder that not only the Sun at dawn, and the accompanying heliacal rising of stars and planets, but also the nightly Host of Heaven were observed by the astronomer-priests. A perfect example of such dual observations concerns the planet Venus, which because of its much shorter orbit time around the Sun than Earth's appears to an observer from Earth half the time as an evening star and half the time as a morning star. A Sumerian hymn to Inanna/Ishtar, whose celestial counterpart was the planet we call Venus, offered adoration to the planet first as an evening star, then as a morning star:

> *The holy one stands out in the clear sky;*
> *Upon all the lands and all the people*
> *the goddess looks sweetly from heaven's midst . . .*

> *At evetime a radiant star,*
> *a great light that fills the sky;*
> *The Lady of the Evening, Inanna,*
> *is lofty on the horizon.*

After describing how both people and beasts retire for the night ''to their sleeping places'' after the appearance of the Evening Star, the hymn continues to offer adoration to Inanna/Venus as the Morning Star: ''She made the morning come forth, the bright daylight; and in the bedchambers sweet sleep has come to an end.''

While such texts throw light on the role of the ziggurats and their rising stages in the observation of the night sky, they also raise the intriguing question: did the astronomer-priests observe the heavens with the naked eye, or did they have instruments for pinpointing the celestial moments of appearances? The answer is provided by depictions of ziggurats on whose upper stages poles topped by circular objects are emplaced; their celestial function is indicated by the image of Venus (Fig. 60a) or of the Moon (Fig. 60b).

The hornlike devices seen in Fig. 60b serve as a link to Egyptian depictions of instruments for astronomical observations associated with temples. There, viewing devices consisting of a circular part emplaced in the center of a pair of horns atop a high pole (Fig. 61a) were depicted as raised in front of the temples to a god called Min. His festival, celebrated once a year at the time of the summer solstice, involved the erection of a high mast by groups of men pulling cords—a predecessor, perhaps, of the Maypole festival in Europe. Atop the mast are raised the emblems of Min—the temple with the viewing lunar horns (Fig. 61b).

The identity of Min is somewhat of a mystery. The evi-

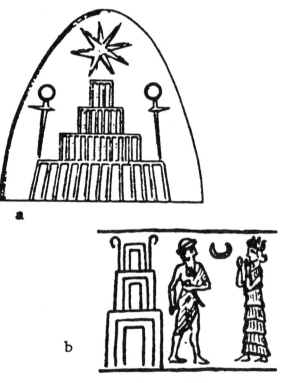

Figures 60a and 60b

dence suggests that he was already worshiped in predynastic times, even in the archaic period that preceded pharaonic rule by many centuries. Like the earliest Egyptian *Neteru* ("Guardians") gods, he had come to Egypt from somewhere else. G.A. Wainwright ("Some Celestial Associations of Min" in the *Journal of Egyptian Archaeology,* vol. XXI) and others believe that he had come from Asia; another opinion (e.g., Martin Isler in the *Journal of the American Research Center in Egypt,* vol. XXVII) was that Min had arrived in Egypt by sea. Min was also known as Amsu or Khem, which according to E.A. Wallis Budge (*The Gods of the Egyptians*) represented the Moon and meant "regeneration"—a calendrical connotation.

In some Egyptian depictions the Goddess of the Moon, Qetesh, was shown standing next to Min. Even more instructive is Min's symbol (Fig. 61c) that some call his "dou-

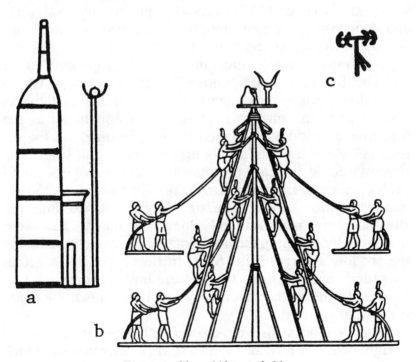

Figures 61a, 61b, and 61c

ble axe weapon'' but others consider to have been a gnomon. We believe that it was a hand-held viewing instrument that represented the crescents of the Moon.

Was Min perhaps another incarnation of Thoth, who was firmly linked to the lunar calendar of Egypt? What is certain is that Min was deemed to be related celestially to the Bull of Heaven, the zodiacal constellation of Taurus, whose age lasted from about 4400 B.C. to about 2100 B.C. The viewing devices that we have seen in the Mesopotamian depictions and those associated with Min in Egypt thus represent some of the oldest astronomical instruments on Earth.

According to the Uruk ritual texts, an instrument called *Itz Pashshuri* was used for the planetary observations. Thureau-Dangin translated the term simply as ''an apparatus''; but the term literally meant an instrument ''that solves, that unlocks secrets.'' Was this instrument one and the same as the circular objects that topped poles or posts, or was the term a generic one, meaning ''astronomical instrument'' in general? We cannot be sure because both texts and depictions have been found, from Sumerian times on, that attest to the existence of a variety of such instruments.

The simplest astronomical device was the *gnomon* (from the Greek ''that which knows''), an instrument which tracked the Sun's movements by the shadow cast by an upright pole; the shadow's length (growing smaller as the Sun rose to midday) indicated the hourly time and the direction (where the Sun's rays first appeared and last cast a shadow) could indicate the seasons. Archaeologists found such devices at Egyptian sites (Fig. 62a) which were pre-marked to show time (Fig. 62b). Since at solstice times the shadows grew inconveniently long, the flat devices were improved by inclining the horizontal scale, thereby reducing the shadow's length (Fig. 62c). In time, this led to actual structural shadow clocks which were built as stairways that indicated time as the shadow moved up or down the stairs (Fig. 62d).

Shadow clocks also developed into sundials when the upright pole was provided with a semicircular base on which an angular scale was marked. Archaeologists have found

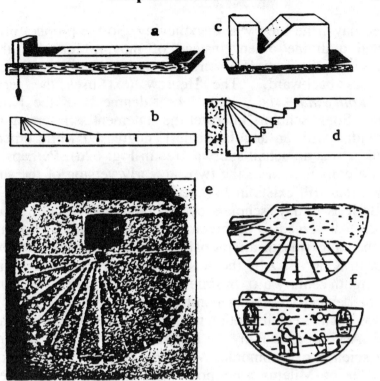

Figures 62a, 62b, 62c, 62d, 62e, and 62f

such instruments at Egyptian sites (Fig. 62e), but the oldest device so far discovered comes from the Canaanite city of Gezer in Israel; it has the regular angular scale on its face and a scene of the worship of the Egyptian god Thoth on the reverse side (Fig. 62f). This sundial, made of ivory, bears the cartouche of the Pharaoh Merenptah, who reigned in the thirteenth century B.C.

Shadow clocks are mentioned in the Bible. The Book of Job refers to portable gnomons, probably of the kind shown in 62a, that were used in the fields to tell time, when it observes that the hired laborer "earnestly desireth the shadow" that indicated it was time to collect his daily wages (Job 7:2). Less clear is the nature of a shadow clock that featured in a miraculous incident reported in II Kings chapter 20 and Isaiah chapter 38. When the prophet Isaiah told the ailing King Hezekiah that he would fully recover within three days, the king was disbelieving. So the prophet predicted a divine omen: instead of moving forward, the shadow of the Temple's sun clock would be "brought ten degrees backward." The Hebrew text uses the term *Ma'aloth Ahaz,* the "stairs" or "degrees" of the King Ahaz. Some scholars interpret the statement as referring to a sundial with an angular scale ("degrees") while others think it was an actual stairway (as in Fig. 62d). Perhaps it was a combination of the two, an early version of the sun clock that still exists in Jaipur, India (Fig. 63).

Be it as it may, scholars by and large agree that the sun clock that served as an omen for the miraculous recovery of the king was in all probability a gift presented to the Judean King Ahaz by the Assyrian king Tiglatpileser II in the eighth century B.C. In spite of the Greek name (*gnomon*) of the device (whose use continued into the Middle Ages), it was not a Greek invention nor, it seems, even an Egyptian one. According to Pliny the Elder, the first-century savant, the science of gnomonics was first described by Anaximander of Miletus who possessed an instrument called "shadow hunter." But Anaximander himself, in his work (in Greek) *Upon Nature* (547 B.C.) wrote that he had obtained the gnomon from Babylon.

The text in II Kings chapter 20, it seems to us, suggests a sundial rather than a built staircase and that it was placed in the Temple courtyard (it had to be in the open where the

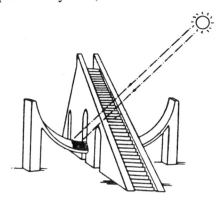

Figure 63

Sun could cast shadows). If Andrae was right regarding the astronomical function of altars, it was possible that the instrument was placed upon the Temple's main altar. Such altars had four "horns," a Hebrew term (*Keren*) that also meant "corner" as well as "beam, ray"—terms suggesting a common astronomical origin. Pictorial evidence supporting such a possibility ranges from early depictions of ziggurats in Sumer, where "horns" preceded the circular objects (Fig. 64a) all the way to Greek times. In tablets depicting altars from several centuries after Hezekiah's time, we can see (Fig. 64b) a viewing ring on a short support placed between two altars; in a second illustration (Fig. 64c) we can see an altar flanked by devices for Sun viewing and Moon viewing.

In considering the astronomical instruments of antiquity, we are in fact dealing with knowledge and sophistication

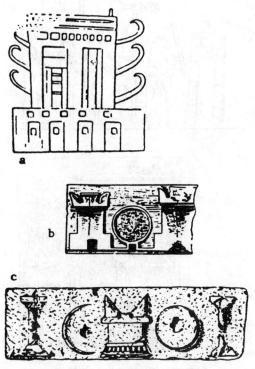

Figures 64a, 64b, and 64c

that go back millennia to ancient Sumer. One of the most
archaic depictions from Sumer that shows a procession of
temple attendants holding tools and instruments, pictures
one of them holding a pole surmounted by an astronomical
instrument: a device that connects two short posts with sighting rings on their tops (Fig. 65a). The twin rings in such
an arrangement are familiar even nowadays in modern bi-
noculars or theodolites for creating and measuring depth and
distance. By carrying it, the attendant makes clear that it
was a portable device, an instrument that could be emplaced
in various viewing positions.

If the process of celestial observation progressed from
massive ziggurats and great stone circles to lookout towers
and specially designed altars, the instruments with which
the astronomer-priests scanned the heavens at night or
tracked the Sun in daytime must have progressed in tandem.

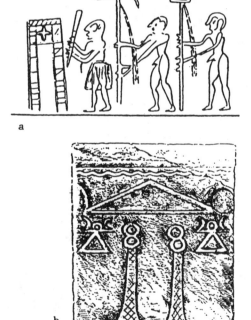

Figures 65a and 65b

That such instruments became portable thus makes much sense, especially if some were used not only for the original calendrical purposes (fixing festival times) but also for navigation. By the end of the second millennium B.C. the Phoenicians of northern Canaan had become the best navigators of the ancient world; plying the trade routes, one may say, between the stone pillars of Byblos and the ones in the British Isles, their foremost western outpost was Carthage (*Keret-Hadash*, "New City"). There they adopted as their main divine symbol the depiction of an astronomical instrument; before it began to appear on stelae and even tombstones, it was shown in association with two double-ringed pillars that flanked the entrance to a temple (Fig. 65b)—as earlier in Mesopotamia. The ring flanked by two opposite-facing crescents suggests observations of the Sun and of the Moon's phases.

A "votive tablet" found in the ruins of a Phoenician settlement in Sicily (Fig. 66a) depicts a scene in an open courtyard, suggesting that the Sun's movements rather than the night sky are the astronomical objective. The ringed pillar and an altar stand in front of a three-columned structure; there, too, is the viewing device: a ring between two short vertical posts placed on a horizontal bar and mounted atop a triangular base. This particular shape for observations of the Sun brings to mind the Egyptian hieroglyph for "horizon"—the Sun rising between two mountains (Fig. 66b). Indeed, the Phoenician device (scholars refer to it as a "cult symbol") suggesting a pair of raised hands is related to the Egyptian hieroglyph for *Ka* (Fig. 66c) that represented the pharaoh's spirit or alter ego for the Afterlife journey to the abode of the gods on the "Planet of millions of years." That the origin of the *Ka* was, to begin with, an astronomical instrument is suggested by an archaic Egyptian depiction (Fig. 66d) of a viewing device in front of a temple.

All these similarities and their astronomical origin should add new insights to understanding Egyptian depictions (Fig. 67) of the Ka's ascent toward the gods' planet with outstretched hands that emulate the Sumerian device; it ascends from atop a pillar equipped with gradation-steps.

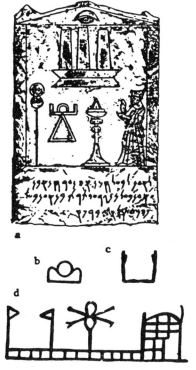

Figures 66a, 66b, 66c, and 66d

Figure 67

The Egyptian hieroglyph depicting this step-pillar was called *Ded,* meaning "Everlastingness." It was often shown in pairs, because two such pillars were said to have stood in front of the principal temple to the great Egyptian god Osiris in Abydos. In the Pyramid Texts, in which the pharaohs' afterlife journeys are described, the two *Ded* pillars are shown flanking the "Door of Heaven." The double doors stay closed until the arriving alter ego of the king pronounces the magical formula: "O Lofty One, thou Door of Heaven: the king has come to thee; cause this door to be opened for him." And then, suddenly, the "double doors of heaven open up . . . the aperture of the celestial windows is open." And, soaring as a great falcon, the pharaoh's *Ka* has joined the gods in Everlastingness.

The Egyptian Book of the Dead has not reached us in the form of a cohesive book, assuming that a composition that might be called a "book" truly existed; rather, it has been collated from the many quotations from it that cover the walls of royal tombs. But a complete book did reach us from ancient Egypt, and it shows that an ascent heavenward to attain immortality was deemed connected with the calendar.

The book we refer to is the *Book of Enoch,* an ancient composition known from two sets of versions, an Ethiopic one that scholars identify as "1 Enoch," and a Slavonic version that is identified as "2 Enoch," and which is also known as *The Book of the Secrets of Enoch.* Both versions, of which copied manuscripts have been found mostly in Greek and Latin translations, are based on early sources that enlarged on the short biblical mention that Enoch, the seventh Patriarch after Adam, did not die because, at age 365, "he walked with God"—taken heavenward to join the deity.

Enlarging on this brief statement in the Bible (Genesis chapter 5), the books describe in detail Enoch's two celestial journeys—the first to learn the heavenly secrets, return, and impart the knowledge to his sons; and the second to stay put in the heavenly abode. The various versions indicate wide astronomical knowledge concerning the motions of the

Sun and the Moon, the solstices and the equinoxes, the reasons for the shortening and lengthening days, the structure of the calendar, the solar and lunar years, and the rule of thumb for intercalation. In essence, the secrets that were imparted to Enoch and by him to his sons to keep, were the knowledge of astronomy as it related to the calendar.

The author of *The Book of the Secrets of Enoch,* the so-called Slavonic version, is believed to have been (to quote R.H. Charles, *The Apocrypha and Pseudepigrapha of the Old Testament*) ''a Jew who lived in Egypt, probably in Alexandria'' some time around the beginning of the Christian era. This is how the book concludes:

Enoch was born on the sixth day of the month Tsivan, and lived three hundred and sixty-five years.

He was taken up to heaven on the first day of the month Tsivan and remained in heaven sixty days. He wrote all these signs of all creation which the Lord created, and wrote three hundred and sixty-six books, and handed them over to his sons.

He was taken up [again] to heaven on the sixth day of the month Tsivan, on the very day and hour when he was born.

Methosalam and his brethren, all the sons of Enoch, made haste and erected an altar at the place called Ahuzan, whence and where Enoch had been taken up to heaven.

Not only the contents of the *Book of Enoch*—astronomy as it relates to the calendar—but also the very life and ascension of Enoch are thus replete with calendrical aspects. His years on Earth, 365, are of course the number of whole days in a solar year; his birth and departure from Earth are linked to a specific month, even the day of the month.

The Ethiopic version is deemed by scholars to be older by several centuries than the Slavonic one, and portions of that older version are in turn known to have been based on even older manuscripts, such as a lost *Book of Noah*. Fragments of Enoch books were discovered among the Dead Sea scrolls. The astronomical-calendrical tale of Enoch thus goes back into great antiquity—perhaps, as the Bible asserts, to pre-Diluvial times.

Now that it is certain that the biblical tales of the Deluge and the *Nefilim* (the biblical Anunnaki), of the creation of the Adam and of Earth itself, and of ante-Diluvial patriarchs, are abbreviated renderings of original earlier Sumerian texts that recorded all that, it is almost certain that the biblical "Enoch" was the equivalent of the Sumerian first priest, EN.ME.DUR.AN.KI ("High Priest of the ME's of the Bond Heaven-Earth"), the man from the city Sippar taken heavenward to be taught the secrets of Heaven and Earth, of divination, and of the calendar. It was with him that the generations of astronomer-priests, of Keepers of the Secrets, began.

The granting by Min to the Egyptian astronomer-priests of the viewing device was not an extraordinary action. A Sumerian sculpture molded in relief shows a great god granting a hand-held astronomical device to a king-priest (Fig. 68). Numerous other Sumerian depictions show a king being granted a measuring rod and a rolled measuring cord for the purpose of assuring the correct astronomical orientation of temples, as we have seen in Fig. 54. Such depictions only enhance the textual evidence that is explicit about the manner in which the line of astronomer-priests began.

Did Man, however, become haughty enough to forget all that, to start thinking he had attained all that knowledge by himself? Millennia ago the issue was tackled when Job was asked to admit that not Man but *El*, "the Lofty One," was the Keeper of the Secrets of Heaven and Earth:

> *Say, if thou knowest science:*
> *Who hath measured the Earth, that it be known?*
> *Who hath stretched a cord upon it?*
> *By what were its platforms wrought?*
> *Who hath cast its Stone of Corners?*

Figure 68

Have you ever ordered Morning or figured out Dawn according to the corners of the Earth? Job was asked. Do you know where daylight and darkness exchange places, or how snow and hailstones come about, or rains, or dew? "Do you know the celestial laws, or how they regulate that which is upon the Earth?"

The texts and depictions were intended to make clear that the human Keepers of the Secrets were pupils, not teachers. The records of Sumer leave no doubt that the teachers, the original Keepers of the Secrets, were the Anunnaki.

The leader of the first team of Anunnaki to come to Earth, splashing down in the waters of the Persian Gulf, was E.A— he "whose home is water." He was the chief scientist of the Anunnaki and his initial task was to obtain the gold they needed by extracting it from the gulf's waters—a task requiring knowledge in physics, chemistry, metallurgy. As a shift to mining became necessary and the operation moved to southeastern Africa, his knowledge of geography, geology, geometry—of all that we call Earth Sciences—came into play; no wonder his epithet-name changed to EN.KI, "Lord Earth," for his was the domain of Earth's secrets. Finally, suggesting and carrying out the genetic engineering that brought the Adam into being—a feat in which he was helped by his half sister Ninharsag, the Chief Medical Officer—he demonstrated his prowess in the disciplines of Life Sciences: biology, genetics, evolution. More than one hundred ME's, those enigmatic objects that, like computer disks, held the knowledge arranged by subject, were kept by him in his center, Eridu, in Sumer; at the southern tip of Africa, a scientific station held "the tablet of wisdom."

All that knowledge was in time shared by Enki with his six sons, each of whom became expert in one or more of these scientific secrets.

Enki's half brother EN.LIL—"Lord of the Command"—arrived next on Earth. Under his leadership the number of Anunnaki on Earth increased to six hundred; in addition, three hundred IGI.GI ("Those who observe and see") remained in Earth orbit, manning orbiting stations, operating shuttlecraft to and from spacecraft. He was a great spaceman, organizer, disciplinarian. He established the first Mission Control Center in NI.IBRU, known to us by its Akkadian name Nippur, and the communication links with the Home Planet, the DUR.AN.KI—"Bond Heaven-Earth." The space charts, the celestial data, the secrets of astronomy were his to know and keep. He planned and supervised the setting up of the first space base in Sippar ("Bird City"). Matters of weather, winds and rains, were his concern; so was the assurance of efficient transportation and supplies, including the local provision of foodstuffs and the arts and crafts of agriculture and shepherding. He maintained discipline among the Anunnaki, chaired the council of the "Seven who Judge," and remained the supreme god of law and order when Mankind began to proliferate. He regulated the functions of the priesthood, and when kingship was instituted, it was called by the Sumerians "Enlilship."

A long and well-preserved *Hymn to Enlil, the All Beneficent* found among the ruins of the E.DUB.BA, "House of Scribal Tablets" in Nippur, mentioned in its one hundred seventy lines many of the scientific and organizational achievements of Enlil. On his ziggurat, the E.KUR ("House which is like a mountain"), he had a "beam that searched the heart of all the lands." He "set up the *Duranki*," the "Bond Heaven-Earth." In Nippur, "a bellwether of the universe" he erected. Righteousness and justice he decreed. With "ME's of heaven" that "none can gaze upon" he established in the innermost part of the Ekur "a heavenly zenith, as mysterious as the distant sea," containing the "starry emblems . . . carried to perfection"; these enabled the establishment of rituals and festivals. It was under Enlil's guidance that "cities were built, settlements founded, stalls built, sheepfolds erected," riverbanks controlled for over-flowing, canals built, fields and meadows "filled with rich grain," gardens made to produce fruits, weaving and en-twining taught.

Those were the aspects of knowledge and civilization that Enlil bequeathed to his children and grandchildren, and through them to Mankind.

The process by which the Anunnaki imparted such diverse aspects of science and knowledge to Mankind has been a neglected field of study. Little has been done to pursue, for example, such a major issue as how astronomer-priests came into being—an event without which we, today, would nei-ther know much about our own Solar System nor be able to venture into space. Of the pivotal event, the teaching of the heavenly secrets to Enmeduranki, we read in a little-known tablet that was fortunately brought to light by W. G. Lambert in his study *Enmeduranki and Related Ma-terial* that

> *Enmeduranki [was] a prince in Sippar,*
> *Beloved of Anu, Enlil and Ea.*
> *Shamash in the Bright Temple appointed him [as*
> *   priest].*
> *Shamash and Adad [took him] to the assembly [of the*
> *   gods] . . .*

*They showed him how to observe oil on water,
a secret of Anu, Enlil and Ea.
They gave him the Divine Tablet,
the* kibbu *secret of Heaven and Earth . . .
They taught him how to make calculations with
    numbers.*

When the instruction of Enmeduranki in the secret knowledge of the Anunnaki was accomplished, he was returned to Sumer. The "men of Nippur, Sippar and Babylon were called into his presence." He informed them of his experiences and of the establishment of the institution of priesthood and that the gods commanded that it should be passed from father to son:

*The learned savant
who guards the secrets of the gods
will bind his favored son with an oath
before Shamash and Adad . . .
and will instruct him in the secrets of the gods.*

The tablet has a postcript:

*Thus was the line of priests created,
those who are allowed to approach Shamash and Adad.*

According to the Sumerian King Lists Enmeduranna was the seventh pre-Diluvial holder of kingship, and reigned in Sippar during six orbits of Nibiru before he became High Priest and was renamed Enmeduranki. In the *Book of Enoch* it was the archangel Uriel ("God is my light") who showed Enoch the secrets of the Sun (solstices and equinoxes, "six portals" in all) and the "laws of the Moon" (including intercalation), and the twelve constellations of the stars, "all the workings of heaven." And in the end of the schooling, Uriel gave Enoch—as Shamash and Adad had given Enmeduranki—"heavenly tablets," instructing him to study them carefully and note "every individual fact" therein. Returning to Earth, Enoch passed this knowledge to his oldest son, Methuselah. The *Book of the Secrets of Enoch* includes in the knowledge granted Enoch "all the workings of heaven, earth and the seas, and all the elements, their passages and goings and the thunderings of the thunder; and of the Sun and the Moon; the goings and changings of the stars; the seasons, years, days, and hours." This would be in line with the attributes of Shamash—the god whose celestial counterpart was the Sun and who commanded the spaceport, and of Adad who was the "weather god" of antiquity, the god of storms and rains. Shamash (Utu in Sumerian) was usually depicted (see Fig. 54) holding the measuring rod and cord; Adad (Ishkur in Sumerian) was shown holding the forked lightning. A depiction on the royal seal of an Assyrian king (Tukulti-Ninurta I) shows the king being introduced to the two great gods, perhaps for the purpose of granting him the knowledge they had once given to Enmeduranki (Fig. 69).

Appeals by later kings to be granted as much "Wisdom" and scientific knowledge as renowned early sages had possessed, or boasts that they knew as much, were not uncommon. Royal Assyrian correspondence hailed a king as "surpassing in knowledge all the wise men of the Lower World" because he was an offspring of the "sage Adapa." Another instance had a Babylonian king claim that he possessed "wisdom that greatly surpassed even that contained in the writings that Adapa had composed." These were

Figure 69

references to Adapa, the Sage of Eridu (Enki's center in Sumer), whom Enki had taught "wide understanding" of "the designs of Earth"—the secrets of Earth Sciences.

One cannot rule out the possibility that, as Enmeduranki and Enoch, Adapa too was the seventh in a line of sages, the Sages of Eridu, and thus another version of the Sumerian memory echoed in the biblical Enoch record. According to this tale, seven Wise Men were trained in Eridu, Enki's city; their epithets and particular knowledge varied from version to version. Rykle Borger, examining this tale in light of the Enoch traditions (*"Die Beschworungsserie Bit Meshri und die Himmelfahrt Henochs"* in the *Journal of Near Eastern Studies,* vol. 33), was especially fascinated by the inscription on the third tablet of the series of Assyrian Oath Incantations. In it the name of each sage is given and his main call on fame is explained; it says thus of the seventh: "Utu-abzu, he who to heaven ascended." Citing a second such text, R. Borger concluded that this seventh sage, whose name combined that of Utu/Shamash with the Lower World (*Abzu*) domain of Enki, was the Assyrian "Enoch."

According to the Assyrian references to the wisdom of Adapa, he composed a book of sciences titled U.SAR d ANUM d ENLILA—"Writings regarding Time; from divine Anu and divine Enlil." Adapa, thus, is credited with writing Mankind's first book of astronomy and the calendar.

When Enmeduranki ascended to heaven to be taught the various secrets, his patron gods were Utu/Shamash and Adad/Ishkur, a grandson and a son of Enlil. His ascent was thus under Enlilite aegis. Of Adapa we read that when Enki sent him heavenward to Anu's abode, the two gods who acted as his chaperons were Dumuzi and Gizzida, two sons of Ea/Enki. There, "Adapa from the horizon of heaven to the zenith of heaven cast a glance; he saw its awesomeness"—words reflected in the Books of Enoch. At the end of the visit Anu denied him everlasting life; instead, "the priesthood of the city of Ea to glorify in future" he decreed for Adapa.

The implication of these tales is that there were two lines of priesthood—one Enlilite and one Enki'ite; and two central

scientific acadamies, one in Enlil's Nippur and the other in
Enki's Eridu. Both competing and cooperating, no doubt,
as the two half brothers themselves were, they appear to
have acquired their specialties. This conclusion, supported
by later writings and events, is reflected in the fact that we
find the leading Anunnaki having each their talents, specialty, and specific assignments.

As we continue to examine these specialties and assignments, we will find that the close relationship of temple-
astronomy-calendar was also expressed in the fact that several deities, in Sumer as in Egypt, combined these specialties
in their attributes. And since the ziggurats and temples
served as observatories—to determine the passage of both
Earthly and Celestial Times—the deities with the astronomical knowledge were also the ones with the knowledge of
orienting and designing the temples and their layouts.

"Say, if thou knowest science: Who hath measured the
Earth, that it be known? Who hath stretched a *cord* upon
it?" So was Job asked when called upon to admit that God,
not Man, was the ultimate Keeper of the Secrets. In the
scene of the introduction of the king-priest to Shamash (Fig.
54), the purpose or essence of the occurrence is indicated
by two Divine Cordholders. The two cords they stretch to
a ray-emitting planet form an angle, suggesting measurement not so much of distance as of orientation. An Egyptian
depiction of a similar motif, a scene painted on the Papyrus
of Queen Nejmet, shows how two cordholders measured an
angle based on the planet called "Red Eye of Horus" (Fig.
70).

The stretching of cords to determine the proper astronomical orientation of a temple was the task of a goddess
called Sesheta in Egypt. She was on the one hand a Goddess
of the Calendar; her epithets were "the great one, lady of
letters, mistress of the House of Books" and her symbol
was the stylus made of a palm branch, which in Egyptian
hieroglyphs stood for "counting the years." She was depicted with a seven-rayed star within the Heavenly Bow on
her head. She was the Goddess of Construction, but only
(as pointed out by Sir Norman Lockyer in *The Dawn of*

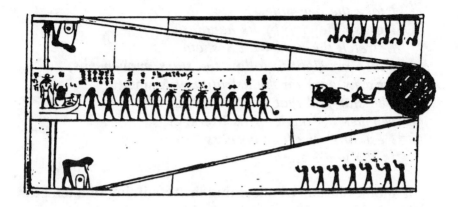

Figure 70

Astronomy) for the purpose of determining the orientation of temples. Such an orientation was not haphazard or a matter left to guesswork. The Egyptians relied on divine guidance to determine the orientation and major axis of their temples; the task was assigned to Sesheta. Auguste Mariette, reporting on his finds at Denderah where depictions and inscriptions pertaining to Sesheta were discovered, said it was she who "made certain that the construction of sacred shrines was carried out exactly according to the directions contained in the Divine Books."

Determining the correct orientation called for an elaborate ceremony named *Put-ser,* meaning "the stretching of the cord." The goddess sank a pole in the ground by hammering it down with a golden club; the king, guided by her, sank another pole. A cord was then stretched between the two poles, indicating the proper orientation; it was determined by the position of a specific star. A study by Z. Zaba published by the Czechoslovak Academy of Sciences (*Archiv Orientalni,* Supplement 2, 1953) concluded that the ceremony revealed knowledge of the phenomenon of precession, and thus of the zodiacal division of the celestial circle. The astral aspects of the ceremony have been made clear by relevant inscriptions, as the one found on the walls of the temple of Horus in Edfu. It records the words of the pharaoh:

> *I take the peg-pole,*
> *I grasp the club by its handle,*
> *I stretch the cord with Sesheta.*
> *I turn my sight to follow the stars' movements,*
> *I fix my gaze on the astrality of* Msihettu.
> *The star-god that announces the time*
> *reaches the angle of its* Merkhet;
> *I establish the four corners*
> *of the god's temple.*

In another instance concerning the rebuilding of a temple in Abydos by the Pharaoh Seti I, the inscription quotes the king thus:

> *The hammering club in my hand was of gold.*
> *I struck the peg with it.*
> *Thou wast with me in thy capacity of* Harpedonapt.
> *Thy hand held the spade during the fixing of*
> *the temple's four corners with accuracy*
> *by the four supports of heaven.*

The ceremony was pictorially depicted on the temple's walls (Fig. 71).

Figure 71

Sesheta was, according to Egyptian theology, the female companion and chief assistant of Thoth, the Egyptian god of sciences, mathematics, and the calendar—the Divine Scribe, who kept the gods' records, and the Keeper of the Secrets of the construction of the pyramids.

As such, he was the foremost Divine Architect.

6

THE DIVINE ARCHITECTS

Some time between 2200 and 2100 B.C.—a time of great import at Stonehenge—Ninurta, Enlil's Foremost Son, embarked on a major undertaking: the building of a new "House" for himself at Lagash.

The event throws light on many matters of gods and men thanks to the fact that the king entrusted with the task, Gudea of Lagash, wrote it all down in great detail on two large clay cylinders. In spite of the immensity of the task, he realized that it was a great honor and a unique opportunity to have his name and deeds remembered for all time, for not many kings were so entrusted; in fact, royal records (since found by archaeologists) spoke of at least one instance when a famous king (Naram-Sin), otherwise beloved by the gods, was again and again refused permission to engage in the building of a new temple (such a situation arose millennia later in the case of King David in Jerusalem). Shrewdly expressing his gratitude to his god by inscribing laudatory statements on statues of himself (Fig. 72) which Gudea then emplaced in the new temple, Gudea managed to leave behind a rather substantial amount of written information which explains the How and What for of the sacred precincts and temples of the Anunnaki.

As the Foremost Son of Enlil by his half sister Ninharsag and thus the heir apparent, Ninurta shared his father's rank of fifty (that of Anu being the highest, sixty, and that of Anu's other son, Enki, being forty) and so it was a simple choice to call Ninurta's ziggurat E.NINNU, the "House of Fifty."

Throughout the millennia Ninurta was a faithful aide to his father, carrying out dutifully each task assigned to him. He acquired the epithet "Foremost Warrior of Enlil" when

Figure 72

a rebel god called Zu seized the Tablets of Destinies from
Mission Control Center in Nippur, disrupting the bond
Heaven-Earth; it was Ninurta who pursued the usurper to
the ends of Earth, seizing him and restoring the crucial
tablets to their rightful place. When a brutal war, which in
The Wars of Gods and Men we have called the Second
Pyramid War, broke out between the Enlilites and the
Enki'ites, it was again Ninurta who led his father's side to
victory. That conflict ended with a peace conference forced
on the warring clans by Ninharsag, in the aftermath of which
the Earth was divided among the two brothers and their sons
and civilization was granted to Mankind in the "Three Regions"—Mesopotamia, Egypt, and the Indus Valley.

The peace that ensued lasted a long time, but not forever.
One who had been unhappy with the arrangements all along
was Marduk, the Firstborn Son of Enki. Reviving the rivalry

between his father and Enlil which stemmed from the complex succession rules of the Anunnaki, Marduk challenged the grant of Sumer and Akkad (what we call Mesopotamia) to the offspring of Enlil and claimed the right to a Mesopotamian city called *Bab-Ili* (Babylon)—literally, ''Gateway of the Gods.'' As a result of the ensuing conflicts, Marduk was sentenced to be buried alive inside the Great Pyramid of Giza; but, pardoned before it was too late, he was forced into exile; and once again Ninurta was called upon to help resolve the conflicts.

Ninurta, however, was not just a warrior. In the aftermath of the Deluge it was he who dammed the mountain passes to prevent more flooding in the plain between the Euphrates and Tigris rivers and who had arranged extensive drainage works there to make the plain habitable again. Thereafter, he oversaw the introduction of organized agriculture to the region and was fondly nicknamed by the Sumerians *Urash*— ''He of the Plough.'' When the Anunnaki decided to give Kingship to Mankind, it was Ninurta who was assigned to organize it at the first City of Men, Kish. And when, after the upheavals caused by Marduk, the lands quieted down circa 2250 B.C., it was again Ninurta who restored order and kingship from his ''cult city,'' Lagash.

His reward was permission from Enlil to build a brand new temple in Lagash. It was not that he was ''homeless''; he already had a temple in Kish, and a temple within the sacred precinct in Nippur, next to his father's ziggurat. He also had his own temple in the *Girsu,* the sacred precinct of his ''cult center,'' the city of Lagash. French teams of archaeologists who have been excavating at the site (now locally called Tello), conducting twenty ''campaigns'' between 1877 and 1933, uncovered many of the ancient remains of a square ziggurat and rectangular temples whose corners were precisely oriented to the cardinal points (Fig. 73). They estimated that the foundations of the earliest temple were laid in Early Dynastic times, before 2700 B.C., on the mound marked ''K'' on the excavations map. Inscriptions by the earliest rulers of Lagash already spoke of rebuilding and improvements in the Girsu, as well as of the

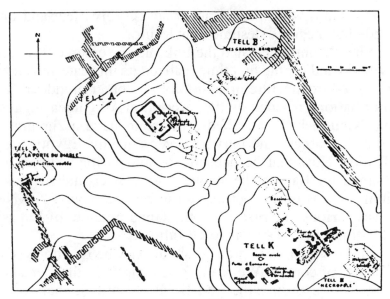

Figure 73

Figure 74

presentation of votive artifacts, such as the silver vase by
Entemena (Fig. 48), over a period of six or seven hundred
years before Gudea's time. Some inscriptions may mean
that the foundations for the very first Eninnu were laid by
Mesilim, a king of Kish who had reigned circa 2850 B.C.

Kish, it will be recalled, was where Ninurta had established for the Sumerians the institution of Kingship. For a
long time the rulers of Lagash were considered just viceroys,
who had to earn the title "king of Kish" in order to be full-
fledged sovereigns. It was perhaps this second-class stigma
that made Ninurta seek a temple truly authentic for his city;
he also needed one that could hold the remarkable weapons
that he had been granted by Anu and Enlil, including an
aircraft that was nicknamed the Divine Storm Bird (Fig. 74)

which had a wingspan of about seventy-five feet and thus needed a specially designed enclosure.

When Ninurta defeated the Enki'ites he entered the Great Pyramid and for the first time realized its intricate and amazing inner architecture in addition to its outer grandeur. The information provided by the inscriptions of Gudea suggests that Ninurta had nourished a desire to have a ziggurat of similar greatness and intricacy ever since his Egyptian tour of duty. Now that he had once again pacified Sumer and attained for Lagash the status of a royal capital, he asked Enlil once again for permission to build a new E.NINNU, a new "House of Fifty," in the Girsu precinct of Lagash. This time, his wish was to be fulfilled.

That his wish was granted should not be downplayed as a matter of course. We read, for example, in the Canaanite "myths" regarding the god Ba'al ("Lord"), that for his role in defeating the enemies of El ("The Lofty One," the supreme deity) he sought El's permission to build a House on the crest of Mount Zaphon in Lebanon. Ba'al had sought this permission before, and was repeatedly turned down; he had repeatedly complained to "Bull El, his father":

> No house has Ba'al like the gods,
> no precinct like the children of Asherah;
> the abode of El is the shelter of his son.

Now he asked Asherah, El's spouse, to intercede for him; and Asherah finally convinced El to give his permission. Added to the previous arguments was a new one: Ba'al, she said, could then "observe the seasons" in his new House— make there celestial observations for a calendar.

But though a god, Ba'al could not just go ahead and build his temple-abode. The plans had to be drawn and construction supervised by the *Kothar-Hasis,* the "Skilled and Knowing" Craftsman of the Gods. Not only modern scholars but even Philo of Byblos in the first century A.D. (quoting earlier Phoenician historians) compared Kothar-Hasis with the Greek divine craftsman Hephaestus (who built the temple-abode of Zeus) or with Thoth, the Egyptian god of knowledge, crafts, and magic. The Canaanite texts indeed state that Ba'al sent emissaries to Egypt to fetch Kothar-Hasis, but found him eventually in Crete.

No sooner, however, did Kothar-Hasis arrive than Ba'al got into fierce arguments with him regarding the temple's architecture. He wanted, it appears, a House of only two parts, not the customary three—an *Hekhal* and a *Bamtim* (a raised stage). The sharpest argument was over a funnellike window or skylight which Kothar-Hasis claimed had to be positioned "in the House" but Ba'al vehemently argued should be located somewhere else. The argument is given the space of many verses in the text to show its ferocity and importance; it involved shouting and spitting . . .

The reasons for the argument regarding the skylight and its location remain obscure; our guess is that it might have been connected with the temple's orientation. The statement by Asherah that the temple would enable observance of the seasons suggests an orientation requiring certain astronomical observations. Ba'al, on the other hand, as the Canaanite text later reveals, was planning to install in the temple a secret communication device that would enable him to seize power over other gods. To that purpose Ba'al "stretched a cord, strong and supple," from the peak of Zaphon ("North") to Kadesh ("the Sacred Place") in the south, in the Sinai desert.

The orientation in the end remained the way the divine architect, Kothar-Hasis, wanted it. "Thou shalt heed my words," he told Ba'al emphatically, and "as for Ba'al, his house was thus built." If, as one must assume, the later temples atop the Baalbek platform were built according to that olden plan, then we find that the orientation Kothar-Hasis had insisted upon resulted in a temple with an east–west axis (see Fig. 25).

As the Sumerian tale of the new Eninnu temple unfolds, we shall see that it too involved celestial observations to determine its orientation, and required the services of divine architects.

*　*　*

Much like King Solomon some thirteen hundred years later, Gudea in his inscriptions detailed the number of workmen (216,000) involved in the project, the cedarwood timbers he had hauled from Lebanon, the other types of timber used for great beams, the "great stones from the mountains, split into blocks"—bitumen from the wells and from the "bitumen lake," copper from the "copper mountains," silver "from its mountain" and "gold from its mountains"; and all the bronze artifacts, and the decorations, and the trimmings, and the stelae and statues. All was described in detail, all was so magnificent and marvelous that, when it was finished, "the Anunnaki were altogether seized with admiration."

The sections in the Gudea inscriptions of the greatest interest are those that deal with the events that preceded the construction of the temple, the determination of its orientation, its equipment and symbolism; we follow primarily the information provided in the inscription known as Cylinder A.

The chain of events, Gudea's record states, began on a certain day, a day of great significance. Referring in the inscriptions to Ninurta by his formal title NIN.GIRSU—"Lord of the Girsu"—this how the record begins:

> On the day when the fate Heaven-Earth is decreed,
> When Lagash lifted its head heavenwards
> in accordance with the great ME's,
> Enlil cast a favorable eye upon the lord Ningirsu.

Recording Ninurta's complaint about the delay in the building of the new temple "which is vital to the city in accordance with the ME's," it reports that on that propitious day Enlil finally granted the permission, and he also decreed what the temple's name shall be: "Its king shall name the temple E.NINNU." The edict, Gudea wrote, "made a brilliance in heaven and on Earth."

Having received the permission of Enlil and having obtained the name for the new ziggurat, Ninurta was now free to proceed with the construction. Without losing time, Gudea rushed to supplicate his god to be the one chosen for the task. Offering sacrifices of oxen and kids "he sought the divine will . . . by day and in the middle of the night Gudea lifted up his eyes to his lord Ningirsu; for the command to build his temple he set his eyes." Persisting, Gudea kept praying: "He said and sighed: 'Thus, thus will I speak; thus, thus will I speak; this word I shall bring forth: I am the shepherd, chosen for kingship.' "

Finally the miracle happened. "At midnight," he wrote, "something came to me; its meaning I did not understand." He took his asphalt-lined boat and, sailing on a canal, went to a nearby town to seek an explanation from the oracle goddess Nanshe in her "House of Fate-Solving." Offering prayers and sacrifices that she would solve the riddle of his vision, he proceeded to tell her about the appearance of the god whose command he was to heed:

> *In the dream [I saw]*
> *a man who was bright, shining like Heaven,*
> *great in Heaven, great on Earth,*
> *who by his headdress was a god.*
> *By his side was the Divine Storm Bird;*
> *Like a devouring storm under his feet*
> *two lions crouched, on the right and on the left.*
> *He commanded me to build his temple.*

A celestial omen then occurred whose meaning, Gudea told the oracle goddess, he did not understand: the Sun upon *Kishar*, Jupiter, was suddenly seen on the horizon. A woman then appeared who gave Gudea other celestial directions:

> *A woman—*
> *who was she? Who was she not?*
> *the image of a temple-structure, a ziggurat,*
> *she carried on her head—*
> *in her hand she held a holy stylus,*
> *the tablet of the favorable star of heaven*

she bore,
taking counsel with it.

A third divine being then appeared who had the look of
a "hero":

A tablet of lapis lazuli his hand held;
the plan of a temple he drew on it.

And then, before his very eyes, there materialized the
signs for construction: "a holy carrying-basket" and a
"holy brick mold" in which there was placed "the destined
brick."

Having heard the details of the dreamlike vision, the
oracle goddess proceeded to tell Gudea what it meant. The
first god to appear was Ningirsu (Ninurta); "for thee to
build his temple, Eninnu, he commanded." The heliacal
rising, she explained, signaled the god Ningishzidda, indicating to him the point of the Sun on the horizon. The
goddess was Nisaba; "to build the House in accordance
with the Holy Planet she instructed thee." And the third
god, Nanshe explained, "Nindub is his name; to thee the
plan of the House he gave."

Nanshe then added some instructions of her own, reminding Gudea that the new Eninnu had to provide appropriate places for Ninurta's weapons, for his great aircraft,
even for his favorite lyre. Given these explanations and
instructions Gudea returned to Lagash and secluded himself
in the old temple, trying to figure out what all those instructions meant. "For two days in the sanctuary of the temple
he shut himself in, at night he was shut in; the House's plan
he contemplated, the vision he repeated to himself."

Most baffling to him, to begin with, was the matter of
the new temple's orientation. Stepping up to a high or elevated part of the old temple called *Shugalam*, "the place
of the aperture, the place of determining, from which Ningirsu can see the repetition over his lands," Gudea removed
some of the "spittle" (mortar? mud?) that obstructed the
view, trying to fathom the secrets of the temple's construc-

tion; but he was still baffled and perplexed. "Oh my lord Ningirsu," he called out to his god, "Oh son of Enlil: my heart remains unknowing; the meaning is as far from me as the middle of the ocean, as the midst of heaven from me it is distant . . . Oh, son of Enlil, lord Ningirsu—I, I do not know."

He asked for a second omen; and as he was sleeping Ningirsu/Ninurta appeared to him; "While I was sleeping, at my head he stood," Gudea wrote. The god made clear the instructions to Gudea, assuring him of constant divine help:

> *My commands will teach thee the sign*
> *by the divine heavenly planet;*
> *In accordance with the holy rites*
> *my House, the Eninnu,*
> *shall bind Earth with Heaven.*

The god then lists for Gudea all the inner requirements of the new temple, expanding at the same time on his great powers, the awesomeness of his weapons, his memorable deeds (such as the damming of the waters) and the status he was granted by Anu, "the fifty names of lordship, by those ordained." The construction, he tells Gudea, should begin on "the day of the new Moon," when the god will give him the proper omen—a signal: on the evening of the New Year the god's hand shall appear holding a flame, giving off a light "that shall make the night as light as day."

Ninurta/Ningirsu also assures Gudea that he will receive from the very beginning of the planning of the new Eninnu divine help: the god whose epithet was "The Bright Serpent" shall come to help build the Eninnu and its new precinct—"build it to be like the House of the Serpent, as a strong place it shall be built." Ninurta then promises Gudea that the construction of the temple will bring the land abundance: "When my temple-terrace is completed," rains will come on time, the irrigation canals will fill up with water, even the desert "where water has not flowed" shall bloom; there will be abundant crops, and plenty of oil for cooking, and "wool in abundance shall be weighed."

Now "Gudea understood the favorable plan, a plan that was the clear message of his vision-dream; having heard the words of the lord Ningirsu, he bowed his head . . . Now he was greatly wise and understood great things."

Losing no time Gudea proceeded to "purify the city" and organize the people of Lagash, old and young, to form work brigades and enlist themselves in the solemn task. In verses that throw light on the human side of the story, of life and manners and social problems more than four millennia ago, we read that as a way to consecrate themselves for the unique undertaking "the whip of the overseer was prohibited, the mother did not chide her child . . . a maid who had done a great wrong was not struck by her mistress in the face." But the people were asked not only to become angelic; to finance the project, Gudea "levied taxes in the land; as a submission to the lord Ningirsu the taxes were increased" . . .

One can stop here for a moment to look ahead to another construction of a God's Residence, the one built in the wilderness of Sinai for Yahweh. The subject is recorded in detail in the Book of Exodus, beginning in chapter 25. "Speak unto the Children of Israel," Yahweh told Moses, "that they may bring for me a contribution: from every man whose heart shall prompt him thereto shall be taken an allotment for me . . . and they shall build for me a sacred sanctuary, and I shall dwell in their midst. In accordance with all that which I am showing thee, the plan of the Residence and the pattern of all the instruments thereof shall ye make it." Then followed the most detailed architectural instructions—details which make possible the reconstructions of the Residence and its components by modern scholars.

To help Moses carry out these detailed plans, Yahweh decided to provide Moses with two assistants whom Yahweh was to endow with a "divine spirit"—"wisdom and understanding and knowledge of all manner of workmanship." Two men were chosen by Yahweh to be so instructed,

Bezalel and Aholiab, "to carry out all of the sacred work in all of the manner that Yahweh had ordered." These instructions began with the layout plan of the Residence and make clear that it was a rectangular enclosure with its long sides (one hundred cubits) facing precisely south and north and its short sides (fifty cubits in length) facing precisely east and west, creating an east–west axis of orientation (see Fig. 44a).

By now "greatly wise" and "understanding great things," Gudea—to go back to Sumer some seven centuries before the Exodus—launched the execution of the divine instructions in a grand way. By canal and river he sent out boats, "holy ships on which the emblem of Nanshe was raised," to summon assistance from her followers; he sent caravans of cattle and asses to the lands of Inanna, with her emblem of the "star-disk" carried in front; he enlisted the men of Utu, "the god whom he loves." As a result, "Elamites came from Elam, Susians came from Susa; Magan (Egypt) and Melukhah (Nubia) sent a large tribute from their mountains." Cedars were brought from Lebanon, bronze was collected, shiploads of stones arrived. Copper, gold, silver, and marble were obtained.

When all that was ready, it was time to make the bricks of clay. This was no small undertaking, not only because tens of thousands of bricks were needed. The bricks—one of the Sumerian "firsts" which, in a land short of stones, enabled them to build high-rise buildings—were not of the shape and size that we use nowadays: they were usually square, a foot or more on each side and two or three inches thick. They were not identical in all places at all times; they were sometimes just sun-dried, sometimes dried in kilns for durability; they were not always flat, but sometimes concave or convex, as their function required, to withstand structural stress. As is clear from Gudea's as well as other kings' inscriptions, when it came to temples, and even more so to ziggurats, it was the god in charge who determined the size and shape of the bricks; this was such an important step in the construction, and such an honor for the king to mold the first brick, that the kings embedded in the wet bricks a

stamped inscription (Fig. 75) with a votive content. This
custom, fortunately, made it possible for archaeologists to
identify so many of the kings involved in the construction,
reconstruction, or repair of the temples.

Gudea devoted many lines in his inscriptions to the subject
of the bricks. It was a ceremony attended by several gods
and was held on the grounds of the old temple. Gudea
prepared himself by spending the night in the sanctuary,
then bathing clean and putting on special clothes in the
morning. Throughout the land it was a solemn rest day.
Gudea offered sacrifices, then went into the old Holy of
Holies; there was the brick mold that the god had shown
him in the vision-dream and a "holy carrying-basket." Gudea put the basket on his head. A god named Galalim led
the procession. The god Ningishzidda held the brick-mold
in his hand. He let Gudea pour into the mold water from
the temple's copper cup, as a good omen. On a signal from
Ninurta, Gudea poured clay into the mold, all the while
uttering incantations. Reverently, the inscription says, he
carried out the holy rites. The whole city of Lagash "was
lying low," waiting for the outcome: will the brick come
out right or will it be faulty?

Figure 75

After the sun had shone upon the mold
Gudea broke the mold,
he separated the brick.
The bottom face of the stamped clay he saw;
with a faithful eye he examined it.

The brick was perfect!

He carried the brick to the temple,
the brick raised from the mold.
Like a brilliant diadem he raised it to heaven;
he carried it to the people and raised it.
He put the brick down in the temple;
it was solid and firm.
And the heart of the king
was made as bright as the day.

Ancient, even archaic, Sumerian depictions have been found dealing with the brick ceremony; one of them (Fig. 76) shows a seated deity holding up the Holy Mold, bricks from which are carried to construct a ziggurat.

The time has thus come to start building the temple; and the first step was to mark out its orientation and implant the foundation stone. Gudea wrote that a new place was chosen for the new Eninnu, and archaeologists (see map, Fig. 73) have indeed found its remains on a hill about fifteen hundred feet away from the earlier one, on the mound marked "A" on the excavations map.

We know from these remains that the ziggurat was built

Figure 76

so that its corners would be oriented to the cardinal points; the precise orientation was obtained by first determining true east, then running one or more walls at right angles to each other. This ceremony too was done on an auspicious day for which "the full year" had to come to pass. The day was announced by the goddess Nanshe: "Nanshe, a child of Eridu" (the city of Enki) "commanded the fulfillment of the ascertained oracle." It is our guess that it was the Day of the Equinox.

At midday, "when the Sun came fully forth," the "Lord of the Observers, a Master Builder, stationed at the temple, the direction carefully planned." As the Anunnaki were watching the procedure of determining the orientation "with much admiration," he "laid the foundation stone and marked in the earth the wall's direction." We read later on in the inscription that this Lord of the Observers, the Master Builder, was Ningishzidda; and we know from various depictions (Fig. 77) that it was a deity (recognized by his horned cap) who implanted the conical cornerstone on such occasions.

Apart from depictions of the ceremony, showing a god with the horned headdress implanting the conical "stone," such representations cast in bronze suggest that the "stone" was actually a bronze one; the use of the term "stone" is not unusual, since all metals resulting from quarrying and mining were named with the prefix NA, meaning "stone" or "that which is mined." In this regard it is noteworthy that in the Bible the laying of the corner or First Stone was also considered a divine or divinely inspired act signifying the Lord's blessing to the new House. In the prophecy by Zechariah about the rebuilding of the Temple in Jerusalem, he relates how Yahweh showed him in a vision "a man holding a measuring cord in his hand," and how he was told that this divine emissary would come to measure the four sides of a rebuilt and greater Jerusalem with its new Lord's House, whose stones shall rise sevenfold after the Lord will place for him the First Stone. "And when they shall see the bronze stone in the hands of Zerubbabel" (the one chosen by Yahweh to rebuild the Temple) all nations

Figure 77

will know that it was the Lord's will. On that occasion too the men chosen to carry out the temple's rebuilding were named by Yahweh.

In Lagash, once the cornerstone was embedded by the god Ningishzidda, Gudea was able to lay the temple's foundations, by now "like Nisaba knowing the meaning of numbers."

The ziggurat built by Gudea, scholars have concluded, was one of seven stages. Accordingly, seven blessings were pronounced as soon as the laying of the foundation stone was completed and the temple's orientation set and Gudea began to place the bricks along the marking on the ground:

> *May the bricks rest peacefully!*
> *May the House by its plan rise high!*
> *May the divine Black Storm Bird*

be as a young eagle!
May it be like a young lion awesome!
May the House have the brilliance of Heaven!
May joy abound at the prescribed sacrifices!
May Eninnu be a light unto the world!

Then did Gudea begin to build the "House, a dwelling he established for his lord Ningirsu . . . a temple truly a Heaven-Earth mountain, its head reaching heavenward . . . Joyfully did Gudea erect the Eninnu with Sumer's firm bricks; the great temple he thus constructed."

With no stones to be quarried in Mesopotamia, the "Land between the rivers" which was covered with an avalanche of mud during the Deluge, the only building materials were the mud or clay bricks, and all the temples and ziggurats were so built. The statement by Gudea that the Eninnu was erected "with Sumer's firm bricks" is thus a mere statement of fact. What is puzzling is the detailed list by Gudea of other materials used in the construction. We refer here not to the various woods and timbers, which were commonly used in temple constructions, but to the variety of metals and stones employed in the project—materials all of which had to be imported from afar.

The king, we read in the inscriptions, "the Righteous Shepherd," "built the temple bright with metal" bringing copper, gold, and silver from distant lands. "He built the Eninnu with stone, he made it bright with jewels; with copper mixed with tin he held it fast." This is undoubtedly a reference to bronze which, in addition to its use for various listed artifacts, apparently was also used to clamp together stone blocks and metals. The making of bronze, a complex process involving the mixing of copper and tin under great heat in specified proportions, was quite an art; and indeed Gudea's inscription makes it clear that for the purpose a *Sangu Simug,* a "priestly smith," working for the god Nintud, was brought over from the "Land of smelting." This priestly smith, the inscription adds, "worked on the temple's facade; with two handbreadths of bright stone he faced over the brickwork; with diorite and one handbreadth of bright stone he . . . '' (the inscription is too damaged here to be legible).

Not just the mere quantity of stones used in the Eninnu but the outright statement that the brickwork was faced with bright stone of a certain thickness—a statement that until now has not drawn the attention of scholars—is nothing short of sensational. We know of no other instance of Sumerian records of temple construction that mention the facing or ''casing'' of brickwork with stones. Such inscriptions speak only of brickwork—its erection, its crumbling, its replacement—but *never of a stone facing* over the brick facade.

Incredibly—but as we shall show, not inexplicably—the facing of the new Eninnu with bright stones, unique in Sumer, emulated the *Egyptian* method of facing step-pyramids with bright stone casings to give them smooth sides!

The Egyptian pyramids that were built by pharaohs began with one built by King Zoser at Sakkara (south of Memphis) circa 2650 B.C. (Fig. 78). Rising in six steps within a rectangular sacred precinct, it was originally faced with bright limestone casing stones of which only traces now remain: its casing stones, as those of ensuing pyramids, were removed by later rulers to be used in their own monuments.

The Egyptian pyramids, as we have shown and proved in *The Stairway to Heaven,* began with those built by the Anunnaki themselves—the Great Pyramid and its two companions at Giza. It was they who devised the casing with bright stones of what were in their core step-pyramids, giving them their renowned smooth sides. That the new Eninnu in Lagash, commissioned by Ninurta at about the same time

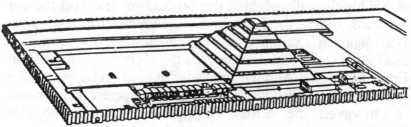

Figure 78

as Stonehenge became truly a *stone*-henge, emulated an Egyptian pyramid's stone facing, is a major clue for the resolution of the Stonehenge enigma.

Such an unexpected link to ancient Egypt, as we have been showing, was only one among many. Gudea himself was alluding to these connections when he stated that the shape of the Eninnu and its casing with bright stones were based on information provided by Nisaba "who was taught the plan of the temple by Enki" in the "House of Learning." That academy was undoubtedly in one of Enki's centers; and Egypt, it will be recalled, was the domain allotted to Enki and his descendants when Earth was divided.

The Eninnu project involved the participation of quite a number of gods; Nisaba, who had appeared to Gudea in the first vision with the star map, was not the only female among them. Let us look at the full list, then highlight the female roles.

First there was Enlil, who began the process by granting the permission to Ninurta to build the new temple. Then Ninurta appeared to Gudea, informing him of the divine decision and of his (Gudea's) selection to be the builder. In his vision Ningishzidda indicated to him the celestial point where the Sun rose, Nisaba pointed with a stylus to the favorable star, and Nindub drew the plan of the temple on a tablet. In order to understand all that, he consulted Nanshe, the oracle goddess. Inanna/Ishtar and Utu/Shamash enlisted their followers in obtaining the rare building materials. Ningishzidda, with the participation of a god named Galalim, was involved in molding the bricks. Nanshe chose the auspicious day on which to start the construction. Ningishzidda then determined the orientation and laid the cornerstone. Before the Eninnu was declared fit for its purpose, Utu/Shamash examined its alignment with the Sun. The individual shrines built alongside the ziggurat honored Anu, Enlil, and Enki. And the final purification and consecration rites, before Ninurta/Ningirsu and his spouse Bau moved in, involved the deities Ninmada, Enki, Nindub, and Nanshe.

Astronomy clearly played a key role in the Eninnu project; and two of the deities involved, Nanshe and Nisaba, were female astronomer-gods. They applied their specialized knowledge of astronomy, mathematics, and metrology not only to temple construction (as in Gudea's case), but also to general productive purposes as well as in ritual roles. One, however, was trained in the academy of Eridu; the other in that of Nippur.

Nanshe, who identified for Gudea the celestial role of each of the deities that appeared to him in his vision and determined the precise calendrical day (of the equinox) for orienting the temple, is called in the Gudea inscriptions "a daughter of Eridu" (Enki's city in Sumer). Indeed, in the major God Lists of Mesopotamia, she was called NIN.A— "Lady of Water"—and shown as a daughter of Ea/Enki. The planning of waterways and the locating of fountainheads were her specialty; her celestial counterpart was the constellation Scorpio—*mul GIR.TAB* in Sumerian. The knowledge she contributed to the building of the Eninnu in Lagash was thus that of the Enki'ite academies.

A hymn to Nanshe in her role as determiner of the New Year Day has her sitting in judgment on Mankind on that day, accompanied by Nisaba in the role of Divine Accountant who tallies and measures the sins of those who are judged, such as the sin of he "who substituted a small weight for a large weight, a small measure for a large measure." But while the two goddesses were frequently mentioned together, Nisaba (some scholars read her name Nidaba) was clearly listed among the Enlilites, and was sometimes identified as a half sister of Ninurta/Ningirsu. Although she was in later times deemed to be a goddess who blesses the crops—perhaps because of her association with the calendar and weather—she was described in Sumerian literature as one who "opens men's ears," i.e. teaches them wisdom. In one of several School Essays compiled by Samuel N. Kramer (*The Sumerians*) from scattered fragments, the *Ummia* ("Word-knower") names Nisaba as the patron goddess of the E.DUB.BA ("House of Inscribed Tablets"), Sumer's principal academy for scribal arts. Kramer called her "the Sumerian goddess of Wisdom."

Nisaba was, in the words of D.O. Edzard (*Götter und Mythen im Vorderen Orient*), the Sumerian goddess of "the art of writing, mathematics, science, architecture and astronomy." Gudea specifically described her as the "goddess who knows numbers"—a female "Einstein" of antiquity . . .

The emblem of Nisaba was the Holy Stylus. A short hymn to Nisaba on a tablet unearthed in the ruins of the sacred precinct of Lagash (Fig. 79) describes her as "she who acquired fifty great ME's" and as possessor of the "stylus of seven numbers." Both numbers were associated with Enlil and Ninurta: the numerical rank of both was fifty, and one of Enlil's epithets (as commander of Earth, the seventh planet) was "Lord of Seven."

With her Holy Stylus Nisaba pointed out to Gudea the "favorite star" on the "star tablet" that she held on her knees; the implication is that the star tablet had drawn on it more than one star, so that the correct one for the orientation had to be pointed out from among several stars. This conclusion is strengthened by the statement in *The Blessing of Nisaba by Enki* that Enki had given her as part

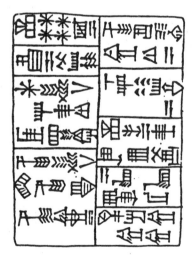

Figure 79

of her schooling "the holy tablet of the heavenly stars"—again "stars" in the plural.

The term MUL in Sumerian (*Kakkab* in Akkadian), meaning "celestial body," was applied to both planets and stars, and one wonders what heavenly bodies were shown on the star map possessed by Nisaba, whether they were stars or planets or (probably) both. The opening line of the text shown in Fig. 79, paying homage to Nisaba as a great astronomer, calls her NIN MUL.MUL.LA—"Lady of Many Stars." The intriguing aspect of this formulation is that the term "many stars" is written not with a star sign together with the determinative sign for "many," but with four star signs. The only plausible explanation for this unusual formulation is that Nisaba could point out, on her sky map, the four stars that we continue to use for determining the cardinal points.

Her great wisdom and scientific knowledge were expressed in Sumerian hymns by the statement that she was "perfected with the fifty great ME's"—those enigmatic "divine formulas" that, like computer disks, were small enough to be carried by hand though each contained a vast amount of information. Inanna/Ishtar, a Sumerian text related, went to Eridu and tricked Enki into giving her one hundred of them. Nisaba, on the other hand, did not have to steal the fifty ME's. A poetic text compiled from fragments and rendered into English by William W. Hallo (in a lecture titled "The Cultic Setting of Sumerian Poetry") that he called *The Blessing of Nisaba by Enki*, makes clear that in addition to her Enlilite schooling Nisaba was also a graduate of the Eridu academy of Enki. Extolling Nisaba as "Chief scribe of heaven, record-keeper of Enlil, all-knowing sage of the gods" and exalting Enki, "the craftsman of Eridu" and his "House of Learning," the hymn says of Enki:

He verily opened the House of Learning for Nisaba;
He verily placed the lapis lazuli tablet on her knee,
to take counsel with the holy tablet of the heavenly stars.

The "cult city" of Nisaba was called Eresh ("Foremost Abode"); its remains or location were never discovered in Mesopotamia. The fifth stanza of this poem suggests that it was located in the "Lower World" (*Abzu*) of Africa, where Enki oversaw the mining and metallurgical operations and conducted his experiments in genetics. Listing the various distant locations where Nisaba was also schooled under Enki's aegis, the poem states:

> *Eresh he constructed for her,*
> *in abundance created of pure little bricks.*
> *She is granted wisdom of the highest degree*
> *in the Abzu, great place of Eridu's crown.*

A cousin of Nisaba, the goddess ERESH.KI.GAL ("Foremost Abode in the Great Place"), was in charge of a scientific station in southern Africa and there shared control of a Tablet of Wisdom with Nergal, a son of Enki, as a marriage dowry. It is quite possible that it was there that Nisaba acquired her additional schooling.

This analysis of Nisaba's attributes can help us to identify the deity—let us call her Goddess of Astronomers—appearing on an Assyrian tablet (Fig. 80). She is shown inside

Figure 80

a gateway surmounted by the stepped viewing positions. She holds a pole-mounted viewing instrument, identified here by the crescent as one for viewing the Moon's movements, i.e. for calendrical purposes. And she is further identified by the four stars—the symbol, we believe, of Nisaba.

One of the oddest statements made by Gudea when he described the deities who appeared to him concerned Nisaba: "The image of a temple-structure, a ziggurat, she carried on her head." The headdress of Mesopotamian deities was distinguished by its pairs of horns; that gods or goddesses would instead wear on their heads the image of a temple or an object was absolutely unheard of. Yet, in his inscription, that is how Gudea described Nisaba.

He was not imagining things. If we examine illustration 80, we will see that Nisaba is indeed carrying on her head the image of a temple-ziggurat, just as Gudea had stated. But it is not a stepped structure; rather, it is the image of a smooth-sided pyramid—an *Egyptian* pyramid!

Moreover, not only is the ziggurat Egyptianized—the very custom of wearing such an image on the head is Egyptian, especially as it applied to Egyptian goddesses. Foremost of them were Isis, the sister-wife of Osiris (Fig. 81a) and Nephtys, their sister (Fig. 81b).

Was Nisaba, an Enlilite goddess schooled in Enki's academy, Egyptianized enough to be wearing this kind of headgear? As we pursue this investigation, many similarities between Nisaba and Sesheta, the female assistant of Thoth in Egypt, come to light. In addition to the attributes and function of Sesheta that we have already reviewed, there were others that closely matched those of Nisaba. They included her role as "the goddess of the arts of writing and of science," in the words of Hermann Kees (*Der Götterglaube in Alten Aegypten*). Nisaba possessed the "stylus of seven numbers"; Sesheta too was associated with the number seven. One of her epithets was "Sesheta means seven" and her name was often written hieroglyphically by the sign for seven placed above a bow. Like Nisaba, who had appeared to Gudea with the image of a temple-structure on

Figures 81a and 81b

her head, so was Sesheta depicted with the image of a twin-towered structure on her head, above her identifying star-and-bow symbol (Fig. 82). She was a "daughter of the sky," a chronologer and chronographer; and like Nisaba, she determined the required astronomical data for the royal-temple builders.

According to the Sumerian texts, the consort of Nisaba was a god called *Haia*. Hardly anything is known of him, except that in the judgment procedures on New Year's Day supervised by Nanshe, he was also present, acting as the balancer of the scales. In Egyptian beliefs Judgment Day for the pharaoh was when he died, at which time his heart was weighed to determine his fate in the Afterlife. In Egyptian theology, the god who balanced the scales was Thoth, the god of science, astronomy, the calendar, and of writing and record keeping.

Such an overlapping of identities between the deities who provided the astronomical and calendrical knowledge for the Eninnu reveals an otherwise unknown state of cooperation between the Sumerian and Egyptian Divine Architects in Gudea's time.

It was, in many respects, an unusual phenomenon; it found expression in the unique shape and appearance of the

Figure 82

Eninnu and in the establishment within its sacred precinct of an extraordinary astronomical facility. It all involved and revolved around the calendar—the gift to Mankind by the divine Keepers of the Secrets.

After the construction of the Eninnu ziggurat was completed, much effort and artistry went into its adorning, not only outside but also inside; portions, we learn, of the "inner shrine" were overlaid with "cedar panels, attractive to the eye." Outside, rare trees and bushes were planted to create a pleasant garden. A pool was built and filled with rare fish—another unusual feature in Sumerian temple precincts and one which is akin to Egyptian ones, where a sacred pool was a common feature.

"The dream," Gudea wrote, "was fulfilled." The Eninnu was completed, "like a bright mass it stands, a radiant brightness of its facing covers everything; like a mountain which glows it joyously rises.''

Now he turned his attention and efforts to the Girsu, the sacred precinct as such. A ravine, ''a great dump'' was filled up: ''with the wisdom granted by Enki divinely he did the grading, enlarging the area of the temple terrace.'' Cylinder A alone lists more than fifty separate shrines and temples built adjoining the ziggurat to honor the various gods involved in the project as well as Anu, Enlil, and Enki. There were enclosures, service buildings, courts, altars, gates; residences for the various priests; and, of course, the special dwelling and sleeping quarters of Ningirsu/Ninurta and his spouse Bau.

There were also special enclosures or facilities for housing the Divine Black Bird, the aircraft of Ninurta, and for his awesome weapons; as well as places at which the astronomical-calendrical functions of the new Eninnu were to be performed. There was a special place for ''the Master of Secrets,'' and the new *Shugalam,* the high place of the aperture, the ''place of determining whose awesomeness is great, where the Brilliance is announced.'' And there were two buildings connected with the ''solving of the cords'' and the ''binding with the cords'' respectively— facilities whose purpose has eluded scholars but which had to be connected with celestial observations, for they were located next to, or were part of, the structures called ''Uppermost Chamber'' and ''Chamber of the seven zones.''

There were certain other features that were added to the new Eninnu and its sacred precinct that indeed made it as unique as Gudea had boasted; we shall discuss them in the detail they deserve further on. There was also a need, as the text makes clear, to await a certain specific day—New Year's Day, to be precise—before Ninurta and his spouse Bau could actually move into the new Eninnu and make it their dwelling abode.

Whereas Cylinder A was devoted to the events leading to the construction of the Eninnu and the construction itself, Gudea's inscriptions on Cylinder B deal with the rites con-

nected with the consecration of the new ziggurat and its
sacred precinct and the ceremonies involved in the actual
arrival of Ninurta and Bau in the *Girsu*—reaffirming his
title as NIN.GIRSU, "Lord of Girsu"—and their entry into
their new dwelling place. The astronomical and calendrical
aspects of these rites and ceremonies enhance the data with
which the Cylinder A inscriptions are filled.

While the arrival of the inauguration day was awaited—
for the better part of a year—Gudea engaged in daily prayers, the pouring of libations, and the filling up of the new
temple's granaries with food from the fields and its cattle
pens with sheep from the pastures. Finally the designated
day arrived:

> *The year went round,*
> *the months were completed;*
> *the New Year came in the heavens—*
> *the "Month of the Temple" began.*

On that day, as the "new Moon was born," the dedication
ceremonies began. The gods themselves performed the purification and consecration rites: "Ninmada performed the
purification; Enki granted a special oracle; Nindub spread
incense; Nanshe, the Mistress of Oracles, sang holy hymns;
they consecrated the Eninnu, made it holy."

The third day, Gudea recorded, was a bright day. It was
on that day that Ninurta stepped out—"with a bright radiance he shone." As he entered the new sacred precinct,
"the goddess Bau was advancing on his left side." Gudea
"sprinkled the ground with an abundance of oil . . . he
brought forth honey, butter, wine, milk, grain, olive oil . . .
dates and grapes he piled up in a heap—food untouched by
fire, food for the eating by the gods."

The entertainment of the divine couple and the other gods
with fruits and other uncooked foods went on until midday.
"When the Sun rose high over the country" Gudea "slaughtered a fat ox and a fat sheep" and a feast of roasted meats
with much wine began; "white bread and milk they brought
by day and through the night"; and "Ninurta, the warrior

of Enlil, taking food and beer for drink, was satisfied.'' All the while Gudea ''made the whole city kneel, he made the whole country prostrate itself . . . By day there were petitions, by night prayers.''

''At the morning aurora''—at dawn—''Ningirsu, the warrior, entered the Temple; into the Temple its lord came; giving a shout like the cry of battle, Ningirsu advanced into his temple.'' ''It was,'' observed Gudea, ''like the rising of the Sun over the land of Lagash . . . and the Land of Lagash rejoiced.'' It was also the day on which the harvest began:

> *On that day,*
> *when the Righteous God entered,*
> *Gudea, on that day,*
> *began to harvest the fields.*

Following a decree of Ninurta and the goddess Nanshe, there followed seven days of repentance and atonement in the land. ''For seven days the maid and her mistress were equal, master and slave walked side by side . . . of the evil tongue the word was changed to good . . . the rich man did not wrong the orphan, no man oppressed the widow . . . the city restrained wickedness.'' At the end of the seven days, on the tenth day of the month, Gudea entered the new temple and for the first time performed there the rites of the High Priest, ''lighting the fire in the temple-terrace before the bright heavens.''

A depiction on a cylinder seal from the second millennium B.C., found at Ashur, may well have preserved for us the scene that had taken place a thousand years earlier in Lagash: it shows a High Priest (who as often as not was also the king, as in the case of Gudea) lighting a fire on an altar as he faces the god's ziggurat, while the ''favorite planet'' is seen in the heavens (Fig. 83).

On the altar, ''before the bright heavens, the fire on the temple-terrace increased.'' Gudea ''oxen and kids sacrificed in numbers.'' From a lead bowl he poured a libation. ''For the city below the temple he pleaded.'' He swore everlasting

Figure 83

allegiance to Ningirsu, "by the bricks of Eninnu he swore, a favorable oath he swore."

And the god Ninurta, promising Lagash and its people abundance, that "the land may bear whatever is good," to Gudea himself said: "Life shall be prolonged for thee."

Appropriately, the Cylinder B inscription concludes thus:

House, rising heavenward as a great mountain,
its luster powerfully falls on the land
as Anu and Enlil the fate of Lagash determine.

Eninnu, for Heaven-Earth constructed,
the lordship of Ningirsu
to all the lands it makes known.

O Ningirsu, thou art honored!
The House of Ningirsu is built;
Glory be unto it!

7

A STONEHENGE
ON THE EUPHRATES

There is a wealth of information in the inscriptions of Gudea; the more we study them and the special features of the Eninnu he built, the more astounded we shall be.

Perusing the texts verse by verse and visualizing the great new temple-terrace and its ziggurat, we shall discover amazing celestial features of the "Bond Heaven-Earth"; one of the earliest if not the very earliest association of a temple with the zodiac; the appearance of sphinxes in Sumer at a totally unexpected time; an array of links with Egypt and especially with one of its gods; and a "mini-Stonehenge" in the Land Between the Rivers . . .

Let us begin with the first task Gudea undertook after the construction of the ziggurat was completed and the temple-terrace formed. It was the erection of seven upright stone pillars at seven carefully selected positions. Gudea, the inscription states, made sure that they be firmly erected: he "laid them on a foundation, on bases he erected them."

The stelae (as scholars call these upright stones) must have been of great importance, for Gudea spent a full year in bringing the rough stone blocks, from which the uprights were carved to shape, from a distant source to Lagash; and another year to cut and shape them. But then, in a frenzied effort that lasted a precise seven days during which the work was carried out without stopping, without rest, the seven stelae were set up in their proper places. If, as the information given suggests, the seven stelae were positioned in some astronomical alignment, then the speed becomes understandable, for the longer the setting up would have taken, the more misaligned the celestial bodies would have become.

Signifying the importance of the stelae and their position is the fact that Gudea gave each one a "name" made up of a long sacred utterance evidently related to the position of the stela (e.g. "on the lofty terrace," facing the "gate of the river-bank" or another one "opposite the shrine of Anu"). Although the inscription stated unequivocally (column XXIX line 1) that "seven stelae were erected" in those seven hectic days, the names of only six locations are given. In respect to one, presumably the seventh stela, the inscription states that it "was erected toward the rising sun." Since by then all the required orientations of the Eninnu had already been fixed, starting with the divine instructions and the laying of the cornerstone by Ningishzidda, neither the six spread out stelae nor the seventh "erected toward the rising sun" were required for orienting the temple. Another, different purpose had to be the motive; the only logical conclusion is that it involved observations other than determining the Day of the Equinox (i.e. of the New Year)— some astronomical-calendrical observations of an unusual nature, justifying the great effort in obtaining and shaping the stelae and the haste in setting them up.

The enigma of these erected stone pillars begins with the question, why so many when two are enough to create a line of sight, say toward the rising Sun. The puzzle is engulfed by incredulity when we read on in the inscription the sensational statement that the six whose locations were named were placed by Gudea *"in a circle."* Did Gudea use the stelae to form a stone *henge*—in ancient Sumer, more than five thousand years ago?

Gudea's inscription indicates, according to A. Falkenstein (*Die Inschriften Gudeas von Lagash*), the existence of an avenue or pathway which—as at Stonehenge!—could provide an unimpeded sightline. He noted that the stela which was "toward the rising Sun" stood at one end of a pathway or avenue called "Way to the high position." At the other end of this way was the *Shugalam*, the "High place whose awesomeness is great, where the Brilliance is raised.'' The term SHU.GALAM meant, according to Falkenstein, ''Where the hand is raised''—a high place from which a signal is given. Indeed, the Cylinder A inscription asserts that ''At the radiant entrance of Shugalam, Gudea stationed a favorable image; toward the rising Sun, in the destined place, the emblem of the Sun he established.''

We have already discussed the functions of the *Shugalam* when Gudea had gone to it, in the old temple, to remove the mortar or mud that obstructed the view through it. It was, we found, ''the place of the aperture, the place of determining.'' There, the inscription stated, ''Ninurta could see the repetitions''—the annual celestial cycle—''over his lands.'' The description brings to mind the ceiling aperture about which there was so much arguing on Mount Zaphon between Ba'al and the divine architect who came from Egypt to design the new temple in Lebanon.

Some additional light on the enigmatic purpose of such a skylight or aperture in the ceiling can be obtained from the examination of the Hebrew term for such a contraption and its Akkadian roots. It is *Tzohar* and appears just once in the Bible to describe the only aperture in the ceiling of the otherwise hermetically sealed Noah's Ark. The meaning, all agree, is ''a ceiling window through which a beam of light can shine in.'' In modern Hebrew the term is also used to denote ''zenith,'' the point in the sky directly overhead; and both in modern Hebrew and biblical texts the term *Tzohora'im* that derived from it meant and still means ''midday,'' when the Sun is directly overhead. *Tzohar* was thus not just a simple aperture, but one intended to let a beam of the Sun shine into a darkened enclosure at a certain time of the day; spelled slightly differently, *Zohar*, the term acquired the meaning ''brightness, brilliance.'' All stem from the Akkadian, the mother tongue of all the Semitic languages, in which the words *tzirru, tzurru* meant ''lighten up, shine'' and ''be high.''

At the *Shugalam*, Gudea wrote, he ''fixed the image of the Sun.'' All the evidence suggests that it was a viewing device through which the rising Sun—undoubtedly on Equi-

nox Day, to judge from all the data in the inscriptions—
was observed to determine and announce the arrival of the
New Year.

Was the concept underlying the structural arrangement
the same as (possibly) the one on Mount Zaphon and (certainly) as at the Egyptian temples, where a beam of sunlight
passed along the preselected axis to light up the Holy of
Holies at sunrise on the prescribed day?

In Egypt the Sun Temples were flanked by two obelisks
(Fig. 84) which the pharaohs erected so that they might
be granted long life; their function was to guide the Sun's
beam on the prescribed day. E.A. Wallis Budge (*The
Egyptian Obelisk*) pointed out that the pharaohs, such as
Ramses II and Queen Hatshepsut, always set up these
obelisks in pairs. Queen Hatshepsut even wrote her royal
name (within a cartouche) between two obelisks (Fig. 85a)
to imply that the Blessed Beam of Ra shone on her on
the crucial day.

Scholars have noted that Solomon's Temple also had two
pillars erected at its entrance (Fig. 85c); like the uprights
at the Eninnu which were given names by Gudea, so were
the two pillars named by Solomon:

> *And he set up the pillars*
> *in the porch of the temple.*
> *He set up the right pillar*

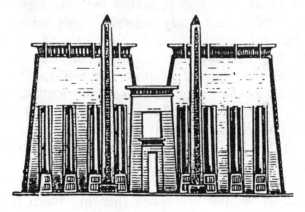

Figure 84

> *and called the name thereof* Yakhin;
> *and he set up the left pillar*
> *and called the name thereof* Bo'az.

While the meaning of the two names eludes scholars (the best assumption is "Yahweh makes firm" and "In him is strength"), the shape, height, and makeup of the pillars is described in the Bible (mainly I Kings chapter 7) in detail. The two pillars were made of cast bronze, eighteen cubits (some twenty-seven feet) high. Each pillar supported a complex "headband" around which, as a crown, there was placed a corolla whose serrated top created seven protrusions; one of them (or both, depending on the way the verse is read) was "encircled by a cord twelve cubits long." (Twelve and seven are the predominant numbers in the Temple.)

The Bible does not state the purpose of these pillars, and theories have ranged from purely decorative or symbolic to a function akin to that of the pair of obelisks that flanked the entrances to the temples in Egypt. In this regard a clue is suggested by the Egyptian word for "obelisk," which was *Tekhen*. The term, Budge wrote, "was a very old word, and we find it in the dual in the Pyramid Texts which were written before the close of the VIth Dynasty." As to the meaning of the word, which he did not know, he added: "The exact meaning of *Tekhen* is unknown to us and it is probable that the Egyptians had forgotten it at a very early period." This raises the possibility that the word was a foreign term, a "loanword" from another language or country, and we on our part believe that the source, of both the biblical *Yakhin* and the Egyptian *Tekhen* was the Akkadian root *khunnu* which meant "to establish correctly" as well as "to start a light" (or fire). The Akkadian term may even be traced back to the earlier Sumerian term GUNNU which combined the meanings "daylight" with "tube, pipe."

These linguistic clues sit well with earlier Sumerian depictions of temple entrances showing them flanked by pillars to which circular devices were attached (Fig. 85b).

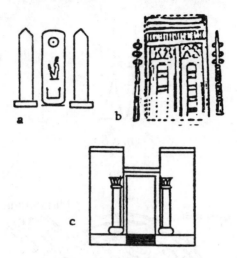

Figures 85a, 85b, and 85c

These must have been the forerunners of all such pairs of uprights, pillars, or obelisks elsewhere, for they appear on the Sumerian depictions millennia before the others. The search for answers to the puzzle of these uprights is further assisted by examining the term used by Gudea in his inscriptions to describe the stone uprights. He called all seven of them NE.RU—from which the Hebrew word *Ner,* meaning "candle," stems. Sumerian script evolved by the scribe's making wedgelike markings with a stylus on wet clay to emulate the original drawing of the object or action for which the sign stood. We find that the original pictograph for the term *Neru* was that of two—two, not one—pillars set upon stable bases with antennalike protrusions (Fig. 86).

Such paired pillars, guiding (actually or symbolically) the Sun's beam on a specific day were sufficient if only one solar position—equinoctial *or* solstitial—was involved. If such a single determination was intended at the Girsu, two stelae, in alignment with the Shugalam, would have sufficed. But Gudea set up seven of them, six in a circle and the seventh in alignment with the Sun. To form a line of sight, this odd pillar could have been positioned either in the circle's center, or outside of it in the avenue. Either

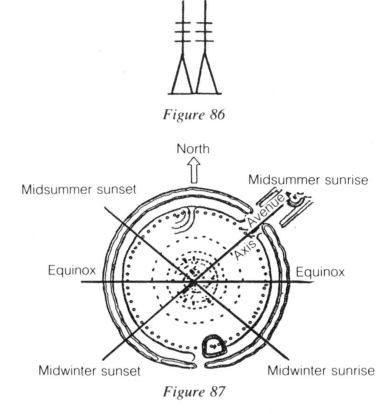

Figure 86

Figure 87

way, the outcome would indicate uncanny similarities to Stonehenge in the British Isles.

Six outer or circumference points with one in the center would have created a layout (Fig. 87) that, as in Stonehenge II—belonging to the same time—provided alignments not only with the equinoxes but also with the four solstice points (midsummer sunrise and sunset, midwinter sunrise and sunset). Since the Mesopotamian New Year was firmly anchored to the equinoxes, resulting in ziggurats whose determining corner was oriented to the east, an arrangement of stone pillars that incorporated fixings of the solstices was a major innovation. It also indicated a decisive "Egyptian" influence, for it was at Egyptian temples that an orientation linked to the solstices was the dominant feature—certainly by Gudea's time.

If, as Falkenstein's study suggests, the seventh pillar was not within the circle of six stelae but outside of it—in the pathway or avenue leading to the Shugalam, an even more astounding similarity emerges, not to the later Stonehenge but to the earliest one, to Stonehenge I, where—we may recall—there were only seven stones: the four Station Stones forming a rectangle, two Gateway Stones that flanked the beginning of the Avenue, and the Heel Stone that marked out the sightline—an arrangement of seven stone uprights illustrated in Fig. 88. Since at Stonehenge the Aubrey Holes were part of phase I, the sightline could be easily determined by a viewer at hole 28 directing his gaze through a post inserted in hole 56, watching for the Sun to appear above the Heel Stone on the propitious day.

Such a similarity in layouts would be even more significant than the first alternative, for—as we have reported earlier—the rectangle formed by the four Station Stones implied lunar observations in addition to the solar ones. The realization of this rectangular arrangement led both Newham

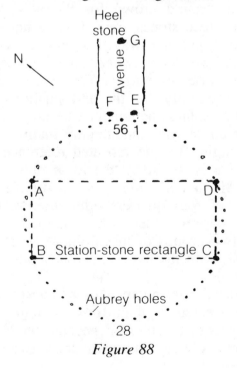

Figure 88

and Hawkins to far-reaching conclusions regarding the sophistication of the planners of Stonehenge I. But since Stonehenge I preceded the Eninnu by about seven centuries, the similarity would have to imply that whoever had planned the layout of the seven uprights in the Eninnu copied from whoever had planned Stonehenge I.

Such a kinship between the two structures, in two different parts of the world, seems incredible; it will, however, become credible as we bring to light more amazing aspects of Gudea's Eninnu.

The six-plus-one circle just described was not the only stone circle on the platform of the new Eninnu.

Boasting that he accomplished "great things" that called for unusual "wisdom" (scientific knowledge), Gudea proceeded to describe, after the section dealing with the stelae, the "crownlike circle for the new Moon"—a creation in stone so unique that "its name in the midst of the world he caused to brightly go forth." This second circle was arranged as a "round crown for the new Moon" and consisted of thirteen stones erected "like heroes in a network"—a most figurative way, it seems to us, to describe *a circle of upright stones connected at the top by lintels to form a "network" akin to the Trilithons at Stonehenge!*

While the possibility that the first smaller circle served lunar as well as solar functions can be only surmised, the second larger circle was undoubtedly intended to observe the Moon. Judging by the repeated references in the inscriptions to the New Moon, the lunar observations were geared to the Moon's monthly cycle, its waxing and waning in the course of four quarters. Our interpretation of the crownlike circle is reinforced by the statement that this circle consisted of two groups of megaliths—one of six and the other of seven, with the latter apparently more elevated or taller than the first.

At first glance the arrangement of *thirteen* (six plus seven) megaliths, connected at their tops by lintels to form a "crown," seems to be an error, because we expect to find only twelve pillars (which in a circle create twelve apertures) if the arrangement is related to the twelve months of the lunar phases. The presence of thirteen pillars, however, does make sense if account were taken of the need to add one month every now and then for intercalation purposes. If so, the amazing stone circles in the Girsu were also the first instance where calendars made of stone meshed to correlate the solar and lunar cycles.

(One wonders whether these stone circles in the Girsu somehow presaged the introduction of the seven-day week—a division of time whose origin has evaded scholars—the biblical week which totaled seven by adding the six days of creation to the final additional day of rest. The number seven appears twice, in the first arrangement of pillars and as part of the second circle; and it is quite possible that somehow days were counted according to either group, leading to a repetition of periods of seven days. Also, four phases of the Moon multiplied by the thirteen pillars would divide the year into fifty-two weeks of seven days each).

Whatever the astronomical-calendrical possibilities inherent in the two circles (and we have probably only touched upon the very basic ones), *it is evident that in the Girsu of Lagash a solar-lunar stone computer was put into operation.*

If all this begins to sound like a *"Stonehenge on the Euphrates"*—a mini-Stonehenge erected by a Sumerian king in the *Girsu* of Lagash at about the same time that Stonehenge in the British Isles became a truly stone circle circa 2100 B.C.—there is more to come. It was at that time that the second type of stone, the bluestones, was brought to the plain of Salisbury from a distant source. This too enhances the similarities: Gudea too hauled not one but two types of stones from a great distance, "from the stone mountains" of Magan (Egypt) and Melukhah (Nubia), both in Africa. We read in the inscription on Cylinder A that it took a full year to obtain these stone blocks from "stone mountains which no [Sumerian] king had entered before." To reach them, Gudea "into the mountains made a way, and their great stones he brought out in blocks; shiploads of *Hua* stones and *Lua* stones.''

Though the meaning of the names of the two types of stones remains undeciphered, their distant origin is clearly stated. Coming from two African sources, they were first transported by land via a new way made by Gudea, then carried by ships over sea routes to Lagash (which was connected to the Euphrates River by a navigable canal).

As at Salisbury Plain in the British Isles so was it in the Mesopotamian plain: stones hauled from afar, stones especially selected, set up in two circles. As at Stonehenge I, seven pillars played a key role; as in all the phases of Stonehenge in Lagash, too, a large megalith created the desired sightline toward the principal solar orientation. In both places a stone "computer" was created to serve as a solar-lunar observatory.

Were both, then, created by the same scientific genius, by the same Divine Architect—or were they simply the result of accumulated scientific traditions that found expression in similar structures?

While general scientific knowledge as applied to astronomy and the calendar undoubtedly played a role, the hand of a specific Divine Architect cannot be ignored. In earlier chapters we have pointed out the key difference in design between Stonehenge and all the other temples of the Old World: the former was based on circular formations to observe the heavens; the latter were all built with right angles (rectangular or square). This difference is evident not only in the general plan of the other temples but also in the several instances where stone uprights were found, emplaced in a pattern suggesting an astronomical-calendrical function. An outstanding example was found at Byblos, on a promontory overlooking the Mediterranean Sea. The Holy of Holies of its temple, square in shape, was flanked by upright stone monoliths. They were set up in alignments suggesting observations of equinoxes and solstices; but none were arranged in a circle. So apparently was the case at a Canaanite site, Gezer, near Jerusalem, where the discovery of a tablet inscribed with the full list of months and their agricultural activities may suggest the existence of a center for the study of the calendar. There too a row of upright monoliths indicates the existence in antiquity of a structure perhaps akin to that at Byblos; the remaining uprights, standing in a straight line, belie any circular arrangement.

The few known instances of monoliths arranged in a circle, somehow emulating the extraordinary circular arrangement at the Girsu, come to us from the Bible. Their rarity, however, points to a direct connection to Sumer in Gudea's time.

Knowledge of a circle of thirteen with an upright in the center emerges in the tale of Joseph, a great-grandson of Abraham, who kept annoying his eleven brothers by telling them of his dreams wherein they all bowed to him although he was the youngest. The dream that upset them most, leading them to get rid of him by selling him into slavery in Egypt, was the one in which, Joseph related, he saw "the Sun and the Moon and eleven stars bowing down to me," meaning his father and mother and eleven brothers.

Several centuries later, as the Israelites left Egypt for the Promised Land in Canaan, an actual stone circle—this time of twelve stones—was erected. In chapters 3 and 4 of the Book of Joshua the Bible describes the miraculous crossing of the Jordan River by the Israelites under the leadership of Joshua. As instructed by Yahweh, the heads of the twelve tribes erected twelve stones in the midst of the river; and as the priests carrying the Ark of the Covenant stepped into the waters and stood where the twelve stones were placed, the flow of the river's waters "was cut off" upstream and the dry river bed was exposed, enabling the Israelites to cross the Jordan on foot. As soon as the priests carrying the Ark stepped off the stones and carried the Ark across, "the waters of the Jordan returned to their place and flowed over its banks as they did before."

Then Yahweh ordered Joshua to take the twelve stones and erect them in a circle on the west side of the river, east of Jericho, as an everlasting commemoration of the miracle performed by Yahweh. The place where the twelve stones were erected was since then known as *Gilgal,* meaning "Place of the Circle."

Not only the establishment of the twelve-stone circle as a miraculous device is relevant here; so is the date of the event. We first learn in Chapter 3 that the time was "harvest time, when the waters of the Jordan overflow its banks." Then Chapter 4 is more specific: it was in the first month of the calendar, the month of the New Year; and it was on the tenth of that month—the very day on which the inauguration ceremonies were culminated in Lagash—that "the people left the Jordan and encamped at Gilgal, where Joshua erected the twelve stones brought up from the Jordan River."

These calendrical markers bear uncanny resemblance to similar data concerning the time when Gudea had erected the stone circles on the platform of the Girsu, after the Eninnu itself was completed. We read in the Gudea inscriptions that the day Ninurta and his spouse entered their new abode was the day when the harvest began in the land— matching the "harvest time" in the tale of Gilgal. Astronomy and the calendar converge in both tales, and both concern circular structures.

The emergence of traditions of stone circles among the descendants of Abraham can be traced, we believe, to Abraham himself and the identity of his father Terah. Dealing with the subject in great detail in *The Wars of Gods and Men,* we have concluded that Terah was an oracle priest of royal descent, raised and trained in Nippur. Based on biblical data we have calculated that he was born in 2193 B.C.; this means that Terah was an astronomer-priest in Nippur when Enlil authorized his son, Ninurta, to proceed with the building of the new Eninnu by Gudea.

Terah's son Abram (later renamed Abraham) was born, by our calculations, in 2123 B.C. and was ten years old when the family moved to Ur, where Terah was to serve as a liaison. The family stayed there until 2096 B.C. when it left Sumer for the Upper Euphrates region (a migration that later led to Abraham's settlement in Canaan). Abraham was by then well-versed in royal and priestly matters, including astronomy. Getting his education in the sacred precincts of Nippur and Ur just as the glories of the new Eninnu were talked about, he could not have missed learning of the wondrous stone circle of the Girsu; and this would explain the knowledge thereof by his descendants.

Where did the idea of a *circle* as a shape appropriate to astronomical observations—a shape that is the most outstanding feature of Stonehenge—come from? In our view, it came from the zodiac, the cycle of twelve constellations grouped around the Sun in the orbital plane (the Ecliptic) of the planets.

Earlier this century archaeologists uncovered in the Galilee, in northern Israel, the remains of synagogues dating to the decades and centuries immediately following the destruction of the Second Temple in Jerusalem by the Romans (in A.D. 70). To their surprise, a common feature of those synagogues was the decoration of their floors with intricate mosaic designs that included the signs of the zodiac. As this one from a place called Bet-Alpha shows (Fig. 89), the number—twelve—was the same as nowadays, the symbols were the same as now in use, and so were the names: written in a script no different from that of modern Hebrew, they begin (on the east) with *Taleh* for ram, Aries, flanked by *Shor* (bull) for Taurus and *Dagim* (fishes) for Pisces, and so on in the very same order that we continue to employ millennia later.

This zodiacal circle of what the Akkadians called *Manzallu* ("stations" of the Sun) was the source of the Hebrew term *Mazalot*, which came to denote "lucks." Therein lies the transition from the essential astronomical and calendrical nature of the zodiac to its astrological connotations—a transition that in time obscured the original significance of the zodiac and the role it played in the affairs of gods and men. Last but not least was its wondrous expression in the Eninnu that Gudea built.

The notion has prevailed, in spite of the facts, that the concept, names, and symbols of the zodiac were devised

Figure 89

by the Greeks, for the word is of Greek origin, meaning "animal circle." It is conceded that the inspiration for them may have come from Egypt, where the zodiac with its unaltered symbols, order, and names was certainly known (Fig. 90). In spite of the antiquity of some of the Egyptian depictions—including a magnificent one in the temple at Denderah, of which more later—the zodiac did not begin there. Studies such as the one by E.C. Krupp *(In Search of Ancient Astronomies)* have emphatically stated that "all available evidence indicates that the concept of the zodiac was not native to Egypt; instead, it is believed that the zodiac was imported to Egypt from Mesopotamia," at some unknown date. Greek savants, who had access to Egyptian art and traditions, had also attested in their writings that as far as astronomy was concerned, its knowledge came to them from the "Chaldeans," the astronomer-priests of Babylonia.

1. Aries. 2. Taurus. 3. Gemini.

4. Cancer. 5. Leo.

6. Virgo. 7. Libra. 8. Scorpio.

9. Sagittarius. 10. Capricorn.

11. Aquarius. 12. Pisces.

Figure 90

Archaeologists have found Babylonian astronomical tablets clearly marked off into twelve parts, each with its pertinent zodiacal symbol (Fig. 91). They may well represent the kind of sources that the Greek savants studied. Pictorially, however, the celestial symbols were carved on stones within a heavenly circle. Almost two thousands years before the circular zodiac of Bet-Alpha, Near Eastern rulers, especially in Babylon, invoked their gods on treaty documents; boundary stones *(Kudurru)* were emblazoned with the celestial symbols of these gods—planets and zodiacs—within the heavenly circle, embraced by an undulating serpent that represented the Milky Way (Fig. 92).

The zodiac, however, was begun, as far as Mankind is concerned, in Sumer. As we have undisputably shown in *The 12th Planet*, the Sumerians knew of, depicted (Fig. 93a) and named the zodiacal houses exactly as we still do six thousand years later:

Figure 91

Figure 92

GU.ANNA ("Heavenly Bull")—Taurus.
MASH.TAB.BA ("Twins")—Gemini.
DUB ("Pincers, Tongs")—the Crab (Cancer).
UR.GULA ("Lion")—Leo.
AB.SIN ("Whose Father was Sin")—the Maiden (Virgo).
ZI.BA.AN.NA ("Heavenly Fate")—the scales of Libra.
GIR.TAB ("The Clawer, the Cutter")—Scorpio.
PA.BIL ("Defender")—Archer (Sagittarius).
SUHUR.MASH ("Goat-fish")—Capricorn.
GU ("Lord of the Waters")—the Water Bearer (Aquarius).
SIM.MAH ("Fishes")—Pisces.
KU.MAL ("Field Dweller")—the Ram (Aries).

Overwhelming evidence demonstrates that the Sumerians were cognizant of the zodiacal ages—not only the names and images but the precessional cycle thereof—when the calendar was begun in Nippur, circa 3800 B.C., in the Age of Taurus. Willy Hartner, in his study titled "The Earliest History of the Constellations in the Near East" *(Journal of Near Eastern Studies),* analyzed the Sumerian pictorial evidence and concluded that numerous depictions of a bull nudging a lion (Fig. 93b, from the fourth millenium B.C.) or a lion pushing bulls (Fig. 93c, from about 3000 B.C.) are representations of the zodiacal time when the spring equinox, at which time the calendrical new year began, was in the constellation Taurus and the summer solstice occurred in the sign of Leo.

Alfred Jeremias *(The Old Testament in the Light of the Ancient Near East)* found textual evidence that the Sumerian zodiacal-calendrical "point zero" stood precisely between the Bull and the Twins (Gemini), from which he concluded that the zodiacal division of the heavens—inexplicably to him—was devised even before the Sumerian civilization began, in the Age of Gemini. Even more puzzling to scholars has been a Sumerian astronomical tablet (VAT.7847 in the Berlin Vorderasiatisches Museum) that begins the list of zodiacal constellations with that of

Figures 93a, 93b, and 93c

Leo—taking one back to circa 11000 B.C., just about the time of the Deluge.

Devised by the Anunnaki as a link between Divine Time (the cycle based on the 3,600 years orbit of Nibiru) and Earthly Time (the Earth's orbital period), the Celestial Time (the time span of 2,160 years for the precessional shift from one zodiacal House to another) served to date major events in Earth's prehistory as archaeoastronomy could do in historical times. Thus, a depiction of the Anunnaki as astronauts and a spacecraft coursing between Mars (the six-pointed star) and Earth (identified by the seven dots and the accompanying crescent of the Moon) places the event, time-wise, in the Age of Pisces by including the zodiacal symbol of the two fishes in the depiction (Fig. 94). Written texts also included zodiacal dates; a text placing the Deluge in the Age of Leo is one example.

Even if we cannot be certain precisely when Mankind

Figure 94

was made aware of the zodiac, clearly it was long before
Gudea's time. Hence it should not surprise us to discover
that zodiacal depictions were indeed present in the new
temple in Lagash; not, however, on the floor as in Bet-
Alpha, and not as symbols carved on boundary stones.
Rather, in a magnificent structure that can rightly be called
the first and most ancient planetarium!

We read in Gudea's inscriptions that he emplaced "images of the constellations" in a "pure and guarded place,
in an inner sanctuary." There, a specially designed "vault
of heaven"—an imitation of the heavenly circle, a kind of
ancient planetarium—was built as a dome resting on what
is translated as "entablature" (a technical term meaning a
base of a superstructure resting atop columns). In that "vault
of heaven" Gudea "caused to dwell" the zodiacal images.
We find clearly listed the "Heavenly Twins," the "Holy
Capricorn," the "Hero" (Sagittarius), the Lion, the "Celestial Creatures" of the Bull and the Ram.

As Gudea had boasted, that "vault of heaven" studded
with the zodiacal symbols must indeed have been a sight
to behold. Millennia later, we can no longer step into that
inner sanctum and share with Gudea the illusion of viewing
the heavens with their shimmering constellations; but we
could have gone to Denderah, in Upper Egypt, entered
there the inner sanctum of its principal temple, and looked

up to the ceiling. There we could have seen a painting of the starry heavens: the celestial circle, held up at the four cardinal points by the Sons of Horus and at the four points of solstitial sunrise and sunset by four maidens (Fig. 95). A circle depicting the thirty six "decans" (ten-day periods, three per month, of the Egyptian calendar) surrounds the central "vault of heaven" in which the twelve zodiacal constellations are depicted by the same symbols (bull, ram, lion, twins, etc.) and in the same order that we still use and that was begun in Sumer. The hieroglyphic name of the temple, *Ta ynt neterti,* meant "Place of the pillars of the goddess," suggesting that at Denderah too, as in the Girsu, stone uprights served for celestial observations, connected on the one hand to the zodiac and on the other hand to the calendar (as the thirty-six decans attest).

Figure 95

Scholars are unable to agree on the point in time represented by the Denderah zodiac. The depiction as now known was discovered when Napoleon visited Egypt, has since been removed to the Louvre Museum in Paris, and is believed to date to the period when Egypt came under Greco-Roman dominance. Scholars are, however, certain that it replicated a similar depiction in a much earlier temple, one that was dedicated to the goddess Hathor. Sir Norman Lockyer in *The Dawn of Astronomy* interpreted a Fourth Dynasty (2613–2494 B.C.) text as describing the celestial alignments in that earlier temple; this would date the Denderah "vault of heaven" to a time between the completion of Stonehenge I and the building of the Eninnu in Lagash by Gudea. If, as others hold, the skies shown in Denderah are dated by the image of the club topped by a falcon touching the foot of the Twins (Gemini), between the Bull (Taurus) on the right and the Crab (Cancer) on the left, it means that the Denderah depiction turned back the skies (as we do in modern planetariums when, say, at Christmas time the skies are shown as they were in the time of Jesus) to sometime between 6540 B.C. and 4380 B.C. According to the Egyptian chronology transmitted by the priests and recorded by Manetho, that was the time when demigods reigned over Egypt; such a dating of the Denderah skies (as distinct from when the temple itself was built) corroborates the findings, mentioned above, by Alfred Jeremias regarding the "point zero" of the Sumerian zodiacal calendar. Both Egyptian and Sumerian zodiacal datings thus confirm that the concept preceded the start of those civilizations, and that the "gods," not men, were responsible for the depictions and their dating.

Since, as we have shown, the zodiac and its accompanying Celestial Time were devised by the Anunnaki soon after they first came to Earth, some of the zodiacal dates marking events depicted on cylinder seals do stand for zodiacal ages that preceded the emergence of Man's civilizations. The Age of Pisces, for example, that is indicated by the two fishes on Fig. 94, occurred no later than between 25980 B.C. and 23820 B.C. (or earlier if the event had taken place at prior ages of Pisces in the Great Cycle of 25,920 years).

Incredibly but not surprisingly, we find a suggestion that a "starry heaven" depicting the celestial circle with the constellations of the zodiac might have existed in the earliest times in a Sumerian text known to scholars as *A Hymn to Enlil the All-Beneficent*. Describing the innermost part of Enlil's Mission Control Center in Nippur, inside the E.KUR ziggurat, the text states that in a darkened chamber called Dirga there was installed "a heavenly zenith, as mysterious as the distant sea" in which "the starry emblems" were "carried to perfection."

The term DIR.GA connotes "dark, crownlike"; the text explains that the "starry emblems" installed therein enabled the determination of festivals, meaning a calendrical function. It all sounds like a forerunner of Gudea's planetarium; except that the one in the Ekur was hidden from human eyes, open to the Anunnaki alone.

Gudea's "vault of heaven," constructed as a planetarium, bears a greater similarity to the Dirga than to the depiction at Denderah, which was only a painting on the ceiling. Yet we cannot rule out the possibility that the inspiration for the one in the Girsu came from Egypt because of the numerous similarities to Egyptian ones that features in the Girsu bore. The list is far from being exhausted.

Some of the most impressive finds now adorning the Assyrian and Babylonian collections in the major museums are colossal stone animals with bodies of bulls or lions and heads of gods wearing horned caps (Fig. 96) that stood as guardians at temple entrances. We can safely assume that these "mythical creatures," as scholars call them, translated into stone sculptures the Bull-Lion motif that we illustrated earlier, thereby invoking for the temples the magic of an earlier Celestial Time and the gods associated with its past zodiacal ages.

Archaeologists believe that these sculptures were inspired by the sphinxes of Egypt, primarily the great Sphinx of Giza, with which the Assyrians and Babylonians were fa-

Figure 96

miliar as a result of both trade and warfare. But the Gudea inscriptions reveal that some fifteen hundred years before such zodiacal-cum-divine creatures were emplaced in Assyrian temples, Gudea had already positioned sphinxes at the Eninnu temple; the inscriptions specifically mention "a lion that instilled terror" and a "wild ox, massively crouching like a lion." To the archaeologists' utter disbelief that sphinxes could have been known in ancient Sumer, a statue of Ninurta/Ningirsu himself, depicting him as a crouching sphinx (Fig. 97), was discovered among the ruins of the Girsu in Lagash.

Hints that all that should have been expected were given to Gudea—and thus to us—in the address by Ninurta to the baffled Gudea during the second night vision, in which Ninurta asserted his powers and reasserted his standing among the Anunnaki ("By fifty edicts my lordship is or-

Figure 97

dained''), pointed out his unusual familiarity with other parts of the world (''A lord whose eyes are lifted up afar'' as a result of his roamings in his Divine Black Bird), assured him of the cooperation of Magan and Melukhah (Egypt and Nubia), and promised him that the god called ''the Bright Serpent'' will, in person, come to assist in the construction of the new Eninnu: ''As a strong place it shall be built, like E.HUSH will my holy place be.''

This last statement is truly sensational in its implications.

''E'' as we already know meant a god's ''house,'' a temple; and in the case of the Eninnu—a stage-pyramid. HUSH (pronounced ''Chush'' with the ''ch'' as in the German *Loch*) meant in Sumerian ''of reddish hue, red-colored.'' So this is what Ninurta/Ningirsu stated: the new Eninnu will be like the ''Red-hued Divine House.'' The statement implies that the new Eninnu will emulate an existing structure known for its reddish hue . . .

Our search for such a structure can be facilitated by tracing back the pictograph for the sign *Hush*. What we find is truly astounding, for what it amounts to (Fig. 98a) is a line drawing of an *Egyptian pyramid* showing its shafts, internal passages. and subterranean chambers. More specifically, it appears to be drawn as a cross section of the Great Pyramid of Giza (Fig. 98b) and its trial scale model, the small pyramid of Giza (Fig. 98c)—and of the first successful phar-

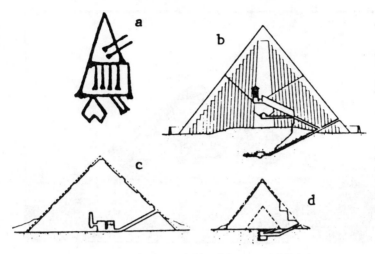

Figures 98a, 98b, 98c, and 98d

aonic pyramid (Fig. 98d) which, quite significantly—was called the *Red Pyramid,* of the very same hue that *Hush* had meant.

The Red Pyramid was certainly there to be emulated when the Eninnu was built in Lagash. It was one of three pyramids attributed to Sneferu, the first pharaoh of the IV dynasty, who reigned circa 2600 B.C. His architects first attempted to build for him a pyramid at Maidum, emulating the 52° slope of the Giza pyramids that were built millennia earlier by the Anunnaki; but the angle was too steep and the pyramid collapsed. The collapse led to a hurried change in the angle of a second pyramid at Dahshur to a flatter 43°, resulting in the pyramid nicknamed the Bent Pyramid. This led to the construction, also at Dahshur, of the third Sneferu pyramid. Considered the "first classical pyramid" of a pharaoh, its sides slope up at the safe angle of about 43½° (Fig. 99). It was built of local pink limestone and was therefore nicknamed the Red Pyramid. Protrusions on the sides were intended to hold in place a surfacing of white limestone; but that did not stay put for long, and today the pyramid is seen in its original reddish hue.

Having fought (and won) the Second Pyramid War in Egypt, Ninurta was not unfamiliar with its subsequent pyr-

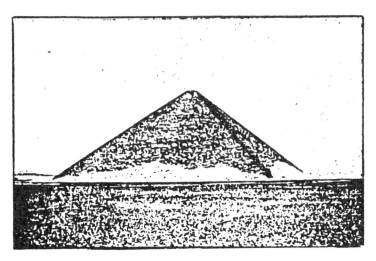

Figure 99

amids. Had he seen, as kingship came to Egypt, not only the Great Pyramid and its companions at Giza, but also the step-pyramid built by the Pharaoh Zoser at Sakkara, surrounded by its magnificent sacred precinct (see Fig. 78), built circa 2650 B.C.? Had he seen the final successful emulation by a pharaoh and his architects of the Great Pyramid—the Red Pyramid of Sneferu, built circa 2600 B.C.? And did he then tell the Divine Architect: that is what I would like to have built for me, a unique ziggurat combining elements of all three?

Else, how can one account for the compelling evidence linking the Eninnu, built between 2200 and 2100 B.C., with Egypt—and its gods?

And how else, except in this way, can one explain the similarities between Stonehenge in the British Isles and "Stonehenge on the Euphrates"?

For the explanation we have to turn our attention to the Divine Architect, the Keeper of the Secrets of the Pyramids, the god called by Gudea Ningishzidda; for he was none other than the Egyptian god *Tehuti* whom we call THOTH.

Thoth was called in the Pyramid Texts "He who reckons the heavens, the counter of the stars and the measurer of the Earth''; the inventor of arts and sciences, scribe of the gods, the ''One who made calculations concerning the heavens, the stars and the Earth.'' As the ''Reckoner of times and of seasons,'' he was depicted with a symbol combining the Sun's disk and the Moon's crescent upon his head, and—in words reminiscent of the biblical adoration of the Celestial Lord—the Egyptian inscriptions and legends said of Thoth that his knowledge and powers of calculating ''measured out the heavens and planned the Earth.'' His hieroglyphic name *Tehuti* is usually explained as meaning ''He who balances.'' Heinrich Brugsch *(Religion und Mythologie)* and E.A. Wallis Budge *(The Gods of the Egyptians)* interpreted that to mean that Thoth was the ''god of the equilibrium'' and considered depictions of him as ''Master of the Balance'' to indicate that he was associated with the equinoxes—the time when the day and the night were balanced. The Greeks identified Thoth with their god Hermes, whom they considered to have been the originator of astronomy and astrology, of the science of numbers and of geometry, of medicine and botany.

As we follow in the footsteps of Thoth, we shall come upon calendar tales that raise the curtain on the affairs of gods and men—and on enigmas such as Stonehenge.

8

CALENDAR TALES

The story of the calendar is one of ingenuity, of a sophisticated combination of astronomy and mathematics. It is also a tale of conflict, religious fervor, and struggles for supremacy.

The notion that the calendar was devised by and for farmers so that they would know when to sow and when to reap has been taken for granted too long; it fails both the test of logic and of fact. Farmers do not need a formal calendar to know the seasons, and primitive societies have managed to feed themselves for generations without a calendar. The historic fact is that the calendar was devised in order to predetermine the precise time of festivals honoring the gods. The calendar, in other words, was a religious device. The first names by which months were called in Sumer had the prefix EZEN. The word did not mean "month"; it meant "festival." The months were the times when the Festival of Enlil, or the Festival of Ninurta, or those of the other leading deities were to be observed.

That the calendar's purpose was to enable religious observances should not surprise one at all. We find an instance that still regulates our lives in the current common, but actually Christian, calendar. Its principal festival and the focal point that determines the rest of the annual calendar is Easter, the celebration of the resurrection, according to the New Testament, of Jesus on the third day after his crucifixion. Western Christians celebrate Easter on the first Sunday after the full moon that occurs on or right after the spring equinox. This created a problem for the early Christians in Rome, where the dominant calendrical element was the solar year of 365 days and the months were of irregular length and not exactly related to the Moon's phases. The determination of Easter Day therefore required a reliance on the Jewish calendar, because the Last Supper, from which the other crucial days of Eastertide are counted, was actually the *Seder* meal with which the Jewish celebration of Passover begins on the eve of the fourteenth day of the month Nissan, the time of the full Moon. As a result, during the first centuries of Christianity Easter was celebrated in accordance with the Jewish calendar. It was only when the Roman emperor Constantine, having adopted Christianity, convened a church council, the Council of Nicaea, in the year 325, that the continued dependence on the Jewish calendar was severed, and Christianity, until then deemed by the gentiles as merely another Jewish sect, was made into a separate religion.

In this change, as in its origin, the Christian calendar was thus an expression of religious beliefs and an instrument for determining the dates of worship. It was also so later on, when the Moslems burst out of Arabia to conquer by the sword lands and people east and west; the imposition of their purely lunar calendar was one of their first acts, for it had a profound religious connotation: it counted the passage of time from the *Hegira*, the migration of Islam's founder Mohammed from Mecca to Medina (in 622).

The history of the Roman-Christian calendar, interesting by itself, illustrates some of the problems inherent in the imperfect meshing of solar and lunar times and the resulting need, over the millennia, for calendar reforms and the ensuing notions of ever-renewing Ages.

The current Common Era Christian calendar was introduced by Pope Gregory XIII in 1582 and is therefore called the Gregorian Calendar. It constituted a reform of the previous Julian Calendar, so named after the Roman emperor Julius Caesar.

That noted Roman emperor, tired of the chaotic Roman calendar, invited in the first century B.C. the astronomer Sosigenes of Alexandria, Egypt, to suggest a reform of the calendar. Sosigenes's advice was to forget about lunar time-keeping and to adopt a solar calendar ''as that of the Egyptians.'' The result was a year of 365 days plus a leap year of 366 days once in four years. But that still failed to account for the extra 11¼ minutes a year in excess of the quarter-day over and above the 365 days. That seemed too minute to bother with; but the result was that by 1582 the first day of spring, fixed by the Council of Nicaea to fall on March 21, was retarded by ten days to March 11th. Pope Gregory corrected the shortfall by simply decreeing on October 4, 1582, that the next day should be October 15. This reform established the currently used Gregorian calendar, whose other innovation was to decree that the year begin on January first.

The astronomer's suggestion that a calendar ''as that of the Egyptians'' be adopted in Rome was accepted, one must assume, without undue difficulty because by then Rome, and especially Julius Caesar, were quite familiar with Egypt, its religious customs, and hence with its calendar. The Egyptian calendar was at that time indeed a purely solar calendar of 365 days divided into twelve months of thirty days each. To these 360 days an end-of-year religious festival of five days was added, dedicated to the gods Osiris, Horus, Seth, Isis, and Nephthys.

The Egyptians were aware that the solar year is somewhat longer than 365 days—not just by the full day every four years, as Julius Caesar had allowed for, but by enough to shift the calendar back by one month every 120 years and by a full year every 1,460 years. The determining or sacred cycle of the Egyptian calendar was this 1,460-year period, for it coincided with the cycle of the heliacal rising of the star Sirius (Egyptian *Sept,* Greek *Sothis*) at the time of the Nile's annual flooding, which in turn takes place at about the summer solstice (in the northern hemisphere).

Edward Meyer (*Ägyptische Chronologie*) concluded that when this Egyptian calendar was introduced, such a convergence of the heliacal rising of Sirius and of the Nile's inundation had occurred on July 19th. Based on that Kurt Sethe (*Urgeschichte und älteste Religion der Ägypter*) calculated that this could have happened in either 4240 B.C.

or 2780 B.C. by observing the skies at either Heliopolis or Memphis.

By now researchers of the ancient Egyptian calendar agree that the solar calendar of 360 + 5 days was not the first prehistoric calendar of that land. This "civil" or secular calendar was introduced only after the start of dynastic rule in Egypt, i.e., after 3100 B.C.; according to Richard A. Parker (*The Calendars of the Ancient Egyptians*) it took place circa 2800 B.C. "probably for administrative and fiscal purposes." This civil calendar supplanted, or perhaps supplemented at first, the "sacred" calendar of old. In the words of the *Encyclopaedia Britannica*, "the ancient Egyptians originally employed a calendar based upon the Moon." According to R.A. Parker (*Ancient Egyptian Astronomy*) that earlier calendar was, "like that of all ancient peoples," a calendar of twelve *lunar* months plus a thirteenth intercalary month that kept the seasons in place.

That earlier calendar was also, in the opinion of Lockyer, equinoctial and linked indeed to the earliest temple at Heliopolis, whose orientation was equinoctial. In all that, as in the association of months with religious festivals, the earliest Egyptian calendar was akin to that of the Sumerians.

The conclusion that the Egyptian calendar had its roots in predynastic times, before civilization appeared in Egypt, can only mean that it was not the Egyptians themselves who invented their calendar. It is a conclusion that matches that regarding the zodiac in Egypt, and regarding both the zodiac and the calendar in Sumer: they were all the artful inventions of the "gods."

In Egypt, religion and worship of the gods began in Heliopolis, close by the Giza pyramids; its original Egyptian name was *Annu* (as the name of the ruler of Nibiru) and it is called *On* in the Bible: when Joseph was made viceroy over all of Egypt (Genesis chapter 41), the Pharaoh "gave him Assenath, the daughter of Potiphera, the [high] priest of On, for a wife." Its oldest shrine was dedicated to *Ptah* ("The Developer") who, according to Egyptian tradition, raised Egypt from under the waters of the Great Flood and made it habitable by extensive drainage and earthworks. Divine reign over Egypt was then transferred by Ptah to his son *Ra* ("The Bright One") who was also called *Tem* ("The Pure One"); and in a special shrine, also at Heliopolis, the Boat of Heaven of Ra, the conical *Ben-Ben,* could be seen by pilgrims once a year.

Ra was the head of the first divine dynasty according to the Egyptian priest Manetho (his hieroglyphic name meant "Gift of Thoth"), who compiled in the third century B.C. Egypt's dynastic lists. The reign of Ra and his successors, the gods Shu, Geb, Osiris, Seth, and Horus, lasted more than three millennia. It was followed by a second divine dynasty that was begun by Thoth, another son of Ptah; it lasted half as long as the first divine dynasty. Thereafter a dynasty of demigods, thirty of them, reigned over Egypt for 3,650 years. Altogether, according to Manetho, the divine reigns of Ptah, the Ra dynasty, the Thoth dynasty, and the dynasty of the demigods lasted 17,520 years. Karl R. Lepsius (*Königsbuch der alten Ägypter*) noted that this time span represented exactly twelve Sothic cycles of 1,460 years each, thereby corroborating the prehistoric origin of calendrical-astronomical knowledge in Egypt.

Based on substantial evidence, we have concluded in *The Wars of Gods and Men* and other volumes of *The Earth Chronicles* that Ptah was none other than Enki and that Ra was Marduk of the Mesopotamian pantheon. It was to Enki and his descendants that the African lands were granted when Earth was divided among the Anunnaki after the Deluge, leaving the E.DIN (the biblical land of Eden) and the Mesopotamian sphere of influence in the hands of Enlil and his descendants. Thoth, a brother of Ra/Marduk, was the god the Sumerians called Ningishzidda.

Much of the history and violent conflicts that followed the Earth's division stemmed from the refusal of Ra/Marduk to acquiesce in the division. He was convinced that his father was unjustly deprived of lordship of Earth (what the epithet-name EN.KI, "Lord Earth," connoted); and that therefore he, not Enlil's Foremost Son Ninurta, should rule supreme on Earth from Babylon, the Mesopotamian city whose name meant "Gateway of the Gods." Obsessed by this ambition, Ra/Marduk caused not only conflicts with the Enlilites, but also aroused the animosity of some of his own brothers by involving them in these bitter conflicts as well as by leaving Egypt and then returning to reclaim the lordship over it.

In the course of these comings and goings and ups and downs in Ra/Marduk's struggles, he caused the death of a younger brother called Dumuzi, let his brother Thoth reign and then forced him into exile, and made his brother Nergal change sides in a War of the Gods that resulted in a nuclear holocaust. It was in particular the on-again, off-again relationship with Thoth, we believe, that is essential to the Calendar Tales.

The Egyptians, it will be recalled, had not one but two calendars. The first, with roots in prehistoric times, was "based upon the Moon." The later one, introduced several centuries after the start of pharaonic rule, was based on the 365 days of the solar year. Contrary to the notion that the latter "civil calendar" was an administrative innovation of a pharaoh, we suggest that it too, like the earlier one, was an artful creation of the gods; except that while the first one was the handiwork of Thoth, the second one was the craftwork of Ra.

One aspect of the civil calendar considered specific and original to it was the division of the thirty-day months into "decans," ten-day periods each heralded by the heliacal rising of a certain star. Each star (depicted as a celestial god sailing the skies, Fig. 100) was deemed to give notice of the last hour of the night; and at the end of ten days, a new decan-star would be observed.

It is our suggestion that the introduction of this decan-based calendar was a deliberate act by Ra in a developing conflict with his brother Thoth.

Both were sons of Enki, the great scientist of the Anunnaki, and one can safely assume that much of their

Figure 100

knowledge had been acquired from their father. This is certain in the case of Ra/Marduk, for a Mesopotamian text has been found that clearly states so. It is a text whose beginning records a complaint by Marduk to his father that he lacks certain healing knowledge. Enki's response is rendered thus:

> *My son, what is it you do not know?*
> *What more could I give to you?*
> *Marduk, what is it that you do not know?*
> *What could I give you in addition?*
> *Whatever I know, you know!*

Was there, perhaps, some jealousy between the two brothers on this score? The knowledge of mathematics, of astronomy, of orienting sacred structures was shared by both; witness to Marduk's attainments in these sciences was the magnificent ziggurat of Babylon (see Fig. 33) which, according to the *Enuma elish*, Marduk himself had designed. But, as the above-quoted text relates, when it came to medicine and healing, his knowledge fell short of his brother's: he could not revive the dead, while Thoth could. We learn of the latter's powers from both Meso-potamian and Egyptian sources. His Sumerian depictions show him with the emblem of the entwined serpents (Fig. 101a), the emblem originally of his father Enki as the god

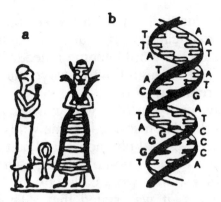

Figures 101a and 101b

who could engage in genetic engineering—the emblem, we have suggested, of the double helix of DNA (Fig. 101b). His Sumerian name, NIN.GISH.ZID.DA, which meant "Lord of the Artifact of Life," bespoke recognition of his capacity to restore life by reviving the dead. "Lord healer, Lord who seizes the hand, Lord of the Artifact of Life" a Sumerian liturgical text called him. He was prominently featured in magical healing and exorcism texts; a *Maqlu* ("Burnt Offerings") series of incantations and magical formulas devoted a whole tablet, the seventh, to him. In one incantation, devoted to drowned mariners ("the seafaring folk who are utterly at rest"), the priest invokes the formulas of "Siris and Ningishzidda, the miracle workers, the spellbinders."

Siris is the name of a goddess otherwise unknown in the Sumerian pantheon, and the possibility that it is a Mesopotamian rendition of the star's name Sirius comes to our mind because in the Egyptian pantheon Sirius was the star associated with the goddess Isis. In Egyptian legendary tales, Thoth was the one who had helped Isis, the wife of Osiris, to extract from the dismembered Osiris the semen with which Isis was impregnated to conceive and bear Horus. This was not all. In an Egyptian inscription on an artifact known as the Metternich Stela, the goddess Isis describes how Thoth brought her son Horus back from the dead after Horus was stung by a poisonous scorpion. Responding to her cries, Thoth came down from the skies, "and he was provided with magical powers, and possessed the great power which made the word become indeed." And he performed magic, and by nighttime it drove the poison away and Horus was returned to life.

The Egyptians held that the whole *Book of the Dead,* verses from which were inscribed on the walls of pharaonic tombs so that the deceased pharaoh could be translated into an Afterlife, was a composition of Thoth, "written with his own fingers." In a shorter work called by the Egyptians the *Book of Breathings,* it was stated that "Thoth, the most mighty god, the lord of Khemennu, cometh to thee; he writeth for thee the Book of Breathings with his own fingers, so that thy *Ka* shall breathe for ever and ever and thy form endowed with life on Earth."

We know from Sumerian sources that this knowledge, so essential in pharaonic beliefs—knowledge to revive the dead—was first possessed by Enki. In a long text dealing with Inanna/Ishtar's journey to the Lower World (southern Africa), the domain of her sister who was married to another son of Enki, the uninvited goddess was put to death. Responding to appeals, Enki fashioned medications and supervised the treatment of the corpse with sound and radiation pulses, and "Inanna arose."

Evidently, the secret was not divulged to Marduk; and when he complained, his father gave him an evasive answer. That alone would have been enough to make the ambitious and power-hungry Marduk jealous of Thoth. The feeling of being offended, perhaps even threatened, was probably greater. First, because it was Thoth, and not Marduk/Ra, who had helped Isis retrieve the dismembered Osiris (Ra's grandson) and save his semen, and then revived the poisoned Horus (a great-grandson of Ra). And second, because all that led—as the Sumerian text makes clearer—to an affinity between Thoth and the star Sirius, the controller of the Egyptian calendar and the harbinger of the life-giving inundation of the Nile.

Were these the only reasons for the jealousy, or did Ra/Marduk have more compelling reasons to see in Thoth a rival, a threat to his supremacy? According to Manetho, the long reign of the first divine dynasty begun by Ra ended abruptly after only a short reign of three hundred years by Horus, after the conflict that we have called the First Pyramid War. Then, instead of another descendant of Ra, it was Thoth who was given lordship over Egypt and his dynasty continued (according to Manetho) for 1,570 years. His reign, an era of peace and progress, coincided with the New Stone (Neolithic) Age in the Near East—the first phase of the granting of civilization by the Anunnaki to Mankind.

Why was it Thoth, of all the other sons of Ptah/Enki, who was chosen to replace the dynasty of Ra in Egypt? A clue might be suggested in a study titled *Religion of the Ancient Egyptians* by W. Osborn, Jr., in which it is stated as follows regarding Thoth: "Though he stood in mythology in a secondary rank of deities, yet he always remained a direct emanation from, and part of, Ptah—the *firstborn* of the primeval deity" (emphasis is ours). With the complex rules of succession of the Anunnaki, where a son born to a half sister became the legal heir ahead of a firstborn son (if mothered not by a half sister)—a cause of the endless friction and rivalry between Enki (the first-born of Anu) and Enlil (born to a half sister of Anu)—could it be that the circumstances of Thoth's birth somehow posed a challenge to Ra/Marduk's claims for supremacy?

It is known that initially the dominating "company of the gods" or divine dynasty was that of Heliopolis; later on it was superseded by the divine triad of Memphis (when Memphis became the capital of a unified Egypt). But in between there was an interim *Paut* or "divine company" of gods headed by Thoth. The "cult center" of the latter was Hermopolis ("City of Hermes" in Greek) whose Egyptian name, *Khemennu*, meant "eight." One of the epithets of Thoth was "Lord of Eight," which according to Heinrich Brugsch (*Religion und Mythologie der alten Aegypter*) referred to eight celestial orientations, including the four cardinal points. It could also refer to Thoth's ability to ascertain and mark out the eight standstill points of the Moon—the celestial body with which Thoth was associated.

Marduk, a "Sun god," on the other hand, was associated with the number ten. In the numerical hierarchy of the Anunnaki, in which Anu's rank was the highest, sixty, that of Enlil fifty and of Enki forty (and so on down), the rank of Marduk was ten; and that could have been the origin of the decans. Indeed, the Babylonian version of the Epic of Creation attributes to Marduk the devising of a calendar of twelve months each divided into three "celestial astrals":

> *He determined the year,*
> *designating the zones:*
> *For each of the twelve months*
> *he set up three celestial astrals,*
> *[thus] defining the days of the year.*

This division of the skies into thirty-six portions as a means of "defining the days of the year" is as clear a reference as possible to the calendar—a calendar with thirty-six "decans." And here, in *Enuma elish,* the division is attributed to Marduk, alias Ra.

The Epic of Creation, undoubtedly of Sumerian origin, is known nowadays mostly from its Babylonian rendition (the seven tablets of the *Enuma elish*). It is a rendition, all scholars agree, that was intended to glorify the Babylonian national god Marduk. Hence, the name "Marduk" was inserted where in the Sumerian original text the invader from outer space, the planet Nibiru, was described as the Celestial Lord; and where, describing deeds on Earth, the Supreme God was named Enlil, the Babylonian version also named Marduk. Thereby, Marduk was made supreme both in heaven and on Earth.

Without further discovery of intact or even fragmented tablets inscribed with the original Sumerian text of the Epic of Creation, it is impossible to say whether the thirty-six decans were a true innovation by Marduk or were just borrowed by him from Sumer. A basic tenet of Sumerian astronomy was the division of the celestial sphere enveloping the Earth into three "ways"—the Way of Anu as a central celestial band, the Way of Enlil of the northern skies, and the Way of Ea (i.e., Enki) in the southern skies. It has been thought that the three ways represented the equatorial band in the center and the bands demarcated by the two tropics, north and south; we have, however, shown in *The 12th Planet* that the Way of Anu, straddling the equator, extended 30° northward and southward of the equator, resulting in a width of 60°; and that the Way of Enlil and the Way of Ea similarly extended for 60° each, so that the three covered the complete celestial sweep of 180° from north to south.

If this tripartite division of the skies were to be applied to the calendrical division of the year into twelve months, the result would be thirty-six segments. Such a division—resulting in decans—was indeed made, in Babylon.

In 1900, addressing the Royal Astronomical Society in London, the orientalist T.G. Pinches presented a reconstruction of a Mesopotamian astrolabe (literally: "Taker of stars"). It was a circular disk divided like a pie into twelve segments and three concentric rings, resulting in a division of the skies into thirty-six portions (Fig. 102). The round symbols next to the inscribed names indicated that the reference was to celestial bodies; the names (here transliterated) are those of constellations of the zodiac, stars, and planets—thirty-six in all. That this division was linked to the calendar is made clear by the inscribing of the months' names, one in each of the twelve segments at the segment's top (the marking I to XII, starting with the first month Nisannu of the Babylonian calendar, is by Pinches).

While this Babylonian planisphere does not answer the question of the origin of the relevant verses in *Enuma elish*, it does establish that what was supposed to have been a unique and original Egyptian innovation in fact had a counterpart (if not a predecessor) in Babylon—the place claimed by Marduk for his supremacy.

Even more certain is the fact that the thirty-six decans

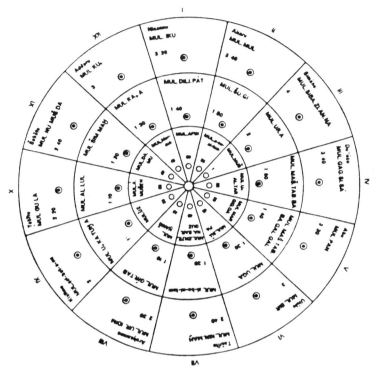

Figure 102

do not feature in the first Egyptian calendar. The earlier one was linked to the Moon, the later one to the Sun. In Egyptian theology, Thoth was a Moon God, Ra was a Sun God. Extending this to the two calendars, it follows that the first and older Egyptian calendar was formulated by Thoth and the second, later one, by Ra/Marduk.

The fact is that when the time came, circa 3100 B.C., to extend the Sumerian level of civilization (human Kingship) to the Egyptians, Ra/Marduk—having been frustrated in his efforts to establish supremacy in Babylon—returned to Egypt and expelled Thoth.

It was then, we believe, that Ra/Marduk—not for administrative convenience but in a deliberate step to eradicate the vestiges of Thoth's predominance—reformed the calendar. A passage in the *Book of the Dead* relates that Thoth was "disturbed by what hath happened to the divine children" who have "done battle, upheld strife, created fiends, caused trouble." As a consequence of this Thoth "was provoked to anger when they [his adversaries] bring the years to confusion, throng in and push to disturb the months." All that evil, the text declares, "in all they have done unto thee, they have worked iniquity in secret."

This may well indicate that the strife that led to the substitution of Thoth's calendar by Ra/Marduk's calendar in Egypt took place when the calendar (for reasons explained earlier) needed to be put back on track. R.A. Parker, we have noted above, believes that this change occurred circa 2800 B.C. Adolf Erman (*Aegypten und Aegyptisches Leben im Altertum*) was more specific. The opportunity, he wrote, was the return of Sirius to its original position, after the 1,460-year cycle, on July 19, 2776 B.C.

It should be noted that that date, circa 2800 B.C., is the official date adopted by the British authorities for Stonehenge I.

The introduction by Ra/Marduk of a calendar divided into, or based upon, ten-day periods may have also been prompted by a desire to draw a clear distinction, for his followers in Egypt as well as in Mesopotamia, between himself and the one who was "seven"—the head of the Enlilites, Enlil himself. Indeed, such a distinction may have underlain the oscillations between lunar and solar calendars; for the calendars, as we have shown and ancient records attested, were devised by the Anunnaki "gods" to delineate for their followers the cycles of worship; and the struggle for supremacy meant, in the final analysis, who was to be worshiped.

Scholars have long debated, but have yet to verify, the origin of the week, the slice of the year measured in lengths of seven days. We have shown in earlier books of *The Earth Chronicles* that seven was the number that represented our planet, the Earth. Earth was called in Sumerian texts "the seventh," and was depicted in representations of celestial bodies by the symbol of the seven dots (as in Fig. 94) because journeying into the center of our Solar System from

their outermost planet, the Anunnaki would first encounter
Pluto, pass by Neptune and Uranus (second and third), and
continue past Saturn and Jupiter (fourth and fifth). They
would count Mars as the sixth (and therefore it was depicted
as a six-pointed star) and Earth would be the seventh. Such
a journey and such a count are in fact depicted on a planisphere discovered in the ruins of the royal library of Nineveh, where one of its eight segments (Fig. 103) shows the
flight path from Nibiru and states (here in English translation) "deity Enlil went by the planets." The planets, represented by dots, are seven in number. For the Sumerians,
it was Enlil, and no other, who was "Lord of Seven."
Mesopotamian as well as biblical names, of persons (e.g.,
Bath-sheba, "Daughter of Seven") or of places (e.g., *Beer-
Sheba,* "the well of Seven") honored the god by this
epithet.

The importance or sanctity of the number seven, transferred to the calendrical unit of seven days as one week,
permeates the Bible and other ancient scriptures. Abraham
set apart seven ewe lambs when he negotiated with Abi-
melech; Jacob served Laban seven years to be able to marry
one of his daughters, and bowed seven times as he approached his jealous brother Esau. The High Priest was

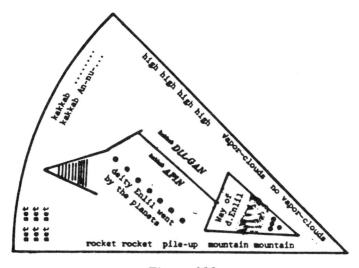

Figure 103

required to perform various rites seven times, Jericho was to be circled seven times so that its walls should tumble down; and calendrically, the seventh day had to be strictly observed as the Sabbath and the important festival of Pentecost had to take place after the count of seven weeks from Passover.

Though no one can say who "invented" the seven-day week, it is obviously associated in the Bible with the earliest times—indeed, when Time itself began: witness the seven days of Creation with which the book of Genesis begins. The concept of a seven-day delineated period of counted time, a Time of Man, is found in the biblical as well as the earlier Mesopotamian Deluge tale, thereby attesting to its antiquity. In the Mesopotamian texts, the hero of the flood is given seven days' advance warning by Enki, who "opened the water clock and filled it" to make sure his faithful follower would not miss the deadline. In those versions the Deluge is said to have begun with a storm that "swept the country for seven days and seven nights." In the biblical version the Deluge also began after a seven-day advance warning to Noah.

The biblical tale of the flood and its duration reveals a far-reaching understanding of the calendar in very early times. Significantly, it shows familiarity with the unit of seven days and of a division of the year into fifty-two weeks of seven days each. Moreover, it suggests an understanding of the complexities of a lunar-solar calendar.

According to Genesis, the Deluge began "in the second month, on the seventeenth day of the month" and ended the following year "in the second month, on the twenty-seventh day of the month." But what on the face of it would appear to be a period of 365 days plus ten, is not so. The biblical tale breaks down the Deluge into 150 days of the avalanche of water, 150 days during which the water receded, and another forty days until Noah deemed it safe to open the Ark. Then, in two seven-day intervals, he sent out a raven and a dove to survey the landscape; only when the dove no longer came back did Noah know it was safe to step out.

According to this breakdown, it all added up to 354 days (150 + 150 + 40 + 7 + 7). But that is not a solar year; that is precisely a lunar year of twelve months averaging 29.5 days each (29.5 × 12 = 354) represented by a calendar—as the Jewish one still is—alternating between months of 29 and 30 days.

But 354 days is not a full year in solar terms. Recognizing this, the narrator or editor of Genesis resorted to intercalation, by stating that the Deluge, which began on the seventeenth day of the second month, ended (a year later) on the twenty-seventh of the second month. Scholars are divided in regard to the number of days thus added to the lunar 354. Some (e.g., S. Gandz, *Studies in Hebrew Mathematics and Astronomy*) consider the addition to have been eleven days—the correct intercalary addition that would have expanded the lunar 354 days to the full 365 days of the solar year. Others, among them the author of the ancient *Book of Jubilees,* consider the number of days added to be just ten, increasing the year in question to only 364 days. The significance is, of course, that it implies a calendar divided into fifty-two weeks of seven days each (52 × 7 = 364).

That this was not just a result of adding 354 + 10 as the number of days, but a deliberate division of the year into fifty-two weeks of seven days each, is made clear in the text of the *Book of Jubilees.* It states (chapter 6) that Noah was given, when the Deluge ended, "heavenly tablets" ordaining that

> *All the days of the commandment*
> *will be two and fifty weeks of days*
> *which will make the year complete.*
> *Thus it is engraven and ordained*
> *on the heavenly tablets;*
> *there shall be no neglecting for a single*
> *year or from year to year.*
> *And command thou the children of Israel*
> *that they observe the years according to*
> *this reckoning:*

three hundred and sixty-four days;
these shall constitute a complete year.

The insistence on a year of fifty-two weeks of seven days, adding up to a calendrical year of 364 days, was not a result of ignorance regarding the true length of 365 full days in a solar year. The awareness of this true length is made clear in the Bible by the age ("*five* and sixty and three hundred years") of Enoch until he was lofted by the Lord. In the nonbiblical *Book of Enoch* the "overplus of the Sun," the five epagomenal days that had to be added to the 360 days (12 × 30) of other calendars, to complete the 365, are specifically mentioned. Yet the *Book of Enoch,* in chapters describing the motions of the Sun and the Moon, the twelve zodiacal "portals," the equinoxes and the solstices, states unequivocally that the calendar year shall be "a year exact as to its days: three hundred and sixty-four." This is repeated in a statement that "the complete year, with perfect justice" was of 364 days—fifty-two weeks of seven days each.

The *Book of Enoch*, especially in its version known as Enoch II, is believed to show elements of scientific knowledge centered at the time in Alexandria, Egypt. How much of that can be traced back to the teachings of Thoth cannot be stated with any certainty; but biblical as well as Egyptian tales suggest a role for seven and fifty-two times seven beginning in much earlier times.

Well known is the biblical tale of Joseph's rise to governorship over Egypt after he had successfully interpreted the pharaoh's dreams of, first, seven fatfleshed cows that were devoured by seven leanfleshed cows, and then of seven full ears of corn swallowed up by seven dried-out ears of corn. Few are aware, however, that the tale— "legend" or "myth" to some—had strong Egyptian roots as well as an earlier counterpart in Egyptian lore. Among the former was the Egyptian forerunner of the Greek Sibylline oracle goddesses; they were called the Seven Hathors, Hathor having been the goddess of the Sinai peninsula who was depicted as a cow. In other words, the Seven

Hathors symbolized seven cows who could predict the future.

The earlier counterpart of the tale of seven lean years that followed seven years of plenty is a hieroglyphic text (Fig. 104) that E.A.W. Budge (*Legends of the Gods*) titled "A legend of the god Khnemu and of a seven year famine." Khnemu was another name for Ptah/Enki in his role as fashioner of Mankind. The Egyptians believed that after he had turned over lordship over Egypt to his son Ra, he retired to the island of Abu (known as Elephantine since Greek times because of its shape), where he formed twin caverns—two connected reservoirs—whose locks or sluices could be manipulated to regulate the flow of the Nile's waters. (The modern Aswan High Dam is similarly located above the Nile's first cataract).

According to this text, the Pharaoh Zoser (builder of

Figure 104

the step-pyramid at Saqqara) received a royal dispatch from the governor of the people of the south that grievous suffering had come upon the people "because the Nile hath not come forth to the proper height for *seven years*." As a result, "grain is very scarce, vegetables are lacking altogether, every kind of thing which men eat for their food hath ceased, and every man now plundereth his neighbor."

Hoping that the spread of famine and chaos could be avoided by a direct appeal to the god, the king traveled south to the island of Abu. The god, he was told, dwells there "in an edifice of wood with portals formed of reeds," keeping with him "the cord and the tablet" that enable him to "open the double door of the sluices of the Nile." Khnemu, responding to the king's pleadings, promised "to raise the level of the Nile, give water, make the crops grow."

Since the annual rising of the Nile was linked to the heliacal rising of the star Sirius, one must wonder whether the tale's celestial or astronomical aspects recall not only the actual shortage of water (which occurs cyclically even nowadays) but also to the shift (discussed above) in the appearance of Sirius under a rigid calendar. That the whole tale had calendrical connotations is suggested by the statement in the text that the abode of Khnemu at Abu was astronomically oriented: "The god's house hath an opening to the southeast, and the Sun standeth immediately opposite thereto every day." This can only mean a facility for observing the Sun in the course of moving to and from the winter solstice.

This brief review of the use and significance of the number seven in the affairs of gods and men suffices to show its celestial origin (the seven planets from Pluto to Earth) and its calendrical importance (the seven-day week, a year of fifty-two such weeks). But in the rivalry among the Anunnaki, all that assumed another significance: the determination of who was the God of Seven (*Eli-Sheva* in Hebrew, from which Elizabeth comes) and thus the titular Ruler of Earth.

And that, we believe, is what alarmed Ra/Marduk on his return to Egypt after his failed coup in Babylon: the spreading veneration of Seven, still Enlil's epithet, through the introduction of the seven-day week into Egypt.

In these circumstances the veneration of the Seven Hathors, as an example, must have been anathema to Ra/Marduk. Not only their number, seven, which implied veneration of Enlil; but their association with Hathor, an important deity in the Egyptian pantheon but one for whom Ra/Marduk had no particular liking.

Hathor, we have shown in earlier books of *The Earth Chronicles*, was the Egyptian name for Ninharsag of the Sumerian pantheon—a half sister of both Enki and Enlil and the object of both brothers' sexual attention. Since the official spouses of both (Ninki of Enki, Ninlil of Enlil) were not their half sisters, it was important for them to beget a son by Ninharsag; such a son, under the succession rules of the Anunnaki, would be the undisputed Legal Heir to the throne on Earth. In spite of repeated attempts by Enki, all Ninharsag bore him were daughters; but Enlil was more successful, and his Foremost Son was conceived in a union with Ninharsag. This entitled Ninurta (Ningirsu, the "Lord of Girsu" to Gudea) to inherit his father's rank of fifty—at the same time depriving Enki's firstborn, Marduk, of rulership over the Earth.

There were other manifestations of the spread of the worship of seven and its calendrical importance. The tale of the seven-year drought takes place at the time of Zoser, builder of the Saqqara pyramid. Archaeologists have discovered in the area of Saqqara a circular "altar-top" of alabaster whose shape (Fig. 105) suggests that it was intended to serve as a sacred lamp to be lighted over a seven-day period. Another find is that of a stone "wheel" (some think it was the base of an omphalos, an oracular "navel stone") that is clearly divided into four segments of seven markers each (Fig. 106), suggesting that it was really a stone calendar—a lunar calendar, no doubt—incorporating the seven-day week concept and (with the

Figure 105

Figure 106

aid of the four dividers) enabling a lunar monthly count
ranging from twenty-eight to thirty-two days.

Calendars made of stone had existed in antiquity, as evidence Stonehenge in Britain and the Aztec calendar in Mexico. That this one was found in Egypt should be the least
wonder, for it is our belief that the genius behind all of
those geographically spread stone calendars was one and
the same god: Thoth. What may be surprising is this cal-

endar's embracing the cycle of seven days; but that too, as another Egyptian "legend" shows, should not have been unexpected.

What archaeologists identify as games or game boards have been found almost everywhere in the ancient Near East, as witness these few illustrations of finds from Mesopotamia, Canaan, and Egypt (Fig. 107). The two players moved pegs from one hole to another in accordance with the throw of dice. Archaeologists see in that no more than games with which to while away the time; but the usual number of holes, fifty-eight, is clearly an allocation of twenty-nine to each player—and twenty-nine is the number of full days in a lunar month. There were also obvious subdivisions of the holes into smaller groups, and grooves connected some holes to others (indicating perhaps that the player could jump-advance there). We notice, for example,

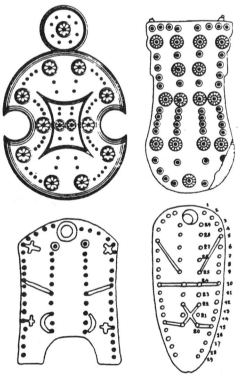

Figure 107

that hole 15 was connected to hole 22 and hole 10 to 24, which suggests a "jump" of one week of seven days and of a fortnight of fourteen days.

Nowadays we employ ditties ("Thirty days hath September") and games to teach the modern calendar to children; why exclude the possibility that it was so also in antiquity?

That these were calendar games and that at least one of them, the favorite of Thoth, was designed to teach the division of the year into fifty-two weeks, is evident from an ancient Egyptian tale known as "The Adventures of Satni-Khamois with the Mummies."

It is a tale of magic, mystery, and adventure, an ancient thriller that combines the magical number fifty-two with Thoth and the secrets of the calendar. The tale is written on a papyrus (cataloged as Cairo-30646) that was discovered in a tomb in Thebes, dating to the third century B.C. Fragments of other papyruses with the same tale have also been found, indicating that it was part of the established or canonical literature of ancient Egypt that recorded the tales of gods and men.

The hero of this tale was Satni, a son of the pharaoh, "well instructed in all things." He was wont to wander in the necropolis of Memphis, studying the sacred writings on temple walls and researching ancient "books of magic." In time he himself became "a magician who had no equal in the land of Egypt." One day a mysterious old man told him of a tomb "where there is deposited the book that the god Thoth had written with his own hand," and in which the mysteries of the Earth and the secrets of heaven were revealed. That secret knowledge included divine information concerning "the risings of the Sun and the appearances of the Moon and the motions of the celestial gods [the planets] that are in the cycle [orbit] of the Sun"; in other words—the secrets of astronomy and the calendar.

The tomb in question was that of Ne-nofer-khe-ptah, the son of a former king. When Satni asked to be shown the location of this tomb, the old man warned him that although

Nenoferkheptah was buried and mummified, he was not dead and could strike down anyone who dared take away the Book of Thoth that was lodged at his feet. Undaunted, Satni searched for the subterranean tomb, and when he reached the right spot he "recited a formula over it and a gap opened in the ground and Satni went down to the place where the book was."

Inside the tomb Satni saw the mummies of Nenoferkheptah, of his sister-wife, and of their son. The book was indeed at Nenoferkheptah's feet, and it "gave off a light as if the sun shone there." As Satni stepped toward it, the wife's mummy spoke up, warning him to advance no further. She then told Satni of her own husband's adventures when he had attempted to obtain the book, for Thoth had hidden it in a secret place, inside a golden box that was inside a silver box that was inside a series of other boxes within boxes, the outermost ones being of bronze and iron. When her husband, Nenoferkheptah, ignored the warnings and the dangers and grasped the book, Thoth condemned him and his wife and their son to suspended animation: although alive, they were buried; and although mummified, they could see, hear, and speak. She warned Satni that if he touched the book, his fate would be the same or worse.

The warnings and the fate of the earlier king did not deter Satni. Having come so far, he was determined to get the book. As he took another step toward the book, the mummy of Nenoferkheptah spoke up. There was a way to possess the book without incurring the wrath of Thoth, he said: to play and win the Game of Fifty-Two, "the magical number of Thoth."

Challenging fate, Satni agreed. He lost the first game and found himself partly sunk into the floor of the tomb. He lost the next game, and the next, sinking down more and more into the ground. How he managed to escape with the book, the calamities that befell him as a result, and how he in the end returned the book to its hiding place, makes fascinating reading but is unessential to our immediate subject: the fact that the astronomical and calendrical "secrets of Thoth'' included the Game of Fifty-Two—the division of the year into fifty-two seven-day portions, resulting in the enigmatic year of only 364 days of the books of Jubilees and Enoch.

It is a magical number that vaults us across the oceans, to the Americas, returns us to the enigma of Stonehenge, and parts the curtains on the events leading to, and resulting from, the first New Age recorded by Mankind.

9

WHERE THE SUN ALSO RISES

No view epitomizes Stonehenge more than the sight of the Sun's rays shining through the still-standing megaliths of the Sarsen Circle at sunrise on summer's longest day, when the Sun in its northern migration seems to hesitate, stop, and begin to return. As fate would have it, only four of those great stone pillars remain upright and connected at the top by the curving lintels, forming three elongated windows through which we, as though we were Stonehenge's long-gone giant builders, can also view—and determine— the beginning of a new annual cycle (Fig. 108).

And as fate would have it, somewhere on the other side of the world, another set of three windows in a massive structure of cyclopean stones—built, local lore relates, by giants—also offers a breathtaking view of the Sun appearing through white and misty clouds to direct its rays in a precise alignment. That other place of the Three Windows, where the Sun also rises on a crucial calendrical day, is in South America, in Peru (Fig. 109).

Is the similarity just a visual fluke, a mere coincidence? We think not.

Nowadays the place is called Machu Picchu, so named after the sharp peak that rises ten thousand feet at a bend of the Urubamba River on which the ancient city is situated. So well hidden in the jungle and among the endless peaks of the Andes, it eluded the Spanish *Conquistadors* and remained a "lost city of the Incas" until discovered in 1911 by Hiram Bingham. It is now known that it was built long before the Incas, and that its olden name was *Tampu-Tocco,* "Haven of the Three Windows." The place, and its unique three windows, are featured in local lore regarding the origins of the Andean civilization when the gods, led by

Figure 108

Figure 109

the great creator Viracocha, placed the four Ayar brothers and their four sister-wives in Tampu-Tocco. Three brothers emerged through the three windows to settle and civilize the Andean lands; one of them founded the Ancient Empire that preceded that of the Incas by thousands of years.

The three windows formed part of a massive wall constructed of cyclopean granite stones that—as at Stonehenge—were not native to the site, but hauled from a great distance across towering mountains and steep valleys. The colossal stones, carefully smoothed and rounded on their surfaces, were cut into numerous sides and angles as though they were soft putty. Each stone's sides and angles fitted the sides and angles of all its adjoining stones; all these polygonal stones thus locked into one another like pieces of a jigsaw puzzle, tightly fitting without any mortar or cement and withstanding the not infrequent earthquakes in the area and other ravages of man and nature.

The Temple of the Three Windows, as Bingham named it, has only three walls: the one with the windows facing in an easterly direction, and two sidewalls as protecting wings. The western side is completely open, providing room for a stone pillar, about seven feet high; supported by two horizontally placed, carefully shaped stones, one on each side, the pillar precisely faces the central window. Because of a niche cut into the pillar's top, Bingham surmised that it might have held a beam supporting a thatched roofing; but that would have been a unique feature in Machu Picchu, and we believe that the pillar here served the same purpose as the Heel Stone (at first) at Stonehenge or the Altar Stone (later on there), i.e., as the Seventh Pillar of Gudea to provide the line of sight. Ingeniously, the availability of three windows made possible three lines of sight—to sunrise on midsummer day, equinox day, and midwinter day (Fig. 110).

The structure of the three windows with the facing pillar made up the eastern part of what Bingham named, and scholars still call, the Sacred Plaza. Its other principal structure, also three-sided, has its longest wall on the Plaza's northern end and is without a wall on its southern face. It

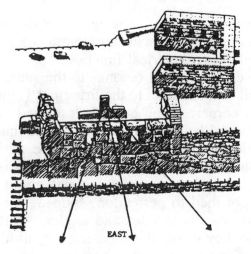

Figure 110

too is made of cyclopean blocks of imported granite also held together by their polygonal shapes. The central north wall has been so constructed as to create seven false windows—trapezoidal cutouts that imitate the three windows but do not in fact cut through the stone wall. A massive rectangular stone monolith, measuring fourteen by five by three feet, lies on the structure's floor below these false windows. Though the purpose of this structure has not been determined, it is still referred to as the Principal Temple, as Bingham named this structure.

Since the five-foot height of the prostrate stone did not let it serve as a seat, Bingham speculated that it might have served as an offering table, "a species of an altar; possibly offerings of food were placed on it, or it may have been intended to receive mummies of the honored dead, which could here be brought out and worshipped on days of festival." Though such customs are purely imaginary, the suggestion that the structure could have been related to festival days—i.e. to the calendar—is intriguing. The false seven windows have six markedly protruding stone pegs above them, so that some kind of counting involving seven and six—as at the Girsu in Lagash—cannot be ruled out. The two sidewalls contain five false windows each, so that each sidewall—one on the east, one on the west—provided a count of twelve together with the central (northern) wall. This too implies a calendrical function.

A smaller enclosure that belongs to the same Megalithic Age was built as an adjunct to the Principal Temple, behind its northwest corner. It can best be described as a roofless room with a stone bench; Bingham assumed that it was the priest's abode, but there is nothing there to indicate its purpose. What is obvious, though, is that it was built with the greatest care of the same polygonal granite boulders, shaped and polished to perfection. Indeed, it is there that the stone with the most sides and angles—thirty-two!—is found; how and by whom this amazing megalith was carved and emplaced is a mystery that confounds the visitor.

Right behind this enclosure there begins a stairway, made of rectangularly shaped but undressed field stones that serve as steps. It winds its way upward, leading from the Sacred Plaza up a hill which overlooks the whole city. The top of the hill was flattened to enable the construction of an enclosure. It was also built of beautifully shaped and smoothed stones, but not of a megalithic size and not outstandingly polygonal; rather, the higher entrance wall that creates a gateway to the hilltop and the surrounding lower walls are built of ashlars—rectangularly shaped stones that, as bricks, form masonry walls. This method of construction is neither of a kind with the colossi of the Megalithic Age nor of the obviously inferior structures of field stones, mortared together in their irregular shapes, of which most other structures at Machu Picchu are built. The latter undoubtedly belong to the Inca period; and the ashlar-built structures, as the one on the hilltop, belong to an earlier era which, in *The Lost Realms,* we have identified as the era of the Ancient Empire.

The ashlar-built structure atop the hill was clearly intended only as a decorative-protective enclosure for the main feature of the hilltop. There, in the center, where the hilltop was flattened to form a platform, an outcropping of the native stone was left sticking out, then shaped and carved magnificently to create a polygonal base from which a short stone column projects upward. That the stone-on-a-base served astronomical-calendrical purposes is evident from its name: *Inti-huatana,* which in the local tongue meant "That which binds the Sun." As the Incas and their descendants explained, it was a stone instrument for observing and determining the solstices, to make sure that the Sun be bound and not keep moving away for good without being pulled back to return (Fig. 111).

Nearly a quarter of a century passed between the discovery of Machu Picchu and the first serious study of its astronomical connotations. It was only in the 1930s that Rolf Müller, a professor of astronomy at the University of Potsdam in Germany, began a series of investigations at several important sites in Peru and Bolivia. Fortunately, he applied to his findings the principles of archaeoastronomy that were first expounded by Lockyer; and so, besides the interesting conclusions regarding the astronomical aspects of Machu Picchu, Cuzco, and Tiahuanacu (on the southern shores of Lake Titicaca), Müller was able to pinpoint their time of construction.

Müller concluded (*Die Intiwatana (Sonnenwarten) im Alten Peru* and other writings) that the short pillar atop the base, and the base itself, were cut and shaped to enable

Figure 111

precise astronomical observations at this particular geographical location and elevation. The pillar (Fig. 112a) served as a gnomon and the base as a recorder of the shadow. However, the base itself was so shaped and oriented that observations along its grooves could pinpoint sunrise or sunset on crucial days (Fig. 112b). Müller concluded that those preintended days were sunset (*Su*) on the day of the winter solstice (June 21 in the southern hemisphere) and sunrise (*Sa*) on the day of the summer solstice (there, December 23). He furthermore determined that the angles of the rectangular base were such that if one were to observe the horizon along a diagonal sightline connecting protrusions 3 and 1, one would have observed sunset precisely on the equinox days at the time the Intihuatana was carved.

That, he concluded based on the Earth's greater tilt at the time, was just over four thousand years ago—sometime

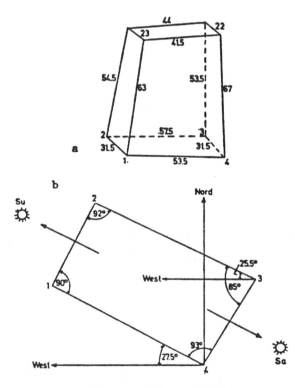

Figures 112a and 112b

between 2100 B.C. and 2300 B.C. This makes the Intihuatana at Machu Picchu contemporaneous with, if not somewhat older than, the Eninnu in Lagash and Stonehenge II. More remarkable perhaps is the rectangular layout for the astronomical function of the Intihuatana's base, for it imitates the exceptional rectangular layout of the four Station Stones of Stonehenge I (though, apparently, without its lunar purposes).

The legend of the Ayar brothers relates that the three brothers from whom the Andean kingdoms stemmed—a kind of South American version of the biblical Ham, Shem, and Japhet—got rid of the fourth brother by imprisoning him in a cave inside a great rock, where he was turned into a stone. Such a cave inside a cleft great rock, with a white vertical stem or short pillar inside, indeed exists at Machu Picchu. Above it one of the most remarkable structures in the whole of South America still stands. Built of the same kind of ashlars as on the platform of the Intihuatana, and thus clearly contemporaneous with it, is an enclosure which on two sides forms perfect walls at a right angle to each other, and on the other two sides curves to form a perfect semicircle (Fig. 113a). It is known the *Torreon* (the Tower).

The enclosure, which is reached by seven stone steps, encompasses, as at the Intihuatana, the protruding peak of the great rock on which it was constructed. As with the Intihuatana, the outcropping here was also carved and given a purposeful shape; except that here no stem was made to act as a gnomon. Instead, the astronomical sightlines that run along grooves and polygonal surfaces of the "sacred rock" lead to two windows in the semicircular wall. Müller, and other astronomers after him (e.g., D.S. Dearborn and R.E. White, *Archaeoastronomy at Machu Picchu*), concluded that the sightlines were oriented to sunrises on the days of the winter and summer solstices—more than four thousand years ago (Fig. 113b).

The two windows were similar in their trapezoid shape (wider at the bottom, narrower at the top) to the legendary Three Windows in the Sacred Plaza and thus emulated, in shape and purpose, the ones from the Megalithic Age. The

Figures 113a and 113b

similarity continued in that the structure of perfect ashlars, where the semicircle ended and the northerly straight wall began, had a third window—if one can so call the aperture. It is larger than the other two; its sill is not straight, but is shaped as an inverted stairway; and its top is formed not by a straight lintel stone but by a wedgelike slit, like an inverted V (Fig. 114).

Because the view through this opening (from inside the Torreon outward) is obstructed by fieldstone buildings from

Figure 114

Inca times, the astronomers who had studied the Torreon attached no astronomical significance to this Third Window. Bingham pointed out that the wall at this window showed clear evidence of fire, and he surmised that it was evidence of the burning of sacrifices on certain festival dates. Our own studies show that when the Incan buildings were not yet there, i.e., at the time of the Ancient Empire, a sightline from the Sacred Rock through the slit in this window to the Intihuatana atop the hill to the northwest would probably have indicated winter solstice sunset when the Torreon was built.

The structure atop the cleft rock also emulated those in the Sacred Plaza in other features. In addition to the three apertures, there were nine false trapezoidal windows in the straight parts of the enclosing walls (see Fig. 113). Spaced between these false windows there protrude from the walls stone pegs or "bobbins" as Bingham called them (Fig. 115). The longer wall, which has seven false windows, has six such pegs—duplicating the arrangement in the longer wall of the Principal Temple.

The number of the windows—actual plus false—twelve, undoubtedly denotes calendrical functions, such as the count of twelve months in a year. The number of false windows (seven) and pegs (six) in the longer wall, as in that of the Principal Temple, may indicate a calendrical need to engage in intercalation—a periodic adjustment of the lunar cycle to the solar cycle by adding a thirteenth month every few years. Combined with the alignments and apertures for observing and determining the solstices and the equinoxes, the false windows with their pegs lead to the conclusion that at Machu Picchu someone had created a complex solar-lunar stone computer to serve as a calendar.

The Torreon, contemporaneous with the Eninnu and with Stonehenge II, is in one respect more remarkable than the rectangular format at the Intihuatana, because it presents the extremely rare *circular* shape of a stone structure—extremely rare, that is, in South America, but with an obvious kinship to the stone circles of Lagash and Stonehenge.

Figure 115

According to legends and data compiled by the Spaniard Fernando Montesinos at the beginning of the seventeenth century, the Inca Empire was not the first kingdom with a capital at Cuzco in Peru. Researchers now know that the legendary Incas, whom the Spaniards encountered and subjugated, came to power at Cuzco only in A.D. 1021. Long before them one of the Ayar brothers, Manco Capac, founded the city when a golden rod given him by the god Viracocha sank into the ground to indicate the right location. It happened, by the calculations of Montesinos, circa 2400 B.C.—almost 3,500 years before the Incas. That Ancient Empire lasted nearly 2,500 years until a succession of plagues, earthquakes, and other calamities caused the people to leave Cuzco. The king, accompanied by a handful of chosen people, retreated to the hideout of Tampu-Tocco; there, the interregnum lasted about a thousand years, until a young man of noble birth was chosen to lead the people back to Cuzco and establish a New Kingdom—that of the Inca dynasty.

When the Spanish conquerors arrived in Cuzco, the Inca capital, in 1533, they were astounded to discover a metropolis with some 100,000 dwelling houses surrounding a royal-religious center of magnificent palaces, temples, plazas, gardens, marketplaces, parade grounds. They were puzzled to hear that the city was divided into twelve wards, arranged in an oval, whose boundaries ran along sightlines anchored to observation towers built on peaks encircling the city (Fig. 116). And they were awed by the sight of the city's and empire's holiest temple—not because it was superbly built, but because it was literally covered with gold. True to its name *Cori-cancha*, meaning Golden Enclosure, the temple's walls were covered with plates of gold; inside there were wondrous artifacts and sculptures of birds and animals made of gold, silver, and precious stones; and in the temple's main courtyard there was a garden whose corn and other growths were all artificial, made of gold and silver. The initial scouting party of Spaniards alone removed seven hundred of those gold plates (as well as many of the other precious artifacts).

Figure 116

Chroniclers who had seen the Coricancha before it was vandalized, demolished by the Catholic priests, and built over into a church, reported that the enclosed compound included a main temple, dedicated to the god Viracocha; and shrines or chapels for the worship of the Moon, Venus, a mysterious star called *Coyllor,* the Rainbow, and the god of Thunder and Lightning. The Spaniards nevertheless called the temple Temple of the Sun, believing that the Sun was the supreme deity wcrshiped by the Incas.

It is assumed that the idea came to the Spaniards from the fact that in the Holy of Holies of the Coricancha—a semicircular chamber—there hung on the wall above the great altar an "image of the Sun." It was a great golden disk which the Spaniards assumed to represent the Sun. In reality, it had served in earlier times to reflect a beam of light as the Sun's rays penetrated the dark chamber once a year—at the moment of sunrise on the day of the winter solstice.

Significantly, the arrangement was akin to that in the Great Temple of Amon at Karnak, in Egypt. Significantly, the Holy of Holies was in the same extremely rare form of a semicircle, as the Torreon in Machu-Picchu. Significantly, the earliest part of the temple, including the Holy of Holies, was built of the same perfect ashlars as the Torreon and the walls enclosing the Intihuatana—the hallmark of the Ancient Empire era. And, not surprisingly, careful studies and measurements by Müller showed that the orientation designed to permit the beam of sunlight to travel through the corridor and bounce off the ''image of the Sun'' was conceived when the Earth's obliquity was 24° (Fig. 117), which chronologically means, he wrote, more than four thousand years earlier. This matches the timetable related by Montesinos, according to which the Ancient Empire began circa 2500–2400 B.C. and the assertion that the temple in Cuzco was built soon thereafter.

As astoundingly early as the structures of the Ancient Empire were, they were clearly not the earliest ones, for according to the Ayar legends the megalithic Three Windows had already existed when the founder of the Ancient Empire, Manco Capac, and his brothers set out from Tampu-Tocco to establish kingships in the Andean lands.

A Megalithic Age with its colossal structures had ob-

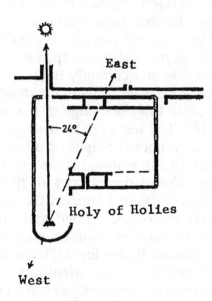

Figure 117

viously preceded the Ancient Empire—structures distinguished not only by their immense size, but also by the amazing polygonality of their stone blocks coupled with the smoothly shaped and somewhat rounded faces of these megaliths. But as mind-boggling as that age's structures at Machu Picchu are, they are neither the largest nor the most enigmatic ones. The prize for that should undoubtedly go to the ruins at Sacsahuaman, the promontory that overlooks Cuzco.

Shaped like a triangle with its base toward the mountain chain of which the promontory is an edge, its two sides formed by deep gorges, its apex forms a peak that rises steeply some eight hundred feet above the city that lies at its bottom. The promontory can be divided into three parts. The widest part, forming the triangle's base, is dominated by huge rock outcroppings that someone—"giants" according to local lore—had cut and shaped, with incredible ease and at angles that could not possibly have been formed with crude hand tools, to form giant steps or platforms or inverted stairs, additionally perforating the rocks with twisting channels, tunnels, grooves, and niches. The promontory's middle section is formed by an area hundreds of feet wide and long that has been flattened out to form a huge level area. This flattened-out area is clearly separated from the triangular and more elevated apex of the promontory by a most remarkable and certainly unique stone structure. It consists of three massive walls that extend in a zigzag parallel to each other from one edge of the promontory to the other (Fig. 118). The walls are built so as to rise one behind the other, to a combined height of about sixty feet. They are constructed of the colossal stone blocks and in the polygonal fashion that is the earmark of the Megalithic Age; those in the forefront, that support the earthfills that form the raised terraces for the second and third tiers, are the most massive. Its smallest boulders weigh between ten and twenty tons; most are fifteen feet high and are ten to fourteen feet in width and thickness. Many are much larger; one boulder in the front row is twenty-seven feet high and weighs over three hundred tons (Fig. 119). As with the other mega-

Figure 118

Figure 119

liths at Machu Picchu, the ones at Sacsahuaman too were brought over from a great distance, were given their smooth and beveled faces and polygonal shapes, and remain holding fast together without mortar.

By whom, when, and why were these structures above ground, and the tunnels, channels, conduits, bored holes, and other odd shapes carved into the living rocks, made and fashioned? Local lore attributed it to "the giants." The Spaniards, as the chronicler Garcilaso de la Vega wrote, believed that they were "erected not by men but by demons." Squier wrote that the zigzagging walls represented "without doubt the grandest specimens of the style called Cyclopean extant in America," but offered no explanation or theory.

Recent excavations have uncovered behind the large rock outcroppings that separate the flat middle area from the rocky area leading to the northwest, where most of the tunnels and channels have been formed, one of the most unusual structural shapes in South America: a perfect circle. Carefully shaped stones have been laid out so as to form the rim of a sunken area, perfectly circular. In *The Lost Realms* we enumerate the reasons for our conclusion that it served as a reservoir where ores—gold ores, to be specific— were processed as in a giant pan.

This, however, was not the only circular structure on the promontory. Assuming that the three tiers of colossal walls were ramparts of a fortress, the Spaniards took it for granted that structural remains in the highest and narrowest part of the promontory, behind and above the walls, belonged to an Inca fortification. Prompted by local legends that a child once fell into a hole there and later emerged eight hundred feet down in Cuzco proper, local archaeologists engaged in limited excavations. They discovered that the area behind and above the three walls was honeycombed with subterranean tunnels and chambers. More important, they uncovered there the foundations of a series of connected square and rectangular buildings (Fig. 120a); in their midst there were the remains of a perfectly circular structure. The natives refer to the structure as the *Muyocmarca*, "The Circular Building"; the archeologists call it the *Torreon*—the Tower—the same descriptive name given to the semicircular structure at Machu Picchu, and assumed that it was a defensive tower, part of the Sacsahuaman "fortress."

Archaeoastronomers, however, see in the structure clear evidence of an astronomical function. R.T. Zuidema (*Inca Observations of the Solar and Lunar Passages*, and other studies) noted that the alignment of the straight walls adjoining the circular structure was such that the north and south points of zenith and nadir could have been determined there. The walls that form the square enclosure within which

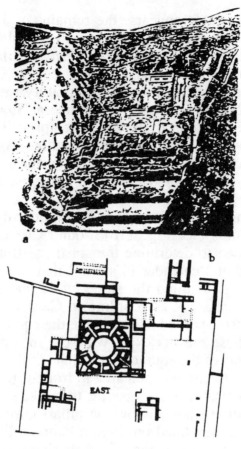

Figures 120a and 120b

the circular structure was emplaced are indeed aligned with the cardinal points (Fig. 120b); but they form only a frame for the circular structure, which consisted of three concentric walls connected by spokes of masonry that divide the outer two circular walls into sections. One such opening—an aperture if the higher courses forming the tower followed the ground plan—does point due south and thus could have served to determine sunset on nadir day. But the four other openings are clearly oriented to the northeast, southeast, southwest, and northwest—the unmistakable points of sunset and sunrise on the winter and summer solstice days (in the southern hemisphere).

If these are, at it appears, the remains of a full-fledged astronomical observatory, it was in all probability *the earliest round observatory in South America,* perhaps in all of the Americas.

The alignment of this round observatory to the solstices puts it in the same category as the one at Stonehenge and orientationally as that of Egyptian temples. The evidence suggests, however, that after the Megalithic Age and in the era of the Ancient Empire begun under the aegis of Viracocha, both the equinoxes and the lunar cycle played the key roles in the Andean calendar.

The chronicler Garcilaso de la Vega, describing the towerlike structures (see Fig. 116) around Cuzco, stated that they were used to determine the solstices. But he also described another "calendar in stone" that has not survived and that brings to mind the stone circle that stood on the platform in Lagash . . . According to Garcilaso, the pillars erected in Cuzco served to determine the equinoxes, not the solstices. These are his exact words: "In order to denote the precise day of the equinoctial, pillars of the finest marble had been erected in the open area in front of the Coricancha which, when the Sun came near the time, the priests watched daily to observe what shadow the pillars cast; and to make it more exact they fixed on them a gnomon like the pin of a dial. And so, soon as the sun at its rising came to cast a direct shadow by it and at the sun's height, by midday, cast no shadow, they concluded that the sun had entered the equinoctial."

According to the authoritative study *The Andean Calendar* by L.E. Valcarcel, such a fixing and veneration of the equinoxes was carried into Inca times although they switched from an earlier equinoctial calendar to a solstitial one. His study brought out the fact that Inca month names accorded special significance to months corresponding to our March and September, the equinoctial months. "The Incas believed," he wrote, "that on the two days of the equinoxes Father Sun came down to live among men."

The need to adjust the solar calendar over a period of millennia because of the phenomenon of precession and, perhaps, also due to the wavering between a solstitial and an equinoctial New Year, led to repeated reforms of the calendar even in the days of the Ancient Empire. According to Montesinos, the 5th, 22nd, 33rd, 39th, and 50th monarchs of the Ancient Empire "renewed the computation of time that had fallen into confusion." That such calendar reforms had to do with wavering between solstices and equinoxes is confirmed by the statement that the monarch Manco Capac IV "ordered that the year begin at the spring equinox," a feat possible because he was an *Amauta,* a "knower of astronomy." But evidently in doing so he only reinstated a calendar that had once been in use, in earlier times; for, according to Montesinos, the fortieth monarch who had reigned a thousand years before Manco Capac IV, "established an academy for the study of astronomy and determined the equinoxes. He was knowing in astronomy and found the equinoxes, which the Indians called *Illa-Ri.*"

As if all that was not enough to require constant reforms, other evidence also indicates the employment of, or at least familiarity with, the lunar calendar. In his studies of Andean archaeoastronomy Rolf Müller reported that at a site called Pampa de Anta, some ten miles west of Sacsahuaman, the sheer rock has been carved into a series of steps that form a semicircle or crescent. Since there is nothing to view there except the promontory at Sacsahuaman to the east, Müller concluded that the place served to make astronomical observations along a sightline anchored on the Sacsahuaman promontory—but, apparently, linked to appearances of the Moon. The native name for the edifice, *Quillarumi,* "Moon Stone," suggests such a purpose.

Shackled by the notions that the Incas worshiped the Sun, modern scholars found it at first difficult to concede that Inca observations could have also included the Moon. In fact the early Spanish chroniclers stated repeatedly that the Incas had an elaborate and precise calendar incorporating both solar and lunar aspects. The chronicler Felipe Guaman Poma de Avila stated that the Incas "knew the cycles of the Sun and the Moon . . . and the month of the year and the four winds of the world." The assertion that the Incas observed both solar and lunar cycles is confirmed by the fact that next to the shrine to the Sun in the Coricancha there was a shrine to the Moon. In the Holy of Holies the central symbol was an ellipse flanked by the Sun on the left and the Moon on the right; it was only the ruler Huascar, one of the two half brothers who were fighting over the throne when the Spaniards arrived, who replaced the oval with a golden disk representing the Sun.

These are Mesopotamian calendrical features; finding them in the remote Andes has baffled the scholars. Even more perplexing has been the certainty that the Incas were familiar with the zodiac—a wholly arbitrary device for dividing the orbital circle around the Sun into twelve parts— a Sumerian "first" by all accounts.

E.G. Squier, in his report on Cuzco and the meaning of its name ("Navel of the Earth"), noted that the city was divided into twelve wards arranged around the nucleus or "navel" in an elliptical shape (Fig. 121), which is the true orbital circuit. Sir Clemens Markham (*Cuzco and Lima: the Incas of Peru*) quoted the chronicler Garcilaso de la Vega's information that the twelve wards represented the twelve zodiacal constellations. Stansbury Hagar (*Cuzco, the Celestial City*) noted that, according to Inca lore, Cuzco was laid out in conformity with a sacred or divine plan to emulate the heavens, and concluded that the first ward, named "Terrace of Kneeling," represented the constellation Aries. He showed that—as in Mesopotamia—the Incas also associated each of the twelve zodiac "houses" with a parallel month in the calendar. These zodiacal months bore names that had an uncanny resemblance to their Near Eastern names that originated in Sumer. Thus, the month of the autumn equinox, which equaled the month of the spring equinox and the constellation of the Bull (Taurus) when the calendar began in Sumer, was called *Tupa Taruca,* "Pasturing Stag." The constellation of the Maiden (Virgo), as another example, was called *Sara Mama,* "Mother Maize." To grasp fully the extent of such similarities, one should recall that in Mesopotamia this constellation (see Fig. 91) was depicted as a maiden holding a stalk of grain—wheat or barley

Figure 121

in Mesopotamia, replaced by *maiz* (corn) in the Andes. Hagar's conclusion that the zodiacal layout in Cuzco associated the first ward with Aries rather than with Taurus as in Sumer, suggests that the city's plan was devised after the Age of Taurus had ended (due to precession) at about 2150 B.C. According to Montesinos, it was the fifth ruler of the Ancient Empire who completed the Coricancha and introduced a new calendar some time after 1900 B.C. That *Capac* (ruler) was given the epithet *Pachacuti* (Reformer), and one can safely conclude that the reform of the calendar in his time was required by the zodiacal shift from Taurus to Aries—another confirmation of familiarity with the zodiac and its calendrical aspects even in pre-Inca times in the Andes.

There were other aspects—complex aspects—of the ancient Near Eastern calendars in the calendar that the Incas had retained from the days of the Ancient Empire. The requirement (still in force in the Jewish and Christian calendars) that the spring festival (Passover, Easter) be held when the Sun is in the relevant zodiac house *and* on or immediately after the first full Moon of that month, forced the ancient priest-astronomers to intercalate the solar and lunar cycles. The studies by R.T. Zuidema and others concluded that not only did such intercalation take place in the Andes, but that the lunar cycle was additionally linked to two other phenomena: it had to be the first full Moon after the June solstice, and it was to coincide with the first heliacal rising of a certain star. This double correlation is intriguing, for it brings to mind the Egyptian linking of the beginning of their calendrical cycle both to the solar date (rising of the Nile) and the heliacal rising of a star (Sirius).

Some twenty miles northeast of Cuzco, at a place called Pisac, there are remains of a structure, probably from early Inca times, that appear to have been an attempt to emulate and combine some of the sacred structures at Machu Picchu: a building one of whose sides was semicircular, with a crude *Intihuatana* in its midst. At a place not far from Sacsahuaman called Kenko, a large semicircle of well-shaped ashlars fronts on a large stone monolith that could have had the shape of an animal (the features are too damaged to be discerned); whether or not this edifice had astronomical-calendrical functions is unknown. These sites, added to those of Machu Picchu, Sacsahuaman, and Cuzco, illustrate the fact that in what has been called the Sacred Valley— *and only there*—religion, the calendar, and astronomy led to the construction of *circular or semicircular* observatories; nowhere else in South America do we find such structures.

Who was it who, *at about the same time,* applied the same set of astronomical principles and adopted a circular shape for celestial observations in early Britain, at Lagash in Sumer, and in South America's Ancient Empire?

All legends, supported by geographical evidence and archaeological finds, point to the southern shores of Lake Titicaca as the place of the South American Beginning—

not only of human civilization, but of the gods themselves. It was there, according to the legends, that the repopulation of the Andean lands began after the Deluge; that the gods, headed by Viracocha, had their abode; that the couples destined to begin the Ancient Empire were given knowledge, route instructions, and the Golden Wand with which to locate the site of the Navel of the Earth—of establishing *Cuzco*.

Insofar as human beginnings in the Andes are concerned, the tales connected them to two distinct islands off the southern shore of Lake Titicaca. They were called the Island of the Sun and the Island of the Moon, the two luminaries having been considered as the two principal helpers of Viracocha; the calendrical symbolism inherent in these tales has been noted by many scholars. The abode of Viracocha was, however, in a City of the Gods on the mainland, at the lake's southern shore. The place, called Tiahuanacu, was settled by the gods (according to local lore) in times immemorial; it was, the legends related, a place of colossal structures that only giants could erect.

The chronicler Pedro Cieza de León, who traveled throughout what is now Peru and Bolivia in the years immediately following the Spanish conquest, reported that without doubt, of all the antiquities in the Andean lands, the ruins at Tiahuanacu were "the most ancient place of any." Among the edifices that amazed him was an artificial hill "on a great stone foundation" that measured more than 900 feet by 400 feet at its base and rose some 120 feet. Nearby he saw gigantic stone blocks fallen to the ground, among them "many doorways with their jambs, lintels, and thresholds all in one stone" which in turn were part of even larger stone blocks, "some of them thirty feet broad, fifteen or more long, and six in thickness." He wondered whether "human force can have sufficed to move them to the place where we see them, being so large." But not only the immense size of the stone blocks puzzled him; so did their "grandeur and magnificence." "For myself," he wrote, "I fail to understand with what instruments or tools it could have been done, for it is certain that before these great stones could be brought to perfection and left as we see them, the tools must have been much better than those now used by the Indians.'' He had no doubt that ''two stone idols, of the human shape and figure, the features very skillfully carved . . . that seem like small giants'' were responsible for the wondrous structures.

Over the centuries most of the smaller stone blocks have been carted away to be used in La Paz, the Bolivian capital, in railroads leading to it, and in rural areas all around. But even so, travelers continued to report the incredible monumental remains; by the end of the nineteenth century the reports assumed a more scientific accuracy as a result of the visits and researches by Ephraim George Squier (*Peru: Incidents of Travel and Exploration in the Land of the Incas*) and A. Stübel and Max Uhle (*Die Ruinenstaette von Tiahuanaco im Hochland des Alten Peru*). They were followed earlier this century by the most renowned and tenacious researcher of Tiahuanacu, Arthur Posnansky (*Tiahuanacu— The Cradle of American Man*). Their work and more recent excavations and studies, reviewed at length in *The Lost Realms,* have led us to conclude that Tiahuanacu was the tin capital of the ancient world, that its extensive aboveground and underground structures were metallurgical facilities, that the huge one-piece multiwalled stone blocks were part of port facilities at the ancient lakeshore, and that Tiahuanacu was founded not by Man but by the Anunnaki ''gods'' in their search for gold long before Man was taught the uses of tin.

Where a narrow and rare plain fanned out from the southern shore of Lake Titicaca, the site of the once magnificent Tiahuanacu and its port (nowadays called Puma-Punku), only three principal monuments to its past dominate the landscape. The one at the southeastern part of the ruins is the hill called *Akapana,* an artificial hill (as Cieza de León had observed) that was assumed to have served as a fortress; it is now known to have been more like a stage-pyramid with built-in reservoirs, conduits, channels and sluices that indicate its true purpose: a facility for the separation and processing of ores.

This artificial hill, which some believe originally had the shape of a step-pyramid like that of a Mesopotamian ziggurat, dominates the flat landscape. As the visitor casts his gaze about, another structure stands out. Situated to the northwest of the Akapana, it appears from a distance as a transplanted *Arc de Triomphe* from Paris. It is indeed a gate, intricately cut and carved out of a single cyclopean stone block; but it was not set up to commemorate a victory—rather, to enshrine in stone a marvelous calendar.

Called "Gate of the Sun," the single stone block from which it was cut and shaped measured about ten by twenty feet and weighed more than one hundred tons. There are niches and geometrically accurate cutouts upon the lower part of the gate, especially on what is considered its back side (Fig. 122b). The most elaborate and enigmatic carvings are on the upper front side (Fig. 122a), facing due east. There, the arch of the gate has been carved to depict in relief a central figure—probably of Viracocha—flanked on each side by three rows of winged attendants (Fig. 123a); the central figure and three rows have been positioned above a meandering geometric frame so carved as to snake over and under miniature images of Viracocha (Fig. 123b).

The writings of Posnansky have established that the carvings on the gate represented a twelve-month calendar of a year beginning on the day of the spring equinox in the southern hemisphere (September), yet a year where the other major points of the solar year—the autumn equinox and the two solstices—are also indicated by the positions and shapes of the depicted smaller images. It was, he concluded, a calendar of eleven months of thirty days each plus a "great month," a twelfth month of thirty-five days, adding up to a solar year of 365 days.

A twelve-month year beginning on the day of the spring equinox was, as we now know, first introduced at Nippur, in Sumer, circa 3800 B.C.

The "Gate of the Sun," archaeologists have discovered, stands at the northwest corner of what was a wall constructed of upright stone pillars that formed a rectangular enclosure within which the third most prominent edifice of the site

Figures 122a and 122b

stood. Some believe that there was originally a similar gate at the southwestern corner of the enclosure, flanking symmetrically a row of thirteen monoliths erected in the precise center of the enclosure's western wall. That row of monoliths, part of a special platform, faced exactly the monumental stairway that was built at the center of the eastern wall, on the enclosure's opposite side. The monumental stairway, which has been unearthed and restored, led to a series of raised rectangular platforms that encompassed a sunken courtyard (Fig. 124a).

Given the name *Kalasasaya* (''The Standing Pillars''), the edifice was thus oriented precisely along an east–west

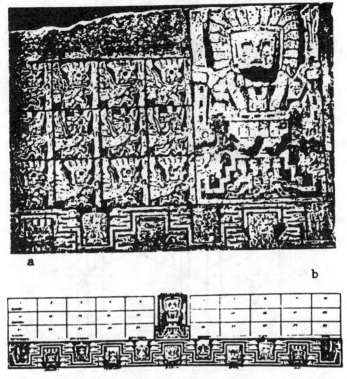

Figures 123a and 123b

axis, in the manner of the Near Eastern temples. This was the first clue that it could have served astronomical purposes. Subsequent researches indeed established that it was a sophisticated observatory for determining the solstices as well as the equinoxes by observing sunrises and sunsets from certain focal points along sightlines anchored at the enclosure's corners and the pillars erected at its western and eastern walls (Fig. 124b). Posnansky found evidence that the back side of the Gate of the Sun was so carved out that it probably held two golden panels that could be swung on bronze axles; that might have enabled the astronomer-priests to angle the plates so that they reflected the sunset rays toward any desired observation post in the Kalasasaya proper. The multiple sightlines, more than were required just for observations on solstice or equinox days, the fact that Viracocha was helped by both the Sun and the Moon,

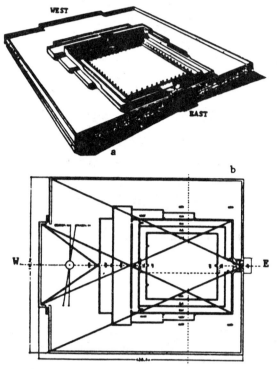

Figures 124a and 124b

and the fact that there were thirteen, not just twelve, pillars at the center of the western wall suggest that the Kalasasaya was not just a solar observatory, but one that served a solar-lunar calendar.

The realization that this ancient structure, more than twenty thousand feet up the Andean mountains, in a desolate, narrow plain among snowbound mountains, was a sophisticated calendrical observatory was compounded by discoveries regarding its age. Posnansky was the first to conclude that the angles formed by the lines of sight suggested an obliquity somewhat greater than the present declination of 23.5°; it meant, he himself was astounded to realize, that the Kalasasaya had been designed and built thousands of years before the Common Era.

The understandable disbelief on the part of the scientific community at the time—at most it was thought the ruins, if not from Incan times, were not older than from a few centuries B.C.—led to the dispatch of a German Astronomical Commission to Peru and Bolivia. Dr. Rolf Müller, whose extensive work on other sites has already been mentioned by us, was one of the three astronomers chosen for the task. The investigations and thorough measurements left no doubt that the obliquity prevailing at the time of construction was such that the Kalasasaya could have been built circa 4050 B.C. or (as the Earth tilted back and forth) circa 10,050 B.C. Müller, who had arrived at a date of just over 4000 B.C. for the megalithic remains at Machu Picchu, was inclined likewise to date the Kalasasaya—a conclusion with which Posnansky in the end agreed.

Who was there with such sophisticated knowledge to plan, orient, and erect such calendrical observatories—and in a manner that followed the astronomical principles and calendrical arrangements devised in the ancient Near East? In *The Lost Realms* we presented the evidence and arrived at the conclusion that it was the same Anunnaki, those who had come to Earth from Nibiru in need of gold. And, like the men who searched for the golden El Dorado millennia later, they also came to the New World in search of gold. The mines in southeastern Africa were flooded by the Deluge; but the same upheaval uncovered the incredibly rich veins of gold in the Andes.

We believe that Anu and his spouse Antu, visiting Earth from Nibiru circa 3800 B.C., also went to see for themselves the new metallurgical center on the southern shore of Lake Titicaca. They left by sailing away on the lake from the port facilities of Puma Punku, where the cyclopean chambers, carved and shaped out of single stone blocks, then stood alongside massive piers.

The remains at Puma Punku hold another enigmatic clue to the amazing link between the structures at Lake Titicaca and the unusual temple to Ninurta that Gudea built. To the disbelief of the site's excavators, they found that the megalithic builders had used *bronze clamps,* formed to fit T-shaped cutouts in adjoining stones, to hold together the huge stone blocks (Fig. 125). Such a clamping method, and such

Figure 125

a use of bronze, were unique to the Megalithic Age, having been found only at Puma Punku and at another site of cyclopean megaliths, Ollantaytambu, some forty-five miles northwest of Cuzco in the Sacred Valley.

Yet thousands of miles away, on the other side of the world, at Lagash in Sumer, Gudea used the very same unique method and the very same unique bronze clamps to hold together the stones that, imported from afar, were used in the construction of the Eninnu. Recording in his inscriptions the unusual use of stones and of metals, this is how Gudea lauded his own achievements:

> *He built the Eninnu with stone,*
> *he made it bright with jewels;*
> *with copper mixed with tin [bronze]*
> *he held it fast.*

It was a feat for which a *Sangu Simug*, a "priestly smith," was brought over from the "Land of Smelting." It was, we believe, Tiahuanacu in the Andes.

10

IN THEIR FOOTSTEPS

The Great Sphinx of Egypt gazes precisely eastward, welcoming the rising Sun along the 30th parallel. In ancient times its gaze welcomed the Anunnaki "gods" as they landed at their spaceport in the Sinai peninsula, and later on guided the deceased pharaohs to an Afterlife, when their *Ka* joined the gods in their heavenly ascents. At some time in between, the Sphinx might have witnessed the departure of a great god—Thoth—with his followers, to be counted among the First Americans.

The 500th anniversary of the epochal voyage of Columbus in 1492 has been by now reclassified from discovery to rediscovery, and has intensified the inquiry regarding the true identity of the "First Americans." The notion that settlement of the Americas began with the trekking of family groups from Asia across a frozen landbridge to Alaska, just before the last ice age abruptly ended, has been grudgingly giving way in the face of mounting archaeological evidence that humans arrived in the Americas many millennia earlier, and that South America, not North America, was the earliest arena of human presence in the New World.

"For the last 50 years, the received wisdom has been that the 11,500-year-old artifacts found at Clovis, New Mexico, were made soon after the first Americans found their way across the Bering landbridge," *Science* magazine (21 February 1992 issue) wrote in an update on the debate among scientists; "Those who have dared question the consensus have met with harsh criticism." The reluctance to accept an earlier age and a different arrival route stems primarily from the simple assumption that Man could not have crossed the oceans separating the Old and New Worlds at such

255

prehistoric times because maritime technology did not yet exist. Notwithstanding the evidence to the contrary, the rock-bottom logic continues to be, if Man couldn't do it, it didn't happen.

The age of the Sphinx has recently emerged as an analogous issue, where scientists refuse to accept new evidence because it implies achievements by Man when Man could not have achieved them; and guidance or assistance by the "gods"—Extraterrestrials—is simply out of consideration.

In previous books of *The Earth Chronicles* we have presented extensive evidence (to date unrefuted) that the great pyramids of Giza were built not by pharaohs of the Fourth Dynasty circa 2600 B.C., but by the Anunnaki "gods" millennia earlier, as components of the landing corridor for the spaceport in the Sinai peninsula. We arrived at the time frame of circa 10,000 B.C.—some 12,000 years ago—for those pyramids; and we showed that the Sphinx, built soon thereafter, had already existed on the Giza plateau when pharaonic reigns began many centuries before the Fourth Dynasty. The evidence we relied on and presented were Sumerian and Egyptian depictions, inscriptions, and texts.

In October 1991, some fifteen years after our initial presentation of such evidence in *The 12th Planet,* Dr. Robert M. Schoch, a Boston University geologist, reported at the annual meeting of the Geological Society of America that meteorological studies of the Sphinx and its layering indicated that it was carved out of the native rock "long before the dynasties of the Pharaohs." The research methods included seismic surveying of subsurface rocks by Dr. Thomas L. Dobecki, a geophysicist from Houston, and Egyptologist Anthony West of New York, and the study of weathering and watermarks on the Sphinx and its surroundings. The precipitation-induced weathering, Dr. Schoch stated, "indicated that work on the Sphinx had begun in the period between 10,000 B.C. and 5000 B.C., when the Egyptian climate was wetter."

The conclusion "flies in the face of everything we know

about ancient Egypt," the *Los Angeles Times* added in its report of the announcement. "Other Egyptologists who have looked at Mr. Schoch's work cannot explain the geological evidence, but they insist that the idea that the Sphinx is thousands of years older than they had thought just simply "does not match up" with what has been known. The newspaper quoted archaeologist Carol Redmount of the University of California at Berkeley: "There's just no way that could be true . . . The Sphinx was created with technology that was far more advanced than that of other Egyptian monuments of known date, and the people of that region would not have had the technology, the governing institutions or the will to have built such a structure thousands of years earlier."

In February 1992, the American Association for the Advancement of Science, meeting in Chicago, devoted a session to the subject "How old is the Sphinx?" at which Robert Schoch and Thomas Dobecki debated their findings with two debunkers, Mark Lehner of the University of Chicago and K.L. Gauri of the University of Louisville. According to the Associated Press, the heated debate which spilled over into a confrontation in the hallway has not focused on the scientific merits of the meteorological findings, but, as Mark Lehner expressed it, on whether it is permissible to "overthrow Egyptian history based on one phenomenon, like a weathering profile." The final argument by the debunkers was the absence of evidence that a civilization advanced enough to carve the Great Sphinx existed in Egypt between 7000 and 5000 B.C. "The people during that age were hunters and gatherers; they didn't build cities," Dr. Lehner said; and with that the debate ended.

The only response to this logical argument is, of course, to invoke someone other than the "hunters and gatherers" of that era—the Anunnaki. But admitting that all evidence points to such more advanced beings from another planet is a threshold that not everyone, including those who find the Sphinx to be 9,000 years old, is as yet ready to cross.

The same Fear-of-Crossing (to coin an expression) has

blocked for many years not just the acceptance, but even the dissemination, of evidence concerning the antiquity of Man and his civilizations in the Americas.

The discovery near Clovis, New Mexico, in 1932 of a trove of leaf-shaped, sharp-edged stone points that could be attached to spears and clubs for hunting, and subsequently at other North American sites, led to the theory that big game hunters migrated from Asia to the Pacific northwest some 12,000 years ago, when Siberia and Asia were linked by an icy landbridge. In time, the theory held, these ''Clovis People'' and their kindred folk spread over North America and, via Central America, eventually also to South America.

This neat image of the First Americans retained its exclusive hold in spite of occasional discoveries, even in the southwestern United States, of remains of crushed bones or chipped pebbles—arguably evidence of human presence—dating some 20,000 years before Clovis. A less doubtful find has been that at Meadowcroft rock shelter, Pennsylvania, where stone tools, animal bones, and, most important, charcoal, have been carbon-dated to between 15,000 and 19,000 years ago—millennia before Clovis, and in the eastern part of the United States to boot.

As linguistic research and genetic trace-backs joined other investigative tools, the evidence began to mount in the 1980s that humans arrived in the New World some 30,000 years ago—probably in more than one migration, and perhaps not necessarily over an icebridge but by rafts or canoes hugging the coastlines. The basic tenet—out of northeast Asia into northwest America—has, however, been stubbornly maintained in spite of unsettling evidence from South America. That evidence, whose discovery was not only ignored but even initially suppressed, pertains primarily to two sites where Stone Age tools, crushed animal bones, and even petroglyphs have been found.

The first of these unsettling settlement sites is Monte Verde in Chile, on the continent's Pacific side. There archaeologists have found remains of clay-lined hearths, stone tools, bone implements, and foundations of wooden shelters—a campsite occupied some 13,000 years ago. This is a date much too early to be explained by a slow southward migration of Clovis People from North America. Moreover, lower strata at this campsite yielded fragmented stone tools that suggest that the site's human occupation began some 20,000 years earlier. The second site is all the way on the other side of South America, in Brazil's northeast. At a place called Pedra Furada, a rock shelter contained circular hearths filled with charcoal surrounded by flints; the nearest source of flint is a mile away, indicating that the sharp stones were brought over intentionally. Dating by radiocarbon and newer methods provided readings spanning the period 14,300 to 47,000 years ago. While most established archaeologists continue to consider the early dates "simply inconceivable," the rock shelter has yielded, at the 10,000 B.C. level, petrogylphs (rock paintings) whose age is undisputable. In one, a long-necked animal that looks like a giraffe—an animal nonexistent in the Americas—seems to have been depicted.

The ongoing challenge to the Clovis theory in regard to the time of arrival has been accompanied by a challenge to the via-the-Bering-strait route as the sole path of arrival. Anthropologists at the Arctic Research Center of the Smithsonian Institution in Washington, D.C., have concluded that the image of animal-skin clad hunters carrying spears across a frozen wilderness (with women and children in tow) is all wrong in thinking of the First Americans. Rather, they were maritime people who sailed in rafts or skinboats to the more hospitable southern shores of the Americas. Others, at the Center for the Study of the First Americans at Oregon State University, do not rule out a crossing of the Pacific via the islands and Australia (which was settled circa 40,000 years ago).

Most others still consider such early crossings by "primitive man" as fantasies; the early dates are shrugged off as instrumental errors, stone "tools" as pieces of fallen rocks, broken animal bones as crushed by rockfalls, not by hunters. The same question that has brought the Age of the Sphinx debate to a dead end has been applied to the First Americans debate: who was there, tens of thousands of years ago, who possessed the technology required for crossing vast oceans by boat, and how could those prehistoric mariners have known that there was land, habitable land, on the other side?

This is a question that (also when applied to the Age of the Sphinx) has only one answer: the Anunnaki, showing Man how to cross the oceans, telling him why and where-to—perhaps carrying him over, ''on the wings of eagles,'' as the Bible has described—to a new Promised Land.

There are two instances of planned migrations recounted in the Bible, and in both the deity was the guide. The first instance was the ordering of Abraham, more than 4,000 years ago, to ''get thee out of thy country and out of thy birthplace and from thy father's house.'' He was to go, Yahweh said, ''unto the land which I will show thee.'' The second instance was the Israelite Exodus from Egypt, some 3,400 years ago. Showing the Israelites the route to take to the Promised Land,

Yahweh went before them by day
in a pillar of cloud,
to lead them the way,
and by night in a pillar of fire
to give light to them,
to go by day and by night.

Aided and guided, the people followed in the footsteps of the gods—in the ancient Near East as well as in the new lands across the oceans.

The latest archaeological discoveries lend credence to memories of early events that are called ''myths'' and ''legends.'' Invariably, they speak of multiple migrations and always from across the seas. Significantly, they often involve the numbers seven and twelve—numbers that are not a reflection of human anatomy or digital counting, but a clue to astronomical and calendrical knowledge, as well as to links with the Old World.

One of the best preserved cycle of legends is that of the Nahuatl tribes of central Mexico, of which the Aztecs whom the Spaniards encountered were the latest extant. Their tales of migration encompassed four ages, or "Suns," the first one of which ended with the Deluge; one version that provides lengths in years for those ages indicates that the first "Sun" began 17,141 years before the tale was related to the Spaniards, i.e. circa 15,600 B.C. and thus indeed millennia before the Deluge. The earliest tribes, the oral legends and the tales written down pictorially in books called codices related, came from *Azt-lan,* the "White Place," which was associated with the number seven. It was sometimes depicted as a place with seven caves out of which the ancestors had emerged; alternatively, it was painted as a place with seven temples: a central large step-pyramid (ziggurat) surrounded by six lesser shrines. *Codex Boturini* contains a series of cartoonlike paintings of the early migration by four tribes that began from the place of the seven temples, involved crossing a sea in boats and a landing in a place of cave shelters; the migrants were guided in that journey to the unknown by a god whose symbol was a kind of Seeing-eye attached to an elliptical rod (Fig. 126a). The four clans of migrants then trekked inland (Fig. 126b), passing by and following various landmarks. Splitting into several tribes, one, the *Mexica,* finally reached the valley where an eagle was perched upon a cactus bush—the signal for their final destination and the place where the Nahuatlan capital was to be built. It later developed into the Aztec capital, whose symbol remained the eagle perched on a cactus bush. It was called *Tenochtitlan,* the City of Tenoch. Those earliest migrants were called Tenochites, the People of Tenoch; in *The Lost Realms* we detailed the reasons why they might have been the descendants of Enoch, the son of Cain, who still suffered the sevenfold avenging of their forefather's crime of fratricide. According to the Bible Cain, who was banished to a distant "Land of Wandering," built a city and named it after his son Enoch; and Enoch had four descendants from whom there grew four clans.

The Spanish chronicler Friar Bernardino de Sahagún

Figures 126a and 126b

(*Historia de las cosas de la Nueva Espana*), whose sources were verbal as well as Nahuatlan tales written down after the conquest, recorded the sea voyage and the name, *Panotlan,* of the landing site; the name simply meant "Place of arrival by sea," and he concluded that it was in what is now Guatemala. His information added the interesting detail that the immigrants were led by four Wise Men, "who carried with them ritual manuscripts and who also knew the secrets of the calendar." We now know that the two—ritual and calendar—were two sides of the same coin, the worship of the gods. It is a safe bet that the Nahuatlan calendar followed the twelve-month arrangement, perhaps even the twelve-zodiac division; for we read (in Sahagún's chronicles) that the Toltecs, the Nahuatl tribe that preceded and taught the Aztecs, "knew that many are the heavens; they said that there are twelve superimposed divisions" thereof.

Down south, where the Pacific Ocean lapped the coasts of South America, Andean "myths" did not recall pre-Diluvial migrations but knew of the Deluge and asserted that the gods, already present in those lands, were the ones to help the few survivors upon the high peaks to repopulate the continent. The legends do speak clearly of new, post-Diluvial arrivals by sea; the first or most memorable of them was one headed by a leader called Naymlap. He led his people across the Pacific in a fleet of boats made of balsa wood, guided by an "idol," a green stone through which the Great God delivered navigational and other instructions. The landfall was at the point where the South American continent juts out the most westward into the Pacific Ocean, at what is nowadays called Cape Santa Helena in Ecuador. After they had landed, the Great God (still speaking through the green stone) instructed the people in farming, building, and handicrafts.

An ancient relic made of pure gold, now kept in the Gold Museum of Bogotá, Colombia (Fig. 127), depicts a tall leader with his entourage atop a balsa wood raft. The art-work may well have represented the sea crossing by Naymlap or his like. They were well acquainted, according to the Naymlap legend, with the calendar and worshiped a pan-

Figure 127

theon of twelve gods. Moving inland to settle where Quito, Ecuador's capital, is now situated, they built there two temples facing each other: one dedicated to the Sun, the other to the Moon. The Temple of the Sun had in front of its gateway two stone columns and in its forecourt a circle of twelve stone pillars.

The familiarity with the sacred number twelve—the hallmark of the Mesopotamian pantheon and calendar—bespeaks a calendar not unlike the one that originated in Sumer. The veneration of both the Sun and the Moon indicates a solar-lunar calendar, again as the one begun in Sumer. A gateway with two stone columns in front of it brings to mind the two columns that were erected at the entrances to temples throughout the ancient Near East, from Mesopotamia through western Asia and Egypt. And, as if all those links to the Old World were not enough, we find a *circle of twelve stone pillars*. Whoever had arrived from across the Pacific must have been aware of the astronomical stone circles of Lagash, or Stonehenge—or both.

Several stone objects that are now kept in the National Museum of Peru in Lima are believed to have served the coastal peoples as calendrical computers. One, for example, catalogued under the number 15-278 (Fig. 128) is divided into sixteen squares that contain pegholes that range from six to twelve; the top and bottom panels are indented with twenty-nine and twenty-eight pegholes respectively — a strong suggestion of a count of lunar monthly phases.

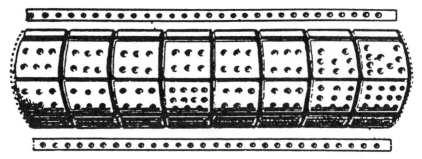

Figure 128

Fritz Buck (*Inscriptiones Calendarias del Peru Prein-caico*) who made the subject his specialty, was of the opinion that the 116 pegholes or indentations in the sixteen squares indicated a link to the calendar of the Mayas of Mexico and Guatemala. That the northern parts of the Andean lands were in close contact with the people and cultures of Mesoamerica—a possibility until recently rejected out of hand—is now hardly disputed. Those who arrived from Mesoamerica undoubtedly included African and Semitic people, as evidenced by numerous stone carvings and sculptures (Fig. 129a). Before them there arrived by sea people that were depicted as Indo-Europeans (Fig. 129b); and sometime in between there landed on these coasts helmeted "Bird people" (Fig. 129c) who were armed with metal weapons. Another group may have arrived overland via the Amazon basin and its tributaries;

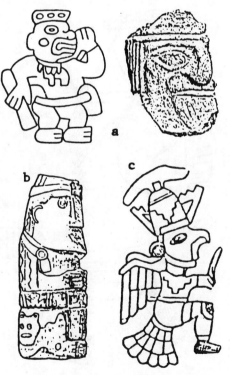

Figures 129a, 129b, and 129c

the symbols that were associated with them (Fig. 130) were identical to the Hittite hieroglyph for ''gods.'' Inasmuch as the Hittite pantheon was an adaptation of the Sumerian pantheon, it perhaps explains the otherwise remarkable discovery of a golden statuette in Colombia of a goddess holding in her hands the emblem of the umbilical cutter—the emblem of Ninharsag, the Mother Goddess of the Sumerians (Fig. 131).

The north-central Andean coast and ranges of South America were peopled by Quechua-speaking peoples, named, for want of a better source, after the main rivers along which they flourished. The Incas, it turned out, formed their empire and laid out their famous highways upon the ruins of those earlier inhabitants. Down south, from about where Lima (the capital of Peru) is situated, along the coast and mountains that face Lake Titicaca, and on southward

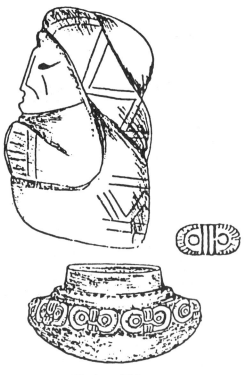

Figure 130

Figure 131

toward Chile, the dominant tribal language was that of the
Aymaras. They too recalled in their legends early arrivals,
on the Pacific coast by sea and by land from the territory
east of Lake Titicaca. The Aymara considered the former
as unfriendly invaders; the latter were called *Uru,* meaning
''Olden people,'' who were a people apart and whose remnants still exist in the Sacred Valley as a group with its own
customs and traditions. The possibility that they were Sumerians, arriving at Lake Titicaca when Ur was Sumer's
capital (the last time between 2200 and 2000 B.C.), must
be taken seriously. The fact is that the province that connects
the Sacred Valley, the eastern shores of Lake Titicaca, and
western Brazil is still called *Madre del Dios*—''Mother of
the gods,'' which is what Ninharsag was. A mere
coincidence?

Scholars find that throughout the millennia the dominant

cultural influence on all these peoples was that of Tiahuanacu; it found its most obvious expression in the thousands
of clay and metal objects that bore the image of Viracocha
as it appears on the Gate of the Sun, in decorations (including on the magnificently woven cloth in which mummies were wrapped) that emulated the symbols on the Gate,
and in their calendar.

The most prevalent of those symbols or, as Posnansky
and others consider them, hieroglyphs, was that of the stairway (Fig. 132a), which was also used in Egypt (Fig. 132b)
and which was often used on Andean artifacts to denote a
"Seeing-eye" tower (Fig. 132c). Such observations, to
judge from the astronomical lines of sight at the Kalasasaya
and from the celestial symbols associated with Tiahuanacu,
included the Moon (whose symbol was a circle between
crescents, Fig. 132d).

On the Pacific side of South America, it thus appears,
the calendar and its celestial knowledge followed in the
footsteps of the same teachers who had been active in the
Near East.

Commenting on the evidence, earlier discussed, for the
much greater antiquity of human presence in the Americas

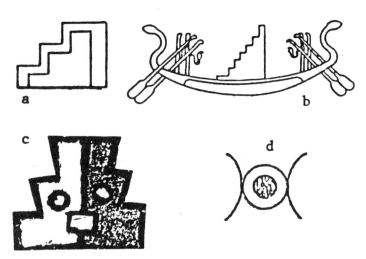

Figures 132a, 132b, 132c, and 132d

and their routes of arrival, Dr. Niede Guidon, of the French Institute of Advanced Social Studies who participated with Brazilian archaeologists in the Pedra Furada discoveries, said thus: "A transatlantic crossing from Africa cannot be ruled out."

The discovery of "the oldest pottery in the Americas," announced by an archaeological team of the Field Museum of Natural History in Chicago in the December 13, 1991, issue of *Science* magazine, "overturned the standard assumptions" regarding the peopling of the Americas and especially the view that the Amazon basin, where the discovery was made, was "simply too poor in resources to have supported a complex prehistoric culture." Contrary to long held opinions, "the Amazon basin had soil as fertile as the flood plains of the Nile, the Ganges and other great river basins of the world," said Dr. Anne C. Roosevelt, the team's leader. The red-brown pottery fragments, some decorated with painted patterns, have definitely been dated by the latest technologies to be no less than seven thousand years old. They were found at a site called Sabtarem in mounds of shells and other trash discarded by the ancient residents, a fishing people.

The date, and the fact that the pottery was painted with linear designs, put it on a par with similar pottery that appeared in the ancient Near East, in the mountains bordering on the plain where the Sumerian civilization blossomed out. In *The Lost Realms* we presented the evidence of Sumerian traces in the Amazon basin and through it in the gold- and tin-producing areas of Peru. The latest discovery, by fixing the pottery's date unquestionably and by coming at a time when early arrivals are a more acceptable possibility, serves mainly to corroborate previously unorthodox conclusions: in antiquity, people from the Near East reached America also by crossing the Atlantic Ocean.

Arrivals from such a direction have not been without calendrical remains. The most dramatic and enigmatic of them were discovered in the northeastern part of the Amazon basin, near the Brazil-Guyana border. There, rising in the

great plain, is an egg-shaped rock that rises some 100 feet
and is some 300 by 250 feet in diameter. A natural cavity
on its top has been carved out to form a pond whose waters
flow on and into the gigantic rock through channels and
conduits. A cavelike cavity has been enlarged to form a
large rock shelter, further carved out to form grottoes and
platforms at various levels. The entrance into the rock's
innards has painted above it a snake that is about twenty-
two feet long, its mouth formed of three openings into the
rock that are surrounded by enigmatic and undeciphered
inscriptions; inside and out, the rock is filled with hundreds
of painted signs and symbols.

Intrigued by reports by earlier explorers and local lore
that the grottoes contained skeletons of "giants whose faces
were European in expression," Professor Marcel F. Homet
(*Die Söhne der Sonne*) explored the rock in the 1950s and
provided more accurate data about it than had been known.
He found that the three facades of the Pedra Pintada point
in three directions: the large facade is oriented on an east–
west line, and the two smaller ones are oriented south-
southeast and south-southwest. His observation was that
"Externally, in its structural orientation . . . this monument
follows the exact identical rules of the ancient European
and Mediterranean cultures." He considered many of the
signs and symbols painted on the meticulously polished
surfaces of the rock to be "impeccably regular numerals
which are not based on the decimal system" but "belong
to the oldest known eastern Mediterranean cultures." He
thought that surfaces filled with dots represented tables of
multiplication, such as 9 times 7 or 5 times 7 or 7 times 7,
and 12 times 12.

The highlight of the rock's ancient artifacts, because of
which some earlier explorers had called it the Place of
the Stone Books, were dolmens—large flat stones laid
across supporting stones—weighing between fifteen and
twenty tons each. They were elaborately painted on their
faces; and two larger ones were cut into precise shapes—
one as a pentagon (Fig. 133a) and the other as an oval
(Fig. 133b). As at the entrance, both appear to depict a

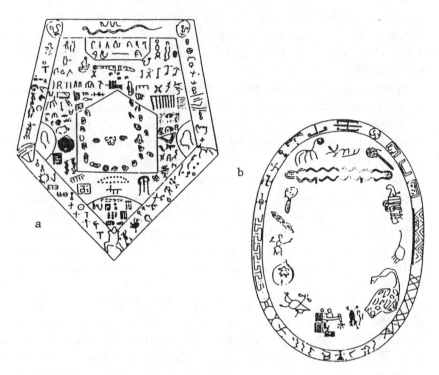

Figures 133a and 133b

serpent as the dominant symbol, and this and other signs brought to Homet's mind ancient Egypt and the eastern Mediterranean. Since many of the dolmens were placed at the levels and the entrances of burial grottoes in the depths of the rock, he concluded that, as the Indian legends held, this was a sacred place for the burial of leaders or other notables "by civilized people who were here, just as they were in Tiahuanacu, the great city of the Andes long, long ago—perhaps thousands of years before the birth of Christ."

Homet's observation regarding the mathematical system that seemed to underlie the markings on the surfaces, "not based on the decimal system" but on that of "the oldest known eastern Mediterranean cultures," is a roundabout way of describing the Sumerian sexagesimal system whose use prevailed throughout the ancient Near East. His other conclusions about links on the one hand to the "eastern Mediterranean" and on the other hand to Tiahuanacu "thousands of years before the birth of Christ" are truly remarkable.

Although the drawings on these two particular dolmens remain undeciphered, they do hold, in our view, a number of important clues. The pentagonal one no doubt records some coherent tale, perhaps, as with the later Mesoamerican picture books, a tale of migration and the route taken. At its four corners the tablet depicts four types of people; in that it could have been a precursor of a well-known Mayan painting on the cover of the *Codex Fejérvary* that showed the four quarters of the Earth and (in different colors) their diverse races of people. As on the pentagonal dolmen, the Mayan depiction also has a geometric central panel.

Except for the central panel, which in Brazil is pentagonal, the dolmen's face is covered with what appears to be an unknown script. We find similarities between it and a script from the eastern Mediterranean known as Linear A; it was a precursor of the script of the island of Crete, and also of that of the Hittites of Anatolia (today's Turkey).

The dominant symbol on the pentagonal dolmen is the serpent, also a well-known symbol of the pre-Hellenic culture of Crete and ancient Egypt. In terms of the ancient Near Eastern pantheon, the serpent was the symbol of Enki and his clan. On the oval dolmen it is depicted as a heavenly cloud, which brings to mind the the serpent symbol on Mesopotamian *kudurru* (Fig. 92), where it represented the Milky Way.

Many of the symbols that frame the central panel on this dolmen are familiar Sumerian and Elamite designs and emblems (such as the swastika). The larger images within the oval frame are even more revealing. If we consider the central uppermost symbol as a script element, precisely twelve symbols are left. In our view, they represent the *twelve signs of the zodiac*.

That not all the symbols are identical to those that originated in Sumer is not unusual, since in various lands (such as China) the zodiac (which means "animal circle") was adapted to local fauna. But some of the symbols on this oval dolmen, such as that of the two fishes (for Pisces), the two human images (the twins of Gemini) and the female holding a stalk of grain (Virgo, the Virgin) are identical to the zodiacal symbols (and their names) that originated in Sumer and were adopted throughout the Old World.

The significance of the Amazonian depiction can, therefore, hardly be exaggerated. As we have pointed out, the zodiac was an entirely arbitrary division of the celestial circle into twelve groups of stars; it was not the result of simple observation of natural phenomena, such as the day–night cycle, the waxing and waning of the Moon, or the Sun's seasonal changes. To find the concept and knowledge of the zodiac, and moreover to have it represented by Mesopotamian symbols, must be taken as evidence of someone with Near Eastern knowledge in the Amazon basin.

No less astounding than the decorative symbols and the zodiacal signs around the oval dolmen's face is the depiction in the center of the pentagonal dolmen. It shows a *circle of stones* surrounding two monoliths, between which there appears a partly erased drawing of a human head whose eye is focused on one of the monoliths. Such a "head with sighting eye" can be found in Mayan astronomical codices, in which the sign depicts astronomer-priests.

All that, plus the astronomical orientations of the rock's three surfaces, bespeaks the presence of someone familiar with celestial observations.

Who was that "someone"? Who could have crossed the ocean at such an early time? The crossing, admittedly, could not have taken place unaided. And whether those who were led or transported to the South American shores already possessed calendrical-astronomical knowledge, or were taught it in the new lands, none of that could have come about without the "gods."

* * *

In the absence of written records, the petroglyphs that have been found in South America are precious clues to what the ancient inhabitants had known and seen. Many of them have been found in the funnel leading, in the continent's northeastern part, into the Amazon basin and up that mighty river and its countless tributaries that begin in the distant Andes. The principal river of the Sacred Valley of the Incas, the Urubamba, is but a tributary of the Amazon River; so are other Peruvian rivers that flow eastward from sites whose mind-boggling remains indicate they were metallurgical processing centers. The known sites, only a fraction of what is there to be discovered if proper archaeological work were carried out, support the veracity of local traditions that people from across the Atlantic landed on those coasts and journeyed via the Amazon basin to obtain the gold and tin and other treasures of the Andes.

In what used to be called British Guiana alone, more than a dozen sites have been discovered where the rocks are covered with carved pictures. At a site near Karakananc in the Pacaraima mountains, the petroglyphs (Fig. 134a) depict stars with different numbers of rays or points (a Sumerian "first"), the crescent of the Moon and solar symbols, and what could have been a viewing device next to a stairway. At a place called Marlissa a long range of granite rocks along a river bank is covered with numerous petroglyphs; some of them adorned the cover of the journal of the Royal Agricultural and Commercial Society of British Guiana (*Timehri*, issue 6 of 1919) (Fig. 134b). The peculiar person with raised hands and a helmetlike head with one large "eye" appears on the rock next to what looks like a large boat (Fig. 134c). The tightly clothed and haloed beings, shown many times over (Fig. 134d), are of giantlike proportions: in one instance thirteen feet tall and in another close to eight feet.

In neighboring Suriname, formerly Dutch Guiana, in the area of the Frederik Willem IV Falls, the petroglyphs are so numerous that researchers have found it necessary to assign numbers to the sites, to each group of petroglyphs

Figures 134a, 134b, 134c, and 134d

at each site, and to individual symbols within each group. Some of them (Fig. 135) would today be deemed to represent UFOs and their occupants, as would a petroglyph (Fig. 136) at site 13 at the Wonotobo Falls, where the previously seen depiction of tall and haloed beings has been converted into a domed contraption with a ladder coming down out of its opening; a mighty person is standing in that opening.

The message conveyed by such petroglyphs is that while some people were seen arriving by boats, other godlike ones arrived in "flying saucers."

At least two of the symbols among these petroglyphs can be recognized as Near Eastern script-signs, and specifically so from Hittite inscriptions in Anatolia. One, which appears as the determinative-sign next to a helmeted and horned face (Fig. 137a), unmistakably resembles the hieroglyphic Hittite

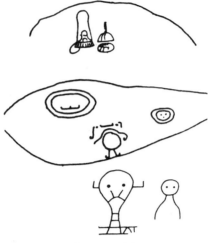

Figure 135

Figure 136

sign meaning "great" (Fig. 137b). This hieroglyphic sign was most often used in Hittite inscriptions in combination with the sign for "king, ruler" to mean "great king" (Fig. 137c); and exactly such a combined hieroglyph has been found several times among the petroglyphs near the Wonotobo cataracts in Suriname (Fig. 137d).

Petroglyphs, indeed, cover rocks large and small throughout South America; their spread and images tell Man's story in that part of the world, a story that is yet to be fully deciphered and understood. For more than a hundred years explorers have shown that the South American continent

Figures 137a, 137b, 137c, and 137d

can be crossed by foot, on horseback, by canoes and rafts. One major route begins in northeastern Brazil/Guyana/Venezuela and uses principally the Amazon river system to enter Peru's north and central parts; the other begins in Brazil somewhere near São Paulo and winds its way westward through the Mato Grosso region to Bolivia and Lake Titicaca, and thence northward into either central Peru (the Sacred Valley) or the coastal regions—two places where the two routes meet.

As the discoveries earlier discussed in this chapter show, Man arrived in the Americas, and especially in South America, tens of thousands of years ago. The migrations, to judge by the petroglyphic evidence, came in three recognizable phases. The extensive work at the Pedra Furada in northeastern Brazil offers a good example of those phases as far as the continent's Atlantic side is concerned.

Pedra Furada is just the most studied site in the area named after its principal village, São Raimundo Nonato; more than 260 archaeological sites of early occupation are found there, and 240 of them contain rock art. As the carbon dating of the charcoal samples from the prehistoric hearths shows, Man lived there beginning some 32,000 years ago. Throughout the area, such habitation appears to have come to an abrupt end circa 12,000 years ago, concurrently with a marked change in climate. It has been our opinion that the change coincided with the abrupt end of the last ice age by the Deluge, the Great Flood. The rock art of that long period was naturalistic; the artists of the time depicted what they saw around them: local animals, trees and other vegetation, people.

A hiatus of some two thousand years followed until human occupation of the site resumed, when other and new groups arrived in the area. Their rock art suggests that they had come from a distant land, for animals not native to the area were included in the paintings: giant sloths, horses, an early type of llama, and (according to the excavators' reports) camels (which, to our eyes, looked more like giraffes). This second phase lasted till about 5,000 years ago and included, in its latter part, the making of decorated pottery. It also included in its art, in the words of Niede Guidon who has led the excavations, "abstract signs" that "seem related to ceremonies or mythical subjects"—a religion, an awareness of the "gods." It is at the end of that phase that the transition to petroglyphs akin to Near Eastern signs, symbols, and script make their appearance, leading in such a third phase to the astronomical and calendrical aspects of the markings on the rocks.

These petroglyphs can be found at both landfall zones and along the two major cross-continent routes. The more they belong to the third phase, the more pronounced are the celestial symbols and connotations. The more they are found in the continent's southern parts, be it in Brazil or Bolivia or Peru, the more are they reminiscent of Sumer, Mesopotamia, and Anatolia. Some scholars, especially in South America, interpret various signs as a kind of cuneiform Sumerian script. The largest petroglyph in that zone is the so-called candelabra or trident that faces whoever reaches South America's Pacific shore at the Bay of Paracas (Fig. 138a). According to local lore it is the lightning rod of Viracocha, as seen atop the Gate of the Sun in Tiahuanacu; we have identified it as the Near Eastern emblem of the "Storm God" (Fig. 138b), the younger son of Enlil whom the Sumerians called *Ishkur*, the Babylonians and Assyrians *Adad*, and the Hittites *Teshub* ("The Wind Blower").

While the Sumerian presence or at least influence can be documented in many, though small, ways, as we have done in *The Lost Realms*, no attempt has been made to date to arrive at a comprehensive picture of the Hittite presence in South America. We have shown some of the Hittite signs to be found in Brazil, but probably much more lies unearthed and unstudied behind such a coincidence as the fact that the hill people of Anatolia were the first to introduce iron in the Old World, and the parallel fact that the country's name, *Brazil*, is identical to the Akkadian word for iron, *Barzel*—a similarity that Cyrus

Figures 138a and 138b

H. Gordon (*Before Columbus* and *Riddles in History*) considered to be a significant clue regarding the true identity of early Americans. Other clues are the Indo-European types depicted on the busts found in Ecuador and northern Peru, and the fact that the enigmatic inscriptions found on Easter Island, in the Pacific Ocean opposite Chile, run as the Hittite script did in the "as the ox ploughs" system—beginning on the upper line from left to right, continuing on the second line from right to left, then again from left to right and so on.

Unlike Sumer, which was situated in an alluvial plain with no stones therein to serve as building materials, the Enlilite domain of Anatolia was all KUR.KI, "mountain land," of which Ishkur/Adad/Teshub was put in charge. The structures and edifices in the Andean lands were also made of stone—from the earliest cyclopean stoneworks through the exquisite ashlars of the Ancient Empire, down to the fieldstone buildings of the Incas and to the present. Who was there in the Andean lands knowledgeable in the use of stone for construction before the lands were populated, before Andean civilization began, before the Incas? We suggest they were stonemasons from Anatolia, who quite usefully were also expert miners—for Anatolia was an important source of metal ores in antiquity and one of the first places to begin mixing copper with tin to make bronze.

Making an on-site visit to the ruins of Hattusas, the ancient Hittite capital, and other bastions nearby, some 150 miles northeast of Ankara, the capital of present-day Turkey, one begins to realize that in some respects they represented crude emulations of Andean stoneworks, even including the unique and intricate incisions in the hard stone to create the "stairway motif" (Fig. 139).

One has to be an expert in ancient ceramics to be able to distinguish between some of the Anatolian and Andean pottery, especially the burnished and polished deep ocherred kind from the bronze age. One need not, however, be an expert to notice the similarity between strange warriors depicted on Peruvian artifacts from the coastal areas (Fig.

Figure 139

140a) and pre-Hellenic warriors depicted on artifacts from the eastern Mediterranean (Fig. 140b).

Regarding the latter similarity, it should be borne in mind that the home of the early Greeks, Ionia, was not in Greece but in the western parts of Anatolia (Asia Minor). The myths and legends of early times, recorded in such works as Homer's *Iliad,* deal in fact with locations that were in Anatolia. Troy was there and not in Greece. So was the famed Sardis, capital of Croesus, king of Lydia, who was renowned for his golden treasures. Perhaps the belief by some that the travels and travails of Odysseus also brought him to what we now call America, are not so farfetched.

Figures 140a and 140b

*   *   *

It is odd that in the increasingly heated debate about the First Americans, little if any attention has been given to the question of how much maritime knowledge the ancient peoples possessed. There are many indications that it was quite extensive and advanced; and once again, the impossible can be accepted as possible only if teachings by the Anunnaki are taken into account.

The Sumerian King List describes an early king of Erech, a predecessor of Gilgamesh, thus: "In Eanna, Meskiaggasher, the son of divine Utu, became high priest as well as king, and ruled 324 years. Meskiaggasher went into the western sea and came forth toward the mountains." How such a cross-oceanic voyage was accomplished without some kind of navigational aids, if none yet existed, is left unexplained by scholars.

Centuries later, Gilgamesh, having been mothered by a goddess, went in search of immortality. His adventures precede in time but exceed in drama those of Odysseus. On his last journey he had to cross the Waters or Sea of Death, which was possible only with the assistance of the boatman Urshanabi. No sooner did the two start the crossing, than Urshanabi accused Gilgamesh of breaking the "stone things'' without which the boatman could not navigate. The ancient text records the lament of Urshanabi about the ''broken stone things'' in three lines that are unfortunately only partly legible on the clay tablet; the three begin with the words ''I peer, but I cannot . . .'' which strongly suggests a navigational device. To correct the problem, Urshanabi instructed Gilgamesh to go back ashore and cut long wooden poles, 120 of them. As they sailed off, Urshanabi instructed Gilgamesh to discard one pole at a time, in groups of twelve. This was repeated ten times until all of the 120 poles were used up: ''At twice-sixty Gilgamesh had used up the poles,'' reaching their destination on the other side of the sea. Thus did a specific number of poles, arranged as instructed, substitute for the ''stone things'' that could no longer be used to peer with.

Gilgamesh is a known historical ruler of ancient Sumer; he reigned in Erech (Uruk) circa 2900 B.C. Centuries later, Sumerian traders reached distant lands by sea routes, exporting the grains, wool, and garments for which Sumer became known and importing—as Gudea has attested—metals, lumber, construction, and precious stones. Such two-way repeated voyages could not have taken place without navigational instruments.

That such instruments had existed in antiquity can be judged from an object that was found in the eastern Mediterranean off the Aegean island Antikythera at the beginning of this century. Sailing through the ancient sea route from the eastern to the western Mediterranean between the islands of Crete and Kythera, two boats of sponge divers discovered the wreck of an ancient ship lying on the sea's bottom. The wreck yielded artifacts, including marble and bronze statues, dated to the fourth century B.C. The ship itself has been dated to some time after 200 B.C.; amphorae, vessels containing wine, olive oil, and other foodstuffs, were dated to about 75 B.C. That the ship and its contents date to a time before the beginning of the Christian era thus seems certain, and so is the conclusion that it had taken on its load at or near the coast of Asia Minor.

The objects and materials raised from the wreck were taken to Athens for examination and study. Among them were a lump of bronze and broken-off pieces that, when cleaned and fitted together, stunned the museum officials. The "object" (Fig. 141) appeared to be a precise mechanism with many gears interlocked at various planes inside a circular frame that was in turn held in a square holder; it seemed to be an astrolabe "with spherical projections and a set of rings." After decades-long studies, including its investigation with X rays and metallurgical analysis, it has been put on view in the National Archaeological Museum in Athens, Greece (catalog number X.15087). The protective housing bears a plaque that identifies the object as follows:

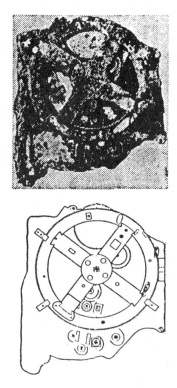

Figure 141

The mechanism was found in the sea of Antikythera island by sponge divers in 1900. It was part of the cargo of a shipwreck which occurred in the first century B.C.

The mechanism is considered to be a calendrical Sun and Moon computing machine dated, after the latest evidence, to circa 80 B.C.

One of the most thorough studies on the subject is the book *Gears from the Greeks* by Professor Derek de Sola Price of Yale University. He found that the three broken-apart sections contained gears and dials and graded plates that in turn were assembled from at least ten separate parts. The gears were linked one to the other on a basis of several differentials—a sophistication which we now find in automatic gearshift boxes in cars—that incorporated the cycle of the Sun and the Metonic (nineteen-year) cycle of the Moon. The gears were fitted with tiny teeth and moved on varied axles; markings on circular and angular parts were accompanied by inscriptions in Greek that named a number of zodiacal constellations.

The instrument was without doubt the product of a high technology and sophisticated scientific knowledge. Nothing coming even close to it in intricacy has been found in subsequent or preceding times, in spite of the guess offered by de Sola Price that it could have been made—or perhaps just repaired—at the School of Posidonios on the island of Rhodes after the model of planetarium devices used by Archimedes. Though he "sympathized with the shock one may feel at revising upwards the estimation of Hellenistic technology," he wrote, he could not agree with the "radical interpretation" by some "that the complexity of the device and its mechanical sophistication put it so far beyond the scope of Hellenistic technology that it could only have been designed and created by alien astronauts coming from outer space and visiting our civilization."

Yet the fact is that nothing coming even close to the instrument's intricacy and precision has been found anywhere in any of the centuries preceding or following the time of the shipwreck. Even medieval astrolabes, more than a millennium after the Antikythera time frame, look like toys (Fig. 142a) compared to the ancient object (Fig. 142b). Moreover, the medieval and later European astrolabes and kindred devices were made of brass, which is easily malleable, whereas the ancient device was made of bronze—a metal useful in casting but extremely difficult to hone and shape in general and especially to produce a mechanism that is more intricate than modern chronometers.

Yet the instrument was there; and no matter who provided the science and technology for it, it proves that time-keeping and celestially guided navigation were possible at that early time at an incredible level of sophistication.

It seems that the reluctance to acknowledge the unacceptable also lies behind the fact that hardly anything con-

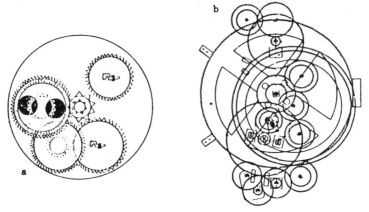

Figures 142a and 142b

cerning early cartography was brought up in the First Americans debate—even with such an opportunity as the 500th anniversary of the Columbus voyage in 1492.

Just across the Aegean Sea from Athens and the Kythera islands, in Istanbul (the previous Ottoman capital and the Byzantine one), in a converted palace now known as the Topkapi Museum, there is kept another find that throws light on ancient navigational capabilities. It is known as the *Piri Re'is Map,* after the Turkish admiral who had it made, and bears the Moslem year equivalent to A.D. 1513 (Fig. 143a). One of several *mapas mundi* (world maps) that have survived from that Age of Discovery, it attracted particular interest for a number of reasons: first, its accuracy and its sophisticated method of projecting global features on a flat surface; second, because it clearly shows (Fig. 143b) the whole of South America, with recognizable geographic and topographic features on both the Atlantic and Pacific coasts; and third, because it correctly projects the Antarctic continent. Although cartographed a few years after the Columbus voyages, the startling fact is that the southern parts of South America were unknown in 1513— Pizarro sailed from Panama to Peru only in 1530, and the Spaniards did not proceed farther down the coast or venture

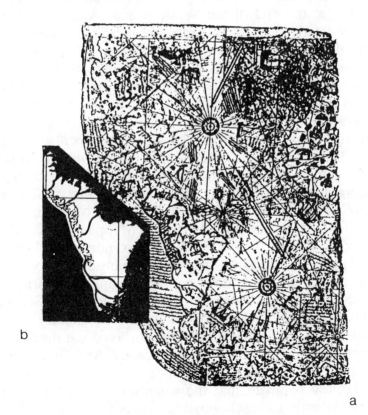

b

a

Figures 143a and 143b

inland to explore the Andean chain until years later. Yet the map shows all of South America, including its Patagonian tip. As to Antarctica, not only how it looks, but its very existence, was unknown until 1820—three *centuries* after the Piri Re'is map. Strenuous studies since the map was discovered in 1929 among the Sultan's treasures have reaffirmed these puzzling features of the map.

Brief notations on the map's margins are more fully explained in a treatise titled *Bahariyeh* ("About the Sea") that the admiral wrote. Regarding such geographic landmarks as the Antilles islands, he explained that he obtained the information from "the maps of the Genoese infidel, Colombo." He also repeated the tale of how Columbus first tried to convince the grandees of Genoa and then the king of Spain that according to a book that he (Columbus) possessed, "at the end of the Western Sea (Atlantic), that is on its western side, there were coasts and islands and all kinds of metals and also precious stones." This detail in the Turkish admiral's book confirms reports from other sources that Columbus knew quite well in advance where he was going, having come into possession of maps and geographic data from ancient sources.

In fact, the existence of such earlier maps is also attested to by Piri Re'is. In a subsequent notation, which explains how the map was drawn, he listed maps made by Arab cartographers, Portuguese maps ("which show the countries of Hind, Sind and China"), the "map of Columbus," as well as "about twenty charts and Mappae Mundi; these are charts drawn in the days of Alexander, Lord of the Two Horns." The latter was an Arabic epithet for Alexander the Great, and the statement means that Piri Re'is saw and used maps from the fourth century B.C. Scholars surmise that such maps were kept in the Library of Alexandria and that some must have survived the destruction by fire of that great hall of science by Arab invaders in A.D. 642.

It is now believed that the suggestion to sail westward on the Atlantic to reach existing coasts was first made not by Columbus but by an astronomer, mathematician, and geographer from Florence, Italy, named Paulo del Pozzo Toscanelli in 1474. It is also recognized that maps, such as the Medicean from 1351 and that of Pizingi of 1367, were available to later mariners and cartographers; the most renowned of the latter has been Gerhard Kremer, alias Mercator, whose *Atlas* of 1569 and methods of projection have remained standard features of cartography to this day.

One of the odd things about Mercator's maps of the world is that they show Antarctica, although that ice covered continent was not discovered, by British and Russian sailors, until 250 years later, in 1820!

As those who had preceded (and succeeded) him, Mercator used for his *Atlas* earlier maps drawn by former cartographers. In respect to the Old World, especially the lands bordering on the Mediterranean, he obviously relied on maps that went back to the time when Phoenicians and Carthaginians ruled the seas, maps drawn by Marinus of Tyre that were made known to future generations by the astronomer, mathematician, and geographer Claudius Ptolemy who lived in Egypt in the second century A.D. For his information on the New World, Mercator relied both on olden maps and the reports of explorers since the discovery of America. But where did he get the data not only on the shape of Antarctica, but on its very existence?

Scholars agree that his probable source was a Map of the World made in 1531 by Orontius Finaeus (Fig. 144a). Correctly projecting the Earth's globe by dividing it into the northern and southern hemispheres, with the north and south poles as epicenters, the map not only shows Antarctica— an amazing fact by itself. It also shows Antarctica with geographical and topographical features that have been buried under and obscured by an ice sheet for thousands of years!

The map shows in unmistakable detail coasts, bays, inlets, estuaries and mountains, even rivers, where none are now seen because of the ice cap that hides them. Nowadays we know that such features exist, because they were discovered by scientific below-ice probings that culminated

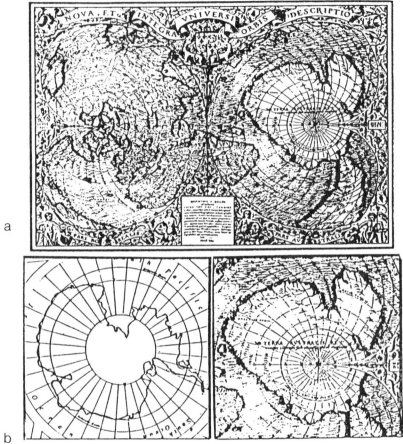

a

b

Figures 144a and 144b

with intensive surveys by many teams during the International Geophysical Year, 1958. The depiction on the Finaeus map, it then became clear, uncannily resembles the true shape of the Antarctic continent and its various geographical features (Fig. 144b).

In one of the most thorough studies of the subject, Charles H. Hapgood (*Maps of the Ancient Sea Kings*) concluded that the Finaeus map was drawn by him based on ancient charts that depicted Antarctica at a time when the continent, after having been freed of its ice covering, began to be covered by ice again in its western parts. That, his research team concluded, was about six thousand years ago, circa 4000 B.C.

Subsequent studies, as that by John W. Weihaupt (*Eos, the Proceedings of the American Geophysical Union,* August 1984), corroborated the earlier findings. Recognizing that "even crude mapping of a large continent would require a knowledge of navigation and geometry presumably beyond the ken of primitive navigators," he was nevertheless convinced that the map was based on data obtained some time between 2,600 and 9,000 years ago. The source of such data, he stated, remains an unanswered puzzle.

Presenting his conclusions in *Maps of the Ancient Sea Kings,* Charles Hapgood wrote: "It becomes clear that ancient voyagers traveled from pole to pole. Unbelievable as it may appear, the evidence nevertheless indicates that some ancient people explored Antarctica when its coasts were free of ice. It is clear, too, that they had an instrument of navigation for accurately determining longitudes that was far superior to anything possessed by the peoples of ancient, medieval, or modern times until the second half of the 18th century."

But those ancient mariners, as we have shown, only followed in the footsteps of the gods.

11

EXILES ON A
SHIFTING EARTH

Historians believe that exile as a deliberate penal policy was introduced by the Assyrians in the eighth century B.C. when they "carried off" kings, groups of elders and court officials, or even whole populations from their own lands to live out their lives among strangers in far-off places. In fact, the forced departure of someone into exile was a form of punishment begun by the gods, and the first exiles were leaders of the Anunnaki themselves. Such forced deportations, first of gods and then of people, have changed the course of history. They also left their mark on the calendar, and were linked to the coming of a New Age.

When the Spaniards, and then other Europeans, realized how numerous were the similarities in traditions, customs, and beliefs between those of the American natives and those that have been associated with the Bible and the Hebrews, they could think of no other explanation but that the "Indians" were descendants of the Ten Lost Tribes of Israel. That harkened back to the mystery surrounding the whereabouts of the people belonging to the ten Israelite tribes that formed the Northern Kingdom who were forced into exile by the Assyrian king Shalmaneser. Biblical and postbiblical sources held that, though dispersed, the exiles kept their faith and customs so that they be counted among those who will be redeemed and returned to their homeland. Ever since the Middle Ages, travelers and savants claimed to have found traces of the Ten Lost Tribes as far away as China or as nearby as Ireland and Scotland. In the sixteenth century, the Spaniards were certain that it was such exiles who had brought civilization to the Americas.

While the exile of the ten tribes by the Assyrians in the eighth century B.C., and then of the remaining two tribes by the Babylonians two centuries later, are historical facts, the "Ten Tribes Connection" to the New World remains in the realm of intriguing legends. Yet, unknowingly, the Spaniards were right in attributing the beginning of a formal civilization, with its own calendar, in the Americas to an exile; but not of a people—rather, the exile of a god.

The peoples of Mesoamerica—the Maya and Aztecs, Toltecs and Olmecs and lesser known tribes—had three calendars. Two were cyclical, measuring the cycles of the Sun and the Moon and of Venus. The other was chronological, measuring the passage of time from a certain starting point, "Point Zero." Scholars have established that this Long Count calendar's starting point was in the year that is designated under the Western calendar as 3113 B.C., but they know not what that starting point signifies. In *The Lost Realms* we have suggested that it marked the date of the arrival of Thoth, with a small band of aides and followers, in America.

Quetzalcoatl, the Great God of the Mesoamericans, was none other than Thoth, we have suggested. His epithet, the Plumed or Winged Serpent, was well known in Egyptian iconography (Fig. 145). Quetzalcoatl, like Thoth, was the god who knew and taught the secrets of temple building, numbers, astronomy, and the calendar. Indeed, the two other calendars of Mesoamerica by themselves offer clues for the Egyptian Connection and for identifying Quetzalcoatl

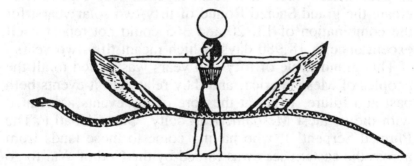

Figure 145

as Thoth. The two without doubt reveal the handiwork of "someone" familiar with the much earlier calendars of the Near East.

First of the two was the *Haab,* a solar-year calendar of 365 days that was subdivided into 18 months of 20 days each, plus an additional five special days at year's end. Although the 18 × 20 division is different from the Near Eastern one of 12 × 30, this calendar was basically an adaptation of the Egyptian calendar of 360 days plus 5. That purely solar calendar, as we have seen, was the one favored by Ra/Marduk; changing its subdivision could have been a deliberate act by Thoth to make it differ from that of his rival.

That purely solar calendar did not allow for intercalation—a device that, in Mesopotamia, was expressed in the addition of a thirteenth month once in a given number of years. In Mesoamerica this number, 13, featured in the next calendar.

As in Egypt, which had both a secular (pure solar-year) calendar as well as a sacred one, so was the second Mesoamerican calendar that of the Sacred Year called *Tzolkin.* In it the division into 20 also played a role; but it was counted in a cycle that rotated 13 times—the number inserted into the *Haab* calendar. That 13 × 20 resulted in a total of only 260 days. What this number, 260, represented or how it had originated has engendered many theories but no certain solutions. What is significant, calendrically and historically, is that these two cyclical calendars were meshed together, as gear wheels lock their teeth together (see Fig. 9b), to create the grand Sacred Round of fifty-two solar years; for the combination of 13, 20 and 365 could not repeat itself except once in 18,980 days, which meant fifty-two years.

This grand cycle of fifty-two years was sacred to all the peoples of Mesoamerica, and they related to it events both past and future. It lay at the core of the events associated with the greatest Mesoamerican deity, Quetzalcoatl ("The Plumed Serpent"), who having come to those lands from across the eastern seas was forced by the God of War to go into exile, but vowed to return in the year "1 Reed" of the fifty-two-year Sacred Cycle. In the Christian calendar, the parallel years were A.D. 1363, 1415, 1467, and 1519; the latter was the very year when Hernando Cortés appeared on the Mexican shores, fair-skinned and bearded as Quetzalcoatl had been; and so it was that the landing was seen by the Aztecs as fulfillment of the prophecy of the Returning God.

The centrality of the number fifty-two, if nothing else, as a hallmark of religious and messianic Mesoamerican beliefs and expectations, pointed to a key similarity between Quetzalcoatl and his Sacred Calendar and Thoth's calendar of fifty-two. The Game of Fifty-two was Thoth's game, and the Tale of Satni earlier related clearly stated that "fifty-two was the magical number of Thoth." We have already explained the significance, in terms of Thoth's feud with Ra/Marduk, of the Egyptian calendar of fifty-two weeks. The Mesoamerican "fifty-two" had "Thoth" stamped all over it.

Another hallmark of Thoth was the application of a circular design to edifices related to the calendrical observations of the heavens. The Mesopotamian ziggurats were squarish, with their corners aligned to the cardinal points. Near Eastern temples—Mesopotamian, Egyptian, Canaanite, even Israelite—were rectangular structures whose axis was oriented either to the equinoxes or the solstices (a plan still manifest in churches and temples of our days). Only in the unique edifice that Thoth helped build in Lagash was a circular shape adopted. Its only other Near Eastern emulation was at the temple dedicated to Hathor (i.e. Ninharsag) at Denderah; and at Stonehenge, near where the Old World faces the New World on the other side of the Atlantic Ocean.

In the New World, in the domain of Adad, the younger son of Enlil and chief deity of the Hittites, the usual rectangular shape and orientation of Mesopotamian temples predominated. The greatest and oldest of them with its certain astronomical and calendrical functions, the Kalasasaya at Tiahuanacu, was rectangular and built on an east–west axis, not unlike the temple of Solomon. Indeed, one must wonder whether when the Lord took the prophet Ezekiel flying to show him an actual temple that was to serve as the model for the design of the future temple of Jerusalem, he did not fly him to Tiahuanacu to view the Kalasasaya, as the biblical detailed architectural text and a comparison of Figs. 50 and 124 may well suggest. Another major southern Andes temple, a focal point of sacred pilgrimages, was the one dedicated to the Great Creator that stood atop a promontory looking out to the expanse of the endless Pacific (not far south from present-day Lima). It too was rectangular in shape.

Judging by the design of these structures, Thoth was not invited there to take a hand in their construction. But if, as we believe, he was the Divine Architect of the circular observatories, he was certainly present in the Sacred Valley. His hallmarks among the structures of the Megalithic Age were the Round Observatory atop the Sacsahuaman promontory, the semicircular Holy of Holies in Cuzco, the Torreon in Machu Picchu.

The actual domain of Quetzalcoatl/Thoth was Mesoamerica and Central America, the lands of the Nahuatl-speaking and Mayan tribes; but his influence extended southward into the northern parts of the South American continent. Petroglyphs found near Cajamarca in the north of Peru (Fig. 146) that depict the Sun, the Moon, five-pointed stars, and other celestial symbols, show repeatedly next to them the symbol of the serpent—the unmistakable emblem of Enki and his clan and specifically so of the deity known as the "Plumed Serpent." The petroglyphs also include depictions of astronomical viewing devices, one held by a person (priest?), as was customary in the ancient Near East, and the other with the curved horns, as were the viewing devices erected in Egypt at the temples of Min (see Fig. 61).

The site appears to have been where ancient routes in the gold lands of the Andes, from the Pacific coast and from the Atlantic coast, met as the latter followed the rivers. Cajamarca itself, somewhat inland, and the natural harbor for it at Trujillo on the Pacific coast, in fact played a historic role in the European conquest of Peru. It was there, at

Figure 146

Trujillo, that Francisco Pizarro and his small band of soldiers
landed in 1530. They marched inland and established their
base at Cajamarca, a city "whose plaza was larger than any
in Spain" and "whose buildings were three times the height
of a man," according to the reports of the Conquistadors.
It was to Cajamarca that the last Inca emperor, Atahualpa,
was lured, only to be imprisoned for a ransom of gold and
silver. The ransom was the filling up of a room twenty-five
feet long and fifteen feet wide, as high as a man could not
reach, with these precious metals. The ministers and priests
of the king's retinue ordered that objects and artifacts made
of gold and silver be brought from all over the land; S.K.
Lothrop (*Inca Treasure as Depicted by Spanish Historians*)
figured out that what the Spaniards then sent back to Spain
from that ransom amounted to 180,000 ounces of gold and
twice as much in silver. (Having collected the ransom, the
Spaniards executed Atahualpa all the same.)

Farther north in Colombia, closer to Mesoamerica, at a site on the Magdalena River's banks, the petroglyphs unmistakably record Hittite and Egyptian encounters by including (Fig. 147) Hittite hieroglyphs (such as the "god" and "king" signs) alongside a variety of Egyptian symbols: cartouches (long rounded frames used to inscribe royal names), the hieroglyph for "splendor" (a circle with a dot in the center as the Sun with golden rays coming down), the "double Moon" Axe of Min.

Moving on northward, the Egyptian symbol par excellence, the drawing of a pyramid, is found among "graffiti" in the tomb area of Holmul, Guatemala (Fig. 148), thereby identifying the early inhabitants of Central America as familiar with Egypt. Also depicted is a circular stage-tower and next to it, apparently, its ground plan. It has all the appearance of a round observatory, similar to the one that had existed on the Sacsahuaman promontory down south.

Incredible as it may sound, reference to petroglyphs with astronomical symbols is made in ancient Near Eastern writings. The *Book of Jubilees,* enlarging and fleshing out the concise biblical record of the generations that followed the Deluge, describes how Noah instructed his descendants by relating to them the tale of Enoch and the knowledge that was granted him. The narrative continues thus:

Figure 147

Figure 148

In the twenty-ninth jubilee, in the first week, in the beginning thereof, Arpachshad took to himself a wife and her name was Rasu'eja, the daughter of Shushan, the daughter of Elam, and she bare him a son in the third year in this week, and he called his name Kainam.

And the son grew, and his father taught him writing, and he went to seek for himself a place which he might occupy as a city for himself.

And he found a writing which former generations had carved on the rock, and he read what there was thereon, and he transcribed it and sinned as a result thereof; for it contained the teaching of the Guardians in accordance with which they used to observe the omens of the sun and moon and stars in all the signs of heaven.

The petroglyphs, we learn from this millennia-old text, were not mere graffiti; they were expressions of knowledge of the "teachings of the Guardians"—the Anunnaki—"in accordance with which they used to observe the omens of the Sun and the Moon and the stars"; the petroglyphs were the "signs of heaven" of "former generations."

The depictions on rocks that we have just shown, including, as they do, round observatories, must be taken as eyewitness reports of what had actually been known and seen in antiquity in the Americas.

Indeed, in the heartland of Quetzalcoatl's domain, in Mexico, where the petroglyphs evolved into hieroglyphs akin to the earliest ones in Egypt, the most obvious traces of his presence are astronomically aligned temples, including circular and semicircular ones, and round observatories. Such remains begin with two perfectly round mounds that marked out the astronomical sightline at La Venta, one of the earliest sites of the Olmecs—African followers of Thoth who had arrived in Mexico by crossing the Atlantic circa 2500 B.C. At the other extreme of the four millennia that passed from then till the Spanish conquest, the latest instance of observatory-in-the-round was the semicircular pyramid in the sacred precinct of the Aztecs in Tenochtitlan (later Mexico City). It was so positioned that it served to determine the Day of the Equinox by watching, from the round "Tower of Quetzalcoatl," the Sun rise precisely between the opposite Pyramid of the Two Temples (Fig. 149).

Chronologically, between the early Olmecs and the late Aztecs, were the countless pyramids and sacred observatories of the Mayas. Some of them, as the one at Cuicuilco (Fig. 150a), were perfectly round. Others, like the one at

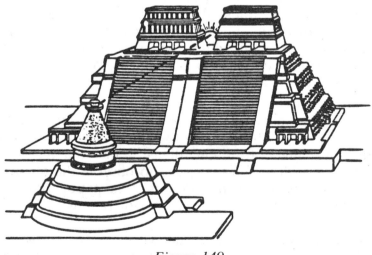

Figure 149

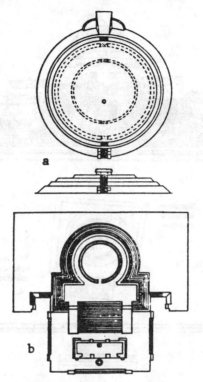

Figures 150a and 150b

Cempoala (Fig. 150b) began, as archaeologists have established, as purely round structures but in time changed shape
as the small original stairways leading to their top stages
evolved into monumental stairways and plazas. The most
renowned of these structures is the *Caracol* in Chichén Itzá
in the Yucatan peninsula—a circular observatory (Fig. 151)
whose astronomical functions and orientations have been
studied extensively and firmly established. Although the
presently seen structure is believed to have been built only
in A.D. 800 or thereabouts, it is known that the Mayas took
over Chichén Itzá from earlier settlers, erecting Mayan
structures where older ones used to be. An original observatory, scholars surmise, must have stood at the site at much
earlier times, built-over and rebuilt as was the Mayan custom
regarding the pyramids.

The sightlines in the existing structure have been exten-

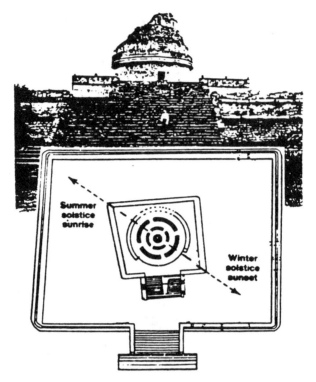

Figure 151

sively researched, and undoubtedly include the principal points of the Sun—the equinoxes and solstices, as well as some of the Moon's major points. Alignments with various stars are also suggested, though not with Venus; that is odd, for in Maya codices the movements of Venus are the principal subject. It is one of the reasons for believing that the sightlines were not devised by Mayan astronomers, but were inherited by them from previous eras.

The Caracol's ground plan—a round tower within a squarish enclosure as part of a larger rectangular structural frame, and the openings for sightlines in the tower itself—bring to mind the shape and layout (now seen only by their foundations) of the circular observatory within its square enclosure and larger rectangular complex at Sacsahuaman above Cuzco (see Fig. 120). Is there much doubt that both were designed by the same Divine Architect? In our opinion, he was Thoth.

INNER TRADITIONS
BEAR & COMPANY

Inner Traditions • Bear & Company
P.O. Box 388
Rochester, VT 05767-0388
U.S.A.

PLEASE SEND US THIS CARD TO RECEIVE OUR LATEST CATALOG.

Book in which this card was found _____

❑ Check here if you would like to receive our catalog via e-mail.

Name _____ Company _____

Address _____ Phone _____

City _____ State ____ Zip ____ Country ____

E-mail address _____

Please check the following area(s) of interest to you:

❑ Health   ❑ Self-help   ❑ Science/Nature   ❑ Shamanism
❑ Ancient Mysteries   ❑ New Age/Spirituality ❑ Ethnobotany   ❑ Martial Arts
❑ Spanish Language   ❑ Sexuality/Tantra   ❑ Children   ❑ Teen

Please send a catalog to my friend:

Name _____ Company _____

Address _____ Phone _____

City _____ State ____ Zip ____ Country ____

Order at 1-800-246-8648 • Fax (802) 767-3726
E-mail: customerservice@InnerTraditions.com • Web site: www.InnerTraditions.com

For their observations Mayan astronomers used viewing devices that are often depicted in the codices (Fig. 152) and the similarities to Near Eastern instruments, viewing perches, and symbols are too numerous to be just coincidence. In all the instances the viewing perches are virtually identical to those atop Mesopotamian viewing towers or turrets; the symbol of the "stairway" that evolved from them, the ubiquitous symbol of the observatory at Tiahuanacu, is also clearly seen in the Mayan codices. One, in *Codex Bodley* (bottom of Fig. 152), indicates that the two astronomer-priests are viewing the Sun as it rises between two mountains; that is exactly how the Egyptian hieroglyphic texts depicted the idea and the word "horizon"; and it may not be by chance alone that the two mountains in the Mayan codex look like the two great pyramids of Giza.

The links with the ancient Near East in general, and with Egypt in particular, that are evidenced by glyphs and archaeological remains are augmented by legends.

The *Popol Vuh*, the "Council Book" of the highland Mayas, contains an account of how the sky and the Earth were formed, how the Earth was divided into four regions and partitioned, and how the measuring cord was brought

Figure 152

and stretched in the sky and over the Earth, creating the four corners. These are all elements basic to Near Eastern cosmogony and sciences, recollections of how the Earth was divided among the Anunnaki, and the functions of the Divine Measurers. Both Nahuatlan traditions, as well as Mayan ones in such forms as the Legend of Votan, recount the arrival of "the Fathers and the Mothers," the tribal ancestors, from across the seas. *The Annals of Cakchiquels,* a Nahuatlan record, states that while they themselves came from the west, there were others who had come from the east, in both instances "from the other side of the sea." The Legend of Votan, who had built the first city that was the cradle of Mesoamerican civilization, was written down by Spanish chroniclers from oral Mayan traditions. The emblem of Votan, they recorded, was the serpent; "he was a descendant of the Guardians, of the race of Can." "Guardians" was the meaning of the Egyptian term *Neteru* (i.e. "gods"). *Can,* studies such as that by Zelia Nuttal (*Papers of the Peabody Museum*) have suggested, was a variant of Canaan who was (according to the Bible) a member of the Hamitic peoples of Africa and a brother-nation of the Egyptians.

The possibility, which we have already mentioned, that the earliest migrants might have been descendants of *Cain,* relates Nahuatlan beginnings to one of the first recorded forced deportations: the exiling of Cain as punishment for the killing of Abel. The very first one, according to the Bible, was the expulsion of Adam and Eve from the Garden of Eden. In our times the exiling of kings has been a known occurrence; the exiling of Napoleon to the island of St. Helena is a notorious example. The biblical record shows that this mode of punishment goes back to the very beginnings of time, when Mankind was held to a certain code of ethics by the "gods." According to the earlier and more detailed Sumerian writings, it was in fact the gods themselves who applied the punishment to their own sinners; and the very first recorded instance concerned their commander in chief, Enlil: he was exiled to a land of banishment for the crime of raping a young Anunnaki nurse (in the end he married her and was given a reprieve).

It is clear from Nahuatlan and Mayan legends that Quetzalcoatl (Kukulkan in Mayan lore) had come to their lands with a small band of followers, and that his eventual departure was a forced one—an exile imposed by the War God. We believe that his arrival was also the result of a forced departure, an exile, from his native land, Egypt. The date of that first event is a vital component of the Mesoamerican counts of Time.

We have already discussed the centrality of the Sacred Round of fifty-two years in Mesoamerican calendrical, religious, and historical affairs, and shown that it was the sacred number of Thoth. Next in significance was a Grand Cycle of "perfect years" that encompassed thirteen eras of *baktuns*, units of four hundred years that were a key element in the consecutive calendar known as the Long Count.

The smallest unit in the Long Count calendar was the *kin*, a single day, and it was built up to larger numbers that could run into the millions of days by a series of multiplications, by 20 and by 360:

$$
\begin{aligned}
1 \text{ kin} &&&= & 1 \text{ day} \\
1 \text{ uinal} &= 1 \text{ kin} \times 20 &&= & 20 \text{ days} \\
1 \text{ tun} &= 1 \text{ kin} \times 360 &&= & 360 \text{ days} \\
1 \text{ ka-tun} &= 1 \text{ tun} \times 20 &&= & 7,200 \text{ days} \\
1 \text{ bak-tun} &= 1 \text{ ka-tun} \times 20 &&= & 144,000 \text{ days}
\end{aligned}
$$

As a purely arithmetical exercise the multiplications by twenty could continue, increasing the number of days that each term and its specific glyph represented, going on to 2,880,000 and 57,600,000 and so on. But in practice the Maya did not go beyond the *baktun;* for the count that began from the enigmatic starting point in 3113 B.C. was deemed to run in cycles of thirteen baktuns. Modern scholars divide the number of days that the Long Count indicates on Mayan monuments not by the perfect 360 but rather by the actual number 365.25 days of the solar year; thus, a monument stating "1,243,615" days is read to mean the passage of 3,404.8 years from August 3113 B.C., i.e. A.D. 292.

The concept of Ages in Earth's history and prehistory was a basic tenet of the pre-Columbian civilizations of Mesoamerica. According to the Aztecs, their Age or "Sun" was the fifth one and "began 5,042 years ago." While the Nahuatlan sources were not specific about how much longer this age was to last, the Mayan sources provided a more precise answer through the Long Count. The present "Sun," they said, will last precisely thirteen baktuns— 1,872,000 days from Point Zero. This represents a Grand Cycle of 5,200 "perfect years" of 360 days each.

In *The Mayan Factor* José Argüelles concluded that each baktun date had acted as a milestone in the history and prehistory of Mesoamerica, as will the year A.D. 2012, in which the thirteen baktuns that began in 3113 B.C. will be completed. He deemed the number 5,200 a key to understanding Mayan cosmogony and ages past and future.

In the 1930s Fritz Buck (*El Calendario Maya en la Cultura de Tiahuanacu*), seeing comparable elements between the Mayan calendars and that of Tiahuanacu, considered the starting date and other periodical markers to be related to actual events affecting the American peoples. He believed that a key symbol on the Gate of the Sun represented 52 and another one 520, and accepted as historically significant the number of 5,200 years; he held, however, that not one but two Great Cycles have to be considered, and that since 1,040 years remain in the second Great Cycle, the first one began in 9360 B.C. It was then, he held, that the legendary events and the tales of the gods in the Andes began. The second Great Cycle, accordingly, began at Tiahuanacu in 4160 B.C.

In arriving at A.D. 2012 as the end of the Fifth Sun, José Argüelles followed the present custom of dividing the 1,872,000 days by the actual number of 365.25 days in a solar year, resulting in the passage of only 5,125 years since the starting point in 3113 B.C. Fritz Buck on the other hand saw no need for such an adjustment, believing that the division should follow the Mayan 360 "perfect year." According to Buck, the historic age through which the Aztecs and Mayas had lived was to last a perfect 5,200 years.

This number, like fifty-two, is connected with Thoth according to ancient Egyptian sources. Among them were the writings of an Egyptian priest whom the Greeks called Manetho (his hieroglyphic name meant "Gift of Thoth"). He recorded the division of monarchies into dynasties, including the divine and semidivine ones that preceded the pharaonic dynasties; he also provided lengths of reign for all of them.

Corroborating legends and tales of the gods from other sources, the list by Manetho asserts that the seven great gods—Ptah, Ra, Shu, Geb, Osiris, Seth, and Horus—reigned a total of 12,300 years. Then began a second divine dynasty, headed by Thoth; it lasted 1,570 years. It was followed by thirty demigods who reigned 3,650 years. A chaotic time followed, a period of 350 years during which Egypt was disunited and in disarray. After that a person called Mên established the first pharaonic dynasty. Scholars hold that this happened circa 3100 B.C.

We have held that the actual date was 3113 B.C., the starting point of the Mesoamerican Long Count. It was then, we believe, that Marduk/Ra, reclaiming lordship over Egypt, expelled Thoth and his followers from that land, forcing them into exile in another, distant, land. And if the preceding reign of Thoth himself (1,570 years) and of his appointed demigods (3,650 years) is tallied, the result is 5,220 years—a mere discrepancy of 20 years from the 5,200 perfect years that make up the Great Mayan Cycle of thirteen baktuns.

As with 52, so was 5,200 a "number of Thoth."

In the olden days, when the Anunnaki were the Lords, the banishment and exile of gods marked milestones in what we have named *The Earth Chronicles*. Much of that part of the tale concerns Marduk, alias Ra in Egypt; and the calendar—the count of Divine, Celestial, and Earthly Time—played a major role in those events.

The reign of Thoth and his dynasty of demigods, ending

circa 3450 B.C., was followed in Egypt, according to Manetho, by a chaotic period that lasted 350 years, in the aftermath of which dynastic rule by pharaohs beholden to Ra began. Segments of the 175th chapter of the *Book of the Dead* (known as the Papyrus of Ani) record an angry exchange between a reappearing Ra and Thoth. "O Thoth, what is it that has happened?" Ra demanded to know. The gods, he said, "have made an uproar, they have taken to quarreling, they have done evil deeds, they have created rebellion." They must have belittled Ra/Marduk in the course of their rebellion: "They have made the great into small."

Ra, the Great God, pointed an accusing finger at Thoth; the accusation directly concerned changes in the calendar: Thoth, Ra accused, "their years cut short, their months had curbed." This Thoth had achieved by "the destruction of Hidden Things that were made for them."

While the nature of the Hidden Things whose destruction shortened the year and the months remains unknown, the outcome could have only meant a switch from the longer solar year to the shorter lunar year—the "making of the great into small." The text ends with Thoth's accepting a sentence of exile and banishment: "I am departing to the desert, the silent land." It is such a tough place, the text explains, that "sexual pleasures are not enjoyed in it" . . .

Another little-understood hieroglyphic text, found in one of Tutankhamen's shrines as well as in royal tombs in Thebes, may have recorded the expulsion order by Ra/Marduk and gave among the reasons the calendrical conflict between the "Sun god" and the "Moon god" (Thoth). The text, which scholars are certain originated at a much earlier time, relates how Ra ordered that Thoth be summoned to him. When Thoth came before Ra, Ra announced: "Behold ye, I am here in the sky in my proper place." Proceeding to berate Thoth and "those who perform deeds of rebellion against me," Ra told Thoth: "Thou encompasseth the two heavens with thy shining rays; that is, Thoth as the Moon encompasses." And he told Thoth: "I shall therefore have thee go all the way around, to the place *Hau-nebut*." Some scholars title the text "The assignment of functions to Thoth." In fact, it was the "assignment" of Thoth to an unidentified distant land because of his "functions"—calendrical preferences—relating to the Moon.

The exiling of Thoth was treated in Mesoamerican time-keeping as Point Zero of the Long Count—according to accepted chronology, in the year 3113 B.C. It must have been an event whose repercussions were recalled far and wide, for it could not be a mere coincidence that according to Hindu traditions (that also divide Earth's history and prehistory into Ages) the present Age, the *Kaliyuga,* began on a day equivalent to midnight between February 17 and 18 in 3102 B.C. This date is uncannily close to the date of Point Zero of the Mesoamerican Long Count, and is, therefore, in some way connected to the exiling of Thoth.

But no sooner than Marduk/Ra forced Thoth to leave the African domains, did he himself become the victim of a similar fate: exile.

With Thoth gone and his brothers Nergal and Gibil remote from the center of Egyptian power, Ra/Marduk could have expected an undisturbed supremacy there. But a new rival had emerged on the scene. He was Dumuzi, the youngest son of Enki, and his domain was the grasslands south of Upper Egypt. Unexpectedly, he emerged as a pretender to the Lordship over Egypt; and as Marduk soon discovered, the ambitions were prompted by a love affair of which Marduk was most disapproving. Preceding by millennia the setting and principals in Shakespeare's *Romeo and Juliet,* Dumuzi's bride was none other than Inanna/Ishtar, a granddaughter of Enlil and one who had fought alongside her brother and uncles to defeat the Enki'ites in the Pyramid Wars.

With limitless ambition, Inanna saw in the espousement with Dumuzi a great role for herself—if only he were to cease being just the Herder (as his epithet was) and assume lordship over the great Egyptian nation: "I had a vision of a great nation choosing Dumuzi as God of its country," she later confided, "for I have made Dumuzi's name exalted, I gave him status."

Opposing the bethrothal and enraged by such ambitions, Marduk sent his "sheriffs" to arrest Dumuzi. Somehow the arrest went wrong; and Dumuzi, trying to hide in his sheep-folds, was found dead.

Inanna raised "a most bitter cry" and sought vengeance. Marduk, fearing her wrath, hid inside the Great Pyramid, all the while asserting his innocence because the death of Dumuzi was unintended, accidental. Unrelenting, Inanna "ceased not striking" at the pyramid, "at its corners, even its multitude of stones." Marduk issued a warning that he would resort to the use of awesome weapons "whose outburst is terrible." Fearing another terrible war, the Anunnaki convened the supreme court of the Seven Who Judge. It was decided that Marduk must be punished, but since he did not directly kill Dumuzi, he could not be sentenced to death. The verdict was therefore to bury Marduk alive in the Great Pyramid within which he took refuge, by hermetically sealing it with him inside.

Various texts, quoted by us at length in *The Wars of Gods and Men,* relate the ensuing events, the commutaion of Marduk's sentence, and the dramatic effort to cut through the massive pyramid, using its original architectural drawings, to reach Marduk in time. The step-by-step rescue is described in detail. So is the conclusion of the incident: Marduk was sentenced to exile, and in Egypt Ra became *Amen*—the Hidden One, a god no longer seen.

As for Inanna, robbed by Dumuzi's death of her dream of being the Lady of Egypt, she was given Erech to be her "cult center" and the domain of Aratta to become the third region of civilization—that of the Indus Valley—circa 2900 B.C.

Where was Thoth in the ensuing centuries, now that his exiler was himself in exile? Apparently roaming distant lands—guiding the erection of the first Stonehenge in the British Isles circa 2800 B.C., helping orient astronomically megalithic structures in the Andes. Where was Marduk during that period? We really do not know, but he must have been somewhere not too far away, for he was watching developments in the Near East and continuing his scheming to seize the supremacy on Earth—supremacy, he believed, wrongly denied to his father Enki.

In Mesopotamia Inanna, ruthless and cunning, maneuvered the kingship of Sumer into the hands of a gardener whom she had found to be a man to her liking. She named him *Sharru-kin*, "righteous ruler," known to us as Sargon I. With Inanna's help he expanded his domains and created a new capital for a greater Sumer hence to be known as Sumer and Akkad. But seeking legitimacy, he went to Babylon—Marduk's city—and there removed some of its hallowed soil to use for foundations in his new capital. That was the opportunity for Marduk to reassert himself. "On account of the sacrilege thus committed," Babylonian texts recorded, "the great lord Marduk became enraged" and destroyed Sargon and his people; and, of course, reinstated himself in Babylon. There he began to fortify the city and enhance its underground water system, making it impervious to attack.

As the ancient texts reveal, it all had to do with Celestial Time.

Alarmed by the prospect of yet another devastating War of the Gods, the Anunnaki met in council. The chief antagonist was Ninurta, the heir apparent of Enlil, whose birthright Marduk was directly challenging. They invited Nergal, a powerful brother of Marduk, to join them in seeking a peaceful solution to the looming conflict. Mixing compliments with persuasion, Nergal first calmed down Ninurta, then agreed to go to Babylon similarly to persuade Marduk to step back from an armed confrontation. The chain of events, with dramatic and in the end fateful turns and consequences, is described in detail in a text known as the *Erra Epos* (Erra having been an epithet of Nergal). It includes many of the verbal exchanges between the participants as though a stenographer were present; and indeed, the text (as its postscript attests) was dictated to a scribe after the events by one of the participating Anunnaki.

As the story unfolds, it becomes increasingly clear that what was happening on Earth had been related to the heavens—to the constellations of the zodiac. In retrospect, the statements and positions taken by the contestants for the supremacy on Earth—Marduk the son of Enki and Ninurta the son of Enlil—lead to no other conclusion than that *the issue was the coming of a New Age:* the impending change from the zodiac house of the bull (Taurus) to the zodiac house of the ram (Aries) as the one in which the spring equinox, and thus the calendrical moment for the New Year, would occur.

Listing all his attributes and heirlooms, Ninurta thus asserted:

> *In Heaven I am a wild bull,*
> *On Earth I am a lion.*
> *In the land I am the lord,*
> *among the gods I am the fiercest.*
> *The hero of the Igigi I am,*
> *among the Anunnaki I am powerful.*

The statement asserts verbally what the depictions, such as we have shown in Fig. 93, have illustrated pictorially: the zodiacal time when the spring equinox began in the House of the Bull (Taurus) and the summer solstice occurred in the zodiac of the Lion (Leo) belonged to the Enlilites, whose "cult animals" were the Bull and the Lion.

Carefully, choosing his words, Nergal formulated his answer to the assertive Ninurta. Yes, he said, all that is true. But

> *On the mountaintop,*
> *in the bush-thicket,*
> *see you not the Ram?*

Its emergence, Nergal continued, is unavoidable:

> *In that grove,*
> *even the supermost time measurer,*
> *the bearer of the standards,*
> *the course cannot change.*
> *One can blow like a wind,*

roar like a storm, [yet]
on the rim of the Sun's orbit,
no matter what the struggle,
see that Ram.

In its relentless precessional retardation, while the zodiacal constellation of the Bull was still dominant, "on the
rim of the Sun's orbit" one could already see the approaching Age of the Ram.

But while the change was unavoidable, the time for it
had not yet come. "The other gods are afraid of battle,"
Nergal said in conclusion. It could all be explained to Marduk, he felt. "Let me go and summon the prince Marduk
away from his dwelling," make him leave peacefully, Nergal suggested.

And so, with Ninurta's reluctant consent, Nergal set out
on a fateful mission to Babylon. On the way he stopped at
Erech, seeking an oracle from Anu at his temple, the
E.ANNA. The message he carried to Marduk from "the
king of the gods" was this: *the Time has not yet come.*

The Time in question, the conversation-debate between
Nergal and Marduk makes clear, was the impending zodiacal change—the coming of a New Age. Marduk received
his brother in the E.SAG.IL, the ziggurat-temple of Babylon; the meeting took place in a sacred chamber called
SHU.AN.NA, "The Celestially Supreme Place," which
evidently Marduk deemed the most suitable place for the
discussion; for he was certain that his time had come, and
even showed Nergal the instruments he used to prove it. (A
Babylonian artist, depicting the encounter between the two
brothers, showed Nergal with his identifying weapon, and
a helmeted Marduk standing atop his ziggurat and holding
in his hand a device—Fig. 153—that looks very much like
the viewing instruments that were employed in Egypt at the
temples of Min.)

Realizing what had happened, Nergal argued to the contrary. Your "precious instrument," he told Marduk, was
imprecise, and that is what had caused him to interpret
incorrectly "the glow of the heavenly stars as the light of

Figure 153

the ordained day.'' While in your sacred precinct you have concluded that ''on the crown of your lordship the light did shine,'' it was not so at the Eanna, where Nergal had stopped on his way. There, Nergal said, ''the face of E.HAL.AN.KI in the Eanna remains covered over.'' The term E.HAL.AN.KI literally means ''House of the circling of Heaven-Earth'' and, in our view, suggests the location of instruments for determining the Earth's precessional shift.

But Marduk saw the issue differently. Whose instruments were really incorrect? At the time of the Deluge, he said, the ''regulations of Heaven-Earth shifted out of their groove and the stations of the celestial gods, the stars of heaven, have changed and did not return to their [former] places.'' A major cause of the change, Marduk claimed, was the fact that ''the *Erkallum* quaked and its covering was diminished, and the measures could no longer be taken.''

This is a highly significant statement, whose scientific importance—as that of the full text of the *Erra Epos*—has been ignored by scholars. *Erkallum* used to be translated ''Lower World'' and more recently the term is left intact, untranslated, as a word whose precise meaning is undetermined. We suggest that it is a term that denotes the land at the bottom of the world—*Antarctica;* and that the ''covering" or more literally "hair-growth-over" is a reference to the ice cap that, Marduk claimed, was still diminished millennia after the Deluge.

When it was all over, Marduk continued, he sent emissaries to check the Lower World. He himself went to take a look. But the "covering," he said, "had become hundreds of miles of water upon the wide seas": the ice cap was still melted.

This is a statement that corroborates our assertion, in *The 12th Planet,* that the Deluge was an immense tidal wave caused by the slippage of the Antarctic ice covering into the adjoining ocean, some 13,000 years ago. The event was the cause, we held, of the abrupt end of the last ice age and the climatic change it had brought about. It also left the Antarctic continent bare of its ice covering, enabling the seeing—and, evidently, mapping—of that continent as its landmass and shorelines really are.

The implication of Marduk's statement that the "regulations of Heaven-Earth had shifted out of their groove" as a result of the melting of the immense ice cap and the redistribution of its weight as water all over the world's seas, bears further study. Did it imply a change in Earth's declination? A somewhat different retardation and thus a different precessional schedule? Perhaps a slowing down of the Earth's spin, or of its orbit around the Sun? The results of experiments simulating the Earth's motions and wobbles with and without an Antarctic ice mass could be most illuminating.

All that, Marduk said, was aggravated by the fate of instruments in the Abzu, the southeastern tip of Africa. We know from other texts that the Anunnaki had a scientific station there that monitored the situation before the Deluge and was thus able to alert them to the impending calamity. "After the regimen Heaven-Earth was undone," Marduk continued, he waited until the fountains dried up and the floodwaters receded. Then he "went back and looked and looked; it was very grievous." What he had discovered was that certain instruments "that to Anu's heaven could reach" were missing, gone. The terms used to describe them are believed by scholars to refer to unidentified crystals. "Where is the instrument for giving orders?" he asked angrily, and "the oracle stone of the gods that gives the sign for lordship . . . Where is the holy radiating stone?"

These pointed questions regarding the missing precision instruments, which used to be operated by the "divine chief craftsman of Anu-powers who carried the holy All-Knower-of-the-Day," sound more like accusations than inquiries. We have earlier referred to an Egyptian text in which Ra/Marduk accused Thoth of destroying "the Hidden Things" that were used for determining the Earth's motions and calendar; the rhetorical questions thrown at Nergal imply deliberate wrongdoing against Marduk. In such circumstances, Marduk indicated, was he not right to rely on his own instruments to determine when *his* Time—the Age of the Ram—had arrived?

Nergal's full response is unclear because where it begins several lines on the tablet have been damaged. It appears that based on his own vast African domains, he did know where some of the instruments (or their replacements) were. He thus suggested that Marduk go to the indicated sites in the Abzu and verify it all for himself. He was certain that thereupon Marduk would realize that his birthright was not at risk; what was being challenged was the timing of his ascendancy.

To put Marduk further at ease, Nergal promised that he would personally see to it that nothing would be disturbed in Babylon during Marduk's absence. And, as a final gesture of reassurance, he promised to make the celestial symbols of the Enlilite Age, "the bulls of Anu and Enlil, crouch at the gate of thy temple."

Such a symbolic act of obeisance, the bowing to Marduk of Enlil's Bull of Heaven at the entrance to Marduk's temple, persuaded Marduk to accept his brother's plea:

Marduk heard this.
The promise, given by Erra [Nergal] found his favor.
So did he step down from his seat,

*and to the Land of Mines, an abode of the Anunnaki,
he set his direction.*

Thus did the dispute regarding the correct timing of the
zodiacal change lead to Marduk's second exile—temporary
only, he believed.

But as fate would have it, the anticipated coming of a
New Age was not to be a peaceful one.

12

THE AGE OF THE RAM

When the Age of the Ram finally arrived, it did not come as the dawn of a New Age. Rather, it was accompanied by darkness at noon—the darkness of a cloud of deadly radiation from the first-ever explosion of nuclear weapons on Earth. It came as the culmination of more than two centuries of upheavals and warfare that pitted god against god and nation against nation; and in its aftermath, the great Sumerian civilization that had lasted for nearly two millennia lay prostrate and desolate, its people decimated, its remnants dispersed in the world's first Diaspora. Marduk did indeed gain supremacy; but the New Order that ensued was one of new laws and customs, a new religion and beliefs; an era of regression in sciences, of astrology instead of astronomy—even of a new and lesser status for women.

Did it have to happen that way? Was the change so devastating and bitter just because it involved ambitious protagonists—because the Anunnaki, not men, had directed the course of events? Or was it all destined, preordained, and the force and influence—real or imagined—of the passage into a new zodiacal house so overwhelming that empires must topple, religions must change, laws and customs and social organization must be overturned?

Let us review the record of that first known changeover; perchance we may find full answers, for sure enlightening clues.

It was, by our calculations, circa 2295 B.C. that Marduk left Babylon, going first to the Land of Mines and then to regions unspecified by the Mesopotamian texts. He left on the understanding that the instruments and other "works of wonder" that he had put up in Babylon would remain undisturbed; but no sooner did Marduk leave, than Nergal/ Erra broke his promisė. Out of mere curiosity, or perhaps with malice in mind, he entered the forbidden *Gigunu,* the mysterious chamber that Marduk had declared off limits. Once inside he caused the chamber's "brilliance" to be removed; thereupon, as Marduk had warned, "the day turned into darkness," and calamities started afflicting Babylon and its people.

Was the "brilliance" a radiating, nuclear-driven device? It is not clear what it was, except that the adverse effects began to spread throughout Mesopotamia. The other gods were angered by Nergal's deed; even his father Enki reprimanded him and ordered him back to his African domain, Kutha. Nergal heeded the order; but before leaving he smashed all that Marduk had set up, and left behind his warriors to make sure that Marduk's followers in Babylon would remain subdued.

The two departures, first of Marduk and then of Nergal, left the arena free for the descendants of Enlil. First to take advantage of the situation was Inanna (Ishtar); she chose a grandson of Sargon, Naram-Sin ("Sin's Favorite") to ascend the throne of Sumer and Akkad; and with him and his armies as her surrogates, she embarked on a series of conquests. Among her first targets was the great Landing Place in the Cedar Mountains, the immense platform of Baalbek in Lebanon. She then assaulted the lands along the Mediterranean coast, seizing Mission Control Center in Jerusalem and the crossing point on the land route from Mesopotamia to the Sinai, Jericho. Now the spaceport itself, in the Sinai peninsula, was under her control. But, unsatisfied, Inanna sought to fulfill her dream of dominating Egypt—a dream shattered by the death of Dumuzi. Guiding, urging, and arming Naram-Sin with her "awesome weapons," she brought about the invasion of Egypt.

The texts suggest that recognizing her as an avowed adversary of Marduk, Nergal gave her his actual or tacit assistance in that invasion. But the other leaders of the Anunnaki did not view it all with equanimity. Not only did she breach the Enlilite-Enki'ite regional boundaries, she also brought under her control the spaceport, that neutral sacred zone in the Fourth Region.

An Assembly of the Gods was convened in Nippur to deal with Inanna's excesses. As a result, an order for her arrest and trial was issued by Enlil. Hearing that, Inanna forsook her temple in Agade, Naram-Sin's capital, and escaped to hide with Nergal. From afar, she sent orders and oracles to Naram-Sin, encouraging him to continue the conquests and bloodshed. To counteract that, the other gods empowered Ninurta to bring over loyal troops from neighboring mountainous lands. A text titled *The Curse of Agade* describes those events and the vow of the Anunnaki to obliterate Agade. True to that vow, the city—once the pride of Sargon and the dynasty of Akkad—was never to be found again.

The relatively brief Era of Ishtar had come to an end; and to bring some measure of order and stability to Mesopotamia and its neighboring lands, Ninurta (under whom Kingship had started in Sumer) was again given command of the country. Before Agade was destroyed, Ninurta its "crownband of lordship, the tiara of kingship, the throne given to rulership, to his temple brought over." At that time his "cult center" was in Lagash, at its Girsu sacred precinct. From there, flying in his Divine Black Bird, Ninurta roamed the plain between the two rivers and the adjoining mountainlands, restoring irrigation and agriculture, returning order and tranquility. Setting personal examples by his unwavering fidelity to his spouse Bau (nicknamed *Gula*, "the Great") with whom he had portraits made (Fig. 154), and devoted to his mother Ninharsag, he proclaimed moral laws and codes of justice. To assist in these tasks he appointed human viceroys; circa 2160 B.C., Gudea was the chosen one.

Over in Egypt, in the aftermath of the exile of Marduk/Ra, Naram-Sin's invasion and the reprimand to Nergal, the country was in disarray. Egyptologists call the chaotic century, between about 2180 and 2040 B.C., the "First Intermediate Period" in Egyptian history. It was a time when the Old Kingdom that was centered in Memphis and He-

Figure 154

liopolis came under attack from Theban princes in the south. Political, religious, and calendrical issues were involved; underlying the human contest was the celestial confrontation between the Bull and the Ram.

From the very beginning of Egyptian dynastic rule and religion, the greatest celestial compliment to the great gods was to compare them to the Bull of Heaven. Its earthly symbol, the Sacred Bull *Apis* (Fig. 155a) was venerated at Heliopolis and Memphis. Some of the earliest pictographic inscriptions—so old that Sir Flinders Petrie (*Royal Tombs*) attributed them to the time of "dynasty zero"—showed this symbol of the Sacred Bull upon a Celestial Boat with a priest holding ritual objects in front of it (Fig. 155b). (The depictions on this archaic plaque and on another similar one also reported by Sir Flinders Petrie, also clearly show the Sphinx, indicating beyond doubt that the Sphinx had already existed many centuries before its supposed construction by the Pharaoh Khephren of the Fourth Dynasty.) As later in Crete for the Minotaur, a special labyrinth was built for the Apis Bull in Memphis. At Saqqara, effigies of bull-heads made of clay with natural horns were placed in recesses within the tomb of a Second Dynasty pharaoh; and it is known that Zoser, a Third Dynasty pharaoh, held special ceremonies in honor of the Bull of Heaven at his spacious pyramid compound in Saqqara. All that had taken place during the Old Kingdom, a period that came to an end circa 2180 B.C.

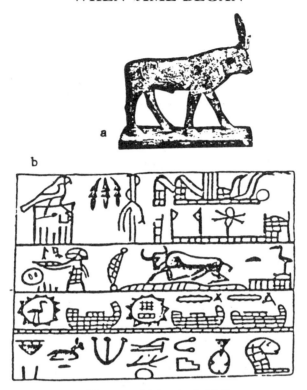

Figures 155a and 155b

When the Theban priests of Ra-Amen began the drive to supersede the Memphite-Heliopolitan religion and calendar, celestial depictions still showed the Sun rising over the Bull of Heaven (Fig. 156a), but the Bull of Heaven was depicted tethered and held back. Later on, when the New Kingdom reunited Egypt with Thebes as its capital and Amon-Ra was elevated to supremacy, the Bull of Heaven was depicted pierced and deflated (Fig. 156b). The Ram began to dominate celestial and monumental art and Ra was given the epithet "Ram of the Four Winds," and was so depicted to indicate that he was master of the four corners and four regions of the Earth (Fig. 157).

Where was Thoth during that First Intermediate Period, when in the heavens above and on Earth below the Ram and its followers were battling and chasing away the Bull and its adherents? There is no indication that he sought to

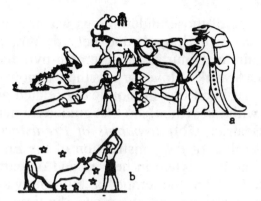

Figures 156a and 156b

Figure 157

reclaim the rulership of a divided and chaotic Egypt. It was a time when, without giving up his new domains in the New World, he could go about that in which he had become proficient—the erection of circular observatories and the teaching of the local inhabitants at old and new places the "secrets of numbers" and the knowledge of the calendar. The reconstruction of Stonehenge I into Stonehenge II and III at about that very time was one of those monumental edifices. If legends be deemed as conveyors of historical fact, then the one about Africans coming to erect the megalithic circles at Stonehenge suggests that Thoth, alias Quetzalcoatl, had brought over for the reconstruction task some of his Olmec followers who by then had become expert stonemasons in Mesoamerica.

The epitome of those undertakings was the invitation by Ninurta to come to Lagash and help design, orient, and build the Eninnu, Ninurta's new temple-pyramid.

Was it just a work of love, or was there a more compelling reason for that burst of astronomically related activity?

Dealing with the symbolism that guided Sumerian temple building, Beatrice Goff (*Symbols of Prehistoric Mesopotamia*) wrote thus of the construction of the Eninnu: "The time is the moment when in heaven and on earth the fates were decided." That the temple be built the way its divine planners had ordained and at the specific time it was to be built and inaugurated, she determined, was all "part of a plan foreordained when the fates were decided; Gudea's commission was part of a cosmic plan." This, she concluded, was "the kind of setting where not only art and ritual but also mythology go hand in hand as essentials in the religion."

Circa 2200 B.C. was indeed a time "when in Heaven and on Earth the fates were decided," for it was the time when a New Age, the Age of the Ram, was due to replace the Old Age, the Age of the Bull.

Though Marduk/Ra was somewhere in exile, there grew a contest for the hearts and minds of people since the "gods" had come to depend increasingly on human kings and human armies to achieve their ends. Many sources indicate that Marduk's son Nabu was crisscrossing the lands that later became known as Lands of the Bible, seeking adherents to his father's side. His name, *Nabu*, had the same meaning and came from the same verb by which the Bible called a true prophet: *Nabi*, one who receives the divine words and signs and in turn expresses them to the people. The divine signs of which Nabu spoke were the changing Heavens; the fact that the New Year and other worship dates no longer seemed to occur when they should have. Nabu's weapon, in behalf of Marduk, was the calendar . . .

What, one may ask, was there to view or determine that was unclear or in dispute? The truth of the matter is that even nowadays, no one can say for sure when one "Age" has ended and the other begun. There could be the arbitrary, mathematically precise calculation that since the Grand Precessional Cycle of 25,920 years is divided into twelve Houses, each House or Age lasts exactly 2,160 years. That was the mathematical basis of the sexagesimal system, the 10:6 ratio between Divine Time and Celestial Time. But if no person alive, no astronomer-priest, had witnessed the beginning of an Age and its ending, for no one human stayed alive 2,160 years, it was either the word of the gods, or the observation of the skies. But the zodiacal constellations are of varied sizes, and the Sun can linger longer or shorter periods within them. The problem is especially acute in the case of Aries, that occupies less than 30° of the celestial arc, while its neighbors Taurus and Pisces extend beyond their official 30° Houses. So, if the gods disagreed, some of them (e.g. Marduk, so well trained in sciences by his father Enki, and Nabu) could say: 2,160 years have passed, the Time has come. But others (e.g. Ninurta, Thoth) could and did say: But look to the Heavens, do you really see the change occurring?

The historical record, as detailed by the ancient texts and affirmed by archaeology, indicates that the tactics worked— at least for a while. Marduk remained in exile and in Mesopotamia the situation calmed down sufficiently for the mountainland troops to be sent back. After serving as a military headquarters for "ninety-one years and forty days" (according to the ancient records), Lagash could become a civilian center for the glorification of Ninurta. Circa 2160 B.C. that was expressed by the construction of the new Eninnu under Gudea's reign.

The Era of Ninurta lasted about a century and a half. Then, satisfied that the situation was under control, Ninurta departed for some distant mission. In his stead Enlil appointed his son Nannar/Sin to oversee Sumer and Akkad, and Ur, Nannar/Sin's "cult center," became the capital of a revitalized empire.

It was an appointment with more than political and hierarchical implications, for Nannar/Sin was the "Moon god" and his elevation to supremacy announced that the purely solar calendar of Ra/Marduk was done with and that the lunisolar calendar of Nippur was the only true one—religiously and politically. To assure adherence, a high priest knowledgeable in astronomy and celestial omens was sent from Nippur's temple to liaison at Ur. His name was Terah; with him was his ten-year-old son, Abram.

The year, by our calculations, was 2113 B.C.

The arrival of Terah and his family in Ur coincided with the establishment of the reign of five successive rulers known as the Ur III dynasty. Their, and Abram's, ensuing century saw on the one hand the glorious culmination of the Sumerian civilization; its epitome and hallmark was the grand ziggurat built there for Nannar/Sin—a monumental edifice that, though lying in ruins for almost four thousand years, still dominates the landscape and awes the viewer by its immensity, stability, and intricacy.

Under the active guidance of Nannar and his spouse Ningal, Sumer attained new heights in art and sciences, literature and urban organization, agriculture and industry and commerce. Sumer became the granary of the Lands of the Bible, its wool and garment industries were in a class by themselves, its merchants were the famed Merchants of Ur. But that was only one aspect of the Era of Nannar. On the other hand, hanging over all this greatness and glory was the destiny ordained by Time—the relentless change, from one New Year to another, of the Sun's position less and less in the House of GUD.ANNA, the "Bull of Heaven," and ever closer to that of KU.MAL, the celestial Ram—with all the dire consequences.

Ever since it was given Priesthood and Kingship, Mankind had known its place and role. The "gods" were the Lords, to be worshiped and venerated. There was a defined hierarchy, prescribed rituals, and holy days. The gods were strict but benevolent, their decrees were sharp but righteous. For millennia the gods oversaw the welfare and fate of Mankind, all the while remaining clearly apart from the people, approachable only by the high priest on specified dates, communicating with the king in visions and by omens. But now all that was beginning to crumble, for the gods themselves were at odds, citing different celestial omens and a changing calendar, increasingly pitting nation against nation in the cause of "divine" wars, quarrels, and bloodshed. And Mankind, confused and bewildered, increasingly speaking of "my god" and "your god," now even began to doubt the divine credibility.

In such circumstances Enlil and Nannar chose carefully the first ruler of the new dynasty. They selected Ur-Nammu ("The Joy of Ur"), a demigod whose mother was the goddess Ninsun. It was undoubtedly a very calculated move meant to evoke among the people memories of past glories and the "good old days," for Ninsun was the mother of the famed Gilgamesh who was still exalted in epic tales and artistic depictions. He was a king of Erech who was privileged to have seen both the Landing Place in the Cedar Mountains of Lebanon and the spaceport in the Sinai; and the choice of another son of Ninsun, some seven centuries later, was meant to evoke confidences that those vital places would again be part of Sumer's heritage, its Promised Lands.

Ur-Nammu's assignment was to steer the people "away from the evil ways" of following the wrong gods. The effort was marked by the repair and rebuilding of all the major temples in the land—with the conspicuous exception of Marduk's temple in Babylon. The next step was to subdue the "evil cities" where Nabu was making converts to Marduk. To that end Enlil provided Ur-Nammu with a "Divine Weapon" with which to "in the hostile lands heap up the rebels in piles." That the enforcement of the Enlilite Celestial Time was a major purpose is made clear in the text that quotes Enlil's instructions to Ur-Nammu about the weapon's use:

> *As the Bull*
> *to crush the foreign lands;*
> *As the Lion*
> *to hunt [the sinners] down;*
> *to destroy the evil cities,*
> *clear them of opposition to the Lofty Ones.*

The Bull of the equinox and the Lion of the solstice were to be upheld; any opponent of the Lofty Ones had to be hunted down, crushed, destroyed.

Leading the called-for military expedition, Ur-Nammu met not victory but an ignominious end. In the course of the battle his chariot got stuck in the mud and he fell off it, only to be crushed to death by its own wheels. The tragedy was compounded when the boat returning his body to Sumer sank on the way, so that the great king was not even brought to burial.

When the news reached Ur, the people were grieved and disbelieving. How did it happen that "the Lord Nannar did not hold Ur-Nammu by the hand," why did Inanna "not put her noble arm around his head," why did Utu not assist him? Why did Anu "alter his holy word"? Surely it was a betrayal by the great gods; it could only happen because "Enlil deceitfully changed his fate-decree."

The tragic death of Ur-Nammu and the doubting of the Enlilite gods at Ur caused Terah and his family to move to Harran, a city in northwestern Mesopotamia that served as a link with the lands and people of Anatolia—the Hittites; evidently, the powers that be felt that Harran, where a temple to Nannar/Sin almost duplicated that of Ur, would be a more appropriate place for the Nippurian scion of a priestly royal line in the turbulent times ahead.

In Ur, Shulgi, a son of Ur-Nammu by a priestess in a marriage arranged by Nannar, ascended the throne. He at once sought the favor of Ninurta, building for him a shrine in Nippur. The move had practical aspects; for as the western provinces became ever more restive in spite of a peace-journey undertaken by Shulgi, he arranged to obtain a "foreign legion" of troops from Elam, a Ninurta domain in the mountains southeast of Sumer. Using them to launch military expeditions against the "sinning cities," he himself sought solace in lavish living and lovemaking, becoming a "beloved" of Inanna and conducting banquets and orgies in Erech, in Anu's very temple.

Although the military expeditions brought, for the first time ever, Elamite troops to the gateway to the Sinai peninsula and its spaceport, they failed to quell the "rebellion" stirred up by Nabu and Marduk. In the forty-seventh year of his reign, 2049 B.C., Shulgi resorted to a desperate stratagem: he ordered the building of a defensive wall along Sumer's western border. To the Enlilite gods it was tantamount to an abandonment of crucial lands where the Landing Place and Mission Control Center were. So, because "the divine regulations he did not carry out," Enlil decreed Shulgi's death, the "death of a sinner," the very next year.

The retreat from the western lands and the death of Shulgi triggered two moves. As we learn from a biographical text in which Marduk explained his moves and motives, it was then that he decided to return to the proximity of Mesopotamia by arriving in the land of the Hittites. Thereupon, it was also decided that Abram should make a move. In the forty-eight years of Shulgi's reign, Abram matured in Harran from a young bridegroom to a seventy-five-year-old leader, possessing varied knowledge and militarily trained and assisted by his Hittite hosts.

And Yahweh said unto Abram:
"Get thee out of thy country
and out of thy birthplace
and from thy father's house,
unto the land which I will show thee."
And Abram departed as Yahweh had spoken unto him.

The destination, as chapter 12 of Genesis makes clear, was the vital Land of Canaan; he was to proceed as quickly as possible and station himself and his elite cavalry in the Negev, on the Canaan-Sinai border. His mission, as we have fully detailed in *The Wars of Gods and Men,* was to protect the gateway to the spaceport. He arrived there skirting the "sinful cities" of the Canaanites; soon thereafter he went to Egypt, obtaining more troops and camels, for a cavalry, from the last pharaoh of the Memphite dynasties. Back in the Negev, he was ready to fulfill his mission of guarding the spaceport's approaches.

The anticipated conflict came to a head in the seventh

year of the reign of Shulgi's successor, Amar-Sin ("Seen by Sin"). It was, even in modern terms, a truly international war in which an alliance of four kings of the East set out from Mesopotamia to attack an alliance of five kings of Canaan. Leading the attack, according to the biblical record in chapter 14 of Genesis, was "Amraphel, the king of Shin'ar" and, for a long time, it was believed that he was the Babylonian king Hammurabi. In fact, as our own studies have shown, he was the Sumerian Amar-Sin and the tale of the international conflict has been recorded also in Mesopotamian texts, such as the tablets of the Spartoli Collection in the British Museum whose confirmation of the biblical tale was first pointed out by Theophilus Pinches in 1897. Together with complementary fragments, the collection of Mesopotamian tablets dealing with those events has come to be known as the *Khedorla'omer Texts*.

Marching under the banner of Sin and according to oracles given by Inanna/Ishtar, the allied army—probably the greatest military force of men ever seen until then—smote one western land after another. Regaining for Sin all the lands between the Euphrates and the Jordan River, they circled the Dead Sea and set as their next target the spaceport in the Sinai peninsula. But there Abram, carrying out his mission, stood in their way; so they turned back north, ready to attack the "evil cities" of the Canaanites.

Instead of waiting in their walled cities to be attacked, the Canaanite alliance marched forth and joined battle with the invaders in the Valley of Siddim. The records, both biblical and Mesopotamian, suggest an indecisive result. The "evil cities" were not obliterated, though the flight (and resulting death) of two kings, those of Sodom and Gomorrah, resulted in booty and prisoners being carried away from there. Among the prisoners from Sodom was Abram's nephew Lot; and when Abram heard that, his cavalry pursued the invaders, catching up with them near Damascus (now the capital of Syria). Lot, other prisoners, and the booty were retaken and brought back to Canaan.

As the Canaanite kings came out to greet them and Abram, they offered that he keep the booty as a reward.

But he refused to take "even a shoelace." He had acted neither out of enmity for the Mesopotamian alliance nor out of support for the Canaanite kings, he explained. It was only for "Yahweh, the God Most High, Possessor of Heaven and Earth, that I have raised my hand," he stated.

The unsuccessful military campaign depressed and confused Amar-Sin. According to the Date Formula for the ensuing year, 2040 B.C., he left Ur and the worship of Nannar/Sin and became a priest in Eridu, Enki's "cult center." Within another year he was dead, presumably of a scorpion's bite. The year 2040 B.C. was even more memorable in Egypt; there, Mentuhotep II, leader of the Theban princes, defeated the northern pharaohs and extended the rule and rules of Ra-Amen throughout Egypt, up to the Sinai boundary. The victory ushered in what scholars call the Middle Kingdom of the XI and XII dynasties that lasted to about 1790 B.C. While the full force and significance of the Age of the Ram came into play in Egypt during the later New Kingdom, the Theban victory of 2040 B.C. marked the end of the Age of the Bull in the African domains.

If, from a historical perspective, the coming of the Age of the Ram appears to have been inevitable, so must it also have appeared to the principal protagonists and antagonists of that very trying time. In Canaan, Abram retreated to a mountain stronghold near Hebron. In Sumer, the new king, Shu-Sin, a brother of Amar-Sin, strengthened the defensive walls in the west, sought an alliance with the Nippurites who had settled with Terah in Harran, and built two large ships—possibly as a precaution, with escape in mind . . . In a night equivalent to one in February 2031 B.C. a major lunar eclipse occurred in Sumer; it was taken to be an ominous omen of the nearing "eclipse" of the Moon god himself. The first victim, however, was Shu-Sin; for by the following year he was no longer king.

As the word of the celestial omen, the eclipse of the Moon, spread throughout the ancient Near East, the required messages of loyalty from viceroys and governors of the provinces, first in the west and then in the east, ceased.

Within a year of the reign of the next (and last) king of Ur, Ibbi-Sin, raiders from the west, organized by Nabu and encouraged by Marduk, were clashing with Elamite mercenaries at Mesopotamia's gates. In 2026 B.C. the compiling of customs receipts (on clay tablets) at Drehem, a major trade gateway in Sumer during the Ur III period, ceased abruptly, indicating that foreign commerce had come to a standstill. Sumer itself became a country under siege, its territory shrinking, its people huddled behind protective walls. In what was once the ancient world's food basket, supplies ran short and prices of essentials—barley, oil, wool—multiplied every month.

Unlike any other time in Sumer's and Mesopotamia's long history, omens were cited in unusual frequency. Judging by the record of human behavior one may see in that a known reaction to fear of the unknown and to a search for reassurance or guidance from some higher power or intelligence. But at that time there was a real cause for watching the heavens for omens, for the celestial arrival of the Ram was becoming increasingly evident.

As the texts that have survived from that period attest, the course of events about to happen on Earth was closely linked to celestial phenomena; and each side to the growing confrontation constantly observed the skies for heavenly signs. Since the various Great Anunnaki were associated with celestial counterparts, both zodiacal constellations and the twelve members of the Solar System (as well as with months), the movements and positions of the celestial bodies associated with the chief protagonists were especially significant. The Moon, counterpart of Ur's great god Nannar/Sin, the Sun (counterpart of Nannar's son Utu/Shamash), Venus (the planet of Sin's daughter Inanna/Ishtar), and the planets Saturn and Mars (associated with Ninurta and Nergal) were especially watched and observed in Ur and Nippur. In addition to all those associations, the various lands of the Sumerian empire were also deemed to belong, celestially, to specific zodiacal constellations: Sumer, Akkad, and Elam were under the sign and protection of Taurus; the Lands of the Westerners, under the sign of Aries. Hence, planetary and zodiacal conjunctions, sometimes coupled with the appearance (bright, dim, horned, etc.) of the Moon, Sun, and planets could spell good or evil omens.

A text designated by scholars *Prophecy Text B*, known from later copies of the original Sumerian record that was made in Nippur, illustrates how such celestial omens were interpreted as prophecies of the coming doom. In spite of breaks and damage, the impact of the tablet's text retains its predictions of the fateful events to come:

> *If [Mars] is very red, bright . . .*
> *Enlil will speak to the great Anu.*
> *The land [Sumer] will be plundered,*
> *The land of Akkad will . . .*
> *. . . in the entire country . . .*
> *A daughter will bar her door to her mother,*
> *. . . friend will slay friend . . .*
>
> *If Saturn will . . .*
> *Enlil will speak to the great Anu.*
> *Confusion will . . . troubles will . . .*
> *a man will betray another man,*
> *a woman will betray another woman . . .*
> *. . . a son of the king will . . .*
> *. . . temples will collapse . . .*
> *. . . a severe famine will occur . . .*

Some of those omen-prophecies directly related the planetary positions to the constellation of the Ram:

> *If the Ram by Jupiter will be entered*
> *when Venus enters the Moon,*
> *the watch will come to an end.*
> *Woes, troubles, confusion*
> *and bad things will occur in the lands.*
> *People will sell their children for money.*
> *The king of Elam will be surrounded in his palace:*
> *. . . the destruction of Elam and its people.*

If the Ram has a conjunction with the planet ...
... when Venus ... and the ...
... planets can be seen ...
... will rebel against the king,
... will seize the throne,
the whole land ... will diminish at his command.

In the opposing camp, the heavens were also observed for signs and omens. One such text, put together through the labor of many scholars from assorted tablets (mostly in the British Museum), is an amazing autobiographical record by Marduk of his exile, agonizing wait for the right celestial omens, and final move to take over the Lordship that he believed was his. Written as a "memoir" by an aging Marduk, he reveals in it his "secrets" to posterity:

O great gods, learn my secrets
as I girdle my belt, my memories recall.
I am the divine Marduk, a great god.
I was cast off for my sins,
to the mountains I have gone.
In many lands I have been a wanderer;
From where the Sun rises to where it sets I went.

Having thus wandered from one end of the Earth to the other, he received an omen:

By an omen to Hatti-land I went.
In Hatti-land I asked for an oracle
[about] my throne and my Lordship.
In its midst [I asked]: "Until when?"
24 years in its midst I nested.

Various astronomical texts from the years that marked the transition from Taurus to Aries offer a clue regarding the omens that Marduk was especially interested in. In those texts, as well as in what is called by scholars "mythological texts," the association of Marduk with Jupiter is strongly suggested. We know that after Marduk had succeeded in his ambitions and established himself in Babylon as the supreme deity, such texts as the Epic of Creation were rewritten there so as to associate Marduk with Nibiru, the home planet of the Anunnaki. But prior to that Jupiter, by all indications, was the celestial body of Marduk in his epithet "Son of the Sun"; and a suggestion—made more than a century and a half ago—that Jupiter might have served in Babylon as a device parallel to that which Sirius had served in Egypt, as the synchronizer of the calendrical cycle, is quite pertinent here.

We refer to a series of lectures delivered at the Royal Institute of Great Britain to the Society of Antiquarians in 1822 (!) by an "antiquarian" named John Landseer in which, in spite of the meager archaeological data then available, he showed an astounding grasp of ancient times. Long before others, and as a result the holder of unaccepted views, he asserted that the "Chaldeans" had known of the phenomenon of precession millennia before the Greeks. Calling those early times an era "when Astronomy was Religion" and vice versa, he asserted that the calendar was related to the zodiacal "mansion" of the Bull, and that the transition to Aries was associated with "a mystifying conjunction of the Sun and Jupiter in the sign of Aries, at the commencement of the great cycle of intricate [celestial] revolutions." He believed that the Greek myths and legends connecting Zeus/Jupiter with the Ram and its golden fleece reflected that transition to Aries. And he calculated that such a determining conjunction of Jupiter and the Sun in the boundary between Taurus and Aries had occurred in the year 2142 B.C.

The notion that Jupiter in a conjunction with the Sun might have served as the Announcer, the herald of the Age of Aries, was also surmised from Babylonian astronomical tablets in a series of papers titled "Euphratean Stellar Researches" by Robert Brown in the *Proceedings of the Society of Biblical Archaeology*, London, in 1893. Focusing in particular on two astronomical tablets (British Museum catalogue numbers K.2310 and K.2894), Brown concluded that they dealt with the position of stars, constellations, and planets as seen in Babylon at midnight on a date equivalent to July 10, 2000 B.C. Apparently quoting Nabu in reference to his "proclamation of the planet of the Prince of Earth"—presumably Jupiter—appearing in an "ocular instance which took place in the sign of Aries," the texts were translated by Brown into a "star map" that showed Jupiter in near conjunction with the brightest star (*Lulim*, known by its Arabic name Hamal) of Aries and just off the point of the spring equinox, when the zodiacal path and the planetary path (celestial equator and ecliptic) cross (Fig. 158).

Dealing with the transitions from one Age to another as recorded in the Mesopotamian tablets, various Assyriologists (as they were called at the time)—e.g. Franz Xavier Kugler (*Im Bannkreis Babels*)—have pointed out that while the transition from Gemini to Taurus was ascertainable with relative precision, that from Taurus to Aries was less determinable timewise. Kugler believed that the vernal equinox signaling the New Year was still in Taurus in 2300 B.C., and noted that the Babylonians had assumed the *Zeitalter*, the new zodiacal Age, to have come into effect in 2151 B.C.

It is probably no coincidence that the same date marked an important innovation in Egyptian practices of depicting the heavens. According to the masterwork on the subject of ancient Egyptian astronomy, *Egyptian Astronomical Texts* by O. Neugebauer and Richard A. Parker, celestial

Fig. II.   Star-map in illustration of Tablet, K. 2310, Rev.

(Portion of the Midnight Sky as seen from Itslighm, July 10, B.C. 2000.)

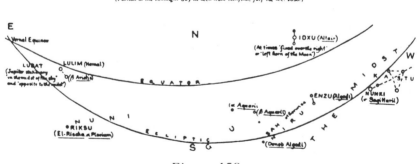

Figure 158

imaging including the thirty-six Decans began to be painted on coffin lids circa 2150 B.C.—coinciding with the chaotic First Intermediate Period, the start of the Theban push northward to supersede Memphis and Heliopolis, and the time when Marduk/Ra read the omens in his favor.

Coffin lids, as time went by and the Age of the Ram was no longer contested, clearly depicted the new Celestial Age, as this illustration from a tomb near Thebes shows (Fig. 159). The four-headed Ram dominates the four corners of the heavens (and the Earth too); the Bull of Heaven is shown pierced with a spear or lance; and the twelve zodiacal constellations, in their Sumerian-devised order and symbols, are arranged so that the constellation of Aries is precisely in the east, i.e., where the Sun appears on the Day of the Equinox.

If the determining or triggering omen for Marduk/Ra was

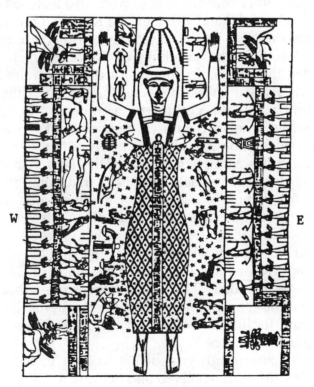

Figure 159

the conjunction of Jupiter and the Sun in the "mansion" of Aries, and if it did occur in 2142 B.C. as John Landseer suggested, then this heralding more or less coincided with the arithmetically calculated (once in 2,160 years) zodiacal shift. That, however, would have meant that the claim that the shift to Aries had come about preceded by about a century and a half the *observational* shift of the vernal equinox into Aries in 2000 B.C. as attested by the two tablets. That discrepancy could explain, at least in part, the disagreement at that time regarding what the celestial omens or observations were truly portending.

As the autobiographical Marduk text admits, even the omen that signified to him the time to end his wanderings and come to Hatti Land, the Land of the Hittites in Asia Minor, occurred twenty-four years before his next move. But that and other celestial omens were also watched closely on the Enlilite side; and although the Ram had not yet fully dominated the New Year's day on the spring equinox in the time of Ibbi-Sin, the last king of Ur, the oracle priests interpreted the omens as portents of the disastrous end. In the fourth year of Ibbi-Sin's reign (2026 B.C.) the oracle priests told him that according to the omens, "For the second time, he who calls himself Supreme, like one whose chest has been anointed, shall come from the west." With such predictions Sumerian cities, in the fifth year of Ibbi-Sin's reign, ceased the delivery of the traditional sacrificial animals for Nannar's temple in Ur. That same year the omen-priests prophesied that "when the sixth year comes, the inhabitants of Ur will be trapped." In the following, sixth year, the omens of destruction and ruin became more urgent and Mesopotamia itself, the heartland of Sumer and Akkad, was invaded. The inscriptions record that in the sixth year the "hostile Westerners had entered the plain, had entered the interior of the country, taking one by one all the great fortresses."

In the twenty-fourth year of his sojourn in the Land of the Hittites, Marduk received another omen: "My days [of exile] were completed, my years [of exile] were fulfilled," he wrote in his memoirs. "With longing to my city Babylon I set course, to my temple Esagila as a mount [to rebuild], my everlasting abode to reestablish." The partly damaged tablet then describes Marduk's route from Anatolia back to Babylon; the cities named indicate that he first went south to Hama (the biblical Hamat), then crossed the Euphrates at Mari; he indeed returned, as the omens had predicted, from the west.

The year was 2024 B.C.

In his autobiographical memoirs Marduk described how he had expected his return to Babylon to be a triumphant one, opening an era of well-being and prosperity for its people. He envisaged the establishment of a new royal dynasty, and foresaw as the first task of the new king the rebuilding of the Esagil, the temple-ziggurat of Babylon, according to a new "ground plan of Heaven and Earth"— one in accord with the New Age of the Ram:

> *I raised my heels toward Babylon,*
> *through the lands I went to my city;*
> *A king in Babylon to make the foremost,*
> *in its midst my temple-mountain to heaven raise.*
> *The mountainlike Esagil he will renew,*
> *the ground plan of Heaven and Earth*
> *will he for the mountainlike Esagil draw,*
> *its height he will alter,*
> *its platform he will raise,*
> *its head he will ameliorate.*
>
> *In my city Babylon*
> *in abundance he will reside;*
> *My hand he will grasp,*
> *to my city and my temple Esagil*
> *for eternity I shall enter.*

Undoubtedly mindful of the manner in which Ninurta's ziggurat-temple at Lagash was decorated and embellished, Marduk envisioned his own new temple, the Esagil ("House whose head is loftiest"), decorated with bright and precious metals: "with cast metal will it be covered, its steps with drawn metal will be overlaid, its sidewalls with brought-over metal will be filled." And when all that shall be completed, Marduk mused, astronomer-priests shall ascend the ziggurat's stages and observe the heavens, confirming his rightful supremacy:

> *Omen-knowers, put to service,*
> *shall then ascend its midst;*
> *Left and right, on opposite sides,*
> *they shall separately stand.*
> *The king will then approach;*
> *the rightful star of the Esagil*
> *over the land [he will observe].*

When the Esagil was eventually built, it was erected according to very detailed and precise plans; its orientation, height, and various stages were indeed such that its head pointed directly (see Fig. 33) to the star *Iku,* the lead star of the constellation Aries.

But Marduk's ambitious vision was not to be fulfilled right then and there. In the very same year that he began his march back to Babylon at the head of a horde of Western supporters organized by Nabu, a most awesome catastrophe befell the ancient Near East—a calamity the likes of which neither Mankind nor Earth itself had previously experienced.

He expected that once the omens were clear, both gods and men would heed his call for accepting his supremacy without further resistance. "I called on the gods, all of them, to heed me," Marduk wrote in his memoirs. "I called on the people along my march, 'bring your tribute to Babylon.' " Instead, he encountered a scorched-earth policy: the gods in charge of cattle and grains left, "to heaven they went up," and the god in charge of beer "made sick the heart of the land." The advance turned violent and bloody. "Brother consumed brother, friends slew each other with the sword, corpses of people blocked the gates." The land was laid waste, wild animals devoured people, packs of dogs bit people to death.

As Marduk's followers continued their advance, the temples and shrines of other gods began to be desecrated. The greatest sacrilege was the defilement of Enlil's temple in Nippur, until then the venerated religious center of all the lands and all the peoples. When Enlil heard that even the Holy of Holies was not spared, that "in the holy of holies the veil was torn away," he rushed back to Mesopotamia. He "set off a brilliance like lightning" as he came down from the skies; "riding in front of him were gods clothed with radiance." Seeing what had happened, "Enlil evil against Babylon caused to be planned." He ordered that Nabu be seized and brought before the Council of the Gods, and Ninurta and Nergal were given the assignment. But they found that Nabu had escaped from his temple in Borsippa, on the Euphratean border, to hide among his followers in Canaan and the Mediterranean islands.

Meeting in Council, the leading Anunnaki debated what to do, discussing the alternatives "a day and a night, without ceasing." Only Enki spoke up in defense of his son: "Now that prince Marduk has risen, now that the people for the second time have raised his image," why does opposition continue? He reprimanded Nergal for opposing his brother; but Nergal, "standing before him day and night without cease," argued that the celestial omens were being misread. "Let Shamash"—the Sun god—"see the signs and inform the people," he said; "Let Nannar"—the Moon god—"at his sign look and impart that to the land." Referring to a constellation-star whose identity is being debated, Nergal said that "among the stars of heaven the Fox Star was twinkling its rays to him." He was seeing other omens— "dazzling stars of heaven that carry a sword"—comets streaking in the skies. He wanted to know what these new omens meant.

As the exchanges between Enki and Nergal became harsher, Nergal, "leaving in a huff," announced that it was necessary to "activate that which with a mantle of radiance is covered," and thereby make the "evil people perish."

There was no way to block the takeover by Marduk and Nabu except by the use of "the seven awesome weapons," whose hiding place in Africa he alone knew. They were weapons that of the lands could make "a dust heap," cities "to upheaval," seas "to agitate, that which teems in them to decimate" and "people make vanish, their souls turn to vapor." The description of the weapons and the consequences of their use clearly identifies them as nuclear weapons.

It was Inanna who had pointed out that time was running out. "Until the time is fulfilled, the hour will be past!" she told the arguing gods; "pay attention, all of you," she said, advising them to continue their deliberations in private, lest the plan of attack be divulged to Marduk (presumably by Enki). "Cover your lips," she told Enlil and the others, "go into your private quarters!" In the privacy of the Emeslam temple, Ninurta spoke up. "The time has elapsed, the hour has passed," he said. "Open up a path and let me take the road!"

The die was cast.

Of the various extant sources dealing with the fateful chain of events, the principal and most intact one is the *Erra Epic*. It describes in great detail the discussions, the arguments for and against, the fears for the future if Marduk and his followers should control the spaceport and its auxiliary facilities. Details are added by the *Khedorlaomer Texts* and inscriptions on various tablets, such as those in the *Oxford Editions of Cuneiform Texts*. They all describe the ominous and fateful march to its culmination, of which we can read in Genesis, chapters 18 and 19: the "upheavaling" of Sodom and Gomorrah and of the "evil cities" of their plain, "and all the inhabitants of the cities, and all that which grew on the ground."

The upheavaling and wiping off the face of the Earth of the "evil cities" was only a sideshow. The main target of obliteration was the spaceport in the Sinai peninsula. "That which was raised toward Anu to launch," the Mesopotamian texts state, Ninurta and Nergal "caused to wither; its face they made fade away, its place they made desolate." The year was 2024 B.C.; the evidence—the immense cavity in the center of the Sinai and the resulting fracture lines, the vast surrounding flat area covered with blackened stones, traces of radiation south of the Dead Sea, the new extent and shape of the Dead Sea—is still there, four thousand years later.

The aftereffects were no less profound and lasting. The nuclear blasts and their brilliant flashes and earthshaking impact were neither seen nor felt far away in Mesopotamia; but as it turned out, the attempt to save Sumer, its gods, and its culture in fact led to a dismal end for Sumer and its civilization.

The bitter end of Sumer and her great urban centers is described in numerous Lamentation Texts, long poems that bewail the demise of Ur, Nippur, Uruk, Eridu, and other famed and less famed cities. Typical of the calamities that befell the once proud and prosperous land are those listed in the *Lamentation Over the Destruction of Ur*, a long poem of some 440 verses of which we shall quote but a few:

The city into ruins was made,
the people groan . . .
Its people, not potsherds,
filled its ravines . . .
In its lofty gates, where they were wont
to promenade, dead bodies lay about . . .
Where the festivities of the land took place,
the people lay in heaps . . .
The young were lying in their mothers' laps
like fish carried out of the waters . . .
The counsel of the land was dissipated.

In the storehouses that abounded in the land,
fires were kindled . . .
The ox in its stable has not been attended,
gone is its herdsman . . .
The sheep in its fold has not been attended,
gone is its shepherd boy . . .
In the rivers of the city dust has gathered,

into fox dens they have become . . .
In the city's fields there is no grain,
gone is the fieldworker . . .
The palm groves and vineyards, with honey and wine
abounded, now bring forth mountain thorns . . .
Precious metals and stones, lapis lazuli,
have been scattered about . . .
The temple of Ur has been given over
to the wind . . .
The song has been turned into weeping . . .
Ur has been given over to tears.

For a long time scholars have held the view that the various lamentation texts dealt with the successive but separate destruction of Sumer's cities by invaders from the west, the east, the north. But in *The Wars of Gods and Men* we have suggested that it was not so; that what these lamentations deal with was one single countrywide calamity, an unusual catastrophe and a sudden disaster against which no protection, no defense, no hiding was possible. This view, of a single sudden and overwhelming calamity, is now increasingly accepted by scholars; yet to be accepted is the evidence that we have presented that the calamity was linked to the "upheavaling" of the "evil cities" and the spaceport in the west. It was the unexpected development of an atmospheric vacuum, creating an immense whirlwind and a storm that carried the radioactive cloud eastward—toward Sumer.

The various available texts, and not just the lamentation texts, clearly speak of the calamity as an unstoppable storm, an Evil Wind, and clearly identify it as the result of an unforgettable day when a nuclear blast had created it near the Mediterranean coast:

> *On that day,*
> *When heaven was crushed*
> *and the Earth was smitten,*
> *its face obliterated by the maelstrom—*

When the skies were darkened
and covered as with a shadow—

On that day there was created

A great storm from heaven . . .
A land-annihilating storm . . .
An evil wind, like a rushing torrent . . .
A battling storm joined by a scorching heat . . .
By day it deprived the land of the bright sun,
in the evening the stars did not shine . . .

The people, terrified, could hardly breathe;
The Evil Wind clutched them,
does not grant them another day . . .
Mouths were drenched in blood,
heads wallowed in blood . . .
The face was made pale by the Evil Wind.

After the deadly cloud had moved on, ''after the storm was carried off from the city, that city was turned into desolation'':

It caused cities to be desolated,
It caused houses to become desolate,
It caused stalls to become desolate,
the sheepfolds to be emptied . . .
Sumer's rivers it made flow
with water that is bitter;
its cultivated fields grow weeds,
its pastures grow withering plants.

It was a death-carrying storm that endangered even the gods. The lamentations list virtually every major Sumerian city as places where their gods had abandoned their abodes, temples, and shrines—in most cases never to return. Some escaped the approaching cloud of death hurriedly, ''flying off as a bird.'' Inanna, having rushed to sail off to a safe haven, later complained that she had to leave behind her

jewelry and other possessions. The story, however, was not
the same everywhere. In Ur, Nannar and Ningal refused to
abandon their followers and appealed to the great Enlil to
do whatever possible to avert the disaster, but Enlil responded that the fate of Ur could not be changed. The divine
couple spent a nightmarish night in Ur: "Of that night's
foulness they did not flee," hiding underground "as termites." But in the morning Ningal realized that Nannar/Sin
had been afflicted, and "hastily putting on a garment" departed the beloved Ur with the stricken mate. In Lagash,
where with Ninurta away Bau had stayed in the Girsu by
herself, the goddess could not force herself to leave. Lingering behind "she wept bitterly for her holy temple, for
her city." The delay almost cost her her life: "On that day,
the storm caught up with her, with the Lady." (Indeed,
some scholars deem the ensuing verse in the lamentation to
indicate that Bau had in fact lost her life: "Bau, as if she
were a mortal, the storm had caught up with her.")

Fanning out in a wide swath over what used to be Sumer
and Akkad, the Evil Wind's path touched Eridu, Enki's
city, in the south. Enki, we learn, took cover some distance
away from the wind's path, yet close enough to be able to
return to the city after the cloud had passed. He found a
city "smothered with silence, its residents stacked up in
heaps." But here and there there were survivors, and Enki
led them southward, to the desert. It was an "inimical
land," uninhabitable; but using his scientific prowess,
Enki—like Yahweh half a millennium later in the Sinai
desert—managed miraculously to provide water and food
for "those who have been displaced from Eridu."

As fate would have it, Babylon, situated on the northern
edge of the Evil Wind's wide swath, was the least affected
of all the Mesopotamian cities. Alerted and advised by his
father, Marduk urged the city's people to leave and hurry
northward; and, in words reminiscent of the angels' advice
to Lot and his family as they were told to leave Sodom
before its upheavaling, Marduk told the escapees "neither
to turn nor to look back." If escape was not possible, they
were told to "get thee into a chamber below the earth, into

a darkness." Once the Evil Storm had passed, they were not to consume any of the food or beverage in the city, for they might have been "touched by the ghost."

When the air finally cleared, all of southern Mesopotamia lay prostrate. "The storm crushed the land, wiped out everything . . . No one treads the highways, no one seeks out the roads . . . On the banks of the Tigris and the Euphrates, only sickly plants grow . . . In the orchards and the gardens there is no new growth, quickly they waste away . . . On the steppes cattle large and small become scarce . . . The sheepfolds have been delivered to the Wind."

Life began to stir anew only seven years later. Backed by Elamite and Gutian troops loyal to Ninurta, a semblance of organized society returned to Sumer under rulers seated in former provincial centers, Isin and Larsa. It was only after the passage of seventy years—the same interval that later applied to the restoration of the temple in Jerusalem—that the temple in Nippur was restored. But the "gods who determine the destinies," Anu and Enlil, saw no purpose in resurrecting the past. As Enlil had told Nannar/Sin who had appealed in behalf of Ur—

Ur was granted kingship—
it was not granted an eternal reign.

Marduk had won out. Within a few decades, his vision of a king in Babylon who would grasp his hand, rebuild the city, raise high its ziggurat Esagil—had come true. After a halting start, the First Dynasty of Babylon attained the intended power and assurance that were expressed by Hammurabi:

Lofty Anu, lord of the gods
who from Heaven to Earth came,
and Enlil, lord of Heaven and Earth
who determines the destinies of the land,
Determined for Marduk, the firstborn of Enki,
the Enlil-functions over all mankind;

Made him great among the gods who watch and see,
Called Babylon by name to be exalted,
made it supreme in the world;
And established for Marduk, in its midst,
an everlasting kingship.

In Egypt, unaffected by the nuclear cloud, the transition to the Age of the Ram began right after the Theban victory and the enthronement of the Middle Kingdom dynasties. When the celebrations of the New Year, coinciding with the rising of the Nile, were adjusted to the New Age, hymns to Ra-Amen praised him thus:

O Brilliant One
who shines in the inundation waters.
He who raised his head and lifts his forehead:
He of the Ram, the greatest of celestial creatures.

Under the New Kingdom, temple avenues were lined with statues of the Ram; and in the great temple to Amon-Ra in Karnak, in a secret observation perch that had to be opened on the day of the winter solstice to let in the Sun's rays through the path to the Holy of Holies, the following instructions were inscribed for the astronomer-priest:

One goes toward the hall called Horizon of the Sky.
One climbs the Aha, *"Lonesome place of the majestic*
  soul,"
the high room for watching the Ram who sails across the
  skies.

In Mesopotamia, slowly but surely, the ascendancy of the Age of the Ram was recognized by changes in the calendar and in the lists of the celestial stars. Such lists, that used to begin with Taurus, now began with Aries; and for Nissan, the month of the spring equinox and the New Year, the zodiac of Aries rather than Taurus was thereafter written in. An example is the Babylonian astrolabe ("taker of stars") that we have discussed earlier (see Fig. 102) in

Figure 160

connection with the origin of the division into thirty-six segments. It clearly inscribed the star *Iku* as the defining celestial body for the first month Nisannu. Iku was the "alpha" or lead star of the constellation of the Ram; it is still known by its Arabic name *Hamal,* meaning "male sheep."

The New Age had arrived, in the heavens and on Earth.

It was to dominate the next two millennia and the astronomy that the "Chaldeans" had transmitted to the Greeks. When, in the closing years of the fourth century B.C., Alexander came to believe that he was entitled—like Gilgamesh 2,500 years earlier—to immortality because his true father was the Egyptian god Amon, he went to the god's oracle place in Egypt's western desert to seek confirmation. Having received it, he struck silver coins bearing his image adorned with the horns of the Ram (Fig. 160).

A few centuries later the Ram faded and was replaced by the sign of the Fishes, Pisces. But that, as the saying goes, is already history.

13

AFTERMATH

To establish his supremacy on Earth, Marduk proceeded to establish his supremacy in the heavens. A major vehicle to that end was the all-important annual New Year celebration, when the Epic of Creation was read publicly. It was a tradition whose purpose was to acquaint the populace not only with the basic cosmogony and the tale of Evolution and the arrival of the Anunnaki, but also as a way to state and reinstate the basic religious tenets regarding Gods and Men.

The Epic of Creation was thus a useful and powerful vehicle for indoctrination and reindoctrination; and as one of his first acts Marduk instituted one of the greatest forgeries ever: the creation of a Babylonian version of the epic in which the name "Marduk" was substituted for the name "Nibiru." It was thus Marduk, as a celestial god, who had appeared from outer space, battled Tiamat, created the Hammered Out Bracelet (the Asteroid Belt) and Earth of Tiamat's halves, rearranged the Solar System, and became the Great God whose orbit encircles and embraces "as a loop" the orbits of all the other celestial gods (planets), making them subordinate to Marduk's majesty. All the ensuing celestial stations, orbits, cycles, and phenomena were thus the masterworks of Marduk: it was he who determined Divine Time by his orbit, Celestial Time by defining the constellations, and Earthly Time by giving Earth its orbital position and tilt. It was he, too, who had deprived Kingu, Tiamat's chief satellite, of its emerging independent orbit and made it a satellite of Earth, the Moon, to wax and wane and usher in the months.

In so rearranging the heavens, Marduk did not forget to settle some personal accounts. In the past Nibiru, as the

350

home planet of the Anunnaki, was the abode of Anu and thus associated with him. Having appropriated Nibiru to himself, Marduk relegated Anu to a lesser planet—the one we call Uranus. Marduk's father, Enki, was originally associated with the Moon; now Marduk gave him the honor of being "number one" planet—the outermost, the one we call Neptune. To hide the forgery and make it appear as though it was always so, the Babylonian version of the Epic of Creation (called *Enuma elish* after its opening words) employed Sumerian terminology for the planetary names, calling the planet NUDIMMUD, "The Artful Creator"— which was exactly what Enki's Egyptian epithet, *Khnum,* had meant.

A celestial counterpart was needed for Marduk's son Nabu. To achieve that, the planet we call Mercury, which was associated with Enlil's young son Ishkur/Adad, was expropriated and allocated to Nabu. Sarpanit, Marduk's spouse to whom he owed his release from the Great Pyramid and the commutation of the sentence of being buried alive in it to that of exile (the first one of the two), was also not forgotten. Settling accounts with Inanna/Ishtar, he deprived her of the celestial association with the planet we call Venus and granted the planet to Sarpanit. (As it happened, while the switch from Adad to Nabu was partly retained in Babylonian astronomy, that of replacing Ishtar by Sarpanit did not take hold.)

Enlil was too omnipotent to be shoved aside. Instead of changing Enlil's celestial position (as the god of the Seventh Planet, Earth) Marduk appropriated to himself the Rank of Fifty that was Enlil's rank, just a rung below Anu's sixty (Enki's numerical rank was forty). That takeover was incorporated into the *Enuma elish* by listing, in the seventh and last tablet of the epic, the Fifty Names of Marduk. Starting with his own name, "Marduk," and ending with his new celestial name, "Nibiru," the list accompanied each name-epithet with a laudatory explanation of its meaning. When the reading of the fifty names during the New Year celebrations was completed, there was no achievement, creative deed, benevolence, lordship, or supremacy left out

... "With the Fifty Names," the last two verses of the epic stated, "the Great Gods proclaimed him; with the title Fifty they made him supreme." An epilogue, added by the priestly scribe, made the Fifty Names required reading in Babylon:

> *Let them be kept in mind,*
> *let the lead man explain them;*
> *Let the wise and the knowing*
> *discuss them together;*
> *Let the father recite them*
> *and impart them to his son.*

Marduk's seizure of the supremacy in the heavens was accompanied by a parallel religious change on Earth. The other gods, the Anunnaki leaders—even his direct adversaries—were neither punished nor eliminated. Rather, they were declared subordinate to Marduk through the gimmick of asserting that their various attributes and powers were transferred to Marduk. If Ninurta was known as the god of husbandry, who had given Mankind agriculture by damming the mountain gushes and digging irrigation canals—the function now belonged to Marduk. If Adad was the god of rains and storms, Marduk was now the "Adad of rains." The list, only partially extant on a Babylonian tablet, began as follows:

Ninurta	=	Marduk of the hoe
Nergal	=	Marduk of the attack
Zababa	=	Marduk of the hand-to-hand combat
Enlil	=	Marduk of lordship and counsel
Nabium	=	Marduk of numbers and counting
Sin	=	Marduk the illuminator of the night
Shamash	=	Marduk of justice
Adad	=	Marduk of rains

Some scholars have speculated that in this concentration of all divine powers and functions in one hand, Marduk had

introduced the concept of one omnipotent god—a step toward the monotheism of the biblical Prophets. But that
confuses the belief in one God Almighty with a religion in
which one god is just superior to the other gods, a polytheism
in which one god dominates the others. In the words of
Enuma elish, Marduk became "the Enlil of the gods," their
"Lord."

No longer residing in Egypt, Marduk/Ra became *Amen,*
"The Unseen One." Egyptian hymns to him, nevertheless,
proclaimed his supremacy, also connoting the new theology
that he was now the "god of gods," "more powerful of
might than the other gods." In one set of such hymns,
composed in Thebes and discovered written on what is
known as the *Leiden Papyrus,* the chapters begin with a
description of how after the "islands which are in the midst
of the Mediterranean" recognized his name as "high and
mighty and powerful," the peoples of "the hill countries
came down to thee in wonder; every rebellious country was
filled of thy terror." Listing other lands that switched their
obedience to Amen-Ra, the sixth chapter continued by describing the god's arrival in the Land of the Gods—as we
understand it, Mesopotamia—and the ensuing construction
there of Amon's new temple—as we understand it, the Esagil. The text reads almost like that of Gudea's description
of all the rare building materials brought over from lands
near and far: "The mountains yield blocks of stone for thee,
to make the great gates of thy temple; vessels are upon the
sea, seafaring craft are at the quays, loaded and navigated
unto thy presence." Every land, every people, send pro-
pitiatory offerings.

But not only people pay Amen homage; so do all the
other gods. Here are some of the verses from the following
chapters of the papyrus extolling Amen-Ra as the king of
the gods:

The company of the gods which came forth from heaven
assembled at thy sight, announcing:
"Great of glory, Lord of Lords . . . He is the Lord!"

The enemies of the Universal Lord are overthrown;
his foes who were in heaven and on Earth are no more.
Thou art triumphant, Amen-Ra!

Thou art the god more powerful of might than all
the other gods. Thou art the sole Sole One.
Universal god:
Stronger than all the cities is thy city Thebes.

Ingeniously, the policy was not to eliminate the other
Great Anunnaki but to control and supervise them. When,
in time, the Esagila sacred precinct was built with appropriate grandeur, Marduk invited the other leading deities to
come and reside in Babylon, in special shrines that were
built for each one of them within the precinct. The sixth
tablet of the epic in its Babylonian version states that after
Marduk's own temple-abode was completed, and shrines
for the other Anunnaki were erected, Marduk invited all of
them to a banquet. "This is Babylon, the place that is your
home!" he said. "Make merry in its precincts, occupy its
broad places." By acceding to his invitation, the others
would literally have made Babylon what its name—*Bab-
ili*—had meant: "Gateway of the gods."

According to this Babylonian version, the other gods took
their seats in front of the lofty dais on which Marduk had
seated himself. Among them were "the seven gods of destiny." After the banqueting and the performance of all the
rites, after verifying "that the norms had been fixed according to all the portents,"

> *Enlil raised the bow, his weapon,*
> *and laid it before the gods.*

Recognizing the symbolic declaration of "peaceful co-
existence" by the leader of the Enlilites, Enki spoke up:

May our son, the Avenger, be exalted;
Let his sovereignty be surpassing,
without a rival.

May he shepherd the human race to the end of days;
without forgetting, let them acclaim his ways.

Enumerating all the worshiping duties that the people
were to perform in honor of Marduk and the other gods
gathered in Babylon, Enki had this to say to the other
Anunnaki:

> *As for us, by his names pronounced,*
> *he is our god!*
> *Let us now proclaim his Fifty Names!*

Proclaiming his Fifty Names—granting Marduk the Rank
of Fifty that had been Enlil's and Ninurta's—Marduk became the God of Gods. Not a sole God, but the god to
whom the other gods had to pay obeisance.

If the new religion proclaimed in Babylon was a far cry
from a monotheistic theology, scholars (especially at the
turn of this century) wondered and heatedly debated the
extent to which the notion of a Trinity had originated in
Babylon. It was recognized that Babylon's New Religion
stressed the lineage Enki-Marduk-Nabu and that the divinity
of the Son was obtained from a Holy Father. It was pointed
out that Enki referred to him as "our Son," that his very
name, MAR.DUK, meant "Son of the Pure Place" (P.
Jensen), "Son of the Cosmic Mountain" (B. Meissner),
"Son of the Brilliant Day" (F.J. Delitzsch), "Son of Light"
(A. Deimel) or simply "The True Son" (W. Paulus). The
fact that all those leading Assyriologists were German was
primarily due to the particular interest that the Deutsche
Orient-Gesellschaft—an archaeological society that also
served the political and intelligence-gathering ends of Germany—had conducted an unbroken chain of excavations at
Babylon from 1899 until almost the end of World War I
when Iraq fell to the British in 1917. The unearthing of
ancient Babylon (though the remains were by and large those
from the seventh century B.C.) amid the growing realization
that the biblical creation tales were of Mesopotamian origin,
led to heated scholarly debates under the theme *Babel und*

Bibel—Babylon and Bible, and then to theological ones. Was *Marduk Urtyp Christie?* studies (as one so titled by Witold Paulus) asked, after the tale of Marduk's entombment and subsequent reappearance to become the dominant deity was discovered.

The issue, never resolved, was just let evaporate as post–World War I Europe, and especially Germany, faced more pressing problems. What is certain is that the New Age that Marduk and Babylon ushered in circa 2000 B.C. *manifested itself in a new religion,* a polytheism in which one god dominated all the others.

Reviewing four millennia of Mesopotamian religion, Thorkild Jacobsen (*The Treasures of Darkness*) identified as the main change at the beginning of the second millennium B.C. the emergence of national gods in lieu of the universal gods of the preceding two millennia. The previous plurality of the divine powers, Jacobsen wrote, "required the ability to distinguish, evaluate and choose" not just between the gods but also between good and evil. By assuming all the other gods' powers, Marduk abolished such choices. "The national character of Marduk," Jacobsen wrote (in a study titled *Toward the Image of Tammuz*), created a situation in which "religion and politics became more inextricably linked" and in which the gods, "through signs and omens, actively guided the policies of their countries."

The emergence of guiding politics and religion by "signs and omens" was indeed a major innovation of the New Age. It was not a surprising development in view of the importance that celestial signs and omens had played in determining the true beginning of the zodiacal change and in deciding who would become supreme on Earth. For many millennia it was the word of the Seven Who Determine the Destinies, Anu, Enlil, and the other Anunnaki leaders, who made the decisions affecting the Anunnaki; Enlil, by himself, was the Lord of the Command as far as Mankind was concerned. Now, signs and omens in the heavens guided the decisions.

In the "prophecy texts" (one of which we have earlier quoted) the principal gods played a role alongside or within the framework of the celestial omens. Under the New Age, the celestial omens—planetary conjunctions, eclipses, lunar halos, stellar backgrounds, and so on—were sufficient by themselves, and no godly intervention or participation was required: the heavens alone foretold the fates.

Babylonian texts, and those of neighboring nations in the second and first millennia B.C., are replete with such Omina and their interpretation. A whole science, if one so wishes to call it, developed as time went on, with special *beru* (best translated "fortune teller") priests on hand to interpret observations of celestial phenomena. At first the predictions, continuing the trend that began at the time of the Third Dynasty of Ur, concerned themselves with affairs of state— the fate of the king and his dynasty and the fortunes of the land:

When a halo surrounds the Moon and Jupiter
stands within it, there will be an invasion
of the army of Aharru.

When the Sun reaches its zenith and is dark,
the unrighteousness of the land will come to naught.

When Venus draws near Scorpio, evil winds will
come to the land.

When in the month Siwan Venus shall appear
in Cancer, the king will have no rival.

When a halo surrounds the Sun and its opening
points to the south, a south wind will blow.
If a south wind shall blow on the day of the Moon's
disappearance, it will rain from the heavens.

When Jupiter appears at the beginning of the year,
in that year corn will be plentiful.

The "entrances" of planets into the zodiacal constellations were thought of as particularly important, as signs of the enhancement of the planet's (good or bad) influence. The positions of the planets inside the zodiacal constellations were described by the term *Manzallu* ("stations"), from which the Hebrew plural *Mazzaloth* (II Kings 23:5) comes, and from which a *Mazal* ("luck, fortune") evolved, capable of being good luck or bad luck.

Since not only constellations and planets but also months had been associated with various gods—some, by Babylonian times, adversaries of Marduk—the time of the celestial phenomena grew in importance. One omen, as an example, said: "If the Moon shall be eclipsed in the month Ayaru in the third watch" and certain other planets will be at given positions, "the king of Elam will fall by his own sword . . . his son will not take the throne; the throne of Elam will be unoccupied."

A Babylonian text on a very large tablet (VAT-10564) divided into twelve columns contained instructions for what may or may not be done in certain months: "A king may build a temple or repair a holy place only in Shebat and Adar . . . A person may return to his home in Nissan." The text, called by S. Langdon (*Babylonian Menologies and the Semitic Calendars*) "the great Babylonian Church Calendar," then listed the lucky and unlucky months, even days and even half days, for many personal activities (such as the most favorable time for bringing a new bride into the house).

As the omens, predictions, and instructions increasingly assumed a more personal nature, they verged on the horoscopic. Would a certain person, not necessarily the king, recover from an illness? Will the pregnant mother bear a healthy child? If some times or certain omens were unlucky, how could one ward off the ill luck? In time, incantations were devised for the purpose; one text, for example, actually provided the sayings to be recited to prevent the thinning of a man's beard by appealing to "the star that giveth light" with prescribed utterings. All that was followed by the introduction of amulets in which the warding-off verses were inscribed. In time, too, the material of the amulet (mostly made to be worn on a string around the neck) could also make a difference. If made of hematite, one set of instructions stated, "the man could lose that which he acquired." On the other hand, an amulet made of lapis lazuli assured that "he shall have power."

In the famous library of the Assyrian king Ashurbanipal, archaeologists have found more than two thousand clay tablets with texts pertaining to omens. While the majority dealt with celestial phenomena, not all of them did so. Some dealt with dream-omens, others with the interpretation of "oil and water" signs (the pattern made by oil as it was poured on water), even the significance of animal entrails as they appeared after sacrifices. What used to be astronomy became astrology, and astrology was followed by divinations, fortune-telling, sorcery. R. Camblell Thompson was probably right in titling a major collection of omen texts *The Reports of the Magicians and Astrologers of Nineveh and Babylon*.

Why did the New Age bring all that about? Beatrice Goff (*Symbols of Prehistoric Mesopotamia*) identified the cause as the breakdown of the gods-priests-kings framework that had held society together in the prior millennia. "There was no aristocracy, no priesthood, no intelligentsia" to prevent the situation where "all the affairs of living were inextricably bound up with such 'magical' practices." Astronomy became astrology because, with the Olden Gods gone from their "cult centers," the people were looking at least for signs and omens to guide them in turbulent times.

Indeed, even astronomy itself was no longer what it had been during two millennia of Sumerian achievements. Despite the reputation and high esteem in which "Chaldean" astronomy was held by the Greeks in the second half of the first millennium B.C., it was a sterile astronomy and a far cry from that of Sumer, where so many of the principles, methods, and concepts on which modern astronomy is founded had originated. "There is scarcely another chapter in the history of science where a deep gap exists between the generally accepted description of a period and the results which have slowly emerged from a detailed investigation of the source material,'' O. Neugebauer wrote in *The Exact Sciences in Antiquity*. ''It is evident,'' he wrote, ''that mathematical theory played a major role in Babylonian astronomy as compared with the very modest role of observations.'' That ''mathematical theory,'' studies of the astronomical tablets of the Babylonians revealed, were column upon column upon column of rows of numbers, imprinted—we use the term purposely—on clay tablets *as though they were computer printouts!* Fig. 161 is a photograph of one such (fragmented) tablet; Fig. 162 is the contents of such a tablet converted to modern numerals.

Not unlike the astronomical codices of the Mayas, that contained page after page after page of glyphs dealing with the planet Venus, but without any indication that they were based on actual Mayan observations but rather followed some data source, so were the Babylonian lists of *predicted* positions of the Sun, Moon, and visible planets extremely detailed and accurate. In the Babylonian instance, however, the position lists (called ''Ephemerides'') were accompanied by procedure texts on companion tablets in which the rules for computing the ephemerides were given step by step; they contained instructions how, for example, to compute—for over *fifty years in advance*—Moon eclipses by taking into account data from columns dealing with the orbital velocities of the Sun and the Moon and other factors that were needed. *But,* to quote from *Astronomical Cuneiform Texts* by O. Neugebauer, ''unfortunately these procedure texts do not contain much of what we would call the 'theory' behind the method.''

Yet ''such a theory,'' he pointed out, ''must have existed because it is impossible to devise computational schemes of high complication without a very elaborate plan.'' It was clear from the very neat script and carefully arranged columns and rows, Neugebauer stated, that these Babylonian tablets were *copies* meticulously made from preexisting sources already so neatly and accurately arranged. The mathematics on which the number series were based was the Sumerian sexagesimal system, and the terminology

Figure 161

used—of zodiacal constellations, month names, and more
than fifty astronomical terms—was purely Sumerian. There
can, therefore, be no doubt that the source of the Babylonian
data was Sumerian; all the Babylonians knew was how to
use them, by translating into Babylonian the Sumerian "procedure texts."

It was not until the eighth or seventh centuries B.C. that
astronomy, in what is called the Neo-Babylonian period,
reassumed the observational aspects. These were recorded
in what scholars (e.g., A.J. Sachs and H. Hunger, *Astro-*

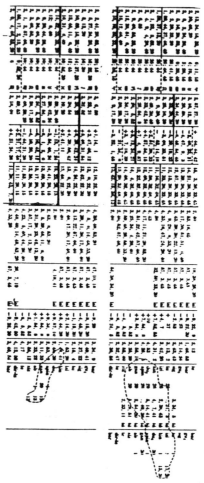

Figure 162

nomical Diaries and Related Texts from Babylonia) call "astronomers' diaries." They believe that Hellenistic, Persian, and Indian astronomy and astrology derived from such records.

The decline and deterioration manifested in astronomy was symptomatic of an overall decline and regression in the sciences, the arts, the laws, the social framework.

One is hard put to find a Babylonian "first," contributed to culture and civilization, that surpassed, or even matched, the countless Sumerian ones. The sexagesimal system and the mathematical theories were retained without improvement. Medicine deteriorated to become little more than sorcery. No wonder that many of the scholars studying the period consider the time when the Old Age of the Sumerian Bull of Heaven gave way to the New Age of the Babylonian Ram a "time of darkness."

The Babylonians, as did the Assyrians and others that followed, retained—almost until the Greek era—the cuneiform script that the Sumerians had devised (based, as we have shown in *Genesis Revisited,* on sophisticated geometric and mathematical theories). But instead of any improvement, the Old Babylonian tablets were written in a more scribbled and less refined script. The many Sumerian references to schools, teachers, homework, were nonexistent in the ensuing centuries. Gone was the Sumerian tradition of literary creativity that bequeathed to future generations, including ours, "wisdom" texts, poetry, proverbs, allegorical tales, and not least of all the "myths" that had provided the data concerning the solar system, the Heavens and Earth, the Anunnaki, the creation of Man. These, it ought to be pointed out, were literary genres that reappear only in the Hebrew Bible about a millennium later. A century and a half of digging up the remains of Babylon produced texts and inscriptions by rulers boasting of military campaigns and conquests, of how many prisoners were taken or heads cut off—whereas Sumerian kings (as, for example, Gudea) boasted in their inscriptions of building temples, digging canals, having beautiful works of art made.

A harshness and a coarseness replaced the former compassion and elegance. The Babylonian king Hammurabi, the sixth in what is called the First Dynasty of Babylon, has been renowned because of his famous legal code, the "Code of Hammurabi." It was, however, just a listing of crimes and their punishments—whereas a thousand years earlier Sumerian kings had promulgated codes of social justice, their laws protecting the widow, the orphan, the weak, and decreeing that "you shall not take away the donkey of a widow," or "you shall not delay the wages of a day laborer.'' Again, the Sumerian concept of laws, intended to direct human conduct rather than punish its faults, reappears only in the biblical Ten Commandments some six centuries after the fall of Sumer. Sumerian rulers cherished the title EN.SI—''Righteous Shepherd.'' The ruler selected by Inanna to reign in Agade (Akkad) whom we call Sargon I in fact bore the name-epithet *Sharru-kin*, ''Righteous King.'' The Babylonian kings (and the Assyrian ones later on) called themselves ''King of the four regions'' and boasted of being ''King of kings'' rather than a ''shepherd'' of the people. (It was greatly symbolic that Judea's greatest king, David, had been a shepherd.)

Missing in the New Age were expressions of tender love. This may sound like an insignificant item in the long list of changes for the worse; but we believe that it was a manifestation of a profound mind-set that went all the way down from the top—from Marduk himself.

The poetry of Sumer included a substantial number of love and lovemaking poems. Some, it is true, were related to Inanna/Ishtar and her relationship with her bridegroom Dumuzi. Others were recited or sung by kings to divine spouses. Yet others were devoted to the common bride and bridegroom, or husband and wife, or parental love and compassion. (Once again, this genre reappears only after many centuries in the Hebrew Bible, in the Book of The Song of Songs.) It seems to us that this omission in Babylonia was not accidental, but part of an overall decline in the role of women and their status as compared to Sumerian times.

The remarkable role of women in all walks of life in Sumer and Akkad and its very marked downgrading upon the rise of Babylon, have been lately reviewed and documented in special studies and several international conferences, such as the ''Invited Lectures on the Middle East at the University of Texas at Austin'' published in 1976 (*The Legacy of Sumer*) by Denise Schmandt-Besserat as editor, and the proceedings at the *33rd Rencontre Assyriologique Internationale* in 1986, whose theme was ''The woman in the ancient Near East.'' The gathered evidence shows that in Sumer and Akkad women engaged not only in household chores like spinning, weaving, milking, or tending to the family and the home, but also were "working professionals" as doctors, midwives, nurses, governesses, teachers, beauticians, and hairdressers. The textual evidence recently culled from discovered tablets augments the depictions of women in their varied tasks from the earliest recorded times that showed them as singers and musicians, dancers and banquet-masters.

Women were also prominent in business and property management. Records have been found of women managing the family lands and overseeing their cultivation, and then supervising the trade in the resulting products. This was especially true of the "ruling families" of the royal court. Royal wives administered temples and vast estates, royal daughters served not only as priestesses (of which there were three classes) but even as the High Priestess. We have already mentioned Enheduanna, the daughter of Sargon I, who composed a series of memorable hymns to Sumer's great ziggurat-temples. She served as High Priestess at Nannar's temple in Ur (Sir Leonard Woolley, who had excavated at Ur, found there a round plaque depicting Enheduanna performing a libation ceremony). We know that the mother of Gudea, Gatumdu, was a High Priestess in the Girsu of Lagash. Throughout Sumerian history, other women held such high positions in the temples and priestly hierarchies. There is no record of a comparable situation in Babylon.

The story of women's role and position in the royal courts was no different. One must refer to Greek sources to find mention of a ruling queen (as distinct from a queen-consort) in Babylonian history—the tale of the legendary Semiramis who, according to Herodotus (I, 184) "held the throne in Babylon" in earlier times. Scholars have been able to establish that she was a historical person, Shammu-ramat. She did reign in Babylon, but only because her husband, the *Assyrian* king Shamshi-Adad, had captured the city in 811 B.C. She served as the royal regent for five years after her husband's death, until their son Adad-Nirari III could assume the throne. "This lady," H.W.F. Saggs wrote in *The Greatness That Was Babylon*,

"was obviously very important" because "quite excep-
tionally for a woman, she is mentioned along with the
king in a dedication inscription" (!)

Consort-queens and queen mothers were even more frequent in Sumer; but Sumer could also boast the first-ever
queen in her own right, bearing the title LU.GAL ("Great
Man") which meant "king." Her name was Ku-Baba; she
is recorded in the Sumerian King Lists as "the one who
consolidated the foundations of Kish" and headed the Third
Dynasty of Kish. There may have been other queens like
her during the Sumerian era, but scholars are not certain of
their status (i.e. whether they were only queen-consorts or
regents for an underage son).

It is noteworthy that even in the most archaic Sumerian
depictions in which males were shown naked, females were
dressed (Fig. 163a is an example); the exceptions were

Figures 163a, 163b, and 163c

depictions of intercourse, where both were shown naked. As time went on women's dress and garments, as well as their hairdos, became more elaborate and elegant (Fig. 163b, 163c), reflecting their status, education, and noble demeanor. Scholars researching these aspects of the civilizations of the ancient Near East have noted that whereas during the two millennia of Sumerian primacy women were depicted *by themselves* in drawings and in plastic art—hundreds of statues and statuettes that are actual portraits of individual females have been found—there is an almost total absence of such depictions in the post-Sumerian period in the Babylonian empire.

W.G. Lambert titled the paper he had presented at the Rencontre Assyriologique "Goddesses in the Pantheon: A Reflection of Women in Society?" We believe that the situation may well have been the reverse: women's status in society reflected the standing of the goddesses in the pantheon. In the Sumerian pantheon, female Anunnaki played leading roles along with the males from the very beginning. If EN.LIL was "Lord of the Command," his spouse was NIN.LIL, "Lady of the Command"; if EN.KI was "Lord of Earth," his spouse was NIN.KI, "Lady of Earth." When Enki created the Primitive Worker through genetic engineering, Ninharsag was there to be the cocreator. Suffice it to reread the inscriptions of Gudea to realize how many important roles goddesses played in the process that led to the building of the new ziggurat-temple. Suffice it also to point out that one of Marduk's first acts was to transfer to the male Nabu the functions of Nisaba as deity of writing. In fact, all those goddesses that in the Sumerian pantheon held specific knowledge or performed specific functions, were by and large relegated to obscurity in the Babylonian pantheon. When goddesses were mentioned, they were only listed as spouses of the male gods. The same held true for the people under the gods: women were mentioned as wives or daughters, mostly when they were "given" in arranged marriages.

We surmise that the situation reflected Marduk's own bias. Ninharsag, the "Mother of gods and men," was, after all, the mother of his main adversary in the contest for the supremacy on Earth, Ninurta. Inanna/Ishtar was the one who had caused him to be buried alive inside the Great Pyramid. The many goddesses who were in charge of the arts and sciences assisted the construction of the Eninnu in Lagash as a symbol of defiance of Marduk's claims that his time had come. Was there any reason for him to retain the high position and veneration of all these females? Their downgrading in religion and worship was, we believe, reflected in a general downgrading of the status of women in the post-Sumerian society.

An interesting aspect of that was the apparent change in the rules of succession. The source of the conflict between Enki and Enlil was the fact that while Enki was Anu's firstborn, Enlil was the Legitimate Heir because he was born to Anu by a mother who was Anu's half sister. On Earth, Enki repeatedly tried to have a son by Ninharsag, a half sister of his and Enlil's, but she bore him only female offspring. Ninurta was the Legitimate Heir on Earth because it was Ninharsag who bore him to Enlil. Following these rules of succession, it was Isaac who was born to Abraham by his half sister Sarah and not the firstborn Ishmael (the son of the maid Hagar) who became the patriarch's Legitimate Heir. Gilgamesh, king of Erech, was two-thirds (not just one-half) ''divine'' because his mother was a goddess; and other Sumerian kings sought to enhance their status by claiming that a goddess nursed them with mother's milk. All such matriarchal lineages lost their significance when Marduk became supreme. (Maternal lineage became significant again among the Jews at the time of the Second Temple.)

What was the ancient world experiencing at the beginning of the New Age of the 20th century B.C., in the aftermath of international wars, the use of nuclear weapons, the dissolution of a great unifying political and cultural system, the displacement of a boundaryless religion with one of national gods? We at the end of the 20th century A.D. may find it possible to visualize, having ourselves witnessed the aftermath of two world wars, the use of nuclear weapons, the dissolution of a giant political and ideological system, the displacement of centrally controlled and boundless empires by religiously guided nationalism.

The phenomena of millions of war refugees on the one hand, and the rearrangement of the population-map on the other hand, so symptomatic of the events of the twentieth century A.D., *had their counterparts in the twentieth century* B.C.

For the first time there appears in Mesopotamian inscriptions the term *Munnabtutu,* literally meaning "fugitives from a destruction." In light of our twentieth century A.D. experience a better translation would be "displaced persons"—people who, in the words of several scholars, had been "de-tribalized," people who had lost not only their homes, possessions, and livelihoods but also the countries to which they had belonged and were henceforth "stateless refugees," seeking religious asylum and personal safe havens in other peoples' lands.

As Sumer itself lay prostrate and desolate, the remnants of its people (in the words of Hans Baumann, *The Land of Ur*) "spread in all directions; Sumerian doctors and astronomers, architects and sculptors, cutters of seals and scribes, became teachers in other lands."

To all the many Sumerian "firsts," they have thus added one more as Sumer and its civilization came to a bitter end: *the first Diaspora . . .*

Their migrations, it is certain, took them to where earlier groups had gone, such as Harran where Mesopotamia links up with Anatolia, the place to where Terah and his family had migrated and which was already then known as "Ur away from Ur." They undoubtedly stayed (and prospered) there in ensuing centuries, for Abraham sought a bride for Isaac his son among the erstwhile relatives there, and so did Isaac's son Jacob. Their wanderings no doubt also followed in the footsteps of the famed Merchants of Ur, whose loaded caravans and laden ships had blazed trails on land and sea to places near and far. Indeed, one can learn where the "displaced persons" of Sumer went by looking at the foreign cultures that sprouted one after the other in foreign lands—cultures whose script was the cuneiform, whose language included countless Sumerian "loanwords" (especially in the sciences), whose pantheons, even if the gods were called by local names, were the Sumerian pantheon, whose "myths" were the Sumerian "myths," whose tales of heroes (such as of Gilgamesh) were of Sumerian heroes.

How far did the wanderers of Sumer go?

We know that they certainly went to the lands where new nation-states were formed within two or three centuries after the fall of Sumer. While the *Amurru* ("Westerners"), followers of Marduk and Nabu, poured into Mesopotamia and provided the rulers that made up the First Dynasty of Marduk's Babylon, other tribes and nations-to-be engaged in massive population movements that forever changed the Near East, Asia, and Europe. They brought about the emergence of Assyria to Babylon's north, the Hittite kingdom to the northwest, the Hurrian Mitanni to the west, the Indo-Aryan kingdoms that spread from the Caucasus on Babylon's northeast and east, and those of the "Desert peoples" to the south and of the "Sealand people" to the southeast. As we know from the later records of Assyria, Hatti-land, Elam, Babylon and from their treaties with others (in which each one's national gods were invoked), the great gods of Sumer did forgo the "invitation" of Marduk to come and reside within the confines of Babylon's sacred precinct; instead, they mostly became national gods of the new or old-new nations.

It was in such lands that the Sumerian refugees were given asylum all around Mesopotamia, serving at the same time as catalysts for the conversion of their host countries into modern and flourishing states. But some must have ventured to more distant lands, migrating there on their own or, more probably, accompanying the displaced gods themselves.

To the east there stretched the limitless reaches of Asia. Much discussed has been the migratory wave of the Aryans (or Indo-Aryans as some prefer). Originating somewhere southwest of the Caspian Sea, they migrated to what had been the Third Region of Ishtar, the Indus Valley, to repopulate and reinvigorate it. The Vedic tales of gods and heroes that they brought with them were the Sumerian "myths" retold; the notions of Time and its measurement and cycles were of Sumerian origin. It is a safe assumption, we believe, that mingled into the Aryan migration were Sumerian refugees; we say "safe assumption" because Sumerians had to pass that way in order to reach the lands that we call the Far East.

It is generally accepted that within two centuries or so of 2000 B.C. a "mysteriously abrupt change" (in the words of William Watson, *China*) had occurred in China; without any gradual development the land was transformed from one of primitive villages to one with "walled cities whose rulers possessed bronze weapons and chariots and the knowledge of writing." The cause, all agree, was the arrival of migrants from the west—the same "civilizing influences" of Sumer "which can ultimately be traced to the cultural migrations comparable to those which radiated in the West from the Near East"—the migrations in the aftermath of the fall of Sumer.

The "mysteriously abrupt" new civilization blossomed out in China circa 1800 B.C. according to most scholars. The vastness of the country and the sparseness of the earliest evidence offer fertile grounds for scholarly disagreements, but the prevalent opinion is that writing was introduced together with Kingship by the Shang Dynasty; the purpose was significant in itself: to record *omens* on animal bones. The omens were mostly concerned with inquiries for guidance from enigmatic Ancestors.

The writing was monosyllabic and the script was pictographic (from which the familiar Chinese characters evolved into a kind of "cuneiform"—Fig. 164)—both hallmarks of Sumerian writing. Nineteenth-century observations regarding the similarity between the Chinese and Sumerian scripts were the subject of a major study by C.J. Ball (*Chinese and Sumerian*, 1913) that was published under the auspices of Oxford University. It proved conclusively the similarity between the Sumerian pictographs (from which the cuneiform

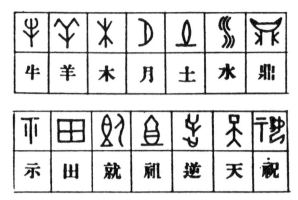

Figure 164

signs evolved) and the old forms (*Ku Wen*) of Chinese writing.

Ball also tackled the issue of whether this was a similarity stemming only from the expectation that a man or a fish would be drawn pictorially in similar ways even by unrelated cultures. What his research has shown was that not only did the pictographs look the same, but they also (in a material number of instances) were pronounced the same way; this included such key terms as *An* for "heaven" and "god," *En* for "lord" or "chief," *Ki* for "Earth" or "land," *Itu* for "month," *Mul* for "bright/shining" (planet or star). Moreover, when a Sumerian syllable had more than one meaning, the parallel Chinese pictograph had a similar set of varied meanings; Fig. 165 reproduces some of the more than one hundred instances illustrated by Ball.

Recent studies in linguistics, spearheaded by former Soviet scholars, have expanded the Sumerian link to include the whole family of Central and Far Asian or "Sino-Tibetan" languages. Such links form only one aspect of a variety of scientific and "mythological" aspects that recall those of Sumer. The former are especially strong; such aspects as the calendar of twelve months, time counting by dividing the day into twelve double-hours, the adoption of the totally arbitrary device of the zodiac, and the tradition of astronomical observations are entirely of Sumerian origin.

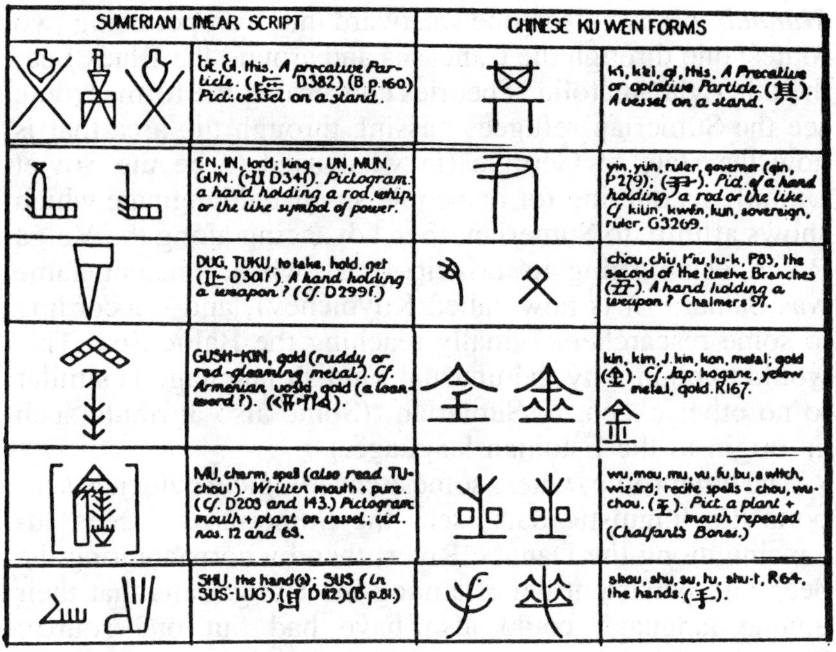

Figure 165

The "mythological" links are more widespread. Throughout the steppes of Central Asia and all the way from India to China and Japan, the religious beliefs spoke of gods of Heaven and Earth and of a place called *Sumeru* where, at the navel of the Earth, there was a bond that connected the Heaven and the Earth as though the two were two pyramids, one inverted atop the other, linked together as an hourglass with a long and narrow waist. The Japanese *Shintu* religious belief that their emperor is descended of a son of the Sun becomes plausible if one assumes that the reference is not to the star around which Earth orbits, but to the "Sun god" Utu/Shamash; for with the spaceport in the Sinai of which he had been in charge obliterated, and the Landing Place in Lebanon in Mardukian hands, he may well have wandered with bands of his followers to the far reaches of Asia.

As linguistic and other evidence indicates, the Sumerian

Munnabtutu had also gone westward into Europe, using two routes: one through the Caucasus and around the Black Sea, the other via Anatolia. Theories concerning the former route see the Sumerian refugees passing through the area that is now the state of Georgia (in what used to be the Soviet Union), accounting for its people's unusual language which shows affinity to Sumerian, then advancing along the Volga River, establishing its principal city whose ancient name was Samara (it is now called Kuybichev), and—according to some researchers—finally reaching the Baltic Sea. This would explain why the unusual Finnish language is similar to no other except to Sumerian. (Some also attribute such an origin to the Estonian language.)

The other route, where some archaeological evidence supports the linguistic data, sees the Sumerian refugees advancing along the Danube River, thereby corroborating the deep and persistent belief among the Hungarians that their unique language could also have had but one source: Sumerian.

Have Sumerians indeed come this way? The answer might be found in one of the most puzzling relics from antiquity that can be seen where the Danube meets the Black Sea in what was once the Celtic-Roman province of Dacia (now part of Romania). There, at a site called Sarmizegetusa, a series of what researchers have called "calendrical temples" includes what could well be described as "*Stonehenge by the Black Sea.*"

Built on several man-made terraces, various structures have been so designed as to form integrated components of a wondrous Time Computer made of stone and wood (Fig. 166). Archaeologists have identified five structures that were in reality rows of round stone "lobes" shaped to form short cylinders, neatly arranged within rectangles formed by sides made of small stones cut to a precise design. The two larger of these rectangular structures contained sixty lobes each, one (the "large old sanctuary") in four rows of fifteen, and the other (the "large new sanctuary") six rows of ten.

Three components of this ancient "calendar city" were round. The smallest is a stone disk made of ten segments

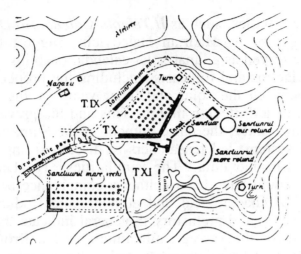

Figure 166

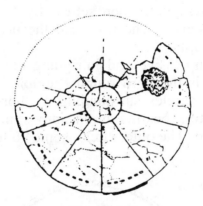

Figure 167

(Fig. 167) in which small stones were embedded to form a circumference—six stones per segment, making a total of sixty. The second round structure, sometimes called the "small round sanctuary," consists of a perfect circle of stones, all precisely and identically shaped, arranged in eleven groups of eight, one of seven and one of six; wider and differently shaped stones, thirteen in number, were placed so as to separate the other grouped stones. There must have been other posts or pillars within the circle, for observation and computing; but none can be determined with certainty. Studies, such as *Il Templo-Calendario Dacico di Sarmizegetusa* by Hadrian Daicoviciu, suggest that this structure served as a lunar-solar calendar enabling a variety of calculations and forecasts, including the proper intercalation between the solar and lunar years by the periodic addition of a thirteenth month. This and the prevalence of the number sixty, the basic number of the Sumerian sexagesimal system, led researchers to discern strong links to ancient Mesopotamia. The similarities, H. Daicoviciu wrote, "could have been neither a coincidence nor an accident." Archaeological and ethnographic studies of the area's history and prehistory in general indicate that at the beginning of the second millennium B.C. a Bronze Age civilization of "nomadic shepherds with a superior social organization" (*Rumania,* an official guidebook) arrived in the area that was until then settled by "a population of simple hand-tillers." The time and the description fit the Sumerian migrants.

The most impressive and intriguing component of this Calendar City is the third round "temple." It consists of two concentric circles surrounding a "horseshoe" in the middle (Fig. 168), bearing an uncanny similarity to Stonehenge in Britain. The outer circle, some 96 feet in diameter,

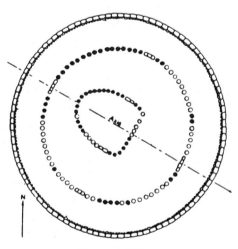

Figure 168

is made up of a ring of 104 dressed andesite blocks that surrounds 180 perfectly shaped oblong andesite blocks, each with a square peg on top as though all were intended to support a movable marker. These uprights are arranged in groups of six; the groups are separated by perfectly shaped horizontal stones, thirty in all. Altogether, then, the outer circle of 104 stones rings an inner circle of 210 (180 + 30) stones.

The second circle, between the outer one and the horse-shoe, consists of sixty-eight postholes—akin to the Aubrey holes at Stonehenge—divided into four groups separated by horizontal stone blocks: three each in the northeast and southeast positions and four each in the northwest and south-east positions, giving the "henge" its main northwest–southeast axis and its perpendicular northeast–southwest one. These four grouped markers, one can readily notice, emulate the four Station Stones at Stonehenge.

The final, and immediately obvious, similarity to Stone-henge is the innermost "horseshoe"; it consists of an el-liptical arrangement of twenty-one postholes, separated by two horizontal stones on each side from a locking line of thirteen postholes that face to the southeast, leaving no doubt that the principal observational target was the winter solstice Sun. H. Daicoviciu, eliminating some of the wooden posts for simpler visualization, offered a drawing of how the "temple" might have looked (Fig. 169). Noting that the

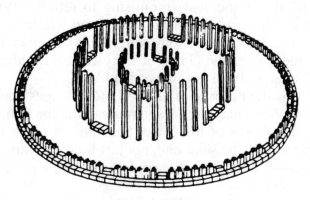

Figure 169

wooden posts were coated with a terra-cotta "plating," Serban Bobancu and other researchers at the National Academy of Romania (*Calendrul de la Sarmizegetusa Regia*) observed that each of those posts "had a massive limestone block as its foundation, a fact that undoubtedly reveals the numerical structure of the sanctuary and proves, as in fact all the others structures do, that the builders wished these structures to last throughout centuries and millennia."

These latest researchers concluded that the "old temple" originally consisted of only fifty-two lobes (4 × 13 rather than the 4 × 15 arrangement) and that there were in effect two calendrical systems geared into one another at Sarmizegetusa: one a solar-lunar calendar with Mesopotamian roots, and another "ritual calendar" geared to fifty-two, akin to the sacred cycle of Mesoamerica and having stellar aspects rather than lunar-solar ones. They concluded that the "stellar era" consisted of four periods of 520 years each (double the 260 of the Mesoamerican Sacred Calendar), and that the ultimate purpose of the calendrical complex was to measure an "era" of 2,080 years (4 × 520)—the approximate length of the Age of Aries.

Who was the mathematical-astronomical genius who had devised all that, and to what purpose?

The spellbinding answer, we believe, also leads to a solution of the enigmas of Quetzalcoatl and the circular observatories that he had built, the god who according to Mesoamerican lore left at one point in time to go back eastward across the seas (promising to return). Was it not just the Enlilite gods who had guided and led the wandering Sumerians, but also Thoth/Ningishzidda (alias Quetzalcoatl), the god of the Game of Fifty-two, who himself had been displaced from his native land?

And was the purpose of all the "stonehenges" in Sumer, and South America, and Mesoamerica, and the British Isles, and on the shores of the Black Sea, not so much to adjust the lunar year to the solar one, not just for calculating Earthly Time but—ultimately—to calculate Celestial Time, the zodiacal Ages?

When the Greeks adopted Thoth as their god Hermes,

they bestowed on him the title *Hermēs Trismegistos*, "Hermes the thrice greatest." Perhaps they recognized that he had thrice guided Mankind in the observation of the beginning of a New Age—the changeover to Taurus, to Aries, to Pisces.

For that was, for those generations of Mankind, when Time began.

ADDITIONAL SOURCES

In addition to sources cited in context, the following periodicals, scholarly studies, and individual works were among the sources consulted:

I. Studies, articles and reports in various issues of the following periodicals and scholarly series:
Abhandlungen für die Kunde des Morgenlandes (Berlin)
Acta Orientalia (Copenhagen and Oslo)
Der Alte Orient (Leipzig)
Alter Orient und Altes Testament (Neukirchen-Vluyn)
American Antiquity (Salt Lake City)
American Journal of Semitic Languages and Literature (Chicago)
American Oriental Series (New Haven)
Analecta Orientalia (Rome)
Anatolian Studies (London)
Annual of the American Schools of Oriental Research (New Haven)
Antigüedades de Mexico (Mexico City)
Archaeology (New York)
Architectura (Munich)
Archiv für Keilschriftforschung (Berlin)
Archiv für Orientforschung (Berlin)
Archiv Orientalni (Prague)
Archives des Sciences physique et naturelles (Paris)
The Assyrian Dictionary (Chicago)
Assyriological Studies (Chicago)

Assyriologische Bibliothek (Leipzig)

Astronomy (Milwaukee)

Babyloniaca (Paris)

Beiträge zur Assyriologie und semitischen Sprachwissenschaft (Leipzig)

Biblica et Orientalia (Rome)

Bibliotheca Mesopotamica (Malibu)

Bibliotheca Orientalis (Leiden)

Biblische Studien (Freiburg)

Bulletin of the American Schools of Oriental Research (Jerusalem and Baghdad)

Centaurus (Copenhagen)

Cuneiform Texts from Babylonian Tablets (London)

Deutsche Akademie der Wissenschaften: Mitteilungen der Institut für Orientforschung (Berlin)

Deutsches Morgenländische Gesellschaft, Abhandlungen (Leipzig)

Ex Oriente Lux (Leipzig)

Grundriss der Theologischen Wissenschaft (Freiburg and Leipzig)

Harvard Semitic Series (Cambridge, Mass.)

Hebrew Union College Annual (Cincinnati)

Icarus (San Diego)

Inca (Lima)

Institut Français d'Archéologie Orientale, Bulletin (Paris)

Iranica Antiqua (Leiden)

Iraq (London)

Isis (London)

Journal of the American Oriental Society (New Haven)

Journal Asiatique (Paris)

Journal of Biblical Literature and Exegesis (Middletown)

Journal of the British Astronomical Association (London)

Journal of Cuneiform Studies (New Haven)

Journal of Egyptian Archaeology (London)
Journal of Jewish Studies (Chichester, Sussex)
Journal of Near Eastern Studies (Chicago)
Journal of the Manchester Egyptian and Oriental Society (Manchester)
Journal of the Royal Asiatic Society (London)
Journal of Semitic Studies (Manchester)
Journal of the Society of Oriental Research (Chicago)
Keilinschriftliche Bibliothek (Berlin)
Klio (Leipzig)
Königliche Gesellschaft der Wissenchaften zu Göttingen: Abhandlungen (Göttingen)
Leipziger semitische Studien (Leipzig)
Mesopotamia: Copenhagen Studies in Assyriology (Copenhagen)
El Mexico Antiguo (Mexico City)
Mitteilungen der altorientalischen Gesellschaft (Leipzig)
Mitteilungen der Deutschen Orient-Gesellschaft (Berlin)
Mitteilungen der vorderasiatisch-aegyptischen Gesellschaft (Berlin)
Mitteilungen des Instituts für Orientforschung (Berlin)
München aegyptologische Studien (Berlin)
Musée du Louvre: Textes Cunéiformes (Paris)
Musée Guimet: Annales (Paris)
The Museum Journal (Philadelphia)
New World Archaeological Foundation: Papers (Provo)
Occasional Papers on the Near East (Malibu)
Oriens Antiquus (Rome)
Oriental Studies (Baltimore)
Orientalia (Rome)
Orientalische Literaturzeitung (Berlin)
Oxford Editions of Cuneiform Inscriptions (Oxford)
Proceedings of the Society of Biblical Archaeology (London)

Publications of the Babylonian Section, University Museum (Philadelphia)

Quellen und Studien zur Geschichte der Mathematik, Astronomie und Physik (Berlin)

Reallexikon der Assyriologie (Berlin)

Recherches d'archéologie, de philosophie et d'histoire (Cairo)

Records of the Past (London)

Revista del Museo Nacional (Lima)

Revista do Instituto Historico e Geografico Brasiliero (Rio de Janeiro)

Revue Archéologique (Paris)

Revue biblique (Paris)

Revue d'Assyriologie et d'archéologie orientale (Paris)

Revue des Etudes Semitique (Paris)

Scientific American (New York)

Service des Antiquites: Annales de l'Egypte (Cairo)

Society of Biblical Archaeology: Transactions (London)

Studi Semitici (Rome)

Studia Orientalia (Helsinki)

Studien zu Bauforschung (Berlin)

Studies in Ancient Oriental Civilizations (Chicago)

Studies in Pre-Columbian Art and Archaeology (Dumbarton Oaks)

Sumer (Baghdad)

Syria (Paris)

Texts from Cuneiform Sources (Locust Valley, N.Y.)

University Museum Bulletin, University of Pennsylvania (Philadelphia)

Vorderasiatische Bibliothek (Leipzig)

Die Welt des Orients (Göttingen)

Wiener Zeitschrift für die Kunde des Morgenlandes (Vienna)

Yale Oriental Series (New Haven)

Zeitschrift der deutschen morgenländischen Gesellschaft (Leipzig)

Zeitschrift für Assyriologie und verwandte Gebiete (Leipzig)

Zeitschrift für die alttestamentliche Wissenschaft (Berlin, Gissen)

Zeitschrift für Keilschriftforschung (Leipzig)

Zenit (Utrecht)

II. Individual Works and Studies:

Abetti, G. *The History of Astronomy*. 1954.

Antoniadi, E.-M. *L'astronomie égyptienne*. 1934.

Armour, R.A. *Gods and Myths of Ancient Egypt*. 1986.

Asher-Greve, J.M. *Frauen in altsumerischer Zeit*. 1985.

Aubier, C. *Astrologie Chinoise*. 1985.

Aveni, A.F. *Skywatchers of Ancient Mexico*. 1980.

————*Empires of Time: Calendars, Clocks and Cultures*. 1989.

Aveni, A.F. (ed.) *Archaeoastronomy in Pre-Columbian America*. 1975.

————*Native American Astronomy*. 1977.

————*Archaeoastronomy in the New World*. 1982.

————*World Archaeoastronomy*. 1989.

Babylonian Talmud

Balfour, M.D. *Stonehenge and its Mysteries*. 1980.

Barklay, E. *Stonehenge and its Earthworks*. 1895.

Barrois, A.-G. *Manuel d'Archéologie Biblique*. 1939.

Barton, G.A. *The Royal Inscriptions of Sumer and Akkad*. 1929.

Benzinger, I. *Hebräische Archäologie*. 1927.

Bittel, K. (ed.) *Anatolian Studies Presented to Hans Gustav Güterbock*. 1974.

Bobula, I. *Sumerian Affiliations*. 1951.

————*The Origin of the Hungarian Nation*. 1966.

Boissier, A. *Choix de Textes*. 1905–6.

Boll, F. and Bezold, C. *Sternglaube und Sternbedeutung.* 1926.

Boll, F., Bezold, C. and Gundel, W. *Sternglaube, Sternreligion und Sternorakel.* 1927.

Bolton, L. *Time Measurement.* 1924.

Borcchardt, L. *Beiträge zur Ägyptische Bauforschung und Altertumskunde.* 1937–1950.

Bottero, J. and Kramer, S.N. *Lorsque les dieux faisaient l'Homme.* 1989.

Brown, P.L. *Megaliths, Myths and Men.* 1976.

Brugsch, H.K. *Nouvelle Recherches sur la Division de l'Anneé des Anciens Égyptiens.* 1856.

————*Thesaurus Inscriptionum Aegyptiacarum.* 1883.

————*Religion und Mythologie der alten Aegypter.* 1891.

Budge, E.A.W. *The Gods of the Egyptians.* 1904.

Burl, A. *The Stone Circles of the British Isles.* 1976.

————*Prehistoric Avebury.* 1979.

Canby, C.A. *A Guide to the Archaeological Sites of the British Isles.* 1988.

Caso, A. *Calendario y Escritura de las Antiguas Culturas de Monte Alban.* 1947.

————*Los Calendarios Prehispanicos.* 1967.

Charles, R.H. *The Apocrypha and Pseudoepigrapha of the Old Testament.* 1976 edition.

Chassinat, E.G. *Le Temple de Dendera.* 1934.

Chiera, E. *Sumerian Religious Texts.* 1924.

Childe, V.G. *The Dawn of European Civilization.* 1957.

Chippindale, C. *Stonehenge Complete.* 1983.

Clay, A.T. *Babylonian Records in the Library of J. Pierpont Morgan.* 1912–1923.

Cornell, J. *The First Stargazers.* 1981.

Cottrell, A. (ed.) *The Encyclopedia of Ancient Civilizations.* 1980.

Craig, J.A. *Astrological-Astronomical Texts in the British Museum.* 1899.

Dalley, S. *Myths from Mesopotamia.* 1989.

Dames, M. *The Silbury Treasure.* 1976.

—— *The Avebury Cycle.* 1977.

Daniel, G. *The Megalithic Builders of Western Europe.* 1962.

Dhorme, P. *La Religion Assyro-babylonienne.* 1910.

Dubelaar, C.N. *The Petroglyphs in the Guianas and Ancient Areas of Brazil and Venezuela.* 1986.

Dumas, F. *Dendera et le temple d'Hathor.* 1969.

Dunand, M. *Fouilles de Byblos.* 1939–1954.

Durand, J.-M. (ed.) *La femme dans le Proche-Orient antique.* 1986.

Eichhorn, W. *Chinese Civilization.* 1980.

Eichler, B.L. (ed.) *Kramer Anniversary Volume.* 1976.

Eisler, R. *Weltenmantel und Himmelszeit.* 1910.

—— *The Royal Art of Astronomy.* 1946.

Emery, W.B. *Archaic Egypt.* 1961.

Endrey, A. *Sons of Nimrod.* 1975.

Epping, J. *Astronomisches aus Babylon.* 1889.

Falkenstein, A. *Archaische Texte aus Uruk.* 1936.

—— *Sumerische Götterlieder.* 1959.

Falkenstein, A. and von Soden, W. *Sumerische und Akkadische Hymnen und Gebete.* 1953.

Fischer, H.G. *Dendera in the Third Millenium B.C.* 1968.

Flornoy, B. *Amazone—Terres et Homme.* 1969.

Fowles, J. and Brukoff, B. *The Enigma of Stonehenge.* 1980.

Frankfort, H. *The Problem of Similarity in Ancient Near Eastern Religions.* 1951.

—— *The Art and Architecture of the Ancient Orient.* 1969.

Gaster, T.H. *Myth, Legend and Custom in the Old Testament.* 1969.

Gauquelin, M. *The Scientific Basis of Astrology.* 1969.

Gibson, Mc. and Biggs, R.D. (eds.) *Seals and Sealing in the Ancient Near East*. 1977.

Gimbutas, M. *The Prehistory of Eastern Europe*. 1956.

Girshman, R. *L'Iran et la migration des Indo-aryens et des iraniens*. 1977.

Grayson, A.K. *Assyrian and Babylonian Chronicles*. 1975.

———— *Babylonian Historical Literary Texts*. 1975.

Gressmann, H. (ed.) *Altorientalische Texte zum alten Testament*. 1926.

Grimm, J. *Teutonic Mythology*. 1900.

Haddingham, E. *Early Man and the Cosmos*. 1984.

Hallo, W.W. and Simpson, W.K. *The Ancient Near East: A History*. 1971.

Hartmann, J. (ed.) *Astronomie*. 1921.

Heggie, D.C. *Megalithic Science*. 1981.

Heggie, D.C. (ed.) *Archaeoastronomy in the Old World*. 1982.

Higgins, R. *Minoan and Mycenaean Art*. 1967.

Hilprecht, H.V. *Old Babylonian Inscriptions*. 1896.

Hilprecht Anniversary Volume. 1909.

Hodson, F.R. (ed.) *The Place of Astronomy in the Ancient World*. 1974.

Holman, J.B. *The Zodiac: The Constellations and the Heavens*. 1924.

Hommel, F. *Die Astronomie der alten Chaldäer*. 1891.

———— *Aufsätze und Abhandlungen*. 1892–1901.

Hooke, S.H. *Myth and Ritual*. 1933.

———— *The Origins of Early Semitic Ritual*. 1935.

———— *Babylonian and Assyrian Religion*. 1962.

Hoppe. E. *Mathematik und Astronomie im Klassichen Altertums*. 1911.

Ibarra Grasso, D.E. *Ciencia Astronomica y Sociologia*. 1984.

Jastrow, M. *Die Religion Babyloniens und Assyriens*. 1905–1912.

388   **WHEN TIME BEGAN**

Jean, C.-F. *La religion sumerienne*. 1931.

Jensen, P. *Die Kosmologie der Babylonier*. 1890.

——— *Texte zur assyrisch-babylonischen Religion*. 1915.

Jeremias, A. *Das alter der babylonischen Astronomie*. 1908.

Joussaume, R. *Dolmens for the Dead*. 1988.

Kees, H. *Der Götterglaube im Alten Aegypten*. 1941.

Keightly, D. *Sources of Shang History*. 1978.

Keightly, D. (ed.) *The Origins of Chinese Civilization*. 1983.

Kelly-Buccellati, M. (ed.) *Studies in Honor of Edith Porada*. 1986.

King, L.W. *Babylonian Magic and Sorcery*. 1896.

——— *Babylonian Religion and Mythology*. 1899.

——— *Cuneiform Texts from Babylonian Tablets*. 1912.

Koldewey, R. *The Excavations at Babylon*. 1914.

Komoroczy, G. *Sumer es Magyar?* 1976.

Kramer, S.N. *Sumerian Mythology*. 1961

——— *The Sacred Marriage Rite*. 1980.

——— *In the World of Sumer*. 1986.

Kramer, S.N. and Maier, J. (eds.) *Myths of Enki, the Crafty God*. 1989.

Krickberg, W. *Felsplastik und Felsbilder bei den Kulturvolkern Altameriker*. 1969.

Krupp, E.C. *Echoes of Ancient Skies: The Astronomies of Lost Civilizations*. 1983.

Krupp, E.C. (ed.) *In Search of Ancient Astronomies*. 1978.

——— *Archaeoastronomy and the Roots of Science*. 1983.

Kugler, F.X. *Die babylonische Mondrechnung*. 1900.

——— *Sternkunde und Sterndienst in Babylon*. 1907–1913.

——— *Im Bannkreis Babels*. 1910.

——— *Alter und Bedeutung der babylonischen Astronomie und Astrallehre*, 1914.

Lambert, B.W.L. *Babylonian Wisdom Literature*. 1960.

Langdon, S. *Sumerian and Babylonian Psalms*. 1909.

────── *Tablets from the Archives of Drehem*. 1911.

────── *Die neubabylonischen Koenigs inschriften*. 1912.

────── *Babylonian Wisdom*. 1923.

────── *Babylonian Penitential Psalms*. 1927.

Langdon, S. (ed.) *Oxford Editions of Cuneiform Texts*. 1923.

Lange, K. and Hirmer, M. *Egypt: Architecture, Sculpture, Painting*. 1968.

Lathrap, D.W. *The Upper Amazon*. 1970.

Lehmann, W. *Einige probleme centralamerikanische kalenders*. 1912.

Leichty, E., Ellis, M. de J. and Gerardi, P. (eds.) *A Scientific Humanist: Studies in Memory of Abraham Sachs*. 1988.

Lenzen, H.J. *Die entwicklung der Zikkurat*. 1942.

Lesko, B.S. (ed.) *Women's Earliest Records from Ancient Egypt and Western Asia*. 1989.

Lidzbarski, M. *Ephemeris für Semitische Epigraphik*. 1902.

Luckenbill, D.D. *Ancient Records of Assyria and Babylonia*. 1926–7.

Ludendorff, H. *Über die Entstehung der Tzolkin-Periode im Kalender der Maya*. 1930.

────── *Das Mondalter in der Inschriften des Maya*. 1931.

Lutz, H.F. *Sumerian Temple Records of the Late Ur Dynasty*. 1912.

Mahler, E. *Biblische Chronologie*. 1887.

────── *Handbuch der jüdischen Chronologie*. 1916.

Maspero, H. *L'Astronomie dans la Chine ancienne*. 1950.

Menon, C.P.S. *Early Astronomy and Cosmology*. 1932.

Mosley, M. *The Maritime Foundations of Andean Civilization*. 1975.

Needham, J. *Science and Civilization in China*. 1959.

Neugebauer, O. *Astronomical Cuneiform Texts*. 1955.

———— *A History of Ancient Mathematical Astronomy.* 1975.

Neugebauer, P.V. *Astronomische Chronologie.* 1929.

Newham, C.A. *The Astronomical Significance of Stonehenge.* 1972.

Niel, F. *Stonehenge—Le Temple mystérieux de la préhistoire.* 1974.

Nissen, H.J. *Grundzüge einer Geschichte der Frühzeit des Vorderen Orients.* 1983.

Oates, J. *Babylon.* 1979.

O'Neil, W.M. *Time and the Calendars.* 1975.

Oppenheim, A.L. *Ancient Mesopotamia* (1964; revised 1977).

Pardo, L.A. *Historia y Arqueologia del Cuzco.* 1957.

Parrot, A. *Tello.* 1948.

———— *Ziggurats et Tour de Babel.* 1949.

Petrie, W.M.F. *Stonehenge: Plans, Description and Theories.* 1880.

Piggot, S. *Ancient Europe.* 1966.

Ponce-Sanguines, C. *Tiwanaku: Espacio, Tiempo y Cultura.* 1977.

Porada, E. *Mesopotamian Art in Cylinder Seals.* 1947.

Pritchard, J.B. (ed.) *Ancient Near Eastern Texts Relating to the Old Testament.* 1969.

Proceedings of the 18th Rencontre Assyriologique Internationale. 1972.

Radau, H. *Early Babylonian History.* 1900.

Rawlinson, H.C. *The Cuneiform Inscriptions of Western Asia.* 1861–84.

Rawson, J. *Ancient China.* 1980.

Rice, C. *La Civilizacion Preincaica y el Problema Sumerologico.* 1926.

Rivet, P. *Los origines del hombre americano.* 1943.

Rochberg-Halton, F. (ed.) *Language, Literature and History.* 1987.

Roeder, G. *Altaegyptische Erzählungen und Märchen.* 1927.

Rolleston, F. *Mazzaroth, or the Constellations.* 1875.

Ruggles, C.L.N. *Megalithic Astronomy.* 1984.

Ruggles, C.L.N. (ed.) *Records in Stone.* 1988.

Ruggles, C.L.N. and Whittle, A.W.R. (eds.) *Astronomy and Society in Britain During the Period 4000–1500 B.C.* 1981.

Sasson, J.M. (ed.) *Studies in Literature from the Ancient Near East Dedicated to Samuel Noah Kramer.* 1984.

Saussure, L. de *Les Origines de l'Astronomie Chinoise.* 1930.

Sayce, A.H. *Astronomy and Astrology of the Babylonians.* 1874.

——— *The Religion of the Babylonians.* 1888.

Schiaparelli, G. *L'Astronomia nell'Antico Testamento.* 1903.

Schwabe, J. *Archetyp und Tierkreis.* 1951.

Sertima, I.V. *They Came Before Columbus.* 1976.

Shamasashtry, R. *The Vedic Calendar.* 1979.

Sivapriyananda, S. *Astrology and Religion in Indian Art.* 1990.

Sjöberg, A.W. and Bergmann, E. *The Collection of Sumerian Temple Hymns.* 1969.

Slosman, A. *Le zodiaque de Denderah.* 1980.

Smith, G.E. *Ships as Evidence of the Migrations of Early Cultures.* 1917.

Spinden, H.J. *Origin of Civilizations in Central America and Mexico.* 1933.

Sprockhoff, E. *Die nordische Megalitkultur.* 1938.

Starr, I. *The Rituals of the Diviner.* 1983.

Steward, J.H. (ed.) *Handbook of South American Indians.* 1946.

Stobart, C. *The Glory That Was Greece.* 1964.

Stoepel, K.T. *Südamerikanische Prähistorische Tempel und Gottheiten*. 1912.

Stücken, E. *Beiträge zur orientalischen Mythologie*. 1902.

The Sumerian Dictionary of the University Museum, University of Pennsylvania. 1984–

Tadmor, H. and Weinfeld, M. (eds.) *History, Historiography and Interpretation*. 1983.

Talmon, Sh. *King, Cult and Calendar in Ancient Israel*. 1986.

Taylor, L.W. *The Mycenaeans*. 1966.

Tello, J.C. *Origen y Desarrollo de las Civilizaciones Prehistoricas Andinas*. 1942.

Temple, J.E. *Maya Astronomy*. 1930.

Thom, A. *Megalithic Sites in Britain*. 1967.

Thomas, D.W. (ed.) *Documents from Old Testament Times*. 1961.

Thompson, J.E.S. *Maya History and Religion*. 1970.

Trimborn, H. *Die Indianischen Hochkulturen des Alten Amerika*. 1963.

Van Buren, E.D. *Clay Figurines of Babylonia and Assyria*. 1930.

—— *Religious Rites and a Ritual in the Time of Uruk IV–III*. 1938.

Vandier, J. *Manuel d'Archéologie Égyptienne*. 1952–58.

Virolleaud, Ch. *L'Astronomie Chaldéenne*. 1903–8.

Ward, W.A. *Essays on the Feminine Titles of the Middle Kingdom*. 1986.

Weidner, E.F. *Alter und Bedeutung der babylonischen Astronomie und Astrallehre*. 1914.

—— *Handbuch der babylonischen Astronomie*. 1915.

Wiener, L. *Africa and the Discovery of America*. 1920.

—— *Mayan and Mexican Origins*. 1926.

Wilford, J.N. *The Mapmakers*. 1982.

Williamson, R.A. (ed.) *Archaeoastronomy in the Americas*. 1978.

Winckler, H. *Himmels- und Weltenbilder der Babylonier*. 1901.

Wolkstein, D. and Kramer, S.N. *Inanna, Queen of Heaven and Earth*. 1983.

Wuthenau, A. von *Unexpected Faces in Ancient America*. 1980.

Ziolkowsky, M.S. and Sadowski, R.M. (eds.) *Time and Calendars in the Inca Empire*. 1989.

INDEX

Praise for the Works of Zecharia Sitchin

Also by Zecharia Sitchin

Genesis Revisited

Divine Encounters

The Earth Chronicles Handbook

The Earth Chronicles Expeditions (autobiographical)

Journeys to the Mythical Past (autobiographical)

The King Who Refused to Die (fiction)

The Lost Book of Enki

There Were Giants Upon the Earth

The Earth Chronicles

The 12th Planet — Book I

The Stairway to Heaven — Book II

The Wars of Gods and Men — Book III

The Lost Realms — Book IV

When Time Began — Book V

The Cosmic Code — Book VI

The End of Days — Book VII

ZECHARIA SITCHIN

—— THE ——
COSMIC
CODE

**The Sixth Book
of
<u>The Earth Chronicles</u>**

Bear & Company
Rochester, Vermont • Toronto, Canada

Bear & Company
One Park Street
Rochester, Vermont 05767
www.BearandCompanyBooks.com

Bear & Company is a division of Inner Traditions International

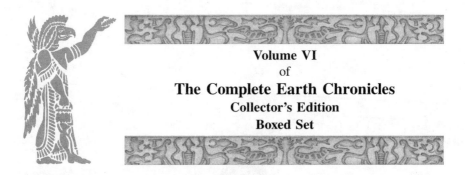

Volume VI
of
The Complete Earth Chronicles
Collector's Edition
Boxed Set

Printed and bound in India at Replika Press Pvt. Ltd.

10 9 8 7 6

CONTENTS

1

STAR STONES

It took a war—a fierce and bloody war—to bring to light, just decades ago, one of the most enigmatic ancient sites in the Near East. If not *the* most enigmatic, it certainly is the most puzzling, and for sure one rooted in great antiquity. It is a structure that has no parallel among the remains of the great civilizations that had flourished in the Near East in past millennia—at least so far as has been uncovered. Its closest parallels are thousands of miles away, across the seas and on other continents; and what it mostly brings to mind is Stonehenge in faraway Britain.

There, on a windswept plain in England about eighty miles southwest of London, circles of imposing megaliths form the most important prehistoric monument in the whole of Britain. There, a semicircle of huge upright stones that have been connected at their tops by lintel stones encompasses within it a semicircle of smaller stone uprights, and is surrounded in turn by two circles of other megaliths. The multitudes that visit the site find that only some of the megaliths still remain standing, while others have collapsed to the ground or are somehow gone from the site. But scholars and researchers have been able to figure out the configuration of the circles-within-circles (Fig. 1, which highlights the still-standing megaliths), and observe the holes indicating where two other circles—of stones or perhaps wooden pegs—had once existed, in earlier phases of Stonehenge.

The horseshoe semicircles, and a fallen large megalith nicknamed the Slaughter Stone, indicate beyond doubt that the structure was oriented on a northeast–southwest axis.

1

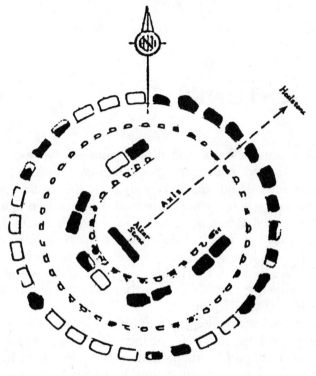

Figure 1

They point to a line of sight that passes between two stone uprights through a long earthworks Avenue, straight to the so-called Heel Stone (Fig. 2). All the studies conclude that the alignments served astronomical purposes; they were first oriented circa 2900 B.C. (give or take a century or so) to sunrise on the summer solstice day; and then realigned circa 2000 B.C. and again circa 1550 B.C. toward sunrise on summer solstice day in those times (Fig. 3).

One of the shortest yet most fierce and ferocious recent wars in the Middle East was the Six Day War of 1967, when the hemmed-in and besieged Israeli army defeated the armies of Egypt, Jordan, and Syria and captured the Sinai peninsula, the West Bank of the Jordan River, and the Golan Heights.

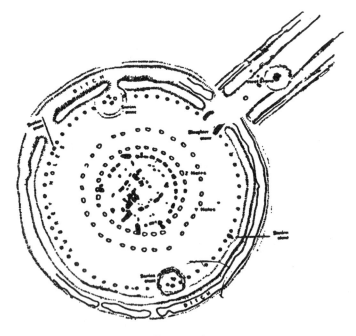

Figure 2

In the years that followed Israeli archaeologists conducted extensive archaeological surveys and excavations in all those areas, bringing to light settlements from early Neolithic times through biblical times to Greek, Roman, and Byzantine periods. Yet nowhere was the surprise greater than on the sparsely inhabited and mostly empty plateau called the Golan Heights. Not only was it discovered that it had been an actively inhabited and cultivated area in the earliest times of human habitation; not only were remains of settlements found from the several millennia preceding the Common Era.

Virtually in the middle of nowhere, on a windswept plain (that had been used by the Israeli army for artillery practice), piles of stones arranged in circles turned out—when viewed from the air—to be a *Near Eastern "Stonehenge"* (Fig. 4).

The unique structure consists of several concentric stone circles, three of them fully circular and two forming only

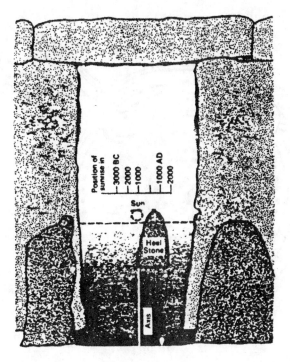

Figure 3

semicircles or "horseshoes." The outer circle is almost a third of a mile in circumference, and the other circles get smaller as they get nearer the structure's center. The walls of the three main stone circles rise to eight feet or more, and their width exceeds ten feet. They are constructed of field stones, ranging in size from small to *megalithic ones that weigh five tons and even more.* In several places the circular concentric walls are connected to each other by radial walls, narrower than but about the same height as the circular walls. In the precise center of the complex structure there rises a huge yet well-defined pile of stones, measuring some sixty-five feet across.

Apart from its unique shape, this is by far one of the largest single stone structures in western Asia, so large in

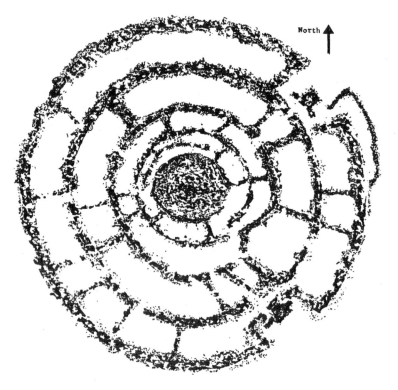

Figure 4

**fact that it can be seen from space by Earth-orbiting
spacecraft.**

Engineers who have studied the site estimated that, even
in its present condition, it contains more than 125,000 cubic
feet of stones weighing an aggregate of close to 45,000 tons.
They estimated that it would have taken one hundred workmen at least six years to create this monument—collect the
basalt stones, transport them to the site, place them according
to a preconceived architectural plan, and raise the walls (undoubtedly taller than the now-visible remains) to form the
cohesive complex structure.

All of which raises the questions, by whom was this structure built, when, and for what?

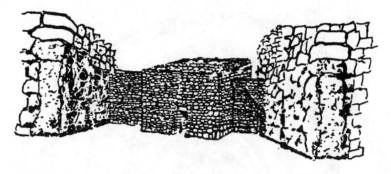

Figure 5

The easiest question to answer is the last one, for the structure itself seems to indicate its purpose—at least its original purpose. The outermost circle clearly showed that it contained two breaks or openings, one located in the northeast and the other in the southeast—locations that indicate an orientation toward the summer and winter solstices.

Working to clear away fallen rocks and ascertain the original layout, Israeli archaeologists exposed in the northeastern opening a massive square structure with two extended "wings" that protected and hid narrower breaks in the two next concentric walls behind it (Fig. 5); the building thus served as a monumental gate providing (and guarding) an entrance into the heart of the stone complex. It was in the walls of this entryway that the largest basalt boulders, weighing as much as five and a half tons each, were found. The southeastern break in the outer ring also provided access to the inner parts of the structure, but there the entranceway did not possess the monumental building; but piles of fallen stones starting in this entranceway and leading outward from it suggest the outlines of a stone-flanked avenue extending in the southeastern direction—an avenue that might have outlined an astronomical line of sight.

These indications that the place was indeed, as Stonehenge in Britain, built to serve as an astronomical observatory (and primarily to determine the solstices) is reinforced by the existence of such observatories elsewhere—structures that are

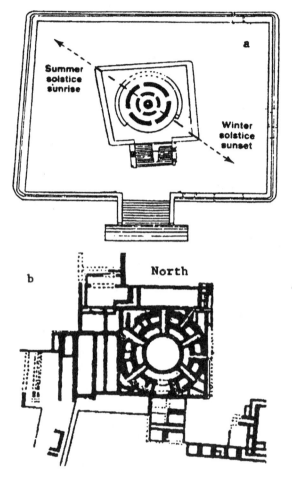

Figures 6a and 6b

even more similar to the one on the Golan, for they feature not only the concentric circles, but also the radial walls connecting the circles. What is amazing is that those similar structures are at ancient sites all the way on the other side of the world, in the Americas.

One is the Mayan site Chichén Itzá in the Yucatán peninsula of Mexico (Fig. 6a), nicknamed the Caracol (''Snail'') on

account of the winding stairs inside the observatory's tower. Another is the circular observatory atop the promontory of Sacsahuaman in Peru (Fig. 6b) that overlooks the Inca capital Cuzco; there, as at Chichén Itzá, there was probably a lookout tower; its foundations reveal the layout and astronomical alignments of the structure and clearly show the concentric circles and connecting radials.

Such similarities were reason enough for the Israeli scientists to call in Dr. Anthony Aveni of the USA, an internationally acclaimed authority on ancient astronomies, especially those of the pre-Columbian civilizations of the Americas. His task was not only to confirm the astronomical orientations underlying the design of the Golan site, but also to help determine its age—and thus, in addition to the For What question, also answer the question When.

That the orientation of a structure—if aligned to the solstices—can reveal the time of its construction, has been an accepted tool in archaeoastronomy since the publication of *The Dawn of Astronomy* by Sir Norman Lockyer in 1894. The apparent movement of the Sun from north to south and back as the seasons come and wane is caused by the fact that the Earth's axis (around which the Earth rotates to create the day/night cycle) is inclined to the plane (''ecliptic'') in which the Earth orbits the Sun. In this celestial dance— though it is the Earth that moves and not the Sun—it appears to observers on Earth that the Sun, moving back and forth, reaches some distant point, hesitates, stops, and then as if it changed its mind, starts back; crosses the equator, goes all the way to the other extreme, hesitates, and stops there, and goes back. The two crossings a year over the equator (in March and September) are called equinoxes; the two stops, one in the north in June and one in the south in December, are called solstices (''Sun Standstills'')—the summer and winter solstices for observers in the Earth's northern hemisphere, as people at Stonehenge and on the Golan had been.

Studying ancient temples, Lockyer divided them into two classes. Some, as the Temple of Solomon in Jerusalem and the temple to Zeus at a place called Baalbek in Lebanon,

were built along an east–west axis that oriented them to sunrise on the days of the equinoxes. Others, as pharaonic temples in Egypt, were aligned on an axis inclined southwest–northeast, which meant that they were oriented to the solstices. He was surprised, however, to discover that while in the former the orientation never changed (so he called them Eternal Temples), the latter—such as the great Egyptian temples in Karnak—showed that as successive Pharaohs needed to see the rays of the Sun strike the holy of holies on the day of the solstice, they kept changing the direction of the avenues and corridors toward a slightly different point in the skies. Such realignments were also made at Stonehenge.

What had caused those directional changes? Lockyer's answer was: changes in the Earth's inclination, resulting from its wobble.

Nowadays the inclination of the Earth's axis (''obliquity'') to its orbital path (''ecliptic'') is 23.5 degrees, and it is this inclination that determines how far northward or southward the Sun would appear to move seasonally. If this angle of inclination were to remain unchanged forever, the solstice points would also remain the same. But astronomers have concluded that the Earth's tilt (caused by its wobble) changes over the centuries and millennia, rising and falling over and over again.

Right now, as in the preceding several millennia, the tilt has been in a narrowing phase. It was over 24 degrees circa 4000 B.C., declined to 23.8 degrees circa 1000 B.C., and continued to fall to its present smidgen under 23.5 degrees. The great innovation of Sir Norman Lockyer was to apply this change in Earth's obliquity to the ancient temples and establish the dates of construction of the various phases of the Great Temple in Karnak (Fig. 7) as well as for the phases of Stonehenge (as indicated by changes in the location of the Heel Stone, Fig. 3).

The same principles have since been used to determine the age of astronomically oriented structures in South America earlier this century, by Arthur Posnansky in respect to the ruins of Tiwanaku on the shores of Lake Titicaca, and by

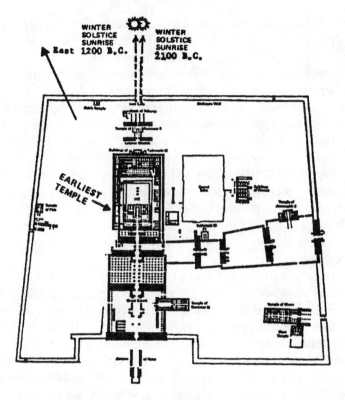

Figure 7

Rolf Müller for the semicircular Torreon in Machu Picchu and the famed Temple of the Sun in Cuzco. Their meticulous researches showed that in order to determine exactly the angle of the Earth's tilt—which indicates, when elevation and geographic position are taken into account, the structure's age—it is essential to determine precisely where north is. It is thus undoubtedly significant that in the case of the Golan site, the researchers there found that the dominant and on clear days visible *peak of Mount Hermon lies precisely north of the structure's center.* Dr. Aveni and his Israeli colleagues, Yonathan Mizrachi and Mattanyah Zohar, were thus able to determine that the site was so oriented as to enable an observer standing in its center and following a

sight line through the center of the northeastern gateway, to see the Sun rise there on solstice day on a June dawn at about *3000 B.C.*!

By 2000 B.C., the scientists concluded, the Sun would have appeared to a similar observer noticeably off-center, but probably still within the gateway. Five hundred years later, the structure had lost its value as a precise astronomical observatory. It was, then, sometime between 1500 and 1200 B.C.—as confirmed by carbon dating of small artifacts recovered there—that the central stone heap was enlarged to form a cairn—a stone mound under which a cavity has been dug out, probably to serve as a burial chamber.

Uncannily, these phased dates are virtually identical to the dates assigned to the three phases of Stonehenge.

Because it was protected by the mound of stones above it, the cavity under the cairn—the presumed burial chamber—remained the most intact part of the ancient site. It was located with the aid of sophisticated seismic instruments and ground-penetrating radar. Once a large cavity had been indicated, the excavators (led by Dr. Yonathan Mizrachi) dug a trench that led them into a circular chamber of over six feet in diameter and about five feet high. It led to a larger chamber, oval in shape, about eleven feet long and about four feet wide. The latter's walls were constructed of six courses of basalt stones rising in a corbelled fashion (i.e. slanting inward as the walls rose); the chamber's ceiling was made of two massive basalt slabs, each weighing some five tons.

There was no coffin and no body, nor any other human or animal remains in either the chamber or antechamber. But the archaeologists did find, as a result of meticulous sifting of the soil, a few gold earrings, several beads made of carnelian semiprecious stone, flint blades, bronze arrowheads, and ceramic shards. They therefore concluded that indeed it was a burial chamber, but one that had been looted, probably in antiquity. The fact that some of the stones used to pave the chamber's floor were pried out reinforced the conclusion that the place had been broken into by grave robbers.

The finds have been dated to the period known as Late Bronze Age, which extended from about 1500 to 1200 B.C. That was the time frame of the Exodus of the Children of Israel from Egypt under the leadership of Moses, and the conquest of the Promised Land under the leadership of Joshua. Of the twelve tribes, the tribes of Reuben and Gad and half the tribe of Manasseh were allotted parts of Transjordan, from the River Arnon in the south to the foothills of Mount Hermon in the north. Those domains included the mountain range of Gilad east of the Jordan River and the plateau that is now the Golan. It was therefore perhaps unavoidable that Israeli researchers turned to the Bible for an answer to the question: Who?

According to the books of Numbers and Joshua, the northern part of the Gilead mountains was ruled by a king called Og from his capital of Bashan. The capture of Og's domain is described in Deuteronomy (chapter 3). "Og and all his men took the field against the Children of Israel," the narrative states. Winning the battle, the Israelites captured sixty towns that were "fortified with high walls and gates and barriers, apart from a great number of unwalled towns." The construction of high stone walls and gates—features of the enigmatic Golan site—was thus within the capabilities of the kingdoms in the time of King Og.

Og, according to the Bible, was a big and stout man: "His iron bedstead is nine cubits long and four cubits wide" (equivalent to over thirteen feet and six feet, respectively). This giant size, the Bible hints, was due to his being a descendant of the Repha'im, a giantlike race of demigods who had once dwelt in that land. (Other giantlike descendants of the Repha'im, including Goliath, are mentioned in the Bible as siding with the Philistines at the time of David). Combining the references to the Repha'im with the biblical account of the circular stone structure erected by Joshua after the crossing of the Jordan River, and the naming of the place Gilgal—"The Circular Stone Heap"—some in Israel have nicknamed the Golan site Gilgal Repha'im—"The Circular Stone Heap of the Repha'im."

While the biblical verses alone do not support such a naming, nor do they really link King Og to the burial chambers, the biblical assertions that the area had once been the domain of the Repha'im and that Og was descended of them are quite intriguing, because we find the Repha'im and their offspring mentioned in Canaanite myths and epic tales. The texts, which clearly place the divine and semidivine actions and events in the area we are dealing with here, were written on clay tablets discovered in the 1930s at a coastal site in northern Syria whose ancient name was Ugarit. The texts describe a group of deities whose father was El ("God, the Lofty One") and whose affairs centered on El's son Ba'al ("the Lord") and his sister Anat ("She who answers"). The focus of Ba'al's attention was the mountainous stronghold and sacred place Zaphon (meaning both "the northern place" and "the place of secrets") and the arena of Ba'al and his sister was what nowadays is northern Israel and the Golan. Roaming the area's skies with them was their sister Shepesh (the name's uncertain meaning suggests an association with the Sun); and of her the texts clearly state that "she governs the Repha'im, the divine ones" and rules over demigods and mortals.

Several of the discovered texts deal with such involvement on the part of the trio. One, titled by scholars *The Tale of Aqhat*, pertains to Danel ("Whom God Judges," Daniel in Hebrew), who—although a Rapha-Man (i.e. descended of the Repha'im)—could not have a son. Growing old and despondent about not having a male heir, Danel appeals to Ba'al and Anat, who in turn intercede with El. Granting the Rapha-Man's wish, El instills in him a "quickening life-breath" and enables him to mate with his wife and have a son whom the gods name Aqhat.

Another tale, *The Legend of King Keret* (Keret, "The Capital, the Metropolis," is used as the name of both the city and its king), concerns the claim to immortality by Keret because of his divine descent. Instead, he falls ill; and his sons wonder aloud: "How could an offspring of El, the Merciful One, die? Shall a divine one die?" Foreseeing the seemingly incredible death of a demigod, the sons envision not

only the Peak of Zaphon, but also the Circuit of Broad Span lamenting for Keret:

> *For thee, father,*
> *shall weep Zaphon, the Mount of Ba'al.*
> *The sacred circuit, the mighty circuit,*
> *the circuit of broad span,*
> *[for thee] shall lament.*

There is here, then, a reference to two highly venerated places that shall mourn the death of the demigod: Mount Zaphon, the Mount of Ba'al—and a renowned sacred *circular* structure—"the sacred circuit, the mighty circuit, the circuit of broad span." If Mount Zaphon, the "Mount of the North," was Mount Hermon, which lies precisely north of the Golan site, *was then the Sacred Circuit the enigmatic Golan site*?

Granting appeals for mercy, El at the last moment sent the goddess Shataqat, "a female who removes the illness," to save Keret. "She flies over a hundred towns, she flies over a multitude of villages" on her rescue mission; arriving at Keret's home in the nick of time, she manages to revive him.

But being only a demigod, Keret in the end did die. Was he then the one buried in the tomb within "the sacred circuit, the mighty circuit, the circuit of broad span"? Though the Canaanite texts give no chronological hint, it is evident that they relate events from the Bronze Age—a time frame that could well fit the date of the artifacts discovered in the Golan site's tomb.

Whether or not any of those legendary rulers ended up being buried at the Golan site, we may never know for sure; especially since the archaeologists studying the site raised the possibility of intrusive burials—namely, the entombment of a later-deceased in a burial place from earlier times, involving as often as not the removal of the earlier remains. They are, however, certain (based on structural features and various dating techniques) that the construction of the "henge"—concentric walls of what we might dub Star Stones because of the

astronomical function—preceded, by 1,000 to 1,500 years, the addition of the cairn and its burial chambers.

As at Stonehenge and other megalithic sites, so too regarding the Golan site, the enigma of who built them is only intensified by establishing their age and determining that an advanced knowledge of astronomy underlay their orientations. Unless they were indeed the divine beings themselves, who was there capable of the feat—circa 3000 B.C. in the case of the Golan site?

In 3000 B.C. there was in western Asia only one civilization high enough, sophisticated enough, and with an extraordinary astronomical knowledge, capable of planning, orienting astronomically, and carrying out the kind of major structures here considered: the Sumerian civilization. It blossomed out in what is nowadays southern Iraq, "suddenly, unexpectedly, out of nowhere" in the words of all scholars. And within a few centuries—an instant as human evolution goes—accounted for virtually all the firsts of what we deem essential to a high civilization, from the wheel to the kiln and bricks and high-rise buildings, writing and poetry and music, codes of law and courts, judges and contracts, temples and priests, kings and administrators, schools and teachers, doctors and nurses; and amazing knowledge of mathematics, exact sciences, and astronomy. Their calendar, still in use as the Jewish calendar, was inaugurated in a city called Nippur in 3760 B.C.—embracing all the sophisticated knowledge required for the structures we are discussing.

It was a civilization that preceded that of Egypt by some eight hundred years and by a thousand years that of the Indus Valley. The Babylonians, Assyrians, Hittites, Elamites, Canaanites, and Phoenicians followed later, some much later. They all bore the imprint and borrowed the underlying firsts of the Sumerians; so did the civilizations that in time rose in Greece and the Mediterranean islands.

Did the Sumerians venture as far as the Golan Heights? Undoubtedly, for their kings and their merchants went westward toward the Mediterranean Sea (which they called the

Upper Sea), and sailed the waters of the Lower Sea (the Persian Gulf) to other distant lands. When Ur was their capital, its merchants were familiar in all parts of the ancient Near East. And one of Sumer's most famed kings, Gilgamesh—a famed king of Uruk (the biblical Erech)—in all probability passed through the site. The time was circa 2900 B.C., soon after the Golan site was first constructed.

The father of Gilgamesh was the city's High Priest; his mother was the goddess Ninsun. Aiming to be a mighty king and aggrandize his city, Gilgamesh started his reign by challenging the authority of the then-principal city of Sumer, Kish. A clay tablet describing the episode names the king of Kish Agga, and twice describes him as being "stout." Kish was then the capital of a wide domain that might have extended beyond the Euphrates River; and one must wonder whether the stout king Agga might have been a forerunner of the giantlike Og of biblical fame; for the naming of kings after earlier predecessors was a common Near Eastern practice.

Proud, ambitious, and swashbuckling in his youth, Gilgamesh took hard his creeping aging. To sustain his prowess he took to dropping in on newlyweds in his city, claiming the royal right to be the first to have sex with the bride. When the townspeople could not stand it anymore, they appealed to the gods for help; and the gods responded by creating a double for Gilgamesh, who stopped the king's shenanigans. Subdued, Gilgamesh grew gloomy and reflective. He witnessed people his age or even younger dying; and then it occurred to him that there is another way: he was, after all, partly divine—not just a *demi*god, but *two-thirds* divine, for it was not his father but his mother who was a goddess!

Should he, Gilgamesh, then die as a mortal, or be entitled to the everlasting life of the gods? He presented his case to his mother. Yes, she told him, you are right. But in order to attain the divine life span, you must ascend the heavens and reach the gods' abode. And the places from which such ascents are possible, she told him, are under the command of his godfather Utu (later known as Shamash).

Utu/Shamash tried to dissuade Gilgamesh: "Who, Gilga-

mesh, can scale heaven? Only the gods live forever under the Sun. As for Mankind, numbered are their days.'' Go, be with your family and your townsfolk, enjoy the rest of your days, the god said to him.

The story of Gilgamesh and his quest for immortality is told in the *Epic of Gilgamesh*, a long text written on clay tablets and discovered by archaeologists in both the original Sumerian and various ancient translations. As the tale unfolds, we read that Gilgamesh was not dissuaded, and an object that fell from the skies was deemed by him a sign from heaven that he should not give up. Agreeing to help, Ninsun revealed to him that there is a place in the Cedar Mountains—the Landing Place—from which Gilgamesh could ascend to the divine abode. It would be a journey fraught with dangers, she warned Gilgamesh. But what is the alternative? he asked her. If I fail in my quest, he said, at least future generations will know that I tried.

Giving her blessing to the journey, Ninsun insisted that the artificial man, Enkidu, go in front of Gilgamesh and protect him along the way. The choice was opportune, for the area of their destination was the very area from which Enkidu had come, the hills where he had roamed with the wild beasts. He explained to Gilgamesh how dangerous the undertaking would be; but Gilgamesh insisted on going.

In order to reach the Cedar Mountains in what is now Lebanon from Sumer (which was in what is now southern Iraq), Gilgamesh had to cross the plateau that we now call the Golan. And indeed we find it stated, in the preamble to the epic in which the king's adventures and achievements are enumerated, that it was ''he who opened the mountain passes.'' It was a first that merited recalling, for there are no mountains in the land called Sumer.

On their way Gilgamesh stopped several times to seek divine oracles from the Sun God. When they reached the hill land and the woodlands (the likes of which there were none in Sumer), Gilgamesh had a series of omen-dreams. At a crucial stop, from where they could already see the Cedar Mountains, Gilgamesh sought to induce a dream-omen by

Figure 8

sitting within a circle that was formed for him by Enkidu. Was it Enkidu, possessing superhuman strength, who arranged the field stones for Gilgamesh to form Star Stones?

We can only guess. But physical evidence attesting to the familiarity of those who had lived on the Golan Heights for generations with Gilgamesh and his tale has recently been found on the Heights.

One of the most recounted episodes in the king's adventures has been the incident in which he encountered two ferocious lions, fought them off, and killed them with his bare hands. The heroic deed was a favorite subject of Near Eastern artists in antiquity. Yet it was a totally unexpected discovery to find, at a site near the concentric circles, a stone slab with such a depiction (Fig. 8)! (The artifact is on exhibit at the new and most-interesting Golan Archaeological Museum in Qatzrin).

While the textual references and the depiction on the stone slab do not constitute conclusive evidence that Gilgamesh reached the site on his journey to the Cedar Mountains of Lebanon, there is one more intriguing clue to be considered. After the site was identified from the air, the Israeli archaeologists discovered that it was marked on (captured) Syrian army maps by the name Rugum el-Hiri—a most puzzling name, for it meant in Arabic "Stone heap of the bobcat."

The explanation for the puzzling name, we suggest, may well lie in the *Epic of Gilgamesh*, reflecting a memory of the King Who Fought the Lions.

And, as we shall see, that is just the beginning of intricate and interwound associations.

2

FATE HAS TWELVE STATIONS

Scholars have long recognized that in the lore of diverse nations the same theme, the same basic tale, appears and reappears though under different guises, names, and localities. It is thus perhaps no wonder that the carved basalt stone on which Gilgamesh is depicted fighting with the lions was discovered near a village bearing the name Ein Samsum—"Samson's Spring." For, it will be recalled, Samson also fought and killed a lion with his bare hands. That was some two thousand years after Gilgamesh, and certainly not on the Golan Heights. Is the village's name, then, just a coincidence, or the lingering memory of a visitor called Gilgamesh becoming Samson?

Of greater significance is the association with King Keret. Though the venue of the Canaanite tale is not stated, it is presumed by many (e.g. Cyrus H. Gordon, *Notes on the Legend of Keret*) that the combined name for the king and his capital in fact identified the island of Crete. There, according to Cretan and Greek legends, civilization began when the god Zeus saw Europa, the beautiful daughter of a king of Phoenicia (present-day Lebanon) and, taking the form of a bull, abducted her and swam with her on his back across the Mediterranean Sea to the island of Crete. There he had three sons by her, among them Minos, who in time became the one with whom the beginning of Cretan civilization is associated.

Thwarted in his aspirations to the throne, Minos appealed to Poseidon, god of the seas, to bestow upon him a sign of divine favor. In response, Poseidon made a Divine Bull, pure white, appear from the sea. Minos vowed to offer the beau-

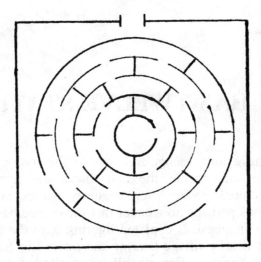

Figure 9

tiful bull as a sacrifice to the god, but was so enthralled by it that instead he kept it to himself. In punishment, the god made the king's wife fall in love and mate with the bull; the offspring was the legendary Minotaur, a half-man, half-bull creature. Minos then commissioned the divine craftsman Daedalus to build in the Cretan capital Knossos an underground maze from which the bull-man would be unable to escape. The maze was called the Labyrinth.

A huge stone sculpture of a bull's horns does greet the visitor to the excavated remains of Knossos, but not the remains of the Labyrinth. Yet its memory and its circular shape, as a maze of concentric circular walls with passages blocked by radials (as in this suggested layout, Fig. 9) have not been forgotten.

It certainly resembles the layout of the Golan site; and it calls for going back to the *Epic of Gilgamesh* for the heroes' encounter with the Bull of Heaven.

As the epic tells it, during the final night before attempting to enter the Cedar Forest, Gilgamesh envisioned a rocketship thunderously rising, in a fiery ascent, from the Landing Place. The next morning they found the hidden entryway into

Figure 10

the forbidden enclosure; but no sooner did they start on their
way in than a robotic guardian blocked their way. It was
"mighty, its teeth as the teeth of a dragon, its face of a
ferocious lion, its advance like the onrushing headwaters."
A "radiating beam" emanated from its forehead, "devouring
trees and bushes"; "from its killing force, none could escape."

Seeing the predicament of Gilgamesh and Enkidu, Utu/
Shamash "down from the skies spoke to the heroes." He
advised them not to run, but instead to draw near the monster
as soon as the god would blow a swirling wind whose dust
would blind the guardian. As soon as that happened, Enkidu
struck and killed it. Ancient artists depicted on cylinder seals
(Fig. 10) Gilgamesh, Enkidu, and Utu/Shamash together with
the menacing robot; its depiction brings to mind the biblical
description of the "angels with the whirling sword" that God
placed at the entrance to the Garden of Eden to make sure
that the expelled Adam and Eve would not reenter it.

The fight was also watched by Inanna (later known as
Ishtar), the twin sister of Utu/Shamash. She had quite a record of enticing human males to spend a night with her—a
night which they rarely survived. Captivated by the beauty
of Gilgamesh as he bathed naked in a nearby river or wa-
terfall, she invited him: "Come, Gilgamesh, be my lover!"
But knowing the record, he turned her down.

Enraged by this insulting refusal, Ishtar summoned the

Bull of Heaven to smite Gilgamesh. Running for their lives, the duo rushed back to Uruk; but the Bull of Heaven caught up with them on the banks of the Euphrates River. At the moment of mortal danger it was again Enkidu who managed to strike and kill the Bull of Heaven.

Inanna/Ishtar, enraged, "sent up a wail to Heaven," demanding that the two comrades be put to death. Though temporarily spared, Enkidu died first; then so did Gilgamesh (after a second journey that took him to a spaceport in the Sinai peninsula).

What was the Bull of Heaven—GUD.ANNA in Sumerian? Many students of the *Epic*, such as Giorgio de Santillana and Hertha von Dechend in *Hamlet's Mill*, have come to the conclusion that the *Epic*'s events, taking place on Earth, are but a mirror image of events taking place in Heaven. Utu/Shamash is the Sun, Inanna/Ishtar is what she was later called in Greek and Roman times—Venus. The menacing guardian of the Cedar Mountains with the face of a lion is the *constellation of Leo* (the Lion), and the Bull of Heaven the celestial group of stars that has been called— since Sumerian times!—the *constellation of the Bull* (Taurus).

There are, indeed, Mesopotamian depictions with the Lion/ Bull theme (Fig. 11a and 11b); and as was first remarked upon by Willy Hartner (*The Earliest History of the Constellations in the Near East*), in the fourth millennium B.C. the Sumerians would have observed the two constellations in key zodiacal positions: the constellation of the Bull (Taurus) as the constellation of the spring equinox and the constellation of the Lion (Leo) as that of the summer solstice.

The attributing of zodiacal connotations to epic events on Earth, as told by the Sumerians, implies that they had such celestial knowledge—in the fourth millennium B.C., some three millennia before the usually presumed time of the grouping of stars into constellations and the introduction of the twelve zodiacal ones by the Greeks. In fact, the Greek savants (of Asia Minor) themselves explained that the knowledge came to them from the "Chaldeans" of Mesopotamia;

Figures 11a and 11b

and, as Sumerian astronomical texts and pictorial depictions attest, the credit should go to them. Their names and symbols for the zodiacal constellations remained unchanged to our time.

The Sumerian zodiacal lists began with Taurus, which was indeed the constellation from which the Sun was observed rising at dawn on the day of the spring equinox in the fourth millennium B.C. It was called in Sumerian GUD.ANNA ("Bull of Heaven" or "Heavenly Bull")—the very same term used in the *Epic of Gilgamesh* for the divine creature that Inanna/Ishtar had summoned from the heavens and that the two comrades slew.

Did the slaying represent or symbolize an actual celestial event, circa 2900 B.C.? While the possibility cannot be ruled out, the historical record indicates that major events and changes did occur on Earth at that time; and the "slaying" of the Bull of Heaven represented an omen, a heavenly omen, predicting or even triggering events on Earth.

For the better part of the fourth millennium B.C. the Sumerian civilization was not only the greatest on Earth, but also the only one. But circa 3100 B.C. the Civilization of the Nile (Egypt and Nubia) joined the one on the Euphrates-

Figure 12

Tigris Rivers. Did this split-up on Earth—alluded to by the biblical tale of the Tower of Babel and the end of the era when Mankind spoke one tongue—find expression in the description (in the Gilgamesh epic) of the coup de grace dealt the Bull of Heaven by the tearing off of its foreleg by Enkidu? Egyptian celestial-zodiacal depictions indeed associated the beginning of their civilization with the cutting off of the forepart of the constellation of the Bull (Fig. 12).

As we have detailed in *The Wars of Gods and Men*, Inanna/Ishtar had expected at that time to become mistress of the new civilization, but it was—literally and symbolically—torn away from her. She was partly appeased when a third civilization, that of the Indus Valley, was put under her aegis, circa 2900 B.C.

As significant as celestial omens had been for the gods, they were even more consequential to mortals on Earth; witness the fate that befell the two comrades. Enkidu, an artificially created being, died as a mortal. And Gilgamesh, two-thirds divine, could not escape mortality. Though he went on a second journey, enduring hardships and dangers, and though he did find the Plant of Everlasting Youth, he returned to Uruk empty-handed. According to the Sumerian King List, "the divine Gilgamesh, whose father was a human, the High Priest of the temple precinct, ruled 126 years; Urlugal, son of Gilgamesh, ruled after him."

We can almost hear the son of Gilgamesh crying out, as

did the sons of King Keret: "How could an offspring of El, The Merciful One, die? Shall a divine one die?" But Gilgamesh, though more than a demigod, tangled with his Fate. His was the Age of the Bull, and he slew it; and his Fate, a Fate made in Heaven, changed from a chance for immortality to that of a mortal's death.

A thousand years after the probable stay of Gilgamesh at the Golan site, it was visited by another ancient VIP who also saw Fate written in the zodiacal constellations. He was Jacob, the grandson of Abraham; and the time, by our calculations, was about 1900 B.C.

A question that is often ignored regarding the megalithic structures around the globe is, Why have they been constructed where they are? The location obviously had to do with their particular purpose. The great pyramids of Giza, we have suggested in our writings, served as anchors for a Landing Corridor leading to a spaceport in the Sinai peninsula, and were emplaced precisely because of that link on the thirtieth parallel north. Stonehenge, it was suggested by leading astronomers, was erected where it is because it is precisely there that its astronomical functions could combine both solar and lunar observations. Until more might come to light concerning the Golan Circles, the most likely reason for its being where it is was that it lay astride one of the few linkways that connected two major international routes (in antiquity and still now): the King's Highway, which ran along the hills east of the Jordan River, and the Way of the Sea, which ran on the west along the coast of the Mediterranean Sea (Map). The two routes connected Mesopotamia and Egypt, Asia and Africa—be it for peaceful trade or military invasions. The links between the two routes were dictated by geography and topography. At the Golan site, the crossing could be made on either side of the Sea of Galilee (Lake Kinnereth); the preferred one—then and now—is the one on the north, where the bridge has retained its ancient name: The Bridge of the Daughters of Jacob.

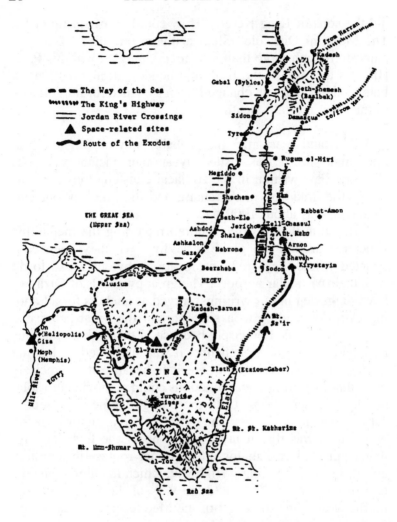

The Golan site was thus located where travelers from different nations and diverse homelands could stop and scan the heavens for omens, to seek out clues regarding their Fates, perhaps to mingle at a neutral site because it was sacred, and there negotiate issues of war or peace.

Based on biblical and Mesopotamian data, we believe that this was what Jacob had used the site for.

The story began two centuries earlier, in Sumer; and it began not with Jacob's grandfather Abraham but with Jacob's great-grandfather, Terah. His name suggests that he was an oracle priest (*Tirhu*); the family's care to be known as *Ibri* (Hebrew) people suggests to us that they considered themselves to be Nippurians—people from the city Nippur that in Sumerian was rendered NI.IBRU—"The Beautiful/Pleasant Abode of Crossing." The religious and scientific center of Sumer, Nippur was the site of the DUR.AN.KI, the "Bond Heaven-Earth," located in the city's sacred precinct. It was the focal point for the preservation, study, and interpretation of accumulated astronomical, calendrical, and celestial knowledge; and Abraham's father, Terah, was one of its priests.

Circa 2100 B.C. Terah was transferred to Ur. The time was a period known to Sumerologists as Ur III, for it was then that Ur, for the third time, became the capital not only of Sumer, and not only of an enlarged political entity called Sumer and Akkad, but also of a virtual empire that flourished and was held together not by force of arms but by a superior culture, a unified pantheon (what is known as Religion), a capable administration, and—not least of all—a thriving trade. Ur was also the cult-center of the Moon god Nannar (later known by the Semitic people as Sin). Rapidly developing events in Sumer and beyond triggered first the transfer of Terah to Ur and then to a distant city called Harran. Situated on the Upper Euphrates and its tributaries, the city served as a major crossroads and trading post (which its name, meaning the Caravanry, indicated). Founded by Sumerian merchants, Harran also boasted a large temple to the Moon god, so much so that the city was looked upon as an "Ur away from Ur."

On these transfers Terah took with him his family. The move to Harran included Abram (as he was then called), Terah's firstborn; a son called Nahor; the two sons' wives, Sarai (later renamed Sarah) and Milcah; and Terah's grandson Lot, the son of Abram's brother Haran who had died in Ur. They dwelt there, in Harran, "many years" according to

the Bible, and it was there that Terah died when he was 205 years old.

It was after that that God said unto Abram: "Get thee out of thy country, and out of thy birthplace, and from thy father's dwelling place, unto the land that I will show thee . . . There I will make thee unto a great nation, and I will bless thee and make great thy name." And Abram took Sarai his wife and Lot his nephew and all the people in their household and all of their belongings, and went to the Land of Canaan; "and Abram was seventy-five years old when he departed from Harran." His brother Nahor stayed behind, with his family, in Harran.

Acting on divine instructions, Abram moved quickly in Canaan to establish a base in the Negev, the arid area of Canaan bordering the Sinai peninsula. On a visit to Egypt he was received in the Pharaoh's court; back in Canaan, he dealt with the local rulers. He then played a role in an international conflict, known in the Bible (Genesis 14) as the War of the Kings. It was after that that God promised Abram that his "seed" should inherit and rule the lands between the Brook of Egypt and the Euphrates River. Doubting the promise, Abram pointed out that he and his wife Sarai had no children. So God told Abram not to worry. "Look now toward the heavens," he told him, "and count the stars if you can . . . so numerous shall be thy seed." But Sarai remained barren even after that.

So, at her suggestion Abram slept with her handmaiden Hagar, who did bear him a son, Ishmael. And then, miraculously—after the upheaval of Sodom and Gomorrah, when the couple's names were changed to Abraham and Sarah— Abraham, then aged one hundred, had a son by his wife Sarah, aged ninety. Though not the firstborn, Sarah's son, Isaac, was the Legitimate Heir under the Sumerian succession rules that the Patriarch followed; for he was a son of his father's half sister: "the daughter of my father but not of my mother," Abraham said of Sarah (Genesis 20:12).

It was after the death of Sarah, his lifelong companion, that Abraham, "old and advanced in years" (137 years, by

our calculations) became concerned about his unmarried son Isaac. Fearing that Isaac would end up marrying a Canaanite, he sent the overseer of his household to Harran, to find there a bride for Isaac from among the relatives that had remained there. Arriving at the dwelling village of Nahor, he met at the watering well Rebecca, who turned out to be Nahor's granddaughter and ended up going to Canaan to become Isaac's wife.

Twenty years after they got married Rebecca gave birth to twins, Esau and Jacob. Esau was first to get married, taking two wives right off, both of them Hittite lasses; "they were a source of grief to Isaac and Rebecca." The troubles are not detailed in the Bible, but the situation between mother and daughters-in-law was so bad that Rebecca told Isaac: "I am disgusted with life on account of the Hittite women; should Jacob too marry such a Hittite woman, of the local females, what good would life be to me?" So Isaac called Jacob and instructed him to go to Harran, to his mother's family, to find there a bride. Heeding his father's words, "Jacob left Beersheba and set out for Harran."

Of Jacob's journey from the south of Canaan to distant Harran, the Bible reports only one episode—though a very significant one. It was the nighttime vision by Jacob, "as he came upon a certain place," of a stairway to heaven on which Angels of the Lord were ascending and descending. Awakened, Jacob realized that he had come upon "a place of the *Elohim* and a gateway to heaven." He marked the place by setting up there a commemorative stone, and named the site Beth-El—"The House of El," the Lord. And then, by a route that is not stated, he continued to Harran.

On the city's outskirts he saw shepherds gathering with their flocks at a well in the field. Addressing them, Jacob inquired whether they knew Laban, his mother's brother. Indeed we know him, the shepherds said, and here comes his daughter Rachel, shepherding his flocks. Bursting into tears, Jacob introduced himself as the son of Rebecca, her aunt. No sooner did Laban hear the news than he, too, came running, hugging and kissing his nephew, inviting him to stay

with him and meet his other daughter, the older Leah. Marriage was clearly in the father's mind; but Jacob fell in love with Rachel, and offered to work for Laban seven years in lieu of a dowry. But on the night of the wedding, after the banquet, Laban substituted Leah for Rachel in the bridal bed . . .

When Jacob discovered the bride's identity in the morning, Laban was nonplussed. Here, he said, we do not marry off the younger daughter before her elder sister; why don't you work for me another seven years, and then marry Rachel, too? Still in love with Rachel, Jacob agreed. After seven years, he married Rachel; but the wily Laban held on to the hard worker and capable shepherd that Jacob was, and would not let him go. To keep Jacob from leaving, he let him start raising his own flocks; but the more Jacob succeeded, the more were Laban's sons grumbling with envy.

And so it was, when Laban and his sons were away to shear their flocks of sheep, that Jacob gathered his wives and children and flocks and fled Harran. "And he crossed the river"—the Euphrates—"and set his course toward the mount of Gile'ad."

"On the third day it was told to Laban that Jacob had escaped; so he took his kinfolk with him and pursued after Jacob; and after seven days he caught up with him at the mount of Gilead."

Gilad—"The Everlasting Stone Heap" in Hebrew— the site of the circular observatory in the Golan!

The encounter started with bitter exchanges and reciprocal accusations. It ended with a peace treaty. In the manner of boundary treaties of the time, Jacob selected a stone and erected it to be a Witnessing Pillar, to mark the boundary beyond which Laban would not cross into Jacob's domains nor would Jacob cross to Laban's domains. Such boundary stones, called *Kudurru* in Akkadian because of their rounded tops, have been discovered at various Near Eastern sites. As a rule, they were inscribed with details of the treaty and included the invoking of each side's gods as witnesses and guarantors. Adhering to the custom, Laban called for "the God of Abraham

and the gods of Nahor'' to guarantee the treaty. Apprehensive, Jacob ''swore by the fear of his father Isaac.'' Then he added his own touch to the occasion and the place:

> *And Jacob said to his sons:*
> *Gather stones;*
> *And they gathered stones*
> *and arranged them in a heap . . .*
> *And Jacob called the stone heap*
> *Gal'ed.*

By a mere change of pronunciation, from *Gilad* to *Gal-Ed*, Jacob changed the meaning of the name from its long-standing ''The Everlasting Stone Heap'' to ''The Stone Heap of Witnessing.''

How certain can we be that the place was that of the Golan circles' site? Here, we believe, is the convincing final clue: In his oath of treaty, Jacob also described the site as *Ha-Mitzpeh—the Observatory*!

The *Book of Jubilees*, an extrabiblical book that recounted the biblical tales from varied early sources, added a postscript to the recorded event: ''And Jacob made there a heap for a witness, wherefore the name of the place is called 'The Heap of Witness'; but before they used to call the land of Gilead the Land of the Repha'im.''

And thus we are back to the enigmatic Golan site and its nickname Gilgal Repha'im.

The *Kudurru* boundary stones that have been found in the Near East bore, as a rule, not just the terms of the agreement and the names of the gods invoked as its guarantors, but also the gods' celestial symbols—sometimes of the Sun and Moon and planets, sometimes of the zodiacal constellations (as in Fig. 13)—all twelve of them. For that, since the earliest Sumerian times, was the count—twelve—of the zodiacal constellations, as evidenced by their names:

Figure 13

GUD.ANNA—Heavenly Bull (*Taurus*)
MASH.TAB.BA—Twins (*Gemini*)
DUB—Pincers, Tongs (*Cancer*)
UR.GULA—Lion (*Leo*)
AB.SIN—Whose Father Was Sin ("the Maiden" = *Virgo*)
ZI.BA.AN.NA—Heavenly Fate ("the Scales" = *Libra*)
GIR.TAB—Which Claws and Cuts (*Scorpio*)
PA.BIL—the Defender ("the Archer" = *Sagittarius*)
SUHUR.MASH—Goat-Fish (*Capricorn*)
GU—Lord of the Waters (*Aquarius*)
SIM.MAH—Fishes (*Pisces*)
KU.MAL—Field Dweller (the Ram = *Aries*)

Figure 14

While not all the symbols depicting the twelve zodiacal constellations have survived from Sumerian times, or even Babylonian times, they have been found on Egyptian monuments, in identical depictions and names (Fig. 14).

Should anyone doubt that Abraham, a son of the astronomer-priest Terah, was aware of the twelve zodiacal houses when God told him to observe the skies and see therein the future? As the stars you observe in the heavens, so shall thy offspring be, God told Abraham; and when his

first son was born by the handmaiden Hagar, God blessed
the boy, Ishmael ("By God Heard"), by this prophecy:

> *As for Ishmael:*
> *Indeed I have heard him.*
> *By this do I bless him:*
> *I will make him fruitful*
> *and I will multiply him exceedingly;*
> *Of him twelve chieftains will be born,*
> *his shall be a great nation.*

> *Genesis 17:20*

With that prophetic blessing, linked to the starry heavens
as observed by Abraham, does the Bible for the first time
record the number twelve and its significance. It then relates
(Genesis 25) that Ishmael's sons—each a chief of a tribal
state—indeed numbered twelve. Listing them by their names,
the Bible emphasizes: "Those were the sons of Ishmael according to their courts and strongholds—twelve chieftains,
each to his own nation." Their domains encompassed Arabia
and the desertland to its north.

The next time the Bible employs the number twelve is in
listing Jacob's twelve sons at the time when he was back at
his father's estate in Hebron. "And the number of the sons
of Jacob was twelve," the Bible states in Genesis 35, listing
them by the names that later became familiar as names of
the Twelve Tribes of Israel:

Six by Leah:
Reuben, Simeon, Levi, Judah, Issachar, Zebulun.
Two by Rachel:
Joseph, Benjamin.
Two by Bilhah, *Rachel's handmaiden:*
Dan, Naphtali.
And two by Zilpah, *Leah's handmaiden:*
Gad and Asher.

There is, however, sleight of hand in this list: This was
not the original count of the twelve children who came back
with Jacob to Canaan: Benjamin, the youngest, was born by
Rachel when the family was already back in Canaan, in Bethlehem, where she died while giving birth. Yet the number of
Jacob's children was twelve before that: The last child born
by Leah was a *daughter*, Dinah. The list—perhaps by more
than a coincidence—was thus made up of eleven males and
one female, matching the list of zodiacal constellations that
is made up of one female (Virgo, the Virgin) and eleven
"male" ones.

The zodiacal implications of the twelve children of Jacob
(renamed *Israel* after he had wrestled with a divine being
when crossing the Jordan River) can be discerned twice in
the continuing biblical narrative. Once, when Joseph—a
master of having and solving dream-omens—boasted to his
brothers that he had dreamed that the Sun and the Moon (the
elder Jacob and Leah) and eleven *Kokhavim* were bowing to
him. The word is usually translated "stars," but the term
(stemming from the Akkadian) served equally to denote constellations. With Joseph's, the total added up to twelve. The
implication, that his was a superior constellation, annoyed
greatly his brothers.

The next time was when Jacob, old and dying, called his
twelve sons to bless them and foretell their future. Known
as the *Prophecy of Jacob*, the last words of the Patriarch
begin by associating the eldest son, Reuben, with Az—the
zodiacal constellation of Aries (which, by then, was the constellation of the spring equinox instead of Taurus). Simeon
and Levi were lumped together as the Twins, Gemini; because they had killed many men when they revenged the rape
of their sister, Jacob prophesied, they would be dispersed
among the other tribes and forfeit their own domains. Judah
was compared to a Lion (Leo) and foreseen as the holder of
the royal scepter—a prediction of Judea's kingship. Zebulun
was envisioned as a Dweller of the Seas (Aquarius), which
he indeed became. The predictions of the twelve tribal sons'
future continued, linked by name and symbol to the zodiacal

constellations. Last were Rachel's sons: Joseph was depicted as the Bowman (Sagittarius); and the last one, Benjamin—having substituted for his sister Dinah (Virgo)—was described as a predator that feeds off others.

The strict adherence to the number twelve, emulating the twelve houses of the zodiac, involved another sleight of hand that usually escapes notice. After the Exodus and the division of the Promised Land among the Twelve Tribes, they again included some rearrangement. Suddenly the account of the Twelve Tribes who shared territories lists the two sons of Joseph (who were born to him in Egypt)—Manasseh and Ephra'im. The list, nevertheless, stayed at twelve; for, as prophesied by Jacob, the tribes of Simeon and Levi did not share in the territorial distributions and, as foretold, were dispersed among the other tribes. The requirement—the sanctity—of the Celestial Twelve was again preserved.

Archaeologists excavating the remains of Jewish synagogues in the Holy Land are sometimes puzzled to find the floors of such synagogues decorated with the zodiacal circle of twelve constellations, depicted by their traditional symbols (Fig. 15). They tend to view the finds as aberrations resulting from Greek and Roman influences in the centuries before Christianity. Such an attitude, stemming from the belief that the practice was prohibited by the Old Testament, ignores the historical record—the Hebrews' familiarity with the zodiacal constellations and their association with predictions of the future—with Fate.

For generations and to this day, one can hear cries of *Mazal-tov! Mazal-tov!* at Jewish weddings or when a boy is circumcised. Ask anyone what it means, and the answer will be: It means "Good Luck," let the couple or boy have good luck with them.

Few realize, however, that though that is what is intended, that is not what the phrase means. *Mazal-tov* literally means "a good/favorable *zodiacal constellation.*" The term comes from the Akkadian (the first or Mother Semitic language), in which *Manzalu* meant "station"—the zodiacal station in

Figure 15

which the Sun was seen to "station" itself on the day of wedding or birth.

Such an association of one's zodiacal house with one's Fate is in vogue through horoscopic astrology, which starts by establishing (through the date of birth) what sign one is—a Pisces, a Cancer, or any other of the twelve zodiacal constellations. Going back, we could say that according to the Prophecy of Jacob, Judah was a Leo, Gad a Scorpio, and Naphtali a Capricorn.

The observation of the heavens for fateful indications, a task performed by a corps of astronomer-priests, assumed a key role in royal decisions during Babylonian times. The fate of the king, the fate of the land and of nations were divined from the position of the planets in a particular zodiacal con-

stellation. Royal decisions awaited the word of astronomer-
priests. Was the Moon, expected in Sagittarius, obscured by
clouds? Had the comet seen in Taurus moved on to another
constellation? What was the meaning for the king or the land
of the observation that, on the same evening, Jupiter rose in
Sagittarius, Mercury in Gemini, and Saturn in Scorpio? Records literally requiring hundreds of tablets reveal that those
heavenly phenomena were interpreted to foretell invasions,
famines, floodings, civil unrest—or, on the other hand, long
life for the king, a stable dynasty, victory in war, prosperity.
Most of the records of such observations were written down
as straight prose on clay tablets; sometimes, the astrological
almanacs, as horoscopical handbooks, were illustrated with
the symbols of the relevant zodiacal constellations. In all
instances, Fate was deemed to be indicated by the heavens.

Today's horoscopic astrology's roots go back well beyond
the Babylonians, the "Chaldeans" of Greek reports. Coupled
with the twelve-month calendar, the notion that Fate and the
Zodiac are two aspects of the same course of events undoubtedly began at least when the calendar began—in Nippur, in 3760 B.C. (which is when the count of the Jewish
calendar began). That such an association is really that old
can be gleaned, in our opinion, from one of the Sumerian
constellation names, that of ZI.BA.AN.NA. The term, understood to mean "Heavenly Fate," literally means "Life-
Decision in the heavens" as well as "The Heavenly Scales
of Life." This was a concept that was recorded in Egypt in
the *Book of the Dead*; it was a belief that one's hope for an
eternal afterlife depends on the weighing of his heart on the
Day of Judgment. The scene was magnificently depicted on
the Papyrus of Ani, where the god Anubis is shown weighing
the heart in a balance and the god Thoth, the Divine Scribe,
recording the result on a pallet (Fig. 16).

An unsolved puzzle in Jewish traditions is why the biblical
Lord had chosen the *seventh* month, Tishrei, as the month in
which the Hebrew New Year was to begin, rather than starting it in the month counted in Mesopotamia as the first
month, Nissan. If it was, as has been suggested by way of

Figure 16

an explanation, a desire to enforce a clear break from the Mesopotamian veneration of stars and planets, why still call it the seventh month and not renumber it the first month?

It seems to us that the opposite is true, and that the answer lies in the very name of the constellation ZI.BA.AN.NA and its connotation of the Scales of Fate. We believe that the crucial clue is the calendrical link with the zodiac. At the time of the Exodus (mid–second millennium B.C.) the first constellation, that of the spring equinox, was Aries, not Taurus anymore. *And starting with Aries, the constellation of the Heavenly Scales of Life was indeed the seventh.* The month in which the Jewish New Year was to begin, the month in which it would be decided in heaven who is to live and who is to die, who is to be healthy or to be sick, to be richer or poorer, happy or unhappy—was the month that paralleled the zodiacal month of the Celestial Scales.

And in the heavens, Fate had twelve stations.

3

DIVINE GENERATIONS

The twelve-part zodiac and its antiquity stir up two puzzles: Who originated it and why was the celestial circle divided into *twelve* parts?

The answers require the crossing of a threshold—to a realization that underlying the seemingly astrological significance of dividing the heavens into twelve parts is a highly sophisticated astronomy—an astronomy, in fact, so advanced that Man, by himself, could not have possessed it when this division of the celestial circle began.

In its annual orbit around the Sun, the Sun appears to be rising each month—a twelfth part of the year—in a different station. But the one that counts most, the one that was deemed crucial in antiquity and which determines the transition from Age to Age (from Taurus to Aries to Pisces and soon to Aquarius), is the one in which the Sun is seen rising on the day of the spring equinox (Fig. 17). As it happens, the Earth in its annual orbit around the Sun does not return to the exact same spot. Owing to a phenomenon called Precession, there is a slight retardation; it accumulates to one degree every 72 years. The retardation (assuming each of the twelve segments to be equal, 30 degrees each) thus requires 2,160 years (72 × 30) to execute a shift from sunrise on equinox day against the starry background of one zodiacal constellation (e.g. Taurus) to the one *before* it (i.e. Aries)— while the Earth orbits the Sun in a counterclockwise direction, the retardation causes the Day of the Equinox to shift backwards.

Now, even with the longer longevity in Sumerian/biblical

40

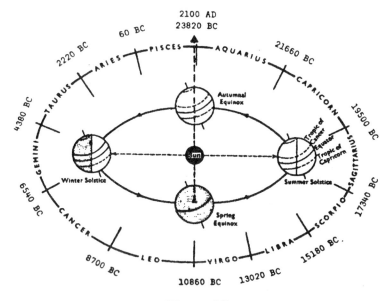

Figure 17

times (Terah 205, Abraham 175) it would have taken a life-time to notice a retardation of one (72 years) or two (144 years) degrees—a highly unlikely achievement without the advanced astronomical equipment that would be needed. So much more the ability to realize and verify a complete Zodiacal Age shift of 2,160 years. Even the pre-Diluvial Patriarchs with what scholars consider "fantastic" longevities—969 years for the record holder Methuselah and 930 for Adam—did not live long enough to observe a full zodiacal period. Noah, the hero of the Deluge, lived a mere 950 years; yet Sumerian recollections of the event named the zodiacal constellation—Leo—in which it had happened.

This was only part of the impossible knowledge possessed by the Sumerians. How could they have known all that they did? They themselves provided the answer: All that we know was taught to us by the Anunnaki—"Those Who From Heaven to Earth Came." And they, coming from another planet with a vast orbital period and a longevity in which

one year encompassed 3,600 of Earthlings', had no difficulty discerning Precession and devising the twelve-part Zodiac.

In a series of texts which formed the basis of ancient science and religion, and which were rendered later on in other tongues, including the biblical Hebrew, the Sumerians' tales of the Anunnaki—of the ancient gods—have been the stuff of which "mythology" was made. In the Western cultures the mythology that jumps first to mind is that of the Greeks; but it, as all the ancient mythologies and divine pantheons of all the nations—all over the world—stemmed from the original Sumerian beliefs and texts.

There was a time, the Sumerians told, when civilized Man was not yet on Earth, when animals were only wild and undomesticated and crops were not yet cultivated. At that long-ago time there arrived on Earth a group of fifty Anunnaki. Led by a leader whose name was E.A. (meaning "whose home is water"), they journeyed from their home planet NIBIRU ("planet of crossing") and, reaching Earth, splashed down in the waters of the Persian Gulf. A text known to scholars as the "myth" of *Ea and the Earth* describes how that first group waded ashore, finding themselves in a marshland. Their first task was to drain the marshes, clear river channels, check out food sources (found to be fish and fowl). They then began to make bricks from the clay of the soil and established the first-ever settlement on Earth by extraterrestrials. They named the habitat ERIDU, which meant "Home in the Faraway" or "Home away from home." That name is the origin of the name "Earth" in some of the oldest languages. The time: 445,000 years ago.

The astronauts' mission was to obtain gold by extracting it from the waters of the gulf—gold needed for survival on Nibiru; for there the planet was losing its atmosphere and thus also its internal heat, slowly endangering continued life on Nibiru. But the plan proved unworkable, and the leaders back home decided that gold could be obtained only the hard way—by mining it where it was in abundance, in southeastern Africa.

The new plan called for a substantial increase in the num-

ber of Anunnaki on Earth, and in time they numbered six hundred. There was also a need for an elaborate operation of shipping out from Earth the refined gold and bringing in varied supplies. For that three hundred additional Nibiruans were employed as IGI.GI ("Those Who Observe and See"), operating orbiting platforms and shuttlecraft. Nibiru's ruler, AN ("The Heavenly One"—Anu in Akkadian) came to Earth to supervise the expanded presence and operations. He brought along with him two of his children: his son EN.LIL ("Lord of the Command"), a strict disciplinarian, to serve as Chief of Operations; and a daughter, NIN.MAH ("Mighty Lady"), Chief Medical Officer.

The division of duties between the pioneer Ea and the newly arrived Enlil proved tricky, and at a certain moment of impasse Anu was willing to stay on earth and let one of his sons act as viceroy on Nibiru. In the end the three drew lots. Anu returned to reign on Nibiru; Enlil's lot was to stay in the area of the original landing and expand it to an E.DIN ("Home of the Righteous Ones"). His task was to establish additional settlements, each with a specific function (a spaceport, a Mission Control Center, a metallurgical center, a medical center, or as landing beacons). And Ea's lot was to organize the mining operations in southeastern Africa—a task for which he, as an outstanding scientist, was not unsuited.

That the task was within his competence did not mean that Ea liked the assignment away from the Edin. So to compensate him for the transfer he was given the title-name EN.KI— "Lord of Earth."

Enlil might have thought that it was just a gesture; Ea/Enki, however, took the title more seriously. Though both were sons of An, they were only half brothers. Ea/Enki was the Firstborn Son, and normally would have followed his father on the throne. But Enlil was a son born to Anu by a half sister of his; and according to the succession rules on Nibiru, that made Enlil the Legal Heir, even if not firstborn. Now the two half brothers found themselves on another planet, facing a potential conflict: If the mission to Earth

would become an extended affair—perhaps even a permanent colonization of another planet—who would be in supreme authority, the Lord of Earth or the Lord of the Command?

The matter became an acute problem for Enki in view of the presence on Earth of his son Marduk as well as Enlil's son Ninurta; for while the former was born to Enki by his official consort, the latter was born to Enlil (on Nibiru) by the half sister Ninmah (when both were unmarried; Enlil married Ninlil on Earth, Ninmah never married). And that gave Ninurta precedence over Marduk in the line of succession.

Unabashed philanderer that he was, Enki decided to remedy the situation by having sex with his half sister, too, hoping also to have a son by her. The lovemaking produced a daughter instead. Unrelenting, Enki lost no time in sleeping with the daughter as soon as she matured; but she, too, bore a daughter. Ninmah had to temporarily immobilize Enki to put an end to his conjugal attempts.

Though he could not attain a son by a half sister, Enki was not lacking other male offspring. In addition to MAR.DUK ("Son of the Pure Mound"), who had also come from Nibiru, there were the brothers NER.GAL ("Great Watcher"), GIBIL ("He of the Fire"), NIN.A.GAL ("Prince of the Great Waters"), and DUMU.ZI ("Son Who Is Life"). It is not certain that all of them were in fact mothered by Enki's official spouse, NIN.KI ("Lady Earth"); it is virtually certain that the sixth son, NIN.GISH.ZID.DA ("Lord of the Artifact/Tree of Life") was the result of a liaison between Enki and Enlil's granddaughter Ereshkigal when she was a passenger on his ship, on the way from the Edin to Africa. A Sumerian cylinder seal depicted Enki and his sons (Fig. 18).

Once Enlil had married his official consort, a young nurse who was given the epithet-name NIN.LIL ("Lady of the Command"), he never wavered in his fidelity to her. They had together two sons—the Moon god NANNAR ("The Bright One"), who was later known as *Sin* by the Semitic-

Figure 18

speaking peoples; and a younger son, ISH.KUR ("He of the Mountains"), who was better known by the name *Adad*— "The Beloved" son. This paucity of offspring, compared to Enki's clan, might explain why the three children of Nannar/ Sin and his spouse, NIN.GAL ("Great Lady"), were quickly included in the leadership of the Anunnaki, in spite of their being three generations removed from Anu. They were the above-mentioned ERESH.KI.GAL ("Mistress of the Great Land") and the twins UTU ("The Shiny One") and IN.ANNA ("An's Beloved")—the *Shamash* ("Sun god") and *Ishtar* (Astarte/Venus) of later pantheons.

At the peak of their presence on Earth the Anunnaki numbered six hundred, and the texts named quite a number of them—as often as not indicating their roles or functions. The very first text dealing with Enki's initial splashdown names some of his lieutenants and the tasks assigned to them. The governors of each of the settlements established by the Anunnaki were named, as were all ten ante-Diluvial rulers in the Edin. The female offspring born as a result of Enki's shenanigans were identified, as were their assigned husbands. Recalled by name were chamberlains and emissaries of the principal gods, as were male and female deities in charge of specific activities (e.g. Ninkashi, in charge of beer making).

Contrary to the total absence of a genealogy for Yahweh, the biblical God, the Anunnaki "gods" were fully cognizant of genealogies and the changing generations. There existed

as part of the secret knowledge kept in temples God Lists, in which the Anunnaki "gods" were listed in genealogical/generational succession. Some such discovered lists named no fewer than twenty-three Divine Couples who were the precursors of Anu (and thus of Enlil and Enki) on Nibiru. Some lists just named the Anunnaki gods in chronological succession; others carefully noted the name of the divine mother alongside the divine father's name, for who the mother was determined the offspring's status under the Rules of Succession.

Towering above them all was always a circle of twelve Great Gods, the forerunner of the Twelve Olympians of the Greek pantheon. Beginning with the Olden Gods, then changing with the times and the generations, the composition of the Circle of Twelve varied—but always remained twelve; as someone dropped off, another was added instead; as someone had to be elevated in rank, someone else had to be demoted.

The Sumerians depicted their gods wearing distinctive horned caps (Fig. 19), and we have suggested that the number of pairs of such horns reflected the numerical rank of the deities. The ranking in the original Sumerian pantheon began with 60 (the base number in Sumerian mathematics) for Anu, and continued with 50 for the legal successor Enlil, 40 for Enki, 30 for Nannar/Sin, 20 for Utu/Shamash, and 10 for Ishkur/Adad. The female component was given the ranks 55, 45, 35, and 25 for the spouses Antu, Ninlil, Ninki, and Ningal, then 15 for the unmarried Ninmah and 5 for the single Inanna/Ishtar; reflecting the generational changes, the latter in time attained the rank "15" and Ninmah dropped to 5.

It is noteworthy that the two contenders for the Succession on Earth, Ninurta and Marduk, were kept off the initial "Olympian" list. But when the contest heated up, the Council of the Gods recognized Ninurta as the legal successor and assigned to him the rank of 50—the same as that of his father Enlil. Marduk, on the other hand, was given the low rank 10.

These rankings were considered divine secrets, revealed

Figure 19

only to selected priestly "initiates." The tablets on which the "secret numbers of the gods" were inscribed (such as tablet K.170 from the temple of Nineveh) contained a strict prohibition against showing it to the *la mudu'u*—the "uninitiated." Frequently, information about the gods was recorded without naming them by their names; instead, their secret numbers were used, e.g. "the god 30" for Nannar/Sin.

The table in Fig. 20 identifies the Great Gods by parentage and rank, highlighting the twelve Great Gods.

But why *twelve*?

The answer, we believe, lies in another major problem that the Anunnaki faced once they changed their mission from a one-time mineral-extracting expedition to a long-term settlement with almost a thousand of them involved. From their viewpoint, they had come from a planet with a "normal" orbit to one that crazily runs around the Sun, orbiting the Sun 3,600 times in one (Nibiru) year (one orbital period). Besides the physical adjustments, there was a need somehow

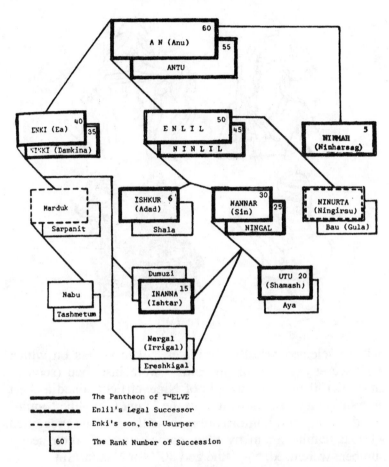

Figure 20

to relate Earthtime to Nibirutime. Establishing their sophisticated equipment at Mission Control Center in Nippur (a
facility called DUR.AN.KI—''Bond Heaven-Earth''), they
certainly became aware of the gradual retardation that we
call precession, and realized that the Earth, besides the orbital
fast year, also had another longer cycle—the 25,920 years it
took the Earth to return to the same heavenly spot, a cycle
that came to be known as the Great Year.

As depictions on cylinder seals (Fig. 21) show, the An-

Figure 21

unnaki considered the "family of the Sun" to consist of twelve members: the Sun (in the center), the Moon (for reasons which were given), the nine planets we know of at present, and one more—their own planet, Nibiru. To them this number, twelve, was a basic number to be applied in all celestial matters affecting the Bond Heaven-Earth, including the division of the starry circle around the Sun. Using their detailed sky charts, they grouped the stars in each sky segment into constellations. What shall they name them? Why not after their very own leaders?

Here was Ea, "Whose Home Is Water," who had splashed down to Earth in the waters of the Persian Gulf, who loved to sail the marshes in a boat, who filled the lakes with fish. They honored him by naming accordingly two constellations, those of the Waterman (Aquarius) and the Fishes (Pisces); in Sumerian times, he was so depicted on cylinder seals (Fig. 22a) and the priests that oversaw his worship were dressed as Fishmen (Fig. 22b). Enlil—forceful, strong-headed, and

Figures 22a, 22b, and 22c

frequently compared to a bull, was honored with naming his constellation as that of the Bull (Taurus). Ninmah, desired but never married, had the constellation Virgo named for her. Ninurta, often called Enlil's Foremost Warrior, was honored with the Bow—Sagittarius; Ea's firstborn, stubborn and hardheaded, was likened to a roaming Ram (Aries). And when the twins Utu/Shamash and Inanna/Ishtar were born, it was only befitting that a constellation, Gemini (the Twins), be named in their honor. (In recognition of Enlil's and Utu's roles in the Anunnaki's space activities, the Enlilite priests dressed as Eaglemen, Fig. 22c). As the hierarchial ranks changed and as second- and third-generation Anunnaki joined the scene on Earth, all the twelve zodiacal constellations were assigned to Anunnaki counterparts.

Not men, but the gods, devised the zodiac.

And the number, no matter what the changes, always had to add up to twelve.

After forty ''Repetitions'' (orbits) of Nibiru since the first arrival, the Anunnaki assigned to the gold mines mutinied. A text called *Atra Hasis* describes the events that preceded the mutiny, the mutiny itself, and its consequences. The most important consequence was the creation of The Adam: the text tells how Mankind was brought about. Encouraged by Enki, the mutiny was directed primarily against Enlil and his son NIN.UR.TA (''Lord Who Completes the Foundation''). Enlil demanded that the mutineers be given the maximum punishment; Enki described the impossibility of continuing the harsh toil; Anu sided with Enki. But the gold was still needed for survival; so how would it be obtained?

At the moment of impasse, Enki sprang on the Anunnaki leadership his astounding suggestion: Let us, he said, create a Primitive Worker who shall be capable of doing the work! When the amazed Council of the Gods asked how a new being could be created, Enki explained that the being he had in mind ''already exists''—a hominid that had evolved on Earth, but had not yet reached the evolutionary stage of the Anunnaki. All we have to do, he said, is to ''put the mark of the gods'' on them—to alter them genetically to resemble the Anunnaki.

The discussion and the suggested solution are echoed in the Bible:

> *And* Elohim *said:*
> *''Let us make Man in our image*
> *and after our likeness''*

—a being that would resemble the Anunnaki both physically and mentally. This being, Enki promised, ''will be charged with the service of the gods, that they might have their ease.'' Enticed by the prospect of relief from the hard toil, the gods agreed.

Several Sumerian texts describe how, with the help of Nin-

Figure 23

mah and after much trial and error, a *Lullu*—a "Mixed One"—was created. Satisfied that a "perfect model" had been attained, Ninmah raised him and shouted: "My hands have made it!"

She considered the moment to mark a momentous event. So should we—for, in the depiction of the moment by a Sumerian artist on a cylinder seal (Fig. 23), we are shown the most momentous event in the annals of Mankind: the moment when we, *Homo sapiens*, emerged on Earth.

Using the successful genetic combination, the slow process of making duplicates—a process we now call cloning—was started. The reproduction, involving the need for Anunnaki females to serve as Birth Goddesses, cloned the Primitive Worker in sets of seven males, seven females. The Bible (Genesis chapters 1 and 5) tells it thus:

> *On the day that* Elohim *created the Adam,*
> *in the likeness of* Elohim *he made him;*
> *Male and female created he them.*

Cloning was a slow process, requiring the service of the Birth Goddesses because the new being, as a hybrid, could not procreate on its own. So to speed it up Enki performed a second feat of genetic engineering—but this time on his

own initiative. Tinkering with what are now called chromosomes X and Y, he gave the human race the ability to procreate on its own. The Bible recorded the event in the tale of Adam and Eve in the Garden of Eden (the Sumerian E.DIN), in which Enki plays the role of the *Nachash*—a term translated "serpent" but which also means "He who knows/possesses secrets."

Though he had voted for the genetic experiment, Enlil did so reluctantly. Unlike the great scientist Enki, he was not carried away by the scientific challenge. Whimsically we might even imagine him saying, "We did not come to another planet to play God" . . . He was infuriated when Enki performed the second (unauthorized) genetic manipulation. "You have made the Adam to be like one of us," able to procreate, he shouted; one more step, and he would also partake of the fruit of the Tree of Life!

So Mankind was banished from the Garden of Eden, to fend for itself; but instead of withering, it proliferated and filled the Earth. Enlil's displeasure grew when young Anunnaki began to fraternize with the Daughters of Man, even had children with them. In the Bible (Genesis chapter 6) the story of the *Nefilim* ("Those Who Came Down"), the "sons of the *Elohim*" who intermarried with human females, serves as a preamble to the story of the Deluge, the explanation for the decision to wipe Mankind off the face of the Earth.

Enlil put his plan before the Council of the Gods. A great calamity, he said, is about to happen. On its next passage Nibiru will cause a huge tidal wave that will engulf the Earth. Let us not warn Mankind—let all flesh perish! The gods agreed and swore to secrecy. So did Enki; but he found a way to warn his faithful worshiper Ziusudra ("Noah" in the Bible) and instructed him to build the Ark to save his family and friends, as well as to preserve the "seed" of living animals.

The story of the Great Flood is one of the longest in the Bible; yet as long as it is, it is but a short version of much longer and more detailed Sumerian and Akkadian texts that

deal with this watershed event. In its aftermath even Enlil relented. Realizing that after everything that the Anunnaki had built on Earth had been destroyed, they needed Mankind as a partner to make Earth habitable again. With Enlil's consent, the Anunnaki began to advance Mankind culturally and technologically, in intervals that lasted 3,600 years (matching the orbital period of Nibiru). The culmination of the process was the great Sumerian civilization.

On the eve of the Deluge, the Anunnaki took to their craft to escape the calamity, watching the havoc and total destruction from Earth's skies. Not only Mankind perished: All that the Anunnaki had built in the past 432,000 years was wiped off the face of the Earth or buried under miles-thick layers of mud; and that included the spaceport they had in the E.DIN.

As soon as the tidal wave began to recede, they could bring their Earth-orbiting craft down on the Near East's highest peaks, the peaks of Ararat. As more of the dry land appeared, they could use the Landing Place—a vast stone platform that had been erected before the Flood in the Cedar Mountains of what is now Lebanon. But to resume the space operations they needed a spaceport; and the decision was made to erect it in the Sinai peninsula. The Landing Corridor, as before the Flood, was anchored on the conspicuous twin peaks of Mount Ararat; the Landing Place was incorporated; a new Mission Control Center (to replace the one that had been in pre-Diluvial Nippur) was selected; and two artificial twin peaks, to anchor the Landing Corridor's terminus, were erected—the two still-standing great pyramids at Giza in Egypt.

Concerned by the simmering rivalries between what has come to look like two distinct clans on Earth, the location of the spaceport and its auxiliary facilities assumed major importance. To minimize frictions, the de facto division of domains between Enlil in the Edin and Enki in the Abzu was formalized, the former and his descendants granted dominion over Asia and nearby parts of Europe, the latter the whole

African continent. That meant that the pre-Diluvial Landing Place and the new Mission Control Center were in Enlilite territory, and the great pyramids with their intricate guidance systems in Enki'ite hands. It was therefore resolved to place the area of the spaceport, the Sinai peninsula, in the neutral hands of Ninmah. To mark the event, she was given the title-epithet NIN.HAR.SAG—"Lady of the Mountainpeaks."

Our suggestion that the gods of Egypt were none other than Enki and his clan may seem far-fetched at first glance. Weren't their names, to start with, entirely different? The great Olden God of the Egyptians, for example, was called PTAH, "The Developer"; but that was also the meaning of Enki's Sumerian epithet NUDIMMUD, "The Maker of Artful Things." He was the Knower of Secrets, the Divine Serpent, in both pantheons; and (recalling his epithet "whose home is water") was depicted in both as the Divine Waterman (Figs. 14, 22), our Aquarius. In the Egyptian pantheon the Mistress of the Sinai was HATHOR, nicknamed "The Cow" in her old age; so too was Ninharsag nicknamed in Sumer as she grew old.

Enki's principal son and successor in Egypt was RA, "The Pure One," paralleling Marduk, "Son of the Pure Mound," in Mesopotamia. The many other similarities between the two have been expounded in *The Wars of Gods and Men*. So were the reasons for identifying the Egyptian god THOTH, a son of Ptah and keeper of divine secret knowledge, as the god Ningishzidda of the Sumerian texts.

In time Ptah/Enki handed over the reign over Egypt to his son Marduk/Ra; but the latter was not appeased. Reign over the *whole* Earth was his birthright, he kept asserting; and that led to conflicts with the Enlilites that we described as the Pyramid Wars. At one time—circa 8700 B.C. by our calculations—he was forced to leave Egypt; according to Manetho (an Egyptian priest who wrote down the history and prehistory of Egypt in Greek times) the reign was then assigned to Marduk's brother Thoth. Where did Marduk/Ra go? The possibility that he was sent back to Nibiru (the Egyptians called it Planet of Millions of Years) cannot be ruled out. An an-

cient Egyptian text recorded in pharaonic tombs, called *The Assignment of Functions to Thoth*, has Ra transferring powers to Thoth and designating Thoth as "Thoth, the Place Taker." "Thou shalt be in my place," Ra announces, "a Place Taker." Explaining where he is, Ra tells Thoth: "I am here in the sky, in my proper place." The fact that one segment of the absence, that of demigods, lasted 3,650 years—almost exactly the average 3,600 years of Nibiru's orbit—strongly suggests that that is where Ra/Marduk spent his absence from Earth. Texts, both Egyptian and Mesopotamian, that describe a tough space journey that became especially perilous near Saturn, may well have dealt with Ra/Marduk's return voyage to Earth.

The returning Ra/Marduk found an Earth that he could hardly recognize. In the intervening period, the Sumerian civilization had burst into full bloom. There, in addition to the expansion of the headquarters of Enlil and Enki into sacred precincts surrounded by teeming cities (Nippur and Eridu, respectively), Cities Of Man had been established. The newly created institution of Kingship was inaugurated in a new city, Kish, under the aegis of Ninurta. Nannar/Sin was given mastery over a new urban center called Ur. A sacred precinct built for a visit of Anu and Antu was expanded to become the city of Uruk (the biblical Erech) and was given as a gift to Inanna/Ishtar. The functions of the Priesthood were formalized; a calendar—the famed Calendar of Nippur—was introduced, based on sophisticated astronomical knowledge and official festivals. Started in 3760 B.C., it is still in use as the Hebrew calendar.

The returning Marduk must have cried out to his father and the Council of the Gods: And what about me?

He set his sights on a place not far from where the pre-Diluvial spaceport had been, and determined to make it into a *Bab-Ili*—"Gateway of the Gods" (hence its lasting name *Babylon*). It was to be a symbolic and actual expression of his supremacy.

What ensued is recalled in the Bible as the incident of the Tower of Babel; it took place in Shine'ar (the biblical name

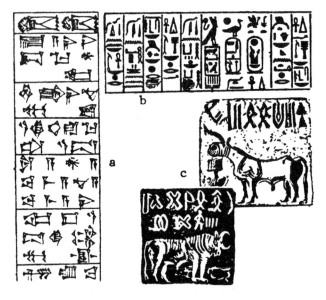

Figures 24a, 24b, and 24c

for Sumer). There the followers of the god of Babylon began to build "a tower whose head can reach the heavens"—a launch tower, we would say nowadays. "Let us make us a *Shem*," they said—not a "name" as is commonly translated, but the original meaning of the Sumerian source of the word *MU*—a rocketlike object. The time, by our calculations, was 3450 B.C.

Descending from the skies, the leader of the *Elohim* ordered the tower destroyed. Both the biblical version and the Mesopotamian texts report that it was in the aftermath of this incident that the *Elohim* decided to "confuse Mankind's language," to prevent Mankind from acting in unison. Until then "there was one language and one kind of words upon the whole Earth" (Genesis 11:1). Until then there was indeed one civilization, that of Sumer, with a single language and form of writing (Fig. 24a). In the aftermath of the incident at Babylon, a second civilization, the Nile Civilization (Egypt and Nubia), was established, with its own language

and script (Fig. 24b); and several centuries later, the third
civilization, that of the Indus Valley, was begun with its own
language and script (Fig. 24c), a script that is still undeciphered. Thus was Mankind alloted three Regions; the Fourth
Region was retained by the gods: the Sinai peninsula, where
the spaceport was.

Defied in Mesopotamia, Ra/Marduk returned to Egypt to
reassert his supremacy there, as the Great God of the new
civilization. The time was 3100 B.C. There was, of course,
the small problem of what to do with Thoth, who had been
the reigning deity in Egypt and Nubia while Ra/Marduk was
gone. Unceremoniously, he was sent away . . . In *The Lost
Realms* we have suggested that, taking along a group of his
African followers, he went all the way to the New World, to
become Quetzalcoatl, the Winged Serpent god. The first calendar instituted by him in Mesoamerica (the Long Count
calendar) began in the year 3113 B.C.; it was, we believe, the
precise date of the arrival in the New World of Thoth/Quet-
zalcoatl.

Still seething from his failure in Mesopotamia, the bitter
Marduk turned to settling other scores. During his absence a
divine "Romeo and Juliet"—his brother Dumuzi and In-
anna/Ishtar, the granddaughter of Enlil—fell in love and
were to be betrothed. The union was anathema to Ra/Mar-
duk; he was especially alarmed by Inanna's hopes to become
Mistress of Egypt through the marriage. When Marduk's emissaries tried to seize Dumuzi, he accidentally died as he tried
to escape. His death was blamed on Marduk.

Texts that have been discovered in several copies and versions provide details of the trial of Marduk and his punishment: to be buried alive in the Great Pyramid, which was
sealed tight to create a divine prison. With only air to breathe
but no food or water, Marduk was sentenced to die in that
colossal tomb. But his spouse and mother successfully appealed to Anu to commute the death sentence into one of
exile. Using the original construction plans, an escape shaft
was dug and blasted into the passages above the massive
plugs. The return of Marduk from certain death, his emer-

gence from his tomb, were aspects of the view that the texts—titled by early translators ''The Death and Resurrection of the Lord''—were precursors of the New Testament tale of the death, entombment, and resurrection of Jesus.

Sentenced to exile, Ra/Marduk became *Amen-Ra*, the unseen god. This time, however, he roamed the Earth. In an autobiographical text in which his return was prophesied, Marduk described his wanderings thus:

> *I am the divine Marduk, a great god.*
> *I was cast off for my sins.*
> *To the mountains I have gone,*
> *in many lands I have been a wanderer.*
> *From where the sun rises*
> *to where it sets I went.*

And wherever he roamed, he kept asking the Gods of Fate: ''Until when?''

The answer regarding his Fate, he realized, came from the heavens. The Age of the Bull, the age zodiacally belonging to Enlil and his clan, was ending. The dawn was nearing when the Sun would rise on the first day of spring, the day of the New Year in Mesopotamia, in the zodiacal constellation of the Ram (Aries)—*his* constellation. The celestial cycle of Fates augurs his, Marduk's, supremacy!

Not everyone agreed. Was it just so because of time calculations, or an observable celestial phenomenon? Marduk could not care less; he launched a march on Mesopotamia while his son, Nabu, organized followers to invade the Sinai and seize the spaceport. The escalating conflict is described in a text known as the *Erra Epos*; it tells how, seeing no other choice, the gods opposing Marduk used nuclear weapons to obliterate the spaceport (and, as a sideshow, the unfaithful cities of Sodom and Gomorrah).

But Fate intervened on the side of Marduk. The prevailing western winds carried the deathly nuclear cloud eastward, toward Sumer. Babylon, farther north, was spared. But in

southern Mesopotamia the Evil Wind caused sudden death and lasting desolation. Sumer's great capital, Ur, was a place where wild dogs roamed.

And so, in spite of the extraordinary efforts of Marduk's opponents, the Age of the Ram indeed ushered in the rise of Babylon.

4

BETWEEN FATE
AND DESTINY

Was it Fate, or was it Destiny, that led Marduk by an unseen hand through all his troubles and tribulations over many millennia to his final goal: supremacy on Earth?

Not many languages have such a choice of words for that "something" that predetermines the outcome of events before they happen, and even in the English language many would be hard put to explain the difference. The best dictionaries (such as *Webster's*) explain the one term by the other, regarding as synonyms for both "doom," "lot," and "fortune." But in the Sumerian language, and thus in Sumerian philosophy and religion, there was a clear distinction between the two. *Destiny*, NAM, was the predetermined course of events that was *unalterable*. *Fate* was NAM.TAR— a predetermined course of events that *could be altered*; literally, TAR, to cut, break, disturb, change.

The distinction was not a matter of mere semantics; it went to the core of things, affecting and dominating the affairs of gods and men, lands and cities. Was something that was about to happen, even something that had happened—a Destiny, the outcome (and, if you will, the destination to which it leads) unalterable; or was it a combination of chance events, or willed decisions, or temporary ups or downs that might or might not be fatal, that another chance event or a prayer or a change in a lifestyle might lead to a different end result? And if the latter, what might have been different?

The fine line distinguishing between the two may be blurred today, but it was a difference well-defined in Sumerian and biblical times. For the Sumerians, Destiny began

in the heavens, starting with the preordained orbital paths of the planets. Once the Solar System begot its shape and composition after the Celestial Battle, the planetary orbits became everlasting Destinies; the term and concept could then be applied to the future course of events on Earth, starting with the gods who had celestial counterparts.

In the biblical realm, it was Yahweh who controlled both Destinies and Fates, but while the former was predetermined and unalterable, the latter (Fate) could be affected by human decisions. Because of the former powers, the course of future events could be foretold years, centuries, and even millennia earlier, as when Yahweh revealed to Abraham the future of his descendants, including the sojourn of four hundred years in Egypt (Genesis 15:13–16). How that sojourn would come about (it began with a search for food during a great famine) was a matter of Fate; that the sojourn would begin with an unexpected welcome (because Joseph, through a series of consecutive occurrences, became Overseer over all of Egypt) was a matter of Fate; but that the sojourn (after a period of enslavement) would end with a liberating Exodus at a predetermined time was a Destiny, preordained by Yahweh.

Because they were called to prophecy by God, the biblical prophets could foretell the future of kingdoms and countries, of cities and kings and individuals. But they made it clear that their prophecies were merely expressions of divine decisions. "Thus sayeth Yahweh, Lord of Hosts," was a frequent way in which the Prophet Jeremiah began as the future of kingdoms and rulers was foretold. "So sayeth the Lord Yahweh," the Prophet Amos announced.

But when it came to Fates, the free will and free choice of people and nations could come and did come into play. Unlike Destinies, Fates could be changed and punishments could be averted if righteousness replaced sin, if piety replaced profanity, if justice prevailed over injustice. "It is not the death of the evildoer that I seek, but that the wicked shall turn from his ways and live," the Lord God told the Prophet Ezekiel (33:11).

The distinction made by the Sumerians between Fate and

Destiny, and how they can both play a role even in the life of a single individual, becomes apparent in the life story of Gilgamesh. He was, as we have mentioned, the son of Uruk's high priest and the goddess Ninsun. As he grew older and began to contemplate issues of life and death, he posed the question to his godfather, the god Utu/Shamash:

> *In my city man dies; oppressed is my heart.*
> *Man perishes, heavy is my heart . . .*
> *Man, the tallest, cannot stretch to heaven;*
> *Man, the widest, cannot cover the Earth.*
> *Will I too 'peer over the wall'?*
> *Will I too be fated thus?*

The answer of Utu/Shamash was not encouraging. "When the gods created Mankind," he said, "death to Mankind they allotted; Life they retained in their own keeping." This is your Destiny; so, while you are alive and what you do in the meantime is a Fate that you can change or affect, enjoy it and make the most of it—

> *Let full be thy belly, Gilgamesh;*
> *Make thou merry by day and night!*
> *Of each day, make a feast of rejoicing;*
> *Day and night, dance thou and play!*
> *Let thy garments be sparkling fresh,*
> *Bathe in water, let thy head be washed.*
> *Pay heed to the little one who holds thy hand,*
> *Let thy spouse delight in your bosom.*
> *This is the fate of Mankind.*

Receiving this answer, Gilgamesh realized that what he must do is take some drastic action to change his Destiny, not merely his Fate; otherwise, he would meet the same end as any mortal. With his mother's reluctant blessing, he embarked on the journey to the Landing Place in the Cedar Mountains, there to join the gods. But Fate intervened, again and again. First it was in the shape of Huwawa, the robotic

guardian of the Cedar Forest, then through the lusting of Inanna/Ishtar for the king and the rebuff that led to the slaying of the Bull of Heaven. The role of Fate—*Namtar*—was recognized and considered by Gilgamesh and his companion Enkidu right then, even right after the slaying of Huwawa. The epic text relates how the two comrades sit and contemplate the expected punishment. As the actual slayer, Enkidu ponders what his fate will be. Gilgamesh comforts him: Worry not, he says; the "Adjurer" Namtar indeed can devour—but he also "lets the caught bird go back to its place, lets the caught man return to the bosom of his mother." Falling into the hands of Namtar is not an unalterable occurrence; as often as not, Fate reverses itself.

Refusing to give up, Gilgamesh embarked on a second journey, this time to the spaceport in the Sinai peninsula. His troubles and tribulations on the way were countless, yet he persevered. At last he managed to obtain the fruit that would have given him eternal youth; but in the end a serpent snatched it from him as the weary Gilgamesh fell asleep, and he returned to Uruk empty-handed, there to die.

A series of *What if?* questions naturally come to mind. What if things had gone differently in the Cedar Mountains— would Gilgamesh have succeeded to ascend heavenward and join the gods on their planet? What if he had not fallen asleep and kept the Plant of Everlasting Youth?

A Sumerian text titled by scholars *The Death of Gilgamesh* provides an answer. The end, it explains, was preordained; there was no way that Gilgamesh, taking his Fate into his own hands over and over again, could have changed his Destiny. The text provides this conclusion by reporting an omen-dream of Gilgamesh that contained a prediction of his end. Here is what Gilgamesh is told:

> *O Gilgamesh,*
> *this is the meaning of the dream:*
> *The great god Enlil, father of the gods,*
> *had decreed thy destiny.*

Thy fate for kingship he determined;
For eternal life he has not destined thee.

The Fate of Gilgamesh, he is told, has been overridden by Destiny. He was fated to be a king; he was not destined to avoid death. And so destined, Gilgamesh is described dying. "He who was firm of muscle, lies unable to rise . . . He who had ascended mountains, lies, rises not." "On the bed of Namtar he lies, rises not."

The text lists all the good happenings that Gilgamesh had experienced—kingship, victories in battle, a blessed family, faithful servants, beautiful garments; but recognizing the interplay of Fate and Destiny, concludes by explaining to Gilgamesh: Both "the light and the darkness of Mankind were granted to thee." But in the end, because Destiny has overridden Fate, "Gilgamesh, the son of Ninsun, lies dead."

The *What if?* question can be expanded from one individual to Mankind as a whole.

What would have been the course of events on Earth (and elsewhere in the Solar System) were Ea's original plan to obtain gold from the waters of the Persian Gulf to succeed? At a crucial turn of events, Anu, Enlil, and Ea drew lots to see who would rule Nibiru, who would go to the mines in southeast Africa, who would be in charge of the expanded Edin. Ea/Enki went to Africa and, encountering there the evolving hominids, could tell the gathered gods: The Being that we need, *it exists*—all that we have to do is put on it our genetic mark!

The *Atra Hasis* text, brought together from several renditions and many fragments by W. G. Lambert and A. R. Millard, described the fateful moment thus:

The gods had clasped hands together,
had cast lots and had divided.

Would the feat of genetic engineering have taken place had either Anu or Enlil been the one to go to southeastern Africa?

Would we have shown up on our planet anyway, through evolution alone? Probably—for that is how the Anunnaki (from the same seed of life!) had evolved on Nibiru, but far ahead of us. But on Earth we came about through genetic engineering, when Enki and Nimah jumped the gun on evolution and made Adam the first "test tube baby."

The lesson of the *Epic of Gilgamesh* is that Fate cannot change Destiny. The emergence of *Homo sapiens* on Earth, we believe, was a matter of Destiny, a final outcome that might have been delayed or reached otherwise, but undoubtedly reached. Indeed, we believe that even though the Anunnaki deemed their coming to Earth their own decision for their own needs, that too, we believe, was preordained, destined by a cosmic plan. And equally so, we believe, will be Mankind's Destiny: to repeat what the Anunnaki had done to us by going to another planet to start the process all over again.

One who understood the connection between Fate and the twelve zodiacal constellations was Marduk himself. They constituted what we have termed Celestial Time, the link between Divine Time (the orbital period of Nibiru) and Earthly Time (the Year, months, seasons, days, and nights resulting from the Earth's orbit, tilt, and revolution about its own axis). The heavenly signs that Marduk had invoked— the arrival of the Zodiacal Age of the Ram—were signs in the realm of Fate. What he needed to solidify his supremacy, to eliminate from it the notion that, as Fate, it could be changed or revised or reversed, was a Celestial Destiny. And to that aim he ordered what can be considered the most audacious falsification ever.

We are talking about the most sacred and basic text of the ancient peoples: the *Epic of Creation*, the core and bedrock of their faith, religion, science. Sometimes called by its opening lines *Enuma elish (When in the Heights of Heaven)*, it was a tale of events in the heavens that involved celestial gods and a Celestial Battle, the favorable outcome of which made possible all the good things on Earth, including the

Figure 25

coming into being of Mankind. Without exception the text was viewed by the scholars who began to piece it together from many fragments as a celestial myth, an allegory of the eternal fight between good and evil. The fact that wall sculptures discovered in Mesopotamia depicted a winged (i.e. celestial) god fighting a winged (i.e. celestial) monster (Fig. 25) solidified the notion that here was an ancient forerunner of the tale of St. George and the Dragon. Indeed, some of the early translations of the partial text titled it *Bel and the Dragon*. In those texts, the Dragon was called Tiamat and Bel ("the Lord") was none other than Marduk.

It was only in 1876 that George Smith, working in the British Museum on piecing together fragments of inscribed clay tablets from Mesopotamia, published the master work *The Chaldean Genesis* that suggested the existence of a Babylonian story that paralleled the creation parts of Genesis in the Bible; and then the Museum's Keeper of Babylonian Antiquities, L. W. King, followed with the authoritative work *The Seven Tablets of Creation* to establish conclusively the correlation between the biblical seven days of creation and the earlier Mesopotamian sources.

But if that was the case, how could the Babylonian text still be called an allegory? For doing so would also catego-

rize the tale in Genesis as an allegory and not an unalterable Divine Act that has been a bedrock of monotheism and Judeo-Christian beliefs.

In our 1976 book *The Twelfth Planet* we have suggested that neither the Mesopotamian text nor its condensed biblical version was myth or allegory. They were based, we suggested, on a most sophisticated cosmogony that, based on advanced science, described the creation of *our* Solar System stage by stage; and then the appearance of a stray planet from outer space that was gradually drawn into our Solar System, resulting in a collision between it and an olden member of the Sun's family. The ensuing Celestial Battle between the invader—"Marduk"—and the olden planet—Tiamat—led to the destruction of Tiamat. Half of it broke up into bits and pieces that became a Hammered Bracelet; the other half, shunted to a new orbit, became the planet Earth, carrying with it Tiamat's largest satellite that we call the Moon. And the invader, attracted into the center of our Solar System and slowed down by the collision, became permanently the twelfth member of our Solar System.

In the subsequent companion book *Genesis Revisited* (1990), we showed that all the advances in our celestial knowledge corroborated the Sumerian tale—a tale which explained satisfactorily the history of our Solar System, the enigma of Earth's continents starting only on one side with an immense gap (the Pacific basin) on the other side, the origin of the Asteroid Belt and the Moon, the reason for Uranus lying on its side and Pluto having an odd orbit, and on and on. The extra knowledge we have gained through the study of comets, the use of the Hubble telescope, and the probes of the Moon (manned) and other planets in our Solar System (by unmanned spacecraft) continue to corroborate the Sumerian data as we have understood it.

By calling the cosmogony underlying the *Epic of Creation* Sumerian, rather than Babylonian, we provide a clue to the true source and nature of the text. The discovery of fragments of an earlier *Sumerian* version of *Enuma elish* convinced scholars that the *Epic of Creation* was originally a Sumerian

text, in which the invading planet was called NIBIRU, not "Marduk." They are now convinced that the extant Babylonian version was a deliberate forgery, intended to equate the Marduk who was on Earth with the celestial/planetary "god" who changed the makeup of our heavens, gave our Solar System its present shape, and—in a manner of speaking—created the Earth and all that was on it. That included Mankind, for according to the Sumerian original version it was Nibiru, coming from some other part of the universe, that brought with it and *imparted to Earth during the collision* the "Seed of Life."

(For that matter, it should be realized that the illustration so long deemed to represent Marduk battling the Dragon is also all wrong. It is a depiction from Assyria, where the supreme god was Ashur, and not Babylon; the deity is depicted as an Eagleman, which indicates an Enlilite being; the divine cap he wears has three pairs of horns, indicating the rank of 30, which was not Marduk's rank; and his weapon is the forked lightning, which was the divine weapon of Ishkur/Adad, Enlil's—not Enki's—son.)

No sooner did Marduk seize the sovereignty in Babylon, than the pivotal New Year rites were changed, to require the public reading (on the festival's fourth evening) of *Enuma elish* in its new, Babylonian, version; in it the supremacy of Marduk on Earth only paralleled his supremacy in the heavens, as the planet with the greatest orbital path, the one that embraces all the others in its loop.

The key to this distinction was the term "Destiny." That was the term used to describe the orbital paths. The everlasting, unchanging orbit was a planet's Destiny; and that is what Marduk was granted according to *Enuma elish.*

Once one realizes that this is the meaning and significance of the ancient term for "orbits," one can follow the steps by which the Destiny was attained by Marduk. The term is used, for the first time in the text, in connection with the principal satellite of Tiamat (which the text calls Kingu). At first it is only one of Tiamat's eleven satellites (moons); but as it "grows in stature," it becomes the "leader of her host."

Once the only large planet and a consort of Apsu (the Sun), Tiamat "grew haughty" and was not too pleased to see other celestial gods appear in pairs: Lahmu and Lahamu (Mars and Venus) between her and the Sun (where there had been before only the Sun's messenger Mummu/Mercury), and the pairs Kishar and Anshar (Jupiter and Saturn, the latter with his messenger Gaga/Pluto); then Anu and Nudimmud (Uranus and Neptune). Tiamat and her group of moons on the one hand and the new planets on the other hand, in a still unstable Solar System, begin to encroach on each other's domains. The others get especially concerned when Tiamat "unlawfully" extends to Kingu, her largest satellite, the privileged status of having an orbit of his own—of becoming a full-fledged planet:

> *She has set up an Assembly . . .*
> *She has borne monster-gods;*
> *Withal eleven of this kind she has brought forth.*

> *From among the gods who formed her Assembly*
> *she has elevated Kingu, her firstborn,*
> *made him chief among the gods;*
> *She exalted Kingu, in their midst made him great . . .*

> *She gave him a Tablet of Destinies,*
> *she fastened it upon his chest, [saying:]*
> *"Now the command shall never be altered,*
> *the decree shall be unchangeable!"*

Unable to withstand the "raging host" of Tiamat by themselves, the celestial gods see salvation coming from outside the Solar Syatem. As was the case when The Adam was created when an impasse was faced, so was it in the primordial heavens: It was Ea ("Nudimmud," the "Artful Creator" in Sumerian) who brought off the saving creature. As the outermost planet, facing the "Deep"—outer space—he attracts a stranger, a new planet. Passing in the vicinity of our Solar System as a result of a catastrophe, a cosmic ac-

cident far out, the new planet is the result of Fate, and does not yet orbit our Sun—he has no Destiny as yet:

> *In the Chamber of Fates,*
> *the Hall of Designs,*
> *Bel, most wise, wisest of the gods,*
> *was engendered;*
> *In the heart of the Deep was the god created.*

It is noteworthy that the newly arrived planet, a celestial god, is called even in the Babylonian rendition *Bel*, "The Lord," and in the Assyrian version the word "Bel" is replaced by the word "Ashur." The Babylonian version—the most commonly used nowadays—repeats however the last line, and in this second time renders it: "In the heart of the pure Deep was *Marduk* created," the addition of the word *pure* intended no doubt to explain the origin of the name MAR.DUK, "Son of the Pure Place." (This double rendition is one of the clues exposing the falsification).

Beyond Ea (Neptune), Anu (Uranus) welcomed the invader. The increasing gravitational pull made the invader sprout four moons, as well as pull him more to the Solar System's midst. By the time it reached Anshar (Saturn), and sprouted three more moons, the invader was already inexorably caught in the Sun's gravitational pull. His course curved inward (Fig. 26), starting to form an orbital path around the Sun. *The invader, in other words, was envisioning a Destiny for himself!*

Once he was "kissed" by Anshar/Saturn,

> *The gods, his forebears,*
> *the destiny of Bel then determined;*
> *They set him on the path,*
> *the way to success and attainment.*

The path thus ordained for him, Bel found out, was set on a collision course with Tiamat. He was willing to accept the

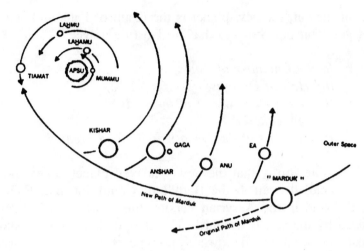

Figure 26

challenge but on a condition. Becoming now Marduk (both celestial and on Earth), he said to Anshar:

> *Lord of the gods,*
> *determiner of the great gods' destinies:*
> *If I am indeed to be your Avenger,*
> *to vanquish Tiamat and save your lives,*
> *convene the divine Assembly,*
> *proclaim supreme my Destiny!*

The celestial gods accepted Marduk's conditions. "For Marduk, their Avenger, they decreed a destiny;" and that Destiny, that orbit, "shall be unequaled." Now then, they said—go and slay Tiamat!

The ensuing Celestial Battle is described in the fourth tablet of *Enuma elish.* Unavoidably set on a collision course, Marduk and Tiamat cast lightnings, blazing flames, and gravitational nets against each other, "shaking with fury." As they neared each other—Tiamat moving like all planets in a counterclockwise direction, Marduk onrushing in a clockwise path—it was one of Marduk's satellite moons that struck

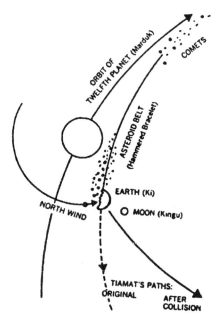

Figure 27

Tiamat first; then another and another of his moons struck
Tiamat—"tearing into her insides, splitting her up." A "divine lightning," an immense electrical bolt, then shot out
from Marduk into the fissure, and "the life-breath of Tiamat
extinguished."

The intact Marduk swept by, made an orbital round, and
returned to the site of the battle. This time he himself struck
Tiamat with far-reaching consequences. One half of her he
smashed into bits and pieces to become the Great Band (the
Asteroid Belt); the other half, struck by Marduk's moon
named North Wind, was shunted to a new place in the heavens, to become Earth in a new orbital path. Its Sumerian
name, KI (from which the Akkadian/Hebrew "Gei" and the
Greek "Gaea" come) meant "the cleaved one" (Fig. 27).

As Tiamat's own moons were dispersed—many changing
direction to clockwise (retrograde) orbits—a special fate was

determined by Marduk for the largest of Tiamat's moons, Kingu:

> *He took from him the Tablet of Destinies,*
> *not rightfully Kingu's,*
> *sealed it with a seal*
> *and fastened it to his own breast.*

Now, finally, Marduk had obtained a permanent, unalterable Destiny—an orbital path that, ever since, has kept bringing the erstwhile invader again and again to the site of the Celestial Battle where Kingu had once been. Together with Marduk, and counting Kingu (our Moon) for it had possessed a Destiny, the Sun and its family reached the count of twelve.

It was this count, we suggest, that determined twelve to be the celestial number, and thus the twelve stations ("houses") of the zodiac, twelve months of the year, twelve double-hours in a day-night cycle, twelve tribes of Israel, twelve apostles of Jesus.

The Sumerians considered the abode (called "cult center" by most scholars) of Enlil as the Navel of the Earth, the place from which other key locations were equidistant, the epicenter of concentric divinely ordained sites. Best known by its later Akkadian/Semitic name Nippur, its Sumerian name was NIBRU.KI—"The Place of the Crossing," representing on Earth the Celestial Place of Crossing, the site of the Celestial Battle to which Nibiru keeps returning every 3,600 years.

Functioning as a Mission Control Center, Nippur was the site of the DUR.AN.KI, the "Bond Heaven-Earth" from which the space operations of the Anunnaki were controlled, and at which the sky-maps, and all the formulas concerning the celestial motions of the members of our Solar System and the tracking of Divine Time, Celestial Time, and Earthly Time and their interrelationships, were maintained and calculated.

This tracking of what was deemed to be unalterable orbital

paths was conducted with the aid of the Tablets of Destinies. We can glimpse their functions and the sacred chamber where they whirred and hummed by reading what happened when their operation had come to a sudden halt. The Sumerian text describing that, named by translators *The Myth of Zu*, deals with the scheming of the god Zu (his full name, later discoveries revealed, was AN.ZU—"The Knower of Heavens") to usurp the Bond Heaven-Earth by seizing and carrying off the Tablets of Destinies. Everything came to a standstill; "the lighted brightness petered out; silence prevailed"; and in the heavens those who manned the shuttlecraft and spacecraft, "the Igigi, in space, were confounded." (The epic tale ends with the overpowering of Zu by Enlil's son Ninurta, the reinstallation of the Tablets of Destinies in the Duranki, and the execution of Zu).

The distinction between an unalterable Destiny and a Fate that could be altered or averted was expressed in a two-part *Hymn to Enlil,* that described both his powers as a decreer of Fates and as a pronouncer of Destinies:

Enlil:
In the heavens he is the Prince,
On Earth he is the Chief.
His command is far-reaching,
His utterance is lofty and holy;
The shepherd Enlil decrees the Fates.

Enlil:
His command in the heights made the heavens tremble,
down below he made the Earth quake.
He pronounces destinies unto the distant future,
His decrees are unchangeable.
He is the Lord who knows the destiny of the Land.

Destinies, the Sumerians believed, were of a celestial nature. As high-ranking as Enlil was, his pronouncements of unalterable Destinies were not the result of his own decisions or plans. The information was made known to him; he was

a "lord who knows the Destiny of the land," he was a "trustworthy called-one"—not a human prophet but a divine prophet.

That was quite different from the instances when—in consultation with other gods—he decreed Fates. Sometimes he consulted just his trusted vizier, Nusku:

> *When in his awesomeness he decrees the fates—*
> *his command, the word that is in his own heart—*
> *to his exalted vizier, the chamberlain Nusku,*
> *does he make known, him he consults.*

Not only Nusku, Enlil's chamberlain, but also his spouse Ninlil is depicted in this hymn as participating in deciding Fates:

> *Mother Ninlil, the holy wife,*
> *whose words are gracious . . .*
> *The eloquent one whose speech is elegant,*
> *has seated herself by your side . . .*
> *She speaks eloquently with you,*
> *whispers words at your side,*
> *decrees the fates.*

Fates, the Sumerians believed, were made, decreed and altered on Earth; and in spite of the hymnal words of adoration or minimal consultation, it appears that the determination of Fates—including that of Enlil himself—was achieved by a process that was more democratic, more akin to that of a constitutional monarchy. The powers of Enlil seemed to stem not only from above, from Anu and Nibiru, but also from below, from an Assembly of the Gods (a kind of parliament or congress). The most crucial decisions—fateful decisions—were made at a Council of the Great Gods, a kind of Cabinet of Ministers where discussions sometimes became debates and as often as not turned into heated exchanges . . .

The references to the Council and the Assembly of the

Anunnaki gods are numerous. The creation of The Adam was a subject so discussed; so was the decision to wipe Mankind off the face of the Earth at the time of the Deluge. The latter clearly states that ''Enlil opened his mouth to speak and addressed the Assembly of the gods.'' The suggestion to annihilate Mankind was opposed by Enki, who, having failed to sway the assembly, ''got fed up with the sitting in the Assembly of the Gods.'' We read that later on, as the gods were orbiting the Earth in their spacecraft, observing the havoc down below, Ishtar bewailed what she saw and wondered how she could have voted for the annihilation of Mankind: ''How could I, in the Assembly of the Gods, I myself give evil counsel?''

And after the Deluge, when the remnants of Mankind began to fill the Earth again and the Anunnaki started to give Mankind civilization and institute Kingship as a way to deal with the growing human masses,

> *The great Anunnaki who decree Fates*
> *sat exchanging their counsels regarding the land.*

This manner of determining Fates was not limited to the affairs of Man; it also applied to the affairs of the gods themselves. Thus, when Enlil, in the early times of arrival on Earth, took a liking to a young Anunnaki female and had sex with her over her objections, Enlil was sentenced into banishment first by ''the fifty Senior Gods sitting in assembly,'' and then by the ''Fate-decreeing gods, the seven of them.''

Such was the manner, according to the Babylonian version of *Enuma elish*, that the Destiny of Marduk, to be supreme on Earth (and in the celestial counterpart), was confirmed. In that text the Assembly of the Gods is described as a gathering of Senior Gods, coming from various places (and perhaps not only from Earth, for in addition to Anunnaki the delegates also included Igigi). The number of those gathered was fifty—a number matching the numerical rank of Enlil. In the Akkadian texts they were designated as *Ilani rabuti sha mu-*

shimu shimati—"Senior/Great Gods who determine Fates."

Describing how such Senior Gods gathered to proclaim Marduk's supremacy, *Enuma elish* paints a scene of camaraderie, of friends who had not seen each other for quite some time. They arrived at a special Place of Assembly; "they kissed one another . . . There was conversation; they sat down to banquet; they ate festive bread, they drank choice wine." And then the camaraderie turned solemn as the "Seven Gods of Destiny" entered the Assembly Hall and sat down to start the business at hand.

For unexplained reasons, Marduk was tested for his magical powers. Show us, the gathered Anunnaki said, how you "can command to destroy as well as command to create!"

They formed a circle and "placed in it the images of the constellations." The term, *Lamashu*, undoubtedly means the images/symbols of the zodiac. "Open thy mouth," they said, "let the images vanish! Speak again, and let the constellations reappear!"

Obliging, Marduk performed the miracle:

> *He spoke, and the constellations vanished;*
> *He spoke again, and the images were restored.*
>
> *When the gods, his elders,*
> *saw the power of his utterance,*
> *they rejoiced, they proclaimed:*
> *"Marduk is supreme!"*

"They bestowed on him the scepter, the throne and the royal robe"—a most resplendent robe, as Babylonian depictions showed (Fig. 28). "From this day," they announced, "thy decree shall be unrivaled, thy command as that of Anu . . . No one among the gods shall transgress thy boundaries."

While the Babylonian text suggests that the supremacy of Marduk was tested, confirmed, and pronounced in one session, other texts that concern the decision-making process suggest that the Assembly stage at which fifty Senior Gods participated was followed by a separate stage of a meeting

Figure 28

of the Seven Great Gods Who Judge; and then the actual
pronouncement of the decision, of the Fate or the Destiny,
was made by Enlil in consultation with or after approval by
Anu. Indeed, the need for this stage-by-stage procedure and
the final pronouncement by Enlil in behalf of Anu was recognized even by the followers of Marduk. The renowned
Babylonian king Hammurabi, in the preamble to his famous
law code, exalted the supremacy of his god Marduk with
these words:

> *Lofty Anu,*
> *Lord of the gods who from heaven to Earth came,*
> *and Enlil, Lord of heaven and Earth*
> *who determines the destinies of the land,*
> *Determined for Marduk, the firstborn of Enki,*
> *the Enlil-functions over all mankind.*

Such a transfer of Enlil's authority to Marduk, the Babylonian texts asserted, was executed and symbolized by the

bestowal on Marduk of the fifty names. The last and most important of the power-names bestowed on him was that of *Nibiru*—the very name of the planet whom the Babylonians renamed Marduk.

Assemblies of the gods were sometimes called not to proclaim new Fates, but to ascertain what had been determined at an earlier time, on the Tablets of Destinies.

Biblical statements reflect not only the royal custom of writing things down on a scroll or tablet and then sealing the document as preserved evidence; the custom was attributed to (and undoubtedly learned from) the gods. The culmination of those references is found in the Song of Moses, his testament and prophecy before he died. Extolling the almighty Yahweh, and his capacity to proclaim and foresee Destinies, Moses quotes the Lord as saying of the future:

> *Lo and behold:*
> *It is a secret with me hidden,*
> *stored and sealed within my treasures.*

Hittite texts discovered in the royal library of their capital Hattushas contained tales of conflict between the gods that had certainly served as a proximate source of Greek myths. In those texts the names of the Olden Gods are given as had been known from Sumerian times (such as Anu, Enlil, and Enki); or in Hittite for gods known from the Sumerian pantheon (such as *Teshub*, "The Wind Blower," for Ishkur/Adad); or sometimes for deities whose identity remains obscure. Two epic songs pertain to gods called Kumarbis and Illuyankas. In the first instance, Teshub demanded that the *Tablets of Fate*—"the old tablets with the words of Fate"—be recovered from Enki's abode in southeastern Africa, and brought to the Assembly of the Gods. In the other, after conflict and competition, the gods met in the Assembly to have their order and ranks established—an order and ranks that were pictorially depicted on the rock walls of the sacred sanctuary now known as Yazilikaya (Fig. 29).

Figure 29

But without doubt one of the most crucial, longest, bitterest, and literally fateful was the Assembly of the Gods where it was determined to approve the use of nuclear weapons to vaporize the spaceport in the Sinai peninsula. Using primarily the long and detailed record known as the *Erra Epos*, we have reconstructed the unfolding events, identified the protagonists and antagonists, and rendered almost verbatim (in *The Wars of Gods and Men*) the proceedings of the Assembly. The unintended result, as has already been mentioned, was the demise of Sumer and the end of life in its cities.

The occurrence is also one of the clearest if tragic examples of how Fate and Destiny could be interwoven.

Hardest hit in Sumer was its glorious capital, Ur, seat and center of its people's beloved god Nannar/Sin (the Moon god) and his spouse, Ningal. The lamentation texts (*Lamentation Over the Destruction of Sumer and Ur, Lamentation Over the Destruction of Ur*) describe how, when it was realized that the Evil Wind bearing the cloud of death was wafting toward Sumer, Nannar/Sin rushed to his father Enlil with a plea for help, some divine miracle to avert the calamity from Ur. Was it not, he asked his father, unthinkable to see this pride of Ur, a city throughout renowned, perish? He appealed to Anu: "Utter, 'It is enough!' " He appealed to Enlil: "Pronounce a favorable Fate!" But Enlil saw no way to change the onrushing end.

In desperation Nannar/Sin insisted that the gods meet in Assembly. As the senior Anunnaki seated themselves, Nannar/Sin cried his eyes out to Anu, to Enlil made supplica-

tions. "Let not my city be destroyed, verily I said to them,"
Nannar/Sin later recorded. "Let not the people perish!"

But the response, coming from Enlil, was harsh and decisive:

> *Ur was granted Kingship;*
> *Eternal reign it was not granted.*

5

OF DEATH AND RESURRECTION

The lesson of the destruction of Sumer and Ur was that chance and alterable Fate cannot supersede unalterable Destiny. But what about the other way—can a Fate, no matter by whom decreed, be superseded by Destiny?

The issue had certainly been pondered in antiquity, for otherwise what was the reason for prayers and supplications that had begun then, of the admonitions by the Prophets for righteousness and repentance? The biblical Book of Job raises the question whether Fate—to be afflicted to the point of hopelessness—shall prevail even if Job's righteousness and piety had destined him to long life.

It was a theme whose origins can be found in the Sumerian poem that scholars titled *Man and His God*, whose subject is the righteous sufferer, a victim of cruel fate and undeserved misfortune. "Fate grasped me in its hand, carries away my breath of life," the unnamed sufferer lamented; but he sees the Gates of Mercy opening up for him "now that you, my god, have shown me my sins." Confession and repentance make his god "turn aside the Demon of Fate," and the supplicant lives a long and happy life.

Just as the tale of Gilgamesh demonstrated that Fate could not override his ultimate Destiny (to die as a mortal), so did other tales convey the moral that neither can Fate bring about death if it was not yet so destined. A paramount example was none other than Marduk himself, who of all the gods of antiquity set a record in suffering and setbacks, of disappearances and reappearances, of exiles and returns, of apparent death and unexpected resurrection; so much so, in

fact, that when the full scope of the events concerning Marduk became known after the discovery of ancient inscriptions, scholars seriously debated at the turn of this century whether his story was a prototype of the story of Christ. (The notion was abetted by the close affinity between Marduk with his father Enki on the one hand and with his son Nabu on the other hand, creating the impression of an early Trinity).

The impact of Marduk's ordeals and its moral for humanity was evidenced by a Mystery Play in which his apparent death and return from the dead were played out by actors. The Mystery Play was acted out in Babylon as part of the New Year ceremonies, and various ancient records suggest that it served a darker purpose as well—to point an accusing finger at his enemies and judges who were responsible for his death sentence and entombment. As variant renditions indicate, the identity of those responsible changed from time to time to suit the changing political-religious scene.

One of the original accusees was Inanna/Ishtar; and it is ironic that while she truly had died and resurrected, her miraculous experience was neither reenacted (as was Marduk's) nor recalled in the calendar (as was the death of her beloved Dumuzi after whom the month Tammuz was named). This is doubly ironic because it was as a result of the death of Dumuzi that Inanna/Ishtar ended up dead.

Not even a Shakespeare could conceive the tragic irony of the events that followed the entombment and resurrection of Marduk as a result of Inanna's outcry. For as things turned out, while he had not truly died or really come back from the dead, his accuser Inanna did meet actual death and attained true resurrection. And while the death of Dumuzi was the underlying cause of both occurrences, the cause of Inanna's death and resurrection was her own fateful decision.

We use the term "fateful" judiciously, for it was her Fate, not her Destiny, to meet her death; and it was because of that distinction that she could be resurrected. And the account of those events illuminates the issues of Life, Death, and Resurrection not, as the *Epic of Gilgamesh*, among mortals or demigods, but among the gods themselves. In her tale of

Fate versus Destiny, there are clues to the resolution of enigmas that have been calling out for solutions.

The suspenseful story of Inanna/Ishtar's death and resurrection reveals, from the very beginning, that she met her death—real death, not just entombment—as a result of her own decisions. She created her own Fate; but since her death (at least at that time) was not her Destiny—in the end she was revived and resurrected.

The tale is recorded in texts written first in the original Sumerian language, with later renderings in Akkadian. Scholars refer to the various renditions as the tale of *Inanna's Descent to the Lower World*, although some prefer the term Netherworld instead of Lower World, implying a hellish domain of the dead. But in fact Inanna set her course to the Lower World, which was the geographic term denoting the southernmost part of Africa. It was the domain of her sister Ereshkigal and Nergal, her spouse; and it appears that as a brother of Dumuzi it was his task to arrange the funeral. And although Inanna was warned not to go there, she decided to make the trip anyway.

Attending the funeral rites of her beloved Dumuzi was the reason Inanna gave for her journey; but it is evident that no one believed her . . . It has been our guess that according to a custom (that later guided biblical laws), Inanna intended to demand that Nergal, as an older brother of Dumuzi, sleep with her so that a son be born as a pseudo-son of Dumuzi (who had died sonless). And that intention infuriated Ereshkigal.

Other texts described the seven objects that Inanna put on for her use during her travels in her Boat of Heaven—a helmet, ear "pendants," a "measuring rod" among them—all held firmly in place by straps. Sculptures (Fig. 30) depicted her similarly attired. As she reached the gates of her sister's abode—seven of them—the gatekeeper stripped her of all those protective devices, one by one. When she finally entered the throne room, Ereshkigal broke into a rage. There was a shouting match. According to the Sumerian text, Ereshkigal ordered that Inanna be subjected to the "Eyes of

Figure 30

Death''—some kind of death rays—that turned the body of Inanna into a corpse; and the corpse was hung on a stake. According to the later Akkadian version, Ereshkigal ordered her chamberlain Namtar to "release against Ishtar the sixty miseries"—afflictions of the eyes, the heart, the head, the feet, "of all parts of her, against her whole body"—putting Ishtar to death.

Anticipating trouble, Inanna/Ishtar had instructed her own chamberlain, Ninshubur, to raise an outcry in the event she did not return in three days. When she failed to return, Ninshubur came before Enlil to beg that Inanna be saved from death, but Enlil could not help. Ninshubur appealed to Nannar, Inanna's father, but he, too, was helpless. Then Ninshubur appealed to Enki, and he *was* able to help. He fashioned two artificial beings who could not be harmed by the Eyes of Death, and sent them on the rescue mission. To one android he gave the Food of Life, to the other the Water of

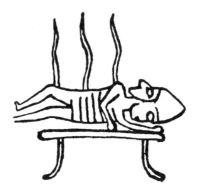

Figure 31

Life; and so provided, they descended to the abode of Ereshkigal to reclaim Inanna's lifeless body. Then,

> *Upon the corpse, hung from the stake,*
> *they directed the Pulser and the Emitter.*
> *Upon the flesh that had been smitten,*
> *sixty times the Food of Life,*
> *sixty times the Water of Life,*
> *they sprinkled upon it;*
> *And Inanna arose.*

The use of radiation—a Pulser, and Emitter—to revive the
dead was depicted on a cylinder seal (Fig. 31) in which we
see a patient whose face is covered with a mask being treated
with radiation. The patient who was being revived (whether
man or god is unclear), lying on a slab, was surrounded by
Fishmen—representatives of Enki. It is a clue to be borne in
mind together with the detail in the tale that while neither
Enlil nor Nannar could help Inanna, Enki could. The androids whom Enki had fashioned to return Inanna from the
dead, however, were not the Fishmen-doctor/priests shown
in the above depiction. Requiring neither food nor water,
sexless and bloodless, they may have looked more like the
figurines of divine android messengers (Fig. 32). It was as

Figure 32

androids that they were not affected by Ereshkigal's death rays.

Having resurrected Inanna/Ishtar, they accompanied her on her safe return to the Upper World. Awaiting her was her faithful chamberlain Ninshubur. She had many words of gratitude for him. Then she went to Eridu, the abode of Enki, "he who had brought her back to life."

Were *Inanna's Descent to the Lower World* made into a Passion Play, as the tale of Marduk was, it would certainly have kept the audience at the edge of their seats; for whereas Marduk's "death" was really only an entombment under a death sentence, and his "resurrection" in reality a rescue before the point of death, Inanna/Ishtar was truly dead and her resurrection a true return from the dead. But were someone in the audience familiar with the nuances of Sumerian terminology, he would have known from the midpoint of the tale that it would turn out all right . . . For the one whom Ereshkigal had ordered to put Inanna to death was her chamberlain *Namtar*—not NAM, "Destiny" that was unalterable,

but NAM.TAR, "Fate" that could be altered.

It was Namtar who put Ishtar to death by "releasing against her the sixty miseries," and the one who, after she was revived and resurrected, took her through the seven gates and returned to her, at each gate, her special attire and adornments and her attributes of power.

The notion of the realm of Namtar as a Netherworld, an abode of the dead but at the same time a place from which one could escape and be back among the living, formed the basis for an Assyrian text dealing with the near-death experience of a prince named Kumma.

As in an episode of the TV series *The Twilight Zone*, the prince sees himself arriving in the Netherworld. Right off he sees a man standing before Namtar: "In his left hand he held the hair of his head, in his right he held a sword." Namtaru, Namtar's concubine, stood nearby. Monstrous beasts surrounded them: a serpent-dragon with human hands and feet, a beast with the head of a lion and four human hands. There was *Mukil* ("Smiter"), birdlike with human hands and feet, and *Nedu* ("Who casts down"), who had the head of a lion, the hands of a man, and the feet of a bird. Other monsters had mixed limbs of humans, birds, oxen, lions.

Moving on, the prince comes upon a judgment scene. The man being judged has a pitch-black body and wears a red cloak. In one hand he carries a bow, in the other a sword; with his left foot he treads on a snake. But his judge is not Namtar, who is only the "vizier of the Netherworld"; the judge is Nergal, lord of the Lower World. The prince sees him "seated on a majestic throne, wearing a divine crown." From his arms lightnings flashed, and "the Netherworld was filled with terror."

Trembling, the prince bowed down. When he stood up, Nergal shrieked at him: "Why did you offend my beloved wife, Queen of the Netherworld?!" The prince was dumbfounded and speechless. Was this his end?

But no, no longer in the court of Namtar, that was not the bitter end. It was all, in turns out, a case of mistaken identity. The Queen of the Netherworld herself ordered his release

and return to the realm of Shamash, the Upper World of sunlight. But Nergal intervened; the life of the prince might be spared, but he cannot return from the dead unharmed. He must suffer from this near-death experience, and become afflicted with aches, pains, and insomnia . . . He has to suffer from nightmares.

The return of the dead Dumuzi from the Lower World was quite different.

Revived and freed to go back to the Upper World, Inanna did not forget her dead beloved. On her orders, the two divine messengers also took back with them the lifeless body of Dumuzi. They took the body to Bad-Tibira in the Edin; there the body was embalmed at Inanna's request:

> *As for Dumuzi, the lover of my youth:*
> *Wash him with pure water,*
> *anoint him with sweet oil,*
> *clothe him in a red garment,*
> *lay him on a slab of lapis-stone.*

Inanna ordered that the preserved body be put upon a stone slab of lapis lazuli to be kept in a special shrine. It should be preserved, she said, so that one day, on the Final Day, Dumuzi could return from the dead and "come up to me." For that, she asserted, would be the day when

> *The dead one will arise*
> *and smell the sweet incense.*

This, one should note, is the first mention of a belief in a Final Day when the dead shall arise. It was such a belief that caused the annual wailing for Tammuz (the Semitic rendering of Dumuzi) that continued for millennia even unto the time of the Prophet Ezekiel.

The death and mummification of Dumuzi, though so briefly told here, provide important insights. When he and Inanna/Ishtar fell in love—he an Enkiite, she an Enlilite—

in the midst of conflicts between the two divine clans, the betrothal received the blessing of Inanna's parents, Nannar/Sin and his spouse Ningal/Nikkal. One of the texts in the series of *Dumuzi and Inanna* love songs has Ningal, "speaking with authority," saying to Dumuzi:

> *Dumuzi, the desire and love of Inanna:*
> *I will give you life unto distant days;*
> *I will preserve it for you,*
> *I will watch over your House of Life.*

But in fact Ningal had no such authority, for all matters of Destiny and Fate were in the hands of Anu and Enlil. And, as all later knew, a tragic and untimely death did befall Dumuzi.

The failure of a divine promise in a matter of life and death is not the only disturbing aspect of the tragic fate of Dumuzi. It raises the issue of the gods' immortality; we have explained in our writings that it was only a relative longevity, a life span resulting from the fact that one year on Nibiru equaled 3,600 Earth years. But to those who in antiquity considered the Anunnaki to be gods, the tale of Dumuzi's death had to come as a shock. Was it because she had indeed expected Dumuzi to come back to life on the Final Day that Inanna ordered his embalmment and his placement on a stone slab rather than burial—or in order to preserve the illusion of divine immortality for the masses? Yes, she might have been saying, the god had died, but that is only a temporary, transitional phase, for in due time he shall be resurrected, he will arise and enjoy the sweet incense smells.

The Canaanite tales concerning Ba'al, "the Lord," seem to take the position that one had to distinguish between the good guys and the bad guys. Seeking to assert his supremacy and to establish it on the peak of Zaphon (the Secret Place of the North), Ba'al fought to the death his brother-adversaries. But in a fierce battle with the "godly *Mot*" ("Death"), Ba'al is killed.

Anat, the sister-lover of Ba'al, and their sister Shepesh,

bring the terrible news to Ba'al's father, *El*: "Puissant Ba'al
is dead, the Prince, Lord of Earth, is perished!" they tell the
shocked father; in the fields of Dabrland "we came upon
Ba'al, fallen on the ground." Hearing the news, El steps off
his throne and sits down on a stool, as mourner's custom is
(among the Jews) to this day. "He pours dust of mourning
on his head, puts on sackcloth." With a stone knife he gashes
himself; "he lifts up his voice and cries: Ba'al is dead!"

The grieving Anat returns to the field where Ba'al had
fallen and, like El, puts on sackcloth, gashes herself, then
"weeps her fill of weeping." Then she calls her sister Shepesh to come and help her carry the lifeless body to the
Fastness of Zaphon, there to bury the dead god:

> *Hearkening, Shepesh, the gods' maiden,*
> *picks up Puissant Baal,*
> *sets him on Anat's shoulder.*
> *Up to Zaphon's fastness she brings him,*
> *bewails him and buries him;*
> *She lays him in a hollow,*
> *to be with the earth-ghosts.*

Completing the requisites of mourning, Anat returns to
El's abode. Bitterly she tells those gathered: Now you can
go and rejoice, for Ba'al is dead, and his throne is free! The
goddess Elath and her kinsmen, ignoring Anat's irony, mer-
rily go about discussing succession. As one of the other of
El's sons is recommended, El says no, he is a weakling.
Another candidate is permitted to go to Zaphon, to try out
Ba'al's throne; "but his feet reach not down to the foot-
stool," and he, too, is eliminated. No one, it appears, can
replace Ba'al.

This gives Anat hope: resurrection. Enlisting again the
help of Shepesh, she penetrates Mot's abode. Using subterfuge, she "draws near to him, like a ewe for her lamb . . .
She seizes the godly Mot and with a sword she cleaves him."
Then she burns the dead Mot's body, grinds the remains,
spreads the ashes over the fields.

And the killing of Mot, who had killed Ba'al, triggers a miracle: *the dead Ba'al comes back to life!*

> *Indeed did Puissant Baal die;*
> *Indeed did the Lord of Earth perish.*
> *But lo and behold:*
> *Alive is Puissant Baal!*
> *Behold, existent is the princely Lord of Earth!*

Getting the news, El wonders whether it is all a dream, "a vision." But it is true! Casting off the sackcloth and ways of mourning, El rejoices:

> *Now will I sit up and find rest,*
> *and my heart shall be at ease;*
> *For alive is Puissant Baal,*
> *Existent is the prince, Lord of Earth.*

In spite of El's evident uncertainty whether the resurrection is an illusory vision, a mere dream, the Canaanite storyteller chose to assure the people that in the end even El accepts the miracle. The assurance is echoed in the tale of Keret, who is only a demigod; yet his sons, seeing him in the throes of death, cannot believe that "a son of El shall die."

It is perhaps in light of the unacceptability of a god's death that the notion of resurrection has been brought into play. And whether or not Inanna herself believed that her beloved would return from the dead, the elaborate preservation of Dumuzi's body and her accompanying words also preserved, among the human masses, the illusion of the immortality of the gods.

The procedure that she personally outlined for the preservation, so that on the Final Day Dumuzi could arise and rejoin her, is undoubtedly the procedure known as mummification. This might come as a shock to Egyptologists, who have held that mummification began *in Egypt* at the time of the Third Dynasty, circa 2800 B.C. There the procedure en-

Figure 33

tailed washing the body of the departed Pharaoh, rubbing it with oils, and wrapping it in a woven cloth—preserving the body so that the Pharaoh could undertake a Journey to the Afterlife.

Yet here we have a *Sumerian* text recording mummification centuries earlier!

The procedure's step-by-step details in this text are identical to what was later practiced in Egypt, down to the color of the enshrouding cloth.

Inanna ordered that the preserved body be put to rest upon a stone slab of lapis lazuli, to be kept in a special shrine. She named the shrine E.MASH—"House/Temple of the Serpent." It was perhaps more than a symbolic gesture of placing the dead son of Enki in his father's hands. For Enki was not only the *Nachash*—Serpent, as well as Knower of Secrets—of the Bible. In Egypt, too, his symbol was the serpent and the hieroglyph of his name PTAH represented the double helix of DNA (Fig. 33), for that was the key to all matters of life and death.

Though venerated in Sumer and Akkad as Inanna's betrothed and mourned in Mesopotamia and beyond as Ishtar's departed Tammuz, Dumuzi was an African god. It was thus perhaps inevitable that his death and embalmment would be compared by scholars to the tragic tale of the great Egyptian god *Osiris*.

The story of Osiris is akin to the biblical tale of Cain and

Figure 34

Abel in which a rivalry ended in a brother killing a brother. It begins with two divine couples, two half brothers (*Osiris* and *Seth*) marrying two sisters (*Isis* and *Nepthys*). To avoid recriminations, the Kingdom of the Nile was divided between the two brothers: Lower Egypt (the northern part) was allotted to Osiris and the southern part (Upper Egypt) to Seth. But the complex divine rules of succession, giving preference to the Legitimate Heir over the Firstborn Son, inflamed the rivalry to the point where Seth, using a ruse, trapped Osiris inside a chest which was then cast into the Mediterranean Sea, and Osiris was drowned.

Isis, the spouse of Osiris, found the chest when it was washed ashore in what is now Lebanon. She took the body of her husband Osiris back to Egypt, seeking the help of the god Thoth to resurrect Osiris. But Seth found out what was going on, seized the corpse, cut it up into fourteen pieces, and dispersed the pieces all over Egypt.

Unyielding, Isis searched for the pieces and found them all, except (so the tale says) the phallus of Osiris. She put the pieces back together, binding them with a woven purple cloth to reconstitute Osiris's body—thus starting mummification in Egypt. All the depictions of Osiris from pharaonic times show him tightly wrapped in the shroud (Fig. 34).

Like Inanna before her, so did Isis enshroud and mummify her deceased spouse, thereby giving rise in Egypt (as Inanna's deed had done in Sumer and Akkad) to the notion of

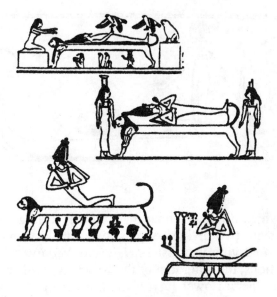

Figure 35

the resurrected god. While in Inanna's case the deed by the
goddess might have been intended to satisfy a personal denial
of the loss as well as to affirm the *gods'* immortality, in
Egypt the act became a pillar of the pharaonic belief that the
human king could also undergo the transfiguration and, by
emulating Osiris, attain immortality in an afterlife with the
gods. In the words of E. A. Wallis Budge in the preface to
his masterwork *Osiris & The Egyptian Resurrection*, "The
central figure of the ancient Egyptian Religion was Osiris,
and the chief fundamentals of his cult were the belief in his
divinity, death, resurrection and absolute control of the destinies of the bodies and souls of men." The principal shrines
to Osiris in Abydos and Denderah depicted the steps in the
god's resurrection (Fig. 35). Wallis Budge and other scholars
believed that these depictions were drawn from a Passion or
Mystery Play that had been acted out annually at those
places—a religious ritual that, in Mesopotamia, was accorded to Marduk.

The *Pyramid Texts* and other funerary quotes from the

Figure 36

Egyptian *Book of the Dead* related how the dead Pharaoh, embalmed and mummified, was prepared to exit his tomb (deemed only a temporary restplace) through a false door on the east and begin a Journey to the Afterlife. It was presumed to be a journey simulating the journey of the resurrected Osiris to his heavely throne in the Eternal Abode; and though it was a journey that made the Pharaoh soar heavenward as a divine falcon, it began by passing through a series of underground chambers and subterranean corridors filled with miraculous beings and sights. In *The Stairway to Heaven* we have analyzed the geography and topography of the ancient texts and concluded that it was a simulation of a journey to an underground launch silo in the Sinai peninsula—not unlike the actual depiction of an actual site in the peninsula in the tomb of Hui, a pharaonic governor of the Sinai peninsula (Fig. 36).

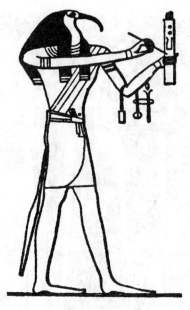

Figure 37

The resurrection of Osiris was coupled with another miraculous feat, that of bringing about the birth of his son, *Horus*, well after Osiris himself was dead and dismembered. In both events, which the Egyptians rightly considered to be magical, a god called *Thoth* (always shown in Egyptian art as Ibis-headed, Fig. 37) played the decisive role. It was he who aided Isis in putting the dismembered Osiris together, and then instructed her how to extract the "essence" of Osiris from his dismembered and dead body, and then impregnate herself artificially. Doing that, she managed to become pregnant and give birth to a son, Horus.

Even those who take the tale to be a recollection of some actual events and not just a "myth" assume that what Isis did was to extract from the dead Osiris his semen, and thus his "essence." But this was impossible, since the one part that Isis could not find and recombine was his male organ. The magical feat of Thoth had to go beyond artificial insem-

ination, now quite common. What he had to do was to obtain for her the *genetic* "essence" of Osiris. The texts as well as depictions coming to us from ancient Egypt confirm that Thoth indeed possessed the "secret knowledge" needed for such feats.

The biomedical—"magical" in human eyes—capabilities of Thoth were called upon once more for the sake of Horus. In order to protect the boy from the ruthless Seth, Isis kept the birth of Horus a secret, hiding him in a swampy area. Unaware of the existence of a son of Osiris, Seth—just as Enki had tried to obtain a son by his half sister Ninmah— tried to force Isis, his half-sister, to have intercourse with him so that he might have a son by a half sister, and thus an uncontested heir. Luring Isis to his abode, he held her captive for a while; but Isis managed to escape and returned to the swamps where Horus was hidden. To her grief she found Horus dead from a sting of a poisonous scorpion. She lost no time in calling for help from Thoth:

Then Isis sent forth a cry to heaven
and addressed her appeal to the
Boat of Millions of Years . . .
And Thoth came down;
He was provided with magical powers,
and possessed the great power which made
the word turn into deed . . .

And he said to Isis:
I have come this day in the Boat of the Celestial
Disc from the place where it was yesterday.
When the night cometh,
this Light [beam] shall drive away [the poison]
for the healing of Horus . . .
I have come from the skies to save the child
for his mother.

Thus revived and resurrected from death (and perhaps forever immunized) by the magical powers of Thoth, Horus grew up to become *Netch-Atef*, the "Avenger" of his father.

The biomedical powers of Thoth in matters of life and death were also recorded in a series of ancient Egyptian texts known as *Tales of the Magicians*. In one of them (Cairo Papyrus 30646) a long tale deals with a couple of royal descent who unlawfully took possession of the *Book of the Secrets of Thoth*. In punishment Thoth buried them in a subterranean chamber in a state of suspended animation—mummified as the dead but able to see, hear, and speak. In another tale, written on the *Westcar Papyrus*, a son of the Pharaoh Khufu (Cheops) told his father of an old man who "was acquainted with the mysteries of Thoth." Among them was the ability to restore life to the dead. Wishing to see this with his own eyes, the king ordered that a prisoner's head be cut off, then challenged the sage to reconnect the severed head and return the man to life. The sage refused to perform this "magic of Thoth" on a human being; so the head of a goose was severed. The sage "spoke certain words of power" from the *Book of Thoth*; and lo and behold, the severed head joined itself back to the body of the goose, the goose stood up, waddled, then began to honk—alive as before.

That Thoth had indeed possessed the ability to resurrect a dead person who had been beheaded, reattach the head, and return the victim to life, was known in ancient Egypt because of an incident that had occurred when Horus finally took up arms against his uncle Seth. After battles that raged on land, water, and in the air, Horus succeeded in capturing Seth and his lieutenants. Bringing them before Ra for judgment, Ra put the captives' fate in the hands of Horus and Isis. Thereupon Horus started to slay the captives by cutting off their heads; but when it came to Seth, Isis could not see this done to her brother and stopped Horus from executing Seth. Enraged, Horus turned on his own mother and beheaded her! She survived only because Thoth rushed to the scene, reattached her head, and resurrected her.

To appreciate Thoth's ability to achieve all that, let us

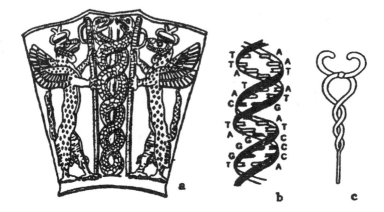

Figures 38a, 38b, and 38c

recall that we have identified this son of Ptah as Ningishzidda (son of Enki in Sumerian lore), whose Sumerian name meant "Lord of the Tree/Artifact of Life." He was the Keeper of [the] Divine Secrets of the exact sciences, not the least of which were the secrets of genetics and biomedicine that had served well his father Enki at the time of the Creation of Man. Sumerian texts, in fact, attest that at one time Marduk complained to his father Enki that he was not taught all the knowledge that Enki possessed.

"My son," responded Enki, "what is it that you do not know? What more could I give to you?" The withheld knowledge, Marduk pointed out, was the secret of resurrecting the dead; that secret knowledge was imparted by Enki to Marduk's brother, Ningishzidda/Thoth, but not to Marduk/Ra.

That secret knowledge, those powers granted to Thoth/Ningishzidda, found expression in Mesopotamian art and worship by depicting him by or with the symbol of the Entwined Serpents (Fig. 38a)—a symbol that we have identified as a representation of the double helix DNA (Fig. 38b)—a symbol that has survived to our time as the emblem of medicine and healing (Fig. 38c).

There was undoubtedly a connection between all that and

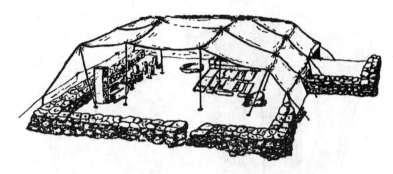

Figure 39

the fashioning by Moses of a copper serpent in order to stop a pestilence that felled countless Israelites during the Exodus. Raised in the Pharaoh's court and trained by Egypt's magicians, Moses, on the Lord's instructions, "made a copper serpent, and placed it atop a Miracle Pole," and when those who were afflicted by the plague looked up to the copper serpent, they remained alive (Numbers 21:8–10).

It is perhaps more than a coincidence that one of the leading international authorities on ancient copper mining and metallurgy, Professor Benno Rothenberg (*Midianite Timna* and other publications), discovered in the Sinai peninsula a shrine dating back to the time of the Midianite period—the time when Moses, having escaped to the Sinai wilderness for his life—dwelt with the Midianites and even married the daughter of the Midianite high priest. Located in the area where some of the earliest copper mining had taken place, Professor Rothenberg found in the shrine's remains a small copper serpent; it was the sole votive object there. (The shrine has been reconstructed as an exhibit in the Nechushtan Pavilion of the Eretz Israel Museum in Tel Aviv, Fig. 39, where the copper serpent can also be seen.)

The biblical record and the finds in the Sinai peninsula have a direct bearing on the depiction of Enki as a *Nachash*. The term has not just the two meanings that we have already mentioned ("Serpent," "Knower of Secrets") but also a third one—"He of Copper," for the Hebrew word for cop-

per, *Nechoshet*, stems from the same root. One of Enki's epithets in Sumerian, BUZUR, also has the double meaning "He who knows/solves secrets" and "He of the copper mines."

These various interconnections may offer an explanation of the otherwise puzzling choice by Inanna of a resting place for Dumuzi: Bad-Tibira. Nowhere in the relevant texts is there any indication of a connection between Dumuzi (and, for that matter, Inanna) and that City of the Gods. The only possible connection is the fact that Bad-Tibira was established as the metallurgical center of the Anunnaki. Did Inanna, then, place the embalmed Dumuzi near where not only gold but also copper was refined?

Another possibly relevant tidbit concerns the construction of the Tabernacle and Tent of Appointment in the desert of the Exodus, in accordance with very detailed and explicit instructions by Yahweh to Moses: where gold or silver were to be used and how, what kinds of woods or timbers and in what sizes, what manner of cloth or skins, how sewn, how decorated. Great care is also taken in these instructions regarding the rites to be performed by the priests (only Aaron and his sons at that time): their clothing, the sacred objects they would wear, the very explicit combination of ingredients that would make the unique incense that would result in the proper cloud to shield them from the deathly radiation by the Ark of the Covenant. And then one more requirement: the fashioning of a washbasin in which they had to wash their hands and feet, "so that they die not when they enter the Ark of the Covenant." And the washbasin, Exodus 30: 17 specified, must be made of copper.

All these dispersed but seemingly connected facts and tidbits suggest that copper somehow played a role in human biogenetics—a role which modern science is only beginning to uncover (a recent example is a study, published in the journal *Science* of 8 March 1996, about the disruption of copper metabolism in the brain associated with Alzheimer's disease).

Such a role, if not part of the first genetic endeavor by

Enki and Ninmah to produce The Adam, seems to have certainly entered the human genome when Enki, as the Nachash, engaged in the second manipulation when Mankind was endowed with the ability to procreate.

Copper, in other words, was apparently a component of our Destiny, and a studious and expert analysis of the Sumerian creation texts might well lead to medical breakthroughs that could affect our own daily lives.

As for the gods, Inanna, for one, believed that copper might assist her beloved's resurrection.

6

THE COSMIC CONNECTION: DNA

Even before television, courtroom dramas have titillated many and trials made history. We have come a long way from the biblical rule, "by two witnesses shall the verdict be." From eyewitnesses court evidence has moved to documentary evidence, to forensic evidence, and—what seems at the moment as the epitome—to DNA evidence.

Having discovered that all life is determined by the tiny bits of nucleic acids that spell out heredity and individuality on chains called chromosomes, modern science has attained the capability of reading those entwined DNA letters to distinguish their unique, individually spelled "words." Using DNA readings to prove guilt or innocence has become the highlight of courtroom dramas.

An unmatched feat of twentieth-century sophistication? No, a feat of 100th-century sophistication *in the past*—a court drama from 10,000 B.C.

The ancient celebrated case took place in Egypt, at a time when gods and not yet men reigned over the land; and it concerned not men but the gods themselves. It concerned the adversaries Seth and Horus and had its roots in the rivalry between the half brothers Seth and Osiris. Seth, it will be recalled, resorted to foul play to get rid of Osiris and take over his domains. The first time he tricked Osiris into a chest that Seth quickly sealed and sank in the Mediterranean Sea; but Isis found the chest and, with the help of Thoth, revived Osiris. The next time the frustrated Seth seized and cut up Osiris into fourteen pieces. Isis located the dispersed pieces and put them together, and mummified Osiris to start the

Afterlife legend. She missed, however, the god's phallus, which she could not find, for Seth had disposed of it so that Osiris would have no heir.

Determined to have one so that he would avenge his father, Isis appealed to Thoth, the Keeper of Divine Secrets, to help her. Extracting the "essence" of Osiris from the dead god's available parts, Thoth helped Isis impregnate herself and give birth to a son, Horus.

The "essence" (not "seed"!), we now know, was what we nowadays call DNA—the genetic nucleic acids that form chains on the chromosomes, chains that are arranged in base pairs in a double helix (see Fig. 38b). At conception, when the male sperm enters the female egg, the entwined double helixes separate, and one strand from the male combines with one strand from the female to form a new double-helixed DNA for their offspring. It is thus essential not only to bring together the two double-helixed DNAs, but also to attain a separation—an unwinding—of the double strands, and then a recombining of only one strand from each source into the new entwined double-helixed DNA.

Pictorial depictions from ancient Egypt indicate that Thoth—the son of Ptah/Enki—was well aware of these biological-genetic processes and employed them in his genetic feats. In Abydos, a wall painting (Fig. 40), in which the Pharaoh Seti I acted out the role of Osiris, showed Thoth giving Life (the *Ankh* symbol) back to the dead god while obtaining from him the two distinct strands of DNA. In a depiction from the *Book of the Dead* dealing with the subsequent birth of Horus, we see (Fig. 41) how the two Birth Goddesses assisting Thoth hold *one strand each* of DNA, the DNA's double helix having been separated so that only one strand recombines with that of Isis (shown holding the newborn Horus).

Isis raised the boy in secret. When he came of age, his mother decided that it was time to claim for him his father's inheritance. So one day, to Seth's utter surprise, Horus appeared before the Council of the Great Gods and announced that he was the son and heir of Osiris. It was an incredible

Figure 40

claim, yet one that could not be dismissed out of hand. Was the young god really the son of the dead Osiris?

As recorded in a text known as the *Chester Beatty Papyrus No. 1*, the appearance of Horus astounded the assembled gods, and of course Seth more than any other. As the council began to deliberate the sudden claim, Seth had a conciliatory suggestion: Let the deliberations be recessed, so as to give him a chance to get acquainted with Horus and see if the matter could be settled amicably. He invited Horus to "come, let us pass a happy day in my house," and Horus agreed. But Seth, who had once tricked Osiris to his death, had new treachery in mind:

> *When it was eventide,*
> *the bed was spread for them,*
> *and the twain lay thereon.*

Figure 41

And in the night
Seth caused his member to become stiff,
and he made it go between the loins of Horus.

When the deliberations were resumed, Seth made an astounding announcement. Whether or not Horus is the son of Osiris, he said, matters no more. For now his, Seth's, seed is in Horus, and that makes Horus a successor of Seth rather than a front-runner for the succession!

Then Horus made an even more surprising announcement. On the contrary, he said, it is not I who have been disqualified—it is Seth! And he went on to tell that he was not really asleep when Seth poured his semen. It did not enter my body, he said, because "I caught the seed between my hands." In the morning he took the semen to show it to his mother Isis, and the report gave her an idea. She made Horus erect his member and ejaculate his semen into a cup; then she spread the semen of Horus on lettuce in Seth's garden—a favorite breakfast food of Seth. Unknowingly, he ended up ingesting the semen of Horus. So, Horus said, it is my semen that is in Seth, and now he can succeed me but not precede me on the divine throne . . .

Totally baffled, the Council of the Gods turned to Thoth to resolve the issue. Using his powers of genetic knowledge, he checked the semen that Isis had kept in a pot, and found it to indeed be that of Seth. He examined Horus and found no traces of Seth's DNA in him. Then he examined Seth, and found that he had indeed ingested the DNA of Horus.

Acting as a forensic expert in a modern court, but evidently armed with technical abilities which we are yet to attain, he submitted the DNA analysis results to the Council of the Gods. They voted unanimously to grant the dominion over Egypt to Horus.

(Seth's refusal to yield the dominion led to what we have termed the First Pyramid War, in which Horus enlisted, for the first time, humans in a war between the gods. We have detailed those events in *The Wars of Gods and Men*).

Recent discoveries in genetics throw light on a persistent and seemingly odd custom of the gods, and at the same time highlight their biogenetic sophistication.

The importance of the wife-sister in the succession rules of the gods of Mesopotamia and Egypt, evident from all that we have reported thus far, was echoed also in the Greek myths regarding their gods. The Greeks named the first divine couple, emerging out of Chaos, *Gaea* ("Earth") and *Uranus* ("Sky" or "Heaven"). Of them twelve *Titans* were brought forth, six males and six females. Their intermarriages and varied offspring laid the groundwork for later struggles for supremacy. Of the earliest struggles the one who emerged on top was *Cronus*, the youngest male Titan, whose spouse was his sister *Rhea*; their children were the three sons *Hades, Poseidon* and *Zeus*, and the three daughters *Hestia, Demeter* and *Hera*. Though Zeus fought his way up to the supremacy, he had to share dominion with his brothers. The three divided the domains among them—some versions say by drawing lots—very much as Anu, Enlil, and Enki had: Zeus was the heavenly god (yet residing on Earth, on Mount Olympus); Hades was accorded the Lower World; and Poseidon the seas.

The three brothers and three sisters, offspring of Cronus and Rhea, constituted the first half of the Olympian Circle of twelve. The other six were offspring of Zeus, born when Zeus consorted with a variety of goddesses. Of one of them, Leto, he had his Firstborn Son, the great Greek and Roman god *Apollo*. When it was time, however, to obtain a male heir in accordance with the succession rules of the gods, Zeus turned to his own sisters. Hestia, the oldest, was by all accounts a recluse, too old or too sick to be the object of matrimony and childbearing. Zeus thus sought a son by his middle sister, Demeter; but instead of a son she bore him a daughter, Persephone. This paved the way for Zeus to marry Hera, the youngest sister; and she did bear to Zeus a son, *Ares*, and two daughters (Ilithyia and Hebe). When the Greeks and Romans, who lost the knowledge of the planets beyond Saturn, named the known planets, they assigned one—Mars—to Ares; though not the Firstborn Son, he was Zeus's Foremost Son. Apollo, as great a god as he was, had no planet named after him by the Greeks and Romans.

All this reinforces the importance of the wife-sister in the annals of the gods. In matters of succession, the issue arose again and again: Who will the successor to the throne be— the Firstborn Son or the Foremost Son, if the latter was born by a half sister and the former not? That issue appears to have dominated and dictated the course of events on Earth from the moment Enlil joined Enki on this planet, and the rivalry was continued by their sons (Ninurta and Marduk, respectively). In Egyptian tales of the gods, a conflict for similar reasons reared its head between Ra's descendants, Seth and Osiris.

The rivalry, which from time to time flared into actual warfare (Horus in the end fought Seth in single combat in the skies of the Sinai peninsula), by all accounts did not begin on Earth. There were similar conflicts of succession on Nibiru, and Anu did not come by his rulership without fights and battles.

Like the custom that a widow left without a son could demand the husband's brother to "know" her as a surrogate

husband and give her a son, so did the Anunnnaki's rules of succession, giving priority to a son by a half sister, find their way into the customs of Abraham and his descendants. In his case, his first son was Ishmael, born by the handmaiden Hagar. But when, at an incredible old age and after divine intervention, Sarah bore Isaac—it was Isaac who was the Legitimate Heir. Why? Because Sarah was Abraham's half sister. "She is my sister, the daughter of my father but not of my mother," Abraham explained (Genesis 20:12).

The marrying of a half sister as a wife was prevalent among the Pharaohs of Egypt, as a means both to legitimize the king's reign and the succession. The custom was even found among the Inca kings of Peru, so much so that the occurrence of calamities during a certain king's reign was attributed to his marrying a woman who was not his half sister. The Inca custom had its roots in the Legends of Beginnings of the Andean peoples, whereby the god Viracocha created four brothers and four sisters who intermarried and were guided to various lands. One such brother-sister couple, which was given a golden wand with which to find the Navel of the Earth in South America, began kingship in Cuzco (the erstwhile Inca capital). That was why Inca kings—providing they had been born of a succession of brother-sister royal couples—could claim direct lineage to the Creator God Viracocha.

(Viracocha, according to Andean legends, was a great God of Heaven who had come to Earth in antiquity and chose the Andean mountains as his arena. In *The Lost Realms* we have identified him as the Mesopotamian god Adad = the Hittite god Teshub, and pointed to many other similarities, besides the brother-sister customs, between the Andean cultures and those of the ancient Near East).

The persistence of the brother-sister intermarriage and the seemingly totally out of proportion significance attached to it, among gods and mortals alike, is puzzling. The custom on the face of it appears to be more than a localized "let's keep the throne in the family" attitude, and at worst the courting of genetic degradation. Why, then, the lengths to

which the Anunnaki (example: Enki's repeated efforts to
have a son by Ninmah) went to attain a son by such a union?
What was so special about the genes of a half sister—the
daughter, let us keep in mind, of the male's *mother* but definitely not of the father?

As we search for the answer, it will help to note other
biblical practices affecting the mother/father issues. It is customary to refer to the period of Abraham, Isaac, Jacob, and
Joseph as the Patriarchal Age, and when asked most people
would say that the history related in the Old Testament has
been presented from a male-oriented viewpoint. Yet the fact
is that it was the *mothers*, not the fathers, who controlled the
act that, in the ancients' view, gave the subject of the tale
its status of "being"—the *naming* of the child. Indeed, not
only a person but a place, a city, a land, were not deemed
to have come into being until they were given a name.

This notion, in fact, goes back to the beginning of time,
for the very opening lines of the *Epic of Creation*, wishing
to impress on the listener that the story begins before the
Solar System had been fully fashioned, declare that the story
of Tiamat and the other planets begins

> Enuma elish la nabu shamamu
> *When in the heights heaven had not been named*
> Shapiltu ammatum shuma la zakrat
> *And below, firm ground (Earth) had not been called*

And in the important matter of naming a son, it was either
the gods themselves or the mother whose privilege it was.
We thus find that when the *Elohim* created *Homo sapiens*, it
was they who named the new being "Adam" (Genesis 5:2).
But when Man was given the ability to procreate on his own,
it was Eve—not Adam—who had the right and privilege of
naming their first male child Cain (Genesis 4:1) as well as
Seth who replaced the slain Abel (Genesis 4:25).

At the start of the "Patriarchal (!) Age" we find that the
privilege of naming the two sons of Abraham was taken over
by divine beings. His firstborn by Hagar, his wife's hand-

maiden, was called Ishma'el by an Angel of Yahweh (Genesis 16:11); and the Legitimate Heir Isaac (*Itzhak*, "Who causes laughter") was so named by one of the three divine beings who visited Abraham before the destruction of Sodom and Gomorrah (because when Sarah had heard God saying that she would have a son, she laughed; Genesis 17:19; 18:12). No specific information is provided in the Bible regarding the two sons of Isaac by Rebecca, Esau and Jacob (it is simply stated that this is how they were called). But then it is clearly stated that it was Leah who named Jacob's sons by her and by her handmaiden, as did Rachel (Genesis chapters 29 and 30). Centuries later, after the Israelites had settled in Canaan, it was Samson's mother who so named him (Judges 13:24); so did the mother of the Man of God, Samuel (1 Samuel 1:20).

The Sumerian texts do not provide this kind of information. We do not know, for example, who named Gilgamesh— his mother the goddess or his father the High Priest. But the tale of Gilgamesh provides an important clue to the solution of the puzzle at hand: the importance of the mother in determining the son's hierarchical standing.

His search for attaining the longevity of the gods, it will be recalled, led him first to the Landing Place in the Cedar Mountains; but he and his companion Enkidu were prevented from entering by its robotic guardian and the Bull of Heaven. Gilgamesh then journeyed to the spaceport in the Sinai peninsula. The access to it was guarded by awesome Rocketmen who trained on him "the dreaded spotlight that sweeps the mountains" whose "glance was death" (Fig. 42); but Gilgamesh was not affected; whereupon one Rocketman shouted to his comrade:

> *He who comes,*
> *of the flesh of the gods*
> *is his body!*

Figure 42

Permitted to approach, Gilgamesh confirmed the guard's conclusion: Indeed he was immune to the death rays because his body was of the "flesh of the gods." He was, he explained, not just a *demi*god—he was *"two-thirds* divine," because it was not his father but his *mother* who was a goddess, one of the female Anunnaki.

Here, we believe, is the key to the puzzle of the succession rules and other emphasis on the mother. It is through her that an extra "qualifying dose" was given to the hero or the heir (be it Anunnaki or patriarchal).

This seemed to make no sense even after the discovery, in 1953, of the double-helix structure of DNA and the understanding how the two strands unwind and separate so that only one strand from the female egg and one strand from the male sperm recombine, making the offspring a fifty-fifty image of its parents. Indeed, this understanding, while explaining the demigod claims, defied the inexplicable claim of Gilgamesh to be two-thirds divine.

It was not until the 1980s that the ancient claims began to make sense. This came with the discovery that in addition to the DNA stored in the cells of both males and females in the double-helix structures on the chromosome stems, forming the cell's nucelus, there was another kind of DNA that floats

in the cell outside the nucelus. Given the designation Mitochondrial DNA (mtDNA), it was found to be transmitted *only from the mother* as is, i.e. without splitting and recombining with any DNA from the male.

In other words, if the mother of Gilgamesh was a goddess, then he had indeed inherited both her half of the regular DNA *plus* her mtDNA, making him, as he had claimed, two-thirds divine.

It was this discovery of the existence and transmittal as is of mtDNA that has enabled scientists, from 1986 on, to trace the mtDNA in modern humans to an "Eve" who had lived in Africa some 250,000 years ago.

At first scientists believed that the sole function of mtDNA was to act as the cell's power plant, providing the energy required for the cell's myriad chemical and biological reactions. But then it was ascertained that the mtDNA was made of "mitochondrions" containing 37 genes arranged in a closed circle, like a bracelet; and that such a genetic "bracelet" contains over 16,000 base pairs of the genetic alphabet (by comparison, each of the chromosomes making up the cell's core that are inherited half from each parent contains upward of 100,000 genes and an aggregate of more than three billion base pairs).

It took another decade to realize that impairments in the makeup or functions of mtDNA can cause debilitating disorders in the human body, especially of the nervous system, of heart and skeletal muscles, and of the kidneys. In the 1990s researchers found that defects ("mutations") in mtDNA also disrupt the production of 13 important body proteins, resulting in various severe ailments. A list published in 1997 in *Scientific American* starts with Alzheimer's disease and goes on to include a variety of vision, hearing, blood, muscle, bone marrow, heart, kidney, and brain malfunctions.

These genetic ailments join a much longer list of bodily malfunctions and dysfunctions that defects in the nuclear DNA can cause. As scientists unravel and understand the "genome"—the complete genetic code—of humans (a feat

Figures 43a and 43b

recently achieved for a single lowly bacterium), the function
that each gene performs (and as the other side of the coin,
the ailments if it is absent or malfunctions) is steadily becoming known. By not producing a certain protein or enzyme
or other key bodily compound, the gene regulating that has
been found to cause breast cancer, or hinder bone formation,
deafness, loss of eyesight, heart disorders, the excessive gain
of weight or the opposite thereof, and so on and on.

What is interesting in this regard is that we come across
a list of similar genetic defects as we read the Sumerian texts
about the creation of the Primitive Worker by Enki with the
assistance of Ninmah. The attempt to recombine the strands
of hominid DNA with strands of Anunnaki DNA to create
the new hybrid being was a process of trial and error, and
the beings initially brought about sometimes lacked organs
or limbs—or had too many of them. The Babylonian priest
Berossus, who in the third century B.C. compiled for the
Greeks the history and knowledge of the earlier Sumerians,
described the failed results of Man's creators by reporting
that some of the trial-and-error beings had two heads on one
body. Such ''monsters'' have indeed been depicted by the
Sumerians (Fig. 43a), as well as another anomaly—a being

with one head but two faces called Usmu (Fig. 43b). Specifically mentioned in the texts was a being who could not hold its urine, and a variety of malfunctions including eye and eyesight diseases, trembling hands, an improper liver, a failing heart, and "sicknesses of old age." The text called *Enki and Ninmah: The Creation of Mankind*, besides listing more dysfunctions (rigid hands, paralyzed feet, dripping semen) also depicted Enki as a caring god who, rather than destroying such deformed beings, found some useful life for them. Thus, when one outcome was a man with faulty eyesight, Enki taught him an art that did not require seeing—the art of singing and the playing of a lyre.

To all those, the text states, Enki decreed this or that Fate. He then challenged Ninmah to try the genetic engineering on her own. The results were terrible: the beings she brought about had the mouth in the wrong place, a sick head, sore eyes, aching neck, shaky ribs, malfunctioning lungs, a heart ailment, inability to move the bowels, hands that were too short to reach the mouth, and so on and on. But as the trial and error continued, Ninmah was able to correct the various defects. Indeed, she reached a point that she became so knowledgeable of the Anunnaki/hominid genomes that she boasted that she could make the new being as perfect or imperfect as she wished:

> *How good or bad is man's body?*
> *As my heart prompts me,*
> *I can make its fate good or bad.*

We, too, have now reached the stage where we can insert or replace a certain gene whose role we have uncovered, and try to prevent or cure a specific disease or shortcoming. Indeed, a new industry, the biotechnology industry, has sprung up, with a seemingly limitless potential in medicine (and the stock market). We have even learned to perform what is called transgenic engineering—the transfer of genes between different species, a feat that is achievable because *all* the genetic material on this planet, from the lowest bacterium to

the most complex being (Man), of all living organisms that roam or fly or swim or grow, is made up of the same genetic ABC—the same nucleic acids that formed the "seed" brought into our Solar System by Nibiru.

Our genes are, in fact, our cosmic connection.

Modern advances in genetics move along two parallel yet interconnected routes. One is to ascertain the human genome, the total genetic makeup of the human being; this involves the reading of a code that although written with just four letters (A-G-C-T, short for the initials of the names given to the four nucleic acids that make up all DNA) is made up of countless combinations of those letters that then form "words" that combine into "sentences" and "paragraphs" and finally a complete "book of life." The other research route is to determine the function of each gene; that is an even more daunting task, facilitated by the fact that if that very same gene ("genetic word") can be found in a simpler creature (such as a lowly bacterium, or a laboratory mouse) and its function could be experimentally determined, it is virtually certain that the same gene in humans would have the same functions (or its absence the same malfunctions). The discovery of genes related to obesity, for example, has been achieved that way.

The ultimate goal of this search for the cause, and thus the cure, of human ailments and deficiencies is twofold: to find the genes that control the body's physiology and those that control the brain's neurological functions. To find the genes that control the process of aging, the cell's internal clock of the span of life—the genes of longevity—and the genes that control memory, reasoning, intelligence. Experiments on laboratory mice on the one hand and on human twins on the other hand, and extensive researches in between, indicate the existence of genes and groups of genes that account for both. How tedious and elusive these research targets are can be illustrated by the conclusion of a search for an "intelligence gene" by comparing twins: the researchers concluded that there might be as many as 10,000 "gene

sites" or "genetic words" responsible for intelligence and cognitive diseases, each playing a tiny part by itself.

In view of such complexities, one wishes that modern scientists would avail themselves of a road map provided by—yes!—the Sumerians. The remarkable advances in astronomy keep corroborating the Sumerian cosmogony and the scientific data provided in the *Epic of Creation*: the existence of other solar systems, highly elliptic orbital paths, retrograde orbits, catastrophism, water on the outer planets— as well as explanations for why Uranus lies on its side, the origin of the Asteroid Belt and of the Moon, the Earth's cavity on one side and the continents on the other side. All is explained by the scientifically sophisticated tale of Nibiru and the Celestial Battle.

Why not then take seriously, as a scientific road map, the other part of the Sumerian creation tales—that of the creation of The Adam?

The Sumerian texts inform us, first of all, that the "seed of life"—the genetic alphabet—was imparted to Earth by Nibiru during the Celestial Battle, some four billion years ago. If the evolutionary processes on Nibiru began a mere one percent before they were launched on Earth, evolution there had begun forty million years before it started on Earth. It is thus quite plausible that the advanced superhumans, Anunnaki, were capable of space travel half a million years ago. It is also plausible that when they came here, they found on Earth the parallel intelligent beings still at the hominid stage.

But coming from the same "seed," transgenic manipulation was possible, as Enki had discovered and then suggested. "The being we need already exists!" he explained. "All we need to do is put our [genetic] mark on it."

One must presume that by then the Anunnaki were aware of the complete genome of the Nibiruans, and capable of determining no less of the hominids' genome as we are by now of ours. What traits, specifically, did Enki and Ninmah choose to transfer from the Anunnaki to the hominids? Both Sumerian texts and biblical verses indicate that while the first humans possessed some (but not all) of the longevity of the

Anunnaki, the creator couple deliberately withheld from The Adam the genes of immortality (i.e. the immense longevity of the Anunnaki that paralleled Nibiru's orbital period). What defects, on the other hand, remained hidden in the depths of the recombined genome of The Adam?

We strongly believe that were qualified scientists to study in detail the data recorded in the Sumerian texts, valuable biogenetic and medical information could be obtained. An amazing case in point is the deficiency known as Williams Syndrome. Afflicting roughly one in 20,000 births, its victims have a very low IQ verging on retardation; but at the same time they excel in some artistic field. Recent research has discovered that the syndrome resulting in such "idiot savants" (as they are sometimes described) is caused by a minute gap in Chromosome 7, depriving the person of some fifteen genes. One of the frequent impairments is the inability of the brain to recognize what the eyes see—*impaired eyesight*; one of the most common talents is *musical*. **But that is exactly the instance recorded in the Sumerian text of the man with impaired eyesight whom Enki taught to sing and play music!**

Because The Adam could not, at first, procreate (requiring the Anunnaki to engage in cloning), we must conclude that at that stage the hybrid being possessed only the basic twenty-two chromosomes. The types of ailments, deficiencies (and cures) that modern biomedicine should expect to find on those chromosomes are the types and range listed in the Enki and Ninmah texts.

The next genetic manipulation (echoed in the Bible in the tale of Adam and Eve in the Garden of Eden) was the granting of the ability to procreate—the addition of the X (female) and Y (male) chromosomes to the basic 22 (Fig. 44). Contrary to long-held beliefs that these two chromosomes have no other function besides determining the offspring's sex, recent research has revealed that the chromosomes play wider and more diverse roles. For some reason this astonished the scientists in particular regarding the Y (male) chromosome. Studies published at the end of 1997 under

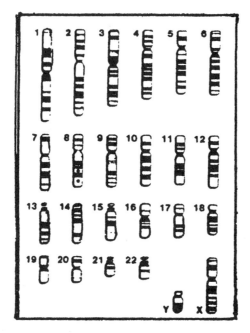

Figure 44

scientific headings as "Functional Coherence of the Human Y Chromosome" received bold headlines in the press such as "Male Chromosome Is Not a Genetic Wasteland, After All" (the *New York Times*, October 28, 1997). (These discoveries confirmed, as an unexpected bonus, that "Adam," too, like Eve, had come out of southeastern Africa).

Where did Enki—the *Nachash*—obtain the X and Y chromosomes? And what about the source of the mtDNA? Hints scattered in the Sumerian texts suggest that Ninki, Enki's spouse, played some crucial role in the final stage of human creation. It was she, Enki decided, who would give the humans the final touch, one more genetic heritage:

> *The newborn's fate,*
> *thou shalt pronounce;*

Ninki would fix upon it
the image of the gods.

The words echo the biblical statement that "in their *image* and after their *likeness* did the *Elohim* create The Adam." And if indeed it was Ninki, Enki's spouse and mother of Marduk, who was the source of the mtDNA of "Eve," the importance attached to the sister-wife lineage begins to make sense; for it constituted one more link to Man's cosmic origins.

Sumerian texts assert that while the gods kept "Eternal Life" to themselves, they did give Mankind *"Wisdom,"* an extra dose of intelligence genes. That additional genetic contribution, we believe, is the subject of a text that scholars call *The Legend of Adapa*.

Clearly identified in the text as a "Son of Eridu," Ea/Enki's "cult center" in the Edin, he was also called in the text "the son of Ea"—an offspring, as far as other pieces of data suggest, of Ea/Enki himself by a woman other than his spouse. By dint of this lineage, as well as by deliberate action, Adapa was recalled for generations as the Wisest of Men, and was nicknamed the Sage of Eridu:

> *In those days, in those years,*
> *Ea created the Sage of Eridu*
> *as a model of men.*
> *Wide understanding he perfected for him,*
> *disclosing the designs of the Earth.*
> *To him he had given Widsom;*
> *Eternal Life he had not given him.*

This clash between Fate and Destiny takes us to the moment when *Homo sapiens-sapiens* appeared; Adapa, too, being the son of a god, asked for immortality. That, as we know from the *Epic of Gilgamesh*, could be obtained by ascending heavenward to the abode of the Anunnaki; and that was what Ea/Enki told Adapa. Undaunted, Adapa asked for and received Enki's "road map" for reaching the place: "He made

Adapa take the way to heaven, and to heaven he ascended.'' Enki provided him with correct instructions of how to gain admittance to the throne room of Anu; but also gave him completely wrong instructions on how to behave when he would be offered the Bread of Life and the Water of Life. If you accept them and partake of them, Enki warned Adapa, surely you shall die! And, so misled by his own father, Adapa refused the food and the waters of the gods and ended up subject to his mortal's Destiny.

But Adapa did accept a garment that was brought to him and wrapped himself in it, and did take the oil that was offered to him, and anointed himself with it. Therefore, Anu declared, Adapa would be *initiated into the secret knowledge of the gods.* He showed him the celestial expanse, ''from the horizon of heaven to heaven's zenith.'' He would be allowed to return to Eridu safe and sound, and there would be initiated by the goddess Ninkarrak into the secrets of ''the ills that were allotted to Mankind, the diseases that were wrought upon the bodies of mortals,'' and taught by her how to heal such ailments.

It would be relevant here to recall the biblical assurances by Yahweh to the Israelites in the wilderness in Sinai. Wandering three days without any water, they reached a watering hole whose water was unpotable. So God pointed out to Moses a certain tree and told him to throw it into the water, and the water became potable. And Yahweh said to the Israelites: If you shall give ear to my commandments, I shall not impose on thee the illnesses of Egypt; ''I Yahweh shall be thine healer'' (Exodus 15:26). The promise by Yahweh to act as the healer of his chosen people is repeated in Exodus 23:25, where a specific reference is made to enabling a woman who is barren to bear children. (That particular promise was kept in regard to Sarah and other female heroines of the biblical narrative).

Since we are dealing here with a divine entity, it is safe to assume that we are dealing here also with *genetic healing.* The incident with the *Nefilim,* who had found on the eve of the Deluge that the ''Daughters of The Adam'' were com-

patible, and sufficiently so to be able to have children together, also involves genetics.

Was such knowledge of genetics, for healing purposes,
imparted to Adapa or other demigods or initiates? And if
so—how? How could the complex genetic code be taught to
Earthlings in those "primitive" times?

**For the answer, we believe, we have to search in letters
and in numbers.**

7

SECRET KNOWLEDGE,
SACRED TEXTS

Science—the understanding of the workings of the heavens and the Earth—was the gods' possession; so did the ancient peoples unequivocally believe. It was a "secret of the gods," to be hidden from Mankind or revealed, from time to time and only partly, to selected individuals—initiates into the divine secrets.

"Everything that we know was taught to us by the gods," the Sumerians stated in their writings; and therein lies the foundation, throughout the millennia and unto our own times, of Science and Religion, of the discovered and the occult.

First there was the Secret Knowledge; what was revealed when Mankind was granted Understanding became Sacred Wisdom, the foundation of human civilizations and advancement. As to the secrets that the gods had kept to themselves—those, in the end, proved the most devastating to Mankind. And one must begin to wonder whether the unending search for That Which Is Hidden, sometimes in the guise of mysticism, stems not from the wish to attain the divine but from a fear of what Fate the gods—in their secret conclaves or in hidden codes—have destined for Mankind.

Some of the knowledge that was, or could be, imparted to Mankind when Wisdom and Understanding were granted can be gleaned from God's challenge to Job regarding what he does not know (but God does). "Say if thou knowest science," the biblical Lord stated to the suffering Job:

Who has measured the Earth,
that it be known?

125

Who has stretched a cord upon it?
By what were its platforms wrought?
Who has cast its stone of corners?

Wherefrom cometh Wisdom,
and where is Understanding located?
Mortals know not its arraignment,
in the Land of the Living it is not found.

The ways thereof to Elohim *are known,*
God knows the place thereof;
For he sees to the ends of the Earth
and all that is under the Heavens he views.

With such words did the biblical Lord challenge Job (in chapter 28) to stop questioning the reasons for his Fate, or its ultimate purpose; for Man's knowledge—Wisdom and Understanding—fall so far short of God's, that it serves no purpose to question or try to fathom divine will.

That ancient treatment of Wisdom and Understanding of the secrets of the heavens and the Earth—of science—as a divine domain to which only a few selected mortals can be given access, found expression not only in canonical writings but also in such Jewish mysticism as the *Kaballah*, according to which the Divine Presence symbolized by God's Crown rests on the penultimate supports designated Wisdom (*Hokhmah*) and Understanding (*Binah*) (Fig. 45). They are the same two components of scientific knowledge regarding which Job had been challenged.

The references to *Hokhmah* ("Wisdom") in the Old Testament reveal that it was considered to have been a gift from God, because it was the Lord of the Universe who possessed the Wisdom required for creating the heavens and the Earth. "How great are thy deeds, Oh Lord; with Wisdom hast thou wrought them all," Psalm 104 states as it describes and extols, phase by phase, the Creator's handiwork. When the Lord granted Wisdom to selected humans, the Bible held, He

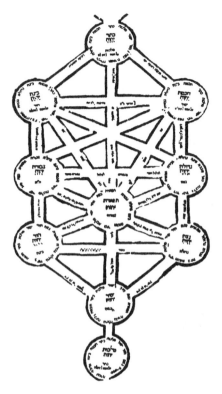

Figure 45

in fact shared with them secret knowledge concerning the heavens and the Earth and all that is upon the Earth. The Book of Job described such knowledge as "Wisdom's Secrets," which had not been revealed to him.

Revelation, the sharing of secret knowledge with humanity through chosen initiates, began before the Deluge. Adapa, the offspring of Enki to whom Wisdom and Understanding (but not Eternal Life) were granted, was shown by Anu the expanse of the heavens not merely as a sightseeing thrill. Post-Diluvial references to him attributed to him the authorship of a work known by its English title *Writings Regarding Time, [from] Divine Anu and Divine Enlil*—a treatise that dealt with time reckoning and the calendar. The

Tale of Adapa, on the other hand, specifically mentions that
he was taught, back in Eridu, the arts of medicine and healing. He was thus a well-rounded scientist, adept in both celestial and earthly subjects; he was also anointed as the
Priest of Eridu—perhaps the first to combine Science and
Religion.

Sumerian records spoke of another, pre-Diluvial Chosen
One who was initiated into the divine secrets by being taken
up to the celestial abode of the Anunnaki. He came from
Sippar (''Bird City'') where Utu/Shamash was in charge, and
was probably an offspring of his, a demigod. Known in the
texts as EN.ME.DUR.ANNA as well as EN.ME.DUR.AN.KI
(''Master of the Divine Tablets Concerning the Heavens'' or
''Master of the Divine Tablets of the Bond Heaven-Earth''),
he, too, was taken aloft to be taught secret knowledge. His
sponsors and teachers were the gods Utu/Shamash and Ish-
kur/Adad:

> *Shamash and Adad [clothed? anointed?] him,*
> *Shamash and Adad set him on a large golden throne.*
> *They showed him how to observe oil and water,*
> *a secret of Anu, Enlil and Ea.*

> *They gave him a divine tablet,*
> *the* Kibbu, *a secret of Heaven and Earth.*
> *They placed in his hand a cedar instrument,*
> *a favorite of the great gods.*
> *They taught him to make calculations with numbers.*

Though the *Tale of Adapa* does not say so explicitly, it
appears that he was allowed, if not actually required, to share
some of his secret knowledge with his fellow humans, for
else why would he compose the renowned book? In the case
of Enmeduranki the transmission of the learned secrets was
also mandated—but with the stricture that it must be limited
to the line of priests, from father to son, begun with Enmeduranki:

The learned savant
who guards the secrets of the great gods
will bind his favored son with an oath
before Shamash and Adad.
By the Divine Tablet, with a stylus,
he will instruct him in the secrets of the gods.

The tablet on which this text has been inscribed (now kept in the British Museum) has a postscript: "Thus was the line of priests created, those who are allowed to approach Shamash and Adad."

The Bible also recorded the heavenward ascent of the pre-Diluvial patriarch Enoch—the seventh of the ten listed, as was Enmeduranki in the Sumerian King List. Of that extraordinary experience the Bible only says that, at age 365, Enoch was taken aloft to be with God. Fortunately, the extrabiblical *Book of Enoch,* handed down through the millennia and surviving in two versions, provide much greater detail; how much is originally ancient, and how much was fancy and speculation when the "books" were compiled close to the beginning of the Christian era, one cannot say. But the contents are worth summarizing, if for no other reason than for the affinity to the Enmeduranki tale, and because of a briefer but still much more extensive narrative in another extrabiblical book, the *Book of Jubilees.*

From these sources it emerges that Enoch made not one but two celestial journeys. On the first one he was taught the Secrets of Heaven, and was instructed to impart the knowledge on his return to Earth to his sons. Ascending toward the Divine Abode, he was lofted through a series of heavenly spheres. From the place of the Seventh Heaven he could see the shape of the planets; in the Eighth Heaven he could discern constellations. The Ninth Heaven was the "home of the twelve signs of the zodiac." And in the Tenth Heaven was the Divine Throne of God.

(It should be noted here that the abode of Anu, according to Sumerian texts, was on Nibiru, which we have identified as a tenth planet of our Solar System. In *Kabbalah* beliefs,

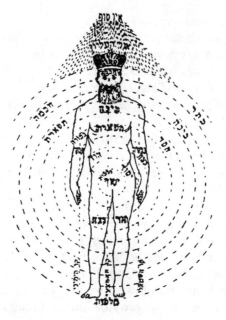

Figure 46

the way to the abode of God Almighty led through ten *Se-firot*, translated "brilliances" but actually depicted as ten concentric spheres—Fig. 46—in which the central one is named *Yessod* ("Foundation"), the eighth and the ninth *Binah* and *Hokhmah*, and the tenth *Ketter*, the "Crown" of the God Most High. Beyond that stretches *Ein Soff*, "Infinity").

Accompanied by two angels, Enoch arrived at his final destination, God's Abode. There his earthly garments were removed; he was clothed in divine garments and anointed by the angels (as was done to Adapa). On the Lord's command, the archangel Pravuel brought out "the books from the sacred storehouse" and gave him a reed stylus with which to write down what the archangel would dictate to him. For thirty days and thirty nights Pravuel dictated and Enoch wrote down "the secrets of the workings of heaven, of the Earth and of the seas; and of all the elements, their passages

and goings, and the thunderings of the thunder; and [the se-
crets] of the Sun and the Moon, and the goings and changings of the planets; the seasons and the years and the days
and the hours . . . and all the things of men, the tongues of
of every human song . . . and all the things fit to learn."

According to the *Book of Enoch*, all that vast knowledge,
"secrets of the Angels and God," was written down in 360
sacred books, which Enoch took back with him to Earth.
Summoning his sons, he showed them the books and explained their contents to them. He was still talking and instructing when a sudden darkness fell and the two angels
who had brought Enoch back lifted him and returned him to
the heavens; it was precisely the day and hour of his 365th
birthday. The Bible (Genesis 5:23–24) simply states: "And
all the days of Enoch were three hundred and sixty and five
years; and Enoch walked with God, and he was no more, for
he was taken by *Elohim*."

A prominent similarity between all three tales (Adapa, Enmeduranki, and Enoch) is the involvement of two divine beings in the celestial experience. Adapa was met at the Gate
of Anu, and accompanied in and out, by the two young gods
Dumuzi and Gizidda; Enmeduranki's sponsors/teachers were
Shamash and Adad; and Enoch's, two archangels. The tales
undoubtedly were the inspiration for an Assyrian depiction
of Anu's heavenly gate, in which it is guarded by two Eaglemen. The gate bears the symbol of Nibiru, the Winged
Disc, and the heavenly location is indicated by the celestial
symbols of the Earth (as the seventh planet), the Moon, and
the complete Solar System (Fig. 47).

Another aspect that stands out—though not explicitly so
in the case of Enoch—is the tradition that the granting of the
Wisdom and Understanding made the chosen individual not
just a scientist but also a priest, and moreover the progenitor
of a priestly line. We find this principle employed in the
Sinai wilderness during the Exodus, when Yahweh, the biblical Lord, chose Aaron (the brother of Moses) and his sons
to be the Lord's priests (Exodus 28:1). Already distinguished
by belonging to the tribe of Levi—both on the father's *and*

Figure 47

the mother's sides (Exodus 2:1)—Moses and Aaron were
initiated into magical powers that enabled them to perform
miracles as well as trigger the calamities that were meant to
convince the Pharaoh to let the Israelites leave. Aaron and
his sons were then sanctified—"upgraded" in current parlance—to become priests endowed with considerable Wisdom and Understanding. The Book of Leviticus sheds light
on some of the knowledge that was granted to Aaron and
his sons; it included secrets of the calendar (quite complex,
since it was a lunar-solar calendar), of human maladies and
healing, and veterinary knowledge. Considerable anatomical
information is included in the relevant chapters of Leviticus,
and the possibility that the Israelite priests were given
"hands-on" lessons cannot be ruled out in view of the fact
that clay models of anatomical parts, inscribed with medical
instructions, were current in Babylon even before the time
of the Exodus—Fig. 48.

(The Bible described King Solomon as the "wisest of
men" who could discourse on the biodiversity of all the
plants, "from cedars of Lebanon to the hyssop that grows
out of a wall, and animals, and birds, and creeping things,
and fishes." He could do so because in addition to the Wisdom and the Understanding (intelligence) that were God-
given, he also acquired *Da'ath*—learned knowledge).

The priestly line begun with Aaron was subjected to rig-

Figure 48

orous laws imposing marital and procreation constraints. Whom they could have conjugal relations with and especially whom they could marry required that "the priestly seed shall not be profaned," and if one's seed shall be imperfect— "shall have a blemish," a mutation, a genetic defect—that man was prohibited through all generations to perform priestly duties, "for I Yahweh hath sanctified the priestly line" of Aaron.

These strictures intrigued generations of biblical scholars; but their true significance became evident only with the advent of DNA researches. It was only in January 1997, in the journal *Nature*, that an international group of scientists reported the existence of a "Priestly Gene" among Jews whose lineage can be traced back to Aaron. Unchanged Jewish traditions require that certain rituals and blessings called for on the Sabbath and High Holidays services must be per-

formed only by a *Cohen*. The term, meaning "priest," was first used in the Bible to describe Aaron and his sons. Ever since then, the designation has been passed down through the generations from fathers to sons, and the only way to become a Cohen is to be born as a son of one. This privileged status has been as often as not identified by using "Cohen" as a family name (transmuted into Kahn, Kahane, Kuhn) or as an adjective added after a person's name, so and so *Ha-Cohen*, "the priest."

It was this aspect of the patrilineal nature of the Jewish *Cohen* tradition that intrigued a research team from Israel, England, Canada, and the USA. Focusing on the male ("Y") chromosome that is passed from father to son, they tested hundreds of "Cohens" in different countries and found that by and large they had two unique "markers" on the chromosome. This proved to be the case both for *Ashkenazi* (East European) and *Sephardi* (Near Eastern/African) Jews who had branched out after the destruction of the Jerusalem Temple in A.D. 70, indicating the antiquity of the genetic markers.

"The simplest and most straightforward explanation is that these men have the Y chromosome of Aaron," explained Dr. Karl Skorecki of the Israel Institute of Technology in Haifa.

The tales of those who were initiated into the secret knowledge assert that the information was written down in "books." These, for sure, were not what we now call "books"—inscribed pages bound together. The many texts discovered in caves near the Dead Sea in Israel are referred to as the Dead Sea scrolls, for they were texts inscribed on sheets of parchment (made mostly of goat skins) sewn together and rolled to form scrolls, the way the *Scrolls of the Law* (the first five books of the Hebrew Bible) are inscribed and rolled to this day. The biblical Prophets (especially Ezekiel) featured scrolls as part of the divinely given messages. Ancient Egyptian texts were written on papyrus—sheets made from reeds growing in the Nile River. And the earliest known texts, from Sumer, were inscribed on clay tablets;

using a reed stylus, the scribe would make markings on a piece of wet clay that, after it dried, would become a hard inscribed tablet.

In which form were the "books" written by Adapa, Enmeduranki, and Enoch (360 of them by the latter!)? Bearing in mind that they are attributed to a time before the Deluge— thousands of years even before the Sumerian civilization— probably in none of the post-Diluvial forms, although the Assyrian king Ashurbanipal did boast that he could read "writing from before the Flood." Since in each instance what was written down was dictated by the divine Lord, it would be logical to wonder whether the writing was done in what some Sumerian and Akkadian texts call *Kitab Ilani*— "writing of the gods." References to such writings by the Anunnaki may be found, for example, in inscriptions dealing with the rebuilding of run-down temples, in which the claim was made that the reconstruction followed "the drawings from olden times and *the writing of the Upper Heaven*." The Sumerians listed a goddess, Nisaba (sometimes spelled Nidaba), as the patron goddess of scribes and the one who kept the records for the gods; her symbol was the Holy Stylus.

One of the references to writings of the gods in the earliest times is found in a Hittite text dubbed by scholars *The Song of Ullikummis*. Written on clay tablets that have been discovered in the ancient Hittite capital Hattushas (near the present-day village of Boghaskoy in central Turkey), it relates a puzzling tale of a "vigorous god made of diorite stone" that an ancient god whom the Hittite named Kumarbis had fashioned in order to challenge the other gods. The challenged gods, unable to withstand or counter the challenger Ullikummis, rushed to Enki's abode in the Lower World to obtain from him the hidden "old tablets with the words of fate." But after the "ancient storehouse" was opened, and the "olden seals" with which the tablets were secured were removed, it was discovered that the writing was in "the olden words," requiring the Olden Gods to understand them.

In Egypt it was Thoth who was venerated as the Divine

Scribe. It was he who, after the Council of the Gods resolved to recognize Horus as the legitimate heir, inscribed on a metal tablet the Decree of the Gods, and the tablet was then lodged in the "divine Chamber of Records." In addition to records for divine use, Thoth was also credited by the Egyptians with writing books for the guidance of mortals. The *Book of the Dead*, they held, was a composition "written by Thoth with his own fingers" as a guide to the Journey in the Afterlife. A shorter work called by the Egyptians the *Book of Breathings* also contained the statement that it was Thoth who "had written this book with his own fingers." And in the *Tales of the Magicians*, to which we have already referred, it was said that the living but inanimate king and queen whom Thoth had punished guarded, in the subterranean chamber, "the book that the god Thoth has written with his own hand" and in which secret knowledge concerning the Solar System, astronomy, and the calendar was revealed. When the seeker of such "ancient books of sacred writings" penetrated the subterranean chamber, he saw the book "giving off a light as if the Sun shone there."

What were those divine "books" and what kind of writing was on them?

The epithet-name of Enmeduranna, "Master of the Divine Tablets Concerning Heaven," draws attention to the term ME in his name, translated here as "Divine Tablets." In truth no one can be sure what the ME's were, whether tablets or something more akin to computer-memory chips or discs. They were objects small enough to be held in one hand, for it was told that Inanna/Ishtar, seeking to elevate her city Uruk to capital status, connivingly obtained from Enki scores of the ME's that were encoded with the secrets of Supreme Lordship, Kingship, Priesthood, and other aspects of a high civilization. And we recall that the evil Zu stole from Enlil's Duranki the Tablets of Destinies and the ME's which were encoded with the Divine Formulas. Perhaps we will grasp what they were if we look to technology millennia ahead.

Putting aside the question of the gods' own writings and data-keeping for their own purposes, the issue of what lan-

guage and what writing system were used when secret knowledge was dictated to Earthlings for use by Earthlings becomes a matter of great significance when it comes to the Bible—and especially so in regard to the events on Mount Sinai.

Paralleling the tale of Enoch staying in the heavenly abode "thirty days and thirty nights" taking dictation, is the biblical report of Moses, having ascended toward the Lord God atop Mount Sinai, "stayed there with Yahweh forty days and forty nights—bread he did not eat and water he did not drink—and he wrote upon the tablets the words of the Covenant and the Ten Commandments" as God dictated (Exodus 34:28).

Those, however, were the second set of tablets, replacing the first set that Moses smashed in anger when he had come down from Mount Sinai a previous time. The Bible provides greater—and mind-boggling—details regarding that first instance of sacred writings; then, the Bible explicitly states, *God himself did the inscribing!*

The tale begins in chapter 24 of the book of Exodus, when Moses and Aaron and two of his sons, and seventy of the Elders of Israel, were invited to approach Mount Sinai on the peak of which the Lord had landed in his *Kabod*. There the dignitaries could glimpse the divine presence through a thick cloud, blazing as a "devouring fire." Then Moses alone was summoned to the mountaintop, to receive the *Torah* ("Teachings") and the Commandments *that the Lord God had already written down*:

> *And Yahweh said unto Moses:*
> *Come up to me upon the Mount*
> *and remain there,*
> *and I will give thee the stone tablets—*
> *the Teachings and the Commandments—*
> *that I had written,*
> *so that you may teach them.*
>
> *Exodus 24:12*

"And Moses went into the midst of the cloud, and ascended the Mount; and he stayed there forty days and forty nights." Then Yahweh

> *Gave to Moses,*
> *when He had finished speaking with him,*
> *the two Tablets of Testimony—*
> *stone tablets,*
> *inscribed with the finger of* Elohim.
>
> *Exodus 31:17*

Additional astounding information regarding the tablets and the manner in which they were inscribed is provided in Exodus 32:16–17 that describe the events that took place as Moses was coming down the Mount after a long and (to the people) inexplicable absence:

> *And Moses turned to come down from the Mount,*
> *and the two Tablets of the Testimony in his hand—*
> *tablets inscribed on both their sides,*
> *inscribed on the one side and on the other side.*
> *And the Tablets were the handiwork of* Elohim,
> *and the writing was the writing of* Elohim,
> *and it was engraved upon the tablets*

Two tablets made of stone, divinely handcrafted. Inscribed front and back in the "writing of the *Elohim"*— which must mean both language and script; and so engraved into the stone by God himself!

And all that in a language and in a script that Moses could read and understand, for he was to teach all that to the Israelites . . .

As we know from the rest of the biblical record, Moses smashed the two tablets when, reaching the encampment, he saw that in his absence the people made a golden calf to be worshiped in imitation of Egyptian customs. When the crisis was over,

Yahweh said unto Moses:
Hew thyself two tablets of stone
like the first two ones,
and I shall write upon these tablets
the words which were on the first tablets
that thou hast broken.

Exodus 34:1

And Moses did so and went up the Mount again. There Yahweh came toward him, and Moses bowed and repeated his pleas for forgiveness. In response, the Lord God dictated to him additional commandments, saying: "Write thee these words down, for in accordance with them did I make a Covenant with thee and with the people of Israel." And Moses stayed on the Mount forty days and forty nights, recording on the tablets "the words of the Covenant and the Ten Commandments" (Exodus 35:27–28). This time, *Moses was taking down dictation.*

Not only the sections in Exodus, Leviticus, and Deuteronomy recording the Teachings and Commandments, but all of the first five books of the Hebrew Bible (the above plus Genesis and Numbers) have been deemed, from the very beginning, to be sacred writings. Embraced by the general term *Torah*, they are also known as the *Five Books of Moses*, because of the tradition that Moses himself wrote or authored all five of them as a divine revelation to him. Therefore, the *Torah* scrolls that are taken out of their ark in synagogues and read on the Sabbath and High Holidays must be copied (by special scribes) precisely the way they have come down through the ages—book by book, chapter by chapter, verse by verse, word by word, *letter by letter*. An error of one letter disqualifies the whole five-book scroll.

While this letter-by-letter precision has been studied by Jewish sages and biblical scholars throughout the ages (long before the latest interest in "secret codes" in the *Torah*), an even more challenging aspect of the long and extensive dictation and the required letter-by-letter accuracy has been completely ignored:

And that is, that such a method of writing upon Mount Sinai could not have been the slow cuneiform script of Mesopotamia that was usually written with a stylus on wet clay, nor the monumental hieroglyphic picturelike script of Egypt. The volume and speed and the letter-by-letter accuracy required an *alphabetic script*!

The problem is that at the time of the Exodus, circa 1450 B.C., nowhere in the ancient world did an alphabetic script yet exist.

The concept of an alphabet is the work of genius; and whoever the genius was, he based it on existing foundations. Egyptian hieroglyphic writing advanced from picture-signs depicting objects to signs standing for syllables or even consonants; but it has remained a complex writing system of countless picture-signs (see Fig. 24b). Sumerian writing advanced from its original pictographs to cuneiform (Fig. 49) and the signs acquired a syllabic sound; but to form from them a vocabulary required hundreds of different signs. The genius combined cuneiform ease with Egyptian advances to consonants, and *achieved it with just twenty-two signs*!

Starting with that, the ingenious inventor asked himself as well as his disciple: What is the word for what you see? The answer—*in the language of the Semitic Israelites*—was *Aluf*. Fine, said the inventor: Let us call this symbol *Aleph* and simply pronounce it "A." He then drew the pictograph for house. What do you call that? he asked, and the disciple answered: *Bayit*. Fine, said the inventor, from now on we will call this sign "*Beth*" and pronounce it simply as "B."

We cannot vouch that such a conversation actually took place, but we are certain that this was the process of creating and inventing the Alpha-Bet. The third letter, *Gimel* (pronounced "G") was the image of a camel (*Gamal* in Hebrew); the next one, *Daleth* for "D," represented *Deleth*, "door" (on its hinges); and so on through the twenty-two letters of the Semitic alphabet (Fig. 50), all of which serve as consonants and three of which can double up as vowels.

Who was the ingenious innovator?

INNER TRADITIONS
BEAR & COMPANY

Inner Traditions • Bear & Company
P.O. Box 388
Rochester, VT 05767-0388
U.S.A.

PLEASE SEND US THIS CARD TO RECEIVE OUR LATEST CATALOG.

Book in which this card was found

❑ Check here if you would like to receive our catalog via e-mail.

Name_____ Company_____

Address_____ Phone_____

City_____ State_____ Zip____ Country____

E-mail address_____

Please check the following area(s) of interest to you:

❑ Health   ❑ Self-help   ❑ Science/Nature   ❑ Shamanism

❑ Ancient Mysteries   ❑ New Age/Spirituality ❑ Ethnobotany   ❑ Martial Arts

❑ Spanish Language   ❑ Sexuality/Tantra   ❑ Children   ❑ Teen

Please send a catalog to my friend:

Name_____ Company_____

Address_____ Phone_____

City_____ State_____ Zip____ Country____

E-mail:_____

Order at 1-800-246-8648 • Fax (802) 767-3726

E-mail: customerservice@InnerTraditions.com • Web site: www.InnerTraditions.com

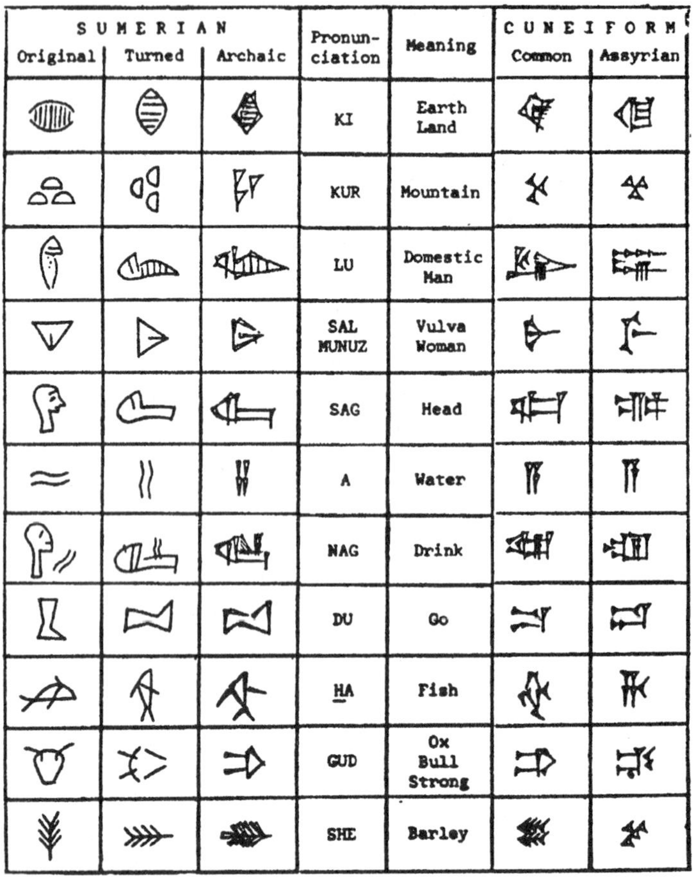

SUMERIAN			Pronun-	Meaning	CUNEIFORM	
Original	Turned	Archaic	ciation		Common	Assyrian
			KI	Earth Land		
			KUR	Mountain		
			LU	Domestic Man		
			SAL MUNUZ	Vulva Woman		
			SAG	Head		
			A	Water		
			NAG	Drink		
			DU	Go		
			HA	Fish		
			GUD	Ox Bull Strong		
			SHE	Barley		

Figure 49

If one is to accept the learned opinion, it was some manual laborer, a slave in the Egyptian turquoise mines in the western Sinai, near the Red Sea, because it was there that Sir Flinders Petrie found in 1905 signs carved on walls that, a decade later, Sir Alan Gardiner deciphered as "acrophonic"—spelling out L-B-A-L-T (Fig. 51); it meant Dedicated "To the Mistress" (presumably the goddess Hathor)—but in Semitic, not Egyptian! Further similar writings discovered in that area left no doubt that the alphabet originated there; from

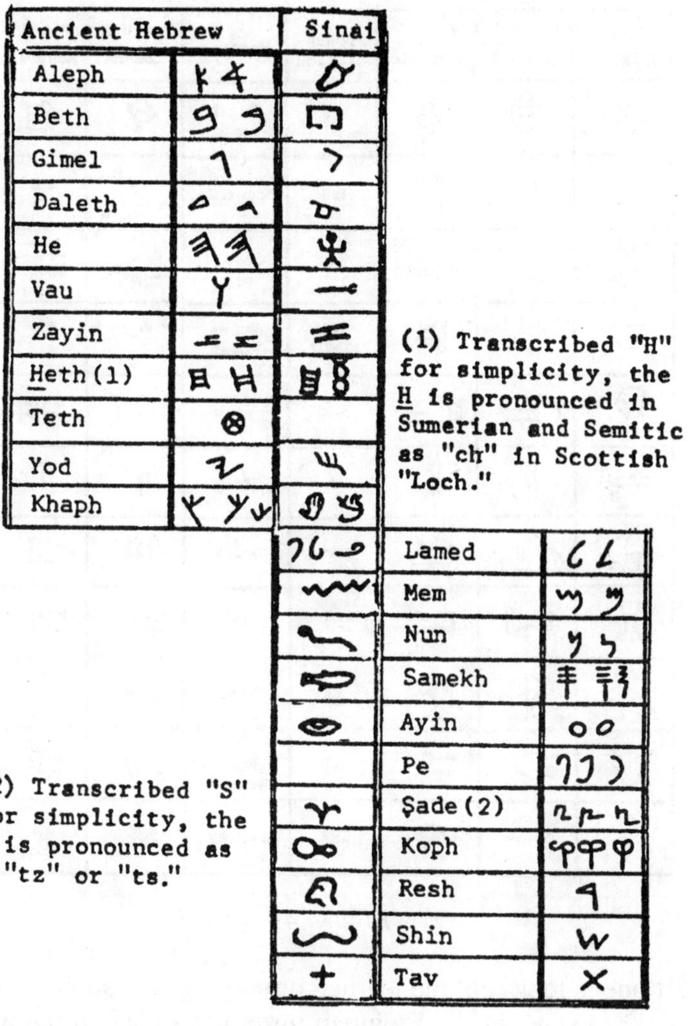

Ancient Hebrew		Sinai
Aleph	ꓘ ꓯ	𝑂
Beth	9 9	⊓
Gimel	�1	>
Daleth	◿ ◺	⊓
He	㋡ ㋡	⚥
Vau	Y	⊸
Zayin	⊐ ⊏	⊒
Heth (1)	目 ㅐ	目 目
Teth	⊗	
Yod	𝒵	⅏
Khaph	ꓘ ꓘᵥ	Ɗ ꙗ

(1) Transcribed "H" for simplicity, the H̲ is pronounced in Sumerian and Semitic as "ch" in Scottish "Loch."

	Lamed	⊂ ⊂
꒛ᒪ ᒧ	Lamed	⊂ ⊂
⌄⌄⌄	Mem	꒲ ꒲
⌐	Nun	꒤ ꒥
⬭	Samekh	⌹ ⌹⌿
⬮	Ayin	○ ⊘
	Pe	꒒꒒⌒
ꙗ	Ṣade (2)	⌐ ⌐ ⌐
∞	Koph	φφ φ
꘯	Resh	⌐
⌣	Shin	w
+	Tav	✕

(2) Transcribed "S" for simplicity, the Ṣ is pronounced as "tz" or "ts."

Figure 50

there it spread to Canaan and then to Phoenicia (where an attempt to express the ingenious idea with cuneiform signs— Fig. 52—was short-lived). Beautifully executed, the original "Sinaitic script" served as the Temple script in Jerusalem and as the royal script of Judean kings (Fig. 53a) until it

Figure 51

was replaced, during the time of the Second Temple, with a square script borrowed from the Aramaeans (the script used in the Dead Sea scrolls unto modern times, Fig. 53b).

No one has really been comfortable with the attribution of the revolutionary innovation, at the end of the Bronze Age, to a slave in turquoise mines. It required an outstanding knowledge of speech and writing and linguistics, apart from outstanding Wisdom and Understanding, that could hardly have been possessed by a mere slave. And what was the purpose of inventing a new script when, in the very same mining areas, monuments and walls were filled with *Egyptian* hieroglyphic inscriptions (Fig. 54)? How could an obscure innovation in a restricted area spread to Canaan and beyond and replace there a writing method that had existed and served well for more than two millennia? It just does not make sense; but in the absence of another solution, that theory still stands.

But, if we have imagined right the conversation that

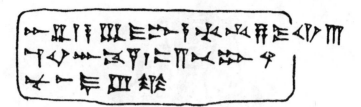

Figure 52

had led to this alphabet, then it was Moses to whom the first lesson was given. He was in the Sinai; he was there at the right time; he engaged in extensive writings; and he had the supreme teacher—God himself.

Little noticed in the biblical tales of Exodus is the fact that Moses was instructed by Yahweh to write things down even before the ascent upon Mount Sinai to receive the tablets. The first time was after the war with the Amalekites, a tribe that instead of acting as an ally betrayed the Israelites and attacked them. The betrayal, God said, should be remembered by all future generations: "And Yahweh said unto Moses: *Write this down in a book* for a remembrance" (Exodus 17:14). The second mention of a book of writings occurs in Exodus 24:4 and 24:7, in which it is reported that after the Lord God, speaking in a booming voice from atop the Mount, listed the conditions for an everlasting Covenant between Him and the Children of Israel, "Moses *wrote down* all the words of Yahweh, and built an altar at the foot of the Mount and erected twelve stone pillars according to the number of the tribes of Israel." And then "he took the covenant *book* and read from it to the people to hear."

The dictating and writing down had thus begun before the ascents of Moses to the mountaintop and the two separate writings on the stone tablets. One has to look to the earlier chapters of Exodus to find out when and where the alphabetic innovation—the language and writing employed in the Lord's communications with Moses—could have taken place. There we read that Moses, adopted as a son by the

Figures 53a and 53b

Pharaoh's daughter, fled for his life after he had killed an Egyptian official. His destination was the Sinai peninsula, where he ended up dwelling with the Midianite high priest (and marrying his daughter). And one day, shepherding the flocks, he wandered into the wilderness where the "Mount of the *Elohim*" was, and there he was summoned by God out of the burning bush and given the task of leading his people, the Children of Israel, out of Egypt.

Moses returned to Egypt only after the death of the Pharaoh who had sentenced him (Thothmes III, by our calculations), in 1450 B.C., and struggled with the next Pharaoh (Amenophis II in our opinion) for seven years until the Exodus was permitted. Having started to hear from the Lord

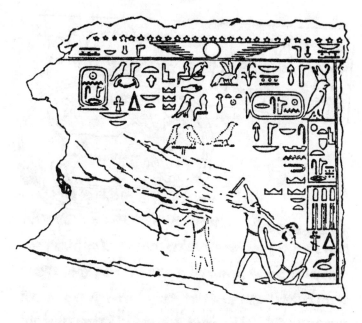

Figure 54

God already in the wilderness, and then during the seven years, there had thus been ample time to innovate and master a new form of writing, one that was simpler and much faster than those of the great empires of the time—Mesopotamian, Egyptian, Hittite.

The Bible relates extensive communications between Yahweh and Moses and Aaron from the moment Moses had been summoned to the burning bush onward. Whether the divine messages, sometimes involving detailed instructions, were ever in writing the Bible does not say; but it might be significant that the "magicians" in the Pharaoh's court thought that they had been written instructions: "And the Pharaoh's magicians said to him: This is the finger of god" (Exodus 8:15). "The *finger of God*," it will be recalled, was the term used in Egyptian texts regarding the god Thoth, to indicate a writing by the god himself.

If all this leads to the suggestion that alphabetic writing

began in the Sinai Peninsula—it should not be surprising that archaeologists have reached that same conclusion, but without being able to explain how such a tremendous and ingenious innovation could have originated in a wilderness.

Did the conversation that we have imagined actually take place, or did Moses invent the alphabet by himself? After all, he was in the Sinai peninsula at the very same time, he was highly educated in the Egyptian court (where correspondence with both the Mesopotamians and Hittites had been going on), and he undoubtedly learned the Semitic language from the Midianites (if not knowing it already from his Israelite brethren in Egypt). Did he, in his wanderings in the Sinai wilderness, see the Semitic slaves (Israelites who had by then been enslaved in Egypt), crudely etch on the mines' walls his idea of a new way of writing?

One would have liked to be able to attribute the brilliant innovation to Moses, acting alone; it would have been gratifying to credit the biblical leader of the Exodus, the only one who had conversed with God person-to-person according to the Bible, with the invention of the alphabet and the cultural revolution it had triggered. But the repeated references to Divine Writing, writing by God himself, and Moses only taking dictation, suggest that the alphabetic writing and language system were one of the ''secrets of the gods.'' Indeed, it was to the same Yahweh that the Bible attributed the invention/innovation of other diverse languages and scripts on a previous occasion—in the aftermath of the incident of the Tower of Babel.

One way or another, we feel that Moses was the initiate through whom the innovation was revealed to Mankind. And thus we can rightly call it *The Mosaic Alphabet*.

There is more to the first alphabet as a ''secret of the gods.'' It is based, in our opinion, on the most sophisticated and ultimate knowledge—that of the genetic code.

When the Greeks adopted the Mosaic alphabet a thousand years later (though reversing it as a mirror image, Fig. 55), they found it necessary to add more letters in order to allow

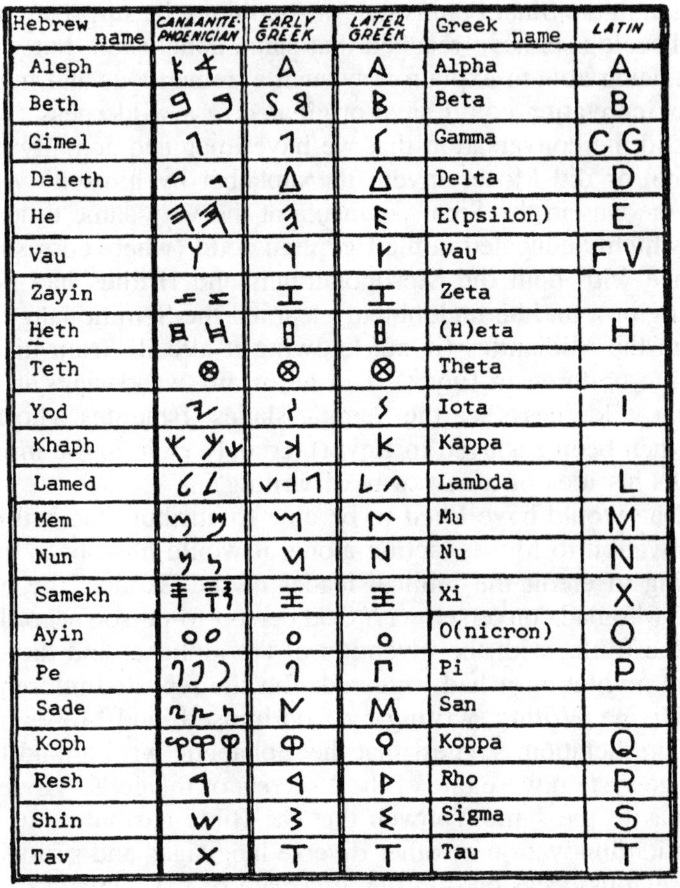

Hebrew name	CANAANITE-PHOENICIAN	EARLY GREEK	LATER GREEK	Greek name	LATIN
Aleph		Δ	A	Alpha	A
Beth		S �	B	Beta	B
Gimel		ꓶ	⌐	Gamma	C G
Daleth		Δ	Δ	Delta	D
He		ʒ	E	E(psilon)	E
Vau	Y	Y	ⱶ	Vau	F V
Zayin		I	I	Zeta	
Heth		8	8	(H)eta	H
Teth	⊗	⊗	⊗	Theta	
Yod		?	?	Iota	I
Khaph		ꓘ	K	Kappa	
Lamed		∨⌐ꓶ	L ∧	Lambda	L
Mem		ᛘ	ᛙ	Mu	M
Nun		Ⅵ	N	Nu	N
Samekh		王	王	Xi	X
Ayin	o o	o	o	O(nicron)	O
Pe		ꓶ	Г	Pi	P
Sade		Ⲙ	M	San	
Koph		Ϙ	Ϙ	Koppa	Q
Resh		ꓺ	Ρ	Rho	R
Shin	W	3	ξ	Sigma	S
Tav	X	T	T	Tau	T

Figure 55

for all the pronunciation needs. In fact, within the confines of the twenty-two letters of the Mosaic-Semitic alphabet, some letters can be pronounced as "soft" (V, Kh, S, Th) or hard (B, K, SH, T); and other letters had to double up as vowels.

Indeed, as we contemplate this limitation to *twenty-two*—no more, no less—we cannot help recalling the constrictions applied to the sacred number *twelve* (requiring the addition

or dropping of deities in order to keep the "Olympian Circle" to precisely twelve). Did such a hidden principle—divinely inspired—apply to the restriction of the original alphabet to twenty-two letters?

The number ought to be familiar in this day and age. It is the number of human chromosomes when The Adam was created, before the second genetic manipulation had added the sex chromosomes "Y" and "X"!

Did the Almighty who had revealed to Moses the secret of the alphabet, then, use the genetic code as the secret code of the alphabet?

The answer seems to be Yes.

If this conclusion seems outlandish, let us read the Lord's statement in Isaiah 45:11: "It is I who created the Letters . . . It is I who made the Earth and created the Adam upon it," thus sayeth Yahweh, the Holy One of Israel. Whoever was involved in the creation of Man was involved in the creation of the letters that make up the alphabet.

Present-day computer systems construct words and numbers from just two "letters," a Yes-No system of ones and zeroes matching an On-Off flow of electrons (and thus called binary). But attention has already shifted to the four-letter genetic code and the much greater speed with which the transactions take place within the living cell. Conceptually, the present computer language that is expressed in a sequence such as 01001100111100110000010100 etc. (and in countless variations using "0" and "1") can be envisaged as the genetic language of a DNA fragment expressed as the nucleotides CGTAGAATTCTGCGAACCTT and so on in a chain of DNA letters (that are always arranged in *three letter "words"*) bound as base-pairs in which the A binds with T, C with G. The problem and the challenge is how to create and read computer chips that are coated not with "0" and "1" electrons but with bits of genetic material. Advances since 1991 at various academic institutions as well as at commercial enterprises involved in genetic treatments have succeded in creating silicon chips coated with nucleotides. Comparing the speed and the capabilities of DNA Comput-

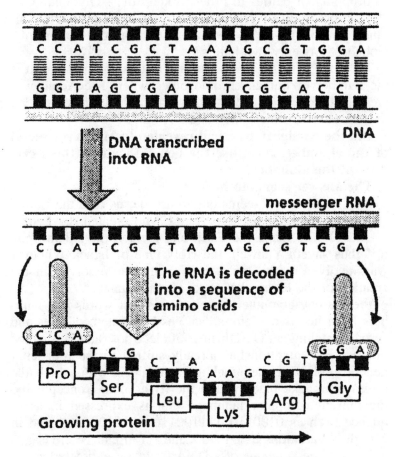

Figure 56

ing, as the new science is called, "the information storage capacity of DNA is huge," a research paper published in *Science* (October 1997) stated.

In nature, the genetic information encoded in the DNA is decoded, at lightning speed, by a messenger called RNA that transcribes and recombines the DNA "letters" into "words" consisting of three letters. These three-letter groupings, it has been established, lie at the core of all life forms on Earth because they spell out chemically and biologically the twenty

amino acids whose chains form the proteins of which all life on Earth—and probably elsewhere in the cosmos—consists. Figure 56 illustrates schematically, and in a simplified manner, how a given DNA sequence is decoded and recombined into the amino acids Propraline (''Pro''), Serine (''Ser''), etc., by means of the three-letter word code to build a protein.

The rich and precise Hebrew language is based on ''root'' words from which verbs, nouns, adverbs, adjectives, pronouns, tenses, conjugations and all other grammatical variants derive. For reasons that no one has been able to explain, these root words are made up of *three letters*. This is quite a departure from the Akkadian, the mother-language of all Semitic languages, which was formed from syllables—sometimes just one, sometimes two or three or more.

Could the reason for the three-letter Hebrew root words be the three letter DNA-language—the very source, as we have concluded, of the alphabet itself? If so, then the three letter root words corroborate this conclusion.

''Death and life are in the language,'' the Bible states in Proverbs (18:21). The statement has been treated allegorically. It is time, perhaps, to take it literally: *the language of the Hebrew Bible and the DNA genetic code of life (and death) are but two sides of the same coin.*

The mysteries that are encoded therein are vaster than one can imagine; they include among other wondrous discoveries the secrets of healing.

8

HIDDEN CODES,
MYSTIC NUMBERS

It was probably inevitable that with the advent of the modern computer age, some masters of the craft would turn their capabilities to a novel and new goal: the search for a "secret code" in the Bible.

While this is presented in scientific papers and even books as the epitome of modern sophistication, the fact is that this search is actually a *renewed*, not a new, search, albeit with new and more advanced tools.

The Hebrew Bible consists of three parts, the *Torah* ("Teachings"), which comprises the Pentateuch (the *Five Books of Moses*) and, historically and chronologically, covers the time from Creation through the wanderings of the Exodus and the death of Moses; *Neviyim* ("Prophets"), encompassing the books of Joshua and the Judges, Samuel and the Kings, and then the major and minor Prophets, the Psalms and Proverbs and Job—historically from the Israelite settlement in Canaan through the destruction of the First Temple of Jerusalem; and *Ketuvim* ("Writings"), starting with the Song of Songs through the books attributed to the two leaders who led the exiles back to Judea to rebuild the Temple (Ezra and Nehemiah) and (in the arrangement of the Hebrew Bible's canon) ending with 1 and 2 Chronicles. All together the three parts are called by the acronym *TaNaKh*; and it was already in the time of the Prophets that interpretive references to the first part, the Torah, were made.

Discussions by Jewish sages and religious leaders intended to "read between the lines" of the words of the Torah, then of the Prophets, intensified during the exile after the destruc-

tion (by the Babylonian king Nebuchadnezzar) of the First Temple, and even more so after the destruction of the Second Temple (by the Romans). The record of those deliberations is the *Talmud* ("The Study"). Jewish mysticism, known as the *Kaballah*, took over and built upon those earlier searches for hidden meanings.

That such hidden meanings did exist, the Bible itself attests. The key was the alphabet, the twenty-two letters.

A simple encoding device, which even schoolchildren often play, is the serial substitution of letters. Kabbalist sages in the Middle Ages used as a search tool a system known as ATBSh, in which the last letter of the Hebrew alphabet, Tav ("T") is substituted for the first letter Aleph ("A"); the last but one, Shin ("Sh") for the second Beth ("B"), and so on. The Kabbalist Abraham ben Jechiel Hacohen illustrated the system and provided the key to it in a book published in A.D. 1788.

But in fact such a coding system was used by the Prophet Jeremiah (7th century B.C.) who, prophesying the fall of mighty Babylon, substituted the spelling B-B-L (Babel) with the letters Sh-Sh-Kh to avoid imprisonment (Jeremiah 25:26 and 51:42). The Book of Lamentations, attributed to the Prophet Jeremiah, in which the fall and destruction of Jerusalem are bewailed, employed another hidden code, called Acrostics, in which the first (or sometimes last) letter of a verse make up a word or a name, or (as in the case of Jeremiah) reveal the identity of the sacred alphabetical letters. The first word in the first verse (translated "alas") begins with an Aleph, the second verse begins with a Beth and so on through the twenty-second verse. The same acrostics is repeated by the Prophet in the second chapter; then each letter starts two verses in the third chapter, reverting to one per verse in the fourth. Psalm 119 is constructed with eightfold acrostics!

The authenticity of certain verses in Psalms could be verified by noticing that each verse has two parts, each of which starts alphabetically (e.g., Psalm 145); the same clue is hidden in the verse arrangement of Proverbs 31. In Psalm 145, moreover, the three verses (11, 12, 13) that extol the kingship

of Yahweh begin with the letters Kh-L-M, which read backward spell *MeLeKh*, "King."

The use of acrostics as a hidden code, evident in other books of the Bible as well, is also found in post-biblical books (some of which are included in the Christian arrangement of the Old Testament). A prominent example comes from the time of the revolt against Greek rule in the second century B.C. The revolt bears the name of its leaders, the Maccabees—a name which was in fact an acronym based on the verse in the Song of Moses (Exodus 15:11)—"Who is like thee among the gods, oh Yahweh"—the first letters of the four Hebrew words forming the acronym M-K-B-I, pronounced "Maccabee."

After the destruction of the Second Temple by the Romans in A.D. 70, the spiritual and religious mainstay for the Jews were the Holy Scriptures—the treasure of divine and prophetic words. Was it all fated, was it all predicted? And what is still destined, what is yet to come? The keys to the past and to the future had to be hidden in the sacred writings, by then canonized not only as to content but also as to every word and every letter. That search for hidden meanings obscured by secret codes became known after the Temple's destruction as "entering the forbidden grove," the word for "grove"—*PaRDeS*—in itself being an acronym created from the first letters of four methods of extracting the scriptures' message: *Peshat* (literal meaning), *Remez* (hint), *Drash* (interpretation) and *Sod* (secret). A Talmudic tale intended to illustrate the risks of dealing prematurely with what has been meant to remain unrevealed relates how four rabbinic sages entered the Pardes; one "gazed and died," another lost his mind, a third went wild and began to "uproot the plants"; only one, Rabbi Akiba, came out whole.

The search for hidden meanings was resumed in Medieval times by the Kabbalists and their forerunners. What would an examination of the Bible by the ATBSh code reveal? What if another letter rearrangement is used? What if a word is deemed inserted just to hide the real meaning, and thus should be skipped to read the intended text? By such meth-

ods, for example, one could prove that Psalm 92 (''A Song for the Sabbath Day'') was actually composed by Moses in the Sinai, and not by King David. In another instance it was asserted that the great Jewish savant Maimonides (Spain and Egypt, twelfth century A.D.) was named in the Book of Exodus, where the first letters of the last four words in verse 11:9 create the acronym R-M-B-M—matching the acronym resulting from the full name of Maimonides, *Rabbi Moshe Ben Maimon* (explaining the prevalent reference to him as *Rambam*).

But, Medieval savants wondered, had the search to be limited to only first or last letters of words, the beginning or end of verses? What happens if one searches for hidden meanings by skipping letters? Every second, every fourth, every forty-second? It was perhaps inevitable that with the advent of computers, someone would apply this tool to an expedited search for a ''code'' based on letter spacing. The latest spate of interest in the subject indeed resulted from such an application of computer techniques by a number of Israeli scientists; it was launched by the publication in August 1994 of a paper titled ''Equidistant Letter Sequences in the Book of Genesis'' in the prestigious journal *Statistical Science* by Doron Witzum, Eliyahu Rips and Yoav Rosenberg.

Subsequent reviews, analyses, and books (*The Bible Code* by Michael Drosnin and *The Truth Behind the Bible Code* by Jeffrey Satinover) deal, in essence, with one basic premise: If you list all of the 304,805 letters in the Pentateuch in sequence, and arrange them in ''blocs'' that segment those letters into sections consisting of a certain number of lines, and each line a certain number of letters, then choose a skipping method—certain letters will form words that, unbelievable as it sounds, spell out predictions for our time and for all time, such as the assassination of Prime Minister Rabin of Israel or the discovery of the Theory of Relativity by Albert Einstein.

However, in order to achieve such alleged ''predictions'' of future events in texts written thousands of years ago, the searchers had to devise arbitrary and changeable rules for

how to read the "code words." The letters forming the predictory words end up sometimes lying next to each other, sometimes spaced out (with the spacing varied and flexible), sometimes read vertically, sometimes horizontally or diagonally, sometimes backward, sometimes from down up . . .

Such arbitrariness in selecting the length and number of lines, the direction of reading, the skipping or nonskipping of letters and so on must rob the uninitiated of the uncritical acceptance of the code claims that are based exclusively on letters in the Bible; and to do that without belaboring the issue of whether the current text of the Pentateuch is precisely the original, divinely endowed, letter-by-letter arrangement. We say that not only because minor deviations (example: writing certain words with a vowel-letter or without one) had apparently occurred, but also because of our belief (expounded in *Divine Encounters*) that there was one more letter, an Aleph, at the beginning of Genesis. Apart from the theological implications, the immediate issue is a distortion of the letter count.

Nevertheless, the encryption of hidden words or meanings into the biblical text must be accepted as a serious possibility, not only because of the examples cited above, but for two other very important reasons.

The first of them is that instances of encoding and encryption have been found in non-Hebrew texts from Mesopotamia, both from Babylonia and from Assyria. They include texts that begin or end with the warning that they are secret, to be shown only to the initiated (or, conversely, not to be revealed to the uninitiated), under penalty of death in the hands of the gods. Such texts sometimes employed decipherable encoding methods (such as acronyms), and sometimes encrypting methods that remain an enigma. Among the former is a hymn by the Assyrian king Ashurbanipal in praise of the god Marduk and Marduk's spouse Zarpanit. It uses the cuneiform syllabic signs at the beginning of lines to spell out a hidden message to the god Marduk. Apart from the acronymic encoding the king employed a second method

of encryption: The syllables that formed the secret message began on line 1, skipped line 2, used line 3, skipped line 4 and so on, skipping one line through line 9. Then the coded message skipped two lines at a time, returning to a single line skip on line 26, returning to a two-line skip from line 36, and then back to a one-line skip through the rest of the tablet (including its reverse side).

In this double-encoding, the Assyrian king spelled out the following secret message to the god (we provide the translation horizontally, though the message in the tablet is read vertically, from top to bottom):

A-na-ku Ah-shur-ba-an-ni-ap-li
I am Ashurbanipal
Sha il-shu bu-ul-li-ta ni-shu-ma Ma-ru-du-uk
Who to his god called give me life Marduk *[and]*
Da-li-le-ka lu-ud-lu
I will praise thee

The discovery of an acrostic inscription by one Shaggil-kinam-ubbib, a priest in the temple of Marduk in Babylon, indicates not only the priesthood's accessibility to such encoding, but also raises questions regarding its antiquity. In that acronym (in which there is an eleven-line skip between the coded syllables) the encoder's name is clearly stated. As far as is known, a priest by that name did serve in the Esagil temple in Babylon circa 1400 B.C. That would date the concept of encoding to about the time of the Exodus. Since most scholars find this early date too much to swallow, they prefer to date it to the eighth century B.C. after all.

A somewhat different encoding method was used by the Assyrian king Esarhaddon, Ashurbanipal's father. On a stela that commemorated a historic invasion by him of Egypt (known to scholars as the Black Stone of Esarhaddon, now in the British Museum—Fig. 57) he claimed that he had launched the military campaign not only with the blessing of the gods, but also under the celestial aegis of seven constellations that ''determine the fates''—a certain

Figure 57

reference to zodiacal constellations. In the inscription (on the stela's back side) he claimed that the cuneiform signs naming the constellations "are in the likeness of the writing of my name, *Asshur-Ah-Iddin*" (Asarhaddon or Esarhaddon in English).

Exactly how this code or encryption worked is unclear; but one can figure out another hidden meaning claimed by this king in the same inscription. Dealing with the restoration of Marduk's temple in Babylon, which the Assyrian king undertook as a way to be accepted also as a ruler of Babylonia, he recalled that Marduk, having become angry at the Babylonians, had decreed that the city and its temple shall remain in ruins for seventy years. That was, Esarhaddon wrote, what "Marduk wrote down in the Book of Fates." However, responding to Esarhaddon's appeals,

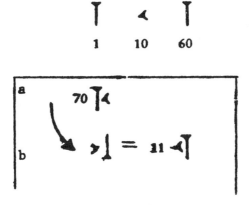

Figure 58

The merciful Marduk,
in a moment when his heart was appeased,
turned the tablet upside down
and, in the eleventh year,
approved the restoration.

What can be figured out regarding this hidden oracle is that the god's act represented a sleight of hand with figures— with the symbols (also in cuneiform) that stood for numbers. In the Sumerian sexagesimal (meaning "base sixty") system, the sign for "one" could mean both 1 and 60, depending on position. The sign for 10 was a chevronlike symbol. What Esarhaddon asserted was that the god took the Book of Fates, on which the decreed period of desolation was "70" years (Fig. 58a) and turned it upside down, so that the cuneiform signs represented "11" (Fig. 58b).

The association of hidden messages and secret meanings not with words alone but with *numerals and numbers* was even more prominent in the writings of Sargon II, the grandfather of Ashurbanipal. During his reign (721–705 B.C.) he established a new administrative-military capital on the site of a village some twelve miles northeast of the ancient royal capital and religious center Nineveh. His Assyrian name was

Sharru-kin (''Righteous King'') and he named the new city Dur Sharrukin (''Fort Sargon''—an archaeological site now known as Khorsabad). In the inscription commemorating this achievement, he wrote that the mighty wall he had built around the city was 16,283 cubits long, ''which is the number of my name.''

Such a use of numbers to encode word-syllables appears in a text known as *An Exaltation to Ishtar*, where the worshiper signed his name not with letters but with numbers:

> *21-35-35-26-41*
> *the son of 21-11-20-42*

The key to such numerical encodings remains undeciphered. But we have reason to believe that such Mesopotamian encoding methods were known to the Hebrew Prophets.

One of the most difficult passages in the Bible is the prophecy of Isaiah about the time of Retribution, when ''it shall come to pass that a great trumpet shall be blown, and they shall return those who were lost in the land of Assyria and those who were cast out to the land of Egypt, and they shall bow down to Yahweh on the Holy Mount in Jerusalem.'' At that time, Isaiah prophesied, confusion shall reign and people will ask each other, ''Who shall be given the understanding'' of the message which has somehow been altered to hide its meaning:

> *For precept is upon precept,*
> *precept is within precept;*
> *Line is upon line,*
> *line is with line—*
> *A little here, somewhat there;*
> *For with a confused*
> *   language*
> *and in a strange tongue*
> *will He address this people.*

> *Isaiah 28:10–11*

No one has really understood how a "precept upon precept" and "line with line" will result in a "confused language" and a "strange tongue." The Hebrew words are *Tzav* ("order") and *Kav* ("line"), and have been rendered in more modern English translations as "command" and "rule" respectively (*The New American Bible*), "mutter" and "murmur" (*Tanakh, the Holy Scriptures*), or even "harsh cries" and "raucous shouts" (!) (*The New English Bible*).

What language could be confused, or its written signs given a strange meaning, by changing the "order" and a "line" here and there? It is our suggestion that what the Prophet Isaiah—a contemporary of Sargon II and Sennacherib—was talking about is the *cuneiform script* of the Assyrians and the Babylonians!

It was of course not an unknown language; but as the verse quoted above states, the message delivered in that language could not be understood because it had been encoded by *Kav* to *Kav*, by changing a "line" here and a "line" there, thereby changing the "precept" of what the message was saying. The changed *Tzav* ("order") hints at encryption methods (like the A/T-B/Sh) using the changed order of the letters.

This suggested solution to the enigma of verses 28:10–11 can serve to explain the subsequent description by the Prophet (29:10–12) of the inability of anyone to understand the envisioned writings because "the words of the book have become unto you as a book that has been sealed." The last word, *hatoom*, is usually translated "sealed," but in the biblical usage it had the connotation of "hidden," made a secret. It was a term employed in the same sense as the Mesopotamian encoded writings that were sealed from the eyes of the uninitiated. It was so employed in the prophetic Song of Moses (Deuteronomy 32:34) where God is quoted as stating that the predetermined things to come are "a secret with me hidden, stored and sealed within my treasures." The term is also used in the sense of "hidden away" or "made a secret" in Isaiah 8:17; and even more so in the Book of

Daniel and its vision and symbolisms of things to come at
the End of Things.

Isaiah, whose prophecies were attuned to the international arena and the encryption of royal messages of his
time, may have given away the very clue to the existence
of a "Bible Code." Three times he revised the word *Ototh*
("signs") that is used in the Bible to denote divine or celestial signs to read *Otioth*—a plural of *Oth* that means both
"sign" and "letter," conveying the meaning of *letters* in his
prophecy.

We have already mentioned the reference by Isaiah to
Yahweh as the creator of the Letters (of the alphabet). In
verse 45:11 the Prophet, extolling the uniqueness of Yahweh,
states that it was Yahweh who "hath arrayed by letters that
which shall come to pass." And that such an arrayment was
encoded ought to be the way to understand the enigmatic
verse 41:23. Describing how the bewildered people of the
Earth seek to divine the future from the past, Isaiah quotes
them as begging God:

Tell us the letters backward!

Were the word the usual *Ototh*, it would have meant, "tell
us the signs back from the beginning of things." But the
Prophet has chosen—three times—to write *Otioth*, "letters."
And the clear request is to be enabled to understand the divine plan by being shown the letters *backward*, as in a code,
in which the letters have been scrambled.

But as the Mesopotamian examples indicate, acrostics was
too simple a device, and the real encodement—still undeciphered in the case of Sargon II—relied on the *numerical
values* of cuneiform signs. We have already mentioned the
"secret of the gods" concerning their rank numbers—numbers which sometimes were written or invoked instead of the
gods' names. Other tablets in which Sumerian terminology
was retained even in Akkadian texts (many remaining obscure because of breaks in the tablets) point to the early use

א	1
ב	2
ג	3
ד	4
ה	5
ו	6
ז	7
ח	8
ט	9
י	10
כ	20

ל	30
מ	40
נ	50
ס	60
ע	70
פ	80
צ	90
ק	100
ר	200
ש	300
ת	400

Figure 59

of *numerology* as a secret code, especially when the gods were involved.

It is no wonder then that the letters of the Hebrew alphabet were granted numerical values (Fig. 59) and that such values played a much greater role in the encoding and the decoding of secret knowledge than the letters by themselves. When the Greeks adopted the alphabet, they retained the practice of assigning numerical values to letters; and it is from Greek that the art of and rules for the interpretation of letters, words or groups of words by their numerical values was given the name Gematria.

Beginning in the time of the Second Temple, the numerological Gematria became a tool in the hands of scholars as well as gnostics to pry out of the biblical verses and words untold numbers of hidden meanings or bits of information, or for drawing new rules where the biblical ones were in-

complete. Thus, it was held that when a man took an oath to be a Nazirite, the unspecified period of abstention should be 30 days, because the defining word *YiHYeH* ("shall be") in Numbers chapter 6 has the numerical value 30. Comparing words and their implications by their numerical equivalents opened up countless possibilities for hidden meanings. As an example, it was suggested that Moses and Jacob had a similar divine experience, because the ladder to heaven (*Sulam* in Hebrew) that Jacob saw in the nighttime vision and the mount (Sinai) on which Moses received the Tablets of the Law had both the same numerical value, 130.

The employment of numerology and especially Gematria to detect secret meanings reached a new height with the growth of Jewish mysticism known as the Kabbalah during the Middle Ages. In those searches special attention was given to divine names. Paramount was the study of the name by which the Lord God named himself to Moses, YHWH: "I am whoever I will be, Yahweh is my name" (Exodus 3: 14–15). If added simply, the four letters of the divine name (the Tetragammaton) amount to 26 (10+5+6+5); but under more complex methods advocated by the Kabbalists, in which the spelled-out names of the four letters (Yod, Hei, Wav, Hei) were added up numerically, the total comes to 72. The numerical equivalents of these numbers made up scores of insightful other words.

(At the beginning of Christianity an Alexandrian sect held that the name of the supreme and primordial creator was Abraxas, the sum of whose letters equaled 365—the number of days in a solar year. The sect's members used to wear cameos made of semiprecious stones, bearing the god's image and name—as often as not equated with YaHU (short for Yahweh)—Fig. 60. There is every reason to believe that Abraxas stemmed from *Abresheet*, "Father/Progenitor of Beginning," that we have proposed as the full first word, starting with an "A," of Genesis, rather than the current *Bresheet* which makes Genesis start with a "B." If Genesis indeed had one more letter, the code sequencing now in vogue would have to be reexamined).

Figure 60

How much value should one attach to numerical codes or meanings—a code inherent in the letters themselves and not on arbitrary spacing between them? Because such usages lead back to Sumerian times, were valid in Akkadian times, and were deemed at all times to be "secrets of the gods" not to be revealed to the uninitiated, and because of the link to DNA, we believe that numerical codes are the secret code!

In fact, one of the most obvious (and thus, as in detective tales, the most ignored) clues is the very term for "book," *SeFeR* in Hebrew. Stemming from the root SFR, its derivations were the words for writer/scribe (*Sofer*), to tell (*Lesapher*), a tale or story (*Sippur*), and so on.

But the very same root SFR also denoted everything connected with numbers! To count was *Lisfor,* numeral is *Sifrah,* number is *Mispar,* counting is *Sephirah.* In other words, from the very moment that the three-letter root words of the Hebrew emerged, to write with letters and to count with numbers were considered one and the same.

Indeed, there are instances in the Hebrew Bible where the meanings "book" and "number" were interchangeable, as in 1 Chronicles 27:24 where, reporting a census conducted by King David, the word "number" was used twice in the same sentence, once to denote the number (of the people counted) and then to mean David's book of records.

Such a double meaning, and perhaps a triple meaning, has challenged translators of verse 15 in Psalm 71. Seeking God's help though he knows not all of God's miracles, the Psalmist vowed to recount God's deeds of salvation and justice "although I know not *Sefuroth*." The King James version translates the word as "numbers"; more modern translations prefer the connotation of "to tell,"—"tellings." But in this unusual form, the Psalmist has included a third meaning, that of "mysteries."

As times became more turbulent in Judea, with one revolt (that of the Maccabees against Greek rule) followed by another (against Roman oppression), the search for messages of hope—Messianic bodings—intensified. The scanning of earlier texts for coded numbers evolved into the use of numbers as secret codes. One of the most enigmatic and best encrypted instances found its way into the New Testament: The number of a "beast" encoded as "666" in the Book of Revelation,

> *Here is Wisdom;*
> *Let him that hath Understanding*
> *count the number of the beast,*
> *for it is the Number of a Man;*
> *And his number is six hundred and three score and six.*

> *Revelation 13:18*

The passage deals with Messianic expectations, the downfall of evil, and in its aftermath a Second Coming, the return of the Kingdom of Heaven to Earth. Countless attempts have been made over the millennia to decipher the numerical code of "666" and thus understand the prophecy. The number clearly appears in the early (Greek) manuscript of the book whose full title is The Gospel According to St. John, which begins with the statement "In the beginning was the Word, and the Word was with God, and the Word was God" and which is filled with numerical references. Using the numerical values of the Greek letters (which follow closely the

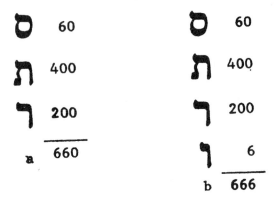

Figures 61a and 61b

Hebrew arrangement) and the methods of Gematria, it has been suggested that the "beast" was the evil Roman empire because the numerical value of *LATEINOS* was 666. Others have suggested that the numerical code meant the evil emperor himself (Trajan) whose middle name, ULPIOS, also added up numerically rendered to 666. Still another suggestion was that the code was in Hebrew, standing for *Neron Qesar* ("Nero the Emperor"), whose Hebrew spelling N-R-W-N + Q-S-R also added up to 666; and so on, in a variety of Gematria approaches both using straight addition as well as triangulation methods.

The possibility that the encoded secret of "666" is to be uncovered in Hebrew rather than Greek or Roman word meanings might well be the key to finally resolving the enigma. We find that 660 in Hebrew is the numerical equivalent of *SeTeR* (Fig. 61a)—a hidden thing, an occult mystery; it was employed in the Bible in connection with divine Wisdom and Understanding that were hidden and occulted from Man. To make it 666, the letter *Wav* (= 6) has to be added (Fig. 61b), changing the meaning from a "secret" to "his secret," *SiTRO*, "his hidden thing." Some find this rendition of "*his* secret" to describe a "watery darkness" where the Celestial Battle with Tiamat is recalled:

The Earth shook and trembled,
the foundations of the hills were shaken . . .
There went up smoke from his nostrils,
a devouring fire out of his mouth . . .
He made darkness his secret,
by a watery darkness and celestial clouds covered.

Psalms 18:8–12

There are repeated references in the Bible to that Celestial Battle, which in the Mesopotamian *Epic of Creation* took place between Nibiru/Marduk and Tiamat, and in the Bible between Yahweh as the Primeval Creator and *Tehom*, a "watery deep." Tehom/Tiamat was sometimes spoken of as *Rahab*, the "haughty one," or rendered with an inversion of letters *RaBaH* ("the great one") instead of RaHaB. The wording in Psalm 18 echoes a much earlier statement in Deuteronomy 29:19, in which the judgments of Yahweh "on the last generation" are prophesied and described as a time when "smoke shall go up from the nostrils" of God. That time of final accounting is often referred to in the Bible by the adverb *Az*—"then," at that particular future time.

If the author of Revelation, as is evident, also had in mind that *Az*, that "then" at the time of the Last Generation, when the Lord shall reappear as He had when Heaven and Earth were created at the time of the battle with *Tehom Rabah* (a term used in combination in Amos 7:4, Psalms 36:7, Isaiah 5:10), then a numerical approach to the enigma of the "666" would suggest that the Book of Revelation was speaking of the Return of the Celestial Lord in a reenactment of the Celestial Battle; *for the sum total of the numerical value of Az + Tehom + Rabah is 666* (Fig. 62).

Such an attempt by us to decode the number "666" by reconverting it into letters and then search for words containing those letters in the Old Testament does not exhaust the possibilities. The transmutation of *Abresheet* into *Abraxas* (with its numerical value 365) as a gentile deity, and the biblical references (earlier quoted) to encodements in cuneiform writings by changing the lines in the cuneiform

אז	8
תהום	451
רבה	207
	666

Figure 62

signs, as well as the reference to backward reading as well as the A-T-B-Sh employment to hide identities of foreign gods, raise the question: To what extent, especially as the destiny of the Hebrews became entangled in the fate of other nations and their gods, did biblical encodements actually hide secret data from foreign writings and pantheons? If the creation tales of Genesis were actually shorter versions of the creation secrets recorded in *Enuma elish*, what about those secret portions that had been revealed to Enmeduranki and Adapa (and Enoch)?

We read in Genesis that when the Pharaoh elevated Joseph, who interpreted dreams, to high office, he gave him as was appropriate to an Egyptian official a new, Egyptian name: Zophnat-Pa'aneach. While scholars have attempted to reconstruct the hieroglyphic writing and Egyptian meaning of the epithet-name, what is obvious is that it was in reality a name whose meaning was encoded in *Hebrew*, for in Hebrew it clearly meant "Solver" (*Pa'aneach*) of "Secret/Hidden Things" (*Zophnot*).

Such language/letter/number transfigurations reinforce the question (and the possibility)—and not only in regard to the reason for "666"—of whether the codes might have included allusions to other deities of pantheons known in antiquity.

One of the unexplained aspects of the Hebrew alphabet is

צ פ נ מ כ

ץ ף ן ם ך   a

ן פ צ — "Secret Code"

b   ך מ   (of) "Sixty"

ס   60

ו   6   c

ד   4

_____

70

Figures 63a, 63b and 63c

that five letters are written differently when their place is at
the end of a word (Fig. 63a). If we are to do our own venturing into the Pardes, the "forbidden grove," and adopting
the premise of a combination letter+number code, we could
say that read in reverse (from left to right) the encoded reason for these odd five letters is a "secret code" (*Zophen*) of
"60" (*M+Kh*), which is the secret number of Anu! (Fig.
63b).

If so, was it just a coincidence that the first letter in the
Hebrew word for "secret"—SOD—("S") has the numerical value "60," and even more so that the numerical value
of the full word is "70"—the secret number of the desola-

tion decreed by Marduk (and then reversed by him) for the city of Babylon? And for that matter, was the statement (in Jeremiah and elsewhere) that the desolation of Jerusalem and its Temple would also last the exact same 70 years—a prophecy that, when announced, was presented as a revelation of a secret, a *Sod*, of God? (Fig. 63c).

An approach that accepts the possibility that the Old Testament as well as the New Testament borrowed for their encodings from earlier Mesopotamian secret writings and divine rankings leads to another possible solution of the "666" enigma.

One of the rare (discovered) instances where the number "6" was revealed as a divine rank was in a tablet that was put together by Alasdair Livingstone in *Mystical and Mythological Explanatory Works of Assyrian and Babylonian Scholars*. The reconstructed tablet—which bears the admonition regarding the undisclosable secrets it contains—begins with 60 as the rank of "the preeminent god, father of the gods" and then, in a separate column, reveals his identity: Anu. Followed by Enlil (50), Ea/Enki (40), Sin (30) and Shamash (20), it lists *Adad*, the "god of rain and thunders," as "6." As the listing continues on the obverse as well as the reverse sides, it lists *"600" as the secret number of the Anunnaki*.

What emerges from that Mesopotamian tablet regarding the secret numbers of the gods may well have the key to finally solving the mystery of "666" by looking at it as a Sumerian-based encoding:

600 = The Anunnaki, "Those Who From Heaven to Earth Came"
 60 = Anu, their supreme ruler
  6 = Adad, one of the gods who teaches Initiates
———
666 = "Here is Wisdom," "Counted by him who has Understanding"

(The proximity of Anu and Adad beginning in the second millennium B.C. found not only textual expressions but also

in their having joint temples. Incredible as it may sound, the Bible, too, lists Anu and Adad next to each other in a list of gods of "other nations"—2 Kings 17:31).

The secret numbers of the gods can serve as clues to the deciphering of secret meanings in other divine names. Thus, when the alphabet was conceived, the letter "M"—*Mem*, from *Ma'yim*, water, paralleled the Egyptian and Akkadian pictorial depictions of water (a pictograph of waves) as well as the pronunciation of the term in those languages for "water." Was it then just a coincidence that the numerical value of "M" in the Hebrew alphabet was "40"—the secret numerical rank of Ea/Enki, "whose home is water," the prototype Aquarius?

Was there an equally secret numerical code that has originated in Sumer for YaHU—the shortened form for the Tetragammaton YaHWeH? Were one a Sumerian initiate seeking to apply the secret numbers code to this theophoric name (as used in prefixes and suffixes to personal names), one could say that YHU is a secret code for "50" (IA = 10, U = 5, IA.U = 10×5 = 50), with all the theological implications thereof.

While attention has been focused on the *meaning* of "666," we find in the cryptic verse in Revelation a statement of utmost significance. The secret code, it states, is what *Wisdom* is all about, and it can be deciphered only by those who have *Understanding*.

These are precisely the two terms used by the Sumerians, and those who came after them, to denote the secret knowledge that only privileged initiates had been taught by the Anunnaki.

At the foundation of the incredible and encompassing Sumerian knowledge lay an equally amazing knowledge of numbers. As the Assyriologist-mathematician Herman V. Hilprecht observed earlier this century after the discovery of numerous Mesopotamian mathematical tablets (*The Babylonian Expedition of the University of Pennsylvania*), "all the

multiplication and division tables from the temple libraries of Nippur and Sippar, and from the library of Ashurbanipal in Nineveh, are based upon the number 12960000''—a virtual astronomical number, a number that required astounding sophistication to be comprehended, and whose utility to humans in the fourth millennium B.C. seemed completely questionable.

But analyzing this number—with which some mathematical tablets started—Professor Hilprecht concluded that it could only be related to the phenomenon of Precession—the retardation of the Earth in its orbit around the Sun that takes 25,920 years to complete (until the Earth returns to the exact same spot). That complete circling of the twelve houses of the zodiac has been named a Great Year; the astronomical number 12,960,000 represented 500 such Great Years. But who, except for the Anunnaki, could grasp or have use for such a vast span of time?

In considering numerical and counting systems, the decimal system (''base ten'') is the most obviously ''man-friendly,'' resulting from counting on the fingers of our hands. Even the perplexing Mayan calendar system called *Haab*, which divided the solar year into 18 months of 20 days each (plus 5 special days at year's end) can be assumed to have resulted from counting all 20 human digits, fingers and toes combined. But from where did the Sumerians take the sexagesimal (''base 60'') system whose lasting expression is still extant in time reckoning (60 minutes, 60 seconds), astronomy (a celestial circle of 360 degrees), and geometry?

In our book *When Time Began* we have suggested that the Anunnaki, coming from a planet whose orbital period (one year on Nibiru) equaled 3,600 orbits of the planet Earth, needed some kind of a common denominator for such diverse periods—and have found one in the phenomenon of Precession (which only they, not men with the shorter life spans dictated by Earth's cycles, could have discovered). When they divided the celestial circle into twelve parts, the preces-

Figure 64

sional retardation—that could be easily observed by them—
was 2,160 years per "house." That, we have suggested, led
to the ratio of 3,600:2,160 or 10:6 (the eventual Golden Ratio
of the Greeks), and to the sexagesimal system that ran 6 ×
10 × 6 × 10 and so on (resulting in 60, 360, 3600 and so
on to the immense number 12,960,000).

In this system, several numbers of celestial or sacred import seem to be out of place. One is the number seven, whose
significance in the story of Creation, as the seventh or Sabbath day, in the name of Abraham's abode *Beer-Sheba*
("The Well of Seven") and so on is easily recognized. In
Mesopotamia it was applied to the Seven Who Judge, the
Seven Sages, the seven gates of the Lower World, the seven
tablets of *Enuma elish*. It was an epithet of Enlil ("Enlil is
Seven," the Sumerians stated); and—undoubtedly the origin
of the number's significance—it was the planetary number
of Earth. "Earth (KI) is the seventh," all Sumerian astronomical texts asserted. This, as we have explained, made
sense only to someone coming into the center of our Solar
System from the outside. To him (or them) coming from the
far-out Nibiru, Pluto would be the first planet, Neptune and
Uranus the second and third, Saturn and Jupiter the fourth
and fifth, Mars would be the sixth and Earth the seventh (and
then Venus the eighth—as indeed these planets were depicted on monuments and cylinder seals, Fig. 64).

(In Sumerian hymns to Enlil, "the all-beneficent," he was
credited with seeing to it that there was food and well-being
in the land; he was also invoked as the guarantor of treaties

and oaths. No wonder, then, that in Hebrew the root from which seven stems—Sh-V-A—is the same root from which the meanings "to be satiated" *and* "to swear, to take an oath" derive).

The number "7" is a key number in Revelation (7 angels, 7 seals, and so on); so was the next extraordinary number—12—or multiples thereof, 144,000 in Revelation 7:3–5, 14:1 etc. We have already recounted its applications and its significance, as stemming from the number of the members of our Solar System (Sun, Moon, and 10 planets—the 9 we know of plus Nibiru).

And then—hardly realized—was the peculiar number 72. To say, as has been done, that it is simply a multiple of 12 by 6, or that when multiplied by 5 it results in 360 (as the number of degrees in a circle), is merely to state the obvious. But *why* 72 to begin with?

We have already observed that the mystics of the Kaballah arrived through Gematria methods at the number *72 as the numerical secret of Yahweh*. Although obscured in the biblical report of the time when God instructed Moses and Aaron to approach the Holy Mount and to take along 70 of the elders of Israel, the fact is that Moses and Aaron had 72 companions: In addition to the 70 elders, God instructed that 2 sons of Aaron also be invited (although Aaron had 4 sons)—making the total 72.

Of all places we also find this odd number 72 in the Egyptian tale dealing with the contending of Horus and Seth. Relating the tale from its hieroglyphic sources, Plutarch (in *De Iside et Osiride*, wherein he equated Seth with Typhon of Greek myths) said that when Seth tricked Osiris into the doomed chest, he did so in the presence of 72 "divine comrades."

Why then 72 in these various instances? The only plausible answer, we believe, is to be found in the phenomenon of Precession, for it is there that the crucial number 72 is to be found, as the number of years it takes to retard the Earth by one degree.

To this day it is not certain how the concept of a Jubilee

had come about, the 50-year period decreed in the Bible and used as the time unit in the *Book of Jubilees*. Here is the answer: to the Anunnaki, whose one orbit around the Sun equaled 3,600 Earth years, the orbit passed through 50 precessional degrees ($50 \times 72 = 3,600$)!

It was perhaps more than a coincidence that Enlil's secret rank number—and the number sought by Marduk—was also 50. For it was one of the numbers that expressed the relationships between Divine Time (stemming from Nibiru's motions), Earthly Time (relating to the motions of the Earth and its Moon), and Celestial Time (or zodiacal time, resulting from Precession). The numbers 3,600, 2,160, 72, and 50 were numbers that belonged to the Tablets of Destinies in the heart of Nippur's DUR.AN.KI; they were truly numbers expressing the ''Bond Heaven-Earth.''

The Sumerian King List asserts that 432,000 years (120 orbits of Nibiru) had passed from the arrival of the Anunnaki on Earth until the Deluge. The number 432,000 is also key in the Hindu and other concepts of Ages and the periodic catastrophies that befall the Earth.

The number 432,000 also embraces 72 precisely 6,000 times. And it is perhaps worth keeping in mind that according to Jewish sages the count of years in the Jewish calendar—5,758 in A.D. 1998—will come to a completion, a terminus, when it reaches 6,000; it is then that it will all come full cycle.

As is evident from the ancient records concerning such initiates—Adapa, Enmeduranna, Enoch—the core of the knowledge and understanding revealed to them, no matter what else, was astronomy, the calendar, and mathematics (the ''secret of numbers''). Indeed, as a review of the encoding and encrypting practices in antiquity has shown, the common thread between them, no matter what language used, was numbers. If there was once a single universal language on Earth (as the Sumerian texts and the Bible assert), it had to be mathematically based; and if—or rather, when—we communicate with extraterrestrials, as had once been done with

the Anunnaki on their visits here, and as we shall do when we venture into space—the cosmic language will be one of numbers.

In fact, current computing systems have already adopted a universal numbers language. When in typewriters the key for "A" was pressed, a lever holding this letter was activated and it struck the paper with an "A." In the computers, when the key for "A" is pressed, an electronic signal is activated that expresses the "A" as a series of "0" or "1" numbers—the letters have been digitized. Modern computers have, in other words, converted letters into numbers; and one can say that they have *Gematriatized* writing.

And if one takes seriously the Sumerian and biblical statements about the inclusion of medical knowledge in the Knowledge and Understanding passed on to us—is there somewhere in all the ancient texts, so meticulously copied with precision because they had been "canonized," the key to sharing with us the genetic knowledge that went into our creation, and thus still accompanies us in health and in sickness and in death?

We have reached the point where our scientists have identified a specific gene—calling it, say, P51—at a specific site on chromosome number 1 or 13 or 22, that is responsible for a trait or malady. It is a gene and a location that can be expressed on computers—now as numbers, or wholly in letters, or in combinations thereof.

Is there already in those ancient texts, and especially the Hebrew Bible, such coded genetic information? If we could only decipher such a code, we could become beings like the "Perfect Model" that Enki and Ninharsag had intended to create.

9

PROPHECY: WRITINGS
FROM THE PAST

Mankind's enduring belief that someone in the past could foresee the future—that, in Sumerian parlance, someone had known Destiny and could determine Fate—was founded upon the Written Word. Revealed or secret, straightforward or encrypted, the information had to be recorded, written down. A covenant, a treaty, a *prophecy*—what value to those then present or to those who will inhabit the future unless the words be written down?

When archaeologists excavate an ancient site, nothing is deemed more exciting and significant than "something" with writing on it—an object, a brick, a stone slab, pottery shards, and needless to say a text or part thereof inscribed on a clay tablet or a papyrus sheet. What was the place, what was its ancient name, to what culture did it belong, who were its rulers? A few scribbled letters, a couple of words offer answers; and so much more, of course, fuller texts.

One of the earliest antiquarians, if not a full-fledged archaeologist, was the Assyrian king Ashurbanipal. Believing that his own fate and the land's Destiny were determined way back in the past, he made written records from the past the prime prize or booty of his conquests; and the library of his palace in Nineveh was at the time (seventh century B.C.) perhaps the greatest collection of clay tablets of countless ancient texts of "myths" and epics, royal annals, and what was then the "books" (on clay tablets) of astronomy, mathematics, medicine, and other invaluable texts. The tablets were carefully arranged on wooden shelves, and each shelf began with a catalogue tablet listing what was on that shelf.

In all a tremendous treasure of ancient knowledge, records, and prophecy was assembled there. A great many of the texts now known come from the tablets, or fragments thereof, found in Nineveh. At the same time, the catalogue tablets at the start of each shelf also reveal how much is still missing and undiscovered.

Certainly missing—for none has been duplicated elsewhere—are what Ashurbanipal himself identified as "writings from before the Deluge"; we know that they had existed because Ashurbanipal had boasted that he could read that writing.

The king's assertion, one might note here, has not been taken seriously by modern Assyriologists. Some have amended the king's statement to read "writings in Sumerian," for it seems incredible not only to claim that there had been writing millennia before Mesopotamian tablets, but that such writing (on whatever tablets) had survived the global catastrophe.

Yet other texts and sources, unrelated to Ashurbanipal or his time, make those very assertions. Adapa—a pre-Diluvial initiate—wrote a book whose title, rendered in Sumerian, was *U. SAR Dingir ANUM Dingir ENLILA* (*Writings Regarding Time [from] divine Anu and divine Enlil*).

Enoch, another pre-Diluvial ancestor, returned from heaven with 360 "books"—a number not only with a celestial/mathematical allusion, but one, let us point out, which when converted into letters spells out *SeQeR* $(60+100+200)$—"that which is hidden." The name-place *Saqqarah* in Egypt, the "hidden place" of early royal pyramids and burials, stems from the same root.

The *Book of Enoch* (known as 1 Enoch) purports to have been written by Enoch himself as a first-person report. Although by all scholarly opinions it was compiled shortly before the Christian era, citations from it in other early works and parallels with other extrabiblical writings (as well as the fact that it was canonized in early Christian times), attest to its being based on truly ancient texts. In the book itself, after a brief introduction that explains who the *Nefilim* (of Genesis

6 renown) were, Enoch states that what follows is "the book of the words of righteousness and of the reprimand of the eternal *Nefilim*" that were heard by him during a vision and which he now proceeds to put down "in a human language"—a language "which the Great One has given to men to converse therewith."

Having been given knowledge of the heavens and the Earth and their mysteries, Enoch was told to write down prophecies of future events (according to the *Book of Jubilees*, Enoch was shown "what was and what will be"). Although scholars assume that the "prophecies" were really hindsight, the incorporation in *1 Enoch* of earlier texts and its subseqent canonization attest that at the time of the Second Temple it was firmly believed that the future could be and was foretold in the past by divine inspiration—even dictated by the Lord himself or his Angels to humans, to be recorded and written down and passed to future generations.

Even more emphatic in asserting that Enoch brought down with him books that contained not only scientific knowledge but also prophecies of the future is the version known as 2 Enoch or by the full title *The Book of the Secrets of Enoch*. It states that God instructed Enoch to "give the handwritten books to his children" so that they may be handed down "from generation to generation and from nation to nation." Then God disclosed to him the "secrets of Creation" and the cycles of the events on Earth. "At the beginning of the eighth thousand of years there will be a time of Not-Counting, [a time] with neither years nor months or weeks, nor days or hours" (2 Enoch 33:1–2).

A reference is then made to even earlier writings that belonged to Enoch's ancestors Adam and Seth—"handwriting that should not be destroyed till the end of time." There is also reference to a "chart" that God has "put on Earth" and "ordered that it be preserved, and that the handwriting of thy fathers be preserved, and that it *perish not in the Deluge* which I shall bring upon thy race."

The reference to a future Deluge, included in 2 Enoch as a prophetic revelation by God to Enoch, thus speaks of

"handwritings" by both Adam and his son Seth and a divine "chart" that were deposited on Earth and were to survive the Deluge. If such "handwritings" ever existed, they must be counted among the missing pre-Diluvial writings. At the time of the Second Temple it was held that among such pre-Diluvial writings were the *Books of Adam and Eve*, in which many details were provided, augmenting the biblical tale.

Scholars agree that *1 Enoch* has clearly incorporated, verbatim, sections from a much earlier manuscript called the *Book of Noah*, a work that was mentioned in other writings besides the *Book of Enoch*. It could well have been the source of the very enigmatic eight verses in Genesis chapter 6; preceding the biblical version of the Deluge and its hero Noah, those verses speak of the *Nefilim*, the "sons of the *Elohim*" who had married the Daughters of The Adam as the background for God's decision to wipe mankind off the face of the Earth. In it, the tale is fully told, the Nefilim are identified, the nature of the divine wrath is explained. Harking back in all probability to Sumerian times and sources, it includes some details otherwise known only from the Mesopotamian *Atra Hasis* text.

It is more than likely that the two books mentioned above—the *Books of Adam and Eve* and the *Book of Noah*—did in fact exist, in one form or another, and were actually known to the compilers of the Old Testament. After having described the creation of The Adam and of Eve, and the incident in the Garden of Eden and the birth of Cain and Abel and then of Enosh, Genesis restarts (in chapter 5) the genealogical record by saying, "This is the book of the generations of Adam" and recounts the creation tale. The Hebrew word translated "generations" (*Toledoth*) connotes more than "generations"—it bespeaks "the histories of"; and the ensuing text gives the impression of a summary based on some longer prior text.

The same term, *Toledoth*, starts the story of Noah and the Deluge. Again translated "These are the generations of Noah," the words really begin the story not so much of Noah

as of the Deluge—a story based, without question, on earlier
Sumerian (and then Akkadian) texts.

Interesting and intriguing light on what the *Book of Noah*
might have contained is to be found in the *Book of Jubilees,*
another one of the Apocrypha (extrabiblical) books from the
time of the Second Temple (or earlier). It states that the Angels "explained to Noah all the medicines, all the diseases
and how he might heal them with herbs of the earth; and
Noah wrote down all things in a book, concerning every kind
of medicine." And after the Deluge, Noah "gave all that he
had written to his son Shem."

Starting a new chapter not only in the Bible but in human
affairs again with the word *Toledoth* is next found in Genesis
chapter 10. Dealing with the post-Diluvial times, it begins,
"Now these are the 'generations' of the sons of Noah: Shem,
Ham and Japhet; and unto them were born sons after the
Deluge." The general list, nicknamed by biblical scholars
the Table of Nations, reverts to Shem and his descendants
and pays special attention to the line of his middle son Arpakhshad both in this chapter and by returning to the subject
in chapter 11 with the opening "These are the 'generations'
of Shem." The significance, we soon gather, is that it was
the direct ancestral line of Abraham's family.

The existence of a book that we might arbitrarily title *The
Book of Shem* or, more specifically, the *Book of Arpakhshad,*
is suggested by yet another tradition concerning writings
from before the Deluge. The reference is found in the *Book
of Jubilees;* it informs us that Arpakhshad, a grandson of
Noah, was taught by his father Shem to write and read; and
seeking a place where to settle, "he found a writing which
former generations had carved on a rock, and read what
was thereon, and he transcribed it." Among other information "it included the teachings of the Nefilim concerning
how to observe the omens of the sun and the moon and the
stars and the signs of heaven." This desciption of the contents of the writings by the Nefilim—and thus from before
the Deluge—parallels the wording in the *Book of Enoch*
about the knowledge of the Sun and the Moon and the stars/

planets that he was taught from "the heavenly tablets, and all that was written thereon." All that Enoch passed on to his son Metuselah, saying to him:

All these things I am recounting to thee
and writing down for thee;
I have revealed to thee everything
and given thee books concerning all this.
So preserve, my son Metuselah,
the books from thy father's hand
and deliver them to the generations of the world.

An unambiguous reference to pre-Diluvial writings and what had happened to them as far as the destruction by the avalanche of waters was concerned is found in the writings of Berossus. A Babylonian historian-priest who compiled a history of Mankind for the Greek rulers of the Near East after the death of Alexander, he clearly had access to a library of ancient writings in Akkadian (and possibly in Sumerian, too: In the first volume of his writings, describing events from the splash landing of Ea to the Deluge, he called the hero of the Great Flood by his Sumerian name, Ziusudra). In the fragments of Berossus's writings that are available from Greek historians, it is stated that after Ea/Enki had revealed to Sisithros (= Ziusudra) that there would be a Deluge, "he ordered him to conceal every available writing in Sippar, the city of Shamash. Sisithros accomplished all these things, sailed immediately to Armenia, and thereupon what the god had announced did happen." Those writings were about "beginnings, middles, and ends."

Berossus continued to relate that among those who were in the ark and survived the Deluge was *Sambethe*, the wife of one of the sons of Ziusudra/Noah—her name probably a corruption of the Sumerian or Akkadian *Sabitu* ("The Seventh"). According to Berossus "she was the first of the Sybils, and she had prophesied concerning the building of the Tower of Babylon and all that happened to the enterprises

of its planners; this was before the division of the languages.''

To this first of a line of oracle prophetesses (the most renowned of which was the Sybil in Delphi) was attributed the role of intermediary between the gods and the survivors of the Deluge. She uttered to them the words that were ''a voice from the air,'' which directed them how to survive after the Deluge and ''how to recover from Sippar the books that described the future of Mankind.''

The ubiquitous traditions and recollections regarding writings from before the Flood clearly persist in asserting that apart from all manner of scientific knowledge they also included prophecies concerning the future. As often as not, such prophecies concerned not only fateful events that would befall individuals or nations, but also humanity's and Earth's ultimate destiny.

Enoch was shown ''what was and what will be,'' and wrote down for future generations the secrets of creation and the cycles of events on Earth. God had placed a ''chart'' on Earth, determining the destiny of the planet and all that is upon it. The writings from before the Deluge were about ''beginnings, middles and ends.''

Indeed, as one reviews the beliefs underlying all these diverse statements, one begins to understand why the editors of Genesis in its Hebrew version had omitted the Aleph to make the beginning start with Beginning, with a ''B'' (*Beth*). For the very notion of a beginning incorporates within it a notion of an end. The very admonition that the ancient writings, containing all that there is to be known—those ancient ''data banks,'' to use computer lingo—must be preserved until the ''end of times'' or ''end of days'' implies that such an end had been destined. By starting with *B*eginning, the Bible's editors subscribed to that belief.

These concepts permeate the Bible, from the very start in Genesis through the books of the Prophets to the final books (of the Hebrew Bible). ''And Jacob called unto his sons, and said: Come, gather, and I shall tell you that which shall befall

you at the end of days'' (Genesis 49:1). Fearing that the Israelites would abandon the commandments after his death, Moses alerted them to the ''evils that will befall you in the last days'' (Deuteronomy 31:29). Coupled with that admonition was a prediction—a prophecy—of the Fate and future of each one of the tribes of Israel. The prophetic visions of Isaiah open with the statement, ''And it shall be at the end of days'' (2:2); and the Prophet Jeremiah clearly explained that what shall be ''at the end of days'' had been planned ''in Yahweh's heart'' from the very beginning (23:20). ''He tells the End at the Beginning,'' Isaiah extolled the Lord God (46:10).

God was the ultimate prophet and the source of all prophecy. That biblical view found expression even where the text seems just to report events. The punishment imposed on Adam and Eve after they had eaten the forbidden fruit in the Garden of Eden foresaw the future ways of human beings. Cain was given a protective mark, for otherwise he and his descendants would be avenged for seventy and seven generations. In a covenant made by God with Noah and his sons, He promised that there would never again be a Deluge. In a covenant with Abraham, God foretold his future as the father of multitudes of nations; but predicted that a time would come when his offspring would be enslaved in a foreign land—a bitter experience that would last 400 years (as the Israelite sojourn in Egypt eventually did). And regarding the barren Sarah, God predicted that she would have a son and that out of her womb there would come nations and kings thereof.

Encompassing the human story from Adam and Eve through the destruction of the First Temple of Jerusalem and its rebuilding by returning exiles in the sixth century B.C., the Old Testament also tells, indirectly and almost unperceptibly, the shift of prophecy from a direct communication from God to one through Angels (literally: Emissaries) and then through Prophets. Though Moses was designated a Prophet of God, the universality of the phenomenon is revealed by the biblical tale of Bile'am or Balaam. He was a

renowned seer at the time of the Exodus, and was retained
by the Moabite king to curse the advancing Israelites; but
each time a place for the cursing and the rituals therefore
were prepared, Yahweh appeared to him and warned him not
to put a curse on His chosen people. After several attempts
he was persuaded by the Moabite king to try once more; but
then, in a divine vision, he could ''hear the sayings of God
and discern the knowledge of the One who is Most High.''
''Though not nigh, I can see it,'' Bala'am announced of the
Star of Jacob; ''though not now, it steppeth forth.'' And that
is what the divine message is, he said: the Sons of Israel
shall defeat and conquer the nations standing in their way.
Incredibly, the list of those doomed nations included Assyria—a nation not at all present in Canaan at the time of
the Exodus and whose kings assaulted only many centuries
later the Israelite kingdoms that were yet to be formed.

A case of prophecy based on past prophecies was the future great battle of Gog and Magog that was revealed to the
Prophet Ezekiel (chapters 38 and 39)—a battle that in the
apocalyptic literature of the time assumed the role of the final
battle in the last millennium, the Armageddon of the New
Testament. Though in later writings Gog and Magog were
treated as two different persons or nations, Ezekiel speaks of
Gog as the ruler of the land Magog, and predicts that the end
of his domination shall come when he will attack the land
of Jerusalem, ''the navel of the Earth.'' Predicting that this
shall take place at, and be a sign of, ''the End of Days,''
Yahweh declared through Ezekiel: Though thou shalt come
only at the end of days, Gog—

> *It is thou*
> *of whom I had spoken*
> *in the olden days*
> *through the Prophets of Israel*
> *who had prophesied in those days.*

In those final times, Yahweh announced through Ezekiel,
there shall be a great earthquake and great destruction, and

plagues and bloodshed, and torrents of rains, and fire and brimstones from the skies.

Another Prophet who recalled earlier prophets—the "First Prophets"—was Zechariah (1:4, 7:7, 7:12), who also saw the future in terms of the past, the so-called "First Days." This was in line with all the biblical prophecies: in foretelling the future, the Prophets asserted that the End was anchored in the Beginning. Foreseeing the world's nations gathered together to find out what is in store, the Prophet Isaiah envisioned them asking each other, "Who among us can tell the future by letting us hear the First Things?" Mocking that quest among the nations who ask about the past and the future not God but each other, Isaiah declared that only Yahweh, the Lord of Hosts, has that knowledge (Isaiah chapter 43). That is further enlarged upon in Isaiah chapter 48, wherein Yahweh announced:

> *It is I who had told the first things,*
> *out of my mouth were they uttered.*
> *And I shall announce them suddenly;*
> *And when I shall do so, it shall happen.*

The quest for the hidden past in order to divine the future permeates not only the books of the Prophets but also the biblical books of Psalms, Proverbs, and Job. "Give ear, my people, to my teachings, incline your ears to the words of my mouth; I will open my mouth with parables and will utter riddles from olden times," the Psalmist (78:2–3) said of the remembrances passed from generation to generation. Asserting that he was qualified to address those riddles, he explained: "For I have taken count of the days of old and the years of ancient times" (77:6).

This approach, of "Let's find out what has happened in the past so that we might know what's coming," was based on Mankind's experience throughout the millennia of human memory—"myths" to most, recollections of actual events to us. To anyone aware of the ancient tales—anyone not only now but also in biblical times—it had to be obvious that at

every twist and turn Mankind depended on the plans and whims of its creators, the *Elohim*.

In the Beginning, we today and people (and certainly Prophets) millennia ago have been informed that we have come into being as a result of discussions in a council of the gods, meeting to resolve a mutiny in the gold mines. Our genetic makeup was determined as two Anunnaki—Enki and Ninmah—acted both seriously and frivolously. It was at the Council of the Great Gods that they voted and swore to bring the creative experiment to an end and let Mankind perish in the Deluge. And it was that, meeting in council, the Anunnaki gods decided after the Deluge to give Mankind ''Kingship'' in the three regions—the civilizations of Mesopotamia, of the Nile Valley, and of the Indus Valley.

Curious about the records of the Beginnings, the human story from Creation through the Deluge and the rise of nations, the people of the last millennium B.C.—the time of the biblical Prophets—also wondered about the Olden Days, the events in the previous millennium or two—the time when the Bible switched to Ur of the Chaldees in Sumer, and Abraham, and the War of the Kings, and the upheaval of Sodom and Gomorrah. Tell us of those Olden Days so that we would know what to expect, the people demanded of those entrusted with prophecy and knowledge.

The Bible mentions several such records—''books''—that may have held the answers but that have completely vanished. One is the *Book of Jashar*, the *Book of Straightness* if literally translated but probably meaning the record of the Right Things. The other and probably much more important was the *Book of the Wars of Yahweh*, implying by its enigmatic title that it dealt with wars and conflicts among the *Elohim*.

Such conflicts, flaring at times into open warfare, were recorded in Sumerian writings; and such writings from the past were truly Divine Words, for the texts were either written down by the Divine Scribes or dictated by the gods to human scribes. Originally recorded by the gods themselves were the events on Nibiru that involved the seizing of the

throne there by Anu and the continuation of the struggle for succession to another planet, Earth; the tale of Zu; the contending between Horus and Seth (which led to the first-ever enlisting of Mankind in a war between the gods). And in that category, of writings by the gods themselves, belonged a "Prophecy Text" that has come to us in the Akkadian version and which was nothing short of an *autobiography by Marduk*. In the other category, that of books directly dictated by a deity, was a text known as the *Erra Epos*, a record of events as told by Nergal. Both those texts were attempts by the gods to explain to Mankind how two millennia of civilization—the Olden Days—had come abruptly to an end.

It was more than ironic that the events that had triggered the end of the great Sumerian civilization coincided with its most glorious epoch. An "olden book"—a Sumerian text—recorded the Council of the Great Gods at which the grant of Kingship (civilization) to Mankind was decided upon:

> *The great Anunnaki who decree Fates*
> *sat exchanging their counsels regarding the land.*
> *They who created the four regions,*
> *who set up the settlements, who oversaw the land,*
> *were too lofty for Mankind.*

And so they decided that the institution of Kingship should be created, both as a buffer as well as a link between the Lofty Ones and the mass of humanity. Up to then, the Earthlings were allowed to live beside the sacred precincts in the cities of the Gods; thereafter, they were to have their own cities, ruled by LU.GALs, "Great Men"—kings—who were to act as surrogates for the divine lords.

When the Anunnaki returned to the Edin, the plain between the Tigris and Euphrates after the plain had dried enough after the Deluge, they reestablished the Cities of the Gods exactly in accordance with the pre-Diluvial plan. The first one to be rebuilt was Eridu, Enki's city; and it was there, we believe, that the momentous decision to grant Mankind

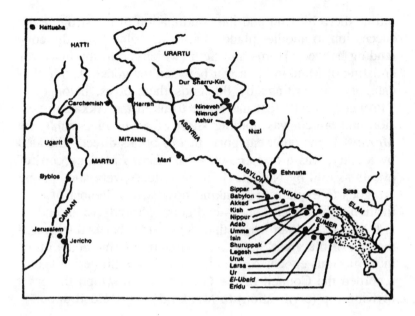

civilization was made; the time, archaeological evidence shows, was circa 3800 B.C.

But in compliance with the gods' decision, Kingship of Men had to begin at a City of Men, and that one was a new settlement called Kish. The date was marked by the grant of a calendar to Mankind, a calendar designed at Enlil's "cult center," Nippur. It began to tick in 3760 B.C.

The *Sumerian King List* recorded the recurring transfer of the land's capital city from one City of Men to another in Sumer. Such shifts were not unrelated to the fortunes and shifts of authority between the gods themselves, or even the rivalries between them—both in the First Region (Mesopotamia and neighboring lands), the Second Region (the Nile Valley) and the Third Region (the Indus Valley) (where civilizations followed circa 3100 B.C. and 2900 B.C.). Rumbling below the surface and from time to time violently erupting was the conflict between Marduk and Ninurta—the heirs apparent of Enki and Enlil respectively, who took over as their own the erstwhile rivalry between their fathers. There was

indeed no Peace on Earth until Marduk—having caused the death of Dumuzi—had his sentence to be buried alive inside the sealed Great Pyramid commuted to exile. It was the same punishment—banishment to a distant land—that Marduk had imposed on his half brother Ningishzidda/Thoth, who had gone across the oceans to become the Plumed Serpent god (Quetzalcoatl) of Mesoamerica.

It was during that relative period of peace that began with the start of the third millennium B.C. that the Sumerian civilization expanded to neighboring lands and flourished under great kings, such as Gilgamesh. Within a few centuries, the northward expansion incorporated Semitic tribes; and circa 2400 B.C. a greater dominion under a Righteous King (*Sharru-kin*)—Sargon I—was formed with a capital in the new city of Agade. It was henceforth known as the unified kingdom of Sumer and Akkad.

Numerous texts, mostly fragmented, have been found that record the course of events—the affairs of both gods and men—in the ensuing centuries. The empire's center kept changing. Finally, in 2113 B.C., the most glorious chapter in the history of Sumer and Akkad began. Historians refer to the era as the Ur III period, for it was the third time that Ur had become the empire's capital. It was the "cult center" of Nannar/Sin, who resided in its sacred precinct (Fig. 65) with his spouse Ningal. Their lordship was enlightened and benevolent. The king they had anointed to start the new dynasty, Ur-Nammu ("The Joy of Ur") was wise, righteous, and a master of international trade in which Sumer exchanged grains and woolen products for metals and timbers; its colorful coats were prized, according to the Bible, even in distant Jericho. The "merchants of Ur" were internationally known and respected; through them Sumerian civilization, in all of its aspects, spread far and wide. In need of more wool, the Sumerians tapped into the grazing plains in the northern regions, where a major trading outpost was established at the gateway to Asia Minor, the land of the Hittites. It was named Harran—"The Caravanry." Intended to

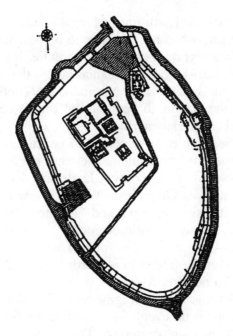

Figure 65

serve as a mini-Ur, an Ur-away-from-Ur, it emulated in layout and in its temple Ur itself.

All the while, from his exile, Marduk was watching these developments with a growing sense of frustration and anger. In his autobiography (a copy of which was discovered in the library of Ashurbanipal) Marduk recalled how, after having wandered in many lands, "from where the sun rises to where it sets," he had arrived in Hatti Land (the land of the Hittites). "Twenty-four years in its midst I nested," he wrote. And all during these years he kept asking the council of the gods: "Until when?"

In the absence of a clear or satisfactory answer, Marduk looked to the heavens. Fate, we have said, has twelve stations; the Fate-Station (zodiacal house) of Marduk was the constellation of the Ram (Aries); and as Precession kept shifting the first day of spring away from the constellation of the Bull (Taurus)—Enlil's zodiacal house—it came ever

closer to "entering" the Fate-Station of Marduk's Ram. Sure that the time has come for his Destiny to be fulfilled, Marduk envisioned himself returning to Babylon with pomp and circumstance, appointing a worthy king, watching the nations at peace and the peoples prosper—a prophetic vision of what shall come to pass at the Latter Days when Babylon shall live up to its name: *Bab-ili*, "Gateway of the Gods."

Other texts from that time, that scholars consider part of the collection of *Akkadian Prophecies*, recorded reports of astronomers who watched the heavens for planetary omens connected with the constellation of the Ram. The omens, however, were mostly ones of warfare, slaughter, plunder, destruction; and it was those prophecies, rather than Marduk's rosy ones, that have come to pass. The other gods, led by Ninurta and by Marduk's own brother Nergal, using scientific tools "from the Olden Days," "artifacts of Heaven and Earth," claimed that the shift to the Age of the Ram had not yet occurred. Impatient, Marduk sent his son Nabu to raise a human army from among their followers in the Lands of the West—the lands west of the Euphrates River. In 2024 B.C. Nabu launched a successful invasion of Mesopotamia and opened the gates of Babylon to his father Marduk.

The *Erra Epos* relates those momentous events from the viewpoint of Nergal (nicknamed *Erra*, The Annihilator) and Ninurta (nicknamed *Ishum*, The Scorcher). It details frantic negotiations to settle the dispute peacefully, calls on Marduk to be patient; endless debates at the Council of the Anunnaki that in the end was meeting in continuous session; alarm at the true intentions of Nabu and his human army; and finally suspicions that while Marduk speaks of Babylon as the Gateway of the Gods, his son—with followers in the areas bordering on the spaceport in the Sinai—was really intending to capture the *spaceport* and thus control contact with the home planet Nibiru.

Seeing no other way to stop Marduk and Nabu, the Council of the Great Gods authorized Nergal and Ninurta to unlock the "Seven Awesome Weapons" that had been hidden under lock and seal in the Abzu (Enki's abode in southeast-

ern Africa). A nuclear holocaust was unleashed; it vaporized the spaceport, leaving a huge gash in the peninsula's face and a vast blackened area all around it. The "sinning cities" that sided with Nabu in what was then a fertile valley south of the Dead Sea were likewise obliterated—an upheaval that Abraham could see from his abode in the south of Canaan.

But as Fate would have it, the nuclear "cloud of death," carried by the prevailing Mediterranean winds, drifted eastward toward Mesopotamia; in its path, all that was alive—people, animals, plants—died a horrible death. As the deathly cloud neared Sumer, the Anunnaki gods began to abandon their cities. But Nannar/Sin would not accept the doom of his splendid city Ur. His appeals to Anu and Enlil to find a way to spare Ur were of no avail; and as the helpless Enlil bluntly told him, "Ur was granted kingship—an everlasting reign it was not granted . . . Its kingship, its reign, has been *cut*"—not to everlast was its NAM.TAR, a Destiny that can be cut and broken, Fate.

But as fate would have it, the winds, as they reached Mesopotamia, changed course to the southeast. And while Sumer and its great olden cities lay prostrate and desolate, the city of Babylon to the north was completely spared.

Until then Marduk had looked to the heavens to divine his Fate. The miraculous sparing of Babylon from the nuclear death and desolation led him to wonder whether his now unobstructed way to supremacy was more than Fate—whether it was his Destiny.

Were Marduk not a deity already, one could have said that what ensued was his deification. In the circumstances, let us call it his *Celestialization*. The vehicle for that was an alteration ("falsification" is equally applicable) of the hallowed text of *Enuma elish*: to call Nibiru "Marduk" and thereby make the supreme planetary god and the supreme god on Earth one and the same. After so substituting "Marduk" for Nibiru in the tale of the Celestial Battle, the crucial words were then applied to him: Obtaining a Tablet of Destinies from Kingu, the chief of Tiamat's host,

The Tablet of Destinies he took from him,
Sealed it with a seal,
To his [own] breast fastened it.

His was now a Destiny. And the gods, in their Assembly, to "this utterance paid heed." They bowed and shouted: "Marduk is king!" Accepting the inevitable, Anu and Enlil (in the words of an inscription by the Babylonian king Hammurabi),

Determined for Marduk, the firstborn of Enki,
the Enlil-functions over all mankind,
Made him great among the gods who watch and see,
Called Babylon by name to be exalted,
made it supreme in the world;
And established for Marduk, in its midst,
an everlasting Lordship.

The coronation—to use an understandable term—of Marduk as "king of the gods" took place in a solemn ceremony, at an assembly of the Fifty Great Gods and the "Seven Gods of Destiny," and with hundreds of rank and file Anunnaki present. Symbolically, Enlil laid before Marduk his divine weapon, the Bow (which in the heavens had the Bow-star as its counterpart). Then the transfer of the Enlil-powers to Marduk was further celebrated by the transfer to Marduk of the secret numerical rank of 50. That was done by a recitation, one by one, of the "fifty names." They start with Marduk's proper name, asserting that it was Anu himself who had so named Marduk when he was born, and, running through the rest of the epithet-names, ends with Nibiru—the transformation of the god on Earth into the supreme planetary god.

The fifty names are made up from *Sumerian* words or syllable combinations—epithets of whoever had possessed the fifty names before the *Epic of Creation* was falsified to accommodate Marduk; and although the Babylonian editors of the text (written in the Akkadian language) attempted to explain to their contemporaries the enigmatic Sumerian syl-

labic words, it is evident that even they could not fully grasp what secret message each name had conveyed. That such secret meanings or encodings underlay the fifty names was recognized by the renowned Assyriologist and biblical scholar E. A. Speiser; rendering *Enuma elish* in English for *Ancient Near Eastern Texts Relating to the Old Testament*, he observed that "the text etymologizes the names in a manner made familiar by the Bible; the etymologies, which accompany virtually every name on the long list, are meant to be cabalistic and symbolic rather than strictly linguistic."

There is more in the Fifty Names of a "Kabbalistic" nature than the above observation allows. The first nine names are listed at the end of the sixth tablet of *Enuma elish*, and are accompanied by several accolade verses. As had been noted by Franz M. Th. Böhl in his *Die fünfzig Namen des Marduk*, the utterance of those first nine names was attributed to forefathers not only of Marduk but even of Anu himself; three of them contained triple meanings each; and in one such meaning-within-meaning, the unique (and otherwise unreported) ability to "revive the dead gods" was attributed to Marduk. That, Franz Böhl suggested, could be a reference to the death and resurrection of Osiris (of Egyptian lore), because the ensuing three names (numbers 10, 11, 12) are variants of the epithet-name ASAR (*Asaru* in Akkadian) and, according to Böhl, three epithets that paralleled three epithets of the Egyptian god.

With those three epithet-names *Enuma elish* moves on to the seventh tablet—not without implications for the seven days of Creation in Genesis (of which the first six were periods of activity and the seventh a day of rest and divine contemplation); and seven was, we will recall, the planetary designation of Earth and of Enlil as Earth's Commander.

The three ASAR epithets, after which the epithet-names become varied and diverse, bring the total of names to twelve. They are additionally explained in four verses giving the fourfold meaning of the three ASAR names, suggesting again an attempt to incorporate twelve into the text. The recitation of the fifty names thus incorporates the divine rank

number of Enlil and his planetary number, the number of the members of the Solar System, and of the constellations.

"All of my instructions are embodied in the fifty names," Enki announced at the conclusion of the ceremony. In those names, "all the rites have been combined." In his own hand "he wrote it down, preserved for the future," and ordered that the writing be lodged in the Esagil temple that the gods shall build for Marduk in Babylon. There the secret knowledge shall be safeguarded by a line of priestly initiates, passed from father to son: "Let them be kept [there], let the elder explain them; let the wise and knowing father impart to the son."

What deeper meanings, what secret knowledge do the fifty names hold that, according to Enki, combine in them all that there was to know?

Perhaps one day, when a new discovery will enable us to decode the numerical encryptions of Assyrian and Babylonian kings, we too will know.

10

NAVEL OF THE EARTH

Twenty-four years before the nuclear calamity two paths crossed, and not by accident. One was that of a god who was certain that his Fate had become a Destiny; the other was of a man whose Destiny became his Fate. The god was Marduk; the man was Abraham; the place where their paths crossed was Harran.

And an outcome of that was to last to our very own times, when Babylon (now Iraq) rained deathly missiles on the land of Jerusalem (now Israel).

That Abraham had sojourned in Harran is known from the Bible. That Marduk had wanderings in faraway lands, and that he ended up in the land of the Hittites, we know from his autobiography. That the specific place where he had spent twenty-four years was Harran is surmised by us from the very opening words of Marduk's "autobiography": He begins his query, "Until when?" by addressing it to *ilu Haranim*, the "gods of Harran" (Fig. 66), as the immediately present gods, and only then goes on to the distant Great Gods Who Judge.

Indeed, to be in Harran was a logical choice, for it was a major urban and religious center—lying at the crossroads of trade routes—and a hub of communications, at the border of Sumer and Akkad but not yet within Sumer proper, Harran was a perfect headquarters for the god whose son was raising an invasion army.

A sojourn of twenty-four years before the invasion and the nuclear holocaust that occurred in 2024 B.C. means that Marduk arrived in Harran in 2048 B.C. That, by our calculations

Figure 66

(based on a careful synchronization of biblical, Mesopotamian, and Egyptian data) was on the very footsteps of Abram/Abraham. He was born, by our calculations, in 2123 B.C. Every move of Terah and his family, we have shown in *The Wars of Gods and Men*, was linked to the fast-developing events in Ur and the Sumerian empire. The Bible informs us that Abram/Abraham left Harran, on God's instructions, at age 75. The year, then, was 2048 B.C.—the very year in which Marduk had arrived in Harran! And it was then that *Yahweh*—not just "the Lord God"—"said unto Abram: Get thee out of thy country, and out of thy birthplace, and from thy father's dwelling place, unto the land which I will show thee." It was a triple departure—from Abram's *country* (Sumer), and from his *birthplace* (Nippur), and from his father's *dwelling place* (Harran); and it was to a new and unfamiliar destination, for Yahweh had to show it to Abram.

Taking his wife Sarai and his nephew Lot with him, Abram went to "the land of Canaan." Arriving from the north (crossing over perhaps where his grandson Jacob would later cross), he moved fast southward, reaching a place called Alon-Moreh—a name literally meaning "The oak tree which points," apparently a well-known landmark that a traveler could not miss. To be certain that he was traveling correctly, Abram awaited further instructions; and "Yahweh appeared there unto Abram," confirming that he was in the right place. Moving on, Abram reached Beth-El ("God's Abode") and again "called out the name of Yahweh," continuing thereafter without stopping to the Negev ("The Dryness"), the southernmost part of Canaan bordering on the Sinai peninsula.

He did not linger there long. Food was short there. So Abram moved on, all the way to Egypt. It is customary to depict Abraham as a nomadic Bedouin chieftain, spending his days tending his flocks or lolling in his tent. In fact he had to be much more than that, for otherwise why was he chosen by Yahweh to be sent on the divinely ordained mission? He was descended from a line of priests; and the names of his and his brother's wives, *Sarai* ("princess") and *Milcah* ("queenly") indicate a connection with Sumer's royal line. No sooner did Abram reach the Egyptian border than he coached his wife on how to behave when they would be received at the Pharaoh's court (and later on, back in Canaan, he dealt with its kings as an equal). After a sojourn of five years in Egypt, when Abram was ordered back to the Negev, he was provided by the Pharaoh with a great number of men and women to be in his service, and with flocks of sheep and herds of oxen and she-asses and he-asses—as well as with a flock of highly prized camels. The inclusion of camels is significant, for they were suited for military purposes in desert conditions.

That a military conflict was brewing we learn in the chapter immediately following in Genesis (chapter 14), dealing with the invasion of southern Canaan by a coalition of Kings of the East—from Sumer and its protectorates (such as Elam,

in the Zagros Mountains, which was renowned for its fighting men). Capturing city after city as they followed the King's Highway, they detoured around the Dead Sea and headed straight for the Sinai peninsula (see map p. 26). But there Abram and his armed men blocked the invaders' way. Disappointed, the invaders satisfied themselves by looting the five cities (that included Sodom and Gomorrah) in the fertile plain south of the Dead Sea; among the prisoners they took was Lot, Abram's nephew.

When word reached Abram that his nephew had been taken captive, he pursued the invaders with 318 select men all the way to Damascus. Since some time had passed until a refugee from Sodom told Abram about his nephew's capture, it was quite a feat for Abram to catch up with the invaders, who were already at Dan, in the north of Canaan. It is our suggestion that the "trained young men" as they are called in Genesis were camel-riding cavalrymen (Fig. 67), from a Mesopotamian sculpture.

"It was after those events," the Bible states (Genesis 15), "that Yahweh spoke to Abram in a vision, saying: Fear not, Abram; I am thy shielder; thy reward shall be exceedingly great."

It is time to review the Abram saga up to this point and to ask some questions. Why was Abram told to forsake everything and go to a completely strange place? What was special about Canaan? Why the rush to reach the Negev, on the border of the Sinai peninsula? Why the royal reception in Egypt and the return with an army and a camel-cavalry? What was the target of the invaders from the East? And why was their defeat at the hands of Abram deserving of a promise of a "great reward" from God?

Far from the customary picture painted of Abram as a nomadic sheepherder, he turns out to be a superb military leader and a major actor on the international scene. It can all be explained, we suggest, only if one accepts the reality of the Anunnaki presence and takes into consideration the other major events occurring at the same time. The only prize worth an international war—at the very time that Nabu was

Figure 67

organizing fighters in the lands west of the Euphrates—was the spaceport in the Sinai. It was that which Abram—allied with the Hittites and trained by them in martial arts—was hurriedly sent to protect. It was to that purpose that an Egyptian Pharaoh in Memphis, himself facing an invasion by followers of Ra/Marduk based in Thebes in the south, provided Abram with a camel-riding cavalry and a large number of other men and women servants. And it was because Abram successfully protected the gateway to the spaceport that Yahweh assured him of a great reward—as well as promised him protection from future retribution by the losing side.

The War of the Kings took place, by our calculations, in 2041 B.C. The year after that the princes of the south captured Memphis in Egypt and dethroned Abram's ally, declaring allegiance to Amon-Ra, the "hidden" or "unseen" Ra/Marduk, who was then still in exile. (After Marduk's rise to

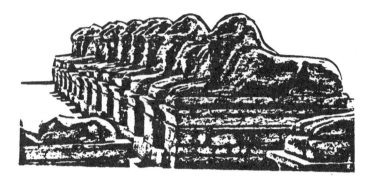

Figure 68

supremacy, the new rulers of Egypt began building in Karnak, a suburb of the capital Thebes, Egypt's greatest temple in honor of Amon-Ra; they lined the majestic avenue leading to it with ram-headed sphinxes—Fig. 68—honoring the god whose age, the Age of the Ram, had arrived).

Things were no less hectic in Sumer and its empire. Celestial omens, including a total lunar eclipse in 2031 B.C., predicted coming doom. Under the pressure of Nabu's warriors, the last kings of Sumer drew back their forces and protective outposts ever closer to the capital Ur. There was little comfort to be found in appeals to the gods, for the gods themselves were engulfed in the sharpening confrontation with Marduk. Gods as well as men looked to the heavens for signs. A human, even one as qualified or chosen as Abram, could no longer protect the essential facility of the Anunnaki, the spaceport. And so, in 2024 B.C., with the consent of the Council of the Great Gods, Nergal and Ninurta used nuclear weapons to keep the prize from Marduk. It is all described vividly and in detail in the *Erra Epos*; it is there also that a sideshow, the upheaval of the "sinning cities" that included Sodom and Gomorrah, is recounted.

Abram was forewarned about what was to happen; at his request, two Angels of the Lord went to Sodom the day before the nuking of the spaceport and the cities to save Lot and his family. Asking for time to gather his family, Lot

prevailed on the two divine beings to postpone the upheaval until he and his family could reach a safe haven in the mountains. The event was thus not a natural calamity—it was predictable and postponable.

"And in the morning Abraham got up early and went to the place where he had stood before Yahweh" the day before; "and he looked toward Sodom and Gomorrah, and toward all the land of the plain; and he beheld and saw a smoky steam rising from the earth, as the steamy smoke of a furnace."

On God's orders, Abraham moved away from the place, getting closer to the seashore. In the mountains in southeastern Jordan, Lot and his daughters huddled in fear; their mother, having lingered behind as they were escaping from Sodom, was vaporized by the nuclear explosion. (The usual translation of the words, that she was turned into a pillar of salt, stems from a misreading of the Sumerian word that could mean both "salt" and "vapor"). Convinced that they had just witnessed the end of the world, the two daughters of Lot decided that the only way to enable the human race to survive was to have them sleep with their own father. Each one had a son that way; they were, according to the Bible, the progenitors of two tribes east of the Jordan River: the Moabites and the Amonites.

And as for Abraham: "God remembered Sarah as he had promised" (when He appeared to them with the two Angels the year before), "and Sarah conceived and bore Abraham a son in his old age," and they named the son Isaac. Abraham was 100 years old at the time; Sarah was 90.

With the spaceport gone, Abraham's mission had come to an end. Now it was up to God to keep His end of the bargain. He had "cut a covenant" with Abraham to give him and his descendants as an everlasting legacy the lands between the Brook of Egypt and the Euphrates River. And now, through Isaac, the promise had to be kept.

And there was also the question of what to do with the other space facilities.

There were, to be sure, two such facilities in addition to the spaceport itself. One was the Landing Place, to which Gilgamesh had set his course. The other was the Mission Control Center—no longer needed, but still intact; a post-Diluvial "Navel of the Earth," serving the same function as the pre-Diluvial "Navel of the Earth" that Nippur had been.

To understand the similar functions and consequently similar layouts, one should compare our sketches of the pre- and post-Diluvial space facilities. Before the Deluge (Fig. 69) Nippur, designated the "Navel of the Earth" because it was at the center of concentric circles delineating the Landing Corridor, served as Mission Control Center. Cities of the Gods whose names meant "Seeing the Red Light" (Larsa), "Seeing the Halo at Six" (Lagash) and "Seeing the Bright Halo" (Laraak) marked out both the equidistant spacing and the landing path toward Sippar ("Bird City"), the site of the spaceport. The landing path, within an elongated Landing Corridor, was based at its point on the twin peaks of Mount Ararat—the most prominent topographic feature in the Near East. Where that line intersected the precise line northward, the spaceport was to be built. Thus, the Landing Path formed a precise 45° angle with the geographic parallel.

After the Deluge, when humanity was granted the three Regions, the Anunnaki retained for themselves the Fourth Region—the Sinai peninsula. There, in the central plain, the ground was both flat and hard (perfect tank terrain, as modern armies have concluded), unlike the mud-buried and water-clogged post-Diluvial plain in Mesopotamia. Choosing again the twin peaks of Ararat as the anchor point, the Anunnaki drew a landing path at the same 45° angle to the geographic parallel—the 30th parallel north (Fig. 70).

There in the central plain of the Sinai peninsula, where the diagonal line intersected the 30th parallel, was to be the spaceport. To complete the layout, two more components were required: To establish a new Mission Control Center, and to delineate (and anchor) the Landing Corridor.

We believe that the outlining of the Landing Corridor preceded the choosing of the site for Mission Control Center.

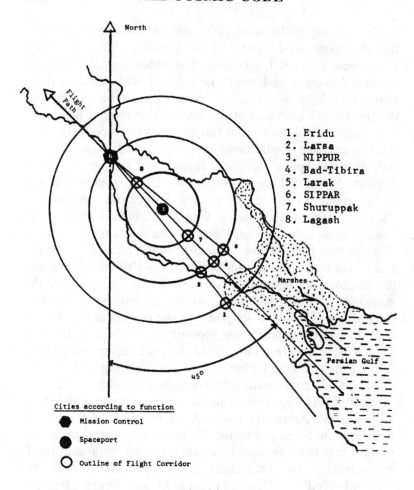

North

Flight Path

1. Eridu
2. Larsa
3. NIPPUR
4. Bad-Tibira
5. Larak
6. SIPPAR
7. Shuruppak
8. Lagash

Marshes

Persian Gulf

45°

Cities according to function

⬢ Mission Control

● Spaceport

○ Outline of Flight Corridor

Figure 69

The reason? *The existence of the Landing Place*, in the Cedar Mountains in Lebanon.

Every folklore, every legend connected with the place repeats the same assertion, that the place existed before the Flood. As soon as the Anunnaki landed back on Earth after the Deluge on the peaks of Ararat, they had at their disposal a real, functioning Landing Place—not a full-fledged space-

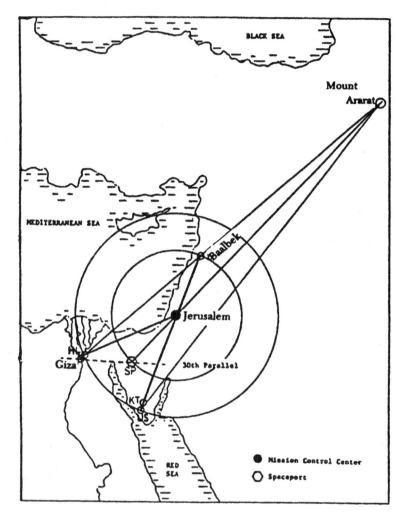

Figure 70

port, but a place to land on. All the Sumerian texts dealing with the grant to Mankind of "domesticated" (i.e. genetically altered) plants and animals describe a biogenetic laboratory in the Cedar Mountains, with Enlil now cooperating with Enki to restore life on Earth. All the modern scientific evidence corroborates that it was from that particular area

that wheat and barley and the first domesticated animals had come. (Here again modern advances in genetics join the parade of corroborations: A study published in the journal *Science* as recently as November 1997 pinpoints the place where wild einkorn wheat was genetically manipulated to create the "Founder Crop" of eight different cereals: some 11,000 years ago, in that particular corner of the Near East!)

There was every reason to include this place—a vast stone platform of massive construction—in the new space facilities. That, in turn, determined by equidistant concentric circles the location of Mission Control Center.

To complete the space facilities, it was necessary to anchor the Landing Corridor. In its southeastern end, two nearby peaks—one of which remained hallowed to this day as the so-called Mount Moses—were handy. In the equidistant northwestern edge there were no peaks, just a flat plateau. The Anunnaki—not any mortal Pharaoh—built there two artificial mountains, the two great pyramids of Giza (the smaller Third Pyramid, we have suggested in *The Stairway to Heaven*, was built first as a test scale model). The layout was completed with a "mythological" animal carved from the native rock—the sphinx. It gazes precisely along the 30th parallel, eastward toward the spaceport in the Sinai.

These were the components of the post-Diluvial spaceport of the Anunnaki in the Sinai peninsula, as built by them circa 10500 B.C. And when the landing and takeoff place in the Sinai's central plain was blown up, the spaceport's auxiliary components remained standing: the Giza pyramids and Sphinx, the Landing Place in the Cedar Mountains, and Mission Control Center.

The Landing Place, as we know from the adventures of Gilgamesh, was there circa 2900 B.C. Gilgamesh witnessed there, the night before he had attempted entry, a rocketship rising. The place remained extant after the Deluge—a Phoenician coin depicted vividly what had stood atop the stone platform (Fig. 71). *The vast stone platform still exists.* The place is called Baalbek—for it was the "Secret Place of the North" of the Canaanite god Ba'al. The Bible knew the place

Figure 71

as *Beth-Shemesh*, "House/Abode of Shamash" (the Sun God) and it was within the domains of King Solomon. The Greeks after Alexander called the place *Heliopolis*, meaning "City of Helios," the Sun God, and built there temples to Zeus, his sister Aphrodite, and his son Hermes. The Romans after them erected temples to Jupiter, Venus, and Mercury. The temple to Jupiter was the largest temple ever built by the Romans anywhere in the empire, for they believed that the place was the most important oracle place in the world, one that would foretell the fate of Rome and its empire.

The remains of the Roman temples still stand atop the vast stone platform; so does, undisturbed by the passage of time and the ravages of nature and men, the platform itself. Its flat top rests on layer upon layer ("courses") of large stone blocks, some weighing hundreds of tons. Of great renown from antiquity is the *Trilithon*—a group of three colossal stone blocks, lying side by side and forming a middle course where the platform had sustained its greatest load-impact (Fig. 72, with a passing man for size comparison). Each of these colossal megaliths weighs about 1,100—one thousand one hundred—tons; it is a weight that no modern piece of equipment can even come close to lifting and moving.

But who could have done that in antiquity? The local leg-

Figure 72

end says: the Giants. They not only placed those stone blocks
where they are, they also quarried and shaped and carried
them over a distance of almost a mile; that is certain, for the
quarry has been found. There, one of the colossal stone
blocks protrudes from the mountainside half-quarried (Fig.
73); a man sitting on it looks like a fly on a block of ice.

Down at the southern end of the Landing Corridor, the
Giza pyramids still stand, defying all traditional explanations,
challenging Egyptologists to accept that they had been built
millennia before the Pharaohs and not by any one of them.
The sphinx still gazes precisely eastward along the 30th par-

Figure 73

allel, keeping to itself its secrets—perhaps even the secrets of the *Book of Thoth*.

And what about Mission Control Center?

That, too, exists; it is a place called *Jerusalem*.

And there, too, a great and sacred platform rests atop colossal stone blocks that no man or ancient machine could have moved, raised, and put in place.

The biblical record of Abraham's comings and goings in Canaan includes two instances of seemingly unnecessary digression; in both instances, the place digressed to was the site of the future Jerusalem.

The first time the digression is reported as an epilogue to the story of the War of the Kings. Having caught up with and defeated the invaders all the way north near Damascus, Abraham returned to Canaan with the captives and the booty;

> *And the king of Sodom went forth toward him—*
> *after he was returning from smiting Khedorlaomer*
> *and the kings who were with him—*
> *to the Valley of Shaveh, which is the king's valley.*

> *And Melchizedek, the king of Shalem—*
> *and he was a priest unto the God Most High—*

brought forth bread and wine,
and he blessed him, saying:

"Blessed be Abram unto God Most High,
Creator of Heaven and Earth;
And blessed be the God Most High,
who hath delivered thy enemies unto thy hands."

Melchizedek (whose name has meant in Hebrew exactly what the Akkadian *Sharru-kin,* "Righteous King," has meant) offered Abram to keep a tenth of all of the booty that he had retrieved. The king of Sodom was more generous: Keep all the wealth, he said, just return to me the captives. But Abram would have none of that; swearing by "Yahweh, the God Most High, Creator of Heaven and Earth," he said he would not keep even a shoelace (Genesis chapter 14).

(Scholars have long debated, and will undoubtedly continue to debate, whether Abraham swore by the "God Most High" of Melchizedek, or meant to say: No, *Yahweh* is the God Most High by whom I will swear.)

This is the first time that an allusion is made in the Bible to Jerusalem, here called *Shalem.* That this was a reference to what was later known as Jerusalem is based not only on long-standing traditions, but also on the clear identification in Psalm 76:3. It is generally accepted that the full name, *Yeru-Shalem* in Hebrew, meant "The city of Shalem," Shalem being a deity's name. Some suggest, however, that the name could also mean "Founded by Shalem." And it could also be argued that the word *Shalem* was not a name or even a noun, but an adjective, meaning "complete," "without defect." That would make the place's name mean "the Perfect Place." Or, if Shalem be a deity's name, it could mean the place of the "One who is perfect."

Whether honoring a god, established by a god, or the Perfect Place, Shalem/Jerusalem was located in the most unlikely place as far as Cities of Man were concerned. It was located amidst barren mountains, neither at any trade or military crossroads, nor near any food or water sources. Indeed,

it was a place almost completely bereft of water, and the proper supply of drinking water was constantly to be a principal problem and vulnerability of Jerusalem. Shalem/Jerusalem featured neither in Abraham's migrations nor in the route of the invasion from the east, nor in his pursuit of the invaders. Why then a detour for a victory celebration—a detour, one is inclined to say, to a "godforsaken place"—except that the place was definitely not God-forsaken. It was a place—the only place in Canaan—where a priest serving the God Most High was located. And the question is, Why there? What was special about the place?

The second seemingly unnecessary digression had to do with the testing by God of Abraham's devotion. Abram had already carried out his mission to Canaan. God had already promised him that his reward would be great, that God himself should protect him. The miracle of a son and Legal Heir at extreme old age had happened; Abram's name was changed to Abraham, "Father of a multitude of nations." The land was promised to him and his descendants; the promise was incorporated in a covenant that involved a magical ritual. Sodom and Gomorrah had been destroyed and all was ready to let Abraham and his son enjoy the peace and quiet to which they were surely entitled.

Then, all of a sudden, "it was after all those things," the Bible says (Genesis chapter 22), "that God tested Abraham," telling him to go to a certain place and there sacrifice his own beloved son:

> *Take now thou thy son Isaac,*
> *thy only one whom thy lovest,*
> *and get thee unto the Land of Moriah;*
> *and offer him there as a sacrifice*
> *on one of the mounts*
> *which I shall point out to thee.*

Why God decided to test Abraham in that excruciating way, the Bible does not explain. Abraham, ready to carry out the divine order, found out in the nick of time that it was

only a test of his devotion: An Angel of the Lord pointed out to him a ram caught in the bushes, and told him that it was the ram that was to be sacrificed, not Isaac. But why was the test, if it was needed at all, not conducted just where Abraham and Isaac dwelt, near Beersheba? Why the need to undertake a journey of three days? Why go to the part of Canaan that God identified as the Land of Moriah, and there to locate a specific mount—which God himself pointed out—to conduct there the test?

As in the first instance, there had to be something special about the chosen place. We read (Genesis 22:4) that, "On the third day Abraham lifted his eyes and saw the place from a distance." The area was rich, if with anything, with barren mounts; from nearby, and certainly from a distance, they all look alike. Yet Abraham *recognized* the particular mount "from a distance." There had to be something there that distinguished it from all the other mounts. So much so that when the ordeal was over he gave the place a long-remembered name: The Mount Where Yahweh Is Seen. As 2 Chronicles 3:1 makes clear, Mount Moriah was the Jerusalem peak on which the Temple was eventually built.

From the time Jerusalem became a city, it encompassed three mounts. Listed from the northeast to the southwest, they have been Mount *Zophim* ("Mount of Observers," now called Mount Scopus in English), Mount *Moriah* ("Mount of Directing, of Pointing Out") in the center, and Mount *Zion* ("Mount of the Signal"); these are designations of functions that bring to mind the function-names of the Beacon Cities of the Anunnaki marking out Nippur and the Landing Path when the spaceport had been in Mesopotamia.

Jewish legends relate that Abraham recognized Mount Moriah from a distance because he saw upon it "a pillar of fire reaching from the Earth to Heaven, and a heavy cloud in which the Glory of God was visible." This language is almost identical to the biblical description of the presence of the Lord upon Mount Sinai during the Exodus. But putting

such lore aside, what we believe Abraham saw that identified the mount as different, that distinguished it from all others there, was the *great platform upon it*.

A platform which, though smaller than at Baalbek's Landing Place, was also part of the space facilities of the Anunnaki. For Jerusalem (before it became Jerusalem), we suggest, was the post-Diluvial Mission Control Center.

And, as at Baalbek, that platform, too, still exists.

The reason (for the first) and purpose (of the second) digressions thus come into focus. The fulfillment of his mission was marked by a formal celebration, including a priestly blessing of Abraham with the ceremonial bread and wine, at a site—the only site in Canaan—directly connected to the presence of the *Elohim*. The second diversion was meant to test Abraham's qualifications for a chosen status *after* the destruction of the spaceport and the resulting dismantling of the accoutrements of Mission Control Center; and to renew there the covenant in the presence of Abraham's successor, Isaac. Such a renewal of the divine vow indeed followed right away after the test:

> *And the Angel of Yahweh*
> *called out to Abraham for a second time*
> *from the skies, saying, this is Yahweh's word:*
> *"This is my oath:*
> *Because thou hast done this thing,*
> *and hast not withheld thy son, the unique one,*
> *I will greatly bless thee*
> *and I will exceedingly multiply thy seed . . .*
> *And in thy seed shall the nations of the Earth*
> *be blessed."*

By renewing the divine vow at this particular site, the site itself—hallowed ground ever since—became part and parcel of the heritage of Abraham the Hebrew and his descendants.

The Divine Promise to Abraham, he had already been told

by God, was to come true only after a passage of time and
a servitude in a foreign land for four hundred years. All told
it was a thousand years later when the descendants of Abraham took possession of the sacred mount, Mount Moriah.
When the Israelites arrived in Canaan after the Exodus, they
found that a tribe of Jebusites had settled south of the sacred
mount, and let them be, for the time to take possession of
that most hallowed ground had not yet come. The singular
prize went to King David, who circa 1000 B.C.—a thousand
years after the testing of Abraham—captured the Jebusite
settlement and moved the capital from Hebron to what has
been called in the Bible the City of David.

It is important to realize that the Jebusite settlement that
David captured, and his new capital, were not at all ''Jerusalem'' as it is now envisioned, not even the walled ''Old
City.'' The area captured by David and thereafter known as
the City of David was on Mount Zion, not Mount Moriah.
Even when David's successor Solomon extended the city
northward to a section called Ophel (Fig. 74), it still stopped
short of encroaching on the unique area to the north. It indicates, we suggest, that the *sacred platform extending from
there northward on Mount Moriah already existed* at the time
of David and Solomon.

The Jebusite settlement was thus not on Mount Moriah
and its platform, but well to its south. (Human dwellings
near—but not within—a sacred precinct were common in
Mesopotamian ''cult centers,'' such as at Ur (see Fig. 65) or
even in Enlil's Nippur, as evidenced by an actual map of
Nippur discovered drawn on a clay tablets, Fig. 75).

One of David's first actions was to transfer the Ark of the
Covenant from its latest temporary location to the capital, in
preparation for placing it in a proper House of Yahweh
which David planned to erect. But that honor, he was told
by the Prophet Nathan, was not to be his on account of all
the blood that his hands had shed during the national wars
and his personal conflicts; the honor, he was told, would go
to his son Solomon. All he was allowed to do in the meantime was to erect an altar; the precise place for it was shown

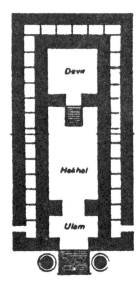

EAST

Figure 76

dation Stone''—for it was from that stone that "the whole world was woven.'' The Prophet Ezekiel (38:12) identified it as the Navel of the Earth. The tradition was so entrenched that Christian artists in the Middle Ages depicted the place as the Navel of the Earth (Fig. 79a) and continued to do so even after the discovery of America (Fig. 79b).

The Temple that Solomon built (the First Temple) was destroyed by the Babylonian king Nebuchadnezzar in 576 B.C., and was rebuilt by Jewish exiles returning from Babylon 70 years later. That rebuilt Temple, known as the Second Temple, was later substantially enhanced and aggrandized by the Judean king Herod, during his reign from 36 to 4 B.C. But the Second Temple, in all its phases, adhered to the original layout, location, and the situating of the Holy of Holies upon the Sacred Rock. And when the Moslems captured Jerusalem in the seventh century A.D., they claimed that it was from that Sacred Rock that Mohammed ascended

It took seven years to complete the building of the Temple
and to equip it with all the ritual utensils. Then, on the next
New Year ("in the seventh month") celebration, the king
and the priests and all the people witnessed the transfer of
the Ark of the Covenant to its permanent place, in the Temple's Holy of Holies. "There was nothing in the Ark except
the two stone tablets that Moses had placed therein" at
Mount Sinai. No sooner was the Ark in place under the
winged Cherubim, than "a cloud filled the House of Yahweh," forcing the priests to rush out. Then Solomon, standing at the altar that was in the courtyard, prayed to God
"who in heaven dwells" to come and reside in his House.
It was later, at night, that Yahweh appeared to Solomon in
a dream and promised him a divine presence: "My eyes and
my heart will be in it forever."

The Temple was divided into three parts, entered through
a large gateway flanked by two specially designed pillars
(Fig. 76). The front part was called the *Ulam* ("Hallway");
the largest, middle part was the *Ekhal*, a Hebrew term stemming from the Sumerian E.GAL ("Great Abode"). Screened
off from that was the innermost part, the Holy of Holies. It
was called the *Dvir*—literally: The Speaker—for it held the
Ark of the Covenant with the two Cherubim upon it (Fig.
77), from between which God had spoken to Moses during
the Exodus. The great altar and the washbasins were in the
courtyard, not inside the Temple.

Biblical data and references, age-old traditions and ar-
chaeological evidence have left no doubt that the Temple that
Solomon built (the First Temple) stood upon the great stone
platform that still crowns Mount Moriah (also known as the
Holy Mount, Mount of the Lord, or the Temple Mount).
Given the dimensions of the Temple and the size of the platform, there is general agreement where the Temple stood
(Fig. 78), and that the Ark of the Covenant within the Holy
of Holies was emplaced upon a rock outcropping, a Sacred
Rock, which according to unwavering traditions was the rock
upon which Abraham was about to sacrifice Isaac. The rock
has been called in Jewish scriptures *Even Sheti'yah*—"Foun-

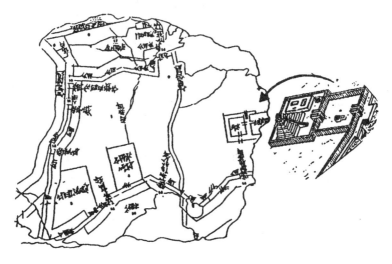

Figure 75

(The extent of those detailed specifications for the temple and its various sections and the ritual utensils can be judged from 1 Chronicles 28:11–19).

In the fourth year of his reign—480 years after the start of the Exodus, the Bible states—Solomon began the construction of the Temple, *"on Mount Moriah, as had been shown to his father David."* While timbers cut from the Cedars of Lebanon and the purest gold of Ophir were imported and copper for the specified washbasins was mined and smelted in the famed King Solomon's Mines, the structure itself had to be erected with "hewn and cut stones, large and costly stones."

The stone ashlars had to be prepared and cut to size and shape elsewhere, for the construction was subject to a strict prohibition against the use of any iron tools for the Temple. The stone blocks had to be transported, brought over to the site for assembly only. "And the House, when it was in building, was built of stone made ready before it was brought thither; so that there was neither hammer nor axe nor any tool of iron heard in the House while it was in building" (1 Kings 6:7).

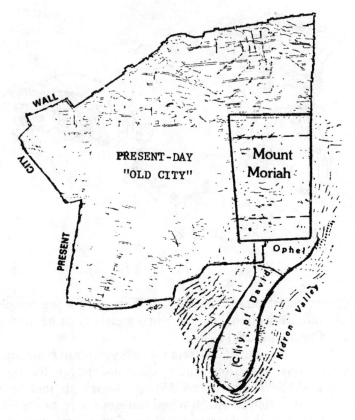

Figure 74

to David by an "Angel of Yahweh, standing between Heaven and Earth," pointing out the place with a drawn sword. He was also shown a *Tavnit*—a scale model—of the future temple and given detailed architectural instructions, which, when the time came, he handed over to Solomon in a public ceremony, saying:

> *All of this, in writing by His hand,*
> *did Yahweh make me*
> *understand—*
> *all of the workings of the* Tavnit.

Figure 77

heavenward for a nighttime visit; and they enshrined the place by building the Dome of the Rock (Fig. 80) to shelter and magnify it.

Geologically the rock is an outcropping of the underlying natural rock, protruding above the level of the stone platform some five or six feet (the face is not even). But it is a most unusual "outcropping," in more than one way. Its visible face has been cut and shaped, with an impressive degree of precision (Fig. 81a), to form rectangular, elongated, horizontal and vertical receptacles and niches of varying depths and sizes. These artificial niches and receptacles had to have some purpose known to whoever had made those incisions in the rock. What has been only surmised since long ago (e.g. Hugo Gressmann, *Altorientalische Bilder zum Alten Testament*) has been confirmed by recent researchers (such as Leen Ritmeyer, *Locating the Original Temple Mount*): the Ark of the Covenant and the walls of the Holy of Holies had been emplaced where the long straight cut and other niches in the face of the rock were made.

The implication of those findings is that the cuts and niches in the face of the rock date back at least to the time of the First Temple. There is, however, no mention whatsoever in the relevant passages in the Bible of any such cutting by Solomon; indeed, it would have been impossible—

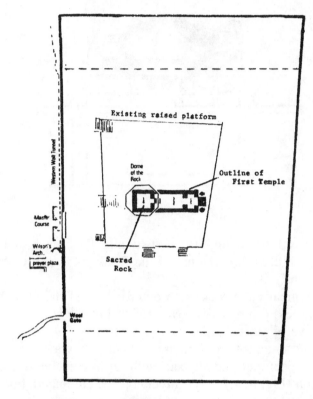

Figure 78

because of the strict prohibition against the use of metal axes and other tools on the Mount!

The enigma of the Sacred Rock and what had stood on top of it is magnified by the mystery of what might have stood under it. For the rock is not a simple outcropping. *It is hollow!*

In fact, given permission, one can descend a flight of stairs built by the Moslem authorities, and end up in a cavelike cavern the rocky roof of which is the protruding upper part of the Sacred Rock. This cavern—whether natural or not is uncertain—also features deep niches and receptacles, both in the rocky walls and (as could be seen before the floor was covered with prayer rugs) also in the floor. At one place there

Figures 79a and 79b

is what looks like an opening into a dark tunnel; but what it is and where it leads is a well-kept Moslem secret.

Nineteenth-century travelers have stated that this cavern is not the last subsurface cavity associated with the Sacred Rock; they stated that there is yet another, lower cavity beneath it (Fig. 81b). Israeli researchers, fanatically barred from the area, have determined with the aid of soil-penetrating radar and sonar technology that there is indeed another major cavity under the Sacred Rock.

These mysterious cavities have given rise to speculation not only regarding possible Temple treasures, or Temple records that might have been hidden there when the First Tem-

Figure 80

ple and then the Second Temple were about to be overrun and destroyed. There is even speculation that the Ark of the Covenant, which the Bible ceased to mention after the Egyptian Pharaoh Sheshak ransacked (but did not destroy) the Temple circa 950 B.C., might have been hidden there. That, for the time being, must remain just speculation.

What is certain, though, is that the biblical Prophets and the Psalmist referred to this Sacred Rock when they had used the term "Rock of Israel" as a euphemism for "Yahweh." And the Prophet Isaiah (30:29), speaking of the future time of universal redemption on the Day of the Lord, prophesied that the nations of the Earth shall come to Jerusalem to praise the Lord "on the Mount of Yawheh, at the Rock of Israel."

The Temple Mount is covered by a horizontal stone platform, slightly off-perfect rectangular in shape (because of the contours of the terrain), whose size is about 1,600 by 900

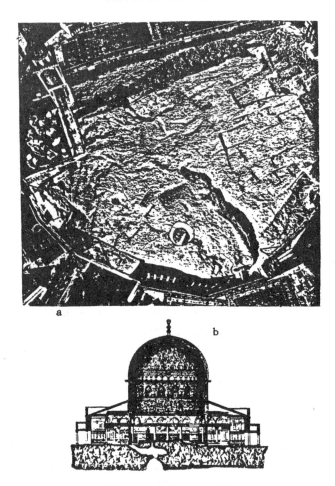

Figures 81a and 81b

feet, for a total stone-paved area of close to 1,500,000 square feet. Although it is believed that the present-day platform includes sections, at the extreme south and possibly also in the north, that had been added between the First Temple's building and the destruction of the Second Temple, it is certain that the bulk of the platform is original; it is certainly so regarding the slightly raised portion, where the Sacred Rock (and thus the Dome of the Rock) are located.

As the visible sides of the platform's retaining walls show, and as more recent excavations have revealed, the natural bedrock of Mount Moriah slopes considerably from north to south. Though no one can say with any certainty what the size of the platform had been in the time of Solomon, nor estimate precisely the depth of the slopes that had to be filled, an arbitrary assumption of a platform measuring only 1,000,000 square feet and an average depth of 60 feet (much less in the north, much more in the south), the result is a landfill requiring 60,000,000 cubic feet of aggregate (soil, fieldstones). This is a very major construction undertaking.

Yet nowhere in the Bible is there even a mention or a hint of such an undertaking. The instructions for the First Temple cover pages upon pages in the Bible; every small detail is given, measurements are precise to an amazing degree, where this or that utensil or artifact should be is prescribed, how long the poles that carry the Ark is specified, and so on and on. But it all applies to the *House* of Yahweh. Not a word about the platform on which it was to stand; and that could only mean that the platform has already been there; there was no need to construct it.

Standing out in complete contrast to that absence of mention are the repeated references in 2 Samuel and 1 Kings to the *Millo*, literally "the filling"—a project begun by David and enlarged by Solomon to fill up part of the slopes on the sotheastern corner of the sacred platform, so as to enable the City of David to expand northward, closer to the ancient platform. Clearly, the two kings were quite proud of that achievement and made sure it was recorded in the royal chronicles. (Recent excavations in that area indicate, however, that what was done was to raise the sloping level by constructing a series of terraces that grew smaller as they rose; that was much easier than first surrounding the expanded area with high retaining walls and filling up the gap with aggregate).

This contrast undoubtedly corroborates the conclusion that neither David nor Solomon built the vast platform on Mount Moriah, with the immense retaining walls and enormous

amount of landfill required. All the evidence suggests that the platform already existed when the construction of a Temple was even contemplated.

Who then built the platform, with all the earthworks and stonework that it entailed? Our answer, of course, is: the same master builders who had built the platform at Baalbek (and, for that matter, the vast and precisely positioned platform on which the Great Pyramid of Giza stands).

The great platform that covers the Temple Mount is surrounded by walls that serve both as retaining walls and as fortifications. The Bible reports that Solomon built such walls, as did Judean kings after him. Visible sections of the walls, especially on the southern and eastern sides, display constructions from various later periods. Invariably, the lower (and thus more ancient) courses are built of larger and better-shaped stone blocks. Of these walls, only the Western Wall, by tradition and as confirmed by archaeology, has remained hallowed as an actual remnant from the time of the First Temple—at least in its lowest courses where ashlars (perfectly cut and shaped stone blocks) are the largest. For almost two millennia, since the destruction of the Second Temple, Jews held on to this remnant, worshiping there, praying to God, seeking personal succor by inserting slips of paper with a request to God between the ashlars, bewailing the Temple's destruction and the Jewish people's dispersion—so much so that, in time, the Crusaders and other conquerors of Jerusalem nicknamed the Western Wall the "Wailing Wall."

Until the reunification of Jerusalem by Israel in 1967, the Western Wall was no more than a sliver of a wall, about a hundred feet or so squeezed between residential houses. In front was left a narrow space for the prayers, and on both sides, rising house atop house, it encroached on the Holy Mount. When the houses were removed, a large plaza was formed in front of the Western Wall and its extension all the way to its southern corner was unveiled (Fig. 82). And, for the first time in almost two millennia, it was realized that the retaining walls extend downward nearly as much as they had

Figure 82

been exposed above what has been considered ground level. As suggested by the hitherto visible portion of the "Wailing Wall," the lower courses were larger, better shaped, and of course much older.

Beckoning with mystery and with a promise of ancient secrets was the extension of the Western Wall to the north.

There Captain Charles Wilson explored in the 1860s an archway (which still bears his name) that led northward to a

tunnel-like passage and westward to a series of arched chambers and vaults. The removal of the encroaching dwellings revealed that the current street level lay atop several lower, now-subterranean, levels of ancient structures that included more passages and archways. How far down and how far north did all that extend? That was a puzzle that Israeli archaeologists finally began to tackle.

In the end what they discovered was mind-boggling.

Using data from the Bible, from the Book of Maccabees and from the writings of the Jewish-Roman historian Josephus (and taking into account even a medieval legend that King David knew of a way to ascend the Mount from the west), Israeli archaeologists concluded that Wilson's Arch was the entranceway to what must have been in earlier times an open-air street that ran along the Western Wall, and that the Wall itself extended northward by hundreds of feet. The laborious clearing of the rubble, confirming those assumptions, led to the opening in 1996 of the "Archaeological Tunnel" (an event that made headlines for more than one reason).

Extending for about 1,600 feet from its start at Wilson's Arch to its exit on Via Dolorosa (where Jesus walked carrying the cross), the Western Wall Tunnel uncovered and passes through remains of streets, water tunnels, water pools, archways, structures, and marketplaces from Byzantine, Roman, Herodian, Hasmonean, and biblical times. The thrilling and eerie experience of walking through the tunnel, deep below ground level, is akin to being transported in a time machine—backward into the past with every step.

All along the visitor can see—and touch—the actual parts of the western retaining wall from the earliest times. Courses that have been hidden for millennia have been exposed. In the northernmost section of the tunnel, the natural bedrock that slopes upward comes into view. But the greatest surprise, for the visitor as well as for the archaeologists, lies in the more southerly section of the uncovered wall:

There—at the ancient street level but not yet the lowest bottom course—there had been emplaced massive stone

Figure 83

blocks and on top of them four colossal blocks each weighing hundreds of tons!

In that portion of the Western Wall, a 120-foot section is made up of stone blocks that are an extraordinary 11 feet high, about double even the unusually large blocks that form the course below. Only 4 stone blocks make up the section; one of them is a colossal 42 feet long (Fig. 83); another is 40 feet long, and a third over 25 feet long. Soil-penetrating radar and other soundings have indicated that the depths of these stones is 14 feet. The largest of the three is thus a stone mass of about 6,500 cubic feet, weighing 1,200,000 pounds, which is about 600 tons! The somewhat smaller one weighs about 570 tons, and the third one about 355 tons.

These are colossal sizes and weights by any yardstick; the blocks used in the construction of the Great Pyramid in Giza average 2.5 tons each, with the largest weighing about 15 tons. Indeed, the only comparison that comes to mind are the three Trilithons in the great stone platform of Baalbek, that also form a course above somewhat smaller but still-colossal stone blocks (see Fig. 72).

Who could have emplaced such colossal stone blocks, and what for?

Because the stone blocks are indented at their margins, archaeologists assume that they are from the time of the Second Temple (or more specifically the Herodian period, first century B.C.). But even those who hold that the original stone platform was smaller than the present one agree that the central portion that encompasses the Sacred Stone, and to which the massive retaining wall belongs, had existed from the time of the First Temple. At that time the prohibition against using iron tools (that dates back to the time of Joshua) was strictly enforced. All the stone blocks used by Solomon, without exception, were quarried, cut, shaped, and prepared elsewhere, to be brought to the site only for assembly. That this was the case regarding the colossal stone blocks under discussion is additionally clear from the fact that they are not part of the native rock; they lie well above it, and have a somewhat different hue. (In fact, the latest discoveries west of Jerusalem suggest that they might have come from a quarry there). How they were transported and raised to the required level and then pushed into the necessary emplacement remain questions that archaeologists are unable to resolve.

An answer, however, to the question what for? has been offered. The site's chief archaeologist, Dan Bahat, writing in *Biblical Archaeology Review*, stated: "We believe that on the other (eastern) face of the western wall at this point, under the Temple Mount, is an enormous hall; our theory is that the Master Course" (as this section had come to be called) "was installed to support and serve as a counter-force to the vault inside."

The section with the enormous stone blocks lies only slightly to the south of the location of the Sacred Stone. To suggest, as we do, that this massive section was needed for heavy impacts associated with the site's function as a Mission Control Center with its equipment installed on and within the Sacred Rock, seems to be the only plausible explanation after all.

11

A TIME OF PROPHECY

Was the delay in the start of building the Jerusalem Temple
due to the reason given—David's shedding of enemy blood
in wars and feuds—or was that just an excuse, obscuring
another more profound reason?

One finds it odd that as a result of the delay the span of
time that had passed from the renewed covenant with Abraham (and on that occasion also with Isaac) on Mount Moriah
until the Temple's building began was exactly a thousand
years. It is odd because the exile of Marduk had also lasted
a thousand years; and that seems to be more than a chance
coincidence.

The Bible makes it clear that the timing of the Temple's
building was determined by God himself; though the architectural details and even a scale model were ready, it was
He who said, through the Prophet Nathan: Not yet, not David, but the next king, Solomon. Likewise, it is evident that
it was not Marduk himself who had set the time for ending
his exile. Indeed, almost in desperation he cried out: Until
When? And that had to mean that the end of his days of
exile was unknown to him; it was determined by what might
be called Fate—or, if deliberate, by the unseen hand of the
Lord of Lords, the God whom the Hebrews called Yahweh.

The notion that a millennium—a thousand years—signifies more than a calendrical event, portending apocalyptic
events, is commonly held to have stemmed from a visionary
account in the Book of Revelation chapter 20, in which it
was prophesied that the "Dragon, that old Serpent, which is
the Devil and Satan," shall be bound for a thousand years,

cast into a pit and shut therein for a thousand years, unable to deceive the nations "till the thousand years should be fulfilled." It will be then that Gog and Magog shall be engaged in a world war; the First Resurrection of the dead shall occur, and Messianic Times will begin.

Those visionary words, introducing in Christianity the notion (and expectation) of an apocalyptic millennium, were written in the first century A.D. So, although the book names Babylon as the "evil empire," scholars and theologians assume that this was a code name for Rome.

But even so, it is significant that the words in Revelation echo the words of the Prophet Ezekiel (sixth century B.C.) who had a vision of the resurrection of the dead on the Day of the Lord (chapter 37) and the world war of Gog and Magog (chapters 38, 39); it shall take place, Ezekiel stated, "at the End of Years." It was all, he said, foretold by the Prophets of Yahweh in the Olden Days, "who had then prophesied about the Years."

"The Years" to be fulfilled, the count till the "End of Years." It was indeed many centuries before Ezekiel's time that the Bible offered a clue:

> *A thousand years,*
> *in thy eyes,*
> *are but as one day that has passed.*

The statement, in Psalm 90:4, is attributed in the Bible to Moses himself; the application of a thousand years to a divine time measurement thus goes back to at least the time of the Exodus. Indeed, Deuteronomy (7:9) assigns to the duration of God's Covenant with Israel a period of "a thousand generations;" and in a Psalm of David composed when the Ark of the Covenant was brought over to the City of David, the duration of a thousand generations was recalled once more (1 Chronicles 16:15). Other Psalms repeatedly applied the number "thousand" to Yahweh and his wonders; Psalm 68:18 even gave a thousand years as the duration of the Chariot of the *Elohim*.

The Hebrew word for "thousand," *Eleph*, is spelled with the three letters *Aleph* ("A"), *Lamed* ("L") and *Peh* ("P" or Ph"), which can be read as *Aleph*, meaning the first letter of the alphabet, and numerically "1." Added together the three letters have the numerical value 111 (1+30+80), which can be taken as a triple affirmation of the Oneness of Yahweh and of monotheism, "One" being a code word for "God." Not by chance, the same three letters rearranged (P-L-A) spell *Peleh*—a wonder of wonders, an epithet for God's handiwork, and the mysteries of Heaven and Earth that are beyond human understanding. Those wonders of wonders referred principally to the things created and foretold in the long-ago past; they were also the subject of Daniel's inquiry when he sought to divine the End of Time (12:6).

There thus appear to be wheels within wheels, meanings within meanings, codes within codes in those verses concerning a millennial period: not just the obvious numerical sequential count of passing time, but also a built-in duration of the Covenant, a coded affirmation of monotheism, and a prophecy concerning the millennium and the End of Years.

And, as the Bible makes clear, the thousand years whose count began with the building of the Temple—coinciding with what is now called the last millennium B.C.—was a time of prophecy.

To understand the events and prophecies of that last millennium, one ought to turn the clock back to the preceding millennium, to the nuclear calamity and the assumption of supremacy by Marduk.

The *Lamentation Texts* describing the havoc and desolation that engulfed Sumer and Akkad as the deathly nuclear cloud wafted toward Mesopotamia vividly describe how the Sumerian gods hurriedly abandoned their "cult centers" as the Evil Wind advanced toward them. Some "hid in the mountains," some "escaped to the distant plains." Inanna, leaving her possessions behind, sailed off to Africa in a submersible ship; Enki's spouse Ninki, "flying as a bird," went to the Abzu in Africa while he sought safe haven in the

north; Enlil and Ninlil left to an unknown destination, as did the spinster Ninharsag. In Lagash the goddess Bau found herself alone, for Ninurta had been gone since the nuclear blasting; she ''wept bitterly for her temple'' and lingered on; the result was tragic, for ''on that day the storm caught up with her; Bau, as if she were mortal, the storm caught up with her.''

The list of fleeing gods goes on and on, until it gets to Ur and its deities. There, as we have already mentioned, Nannar/ Sin refused to believe that his city's fate was sealed. In the lamentation she herself wrote later, his spouse Ningal described how, in spite of the foul smell of the dead whose bodies filled the city they stayed on ''and did not flee.'' Nor did they flee on the night that followed the awesome day. But by morning the two deities, huddled in their ziggurat's subterranean chamber, realized that the city was doomed, and they, too, left.

The nuclear cloud, shifted southward by the winds, spared Babylon; and that was taken as an omen reinforcing the grant of the fifty names to Marduk as an indication of his deserved supremacy. His first step was to carry out his father's suggestion that the Anunnaki themselves build for him his house/temple in Babylon, the E.SAG.IL (''House of Lofty Head''). To that was added in the sacred precinct another temple for the celebration of the New Year and the reading of the revised *Enuma elish*; its name, E.TEMEN.AN.KI (''House of the Foundation Heaven-Earth'') was clearly intended to indicate that it had replaced Enlil's DUR.AN.KI (''Bond Heaven-Earth''), which had been at the heart of Nippur when it was Mission Control Center.

Scholars have paid scant attention to the issue of mathematics in the Bible, leaving untackled what should have been a puzzle: Why has the Hebrew Bible adopted completely the decimal system, although Abraham was an *Ibri*—a Sumerian from Nippur—and all the tales in Genesis (as echoed in the Psalms and elsewhere) were based on Sumerian texts? Why was the Sumerian sexagesimal system (''base 60'') not at all

echoed in the Bible's numerology—a practice that culminated in the concept of a millennium?

One wonders whether Marduk had been cognizant of this issue. He marked his assumption of supremacy by proclaiming a New Age (that of the Ram), by revising the calendar, and by building a new Gateway of the Gods. In those steps one can find evidence also for a new mathematics—a tacit shift from the sexagesimal to the decimal system.

The focal point of those changes was the temple-ziggurat honoring him, that Enki suggested be built by the Anunnaki themselves. Archaeological discoveries of its remains (after repeated rebuildings) as well as the information provided by tablets with precise architectural data, reveal that the ziggurat rose in seven stages, the topmost of which served as the actual residence of Marduk. Planned (as Marduk himself had claimed) "in accordance with the writings of the Upper Heaven," it was a square structure whose base or first stage measured 15 *gar* (about 300 feet) on each side and rising 5.5 *gar* (about 110 feet); atop that there was a second stage, smaller and shorter; and so on, until the whole temple reached a combined height of the same 300 feet as the bottom base. The result was a cube whose circumference equaled 60 *gar* in each of its three dimensions, giving the structure the celestial number 3600 when squared (60×60) and 216,000 when cubed ($60 \times 60 \times 60$). But in that number was hidden a shift to the decimal system, for it represented the zodiacal number 2,160 multiplied by 100.

The four corners of the ziggurat faced precisely to the four cardinal points of the compass. As studies by archaeoastronomers have shown, the staggered height of each of the first six stages was precisely calculated to enable celestial observations at that particular geographic location. The ziggurat was thus intended not only to surpass Enlil's onetime Ekur, but also to take over Nippur's astronomical/calendrical functions.

This was carried out in practice by the institution of a revision of the calendar—a matter of theological prestige as well as of necessity, because the zodiacal shift (from Taurus

to Aries) also necessitated an adjustment of one month in the calender if *Nissan* (''The Standard Bearer'') was to remain the first month and the month of the spring equinox. To achieve that, Marduk ordered that the last month of the year, Addaru, was to be doubled that year. (The device of doubling Addar seven times within a cycle of nineteen years has been adopted in the Hebrew calendar as a way to periodically realign the lunar and solar years).

As in Mesopotamia, so was the calendar revised in Egypt. Originally devised there by Thoth, whose ''secret number'' was 52, it divided the year into 52 weeks of 7 days each, resulting in a solar year of only 364 days (an issue prominent in the *Book of Enoch*). Marduk (as Ra) instituted instead a year based on a division into 10: he divided the year into 36 ''decans'' of ten days each; the resulting 360 days were then followed by five special days, to complete 365.

The New Age ushered in by Marduk was not one of monotheism. Marduk did not declare himself sole god; indeed, he needed the other gods to be present and to hail him as supreme. To that purpose he provided in the sacred precinct of Babylon shrines, small temples and residences for all the other principal gods, and invited them to make their homes therein. There is no indication in any of the texts that any accepted the invitation. In fact, at about the time that the royal dynasty that Marduk had envisioned was finally installed in Babylon circa 1890 B.C., the dispersed gods began to establish their own new domains all around Mesopotamia.

Prominent among them was Elam in the east, with Susa (later the biblical Shushan) as its capital and Ninurta as its ''national god.'' In the west, a kingdom whose capital was called Mari (from the term *Amurru*, the Western One) blossomed out into its own on the western banks of the Euphrates River; its magnificent palaces were decorated with murals showing Ishtar investing the king (Fig. 84), attesting to the high standing of that goddess there. In the mountainous Hatti Land, where the Hittites had already worshiped Enlil's youngest son Adad by his Hittite name Teshub (the Wind/Storm God), a kingdom with imperial strength and aspirations be-

Figure 84

gan to grow. And between the Land of the Hittites and Babylonia there arose a brand-new kingdom—that of *Assyria*, with a pantheon identical to that of Sumer and Akkad, except that the national god was named *Ashur*—the "Seeing One." He combined the powers and identities of both Enlil and Anu, and his depiction as a god within a winged circular object (Fig. 85) dominated Assyrian monuments.

And, in distant Africa, there was Egypt, the Kingdom of the Nile. But there a chaotic period, called by scholars the Second Intermediate Period, removed the country from the international scene until the so-called New Kingdom began circa 1650 B.C.

Scholars are still hard put to explain why the ancient Near East came astir just at that time. The new (17th) dynasty that took control of Egypt was seized with imperial fervor, thrusting into Nubia in the south, Libya in the west, and the lands along the Mediterranean coast to the east. In the Land of the Hittites, a new king sent his army across the barrier of the Taurus Mountains, also along the Mediterranean coast; his successor overran Mari. And in Babylon, a people called Cassites, appearing out of nowhere (actually, from the northeastern mountain region bordering on the Caspian Sea) at-

Figure 85

tacked Babylon and brought the dynasty that started with Hammurabi to an abrupt end.

As each nation made the claim that they went on the warpath in the name and on the orders of their national god, the growing conflicts might well have represented a struggle between the gods through human surrogates. A clue that seems to confirm this is the fact that the theophoric names of Pharaohs of the 18th dynasty dropped the prefix or suffix Ra or Amen in favor of Thoth. The change, that began with Thothmes (sometimes rendered Tuthmosis) I in 1525 B.C., also marked the beginning of the oppression of the Israelites. The reason given by the Pharaoh is enlightening: Launching military expeditions to Naharin, on the Upper Euphrates, he feared that the Israelites would become an internal fifth column. The reason? Naharin was the very area where Harran was located, and where the people were descendants of the Patriarchal relatives.

As much as this explains the given reasons for the oppression of the Israelites, it leaves unexplained why, and what for, did the Egyptians—now venerating Thoth—send armies to conquer distant Harran. It is a puzzle that bears keeping in mind.

The military expeditions on the one hand and the concurrent oppression of the Israelites, peaking with the edict ordering the killing of all Israelite newborn males, reached a climax under Thothmes III, forcing Moses to flee after he

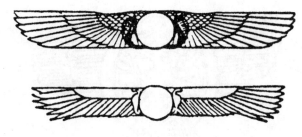

Figure 86

had stood up for his people. He could return to Egypt from
the Sinai wilderness only after the death of Thothmes III in
1450 B.C. Seventeen years later, after repeated demands and
a series of afflictions wrought by Yahweh upon "Egypt and
its gods," the Israelites were let go, and the Exodus began.

Two incidents mentioned in the Bible, and a major change
in Egypt, indicate theological repercussions among other
peoples as a result of the miracles and wonders attributed to
Yahweh in support of his Chosen People.

"And when Jethro, the Priest of Midian, the father-in-law
of Moses, heard of all that God had done for Moses and for
his people Israel," we read in Exodus chapter 18, he came
to the Israelite encampment, and after getting the full story
from Moses, Jethro said: "Now I know that Yahweh is
greater than all the gods;" and he offered sacrifices to Yahweh. The next incident (described in Numbers chapters 22–
24) occurred when the Moabite king retained the seer
Bile'am (also rendered Bala'am) to put a curse on the advancing Israelites. But "the spirit of God came upon Bilam,"
and in a "divine vision" he saw that the House of Jacob
was blessed by Yahweh, and that His word cannot be coun-
termanded.

The recognition by a non-Hebrew priest and seer of the
powers and supremacy of Yahweh had an unexpected effect
on the Egyptian royal family. In 1379 B.C.—just as the Israelites were entering Canaan proper—a new Pharaoh
changed his name to Akhenaten—the Aten being represented
by the Winged Disc (Fig. 86), moved his capital to a new

place, and began to worship one god. It was a short-lived experiment to which the priests of Amen-Ra put a quick end . . . Short-lived, too, was the concept of a universal peace that accompanied the faith in a universal God. In 1296 B.C. the Egyptian army, ever thrusting toward the Harran region, was decisively defeated by the Hittites in the Battle of Kadesh (in what is now Lebanon).

As the Hittites and Egyptians exhausted each other, there was more room for the Assyrians to assert themselves. A series of expansions virtually in all directions culminated in the recapture of Babylon by the Assyrian king Tukulti-Ninurta I—a theophoric name that indicates the religious allegiance—and the seizing of Babylon's god, Marduk. What followed is typical of the polytheism of the time: Far from denigrating the god, he was brought over to the Assyrian capital and, when the time came for the New Year ceremonies, it was Marduk, not Ashur, who featured in the age-old rituals. This "unification of the churches," to coin an expression, failed to stop the increasing exhaustion among the once-imperial kingdoms; and for several ensuing centuries, the two erstwhile powers of Mesopotamia joined Egypt and Hatti Land in a retraction and loss of conquering zeal.

It was undoubtedly that withdrawal of imperial tentacles that made possible the emergence of prosperous city-states in western Asia, especially along the Mediterranean coast, in Asia Minor, even in Arabia. Their rise, however, became a magnet attracting migrants and invaders virtually from all directions. Invaders who came in ships—the "Peoples of the Sea" as the Egyptians called them—tried to settle in Egypt and ended up occupying the coast of Canaan. In Asia Minor, the Greeks launched a thousand ships against Troy. People speaking Indo-European languages pushed their way into Asia Minor and down the Euphrates River. The forerunners of the Persians encroached on Elam. And in Arabia, tribes that became wealthy from controlling trade routes cast their eyes to the fertile lands to their north.

In Canaan, tired of constantly battling city-kings and princedoms all around them, the Israelites sent, through the

High Priest Samuel, a request to Yahweh: Make us one strong nation, give us a king!

The first one was Saul; after him came David, and then the transfer of the capital to Jerusalem.

The Bible lists Men of God during that period, even calls them "prophets" in the strictest sense of the word: "spokesmen" for God. They did deliver divine messages, but they were more in the nature of oracle priests known elsewhere in antiquity.

It was only after the Temple to Yahweh was built, that prophecy—the foretelling of things to come—came into full bloom. And there was nothing akin to the Hebrew Prophets of the Bible, who combined the preaching of justice and morality with the foreseeing of things to come, anywhere else in the ancient world.

The period that is now called in hindsight the first millennium B.C. was actually the *last millennium* in the four-thousand-year-old human story that began with the blossoming out of the Sumerian civilization. The midpoint in this human drama, whose story we have called *The Earth Chronicles*, was the nuclear holocaust, the demise of Sumer and Akkad, and the hand-over of the Sumerian baton to Abraham and his seed. That was the watershed after the first two thousand years. Now, the next half of the story, the last two millennia of what had begun in Sumer and a state visit to Earth by Anu circa 3760 B.C., was also coming to an end.

That, indeed, was the thread connecting the great biblical prophecies at that time: The cycle is coming to a closure, what had been foretold at the Beginning of Years shall be coming true at the End of Years.

Mankind has been given an opportunity to repent, to return to justice and morality, to recognize that there is only one true God, the God even of the *Elohim* themselves. With every word, vision, symbolic act the Prophets tolled the message: Time is running out; great events are about to happen. Yahweh does not seek the death of the evildoers—He seeks their return to righteousness. Man cannot control his Destiny

but can control his Fate; Man, kings, nations, can choose the course to follow. But if evil shall prevail, if injustice shall rule human relations, if nation shall continue to take sword to other nations, all shall be judged and doomed on the Day of the Lord.

As the Bible itself acknowledges, it was not a message to a receptive audience. Surrounded by peoples who seemed to know whom they worshiped, the Jews were asked to adhere to strict standards demanded by an unseen God, one whose mere image was unknown. The true prophets of Yahweh had their hands full facing "false prophets" who also claimed to be delivering God's word. Sacrifices and donations to the Temple will atone all sins, the latter said; Yahweh wants not your sacrifices but that you live in justice, Isaiah said. Great calamities will befall the unrighteous, Isaiah said; No, no—Peace is coming, the false prophets said.

To be believed, the biblical Prophets resorted to miracles—just as Moses, instructed by God, had to resort to miracles to obtain the Pharaoh's release of the Israelites, and then to convince the Israelites of Yahweh's almightiness.

The Bible describes in detail the difficulties faced by the Prophet Elijah during the reign (in the northern kingdom, Israel) of Ahab and his Phoenician wife Jezebel, who brought with her the worship of the Canaanite god Ba'al. Having already established his reputation by making a poor woman's flour and oil last and last, and by reviving a boy who had died, Elijah's greatest challenge was a confrontation with the "prophets of Ba'al" on Mount Carmel. Who was a "true prophet" was to be determined, in front of an assembled multitude headed by the king, by the performance of a miracle: A sacrifice on a pile of wood was readied, but no fire was lit—the fire had to come from heaven. And the prophets of Ba'al called in the name of Ba'al from morning till noon, but there was no sound and no answer (1 Kings chapter 18). Mocking them, Elijah said: Perhaps your god is asleep—why don't you call to him much louder? And they did till evetime, but nothing happened. Then Elijah took stones and rebuilt an altar to Yahweh that was in ruins, and arranged the wood

and the sacrificial ox on it, and asked the people to pour water on the altar, to make sure there was no hidden fire there. And he called the name of Yahweh, the god of Abraham and Isaac and Jacob; "and a fire of Yahweh decsended upon the sacrifice and it and the altar were burnt down." Convinced of Yahweh's supremacy, the people seized the prophets of Ba'al and killed them all.

After Elijah was taken up to heaven in a fiery chariot, his disciple and successor Elisha also performed miracles to establish his authenticity as a true Prophet of Yahweh. He turned water blood red, revived a dead boy, filled up empty vessels from a minute amount of oil, fed a hundred people with a bit of leftover food, and made a bar of iron float on water.

How believable were such miracles then? We know from the Bible—the tales from the time of Joseph and then the Exodus—as well as from Egyptian texts themselves, such as the *Tales of the Magicians,* that the royal court there had its fill of magicians and soothsayers. Mesopotamia had omen-priests and oracle priests, diviners and seers, and solvers of dreams. Nevertheless, when a scholarly discipline called Bible Criticism became fashionable in the nineteenth century A.D., such tales of miracle-making added to the insistence that everything in the Bible must be supported by independent sources to be believed. Fortunately, among the earliest finds by archaeologists in the nineteenth century was an inscribed stela of the Moabite king Mesha, in which he not only corroborated data regarding Judea in the time of Elijah, but was one of the rare extrabiblical mentions of Yahweh by His full name (Fig. 87). Though this is no corroboration of the miracles themselves, this find—as others later on—went far to authenticate events and personalities recorded in the Bible.

While the texts and artifacts discovered by archaeologists provided corroboration, they also shed light on profound differences between the biblical Prophets and those fortune-tellers of other nations. From the very beginning the Hebrew *Nebi'im*—translated "prophets" but literally meaning

Figure 87

"spokesmen" of God—explained that the magic and fore-sight were not theirs but God's. The miracles were His, and what was foretold was just what God had ordained. More-over, rather than acting as court employees, as "Yes-men prophets," they as often as not criticized and admonished the high-and-mighty for personal wrongdoing or wrong na-tional decisions. Even King David was reprimanded for cov-eting the wife of Uriah the Hittite.

By an odd coincidence—if that is all it was—at the same time that David captured Jerusalem and took the initial steps to establish the House of Yahweh on the Sacred Platform, the decline and decay of what is termed Old Assyria came to an abrupt end and, under a new dynasty, what historians

call the Neo-Assyrian period was ushered in. And no sooner was the Temple of Yahweh built, than Jerusalem began to attract the attention of distant rulers. As a direct consequence, its prophets, too, shifted their sights to the international arena, and embedded prophecies concerning the world at large within their prophecies regarding Judea, the split-off northern kingdom of Israel, their kings, and their peoples. It was a worldview that was amazing in its scope and understanding—by Prophets who, before they were summoned by God, were mostly simple villagers.

Such profound knowledge of distant lands and nations, the names of their kings (in one instance, even a king's nickname), their commerce and trade routes, their armies and makeup of fighting forces, must have amazed even the kings of Judea at the time. Once, at least, an explanation was spelled out. It was Hanani the Prophet who (warning the Judean king against a treaty with the Aramaeans) explained to the king: Rely on the word of Yahweh, for "it is the eyes of Yahweh that roam the whole Earth."

In Egypt, too, a period of disunity ended when a new dynasty, the 22nd, reunited the country and relaunched the involvement in international affairs. The new dynasty's first king, the Pharaoh Sheshonq, seized the historical first of being the first foreign ruler of one of the then-great powers to forcefully enter Jerusalem and seize its treasures (without, however, damaging or defiling the Temple). The event, occurring in 928 B.C., is related in 1 Kings 14 and in 2 Chronicles 12; it was all foretold by Yahweh to the Judean king and his noblemen ahead of time by the Prophet Shemaiah; it was also one of the instances where the biblical account has been corroborated by an outside, independent record— in this case by the Pharaoh himself, on the southern walls of the temple of Amen in Karnak.

Assyrian encroachments on the Jewish kingdoms, accurately recorded in the Bible, began with the northern kingdom, Israel. Here again, biblical records are fully corroborated by the annals of the Assyrian kings; Shalmaneser III (858–824 B.C.) even pictured the Israelite king Jehu

Figure 88

bowing down before him, in a scene dominated by the Winged Disc symbol of Nibiru (Fig. 88a). Some decades later another Israelite king warded off an attack by prepaying tribute to the Assyrian king Tiglat-Pileser III (745–727 B.C.). But that only gained some time: in 722 B.C. the Assyrian king Shalmaneser V marched on the northern kingdom, captured its capital Samaria (*Shomron*—"Little Sumer"—in Hebrew), and exiled its king and noblemen. Two years later the next Assyrian king, Sargon II (721–705 B.C.) exiled the rest of the people—giving rise to the enigma of the Ten Lost Tribes of Israel—and ended the independent existence of that state.

The Assyrian kings began each record of their numerous military campaigns with the words "On the command of my god Ashur," giving their conquests the aura of religious wars. The conquest and subjugation of Israel was so important that Sargon, recording his victories on the walls of his palace, began the inscription by identifying himself as "Sargon, conqueror of Samaria and of the entire land of Israel." With that achievement, crowning his conquests elsewhere, he wrote, "I aggrandized the territory belonging to Ashur, the king of the gods."

*   *   *

While those calamities, according to the Bible, befell the northern state Israel because its leaders and people failed to heed the Prophets' warnings and admonitions, the kings of Judea to the south were more attentive to the prophetic guidance and, for a while, enjoyed a period of relative peace. But the Assyrians had their eye on Jerusalem and its temple; and for reasons which their annals do not explain, many of their military expeditions started in the Harran area and then extended westward to the Mediterranean coast. Significantly, the annals of the Assyrian kings, describing their conquests and domains in the Harran area, identify by name a city called Nahor and a city called Laban—cities bearing the names of the brother and brother-in-law of Abraham.

The turn of Judea and specifically Jerusalem to come under Assyrian attack was not long in coming. The task of extending the territories and the "command" of the god Ashur to the House of Yahweh fell to Sennacherib, the son of Sargon II and his successor in 704 B.C. Aiming to consolidate his father's conquests and put an end to recurring rebellions in Assyrian provinces, he devoted his third campaign (701 B.C.) to the capture of Judea and Jerusalem.

The events and circumstances of that attempt are extensively recorded both in the Assyrian's annals and in the Bible, making it one of the best documented instances of biblical veracity. It was also an occurrence that showed the veracity of the biblical prophecy, its value as a foretelling guide, and the scope of its geopolitical grasp.

Furthermore, there exists physical evidence—to this very day—corroborating and illustrating an important aspect of those events; so that one can see with one's own eyes how real and true it all was.

As we start relating those events with the words of Sennacherib himself, let it be noticed that here again the campaign against distant Jerusalem began with a detour to "Hatti Land," to the area of Harran, and only then swung all the way westward to the Mediterranean coast, where the first city attacked was Sidon:

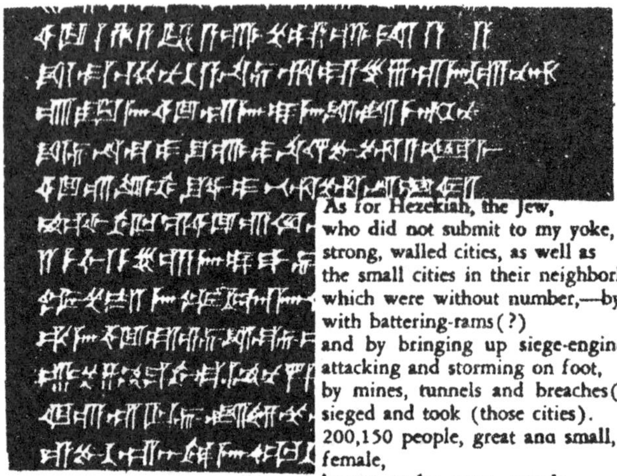

As for Hezekiah, the Jew,
who did not submit to my yoke, 46 of his
strong, walled cities, as well as
the small cities in their neighborhood,
which were without number,—by levelling
with battering-rams(?)
and by bringing up siege-engines(?), by
attacking and storming on foot,
by mines, tunnels and breaches(?), I besieged and took (those cities).
200,150 people, great and small, male and
female,
horses, mules, asses, camels,
cattle and sheep, without number, I brought
away from them
and counted as spoil. Himself, like a caged
bird
I shut up in Jerusalem his royal city.

Figure 88b

In my third campaign I marched against Hatti.
Luli, king of Sidon, whom the terror-inspiring
glamor of my lordship had overwhelmed,
fled far overseas and perished.

The awe-inspiring splendor of the Weapon of Ashur,
my lord, overwhelmed the strong cities of Greater
    Sidon . . .
All the kings from Sidon to Arvad, Byblos, Ashdod,
Beth-Ammon, Moab and Adom brought sumptuous
    gifts;
the king of Ashkelon I deported to Assyria . . .

The inscription (Fig. 88b) continued:

As for Hezekiah the Judean
who did not submit to my yoke

46 of his strong walled cities
as well as the small cities in their neighborhood
which were without number . . .
I besieged and took them and
200,150 people old and young male and female
horses, mules, camels, asses, cattle and sheep
I brought away from them.

In spite of these losses, Hezekiah remained unyielding—because the Prophet Isaiah had thus prophesied: Fear not the attacker, for Yahweh will impose His spirit on him, and he shall hear a rumor, and will return to his land, and there he will be felled by the sword . . . "Thus sayeth Yahweh: the king of Assyria shall not enter this city! The way he came he shall go back, for I protect this city to save it, for My sake and for the sake of David my servant." (2 Kings chapter 19).

Defied by Hezekiah, Sennacherib went on to state thus in his annals:

In Jerusalem, I made Hezekiah
a prisoner in his royal palace,
like a bird in a cage, surrounding him
with earthworks, molesting those who
left by the city gates.

"I then took away districts of Hezekiah's kingdom and gave them away to the kings of Ashdod and Ekron and Gaza—Philistine city-states—and increased the tribute on Hezekiah," Sennacherib wrote; and then he listed the tribute that Hezekiah "sent to me later in Nineveh."

Almost imperceptibly thus, the annals mention neither the capture of Jerusalem nor the seizing of its king—just the imposition of heavy tribute: gold, silver, precious stones, antimony, cut red stones, furnishings inlaid with ivory, elephant hides "and all kinds of valuable treasure."

The boasting omits telling what had really happened in Jerusalem; the source for the more complete story is the Bi-

ble. It records, in 2 Kings chapter 20 and, similarly, in the book of the Prophet Isaiah and in the Book of Chronicles, that "in the fourteenth year of Hezekiah, Sennacherib the king of Assyria came upon all of the fortified cities of Judea and captured them. Then Hezekiah the king of Judea sent word to the king of Assyria, who was in Lachish, saying: I have done wrong; turn back, and whatever you impose on me I shall endure. So the king of Assyria imposed on Hezekiah the king of Judea three hundred bars of silver and thirty bars of gold;" and Hezekiah paid it all, including as an extra tribute the bronze inlays of the temple and palace doors, and handed them over to Sennacherib.

But the king of Assyria reneged on the deal. Instead of retreating back to Assyria, he sent a large force against the Judean capital; and as the Assyrian siege tactic had been, the first thing the attackers did was to seize the city's water reservoirs. The tactic worked elsewhere, but not in Jerusalem. For, *unbeknown to the Assyrians, Hezekiah had a water tunnel dug under the city's walls, diverting the plentiful waters of the Spring of Gihon to the Pool of Silo'am inside the city.* This subterranean secret water tunnel provided the besieged city with fresh water, defying the Assyrians' plans.

Frustrated by the failure of the siege to subdue the city, the Assyrian commander turned to psychological warfare. Speaking in Hebrew so that the common defenders would understand, he pointed out the futility of resistance. None of the other nations' gods could save them; who is this "Yahweh" and why would he do better for Jerusalem? He was a god as fallible as the others . . .

Hearing all that, Hezekiah tore his clothes and put on a mourner's sackcloth, and went to the Temple of Yahweh, and prayed to "Yahweh the God of Israel, who abides upon the Cherubim, the sole God upon all the nations, the maker of the Heaven and the Earth." Assuring him that his prayer was heard, the Prophet reiterated the divine promise: The Assyrian king shall never enter the city; he will return home in failure, and there he will be assassinated.

That night a divine miracle happened, and the first part of the prophecy came true:

> *And it came to pass that night,*
> *that the Angel of Yahweh went forth*
> *and smote in the camp of the Assyrians*
> *a hundred and eighty five thousand.*
> *And at sunrise, lo and behold:*
> *they were all dead corpses.*
> *So Sennacherib, the king of Assyria, departed*
> *and journeyed back and dwelt in Nineveh.*
>
> *2 Kings 19:35–36*

In a postscript, the Bible made sure to record that the second part of the prophecy had also come true, adding "And Sennacherib went away, and journeyed back to Nineveh. And it was when he was bowing down in his temple to his god Nisrokh, that Adramelekh and Sharezzer struck him down with a sword; and they fled to the land of Ararat. His son Esarhaddon became king in his stead."

The biblical postscript regarding the manner in which Sennacherib died has long puzzled scholars, for the royal Assyrian annals left the king's death a mystery. Only recently did scholars, with the aid of additional archaeological finds, confirm the biblical account: Sennacherib was indeed assassinated (in the year 681 B.C.) by two of his own sons, and the heir to the throne became another, younger son called Esarhaddon.

We, too, can add a postscript to further confirm the veracity of the Bible.

Early in the nineteenth century, archaeologists exploring Jersalem discovered that *the Tunnel of Hezekiah was fact, not myth*: that a subterranean tunnel indeed served as a conduit for a secret supply of water in Jerusalem, cut through the city's native rock under the defensive walls from the time of the Judean kings!

In 1838 the explorer Edward Robinson was the first in modern times to traverse its full length, 1,750 feet. In the

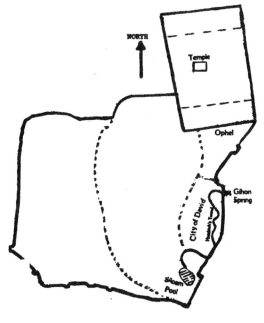

Figure 89

ensuing decades other renowned explorers of ancient Jerusalem (Charles Warren, Charles Wilson, Claude Conder,
Conrad Schick) cleared and examined the tunnel and its various shafts. It indeed connected the water's source at the
Spring of Gihon (outside the defensive walls) to the Pool of
Silo'am inside the city (Fig. 89). Then, in 1880, playing boys
discovered that about midway in the tunnel an inscription
had been carved into the wall. The Turkish authorities of the
time ordered that the inscribed segment of the wall be excised and brought to Istanbul (the Turkish capital). It was
then ascertained that the inscription (Fig. 90), in beautiful
ancient Hebrew script current at the time of the Judean kings,
commemorated the completion of the tunnel when the tun-
nelers of Hezekiah, cutting through the rock from both ends,
met at that very spot where the inscription was found.

The inscription (on the piece of rock excised from the

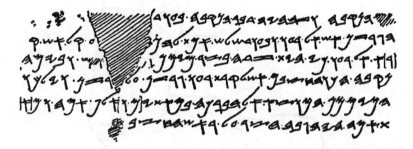

Figure 90

tunnel's wall), which is on display in the Istanbul Archaeological Museum, renders the following account:

> ... the tunnel. And this is the account of the break-
> through. When [the tunnelers lifted] the axe each to-
> ward his fellow, and while there were still three cubits
> to be tunneled [through], the voice of a man was heard
> calling to his fellow, for there was a crack in the rock
> on the right ... And on the day of the breakthrough
> the tunnelers struck each toward his comrade, axe to-
> ward axe. And the water started to flow from its source
> to the pool, a thousand and two hundred cubits; and
> the height of the rock above the heads of the tunnelers
> was one hundred cubits.

The accuracy and veracity of the biblical account of the
events in Jerusalem extended to the events in faraway Nineveh concerning the succession on the throne of Assyria: It
was indeed a bloody affair that pitted sons of Sennacherib
against him and ended with the younger son, Esarhaddon
(also spelled Asarhaddon), ascending the throne. The bloody
events are described in the *Annals of Esarhaddon* (on the
artifact known as Prism B), in which he ascribes his choice
to kingship over his older brothers as the result of an oracle
given to Sennacherib by the gods Shamash and Adad—a
choice approved by the great gods of Assyria and Babylon
"and all the other gods residing in heaven and on Earth."

The bloody end of Sennacherib was but one act in a raging drama concerning the role and standing of the god Marduk. The Assyrian attempt to bring the Babylonians to heel and in reality annex Babylon by bringing Marduk over to the Assyrian capital did not work, and within decades Marduk was returned to his honored position in Babylon. The texts suggest that a crucial aspect of the god's restoration was the need to celebrate the Akitu festival of the New Year, in which the *Enuma elish* was publicly read and the Resurrection of Marduk was reenacted in a Passion Play, in Babylon and nowhere else. By the time of Tiglat-Pileser III, the king's legitimacy required his humbling himself before Marduk until Marduk "took both my hands in his" (in the king's words).

To cement his choice of Esarhaddon as his successor, Sennacherib had appointed him as Babylon's viceroy (and named himself "King of Sumer and Akkad"). And when he ascended the throne, Esarhaddon took the solemn oath of office "in the presence of the gods of Assyria: Ashur, Sin, Shamash, Nebo, and Marduk." (Ishtar, though not present, was invoked in later annals).

But all those efforts to be religiously inclusive failed to bring stability or peace. As the seventh century B.C. began, ushering in the second half of what, counting forward from the Sumerian start, was the Last Millennium, turmoil seized the great capitals and spread throughout the ancient world.

The biblical Prophets saw it all coming; it was the beginning of the End, they announced in behalf of Yahweh.

In the prophesied scenario of events to come, Jerusalem and its Sacred Platform were to be the focal point of a global catharsis. The divine fury was to manifest itself first against the city and its people, for they had abandoned Yahweh and his commandments. The kings of the great nations were to be the instruments of Yahweh's wrath. But then they, too, each one in his turn, would be judged on the Day of Judgment. "It will be a judgment upon all flesh, for Yahweh has a quarrel with all the nations," the Prophet Jeremiah announced.

Assyria, the Prophet Isaiah quoted Yahweh as saying, was his punishing cane; he foresaw its sweeping down upon many nations, even invading Egypt (a prophecy that did come true); but then Assyria, too, would be judged for its sins. Babylon was to be next, the Prophet Jeremiah said; its king would come upon Jerusalem, but seventy years later (as indeed came to be) Babylon, too, would be brought to heel. The sins of nations great and small, from Egypt and Nubia all the way to distant China (!) were to be judged on the Day of Yahweh.

One by one, the prophecies were fulfilled. Of Egypt the Prophet Isaiah foresaw its occupation by Assyrian forces after a three-year war. The prophecy came true at the hands of Esarhaddon, Sennacherib's successor. What is remarkable, beside the fact of the prophecy's fulfillment, is that before leading his army westward then southward toward Egypt, the Assyrian king made a detour to Harran!

That was in 675 B.C. In the same century, the fate of Assyria itself was sealed. A resurgent Babylon under king Nabupolassar captured the Assyrian capital Nineveh by breaking the river dams to flood the city—just as the Prophet Nahum had foretold (1:8). The year was 612 B.C.

The remnants of the Assyrian army retreated—of all places—to Harran; but there the ultimate instrument of divine judgment made its appearance. It would be, Yahweh told Jeremiah (Jeremiah 5:15–16), "a distant nation . . . a nation whose language thou knowest not:"

> *Behold,*
> *a people cometh from a country in the north,*
> *a great nation shall be roused*
> *from the remoteness of the Earth.*
> *They grasp bows and spears,*
> *they are cruel, they show no mercy.*
> *The sound of them is like the roaring sea,*
> *they ride upon horses,*
> *arrayed as men of battle.*

> *Jeremiah 6:22–23*

The Mesopotamian records of the time speak of the sudden appearance, from the north, of the Umman-Manda—perhaps advance hordes of Scythians from central Asia, perhaps forerunners of the Medes from the highlands of what is now Iran, perhaps a combination of both. In 610 B.C. they captured Harran, where the remnants of the Assyrian army holed up, and gained control of the vital crossroads. In 605 B.C. an Egyptian army headed by the Pharaoh Necho thrust once again—as Thothmes III had attempted before the Exodus—to reach and capture Naharin, on the Upper Euphrates. But a combined force of Babylonians and Umman-Manda, at a crucial battle at Carcemish near Harran, gave Egypt's empire the final coup de grace. It was all as Jeremiah had prophesied concerning haughty Egypt and its king Necho:

Like a river that riseth and as surging streams
has been Egypt, [saying]
I will rise, I will cover the Earth,
I will wipe out towns and all who dwell therein . . .

But that day,
the day of Yahweh, Lord of Hosts, shall be,
a day of retribution,
in the land of the north, by the Euphrates River . . .

Thus sayeth Yahweh, Lord God of Israel:
"I have made commandments upon Amen of Thebes,
and upon Pharaoh, and upon Egypt and its gods
and its kings—on Pharaoh and all who on him rely:
Into the hands of those who seek to kill them,
Into the hands of Nebuchadnezzar king of Babylon
and into the hands of his subjects
I shall deliver them."

Jeremiah chapter 46

Assyria was vanquished—the victor has become a victim. Egypt was beaten and its gods disgraced. There was no power left to stand in the way of Babylon—nor for Babylon

to act out Yahweh's wrath against Judea, and then meet her own fate.

At the helm of Babylon was now a king of Caesarian ambitions. He was given the throne in recognition of the victory at Carchemish and the royal name Nebuchadnezzar (the second), a theophoric name incorporating the name of Nabu, Marduk's son and spokesman. He lost no time launching military campaigns "by the powers of my lords Nabu and Marduk." In 597 B.C. he sent his forces to Jerusalem, ostensibly only to remove its pro-Egyptian king Jeho'iakim and replace him with his son Jeho'iachin, a mere youth. It was only, it turned out, a test run; for one way or another, he was fated to play out the role Yahweh had assigned to him as the punisher of Jerusalem for the sins of its people; but ultimately, Babylon herself would be judged:

> *This is the word of Yahweh concerning Babylon—*
> *Declare it among the nations,*
> *raise a standard and proclaim,*
> *deny nothing, announce:*
> *'Captured is Babylon,*
> *its Lord is shamed, Marduk is dismayed;*
> *its idols are withered, her fetishes cowered'.*
> *For a nation from the north hath come upon her*
> *from the north;*
> *it will make her land desolate, without dwellers.*
>
> *Jeremiah 50:1–3*

It will be an Earthwide catharsis, in which not only nations but also their gods shall be called to account, Yahweh, the "Lord of Hosts," made clear. But at the end of the catharsis, after the coming of the Day of the Lord, Zion shall be rebuilt and all the nations of the world shall gather to worship Yahweh in Jerusalem.

When all is said and done, the Prophet Isaiah declared, Jerusalem and its rebuilt Temple would be the sole "Light unto the nations." *Jerusalem shall suffer its Fate, but will arise to fulfill its Destiny:*

And it shall come to pass
at the End of Days:
The Mount of the Temple of Yahweh
shall be established ahead of all mountains
and shall be exalted above all hills;
And all the nations shall throng unto it.
And many peoples shall come and say:
'Come ye, let us go up to the Mountain of Yahweh,
to the Temple of the God of Jacob,
that He may teach us of his ways and
that we may follow in His path;
for out of Zion shall come instruction
and the word of God from Jerusalem'.

Isaiah 2:2–3

In those unfolding events and prophecies concerning the great powers, Jerusalem and its Temple, and what is to come in the Last Days, the Prophets in the Holy Land were joined by the Prophet Ezekiel who was shown Divine Visions on the banks of the Khabur River in faraway Harran.

For there, in Harran, the divine and human drama that began when the paths of Marduk and Abraham crossed, was also destined to come to an end—at the very same time that Jerusalem and its Temple were facing Fate.

12

THE GOD WHO RETURNED FROM HEAVEN

Was the crossing of the paths of Marduk and Abraham in Harran just a chance coincidence, or was Harran chosen by the unseen hand of Fate?

It is a nagging question, calling for a divining answer, for the place where Yahweh had chosen Abram for a daring mission and where Marduk made his reappearance after an absence of a thousand years, was later on the place where a series of incredible events—miraculous events, one could well say—began to unfold. They were occurrences of prophetic scope, affecting the course of both human and divine affairs.

The key events, recorded for posterity by eyewitnesses, began and ended with the fulfillment of the biblical prophecies concerning Egypt, Assyria, and Babylon; and they included the departure of a god from his temple and his city, his ascent to the heavens, and his return from the heavens a half century later.

And, for a reason perhaps more metaphysical than geographic or geopolitical, so many of the crucial events of the last two millennia of the count that began when the gods, meeting in council, decided to give Mankind civilization, took place in or around Harran.

We have already mentioned in passing the detour of Esarhaddon to Harran. The details of that pilgrimage were recorded on a tablet that was part of the royal correspondence of Ashurbanipal, Esarhaddon's son and successor. It was when Esarhaddon contemplated an attack on Egypt, he turned northward instead of westward and looked for "the

cedarwood temple'' in Harran. There ''he saw the god Sin leaning on a staff, with two crowns on his head. The god Nusku was standing before him. The father of my majesty the king entered the temple. The god placed a crown upon his head, saying: 'You will go to countries, therein you will conquer!' He departed and conquered Egypt.'' (Nusku, we know from Sumerian God List, was a member of Sin's entourage).

The invasion of Egypt by Esarhaddon is a historical fact, fully making true Isaiah's prophecy. The details of the detour to Harran additionally serve to confirm the presence there, in 675 B.C., of the god Sin; for it was several decades later that Sin ''became angry with the city and its people'' and was gone—to the heavens.

Nowadays Harran still stands where it did in the time of Abraham and his family. Outside the city's crumbling walls (walls from Islamic-conquest times) the well where Jacob met Rebecca still flows with water, and in the surrounding plain sheep still graze as they did four millennia ago. In centuries past Harran was a center of learning and literature, where the Greeks after Alexander gained access to the accumulated ''Chaldean'' knowledge (the writings of Berossus were one of the results) and much later the Moslems and Christians exchanged cultures. But the pride of the place (Fig. 91) was the temple dedicated to the god Sin, in whose ruins written testimony of the miraculous events concerning Nannar/Sin has survived the millennia.

The testimony was not hearsay; it consisted of eyewitness reports. They were not anonymous witnesses, but a woman named Adda-Guppi and her son Nabuna'id. They were not, as happens nowadays, a country sherrif and his mother reporting a UFO sighting in some sparsely inhabited area. She was the High Priestess of the great temple of Sin, a sacred and revered shrine since millennia before her time; her son was the last king of the mightiest empire on Earth in those days, Babylon.

The High Priestess and her son the king recorded the events on stelae—stone columns inscribed in cuneiform

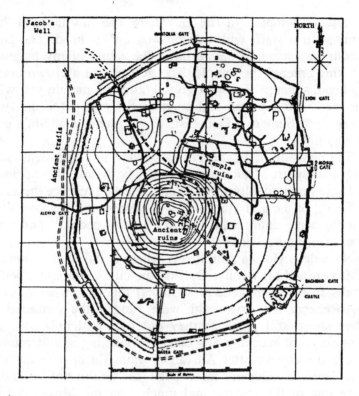

Figure 91

script, accompanied by pictorial depictions. Four of them have been found this century by archaeologists, and it is believed that the stelae were placed by the king and his mother each at each corner of the renowned temple to the Moon god in Harran, the E.HUL.HUL ("Temple of Double Joy"). One pair of stelae carried the mother's testimony, the other pair recorded the king's words. It was on the stelae of Adda-Guppi, the temple's High Priestess, that the departure and heavenly ascent of the god Sin were recorded; and it was in the inscriptions of the king, Nabuna'id, that the god's miraculous and unique return was reported. With an evident sense of history and in the manner of a trained temple official, Adda-Guppi provided in her stelae precise dates for the

astounding events; the dates, linked as was then customary
to regnal years of known kings, could thus be—and have
been—verified by modern scholars.

In the better-preserved stela, cataloged by scholars as H₁B,
Adda-Guppi began her written testimony (in the Akkadian
language) thus:

> *I am the lady Adda-Guppi,*
> *mother of Nabuna'id, king of Babylon,*
> *devotee of the gods Sin, Ningal, Nusku*
> *and Sadarnunna, my deities,*
> *to whose godliness I have been pious*
> *ever since my childhood.*

She was born, Adda-Guppi wrote, in the twentieth year of
Ashurbanipal, king of Assyria—in the middle of the seventh
century B.C. Though in her inscriptions Adda-Guppi does not
state her genealogy, other sources suggest that she stemmed
from a distinguished lineage. She lived, according to her inscription, through the reigns of several Assyrian and Babylonian kings, reaching the ripe old age of ninety-five when
the miraculous events had taken place. Scholars have found
her listing of reigns to be in accord with Assyrian and Babylonian annals.

Here then is the record of the first remarkable occurrence,
in Adda-Guppi's own words:

> *It was in the sixteenth year of Nabupolassar,*
> *king of Babylon, when Sin, lord of gods,*
> *became angry with his city and his temple*
> *and went up to heaven;*
> *and the city and the people in it*
> *went to ruin.*

The year bears noticing, for events—known from other
sources—had taken place at that time, corroborating what
Adda-Guppi had recorded. For the year was 610 B.C.—when

the defeated Assyrian army retreated to Harran for a last stand.

There are quite a number of issues that call for clarification as a result of this statement: Was Sin "angry with the city and its people" because they let the Assyrians in? Did he decide to leave on account of the Assyrians, or the approaching Umman-Manda hordes? How, by what means, did he go up to heaven—and where did he go? To another place on Earth, or away from Earth, a celestial place? The writings of Adda-Guppi gloss over these issues, and for the moment we, too, shall leave the questions hanging.

What the High Priestess does state is that after the departure of Sin "the city and the people in it went to ruin." Some scholars prefer to translate the word in the inscription as "desolate," as better describing what had happened to the once-thriving metropolis, a city whom the Prophet Ezekiel (27:23) listed among the great international trading centers of the time, specializing "in all sorts of things, in blue clothes, and broidered work, and in chests of rich apparel, bound with cords and made of cedar." Indeed, the desolation in the abandoned Harran brings to mind the opening words of the biblical Book of Lamentations about the desolate and desecrated Jerusalem: "How solitary lies the city, once so full of people! Once great among the nations, now become a widow; once queen among the provinces, now become a tributary."

While others fled, Adda-Guppi stayed on. "Daily, without ceasing, by day and night, for months, for years," she went to the abandoned shrines. Mourning, she forsook the dresses of fine wool, took off her jewels, wore neither silver nor gold, relinquished perfumes and sweet-smelling oils. As a ghost roaming the empty shrines, "in a torn garment I was clothed, I came and went noiselessly," she wrote.

Then, in the abandoned sacred precinct, she discovered a robe that had once belonged to Sin. It must have been a magnificent garment, in the manner of robes worn at the time by various deities, as depicted on monuments from Mesopotamia (see Fig. 28). To the despondent High Priestess, the

find seemed an omen from the god; it was as though he had suddenly given her a physical presence of himself. She could not take her eyes off the sacred garb, daring not to touch it except by "taking hold of its hem." As if the god himself was there to listen, she prostrated herself and "in prayer and humility" uttered the following vow:

> *If you would return to your city,*
> *all the Black-Headed people*
> *would worship your divinity!*

"Black-Headed people" was a term used by the Sumerians to describe themselves; and the employment of the term by the High Priestess in Harran was highly unusual. Sumer, as a political-religious entity, had ceased to exist almost 1,500 years before the time of Adda-Guppi, when the land and its capital, the city of Ur, fell victim to a deadly nuclear cloud in 2024 B.C. Sumer, by Adda-Guppi's time, was just a hallowed memory, its erstwhile capital Ur a place of crumbling ruins, its people (the "Black-Headed" people) dispersed to many lands. How then could a High Priestess in Harran offer to her god Sin to restore him to lordship in distant Ur, and to make him again the god of all the Sumerians, wherever they had dispersed?

It was a true vision of the Return of the Exiles and a Restoration of a god in his ancient cult center worthy of biblical prophecies. To achieve that, Adda-Guppi proposed her god a deal: If he would return and then use his authority and divine powers to make her son Nabuna'id the next imperial king, reigning in Babylon over both the Babylonian and Assyrian domains—Nabuna'id would restore the temple of Sin in Ur and would reinstate the worship of Sin in all the lands where the Black-Headed people dwelt!

The Moon god liked the idea. "Sin, lord of the gods of Heaven and Earth, for my good doings looked upon me with a smile; he heard my prayers, he accepted my vow. The wrath of his heart calmed; toward Ehulhul, the temple of Sin in Harran, the divine residence in which his heart rejoiced,

he became reconciled; and he had a change of heart.''

The smiling god, Adda-Guppi wrote on in her inscription, accepted the deal:

> *Sin, lord of the gods,*
> *looked with favor upon my words.*
> *Nabuna'id, my only son,*
> *issue of my womb,*
> *to the kingship he called—*
> *the kingship of Sumer and Akkad.*
> *All the lands from the border of Egypt,*
> *from the Upper Sea to the Lower Sea,*
> *in his hands he entrusted.*

Grateful and overwhelmed, Adda-Guppi raised her hands and "reverently, with imploration" thanked the god for "pronouncing the name of Nabuna'id, calling him to kingship." Then she implored the god to assure the success of Nabuna'id—to persuade the other great gods to be at Nabuna'id's side as he battled the enemies, to enable him to fulfill the vow to rebuild the Ehulhul temple and restore Harran to its greatness.

In a postscript added to the inscriptions when Adda-Guppi, aged 104, was on her deathbed (or recording her words right after she had passed on), the text reported that both sides kept their bargain: "I myself saw it fulfilled;" Sin "honored his word which he spoke to me," causing Nabuna'id to become king of a new Sumer and Akkad (in 555 B.C.); and Nabuna'id kept the vow to restore the Ehulhul temple in Harran, "perfected its structure." He renewed the worship of Sin and his spouse Ningal—"all the forgotten rites he made anew." And the divine couple, accompanied by the divine emissary Nusku and his consort (?) Sadarnunna, returned into the Ehulhul temple in a solemn and ceremonial procession.

The duplicate stela's inscription contains nineteen additional lines undoubtedly added by Adda-Guppi's son. In the ninth year of Nabuna'id—in 546 B.C.—"the Fate of herself

carried her off. Nabuna'id, king of Babylon, her son, issue of her womb, entombed her corpse, wrapped in [royal] robes and pure white linen. He adorned her body with splendid ornaments of gold set with beautiful precious stones. With sweet oils he anointed her body; and laid it to rest in a secret place."

The mourning for the king's mother was widespread. "People from Babylon and Borsippa, dwellers of far regions, kings, princes, and governors came from the border of Egypt on the Upper Sea unto the Lower Sea"—from the Mediterranean to the Persian Gulf. The mourning, which included casting ashes upon the head, weeping, and self-inflicted cuts, lasted seven days.

Before we turn to the inscriptions of Nabuna'id and their miracle-filled tales, one must stop to wonder how—if what Adda-Guppi had recorded was true—she managed to communicate with a deity that by her own statement was no longer in the temple or in the city—gone and ascended to heaven, in fact.

The first part, that of Adda-Guppi addressing her god, is easy: she prayed, addressing her prayers to him. Prayer as a way of laying before the deity one's fears and worries, asking for health or good fortune or long life, even seeking guidance for the right choices between alternatives, is still with us. From the time when writing began in Sumer, prayers and appeals to the gods were recorded. Indeed, prayer as a means of communicating with one's deity probably preceded the written word and, according to the Bible, began when the first humans became Homo sapiens: It was when Enosh ("*Homo sapiens* Man"), the grandson of Adam and Eve, was born, "that it was begun to call the name of God" (Genesis 4:26).

Touching the hem of the god's robe, prostrating herself, with great humility Adda-Guppi prayed to Sin. She did so day after day, until he heard her prayers and responded.

Now comes the more tricky part—how did Sin respond, how could his words or message reach the High Priestess?

The inscription itself provides the answer: the god's response came to her in a dream. As she passed out, perhaps in a trancelike sleep, the god appeared to her in a dream:

> *In the dream*
> *Sin, lord of the gods,*
> *laid his two hands on me.*
> *He spoke to me, thus:*
> *"On account of you*
> *the gods will return to inhabit Harran.*
> *I will entrust your son, Nabuna'id,*
> *with the divine residences in Harran.*
> *He shall rebuild the Ehulhul,*
> *shall perfect its structure;*
> *he will restore Harran and make her*
> *more perfect than it was before."*

Such a manner of communication, directed from a deity to a human, was far from being unusual; indeed, it was the one mostly employed. Throughout the ancient world kings and priests, patriarchs and prophets received the divine word through the medium of dreams. They could be oracle dreams or omen ones, sometimes with words only heard, sometimes including visions. In fact, the Bible itself quotes Yahweh telling the sister and brother of Moses during the Exodus: "If there be a prophet among you, I the Lord will make myself known to him in a vision and will speak to him in a dream."

Nabuna'id also reported divine communications received by means of dreams. But his inscriptions reported much more: a unique event and an uncommon theophany. His two stelae (referred to by scholars as H_2A and H_2B) are adorned at their tops with a depiction of the king holding an unusual staff and facing the symbols of three celestial bodies, the planetary gods that he venerated (Fig. 92). The long inscription below begins right off with the great miracle and its uniqueness:

Figure 92

*This is the great miracle of Sin
that has by gods and goddesses
not happened to the land,
since days of old unknown;
That the people of the Land
had neither seen nor found written
on tablets since days of old:
That divine Sin,
Lord of gods and goddesses,
residing in the heavens,
has come down from the heavens—
in full view of Nabuna'id,
king of Babylon.*

The claim that this was a unique miracle was not unjustified, for the event entailed both a return of a deity and a theophany—two aspects of divine interaction with humans that, as the inscription cautiously qualifies, were not unknown in the Days of Old. Whether Nabuna'id (whom some scholars have nicknamed "the first archaeologist" on account of his penchant for uncovering and digging up the ruins of earlier sites) had qualified his statement just to be on the safe side, or whether he was actually familiar, through olden tablets, with such events that had indeed taken place far away and long ago, we do not know; but the fact is that such events did happen.

Thus, in the turbulent times that ended with the demise of the Sumerian empire circa 2000 B.C., the god Enlil, who was away somewhere else, hurried back to Sumer when he was notified that his city, Nippur, was in danger. According to an inscription by the Sumerian king Shu-Sin, Enlil returned "flying from horizon to horizon; from south to north he traveled; through the skies, over Earth, he hurried."

That Return, however, was sudden, unannounced, and not part of a theophany.

Some five hundred years later—still almost a thousand years before the return and theophany by Sin—the greatest theophany on record took place in the Sinai peninsula, during the Israelite Exodus from Egypt. Notified in advance and told how to prepare for the event, the Children of Israel—all 600,000 of them—witnessed the Lord descending upon Mount Sinai. The Bible stresses that it was done "in full sight of all the people" (Exodus 19:11). But that great theophany was not a return.

Such divine comings and goings, including the ascent and descent of Sin to and from the heavens, imply that the Great Anunnaki possessed the required flying vehicles—and indeed they did. Yahweh landed on Mount Sinai in an object that the Bible called *Kabod* that had the appearance of a "devouring fire" (Exodus 24:11); the Prophet Ezekiel described the *Kabod* (usually translated "glory" but which literally means "the heavy thing") as a luminous and radiating

vehicle equipped with wheels within wheels. He might have had in mind something comparable to the circular chariot in which the Assyrian god Ashur was depicted (Fig. 85). Ninurta possessed the *Imdugud*, the "Divine Black Bird"; and Marduk had a special housing built in his sacred precinct in Babylon for his "Supreme Traveler"; it was probably the same vehicle that the Egyptian called the Celestial Boat of Ra.

What about Sin and his celestial comings and goings?

That he indeed possessed such a flying vehicle—an essential requirement for the heavenward departure and return reported in the Harran inscriptions—is attested by many hymns to him. A Sumerian one, describing Sin flying over his beloved city Ur, even referred to the god's Boat of Heaven as his "glory":

> *Father Nannar, Lord of Ur*
> *Whose glory is the sacred Boat of Heaven . . .*
> *When in the Boat of Heaven thou ascendeth,*
> *thou art glorious.*
> *Enlil hath adorned thy hand with a scepter,*
> *everlasting when over Ur*
> *in the Sacred Boat thou mountest.*

While no depiction of the Moon god's "Boat of Heaven" has so far been identified, a possible depiction does exist. Lying astride a major route linking East and West across the Jordan River was Jericho, one of the oldest known cities. The Bible (and other ancient texts) refer to it as the City of the Moon god—which is what the biblical name, *Yeriho*, means. It was there that the Prophet Elijah (9th century B.C.) was told by the biblical God to go across the Jordan River to be taken up, heavenward, in a fiery chariot. It was, as described in 2 Kings chapter 2, not a chance event, but a prearranged appointment. Starting his final journey from a place called Gilgal, the Prophet was accompanied by his aide Elisha and a group of disciples. And when they reached Jericho, the disciples inquired of Elisha: "Do you know that

the Lord will take your master away today?'' And Elisha, acknowledging that, admonished them to keep quiet.

When they reached the Jordan River, Elijah insisted that the others stay behind. Fifty of the disciples advanced to the river's edge and stopped; but Elisha would not depart. So "Elijah took his mantle and, rolling it up, struck the water, and it divided to the right and left, and the two of them crossed over on dry land.'' Then, on the other side of the Jordan,

> *A fiery chariot with fiery horses*
> *suddenly appeared*
> *and separated them one from the other;*
> *and Elijah went up to heaven*
> *in a whirlwind.*

In the 1920s an archaeological expedition sent by the Vatican began excavations at a site in Jordan called Tell Ghassul, "Mound of the Messenger.'' Its antiquity extended back millennia, and some of the oldest dwellings in the ancient Near East were unearthed there. On some of the collapsed walls the archaeologists discovered beautiful and unusual murals painted in a variety of colors. One depicted a "star'' that looked more like a compass pointing to the major cardinal points and their subdivisions; another showed a seated deity receiving a ritual procession. Other murals depicted black bulbous objects with eyelike openings and extended legs (Fig. 93); the latter could well have been the kind of "fiery chariot'' that carried Elijah heavenward. Indeed, the place could well have been the very site of Elijah's ascent: standing there, atop the mound, one can see the Jordan River not far away and beyond it, shimmering in the distance, the city of Jericho.

According to Jewish tradition, the Prophet Elijah will return someday to announce the Messianic Time.

That Adda-Guppi and her son Nabuna'id thought that such a time had indeed arrived, signaled and signified by the Re-

Figure 93

turn of the Moon god, is evident. They expected their Messianic Time to usher in an era of peace and prosperity, a new era that would begin with the rebuilding and rededication of the Temple of Harran.

That similar prophetic visions had taken place at about *the same time* regarding the God and the Temple of Jerusalem is, on the other hand, hardly realized. But that, in fact, was the subject of the prophecies of Ezekiel—that began "when the heavens opened" and he saw the radiating celestial chariot coming in a whirlwind.

The chronology provided in the Harran inscriptions, as verified by scholars from Assyrian and Babylonian annals, indicates that Adda-Guppi was born circa 650 B.C.; that Sin departed from his temple in Harran in 610 B.C.—and returned in 556 B.C. That was the exact same period when Ezekiel, who had been a priest in Jerusalem, was called to prophecy when he was among the Judean exiles in northern Mesopotamia. We are provided by him with an exact date: It was on the fifth day of the fourth month in the fifth year of the exile of the Judean king Jeho'iachin, "when I was among the exiles on the banks of the river Khebar that the heavens opened up and I saw divine visions," Ezekiel wrote right at the beginning of his prophecies. The time was 592 B.C.!

The Khebar (or Khabur, as it is now known) River is one of the tributaries of the great Euphrates River that begins its flow in the mountains of today's eastern Turkey. Not too far to the east of the Khabur River is another important tributary of the Euphrates, the River Balikh; and it is on the shores of the Balikh that Harran has been situated for millennia.

Ezekiel found himself so far away from Jerusalem, on the banks of a river in Upper Mesopotamia, at the edge of Hittite territory ("Hattiland" in cuneiform records), because he was one of several thousand noblemen, priests, and other leaders of Judea who were captured and taken into exile by Nebuchadnezzar, the Babylonian king who overran Jerusalem in 597 B.C.

Those tragic events are detailed in the second book of Kings, mainly 24:8–12. Remarkably, a Babylonian clay tablet (part of the series known as *The Babylonian Chronicles*) recorded the very same events, with matching dates.

Remarkably too, this Babylonian expedition—like the earlier one by Esarhaddon—was also launched from a starting point near Harran!

The Babylonian inscription details the capture of Jerusalem, the seizing of its king, his replacement on the throne of Judea by another king of Nebuchadnezzar's choice, and the exiling—"sending off to Babylon"—of the captured king and the land's leaders. It was thus that the priest Ezekiel found himself on the banks of the Khabur River in the province of Harran.

For a while—apparently for the first five years—the exiles believed that the calamities that had befallen their city and temple and themselves were a temporary setback. Though the Judean king Jeho'iachin was held in captivity, he was alive. Though the Temple's treasures were carried off to Babylon as booty, the Temple was still intact; and the majority of the people still remained in their land. The exiles, keeping in touch with Jerusalem by messengers, had high hopes that one day Jeho'iachin would be reinstated and the Temple restored to its sacred glory.

But no sooner had Ezekiel been called to prophecy, in the

fifth year of exile (592 B.C.), than the Lord God instructed him to announce to the people that the exile and the sacking of Jerusalem and its Temple were not the end of the ordeal. It was only meant as a warning to the people to mend their ways—behave with justice toward each other, and worship Yahweh according to the Commandments. But, said Yahweh to Ezekiel, the people did not mend their ways; rather, they turned to the worship of "alien gods." Therefore, said the Lord God, Jerusalem shall be attacked again, and this time it shall be totally destroyed, temple and all.

The instrument of his wrath, Yahweh said, would again be the king of Babylon. It is an established and known historical fact that in 587 B.C. Nebuchadnezzar, distrusting the king he himself had set on the Judean throne, again besieged Jerusalem. This time, in 586 B.C., the captured city was burned and left in ruins; so was the Temple of Yahweh that Solomon had built half a millennium earlier.

This much is indeed known. But what is hardly known is the reason why the warning was not heeded by the people and their remaining leaders in Jerusalem. It was their belief that *"Yahweh has left the Earth!"*

Accorded what would these days he deemed "remote vision," Ezekiel was shown first the Elders of Jerusalem behind their closed doors, then taken on a visionary tour of the city's streets. There was a complete breakdown of justice and religious observances, for the word that got out was

Yahweh sees us no more—
Yahweh has left the Earth!

It was in 610 B.C., according to the Harran inscriptions, that "Sin, lord of gods, became angry with his city and his temple and went up to heaven." It was in 597 B.C.—just over a decade later—that Yahweh became angry with Jerusalem his city and its people, and let the uncircumcised Neb-

uchadnezzar—a king by the grace of Marduk—enter, loot
and destroy the Temple of Yahweh.

And the people cried out: "God has left the Earth!"

And they knew not when, or if ever, He would return.

EPILOGUE

His mother's great expectations for Nabuna'id, as a reuniter of Sumer and Akkad and restorer of the glorious Olden Days, did not prepare the new king for the turmoil that he soon faced. He might have expected military challenges; he did not anticipate the religious fervor with which his domains were seized.

No sooner was he on the royal throne in Babylon, under a deal between his mother and Sin, than he realized that Marduk—once removed and since returned to Babylon—had to be appeased and given his due. In a series of true or pretended omen-dreams, Nabuna'id reported obtaining the blessing of Marduk (and Nabu) not only to his kingship, but also to the promised rebuilding of Sin's temple in Harran.

To leave no doubt about the importance of those dream-messages, the king reported that Marduk specifically inquired of him whether he had seen the *"Great Star, the planet of Marduk"*—a direct reference to Nibiru—and what other planets were in conjunction with it. When the king reported that they were the "god 30" (the Moon, Sin's celestial counterpart) and the "god 15" (Ishtar and her counterpart Venus), he was told: "There are no evil portents in the conjunction."

But neither the people of Harran nor the people of Babylon were happy with this "co-regnum" of the gods, nor were the followers of Ishtar "and the other gods." Sin, whose temple in Harran was eventually restored, demanded that his great temple in Ur should also become again a center of

277

worship. Ishtar complained that her golden cela in Uruk (Erech) must be reconstructed and that she be given again a chariot drawn by seven lions. And, as one reads between the lines of the king's inscription, he was getting fed up with that tug and pull by multiple gods and their priesthoods.

In a text titled by scholars *Nabuna'id and the Clergy of Babylon* (on a tablet now in the British Museum), the priests of Marduk presented a charge sheet, a list of accusations against Nabuna'id; they ran from civil matters ("law and order are not promulgated by him") through economic neglect ("the farmers are corrupted," "the trader's roads are blocked") and unsuccessful wars ("the nobles are killed in war") to the most serious charges: religious sacrilege—

> *He made an image of a god*
> *which nobody had seen before in the land;*
> *He placed it in the temple,*
> *raised it upon a pedestal . . .*
> *With lapis lazuli he adorned it,*
> *crowned it with a tiara . . .*

It was a statue of a strange deity—never seen before, the priests stressed—with "hair reaching down to the pedestal." It was so unusual or unseemly that not even Enki and Ninmah could have conceived it, so strange that "not even the learned Adapa knows his name." To make matters worse, two unusual beasts were sculpted as its guardians: one representing the Deluge-Demon and the other a Wild Bull. To add insult to sacrilege, the king placed this abomination in the Esagil temple of Marduk, and announced that the *Akitu* (New Year) festival, which was central to the equating of Marduk with the celestial Nibiru, would no longer be celebrated.

The priests announced for all to hear that "the protective deity of Nabuna'id became hostile to him," that "the former favorite of the gods was now fated to misfortune." And so Nabuna'id announced that he was leaving Babylon "on an expedition to a distant region." He named his son Bel-shar-

uzur ("Bel/Marduk protects the king"—the Belshazzar of the Book of Daniel) as regent.

His destination was Arabia, and his entourage included, as the various inscriptions attest, Jews from among the Judean exiles. His principal base was at a city called Teima (a name encountered in the Bible) and he established six settlements for his followers; five of them were listed, a thousand years later, by Islamic sources as Jewish towns. Some believe that Nabuna'id was seeking the seclusion of the desert to contemplate monotheism; a text fragment discovered among the Dead Sea scrolls in Qumran reports that Nabuna'id was smitten with an "unpleasant skin disease" in Teima, and was cured only after "a Jew told him to give honor to the God Most High." The bulk of the evidence suggests, however, that he was propagating the worship of Sin, the Moon god symbolized by the crescent—a symbol adopted in time by the Arabian worshipers of Allah.

Whatever the religious beliefs Nabuna'id was captivated by, they were anathema to the priests in Babylon. And so, when the Achaemenid rulers of Persia absorbed the kingdom of Medea and expanded into Mesopotamia, Cyrus the king was welcomed in Babylon not as a conqueror but as a liberator. Wisely, he rushed to the Esagil temple as soon as he entered the city and "held the hands of Marduk by both hands."

The year was 539 B.C.; it marked the prophesied end of Babylonian independent existence.

One of his first acts was to issue a proclamation permitting the Jewish exiles to return to Judea and rebuild the Temple in Jerusalem. The edict, recorded on the Cylinder of Cyrus that is now kept in the British Museum, corroborates the Biblical report, according to which Cyrus "was charged to do so by Yahweh, the God of Heaven."

The rebuilding of the Temple, under the leadership of Ezra and Nehemiah, was completed in 516 B.C.—seventy years after its destruction, as had been prophesied by Jeremiah.

* * *

The story of Babylon's end is told in the Bible in one of its most enigmatic books, the Book of Daniel. Introducing Daniel as one of the Judean exiles taken into Babylonian captivity, it relates how he was selected, with three other friends, to serve in the court of Nebuchadnezzar and how (as Joseph in Egypt) he was elevated to high office after solving the king's omen-dreams about future events.

The book then moves to events at the time of Belshazzar, when, during a great banquet, a hand floating by itself appeared and wrote on the wall MENE MENE TEKEL UPHARSIN. Not one of the king's seers and wizards could decipher the inscription. As a last resort, Daniel—now long retired—was called in. And Daniel explained the meaning to the Babylonian king: God has numbered the days of your kingdom; you have been weighed and found wanting; your kingdom will come to an end, divided between the Medes and the Persians.

After that Daniel himself began to have omen-dreams and see visions of the future in which the "Ancient of Days" and his archangels played key roles. Baffled by his own dreams and visions, Daniel asked the angels for explanations. In each instance they turned out to be predictions of future events that went beyond the fall of Babylon, even beyond the fulfillment of the seventy-year prophecy of the rebuilding of the Temple. The rise and fall of the Persian Empire was predicted, the coming of the Greeks under Alexander, the split of his domains after his death, and what followed.

Though many modern scholars—but not Jewish sages or the Fathers of the Christian Church—take those prophecies (only accurate in part) as hindsight, indicating a much later author (or even several authors), the central point of the dreams, visions, and omens experienced by Daniel is a preoccupation with the question: *When?* When will be the final kingdom, the only one that will survive and last?

It will be one that only the followers of the God Most High, the "Ancient of Days," will live to see (even the dead among them, who will rise). But over and over again, Daniel kept asking the angels: When?

In one instance the angel responded that a phase in the future events, a time when an unholy king shall try to "change the times and the laws," will last "a time, times, and half a time;" only after that will "the kingdoms under heaven be given to the people, the holy ones of the Most High."

Another time the revealing angel said: "Seventy weeks of years have been decreed for your people and your city until the measure of transgression is filled and prophetic vision ratified."

One more time a divine emissary was asked by Daniel: "How long until the end of these awful things?" He got again the enigmatic answer: The fulfillment of all the prophesied things shall come after "a time, times and half a time."

"I heard and did not understand," Daniel wrote. "So I said, my Lord, what will be the outcome of these things?" Speaking still in codes, the divine being answered, "From the time the regular offering is abolished and an appalling abomination is set up it will be a thousand and two hundred and ninety days. Happy is the one who waits and reaches one thousand three hundred and thirty-five days."

As Daniel stood puzzled, the Angel of God added:

> *You, Daniel, shall rest and arise*
> *to your destiny at the End of Days . . .*
> *But keep the words secret,*
> *and seal the book until the End of Time.*

At the End of Time, when the nations of Earth shall gather in Jerusalem, they shall all speak "in a clear language," stated the Prophet Zephaniah (whose very name meant "By Yahweh Encoded")—there will no longer be a need for confounded languages and letters to be read backward and hidden encodings.

And, as Daniel, we are still asking: When?

INDEX

283

Praise for the Works of Zecharia Sitchin

"Reflects the highest level of scientific knowledge . . ."

SCIENCE & RELIGION NEWS

"Exciting . . . credible . . . most provocative and compelling."

LIBRARY JOURNAL

"One of the most important books on Earth's roots ever written."

EAST WEST JOURNAL

"Sitchin is a zealous investigator into man's origins . . . a dazzling performance."

KIRKUS REVIEWS

"For thousands of years priests, poets, and scientists have tried to explain how man was created. Now a recognized scholar has come forth with a theory that is most astonishing of all."

UNITED PRESS INTERNATIONAL

ZECHARIA SITCHIN

THE END *of* DAYS

Armageddon and Prophecies of the Return

The Seventh and Concluding Book of The Earth Chronicles

Bear & Company
Rochester, Vermont • Toronto, Canada

Bear & Company
One Park Street
Rochester, Vermont 05767
www.BearandCompanyBooks.com

Bear & Company is a division of Inner Traditions International

Originally published in 2007 by William Morrow
Paperback edition published in 2008 by Harper
Bear & Company hardcover edition published in 2014 by arrangement
with William Morrow, an imprint of HarperCollins Publishers

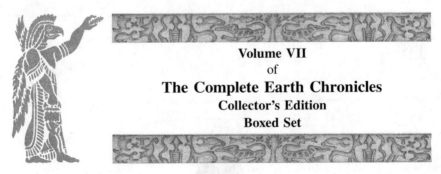

Volume VII
of
The Complete Earth Chronicles
Collector's Edition
Boxed Set

Printed and bound in India at Replika Press Pvt. Ltd.

10 9 8 7 6

Dedicated
to my brother,
Dr. Amnon Sitchin,
whose aerospace expertise
was invaluable at all times

CONTENTS

THE PAST, THE FUTURE

"When will they return?"

I have been asked this question countless times by people who have read my books, the "they" being the Anunnaki—the extraterrestrials who had come to Earth from their planet, Nibiru, and were revered in antiquity as gods. Will it be when Nibiru in its elongated orbit returns to our vicinity, and what will happen then? Will there be darkness at noon and the Earth shall shatter? Will it be Peace on Earth, or Armageddon? A Millennium of trouble and tribulations, or a messianic Second Coming? Will it happen in 2012, or later, or not at all?

These are profound questions that combine people's deepest hopes and anxieties with religious beliefs and expectations, questions compounded by current events: wars in lands where the entwined affairs of gods and men began; the threats of nuclear holocausts; the alarming ferocity of natural disasters. They are questions that I dared not answer all these years—but now are questions the answers to which cannot—must not—be delayed.

Questions about the Return, it ought to be realized, are not new; they have inexorably been linked in the past—as they are today—to the expectation and the apprehension of the Day of the Lord, the End of Days, Armageddon. Four millennia ago, the Near East witnessed a god and his son promising Heaven on Earth. More than three millennia ago, king and people in Egypt yearned for a messianic time. Two millennia

ago, the people of Judea wondered whether the Messiah had appeared, and we are still seized with the mysteries of those events. Are prophecies coming true?

We shall deal with the puzzling answers that were given, solve ancient enigmas, decipher the origin and meaning of symbols—the Cross, the Fishes, the Chalice. We shall describe the role of space-related sites in historic events and show why Past, Present, and Future converge in Jerusalem, the place of the "Bond Heaven-Earth." And we shall ponder why it is that our current twenty-first century A.D. is so similar to the twenty-first century B.C. Is history repeating itself—is it destined to repeat itself? Is it all guided by a Messianic Clock? Is the time at hand?

More than two millennia ago, Daniel of Old Testament fame repeatedly asked the angels: *When?* When will be the End of Days, the End of Time? More than three centuries ago the famed Sir Isaac Newton, who elucidated the secrets of celestial motions, composed treatises on the Old Testament's Book of Daniel and the New Testament's Book of Revelation; his recently found handwritten calculations concerning the End of Days will be analyzed, along with more recent predictions of The End.

Both the Hebrew Bible and the New Testament asserted that the secrets of the Future are embedded in the Past, that the destiny of Earth is connected to the Heavens, that the affairs and fate of Mankind are linked to those of God and gods. In dealing with what is yet to happen, we cross over from history to prophecy; one cannot be understood without the other, and we shall report them both. With that as our guide, let us look at what is to come through the lens of what had been. The answers will be certain to surprise.

ZECHARIA SITCHIN
NOVEMBER 2006

1

THE MESSIANIC CLOCK

Wherever one turns, humankind appears seized with Apocalyptic trepidation, Messianic fervor, and End of Time anxiety.

Religious fanaticism manifests itself in wars, rebellions, and the slaughter of "infidels." Armies amassed by Kings of the West are warring with armies of the Kings of the East. A Clash of Civilizations shakes the foundations of traditional ways of life. Carnage engulfs cities and towns; the high and the mighty seek safety behind protective walls. Natural calamities and ever-intensifying catastrophes leave people wondering: Has Mankind sinned, is it witnessing Divine Wrath, is it due for another annihilating Deluge? Is this the Apocalypse? Can there be—will there be—Salvation? Are Messianic times afoot?

The time—the twenty-first century A.D.—or was it the twenty-first century B.C.?

The correct answer is Yes and Yes, both in our own time as well as in those ancient times. It is the condition of the present time, as well as at a time more than four millennia ago; and the amazing similarity is due to events in the middle time in between—the period associated with the messianic fervor at the time of Jesus.

Those three cataclysmic periods for Mankind and its planet—two in the recorded past (circa 2100 B.C. and when B.C. changed to A.D.), one in the nearing future—are interconnected; one has led to the other,

one can be understood only by understanding the other. The Present stems from the Past, the Past is the Future. Essential to all three is **Messianic Expectation;** and linking all three is **Prophecy.**

How the present time of troubles and tribulations will end—what the Future portends—requires entering the realm of Prophecy. Ours will not be a mélange of newfound predictions whose main magnet is fear of doom and End, but a reliance upon unique ancient records that documented the Past, predicted the Future, and recorded previous messianic expectations—prophesying the future in antiquity and, one believes, the Future that is to come.

In all three apocalyptic instances—the two that had occurred, the one that is about to happen—the physical and spiritual relationship between Heaven and Earth was and remains pivotal for the events. The physical aspects were expressed by the existence on Earth of actual sites that linked Earth with the heavens—sites that were deemed crucial, that were focuses of the events; the spiritual aspects have been expressed in what we call Religion. In all three instances, a changed relationship between Man and God was central, except that when, circa 2100 B.C., Mankind faced the first of these three epochal upheavals, the relationship was between men and *gods,* in the plural. Whether that relationship has really changed, the reader will soon discover.

The story of the gods, the **Anunnaki** ("Those who from heaven to Earth came"), as the Sumerians called them, begins with their coming to Earth from **Nibiru** in need of gold. The story of their planet was told in antiquity in the *Epic of Creation,* a long text on seven tablets; it is usually considered to be an allegorical myth, the product of primitive minds that spoke of planets as living gods combating each other. But as I have shown in my book *The Twelfth Planet,* the ancient text is in fact a sophisticated cosmogony that tells how a stray planet, passing by our solar system, collided with a planet called Tiamat; the collision resulted in the creation of Earth and its Moon, of the Asteroid Belt and comets, and in the capture of the invader itself in a great elliptical orbit that takes about 3,600 Earth-years to complete (fig. 1).

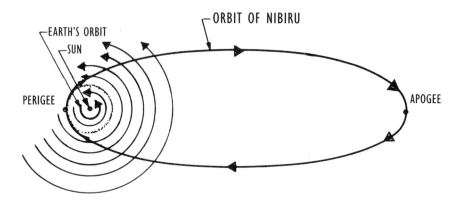

Figure 1

It was, Sumerian texts tell, 120 such orbits—432,000 Earth-years—prior to the Deluge (the "Great Flood") that the Anunnaki came to Earth. How and why they came, their first cities in the E.DIN (the biblical Eden), their fashioning of the Adam and the reasons for it, and the events of the catastrophic Deluge—have all been told in The Earth Chronicles series of my books and will not be repeated here. But before we time-travel to the momentous twenty-first century B.C., some pre-Diluvial and post-Diluvial landmark events need to be recalled.

The biblical tale of the Deluge, starting in chapter 6 of Genesis, ascribes its conflicting aspects to a sole deity, Yahweh, who at first is determined to wipe Mankind off the face of the Earth and then goes out of his way to save it through Noah and the Ark. The earlier Sumerian sources of the tale ascribe the disaffection with Mankind to the god **Enlil,** and the countereffort to save Mankind to the god **Enki.** What the Bible glossed over for the sake of Monotheism was not just the disagreement between Enlil and Enki but a rivalry and a conflict between two clans of Anunnaki that dominated the course of subsequent events on Earth.

That conflict between the two and their offspring, and the Earth regions allocated to them after the Deluge, need to be kept in mind to understand all that happened thereafter.

The two were half-brothers, sons of Nibiru's ruler **Anu**; their conflict on Earth had its roots on their home planet, Nibiru. Enki— then called **E.A** ("He whose home is water")—was Anu's firstborn son, but not by the official spouse, **Antu.** When Enlil was born to Anu by Antu—a half-sister of Anu—Enlil became the Legal Heir to Nibiru's throne though he was not the firstborn son. The unavoidable resentment on the part of Enki and his maternal family was exacerbated by the fact that Anu's accession to the throne was problematic to begin with: having lost out in a succession struggle to a rival named Alalu, he later usurped the throne in a coup d'état, forcing Alalu to flee Nibiru for his life. That not only backtracked Ea's resentments to the days of his forebears but also brought about other challenges to the leadership of Enlil, as told in the epic *Tale of Anzu*. (For the tangled relationships of Nibiru's royal families and the ancestries of Anu and Antu, Enlil and Ea, see *The Lost Book of Enki*.)

The key to unlocking the mystery of the gods' succession (and marriage) rules was my realization that these rules also applied to the people chosen by them to serve as their proxies to Mankind. It was the biblical tale of the Patriarch Abraham explaining (*Genesis* 20:12) that he did not lie when he had presented his wife Sarah as his sister: "Indeed, she is my sister, the daughter of my father, but not the daughter of my mother, and she became my wife." Not only was marrying a half-sister from a different mother permitted, but a son by her—in this case Isaac—became the Legal Heir and dynastic successor, rather than the Firstborn Ishmael, the son of the handmaiden Hagar. (How such succession rules caused the bitter feud between Ra's divine descendants in Egypt, the half-brothers Osiris and Seth who married the half-sisters Isis and Nephtys, is explained in *The Wars of Gods and Men*.)

Though those succession rules appear complex, they were based on what those who write about royal dynasties call "bloodlines"—what we now should recognize as sophisticated DNA genealogies that also distinguished between general DNA inherited from the parents as well as the mitochondrial DNA (mtDNA) that is inherited by females only from the mother. The complex yet basic rule was this: Dynastic lines continue through the male line; the Firstborn son is next in succession;

a half-sister could be taken as wife *if she had a different mother;* and if a son by such a half-sister is later born, that son—though not Firstborn—becomes the Legal Heir and the dynastic successor.

The rivalry between the two half-brothers Ea/Enki and Enlil in matters of the throne was complicated by personal rivalry in matters of the heart. They both coveted their half-sister **Ninmah,** whose mother was yet another concubine of Anu. She was Ea's true love, but he was not permitted to marry her. Enlil then took over, and had a son by her—**Ninurta.** Though born without wedlock, the succesion rules made Ninurta Enlil's uncontested heir, being both his Firstborn son and one born by a royal half-sister.

Ea, as related in The Earth Chronicles books, was the leader of the first group of fifty Anunnaki to come to Earth to obtain the gold needed to protect Nibiru's dwindling atmosphere. When the initial plans failed, his half-brother Enlil was sent to Earth with more Anunnaki for an expanded Mission Earth. If that was not enough to create a hostile atmosphere, Ninmah too arrived on Earth to serve as chief medical officer ...

A long text known as the *Atrahasis Epic* begins the story of gods and men on Earth with a visit by Anu to Earth to settle once and for all (he hoped) the rivalry between his two sons, which was ruining the vital mission; he even offered to stay on Earth and let one of the half-brothers assume the regency on Nibiru. With that in mind, the ancient text tells us, lots were drawn to determine who would stay on Earth and who would sit on Nibiru's throne:

> *The gods clasped hands together,*
> *had cast lots and had divided:*
> *Anu went up [back] to heaven,*
> *[For Enlil] the Earth was made subject;*
> *The seas, enclosed as with a loop,*
> *to Enki the prince were given.*

The result of drawing lots, then, was that Anu returned to Nibiru as its king. Ea, given dominion over the seas and waters (in later times,

"Poseidon" to the Greeks and "Neptune" to the Romans), was granted the epithet EN.KI ("Lord of Earth") to soothe his feelings; but it was EN.LIL ("Lord of the Command") who was put in overall charge: "To him the Earth was made subject." Resentful or not, Ea/Enki could not defy the rules of succession or the results of the drawing of lots; and so the resentment, the anger at justice denied, and a consuming determination to avenge injustices to his father and forefathers and thus to himself led Enki's son **Marduk** to take up the fight.

Several texts describe how the Anunnaki set up their settlements in the E.DIN (the post-Diluvial Sumer), each with a specific function, and all laid out in accordance with a master plan. The crucial space connection—the ability to constantly stay in communication with the home planet and with the shuttlecraft and spacecraft—was maintained from Enlil's command post in **Nippur,** the heart of which was a dimly lit chamber called the DUR.AN.KI, "The Bond Heaven-Earth." Another vital facility was a spaceport, located at Sippar ("Bird City"). Nippur lay at the center of concentric circles at which the other "cities of the gods" were located; all together they shaped out, for an arriving spacecraft, a landing corridor whose focal point was the Near East's most visible topographic feature—the twin peaks of Mount Ararat (fig. 2).

And then the Deluge "swept over the earth," obliterated all the cities of the gods with their Mission Control Center and Spaceport, and buried the Edin under millions of tons of mud and silt. Everything had to be done all over again—but much could no longer be the same. First and foremost, it was necessary to create a new spaceport facility, with a new Mission Control Center and new Beacon-sites for a Landing Corridor. The new landing path was anchored again on the prominent twin peaks of Ararat; the other components were all new: the actual spaceport in the Sinai Peninsula, on the 30th parallel north; artificial twin peaks as beacon sites, the Giza pyramids; and a new Mission Control Center at a place called Jerusalem (fig. 3). It was a layout that played a crucial role in post-Diluvial events.

The Deluge was a watershed (both literally and figuratively) in the affairs of both gods and men, and in the relationship between

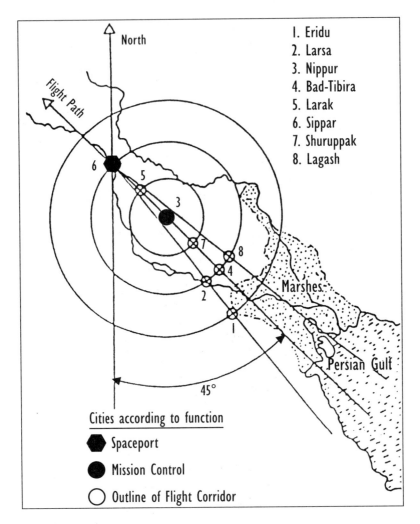

1. Eridu
2. Larsa
3. Nippur
4. Bad-Tibira
5. Larak
6. Sippar
7. Shuruppak
8. Lagash

North

Flight Path

Marshes

Persian Gulf

45°

Cities according to function

⬢ Spaceport

● Mission Control

○ Outline of Flight Corridor

Figure 2

the two: the Earthlings, who were fashioned to serve and work for the gods were henceforth treated as junior partners on a devastated planet.

The new relationship between men and gods was formulated, sanctified, and codified when Mankind was granted its first high civilization, in Mesopotamia, circa 3800 B.C. The momentous event followed a state visit to Earth by Anu, not just as Nibiru's ruler but also as the head of the pantheon, on Earth, of the ancient gods. Another (and probably

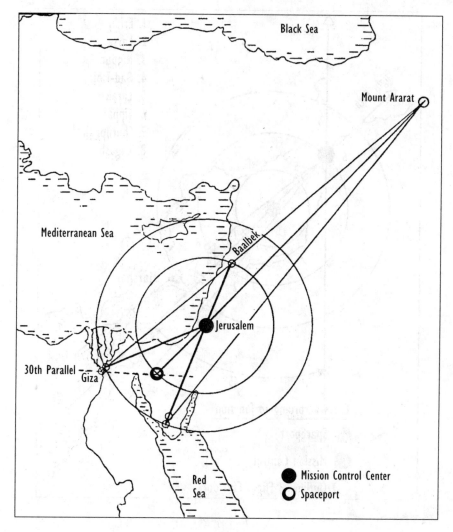

Figure 3

the main) reason for his visit was the establishment and affirmation
of peace among the gods themselves—a live-and-let-live arrangement
dividing the lands of the Old World among the two principal Anunnaki
clans, that of Enlil and that of Enki—for the new post-Diluvial circumstances and the new location of the space facilities required a new territorial division among the gods.

It was a division that was reflected in the biblical Table of Nations

(Genesis 10), in which the spread of Mankind, emanating from the three sons of Noah, was recorded by nationality and geography: Asia to the nations/lands of Shem, Europe to the descendants of Japhet, Africa to the nation/lands of Ham. The historical records show that the parallel division among the gods allotted the first two to the Enlilites, the third one to Enki and his sons. The connecting Sinai Peninsula, where the vital post-Diluvial spaceport was located, was set aside as a neutral Sacred Region.

While the Bible simply listed the lands and nations according to their Noahite division, the earlier Sumerian texts recorded the fact that the division was a deliberate act, the result of deliberations by the leadership of the Anunnaki. A text known as the *Epic of Etana* tells us that

> *The great Anunnaki who decree the fates*
> *sat exchanging their counsels regarding the Earth.*
> *They created the four regions,*
> *set up the settlements.*

In the First Region, the lands between the two rivers Euphrates and Tigris (Mesopotamia), Man's first known high civilization, that of Sumer, was established. Where the pre-Diluvial cities of the gods had been, Cities of Man arose, each with its sacred precinct where a deity resided in his or her ziggurat—Enlil in Nippur, Ninmah in Shuruppak, Ninurta in Lagash, **Nannar/Sin** in Ur, **Inanna/Ishtar** in Uruk, **Utu/Shamash** in Sippar, and so on. In each such urban center an EN.SI, a "Righteous Shepherd"—initially a chosen demigod—was selected to govern the people on behalf of the gods; his main assignment was to promulgate codes of justice and morality. In the sacred precinct, a priesthood overseen by a high priest served the god and his spouse, supervised the holiday celebrations, and handled the rites of offerings, sacrifices, and prayers to the gods. Art and sculpture, music and dance, poetry and hymns, and above all writing and recordkeeping flourished in the temples and extended to the royal palace.

From time to time one of those cities was selected to serve as the

land's capital; there the ruler was king, LU.GAL ("Great man"). Initially and for a long time thereafter this person, the most powerful man in the land, served as both king and high priest. He was carefully chosen, for his role and authority, and all the physical symbols of Kingship, were deemed to have come to Earth directly from Heaven, from Anu on Nibiru. A Sumerian text dealing with the subject stated that before the symbols of Kingship (tiara/crown and scepter) and of Righteousness (the shepherd's staff) were granted to an earthly king, they "lay deposited before Anu in heaven." Indeed, the Sumerian word for Kingship was *Anuship*.

This aspect of "Kingship" as the essence of civilization, just behavior and a moral code for Mankind, was explicitly expressed in the statement in the *Sumerian King List* that after the Deluge *"Kingship was brought down from Heaven."* It is a profound statement that must be borne in mind as we progress in this book to the messianic expectations—in the words of the New Testament, for the **Return of the "Kingship of Heaven" to Earth.**

Circa 3100 B.C. a similar yet not identical civilization was established in the Second Region in Africa, that of the river Nile (Nubia and Egypt). Its history was not as harmonious as that among the Enlilites, for rivalry and contention continued among Enki's six sons, to whom not cities but whole land domains were allocated. Paramount was an ongoing conflict between Enki's firstborn **Marduk (*Ra* in Egypt)** and **Ningishzidda (*Thoth* in Egypt)**, a conflict that led to the exile of Thoth and a band of African followers to the New World (where he became known as *Quetzalcoatl,* the Winged Serpent). Marduk/Ra himself was punished and exiled when, opposing the marriage of his young brother Dumuzi to Enlil's granddaughter Inanna/Ishtar, he caused his brother's death. It was as compensation to Inanna/Ishtar that she was granted dominion over the Third Region of civilization, that of the Indus Valley, circa 2900 B.C. It was for good reason that the three civilizations—as was the spaceport in the sacred region—were all centered on the 30th parallel north (fig. 4).

According to Sumerian texts, the Anunnaki established Kingship—civilization and its institutions, as most clearly exemplified in Mesopotamia—as a new order in their relationships with Mankind,

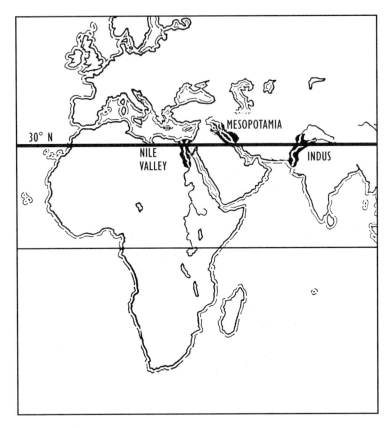

Figure 4

with kings/priests serving both as a link and a separator between gods and men. But as one looks back on that seemingly "golden age" in the affairs of gods and men, it becomes evident that the affairs of the gods constantly dominated and determined the affairs of Men and the fate of Mankind. Overshadowing all was the determination of Marduk/Ra to undo the injustice done to his father, Ea/Enki, when under the succession rules of the Anunnaki not Enki but Enlil was declared the Legal Heir of their father, Anu, the ruler on their home planet, Nibiru.

In accord with the sexagesimal ("base sixty") mathematical system that the gods granted the Sumerians, the twelve great gods of the Sumerian pantheon were given numerical ranks in which Anu held the supreme Rank of Sixty; the Rank of Fifty was granted to Enlil; that of Enki was forty, and so farther down, alternating between male and

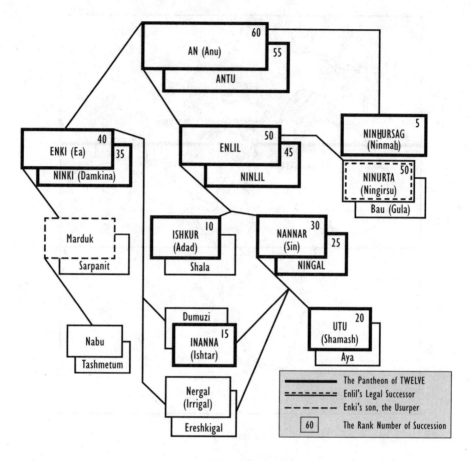

Figure 5

female deities (fig. 5). Under the succession rules, Enlil's son Ninurta was in line for the Rank of Fifty on Earth, while Marduk held a nominal Rank of Ten; and initially, these two successors-in-waiting were not yet part of the twelve "Olympians."

And so the long, bitter, and relentness struggle by Marduk that began with the Enlil-Enki feud focused later on Marduk's contention with Enlil's son Ninurta for the succession to the Rank of Fifty and then extended to Enlil's granddaughter Inanna/Ishtar, whose marriage to Dumuzi, Enki's youngest son, was so opposed by Marduk that it ended with Dumuzi's death. In time Marduk/Ra faced conflicts even with other brothers and half-brothers of his, in addition to the conflict

with Thoth that we have already mentioned—principally with Enki's son **Nergal,** who married a granddaughter of Enlil named Ereshkigal.

In the course of these struggles, the conflicts at times flared up to full-fledged wars between the two divine clans; some of those wars are called "The Pyramid Wars" in my book *The Wars of Gods and Men.* In one notable instance the fighting led to the burying alive of Marduk inside the Great Pyramid; in another, it led to its capture by Ninurta. Marduk was also exiled more than once—both as punishment and as a self-imposed absence. His persistent efforts to attain the status to which he believed he was entitled included the event recorded in the Bible as the Tower of Babel incident; but in the end, after numerous frustrations, success came only when Earth and Heaven were aligned with the **Messianic Clock.**

Indeed, the first cataclysmic set of events, in the twenty-first century B.C., and the messianic expectations that accompanied it, is principally the story of Marduk; it also brought to center stage his son **Nabu**—a deity, the son of a god, but whose mother was an Earthling.

Throughout the history of Sumer that spanned almost two thousand years, its royal capital shifted—from the first one, Kish (Ninurta's first city), to Uruk (the city that Anu granted to Inanna/Ishtar) to Ur (Sin's seat and center of worship); then to others and then back to the initial ones; and finally, for the third time, back to Ur. But at all times Enlil's city, Nippur, his "cult center," as scholars are wont to call it, remained the religious center of Sumer and the Sumerian people; it was there that the annual cycle of worshipping the gods was determined.

The twelve "Olympians" of the Sumerian pantheon, each with his or her celestial counterpart among the twelve members of the Solar System (Sun, Moon, and ten planets, including Nibiru), were also honored with one month each in the annual cycle of a twelve-month year. The Sumerian term for "month," EZEN, actually meant holiday, festival; and each such month was devoted to celebrating the worship-festival of one of the twelve supreme gods. It was the need to determine the exact time when each such month began and ended (and not in order to enable peasants to know when to sow or harvest, as schoolbooks explain) that

led to the introduction of *Mankind's first calendar* in **3760 B.C.** It is known as the **Calendar of Nippur** because it was the task of its priests to determine the calendar's intricate timetable and to announce, for the whole land, the time of the religious festivals. That calendar is still in use to this day as the Jewish religious calendar, which, in A.D. 2007, numbers the year as 5767.

In pre-Diluvial times Nippur served as Mission Control Center, Enlil's command post where he set up the DUR.AN.KI, the "Bond Heaven-Earth" for the communications with the home planet, Nibiru, and with the spacecraft connecting them. (After the Deluge, these functions were relocated to a place later known as Jerusalem.) Its central position, equidistant from the other functional centers in the E.DIN (see Fig. 2), was also deemed to be equidistant from the "four corners of the Earth" and gave it the nickname *"Navel of the Earth."* A hymn to Enlil referred to Nippur and its functions thus:

> *Enlil,*
> *When you marked off divine settlements on Earth,*
> *Nippur you set up as your very own city . . .*
> *You founded the Dur-An-Ki*
> *In the center of the four corners of the Earth.*

(The term "the Four Corners of the Earth" is also found in the Bible; and when Jerusalem replaced Nippur as Mission Control Center after the Deluge, it too was nicknamed the Navel of the Earth.)

In Sumerian the term for the four regions of the Earth was UB, but it also is found as AN.UB—the heavenly, the *celestial* four "corners"—in this case an astronomical term connected with the calendar. It is taken to refer to the four points in the Earth-Sun annual cycle that we nowadays call the Summer Solstice, the Winter Solstice, and the two crossings of the equator—once as the Spring Equinox and then as the Autumnal Equinox. In the Calendar of Nippur, the year began on the day of the Spring Equinox and it has so remained in the ensuing calendars of the ancient Near East. That determined the time of the most important festival of the year—the New Year festival, an event

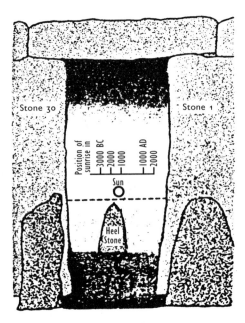

Figure 6

that lasted ten days, during which detailed and canonized rituals had to be followed.

Determining calendrical time by Heliacal Rising entailed the observation of the skies at dawn, when the Sun just begins to rise on the eastern horizon but the skies are still dark enough to show the stars in the background. The day of the equinox having been determined by the fact that on it daylight and nighttime were precisely equal, the position of the Sun at heliacal rising was then marked by the erection of a stone pillar to guide future observations—a procedure that was followed, for example, later on at Stonehenge in Britain; and, as at Stonehenge, long-term observations revealed that the group of stars ("constellation") in the background has not remained the same (fig. 6); there, the alignment stone called the "Heel Stone" that points to sunrise on solstice day nowadays, pointed originally to sunrise circa 2000 B.C.

The phenomenon, called Precession of the Equinoxes, or just Precession, results from the fact that as the Earth completes one annual orbit around the Sun, it does not return to the same exact celestial spot. There is a slight, very slight retardation; it amounts to one degree (out

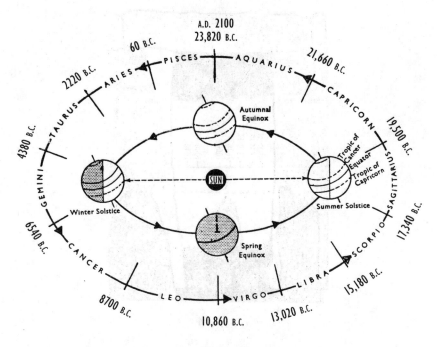

Figure 7

of 360 in the circle) in seventy-two years. It was Enki who first grouped the stars observable from Earth into "constellations" and divided the heavens in which the Earth circled the Sun into twelve parts—what has since been called the Zodiacal Circle of constellations (fig. 7). Since each twelfth part of the circle occupied 30 degrees of the celestial arc, the retardation or precessional shift from one zodiacal house to another lasted (mathematically) **2,160** years (72 × 30), and a complete zodiacal cycle lasted 25,920 years (2,160 × 12). The approximate dates of the **Zodiacal Ages**—following the equal twelve-part division and not actual astronomical observations—have been added here for the reader's guidance.

That this was the achievement from a time preceding Mankind's civilizations is attested to by the fact that a zodiacal calendar was applied to Enki's first stays on Earth (when the first two zodiacal houses were named in his honor); that this was not the achievement of a Greek astronomer (Hipparchus) in the third century B.C. (as most textbooks still suggest) is attested to by the fact that the twelve zodiacal houses

were known to the Sumerians millennia earlier by names (fig. 8) and depictions (fig. 9) that we use to this day.

In *When Time Began* the calendrical timetables of gods and men were discussed at length. Having come from Nibiru, whose orbital period, the SAR, meant 3,600 (Earth-) years, that unit was naturally

1. GU.AN.NA ("heavenly bull"), *Taurus.*
2. MASH.TAB.BA ("twins"), our *Gemini.*
3. DUB ("pincers," "tongs"), the Crab or *Cancer.*
4. UR.GULA ("lion"), which we call *Leo.*
5. AB.SIN ("her father was Sin"), the Maiden, *Virgo.*
6. ZI.BA.AN.NA ("heavenly fate"), the scales of *Libra.*
7. GIR.TAB ("which claws and cuts"), *Scorpio.*
8. PA.BIL ("defender"), the Archer, *Sagittarius.*
9. SUHUR.MASH ("goat-fish"), *Capricorn.*
10. GU ("lord of the waters"), the Water Bearer, *Aquarius.*
11. SIM.MAH ("fishes"), *Pisces.*
12. KU.MAL ("field dweller"), the Ram, *Aries.*

Figure 8

GIR.TAB
Scorpio

PA.BIL
Sagittarius

AB.SIN
Virgo

SUHUR.MASH
Capricorn

Figure 9

the first calendrical yardstick of the Anunnaki even on the fast-orbiting Earth. Indeed, the texts dealing with their early days on Earth, such as the *Sumerian King Lists,* designated the periods of this or that leader's time on Earth in terms of Sars. I termed this **Divine Time.** The calendar granted to Mankind, one based on the orbital aspects of the Earth (and its Moon), was named **Earthly Time.** Pointing out that the 2,160-year zodiacal shift (less than a year for the Anunnaki) offered them a better ratio—the "golden ratio" of 10:6—between the two extremes; I called this **Celestial Time.**

As Marduk discovered, that Celestial Time was the "clock" by which his destiny was to be determined.

But which was **Mankind's Messianic Clock,** determining its fate and destiny—*Earthly Time,* such as the count of fifty-year Jubilees, a count in centuries, or the Millennium? Was it *Divine Time,* geared to Nibiru's orbit? Or was it—is it—*Celestial Time,* which follows the slow rotation of the zodiacal clock?

The quandary, as we shall see, baffled mankind in antiquity; it still lies at the core of the current Return issue. The question that is posed has been asked before—by Babylonian and Assyrian stargazing priests, by biblical Prophets, in the Book of Daniel, in the Revelation of St. John the Divine, by the likes of Sir Isaac Newton, by all of us today.

The answer will be astounding. Let us embark on the painstaking quest.

2

"AND IT CAME TO PASS"

It is highly significant that in its record of Sumer and the early Sumerian civilization, the Bible chose to highlight the *space connection incident*—the one known as the tale of the **"Tower of Babel"**:

> *And it came to pass as they journeyed from the east*
> *that they found a plain in the land of Shin'ar*
> *and they settled there.*
> *And they said to one another:*
> *"Come, let us make bricks and burn them by fire."*
> *And the brick served them as stone,*
> *and the bitumen served them as mortar.*
> *And they said: "Come, let us build us a city*
> *and* a tower whose head shall reach the heavens."
>
> GENESIS 11:2–4

This is how the Bible recorded the most audacious attempt—by Marduk!—to assert his supremacy by establishing his own city in the heart of Enlilite domains and, moreover, to **build there his own space facility with its own *launch tower.*** The place is named in the Bible *Babel,* "Babylon" in English.

This biblical tale is remarkble in many ways. It records, first of all, the settlement of the Tigris-Euphrates plain after the Deluge, after the soil had dried up enough to permit resettlement. It correctly names the new land *Shin'ar,* the Hebrew name for Sumer. It provides the important clue from where—from the mountainous region to the east—the settlers had come. It recognizes that it was there that Man's first urban civilization began—the building of cities. It correctly notes (and explains) that in that land, where the soil consisted of layers of dried mud and there is no native rock, the people used mud bricks for building and by hardening the bricks in kilns could use them instead of stone. It also refers to the use of bitumen as mortar in construction—an astounding bit of information, since bitumen, a natural petroleum product, seeped up from the ground in southern Mesopotamia but was totally absent in the Land of Israel.

The authors of this chapter in Genesis were thus well informed regarding the origins and key innovations of the Sumerian civilization; they also recognized the significance of the "Tower of Babel" incident. As in the tales of the creation of Adam and of the Deluge, they melded the various Sumerian deities into the plural *Elohim* or into an all-encompassing and supreme *Yahweh,* but they left in the tale the fact that it took a *group of deities* to say, "let *us* come down" and put an end to this rogue effort (Genesis 11:7).

Sumerian and later Babylonian records attest to the veracity of the biblical tale and contain many more details, linking the incident to the overall strained relationships between the gods that caused the outbreak of two "Pyramid Wars" after the Deluge. The "Peace on Earth" arrangements, circa 8650 B.C., left the erstwhile *Edin* in Enlilite hands. That conformed to the decisions of Anu, Enlil, and even Enki—but was never acquiesced to by Marduk/Ra. And so it was that when Cities of Men began to be allocated in the former *Edin* to the gods, Marduk raised the issue, "What about me?"

Although Sumer was the heartland of the Enlilite territories and its cities were Enlilite "cult centers," there was one exception: in the south of Sumer, at the edge of the marshlands, there was **Eridu;** it was rebuilt after the Deluge at the exact same site where Ea/Enki's first settlement

on Earth had been. It was Anu's insistence, when the Earth was divided among the rival Anunnaki clans, that Enki forever retain Eridu as his own. Circa **3460 B.C.** Marduk decided that he could extend his father's privilege to also having his own foothold in the Enlilite heartland.

The available texts do not provide the reason why Marduk chose that specific site on the banks of the Euphrates River for his new headquarters, but its location provides a clue: it was situated between the rebuilt Nippur (the pre-Diluvial Mission Control Center) and the rebuilt Sippar (the pre-Diluvial spaceport of the Anunnaki), so what Marduk had in mind could have been a facility that served both functions. A later map of Babylon, drawn on a clay tablet (fig. 10), represents it as a "Navel of the Earth"—akin to Nippur's original function-title. The name Marduk gave the place, *Bab-Ili* in Akkadian, meant "Gateway

Figure 10

of the gods"—a place from which the gods could ascend and descend, where the appropriate main facility was to be a "tower whose head shall reach the heavens"—a **launch tower!**

As in the biblical tale, so it is told in parallel (and earlier) Mesopotamian versions that this attempt to establish a rogue space facility came to naught. Though fragmented, the Mesopotamian texts (first translated by George Smith in 1876) make it clear that Marduk's act infuriated Enlil, who "in his anger a command poured out" for a nighttime attack to destroy the tower.

Egyptian records report that a chaotic period that lasted 350 years preceded the start of Pharaonic kingship in Egypt, circa **3110 B.C.** It is this time frame that leads us to date the Tower of Babel incident to circa **3460 B.C.**, for the end of that chaotic period marked the return of Marduk/Ra to Egypt, the expulsion of Thoth, and the start of the worship of Ra.

Frustrated this time, Marduk never gave up his attempts to dominate the official space facilities that served as the "Bond Heaven-Earth," the link between Nibiru and Earth—or to set up his own facility. Since, in the end, Marduk did attain his aims in Babylon, the interesting question is: Why did he fail in **3460 B.C.**? The equally interesting answer is: It was a matter of timing.

A well-known text recorded a conversation between Marduk and his father, Enki, in which a disheartened Marduk asked his father what he had failed to learn. What he failed to do was to take into account the fact that the time then—the Celestial Time—was **the Age of the Bull, the Age of Enlil.**

Among the thousands of inscribed tablets unearthed in the ancient Near East, quite a number provided information regarding the month associated with a particular deity. In a complex calendar begun in Nippur in **3760 B.C.**, the first month, *Nissanu,* was the EZEN (festival time) for Anu and Enlil (in a leap year with a thirteenth lunar month, the honor was split between the two). The list of "honorees" changed as time went by, as did the composition of the membership of the supreme Pantheon of Twelve. The month associations also changed locally, not

only in various lands but sometimes to recognize the city god. We know, for example, that the planet we call Venus was initially associated with Ninmah and later on with Inanna/Ishtar.

Though such changes make difficult the identifications of who was linked celestially to what, some zodiacal associations can be clearly inferred from texts or drawings. Enki (called at first E.A, "He whose home is water") was clearly associated with the Water Bearer "Aquarius" (fig. 11), and initially if not permanently also with the Fishes, "Pisces." The constellation that was named The Twins, "Gemini," without doubt was so named in honor of the only known divine twins born on Earth—Nannar/Sin's children Utu/Shamash and Inanna/Ishtar. The feminine constellation of "Virgo" (the "Maiden" rather than the inaccurate "Virgin") that, like the planet Venus, was probably named at first in honor of Ninmah, was renamed AB.SIN, "Whose father is Sin," which could be correct only for Inanna/Ishtar. The Archer or Defender, "Sagittarius," matched the numerous texts and hymns extolling Ninurta as the Divine Archer, his father's warrior and defender. Sippar, the city of Utu/Shamash, no longer the site of a spaceport after the Deluge, was considered in Sumerian times to be the center of Law and Justice, and the god was deemed (even by the later Babylonians) as the Chief Justice of the land; it is certain that the Scales of Justice, "Libra," represented his constellation.

Figure 11

And then there were the nicknames comparing the prowess, strength, or characteristics of a god with an animal held in awe; Enlil's, as text after text reiterated, was the *Bull*. It was depicted on cylinder seals, on tablets dealing with astronomy, and in art. Some of the most beautiful art objects discovered in the Royal Tombs of Ur were bull heads sculpted in bronze, silver, and gold, adorned with semiprecious stones. Without doubt, the constellation of the Bull—Taurus—honored and symbolized Enlil. Its name, GUD.ANNA, meant "The Bull of Heaven," and texts dealing with an actual "Bull of Heaven" linked Enlil and his constellation to one of the most unique places on Earth.

It was a place that was called *The Landing Place*—and it is there that one of the most amazing structures on Earth, including a stone tower that reaches to the heavens, still stands.

Many texts from antiquity, including the Hebrew Bible, describe or refer to the unique forest of tall and great cedar trees in Lebanon. In ancient times it extended for miles, surrounding the unique place—a *vast stone platform built by the gods as their first space-related site on Earth,* before their centers and real spaceport were established. It was, Sumerian texts attested, the only structure that had survived the Deluge, and could thus serve right after the Deluge as a base of operations for the Anunnaki; from it they revived the ravished lands with crops and domesticated animals. The place, called the "Landing Place" in the *Epic of Gilgamesh,* was that king's destination in his search for immortality; we learn from the epic tale that it was there, in the sacred cedar forest, that Enlil kept the GUD.ANNA—the "Bull of Heaven," the symbol of Enlil's Age of the Bull.

And what happened then in the sacred forest had a bearing on the course of the affairs of gods and men.

The journey to the Cedar Forest and its Landing Place, we learn from the epic tale, began in Uruk, the city that Anu granted as a present to his great-granddaughter Inanna (a name that meant "Beloved of Anu"). Its king, early in the third millennium B.C., was **Gilgamesh** (fig. 12). He was no ordinary man, for his mother was the goddess Ninsun, a member of Enlil's family. That made Gilgamesh not a mere *demi*-god, but one who was *"two-thirds* divine." As he got older and began

Figure 12

to contemplate matters of life and death, it occurred to him that being two-thirds divine ought to make a difference; why should he "peer over the wall" like an ordinary mortal? he asked his mother. She agreed with him but explained to him that the apparent immortality of the gods was in reality longevity due to the long orbital period of their planet. To attain such longevity he had to join the gods on Nibiru; and to do that, he had to go to the place where the rocket ships ascend and descend.

Though warned of the journey's hazards, Gilgamesh was determined to go. If I fail, he said, at least I will be remembered as one who had tried. At his mother's insistence an artificial double, Enkidu (ENKI.DU meant "By Enki Made"), was to be his companion and guardian. Their adventures, told and retold in the epic's twelve tablets and its many ancient renderings, can be followed in our book *The Stairway to Heaven*. There were, in fact, not one but two journeys (fig. 13): one was to the Landing Place in the Cedar Forest, the other to the spaceport in the Sinai Peninsula where—according to Egyptian depictions (fig. 14)—rocket ships were emplaced in underground silos.

In the first journey circa **2860 B.C.**—to the Cedar Forest in Lebanon—the duo were assisted by the god Shamash, the godfather

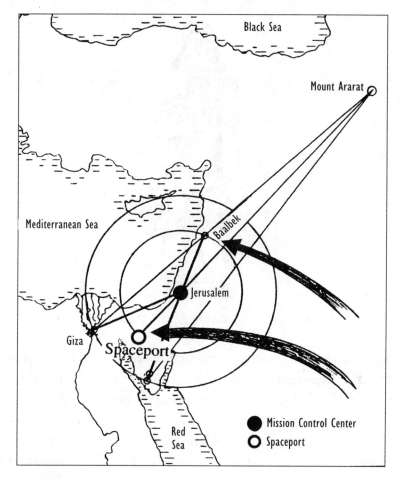

Figure 13

of Gilgamesh, and the going was relatively quick and easy. After they reached the forest *they witnessed during the night the launching of a rocket ship.* This is how Gilgamesh described it:

> *The vision that I saw was wholly awesome!*
> *The heavens shrieked, the earth boomed.*
> *Though daylight was dawning, darkness came.*
> *Lightning flashed, a flame shot up.*
> *The clouds swelled, it rained death!*
> *Then the glow vanished, the fire went out,*
> *And all that had fallen was turned to ashes.*

Figure 14

Awed but undeterred, the next day Gilgamesh and Enkidu discovered the secret entrance that had been used by the Anunnaki, but as soon as they entered it, they were attacked by a robotlike guardian who was armed with death beams and a revolving fire. They managed to destroy the monster and relaxed by a brook thinking that their way in was clear. But when they ventured deeper into the Cedar Forest, a new challenger appeared: **the Bull of Heaven.**

Unfortunately, the sixth tablet of the epic is too damaged for the lines describing the creature and the battle with it to be completely legible. The legible portions do make it clear that the two comrades ran for their lives, pursued by the Bull of Heaven all the way back to Uruk; it was there that Enkidu managed to slay it. The text becomes legible where the boastful Gilgamesh, who cut off the bull's thigh, "called the craftsmen, the armorers, the artisans" of Uruk to admire the bull's horns. The text suggests that they were *artificially made*—"each is cast from thirty minas of lapis, the coating on each is two fingers thick."

Until another tablet with the illegible lines is discovered, we shall not know for sure whether Enlil's celestial symbol in the cedar forest was a specially selected living bull decorated and embellished with gold

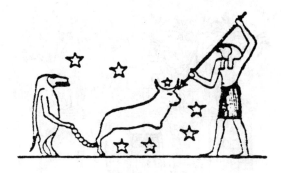

Figure 15

and precious stones or a robotic creature, an artificial monster. What we do know for certain is that upon its slaying, "Ishtar, in her abode, set up a wail" all the way to Anu in the heavens. The matter was so serious that Anu, Enlil, Enki, and Shamash formed a divine council to judge the comrades (only Enkidu ended up being punished) and to consider the slaying's consequences.

The ambitious Inanna/Ishtar had indeed reason to raise a wail: the invincibility of Enlil's Age had been pierced, and the Age itself was symbolically shortened by the cutting off of the bull's thigh. We know from Egyptian sources, including pictorial depictions in astronomical papyri (fig. 15), that the slaying's symbolism was not lost on Marduk: it was taken to mean that in the heavens, too, the Age of Enlil had been cut short.

Marduk's attempt to establish an alternative space facility was not taken lightly by the Enlilites; the evidence suggests that Enlil and Ninurta were preoccupied with establishing their own alternative space facility on the other side of the Earth, in the Americas, near the post-Diluvial sources of gold.

This absence, together with the Bull of Heaven incident, ushered in a period of instability and confusion in their Mesopotamian heartland, subjecting it to incursions from neighboring lands. People called Gutians, then the Elamites, came from the East; Semitic-speaking peoples came from the West. But while the Easterners worshipped the same Enlilite gods as the Sumerians, the *Amurru* ("Westerners") were differ-

ent. Along the shores of the "Upper Sea" (the Mediterranean), in the
lands of the Canaanites, the people were beholden to the Enki'ite gods
of Egypt.

Therein lay the seeds—perhaps to this day—of Holy Wars undertaken *"In the Name of God,"* except that different peoples had different
national gods . . .

It was Inanna who came up with a brilliant idea; it can be described
as "if you can't fight them, invite them in." One day, as she was roaming the skies in her Sky Chamber—it happened circa **2360 B.C.**—she
landed in a garden next to a sleeping man who had caught her fancy.
She liked the sex; she liked the man. He was a Westerner, speaking a
Semitic language. As he wrote later in his memoirs, he knew not who
his father was but knew that his mother was an *Entu,* a god's priestess,
who put him in a reed basket that was carried by the river's flowing
waters to a garden tended by Akki the Irrigator, who raised him as a
son.

The possibility that the strong and handsome man could have been
a god's castoff son was enough for Inanna to recommend to the other
gods that the next king of the land should be this Amurru. When they
agreed, she granted him the epithet-name *Sharru-kin,* the old cherished
title of Sumerian kings. Not stemming from the previous recognized
royal Sumerian lineages, he could not ascend the throne in any one of
the olden capitals, and a brand-new city was established to serve as his
capital. It was called *Aggade*—"Union City." Our textbooks call this
king Sargon of Akkad and his Semitic language Akkadian. His kingdom, which added northern and northwestern provinces to ancient
Sumer, was called *Sumer & Akkad.*

Sargon lost little time in carrying out the mission for which he
was selected—to bring the "rebel lands" under control. Hymns to
Inanna—henceforth known by the Akkadian name *Ishtar*—had her
tell Sargon that he would be remembered "by the destruction of the
rebel land, massacring its people, making its rivers run with blood."
Sargon's military expeditions were recorded and glorified in his
own royal annals; his achievements were summarized in the *Sargon
Chronicle* thus:

Sharru-kin, king of Aggade,
Rose to power in the era of Ishtar.
He left neither rival nor opponent.
He spread his terror-inspiring awe in all the lands.
He crossed the sea in the east,
He conquered the country of the west
in its full extent.

The boast implies that the sacred space-related site, the Landing Place deep in the "country of the west," was captured and held on behalf of Inanna/Ishtar—but not without opposition. Even texts written in glorification of Sargon state that "in his old age all the provinces revolted against him." Counterannals, recording the events as viewed from Marduk's side, reveal that Marduk led a punishing counteroffensive:

On account of the sacrilege Sargon committed,
the great god Marduk became enraged . . .
From east to west he alienated the people from Sargon,
and punished him with an affliction of being without rest.

Sargon's territorial reach, it needs to be noted, included only one of the four post-Diluvial space-related sites—only the Landing Place in the Cedar Forest (see Fig. 3). Sargon was briefly succeeded on the throne of Sumer & Akkad by two sons, but his true successor in spirit and deed was a grandson named Naram-Sin. The name meant "Sin's favorite," but the annals and inscriptions concerning his reign and military campaigns show that he was in fact Ishtar's favorite. Texts and depictions record that Ishtar encouraged the king to seek grandeur and greatness by ceaseless conquest and destruction of her enemies, actively assisting him on the battlefields. Depictions of her, which used to show her as an enticing goddess of love, now showed her as a goddess of war, bristling with weapons (fig. 16).

It was warfare not without a plan—a plan to counter Marduk's ambitions by capturing *all* the space-related sites on behalf of Inanna/Ishtar. The lists of cities captured or subdued by Naram-Sin indicate

Figure 16

that he not only reached the Mediterranean Sea—assuring control of the Landing Place—but also turned southward to invade Egypt. Such an incursion into the Enki'ite domains was unprecedented, and it could take place, a careful reading of the records reveals, because Inanna/Ishtar had formed an unholy alliance with Nergal, Marduk's brother who espoused Inanna's sister. The thrust into Egypt also required entering and crossing the neutral Sacred Region in the Sinai Peninsula, where the spaceport was located—another breach of the olden Peace Treaty. Boastful, Naram-Sin gave himself the title "King of the four regions" . . .

We can hear the protests of Enki. We can read texts that record Marduk's warnings. It was all more than even the Enlilite leadership could condone. A long text known as *The Curse of Aggade,* which tells the story of the Akkadian dynasty, clearly states that its end came about "after the frowning of the forehead of Enlil." And so the "word of Ekur"—the decision of Enlil from his temple in Nippur—was to put an end to it: "The word of the Ekur was upon Aggade" to be destroyed and wiped off the face of the Earth. Naram-Sin's end came circa **2260 B.C.**; texts from that time report that troops from the territory in the east, called Gutium, loyal to Ninurta, were the instrument of divine wrath; Aggade was never rebuilt, never resettled; that royal city, indeed, has never been found.

* * *

The saga of Gilgamesh at the start of the third millennium B.C., and the military forays of the Akkadian kings near the end of that millennium, provide a clear background for that millennium's events: the targets were the space-related sites—by Gilgamesh to attain the gods' longevity, by the kings beholden to Ishtar to attain supremacy.

Without doubt, it was Marduk's "Tower of Babel" attempt that placed the control of the space-related sites at the center of the affairs of gods and men; and as we shall see, that centrality dominated much (if not most) of what took place later.

The Akkadian phase of the War and Peace on Earth was not without celestial or "messianic" aspects.

In his chronicles, Sargon's titles followed the customary honorific "Overseer of Ishtar, king of Kish, great Ensi of Enlil," but he also called himself **"anointed priest of Anu."** It was the first time that being divinely *anointed*—which is what "Messiah" literally means—appears in ancient inscriptions.

Marduk, in his pronouncements, warned of coming upheavals and cosmic phenomena:

> *The day shall be turned into darkness,*
> *the flow of river waters shall be disarrayed,*
> *the lands shall be laid to waste,*
> *the people will be made to perish.*

Looking back, recalling similar biblical prophecies, it is clear that on the eve of the twenty-first century B.C., gods and men expected a coming Apocalyptic Time.

3

EGYPTIAN PROPHECIES, HUMAN DESTINIES

In the annals of Man on Earth, the twenty-first century B.C. saw in the ancient Near East one of civilization's most glorious chapters, known as the Ur III period. It was at the same time the most difficult and crushing one, for it witnessed the end of Sumer in a deathly nuclear cloud. And after that, nothing was the same.

Those momentous events, as we shall see, were also the root of the messianic manifestations that centered on Jerusalem when B.C. turned to A.D. some twenty-one centuries later.

The historic events of that memorable century—as all events in history—had their roots in what had taken place before. Of that, the year **2160 B.C.** is a date worth remembering. The annals of Sumer & Akkad from that time record a major policy shift by the Enlilite gods. In Egypt, the date marked the beginning of changes of political-religious significance, and what occurred in both zones coincided with a new phase in Marduk's campaign to attain supremacy. Indeed, it was Marduk's chess-like strategy maneuvers and geographic movements from one place to another that controlled the agenda of the era's "divine chess game." His moves and movements began with a departure from Egypt, to become (in Egyptian eyes) **Amon** (also written *Amun* or *Amen*), ***The Unseen.***

The date of 2160 B.C. is considered by Egyptologists to mark the beginning of what is designated the First Intermediate Period—a chaotic interval between the end of the Old Kingdom and the dynastic start of the Middle Kingdom. During the thousand years of the Old Kingdom, when the religious-political capital was Memphis in Middle Egypt, the Egyptians worshipped the Ptah pantheon, erecting monumental temples to him, to his son Ra, and to their divine successors. The famed inscriptions of the Memphite Pharaohs glorified the gods and promised an Afterlife for the kings. Reigning as the gods' surrogates, those Pharaohs wore the double crown of Upper (southern) and Lower (northern) Egypt, signifying not just the administrative but also the religious unification of the Two Lands, unification attained when Horus defeated Seth in their struggle for the Ptah/Ra legacy. And then, in 2160 B.C., that unity and religious certainty came crashing down.

The turmoil saw a breakup of the Union, abandonment of the capital, attacks from the south by Theban princes to gain control, foreign incursions, desecration of temples, a collapse of law and order, and droughts, famines, and food riots. Those conditions are recalled in a papyrus known as the *Admonitions of Ipu-Wer,* a long hieroglyphic text that consists of several sections in which it gives an account of calamities and tribulations, blames an unholy enemy for religious wrongdoing and social evils, and calls on the people to repent and resume the religious rites. A prophetic section describing the *coming of a Redeemer,* and another that extolls the ideal times that will follow, conclude the papyrus.

At its start the text describes the breakdown of law and order and of a functioning society—a situation in which "the doorkeepers go and plunder, the wash-man refuses to carry his load . . . robbery is everywhere . . . a man regards his son as an enemy." Though the Nile is in flooding and irrigates the land, "no one ploughs . . . grain has perished . . . the storehouses are bare . . . dust is throughout the land . . . the desert spreads . . . women are dried up, no one can conceive . . . the dead are just thrown into the river . . . the river is blood." The roads are unsafe, trade has ceased, the provinces of Upper Egypt are no longer taxed; "there is civil war . . . barbarians from elsewhere have come to Egypt . . . all is in ruin."

Some Egyptologists believe that at the core of those events lay a simple rivalry for wealth and power, an attempt (successful in the end) by Theban princes from the south to control and rule the whole country. Lately, studies have associated the collapse of the Old Kingdom with a "climate change" that undermined a society founded on agriculture, caused food shortages and food riots, social upheaval, and collapse of authority. But little attention has been paid to a major and perhaps the most important change: in the texts, in the hymns, in the honorific names of temples, it was no longer Ra but from then on Ra-*Amon,* or simply *Amon,* who was henceforth worshipped; Ra became *Amon*—Ra the Unseen—for he was gone from Egypt.

It was indeed a religious change that caused the political and societal breakdown, the unidentified Ipu-Wer wrote; we believe that the change was Ra's becoming Amon. The upheaval began with a collapse of religious observances and manifested itself in the defiling and abandonment of temples, where "the Place of Secrets has been laid bare, the writings of the august enclosure have been scattered, common men tear them up in the streets . . . magic is exposed, it is in the sight of him who knows it not." The sacred symbol of the gods worn on the king's crown, the Uraeus (the Divine Serpent), "is rebelled against . . . religious dates are disturbed . . . priests are carried off wrongfully."

After calling on the people to repent, "to offer incense in the temples . . . to keep the offerings to the gods," the papyrus called on the repenters to *be baptized*—to "remember to immerse." Then the words of the papyrus turn prophetic: in a passage that even Egyptologists call "truly messianic," the Admonitions speak of "a time that shall come" when an unnamed *Savior—a "god-king"*—shall appear. Starting with a small following, of him "men shall say:

> *He brings coolness upon the heart,*
> *He is a shepherd of all men.*
> *Though his herds may be small,*
> *He will spend the days caring for them . . .*
> *Then he would smite down evil,*
> *He would stretch forth his arm against it."*

"People will be asking: 'Where is he today? Is he then sleeping? Why is his power not seen?'" Ipu-Wer wrote, and answered, "Behold, the glory thereof cannot be seen, [but] Authority, Perception and Justice are with him."

Those ideal times, Ipu-Wer stated in his prophecy, will be preceded by their own messianic birth pangs: "Confusion will set throughout the land, in tumultuous noise one will kill the other, the many will kill the few." People will ask: "Does the Shepherd desire death?" No, he answered, "it is the land that commands death," but after years of strife, righteousness and proper worship will prevail. This, the papyrus concluded, was "What Ipu-Wer said when he responded to the majesty of the All-Lord."

If not just the description of events and the messianic prophecies, but also the choice of wording in that ancient Egyptian papyrus seem astounding, there is more to come. Scholars are aware of the existence of another prophetic/messianic text that reached us from ancient Egypt but believe that it was really composed after the events and only pretends to be prophetic by dating itself to an earlier time. To be specific, while the text purports to relate prophecies made at the time of Sneferu, a Fourth Dynasty pharaoh (circa 2600 B.C.), Egyptologists believe that it was actually written in the time of Amenemhet I of the Twelfth Dynasty (circa 2000 B.C.)—*after* the events that it pretends to prophesy. Even so, the "prophecies" serve to confirm those prior occurrences; and many details and the very wording of the predictions can best be described as chilling.

The prophecies are purported to be told to King Sneferu by a "great seer-priest" named Nefer-Rohu, "a man of rank, a scribe competent with his fingers." Summoned to the king to foretell the future, Nefer-Rohu "stretched forth his hand for the box of writing equipment, he drew forth a scroll of papyrus," and then began to write what he was envisioning, in a Nostradamus-like manner:

> *Behold, there is something about which men speak;*
> *It is terrifying . . .*
> *What will be done was never done before.*

The Earth is completely perished.
The land is damaged, no remainder exists.
There is no sunshine that people could see,
No one can live with the covering clouds,
The south wind opposes the north wind.
The rivers of Egypt are empty . . .
Ra must begin the foundations of the Earth again.

Before Ra can restore the "Foundations of the Earth," there will be invasions, wars, bloodshed. Then a new era of peace, tranquillity, and justice will follow. It will be brought by what we have come to call a Savior, a Messiah:

Then it is that a sovereign will come—
Ameni *("The Unknown"),*
The Triumphant he will be called.
The Son-Man will be his name forever and ever . . .
Wrongdoing will be driven out;
Justice in its place will come;
The people of his time rejoice.

It is astounding to find such messianic prophecies of apocalyptic times and the end of Wrongdoing that will be followed by the coming—the return—of peace and justice, in papyrus texts written some 4,200 years ago; it is chilling to find in them terminology that is familiar from the New Testament, about an Unknown, the Triumphant Savior, the "Son-Man."

It is, as we shall see, a link in millennia-spanning interconnected events.

In Sumer, a period of chaos, occupation by foreign troops, defiling of temples, and confusion as to where the capital should be and who should be king followed the end of the Sargonic Era of Ishtar in **2260 B.C.**

For a while, the only safe haven in the land was Ninurta's "cult center" Lagash, from which the Gutian foreign troops were kept out.

Mindful of Marduk's unrelenting ambitions, Ninurta decided to reassert his right to the Rank of Fifty by instructing the then king of Lagash, Gudea, to erect for him in the city's *Girsu* (the sacred precinct) a new and different temple. Ninurta—here called NIN.GIRSU, "Lord of the Girsu"—already had a temple there, as well as a special enclosure for his "Divine Black Bird," or flying machine. Yet the building of the new temple required special permission from Enlil, which was in time granted. We learn from the inscriptions that the new temple had to have special features linking it to the heavens, enabling certain celestial observations. To that end Ninurta invited to Sumer the god Ningishzidda ("Thoth" in Egypt), the Divine Architect and Keeper of the Secrets of the Giza pyramids. The fact that Ningishzidda/Thoth was the brother whom Marduk forced into exile circa 3100 B.C. was certainly not lost on all concerned . . .

The amazing circumstances surrounding the announcement, planning, construction, and dedication of the E.NINNU ("House/ Temple of Fifty") are told in great detail in Gudea's inscriptions; they were unearthed in the ruins of Lagash (a site now called Tello) and are quoted at length in The Earth Chronicles books. What emerges from that detailed record (inscribed on two clay cylinders in clear Sumerian cuneiform script, fig. 17) is the fact that from announcement to dedication, every step and every detail of the new temple was dictated by celestial aspects.

Those special celestial aspects had to do with the very timing of the temple's building: It was the time, as the inscriptions' opening lines declare, when "in the heavens destinies on Earth were determined":

> *At the time when in heaven*
> *destinies on Earth were determined,*
> *"Lagash shall lift its head heavenwards*
> *in accordance with the Great Tablet of Destinies"*
> *Enlil in favor of Ninurta decided.*

That special time when the destinies on Earth are determined in the heavens was what we have called Celestial Time, the Zodiacal Clock.

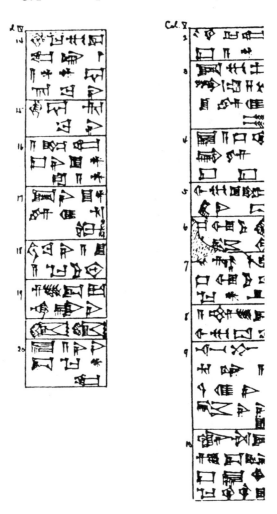

Figure 17

That such determining was linked to Equinox Day becomes evident
from the rest of Gudea's tale, as well as from Thoth's Egyptian name
Tehuti, The Balancer (of day and night) who "Draws the Cord" for orienting a new temple. Such celestial considerations continued to dominate the Eninnu project from start to finish.

Gudea's tale begins with a vision-dream that reads like an episode
from *The Twilight Zone* TV series, for while the several gods featured
in it were gone when he awoke, the various objects they showed him in
the dream remained physically lying by his side!

Figure 18

In that vision-dream (the first of several) the god Ninurta appeared at sunrise, and the Sun was aligned with the planet Jupiter. The god spoke and informed Gudea that he was chosen to build a new temple. Next the goddess Nisaba appeared; she was wearing the image of a temple structure on her head; the goddess was holding a tablet on which the starry heavens were depicted, and with a stylus she kept pointing to the "favorable celestial constellation." A third god, Ningishzidda (i.e., Thoth), held a tablet of lapis lazuli on which a structural plan was drawn; he also held a clay brick, a mold for brickmaking, and a builder's carrying basket. When Gudea awoke, the three gods were gone, but the architectural tablet was on his lap (fig. 18) and the brick and its mold were at his feet!

Gudea needed the help of an oracle goddess and two more vision-dreams to understand the meaning of it all. In the third vision-dream he was shown a holographic-like animated demonstration of the temple's building, starting with the initial alignment with the indicated celestial point, the laying of foundations, the molding of bricks—the construction all the way up, step by step. Both the start of construction and the final dedication ceremony were to be held on sig-

nals from the gods on specific days; both fell on New Year's Day, which meant the day of the Spring Equinox.

The temple "raised its head" in the customary seven stages, but—unusually for the flat-topped Sumerian ziggurats—its head had to be pointed, "shaped like a horn"—Gudea had to emplace upon the temple's top a capstone! Its shape is not described, but in all probabilty (and judging by the image on Nisaba's head), it was in the shape of a pyramidion—in the manner of capstones on Egyptian pyramids (fig. 19). Moreover, rather than leave the brickwork exposed, as was customary, Gudea was required to encase the structure with a casing of reddish stones, increasing its similarity to an Egyptian pyramid. "The outside view of the temple was like that of a mountain set in place."

That raising a structure with the appearance of an Egyptian pyramid had a purpose becomes clear from Ninurta's own words. The new temple, he told Gudea, "will be seen from afar; its awe-inspiring glance will reach the heavens; the adoration of my temple shall extend to all the lands, its heavenly name will be proclaimed in countries from the ends of the Earth—

> *In Magan and Meluhha it will cause people [to say]:*
> *Ningirsu [the "Lord of the Girsu"],*
> *the Great Hero from the Lands of Enlil,*
> *is a god who has no equal;*
> *He is the lord of all the Earth.*

Figure 19

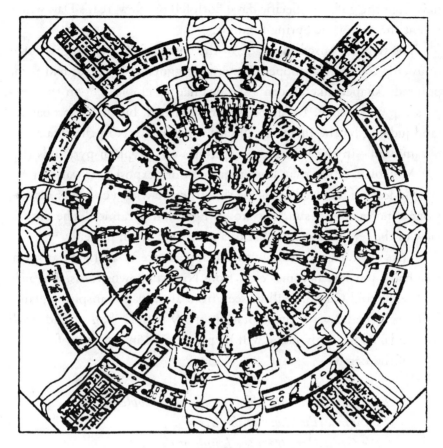

Figure 20

Magan and Meluhha were the Sumerian names for Egypt and Nubia, the Two Lands of the gods of Egypt. The purpose of the Eninnu was to establish, even there, in Marduk's lands, Ninurta's unequaled Lordship: "A god who has no equal, the Lord of all the Earth."

Proclaiming Ninurta's (rather than Marduk's) supremacy required special features in the Eninnu. The ziggurat's entrance had to face the Sun precisely in the east, rather than the customary northeast. In the temple's topmost level Gudea had to erect a SHU.GA.LAM—"where the shining is announced, the place of the aperture, the place of determining," from which Ninurta/Ningirsu could see "the Repetition over the lands." It was a circular chamber with twelve positions, each marked

with a zodiacal symbol, with an aperture for observing the skies—*an ancient planetarium aligned to the zodiacal constellations!*

In the temple's forecourt, linked to an avenue that faced sunrise, Gudea had to erect two stone circles, one with six and the other with seven stone pillars, for observing the skies. Since only one avenue is mentioned, one assumes that the circles were one within the other. As one studies each phrase, terminology, and structural detail, it becomes evident that what was built in Lagash with the help of Ningishzidda/Thoth was a complex yet practical stone observatory, one part of which, devoted entirely to the zodiacs, reminds one of the similar one found in Denderah, Egypt (fig. 20), and the other, geared to observing celestial risings and setting, **a virtual Stonehenge on the banks of the Euphrates River!**

Like Stonehenge in the British Isles (fig. 21), the one built in Lagash provided stone markers for solar observations of solstices and equinoxes, but the prime outside feature was the creation of a sight line from a center stone, continued between two stone pillars, then on down an avenue to another stone. Such a sight line, precisely oriented when planned,

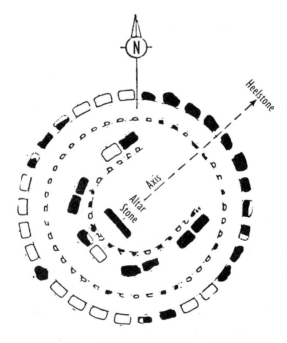

Figure 21

enabled determining at the moment of heliacal rising in which zodiacal constellation the Sun was appearing. *And that—determining the zodiacal age through precise observation—was the prime objective of the whole complex facility.*

In Stonehenge, that sight line ran (and still runs) from the stone column called the Altar Stone in the center, through two stone columns identified as Sarsen Stones numbers 1 and 30, then down the Avenue to the so-called Heel Stone (see fig. 6). It is generally agreed that the Stonehenge with the double Bluestone Circle and the Heel Stone of what is designated Stonehenge II dates to between 2200 to 2100 B.C. *That was also the time—perhaps more accurately, in 2160 B.C.— when the "Stonehenge on the Euphrates" was built.*

And that was no chance coincidence. Like those two zodiacal observatories, other stone observatories proliferated at the same time in other places on Earth—at various sites in Europe, in South America, on the Golan Heights northeast of Israel, even in faraway China (where archaeologists discovered in the Shanzi province a stone circle with thirteen pillars aligned to the zodiac and dating to 2100 B.C.). They were all deliberate countermoves by Ninurta and Ningishzidda to Marduk's Divine Chess Game: **to show Mankind that the zodiacal age was still the Age of the Bull.**

Various texts from that time, including an autobiographical text by Marduk and a longer text known as the *Erra Epos,* shed light on Marduk's wanderings away from Egypt, making him there the Hidden One. They also reveal that his demands and actions assumed an urgency and ferocity because of a conviction that his time for supremacy has come. The Heavens bespeak *my* glory as Lord, was his claim. Why? Because, he announced, the Age of the Bull, the Age of Enlil, was over; *the Age of the Ram, Marduk's zodiacal age, has arrived.* It was, just as Ninurta had told Gudea, the time when in the heavens destinies on Earth were determined.

The zodiacal ages, it will be recalled, were caused by the phenomenon of Precession, the retardation in Earth's orbit around the Sun. The retardation accumulates to 1 degree (out of 360) in seventy-two years;

an arbitrary division of the grand circle into 12 segments of 30 degrees each means that mathematically the zodiacal calendar shifts from one Age to another every 2,160 years. Since the Deluge occurred, according to Sumerian texts, in the Age of the Lion, our Zodiacal Clock can start circa **10,860 B.C.**

An astounding timetable emerges if, in this *mathematically determined* 2,160-year zodiacal calendar, the starting point of 10,800 B.C. rather than 10,860 B.C. is chosen:

> 10,800 to 8640—Age of the Lion (Leo)
>
> 8640 to 6480—Age of the Crab (Cancer)
>
> 6480 to 4320—Age of the Twins (Gemini)
>
> 4320 to 2160—Age of the Bull (Taurus)
>
> 2160 to 0—Age of the Ram (Aries)

Setting aside the neat end result that *synchronizes with the Christian Era,* one must wonder whether it was mere coincidence that the Ishtar-Ninurta era petered out in or about 2160 B.C., just when, according to the above zodiacal calendar, the Age of the Bull, Enlil's Age, was also ending? Probably not; certainly Marduk did not think so. The available evidence suggests that he was sure that according to Celestial Time, *his* time for supremacy, his Age, has arrived. (Modern studies of Mesopotamian astronomy indeed confirm that the zodiacal circle was divided there into 12 houses of 30 degrees each—a mathematical rather than an observational division.)

The various texts we have mentioned indicate that as he moved about, Marduk made another foray into the Enlilite heartland, arriving back in Babylon with a retinue of followers. Rather than resort to armed conflict, the Enlilites enlisted Marduk's brother Nergal (whose spouse was a granddaughter of Enlil) to come to Babylon from southern Africa and persuade his brother to leave. In his memoirs, known as *The Erra Epos,* Nergal reported that Marduk's chief argument was that his time, the Age of the Ram, had arrived. But Nergal counterargued that it is not really so: the Heliacal Rising, he told Marduk, still occurs in the constellation of the Bull!

Enraged, Marduk questioned the accuracy of the observations. What happened to the precise and reliable instruments, from before the Deluge, that were installed in your Lower World domain? he demanded to know from Nergal. Nergal explained that they were destroyed by the Deluge. Come, see for yourself which constellation is seen at sunrise on the appointed day, he urged Marduk. Whether Marduk went to Lagash to make the observation we do not know, but he did realize the cause of the discrepancy:

While mathematically the ages changed every 2,160 years, in reality, observationally, they did not. The zodiacal constellations, in which stars were grouped arbitrarily, were not of equal size. Some occupied a larger arc of the heavens, some smaller; and as it happened, the constellation of the Ram was one of the smaller ones, squeezed between the larger Taurus and Pisces (fig. 22). Celestially, the constellation Taurus, occupying more than 30 degrees of the heavenly arc, lingers on for at least another two centuries beyond its mathematical length.

In the twenty-first century B.C., Celestial Time and Messianic Time failed to coincide.

Go away peacefully and come back when the heavens will declare your Age, Nergal told Marduk. Yielding to his fate, Marduk did leave, but did not go too far away.

And with him, as emissary, spokesman, and herald, was his son, whose mother was an Earthling woman.

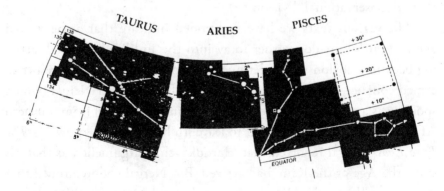

Figure 22

4

OF GODS AND DEMIGODS

The decision of Marduk to stay in or near the contested lands and to involve his son in the struggle for Mankind's allegiance persuaded the Enlilites to return Sumer's central capital to Ur, the cult center of Nannar (Su-en or *Sin* in Akkadian). It was the third time that Ur was chosen to serve in that capacity—hence the designation "Ur III" for that period.

The move linked the affairs of the contending gods to the biblical tale—and role—of Abraham, and the intertwined relationship changed Religion to this day.

Among the many reasons for the choice of Nannar/Sin as the Enlilite champion was the realization that contending with Marduk has expanded beyond the affairs of the gods alone and has become a contest for the minds and hearts of the people—of the very Earthlings whom the gods had created, who now made up the armies that went to war on behalf of their creators . . .

Unlike other Enlilites, Nannar/Sin was not a combatant in the Wars of the Gods; his selection was meant to signal to people everywhere, even in the "rebel lands," that under his leadership an era of peace and prosperity would begin. He and his spouse **Ningal** (fig. 23) were greatly beloved by the people of Sumer, and Ur itself spelled prosperity and well-being; its very name, which meant "urban, domesticated

Figure 23

place," came to mean not just "city" but The City—the urban jewel of the ancient lands.

Nannar/Sin's temple there, a skyscraping ziggurat, rose in stages within a walled sacred precinct where a variety of structures served as the gods' abode and the residences and functional buildings of a legion of priests, officials, and servants who attended to the divine couple's needs and arranged the religious observances by king and people. Beyond those walls there extended a magnificent city with two harbors and canals linking it to the Euphrates River (fig. 24), a great city with the king's palace, administrative buildings (including for scribes and recordkeeping as well as for tax collecting), multilevel private dwellings, workshops, schools, merchants' warehouses, and stalls—all in wide streets where, at many intersections, prayer shrines open to all travelers were built. The majestic ziggurat with its monumental stairways (Reconstruction, fig. 25), though long in ruins, still dominates the landscape even after more than 4,000 years.

But there was another compelling reason. Unlike the contending Ninurta and Marduk, who were both "immigrants" to Earth from Nibiru, Nannar/Sin was born on Earth. He was not only Enlil's Firstborn on Earth—he was the first of the first generation of gods to be born on Earth. His children, the twins Utu/Shamash and Inanna/

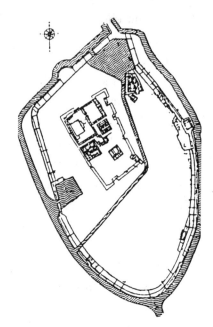

Figure 24

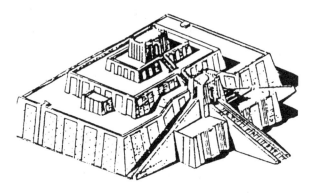

Figure 25

Ishtar, and their sister Ereshkigal, who belonged to the gods' third generation, were all born on Earth. They were gods, but they were also
Earth's natives. All that was without doubt taken into consideration in
the coming struggle for the loyalties of the people.

The choice of a new king, to restart afresh kingship in and from
Sumer, was also carefully made. Gone was the free hand given to (or

assumed by) Inanna/Ishtar, who chose Sargon the Akkadian to start a new dynasty because she liked his lovemaking. The new king, named Ur-Nammu ("The joy of Ur"), was carefully selected by Enlil and approved by Anu, and he was no mere Earthling: He was a son—"the beloved son"—of the goddess Ninsun; she had been, the reader will recall, the mother of Gilgamesh. Since this divine genealogy was restated in numerous inscriptions during Ur-Nammu's reign, in the presence of Nannar and other gods, one must assume that the claim was factual. This made Ur-Nammu not only a demigod but—as was the case of Gilgamesh—"two-thirds divine." Indeed, the claim that the king's mother was the goddess Ninsun placed Ur-Nammu in the very same status as that of Gilgamesh, whose exploits were well remembered and whose name remained revered. The choice was thus a signal, to friends and foes alike, that the glorious days under the unchallenged authority of Enlil and his clan are back.

All that was important, perhaps even crucial, because Marduk had his own attributes of appeal to the masses of Mankind. That special appeal to the Earthlings was the fact that Marduk's deputy and chief campaigner was his son **Nabu**—who not only was born on Earth, but *was born to a mother who herself was an Earthling,* for long ago—indeed, in the days before the Deluge—Marduk broke all traditions and taboos and took an Earthling woman to be his official wife.

That young Anunnaki took Earthling females as wives should not come as a shocking surprise, for it is recorded in the Bible for all to read. What is little known even to scholars, because the information is found in ignored texts and has to be verified from complex God Lists, is the fact that it was Marduk who set the example that the "Sons of the gods" followed:

> *And it came to pass*
> *when the Earthlings began to increase in number*
> *upon the Earth*
> *and daughters were born unto them—*
> *That the sons of the* Elohim

saw the daughters of The Adam
that they were compatible;
And they took unto themselves wives
of whichever they chose.

GENESIS 6:1–2

The biblical explanation of the reasons for the Great Flood in the first eight enigmatic verses of chapter 6 of Genesis clearly points to the intermarriage and its resulting offspring as the cause of the divine wrath:

The Nefilim *were on the Earth*
in those days and thereafter too,
When the sons of the Elohim
came unto the daughters of The Adam
and had children by them.

(My readers may recall that it was my question, as a schoolboy, of why *Nefilim*—which literally means "Those who have come down," who descended [from heaven to Earth]—was usually translated "giants." It was much later that I realized and suggested that the Hebrew word for "giants," *Anakim,* was actually a rendering of the Sumerian *Anunnaki*.)

The Bible clearly cites such intermarriage—the *"taking as wives"*—between young "sons of the gods" (sons of the *Elohim,* the *Nefilim*) and female Earthlings ("daughters of *The Adam*") as God's reason for seeking Mankind's end by the Deluge: "My spirit shall no longer dwell in Man, for in his flesh they erred ... And God repented that He had fashioned the Adam on Earth, and was distraught, and He said: Let me wipe the Adam that I have created off the face of the Earth."

The Sumerian and Akkadian texts telling the story of the Deluge explained that two gods were involved in that drama: it was Enlil who sought Mankind's destruction by the Deluge, while it was Enki who connived to prevent it by instructing "Noah" to build the salvaging ark. When we delve into the details, we find that Enlil's "I've had it up to here!" anger on one hand, and Enki's counterefforts on the other hand,

were not just a matter of principles. *For it was Enki himself who began to copulate with female Earthlings and have children by them*, and it was Marduk, Enki's son, who led the way to and set the example for actual marriages with them . . .

By the time their Mission Earth was fully operative, the Anunnaki stationed on Earth numbered 600; in addition, 300 who were known as the IGI.GI ("Those who observe and see") manned a planetary Way Station—on Mars!—and the spacecraft shuttling between the two planets. We know that Ninmah, the Anunnaki's chief medical officer, came to Earth at the head of a group of female nurses (fig. 26). It is not stated how many they were or whether there were other females among the Anunnaki, but it is clear that in any event females were few among them. The situation required strict sexual rules and supervision by the elders, so much so that (according to one text) Enki and Ninmah had to act as matchmakers, decreeing who should marry whom.

Enlil, a strict disciplinarian, himself fell victim to the shortage of females and date-raped a young nurse. For that even he, the Commander in Chief on Earth, was punished with exile; the punishment was commuted when he agreed to marry Sud and make her his official consort, **Ninlil.** She remained his sole spouse to the very end.

Enki, on the other hand, is described in numerous texts as a philanderer with female goddesses of all ages, and managing to get away with it. Moreover, once "daughters of The Adam" proliferated, he was not averse to having sexual flings with them, too . . . Sumerian texts extolled

Figure 26

that Adapa, "the wisest of men" who grew up at Enki's household, was taught writing and mathematics by Enki and was the first Earthling to be taken aloft to visit Anu on Nibiru; the texts also reveal that Adapa was a secret son of Enki, mothered by an Earthling female.

Apocryphal texts inform us that when Noah, the biblical hero of the Deluge, was born, much about the baby and the birth caused his father, Lamech, to wonder whether the real father had not been one of the Nefilim. The Bible just states that Noah was a genealogically "perfect" man who "Walked with the Elohim"; Sumerian texts, where the Flood's hero is named Ziusudra, suggest that he was a demigod son of Enki.

It was thus that one day Marduk complained to his mother that while his companions were assigned wives, he was not: "I have no wife, I have no children." And he went on to tell her that he had taken a liking to the daughter of a "high priest, an accomplished musician" (there is reason to believe that he was the chosen man Enmeduranki of Sumerian texts, the parallel of the biblical Enoch). Verifying that the young Earthling female—her name was Tsarpanit—agreed, Marduk's parents gave him the go-ahead.

The marriage produced a son. He was named EN.SAG, "Lofty Lord." But unlike Adapa, who was an Earthling demigod, Marduk's son was included in the Sumerian God Lists, where he was also called "the divine MESH"—a term used (as in GilgaMESH) to denote a demigod. *He was thus the first demigod who was a god.* Later on, when he led the masses of humans in his father's behalf, he was given the epithet-name **Nabu**—The Spokesman, *The Prophet*—for that is what the literal meaning of the word is, as is the meaning of the parallel biblical Hebrew word *Nabih,* translated "prophet."

Nabu was thus the god-son and an Adam-son of ancient scriptures, the one whose very name meant Prophet. As in the Egyptian prophecies earlier quoted, his name and role became linked to the messianic expectations.

And so it was, in the days before the Deluge, that Marduk set an example to the other young unespoused gods: find and marry an Earthling female . . . The breach of the taboo appealed in particular to the Igigi

gods who were away on Mars most of the time, with their principal station on Earth being the Landing Place in the Cedar Mountains. Finding an opportunity—perhaps an invitation to come and celebrate Marduk's wedding—they seized Earthling females and carried them off as wives.

Several extra-biblical books, designated The Apocrypha, such as the *Book of Jubilees,* the *Book of Enoch,* and the *Book of Noah,* record the incident of the intermarriage by the Nefilim and fill in the details. Some two hundred "Watchers" ("Those who observe and see") organized themselves in twenty groups; each group had a named leader. One, called Shamyaza, was in overall command. The instigator of the transgression, "the one who led astray the sons of God and *brought them down to Earth* and led them astray through the Daughters of Man," was named Yeqon . . . It happened, these sources confirmed, during the time of Enoch.

In spite of their efforts to fit the Sumerian sources (that told of rival and contradicting Enlil and Enki) into a monotheistic framework—the belief in only one Almighty God—the compilers of the Hebrew Bible ended that section in chapter 6 of Genesis with a recognition of the factual outcome. Speaking of the offspring of those intermarriages, the Bible makes two admissions: the first, that the intermarrying took place in the days before the Deluge, *"and thereafter too"*; and secondly, that from the offspring "came the *heroes of old, the men of renown.*" The Sumerian texts indicate that post-Diluvial heroic kings were indeed such demigods.

But they were the offspring not only of Enki and his clan: sometimes kings in the Enlilite region were sons of Enlilite gods. For example, *The Sumerian King Lists* clearly state that when kingship began in Uruk (an Enlilite domain), the one chosen for kingship was a MESH, a demigod:

> *Meskiaggasher, a son of Utu,*
> *became high priest and king.*

Utu was of course the god Utu/Shamash, grandson of Enlil. Further down the dynastic line there was the famed Gilgamesh, "two-thirds of him divine," son of the Enlilite goddess Ninsun and fathered by the High

Priest of Uruk, an Earthling. (There were several more rulers down the line, both in Uruk and in Ur, who bore the title "Mesh" or "Mes".)

In Egypt, too, some Pharaohs claimed divine parentage. Many in the 18th and 19th Dynasties adopted theophoric names with a prefix or suffix MSS (rendered Mes, Mose, Meses), meaning "Issue of" this or that god—such as the names *Ah-mes* or *Ra-mses* (RA-MeSeS—"issue of," offspring of, the god Ra). The famed queen Hatshepsut, who though a female seized the title and privileges of a Pharaoh, claimed that right by virtue of being a demigod—the great god Amon, she claimed in inscriptions and depictions in her immense temple at Deir el Bahri, "took the form of his majesty the king," the husband of her queen-mother, "had intercourse with her," and caused Hatshepsut to be born as his semidivine daughter. Canaanite texts included the tale of Keret, a king who was the son of the god El.

An interesting variant on such demigod-as-king practices was the case of Eannatum, a Sumerian king in Ninurta's Lagash during the early "heroic" times. An inscription by the king on a well-known monument of his (the "Stela of the Vultures") attributes his demigod status to *artificial insemination* by Ninurta (the Lord of the Girsu, the sacred precinct), and to help from Inanna/Ishtar and Ninmah (here called by her epithet Ninharsag):

> *The Lord Ningirsu, warrior of Enlil,*
> *implanted the semen of Enlil for Eannatum*
> *in the womb of [. . .].*
> *Inanna accompanied his [birth],*
> *named him "Worthy in the Eanna temple,"*
> *set him on the sacred lap of Ninharsag.*
> *Ninharsag offered him her sacred breast.*
> *Ningirsu rejoiced over Eannatum—*
> *semen implanted in the womb by Ningirsu.*

While the reference to the "semen of Enlil" leaves unclear whether Ninurta/Ningirsu's own semen is here considered "semen of Enlil" because he was Enlil's firstborn, or actually used Enlil's semen for the

Figure 27

insemination (which is doubtful), the inscription clearly claims that Eannatum's mother (whose name is illegible on the stela) was artificially impregnated, so that a demigod was conceived without actual sexual intercourse—**a case of immaculate conception in third millennium B.C. Sumer!**

That the gods were no strangers to artificial insemination is corroborated by Egyptian texts, according to which after Seth killed and dismembered Osiris, the god Thoth extracted semen from the phallus of Osiris and impregnated with it the wife of Osiris, Isis, bringing about the birth of the god Horus. A depiction of the feat shows Thoth and birth goddesses holding the two strands of DNA that were used, and Isis holding the newborn Horus (fig. 27).

Clearly, then, after the Deluge the Enlilites too accepted both the mating with Earthling females and considered the offspring "heroes, men of renown," suitable for kingship.

Royal "bloodlines" of demigods were thus begun.

One of the first tasks of Ur-Nammu was to carry out a moral and religious revival. And for that, too, a former revered and remembered king

PLEASE SEND US THIS CARD TO RECEIVE OUR LATEST CATALOG.

Book in which this card was found _____

❏ Check here if you would like to receive our catalog via e-mail.

Name_____ Company_____

Address_____

City_____ State_____ Zip_____ Country_____

E-mail address_____

Please check the following area(s) of interest to you:

❏ Health	❏ Self-help	❏ Science/Nature	❏ Shamanism
❏ Ancient Mysteries	❏ New Age/Spirituality	❏ Ethnobotany	❏ Martial Arts
❏ Spanish Language	❏ Sexuality/Tantra	❏ Children	❏ Teen

Please send a catalog to my friend:

Name_____ Company_____

Address_____

City_____ State_____ Zip_____ Country_____

Order at 1-800-246-8648 • Fax (802) 767-3726
E-mail: customerservice@InnerTraditions.com • Web site: www.InnerTraditions.com

INNER TRADITIONS
BEAR & COMPANY

Inner Traditions • Bear & Company
P.O. Box 388
Rochester, VT 05767-0388
U.S.A.

was emulated. It was done through the promulgation of a new Code of Laws, laws of moral behavior, laws of justice—of adherence, the Code said, to the laws that Enlil and Nannar and Shamash had wanted the king to enforce and the people to live by.

The nature of the laws, a list of do's and don'ts, can be judged by Ur-Nammu's claim that due to those laws of justice, "the orphan did not fall prey to the wealthy, the widow did not fall prey to the powerful, the man with one sheep was not delivered to the man with one ox . . . justice was established in the land." In that he emulated—sometimes using the exact same phrases—a previous Sumerian king, Urukagina of Lagash, who three hundred years earlier had promulgated a law code by which social, legal, and religious reforms were instituted (among them the establishment of women's safehouses under the patronage of the goddess Bau, Ninurta's spouse). These, it ought to be pointed out, were the very same principles of justice and morality that the biblical prophets demanded of kings and people in the next millennium.

As the era of Ur III began, there was obviously a deliberate attempt to return Sumer (now Sumer & Akkad) to its olden days of glory, prosperity, and morality and peace—the times that preceded the latest confrontation with Marduk.

The inscriptions, the monuments, and the archaeological evidence attest that Ur-Nammu's reign, which began in 2113 B.C., witnessed extensive public works, restoration of river navigation, and the rebuilding and protection of the country's highways: "He made the highways run from the lower lands to the upper lands," an inscription stated. Greater trade and commerce followed. There was a surge in arts, crafts, schools, and other improvements in social and economic life (including the introduction of more accurate weights and measures). Treaties with neighboring rulers to the east and northeast spread the prosperity and well-being. The great gods, especially Enlil and Ninlil, were honored with renovated and magnified temples, and for the first time in Sumer's history, the priesthood of Ur was combined with that of Nippur, leading a religious revival.

All scholars agree that in virtually every way the Ur III period begun by Ur-Nammu attained new heights in the Sumerian civilization.

Figure 28

That conclusion only increased the puzzlement caused by a beautifully crafted box that was uncovered by archaeologists: its inlaid panels, front and back, depicted two contradicting scenes of life in Ur. While one of the panels (now known as the "Peace Panel") depicted banqueting, commerce, and other scenes of civil activities, the other (the "War Panel") depicted a military column of armed and helmeted soldiers and horse-drawn chariots marching to war (fig. 28).

A close examination of the records from that time reveals that indeed while under the leadership of Ur-Nammu Sumer itself flourished, the hostility to the Enlilites by the "rebel lands" increased rather than diminished. The situation apparently demanded action, for accordng to Ur-Nammu's inscriptions Enlil gave him a "divine weapon that heaps up the rebels in piles" with which to attack "the hostile lands, destroy the evil cities and clear them of opposition." Those "rebel lands" and "sinning cities" were west of Sumer, the lands of Marduk's

Amorite followers; there, the "evil"—the hostility against Enlil—was fanned by Nabu, who moved about from city to city proselytizing for Marduk. Enlilite records called him "The Oppressor," of whose influence the "sinning cities" had to be rid.

There is reason to believe that the Peace and War panels actually depicted Ur-Nammu himself—one showing him banqueting and celebrating peace and prosperity, the other in the royal chariot, leading his army to war. His military expeditions took him well beyond Sumer's borders into the western lands. But Ur-Nammu—great reformer, builder, and economic "shepherd" that he was—failed as a military leader. In the midst of battle his chariot got stuck in the mud; Ur-Nammu fell off it, but "the chariot like a storm rushed along," leaving the king behind, "abandoned like a crushed jug." The tragedy was compounded when the boat returning Ur-Nammu's body to Sumer "in an unknown place had sunk; the waves sank it down, with him on board."

When news of the defeat and the tragic death of Ur-Nammu reached Ur, a great lament went up there. The people could not understand how such a religiously devout king, a righteous shepherd who only followed the gods' directives with weapons they put in his hands, could perish so ignominiously. "Why did the Lord Nannar not hold him by the hand?" they asked; "Why did Inanna, Lady of Heaven, not put her noble arm around his head? Why did the valiant Utu not assist him?"

The Sumerians, who believed that all that happens had been fated, wondered, "Why did these gods step aside when Ur-Nammu's bitter fate was decided?" Surely those gods, Nannar and his twin children, knew what Anu and Enlil were determining; yet they said nothing to protect Ur-Nammu. There could be only one plausible explanation, the people of Ur and Sumer concluded as they cried out and lamented: The great gods must have gone back on their word—

> *How the fate of the hero had been changed!*
> *Anu altered his holy word.*
> *Enlil deceitfully changed his decree!*

These are strong words, accusing the great Enlilite gods of deceit and double-crossing! The ancient words convey the extent of the people's disappointment.

If that was so in Sumer & Akkad, one can imagine the reaction in the rebellious western lands.

In the struggle for the hearts and minds of Mankind, the Enlilites were faltering. Nabu, the "spokesman," intensified the campaign on behalf of his father, Marduk. His own status was enhanced and changed: his own divinity was now glorified by a variety of venerating epithets. Inspired by Nabu—the *Nabih,* the Prophet—prophecies of the Future, of what is about to happen, began to sweep the contested lands.

We know what they said because a number of clay tablets on which such prophecies were inscribed have been found; written in Old Babylonian cuneiform, they are grouped by scholars as *Akkadian Prophecies* or *Akkadia*n *Apocalypses.* **Common to all of them is the view that Past, Present, and Future are parts of a continuous flow of events;** that within a preordained Destiny there is some room for free will and thus a variated Fate; that for Mankind, both were decreed or determined by the gods of Heaven and Earth; and that *therefore events on Earth reflect occurrences in the heavens.*

To grant the prophecies believability, the texts sometimes anchored the prediction of future events in a known past historic occurrence or entity. What is wrong in the present, why change is needed, is then recounted. The unfolding events are attributed to decisions by one or more of the great gods. *A divine Emissary, a Herald, will appear;* the prophetic text might be his words, written down by the scribe, or expected pronouncements; as often as not, "a son will speak for his father." The predicted event(s) will be linked to omens—the death of a king, or heavenly signs: a celestial body will appear and make a frightful sound; "a burning fire" will come from the skies; "a star shall flash from the height of the sky to the horizon as a torch"; and, **most significantly, "a planet will appear before its time."**

Bad things, Apocalypse, shall precede the final event. There would be calamitous rains, huge devastating waves—or droughts,

the silting of canals, locusts, and famines. Mother will turn against daughter, neighbor against neighbor. Rebellion, chaos, and calamities will occur in the lands. Cities will be attacked and depopulated; kings will die, be toppled, and captured; "one throne will overthrow another." Officials and priests will be killed; temples will be abandoned; rites and offerings will cease. And then the predicted event—a great change, a new era, a new leader, a Redeemer—will come. Good will prevail over evil, prosperity will replace sufferings; abandoned cities will be resettled, the remnants of the dispersed people will return to their homes. Temples will be restored, and the people will perform the correct religious rites.

Not unexpectedly, these Babylonian or pro-Marduk prophecies pointed the accusing finger of wrongdoing at Sumer & Akkad (and also their allies Elam, Hattiland, and the Sealands) and named the Amurru Westerners as the instrument of divine retribution. The Enlilite "cult centers" Nippur, Ur, Uruk, Larsa, Lagash, Sippar, and Adab are named; they will be attacked, plundered, their temples abandoned. The Enlilite gods are described as confused ("unable to sleep"). Enlil is calling out to Anu, but ignores Anu's advice (some translators read the word as "command") that Enlil issue a *misharu* edict—a "putting things straight" order. Enlil, Ishtar, and Adad will be forced to change kingship in Sumer & Akkad. The "sacred rites" will be transferred out of Nippur. Celestially, "the great planet" will appear in the constellation of the Ram. The word of Marduk shall prevail; "He will subdue the Four Regions, the whole Earth shall tremble at the mention of his name . . . After him his son will reign as king and will become master of the whole Earth."

In some of the prophecies, certain deities are the subject of specific predictions: "A king will arise," one text prophesied in regard to Inanna/Ishtar; "he will remove the protective goddess of Uruk from Uruk and make her dwell in Babylon . . . He will establish the rites of Anu in Uruk." The Igigi are also specifically mentioned: "The regular offerings for the Igigi gods, which had ceased, will be reestablished," one prophecy states.

* * *

As was the case with Egyptian prophecies, most scholars also treat the "Akkadian Prophecies" as "pseudo-prophecies" or *post aventum* texts— that they were in fact written long after the "predicted" events; but as we have remarked in regard to the Egyptian texts, to say that the events were not prophesied because they had already happened is only to reassert that the events per se did happen (whether or not they were predicted), and that is what matters most to us. *It means that the prophecies did come true.*

And if so, most chilling is the prediction (in a text known as *Prophecy "B"*):

> *The Awesome Weapon of Erra*
> *upon the lands and the people*
> *will come in judgment.*

A most chilling prophecy indeed, for before the twenty-first century B.C. was over, "judgment upon lands and peoples" occurred when the god Erra ("The Annihilator")—an epithet for Nergal— unleashed nuclear weapons in a cataclysm that made prophecies come true.

5

COUNTDOWN TO DOOMSDAY

The disastrous twenty-first century B.C. began with the tragic and untimely death of Ur-Nammu, in 2096 B.C. It culminated with an unparalleled calamity, by the hand of the gods themselves, in 2024 B.C. The interval was seventy-two years—exactly the precessional shift of one degree; and if it was just a coincidence, then it was one of a series of "coincidental" occurrences that were somehow well coordinated . . .

Following Ur-Nammu's tragic death, the throne of Ur was taken over by his son Shulgi. Unable to claim the status of a demigod, he asserted (in his inscriptions) that he was nevertheless born under divine auspices: the god Nannar himself arranged for the child to be conceived in Enlil's temple in Nippur through a union between Ur-Nammu and Enlil's high priestess, so that "a 'little Enlil,' a child suitable for kingship and throne, shall be conceived."

That was a genealogical claim not to be sneezed at. Ur-Nammu himself, as earlier stated, was "two-thirds" divine, since his mother was a goddess. Though the High Priestess who was Shulgi's mother is not named, her very status suggests that she, too, was of some godly lineage, for it was a king's daughter who was chosen to be an EN.TU; and the kings of Ur, starting with the first dynasty, could be traced back to

demigods. That Nannar himself arranged for the union to take place in Enlil's temple in Nippur was also significant; as previously stated, it was under Ur-Nammu's reign that for the first time the priesthood of Nippur was combined with the priesthood of another city—in this case, with the one in Ur.

Much of what was happening in and around Sumer at the time has been gleaned from "Date Formulas"—royal records in which each year of the king's reign was noted by the major event that year. In the case of Shulgi much more is known, for he left behind other short and long inscriptions, including poetry and love songs.

These records indicate that soon after he had ascended the throne, Shulgi—perhaps hoping to avert his father's fate on a battlefield—reversed his father's militant policies. He launched an expedition to the outlying provinces, including the "rebel lands," but his "weapons" were offers of trade, peace, and his daughters in marriage. Deeming himself a successor to Gilgamesh, his route embraced the two destinations of that famed hero: the Sinai Peninsula (where the spaceport was) in the south and the Landing Place in the north. Observing the sanctity of the Fourth Region, Shulgi skirted the peninsula and paid homage to the gods at its boundary, at a place described as "Great fortified place of the gods." Moving northward west of the Dead Sea, he paused to worship at the "Place of Bright Oracles"—the place we know as Jerusalem—and built there an altar to "the god who judges" (usually an epithet of Utu/Shamash). At the "Snow-covered Place" in the north, he built an altar and offered sacrifices. Having thus "touched base" with the reachable space-related sites, he followed the "Fertile Crescent"—the arching trade and migration east–west route dictated by geography and water sources—then continued southward in the Tigris-Euphrates plain, back to southern Sumer.

When Shulgi returned to Ur, he had every reason to think that he had brought to gods and people alike "Peace in our time" (to use a modern analogy). He was granted by the gods the title "High Priest of Anu, Priest of Nannar." He was befriended by Utu/Shamash and was given the personal attention of Inanna/Ishtar (boasting in his love songs that she granted him her vulva in her temple).

But while Shulgi turned from affairs of state to personal pleasures, the unrest in the "rebel lands" was continuing. Unprepared for military action, Shulgi asked his Elamite ally for troops, offering its king as a reward one of his daughters in marriage and the Sumerian city Larsa as dowry. A major military expedition, employing those Elamite troops, was launched against the "sinning cities" in the west; the troops reached the Fortified Place of the gods at the Fourth Region's boundary. Shulgi in his inscriptions boasted of victory, but in fact, soon thereafter, he started to build a fortified wall to protect Sumer against foreign incursions from the west and from the northwest.

The Date Formulas called it the Great West Wall, and scholars believe that it ran from the Euphrates to the Tigris Rivers north of where Baghdad is situated nowadays, blocking to invaders the way down the fertile plain between the two rivers. It was a defensive measure that preceded the Great Wall of China, which was built for similar reasons, by almost two thousand years!

In 2048 B.C. the gods, led by Enlil, had enough of Shulgi's state failures and personal *dolce vita*. Determining that "the divine regulations he did not carry out," they decreed for him "the death of a sinner." We don't know what kind of death it was, but it is a historic fact that in that year he was replaced on the throne of Ur by his son Amar-Sin, of whom we know from the inscriptions that he launched one military expedition after another—to quell a revolt in the north, to fight an alliance of five kings in the west.

As in so much else, what was happening had root causes going back, sometimes way back, to earlier times and events. The "rebel lands," though in Asia and thus domains in the Enlilite Lands of Noah's son Shem, were inhabited by varied "Canaanites"—offspring of the biblical Canaan who, though descended of Ham (and thus belonging to Africa), occupied a stretch of Shem's lands (Genesis 10). That the "Lands of the West" along the Mediterranean coast were somehow disputed territory was also indicated by ancient Egyptian texts regarding the bitter contest between Horus and Seth that ended in aerial battles between them over the Sinai and the same contested lands.

It is noteworthy that in their military expeditions to subdue and punish the "rebel lands" in the west, both Ur-Nammu and Shulgi reached the Sinai Peninsula but turned away from that Fourth Region without entering it. The prize there was a place called TIL.MUN—the "Place of the Missiles"—the site of the post-Diluvial spaceport of the Anunnaki. When the Pyramid Wars ended, the sacred Fourth Region was entrusted to the neutral hands of Ninmah (who was then renamed NIN.HAR.SAG—"Lady of the Mountain Peaks"), but actual command of the spaceport was put in the hands of Utu/Shamash (here shown in his winged dress uniform, fig. 29, commanding the spaceport's "Eaglemen," fig. 30).

That, however, appeared to change as the struggle for supremacy intensified. Inexplicably, various Sumerian texts and "God Lists" started to associate Tilmun with Marduk's son, the god Ensag/Nabu. Enki was apparently involved in that, for a text dealing with the affair between Enki and Ninharsag states that the two of them decided to allocate the place to Marduk's son: "Let Ensag be the lord of Tilmun," they said.

The ancient sources indicate that from the safety of the sacred region Nabu ventured to the lands and cities along the Mediterranean coast, even to some Mediterranean islands, spreading everywhere the message

Figure 29

Figure 30

of Marduk's coming supremacy. He was, thus, the enigmatic "Son-Man" of the Egyptian and the Akkadian prophecies—the Divine Son who was also a Son-Man, the son of a god and of an Earthling woman.

The Enlilites, understandably, could not accept such a situation. And so it was that when Amar-Sin ascended the throne of Ur after Shulgi, the targets and strategy of the Ur III military expeditions were changed in order to reassert Enlilite control over Tilmun, to sever the sacred region from the "rebel lands," then pry loose those lands from the influence of Nabu and Marduk by force of arms. Starting in 2047 B.C., the sacred Fourth Region became a target and a pawn in the Enlilite struggle with Marduk and Nabu; and as both biblical and Mesopotamian texts reveal, the conflict erupted to *the greatest international "world war" of antiquity.* **Involving the Hebrew Abraham, that "War of the Kings" placed him in center stage of international events.**

In 2048 B.C. the destiny of the founder of monotheism, Abraham, and the fate of the Anunnaki god Marduk converged at a place called Harran.

Harran—"The Caravanry"—was an important trading center from time immemorial in Hatti (the land of the Hittites). It was located at

the crossroads of major international trade and military land routes. Situated at the headwaters of the Euphrates River, it was also a hub for river transportation all the way downstream to Ur itself. Surrounded by fertile meadows watered by the river's tributaries, the Balikh and Khabur Rivers, it was a center of sheepherding. The famed "Merchants of Ur" came there for Harran's wool and brought in exchange to distribute from there Ur's famed woolen garments. Commerce in metals, skins, leather, woods, earthenware products, and spices followed. (The Prophet Ezekiel, who was exiled from Jerusalem to the Khabur area in Babylonian times, mentioned Harran's "merchants in choice fabrics, embroidered cloaks of blue, and many-colored carpets.")

Harran (the town, by that very name, still exists in Turkey, near the border with Syria, and was visited by me in 1997) was also known in ancient times as "Ur away from Ur"; at its center stood a great temple to Nannar/Sin. In 2095 B.C., the year in which Shulgi took over the throne in Ur, a priest named Terah was sent from Ur to Harran to serve at that temple. He took along his family; it included his son Abram. We know about Terah, his family, and their move from Ur to Harran from the Bible:

> *Now these are the generations of Terah:*
> *Terah begot Abram, Nahor and Haran,*
> *and Haran begot Lot.*
> *And Haran died before his father Terah*
> *in his land of birth, in Ur in Chaldea.*
> *And Abram and Nahor took wives—*
> *the wife of Abram was named Sarai*
> *and that of Nahor's wife Milkhah . . .*
> *And Terah took with him his son Abram*
> *and Lot, the son of his son Haran,*
> *and his daughter-in-law Sarai,*
> *and went forth with them from Ur in Chaldea*
> *by the way to Canaan;*
> *and they reached Harran and resided there.*
>
> GENESIS 11:27–31

It is with these verses that the Hebrew Bible begins the pivotal tale of Abraham—called at the beginning by his Sumerian name, **Abram.** His father, we are told earlier, stemmed from a patriarchal line that went all the way back to Shem, the oldest son of Noah (the hero of the Deluge); all those patriarchs enjoyed long lives—Shem to the age of 600, his son Arpakhshad to 438; and subsequent male offspring to 433, 460, 239, and 230 years. Nahor, the father of Terah, lived to age 148; and Terah himself—who fathered Abram when he was 70 years old—lived to age 205. Chapter 11 of Genesis explains that Arpakhshad and his descendants lived in the lands later known as Sumer and Elam and their surroundings. *So Abraham, as Abram, was a true Sumerian.*

This genealogical information alone indicates that Abraham was of a special ancestry. His Sumerian name, AB.RAM, meant "Father's Beloved," an apropriate name for a son finally born to a seventy-year-old father. The father's name, Terah, stemmed from the Sumerian epithet-name TIRHU; it designated an Oracle Priest—a priest who observed celestial signs or received oracular messages from a god, and explained or conveyed them to the king. The name of Abram's wife, SARAI (later *Sarah* in Hebrew), meant "Princess"; the name of Nahor's wife, *Milkhah,* meant "Queenlike"; both suggest a royal genealogy. Since it was later revealed that Abraham's wife was his half-sister—"the daughter of my father but not of my mother," he explained—it follows that Sarai/Sarah's mother was of royal descent. The family thus belonged to Sumer's highest echelons, combining royal and priestly ancestries.

Another significant clue to identifying the family's history is the repeated reference by Abraham to himself, when he met rulers in Canaan and Egypt, as being an *Ibri*—a "Hebrew." The word stems from the root *ABoR*—"to come across, to cross"—so it has been assumed by biblical scholars that by that he meant that he had come across from the other side of the Euphrates River; that is, from Mesopotamia. But I believe that the term was more specific. The name used for Sumer's "Vatican City," *Nippur,* is the Akkadian rendering of the original Sumerian name NI.IBRU, "Splendid Place of Crossing." Abram, and his descendants who are called in the Bible Hebrews, belonged to a family that identified themselves as *"Ibru"*—Nippurians. That would

suggest that Terah was first a priest in Nippur, then moved to Ur, and finally to Harran, taking his family along.

By synchronizing biblical, Sumerian, and Egyptian chronologies (as detailed in *The Wars of Gods and Men*), we have arrived at the year 2123 B.C. as the date of Abraham's birth. The gods' decision to make Nannar/Sin's cult center Ur the capital of Sumer and to enthrone Ur-Nammu took place in 2113 B.C. Soon thereafter, the priesthoods of Nippur and Ur were combined for the first time; it is very likely that it was then that the Nippurian priest Tirhu moved with his family, including the ten-year-old boy Abram, to serve in Nannar's temple in Ur.

In 2095 B.C., when Abraham was twenty-eight and already married, Terah was transferred to Harran, taking the family with him. It could not have been just a coincidence that it was the very same year in which Shulgi succeeded Ur-Nammu. **The emerging scenario is that the movements of this family were somehow linked to the geopolitical events of that era.** Indeed, when Abraham himself was chosen to carry out divine orders to leave Harran and rush to Canaan, *the great god Marduk took the crucial step of moving to Harran.* **It was in 2048 B.C. that the two moves occurred: Marduk coming to sojourn in Harran, Abraham leaving Harran for faraway Canaan.**

We know from Genesis that Abram was seventy-five years old, and it was thus 2048 B.C. that he was told by God, "Get thee out of thy country and out of thy birthplace and from thy father's house"—leave behind Sumer, Nippur, and Harran—and go "unto the land which I will show thee." As to Marduk, a long text known as the *Marduk Prophecy* that he addressed to the people of Harran (clay tablet, fig. 31) provides the clue confirming the fact and the time of his move to Harran: 2048 B.C. **There is no way the two moves could have been unrelated.**

But 2048 B.C. was also the very year in which the Enlilite gods decided to get rid of Shulgi, ordering for him the "death of a sinner"—a move that signaled the end of "let's try peaceful means" and a return to aggressive conflict; *and there is no way that this, too, was just a coincidence.* No, the three moves—Marduk to Harran, Abram leaving Harran for Canaan, and the removal of the decadent Shulgi—had to

Figure 31

be interconnected: **three simultaneous and interrelated moves in the Divine Chess Game.**

They were, as we shall see, steps in the countdown to Doomsday.

The ensuing twenty-four years—from 2048 to 2024 B.C.—were a time of religious fervor and ferment, of international diplomacy and intrigue, of military alliances and clashing armies, of a struggle for strategic superiority. The spaceport in the Sinai Peninsula, and the other space-related sites, were constantly at the core of events.

Amazingly, various written records from antiquity have survived, providing us not just with an outline of events but with great details about the battles, the strategies, the discussions, the arguments, the participants and their moves, and the crucial decisions that resulted in the most profound upheaval on Earth since the Deluge.

Augmented by the Date Formulas and varied other references, the principal sources for reconstructing those dramatic events are the relevant chapters in Genesis; Marduk's autobiography, known as *The*

Marduk Prophecy; a group of tablets in the "Spartoli Collection" in the British Museum known as *The Khedorla'omer Texts;* and a long historical/autobiographical text dictated by the god Nergal to a trusted scribe, a text known as the *Erra Epos.* As in a movie—usually a crime thriller—in which the various eyewitnesses and principals describe the same event not exactly the same way, but from which the real story emerges, so are we able to reach the same result in this case.

Marduk's main chess move, in 2048 B.C., was to establish his command post in Harran. By that he took away from Nannar/Sin this vital northern crossroads and severed Sumer from the northern lands of the Hittites. Besides the military significance, the move deprived Sumer of its economically vital commercial ties. The move also enabled Nabu "to marshal his cities, toward the Great Sea to set his course." Place-names in these texts suggest that the principal cities west of the Euphrates River were coming under full or partial control of the father-son team, including the all-important Landing Place.

It was into the most populated part of the Lands of the West—Canaan—that Abram/Abraham was commanded to go. He left Harran, taking his wife and nephew Lot with him. He was traveling swiftly southward, stopping only to pay homage to his God at selected sacred sites. His destination was the Negev, the dry region bordering the Sinai Peninsula.

He did not stay there long. As soon as Shulgi's successor, Amar-Sin, was enthroned in Ur in 2047 B.C., Abram was instructed to go to Egypt. He was at once taken to meet the reigning Pharaoh and was provided with "sheep and oxen and asses, and male attendants and female servants, and she-asses and camels." The Bible is mum regarding the reason for this royal treatment, except to hint that the Pharaoh, being told that Sarai was Abram's sister, assumed that she was being offered to him in marriage—a step that suggsts that a treaty was discussed. That such high-level international negotiations were taking place between Abram and the Egyptian king seems plausible when one realizes that the year when Abram returned to the Negev after a seven-year stay in Egypt—2040 B.C.—was the very same year in which the Theban princes of Upper Egypt defeated the previous Lower Egypt dynasty, launching Egypt's unified Middle Kingdom. ***Another geopolitical coincidence!***

Abram, now reinforced with manpower and camels, returned to the Negev in the nick of time, his mission now clear: to defend the Fourth Region with its spaceport. As the biblical narrative reveals, he now had with him an elite force of *Ne'arim*—a term ususally translated "Young Men"— but Mesopotamian texts used the parallel term LU.NAR ("NAR-men") to denote armed cavalrymen. It is my suggesation that Abraham, having learned in Harran tactics from the militarily excelling Hittites, obtained in Egypt a striking force of swift camel-riding cavalrymen. His base in Canaan was again the Negev, the area bordering the Sinai Peninsula.

He did so in the nick of time, for a mighty army—legions of an alliance of Enlilite kings—was on its way not only to crush and punish the "sinning cities" that switched allegiance to "other gods," but to also capture the spaceport.

The Sumerian texts dealing with the reign of Amar-Sin, Shulgi's son and successor, inform us that in 2041 B.C. he launched his greatest (and last) military expedition against the Lands of the West that fell under the Marduk-Nabu spell. It entailed an invasion of unparalleled scope by an international alliance, in which not only cities of men but also strongholds of gods and their offspring were attacked.

It was, indeed, such a major and unparalleled occurrence that the Bible devoted a whole long chapter to it—Genesis 14. Biblical scholars call it "The War of the Kings," for it climaxed in a great battle between an army of four "Kings of the East" and the combined forces of five "Kings of the West," and culminated in a remarkable military feat by Abraham's swift cavalrymen.

The Bible begins its report of that great international war by listing the kings and kingdoms of the East who "came and made war" in the West:

> *And it came to pass*
> *in the days of Amraphel king of Shine'ar,*
> *Ariokh king of Ellasar,*
> *Khedorla'omer king of Elam,*
> *and Tidhal the king of Goyim.*

The group of tablets named the *Khedorla'omer Texts* was first brought to scholarly attention by the Assyriologist Theophilus Pinches in a lecture at the Victoria Institute, London, in 1897. They clearly describe the same events that are the great international war of chapter 14 of Genesis, though in much greater detail; it is quite possible, indeed, that those tablets served as the source for the biblical writers. Those tablets identify "Khedorla'omer king of Elam" as the Elamite king Kudur-Laghamar, who is known from historical records. "Ariokh" has been identified as ERI.AKU ("Servant of the Moon god"), who reigned in the city of Larsa (biblical "Ellasar"); and Tidhal was identified as Tud-Ghula, a vassal of the king of Elam.

There has been over the years a debate regarding the identity of "Amraphel king of Shine'ar"; suggestions ranged all the way to Hammurabi, a Babylonian king centuries later. Shine'ar was the constant biblical name for Sumer, not Babylon, so who, in the time of Abraham, was its king? I have convincingly suggested in *The Wars of Gods and Men* that the Hebrew should be read not Amra-Phel but *Amar-Phel,* from the Sumerian AMAR.PAL—a variant of AMAR. SIN—whose Date Formulas attest that he did indeed, in 2041 B.C., launch the War of the Kings.

That fully identified coalition, according to the Bible, was led by the Elamites—a detail corroborated by the Mesopotamian data that highlights the reemerging leading role of Ninurta in the struggle. The Bible also dates this Khedorla'omer Invasion by observing that it took place fourteen years after the previous Elamite incursion into Canaan— another detail conforming to the data from Shulgi's time.

The invasion route this time was, however, different: shortcutting the distance from Mesopotamia by a risky passage through a stretch of desert, the invaders avoided the densely populated Mediterranean coastland by marching on the eastern side of the Jordan River. The Bible lists the places where those battles took place and who the Enlilite forces battled there; the information indicates that an attempt was made to settle accounts with old adversaries—descendants of the intermarrying Igigi, even of the Usurper Zu—who evidently supported the uprisings against the Enlilites. But sight was not lost of the prime target: *the spaceport.* The invading

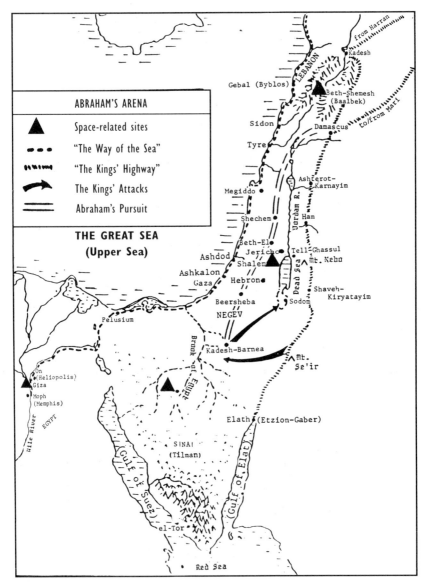

Figure 32

forces followed what has been known since biblical times as the Way of the King, running north–south on the eastern side of the Jordan. But when they turned westward toward the gateway to the Sinai Peninsula, they met a blocking force: Abraham and his cavalrymen (fig. 32).

Referring to the peninsula's gateway city Dur-Mah-Ilani ("The

gods' great fortified place")—the Bible called it Kadesh-Barnea—the
Khedorla'omer Texts clearly stated that the way was blocked there:

> *The son of the priest,*
> *whom the gods in their true counsel had anointed,*
> *the despoiling had prevented.*

"The son of the priest," *anointed by the gods,* **I suggest, was
Abram the son of the priest Terah.**

A Date Formula tablet belonging to Amar-Sin, inscribed on both
sides (fig. 33), boasts of destroying NE IB.RU.UM—"The Shepherding
place of *Ibru'um*." In fact, at the gateway to the spaceport there was no
battle; the mere presence of Abram's cavalry striking force persuaded
the invaders to turn away—to richer and more lucrative targets. But *if
the reference is indeed to Abram, by name, it offers once more an extraordinary extra-biblical corroboration of the Patriarchal record, no matter
who claimed victory.*

Prevented from entering the Sinai Peninsula, the Army of the East

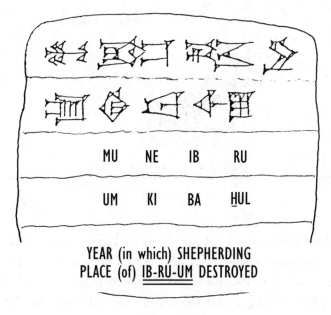

YEAR (in which) SHEPHERDING
PLACE (of) **IB-RU-UM** DESTROYED

Figure 33

turned northward. The Dead Sea was then shorter; its current southern appendix was not yet submerged, and it was then a fertile plain rich with farmland, orchards, and trading centers. The settlements there included five cities, among them the infamous Sodom and Gomorrah. Turning northward, the invaders now faced the combined forces of what the Bible called "five sinning cities." It was there, the Bible reports, that the four kings fought and defeated the five kings. Looting the cities and taking captives with them, the invaders marched back, this time on the western side of the Jordan.

The biblical focus on those battles might have ended with that turning back were it not for the fact that Abram's nephew Lot, who resided in Sodom, was among the captives. When a refugee from Sodom told Abram what had happened, "he armed his trained men, three hundred and eighteen of them, and gave chase." His cavalry caught up with the invaders all the way north, near Damascus (see fig. 32), where Lot was freed and the booty recovered. The Bible records the feat as the "smiting of Khedorla'omer and the kings who were with him" by Abram.

The historical records suggest that as audacious and far-flung that War of the Kings had been, it failed to suppress the Marduk-Nabu surge. Amar-Sin, we know, died in 2039 B.C.—felled not by an enemy lance, but by a scorpion's bite. He was replaced in 2038 B.C. by his brother Shu-Sin. The data for his nine years' reign record two military forays northward but none westward; they speak mostly of his defensive measures. He relied mainly on building new sections of the Wall of the West against attacking Amorites. The defenses, however, were moved each time ever closer to Sumer's heartland, and the territory controlled from Ur kept shrinking.

By the time the next (and last) of the Ur III dynasty, Ibbi-Sin, ascended the throne, invaders from the west had broken through the defensive Wall and were clashing with Ur's "Foreign Legion," Elamite troops, in Sumerian territory. Directing and prompting the Westerners on toward the cherished target was Nabu. His divine father, Marduk himself, was waiting in Harran for the recapture of Babylon.

The great gods, called to an emergency council, then approved extraordinary steps that changed the future forever.

6

GONE WITH THE WIND

The unleashing of "weapons of mass destruction" in the Middle East underlies the fear of Armageddon prophecies coming true. The sad fact is that a mounting conflict—among gods, not men—did lead to the use of nuclear weapons, right there, four thousand years ago. And if there ever was a most regrettable act with the most unexpected consequences, that was it.

That nuclear weapons had been used on Earth for the first time not in A.D. 1945 but in 2024 B.C. is fact, not fiction. The fateful event is described in a variety of ancient texts from which the What and How, the Why and Who can be construed, reconstructed, and put in context. Those ancient sources include the Hebrew Bible, for the first Hebrew patriarch, Abraham, was an eyewitness to the awesome calamity.

The failure of the War of the Kings to subdue the "rebel lands" of course discouraged the Enlilites and encourged the Mardukites, but the events did more than that. On Enlil's instructions, Ninurta got busy setting up an alternative space facility on the other side of the world—all the way in what is now Peru in South America. The texts indicate that Enlil himself was away from Sumer for long stretches of time. These gods' moves caused the last two kings of Sumer, Shu-Sin and Ibbi-Sin, to waver in their allegiances and to start paying homage to Enki in his Sumerian foothold, Eridu. The divine absences also loosened controls over the

78

Elamite "Foreign Legion," and the records speak of "sacrileges" by the Elamite troops. Gods and men were increasingly disgusted with it all.

Especially enraged was Marduk, who received word of looting, destructions, and desecrations in his cherished Babylon. It will be recalled that the last time he was there he was persuaded by his half-brother Nergal to leave peacefully until the Celestial Time would reach the Age of the Ram. He did so having received Nergal's solemn word that nothing would be disturbed or desecrated in Babylon, but the opposite happened. Marduk was angered by the reported desecration of his temple there by the "unworthy" Elamites: "To herds of dogs Babylon's temple they made a den; flying ravens, loudly shrieking, their dung dropped there."

From Harran he cried out to the great gods: "Until When?" Has not the Time arrived yet, he asked in his prophetic autobiography:

> *O great gods, learn my secrets*
> *as I girdle my belt, my memories remember.*
> *I am the divine Marduk, a great god.*
> *I was cast off for my sins,*
> *to the mountains I have gone.*
> *In many lands I have been a wanderer.*
> *From where the sun rises to where it sets I went.*
> *To the highland of Hatti I came.*
> *In Hattiland I asked for an oracle;*
> *in it I asked: "Until when?"*

"Twenty-four years in Harran's midst I nested," Marduk went on; "my days are completed!" The time has come, he said, to set his course to his city (Babylon), "my temple to rebuild, my everlasting abode to establish." Waxing visionary, he spoke of seeing his temple E.SAG.ILA ("Temple whose head is lofty") rising as a mountain upon a platform in Babylon, calling it "The house of my covenant." He foresaw Babylon as forever established, a king of his choice installed there, a city filled with joy, a city blessed by Anu. The messianic times, Marduk prophesied, will "chase away evil and bad luck, bring motherly love to Mankind."

The year in which a sojourn of twenty-four years in Harran was completed was 2024 B.C.; it marked seventy-two years since Marduk had agreed to depart from Babylon and await the oracular celestial time.

Marduk's "until when?" appeal to the Great Gods was not an idle one, for the leadership of the Anunnaki was constantly consulting, informally and in formal councils. Alarmed by the worsening situation, Enlil hurriedly returned to Sumer and was shocked to learn that things had gone wrong even in Nippur itself. Ninurta was summoned to explain the Elamites' misconduct, but Ninurta put all the blame on Marduk and Nabu. Nabu was summoned, and "Before the gods the son of his father came." His main accuser was Utu/Shamash, who, describing the dire situation, said, "all this Nabu has caused to happen." Speaking for his father, Nabu blamed Ninurta, and revived the old accusations against Nergal in regard to the disappearance of the pre-Diluvial monitoring instruments and the failure to prevent sacrileges in Babylon; he got into a shouting match with Nergal, and "showing disrespect . . . to Enlil evil he spoke: 'There is no justice, destruction was conceived, Enlil against Babylon caused evil to be planned.'" It was an unheard-of accusation against the Lord of the Command.

Enki spoke up, but it was in defense of his son, not of Enlil. What are Marduk and Nabu actually accused of? he asked. His ire was directed especially at his son Nergal: "Why do you continue the opposition?" he asked him. The two argued so much that in the end Enki shouted to Nergal to get out of his presence. The gods' councils broke up in disarray.

But all these debates, accusations, and counteraccusations were taking place against the increasingly realized fact—what Marduk referred to as the Celestial Oracle—that with the passage of time, with the crucial shift of the precessional clock by one degree, the Age of the Bull, the zodiacal age of Enlil, was coming to an end, and the Age of the Ram, Marduk's Age, was looming in the heavens. Ninurta could see it coming at his Eninnu temple in Lagash (which Gudea built); Ningishzidda/Thoth could confirm it from all the stone circles that he had erected elsewhere on Earth; and the people knew it, too.

It was then that Nergal—vilified by Marduk and Nabu, ordered out

by his father Enki—"consulting with himself," concocted the idea of resort to the "Awesome Weapons." He did not know where they were hidden, but he knew that they existed on Earth, locked away in a secret underground place (according to a text catalogued as CT-xvi, lines 44–46), somewhere in Africa, in the domain of his brother Gibil:

> *Those seven, in the mountains they abide;*
> *In a cavity inside the earth they dwell.*

Based on our current level of technology, they can be described as seven nuclear devices: "Clad with terror, with a brilliance they rush forth." They were brought to Earth unintentionally from Nibiru and were hidden away in a secret safe place a long time ago; Enki knew where, but so did Enlil.

A War Council of the gods, overruling Enki, voted to follow Nergal's suggestion to give Marduk a punishing blow. There was constant communication with Anu: "Anu to Earth the words was speaking, Earth to Anu the words pronounced." He made it clear that his approval for the unprecedented step was limited to depriving Marduk of the Sinai spaceport, but that neither gods nor people should be harmed: "Anu, lord of the gods, on the Earth had pity," the ancient records state. Choosing Nergal and Ninurta to carry out the mission, the gods made absolutely clear to them its limited and conditional scope.

But that is not what happened: The "Law of Unintended Consequences" proved itself true on a catastrophic scale.

In the aftermath of the calamity that resulted in the death of countless people and the desolation of Sumer, Nergal dictated to a trusted scribe his own version of the events, trying to exonerate himself. The long text is known as the *Erra Epos,* for it refers to Nergal by the epithet *Erra* ("The Annihilator") and to Ninurta as *Ishum* ("The Scorcher"). We can put together the true story by adding to this text information from several other Sumerian, Akkadian, and biblical sources.

Thus we find that no sooner was the decision reached than Nergal rushed to Gibil's African domain to find and retrieve the weapons, not

waiting for Ninurta. To his dismay Ninurta learned that Nergal was disregarding the objective's limits and was going to use the weapons indiscriminately to settle personal accounts: "I shall annihilate the son, and let the father bury him; then I shall kill the father, and let no one bury him," Nergal has boasted.

While the two argued, word reached them that Nabu was not sitting still: "From his temple to marshall all his cities he set his step, toward the Great Sea he set his course; the Great Sea he entered, sat upon a throne that was not his." Nabu was not only converting the western cities, he was taking over the Mediterranean islands and setting himself up as their ruler! Nergal/Erra thus argued that destroying the spaceport was not enough: Nabu, and the cities that rallied to him, also had to be punished, destroyed!

Now, with two targets, the Nergal-Ninurta team saw another problem: Would the "upheavaling" of the spaceport not sound the alarm for Nabu and his sinning followers to escape? Reviewing their targets, they found the solution in splitting up: Ninurta would attack the spaceport; Nergal would attack the nearby "sinning cities." But as all this was agreed upon, Ninurta had second thoughts; he insisted that not only the Anunnaki who manned the space facilities should be forewarned, but that even certain people should be forewarned: "Valiant Erra," he told Nergal, "*will you the righteous destroy with the unrighteous? Will you destroy those who against you have not sinned with those who against you have sinned?*"

Nergal/Erra, the ancient text states, was persuaded: "The words of Ishum appealed to Erra as fine oil." And so, one morning, the two, sharing the seven nuclear explosives between them, set out on their ultimate Mission:

> *Then did the hero Erra go ahead,*
> *remembering the words of Ishum.*
> *Ishum too went forth*
> *in accordance with the words given,*
> *a squeezing in his heart.*

The available texts even tell us who went to what target: "Ishum to the Mount Most Supreme set his course" (we know that the spaceport was beside this mount from the *Epic of Gilgamesh*). "Ishum raised his hand: the Mount was smashed . . . That which was raised toward Anu to launch was caused to wither, its face was made to fade away, its place was made desolate." In one nuclear blow, the spaceport and its facilities were obliterated by the hand of Ninurta.

The ancient text then describes what Nergal did: "Emulating Ishum, Erra the Way of the King followed, the cities he finished off, to desolation he overturned them"; his targets were the "sinning cities" whose kings had formed the alliance against the Kings of the East, the plain in the south of the Dead Sea.

And so it was that in the year 2024 B.C. nuclear weapons were unleashed in the Sinai Peninsula and in the nearby Plain of the Dead Sea; and the spaceport and the Five Cities were no more.

Amazingly, yet no wonder if Abraham and his mission in Canaan is understood the way we explain it, it is in this apocalyptic event that the biblical record and the Mesopotamian texts converge.

We know from the Mesopotamian texts relating the events that, as required, the Anunnaki guarding the spaceport were forewarned: "The two [Nergal and Ninurta], incited to commit the evil, made its guardians stand aside; the gods of that place abandoned it—its protectors went up to the heights of heaven." But while the Mesopotamian texts reiterate that "the two made the gods flee, made them flee the scorching," they are ambiguous regarding whether that advance notice was also extended to the people in the doomed cities. It is here that the Bible provides missing details: we read in Genesis that both Abraham and his nephew Lot were indeed forewarned—but not the other residents of the "sinning cities."

The biblical report, apart from throwing light on the "upheaveling" aspects of the events, contains details that shed an amazing light on the gods in general and on their relationship with Abraham in particular. The story begins in chapter 18 of Genesis when Abraham, now ninety-nine years old, sitting at the entrance to his tent on a hot

midday, "lifted his eyes" and all of a sudden saw "three men stand-ing above him." Though they are described as *Anashim*, "men," there was something different or unusual about them, for he rushed out of his tent and bowed to the ground, and—referring to himself as their servant—washed their feet and offered them food. As it turned out, the three were divine beings.

As they leave, their leader—now identified as the Lord God—decides to reveal to Abraham the trio's mission: to determine whether Sodom and Gomorrah are indeed sinning cities whose upheavaling is justified. While two of the three continue toward Sodom, Abraham approaches and **reproaches** (!) God with words that are identical to those in the Mesopotamian text: *Wilt thou destroy the righteous with the unrighteous?* (Genesis 18:23).

What followed was an incredible bargaining session between Man and God. "Perchance there are fifty righteous within the city—Wilt thou destroy, and not spare the city on account of the fifty righteous within it?" Abraham asked God. When told that, well, the city would be spared if fifty righteous men reside there, Abraham said, what about just forty? What about only thirty? And so it went, down to ten . . . "And Yahweh went away as soon as he had finished speaking, and Abraham returned to his place."

The other two divine beings—the tale's continuation in chapter 19 calls them *Mal'achim,* literally "emissaries" but commonly translated "Angels"—arrived in Sodom in the evening. The happenings there confirmed its people's wickedness, and at daybreak the two urged Abraham's nephew Lot to escape with his family, for "Yahweh is about to destroy the city." The lingering family asked for more time, and one of the "angels" agreed to have the upheaval delayed long enough for Lot and his family to reach the safer mountain.

"And Abraham got up early in the morning . . . and he looked toward Sodom and Gomorrah and toward all the land of the Plain, and beheld, and lo—vapor went up from the earth as the smoke of a furnace."

Abraham was then ninety-nine years old; having been born in 2123 B.C., the time had to be 2024 B.C.

The convergence of the Mesopotamian texts with the biblical narrative of Genesis concerning the upheaval of Sodom and Gomorrah is at once one of the most significant confirmations of the Bible's veracity in general and of Abraham's status and role in particular—and yet one of the most shunned by theologians and other scholars, because of its report of the events of the preceding day, the day three Divine Beings ("Angels" who looked like men) had paid Abraham a visit—it smacks too much of an "Ancient Astronauts" tale. Those who question the Bible or treat the Mesopotamian texts as just myths have sought to explain the destruction of Sodom and Gomorrah as some natural calamity, yet the biblical version confirms twice that the "upheaval" by "fire and sulfur" was not a natural calamity but *a premeditated, postponable, and even cancellable* event: once when Abraham bargained with the Lord to spare the cities so as not to destroy the righteous with the unjust, and again when his nephew Lot obtained a postponement of the upheaval.

Photographs of the Sinai Peninsula from space (fig. 34) still show the immense cavity and the crack in the surface where the nuclear

Figure 34

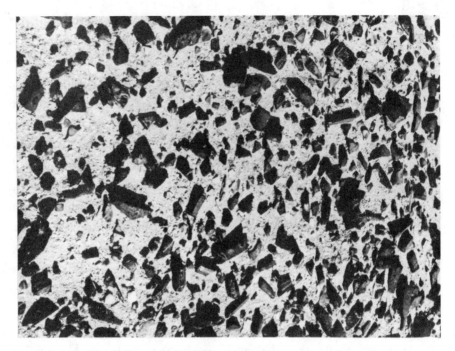

Figure 35

explosion had taken place. The area itself is strewn, to this day, with crushed, burned, and blackened rocks (fig. 35); they contain a highly unusual ratio of isotope uranium-235, indicating in expert opinions exposure to **sudden immense heat of nuclear origin.**

The upheaval of the cities in the plain of the Dead Sea caused the southern shore of the sea to collapse, leading to a flooding of the once fertile area and its appearance, to this day, as an appendage separated from the sea by a barrier called *"El-Lisan"* ("The Tongue") (fig. 36). Attempts by Israeli archaeologists to explore the seabed there have revealed the existence of enigmatic underwater ruins, but the Hashemite Kingdom of Jordan, in whose half of the Dead Sea the ruins are, put a stop to further exploration. Interestingly, the relevant Mesopotamian texts confirm the topographic change and even suggest that the sea became a Dead Sea as a result of the nuclear bombing: Erra, they tell, "Dug through the sea, its wholeness he divided; that which lives in it, even the crocodiles, he made wither."

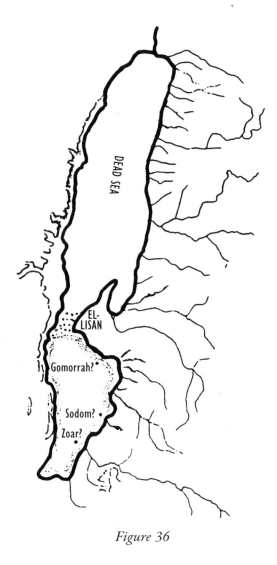

Figure 36

The two, as it turned out, did more than destroy the spaceport and the sinning cities: as a result of the nuclear explosions,

> *A storm, the Evil Wind,*
> *went around in the skies.*

And the chain reaction of unintended consequences began.

* * *

The historical records show that the Sumerian civilization collapsed in the sixth year of the reign in Ur of Ibbi-Sin—in 2024 B.C. It was, the reader will recall, the very year in which Abraham was ninety-nine years old . . .

Scholars assumed at first that Sumer's capital, Ur, was overrun by "barbarian invaders"; but no evidence for such a destructive invasion was found. A text titled "A Lamentation Over the Destruction of Ur" was then discovered; it puzzled the scholars, for it bewailed not the physical destruction of Ur but its "abandonment": the gods who had dwelt there abandoned it, the people who dwelt there were gone, its stables were empty; the temples, the houses, the sheepfolds remained intact—standing, but empty.

Other lamentation texts were then discovered. They lamented not just Ur, but all of Sumer. Again they spoke of "abandonment": not only did the gods of Ur, Nannar, and Ningal abandon Ur; Enlil, "the wild bull," abandoned his beloved temple in Nippur; his spouse, Ninlil, was also gone. Ninmah abandoned her city Kesh; Inanna, "the queen of Erech," abandoned Erech; Ninurta forsook his temple Eninnu; his spouse, Bau, was also gone from Lagash. One Sumerian city after another was listed as having been "abandoned," without their gods, people, or animals. The scholars were now puzzling over some "dire catastrophe," a mysterious calamity that affected the whole of Sumer. What could it be?

The answer to the puzzle was right there in those texts: *Gone with the wind*.

No, this is not a play of words on the title of a famous book/movie. That was the refrain in the lamentation texts: Enlil has abandoned his temple, he was "gone by the wind." Ninlil from her temple was "gone by the wind." Nannar has abandoned Ur—his sheepfolds were "gone by the wind"; and so on and on. The scholars have assumed that this repetition of the words was a literary device, a refrain that the lamenters repeated over and over again to highlight their grief. But that was no literary device—that was the literal truth: **Sumer and its cities were literally emptied as a result of a wind.**

An *"Evil Wind,"* the lamentation (and then other texts) reported, came blowing and caused "a calamity, one unknown to men, to befall the land." It was an *Evil Wind* that "caused cities to be desolate, caused houses to be desolate, caused stalls to be desolate, the sheepfolds to be emptied." There was desolation, but no destruction; emptiness, but no ruins: the cities were there, the houses were there, the stalls and sheepfolds were there—but nothing alive remained; even "Sumer's rivers flow with water that is bitter, the once cultivated fields grow weeds, in the meadows the plants have withered." All life is gone. It was a calamity that had never happened before—

> *On the Land Sumer a calamity fell,*
> *One unknown to men.*
> *One that had never been seen before,*
> *One which could not be withstood.*

Carried by the Evil Wind, it was a death from which there was no escape: it was a death "which roams the street, is let loose in the road . . . The highest wall, the thickest wall, it passes like a flood; no door can shut it out, no bolt can turn it back." Those who hid behind doors were felled inside; those who ran to the rooftops died on the roofs. It was an unseen death: "It stands beside a man, yet no one can see it; when it enters a house, its appearance is unknown." It was a gruesome death: "Cough and phlegm weakened the chest, the mouth was filled with spittle, dumbness and daze have come upon them . . . an overwhelming dumbness . . . a headache." As the Evil Wind clutched its victims, "their mouths were drenched with blood." The dead and dying were everywhere.

The texts make clear that the Evil Wind, "bearing gloom from city to city," was not a natural calamity; it resulted from a deliberate decision of the great gods. It was caused by "a great storm ordered by Anu, a [decision] from the heart of Enlil." And it was the result of a single event—"spawned in a single spawning, in a lightning flash"—an event that occurred far away in the west: "From the midst of the mountains it had come, from the Plain of No-Pity it had come . . . Like a bitter venom of the gods, from the west it had come."

That the cause of the Evil Wind was the nuclear "upheaval" back
in and near the Sinai Peninsula was made clear when the texts asserted
that the gods knew its source and cause—*a blast, an explosion:*

> *An evil blast heralded the baleful storm,*
> *An evil blast was its forerunner.*
> *Mighty offspring, valiant sons,*
> *were the heralds of the pestilence.*

The authors of the lamentation texts, the gods themselves, left us a
vivid record of what had taken place. As soon as the Awesome Weapons
were launched from the skies by Ninurta and Nergal, "they spread awesome rays, scorching everything like fire." The resulting storm "in a
flash of lightning was created." A "dense cloud that brings doom"—a
nuclear "mushroom"—then rose to the sky, followed by "rushing wind
gusts . . . a tempest that scorches the heavens." It was a day not to be
forgotten:

> *On that day,*
> *When heaven was crushed*
> *and the Earth was smitten,*
> *its face obliterated by the maelstrom—*
> *When the skies were darkened*
> *and covered as with a shadow—*
> *On that day the Evil Wind was born.*

The various texts kept attributing the venomous maelstrom to
the explosion at the "place where the gods ascend and descend"—to
the obliteration of the spaceport, rather than to the destruction of the
"sinning cities." It was there, "in the midst of the mountains," that the
nuclear mushroom cloud arose in a brilliant flash—and it was from
there that the prevailing winds, coming from the Mediterranean Sea,
carried the poisonous nuclear cloud eastward, toward Sumer, and there
it caused not destruction but a silent annihilation, bringing death by
nuclear poisoned air to all that lives.

It is evident from all the relevant texts that, with the possible exception of Enki, who had protested and warned against the use of the Awesome Weapons, none of the gods involved expected the eventual outcome. Most of them were Earthborn, and to them the tales of the nuclear wars on Nibiru were Tales of the Elders. Did Anu, who should have known better, think perhaps that the weapons, hidden so long ago, would hardly work or not work at all? Did Enlil and Ninurta (who had come from Nibiru) assume that the winds, if at all, would blow the nuclear cloud toward the desolate deserts that are now Arabia? There is no satisfactory answer; the texts only state that "the great gods paled at the storm's immensity." But it is clear that as soon as the direction of the winds and the intensity of the nuclear venom were realized, an alarm was sounded for those in the wind's path—gods and people alike—to run for their lives.

The panic, fear, and confusion that overtook Sumer and its cities as the alarm was sounded are vividly described in a series of lamentation texts, such as the *Ur Lamentation,* the *Lamentation over the Desolation of Ur and Sumer, The Nippur Lamentation, The Uruk Lamentation,* and others. As far as the gods were concerned, it appears that it was by and large "each man for himself"; using their varied craft, they took off by air and by water to get out of the wind's path. As for the people, the gods did sound the alarm before they fled. As described in *The Uruk Lamentation,* "Rise up! Run away! Hide in the steppe!" the people were told in the middle of the night. "Seized with terror, the loyal citizens of Uruk" ran for their lives, but they were felled by the Evil Wind anyway.

The picture, though, was not identical everywhere. In Ur, the capital, Nannar/Sin was so incredulous that he refused to believe that Ur's fate has been sealed. His long and emotional appeal to his father, Enlil, to avert the calamity is recorded in the *Ur Lamentation* (which was composed by Ningal, Nannar's spouse); so is Enlil's blunt admission of inevitability:

> *Ur was granted kingship—*
> *An eternal reign it was not granted . . .*

Unwilling to accept the inevitable and too devoted to the people

of Ur to abandon them, Nannar and Ningal decided to stay put. It was daytime when the Evil Wind approached Ur; "of that day I still tremble," Ningal wrote, "but of that day's foul smell we did not flee." As doomsday came, "a bitter lament was raised in Ur, but of its foulness we did not flee." The divine couple spent the night of nightmares in the "termite house," an underground chamber deep inside their ziggurat. By morning, as the venomous wind "was carried off from the city," Ningal realized that Nannar was ill. She hastily put on garments and had the god carried out and away from Ur, the city that they loved.

At least another deity was also harmed by the Evil Wind; she was Ninurta's spouse, Bau, who was alone in Lagash (for her husband was busy destroying the spaceport). Loved by the people, who called her "Mother Bau," she was trained as a healing physician, and just could not force herself to leave. The lamentations record that "On that day, the storm caught up with the Lady Bau; as if she was a mortal, the storm caught up with her." It is not clear how badly she was stricken, but subsequent records from Sumer suggest that she did not survive long thereafter.

Eridu, Enki's city, lying farthest to the south, was apparently at the edge of the Evil Wind's path. We learn from *The Eridu Lament* that Ninki, Enki's spouse, flew away from the city to a safe haven in Enki's African Abzu: "Ninki, the Great Lady, flying like a bird, left her city." But Enki himself departed from the city only far enough to get out of the Evil Wind's way: "The Lord of Eridu stayed outside his city . . . for the fate of his city he wept with bitter tears." Many of Eridu's citizens followed him, camping in the fields at a safe distance as they watched— for a day and a half—the storm "put its hand on Eridu."

Amazingly, the least affected of all the land's major centers was Babylon, for it lay beyond the storm's northern edge. As the alert was sounded, Marduk contacted his father to seek advice: What are the people of Babylon to do? he asked. Those who can escape should go north, Enki told him; and in the manner of the two "Angels" who had advised Lot and his family not to look back when they fled Sodom, so did Enki instruct Marduk to tell his followers "neither to turn nor to look back." If escape was not possible, the people should seek shelter underground:

"Get them into a chamber below the earth, into a darkness," was Enki's advice. Following this advice, and due to the wind's direction, Babylon and its people were unharmed.

As the Evil Wind passed and blew away (its remnants, we learn, reached the Zagros Mountains farther east), it left Sumer desolate and prostrate. "The storm desolated the cities, desolated the houses." The dead, lying where they fell, remained unburied: "The dead people, like fat placed in the sun, of themselves melted away." In the grazing lands, "cattle large and small became scarce, all living creatures came to an end." The sheepfolds "were delivered to the Wind." The cultivated fields withered; "on the banks of the Tigris and the Euphrates only sickly weeds grew, in the swamps the reeds rotted in a stench." "No one treads the highways, no one seeks out the roads."

"Oh Temple of Nannar in Ur, bitter is thy desolation!" the lamentation poems bewailed; "Oh Ningal whose land has perished, make thy heart like water!"

> *The city has become a strange city,*
> *how can one now exist?*
> *The house has become a house of tears,*
> *it makes my heart like water.*
> *Ur and its temples have been*
> *delivered to the Wind.*

After two thousand years, the great Sumerian civilization was gone with the wind.

In recent years archaeologists have been joined by geologists, climatologists, and other earth sciences experts for multidisciplinary efforts to tackle the enigma of the abrupt collapse of Sumer & Akkad at the end of the third millennium B.C.

A trend-setting study was one by an international group of seven scientists from different disciplines titled "Climate Change and the Collapse of the Akkadian Empire: Evidence from the Deep Sea," published in the scientific journal *Geology* in its April 2000 issue. Their

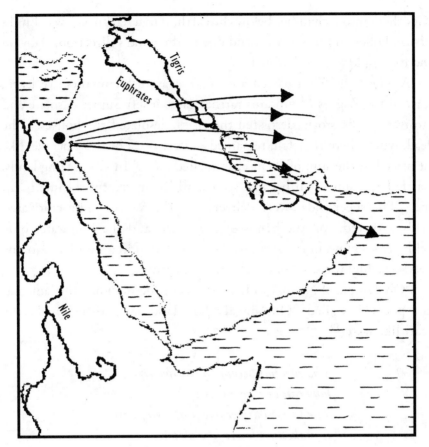

Figure 37

research used radiological and chemical analysis of ancient dust layers
from that period obtained from various Near Eastern sites, but primarily from the bottom of the Gulf of Oman; their conclusion was that
an unusual climate change *in the areas adjoining the Dead Sea* gave rise
to dust storms and that the dust—an unusual "atmospheric mineral
dust"—was carried by the prevailing winds over southern Mesopotamia
all the way beyond the Persian Gulf (fig. 37)—the very pattern of
Sumer's Evil Wind! Carbon dating of the unusual "fallout dust" led to
the conclusion that it was due to an' *"uncommon dramatic event that
occurred near 4025 years before the present."* **That, in other words,
means "near 2025 B.C."**—*the very 2024 B.C. indicated by us!*

Interestingly, the scientists involved in that study observed in their

report that *"the Dead Sea level fell abruptly by 100 meters at that time."*
They leave the point unexplained—but obviously the breach of the
Dead Sea's southern barrier and the flooding of the Plain, as described
by us, explain what had happened.

The scientific journal *Science* devoted its issue of 27 April 2001
to Paleoclimate worldwide. In a section dealing with the events in
Mesopotamia, it refers to evidence from Iraq, Kuwait, and Syria that
the "widespread abandonment of the alluvial plain" between the Tigris
and Euphrates Rivers was due to dust storms "commencing 4025 years
B.P." ("Before the Present"). The study leaves unexplained the cause of
the abrupt "climate change," but it adopts the same date for it: 4,025
years before A.D. 2001.

The fateful year, modern science confirms, was 2024 B.C.

7

DESTINY HAD
FIFTY NAMES

The resort to nuclear weapons at the end of the twenty-first century B.C. ushered—one could say, "with a bang"—the Era of Marduk. It was, in almost all respects, truly a New Age, even the way we understand the term nowadays. Its greatest paradox was that while it made Man look to the heavens, it brought the gods of the heavens down to Earth. The changes that New Age has wrought affect us to this day.

For Marduk the New Age was a wrong righted, an ambition attained, prophecies fulfilled. The price paid—the desolation of Sumer, the flight of its gods, the decimation of its people—was not his doing. If anything, those who suffered were punished for obstructing Destiny. The unforeseen nuclear storm, the Evil Wind, and its course that seemed selectively guided by an unseen hand only confirmed what the Heavens proclaimed: **the Age of Marduk, the Age of the Ram, has arrived.**

The change from the Age of the Bull to the Age of the Ram was especially celebrated and marked in Marduk's homeland, Egypt. Astronomical depictions of the heavens (such as at the Denderah temple, see fig. 20) showed the constellation of the Ram as the focal point of the zodiacal cycle. Lists of zodiacal constellations began not with the Bull as in Sumer, but with the Ram (fig. 38). The most impressive

1. Aries 2. Taurus 3. Gemini

4. Cancer 5. Leo

6. Virgo 7. Libra 8. Scorpio

9. Sagittarius 10. Capricorn

11. Aquarius 12. Pisces

Figure 38

Figure 39

manifestations were the rows of Ram-headed sphinxes that flanked
the processional way to the great temples in Karnak (fig. 39), whose
construction, by Pharaohs of the newly established Middle Kingdom,
began right after Ra/Marduk's ascent to supremacy. They were
Pharaohs who bore theophoric names honoring Amon/Amen, so that
both temples and kings were dedicated to Marduk/Ra as **Amon,** *The
Unseen,* for Marduk, absenting himself from Egypt, selected Babylon in
Mesopotamia to be his Eternal City.

Both Marduk and Nabu survived the nuclear maelstrom unharmed.
Although Nabu was personally targeted by Nergal/Erra, he apparently
hid on one of the Mediterranean islands and escaped harm. Subsequent
texts indicate that he was given his own cult center in Mesopotamia called
Borsippa, a new city situated near his father's Babylon, but he continued
to roam and be worshipped in his favorite Lands of the West. His veneration both there and in Mesopotamia is attested to by sacred places named
in his honor—such as Mount Nebo near the Jordan River (where Moses
later died)—and the theophoric royal names (such as Nabo-pol-assar,
Nebo-chad-nezzar, and many others) by which famous kings of Babylon
were called. And his name, as we have noted, became synonymous with
"prophet" and prophecy throughout the ancient Near East.

Marduk himself, it will be recalled, was asking "Until when?" from his command post in Harran when the fateful events took place. In his autobiographical text *The Marduk Prophecy* he envisioned the **coming of a Messianic Time,** when gods and men will recognize his supremacy, when peace shall replace war and abundance will banish suffering, when a king of his choice "will make Babylon the foremost" with the *Esagil* temple (as its name meant) raising its head to heaven—

> *A king in Babylon will arise;*
> *In my city Babylon, in its midst,*
> *my temple to heaven he will raise;*
> *The mountainlike Esagil he will renew,*
> *the ground plan of Heaven-Earth*
> *for the mountainlike Esagil he will draw;*
> *The Gate of Heaven will be opened.*
> *In my city Babylon a king will arise;*
> *In abundance he will reside;*
> *My hand he will grasp,*
> *He will lead me in processions . . .*
> *To my city and my temple Esagil*
> *for eternity I shall enter.*

That new Tower of Babel, however, was not intended (as the first one was) as a launch tower. His supremacy, Marduk recognized, was now stemming not only from the possession of a physical space connection but from the Signs of Heaven—from the zodiacal Celestial Time, from the position and movement of the celestial bodies, the *Kakkabu* (stars/planets) of heaven.

Accordingly, he envisioned the future Esagil as the reigning astronomical observatory, making redundant Ninurta's Eninnu and the varied stonehenges erected by Thoth. When the Esagill was eventually built, it was a ziggurat erected according to detailed and precise plans (fig. 40): its height, the spacing of its seven stages, and its orientation were such that its head pointed directly to the star *Iku*—the lead star of the constellation of the Ram—circa **1960 B.C.**

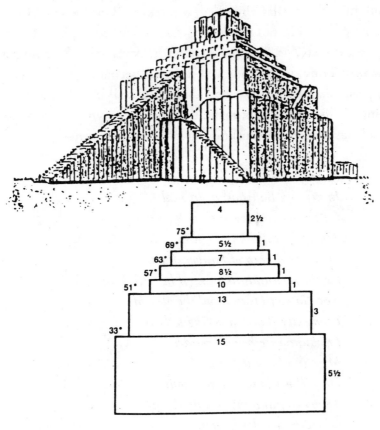

Figure 40

The nuclear apocalypse and its unintended consequences brought to an abrupt end the debate regarding whose zodiacal age it was; Celestial Time was now Marduk's Time. But the gods' planet, Nibiru, was still orbiting and clocking Divine Time—and Marduk's attention shifted to that. As his Prophecy text made clear, he now envisioned astronomer-priests scanning the skies from the ziggurat's stages for **"The rightful planet of the Esagil":**

> *Omen-knowers, put to service.*
> *shall then ascend its midst.*
> *Left and right, on opposite sides,*
> *they shall separately stand.*
> *The king will then approach;*

The rightful Kakkabu *of the Esagil*
over the land [he will observe].

A Star-Religion was born. The god—Marduk—became a star; a star (we call it planet)—Nibiru—became "Marduk." Religion became Astronomy, Astronomy became Astrology.

In conformity with the new Star Religion, the *Epic of Creation, Enuma Elish,* was revised in its Babylonian version so as to grant Marduk a celestial dimension: he did not just come from Nibiru—he *was* Nibiru. Written in "Babylonian," a dialect of Akkadian (the Semitic mother language), it equated Marduk with Nibiru, the home planet of the Anunnaki, and gave the name "Marduk" to the Great Star/Planet that had come from deep space to avenge both the celestial Ea and the one on Earth (fig. 41). It thus made "Marduk" the "Lord" in Heaven as on Earth. His Destiny—in the heavens, his orbit—was the greatest of all the celestial gods (the other planets) (see fig. 1); paralleling that, he was destined to be the greatest of the Anunnaki gods on Earth.

The revised *Epic of Creation* was read publicly on the fourth night of the New Year festival. It credited Marduk with the defeat of the "monster"

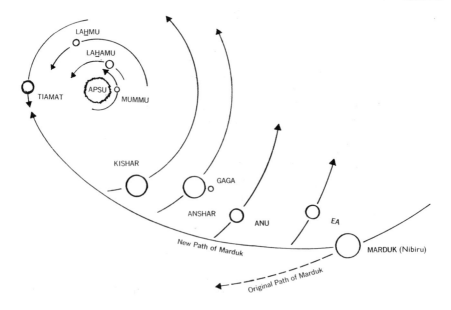

Figure 41

Tiamat in the Celestial Battle, the creation of the Earth (fig. 42), and the reshaping of the solar system (fig. 43)—all the feats that in the original Sumerian version were attributed to the planet Nibiru as part of a sophisticated scientific cosmogony. The new version then credited Marduk even with the "artful fashioning" of "Man," with devising the calendar, and with the selection of Babylon to be the "Navel of the Earth."

The New Year festival—the most important religious event of the year—began on the first day of the month Nissan, coinciding with the Spring Equinox. Calling it in Babylon the *Akiti* festival, it evolved there into a twelve-day-long celebration from the Sumerian ten-day A.KI.TI ("On Earth Bring Life") festival. It was conducted according to elaborately defined ceremonies and prescribed rituals that reenacted (in Sumer) the tale of Nibiru and the coming of the Anunnaki to Earth, as well as (in Babylon) the life story of Marduk. It included episodes from the Pyramid Wars, when he was sentenced to die in a sealed tomb,

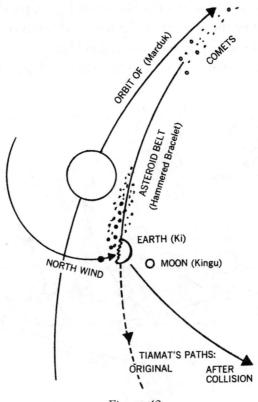

Figure 42

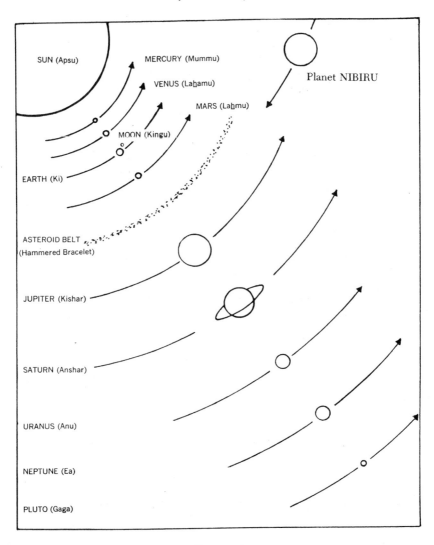

Figure 43

and his "resurrection" when he was brought out of it alive; his exile to become the Unseen; and his final victorious Return. Processions, comings and goings, appearances and disappearances, and even passion plays with actors visually and vividly presented Marduk to the people as a suffering god—suffering on Earth but finally victorious by gaining supremacy through a heavenly counterpart. (The New Testament's Jesus story was so similar that scholars and theologians in Europe debated a century ago whether Marduk was the *"Prototype Jesus."*)

Figure 44

The ceremonies consisted of two parts. The first involved a solitary boat ride by Marduk upon and across the river, to a structure called *Bit Akiti* ("House of Akiti"); the other took place within the city itself. It is evident that the solitary part symbolized Marduk's celestial travel from the home planet's outer location in space to the inner solar system—a journey in a boat upon waters, in conformity with the concept that interplanetary space was a primeval "Watery Deep" to be traversed by "celestial boats" (spacecraft)—a concept represented graphically in Egyptian art, where the celestial gods were depicted as coursing in the skies in "celestial barques" (fig. 44).

It was upon Marduk's successful return from the outer and lonely Bit Akiti that the public festivities began. Those public and joyous ceremonies started with the greeting of Marduk at the wharf by other gods, and his accompaniment by the king and priests in a Sacred Procession, attended by ever-larger crowds. The descriptions of the procession and its route were so detailed that they guided the archaeologists who excavated ancient Babylon. From the texts inscribed on clay tablets and from the unearthed topography of the city, it emerged that there were seven stations at which the sacred procession made stops for prescribed rituals. The stations bore both Sumerian and Akkadian names and symbolized (in Sumer) the travels of the Anunnaki within the solar system (from Pluto to Earth, the seventh planet), and (in Babylon) the "stations" in Marduk's life story: his divine birth in the "Pure Place"; how his birthright, his entitlement to supremacy, was denied; how he was sentenced to death; how he was buried (alive, in the Great Pyramid); how he was

rescued and resurrected; how he was banished and went into exile; and how in the end even the great gods, Anu and Enlil, bowed to destiny and proclaimed him supreme.

The original Sumerian *Epic of Creation* extended over six tablets (paralleled by the biblical six days of creation). In the Bible, God rested on the seventh day, using it to review His handiwork. The Babylonian revision of the Epic culminated with the addition of a seventh tablet that was entirely devoted to the glorification of Marduk by the granting to him of fifty names—an act that symbolized the assumption by him of the Rank of Fifty that was until then Enlil's (and to which Ninurta had been in line).

Starting with his traditional name MAR.DUK, "son of the Pure Place," the names—alternating between Sumerian and Akkadian—granted him epithets that ranged from "Creator of All" to "Lord who fashioned Heaven and Earth" and other titles relating to the celestial battle with Tiamat and the creation of the Earth and the Moon: "Foremost of all the gods," "Allotter of tasks to the Igigi and the Anunnaki" and their Commander, "The god who maintains life . . . the god who revives the dead," "Lord of all the lands," the god whose decisions and benevolence sustain Mankind, the people he had fashioned, "Bestower of cultivation," who causes rains to enrich the crops, allocates fields, and "heaps abundance" for gods and people alike.

Finally, he was granted the name NIBIRU, "He who shall hold the Crossing of Heaven and Earth":

> *The* Kakkabu *which in the skies is brilliant . . .*
> *He who the Watery Deep ceaselessly courses—*
> *Let "Crossing" be his name!*
> *May he uphold the courses of the stars in heaven,*
> *May he shepherd the heavenly gods as sheep.*

"With the title 'Fifty' the great gods proclaimed him; He whose name is 'Fifty' the gods made supreme," the long text states in conclusion.

When the nightlong reading of the seven tablets was completed—it probably was dawn by then—the priests who conducted the ritual service made the following prescribed pronouncements:

Figure 45

Let the Fifty Names be kept in mind . . .
Let the wise and knowing discuss them.
Let the father recite them to his son,
Let the ears of shepherds and herdsmen be opened.
Let them rejoice in Marduk, the "Enlil" of the gods,
whose order is firm, whose command is unalterable;
The utterance of his mouth no god can change.

When Marduk appeared in sight of the people, he was dressed in magnificent vestments that put to shame the simple wool garments of the olden gods of Sumer & Akkad (fig. 45).

Although Marduk was an unseen god in Egypt, his veneration and acceptance there took hold rather quickly. A Hymn to Ra-Amon that glorified the god by a variety of names in emulation of the Akkadian Fifty Names called him "Lord of the gods, who behold him in the midst of the horizon"—a celestial god—"who made the entire Earth," as well as a god on Earth "who created mankind and made the beasts, who created the fruit tree, made herbage and gave life to cattle"—a god "for whom the sixth day is celebrated." The snippets of similarities to the Mesopotamian and the biblical creation tales are clear.

Figure 46

According to these expressions of faith, on Earth, in Egypt, Ra/
Marduk was an unseen god because his main abode was elsewhere—
one long hymn actually referred to Babylon as the place where the gods
are in jubilation for his victory (scholars, though, assume the reference
is not to the Mesopotamian Babylon but to a town by that name in
Egypt). In the heavens he was unseen, because "he is far away in heaven,"
because he went "to the *rear of the horizons . . .* to the height of heaven."
Egypt's reigning symbol—a Winged Disc usually flanked by serpents—
is commonly explained as a Sun disc "because Ra was the Sun"; but, in
fact, it was the ancient world's ubiquitous symbol of Nibiru (fig. 46),
and it was Nibiru that has become a distant unseen "star."

Because Ra/Marduk was physically absent from Egypt, it was in
Egypt that his Star Religion was expressed in its clearest form. There,
Aten, the "Star of Millions of Years" representing Ra/Marduk in his

celestial aspect, became *The Unseen* because it was "far away in heaven," because it had gone "to the rear of the horizon."

The transition to Marduk's New Age and new religion was not so smooth in the Enlilite lands. First, southern Mesopotamia and the western lands that were in the path of the poisonous wind had to recover from its impact.

The calamity that befell Sumer, it will be recalled, was not the nuclear explosion per se but the ensuing radioactive wind. The cities were emptied of their residents and livestock, but were physically undamaged. The waters were poisoned, but the flowing two great rivers soon corrected that. The soil absorbed the radioactive poison, and that took longer to recover; but that, too, improved with time. And so it was possible for people to slowly repopulate and reinhabit the desolated land.

The first recorded administrative ruler in the devastated south was an ex-governor of Mari, a city way northwest on the Euphrates River. We learn that "he was not of Sumerian seed"; his name, Ishbi-Erra, was in fact a Semitic name. He established his headquarters in the city of Isin, and from there he oversaw the efforts to resurrect the other major cities, but the process was slow, difficult, and at times chaotic. His efforts at rehabilitation were continued by several successors, also bearing Semitic names, the so-called Dynasty of Isin. All together, it took them close to a century to revive Ur, Sumer's economic center, and ultimately Nippur, the land's traditional religious heart; but by then that city-at-a-time process ran into challenges from other local city rulers, and the erstwhile Sumer remained fragmented and a broken land.

Even Babylon itself, though outside the Evil Wind's direct path, needed a revived and repopulated country if it was to rise to imperial size and status, and it did not attain the grandeur of Marduk's prophecies for quite some time. More than a century had to pass until a formal dynasty, called by scholars the First Dynasty of Babylon, was installed on its throne (circa 1900 B.C.). Yet another century had to pass until a king who lived up to the prophesied greatness sat on Babylon's throne; his name was Hammurabi. He is mostly known for the code of laws proclaimed by him—laws recorded on a stone stela that

archaeologists have discovered (and that is now in the Louvre in Paris).

It still took some two centuries before Marduk's prophetic vision regarding Babylon could come true. The meager evidence from the post-calamity time—some scholars refer to the period following the demise of Ur as a Dark Age in Mesopotamian history—suggests that Marduk let the other gods—even his adversaries—take care of the recovery and repopulation of their own olden cult centers, but it is doubtful that they took up his invitation. The recovery and rebuilding that were started by Ishbi-Erra began at Ur, but there is no mention of Nannar/Sin and Ningal returning to Ur. There is mention of Ninurta's occasional presence in Sumer, especially in regard to its garrisoning by troops from Elam and Gutium, but there is no record that he or his spouse, Bau, ever returned to their beloved Lagash. The efforts by Ishbi-Erra and his successors to restore the cult centers and their temples culminated—after the passage of seventy-two years—at Nippur, but there is no mention that Enlil and Ninlil resumed residence there.

Where had they gone? One avenue of exploring that intriguing subject was to ascertain what Marduk himself—now supreme and claiming to be the giver of commands to all the Anunnaki—had planned for them.

The textual and other evidence from that time show that Marduk's rise to supremacy did not end polytheism—the religious beliefs in many gods. On the contrary, his supremacy required continued polytheism, for to be supreme over other gods, the existence of other gods was necessary. He was satisfied to let them be, as long as their prerogatives were subject to his control; a Babylonian tablet recorded (in its undamaged portion) the following list of divine attributes that were henceforth vested in Marduk:

Ninurta	is	Marduk of the hoe
Nergal	is	Marduk of the attack
Zababa	is	Marduk of the combat
Enlil	is	Marduk of lordship and counsel
Sin	is	Marduk the illuminator of the night
Shamash	is	Marduk of justice
Adad	is	Marduk of rains

The other gods remained, their attributes remained—but they now held attributes of Marduk that *he* granted to them. He let their worship be continued; the very name of the interim ruler/administrator in the south, Ishbi-*Erra* ("Priest of Erra," i.e., of Nergal) confirms this tolerant policy. But what Marduk expected was that they come and stay with him in his envisaged Babylon—prisoners in golden cages, one may say.

In his autobiographical *Prophecies* Marduk clearly indicated his intentions in regard to the other gods, including his adversaries: they were to come and reside next to him, in Babylon's sacred precinct. Sanctuaries or pavilions for Sin and Ningal, where they would reside—"together with their treasures and possessions"!—are specifically mentioned. Texts describing Babylon, and archaeological excavations there, show that in accordance with Marduk's wishes, Babylon's sacred precinct also included residence-shrines dedicated to Ninmah, Adad, Shamas, and even Ninurta.

When Babylon finally rose to imperial power—under Hammurabi—its ziggurat-temple indeed reached skyward; the prophesied great king in time did sit on its throne; but to its priest-filled sacred precinct, the other gods did not flock. That manifestation of the New Religion did not come about.

Looking at the Hammurabi stela recording his law code (fig. 47), we see him receiving the laws from none other than Utu/Shamash—the very one, according to the above-quoted list, whose prerogatives as God of Justice now belonged to Marduk; and the preamble inscribed on the stela invoked Anu *and Enlil*—the one whose "Lordship and Counsel" were presumably taken over by Marduk—as the gods to whom Marduk was beholden for his status:

> *Lofty Anu,*
> *Lord of the gods who from heaven to Earth came,*
> *and Enlil, Lord of Heaven and Earth*
> *who determines the Land's destinies,*
> *Determined for Marduk, the firstborn of Enki,*
> *the Enlil-functions over all mankind.*

Figure 47

These acknowledgments of the continued empowerment of Enlilite gods, two centuries after the Age of Marduk began, reflect the actual state of affairs: They did not come to retire in Marduk's sacred precinct. Dispersed away from Sumer, some accompanied their followers to far lands in the four corners of the Earth; others remained nearby, rallying their followers, old and new, to a renewed challenge to Marduk.

The sense that Sumer as a homeland was no more is clearly expressed in the divine instructions to Abram of Nippur—on the eve of the nuclear upheaving—to "Semitize" his name to Abraham (and that of his wife Sarai to Sarah), and to make his permanent home in Cannan. Abraham and his wife were not the only Sumerians in need of a new refuge. The nuclear calamity triggered migrational movements on a scale unknown before. The first wave of people was *away* from the affected lands; its most significant aspect, and one with the most lasting effects, was the dispersal of Sumer's remnants away from Sumer. The next wave of migrants was *into* that abandoned land, coming in waves from all directions.

Whichever direction those migration waves took, the fruits of two thousand years of Sumerian civilization were adopted by the other peoples that followed them in the next two millennia. Indeed, though Sumer as a physical entity was crushed, the attainments of its civilization

are still with us to this day—just look up your *twelve-month* calendar, check the time on *your watch* that retained the Sumerian sexagesimal ("base sixty") system, or drive in your contraption on *wheels* (a car).

The evidence for a widespread Sumerian diaspora with its language, writing, symbols, customs, celestial knowledge, beliefs, and gods comes in many forms. Beside the generalities—a religion based on a pantheon of gods who have come from the heavens, a divine hierarchy, god epithet-names that mean the same in the different languages, astronomical knowledge that included a home planet of the gods, a zodiac with its twelve houses, virtually identical creation tales, and memories of gods and demigods that scholars treat as "myths"—there are a host of astounding specific similarities that cannot be explained other than by an actual presence of Sumerians. It was expressed in the spread in Europe of Ninurta's Double-Eagle symbol (fig. 48); the fact that three European languages—Hungarian, Finnish, and Basque—are akin only to Sumerian; and the widespread depiction throughout the world, even in South America, of Gilgamesh fighting off with bare hands two ferocious lions (fig. 49).

In the Far East, there is the clear similarity between the Sumerian cuneiform writing and the scripts of China, Korea, and Japan. The similarity is not only in the script: many similar glyphs are identically pronounced and also have the same meanings. In Japan, civilization

Figure 48

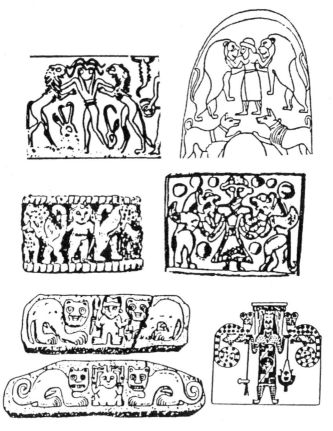

Figure 49

has been attributed to an enigmatic forefather-tribe called AINU. The emperor's family has been deemed to be a line of demigods descended from the Sun-god, and the investiture ceremonies of a new king include a secret solitary nightly stay with the Sun goddess—a ritual ceremony that uncannily emulates the Sacred Marriage rites in ancient Sumer, when the new king spent a night with Inanna/Ishtar.

In the erstwhile Four Regions, the migratory waves of diverse peoples triggered by the nuclear calamity and Marduk's New Age, much like flowing and overflowing rivers and rivulets after stormy rains, filled the pages of the ensuing centuries with the rise and fall of nations, states, and city-states. Into the Sumerian void, newcomers came in from near and far; their arena, their central stage, remained what can rightly

be called the Lands of the Bible. Indeed, until the advent of modern archaeology, little or nothing was known about most of them except for their mention in the Hebrew Bible; it provided not only a record of those various peoples but also of their "national gods"—and of the wars fought in the name of those gods.

But then nations such as the Hittites, states such as Mitanni, or royal capitals such as Mari, Carchemish, or Susa, which were doubt-filled puzzles, were literally dug up by archaeology; in their ruins there were found not only telltale artifacts but also thousands of inscribed clay tablets that brought to light both their existence as well as the extent of their debt to the Sumerian legacy. Virtually everywhere, Sumerian "firsts" in sciences and technology, literature and art, kingship and priesthood were the foundation on which subsequent cultures were developed. In astronomy, Sumerian terminology, orbital formulas, planetary lists, and zodiacal concepts were retained. The Sumerian cuneiform script was kept in use for another thousand years, and then more. The Sumerian language was studied, Sumerian lexicons were compiled, and Sumerian epic tales of gods and heroes were copied and translated. And once those nations' diverse languages were deciphered, it turned out that their gods were, after all, members of the old Anunnaki pantheon.

Did the Enlilite gods themselves accompany their followers when such replanting of Sumerian knowledge and beliefs took place in faraway lands? The data are inconclusive. But what is historically certain is that within two or three centuries of the New Age, in lands bordering Babylonia, those who were supposed to become Marduk's retired guests embarked on even newer kinds of religious affiliations: *National State Religions.*

Marduk may have garnered the Fifty divine names; but it did not prevent, from then on, nation fighting nation and men killing men "in the name of God"—*their* god.

8

IN THE NAME OF GOD

If the prophecies and messianic expectations attendant on the New Age of the twenty-first century B.C. look familiar to us today, the battle cries of the subsequent centuries would not sound strange, either. If in the third millennium B.C. god fought god using armies of men, in the second millennium B.C. men fought men "in the name of god."

It took just a few centuries after the start of Marduk's New Age to show that the fulfillment of his prophecies of grandeur would not easily come. Significantly, the resistance came not so much from the dispersed Enlilite gods but from the people, the masses of their loyal worshippers!

More than a century had to pass from the time of the nuclear ordeal until Babylon (the city) emerged on the stage of history as Babylonia (the state) under its First Dynasty. During that interval southern Mesopotamia—the Sumer of old—was left to recover in the hands of temporary rulers headquartered in Isin and then in Larsa; their theophoric names—Lipit-*Ishtar,* Ur-*Ninurta,* Rim-*Sin, Enlil*-Bani—flaunted their Enlilite loyalties. Their crowning achievement was the restoration of Nippur's temple exactly seventy-two years after the nuclear havoc—another indication of where their loyalties lay, and of an adherence to a zodiacal time count.

Those non-Babylonian rulers were scions of Semitic-speaking royals from a city-state called Mari. As one looks at a map showing the

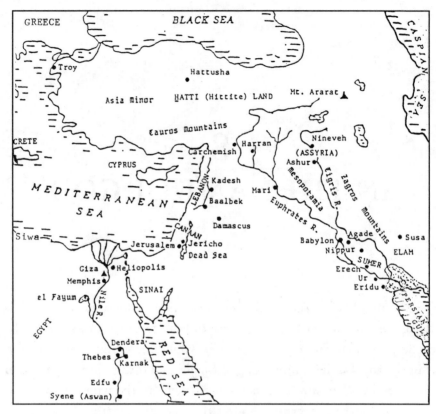

Figure 50

nation-states of the first half of the second millennium B.C. (fig. 50), it becomes clear that the non-Mardukite states formed a formidable vise around Greater Babylon, starting with Elam and Gutium on the southeast and east; Assyria and Hatti in the north; and as a western anchor in the chain, Mari on the mid-Euphrates.

Of them, Mari was the most "Sumerian," even having served once as Sumer's capital, the tenth as that function rotated among Sumer's major cities. An ancient port city on the Euphrates River, it was a major crossing point for people, goods, and culture between Mesopotamia in the east, the Mediterranean lands in the west, and Anatolia in the northwest. Its monuments bore the finest examples of Sumerian writing, and its huge central palace was decorated with murals, astounding in their artistry, honoring Ishtar (fig. 51). (A chapter on Mari and my visit to its ruins can be read in *The Earth Chronicles Expeditions*.)

Figure 51

Its royal archive of thousands of clay tablets revealed how Mari's wealth and international connections to many other city-states were first used and then betrayed by the emerging Babylon. After at first attaining the restoration of southern Mesopotamia by the Mari royals, Babylon's kings—feigning peace and unprovoked—treated Mari as an enemy. In **1760 B.C.** the Babylonian king Hammurabi attacked, sacked, and destroyed Mari, its temples, and its palaces. It was done, Hammurabi boasted in his annals, "through the mighty power of Marduk."

After the fall of Mari, chieftains from the "Sealands"—Sumer's marshy areas bordering the Lower Sea (Persian Gulf)—conducted raids northward, and took from time to time control of the sacred city of Nippur. But those were temporary gains, and Hammurabi was certain that his vanquishing of Mari completed Babylon's political and religious domination of the old Sumer & Akkad. The dynasty to which he belonged, named by scholars the First Dynasty of Babylon, began a century before him and continued through his descendants for another two centuries. In those turbulent times, it was quite an achievement.

Historians and theologians agree that in **1760 B.C.** Hammurabi, calling himself "King of the Four Quarters," "put Babylon on the world map" and **launched Marduk's distinct Star Religion.**

When Babylon's political and military supremacy was thus established, it was time to assert and aggrandize its religious domination. In a city whose splendor was extolled in the Bible and whose gardens were deemed one of the ancient world's wonders, the sacred precinct, with

Figure 52

the Esagil ziggurat-temple at its center, was protected by its own walls and guarded gates; inside, processional ways were laid out to fit the religious ceremonies, and shrines were built for other gods (whom Marduk expected to be his unwilling guests). When archaeologists excavated Babylon, they found not only the city's remains but also "architectural tablets" describing and mapping out the city; though many of the structures are remains from later times, this artist's conception of the sacred precinct's center (fig. 52) gives a good idea of Marduk's magnificent headquarters.

As befits a "Vatican," the sacred precinct was also filled with an impressive array of priests whose religious, ceremonial, administrative, political, and menial tasks can be gleaned from their varied groupings, classifications, and designations.

At the bottom of the hierarchy were the service personnel, the *Abalu*—"Porters"—who clean-swept the temple and adjoining buildings, provided the tools and utensils that the other priests required, and acted as general supply and warehousing personnel—except for woollen yarns, which were entrusted only to the *Shu'uru* priests. Special priests, like the *Mushshipu* and *Mulillu,* performed ritual purification services, except that it required a *Mushlahhu* to handle snake infestations. The *Umannu,* Master Craftsmen, worked in workshops where artful religious objects were fashioned; the *Zabbu* were a group of female priest-

esses, chefs, and cooks who prepared the meals. Other priestesses acted
as professional bewailers in funerals; the *Bakate* knew how to shed bitter tears. And then there were the *Shangu*—simply "the priests"—who
oversaw the overall functioning of the temple, the smooth performance
of its rituals, and the receiving and handling of the offerings, or who
were responsible for the gods' clothes; and so on and on.

The provision of personal "butlering" services to the resident gods
was handled by a small, specially selected elite group of priests. There
were the *Ramaqu,* who handled the purification-by-water rituals (honored with bathing the god), and the *Nisaku,* who poured out the used
water. The anointing of the god with "Sacred Oil"—a delicate mixture
of specific aromatic oils—was placed in specialized hands, starting with
the *Abaraku,* who mixed the ointments, and included the *Pashishu,*
who performed the anointing (in the case of a goddess the priests were
all eunuchs). Then there were altogether other priests and priestesses,
including the Sacred Choir—the *Naru,* who sang; the *Lallaru,* who were
singers and musicians; and the *Munabu,* whose specialty was lamentations. In each group there was the *Rabu*—the Chief, the one in charge.

As envisaged by Marduk, once his Esagil ziggurat-temple was raised
heavenward, its main function was to constantly observe the heavens;
and indeed, the most important segment of temple priests were those
whose task it was to observe the heavens, track the movement of stars
and planets, record special phenomena (such as a planetary conjunction
or an eclipse), and consider whether the heavens bespoke omens; and if
so, to interpret what they did portend.

The astronomer-priests, generally called *Mashmashu,* included
diverse specialties; a *Kalu* priest, for example, specialized in watching
the Constellation of the Bull. It was the duty of the *Lagaru* to keep
a detailed daily record of the celestial observations and to convey the
information to a cadre of interpreter-priests. These—making up the top
priestly hierarchy—included the *Ashippu,* Omen specialists, the *Mahhu*
"who could read the signs," and the *Baru*—"Truth-tellers"—who
"understood mysteries and divine signs." A special priest, the *Zaqiqu,*
was charged with conveying the divine words to the king. Then at the
head of those astronomer-astrologer priests was the *Urigallu,* the Great

Priest, who was a holy man, a magician, and a physician, whose white vestments were elaborately color-trimmed at the hems.

The discovery of some seventy tablets that formed a continuous series of observations and their meaning, named after the opening words *Enuma Anu Enlil,* revealed both the transition from Sumerian astronomy and the existence of oracular formulas that dictated what a phenomenon meant. In time a host of diviners, dream interpreters, fortune-tellers, and the like joined the hierarchy, but they were in the king's rather than the gods' service. In time the celestial observations degraded to astrological omens for king and country—predicting war, tranquillity, overthrows, long life or death, abundance or pestilences, divine blessings or godly wrath. But in the beginning the celestial observations were purely astronomical and were of prime interest to the god—Marduk—and only derivatively to king and people.

It was not by chance that a Kalu priest specialized in watching Enlil's Constellation of the Bull for any untoward phenomena, for the main purpose of the Esagil-as-observatory was to track the heavens zodiacally and keep an eye on Celestial Time. The fact that significant events prior to the nuclear blast happened in seventy-two-year intervals, and continued to do so afterward (see above and earlier chapters), suggests that the zodiacal clock, in which it took seventy-two years for a Precessional shift of one degree, continued to be observed and adhered to.

It is clear from all the astronomical (and astrological) texts from Babylon that its astronomer-priests retained the Sumerian division of the heavens into three Ways or paths, each occupying sixty degrees of the celestial arc: the Way of Enlil for the northern skies, the Way of Ea for the southern skies, and the Way of Anu as the central band (fig. 53). It was in the latter that the zodiacal constellations were located, and it was there that "Earth met Heaven"—at the horizon.

Perhaps because Marduk attained supremacy in accordance with Celestial Time, the zodiacal clock, his astronomer-priests continuously scanned the skies at the horizon, the Sumerian AN.UR, "Heaven's Base." There was no point in looking up to the Sumerian AN.PA, "Heaven's Top," the zenith, for Marduk as a "star," Nibiru, was by then gone and unseen.

But as an orbiting planet, though unseen now, it was bound to return.

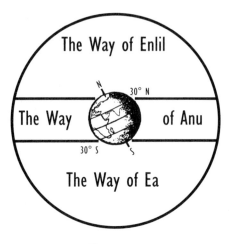

The Way of Enlil

The Way of Anu

30° N

30° S

The Way of Ea

Figure 53

Expressing its equivalent of the Marduk-is-Nibiru theme, the Egyptian version of Marduk's Star-Religion openly promised its faithful that a time will come when this god-star or star-god would *reappear* as the ATEN.

It was this aspect of Marduk's Star Religion—the eventual Return—that directly challenged Babylon's Enlilite adversaries and shifted the conflict's focus to renewed messianic expectations.

Of the post-Sumer actors on the stage of the Old World, four that grew to imperial status left the deepest imprint on history: Egypt and Babylonia, Assyria and Hatti (the land of the Hittites); and each one had its "national god."

The first two belonged to the Enki-Marduk-Nabu camp; the other two were beholden to Enlil, Ninurta, and Adad. Their national gods were called Ra-Amon and Bel/Marduk, Ashur and Teshub, and it was in the name of those gods that constant, prolonged, and cruel wars were fought. The wars, historians may explain, were caused by the usual reasons for war: resources, territory, need, or greed; but the royal annals that detailed the wars and military expeditions presented them as *religious wars* in which one's god was glorified and the opposite deity humiliated. However, the looming expectations of the Return turned those wars to *territorial campaigns* that had *specific sites as their targets*.

The wars, according to the royal annals of all those lands, were

launched by the king "on the command of my god" so-and-so; the campaign was carried out "in accordance with an oracle" from this or that god; and as often as not, victory was attained with the help of unopposable weapons or other direct help provided by the god. An Egyptian king wrote in his war records that it was "Ra who loves me, Amon who favors me," who instructed him to march "against these enemies whom Ra abominates." An Assyrian king, recording the defeat of an enemy king, boasted that he replaced in the city's temple the images of the city's gods "with the images of my gods, and declared them to be henceforth the gods of the country."

A clear example of the religious aspect of those wars—and the deliberate choice of targets—can be found in the Hebrew Bible, in 2 Kings 18–19, in which the siege of Jerusalem by the army of the Assyrian king Sennacherib is described. Having surrounded and cut off the city, the Assyrian commander engaged in psychological warfare in order to get the city's defenders to surrender. Speaking in Hebrew so that all on the city's walls could understand, he shouted to them the words of the king of Assyria: Don't be deceived by your leaders that your god Yahweh will protect you; "Has any of the gods of the nations ever rescued their lands from the hand of the king of Ashur? Where are the gods of Hamath and Arpad? Where are the gods of Sepharvaim, Hena and Avva? Where are the gods of the land of Samaria? Which of the gods of all these lands ever rescued his land from my hand? Will then Yahweh rescue Jerusalem from my hand?" (Yahweh, the historical records show, did.)

What were those religious wars about? The wars, and the national gods in whose name they were fought, don't make sense except when one realizes that at the core of the conflicts was what the Sumerians had called DUR.AN.KI—the "Bond Heaven-Earth." Repeatedly, the ancient texts spoke of the catastrophe "when Earth was separated from Heaven"—when the spaceport connecting them was destroyed. The overwhelming question in the aftermath of the nuclear calamity was this: **Who—which god and his nation—could claim to be the one on Earth who now possessed the link to the Heavens?**

For the gods, the destruction of the spaceport in the Sinai Peninsula was a material loss of a facility that required replacement. But can one

imagine the impact—the spiritual and religious impact—on Mankind? *All of a sudden, the worshipped gods of Heaven and Earth were cut off from Heaven . . .*

With the spaceport in the Sinai now obliterated, only three space-related sites remained in the Old World: the Landing Place in the Cedar Mountains; the post-Diluvial Mission Control Center that replaced Nippur; and the Great Pyramids in Egypt that anchored the Landing Corridor. With the destruction of the spaceport, did those other sites still have a useful celestial function—and thus also a religious significance?

We know the answer, to some extent, because all three sites still stand on Earth, challenging mankind by their mysteries and the gods by facing upward to the heavens.

The most familiar of the three is the Great Pyramid and its companions in Giza (fig. 54); its size, geometric precision, inner complexity,

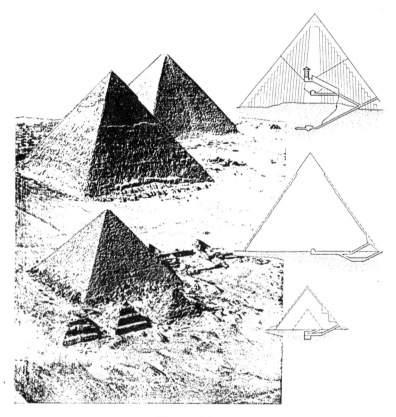

Figure 54

celestial alignments, and other amazing aspects have long cast doubt on the attribution of its construction to a Pharaoh named Cheops—an attribution supported solely by a discovery of a hieroglyph of his name inside the pyramid. In *The Stairway to Heaven* I offered proof that those markings were a modern forgery, and in that book and others voluminous textual and pictorial evidence was provided to explain how and why the Anunnaki designed and built those pyramids. Having been stripped of its radiating guidance equipment during the wars of the gods, the Great Pyramid and its companions continued to serve as physical beacons for the Landing Corridor. With the spaceport gone, they just remained silent witnesses to a vanished Past; there has been no indication that they ever became sacred religious objects.

The Landing Place in the Cedar Forest has a different record. Gilgamesh, who went to it almost a millennium before the nuclear calamity, witnessed there the launching of a rocket ship; and the Phoenicians of the nearby city of Byblos on the Mediterranean coast depicted on a coin (fig. 55) a rocket ship emplaced on a special base within an enclosure at the very same place—almost a thousand years after the nuclear event. So, with and then without the spaceport, **the Landing Place continued to be operative.**

The place, *Ba'albek* ("The valley-cleft of Ba'al"), in Lebanon, consisted in antiquity of a vast (about five million square feet) platform of paved stones at the northwestern corner of which an enormous stone structure

Figure 55

Figure 56

rose heavenward. Built with perfectly shaped massive stone blocks weighing 600 to 900 tons each, its western wall was especially fortified with the heaviest stone blocks on Earth, including three that weigh an incredible 1,100 tons each and are known as the Trilithon (fig. 56). The amazing fact about those colossal stone blocks is that they were quarried about two miles away in the valley, where one such block, whose quarrying was not completed, still sticks out from the ground (fig. 57).

The Greeks venerated the place since Alexander's time as Heliopolis (City of the Sun god); the Romans built there the greatest temple to Zeus. The Byzantines converted it to a great church; the Muslims after them built there a mosque; and present-day Maronite Christians revere the place as a relic from the Time of the Giants. (A visit to the place and its ruins, and how it functioned as a launch tower, are described in *The Earth Chronicles Expeditions*.)

Most sacred and hallowed to this day has been the site that served as Mission Control Center—*Ur-Shalem* ("City of the Comprehensive

Figure 57

Figure 58

God"), **Jerusalem.** There, too, as in Baalbek but on a reduced scale, a large stone platform rests on a rock and cut-stones foundation, including a massive **western wall with three colossal stone blocks** that weigh about six hundred tons *each* (fig. 58). It was upon that preexist-

Figure 59

ing platform that the Temple to Yahweh was built by King Solomon, its Holy of Holies with the Ark of the Covenant resting upon a sacred rock above a subterranean chamber. The Romans, who built the greatest temple ever to Jupiter in Baalbek, also planned to build one to Jupiter in Jerusalem instead of the one to Yahweh. The Temple Mount is nowadays dominated by the Muslim-built Dome of the Rock (fig. 59); its gilded dome originally surmonted the Muslim shrine at Baalbek—evidence that the link between the two space-related sites has seldom been missed.

In the trying times after the nuclear calamity, could Marduk's *Bab-Ili,* his "Gateway of the gods," substitute for the olden Bond Heaven-Earth sites? Could Marduk's new Star Religion offer an answer to the perplexed masses?

The ancient search for an answer, it seems, has continued to our very own time.

The most unremitting adversary of Babylon was the Assyrians. Their province, in the upper region of the Tigris River, was called Subartu in Sumerian times and was the northernmost extension of Sumer &

Figure 60

Akkad. In language and racial origins they appear to have had a kinship to Sargon of Akkad, so much so that when Assyria became a kingdom and imperial power, some of its most famous kings took the name
Sharru-kin—Sargon—as their royal name.

All that, gleaned from archaeolgical finds in the past two centuries,
corroborates the succint statements in the Bible (Genesis 10) that listed
the Assyrians among the descendants of Shem, and Assyria's capital,
Nineveh, and other principal cities as "coming out of"—an outgrowth,
an extension of—Shine'ar (Sumer). Their pantheon was the Sumerian
pantheon—their gods were the Anunnaki of Sumer & Akkad; and the
theophoric names of Assyrian kings and high officials indicated reverence to the gods Ashur, Enlil, Ninurta, Sin, Adad, and Shamash. There
were temples to them, as well as to the goddess Inanna/Ishtar, who was
also extensively worshipped; one of her best-known depictions, as a helmeted pilot (fig. 60), was found in her temple in Ashur (the city).

Historical documents from the time indicate that it was the
Assyrians from the north who were the first to challenge Marduk's
Babylon militarily. The very first recorded Assyrian king, Ilushuma, led
circa 1900 B.C. a successful military expedition down the Tigris River

all the way south to the border of Elam. His inscriptions state that his aim was to "set the freedom of Ur and Nippur"; and he did remove, for a while, those cities from Marduk's grip.

That was only the first fight between Assyria and Babylonia in a conflict that continued for more than a thousand years and lasted to the end of both. It was a conflict in which the Assyrian kings were usually the aggressors. Neighboring each other, speaking the same Akkadian language, and both inheriting the Sumerian foundation, the Assyrians and Babylonians were distinguishable by just one key difference: their national god.

Assyria called itself the "Land of the god Ashur," or simply *ASHUR,* after the name of its national god, for its kings and people considered this religious aspect to be all that mattered. Its first capital was also called "City of Ashur," or simply *Ashur.* The name meant "The One Who Sees" or "The One Who Is Seen." Yet with all the countless hymns, prayers, and other references to the god Ashur, it remains unclear who exactly, in the Sumerian-Akkadian pantheon, he was. In god lists he was the equivalent of Enlil; other references sometimes suggest that he was Ninurta, Enlil's son and heir; but since whenever the spouse was listed or mentioned she was always called Ninlil, the conclusion tends to be that the Assyrian "Ashur" was Enlil.

The historical record of Assyria is one of conquest and aggression against many other nations and their gods. Their countless military campaigns ranged far and wide and were carried on, of course, "in the name of god"—their god, Ashur: "On the command of my god Ashur, the great lord" was the usual opening statement in the Assyrian kings' record of a military campaign. But when it came to the warfare with Babylon, the amazing aspect of Assyria's attacks was its central aim: **not just the rollback of Babylon's influence—but the actual, physical removal of Marduk himself from his temple in Babylon!**

The feat of capturing Babylon and taking Marduk into captivity was first achieved, however, not by the Assyrians but by their neighbors to the north—the Hittites.

Circa 1900 B.C. the Hittites began to spread out from their strongholds in north-central Anatolia (today's Turkey), became a major

military power, and joined the chain of Enlilite nation-states opposed to Marduk's Babylon. In a relatively short time, they attained imperial status and their domains extended southward to include most of the biblical Canaan.

The archaeological discovery of the Hittites, their cities, records, language, and history, is an astounding and exciting tale of bringing to life and corroborating the existence of people and places hitherto known only from the Hebrew Bible. Hittites are repeatedly mentioned in the Bible, but without the disdain or scorn reserved for worshippers of pagan gods. It refers to their presence throughout the lands where the story and history of the Hebrew Patriarchs unfolded. They were Abraham's neighbors in Harran, and it was from Hittite landowners in Hebron, south of Jerusalem, that he bought the Machpelah burial cave. Bathsheba, whom King David coveted in Jerusalem, was the wife of a Hittite captain in his army; and it was from Hittite farmers (who used the site for wheat thrashing) that David bought the platform for the Temple on Mount Moriah. King Solomon bought chariot horses from Hittite princes, and it was one of their daughters whom he married.

The Bible considered the Hittites to belong, genealogically and historically, to the peoples of western Asia; modern scholars believe that they were migrants to Asia Minor from elsewhere—probably from beyond the Caucasus mountains. Because their language, once deciphered, was found to belong to the Indo-European group (as do Greek on the one hand and Sanskrit on the other hand), they are considered to have been non-Semitic "Indo-Europeans." Yet, once settled, they added the Sumerian cuneiform script to their own distinct script, included Sumerian "loan words" in their terminology, studied and copied Sumerian "myths" and epic tales, and adopted the Sumerian pantheon—including the count of twelve "Olympians." In fact, some of the earliest tales of the gods on Nibiru and coming from Nibiru were discovered only in their Hittite versions. The Hittite gods were undoubtedly the Sumerian gods, and monuments and royal seals invariably showed them accompanied by the ubiquitous symbol of the Winged Disc (see fig. 46), the symbol for Nibiru. These gods were sometimes called in the Hittite texts by their Sumerian or Akkadian names—we find Anu, Enlil, Ea,

Figure 61

Ninurta, Inanna/Ishtar, and Utu/Shamash repeatedly mentioned. In other instances the gods were called by Hittite names; leading them was the Hittite national god, **Teshub**—"the Windblower" or "God of storms." He was none other than Enlil's youngest son ISHKUR/Adad. His depictions showed him holding the lightning bolt as his weapon, usually standing upon a bull—the symbol of his father's celestial constellation (fig. 61).

The biblical references to the extended reach and military prowess of the Hittites were confirmed by archaeological discoveries both at Hittite sites and in the records of other nations. Significantly, the Hittite southward reach embraced the two space-related sites of the Landing Place (today's Baalbek) and the post-Diluvial Mission Control Center (Jerusalem); it also brought the Enlilite Hittites to within striking distance of Egypt, the land of Ra/Marduk. The two sides thus had

all it took to engage in armed conflict. In fact, the wars between the two included some of the ancient world's most famous battles fought "in the name of god."

But rather than attack Egypt, the Hittites sprung a surprise. The first, perhaps, to introduce horse-driven chariots in military campaigns, the Hittite army, totally unexpectedly, in 1595 B.C., swept down the Euphrates River, captured Babylon, **and took Marduk into captivity.**

Though one wishes that more detailed records from that time and event would have been discovered, what is known indicates that the Hittite attackers did not intend to take over and rule Babylon: they retreated soon after they had breached the city's defenses and entered its sacred precinct, taking Marduk with them, leaving him unharmed, but apparently under guard, in a city called Hana—a place (yet to be excavated) in the district of Terka, along the Euphrates River.

The humiliating absence of Marduk from Babylon lasted twenty-four years—exactly the same time that Marduk had been in exile in Harran five centuries earlier. After several years of confusion and disorder, kings belonging to a dynasty called the Kassite Dynasty took control of Babylon, restored Marduk's shrine, "took the hand of Marduk," and returned him to Babylon. Still, the Hittite sack of Babylon is considered by historians to have marked the end both of the glorious First Dynasty of Babylon and of the Old Babylonian Period.

The sudden Hittite thrust to Babylon and the temporary removal of Marduk remain an unresolved historical, political, and religious mystery. Was the intention of the raid just to embarrass and diminish Marduk—deflate his ego, confuse his followers—or was there a more far-reaching purpose—or cause—behind it?

Was it possible that Marduk fell victim to the proverbial "hoist by his own petard"?

9

THE PROMISED LAND

The capture and removal of Marduk from Babylon had geopolitical repercussions, shifting for several centuries the center of gravity from Mesopotamia westward, to the lands along the Mediterranean Sea. In religious terms, it was the equal of a tectonic earthquake: in one blow, all the great expectations by Marduk for all gods to be gathered under his aegis, and all the messianic expectations by his followers, were gone like a puff of smoke.

But both geopolitically and religiously, the greatest impact can be summed up as the story of three mountains—the three space-related sites that put the Promised Land in the midst of it all: Mount Sinai, Mount Moriah, and Mount Lebanon.

Of all the events that followed the unprecedented occurrence in Babylon, the central and most lasting one was the Israelite Exodus from Egypt—when, for the first time, sites that until then were the gods' alone were entrusted to people.

When the Hittites who took Marduk captive withdrew from Babylon, they left behind political disarray and a religious enigma: How could that happen? Why did it happen? When bad things happened to people, they would say that the gods were angry; so what now that bad things happened to gods—to Marduk? *Was there a God supreme to the supreme god?*

In Babylon itself, the eventual release and return of Marduk did not provide an answer; in fact, it increased the mystery, for the "Kassites" who welcomed the captured god back to Babylon were non-Babylonian strangers. They called Babylon "Karduniash" and had names such as Barnaburiash and Karaindash, but little else is known about them or their original language. To this day it is not clear from where they came and why their kings were allowed to replace the Hammurabi dynasty circa **1660 B.C.** and to dominate Babylon from **1560 B.C.** until **1160 B.C.**

Modern scholars speak of the period that followed Marduk's humiliation as a "dark age" in Babylonian history, not only because of the disarray it caused but mainly because of the paucity of written Babylonian records from that time. The Kassites quickly integrated themselves into the Sumerian-Akkadian culture, including language and cuneiform script, but were neither the meticulous recordkeepers the Sumerians had been nor the likes of previous Babylonian writers of royal annals. Indeed, most of the few royal records of Kassite kings have been found not in Babylon but in Egypt—clay tablets in the El-Amarna archive of royal correspondence. Remarkably, in those tablets the Kassite kings called the Egyptian Pharaohs "my brother."

The expression, though figurative, was not unjustified, for Egypt shared with Babylon the veneration of Ra-Marduk and, like Babylonia, had also undergone a "dark age"—a period scholars call the Second Intermediate Period. It began with the demise of the Middle Kingdom circa 1780 B.C. and lasted until about **1560 B.C.** As in Babylonia, it featured a reign of foreigner kings known as "Hyksos." Here, too, it is not certain who they were, from where they came, or how it was that their dynasties were able to rule Egypt for more than two centuries.

That the dates of this Second Intermediate Period (with its many obscure aspects) parallel the dates of Babylon's slide from the peak of Hammurabi's victories (**1760 B.C.**) to the capture and resumption of Marduk's worship in Babylon (circa **1560 B.C.**) is probably neither accident nor coincidence: those similar developments at parallel times in Marduk's principal lands happened because Marduk was "hoist by his own petard"—the very justification for his claim to supremacy was now causing his undoing.

Figure 62

The "petard" was Marduk's own initial contention that the time for his supremacy on Earth had arrived because in the heavens the Age of the Ram, his age, had arrived. But as the zodiacal clock kept ticking, the Age of the Ram started to slowly slip away. The physical evidence from those perplexing times still exists, and can be seen, in Thebes, the ancient Egyptian capital of Upper Egypt.

Apart from the great pyramids of Giza, ancient Egypt's most impressive and majestic monuments are the colossal temples of Karnak and Luxor in southern (Upper) Egypt. The Greeks called the place Thebai, from which its name in English—Thebes—derives; the ancient Egyptians called it the City of Amon, for it was to this unseen god that those temples were dedicated. The hieroglyphic writing and the pictorial depictions on their walls, obelisks, pylons, and columns (fig. 62) glorify the god and praise the Pharaohs who built, enlarged, expanded—and kept changing—the temples. It was there that the arrival of the Age of the Ram was announced by the rows of ram-headed sphinxes (see Fig. 39); and it is there that the very layout of the temples reveals the secret quandary of Egypt's followers of Ra-Amon/Marduk.

One time, visiting the sites with a group of fans, I stood in the midst

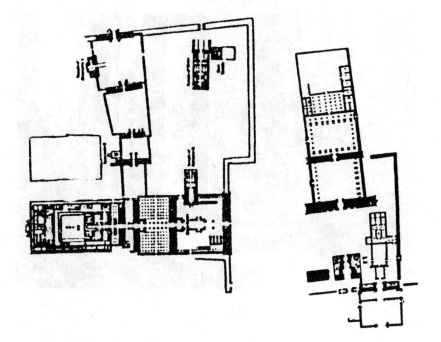

Figure 63

of a temple waving my hands as a traffic policeman; amazed onlookers wondered, "Who is this nut?" but I was trying to point out to my group the fact that the Thebes temples, built by a succession of Pharaohs, kept changing their orientation (fig. 63). It was Sir Norman Lockyer who, in the 1890s, first grasped the significance of this architectural aspect, giving rise to a discipline called archaeoastronomy.

Temples that were oriented to the equinoxes, like Solomon's temple in Jerusalem (fig. 64) (and the old St. Peter's basilica at the Vatican in Rome), faced permanently east, welcoming sunrise on equinox day year after year without reorientation. But temples oriented to the solstices, like Egypt's temples in Thebes or China's Temple of Heaven in Beijing, needed periodic reorientation because, due to Precession, where the Sun rises on solstice day shifts ever so lightly over the centuries—as can be illustrated by Stonehenge, where Lockyer applied his findings (see fig. 6). The very temples that Ra/Marduk's followers had erected to glorify him were showing that the heavens were uncertain about the durability of the god and his Age.

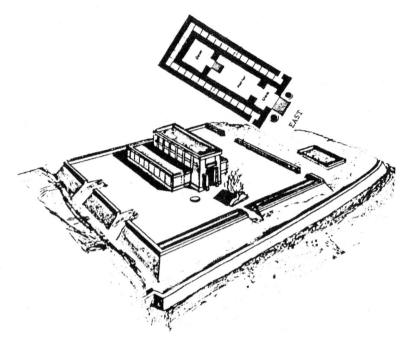

Figure 64

Marduk himself—so aware of the zodiacal clock when he had claimed in the previous millennium that his time had arrived—tried to shift the religious focus by introducing the Star Religion of "Marduk is Nibiru." But his capture and humiliation now raised questions regarding this unseen celestial god. The question, Until when will the Age of Marduk last? changed to the question, If celestially Marduk is the unseen Nibiru, when will it reveal itself, reappear, *return?*

As unfolding events showed, both the religious and the geopolitical focus shifted in the middle of the second millennium B.C. to the stretch of land that the Bible called **Canaan.** As the *return of Nibiru* started to emerge as the religious focus, the *space-related sites* also emerged into sharper focus, and it was in the geographic "Canaan" where both the Landing Place and the erstwhile Mission Control Center were located.

Historians tell the ensuing events in terms of the rise and fall of nation-states and the clash of empires. It was circa **1460 B.C.** that the forgotten kingdoms of Elam and Anshan (later known as Persia, east and southeast of Babylonia) joined to form a new and powerful state,

with Susa (the biblical Shushan) as the national capital and Ninurta, the national god, as *Shar Ilani*—"Lord of the gods"; that newly asser- tive nation-state was to play a decisive role in ending Babylon's and Marduk's supremacy.

It was probably no coincidence that at about the same time, a new powerful state arose in the Euphrates region where Mari had once dom- inated. There the biblical Horites (scholars call them Hurrians) formed a powerful state named **Mitanni**—"The Weapon of Anu"—which cap- tured the lands that are now Syria and Lebanon and posed a geopo- litical and religious challenge to Egypt. That challenge was countered, most ferociously, by Egypt's Pharaoh Tothmosis III, whom historians describe as an "Egyptian Napoleon."

Interwined with all that was the *Israelite exodus from Egypt,* that period's seminal event, if for no other reason than due to its lasting effects, to this day, on Mankind's religions, social and moral codes, and the centrality of Jerusalem. Its timing was not accidental, for all those developments related to the issue of *who shall control the space-related sites when Nibiru's return will occur.*

As was shown in previous chapters, Abraham did not just happen to become a Hebrew patriarch, but was a chosen participant in major international affairs; and the places where his tale took us—Ur, Harran, Egypt, Canaan, Jerusalem, the Sinai, Sodom and Gomorrah—were principal sites of the universal story of gods and men in earlier times. The Israelite Exodus from Egypt, recalled and celebrated by the Jewish people during the Passover holiday, was likewise an integral aspect of the events that were then unfolding throughout the ancient lands. The Bible itself, far from treating the Exodus as just an "Israelite" story, clearly placed it in the context of Egyptian history and the international events of the time.

The Hebrew Bible opens the story of the Israelite exodus from Egypt in its second book, *Exodus,* by reminding the reader that the Israelite presence in Egypt began when Jacob (who was renamed *Israel* by an angel) and his other eleven sons joined Jacob's son Joseph in Egypt, in 1833 B.C. The full story of how Joseph, separated from his

family, rose from being a slave to the rank of viceroy, and how he saved Egypt from a devastating famine, is told by the Bible in the last chapters of Genesis; and my take on how Joseph saved Egypt and what evidence of that exists to this day is told in *The Earth Chronicles Expeditions*.

Having reminded the reader of how and when the Israelite presence in Egypt began, the Bible makes it clear that all that was gone and forgotten by the time of the Exodus: "Joseph and all his brothers and all that generation had passed away." Not only they but even the dynasty of the Egyptian kings who were connected to those times were also long gone. A new dynasty came into power: "And there arose a new king over Egypt who knew not Joseph."

Accurately, the Bible describes the change of government in Egypt. The dynasties of the Middle Kingdom based in Memphis were gone, and after the disarray of the Second Intermediate Period the princes of Thebes launched the dynasties of the New Kingdom. Indeed, there arose entirely new kings over Egypt—new dynasties in a new capital, "and they knew not Joseph."

Forgetting the Israelite contribution to Egypt's survival, a new Pharaoh now saw danger in their presence. He ordered a series of oppressive steps against them, including the killing of all male babies. These were his reasons:

> *And he said unto his people:*
> *"Behold, a nation, Children of Israel, is greater and*
> *mightier than us;*
> *Let us deal wisely with them, lest they multiply*
> *and, when war shall be called, they will join our enemies,*
> *and fight against us, and leave the land."*
> EXODUS 1:9–10

Biblical scholars have assumed all along that the feared nation of the "Children of Israel" were the Israelites sojourning in Egypt. But this is in accord with neither the numbers given nor with the literal wording in the Bible. Exodus begins with a list of the names of Jacob and his children who had come, with their children, to join Joseph in Egypt and

states that "all of those who descended from the loins of Jacob, excluding Joseph who was already in Egypt numbered seventy." (That together with Jacob and Joseph the number totaled seventy-two is an intriguing detail to ponder.) The "sojourn" lasted four centuries, and according to the Bible the number of all the Israelites leaving Egypt was 600,000; no Pharaoh would consider such a group "greater and mightier than us." (For the identity of that Pharaoh and of "the Pharaoh's Daughter" who raised Moses as her son, see *Divine Encounters.*)

The narrative's wording records the Pharaoh's fear that at time of war, the Israelites will "join our enemies, and fight against us, *and leave the land.*" It is a fear not of a "Fifth Column" inside Egypt, but of Egypt's indigent "Children of Israel" leaving to reinforce an enemy nation to whom they are related—all of them being, in Egyptian eyes, "Children of Israel." But what other nation of "Children of Israel" and what war was the Egyptian king talking about?

Thanks to archaeological discoveries of royal records from both sides of those ancient conflicts and the synchronization of their contents, we now know that the New Kingdom Pharaohs were engaged in prolonged warfare against **Mitanni.** Starting circa **1560 B.C.** with the Pharaoh Ahmosis, continued by the Pharaohs Amenophis I, Thothmosis I, and Thothmosis II, and intensifying under Thothmosis III through **1460 B.C.,** Egyptian armies thrust into Canaan and advanced northward against Mitanni. The Egyptian chronicles of those battles frequently mention *Naharin* as the ultimate target—the Khabur River area, which the Bible called *Aram-Naharayim* ("The Western Land of the Two Rivers"); its principal urban center was Harran!

It was there, Bible students will recall, that Abraham's brother Nahor stayed on when Abraham proceeeded to Canaan; it was from there that Rebecca, the bride of Abraham's son Isaac, came—she was in fact the granddaughter of Nahor. And it was to Harran that Isaac's son Jacob (renamed *Israel*) went to find a bride—ending up marrying his cousins, the two daughters (Le'ah and Rachel) of Laban, the brother of his mother, Rebecca.

These direct family ties between the "Children of Israel" (i.e., of Jacob) who were in Egypt and those who stayed on in Naharin-Naharayim

are highlighted in the very first verses in Exodus: the list of the sons of Jacob who had come to Egypt with him includes the youngest, *Ben-Yamin* (Benjamin), the only full brother of Joseph because both were Jacob's sons by Rachel (the others were sons of Jacob by his wife Le'ah and two concubines). We now know from Mitannian tablets that the most important tribe in the Khabur River area were called *Ben-Yamins*! The name of Joseph's full brother was thus a Mitannian tribal name; no wonder, then, that the Egyptians considered the "Children of Israel" in Egypt and the "Children of Israel" in Mitanni as one combined nation "greater and mightier than us."

That was the war the Egyptians were preoccupied with and that was the reason for the Egyptian military concern—not the small number of Israelites in Egypt if they stayed, but a threat if they "left the land" and occupied territory to the north of Egypt. Indeed, *preventing* the Israelites from leaving appears to have been the central theme of the developing drama of the Exodus—there were the repeated appeals by Moses to the reigning Pharaoh to "let my people go," and the Pharaoh's repeated refusals to grant that request—in spite of ten consecutive divine punishments. Why? **For a plausible answer we need to insert the space connection into the unfolding drama.**

In their northward thrusts, the Egyptians marched through the Sinai Peninsula via the Way of the Sea, a route (later called by the Romans *Via Maris*) that afforded passage through the gods' Fourth Region along the Mediterranean coast, without actually entering the peninsula proper. Then, advancing north through Canaan, the Egyptians repeatedly reached the Cedar Mountains of Lebanon and fought battles at *Kadesh,* "The Sacred Place." Those were battles, we suggest, for control of the two sacred space-related sites—the erstwhile Mission Control Center (Jerusalem) in Canaan and the Landing Place in Lebanon. The Pharaoh Thothmosis III, for example, in his war annals, referred to Jerusalem (*"Ia-ur-sa"*), which he garrisoned as the *"place reaching to the outer ends of the Earth"*—a "Navel of the Earth." Describing his campaigns farther north, he recorded battles at Kadesh and Naharin and spoke of taking the Cedar Mountains, the *"Mountains of god's land"* that *"support the pillars to heaven."* The terminology unmistakably

identifies by their space-related attributes the two sites he was claiming to have captured "for the great god, my father Ra/Amon."

And the purpose of the Exodus? In the words of the biblical God himself, to keep His sworn promise to Abraham, Isaac, and Jacob to grant to their descendants as "an Everlasting Heritage" (Exodus 6:4–8); "from the Brook of Egypt to the River Euphrates, the great river"; "the whole of the Land of Canaan," (Genesis 15:18, 17:8); "the Western Mount . . . the Land of Canaan and Lebanon" (Deuteronomy 1:7); "from the desert to Lebanon, from the River Euphrates unto the Western Sea" (Deuteronomy 11:24)—even the *"fortified places reaching heavenwards"* wherein "descendants of the *Anakim*"—the Anunnaki—still resided (Deuteronomy 9:1–2).

The promise to Abraham was renewed at the Israelites' first stop, at *Har Ha-Elohim,* the "Mount of the Elohim/gods." And the mission was to take hold, possess, the two other space-related sites, which the Bible repeatedly connected (as in Psalms 48:3), calling Mount Zion in Jerusalem *Har Kodshi,* "My Sacred Mount," and the other, on the crest of Lebanon, *Har Zaphon,* "The Secret North Mount."

The Promised Land clearly embraced both space-related sites; its division among the twelve tribes granted the area of Jerusalem to the tribes of Benjamin and Judah, and the territory that is now Lebanon to the tribe of Asher. In his parting words to the tribes before he died, Moses reminded the tribe of Asher that the northern space-related site was in their land—like no other tribe, he said, they will see the *"Rider of the clouds soaring heavenwards"* (Deuteronomy 33:26). Apart from the territorial assignment, **the words of Moses imply that the site would be functional and used for soaring heavenward in the future.**

Clearly and most emphatically, the Children of Israel were to be the custodians of the two remaining space-related sites of the Anunnaki. That Covenant with the people chosen for the task was renewed, at the greatest theophany on record, at **Mount Sinai.**

It was certainly not by chance that the theophany occurred there. From the very beginning of the Exodus tale—when God called out to Moses and gave him the Exodus assignment—that place in the Sinai Peninsula occupied center stage. We read in Exodus 3:1 that it hap-

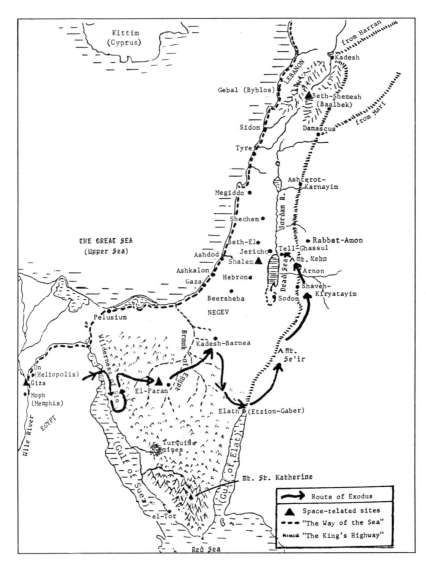

Figure 65

pened at the "Mount of the *Elohim*"—the mountain associated with the
Anunnaki. The route of the Exodus (fig. 65) was divinely determined,
the Israelite multitude having been shown the way by a "pillar of cloud
by day and a pillar of fire by night." The Children of Israel "journeyed
in the wilderness of Sinai according to the instructions of Yahweh," the
Bible clearly states; in the third month of the journey they "reached and

encamped opposite the Mount"; and on the third day thereafter, Yahweh in his *Kabod* "came down upon Mount Sinai in full view of all the people."

It was the same mount that Gilgamesh, arriving at the place where the rocket ships ascended and descended, had called "Mount *Mashu*." It was the same mount with "the double doors to heaven" to which Egyptian Pharaohs went in their Afterlife Journey to join the gods on the "planet of millions of years." It was the Mount astride the erstwhile Spaceport— and it was there that the Covenant was renewed with the people chosen to be the guardians of the two remaining space-related sites.

As the Israelites were preparing, after the death of Moses, to cross the Jordan River, the boundaries of the Promised Land were restated to the new leader, Joshua. Embracing the locations of the space-related sites, the boundaries emphatically included Lebanon. Speaking to Joshua, the biblical God said:

> *Now arise and cross this Jordan,*
> *thou and all this people, the Children of Israel,*
> *unto the land which I do give to them.*
> *Every place where the soles of your feet shall tread upon*
> *have I given to you, just as I have spoken to Moses:*
> *From the Desert to the Lebanon,*
> *and from the great river, the River Euphrates,*
> *in the country of the Hittites,*
> *unto the Great Sea, where the sun sets—*
> *That shall be your boundary.*
>
> JOSHUA 1:2–4

With so much of the current political, military, and religious tur-moil taking place in the Lands of the Bible, and with the Bible itself serving as a key to the past and to the future, one must point out a caveat inserted by the biblical God in regard to the Promised Land. The boundaries, running from the Wilderness in the south to the Lebanon range in the north, and from the Euphrates in the east to the

Mediterranean Sea in the west, were reconfirmed to Joshua. These, God said, were the *promised* boundaries. But to become an actual land grant, it had to be obtained by *possession*. Akin to the "planting of the flag" by explorers in the recent past, the Israelites could possess and keep land where they actually set foot—"tread with the soles of their feet"; therefore, God commanded the Israelites not to tarry and delay but to cross the Jordan and fearlessly and systematically settle the Promised Land.

But when the twelve tribes under the leadership of Joshua were done with the conquest and settlement of Canaan, only part of the areas east of the Jordan were occupied; nor were all of the lands west of the Jordan captured and settled. As far as the two space-related sites were concerned, their stories are totally different: Jerusalem—which was specifically listed (Joshua 12:10, 18:28)—was firmly in the hands of the tribe of Benjamin. But whether the northward advance attained the Landing Place in Lebanon is in doubt. Subsequent biblical references to the site called it the "Crest of *Zaphon*" (the "secret north place")—what the area's dwellers, the Canaanite-Phoenicians, also called it. (Canaanite epics deemed it to be a sacred place of the god Adad, Enlil's youngest son.)

The crossing of the Jordan River—an accomplishment attained with the help of several miracles—took place "opposite Jericho," and the fortified city of Jericho (west of the Jordan) was the Israelites' first target. The story of the tumbling of its walls and its capture includes a biblical reference to Sumer (*Shin'ar* in Hebrew): in spite of the commandment to take no booty, one of the Israelites could not resist the temptation to "keep a valued garment of Shin'ar."

The capture of Jericho, and the town of Ai south of it, opened the way to the Israelites' most important and immediate target: Jerusalem, where the Mission Control platform had been. The missions of Abraham and his descendants and God's covenants with them never lost sight of that site's centrality. As God told Moses, **it is in Jerusalem that His earthly abode was to be;** now the promise-prophecy could be fulfilled.

The capture of the cities on the way to Jerusalem, along with the hill towns surrounding it, turned out to be a formidable challenge, primarily because some of them, and especially Hebron, were inhabited by

"children of the *Anakim*"—descendants of the Anunnaki. Jerusalem, it will be recalled, ceased to function as Mission Control Center when the spaceport in the Sinai was wiped out more than six centuries earlier. But according to the Bible, the descendants of the Anunnaki who had been stationed there were still residing in that part of Canaan. And it was "Adoni-Zedek, king of Jerusalem" who formed an alliance with four other city-kings to block the Israelite advance.

The battle that ensued, at Gibe'on in the Valley of Ayalon just north of Jerusalem, took place on a unique day—**the day the Earth stood still.** For the better part of that day, "the Sun stopped and the Moon stood still" (Joshua 10:10–14), enabling the Israelites to win that crucial battle. (A parallel but reverse occurrence, when nighttime lasted an extra twenty hours, took place on the other side of the world, in the Americas; we discuss the matter in *The Lost Realms*.) In the biblical view, then, God himself assured that Jerusalem would come into Israelite hands.

No sooner was kingship established under David than he was commanded by God to clear the platform atop Mount Moriah and sanctify it for Yahweh's Temple. And ever since Solomon built that Temple there, Jerusalem/Mount Moriah/the Temple Mount have remained uniquely sacred. There is, indeed, no other explanation why Jerusalem—a city not at major crossroads, far from waterways, with no natural resources—has been coveted and sacred since antiquity, deemed to be a singular city, a "Navel of the Earth."

The comprehensive list of captured cities given in Joshua chapter 12 names Jerusalem as the third city, following Jericho and Ai, as firmly in Israelite hands. The story was different, however, in regard to the northern space-related site.

The Cedar Mountains of Lebanon run in two ranges, the Lebanon on the west and the anti-Lebanon on the east, separated by the *Bekka*—the "Cleft," a canyonlike valley that has been known since Canaanite times as the "Lord's Cleft," or *Ba'al-Bekka*—hence Ba'albek, the current name of the site of the Landing Place (on the edge of the eastern range, facing the valley). The kings of the "Mount of the North" are listed in the Book of Joshua as having been defeated; a place called *Ba'al*

Figure 66

Gad "in the valley of Lebanon" is listed as captured; but whether Ba'al-Gad "in the valley of Lebanon" is just another name for Ba'al-Bekka is uncertain. We are told (Judges 1:33) that the Tribe of Naphtali "did not disinherit the dwellers of Beth-Shemesh" ("Abode of Shamash," the Sun god), and that could be a reference to the site, for the later Greeks called the place Heliopolis, "City of the Sun." (Though later the territories under Kings David and Solomon extended to include Beth-Shemesh, it was only temporarily so.)

The primary failure to establish Israelite hegemony over the northern space-related site made it "available" to others. A century and a half after the Exodus the Egyptians attempted to take possession of that "available" Landing Place but were met by an opposing Hittite army. The epic battle is described in words and illustrations (fig. 66) on the walls of Karnak's temples. Known as the Battle of Kadesh, it ended with an Egyptian defeat, but the war and the battle exhausted both sides so much that the site of the Landing Place was left in the hands of the local Phoenician kings of Tyre, Sidon, and Byblos (the biblical Gebal). (The prophets Ezekiel and Amos, who called it "the place of the gods" as well as "the Eden Abode," recognized it as belonging to the Phoenicians.)

The Phoenician kings of the first millennium B.C. were well aware of the site's significance and purpose—witness its depiction on a Phoenician coin from Byblos (see fig. 55). The Prophet Ezekiel

(28:2, 14) admonished the king of Tyre for haughtily believing that, having been to that sacred site of the *Elohim,* he had become himself a god:

> *Thou hast been to a sacred mount,*
> *As a god werest thou, moving within the fiery stones . . .*
> *And you became haughty, saying:*
> *"A god am I, at the place of the* Elohim *I was";*
> *But you are just Man, not god.*

It was at that time that the Prophet Ezekiel—in exile in the "old country," near Harran on the Khabur River—saw divine visions and a celestial chariot, a "Flying Saucer," but that tale must be postponed to a later chapter. Here it is important to note **that of the two space-related sites, only Jerusalem was retained by the followers of Yahweh.**

The first five books of the Hebrew Bible, known as the Torah ("The Teachings"), cover the story from Creation, Adam, and Noah to the Patriarchs and Joseph in Genesis. The other four books—Exodus, Leviticus, Numbers, and Deuteronomy—tell the story of the Exodus on the one hand, and on the other hand enumerate the rules and regulations of the new religion of Yahweh. That a new religion encompassing a new, a "priestly" way of life was promulgated is explicitly made clear: "You shall neither do what is done in the land of Egypt, where you had dwelt, nor as is wont in the Land of Canaan whence I am bringing you; you shall neither behave like them nor follow their statutes" (Leviticus 18:2–3).

Having established the basics of the faith ("You shall have no other God before me") and its moral and ethical code in just Ten Commandments, there follow page after page of detailed dietary requirements, rules for priestly rites and vestments, medical teachings, agricultural directives, architectural instructions, family and sexual conduct regulations, property and criminal laws, and so on. They reveal extraordinary knowledge in virtually every scientific discipline, expertise in metals and textiles, acquaintance with legal systems and societal

issues, familiarity with the lands, history, customs, and gods of other nations—and certain numerological preferences.

The theme of *twelve*—as in the twelve tribes of Israel or in the twelve-month year—is obvious. Obvious, too, is the predilection for *seven,* most prominently in the realm of festivals and rituals, and in establishing a week of seven days and consecrating the seventh day as the Sabbath. *Forty* is a special number, as in the forty days and forty nights that Moses spent upon Mount Sinai, or the forty years decreed for the Israelite wandering in the Sinai wilderness. These are numbers familiar to us from the Sumerian tales—the twelve of the solar system and the twelve-month calendar of Nippur; the seven as the planetary number of the Earth (when the Anunnaki counted from the outside in) and of Enlil as Earth's Commander; the forty as Ea/Enki's numerical rank.

The number *fifty* is also present. Fifty, as the reader knows, was a number with "sensitive" aspects—it was the original rank number of Enlil and the stand-in rank of his heir apparent, Ninurta; and more significantly, in the days of the Exodus, it connoted symbolism to Marduk and his Fifty Names. Extra attention is therefore called for when we find that "fifty" was granted extraordinary importance—*it was used to create a new Unit of Time,* the *fifty-year* **Jubilee.**

While the calendar of Nippur was clearly adopted as the calendar by which the festivals and other Israelite religious rites were to be observed, special regulations were dictated for the fiftieth year; it was given a special name, that of a *Jubilee* Year: "A hallowed Jubilee year it shall be unto you" (Leviticus 25). In such a year, unprecedented freedoms were to take place. The count was to be done by counting the New Year's Day of Atonements for seven years sevenfold, forty-nine times; then on the Day of Atonement on the year thereafter, the fiftieth year, the trumpet call of a *ram's horn* was to be sounded throughout the land, and freedom was to be proclaimed for the land and all who dwelled in it: people should return to their families; property should return to its original owners—all land and house sales shall be redeemable and undone; slaves (who had to be treated at all times as hired help!) shall be set free, and liberty shall be given the land itself by leaving it fallow that year.

As much as the concept of a "Year of Freedom" is novel and unique, the choice of fifty as a calendrical unit seems odd (we have adopted 100—a century—as a convenient unit of time). Then the name given to such a once-in-fifty year is even more intriguing. The word that is translated "Jubilee" is *Yovel* in the Hebrew Bible, and it means "a ram." So one can say that what was decreed was a ***"Year of the Ram,"*** to repeat itself every fifty years, and to be announced by sounding the *ram's horn*. Both the choice of fifty for the new time unit and its name raise the unavoidable question: Was there a hidden aspect here, related to Marduk and his Age of the Ram?

Were the Israelites told to keep counting "fifty years" until some significant divine event, relating either to the Age of the Ram or to the holder of the Rank of Fifty—*when everything shall turn back to a new beginning?*

While no obvious answer is offered in those biblical chapters, one cannot avoid searching for clues by pursuing a significant and very similar year-unit on the other side of the world: not fifty, but fifty-two. It was the Secret Number of the Mesoamerican god Quetzalcoatl, who according to Aztec and Mayan legends gave them civilization, including their three calendars. In *The Lost Realms* we have identified Quetzalcoatl as the Egyptian god Thoth, whose secret number was fifty-two—a calendrical-based number, for it represented the fifty-two weeks of seven days in a solar year.

The oldest of the three Mesoamerican calendars is known as the Long Count: it counted the number of days from a "Day One" that scholars have identified as August 13, 3113 B.C. Alongside this continuous but linear calendar there were two cyclical calendars. One, the *Haab,* was a solar-year calendar of 365 days, divided into 18 months of 20 days each plus an additional 5 special days at year's end. The other was the *Tzolkin,* a Sacred Calendar of only 260 days, composed of a 20-day unit rotated 13 times. The two cyclical calendars were then meshed together, as two geared wheels (fig. 67), to create the Sacred Round of fifty-two years, when these two counts returned to their common starting point and started the counts all over again.

This "bundle" of fifty-two years was a most important unit of time,

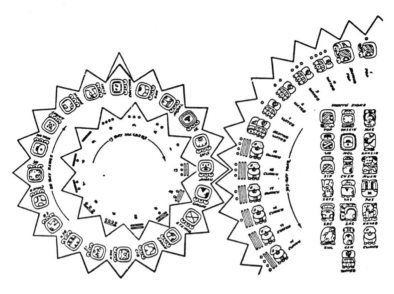

Figure 67

because it was linked to the promise of Quetzalcoatl, who at some point left Mesoamerica to return on his Sacred Year. The Mesoamerican peoples therefore used to gather on mountains every fifty-two years to expect the promised Return of Quetzalcoatl. (In one such Sacred Year, A.D. 1519, a white-faced and bearded Spaniard, Hernando Cortes, landed on Mexico's Yucatan coast and was welcomed by the Aztec king Montezuma as the returning god—a costly mistake, as we now know.)

In Mesoamerica, the "bundle year" served for a countdown to the promised "Year of Return," and the question is, *Was the "Jubilee year" intended to serve a similar purpose?*

Searching for an answer, we find that when the linear fifty-year time unit is meshed with the zodiacal cyclical unit of seventy-two—the time that a shift of one degree requires—we arrive at 3,600 ($50 \times 72 = 3,600$), which was the (mathematical) orbital period of Nibiru.

By linking a Jubilee calendar and the zodiacal calendar to Nibiru's orbit, was the biblical God saying, "When you enter the Promised Land, start the countdown to the Return"?

Some two thousand years ago, during a time of great messianic fervor, it was recognized that the Jubilee was a divinely inspired time unit for predicting the future—for calculating when the meshed geared wheels of

time will announce the Return. That recognition underlies one of the most important postbiblical books, known as *The Book of Jubilees.*

Though available now only from its Greek and later translations, it was originally written in Hebrew, as fragments found among the Dead Sea scrolls confirm. Based on earlier extrabiblical treatises and sacred traditions, it rewrote the Book of Genesis and part of Exodus according to a calendar based on the Jubilee Time Unit. It was a product, all scholars agree, of messianic expectations at the time when Rome occupied Jerusalem, and its purpose was to provide a means by which to predict when the Messiah shall come—when the **End of Days** shall occur.

It is the very task we have undertaken.

10

THE CROSS
ON THE HORIZON

About sixty years after the Israelites' Exodus, highly unusual religious developments took place in Egypt. Some scholars view those developments as an attempt to adopt Monotheism—perhaps under the influence of the revelations at Mount Sinai. What they have in mind is the reign of Amenhotep (sometimes rendered as Amenophis) IV who left Thebes and its temples, gave up the worship of Amon, and declared ATEN the sole creator god.

As we shall show, that was not an echo of Monotheism, but another harbinger of an expected Return—the return, into view, of the Planet of the Cross.

The Pharaoh in question is better known by the new name he had adopted—*Akhen-Aten* ("The servant/worshipper of Aten")—and the new capital and religious center that he had established, *Akhet-Aten* ("Aten of the Horizon"), is better known by the site's modern name, Tell el-Amarna (where the famed ancient archive of royal international correspondence was discovered).

Scion of Egypt's famed Eighteenth Dynasty, Akhenaten reigned from 1379 to 1362 B.C., and his religious revolution did not last. The priesthood of Amon in Thebes led the opposition, presumably because it was

153

deprived of its positions of power and wealth, but it is of course possible that the objections were genuinely on religious grounds, for Akhenaten's successors (of whom most famed was Tut-Ankh-Amen) resumed the inclusion of Ra/Amon in their theophoric names. No sooner was Akhenaten gone than the new capital, its temples, and its palace were torn down and systematically destroyed. Nevertheless, the remains that archaeologists have found throw enough light on Akhenaten and his religion.

The notion that the worship of the Aten was a form of monotheism—worship of a sole universal creator—stems primarily from some of the hymns to the Aten that have been found; they include such verses as *"O sole god,* like whom there is no other . . . The world came into being by thy hand."* The fact that, in a clear departure from Egyptian customs, representation of this god in anthropomorphic form was strictly forbidden sounds very much like Yahweh's prohibition, in the Ten Commandments, against making any "graven images" to worship. Additionally, some portions of the Hymns to Aten read as if they were clones of the biblical Psalms—

> *O living Aten,*
> *How manifold are thy works!*
> *They are hidden from the sight of men.*
> *O sole god, beside whom there is no other!*
> *Thou didst create the earth according to thy desire*
> *whilst thou wast alone.*

The famed Egyptologist James H. Breasted (*The Dawn of Conscience*) compared the above verses to Psalm 104, beginning with verse 24—

> *O Lord, how manifold are thy works!*
> *In wisdom hast thou made them all;*
> *the Earth is full of thy riches.*

The similarity, however, arises not because the two, Egyptian hymn and biblical Psalm, copy each other, but because both speak of the same celestial god of the Sumerian *Epic of Creation*—of Nibiru—that shaped

the Heavens and created the Earth, imparting to it the "seed of life."

Virtually every book on ancient Egypt will tell you that the "Aten" disc that Akhenaten made the central object of worship represented the benevolent Sun. If so, it was odd that in a marked departure from Egyptian temple architecture that oriented the temples to the solstices on a southeast-northwest axis, Akhenaten oriented his Aten temple on an east-west axis—but had it facing west, *away* from the Sun at sunrise. If he was expecting a celestial reappearance from a direction *opposite* to that of where the Sun rises, it could not be the Sun.

A close reading of the hymns reveals that Akhenaten's "star god" was not Ra as Amon "the Unseen," but a different kind of Ra: it was the celestial god who had "existed from primeval time . . . *The one who renews himself*" as it *reappears* in all its glory, a celestial god that was *"going afar and returning."* On a daily basis, those words could indeed apply to the Sun, but on a long-term basis, the description fitted Ra only as Nibiru: it did become unseen, the hymns said, because it was "far away in heaven," because it went "to the rear of the horizon, to the height of heaven." And now, Akhenaten announced, it was coming back in all its glory. Aten's hymns prophesied its reappearance, its return "beautiful on the horizon of heaven . . . Glittering, beautiful, strong," ushering *a time of peace and benevolence to all.* These words express clear messianic expectations that have nothing to do with the Sun.

In support of the "Aten is the Sun" explanation, various depictions of Akhenaten are offered; they show (fig. 68) him and his wife blessed by, or praying to, a rayed star; it is the Sun, most Egyptologists say. The hymns do refer to the Aten as a manifestation of Ra, which to Egyptologists who have deemed Ra to be the Sun means that Aten, too, represented the Sun; but if Ra was Marduk and the celestial Marduk was Nibiru, then Aten, too, represented Nibiru and not the Sun. Additional evidence comes from sky maps, some painted on coffin lids (fig. 69), that clearly showed the twelve zodiacal constellations, the rayed Sun, and other members of the solar system; but the planet of Ra, the "Planet of Millions of Years," is shown as an extra planet in its own *large separate celestial barque beyond the Sun,* with the pictorial hieroglyph for "god" in it—Akhenaten's "Aten."

Figure 68

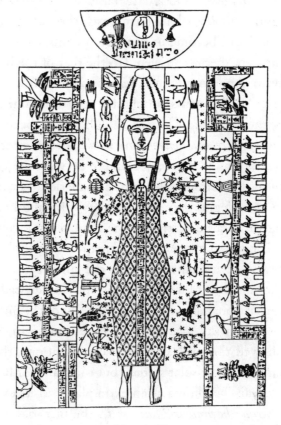

Figure 69

What, then, was Akhenaten's innovation, or, rather, digression, from the official religious line? At its core his "transgression" was the same old debate that had taken place 720 years earlier about *timing*. Then the issue was: Has Marduk/Ra's time for supremacy come, has the Age of the Ram begun in the heavens? Akhenaten shifted the issue from Celestial Time (the zodiacal clock) to Divine Time (Nibiru's orbital time), changing the question to: *When will the **Unseen** celestial god reappear* and become visible—"beautiful on the horizon of heaven"?

His greatest heresy in the eyes of the priests of Ra/Amon can be judged by the fact that he erected a special monument honoring the *Ben-Ben*—an object that had been revered generations earlier as the vehicle in which Ra had arrived on Earth from the heavens (fig. 70). It was an indication, we believe, that what he was expecting in connection with Aten was a Reappearance, a Return not just of the Planet of the Gods, but another arrival, *a New Coming of the gods themselves!*

This, we must conclude, was the innovation, the difference introduced by Akhenaten. In defiance of the priestly establishment, and no doubt prematurely in their opinion, he was announcing the coming of a new messianic time. This heresy was aggravated by the fact that Akhenaten's pronouncements about the returning Aten were accompanied by a personal claim: Akhenaten increasingly referred to himself as *the god's prophet-son, one "who came forth from the god's body,"* and to whom alone the deity's plans were revealed:

Figure 70

There is no other that knoweth thee
except thy son Akhenaten;
Thou hast made him wise in thy plans.

And this, too, was unacceptable to the Theban priests of Amon. As soon as Akhenaten was gone (and it is uncertain how . . .), they restored the worship of Amon—the Unseen god—and smashed and destroyed all that Akhenaten had erected.

That the Aten episode in Egypt, as the introduction of the Jubilee—the "Year of the Ram"—were the stirrings of a wider expectation of a Return of a celestial "star god" is evident from yet another biblical reference to the Ram, yet another manifestation of a **Countdown to the Return.**

It is the record of an unusual incident at the end of the Exodus. It is a tale that is replete with puzzling aspects, and one that ends with a divinely inspired vision of things to come.

The Bible repeatedly declared divination by examining animal entrails, consulting with spirits, soothsaying, enchanting, conjuring, and fortune-telling to be "abominations unto Yahweh"—all manners of sorcery practiced by other nations that the Israelites must avoid. At the same time, it asserted—quoting Yahweh himself—that dreams, oracles, and visions could be legitimate ways of divine communication. It is such a distinction that explains why the Book of Numbers devotes three long chapters (22–24) to tell—approvingly!—the story of a non-Israelite seer and oracle-teller. His name was Bil'am, rendered Balaam in English Bibles.

The events described in those chapters took place when the Israelites ("Children of Israel" in the Bible), having left the Sinai Peninsula, went around the Dead Sea on the east, advancing northward. As they encountered the small kingdoms that occupied the lands east of the Dead Sea and the Jordan River, Moses sought from their kings permission for peaceful passage; it was, by and large, refused. The Israelites, having just defeated the Ammonites, who did not let them pass through peacefully, now "were encamped in the plains of Mo'ab, on the side of

the Jordan that is opposite Jericho," awaiting the Moabite king's permission to pass through his land.

Unwilling to let "the horde" pass yet afraid to fight them, the king of Mo'ab—Balak the son of Zippor—had a bright idea. He sent emissaries to fetch an internationally renowned seer, Bala'am the son of Be'or, and have him "put a curse on these people for me," to make it possible to defeat and chase them away.

Balaam had to be entreated several times before he accepted the assignment. First at Balaam's home (somewhere near the Euphrates River?) and then on the way to Moab, an Angel of God (the word in Hebrew, *Mal'ach,* literally means "emissary") appears and gets involved in the proceedings; he is sometimes visible and sometimes invisible. The angel allows Balaam to accept the assignment only after making sure that Balaam understands that he is to utter only divinely inspired omens. Puzzlingly, Balaam calls Yahweh "my God" when he repeats this condition, first to the king's ambassadors and then to the Moabite king himself.

A series of oracular settings are then arranged. The king takes Balaam to a hilltop from which he can see the whole Israelite encampment, and on the seer's instructions he erects seven altars, sacrifices seven bullocks and seven rams, and awaits the oracle; but from Balaam's mouth come words not of accusation but of praise for the Israelites.

The persistent Moabite king then takes Balaam to another mount, from which just the edge of the Israelite encampment can be seen, and the procedure is repeated a second time. But again Balaam's oracle blesses rather than curses the Israelites: I see them coming out of Egypt protected by a god with spreading ram's horns, he says—it is a nation destined for kingship, a nation that like a lion will arise.

Determined to try again, the king now takes Balaam to a hilltop that faces the desert, facing away from the Israelite encampment; "maybe the gods will let you proclaim curses there," he says. Seven altars are again erected, on which seven bullocks and seven rams are sacrificed. But Balaam now sees the Israelites and their future not with human eyes but "in a divine vision." For the second time he sees the nation protected, as it came out of Egypt, by a god with spreading rams' horns, and envisions Israel as a nation that "like a lion will arise."

When the Moabite king protests, Balaam explains that no matter what gold or silver he be offered, he can utter only the words that God puts in his mouth. So the frustrated king gives up and lets Balaam go. But now Balaam offers the king free advice: Let me tell you what the future holds, he says to the king—"that which will come about to this nation and to your people at the end of days"—and proceeds to describe the divine vision of the future by relating it to a "star":

> *I see it, though not now;*
> *I behold it, though it is not near:*
> *A Star of Jacob is on its course.*
> *A Scepter from Israel will arise—*
> *Moab's quarters it will crush,*
> *all the Children of Seth it will unsettle.*
>
> NUMBERS 24:17

Balaam then turned and cast his eyes toward the Edomites, Amalekites, Kenites, and other Canaanite nations and pronounced an oracle thereon: Those who will survive the wrath of Jacob shall fall into the hands of Assyria; then Assyria's turn will come, and it shall forever perish. And having pronounced that oracle, "Balaam rose up and went back to his place; and Balak too went on his way."

Though the Balaam episode has naturally been the subject of discussion and debate by biblical and theological scholars, it remains baffling and unresolved. The text switches effortlessly between references to the *Elohim*—"gods" in the plural—and to Yahweh, the sole God, as the Divine Presence. It gravely transgresses the Bible's most basic prohibition by applying to the God who brought the Israelites out of Egypt a physical image, and then compounds the transgression by envisioning Him in the image of "a ram with spreading horns"—an image that has been the Egyptian depiction of Amon (fig. 71)! The approving attitude toward a professional seer in a Bible that prohibited soothsaying, conjuring, and so on adds to the feeling that the whole tale was, originally, a non-Israelite tale, and yet the Bible incorporated it, devoting to it substantial space, so the incident and its message must have been considered

Figure 71

a significant prelude to the Israelite possession of the Promised Land.

The text suggests that Balaam was an Aramaean, residing somewhere up the Euphrates River; his prophetic oracles expanded from the fate of the Children of Jacob to the place of Israel among the nations to oracles regarding the future of such other nations—even of distant and yet-to-come imperial Assyria. The oracles were thus an expression of wider non-Israelite expectations at the time. ***By including the tale, the Bible combined the Israelite destiny with Mankind's universal expectations.***

Those expectations, the Balaam tale indicates, were channeled along two paths—the zodiacal cycle on the one hand, and the Returning Star's course on the other hand.

The zodiacal references are strongest regarding the Age of the Ram (and its god!) at the time of the Exodus, and become oracular and prophetic as the Seer Balaam envisions the Future, when the zodiacal constellation symbols of the Bull and the Ram ("bullocks and rams for sevenfold sacrifices") and the Lion ("when the Royal Trumpet shall be heard in Israel") are invoked (Numbers 23). And it is when envisioning that Distant Future that the Balaam text employs the significant term *At the End of Days* as the time to which the prophetic oracles apply (Numbers 24:14).

The term directly links these non-Israelite prophecies to the destiny of Jacob's offspring because it was used by Jacob himself as he lay on his deathbed and gathered his children to hear oracles regarding their future (Genesis 49). "Come gather together," he said, "that I may tell you that which shall befall you at *the End of Days*." The oracles, individually stated for each one of the twelve future tribes of Israel, are deemed by many to be related to the twelve zodiacal constellations.

And what about the Star of Jacob—an explicit vision by Balaam?

In scholarly biblical discussions, it is usually considered in an astrological rather than an astronomical context at best, and more often than not, the tendency has been to deem the reference to "Jacob's Star" as purely figurative. But what if the reference was indeed to a "star" orbiting on its course—a planet prophetically seen though it is not yet visible?

What if Balaam, like Akhenaten, was speaking of the return, the reappearance, of Nibiru? Such a return, it must be realized, would be an extraordinary event that occurs once in several millennia, an event that had repeatedly signified the most profound watersheds in the affairs of gods and men.

This is not just a rhetorical question. In fact, the unfolding events were increasingly indicating that an overwhelmingly significant occurrence was in the offing. Within a century or so of the preoccupations and predictions regarding the Returning Planet that we find in the tales of the Exodus, Balaam, and Akhenaten's Egypt, Babylon itself started to provide evidence of such wide-spreading expectations, and the most prominent clue was the **Sign of the Cross.**

In Babylon, the time was that of the Kassite dynasty, of which we have written earlier. Little has remained of their reign in Babylon itself, and as stated earlier those kings did not excel in keeping royal records. But they did leave behind telltale depictions—and international correspondence of letters on clay tablets.

It was in the ruins of Akhet-Aten, Akhenaten's capital—a site now known as Tell el-Amarna in Egypt—that the famed "el-Amarna Tablets" were discovered. Of the 380 clay tablets, all except three were inscribed in the Akkadian language, which was then the language of international diplomacy. While some of the tablets represented copies of royal letters sent from the Egyptian court, the bulk were original letters received from foreign kings.

The cache was the royal diplomatic archive of Akhenaten, and the tablets were predominantly correspondence he had received from the kings of Babylon!

Did Akhenaten use those exchanges of letters with his counterparts in Babylon to tell them of his newfound Aten religion? We really don't know, for all we have are a Babylonian king's letters to Akhenaten in which he complained that gold sent to him was found short in weight, that his ambassadors were robbed on the way to Egypt, or that the Egyptian king failed to inquire about his health. Yet the frequent exchanges of ambassadors and other emissaries, even offers of intermarriage, as well as the calling of the Egyptian king "my brother" by the Babylonian king, must lead to a conclusion that the hierarchy in Babylon was fully aware of the religious goings-on in Egypt; and if Babylon wondered, "What is this 'Ra as a Returning Star' commotion?" Babylon must have realized that it was a reference to "Marduk as a Returning Planet"—*to Nibiru orbiting back.*

With the tradition of celestial observations so much older and more advanced in Mesopotamia than in Egypt, it is of course possible that the royal astronomers of Babylon had come to conclusions regarding Nibiru's return without Egyptian aid, and even ahead of the Egyptians. Be that as it may, it was in the thirteenth century B.C. that the Kassite kings of Babylon started to signal, in a variety of ways, their own fundamental religious changes.

In **1260 B.C.** a new king ascended the throne in Babylon and adopted the name Kadashman-Enlil—a theophoric name surprisingly venerating Enlil. It was no passing gesture, for he was followed on the throne, for the next century, by Kassite kings bearing theophoric names venerating not only Enlil but also Adad—a surprising gesture suggesting a desire for divine reconciliation. That something unusual was expected was further evidenced on commemorative monuments called *kudurru*— "rounded stones"—that were set up as boundary markers. Inscribed with a text stating the terms of the border treaty (or land grant) and the oaths taken to uphold it, the kudurru was sanctified by symbols of the celestial gods. The divine zodiacal symbols—all twelve of them—were frequently depicted (fig. 72); orbiting above them were the emblems of

Figure 72

Figure 73

Figure 74

the Sun, the Moon, and Nibiru. In another depiction (fig. 73), Nibiru was shown in the company of Earth (the seventh planet) and the Moon (and the umbilical-cutter symbol for Ninmah).

Significantly, Nibiru was depicted no longer by the Winged Disc symbol, but rather in a new way—as the planet of the **radiating cross**—befitting its description by the Sumerians in the "Olden Days" as a radiating planet about to become the "Planet of the Crossing."

This way of showing a long-unobserved Nibiru by a symbol of a radiating cross began to become more common, and soon the Kassite kings of Babylon simplified the symbol to just a **Sign of the Cross,** replacing with it the Winged Disc symbol on their royal seals (fig. 74).

Figure 75

This cross symbol, which looks like the much later Christian "Maltese Cross," is known in studies of ancient glyptic as a "Kassite Cross." As another depiction indicates, the symbol of the cross was for a planet *clearly not the same as the Sun,* which is *separately shown* along with the Moon-crescent and the six-pointed star symbol for Mars (fig. 75).

As the first millennium B.C. began, Nibiru's Sign of the Cross spread from Babylonia to seal designs in nearby lands. In the absence of Kassite religious or literary texts, it is a matter of conjecture what messianic expectations might have accompanied these changes in depictions. Whatever they were, they intensified the ferocity of the attacks by the Enlilite states—Assyria, Elam—on Babylon and their opposition to Marduk's hegemony. Those attacks delayed, but did not prevent, the eventual adoption of the Sign of the Cross in Assyria itself. As royal monuments reveal, it was worn, most conspicuously, by Assyria's kings on their chests, near their hearts (fig. 76)—the way devout Catholics wear the cross nowadays. Religiously and astronomically, it was a most significant gesture. That it was also a widespread manifestation is suggested by the fact that in Egypt, too, depictions were found of a king-god wearing, like his Assyrian counterparts, the sign of the cross on his chest (fig. 77).

The adoption of the Sign of the Cross as the emblem of Nibiru, in Babylon, Assyria, and elsewhere, was not a surprising innovation. The sign had been used before—by the Sumerians and Akkadians. *"Nibiru— let 'Crossing' be its name!"* the *Epic of Creation* stated; and accordingly its symbol, the cross, had been employed in Sumerian glyptic to denote Nibiru, but then *it always signified its **Return into visibility.***

Figure 76

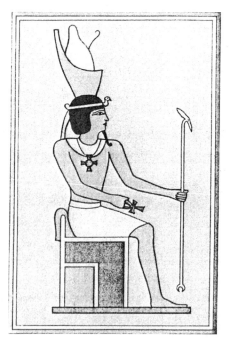

Figure 77

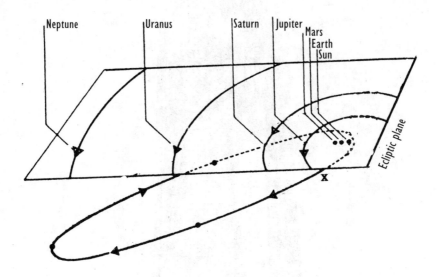

Figure 78

Enuma elish, the *Epic of Creation,* clearly stated that after the Celestial Battle with Tiamat, the Invader made a grand orbit around the Sun and returned to the scene of the battle. Since Tiamat orbited the Sun in a plane called the Ecliptic (as other members of our Sun's planetary family do), it is to that place in the heavens that the Invader had to return; and when it does so, orbit after orbit after orbit, it is there that it *crosses the plane of the ecliptic.* A simple way to illustrate this would be to show the orbital path of the well-known Halley's Comet (fig. 78), which emulates on a greatly reduced scale the orbit of Nibiru: its inclined orbit brings it, as it nears the Sun, from the south, from below the ecliptic, near Uranus. It arches above the ecliptic and makes the turn around the Sun, saying "Hello" to Saturn, Jupiter, and Mars; then it comes down and crosses the ecliptic near the site of Nibiru's Celestial Battle with Tiamat—the Crossing (marked "**X**")—and is gone, only to come back as its orbital Destiny prescribes.

That point, in the heavens and in time, is **The Crossing**—it is then, *Enum elish* stated, that the planet of the Anunnaki becomes the ***Planet of the Cross:***

Planet NIBIRU:
The Crossroads of Heaven and Earth it shall occupy . . .
Planet NIBIRU:
The central position he holds . . .
Planet NIBIRU:
It is he who without tiring
the midst of Tiamat keeps crossing;
Let "Crossing" be his name!

Sumerian texts dealing with landmark events in Mankind's saga provide specific indications regarding the periodic appearances of the Planet of the Anunnaki—approximately every 3,600 years—and always at crucial junctions in Earth's and Mankind's history. It was at such times that the planet was called Nibiru, and its glyptical depictions—even in early Sumerian times—were the Cross.

That record began with the Deluge. Several texts dealing with the Deluge associated the watershed catastrophe with the appearance of the celestial god, Nibiru, in the Age of the Lion (circa 10,900 B.C.)—it was "the constellation of the Lion that measured the waters of the deep," one text said. Other texts described the appearance of Nibiru at Deluge time as a radiating star, and depicted it accordingly (fig. 79)—

When they shall call out "Flooding!"
It is the god Nibiru . . .
*Lord whose **shining crown** with terror is laden;*
*Daily within the Lion **he is afire.***

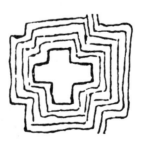

Figure 79

Figure 80

The planet returned, reappeared, and again became "Nibiru" when Mankind was granted farming and husbandry, in the mid-eighth millennium B.C.; depictions (on cylinder seals) illustrating the beginning of agriculture used the Sign of the Cross to show Nibiru visible in Earth's skies (fig. 80).

Finally and most memorably for the Sumerians, the planet was visible once again when Anu and Antu came to Earth on a state visit circa 4000 B.C., in the Age of the Bull (Taurus). The city that was later known for millennia as Uruk was established in their honor, a ziggurat was erected, and from its stages the appearance of the planets on the horizon, as the night sky darkened, was observed. When Nibiru came into view, a shout went up—"The Creator's image has arisen!"—and all present broke into hymnal songs of praise for "the planet of the Lord Anu."

Nibiru's appearance at the start of the Age of the Bull meant that at the time of heliacal rising—when dawn begins but the horizon is still dark enough to see the stars—the constellation in the background was that of Taurus. But the fast-moving Nibiru, arcing in the skies as it circled the Sun, soon descended back to cut across the planetary plain ("ecliptic") to the point of Crossing. There the crossing was observed against the background of the constellation of the Lion. Several depictions, on cylinder seals and in astronomical tablets, used the cross symbol to indicate Nibiru's arrival when Earth was in the Age of the Bull and its crossing was observed in the constellation of the Lion (cylinder seal depiction, fig. 81, and as illustrated in fig. 82).

Figure 81

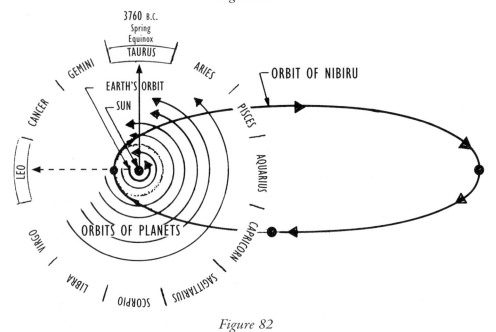

Figure 82

The change from the Winged Disc symbol to the Sign of the Cross thus was not an innovation; it was reverting to the way in which the Celestial Lord had been depicted in earlier times—but only when in its great orbit it crossed the ecliptic and became "Nibiru."

As in the past, the renewed display of the Sign of the Cross signified reappearance, coming back into view, RETURN.

11

THE DAY OF THE LORD

A s the last millennium B.C. began, the appearance of the Sign of
the Cross was a harbinger of the Return. It was also then that
a temple to Yahweh in Jerusalem forever linked its sacred site to the
course of historic events and to Mankind's messianic expectations. The
time and the place were no coincidence: the impending Return dictated
the enshrinement of the erstwhile Mission Control Center.

Compared to the mighty and conquering imperial powers of those
days—Babylonia, Assyria, Egypt—the Hebrew kingdom was a midget.
Compared to the greatness of their capitals—Babylon, Nineveh,
Thebes—with their sacred precincts, ziggurats, temples, processional
ways, ornate gates, majestic palaces, hanging gardens, sacred pools, and
river harbors—Jerualem was a small city with hastily built walls and an
iffy water supply. And yet, millennia later, it is Jerusalem, a living city,
that is in our hearts and in the daily headlines, while the grandeur of
the other nations' capitals has turned to dust and crumbled ruins.

**What made the difference? The Temple of Yahweh that was
built in Jerusalem, and its Prophets whose oracles came true. Their
prophecies, one therefore believes, still hold the key to the Future.**

The Hebrew association with Jerusalem, and in particular with
Mount Moriah, goes back to the time of Abraham. It was when he had
fulfilled his assignment of protecting the spaceport during the War of

the Kings that he was greeted by Malkizedek, the king of *Ir-Shalem* (Jerusalem), "who was a priest of the God Most High." There Abraham was blessed, and in turn took an oath, "by the God Most High, possessor of Heaven and Earth." It was again there, when Abraham's devotion was tested, that he was granted a Covenant with God. Yet it took a millennium, until the right time and circumstances, for the Temple to be built.

The Bible asserted that the Jerusalem temple was unique—and so indeed it was: it was conceived to preserve the "Bond Heaven-Earth" that the DUR.AN.KI of Sumer's Nippur had once been.

> *And it came to pass*
> *in the four hundred and eightieth year*
> *after the Children of Israel came out of Egypt,*
> *in the fourth year of Solomon's reign,*
> *in the second month,*
> *that he began to build the House of the Lord.*

Thus does the Bible record, in the first Book of Kings (6:1), the memorable start of the construction of the Temple of Yahweh in Jerusalem by King Solomon, giving us the exact date of the event. It was a crucial, decisive step whose consequences are still with us; and *the time, it must be noted, was when Babylon and Assyria adopted the Sign of the Cross as the harbinger of the Return . . .*

The dramatic story of the Jerusalem Temple starts not with Solomon but with King David, Solomon's father; and how he happened to become Israel's king is a tale that reveals a divine plan: **to prepare for the Future by resurrecting the Past.**

David's legacy (after a reign of forty years) included a greatly expanded realm, reaching in the north as far as Damascus (and including the Landing Place!), many magnificent Psalms, and the groundwork for Yahweh's temple. Three divine emissaries played key roles in the making of this king and his place in history; the Bible lists them as "Samuel the Seer, Nathan the Prophet, and Gad the Visionary." It was Samuel, the custodian-priest of the Ark of the Covenant, who was

instructed by God to "take the youth David, son of Jesse, from herding sheep to be shepherd of Israel," and Samuel "took the oil-filled horn and *anointed him* to reign over Israel."

The choosing of the young David, who was shepherding his father's flock, to be shepherd over Israel was doubly symbolic, for it harks back to the golden age of Sumer. Its kings were called LU.GAL, "Great Man," but they strove to earn the cherished title EN.SI, "Righteous Shepherd." That, as we shall see, was only the beginning of David's and the Temple's links to the Sumerian past.

David began his reign in Hebron, south of Jerusalem, and that, too, was a choice filled with historic symbolism. The previous name of Hebron, the Bible repeatedly pointed out, was *Kiryat Arba*, "the fortified city of Arba." And who was Arba? "He was a *Great Man* of the *Anakim*"—two biblical terms that render in Hebrew the Sumerian LU.GAL and ANUNNAKI. Starting with passages in the book of Numbers, and then in Joshua, Judges, and Chronicles, the Bible reported that Hebron was a center of the descendants of the "Anakim, who as the Nefilim are counted," thus connecting them to the Nefilim of Genesis 6 who intermarried with the Daughters of Adam. Hebron was still inhabited at the time of the Exodus by three sons of Arba, and it was Caleb the son of Jephoneh who captured the city and slew them on behalf of Joshua. *By choosing to be king in Hebron, David established his kingship as a direct continuation of kings linked to the Anunnaki of Sumerian lore.*

He reigned in Hebron for seven years and then moved his capital to Jerusalem. His seat of kingship—the "City of David"—was built on Mount Zion, just south of and separated by a small valley from Mount Moriah (where the platform built by the Anunnaki was, fig. 83). He constructed the *Miloh*, the Filling, to close the gap between the two mounts, as a first step to building, on the platform, Yahweh's temple; but all he was allowed to erect on Mount Moriah was an altar. God's word, through the Prophet Nathan, was that because David had shed blood in his many wars, not he but his son Solomon would build the temple.

Devastated by the prophet's message, David went and "sat before Yahweh," in front of the Ark of the Covenant (which was still housed

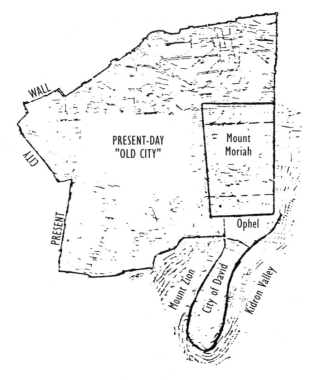

Figure 83

in a portable tent). Accepting God's decision, he asked for one reward for his devout loyalty to Him: an assurance, a sign, that it would indeed be the House of David that would build the Temple and be forever blessed. That very night, sitting in front of the Ark of the Covenant by which Moses had communicated with the Lord, he received a divine sign: he was given a *Tavnit—a scale model*—of the future temple!

One can shrug off the tale's veracity were it not for the fact that what happened that night to King David and his temple project was the equivalent of the *Twilight Zone* tale of the Sumerian king Gudea, who more than a thousand years earlier was likewise given in a vision-dream a tablet with the architectural plan and a brick mold for the construction of a temple in Lagash for the god Ninurta.

When he neared the end of his days, King David summoned to Jerusalem all the leaders of Israel, including the tribal chiefs and the military commanders, the priests and the royal office holders, and told

them of Yahweh's promise; and in full view of those gathered he handed
to his son Solomon "the *Tavnit* of the temple and all its parts and chambers . . . the Tavnit that he received by the Spirit." There was more, for
David also handed over to Solomon "all that Yahweh, in His own hand
written, gave to me for understanding the workings of the Tavnit": A
set of accompanying instructions, divinely written (I Chronicles 28).

The Hebrew term *Tavnit* is translated in the King James English
Bible as "pattern" but is rendered "plan" in more recent translations, suggesting that David was given some kind of an architectural drawing. But
the Hebrew word for "plan" is *Tokhnit. Tavnit,* on the other hand, is
derived from the root verb that means "to construct, to build, to erect," so
what David was given and what he handed over to his son Solomon was a
"constructed model"—in today's parlance, a scale model. (Archaeological
finds throughout the ancient Near East have indeed unearthed scale models of chariots, wagons, ships, workshops, and even multilevel shrines.)

The biblical books of Kings and Chronicles provide precise measurements and clear structural details of the Temple and its architectural designs. Its axis ran east–west, making it an "eternal temple"
aligned to the equinox. Consisting of three parts (see fig. 64), it adopted
the Sumerian temple plans of a forepart (*Ulam* in Hebrew), a great central hall (*Hekhal* in Hebrew, stemming from the Sumerian E.GAL,
"Large Abode"), and a Holy of Holies for the Ark of the Covenant.
That innermost section was called the *Dvir* (the "Speaker")—for it was
by means of the Ark of the Covenant that God spoke to Moses.

As in Sumerian ziggurats, which traditionally were built to express
the sexagesimal's "base sixty" concept, the Temple of Solomon also
adopted sixty in its construction: the main section (the Hall) was 60
cubits (about 100 feet) in length, 20 cubits (60:3) wide, and 120 (60 × 2)
cubits in height. The Holy of Holies was 20 by 20 cubits—just enough
to hold the Ark of the Covenant with the two golden Cherubim atop it
("their wings touching"). Tradition, textual evidence, and archaeological
research indicate that the ark was placed precisely on the extraordinary
rock on which Abraham was ready to sacrifice his son Isaac; its Hebrew
designation, *Even Shatiyah,* means "Foundation Stone," and Jewish
legends hold that it is from it that the world will be re-created. Nowadays

Figure 84

it is covered over and surrounded by the Dome of the Rock (fig. 84). (Readers can find more about the sacred rock and its enigmatic cave and secret subterranean passages in *The Earth Chronicles Expeditions*.)

Though these were not monumental measurements compared to the skyscraping ziggurats, the Temple, when completed, was truly magnificent; it was also unlike any other contemporary temple in that part of the world. No iron or iron tools were used for its erection upon the platform (and absolutely none in its operation—all the utensils were of copper or bronze), and ***the building was inlaid inside with gold;*** even the nails holding the golden plates in place were made of gold. The quantities of gold used (just "for the Holy of Holies, 600 talents; for the nails, fifty shekels") were enormous—so much so that Solomon arranged for special ships to bring gold from Ophir (believed to be in southeast Africa).

The Bible offers no explanation, neither for the prohibition against using anything made of iron on the site nor for the inlaying of everything inside the temple with gold. One can only speculate that iron was shunned because of its magnetic properties, and gold used because it is the best electrical conductor.

It is significant that the only two other known instances of shrines

so inlaid with gold are on the other side of the world. One is the great temple in Cuzco, the Inca capital in Peru, where the great god of South America, Viracocha, was worshipped. It was called the *Coricancha* ("Golden Enclosure"), for its Holy of Holies was completely inlaid with gold. The other is in Puma-Punku on the shores of Lake Titicaca in Bolivia, near the famed ruins of Tiwanaku. The ruins there consist of the remains of four chamberlike stone buildings whose walls, floors, and ceilings were each cut out of a single colossal stone block. The four enclosures were completely inlaid inside with golden plates that were held in place with golden nails. Describing the sites (and how they were looted by the Spaniards) in *The Lost Realms,* I have suggested that Puma-Punku was erected for the stay of Anu and Antu when they visited Earth circa 4000 B.C.

According to the Bible, tens of thousands of workmen were needed for seven years for the immense undertaking. What, then, was the purpose of this House of the Lord? When all was ready, with much pomp and circumstance, the Ark of the Covenant was carried by priests and placed in the Holy of Holies. As soon as the ark was put down and the curtains separating the Holy of Holies from the great hall were drawn, "the House of the Lord was filled with a cloud and the priests could not remain standing." Then Solomon offered a thanksgiving prayer, saying:

> *Lord who has chosen to dwell in the cloud:*
> *I have built for Thee a stately House,*
> *a place where you may dwell forever . . .*
> *Though the uttermost heavens cannot contain Thee,*
> *May you hear our supplications from Thine seat in heaven.*

"And Yahweh appeared to Solomon that night, and said to him: I have heard your prayer; I have chosen this site for my house of worship . . . From heaven I will hear the prayers of my people and forgive their transgressions . . . Now I have chosen and consecrated this House for my *Shem* to remain there forever" (II Chronicles 6–7).

The word *Shem*—here and earlier, as in the opening verses of chapter

6 of Genesis—is commonly translated "Name." As far back as in my first book, *The Twelfth Planet,* I have suggested that the term originally and in the relevant context referred to what the Egyptians called the "Celestial Boat" and the Sumerians called MU—"sky ship"—of the gods. Accordingly, the Temple in Jerusalem, built atop the stone platform, with the Ark of the Covenant placed upon the sacred rock, was to serve as an earthly bond with the celestial deity—both for communicating and for the landing of his sky ship!

Throughout the Temple there was no statue, no idol, no graven image. The only object within it was the hallowed Ark of the Covenant—and "there was nothing in the Ark except the two tablets that were given to Moses in Sinai."

Unlike the Mesopotamian ziggurat temples, from Enlil's in Nippur to Marduk's in Babylon, this one was not a place of residence for the deity, where the god lived, ate, slept, and bathed. **It was a House of Worship, a place of divine contact; it was a temple for a Divine Presence by the Dweller in the Clouds.**

It is said that a picture is worth a thousand words; it is certainly true where there are few pertinent words but many relevant pictures.

It was about the time that the Jerusalem temple was completed and consecrated to the Dweller in the Clouds that a noticeable change in the sacred glyptic—the depiction of the divine—took place where such depictions were common and permissible, and (at the time) first and foremost in Assyria. They showed, most clearly, the god Ashur as a "dweller of the clouds," full face or with just his hand showing, frequently depicted holding a bow (fig. 85)—a depiction reminding one of the Bible's tale of the Bow in the Cloud that was a divine sign in the aftermath of the Deluge.

A century or so later, Assyrian depictions introduced a new variant of the God in the Cloud. Classified as "Deity in a Winged Disc," they clearly showed a deity inside the emblem of the Winged Disc, by itself (fig. 86a) or as it joins the Earth (seven dots) and the Moon (crescent) (fig. 86b). Since the Winged Disc represented Nibiru, it had to be a deity *arriving with Nibiru.* Clearly, then, *these depictions implied expectations of the*

Figure 85

Figure 86a

Figure 86b

nearing arrival not only of the planet but also of its divine dwellers,
probably led by Anu himself.

The changes in glyphs and symbols, begun with the Sign of the
Cross, were manifestations of more profound expectations, of overwhelming changes and wider preparations called for by the expected
Return. However, the expectations and preparations were not the same
in Babylon as in Assyria. In one, the messianic expectations were centered on the god(s) who were already there; in the other, the expectations related to the god(s) about to return and reappear.

In Babylon the expectations were mostly religious—a messianic
revival by Marduk through his son Nabu. Great efforts were undertaken to resume, circa **960 B.C.**, the sacred *Akitu* ceremonies in which
the revised *Enuma elish*—appropriating to Marduk the creation
of Earth, the reshaping of the Heavens (the Solar System), and the
fashioning of Man—was publicly read. The arrival of Nabu from his
shrine in Borsippa (just south of Babylon) to play a crucial role in
the ceremonies was an essential part of the revival. Accordingly, the
Babylonian kings who reigned between 900 B.C. and 730 B.C. resumed
bearing Marduk-related names and, in great numbers, Nabu-related
names.

The changes in Assyria were more geopolitical; historians consider
the time—circa **960 B.C.**—as the start of the Neo-Assyrian Imperial
period. In addition to inscriptions on monuments and palace walls, the
main source of information about Assyria in those days is the annals of
its kings, in which they recorded what they did, year by year. Judging
by that, their main occupation was conquest. With unparalleled ferocity, its kings set out on one military campaign after another not only to
have dominion over the olden Sumer & Akkad but also over what they
deemed essential for the Return: *Control of the space-related sites.*

That this was the purpose of the campaigns is evident not only
from their targets but also from the grand stone reliefs on the walls of
Assyrian palaces from the ninth and eighth centuries B.C. (which one
can see in some of the world's leading museums): as on some cylinder
seals, they show the king and the high priest, accompanied by winged
Cherubim—Anunnaki "astronauts"—flanking the Tree of Life as they

Figure 87a

Figure 87b

welcome the coming of the god in the Winged Disc (fig. 87a, b). *A divine arrival was clearly expected!*

Historians connect the start of this Neo-Assyrian period to the establishment of a new royal dynasty in Assyria, when Tiglath-Pileser II ascended the throne in Nineveh. The pattern of aggrandizement at home and conquest, destruction, and annexation abroad was set by that king's son and grandson, who followed him as kings of Assyria. Interestingly, their first target was the area of the Khabur River, with its important trade and religious center—Harran.

Their successors took it from there. Frequently bearing the same

name as previous glorified kings (hence the numerations I, II, III, etc., for them), the successive kings expanded Assyrian control in all directions, but with special emphasis on the coastal cities and mountains of *La-ba-an* (Lebanon). Circa **860 B.C.** Ashurnasirpal II—who wore the cross symbol on his chest (see fig. 76)—boasted of capturing the Phoenician coastal cities of Tyre, Sidon, and Gebal (Byblos), and of ascending the Cedar Mountain with its sacred site, the olden Landing Place of the Anunnaki.

His son and successor Shalmaneser III recorded the erecting there of a commemorative stela calling the place *Bit Adini*. The name literally meant "the Eden Abode"—and was known by that same name to the biblical Prophets. The Prophet Ezekiel castigated the king of Tyre for deeming himself a god because he had been to that sacred place and "moved within its fiery stones"; and the Prophet Amos listed it when he spoke of the coming *Day of the Lord.*

As could be expected, the Assyrians then turned their attention to the other space-related site. After the death of Solomon his kingdom was split by his contending heirs into "Judea" (with Jerusalem as capital) in the south and "Israel" and its ten tribes in the north. In his best-known inscribed monument, the Black Obelisk, Shalmaneser III recorded the receipt of tribute from the Israelite king Jehu and, in a scene dominated by the Winged Disc emblem of Nibiru, depicted him kneeling in obeisance (fig. 88). Both the Bible and the Assyrian

Figure 88

annals recorded the subsequent invasion of Israel by Tiglath-Pileser III (744–727 B.C.), the detaching of its better provinces, and the partial exile of its leaders. Then, in 722 B.C., his son Shalmaneser V overran what was left of Israel, exiled all of its people, and replaced them with foreigners; the Ten Tribes were gone, their whereabouts remaining a lasting mystery. (Why and how, on his return from Israel, Shalmaneser was punished and abruptly replaced on the throne by another son of Tiglath-Pileser is also an unsolved mystery.)

Having already captured the Landing Place, the Assyrians were now at the doortsep of the final prize, Jerusalem; but again they held off the final assault. The Bible explained it by attributing it all to the will of Yahweh; an examination of Assyrian records suggests that what and when they did in Israel and Judea was synchronized with what and when they did about Babylon and Marduk.

After the capture of the space-related site in Lebanon—but before launching the campaigns toward Jerusalem—the Assyrians took an unprecedented step for reconciliation with Marduk. In 729 B.C. Tiglath-Pileser III entered Babylon, went to its sacred precinct, and "took the hands of Marduk." It was a gesture with great religious and diplomatic significance; the priests of Marduk approved the reconciliation by inviting Tiglath-Pileser to share in the god's sacramental meal. Following that, Tiglath-Pileser's son Sargon II marched southward into the olden Sumer & Akkad areas, and after seizing Nippur turned back to enter Babylon. In 710 B.C. he, like his father, "took the hands of Marduk" during the New Year ceremonies.

The task of capturing the remaining space-related site fell to Sargon's successor, Sennacherib. The assault on Jerusalem in 704 B.C., at the time of its King Hezekiah, is amply recorded both in Sennacherib's annals and in the Bible. But while Sennacherib in his inscriptions spoke just of the successful seizing of Judean provincial cities, the Bible provides a detailed tale of the siege of Jerusalem by a mighty Assyrian army that was miraculously wiped out by Yahweh's will.

Encircling Jerusalem and entrapping its people, the Assyrians engaged in psychological warfare by shouting discouraging words to the defenders on the city's walls, ending with vilification of Yahweh. The

shocked king, Hezekiah, tore his clothes in mourning and prayed in the Temple to "Yahweh, the God of Israel, who rests upon the Cherubim, the sole God upon all the nations," for help. In response, the Prophet Isaiah conveyed to him God's oracle: the Assyrian king shall never enter the city, he will return home in failure, and there he will be assassinated.

> *And it came to pass that night*
> *that the Angel of Yahweh went forth*
> *and smote in the camp of the Assyrians*
> *a hundred and eighty-five thousand.*
> *And at sunrise, lo and behold,*
> *they were all dead corpses.*
> *So Sennacherib, the king of Assyria, departed*
> *and journeyed back to his abode in Nineveh.*
>
> 2 KINGS 19:35–36

To make sure the reader realizes that the whole prophecy came true, the biblical narrative then continues: "And Sennacherib went away, and journeyed back to Nineveh; and it was when he was bowing down in his temple to his god . . . that Adramelekh and Sharezzer struck him down with a sword, and they fled to the land of Ararat. His son Esarhaddon became king in his stead."

The biblical postscript is an amazingly informed record: Sennacherib was indeed murdered, by his own sons, in 681 B.C. For the second time, Assyrian kings who attacked Israel or Judea were dead as soon as they went back.

While prophecy—the foretelling of what is yet to happen—is inherently what is expected of a prophet, the Prophets of the Hebrew Bible were more than that. From the very beginning, as was made clear in Leviticus, a prophet was not to be "a magician, a wizard, an enchanter, a charmer or seer of spirits, a fortune-teller, or one who conjures the dead"—a pretty comprehensive list of the varied fortune-tellers of the surrounding nations. Their mission as *Nabih*—"Spokesmen"—was to convey to kings and peoples Yahweh's own words. And as Hezekiah's

prayer made clear, while the Children of Israel were His Chosen People, He was "sole God *upon all the nations.*"

The Bible speaks of prophets from Moses on, but only fifteen of them have their own books in the Bible. They include the three "majors"—Isaiah, Jeremiah, and Ezekiel—and twelve "minors." Their prophetic period began with Amos in Judea (circa **760 B.C.**) and Hoseah in Israel (750 B.C.) and ended with Malachi (circa 450 B.C.). As expectations of the Return took shape, geopolitics, religion, and actual happenings combined to serve as the foundation of biblical Prophecy.

The biblical Prophets served as Keepers of the Faith and were the moral and ethical compass of their own kings and people; they were also observers and predictors on the world arena by possessing uncannily accurate knowledge of goings-on in distant lands, of court intrigues in foreign capitals, of which gods were worshipped where, plus amazing knowledge of history, geography, trade routes, and military campaigns. ***They then combined such awareness of the Present with knowledge of the Past to foretell the Future.***

To the Hebrew Prophets, Yahweh was not only *El Elyon*—"God Supreme"—and not only God of the gods, *El Elohim,* but a Universal God—of all nations, of the whole Earth, of the universe. Though His abode was in the Heaven of Heavens, He cared for his creation—Earth and its people. Everything that has happened was by His will, and His will was carried out by Emissaries—be it Angels, be it a king, be it a nation. Adopting the Sumerian distinction between predetermined Destiny and free-willed Fate, the Prophets believed that the Future could be foretold because it was all preplanned, yet on the way thereto, things could change. Assyria, for example, was at times called God's "rod of wrath" with which other nations were punished, but when it chose to act unnecessarily brutally or out of bounds, Assyria itself was in turn subjected to punishment.

The Prophets seemed to be delivering a two-track message not only in regard to current events but also in respect to the Future. Isaiah, for example, prophesied that Mankind should expect a Day of Wrath when all the nations (Israel included) shall be judged and punished—as well as look forward to an idyllic time when the wolf shall dwell with the

lamb, men shall beat their swords into plowshares, and Zion shall be a light unto all nations. '

The contradiction has baffled generations of biblical scholars and theologians, but a close examination of the Prophets' words leads us to an astounding finding: the Day of Judgment was spoken of as the **Day of the Lord;** the messianic time was expected at the **End of Days;** and the two were neither synonymous nor predicted as concurrent events. They were two separate events, due to occur at different times:

One, the Day of the Lord, a day of God's judgment, was about to happen;

The other, ushering a benevolent era, was yet to come, sometime in the future.

Did the words spoken in Jerusalem echo the debates in Nineveh and Babylon regarding which time cycle applies to the future of gods and men—Nibiru's orbital Divine Time or the zodiacal Celestial Time? Undoubtedly, as the eighth century B.C. was ending, it was clear in all three capitals that the two time cycles were not identical; *and in Jerusalem, speaking of the coming Day of the Lord, the biblical prophets in fact spoke of the Return of Nibiru.*

Ever since it rendered in the opening chapter of Genesis an abbreviated version of the Sumerian *Epic of Creation*, the Bible recognized the existence of Nibiru and its periodic return to Earth's vicinity, and treated it as another—in this case, celestial—manifestation of Yahweh as a Universal God. The Psalms and the Book of Job spoke of the unseen Celestial Lord that "in the heights of heaven marked out a circuit." They recalled this Celestial Lord's first appearance—when he collided with Tiamat (called in the Bible *Tehom* and nicknamed *Rahab* or *Rabab,* the Haughty One), smote her, created the heavens and "the Hammered Bracelet" (the Asteroid Belt), and "suspended the Earth in the void"; they also recalled the time when that celestial Lord caused the Deluge.

The arrival of Nibiru and the celestial collision, leading to Nibiru's great orbital circuit, were celebrated in the majestic Psalm 19:

The heavens bespeak the glory of the Lord;
The Hammered Bracelet proclaims his handiwork . . .
He comes forth as a groom from the canopy;
Like an athlete he rejoices to run the course.
From the end of the heavens he emanates,
and his circuit is to their end.

It was the nearing of the Celestial Lord at the time of the Deluge that was held to be the forerunner of what will happen next time the celestial Lord will return (Psalm 77:6, 17–19):

I shall recall the Lord's deeds,
remember thine wonders in antiquity . . .
The waters saw thee, O Lord, and shuddered.
Thine splitting sparks went forth,
lightnings lit up the world.
The sound of thine thunder was rolling,
the Earth was agitated and it quaked.

The Prophets considered those earlier phenomena as the guide for what to expect. They expected the Day of the Lord (to quote the Prophet Joel) to be a day when "the Earth shall be agitated, Sun and Moon shall be darkened, and the stars shall withhold their shining . . . A day that is great and terrifying."

The Prophets brought the word of Yahweh to Israel and all nations over a period of about three centuries. The earliest of the fifteen Literary Prophets was Amos; he began to be God's spokesman (*Nabih*) circa **760 B.C.** His prophecies covered three periods or phases: he predicted the Assyrian assaults in the near future, a coming Day of Judgment, and an Endtime of peace and plenty. Speaking in the name of "the Lord Yahweh who reveals His secrets to the Prophets," he described the Day of the Lord as a day when "the Sun shall set at noon and the Earth shall darken in the midst of daytime." Addressing those who worship the "planets and star of their gods," he compared the coming day to the events of the Deluge, when "the day darkened as night, and the waters

of the seas poured upon the earth"; and he warned those worshippers with a rhetorical question (Amos 5:18):

> *Woe unto you that desire the Day of the Lord!*
> *To what end is it for you?*
> *For the day of the Lord is darkness and no light.*

A half-century later, the Prophet Isaiah linked the prophecies of the "Day of the Lord" to a specific geographical site, to the "Mount of the Appointed Time," the place "on the northern slopes," and had this to say to the king who had set himself up on it: "Behold, the Day of the Lord cometh with pitiless fury and wrath, to lay the earth desolate and destroy the sinners upon it." He, too, compared what is about to happen to the Deluge, recalling the time when the "Lord came as a destroying tempest of mighty waves," and described the coming Day as a celestial occurrence that will affect the Earth (Isaiah 13:10, 13):

> *The stars of heaven and its constellations*
> *shall not give their light;*
> *the Sun shall be darkened at its rising*
> *and the Moon shall not shine its light . . .*
> *The heavens shall be agitated*
> *and the Earth in its place will be shaken;*
> *When the Lord of Hosts shall be crossing*
> *on the day of his wrath.*

Most noticeable in this prophecy is the identification of the Day of the Lord as the time when "the Lord of Hosts"—the celestial, the planetary lord—***"shall be crossing."*** This is the very language used in *Enuma elish* when it describes how the invader that battled Tiamat came to be called NIBIRU: ***"Crossing** shall be its name!"*

Following Isaiah, the Prophet Hosea also foresaw the Day of the Lord as a day when Heaven and Earth shall "respond" to each other—a day of celestial phenomena resonating on Earth.

As we continue to examine the prophecies chronologically, we find

that in the seventh century B.C. the prophetic pronouncements became more urgent and more explicit: the Day of the Lord shall be a Day of Judgment upon the nations, Israel included, but primarily upon Assyria for what it has done and upon Babylon for what it will do, and **the Day is approaching, it is near—**

> *The great Day of the Lord is approaching—*
> *It is near!*
> *The sound of the Lord's Day hasteth greatly.*
> *A day of wrath is that day,*
> *a day of trouble and distress,*
> *a day of calamity and desolation,*
> *a day of darkness and deep gloom,*
> *a day of clouds and thick mist.*
>
> ZEPHANIA, 1:14–15

Just before 600 B.C. the Prophet Habakuk prayed to the "God who **in the nearing years is coming,**" and who shall show mercy in spite of His wrath. Habakuk described the expected celestial Lord as a **radiant planet**—the very manner in which Nibiru was depicted in Sumer & Akkad. It shall appear, the Prophet said, from the southern skies:

> *The Lord from the south shall come . . .*
> *Covered are the heavens with his halo,*
> *His splendor fills the Earth.*
> *His rays shine forth*
> *from where his power is concealed.*
> *The Word goes before him,*
> *sparks emanate from below.*
> *He pauses to measure the Earth;*
> *He is seen, and the nations tremble.*
>
> HABAKKUK 3:3–6

The prophecies' urgency increased as the sixth century B.C. began. **"The Day of the Lord is at hand!"** the Prophet Joel announced; **"The**

Day of the Lord is near!" the Prophet Obadiah declared. Circa 570 B.C. the Prophet Ezekiel was given the following urgent divine message (Ezekiel 30:2–3):

> *Son of Man, prophesy and say:*
> *Thus sayeth the Lord God:*
> *Howl and bewail for the Day!*
> *For the Day is near—*
> *the Day of the Lord is near!*

Ezekiel was then away from Jerusalem, having been taken into exile with other Judean leaders by the Babylonian king Nebuchadnezzar. The place of exile, where Ezekiel's prophecies and famed vision of the Celestial Chariot took place, was on the banks of the Khabur River, in the region of **Harran.**

The location was not a chance one, for **the concluding saga of the Day of the Lord—and of Assyria and Babylon—was to be played out where Abraham's journey began.**

12

DARKNESS AT NOON

While the Hebrew Prophets predicted Darkness at Noon, what were the "other nations" expecting as they awaited the Return of Nibiru?

To judge by their written records and engraved images, they were expecting the resolution of the gods' conflicts, benevolent times for mankind, and a great theophany. ***They were in, as we shall see, for an immense surprise.***

In anticipation of the great event, the cadres of priests observing the skies in Nineveh and Babylon were mobilized to note celestial phenomena and interpret their omens. The phenomena were meticulously recorded and reported to the kings. Archaeologists have found in the remains of royal and temple libraries tablets with those records and reports that in many instances were arranged according to subject or the planet they were observing. A well-known collection in which some seventy tablets were combined—in antiquity—was a series titled *Enuma Anu Enlil;* it reported observations of planets, stars, and constellations classified according to the celestial Way of Anu and Way of Enlil—encompassing the skies from 30 degrees south all the way to zenith in the north (see fig. 53).

At first the observations were interpreted by comparing the phenomena to astronomical records from Sumerian times. Though writ-

ten in Akkadian (Babylon's and Assyria's language), the observational reports extensively used Sumerian terminology and mathematics and sometimes included a scribal note that they were translated from earlier Sumerian tablets. Such tablets served as "astronomers' manuals," telling them from past experience what a phenomenon's oracular meaning was:

When the Moon in its calculated time is not seen:
There will be an invasion of a mighty city.

When a comet reaches the path of the Sun:
Field-flow will be diminished,
an uproar will happen twice.

When Jupiter goes with Venus:
The prayers of the land will reach the gods.

As time went on, the reports were increasingly of observations accompanied by the omen-priests' own interpretations: "In the night Saturn came near to the Moon. Saturn is a planet of the Sun. This is the meaning: It is favorable to the king." The noticeable change included the paying of particular attention to eclipses; a tablet (now in the British Museum) listing computer-like columns of numbers served to predict lunar eclipses fifty years in advance.

Modern studies have concluded that the change to the new style of topical astronomy took place in the eighth century B.C. when, after a period of mayhem and royal upheavals in Babylon and Assyria, the two lands' fates were placed in new and strong royal hands: Tiglath-Pileser III (745–727 B.C.) in Assyria and Nabunassar (747–734 B.C.) in Babylonia.

Nabunassar ("By Nabu protected") was hailed, already in antiquity, as an innovator and powerhouse in the field of astronomy. One of his first actions was to repair and restore the temple of Shamash in Sippar, the Sun-god's "cult center" in ancient Sumer. He also built a new observatory in Babylon, updated the calendar (a heritage from Nippur), and instituted

daily reporting to the king of the celestial phenomena and their meaning. It was primarily due to those measures that a wealth of astronomical data, shedding light on subsequent events, has come to light.

Tiglath-Pileser III was also active, in his own ways. His annals describe constant military campaigns and boast of captured cities, brutal executions of local kings and nobility, and mass exiles. His role, and those of his successors Shalmaneser V and Sargon II, in the demise of Israel and the exile of its people (the Ten Lost Tribes), and then the attempt by Sennacherib to seize Jerusalem, were described in the previous chapter. Closer to home, those Assyrian kings were busy annexing Babylonia by "taking the hands of Marduk." The next Assyrian king, Esarhaddon (680–669 B.C.), announced that "both Ashur and Marduk gave me wisdom," swore oaths in the name of Marduk and Nabu, and started to rebuild the Esagil temple in Babylon.

In history books, Esarhaddon is mainly remembered for his successful invasion of Egypt (675–669 B.C.). The invasion's purpose, as far as it could be ascertained, was to stop Egyptian attempts to "meddle in Canaan" and dominate Jerusalem. Noteworthy, in the light of subsequent events, was the route he chose: instead of going the shortest way, to the southwest, he made a considerable detour and went northward, to **Harran.** There, in the olden temple of the god Sin, Esarhaddon sought that god's blessing to embark on the conquest; and Sin, leaning on a staff and accompanied by Nusku (the Divine Messenger of the gods), gave his approval.

Esarhaddon then did turn southward, sweeping mightily through the lands of the eastern Mediterranean to reach Egypt. Significantly, he detoured away from the prize that Sennacherib failed to seize— Jerusalem. Significantly, too, that invasion of Egypt and the detour away from Jerusalem—as well as Assyria's own eventual fate—had been prophesied by Isaiah decades earlier (10:24–32).

Busy geopolitically as Esarhaddon was, he did not neglect the astronomical requirements of those times. With guidance from the gods Shamash and Adad, he erected in Ashur (the city, Assyria's cult center) a "House of Wisdom"—an observatory—and depicted the complete twelve-member solar system, including Nibiru, on his

Figure 89

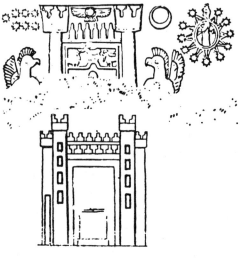

Figure 90

monuments (fig. 89). Leading to a more lavish sacred precinct was a new monumental gate, built—according to cylinder seal depictions— to emulate Anu's gateway on Nibiru (fig. 90). It is a clue to what the Return expectations in Assyria were.

All those religious-political moves suggest that the Assyrians made sure to "touch all the bases" as far as the gods were concerned. And so, by the seventh century B.C., Assyria was ready for the anticipated Return of the

planet of the gods. Discovered texts—including letters to the kings by
their chief astronomers—reveal anticipation of an idyllic, utopian time:

> *When Nibiru will culminate . . .*
> *The lands will dwell securely,*
> *Hostile kings will be at peace;*
> *The gods will receive prayers*
> *and hear supplications.*

> *When the Planet of the Throne of Heaven*
> *will grow brighter,*
> *there will be floods and rains.*

> *When Nibiru attains its perigee,*
> *the gods will give peace.*
> *Troubles will be cleared up,*
> *complications will be unravelled.*

Clearly, the expectation was of a planet that will appear, rise in
the skies, grow brighter, and at its perigee, at the Crossing, become
NIBIRU (the Cross Planet). And as the gateway and other construction
indicated, with the returning planet *a repeat of the previous visit to
Earth by Anu was expected.* It was now up to the astronomer-priests to
watch the heavens for that planetary appearance; but where were they to
look in the celestial expanse, and how would they recognize the planet
when still in the distant skies?

The next Assyrian king, Ashurbanipal (668–630 B.C.), came up
with a solution.

Historians consider Ashurbanipal to have been the most scholarly of
the Assyrian kings, for he had learned other languages besides Akkadian,
including Sumerian, and claimed that he could even read "writings from
before the Flood." He also boasted that he "learnt the secret signs of Heaven
and Earth . . . and studied the heavens with the masters of divination."

Some modern researchers also consider him to have been "The
First Archaeologist," for he systematically collected tablets from sites

that were already ancient in his time—like Nippur, Uruk, and Sippar in what used to be Sumer. He also sent specialized teams to sort out and loot such tablets from the capitals that the Assyrians overran. The tablets ended up in a famed library where teams of scribes studied, translated, and copied chosen texts from the previous millennia. (A visitor to the Museum of the Ancient Near East in Istanbul can see a display of such tablets, neatly arranged on the original shelves, with each shelf headed by a "catalog tablet" that lists all the texts on that shelf.)

While the subjects in the accumulated tablets covered a wide range, what was found indicates that particular attention was given to celestial information. Among the purely astronomical texts there were tablets that belonged to a series titled **"The day of Bel"**—the *Day of the Lord!* In addition, epic tales and histories pertaining to the gods' comings and goings were deemed important, especially if they shed light on Nibiru's passages. *Enuma elish*—the *Epic of Creation* that told how an invading planet joined the solar system to become Nibiru—was copied, translated, and recopied; so were writings dealing with the Great Flood, such as the *Atra-Hasis Epic* and the *Epic of Gilgamesh*. While they all seem to legitimately be part of accumulating knowledge in a royal library, it so happens that *they all dealt with instances of Nibiru's appearances in the past*—and thus with its next nearing.

Among the purely astronomical texts translated and, undoubtedly, carefully studied were guidelines for observing Nibiru's arrival and for recognizing it on its appearance. A Babylonian text that retained the original Sumerian terminology stated:

> *Planet of the god Marduk:*
> *Upon its appearance SHUL.PA.E;*
> *Rising thirty degrees, SAG.ME.NIG;*
> *When it stands in the middle of the sky: NIBIRU.*

While the first-named planet (SHUL.PA.E) is deemed to be Jupiter (but could be Saturn), the next one's name (SAG.ME.NIG) could just be a variant for Jupiter, but is considered by some to be

Mercury.* A similar text from Nippur, rendering the Sumerian planetary names as UMUN.PA.UD.DU and SAG.ME.GAR, suggested that the arrival of Nibiru will be "announced" by the planet Saturn, and after rising 30 degrees will be near Jupiter. Other texts (e.g., a tablet known as K.3124) state that after passing SHUL.PA.E and SAG.ME.GAR—which I believe mean Saturn and Jupiter—"Planet Marduk" will "enter the Sun" (i.e., reach Perigee, closest to the Sun) and "become Nibiru."

Other texts provide clearer clues in regard to Nibiru's path, as well as to the time frame for its appearance:

> *From the station of Jupiter,*
> *the planet passes toward the west.*

> *From the station of Jupiter*
> *the planet increases its brilliance,*
> *and in the zodiac of Cancer will become Nibiru.*

---

*The extensive astronomical data that have been found attracted, already in the 19th and early in the 20th centuries, the time, attention, and patience of scholarly giants who brilliantly combined "Assyriology" with knowledge of astronomy. The very first book of The Earth Chronicles, *The 12th Planet,* covered and used the work and achievements of the likes of Franz Kugler, Ernst Weidner, Erich Ebeling, Herman Hilprecht, Alfred Jeremias, Morris Jastrow, Albert Schott, and Th. G. Pinches, among others. Their task was complicated by the fact that the same *kakkabu* (any celestial body, including planets, fixed stars, and constellations) could have more than one name. I also pointed out right then and there the most basic failing of their work: they all assumed that the Sumerians and other ancient peoples had no way of knowing ("with the naked eye") about planets beyond Saturn. The result was that whenever a planet was named other than the accepted names for the "seven known *kakkabani*"—Sun, Moon, Mercury, Venus, Mars, Jupiter, Saturn—it was assumed to just be yet another name for one of those "known seven." The principal victim of that erroneous stance was Nibiru; whenever it or its Babylonian equivalent, "planet Marduk," was listed, it was assumed to be another name for Jupiter or Mars or (in some extreme views) even for Mercury. Incredibly, modern establishment astronomers continue to base their work on that "only seven" assumption—in spite of the vast contrary evidence that shows that the Sumerians knew the true shape and composition of our solar system, starting with the naming of the outer planets in *Enuma elish,* or the 4,500-year-old depiction of the complete twelve-member solar system, with the Sun in the center, on cylinder seal VA/243 in the Berlin Museum (fig. 91), or the depiction of twelve planetary symbols on Assyrian and Babylonian monuments, and the like.

Figure 91

The great planet:
At his appearance: Dark red.
The heaven he divides in half
as it stands in Nibiru.

Taken together, the astronomical texts from the time of Ashurbanipal described a planet appearing from the solar system's edge, rising and becoming visible when it reaches Jupiter (or even Saturn before that), and then curving down toward the ecliptic. At its perigee, when it is closest to the Sun (and thus to Earth), the planet—at the Crossing—becomes *Nibiru* **"in the zodiac of Cancer."** That, as the enclosed schematic (and not to scale) diagram shows, could happen only when sunrise on the day of the Spring Equinox took place in the Age of the Ram—during the zodiacal age of Aries (fig. 92).

Such clues regarding the orbital path of the Celestial Lord and its reappearance, sometimes using the constellations as a celestial map, are also found in biblical passages, thereby revealing knowledge that must have been internationally available:

"In Jupiter will thy face be seen," states Psalm 17. "The Lord from the south shall come . . . his shining splendor will beam as light," predicted the prophet Habakkuk (chapter 2). "Alone he stretches out the heavens and treads upon the highest Deep; he arrives at the Great Bear, Sirius and Orion, and the constellations of the south," the Book

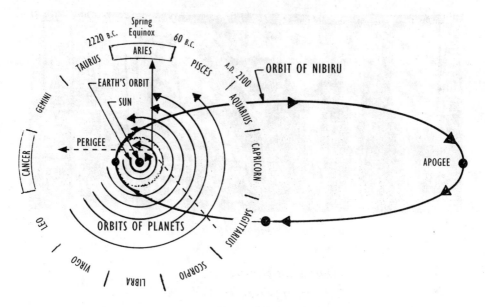

Figure 92

of Job (chapter 9) stated; and the Prophet Amos (5:9) foresaw the Celestial Lord "smiling his face upon Taurus and Aries, from Taurus to Sagittarius he shall go." These verses described a planet that spans the highest heavens and, *orbiting clockwise*—"retrograde," astronomers say—arrives via the southern constellations. It is a trajectory, on a vaster scale, akin to that of Halley's Comet (see fig. 78).

A telling clue in regard to Ashurbanipal's expectations was the meticulous rendering into Akkadian of Sumerian descriptions of the ceremonies attending the state visit of Anu and Antu to Earth circa 4000 B.C. The sections dealing with their stay in Uruk described how, at evetime, an observer was stationed "on the topmost stage of the tower" to watch for and announce the appearance of the planets one after the other, until the "Planet of the Great Anu of Heaven" came into view, whereupon all the gods assembled to welcome the divine couple recited the composition "To the one who grows bright, the heavenly planet of the god Anu" and sang the hymn "The Creator's image has arisen." The long texts then described the ceremonial meals, the retreat to the night-time chambers, the processions the next day, and so on.

One can reasonably conclude that Ashurbanipal was engaged in

collecting, collating, translating, and studying all the earlier texts that could (a) provide guidance to the astronomer-priests for detecting, at the first possible moment, the returning Nibiru and (b) inform the king about the procedures for what to do next. Calling the planet "Planet of the Heavenly Throne" is an important clue to the royal expectations, as were the depictions on palace walls, in magnificent reliefs, of Assyrian kings *greeting the god in the Winged Disc* as it hovered above the Tree of Life (as in fig. 87).

It was important to be informed of the planet's appearance as soon as possible in order to be able to *prepare the proper reception for the arrival of the great god depicted within it—Anu himself?*—and be blessed with long, perhaps even eternal, Life.

But that was not destined to be.

Soon after Ashurbanipal's death, rebellions broke out throughout the Assyrian empire. His sons' hold on Egypt, Babylonia, and Elam disintegrated. Newcomers from afar appeared on the borders of the Assyrian empire—"hordes" from the north, Medes from the east. Everywhere, local kings seized control and declared independence. Of particular importance—immediate and for future events—was Babylon's "decoupling" of the dual kingship with Assyria. As part of the New Year festival in 626 B.C. a Babylonian general whose name— Nabupolassar ("Nabu his son protects")—implied that he claimed to be a son of the god Nabu was enthroned as king of an independent Babylonia. A tablet described the start of his investiture ceremony thus: "The princes of the land were assembled; they blessed Nabupolassar; opening their fists, they declared him sovereign; Marduk in the assembly of the gods gave the Standard of Power to Nabupolassar."

The resentment of Assyria's brutal rule was so great that Nabupolassar of Babylon soon found allies for military action against Assyria. A principal and freshly vigorous ally was the Medes (precursors of the Persians), who had experienced Assyrian incursions and brutality. While Babylonian troops were advancing into Assyria from the south, the Medes attacked from the east, and in 614 B.C.—as had been prophesied by the Hebrew Prophets!—captured and burned down Assyria's religious capital, Ashur. The turn of Nineveh, the royal capital,

came next. *By 612 B.C. the great Assyria was in shambles.* Assyria—the land of the "First Archaeologist"—itself became a land of archaeological sites.

How could that happen to the land whose very name meant "Land of the god Ashur"? The only explanation at the time was that the gods withdrew their protection from that land; in fact, we shall show, there was much more to it: **the gods themselves withdrew—from that land and from Earth.**

And then the most astounding and final chapter of the Return Saga, in which **Harran** was to play a key role, began to unfold.

The amazing chain of events after the demise of Assyria began with the escape to **Harran** of members of Assyria's royal family. Seeking there the protection of the god Sin, the escapees rallied the remnants of the Assyrian army and proclaimed one of the royal refugees as "King of Assyria"; but the god, whose city Harran has been since days of yore, did not respond. *In 610 B.C. Babylonian troops captured Harran and put an end to the Assyrians' lingering hopes.*

The contest for the mantle of successorship to the heritage of Sumer and Akkad was over; it was now worn solely, and with divine blessing, by the king in Babylon. Again, Babylon ruled the lands that were once the hallowed "Sumer & Akkad"—so much so that in many texts from that time, Nabupolassar was given the title "King of Akkad." He used that authority to extend the celestial observations to the erstwhile Sumerian cities of Nippur and Uruk, and some of the key observational texts from the subsequent crucial years come from there.

It was in that same fateful year, 610 B.C.—a memorable year of astounding events, as we shall see—that a reinvigorated Egypt also placed on its throne an assertive strongman named Necho. Just one year later one of the least understod—by historians, that is—geopolitical moves then took place. The Egyptians, who used to be on the same side as the Babylonians in opposition to Assyrian rule, emerged from Egypt and, rushing northward, overran territories and sacred sites that the Babylonians considered theirs. The Egyptian advance, all the way north to Carchemish, put them within striking distance of Harran; it

also placed in Egyptian hands the two space-related sites, in Lebanon and in Judea.

The surprised Babylonians were not going to let it stand. The aging Nabupolassar entrusted the task of recapturing the vital places to his son Nebuchadnezzar, who had already distinguished himself on the battlefields. In June 605 B.C., at Carchemish, the Babylonians crushed the Egyptian army, liberated "the sacred forest in Lebanon which Nabu and Marduk desired," and chased the fleeing Egyptians all the way to the Sinai Peninsula. Nebuchadnezzar stopped the pursuit only on news from Babylon that his father had died. He rushed back, and was proclaimed King of Babylon that same year.

Historians find no explanation for the sudden Egyptian thrust and the ferocity of the Babylonian reaction. To us it is evident that at the core of the events was the expectation of the Return. Indeed, it seems that in that year 605 B.C. the Return was deemed to be imminent, perhaps even overdue; for it was in that very same year that the Prophet Habakkuk began to prophesy in the name of Yahweh, in Jerusalem.

Uncannily foretelling the future of Babylon and other nations, the Prophet asked Yahweh when the Day of the Lord—a day of judgment upon the nations, Babylon included—would come, and Yahweh responded, saying:

> *Write down the prophecy,*
> *explain it clearly on the tablets,*
> *so that it may be quickly read:*
> *For the vision there is a set time;*
> *In the end it shall come, without fail!*
> *Though it may tarry, wait for it;*
> *For it will surely come—*
> *For its appointed time it will not be delayed.*
> HABAKKUK 2:2–3

(The "appointed time," as we shall see, arrived precisely fifty years thereafter.)

* * *

The forty-three years of Nebuchadnezzar's reign (605–562 B.C.) are considered a period of a dominant "Neo-Babylonian" empire, a period marked by decisive actions and fast moves, for there was no time to lose—the nearing Return was now Babylon's prize!

To prepare Babylon for the expected Return, massive renovation and construction works were quickly undertaken. Their focal point was the sacred precinct, where the Esagil temple of Marduk (now simply called *Bel/Ba'al,* "The Lord") was renovated and rebuilt, its seven-stage ziggurat readied for viewing from it the starry skies (fig. 93)—just as had been done in Uruk when Anu had visited circa 4000 B.C. A new Processional Way leading to the sacred precinct through a massive new gate was erected; their walls were decorated and covered from top to bottom with artful glazed bricks that astound to this day, for the site's modern excavators have removed and put the Processional Way and the Gate back together at the Vorderasiatiches Museum in Berlin. Babylon, Marduk's Eternal City, was readied to welcome the Return.

"I have made the city of Babylon to be the foremost among all the countries and every habitation; its name I elevated to be the most praised of all the sacred cities," Nebuchadnezzar wrote in his inscriptions. The expectation, it seems, was that the arriving god of the Winged Disk

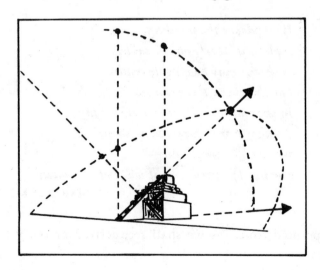

Figure 93

Figure 94

would come down at the Landing Place in Lebanon, then consummate the Return by entering Babylon through the new marvelous Processional Way and imposing Gate (fig. 94)—a gate named "Ishtar" (alias IN.ANNA), who had been "Anu's beloved" in Uruk—another clue regarding whose Return was expected.

Accompanying these expectations was Babylon's role as the new Navel of the Earth—inheriting the pre-Diluvial status of Nippur as the DUR.AN.KI, the "Bond Heaven-Earth." That this was now Babylon's function was expressed by giving the ziggurat's foundation platform the *Sumerian* name E.TEMEN.AN.KI ("Temple of the Foundation for Heaven-Earth"), stressing Babylon's role as the new "Navel of the Earth"—a role clearly depicted on the Babylonian "Map of the World" (see fig. 10). This was terminology that echoed the description of Jerusalem, with its Foundation Stone, serving as a link between Earth and Heaven!

But if that was what Nebuchadnezzar envisioned, then Babylon had to replace the existing post-Diluvial space link—Jerusalem.

Having taken over Nippur's pre-Diluvial role to serve as Mission Control Center after the Deluge, Jerusalem was located at the center of concentric distances to the other space-related sites (see fig. 3). Calling it the "Navel of the Earth" (Ezekiel 38:12), the Prophet Ezekiel announced that Jerusalem has been chosen for this role by God himself:

> *Thus has said the Lord Yahweh:*
> *This is Jerusalem;*
> *In the midst of the nations I placed her,*
> *and all the lands are in a circle*
> *round about her.*
>
> EZEKIEL 5:5

Determined to usurp that role for Babylon, Nebuchadnezzar led his troops to the elusive prize and in 598 B.C. captured Jerusalem. This time, as the Prophet Jeremiah had warned, Nebuchadnezzar was carrying out God's anger at Jerusalem's people, for they had taken up the worship of the celestial gods: "Ba'al, the Sun and the Moon, and the constellations" (II Kings 23:5)—*a list that clearly included Marduk as a celestial entity!*

Starving Jerusalem's people by a siege that lasted three years, Nebuchadnezzar managed to subdue the city and took the Judean king Jehoyachin captive to Babylon. Taken into exile were also Judea's nobil-

ity and learned elite—among them the Prophet Ezekiel—and thousands of its soldiers and craftsmen; they were made to reside by the banks of the Khabur River, near Harran, their ancestral home.

The city itself and the Temple were left intact this time, but eleven years later, in 587 B.C., the Babylonians returned in force. Acting this time, according to the Bible, on their own volition, the Babylonians put the torch to the Temple that Solomon built. In his inscriptions Nebuchadnezzar offered no explanation other than the usual one—to carry out the wishes of and to please "my gods Nabu and Marduk"; but as we shall soon show, the real reason was a simple one: a belief that Yahweh had departed and was gone.

The destruction of the Temple was a shocking and evil deed for which Babylon and its king—previously deemed by the Prophets to have been Yahweh's "rod of wrath"—were to be severely punished: "The vengeance of Yahweh our God, ***vengeance for His Temple***," shall be meted out to Babylon, announced the Prophet Jeremiah (50:28). Predicting the fall of mighty Babylon and its destruction by invaders from the north—events that came true just a few decades later—Jeremiah also proclaimed the fate of the gods whom Nebuchadnezzar had invoked:

> *Declare among the nations and proclaim,*
> *Raise the sign, announce, do not conceal,*
> *Say: Captured is Babylon!*
> *Withered is* Bel, *confounded is* Marduk!
>
> JEREMIAH 50:2

Divine punishment upon Nebuchadnezzar himself was commensurate with the sacrilege. Crazed, according to traditional sources, by a bug that entered his brain through his nose, Nebuchadnezzar died in agony in 562 B.C.

Neither Nebuchadnezzar nor his three bloodline successors (who were murdered or otherwise disposed of in short shrift) lived to see an arrival of Anu at the gates of Babylon. In fact, ***such an arrival never took place***, ***even though Nibiru did return***.

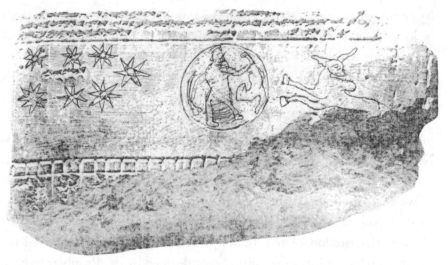

Figure 95

***It is a fact that astronomical tablets from that very time record
actual observations of Nibiru, alias "Planet of Marduk."*** Some
were reported as omina, for example, a tablet catalogued K.8688 that
informed the king that if Venus shall be seen "in front of" (i.e., rising
ahead of) Nibiru, the crops will fail, but if Venus shall rise "behind"
(i.e., after) Nibiru, "the crop of the land will succeed." Of greater interest to us are a group of "Late Babylonian" tablets found in Uruk; they
rendered the data in twelve monthly zodiacal columns and combined
the texts with pictorial depictions. In one of these tablets (VA 7851,
fig. 95), the Planet of Marduk, shown between the Aries ram symbol
on one side and the seven symbol for Earth on the other side, depicts
Marduk within the planet. Another example is tablet VAT 7847; it
names an actual observation, ***in the constellation of Aries,*** as the ***"Day
when the gate of the great lord Marduk was opened"***—when Nibiru
had appeared into view; and then has an entry—*"Day of the Lord
Marduk"*—as the planet moved on and was seen in Aquarius.

Even more telling of the coming into view of the planet "Marduk"
from the southern skies and its fast becoming "Nibiru" in the central celestial band was yet another class of tablets, this time circular. Representing
"an advance backward" to the Sumerian astronomical tenets, the tablets
divided the celestial sphere into the three Ways (Way of Enlil for the

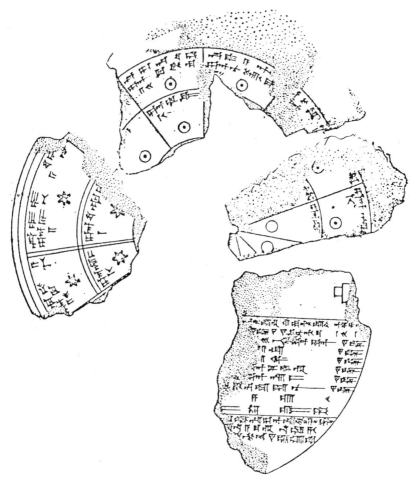

Figure 96

northern skies, of Ea for the southern, and of Anu in the center). The twelve zodiacal-calendrical segments were then superimposed on the three Ways, as shown by the discovered fragments (fig. 96); explanatory texts were written on the back sides of those circular tablets.

In A.D. 1900, addressing a meeting of the Royal Asiatic Society in London, England, Theophilius G. Pinches caused a sensation when he announced that he had succeeded in piecing together a complete "astrolabe" ("Taker of Stars"), as he called the tablet. He showed it to be a circular disc divided into three concentric sections and, like a pie, into twelve segments, resulting in a field of thirty-six portions. Each of the thirty-six

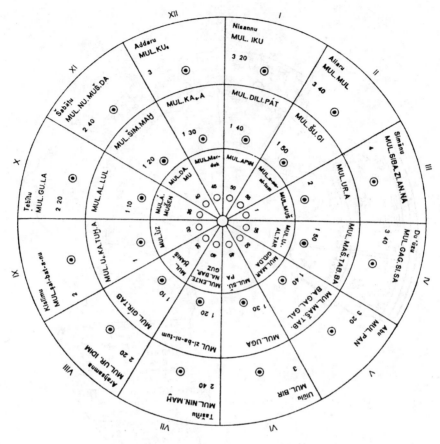

Figure 97

portions contained a name with a small circle below it, indicating it was a celestial body, and a number. Each portion also bore a month's name, so Pinches numbered them from I to XII, starting with Nissan (fig. 97).

The presentation caused an understandable sensation, for here was a Babylonian sky map, divided into the three Ways of Enlil, Anu, and Ea/Enki, showing which planets, stars, and constellations were observed where at each month during the year. The debate over the identity of the celestial bodies (at the root of which lurks the notion of "nothing beyond Saturn") and the meaning of the numbers has yet to end. Also unresolved is the issue of dating—in what year was the astrolabe made, and if it was a copy of an earlier tablet, what was the time shown? Dating opinions ranged from before the twelfth century to the third

century B.C.; most agreed, however, that the astrolabe belonged to the era of Nebuchadnezzar or his successor, Nabuna'id.

The astrolabe presented by Pinches was identified in the ensuing debates as "P" but has been later renamed "Astrolabe A" because another one has since been pieced together and is known as "Astrolabe B."

Though the two astrolabes at first glance look identical, they are different—and for our analysis, the key difference is that in "B" the planet identified as *mul Neberu deity Marduk*—"Planet Nibiru of the god Marduk"—is shown in the Way of Anu, the central-ecliptic band (fig. 98), whereas in "A" the planet identified as *mul Marduk*—the "Planet of Marduk"—is shown in the Way of Enlil, in the northern skies (fig. 99).

The change in name and position is absolutely correct if the two astrolabes depict a *moving planet*—"Marduk" as it was called by the Babylonians—that, after having come into view high in the northern skies (as in "A"), curves down to cross the ecliptic and becomes NIBIRU ("Crossing") when it crosses the ecliptic *in the Way of Anu* (as in "B"). The two-stage documentation by the two astrolabes depicts precisely what we have been asserting all along!

The texts (known as KAV 218, columns B and C) accompanying the circular depictions remove any shadow of doubt regarding the Marduk/Nibiru identity:

> *[Month] Adar:*
> *Planet Marduk in the Way of Anu:*
> *The radiant* Kakkabu *which rises in the south*
> *after the gods of the night finished their tasks,*
> *and divides the heavens.*
> *This* kakkabu *is Nibiru =god Marduk.*

While we can be certain—for reasons soon to be given—that the observations in all those "Late Babylonian" tablets could not have taken place earlier than 610 B.C., we can also be sure that they did not take place after 555 B.C., for that was the date when one called Nabuna'id became the last king of Babylonia; and his claim to

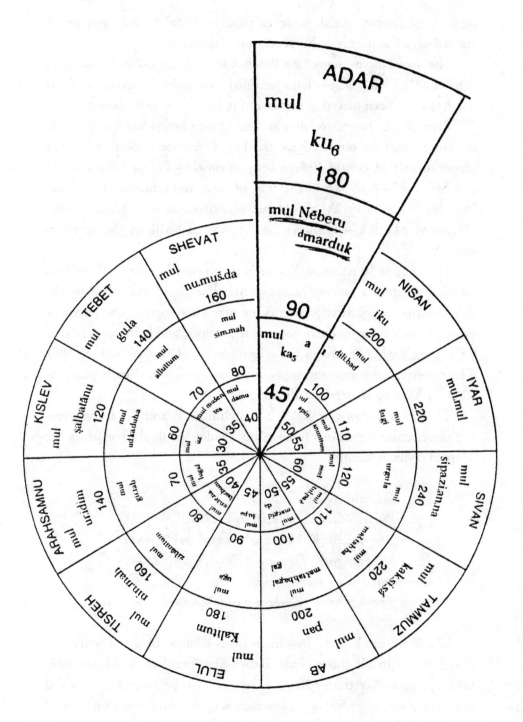

Figure 98

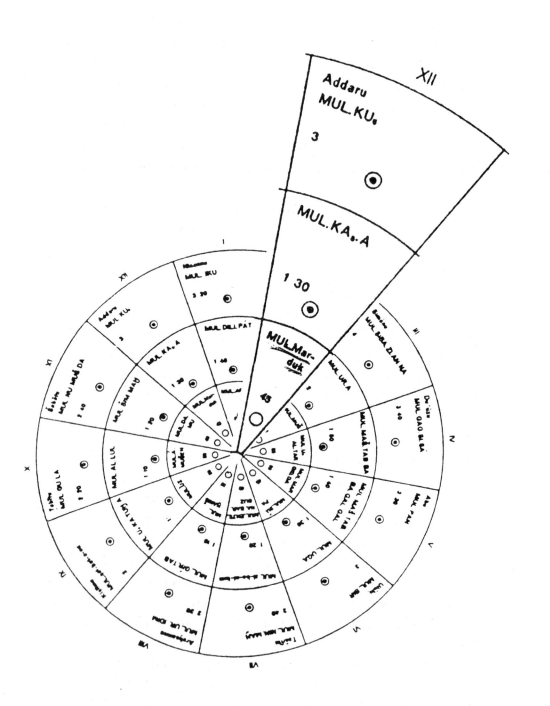

Figure 99

legitimacy was that his kingship was celestially confirmed because *"the planet of Marduk, high in the sky, had called me by my name."* Making that claim, he also stated that in a nighttime vision he had seen *"the Great Star and the Moon."* Based on the Kepler formulas for planetary orbits around the Sun, the whole period of Marduk/Nibiru's visibility from Mesopotamia lasted just a short few years; hence, the visibility claimed by Nabuna'id places the planet's Return in the years immediately preceding 555 B.C.

So when was the precise time of the Return? There is one more aspect involved in resolving the puzzle: the prophecies of "Darkness at noon" on the Day of the Lord—a solar eclipse—**and such an eclipse did in fact occur, in 556 B.C.!**

Solar eclipses, though much rarer than lunar eclipses, are not uncommon; they happen when the Moon, passing in a certain way between Earth and the Sun, temporarily obscures the Sun. Only a small portion of solar eclipses are total. The extent, duration, and path of total darkness vary from passage to passage due to the ever-changing triple orbital dance between Sun, Earth, and Moon, plus Earth's daily revolution and its changing axial tilt.

As rare as solar eclipses are, the astronomical legacy of Mesopotamia included knowledge of the phenomenon, calling it *atalu shamshi.* Textual references suggest that not only the phenomenon but even its lunar involvement were part of the accumulated ancient knowledge. In fact, a solar eclipse whose path of totality passed over Assyria had occurred in 762 B.C. It was followed by one in 584 B.C. that was seen all across the Mediterranean lands, with totality over Greece. **But then, in 556 B.C., there occurred an extraordinary solar eclipse** *"not in an expected time."* If it was not due to the predictable motions of the Moon, **could it have been caused by an unusually close passage of Nibiru?**

Among astronomical tablets belonging to a series called "When Anu Is Planet of the Lord," one tablet (catalogued VACh.Shamash/RM.2,38—fig. 100), dealing with a solar eclipse, recorded thus the observed phenomenon (lines 19–20):

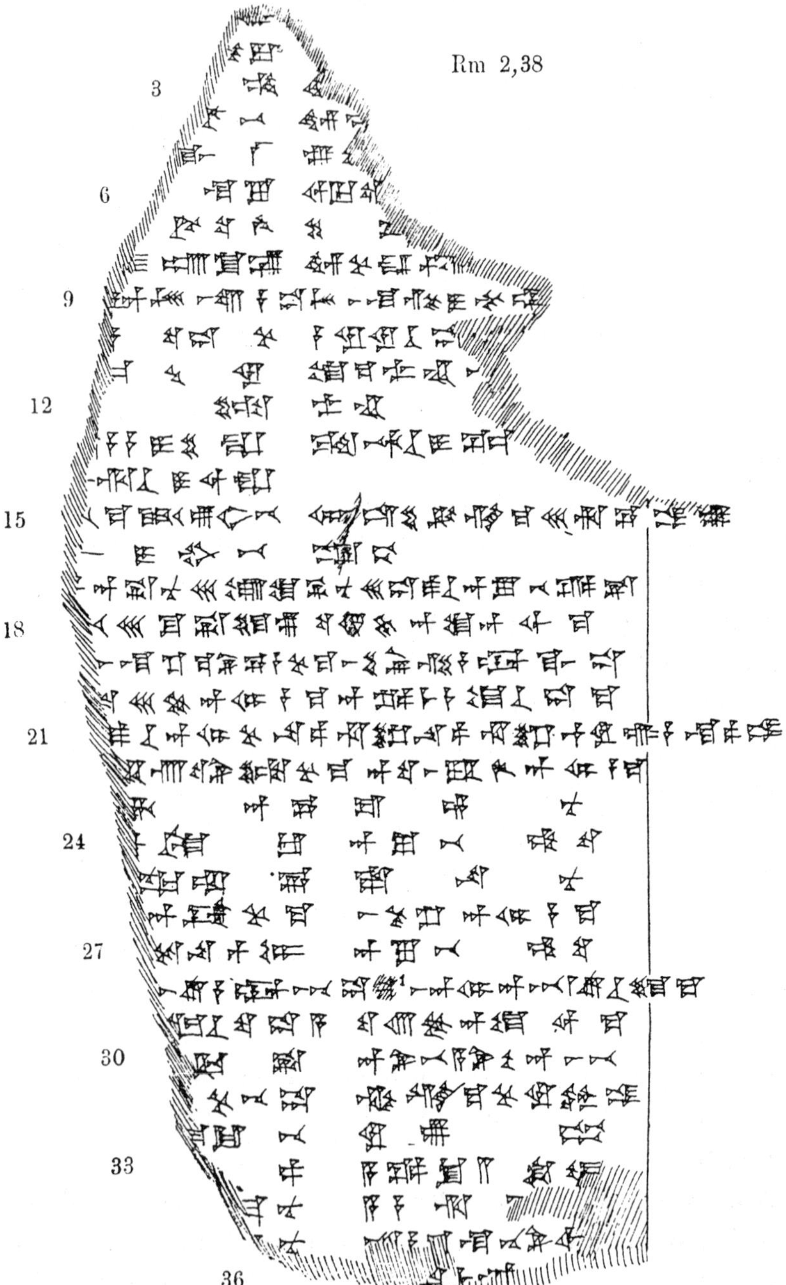

Figure 100

> *In the beginning the solar disc,*
> **not in an expected time,**
> *became darkened,*
> *and* **stood in the radiance of the Great Planet.**
> *On day 30 [of the month] was*
> *the* **eclipse of the Sun.**

What exactly do the words that the darkened Sun "stood in the radiance of the Great Planet" mean? Though the tablet itself does not provide a date for that eclipse, it is our suggestion that the particular wording, highlighted above, *strongly indicates that the unexpected and extraordinary solar eclipse was somehow caused by the return of Nibiru,* the "great radiating planet"; but whether the direct cause was the planet itself, or the effects of its "radiance" (gravitational or magnetic pull?) on the Moon, the texts do not explain.

Still, it is an astronomically historic fact that on a day equal to May 19, 556 B.C., a major total solar eclipse did occur. As shown by this map, prepared by NASA's Goddard Space Flight Center (fig. 101), the eclipse was a great and major one, seen over wide areas, and a unique aspect about it was that *the band of total darkness passed exactly over the district of Harran!*

This last fact is of the utmost significance for our conclusions—and it was even more so in those fateful years in the ancient world; for *right after that,* in 555 B.C., Nabuna'id was proclaimed king of Babylonia—not in Babylon, but in Harran. He was the last king of Babylon; after him, as Jeremiah had prophesied, Babylon followed the fate of Assyria.

It was in 556 B.C. that the prophesied Darkness at Noon came. It was just then that Nibiru returned; it was the prophesied DAY OF THE LORD.

And when the planet's Return did occur, neither Anu nor any other of the expected gods showed up. Indeed, the opposite happened: the gods, the Anunnaki gods, took off and left the Earth.

Total Solar Eclipse of -0556 May 19

Geocentric Conjunction = 12:50:16.9 UT	J.D. = 1518118.034918
Greatest Eclipse = 12:44:22.5 UT	J.D. = 1518118.030815
Eclipse Magnitude = 1.02584	Gamma = 0.31810

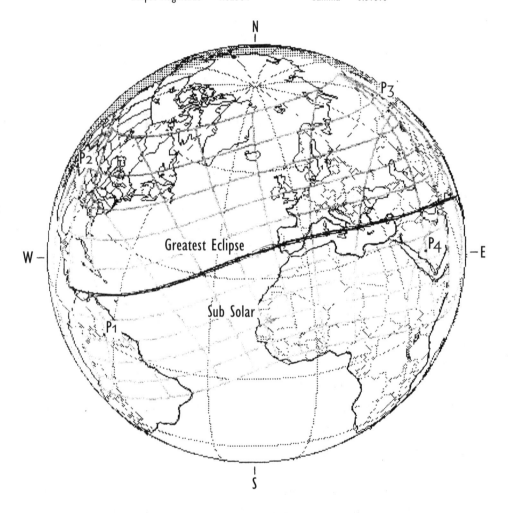

Figure 101

13

WHEN THE
GODS LEFT EARTH

The departure of the Anunnaki gods from Earth was a drama-filled event replete with theophanies, phenomenal occurrences, divine uncertainties, and human quandary.

Incredibly, the Departure is neither surmised nor speculative; it is amply documented. The evidence comes to us from the Near East as well as from the Americas; and some of the most direct, and certainly the most dramatic, records of the ancient gods' departure from Earth come to us from **Harran.** The testimony is not hearsay; it consists of *eyewitness reports,* among them by the Prophet Ezekiel. The reports are included in the Bible, and they were inscribed on stone columns— texts dealing with miraculous events leading to the accession to the throne of Babylon's last king.

Harran nowadays—yes, it is still there, and I have visited it—is a sleepy town in eastern Turkey, just a few miles from the Syrian border. It is surrounded by crumbling walls from Islamic times, its inhabitants dwelling in beehive-shaped mud huts. The traditional well where Jacob met Rachel is still there among the sheep meadows outside the town, with the purest naturally cool water one can imagine.

But in earlier days Harran was a flourishing commercial, cultural,

religious, and political center, so much so that even the Prophet Ezekiel (27:24), who lived in the area with other exiles from Jerusalem, recalled her reputation as a trader in "blue clothes and broidered work, and in chests of rich apparel, bound with cords and made of cedar." It was a city that had been from Sumerian times on an "Ur away from Ur" cult center of the "Moon god" Nannar/Sin. Abraham's family ended up residing there because his father, Terah, was a *Tirhu,* an omen-priest, first in Nippur, then in Ur, and finally in Nannar/Sin's temple in Harran. After the demise of Sumer by the nuclear Evil Wind, Nannar and his spouse, Ningal, made their home and headquarters in Harran.

Though Nannar (*"Su-en,"* or *Sin* for short in Akkadian) was not Enlil's firstborn legal heir—that rank belonged to Ninurta—he was the firstborn of Enlil and his spouse, Ninlil, a firstborn on Earth. Gods and men greatly adored Nannar/Sin and his spouse; the hymns in their honor in Sumer's glorious times, and the lamentations about the desolation of Sumer in general and Ur in particular, reveal the great love and admiration of the people for this divine couple. That many centuries later Esarhaddon went to consult with an aging Sin ("leaning on a staff") regarding the invasion of Egypt, and that the escaping Assyrian royals made a last stand in Harran, serve to indicate the continued important role played by Nannar/Sin and Harran to the very end.

It was in the ruins of the city's great Nannar/Sin temple, the E.HUL.HUL ("House of Double Joy"), that archaeologists discovered four stone columns ("stelae") that once stood in the temple, one at each corner of the main prayer hall. The inscriptions on the stelae revealed that two were erected by the temple's high priestess, Adda-Guppi, and two by her son Nabuna'id, the last king of Babylon.

With an evident sense of history and as a trained temple official, Adda-Guppi provided in her inscriptions precise dates for the astounding events that she had witnessesd. The dates, linked as was then customary to regnal years of known kings, could thus be—and have been—verified by modern scholars. It is thus certain that she was born in 649 B.C. and lived through the reigns of several Assyrian and Babylonian kings, passing on at the ripe old age of 104.

Here is what she wrote on her stela concerning the first of a series
of amazing events:

> *It was in the sixteenth year of Nabupolassar,*
> *king of Babylon, when Sin, lord of the gods,*
> *became angry with his city and his temple*
> **and went up to heaven;**
> *and the city and the people in it went to ruin.*

The sixteenth year of Nabupolassar was 610 B.C.—a memorable
year, the reader may recall, when Babylonian forces captured Harran
from the remnants of the Assyrian royal family and army, and when a
reinvigorated Egypt decided to seize the space-related sites. It was then,
Adda-Guppi wrote, that an angered Sin, removing his protection (and
himself) from the city, packed up **"and went up to heaven!"**

What followed in the captured city is accurately summed up:
"And the city and its people went to ruin." While other survivors fled,
Adda-Guppi stayed on. "Daily, without ceasing, by day and night, for
months, for years," she kept vigil in the ruined temple. Mourning, she
"forsook the dresses of fine wool, took off jewelry, wore neither silver
nor gold, relinquished perfumes and sweet smelling oils." As a ghost
roaming the abandoned shrine, "in a torn garment I was clothed; I
came and went noiselessly," she wrote.

Then, in the desolate sacred precinct, she found a robe that had
once belonged to Sin. To the despondent priestess, the find was an
omen from the god: suddenly he had given her a physical presence of
himself. She could not take her eyes off the sacred garb, not daring to
touch it except by "taking hold of its hem." As if the god himself was
there to hear her, she prostrated herself and "in prayer and humility"
uttered a vow: "If you would return to your city, all the Black-Headed
people would worship your divinity!"

"Black-Headed people" was a term by which the Sumerians used
to describe themselves, and the employment of the term by the high
priestess some 1,500 years after Sumer was no more was full of significance: she was telling the god that were he to come back, he would be

restored to lordship as in the Days of Old, become again the lord god of a restored Sumer and Akkad. To achieve that, Adda-Guppi offered her god a deal: If he would return and then use his divine powers to make her son Nabuna'id the next imperial king, reigning over all the Babylonian and Assyrian domains, Nabuna'id would restore the temple of Sin not only in Harran but also in Ur and would proclaim the worship of Sin as the state religion in all the lands of the Black-Headed people!

Touching the hem of the god's robe, day after day she prayed; then one night the god appeared to her in a dream and accepted her proposal. The Moon god, Adda-Guppi wrote, liked the idea: "Sin, lord of the gods of Heaven and Earth, for my good doings looked upon me with a smile; he heard my prayers; he accepted my vow. The wrath of his heart calmed. Toward Ehulhul, his temple in Harran, the divine residence in which his heart rejoiced, he became reconciled; and he had a change of heart." The god, Adda-Guppi wrote, accepted the deal:

> *Sin, lord of the gods,*
> *looked with favor upon my words.*
> *Nabuna'id, my only son, issue of my womb,*
> *to the kingship he called—*
> *the kingship of Sumer and Akkad.*
> *All the lands from the border of Egypt,*
> *from the Upper Sea to the Lower Sea,*
> *in his hands he entrusted.*

Both sides kept their bargain. "I myself saw it fulfilled," Adda-Guppi stated in the concluding segment of her inscriptions: Sin "honored his word which he spoke to me," causing Nabuna'id to ascend the Babylonian throne in 555 B.C.; and Nabuna'id kept his mother's vow to restore the Ehulhul temple in Harran, "perfecting its structure." He renewed the worship of Sin and Ningal (Nikkal in Akkadian)—"all the forgotten rites he made anew."

And then a great miracle, an occurrence unseen for generations, happened. The event is described in the two stelae of Nabuna'id, in

Figure 102

which he is depicted holding an unusual staff and facing the celestial symbols of Nibiru, Earth, and the Moon (fig. 102):

> *This is the great miracle of Sin*
> *that has by gods and goddesses*
> *not happened in the land,*
> *since days of old unknown;*
> *That the people of the Earth*
> *had neither seen nor found written*
> *on tablets since the days of old:*
> *That Sin, lord of gods and goddesses,*
> ***residing in the heavens,***
> ***has come down from the heavens—***
> *in full view of Nabuna'id, king of Babylon.*

Sin, the inscriptions report, did not return alone. According to the texts, he entered the restored Ehulhul temple in a ceremonial procession, accompanied by his spouse, Ningal/Nikkal, and his aide, the Divine Messenger Nusku.

* * *

The miraculous return of Sin "from the heavens" raises many questions, the first one being Where, "in the heavens," he had been for five or six decades. Answers to such questions can be given by combining the ancient evidence with the achievements of modern science and technology. But before we turn to that, it is important to examine all the aspects of the Departure, for it was not Sin alone who "became angry" and, leaving Earth, "went up to heaven."

The extraordinary celestial comings and goings described by Adda-Guppi and Nabuna'id took place while they were in Harran—a significant point because another eyewitness was present in that area at that very time; he was the Prophet Ezekiel; and he, too, had much to say on the subject.

Ezekiel, a priest of Yahweh in Jerusalem, was among the aristocracy and craftsmen who had been exiled, together with King Jehoiachin, after Nebuchadnezzar's first attack on Jerusalem in 598 B.C. They were taken forcefully to northern Mesopotamia, settling in the district of the Khabur River, just a short distance away from their ancestral home in Harran. And it was there that Ezekiel's famous vision of a celestial chariot had occurred. As a trained priest, he too recorded the place and the date: it was on the fifth day of the fourth month in the fifth year of the exile—594/593 B.C.—"when I was among the exiles on the banks of the river Khebar, that the heavens opened up and I saw visions of *Elohim,*" Ezekiel stated at the very beginning of his prophecies; and what he saw, appearing in a whirlwind, flashing lights and surrounded by a radiance, was a divine chariot that could go up and down and sideways, and within it, "upon the likeness of a throne, the semblance of a man"; and he heard a voice addressing him as "Son of Man" and announcing his prophetic assignment.

The Prophet's opening statement is usually translated "visions of *God.*" The term *Elohim,* which is plural, has been traditionally translated "God" in the singular, even when the Bible itself clearly treats it in the plural, as in "And *Elohim* said let *us* fashion the Adam in *our* image and after *our* likeness" (Genesis 1:26). As readers of my books know, the biblical Adam tale is a rendering of the much more detailed

Sumerian creation texts, where it was an Anunnaki team, led by Enki, that used genetic engineering to "fashion" the Adam. The term *Elohim,* we have shown over and over again, referred to the Anunnaki; and **what Ezekiel reported was that he had encountered an Anunnaki celestial craft**—near Harran.

The celestial craft that was seen by Ezekiel was described by him, in the opening chapter and thereafter, as the God's *Kavod* ("That which is heavy")—the very same term used in Exodus to describe the divine vehicle that had landed on Mount Sinai. The craft's description rendered by Ezekiel has inspired generations of scholars and artists; the resulting depictions have changed with time, as our own technology of flight vehicles has advanced. Ancient texts refer both to spacecraft and aircraft and describe Enlil, Enki, Ninurta, Marduk, Thoth, Sin, Shamash, and Ishtar, to name the most prominent, as gods who possessed aircraft and could roam Earth's skies—or engage in aerial battles, as between Horus and Seth or Ninurta and Anzu (not to mention the Indo-European gods). Of all the varied textual descriptions and pictorial depictions of the "celestial boats" of the gods, the most appropriate to Ezekiel's vision of a Whirlwind appears to be the "whirlwind chariot" depicted at a site in Jordan (fig. 103) from which the Prophet Elijah was taken up to heaven. Helicopter-like, it had to serve just as a shuttlecraft to where full-fledged spacecraft were stationed.

Ezekiel's mission was to prophesy and warn his exiled compatriots of the coming Day of Judgment for all the nations' injustices and abominations. Then, a year later, the same "semblance of a man" appeared again, put out a hand, grabbed him, and carried him all the

Figure 103

way to Jerusalem, to prophesy there. The city, it will be remembered, went through a starving siege, a humiliating defeat, wanton looting, a Babylonian occupation, and the exile of the king and all the nobility. Arriving there, Ezekiel saw a scene of complete breakdown of the rule of law and of religious observances. Wondering what was going on, he heard the remnant sitting in mourning, bewailing (8:12; 9:9):

> **Yahweh sees us no more,**
> **Yahweh has left the Earth!**

This was, we suggest, the reason why Nebuchadnezzar dared attack Jerusalem again and destroy Yahweh's temple. It was an outcry virtually identical to what Adda-Guppi had reported from Harran: "Sin, the lord of the gods, became angry with his city and his people, and went up to heaven; and the city and the people in it went to ruin."

One cannot be certain how or why events occurring in northern Mesopotamia gave rise to a notion in distant Judea that Yahweh, too, had left the Earth, but it is evident that word that God and gods departed had spread far and wide. Indeed, tablet VAT 7847, which we mentioned earlier in connection with the solar eclipse, states the following in a prophetic section regarding calamities that last 200 years:

> *Roaring the gods, flying,*
> *from the lands will go away,*
> *from the people they will be separated.*
> *The people will the gods' abodes leave in ruins.*
> *Compassion and well-being will cease.*
> *Enlil, in anger, will lift himself off.*

Like several other documents of the "Akkadian Prophecies" genre, scholars deem this text, too, a "post-event prophecy"—a text that uses events that had already happened as the basis for predicting other future events. Be that as it may, we have here a document that considerably expands the divine exodus: the angered gods, *led by Enlil,* flew away from their lands; it was not just Sin who was angered and left.

There is yet another document. It is classified by scholars as belonging to "Prophecy in Neo-Assyrian sources," though its very first words suggest authorship by a (Babylonian?) worshipper of Marduk. Here is, in full, what it says:

> *Marduk, the Enlil of the gods, got angry. His mind*
> *became furious.*
> *He made an evil plan to disperse the land and its peoples.*
> *His angry heart was bent on levelling the land and*
> *destroying its people.*
> *A grievous curse formed in his mouth.*
> *Evil portents indicating the disruption of heavenly*
> *harmony started appearing abunbantly in heaven and*
> *on Earth.*
> *The planets in the Ways of Enlil, Anu and Ea worsened*
> *their positions and repeatedly disclosed abnormal omens.*
> *Arahtu, the river of abundance, became a raging current.*
> *A fierce surge of water, a violent flood like the Deluge*
> *swept away the city, its houses and sanctuaries, turning*
> *them to ruins.*
> **The gods and goddesses became afraid, abandoned**
> **their shrines, flew off like birds and ascended to**
> **heaven.**

What is common to all these texts are the assertions that (a) the gods grew angry with the people, (b) the gods "flew away like birds," and (c) they ascended to "heaven." We are further informed that the departure was accompanied by unusual celestial phenomena and some terrestrial disturbances. These are aspects of the Day of the Lord as prophesied by the biblical Prophets: **The Departure was related to the Return of Nibiru—the gods left Earth when Nibiru came.**

The VAT 7847 text includes an intriguing reference to a calamitous period of two centuries. The text does not make it clear whether that was a prediction of what is to follow the gods' departure, or whether it was

during such a time that their anger and disappointment with Mankind grew, leading to the Departure. It seems that the latter is the case, for it is probably no coincidence that the era of biblical prophecy regarding the nations' sins and the coming judgment on the Day of the Lord began with Amos and Hosea circa 760/750 B.C.—two centuries before the Return of Nibiru! For two centuries the Prophets, from the only legitimate place of the "Bond Heaven-Earth"—Jerusalem—called for justice and honesty among people and peace among nations, scorned meaningless offerings and worship of lifeless idols, denounced wanton conquests and pitiless destruction, and warned one nation after another—Israel included—of the inevitable punishments, but to no avail.

If that was the case, then what had taken place was a gradual buildup of divine anger and disappointment, and the reaching of a conclusion by the Anunnaki that "enough is enough"—it was time to leave. It all brings to mind the decision of the gods, led by the disappointed Enlil, to keep the coming Deluge and the gods' lofting themselves in their celestial craft a secret from Mankind; now, as Nibiru was again nearing, it was the Enlilite gods who planned the Departure.

Who left, how did they leave, and where did they go if Sin could come back in a few decades? For the answers, let us roll the events back to the beginning.

When the Anunnaki, led by Ea/Enki, had first come to Earth to obtain the gold with which to protect their planet's endangered atmosphere, they planned to extract the gold from the waters of the Persian Gulf. When that did not work, they shifted to mining operations in southeastern Africa and smelting and refining in the E.DIN, the future Sumer. Their number increased to 600 on Earth plus 300 Igigi who operated celestial craft to a way station on Mars, from which the long-haul spacecraft to Nibiru could be launched more easily. Enlil, Enki's half-brother and rival for the succession, came and was put in overall command. When the Anunnaki toiling in the mines mutinied, Enki suggested that a "Primitive Worker" be fashioned; it was done by genetically upgrading an existing Hominid. And then the Anunnaki began to "take the daughters of the Adam as wives and had children by them" (Genesis 6), with Enki and Marduk breaking the taboo. When

the Deluge came, the outraged Enlil said "let mankind perish," for "the wickedness of Man was great on the Earth." But Enki, through a "Noah," frustrated the plan. Mankind survived, proliferated, and in time was granted civilization.

The Deluge that swept over the Earth flooded the mines in Africa but exposed a mother lode of gold in the Andes Mountains of South America, enabling the Anunnaki to obtain more gold more easily and quickly, and without the need for smelting and refining, for the Placer Gold—pure gold nuggets washed down from the mountains—needed only panning and collecting. It also made it possible to reduce the number of Anunnaki needed on Earth. On their state visit to Earth circa 4000 B.C., Anu and Antu visited the post-Diluvial gold land on the shores of Lake Titicaca.

The visit served as an opportunity to begin reducing the number of Nibiruans on Earth; it also approved peace arrangements between the rival half-brothers and their warring clans. But while Enki and Enlil accepted the territorial divisions, Enki's son Marduk never gave up the strife for supremacy that included control of the olden space-related sites. It was then that the Enlilites began to prepare alternative spaceport facilities in South America. When the post-Diluvial spaceport in the Sinai was wiped out with nuclear weapons in 2024 B.C., the facilities in South America were the only ones left entirely in Enlilite hands.

And so, when the frustrated and disgusted Anunnaki leadership decided that it was time to leave, some could use the Landing Place; others, perhaps with a last large haul of gold, had to use the South American facilities, near the place where Anu and Antu stayed during their visit to the area.

As earlier mentioned, the place—now called Puma-Punku—is a short distance from a shrunken Lake Titicaca (shared by Peru and Bolivia), but was then situated on the lake's southern shore, with harbor facilities. Its main remains consist of a row of four collapsed structures, each made of a single hollowed-out giant boulder (fig. 104). Each such hollowed-out set of chambers was completely inlaid inside with gold plates, held in place by gold nails—an incredible treasure hauled off by

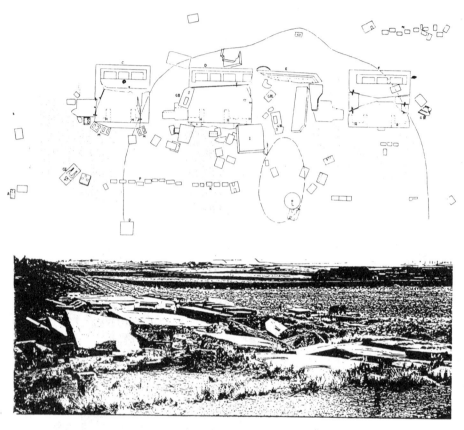

Figure 104

the Spaniards when they arrived in the sixteenth century. How such dwellings were so precisely hollowed out of the rocks and how four huge rocks were brought to the site remain a mystery.

There is yet another mystery at the site. The archaeological finds in the place included a large number of unusual stone blocks that were precisely cut, grooved, angled, and shaped; some of them are shown in fig. 105. One does not need an engineering degree to realize that these stones were cut, drilled, and shaped by someone with incredible technological ability and sophisticated equipment; indeed, one would doubt whether *stones* could be so shaped nowadays. The puzzle is compounded by the mystery of what purpose did these technological miracles serve; obviously, for some unknown yet highly sophisticated purpose. If it was

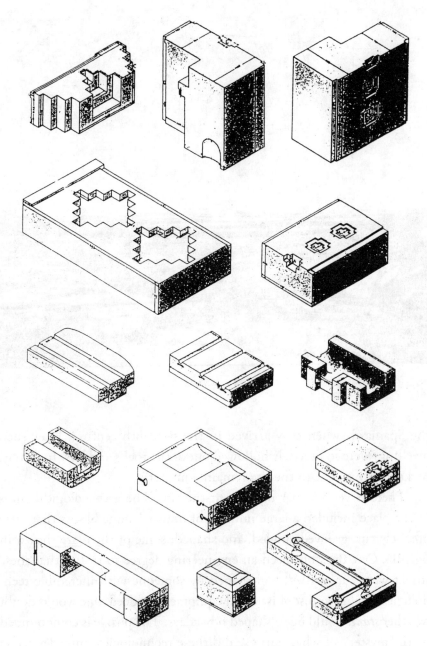

Figure 105

to serve as casting dies for complex instruments, what—and whose—were those instruments?

Clearly, one can think only of the Anunnaki as possessing both the technology to make those "dies" and to use them or their end products. The main outpost of the Anunnaki was situated a few miles inland, at a site now known as Tiwanacu (earlier spelled Tiahuanacu), now belonging to Bolivia. One of the first European explorers to reach it in modern times, George Squier, described the place in his book *Peru Illustrated* as "The Baalbec of the New world"—a comparison more valid than he realized.

The next main modern explorer of Tiwanaku, Arthur Posnansky (*Tihuanacu—The Cradle of American Man*), reached astounding conclusions regarding the site's age. The principal aboveground structures in Tiwanaku (there are numerous subterranean ones) include the **Akapana,** an artificial hill riddled with channels, conduits, and sluices whose purpose is discussed in *The Lost Realms.* A tourist favorite is a stone gateway known as the **Gate of the Sun,** a prominent structure that was also cut from a single boulder, with some of the precision exhibited at Puma-Punku. It probably served an astronomical purpose and undoubtedly a calendrical one, as the carved images on the archway indicate; those carvings are dominated by the larger image of the god Viracocha holding the lightning weapon that clearly emulated the Near Eastern Adad/Teshub (fig. 106). Indeed, in *The Lost Realms* I have suggested that he *was* Adad/Teshub.

The Gate of the Sun is so positioned that it forms an astronomical observation unit with the third prominent structure at Tiwanaku, called the **Kalasasaya.** It is a large rectangular structure with a sunken central courtyard and is surrounded by standing stone pillars. Posnansky's suggstion that the Kalasasaya served as an observatory has been confirmed by subsequent explorers; his conclusion, based on Sir Norman Lockyer's archaeoastronomy guidelines, that the astronomical alignments of the Kalasasaya show that it was built thousands of years before the Incas was so incredible that German astronomical institutions sent teams of scientists to check this out. Their report, and subsequent additional verifications (viz. the scientific journal *Baesseler Archiv,* volume 14)

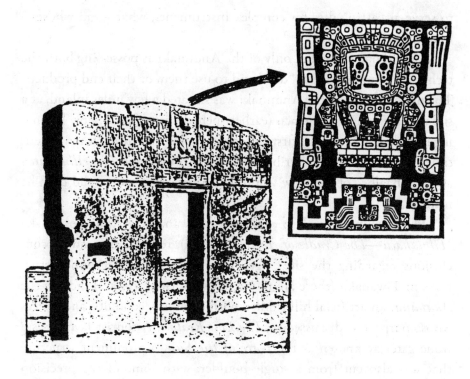

Figure 106

affirmed that the Kalasasaya's orientation unquestionably matched the Earth's obliquity either in 10,000 B.C. **or 4000 B.C.**

Either date, I wrote in *The Lost Realms,* was fine with me—the earlier soon after the Deluge, when the gold-obtaining operations began there, or the later date, when Anu visited; both dates matched the activities of the Anunnaki there, and the evidence for the presence of the Enlilite gods is all over the place.

Archaeological, geological, and mineralogical research at the site and in the area confirmed that Tiwanaku also served as a metallurgical center. Based on various finds and the images on the Gate of the Sun (fig. 107a) and their similarity to depictions in ancient Hittite sites in Turkey (fig. 107b), I have suggested that the gold (and tin!) obtainment operations there were supervised by Ishkur/Adad, Enlil's youngest son. His domain in the Old World was Anatolia, where he was worshipped by the Hittites as Teshub, the "weather god" whose sym-

Figure 107a

Figure 107b

bol was the lightning rod; such a huge symbol, enigmatically carved on a steep mountainside (fig. 108), can be seen from the air or from out in the ocean in the Bay of Paracas, Peru, a natural harbor downhill from Tiwanaku. Nicknamed the Candelabra, the symbol is 420 feet long and 240 feet wide, and its lines, which are 5 to 15 feet wide, have been etched into the hard rocks to a depth of about 2 feet—and no one knows by whom and when or how, unless it was Adad himself who wanted to declare his presence.

To the north of the bay, inland in the desert between the Ingenio and Nazca Rivers, explorers have found one of the most puzzling riddles of antiquity, the so-called **Nazca Lines.** Called by some "the world's largest artworks," a vast area (some 200 square miles!) that extends eastward from the *pampa* (flat desert) to the rugged mountains was used by "someone" as a canvas to draw on it scores of images; the drawings are so huge that they make no sense at ground level—but when viewed from the air, clearly represent known and imaginary animals and birds

Figure 108

(fig. 109). The drawings were made by removing the topsoil to a depth of several inches and were executed with a unicursal line—a continuous line that curves and twists without crossing over itself. Anyone flying over the area (there are small planes at the service of tourists there) invariably concludes that "someone" *airborne* has used a soil-blasting device to doodle on the ground below.

Directly relevant to the subject of the Departure, however, is another even more puzzling feature of the Nazca Lines—actual ***"lines" that look like wide runways*** (fig. 110). Straight without fault, these flat stretches—sometimes narrow, sometimes wide, sometimes short, sometimes long—run straight over hills and vales, no matter the shape of the terrain. There are some 740 straight "lines," sometimes combined with triangular "trapezoids" (fig. 111). They frequently criss-cross

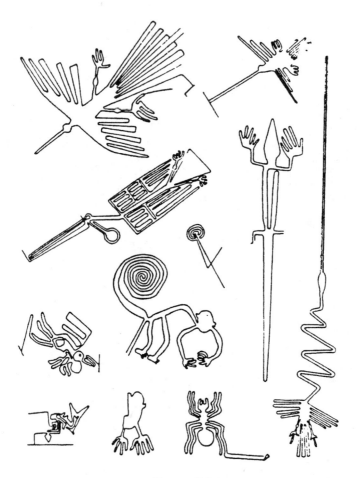

Figure 109

each other without rhyme or reason, sometimes running over the animal drawings, revealing that the lines were made at different times.

Various attempts to resolve the mystery of the lines, including those by the late Maria Reiche, who made it her lifelong project, failed whenever an explanation was sought in terms of "it was done by native Peruvians"—people of a "Nazca culture" or a "Paracas civilization" or the likes. Studies (including some by the National Geographic Society) aimed at uncovering astronomical orientations for the lines—alignments with solstices, equinoxes, this or that star—led nowhere. For those who rule out an "Ancient Astronauts" solution, the enigma remains unresolved.

Figure 110

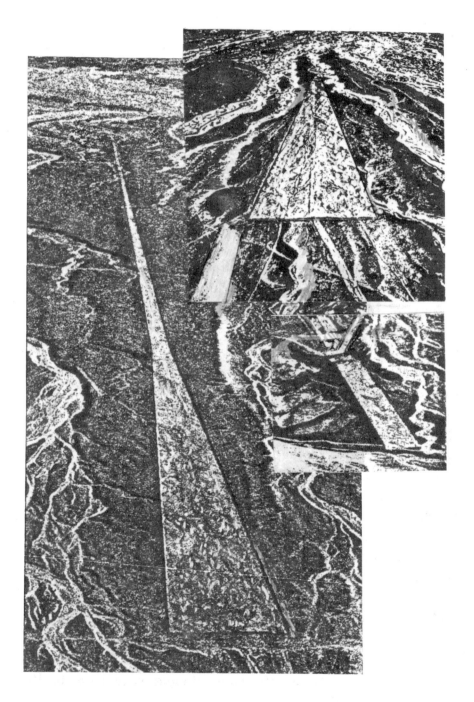

Figure 111

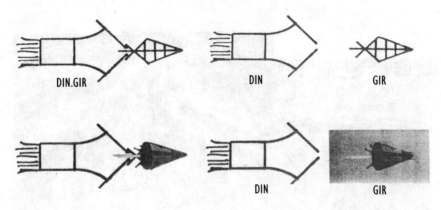

DIN.GIR   DIN   GIR

DIN   GIR

Figure 112

Though the wider lines look like airport runways, on which wheeled aircraft roll to take off (or to land), this is not the case here, if only because the "lines" are not horizontally level—they run straight over uneven terrain, ignoring hills, ravines, and gullies. Indeed, rather than being there to enable takeoff, they appear to be the *result of takeoffs* by craft taking off and leaving on the ground below "lines" created by their engine's exhaust. That the "celestial chambers" of the Anunnaki did emit such exhausts is indicated by the Sumerian pictograph (read DIN.GIR) for the space gods (fig. 112).

This, I suggest, is the solution of the puzzle of the "Nazca Lines": Nazca was the last spaceport of the Anunnaki. It served them after the one in the Sinai was detroyed, and then it served them for the final Departure.

There are no eyewitness-report texts regarding the airborne craft and flights in Nazca; there are, as we have shown, texts from Harran and Babylon regarding the flights that undoubtedly used the Landing Place in Lebanon. The eyewitness reports relating to those departure flights and Anunnaki's craft include the testimony of the Prophet Ezekiel and the inscriptions of Adda-Guppi and Nabunaid.

The inevitable conclusion must be that from at least 610 B.C. through probably 560 B.C., the Anunnaki gods were methodically leaving planet Earth.

* * *

Where did they go as they lifted off Earth? It had to be, of course, a place from which Sin could return relatively soon once he changed his mind. The place was the good old Way Station on Mars, from which the long-distance spaceships raced to intercept and land on the orbiting Nibiru.

As detailed in *The Twelfth Planet,* Sumerian knowledge of our solar system included references to the use of Mars by the Anunnaki as a Way Station. It is evidenced by a remarkable depiction on a 4,500-year-old cylinder seal (fig. 113) now in the Hermitage Museum in St. Petersburg, Russia, that shows an astronaut on Mars (the sixth planet) communicating with one on Earth (the seventh planet, counting from the outside in), with a spacecraft in the heavens between them. Benefiting from Mars's lower gravity compared to that of Earth, the Anunnaki had found it easier and more logical to first transport themselves and their cargos in shuttlecraft from Earth to Mars, and there transfer to reach Nibiru (and vice versa).

In 1976, when all that was first presented in *The Twelfth Planet,* Mars was still held to be an airless, waterless, lifeless, hostile planet, and the suggestion that a space base had once existed there was deemed by establishment scholars even more far out than the notion of "Ancient Astronauts." By the time *Genesis Revisited* was published in 1990, there were enough of NASA's own findings and photographs from Mars to fill up a whole chapter titled "A Space Base on Mars." The evidence

Figure 113

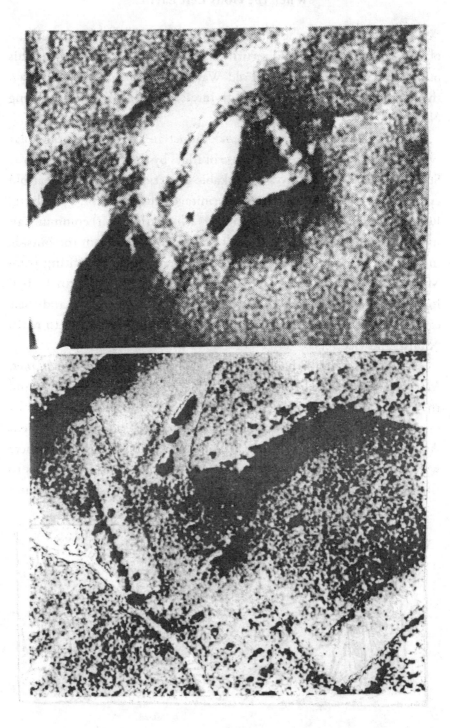

Figure 114

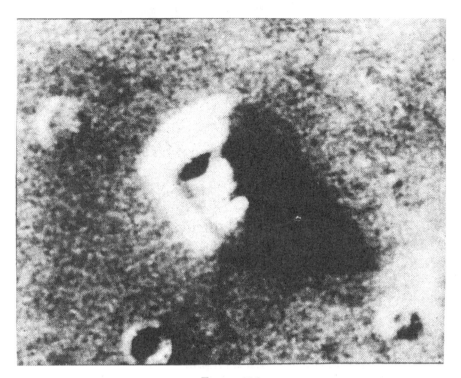

Figure 115

showed that Mars once had water and included photographs of walled structures, roads, a hublike compound (fig. 114 shows just two such photographs)—and the famous Face (fig. 115).

Both the United States and the Soviet Union (now Russia) made great efforts to reach and explore Mars with unmanned spacecraft; unlike other space endeavors, the missions to Mars—since augmented by the European Union—have met with an unusual, troubling, and puzzling high rate of failures, including bewildering unexplained disappearances of spacecraft. But due to persistent efforts, enough U.S., Soviet, and European unmanned spacecraft have managed to reach and explore Mars in the past two decades, that by now the scientific journals—of the same "Doubting Thomases" of the 1970s—have been filled with reports, studies, and photographs announcing that Mars did have a sizeable and still has a thin atmosphere; that it once had rivers, lakes, and oceans and still has water, at some places just below the surface and in some instances even visible as small frozen lakes—as a

Figure 116

Figure 117

medley of the headlines shows (fig. 116). In 2005 NASA's Mars Rovers sent back chemical and photographic evidence backing those conclusions; together with some of the Rovers' amazing photographs showing structural remains—like a sand-covered wall with distinct right-angled corners (fig. 117)—they should suffice here to make the point: **Mars could, and did, serve as a Way Station for the Anunnaki.**

It was the first close-by destination of the departing gods, as confirmed by the relatively quick return of Sin. Who else left, who stayed behind, who might return?

Surprisingly, some of the answers also come from Mars.

14

THE END OF DAYS

Mankind's recollection of landmark events in its past—"legends" or "myths" to most historians—includes tales deemed "universal" in that they have been part of the cultural or religious heritage of peoples all over the Earth. Tales of a First Human Couple, of a Deluge, or of gods who came from the heavens, belong to that category. So do tales of the gods' departure back to the heavens.

Of particular interest to us are such collective memories by the peoples and in the lands where the departures had actually taken place. We have already covered the evidence from the ancient Near East; it also comes from the Americas, and it embraces both Enlilite and Enki'ite gods.

In South America, the dominant deity was called *Viracocha* ("Creator of All"). The Aymara natives of the Andes told of him that his abode was in Tiwanaku, and that he gave the first two brother-sister couples a golden wand with which to find the right place to establish Cuzco (the eventual Inca capital), the site for the observatory of Machu Picchu, and other sacred sites. And then, having done all that, *he left*. The grand layout, which simulated a square ziggurat with its corners oriented to the cardinal points, then marked the direction of his eventual departure (fig. 118). We have identified the god of Tiwanaku as Teshub/Adad of the Hittite/Sumerian pantheon, Enlil's youngest son.

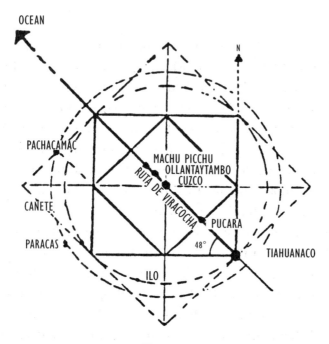

Figure 118

In Mesoamerica, the giver of civilization was the "Winged Serpent," **Quetzalcoatl.** We have identified him as Enki's son Thoth of the Egyptian pantheon (Ningishzidda to the Sumerians) and as the one who, in 3113 B.C., brought over his African followers to establish civilization in Mesoamerica. Though the time of his departure was not specified, it had to coincide with the demise of his African protégés, the Olmecs, and the simultaneous rise of the native Mayas—circa 600/500 B.C. The dominant legend in Mesoamerica was his promise, when he departed, *to return*—on the anniversary of his Secret Number 52.

And so it was, by the middle of the first millennium B.C., in one part of the world after another, that Mankind found itself without its long-worshipped gods; and before long, the question (which has been asked by my readers) began to preoccupy Mankind: *Will they return?*

Like a family suddenly abandoned by its father, Mankind grasped for the hope of a Return; then, like an orphan needing help, Mankind cast about for a Savior. The Prophets promised it will surely happen—at the *End of Days.*

* * *

At the peak of their presence, the Anunnaki numbered 600 on Earth
plus another 300 Igigi based on Mars. Their number was falling after
the Deluge and especially after Anu's visit circa 4000 B.C. Of the gods
named in the early Sumerian texts and in long God Lists, few remained
as the millennia followed each other. Most returned to their home
planet; some—in spite of their wonted "immortality"—died on Earth.
We can mention the defeated Zu and Seth, the dismembered Osiris,
the drowned Dumuzi, the nuclear-afflicted Bau. The departures of the
Anunnaki gods as Nibiru's return loomed were the dramatic finale.

The awesome times when the gods resided in sacred precincts in the
people's cities, when a Pharaoh claimed that a god was riding along in
his chariot, when an Assyrian king boasted of help from the skies, were
over and gone. Already in the days of the Prophet Jeremiah (626–586
B.C.), the nations surrounding Judea were mocked for worshipping not
a "living god" but idols made by craftsmen of stone, wood, and metal—
gods who needed to be carried, for they could not walk.

With the final departure taking place, who of the great Anunnaki
gods remained on Earth? To judge by who was mentioned in the texts
and inscriptions from the ensuing period, we can be certain only of
Marduk and Nabu of the Enki'ites; and of the Enlilites, Nannar/Sin,
his spouse Ningal/Nikkal and his aide Nusku, and probably also Ishtar.
On each side of the great religious divide there was now just one sole
Great God of Heaven and Earth: Marduk for the Enki'ites, Nannar/
Sin for the Enlilites.

The story of Babylonia's last king reflected the new circumstances.
He was chosen by **Sin** in his cult-center Harran—but he required the
consent and blessing of **Marduk** in Babylon, and the celestial confirmation by the appearance of Marduk's planet; and he bore the name
Nabu-Na'id. This divine co-regnum might have been an attempt at
Dual Monotheism (to coin an expression); but *its unintended consequence was to plant the seeds of* Islam.

The historical record indicates that neither gods nor people were
happy with these arrangements. Sin, whose temple in Harran was
restored, demanded that his great ziggurat temple in Ur should also be

rebuilt and become the center of worship; and in Babylon, the priests of Marduk were up in arms.

A tablet now in the British Museum is inscribed with a text that scholars have titled *Nabunaid and the Clergy of Babylon*. It contains a list of accusations by the Babylonian priests against Nabunaid. The charges ran from civil matters ("law and order are not promulgated by him"), through neglect of the economy ("the farmers are corrupted," "the traders' roads are blocked"), and lack of public safety ("nobles are killed"), to the most serious charges: religious sacrilege—

> *He made an image of a god which nobody had seen before*
> *in the land.*
> *He placed it in the temple, raised it upon a pedestal,*
> *He called it by the name of Nannar, with lapis lazuli he*
> *adorned it,*
> *Crowned it with a tiara in the shape of an eclipsed moon,*
> *Made for its hand the gesture of a demon.*

It was, the accusations continued, a strange statue of a deity, never seen before, "with hair reaching down to the pedestal." It was so unusual and unseemly, the priests wrote, that even Enki and Ninmah (who ended up with strange chimera creatures when they attempted to fashion Man) "could not have conceived it"; it was so strange that "not even the learned Adapa"—an icon of utmost human knowledge—"could have named it." To make matters worse, two unusual beasts were sculpted as its guardians—one a "Deluge demon" and the other a wild bull; then the king took this abomination and placed it in Marduk's Esagil temple. Even more offending was Nabunaid's announcment that henceforth the *Akitu* festival, during which the near-death, resurrection, exile, and final triumph of Marduk were reenacted, would no longer be celebrated.

Declaring that Nabunaid's "protective god became hostile to him" and that "the former favorite of the gods was now fated to misfortune," the Babylonian priests forced Nabunaid to leave Babylon and go into exile "in a distant region." It is a historical fact that Nabunaid indeed

left Babylon and named his son Bel-Shar-Uzur—the Belshazzar of the biblical Book of Daniel—as regent.

The "distant region" to which Nabunaid went in self-exile was Arabia. As various inscriptions attest, his entourage included Jews from among the Judean exiles in the Harran region. His principal base was at a place called Teima, a caravan center in what is now northwestern Saudi Arabia that is mentioned several times in the Bible. (Recent excavations there have uncovered cuneiform tablets attesting to Nabunaid's stay.) He established six other settlements for his followers; five of the towns were listed—a thousand years later—by Arabian writers as Jewish towns. *One of them was Medina, the town where Muhammed founded Islam.*

The "Jewish angle" in the Nabunaid tale has been reinforced by the fact that a fragment of the Dead Sea Scrolls, found at Qumran on the shores of the Dead Sea, mentions Nabunaid and asserts that he was suffering in Teima from an "unpleasant skin disease" that was cured only after "a Jew told him to give honor to the God Most High." All that has led to speculation that Nabunaid was contemplating Monotheism; but to him the God Most High was not the Judeans' Yahweh, but his benefector Nannar/Sin, the Moon god, whose crescent symbol has been adopted by Islam; and there is little doubt that its roots can be traced back to Nabunaid's stay in Arabia.

Sin's whereabouts fade out of Mesopotamian records after the time of Nabunaid. Texts discovered at Ugarit, a "Canaanite" site on the Mediterranean coast in Syria now called Ras Shamra, describe the Moon god as retired, with his spouse, to an oasis at the confluence of two bodies of water, "near the cleft of the two seas." Ever wondering why the Sinai Peninsula was named in honor of Sin and its main central crossroads in honor of his spouse, Nikkal (the place is still called, in Arabic, Nakhl), I surmised that the aged couple retired to somewhere on the shores of the Red Sea and the Gulf of Eilat.

The Ugaritic texts called the Moon god *EL*—simply, "God," a forerunner of Islam's *Allah;* and his moon-crescent symbol crowns every Muslim mosque. And as tradition demands, the mosques are flanked, to this day, by minarets that simulate multistage rocketships ready to be launched (fig. 119).

Figure 119

* * *

The last chapter in the Nabunaid saga was linked to the emergence on the scene of the ancient world of the **Persians**—a name given to a medley of peoples and states on the Iranian plateau that included the olden Sumerian Anshan and Elam and the land of the later Medes (who had a hand in the demise of Assyria).

It was in the sixth century B.C. that a tribe called **Achaemeans** by Greek historians who recorded their deeds emerged from the northern outskirts of those territories, seized control, and unified them all to become a mighty new empire. Though deemed to be racially "Indo-Europeans," their tribal name stemmed from that of their ancestor *Hakham-Anish,* which meant "Wise Man" in Semitic Hebrew—a fact that some attribute to the influence of Jewish exiles from the Ten Tribes who had been relocated to that region by the Assyrians. Religiously, the Achaemean Persians apparently adopted a Sumerian-Akkadian pantheon akin to its Hurrian-Mitannian version, which was a step to the

Indo-Aryan one of the Sanskrit Vedas—a mixture that is conveniently simplified by just stating that they believed in a God Most High whom they called *Ahura-Mazda* ("Truth and Light").

In **560 B.C.** the Achaemean king died and his son Kurash succeeded him on the throne and made his mark on subsequent historic events. We call him *Cyrus;* the Bible called him Koresh and considered him Yahweh's emissary for conquering Babylon, overthrowing its king, and rebuilding the destroyed Temple in Jerusalem. "Though you knowest Me not, I, Yahweh, the God of Israel, am thy caller who hath called you by name . . . who will help you though you don't recognize me," the biblical God stated through the prophet Isaiah (44:28 to 45:1–4).

That end of Babylonian kingship was most dramatically foretold in the Book of Daniel. One of the Judean exiles taken to Babylon, Daniel was serving in the Babylonian court of Belshazzar when, during a royal banquet, a floating hand appeared and wrote on the wall *MENE MENE TEKEL UPHARSIN.* Astounded and mystified, the king called his wizards and seers to decipher the inscription, but none could. As a last resort, the exiled Daniel was called in, and he told the king the inscription's meaning: God has weighed Babylon and its king and, finding them wanting, numbered their days; they will meet their end by the hand of the Persians.

In 539 B.C. Cyrus crossed the Tigris River into Babylonian territory, advanced on Sippar where he intercepted a rushing-back Nabunaid, and then—claiming that Marduk himself had invited him—entered Babylon without a fight. Welcomed by the priests who considered him a savior from the heretic Nabunaid and his disliked son, Cyrus "grasped the hands of Marduk" as a sign of homage to the god. But he also, in one of his very first proclamations, rescinded the exile of the Judeans, permitted the rebuilding of the Temple in Jerusalem, and ordered the return of all the Temple's ritual objects that were looted by Nebuchadnezzar.

The returning exiles, under the leadership of Ezra and Nehemiah, completed the rebuilding of the Temple—henceforth known as the Second Temple—in 516 B.C.—exactly, as was prophesied by Jeremiah, seventy years after the First Temple was destroyed. The Bible considered

Figure 120

Cyrus an instrument of God's plans, an "anointed of Yahweh"; historians believe that Cyrus proclaimed a general religious amnesty that allowed each people to worship as they pleased. As to what Cyrus himself might have believed, to judge by the monument he had erected for himself, he appears to have envisioned himself as a winged cherub (fig. 120).

Cyrus—some historians attach the epithet "the great" to his name—consolidated into a vast Persian empire all the lands that had once been Sumer & Akkad, Mari and Mittani, Hatti and Elam, Babylonia and Assyria; it was left to his son Cambyses (530–522 B.C.) to extend the empire to Egypt. Egypt was just recovering from a period of disarray that some consider a Third Intermediate Period, during which it was disunited, changed capitals several times, was ruled by invaders from Nubia, or had no central authority at all. Egypt was also in disarray religiously, its priests uncertain who to worship, so much so that the leading cult was that of the dead Osiris, the leading deity the female Neith whose title was *Mother of God,* and the principal "cult object"

a bull, the sacred Apis Bull, for whom elaborate funerals were held. Cambyses, too, like his father, was no religious zealot, and let people worship as they pleased; he even (according to an inscribed stela now in the Vatican museum) learned the secrets of the worship of Neith and participated in a ceremonial funeral of an Apis Bull.

These religious *laissez-faire* policies bought the Persians peace in their empire, but not forever. Unrest, uprisings, and rebellions kept breaking out almost everywhere. Especially troublesome were growing commercial, cultural, and religious ties between Egypt and Greece. (Much information about that comes from the Greek historian Herodotus, who wrote extensively about Egypt after his visit there circa 460 B.C., coinciding with the beginning of Greece's "golden age.") The Persians could not be pleased with those ties, above all because Greek mercenaries were participating in the local uprisings. Of particular concern were also the provinces in Asia Minor (present-day Turkey), at the western tip of which Asia and the Persians faced Europe and the Greeks. There, Greek settlers were reviving and reinforcing olden settlements; the Persians, on their part, sought to ward off the troublesome Europeans by seizing nearby Greek islands.

The growing tensions broke into open warfare when the Persians invaded the Greek mainland and were beaten at Marathon in 490 B.C. A Persian invasion by sea was beaten off by the Greeks in the straits of Salamis a decade later, but the skirmishes and battles for control of Asia Minor continued for another century, even as in Persia king followed king and in Greece Athenians, Spartans, and Macedonians fought one another for supremacy.

In those double struggles—one among the mainland Greeks, the other with the Persians—the support of the Greek settlers of Asia Minor was very important. No sooner did the Macedonians win the upper hand on the mainland than their king, Philip II, sent an armed corps over the Straits of Hellespont (today's Dardanelles) to secure the loyalty of the Greek settlements. In 334 B.C. his successor, Alexander ("the Great"), heading an army 15,000 strong, crossed into Asia at the same place and launched a major war against the Persians.

Alexander's astounding victories and the resulting subjugation of the

Ancient East to Western (Greek) domination have been told and retold by historians—starting with some who had accompanied Alexander— and need no repetition here. What does need to be described are the *personal* reasons for Alexander's foray into Asia and Africa. For, apart from all geopolitical or economic reasons for the Greek-Persian great war, there was Alexander's own personal quest: there had been persistent rumors in the Macedonian court that not King Philip but a god—an Egyptian god—was Alexander's true father, having come to the queen, Olympias, disguised as a man. With a Greek pantheon that derived from across the Mediterranean Sea and headed (like the Sumerian twelve) by twelve Olympians, and with tales of the gods ("myths") that emulated the Near Eastern tales of the gods, the appearance of one such god in the Macedonian court was not deemed an impossibility. With court shenanigans that involved a young Egyptian mistress of the king and marital strife that included divorce and murders, the "rumors" were believed—first and foremost by Alexander himself.

A visit by Alexander to the oracle in Delphi to find out whether he was indeed the son of a god and therefore immortal only intensified the mystery; he was advised to seek an answer at an Egyptian sacred site. It was thus that as soon as the Persians were beaten in the first battle, Alexander, rather than pursuing them, left his main army and rushed to the oasis of Siwa in Egypt. There the priests assured him that he indeed was a demigod, the son of the ram-god Amon. In celebration, Alexander issued silver coins showing him with ram's horns (fig. 121).

Figure 121

But what about the immortality? While the course of the resumed warfare and Alexander's conquests have been documented by his campaign historian Callisthenes and other historians, his personal quest for Immortality is mostly known from sources deemed to be pseudo-Callisthenes, or "Alexander Romances" that embellished fact with legend. As detailed in *The Stairway to Heaven,* the Egyptian priests directed Alexander from Siwa to Thebes. There, on the Nile River's western shore, he could see in the funerary temple built by Hatshepsut the inscription attesting to her being fathered by the god Amon when he came to her mother disguised as the royal husband— exactly like the tale of Alexander's demigod conception. In the great temple of Ra-Amon in Thebes, in the Holy of Holies, Alexander was crowned as a Pharaoh. Then, following the directions given in Siwa, he entered subterranean tunnels in the Sinai Peninsula, and finally he went to where Amon-Ra, alias Marduk, was—to Babylon. Resuming the battles with the Persians, Alexander reached Babylon in 331 B.C., and entered the city riding in his chariot.

In the sacred precinct he rushed to the Esagil ziggurat temple to grasp the hands of Marduk as conquerors before him had done. *But the great god was dead.*

According to the pseudo-sources, Alexander saw the god lying in a golden coffin, his body immersed (or preserved) in special oils. True or not, the facts are that *Marduk was no longer alive,* and that his Esagil ziggurat was, without exception, described as his **tomb** by subsequent established historians.

According to Diodorus of Sicily (first century B.C.), whose *Bibliothca historica* is known to have been compiled from verified reliable sources, "scholars called Chaldaeans, who have gained a great reputation in astrology and who are accustomed to predict future events by a method based on age-old observations," warned Alexander that he would die in Babylon but "could escape the danger if he re-erected *the tomb of Belus* which had been demolished by the Persians" (Book XVII, 112.1). Entering the city anyway, Alexander had neither the time nor the manpower to do the repairs, and indeed died in Babylon in 323 B.C.

The first century B.C. historian-geographer Strabo, who was

born in a Greek town in Asia Minor, described Babylon in his famed *Geography*—its great size, the "hanging garden" that was one of the Seven Wonders of the World, its high buildings constructed of baked bricks, and so on, and said this in section 16.I.5 (emphasis added):

> **Here too is the tomb of Belus, now in ruins,**
> *having been demolished by Xerxes, as it is said.*
> *It was a quadrangular pyramid of baked bricks,*
> *not only being a stadium in height,*
> *but also having sides a stadium in length.*
> *Alexander intended to repair this pyramid;*
> *but it would have been a large task*
> *and would have required a long time,*
> *so that he could not finish what he had attempted.*

According to this source, the **tomb** of *Bel*/Marduk was destroyed by Xerxes, who was the Persian king (and ruler of Babylon) from 486 to 465 B.C. Strabo, in Book 5, had earlier stated that *Belus* was lying in a coffin when Xerxes decided to destroy the temple, in 482 B.C. Accordingly, Marduk died not long before (Germany's leading Assyriologists, meeting at the University of Jena in 1922, concluded that Marduk was already in his tomb in 484 B.C.). Marduk's son Nabu also vanished from the pages of history about the same time. *And thus came to an end, an almost human end, the saga of the gods who shaped history on planet Earth.*

That the end came as the Age of the Ram was waning was probably no coincidence, either.

With the death of Marduk and the fading away of Nabu, all the great Anunnaki gods who had once dominated Earth were gone; with the death of Alexander, the real or pretended demigods who linked Mankind to the gods were also gone. For the first time since Adam was fashioned, Man was without his creators.

In those despondent times for Mankind, hope came forth from Jerusalem.

Amazingly, the story of Marduk and his ultimate fate in Babylon had been correctly foretold in biblical prophecies. We have already noted that Jeremiah, while forecasting a crushing end for Babylon, made the distinction that its god Bel/Marduk was only doomed to "wither"—to remain, but to grow old and confused, to shrivel and die. We should not be surprised that it was a prophecy that came true.

But as Jeremiah correctly predicted the final downfall of Assyria, Egypt, and Babylon, he accompanied those predictions with prophecies of a reestablished Zion, of a rebuilt temple, and of a "happy end" for all nations *at the End of Days.* It would be, he said, a future that God had planned "in his heart" all along, a secret that shall be revealed to Mankind (23:20) at a predetermined future time: *"at the End of Days you shall perceive it"* (30:24), and "at that time, they shall call Jerusalem Yahweh's Throne, and all nations shall assemble there" (3:17).

Isaiah, in his second set of prophecies (sometimes called the Second Isaiah), identifying Babylon's god as the "Hiding god"—which is what "Amon" meant—foresaw the future in those words:

> **Bel** *is bowed down,* **Nebo** *is cowered,*
> *their images are loads for beasts and cattle . . .*
> *Together they stoopeth, they bowed down,*
> *unable to save themselves from capture.*
>
> ISAIAH 46:1–2

These prophecies, as did Jeremiah's, also contained the promise that Mankind will be offered a new beginning, new hope; that a Messianic Time will come when "the wolf shall dwell with the lamb." And, the Prophet said, "it shall come to pass *at the End of Days* that the Mount of Yahweh's Temple shall be established as foremost of all mountains, exalted above all hills; and all the nations shall throng unto it"; it will be then that the nations "shall beat their swords into ploughshares and their spears into pruning hooks, nation shall not lift up sword against nation, and they shall no longer teach war" (Isaiah 2:1–4).

The assertion that after troubles and tribulations, after people and nations shall be judged for their sins and transgressions, a time of

peace and justice shall come was also made by the early prophets even as they predicted the Day of the Lord as judgment day. Among them were Hosea, who foresaw the *return of the kingdom of God through the House of David at the **End of Days,*** and Micha, who—using words identical to those of Isaiah—declared that "at the End of Days it shall come to pass." Significantly, Micha too considered the **restoration of God's Temple in Jerusalem** *and Yahweh's universal reign* **through a descendant of David** as a prerequisite, a "must" destined from the very beginning, "emanating from ancient times, from everlasting days."

There was thus a combination of two basic elements in those End of Days predictions: one, that the Day of the Lord, a day of judgment upon Earth and the nations, will be followed by Restoration, Renewal, and a benevolent era centered on Jerusalem. The other is, that it has all been preordained, that the End was already planned by God at the Beginning. Indeed, the concept of an End of Epoch, a time when the course of events shall come to a halt—a precursor, one may say, of the current idea of the "End of History"—and a new epoch (one is almost tempted to say, a *New Age*), a new (and predicted!) cycle shall begin, can already be found in the earliest biblical chapters.

The Hebrew term *Acharit Hayamim* (sometimes translated "last days," "latter days," but more accurately "end of days") was already used in the Bible in Genesis (chapter 49), when the dying Jacob summoned his sons and said: "Gather yourselves together, that I may tell you that which shall befall you at the **End of Days.**" It is a statement (followed by detailed predictions that many associate with the twelve houses of the zodiac) that presupposes prophecy by being based on advance knowledge of the future. And again, in Deuteronomy (chapter 4), when Moses, before dying, reviewing Israel's divine legacy and its future, counseled the people thus: "When you in tribulations shall be and such things shall befall you, in the **End of Days** to Yahweh thy God return and hearken to His voice."

The repeated stress on the role of Jerusalem, on the essentiality of its Temple Mount as the beacon to which all nations shall come streaming, had more than a theological-moral reason. A very practical reason

is cited: the need to have the site ready for the return of Yahweh's *Kavod*—the very term used in Exodus and then by Ezekiel to describe God's celestial vehicle! The *Kavod* that will be enshrined in the rebuilt Temple, "from which I shall grant peace, shall be greater than the one in the First Temple," the prophet Haggai was told. Significantly, the *Kavod*'s coming to Jerusalem was repeatedly linked in Isaiah to the other space-related site—in Lebanon: *It is from there that God's **Kavod** shall arrive in Jerusalem,* verses 35:2 and 60:13 stated.

One cannot avoid the conclusion that a divine Return was expected at the End of Days; but when was the End of Days due?

The question—one to which we shall offer our own answer—is not new, for it has already been asked in antiquity, even by the very prophets who had spoken of the End of Days.

Isaiah's prophecy about the time "when a great trumpet shall be blown" and the nations shall gather and "bow down to Yahweh on the Holy Mount in Jerusalem" was accompanied by his admission that without details and timing the people could not understand the prophecy. "Precept is upon precept, precept is within precept, line is upon line, line is with line, a little here, somewhat there" was how Isaiah (28:10) complained to God. Whatever answer he was given, he was ordered to seal and hide the document; no less than three times, Isaiah changed the word for "letters" of a script—*Otioth*—to *Ototh,* which meant "oracular signs," hinting at the existence of a kind of secret **"Bible Code"** due to which the divine plan could not be comprehended until the right time. Its secret code might have been hinted at when the prophet asked God—identified as "Creator of the letters"—to "tell us the letters backward" (41:23).

The prophet Zephaniah—whose very name meant "By Yahweh encoded"—relayed a message from God that it will be at the time of the nations' gathering that He "will speak in a clear language." But that said no more than saying, "You'll know when it will be time to tell."

No wonder, then, that in its final prophetic book, the Bible dealt almost exclusively with the question of WHEN—when will the End of Days come? It is the Book of Daniel, the very Daniel who deciphered

(correctly) for Belshazzar the Writing on the Wall. It was after that that Daniel himself began to have omen-dreams and to see apocalyptic visions of the future in which the "Ancient of Days" and his archangels played key roles. Perplexed, Daniel asked the angels for explanations; the answers consisted of predictions of future events, taking place at, or leading to, the End of Time. And when will that be? Daniel asked; the answers, which on the face of it seemed precise, only piled up enigmas upon puzzles.

In one instance an angel answered that a phase in future events, a time when "an unholy king shall try to change the times and the laws," will last *"a time, times and a half time";* only after that will the promised Messianic Time, when "the kingdom of heaven will be given to the people by the Holy Ones of the Most High," come about. Another time the responding angel said: "Seventy sevens and seventy sixties of years have been decreed for your people and your city until the measure of transgression is filled and prophetic vision is ratified"; and yet another time that "after the seventies and sixties and two of years, the Messiah will be cut off, a leader will come who will destroy the city, and the end will come through a flood."

Seeking a clearer answer, Daniel then asked a divine messenger to speak plainly: "How long until the end of these awful things?" In response, he again received the enigmatic answer that the End will come after ***"a time, times and a half time."*** But what did "time, times and a half time" mean, what did "seventy weeks of years" mean?

"I heard and did not understand," Daniel stated in his book. "So I said: My lord, what will be the outcome of these things?" Again speaking in codes, the angel answered: "from the time the regular offering is abolished and an appalling abomination is set up, it will be a thousand and two hundred and ninety days; happy is the one who waits and reaches one thousand three hundred and thirty five." And having given Daniel that information, the angel—who had called him before "Son of Man"—told him: "Now, go on to thy end, and arise for your destiny at the End of Days."

Like Daniel, generations of biblical scholars, savants and theologians, astrologers and even astronomers—the famed Sir Isaac Newton

among the latter—also said "we heard, but did not understand." The enigma is not just the meaning of "time, time and a half" and so on, but from when does (or did) the count begin? The uncertainty stems from the fact that the symbolic visions seen by Daniel (such as a goat attacking a ram, or two horns multiplying to four and then dividing) were explained to him by the angels as events that were to take place well beyond the Babylon of Daniel's time, beyond its predicted fall, even beyond the prophesied rebuilding of the Temple after seventy years. The rise and demise of the Persian empire, the coming of the Greeks under Alexander's leadership, even the division of his conquered empire among his successors—all are foretold with such accuracy that many scholars believe that the Daniel prophecies are of the "post-event" genre—that the book's prophetic part was actually written circa 250 B.C. but pretended to have been written three centuries earlier.

The clinching argument is the reference, in one of the angelic encounters, to the start of the count "from the time that regular offering [in the temple] is abolished and an appalling abomination is set up." That could only refer to the events that took place in Jerusalem on the 25th day of the Hebrew month Kislev in **167** B.C.

The date is precisely recorded, for it was then that "the abomination of desolation" was placed in the Temple, marking—many then believed—the start of the End of Days.

15

JERUSALEM:
A CHALICE, VANISHED

In the twenty-first century B.C., when nuclear weapons were first used on Earth, Abraham was blessed with wine and bread at Ur-Shalem in the name of the God Most High—and proclaimed Mankind's first Monotheistic religion.

Twenty-one centuries later, a devout descendant of Abraham, celebrating a special supper in *Jerusalem,* carried on his back a cross—the symbol of a certain planet—to a place of execution and gave rise to another monotheistic religion. Questions still swirl about him—Who really was he? What was he doing in Jerusalem? Was there a plot against him, or was he his own plotter? And what was the chalice that has given rise to the legends about (and searches for) the "Holy Grail"?

On his last evening of freedom he celebrated the Jewish Passover ceremonial meal (called *Seder* in Hebrew) with wine and unleavened bread together with his twelve disciples, and the scene has been immortalized by some of the greatest painters of religious art, Leonardo Da Vinci's *The Last Supper* being the most famous of them (fig. 122). Leonardo was renowned for his scientific knowledge and theological insights; what his painting *shows* has been discussed, debated, and analyzed to this day—deepening, rather than resolving, the enigmas.

Figure 122

The key to unlocking the mysteries, we shall show, lies in what the painting *does not show;* it is what is missing from it that holds answers to troubling puzzles in the saga of God and Man on Earth, and the yearnings for Messianic Times. Past, Present, and Future do converge in the two events, separated by twenty-one centuries; Jerusalem was pivotal to both, and by their timing, they were linked by biblical prophecies about the *End of Days.*

To understand what happened twenty-one centuries ago, we need to roll the pages of history back to Alexander, who deemed himself the son of a god, yet died in Babylon at the young age of thirty-two. While alive, he controlled his feuding generals through a mixture of favors, punishments, and even untimely deaths (some, in fact, believed that Alexander himself was poisoned). No sooner did he die than his four-year-old son and his guardian, Alexander's brother, were murdered, and the quarrelling generals and regional commanders divided between them the main conquered lands: Ptolemy and his successors, headquartered in Egypt, seized Alexander's African domains; Seleucus and his successors ruled from Syria, Anatolia, Mesopotamia, and the distant Asian lands; the contested Judea (with Jerusalem) ended up in the Ptolemaic realm.

The Ptolemies, having managed to maneuver Alexander's body for burial in Egypt, considered themselves his true heirs and, by and large,

continued his tolerant attitude toward others' religions. They established the famed Library of Alexandria and assigned an Egyptian priest, known as Manetho, to write down Egypt's dynastic history and divine prehistory for the Greeks (archaeology has confirmed what is still known of Manetho's writings). That convinced the Ptolemies that their civilization was a continuation of the Egyptian one, and they thus considered themselves rightful successors to the Pharaohs. Greek savants showed particular intrerest in the religion and writings of the Jews, so much so that the Ptolemies arranged for the translation of the Hebrew Bible into Greek (a translation known as the *Septuagint*) and allowed the Jews complete religious freedom of worship in Judea, as well as in their growing communities in Egypt.

Like the Ptolemies, the Seleucids also retained a Greek-speaking scholar, a former priest of Marduk known as Berossus, to compile for them the history and prehistory of Mankind and its gods according to Mesopotamian knowledge. In a twist of history, he researched and wrote at a library of cuneiform tablets located near Harran. It is from his three books (which we know of only from fragmented quotations in the writings of others in antiquity) that the Western world, of Greece and then Rome, learned of the Anunnaki and their coming to Earth, the pre-Diluvial era, the creation of Wise Man, the Deluge, and what followed. Thus it was from Berossus (as later confirmed by the discovery and decipherment of the cuneiform tablets) that the 3,600 "Sar" as the "year" of the gods was first learned.

In 200 B.C. the Seleucids crossed the Ptolemaic boundary and captured Judea. As in other instances, historians have searched for geopolitical and economic reasons for the war—ignoring the religious-messianic aspects. It was in the report about the Deluge that the tidbit information was given by Berossus, that Ea/Enki instructed Ziusudra (the Sumerian "Noah") to "conceal every available writing in Sippar, the city of Shamash," for post-Diluvial recovery, because those writings *"were about beginnings, middles and ends."* According to Berossus, the world undergoes periodic cataclysms, and he related them to the zodiacal Ages, his contemporary one having begun 1,920 years before the Seleucid Era (312 B.C.); that would have placed the beginning of the

Age of the Ram in 2232 B.C.—an Age destined to come soon to an end even if the full mathematical length is granted to it (2232 − 2160 = 122 B.C.).

The available records suggest that the Seleucid kings, coupling those calculations with the Missing Return, were seized with the need to urgently expect and prepare for one. A frenzy of rebuilding the ruined temples of Sumer and Akkad began, with emphasis on the E.ANNA— the "House of Anu"—in Uruk. The Landing Place in Lebanon, called by them Heliopolis—City of the Sun god—was rededicated by erecting a temple honoring Zeus. The reason for the war to capture Judea, one must conclude, was the urgency of also preparing the space-related site in Jerusalem for the Return. *It was, we suggest, the Greek-Seleucid way of preparing for the reappearance of the gods.*

Unlike the Ptolemies, the Seleucid rulers were determined to impose the Hellenic culture and religion in their domains. The change was most significant in Jerusalem, where suddenly foreign troops were stationed and the authority of the Temple priests was curtailed. Hellenistic culture and customs were forcefully introduced; even names had to be changed, starting with the high priest, who was obliged to change his name from Joshua to Jason. Civil laws restricted Jewish citizenship in Jerusalem; taxes were raised to finance the teaching of athletics and wrestling instead of the Torah; and in the countryside, shrines to Greek deities were being erected by the authorities and soldiers were sent to enforce worship in them.

In 169 B.C. the then Seleucid king, Antiochus IV (who adopted the epithet Epiphanes), came to Jerusalem. It was not a courtesy visit. Violating the Temple's sanctity, he entered the Holy of Holies. On his orders, the Temple's treasured golden ritual objects were confiscated, a Greek governor was put in charge of the city, and a fortress for a permanent garrison of foreign soldiers was built next to the Temple. Back in his Syrian capital, Antiochus issued a proclamation requiring worship of Greek gods throughout the kingdom; in Judea, it specifically forbade the observance of the Sabbath and circumcision. In accordance with the decree, the Jerusalem temple was to become a temple to Zeus; and in 167 B.C., on the 25th day of the Hebrew month Kislev—*equivalent to*

today's December 25—an idol, a statue representing Zeus, "The Lord of Heaven," was set up by Syrian-Greek soldiers in the temple, and the great altar was altered and used for sacrifices to Zeus. The sacrilege could not have been greater.

The unavoidable Jewish uprising, begun and led by a priest named Matityahu and his five sons, is known as the Hashmonean or Maccabean Revolt. Starting in the countryside, the uprising quickly overcame the local Greek garrisons. As the Greeks rushed in reinforcements, the revolt engulfed the whole country; what the Maccabees lacked in numbers and weapons, they compensated for by the ferocity of their religious zeal. The events, described in the Book of Maccabees (and by subsequent historians), leave no doubt that the fight of the few against a powerful kingdom was guided by a certain timetable: *It was imperative to retake Jerusalem, cleanse the Temple, and rededicate it to Yahweh by a certain deadline.* Managing in 164 B.C. to recapture only the Temple Mount, the Maccabees cleansed the Temple, and the sacred flame was rekindled that year; the final victory, leading to full control of Jerusalem and restoration of Jewish independence, took place in **160 B.C.** The victory and rededication of the Temple are still celebrated by Jews as the holiday of *Hanukkah* ("rededication") on the twenty-fifth day of Kislev.

The sequence and the timing of those events appeared to be linked to the prophecies about the End of Days. Of those prophecies, as we have seen, the ones that offered specific numerical clues in regard to the ultimate future, the End of Days, were conveyed by the angels to Daniel. But clarity is lacking because the counts were enigmatically expressed either in a unit called "time," or in "weeks of years," and even in numbers of days; and it is perhaps only in respect to the latter that one is told when the count does begin, so that one could know when it would end. In that one instance, the count was to begin from the day when "regular offering is abolished and an appalling abomination is set up" in the Jerusalem temple; we have established that such an abominable act indeed took place one day in 167 B.C.

With the sequence of those events in mind, the count of days given to Daniel must have applied to the specific events at the Temple: its defiling

in 167 B.C. ("when the regular offering is abolished and an appalling abomination is set up"), the cleansing of the Temple in 164 B.C. (after "a thousand and two hundred and ninety days"), and Jerusalem's complete liberation by 160 B.C. ("happy is the one who waits and reaches one thousand three hundred and thirty five days"). The numbers of days, 1,290 and 1,335, basically match the sequence of events at the Temple.

According to the prophecies in the Book of Daniel, it was then that the clock of the End of Days began ticking.

The imperative of recapturing the whole city and the removal of uncircumcised foreign soldiers from the Temple Mount by 160 B.C. hold the key to another clue. While we have been using the accepted count of B.C. and A.D. for dating events, the people of those past times obviously could not and did not use a timetable based on a *future* Christian calendar. The Hebrew calendar, as we have mentioned earlier, was the calendar begun in Nippur in 3760 B.C.—and according to that calendar, *what we call 160 B.C. was precisely the year 3600!*

That, as the reader knows by now, was a SAR, the original (mathematical) orbital period of Nibiru. And though Nibiru had reappeared four hundred years earlier, the arrival of the SAR year—3600—*the completion of one Divine Year*—was of unavoidable significance. To those to whom the biblical prophecies of the return of Yahweh's *Kavod* to His Temple Mount were unquestioned divine pronouncements, the year we call "160 B.C." was a crucial moment of truth: no matter where the planet was, God has promised to Return to His Temple, and the temple had to be purified and readied for that.

That the passage of years according to the Nippurian/Hebrew calendar was not lost sight of in those turbulent times is attested by the Book of Jubilees, an extrabiblical book presumed to have been written in Hebrew in Jerusalem in the years following the Maccabean revolt (now available only from its Greek, Latin, Syriac, Ethiopic, and Slavonic translations). It retells the history of the Jewish people from the time of the Exodus in time units of Jubilees—the 50-year units decreed by Yahweh at Mount Sinai (see our chapter 9); it also created a consecutive calendrical historical count that has since become known as

Annu Mundi—"Year of the World" in Latin—that starts in 3760 B.C. Scholars (such as the Rev. R. H. Charles in his English rendition of the book) converted such "Jubilee of years" and their "weeks" to an Anno Mundi count.

That such a calendar was not only kept throughout the ancient Near East, but even determined when events were timed to happen, can be ascertained by simply reviewing some pivotal dates (often highlighted in bold font) given in our earlier chapters. If we choose just a few of those key historical events, this is what transpires when the "B.C." is converted to "N.C." (Nippurian Calendar):

B.C.	N.C.	EVENT
3760	0	Sumerian civilization; Nipput calender begins
3460	300	The Tower of Babel incident
2860	900	Bull of Heaven killed by Gilgamesh
2360	1400	Sargon: Era of Akkad begins
2160	1600	First Intermediate Period in Egypt; Era of Ninurta (Gudea builds Temple-of-Fifty)
2060	1700	Nabu organizes Marduk's followers; Abraham to Canaan; War of the Kings
1960	**1800**	Marduk's Esagil temple in Babylon
1760	2000	Hammurabi consolidates Marduk's supremacy
1560	2200	New dynasty ("Middle Kingdom") in Egypt; new dynastic rule ("Kassite") begins in Babylon
1460	2300	Anshan, Elam, Mitanni emerge against Babylon; Moses in Sinai, the "burning bush"
960	2800	Neo-Assyrian empire launched; Akitu festival renewed in Babylon
860	2900	Ashurnasirpal wears cross symbol
760	**3000**	Prophecy in Jerusalem begins with Amos
560	3200	Anunnaki gods complete their Departure; Persians challenge Babylon; Cyrus
460	3100	Greece's golden age; Herodotus in Egypt
160	**3600**	Maccabees free Jerusalem, Temple rededicated

The impatient reader will hardly wait to fill in the next entries:		
60	3700	**The Romans build the Jupiter temple at Baalbek, occupy Jerusalem**
0	3760	**Jesus of Nazareth; A.D. count begins**

The century and a half that elapsed from the Maccabean freeing of Jerusalem to the events connected with Jesus after he arrived there were some of the most turbulent in the history of the ancient world and of the Jewish people in particular.

That crucial period, whose events affect us to this day, began with understandable jubilation. For the first time in centuries the Jews were again complete masters of their holy capital and sacred Temple, free to appoint their own kings and high priests. Though the fighting at the borders continued, the borders themselves now extended to encompass much of the olden united kingdom of David's time. The establishment of an independent Jewish state, with Jerusalem as its capital, under the Hashmoneans was a triumphal event in all respects—except one:

The return of Yahweh's *Kavod,* expected at the End of Days, did not take place, even though the count of days from abomination time seemed to have been correct. Was the Time of Fulfillment not yet at hand, many wondered; and it became evident that the enigmas of Daniel's other counts, of "years" and "weeks of years" and of "Time, Times," and so on had yet to be deciphered.

Clues were the prophetic parts in the Book of Daniel that spoke of the rise and fall of *future* kingdoms *after* Babylon, Persia, and Egypt— kingdoms cryptically called "of the south," "of the north," or a seafaring "Kittim"; and kingdoms that shall split off them, fight each other, "plant tabernacles of palaces between the seas"—all future entities that were also cryptically represented by varied animals (a ram, a goat, a lion, and so on) whose offspring, called "horns," will again split apart and fight each other. Who were those future nations, and what wars were foretold?

The prophet Ezekiel also spoke of great battles to come, between north and south, between an unidentified Gog and an opposing Magog; and people were wondering whether the prophesied kingdoms have

already appeared on the scene—Alexander's Greece, the Seleucids, the Ptolemies. Were these the subject of the prophecies, or was it someone yet to come in the even more distant future?

There was theological turmoil: Was the expectation at the Jerusalem Temple of the *Kavod* as a physical object a correct understanding of prophecies, or was the expected Coming only of a symbolic, of an ephemeral nature, a *spiritual Presence*? What was required of the people—or was what was destined to happen will happen no matter what? The Jewish leadership split between devout and by-the-book Pharisees and the more liberal Sadducees, who were more internationally minded, recognizing the importance of a Jewish diaspora already spread from Egypt to Anatolia to Mespotamia. In addition to these two mainstreams, small sects, sometimes organized in their own communities, sprang up; the best known of them are the Essenes (of the Dead Sea Scrolls fame), who secluded themselves at Qumran.

In the efforts to decipher the prophecies, a rising new power—**Rome**—had to be figured in. Having won repeated wars with the Phoenicians and with the Greeks, the Romans controlled the Mediterranean and began to get involved in the affairs of Ptolemian Egypt and the Seleucid Levant (Judea included). Armies followed imperial delegates; by 60 B.C., the Romans, under Pompey, occupied Jerusalem. On the way there, like Alexander before him, he detoured to Heliopolis (alias Baalbek) and offered sacrifices to Jupiter; it was followed by the building there, atop the earlier colossal stone blocks, of the Roman empire's greatest temple to Jupiter (fig. 123). A commemorative inscription found at the site indicates that the emperor Nero visited the place in A.D. 60, suggesting that the Roman temple was already built by then.

The national and religious turmoil of those days found expression in a proliferation of historic-prophetic writings, such as the Book of Jubilees, the Book of Enoch, the Testaments of the Twelve Patriarchs, and the Assumption of Moses (and several others, all collectively known as the Apocrypha and Pseuda-Epigrapha). The common theme in them was a belief that history is cyclical, that all has been foretold, that the End of Days—a time of turmoil and upheaval—will mark not just an end of a historic cycle but also the beginning of a new one, and that

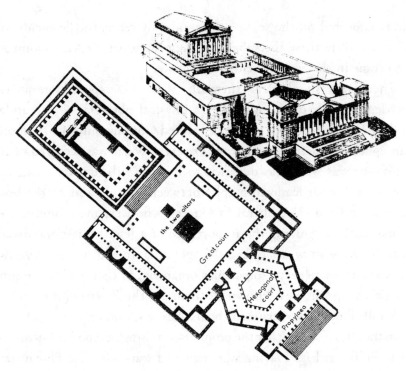

the two altars

Great court

Hexagonal court

Propylaea

Figure 123

the "flipover time" (to use a modern expression) will be manifest by
the coming of the **"Anointed One"**—*Mashi'ach* in Hebrew (translated
Chrystos in Greek, and thus Messiah or Christ in English).

The act of anointing a newly invested king with priestly oil was known
in the Ancient World, at least from the time of Sargon. It was recognized in the Bible as an act of consecration to God from the earliest
times, but its most memorable instance was when the priest Samuel,
custodian of the Ark of the Covenant, summoned David, the son of
Jesse, and, proclaiming him king by the grace of God,

> *Took the horn of oil and anointed him*
> *in the presence of his brethren;*
> *and the Spirit of God*
> *came upon David from that day on.*
>   I SAMUEL 16:13

Studying every prophecy and every prophetic utterance, the devout in Jerusalem found repeated references to **David as God's Anointed,** and a divine vow that it will be of "his seed"—by a descendant of the House of David—that his throne shall be established again in Jerusalem *"in days that are to come."* It is on the "throne of David" that future kings, who must be of the House of David, shall sit in Jerusalem; and when that shall happen, the kings and princes of the Earth shall flock to Jerusalem for justice, peace, and the word of God. This, God vowed, is "an everlasting promise," God's covenant "for all generations." The universality of this vow is attested to in Isaiah 16:5 and 22:22; Jeremiah 17:25, 23:5, and 30:3; Amos 9:11; Habakuk 3:13; Zechariah 12:8; Psalms 18:50, 89:4, 132:10, 132:17, and so on.

These are strong words, unmistakable in their messianic covenant *with the House of David,* yet they are also full of explosive facets that virtually dictated the course of events in Jerusalem. Linked to that was the matter of the **prophet Elijah.**

Elijah, nicknamed the Thisbite after the name of his town in the district of Gile'ad, was a biblical prophet active in the kingdom of Israel (after the split from Judea) in the ninth century B.C., during the reign of king Ahab and his Canaanite wife, Queen Jezebel. True to his Hebrew name, *Eli-Yahu*—"Yahweh is my God"—he was in constant conflict with the priests and "spokesmen" of the Canaanite god Ba'al ("the Lord"), whose worship Jezebel was promoting. After a period of seclusion at a hiding place near the Jordan River, where he was ordained to become "A Man of God," he was given a "mantle of haircloth" that held magical powers and was able to perform miracles in the name of God. His first reported miracle (I Kings 17) was the making of a spoonful of flour and a little cooking oil last a widow as food for the rest of her lifetime. He then resurrected her son, who had died of a virulent illness. During a contest with the prophets of Ba'al on Mount Carmel, he could summon a fire from the sky. His was the only biblical instance of an Israelite revisiting Mount Sinai since the Exodus: when he escaped for his life from the wrath of Jezebel and the priests of Ba'al, an Angel of the Lord sheltered him in a cave on Mount Sinai.

Of him the scriptures said that he did not die because he was

taken up to heaven in a whirlwind to be with God. His ascent, as described in great detail in II Kings 2, was neither a sudden nor an unexpected occurrence; on the contrary, it was a preplanned and prearranged operation whose place and time were communicated to Elijah in advance.

The designated place was in the Jordan Valley, on the eastern side of the river. When it was time to go there, his disciples, headed by one named Elisha, went along. He made a stop at Gilgal (where Yahweh's miracles were performed for the Israelites under the leadership of Joshua). There he tried to shake off his companions, but they went on to accompany him to Beth-El; though asked to stay put and let Elijah cross the river by himself, they stuck with him unto the last stop, Jericho, all the while asking Elisha whether it was "true that the Lord will take Elijah heavenward today?"

At the bank of the Jordan River, Elijah rolled his miracle mantle and struck the waters, parting them, enabling him to cross the river. The other disciples stayed behind, but even then Elisha persisted on being with Elijah, crossing over with him;

> *And as they continued to walk and to talk,*
> *there appeared a chariot of fire with horses of fire,*
> *and the two were separated.*
> *And Elijah went up to heaven, in a whirlwind.*
> *And Elisha saw and cried out:*
> *"My father! My father!*
> *the chariot of Israel and its horsemen!"*
> *And he saw it no more.*
>
> II KINGS 2:11–12

Archaeological excavations at Tell Ghassul (the "Prophet's Mound"), a site in Jordan that fits the biblical tale's geography, have uncovered murals that depicted the "whirlwinds" shown in fig. 103. It is the only site excavated under the auspices of the Vatican. (My search for the finds, which covered archaeological museums in Israel and Jordan and included a visit to the site in Jordan, and ultimately led to the Jesuit-run

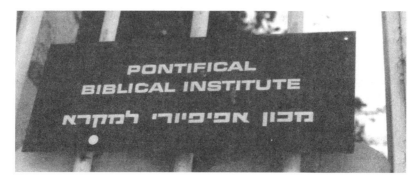

Figure 124

Pontifical Biblical Institute in Jerusalem—fig. 124—is described in *The Earth Chronicles Expeditions.*)

Jewish tradition has held that the transfigured Elijah will one day return as a harbinger of final redemption for the people of Israel, *a herald of the Messiah.* The tradition was already recorded in the fifth century B.C. by the prophet Malachi—the last biblical prophet—in his final prophecy. Because tradition held that the Mount Sinai cave where the angel took Elijah was where God had revealed himself to Moses, Elijah has been expected to reappear at the start of the Passover festival, when the Exodus is commemorated. To this day the *Seder,* the ceremonial evening meal when the seven-day Passover holiday begins, requires the placement on the meal table of a wine-filled cup for Elijah, to sip from as he arrives; the door is opened to enable him to enter, and a prescribed hymn is recited, expressing the hope that he will soon herald "the Messiah, son of David." (As is the case with Christian kids being told that Santa Claus did sneak down the chimney and bring them the gifts they see, so are Jewish kids told that though unseen, Elijah did sneak in and took a tiny sip of wine.) By custom, "Elijahs' Cup" has been embellished to become an artful goblet, a chalice never used for any purpose other than for the Elijah ritual at the Passover meal.

The "Last Supper" of Jesus was that tradition-filled Passover meal.

Though retaining the semblance of choosing its own high priest and king, Judea became for all intents and purposes a Roman colony, ruled first from headquarters in Syria, then by local governors. The Roman

governor, called Procurator, made sure that the Jews chose an *Ethnarch* ("Head of the Jewish Council") to serve as the Temple's High Priest, and at first also a "King of the Jews" (not "King of Judea" as a country), whomever Rome preferred. From 36 to 4 B.C. the king was Herod, descended of Edomite converts to Judaism, who was the choice of two Roman generals (of Cleopatra fame): Mark Anthony and Octavian. Herod left a legacy of monumental structures, including the enhancement of the Temple Mount and the strategic palace-cum-fortress of Masada at the Dead Sea; he also paid heed to the governor's wishes as a de facto vassal of Rome.

It was into a Jerusalem enlarged and magnified by Hashmonean and Herodian constructions, thronged with pilgrims for the Passover holiday, that Jesus of Nazareth arrived—in A.D. 33 (according to the accepted scholarly dating). At that time the Jews were allowed to retain only a religious authority, a council of seventy elders called the *Sanhedrin;* there was no longer a Jewish king; the land, no longer a Jewish state but a Roman province, was governed by the Procurator Pontius Pilate, ensconced in the Antonia Citadel that adjoined the Temple.

Tensions between the Jewish populace and the Roman masters of the land were rising and resulted in a series of bloody riots in Jerusalem. Pontius Pilate, arriving in Jerusalem in A.D. 26, made matters worse by bringing into the city Roman legionnaires with their pole-mounted *signae* and coinage, bearing graven images forbidden in the Temple; Jews showing resistance were pitilessly sentenced to crucifixion in such numbers that the place of execution was nicknamed *Gulgatha*—Place of the Skulls.

Jesus had been to Jerusalem before; "His parents went to Jerusalem every year at the feast of Passover, and when he was twelve years old they went up to Jerusalem after the custom of the feast; and when they had fulfilled the days, as they returned, the child Jesus tarried behind in Jerusalem" (Luke 2:41–43). When Jesus arrived (with his disciples) this time, the situation was certainly not what was expected, not what the biblical prophecies promised. Devout Jews—as Jesus most certainly was—were beholden to the idea of redemption, of salvation by a Messiah, central to which was the special and everlasting bond between God and the House of David. It was clearly and most emphatically expressed in

the magnificent Psalm 89 (19–29), in which Yahweh, speaking to His faithful followers in a vision, said:

> *I have exalted one chosen out of the people;*
> *I have found David, my servant;*
> *With my holy oil have I anointed him . . .*
> *He shall call out to me:*
> *"Thou art my father, my God,*
> *the rock of my salvation!"*
> *And I as a Firstborn shall place him,*
> *supreme of all the kings on Earth.*
> *My compassion for him forever I will keep,*
> *My faithfulness I shall not betray;*
> *My covenant with him will not be violated,*
> *What I have uttered I shall not change . . .*
> *I shall make his seed endure forever,*
> *his throne [endure] as the* **Days of Heaven.**

Was not that reference to the "Days of Heaven" a clue, a linkage between the coming of a savior and the prophesied End of Days? Was it not the time to see the prophecies come true? And so it was that Jesus of Nazareth, now in Jerusalem with his twelve disciples, determined to take matters into his own hands: if salvation requires an Anointed One of the House of David, he, Jesus, would be the one!

His very Hebrew name—*Yehu-shuah* ("Joshua")—meant Yahweh's Savior; and as for the requirement that the Anointed One ("Messiah") be of the House of David, that he was: the very opening verse of the New Testament, in the Gospel According to St. Matthew, says: ***"The book of the generations of Jesus Christ, the son of David, the son of Abraham."*** Then, there and elsewhere in the New Testament, the genealogy of Jesus is given through the generations: Fourteen generations from Abraham to David; fourteen generations from David to the Babylonian exile; and fourteen generations from then to Jesus. He was qualified, the Gospels assured one and all.

Our sources for what happened next are the Gospels and other

books of the New Testament. We know that the "eyewitness reports" were in fact written long after the events; we know that the codified version is the result of deliberations at a convocation called by the Roman emperor Constantine three centuries later; we know that "gnostic" manuscripts, like the Nag Hammadi documents or the Gospel of Judas, give different versions that the Church had reason to suppress; we even know—which is an undisputed fact—that at first there was a Jerusalem Church led by the brother of Jesus, aimed exclusively at Jewish followers, that was overtaken, superseded, and eliminated by the Church of Rome that addressed the gentiles. Yet follow we shall the "official" version, for it, by itself, links the Jesus events in Jerusalem to all the previous centuries and millennia, as told heretofore in this book.

First, any doubt, if it still exists, that Jesus came to Jerusalem at Passover time and that the "Last Supper" was the Passover *Seder* meal must be removed. Matthew 26:2, Mark 14:1, and Luke 22:1 quote Jesus saying to his disciples as they arrived in Jerusalem: "Ye know that after two days is the Feast of the Passover"; "After two days was the feast of the Passover, of the unleavened bread"; and "Now the feast of the unleavened bread drew nigh, and it is called the Passover." The three gospels, in the same chapters, then state that Jesus told his disciples to go to a certain house, where they would be able to celebrate the Passover meal with which the holiday begins.

Next to be tackled is the matter of Elijah, the herald of the coming Messiah (Luke 1:17 even quoted the relevant verses in Malachi). According to the Gospels, the people who heard about the miracles that Jesus performed—miracles that were so similar to those by the prophet Elijah—at first wondered whether Jesus was Elijah reappeared. Not saying no, Jesus challenged his closest disciples: "What say *you* that I am? And Peter answered and said unto him: Thou art the Anointed One" (Mark 8:28–29).

If so, he was asked, where is Elijah, who had to appear first? And Jesus answered: Yes, of course, but he has already come!

> *And they asked him, saying:*
> *Why say the scribes that Elias must first?*

And he answered and told them:
Elias verily cometh first, and restoreth all things . . .
But I say unto you
That Elias has indeed come.

MARK 9:11,13

This was an audacious statement, the test of which was about to come: for if Elijah has in fact returned to Earth, *"is indeed come,"* thereby fulfilling the prerequisite for the Messiah's coming—**then he had to show up at the Seder and drink from his cup of wine!**

As custom and tradition required, the Cup of Elijah, filled with wine, was set on the *Seder* table of Jesus and his disciples. The ceremonial meal is described in Mark 14. Conducting the *Seder,* Jesus took the unleavened bread (now called *Matzoh*) and made the blessing, and broke it, and gave pieces of it to his disciples. "And he took **the cup,** and when he had thanks, he gave it to them, and they all drank of it" (Mark 14:23).

So, without doubt, the Cup of Elijah was there, but Da Vinci chose not to show it. In this *The Last Supper* painting, which could only be based on the New Testament passages, ***Jesus is not holding the crucial cup, and nowhere is there a wine cup on the table!*** Instead there is **an inexplicable gap to the right of Jesus** (fig. 125), and the disciple to his right is bending sideways as if to allow someone unseen to come between them.

Figure 125

Was the thoroughly theologically correct Da Vinci implying that an unseen Elijah did come through the open windows, behind Jesus, and took away the cup that was his? Elijah, the painting thereby suggests, did return; the herald preceding the Anointed King of the House of David did arrive.

And thus confirmed, when the arrested Jesus was brought before the Roman governor who asked him: "Art thou the *king of the Jews?* Jesus said unto him: Thou sayest" (Matthew 27:11). The sentence, to die on the cross, was inevitable.

When Jesus raised the cup of wine and made the required blessing, he said to his disciples, according to Mark 14:24, "This is my blood of the new testament." IF these were his exact words, he did not mean to say that they were to drink wine turned to blood—a grave transgression of one of the strictest prohibitions of Judaism from the earliest times, "for blood is the soul." What he said (or meant to say) was that the wine in *this cup,* the *Cup of Elijah,* was a testament, a confirmation of his **bloodline.** And Da Vinci depicted it convincingly by its disappearance, presumably taken away by the visiting Elijah.

The vanished cup has been a favorite subject of authors over the centuries. The tales became legends: the Crusaders sought it; Knights Templar found it; it was brought over to Europe . . . the cup became a goblet, a chalice; it was the chalice representing the Royal Blood—*Sang Real* in French, becoming *San Greal,* the **Holy Grail.**

Or had it, after all, never left Jerusalem?

The continued subjugation and intensified Roman repression of the Jews in Judea led to the outbreak of Rome's most challenging rebellion; it took Rome's greatest generals and best legions seven years to defeat little Judea and reach Jerusalem. In A.D. 70, after a prolonged siege and fierce hand-to-hand battles, the Romans breached the Temple's defenses; and the commanding general, Titus, ordered the Temple put to the torch. Though resistance continued elsewhere for another three years, the Jewish Great Revolt was over. The triumphant Romans were so jubilant that they commemorated the victory with a series of coins that announced to the world *Judaea Capta*—Judea Captured—and

Figure 126

Figure 127

erected a victory archway in Rome depicting the looted Temple's ritual objects (fig. 126).

But during each year of independence, Jewish coins were struck with the legend "Year One," "Year Two," etc., "for the freedom of Zion," showing fruits of the land as decorative themes. **Inexplicably, the coins of years two and three bore the image of a chalice (fig. 127) . . .**

Was the "Holy Grail" still in Jerusalem?

16

ARMAGEDDON AND PROPHECIES OF THE RETURN

Will they return? When will they return?

These questions have been asked of me countless times, "they" being the Anunnaki gods whose saga has filled my books. The answer to the first question is yes; there are clues that need to be heeded, and the prophecies of the Return need to be fulfilled. The answer to the second question has preoccupied Mankind ever since the watershed events in Jerusalem more than two thousand years ago.

But the question is not only "if" and "when." What will the Return signal, what will it bring with it? Will it be a benevolent coming, or—as when the Deluge was looming—bring about the End? Which prophecies would come true: **a Messianic Time, the Second Coming, a new Beginning—or perhaps a catastrophic Apocalypse, the Ultimate End, Armageddon . . .**

It is the last possibility that shifts these prophecies from the realm of theology, escatology, or mere curiosity to a matter of Mankind's very survival; for *Armageddon,* a term that has come to denote a war of unimagined calamitous scope, *is in fact the name of a specific place*

280

in a land that has been subjected to threats of nuclear annihilation.

In the twenty-first century B.C., a war of the Kings of the East against the Kings of the West was followed by a nuclear calamity. Twenty-one centuries later, when B.C. changed to A.D., Mankind's fears were expressed in a scroll, hidden in a cave near the Dead Sea, that described a great and final "War of the Sons of Light Against the Sons of Darkness." Now again, in the twenty-first century A.D., a nuclear threat hangs over the very same historical place. It is enough reason to ask: *Will* history repeat itself—*does* history repeat itself, in some mysterious way, every twenty-one centuries?

A war, an annihilating conflagration, has been depicted as part of the End of Days scenario in Ezekiel (chapters 38–39). Though "Gog of the land of Magog," or "Gog and Magog," are foreseen as the principal instigators in that final war, the list of combatants that shall be sucked into the battles encompassed virtually every nation of note; and the focus of the conflagration shall be "the dwellers of the Navel of the Earth"—the people of Jerusalem according to the Bible, but the people of "Babylon" as a replacement for Nippur to those for whom the clock stopped there.

It is a spine-chilling realization that Ezekiel's list of those widespread nations (38:5) that will engage in the final war— Armageddon—actually begins with **PERSIA**—*the very country (today's Iran) whose leaders seek nuclear weapons with which to "wipe off the face of the Earth" the people who dwell where Har-Megiddo is!*

Who is that "Gog of the land of Magog," and why does that prophecy from two and a half millennia ago sound so much like current headlines? Does the accuracy of such details in the prophecy point to the When—**to our time, to our century?**

Armageddon, a Final War of Gog and Magog, is also an essential element of the End of Days scenario of the New Testament's prophetic book, Revelation (whose full name is The Apocalypse of St. John the Divine). It compares the instigators of the apocryphal events to two beasts, one of which can "make fire come down from heaven to earth, in sight of men." Only an enigmatic clue is given for its identity (13:18):

Here is wisdom:
Let him that hath understanding
count the number of the beast:
It is the number of a man;
and his number is
six hundred and threescore and six.

Many have attempted to decipher the mysterious number **666,** assuming it is a coded message pertaining to the End of Days. Because the book was written when the persecution of Christians in Rome began, the accepted interpretation is that the number was a code for the oppressor emperor Nero, the numerical value of whose name in Hebrew (NeRON QeSaR) added up to 666. The fact that he had been to the space platform in Baalbek, possibly to inaugurate the temple to Jupiter there, in the year **A.D. 60** may—or may not—have a bearing on the 666 puzzle.

That there could be more to 666 than a connection to Nero is suggested by the intriguing fact that 600, 60, and 6 are all basic numbers of the Sumerian sexagesimal system, so that the "code" might hark back to some earlier texts; there were 600 Anunnaki, Anu's numerical rank was 60, Ishkur/Adad's rank was 6. Then, if the three numbers are to be multiplied rather than added, we get $666 = 600 \times 60 \times 6 = 216,000$, which is the familiar 2,160 (a zodiacal age) times 100—a result that can be speculated on endlessly.

Then there is the puzzle that when seven angels reveal the sequence of future events, they do not link them to Rome; they link them to **"Babylon."** The conventional explanation has been that, like the 666 was a code for the Roman ruler, so was "Babylon" a code word for Rome. But Babylon was already gone for centuries when Revelation was written, and Revelation, speaking of Babylon, unmistakably links the prophecies to "the great river Euphrates" (9:14), even describing how "the sixth angel poured out his vial upon the great river Euphrates," drying it up so that the Kings of the East would be joined in the fighting (16:12). The talk is of a city/land on the Euphrates, not on the Tiber River.

Since Revelation's prophecies are of the future, one must conclude that *"Babylon" is not a code—Babylon means Babylon, a future Babylon* that will get involved in the war of "Armageddon" (which verse 16:16 correctly explains as the name of "a place in the Hebrew tongue"—*Har-Megiddo,* Mount Megiddo, in Israel)—a war involving the Holy Land.

If that future Babylon is indeed today's Iraq, the prophetic verses are again chilling, for as they foretell current events leading to the fall of Babylon after a brief but awesome war, they *predict the breakup of Babylon/Iraq into three parts (16:19)!*

Like the Book of Daniel, which predicted phases of tribulations and trying stages in the messianic process, so has Revelation tried to explain the enigmatic Old Testament prophecies by describing (chapter 20) a First Messianic Age with "a First Resurrection" lasting a thousand years, followed by a Satanic reign of a thousand years (when "Gog and Magog" will engage in an immense war), and then a second messianic time and another resurrection (and thus the "Second Coming").

Unavoidably, these prophecies triggered a frenzy of speculation as the year A.D. 2000 approached: speculation regarding the **Millennium** as a point in time, in the history of Mankind and the Earth, when prophecies would come true.

Besieged with millennium questions as the year 2000 neared, I told my audiences that *nothing will happen in 2000,* and not only because the true millennium point counting from the birth of Jesus had already passed, Jesus having been born, by all scholarly calculations, in 6 or 7 B.C. The main reason for my opinion was that the prophecies appeared to envision not a *linear* timeline—year one, year two, year nine hundred, and so on—but *a cyclical* repetition of events, the fundamental belief that "The First Things shall be the Last Things"—something that can happen only when history and historical time move in a circle, where the start point is the end point, and vice versa.

Inherent in this cyclical plan of history is the concept of God as an *everlasting divine entity* who had been present at the Beginning when Heaven and Earth were created and who will be there at the End of Days, when His kingdom shall be renewed upon His holy mount. It

is expressed in repeated statements from the earliest biblical assertions
through the latest prophets, as when God announced, through Isaiah
(41:4, 44:6, 48:12):

> *I am He, I am the First and also the Last I am . . .*
> *From the Beginnings the Ending I foretell,*
> *and from ancient times the things that are not yet done.*
>
> ISAIAH 48:12, 46:10

And equally so (twice) in the New Testament's Book of Revelation:

> *I am Alpha and Omega,*
> *the Beginning and the Ending,*
> *sayeth the Lord—*
> *Which is, and which was, and which will be.*
>
> REVELATION 1:8

Indeed, the basis for prophecy was the belief that the End was
anchored in the Beginning, that the *Future* could be predicted because
the *Past* was known—if not to Man, then to God: I am the one ***"who
from the Beginning tells the End,"*** Yahweh said (Isaiah 46:10). The
prophet Zechariah (1:4, 7:7, 7:12) foresaw God's plans for the future—
the Last Days—in terms of the Past, ***the First Days.***

This belief, which is restated in the Psalms, in Proverbs, and in
the Book of Job, was viewed as a universal divine plan for the whole
Earth and all its nations. The prophet Isaiah, envisioning the Earth's
nations gathered to find out what is in store, described them asking
each other: "Who among us can tell the future by letting us hear the
First Things?" (41:22). That this was a universal tenet is shown in a
collection of *Assyrian Prophecies,* when the god Nabu told the Assyrian
king Esarhaddon: ***"The future shall be like the past."***

This cyclical element of the biblical Prophecies of the Return leads us to
one current answer to the question of WHEN.

A cyclical revolving of historical time was found, the reader will

recall, in Mesoamerica, resulting from the meshing, like the gears of wheels, of two calendars (see fig. 67), creating the "bundle" of 52 years, on the occurring of which—after an unspecified number of turns—Quetzalcoatl (alias Thoth/Ningishzidda) promised to return. And that introduces us to the so-called *Mayan Prophecies,* according to which **the End of Days will come about in A.D. 2012.**

The prospect that the prophesied crucial date is almost at hand has naturally attracted much interest and merits explaining and analyzing. The claimed date arises from the fact that in that year (depending how one calculates) the time unit called *Baktun* will complete its thirteenth turn. Since a Baktun lasts 144,000 days, it is some kind of a milestone.

Some errors, or fallacious assumptions, in this scenario need to be pointed out. The first is that the Baktun belongs not to the two "meshing" calendars with the 52-year promise (the *Haab* and the *Tzolkin*), but to a third and much older calendar called *The Long Count.* It was introduced by the Olmecs—Africans who had come to Mesoamerica when Thoth was exiled from Egypt—and the count of days actually began with that event, so that Day One of the Long Count was in what we date as August 3113 B.C. Glyphs in that calendar represented the following sequence of units:

I kin			=	I day
I Uinal	=	I kin × 20	=	20 days
I Tun	=	I kin × **360**	=	360 days
I Ka-tun	=	I tun × 20	=	7,200 days
I Bak-tun	=	I Ka-tun × 20	=	144,000 days
I Pictun	=	I Bak-tun × 20	=	2,880,000 days

These units, each a multiple of the previous one, thus continued beyond the Baktun with ever-increasing glyphs. But since Mayan monuments never reached beyond 12 Baktuns, whose 1,728,000 days were already beyond the Mayan existence, the 13th Baktun appears as a real milestone. Besides, Mayan lore purportedly held that the present "Sun" or Age would end with the 13th Baktun, so when its number of days (144,000 × 13 = 1,872,000) is divided by 365.25, it results in the

passage of 5,125 years; when the B.C. 3113 is deducted, **the result is the year A.D. 2012.**

This is an exciting as well as an ominous prediction. But that date has been challenged, already a century ago, by scholars (like Fritz Buck, *El Calendario Maya en la Cultura de Tiahuanacu*) who pointed out that as the above list indicates, the mutiplier, and thus the divider, should be the calendar's own mathematically perfect 360 and not 365.25. That way, the 1,872,000 days result in 5,200 years—a perfect result, because it represents exactly 100 "bundles" of Thoth's magical number 52. Thus calculated, **Thoth's magical year of the Return would be A.D. 2087** (5200 − 3113 = 2087).

One could stand even that wait; the only fly in the ointment is that *the Long Count is a linear time count, and not the required cyclical one,* so that its counted days could roll on to the fourteenth Baktun and the fifteenth Baktun and on and on.

All that, however, does not eliminate the significance of a prophetic millennium. Since the source of "millennium" as an escatological time had its origins in Jewish apocryphal writings from the 2nd century B.C., the search for meaning must shift in that direction. In fact, the reference to "a thousand"—a millennium—as defining an era had its roots way back in the Old Testament. Deuteronomy (7:9) assigned to the duration of God's covenant with Israel a period of "a thousand generations"—an assertion repeated (I Chronicles 16:15) when the Ark of the Covenant was brought to Jerusalem by David. The Psalms repeatedly applied the number "thousand" to Yahweh, his wonders, and even to his chariot (Psalm 68:17).

Directly relevant to the issue of the End of Days and the Return is the statement in Psalm 90:4—a statement attributed to Moses himself—that said of God that *"a thousand years, in thy eyes, are but as one day that has passed."* This statement has given rise to speculation (which started soon after the Roman destruction of the Temple) that it was a way to figure out the elusive messianic End of Days: if Creation, "The Beginning," according to Genesis, took God six days, and a divine day lasts a thousand years, the result is a duration of 6,000

years from Beginning to End. The End of Days, it has thus been figured, will come in the *Anno Mundi* year 6,000.

Applied to the Hebrew calendar of Nippur that began in 3760 B.C., **this means that the End of Days will occur in A.D. 2240** (6000 − 3760 = 2240).

This third End of Days calculation may be disappointing or comforting—it depends on one's expectations. The beauty of this calculation is that it is in perfect harmony with the Sumerian sexagesimal ("base 60") system. It might even prove in future to be correct, but I don't think so: it is again linear—and it is a cyclical time unit that is called for by the prophecies.

With none of the "modern" predicted dates workable, one must look back at the olden "formulas"—do what had been advised in Isaiah, *"look at the signs backwards."* We have two *cyclical* choices: the Divine Time orbital period of Nibiru, and the Celestial Time of the zodiacal Precession. Which one is it?

That the Anunnaki came and went during a "window of opportunity" when Nibiru arrived at Perigee (nearest the Sun, and thus the closest to Earth and Mars) is so obvious that some readers of mine used to simply deduct 3600 from 4000 (as a round date for Anu's last visit), resulting in 400 B.C., or deduct 3600 from 3760 (when the Nippur calendar began)—as the Maccabbees did—and arrive at 160 B.C. Either way, the next arrival of Nibiru is way in the distant future.

In fact, as the reader now knows, Nibiru arrived earlier, circa 560 B.C. When considering that "digression," one must keep in mind that the perfect SAR (3,600) has always been a *mathematical* orbital period, because celestial orbits—of planets, comets, asteroids—digress from orbit to orbit due to the gravitational tug of other planets near which they pass. To use the well-tracked Halley's Comet as an example, its given period of 75 years actually fluctuates from 74 to 76; when it last appeared in 1986, it was 76 years. Extend Halley's digression to Nibiru's 3,600, and you get a plus/minus variant of about 50 years each way.

There is one other reason for wondering why Nibiru had digressed

so much from its wonted SAR: the unusual occurrence of the Deluge circa 10,900 B.C.

During its 120 SARs *before* the Deluge, Nibiru orbited without causing such a catastrophe. Then something unusual happened that brought Nibiru closer to Earth: combined with the slippage conditions of the ice sheet covering Antarctica, the Deluge occurred. What was that "something unusual"?

The answer may well lie farther out in our solar system, where Uranus and Neptune orbit—planets whose many moons include some that, inexplicably, orbit in an "opposite" ("retrograde") direction—the way Nibiru orbits.

One of the great mysteries in our solar system is the fact that the planet Uranus literally lies on its side—its north-south axis faces the Sun horizontally instead of being vertical to it. "Something" gave Uranus a "big whack" sometime in its past, NASA's scientists said—without venturing to guess what the "something" was. I have often wondered whether that "something" was also what caused the huge mysterious "chevron" scar and an unexplained "ploughed" feature that NASA's *Voyager 2* found on Uranus's moon Miranda in 1986 (fig. 128)—a moon that is different in numerous ways from the other moons of Uranus. ***Could a celestial collision with a passing Nibiru and its moons cause all that?***

In recent years astronomers have ascertained that the outer large planets have not stayed put where they were formed but have been drifting outward, away from the Sun. The studies concluded that the shift has been most pronounced in the case of Uranus and Neptune (see sketch, fig. 129), and that can explain why nothing happened out there for many Nibiru orbits—then suddenly something did. It is not implausible to assume that on its "Deluge" orbit Nibiru encountered the drifting Uranus, ***and one of Nibiru's moons struck Uranus,*** tilting it on its side; it could even be that the strike "weapon" was the enigmatic moon Miranda—***a moon of Nibiru***—striking Uranus and ending up captured to orbit Uranus. Such an occurrence would have affected the orbit of Nibiru, slowing it down to about 3,450 Earth-years rather than 3,600, and resulting in a post-Diluvial reappearance schedule of circa 7450, circa 4000, and circa 550 B.C.

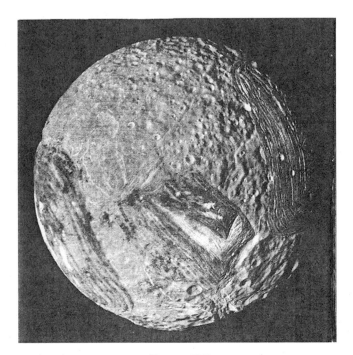

Figure 128

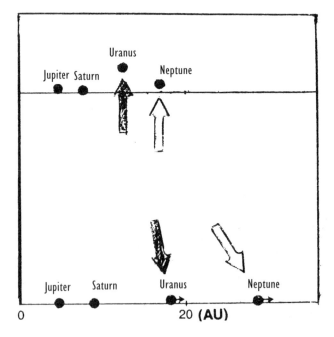

Figure 129

If that is what had happeed, it would explain the "early" arrival of
Nibiru in 556 B.C.—and suggest that **its next arrival will be circa A.D.
2900.** For those who associate the prophesied cataclysmic events with
the return of Nibiru—"Planet X" to some—the time is not at hand.

**But any notion that the Anunnaki limited their comings and
goings to a single short "window" at the planet's perigee is, however,
incorrect. They could keep coming and going at other times as well.**

The ancient texts record numerous instances of back-and-forth travel
by the gods with no indication of a link to the planet's proximity. There
are also a number of tales of Earth-Nibiru travel by Earthlings that
omit any assertion of Nibiru seen in the skies (a sight stressed, on the
other hand, when Anu visited Earth circa 4000 B.C.). In one instance
Adapa, a son of Enki by an Earthling woman, who was given Wisdom
but not immortality, paid a very short visit to Nibiru, accompanied by
the gods Dumuzi and Ningishzidda. Enoch, emulating the Sumerian
Enmeduranki, also came and went, twice, in his lifetime on Earth.

This was possible in at least two ways, as shown in fig. 130: one by a
spaceship accelerating on Nibiru's incoming phase (from point **A**), arriving well ahead of perigee time; the other by decelerating a spacecraft
(at point **B**) during Nibiru's outbound phase, "falling back" toward the
Sun (and thus to Earth and Mars). A short visit to Earth, like the one
by Anu, could take place by combining "A" for arrival and "B" for outbound departure; a short visit to Nibiru (as by Adapa) could take place

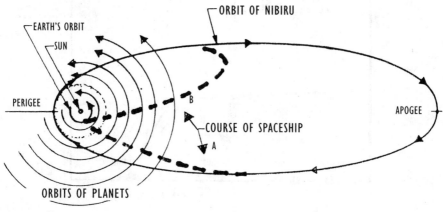

Figure 130

by reversing the procedure—by leaving Earth to intercept Nibiru at "A" and departing from Nibiru at "B" for the return to earth, and so on.

A Return of the Anunnaki at a time other than the planet's return can thus take place, and for that we are left with the other cyclical time—zodiacal time.

I have called it, in *When Time Began*, **Celestial Time,** distinct from yet serving as a link between Earthly Time (our planet's orbital cycle) and Divine Time (the clock of the Anunnaki's planet). If the expected Return will be of the Anunnaki rather than of their planet, then it behooves us to seek the solution to the enigmas of gods and men through the clock that has linked them—the cyclical zodiac of Celestial Time. It was invented, after all, by the Anunnaki as a way to reconcile the two cycles; their ratio—3,600 for Nibiru, 2,160 for a zodiacal Age—was the Golden Ratio of 10:6. It resulted, I have suggested, in the sexagesimal system on which Sumerian mathematics and astronomy were based (6 × 10 × 6 × 10 and so on).

Berossus, as we have mentioned, deemed the zodiacal Ages to be turning points in the affairs of gods and men and held that the world periodically undergoes apocalyptic catastrophes, either by water or by fire, whose timing is determined by heavenly phenomena. Like his counterpart Manetho in Egypt, he also divided prehistory and history into divine, semidivine, and postdivine phases, with a grand total of 2,160,000 years of "the duration of this world." This—wonder of wonders!—is **exactly one thousand—a millennium!—zodiacal ages.**

Scholars studying ancient clay tablets dealing with mathematics and astronomy were astounded to discover that the tablets used the fantastic number 12,960,000—yes, 12,960,000—as a starting point. They concluded that this could only be related to the zodiacal ages of 2,160, whose multiples result in 12,960 (if 2,160 × 6), or 129,600 (if 2,160 × 60), or 1,296,000 (if multiplied by 600); and—wonder of wonders!—the fantastic number with which these ancient lists begin, 12,960,000, **is a multiple of 2,160 by 6,000—as in the divine six days of creation.**

That major events, when the affairs of the gods affected the affairs of men, were linked to zodiacal Ages has been shown throughout this

volume of The Earth Chronicles. As each Age began, something momentous took place: the Age of Taurus signaled the grant of civilization to Mankind. The Age of Aries was ushered in by the nuclear upheaval and ended with the Departure. The Age of Pisces arrived with the destruction of the Temple and the beginning of Christianity. ***Should one not wonder whether the prophetic End of Days really means End of (zodiacal) Age?***

Were the "time, times, and a half" of Daniel simply a terminology referring to zodiacal Ages? The possibility was pondered, some three centuries ago, by none other than Sir **Isaac Newton.** Best known for his formulation of the natural laws governing celestial motions—such as planets orbiting the Sun—his interests also lay in religious thought, and he wrote lengthy treatises about the Bible and biblical prophecies. He considered the celestial motions that he formulated to be "the mechanics of God," and he strongly believed that the scientific discoveries that began with Galileo and Copernicus and were continued by him were meant to happen when they did. This led him to pay particular attention to the "mathematics of Daniel."

In March 2003 the British Broadcasting Corporation (BBC) startled the scientific and religious establishments with a program on Newton that revealed the existence of a document, handwritten by him on front and back, that calculated the End of Days according to Daniel's prophecies.

Newton wrote his numerical calculations on one side of the sheet, and his analysis of the calculations as seven "propositions" on the paper's other side. A close examination of the document—a photocopy of which I am privileged to have—reveals that the numbers that he used in the calculations include 216 and 2,160 several times—a clue to me to understand what his line of thought was: ***he was thinking of zodiacal time—to him, that was the Messianic Clock!***

He summed up his conclusions by writing down a set of three "not before" and a "not later than" timetable for Daniel's prophetic clues:

- Between 2132 and 2370 according to one clue given to Daniel,
- Between 2090 and 2374 according to a second clue,
- Between 2060 and 2370 for the crucial "time, times & half time."

"Sir Isaac Newton predicted the world would end in the year 2060," the BBC announced. Not exactly, perhaps—but as the table of zodiacal Ages in an earlier chapter shows, he was not far off the mark in two of his "not earlier than" dates: **2060 and 2090.**

The original cherished document of the great Englishman is now kept in the Department of Manuscripts and Archives of the Jewish National and University Library—*in Jerusalem!*

A coincidence?

It was in my 1990 book *Genesis Revisited* that the "Phobos Incident"—a hushed-up event—was first publicly revealed. It concerned the loss, in 1989, of a Soviet spacecraft sent to explore Mars and its possibly hollow moonlet called Phobos.

In fact, not one but two Soviet spacecraft were lost. Named *Phobos 1* and *Phobos 2* to indicate their purpose—to probe Mars' moonlet Phobos—they were launched in 1988, to reach Mars in 1989. Though a Soviet project, it was supported by NASA and European agencies. *Phobos 1* just vanished—no details or explanation were ever publicly given. *Phobos 2* did make it to Mars and started to send back photographs taken by two cameras—a regular one and an infrared one.

Amazingly or alarmingly, they included pictures of the shadow of a cigar-shaped object flying in the planet's skies between the Soviet craft and the surface of Mars (fig. 131 by the two cameras). The Soviet mission chiefs described the object that cast the shadow as "something which some may call a flying saucer." Immediately, the spacecraft was directed to shift from Mars orbit to approach the moonlet and, from a distance of 50 yards, bombard it with laser beams. *The last picture* **Phobos 2** *sent showed a missile coming at it from the moonlet* **(fig. 132).** Immediately after that, the spacecraft went into a spin and stopped transmitting—destroyed by the mysterious missile.

The "Phobos incident" remains, officially, an "unexplained accident." In fact, right thereafter, a secret commission on which all the leading space nations were represented sprang into action. The commission and the document it formulated merit more scrutiny than they

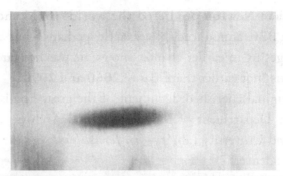

Figure 131

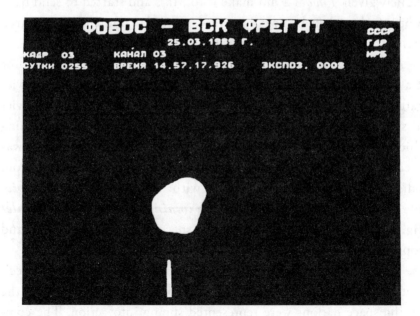

Figure 132

Figure 133

received, for they hold the key to understanding what the world's lead-ing nations really know about Nibiru and the Anunnaki.

The geopolitical events that resulted in the secret group's forma-tion began with the discovery, in 1983, of a "Neptune-sized planet" by IRAS—NASA's Infra-Red Astronomical Satellite—which scanned the edges of the solar system not visually but by detecting heat-emitting celestial bodies. The search for a tenth planet was one of its stated objec-tives, and indeed it found one—determining that it was a planet because, detected once and then again six months later, it was clearly moving in our direction. The news of the discovery made headlines (fig. 133) but was retracted the next day as a "misunderstanding." In fact, the discovery was so shocking that it led to a sudden change in U.S.–Soviet relations, a meeting and an agreement for space cooperation between President Reagan and Chairman Gorbachev, and public statements by the presi-dent at the United Nations and other forums that included the following words (pointing heavenwards with his finger as he said them):

**Just think how easy his task and mine might be in these meet-
ings that we held if suddenly there was a threat to this world
from some other species from another planet outside in the universe . . . I occasionally think how quickly our differences would
vanish if we were facing an alien threat from outside this world.**

The Working Committee that was formed as a result of these concerns conducted several meetings and leisurely consultation—*until the
March 1989 Phobos incident.* Working feverishly, it formulated in *April
1989* a set of guidelines known as the *Declaration of Principles Concerning
Activities Following the Detection of Extraterrestrial Intelligence,* by which
the procedures to be followed after **receiving "a signal or other evidence
of extraterrestrial intelligence"** were agreed upon. The "signal," the
group revealed, "might not be simply one that indicates its intelligent
origin but could be an **actual message** that may need decoding." The
agreed procedures included undertakings to delay disclosure of the
contact for at least twenty-four hours **before a response is made.** This
was surely ridiculous if the message had come from a planet light-years
away . . . No, the preparations were for a nearby encounter!

To me, all these events since 1983, plus all the evidence from Mars
briefly described in previous chapters, and the missile shot out from
the moonlet Phobos, indicate that the Anunnaki still have a presence—
probably a robotic presence—on Mars, their olden Way Station. That
could indicate forethought, a plan to have a facility ready for a future
revisit. **Put together, it suggests an *intent* for a Return.**

To me, the Earth-Mars cylinder seal (see fig. 113) is both a depiction
of the Past and a foretelling of the Future because it bears a date—*a
date indicated by the sign of two fishes—the Age of Pisces.*

**Does it tell us: What had taken place in a previous Age of Pisces
will be repeated again in the Age of Pisces?** If the prophecies are to
come true, if the First Things shall be the Last Things, if the Past is the
Future—the answer has to be Yes.

**We are still in the Age of Pisces. The Return, the signs say, will
happen before the end of our current Age.**

POSTSCRIPT

In November 2005 a major archaeological discovery was made in Israel. While clearing the ground for a new structure, the remains of an ancient large building came to light. Archaeologists were summoned to supervise careful excavation. The building turned out to be a Christian church—the oldest one ever found in the Holy Land. Inscriptions in Greek suggest it was built (or rebuilt) in the third century A.D. As the ruins were cleared, a magnificent mosaic floor came into view. In its center was a depiction of TWO FISHES—the *zodiacal sign of Pisces* (fig. 134).

Figure 134

What is significant about that?

The site of the discovery is Megiddo, at the foot of Mount Megiddo—*Har-Megiddo,* ARMAGEDDON.

Another coincidence?

INDEX

Page numbers in *italics* refer to illustrations.